The new 1987 edition
provides fast access to
the answers—

- What's happening in
  world affairs

- The latest scientific
  information

- The earth's vital
  statistics

- Special articles by
  experts

- More sports pages
  than any other
  almanac

- Plus history, religion,
  taxes, cities and states,
  calendars, celebrities,
  travel, and much more!

If you need to know, turn to

# INFORMATION PLEASE!

## Ordering Information Please Almanac by Mail

*Information Please Almanac* is available in bookstores everywhere. Copies of the *Almanac* may also be ordered directly by mail from the publisher.

To order, write to: Customer Service Department, Houghton Mifflin Publishing Company, Burlington, Massachusetts 01803. Readers may phone Customer Service, Toll-Free (800) 225-3362 for the latest price and shipping information. In Massachusetts, telephone 272-1500.

Other reference books published by Houghton Mifflin Company are: *The American Heritage Dictionary, Webster's II New Riverside University Dictionary, The Professional Secretary's Handbook,* and *Roget's II: The New Thesaurus.*

# INFORMATION
# PLEASE
# ALMANAC®
## ATLAS & YEARBOOK

## 40TH EDITION

# HOUGHTON MIFFLIN COMPANY BOSTON

1987

**Executive Editor**
*Otto Johnson*
**Associate Editor**
*Vera Dailey*
**Contributing Editors**
*Arthur Reed, Jr. (Current Events)*
*William E. Bruno (World Countries)*
*Dennis M. Lyons (Sports)*
**Staff**
*Editorial Assistant:*
*Keith Powell*
**Maps**
*Maps copyright © Hammond Incorporated.*
*Requests for map use should be sent to Hammond Incorporated, Maplewood, New Jersey 07040.*

The Information Please Almanac invites comments and suggestions from readers. Because of the many letters received, however, it is not possible to respond personally to every correspondent. Nevertheless, all suggestions are most welcome, and the editors will consider them carefully. (Information Please Almanac does not rule on bets or wagers.)

ISBN (Hardcover): 0–395–42502–6
ISBN (Paperback): 0–395–42503–4
ISSN: 0073–7860

Previous editions of INFORMATION PLEASE were published in 1985 and 1984 by Houghton Mifflin Company, in 1982 by A&W Publishing Company, and in 1981, 1980, and 1979 by Simon & Schuster, in 1978 and 1977 by Information Please Publishing, Inc., and from 1947–1976 by Dan Golenpaul Associates.

Copies of Information Please Almanac may be ordered directly by mail from:
Customer Service Department
Houghton Mifflin Company
Burlington, Ma 01803
Phone toll-free, (800) 225-3362 for price and shipping information. In Massachusetts phone: 272-1500.

INFORMATION PLEASE ALMANAC®
Editorial Office
Houghton Mifflin Company
52 Vanderbilt Avenue
New York, N.Y. 10017

Printed in the United States of America

WP Pa    BP Hbd 10 9 8 7 6 5 4 3 2 1

# CONTENTS

## SPECIAL FEATURE ARTICLES

Because we recognize the need to go beyond the traditional almanac compilation of data, this new section offers readers a wealth of additional information about subjects covered and topics not discussed in the Information Please Almanac. General Information has been organized as a mini-encyclopedia containing 500 illuminating entries.

Almost 50 pages of selected ideas and beliefs which people have held in different periods of human history that have influenced mankind. Whether these beliefs are true or false, meaningful or meaningless, they are worth serious study. This new section will enable readers to gain a better understanding of the present through a better understanding of the past.

# TABLE OF CONTENTS

# COMPREHENSIVE INDEX

# Ordering Information Please Almanac by Mail

*Information Please Almanac* is available in bookstores everywhere. Copies of the *Almanac* may also be ordered directly by mail from the publisher.

To order, write to: Customer Service Department, Houghton Mifflin Publishing Company, Burlington, Massachusetts 01803. Readers may phone Customer Service, Toll-Free (800) 225-3362 for the latest price and shipping information. In Massachusetts, telephone 272-1500.

Other reference books published by Houghton Mifflin Company are: *The American Heritage Dictionary, Webster's II New Riverside University Dictionary, The Professional Secretary's Handbook,* and *Roget's II: The New Thesaurus.*

# Special Features

## The Danger of Nuclear Terrorism

*By Yonah Alexander*

### Nuclear-Related Incidents 1966-85, By Region

| Country | 1966-70 | 1971-75 | 1976-80 | 1981-85 |
|---|---|---|---|---|
| Asia | 0 | 1 | 2 | 8 |
| Africa | 0 | 0 | 3 | 5 |
| Australia | 0 | 1 | 1 | 1 |
| Eastern Europe and Soviet Union | 0 | 0 | 0 | 1 |
| Latin America | 0 | 1 | 3 | 3 |
| Middle East | 0 | 0 | 2 | 5 |
| North America | 4 | 22 | 38 | 36 |
| Western Europe | 1 | 9 | 108 | 76 |
| TOTAL | 5 | 34 | 157 | 135 |

*Source:* Compiled by the Nuclear Control Institute in cooperation with SUNY's Institute for Studies in International Terrorism, 1986.

Terrorism, as an expedient tactical and strategic tool of politics in the struggle for power within and among nations, is not new in history. From time immemorial, both established regimes and opposition groups, functioning under varying degrees of stress, have intentionally utilized extra-legal instruments of psychological and physical force—including intimidation, coercion, repression and, ultimately, destruction of lives and property—for the purpose of attaining real or imaginary ideological, political, social, and economic goals.

Unlike their historical counterparts, present-day terrorists have introduced into contemporary life a new breed of violence in terms of technology, victimization, threat, and response. The globalization and brutalization of modern violence make it abundantly clear that we have entered a new "Age of Terrorism" with all its frightening ramifications.

The statistics of terrorist violence are, indeed, staggering. From 1970 to 1985, some 24,722 domestic and international terrorist incidents occurred. A total of 45,906 individuals have been killed and another 27,901 wounded with property

Dr. Yonah Alexander is Professor and Director, The Institute for Studies in International Terrorism, State University of New York. He is also a member of the senior research team, The Center for Strategic and International Studies, Georgetown University. He is the editor of *Terrorism: An International Journal* as well as *Political Communications and Persuasion: An International Journal*. He has authored, edited, and co-edited a number of books on terrorism.

damage estimated at billions of dollars. The number of terrorist incidents involving fatalities has been increasing about 20 percent a year since the early 1970s.

Although, at least thus far, no catastrophic disruptions or casualties have resulted from a single terrorist attack, future incidents could be much more costly. The prospect of the use of mass-destruction weapons is seen by many experts as plausible and by others as inevitable.

Thus, terrorists could "go nuclear" by stealing nuclear materials, by making or stealing a bomb, by sabotaging or holding for ransom a nuclear device or nuclear material. A current poll by George Gallup of opinion leaders in the United States indicates that a nuclear incident in the United States involving terrorists is viewed as a more imminent danger than a nuclear war between the superpowers. Moreover, according to the 1986 report of the International Task Force on Prevention of Nuclear Terrorism, a project of the Nuclear Control Institute co-sponsored by the Institute for Studies in International Terrorism of the State University of New York, terrorists might be more willing than nations to use acquired nuclear weapons. Deterrence may not work against terrorists who go to the lengths of "going nuclear." In this sense, nuclear terrorism could be the most dangerous variant of nuclear proliferation and non-nuclear terrorism. While the probability of nuclear terrorism remains low, the consequences for urban and industrial societies could be catastrophic. An explosion would breach the critical post-war moratorium on use of nuclear weapons; in a worst-case situation it conceivably could spark an inadvertent nuclear exchange between the superpowers. Thus, the potential for nuclear terrorism poses an exceptional global danger.

Clearly, the probability of nuclear terrorism is increasing. This is due to a confluence of factors:

1. the growing incidence, sophistication and lethality of conventional forms of terrorism, often to increase shock value;

2. apparent evidence of state support, even sponsorship, of terrorist groups;

3. the storing and deploying of nuclear weapons in areas of intense terrorist activity;

4. an increasing number of potential targets in civil nuclear programs—in particular facilities and shipments in which plutonium and uranium, in forms suitable for use in weapons, are present;

5. potential black and gray markets in nuclear equipment and materials.

It should be emphasized, however, that much can be done to reduce the dangers; the current situation does not call for hopelessness or despair. Nuclear terrorism is possible, but not necessarily imminent or inevitable. The highest priority should be given to protecting nuclear weapons against theft, preventing the detonation of nuclear weapons in the event they are stolen, and recovering stolen weapons.

In the U.S. a federal plan exists for responding to various forms of nuclear terrorism. For example, the Nuclear Emergency Search Team (NEST), operated by the U.S. Department of Energy (with headquarters in Las Vegas, Nevada; and with a secondary arm at Andrews Air Force Base, Maryland) is assigned to find and render harmless stolen nuclear weapons or improvised nuclear devices. During its 11 years of existence, NEST has responded to close to 100 threats, none of which proved to be genuine.

To be sure, NEST is an efficient unit for finding stolen or improvised nuclear weapons if the approximate location of the bomb is known. However, NEST is small and has a limited capability for finding well-shielded sources of radiation. In a large urban area, for example, it would be next to impossible to locate such a device within a limited period of time unless the general vicinity of its concealment were known. NEST's limited technical capability is further reason to upgrade protection of weapons and of materials usable in weapons to make theft all but impossible.

As far as international approaches to prevent nuclear terrorism, the United States and the Soviet Union have several relevant agreements. These include pacts on nuclear weapons proliferation, nuclear weapons protection, the Hot Line, accidental firing of nuclear weapons, and the protection of international transport of fissile material. The two countries have also shared satellite intelligence on potential nuclear disasters and the clandestine activities of non-nuclear weapon states. In the aftermath of the Chernobyl accident, it is likely that the two superpowers will renew their concern for the threat of nuclear terrorism.

In sum, the advances of science and technology are slowly turning the entire modern society into a potential victim of terrorism, with no immunity for the noncombatant segment of the world population or for those nations and peoples who have

## Nuclear-Related Incidents 1966-85, by Type of Incident

| Incident | North America | Western Europe | Others |
|---|---|---|---|
| Kidnapping and assassination | 0 | 8 | 0 |
| Theft and smuggling | 5 | 8 | 11 |
| Bombing, on-site[1] | 9 | 24 | 9 |
| Bombing, off-site[1] | 1 | 99 | 5 |
| Other attacks[2], on-site[1] | 79 | 30 | 4 |
| Other attacks, off-site[1] | 5 | 19 | 1 |
| Other incidents | 1 | 6 | 7 |

1. The term "on-site" is used here to refer to incidents at locations where nuclear materials and equipment are present. "Off-site" incidents are those which took place at utility headquarters, residences of nuclear officials, etc. 2. The term "attacks" includes arson, sabotage, forced entry, etc. Demonstrations which resulted in injuries or property damage are included in this category. SOURCE: Compiled by the Nuclear Control Institute in cooperation with SUNY's Institute for Studies in International Terrorism, 1986.

no direct connection to particular conflicts, or to specific grievances that motivate acts of violence.

Acts of nuclear sabotage and theft and the technical resources needed for construction of a crude nuclear device are within reach of modern terrorist organizations with sufficient resources. Nuclear terrorism, although it may appear improbable, should not be discounted or dismissed. It should be seen as a real threat to civilization.

# Redefining National Security

### By Lester R. Brown

"National security" has become a commonplace expression, a concept regularly appealed to. It is used to justify the maintenance of armies, the development of new weapon systems, and the manufacture of armaments. . . .

Since World War II, the concept of national security has acquired an overwhelmingly military character, rooted in the assumption that the principal threat to security comes from other nations. Commonly veiled in secrecy, considerations of military threats to the security of nations, threats with which military forces cannot cope, are being ignored.

The new sources of danger arise from oil depletion, soil erosion, land degradation, shrinking forests, deteriorating grasslands, and climate alteration. These developments, affecting the natural resources and systems on which the economy depends, threaten not only national economic and political security, but the stability of the international economy itself.

## Militarization of the World Economy

. . . .The principal force driving global militarization is the ideological conflict between the Soviet Union, with its socialist allies, and the United States, in alliance with the industrial democracies. In addition, alignment of the Third World states with the two military superpowers, has made militarization a global phenomenon, independent of the level of economic development. The continued striving for an advantage has led to enormous growth in military expenditures in both camps. . . .

\* \* \*

Over the past quarter-century, the international commerce in arms has soared, largely because of the militarization of Third World economies that lack their own arms manufacturing capacity. Expenditures on arms imports have eclipsed those on other goods, including grain. For example, although world grain trade expanded at nearly 12 percent per year from 1970 to 1984, it was overtaken during the eighties by arms dealings, which grew at over 13 percent annually during the same period. As of 1984, world arms imports totaled $35 billion per year, compared with $33 billion worth of grain, putting guns ahead of bread in world commerce. . . .

## Costs to the Two Superpowers

The cost of the arms race to the superpowers goes beyond any mere fiscal reckoning. It is draining their treasuries, weakening their economies, and lowering their position in the international economic hierarchy. This long, drawn-out conflict is contributing to a realignment of the leading industrial countries, with Japan assuming a dominant position in the world economy. One of the keys to Japan's emergence as an economic superpower is its negligible level of military expenditures—less than 1 percent of GNP. . . .

## New Threats to Security

The extensive deterioration of natural support systems and the declining economic conditions evident in much of the Third World pose threats to national security that now rival the traditional military ones. . . .

The first resource scarcity that dramatically affected the global economy was that of oil. The 1973 price hike sent shock waves throughout the world, the reverberations of which are still being felt more than a decade later. These and other consequences of oil reserve depletion have dominated headlines over the past dozen years, but the depletion of forests, grasslands, and topsoil and the alteration of the hydrological cycle are of greater consequence over the long term.

\* \* \*

Sudan, on the brink of famine in 1985, illustrates the complex relationship between ecological deterioration, declining per capita food production, and soaring external debt. As 1 of 14 countries in which farmland productivity is lower today than it was a generation ago, mainly agrarian Sudan will obviously find it difficult to honor its external financial obligations, however well intentioned its leaders may be.

---

Lester R. Brown is the President of Worldwatch Institute, 1776 Massachusetts Ave., N.W., Washington, D.C. Worldwatch is an independent, nonprofit research organization that was established to inform policy makers and the general public about the interdependence of the world economy and its environmental support systems. This article was excerpted from a report of the same title with permission from *State of The World 1986*, copyright © 1986 by the Worldwatch Institute. The annual *State of The World* may be ordered from Worldwatch or through bookstores in the United States or directly from the publishers, W.W. Norton & Company, Inc., 500 Fifth Ave., New York, N.Y. 10110. A list of other publications is available from Worldwatch.

\* \* \*

Assessments of Third World debt repayment prospects are grim, but they would be even grimmer if financial analysts understood what is happening to the environmental support systems underpinning most Third World economies. It is not a matter of an occasional country here or there experiencing deforestation, soil erosion, or land degradation. The great majority of Third World countries have crossed the sustainable yield thresholds of their basic support systems. . . .

A few governments have begun to redefine national security, putting more emphasis on economic progress and less on buying arms. At a time when global military expenditures are rising, some countries are actually cutting military outlays. A handful are reducing them sharply, not only as a share of GNP but in absolute terms as well. Among them are China, Argentina, and Peru. . . .

## The Challenge

. . . . Understanding the new threats to national security and economic progress will challenge the analytical skills of governments. Sadly, the decision-making apparatus in most governments is not organized to balance threats of a traditional military nature with those of ecological and economic origin. Nonmilitary threats are much less clearly defined. They are the result of cumulative processes that ultimately lead to the collapse of biological systems. These processes are seldom given much thought until they pass a critical threshold, and disaster strikes. Thus it is easier in the government councils of developing countries to justify expenditures for the latest-model jet fighters than for family planning to slow the population growth that is destroying the economy's environmental underpinnings.

\* \* \*

The key to demilitarizing the world economy and shifting resources is a defusing of the arms race between the United States and the Soviet Union. Whether this can be achieved in the foreseeable future remains to be seen. But as the costs of maintaining the arms race multiply, both for the superpowers and for the world at large, the likelihood of reducing tensions may be improving.

\* \* \*

If demilitarization could replace militarization, national governments would be free to reorder their priorities, and could return to paths of sustained progress.

Ironically, for the United States and the Soviet Union, maintaining a position of leadership may now depend on reducing military expenditures to strengthen their faltering economies. Acting thus in their own interests, they could set the stage for demilitarizing the world economy. . . . Once it starts, demilitarization—like militarization—could feed on itself.

# The Changed World Economy

## By Peter F. Drucker

The talk today is of the "changing world economy." I wish to argue that the world economy is not "changing"; it has *already changed*—in its foundations and in its structure—and in all probability the change is irreversible.

Within the last decade or so, three fundamental changes have occurred in the very fabric of the world economy:

—The primary-products economy has come "uncoupled" from employment.

—In the industrial economy itself, production has come "uncoupled" from employment.

—Capital movements rather than trade (in both goods and services) have become the driving force of the world economy. The two have not quite come uncoupled, but the link has become loose, and worse, unpredictable.

\* \* \*

First, consider the primary-products economy. The collapse of non-oil commodity prices began in 1977 and has continued, interrupted only once (right after the 1979 petroleum panic), by a speculative burst that lasted less than six months; it was followed by the fastest drop in commodity prices ever registered. By early 1986 raw material prices were at their lowest levels in recorded history in relation to the prices of manufactured goods and services—in general as low as at the depths of the Great Depression, and in some cases (e.g., lead and copper) lower than their 1932 levels.[1]

This collapse of prices and the slowdown of demand stand in startling contrast to what had been confidently predicted. Ten years ago the Club of Rome declared that desperate shortages for *all* raw materials were an absolute certainty by the year 1985. In 1980 the Carter Administration's *Global 2000 Report to the President: Entering the Twenty-First Century* concluded that world demand for food would increase steadily for at least 20 years; that worldwide food production would fall except in developed countries; and that real food prices would double. . . .

Contrary to all these expectations, global agricultural output actually rose almost one-third between 1972 and 1985 to reach an all-time high. It rose the fastest in less-developed countries. Similarly, production of practically all forest products, metals, and minerals has gone up between 20 and 35 percent in the last ten years—again with the greatest increases in less-developed countries. There is not the slightest reason to believe that the growth rates will slacken despite the collapse of commodity prices. . . .

Perhaps even more amazing than the contrast between such predictions and what has happened

is that the collapse in the raw materials economy seems to have had almost no impact on the world industrial economy. If there was one thing considered "proven" beyond doubt in business cycle theory, it is that a sharp and prolonged drop in raw material prices inevitably, and within 18 to 30 months, brings on a worldwide depression in the industrial economy.[2] While the industrial economy of the world today is not "normal" by any definition of the term, it is surely not in a depression. Indeed, industrial production in the developed noncommunist countries has continued to grow steadily, albeit at a somewhat slower rate in Western Europe.

Of course, a depression in the industrial economy may only have been postponed and may still be triggered by a banking crisis caused by massive defaults on the part of commodity-producing debtors, whether in the Third World or in Iowa. But for almost ten years the industrial world has run along as though there were no raw material crisis at all. The only explanation is that for the developed countries—excepting only the Soviet Union—the primary-products sector has become marginal where before it had always been central.

\* \* \*

The raw material economy has thus come uncoupled from the industrial economy. This is a major structural change in the world economy, with tremendous implications for economic and social policy as well as economic theory, in developed and developing countries alike.

\* \* \*

What accounts for this change?

Demand for food has actually grown almost as fast as the Club of Rome and the *Global 2000 Report* anticipated. But the supply has grown much faster; it not only has kept pace with population growth, it has steadily outrun it. One cause of this, paradoxically, is surely the fear of worldwide food shortages, if not world famine, which resulted in tremendous efforts to increase food output. The United States led the parade with a farm policy of subsidizing increased food production. The European Economic Community followed suit, and even more successfully. The greatest increases, both in absolute and in relative terms, however, have been in developing countries: in India, in post-Mao China and in the rice-growing countries of Southeast Asia.

And there is also the tremendous cut in waste. In the 1950s, up to 80 percent of the grain harvest of India fed rats and insects rather than human beings. Today in most parts of India the wastage is down to 20 percent. . . .

\* \* \*

Import markets for food have all but disappeared. As a result of its agricultural drive, Western Europe has become a substantial food exporter plagued increasingly by unsalable surpluses of all kinds of foods, from dairy products to wine, from wheat to beef. China, some observers predict, will

---

1. When the price of petroleum dropped to $15 a barrel in February 1986, it was actually below its 1933 price (adjusted for the change in the purchasing power of the dollar). It was still, however, substantially higher than its all-time low in 1972-73, which in 1986 dollars amounted to $7-$8 a barrel.

2. The business cycle theory was developed just before World War I by the Russian mathematical economist, Nikolai Kondratieff, who made comprehensive studies of raw material price cycles and their impacts all the way back to 1797.

Peter F. Drucker is Clarke Professor of Social Science and Management at the Claremont Graduate School, California. This article is excerpted and reprinted by permission of *Foreign Affairs*, Spring 1986. Copyright, 1986, by the Council on Foreign Relations, Inc.

have become a food exporter by the year 2000. . . .

The only remaining major food buyer on the world market may then be the Soviet Union—and its food needs are likely to grow.[3] However, the food surpluses in the world are so large—maybe five to eight times what the Soviet Union would ever need to buy—that its food needs are not by themselves enough to put upward pressure on world prices. On the contrary, the competition for access to the Soviet market among the surplus producers—the United States, Europe, Argentina, Australia, New Zealand (and probably India within a few years)—is already so intense as to depress world food prices.

\* \* \*

The second major change in the world economy is the uncoupling of manufacturing production from manufacturing employment. Increased manufacturing production in developed countries has actually come to mean *decreasing* blue-collar employment. As a consequence, labor costs are becoming less and less important as a "comparative cost" and as a factor in competition.

There is a great deal of talk these days about the "deindustrialization" of America. In fact, manufacturing production has risen steadily in absolute volume and has remained unchanged as a percentage of the total economy. Since the end of the Korean War, that is, for more than 30 years, it has held steady at 23-24 percent of America's total GNP. It has similarly remained at its traditional level in all of the other major industrial countries.

It is not even true that American industry is doing poorly as an exporter. To be sure, the United States is importing from both Japan and Germany many more manufactured goods than ever before. But it is also exporting more, despite the heavy disadvantages of an expensive dollar, increasing labor costs, and the near-collapse of a major industrial market, Latin America. In 1984—the year the dollar soared—exports of American manufactured goods rose by 8.3 percent; and they went up again in 1985. The share of U.S.-manufactured exports in world exports was 17 percent in 1978. By 1985 it had risen to 20 percent—while West Germany accounted for 18 percent and Japan 16. The three countries together thus account for more than half of the total.

Thus it is not the American economy that is being "deindustrialized." It is the American labor force.

Between 1973 and 1985, manufacturing production (measured in constant dollars) in the United States rose by almost 40 percent. Yet manufacturing employment during that period went down steadily. There are now five million fewer people employed in blue-collar work in American manufacturing industry than there were in 1975.

Yet in the last 12 years total employment in the United States grew faster than at any time in the peacetime history of any country—from 82 to 110 million between 1973 and 1985—that is, by a full one-third. The entire growth, however, was in non-

manufacturing, and especially in non-blue-collar jobs.

\* \* \*

The third major change that has occurred in the world economy is the emergence of the "symbol" economy—capital movements, exchange rates, and credit flows—as the flywheel of the world economy, in place of the "real" economy—the flow of goods and services. The two economies seem to be operating increasingly independently. This is both the most visible and the least understood of the changes.

World trade in goods is larger, much larger, than it has ever been before. And so is the "invisible trade," the trade in services. Together, the two amount to around $2.5 trillion to $3 trillion a year. But the London Eurodollar market, in which the world's financial institutions borrow from and lend to each other, turns over $300 billion each working day, or $75 trillion a year, a volume at least 25 times that of world trade.[4]

In addition, there are the foreign exchange transactions in the world's main money centers, in which one currency is traded against another. These run around $150 billion a day, or about $35 trillion a year—12 times the worldwide trade in goods and services.

Of course, many of these Eurodollars, yen and Swiss francs are just being moved from one pocket to another and may be counted more than once. A massive discrepancy still exists, and there is only one conclusion: capital movements unconnected to trade—and indeed largely independent of it—greatly exceed trade finance.

There is no one explanation for this explosion of international—or, more accurately, transnational—money flows. The shift from fixed to floating exchange rates in 1971 may have given an initial impetus (though, ironically, it was meant to do the exact opposite) by inviting currency speculation. The surge in liquid funds flowing to petroleum producers after the two oil shocks of 1973 and 1979 was surely a major factor.

\* \* \*

Without it Washington could not finance its budget deficit, at least not without the risk of explosive inflation.

The way major countries have learned to use the international economy to avoid tackling disagreeable domestic problems is unprecedented: the United States has used high interest rates to attract foreign capital and avoid confronting its domestic deficit; the Japanese have pushed exports to maintain employment despite a sluggish domestic economy. This politicization of the international economy is surely also a factor in the extreme volatility and instability of capital flows and exchange rates.

Whichever of these causes is judged the most important, together they have produced a basic change; in the world economy of today, the "real" economy of goods and services and the "symbol" economy of money, credit, and capital are no longer bound tightly to each other; they are, indeed, moving further and further apart.

---

3. Although the African famine looms large in our consciousness, the total population of the affected areas is far too small to make any dent in world food surpluses.

4. A Eurodollar is a U.S. dollar held outside the United States.

# College Degrees by Mail or Modem

*By John Bear, Ph.D.*

The rapidly growing trend toward "non-traditional" degree programs, or ways and means of earning bachelor's, master's, doctorates, and law degrees entirely, or almost entirely, by home study just keeps on growing. For example:

* The University of the State of New York and other fully accredited state universities offer bachelor's degrees that can be earned totally by correspondence at a cost that can be under $500.

* City University in Seattle is offering its M.B.A. electronically; you can complete the degree without ever getting up from your IBM, Apple, or Commodore computer, wherever in the world you live.

* The University of London and several other major international universities have Ph.D. programs that can be completed entirely by correspondence study, plus an exam taken at the nearest embassy or consulate.

* Hundreds of people have passed various Bar Exams and entered the practice of law without ever setting foot in a law school; all their work was done at home by mail, telephone, or computer modem.

What makes it all possible is the still-controversial concept of credit for life experience learning. Proponents of this notion claim that if you know something, it doesn't matter how you learned it; you should get college credit for it. If you are fluent in German, they say, what difference does it make whether you learned it in college classes, from your grandmother, from Berlitz, or because you once lived in Germany? You deserve the same number of credits as if you had attended German classes at the state university for four years.

On the other hand, some people insist that meaningful learning can take place only in a college classroom. They allow that *some* credit could be given for off-campus learning, but to award an entire degree for work done at home or on the job somehow subverts the educational process (and cuts down on attendance at the football games).

Only three accredited schools will award degrees based entirely on things you did before you enrolled: the University of the State of New York, Edison State College in New Jersey, and Charter Oak College in Connecticut. But scores of other schools have programs that offer generous credit for prior learning, and then require as little as one semester of new work, either on campus or by correspondence, to earn a degree.

These are some of the best programs available.

## Bachelor's Degrees

* University of the State of New York, Regents College, Cultural Education Center, Albany, N.Y. 12230. No faculty. No campus. No courses. No library. No football team. Just universally accepted, accredited associate's and bachelor's degrees in almost any subject based on prior coursework, exams, correspondence courses, and/or assessment of nonschool learning experiences. One hundred percent by correspondence.

* University of London, Senate House, Malet St., London WC1E 7HU, England. Nonresident degrees have been offered for over 140 years. For the bachelor's degree you enroll, wait three years, then take a day or two of exams at your nearest consulate. The university doesn't care what you do during those three years. You can take classes elsewhere, study privately, etc. As long as you can pass the exams (usually just in one field), you get the degree. They also have external master's degrees and doctorates, but you have to earn *their* bachelor's first.

* Thomas Edison State College, 101 W. State St., Trenton, N.J. 08625. Almost the same model as New York, with the added option of completing most or all of the required work using your home computer.

* American Open University, 21 Chestnut St., Greenvale, N.Y. 11548. Bachelor's degrees in business, behavioral science, and general studies totally by home study, including correspondence course modules, challenge exams, and credit for life experience learning.

## Master's Degrees

* California State University, Dominguez Hills, 1000 E. Victoria St., Dominguez Hills, Calif. 90747. The External Degree Program in Humanities is a home study degree in history, philosophy, religion, music, or art.

* Empire State College of the State University of New York, 2 Union Ave., Saratoga Springs, N.Y. 12866. The Center for Distance Learning has nonresident master's degrees in a variety of fields, all related to policy studies: business, labor, culture, etc.

* City University, 16661 Northup Way, Bellevue, Wash. 98008. The M.B.A. degree can be completed entirely over your home computer through the auspices of a clearinghouse called Electronic University. E.U., located in San Francisco, (505 Beach St., San Francisco, Calif. 94133) intends to facilitate a wide range of accredited computerized degrees; this one is the first.

## Doctorates

* Union Graduate School, P.O. Box 85315, Cincinnati, Ohio 45201. Union offers the opportunity to earn an accredited Ph.D. in almost any field, almost entirely by independent study. Roughly 35 days of attendance at short seminars (held in various locations around the U.S.) are required. The main activity is production of a "project demonstrating excellence"—something showing that you are very good at what you do.

* University of South Africa, P.O. Box 392, Muckleneuk Ridge, 0001 Pretoria, South Africa. The largest correspondence university in the world of-

John Bear has been researching and writing about ways and means of earning degrees for more than twenty years. He encourages people to ask those who use degrees (especially doctorates) in public, where they got their degree. Dr. Bear's Ph.D. was earned with highest honors at Michigan State University in 1966. He is the author of the best-selling book in this field, *Bear's Guide to Non-Traditional College Degrees*, published by Ten Speed Press, and available in bookstores or directly from the author at P.O. Box 11447, Marina del Rey, Calif. 90295.

Copyright © 1985 by POINT. Reprinted with permission from *Whole Earth Review*, Spring 1986, and permission of the author.

fers students the opportunity to earn extremely inexpensive bachelor's/master's degrees and doctorates without having to visit that beleaguered land. Many people will avoid UNISA on political grounds. Others will note that it has more black students than any other university in the world (including, in past years, Nelson Mandela, and Robert Mugabe of Zimbabwe, who earned his doctorate there).

* Nova University, 3301 College Ave., Fort Lauderdale, Fla. 33314. Master's degrees and doctorates in education, business, computer science and related areas can be earned through a combination of independent study and attendance at a series of weekend and one-week seminars, held in 30 or more locations around the world each summer, as well as through teleconferencing. The programs are designed for mid-career professionals, who can earn the degrees with minimal time away from their full-time jobs.

## Law Degrees

California is the only state where Abe Lincoln could qualify for the Bar Exam using the "study-by-the-fire" method. You study at home for one year, take a "Baby Bar" exam to see if you're on track, study for three more years (864 hours a year), and then take the regular Bar. Only 10 percent of home-study students pass the first time (compared with 60 percent for traditional law schools), but that 10 percent wouldn't have it any other way. A current list of recognized correspondence schools is available from the State Bar of California, P.O. Box 7908, San Francisco, Calif. 94129.

## Unaccredited Schools

More than 200 unaccredited universities offer nonresident degrees of all kinds. Some are serious endeavors whose degrees require substantial amounts of work and are widely (though not universally) accepted in the academic marketplace. Others are "one-room schoolhouses" that do little more than look at your resume and say, in effect, "Oh, that's wonderful. Hand over 2,000 bucks, and

we'll award you our Ph.D." The FBI has been extremely active in recent years exposing and closing down diploma mills through its "DipScam" operation, but the wheels of justice grind slowly, and dozens of fraudulent schools are still operating in the U.S. and Europe.

To get an idea of the kinds of degrees and programs offered by some of the better unaccredited schools, request the literature of Fairfax University (622 Baronne St., New Orleans, La. 70113); Walden University (430 Marquette Ave., Suite 408, Minneapolis, Minn. 55401); International Institute for Advanced Studies (8000 Bonhomme Ave., Clayton, Mo. 63105); Pacific Western University (600 N. Sepulveda Blvd., Los Angeles, Calif. 90049); or Columbia Pacific University (1415 Third St., San Rafael, Calif. 94901).

## Four Things To Do Before Sending Any Money to Any School

1. Check out the degree with any relevant gatekeepers. If a degree will help with job advancement, salary increments, state licensing, graduate school admission, etc., be certain in advance that the degree in question will meet that need. Don't rely on assurances from the schools.

2. Check out the school with the agency in its state that oversees higher education, and with the Better Business Bureau in its city.

3. If an accreditation claim is made, independently verify that it is correct, and that the accrediting agency is one recognized either by the U.S. Department of Education or the Council on Postsecondary Accreditation.

There are more than 100 accrediting agencies, including at least 20 unrecognized ones, set up by schools for the purpose of accrediting themselves.

4. Ask the school these questions: How many degrees in my field have you awarded in the last year? May I have the names and addresses of some recent graduates? May I examine work done by your students? Which faculty member(s) will supervise my work? What are their credentials? Are they full-time employees or is this a sideline for them?

# ELECTIONS

## The Hundredth Congress

### Composition of 99th and 100th Congresses

Unofficial results as of Nov. 5, 1986

| | 99th Congress | | | | 100th Congress | | | |
|---|---|---|---|---|---|---|---|---|
| | Dem. | Rep. | Male | Female | Dem. | Rep. | Male | Female |
| Senate | 47 | 53 | 98 | 2 | 55 | 45 | 98 | 2 |
| House | 253 | 182 | 411 | 24 | 261* | 174* | 411 | 24 |

*Pending outcome of undecided races.

## The Senate

Senior Senator is listed first. The dates in the first column indicate period of service. The date in parentheses after the Senator's name is year of birth. All terms are for six years and expire in January. Mailing address of Senators: The Senate, Washington, D.C. 20510.

**ALABAMA**
1979–91 Howell T. Heflin (D) (1921)
1987–93 Richard C. Shelby (D) (1934)
**ALASKA**
1968–91 Ted Stevens (R) (1923)
1981–93 Frank H. Murkowski (R) (1933)
**ARIZONA**
1977–89 Dennis DeConcini (D) (1937)
1987–93 John McCain (R) (1936)
**ARKANSAS**
1975–93 Dale Bumpers (D) (1925)
1979–91 David H. Pryor (D) (1934)
**CALIFORNIA**
1969–93 Alan Cranston (D) (1914)
1983–89 Pete Wilson (R) (1933)
**COLORADO**
1979–91 William L. Armstrong (R) (1937)
1987–93 Timothy E. Wirth (D) (1939)
**CONNECTICUT**
1971–89 Lowell P. Weicker, Jr. (R) (1931)
1981–93 Christopher J. Dodd (D) (1944)
**DELAWARE**
1971–89 William V. Roth (R) (1921)
1973–91 Joseph R. Biden, Jr. (D) (1942)
**FLORIDA**
1971–89 Lawton Chiles (D) (1930)
1987–93 Bob Graham (D) (1936)
**GEORGIA**
1972–91 Sam Nunn (D) (1938)
1987–93 Wyche Fowler, Jr. (D) (1940)
**HAWAII**
1963–93 Daniel K. Inouye (D) (1924)
1977–89 Spark M. Matsunaga (D) (1916)
**IDAHO**
1973–91 James A. McClure (R) (1924)
1981–93 Steven D. Symms (R) (1938)
**ILLINOIS**
1981–93 Alan J. Dixon (D) (1927)
1985–91 Paul Simon (D) (1928)
**INDIANA**
1977–89 Richard G. Lugar (R) (1932)
1981–93 Dan Quayle (R) (1947)
**IOWA**
1981–93 Charles E. Grassley (R) (1933)
1985–91 Tom Harkin (D) (1939)
**KANSAS**
1969–93 Robert J. Dole (R) (1923)
1978–91 Nancy Landon Kassebaum (R) (1932)
**KENTUCKY**
1975–93 Wendell H. Ford (D) (1924)
1985–91 Mitch McConnell (R) (1942)
**LOUISIANA**
1971–91 J. Bennett Johnson (D) (1932)
1987–93 John B. Breaux (D) (1944)

**MAINE**
1979–91 William S. Cohen (R) (1940)
1980–89 George J. Mitchell (D) (1933)
**MARYLAND**
1977–89 Paul S. Sarbanes (D) (1933)
1987–93 Barbara A. Mikulski (D) (1936)
**MASSACHUSETTS**
1962–89 Edward M. Kennedy (D) (1932)
1985–91 John F. Kerry (D) (1943)
**MICHIGAN**
1977–89 Donald W. Riegle, Jr. (D) (1938)
1979–91 Carl Levin (D) (1934)
**MINNESOTA**
1978–89 David F. Durenberger (R) (1943)
1979–91 Rudy Boschwitz (R) (1930)
**MISSISSIPPI**
1947–89 John C. Stennis (D) (1901)
1978–91 Thad Cochran (R) (1937)
**MISSOURI**
1977–89 John C. Danforth (R) (1936)
1987–93 Christopher S. (Kit) Bond (R) (1939)
**MONTANA**
1977–89 John Melcher (D) (1924)
1979–91 Max Baucus (D) (1941)
**NEBRASKA**
1977–89 Edward Zorinsky (D) (1928)
1979–91 J. James Exon (D) (1921)
**NEVADA**
1983–89 Chic Hecht (R) (1928)
1987–93 Harry M. Reid (D) (1939)
**NEW HAMPSHIRE**
1979–91 Gordon J. Humphrey (R) (1940)
1981–93 Warren B. Rudman (R) (1930)
**NEW JERSEY**
1979–91 Bill Bradley (D) (1943)
1983–89 Frank R. Lautenberg (D) (1924)
**NEW MEXICO**
1973–91 Pete V. Domenici (R) (1932)
1983–89 Jeff Bingaman (D) (1943)
**NEW YORK**
1977–89 Daniel P. Moynihan (D) (1927)
1981–93 Alfonse M. D'Amato (R) (1937)
**NORTH CAROLINA**
1973–91 Jesse Helms (R) (1921)
1987–93 Terry Sanford (D) (1917)
**NORTH DAKOTA**
1960–89 Quentin N. Burdick (D) (1908)
1987–93 Kent Conrad (D) (1948)
**OHIO**
1975–93 John H. Glenn, Jr. (D) (1921)
1977–89 Howard M. Metzenbaum (D) (1917)
**OKLAHOMA**
1979–91 David L. Boren (D) (1941)
1981–93 Don Nickles (R) (1948)

**OREGON**
1967–91 Mark O. Hatfield (R) (1922)
1969–93 Bob Packwood (R) (1932)
**PENNSYLVANIA**
1977–89 John Heinz (R) (1938)
1981–93 Arlen Specter (R) (1930)
**RHODE ISLAND**
1961–91 Claiborne Pell (D) (1918)
1977–89 John H. Chafee (R) (1922)
**SOUTH CAROLINA**
1956–91 Strom Thurmond (R) (1902)
1966–93 Ernest F. Hollings (D) (1922)
**SOUTH DAKOTA**
1979–91 Larry Pressler (R) (1942)
1987–93 Thomas A. Daschle (D) (1947)
**TENNESSEE**
1977–89 James R. Sasser (D) (1936)
1985–91 Albert Gore, Jr. (D) (1948)
**TEXAS**
1971–89 Lloyd M. Bentsen (D) (1921)
1985–91 Phil Gramm (R) (1942)

**UTAH**
1975–93 E.J. (Jake) Garn (R) (1932)
1977–89 Orrin G. Hatch (R) (1934)
**VERMONT**
1971–89 Robert T. Stafford (R) (1913)
1975–93 Patrick J. Leahy (D) (1940)
**VIRGINIA**
1971–91 John W. Warner (R) (1927)
1983–89 Paul S. Trible, Jr. (R) (1946)
**WASHINGTON**
1983–89 Daniel L. Evans (R) (1925)
1987–93 Brock Adams (D) (1927)
**WEST VIRGINIA**
1959–89 Robert C. Byrd (D) (1918)
1985–91 John D. (Jay) Rockefeller IV (D) (1937)
**WISCONSIN**
1957–89 William Proxmire (D) (1915)
1981–93 Robert W. Kasten, Jr. (R) (1942)
**WYOMING**
1977–89 Malcom Wallop (R) (1933)
1979–91 Alan K. Simpson (R) (1931)

# The House of Representatives
### *Results undecided as of Nov. 5, 1986

The numerals indicate the Congressional Districts of the states; the designation AL means At Large. All terms end January 1989. Mailing address of Representatives: House of Representatives, Washington, D.C. 20515

**ALABAMA**
*(7 Representatives)*
1. H.L. (Sonny) Callahan (R)
2. William L. Dickinson (R)
3. William Nichols (D)
4. Thomas Bevill (D)
5. Ronald G. Flippo (D)
6. Ben Erdreich (D)
7. Claude Harris (D)

**ALASKA**
*(1 Representative)*
AL Don Young (R)

**ARIZONA**
*(5 Representatives)*
1. John J. Rhodes III (R)
2. Morris K. Udall (D)
3. Bob Stump (R)
4. Jon Kyl (R)
5. Jim Kolbe (R)

**ARKANSAS**
*(4 Representatives)*
1. Bill Alexander (D)
2. Tommy F. Robinson (D)
3. John Paul Hammerschmidt (R)
4. Beryl Anthony, Jr. (D)

**CALIFORNIA**
*(45 Representatives)*
1. Douglas H. Bosco (D)
2. Wally Herger (R)
3. Robert T. Matsui (D)
4. Vic Fazio (D)
5. Sala Burton (R)
6. Barbara Boxer (D)
7. George Miller (D)
8. Ronald V. Dellums (D)
9. Fortney H. (Pete) Stark (D)
10. Don Edwards (D)
11. Tom Lantos (D)
12. Ernest L. Konnyu (R)
13. Norman Y. Mineta (D)
14. Norman D. Shumway (R)
15. Tony Coelho (D)
16. Leon E. Panetta (D)
17. Charles Pashayan, Jr. (R)
18. Richard H. Lehman (D)
19. Robert J. Lagomarsino (R)
20. William M. Thomas (R)
21. Elton Gallegly (R)
22. Carlos J. Moorhead (R)
23. Anthony C. Beilenson (D)
24. Henry A. Waxman (D)
25. Edward R. Roybal (D)
26. Howard L. Berman (D)
27. Mel Levine (D)
28. Julian C. Dixon (D)
29. Augustus F. Hawkins (D)
30. Matthew G. Martinez (D)
31. Mervyn M. Dymally (D)
32. Glenn M. Anderson (D)
33. David Dreier (R)
34. Esteban Edward Torres (D)
35. Jerry Lewis (R)
36. George E. Brown, Jr. (D)
37. Al McCandless (R)
38. Robert K. Dornan (R)
39. William E. Dannemeyer (R)
40. Robert E. Badham (R)
41. William Lowery (R)
42. Dan Lungren (R)
43. Ron Packard (R)
44. James Bates (D)
45. Duncan L. Hunter (R)

**COLORADO**
*(6 Representatives)*
1. Patricia Schroeder (D)
2. David E. Skaggs (D)
3. Ben Nighthorse Campbell (D)
4. Hank Brown (R)
5. Joel Hefley (R)
6. Daniel L. Schaefer (R)

**CONNECTICUT**
*(6 Representatives)*
1. Barbara B. Kennelly (D)
2. Sam Gejdenson (D)
3. Bruce A. Morrison (D)
4. Stewart B. McKinney (R)
5. John G. Rowland (R)
6. Nancy L. Johnson (R)

**DELAWARE**
*(1 Representative)*
AL Thomas R. Carper (D)

**FLORIDA**
*(19 Representatives)*
1. Earl Hutto (D)
2. William Grant (D)
3. Charles E. Bennett (D)
4. William Chappell, Jr. (D)
5. Bill McCollum (R)
6. Kenneth H. MacKay (D)
7. Sam Gibbons (D)
8. C.W. Bill Young (R)
9. Michael Bilirakis (R)
10. Andy Ireland (D)
11. Bill Nelson (D)
12. Tom Lewis (R)
13. Connie Mack (R)
14. Daniel A. Mica (D)
15. E. Clay Shaw, Jr. (R)
16. Larry Smith (D)
17. William Lehman (D)
18. Claude Pepper (D)
19. Dante B. Fascell (D)

**GEORGIA**
*(10 Representatives)*
1. Robert Lindsay Thomas (D)
2. Charles Hatcher (D)
3. Richard Ray (D)
4. Patrick Lynn Swindall (R)
5. John Lewis (D)
6. Newt Gingrich (R)
7. George (Buddy) Darden (D)
8. J. Roy Rowland (D)
9. Edgar L. Jenkins (D)
10. Doug Bernard, Jr. (D)

**HAWAII**
*(2 Representatives)*
1. Patricia Saiki (R)
2. Daniel K. Akaka (D)

**IDAHO**
*(2 Representatives)*
1. Larry E. Craig (R)
2. Richard H. Stallings (D)

**ILLINOIS**
*(22 Representatives)*
1. Charles A. Hayes (D)
2. Gus Savage (D)
3. Marty Russo (D)
4. Jack Davis (R)
5. William O. Lipinski (D)
6. Henry J. Hyde (R)
7. Cardiss Collins (D)
8. Dan Rostenkowski (D)
9. Sidney R. Yates (D)
10. John Edward Porter (R)
11. Frank Annunzio (D)
12. Philip M. Crane (R)
13. Harris W. Fawell (R)
14. J. Dennis Hastert (R)
15. Edward R. Madigan (R)
16. Lynn Martin (R)
17. Lane Evans (D)
18. Robert H. Michel (R)
19. Terry L. Bruce (D)

20. Richard J. Durbin (D)
21. Melvin Price (D)
22. Kenneth J. Gray (D)

**INDIANA**
*(10 Representatives)*
1. Peter J. Visclosky (D)
2. Philip R. Sharp (D)
3. Thomas W. Ward (D)
4. Daniel Coats (R)
5. Jim Jontz (D)
6. Daniel Burton (R)
7. John T. Myers (R)
8. Frank McClosky (D)
9. Lee H. Hamilton (D)
10. Andrew Jacobs, Jr. (D)

**IOWA**
*(6 Representatives)*
1. Jim Leach (R)
2. Thomas J. Tauke (R)
3. Dave R. Nagle (D)
4. Neal Smith (D)
5. Jim Ross Lightfoot (R)
6. Fred Grandy (R)

**KANSAS**
*(5 Representatives)*
1. Pat Roberts (R)
2. James Slattery (D)
3. Jan Meyers (R)
4. Dan Glickman (D)
5. Bob Whittaker (R)

**KENTUCKY**
*(7 Representatives)*
1. Carroll Hubbard, Jr. (D)
2. William H. Natcher (D)
3. Romano L. Mazzoli (D)
4. Jim Bunning (R)
5. Harold Rogers (R)
6. Larry J. Hopkins (R)
7. Carl C. Perkins (D)

**LOUISIANA**
*(8 Representatives)*
1. Robert L. Livingston, Jr. (R)
2. Corrine C. (Lindy) Boggs (D)
3. W.J. (Billy) Tauzin (D)
4. Buddy Roemer (D)
5. Thomas J. Huckaby (D)
6. Richard Baker (R)
7. Jimmy Hayes (D)
8. Clyde Holloway (R)

**MAINE**
*(2 Representatives)*
1. Joseph E. Brennan (D)
2. Olympia J. Snowe (R)

**MARYLAND**
*(8 Representatives)*
1. Roy Dyson (D)
2. Helen Delich Bentley (R)
3. Benjamin L. Cardin (D)
4. Thomas McMillen (D)*
4. Robert R. Neall (R)*
5. Steny H. Hoyer (D)
6. Beverly B. Byron (D)
7. Kweisi Mfume (D)
8. Constance A. Morella (R)

**MASSACHUSETTS**
*(11 Representatives)*
1. Silvio O. Conte (R)
2. Edward P. Boland (D)
3. Joseph D. Early (D)
4. Barney Frank (D)
5. Chester G. Atkins (D)
6. Nicholas Mavroules (D)
7. Edward J. Markey (D)
8. Joseph P. Kennedy II (D)
9. Joe Moakley (D)
10. Gerry E. Studds (D)
11. Brian J. Donnelly (D)

**MICHIGAN**
*(18 Representatives)*
1. John Conyers, Jr. (D)
2. Carl D. Pursell (R)
3. Howard Wolpe (D)
4. Fred Upton (R)
5. Paul B. Henry (R)
6. Bob Carr (D)
7. Dale E. Kildee (D)
8. Bob Traxler (D)
9. Guy Vander Jagt (R)
10. Bill Schuette (R)
11. Robert W. Davis (R)
12. David E. Bonior (D)
13. George W. Crockett, Jr. (D)
14. Dennis M. Hertel (D)
15. William D. Ford (D)
16. John D. Dingell (D)
17. Sander M. Levin (D)
18. William S. Broomfield (R)

**MINNESOTA**
*(8 Representatives)*
1. Timothy J. Penny (D)
2. Vin Weber (R)
3. Bill Frenzel (R)
4. Bruce F. Vento (D)
5. Martin Olav Sabo (D)
6. Gerry Sikorski (D)
7. Arlan Stangeland (R)*
7. Collin C. Peterson (D)*
8. James L. Oberstar (D)

**MISSISSIPPI**
*(5 Representatives)*
1. Jamie L. Whitten (D)
2. Mike Espy (D)
3. G.V. (Sonny) Montgomery (D)
4. Wayne Dowdy (D)
5. Trent Lott (R)

**MISSOURI**
*(9 Representatives)*
1. William L. Clay (D)
2. Jack Buechner (R)
3. Richard A. Gephardt (D)
4. Ike Skelton (D)
5. Alan Wheat (D)
6. E. Thomas Coleman (R)
7. Gene Taylor (R)
8. William Emerson (R)
9. Harold L. Volkmer (D)

**MONTANA**
*(2 Representatives)*
1. Pat Williams (D)
2. Ron Marlenee (R)

**NEBRASKA**
*(3 Representatives)*
1. Douglas K. Bereuther (R)
2. Hal Daub (R)
3. Virginia Smith (R)

**NEVADA**
*(2 Representatives)*
1. James H. Bilbray (D)
2. Barbara F. Vucanovich (R)

**NEW HAMPSHIRE**
*(2 Representatives)*
1. Robert C. Smith (R)
2. Judd Gregg (R)

**NEW JERSEY**
*(14 Representatives)*
1. James J. Florio (D)
2. William J. Hughes (D)
3. James J. Howard (D)
4. Christopher H. Smith (R)
5. Marge Roukema (R)
6. Bernard J. Dwyer (D)
7. Matthew J. Rinaldo (R)
8. Robert A. Roe (D)
9. Robert G. Torricelli (D)

10. Peter W. Rodino, Jr. (D)
11. Dean A. Gallo (R)
12. Jim Courter (R)
13. H. James Saxton (R)
14. Frank J. Guarini (D)

**NEW MEXICO**
*(3 Representatives)*
1. Manuel Lujan, Jr. (R)
2. Joseph R. Skeen (R)
3. William Richardson (D)

**NEW YORK**
*(34 Representatives)*
1. George J. Hochbreuckner (D)
2. Thomas J. Downey (D)
3. Robert J. Mrazek (D)
4. Norman F. Lent (R)
5. Raymond J. McGrath (R)
6. Floyd H. Flake (D)
7. Gary L. Ackerman (D)
8. James H. Scheuer (D)
9. Thomas J. Manton (D)
10. Charles E. Schumer (D)
11. Edolphus Towns (D)
12. Major R. Owens (D)
13. Stephen J. Solarz (D)
14. Guy V. Molinari (R)
15. Bill Green (R)
16. Charles B. Rangel (D)
17. Ted Weiss (D)
18. Robert Garcia (D)
19. Mario Biaggi (D)
20. Joseph J. DioGuardi (R)
21. Hamilton Fish, Jr. (R)
22. Benjamin A. Gilman (R)
23. Samuel S. Stratton (D)
24. Gerald B.H. Solomon (R)
25. Sherwood Boehlert (R)
26. David O'B. Martin (R)
27. George C. Wortley (R)*
27. Rosemary S. Pooler (D)*
28. Matthew F. McHugh (D)
29. Frank Horton (R)
30. Louise M. Slaughter (D)
31. Jack F. Kemp (R)
32. John J. LaFalce (D)
33. Henry J. Nowak (D)
34. Amory Houghton, Jr. (R)

**NORTH CAROLINA**
*(11 Representatives)*
1. Walter B. Jones (D)
2. Tim Valentine (D)
3. Martin Lancaster (D)
4. David E. Price (D)
5. Stephen L. Neal (D)
6. Howard Coble (R)*
6. Robin Britt (D)*
7. Charlie Rose (D)
8. W.G. (Bill) Hefner (D)
9. J. Alex McMillan (R)
10. Cass Ballenger (R)
11. James McClure Clarke (D)

**NORTH DAKOTA**
*(1 Representative)*
AL Byron L. Dorgan (D)

**OHIO**
*(21 Representatives)*
1. Thomas A. Luken (D)
2. Willis D. Gradison (R)
3. Tony P. Hall (D)
4. Michael G. Oxley (R)
5. Delbert L. Latta (R)
6. Bob McEwen (R)
7. Michael DeWine (R)
8. Donald E. (Buz) Lukens (R)
9. Marcy Kaptur (D)
10. Clarence E. Miller (R)
11. Dennis E. Eckart (D)
12. John R. Kasich (R)
13. Don J. Pease (D)
14. Tom Sawyer (D)

# 44 Congress of the U.S.

15. David L. Jackson (D)
16. Ralph Regula (R)
17. James A. Traficant, Jr. (D)
18. Douglas Applegate (D)
19. Edward F. Feighan (D)
20. Mary Rose Oakar (D)
21. Louis Stokes (D)

**OKLAHOMA**
*(6 Representatives)*
1. James M. Inhofe (R)
2. Mike Synar (D)
3. Wesley W. Watkins (D)
4. Dave McCurdy (D)
5. Mickey Edwards (R)
6. Glenn English (D)

**OREGON**
*(5 Representatives)*
1. Les AuCoin (D)
2. Robert F. Smith (R)
3. Roland L. Wyden (D)
4. Peter A. DeFazio (D)
5. Denny Smith (R)

**PENNSYLVANIA**
*(23 Representatives)*
1. Thomas M. Foglietta (D)
2. William H. Gray III (D)
3. Robert A. Borski (D)
4. Joseph P. Kolter (D)
5. Richard T. Schulze (R)
6. Gus Yatron (D)
7. Curt Weldon (R)
8. Peter H. Kostmayer (D)
9. Bud Shuster (R)
10. Joseph M. McDade (R)
11. Paul E. Kanjorski (D)
12. John P. Murtha (D)
13. Lawrence Coughlin (R)
14. William J. Coyne (D)
15. Don Ritter (R)
16. Robert S. Walker (R)
17. George W. Gekas (R)
18. Doug Walgren (D)
19. William F. Goodling (R)
20. Joseph M. Gaydos (D)
21. Tom Ridge (R)
22. Austin J. Murphy (D)
23. William F. Clinger, Jr. (R)

**RHODE ISLAND**
*(2 Representatives)*
1. Fernand J. St. Germain (D)
2. Claudine J. Schneider (R)

**SOUTH CAROLINA**
*(6 Representatives)*
1. Arthur Ravenel, Jr. (R)
2. Floyd Spence (R)
3. Butler Derrick (D)
4. Elizabeth J. Patterson (D)
5. John M. Spratt, Jr. (D)
6. Robin Tallon (D)

**SOUTH DAKOTA**
*(1 Representative)*
AL Tim Johnson (D)

**TENNESSEE**
*(9 Representatives)*
1. James H. Quillen (R)
2. John J. Duncan (R)
3. Marilyn Lloyd (D)
4. James Cooper (D)
5. William H. Boner (D)
6. Bart Gordon (D)
7. Don Sundquist (R)
8. Ed Jones (D)
9. Harold E. Ford (D)

**TEXAS**
*(27 Representatives)*
1. Jim Chapman (D)
2. Charles Wilson (D)
3. Steven Bartlett (R)
4. Ralph M. Hall (D)
5. John Bryant (D)
6. Joe L. Barton (R)
7. Bill Archer (R)
8. Jack Fields (R)
9. Jack Brooks (D)
10. J.J. Pickle (D)
11. Marvin Leath (D)
12. Jim Wright (D)
13. Beau Boulter (R)
14. Mac Sweeney (R)
15. E. (Kika) de la Garza (D)
16. Ronald D. Coleman (D)
17. Charles W. Stenholm (D)
18. George T. (Mickey) Leland (D)
19. Larry Combest (R)
20. Henry B. Gonzalez (D)
21. Lamar Smith (R)
22. Thomas D. DeLay (R)
23. Albert G. Bustamante (D)
24. Martin Frost (D)
25. Michael A. Andrews (D)
26. Richard Armey (R)
27. Solomon R. Ortiz (D)

**UTAH**
*(3 Representatives)*
1. James V. Hansen (R)
2. Wayne Owens (D)
3. Howard C. Nielson (R)

**VERMONT**
*(1 Representative)*
AL James M. Jeffords (R)

**VIRGINIA**
*(10 Representatives)*
1. Herbert H. Bateman (R)
2. Owen B. Pickett (D)
3. Thomas J. Bliley, Jr. (R)
4. Norman Sisisky (D)
5. Dan Daniel (D)
6. James R. Olin (D)
7. D. French Slaughter, Jr. (R)
8. Stan Parris (R)
9. Frederick C. Boucher (D)
10. Frank R. Wolf (R)

**WASHINGTON**
*(8 Representatives)*
1. John R. Miller (R)
2. Al Swift (D)
3. Don L. Bonker (D)
4. Sid W. Morrison (R)
5. Thomas S. Foley (D)
6. Norman D. Dicks (D)
7. Mike Lowry (D)
8. Rodney Chandler (R)

**WEST VIRGINIA**
*(4 Representatives)*
1. Alan B. Mollohan (D)
2. Harley O. Staggers, Jr. (D)
3. Robert Wise (D)
4. Nick J. Rahall II (D)

**WISCONSIN**
*(9 Representatives)*
1. Les Aspin (D)
2. Robert W. Kastenmeier (D)
3. Steve Gunderson (R)
4. Gerald D. Kleczka (D)
5. James Moody (D)
6. Thomas E. Petri (R)
7. David R. Obey (D)
8. Toby Roth (R)
9. F. James Sensenbrenner, Jr. (R)

**WYOMING**
*(1 Representative)*
AL Dick Cheney (R)

## Facts About Elections

**Candidate with highest popular vote:** Reagan (1984), 54,455,075.
**Candidate with highest electoral vote:** Reagan (1984), 525.
**Candidate carrying most states:** Nixon (1972), and Reagan (1984), 49.
**Candidate running most times:** Norman Thomas, 6 (1928, 1932, 1936, 1940, 1944, 1948).
**Candidate elected, defeated, then reelected:** Cleveland (1884, 1888, 1892).

## Annual Salaries of Federal Officials

| | | | |
|---|---|---|---|
| President of the U.S. | $200,000 [1] | Secretaries of the Army, Navy, Air Force | 75,100 |
| Vice President of the U.S. | 97,900 [2] | Senators and Representatives | 75,100 |
| Cabinet members | 86,200 | President Pro Tempore of Senate | 85,000 |
| Under secretaries of executive departments | 68,700 | Majority and Minority Leader of the Senate | 85,000 |
| Deputy Secretaries of State, Defense, Treasury | 75,100 | Majority and Minority Leader of the House | 85,000 |
| Deputy Attorney General | 75,100 | Speaker of the House | 97,900 |
| Under Secretary of Transportation | 75,100 | Chief Justice of the United States | 104,700 |
| | | Associate Justices of the Supreme Court | 100,600 |

1. Plus taxable $50,000 for expenses and a nontaxable sum (not to exceed $100,000 a year) for travel expenses. 2. Plus taxable $10,000 for expenses. NOTE: All salaries shown above are taxable. Data are as of 1986.

# Senate and House Standing Committees, 99th Congress

## Committees of the Senate

**Agriculture, Nutrition, and Forestry** (17 members)
*Chairman:* Jesse Helms (N.C.)
*Ranking Dem.:* Edward Zorinsky (Neb.)
**Appropriations** (29 members)
*Chairman:* Mark O. Hatfield (Ore.)
*Ranking Dem.:* John C. Stennis (Miss.)
**Armed Services** (19 members)
*Chairman:* Barry Goldwater (Ariz.)
*Ranking Dem.:* Sam Nunn (Ga.)
**Banking, Housing, and Urban Affairs** (15 members)
*Chairman:* E.J. (Jake) Garn (Utah)
*Ranking Dem.:* William Proxmire (Wis.)
**Budget** (22 members)
*Chairman:* Pete V. Domenici (N.M.)
*Ranking Dem.:* Lawton Chiles (Fla.)
**Commerce, Science, and Transportation** (17 members)
*Chairman:* John C. Danforth (Mo.)
*Ranking Dem.:* Ernest F. Hollings (S.C.)
**Energy and Natural Resources** (18 members)
*Chairman:* James A. McClure (Idaho)
*Ranking Dem.:* J. Bennett Johnston (La.)
**Environment and Public Works** (15 members)
*Chairman:* Robert T. Stafford (Vt.)
*Ranking Dem.:* Lloyd M. Bentsen (Tex.)
**Finance** (20 members)
*Chairman:* Bob Packwood (Ore.)
*Ranking Dem.:* Russell B. Long (La.)
**Foreign Relations** (17 members)
*Chairman:* Richard G. Lugar (Ind.)
*Ranking Dem.:* Claiborne Pell (R.I.)
**Governmental Affairs** (13 members)
*Chairman:* William V. Roth, Jr. (Del.)
*Ranking Dem.:* Thomas F. Eagleton (Mo.)
**Judiciary** (18 members)
*Chairman:* Strom Thurmond (S.C.)
*Ranking Dem.:* Joseph R. Biden, Jr. (Del.)
**Labor and Human Resources** (16 members)
*Chairman:* Orrin G. Hatch (Utah)
*Ranking Dem.:* Edward M. Kennedy (Mass.)
**Rules and Administration** (15 members)
*Chairman:* Charles McC. Mathias, Jr. (Md.)
*Ranking Dem.:* Wendell H. Ford (Ky.)
**Small Business** (19 members)
*Chairman:* Lowell P. Weicker, Jr. (Conn.)
*Ranking Dem.:* Dale Bumpers (Ark.)
**Veterans' Affairs** (12 members)
*Chairman:* Frank H. Murkowski (Alas.)
*Ranking Dem.:* Alan Cranston (Calif.)

## Select and Special Committees

**Aging** (19 members)
*Chairman:* John Heinz (Pa.)
*Ranking Dem.:* John H. Glenn (Ohio.)
**Ethics** (6 members)
*Chairman:* Warren Rudman (N.H.)
*Vice Chairman:* Howell T. Heflin (Ala.)
**Indian Affairs** (9 members)
*Chairman:* Mark Andrews (N.D.)
*Ranking Dem.:* John Melcher (Mont.)
**Intelligence** (15 members)
*Chairman:* David Durenberger (Minn.)
*Vice Chairman:* Patrick L. Leahy (Vt.)

## Committees of the House

**Agriculture** (43 members)
*Chairman:* E. (Kika) de la Garza (Tex.)
*Ranking Repub.:* Edward R. Madigan (Ill.)
**Appropriations** (57 members)
*Chairman:* Jamie L. Whitten (Miss.)
*Ranking Repub.:* Silvio O. Conte (Mass.)
**Armed Services** (46 members)
*Chairman:* Les Aspin (Wis.)
*Ranking Repub.:* William L. Dickinson (Ala.)
**Banking, Finance, and Urban Affairs** (49 members)
*Chairman:* Fernand J. St. Germain (R.I.)
*Ranking Repub.:* Chalmers P. Wylie (Ohio)
**Budget** (33 members)
*Chairman:* William H. Gray, 3d (Pa.)
*Ranking Repub.:* Delbert L. Latta (Ohio)
**District of Columbia** (11 members)
*Chairman:* Ronald V. Dellums (Calif.)
*Ranking Repub.:* Stewart B. McKinney (Conn.)
**Education and Labor** (32 members)
*Chairman:* Augustus F. Hawkins (Cal.)
*Ranking Repub.:* James M. Jeffords (Vt.)
**Energy and Commerce** (42 members)
*Chairman:* John D. Dingell (Mich.)
*Ranking Repub.:* James T. Broyhill (N.C.)
**Foreign Affairs** (42 members)
*Chairman:* Dante B. Fascall (Fla.)
*Ranking Repub.:* William S. Broomfield (Mich.)
**Government Operations** (39 members)
*Chairman:* Jack Brooks (Tex.)
*Ranking Repub.:* Frank Horton (N.Y.)
**House Administration** (19 members)
*Chairman:* Frank Annunzio (Ill.)
*Ranking Repub.:* Bill Frenzel (Minn.)
**Interior and Insular Affairs** (42 members)
*Chairman:* Morris K. Udall (Ariz.)
*Ranking Repub.:* Don Young (Alas.)
**Judiciary** (35 members)
*Chairman:* Peter W. Rodino, Jr. (N.J.)
*Ranking Repub.:* Hamilton Fish, Jr. (N.Y.)
**Merchant Marine and Fisheries** (42 members)
*Chairman:* Walter B. Jones (N.C.)
*Ranking Repub.:* Norman F. Lent (N.Y.)
**Post Office and Civil Service** (21 members)
*Chairman:* William D. Ford (Mich.)
*Ranking Repub.:* Gene Taylor (Miss.)
**Public Works and Transportation** (48 members)
*Chairman:* James J. Howard (N.J.)
*Ranking Repub.:* Gene Snyder (Ky.)
**Rules** (13 members)
*Chairman:* Claude Pepper (Fla.)
*Ranking Repub.:* James H. Quillen (Tenn.)
**Science and Technology** (42 members)
*Chairman:* Don Fuqua (Fla.)
*Ranking Repub.:* Manuel Lujan, Jr. (N.M.)
**Small Business** (40 members)
*Chairman:* Parren J. Mitchell (Md.)
*Ranking Repub.:* Joseph M. McDade (Pa.)
**Standards of Official Conduct** (12 members)
*Chairman:* Julian C. Dixon (Calif.)
*Ranking Repub.:* Floyd D. Spence (S.C.)
**Veterans' Affairs** (33 members)
*Chairman:* G.V. (Sonny) Montgomery (Miss.)
*Ranking Repub.:* John P. Hammerschmidt (Ark.)
**Ways and Means** (35 members)
*Chairman:* Dan Rostenkowski (Ill.)
*Ranking Repub.:* John J. Duncan (Tenn.)

## Select Committees

**Aging** (60 members)
*Chairman:* Edward Roybal (Calif.)
*Ranking Repub.:* Matthew J. Rinaldo (N.J.)

**Intelligence** (16 members)
  *Chairman:* Lee H. Hamiliton (Ind.)
  *Ranking Repub.:* Bob Stump (Ariz.)

**Narcotics Abuse and Control** (25 members)
  *Chairman:* Charles B. Rangel (N.Y.)
  *Ranking Repub.:* Lawrence Coughlin (Pa.)

## Speakers of the House of Representatives

| Dates served | Congress | Name and state | Dates served | Congress | Name and state |
|---|---|---|---|---|---|
| 1789–1791 | 1 | Frederick A. C. Muhlenberg (Pa.) | 1863–1869 | 38–40 | Schuyler Colfax (Ind.) |
| 1791–1793 | 2 | Jonathan Trumbull (Conn.) | 1869–1869 | 40 | Theodore M. Pomeroy (N.Y.)[5] |
| 1793–1795 | 3 | Frederick A. C. Muhlenberg (Pa.) | 1869–1875 | 41–43 | James G. Blaine (Me.) |
| 1795–1799 | 4–5 | Jonathan Dayton (N.J.)[1] | 1875–1876 | 44 | Michael C. Kerr (Ind.)[6] |
| 1799–1801 | 6 | Theodore Sedgwick (Mass.) | 1876–1881 | 44–46 | Samuel J. Randall (Pa.) |
| 1801–1807 | 7–9 | Nathaniel Macon (N.C.) | 1881–1883 | 47 | J. Warren Keifer (Ohio) |
| 1807–1811 | 10–11 | Joseph B. Varnum (Mass.) | 1883–1889 | 48–50 | John G. Carlisle (Ky.) |
| 1811–1814 | 12–13 | Henry Clay (Ky.)[2] | 1889–1891 | 51 | Thomas B. Reed (Me.) |
| 1814–1815 | 13 | Langdon Cheves (S.C.) | 1891–1895 | 52–53 | Charles F. Crisp (Ga.) |
| 1815–1820 | 14–16 | Henry Clay (Ky.)[3] | 1895–1899 | 54–55 | Thomas B. Reed (Me.) |
| 1820–1821 | 16 | John W. Taylor (N.Y.) | 1899–1903 | 56–57 | David B. Henderson (Iowa) |
| 1821–1823 | 17 | Philip P. Barbour (Va.) | 1903–1911 | 58–61 | Joseph G. Cannon (Ill.) |
| 1823–1825 | 18 | Henry Clay (Ky.) | 1911–1919 | 62–65 | Champ Clark (Mo.) |
| 1825–1827 | 19 | John W. Taylor (N.Y.) | 1919–1925 | 66–68 | Frederick H. Gillett (Mass.) |
| 1827–1834 | 20–23 | Andrew Stevenson (Va.)[4] | 1925–1931 | 69–71 | Nicholas Longworth (Ohio) |
| 1834–1835 | 23 | John Bell (Tenn.) | 1931–1933 | 72 | John N. Garner (Tex.) |
| 1835–1839 | 24–25 | James K. Polk (Tenn.) | 1933–1934 | 73 | Henry T. Rainey (Ill.)[7] |
| 1839–1841 | 26 | Robert M. T. Hunter (Va.) | 1935–1936 | 74 | Joseph W. Byrns (Tenn.)[8] |
| 1841–1843 | 27 | John White (Ky.) | 1936–1940 | 74–76 | William B. Bankhead (Ala.)[9] |
| 1843–1845 | 28 | John W. Jones (Va.) | 1940–1947 | 76–79 | Sam Rayburn (Tex.) |
| 1845–1847 | 29 | John W. Davis (Ind.) | 1947–1949 | 80 | Joseph W. Martin, Jr. (Mass.) |
| 1847–1849 | 30 | Robert C. Winthrop (Mass.) | 1949–1953 | 81–82 | Sam Rayburn (Tex.) |
| 1849–1851 | 31 | Howell Cobb (Ga.) | 1953–1955 | 83 | Joseph W. Martin, Jr. (Mass.) |
| 1851–1855 | 32–33 | Linn Boyd (Ky.) | 1955–1961 | 84–87 | Sam Rayburn (Tex.)[10] |
| 1855–1857 | 34 | Nathaniel P. Banks (Mass.) | 1962–1971 | 87–91 | John W. McCormack (Mass.)[11] |
| 1857–1859 | 35 | James L. Orr (S.C.) | 1971–1977 | 92–94 | Carl Albert (Okla.)[12] |
| 1859–1861 | 36 | Wm. Pennington (N.J.) | 1977–1987 | 95–99 | Thomas P. O'Neill, Jr. (Mass.)[13] |
| 1861–1863 | 37 | Galusha A. Grow (Pa.) | | | |

1. George Dent (Md.) was elected Speaker pro tempore for April 20 and May 28, 1798. 2. Resigned during second session of 13th Congress. 3. Resigned between first and second sessions of 16th Congress. 4. Resigned during first session of 23rd Congress. 5. Elected Speaker and served the day of adjournment. 6. Died between first and second sessions of 44th Congress. During first session, there were two Speakers pro tempore: Samuel S. Cox (N.Y.), appointed for Feb. 17, May 12, and June 19, 1876, and Milton Sayler (Ohio), appointed for June 4, 1876. 7. Died in 1934 after adjournment of second session of 73rd Congress. 8. Died during second session of 74th Congress. 9. Died during third session of 76th Congress. 10. Died between first and second sessions of 87th Congress. 11. Not a candidate in 1970 election. 12. Not a candidate in 1976 election. 13. Not a candidate in 1986 election. *Source: Congressional Directory.*

## Floor Leaders of the Senate

| Democratic | Republican |
|---|---|
| Gilbert M. Hitchcock, Neb. (Min. 1919–20) | Charles Curtis, Kan. (Maj. 1925–29) |
| Oscar W. Underwood, Ala. (Min. 1920–23) | James E. Watson, Ind. (Maj. 1929–33) |
| Joseph T. Robinson, Ark. (Min. 1923–33, Maj. 1933–37) | Charles L. McNary, Ore. (Min. 1933–44) |
| Alben W. Barkley, Ky. (Maj. 1937–46, Min. 1947–48) | Wallace H. White, Jr., Me. (Min. 1944–47, Maj. 1947–48) |
| Scott W. Lucas, Ill. (Maj. 1949–50) | Kenneth S. Wherry, Neb. (Min. 1949–51) |
| Ernest W. McFarland, Ariz. (Maj. 1951–52) | Styles Bridges, N. H. (Min. 1951–52) |
| Lyndon B. Johnson, Tex. (Min. 1953–54, Maj. 1955–60) | Robert A. Taft, Ohio (Maj. 1953) |
| Mike Mansfield, Mont. (Maj. 1961–77) | William F. Knowland, Calif. (Maj. 1953–54, Min. 1955–58) |
| Robert C. Byrd, W. Va. (Maj. 1977–81, Min. 1981– ) | Everett M. Dirksen, Ill. (Min. 1959–69) |
| | Hugh Scott, Pa. (Min. 1969–1977) |
| | Howard H. Baker, Jr., Tenn. (Min. 1977–81, Maj. 1981–84) |
| | Robert J. Dole, Kan. (Maj. 1985– ) |

NOTE: Min. = Minority Leader; Maj. = Majority Leader. *Source:* United States Senate, Secretary for the Majority.

## Plurality and Majority

In order to win a plurality, a candidate must receive a greater number of votes than anyone running against him. If he receives 50 votes, for example, and two other candidates receive 49 and 2, he will have a plurality of one vote over his closest opponent.

However, a candidate does not have a majority unless he receives more than 50% of the total votes cast. In the example above, the candidate does not have a majority, because his 50 votes are less than 50% of the 101 votes cast.

# Presidential Election of 1984
## Principal Candidates for President and Vice President
### Republican: Ronald W. Reagan; George Bush
### Democratic: Walter F. Mondale; Geraldine A. Ferraro

| State | Total | *Reagan* Rep. | Per-cent | *Mondale* Dem. | Per-cent | Plurality | Electoral vote R | D |
|---|---|---|---|---|---|---|---|---|
| Alabama | 1,441,713 | 872,849 | 60.5 | 551,899 | 38.2 | 320,950 | 9 | — |
| Alaska | 209,605 | 138,377 | 66.6 | 62,007 | 29.8 | 76,370 | 3 | — |
| Arizona | 1,025,897 | 681,416 | 66.4 | 333,854 | 32.5 | 347,562 | 7 | — |
| Arkansas | 884,406 | 534,774 | 60.4 | 338,646 | 38.2 | 196,128 | 6 | — |
| California | 9,505,423 | 5,467,009 | 57.5 | 3,922,519 | 41.2 | 1,544,490 | 47 | — |
| Colorado | 1,295,380 | 821,817 | 63.4 | 454,975 | 35.1 | 366,842 | 8 | — |
| Connecticut | 1,466,900 | 890,877 | 60.7 | 569,597 | 38.8 | 321,280 | 8 | — |
| Delaware | 254,572 | 152,190 | 59.7 | 101,656 | 39.9 | 50,534 | 3 | — |
| D.C. | 211,288 | 29,009 | 13.7 | 180,408 | 85.3 | 151,399 | — | 3 |
| Florida | 4,180,051 | 2,730,350 | 65.3 | 1,448,816 | 34.6 | 1,281,534 | 21 | — |
| Georgia | 1,776,120 | 1,068,722 | 60.1 | 706,628 | 39.7 | 362,094 | 12 | — |
| Hawaii | 335,846 | 185,050 | 55.1 | 147,154 | 43.8 | 37,896 | 4 | — |
| Idaho | 411,144 | 297,523 | 72.3 | 108,510 | 26.3 | 189,013 | 4 | — |
| Illinois | 4,819,088 | 2,707,103 | 56.1 | 2,086,499 | 43.3 | 620,604 | 24 | — |
| Indiana | 2,233,069 | 1,377,230 | 61.6 | 841,481 | 37.6 | 535,749 | 12 | — |
| Iowa | 1,319,805 | 703,088 | 53.2 | 605,620 | 45.8 | 97,468 | 8 | — |
| Kansas | 1,021,991 | 677,296 | 66.2 | 333,149 | 32.6 | 344,147 | 7 | — |
| Kentucky | 1,369,345 | 821,702 | 60.1 | 539,539 | 39.4 | 282,163 | 9 | — |
| Louisiana | 1,706,822 | 1,037,299 | 60.7 | 651,586 | 38.1 | 385,713 | 10 | — |
| Maine | 553,144 | 336,500 | 60.8 | 214,515 | 38.7 | 121,985 | 4 | — |
| Maryland | 1,675,873 | 879,918 | 52.5 | 787,935 | 47.0 | 91,983 | 10 | — |
| Massachusetts | 2,559,453 | 1,310,936 | 51.2 | 1,239,606 | 48.4 | 163,313 | 13 | — |
| Michigan | 3,801,658 | 2,251,571 | 67.7 | 1,529,638 | 31.8 | 721,933 | 20 | — |
| Minnesota | 2,084,449 | 1,032,603 | 49.5 | 1,036,364 | 49.7 | 3,761 | — | 10 |
| Mississippi | 941,104 | 582,377 | 61.8 | 352,192 | 37.4 | 230,185 | 7 | — |
| Missouri | 2,122,783 | 1,274,188 | 60.0 | 848,583 | 39.9 | 425,605 | 11 | — |
| Montana | 384,377 | 232,450 | 60.4 | 146,742 | 38.1 | 85,708 | 4 | — |
| Nebraska | 652,090 | 460,054 | 70.5 | 187,866 | 28.8 | 272,188 | 5 | — |
| Nevada | 286,667 | 188,770 | 66.8 | 91,655 | 31.9 | 97,115 | 4 | — |
| New Hampshire | 389,066 | 267,051 | 68.6 | 120,395 | 30.9 | 146,656 | 4 | — |
| New Jersey | 3,217,862 | 1,933,630 | 60.0 | 1,261,323 | 39.2 | 672,307 | 16 | — |
| New Mexico | 514,370 | 307,101 | 59.7 | 201,769 | 39.2 | 105,332 | 5 | — |
| New York[1] | 6,806,810 | 3,664,763 | 53.8 | 3,119,609 | 45.8 | 545,154 | 36 | — |
| North Carolina | 2,175,361 | 1,346,481 | 61.9 | 824,287 | 37.8 | 522,194 | 13 | — |
| North Dakota | 308,971 | 200,336 | 64.8 | 104,429 | 33.8 | 95,907 | 3 | — |
| Ohio | 4,547,619 | 2,678,560 | 58.9 | 1,825,440 | 40.1 | 853,120 | 23 | — |
| Oklahoma | 1,255,676 | 861,530 | 68.6 | 385,080 | 30.6 | 476,450 | 8 | — |
| Oregon | 1,226,527 | 685,700 | 55.9 | 536,479 | 43.7 | 149,221 | 7 | — |
| Pennsylvania | 4,844,903 | 2,584,323 | 53.3 | 2,228,131 | 45.9 | 356,192 | 25 | — |
| Rhode Island | 410,492 | 212,080 | 51.6 | 197,106 | 48.0 | 14,974 | 4 | — |
| South Carolina | 968,529 | 615,539 | 63.5 | 344,459 | 35.5 | 271,080 | 8 | — |
| South Dakota | 317,867 | 200,267 | 63.0 | 116,113 | 36.5 | 84,154 | 3 | — |
| Tennessee | 1,711,994 | 990,212 | 57.8 | 711,714 | 41.5 | 278,498 | 11 | — |
| Texas | 5,397,571 | 3,433,428 | 63.6 | 1,949,276 | 36.1 | 1,484,152 | 29 | — |
| Utah | 629,656 | 469,105 | 74.5 | 155,369 | 24.6 | 313,736 | 5 | — |
| Vermont | 234,561 | 135,865 | 57.9 | 95,730 | 40.8 | 40,135 | 3 | — |
| Virginia | 2,146,635 | 1,337,078 | 62.2 | 796,250 | 37.0 | 540,828 | 12 | — |
| Washington | 1,883,910 | 1,051,670 | 55.8 | 807,352 | 42.8 | 244,318 | 10 | — |
| West Virginia | 735,742 | 405,483 | 55.1 | 328,125 | 44.6 | 77,358 | 6 | — |
| Wisconsin | 2,211,689 | 1,198,584 | 54.1 | 995,740 | 45.0 | 202,844 | 11 | — |
| Wyoming | 188,968 | 133,241 | 70.5 | 53,370 | 28.2 | 79,871 | 3 | — |
| **Total** | **92,652,842** | **54,455,075** | **58.7** | **37,577,185** | **40.5** | **16,877,890** | **525** | **13** |

1. Reagan figure is combined Republican and Conservative Party votes; Mondale figure is combined Democratic and Liberal Party votes. NATIONAL TOTALS OF OTHER CANDIDATES FOR PRESIDENT: David Bergland, Libertarian, 227,204; Lyndon H. LaRouche, Jr., Independent, 78,773; Sonia Johnson, Citizens, 71,976; Bob Richards, Populist 66,241; Dennis L. Serrette, Independent Alliance, 46,809; Gus Hall, Communist, 36,225; Mel Mason, Socialist Workers, 24,681; others and write-ins, 68,673. *Source: Federal Elections 84,* Federal Election Commission.

# The Governors of the Fifty States

| State | Governor | Current term[1] | State | Governor | Current term[1] |
|-------|----------|-----------------|-------|----------|-----------------|
| Ala. | Guy Hunt (R) | 1987–91 | Mont. | Tim Schwinden (D) | 1985–89 |
| Alaska | Steve Cowper (D) | 1987–91 | Neb. | Kay A. Orr (R) | 1987–91 |
| Ariz. | Evan Mechan (R) | 1987–91 | Nev. | Richard H. Bryan (D) | 1987–91 |
| Ark. | Bill Clinton (D) | 1987–91 | N.H. | John H. Sununu (R) | 1987–89 |
| Calif. | George Deukmejian (R) | 1987–91 | N.J. | Thomas H. Kean (R) | 1986–90 |
| Colo. | Roy Romer (D) | 1987–91 | N.M. | Garrey E. Carruthers (R) | 1987–91 |
| Conn. | William A. O'Neill (D) | 1987–91 | N.Y. | Mario M. Cuomo (D) | 1987–91 |
| Del. | Michael N. Castle (R) | 1985–89 | N.C. | James G. Martin (R) | 1985–89 |
| Fla. | Bob Martinez (R) | 1987–91 | N.D. | George Sinner (D) | 1985–89 |
| Ga. | Joe Frank Harris (D) | 1987–91 | Ohio | Richard F. Celeste (D) | 1987–91 |
| Hawaii | John Waikee (D) | 1986–90[2] | Okla. | Henry Bellmon (R) | 1987–91 |
| Idaho | Cecil D. Andrus (D) | 1987–91 | Ore. | Neil Goldschmidt (D) | 1987–91 |
| Ill. | James R. Thompson (R) | 1987–91 | Pa. | Robert P. Casey (D) | 1987–91 |
| Ind. | Robert D. Orr (R) | 1985–89 | R.I. | Edward DiPrete (R) | 1987–89 |
| Iowa | Terry E. Branstad (R) | 1987–91 | S.C. | Carroll A. Campbell, Jr. (R) | 1987–91 |
| Kan. | Mike Hayden (R) | 1987–91 | S.D. | George Mickelson (R) | 1987–91 |
| Ky. | Martha Layne Collins (D) | 1983–87[2] | Tenn. | Ned Ray McWherter (D) | 1987–91 |
| La. | Edwin W. Edwards (D) | 1984–88[3] | Tex. | William Clements (R) | 1987–91 |
| Me. | John R. McKernan, Jr. (R) | 1987–91 | Utah | Norman H. Bangerter (R) | 1985–89 |
| Md. | William Donald Schaefer (D) | 1987–91 | Vt. | Madeline M. Kunin (D)* | 1987–89 |
| Mass. | Michael S. Dukakis (D) | 1987–91 | Va. | Gerald L. Baliles (D) | 1986–90 |
| Mich. | James J. Blanchard (D) | 1987–91 | Wash. | Booth Gardner (D) | 1985–89 |
| Minn. | Rudy Perpich (D) | 1987–91 | W. Va. | Arch A. Moore, Jr. (R) | 1985–89 |
| Miss. | Bill Allain (D) | 1984–88 | Wis. | Tommy G. Thompson (R) | 1987–91 |
| Mo. | John Ashcroft (R) | 1985–89 | Wyo. | Mike Sullivan (D) | 1987–91 |

1. Except where indicated all terms begin in January. 2. December. 3. March. *Pending confirmation by state legislature.

# Black Elected Officials

| Year | U.S. and State Legislatures[1] | City and County Offices[2] | Law Enforcement[3] | Education[4] | Total |
|------|-------------------------------|----------------------------|--------------------|--------------|-------|
| 1970 (Feb.) | 182 | 715 | 213 | 362 | 1,472 |
| 1972 (Mar.) | 224 | 1,108 | 263 | 669 | 2,264 |
| 1973 (Apr.) | 256 | 1,264 | 334 | 767 | 2,621 |
| 1974 (Apr.) | 256 | 1,602 | 340 | 793 | 2,991 |
| 1975 (Apr.) | 299 | 1,878 | 387 | 939 | 3,503 |
| 1976 (Apr.) | 299 | 2,274 | 412 | 994 | 3,979 |
| 1977 (July) | 316 | 2,497 | 447 | 1,051 | 4,311 |
| 1978 (July) | 316 | 2,595 | 454 | 1,138 | 4,503 |
| 1979 (July) | 315 | 2,647 | 486 | 1,136 | 4,584 |
| 1980 (July) | 326 | 2,832 | 526 | 1,206 | 4,890 |
| 1981 (July) | 343 | 2,863 | 549 | 1,259 | 5,014 |
| 1982 (July) | 342 | 2,951 | 563 | 1,259 | 5,115 |
| 1983 (July) | 366 | 3,197 | 607 | 1,369 | 5,559 |
| 1984 (Jan.) | 396 | 3,259 | 636 | 1,363 | 5,654 |
| 1985 (Jan.) | 407 | 3,517 | 661 | 1,431 | 6,016[5] |
| 1986 (Jan.) | 420 | 3,824 | 676 | 1,504 | 6,424[5] |

1. Includes elected State administrators. 2. County commissioners and councilmen, mayors, vice mayors, aldermen, regional officials, and other. 3. Judges, magistrates, constables, marshals, sheriffs, justices of the peace, and other. 4. Members of State education agencies, college boards, school boards, and other. 5. Does not include Black elected officials in the Virgin Islands. *Source:* Joint Center for Political Studies, Washington, D.C., *Black Elected Officials: A National Roster,* Copyright.

# A Voting Majority Never Elected a President

In the 1964 election, Lyndon B. Johnson became the only President to almost succeed in receiving a majority of votes. He got 43,130,000 votes or 37.8% of those who were eligible to vote. The number of Americans of voting-age who did not vote that year was 43,445,000 or 38.1%.

The President who received the smallest share of votes from eligible Americans was Martin Van Buren, who obtained 11.4% of the ballots from voting-age Americans.

Since universal suffrage was enacted, Calvin Coolidge claimed the smallest percentage by receiving only 23.7% of the ballots from voting-age citizens.

# BUSINESS & ECONOMY

## Looking at the Future of American Business

*An Interview with Marvin Cetron by Timothy Willard*

**What sort of international competition will U.S. Business face in the future?**

Even America's strong new runners—electronics (principally computers, telecommunications, and semiconductors), biotechnology, and aerospace—will face stiff challenges in the coming years, sometimes from foreign nations that just a few years ago were dark-horse competitors. The U.S. steel and textile industries are in sorry shape, and they will have a tough struggle just to stay in the race with government-subsidized competitors from overseas. And there will be more failures of auto and chemical businesses.

**Just how will foreign nations be challenging U.S. businesses?**

The principal challenge for the United States will come from greater productivity—and therefore lower prices—from overseas. Take the automobile industry as an example. In 1950, nearly 80% of all motor vehicles were produced in the United States. By 1980, Detroit turned out eight million vehicles, the same number as in 1960. But Japan's output multiplied 23-fold from 1960 to 11.3 million vehicles.

The automobiles coming out from Detroit were long designed on the "planned obsolescence" theory; they were built to last only three years. Cars are going to last longer in the future. The average car now lasts for seven years and six months. This figure will increase to ten years by 1990 and to 22 years by the year 2000. At the same time, the number of automobile manufacturing companies will decline sharply. There will be only three or four automobile firms in the world by the year 2000. The auto industry will consolidate into a handful of global giants, with production centered in Korea, Italy, and Latin America.

For the past three decades, the productivity of U.S. workers, though still the best in the world, has paled beside the gains made by workers in Japan and continental Europe. More recently, developing nations like South Korea, Singapore, and Taiwan have been coming on strong. Unless this country's productivity picks up, and quickly, by 1990 the per-person output of the U.S. workforce will be matched and then surpassed in more than one overseas country.

**Where will investment dollars be going in the future?**

After 1995, Africa will emerge as the land of business opportunity. Its natural resources have yet to be exploited fully because of the precarious stability of most African countries augurs against long-term investments. But by the turn of the century, many African states will be more attractive to Western investors, and Africa will likely begin to assume the role of the last frontier for low-cost labor.

Other serious business competitors for investment dollars in the future will be South Korea, Singapore, Taiwan, Hong Kong, China, Indonesia, and Thailand. These countries will have a high level of automation and low wage rates, making them bargain investment spots. At the same time, budget-balancing efforts in the United States will probably drop interest rates, and thus the advantages of investing there will be less.

**Will Japan continue to be the United States' leading business competitor?**

Japan is heading for a nose dive that will continue through the early 1990's, then will level out. Its aggressive trading groups will go on giving fits to competitors, but for the foreseeable future—well into the next century—it won't regain anywhere near the overpowering presence in international circles that it commands today.

The cause of this nose dive will be a mix of internal and external factors, such as growing social service demands from an aging population, the strain of total reliance on imported energy and raw materials, and intensifying competition from Korea and other Pacific Rim nations—and then mainland China. Japan's chief hope of avoiding this slump is to become an innovator in technology, which appears dubious but is still an open issue.

**What can the United States do to better compete with foreign countries?**

As far as I'm concerned, if the United States doesn't balance its budget, we're going to have great difficulty competing with foreign nations, no matter what we do.

Our trade deficit is very large—and it's not because of trade barriers. The reason we can't sell our products overseas is very simple. The dollar is overpriced by 40–50%. This is because the U.S. government is bidding for the same money that corporations are, to service the national debt. This keeps interest rates high even though inflation is relatively low, so our products are overpriced. We can't afford to compete with foreign countries, so we lose jobs.

Marvin J. Cetron is a pioneer and expert in the area of technological forecasting and technological assessment. He is the founder and president of Forecasting International, Ltd., 1001 N. Highland St., Arlington, Va. 22210. Dr. Cetron is the author of numerous books. His most recent is The Future of American Business, co-authored with Alicia Pagano and Otis Port, McGraw-Hill, 1985.

Timothy Willard is Managing Editor of *The Futurist*, a publication of The World Future Society, 4916 St., Elmo Ave., Bethesda, Md. 20814. This interview is excerpted with permission from The *Futurist*, March-April 1986. Copyright © 1986 World Future Society.

The only way we're going to balance the budget is to bring down our defense budget and to bring down our entitlement programs and retire later. Economists can argue all day over this cut or that one in smaller budget categories, but all of the possibilities put together probably won't come to much more than $50 billion over President Reagan's remaining three years. That just won't be enough.

The administration and Congress must think in terms of $200 billion over the next three years; otherwise, the government will keep on bidding for money—and bidding up the interest rate. And as long as interest rates here are substantially higher than in Europe, foreign investments will flow into the United States and American exports will find limited markets.

**You've noted that international competition has reduced the number of jobs in the United States, particularly in areas such as automobile or steel manufacturing. Where will the job growth of the future be coming from?**

The bright spot, at least in terms of domestic job growth, is the service industries. This sector of the economy spans an extremely diverse spectrum. On the "high-tech" end are services such as information processing, writing computer software, and hazardous-waste disposal. Among the more traditional service businesses are banking, insurance, real estate, airlines and travel, fast-food restaurants, nursing homes and rental agencies.

Lumped together, services already account for 70% of all U.S. jobs and 60% of the gross national product. These figures will stand at 92% of jobs and 85% of the gross national product by the year 2000, maybe even higher. Close to half of all service jobs will be in some facet of information processing.

But while a few service jobs pay very well indeed—a Ph.D. in computer science with a specialization in artificial intelligence software practically guarantees a starting salary of $70,000—these jobs are relatively scarce, and the number of qualified applicants still more scarce. Most people in the service sector take home less money than the average unionized factory worker—sometimes a lot less.

The whole education system in the United States will have to be revamped. There's little point to training children to be unquestioningly obedient, to use their brains to do rote memorization, when there's no longer a need for industrial serfs for the country's factories. In the next several decades, companies will do a lot of retraining to help both blue-collar and white-collar workers secure other jobs—or to start up their own businesses.

Companies will retrain their employees—often using the now-underutilized facilities of private schools. These retraining programs will be funded partly by the companies, partly by government, and partly by the labor unions. Special entrepreneurial programs will be given by groups such as the Small Business Administration, designed to help employees start their own businesses. And more and more people will be getting training on their own, both to learn new skills and to keep their current training up to date.

In an increasingly technological society, retraining will be crucial. For example, 50% of what an engineer learns will be obsolete in five years. In ten years, that figure leaps to 90%. Retraining is obviously vital.

As increasing numbers of families have two wage earners—75% are expected by the year 2000—it will be easier for one spouse to return to school while the other continues working. In fact, we estimate that every four or five years one spouse will go back for some sort of retraining.

**Are you optimistic or pessimistic about the future?**

Let me begin by saying I'm not an optimist or a pessimist. I'm a realist. I take a look at the data, put it into a machine, and ask myself what it shows me.

Looking at the data coming out, I get extremely optimistic. We're going to live longer, and we're going to have more for everybody. Internationally, we're becoming more productive. The salary differential between men and women is getting smaller.

Sure, it's better in the United States than overseas. But we've got to bring them up to our level. We're not going down to their level.

## Displaced Workers Face High Unemployment

According to a Congressional study, only 60% of 11.5 million workers who lost jobs because of plant closings or relocations during the period 1979 to 1984 were able to obtain new employment. The typical displaced worker was described as a white, middle-aged male, with a long and stable job history, employed in manufacturing in the Middle West or Northeast. The study also showed that only 42% of blacks who had worked at least three years at their former jobs found employment again.

## Consumer Price Indexes
### (1967 = 100)

| Year | Commod-ities | Ser-vices | Hous-ing | All items | Percent change[1] | Year | Commod-ities | Ser-vices | Hous-ing | All items | Percent change[1] |
|------|-------------|-----------|----------|-----------|-----------|------|-------------|-----------|----------|-----------|-----------|
| 1940 | 40.6 | 43.6 | 52.4 | 42.0 | 1.0 | 1975 | 158.4 | 166.6 | 166.8 | 161.2 | 8.9 |
| 1945 | 56.3 | 48.2 | 59.1 | 53.9 | 2.3 | 1979 | 208.4 | 234.2 | 227.6 | 217.4 | 11.3 |
| 1950 | 78.8 | 58.7 | 72.8 | 72.1 | 1.0 | 1980 | 233.9 | 270.3 | 263.3 | 246.8 | 13.6 |
| 1955 | 85.1 | 70.9 | 82.3 | 80.2 | -0.4 | 1981 | 253.6 | 305.7 | 293.5 | 272.4 | 10.4 |
| 1960 | 91.5 | 83.5 | 90.2 | 88.7 | 1.6 | 1982 | 263.8 | 333.3 | 314.7 | 289.1 | 6.1 |
| 1965 | 95.7 | 92.2 | 94.9 | 94.5 | 1.7 | 1983 | 271.5 | 344.9 | 322.0 | 298.4 | 3.2 |
| 1970 | 113.5 | 121.6 | 118.9 | 116.3 | 5.9 | 1984 | 280.7 | 363.0 | 361.7 | 311.1 | 4.3 |

1. Over previous year. **Source:** Department of Labor, Bureau of Labor Statistics.

# Consumer Price Index for All Urban Consumers
## (1967 = 100)

| Group | Feb. 1986 | Feb. 1985 | Group | Feb. 1986 | Feb. 1985 |
|---|---|---|---|---|---|
| All items | 327.5 | 317.4 | Fuel oil, coal, bottled gas | 591.2 | 623.4 |
| Food | 315.3 | 309.5 | House operation[1] | 249.0 | 246.2 |
| Alcoholic beverages | 238.3 | 225.8 | House furnishings | 199.7 | 200.7 |
| Apparel and upkeep | 204.1 | 201.8 | Transportation | 319.2 | 314.3 |
| Men's and boys' apparel | 196.8 | 192.8 | Medical care | 422.3 | 393.8 |
| Women's and girls' apparel | 163.4 | 164.1 | Personal care | 289.1 | 278.2 |
| Footwear | 207.9 | 210.1 | Tobacco products | 344.7 | 323.2 |
| Housing, total | 356.5 | 343.6 | Entertainment | 272.0 | 266.3 |
| Rent | 273.7 | 258.4 | Personal and educational | | |
| Gas and electricity | 444.5 | 443.3 | expenses | 417.7 | 386.9 |

1. Combines house furnishings and operation. *Source:* Department of Labor, Bureau of Labor Statistics.

# Consumer Price Index for Urban Wage Earners and Clerical Workers
## (1967 = 100)

Effective January 1978, the Consumer Price Index was revised, with two indexes now being produced: A new index for All Urban Consumers covers 80% of the non-institutional population; the other index, the Consumer Price Index for Urban Wage Earners and Clerical Workers, covers about half of those included in the new index and is a major revision of the one that had been published for many years.

| | 1986[1] | 1985 | 1980 | 1975 | 1970 | 1965 | 1960 | 1955 | 1950 |
|---|---|---|---|---|---|---|---|---|---|
| All items | 321.4 | 318.5 | 247.0 | 161.2 | 116.3 | 94.5 | 88.7 | 80.2 | 72.1 |
| Food total | 309.0 | 301.8 | 255.3 | 175.4 | 114.9 | 94.4 | 88.0 | 81.6 | — |
| Apparel and upkeep | 205.1 | 205.0 | 177.4 | 142.3 | 116.1 | 93.7 | 89.6 | 84.1 | 79.0 |
| Housing total | 351.6 | 343.3 | 263.2 | 166.8 | 118.9 | 94.9 | 90.2 | 82.3 | 72.8 |
| Rent | 277.5 | 263.7 | 191.3 | 137.3 | 110.1 | 96.9 | 91.7 | 84.3 | 70.4 |
| Gas and electricity | 443.0 | 451.6 | 301.2 | 169.6 | 107.3 | 99.4 | 98.6 | 87.5 | 81.2 |
| Fuel oil, coal, bottled gas | 499.9 | 622.0 | 557.2 | 253.3 | 110.1 | 94.6 | 89.2 | 82.3 | 72.7 |
| House operation[2] | 246.1 | 243.4 | 202.9 | 158.1 | 113.4 | 95.3 | 93.8 | 89.9 | — |
| House furnishings | 198.4 | 197.6 | 172.6 | 144.4 | 111.4 | 97.1 | 99.3 | 99.2 | 95.5 |
| Transportation | 305.9 | 321.6 | 250.5 | 150.6 | 112.7 | 95.9 | 89.6 | 77.4 | 68.2 |
| Medical care | 427.3 | 401.2 | 267.2 | 168.6 | 120.6 | 89.5 | 79.1 | 64.8 | 53.7 |
| Personal care | 288.6 | 279.6 | 212.7 | 150.7 | 113.2 | 95.2 | 90.1 | 77.9 | 68.3 |
| Entertainment | 267.3 | 260.1 | 203.7 | 144.4 | 113.4 | 95.9 | 87.3 | 76.7 | 74.4 |

1. May 1986. 2. Combines house furnishings and operation. *Source:* Department of Labor, Bureau of Labor Statistics.

# Total Family Income
## (figures in percent)

| | White | | | | Black and other races | | | |
|---|---|---|---|---|---|---|---|---|
| Income range | 1984 | 1980 | 1970 | 1960 | 1984 | 1980 | 1970 | 1960 |
| Families (thousands)[1] | 54,400 | 52,710 | 46,535 | 41,123 | 8,306 | 7,599 | 5,413 | 4,333 |
| Under $2,500 | 1.6 | 1.6 | 5.6 | 15.1 | 4.4 | 5.0 | 15.6 | 39.8 |
| $2,500 to $7,499 | 5.9 | 8.6 | 25.8 | 52.9 | 18.0 | 22.5 | 41.4 | 48.9 |
| $7,500 to $12,499 | 9.7 | 13.1 | 33.4 | 24.6 | 16.1 | 18.5 | 25.6 | 9.9 |
| $12,500 to $14,999 | 5.0 | 6.8 | 11.5 | 3.3 | 6.4 | 7.4 | 6.5 | 0.9 |
| $15,000 to $19,999 | 10.7 | 14.1 | 13.8 | 2.2 | 11.8 | 12.8 | 7.4 | 0.3 |
| $20,000 to $24,999 | 11.0 | 14.2 | 4.9 | 0.9 | 9.2 | 10.6 | 2.1 | 0.3 |
| $25,000 to $34,999 | 19.8 | 20.8 | 3.2 | — | 13.8 | 12.9 | 1.1 | — |
| $35,000 to $49,999 | 19.4 | 13.6 | 1.2 | 1.1 | 12.1 | 7.6 | 0.3 | — |
| $50,000 and over | 16.9 | 7.2 | 0.6 | — | 8.2 | 2.8 | 0.1 | — |
| Median income | $27,686 | $21,904 | $10,236 | $5,835 | $17,098 | $13,843 | $6,516 | $3,230 |

1. As of March 1985. *Source:* Department of Commerce, Bureau of the Census.

# Per Capita Personal Income

| Year | Amount | Year | Amount | Year | Amount | Year | Amount | Year | Amount |
|------|--------|------|--------|------|--------|------|--------|------|--------|
| 1929 | $705 | 1960 | $2,219 | 1968 | 3,433 | 1974 | 5,428 | 1980 | 9,511 |
| 1935 | 474 | 1963 | 2,460 | 1969 | 3,667 | 1975 | 5,851 | 1981 | 10,517 |
| 1940 | 593 | 1964 | 2,592 | 1970 | 3,893 | 1976 | 6,402 | 1982 | 11,100 |
| 1945 | 1,223 | 1965 | 2,773 | 1971 | 4,132 | 1977 | 7,043 | 1983 | 11,675 |
| 1950 | 1,501 | 1966 | $2,987 | 1972 | $4,493 | 1978 | $7,729 | 1984 | 12,700 |
| 1955 | 1,881 | 1967 | 3,167 | 1973 | 4,980 | 1979 | 8,638 | 1985 | 13,451 |

*Source:* Department of Commerce, Bureau of Economic Analysis.

# Median Weekly Earnings of Full-Time Workers by Occupation and Sex

| Occupation | MEN | | WOMEN | | TOTAL | |
|------------|-----|-----|-------|-----|-------|-----|
| | Number of workers (in thousands) | Median weekly earnings | Number of workers (in thousands) | Median weekly earnings | Number of workers (in thousands) | Median weekly earnings |
| Managerial and prof. specialty | 11,281 | 605 | 8,692 | 415 | 19,973 | $504 |
| Executive, admin, and managerial | 5,983 | 614 | 3,753 | 401 | 9,736 | 515 |
| Professional specialty | 5,298 | 596 | 4,939 | 424 | 10,237 | 496 |
| Technical, sales, and admin. support | 9,089 | 423 | 15,174 | 281 | 24,262 | 317 |
| Technicians and related support | 1,553 | 484 | 1,133 | 340 | 2,686 | 413 |
| Sales occupations | 4,523 | 425 | 3,018 | 244 | 7,541 | 355 |
| Administrative support, incl. clerical | 3,012 | 393 | 11,023 | 281 | 14,036 | 296 |
| Service occupations | 3,903 | 287 | 3,974 | 192 | 7,877 | 225 |
| Private household | 21 | ([1]) | 314 | 118 | 334 | 121 |
| Protective service | 1,424 | 395 | 147 | 285 | 1,572 | 386 |
| Service, except private household and protective | 2,459 | 242 | 3,513 | 196 | 5,972 | 211 |
| Precision production, craft, and repair | 9,945 | 418 | 860 | 284 | 10,805 | 409 |
| Mechanics and repairers | 3,664 | 417 | 151 | 438 | 3,815 | 418 |
| Construction trades | 3,423 | 396 | 65 | ([1]) | 3,487 | 395 |
| Other precision production, craft, and repair | 2,859 | 449 | 645 | 265 | 3,503 | 412 |
| Operators, fabricators, and laborers | 10,815 | 336 | 3,373 | 231 | 14,189 | 305 |
| Machine operators, assemblers, and inspectors | 4,449 | 358 | 2,720 | 229 | 7,170 | 298 |
| Transportation and material moving occupations | 3,483 | 370 | 190 | 294 | 3,673 | 365 |
| Handlers, equipment cleaners, helpers, and laborers | 2,883 | 272 | 463 | 222 | 3,346 | 265 |
| Farming, forestry, and fishing | 1,262 | 220 | 140 | 192 | 1,402 | 217 |

1. Data not shown where base is less than 100,000. NOTE: Figures are for the second quarter of 1986. *Source:* U.S. Department of Labor, Bureau of Labor Statistics, "Employment and Earnings," July 1986.

# The Public Debt

| Year | Gross debt | | Year | Gross debt | |
|------|------------|-----------|------|------------|-----------|
| | Amount (in millions) | Per capita | | Amount (in millions) | Per capita |
| 1800 (Jan. 1) | $ 83 | $ 15.87 | 1950 | $256,087 [2] | $1,688.30 |
| 1860 (June 30) | 65 | 2.06 | 1955 | 272,807 [2] | 1,650.63 |
| 1865 | 2,678 | 75.01 | 1960 | 284,093 [2] | 1,572.31 |
| 1900 | 1,263 | 16.60 | 1965 | 313,819 [2] | 1,612.70 |
| 1920 | 24,299 | 228.23 | 1970 | 370,094 [2] | 1,807.09 |
| 1925 | 20,516 | 177.12 | 1975 | 533,189 | 2,496.90 |
| 1930 | 16,185 | 131.51 | 1980 | 907,701 | 3,969.55 |
| 1935 | 28,701 | 225.55 | 1983 | 1,377,210 | 5,857.42 |
| 1940 | 42,968 | 325.23 | 1984 | 1,572,266 | 6,626.57 |
| 1945 | 258,682 | 1,848.60 | 1985 [1] | 1,823,103 | 7,514.51 |

1. Preliminary, Sept. 30, 1985. 2. Adjusted to exclude issues to the international Monetary Fund and other international lending institutions to conform to the budget presentation. *Source:* Department of the Treasury, Financial Management Service.

## Gross National Product or Expenditure

### (in billions)

| Item | 1985 | 1984 | 1983 | 1982 | 1980 | 1970 | 1960 | 1950 | 1929 |
|---|---|---|---|---|---|---|---|---|---|
| Gross national product | $3,988 | $3,774 | $3,304 | $3,073 | $2,626 | $982 | $506 | $286 | $103 |
| GNP in constant (1972) dollars[1] | 3,570 | 3,492 | 1,534 | 1,485 | 1,481 | 1,075 | 737 | 534 | 315 |
| Personal consumption expenditures | 2,582 | 2,423 | 2,155 | 1,992 | 1,673 | 619 | 325 | 192 | 77 |
| Durable goods | 362 | 331 | 279 | 245 | 212 | 85 | 43 | 31 | 9 |
| Nondurable goods | 912 | 872 | 801 | 761 | 676 | 265 | 151 | 98 | 38 |
| Services | 1,309 | 1,220 | 1,074 | 986 | 785 | 269 | 131 | 63 | 30 |
| Gross private domestic investment | 669 | 674 | 471 | 414 | 395 | 141 | 76 | 54 | 16 |
| Residential structures | 186 | 179 | 128 | 91 | 105 | 36 | 24 | 20 | 4 |
| Nonresidential structures | 476 | 428 | 129 | 348 | 109 | 38 | 18 | 9 | 5 |
| Producers' durable equipment | 306 | 280 | 226 | 210.8 | 190 | 64 | 30 | 18 | 6 |
| Change in business inventories | 8 | 67 | −13 | −24 | −6 | 4 | 4 | 7 | 2 |
| Net export of goods and services | −79 | −59 | −8 | 17 | 23 | 4 | 4 | 2 | 1 |
| Government purchases | 815 | 737 | 685 | 649 | 535 | 219 | 100 | 38 | 8 |
| Federal | 355 | 313 | 269 | 649 | 199 | 96 | 54 | 19 | 1 |
| National defense | 261 | 237 | 200 | 259 | 132 | 74 | 44 | 14 | n.a. |
| Other | 93 | 76 | 69 | 179 | 67 | 22 | 9 | 5 | n.a. |
| State and local | 460 | 424 | 415 | 79 | 336 | 123 | 47 | 20 | 7 |
| Implicit price deflator[1] | 111 | 108 | 215 | 415 | 177 | 91 | 69 | 54 | 33 |

1. For 1984 and 1985 GNP in constant (1982) dollars. NOTE: n.a. = not available. *Source:* Department of Commerce, Bureau of Economic Analysis.

## Producer Price Indexes by Major Commodity Groups

### (1967 - 100)

| Commodity | 1985[1] | 1980 | 1975 | 1970 | 1965 | 1960 | 1955 |
|---|---|---|---|---|---|---|---|
| All commodities | 309.5 | 268.8 | 174.9 | 110.4 | 96.6 | 94.9 | 87.8 |
| Farm products | 229.4 | 249.4 | 186.7 | 111.0 | 98.7 | 97.2 | 98.2 |
| Processed foods | 258.8 | 241.2 | 182.6 | 112.1 | 95.5 | 89.5 | 85.0 |
| Textile products and apparel | 210.2 | 183.5 | 137.9 | 107.1 | 99.8 | 99.5 | 98.7 |
| Hides, skins, and leather products | 285.2 | 248.9 | 148.5 | 110.3 | 94.3 | 90.8 | 77.3 |
| Fuels and related products and power | 645.7 | 574.0 | 245.1 | 106.2 | 95.5 | 96.1 | 91.2 |
| Chemicals and allied products | 303.4 | 260.3 | 181.3 | 102.2 | 99.0 | 101.8 | 98.5 |
| Rubber and plastic products | 246.1 | 217.4 | 150.2 | 108.3 | 95.9 | 103.1 | 102.4 |
| Lumber and wood products | 313.8 | 288.9 | 176.9 | 113.6 | 95.9 | 95.3 | 97.1 |
| Pulp, paper, and allied products | 327.0 | 249.2 | 170.4 | 108.2 | 96.2 | 98.1 | 87.8 |
| Metals and metal products | 315.1 | 286.4 | 185.6 | 116.6 | 96.4 | 92.4 | 82.1 |
| Machinery and equipment | 299.1 | 239.8 | 161.4 | 111.4 | 93.9 | 92.0 | 75.7 |
| Furniture and household durables | 221.5 | 187.7 | 139.7 | 107.5 | 96.9 | 99.0 | 93.3 |
| Nonmetallic mineral products | 348.5 | 283.0 | 174.0 | 112.9 | 97.5 | 97.2 | 87.5 |
| Transportation equipment (Dec. 1968—100) | 269.4 | 207.0 | 141.5 | 104.6 | 98.5 | 98.8 | — |
| Miscellaneous products | 300.9 | 258.8 | 147.7 | 109.9 | 95.9 | 93.0 | 86.5 |

1. To June 1985. *Source:* Department of Labor, Bureau of Labor Statistics.

## Life Insurance in Force

### (in millions of dollars)

| As of Dec. 31 | Ordinary | Group | Industrial | Credit | Total |
|---|---|---|---|---|---|
| 1915 | $16,650 | $100 | $4,279 | — | $21,029 |
| 1930 | 78,756 | 9,801 | 17,693 | 73 | 106,413 |
| 1945 | 101,550 | 22,172 | 27,675 | 365 | 151,762 |
| 1950 | 149,071 | 47,793 | 33,415 | 3,844 | 234,168 |
| 1955 | 216,812 | 101,345 | 39,682 | 14,493 | 373,332 |
| 1960 | 341,881 | 175,903 | 39,563 | 29,101 | 586,448 |
| 1965 | 499,638 | 308,078 | 39,818 | 53,020 | 900,554 |
| 1970 | 734,730 | 551,357 | 38,644 | 77,392 | 1,402,123 |
| 1980 | 1,760,474 | 1,579,355 | 35,994 | 165,215 | 3,541,038 |
| 1983 | 2,544,275 | 2,219,573 | 31,354 | 170,659 | 4,965,861 |
| 1984 | 2,887,574 | 2,392,358 | 30,104 | 189,951 | 5,499,987 |
| 1985 | 3,247,289 | 2,561,595 | 28,250 | 215,973 | 6,053,107 |

*Source:* American Council of Life Insurance.

## Farm Indexes

### (1977 - 100)

| Year | Prices paid by farmers[1] | Prices rec'd by farmers[2] | Ratio |
|---|---|---|---|
| 1950 | 37 | 56 | 151 |
| 1955 | 40 | 51 | 128 |
| 1960 | 44 | 52 | 118 |
| 1965 | 49 | 54 | 115 |
| 1970 | 56 | 60 | 109 |
| 1975 | 90 | 101 | 113 |
| 1980 | 137 | 134 | 97 |
| 1983 | 156 | 135 | 84 |
| 1984 | 160 | 142 | 86 |
| 1985 | 160 | 129 | 79 |

1. Commodities, interest, and taxes, and wage rates. 2. All crops and livestock. *Source:* Department of Agriculture, Statistical Reporting Service.

# 54 Business and the Economy

## Consumer Credit
(installment credit outstanding; in billions of dollars, seasonally adjusted)

| Holder | 1985 | 1984 | 1983 | 1982 | 1981 | 1980 | 1979 | 1975 |
|---|---|---|---|---|---|---|---|---|
| Commercial banks | 240.8 | 209.2 | 169.3 | 149.1 | 146.0 | 145.6 | 152.7 | 83.0 |
| Finance companies | 120.1 | 96.1 | 86.2 | 77.0 | 73.1 | 63.8 | 57.1 | 32.7 |
| Credit unions | 75.1 | 66.5 | 53.1 | 46.9 | 45.6 | 43.7 | 46.1 | 25.5 |
| Retailers[1] | 39.2 | 37.1 | 34.2 | 29.4 | 28.5 | 26.1 | 25.6 | 16.7 |
| Other[2] | 59.9 | 44.7 | 33.5 | 24.8 | 21.1 | 18.5 | 15.0 | 9.2 |
| Total | 535.1 | 453.6 | 376.3 | 327.2 | 314.3 | 297.7 | 296.5 | 167.7 |

1. Excludes 30-day charge credit held by retailers, oil and gas companies, and travel and entertainment companies. 2. Includes mutual savings banks, savings and loan associations, and gasoline companies. *Source:* Federal Reserve Bulletin.

## Estimated Annual Retail and Wholesale Sales by Kind of Business
(in millions of dollars)

| Kind of business | 1985 | 1980 |
|---|---|---|
| Retail trade, total | 1,373,941 | 959,561 |
| Building materials, hardware, garden supply, and mobile home dealers | 74,062 | 50,703 |
| Automotive dealers | 312,793 | 164,365 |
| Furniture, home furnishings, and equipment stores | 68,112 | 44,058 |
| General merchandise group stores | 159,456 | 113,905 |
| Food stores | 282,198 | 219,493 |
| Gasoline service stations | 100,767 | 93,811 |
| Apparel and accessory stores | 69,673 | 48,102 |
| Eating and drinking places | 131,035 | 89,924 |
| Drug stores and proprietary stores | 46,014 | 30,707 |
| Liquor stores | 17,802 | 16,799 |
| Merchant wholesale trade, total | 1,374,752 | 1,124,451 |
| Total, (excluding farm-product raw materials) | 1,281,500 | 999,018 |
| Durable goods, total | 630,312 | 483,079 |
| Motor vehicles and automotive parts and supplies | 132,391 | 83,142 |

| Kind of business | 1985 | 1980 |
|---|---|---|
| Furniture and home furnishings | 24,210 | 16,276 |
| Lumber and other construction materials | 46,193 | 36,390 |
| Electrical goods | 88,753 | 48,889 |
| Hardware, plumbing, heating and supplies | 41,263 | 29,109 |
| Machinery, equipment, supplies | 165,820 | 140,680 |
| Scrap and waste materials | (s) | 17,244 |
| Nondurable goods, total | 744,440 | 641,372 |
| Total, (excluding farm-product raw materials) | 651,188 | 515,939 |
| Paper and paper products | 36,798 | 22,608 |
| Drugs, drug proprietaries, and druggists' sundries | 25,095 | 13,607 |
| Apparel, piece goods, and notions | 40,701 | 28,506 |
| Groceries and related products | 217,085 | 155,372 |
| Beer, wine, distilled alcoholic beverages | 39,358 | 31,911 |
| Miscellaneous nondurable goods | 104,008 | 77,501 |
| Tobacco and tobacco products | (s) | 12,158 |

NOTE: (S) = does not meet publication standards. *Source:* Department of Commerce, Bureau of the Census.

## Weekly Earnings of Full-Time Women Workers

| Major occupation group | 1985 weekly earnings | % Men's weekly earnings |
|---|---|---|
| Managerial and professional specialty | $399 | 68.4 |
| Executive, administrative, and managerial | 383 | 64.6 |
| Professional specialty | 408 | 71.4 |
| Technical, sales, and administrative support | 269 | 64.0 |
| Technicians and related support | 331 | 70.1 |
| Sales occupations | 226 | 52.4 |
| Administrative support, including clerical | 270 | 69.0 |
| Service occupations | 185 | 68.0 |
| Precision production, craft, and repair | 268 | 65.7 |
| Operators, fabricators, and laborers | 216 | 66.5 |
| Machine operators, assemblers, and inspectors | 216 | 63.3 |
| Transportation and material moving | 252 | 68.3 |
| Handlers, equipment cleaners, helpers, and laborers | 209 | 80.1 |
| Farming, forestry, and fishing | 185 | 85.6 |
| Total; all occupations | 277 | 68.2 |

1. Median usual weekly earnings. Half the workers earn more and half the workers usually earn less each week. *Source:* U.S. Department of Labor, Bureau of Labor Statistics.

## Median Family Income
(in current dollars)

| Year | Income | Percent change | Year | Income | Percent change |
|---|---|---|---|---|---|
| 1960 | $ 5,620 | — | 1980 | 21,023 | 6.9 |
| 1970 | 9,867 | — | 1981 | 22,388 | 6.5 |
| 1974 | 12,902 | 7.1 | 1982 | 23,433 | 4.7 |
| 1975 | 13,719 | 6.3 | 1983 | 24,580 | 4.9 |
| 1978 | 17,640 | 10.2 | 1984 | 25,948 | 5.1 |
| 1979 | 19,661 | 11.5 | 1985 | 27,144 | 5.0 |

*Source:* U.S. Department of Labor, Bureau of Labor Statistics, *Employment and Earnings.*

## Expenditures for New Plant and Equipment[1]
### (in billions of dollars)

| Year | Manufac- turing | Transpor- tation[2] | Total nonmanu- fac- turing | Total |
|------|------|------|------|------|
| 1950 | $7.73 | $2.87 | $18.08 | $25.81 |
| 1955 | 12.50 | 3.10 | 24.58 | 37.08 |
| 1960 | 16.36 | 3.54 | 32.63 | 48.99 |
| 1965 | 25.41 | 5.66 | 45.39 | 70.79 |
| 1970 | 36.99 | 7.17 | 69.16 | 106.15 |
| 1975 | 53.66 | 9.95 | 108.95 | 162.60 |
| 1978 | 78.58 | 13.36 | 166.76 | 245.34 |
| 1979 | 95.92 | 16.05 | 189.02 | 284.94 |
| 1980 | 112.33 | 16.60 | 202.15 | 314.47 |
| 1981 | 126.54 | 15.84 | 222.72 | 349.26 |
| 1982 | 120.68 | 14.79 | 226.79 | 347.47 |
| 1983 | 116.20 | 13.97 | 227.15 | 343.35 |
| 1985 | 153.15 | 17.97 | 278.07 | 431.21 |

1. Data exclude agriculture. 2. Transportation is included in total nonmanufacturing. NOTE: This series was revised in February 1985. *Source:* Department of Commerce, Bureau of Economic Analysis.

## New Housing Starts[1] and Mobile Homes Shipped
### (in thousands)

| Year | No. of units started | Year | No. of units started | Year | Mobile homes shipped |
|------|------|------|------|------|------|
| 1900 | 189 | 1970 | 1,469 | 1965 | 217 |
| 1910 | 387 | 1975 | 1,171 | 1970 | 401 |
| 1920 | 247 | 1976 | 1,548 | 1975 | 213 |
| 1925 | 937 | 1977 | 2,002 | 1977 | 277 |
| 1930 | 330 | 1978 | 2,036 | 1978 | 276 |
| 1935 | 221 | 1979 | 1,760 | 1979 | 277 |
| 1940 | 603 | 1980 | 1,313 | 1980 | 222 |
| 1945 | 326 | 1981 | 1,100 | 1981 | 241 |
| 1950 | 1,952 | 1982 | 1,072 | 1982 | 240 |
| 1955 | 1,646 | 1983 | 1,712 | 1983 | 296 |
| 1960[1] | 1,296 | 1984 | 1,756 | 1984 | 296 |
| 1965 | 1,510 | 1985 | 1,745 | 1985 | 284 |

1. Prior to 1960, starts limited to nonfarm housing; from 1960 on, figures include farm housing. *Sources:* Department of Commerce, Housing Construction Statistics, 1900–1965, and Construction Reports, Housing Starts, 1970–83, Manufactured Housing Institute, 1965–76; National Conference of States on Building Codes and Standards.

## Shareholders in Public Corporations

| Characteristic | 1985 | 1983 | 1980 | 1975 | 1970 | 1965 | 1959 |
|------|------|------|------|------|------|------|------|
| Individual shareholders (thousands) | 47,040 | 42,360 | 30,200 | 25,270 | 30,850 | 20,120 | 12,490 |
| Owners of shares listed on New York Stock Exchange (thousands) | 25,263 | 26,029 | 23,804 | 17,950 | 18,290 | 12,430 | 8,510 |
| Adult shareowner incidence in population | 1 in 4 | 1 in 4 | 1 in 5 | 1 in 6 | 1 in 4 | 1 in 6 | 1 in 8 |
| Median household income | $36,800 | $33,200 | $27,750 | $19,000 | $13,500 | $9,500 | $7,000 |
| Adult shareowners with household income: under $10,000 (thousands) | 2,151 | 1,460 | 1,742 | 3,420 | 8,170 | 10,080 | 9,340 |
| $10,000 and over (thousands) | 40,999 | 36,261 | 25,715 | 19,970 | 20,130 | 8,410 | 2,740 |
| Adult female shareowners (thousands) | 22,509 | 20,385 | 13,696 | 11,750 | 14,290 | 9,430 | 6,350 |
| Adult male shareowners (thousands) | 22,484 | 19,226 | 14,196 | 11,630 | 14,340 | 9,060 | 5,740 |
| Median age | 44 | 45 | 46 | 53 | 48 | 49 | 49 |

NOTE: n.a. = not available. *Source:* New York Stock Exchange.

## 50 Most Active Stocks in 1985

| Stock | Share volume | Stock | Share volume | Stock | Share volume |
|------|------|------|------|------|------|
| American Tel. & Tel. (1) | 313,019,442 | Phibro-Salomon (27) | 131,577,703 | National Semiconductor (10) | 107,397,300 |
| Int'l Business Machines (2) | 259,650,205 | Sears, Roebuck (14) | 130,902,400 | Reynolds (R.J.) Industries | 106,952,900 |
| Phillips Petroleum (12) | 245,696,850 | Hewlett-Packard (15) | 130,626,602 | Eastman Kodak (26) | 105,740,100 |
| American Express (6) | 179,393,600 | AMR Corp. (11) | 130,303,200 | Citicorp (30) | 103,244,600 |
| Unocal Corp. (21) | 165,214,000 | General Electric (13) | 128,849,500 | Pfizer Inc. (35) | 101,400,700 |
| Beatrice Companies | 161,516,100 | Baxter Travenol (22) | 127,804,800 | United States Steel | 100,515,300 |
| Exxon Corp. (3) | 151,913,800 | Schlumberger, N.V. (24) | 127,436,600 | BankAmerica Corp. | 98,932,700 |
| Ford Motor (5) | 149,366,500 | Chrysler Corporation (7) | 125,959,400 | Dow Chemical (45) | 97,342,300 |
| Mobil Corp. (9) | 148,392,800 | Westinghouse Electric | 124,687,600 | Johnson & Johnson (32) | 96,373,700 |
| Texas Oil & Gas (50) | 148,078,600 | Sperry Corp. | 122,566,300 | TransWorld Airlines | 95,013,800 |
| Merrill Lynch (8) | 147,539,100 | Union Carbide | 116,409,580 | CSX Corp. | 94,782,600 |
| General Motors (4) | 147,329,800 | Digital Equipment (18) | 113,717,500 | Boeing Co. (38) | 94,742,800 |
| Texaco Inc. (23) | 145,980,670 | Federal Nat'l Mortgage (31) | 113,337,500 | K mart Corp. (36) | 91,355,900 |
| Middle South Utilities (43) | 140,913,060 | Commonwealth Edison (41) | 113,004,000 | Southern Co. | 91,239,200 |
| Atlantic Richfield (19) | 140,581,300 | Hospital Corp. of America | 109,775,000 | American Medical Int'l | 90,964,300 |
| Pan Am Corp. | 140,317,600 | RCA Corp. | 108,028,300 | Morris (Philip) | 88,985,800 |
| ITT Corp. (17) | 136,667,600 | Motorola, Inc. (29) | 107,433,300 | | |

NOTE: 1984 rank in parentheses, if among top 50. *Source:* New York Stock Exchange.

# How to Read an Annual Report

*Source:* Reprinted with permission from *Outlooks,* © First Marketing Corporation.

With today's economy, you don't have to be a stockbroker to know that no investment is a "sure thing." By reading an annual report though, you can look below a company's surface. Sales may be rising steadily, but aren't you more interested in actual profits?

## Begin at the End

This may seem unusual, but turn to the back of the report first, to the *certified public accountant's* report. This audit will tell you if the company conforms with "generally accepted accounting principles." Now, also in the back of the report, turn to the footnotes. Sometimes they can tell everything about profits.

## Chairman's Letter

In the front of the report, you'll find a *letter from the chairman or chief executive officer,* usually addressed to "our shareholders." It should tell you how the company fared that year, and more importantly—why. This letter will help you focus on the company's future, and the company's stance on economic and political trends which may affect its future.

## A Review of the Stats

A company's assets and liabilities for a given time are found in the *balance sheet.* All items owned by the company which can be turned to cash quickly are referred to as *current assets.* The debts due in one year which are paid out of current assets are called *current liabilities.*

The figure to pay close attention to is *net working capital.* This is the difference between current assets and liabilities. Keep track of this figure from one report to the next. If the working capital decreases, there could be a problem. The difference between total assets and liabilities is known as *stockholders' equity.* You'll want this number to

grow because it is the presumed dollar value of what stockholders own.

The *income statement* shows gains and losses over the year. But many things can make the earnings appear favorable, such as a budget reduction or the sale of a plant. The *net earnings per share* figure at the bottom of the income statement is not a very good indicator for years ahead.

The important number in the income statement is that which reflects *net sales.* How does it compare to the last statement? Again, the major concern is why. These numbers can be deceiving. Are sales keeping pace with inflation?

## How Much Does the Company Owe?

If you divide long-term liabilities by stockholders' equity, you'll get the *debt-to-equity* radio. When that number is high, it means that the company borrows a lot of money. If that money spurs sales, the stockholders can make their profits—as long as the company can meet its debt payments. If it cannot, there could be serious problems.

## For Further Information

For the potential investor who seeks further information, there are additional publications to consider. Within 90 days after the end of its business year, a company must file a Form 10-K with the Securities and Exchange Commission (SEC). This report can offer additional insight into a company's advertising and research policies, as well as other corporate information.

## Comparison is the Key

Whether you are a veteran at the art of gleaning information from annual reports, or if you are waiting to receive your first edition, each time a report comes out you should take the time to compare it with the last. You will gain better insight into a company's performance and how it may affect your personal interest in the organization.

## Largest Businesses, 1985

### (in thousands of dollars)
*Source:* FORTUNE 500 and SERVICE 500 © 1986 Time Inc. All rights reserved.

#### 50 LARGEST INDUSTRIAL CORPORATIONS

| | Sales | Assets |
|---|---|---|
| General Motors | $96,371,700 | $63,832,800 |
| Exxon | 86,673,000* | 69,160,000 |
| Mobil | 55,960,000 | 41,752,000 |
| Ford Motor | 52,774,400 | 31,603,600 |
| International Business Machines | 50,056,000 | 52,634,000 |
| Texaco | 46,297,000 | 37,703,000 |
| Chevron | 41,741,905 | 38,899,492 |
| American Tel. & Tel. | 34,909,500 | 40,462,500 |
| E.I. du Pont de Nemours | 29,483,000 | 25,140,000 |
| General Electric | 28,285,000 | 26,432,000 |
| Amoco | 27,215,000 | 25,198,000 |
| Atlantic Richfield | 22,357,000 | 20,279,000 |
| Chrysler | 21,255,500 | 12,605,300 |
| Shell Oil | 20,309,000 | 26,528,000 |
| U.S. Steel | 18,429,000 | 18,446,000 |
| United Technologies | 15,748,674 | 10,528,105 |
| Phillips Petroleum | 15,676,000 | 14,045,000 |
| Tenneco | 15,400,000 | 20,437,000 |
| Occidental Petroleum | 14,534,400 | 11,585,900 |
| Sun | 13,769,000 | 12,923,000 |
| Boeing | 13,636,000 | 9,246,000 |
| Procter & Gamble | 13,552,000 | 9,683,000 |
| R.J. Reynolds Industries | 13,533,000 | 16,930,000 |
| Standard Oil | 13,002,000 | 18,330,000 |
| ITT | 12,714,276 | 14,272,499 |
| Beatrice | 12,595,000 | 10,379,000 |
| Philip Morris | 12,149,000 | 17,429,000 |
| Dow Chemical | 11,537,000 | 11,830,000 |
| McDonnell Douglas | 11,477,700 | 7,268,400 |
| Rockwell International | 11,337,600 | 7,332,800 |
| Unocal | 10,738,000 | 10,797,000 |
| Westinghouse Electric | 10,700,200 | 9,681,600 |
| Eastman Kodak | 10,631,000 | 12,142,000 |
| Dart & Kraft | 9,942,300 | 5,501,800 |

| | | |
|---|---:|---:|
| Goodyear Tire & Rubber | 9,896,700 | 6,953,500 |
| Lockheed | 9,535,000 | 4,184,000 |
| Allied-Signal | 9,115,000 | 13,271,000 |
| General Foods | 9,022,418 | 4,553,725 |
| Union Carbide | 9,003,000 | 10,581,000 |
| Xerox | 8,947,600 | 9,816,700 |
| PepsiCo | 8,478,902 | 5,861,160 |
| General Dynamics | 8,410,600 | 4,448,100 |
| LTV | 8,198,800 | 6,306,700 |
| Coca-Cola | 8,138,904 | 6,897,706 |
| Sara Lee | 8,117,206 | 3,215,794 |
| Ashland Oil | 7,891,223 | 3,927,633 |
| Minnesota Mining & Manufacturing | 7,846,000 | 6,593,000 |
| Amerada Hess | 7,653,439 | 6,219,453 |
| W.R. Grace | 7,260,100 | 5,420,900 |
| Coastal | 7,254,300 | 8,294,300 |

## 25 LARGEST RETAILING COMPANIES

| | Sales | Assets |
|---|---:|---:|
| Sears Roebuck | $40,715,300 | $66,416,900 |
| K mart | 22,420,002 | 9,990,682 |
| Safeway Stores | 19,650,542 | 4,840,611 |
| Kroger | 17,123,531 | 4,177,807 |
| American Stores | 13,889,528 | 3,462,513 |
| J.C. Penney | 13,747,000 | 10,522,000 |
| Southland | 12,719,241 | 3,735,544 |
| Federated Department Stores | 9,978,027 | 5,353,643 |
| Lucky Stores | 9,382,282 | 1,932,460 |
| Dayton Hudson | 8,793,372 | 4,417,514 |
| Household International | 8,685,500 | 11,928,500 |
| Wal-Mart Stores | 8,580,910 | 3,103,645 |
| Winn-Dixie Stores | 7,774,480 | 1,238,738 |
| F.W. Woolworth | 5,958,000 | 2,535,000 |
| BATUS | 5,881,408 | 4,517,448 |
| Great Atlantic & Pacific Tea | 5,878,286 | 1,363,101 |
| Montgomery Ward | 5,388,000 | 3,654,000 |
| Supermarkets General | 5,122,633 | 1,103,841 |
| May Department Stores | 5,079,900 | 3,442,300 |
| Albertson's | 5,060,265 | 1,124,617 |
| Melville | 4,805,380 | 1,806,673 |
| Associated Dry Goods | 4,385,019 | 2,288,646 |
| R.H. Macy | 4,368,386 | 2,356,615 |
| Wickes Companies | 4,362,454 | 2,648,298 |
| Marriott | 4,317,900 | 3,663,800 |

## 10 LARGEST TRANSPORTATION COMPANIES

| | Operating revenues | Assets |
|---|---:|---:|
| Burlington Northern | $8,650,927 | $12,511,958 |
| United Parcel Service | 7,686,719 | 4,161,693 |
| CSX | 7,320,000 | 11,494,000 |
| Santa Fe Southern Pacific | 6,438,000 | 11,807,600 |
| UAL | 6,383,405 | 7,874,219 |
| AMR | 6,131,028 | 6,421,101 |
| Eastern Air Lines | 4,815,070 | 3,870,064 |
| Delta Air Lines | 4,684,115 | 3,626,840 |
| Norfolk Southern | 3,825,077 | 9,768,631 |
| Trans World Airlines | 3,725,418 | 2,768,800 |

## 10 LARGEST DIVERSIFIED FINANCIAL COMPANIES

| | Assets | Revenues |
|---|---:|---:|
| Federal National Mortgage Assoc. | $99,086,724 | $10,342,075 |
| American Express | 74,777,000 | 11,850,000 |
| Aetna Life & Casualty | 58,293,600 | 18,612,100 |
| Merrill Lynch | 48,117,032 | 7,116,975 |
| First Boston | 45,531,112 | 888,292 |
| CIGNA | 44,736,200 | 16,196,900 |
| Travelers Corp. | 41,641,800 | 14,594,400 |
| Bear Stearns Companies | 23,918,090 | 1,804,259 |
| E.F. Hutton Group | 21,749,360 | 3,205,186 |
| Loews | 16,119,782 | 6,918,294 |

## 10 LARGEST LIFE INSURANCE COMPANIES

| | Assets | Premium and annuity income |
|---|---:|---:|
| Prudential | $91,139,140 | $14,331,883 |
| Metropolitan | 76,494,165 | 7,316,008 |
| Equitable Life Assurance | 47,989,964 | 2,594,629 |
| Aetna Life | 37,889,119 | 3,594,092 |
| New York Life | 27,977,512 | 3,830,010 |
| John Hancock Mutual | 26,256,393 | 2,351,141 |
| Travelers | 25,571,766 | 4,270,704 |
| Teachers Insurance & Annuity | 23,159,057 | 2,240,201 |
| Connecticut General Life | 22,245,808 | 3,922,072 |
| Northwestern Mutual | 17,897,884 | 2,417,095 |

## 10 LARGEST COMMERCIAL BANKS

| | Assets | Deposits |
|---|---:|---:|
| Citicorp | $173,597,000 | $104,959,000 |
| BankAmerica Corp. | 118,541,125 | 94,210,950 |
| Chase Manhattan Corp. | 87,685,442 | 61,353,049 |
| Manufacturers Hanover Corp. | 76,525,769 | 46,261,146 |
| J.P. Morgan & Co. | 69,375,000 | 39,845,000 |
| Chemical New York Corp. | 56,990,174 | 34,505,315 |
| Security Pacific Corp. | 53,503,239 | 32,873,391 |
| Bankers Trust New York Corp. | 50,581,041 | 28,723,505 |
| First Interstate Bancorp | 48,991,038 | 35,554,486 |
| First Chicago Corp. | 38,892,506 | 27,147,535 |

## 10 LARGEST UTILITIES

| | Assets | Operating revenues |
|---|---:|---:|
| GTE | $26,557,897 | $15,732,361 |
| BellSouth | 25,008,300 | 10,663,900 |
| NYNEX | 20,599,700 | 10,313,600 |
| Bell Atlantic | 19,788,400 | 9,084,200 |
| Pacific Telesis Group | 19,538,300 | 8,498,600 |
| Southwestern Bell | 19,291,100 | 7,925,000 |
| Pacific Gas & Electric | 19,098,003 | 8,430,981 |
| American Information Technologies | 18,148,800 | 9,021,100 |
| U S West | 17,974,700 | 7,812,600 |
| Southern | 16,531,495 | 6,813,927 |

# New Business Concerns and Business Failures

| Formations and Failures | 1984 | 1983 | 1982 | 1981 | 1980 | 1979 | 1975 | 1970 |
|---|---:|---:|---:|---:|---:|---:|---:|---:|
| **Business formations** | | | | | | | | |
| Index, net formations (1967 = 100) | 117.1 | 114.8 | 113.2 | 118.6 | 122.4 | 128.3 | 107.0 | 106.4 |
| New Incorporations (1,000) | 635 | 600 | 567 | 582 | 534 | 525 | 326 | 264 |
| Failures, number (1,000) | n.a. | 31.3 | 24.9 | 16.8 | 11.7 | 7.6 | 11.4 | 10.7 |
| Rate per 10,000 concerns | n.a. | 110 | 88 | 61 | 42 | 28 | 43 | 44 |

NOTE: n.a. = not available. *Sources:* U.S. Bureau of Economic Analysis and Dun & Bradstreet Corporation.

## 50 Leading Stocks in Market Value

| Stock | Market value (millions) | Listed shares (millions) | Stock | Market value (millions) | Listed shares (millions) |
|---|---|---|---|---|---|
| International Business Machines | $95,266 | 614.6 | Ford Motor | 9,861 | 170.8 |
| Exxon Corp. | 49,966 | 906.4 | GTE Corp. | 9,672 | 210.3 |
| General Electric | 33,704 | 463.3 | Hewlett-Packard | 9,540 | 258.7 |
| American Telephone & Telegraph | 26,733 | 1,069.3 | Pacific Telesis | 9,068 | 107.2 |
| General Motors | 22,421 | 318.6 | Bristol-Myers | 9,023 | 135.9 |
| Amoco Corp. | 16,672 | 269.5 | Wal-Mart Stores | 8,933 | 280.3 |
| du Pont de Nemours | 16,328 | 240.6 | American Int'l Group | 8,651 | 81.6 |
| BellSouth Corp. | 15,060 | 307.3 | Dow Chemical | 8,623 | 210.3 |
| Sears, Roebuck | 14,404 | 369.3 | U S WEST | 8,599 | 96.6 |
| Atlantic Richfield | 13,838 | 217.1 | Southwestern Bell | 8,518 | 99.6 |
| Chevron Corp. | 13,086 | 342.1 | Eli Lilly | 8,503 | 76.3 |
| Mobil Corp. | 12,972 | 428.8 | Abbott Laboratories | 8,484 | 124.1 |
| Eastman Kodak | 12,553 | 248.6 | Pfizer Inc. | 8,298 | 163.9 |
| American Express | 11,808 | 223.8 | Texaco Inc. | 8,229 | 274.3 |
| Procter & Gamble | 11,787 | 169.0 | Allied-Signal, Inc. | 8,123 | 173.8 |
| Coca-Cola Co. | 11,614 | 137.4 | Boeing Co. | 8,112 | 155.2 |
| Schlumberger, N.V. | 11,111 | 303.4 | Westinghouse Electric | 8,061 | 180.6 |
| Bell Atlantic | 10,636 | 99.9 | Digital Equipment | 7,747 | 58.5 |
| American Home Products | 10,620 | 168.9 | Reynolds (R.J.) Industries. | 7,612 | 242.6 |
| Minnesota Mining & Manufacturing | 10,591 | 118.0 | McDonald's Corp. | 7,424 | 92.1 |
| Morris (Philip) | 10,540 | 119.3 | Bell Canada Enterprises | 7,230 | 240.0 |
| American Information Technologies (Ameritech) | 10,447 | 98.1 | Dart & Kraft | 7,187 | 164.7 |
| | | | Citicorp | 6,982 | 141.4 |
| Merck & Co. | 10,401 | 75.9 | PepsiCo, Inc. | 6,949 | 95.8 |
| Johnson & Johnson | 10,096 | 191.9 | Pacific Gas & Electric | 6,618 | 330.9 |
| NYNEX Corp. | 9,881 | 101.1 | **Total** | **$678,582** | **11,767.7** |

NOTE: As of Dec. 31, 1985. *Source:* New York Stock Exchange.

## Per Capita Personal Income by States

| State | 1985[1] | 1984 | 1983 | 1980 | State | 1985[1] | 1984 | 1983 | 1980 |
|---|---|---|---|---|---|---|---|---|---|
| Alabama | 10,510 | $ 9,987 | $ 9,242 | $ 7,465 | Montana | 10,728 | 10,607 | 9,949 | 8,342 |
| Alaska | 17,756 | 17,550 | 17,194 | 13,007 | Nebraska | 13,699 | 12,572 | 11,212 | 8,895 |
| Arizona | 12,454 | 11,822 | 10,656 | 8,854 | Nevada | 13,981 | 13,298 | 12,451 | 10,848 |
| Arkansas | 10,180 | 9,734 | 8,967 | 7,113 | New Hampshire | 14,308 | 13,386 | 12,021 | 9,150 |
| California | 15,255 | 14,471 | 13,257 | 11,021 | New Jersey | 16,368 | 15,389 | 14,122 | 10,966 |
| Colorado | 14,413 | 13,848 | 12,770 | 10,143 | New Mexico | 10,741 | 10,256 | 9,640 | 7,940 |
| Connecticut | 17,627 | 16,547 | 14,895 | 11,532 | New York | 15,237 | 14,341 | 12,990 | 10,179 |
| Delaware | 14,337 | 13,692 | 12,665 | 10,059 | North Carolina | 11,314 | 10,852 | 9,787 | 7,780 |
| D.C. | 17,909 | 16,870 | 15,744 | 12,251 | North Dakota | 13,034 | 12,290 | 11,666 | 8,642 |
| Florida | 13,397 | 12,773 | 11,593 | 9,246 | Ohio | 12,979 | 12,326 | 11,216 | 9,399 |
| Georgia | 12,158 | 11,548 | 10,379 | 8,021 | Oklahoma | 12,103 | 11,629 | 10,963 | 9,018 |
| Hawaii | 13,542 | 13,028 | 12,114 | 10,129 | Oregon | 12,165 | 11,613 | 10,740 | 9,309 |
| Idaho | 10,605 | 10,146 | 9,555 | 8,105 | Pennsylvania | 12,959 | 12,292 | 11,448 | 9,353 |
| Illinois | 14,397 | 13,705 | 12,405 | 10,454 | Rhode Island | 13,592 | 12,860 | 11,670 | 9,227 |
| Indiana | 12,276 | 11,725 | 10,476 | 8,914 | South Carolina | 10,514 | 10,111 | 9,187 | 7,392 |
| Iowa | 12,779 | 12,123 | 10,705 | 9,226 | South Dakota | 11,207 | 10,904 | 9,847 | 7,800 |
| Kansas | 14,046 | 13,311 | 12,247 | 9,880 | Tennessee | 10,934 | 10,400 | 9,549 | 7,711 |
| Kentucky | 10,585 | 10,232 | 9,397 | 7,679 | Texas | 13,165 | 12,575 | 11,685 | 9,439 |
| Louisiana | 11,015 | 10,741 | 10,270 | 8,412 | Utah | 10,166 | 9,715 | 8,993 | 7,671 |
| Maine | 11,423 | 10,849 | 9,847 | 7,760 | Vermont | 11,599 | 10,828 | 9,979 | 7,957 |
| Maryland | 15,356 | 14,443 | 12,994 | 10,394 | Virginia | 14,164 | 13,291 | 12,116 | 9,413 |
| Massachusetts | 15,790 | 14,755 | 13,264 | 10,103 | Washington | 13,267 | 12,755 | 12,177 | 10,256 |
| Michigan | 13,298 | 12,621 | 11,466 | 9,801 | West Virginia | 10,112 | 9,708 | 9,159 | 7,764 |
| Minnesota | 14,071 | 13,212 | 11,913 | 9,673 | Wisconsin | 12,883 | 12,378 | 11,352 | 9,364 |
| Mississippi | 9,035 | 8,684 | 8,098 | 6,573 | Wyoming | 12,955 | 12,238 | 11,911 | 11,018 |
| Missouri | 12,784 | 12,075 | 10,969 | 8,812 | **United States** | **13,451** | **12,772** | **11,685** | **9,494** |

1. *Preliminary. Source:* U.S. Department of Commerce, Bureau of Economic Analysis, *Survey of Current Business.*

# National Labor Organizations With Membership Over 100,000

| Members[1] | Union |
|---|---|
| 1,010,000 | Automobile, Aerospace and Agricultural Implement Workers of America, International Union, United |
| 125,000 | Bakery, Confectionary, and Tobacco Workers International Union |
| 119,000 | Boilermakers, Iron Ship Builders, Blacksmiths, Forgers and Helpers, International Brotherhood of |
| 103,000 | Bricklayers and Allied Craftsmen, International Union of |
| 609,000 | Carpenters and Joiners of America, United Brotherhood of |
| 150,000 | Classified School Employees, American Association of (Ind.) |
| 253,000 | Clothing and Textile Workers Union, Amalgamated |
| 573,000 | Communications Workers of America |
| 1,641,354 | Education Association, National (Ind.) |
| 192,000 | Electrical, Radio and Machine Workers, International Union of |
| 162,000 | Electrical, Radio and Machine Workers of America, United (Ind.) |
| 820,000 | Electrical Workers, International Brotherhood of |
| 142,000 | Fire Fighters, International Association of |
| 1,007,000 | Food and Commercial Workers International Union, United |
| 204,000 | Government Employees, American Federation of |
| 154,000 | Graphic Communications Workers |
| 340,000 | Hotel and Restaurant Employees and Bartenders, International Union |
| 140,000 | Iron Workers |
| 444,000 | Laborers' International Union of North America |
| 258,000 | Ladies' Garment Workers' Union, International |
| 175,000 | Letter Carriers, National Association of |
| 116,000 [2] | Longshoremens Association, Itnl. |
| 596,000 | Machinists and Aerospace Workers, International Association of |
| 150,000 | Mine Workers of America, United (Ind.) |
| 131,000 | Musicians, American Federation of |
| 160,357 | Nurses' Association; American (Ind.) |
| 112,793 [2] | Office and Professional Employees International Union |
| 124,000 | Oil, Chemical and Atomic Workers International Union |
| 345,000 [2] | Operating Engineers, International Union of |
| 150,000 | Painters and Allied Trades of the United States and Canada, International Brotherhood of |
| 241,000 | Paper Workers International Union, United |
| 228,000 | Plumbing and Pipe Fitting Industry of the United States and Canada, United Association of Journeymen and Apprentices of the |
| 160,000 | Police, Fraternal Order of (Ind.) |
| 246,000 | Postal Workers Union, American |
| 120,000 | Railway, Airline and Steamship Clerks, Freight Handlers, Express and Station Employees, Brotherhood of |
| 110,000 | Retail, Wholesale and Department Store Union |
| 108,000 | Rubber, Cork, Linoleum and Plastic Workers of America, United |
| 589,000 | Service Employees International Union |
| 144,000 [2] | Sheet Metal Workers' International Association |
| 959,000 | State, County and Municipal Employees of America, American Federation of |
| 707,000 | Steelworkers of America, United |
| 456,000 | Teachers, American Federation of |
| 1,800,000 | Teamsters, Chauffeurs, Warehousemen and Helpers of America, International Brotherhood of (Ind.) |
| 120,000 [2] | Transit Union, Amalgamated |
| 115,000 [2] | Transportation Union, United |

1. Data for independent (Ind.) unions are for 1982. Data for AFL-CIO affiliated unions are based on a 2-year period ending June 1983 unless otherwise indicated. 2. 1982. NOTE: Figures are most recent available.

## Work Stoppages Involving 1,000 Workers or More[1]

| Year | Work stoppages | Workers involved (thousands) | Man-days idle (thousands) | Year | Work stoppages | Workers involved (thousands) | Man-days idle (thousands) |
|---|---|---|---|---|---|---|---|
| 1950 | 424 | 1,698 | 30,390 | 1976 | 231 | 1,519 | 23,962 |
| 1955 | 363 | 2,055 | 21,180 | 1977 | 298 | 1,212 | 21,258 |
| 1960 | 222 | 896 | 13,260 | 1978 | 219 | 1,006 | 23,774 |
| 1965 | 268 | 999 | 15,140 | 1979 | 235 | 1,021 | 20,409 |
| 1970 | 381 | 2,468 | 52,761 | 1980 | 187 | 795 | 20,844 |
| 1971 | 298 | 2,516 | 35,538 | 1981 | 145 | 729 | 16,908 |
| 1972 | 250 | 975 | 16,764 | 1982 | 96 | 656 | 9,061 |
| 1973 | 317 | 1,400 | 16,260 | 1983 | 81 | 909 | 17,461 |
| 1974 | 424 | 1,796 | 31,809 | 1984 | 68 | 391 | 8,499 |
| 1975 | 235 | 965 | 17,563 | 1985 | 61 | 584 | 7,079 |

1. The number of stoppages and workers relate to stoppages that began in the year. Days of idleness include all stoppages in effect. Workers are counted more than once if they were involved in more than one stoppage during the year. *Source:* U.S. Department of Labor, Bureau of Labor Statistics, *Monthly Labor Review, August 1986.*

# Corporate Profits
### (in billions of dollars)

| Item | 1986[1] | 1985 | 1984 | 1983 | 1982 | 1980 | 1975 | 1970 |
|---|---|---|---|---|---|---|---|---|
| Domestic industries | 279.8 | 263.5 | 207.1 | 167.2 | 144.1 | 161.9 | 107.6 | 62.4 |
| Financial | 30.5 | 24.4 | 27.8 | 29.6 | 20.9 | 26.9 | 11.8 | 12.1 |
| Nonfinancial | 249.2 | 239.2 | 179.2 | 137.6 | 123.2 | 134.9 | 95.8 | 50.2 |
| Manufacturing | 69.8 | 76.6 | 85.5 | 65.2 | 59.0 | 72.9 | 52.6 | 26.6 |
| Wholesale and retail trade | 50.5 | 49.4 | 45.9 | 33.4 | 27.6 | 23.6 | 21.3 | 9.5 |
| Other | 20.3 | 15.4 | 20.2 | 16.4 | 36.6 | 38.4 | 21.9 | 14.1 |
| Rest of world | 33.9 | 31.9 | 23.0 | 24.8 | 21.8 | 29.9 | 13.0 | 6.5 |
| Total | 313.7 | 295.5 | 285.7 | 225.2 | 165.9 | 191.7 | 120.6 | 68.9 |

1. Preliminary. *Source:* U.S. Bureau of Economic Analysis, *Survey of Current Business.*

# Foreign Assistance
### (in millions of dollars)

| Calendar years | Non-military programs | | | Military programs | | |
|---|---|---|---|---|---|---|
| | Net new grants | Net new credits | Net other assistance | Net grants | Net credits | Total net assistance |
| 1945–1950 | $18,413 | $8,086 | — | $ 1,981 | — | $28,479 |
| 1951–55 | 10,459 | 550 | $ 541 | 12,830 | $ 7 | 24,386 |
| 1956–60 | 8,291 | 1,462 | 2,226 | 13,269 | 42 | 25,290 |
| 1961–65 | 9,384 | 5,538 | 576 | 8,295 | −16 | 23,777 |
| 1966–70 | 8,808 | 9,238 | −564 | 13,296 | 192 | 30,970 |
| 1971–75 | 12,939 | 5,479 | −725 | 16,940 | 2,044 | 36,677 |
| 1976–80 | 14,268 | 10,781 | −286 | 5,662 | 6,959 | 37,385 |
| 1982 | 4,746 | 2,247 | 4 | 1,369 | 2,527 | 10,893 |
| 1983 | 5,350 | 849 | −4 | 1,357 | 2,719 | 10,272 |
| 1984 | 6,518 | 1,416 | 10 | 2,348 | 2,329 | 12,622 |
| 1985 | 8,241 | 282 | 8 | 3,149 | 1,355 | 13,035 |
| Total postwar period | 111,567 | 48,144 | 1,771 | 81,655 | 20,064 | 263,201 |

1. Excludes investment in international nonmonetary financial institutions of $14,442 million. 2. Includes transactions after V-J Day (Sept. 2, 1945). NOTE: Detail may not add to total due to rounding. *Source:* Department of Commerce, Bureau of Economic Analysis.

# The Federal Budget—Receipts and Outlays
### (in billions of dollars)

| Description | 1987[1] | 1986[1] | 1985 |
|---|---|---|---|
| **RECEIPTS BY SOURCE** | | | |
| Individual income taxes | 386.0 | 353.7 | 334.5 |
| Corporation income taxes | 86.7 | 70.9 | 61.3 |
| Social insurance taxes and contributions: | 302.8 | 280.4 | 265.2 |
| Employment taxes and contributions | 273.7 | 252.1 | 234.6 |
| Unemployment insurance | 23.4 | 23.6 | 25.8 |
| Other retirement contributions | 5.6 | 4.7 | 4.8 |
| Excise taxes | 35.2 | 34.6 | 36.0 |
| Estate and gift taxes | 5.7 | 6.1 | 6.4 |
| Customs duties | 12.9 | 12.4 | 12.1 |
| Miscellaneous receipts | 21.1 | 19.0 | 18.5 |
| Total budget receipts | 850.4 | 777.1 | 734.1 |
| **OUTLAYS BY FUNCTION** | | | |
| National defense | 282.2 | 265.8 | 252.7 |
| International affairs | 18.6 | 17.1 | 16.2 |
| General science, space, and technology | 9.2 | 8.9 | 8.6 |
| Energy | 4.0 | 4.4 | 5.7 |

| Description | 1987[1] | 1986[1] | 1985 |
|---|---|---|---|
| Natural resources and environment | 12.0 | 12.9 | 13.4 |
| Agriculture | 19.5 | 25.9 | 25.6 |
| Commerce and housing credit | 1.4 | 3.8 | 4.2 |
| Transportation | 25.5 | 27.1 | 25.8 |
| Community and regional development | 6.5 | 7.9 | 7.7 |
| Education, training, employment, and social services | 27.4 | 30.7 | 29.3 |
| Health | 35.0 | 35.7 | 33.5 |
| Social security and medicare | 282.4 | 268.8 | 254.4 |
| Income security | 118.4 | 118.1 | 128.2 |
| Veterans benefits and services | 26.4 | 26.6 | 26.4 |
| Administration of justice | 6.9 | 6.8 | 6.3 |
| General government | 6.1 | 6.3 | 5.2 |
| General purpose fiscal assistance | 1.7 | 6.2 | 6.4 |
| Net interest | 148.0 | 142.7 | 129.4 |
| Allowances | 0.8 | — | — |
| Undistributed offsetting receipts | −38.1 | −35.8 | −32.8 |
| Total outlays | 994.0 | 979.9 | 946.3 |
| Total budget deficit | −143.6 | −202.8 | −212.2 |

1. Estimated. NOTE: The fiscal year is from Oct. 1 to Sept. 30. *Source:* Executive Office of the President, Office of Management and Budget.

## National Income by Type
### (in billions of dollars)

| Type of share | 1985 | 1984 | 1983 | 1980 | 1975 | 1970 | 1965 | 1960 | 1950 |
|---|---|---|---|---|---|---|---|---|---|
| National income | $3,211.3 | $3,039.3 | $2,646.9 | $2,121.4 | $1,215.0 | $800.5 | $564.3 | $414.5 | $241.1 |
| Compensation of employees | 2,372.5 | 2,221.3 | 1,990.1 | 1,596.5 | 931.1 | 603.9 | 393.8 | 294.2 | 154.6 |
| Wages and salaries | 1,960.3 | 1,835.2 | 1,664.0 | 1,343.6 | 805.9 | 542.0 | 358.9 | 270.8 | 146.8 |
| Supplements to wages and salaries | 412.2 | 386.2 | 326.1 | 252.9 | 125.2 | 61.9 | 35.0 | 23.4 | 7.8 |
| Proprietors' income | 232.9 | 233.7 | 128.6 | 130.6 | 87.0 | 66.9 | 57.3 | 46.2 | 37.5 |
| Business and professional | 193.0 | 201.6 | 107.6 | 107.2 | 63.5 | 50.0 | 42.4 | 34.2 | 24.0 |
| Farm | 21.2 | 32.1 | 21.0 | 23.4 | 23.5 | 16.9 | 14.8 | 12.0 | 13.5 |
| Rental income of persons | 13.8[1] | 10.8[1] | 54.8 | 31.8 | 22.4 | 23.9 | 19.0 | 15.8 | 9.4 |
| Corporate profits[1][2] | 295.5 | 273.3 | 226.3 | 182.7 | 95.9 | 69.4 | 76.1 | 49.9 | 37.7 |
| Net interest | 287.4 | 300.2 | 247.2 | 179.8 | 78.6 | 36.4 | 18.2 | 8.4 | 2.0 |

1. Includes capital consumption adjustment. 2. Includes inventory valuation adjustment. *Source:* Department of Commerce, Bureau of Economic Analysis.

## Persons in the Labor Force

| Year | Labor force[1] Number (thousands) | % working-age population | Percent of labor force in Farm occupation | Nonfarm occupation | Year | Labor force[1] Number (thousands) | % working-age population | Percent of labor force in Farm occupation | Nonfarm occupation |
|---|---|---|---|---|---|---|---|---|---|
| 1830 | 3,932 | 45.5 | 70.5 | 29.5 | 1910 | 37,371 | 52.2 | 31.0 | 69.0 |
| 1840 | 5,420 | 46.6 | 68.6 | 31.4 | 1920 | 42,434 | 51.3 | 27.0 | 73.0 |
| 1850 | 7,697 | 46.8 | 63.7 | 36.3 | 1930 | 48,830 | 49.5 | 21.4 | 78.6 |
| 1860 | 10,533 | 47.0 | 58.9 | 41.1 | 1940 | 52,966 | 52.4 | 17.4 | 82.6 |
| 1870 | 12,925 | 44.4 | 53.0 | 47.0 | 1950 | 59,671 | 53.4 | 11.6 | 88.4 |
| 1880 | 17,392 | 47.3 | 49.4 | 50.6 | 1960 | 69,877 | 55.3 | 6.0 | 94.0 |
| 1890 | 23,318 | 49.2 | 42.6 | 57.4 | 1970 | 82,049 | 58.2 | 3.1 | 96.9 |
| 1900 | 29,073 | 50.2 | 37.5 | 62.5 | 1980 | 106,085 | 62.0 | 2.2 | 97.8 |

1. For 1830 to 1930, the data relate to the population and gainful workers at ages 10 and over. For 1940 to 1960, the data relate to the population and labor force at ages 14 and over; for 1970 and 1980, the data relate to the population and labor force at age 16 and over. The farm and nonfarm percentages relate only to the experienced civilian labor force. *Source:* Department of Commerce, Bureau of the Census.

## Women in the Civilian Labor Force
### (16 years of age and over; in thousands)

| Labor force status | 1985 | 1984 | 1983 | 1982 | 1981 | 1980 |
|---|---|---|---|---|---|---|
| In the labor force: | 51,050 | 49,709 | 48,503 | 47,755 | 46,696 | 45,487 |
| 16 to 19 years of age | 3,767 | 3,810 | 3,868 | 4,056 | 4,211 | 4,381 |
| 20 years and over | 47,283 | 45,900 | 44,636 | 43,699 | 42,485 | 41,106 |
| Employed | 47,259 | 45,915 | 44,047 | 43,256 | 43,000 | 42,117 |
| 16 to 19 years of age | 3,105 | 3,122 | 3,043 | 3,170 | 3,411 | 3,625 |
| 20 years and over | 44,154 | 42,793 | 41,004 | 40,086 | 39,590 | 38,492 |
| Unemployed | 3,791 | 3,794 | 4,457 | 4,499 | 3,696 | 3,370 |
| 16 to 19 years of age | 661 | 687 | 825 | 886 | 800 | 755 |
| 20 years and over | 3,129 | 3,107 | 3,632 | 3,613 | 2,895 | 2,615 |
| Not in the labor force: | 42,686 | 43,068 | 43,181 | 42,993 | 42,922 | 42,861 |
| Women as percent of labor force | 44.2 | 43.8 | 43.5 | 43.3 | 43.0 | 42.5 |
| Total civilian noninstitutional population | 93,736 | 92,778 | 91,684 | 90,748 | 89,618 | 88,348 |

*Source:* Department of Labor, Bureau of Labor Statistics, 1986.

## Employed Persons 16 Years and Over,
## by Race and Major Occupational Groups
### (number in thousands)

| Race and occupational group | 1985 Number | 1985 Percent distribution | 1984 Number | 1984 Percent distribution |
|---|---|---|---|---|
| **WHITE** | | | | |
| Managerial and professional | 23,561 | 25.1 | 22,702 | 24.6 |
| Executive, administrative, & managerial | 11,256 | 12.0 | 10,704 | 11.6 |
| Professional | 12,305 | 13.1 | 11,998 | 13.0 |
| Technical, sales, & administrative support | 29,553 | 31.5 | 29,082 | 31.6 |
| Technicians & support | 2,823 | 3.0 | 2,783 | 3.0 |
| Sales occupations | 11,669 | 12.4 | 11,673 | 12.7 |
| Administrative support | 15,061 | 16.1 | 14,626 | 15.9 |
| Service occupations | 11,432 | 12.2 | 11,214 | 12.2 |
| Precision production, craft, and repair | 12,107 | 12.9 | 11,844 | 12.9 |
| Operators, fabricators, and laborers | 13,951 | 14.9 | 14,036 | 15.2 |
| Farming, forestry, fishing | 3,132 | 3.3 | 3,242 | 3.5 |
| **Total** | **93,736** | **100.0** | **92,120** | **100.0** |
| **BLACK** | | | | |
| Managerial and professional | 1,514 | 14.4 | 1,422 | 14.1 |
| Executive, administrative, & managerial | 649 | 6.2 | 582 | 5.8 |
| Professional | 865 | 8.2 | 840 | 8.3 |
| Technical, sales, & administrative support | 2,785 | 26.5 | 2,592 | 25.6 |
| Technicians & support | 291 | 2.8 | 262 | 2.6 |
| Sales occupations | 696 | 6.6 | 627 | 6.2 |
| Administrative support | 1,798 | 17.1 | 1,703 | 16.8 |
| Service occupations | 2,522 | 24.0 | 2,478 | 24.5 |
| Precision production, craft, and repair | 946 | 9.0 | 939 | 9.3 |
| Operators, fabricators, and laborers | 2,465 | 23.5 | 2,411 | 23.8 |
| Farming, forestry, and fishing | 269 | 2.6 | 277 | 2.7 |
| **Total** | **10,501** | **100.0** | **10,119** | **100.0** |

*Source:* Department of Labor, Bureau of Labor Statistics.

## Mothers Participating in Labor Force
### (figures in percentage)

| | Mothers with children | | |
|---|---|---|---|
| Year | Under 18 years | 6 to 17 years | Under 6 years[1] |
| 1950 | 21.6 | 32.8 | 13.6 |
| 1955 | 27.0 | 38.4 | 18.2 |
| 1965 | 35.0 | 45.7 | 25.3 |
| 1975 | 47.4 | 54.8 | 38.9 |
| 1977 | 50.7 | 58.3 | 40.9 |
| 1979 | 54.5 | 61.6 | 45.4 |
| 1980 | 56.6 | 64.4 | 46.6 |
| 1981 | 58.1 | 65.5 | 48.9 |
| 1982 | 58.5 | 65.8 | 49.9 |
| 1983 | 58.9 | 66.3 | 50.5 |
| 1984 | 60.5 | 68.2 | 52.1 |
| 1985 | 62.1 | 69.9 | 53.5 |

1. May also have older children. NOTE: For 1950 and 1955 data are for April; for 1965 and 1975–84, data are for March. *Source:* Department of Labor, Bureau of Labor Statistics.

## Women in the Working Population

| Year[1] | Number (thousands) | % Female population aged 10 and over[1] | % of Total working population aged 10 and over[1] |
|---|---|---|---|
| 1900 | 5,319 | 18.8 | 18.3 |
| 1910 | 7,445 | 21.5 | 19.9 |
| 1920 | 8,637 | 21.4 | 20.4 |
| 1930 | 10,752 | 22.0 | 22.0 |
| 1940 | 12,845 | 25.4 | 24.3 |
| 1950 | 18,408 | 33.9 | 29.0 |
| 1960[2] | 23,268 | 37.8 | 32.5 |
| 1970 | 31,580 | 43.4 | 37.2 |
| 1980 | 45,611 | 51.6 | 42.0 |
| 1983 | 48,646 | 53.0 | 43.0 |
| 1984 | 49,855 | 53.7 | 43.3 |
| 1985 | 51,200 | 54.5 | 43.7 |

1. For 1900–1930, data relate to population and gainful workers at ages 10 and over; for 1940, to ages 14 and over; beginning 1950, to population at ages 16 and over. 2. Beginning in 1960, figures include Alaska and Hawaii. *Sources:* Department of Commerce, Bureau of the Census, and Department of Labor, Bureau of Labor Statistics.

## Manufacturing Industries—Gross Average Weekly Earnings and Hours Worked

| Industry | 1985[1] Earnings | Hours worked | 1984[1] Earnings | Hours worked | 1980 Earnings | Hours worked | 1975 Earnings | Hours worked | 1970 Earnings | Hours worked | 1958 Earnings | Hours worked |
|---|---|---|---|---|---|---|---|---|---|---|---|---|
| All manufacturing | $385.56 | 40.5 | $370.78 | 40.7 | $288.62 | 39.7 | $189.51 | 39.4 | $133.73 | 39.8 | $82.71 | 39.2 |
| Durable goods | 415.71 | 41.2 | 400.75 | 41.4 | 310.78 | 40.1 | 205.09 | 39.9 | 143.07 | 40.3 | 89.27 | 39.5 |
| Primary metal industries | 484.72 | 41.5 | 480.06 | 42.0 | 391.78 | 40.1 | 246.80 | 40.0 | 159.17 | 40.5 | 101.11 | 38.3 |
| Iron and steel foundries | 429.62 | 40.8 | 423.26 | 41.7 | 328.00 | 40.0 | 220.99 | 40.4 | 151.03 | 40.6 | 86.86 | 37.6 |
| Nonferrous foundries | 388.74 | 41.8 | 381.43 | 42.1 | 291.27 | 39.9 | 190.03 | 39.1 | 138.16 | 39.7 | 90.85 | 39.5 |
| Fabricated metal products | 398.96 | 41.3 | 385.74 | 41.3 | 300.98 | 40.4 | 201.60 | 40.0 | 143.67 | 40.7 | 89.78 | 39.9 |
| Hardware, cutlery, hand tools | 396.42 | 40.7 | 371.69 | 40.8 | 275.89 | 39.3 | 187.07 | 39.3 | 132.33 | 40.1 | 82.92 | 39.3 |
| Other hardware | 418.61 | 40.8 | 385.40 | 41.3 | 286.21 | 39.1 | 195.42 | 39.4 | 133.46 | 40.2 | 84.32 | 39.4 |
| Structural metal products | 369.00 | 41.0 | 354.16 | 40.2 | 291.85 | 40.2 | 202.61 | 40.2 | 142.61 | 40.4 | 92.63 | 40.1 |
| Electric and electronic equipment | 384.48 | 40.6 | 364.90 | 41.0 | 276.21 | 39.8 | 180.91 | 39.5 | 130.54 | 39.8 | 83.95 | 39.6 |
| Machinery, except electrical | 427.04 | 41.5 | 416.91 | 41.9 | 328.00 | 41.0 | 219.22 | 40.9 | 154.95 | 41.1 | 94.33 | 39.8 |
| Transportation equipment | 542.72 | 42.7 | 522.02 | 43.0 | 379.61 | 40.6 | 242.61 | 40.3 | 163.22 | 40.3 | 100.40 | 40.0 |
| Motor vehicles and equipment | 584.64 | 43.5 | 562.93 | 44.5 | 394.00 | 40.0 | 262.68 | 40.6 | 170.07 | 40.3 | 101.24 | 39.7 |
| Lumber and wood products | 326.36 | 39.8 | 312.83 | 39.8 | 252.18 | 38.5 | 167.35 | 39.1 | 117.51 | 39.7 | 69.09 | 38.6 |
| Furniture and fixtures | 283.29 | 39.4 | 266.34 | 39.4 | 209.17 | 38.1 | 142.13 | 37.9 | 108.58 | 39.2 | 69.95 | 39.3 |
| Nondurable goods | 342.86 | 39.5 | 327.10 | 39.6 | 255.45 | 39.0 | 168.78 | 38.8 | 120.43 | 39.1 | 74.11 | 38.8 |
| Textile mill products | 266.39 | 39.7 | 261.06 | 40.6 | 203.31 | 40.1 | 133.28 | 39.2 | 97.76 | 39.9 | 57.51 | 38.6 |
| Apparel and other textile products | 208.00 | 36.3 | 200.75 | 36.7 | 161.42 | 35.4 | 111.97 | 35.1 | 84.37 | 35.3 | 54.05 | 35.1 |
| Leather and leather products | 217.09 | 37.3 | 205.25 | 36.2 | 169.09 | 36.7 | 120.80 | 37.4 | 92.63 | 37.2 | 57.25 | 36.7 |
| Food and kindred products | 341.60 | 40.0 | 328.94 | 39.3 | 271.95 | 39.7 | 184.17 | 40.3 | 127.98 | 40.5 | 79.15 | 40.8 |
| Tobacco manufactures | 448.26 | 37.2 | 414.77 | 37.0 | 294.89 | 38.1 | 171.38 | 38.0 | 110.00 | 37.8 | 62.17 | 39.1 |
| Paper and allied products | 466.34 | 43.1 | 437.68 | 42.7 | 330.85 | 42.2 | 207.58 | 41.6 | 144.14 | 41.9 | 87.99 | 41.9 |
| Printing and publishing | 365.31 | 37.7 | 353.78 | 38.0 | 279.36 | 37.1 | 198.32 | 37.0 | 147.78 | 37.7 | 94.62 | 38.0 |
| Chemicals and allied products | 484.78 | 41.9 | 456.46 | 41.8 | 344.45 | 41.5 | 219.63 | 40.9 | 153.50 | 41.6 | 93.20 | 40.7 |
| Petroleum and allied products | 603.72 | 43.0 | 584.64 | 44.0 | 422.18 | 41.8 | 267.07 | 41.6 | 182.76 | 42.7 | 111.66 | 40.9 |

1. Preliminary. *Source:* Department of Labor, Bureau of Labor Statistics.

## The Economy in 1995

Imagine spending a million dollars a day for the next 6,000 years. That's the amount projected by the U.S. Bureau of Labor Statistics for the U.S. economy in 1995. Such an economy would employ 125 to 130 million workers—an increase of over 25 million—involve a recovery in the sales of cars and a boom in household appliances, and entail over $100 billion in expenditures for medical services. The unemployment rate will decline to 6.0. In order to make these projections, economists correlated almost 700 variables, including labor force, income, investments, expenditures and trade.

The GNP (Gross National Product) in 1995 will be $2.1 to 2.3 trillion—in 1972 dollars. The largest component of GNP is consumer spending, which is divided among purchases of durable goods, nondurable goods, and services. Purchases of durables are projected to grow strongly. About 12 million new cars will be sold in 1995. Recovery of the housing industry is projected to fuel demand for household appliances. In addition, a new boom in household furnishings will feature consumer electronics. Purchases of home computers, software, video cassette recorders, and other electronic products are foreseen to grow strongly in the next decade. Consumer purchases of nondurables—such as food and clothing—will account for a smaller share of GNP in 1995 than they have in recent years. Drugs and medical sundries are the only category of nondurables expected to show rapid growth.

Purchases of services will continue to grow. Consumers are expected to buy more telephone and telegraph services, including cable TV. Expenditures for medical services will grow, due to the increased number of people over 65.

## Nonmanufacturing Industries—Gross Average Weekly Earnings and Hours Worked

| Industry | 1986[1] Earnings | 1986[1] Hours worked | 1985 Earnings | 1985 Hours worked | 1975 Earnings | 1975 Hours worked | 1970 Earnings | 1970 Hours worked | 1958 Earnings | 1958 Hours worked |
|---|---|---|---|---|---|---|---|---|---|---|
| Bituminous coal and lignite mining | $614.66 | 40.2 | $630.77 | 41.4 | $284.53 | 39.2[2] | $186.41 | 40.8 | $97.57 | 33.3 |
| Metal mining | 551.04 | 41.0 | 547.24 | 40.9 | 250.72 | 42.3 | 165.68 | 42.7 | 94.96 | 38.6 |
| Nonmetallic minerals | 466.65 | 45.0 | 451.68 | 44.5 | 213.09 | 43.4 | 155.11 | 44.7 | 88.33 | 43.3 |
| Telephone communications | 520.70 | 41.0 | 512.52 | 41.1 | 221.18 | 38.4 | 131.60 | 39.4 | 78.72 | 38.4 |
| Radio and TV broadcasting | 398.56 | 36.7 | 381.39 | 37.1 | 214.50 | 39.0 | 147.45 | 38.2 | 100.70 | 38.0 |
| Electric, gas, and sanitary services | 554.61 | 41.7 | 534.59 | 41.7 | 246.79 | 41.2 | 172.64 | 41.5 | 98.57 | 40.9 |
| Local and suburban transportation | 318.59 | 38.2 | 309.85 | 38.3 | 196.89 | 40.1 | 142.30 | 42.1 | 87.29 | 43.0 |
| Wholesale trade | 356.35 | 38.4 | 358.36 | 38.7 | 188.75 | 38.6 | 137.60 | 40.0 | 84.02 | 40.2 |
| Retail trade | 174.60 | 29.1 | 177.31 | 29.7 | 108.22 | 32.4 | 82.47 | 33.8 | 54.10 | 38.1 |
| Hotels, tourist courts, motels | 182.68 | 30.6 | 176.90 | 30.5 | 89.64 | 31.9 | 68.16 | 34.6 | 40.89 | 39.7 |
| Laundries and dry cleaning plants | 203.40 | 34.3 | 198.70 | 34.2 | 106.05 | 35.0 | 77.47 | 35.7 | 45.28 | 38.7 |
| General building contracting | 425.26 | 37.6 | 414.78 | 37.1 | 254.88 | 36.0 | 184.40 | 36.3 | 96.92 | 35.5 |

1. May preliminary. 2. 11-month average. *Source:* Department of Labor, Bureau of Labor Statistics.

## Median Income Comparisons of Year-Round Workers by Educational Attainment 1984
### (persons 25 years and over)

| Years of school completed | Median income Women | Median income Men | Income gap in dollars | Women's income as a percent of men's | Percent men's income exceeded women's |
|---|---|---|---|---|---|
| Elementary school: | | | | | |
| Less than 8 years | $9,828 | $14,624 | $4,796 | 67 | 49 |
| 8 years | 10,848 | 16,812 | 5,964 | 65 | 55 |
| High School: | | | | | |
| 1 to 3 years | 11,843 | 19,120 | 7,277 | 62 | 61 |
| 4 years | 14,569 | 23,269 | 8,700 | 63 | 60 |
| College: | | | | | |
| 1 to 3 years | 17,007 | 25,831 | 8,824 | 66 | 52 |
| 4 years or more | 21,889 | 33,934 | 12,045 | 65 | 55 |

*Source:* Department of Commerce, Bureau of the Census.

## Characteristics of Households With Female Householder, 1985

| Characteristics | Number of households | Income bracket | Number of households |
|---|---|---|---|
| All female householders | 26,763,000 | 3 persons | 3,740,000 |
| **MARITAL STATUS** | | 4 persons or more | 3,716,000 |
| Married, husband present | 2,667,000 | **RELATED CHILDREN UNDER 18** | |
| Married, husband absent | 2,497,000 | No related children | 18,661,000 |
| Widowed | 9,728,000 | 1 or more related children | 8,102,000 |
| Divorced | 6,265,000 | **TOTAL HOUSEHOLD INCOME[2]** | |
| Single (never married) | 5,606,000 | Under $2,500 | 1,173,000 |
| **RACE AND SPANISH ORIGIN** | | $2,500 to $4,999 | 3,362,000 |
| **OF HOUSEHOLDER** | | $5,000 to $7,499 | 3,757,000 |
| White | 21,461,000 | $7,500 to $9,999 | 2,619,000 |
| Black | 4,815,000 | $10,000 to $14,999 | 4,163,000 |
| Spanish origin[1] | 1,526,000 | $15,000 to $24,999 | 5,817,000 |
| **SIZE OF HOUSEHOLD** | | $25,000 to $49,000 | 4,748,000 |
| 1 person | 12,680,000 | $50,000 and over | 1,126,000 |
| 2 persons | 6,628,000 | Median income | 12,764 |
| | | Mean income | 17,397 |

1. Persons of Spanish origin may be of any race. 2. As of March 1985. *Source:* Department of Commerce, Bureau of the Census.

# Occupations of Employed Women
## (16 years of age and over)

| Occupations | Percent | | | | | | |
|---|---|---|---|---|---|---|---|
| | 1985 | 1984[1] | 1983[1] | 1982[1] | 1981[1] | 1980[1] | 1979[1] |
| Managerial and professional | 23.4 | 22.5 | 21.9 | 21.7 | 20.9 | 20.4 | 19.6 |
| Technical, sales, administrative support | 45.5 | 45.6 | 45.8 | 45.7 | 45.9 | 46.0 | 45.8 |
| Service occupations | 18.5 | 18.7 | 18.9 | 19.0 | 18.8 | 18.9 | 19.2 |
| Precision production, craft and repair | 2.4 | 2.4 | 2.3 | 1.9 | 1.9 | 1.9 | 1.8 |
| Operators, fabricators, laborers | 9.1 | 9.6 | 9.7 | 10.3 | 11.1 | 11.4 | 12.2 |
| Farming, forestry, fishing | 1.2 | 1.2 | 1.3 | 1.4 | 1.3 | 1.4 | 1.4 |

1. Annual averages. NOTE: Details may not add up to totals because of rounding. *Source:* Department of Labor, Bureau of Labor Statistics.

# Unemployment by Marital Status, Sex, and Race[1]

| Marital status and race | Men | | Women | |
|---|---|---|---|---|
| | Number | Unemployment rate | Number | Unemployment rate |
| **White, 16 years and over** | 3,820,000 | 6.8 | 2,754,000 | 6.3 |
| Married, spouse present | 1,771,000 | 4.8 | 1,308,000 | 5.2 |
| Widowed, divorced, or separated | 495,000 | 9.2 | 601,000 | 7.2 |
| Single (never married) | 1,555,000 | 10.9 | 844,000 | 7.9 |
| **Black, 16 years and over** | 962,000 | 15.3 | 874,000 | 14.1 |
| Married, spouse present | 234,000 | 7.8 | 185,000 | 7.9 |
| Widowed, divorced, or separated | 125,000 | 13.2 | 196,000 | 11.2 |
| Single (never married) | 603,000 | 26.0 | 493,000 | 23.4 |
| **Total, 16 years and over** | 4,928,000 | 7.6 | 3,739,000 | 7.2 |
| Married, spouse present | 2,081,000 | 5.1 | 1,551,000 | 5.5 |
| Widowed, divorced, or separated | 637,000 | 9.9 | 817,000 | 7.9 |
| Single (never married) | 2,210,000 | 13.0 | 1,371,000 | 10.5 |

1. March 1986. *Source:* U.S. Department of Labor, Bureau of Labor Statistics.

# Earnings Distribution of Year-Round, Full-Time Workers, by Sex, 1984
## (persons 15 years old and over as of March 1985)

| Earnings group | Number | | Distribution (percent) | | Likelihood of a woman in each earnings group (percent)[1] |
|---|---|---|---|---|---|
| | Women | Men | Women | Men | |
| $2,999 or less | 603,000 | 1,019,000 | 2.3 | 2.3 | 1.0 |
| $3,000 to $4,999 | 383,000 | 416,000 | 1.4 | 0.9 | 1.6 |
| $5,000 to $6,999 | 1,184,000 | 1,010,000 | 4.5 | 2.3 | 2.0 |
| $7,000 to $9,999 | 3,584,000 | 2,237,000 | 13.5 | 5.1 | 2.6 |
| $10,000 to $14,999 | 7,762,000 | 5,955,000 | 29.3 | 13.6 | 2.2 |
| $15,000 to $19,999 | 5,834,000 | 6,699,000 | 22.0 | 15.2 | 1.4 |
| $20,000 to $24,999 | 3,594,000 | 6,574,000 | 13.6 | 15.0 | 0.9 |
| $25,000 to $49,999 | 3,311,000 | 16,391,000 | 12.5 | 37.4 | 0.3 |
| $50,000 and over | 213,000 | 3,538,000 | 0.8 | 8.1 | 0.1 |
| Total | 26,466,000 | 43,808,000 | 100.0 | 100.0 | — |

1. Figures obtained by dividing percentages for women by percentages for men. *Source:* Department of Commerce, Bureau of the Census.

## Comparison of Median Earnings of Year-Round, Full-Time Workers 15 Years and Over, by Sex, 1960 to 1984

| Year | Median earnings | | Earnings gap in current dollars | Women's earnings as a percent of men's | Percent men's earnings exceeded women's | Earnings gap in constant 1984 dollars |
|---|---|---|---|---|---|---|
| | Women | Men | | | | |
| 1960 | $3,257 | $5,368 | $2,111 | 60.7 | 64.8 | $7,404 |
| 1965 | 3,828 | 6,388 | 2,560 | 60.0 | 66.9 | 8,428 |
| 1970 | 5,323 | 8,966 | 3,643 | 59.4 | 68.4 | 9,745 |
| 1974 | 6,970 | 11,889 | 4,919 | 58.6 | 70.6 | 10,361 |
| 1975 | 7,504 | 12,758 | 5,254 | 58.8 | 70.0 | 10,140 |
| 1976 | 8,099 | 13,455 | 5,356 | 60.2 | 66.1 | 9,773 |
| 1978 | 9,350 | 15,730 | 6,380 | 59.4 | 68.2 | 10,158 |
| 1979 | 10,169 | 17,045 | 6,876 | 59.7 | 67.6 | 9,840 |
| 1980 | 11,197 | 18,612 | 7,415 | 60.2 | 66.2 | 9,347 |
| 1981 | 12,001 | 20,260 | 8,259 | 59.2 | 68.8 | 9,432 |
| 1982 | 13,014 | 21,077 | 8,063 | 61.7 | 62.0 | 8,677 |
| 1983 | 13,915 | 21,881 | 7,966 | 63.6 | 57.2 | 8,305 |
| 1984 | 14,780 | 23,218 | 8,438 | 63.7 | 57.1 | 8,438 |

*Source:* Department of Commerce, Bureau of the Census.

## Full- and Part-Time Status of the Civilian Labor Force: 1970 to 1984

| ITEM | Full-Time | | | | | Part-Time | | | | |
|---|---|---|---|---|---|---|---|---|---|---|
| | 1984 | 1983 | 1980 | 1975 | 1970 | 1984 | 1983 | 1980 | 1975 | 1970 |
| **Civilian labor force** | 97,632 | 95,736 | 91,295 | 80,117 | 71,069 | 15,912 | 15,814 | 15,644 | 13,659 | 11,703 |
| Percent of total | 86.0 | 85.8 | 85.4 | 85.4 | 85.9 | 14.0 | 14.2 | 14.6 | 14.6 | 14.1 |
| Employed | 90,574 | 86,661 | 85,027 | 73,595 | 67,863 | 14,431 | 14,172 | 14,275 | 12,251 | 10,814 |
| Unemployed | 7,057 | 9,075 | 6,269 | 6,523 | 3,206 | 1,481 | 1,642 | 1,369 | 1,408 | 889 |
| Percent[1] | 7.2 | 9.5 | 6.9 | 8.1 | 4.5 | 9.3 | 10.4 | 8.8 | 10.3 | 7.6 |
| Males, 20 yr. and over | 56,605 | 55,636 | 53,571 | 48,895 | 44,962 | 3,096 | 3,108 | 2,883 | 2,601 | 2,259 |
| Employed | 52,920 | 50,653 | 50,405 | 45,640 | 43,460 | 2,849 | 2,834 | 2,697 | 2,378 | 2,122 |
| Unemployed | 3,685 | 4,982 | 3,167 | 3,255 | 1,502 | 247 | 274 | 186 | 223 | 137 |
| Percent[1] | 6.5 | 9.0 | 5.9 | 6.7 | 3.3 | 8.0 | 8.8 | 6.5 | 8.6 | 6.1 |
| Females, 20 yr and over | 37,001 | 35,854 | 32,722 | 26,359 | 22,226 | 8,898 | 8,782 | 8,383 | 7,052 | 6,074 |
| Employed | 34,445 | 32,812 | 30,588 | 24,148 | 21,149 | 8,347 | 8,192 | 7,904 | 6,578 | 5,803 |
| Unemployed | 2,556 | 3,042 | 2,135 | 2,210 | 1,077 | 551 | 589 | 480 | 474 | 271 |
| Percent[1] | 6.9 | 8.5 | 6.5 | 8.4 | 4.8 | 6.2 | 6.7 | 5.7 | 6.7 | 4.5 |
| Persons, 16–19 yr | 4,026 | 4,247 | 5,001 | 4,864 | 3,881 | 3,918 | 3,924 | 4,377 | 4,005 | 3,370 |
| Employed | 3,210 | 3,196 | 4,035 | 3,807 | 3,254 | 3,235 | 3,146 | 3,676 | 3,295 | 2,889 |
| Unemployed | 816 | 1,051 | 966 | 1,057 | 626 | 683 | 778 | 701 | 709 | 480 |
| Percent[1] | 20.3 | 24.7 | 19.3 | 21.7 | 16.1 | 17.4 | 19.8 | 16.0 | 17.7 | 14.3 |

1. Unemployment as percent of civilian labor force in specified group.

## Advertising Expenditures by Medium

### (in billions)

| Medium | 1985 | | 1984 | | 1980 | | 1975 | | 1970 | | 1960 | |
|---|---|---|---|---|---|---|---|---|---|---|---|---|
| | Amt. | % of total | Amt. | % of total | Amt. | % of total | Amt. | % of total | Amt. | % of total | Amt. | % of total |
| Newspapers | 25.2 | 26.5 | 23.7 | 26.9 | $14.8 | 27.7 | $8.2 | 29.5 | $5.7 | 29.2 | $3.7 | 31.0 |
| Magazines | 5.2 | 5.4 | 4.9 | 5.6 | 3.1 | 5.9 | 1.5 | 5.2 | 1.3 | 6.6 | 0.9 | 7.9 |
| Business Papers | 2.4 | 2.5 | 2.2 | 2.6 | 1.7 | 3.1 | 0.9 | 3.3 | 0.7 | 3.8 | 0.6 | 5.1 |
| Radio | 6.5 | 6.9 | 5.8 | 6.6 | 3.7 | 6.9 | 2.0 | 7.1 | 1.3 | 6.7 | 0.7 | 5.8 |
| Television | 20.8 | 21.9 | 19.8 | 22.6 | 11.4 | 21.2 | 5.3 | 18.9 | 3.6 | 18.4 | 1.6 | 13.3 |
| Direct mail | 15.5 | 16.4 | 13.8 | 15.7 | 7.6 | 14.2 | 4.1 | 14.8 | 2.8 | 14.1 | 1.8 | 15.3 |
| Outdoor | .9 | 1.0 | 0.9 | 1.0 | 0.6 | 1.1 | 0.3 | 1.2 | 0.2 | 1.2 | 0.2 | 1.7 |
| Miscellaneous[1] | 18.2 | 19.2 | 16.7 | 20.0 | 10.7 | 19.9 | 5.6 | 20.0 | 3.9 | 20.0 | 2.4 | 19.8 |
| Total | 94.8 | 100.0 | 88.0 | 100.0 | 53.6 | 100.0 | 27.9 | 100.0 | 19.5 | 100.0 | 11.9 | 100.0 |

1. Includes regional farm papers. *Sources:* McCann-Erickson, Inc., and *Advertising Age.*

# Leading Advertising Agencies in World Billings

(in millions of dollars)

| Agency | 1984 | 1983 |
|---|---|---|
| Young & Rubicam | $3,575.3 | $3,202.1 |
| Ogilvy Group | 3,318.7 | 2,887.9 |
| Ted Bates Worldwide | 3,106.9 | 2,829.2 |
| Saatchi & Saatchi Compton Worldwide | 3,033.1 | 2,301.7 |
| J. Walter Thompson Co. | 3,009.2 | 2,765.3 |
| BBDO International | 2,516.0 | 2,275.0 |
| McCann-Erickson Worldwide | 2,302.8 | 1,949.3 |
| D'Arcy Masius Benton & Bowles | 2,181.3 | 2,314.4 |
| Foote, Cone & Belding Communications | 1,901.0 | 1,802.3 |
| Leo Burnett Co. | 1,868.5 | 1,734.8 |

*Source:* Reprinted with permission from the March 27, 1986, issue of *Advertising Age.* Copyright © 1986 by Crain Communications, Inc.

# Unemployment Rate, 1985

| Race and age | Women[1] | Men[1] |
|---|---|---|
| All races: | 7.4 | 7.0 |
| 16 to 19 years | 17.6 | 19.5 |
| 20 years and over | 6.6 | 6.2 |
| White | 6.4 | 6.1 |
| 16 to 19 years | 14.8 | 16.5 |
| 20 years and over | 5.7 | 5.4 |
| Minority races: | 13.5 | 13.8 |
| 16 to 19 years | 35.8 | 38.4 |
| 20 years and over | 7.0 | 9.0 |

1. Annual averages. *Source:* Department of Labor.

# Unemployment Rate in the Civilian Labor Force

| Year | Unemployment Rate | Year | Unemployment Rate |
|---|---|---|---|
| 1920 | 5.2 | 1974 | 5.6 |
| 1922 | 6.7 | 1976 | 7.7 |
| 1924 | 5.0 | 1978 | 6.0 |
| 1926 | 1.8 | 1979 | 5.8 |
| 1928 | 4.2 | 1980 | 7.1 |
| 1930 | 8.7 | 1981 | 7.6 |
| 1932 | 23.6 | 1982 | 9.7 |
| 1934 | 21.7 | 1983 | 9.6 |
| 1936 | 16.9 | 1984 | 7.5 |
| 1938 | 19.0 | 1985 | 7.2 |
| 1940 | 14.6 | Jan. | 7.4 |
| 1942 | 4.7 | Feb. | 7.3 |
| 1944 | 1.2 | March | 7.3 |
| 1946 | 3.9 | April | 7.3 |
| 1948 | 3.8 | May | 7.3 |
| 1950 | 5.3 | June | 7.3 |
| 1952 | 3.0 | July | 7.3 |
| 1954 | 5.5 | August | 7.1 |
| 1956 | 4.1 | Sept. | 7.1 |
| 1958 | 6.8 | Oct. | 7.1 |
| 1960 | 5.5 | Nov. | 7.0 |
| 1962 | 5.5 | Dec. | 6.9 |
| 1964 | 5.2 | 1986 | |
| 1966 | 3.8 | Jan. | 6.7 |
| 1968 | 3.6 | Feb. | 7.3 |
| 1970 | 4.9 | March | 7.2 |
| 1972 | 5.6 | April | 7.1 |

NOTE: Estimates prior to 1940 are based on sources other than direct enumeration. *Source:* Department of Labor, Bureau of Labor Statistics.

# Employment and Unemployment

(in millions of persons)

| Category | 1986[2] | 1985 | 1980 | 1975 | 1970 | 1959 | 1950 | 1945 | 1941 | 1932 | 1929 |
|---|---|---|---|---|---|---|---|---|---|---|---|
| **EMPLOYMENT STATUS[1]** | | | | | | | | | | | |
| Civilian noninstitutional population | 180.5 | 178.2 | 167.7 | 153.2 | 137.1 | 115.3 | 105.0 | 94.1 | 99.9 | — | — |
| Civilian labor force | 118.1 | 115.5 | 106.9 | 93.8 | 82.8 | 68.4 | 62.2 | 53.9 | 55.9 | — | — |
| Civilian labor force participation rate | 65.4 | 64.8 | 63.8 | 61.2 | 60.4 | 59.3 | 59.2 | 57.2 | 56.0 | | |
| Employed | 109.7 | 107.2 | 99.3 | 85.8 | 78.7 | 64.6 | 58.9 | 52.8 | 50.4 | 38.9 | 47.6 |
| Employment-population ratio | 60.8 | 60.1 | 59.2 | 56.1 | 57.4 | 56.0 | 56.1 | 56.1 | 50.4 | | |
| Agriculture | 3.2 | 3.2 | 3.4 | 3.4 | 3.5 | 5.6 | 7.2 | 8.6 | 9.1 | 10.2 | 10.5 |
| Nonagricultural industries | 106.5 | 104.0 | 95.9 | 82.4 | 75.2 | 59.1 | 51.8 | 44.2 | 41.3 | 28.8 | 37.2 |
| Unemployed | 8.4 | 8.3 | 7.6 | 7.9 | 4.1 | 3.7 | 3.3 | 1.0 | 5.6 | 12.1 | 1.6 |
| Unemployment rate | 7.1 | 7.2 | 7.1 | 8.5 | 4.9 | 5.5 | 5.3 | 1.9 | 9.9 | 23.6 | 3.2 |
| Not in labor force | 62.4 | 62.7 | 60.8 | 59.4 | 54.3 | 47.0 | 42.8 | 40.2 | 44.0 | — | — |
| **INDUSTRY** | | | | | | | | | | | |
| Total nonagricultural employment | 99.8 | 97.6 | 90.4 | 76.9 | 70.9 | 53.3 | 45.2 | 40.4 | 36.5 | 23.6 | 31.3 |
| Goods-producing industries | 24.9 | 24.9 | 25.7 | 22.6 | 23.6 | 20.4 | 18.5 | 17.5 | 16.0 | 8.6 | 13.3 |
| Mining | 0.8 | 0.9 | 1.0 | 0.8 | 0.6 | 0.7 | 0.9 | 0.8 | 1.0 | 0.7 | 1.1 |
| Construction | 4.9 | 4.7 | 4.3 | 3.5 | 3.6 | 3.0 | 2.4 | 1.1 | 1.8 | 1.0 | 1.5 |
| Manufacturing: Durable goods | 11.3 | 11.5 | 12.2 | 10.7 | 11.2 | 9.4 | 8.1 | 9.1 | 7.0 | — | — |
| Nondurable goods | 7.8 | 7.8 | 8.1 | 7.6 | 8.2 | 7.3 | 7.1 | 6.5 | 6.2 | — | — |
| Services-producing industries | 75.0 | 72.7 | 64.7 | 54.3 | 47.3 | 32.9 | 26.7 | 22.9 | 20.6 | 15.0 | 18.0 |
| Transportation and public utilities | 5.2 | 5.2 | 5.1 | 4.5 | 4.5 | 4.0 | 4.0 | 3.9 | 3.3 | 2.8 | 3.9 |
| Trade, Wholesale | 5.8 | 5.7 | 5.3 | 4.4 | 4.0 | 3.1 | 2.6 | 1.9 | 2.0 | — | — |
| Retail | 17.9 | 17.4 | 15.0 | 12.6 | 11.0 | 8.0 | 6.8 | 5.4 | 5.3 | — | — |
| Finance, insurance, and real estate | 6.3 | 6.0 | 5.2 | 4.2 | 3.6 | 2.5 | 1.9 | 1.5 | 1.5 | 1.3 | 1.5 |
| Services | 23.1 | 22.0 | 17.9 | 13.9 | 11.5 | 7.1 | 5.4 | 4.2 | 3.9 | 2.9 | 3.4 |
| Federal government | 2.9 | 2.9 | 2.9 | 2.7 | 2.7 | 2.2 | 1.9 | 2.8 | 1.3 | 0.6 | 0.5 |
| State and local government | 13.8 | 13.5 | 13.4 | 11.9 | 9.8 | 5.9 | 4.1 | 3.1 | 3.3 | 2.7 | 2.5 |

1. For 1929–45, figures on employment status relate to persons 14 years and over; beginning in 1950, 16 years and over.
2. As of June. NOTE: Figures may not add to totals because of rounding. *Source:* Department of Labor, Bureau of Labor Statistics.

## Livestock on Farms (in thousands)

| Type | 1986 | 1985 | 1984 | 1980 | 1975 | 1970 | 1965 | 1960 | 1950 | 1945 |
|---|---|---|---|---|---|---|---|---|---|---|
| Cattle[1] | 105,468 | 109,749 | 113,700 | 111,242 | 132,028 | 112,369 | 109,000 | 96,236 | 77,963 | 85,573 |
| Dairy cows[1] | 11,179 | 10,805 | 11,109 | 10,758 | 11,220 | 13,303 | 16,981 | 19,527 | 23,853 | 27,770 |
| Sheep[1] | 9,932 | 10,443 | 11,487 | 12,699 | 14,515 | 20,423 | 25,127 | 33,170 | 29,826 | 39,609 |
| Swine[2] | 52,298 | 54,073 | 56,694 | 67,318 | 54,693 | 57,046 | 56,106 | 59,026 | 58,937 | 59,373 |
| Chickens[2] | n.a. | 374,008 | 364,880 | 400,585 | 384,101 | 422,000 | 401,000 | 369,000 | 457,000 | 516,000 |
| Turkeys[3] | n.a. | 3,159 | 3,155 | 3,749 | 3,014 | 6,715 | 6,100 | 5,633 | 5,124 | 7,082 |

1. As of Jan. 1. 2. As of Jan. 1 the previous year for 1945–60 and Dec. 1 for 1965–85. 3. Turkey breeder hens for 1975–85 as of Dec. 1 the previous year. *Source:* Department of Agriculture, Statistical Reporting Service, Economic Research Service.

## Agricultural Output by States, 1985 Crops

| State | Corn (1,000 bu) | Wheat (1,000 bu) | Cotton (1,000 ba[1]) | Potatoes (1,000 cwt) | Tobacco (1,000 lb) | Cattle[2] (1,000 head) | Swine[3] (1,000 head) |
|---|---|---|---|---|---|---|---|
| Alabama | 24,375 | 12,800 | 545.0 | 2,252 | — | 1,830 | 345 |
| Alaska | — | — | — | — | — | 9.5 | 2.3 |
| Arizona | 2,205 | 9,804 | 1,036.7 | 1,450 | — | 1,050 | 175 |
| Arkansas | 7,885 | 18,240 | 703.0 | — | — | 1,850 | 436 |
| California | 46,400 | 68,860 | 3,114.0 | 22,945 | — | 4,960 | 145 |
| Colorado | 103,555 | 139,302 | — | 20,140 | — | 3,000 | 225 |
| Connecticut | — | — | — | 350 | 3,315 | 110 | 7.0 |
| Delaware | 19,075 | 2,064 | — | 1,820 | — | 26 | 35 |
| Florida | 12,350 | 4,290 | 32.5 | 7,930 | 16,318 | 2,190 | 158 |
| Georgia | 81,900 | 25,575 | 370.0 | — | 82,080 | 1,750 | 1,150 |
| Hawaii | — | — | — | — | — | 221 | 55 |
| Idaho | 10,000 | 72,030 | — | 102,515 | — | 1,780 | 125 |
| Illinois | 1,534,950 | 36,750 | — | 855 | — | 2,500 | 5,400 |
| Indiana | 756,450 | 37,100 | — | 890 | 14,560 | 1,620 | 4,150 |
| Iowa | 1,707,300 | 5,376 | — | 330 | — | 5,600 | 13,500 |
| Kansas | 140,400 | 433,200 | 0.4 | — | — | 5,860 | 1,520 |
| Kentucky | 159,120 | 10,540 | — | — | 428,409 | 2,580 | 800 |
| Louisiana | 23,370 | 7,140 | 742.0 | 42 | — | 1,320 | 60 |
| Maine | — | — | — | 27,160 | — | 145 | 7.9 |
| Maryland | 70,400 | 6,517 | — | 320 | 28,350 | 390 | 205 |
| Massachusetts | — | — | — | 825 | 781 | 100 | 54 |
| Michigan | 286,650 | 45,000 | — | 15,136 | — | 1,450 | 1,190 |
| Minnesota | 724,500 | 142,426 | — | 15,933 | — | 3,550 | 4,100 |
| Mississippi | 7,820 | 9,300 | 1,655.0 | — | — | 1,588 | 230 |
| Missouri | 272,800 | 49,920 | 204.0 | — | 5,450 | 4,850 | 3,050 |
| Montana | 1,045 | 56,240 | — | 1,890 | — | 2,960 | 135 |
| Nebraska | 953,600 | 89,700 | — | 2,873 | — | 6,100 | 3,900 |
| Nevada | — | 1,770 | — | 3,105 | — | 620 | 15 |
| New Hampshire | — | — | — | — | — | 69 | 8.6 |
| New Jersey | 12,540 | 1,924 | — | 2,464 | — | 102 | 45 |
| New Mexico | 10,075 | 20,520 | 82.8 | 2,860 | — | 1,410 | 38 |
| New York | 68,400 | 8,410 | — | 9,995 | — | 2,000 | 130 |
| North Carolina | 128,375 | 22,040 | 117.0 | 2,575 | 556,522 | 1,175 | 2,350 |
| North Dakota | 40,320 | 323,255 | — | 23,630 | — | 2,050 | 285 |
| Ohio | 511,810 | 58,900 | — | 2,806 | 16,946 | 1,835 | 1,980 |
| Oklahoma | 6,148 | 165,000 | 285.0 | — | — | 5,300 | 200 |
| Oregon | 6,600 | 56,040 | — | 26,701 | — | 1,650 | 125 |
| Pennsylvania | 151,800 | 10,080 | — | 5,720 | 21,900 | 1,960 | 780 |
| Rhode Island | — | — | — | 700 | — | 8.0 | 5.0 |
| South Carolina | 45,760 | 12,470 | 180.0 | — | 98,900 | 620 | 400 |
| South Dakota | 252,000 | 111,215 | — | 1,920 | — | 4,160 | 1,610 |
| Tennessee | 79,380 | 8,000 | 419.0 | 375 | 127,403 | 2,535 | 950 |
| Texas | 156,450 | 187,200 | 3,995.1 | 3,855 | — | 14,100 | 435 |
| Utah | 1,840 | 8,720 | — | 1,658 | — | 800 | 23 |
| Vermont | — | — | — | 66 | — | 350 | 6.4 |
| Virginia | 54,450 | 10,545 | 1.2 | 3,300 | 91,092 | 1,760 | 400 |
| Washington | 21,600 | 128,250 | — | 62,370 | — | 1,470 | 51 |
| West Virginia | 7,665 | 344 | — | — | 3,384 | 580 | 37 |
| Wisconsin | 358,450 | 8,380 | — | 24,130 | 17,560 | 4,440 | 1,250 |
| Wyoming | 5,194 | 5,528 | — | 245 | — | 1,365 | 34 |
| U.S. Total | 8,865,006 | 2,424,765 | 13,432.2 | 404,131 | 1,512,970 | 109,749 | 52,298 |

1. 480-lb net-weight bales. 2. Number on farms as of Jan. 1, 1986. 3. Number on farms as of Dec. 1, 1985. *Source:* Department of Agriculture, Statistical Reporting Service.

## Farm Income
(in millions of dollars)

| Year | Cash receipts from marketings | | Government payments | Total cash income |
|------|-------|-------|-------|-------|
| | Crops | Livestock, livestock products | | |
| 1920 | $6,644 | $5,956 | — | $12,600 |
| 1925 | 5,545 | 5,476 | — | 11,021 |
| 1930 | 3,868 | 5,187 | — | 9,055 |
| 1935 | 2,977 | 4,143 | $573 | 7,693 |
| 1940 | 3,469 | 4,913 | 723 | 9,105 |
| 1945 | 9,655 | 12,008 | 742 | 22,405 |
| 1950 | 12,356 | 16,105 | 283 | 28,744 |
| 1955 | 13,523 | 15,967 | 229 | 29,719 |
| 1960 | 15,259 | 18,989 | 702 | 34,950 |
| 1965 | 17,479 | 21,886 | 2,463 | 41,828 |
| 1970 | 20,977 | 29,532 | 3,717 | 54,226 |
| 1975 | 45,813 | 43,087 | 807 | 89,707 |
| 1978 | 53,925 | 59,162 | 3,030 | 116,117 |
| 1979 | 64,142 | 68,594 | 1,375 | 134,111 |
| 1980 | 72,269 | 67,800 | 1,286 | 141,355 |
| 1981 | 71,326 | 69,215 | 1,932 | 142,473 |
| 1982 | 66,298 | 70,139 | 3,492 | 139,929 |
| 1983 | 74,140 | 69,203 | 9,294[1] | 152,637 |
| 1984 | 69,069 | 72,739 | 8,430 | 150,238 |

1. Includes value of PIK commodities. *Source:* Department of Agriculture, Economic Research Service. NOTE: Figures are latest available.

## Consumption of Principal Foods[1]
(in pounds per capita)

| Foods | 1984 | 1983 | 1982 |
|-------|------|------|------|
| Red meats | 143.5 | 144.2 | 139.4 |
| Poultry | 67.0 | 63.8 | 64.1 |
| Eggs | 33.0 | 33.1 | 33.4 |
| Fluid milk and cream[2] | 243.4 | 240.0 | 242.2 |
| Cheese | 23.3 | 22.4 | 20.1 |
| Butter | 5.0 | 5.1 | 4.5 |
| Margarine | 10.4 | 10.3 | 11.1 |
| Fats and oils | 61.6 | 62.7 | 56.3 |
| Fresh fruits | 86.6 | 87.5 | 83.9 |
| Processed fruits | n.a. | 48.6 | 50.4 |
| Fresh vegetables | 75.5 | 71.0 | 71.2 |
| Processed vegetables | 44.6 | 44.8 | 43.5 |
| Potatoes, sweet potatoes[3] | 125.6 | 125.3 | 119.3 |
| Sugar | 67.5 | 71.0 | 75.2 |
| Corn products[4] | n.a. | 130.2 | 125.6 |
| Wheat flour | 117.8 | 116.0 | 114.0 |
| Coffee | 7.7 | 7.6 | 7.5 |
| Cocoa products | 3.6 | 3.3 | 3.0 |

1. As of August 1985. Except where noted, consumption is from commercial sources and is in terms of retail weight. 2. Includes milk and cream produced and consumed on farms. 3. Farm-weight equivalent of fresh and processed use. 4. Farm-weight equivalent of corn for all food use except fresh. NOTE: n.a. = not available. *Source:* Department of Agriculture, Economic Research Service.

## Government Employment and Payrolls

| Year and function | Employees (in thousands) | | | | October payrolls (in millions) | | | |
|-------------------|-------|----------|-------|-------|-------|----------|-------|-------|
| | Total | Federal[1] | State | Local | Total | Federal[1] | State | Local |
| 1940 | 4,474 | 1,128 | 3,346 | | $566 | 177 | $389 | |
| 1945 | 6,677 | 3,496 | 3,181 | | 1,059 | 591 | 468 | |
| 1950 | 6,402 | 2,117 | 1,057 | 3,228 | 1,528 | 613 | 218 | 696 |
| 1955 | 7,432 | 2,378 | 1,199 | 3,855 | 2,265 | 846 | 326 | 1,093 |
| 1960 | 8,808 | 2,421 | 1,527 | 4,860 | 3,333 | 1,118 | 524 | 1,691 |
| 1965 | 10,589 | 2,588 | 2,028 | 5,973 | 4,884 | 1,484 | 849 | 2,551 |
| 1970 | 13,028 | 2,881 | 2,755 | 7,392 | 8,334 | 2,428 | 1,612 | 4,294 |
| 1972 | 13,759 | 2,795 | 2,957 | 8,007 | 9,950 | 2,710 | 1,937 | 5,303 |
| 1975 | 14,973 | 2,890 | 3,271 | 8,813 | 13,224 | 3,584 | 2,653 | 6,987 |
| 1976 | 15,012 | 2,843 | 3,343 | 8,826 | 13,924 | 3,565 | 2,894 | 7,465 |
| 1977 | 15,459 | 2,848 | 3,491 | 9,120 | 15,338 | 3,918 | 3,195 | 8,225 |
| 1978 | 15,628 | 2,885 | 3,539 | 9,204 | 16,483 | 4,344 | 3,483 | 8,656 |
| 1979 | 15,971 | 2,869 | 3,699 | 9,403 | 18,077 | 4,728 | 3,869 | 9,480 |
| 1980 | 16,213 | 2,898 | 3,753 | 9,562 | 19,935 | 5,205 | 4,285 | 10,445 |
| 1981 | 15,968 | 2,865 | 3,726 | 9,377 | 21,193 | 5,239 | 4,668 | 11,287 |
| 1982 | 15,841 | 2,848 | 3,744 | 9,249 | 23,173 | 5,959 | 5,022 | 12,192 |
| 1983 | 16,034 | 2,875 | 3,816 | 9,344 | 24,525 | 6,302 | 5,346 | 12,878 |
| 1984 | 16,436 | 2,942 | 3,898 | 9,595 | 26,904 | 7,137 | 5,815 | 13,952 |
| 1985, total | 16,690 | 3,021 | 3,984 | 9,685 | 28,945 | 7,580 | 6,329 | 15,036 |
| National defense and international relations | 1,101 | 1,101 | (2) | (2) | 2,898 | 2,898 | (2) | (2) |
| Postal service | 754 | 754 | (2) | (2) | 1,741 | 1,741 | (2) | (2) |
| Education | 7,119 | 15 | 1,764 | 5,340 | 10,722 | 38 | 2,444 | 8,240 |
| Instructional employees | 4,002 | n.a. | 526 | 3,475 | 7,486 | n.a. | 1,096 | 6,390 |
| Highways | 552 | 4 | 252 | 296 | 922 | 14 | 460 | 448 |
| Health and hospitals | 1,653 | 263 | 678 | 712 | 2,774 | 640 | 1,091 | 1,043 |
| Police protection | 760 | 66 | 81 | 613 | 1,516 | 188 | 175 | 1,153 |
| Local fire protection | 317 | (2) | (2) | 317 | 554 | (2) | (2) | 554 |
| Sewerage and sanitation | 221 | n.a. | 1 | 220 | 358 | n.a. | 1 | 358 |
| Parks and recreation | 263 | n.a. | 33 | 230 | 293 | n.a. | 44 | 249 |
| Natural resources | 443 | 241 | 163 | 39 | 906 | 598 | 258 | 50 |
| Financial administration | 438 | 118 | 131 | 190 | 744 | 253 | 229 | 262 |
| All other | 3,069 | 459 | 881 | 1,728 | 5,517 | 1,210 | 1,628 | 2,679 |

1. Civilians only. 2. Not applicable. NOTE: n.a. = not available. *Source:* Department of Commerce, Bureau of the Census.

# Receipts and Outlays of the Federal Government

## (in millions of dollars)

From 1789 to 1842, the federal fiscal year ended Dec. 31; from 1844 to 1976, on June 30; and beginning 1977, on Sept. 30.

| Year | Customs (including tonnage tax)[1] | Income and profits tax | Other | Miscellaneous taxes and receipts | Total receipts | Net receipts[2] |
|---|---|---|---|---|---|---|
| | | **Internal revenue** | | | | |
| | | Receipts | | | | |
| 1789–1791 | $    4 | — | — | — | $    4 | $    4 |
| 1800 | 9 | — | $  −1 | $  1 | 11 | 11 |
| 1810 | 9 | — | — | 1 | 9 | 9 |
| 1820 | 15 | — | — | 3 | 18 | 18 |
| 1830 | 22 | — | — | 3 | 25 | 25 |
| 1840 | 14 | — | — | 6 | 20 | 20 |
| 1850 | 40 | — | — | 4 | 44 | 44 |
| 1860 | 53 | — | — | 3 | 56 | 56 |
| 1865 | 85 | — | 209 | 39 | 334 | 334 |
| 1870 | 195 | — | 185 | 32 | 411 | 411 |
| 1880 | 187 | — | 124 | 23 | 334 | 334 |
| 1890 | 230 | — | 143 | 31 | 403 | 403 |
| 1900 | 233 | — | 295 | 39 | 567 | 567 |
| 1910 | 334 | — | 290 | 52 | 675 | 675 |
| 1915 | 210 | $    80 | 335 | 72 | 698 | 683 |
| 1918 | 180 | 2,314 | 872 | 299 | 3,665 | 3,645 |
| 1929 | 602 | 2,331 | 607 | 493 | 4,033 | 3,862 |
| 1933 | 251 | 746 | 858 | 225 | 2,080 | 1,997 |
| 1939 | 319 | 2,189 | 2,972 | 188 | 5,668 | 4,979 |
| 1943 | 324 | 16,094 | 6,050 | 934 | 23,402 | 21,947 |
| 1944 | 431 | 34,655 | 7,030 | 3,325 | 45,441 | 43,563 |
| 1945 | 355 | 35,173 | 8,729 | 3,494 | 47,750 | 44,362 |
| 1950 | 423 | 28,263 | 11,186 | 1,439 | 41,311 | 36,422 |
| 1956[4] | 705 | 56,639 | 20,564 | 389 | 78,297 | 74,547 |
| 1960 | 1,123 | 67,151 | 28,266 | 1,190 | 97,730 | 92,492 |
| 1965 | 1,478 | 79,792 | 39,996 | 1,598 | 122,863 | 116,833 |
| 1970 | 2,494 | 138,689 | 65,276 | 3,424 | 209,883 | 193,743 |
| 1975 | 3,782 | 202,146 | 108,371 | 6,711 | 321,010 | 280,997 |
| 1980 | 7,482 | 359,927 | 192,436 | 12,797 | 572,641 | 520,050 |
| 1983 | 9,060 | 411,410 | 251,491 | 15,620 | 687,581 | 600,563 |
| 1984 | 11,791 | 434,905 | 286,585 | 16,987 | 750,269 | 666,457 |
| 1985 | 12,079 | 474,074 | 311,092 | 18,576 | 815,821 | 733,996 |

| Year | Department of Defense (Army, 1789–1950) | Department of the Navy | Interest on public debt | All other | Net outlays[3] | Surplus (+) or deficit (−) |
|---|---|---|---|---|---|---|
| | | | **Outlays** | | | |
| 1789–1791 | $    1 | — | $    2 | $  1 | $    4 | — |
| 1800 | 3 | $    3 | 3 | 1 | 11 | — |
| 1810 | 2 | 2 | 3 | 1 | 8 | $  +1 |
| 1820 | 3 | 4 | 5 | 6 | 18 | — |
| 1830 | 5 | 3 | 2 | 5 | 15 | +10 |
| 1840 | 7 | 6 | — | 11 | 24 | −4 |
| 1850 | 9 | 8 | 4 | 18 | 40 | +4 |
| 1860 | 16 | 12 | 3 | 32 | 63 | −7 |
| 1865 | 1,031 | 123 | 77 | 66 | 1,298 | −964 |
| 1870 | 58 | 22 | 129 | 101 | 310 | +101 |
| 1880 | 38 | 14 | 96 | 120 | 268 | +66 |
| 1890 | 45 | 22 | 36 | 215 | 318 | +85 |
| 1900 | 135 | 56 | 40 | 290 | 521 | +46 |
| 1910 | 190 | 123 | 21 | 359 | 694 | −19 |
| 1915 | 202 | 142 | 23 | 379 | 746 | −63 |
| 1918 | 4,870 | 1,279 | 190 | 6,339 | 12,677 | −9,032 |
| 1929 | 426 | 365 | 678 | 1,658 | 3,127 | +734 |
| 1933 | 435 | 349 | 689 | 3,125 | 4,598 | −2,602 |
| 1939 | 695 | 673 | 941 | 6,533 | 8,841 | −3,862 |
| 1943 | 42,526 | 20,888 | 1,808 | 14,146 | 79,368 | −57,420 |

| Year | Department of Defense (Army, 1789–1950) | Department of the Navy | Interest on public debt | All other | Net outlays[3] | Surplus (+) or deficit (−) |
|---|---|---|---|---|---|---|
| | | | **Outlays** | | | |
| 1944 | 49,438 | 26,538 | 2,609 | 16,401 | 94,986 | −51,423 |
| 1945 | 50,490 | 30,047 | 3,617 | 14,149 | 98,303 | −53,941 |
| 1950 | 5,789 | 4,130 | 5,750 | 23,875 | 39,544 | −3,122 |
| 1956[4] | 35,693 | — | 6,787 | 27,981 | 70,460 | +4,087 |
| 1960 | 43,969 | — | 9,180 | 39,075 | 92,223 | +269 |
| 1965 | 47,179 | — | 11,346 | 59,904 | 118,430 | −1,596 |
| 1970 | 78,360 | — | 19,304 | 98,924 | 196,588 | −2,845 |
| 1975 | 87,471 | — | 32,665 | 205,969 | 326,105 | −45,108 |
| 1980 | 136,138 | — | 74,860 | 368,013 | 579,011 | −58,961 |
| 1983 | 207,939 | — | 128,813 | 459,165 | 795,917 | −195,354 |
| 1984 | 223,877 | — | 153,838 | 464,085 | 841,800 | −175,342 |
| 1985 | 244,054 | — | 178,945 | 513,810 | 936,809 | −202,813 |

1. Beginning 1933, tonnage tax is included in "Other receipts." 2. Net receipts equal total receipts less (a) appropriations to federal old-age and survivors' insurance trust fund beginning fiscal year 1939 and (b) refunds of receipts beginning fiscal year 1933. 3. Includes Air Force 1950–65 (in millions): 1950—$3,521; 1956—$16,750; 1960—$19,065; 1965—$18, 471. 4. Beginning 1956, computed on unified budget concepts; not strictly comparable with preceding figures. *Source:* Department of the Treasury, Financial Management Service.

## Contributions to International Organizations
### (for fiscal year 1985 in millions of dollars)

| Organization | Amount[1] | Organization | Amount[1] |
|---|---|---|---|
| United Nations and Specialized Agencies | 356.36 | Special Voluntary Programs | 679.26 |
| United Nations | 180.00 | Consultative Group on International | |
| Food and Agriculture Organization | 49.97 | Agricultural Research | 45.16 |
| International Atomic Energy Agency | 18.10 | Intergovernmental Committee for Migration | 5.30 |
| International Civil Aviation Organization | 6.77 | International Atomic Energy Agency Technical | |
| International Labor Organization | 31.84 | Assistance Fund | 17.98[2] |
| International Telecommunication Union | 2.54 | International Fund for Agricultural Development | 90.00 |
| World Health Organization | 61.15 | OAS Special Development Assistance Fund | 6.00 |
| World Meteorological Organization | 4.60 | OAS Special Multilateral Fund (Education and | |
| Others (8 Programs, less than $1 million) | 1.39 | Science) | 6.50 |
| Peacekeeping Forces | | OAS Special Projects Fund (Mar del Plata) | 2.60 |
| United Nations Force in Cyprus | 8.99 | PAHO Special Health Promotion Funds | 3.00 |
| United Nations Disengagement Observer Force | | United Nations Children's Fund | 52.99 |
| (UNDOF) and UNIFIL | 47.40 | United Nations Development Program | 156.75 |
| Multinational Force and Observers | 28.00 | United Nations Educational and Training Program | |
| Inter-American Organizations | 90.98 | for Southern Africa | 1.00 |
| Organization of American States | 43.13 | United Nations Environment Program | 9.85 |
| Inter-American Institute for Cooperation on | | U.N. Capital Development Fund | 1.99 |
| Agriculture | 12.51 | U.N./FAO World Food Program | 28.60[3] |
| Inter-American Tropical Tuna Commission | 2.38 | U.N. Fund for Drug Abuse Control | 2.73 |
| Pan American Health Organization | 32.42 | U.N. Fund for Population Activities | 36.00 |
| Others (4 Programs, less than $1 million) | .54 | U.N. High Commissioner for Refugees Program: | |
| Regional Organizations | 30.05 | Regular Programs (5) | 82.28 |
| NATO Civilian Headquarters (and MBFR) | 12.87 | Special Programs (4) | 42.67 |
| Organization for Economic Cooperation and | | United Nations Relief and Works Agency: | |
| Development | 16.37 | Regular Program | 74.99 |
| Others (3 Programs, less than $1 million) | .81 | West African Rice Development Association | |
| Other International Organizations | 10.87 | (WARDA) | 2.40 |
| Customs Cooperation Council | 1.08 | WHO Special Programs | 6.00 |
| General Agreement on Tariffs and Trade | 2.92 | WMO Voluntary Cooperation Program | 1.95 |
| International Institute for Cotton | 2.30 | Others (12 Programs, less than $1 million) | 2.52 |
| Others (36 Programs, less than $1 million) | 4.57 | **Total U.S. Contributions** | **$1,251.91** |

1. Estimated. 2. Includes cash, commodities and services and $6.95 million for Safeguards Program. 3. Includes commodities and services. No cash contribution made in fiscal year 1985. *Source:* Department of State.

# Social Welfare Expenditures Under Public Programs
### (in millions of dollars)

| Year and source of funds | Social insur- ance | Public aid | Health and medical pro- grams | Veter- ans' pro- grams | Edu- cation | Hous- ing | Other social welfare | All health and medical care[1] | Total social welfare | Total social welfare as: Percent of gross national product | Percent of total gov't outlays |
|---|---|---|---|---|---|---|---|---|---|---|---|
| **FEDERAL** | | | | | | | | | | | |
| 1950 | $2,103 | $1,103 | $604 | $6,386 | $157 | $15 | $174 | $1,362 | $10,541 | 4.0 | 26.2 |
| 1955 | 6,385 | 1,504 | 1,150 | 4,772 | 485 | 75 | 252 | 1,948 | 14,623 | 3.9 | 22.3 |
| 1960 | 14,307 | 2,117 | 1,737 | 5,367 | 868 | 144 | 417 | 2,918 | 24,957 | 5.0 | 28.1 |
| 1965 | 21,807 | 3,594 | 2,781 | 6,011 | 2,470 | 238 | 812 | 4,625 | 37,712 | 5.7 | 32.6 |
| 1970 | 45,246 | 9,649 | 4,775 | 8,952 | 5,876 | 582 | 2,259 | 16,600 | 77,337 | 8.1 | 40.1 |
| 1975 | 99,715 | 27,205 | 8,513 | 16,570 | 8,629 | 2,541 | 4,264 | 34,645 | 167,436 | 11.5 | 53.8 |
| 1979 | 163,879 | 43,384 | 11,707 | 20,412 | 12,108 | 5,069 | 6,649 | 59,009 | 263,634 | 10.9 | 54.1 |
| 1980 | 191,162 | 48,666 | 12,886 | 21,254 | 13,452 | 6,608 | 8,786 | 68,989 | 303,276 | 11.5 | 53.2 |
| 1981 | 224,574 | 55,946 | 13,596 | 23,229 | 13,372 | 6,045 | 7,304 | 80,505 | 344,066 | 11.6[2] | 54.0[2] |
| 1982 | 250,551 | 52,485 | 14,598 | 24,463 | 11,917 | 7,176 | 6,500 | 90,776 | 367,691 | 12.0[2] | 52.5[2] |
| 1983[2] | 274,263 | 55,895 | 15,637 | 25,561 | 12,090 | 8,087 | 7,046 | 100,263 | 398,578 | n.a. | n.a. |
| **STATE AND LOCAL** | | | | | | | | | | | |
| 1950 | 2,844 | 1,393 | 1,460 | 480 | 6,518 | (3) | 274 | 1,704 | 12,967 | 4.9 | 59.2 |
| 1955 | 3,450 | 1,499 | 1,953 | 62 | 10,672 | 15 | 367 | 2,473 | 18,017 | 4.7 | 55.3 |
| 1960 | 4,999 | 1,984 | 2,727 | 112 | 16,758 | 33 | 723 | 3,478 | 27,337 | 5.5 | 60.1 |
| 1965 | 6,316 | 2,690 | 3,466 | 20 | 25,638 | 80 | 1,254 | 4,911 | 39,464 | 6.0 | 60.4 |
| 1970 | 9,446 | 6,839 | 5,132 | 127 | 44,970 | 120 | 1,886 | 8,791 | 68,519 | 7.1 | 64.0 |
| 1975 | 23,298 | 14,122 | 9,195 | 449 | 72,234 | 631 | 2,683 | 17,847 | 122,612 | 8.4 | 63.7 |
| 1979 | 30,408 | 20,940 | 13,256 | 190 | 97,154 | 424 | 4,192 | 27,814 | 166,563 | 6.9 | 65.6 |
| 1980 | 38,592 | 23,133 | 14,771 | 212 | 107,597 | 601 | 4,813 | 31,309 | 189,720 | 7.2 | 66.5 |
| 1981 | 42,821 | 26,477 | 17,124 | 212 | 114,773 | 688 | 4,679 | 36,327 | 206,774 | 7.0[2] | 63.1[2] |
| 1982 | 52,481 | 28,367 | 19,195 | 245 | 121,957 | 778 | 5,154 | 40,738 | 228,178 | 7.4[2] | 62.6[2] |
| 1983[2] | 56,288 | 29,935 | 21,281 | 266 | 129,416 | 1,003 | 4,944 | 43,941 | 243,132 | n.a. | n.a. |
| **TOTAL** | | | | | | | | | | | |
| 1950 | 4,947 | 2,496 | 2,064 | 6,866 | 6,674 | 15 | 448 | 3,065 | 23,508 | 8.9 | 37.4 |
| 1955 | 9,835 | 3,003 | 3,103 | 4,834 | 11,157 | 89 | 619 | 4,421 | 32,640 | 8.6 | 32.7 |
| 1960 | 19,307 | 4,101 | 4,464 | 5,479 | 17,626 | 177 | 1,139 | 6,395 | 52,293 | 10.5 | 38.4 |
| 1965 | 28,123 | 6,283 | 6,246 | 6,031 | 28,108 | 318 | 2,066 | 9,535 | 77,175 | 11.7 | 42.2 |
| 1970 | 54,691 | 16,488 | 9,907 | 9,078 | 50,846 | 701 | 4,145 | 25,391 | 145,856 | 15.2 | 48.2 |
| 1975 | 123,013 | 41,326 | 17,708 | 17,019 | 80,863 | 3,172 | 6,947 | 52,492 | 290,047 | 20.0 | 57.4 |
| 1979 | 194,288 | 64,324 | 24,963 | 20,602 | 109,262 | 5,493 | 10,841 | 86,823 | 429,710 | 17.8 | 57.8 |
| 1980 | 229,754 | 71,799 | 27,657 | 21,466 | 121,050 | 7,210 | 13,599 | 100,298 | 492,534 | 18.7 | 57.4 |
| 1981 | 267,395 | 82,424 | 30,720 | 23,441 | 128,145 | 6,734 | 11,983 | 116,832 | 550,841 | 18.6[2] | 56.9[2] |
| 1982 | 303,033 | 80,852 | 33,793 | 24,708 | 133,874 | 7,954 | 11,654 | 131,514 | 595,869 | 19.4[2] | 55.7[2] |
| 1983[2] | 330,551 | 85,830 | 36,918 | 25,826 | 141,505 | 9,090 | 11,990 | 144,204 | 641,709 | n.a. | n.a. |
| **PERCENT OF TOTAL, BY TYPE** | | | | | | | | | | | |
| 1950 | 21.0 | 10.6 | 8.8 | 29.2 | 28.4 | 0.1 | 1.9 | 13.0 | 100.0 | (3) | (3) |
| 1955 | 30.1 | 9.2 | 9.5 | 14.8 | 34.2 | 0.3 | 1.9 | 13.5 | 100.0 | (3) | (3) |
| 1960 | 36.9 | 7.8 | 8.5 | 10.5 | 33.7 | 0.3 | 2.2 | 12.2 | 100.0 | (3) | (3) |
| 1965 | 36.4 | 8.1 | 8.1 | 7.8 | 36.4 | 0.4 | 2.7 | 12.4 | 100.0 | (3) | (3) |
| 1970 | 37.5 | 11.3 | 6.7 | 6.2 | 34.9 | 0.5 | 3.0 | 17.2 | 100.0 | (3) | (3) |
| 1975 | 42.4 | 14.2 | 6.1 | 5.9 | 27.9 | 1.1 | 2.4 | 18.1 | 100.0 | (3) | (3) |
| 1979 | 45.2 | 15.0 | 5.8 | 4.8 | 25.4 | 1.3 | 2.5 | 20.2 | 100.0 | (3) | (3) |
| 1980 | 46.6 | 14.6 | 5.6 | 4.4 | 24.6 | 1.5 | 2.8 | 20.4 | 100.0 | (3) | (3) |
| 1981[2] | 48.6 | 15.0 | 5.5 | 4.3 | 23.3 | 1.2 | 2.2 | 21.1 | 100.0 | (3) | (3) |
| 1982[2] | 50.8 | 13.6 | 5.6 | 4.2 | 22.6 | 1.3 | 2.0 | 22.0 | 100.0 | (3) | (3) |
| 1983[2] | 51.5 | 13.4 | 5.8 | 4.0 | 22.1 | 1.4 | 1.9 | 22.5 | 100.0 | (3) | (3) |
| **FEDERAL PERCENT OF TOTAL** | | | | | | | | | | | |
| 1950 | 42.5 | 44.2 | 29.2 | 93.0 | 2.3 | 100.0 | 38.9 | 44.4 | 44.8 | (3) | (3) |
| 1955 | 64.9 | 50.1 | 37.1 | 98.7 | 4.3 | 83.7 | 40.7 | 44.1 | 44.8 | (3) | (3) |
| 1960 | 74.1 | 51.6 | 38.9 | 98.0 | 4.9 | 81.2 | 36.6 | 45.6 | 47.7 | (3) | (3) |
| 1965 | 77.5 | 57.2 | 44.5 | 99.7 | 8.8 | 74.9 | 39.3 | 48.5 | 48.9 | (3) | (3) |
| 1970 | 82.7 | 58.5 | 48.2 | 98.6 | 11.6 | 82.9 | 54.5 | 65.4 | 53.0 | (3) | (3) |
| 1975 | 81.1 | 65.8 | 48.1 | 97.4 | 10.7 | 80.1 | 61.4 | 66.0 | 57.7 | (3) | (3) |
| 1979 | 84.3 | 67.4 | 46.9 | 99.1 | 11.1 | 92.3 | 61.3 | 68.0 | 61.4 | (3) | (3) |
| 1980 | 83.2 | 67.8 | 46.6 | 99.0 | 11.1 | 91.7 | 64.6 | 68.8 | 61.6 | (3) | (3) |
| 1981[2] | 84.0 | 67.8 | 47.5 | 99.1 | 10.4 | 89.8 | 59.6 | 69.9 | 62.6 | (3) | (3) |
| 1982[2] | 82.9 | 64.9 | 45.8 | 99.0 | 8.9 | 90.2 | 53.9 | 69.8 | 61.9 | (3) | (3) |
| 1983[2] | 83.0 | 65.1 | 42.4 | 99.0 | 8.5 | 89.0 | 58.8 | 69.5 | 62.1 | (3) | (3) |

1. Combines health and medical programs with medical services provided in connection with social insurance, public aid, veterans, and other social welfare programs. 2. Preliminary. 3. Not applicable. NOTE: n.a. = not available. Figures are latest available. *Source:* Department of Health and Human Services. *Social Security Bulletin,* December 1984.

# Domestic Freight Traffic by Major Carriers
### (in millions of ton-miles)[1]

| Year | Railroads Ton-miles | % of total | Inland waterways[2] Ton-miles | % of total | Motor trucks Ton-miles | % of total | Oil pipelines Ton-miles | % of total | Air carriers Ton-miles | % of total |
|---|---|---|---|---|---|---|---|---|---|---|
| 1940 | 379,201 | 61.3 | 118,057 | 19.1 | 62,043 | 10.0 | 59,277 | 9.6 | 14 | — |
| 1945 | 690,809 | 67.3 | 142,737 | 13.9 | 66,948 | 6.5 | 126,530 | 12.3 | 91 | — |
| 1950 | 596,940 | 56.2 | 163,344 | 15.4 | 172,860 | 16.3 | 129,175 | 12.1 | 318 | — |
| 1955 | 631,385 | 49.5 | 216,508 | 17.0 | 223,254 | 17.5 | 203,244 | 16.0 | 481 | — |
| 1960 | 579,130 | 44.1 | 220,253 | 16.8 | 285,483 | 21.7 | 228,626 | 17.4 | 778 | — |
| 1965 | 708,700 | 43.3 | 262,421 | 16.0 | 359,218 | 21.9 | 306,393 | 18.7 | 1,910 | 0.1 |
| 1970 | 771,168 | 39.8 | 318,560 | 16.4 | 412,000 | 21.3 | 431,000 | 22.3 | 3,274 | 0.2 |
| 1975 | 759,000 | 36.7 | 342,210 | 16.5 | 454,000 | 22.0 | 507,300 | 24.6 | 3,732 | 0.2 |
| 1978 | 867,982 | 35.1 | 409,316 | 16.6 | 602,000 | 24.4 | 585,800 | 23.7 | 4,630 | 0.2 |
| 1979 | 927,000 | 35.7 | 431,000 | 16.6 | 628,000 | 24.2 | 605,000 | 23.3 | 4,439 | 0.2 |
| 1980 | 932,000 | 37.2 | 420,000 | 16.9 | 567,000 | 22.6 | 588,000 | 23.1 | 4,528 | 0.2 |
| 1981 | 926,000 | 37.5 | 423,000 | 17.1 | 565,000 | 22.9 | 553,000 | 22.4 | 4,657 | 0.2 |
| 1982 | 810,000 | 35.8 | 351,000 | 15.5 | 525,000 | 23.2 | 571,000 | 25.3 | 4,476 | 0.2 |
| 1983 | 841,000 | 36.0 | 359,000 | 15.4 | 575,000 | 24.6 | 556,000 | 23.8 | 5,870 | 0.3 |
| 1984 | 935,000 | 37.5 | 382,000 | 15.3 | 605,000 | 24.2 | 568,000 | 22.7 | 6,600 | 0.3 |
| 1985[3] | 898,000 | 37.2 | 348,000 | 14.4 | 600,000 | 24.9 | 562,000 | 23.3 | 6,390 | 0.3 |

1. Mail and express included, except railroads for 1970. 2. Rivers, canals, and domestic traffic on Great Lakes. 3. Preliminary.
*Sources:* Interstate Commerce Commission; Dept. of Transportation; Association of American Railroads.

# Tonnage Handled by Principal U.S. Ports
### (Over 10 million tons annually; in thousands of tons)

| Port | 1984 | 1983 | Port | 1984 | 1983 |
|---|---|---|---|---|---|
| New York | 161,676 | 147,307 | Huntington, W. Va. | 21,731 | 14,824 |
| New Orleans | 154,220 | 156,272 | Toledo Harbor, Ohio | 20,836 | 17,408 |
| Houston | 96,777 | 88,706 | Seattle | 20,327 | 17,583 |
| Valdez Harbor, Alaska | 92,047 | 93,536 | Boston | 19,888 | 17,036 |
| Baton Rouge, La. | 66,198 | 68,395 | Paulsboro, N.J. | 18,197 | 15,783 |
| Tampa Harbor | 46,517 | 41,434 | Detroit | 17,530 | 14,955 |
| Norfolk Harbor, Va. | 44,897 | 42,967 | Tacoma Harbor, Wash. | 17,383 | 14,458 |
| Corpus Christi Ship Chnl, Tex. | 44,081 | 39,131 | Port Arthur, Tex. | 16,430 | 18,338 |
| Long Beach, Calif. | 42,848 | 41,112 | Richmond, Calif. | 16,341 | 15,803 |
| Corpus Christi, Tex. | 42,281 | 37,455 | Cincinnati | 15,936 | 15,963 |
| Baltimore Harbor | 37,306 | 31,574 | Newport News, Va. | 15,552 | 13,517 |
| Duluth-Superior, Minn. | 37,255 | 30,094 | Freeport, Tex. | 15,122 | 15,671 |
| Mobile, Ala. | 35,718 | 29,690 | Indiana, Ind. | 14,568 | 14,475 |
| Pittsburgh | 34,297 | 26,482 | Cleveland | 12,290 | 11,359 |
| Beaumont, Tex. | 33,004 | 36,001 | Memphis, Tenn. | 12,717 | 12,134 |
| Los Angeles | 31,242 | 28,034 | Conneaut Harbor, Ohio | 12,660 | — |
| Texas City, Tex. | 30,656 | 35,496 | St. Paul | 12,535 | 12,141 |
| Philadelphia | 28,509 | 29,808 | Jacksonville, Fla. | 11,849 | 11,760 |
| Portland, Ore. | 27,302 | 25,749 | Galveston, Tex. | 11,752 | 10,177 |
| Lake Charles, La. | 27,238 | 21,783 | Savannah, Ga. | 11,245 | 10,610 |
| St. Louis (Metropolitan) | 26,976 | 22,657 | San Juan, P. R. | 10,935 | 10,744 |
| Marcus Hook, Pa. | 26,110 | 22,670 | New Haven, Conn. | 10,625 | — |
| Pascagoula, Miss. | 24,153 | 20,237 | Escanaba, Mich. | 10,454 | — |
| Chicago | 23,813 | 24,454 | | | |

*Source:* Department of the Army, Corps of Engineers.

# Annual Railroad Carloadings

| Year | Total | Year | Total | Year | Total | Year | Total |
|---|---|---|---|---|---|---|---|
| 1920 | 33,754,000 | 1945 | 41,918,000 | 1970 | 27,160,000 | 1980 | 22,598,000 |
| 1925 | 34,783,000 | 1950 | 38,903,000 | 1975 | 23,217,000 | 1981 | 21,612,000 |
| 1930 | 30,173,000 | 1955 | 37,636,000 | 1977 | 23,173,000 | 1982 | 18,498,000 |
| 1935 | 22,015,000 | 1960 | 30,441,000 | 1978 | 23,355,000 | 1983 | 18,815,000 |
| 1940 | 36,358,000 | 1965 | 29,248,000 | 1979 | 23,892,000 | 1984 | 20,249,000 |

*Source:* Association of American Railroads.

# Estimated Motor Vehicle Registration, 1985

### (in thousands; including publicly owned vehicles)

| State | Autos[1] | Trucks and buses | Motor-cycles | Total | State | Autos[1] | Trucks and buses | Motor-cycles | Total |
|-------|------|------|------|------|-------|------|------|------|------|
| Alabama | 2,274 | 961 | 69 | 3,235 | Nebraska | 833 | 430 | 45 | 1,263 |
| Alaska | 236 | 146 | 10 | 382 | Nevada | 540 | 215 | 20 | 755 |
| Arizona | 1,500 | 619 | 79 | 2,119 | New Hampshire | 773 | 132 | 58 | 905 |
| Arkansas | 991 | 529 | 29 | 1,520 | New Jersey | 4,412 | 495 | 127 | 4,907 |
| California | 14,274 | 4,010 | 715 | 18,284 | New Mexico | 760 | 457 | 47 | 1,217 |
| Colorado | 2,078 | 773 | 113 | 2,851 | New York | 7,774 | 1,158 | 217 | 8,932 |
| Connecticut | 2,263 | 159 | 77 | 2,422 | N. Carolina | 3,190 | 1,227 | 68 | 4,417 |
| Delaware | 379 | 99 | 10 | 478 | N. Dakota | 434 | 278 | 31 | 712 |
| D.C. | 214 | 19 | 5 | 233 | Ohio | 6,621 | 1,396 | 271 | 8,017 |
| Florida | 7,886 | 1,975 | 244 | 9,861 | Oklahoma | 1,744 | 1,025 | 105 | 2,769 |
| Georgia | 2,979 | 1,627 | 113 | 4,606 | Oregon | 1,599 | 629 | 83 | 2,228 |
| Hawaii | 578 | 84 | 18 | 662 | Pennsylvania | 5,867 | 1,293 | 226 | 7,160 |
| Idaho | 562 | 409 | 49 | 971 | Rhode Island | 554 | 88 | 25 | 642 |
| Illinois | 6,211 | 1,558 | 219 | 7,769 | S. Carolina | 1,644 | 506 | 38 | 2,150 |
| Indiana | 3,014 | 1,032 | 135 | 4,046 | S. Dakota | 411 | 240 | 38 | 651 |
| Iowa | 1,743 | 705 | 255 | 2,448 | Tennessee | 2,864 | 748 | 103 | 3,612 |
| Kansas | 1,476 | 681 | 101 | 2,157 | Texas | 8,681 | 3,961 | 307 | 12,642 |
| Kentucky | 1,769 | 822 | 50 | 2,591 | Utah | 759 | 344 | 57 | 1,103 |
| Louisiana | 2,074 | 941 | 58 | 3,015 | Vermont | 293 | 94 | 22 | 387 |
| Maine | 604 | 222 | 48 | 826 | Virginia | 3,571 | 627 | 82 | 4,198 |
| Maryland | 2,769 | 553 | 70 | 3,322 | Washington | 2,517 | 1,059 | 142 | 3,576 |
| Massachusetts | 3,332 | 470 | 102 | 3,802 | West Virginia | 1,022 | 429 | 35 | 1,451 |
| Michigan | 5,279 | 1,382 | 235 | 6,661 | Wisconsin | 2,382 | 739 | 194 | 3,121 |
| Minnesota | 2,274 | 696 | 166 | 2,970 | Wyoming | 291 | 205 | 22 | 496 |
| Mississippi | 1,047 | 396 | 25 | 1,443 | **TOTAL** | **130,364** | **39,873** | **5,472** | **170,237** |
| Missouri | 2,626 | 949 | 85 | 3,575 | | | | | |
| Montana | 396 | 281 | 29 | 677 | | | | | |

1. Includes taxicabs. NOTE: Figures are latest available. *Source:* Department of Transportation, Federal Highway Administration.

# Passenger Car Production by Make

| Companies and models | 1985 | 1984 | 1980 | 1975 | 1970 | 1965 |
|------|------|------|------|------|------|------|
| American Motors Corporation | 109,919 | 192,196 | 164,725 | 323,704 | 276,127 | 346,367 |
| Chrysler Corporation | | | | | | |
| Plymouth | 369,487 | 378,275 | 293,342 | 443,550 | 699,031 | 679,539 |
| Dodge | 482,388 | 465,851 | 263,169 | 354,482 | 405,699 | 547,531 |
| Chrysler | 414,193 | 403,659 | 82,440 | 102,940 | 158,614 | 224,061 |
| Imperial | — | — | — | 1,930 | 10,111 | 16,422 |
| Total | **1,266,068** | **1,247,785** | **638,974** | **902,902** | **1,273,455** | **1,467,553** |
| Ford Motor Company | | | | | | |
| Ford | 1,098,627 | 1,145,144 | 929,627 | 1,301,414 | 1,647,918 | 2,164,902 |
| Mercury | 374,446 | 461,409 | 324,528 | 405,104 | 310,463 | 355,404 |
| Lincoln | 163,077 | 168,704 | 52,793 | 101,520 | 58,771 | 45,470 |
| Total | **1,636,150** | **1,775,257** | **1,306,948** | **1,808,038** | **2,017,152** | **2,565,776** |
| General Motors Corporation | | | | | | |
| Chevrolet | 1,691,254 | 1,456,733 | 1,737,336 | 1,687,091 | 1,504,614 | 2,587,509 |
| Pontiac | 702,617 | 506,099 | 556,429 | 523,469 | 422,212 | 860,652 |
| Oldsmobile | 1,168,982 | 1,065,528 | 783,225 | 654,342 | 439,632 | 650,801 |
| Buick | 1,001,461 | 987,833 | 783,575 | 535,820 | 459,931 | 653,838 |
| Cadillac | 322,765 | 328,544 | 203,991 | 278,404 | 152,859 | 196,595 |
| Total | **4,887,079** | **4,344,737** | **4,064,556** | **3,679,126** | **2,979,248** | **4,949,395** |
| Checker Motors Corporation | — | — | 3,197 | 3,181 | 4,146 | 6,136 |
| Volkswagen of America | 96,458 | 74,785 | 197,106 | — | — | — |
| Honda | | | | | | |
| Nissan | 145,337 | 138,572 | — | — | — | — |
| Industry total | **8,184,821** | **7,773,332** | **6,375,506** | **6,716,951** | **6,550,128** | **9,335,227** |

*Source:* Motor Vehicle Manufacturers Association of the United States.

## Motor Vehicle Data

|  | 1984 | 1980 | 1970 | 1960 | 1950 |
|---|---|---|---|---|---|
| U.S. passenger cars and taxis registered (thousands) | 127,867 | 121,724 | 89,280 | 61,671 | 40,339 |
| Total mileage of U.S. passenger cars (millions) | 1,254,265 | 1,111,950 | 901,000 | 588,083 | 363,613 |
| Total fuel consumption of U.S. passenger cars (millions of gallons) | 74,042 | 73,375 | 65,784 | 41,169 | 24,305 |
| World registration of cars, trucks, and buses (thousands) | 473,278 | 411,113 | 248,900 | 126,908 | 70,424 |
| U.S. registration of cars, trucks, and buses (thousands) | 168,607 | 155,890 | 108,407 | 73,858 | 49,162 |
| U.S. share of world registration of cars, trucks, and buses | 35.6% | 37.9% | 43.6% | 58.2% | 69.8% |

*Source:* Motor Vehicle Manufacturers Association of the U.S.

## Domestic Passenger Car Sales

| Company and model | 1985 | 1984 | 1983 |
|---|---|---|---|
| American Motors | 123,449 | 190,255 | 193,351 |
| Total Renault | 110,673 | 169,601 | 146,190 |
| Alliance | 71,494 | 100,366 | 126,008 |
| Encore | 39,179 | 69,235 | 20,182 |
| Total AMC | 12,776 | 20,654 | 47,161 |
| Spirit | — | — | 4,441 |
| Concord | — | — | 11,513 |
| Eagle | 12,776 | 20,654 | 31,207 |
| Chrysler Corp. | 1,139,936 | 986,998 | 841,622 |
| Total Plymouth | 329,371 | 289,244 | 265,608 |
| Horizon | 84,500 | 78,298 | 56,763 |
| Turismo | 52,817 | 47,109 | 36,497 |
| Reliant | 138,833 | 138,154 | 157,247 |
| Plymouth | 17,627 | 16,609 | 15,101 |
| Total Chrysler | 375,880 | 328,499 | 260,884 |
| Laser | 50,957 | 53,131 | 11,097 |
| LeBaron GTS | 71,018 | 2,494 | — |
| LeBaron K | 87,482 | 98,830 | 80,309 |
| Cordoba | 0 | 136 | 10,375 |
| New Yorker | 36,490 | 39,303 | 73,729 |
| E-Class | 20,923 | 40,265 | 35,283 |
| Total Imperial | — | — | 1,153 |
| Total Dodge | 434,325 | 369,255 | 313,977 |
| Omni | 71,473 | 67,933 | 50,451 |
| Charger | 57,171 | 51,940 | 45,975 |
| Daytona | 49,533 | 44,717 | 8,761 |
| Aries | 116,284 | 111,984 | 119,400 |
| 600 Coupe/400 | 3,012 | 18,953 | 28,488 |
| Diplomat | 34,919 | 28,623 | 22,603 |
| Mirada/Magnum | 0 | 282[1] | 4,417[1] |
| Dodge 600 | 52,318 | 42,843 | 33,882 |
| Ford Motor | 2,070,392 | 1,957,461 | 1,571,321 |
| Ford Division | 1,386,195 | 1,300,644 | 1,060,315 |
| EXP | 17,927 | 31,213 | 19,574 |
| Escort | 420,690 | 353,578 | 326,333 |
| Mustang | 157,821 | 138,296 | 116,976 |
| Tempo | 281,144 | 236,532 | 136,148 |
| Fairmont | — | — | 37,521 |
| Granada | — | — | 3,751 |
| Thunderbird | 157,209 | 154,865 | 134,710 |
| LTD | 180,514 | 196,907 | 165,396 |
| Crown Victoria | 162,334 | 169,253 | 119,905 |
| L-M Division | 684,197 | 678,673 | 511,007 |
| Total Mercury | 519,059 | 527,198 | 409,433 |
| LN 7 | — | — | 4,694 |
| Lynx | 85,871 | 67,725 | 78,876 |
| Topaz | 73,098 | 73,454 | 41,796 |
| Zephyr | — | — | 11,583 |
| Cougar/Monarch | — | 120,964[4] | 906 |
| Cougar[2] XR 7 | 113,405 | — | 87,027 |
| Capri | 15,389 | 17,739 | 22,708 |
| Marquis | 87,844 | 103,722 | 65,184 |
| Mercury Grand Marquis | 135,202 | 143,594 | 96,659 |

| Company and model | 1985 | 1984 | 1983 |
|---|---|---|---|
| Total Lincoln | 165,138 | 151,475 | 101,574 |
| Continental | 27,679 | 31,110[5] | 13,691[5] |
| Lincoln | 117,606 | 90,869 | 59,626 |
| Mark VII | 19,853 | 29,496 | 28,257 |
| General Motors | 4,607,458 | 4,587,508 | 4,053,561 |
| Buick Division | 845,579 | 941,611 | 845,083 |
| Skyhawk | 85,639 | 121,858 | 72,998 |
| Skylark | 54,513 | 104,589 | 102,763 |
| Century | 234,508 | 217,042 | 150,280 |
| Regal Sedan/Coupe | 112,590 | 182,185 | 234,035 |
| LeSabre | 115,212 | 164,314 | 151,555 |
| Electra | 99,185 | 84,414 | 80,106 |
| Riviera | 48,834 | 53,398 | 53,346 |
| Cadillac Division | 298,762 | 320,017 | 300,337 |
| Cimarron | 23,754 | 18,014 | 19,188 |
| Seville | 29,034 | 35,349 | 33,522 |
| Cadillac | 187,664 | 195,177 | 176,003 |
| Eldorado | 58,310 | 70,577 | 71,624 |
| Chevrolet Division | 1,600,200 | 1,565,143 | 1,347,447 |
| Chevette | 129,927 | 164,917 | 178,759 |
| Nova | 35,594 | — | — |
| Cavalier | 431,031 | 377,446 | 259,397 |
| Citation | 43,677 | 92,174 | 92,379 |
| Camaro | 199,985 | 202,172 | 178,266 |
| Celebrity | 363,619 | 322,198 | 180,354 |
| Malibu | 0 | 881 | 85,421 |
| Monte Carlo | 112,585 | 115,930 | 105,797 |
| Chevrolet | 245,826 | 258,902 | 238,930 |
| Corvette | 37,956 | 30,424 | 28,144 |
| Oldsmobile Division | 1,066,122 | 1,056,053 | 1,007,559 |
| Firenza | 49,580 | 62,456 | 44,753 |
| Omega | 0 | 34,103 | 49,818 |
| Calais | 122,810 | 14,881 | — |
| Cutlass Ciera | 333,585 | 242,209 | 191,720 |
| Cutlass Supreme | 217,504 | 302,087 | 331,179 |
| Olds 88 | 188,129 | 258,297 | 228,770 |
| Olds 98 | 122,421 | 100,419 | 119,526 |
| Toronado | 32,093 | 41,605 | 41,791 |
| Pontiac Division | 796,795 | 704,684 | 553,135 |
| Fiero | 90,303 | 93,485 | 22,591 |
| 1000 | 22,424 | 28,004 | 34,173 |
| 2000/Sunbird | 116,837[3] | 126,916[3] | 88,313 |
| Phoenix | 896 | 13,202 | 24,362 |
| Firebird | 100,610 | 101,414 | 90,777 |
| 6000 | 165,728 | 125,828 | 92,513 |
| Bonneville/LeMans | 52,972[4] | 65,387[4] | 84,122 |
| Grand Prix | 57,153 | 71,609 | 89,355 |
| Parisienne | 69,049 | 62,084 | 26,929 |
| Volkswagen | 77,537 | 73,838 | 85,045 |
| Honda | 145,976 | 133,601 | 50,402 |
| Domestic total | 8,204,547 | 7,951,517 | — |
| Import total | 2,838,116 | 2,440,258 | — |
| **Industry total** | **11,042,658** | **10,391,775** | **9,177,777** |

1. Mirada only. 2. Cougar only. 3. Sunbird only. 4. Bonneville only. *Source: Automotive News, Jan. 9, 1986.*

## Domestic and Export Factory Sales of Motor Vehicles
(in thousands)

| | From plants in United States | | | | | | | | |
| | Passenger cars | | | Motor trucks and buses | | | Total motor vehicles | | |
| Year | Total | Domestic | Exports | Total | Domestic | Exports | Total | Domestic | Exports |
|---|---|---|---|---|---|---|---|---|---|
| 1965 | 9,306 | 9,101 | 205 | 1,752 | 1,616 | 136 | 11,058 | 10,717 | 341 |
| 1970 | 6,547 | 6,187 | 360 | 1,692 | 1,566 | 126 | 8,239 | 7,753 | 486 |
| 1975 | 6,713 | 6,073 | 640 | 2,272 | 2,003 | 269 | 8,985 | 8,076 | 909 |
| 1980 | 6,400 | 5,840 | 560 | 1,667 | 1,464 | 203 | 8,067 | 7,304 | 763 |
| 1981 | 6,255 | 5,749 | 506 | 1,701 | 1,513 | 188 | 7,956 | 7,262 | 694 |
| 1982 | 5,049 | 4,696 | 353 | 1,906 | 1,779 | 127 | 6,955 | 6,475 | 480 |
| 1983 | 6,739 | 6,201 | 538 | 2,414 | 2,260 | 154 | 9,153 | 8,461 | 692 |
| 1984 | 7,621 | 7,030 | 591 | 3,075 | 2,884 | 191 | 10,696 | 9,914 | 782 |
| 1985 | 8,002 | 7,337 | 665 | 3,357 | 3,126 | 231 | 11,359 | 10,463 | 896 |

*Source:* Motor Vehicle Manufacturers Association of the U.S.

## Balance of International Payments
(in billions of dollars)

| Item | 1985 | 1984 | 1983 | 1980 | 1975 | 1970 | 1965 | 1960 | 1955 |
|---|---|---|---|---|---|---|---|---|---|
| Exports of goods and services (excluding transfers under military grants) | $358.5 | $360.1 | $333.6 | $344.7 | $155.7 | $65.7 | $41.1 | $28.9 | $19.9 |
| Merchandise, adjusted, excluding military | 214.4 | 220.0 | 200.7 | 224.0 | 107.1 | 42.5 | 26.5 | 19.7 | 14.4 |
| Transfers under U.S. military agency sales contracts | 9.0 | 10.1 | 12.4 | 8.2 | 3.9 | 1.5 | 0.8 | 0.3 | 0.2 |
| Receipts of income on U.S. investments abroad | 90.0 | 86.2 | 78.0 | 75.9 | 25.4 | 11.8 | 7.4 | 4.6 | 2.6 |
| Other services | 45.0 | 43.9 | 42.4 | 36.5 | 19.3 | 9.9 | 6.4 | 4.3 | 2.7 |
| Imports of goods and services | −461.2 | −454.4 | −365.5 | −333.9 | −132.6 | −60.0 | −32.8 | −23.7 | −17.8 |
| Merchandise, adjusted, excluding military | −339.0 | −332.4 | −262.7 | −249.3 | −98.0 | −39.9 | −21.5 | −14.8 | −11.5 |
| Direct defense expenditures | −12.0 | −12.0 | −12.5 | −10.7 | −4.8 | 4.9 | −3.0 | −3.1 | −2.9 |
| Payments of income on foreign assets in U.S. | −65.0 | −67.4 | −52.6 | −43.2 | −12.6 | −5.5 | −2.1 | −1.2 | −0.5 |
| Other services | −46.0 | −42.5 | −37.5 | −30.7 | −17.2 | −9.8 | −6.2 | −4.6 | −2.8 |
| Unilateral transfers, excluding military grants, net | −15.0 | −12.1 | −8.8 | −7.0 | −4.6 | −3.3 | −2.9 | −2.3 | −2.5 |
| U.S. Government assets abroad, net | −32.4 | −24.0 | −55.0 | −84.8 | −3.5 | −1.6 | −1.6 | −1.1 | −0.3 |
| U.S. private assets abroad, net | −26.0 | −15.0 | −48.8 | −71.5 | −35.4 | −10.2 | −5.3 | −5.1 | −1.3 |
| U.S. assets abroad, official reserve, net | −4.0 | −3.1 | −1.2 | −8.2 | −0.6 | 2.5 | 1.2 | 2.1 | 0.2 |
| Foreign assets in U.S., net | 127.1 | 103.0 | 84.3 | 50.3 | 15.6 | 6.4 | 0.7 | 2.3 | −1.4 |
| Statistical discrepancy | 23.0 | 27.3 | 11.5 | 29.6 | 5.5 | −0.2 | −0.5 | −1.0 | 0.4 |
| Balance on goods and services | −103.0 | −94.3 | −31.9 | 10.8 | 23.1 | 5.7 | 8.3 | 5.1 | 2.2 |
| Balance on goods, services, and remittances | −106.4 | −98.0 | −34.5 | 8.4 | 21.3 | 4.1 | 7.2 | 4.5 | 1.6 |
| Balance on current account | −118.0 | −106.4 | −40.8 | 3.7 | 18.4 | 2.4 | 5.4 | 2.8 | −0.3 |

NOTE: — denotes debits. *Source:* Department of Commerce, Bureau of Economic Analysis.

## Foreign Investors in U.S. Business Enterprises

| | Number | | | | Investment outlays (millions of dollars) | | | |
| | 1985[1] | 1984 | 1983 | 1982 | 1985[1] | 1984 | 1983 | 1982 |
|---|---|---|---|---|---|---|---|---|
| Investments, total | 508 | 764 | 775 | 1,108 | 19,547 | $15,197 | $8,091 | $10,817 |
| Acquisitions | 287 | 315 | 299 | 395 | 17,642 | 11,836 | 4,848 | 6,563 |
| Establishments | 221 | 449 | 476 | 713 | 1,905 | 3,361 | 3,244 | 4,254 |
| Investors, total | 553 | 831 | 850 | 1,218 | 19,547 | 15,197 | 8,091 | 10,817 |
| Foreign direct investors | 226 | 434 | 460 | 720 | 3,805 | 4,181 | 2,528 | 4,129 |
| U.S. affilates | 327 | 397 | 390 | 498 | 15,742 | 11,016 | 5,564 | 8,043 |

1. Figures are preliminary. *Source:* U.S. Department of Commerce, *Survey of Current Business,* May 1986.

# Imports of Leading Commodities
## (value in millions of dollars)

| Commodity | 1985 | 1984 |
|---|---|---|
| Food and live animals | $20,292 | $17,972 |
| Cattle, except for breeding | 301 | 279 |
| Meat and preparations | 2,472 | 2,034 |
| Dairy products and eggs | 446 | 425 |
| Fish | 3,462 | 3,671 |
| Grains and feed for animals | 767 | 614 |
| Vegetables and fruit | 4,619 | 3,891 |
| Sugar, cane or beet | 1,001 | 1,258 |
| Coffee | 3,284 | 3,064 |
| Cocoa beans | 604 | 411 |
| Tea | 184 | 203 |
| Beverages and tobacco | 4,124 | 3,653 |
| Alcoholic beverages | 1,388 | 2,853 |
| Tobacco, unmanufactured | 571 | 625 |
| Crude materials, inedible, except fuels | 11,167 | 11,082 |
| Hides and skins, except fur skins | 76 | 70 |
| Fur skins, undressed | 175 | 160 |
| Crude rubber | 745 | 823 |
| Wood—simply worked | 3,195 | 2,853 |
| Paper base stocks | 1,572 | 1,883 |
| Textile fibers and wastes | 377 | 387 |
| Industrial diamonds | 139 | 123 |
| Ores and metal scrap | 2,564 | 2,890 |
| Iron ore and concentrates | 561 | 534 |
| Nonferrous metal ores and concentrates | 1,418 | 1,606 |
| Precious metal ores and concentrates, except gold | 240 | 355 |
| Mineral fuels and related materials | 55,843 | 60,980 |
| Petroleum products | 51,471 | 55,906 |
| Natural gas | 4,176 | 4,923 |
| Animal and vegetable oils and fats | 730 | 696 |
| Chemicals | 15,321 | 13,697 |
| Organic chemicals | 4,832 | 4,265 |
| Inorganic chemicals | 3,554 | 3,458 |
| Medicinal and pharmaceutical products | 1,108 | 931 |
| Fertilizers, manufactured | 1,049 | 1,142 |
| Machinery and transport equipment | 141,721 | 119,192 |
| Machinery | 77,717 | 68,390 |
| Transport equipment | 64,003 | 50,802 |
| Automobiles, buses, trucks | 47,009 | 36,593 |
| Motor vehicle parts | 10,568 | 8,819 |
| Aircraft and parts | 3,600 | 3,011 |
| Misc. manufactured goods | 51,684 | 42,481 |
| Paper and manufactures | 6,248 | 5,571 |
| Glass, glassware, and pottery | 2,406 | 1,984 |
| Gem diamonds | 3,020 | 2,905 |
| Metals and manufactures | 7,022 | 5,923 |
| Iron and steel-mill products | 10,614 | 10,208 |
| Nonferrous metals | 7,172 | 8,170 |
| Precious metals, except gold | 1,834 | 1,912 |
| Textile yarn and thread | 574 | 4,531 |
| Clothing | 16,056 | 13,497 |
| Footwear | 6,104 | 5,034 |
| Scientific and contolling instruments | 3,298 | 2,696 |
| Printed matter | 1,175 | 980 |
| Clocks and watches | 1,406 | 1,254 |
| Baby carriages, toys, games and sporting goods | 4,451 | 3,329 |
| Artworks and antiques | 2,216 | 2,467 |
| Other transactions | 11,245 | 9,828 |
| **Total** | **$361,626** | **325,726** |

# Exports of Leading Commodities
## (value in millions of dollars)

| Commodity | 1985 | 1984 |
|---|---|---|
| Food and live animals | $19,268 | $24,463 |
| Meat and preparations | 1,153 | 1,208 |
| Dairy products and eggs | 388 | 368 |
| Grains and preparations | 11,050 | 16,076 |
| Wheat, including wheat flour | 3,780 | 6,698 |
| Rice | 664 | 845 |
| Corn | 5,318 | 7,081 |
| Vegetables and fruit | 2,377 | 2,434 |
| Feed for animals | 1,890 | 2,226 |
| Beverages and tobacco | 2,958 | 2,849 |
| Cigarettes | 1,179 | 1,120 |
| Tobacco | 1,520 | 1,511 |
| Crude materials, inedible, except fuels | 16,939 | 20,249 |
| Hides and skins, except fur skins | 1,088 | 1,171 |
| Soybeans | 3,906 | 5,438 |
| Synthetic rubber | 583 | 624 |
| Logs and lumber | 2,036 | 2,042 |
| Pulpwood and wood pulp | 1,945 | 2,144 |
| Raw cotton, excluding wastes | 1,633 | 2,441 |
| Ores and metal scrap | 2,692 | 2,666 |
| Mineral fuels and related materials | 9,970 | 9,310 |
| Coal | 4,553 | 4,219 |
| Petroleum and products | 4,707 | 4,470 |
| Animal and vegetable oils and fats | 1,434 | 1,922 |
| Soybean oil | 439 | 755 |
| Chemicals | 21,758 | 22,336 |
| Chemical elements and compounds | 9,290 | 9,699 |
| Medicines and pharmaceuticals | 2,708 | 2,628 |
| Fertilizers | 2,160 | 1,815 |
| Plastic materials and resins | 3,777 | 4,050 |
| Machinery and transport equipment | 94,278 | 89,973 |
| Machinery | 59,488 | 60,317 |
| Power generating machinery | 9,271 | 9,114 |
| Aircraft engines, parts | 2,232 | 1,798 |
| Automotive engines, parts | 1,290 | 1,415 |
| Agricultural machinery, including tractors, and parts | 1,601 | 1,740 |
| Office machines, computers | 14,927 | 14,592 |
| Metalworking machinery | 1,249 | 1,175 |
| Textile and leather machinery | 498 | 520 |
| Transport equipment | 34,790 | 29,655 |
| Motor vehicles and parts | 19,364 | 17,548 |
| Aircraft, spacecraft, accessories | 14,373 | 10,914 |
| Misc. manufactured goods | 15,338 | 15,699 |
| Tires and tubes | 342 | 392 |
| Paper and manufactures | 2,328 | 2,620 |
| Nonmetallic mineral manufactures | 1,820 | 6,484 |
| Metals and manufactures | 5,958 | 1,348 |
| Iron and steel-mill products | 1,234 | 1,248 |
| Nonferrous base metals | 1,471 | 1,634 |
| Other manufactures of metal | 3,253 | 3,602 |
| Textile yarns and fabrics | 2,366 | 23,819 |
| Clothing | 754 | 807 |
| Scientific instruments | 6,505 | 6,198 |
| Photographic supplies | 1,313 | 1,464 |
| Printed matter | 1,279 | 1,391 |
| Other transactions | 10,970 | 10,116 |
| **Total** | **$213,146** | **$217,888** |

*Source:* Department of Commerce, Bureau of the Census, Foreign Trade Division.

# TAXES

## History of the Income Tax in the United States

*Source: Touche Ross & Co.*

The nation had few taxes in its early history. From 1791 to 1802, the United States Government was supported by internal taxes on distilled spirits, carriages, refined sugar, tobacco and snuff, property sold at auction, corporate bonds, and slaves. The high cost of the War of 1812 brought about the nation's first sales taxes on gold, silverware, jewelry, and watches. In 1817, however, Congress did away with all internal taxes, relying on tariffs on imported goods to provide sufficient funds for running the Government.

In 1862, in order to support the Civil War effort, Congress enacted the nation's first income tax law. It was a forerunner of our modern income tax in that it was based on the principles of graduated, or progressive, taxation and of withholding income at the source. During the Civil War, a person earning from $600 to $10,000 per year paid tax at the rate of 3%. Those with incomes of more than $10,000 paid taxes at a higher rate. Additional sales and excise taxes were added, and an "inheritance" tax also made its debut. In 1866, internal revenue collections reached their highest point in the nation's 90-year history—more than $310 million, an amount not reached again until 1911.

The Act of 1862 established the office of Commissioner of Internal Revenue. The Commissioner was given the power to assess, levy, and collect taxes, and the right to enforce the tax laws through seizure of property and income and through prosecution. His powers and authority remain very much the same today.

In 1868, Congress again focused its taxation efforts on tobacco and distilled spirits and eliminated the income tax in 1872. It had a short-lived revival in 1894 and 1895. In the latter year, the U.S. Supreme Court decided that the income tax was unconstitutional because it was not apportioned among the states in conformity with the Constitution.

By 1913, with the 16th Amendment to the Constitution, the income tax had become a permanent fixture of the U.S. tax system. The amendment gave Congress legal authority to tax income and resulted in a revenue law that taxed incomes of both individuals and corporations. In fiscal year 1918, annual internal revenue collections for the first time passed the billion-dollar mark, rising to $5.4 billion by 1920. With the advent of World War II, employment increased, as did tax collections—to $7.3 billion. The withholding tax on wages was introduced in 1943 and was instrumental in increasing the number of taxpayers to 60 million and tax collections to $43 billion by 1945.

In 1981, Congress enacted the largest tax cut in U.S. history, approximately $750 billion over six years. The tax reduction, however, was offset by two tax acts, in 1982 and 1984, which attempted to raise approximately $265 billion.

## Internal Revenue Service

The Internal Revenue Service (IRS), a bureau of the U.S. Treasury Department, is the federal agency charged with the administration of the tax laws passed by Congress. The IRS functions through a national office in Washington, 7 regional offices, 63 district offices, and 10 service centers.

Operations involving most taxpayers are carried out in the district offices and service centers. District offices are organized into Resources Management, Examination, Collection, Taxpayer Service, Employee Plans and Exempt Organizations, and Criminal Investigation. All tax returns are filed with the service centers, where the IRS computer operations are located.

### Auditing Tax Returns

Most taxpayers' contacts with the IRS arise through the auditing of their tax returns. The Service has been empowered by Congress to inquire about all persons who may be liable for any tax and to obtain for review the books and/or records pertinent to those taxpayers' returns. A wide-ranging audit operation is carried out in the 63 district offices by some 13,700 field agents and 3,500 office auditors.

### Selecting Returns for Audit

The primary method used by the IRS in selecting returns for audits is a computer program that measures the probability of tax error in each return. The data base (established by an in-depth audit of randomly selected returns in various income categories) consists of approximately 200–250 individual items of information taken from each return. These 200–250 variables individually or in combination are weighted as relative indicators of potential tax change. Returns are then scored according to the weights given the combinations of variables as they appear on each return. The higher the score, the greater the tax change potential. Other returns are selected for examination on the basis of claims for refund, multi-year audits, related

## Internal Revenue Service

| | 1985 | 1984 | 1983 | 1970 | 1960 | 1950 |
|---|---|---|---|---|---|---|
| U.S. population (in thousands) | 239,231 | 237,051 | 234,875 | 204,878 | 180,671 | 152,271 |
| Number of IRS employees | 92,254 | 87,635 | 85,379 | 68,098 | 50,199 | 55,551 |
| Cost to govt. of collecting | | | | | | |
| $100 in taxes | $0.48 | $0.48 | $0.47 | $0.45 | $0.40 | $0.59 |
| Tax per capita | $3,105.25 | $2,870.59 | $2,670.56 | $955.31 | $507.96 | $255.84 |
| Collections by principal sources (in thousands of dollars) | | | | | | |
| Total IRS collections | $742,871,541 | $680,475,229 | $627,246,793 | $195,722,096 | $91,744,803 | $38,957,132 |
| Income and profits taxes | | | | | | |
| Individual | 396,659,558 | 362,891,679 | 349,627,967 | 103,651,585 | 44,945,711 | 17,153,308 |
| Corporation | 77,412,769 | 74,179,370 | 61,779,556 | 35,036,983 | 22,179,414 | 10,854,351 |
| Employment taxes | 225,214,568 | 199,210,028 | 173,847,854 | 37,449,188 | 11,158,589 | 2,644,575 |
| Estate and gift taxes | 6,579,703 | 6,116,667 | 6,225,877 | 3,680,076 | 1,626,348 | 706,227 |
| Alcohol taxes | 5,398,100 | 5,402,467 | 5,634,853 | 4,746,382 | 3,193,714 | 2,219,202 |
| Tobacco taxes | 4,483,193 | 4,663,610 | 4,139,810 | 2,094,212 | 1,931,504 | 1,328,464 |
| Manufacturers' excise taxes | 10,020,574 | 10,097,242 | 6,776,023 | 6,683,061 | 4,735,129 | 1,836,053 |
| All other taxes | 17,103,077 | 17,854,167 | 19,214,853 | 2,380,609 | 2,004,394 | 2,214,951 |

NOTE: For fiscal year ending September 30th.

return audits, and other audits initiated by the IRS as a result of informants' information, special compliance programs, and the information document matching program.

In 1985, the IRS recommended additional tax and penalties on 1,104,161 returns, totaling $17.1 billion.

### The Appeals Process

The IRS attempts to resolve tax disputes through an administrative appeals system. Taxpayers who, after audit of their tax returns, disagree with a proposed change in their tax liabilities are entitled to an independent review of their cases. Taxpayers are able to seek an immediate, informal appeal with the Appeals Office. If, however, the dispute arises from a field audit and the amount in question exceeds $2,500, a taxpayer must submit a written protest. Alternatively, the taxpayer can wait for the examiner's report and then request consideration by the Appeals Office and file a protest if necessary. Taxpayers may represent themselves or be represented by an attorney, accountant, or any other advisor authorized to practice before the IRS. Taxpayers can forego their right to the above process and await receipt of a deficiency notice. At this juncture, taxpayers can either (1) not pay the deficiency and petition the Tax Court by a required deadline or (2) pay the deficiency and file a claim for refund with the District Director's office. If the claim is denied, a suit for refund may be brought either in the District Court or the Claims Court within a specified period.

## Federal Individual Income Tax

The Federal individual income tax is levied on the world-wide income of U.S. citizens and resident aliens and on certain types of U.S. source income of non-residents. For a non-itemizer, "tax table income" is adjusted gross income *(see below)* less $1,080 for each personal exemption and the amount of his charitable contributions. If a taxpayer itemizes, tax table income is adjusted gross income minus excess itemized deductions and personal exemptions. Excess itemized deductions are the excess of a taxpayer's itemized deductions *(see below)* over the zero bracket amount. The zero bracket amount is $2,480 for unmarried individuals and heads of household; $3,670 for married individuals filing jointly and for surviving spouses; $1,835 for married individuals filing separately. Taxpayers with taxable income of less than $50,000 are required to use the tax tables. Taxpayers with taxable income of $50,000 or more must use Tax Rate Schedule X, Y, or Z to compute their tax. For this purpose tax rates are graduated, for joint returns, from a minimum of 11% on the first $2,270 of taxable income above $3,670 to a maximum of 50% of taxable income above $175,250 (1986 rates).

### Who Must File a Return[1]

| You must file a return if you are: | and your gross income is at least: |
|---|---|
| Single (legally separated, divorced, or married living apart from spouse with dependent child) and are under 65 | $3,560 |
| Single (legally separated, divorced, or married living apart from spouse with dependent child) and are 65 or older | $4,640 |
| A person who can be claimed as a dependent on your parent's return, and who has taxable dividends, interest, or other unearned income | $1,080 |
| A qualifying widow(er) with a dependent child and under 65 | $4,750 |
| A qualifying widow(er) with a dependent child and are 65 or older | $5,830 |
| Married, filing jointly, living together at end of year (or at date of death of spouse), and both are under 65 | $5,830 |

Married, filing jointly, living together at
end of year (or at date of death of
spouse), and one is 65 or older     $6,910
Married, filing jointly, living together at
end of year (or at date of death of
spouse), and both are 65 or older     $7,990
Married, filing separate return, or married
but not living together at end of year   $1,080
A person with income from sources
within U.S. possessions     $1,080
Self-employed and your net earnings
from self-employment were at least
$400
A person who received any advance
earned income credit payments from
their employer during the year
A person who owes minimum tax,
individual retirement arrangement
tax, investment credit recapture tax
or social security tax on unreported
tips
1. In 1986.

## Adjusted Gross Income

*Gross income* consists of wages and salaries, tips
and gratuities, interest, dividends, annuities, rents
and royalties, up to 1/2 of Social Security Benefits
if the recipient's income exceeds a base amount,
and certain other types of income. Among the
items excluded from gross income, and thus not
subject to tax, are federal and state unemployment
compensation (phased out above a base amount),
public assistance benefits, interest on exempt securities (mostly state and local bonds), and 60 percent
of net capital gains. Net capital gain is the excess
of net long-term capital gain over the net short-
term capital loss for the year. In addition, the first
$100 (up to $200 on a joint return) of eligible dividends received is excluded from gross income. *Adjusted gross income* is determined by subtracting
from gross income certain business-type expenses
considered necessary in earning income, job-
related moving expenses, alimony, payments to an
I.R.A. or Keogh, disability income, penalties on
early withdrawal of savings, and the deduction for
a married couple when both work.

## Itemized Deductions

Taxpayers may itemize deductions or, as previously discussed, take the benefit of the zero bracket
amount incorporated in the tax tables and tax rate
schedules. In itemizing deductions, the following
are the major items that may be deducted (with
limits, in some instances): interest payments; state
and local general sales, income, and property taxes;
medical expenses; charitable contributions; and
casualty losses.

## Personal Exemptions

Personal exemptions are available to the taxpayer, his spouse, and his dependents. The amount
is $1,080 for each individual. Additional exemp-
tions of $1,080 each are granted for persons 65 and
over and for the blind.

## Credits

Taxpayers can reduce their income tax liability
by claiming the benefit of certain tax credits. Each
dollar of tax credit offsets a dollar of tax liability.
The following are a few of the available tax credits:

Certain lower-income households with dependent children may claim an Earned Income Credit
of up to $550 on $5,000 of earned income. This
maximum credit will be reduced if earned income
or adjusted gross income exceeds $6,500, and the
credit will be zero for families with incomes over
$11,000.

A credit for Child and Dependent Care Expenses is available for amounts paid to care for a
child or other dependent so that the taxpayer can
work. The credit is between 20% and 30% (depending on adjusted gross income) of up to $2,400
of employment-related expenses for one qualifying
child or dependent and up to $4,800 of expenses
for two or more qualifying individuals.

The elderly and those under 65 who are retired
under total disability may be entitled to a credit of
up to $750 (if single) or $1,150 (if married and filing
jointly). No credit is available if the taxpayer is single and has adjusted gross income of $17,500 or
more, or $5,000 or more in nontaxable Social Secu-
rity benefits. Similarly, the credit is unavailable to
a married couple if their adjusted gross income exceeds $25,000 or if their nontaxable Social Security
benefits equal or exceed $7,500.

Other tax credits available to taxpayers include
the targeted jobs credit, contributions to candidates for public office credit, the investment tax
credit, and the foreign tax credit.

## Recent Legislation

**Tax Reform Act of 1986.** On Oct. 22, 1986, President Reagan signed into law one of the most far-
reaching reforms of the United States tax system
since the adoption of the income tax. The law attempts to be revenue neutral by increasing business taxes and correspondingly decreasing individual taxes by approximately $120 billion over a five-
year period.

For individuals, the law reduces the current 14
bracket rate structure ranging from 11 percent to
50 percent to two rates of 15 percent and 28 percent. For higher income taxpayers, the 15 percent
bracket is phased out causing a tax rate of 33 percent on a portion of their total income.

The law eliminates the deductions for sales tax,
interest on personal loans (other than interest on
first and second homes), the $200 dividend exclu-
sion, the charitable deduction for nonitemizers,
the capital gains tax exclusion, and the two wage
earner deduction. Deductions for medical expenses, unreimbursed business expenses, union
dues, tax preparation fees, retirement plans known
as 401(k)'s and I.R.A.'s are severely restricted.

Under the law, taxpayers are prohibited from
using "passive losses" from investments such as
limited partnerships to offset their wages, interest,
dividend or other income. In addition, taxpayers
who actively manage rental property are allowed
to deduct losses from the investment of up to $25,-
000 if their income is less than $100,000. The allow-
able loss is further reduced for taxpayers who earn
over $100,000 and is disallowed for taxpayers earn-
ing over $150,000.

The standard deduction is increased to $3,000
for single filers and $5,000 for joint filers. The per-
sonal exemption is raised to $2,000, however, it is
phased out for higher income taxpayers.

For corporations, the top tax rate is scheduled to
drop from 46 percent to 34 percent. In addition,
a new minimum tax will be imposed to prevent
profitable companies from avoiding taxation.

For all businesses, some depreciation schedules would be lengthened, the deduction for business entertainment is restricted to 80 percent of the cost, and numerous tax preferences are removed.

Finally, the investment tax credit is repealed for property placed in service after 1985. Most of the provisions are effective after 1986.

## Federal Income Tax Comparisons
### Taxes at Selected Rate Brackets After Standard Deductions/Zero Bracket Amounts[2]

| Adjusted gross income | Single return listing no dependents | | | | Joint return listing two dependents | | | |
|---|---|---|---|---|---|---|---|---|
| | 1986 | 1980 | 1972[1] | 1967 | 1986 | 1980 | 1972[1] | 1967 |
| $ 5,000 | $ 161 | $ 250 | $ 495 | $ 667 | $ −547[3] | $−500[3] | $ 102 | $ 286 |
| 10,000 | 863 | 1,177 | 1,545 | 1,742 | 96 | 374 | 901 | 1,114 |
| 15,000 | 1,706 | 2,345 | 2,703 | 3,334 | 868 | 1,242 | 1,820 | 2,172 |
| 20,000 | 2,788 | 3,837 | 4,255 | 5,350 | 1,625 | 2,265 | 3,010 | 3,428 |
| 25,000 | 4,067 | 5,562 | 6,090 | 7,730 | 2,493 | 3,497 | 4,380 | 4,892 |
| 30,000 | 5,509 | 7,522 | 8,152 | 10,938 | 3,548 | 4,953 | 6,020 | 6,596 |

1. A 2.5% surcharge was in effect. 2. For comparison purposes, tax rate schedules were used. 3. Refund based on Earned Income credit for families with dependent children.

## Federal Corporation Taxes

Corporations are taxed under a graduated tax rate structure as shown in the chart below. The benefits of the lower rates are phased out for corporations with taxable income between $1,000,000 and $1,405,000 and totally eliminated for corporations with incomes equal to or in excess of $1,405,000.

If the corporation qualifies, it may elect to be an S corporation. If it makes this election, the corporation will not (with certain exceptions) pay corporate tax on its income. Its income is instead passed through and taxed to its shareholders. There are several requirements a corporation must meet to qualify as an S corporation including having 35 or fewer shareholders, and having only one class of stock.

### 1986

| Taxable income | Tax | Percent over excess |
|---|---|---|
| $0 to $25,000 | $ 0 | 15% over $0 |
| $25,000 to $50,000 | $ 3,750 | 18% over $25,000 |
| $50,000 to $75,000 | $ 8,250 | 30% over $50,000 |
| $75,000 to $100,000 | $ 15,750 | 40% over $75,000 |
| $100,000 and over | $ 25,750 | 46% over $100,000 |

# State Corporation Income and Franchise Taxes

All states but Nevada, South Dakota, Texas, Washington, and Wyoming impose a tax on corporation net income. The majority of states impose the tax at flat rates ranging from 2.35% to 11.5%. Several states have adopted a graduated basis of rates for corporations.

Nearly all states follow the federal law in defining net income. However, many states provide for varying exclusions and adjustments.

A state is empowered to tax all of the net income of its domestic corporations. With regard to non-resident corporations, however, it may only tax the net income on business carried on within its boundaries. Corporations are, therefore, required to apportion their incomes among the states where they do business and pay a tax to each of these states. Nearly all states provide an apportionment to their domestic corporations, too, in order that they not be unduly burdened.

Several states tax unincorporated businesses separately.

# Federal Estate and Gift Taxes

A Federal Estate Tax Return must be filed for the estate of every U.S. citizen or resident whose gross estate, if the decedent died in 1986, exceeds $500,000. An estate tax return must also be filed for the estate of a non-resident, if the value of his gross estate in the U.S. is more than $60,000 at the date of death. The estate tax return is due nine months after the date of death of the decedent, but a reasonable extension of time to file may be obtained for good reason. Tax due is to be paid when the return is filed. The executor of an estate with an interest in closely held business that comprises at least 35% of the adjusted gross estate may pay estate tax attributable to the business in from two to ten equal annual installments. In such a case, a 5-year extension for the payment of estate taxes may be exercised for that portion of the tax attributable to a closely held business.

Under the unified federal estate and gift tax structure, individuals who make taxable gifts during the calendar year are required to file a gift tax return by April 15 of the following year.

A unified credit of $155,800 (during 1986) is available to offset both estate and gift taxes. Any part of the credit used to offset gift taxes is not available to offset estate taxes. As a result, although they are still taxable as gifts, lifetime transfers no longer cushion the impact of progressive estate tax rates. Lifetime transfers and transfers made at death are cumulated for estate tax rate purposes. Gift taxes are computed by applying the uniform rate schedule to lifetime taxable transfers (after deducting the unified credit) and subtracting the taxes payable for prior taxable periods. In general, estate taxes are computed by applying the uniform rate schedule to cumulated transfers and subtract-

ing the gift taxes paid. An appropriate adjustment is made for taxes on lifetime transfers—such as certain gifts within three years of death—in a decedent's estate.

Among the deductions allowed in computing the amount of the estate subject to tax are funeral expenditures, administrative costs, claims and bequests to religious, charitable, and fraternal organizations or government welfare agencies, and state inheritance taxes. For transfers made after 1981 during life or death, there is an unlimited marital deduction.

An annual gift tax exclusion is provided that permits tax-free gifts to each donee of $10,000 for each year. A husband and wife who agree to treat gifts to third persons as joint gifts can exclude up to $20,000 a year to each donee. An unlimited exclusion for medical expenses and school tuition paid for the benefit of any donee is also available.

## Federal Estate and Gift Taxes
### Unified Rate Schedule, 1986[1]

| If the net amount is: | | Tentative tax is: | | |
| From | To | Tax + | % | On excess over |
|---|---|---|---|---|
| $ 0 | $ 10,000 | $ 0 | 18 | $ 0 |
| 10,000 | 20,000 | 1,800 | 20 | 10,000 |
| 20,000 | 40,000 | 3,800 | 22 | 20,000 |
| 40,000 | 60,000 | 8,200 | 24 | 40,000 |
| 60,000 | 80,000 | 13,000 | 26 | 60,000 |
| 80,000 | 100,000 | 18,200 | 28 | 80,000 |
| 100,000 | 150,000 | 23,800 | 30 | 100,000 |
| 150,000 | 250,000 | 38,800 | 32 | 150,000 |
| 250,000 | 500,000 | 70,800 | 34 | 250,000 |
| 500,000 | 750,000 | 155,800 | 37 | 500,000 |
| 750,000 | 1,000,000 | 248,300 | 39 | 750,000 |
| 1,000,000 | 1,250,000 | 345,800 | 41 | 1,000,000 |
| 1,250,000 | 1,500,000 | 448,300 | 43 | 1,250,000 |
| 1,500,000 | 2,000,000 | 555,800 | 45 | 1,500,000 |
| 2,000,000 | 2,500,000 | 780,800 | 49 | 2,000,000 |
| 2,500,000 | 3,000,000 | 1,025,800 | 53 | 2,500,000 |
| 3,000,000 and up | — | 1,290,800 | 55 | 3,000,000 |

1. The estate and gift tax rates are combined in the single rate schedule effective for the estates of decedents dying, and for gifts made, after Dec. 31, 1976.

## State General Sales and Use Taxes, July 1985[1]

| State | Percent rate | State | Percent rate | State | Percent rate |
|---|---|---|---|---|---|
| Alabama | 4 | Kentucky | 5 | Ohio | 5 |
| Arizona | 5 | Louisiana | 4 | Oklahoma | 3.25 |
| Arkansas | 4 | Maine | 5 | Pennsylvania | 6 |
| California | 4.75 | Maryland | 5 | Rhode Island | 6 |
| Colorado | 3 | Massachusetts | 5 | South Carolina | 5 |
| Connecticut | 7.5 | Michigan | 4 | South Dakota | 4 |
| D.C. | 6 | Minnesota | 6 | Tennessee | 5.5 |
| Florida | 5 | Mississippi | 6 | Texas | 4.125 |
| Georgia | 3 | Missouri | 4.225 | Utah | 4.59375 |
| Hawaii | 4 | Nebraska | 3.5 | Vermont | 4 |
| Idaho | 5 | Nevada | 5.75 | Virginia | 3 |
| Illinois | 5 | New Jersey | 6 | Washington | 6.5 |
| Indiana | 5 | New Mexico | 4.75 | West Virginia | 5 |
| Iowa | 4 | New York | 4 | Wisconsin | 5 |
| Kansas | 4 | North Carolina | 3 | Wyoming | 3 |
| | | North Dakota | 4 | | |

1. Local and county taxes, if any, are additional. NOTE: Alaska, Delaware, Montana, New Hampshire and Oregon have no statewide sales and use taxes. *Source: Information Please Almanac* questionnaires to the states, and Tax Foundation, Inc.

## Sales Tax Rates in Selected Cities[1]

| City | Percent rate | City | Percent rate | City | Percent rate |
|------|------|------|------|------|------|
| Amarillo, Tex. | 1 | Ithaca, N.Y.[2] | 3 | Richmond, Va. | 1 |
| Anaheim, Calif.[2] | 1.25 | Jefferson City, Mo. | 1 | Roanoke, Va. | 1 |
| Austin, Tex. | 2 | Lincoln, Neb. | 1.5 | Sacramento, Calif.[2] | 1.25 |
| Baton Rouge, La.[3] | 3 | Los Angeles[2] | 1.25 | St. Louis | 1.375 |
| Berkeley, Calif.[2,4] | 1.75 | Lynchburg, Va. | 1 | San Antonio, Tex. | 1.5 |
| Birmingham, Ala. | 2 | Mobile, Ala. | 3 | San Diego, Calif.[2] | 1.25 |
| Boulder, Colo. | 2.15 | Montgomery, Ala. | 3 | San Francisco[2,4] | 1.75 |
| Chicago[2] | 3 | New Orleans[3] | 5.0 | Seattle[2] | 1.4 |
| Dallas | 2 | New York | 4.25 | Shreveport, La.[3] | 3.5 |
| Denver | 3.5 | Nome, Alaska | 3 | Spokane, Wash.[2] | 1.3 |
| Duluth, Minn. | 1 | Norfolk, Va. | 1 | Springfield, Ill.[2] | 2 |
| El Paso | 1 | Oakland, Calif.[2,4] | 1.75 | Topeka, Kan. | 1.0 |
| Fort Worth | 1.25 | Oklahoma City | 2 | Troy, N.Y.[2] | 3 |
| Fresno, Calif.[2] | 1.25 | Omaha, Neb. | 1.5 | Tucson, Ariz. | 2 |
| Glendale, Calif.[2] | 1.75 | Pasadena, Calif.[2] | 1.25 | Tulsa, Okla. | 3 |
| Houston | 2 | Phoenix, Ariz. | 1 | Washington, D.C. | 6 |
| Huntsville, Ala. | 3 | Rapid City, S.D. | 2 | Yonkers, N.Y.[2] | 4 |

1. Excludes state and county sales taxes unless otherwise indicated. 2. Combined city and county rate. 3. Includes Parish School Board tax. 4. Includes 0.5% imposed for public transit. *Source:* Tax Foundation, Inc.

## Income Tax Rates in Selected Cities
### (Population exceeding 50,000)

| City | Percent rate | Year begun | City | Percent rate | Year begun |
|------|------|------|------|------|------|
| Akron, Ohio | 2 | 1962 | Lakewood, Ohio | 1.5 | 1968 |
| Allentown, Pa. | 1 | 1958 | Lancaster, Pa | 0.5 | 1959 |
| Altoona, Pa. | 1 | 1948 | Lansing, Mich | 1 | 1968 |
| Baltimore | ([1]) | 1966 | Lexington, Ky. | 2 | 1952 |
| Bethlehem, Pa. | 1 | 1957 | Lima, Ohio | 1.5 | 1959 |
| Birmingham, Ala. | 1 | 1970 | Lorain, Ohio | 1.5 | 1967 |
| Canton, Ohio | 2 | 1954 | Louisville, Ky. | 2.2 | 1948 |
| Cincinnati | 2 | 1954 | Mansfield, Ohio | 1 | 1966 |
| Cleveland | 2 | 1967 | New York | 0.9–4.3 | 1966 |
| Cleveland Heights, Ohio | 2 | 1968 | Owensboro, Ky. | 1 | 1960 |
| Columbus, Ohio | 2 | 1947 | Parma, Ohio | 2 | 1967 |
| Covington, Ky. | 2.5 | 1956 | Philadelphia | 4.96 | 1939 |
| Dayton, Ohio | 2.25 | 1949 | Pontiac, Mich. | 1 | 1968 |
| Detroit | 3 | 1965 | Reading, Pa. | 1 | 1969 |
| District of Columbia | 2–11 | 1947 | Saginaw, Mich. | 1 | 1965 |
| Elyria, Ohio | 1.5 | 1969 | St. Louis | 1 | 1948 |
| Erie, Pa. | 1 | 1948 | Scranton, Pa. | 3.5 | 1948 |
| Euclid, Ohio | 2 | 1967 | Springfield, Ohio | 2.5 | 1948 |
| Flint, Mich. | 1 | 1965 | Toledo, Ohio | 2.25 | 1946 |
| Gadsden, Ala. | 2 | 1956 | Warren, Ohio | 1.5 | 1952 |
| Grand Rapids, Mich. | 1 | 1967 | Wilkes-Barre, Pa. | 2.5 | 1966 |
| Hamilton, Ohio | 1.75 | 1960 | Wilmington, Del. | 1.25 | 1970 |
| Harrisburg, Pa. | 1 | 1966 | York, Pa. | 1.5 | 1965 |
| Kansas City, Mo. | 1 | 1964 | Youngstown, Ohio | 2 | 1948 |
| Kettering, Ohio | 1.75 | 1968 | | | |

1. Tax is 50% of state income tax. NOTE: Rates are for residents only, except in Kentucky, Ohio, and Pennsylvania cities, where non-resident rate is the same. *Source:* Tax Foundation, Inc.

## U.S. Home Ownership on the Decline

According to the 1985 Home Buyer Survey of the United States League of Savings Institutions, the percentage of American households who own their own homes (63.9%) has fallen in every year in the 1980s after reaching a peak of 65.6% in 1980.

Thus, in spite of the recent improvements in affordability, homeownership is becoming more difficult to achieve.

A second income was an important element in household income for almost 70% of 1985 first-time home buyer households. Moreover, the importance of that second income was growing—for more than half of these households the second income accounted for more than 30% of total household income.

The medium incomes of home buyers increased from $35,987 in 1983 to $42,396 in 1985. In 1985, 68.8% of first-time buyers made a down payment of less than 20% versus 67.9% in 1983.

## State and Local Taxes Paid by a Family of Four in Selected Large Cities, 1984

| City | Total Taxes Paid by Gross Family Income Level | | | Percent of Income by Income Level | | |
|------|---------|---------|---------|---------|---------|---------|
|  | $15,000 | $25,000 | $35,000 | $15,000 | $25,000 | $35,000 |
| Albuquerque | 1,134 | 1,731 | 2,559 | 7.6 | 6.9 | 7.3 |
| Atlanta | 995 | 1,828 | 2,715 | 6.6 | 7.3 | 7.8 |
| Baltimore | 1,678 | 2,991 | 1,126 | 11.2 | 12.0 | 11.9 |
| Boise City | 1,097 | 2,055 | 3,100 | 7.3 | 8.2 | 8.9 |
| Boston | 1,174 | 2,102 | 3,042 | 7.8 | 8.4 | 8.7 |
| Bridgeport | 1,770 | 2,721 | 3,736 | 11.8 | 10.9 | 10.7 |
| Burlington | 1,230 | 2,021 | 2,924 | 8.2 | 8.1 | 8.4 |
| Charlotte | 1,174 | 2,042 | 2,959 | 7.8 | 8.2 | 8.5 |
| Chicago | 1,218 | 2,065 | 2,928 | 8.1 | 8.3 | 8.4 |
| Cleveland | 1,326 | 2,371 | 3,497 | 8.8 | 9.5 | 10.0 |
| Columbia | 1,158 | 2,094 | 3,088 | 7.7 | 8.4 | 8.8 |
| Des Moines | 1,404 | 2,480 | 3,660 | 9.4 | 9.9 | 10.5 |
| Detroit | 1,791 | 3,082 | 4,357 | 11.9 | 12.3 | 12.5 |
| Honolulu | 1,177 | 2,108 | 3,108 | 7.9 | 8.4 | 8.9 |
| Indianapolis | 1,301 | 2,029 | 3,514 | 8.7 | 8.1 | 10.0 |
| Jackson, MS | 815 | 1,374 | 2,103 | 5.4 | 5.5 | 6.0 |
| Milwaukee | 1,981 | 3,351 | 4,836 | 13.2 | 13.4 | 13.8 |
| Minneapolis | 1,204 | 2,836 | 4,911 | 8.0 | 11.3 | 14.0 |
| Newark, NJ | 3,048 | 4,871 | 6,845 | 20.3 | 19.5 | 19.6 |
| New York City | 1,603 | 2,987 | 4,791 | 10.7 | 12.0 | 13.7 |
| Norfolk | 1,190 | 1,987 | 2,831 | 7.9 | 8.0 | 8.1 |
| Omaha | 1,087 | 1,738 | 2,477 | 7.3 | 7.0 | 7.1 |
| Philadelphia | 1,842 | 2,933 | 4,026 | 12.3 | 11.7 | 11.5 |
| Portland, ME | 1,357 | 2,338 | 3,636 | 9.1 | 9.4 | 10.4 |
| Portland, OR | 1,453 | 2,755 | 4,098 | 9.7 | 11.0 | 11.7 |
| Providence | 1,992 | 3,225 | 4,614 | 13.3 | 12.9 | 13.2 |
| Salt Lake City | 1,268 | 2,155 | 3,056 | 8.5 | 8.6 | 8.7 |
| St. Louis | 1,371 | 2,295 | 3,257 | 9.1 | 9.2 | 9.3 |
| Washington, DC | 1,418 | 2,527 | 3,802 | 9.5 | 10.1 | 10.9 |
| Wilmington | 1,747 | 3,085 | 4,521 | 11.7 | 12.3 | 12.9 |
| Median[1] | 1,158 | 1,987 | 2,831 | 7.7 | 8.0 | 8.1 |

1. Median of all 51 cities. For complete list of cities. NOTE: Data based on average family of four (one wage earner, wife or husband, and two school age children) owning their own home and living in a city where taxes apply. Comprises State and local sales, income, auto, and real estate taxes. *Source:* Government of the District of Columbia, Department of Finance and Revenue, *Tax Burdens in Washington, D.C. Compared With Those in The Largest City in Each of the 50 States, 1984.*

## Residential Property Tax Rates in Selected Large Cities by Rank: 1984

| City | Effective Tax Rate Per $100 Rate | Assessment level (percent) | Nominal rate per $100 | City | Effective Tax Rate Per $100 Rate | Assessment level (percent) | Nominal rate per $100 |
|------|------|------|------|------|------|------|------|
| Newark, NJ | 6.29 | 50.0 | 12.58 | Chicago | 1.99 | [2]19.8 | 10.05 |
| Detroit | 4.04 | 49.1 | 8.22 | Omaha | 1.98 | 72.4 | 2.74 |
| Wilmington | 3.47 | 70.0 | 4.95 | Memphis | 1.54 | 22.3 | 6.91 |
| Providence | 3.36 | 48.3 | 6.96 | Boise City | 1.53 | 100.0 | 1.53 |
| Milwaukee | 3.34 | 99.9 | 3.34 | New York City | 1.42 | 15.6 | 9.10 |
| Baltimore | 2.70 | 43.5 | 6.21 | Fargo | 1.40 | 4.5 | 31.20 |
| Des Moines | 2.68 | 72.5 | 3.69 | Louisville | 1.27 | 90.0 | 1.40 |
| Manchester | 2.67 | 33.0 | 8.10 | Atlanta | 1.23 | 24.4 | 5.03 |
|  |  |  |  | Charlotte | 1.20 | 94.5 | 1.27 |
| Philadelphia | 2.62 | 35.0 | 7.48 | Columbia | 1.18 | 4.0 | 29.55 |
| Indianapolis | 2.56 | 20.0 | 12.78 |  |  |  |  |
| Bridgeport | 2.39 | 30.0 | 7.97 | Norfolk | 1.14 | 91.0 | 1.25 |
| Portland, OR | 2.37 | 96.0 | 2.47 | Washington, DC | 1.14 | 93.0 | 1.22 |
| Portland, ME | 2.35 | 90.0 | 2.61 | Jackson, MS | 1.12 | 15.0 | 7.45 |
| Minneapolis | 2.31 | [1]20.4 | 11.30 | Billings | 1.09 | 3.7 | 29.34 |
| Sioux Falls | 2.15 | 31.2 | 6.89 | Charleston, WV | 1.07 | 62.0 | 1.73 |
|  |  |  |  | New Orleans | 1.06 | 10.0 | 10.57 |
| St. Louis | 2.15 | 33.2 | 6.45 | Wichita | 1.02 | 7.8 | 13.11 |

| | | | | | | |
|---|---|---|---|---|---|---|
| Phoenix | 1.00 | 10.0 | 10.02 | Oklahoma City | 1.59 | 13.5 | 11.77 |
| Salt Lake City | 1.00 | 12.0 | 8.31 | | | | |
| | | | | Little Rock | .91 | 11.0 | 8.28 |
| Seattle | .95 | 94.5 | 1.00 | Las Vegas | .80 | 33.7 | 2.36 |
| Cleveland | 1.87 | 35.0 | 5.16 | Anchorage | .78 | 79.0 | .99 |
| Jacksonville | 1.85 | 94.0 | 1.97 | Denver | .70 | 7.8 | 8.99 |
| Albuquerque | 1.80 | 33.3 | 5.39 | | | | |
| | | | | Birmingham | .70 | 10.0 | 6.95 |
| Burlington | 1.79 | 24.0 | 7.44 | Los Angeles | .66 | 61.2 | 1.07 |
| Boston | 1.71 | 100.0 | 1.71 | Honolulu | .61 | 90.0 | .68 |
| Houston | 1.68 | 100.0 | 1.68 | Casper | .59 | 7.4 | 7.90 |

1. Statutory assessment levels: 16% first $27,000, 22% next $27,000, and 28% over $54,000. Level noted is for $75,000.
2. Assessment level of 10.25% × statewide equalization factor of 1.9288.
   *Source:* Government of the District of Columbia, Department of Finance and Revenue, *Tax Burdens in Washington, DC Compared With Those in The Largest City in Each of the 50 States, 1984.*

# Do U.S. Taxpayers Get Better Breaks Than Europeans?

### By Jeffrey Owens

How does the overall tax burden in the United States compare to that in other industrialized countries? Are tax levels increasing? How much money is left with the average taxpayer after the Internal Revenue Service and the Social Security Administration have taken their share?

Two approaches are used. The first looks at the aggregate tax levels and structures; the second examines direct taxes paid by a representative taxpayer. The comparisons use statistics compiled by the Organization for Economic Development (OECD), which groups together 23 major industrialized countries, including all the member states of the European Community. The statistics cover taxes paid to federal, state, and local governments (many European countries have local income and property taxes) and compulsory social security contributions are regarded as a tax on earnings.

The most convenient way of comparing overall tax burdens is to examine the proportion of gross domestic product (GDP) accounted for by taxation. Within the OECD tax-to-GDP ratios range from 15% in Turkey to over 50% in Sweden. The highest taxed countries are Sweden, Denmark, Norway, France, the Netherlands, and Belgium, while the lowest are the United States, Japan, Spain, and Turkey.

The average tax take in the OECD area is 37% of GDP. The equivalent figure for the E.C. countries (excluding Portugal and Spain) is 41%. The United States, which takes less than 30% of GDP in taxation, is a comparatively low-tax country. Japan is the only other major industrial country with such a low level of taxation.

There are, of course, many problems in making such comparisons. Taxes, unlike elephants, can be difficult to define and to identify. When, for example, does a fee for garbage services become a local tax? Countries make varying uses of tax subsidies to implement policies. These tax expenditures re-

Jeffrey Owens works in the fiscal affairs division of OECD. The views expressed in this article are his own, and in no way reflect those of OECD. The article is excerpted and reprinted with permission of *EUROPE* magazine, 1986, published by the Delegation of the Commission of the European Communities, © The Commission of the European Communities, 1985.

duce revenue, yet the degree of government intervention in the economy is much the same as if a direct expenditure were used. In some countries, such as Finland and Switzerland, sickness schemes are operated outside of government, yet employers have a legislative obligation to contribute to them. In many countries, a large part of payroll taxes are *paid by* the government in its role as an employer. Should these taxes be included in tax burden comparisons? The OECD statistics include them, but a case could be made for exclusion (the Swedish tax burden would then fall from 50% to 45% of GDP!).

Interpreting international statistics on tax ratios is also difficult. What does it mean to say that Sweden is a high-tax country? Does it follow that the average Swede is in some way worse off than the average American? Perhaps some Americans would prefer to pay higher taxes if these were matched by a cradle-to-grave welfare system? Economists cannot provide any unambiguous answers to these questions, for any response must depend on how government uses the revenues and on whether incentives to work, save, and invest are seriously distorted in a high-tax economy.

## Sources of Revenue

All taxes are eventually paid by individuals either in the form of lower incomes or higher prices. Nevertheless, it is of some interest to examine which taxes bring in the most money. Though countries levy many kinds of taxes—France levies over 250 taxes—over the last decade around 85% of revenues usually have come from three main sources: personal income taxes, social security contributions, and value-added taxes (VAT) and sales taxes.

A comparison of the tax structure of the United States and of the "average" tax structure in the E.C. shows that the largest single source of revenue in both cases is the personal income tax, but whereas this tax accounts for 37% of revenues in the United States, it accounts for only 27% in the Community. The situation is reversed if general consumption taxes are compared. Europe places a far heavier reliance on these taxes than does the

United States: 19% as opposed to 7%. Much the same applies for excise and other specific consumption taxes. Taxes on property, however, are almost twice as high in the United States than in the E.C.

As regards the other major sources of revenue, social security contributions are somewhat more important in the United States, whereas corporate taxes are less important. The main conclusion that can be drawn is that in comparison to the E.C., the United States places a heavier reliance on direct, rather than indirect forms of taxation.

## A Representative Taxpayer

An alternative approach to comparing tax levels is to examine the tax bill of a representative taxpayer, the so-called average production worker (APW). An APW is defined as an adult working full-time in the manufacturing sector and receiving the average gross earnings of that group. In most countries, personal income taxes are the single most important source of tax revenue. The method of calculating these taxes is similar in all countries. First, the tax allowances applicable to a taxpayer are deducted from gross earnings, the schedule rate is then applied, and the resulting tax liability reduced by any relevant tax credits.

We can also compare the average rate of income tax applicable to a married couple with two children at the income level of an APW. In 1984[1] this rate ranged from over 30% in Denmark and and Sweden to less than 1% in France. The U.S. rate was 15%, whereas the average rate for the E.C. was 12%, a result that may surprise some Americans (the average U.S. industrial wage in 1984[1] was just below $19,500 and on this income $1,640 was paid in federal taxes and $1,320 in state and local taxes).

Compulsory employee social security contributions are the other major determinant of take-home pay. Except for Australia and New Zealand, all OECD countries use social contributions to fi-

1. Latest comparable figures.

nance social benefits. For the most part the employee's share is levied on gross earnings, without any allowances for family situation. There is usually a ceiling on the earnings base, after which the marginal rate of contribution is zero. The employer's share is invariably larger than that of the employee. If employees' social security contributions are added to personal income taxes we get a rough indication of how much money is left in taxpayers' pockets after the payment of these levies. Taken together, these two levies account for more than 35% of earnings in Denmark, Turkey, the Netherlands, and Sweden, but less than 15% in Spain, Greece, France, Luxembourg, Canada, and Japan.

The United States, at 22%, is close to the OECD average, but a little below the average of the E.C. (25%). The typical U.S. manufacturing worker would take home more than 78% of his earnings, whereas his E.C. counterpart would be left with less than 75%. The European worker, however, would be eligible for cash family allowances which would be worth between 2% and 7% of his earnings, and the employee would generally have access to subsidized state medical and welfare services.

## Conclusions

The overall tax burden in the United States compares favorably to European tax burdens and is more or less in line with that of Japan. Direct taxes, however, are heavier, in part because E.C. countries have access to a buoyant VAT (all of the 11 top-ranked countries have a VAT).

At the APW income level, the U.S. worker pays a larger proportion of his earnings in direct taxes than the average worker in the Community. The current tax reform proposals in the United States, if implemented, would narrow this gap. It is unlikely, however, that statistics will convince U.S. taxpayers that they are not too badly off when compared to Europeans. Tax burdens have more to do with perceptions than reality, and, insofar as taxpayers perceive their taxes to be unfair—they are also likely to perceive them as being too heavy.

## Countries Ranked by Overall Tax Burdens as % Of GDP

| | | | |
|---|---|---|---|
| 1. Sweden | 7. Austria | 13. Finland | 19. Australia |
| 2. Denmark | 8. Luxembourg | 14. Canada | 20. United States |
| 3. Norway | 9. Italy | 15. Greece | 21. Japan |
| 4. France | 10. Ireland | 16. Switzerland | 22. Spain |
| 5. Netherlands | 11. United Kingdom | 17. Portugal | 23. Turkey |
| 6. Belgium | 12. Germany | 18. New Zealand | |

*Source:* Revenue Statistics of OECD member countries, Paris 1985. NOTE: Countries are ranked by 1984 figures, except for Australia, Belgium, Greece, Spain and the United States where 1983 figures are used.

## Countries Ranked by Direct Tax Burdens on Income (Income Taxes and Social Security Contributions Paid by Individuals as % of GDP

| | | | |
|---|---|---|---|
| 1. Denmark | 7. Germany | 13. United States | 19. Japan |
| 2. Belgium | 8. Luxembourg | 14. Canada | 20. Greece |
| 3. Sweden | 9. Austria | 15. United Kingdom | 21. Spain |
| 4. Netherlands | 10. Switzerland | 16. Norway | 22. Turkey |
| 5. New Zealand | 11. Ireland | 17. Australia | 23. Portugal |
| 6. Finland | 12. Italy | 18. France | |

*Source:* Revenue Statistics of OECD Member countries, Paris 1985. NOTE: Countries are ranked by 1984 figures, except for Australia, Belgium, Greece, Italy, Japan, Spain, and the United States where 1983 figures are used.

# CAREER PLANNING KIT

## Computer Training: A Little Goes a Long Way

*Source:* Occupational Outlook Quarterly, U.S. Department of Labor, Bureau of Labor Statistics.

Computers are popping up on desks and in workplaces all through American industry like flowers in the spring. They represent the most widespread technological innovation of our time, since they are used virtually in every industry and in 140 occupations. One worker in eight now uses a computer, and this number is growing rapidly.

Yet despite the apprehensions of educators and industrialists that training in this new high-technology field would make great demands on the school system, most workers involved with computers learn to use them very quickly; a few hours to a few weeks of formal training, mostly provided by their employers, is usually enough. Only a small proportion require extensive computer training.

These are the major conclusions of a study by the National Institute for Work and Learning. The study was done for the National Commission for Employment Policy, which initiated it to provide information for planning education for this new technology.

It is difficult to generalize about the diverse situations in so many occupations; each has its own history and traditions, work content, industrial attachments, union or professional organizations, and traditional means of education or training, to which the new skill requirements imposed by the computer must be added. Training methods differ within each occupation. There is usually no standard method. Nevertheless, a few broad patterns of training emerge from this review. Workers using computers fall into three groups with respect to the training they need, as shown in the accompanying table.

### Extensive Training Required

This group includes the engineers and scientists who design the computer equipment and the computer system programmers who write the internal operating programs. Each requires different training, but in each case the training takes years and usually involves a combination of formal schooling and experience.

Altogether, this group accounted for about 0.6 percent of all workers in the United States and about 5 percent of those using computers. These are rapidly growing occupations, but even by 1995, they are projected to amount to only 1 percent of all workers.

### Computer Training Not Always Required

Some workers in these occupations use computers. They usually use software already available for caculating, word processing, modeling, or simulation, but some of them may have to be able to write computer programs or modify existing programs. They are primarily in the scientific and technical occupations. Only a few of these computer users write programs; they account for 5 to 10 percent of all computer users and about 1 percent of all

workers.

Whether or not a worker has to write programs depends on whether the necessary software is already available. In the intensely competitive software market, producers vie with each other to provide user-friendly programs for every application likely to attract customers.

The programming skills required by this group are not nearly at the level required of professional applications programmers, although some of the individuals in this group of occupations may obtain such skill levels.

They write programs mostly in high-level languages such as COBOL, FORTRAN, or BASIC, rather than in assembler languages used by professional programmers. Because programming is an extra skill for them, subordinate to their main professional interests, few have the motivation or time to spend in developing this skill beyond that needed to get the work done.

Members of these occupations have learned programming in a variety of ways, including one-semester or longer courses in vocational or technical schools, or in two-year or four-year colleges, one-to-two-week courses (or a series of several such brief courses) given by the employer or computer manufacturers, self-learning from manuals or computer-based instruction, or just learning from friends. College students in these fields frequently take one or more programming courses in the computer sciences department.

Whatever the method of introductory training, one thing is essential: Experience after training. This experience may be gained in the computer laboratory in school or on the job. Learning is made easier if the student has someone to turn to for help—a friend, colleague, instructor, or supervisor.

### Only Brief Training is Required

Workers in this group require only training in operating computers with software already available. They amount to more than 80 percent of workers who use computers and include most of the managerial, clerical, sales, and industrial process workers who use computers.

These workers can learn their computer skills in anywhere from a few hours to a few weeks of training—a testimony to the ingenuity with which computer manufacturers and software producers have attacked the problem of making the systems "user-friendly." Much of this training is given on the job or in brief courses provided by employers, manufacturers of equipment, unions, or schools.

In addition to the brief formal training that is the most common method of learning, workers need an additional period of working with the computer on the job to perfect their skills. The time required to attain proficiency depends on many factors. The difficulty of the subject matter with which the worker is dealing and his or her familiarity with it; the worker's familiarity, facility, and previous experience with computers; the amount of time the worker spends using the computer and whether the work involves all the operations with frequency, or whether some operations are required only infrequently and are therefore not encountered or learned until a long time after the worker begins using the computer. Because of these variables and because proficiency means different things in different situations, it is difficult to generalize on the number of weeks or months required to attain proficiency.

People planning to enter these occupations can enhance their employability by studying computer-related skills in school. Even in these occupations, at least a few workers in each have probably written a computer program related to their job.

For this reason, the distinction made between group II and III, based on whether some members of the occupation write programs, becomes a little hazy at the edges.

## Additional Information

An excellent book based on this report has been published by Peterson's Guides, Princeton, N.J., entitled "Getting A Job In The Computer Age," and is designed as a career guidance and planning reference for students, teachers, counselors, parents, and workers who are concerned about what computer training is needed and who provides the training in 140 occupations.

# Workers Who Use Computers
## Group I—Extensive Computer Training is Required

| | | |
|---|---|---|
| Computer programmer | Data-processing equipment repairer | Programmer, numerically controlled |
| Computer science teacher, college | Engineers and scientists who design | machine tools |
| Computer systems analyst | computers | Repairer of numerically controlled |
| | | industrial equipment |

## Group II—Computer Programming Training Not Always Required

| **Engineering and related technical occupations** | **Life and physical science occupations** | **Other professional and technical occupations** |
|---|---|---|
| Engineer | Biological and agricultural scientist | Accountant and auditor |
| Engineering technician and | Chemist | Architect |
| technologist | Geologist | Dietician |
| Surveyor and surveying and mapping | Geophysicist | Elementary and secondary school |
| scientist, technician, and | Meteorologist | teacher |
| technologist | Physicist | Forester and conservation scientist |
| | | Medical records administrator |
| | **Mathematical science occupations** | Social scientist |
| | Actuary | Urban and regional planner |
| | Mathematician | |
| | Statistician | |

## Group III—Only Brief Computer Training Required

| **Engineering technician** | **Managerial and administrative occupations** | **Craft and industrial process workers** |
|---|---|---|
| Broadcast technician | | Aircraft mechanic |
| Drafter | | Central office and PBX technician |
| Estimator-analyst, electric utilities | **Sales occupations** | Chemical plant operator |
| | Real estate agent and broker | Electric generating plant operator |
| **Medical occupations** | Sales representative, computer or | Graphic arts occupations |
| Health technician and technologist | software manufacturing | Pattern grader and layout worker, |
| Licensed practical nurse | Securities sales agent | apparel and shoe industry |
| Medical records technician | Travel agent | Petroleum refinery operator |
| Pharmacist | | Systems operator or dispatcher, |
| Physician | **Administrative support occupations** | electric utilities |
| Registered nurse | Airline reservation agent | |
| | Bank teller | **Farm operators and managers** |
| **Other professional and technical occupations** | Bookkeeper and accounting clerk | |
| Air traffic controller | Cashier | |
| Airline pilot | Computer and peripheral equipment | |
| Commercial and graphic artist and | operator | |
| designer | Data-entry keyer | |
| Industrial designer | Directory assistance operator | |
| Lawyer | Postal clerk, letter-sorting machine | |
| Legal assistant | operator | |
| Librarian | Secretary | |
| Library technician | Stenographer and shorthand reporter | |
| Purchasing agent and manager | Traffic, shipping, and receiving clerk | |
| Reporter and correspondent | Typist and word-processing machine | |
| Technical writer | operator | |
| Writer and editor | | |

# How To Write A Successful Résumé

*Source: The Professional Secretary's Handbook,* Copyright © 1984, Houghton Mifflin Company.

## The Résumé

Your personal résumé should be thought of as a marketing tool for selling yourself to a prospective employer. Since you will have limited page space on which to present everything relevant about your work history, you should go back to the "who," "what," "where," "when," "why" formula and be concise and clear in your presentation and format. A lot of people out there are looking for jobs—all of them with résumés in one form or another. An employer may have to look through as many as 100 résumés of applicants for the same job before selecting the people to be interviewed. Therefore, your résumé must be eye-catching and brief so that a person scanning a page can immediately pick out your best assets and work experience.

If you have a career objective, you may want to state it on your résumé. There are two schools of thought on this subject, however. If you state your job objective, you may be limiting or categorizing yourself into a specific job market. There may be a job out there that can combine all of your skills with a title that does not even resemble your career objective. On the other hand, you may have determined in your research that you definitely want the particular type of job atmosphere associated with the title that you are seeking.

## The Format

You may put identical information into several different formats and thereby present totally different images with each. The choice of formats will depend on the way you want to focus attention on your proficiencies.

## Guidelines

The appearance of your résumé is almost as important as its content, for your resume is a reflection of your professionalism. As such, it should project a businesslike image. Here are a few general guidelines for résumé preparation that will help you:

(1) Paper should be 8 1/2″ × 11″ and white or off-white. If you are going to use colored paper, it should be conservative in tone or shade.

(2) Use a high-quality copying process such as offset printing or laser printing.

(3) Don't include personal information other than your name, address, and telephone number. Employers do not need to know your marital status, height, weight, sex, etc. Most of that can be determined at your interview.

(4) Use the active voice throughout and be careful not to change tenses in the body of the résumé.

(5) Try to keep the format pleasing to the eye. Avoid overuse of underlining and capitalization.

(6) Spell out names of organizations and agencies. Titles also should be spelled out.

(7) Proofread your résumé carefully. In fact, have someone else proofread it for you a final time before you have it printed. There is nothing more embarrassing than finding a mistake on your résumé after having given it to a prospective employer.

## The Chronological Résumé

The chronological format is one of the most commonly used. It starts with your latest job experience and works backward. It is easy to follow and focuses on your career development. Since tasks for each position are detailed separately in the chronological format, try not to repeat elements of job descriptions. Only the inclusive years should be used to designate employment dates; there is no need to specify the months. If you want to highlight skills instead of chronological work history, you should not use this format.

## The Functional Résumé

If you want to highlight your skills as opposed to the individual tasks for each position that you have held, you may want to use the functional résumé for your resume. This format details your skills under the specific function areas that you choose to highlight. A disadvantage to the use of this format is the possibility that your interviewer might want to relate your duties to each previously held job. However, this format may give you an opportunity to cover each position in more detail at your interview.

If you have had more than three or four jobs or if your experience looks scattered, this is an excellent format to use. Because the functional résumé focuses on your marketable skills rather than on your job history, it also can be used advantageously if you are worried that a prospective employer will be concerned with too many moves.

## Where To Find Your Niche

**The newspaper.** This is probably the first place that people look when they are trying to get information on available jobs. Look through all the jobs. One suiting all of your qualifications might be listed in any section of the classifieds.

Be sure to keep a file on all of the ads that you have answered so that you do not answer the same ad twice, and also so that you remember what positions you have applied for.

**Trade journals and speciality publications.** If you are looking for a job in a specialized industry, you may want to check out the classifieds in professional trade journals. Your local library will have trade journals and speciality publications available for you to browse through.

**Employment agencies.** If you are going to use an employment agency to find a job, be sure to find one that specializes in the jobs that you are seeking. Agencies screen and test job candidates before sending them on interviews. Hence, an agency interview should be treated exactly like an interview with a prospective employer.

## The Application Cover Letter

When you answer an ad through the mail, you should always send a descriptive cover letter with your résumé. The letter should be brief and formal while at the same time sparking the interest of the prospective employer. Try to give a reason why you should be interviewed for the advertised position. Never prepare a cover letter for photocopying and submission to numerous firms. Such letters indicate that the sender is lazy and uninterested in taking the time to write personally to a prospective employer.

**Résumé**

PROFILE

Margaret E. Longford
321 State Street  Apartment 39
City, US 98765
(800) 555-1212

Experience

November 1975 - December 1983          Allied College Publications, Inc.
                                       College Textbook Division/Science
                                       Associate Editor, Acquisitions

July 1969      - November 1975         Howe & Row Publishers, Inc.
                                       College Textbook Department
                                       Assistant Editor, Life Sciences

March 1967     - July 1969             LangData Incorporated
                                       College Division
                                       Editorial Assistant


Experience Summary

Sixteen years' experience in line editing of college science textbooks . Author
acquisitions . Production & Scheduling . Cost estimation . Budgets . Contracts .
Revisions . Manuscript Review . Liaison with Typesetters, Artists, Designers,
and Printers . Public Relations & Marketing Support . Liaison with Sales Personnel


Education

1964 - 1967        MBA              Taft Graduate School of Business
                                    Management

1960 - 1964        BA (cum laude)   Hartfield College
                                    Major:  Biology

1956 - 1960        diploma          Stonleigh School for Girls


Languages

French (fluent)
German (fluent)
Russian (scientific only)

Publications List

Available upon request

References

Available upon request

# Helpful Hints for the Interview

*Source:* U.S. Department of Labor, Employment and Training Administration

A job interview is your showcase for merchandising your talents. During the interview an employer judges your qualifications, appearance, and general fitness for the job opening. It is your opportunity to convince the employer that you can make a real contribution.

Equally important, it gives you a chance to appraise the job, the employer, and the firm. It enables you to decide if the job meets your career needs and interests and whether the employer is of the type and caliber you want to work for.

Before each interview, though, you should assume that the job you are applying for is precisely the one you want—because it may be. To present your qualifications most advantageously, you will need to prepare in advance. You should have the needed papers ready and the necessary information about yourself firmly in mind; and you should know how to act at the interview to make it an effective device for selling your skills.

## Preparing for the Interview

Assemble all the papers that you may need. The main item will be your background and work experience inventory. It contains all the facts and figures you could possibly be asked—either in filling in the job application form, or in the job interview. Don't forget to take copies of your résumé, even though you may have already submitted one. Take your social security card, recent school records, military separation papers, and union card, if you have one. If your work is the sort you can show in an interview (such as artwork, publications, or procedures), take along a few samples. Be careful not to leave your only copy of something, as it could get lost.

## Additional Pointers

* Learn all you can about the company where you are going for an interview—its product or service, standing in the industry, number and kinds of jobs available, and hiring policies.
* Know what you have to offer—what education and training you have had, what work you have done, and what you can do.
* Know what kind of job you want and why you want to work for the firm where you are applying.
* Bring along the names, addresses, and business affiliations of three persons (not relatives) who are familiar with your work and character. If you are a recent graduate, you can list your teachers. Ask references for permission to use their names.
* As you are filling in the job application, be aware that it in itself offers an excellent opportunity to convince an employer that you are a valuable person to hire. It is not only a chance to describe your accomplishments, but it also shows how clearly you can think and write, and how well you can present important details.
* Learn the area salary scale for the type of work you are seeking. If you have the required skill and experience, don't hesitate to state your salary expectations in filling in the application blank. On the other hand, if for any reason you don't want to commit yourself then, simply write "Open" in the space for salary desired. If asked, say you prefer to wait until the job interview to discuss salary.

* Never take anyone with you to the interview.
* Allow as much uninterrupted time for the interview as may be required. (For example, do not park your car in a limited-time space.)
* Dress conservatively. Avoid either too formal or too casual dress.

## You and the Interview

* Be pleasant and friendly but businesslike.
* Let the employer control the interview. Your answers should be frank and brief but complete, without rambling. Avoid dogmatic statements.
* Be flexible and willing but give the employer a clear idea of your job preferences.
* Stress your qualifications without exaggeration. The employer's questions or statements will indicate the type of person wanted. Use these clues in presenting your qualifications. For example, if you are being interviewed for an engineering position and the employer mentions that the job will require some customer contact work, use this clue to emphasize any work, experience, or courses you have had in this kind of skill.
* If you have not sent your resume in advance, present it, or your work records, references, personal data, work samples, or other materials to support your statements when the employer requests them.
* In discussing your previous jobs and work situations, avoid criticizing former employers or fellow workers.
* Don't discuss your personal, domestic, or financial problems unless you are specifically asked. Answer only what relates to the job.
* Don't be in a hurry to ask questions unless the employer invites them. But don't be afraid to ask what you need to know. If the employer offers you a job, be sure you understand exactly what your duties will be. Also find out what opportunities for advancement will be open. A definite understanding about the nature of your job will avoid future disappointment for either you or your employer.
* Be prepared to state the salary you want, but not until the employer has introduced the subject. Be realistic in discussing salary. But don't sell yourself short.
* If the employer does not definitely offer you a job or indicate when you will hear about it, ask when you may call to learn the decision.
* If the employer asks you to call or return for another interview, make a note of the time, date, and place.
* Thank the employer for the interview. If the firm cannot use you, ask about other employers who may need a person with your qualifications.

## The College Labor Market

According to the Bureau of Labor Statistics, the keen competition that characterized the job market for college graduates in the 1970s and early 1980s is not expected to abate appreciably.

Not since the late 1960s has the supply of college graduates been in rough balance with the number of jobs requiring a college degree.

# Retail Trade

**Millions of jobs, no experience necessary**

*Source: Occupational Outlook.*

The retail trade industry, employing almost 17,000,000 employees, is also the economy's main point of entry for new workers. More young people land their first job in retail trade than in any other industry. Almost three million 16- to 19-year olds hold jobs in retail trade; more than two million of them work part-time (less than 35 hours a week). Millions of older workers also hold retail jobs requiring little or no experience.

Few of these jobs provide high earnings, and many may not be very challenging or interesting. However, for students or others looking for extra income and for people seeking employment for the first time, these jobs may be just right. They sometimes lead to careers in the industry. More commonly, they serve as bridges to better paying or more promising jobs in other industries.

## Flexible Hours, Low Pay

These jobs have many advantages, although the average pay is low. Many people find the hours attractive. Retailers are usually open long hours and can often set up a worker's schedule to fit with school programs, child-care arrangements, or other demands on a person's time. The seasonal nature of some of these jobs—those available only in the summer or during the holiday buying rush—is also appealing to students and others who are not looking for year-round positions. Another attractive feature of many of these jobs is their proximity to the worker's home.

Most of these jobs pay the minimum wage—$3.35 an hour—or only a little more. However, there are some highly paid jobs in retail trade that beginners can move up to with experience or special training. Many cashiers in grocery stores and waiters in expensive restaurants have relatively high earnings. Other higher paying occupations in retail trade include store manager, restaurant manager, sales representative, and buyer.

## Cashiers

Typically, about one-half of all job openings are filled by people 19 years or younger, and almost three-quarters of all cashiers are below the age of 25. About one in four is a student.

Wages for union cashiers working full-time average over $11 an hour; beginners average at least $5.00 an hour. Almost two million people are employed as cashiers.

## Sales Workers

Most of these jobs require little or no special knowledge, although sales workers dealing with some kinds of goods, such as cars or stereo equipment, must be able to explain complex features.

The starting salary for most retail sales workers is the minimum wage; stores that are not covered by minimum wage laws may pay lower salaries. Median weekly earnings of full-time sales workers are $310. Earnings vary considerably according to the type of goods sold, however, ranging from $230 for apparel sales workers to $450 for motor vehicle and boat sales workers. Besides their salary, some sales workers receive a commission based on the value of the goods they sell. Other sales workers receive only a commission; their earnings fluctuate a great deal.

Almost half of all retail sales workers are employed part-time (less than 35 hours a week), but most of those who deal with "big ticket" items work full-time.

## Buyers

This is not an entry-level occupation. Familiarity with merchandise, wholesaling, and retailing is generally required. Experience is most often gained as an assistant buyer or buyer trainee.

Most employers accept college graduates for buyer trainee programs, which combine classroom instruction in merchandising and purchasing with short rotations to various jobs in the store.

Courses in merchandising or marketing may be helpful to applicants but are not essential. Retail trade sales workers may also be accepted as buyer trainees. Most trainees begin as assistant buyers—selling merchandise, supervising sales workers, checking invoices on material received, and keeping account of stock. They gradually assume buying responsibilities, becoming buyers after about a year.

Median annual earnings of buyers are at least $20,000. The top 10 percent earn over $38,480. Their income depends on the amount and type of product purchased, the employer's sales volume, and, to some extent, their seniority. They often earn cash bonuses based on performance and may participate in profit sharing or other incentive plans.

Buyers often operate under great pressure. They frequently work more than a 40-hour week because of special sales and conferences. Substantial traveling is required.

Experienced buyers may advance to merchandise manager and to executive jobs such as general merchandise manager for distributors, department stores, or chain stores.

## Jobs on the Decline

The following 20 occupations are projected by the U.S. Department of Labor to have the largest rate of decline:

Aircraft structure assembler, Butcher and meatcutter, Central telephone office operator, College and University faculty member, Data-entry operator, Faller and bucker, Farm laborer, Farm owner and tenant, Graduate assistant, Postal clerk, Postmaster and mail superintendent, Private household worker, Railroad brake operator, Railroad conductor, Rotary drill operator, Roustabout, Shoemaking machine operative, Stenographer, Taxi driver, and Typesetter and compositor.

Note that some of the above occupations will still have numerous openings in the next decade.

In 1984, the Bureau of Labor Statistics reported that over seven of every ten jobs were in industries that provide services. Industries that produce goods through farming, construction, mining, and manufacturing accounted for fewer than three of every ten jobs.

Information Please Almanac is not responsible and assumes no responsibility for any action undertaken by anyone utilizing the first aid procedures which follow.

## The Heimlich Maneuver[1]

### Food-Choking

**What to look for:** Victim cannot speak or breathe; turns blue; collapses.

**To perform the Heimlich Maneuver when the victim is standing or sitting:**
1. Stand behind the victim and wrap your arms around his waist.
2. Place the thumb side of your fist against the victim's abdomen, slightly above the navel and below the rib cage.
3. Grasp your fist with the other hand and press your fist into the victim's abdomen with a quick upward thrust. Repeat as often as necessary.
4. If the victim is sitting, stand behind the victim's chair and perform the maneuver in the same manner.
5. After the food is dislodged, have the victim seen by a doctor.

**When the victim has collapsed and cannot be lifted:**
1. Lay the victim on his back.
2. Face the victim and kneel astride his hips.
3. With one hand on top of the other, place the heel of your bottom hand on the abdomen slightly above the navel and below the rib cage.
4. Press into the victim's abdomen with a quick upward thrust. Repeat as often as necessary
5. Should the victim vomit, quickly place him on his side and wipe out his mouth to prevent aspiration (drawing of vomit into the throat.)
6. After the food is dislodged, have the victim seen by a doctor.
NOTE: If you start to choke when alone and help is not available, an attempt should be made to self-administer this maneuver.

## Burns[2]

**First Degree: Signs/Symptoms**—reddened skin, **Treatment**—Immerse quickly in cold water or apply ice until pain stops.

**Second Degree: Signs/Symptoms**—reddened skin, blisters. **Treatment**—(1) Cut away loose clothing. (2) Cover with several layers of cold moist dressings or, if limb is involved, immerse in cold water for relief of pain. (3) Treat for shock.

**Third Degree: Signs/Symtoms**—skin destroyed, tissues damaged, charring. **Treatment**—(1) Cut away loose clothing (do not remove clothing adhered to skin). (2) Cover with several layers of sterile, cold, moist dressings for relief of pain and to stop burning action. (3) Treat for shock.

## Poisons[2]

**Treatment**—(1) Dilute by drinking large quantities of water. (2) Induce vomiting except when poison is corrosive or a petroleum product. (3) Call the poison control center or a doctor.

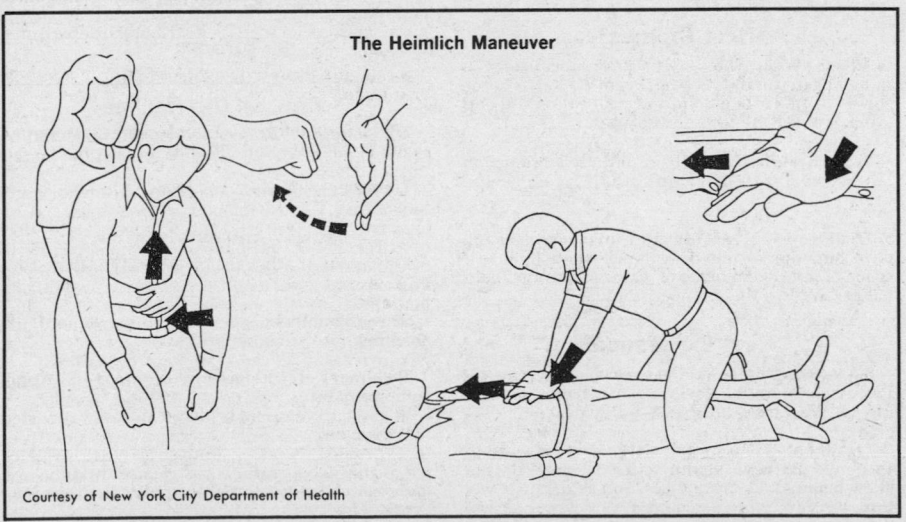

**The Heimlich Maneuver**

Courtesy of New York City Department of Health

## Shock[2]

Shock may accompany any serious injury: blood loss, breathing impairment, heart failure, burns. Shock can kill—treat as soon as possible and continue until medical aid is available.

**Signs/Symptoms**—(1) Shallow breathing. (2) Rapid and weak pulse. (3) Nausea, collapse, vomiting. (4) Shivering. (5) Pale, moist skin. (6) Mental confusion. (7) Drooping eyelids, dilated pupils.

**Treatment**—(1) Establish and maintain an open airway. (2) Control bleeding. (3) Keep victim lying down. Exception: Head and chest injuries, heart attack, stroke, sun stroke. If no spine injury, victim may be more comfortable and breathe better in a semi-reclining position. If in doubt, keep the victim flat. Elevate the feet unless injury would be aggravated. Maintain normal body temperature. Place blankets under and over victim.

## Frostbite[2]

Most frequently frostbitten: toes, fingers, nose, and ears. It is caused by exposure to cold.

**Signs/Symptoms**—(1) Skin becomes pale or a grayish-yellow color. (2) Parts feel cold and numb. (3) Frozen parts feel doughy.

**Treatment**—(1) Until victim can be brought inside, he should be wrapped in woolen cloth and kept dry. (2) Do not rub, chafe, or manipulate frostbitten parts. (3) Bring victim indoors. (4) Place in warm water (102° to 105°) and make sure it remains warm. Test water by pouring on inner surface of your forearm. Never thaw if the victim has to go back out into the cold which may cause the affected area to be refrozen. (5) Do not use hot water bottles or a heat lamp, and do not place victim near a hot stove. (6) Do not allow victim to walk if feet are affected. (7) Once thawed, have victim gently exercise parts. (8) For serious frostbite, seek medical aid for thawing because pain will be intense and tissue damage extensive.

## Heat Cramps[2]

Affects people who work or do strenuous exercises in a hot environment. To prevent it, such people should drink large amounts of cool water and add a pinch of salt to each glass of water

**Signs/Symptoms**—(1) Painful muscle cramps in legs and abdomen. (2) Faintness. (3) Profuse perspiration.

**Treatment**—(1) Move victim to a cool place. (2) Give him sips of salted drinking water (one teaspoon of salt to one quart of water). (3) Apply manual pressure to the cramped muscle.

## Heat Exhaustion[2]

**Signs/Symptoms**—(1) Pale and clammy skin. (2) Profuse perspiration. (3) Rapid and shallow breathing. (4) Weakness, dizziness, and headache.

**Treatment**—(1) Care for victim as if he were in shock. (2) Remove victim to a cool area, do not allow chilling. (3) If body gets too cold, cover victim.

## Heat Stroke[2]

**Signs/Symptoms**—(1) Face is red and flushed. (2) Victim becomes rapidly unconscious. (3) Skin is hot and dry with no perspiration.

**Treatment**—Lay victim down with head and shoulders raised. (2) Reduce the high body temperature as quickly as possible. (3) Apply cold applications to the body and head. (4) Use ice and fan if available. (5) Watch for signs of shock and treat accordingly. (6) Get medical aid as soon as possible.

## Hypothermia[2]
### (Exposure)

Chills the inner core of the body so the body can't generate heat to stay warm.

**Signs/Symtoms**—(1) Entire body affected. (2) Shivering. (3) Numbness. (4) Low body temperature. (5) Drowsiness, mumbling, incoherence. (6) Muscular weakness.

**Treatment**—(1) Bring victim into a warm room as quickly as possible. (2) Remove wet clothing. (3) Wrap victim in prewarmed blankets, put in a warm tub of water, or next to one, or between two people for body warmth. (4) Give artificial respiration, if necessary. (5) If victim is conscious, give warm drink (no alcohol). (6) Get medical help as soon as possible.

## Insect Bites and Stings[2]
(From bees, wasps, yellow jackets, hornets, mosquitoes, ticks, fleas, and bedbugs)

**Signs/Symptoms**—(1) Local irritation and pain. (2) Moderate swelling and redness. (3) Itching and/or burning may be present.

**Treatment**—(1) If stinger is left in the wound, withdraw it. (2) Apply paste of baking soda and water. (3) Immediate application of ice or ice water to the bite or sting relieves pain. (4) For people who are allergic to certain insects, use a constricting bandage (if on an extremity) and ice. Get medical help immediately.

## Strains[2]

Strains are caused by overstretching of a muscle or tendon.

**Signs/Symptoms**—(1) Intense pain. (2) Moderate swelling. (3) Pain and difficulty in moving.

**Treatment**—(1) Rest. (2) Apply mild heat.

## Sprains[2]

Ligaments or other tissues around joints are torn or stretched.

**Signs/Symptoms**—(1) Pain on movement. (2) Swelling. (3) Discoloration.

**Treatment**—(1) Elevate injured part. (2) Apply cold compresses.
Warning: Check with physician to be sure it is not a fracture.

*Sources:* 1. New York City Department of Health. NOTE: Heimlich Maneuver, T.M. Pending. 2. *First Aid,* Mining Enforcement and Safety Administration, U.S. Department of the Interior.

# NUTRITION & HEALTH

## The Growing Use of Irradiation to Preserve Food

*By Chris W. Lecos*

After more than two years of deliberation and the review of thousands of written comments from proponents and opponents, the Food and Drug Administration has given the green light for the expanded uses of irradiation in the U.S. food supply. Food irradiation, at the levels approved, will provide industry with another way to extend the shelf life of food and to protect it against insects without creating any health hazards to consumers, the agency stressed.

A regulation published by FDA in the *Federal Register* April 18, 1986, allows for the first time the use of radiation on fruits and vegetables and increases the level of radiation allowed for dried herbs, spices, and vegetable seasoning. The regulation is the result of a proposal published in 1984 that elicited more than 5,000 public comments, and follows a July 22, 1985, approval by the agency for the use of radiation on pork.

Besides setting maximum radiation levels, the regulation also spells out labeling requirements for irradiated food for the next two years. Labels of packaged foods sold at the retail level will have to state clearly that the products have been treated with radiation. They also must have a logo, or symbol, to inform shoppers that the products have been irradiated. Also, supermarkets and grocery stores will have to identify fresh fruits and vegetables that have been treated with radiation. FDA said this can be done in various ways, such as counter signs, cards, and other displays near the produce bins. Irradiated foods sold on the wholesale market that might be reprocessed must have labeling that advises not to irradiate the product again.

Although the idea of food irradiation is new to most consumers, the latest regulation is the result of more than 40 years of research into the process, much of it by the federal government.

The first approved use of radiation on food occurred when FDA permitted it to kill insects in wheat and wheat products in 1963 and to slow the development of sprouts in potatoes in 1964. However, the process was never adopted by industry for these foods because cheaper methods of preservation were available.

Earlier in 1986, the U.S. Department of Agriculture approved irradiation of fresh pork—at limits set in 1985 by FDA—to control the parasite that can cause trichinosis.

Expanding the uses of irradiation to include fruits and vegetables and increasing the radiation levels for dried herbs and spices were proposed by FDA on Feb. 14, 1984. The regulation published April 18 is the result of that proposal. Specifically, the regulation:

Permits manufacturers to use up to 1 kilogray (kGy) of radiation on fresh fruits and vegetables to inhibit ripening and kill insects, spiders, mites, and other pests that commonly infest these foods. One kilogray is considered a low level for irradiating foods.

Increases the previously permitted irradiated

This international logo will appear on irradiated food in the United States. It consists of a solid circle, representing an energy source, above two petals, which represents the food. The five breaks in the outer circle depict rays from the energy source.

level for spices, herbs, and other dried or dehydrated aromatic foods from plants from 10 kilogray to 30 kilogray. This is regarded as a high dosage level. (Gray is the current term for amount of absorbed radiation, replacing rad. One gray equals 100 rads. One kilogray equals 1,000 gray, which equals 100,000 rads. One kilogray is the maximum level FDA has set for treating fresh fruits and vegetables.)

Requires that labels of irradiated foods sold at the retail level state that they were "treated with radiation" or "treated by irradiation." This is the wording that will be in effect for two years. Similar language would have to be used on packaged wholesale foods, along with the warning that the product should not be irradiated again. A special logo also must be on the label of irradiated foods sold at retail but is optional for wholesale foods.

Establishes record-keeping and other general requirements for manufacturers.

FDA started paving the way for its recent regulation in 1981, when it announced that it was considering how to ensure the safety of irradiated food.

Any safety assessments of irradiated foods, a committee of FDA scientists said, should be based on projected levels of human consumption of those foods; estimates of the "identity, amount, and potential toxicity of new chemical constituents generated in the food" by the irradiation process; and use of the most up-to-date methods of toxicity testing. The committee estimated that "as much as 40 percent of the total diet" theoretically could consist of irradiated foods. However, it estimated that actual consumption probably would not exceed 10 percent of the diet.

## Foods Approved for Irradiation Treatment

| Food | Purpose | Dose limit | Date Approved |
|---|---|---|---|
| Fruits and vegetables | To slow growth and ripening and to control insects | Up to 1 kilogray (kGy) | April 18, 1986 |
| Dry or dehydrated herbs, spices, seeds, teas, vegetables seasonings | To kill insects and control microorganisms | Up to 30 kGy | April 18, 1986 |
| Pork | To control *Trichinella spiralis* (the parasite that causes trichinosis) | Minimum 0.3 kGy to maximum of 1 kGy | July 22, 1985 |
| White potatoes | To inhibit sprout development | 50 to 150 gray | Aug. 8, 1964 |
| Wheat, wheat flour | To control insects | 200 to 500 gray | Aug. 21, 1963 |

The committee reported that food irradiated at doses up to 1 kilogray "is wholesome and safe for human consumption, even where the food that is irradiated may constitute a substantial portion of the diet." The committee added that foods "comprising no more than .01 percent of the daily diet [such as spices] and irradiated at 50 kilogray or less also can be considered safe for human consumption without toxicological testing."

When food is irradiated, most of the radiation passes through the food without being absorbed. The small amount that is absorbed is what kills insects, extends shelf life, and prevents fruits and vegetables from ripening too fast.

Unlike chemical pesticides, irradiation leaves no residue in food. Exposing food to gamma rays, electron beams, or X-rays—common irradiation methods—does not make the food radioactive, nor does it pose any radioactivity danger to consumers. Consumers are not exposed to radiation.

Like other methods of processing, irradiation does cause small chemical changes in food. These changes produce new substances called radiolytic products. Experiments have shown that "very few of these radiolytic products are unique to irradiated food; approximately 90 percent of the radiolytic products . . . are known to be natural components of food." The remaining 10 percent are chemically similar to natural food components.

Responding to contentions that radiolytic products are toxic, FDA said that it disagreed that toxic substances would be produced in food in unsafe amounts under the radiation levels approved. "The agency has no evidence to cause it to change its position that the chemical differences between foods irradiated at the doses allowed by this regulation and nonirradiated foods are too small to cause concern about the safety of the irradiated foods."

Irradiation also can affect the flavor, texture, and to some extent, even the nutrient content of food. But these changes also occur when food is cooked, canned or frozen. The scientific literature, FDA said, indicates that there are no nutritional differences between food that is not irradiated and food irradiated at levels below 1 kilogray.

FDA's labeling requirements are almost the same as those for foods it had approved in the past for irradiation. The logo to identify irradiated foods, however, is a new feature. FDA hopes that consumers will become so familiar with it that eventually it can be used by itself, without any text about irradiation on the label.

In addition to requiring a label statement that a food has been "treated with radiation" or "treated by irradiation," FDA is encouraging manufacturers to state, on the labels of wholesale and retail products, the purpose and type of the irradiation. For example, the label might say "treated with radiation to extend shelf life," or "treated with radiation to inhibit maturation." A label also could state that the product was treated with X-rays, gamma radiation, or electron beams.

As the FDA put it: "The agency recognizes that, because this is a new technology, manufacturers may want to use additional labeling statement as part of a consumer education effort. For example, in addition to the required language, the firm may wish to state that 'this treatment does not induce radioactivity.' The agency will permit such educational statements if they are truthful and not misleading to consumers."

Chris W. Lecos is a member of FDA's public affairs staff. Excerpted from "The Growing Use of Irradiation to Preserve Food," published in *FDA Consumer*, July-August 1986.

## New Rules for Medicated Feeds

As of May 2, 1986, new FDA regulations strengthen the agency's control of medicated animal feeds that leave potentially harmful drug residues in meat, milk, or eggs.

At the same time, the new rules reduce the requirements for approval of medicated feeds that pose little risk.

Under the new regulations, approval of medicated feed applications will be based on the degree of risk from the drug, either in terms of its toxicity or its concentration in the feed.

## Health in 1900: A Look Back

If you were born in 1900, your life expectancy would have been pitifully short by today's standards: 46.6 years if you were a white male and 48.7 years if you were a white female. If you were a member of a non-white group, your life expectancy would have been 15 years shorter!

The first years were the hardest and contributed most to the short life expectancy. Fifteen percent of all infants did not make it to their first birthday. The three biggest killers were (1) pneumonia and the flu, (2) tuberculosis, and (3) infectious intestinal diseases. In addition, typhoid, diphtheria, and diseases of early infancy often took lives. In a word, infectious diseases were the big killers.

# Vaccines: Balancing Risks and Benefits

With all the recent publicity about adverse side effects from vaccines, some parents have become understandably confused about whether their children would be better off with or without the usual immunizations. Many wonder whether the risks of vaccines might outweigh their benefits.

The scientific evidence indicates, however, that for all of the standard childhood vaccines—diphtheria, pertussis (whooping cough), tetanus, measles, mumps, rubella (German measles), and polio—the benefits of immunization substantially exceed the risks.

All medical procedures have some degree of risk, and immunizations are no exception. On rare occasions, they can cause serious or even permanent side effects. However, the diseases they protect against are also dangerous; they can kill or permanently disable a child. This is true even for measles, mumps, and rubella, which most laymen don't think of as potentially serious diseases. Measles and mumps both have serious complications; before vaccines against these diseases were available, substantial numbers of children suffered these complications, since the diseases were practically universal. Rubella is a mild disease in children, but if a pregnant woman catches it, it can cause miscarriage, stillbirth, or serious birth defects. Thus, for all seven of the diseases against which children are routinely immunized, the risk of serious consequences from the disease is far greater than the risk of serious side effects from immunization.

## Polio Vaccine

Public concern about side effects has focused on the vaccines against polio and whooping cough. The use of oral polio vaccine unavoidably causes about five cases of polio in the United States each year, usually in unimmunized adults who come in contact with recently immunized children. This small risk must be weighed against the enorous benefits of polio vaccine. Before the vaccine was available, there were more than 20,000 cases of polio a year in this country. Today, the disease is almost unknown. However, polio still exists and immunization against it is still necessary, as a recent polio outbreak in an unvaccinated religious community tragically demonstrated.

## Whooping Cough Vaccine

The "P" component of DPT vaccine, which protects children against pertussis (whooping cough) has aroused great concern in recent years. Its potential hazards were dramatized in TV documentaries in 1982 and 1985 and in a recently published book, *DPT: A Shot in the Dark*, by Harris L. Coulter and Barbara Loe Fisher. Both the programs and the book have been harshly criticized for presenting only one side of the story. They devoted extensive attention to descriptions of children allegedly injured by the vaccine but almost ignored the disease, pertussis, that the vaccine prevents. Unfortunately, few parents could supply the missing pictures of the devasting effects of pertussis from their own memories, since most were born after this disease was nearly eliminated in the United States.

Pertussis vaccine is indeed the most toxic of the vaccines in current use, causing an estimated one case of brain damage per 310,000 doses. However, the disease it prevents also causes brain damage.

Dr. Paul F. Wehrle of the American Academy of Pediatrics (AAP) noted that "pertussis, the disease, would potentially produce ten times the rate of brain damage as the pertussis vaccine."

Before pertussis vaccine was available, there were more than 250,000 cases of the disease each year, with more than 7,000 deaths. Today, only about 2,000 cases and 5 to 20 deaths are reported each year.

Both *DPT: A Shot in the Dark* and a recent episode of the TV program *20/20* have suggested that pertussis vaccine causes sudden infant death syndrome (SIDS). This is not the case. A major nationwide research study, administered by the National Institute of Child Health and Human Development and completed in 1982, showed no evidence of a link between SIDS and DPT vaccine. The study analyzed more than 800 SIDS cases from all over the country. According to AAP president Dr. Robert J. Haggerty, "Although the entire medical community hopes the cause of SIDS is soon detected, there is still no answer to this tragedy. What we do know, however, is that the pertussis vaccine—as well as any other childhood immunization—is not the cause.

## Risk/Benefit Decisions

Many people think that whenever science comes up with a new vaccine, public health officials will automatically recommend it for the whole population. This is not true. Evaluations and re-evaluations of risks and benefits are constantly being made, and when conditions change, recommendations may also change. For instance, in 1971, the U.S. Public Health Service advised that routine immunization of civilians against smallpox be discontinued, because the chance of contracting the disease in the United States had become remote, and the risks of vaccination had become greater than the benefits. Very recently, an effective vaccine against chickenpox was developed. This vaccine has been lifesaving for children with leukemia, for whom chickenpox can be a fatal disease. However, it is still uncertain whether the vaccine will be recommended for all children. The risks of the vaccine will need to be carefully weighed against the benefit of preventing a disease which is almost always mild in healthy children.

Unlike smallpox, which has been eradicated worldwide, diphteria, pertussis, and tetanus still exist, and when the DPT immunization rate drops, the rates of these discascs rise. Following adverse publicity about the side effects of whooping cough vaccine, immunization rates fell in both England and Japan in the mid-1970s. Both countries have since experienced major epidemics of whooping cough.

## Healthier Lifestyles?

It has been argued that because of today's healthier lifestyles and better medical treatment, the

---

Excerpted from "Vaccines: Balancing Risks and Benefits" published in *ACSH News & Views,* a publication of the American Council on Science and Health, 1995 Broadway, New York, N.Y. 10023.

NOTE: The opinions expressed in this article are those of the author and do not necessarily represent those of *Information Please Almanac* or Houghton Mifflin Company. They are presented to bring this important issue to our readers' attention.

need for immunization against childhood diseases has decreased. This argument is wrong. The experiences of England and Japan have shown that pertussis is still a deadly disease and that epidemics of it can still occur, even in technologically developed countries. The same is true of the other major childhood diseases. Even long-forgotten diphtheria still occurs occasionally in the United States in unvaccinated children. There is still no specific antibiotic for any of the preventable childhood diseases. Thus, prevention of these diseases is preferable to treatment of them.

## Vaccines Are Not Just Kid Stuff

Adults need vaccinations too, and many do not have protection that they should. Although immunization to prevent disease is routine in children, "the medical community has lagged in applying these same principles to adult diseases," according

to Dr. Anthony S. Fauci, director of the National Institute of Allergy and Infectious Disease.

The American College of Physicians is currently conducting a compaign to promote adult vaccination. All adults should be immunized against tetanus and diphtheria, and booster doses are needed every 10 years. If you can't remember when you had your last tetanus/diphtheria shot, you should consult your doctor. Other vaccines are important for specific population groups. Adults who have never had measles should be immunized against it. Women of childbearing age particularly need rubella vaccine. Health care workers and other people at risk of catching hepatitis B should receive this vaccine. Persons over age 65 and those with chronic health problems should be immunized against pneumococcal pneumonia and influenza, since these diseases can be very serious in these individuals.

## Are We Facing Vaccine Shortages?

The "precarious" nature of vaccine supplies in the United States constitutes a "threat to the public's health," and action is "urgently needed" to reduce the uncertainty faced by manufacturers with regard to liability for vaccine-related injury, according to a new report from the National Academy of Sciences Institute of Medicine. The report calls for the creation of a permanent national vaccine commission to coordinate the establishment and attainment of goals in an effort to combat infectious diseases.

In early 1985, the United States experienced an unprecedented temporary shortage of DTP vaccine (the one that protects children against diphtheria, tetanus, and whooping cough [pertussis]). Two of the three manufacturers of this vaccine had withdrawn from the market, so when the remaining manufacturer experienced production problems, the disruption of the vaccine supply was so great that doctors were advised to withhold scheduled immunizations from older children in order to conserve supplies for infants, who are most vulnerable to pertussis.

The withdrawal of vaccine manufacturers from the market was prompted by concern over unpredictable and unavoidable liability costs. Even in the absence of any negligence, a few of the millions of vaccinated individuals will suffer serious adverse effects. No systematic financial compensation is now provided for vaccine victims, and some have resorted to lawsuits against vaccine manufacturers. In a few cases, juries have awarded large sums to the victims even though no negligence or misconduct was involved.

Most of the vaccines of major importance to public health are produced by only one U.S. manufacturer, and no contingency plan exists for dealing with a situation in which no commercial manufacturer is willing to produce a major vaccine. Clearly, the potential exists for shortages even more critical than the one we experienced in 1985. The Institute of Medicine report, which offers a variety of options for resolving the liability problem, could be an important first step toward ending this public health threat. But will it be taken seriously? Other comprehensive reports on this subject from equally distinguished bodies, including the Congressional Office of Technology Assessment, have not led to significant actions. Must we have a major epidemic of a preventable disease, as a result of a

prolonged vaccine shortage, before any real changes are made?

## Tobacco Kills 500,000 Americans a Year

More than half a million Americans die due to the effects of tobacco each year, according to a new study published in *Population and Development Review*, a publication of the Population Council. That's more than one-fourth of *all* deaths from *all* causes.

Included in this half-million figure are 485,000 deaths occurring among cigarette smokers, as well as other deaths due to pipes, cigars, smokeless tobacco, and passive smoking. Dr. R. T. Ravenholt, Director of World Health Surveys, Inc., used the most recent available mortality statistics (1980) and data from large epidemiological studies of smokers to arrive at his estimate of tobacco-related deaths.

In 1964, when the first Surgeon General's Report on Smoking and Health was issued, Dr. Ravenholt estimated that tobacco was killing 250,000 Americans annually. Thus in the 20 years since this landmark report warned the public of the dangers of tobacco, U.S. mortality from this cause has doubled.

According to Dr. Ravenholt's estimates, 35 percent of all cancer deaths are attributable to cigarette smoking. That's 147,000 deaths a year.

In addition, 240,000 cardiovascular disease deaths (24 percent of the total mortality from this cause), 61,000 deaths from chronic bronchitis and emphysema, 14,000 deaths from peptic ulcer and other tobacco-induced digestive diseases, 4,000 deaths in fires and other cigarette-related accidents, and 4,000 infant deaths caused by maternal smoking during pregnancy can be attributed to tobacco.

Dr. Ravenholt says that addiction, in all of its forms, should be regarded as the leading cause of death in America, since nearly one-third of all deaths from all causes are attributable to the use of addictive substances. Tobacco leads the list of dangerous addictive substances, since it is responsible for 25 percent of our annual death toll. An additional five percent can be attributed to alcohol, and one to two percent to other addictive substances.

Reprinted from "Health Watch" in *ACSH News & Views.*

# The Health Hazards of Smokeless Tobacco

### By Cathy Becker Popescu

Smokeless tobacco has come out of the closet.

While snuff dipping and tobacco chewing have traditionally been relegated to the backwoods, the lone prairie, and the outfield, over the past decade or so the smokeless tobacco habit has moved into mainstream America. Colleges from coast to coast now sport tobacco chewing clubs and the circular imprint of a snuff tin on the rear blue jean pocket has become de rigeur for many junior high and high school students across the country.

An estimated 22 million Americans, mostly males, currently use snuff and chewing tobacco. Studies from various parts of the country have indicated that seven to 25 percent of young males use smokeless tobacco. As many as one-third of the members of high school varsity football and baseball teams were chewing, dipping, or both, according to one survey.

For those too young for the real thing, there is Big League Chew, a shredded bubble gum that produces "man size wads" and Chaw, a powdered bubble gum in a box resembling a snuff tin. And for those who are interested in obtaining a little nourishment from their chew, there is even a brand of shredded beef jerky in a snuff-like tin.

## Good Old Fashioned Fun?

While participating in a local tobacco spitting contest or belonging to a collegiate tobacco chewing club may sound like nothing more than good old fashioned fun, there is a darker side to smokeless tobacco use.

Like cigarettes, chewing tobacco and snuff contain nicotine, which can be absorbed through the lining of the mouth. Although the nicotine from smokeless tobacco enters the bloodstream more slowly than that from cigarettes, studies have shown that average blood concentrations in regular users of smokeless tobacco are comparable to those found in smokers. The physiological effects of nicotine, which include increased heart rate and blood pressure, are the same whether the source is smokeless tobacco or a cigarette.

Smokeless tobacco users, like smokers, are likely to become dependent on or addicted to nicotine. Dr. Arden G. Christen, Chairman of the Department of Preventive Dentistry at the Indiana University School of Dentistry, considers nicotine dependency to be the major threat of smokeless tobacco use by young people.

Says Dr. Christen, "The brain makes no distinction between one tobacco habit and another. The number one problem with smokeless tobacco as far as I'm concerned is the possibility that kids who use it will graduate to cigarettes for social and aesthetic reasons as they get older."

Smokeless tobacco use can also cause more immediate problems in young users, as indicated by a recent study conducted at the University of Colorado School of Dentistry. Studying a random sample of 1,119 Colorado high school students, 10 percent of whom were smokeless tobacco users, researchers noted hyperkeratosis (abnormal growth of cells lining the mouth), gum inflammation, and erosion of the teeth.

According to Dr. Christen, gum recession, which is a form of periodontal disease, is one of the earliest and most common signs of smokeless tobacco use. Teeth can also begin to wear down within a few months due to the "grit" in the smokeless tobacco, which acts as a fine sandpaper. Leukoplakia—whitish or grayish patches of cells—often develops at the spot where the tobacco is routinely held. Although leukoplakia is a precancerous condition, it usually goes away when tobacco use is discontinued.

## A Complete Carcinogen

A more long-term and serious consequence of smokeless tobacco use is the risk of oral cancer.

"The juice from tobacco is known to be a complete carcinogen in and of itself," says Dr. Christen. Analysis shows that smokeless tobacco products contain nitrosamines which are capable of producing cancer in laboratory animals. Additional nitrosamines are formed in the mouth as the tobacco is "chewed."

In the Third National Cancer Survey, researchers noted an excess risk for cancers of the gum and mouth among men who used chewing tobacco or snuff.

While not as lethal as lung cancer, oral cancer does have a relatively high mortality rate since it tends to spread quickly to other parts of the body. And unless the disease is detected early, the treatment for oral cancer is generally quite radical and disfiguring.

## A New Generation of Addicts

Concerned over the increasing popularity of smokeless tobacco products and the public's ignorance of the risks, health groups have urged the Federal Trade Commission (FTC) to take action. Doctors Ought to Care (DOC) has petitioned the FTC to require warning labels on all smokeless tobacco products, similar to the ones found on cigarette packages. DOC has also petitioned the FTC to ban all broadcast ads for smokeless tobacco products and to require warnings on printed ads. The Public Citizen Health Research Group has filed a similar petition. The American Dental Association also plans to call for warning labels on smokeless tobacco products, according to Dr. Kenneth Burrell, Assistant Secretary of the Council on Dental Therapeutics of the ADA.

Of course, the dangers of smokeless tobacco are relative. For a cigarette smoker who has been unable to shake his nicotine dependency after several attempts at quitting, smokeless tobacco may be a reasonable alternative. It is not a safe alternative, as some ads imply, but it is certainly safer than smoking.

The large numbers of young people who have begun to chew tobacco and dip snuff represent a cause for serious concern, however. After we have come so far in the war against smoking, it would be a shame to allow a whole new generation to become nicotine addicts.

Cathy Becker Popescu, M.S., is a Research Associate with ACSH. Excerpted from "Tarnishing a Spitting Image: The Health Hazards of Smokeless Tobacco" published in *ACSH News & Views,* a publication of the American Council on Science and Health, 1995 Broadway, New York, N.Y. 10023.

# Aerobic versus Anaerobic Exercise: Which is Better for You?

*By Carol Henderson*

It seems that everybody these days is running off to an aerobic exercise class or building muscles with a weight-lifting routine. What are the benefits of aerobic versus anaerobic exercise and how do they differ?

"Aerobic" literally means with oxygen, while "anaerobic" means without oxygen. Aerobic exercise actually refers to a variety of exercises that stimulate heart and lung activity for a time period that is sufficiently long to produce beneficial changes in the body. These include cycling, swimming, running, walking, and other active sports. All of these exercises have one thing in common. By making the body work hard, they demand plenty of oxygen. That's the basic idea, and that's what makes them aerobic exercises.

The main objective of an aerobic exercise program is to increase the maximum amount of oxygen that the body can process with a given time. This is called your aerobic capacity. This capacity depends on the body's ability to rapidly breathe large amounts of air, forcefully deliver large volumes of blood, and effectively deliver oxygen to all parts of the body. Basically, aerobic exercise depends on efficient lungs, a powerful heart, and a good vascular system. Aerobic capacity is the best index of overall physical fitness as it reflects the conditions of all these vital organs.

The changes induced by aerobic exercise in the various systems and organs of the body are called the "training effect." Aerobic exercise produces this training effect by increasing the body's capacity to utilize oxygen in several ways:

It strengthens the muscles of respiration which facilitates the rapid flow of air in and out of the lungs.

It improves the strength and pumping efficiency of the heart which improves the ability of the body to more rapidly transport life-sustaining oxygen from the lungs to the heart and other parts of the body.

It tones up muscles throughout the body.

It improves general circulation and can lower blood pressure by reducing the work on the heart.

It causes an increase in the total amount of blood circulating through the body, making blood a more efficient oxygen carrier.

Unless the aerobic exercise is of sufficient intensity and duration, it will not produce a training effect and cannot be considered an aerobic exercise.

## Walking as an Exercise

Walking as an aerobic exercise has become increasingly popular due to the number of injuries running and jogging have produced for many people. Among these are ankle and knee injuries, low back strains, fractures, and muscles and ligament problems. Walking, however, is a structurally effortless, automatic process for the body and studies have shown that walking can produce the following positive results:

It lowers the circulating blood fats to the same extent as more strenuous forms of exercise.

It increases the ability of the heart and lungs to distribute oxygen in the body, which builds physical endurance.

It helps in the treatment of hypertension by lowering the blood pressure.

It reduces stress and can rehabilitate patients with peripheral vascular disease.

It increases the elasticity of the blood vessels.

For those who walk one hour, five days a week, it gives the same metabolic benefits as jogging without as much risk.

## Weight-Lifting and Isometrics

In contrast to aerobic exercise, anaerobic exercise, without oxygen, includes exercises such as weight-lifting and isometrics. These exercises, while building strength and muscle tone, actually impair blood flow through the muscles. This happens because one is building up tension in the muscles against heavy resistance, as in the case of weight-lifting.

Since the blood flow to these muscles is impaired during anaerobic exercise, fatigue sets in rapidly, and the exercise cannot be kept up for too long a time. There is a relatively low caloric expenditure in this type of exercise, and there are no cardiovascular benefits as in aerobic exercise. In fact, anaerobic exercise can increase both blood pressure and heart rate because of the body's reflex response to this impaired blood flow. Therefore, this kind of exercise is potentially dangerous, especially for those with a history of high blood pressure or other cardiovascular problems.

The American Council on Science and Health recommends participation in aerobic and anaerobic exercise only after a person's physical fitness capacity has been evaluated by a physician.

Carol Henderson has a master's degree in Public Health and is a freelance writer. Reprinted with permission from *ACSH News & Views,* a publication of the American Council on Science and Health, 1995 Broadway, New York, N.Y. 10023.

## Diet Food Sales Are On an Upswing

Consumers spent over $20 billion on diet foods and beverages in 1985, and sales of those products will reach at least $28.8 billion in 1990, according to a Business Communications Company, Inc., study of the diet foods industry. The market research firm says the maturing of the populace and increased longevity are increasing the market potential for diet foods. For the period 1985 to 1990, the study forecast sales increases of 10.4 percent for reduced-sugar products, 9.5 percent for calorie-controlled foods, 318 percent for reduced-fat foods, and 7.4 percent for reduced-sodium products. Caffeine-free beverage sales will go up by 5.3 percent, and reduced-calorie and reduced-alcohol beverages will jump 8.6 percent, the firm predicts.

# Mean Heights and Weights and Recommended Energy Intake

| Category | Age (years) | Weight (lb) | Weight (kg) | Height (in.) | Height (cm) | Energy needs (with range) (kcal) | Energy needs (with range) (MJ) |
|---|---|---|---|---|---|---|---|
| Infants | 0.0–0.5 | 13 | 6 | 24 | 60 | kg × 115 (95–145) | kg × .48 |
|  | 0.5–1.0 | 20 | 9 | 28 | 71 | kg × 105 (80–135) | kg × .44 |
| Children | 1–3 | 29 | 13 | 35 | 90 | 1300 (900–1800) | 5.5 |
|  | 4–6 | 44 | 20 | 44 | 112 | 1700 (1300–2300) | 7.1 |
|  | 7–10 | 62 | 28 | 52 | 132 | 2400 (1650–3300) | 10.1 |
| Males | 11–14 | 99 | 45 | 62 | 157 | 2700 (2000–3700) | 11.3 |
|  | 15–18 | 145 | 66 | 69 | 176 | 2800 (2100–3900) | 11.8 |
|  | 19–22 | 154 | 70 | 70 | 177 | 2900 (2500–3300) | 12.2 |
|  | 23–50 | 154 | 70 | 70 | 178 | 2700 (2300–3100) | 11.3 |
|  | 51–75 | 154 | 70 | 70 | 178 | 2400 (2000–2800) | 10.1 |
|  | 76 + | 154 | 70 | 70 | 178 | 2050 (1650–2450) | 8.6 |
| Females | 11–14 | 101 | 46 | 62 | 157 | 2200 (1500–3000) | 9.2 |
|  | 15–18 | 120 | 55 | 64 | 163 | 2100 (1200–3000) | 8.8 |
|  | 19–22 | 120 | 55 | 64 | 163 | 2100 (1700–2500) | 8.8 |
|  | 23–50 | 120 | 55 | 64 | 163 | 2000 (1600–2400) | 8.4 |
|  | 51–75 | 120 | 55 | 64 | 163 | 1800 (1400–2200) | 7.6 |
|  | 76 + | 120 | 55 | 64 | 163 | 1600 (1200–2000) | 6.7 |
| Pregnancy |  |  |  |  |  | + 300 |  |
| Lactation |  |  |  |  |  | + 500 |  |

The energy allowances for the young adults are for men and women doing light work. The allowances for the two older age groups represent mean energy needs over these age spans, allowing for a 2% decrease in basal (resting) metabolic rate per decade and a reduction in activity of 200 kcal/day for men and women between 51 and 75 years, 500 kcal for men over 75 years, and 400 kcal for women over 75. The customary range of daily energy output is shown for adults in parentheses, and is based on a variation in energy needs of ± 400 kcal at any one age, emphasizing the wide range of energy intakes appropriate for any group of people. Energy allowances for children through age 18 are based on median energy intakes of children these ages followed in longitudinal growth studies. The values in parentheses are 10th and 90th percentile of energy intake, to indicate the range of energy consumption among children of these ages. NOTE: kg—kilogram; cm—centimeter; kcal—kilocalorie; MJ—megajoule. 1 kcal is equivalent to 4.18 kilojoules. 1 megajoule is equal to 1000 kilojoules. *Source: Recommended Dietary Allowances*, Ninth Edition (1980), with the permission of the National Academy of Sciences, Washington, D.C.

# Desirable Weights[1]

| Height[2] (in.) | Height[2] (cm) | Weight[3] — Men (lb) | Weight[3] — Men (kg) | Weight[3] — Women (lb) | Weight[3] — Women (kg) |
|---|---|---|---|---|---|
| 58 | 147 | — — | — — | 102 (92–119) | 46 (42–54) |
| 60 | 152 | — — | — — | 107 (96–125) | 49 (44–57) |
| 62 | 158 | 123 (112–141) | 56 (51–64) | 113 (102–131) | 51 (46–59) |
| 64 | 163 | 130 (118–148) | 59 (54–67) | 120 (108–138) | 55 (49–63) |
| 66 | 168 | 136 (124–156) | 62 (56–71) | 128 (114–146) | 58 (52–66) |
| 68 | 173 | 145 (132–166) | 66 (60–75) | 136 (122–154) | 62 (55–70) |
| 70 | 178 | 154 (140–174) | 70 (64–79) | 144 (130–163) | 65 (59–74) |
| 72 | 183 | 162 (148–184) | 74 (67–84) | 152 (138–173) | 69 (63–79) |
| 74 | 188 | 171 (156–194) | 78 (71–88) | — — | — — |
| 76 | 193 | 181 (164–204) | 82 (74–93) | — — | — — |

1. Desirable weights for men and women of different heights, based on evidence from insurance statistics of weight in relation to longevity. According to the National Center for Health Statistics, the average American male adult is 70 in. tall (178 cm) and the average female is 64 in. tall (163 cm). Accordingly, the average desirable weights are 154 lb (70 kg) and 120 lb (55 kg) throughout adult life. 2. Without shoes. 3. Without clothes. Average weight ranges in parentheses. *Source: Recommended Dietary Allowances*, 9th Edition (1980), with permission of the National Academy of Sciences, Washington, D.C.

## Sunbathing and Skin Cancer

Scientists agree that ultraviolet radiation from the sun is the leading cause of skin cancer, which is responsible for an estimated 6,500 to 7,500 deaths in the United States every year.

People can reduce the potential hazard from the sun by not exposing themselves to it unnecessarily for extended periods between 10 a.m. and 2 p.m. when most ultraviolet radiation is strongest.

# Recommended Daily Dietary Allowances[1]

### Designed for the maintenance of good nutrition of practically all healthy persons in the U.S. (revised 1980)

| Persons | Age (years) | Wgt. (lbs) | Wgt. (kg) | Hgt. (in.) | Hgt. (cm) | Fat-Soluble Vitamins | | | Water-Soluble Vitamins | | | | |
|---|---|---|---|---|---|---|---|---|---|---|---|---|---|
| | | | | | | Vita-min A µg R.E.[2] | Vita-min D (µg)[3] | Vita-min E (mgα T.E.)[4] | Ascor-bic Acid (mg) | Fola-cin (µg) | Nia-cin[5] (mg) | Ribo-flavin (mg) | Thia-min (mg) |
| Infants | 0.0–0.5 | 13 | 6 | 24 | 60 | 420 | 10 | 3 | 35 | 30 | 6 | 0.4 | 0.3 |
| | 0.5–1.0 | 20 | 9 | 28 | 71 | 400 | 10 | 4 | 35 | 45 | 8 | 0.6 | 0.5 |
| Children | 1–3 | 29 | 13 | 35 | 90 | 400 | 10 | 5 | 45 | 100 | 9 | 0.8 | 0.7 |
| | 4–6 | 44 | 20 | 44 | 112 | 500 | 10 | 6 | 45 | 200 | 11 | 1.0 | 0.9 |
| | 7–10 | 62 | 28 | 52 | 132 | 700 | 10 | 7 | 45 | 300 | 16 | 1.4 | 1.2 |
| Males | 11–14 | 99 | 45 | 62 | 157 | 1,000 | 10 | 8 | 50 | 400 | 18 | 1.6 | 1.4 |
| | 15–18 | 145 | 66 | 69 | 176 | 1,000 | 10 | 10 | 60 | 400 | 18 | 1.7 | 1.4 |
| | 19–22 | 154 | 70 | 70 | 177 | 1,000 | 7.5 | 10 | 60 | 400 | 19 | 1.7 | |
| | 23–50 | 154 | 70 | 70 | 178 | 1,000 | 5 | 10 | 60 | 400 | 18 | 1.6 | 1.4 |
| | 51+ | 154 | 70 | 70 | 178 | 1,000 | 5 | 10 | 60 | 400 | 16 | 1.4 | 1.2 |
| Females | 11–14 | 101 | 46 | 62 | 157 | 800 | 10 | 8 | 50 | 400 | 15 | 1.3 | 1.1 |
| | 15–18 | 120 | 55 | 64 | 163 | 800 | 10 | 8 | 60 | 400 | 14 | 1.3 | 1.1 |
| | 19–22 | 120 | 55 | 64 | 163 | 800 | 7.5 | 8 | 60 | 400 | 14 | 1.3 | 1.1 |
| | 23–50 | 120 | 55 | 64 | 163 | 800 | 5 | 8 | 60 | 400 | 13 | 1.2 | 1.0 |
| | 51+ | 120 | 55 | 64 | 163 | 800 | 5 | 8 | 60 | 400 | 13 | 1.2 | 1.0 |
| Pregnant | — | — | — | — | — | +200 | +5 | +2 | +20 | +400 | +2 | +0.3 | +0.4 |
| Lactating | — | — | — | — | — | +400 | +5 | +3 | +40 | +100 | +5 | +0.5 | +0.5 |

| Persons | Age (years) | Wgt. (lbs) | Wgt. (kg) | Hgt. (in.) | Hgt. (cm) | Water-Soluble Vitamins | | Minerals | | | | | |
|---|---|---|---|---|---|---|---|---|---|---|---|---|---|
| | | | | | | Vita-min B₁ (mg) | Vita-min B₁₂ (µg) | Cal-cium (mg) | Phos-pho-rus (mg) | Io-dine (µg) | Iron (mg) | Mag-nesium (mg) | Zinc (mg) |
| Infants | 0.0–0.5 | 13 | 6 | 24 | 60 | 0.3 | 0.5[6] | 360 | 240 | 40 | 10 | 50 | 3 |
| | 0.5–1.0 | 20 | 9 | 28 | 71 | 0.6 | 1.5 | 540 | 360 | 50 | 15 | 70 | 5 |
| Children | 1–3 | 29 | 13 | 35 | 90 | 0.9 | 2.0 | 800 | 800 | 70 | 15 | 150 | 10 |
| | 4–6 | 44 | 20 | 44 | 112 | 1.3 | 2.5 | 800 | 800 | 90 | 10 | 200 | 10 |
| | 7–10 | 62 | 28 | 52 | 132 | 1.6 | 3.0 | 800 | 800 | 120 | 10 | 250 | 10 |
| Males | 11–14 | 99 | 45 | 62 | 157 | 1.8 | 3.0 | 1,200 | 1,200 | 150 | 18 | 350 | 15 |
| | 15–18 | 145 | 66 | 69 | 176 | 2.0 | 3.0 | 1,200 | 1,200 | 150 | 18 | 400 | 15 |
| | 19–22 | 154 | 70 | 70 | 177 | 2.2 | 3.0 | 800 | 800 | 150 | 10 | 350 | 15 |
| | 23–50 | 154 | 70 | 70 | 178 | 2.2 | 3.0 | 800 | 800 | 150 | 10 | 350 | 15 |
| | 51+ | 154 | 70 | 70 | 178 | 2.2 | 3.0 | 800 | 800 | 150 | 10 | 350 | 15 |
| Females | 11–14 | 101 | 46 | 62 | 157 | 1.8 | 3.0 | 1,200 | 1,200 | 150 | 18 | 300 | 15 |
| | 15–18 | 120 | 55 | 64 | 163 | 2.0 | 3.0 | 1,200 | 1,200 | 150 | 18 | 300 | 15 |
| | 19–22 | 120 | 55 | 64 | 163 | 2.0 | 3.0 | 800 | 800 | 150 | 18 | 300 | 15 |
| | 23–50 | 120 | 55 | 64 | 163 | 3.0 | 3.0 | 800 | 150 | 150 | 18 | 300 | 15 |
| | 51+ | 120 | 55 | 64 | 163 | 2.0 | 3.0 | 800 | 800 | 150 | 10 | 300 | 15 |
| Pregnant | — | — | — | — | — | +0.6 | +1.0 | +400 | +400 | +25 | [7] | +150 | +5 |
| Lactating | — | — | — | — | — | +0.5 | +1.0 | +400 | +400 | +50 | [7] | +150 | +10 |

1. Allowances provide for individual variances among most normal persons living in the United States under usual environmental stresses. 2. Retinol equivalents. 1. Retinol equivalent = 1 µg retinol. 3. As cholecalciferol. 10 µg cholecalciferol = 400 I.U. vitamin D. 4. αtocopherol equivalents. 1 mg d-α-tocopherol = 1 α T.E. 5. 1 NE (niacin equivalent) is equal to 1 mg of niacin or 60 mg of dietary tryptophan. 6. The RDA for vitamin B12 in infants is based on average concentration of the vitamin in human milk. 7. Cannot be met by ordinary diets: use of supplemental iron is recommended. NOTE: mg—milligram; µg—microgram; IU—International Units; lbs—pounds; Wgt.—Weight; Hgt.—Height. *Source: Recommended Dietary Allowances,* Ninth Edition (1980), with the permission of the National Academy of Sciences, Washington, D.C. Most recent. A 1985 revision was not adapted.

# Calories, Minerals, and Vitamins of Selected Foods

| Food and amount | Energy (calories) | Protein (gm) | Fat (gm) | Calcium (mg) | Iron (mg) | Vitamin A (IU) | Vitamin B¹ (thiamin) (mg) | Vitamin B² (riboflavin) (mg) | Vitamin C (ascorbic acid) (mg) |
|---|---|---|---|---|---|---|---|---|---|
| Apple, 1 medium, raw | 80 | — | 1 | 10 | .4 | 120 | .04 | .03 | 6 |
| Applesauce, 1 cup, canned, unsweetened | 100 | — | — | 10 | 1.2 | 100 | .05 | .02 | 2 |
| Bacon, 2 slices, crisp | 85 | 4 | 8 | 2 | .5 | — | .08 | .05 | — |
| Banana, 1 medium | 100 | 1 | — | 10 | .8 | 230 | .06 | .07 | 12 |
| Beans, snap green, 1 cup cooked | 30 | 2 | — | 63 | .8 | 680 | .09 | .11 | 15 |
| Beans, red kidney, 1 cup canned | 230 | 15 | 1 | 74 | 4.6 | 10 | .13 | .10 | — |
| Beans, baked, pork and molasses, 1 cup | 385 | 16 | 12 | 161 | 5.9 | — | .15 | .10 | — |
| Beef cuts, cooked: Chuck, boned, 3 ounces | 245 | 23 | 16 | 10 | 2.9 | 30 | .04 | .18 | — |
| Hamburger, 3 ounces | 235 | 20 | 17 | 9 | 2.6 | 30 | .07 | .17 | — |
| Rib roast, 3 ounces boned | 375 | 17 | 33 | 8 | 2.2 | 70 | .05 | .13 | — |
| Round, 3 ounces boned | 220 | 24 | 13 | 10 | 3.0 | 20 | .07 | .19 | — |
| Sirloin, 3 ounces boned | 330 | 20 | 27 | 9 | 2.5 | 50 | .05 | .15 | — |
| Beef stew with vegetables, 1 cup | 220 | 16 | 11 | 29 | 2.9 | 2,400 | .15 | .17 | 17 |
| Beets, 1 cup cooked | 55 | 2 | — | 24 | .9 | 30 | .05 | .07 | 10 |
| Breads: Cracked wheat, average slice | 65 | 2 | 1 | 22 | .5 | — | .08 | .06 | — |
| Italian, average slice, enriched | 85 | 3 | — | .5 | .7 | — | .12 | .07 | — |
| Raisin, average slice enriched | 65 | 2 | 1 | 18 | .6 | — | .09 | .06 | — |
| Rye (American), average slice | 60 | 2 | — | 19 | .5 | — | .07 | .05 | — |
| White, average slice enriched | 70 | 2 | 1 | 21 | .6 | — | .10 | .06 | — |
| Whole wheat, average slice | 65 | 3 | 1 | 24 | .8 | — | .09 | .03 | — |
| Butter, 1 tbsp | 100 | — | 12 | 3 | — | 430 | — | — | — |
| Cabbage, 1 cup, raw, coarsely shredded | 15 | 1 | — | 34 | .3 | 90 | .04 | .04 | 33 |
| Cake: Sponge, average slice | 195 | 5 | 4 | 20 | 1.1 | 300 | .09 | .14 | — |
| Pound, average slice | 160 | 2 | 10 | 6 | .5 | 80 | .05 | .06 | — |
| Candies: Caramels, 1 ounce | 115 | 1 | 3 | 42 | .4 | — | .01 | .05 | — |
| Chocolate, milk, 1 ounce | 145 | 2 | 9 | 65 | .3 | 80 | .02 | .10 | — |
| Cantaloupe, 1/2 melon | 80 | 2 | — | 38 | 1.1 | 9,240 | .11 | .08 | 90 |
| Carrot, raw, 1 average size | 30 | 1 | — | 27 | .5 | 7,930 | .04 | .04 | 6 |
| Catsup, 1 tbsp | 15 | — | — | 3 | .1 | 210 | .01 | .01 | 2 |
| Cheese: Cheddar, 1 ounce | 115 | 7 | 9 | 204 | .2 | 300 | .01 | .11 | — |
| Cottage, creamed, 1 cup | 235 | 28 | 10 | 135 | .3 | 370 | .05 | .37 | — |
| Cottage, uncreamed, 1 cup | 125 | 25 | 1 | 46 | .3 | 40 | .04 | .21 | — |
| Cream cheese, 1 ounce | 100 | 2 | 10 | 23 | .3 | 400 | — | .06 | — |
| Swiss, natural, 1 ounce | 105 | 8 | 8 | 272 | — | 240 | .01 | .10 | — |
| Swiss, process, 1 ounce | 95 | 7 | 7 | 219 | .2 | 230 | — | .08 | — |
| Chicken, broiled, 3 ounces | 115 | 20 | 3 | 8 | 1.4 | 80 | .05 | .16 | — |
| Chicken, fried, 1/2 breast, 3.3 ounces | 160 | 26 | 5 | 9 | 1.3 | 70 | .04 | .17 | — |
| Chicken, canned, boned, 3 ounces | 170 | 18 | 10 | 18 | 1.3 | 200 | .03 | .11 | 3 |
| Clams, raw, 3 ounces | 65 | 11 | 1 | 59 | 5.2 | 90 | .08 | .15 | 8 |
| Cocoa, 1 cup, homemade | 220 | 9 | 9 | 298 | .8 | 320 | .10 | .44 | 2 |
| Coffee; black, 1 cup | — | — | — | — | — | — | — | — | — |
| Cola, carbonated, 12 ounces | 145 | — | — | — | — | — | — | — | — |
| Corn, average ear | 70 | 2 | 1 | 2 | .5 | 310 | .09 | .08 | 7 |
| Corn flakes, 1 cup | 95 | 2 | — | 3 | .6 | 1,180 | .29 | .35 | 9 |
| Crabmeat, canned, 3 ounces | 85 | 15 | 2 | 38 | .7 | — | .07 | .07 | — |
| Crackers, Graham, 4 | 110 | 2 | 3 | 11 | 1.0 | — | .04 | .16 | — |
| Saltines, 4 | 50 | 1 | 1 | 2 | .5 | — | .05 | .05 | — |
| Cream: Light, table, 1 cup | 470 | 6 | 46 | 231 | .1 | 1,730 | .08 | .36 | 2 |
| Heavy, whipping, 1 cup | 820 | 5 | 88 | 154 | .1 | 3,500 | .05 | .26 | 1 |
| Sour, 1 cup | 495 | 7 | 48 | 268 | .1 | 1,820 | .08 | .34 | 2 |
| Whipped topping (pressurized), 1 cup | 155 | 2 | 13 | 61 | — | 550 | .02 | .04 | — |
| Doughnut, 1 plain | 100 | 1 | 5 | 10 | .4 | 20 | .05 | .05 | — |
| Egg: Raw or cooked in shell, 1 | 80 | 6 | 6 | 28 | 1.0 | 260 | .04 | .14 | — |
| Omelet, scrambled, 1 | 95 | 6 | 7 | 47 | .9 | 310 | .04 | .16 | — |
| Frankfurter, 1 | 170 | 7 | 15 | 3 | .8 | — | .08 | .11 | — |
| Fruit cocktail, 1 cup canned | 195 | 1 | — | 23 | 1.0 | 360 | .05 | .03 | 5 |
| Grapefruit: Raw, 1/2 | 45 | 1 | — | 19 | .5 | 10 | .05 | .02 | 44 |
| Canned, syrup, 1 cup | 180 | 2 | — | 33 | .8 | 30 | .08 | .05 | 76 |
| Juice, fresh, 1 cup | 95 | 1 | — | 22 | .5 | 20 | .10 | .05 | 93 |

| Food and amount | Energy (calories) | Protein (gm) | Fat (gm) | Calcium (mg) | Iron (mg) | Vitamin A (IU) | Vitamin B¹ (thiamin) (mg) | Vitamin B² (riboflavin) (mg) | Vitamin C (ascorbic acid) (mg) |
|---|---|---|---|---|---|---|---|---|---|
| Haddock, breaded, fried, 3 ounces | 140 | 17 | 5 | 34 | 1.0 | — | .03 | .06 | 2 |
| Honey, strained, 1 tbsp. | 65 | — | — | 1 | .1 | — | — | .01 | — |
| Ice cream, 1 cup | 270 | 5 | 14 | 176 | .1 | 540 | .05 | .33 | 1 |
| Jellies, 1 tbsp | 50 | — | — | 4 | .3 | — | — | .01 | 1 |
| Lamb: Rib chop, boned, 4 ounces | 400 | 25 | 33 | 10 | 1.5 | — | .14 | .25 | — |
|   Leg roast, 3 ounces, boned | 235 | 22 | 16 | 9 | 1.4 | — | .13 | .23 | — |
| Lemon, 1 medium | 20 | 1 | — | 19 | .4 | 10 | .03 | .01 | 39 |
| Liver: Beef, fried, 2 ounces | 130 | 15 | 6 | 6 | 5.0 | 30,280 | .15 | 2.37 | 15 |
| Luncheon meat: Boiled ham, 2 ounces | 135 | 11 | 10 | 6 | 1.6 | — | .25 | .09 | — |
|   Canned, spiced or unspiced, 2 ounces | 165 | 8 | 14 | 5 | 1.2 | — | .18 | .12 | — |
| Macaroni, enriched, 1 cup | 155 | 5 | 1 | 11 | 1.3 | — | .20 | .11 | — |
| Macaroni and cheese, 1 cup | 430 | 17 | 22 | 362 | 1.8 | 860 | .20 | .40 | — |
| Margarine, 1 tbsp | 100 | — | 12 | 3 | — | 470 | — | — | — |
| Mayonnaise, 1 tbsp | 100 | — | 11 | 3 | .1 | 40 | — | .01 | — |
| Milk: Whole, 1 cup | 150 | 8 | 8 | 291 | .1 | 310 | .09 | .40 | 2 |
|   Skim (non-fat), 1 cup | 85 | 8 | — | 302 | .1 | 500 | .09 | .34 | 2 |
|   Buttermilk, 1 cup | 100 | 8 | 2 | 285 | .1 | 80 | .08 | .38 | 2 |
| Mushrooms, canned, 1 cup | 40 | 5 | — | 15 | 1.2 | — | .04 | .60 | 4 |
| Nuts: Almonds, 1 cup shelled | 850 | 26 | 77 | 332 | 6.7 | — | .34 | 1.31 | — |
|   Peanuts, roasted, 1 cup | 840 | 37 | 72 | 107 | 3.0 | — | .46 | .19 | — |
| Oatmeal, 1 cup cooked | 130 | 5 | 2 | 22 | 1.4 | — | .19 | .05 | — |
| Oils, salad, cooking, 1 tbsp | 120 | — | 14 | — | — | — | — | — | — |
| Orange, 1 medium | 65 | 1 | — | 54 | .5 | 260 | .13 | .05 | 66 |
| Orange juice, fresh, 1 cup | 110 | 2 | — | 27 | .5 | 500 | .22 | .07 | 124 |
|   Frozen, diluted with 3 parts water, 1 cup | 120 | 2 | — | 25 | .2 | 540 | .23 | .03 | 120 |
| Oysters, raw, 1 cup | 160 | 20 | 4 | 226 | 13.2 | 740 | .34 | .43 | — |
| Pancake, wheat, 1 average | 60 | 2 | 2 | 27 | .4 | 30 | .06 | .07 | — |
| Peach, raw, 1 medium | 40 | 1 | — | 9 | .5 | 1,330 | .02 | .05 | 7 |
| Peanut butter, 1 tbsp | 95 | 4 | 8 | 9 | .3 | — | .02 | .02 | — |
| Peas, green, 1 cup | 110 | 8 | — | 30 | 3.0 | 960 | .43 | .14 | 21 |
| Pie: Apple, 4-inch wedge | 345 | 3 | 15 | 11 | .9 | 40 | .15 | .11 | 2 |
|   Cherry, 4-inch wedge | 350 | 4 | 15 | 19 | .9 | 590 | .16 | .12 | — |
|   Lemon meringue, 4-inch wedge | 305 | 4 | 12 | 17 | 1.0 | 200 | .09 | .12 | 4 |
| Pineapple, raw, 1 cup diced | 80 | 1 | — | 26 | .8 | 110 | .14 | .05 | 26 |
| Pineapple juice, canned, 1 cup | 140 | 1 | — | 38 | .8 | 130 | .13 | .05 | 23 |
| Pizza (cheese), 4 3/4-inch wedge | 145 | 6 | 4 | 86 | 1.1 | 230 | .16 | .18 | 4 |
| Pork: Roast, 3 ounces | 310 | 21 | 24 | 9 | 2.7 | — | .78 | .22 | — |
|   Chop, with bone, 2.7 ounces | 305 | 19 | 25 | 9 | 2.7 | — | .75 | .22 | — |
| Potatoes: Baked, 1 medium | 145 | 4 | — | 14 | 1.1 | — | .15 | .07 | 31 |
|   French fried, deep fat, 10 pieces | 135 | 2 | 7 | 8 | .7 | — | .07 | .04 | 11 |
|   Mashed with milk, 1 cup | 135 | 4 | 2 | 50 | .8 | 40 | .17 | .11 | 21 |
| Potato chips, 10 | 115 | 1 | 8 | 8 | .4 | — | .04 | .01 | 3 |
| Prune juice, 1 cup canned | 195 | 1 | — | 36 | 1.8 | — | .03 | .03 | 5 |
| Rice: White, enriched, 1 cup cooked | 225 | 4 | — | 21 | 1.8 | — | .23 | .02 | — |
|   Puffed, 1 cup | 60 | 1 | — | 3 | .3 | — | .07 | .01 | — |
| Salad dressings: Mayonnaise type, 1 tbsp | 65 | — | 6 | 2 | — | 30 | — | — | — |
|   French, 1 tbsp | 65 | — | 6 | 2 | .1 | — | — | — | — |
|   French, low calorie, 1 tbsp | 15 | — | 1 | 2 | .1 | — | — | — | — |
| Sardines, canned, 3 ounces | 175 | 20 | 9 | 372 | 2.5 | 190 | .02 | .17 | — |
| Spaghetti, 1 cup cooked | 155 | 5 | 1 | 11 | 1.3 | — | .20 | .11 | — |
| Spinach, 1 cup cooked | 40 | 5 | 1 | 167 | 4.0 | 14,580 | .13 | .25 | 50 |
| Sugar, 1 teaspoon | 15 | — | — | — | — | — | — | — | — |
| Tomato juice, canned, 1 cup | 45 | 2 | — | 17 | 2.2 | 1,940 | .12 | .07 | 39 |
| Tuna fish, 3 ounces | 170 | 24 | 7 | 7 | 1.6 | 70 | .04 | .10 | — |
| Veal, 3-ounce cutlet | 185 | 23 | 9 | 9 | 2.7 | — | .06 | .21 | — |
| Yogurt, from lowfat milk, 8-oz. container, plain | 145 | 12 | 4 | 415 | .2 | 150 | .10 | .49 | 2 |

NOTE: GM—gram; MG—milligram; IU—International Unit. A dash indicates little or no basis for assigning value. *Source:* Department of Agriculture, Science and Education Administration.

# HEADLINE HISTORY

In any broad overview of history, arbitrary compartmentalization of facts is self-defeating (and makes locating interrelated people, places, and things that much harder). Therefore, Headline History is designed as a "timeline"—a chronology that highlights both the march of time and interesting, sometimes surprising, juxtapositions.

*Also see* related sections of *Information Please,* particularly Inventions and Discoveries, Countries of the World, etc.

## B.C.
### Before Christ or Before Common Era (B.C.E.)

**5 billion B.C.**   Planet Earth formed.
**3 billion B.C.**   First signs of primeval life (bacteria and blue-green algae) appear in oceans.
**600 million B.C.**   Earliest date to which fossils can be traced.
**1.7 million B.C.**   First discernible hominids (*Australopithecus* and *Homo habilis*). Early hunters and food-gatherers.
**500,000 B.C.**   *Homo erectus* (crude chopping tools).
**70,000 B.C.**   Neanderthal man (use of fire and advanced tools).
**35,000 B.C.**   Neanderthal man being replaced by later groups of *Homo sapiens* (i.e. Cro-Magnon man, etc.).
**18,000 B.C.**   Cro-Magnons being replaced by later cultures.
**15,000 B.C.**   Migrations across Bering Straits into the Americas.
**10,000 B.C.**   Semi-permanent agricultural settlements in Old World.
**10,000–4,000 B.C.**   Development of settlements into cities and development of skills such as the wheel, pottery and improved methods of cultivation in Mesopatamia and elsewhere.

**NOTE:** For futher information on the geographic development in Earth's prehistory, read pages 365-366 in the Science section.

**4500–3000 B.C.**   Sumerians in the Tigris and Euphrates valleys develop a city-state civilization; first phonetic writing (**c.3500 B.C.**). Egyptian agriculture develops. Western Europe is neolithic, without metals or written records. Earliest recorded date in Egyptian calendar (**4241 B.C.**). First year of Jewish calendar (**3760 B.C.**). Copper used by Egyptians and Sumerians.
**3000–2000 B.C.**   Pharaonic rule begins in Egypt. Cheops, 4th dynasty (**2700–2675 B.C.**). The Great Sphinx of Giza. Earliest Egyptian mummies. Papyrus. Phoenician settlements on coast of what is now Syria and Lebanon. Semitic tribes settle in Assyria. Sargon, first Akkadian king, builds Mesopotamian empire. The Gilgamesh epic (**c.3000 B.C.**). Abraham leaves Ur (**c.2000 B.C.**). Systematic astronomy in Egypt, Babylon, India, China.
**2000–1500 B.C.**   Hyksos invaders drive Egyptians from Lower Egypt (**17th century B.C.**). Amosis I frees Egypt from Hyksos (**c.1600 B.C.**). Assyrians rise to power—cities of Ashur and Nineveh. Twenty-four-character alphabet in Egypt. Israelites enslaved in Egypt. Cuneiform inscriptions used by Hittites. Peak of Minoan culture on Isle of Crete—earliest form of written Greek. Hammurabi, king of Babylon, develops oldest existing code of laws (**18th century B.C.**). In Britain, Stonehenge erected on some unknown astronomical rationale.
**1500–1000 B.C.**   Ikhnaton develops monotheistic religion in Egypt (**c.1375 B.C.**). His successor, Tutankhamen, returns to earlier gods. Moses leads Israelites out of Egypt into Canaan—Ten Commandments. Greeks destroy Troy (**c.1193 B.C.**). End of Greek civilization in Mycenae with invasion of Dorians. Chinese civilization develops under Shang dynasty. Olmec civilization in Mexico—stone monuments; picture writing.
**1000–900 B.C.**   Solomon succeeds King David, builds Jerusalem temple. After Solomon's death, kingdom divided into Israel and Judah. Hebrew elders begin to write Old Testament books of Bible. Phoenicians colonize Spain with settlement at Cadiz.
**900–800 B.C.**   Phoenicians establish Carthage (**c.810 B.C.**). The *Iliad* and the *Odyssey,* perhaps composed by Greek poet Homer.
**800–700 B.C.**   Prophets Amos, Hosea, Isaiah. First recorded Olympic games (**776 B.C.**). Legendary founding of Rome by Romulus (**753 B.C.**). Assyrian

Triceratops

Brontosaur

Ra-Horakhte

## Some Ancient Civilizations

| Name | Approximate dates | Location | Major cities |
|---|---|---|---|
| Akkadian | 2350–2230 B.C. | Mesopotamia, parts of Syria, Asia Minor, Iran | Akkad, Ur, Erich |
| Assyrian | 1800–889 B.C. | Mesopotamia, Syria | Assur, Nineveh, Calah |
| Babylonian | 1728–1686 B.C. (old) 625–539 B.C. (new) | Mesopotamia, Syria, Palestine | Babylon |
| Cimmerian | 750–500 B.C. | Caucasus, northern Asia Minor | — |
| Egyptian | 2850–715 B.C. | Nile valley | Thebes, Memphis, Tanis |
| Etruscan | 900–396 B.C. | Northern Italy | — |
| Greek | 900–200 B.C. | Greece | Athens, Sparta, Thebes, Mycenae, Corinth |
| Hittite | 1640–1200 B.C. | Asia Minor, Syria | Hattusas, Nesa |
| Lydian | 700–547 B.C. | Western Asia Minor | Sardis, Miletus |
| Mede | 835–550 B.C. | Iran | Media |
| Minoan | 3000–1100 B.C. | Crete | Knossos |
| Persian | 559-330 B.C. | Iran, Asia Minor, Syria | Persepolis, Pasargadae |
| Phoenician | 1100–332 B.C. | Palestine (colonies: Gibraltar, Carthage Sardinia) | Tyre, Sidon, Byblos |
| Phrygian | 1000–547 B.C. | Central Asia Minor | Gordion |
| Roman | 500 B.C.–A.D. 300 | Italy, Mediterranean region, Asia Minor, western Europe | Rome, Byzantium |
| Scythian | 800–300 B.C. | Caucasus | — |
| Sumerian | 3200–2360 B.C. | Mesopotamia | Ur, Nippur |

**Jupiter**

**Plato**

king Sargon II conquers Hittites, Chaldeans, Samaria (end of Kingdom of Israel). Earliest written music. Chariots introduced into Italy by Etruscans.

**700–600 B.C.** End of Assyrian Empire (**616 B.C.**)—Nineveh destroyed by Chaldeans (Neo-Babylonians) and Medes (**612 B.C.**). Founding of Byzantium by Greeks (**c.660 B.C.**). Building of the Acropolis in Athens. Solon, Greek lawgiver (**640–560 B.C.**). Sappho of Lesbos, Greek poetess, Lao-Tse, Chinese philosopher and founder of Taoism (born **c.604 B.C.**).

**600–500 B.C.** Babylonian king Nebuchadnezzar builds empire, destroys Jerusalem (**586 B.C.**). Babylonian Captivity of the Jews (starting **587 B.C.**). Hanging Gardens of Babylon. Cyrus the Great of Persia creates great empire, conquers Babylon (**539 B.C.**), frees the Jews. Athenian democracy develops. Aeschylus, Greek dramatist (**525–465 B.C.**). Confucius (**551–479 B.C.**) develops philosophy-religion in China. Buddha (**563–483 B.C.**) founds Buddhism in India.

**500–400 B.C.** Greeks defeat Persians: battles of Marathon (**490 B.C.**), Thermopylae (**480 B.C.**), Salamis (**480 B.C.**). Peloponnesian Wars between Athens and Sparta (**431–404 B.C.**)—Sparta victorious. Pericles comes to power in Athens (**462 B.C.**). Flowering of Greek culture during the Age of Pericles (**450–400 B.C.**). Sophocles, Greek dramatist (**496–c.406 B.C.**). Hippocrates, Greek "Father of Medicine" (born **460 B.C.**). Xerxes I, king of Persia (rules **485–465 B.C.**).

**400–300 B.C.** Pentateuch—first five books of the Old Testament evolve in final form. Philip of Macedon assassinated (**336 B.C.**) after conquering Greece; succeeded by son, Alexander the Great (**356–323 B.C.**), who destroys Thebes (**335 B.C.**), conquers Tyre and Jerusalem (**332 B.C.**), occupies Babylon (**330 B.C.**), invades India, and dies in Babylon. His empire is divided among his generals; one of them, Seleucis I, establishes Middle East empire with capitals at Antioch (Syria) and Seleucia (in Iraq). Trial and execution of Greek philosopher Socrates (**399 B.C.**). Dialogues recorded by his student, Plato. Euclid's work on geometry (**323 B.C.**). Aristotle, Greek philosopher (**384–322 B.C.**). Demosthenes, Greek orator (**384–322 B.C.**). Praxiteles, Greek sculptor (**400–330 B.C.**).

**300–251 B.C.** First Punic War (**264–241 B.C.**): Rome defeats the Carthaginians and begins its domination of the Mediterranean. Temple of the Sun at Teotihuacan, Mexico (**c.300 B.C.**). Invention of Mayan calendar in

Yucatán—more exact than older calendars. First Roman gladiatorial games (**264 B.C.**). Archimedes, Greek mathematician (**287–212 B.C.**).

**250–201 B.C.**   Second Punic War (**219–201 B.C.**): Hannibal, Carthaginian general (**246–142 B.C.**), crosses the Alps (**218 B.C.**), reaches gates of Rome (**211 B.C.**), retreats, and is defeated by Scipio Africanus at Zama (**202 B.C.**). Great Wall of China built (**c.215 B.C.**).

**200–151 B.C.**   Romans defeat Seleucid King Antiochus III at Thermopylae (**191 B.C.**)—beginning of Roman world domination. Maccabean revolt against Seleucids (**167 B.C.**).

**150–101 B.C.**   Third Punic War (**149–146 B.C.**): Rome destroys Carthage, killing 450,000 and enslaving the remaining 50,000 inhabitants. Roman armies conquer Macedonia, Greece, Anatolia, Balearic Islands, and southern France. Venus de Milo (**c.140 B.C.**). Cicero, Roman orator (**106–43 B.C.**).

**100–51 B.C.**   Julius Caesar (**100–44 B.C.**) invades Britain (**55 B.C.**) and conquers Gaul (France) (**c.50 B.C.**). Spartacus leads slave revolt against Rome (**71 B.C.**). Romans conquer Seleucid empire. Roman general Pompey conquers Jerusalem (**63 B.C.**). Cleopatra on Egyptian throne (**51–31 B.C.**). Chinese develop use of paper (**c.100 B.C.**). Virgil, Roman poet (**70–19 B.C.**). Horace, Roman poet (**65–8 B.C.**).

**50–1 B.C.**   Caesar crosses Rubicon to fight Pompey (**50 B.C.**). Herod made Roman governor of Judea (**47 B.C.**). Caesar murdered (**44 B.C.**). Caesar's nephew, Octavian, defeats Mark Antony and Cleopatra at Battle of Actium (**31 B.C.**), and establishes Roman empire as Emperor Augustus—rules 27 B.C.—A.D. 14. Birth of Jesus Christ (variously given for **4 B.C.** to **A.D. 7**). Ovid, Roman poet (**43 B.C.—A.D. 18**).

**Marcus Aurelius**

# A.D.
## The Christian or Common Era (C.E.)

**1–49**   After Augustus, Tiberius becomes emperor (dies, **37**), succeeded by Caligula (assassinated, **41**), who is followed by Claudius. Crucifixion of Jesus (probably **30**). Han dynasty in China founded by Emperor Kuang Wu Ti. Buddhism introduced to China.

**50–99** Claudius poisoned (**54**), succeeded by Nero (commits suicide, **68**). Missionary journeys of Paul the Apostle (**34–60**). Jews revolt against Rome; Jerusalem destroyed (**70**). Roman persecutions of Christians begin (**64**). Colosseum built in Rome (**71–80**). Trajan (rules **98–116**); Roman empire extends to Mesopotamia, Arabia, Balkans. First Gospels of St. Mark, St. John, St. Matthew.

**100–149**   Hadrian rules Rome (**117–138**); codifies Roman law, establishes postal system, builds wall between England and Scotland. Jews revolt under Bar Kokhba (**122–135**); final *Diaspora* (dispersion) of Jews begins.

**150–199**   Marcus Aurelius (rules Rome **161–180**). Oldest Mayan temples in Central America (**c.200**)., Mayan civilization develops writing, astronomy, mathematics.

**Jesus Christ**

**200–249**   Goths invade Asia Minor (**c.220**). Roman persecutions of Christians increase. Persian (Sassanid) empire re-established. End of Chinese Han dynasty.

**250–299**   Increasing invasions of the Roman empire by Franks and Goths. Buddhism spreads in China.

**300–349**   Constantine the Great (rules **312–337**) reunites eastern and western Roman empires, with new capital (Constantinople) on site of Byzantium (**330**); issues Edict of Milan legalizing Christianity (**313**); becomes a Christian on his deathbed (**337**). Council of Nicaea (**325**) defines orthodox Christian doctrine. First Gupta dynasty in India (**c.320**).

**350–399**   Huns (Mongols) invade Europe (**c.360**). Theodosius the Great (rules **392–395**)—last emperor of a united Roman empire. Roman empire permanently divided in **395**: western empire ruled from Rome; eastern empire ruled from Constantinople.

**400–449**   Western Roman empire disintegrates under weak emperors. Alaric, king of the Visigoths, sacks Rome (**410**). Attila, Hun chieftain, attacks Roman provinces (**433**). St. Patrick returns to Ireland (**432**). St. Augustine's *City of God* (**411**).

**450–499**   Vandals destroy Rome (**455**). Western Roman empire ends as Odoacer, German chieftain, overthrows last Roman emperor, Romulus Augustulus, and becomes king of Italy (**476**). Ostrogothic kingdom of Italy established by Theodoric the Great (**493**). Clovis, ruler of the Franks, is converted to Christianity (**496**). First schism between western and eastern churches (**484**). Peak of Mayan culture in Mexico (**c.460**).

**500–549**   Eastern and western churches reconciled (**519**). Justinian I, the

**Mayan glyphs**

# ANCIENT EMPIRES

ASIA

Indus R.

Persepolis

Caspian Sea

Mt. Ararat

Ur

Susa

Assur

Babylon

Tigris

Euphrates

ARABIA

Red Sea

Berenice

The Egyptian Empire (1400 BC)

Alexander's Empire (323 BC)

The Roman Empire (120 AD)

Path of the Crusaders (1000-1200 AD)

Damascus

Jerusalem

Antioch

Thebes

Gaza

Memphis

Issus

Tarsus

Tyre

Cyprus

Nile R.

Alexandria

SARMATIA

Black Sea

Sinope

Troy

Smyrna

Crete

Cyrene

Athens

Sparta

Byzantium

MACEDONIA

Mt.

Olympus

Pella

Syracuse

Mediterranean Sea

GERMANIA

EUROPE

Vienna

Danube R.

ETRUSCANS

Florence

Rome

Pompeii

Sicily

Carthage

GAUL

Cologne

Rhine R.

Genoa

Sardinia

New Carthage

Paris

London

Taraco

Valencia

AFRICA

Miles  0   200   400   600

Kilometers 0

Great (483–565), becomes Byzantine emperor (527), issues his first code of civil laws (529), conquers North Africa, Italy, and part of Spain. Plague spreads through Europe (from 542). Arthur, semi-legendary king of the Britons (killed, c.537). Boëthius, Roman scholar (executed, 524).

**550–599**  Beginnings of European silk industry after Justinian's missionaries smuggle silkworms out of China (553). Mohammed, founder of Islam (570–632). Buddhism in Japan (c.560). St. Augustine of Canterbury brings Christianity to Britain (597). After killing about half the population, plague in Europe subsides (594).

**600–649**  Mohammed flees from Mecca to Medina (the *Hegira*); first year of the Muslim calendar (622). Muslim empire grows (634). Arabs conquer Jerusalem (637), destroy Alexandrian library (641), conquer Persians (641). Fatima, Mohammed's daughter (606–632).

**650–699**  Arabs attack North Africa (670), destroy Carthage (697). Venerable Bede, English monk (672–735).

**700–749**  Arab empire extends from Lisbon to China (by 716). Charles Martel, Frankish leader, defeats Arabs at Tours/Poitiers, halting Arab advance in Europe (732). Charlemagne (742–814).

**750–799**  Caliph Harun al-Rashid rules Arab empire (786–809): the "golden age" of Arab culture. Vikings begin attacks on Britain (790), land in Ireland (795). Charlemagne becomes king of the Franks (771). City of Machu Picchu flourishes in Peru.

**Viking warrior**

**800–849**  Charlemagne (Charles the Great) crowned first Holy Roman Emperor in Rome (800). Arabs conquer Crete, Sicily, and Sardinia (826–827). Charlemagne dies (814), succeeded by his son, Louis the Pious, who divides France among his sons (817).

**850–899**  Norsemen attack as far south as the Mediterranean but are repulsed (859), discover Iceland (861). Alfred the Great becomes king of Britain (871), defeats Danish invaders (878). Russian nation founded by Vikings under Prince Rurik, establishing capital at Novgorod (855–879).

**900–949**  Vikings discover Greenland (c.900). Arab Spain under Abd ar-Rahman III becomes center of learning (912–961).

**950–999**  Eric the Red establishes first Viking colony in Greenland (982). Mieczyslaw I becomes first ruler of Poland (960). Hugh Capet elected King of France in 987; Capetian dynasty to rule until 1328. Musical notation systematized (c.990). Vikings and Danes attack Britain (988–999). Holy Roman Empire founded by Otto I, King of Germany since 936, crowned by Pope John XII in 962.

### 11th century A.D.

**c.1000**  Hungary and Scandinavia converted to Christianity. Viking raider Leif Ericson discovers North America, calls it *Vinland.* Chinese invent gunpowder. *Beowulf,* Old English epic.

**1009**  Moslems destroy Holy Sepulchre in Jerusalem.

**1013**  Danes control England. Canute takes throne (1016), conquers Norway (1028), dies (1035); kingdom divided among his sons: Harold Harefoot (England), Sweyn (Norway), Hardecanute (Denmark).

**1040**  Macbeth murders Duncan, king of Scotland.

**1053**  Robert Guiscard, Norman invader, establishes kingdom in Italy, conquers Sicily (1072).

**1054**  Final separation between Eastern (Orthodox) and Western (Roman) churches.

**1055**  Seljuk Turks, Asian nomads, move west, capture Baghdad, Armenia (1064), Syria, and Palestine (1075).

**1066**  William of Normandy invades England, defeats last Saxon king, Harold II, at Battle of Hastings, crowned William I of England ("the Conqueror").

**1073**  Emergence of strong papacy when Gregory VII is elected. Conflict with English and French kings and German emperors will continue throughout medieval period.

**1095**  (*See* special material on "The Crusades.")

### 12th century A.D.

**1150–67**  Universities of Paris and Oxford founded in France and England.

**1162**  Thomas à Becket named Archbishop of Canterbury, murdered by Henry II's men (1170). Troubadours (wandering minstrels) glorify romantic concepts of feudalism.

**1189**  Richard I ("the Lionhearted") succeeds Henry II in England, killed in France (1199), succeeded by King John.

### 13th century A.D.

**1211**  Genghis Khan invades China, captures Peking (1214), conquers Persia (1218), invades Russia (1223), dies (1227).

**Richard the Lion-Hearted**

**Thomas Aquinas**

**1215** King John forced by barons to sign Magna Carta at Runneymede, limiting royal power.

**1233** The Inquisition begins as Pope Gregory IX assigns Dominicans responsibility for combatting heresy. Torture used (**1252**). Ferdinand and Isabella establish Spanish Inquisition (**1478**). Tourquemada, Grand Inquisitor, forces conversion or expulsion of Spanish Jews (**1492**). Forced conversion of Moors (**1499**). Inquisition in Portugal (**1531**). First Protestants burned at the stake in Spain (**1543**). Spanish Inquisition abolished (**1834**).

**1241** Mongols defeat Germans in Silesia, invade Poland and Hungary, withdraw from Europe after Ughetai, Mongol leader, dies.

**1251** Kublai Khan governs China, becomes ruler of Mongols (1259), establishes Yuan dynasty in China (1280), invades Burma (1287), dies (1294).

**1271** Marco Polo of Venice travels to China, in court of Kublai Khan (1275–1292), returns to Genoa (1295) and writes *Travels*.

**1295** English King Edward I summons the Model Parliament.

## 14th century A.D.

**1312-37** Mali Empire reaches its height in Africa under King Mansa Musa.

**1337-1453** Hundred Years' War—English and French kings fight for control of France.

**c.1325** The beginning of the Renaissance in Italy: writers Dante, Petrarch, Boccaccio; painter Giotto. Development of *No* drama in Japan. Aztecs establish capital on site of modern Mexico City. Peak of Moslem culture in Spain. Small cannon in use.

**1347-1351** At least 25 million people die in Europe's "Black Death" (bubonic plague).

**1368** Ming dynasty begins in China.

**1376-82** John Wycliffe, pre-Reformation religious reformer and followers translate Latin Bible into English.

**1378** The Great Schism (to 1417)—rival popes in Rome and Avignon, France, fight for control of Roman Catholic Church.

**c.1387** Chaucer's *Canterbury Tales*.

## 15th century A.D.

**1415** Henry V defeats French at Agincourt. Jan Hus, Bohemian preacher and follower of Wycliffe, burned at stake in Constance as heretic.

**1418-60** Portugal's Prince Henry the Navigator sponsors exploration of Africa's coast.

**1428** Joan of Arc leads French against English, captured by Burgundians (1430) and turned over to the English, burned at the stake as a witch after ecclesiastical trial (1431).

**1438** Inca rule in Peru.

**1450** Florence becomes center of Renaissance arts and learning under the Medicis.

**1453** Turks conquer Constantinople, end of the Byzantine empire. Hundred Years' War between France and England ends.

**Christopher Columbus**

**1455** The Wars of the Roses, civil wars between rival noble factions, begin in England (to 1485). Having invented printing with movable type at Mainz, Germany, Johann Gutenberg completes first Bible.

**1462** Ivan the Great rules Russia until 1505 as first czar; ends payment of tribute to Mongols.

**1492** Moors conquered in Spain by troops of Ferdinand and Isabella. Columbus discovers Caribbean islands, returns to Spain (1493). Second voyage to Dominica, Jamaica, Puerto Rico (1493–1496). Third voyage to Orinoco (1498). Fourth voyage to Honduras and Panama (1502–1504).

**1497** Vasco da Gama sails around Africa and discovers sea route to India (1498). Establishes Portuguese colony in India (1502). John Cabot, employed by England, reaches and explores Canadian coast. Michelangelo's *Bacchus* sculpture.

## THE CRUSADES (1096–1291)

In 1095 at Council of Clermont, Pope Urban II calls for war to rescue Holy Land from Moslem infidels. *First Crusade* (1096)—about 500,000 peasants led by Peter the Hermit prove so troublesome that Byzantine Emperor Alexius ships them to Asia Minor; only 25,000 survive return after massacre by Seljuk Turks. Followed by organized army, led by nobility, which reaches Constantinople (1097), conquers Jerusalem (1099), Acre (1104), establishes Latin Kingdom protected by Knights of St. John the Hospitaller (1100), and Knights Templar (1123). Seljuk Turks start series of counterattacks (1144). *Second Crusade* (1146) led by King Louis VIII of France and Emperor Conrad III. Crusaders perish in Asia Minor (1147).

Saladin controls Egypt (1171), unites Islam in Holy War (*Jihad*) against Christians, recaptures Jerusalem (1187). *Third Crusade* (1189) under kings of France, England, and Germany fails to reduce Saladin's power. *Fourth Crusade* (1200–1204)—French knights sack Greek Christian Constantinople, establish Latin empire in Byzantium. Greeks reestablish Orthodox faith (1262).

*Children's Crusade* (1212)—Only 1 of 30,000 French children and about 200 of 20,000 German children survive to return home. Other Crusades—against Egypt (1217), *Sixth* (1228), *Seventh* (1248), *Eighth* (1270). Mamelukes conquer Acre; end of the Crusades (1291).

## 16th century A.D.

**1501** First black slaves in America brought to Spanish colony of Santo Domingo.

**c.1503** Leonardo da Vinci paints the *Mona Lisa*.

**1506** St. Peter's Church started in Rome; designed and decorated by such artists and architects as Bramante, Michelangelo, da Vinci, Raphael, and Bernini before its completion in **1626**.

**1509** Henry VIII ascends English throne. Michelangelo paints the ceiling of the Sistine Chapel.

**1517** Turks conquer Egypt, control Arabia. Martin Luther posts his 95 theses denouncing church abuses on church door in Wittenberg—start of the Reformation in Germany.

**1519** Ulrich Zwingli begins Reformation in Switzerland. Hernando Cortes conquers Mexico for Spain. Charles I of Spain is chosen Holy Roman Emperor Charles V. Portuguese explorer Fernando Magellan sets out to circumnavigate the globe.

**1520** Luther excommunicated by Pope Leo X. Suleiman I ("the Magnificent") becomes Sultan of Turkey, invades Hungary (**1521**), Rhodes (**1522**), attacks Austria (**1529**), annexes Hungary (**1541**), Tripoli (**1551**), makes peace with Persia (**1553**), destroys Spanish fleet (**1560**), dies (**1566**). Magellan reaches the Pacific, is killed by Philippine natives (**1521**). One of his ships under Juan Sebastián del Cano continues around the world, reaches Spain (**1522**).

**Martin Luther**

**1524** Verrazano, sailing under the French flag, explores the New England coast and New York Bay.

**1527** Troops of the Holy Roman Empire attack Rome, imprison Pope Clement VII—the end of the Italian Renaissance. Castiglione writes *The Courtier*. The Medici expelled from Florence.

**1532** Pizarro marches from Panama to Peru, kills the Inca chieftain, Atahualpa, of Peru (**1533**). Machiavelli's *Prince* published posthumously.

**1535** Reformation begins as Henry VIII makes himself head of English Church after being excommunicated by Pope. Sir Thomas More executed as traitor for refusal to acknowledge king's religious authority. Jacques Cartier sails up the St. Lawrence River, basis of French claims to Canada.

**1536** Henry VIII executes second wife, Anne Boleyn. John Calvin establishes Presbyterian form of Protestantism in Switzerland, writes *Institutes of the Christian Religion*. Danish and Norwegian Reformations. Michelangelo's *Last Judgment*.

**1541** John Knox leads Reformation in Scotland, establishes Presbyterian church (**1560**).

**1543** Publication of *On the Revolution of Heavenly Bodies* by Polish scholar Nicolaus Copernicus—giving his theory that the earth revolves around the sun.

**1545** Council of Trent to meet intermittently until **1563** to define Catholic dogma and doctrine, reiterate papal authority.

**1547** Ivan IV ("the Terrible") crowned as Czar of Russia, begins conquest of Astrakhan and Kazan (**1552**), battles nobles (boyars) for power (**1564**), kills his son (**1580**), dies, and is succeeded by a son who gives power to Boris Godunov (**1584**).

**Albrecht Dürer**

**1553** Roman Catholicism restored in England by Queen Mary I, who rules until **1558**. Religious radical Michael Servetus burned as heretic in Geneva by order of John Calvin.

**1554** Benvenuto Cellini completes the bronze *Perseus*.

**1556** Akbar the Great becomes Mogul emperor of India, conquers Afghanistan (**1581**), continues wars of conquest (until **1605**).

**1558** Queen Elizabeth I ascends the throne (rules to **1603**). Restores Protestantism, establishes state Church of England (Anglicanism). Renaissance will reach height in England—Shakespeare, Marlowe, Spenser.

**1561** Persecution of Huguenots in France stopped by Edict of Orleans. French religious wars begin again with massacre of Huguenots at Vassy. St. Bartholomew's Day Massacre—thousands of Huguenots murdered (**1572**). Amnesty granted (**1573**). Persecution continues periodically until Edict of Nantes (**1598**) gives Huguenots religious freedom (until **1685**).

**1568** Protestant Netherlands revolts against Catholic Spain; independence will be acknowledged by Spain in **1648**. High point of Dutch Renaissance—painters Rubens, Van Dyck, Hals, and Rembrandt.

**1570** Japan permits visits of foreign ships. Queen Elizabeth I excommunicated by Pope. Turks attack Cyprus and war on Venice. Turkish fleet defeated at Battle of Lepanto by Spanish and Italian fleets (**1571**). Peace of Constantinople (**1572**) ends Turkish attacks on Europe.

**René Descartes**

1580 Francis Drake returns to England after circumnavigating the globe. Knighted by Queen Elizabeth I (**1581**). Montaigne's *Essays* published.
1583 William of Orange rules The Netherlands; assassinated on orders of Philip II of Spain (**1584**).
1587 Mary, Queen of Scots, executed for treason by order of Queen Elizabeth I. Monteverdi's *First Book of Madrigals.*
1588 Defeat of the Spanish Armada by English. Henry, King of Navarre and Protestant leader, recognized as Henry IV, first Bourbon king of France. Converts to Roman Catholicism in **1593** in attempt to end religious wars.
1590 Henry IV enters Paris, wars on Spain (**1595**), marries Marie de Medici (**1600**), assassinated (**1610**). Spenser's *The Faerie Queen*, El Greco's *St. Jerome.* Galileo's experiments with falling objects.
1598 Boris Godunov becomes Russian Czar. Tycho Brahe describes his astronomical experiments.

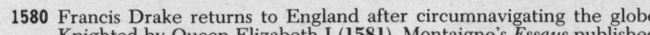

## 17th century A.D.

1600 Giordano Bruno burned as a heretic. Ieyasu rules Japan, moves capital to Edo (Tokyo). Shakespeare's *Hamlet* begins his most productive decade. English East India Company established to develop overseas trade.
1607 Jamestown, Virginia, established—first permanent English colony on American mainland.
1609 Samuel de Champlain establishes French colony of Quebec.
1611 Gustavus Adolphus elected King of Sweden. King James Version of the Bible published in England. Rubens paints his *Descent from the Cross.*
1614 John Napier discovers logarithms.
1618 Start of the Thirty Years' War (to **1648**)—Protestant revolt against Catholic oppression; Denmark, Sweden, and France will invade Germany in later phases of war. Kepler proposes his Third Law of planetary motion.
1620 Pilgrims, after three-month voyage in *Mayflower,* land at Plymouth Rock. Francis Bacon's *Novum Organum.*
1633 Inquisition forces Galileo to recant his belief in Copernican theory.
1642 English Civil War. Cavaliers, supporters of Charles I, against Roundheads, parliamentary forces. Oliver Cromwell defeats Royalists (**1646**). Parliament demands reforms. Charles I offers concessions, brought to trial (**1648**), beheaded (**1649**). Cromwell becomes Lord Protector (**1653**). Rembrandt paints his *Night Watch.*
1644 End of Ming Dynasty in China—Manchus come to power. Descartes' *Principles of Philosophy.* John Milton's *Areopagitica* on the freedom of the press.
1648 End of the Thirty Years' War. German population about half of what it was in **1618** because of war and pestilence.
1658 Cromwell dies; his son, Richard, resigns and Puritan government collapses.
1660 English Parliament calls for the restoration of the monarchy; invites Charles II to return from France.
1661 Charles II is crowned King of England. Louis XIV begins personal rule as absolute monarch; starts to build Versailles.

**George Washington**

## THE FOUNDING OF THE AMERICAN NATION

Colonization of America begins: Jamestown, Va. (**1607**); Pilgrims in Plymouth (**1620**); Massachusetts Bay Colony (**1630**) New Netherland founded by Dutch West India Company (**1623**), captured by English (**1664**). Delaware established by Swedish trading company (**1638**), absorbed later by Penn family. Proprietorships by royal grants to Lord Baltimore (Maryland, **1632**); Captain John Mason (New Hampshire, **1635**); Sir William Berkeley and Sir George Carteret (New Jersey, **1663**); friends of Charles II (the Carolinas, **1663**); William Penn (Pennsylvania, **1682**); James Oglethorpe and others (Georgia, **1732**).

Increasing conflict between colonists and Britain on western frontier because of royal edict limiting western expansion (**1763**), and regulation of colonial trade and increased taxation of colonies (Writs of Assistance allow search for illegal shipments, **1761**; Sugar Act, **1764**; Currency Act, **1764**; Stamp Act, **1765**; Quartering Act, **1765**; Duty Act, **1767**.) Boston Massacre (**1770**). Lord North attempts conciliation (**1770**), followed by punitive measures passed by Parliament—the "Intolerable Acts."

First Continental Congress (**1774**) sends "Declaration of Rights and Grievances" to king, urges colonies to form Continental Association. Paul Revere's Ride and Lexington and Concord battle between Massachusetts minutemen and British (**1775**).

Second Continental Congress (**1775**), while sending "olive branch" to the king, begins to raise army, appoints Washington commander-in-chief, and seeks alliance with France. Some colonial legislatures urge their delegates to vote for independence. Declaration of Independence (**July 4, 1776**).

Major Battles of the Revolutionary War: *Long Island:* Howe defeats Putnam's division of Washington's Army in Brooklyn Heights, but Americans escape across East River (**1776**). *Trenton and Princeton:* Washington defeats Hessians at Trenton. British at Princeton, winters at Morristown (**1776-77**). Howe winters in Philadelphia; Washington at Valley Forge (**1777-78**). Burgoyne surrenders British army to General Gates at *Saratoga* (**1777**).

France recognizes American independence (**1778**). The War moves south: Savannah captured by British (**1778**); Charleston occupied (**1780**); Americans fight successful guerrilla actions under Marion, Pickens, and Sumter. In the West, George Rogers Clark attacks Forts Kaskaskia and Vincennes (**1778-1779**), defeating British in the region. Cornwallis surrenders at *Yorktown,* Virginia (**Oct. 19, 1781**). By **1782**, Britain is eager for peace because of conflicts with European nations. *Peace of Paris* (**1783**): Britain recognizes American independence.

**1664** British take New Amsterdam from the Dutch. English limit "Nonconformity" with re-established Anglican Church. Isaac Newton's experiments with gravity.

**1665** Great Plague in London kills 75,000.

**1666** Great Fire of London. Molière's *Misanthrope*.

**1683** War of European powers against the Turks (to **1699**). Vienna withstands three-month Turkish siege; high point of Turkish advance in Europe.

**1685** James II succeeds Charles II in England, calls for freedom of conscience (**1687**). Protestants fear restoration of Catholicism and demand "Glorious Revolution." William of Orange invited to England and James II escapes to France (**1688**). William III and his wife, Mary, crowned. In France, Edict of Nantes of **1598**, granting freedom of worship to Huguenots (French Protestants), is revoked by Louis XIV; thousands of Protestants flee.

**1689** Peter the Great becomes Czar of Russia—attempts to westernize nation and build Russia as a military power. Defeats Charles XII of Sweden at Poltava (**1709**). Beginning of the French and Indian Wars (to **1763**), campaigns in America linked to a series of wars between France and England for domination of Europe.

**1690** William III of England defeats former King James II and Irish rebels at Battle of the Boyne in Ireland. John Locke's *Human Understanding*.

Hanging of witches

### 18th century A.D.

**1701** War of the Spanish Succession begins—the last of Louis XIV's wars for domination of the continent. The Peace of Utrecht (**1714**) will end the conflict and mark the rise of the British Empire. Called Queen Anne's War in America, it ends with the British taking New Foundland, Acadia, and Hudson's Bay Territory from France, and Gibraltar and Minorca from Spain.

**1704** Deerfield (Conn.) Massacre of English colonists by French and Indians. Bach's first cantata. Jonathan Swift's *Tale of a Tub*. *Boston News Letter*—first newspaper in America.

**1707** United Kingdom of Great Britain formed—England, Wales, and Scotland joined by parliamentary Act of Union.

**1729** J. S. Bach's *St. Matthew Passion*. Isaac Newton's *Principia* translated from Latin into English.

**1735** John Peter Zenger, New York editor, acquitted of libel in New York, establishing press freedom.

**1740** Capt. Vitus Bering, Dane employed by Russia, discovers Alaska.

**1746** British defeat Scots under Stuart Pretender Prince Charles at Culloden Moor. Last battle fought on British soil.

**1751** Publication of the *Encyclopédie* begins in France, the "bible" of the Enlightenment.

**1755** Samuel Johnson's *Dictionary* first published. Great earthquake in Lisbon, Portugal—over 60,000 die.

**1756** Seven Years' War (French and Indian War in America) (to **1763**), in which Britain and Prussia defeat France, Spain, Austria, and Russia. France loses North American colonies; Spain cedes Florida to Britain in exchange for Cuba. In India, over 100 British prisoners die in "Black Hole of Calcutta."

**1757** Beginning of British Empire in India as Robert Clive, British commander, defeats Nawab of Bengal at Plassey.

**1759** British capture Quebec from French. Voltaire's *Candide*. Haydn's *Symphony No. 1*.

**1762** Catherine II ("the Great") becomes Czarina of Russia. J. J. Rousseau's *Social Contract*. Mozart tours Europe as six-year-old prodigy.

**1765** James Watt invents the steam engine.

**1769** Sir William Arkwright patents a spinning machine—an early step in the Industrial Revolution.

**1772** Joseph Priestley and Daniel Rutherford independently discover nitrogen. Partition of Poland—in **1772**, **1793**, and **1795**, Austria, Prussia, and Russia divide land and people of Poland, end its independence.

**1775** The American Revolution (*see* "The Founding of the American Nation"). Priestley discovers hydrochloric and sulfuric acids.

**1776** Adam Smith's *Wealth of Nations*. Edward Gibbon's *Decline and Fall of the Roman Empire*. Thomas Paine's *Common Sense*. Fragonard's *Washerwoman*. Mozart's *Haffner Serenade*.

**1778** Capt. James Cook discovers Hawaii. Franz Mesmer uses hypnotism.

**1781** Immanuel Kant's *Critique of Pure Reason*. Herschel discovers Uranus.

**1783** End of Revolutionary War (*see* special material on "The Founding of

Johann Sebastian Bach

Joseph Haydn

**Wolfgang A. Mozart**

the American Nation"). William Blake's poems. Beethoven's first printed works.

1784 Crimea annexed by Russia. John Wesley's *Deed of Declaration*, the basic work of Methodism.

1785 Russians settle Aleutian Islands.

1787 The Constitution of the United States signed. Lavoisier's work on chemical nomenclature. Mozart's *Don Giovanni*.

1788 French *Parlement* presents grievances to Louis XVI who agrees to convening of Estates-General in 1789—not called since 1613. Goethe's *Egmont*. Laplace's *Laws of the Planetary System*.

1789 French Revolution (*see* special material on the "French Revolution"). In U.S., George Washington elected President with all 69 votes of the Electoral College, takes oath of office in New York City. Vice President: John Adams. Secretary of State: Thomas Jefferson. Secretary of Treasury: Alexander Hamilton.

1790 H.M.S. *Bounty* mutineers settle on Pitcairn Island. Aloisio Galvani experiments on electrical stimulation of the muscles. Philadelphia temporary capital of U.S. as Congress votes to establish new capital on Potomac. U.S. population about 3,929,000, including 698,000 slaves. Lavoisier formulates *Table of 31 chemical elements*.

1791 U.S. Bill of Rights ratified. Boswell's *Life of Johnson*.

1794 Kosciusko's uprising in Poland quelled by the Russians. In U.S., Whiskey Rebellion in Pennsylvania as farmers object to liquor taxes. U.S. Navy and Post Office Department established.

1796 Napoleon Bonaparte, French general, defeats Austrians. In the U.S., Washington's Farewell Address (Sept. 17); John Adams elected President; Thomas Jefferson, Vice President. Edward Jenner introduces smallpox vaccination.

1798 Napoleon extends French conquests to Rome and Egypt.

1799 Napoleon leads coup that overthrows Directory, becomes First Consul—one of three who rule France.

## 19th century A.D.

1800 Napoleon conquers Italy, firmly establishes himself as First Consul in France. In the U.S., Federal Government moves to Washington. Robert Owen's social reforms in England. William Herschel discovers infrared rays. Alessandro Volta produces electricity.

1801 Austria makes temporary peace with France. United Kingdom of Great Britain and Ireland established with one monarch and one parliament; Catholics excluded from voting.

1803 U.S. negotiates Louisiana Purchase from France: For $15 million, U.S. doubles its domain, increasing its territory by 827,000 sq. mi. (2,144,500 sq km), from Mississippi River to Rockies and from Gulf of Mexico to British North America.

1804 Haiti declares independence from France; first black nation to gain freedom from European colonial rule. Napoleon proclaims himself emperor of France, systematizes French law under *Code Napoleon*. In the U.S., Alexander Hamilton is mortally wounded in duel with Aaron Burr. Lewis and Clark expedition begins exploration of what is now northwestern U.S.

1805 Lord Nelson defeats the French-Spanish fleets in the Battle of Trafalgar. Napoleon victorious over Austrian and Russian forces at the Battle of Austerlitz.

1807 Robert Fulton makes first successful steamboat trip on *Clermont* between New York City and Albany.

1808 French armies occupy Rome and Spain, extending Napoleon's empire. Britain begins aiding Spanish guerrillas against Napoleon in Peninsular War. In the U.S., Congress bars importation of slaves. Beethoven's *Fifth* and *Sixth Symphonies* performed.

1812 Napoleon's Grand Army invades Russia in June. Forced to retreat in winter, most of Napoleon's 600,000 men are lost. In the U.S., war with

**Sir Humphrey Davy**

## FRENCH REVOLUTION (1789–1799)

Revolution begins when Third Estate (Commons) delegates swear not to disband until France has a constitution. Paris mob storms Bastille, symbol of royal power (July 14, 1789). National Assembly votes for Constitution, Declaration of the Rights of Man, a limited monarchy, and other reforms (1789–90). Legislative Assembly elected, Revolutionary Commune formed, and French Republic proclaimed (1792). War of the First Coalition—Austria, Prussia, Britain, Nether-lands, and Spain fight to restore French nobility (1792–97). Start of series of wars between France and European powers that will last, almost without interruption, for 23 years. Louis XVI and Marie Antoinette executed. Committee of Public Safety begins Reign of Terror as political control measure. Interfactional rivalry leads to mass killings. Danton and Robespierre executed. Third French Constitution sets up Directory government (1795).

Britain declared over freedom of the seas for U.S. vessels. U.S.S. *Constitution* sinks British frigate. (*See* special material on the "War of 1812.")

**1814** French defeated by allies (Britain, Austria, Russia, Prussia, Sweden, and Portugal) in War of Liberation. Napoleon exiled to Elba, off Italian coast. Bourbon King Louis XVIII takes French throne. George Stephenson builds first practical steam locomotive.

**1815** Napoleon returns: "Hundred Days" begin. Napoleon defeated by Wellington at Waterloo, banished again to St. Helena in South Atlantic. Congress of Vienna: victorious allies change the map of Europe.

**1817** Simón Bolívar establishes independent Venezuela, as Spain loses hold on South American countries. Bolívar named President of Colombia (**1819**). Peru, Guatemala, Panama, and Santo Domingo proclaim independence from Spain (**1821**).

**1820** Missouri Compromise—Missouri admitted as slave state but slavery barred in rest of Louisiana Purchase north of 36°30′ N.

**1822** Greeks proclaim a republic and independence from Turkey. Turks invade Greece. Russia declares war on Turkey (**1828**). Greece also aided by France and Britain. War ends and Turks recognize Greek independence (**1829**). Brazil becomes independent of Portugal. Schubert's *Eighth Symphony* ("The Unfinished").

**Ludwig van Beethoven**

**1823** U.S. Monroe Doctrine warns European nations not to interfere in Western Hemisphere.

**1824** Mexico becomes a republic, three years after declaring independence from Spain. Beethoven's *Ninth Symphony*.

**1825** First passenger-carrying railroad in England.

**1830** French invade Algeria. Louis Philippe becomes "Citizen King" as revolution forces Charles X to abdicate. Mormon church formed in U.S. by Joseph Smith.

**1831** Polish revolt against Russia fails. Belgium separates from the Netherlands. In U.S., Nat Turner leads unsuccessful slave rebellion.

**1833** Slavery abolished in British Empire.

**1834** Charles Babbage invents "analytical engine," precursor of computer. McCormick patents reaper.

**1836** Boer farmers start "Great Trek"—Natal, Transvaal, and Orange Free State founded in South Africa. Mexican army besieges Texans in Alamo. Entire garrison, including Davy Crockett and Jim Bowie, wiped out. Texans gain independence from Mexico after winning Battle of San Jacinto. Dicken's *Pickwick Papers*.

**1837** Victoria becomes Queen of Great Britain. Mob kills Elijah P. Lovejoy, Illinois abolitionist publisher.

**1839** First Opium War (to **1842**) between Britain and China, over importation of drug into China.

**1840** Lower and Upper Canada united.

**1841** U.S. President Harrison dies (**April 4**) one month after inauguration; John Tyler becomes first Vice President to succeed to Presidency.

**1844** Democratic convention calls for annexation of Texas and acquisition of Oregon ("Fifty-four-forty-or-fight"). Five Chinese ports opened to U.S. ships. Samuel F. B. Morse patents telegraph.

**1845** Congress adopts joint resolution for annexation of Texas.

**1846** Failure of potato crop causes famine in Ireland. U.S. declares war on Mexico. California and New Mexico annexed by U.S. Brigham Young leads Mormons to Great Salt Lake. W.T. Morton uses ether as anesthetic. Sewing machine patented by Elias Howe.

**Giuseppe Verdi**

**1848** Revolt in Paris: Louis Philippe abdicates; Louis Napoleon elected President of French Republic. Revolutions in Vienna, Venice, Berlin, Milan, Rome, and Warsaw. Put down by royal troops in **1848–49**. U.S.-Mexico War ends; Mexico cedes claims to Texas, California, Arizona, New Mexico, Utah, Nevada. U.S. treaty with Britain sets Oregon Territory boundary at 49th parallel. Karl Marx and Friedrich Engels' *Communist Manifesto*.

**1849** California gold rush begins.

**1850** Henry Clay opens great debate on slavery, warns South against secession.

**1851** Herman Melville's *Moby Dick*. Harriet Beecher Stowe's *Uncle Tom's Cabin*.

**1852** South African Republic established. Louis Napoleon proclaims himself Napoleon III ("Second Empire").

---

## WAR OF 1812

British interference with American trade, impressment of American seamen, and "War Hawks" drive for western expansion lead to war. American attacks on Canada foiled; U.S. Commodore Perry wins battle of Lake Erie (**1813**). British capture and burn Washington (**1814**) but fail to take Fort McHenry at Baltimore. Andrew Jackson repulses assault on New Orleans after treaty of Ghent ends war (**1815**). War settles little but strengthens U.S. as independent nation.

**Dred Scott**

**1853** Crimean War begins as Turkey declares war on Russia. Commodore Perry reaches Tokyo.

**1854** Britain and France join Turkey in war on Russia. In U.S., Kansas-Nebraska Act permits local option on slavery; rioting and bloodshed. Japanese allow American trade. Antislavery men in Michigan form Republican Party. Tennyson's *Charge of the Light Brigade*. Thoreau's *Walden*.

**1855** Armed clashes in Kansas between pro- and anti-slavery forces. Florence Nightingale nurses wounded in Crimea. Walt Whitman's *Leaves of Grass*.

**1856** Flaubert's *Madame Bovary*.

**1857** Supreme Court, in Dred Scott decision, rules that a slave is not a citizen. Financial crisis in Europe and U.S. Great Mutiny (Sepoy Rebellion) begins in India. India placed under crown rule as a result.

**1858** Pro-slavery constitution rejected in Kansas. Abraham Lincoln makes strong antislavery speech in Springfield, Ill.: ". . . this Government cannot endure permanently half slave and half free." Lincoln-Douglas debates. First trans-Atlantic telegraph cable completed by Cyrus W. Field.

**1859** John Brown raids Harpers Ferry; is captured and hanged. Work begins on Suez Canal. Unification of Italy starts under leadership of Count Cavour, Sardinian premier. Joined by France in war against Austria. Edward Fitzgerald's *Rubaiyat of Omar Khayyam*. Charles Darwin's *Origin of Species*. J. S. Mill's *On Liberty*

**1861** U.S. Civil War begins as attempts at compromise fail (*see* special material on "The Civil War"). Congress creates Colorado, Dakota, and Nevada territories; adopts income tax; Lincoln inaugurated. Serfs emancipated in Russia. Pasteur's theory of germs. Independent Kingdom of Italy proclaimed under Sardinian King Victor Emmanuel II.

**1863** French capture Mexico City; proclaim Archduke Maximilian of Austria emperor.

**1865** Lincoln fatally shot at Ford's Theater by John Wilkes Booth. Vice President Johnson sworn as successor. Booth caught and dies of gunshot wounds; four conspirators are hanged. Joseph Lister begins antiseptic surgery. Gregor Mendel's Law of Heredity. Lewis Carroll's *Alice's Adventures in Wonderland*.

**1866** Alfred Nobel invents dynamite. Seven Weeks' War: Austria defeated by Prussia and Italy.

**1867** Austria-Hungary Dual Monarchy established. French leave Mexico; Maximilian executed. Dominion of Canada established. U.S. buys Alaska from Russia for $7,200,000. South African diamond field discovered. Volume I of Marx's *Das Kapital*. Strauss's *Blue Danube*.

**Abraham Lincoln**

**1868** Revolution in Spain; Queen Isabella deposed, flees to France. In U.S., Fourteenth Amendment giving civil rights to blacks is ratified. Georgia under military government after legislature expels blacks.

**1869** First U.S. transcontinental rail route completed. James Fisk and Jay Gould attempt to control gold market causes Black Friday panic. Suez Canal opened. Mendeleev's periodic table of elements.

**1870** Franco-Prussian War (to 1871): Napoleon III capitulates at Sedan. Revolt in Paris; Third Republic proclaimed.

---

## THE CIVIL WAR
### (The War Between the States or the War of the Rebellion)

Apart from the matter of slavery, the Civil War arose out of both the economic and political rivalry between an agrarian South and an industrial North and the issue of the right of states to secede from the Union.

**1861** After South Carolina secedes **(Dec. 20, 1860),** Mississippi, Florida, Alabama, Georgia, Louisiana, and Texas follow, forming the Confederate States of America, with Jefferson Davis as president **(Jan.-March).** War begins as Confederates fire on Fort Sumter **(April 12).** Lincoln calls for 75,000 volunteers. Southern ports blockaded by superior Union naval forces. Virginia, Arkansas, Tennessee, and North Carolina secede to complete 11-state Confederacy. Union army advancing on Richmond repulsed at first Battle of Bull Run **(July).**

**1862** Edwin M. Stanton named Secretary of War **(Jan.).** Grant wins first important Union victory in West, at Fort Donelson; Nashville falls **(Feb.).** Ironclads, Union's *Monitor* and Confederate's *Virginia (Merrimac)* duel at Hampton Roads **(March).** New Orleans falls to Union fleet under Farragut; city occupied **(April).** Grant's army escapes defeat at Shiloh. Memphis falls as Union gunboats control upper Mississippi **(June).** Confederate general Robert E. Lee victorious at second Battle of Bull Run **(Aug.).** Union army under McClellan halts Lee's attack on Washington in the Battle of Antietam **(Sept.).** Lincoln removes McClellan for lack of aggressiveness. Burnside's drive on Richmond fails at Fredericksburg **(Dec.).** Union forces under Rosecrans chase Bragg through Tennessee; battle of Murfreesboro **(Oct.-Jan. 1863).**

**1863** Lee defeats Hooker at Chancellorsville; "Stonewall" Jackson, Confederate general, dies **(May).** Confederate invasion of Pennsylvania stopped at Gettysburg by George Meade—Lee loses 20,000 men—the greatest battle of the War **(July).** It and the Union victory at Vicksburg mark the war's turning point. Union general George H. Thomas, the "Rock of Chickamauga," holds Bragg's forces on Georgia-Tennessee border **(Sept.).** Sherman, Hooker, and Thomas drive Bragg back to Georgia. Tennessee restored to the Union **(Nov.).**

**1864** Ulysses S. Grant named commander-in-chief of Union forces **(March).** In the Wilderness campaign, Grant forces Lee's Army of Northern Virginia back toward Richmond **(May-June).** Sherman's Atlanta campaign and "march to the sea" **(May-Sept.).** Farragut's victory at Mobile Bay **(Aug.).** Hood's Confederate army defeated at Nashville. Sherman takes Savannah **(Dec.).**

**1865** Sheridan defeats Confederates at Five Forks; Confederates evacuate Richmond **(April).** On April 9, Lee surrenders to Grant at Appomattox.

**1871** France surrenders Alsace-Lorraine to Germany; war ends. German Empire proclaimed with Prussian King as Kaiser Wilhelm I. Fighting with Apaches begins in American West. Boss Tweed corruption exposed in New York. The Chicago Fire, with 250 deaths and $196-million damage. Stanley meets Livingston in Africa.

**1872** Congress gives amnesty to most Confederates. Jules Verne's *Around the World in 80 Days.*

**1873** Economic crisis in Europe. U.S. establishes gold standard.

**1875** First Kentucky Derby.

**1876** Sioux kill Gen. George A. Custer and 264 troopers at Little Big Horn River. Alexander Graham Bell patents the telephone.

**1877** After Presidential election of 1876, Electoral Commission gives disputed Electoral College votes to Rutherford B. Hayes despite Tilden's popular majority. Russo-Turkish war (ends in 1878 with power of Turkey in Europe broken). Reconstruction ends in the American South. Thomas Edison patents phonograph.

**1878** Congress of Berlin revises Treaty of San Stefano ending Russo-Turkish War; makes extensive redivision of southeastern Europe. First commercial telephone exchange opened in New Haven, Conn.

**1880** U.S.-China treaty allows U.S. to restrict immigration of Chinese labor.

**1881** President Garfield fatally shot by assassin; Vice President Arthur succeeds him. Charles J. Guiteau convicted and executed (in 1882).

Geronimo

**1882** Terrorism in Ireland after land evictions. Britain invades and conquers Egypt. Germany, Austria, and Italy form Triple Alliance. In U.S., Congress adopts Chinese Exclusion Act. Rockefeller's Standard Oil Trust is first industrial monopoly. In Berlin, Robert Koch announces discovery of tuberculosis germ.

**1883** Congress creates Civil Service Commission. Brooklyn Bridge and Metropolitan Opera House completed.

**1885** British Gen. Charles G. "Chinese" Gordon killed at Khartoum in Egyptian Sudan.

**1886** Bombing at Haymarket Square, Chicago, kills seven policemen and injures many others. Eight alleged anarchists accused—three imprisoned, one commits suicide, four hanged. (In 1893, Illinois Governor Altgeld, critical of trial, pardons three survivors.) Statue of Liberty dedicated. Geronimo, Apache Indian chief, surrenders.

**1887** Queen Victoria's Golden Jubilee. Sir Arthur Conan Doyle's first Sherlock Holmes story, "A Study in Scarlet."

**1888** Historic March blizzard in Northeast U.S.—many perish, property damage exceeds $25 million. George Eastman's box camera (the Kodak). J.B. Dunlop invents pneumatic tire. Jack the Ripper murders in London.

**1889** Second (Socialist) International founded in Paris. Indian Territory in Oklahoma opened to settlement. Thousands die in Johnstown, Pa., flood. Mark Twain's *A Connecticut Yankee in King Arthur's Court.*

**1890** Congress votes Sherman Antitrust Act. Sitting Bull killed in Sioux uprising.

**1892** Battle between steel strikers and Pinkerton guards at Homestead, Pa.; union defeated after militia intervenes. Silver mine strikers in Idaho fight non-union workers; U.S. troops dispatched. Diesel engine patented.

Samuel Clemens

**1894** Sino-Japanese War begins (ends in 1895 with China's defeat). In France, Capt. Alfred Dreyfus convicted on false treason charge (pardoned in 1906). In U.S., Jacob S. Coxey of Ohio leads "Coxey's Army" of unemployed on Washington. Eugene V. Debs calls general strike of rail workers to support Pullman Company strikers; strike broken, Debs jailed for six months. Thomas A. Edison's kinetoscope given first public showing in New York City.

**1895** X-rays discovered by German physicist, Wilhelm Roentgen.

**1896** Supreme Court's *Plessy v. Ferguson* decision—"separate but equal" doctrine. Alfred Nobel's will establishes prizes for peace, science, and literature. Marconi receives first wireless patent in Britain. William Jennings Bryan delivers "Cross of Gold" speech at Democratic Convention

---

## SPANISH-AMERICAN WAR (1898–1899)

War fires stoked by "jingo journalism" as American people support Cuban rebels against Spain. American business sees economic gain in Cuban trade and resources and American power zones in Latin America. Outstanding events: Submarine mine explodes U.S. battleship *Maine* in Havana Harbor (**Feb. 15**); 260 killed; responsibility never fixed. Congress declares independence of Cuba (**April 19**). Spain declares war on U.S. (**Apr. 24**); Congress (**Apr. 25**) formally declares nation has been at war with Spain since Apr. 21. Commodore

George Dewey wins seven-hour battle of Manila Bay (**May 1**). Spanish fleet destroyed off Santiago, Cuba (**July 3**); city surrenders (**July 17**). Treaty of Paris (ratified by Senate **1899**) ends war. U.S. given Guam and Puerto Rico and agrees to pay Spain $20 million for Philippines. Cuba independent of Spain; under U.S. military control for three years until **May 20, 1902**. Yellow fever is eradicated and political reforms achieved.

in Chicago. First modern Olympic games held in Athens, Greece.

**1898** Chinese "Boxers," anti-foreign organization, established. They stage uprisings against Europeans in **1900;** U.S. and other Western troops relieve Peking legations. Spanish-American War (*see* special material on the "Spanish-American War"). Pierre and Marie Curie discover radium and polonium.

**1899** Boer War (or South African War). Conflict between British and Boers (descendants of Dutch settlers of South Africa). Causes rooted in longstanding territorial disputes and in friction over political rights for English and other "uitlanders" following 1886 discovery of vast gold deposits in Transvaal. (British victorious as war ends in **1902**.) Casualties: 5,774 British dead, about 4,000 Boers. Union of South Africa established in **1908** as confederation of colonies; becomes British dominion in **1910**.

## 20th century A.D.

**1900** Hurricane ravages Galveston, Tex.; 6,000 drown. Sigmund Freud's *The Interpretation of Dreams.*

**1901** Queen Victoria dies; succeeded by son, Edward VII. As President McKinley begins second term, he is shot fatally by anarchist Leon Czolgosz. Theodore Roosevelt sworn in as successor.

**1902** Enrico Caruso's first gramophone recording.

**1903** Wright brothers, Orville and Wilbur, fly first powered, controlled, heavier-than-air plane at Kitty Hawk, N.C. Henry Ford organizes Ford Motor Company.

**1904** Russo-Japanese War—competition for Korea and Manchuria: In **1905**, Port Arthur surrenders to Japanese and Russia suffers other defeats; President Roosevelt mediates Treaty of Portsmouth, N.H., ending war with concessions for Japan. *Entente Cordiale:* Britain and France settle their international differences. General theory of radioactivity by Rutherford and Soddy. New York City subway opened.

Albert Einstein

**1905** General strike in Russia; first workers' soviet set up in St. Petersburg. Sailors on battleship *Potemkin* mutiny; reforms including first Duma (parliament) established by Czar's "October Manifesto." Albert Einstein's special theory of relativity and other key theories in physics. Franz Lehar's *Merry Widow.*

**1906** San Francisco earthquake and three-day fire; 500 dead. Roald Amundsen, Norwegian explorer, fixes magnetic North Pole.

**1907** Second Hague Peace Conference, of 46 nations, adopts 10 conventions on rules of war. Financial panic of **1907** in U.S.

**1908** Earthquake kills 150,000 in southern Italy and Sicily. U.S. Supreme Court, in Danbury Hatters' case, outlaws secondary union boycotts.

**1909** North Pole reached by American explorers Robert E. Peary and Matthew Henson.

**1910** Boy Scouts of America incorporated.

**1911** First use of aircraft as offensive weapon in Turkish-Italian War. Italy defeats Turks and annexes Tripoli and Libya. Chinese Republic proclaimed after revolution overthrows Manchu dynasty. Sun Yat-sen named president. Mexican Revolution: Porfirio Diaz, president since 1877, replaced by Francisco Madero. Triangle Shirtwaist Company fire in New York; 145 killed. Richard Strauss's *Der Rosenkavalier.* Irving Berlin's *Alexander's Ragtime Band.* Amundsen reaches South Pole.

**1912** Balkan Wars (1912–13) resulting from territorial disputes: Turkey defeated by alliance of Bulgaria, Serbia, Greece, and Montenegro; London peace treaty (1913) partitions most of European Turkey among the victors. In second war (1913), Bulgaria attacks Serbia and Greece and is defeated after Romania intervenes and Turks recapture Adrianople. *Titanic* sinks on maiden voyage; over 1,500 drown.

**1913** Suffragettes demonstrate in London. Garment workers strike in New York and Boston; win pay raise and shorter hours. Sixteenth Amendment (income tax) and 17th (popular election of U.S. senators) adopted. Bill creating U.S. Federal Reserve System becomes law. Stravinsky's *The Rite of Spring.*

**1914** World War I begins (*see* special material on "World War I"). Panama Canal officially opened. Congress sets up Federal Trade Commission, passes Clayton Antitrust Act. U.S. Marines occupy Veracruz, Mexico, intervening in civil war to protect American interests.

**1915** U.S. protests German submarine actions and British blockade of Germany. U.S. banks lend $500 million to France and Britain. D. W. Griffith's film *Birth of a Nation.* Albert Einstein's *General Theory of Relativity.*

**1916** Congress expands armed forces. Tom Mooney arrested for San Francisco bombing (pardoned in **1939**). Pershing fails in raid into Mexico in quest of rebel Pancho Villa. U.S. buys Virgin Islands from Denmark for $25 million. President Wilson re-elected with "he kept us out of war" slogan. "Black Tom" explosion at munitions dock in Jersey City, N.J., $40,000,000 damages; traced to German saboteurs. Margaret Sanger opens first birth control clinic. Easter Rebellion in Ireland put down by British troops.

**1917** First U.S. combat troops in France as U.S. declares war (**April 6**). Russian Revolution—climax of long unrest under czars. February Revolution— Czar forced to abdicate, liberal government created. Kerensky becomes prime minister and forms provisional government (**July**). In October Revolution, Bolsheviks seize power in armed coup d'état led by Lenin and Trotsky. Kerensky flees. Revolutionaries execute the czar and his family (**1918**). Reds set up Third International in Moscow (**1919**). Balfour Declaration promises Jewish homeland in Palestine. Sigmund Freud's *Introduction to Psychoanalysis*.

**1918** Russian Civil War between Reds (Bolsheviks) and Whites (anti-Bolsheviks); Reds win in **1920**. Allied troops (U.S., British, French) intervene (**March**); leave in **1919**. Japanese hold Vladivostok until **1922**. World-wide influenza epidemic strikes; by **1920**, nearly 20 million are dead. In U.S. alone, 500,000 perish.

**1919** Third International (Comintern) establishes Soviet control over international Communist movements. Paris peace conference. Versailles Treaty, incorporating Wilson's draft Covenant of League of Nations, signed by Allies and Germany; rejected by U.S. Senate. Congress formally ends war in **1921**. Eighteenth (Prohibition) Amendment adopted. Alcock and Brown make first trans-Atlantic non-stop flight.

**1920** League of Nations holds first meeting at Geneva, Switzerland. U.S. Dept. of Justice "red hunt" nets thousands of radicals; aliens deported. Women's suffrage (19th) amendment ratified. First Agatha Christie mystery. Sinclair Lewis's *Main Street*.

Nikolai Lenin

**1921** Reparations Commission fixes German liability at 132 billion gold marks. German inflation begins. Major treaties signed at Washington Disarmament Conference limit naval tonnage and pledge to respect territorial integrity of China. Irish Free State formed in southern Ireland as self-governing dominion of British Empire. In U.S., Nicola Sacco and Bartolomeo Vanzetti, Italian-born anarchists, convicted of armed robbery murder; case stirs world-wide protests; they are executed in 1927.

**1922** Mussolini marches on Rome; forms Fascist government. Irish Free State officially proclaimed.

**1923** Adolf Hitler's "Beer Hall Putsch" in Munich fails; in **1924** he is sentenced to five years in prison where he writes *Mein Kampf;* released after eight months. Occupation of Ruhr by French and Belgian troops to enforce reparations payments. Widespread Ku Klux Klan violence in U.S. George Gershwin's *Rhapsody in Blue*.

**1924** Death of Lenin; Stalin wins power struggle, rules as Soviet dictator until death in **1953**. Italian Fascists murder Socialist leader Giacomo Matteotti. Interior Secretary Albert B. Fall and oilmen Harry Sinclair and Ed-

## WORLD WAR I (1914–1918)

Imperial, territorial, and economic rivalries lead to the "Great War" between the Central Powers (Austria-Hungary, Germany, Bulgaria, and Turkey) and the Allies (U.S., Britain, France, Russia, Belgium, Serbia, Greece, Romania, Montenegro, Portugal, Italy, Japan). About 10 million combatants killed, 20 million wounded.

**1914** Austrian Archduke Francis Ferdinand and wife assassinated in Sarajevo by Serbian nationalist, Gavrilo Princip (**June 28**). Austria declares war on Serbia (**July 28**). Germany declares war on Russia (**Aug. 1**), on France (**Aug. 3**), invades Belgium (**Aug. 4**). Britain declares war on Germany (**Aug. 4**). Germans defeat Russians in Battle of Tannenberg on Eastern Front (**Aug.**). First Battle of the Marne (**Sept.**). German drive stopped 25 miles from Paris. By end of year, war on the Western Front is "positional" in the trenches.

**1915** German submarine blockade of Great Britain begins (**Feb.**). Dardanelles Campaign—British land in Turkey (**April**), withdraw from Gallipoli (**Dec. to Jan. 1916**). Germans use gas at second Battle of Ypres (**April–May**). *Lusitania* sunk by German submarine—1,198 lost, including 128 Americans (**May 7**). On Eastern Front, German and Austrian "great offensive" conquers all of Poland and Lithuania; Russians lose 1 million men (by **Sept. 6**). "Great Fall Offensive" by Allies results in little change from 1914 (**Sept.–Oct.**). Britain and France declare war on Bulgaria (**Oct. 14**).

**1916** Battle of Verdun—Germans and French each lose about 350,000 men (**Feb.**). Extended submarine warfare begins (**March**). British-German sea battle of Jutland (**May**); British lose more ships, but German fleet never ventures forth again. On Eastern front, the Brusilov offensive demoralizes Russians, costs them 1 million men (**June–Sept.**). Battle of the Somme—British lose over 400,000; French, 200,000; Germans, about 450,000; all with no strategic results (**July–Nov.**). Romania declares war on Austria-Hungary (**Aug. 27**). Bucharest captured (**Dec.**).

**1917** U.S. declares war on Germany (**April 6**). Submarine warfare at peak (**April**). On Italian Front, Battle of Caporetto—Italians retreat, losing 600,000 prisoners and deserters (**Oct.–Dec.**). On Western Front, Battles of Arras, Champagne, Ypres (third battle), etc. First large British tank attack (**Nov.**). U.S. declares war on Austria-Hungary (**Dec. 7**). Armistice between new Russian Bolshevik government and Germans (**Dec. 15**).

**1918** Great offensive by Germans (**March–June**). Americans' first important battle role at Château-Thierry—as they and French stop German advance (**June**). Second Battle of the Marne (**July–Aug.**)—start of Allied offensive at Amiens, St. Mihiel, etc. Battles of the Argonne and Ypres panic German leadership (**Sept.–Oct.**). British offensive in Palestine (**Sept.**). Germans ask for armistice (**Oct. 4**). British armistice with Turkey (**Oct.**). German Kaiser abdicates (**Nov.**). Hostilities cease on Western Front (**Nov. 11**).

**Charles A. Lindbergh**

**Amelia Earhart**

ward L. Doheny are charged with conspiracy and bribery in the Teapot Dome scandal, involving fraudulent leases of naval oil reserves. In 1931, Fall is sentenced to year in prison; Doheny and Sinclair acquitted of bribery. Nathan Leopold and Richard Loeb convicted in "thrill killing" of Bobby Franks in Chicago; defended by Clarence Darrow; sentenced to life imprisonment. (Loeb killed by fellow convict in 1936; Leopold paroled in 1958, dies in 1971.)

1925 Nellie Tayloe Ross elected governor of Wyoming; first woman governor elected in U.S. Locarno conferences seek to secure European peace by mutual guarantees. John T. Scopes convicted and fined for teaching evolution in a public school in Tennessee "Monkey Trial"; sentence set aside. John Logie Baird, Scottish inventor, transmits human features by television. Adolf Hitler publishes Volume I of *Mein Kampf.*

1926 General strike in Britain brings nation's activities to standstill. U.S. marines dispatched to Nicaragua during revolt; they remain until 1933. Gertrude Ederle of U.S. is first woman to swim English Channel.

1927 German economy collapses. Socialists riot in Vienna; general strike follows acquittal of Nazis for political murder. Trotsky expelled from Russian Communist Party. Charles A. Lindbergh flies first successful solo non-stop flight from New York to Paris. Ruth Snyder and Judd Gray convicted of murder of Albert Snyder; they are executed at Sing Sing prison in 1928. *The Jazz Singer,* with Al Jolson, first part-talking motion picture.

1928 Kellogg-Briand Pact, outlawing war, signed in Paris by 65 nations. Alexander Fleming discovers penicillin. Richard E. Byrd starts expedition to Antarctic; returns in 1930.

1929 Trotsky expelled from U.S.S.R. Lateran Treaty establishes independent Vatican City. In U.S., stock market prices collapse, with U.S. securities losing $26 billion—first phase of Depression and world economic crisis. St. Valentine's Day gangland massacre in Chicago.

1930 Britain, U.S., Japan, France, and Italy sign naval disarmament treaty. Nazis gain in German elections. Cyclotron developed by Ernest O. Lawrence, U.S. physicist.

1931 Spain becomes a republic with overthrow of King Alfonso XIII. German industrialists finance 800,000-strong Nazi party. British parliament enacts statute of Westminster, legalizing dominion equality with Britain. Mukden Incident begins Japanese occupation of Manchuria. In U.S., Hoover proposes one-year moratorium of war debts. Harold C. Urey discovers heavy hydrogen. Gangster Al Capone sentenced to 11 years in prison for tax evasion (freed in 1939; dies in 1947).

1932 Nazis lead in German elections with 230 Reichstag seats. Famine in U.S.S.R. In U.S., Congress sets up Reconstruction Finance Corporation to stimulate economy. Veterans march on Washington—most leave after Senate rejects payment of cash bonuses; others removed by troops under Douglas MacArthur. U.S. protests Japanese aggression in Manchuria. Amelia Earhart is first woman to fly Atlantic solo. Charles A. Lindbergh's baby son kidnapped, killed. (Bruno Richard Hauptmann arrested in 1934, convicted in 1935, executed in 1936.)

1933 Hitler appointed German chancellor, gets dictatorial powers. Reichstag fire in Berlin; Nazi terror begins. (*See* special material on "The Holocaust.") Germany and Japan withdraw from League of Nations. Giuseppe Zangara executed for attempted assassination of President-elect

## THE HOLOCAUST (1933–1945)

"Holocaust" is the term describing the Nazi annihilation of about 6 million Jews (two thirds of the pre-World War II European Jewish population), including 4,500,000 from Russia, Poland, and the Baltic; 750,000 from Hungary and Romania; 290,000 from Germany and Austria; 105,000 from The Netherlands; 90,000 from France; 54,000 from Greece, etc.

The Holocaust was unique in its being *genocide*—the systematic destruction of a people solely because of religion, race, ethnicity, or nationality—on an unmatched scale. Along with the Jews, another 9 to 10 million people—Gypsies, Slavs (Poles, Ukrainians, and Belorussians)—were exterminated.

The only comparable act of genocide in modern times was launched in April 1915, when an estimated 600,000 Armenians were massacred by the Turks.

**1933** Hitler named German Chancellor (**Jan.**). Dachau, first concentration camp, established (**March**). Boycotts against Jews begin (**April**).

**1935** Anti-Semitic Nuremberg Laws passed by Reichstag (**Sept.**).

**1937** Buchenwald concentration camp opens (**July**).

**1938** Extenstion of anti-Semitic laws to Austria after annexation (**March**). *Kristallnacht* (Night of Broken Glass)—anti-Semitic riots in Germany and Austria (**Nov. 9**). 26,000 Jews sent to concentration camps; Jewish children expelled from schools (**Nov.**). Expropriation of Jewish property and businesses (**Dec.**).

**1940** As war continues, Nazi acts against Jews extended to German-conquered areas.

**1941** Deportation of German Jews begins; massacres of Jews in Odessa and Kiev—68,000 killed (**Nov.**); in Riga and Vilna—almost 60,000 killed (**Dec.**).

**1942** Unified Jewish resistance in ghettos begins (**Jan.**). 300,000 Jews from Warsaw Ghetto deported to Treblinka death camp (**July**).

**1943** Warsaw Ghetto uprisings (**Jan.** and **April**); Ghetto exterminated (**May**).

**1944** 476,000 Hungarian Jews sent to Auschwitz (**May–June**). D-day (**June 6**). Soviet Army liberates Maidanek death camp (**July**). Nazis try to hide evidence of death camps (**Nov.**).

**1945** Americans liberate Buchenwald, Bergen-Belsen camps (**April**). Nuremberg War Crimes Trial (**Nov. 1945 to Oct. 1946**).

Roosevelt in which Chicago Mayor Cermak is fatally shot. Roosevelt inaugurated ("the only thing we have to fear is fear itself"); launches New Deal. Prohibition repealed. U.S.S.R. recognized by U.S.

**1934** Chancellor Dollfuss of Austria assassinated by Nazis. Hitler becomes Führer. U.S.S.R. admitted to League of Nations. Dionne sisters, first quintuplets to survive beyond infancy, born in Canada.

**1935** Saar incorporated into Germany after plebiscite. Nazis repudiate Versailles Treaty, introduce compulsory military service. Mussolini invades Ethiopia; League of Nations invokes sanctions. Roosevelt opens second phase of New Deal in U.S., calling for social security, better housing, equitable taxation, and farm assistance. Huey Long assassinated in Louisiana.

**1936** Germans occupy Rhineland. Italy annexes Ethiopia. Rome-Berlin Axis proclaimed (Japan to join in **1940**). Trotsky exiled to Mexico. King George V dies; succeeded by son, Edward VIII, who soon abdicated to marry American-born divorcée, and is succeeded by brother, George VI. Spanish civil war begins. (Franco's fascist forces defeat Loyalist forces by **1939**, when Madrid falls.) War between China and Japan begins, to continue through World War II. Japan and Germany sign anti-Comintern pact; joined by Italy in **1937**.

**Adolf Hitler**

**1937** Hitler repudiates war guilt clause of Versailles Treaty; continues to build German power. Italy withdraws from League of Nations. U.S. gunboat *Panay* sunk by Japanese in Yangtze River. Japan invades China, conquers most of coastal area. Amelia Earhart lost somewhere in Pacific on round-the-world flight.

**1938** Hitler marches into Austria; political and geographical union of Germany and Austria proclaimed. Munich Pact—Britain, France, and Italy agree to let Germany partition Czechoslovakia. Douglas "Wrong-Way" Corrigan flies from New York to Dublin.

**1939** Germany occupies Bohemia and Moravia; renounces pacts with Poland and England and concludes 10-year non-aggression pact with U.S.S.R. Russo-Finnish War begins; Finns to lose one-tenth of territory in **1940** peace treaty. World War II begins (*see* special material on "World War II"). In U.S., Roosevelt submits $1,319-million defense budget, proclaims U.S. neutrality, and declares limited emergency. Einstein writes FDR about feasibility of atomic bomb. New York World's Fair opens.

**1940** Trotsky assassinated in Mexico. Estonia, Latvia, and Lithuania annexed by U.S.S.R. U.S. trades 50 destroyers for leases on British bases in Western Hemisphere. Selective Service Act signed.

## WORLD WAR II (1939–1945)

Axis powers (Germany, Italy, Japan, Hungary, Romania, Bulgaria) *vs.* Allies (U.S., Britain, France, U.S.S.R., Australia, Belgium, Brazil, Canada, China, Denmark, Greece, Netherlands, New Zealand, Norway, Poland, South Africa, Yugoslavia).

**1939** Germany invades Poland and annexes Danzig; Britain and France give Hitler ultimatum (**Sept. 1**), declare war (**Sept. 3**). Disabled German pocket battleship *Admiral Graf Spee* blown up off Montevideo, Uruguay, on Hitler's orders (**Dec. 17**). Limited activity ("Sitzkrieg") on Western Front.

**1940** Nazis invade Netherlands, Belgium, and Luxembourg (**May 10**). Chamberlain resigns as Prime Minister; Churchill takes over (**May 10**). Germans cross French frontier (**May 12**) using air/tank/infantry "Blitzkrieg" tactics. Dunkerque evacuation—about 335,000 out of 400,000 Allied soldiers rescued from Belgium by British civilian and naval craft (**May 26–June 3**). Italy declares war on France and Britain; invades France (**June 10**). Germans enter Paris; city undefended (**June 14**). France and Germany sign armistice at Compiègne (**June 22**). Nazis bomb Coventry, England (**Nov. 14**).

**1941** Germans launch attacks in Balkans. Yugoslavia surrenders—General Mihajlovic continues guerrilla warfare; Tito leads left-wing guerrillas (**April 17**). Nazi tanks enter Athens; remnants of British Army quit Greece (**April 27**). Hitler attacks Russia (**June 22**). Atlantic Charter—FDR and Churchill agree on war aims (**Aug. 14**). Japanese attacks on Pearl Harbor, Philippines, Guam force U.S. into war; U.S. Pacific fleet crippled (**Dec. 7**). U.S. and Britain declare war on Japan. Germany and Italy declare war on U.S.; Congress declares war on those countries (**Dec. 11**).

**1942** British surrender Singapore to Japanese (**Feb. 15**). U.S. forces on Bataan peninsula in Philippines surrender (**April 9**). U.S. and Filipino troops on Corregidor island in Manila Bay surrender to Japanese (**May 6**). Village of Lidice in Czechoslovakia razed by Nazis (**June 10**). U.S. and Britain

land in French North Africa (**Nov. 8**).

**1943** Casablanca Conference—Churchill and FDR agree on unconditional surrender goal (**Jan. 14–24**). German 6th Army surrenders at Stalingrad—turning point of war in Russia (**Feb. 1–2**). Remnants of Nazis trapped on Cape Bon, ending war in Africa (**May 12**). Mussolini deposed; Badoglio named premier (**July 25**). Allied troops land on Italian mainland after conquest of Sicily (**Sept. 3**). Italy surrenders (**Sept. 8**). Nazis seize Rome (**Sept. 10**). Cairo Conference: FDR, Churchill, Chiang Kai-shek pledge defeat of Japan, free Korea (**Nov. 22–26**). Teheran Conference: FDR, Churchill, Stalin agree on invasion plans (**Nov. 28–Dec. 1**).

**1944** U.S. and British troops land at Anzio on west Italian coast and hold beachhead (**Jan. 22**). U.S. and British troops enter Rome (**June 4**). D-Day—Allies launch Normandy invasion (**June 6**). Hitler wounded in bomb plot (**July 20**). Paris liberated (**Aug. 25**). Athens freed by Allies (**Oct. 13**). Americans invade Philippines (**Oct. 20**). Germans launch counteroffensive in Belgium—Battle of Bulge (**Dec. 16**).

**1945** Yalta Agreement signed by FDR, Churchill, Stalin—establishes basis for occupation of Germany, returns to Soviet Union lands taken by Germany and Japan; U.S.S.R. agrees to friendship pact with China (**Feb. 11**). Mussolini killed at Lake Como (**April 28**). Admiral Doenitz takes command in Germany; suicide of Hitler announced (**May 1**). Berlin falls (**May 2**). V-E Day—Germany signs unconditional surrender terms at Rheims (**May 7**). Potsdam Conference—Truman, Churchill, Atlee (after **July 28**), Stalin establish council of foreign ministers to prepare peace treaties; plan German postwar government and reparations (**July 17–Aug. 2**). A-bomb blasts Hiroshima (**Aug. 6**). U.S.S.R. declares war on Japan (**Aug. 8**). Nagasaki hit by A-bomb (**Aug. 9**). Japan surrenders (**Aug. 14**). V-J Day—Japanese sign surrender terms aboard battleship *Missouri* (**Sept. 2**).

**D-Day, June 6, 1944**

**Winston Churchill, Franklin D. Roosevelt, and Joseph V. Stalin at Yalta**

**1941** Japanese surprise attack on U.S. fleet at Pearl Harbor brings U.S. into World War II. Manhattan Project (atomic bomb research) begins. Roosevelt enunciates "four freedoms," signs lend-lease act, declares national emergency, promises aid to U.S.S.R.

**1942** Declaration of United Nations signed in Washington. Women's military services established. Enrico Fermi achieves nuclear chain reaction. Japanese and persons of Japanese ancestry moved inland from Pacific Coast. Coconut Grove nightclub fire in Boston kills 491.

**1943** President freezes prices, salaries, and wages to prevent inflation. Income tax withholding introduced.

**1944** G.I. Bill of Rights enacted. Bretton Woods Conference creates International Monetary Fund and World Bank. Dumbarton Oaks Conference—U.S., British Commonwealth, and U.S.S.R. propose establishment of United Nations.

**1945** Yalta Conference (Roosevelt, Churchill, Stalin) plans final defeat of Germany (**Feb.**). Germany surrenders (**May 7**). San Francisco Conference establishes U.N. (**April–June**). FDR dies (April 12). Potsdam Conference (Truman, Churchill, Stalin) establishes basis of German reconstruction (**July–Aug**). Japan surrenders (**Sept. 2**).

**1946** First meeting of U.N. General Assembly opens in London (**Jan. 10**). League of Nations dissolved (**April**). Italy abolishes monarchy (**June**). Verdict in Nuremberg war trial: 12 Nazi leaders (including 1 tried in absentia) sentenced to hang; 7 imprisoned; 3 acquitted (**Oct. 1**). Goering commits suicide a few hours before 10 other Nazis are executed (**Oct. 15**). Winston Churchill's "Iron Curtain" speech warns of Soviet expansion.

**1947** Britain nationalizes coal mines (**Jan. 1**). Peace treaties for Italy, Romania, Bulgaria, Hungary, Finland signed in Paris (**Feb. 10**). Soviet Union rejects U.S. plan for U.N. atomic-energy control (**March 4**). Truman Doctrine proposed—the first significant U.S. attempt to "contain" communist expansion (**March 12**). Marshall Plan for European recovery proposed—a coordinated program to help European nations recover from ravages of war (**June**). (By 1951, this "European Recovery Program" had cost $11 billion.) India and Pakistan gain independence from Britain (**Aug. 15**). Cominform (Communist Information Bureau) founded under Soviet auspices to rebuild contacts among European Communist parties, missing since dissolution of Comintern in 1943 (**Sept.**). (Yugoslav party expelled in 1948 and Cominform disbanded in 1956.)

**1948** Gandhi assassinated in New Delhi by Hindu fanatic (**Jan. 30**). Communists seize power in Czechoslovakia (**Feb. 23–25**). Burma and Ceylon granted independence by Britain. Organization of American States (OAS) Charter signed at Bogotá, Colombia (**April 30**). Nation of Israel proclaimed; British end Mandate at midnight; Arab armies attack (**May 14**). Berlin airlift begins (**June 21**); ends May 12, 1949. Stalin and Tito break (**June 28**). Independent Republic of Korea is proclaimed, following election supervised by U.N. (**Aug. 15**). Verdict in Japanese war trial: Tojo and six others sentenced to hang (hanged Dec. 23); 18 imprisoned (**Nov. 12**). United States of Indonesia established as Dutch and Indonesians settled conflict (**Dec. 27**). Alger Hiss, former U.S. State Department official, indicted on perjury charges after denying passing secret documents to communist spy ring. Convicted in second trial (1950) and sentenced to five-year prison term.

**1949** Cease-fire in Palestine (**Jan. 7**). Truman proposes Point Four Program to help world's backward areas (**Jan. 20**). Israel signs armistice with Egypt (**Feb. 24**). Start of North Atlantic Treaty Organization (NATO)—treaty signed by 12 nations (**April 4**). German Federal Republic (West Germany) established (**Sept. 21**). Truman discloses Soviet Union has set off atomic explosion (**Sept. 23**). Communist People's Republic of China formally proclaimed (**Oct. 1**).

**1950** Truman orders development of hydrogen bomb (**Jan. 31**). Korean War (*see* special material on the "Korean War"). Assassination attempt on

---

## KOREAN WAR (1950–1953)

1950 North Korean Communist forces invade South Korea (June 25). U.N. calls for cease-fire and asks U.N. members to assist South Korea (June 27). Truman orders U.S. forces into Korea (June 27). North Koreans capture Seoul (June 28). Gen. Douglas MacArthur designated commander of unified U.N. forces (July 8). Pusan Beachhead—U.N. forces counterattack and capture Seoul (Aug.–Sept.), capture Pyongyang, North Korean capital (Oct.). Chinese Commu-

nists enter war (**Oct. 26**), force U.N. retreat toward 39th parallel (**Dec.**).

1951 Gen. Matthew B. Ridgeway replaces MacArthur after he threatens Chinese with massive retaliation (April 11). Armistice negotiations (July) continue with interruptions until **June 1953**.

1953 Armistice signed (**June 26**). Chinese troops withdraw from North Korea (**Oct. 26, 1958**), but over 200 violations of armistice noted in **1959**.

President Truman by Puerto Rican nationalists (**Nov. 1**). Brink's robbery in Boston; almost $3 million stolen (**Jan. 17**).

**1951** Six nations agree to Schuman Plan to pool European coal and steel (**March 19**)—in effect Feb. 10, 1953. Julius and Ethel Rosenberg sentenced to death for passing atomic secrets to Russians (**March**). Japanese peace treaty signed in San Francisco by 49 nations (**Sept. 8**). Color television introduced in U.S.

**1952** George VI dies; his daughter becomes Elizabeth II (**Feb. 6**). NATO conference approves European army (**Feb.**). AEC announces "satisfactory" experiments in hydrogen-weapons research; eyewitnesses tell of blasts near Enewetak (**Nov.**).

**1953** Gen. Dwight D. Eisenhower inaugurated President of United States (**Jan. 20**). Stalin dies (**March 5**). Malenkov becomes Soviet Premier; Beria, Minister of Interior; Molotov, Foreign Minister (**March 6**). Dag Hammarskjold begins term as U.N. Secretary-General (**April 10**). Edmund Hillary, of New Zealand, and Tenzing Norkay, of Nepal, reach top of Mt. Everest (**May 29**). East Berliners rise against Communist rule; quelled by tanks (**June 17**). Egypt becomes republic ruled by military junta (**June 18**). Julius and Ethel Rosenberg executed in Sing Sing prison (**June 19**). Korean armistice signed (**July 27**). Moscow announces explosion of hydrogen bomb (**Aug. 20**).

**1954** First atomic submarine *Nautilus*, launched (**Jan. 21**). Five U.S. Congressmen shot on floor of House as Puerto Rican nationalists fire from spectators' gallery; all five recover (**March 1**). Army *vs.* McCarthy inquiry—Senate subcommittee report blames both sides (**Apr. 22–June 17**). Dien Bien Phu, French military outpost in Vietnam, falls to Vietminh army (**May 7**). (*see* special material on the "Vietnam War.") U.S. Supreme Court (in *Brown* v. *Board of Education of Topeka*) unanimously bans racial segregation in public schools (**May 17**). Eisenhower launches world atomic pool without Soviet Union (**Sept. 6**). Eight-nation Southeast Asia defense treaty (SEATO) signed at Manila (**Sept. 8**). West Germany is granted sovereignty, admitted to NATO and Western European Union (**Oct. 23**). Dr. Jonas Salk starts innoculating children against polio. Algerian War of Independence against France begins (**Nov.**); France struggles to maintain colonial rule until 1962 when it agrees to Algeria's independence.

**1955** Nikolai A. Bulganin becomes Soviet Premier, replacing Malenkov (**Feb. 8**). Churchill resigns; Anthony Eden succeeds him (**April 6**). Federal Republic of West Germany becomes a sovereign state (**May 5**). Warsaw

**Jackie Robinson**

## VIETNAM WAR (1950–1975)

U.S., South Vietnam, and Allies versus North Vietnam and National Liberation Front (Viet Cong). Outstanding events:

**1950** President Truman sends 35-man military advisory group to aid French fighting to maintain colonial power in Vietnam.

**1954** After defeat of French at Dienbienphu, Geneva Agreements (**July**) provide for withdrawal of French and Vietminh to either side of demarcation zone (DMZ) pending reunification elections, which are never held. Presidents Eisenhower and Kennedy (from **1954** onward) send civilian advisors and, later, military personnel to support South Vietnamese.

**1960** Communists from National Liberation Front in South.

**1963** Ngo Dinh Diem, South Vietnam's premier, slain in coup (**Nov. 1**).

**1961–1963** U.S. military advisors rise from 2,000 to 15,000.

**1964** North Vietnamese torpedo boats reportedly attack U.S. destroyers in Gulf of Tonkin (**Aug. 2**). President Johnson orders retaliatory air strikes. Congress approves Gulf of Tonkin resolution (**Aug. 7**) authorizing President to take necessary steps to "maintain peace."

**1965** U.S. planes begin combat missions over South Vietnam. In **June**, 23,000 American advisors committed to combat. By end of year over 184,000 U.S. troops in area.

**1966** B-52s bomb DMZ, reportedly used by North Vietnam for entry into South (**July 31**).

**1967** South Vietnam National Assembly approves election of Nguyen Van Thieu as President (**Oct. 21**).

**1968** U.S. has almost 525,000 men in Vietnam. In Tet offensive (**Jan.–Feb.**), Viet Cong guerrillas attack Saigon, Hue, and some provincial capitals. President Johnson orders halt to U.S. bombardment of North Vietnam (**Oct. 31**). Saigon and N.L.F. join U.S. and North Vietnam in Paris peace talks.

**1969** President Nixon announces Vietnam peace offer (**May 14**)—begins troop withdrawals (**June**). Viet Cong forms Provisional Revolutionary Government. U.S. Senate calls for curb on commitments (**June 25**). Ho Chi Minh, 79, North Vietnam president, dies (**Sept. 3**); collective leadership chosen. Some 6,000 U.S. troops pulled back from Thailand and 1,000 marines from Vietnam (announced **Sept. 30**). Massive demonstrations in U.S. protest or support war policies (**Oct. 15**).

**1970** Nixon announces sending of troops to Cambodia (**April 30**). Last U.S. troops removed from Cambodia (**June 29**).

**1971** Congress bars use of combat troops, but not air power, in Laos and Cambodia (**Jan. 1**). South Vietnamese troops, with U.S. air cover, fail in Laos thrust. Many American ground forces withdrawn from Vietnam combat. *New York Times* publishes Pentagon papers, classified material on expansion of war (**June**).

**1972** Nixon responds to North Vietnamese drive across DMZ by ordering mining of North Vietnam ports and heavy bombing of Hanoi-Haiphong area (**April 1**). Nixon orders "Christmas bombing" of north to get North Vietnamese back to conference table (**Dec.**).

**1973** President orders halt to offensive operations in North Vietnam (**Jan. 15**). Representatives of North and South Vietnam, U.S., and N.L.F. sign peace pacts in Paris, ending longest war in U.S. history (**Jan. 27**).

**1974** Both sides accuse each other of frequent violations of cease-fire agreement.

**1975** Full-scale warfare resumes. Communists victorious (**April 30**). South Vietnam Premier Nguyen Van Thieu resigns (**April 21**). American troops evacuated (**April 30**). More than 140,000 Vietnamese refugees leave by air and sea, many to settle in U.S. Provisional Revolutionary Government takes control (**June 6**).

**1976** Election of National Assembly paves way for reunification of North and South.

Pact, east European mutual defense agreement, signed (**May 14**). Argentina ousts Perón (**Sept. 19**). President Eisenhower suffers coronary thrombosis in Denver (**Sept. 24**). Martin Luther King, Jr., leads black boycott of Montgomery, Ala., bus system (**Dec. 1**); desegregated service begun (**Dec. 21**). AFL and CIO become one organization—AFL-CIO (**Dec. 5**).

**1956** Nikita Khrushchev, First Secretary of U.S.S.R. Communist Party, denounces Stalin's excesses (**Feb. 24**). First aerial H-bomb tested over Namu islet, Bikini Atoll—10 million tons TNT equivalent (**May 21**). Worker's uprising against Communist rule in Poznan, Poland, is crushed (**June 28–30**). Egypt takes control of Suez Canal (**July 26**). Israel launches attack on Egypt's Sinai peninsula and drives toward Suez Canal (**Oct. 29**). British and French invade Egypt at Port Said (**Nov. 5**). Cease-fire forced by U.S. pressure stops British, French, and Israeli advance (**Nov. 6**). Revolt starts in Hungary—Soviet troops and tanks crush anti-Communist rebellion (**Nov.**),

**Yuri Gagarin**

**1957** Eisenhower Doctrine calls for aid to Mideast countries which resist armed aggression from Communist-controlled nations (**Jan. 5**). Eisenhower sends troops to Little Rock, Ark., to quell mob and protect school integration (**Sept. 24**). Russians launch *Sputnik I*, first earth-orbiting satellite—the Space Age begins (**Oct. 4**).

**1958** Army's Jupiter-C rocket fires first U.S. earth satellite, *Explorer I*, into orbit (**Jan. 31**). Egypt and Syria merge into United Arab Republic (**Feb. 1**). European Economic Community (Common Market) established by Rome Treaty becomes effective **Jan. 1, 1958**. Khrushchev becomes Premier of Soviet Union as Bulganin resigns (**Mar. 27**). Gen. Charles de Gaulle becomes French premier (**June 1**), remaining in power until 1969. New French constitution adopted (**Sept. 28**), de Gaulle elected president of 5th Republic (**Dec. 21**). Eisenhower orders U.S. Marines into Lebanon at request of President Chamoun, who fears overthrow (**July 15**).

**1959** Cuban President Batista resigns and flees—Castro takes over (**Jan. 1**). Tibet's Dalai Lama escapes to India (**Mar. 31**). St. Lawrence Seaway opens, allowing ocean ships to reach Midwest (**April 25**).

**1960** American U-2 spy plane, piloted by Francis Gary Powers, shot down over Russia (**May 1**). Khrushchev kills Paris summit conference because of U-2 (**May 16**). Powers sentenced to prison for 10 years (**Aug. 19**)—freed in **February 1962** in exchange for Soviet spy. Top Nazi murderer of Jews, Adolf Eichmann, captured by Israelis in Argentina (**May 23**)—executed in Israel in **1962**. Communist China and Soviet Union split in conflict over Communist ideology. Belgium starts to break up its African colonial empire, gives independence to Belgian Congo (Zaire) on **June 30**. Cuba begins confiscation of $770 million of U.S. property (**Aug. 7**).

**1961** U.S. breaks diplomatic relations with Cuba (**Jan. 3**). John F. Kennedy inaugurated President of U.S. (**Jan. 20**). Kennedy proposes Alliance for Progress—10-year plan to raise Latin American living standards (**Mar. 13**). Moscow announces putting first man in orbit around earth, Maj. Yuri A. Gagarin (**April 12**). Cuba invaded at Bay of Pigs by an estimated 1,200 anti-Castro exiles aided by U.S.; invasion crushed (**April 17**). First U.S. spaceman, Navy Cmdr. Alan B. Shepard, Jr., rockets 116.5 miles up in 302-mile trip (**May 5**). Virgil Grissom becomes second American astronaut, making 118-mile-high, 303-mile-long rocket flight over Atlantic (**July 21**). Gherman Stepanovich Titov is launched in Soviet spaceship *Vostok II:* makes 17 1/2 orbits in 25 hours, covering 434,960 miles before landing safely (**Aug. 6**). East Germans erect Berlin Wall between East and West Berlin to halt flood of refugees (**Aug. 13**). U.S.S.R. fires 50-megaton hydrogen bomb, biggest explosion in history (**Oct. 29**).

**1962** Lt. Col. John H. Glenn, Jr., is first American to orbit earth—three times in 4 hr 55 min (**Feb. 20**). Adolf Eichmann hanged in Israel for his part in Nazi extermination of six million Jews (**May 31**). France transfers sovereignty to new republic of Algeria (**July 3**). Cuban missile crisis—U.S.S.R. to build missile bases in Cuba; Kennedy orders Cuban blockade, lifts blockade after Russians back down (**Aug.–Nov.**). James H. Meredith, escorted by Federal marshals, registers in University of Mississippi (**Oct. 1**). Pope John XXIII opens Second Vatican Council (**Oct. 11**)—Council holds four sessions, finally closing Dec. 8, 1965. Cuba releases 1,113 prisoners of 1961 invasion attempt (**Dec. 24**).

**1963** France and West Germany sign treaty of cooperation ending four centuries of conflict (**Jan. 22**). Pope John XXIII dies (**June 3**)—succeeded June 21 by Cardinal Montini, who becomes Paul VI. U.S. Supreme Court rules no locality may require recitation of Lord's Prayer or Bible verses in public schools (**June 17**). Civil rights rally held by 200,000 blacks and whites in Washington, D.C. (**Aug. 28**). Washington-to-Moscow "hot line" communications link opens, designed to reduce risk of accidental war (**Aug. 30**). President Kennedy shot and killed by sniper in Dallas, Tex. Lyndon B. Johnson becomes President same day (**Nov. 22**). Lee Harvey Oswald, accused assassin of President Kennedy, is shot and killed by Jack Ruby, Dallas nightclub owner (**Nov. 24**).

**1964** U.S. Supreme Court rules that Congressional districts should be roughly equal in population (**Feb. 17**). Jack Ruby convicted of murder in slaying of Lee Harvey Oswald; sentenced to death by Dallas jury (**March 14**)—conviction reversed **Oct. 5, 1966**; Ruby dies **Jan. 3, 1967,** before second trial can be held. Three civil rights workers—Schwerner, Goodman, and Cheney—murdered in Mississippi (**June**). Twenty-one arrests result in trial and conviction of seven by Federal jury. President's Commission on the Assassination of President Kennedy issues Warren Report concluding that Lee Harvey Oswald acted alone.

**1965** Rev. Dr. Martin Luther King, Jr., and more than 2,600 other blacks arrested in Selma, Ala., during three-day demonstrations against voter-registration rules (**Feb. 1**). Malcolm X, black-nationalist leader, shot to death at Harlem rally in New York City (**Feb. 21**). U.S. Marines land in Dominican Republic as fighting persists between rebels and Dominican army (**April 28**). Medicare, senior citizens' government medical assistance program, begins (**July 1**). Blacks riot for six days in Watts section of Los Angeles: 34 dead, over 1,000 injured, nearly 4,000 arrested, fire damage put at $175 million (**Aug. 11–16**). Power failure in Ontario plant blacks out parts of eight northeastern states of U.S. and two provinces of southeastern Canada (**Nov. 9**).

John F. Kennedy

**1966** Black teen-agers riot in Watts, Los Angeles; two men killed and at least 25 injured (**March 15**). Michael E. De Bakey implants artificial heart in human for first time at Houston hospital; plastic device functions and patient lives (**April 21**).

**1967** Three Apollo astronauts—Col. Virgil I. Grissom, Col. Edward White II, and Lt. Cmdr. Roger B. Chaffee—killed in spacecraft fire during simulated launch (**Jan. 27**). Israeli and Arab forces battle; six-day war ends with Israel occupying Sinai Peninsula, Golan Heights, Gaza Strip, and east bank of Suez Canal (**June 5**). Red China announces explosion of its first hydrogen bomb (**June 17**). Racial violence in Detroit; 7,000 National Guardsmen aid police after night of rioting. Similar outbreaks occur in New York City's Spanish Harlem, Rochester, N.Y., Birmingham, Ala., and New Britain, Conn. (**July 23**). Thurgood Marshall sworn in as first black U.S. Supreme Court justice (**Oct. 2**). Dr. Christian N. Barnard and team of South African surgeons perform world's first successful human heart transplant (**Dec. 3**)—patient dies 18 days later.

**1968** North Korea seizes U.S. Navy ship *Pueblo;* holds 83 on board as spies (**Jan. 23**). President Johnson announces he will not seek or accept presidential renomination (**March 31**). Martin Luther King, Jr., civil rights leader, is slain in Memphis (**April 4**)—James Earl Ray, indicted in murder, captured in London on **June 8**. In 1969 Ray pleads guilty and is sentenced to 99 years. Sen. Robert F. Kennedy is shot and critically wounded in Los Angeles hotel after winning California primary (**June 5**)—dies **June 6**. Sirhan B. Sirhan convicted **1969**. Czechoslovakia is invaded by Russians and Warsaw Pact forces to crush liberal regime (**Aug. 20**).

Martin Luther King, Jr.

**1969** Richard M. Nixon is inaugurated 37th President of the U.S. (**Jan. 20**). Apollo 11 astronauts—Neil A. Armstrong, Edwin E. Aldrin, Jr., and Michael Collins—take man's first walk on moon (**July 20**). Sen. Edward M. Kennedy pleads guilty to leaving scene of fatal accident at Chappaquiddick, Mass. (**July 18**) in which Mary Jo Kopechne was drowned—gets two-month suspended sentence (**July 25**).

**1970** Biafra surrenders after 32-month fight for independence from Nigeria (**Jan. 12**). Rhodesia severs last tie with British Crown and declares itself a racially segregated republic (**March 1**). Four students at Kent State University in Ohio slain by National Guardsmen at demonstration protesting April 30 incursion into Cambodia (**May 4**). Senate repeals Gulf of Tonkin resolution (**June 24**).

**1971** Supreme Court rules unanimously that busing of students may be ordered to achieve racial desegregation (**April 20**). Anti-war militants attempt to disrupt government business in Washington (**May 3**)—police and military units arrest as many as 12,000; most are later released. Twenty-sixth Amendment to U.S. Constitution lowers voting age to 18. U.N. seats Communist China and expels Nationalist China (**Oct. 25**).

**1972** President Nixon makes unprecedented eight-day visit to Communist China (**Feb.**). Britain takes over direct rule of Northern Ireland in bid for peace (**March 24**). Gov. George C. Wallace of Alabama is shot by Arthur H. Bremer at Laurel, Md., political rally (**May 15**). Five men are apprehended by police in attempt to bug Democratic National Committee headquarters in Washington D.C.'s Watergate complex—start of the Watergate scandal (**June 17**). Supreme Court rules that death penalty is unconstitutional (**June 29**). Eleven Israeli athletes at Olympic Games in Munich are killed after eight members of an Arab terrorist group invade Olympic Village; five guerrillas and one policeman are also killed (**Sept. 5**).

**1973** Great Britain, Ireland, and Denmark enter European Common Market (**Jan. 1**). Nixon, on national TV, accepts responsibility, but not blame, for Watergate; accepts resignations of advisers H. R. Haldeman and John D. Ehrlichman, fires John W. Dean III as counsel. (**April 30**). Greek military junta abolishes monarchy and proclaims republic (**June 1**). U.S. bombing of Cambodia ends, marking official halt to 12 years of combat activity in Southeast Asia (**Aug. 15**). Fourth and biggest Arab-Israeli War begins as Egyptian and Syrian forces attack Israel as Jews mark Yom Kippur, holiest day in their calendar. (**Oct. 6**). Spiro T. Agnew resigns as Vice President and then, in Federal Court in Baltimore, pleads no contest to charges of evasion of income taxes on $29,500 he received in 1967, while Governor of Maryland. He is fined $10,000 and put on three years' probation (**Oct. 10**). In the "Saturday Night Massacre," Nixon fires special Watergate prosecutor Archibald Cox and Deputy Attorney General William D. Ruckelshaus; Attorney General Elliot L. Richardson resigns (**Oct. 20**). Egypt and Israel sign U.S.-sponsored cease-fire accord (**Nov. 11**).

Voyager

**1974** Patricia Hearst, 19-year-old daughter of publisher Randolph Hearst, kidnapped by Symbionese Liberation Army. (**Feb. 5**). House Judiciary Committee adopts three articles of impeachment charging President Nixon with obstruction of justice, failure to uphold laws, and refusal to produce material subpoenaed by the committee (**July 30**). Richard M. Nixon announces he will resign the next day, the first President to do so (**Aug. 8**). Vice President Gerald R. Ford of Michigan is sworn in as 38th President of the U.S. (**Aug. 9**). Ford grants "full, free, and absolute pardon" to ex-President Nixon (**Sept. 8**).

**1975** John N. Mitchell, H. R. Haldeman, John D. Ehrlichman, and Robert C. Mardian found guilty of Watergate cover-up. Mitchell, Haldeman, and Ehrlichman are sentenced on Feb. 21 to 30 months-8 years in jail and Mardian to 10 months-3 years (**Jan. 1**). American merchant ship *Mayaguez*, seized by Cambodian forces, is rescued in operation by U.S. Navy and Marines, 38 of whom are killed (**May 15**). *Apollo* and *Soyuz* spacecraft take off for U.S.-Soviet link-up in space (**July 15**). President Ford escapes assassination attempt in Sacramento, Calif., (**Sept. 5**). President Ford escapes second assassination attempt in 17 days. (**Sept. 22**).

**1976** Supreme Court rules that blacks and other minorities are entitled to retroactive job seniority (**March 24**). Ford signs Federal Election Campaign Act (**May 11**). Supreme Court rules that death penalty is not inherently cruel or unusual and is a constitutionally acceptable form of punishment (**July 3**). Nation celebrates Bicentennial (**July 4**). Israeli airborne commandos attack Uganda's Entebbe Airport and free 103 hostages held by pro-Palestinian hijackers of Air France plane; one Israeli and several Ugandan soldiers killed in raid (**July 4**). Mysterious disease that eventually claims 29 lives strikes American Legion convention in Philadelphia (**Aug. 4**). Jimmy Carter elected U.S. President (**Nov. 2**).

Viking

**1977** First woman Episcopal priest ordained (**Jan. 1**). Scientists identify previously unknown bacterium as cause of mysterious "legionnaire's disease" (**Jan. 18**). Carter pardons Vietnam draft evaders (**Jan. 21**). Scientists report using bacteria in lab to make insulin (**May 23**). Supreme Court rules that states are not required to spend Medicaid funds on elective abortions (**June 20**). Deng Xiaoping, purged Chinese leader, restored to power as "Gang of Four" is expelled from Communist Party (**July 22**). Nuclear-proliferation pact, curbing spread of nuclear weapons, signed by 15 countries, including U.S. and U.S.S.R. (**Sept. 21**).

**1978** President chooses Federal Appeals Court Judge William H. Webster as F.B.I. Director (**Jan. 19**). Rhodesia's Prime Minister Ian D. Smith and three black leaders agree on transfer to black majority rule (**Feb. 15**). Former Italian Premier Aldo Moro kidnapped by left-wing terrorists, who kill five bodyguards (**March 16**); he is found slain (**May 9**). U.S. Senate approves Panama Canal neutrality treaty (**March 16**); votes treaty to turn canal over to Panama by year 2000 (**April 18**). Californians in referendum approve Proposition 13 for nearly 60% slash in property tax revenues (**June 6**). Supreme Court, in Bakke case, bars quota systems in college admissions but affirms constitutionality of programs giving advantage to minorities (**June 28**). Pope Paul VI, dead at 80, mourned (**Aug. 6**); new Pope, John Paul I, 65, dies unexpectedly after 34 days in office (**Sept. 28**); succeeded by Karol Cardinal Wojtyla of Poland as John Paul II (**Oct. 16**). "Framework for Peace" in Middle East signed by

Egypt's President Anwar el-Sadat and Israel Premier Menachem Begin after 13-day conference at Camp David led by President Carter (**Sept. 17**).

**1979** Oil spills pollute ocean waters in Atlantic and Gulf of Mexico (**Jan. 1, June 8, July 21**). Ohio agrees to pay $675,000 to families of dead and injured in Kent State University shootings (**Jan. 4**). Vietnam and Cambodian insurgents it backs announce fall of Phnom Penh, Cambodian capital, and collapse of Pol Pot regime (**Jan. 7**). Shah leaves Iran after year of turmoil (**Jan. 16**); revolutionary forces under Moslem leader, Ayatollah Ruhollah Khomeini take over (**Feb. 1** et seq.). Conservatives win British election; Margaret Thatcher new Prime Minister (**March 28**). Nuclear power plant accident at Three Mile Island, Pa., releases radioactivity (**March 28**). Carter and Brezhnev sign SALT II agreement (**June 14**). China signs three-year trade treaty with U.S. (**July 7**). Nicaraguan President Gen. Anastasio Somoza Debayle resigns and flees to Miami (**July 17**); Sandinists form government (**July 19**). Earl Mountbatten of Burma, 79, British World War II hero, and three others killed by blast on fishing boat off Irish coast (**Aug. 27**); two I.R.A. members accused (**Aug. 30**). Vietnamese start offensive against Pol Pot regime in Cambodia (**Sept. 25**). Park Chung Hee, 62, South Korea president for 18 years, assassinated by intelligence chief (**Oct. 26**). Iranian militants seize U.S. Embassy in Teheran and hold hostages (**Nov. 4**). Soviet invasion of Afghanistan stirs world protests (**Dec. 27**).

**Space Shuttle Columbia**

**1980** Six U.S. Embassy aides escape from Iran with Canadian help (**Jan. 29**). F.B.I.'s two-year undercover operation "Abscam" (for Arab scam) implicates public officials (**Feb. 2**). U.S. breaks diplomatic ties with Iran (**April 7**). Eight U.S. servicemen are killed and five are injured as helicopter and cargo plane collide in abortive desert raid to rescue American hostages in Teheran (**April 25**). Cyrus R. Vance resigns as Secretary of State (**April 28**); Senator Edmund S. Muskie of Maine succeeds him (**April 29**). Supreme Court upholds limits on federal aid for abortions (**June 30**). Justices approve affirmative action for minority contractors in federal works program (**July 2**). Olympic games open in Moscow, boycotted by U.S. and other nations (**July 19**). Shah of Iran dies at 60 (**July 27**). Anastasio Somoza Debayle, ousted Nicaragua ruler, and two aides assassinated in Asunción, Paraguay capital (**Sept. 17**). Iraq troops hold 90 square miles of Iran after invasion (**Sept. 19**). Aleksei N. Kosygin, 79, ailing Soviet Prime Minister, resigns (**Oct. 23**). Ronald Reagan elected President in Republican sweep (**Nov. 4**). Three U.S. nuns and lay worker found slain in El Salvador (**Dec. 4**). John Lennon of Beatles shot dead in New York City (**Dec. 8**).

**1981** U.S.-Iran agreement frees 52 hostages held in Teheran since Nov. 4, 1979 (**Jan. 18**); hostages welcomed back in U.S. (**Jan. 25**). Ronald Reagan takes oath as 40th President (**Jan. 20**). President Reagan wounded by gunman, with press secretary, and two law-enforcement officers (**March 30**). Hunger strikers die in Belfast prison protest (**May 5-July 13**). Pope John Paul II wounded by gunman (**May 14**). Israeli planes destroy Iraqi atomic reactor (**June 8**). Supreme Court rules, 4-4, that former President Nixon and three top aides may be required to pay monetary damages for unconstitutional wiretap of home telephone of former national security aide (**June 22**). Congress supports Reagan's $35.5-billion budget cuts designed to reverse government's expansion (**June 26-July 31**). Reagan nominates Judge Sandra Day O'Connor, 51, of Arizona as first woman on Supreme Court (**July 7**). More than 110 die in collapse of aerial walkways in lobby of Hyatt Regency Hotel in Kansas City; 188 injured (**July 18**). Millions around world view wedding of Prince Charles of Britain, 32, and Lady Diana Spencer, 20 (**July 29**). Air controllers strike, disrupting flights (**Aug. 3**). Government dismisses strikers (**Aug. 11**).

**Sandra Day O'Connor**

**1982** *Philadelphia Bulletin* ceases publication (**Jan. 29**). British overcome Argentina in Falklands war (**April 2-June 15**). British Queen gives Canada its Constitution (**April 17**). Israel completes withdrawal from Sinai (**April 25**). Israel invades Lebanon in attack on P.L.O. (**June 4**). John W. Hinckley, Jr., found not guilty because of insanity in shooting of President Reagan (**June 21**). Princess of Wales gives birth to a boy (**June 21**). Alexander M. Haig, Jr., resigns as Secretary of State (**June 25**). Equal rights amendment fails ratification (**June 30**). Bomb blast kills Lebanon President-elect, Bashir Gemayel (**Sept. 14**). His brother, Amin Gemayel, is elected to succeed him (**Sept. 21**). Lebanese Christian Phalangists kill hundreds of people in two Palestinian refugee camps in West Beirut (**Sept. 15**). Princess Grace, 52, dies of injuries when car plunges off mountain road. Daughter Stephanie, 17, suffers serious injuries (**Sept. 14**). Polish Parliament outlaws Solidarity and all existing labor unions (**Oct. 8**). Leonid I. Brezhnev, Soviet leader, dies at 75 (**Nov. 10**). Yuri V. Andropov, 68, chosen as his successor (**Nov. 15**). Space shuttle *Columbia* lands at Edwards Air Force Base, Calif., after successful five-day inaugural trip (**Nov. 16**). Artificial heart implanted for first time in Dr. Barney B. Clark, 61, at University of Utah Medical Center in Salt Lake City (**Dec. 2**). Barney Clark dies (**March 23, 1983**).

**1983** Jim Thorpe's Olympic gold medals won in 1912 are posthumously returned to him at Los Angeles (**Jan. 18**). George C. Wallace becomes the first man to be inaugurated for fourth term as Governor of Alabama (**Jan. 19**). Pope John Paul II signs new Roman Catholic code incorporating changes brought about by Second Vatican Council (**Jan 25**). Key subatomic "W" particle discovered after 40-year search by scientific team at CERN research center near Geneva (**Jan. 26**). Snowstorm paralyzes Northeast, fourteen deaths reported (**Feb. 12**). Congressional commission charges internment of 120,000 Japanese citizens and resident aliens in World War II was a grave injustice (**Feb. 24**). Queen Elizabeth and Prince Philip arrive at San Diego, Calif., on first stop of North American tour (**Feb. 26**). Supreme Court votes 5–4 to uphold age bias law (**March 2**). Final episode of CBS-TV series, M*A*S*H, draws an estimated 125 million viewers (**March 2**). EPA head, Anne McGill Burford, resigns in dispute over investigation of environmental agency (**March 9**). John Paul II completes visit to seven Central American countries (**March 10**). Employees agree to buy National Steel's Weiton Steel Works for $66 million (**March 13**). OPEC members agree to cut oil prices for first time (**March 14**). Congress votes $4.6 billion for emergency jobs bill (**March 21**). More than 200 people are killed in Popauan, Columbia, earthquake (**March 31**). Thousands of demonstrators in Europe protest nuclear weapons on European soil (**April 1**). U.S. grants asylum to Chinese tennis star, Hu Na, 19, who defected during tournament in California, July 1982 (**April 4**). Second space shuttle *Challenger* makes successful maiden voyage which included the first U.S. space walk in nine years (**April 4**). More than 27,000 people are displaced and at least 10 killed after 20 inches of rain fall in Gulf Coast states (**April 8**). Harold Washington, 60, becomes the first black mayor elected in Chicago (**April 12**). Severe earthquake shakes Coalinga, Calif., injuring 47, and causing an estimated $31 million in property damage (**May 2**). U.S. bishops denounce the testing, manufacture, and deployment of nuclear weapons (**May 3**). West German Interior Ministry declares Hitler diaries published in *Stern* magazine a hoax (**May 6**). New York celebrates 100th anniversary of the Brooklyn Bridge (**May 24**). Lt. Cmdr. Albert Schaufelberger, 3rd, American military advisor in San Salvador, killed by four assassins (**May 25**). Death toll over 200 after a Nile steamer burns and sinks (**May 25**). Earthquake strikes Northern Japan, killing almost 100 people (**May 26**). *Pioneer 10* spacecraft launched March 3, 1972, crosses the orbit of Neptune and departs the planetary system (**June 13**). U.S. Supreme Court declares many local abortion restrictions unconstitutional (**June 15**). Sally K. Ride, 32, becomes the first U.S. woman astronaut in space as a crew member aboard the space shuttle *Challenger* (**June 18**). Supreme court votes, 7–2, to restrict rights of Congress to overrule actions by the Executive Branch (**June 23**). Yasir Arafat, P.L.O. leader, is expelled from Syria by Syrian army head (**June 24**). Proposed anti-abortion constitutional amendment rejected by Senate in 50–40 vote (**June 28**). Supreme Court declares life prison sentence without possibility of parole for minor crime is unconstitutional (**June 28**). Ecuadorean jetliner crashes in mountain near Cuenca, killing 119 (**July 11**). Armenian terrorists explode bomb at Orly Airport, Paris, killing six, and injuring 56 others (**July 15**). Polish government lifts martial law (**July 22**). U.S. admits shielding former Nazi Gestapo chief, Klaus Barbie, 69, the "butcher of Lyons," wanted by French Government for war crimes (**Aug. 15**). Benigno S. Aquino, Jr., 50, political rival of Philippine President Marcos, slain in Manila (**Aug. 21**). Air Force Col. Guion S. Bluford, Jr., 40, becomes the first black astronaut in space shuttle *Challenger* (**Aug. 30**). A South Korean Boeing 747 jetliner bound for Seoul apparently strays off course into Soviet air space and is shot down by a Soviet SU-15 fighter after it had tracked the airliner for two hours; all 269 aboard are killed, including 61 Americans (**Aug. 30**). Brazil assured of $11 billion in credits from International Monetary Fund (**Sept. 26**). Bomb explosion in Burma kills South Korean officials (**Oct. 9**). Terrorist explosion kills 237 U.S. Marines in Beirut (**Oct. 23**). U.S. and Caribbean Allies invade Grenada (**Oct. 25**). Rita Lavelle, former EPA official, guilty of perjury (**Dec. 1**). Lech Walesa's wife accepts his Nobel Peace Prize (**Dec. 10**). Hundreds die in Guinea earthquake (**Dec. 21**).

**1984** Bell System broken up, with its 22 local telephone companies organized into regional holding companies; AT&T divided into AT&T Communications and AT&T Technologies Inc. (**Jan. 1**). France gets first deliveries of Soviet natural gas (**Jan. 1**). Syria frees captured U.S. Navy pilot, Lieut.

Sally K. Ride

Lech Walesa

Robert C. Goodman, Jr., after appeal by Rev. Jesse H. Jackson (**Jan. 3**).
Supreme Military Council named to rule Nigeria (**Jan. 3**). Paul Thayer
resigns as deputy defense secretary amid inquiry into charges of furnishing confidential stock market information (**Jan. 4**). Woman in Australia
is mother of first "test tube" quadruplets (**Jan. 6**). Rita Lavelle sentenced
to six months and $10,000 fine for lying about EPA program to clean
up hazardous waste (**Jan. 9**). U.S. and Vatican exchange diplomats after
116-year hiatus (**Jan. 10**). Former President Reynaldo Bignone arrested
in Argentina in presumed slaying of two Communists (**Jan. 10**). U.S. and
China sign agreements on industrial cooperation and renew accords on
science and technology (**Jan. 12**). Supreme Court, 5-4, upholds use of
video recorders in homes (**Jan. 17**). George Orwell's *1984* becomes
fastest-selling book in U.S. (**Jan. 18**). State Department found to have
revealed in 1947 postwar aid by Vatican to escaped Nazis (**Jan. 26**).
*Challenger* carries out 10th mission in space shuttle program (**Feb. 3-
11**). Reagan orders U.S. marines withdrawn from Beirut international
peacekeeping force (**Feb. 7**). Yuri V. Andropov dies at 69; Konstantin
U. Chernenko, 72, named Soviet Union leader (**Feb. 9**). China and Soviet
Union sign $1.2-billion trade agreement (**Feb. 10**). Italy and Vatican
reach accord ending Roman Catholicism as state religion (**Feb. 18**). Federal judge in Manhattan metes maximum sentences to four convicted
in Brink's armored car robbery (**Feb. 18**). Supreme Court, 6-3, upholds
Reagan stand that rights statute is enforceable only on specific programs
getting Federal education aid (**Feb. 28**). Justices rule, 5-4, that a city can
constitutionally use public funds for Christmas creche (**March 5**). Four
sentenced to prison for 1983 rape of woman in Massachusetts tavern
(**March 17 and 25**). Senate votes down school prayer amendment
(**March 20**). Four armed men seize $21.8 million in Rome, Italy's largest
single theft (**March 24**). Reagan ends U.S. role in Beirut by releasing
Sixth Fleet from peacekeeping force for duty elsewhere in Mediterranean (**March 30**). First baby born from frozen embryo in Australia (**April
10**). Congress rebukes President Reagan on use of federal funds for mining Nicaraguan harbors (**April 10**). Space shuttle *Challenger* ends seven-
day mission on which satellite was repaired in orbit (**April 13**). Gunman
fires from Libyan Embassy into London crowd, killing British police-
woman (**April 17**). Twenty-nine die as Dominican crowd battles police
in rioting over price increases (**April 24**). Robert Kennedy's son, David,
found dead in Florida hotel (**April 25**). U.S. fines Swedish importer $3
million for illegal shipments to Soviet Union (**April 27**). Pope visits Far
East and conducts first canonization outside Rome since Middle Ages
(**May 2-11**). Soviet Union withdraws from summer Olympic Games in
U.S. and other bloc nations follow (**May 7** et seq.). Seven Agent Orange
makers create $180-million fund for Vietnam veterans harmed by her-
bicide (**May 7**). World Court rules against U.S. on mining of Nicaraguan
harbors (**May 10**). Federal judge finds U.S. negligent in 1950 atomic tests
(**May 10**). José Napoleón Duarte, moderate, elected president of El Salvador (**May 11**). Supreme Court refuses to review conviction of Rev. Sun
Myung Moon on income tax charges (**May 14**); he enters prison (**July
21**). Opposition makes strong showing in Philippine elections (**May 23**).
President Reagan visits Ireland and England (**June 4** et seq.). Three hundred slain as Indian Army occupies Sikh Golden Temple in Amritsar
(**June 6**). Summit conference of industrial nations pledges aid to debtor
countries (**June 7**). Italians link Bulgarians to attack on Pope (**June 9**).
Swale, 3-year-old winner of Kentucky Derby and Belmont Stakes, drops
dead (**June 17**). Supreme Court rules states can force Jaycees to admit
women (**July 3**). Justices, 6-3, relax rules on evidence from defective
search warrants (**July 5**). Fire damages York Minster Cathedral in England (**July 9**). Nation's first compulsory seat-belt law enacted in New
York (**July 11**). Thirty-ninth Democratic National Convention, in San
Francisco, nominates Walter F. Mondale and Geraldine A. Ferraro (**July
16-19**). Nude photos cost Vanessa Williams title as Miss America (**July
20-23**). Thirty-third Republican National Convention, at Dallas, renomi-
nates President Reagan and Vice President Bush (**Aug. 20-25**). Russians
successfully test cruise missiles (**Aug. 25**). Thomas C. Reed, former national security official, indicted on stock charges (**Aug. 30**). Brian Mulroney and Conservative party win Canadian election in landslide (**Sept.
4**). British Prime Minister Margaret Thatcher nearly killed by I.R.A. assassination attempt (**Oct. 12**). Indian Prime Minister Indira Gandhi assassinated by two Sikh bodyguards; 1,000 killed in later anti-Sikh riots;
son Rajiv succeeds her (**Oct. 31**). President Reagan re-elected in landslide with 59% of vote (**Nov. 7**). First Sumerian dictionary published
(**Nov. 30**). Toxic gas leaks from Union Carbide plant in Bhopal, India,
killing 2,000 and injuring 150,000 (**Dec. 3**). Bronze Age artifacts uncovered in 3,400-year old shipwreck (**Dec. 4**).

**Geraldine A. Ferraro**

**1985** U.S. and Soviet Union reach compromise agreement on resuming negotiations on limiting and reducing nuclear arms and preventing arms race in space **(Jan. 8)**. Two-thousand refugee Ethiopian Jews perish in Sudan **(Jan. 18)**. Ronald Reagan, 73, takes oath for second term as 40th President **(Jan. 20)**. U.S. Court jury clears *Time* magazine of deliberate falsehood in libel suit brought by Ariel Sharon, Israel leader **(Jan. 24)**. New Zealand bars U.S. ship when Washington refuses to say whether she carries nuclear arms **(Feb. 4)**. President Reagan calls on Congress for major budget reductions **(Feb. 4)**; in State of Union Message he stresses tax revision and economic growth **(Feb. 6)**. Border of Gibraltar reopened under Spain-Britain agreement **(Feb. 5)**. Four Polish security officials convicted in abduction and murder of Rev. Jerzy Popieluszko, pro-Solidarity activist **(Feb. 7)**. Worldwide Conservative Rabbinical Assembly approves women in clergy **(Feb. 14)**. Vietnamese drive Cambodian rebels from last of their bases **(Feb. 15)**. General Westmoreland settles libel action against CBS **(Feb. 18)**. Prime Minister Margaret Thatcher addresses Congress, endorsing Reagan's policies **(Feb. 20)**. I.R.A. terrorists kill nine officers and civilians at Ulster police base **(Feb. 28)**. Uruguay ends military rule after 12 years **(March 1)**. Car bomb kills 62 in Beirut suburb; 200 wounded **(March 6)**. Kidnapped U.S. drug agent and his pilot slain in Mexico **(March 6)**. U.S.S.R. leader Chernenko dies at 73 and is replaced by Mikhail S. Gorbachev, 54 **(March 11)**. Secretary of Labor Raymond J. Donovan, facing New York fraud trial, resigns; first sitting Cabinet member to be indicted **(March 15)**. Civilian rule returns to Brazil after 12 years **(March 15)**. World honors Bach on 300th birthday **(March 21)**. Russian sentry kills U.S. officer on reconnaissance mission in East Germany **(March 25)**. A.H. Robins sets aside $615 million to settle claims over Dalkon Shield, contraceptive device **(April 2)**. Tens of thousands mark 40th anniversary of liberation of Buchenwald death camp **(April 13)**. Reagan target of wide attacks by Jewish leaders and others over visit to Bitburg Cemetary, West Germany, where SS troops are buried **(April 18 et seq.-May 5)**. Illinois Governor commutes convicted rapist's sentence **(May 12)**. Philadelphia police firebomb home of MOVE, organization of armed blacks, and fire spreads to neighboring homes; 11 dead and 200 homeless **(May 13)**. Thirty-eight killed in Brussels football riot **(May 29)**. House votes 248 to 184 to give $27 million in nonmilitary aid to Nicarauguan rebels **(June 12)**. Two Shiite Moslem gunmen capture TWA airliner with 133 aboard, 104 of them Americans **(June 14)**; 39 remaining hostages freed in Beirut **(June 30)**. Supreme Court, 5-4, bars public school teachers from parochial schools **(July 1)**. South Africa decrees state of emergency giving police and army near absolute power in black townships **(July 20)**. President Reagan undergoes surgery for removal of intestinal polyp, found to be noncancerous **(July 13-15)**. China's President Li Ziannian greeted in U.S.; he and Reagan agree on pact for sale of American nuclear equipment **(July 23)**. Arthur James Walker, 50, retired naval officer, convicted by federal judge of participating in Soviet spy ring **(Aug. 9)**. Spy scandal flares up in West Germany as top counterintelligence officer defects to East Germany **(Aug. 23)**. Pentagon scraps Sergeant York antiaircraft weapon after $1.8-billion outlay **(Aug. 27)**. Thousands dead in Mexico earthquake **(Sept. 19)**. French government shaken by scandal over sinking of antinuclear ship off New Zealand **(Sept. 22)**. Israelis bomb P.L.O. headquarters in Tunis in retaliation for slaying of three Israelis in Cyprus **(Oct. 1)**. P.L.O. terrorists hijack *Achille Lauro,* Italian cruise ship, with 80 passengers and crew **(Oct. 7)**; American, Leon Klinghoffer, killed **(Oct. 8)**.

**Ronald W. Reagan and
Mikhail S. Gorbachev**

(For later events, *See* Current Events, pages 962–974).

# WORLD STATISTICS

## Area and Population by Country
### Mid-1986 Estimates

| Country | Area[1] | Population | Country | Area[1] | Population |
|---|---|---|---|---|---|
| Afghanistan | 249,999 | 15,400,000 | Haiti | 10,714 | 5,900,000 |
| Albania | 11,100 | 3,000,000 | Honduras | 43,277 | 4,600,000 |
| Algeria | 919,591 | 22,800,000 | Hungary | 35,919 | 10,600,000 |
| Angola | 481,351 | 8,200,000 | Iceland | 39,768 | 200,000 |
| Antigua and Barbuda | 171 | 100,000 | India[3] | 1,266,595 | 785,000,000 |
| Argentina | 1,068,297 | 31,200,000 | Indonesia | 735,268 | 168,400,000 |
| Australia | 2,967,894 | 15,800,000 | Iran | 636,293 | 46,600,000 |
| Austria | 32,374 | 7,600,000 | Iraq | 167,924 | 16,000,000 |
| Bahamas | 5,380 | 200,000 | Ireland | 27,136 | 3,600,000 |
| Bahrain | 240 | 400,000 | Israel | 7,847 | 4,200,000 |
| Bangladesh | 55,598 | 104,100,000 | Italy | 116,303 | 57,200,000 |
| Barbados | 166 | 300,000 | Ivory Coast | 124,503 | 10,500,000 |
| Belgium | 11,781 | 9,900,000 | Jamaica | 4,232 | 2,300,000 |
| Belize | 8,867 | 200,000 | Japan | 143,750 | 121,500,000 |
| Benin | 43,483 | 4,100,000 | Jordan | 37,737 | 3,700,000 |
| Bhutan | 18,147 | 1,400,000 | Kenya | 224,960 | 21,000,000 |
| Bolivia | 424,162 | 6,400,000 | Korea, North | 46,540 | 20,500,000 |
| Botswana | 231,804 | 1,100,000 | Korea, South | 38,025 | 43,300,000 |
| Brazil | 3,286,472 | 143,000,000 | Kuwait | 6,880 | 1,800,000 |
| Brunei | 2,226 | 200,000 | Laos | 91,429 | 3,700,000 |
| Bulgaria | 42,823 | 9,000,000 | Lebanon | 4,015 | 2,700,000 |
| Burkina Faso[2] | 105,869 | 7,100,000 | Lesotho | 11,720 | 1,600,000 |
| Burma | 261,789 | 37,700,000 | Liberia | 43,000 | 2,300,000 |
| Burundi | 10,747 | 4,900,000 | Libya | 679,359 | 3,900,000 |
| Cambodia | 69,898 | 6,400,000 | Luxembourg | 998 | 400,000 |
| Cameroon | 183,568 | 10,000,000 | Madagascar | 226,657 | 10,300,000 |
| Canada | 3,851,790 | 25,600,000 | Malawi | 45,747 | 7,300,000 |
| Cape Verde | 1,557 | 300,000 | Malaysia | 127,316 | 15,800,000 |
| Central African Republic | 240,534 | 2,700,000 | Maldives | 115 | 200,000 |
| Chad | 495,753 | 5,200,000 | Mali | 478,764 | 7,900,000 |
| Chile | 292,257 | 12,300,000 | Malta | 122 | 400,000 |
| China, People's Republic of | 3,705,390 | 1,050,000,000 | Mauritania | 397,954 | 1,900,000 |
| China, Republic of | 13,885 | 19,600,000 | Mauritius | 790 | 1,000,000 |
| Colombia | 439,735 | 30,000,000 | Mexico | 761,601 | 81,700,000 |
| Comoros | 838 | 500,000 | Mongolia | 604,247 | 1,900,000 |
| Congo | 132,046 | 1,800,000 | Morocco | 172,413 | 23,700,000 |
| Costa Rica | 19,575 | 2,700,000 | Mozambique | 309,494 | 14,000,000 |
| Cuba | 44,218 | 10,200,000 | Nepal | 54,362 | 17,400,000 |
| Cyprus | 3,572 | 700,000 | Netherlands | 15,770 | 14,500,000 |
| Czechoslovakia | 49,370 | 15,500,000 | New Zealand | 103,736 | 3,300,000 |
| Denmark | 16,629 | 5,100,000 | Nicaragua | 50,193 | 3,300,000 |
| Djibouti | 8,494 | 300,000 | Niger | 489,189 | 6,700,000 |
| Dominica | 290 | 100,000 | Nigeria | 356,667 | 105,400,000 |
| Dominican Republic | 18,816 | 6,400,000 | Norway | 125,181 | 4,200,000 |
| Ecuador | 109,483 | 9,600,000 | Oman | 82,030 | 1,300,000 |
| Egypt | 386,660 | 50,500,000 | Pakistan[4] | 310,403 | 101,900,000 |
| El Salvador | 8,260 | 5,100,000 | Panama | 29,208 | 2,200,000 |
| Equatorial Guinea | 10,830 | 400,000 | Papua New Guinea | 178,259 | 3,400,000 |
| Ethiopia | 471,776 | 43,900,000 | Paraguay | 157,047 | 4,100,000 |
| Fiji | 7,055 | 700,000 | Peru | 496,222 | 20,200,000 |
| Finland | 130,119 | 4,900,000 | Philippines | 115,830 | 58,100,000 |
| France | 211,207 | 55,400,000 | Poland | 120,725 | 37,500,000 |
| Gabon | 103,346 | 1,200,000 | Portugal | 35,553 | 10,100,000 |
| Gambia | 4,361 | 800,000 | Qatar | 4,247 | 300,000 |
| Germany, East | 41,768 | 16,700,000 | Romania | 91,699 | 22,800,000 |
| Germany, West | 95,976 | 60,700,000 | Rwanda | 10,169 | 6,500,000 |
| Ghana | 92,099 | 13,600,000 | St. Lucia | 238 | 100,000 |
| Greece | 50,944 | 10,000,000 | St. Vincent and the Grenadines | 150 | 100,000 |
| Grenada | 133 | 100,000 | Saudi Arabia | 829,996 | 11,500,000 |
| Guatemala | 42,042 | 8,600,000 | Senegal | 75,750 | 6,900,000 |
| Guinea | 94,964 | 6,200,000 | Sierra Leone | 27,699 | 3,700,000 |
| Guinea-Bissau | 13,948 | 900,000 | Singapore | 224 | 2,600,000 |
| Guyana | 83,000 | 800,000 | Solomon Islands | 10,983 | 300,000 |

131

| Country | Area[1] | Population | Country | Area[1] | Population |
|---|---|---|---|---|---|
| Somalia | 246,200 | 7,800,000 | Uganda | 91,134 | 15,200,000 |
| South Africa | 471,443 | 33,200,000 | U.S.S.R. | 8,649,496 | 280,000,000 |
| Spain | 194,896 | 38,800,000 | United Arab Emirates | 32,278 | 1,400,000 |
| Sri Lanka | 25,332 | 16,600,000 | United Kingdom | 94,226 | 56,600,000 |
| Sudan | 967,495 | 22,900,000 | United States | 3,615,105 | 241,000,000 |
| Suriname | 63,037 | 400,000 | Uruguay | 68,037 | 3,000,000 |
| Swaziland | 6,704 | 700,000 | Vanuatu | 5,700 | 100,000 |
| Sweden | 173,731 | 8,400,000 | Venezuela | 352,143 | 17,800,000 |
| Switzerland | 15,941 | 6,500,000 | Vietnam | 128,401 | 62,000,000 |
| Syria | 71,498 | 10,500,000 | Western Samoa | 1,097 | 200,000 |
| Tanzania | 364,898 | 22,400,000 | Yemen, People's Democratic | 128,559 | 2,300,000 |
| Thailand | 198,456 | 52,800,000 | Republic of | | |
| Togo | 21,622 | 3,000,000 | Yemen Arab Republic | 75,290 | 6,300,000 |
| Tonga | 270 | 105,000 | Yugoslavia | 98,766 | 23,200,000 |
| Trinidad and Tobago | 1,200 | 1,200,000 | Zaire | 905,563 | 31,300,000 |
| Tunisia | 63,170 | 7,200,000 | Zambia | 290,584 | 7,100,000 |
| Turkey | 301,381 | 52,300,000 | Zimbabwe | 150,803 | 9,000,000 |

1. Square miles. 2. Formerly Upper Volta. 3. Includes the Indian-held part of Jammu and Kashmir. 4. Excludes the Pakistani-held part of Jammu and Kashmir. *Source: 1986 World Population Data Sheet,* Population Reference Bureau, Inc., Washington, D.C.

## Some Large Cities of the World

Census figures and population estimates in the following table are based on data reflecting different years. Some cities include metropolitan areas or contiguous suburbs, while others report only those residing within precise geographical or physical boundaries. Therefore, the ratings in this listing must be considered approximate.

| City | Population | Year | City | Population | Year |
|---|---|---|---|---|---|
| Addis Ababa, Ethiopia | 1,275,000 | 1980E | Chicago | 2,992,472 | 1984E |
| Ahmedabad, India | 2,548,057[1] | 1981E | Chittagong, Bangladesh | 1,388,476[2] | 1981C |
| Alexandria, Egypt | 2,317,705 | 1976C | Chongqing (Chungking), China | 3,890,000 | 1983E |
| Algiers | 2,500,000 | 1982E | Cologne, West Germany | 972,400 | 1984E |
| Amman, Jordon | 750,000 | 1981E | Copenhagen | 1,365,760 | 1984E |
| Amsterdam | 994,062 | 1983E | Cordoba, Argentina | 1,000,000 | 1983E |
| Ankara, Turkey | 2,251,533 | 1985C | Cuenca, Ecuador | 155,000 | 1983E |
| Antwerp, Belgium | 488,425 | 1984C | Dacca, Bangladesh | 3,500,000 | 1982E |
| Athens | 3,027,000 | 1981C | Damascus, Syria | 1,200,000 | 1981E |
| Auckland, New Zealand | 825,000 | 1982E | Delhi, India | 5,729,283[2] | 1981E |
| Baghdad, Iraq | 3,300,000 | 1982E | Dnepropetrovsk, U.S.S.R. | 1,140,000 | 1984E |
| Baku, U.S.S.R. | 1,661,000 | 1984E | Donetsk, U.S.S.R. | 1,055,000 | 1983E |
| Badung, Indonesia | 1,602,000 | 1983E | Dresden, East Germany | 519,607 | 1984E |
| Bangalore, India | 2,921,751[2] | 1981E | Dublin | 550,000 | 1982E |
| Bangkok | 5,174,682 | 1984E | Düsseldorf, West Germany | 570,700 | 1984E |
| Barcelona | 1,750,000 | 1983E | Edinburgh, Scotland | 444,700 | 1982E |
| Barranquilla, Colombia | 924,000 | 1982E | Edmonton, Canada | 657,057 | 1981C |
| Beirut, Lebanon | 750,000 | 1981E | Essen, West Germany | 628,800 | 1984E |
| Belfast, Northern Ireland | 324,900 | 1982E | Florence, Italy | 435,698 | 1984E |
| Belgrade, Yugoslavia | 1,250,000 | 1982E | Frankfurt, West Germany | 604,600 | 1984E |
| Belo Horizonte, Brazil | 2,500,000 | 1980E | Fukuoka, Japan | 1,162,000 | 1985E |
| Berlin[3] | 3,033,900 | 1983E | Geneva | 159,500 | 1984E |
| Bern, Switzerland | 140,600 | 1984E | Genoa, Italy | 738,099 | 1984E |
| Birmingham, England | 1,017,300 | 1982E | Glasgow, Scotland | 761,000 | 1982E |
| Bogotá, Colombia | 4,483,300 | 1982E | Gorky, U.S.S.R. | 1,392,000 | 1984E |
| Bombay | 8,248,405 | 1981E | Guadalajara, Mexico | 3,000,000 | 1980C |
| Brisbane, Australia | 1,146,600 | 1984E | Guatemala City | 1,250,000 | 1982E |
| Brussels | 982,434 | 1984E | Guayaquil, Ecuador | 1,750,000 | 1983E |
| Bucharest | 1,961,189 | 1982E | The Hague | 672,127 | 1983E |
| Budapest | 2,100,000 | 1982E | Haifa, Israel | 227,900 | 1983E |
| Buenos Aires | 3,000,000 | 1983E | Hamburg, West Germany | 1,600,300 | 1984E |
| Cairo | 12,000,000 | 1984E | Harbin, China | 3,730,000 | 1983E |
| Calcutta | 9,194,018 | 1981E | Havana | 1,972,000 | 1983E |
| Calgary, Canada | 592,743[2] | 1981C | Helsinki, Finland | 484,471 | 1983E |
| Cali, Colombia | 1,450,000 | 1982E | Ho Chi Minh City (Saigon), Vietnam | 3,450,000 | 1979E |
| Canton, China | 6,840,000 | 1983E | Hyderabad, India | 2,528,198[2] | 1981C |
| Cape Town, South Africa | 1,000,000 | 1984E | Hyderabad, Pakistan | 795,000[2] | 1981C |
| Caracas, Venezuela | 3,000,000[2] | 1981E | Ibadan, Nigeria | 847,000 | 1975E |
| Casablanca, Morocco | 2,139,204[2] | 1982E | Istanbul | 5,494,916 | 1985C |

| City | Population | Year | City | Population | Year |
|---|---|---|---|---|---|
| Jakarta, Indonesia | 7,636,000 | 1983E | Port-au-Prince, Haiti | 790,000 | 1980E |
| Jerusalem | 431,800 | 1983E | Porto Alegre, Brazil | 2,200,000 | 1980C |
| Johannesburg, South Africa | 1,700,000 | 1984E | Prague | 1,185,000 | 1982E |
| Kanpur, India | 1,639,064 [2] | 1981E | Pusan, South Korea | 3,500,000 | 1985E |
| Karachi, Pakistan | 5,208,100 | 1981C | Pyongyang, North Korea | 1,500,000 | 1982E |
| Kharkov, U.S.S.R. | 1,536,000 | 1984E | Quebec | 576,075 | 1981C |
| Kiev, U.S.S.R. | 2,409,000 | 1984E | Quezon City, Philippines | 1,175,000 | 1981E |
| Kinshasa, Zaire | 2,000,000 | 1982E | Quito, Ecuador | 880,000 | 1983E |
| Kobe, Japan | 1,413,000 | 1985E | Rangoon, Burma | 2,250,000 | 1983E |
| Kuala Lumpur, Malaysia | 1,000,000 | 1980E | Recife, Brazil | 2,300,000 | 1980C |
| Kuilbyshev, U.S.S.R. | 1,251,000 | 1984E | Rio de Janeiro | 9,000,000 | 1980C |
| Lagos, Nigeria | 4,000,000 [2] | 1980E | Riyadh, Saudi Arabia | 1,250,000 | 1980E |
| Lahore, Pakistan | 2,952,700 | 1981C | Rome | 2,826,733 | 1984E |
| La Paz, Bolivia | 954,000 | 1983E | Rosario, Argentina | 950,000 | 1983E |
| Lausanne, Switzerland | 126,200 | 1984E | Rotterdam | 1,025,466 | 1983E |
| Leipzig, East Germany | 557,129 | 1984E | Salvador, Brazil | 1,800,000 | 1980C |
| Leningrad | 4,827,000 | 1984E | San José, Costa Rica | 278,500 | 1984E |
| Liege, Belgium | 203,065 | 1984E | Santiago, Chile | 4,231,500 | 1985E |
| Lima | 4,164,000 | 1981E | Santo Domingo, Dominican Republic | 1,313,170 | 1982E |
| Lisbon | 900,000 | 1982E | São Paulo | 12,600,000 | 1980C |
| Liverpool, England | 510,700 | 1982E | Sapporo, Japan | 1,543,000 | 1985E |
| Lódz, Poland | 850,000 | 1982E | Seoul, South Korea | 9,600,000 | 1985E |
| London | 6,765,100 | 1982E | Seville, Spain | 650,000 | 1983E |
| Los Angeles | 3,096,721 | 1984E | Shanghai | 11,940,000 | 1983E |
| Lyons, France | 410,455 | 1982E | Sheffield, England | 545,800 | 1982E |
| Madras, India | 4,289,347 [2] | 1981E | Shenyang, China | 5,210,000 | 1983E |
| Madrid | 3,175,000 | 1983E | Singapore, Singapore | 2,500,000 | 1983E |
| Managua | 1,000,000 | 1985E | Sofia, Bulgaria | 1,094,000 | 1982E |
| Manchester, England | 458,600 | 1982E | Stockholm | 1,409,000 | 1985E |
| Manila | 1,750,000 | 1981E | Stuttgart, West Germany | 563,200 | 1984E |
| Marseilles, France | 868,435 | 1983E | Surabaja, Indonesia | 2,289,000 | 1983E |
| Mecca, Saudi Arabia | 750,000 | 1980E | Sverdlovsk, U.S.S.R. | 1,286,000 | 1984E |
| Medellin, Colombia | 1,664,000 | 1982E | Sydney | 3,358,000 | 1984E |
| Melbourne | 2,890,700 | 1984E | Taipei, Taiwan | 2,449,702 | 1984E |
| Mexico City | 12,900,000 | 1980C | Tashkent, U.S.S.R. | 1,986,000 | 1984E |
| Milan, Italy | 1,535,722 | 1984E | Tbilisi, U.S.S.R. | 1,140,000 | 1984E |
| Minsk, U.S.S.R. | 1,442,000 | 1984E | Teheran | 6,000,000 | 1982E |
| Monterrey, Mexico | 2,700,000 | 1980C | Tel Aviv, Israel | 330,400 | 1983E |
| Montevideo, Uruguay | 1,325,000 | 1982E | Tianjin (Tientsin), China | 7,850,000 | 1983E |
| Montreal | 2,828,349 [2] | 1981C | Tokyo | 8,425,000 | 1985E |
| Moscow | 8,037,000 | 1984E | Toronto | 2,998,947 [2] | 1981C |
| Munich, West Germany | 1,277,000 | 1984E | Tripoli, Libya | 1,000,000 | 1980E |
| Nagoya, Japan | 2,118,200 | 1985E | Tunis, Tunisia | 600,000 | 1981E |
| Nanjing (Nanking), China | 4,560,000 | 1983E | Turin, Italy | 1,049,997 | 1984E |
| Nantes, France | 237,789 | 1983E | Valparaiso, Chile | 266,900 | 1985E |
| Naples, Italy | 1,206,955 | 1984E | Valencia, Spain | 750,000 | 1983E |
| New York | 7,164,742 | 1984E | Vancouver, Canada | 1,268,183 [2] | 1981C |
| Nice, France | 331,165 | 1983E | Venice | 332,775 | 1981C |
| Novosibirsk, U.S.S.R. | 1,384,000 | 1984E | Vienna | 1,550,000 | 1983E |
| Odessa, U.S.S.R. | 1,097,000 | 1984E | Volgograd, U.S.S.R. | 962,000 | 1983E |
| Osaka, Japan | 2,634,000 | 1985E | Warsaw | 1,625,000 | 1982E |
| Oslo | 447,000 | 1985E | Washington, D.C. | 622,823 | 1984E |
| Ottawa | 717,978 [2] | 1981C | Wellington, New Zealand | 345,000 | 1982E |
| Palermo | 716,149 | 1984E | Winnipeg, Canada | 584,842 [2] | 1981C |
| Panama City, Panama | 400,000 | 1980E | Yokohama, Japan | 2,984,000 | 1985E |
| Paris | 2,150,000 | 1983E | Zurich | 354,500 | 1984E |
| Peking | 9,330,000 | 1983E | | | |

1. E = estimated; C = census. 2. Figure is for metropolitan area and may include suburbs or some rural population. 3. West Berlin, 1,860,900; East Berlin, 1,173,000. NOTE: The population of many other cities will be found throughout the World History section under individual countries. *See* Table of Contents.

## World Population Nearing Peak in Growth

The world population estimate for mid-1986 is 4.942 billion. This figure is nearly double the 2.5 billion count of 1950, at the start of the post-World War II "population explosion" in less developed countries touched off by sharp death rate declines initially unaccompanied by birth rate declines. The rate of global growth has passed its peak, declining from slightly over 2 percent a year in the late 1960s to 1.7 percent today, according to the Population Reference Bureau.

# Expectation of Life by Age and Sex for Selected Countries

| | | Average future lifetime in years at stated age | | | | | | | | | | | |
| | | Males | | | | | | Females | | | | | |
| Country | Period | 0 | 1 | 10 | 20 | 40 | 60 | 0 | 1 | 10 | 20 | 40 | 60 |
|---|---|---|---|---|---|---|---|---|---|---|---|---|---|
| **NORTH AMERICA** | | | | | | | | | | | | | |
| United States | 1983 | 71.0 | 70.9 | 62.1 | 52.6 | 34.1 | 17.8 | 78.3 | 78.0 | 69.2 | 59.5 | 40.2 | 22.6 |
| Canada | 1980-82 | 71.9 | 71.7 | 62.9 | 53.4 | 34.7 | 18.0 | 78.9 | 78.6 | 69.8 | 60.0 | 40.7 | 22.8 |
| Mexico | 1979 | 62.1 | — | — | — | — | — | 66.0 | — | — | — | — | — |
| Trinidad and Tobago | 1970 | 64.1 | 65.6 | 57.3 | 47.8 | 29.5 | 13.6 | 68.1 | 69.3 | 60.9 | 51.3 | 32.7 | 16.3 |
| **CENTRAL AND SOUTH AMERICA** | | | | | | | | | | | | | |
| Brazil | 1960-70 | 57.6 | — | 56.2 | 47.0 | 30.0 | 15.0 | 61.1 | — | 58.9 | 49.7 | 32.5 | 16.6 |
| Chile | 1975-80 | 61.3 | 65.2 | 57.7 | 48.3 | 30.9 | 15.9 | 67.6 | 70.6 | 62.8 | 53.2 | 35.2 | 18.9 |
| Costa Rica | 1972-74 | 66.3 | 69.1 | 61.3 | 51.8 | 33.8 | 17.4 | 70.5 | 72.7 | 64.9 | 55.2 | 36.5 | 19.2 |
| Ecuador[1] | 1974-79 | 59.5 | 63.3 | 57.4 | 48.6 | 32.1 | 16.5 | 61.8 | 65.4 | 59.2 | 50.3 | 33.5 | 17.4 |
| Guatemala | 1972-73 | 53.7 | — | 55.3 | 46.5 | 30.5 | 16.2 | 55.5 | — | 56.6 | 47.8 | 31.6 | 16.6 |
| Panama[2] | 1980-85 | 69.2 | 70.1 | 62.3 | 53.0 | 35.0 | 18.5 | 72.8 | 73.6 | 65.7 | 56.1 | 37.5 | 20.2 |
| Peru[3] | 1980-85 | 56.8 | — | — | — | — | — | 60.5 | — | — | — | — | — |
| Uruguay | 1974-76 | 65.7 | 68.3 | 59.8 | 50.2 | 31.8 | 16.0 | 72.4 | 74.5 | 66.1 | 56.4 | 37.4 | 20.0 |
| Venezulea | 1975-80 | 64.8 | 67.1 | 59.3 | 50.0 | 32.4 | 16.9 | 70.7 | 72.5 | 64.7 | 55.0 | 36.4 | 19.7 |
| **EUROPE** | | | | | | | | | | | | | |
| Austria | 1983 | 69.5 | 69.4 | 60.7 | 51.2 | 32.7 | 16.4 | 76.8 | 76.6 | 67.7 | 57.9 | 38.6 | 20.6 |
| Belgium | 1972-76 | 68.6 | 68.9 | 60.3 | 50.7 | 32.0 | 15.5 | 75.1 | 75.2 | 66.5 | 56.6 | 37.5 | 19.7 |
| Cyprus | 1979-81 | 72.3 | — | 63.8 | 54.0 | 34.6 | 17.3 | 76.0 | — | 67.2 | 57.3 | 37.7 | 19.5 |
| Czechoslovakia | 1982 | 67.1 | 67.4 | 58.8 | 49.2 | 30.5 | 14.8 | 74.4 | 74.4 | 65.9 | 56.0 | 36.6 | 18.9 |
| Denmark[4] | 1982-83 | 71.3 | 71.2 | 62.4 | 52.7 | 33.9 | 17.2 | 77.5 | 77.1 | 68.3 | 58.4 | 39.1 | 21.6 |
| Finland | 1983 | 70.1 | 69.6 | 60.8 | 51.1 | 32.4 | 16.1 | 77.9 | 77.4 | 68.5 | 58.7 | 39.3 | 21.0 |
| France | 1981 | 70.4 | 70.2 | 61.5 | 51.9 | 33.4 | 17.3 | 78.5 | 78.1 | 69.4 | 59.6 | 40.3 | 22.3 |
| Germany, East[5] | 1983 | 69.4 | 69.3 | 60.6 | 51.0 | 32.3 | 15.8 | 75.4 | 75.0 | 66.3 | 56.5 | 37.2 | 19.3 |
| Germany, West[5] | 1981-83 | 70.4 | 70.3 | 61.5 | 51.9 | 33.2 | 16.6 | 77.0 | 76.8 | 68.0 | 58.2 | 38.9 | 20.9 |
| Greece | 1970 | 70.1 | 72.2 | 63.8 | 54.1 | 35.1 | 17.5 | 73.6 | 75.3 | 66.9 | 57.1 | 37.8 | 19.3 |
| Hungary | 1983 | 65.5 | 66.0 | 57.2 | 47.6 | 29.4 | 15.0 | 73.4 | 73.7 | 64.9 | 55.1 | 36.0 | 18.9 |
| Ireland | 1978-80 | 69.4 | 69.4 | 60.8 | 51.1 | 32.2 | 15.6 | 74.9 | 74.8 | 66.0 | 56.2 | 36.8 | 19.1 |
| Italy | 1974-77 | 69.7 | 70.3 | 61.6 | 52.0 | 33.0 | 16.5 | 75.9 | 76.3 | 67.6 | 57.7 | 38.3 | 20.3 |
| Netherlands | 1982-83 | 72.7 | 72.4 | 63.6 | 53.9 | 39.5 | 17.4 | 79.4 | 79.0 | 70.2 | 60.4 | 45.7 | 22.7 |
| Norway | 1982-83 | 72.6 | 72.3 | 63.6 | 53.9 | 35.0 | 17.9 | 79.5 | 79.1 | 70.3 | 60.4 | 40.9 | 22.6 |
| Poland | 1983 | 67.0 | 67.5 | 58.8 | 49.2 | 31.0 | 15.6 | 75.1 | 75.4 | 66.6 | 56.8 | 37.5 | 19.9 |
| Portugal | 1975 | 65.1 | 67.0 | 58.8 | 49.4 | 31.4 | 15.6 | 72.9 | 74.5 | 66.2 | 56.5 | 37.3 | 19.6 |
| Spain | 1975 | 70.4 | 70.9 | 62.3 | 52.6 | 33.8 | 17.1 | 76.2 | 76.5 | 67.8 | 58.0 | 38.6 | 20.6 |
| Sweden | 1983 | 73.6 | 73.1 | 64.3 | 54.5 | 35.5 | 18.2 | 79.6 | 79.1 | 70.2 | 60.4 | 40.9 | 22.6 |
| Switzerland | 1981-82 | 72.7 | 72.3 | 63.6 | 53.9 | 35.3 | 18.1 | 79.6 | 79.1 | 70.3 | 60.5 | 41.2 | 22.9 |
| U.S.S.R. | 1971-72 | 64.0 | — | — | — | — | — | 74.0 | — | — | — | — | — |
| United Kingdom | | | | | | | | | | | | | |
| England and Wales | 1981-83 | 71.3 | 71.2 | 62.4 | 52.7 | 33.5 | 16.5 | 77.3 | 71.0 | 68.2 | 58.4 | 38.9 | 21.1 |
| Northern Ireland[6] | 1983 | 69.2 | 69.3 | 60.5 | 50.9 | 32.1 | 15.6 | 75.6 | 75.4 | 66.6 | 56.8 | 37.4 | 19.0 |
| Scotland | 1981-83 | 69.3 | 69.1 | 60.4 | 50.7 | 31.7 | 15.5 | 75.4 | 75.1 | 66.3 | 56.5 | 37.1 | 19.7 |
| Yugoslavia | 1980-81 | 67.6 | 68.9 | 60.4 | 50.7 | 32.2 | 12.8 | 73.2 | 74.4 | 65.8 | 56.0 | 36.7 | 15.0 |
| **ASIA** | | | | | | | | | | | | | |
| Bangladesh | 1981 | 55.3 | 61.3 | 57.5 | 48.2 | 30.0 | 14.7 | 54.4 | 60.0 | 56.8 | 47.9 | 30.8 | 16.0 |
| India | 1961-70 | 46.4 | 52.3 | 48.8 | 41.1 | 25.9 | 13.6 | 44.7 | 50.2 | 47.7 | 39.9 | 25.4 | 13.8 |
| Iran[3] | 1980-85 | 55.7 | 60.7 | 53.8 | 45.1 | 29.1 | 14.5 | 55.0 | 60.1 | 54.3 | 49.9 | 30.4 | 15.3 |
| Israel[7] | 1983 | 72.5 | 72.6 | 63.9 | 54.2 | 35.1 | 18.0 | 75.9 | 75.9 | 67.2 | 57.4 | 37.9 | 19.7 |
| Japan[8] | 1983 | 72.2 | 73.7 | 64.9 | 55.2 | 36.2 | 19.0 | 79.7 | 79.2 | 70.4 | 60.5 | 41.1 | 22.6 |
| Korea, South | 1978-79 | 62.7 | 63.7 | 55.6 | 46.2 | 28.1 | 12.7 | 69.1 | 71.0 | 63.5 | 53.9 | 35.0 | 17.9 |
| Pakistan | 1976-78 | 59.0 | 66.5 | 61.3 | 52.3 | 34.8 | 19.2 | 59.2 | 65.6 | 60.7 | 52.0 | 35.2 | 19.3 |
| Sri Lanka[3] | 1980-85 | 66.0 | — | — | — | — | — | 69.0 | — | — | — | — | — |
| Syria | 1981 | 63.8 | 66.9 | 59.9 | 50.7 | 32.7 | 16.2 | 64.7 | 67.0 | 60.1 | 50.9 | 32.8 | 16.2 |
| **AFRICA** | | | | | | | | | | | | | |
| Egypt[3] | 1980-85 | 56.4 | — | — | — | — | — | 58.2 | — | — | — | — | — |
| Kenya[3] | 1980-85 | 51.2 | — | — | — | — | — | 54.7 | — | — | — | — | — |
| South Africa[3] | 1980-85 | 51.8 | — | — | — | — | — | 55.2 | — | — | — | — | — |
| **OCEANIA** | | | | | | | | | | | | | |
| Australia[9] | 1983 | 72.0 | 71.8 | 63.1 | 53.5 | 34.7 | 17.6 | 78.7 | 78.4 | 69.6 | 59.7 | 40.3 | 22.3 |
| New Zealand | 1983 | 70.8 | 70.7 | 62.0 | 52.5 | 33.8 | 16.9 | 76.9 | 76.8 | 68.0 | 58.2 | 39.0 | 21.2 |

1. Excluding nomadic Indian tribes. 2. Excluding tribal Indian population. 3. Estimates prepared by the Population Division of the United Nations. 4. Excluding data for Faeroe Islands and Greenland. 5. Including relevant data relating to Berlin. No separate data have been supplied. 6. Provisional. 7. Including data for East Jerusalem and Israeli residents in certain other territories under occupation by Israeli military forces since June 1967. 8. Japanese nationals in Japan only. 9. Excluding full-blooded aborigines. NOTE: Figures are latest available. *Source:* United Nations *Demographic Yearbook, 1984.*

## Estimates of World Population by Regions

### Estimated population in millions

| Year | North America[1] | Latin America[2] | Europe[3] | U.S.S.R. | Asia[4] | Africa | Oceania | World total |
|------|------|------|------|------|------|------|------|------|
| 1650 | 1 | 7 | 103 | (5) | 257 | 100 | 2 | 470 |
| 1750 | 1 | 10 | 144 | (5) | 437 | 100 | 2 | 694 |
| 1850 | 26 | 33 | 274 | (5) | 656 | 100 | 2 | 1,091 |
| 1900 | 81 | 63 | 423 | (5) | 857 | 141 | 6 | 1,571 |
| 1930 | 134 | 108 | 355 | 179 | 1,120 | 164 | 10 | 2,070 |
| 1950 | 166 | 164 | 392 | 180 | 1,380 | 219 | 13 | 2,513 |
| 1960 | 199 | 215 | 425 | 214 | 1,683 | 275 | 16 | 3,027 |
| 1970 | 226 | 283 | 460 | 244 | 2,091 | 354 | 19 | 3,678 |
| 1980 | 252 | 365 | 484 | 266 | 2,618 | 472 | 23 | 4,478 |
| 1981 | 254 | 370 | 487 | 268 | 2,691 | 484 | 23 | 4,577 |
| 1982 | 257 | 381 | 487 | 270 | 2,720 | 501 | 23 | 4,640 |
| 1983 | 259 | 390 | 489 | 272 | 2,771 | 516 | 24 | 4,722 |
| 1984 | 262 | 398 | 491 | 275 | 2,785 | 532 | 24 | 4,766 |
| 1985 | 264 | 410 | 492 | 278 | 2,831 | 566 | 24 | 4,865 |

1. U.S. (including Alaska and Hawaii), Bermuda, Canada, Greenland, and St. Pierre and Miquelon. 2. Mexico, Central and South America, and Caribbean Islands. 3. Includes Russia 1650–1900. 4. Excludes Russia (U.S.S.R.). 5. Included in Europe. NOTE: From 1930 on European Turkey included in Asia not Europe. *Sources:* W.F. Willcox, 1650–1900; United Nations, 1930–79. United States Department of Commerce, Bureau of the Census, 1981, 1982, 1983, 1984.

## Crude Birth and Death Rates for Selected Countries
### (per 1,000 population)

| Country | Birth rates | | | | | Death rates | | | | |
|---------|------|------|------|------|------|------|------|------|------|------|
| | 1984 | 1983 | 1982 | 1980 | 1975 | 1984 | 1983 | 1982 | 1980 | 1975 |
| Australia | 15.1 | 15.8 | 15.8 | 15.3 | 16.9 | 7.1 | 7.3 | 7.6 | 7.4 | 7.9 |
| Austria | 11.7 | 11.9 | 12.5 | 12.0 | 12.5 | 11.6 | 12.3 | 12.0 | 12.2 | 12.8 |
| Belgium | 11.7 | 11.9 | 12.2 | 12.7 | 12.2 | 11.1 | 11.3 | 11.4 | 11.6 | 12.2 |
| Canada | n.a. | 15.0 | 15.1 | 15.4 | 15.8 | n.a. | 7.0 | 7.1 | 7.2 | 7.4 |
| Czechoslovakia | 14.7 | 14.8 | 15.2 | 16.4 | 19.6 | 11.8 | 12.0 | 11.7 | 12.1 | 11.5 |
| Denmark | 10.1 | 9.9 | 10.3 | 11.2 | 14.2 | 11.2 | 11.2 | 10.8 | 10.9 | 10.1 |
| El Salvador | 29.8 | 27.6 | 31.4 | 34.7 | 38.9 | 6.0 | 6.3 | 6.7 | 7.9 | 7.9 |
| Finland | 13.3 | 13.8 | 13.7 | 13.1 | 13.9 | 9.2 | 9.3 | 9.0 | 9.3 | 9.3 |
| France | 13.8 | 13.7 | 14.7 | 14.8 | 14.1 | 9.8 | 10.2 | 10.1 | 10.2 | 10.6 |
| Germany, East | 13.7 | 14.0 | 14.4 | 14.6 | 10.8 | 13.3 | 13.3 | 13.7 | 14.2 | 14.3 |
| Germany, West | 9.5 | 9.7 | 10.1 | 10.0 | 9.7 | 11.3 | 11.7 | 11.6 | 11.6 | 12.1 |
| Greece | 12.8 | 13.6 | 14.3 | 15.4 | 15.7 | 8.9 | 9.1 | 8.7 | 9.1 | 8.9 |
| Hungary | 11.7 | 11.9 | 12.5 | 13.9 | 18.4 | 13.7 | 13.9 | 13.5 | 13.6 | 12.4 |
| Ireland | 18.2 | 19.0 | 20.3 | 21.9 | 21.5 | 9.1 | 9.3 | 9.4 | 9.7 | 10.6 |
| Israel | 23.7 | 24.1 | n.a. | 24.1 | 28.2 | 6.7 | 6.8 | n.a. | 6.7 | 7.1 |
| Italy | 10.3 | 10.6 | 10.9 | 11.2 | 14.8 | 9.3 | 9.9 | 9.4 | 9.7 | 9.9 |
| Japan | 12.5 | 12.7 | 12.9 | 13.7 | 17.2 | 6.2 | 6.2 | 6.1 | 6.2 | 6.4 |
| Luxembourg | 11.5 | 11.5 | 12.0 | 11.5 | 11.2 | 11.2 | 11.3 | 11.6 | 11.5 | 12.2 |
| Malta | 14.8 | 15.0 | 16.0 | 16.0 | 18.3 | 7.9 | 8.3 | 9.5 | 8.8 | 8.8 |
| Mauritius | 19.7 | 20.7 | 22.4 | 27.0 | 25.1 | 6.6 | 6.6 | 6.7 | 7.2 | 8.1 |
| Mexico | n.a. | n.a. | n.a. | n.a. | 37.5 | n.a. | n.a. | n.a. | n.a. | 7.2 |
| Netherlands | 12.1 | 11.8 | 12.0 | 12.8 | 13.0 | 8.3 | 8.2 | 8.2 | 8.1 | 8.3 |
| New Zealand | 16.0 | 15.8 | 15.8 | n.a. | 18.4 | 7.9 | 8.1 | 8.1 | n.a. | 8.1 |
| Norway | 12.1 | 12.1 | 12.4 | 12.5 | 14.1 | 10.3 | 10.2 | 10.0 | 10.1 | 9.9 |
| Panama | 25.5 | 26.4 | 25.5 | 26.8 | 32.3 | n.a. | n.a. | n.a. | n.a. | n.a. |
| Poland | 18.9 | 19.7 | 19.4 | 19.5 | 18.9 | 9.9 | 9.5 | 9.2 | 9.8 | 8.7 |
| Portugal | 13.6 | 14.4 | n.a. | 16.4 | 19.1 | n.a. | 9.3 | n.a. | 9.9 | 10.4 |
| Singapore | 16.4 | 16.2 | 17.3 | 17.3 | 17.8 | 5.2 | 5.3 | 5.2 | 5.2 | 5.1 |
| Spain | n.a. | n.a. | 13.4 | 16.1 | 19.1 | n.a. | n.a. | 7.4 | 7.7 | 8.2 |
| Sweden | 11.3 | 11.0 | 11.1 | 11.7 | 12.6 | 10.9 | 10.9 | 10.9 | 11.0 | 10.8 |
| Switzerland | 11.5 | 11.4 | n.a. | 11.3 | 12.3 | 9.1 | 9.3 | n.a. | 9.2 | 8.7 |
| Tunisia | n.a. | n.a. | n.a. | n.a. | 36.6 | n.a. | n.a. | n.a. | n.a. | n.a. |
| United Kingdom | 12.9 | 13.0 | 12.8 | 13.5 | 12.5 | 11.4 | 11.9 | 11.8 | 11.8 | 11.9 |
| United States | 15.7 | 15.5 | 16.0 | 16.2 | 14.8 | 8.7 | 8.6 | 8.6 | 8.9 | 8.9 |
| Yugoslavia | 16.4 | 16.6 | 14.9 | 17.0 | 18.2 | 9.3 | 9.6 | 8.9 | 9.0 | 8.7 |

NOTE: n.a. = not available. *Source:* United Nations, *Monthly Bulletin of Statistics,* May 1986.

## Cost of Living of United Nations Personnel in Selected Cities as Reflected by Index of Retail Prices, 1985

(New York City, December 1985 = 100)

| City | Index | City | Index | City | Index |
|---|---|---|---|---|---|
| Abu Dhabi | 122[1] | Dar es Salaam | 78[1] | New Delhi | 74 |
| Addis Ababa | 76 | Geneva | 100 | Panama City | 101 |
| Algiers | 88[1] | Guatemala City | 58 | Paris | 88 |
| Amman | 79 | The Hague | 93 | Port-au-Prince | 71 |
| Ankara | 57 | Islamabad | 49 | Quito | 54 |
| Athens | 62 | Jakarta | 75 | Rabat | 51 |
| Baghdad | 114[1] | Kabul | 73 | Rangoon | 66 |
| Bangkok | 58 | Katmandu | 66 | Rio de Janeiro | 46 |
| Beirut | 50 | Kingston | 62 | San Salvador | 61 |
| Belgrade | 60 | Kinshasa | 59[1] | Santiago | 53 |
| Bogota | 56 | La Paz | 43 | Seoul | 75 |
| Bonn | 90 | Lagos | 97[1] | Sofia | 95 |
| Brazzaville | 67[1] | Lima | 54 | Sydney | 68 |
| Brussels | 90 | London | 92 | Tokyo | 123 |
| Budapest | 47 | Madrid | 79 | Tripoli | 131 |
| Buenos Aires | 73 | Managua | 85 | Tunis | 56 |
| Cairo | 102 | Manila | 66 | Valetta | 59 |
| Caracas | 47 | Mexico City | 39 | Vienna | 81 |
| Colombo | 50 | Montevideo | 56 | Vientiane | 87[1] |
| Copenhagen | 98 | Montreal | 69 | Warsaw | 57 |
| Dacca | 62 | Nairobi | 57 | Washington D.C. | 93 |
| Dakar | 78 | Nassau | 106 | | |

1. Calculated on the basis of cost of Government or subsidized housing which is normally lower than prevailing rentals. *Source:* United Nations, *Monthly Bulletin of Statistics, March 1986.*

## Unemployment Figures for Selected Countries: 1980-1985

(In thousands except for percentages)

| Country | 1985 No. | 1985 % | 1984 No. | 1984 % | 1983 No. | 1983 % | 1982 No. | 1982 % | 1981 No. | 1981 % | 1980 No. | 1980 % |
|---|---|---|---|---|---|---|---|---|---|---|---|---|
| Australia | 601.6 | 8.3 | 642.1 | 9.0 | 697.0 | 10.0 | 494.9 | 7.2 | 393.9 | 5.8 | 408.6 | 6.1 |
| Austria[1] | 139.5 | 4.8 | 130.5 | 4.5 | 127.4 | 4.5 | 105.3 | 3.7 | 69.3 | 2.4 | 53.2 | 1.9 |
| Belgium[1][2] | 557.4 | 13.5 | 595.0 | 14.4 | 589.5 | 14.3 | 559.8 | 13.8 | 471.6 | 11.6 | 382.3 | 9.4 |
| Canada | 1,327.9 | 10.5 | 1,399.0 | 11.3 | 1,448.0 | 11.9 | 1,314.0 | 11.0 | 898.0 | 7.5 | 865.0 | 7.5 |
| Chile | 273.4 | 17.0 | 285.0 | 18.4 | 279.0 | 19.0 | 272.1 | 20.0 | 121.3 | 9.0 | 152.4 | 12.0 |
| Cyprus[1] | n.a. | n.a. | 8.0 | 3.3 | 7.8 | 3.3 | 6.4 | 2.8 | 5.9 | 2.6 | 4.3 | 1.9 |
| Denmark[1] | 247.8 | 9.2 | 276.3 | 10.3 | 283.0 | 10.6 | 262.8 | 9.8 | 243.0 | 9.2 | 183.8 | 7.0 |
| Finland[2] | 163.2 | 6.3 | 158.0 | 6.2 | 156.0 | 6.1 | 149.0 | 5.9 | 127.0 | 5.1 | 114.0 | 4.7 |
| Germany, West[1] | 2,304.0 | 9.3 | 2,265.6 | 9.1 | 2,258.2 | 9.1 | 1,833.2 | 7.5 | 1,271.6 | 5.5 | 888.9 | 3.8 |
| Hong-Kong | n.a. | n.a. | 101.0 | 3.9 | 113.9 | 4.5 | 95.6 | 3.8 | 96.4 | 3.9 | 87.5 | 3.8 |
| Ireland[3] | 230.6 | 17.7 | 214.2 | 16.2 | 192.7 | 14.7 | 156.6 | 12.1 | 96.1 | 13.5 | 73.7 | 10.3 |
| Israel | n.a. | n.a. | 85.0 | 5.9 | 63.0 | 4.5 | 68.4 | 5.0 | 68.4 | 5.0 | 64.0 | 4.8 |
| Italy | 2,471.0 | 10.6 | 2,391.0 | 10.4 | 2,264.0 | 9.9 | 2,052.0 | 9.1 | 1,895.0 | 8.4 | 1,684.0 | 7.6 |
| Japan | 1,564.3 | 2.6 | 1,600.0 | 2.7 | 1,560.0 | 2.6 | 1,360.0 | 2.4 | 1,260.0 | 2.2 | 1,140.0 | 2.0 |
| Korea | 619.0 | 4.0 | 567.0 | 3.8 | 614.0 | 4.1 | 656.0 | 4.4 | 661.0 | 4.5 | 749.0 | 5.2 |
| Netherlands[1][2] | 761.0 | 15.6 | 822.4 | 17.6 | 800.6 | 17.1 | 541.7 | 12.6 | 385.3 | 9.1 | 248.0 | 5.9 |
| Norway | 51.0 | 2.5 | 61.0 | 3.0 | 67.0 | 3.3 | 52.0 | 2.6 | 40.0 | 2.0 | 33.0 | 1.7 |
| Philippines | n.a. | n.a. | 1,231.0 | 6.1 | 850.0 | 4.1 | 1,084.0 | 5.5 | 1,008.0 | 5.4 | 856.0 | 4.8 |
| Portugal | n.a. | n.a. | 381.0 | 8.3 | 354.8 | 7.7 | 315.5 | 7.4 | 355.5 | 8.2 | 330.0 | 7.8 |
| Puerto Rico | n.a. | n.a. | 198.0 | 20.7 | 220.0 | 23.4 | 208.0 | 22.8 | 184.0 | 19.9 | 156.0 | 17.1 |
| Sweden | 125.0 | 2.8 | 136.0 | 3.1 | 151.0 | 3.5 | 137.0 | 3.1 | 107.6 | 2.5 | 86.0 | 2.0 |
| Switzerland[1][4] | 30.3 | 1.0 | 35.2 | 1.1 | 26.3 | 0.9 | 13.2 | 0.4 | 6.0 | 0.2 | 6.3 | 0.2 |
| United Kingdom[1] | 3,271.2 | 13.5 | 3,159.8 | 13.1 | 3,104.7 | 12.9 | 3,119.0 | 13.1 | 2,733.8 | 11.1 | 1,794.7 | 7.3 |
| United States | 8,312.0 | 7.2 | 8,539.0 | 7.5 | 10,717.0 | 9.6 | 10,678.0 | 9.7 | 8,273.0 | 7.6 | 7,637.0 | 7.1 |
| Yugoslavia[1] | 1,040.0 | 13.8 | 974.8 | 13.3 | 910.3 | 12.8 | 862.5 | 12.4 | 808.6 | 11.9 | 785.5 | 11.9 |

1. Employment office statistics. All others labor force sample surveys unless otherwise indicated. 2. Scope of series revised as of 1983. 3. Compulsory unemployment insurance statistics. 4. Scope of series revised as of 1984. NOTE: n.a. = not available. *Source:* United Nations, *Monthly Bulletin of Statistics, June 1986.*

# Value of Exports and Imports
## (in millions of U.S. dollars)

| Country | Exports[1] | Imports[1] | Country | Exports[1] | Imports[1] |
|---|---|---|---|---|---|
| Afghanistan | 708[2] | 695[2] | Liberia | 452 | 363 |
| Algeria | 11,886 | 10,289 | Libya | 13,951[2] | 7,175[2] |
| Argentina | 8,107 | 4,583 | Madagascar | 334 | 370 |
| Australia | 23,998 | 23,424 | Malawi | 313 | 269 |
| Austria | 15,741 | 19,631 | Malaysia | 13,917[2] | 13,987[2] |
| Bahamas | 3,393 | 4,098 | Mali | 181 | 368 |
| Bahrain | 3,139 | 3,530 | Malta | 394 | 717 |
| Bangladesh | 934 | 2,042 | Mauritania | 297 | 246 |
| Barbados | 391 | 659 | Mauritius | 373 | 472 |
| Belgium-Luxembourg | 51,779 | 55,303 | Mexico | 23,602 | 11,280 |
| Benin | 24[2] | 464[2] | Morocco | 2,172 | 3,907 |
| Bolivia | 773 | 631 | Netherlands | 65,881 | 62,136 |
| Brazil | 27,005 | 15,210 | New Zealand | 5,358 | 6,010 |
| Bulgaria | 12,850 | 12,714 | Nicaragua | 385 | 826 |
| Burkina Faso | 57[3] | 288[3] | Nigeria | 14,124 | 5,863 |
| Burma | 310 | 239 | Norway | 18,892 | 13,889 |
| Burundi | 98 | 186 | Oman | 4,422 | 2,748 |
| Cameroon | 882 | 1,106 | Pakistan | 2,614 | 5,873 |
| Canada | 86,817 | 73,999 | Panama | 256 | 1,423 |
| Cape Verde | 4[4] | 68[4] | Papua-New Guinea | 895 | 968 |
| Central African Republic | 109[2] | 127[2] | Paraguay | 386 | 563 |
| Chile | 3,657 | 3,481 | Peru | 3,131 | 1,870 |
| Colombia | 3,462 | 4,052 | Philippines | 5,322 | 6,051 |
| Congo | 1,066[3] | 806[3] | Poland | 11,649 | 10,548 |
| Costa Rica | 978 | 1,085 | Portugal | 5,208 | 7,978 |
| Cuba | 6,164 | 8,134 | Qatar | 3,297[3] | 1,456[3] |
| Cyprus | 575 | 1,364 | Romania | 13,241[3] | 9,959[3] |
| Czechoslovakia | 17,153 | 17,078 | Rwanda | 83 | 295 |
| Denmark | 15,959 | 16,585 | Saudi Arabia | 36,834 | 33,696 |
| Dominican Republic | 868 | 1,257 | Senegal | 536 | 1,001 |
| Ecuador | 2,581 | 1,716 | Sierra Leone | 148 | 166 |
| Egypt | 3,140 | 10,766 | Singapore | 24,108 | 28,712 |
| El Salvador | 607 | 1,314 | Solomon Islands | 151 | 107 |
| Ethiopia | 417 | 942 | Somalia | 45 | 109 |
| Fiji | 256 | 450 | Spain | 23,544 | 28,812 |
| Finland | 13,505 | 12,443 | Sri Lanka | 1,454 | 1,845 |
| France | 93,276 | 103,807 | Sudan | 624[3] | 1,354[3] |
| Gabon | 2,018 | 888 | Suriname | 356 | 346 |
| Gambia | 47 | 98 | Sweden | 29,378 | 26,416 |
| Germany, East | 24,836 | 22,940 | Switzerland | 25,863 | 29,469 |
| Germany, West | 169,784 | 151,246 | Syria | 1,853 | 4,116 |
| Ghana | 571 | 591 | Tanzania | 366[3] | 822[3] |
| Greece | 4,811 | 9,434 | Thailand | 7,413 | 10,398 |
| Guatemala | 1,129 | 1,278 | Togo | 191 | 271 |
| Guinea-Bissau | 12[2] | 50[2] | Tonga | 6[3] | 38[3] |
| Guyana | 91 | 601 | Trinidad | 2,194 | 2,101 |
| Haiti | 179 | 472 | Tunisia | 1,797 | 3,218 |
| Honduras | 670[3] | 823[3] | Turkey | 7,086 | 10,822 |
| Hungary | 8,563 | 8,091 | Uganda | 345[4] | 293[4] |
| Iceland | 740 | 839 | U.S.S.R. | 91,652 | 80,680 |
| India | 8,793 | 13,953 | United Arab Emirates | 17,257[2] | 9,419[2] |
| Indonesia | 21,888 | 13,882 | U.K. | 94,502 | 105,961 |
| Iran | 20,247[3] | 18,296[3] | U.S. | 217,888 | 341,177 |
| Iraq | 10,530[5] | 7,903[5] | Uruguay | 925 | 776 |
| Ireland | 9,629 | 9,663 | Vanuatu | 44 | 67 |
| Israel | 5,804 | 8,411 | Venezuela | 14,337 | 6,676 |
| Italy | 73,303 | 84,215 | Western Samoa | 19 | 50 |
| Ivory Coast | 2,698 | 1,340 | Yemen, People's | 430[5] | 673[5] |
| Jamaica | 747 | 1,146 | Yemen Arab | 39[2] | 1,521[2] |
| Japan | 170,107 | 136,522 | Yugoslavia | 9,811 | 11,538 |
| Jordan | 752 | 2,784 | Zaire | 1,004 | 682 |
| Kenya | 1,083 | 1,547 | Zambia | 655 | 608 |
| Korea, South | 29,245 | 30,631 | Zimbabwe | 1,003 | 959 |
| Kuwait | 10,751 | 7,694 | | | |

1. 1984 unless otherwise indicated. 2. 1982. 3. 1983. 4. 1980. 5. 1981. *Source:* United Nations, *Monthly Bulletin of Statistics,* July 1986.

# Energy, Petroleum, and Coal, by Country

| Country | Energy consumed[1] (coal equiv.) Total (mil. metric tons) 1983 | 1980 | Per capita (kilograms) 1983 | 1980 | Electric energy production[2] (bil. kwh) 1983 | 1980 | Crude petroleum production[3] (mil. metric tons) 1983 | 1980 | Coal production[4] (mil. metric tons) 1983 | 1980 |
|---|---|---|---|---|---|---|---|---|---|---|
| Algeria | 12.8 | 24.8 | 624 | 1,327 | 8.5 | 7.1 | 31.6[6] | 47.4 | (Z)[6] | (Z) |
| Argentina | 50.9 | 49.3 | 1,718 | 1,746 | 43.0 | 39.7 | 25.2 | 25.3 | .5 | .4 |
| Australia[7] | 92.0 | 91.2 | 6,006 | 6,195 | 106.3 | 96.1 | 17.7 | 18.9 | 97.8 | 72.5 |
| Austria | 26.7 | 30.5 | 3,564 | 4,058 | 42.6 | 42.0 | 1.3 | 1.5 | — | — |
| Bahrain | 4.8 | 4.4 | 12,113 | 12,651 | 2.0 | 1.7 | 2.0[6] | 2.4 | (NA) | — |
| Bangladesh | 4.6 | 3.8 | 48 | 44 | 3.8 | 2.7 | (Z) | (Z) | (X) | (X) |
| Belgium | 48.9 | 59.1 | 4,950 | 5,997 | 52.7 | 53.6 | (X) | (X) | 7.5 | 6.3 |
| Brazil | 85.7 | 92.5 | 660 | 763 | 162.0 | 139.5 | 16.6 | 9.1 | 6.7 | 5.2 |
| Bulgaria | 50.2 | 47.3 | 5,488 | 5,254 | 42.5 | 34.8 | .3[6] | .3[6] | .2 | .3 |
| Burma | 2.5 | 2.2 | 66 | 62 | 1.9 | 1.3 | 1.5[6] | 1.6 | (Z)[6] | (Z) |
| Canada | 238.6 | 254.2 | 9,546 | 10,547 | 408.4 | 377.5 | 66.4 | 70.4 | 22.6 | 20.2 |
| Chile | 10.6 | 11.4 | 909 | 1,025 | 12.6 | 11.8 | 1.8 | 1.6 | 1.0 | 1.0 |
| China: Mainland | 629.1 | 562.8 | 616 | 571 | 351.4 | 300.6 | 106.1 | 105.9 | 687.6 | 595.8 |
| Taiwan[8] | 41.2 | 37.9 | 2,192 | 2,127 | 47.5 | 42.0 | .1 | .2 | 2.2 | 2.6 |
| Colombia | 25.0 | 23.8 | 909 | 923 | 27.1 | 22.9 | 7.9 | 6.5 | 6.0[6] | 4.9 |
| Cuba | 13.7 | 13.6 | 1,385 | 1,394 | 11.6 | 9.9 | .7 | .3 | (X) | (X) |
| Czechoslovakia | 96.9 | 97.4 | 6,243 | 6,364 | 76.3 | 72.7 | .1 | .1 | 26.9[9] | 28.3[9] |
| Denmark | 22.2 | 26.9 | 4,313 | 5,254 | 22.2 | 27.1 | 2.2 | .3 | (X) | (X) |
| Ecuador | 5.8 | 5.7 | 657 | 708 | 4.3 | 3.4 | 12.0 | 10.4 | (NA) | (NA) |
| Egypt | 25.9 | 20.1 | 582 | 488 | 23.5 | 18.9 | 36.0 | 29.4 | (X) | (X) |
| Ethiopia | .8 | .9 | 24 | 27 | .8 | .7 | (X) | (X) | (NA) | (NA) |
| Finland | 21.6 | 26.4 | 4,460 | 5,514 | 40.2[5] | 38.7[5] | (X) | (X) | (X) | (X) |
| France[10] | 208.2 | 237.3 | 3,832 | 4,409 | 283.4[5] | 246.4[5] | 1.7 | 1.2 | 18.6[9] | 20.2[9] |
| Germany, East | 121.8 | 121.8 | 7,301 | 7,276 | 104.9 | 98.8 | .1[6] | .1 | (Z) | (Z) |
| Germany, West | 339.7 | 359.4 | 5,538 | 5,829 | 373.8 | 368.8 | 4.1 | 4.6 | 89.6 | 94.5 |
| Greece | 21.4 | 20.1 | 2,179 | 2,088 | 22.3 | 22.7 | 1.2 | (Z) | (X) | (X) |
| Hong Kong | 10.2 | 7.3 | 1,884 | 1,448 | 16.5 | 12.6 | (NA) | (NA) | (X) | (X) |
| Hungary | 39.8 | 40.6 | 3,697 | 3,787 | 25.8 | 23.9 | 2.0 | 2.0 | 2.8[9] | 3.1[9] |
| India | 169.3 | 139.4 | 231 | 202 | 148.0 | 119.3 | 25.1 | 9.4 | 133.3 | 109.1 |
| Indonesia | 38.3 | 34.7 | 240 | 230 | 15.3 | 14.2 | 66.0 | 77.6 | .5 | .3 |
| Iran | 47.3 | 45.7[15] | 1,114 | 1,177[15] | 30.0 | 22.4[15] | 123.1 | 72.7[15] | .8[6] | .9[15] |
| Iraq | 9.2 | 10.7 | 630 | 807 | 13.7 | 11.4 | 46.8 | 130.1 | (NA) | (NA) |
| Ireland | 11.2 | 11.1 | 3,185 | 3,268 | 11.2 | 10.9 | (X) | (X) | .1 | .1 |
| Israel | 10.2 | 8.8 | 2,460 | 2,273 | 14.6 | 12.5 | (Z)[6] | (Z) | (X) | (X) |
| Italy[11] | 172.6 | 174.9 | 3,051 | 3,112 | 182.9 | 185.7 | 2.2 | 1.8 | (Z)[6] | (Z)[6] |
| Japan | 403.9 | 434.8 | 3,397 | 3,726 | 602.4 | 577.5 | .4 | .4 | 17.1 | 18.0 |
| North Korea | 52.3 | 48.5 | 2,726 | 2,713 | 41.0 | 35.0 | (X) | (X) | 38.0[6] | 36.0[6] |
| South Korea | 57.8 | 52.3 | 1,454 | 1,373 | 53.0 | 40.1 | (X) | (X) | 19.0 | 18.6 |
| Kuwait[12] | 8.5 | 6.9 | 5,224 | 5,019 | 12.8 | 9.4 | 53.5 | 84.1 | n.a. | n.a. |
| Libya | 19.1 | 7.3 | 5,713 | 2,456 | 7.2 | 4.8 | 52.5[6] | 88.3 | (X) | (X) |
| Malaysia | 13.3 | 12.2 | 896 | 882 | 12.1 | 10.2 | 19.0 | 13.2 | (X) | (X) |
| Mexico | 130.4 | 118.6 | 1,736 | 1,709 | 82.3[5] | 67.0[5] | 138.6 | 99.9 | 7.8[6] | 7.0 |
| Morocco | 6.6 | 6.4 | 301 | 319 | 6.0 | 4.9 | (Z)[6] | (Z) | .8 | .7 |
| Netherlands | 91.9 | 93.0 | 6,380 | 6,543 | 59.6 | 64.8 | 2.6 | 1.3 | (Z) | (Z) |
| New Zealand | 11.7 | 10.0 | 3,605 | 3,152 | 25.5 | 22.0 | .6[6] | .3 | 2.2[6] | 2.0 |
| Nigeria | 17.0 | 11.0 | 191 | 136 | 8.5 | 7.2 | 61.2 | 104.2 | (Z)[6] | .2 |
| Norway[16] | 23.8 | 26.3 | 5,751 | 6,423 | 106.2 | 84.1 | 30.6 | 24.6 | .5 | .3 |
| Pakistan | 21.7 | 16.6 | 226 | 191 | 19.6 | 15.3 | .6 | .5 | 1.9 | 1.5 |
| Peru | 11.8 | 12.0 | 630 | 693 | 9.3 | 9.8 | 8.5 | 9.6 | .1[6] | .1[6] |
| Philippines | 16.3 | 16.7 | 313 | 346 | 20.8 | 17.9 | .7 | .5 | 1.0 | .3 |
| Poland | 161.4 | 176.8 | 4,376 | 4,935 | 125.8 | 121.9 | .2 | .3 | 191.1 | 193.1 |
| Portugal | 13.2 | 11.2 | 1,331 | 1,153 | 18.2 | 15.3 | (X) | (X) | .2 | .2 |
| Romania | 101.4 | 100.0 | 4,462 | 4,505 | 70.3 | 67.5 | 11.6 | 11.5 | 7.8 | 8.1 |
| Saudi Arabia[11] | 37.4 | 25.3 | 3,591 | 2,745 | 32.0 | 18.9 | 252.7 | 495.9 | n.a. | n.a. |
| South Africa[13] | 99.9 | 90.2 | 2,827 | 2,751 | 109.2 | 90.4 | (X) | (X) | 139.6 | 116.6 |
| Soviet Union | 1,611.5 | 1,473.1 | 5,900 | 5,549 | 1,408.1 | 1,293.9 | 616.3 | 603.2 | 486.8 | 492.9 |
| Spain | 81.8 | 88.4 | 2,130 | 2,359 | 115.5 | 110.5 | 3.0 | 1.6 | 15.8[6][9] | 13.1[9] |
| Sudan | 1.6 | 1.5 | 79 | 82 | 1.0 | 1.0 | (X) | (X) | n.a. | n.a. |
| Sweden | 38.8 | 44.5 | 4,681 | 5,376 | 109.6 | 96.7 | (Z) | (Z) | (Z) | (Z) |
| Switzerland[14] | 23.6 | 23.3 | 3,720 | 3,636 | 51.8[5] | 48.1[5] | (X) | (X) | (X) | (X) |
| Syria | 9.1 | 7.3 | 930 | 835 | 6.2 | 3.8 | 9.4 | 8.3 | (X) | (X) |
| Tanzania | .9 | .8 | 43 | 44 | .7 | .7 | (X) | (X) | (Z)[6] | (Z) |
| Thailand | 17.4 | 17.3 | 352 | 372 | 18.9 | 15.1 | (Z)[6] | (Z) | (Z)[6] | (Z) |
| Trinidad and Tobago | 6.4 | 7.5 | 5,830 | 6,992 | 2.3 | 2.0 | 8.3[6] | 11.0 | n.a. | n.a. |

| Country | Energy consumed[1] (coal equiv.) | | | | Electric energy production[2] (bil. kwh) | | Crude petroleum production[3] (mil. metric tons) | | Coal production[4] (mil. metric tons) | |
|---|---|---|---|---|---|---|---|---|---|---|
| | Total (mil. metric tons) | | Per capita (kilograms) | | | | | | | |
| | 1983 | 1980 | 1983 | 1980 | 1983 | 1980 | 1983 | 1980 | 1983 | 1980 |
| Tunisia | 4.3 | 4.1 | 631 | 639 | 3.5 | 2.8 | 5.6 | 5.6 | (X) | (X) |
| Turkey | 35.5 | 31.9 | 744 | 718 | 27.3 | 23.3 | 2.2 | 2.3 | 4.1[6] | 3.6 |
| United Arab Emirates | 23.0 | 16.8 | 19,198 | 17,188 | 7.9 | 6.3 | 53.6[6] | 82.8 | n.a. | n.a. |
| United Kingdom | 260.6 | 271.0 | 4,670 | 4,850 | 276.2 | 284.9 | 111.4 | 78.9 | 119.3[9] | 130.1[9] |
| United States | 2,174.8 | 2,364.5 | 9,304 | 10,386 | 2,368[5] | 2,354[6] | 427.5 | 424.2 | 660.5 | 710.4 |
| Venezuela | 50.1 | 49.0 | 2,903 | 3,140 | 41.7 | 35.9 | 95.2 | 114.8 | (Z) | (Z) |
| Vietnam | 7.2 | 6.6 | 125 | 122 | 4.2 | 3.8 | n.a. | n.a. | 6.0[6] | 5.2 |
| Yugoslavia | 52.9 | 48.0 | 2,313 | 2,152 | 71.6 | 59.4 | 4.1 | 4.2 | .4 | .4 |
| Zaire | 2.1 | 2.0 | 68 | 69 | 4.2 | 4.2 | 1.1[6] | 1.0 | .1 | .1 |
| Zambia | 2.2 | 2.3 | 354 | 403 | 10.1[6] | 9.2 | (X) | (X) | .5 | .6 |
| **World, total** | **8,523.8** | **8,544.3** | **1,820** | **1,919** | **8,797** | **8,247** | **2,648** | **2,979** | **2,829** | **2,728** |

— Represents zero. n.a. = not available. X = Not applicable. Z = Less than 50,000 metric tons. 1. Based on apparent consumption of coal, lignite, petroleum products, natural gas, and hydro, nuclear, and geothermal electricity. 2. Comprises production by utilities generating primarily for public use, and production by industrial establishments generating primarily for own use. Relates to production at generating centers, including station use and transmission losses. 3. Includes shale oil, but excludes natural gasoline. 4. Excludes lignite and brown coal, except as noted. 5. Net production, i.e. excluding station use. 6. United Nations Statistical Office estimate. 7. For year ending June 30 of year shown. 8. Source: U.S. Bureau of the Census. Data from Republic of China publications. 9. Includes slurries. 10. Includes Monaco. 11. Includes San Marino. 12. Includes share of production and consumption in the Neutral Zone. 13. Includes Botswana, Lesotho, Namibia, and Swaziland. 14. Includes Liechtenstein. 15. For the year ending March 20 of year shown. 16. Includes Svalbard and Jan Mayen Islands. *Source:* Except as noted, Statistical Office of the United Nations, New York, N.Y., *Energy Statistics Yearbook, 1983.* (copyright.) From: *Statistical Abstract of the United States 1986.*

# Wheat, Rice, and Corn—Production by Country

(in thousands of metric tons)

| Country | Wheat | | | Rice | | | Corn | | |
|---|---|---|---|---|---|---|---|---|---|
| | 1983 | 1982 | 1981 | 1983 | 1982 | 1981 | 1983 | 1982 | 1981 |
| Afghanistan | 3,750[1] | 2,862 | 2,850 | 650[1] | 473 | 475 | 1,000[1] | 800 | 798[1] |
| Argentina | 11,700 | 15,130 | 8,300 | 277 | 437 | 286 | 8,840 | 9,600 | 12,900 |
| Australia | 21,780 | 8,879 | 16,360 | 522 | 854 | 728 | 95 | 212 | 173 |
| Austria | 1,415 | 1,236 | 1,025 | n.a. | n.a. | n.a. | 1,437 | 1,551 | 1,374 |
| Bangladesh | 1,095 | 967 | 1,093 | 21,700 | 21,322 | 20,444 | 1[1] | 1 | 1 |
| Belgium[3] | 1,084[2] | 1,068 | 926 | n.a. | n.a. | n.a. | 38[2] | 36[1] | 38 |
| Brazil | 2,273 | 1,849 | 2,209 | 7,760 | 9,716 | 8,228 | 18,756 | 21,865 | 21,117 |
| Bulgaria | 3,600 | 4,913 | 4,443 | 72 | 75 | 74 | 3,101 | 3,418 | 2,401 |
| Burma | 183 | 124 | 117 | 14,500[2] | 14,758 | 14,147 | 301 | 206 | 166 |
| Cambodia | n.a. | n.a. | n.a. | 1,700 | 1,400 | 1,160[1] | 60[2] | 46 | 98[2] |
| Canada | 26,914 | 26,790 | 24,802 | n.a. | n.a. | n.a. | 5,875 | 6,513 | 6,673 |
| Chile | 800[2] | 650 | 686 | 107 | 131 | 100 | 512[1] | 425 | 518 |
| China: Mainland[2] | 81,392 | 68,422 | 59,643 | 172,184 | 164,493 | 147,042 | 64,135 | 60,413 | 59,301 |
| Colombia | 73[1] | 69[1] | 62 | 1,780 | 2,018 | 1,799 | 867[1] | 899 | 880 |
| Cuba | n.a. | n.a. | n.a. | 490 | 520 | 461 | 96[2] | 96[2] | 95[2] |
| Czechoslovakia | 5,820[1] | 4,606 | 4,325 | n.a. | n.a. | n.a. | 710[2] | 941 | 706 |
| Denmark | 1,577 | 1,207 | 835 | n.a. | n.a. | n.a. | n.a. | n.a. | n.a. |
| Ecuador | 23[1] | 39 | 41 | 222 | 384 | 434 | 258[1] | 324 | 281 |
| Egypt | 1,996 | 2,017 | 1,938 | 2,440 | 2,441 | 2,236 | 3,510[1] | 3,347 | 3,308 |
| Ethiopia | 950[2] | 917 | 707 | n.a. | n.a. | n.a. | 1,600[2] | 1,603 | 1,200 |
| Finland | 550 | 435 | 235 | n.a. | n.a. | n.a. | n.a. | n.a. | n.a. |
| France | 24,781 | 25,342 | 22,857 | 32 | 27 | 20 | 10,143 | 10,381 | 8,956 |
| Germany, East | 3,470 | 2,739 | 2,942 | n.a. | n.a. | n.a. | 1[1] | 1 | 3 |
| Germany, West | 8,998 | 8,632 | 8,313 | n.a. | n.a. | n.a. | 934 | 1,054 | 832 |
| Greece | 2,026 | 2,983 | 2,780 | 78 | 83 | 78 | 1,622 | 1,448 | 1,337 |
| Hungary | 4,800[2] | 5,762 | 4,614 | 40[2] | 48 | 39 | 7,600[2] | 7,959 | 6,998 |
| India | 42,502 | 37,452 | 36,313 | 90,000[2] | 69,648 | 79,883 | 7,300[2] | 6,274 | 6,897 |
| Indonesia | n.a. | n.a. | n.a. | 34,300 | 34,104 | 32,774 | 4,000[1] | 3,207 | 4,509 |
| Iran | 6,669[2] | 6,500[1] | 6,518[1] | 1,400[2] | 1,400[2] | 1,500[2] | 55[2] | 53[2] | 50[2] |
| Iraq | 1,000 | 965 | 902 | 200[2] | 163 | 162 | 90[2] | 28 | 39 |
| Ireland | 350[1] | 400 | 280 | n.a. | n.a. | n.a. | n.a. | n.a. | n.a. |
| Israel | 335 | 147 | 215 | n.a. | n.a. | n.a. | 28 | 22 | 15[2] |
| Italy | 8,514 | 8,903 | 8,830 | 1,060 | 964 | 893 | 6,900 | 6,847 | 7,197 |

| | | | | | | | | | |
|---|---|---|---|---|---|---|---|---|---|
| Japan | 747 | 742 | 587 | 12,958 | 12,838 | 12,824 | 2 [1] | 2 | 3 |
| Korea, North[2] | 500 | 450 | 400 | 5,200 | 5,000 | 4,900 | 2,500 | 2,330 | 2,250 |
| Korea, South | 112 | 66 | 57 | 7,608 | 7,308 | 7,149 | 101 | 117 | 145 |
| Laos | n.a. | n.a. | n.a. | 1,002 | 1,088 | 1,155 | 39 | 35 | 33 |
| Madagascar | ([4]) | ([4]) | ([4]) | 2,147 | 1,967 | 2,012 | 115 | 113 | 121 |
| Malaysia | n.a. | n.a. | n.a. | 2,000 | 1,832 | 2,177 | 9 [2] | 9 | 8 |
| Mexico | 3,697 | 4,468 | 3,189 | 655 | 600 | 644 | 13,928 | 10,129 | 14,766 |
| Nepal | 657 | 526 | 477 | 2,744 | 1,833 | 2,560 | 768 | 718 | 752 |
| Netherlands | 1,043 | 967 | 882 | n.a. | n.a. | n.a. | ([4]) | 2 [2] | 2 [2] |
| New Zealand | 280 | 321 | 326 | n.a. | n.a. | n.a. | 176 [1] | 214 | 152 |
| Pakistan | 12,414 | 11,304 | 11,474 | 5,210 | 5,167 | 5,145 | 1,000 [1] | 1,005 | 931 |
| Panama | n.a. | n.a. | n.a. | 169 [2] | 176 | 195 | 68 [1] | 62 | 57 |
| Peru | 75 | 101 | 119 | 770 | 765 | 712 | 583 | 625 | 587 |
| Philippines | n.a. | n.a. | n.a. | 8,150 | 7,731 | 8,108 | 3,385 | 3,126 | 3,290 |
| Poland | 5,165 | 4,476 | 4,203 | n.a. | n.a. | n.a. | 64 | 68 | 65 |
| Portugal | 281 | 437 | 315 | 100 [1] | 143 | 112 | 475 [1] | 464 | 419 |
| Romania | 5,000 [1] | 6,460 | 5,310 | 50 | 46 | 49 | 10,500 [2] | 12,620 | 11,892 |
| South Africa | 1,770 | 2,420 | 2,340 | 3 [2] | 3 [2] | 3 [2] | 3,910 | 8,359 | 14,660 |
| Soviet Union[2] | 82,000 | 87,000 | 80,000 | 2,500 | 2,500 | 2,400 | 14,000 | 12,000 | 8,000 |
| Spain | 4,330 | 4,410 | 3,409 | 223 | 402 | 444 | 1,788 | 2,330 | 2,157 |
| Sri Lanka | n.a. | n.a. | n.a. | 2,200 | 2,156 | 2,229 | 25 [2] | 24 [2] | 24 |
| Sweden | 1,721 | 1,490 | 1,066 | n.a. | n.a. | n.a. | n.a. | n.a. | n.a. |
| Switzerland | 436 | 433 | 409 | n.a. | n.a. | n.a. | 136 | 173 | 139 |
| Syria | 1,612 | 1,556 | 2,087 | ([4]) | ([4]) | ([4]) | 70 [1] | 50 | 46 |
| Thailand | n.a. | n.a. | n.a. | 18,535 | 16,878 | 17,774 | 3,552 | 3,002 | 3,449 |
| Turkey | 16,400 | 17,542 | 17,000 | 325 [2] | 350 | 330 | 1,375 [2] | 1,360 | 1,200 |
| United Kingdom | 10,880 | 10,320 | 8,707 | n.a. | n.a. | n.a. | 1 [2] | 1 [2] | 1 [2] |
| United States | 66,010 | 76,538 | 76,169 | 4,523 | 6,967 | 8,289 | 106,781 | 212,338 | 208,330 |
| Uruguay | 450 [1] | 316 | 388 | 332 [1] | 419 | 330 | 103 [1] | 97 | 181 |
| Venezuela | ([4]) | ([4]) | ([4]) | 509 | 670 | 681 | 429 | 501 | 452 |
| Vietnam | n.a. | n.a. | n.a. | 14,500 [2] | 14,500 | 12,570 | 420 [2] | 437 | 460 [2] |
| Yugoslavia | 5,519 | 5,218 | 4,270 | 40 | 42 | 42 | 10,688 | 11,126 | 9,807 |
| **World, total** | 498,182 | 486,423 | 453,821 | 449,827 | 423,464 | 411,814 | 344,103 | 451,080 | 452,030 |

1. Unofficial figure. 2. FAO estimate 3. Includes Luxembourg. 4. None or negligible. NOTES: Rice data cover rough and paddy. Data for each country pertain to the calendar year in which all or most of the crop was harvested. n.a.= not available. *Source: Food and Agriculture Organization of the United Nations, Rome, Italy. 1983 FAO Production Yearbook, vol. 37* (copyright). From: *Statistical Abstract of the United States 1986.*

## Consumer Price Indexes for Selected Countries

### (1967 = 100)

| Country | Total Indexes[1] | | | | Average annual percent change 1980–1984 | Indexes for Selected Items, 1984 | | | |
|---|---|---|---|---|---|---|---|---|---|
| | 1984 | 1983 | 1982 | 1980 | | Food[1] | Clothing | Housing[2] | Transportation |
| Australia | 412.4 | 396.7 | 360.3 | 295.5 | 8.0 | 398.6 | 389.6 | 461.7 | n.a. |
| Austria | 249.9 | 236.6 | 229.0 | 203.3 | 4.9 | 223.3 | 202.8 | 297.5 | 272.1 |
| Canada | 334.9 | 321.0 | 303.4 | 243.5 | 7.6 | 379.2 | 235.6 | 340.6 | 344.4 |
| France | 439.2 | 408.9 | 373.1 | 294.2 | 10.6 | 446.3 | 387.4 | 475.9 | 505.4 |
| Germany, West | 207.9 | 201.9 | 196.1 | 175.8 | 4.2 | 184.3 | 206.8 | 232.5 | 223.6 |
| Italy | 702.7 | 634.2 | 553.2 | 403.2 | 14.9 | 634.3 | 751.8 | 707.6 | 856.5 |
| Japan | 316.4 | 309.4 | 303.8 | 281.8 | 2.8 | 324.3 | 330.8 | 256.6 | 274.8 |
| Netherlands | 284.9 | 276.2 | 268.7 | 237.4 | 4.6 | 230.1 | 285.6 | 323.9 | 271.5 |
| Sweden | 387.5 | 358.8 | 329.3 | 270.6 | 8.9 | 454.2 | 248.1 | 435.5 | n.a. |
| United Kingdom | 565.1 | 538.3 | 514.7 | 423.6 | 5.6 | 596.3 | 320.1 | 592.2 | 584.4 |
| United States | 311.1 | 298.4 | 289.1 | 246.8 | 4.6 | 302.9 | 187.0 | 336.5 | 311.7 |

1. Includes other items not shown separately. 2. Restaurant meals, alcohol, and tobacco are included for some countries, excluded for others. 3. Includes shelter, utilities, and household furnishings and operations. However, actual coverage and measurements vary significantly from country to country. NOTE: n.a. = not available. *Source:* United States Department of Labor, Bureau of Labor Statistics.

## India To Surpass China As Most Populous

China's one-child-per-family campaign, seen by Chinese leaders as being for this generation only, will succeed in its goal of holding the country's population to 1.2 billion in the year 2000. India, on the other hand, is unlikely to come anywhere near its goal of replacement level fertility by 2000. India's population, estimated at 785 million in 1986 and growing by 16 million a year, compared to 9 million in China, will overtake China's as the world's largest by 2020.

## Meat—Production by Country
### (in thousands of metric tons)

| Country | 1982, est. | 1981 | 1980 | Country | 1982, est. | 1981 | 1980 |
|---------|-----------|------|------|---------|-----------|------|------|
| Argentina | 2,927 | 3,302 | 3,267 | Italy | 2,313 | 2,285 | 2,305 |
| Australia[1] | 2,307 | 2,281 | 2,332 | Japan | 1,908 | 1,867 | 1,893 |
| Belgium[2] | 994 | 1,004 | 985 | Mexico | 1,172 | 1,151 | 1,145 |
| Brazil | 3,322 | 3,141 | 3,115 | Netherlands | 1,605 | 1,648 | 1,565 |
| Canada | 1,887 | 1,891 | 1,852 | New Zealand[1] | 1,170 | 1,158 | 1,091 |
| China: Mainland | 20,570 | 19,850 | 19,364 | Pakistan | 704 | 689 | 657 |
| Czechoslovakia | 1,130 | 1,233 | 1,210 | Poland | 2,049 | 1,861 | 2,397 |
| Denmark | 1,223 | 1,232 | 1,218 | Romania | 1,374 | 1,361 | 1,359 |
| France | 3,815 | 3,925 | 3,880 | Soviet Union | 12,562 | 12,657 | 12,609 |
| Germany, East | 1,663 | 1,705 | 1,612 | Spain | 1,640 | 1,579 | 1,545 |
| Germany, West | 4,647 | 4,771 | 4,800 | United Kingdom | 2,187 | 2,263 | 2,307 |
| Hungary | 1,080 | 1,054 | 1,065 | United States | 17,057 | 17,706 | 17,680 |
| India | 707 | 688 | 654 | Yugoslavia | 1,154 | 1,133 | 1,117 |
| Iran | 471 | 462 | 459 | **World, total** | **111,239** | **110,994** | **110,222** |

1. Year ending June 30 for Australia and September 30 for New Zealand. 2. includes Luxembourg. NOTE: Covers beef and veal (incl. buffalo meat), pork (incl. bacon and ham), and mutton and lamb (incl. goat meat). Refers to meat from animals slaughtered within the national boundaries irrespective of origin of animals, and relates to commercial and farm slaughter. In terms of carcass weight. Excludes lard, tallow, and edible offals. NOTE: Data are most recent available. *Source:* Office of the United Nations, New York, NY, *Statistical Yearbook.* (Copyright.) From: *Statistical Abstract of the United States 1986.*

## Crude Steel Production and Consumption

| | Production (mil. metric tons) | | | Consumption | | | | | |
|---|---|---|---|---|---|---|---|---|---|
| | | | | Total (mil. metric tons) | | | Per capita (kilograms) | | |
| Country | 1983 | 1982 | 1981 | 1983 | 1982 | 1981 | 1983 | 1982 | 1981 |
| Argentina | 2.8 | 2.8 | 2.4 | 3.6 | 2.4 | 3.2 | 120 | 84 | 114 |
| Australia | 5.4[4] | 7.3[1] | 8.0[1] | 4.9 | 5.6 | 7.1 | 318 | 367 | 478 |
| Austria | 4.4 | 4.3 | 4.7 | 2.0 | 2.1 | 2.3 | 263 | 279 | 301 |
| Bangladesh | z | n.a. | .1 | .3 | .2 | .3 | 3 | 3 | 3 |
| Belgium | 10.3 | 9.9 | 12.3 | 5.8 | 4.7[2] | 3.3[2] | 564[2] | 461[2] | 319[2] |
| Brazil | 8.2 | 7.7 | 8.4 | 7.9 | 10.7 | 17.4 | 61 | 85 | 141 |
| Bulgaria | 2.8 | 2.6 | 2.5 | 3.2 | 3.0 | 2.8 | 353 | 337 | 319 |
| Canada | 12.8 | 11.9 | 14.8 | 11.0 | 9.1 | 13.5 | 443 | 371 | 553 |
| China: Mainland | 40.1 | 37.2 | 35.6 | 51.7 | 42.1 | 39.4 | 50 | 41 | 39 |
| Czechoslovakia | 15.0 | 15.0 | 15.3 | 11.1 | 11.1 | 11.3 | 719 | 724 | 735 |
| France | 17.6 | 18.4 | 21.3 | 15.0 | 17.2 | 17.5 | 275 | 318 | 325 |
| Germany, East | 7.2 | 7.2 | 7.5 | n.a. | 9.5 | 9.7 | n.a. | 570 | 561 |
| Germany, West | 35.7 | 35.9 | 41.6 | 29.8 | 26.8 | 31.0 | 486 | 436 | 503 |
| Greece | .9[35] | .8[3] | 1.0[3] | 2.0 | 1.5 | 1.5 | 207 | 150 | 157 |
| India | 10.1 | 10.9 | 10.7 | 12.1 | 13.6 | 12.6 | 16 | 18 | 19 |
| Italy | 21.8 | 24.2 | 25.0 | 18.2 | 20.4 | 19.7 | 319 | 360 | 345 |
| Japan | 97.2 | 99.5 | 101.7 | 59.6 | 63.7 | 65.4 | 500 | 538 | 561 |
| Korea, North | 3.5[3] | 3.5[3] | 3.5[3] | 6.1 | 5.8 | 5.6 | 320 | 312 | 304 |
| Korea, South | 5.1 | 5.7 | 5.9 | 8.9 | 7.5 | 13.1 | 222 | 192 | 338 |
| Mexico | 6.7 | 6.9 | 7.4 | 7.5 | 8.5 | 11.7 | 100 | 117 | 164 |
| Netherlands | 2.9 | 3.0 | 4.3 | 3.4 | 3.7 | 3.9 | 237 | 259 | 272 |
| Nigeria | .1[5] | .1 | z | .9 | 1.4 | 1.7 | 10 | 16 | 22 |
| Poland | 16.2 | 14.1 | 15.1 | 14.9 | 14.4 | 15.4 | 406 | 398 | 429 |
| Romania | 12.6 | 13.1 | 13.0 | 10.9 | 11.6 | 11.4 | 482 | 512 | 513 |
| South Africa | 7.0[5] | 8.4 | 9.0 | 4.6 | 5.6 | 6.9 | 130 | 162 | 201 |
| Soviet Union | 152.5 | 147.2 | 148.4 | n.a. | n.a. | n.a. | n.a. | n.a. | n.a. |
| Spain | 13.3 | 13.4 | 12.9 | 9.3 | 9.0 | 8.0 | 244 | 237 | 224 |
| Sweden | 4.2[5] | 3.9 | 3.8 | 3.5 | 3.5 | 3.4 | 419 | 423 | 412 |
| Turkey | 2.5 | 1.9 | 1.5[3] | 4.2 | 3.3 | 3.3 | 88 | 70 | 74 |
| United Kingdom | 15.0 | 13.7 | 15.6 | 14.1 | 14.2 | 14.9 | 249 | 251 | 267 |
| United States | 76.8[4] | 67.7[4] | 109.6[4] | 94.5 | 85.8 | 129.7 | 403 | 263 | 565 |
| Venezuela | 2.2[5] | 2.3 | 1.8 | 2.6 | 3.4 | 3.1 | 158 | 213 | 219 |
| Yugoslavia | 2.0 | 2.0 | 2.3 | 5.3 | 5.2 | 5.0 | 231 | 223 | 223 |
| **World** | **642.0** | **629.0** | **692.1** | n.a. | n.a. | n.a. | n.a. | n.a. | n.a. |

1. Year ending June 30. 2. Luxembourg included with Belgium. 3. Data from U.S. Bureau of Mines. 4. Excludes steel for castings made in foundries operated by companies not producing ingots. 5. Estimated. n.a. = not available. Z less than 50,000 metric tons. NOTE: Production data cover both ingots and steel for castings and exclude wrought (puddled) iron. Consumption data represent apparent consumption (i.e. production plus imports minus exports) and do not take into account changes in stock. *Source:* Statistical Office of the United Nations, New York, NY, *Statistical Yearbook.* (Copyright.)

# Communications
## (telephones, newspapers, radio, and television)

| Country | Tele- phones, in use[1] 1984 (1,000) | Tele- phones per 100 popula- tion, 1984 | Daily newspapers,[2] 1982 Circulation Copies per 1,000 popu- lation | Receiving sets, 1983 TV sets per 1,000 popu- lation | Receiving sets, 1983 Radios per 1,000 popu- lation |
|---|---|---|---|---|---|
| Algeria | n.a. | n.a. | 22 | 65 | 215 |
| Argentina | 3,230 | 10.3 | n.a. | 199 | 540 |
| Australia | 7,400 | 52.0 | 334[7] | 423 | 1,301 |
| Austria | 3,330 | 44.1 | 453[7] | 311[12] | 530[12] |
| Bangladesh | 100[5] | 0.1 | 6 | 1 | 8[12] |
| Belgium | 3,960 | 47.0 | 224 | 303[12] | 468[12] |
| Bolivia | 144 | 2.6 | 46 | 64 | 575 |
| Brazil | 8,540 | 6.3 | 48 | 127 | 386 |
| Bulgaria | n.a. | n.a. | 235 | 189[12] | 230 |
| Burma | 49[6] | 1.0 | 14 | n.a. | 23 |
| Cambodia | n.a. | n.a. | n.a. | 9 | 131 |
| Canada | 16,200 | 67.1 | 226 | 463 | 761 |
| Chile | 595 | 5.0 | 115 | 116 | 304 |
| China, People's Republic of | 5,150 | 1.0[7] | 33 | 7 | 67 |
| China, Republic of | 3,600 | n.a. | n.a. | n.a. | n.a. |
| Colombia | 1,750 | 6.0 | n.a. | 98 | 133 |
| Costa Rica | 265 | 11.0 | 77 | 76 | 86 |
| Cuba | n.a. | n.a. | 118 | 168 | 316 |
| Cyprus | 150 | 20.0 | n.a. | 139 | 611 |
| Czechoslovakia | n.a. | n.a. | 318 | 280[12] | 270[12] |
| Denmark | 3,590 | 70.6 | 356 | 369[12] | 392[12] |
| Dominican Republic | 175 | 3.0 | 42[7] | 92 | 201 |
| Ecuador | 290 | 3.3 | 64 | 62 | 319 |
| Egypt | 600[5] | 1.3 | 78 | 44 | 174 |
| El Salvador | 100 | 2.0 | n.a. | 63 | 362 |
| Ethiopia | n.a. | n.a. | 1 | 1 | 89 |
| Finland | 2,700 | 53.0 | 521 | 357[12] | 987 |
| France | 29,370 | 54.2 | 191[9] | 375 | 860 |
| Germany, East | 3,441 | n.a. | 535 | 358[12] | 384[12] |
| Germany, West | 31,370 | 51.0 | 408 | 360[12] | 401[12] |
| Ghana | 68 | 0.6 | 31[8] | 6 | 173 |
| Greece | 3,110 | 31.6 | n.a. | 173[12] | 406 |
| Guatemala | 97 | 1.6 | n.a. | 25 | 43 |
| Honduras | 33 | 1.0 | 61 | 13 | 49 |
| Hong Kong | 1,500 | n.a. | n.a. | 225 | 510 |
| Hungary | n.a. | n.a. | 249 | 371 | 540 |
| Iceland | 116 | 49.7 | 420 | 293[12] | 586[12] |
| India | 2,600 | 0.4 | 21 | 3[12] | 61[12] |
| Indonesia | 392 | 0.2 | n.a. | 22 | 138 |
| Iran | n.a. | n.a. | n.a. | 55 | 180 |
| Iraq | 500 | 3.9 | n.a. | 55 | 188 |
| Ireland | 779 | 22.2 | 215 | 239 | 456 |
| Israel | 1,302 | 32.1 | n.a. | 256 | 270 |
| Italy | 21,680 | 38.2 | 82 | 243[12] | 250[12] |
| Jamaica | 124 | 6.0 | 46 | 89 | 394 |
| Japan | 58,000 | 49.5 | 575 | 556 | 713 |
| Kenya | 216 | 1.3 | 12 | 4 | 34 |
| Korea, South | 4,800 | 121.0 | n.a. | 175 | 451 |
| Kuwait | 232 | 15.3 | 250 | 258 | 285 |
| Lebanon | 150 | 5.0 | n.a. | 296[13] | 797 |
| Luxembourg | 199 | 54.8 | 358[11] | 251[13] | 644[13] |
| Madagascar | 38 | 0.4 | 6 | 8 | 213 |
| Malaysia | 609 | 5.1 | n.a. | 96 | 437 |
| Mexico | 5,410 | 7.6 | n.a. | 111 | 290 |
| Morocco | 241 | 1.2 | n.a. | 39 | 163 |
| Netherlands | 8,030 | 56.0 | 322 | 450 | 793 |
| New Zealand | 1,700 | 55.0 | 325 | 288 | 890 |
| Nigeria | 155 | 0.2 | 6 | 5 | 79 |
| Norway | 2,200 | 53.5 | 483 | 319[12] | 412 |
| Pakistan | 314 | 0.3 | 14[11] | 12 | 78 |
| Panama | 213 | 10.0 | 61 | 122 | 160 |
| Paraguay | 64 | 2.0 | n.a. | 23 | 75 |
| Peru | 519 | 2.8 | n.a. | 49 | 160 |
| Philippines | 707 | 1.2 | n.a. | 26 | 45 |

| Country | Tele-phones, in use[1] 1984 (1,000) | Tele-phones per 100 popula-tion, 1984 | Daily newspapers,[2] 1982 Circulation Copies per 1,000 popu-lation | Receiving sets, 1983 TV sets per 1,000 popu-lation | Radios per 1,000 popu-lation |
|---|---|---|---|---|---|
| Poland | n.a. | n.a. | 218 | 234[12] | 247[12] |
| Portugal | 1,570 | 14.0 | 49 | 151[12] | 171 |
| Puerto Rico | n.a. | n.a. | 168 | 293 | 731 |
| Romania | n.a. | n.a. | 186 | 173[12] | 143[12] |
| Saudi Arabia | 790 | 8.0 | n.a. | 254 | 295 |
| Singapore | 700 | 26.5 | 286 | 188[12] | 272[12] |
| South Africa | 3,210 | 13.1 | 66[10] | 70[9] | 275[25] |
| Soviet Union | n.a. | n.a. | 405 | 308 | 514 |
| Spain | 13,300 | 35.0 | 79 | 258 | 285 |
| Sri Lanka | 75[5] | 0.5 | 111 | 3 | 117 |
| Sudan | 68 | 0.4 | 5 | 49 | 246 |
| Sweden | 7,130 | 85.5 | 524 | 390[12] | 858 |
| Switzerland | 4,980 | 77.0 | 381 | 378 | 364[12] |
| Syria | 472 | 4.7 | 12 | 44 | 195 |
| Thailand | 496 | 1.1 | n.a. | 17 | 146 |
| Trinidad and Tobago | 86 | 7.0 | 149 | 261 | 309 |
| Tunisia | 188 | 3.0 | 41 | 54 | 163 |
| Turkey | 2,390 | 5.3 | n.a. | 118 | 123 |
| United Kingdom | 29,100 | 51.7 | 421 | 479 | 993 |
| United States | 182,558 | 79.1 | 269 | 790 | 2,043 |
| Uruguay | 294 | 9.9 | n.a. | 124 | 558 |
| Venezuela | 1,380 | 8.5 | 186 | 126 | 405 |
| Vietnam | n.a. | n.a. | n.a. | n.a. | n.a. |
| Yugoslavia | 1,900[7] | n.a. | 103[7] | 203[12] | 238[12] |
| Zimbabwe | 236 | 3.1 | 21 | 12 | 45 |

1. Comprises public and private telephones installed which can be connected to a central exchange. 2. Publications containing general news and appearing at least 4 times a week, may range in size from a single sheet to 50 or more pages. Circulation data refer to average circulation per issue or number of printed copies per issue and include copies sold outside the country. 3. Estimated number of sets in use, except as noted. 4. Data cover estimated number of receivers in use, except as noted, and apply to all types of receivers for radio broadcasts to the public, including receivers connected to a radio "redistribution system" but excluding television sets. 5. Estimated. 6. 1982/83. 7. 1979. 8. 1978. 9. 1976. 10. 33 dailies. 11. 9 dailies. 12. 8 dailies. 13. 1977. 14. 4 dailies. 15. 3 dailies. 16. 26 dailies. 17. 32 dailies. 18. 18 dailies. 19. 17 dailies. 20. Data include non-daily newspapers. 21. 2 dailies. 22. Number of licenses issued. 23. 1980. NOTE: n.a. = not available. *Sources:* Except Taiwan, Statistical Office of the United Nations, New York, NY, *Statistical Yearbook* (copyright) and United Nations Educational, Scientific, and Cultural Organization, Paris, France, *Statistical Yearbook* (copyright); Taiwan, U.S. Bureau of the Census. Data from Republic of China publications. All from *Statistical Abstract of the United States 1985.* Telephone information from *The World Factbook 1985.*

## World's 20 Most Populous Countries: 1986 and 2100

| | 1986 | | | 2100 | |
|---|---|---|---|---|---|
| Rank | Country | Population | Rank | Country | Population |
| 1. | China | 1,050,000,000 | 1. | India | 1,631,800,000 |
| 2. | India | 785,000,000 | 2. | China | 1,571,400,000 |
| 3. | USSR | 280,000,000 | 3. | Nigeria | 508,800,000 |
| 4. | United States | 241,000,000 | 4. | USSR | 375,900,000 |
| 5. | Indonesia | 168,400,000 | 5. | Indonesia | 356,300,000 |
| 6. | Brazil | 143,300,000 | 6. | Pakistan | 315,800,000 |
| 7. | Japan | 121,500,000 | 7. | United States | 308,700,000 |
| 8. | Nigeria | 105,400,000 | 8. | Bangladesh | 297,100,000 |
| 9. | Bangladesh | 104,100,000 | 9. | Brazil | 293,200,000 |
| 10. | Pakistan | 101,900,000 | 10. | Mexico | 195,500,000 |
| 11. | Mexico | 81,700,000 | 11. | Ethiopia | 173,300,000 |
| 12. | Vietnam | 62,000,000 | 12. | Vietnam | 168,100,000 |
| 13. | Germany, West | 60,700,000 | 13. | Iran | 163,800,000 |
| 14. | Philippines | 58,100,000 | 14. | Zaire | 138,900,000 |
| 15. | Italy | 57,200,000 | 15. | Japan | 127,900,000 |
| 16. | United Kingdom | 56,600,000 | 16. | Philippines | 125,100,000 |
| 17. | France | 55,400,000 | 17. | Tanzania | 119,600,000 |
| 18. | Thailand | 52,800,000 | 18. | Kenya | 116,400,000 |
| 19. | Turkey | 52,300,000 | 19. | Burma | 111,700,000 |
| 20. | Egypt | 50,500,000 | 20. | Egypt | 110,500,000 |

From the *1986 World Population Data Sheet* of the Population Reference Bureau, Inc. *Original sources:* 1986, Population Reference Bureau; 2100, World Bank.

# Countries, Territories, and Dependencies

For later developments, *see* Current Events

## AFGHANISTAN

**Democratic Republic of Afghanistan**
**President:** Babrak Karmal (1979)
**Premier:** Sultan Ali Keshtmand (1981)
**Area:** 251,000 sq mi. (650,090 sq km)
**Population (est. mid-1986):** 15,400,000 (average annual growth rate: 2.4%)
**Density per square mile:** 61.35
**Capital:** Kabul
**Largest cities (est. 1983):** Kabul, 750,000; Kandahar, 225,000; Herat, 150,000
**Monetary unit:** Afghani
**Languages:** Pushtu and Dari Persian (both official)
**Religion:** Islam (Sunni, 74%; Shiite, 25%; other 1%)
**National name:** Jamhouri Democratike Afghanistan
**Literacy rate:** 12%
**Economic summary:** Gross national product (1985): $3.0 billion. Average annual growth rate (1976–79): 2.5%. Per capita income (1984): $160. Land used for agriculture: 12%; labor force: 68%; principal products: wheat, grains, cotton, fruits, nuts. Labor force in industry: 10%; major products: carpets and textiles. Natural resources: natural gas, oil, coal, copper, sulfur, lead, zinc, iron, salt, precious and semi-precious stones. Exports: fresh and dried fruits, natural gas, carpets. Imports: petroleum products and food supplies. Major trading partners: U.S.S.R., and Soviet bloc countries.

**Geography.** Afghanistan, approximately the size of Texas, lies wedged between the U.S.S.R., China, Pakistan, and Iran. The country is split east to west by the Hindu Kush mountain range, rising in the east to heights of 24,000 feet (7,315 m). With the exception of the southwest, most of the country is covered by high snow-capped mountains and is traversed by deep valleys.

**Government.** A Marxist "people's republic" was created by the coup of April 27, 1978. In May 1986, a shake-up led to Lt. Gen. Mohammed Najibullah, head of the secret police, becoming general secretary of the Central Committee of the People's Democratic Party of Afghanistan, replacing Babrak Karmal who remained as figurehead President of the 107-member Revolutionary Council.

**History.** Darius I and Alexander the Great were the first conquerors to use Afghanistan as the gateway to India. Islamic conquerors arrived in the 7th century and Genghis Khan and Tamerlane followed in the 13th and 14th centuries.

In the 19th century, Afghanistan became a battleground in the rivalry of imperial Britain and Czarist Russia for the control of Central Asia. The Afghan Wars (1838–42 and 1878–81) fought against the British by Dost Mohammed and his son and grandson ended in defeat.

Afghanistan regained autonomy by the Anglo-Russian agreement of 1907 and full independence by the Treaty of Rawalpindi in 1919. Emir Amanullah founded the kingdom in 1926.

Taraki's attempts to create a Marxist state with Soviet aid brought armed resistance from conservative Muslim opposition.

Taraki was succeeded by Prime Minister Hafizullah Amin. Amin was replaced by Babrak Karmal, who had called for Soviet troops under a mu-

tual defense treaty. Pakistan and other Moslem nations called for a U.N. Security Council session and charged that Amin had been executed on Dec. 27 by Soviet troops already present in Kabul. The Council's call for immediate withdrawal of an estimated 40,000 Soviet troops was vetoed by the U.S. S.R. on Jan. 8, 1980.

The Soviet invasion was met with unanticipated fierce resistance from the Afghan population, resulting in a bloody, dirty and to an extent, secret war that still raged late in 1986. Soviet troops were estimated by Western sources in 1986 to number about 110,000 in Afghanistan, with another 40,000 backing them up just across the Soviet border. Pitted against the Soviets' bombers, helicopter gunships, heavy artillery and mechanized infantry were upward of 30,000 Afghan tribesmen who called themselves "mujahedeen," or "holy warriors." In the early fighting, many of the guerrillas were armed only with 19th-century flintlock rifles, but later they acquired more modern weapons, including rockets that they used to attack Soviet installations.

By 1986, Soviet high-altitude saturation bombing had demolished many villages in several regions of the country. Although there were no available accurate figures, the nation's population was reported to have shrunk by as much as one third, with at least four million having fled to Iran or Pakistan and up to one million killed in the war.

## ALBANIA

**People's Socialist Republic of Albania**
**President of Presidium:** Ramiz Alia (1982)
**Premier:** Adil Carcani (1982)
**Area:** 11,100 sq mi. (28,748 sq km)
**Population (est. mid-1986):** 3,000,000 (average annual growth rate: 2.0%)
**Density per square mile:** 270.3
**Capital and largest city (est. 1983):** Tirana, 200,000
**Monetary unit:** Lek
**Language:** Albanian
**Religions:** Historically Islam 70%; Greek Orthodox, 20%; Roman Catholic, 10%
**National name:** Republika Popullore Socialiste e Shqipërisë
**Literacy rate** 75%
**Economic summary:** Gross national product (1985 est.): $2.7 billion. Average annual growth rate (1970–78): 4.2%. Per capita income (1984 est.): $900. Land used for agriculture: 43%; labor force: 61%; principal products: wheat, corn, potatoes, sugar beets, cotton, tobacco. Labor force in industry: 18%; major products: textiles, timber, construction materials, fuels, semi-processed minerals. Exports: minerals, metals, fuels, foodstuffs, agricultural materials. Imports: machinery, equipment, and spare parts, minerals, metals, fuels, construction materials, foodstuffs. Major trading partner: Yugoslavia

**Geography.** Albania is situated on the eastern shore of the Adriatic Sea, with Yugoslavia to the north and east and Greece to the south. Slightly larger than Maryland, it is a mountainous country, mostly over 3,000 feet (914 m) above sea level, with a narrow, marshy coastal plain crossed by several rivers. The centers of population are contained in the interior mountain plateaus and basins.

**Government.** The last staunchly Stalinist Communist state, Albania is ruled by the Albanian Workers (Communist) Party, headed by a Politburo which hands down all policy decisions. President Ramiz Alia took over as First Secretary of the party and the Politburo upon the death in 1985 of Énver Hoxha, who wielded absolute power in the party posts for four decades.

**History.** Albania proclaimed its independence on Nov. 28, 1912, after a history of Roman, Byzantine, and Turkish domination.

Largely agricultural, Albania is one of the poorest countries in Europe. A battlefield in World War I, after the war it became a republic in which a conservative Moslem landlord, Ahmed Zogu, proclaimed himself President in 1925, and then proclaimed himself King Zog I in a monarchy in 1928. He ruled until Italy annexed Albania in 1939. Communist guerrillas under Enver Hoxha seized power in 1944, near the end of World War II.

His regime closed all of the nation's 2,169 churches and mosques in 1967 in a move to make Albania "the first atheist state in the world."

Hoxha died on April 11, 1985, at the age of 78. His successor as Communist party chief was Ramiz Alia, 59, who had been President since 1982.

# ALGERIA

**Democratic and Popular Republic of Algeria**
**President:** Chadli Bendjedid (1979)
**Prime Minister:** Abdelhamid Brahimi (1984)
**Area:** 919,595 sq mi. (2,381,751 sq km)
**Population (est. mid-1986):** 22,800,000 (average annual growth rate: 3.2%)
**Density per square mile:** 24.8
**Capital:** Algiers
**Largest cities (est. 1982):** Algiers, 2,500,000; Oran, 600,000; Constantine, 500,000; Annaba, 300,000
**Monetary unit:** Dinar
**Languages:** Arabic (official), French
**Religion:** Islam (Sunni)
**National name:** République Algérienne Democratique et Populaire—El Djemhouria El Djazaïria Demokratia Echaabia
**Literacy rate** 46%
**Economic summary:** Gross national product (est. 1984): $51.9 billion. Annual growth rate (1984): 4.0%. Per capita income (1984): $2,430. Land used for agriculture: 3%; labor force: 19%; principal products: wheat, barley, oats, wine, fruits, olives, vegetables, livestock. Labor force in industry: 20%; major products: petroleum, gas, petrochemicals, fertilizers, iron and steel, textiles, transport equipment. Natural resources: petroleum, natural gas, iron ore, phosphates, lead, zinc, mercury. Exports: petroleum and gas. Imports: food, capital and consumer goods. Major trading partners: U.S., West Germany, France, Italy.

**Geography.** Nearly four times the size of Texas, Algeria is bordered on the west by Morocco and on the east by Tunisia and Libya. To the south are Mauritania, Mali, and Niger. Low plains cover small areas near the Mediterranean coast, with 68% of the country a plateau between 2,625 and 5,250 feet (800 and 1,600 m) above sea level. The highest point is Mount Tahat in the Sahara, which rises 9,850 feet (3,000 m).

**Government.** Algeria is governed by the President, whose term runs for 5 years. A new Constitution was approved on Nov. 19, 1976.

A National Popular Assembly of 281 members exercises legislative power, serving for a five-year term. The National Liberation Front, which led the struggle for independence from France, is the only legal party.

**History.** As ancient Numidia, Algeria became a Roman colony at the close of the Punic Wars (145 B.C.). Conquered by the Vandals about A.D. 440, it fell from a high state of civilization to virtual barbarism, from which it partly recovered after invasion by the Moslems about 650.

In 1492 the Moors and Jews, who had been expelled from Spain, settled in Algeria. Falling under Turkish control in 1518, Algiers served for three centuries as the headquarters of the Barbary pirates. The French took Algeria in 1830 and made it a part of France in 1848.

On July 5, 1962, Algeria was proclaimed independent. In October 1963, Ahmed Ben Bella was elected President. He began to nationalize foreign holdings and aroused opposition. He was overthrown in a military coup on June 19, 1965, by Col. Houari Boumediène, who suspended the Constitution and sought to restore financial stability.

Boumediène died in December 1978 after a long illness. Chadli Bendjedid, Secretary-General of the National Liberation Front, took the presidency in a smooth transition of power. On July 4, 1979, he released from house arrest former President Ahmed Ben Bella, who had been confined for 14 years since his overthrow.

Algeria, chosen by Iran to represent it in negotiations in November 1980 with the United States, was able to secure the eventual release of 52 Americans who had been held hostage in the U.S. Embassy in Teheran. The hostages were flown to Algiers on Jan. 20, 1981, and turned over to U.S. custody, ending 444 days in captivity.

# ANDORRA

**Principality of Andorra**
**Episcopal Co-Prince:** Msgr. Joan Martí y Alanis, Bishop of Seo de Urgel, Spain
**French Co-Prince:** François Mitterrand, President of France (1981)
**First Syndic:** Francesc Cerqueda Pasquet (1982)
**Area:** 175 sq mi. (453 sq km)
**Population (est. 1985):** 47,000 (average annual growth rate: 5.4%)
**Density per square mile:** 200.0
**Capital (est. 1983):** Andorra la Vella, 15,000
**Monetary units:** French franc and Spanish peseta
**Languages:** Catalán (official); French, Spanish
**Religion:** Roman Catholic
**National names:** Les Vallées d'Andorre-Valls d'Andorra
**Literacy rate** 100%
**Economic summary:** Land used for agriculture: 4%; labor force: 20%; principal products: oats, barley, cattle, sheep. Labor force in industry: 80%; major products: tobacco products and electric power; tourism. Natural resources: water power, mineral water. Major trading partners: Spain and France.

**Geography.** Andorra lies high in the Pyrenees

Mountains on the French-Spanish border. The country is drained by the Valira River.

**Government.** A General Council of 28 members, elected for four years, chooses the First Syndic and Second Syndic. In 1976 the Andorran Democratic Party, the principality's first political party, was formed.

**History.** An autonomous and semi-independent co-principality, Andorra has been under the joint suzerainty of the French state and the Spanish bishops of Urgel since 1278.

# ANGOLA

**People's Republic of Angola**
**President:** José Eduardo dos Santos (1979)
**Area:** 481,350 sq mi. (1,246,700 sq km)
**Population (est. mid-1986):** 8,200,000 (average annual growth rate: 2.5%)
**Density per square mile:** 17.0
**Capital and largest city (est. 1983):** Luanda, 525,000
**Monetary unit:** Kwanza
**Languages:** Bantu, Portuguese (official)
**Religions:** Roman Catholic, 69%; Protestant, 20%; Animist, 10%
**Literacy rate:** 20%
**Economic summary:** Gross national product (1980): $3.3 billion. Average annual growth rate (1981): 0.1%. Per capita income (1980): $470. Principal agricultural products: coffee, sisal, corn, cotton, sugar, tobacco, bananas. Major industrial products: oil, diamonds, processed fish, tobacco, textiles, cement, processed food and sugar. Natural resources: diamonds, gold, iron, oil. Exports: oil, coffee, diamonds, fish and fish products, iron ore, timber, corn. Imports: machinery and electrical equipment, bulk iron, steel and metals, textiles, clothing. Major trading partners: Brazil, U.S.S.R., Portugal, U.S.

**Geography.** Angola, more than three times the size of California, extends for more than 1,000 miles (1,-609 km) along the South Atlantic in southwestern Africa. Zaire is to the north and east; Zambia to the east, and South-West Africa (Namibia) to the south. A plateau averaging 6,000 feet (1,829 m) above sea level rises abruptly from the coastal lowlands. Nearly all the land is desert or savanna, with hardwood forests in the northeast.

**Government.** A Marxist "people's republic" is the recognized government, but large areas in the east and south are held by the Union for the Total Independence of Angola (Unita), led by Jonas Savimbi. President José Eduardo dos Santos heads the only official party, the Popular Movement for the Liberation of Angola-Workers Party. The Popular Movement won out over Savimbi's group and a third element in an internal struggle after Portugal granted its former colony independence on Nov. 11, 1975. Elections promised at the time of independence have never taken place, and the government relies heavily on Soviet support and Cuban troops, while Savimbi receives aid from South Africa.

**History.** Discovered by the Portuguese navigator Diego Cao in 1482, Angola became a link in trade with India and the Far East. Later it was a major source of slaves for Portugal's New World colony of Brazil. Development of the interior began after the Treaty of Berlin in 1885 fixed the colony's bor-

ders, and British and Portuguese investment pushed mining, railways, and agriculture.

Following World War II, independence movements began but were sternly suppressed by military force. The April revolution of 1974 brought about a reversal of Portugal's policy, and the next year President Francisco da Costa Gomes signed an agreement to grant independence to Angola. The plan called for election of a constituent assembly and a settlement of differences by the MPLA and the National Front for the Liberation of Angola (FNLA) and the National Union for the Total Independence of Angola (UNITA).

The Organization of African Unity, recognized the MPLA government led by Agostinho Neto on Feb. 11, 1976, and the People's Republic of Angola became the 47th member of the organization.

Although militarily victorious, Neto's regime had yet to consolidate its power in opposition strongholds in the east and south.

In March 1977 and May 1978, Zairean refugees in Angola invaded Zaire's Shaba Province, bringing charges by Zairean President Mobutu Sese Seko that the unsuccessful invasions were Soviet-backed with Angolan help. Angola, the U.S.S.R., and Cuba denied complicity.

Neto died in Moscow of cancer on Sept. 10, 1979. The Planning Minister, José Eduardo dos Santos, was named President.

The South-West Africa People's Organization, or Swapo, the guerrillas fighting for the independence of the disputed territory south of Angola also known as Namibia, fought from bases in Angola and the South African armed forces also maintained troops there until early June 1985.

The South African troops left after Angola agreed to try to limit guerrilla activity in the Namibia border region and to patrol the area jointly with South African forces until the withdrawal was complete. However, after their departure, South African troops pursued Swapo guerrillas into Angola and killed 61 of them in late June of 1985.

In February 1986, President Reagan, following a repeal of an earlier ban on military aid to Joseph Savimbi's UNITA rebels, announced that $15 million in aid was being given to them.

# ANTIGUA AND BARBUDA

**Sovereign:** Queen Elizabeth II
**Governor-General:** Sir Wilfred E. Jacobs (1981)
**Prime Minister:** Vere Bird (1981)
**Area:** 170 sq mi. (442 sq km)
**Population (est. mid-1986):** 100,000 (average annual growth rate: 1%)
**Density per square mile:** 588.2
**Capital and largest city (est. 1983):** St. John's, 25,000
**Monetary unit:** East Caribbean dollar
**Language:** English
**Religions:** Anglican and Roman Catholic
**Literacy rate:** 88%
**Member of Commonwealth of Nations**
**Economic summary:** Gross national product (1986): $130 million. Average annual growth rate (1978–82): −5.2%. Per capita income (1983): $1,750. Land used for agriculture: 54%; principal product: cotton. Major industry: tourism. Exports: clothing, rum, lobsters. Imports: fuel, food, machinery. Major trading partners: U.K., U.S.

**Geography.** Antigua, the larger of the two main islands, is low-lying except for a range of hills in the south that rise to their highest point at Boggy Peak (1,330 ft; 405 m). Deforested and without major streams, the island is subject to droughts despite a mean annual rainfall of 44 inches. Barbuda is a coral island, well wooded.

**Government.** Executive power is held by the Cabinet, presided over by Prime Minister Vere C. Bird. A 17-member Parliament is elected by universal suffrage. The Antigua Labour Party, led by Prime Minister Bird, holds 16 seats and the remaining one is held by an independent member, Eric Burton, who has been appointed opposition leader.

**History.** Antigua was discovered by Christopher Columbus in 1493 and named for the Church of Santa Maria la Antigua in Seville. Colonized by Britain in 1632, it joined the West Indies Federation in 1958. With the breakup of the Federation, it became one of the West Indies Associated States in 1967, self-governing in internal affairs. Full independence was granted Nov. 1, 1981.

# ARGENTINA

**Argentine Republic**
**President:** Rául Alfonsín (1983)
**Area:** 1,072,067 sq mi. (2,776,654 sq km)
**Population (est. mid-1986):** 31,200,000 (average annual growth rate: 1.6%)
**Density per square mile:** 29.1
**Capital:** Buenos Aires
**Largest cities (est. 1983):** Buenos Aires, 3,000,000; Córdoba, 1,000,000; Rosario, 950,000; La Plafa, 450,000; San Miguel de Tucumán, 400,000
**Monetary unit:** Austral
**Language:** Spanish
**Religion:** Predominantly Roman Catholic
**National name:** República Argentina
**Literacy rate** 94%
**Economic summary:** Gross national product (1982): $58.2 billion. Average annual growth rate (1970–79): 1.0%. Per capita income (1980): $2,390. Land used for agriculture: 57%; labor force: 19%; principal products: grains, oilseeds, livestock products. Labor force in industry: 25%; major products: processed foods, motor vehicles, consumer durables, textiles, chemicals. Natural resources: minerals, lead, zinc, tin, copper, iron, manganese, oil, uranium. Exports: meats, corn, wheat, wool, hides. Imports: machinery, fuel and lubricating oils, iron and steel. Major trading partners: U.S., Brazil, Italy, West Germany, Netherlands, Soviet Union.

**Geography.** With an area slightly less than one third of the United States and second in South America only to its eastern neighbor, Brazil, in size and population, Argentina is a plain, rising from the Atlantic to the Chilean border and the towering Andes peaks. Aconcagua (23,034 ft.; 7,021 m) is the highest peak in the world outside Asia. It is bordered also by Bolivia and Paraguay on the north, and by Uruguay on the east.

The northern area is the swampy and partly wooded Gran Chaco, bordering on Bolivia and Paraguay. South of that are the rolling, fertile pampas, rich for agriculture and grazing and supporting most of the population. Next southward is Patagonia, a region of cool, arid steppes with some wooded and fertile sections.

**Government.** Argentina is a federal union of 22 provinces, one national territory, and the Federal District. Under the Constitution of 1853 (restored by a Constituent National Convention in 1957), the President and Vice President are elected every six years by popular vote through an electoral college. The President appoints his Cabinet. The Vice President presides over the Senate but has no other powers. The Congress consists of two houses: a 46-member Senate and a 254-member Chamber of Deputies.

President Raúl Alfonsín's civilian government was inaugurated in December 1983. Mid-term elections in November 1985 gave his Radical Union Party more than half the seats in the Chamber.

**History.** Discovered in 1516 by Juan Díaz de Solis, Argentina developed slowly under Spanish colonial rule. Buenos Aires was settled in 1580; the cattle industry was thriving as early as 1600.

Invading British forces were expelled in 1806–07, and when Napoleon conquered Spain, the Argentinian set up their own government in the name of the Spanish King in 1810. On July 9, 1816, independence was formally declared.

As in World War I, Argentina proclaimed neutrality at the outbreak of World War II, but in the closing phase declared war on the Axis on March 27, 1945, and became a founding member of the United Nations. Juan D. Perón, an army colonel, emerged as the strongman of the postwar era, winning the Presidential elections of 1946 and 1951.

Opposition to Perón's increasing authoritarianism, led to a coup by the armed forces that sent Perón into exile in 1955. Argentina entered a long period of military dictatorships with brief intervals of constitutional government.

The former dictator returned to power in 1973 and his wife was elected Vice-President.

After Peron's death in 1974, his widow became the hemisphere's first woman chief of state, but was deposed in 1976 by a military junta.

In December 1981, Lt. Gen. Leopoldo Galtieri, commander of the army, was named president.

On April 2, 1982, Galtieri landed thousands of troops on the Falkland Islands on and reclaimed the Malvinas, their Spanish name, as national territory. By May 21, 5,000 British marines and paratroops landed from the British armada, and regained control of the islands.

Galtieri resigned three days after the surrender of the island garrison on June 14. Maj. Gen. Reynaldo Bignone, took office as President on July 1. Civilian rule was promised by early 1984 and on July 16 Bignone lifted the six-year ban on political parties.

In the presidential election of October 1983, Raúl Alfonsín, leader of the middle-class Radical Civic Union, handed the Peronist Party its first defeat since its founding.

Among the enormous problems facing Alfonsín after eight years of mismanagement under military rule was a $45-billion foreign debt, the developing world's third largest. In some circles, fears were voiced that the new civilian government might repudiate the debt, triggering a wholesale repudiation by debtor countries that could bring on a worldwide financial collapse. But after cliffhanging negotiations with American, European, and Japanese banks representing the country's private creditors, the Alfonsín government agreed on June 29, 1984, to pay $350 million in overdue interest and was moving toward austerity measures.

With the arrears mounting at the rate of $150

million a month, the debt to foreign creditors mounted to $48 billion by mid-1985, and more than $1 billion was past due. On June 11, the Alfonsin government reached agreement with the International Monetary Fund on an austerity program designed to put Argentina into a position to pay its way internationally and keep current with its debt obligations. The agreement opened the door for up to $1.2 billion of new loans to Argentina. A key requirement of the pact was that inflation, which had been running at 1,010%, be brought down to 150% by April 1986.

Three days later, on June 14, President Alfonsin announced an "economy of war" to bring the inflation rate down. The program combined the creation of a new currency—the austral, meaning southern—to replace the peso, wage and price controls and a halt to the government's deficit spending. After a brief bank holiday, banks reopened and exchanged australs for pesos at the rate of 1,000 pesos for one new austral. To maintain the value of the new currency, the government promised to stop printing money to balance its budget.

# AUSTRALIA

**Commonwealth of Australia**
**Sovereign:** Queen Elizabeth II
**Governor-General:** Sir Ninian Stephen (1982)
**Prime Minister:** Robert J. L. Hawke (1983)
**Area:** 2,966,150 sq mi. (7,682,300 sq km)
**Population (est. mid-1986):** 15,800,000 (average annual growth rate: 0.8%)
**Density per square mile:** 5.3
**Capital (est. 1984):** Canberra, 264,400
**Largest cities (est. 1984 for metropolitan area):** Sydney, 3,358,000; Melbourne, 2,890,700; Brisbane, 1,146,-600; Adelaide, 979,600; Perth, 983,400
**Monetary unit:** Australian dollar
**Language:** English
**Religions:** Roman Catholic, 28%; Anglican, 28%; Uniting Church (combined Methodist-Presbyterian), 14%
**Literacy rate:** 99%
**Member of Commonwealth of Nations**
**Economic summary:** Gross national product (1983): $166.2 billion. Average annual growth rate (1970–79): 1.4%. Per capita income (1980): $9,820. Land used for agriculture: 64%; labor force: 6.2% (1984); principal products: wool, meat, cereals, sugar, wine grapes, sheep, cattle, dairy products. Labor force in industry: 25.6% (1984); major products: machinery, motor vehicles, iron and steel, textiles, chemicals. Natural resources: gold, iron ore, bauxite, zinc, lead, tin, coal, oil, gas, copper, nickel, diamonds, uranium, timber. Exports: agricultural products, metal ores, wool, coal. Imports: manufactured raw materials, capital equipment, consumer goods. Major trading partners: Japan, U.S., U.K., New Zealand, West Germany, North Korea, Singapore.

**Geography.** The continent of Australia, with the island state of Tasmania, is approximately equal in area to the United States (excluding Alaska and Hawaii), and is nearly 50% larger than Europe (excluding the U.S.S.R.).

Mountain ranges run from north to south along the east coast, reaching their highest point in Mount Kosciusko (7,308 ft; 2,228 m). The western half of the continent is occupied by a desert plateau that rises into barren, rolling hills near the west coast. It includes the Great Victoria Desert to the south and the Great Sandy Desert to the north. The

Great Barrier Reef, extending about 1,245 miles (2,000 km), lies along the northeast coast.

The island of Tasmania (26,178 sq mi.; 67,800 sq km) is off the southeastern coast.

**Government.** The Federal Parliament consists of a bicameral legislature. The House of Representatives has 148 members elected for three years by popular vote. The Senate has 76 members elected by popular vote for six years. One half of the Senate is elected every three years. Voting is compulsory at 18. Supreme federal judicial power is vested in the High Court of Australia in the Federal Courts, and in the State Courts invested by Parliament with Federal jurisdiction. The High Court consists of seven justices, appointed by the Governor-General in Council. Each of the states has its own judicial system.

The major political parties are the Australian Labor Party (82 seats in the House of Representatives), led by Prime Minister R.J.L. (Bob) Hawke; Liberal Party (45 seats) led by John Howard; National Party (21 seats), led by Ian M. Sinclair.

**History.** Dutch, Portuguese, and Spanish ships sighted Australia in the 17th century; the Dutch landed at the Gulf of Carpentaria in 1606. Australia was called New Holland, Botany Bay, and New South Wales until about 1820.

Captain James Cook, in 1770, claimed possession for Great Britain.

Free settlers established six colonies: New South Wales (1786), Tasmania (then Van Diemen's Land) (1825), Western Australia (1829), South Australia (1834), Victoria (1851), and Queensland (1859).

The six colonies became states and in 1901 federated into the Commonwealth of Australia with a Constitution that incorporated British parliamentary tradition and U.S. federal experience. Australia became known for liberal legislation: free compulsory education, protected trade unionism with industrial conciliation and arbitration, the "Australian" ballot facilitating selection, the secret ballot, women's suffrage, maternity allowances, and sickness and old age pensions.

In the election of 1983, Robert Hawke, head of the Labor Party, became Prime Minister. The Labor government was reelected in a Federal election in December 1984.

By mid-1982, however, world recession was slowing the resources boom and for the first time in years Australia reported a drop in employment and a record $3.4-billion trade deficit for the year ending June 30.

## Australian External Territories

**Norfolk Island** (13 sq mi.; 36.3 sq km) was placed under Australian administration in 1914. Population in 1983 was about 1,800.

**The Ashmore and Cartier Islands** (.8 sq mi.), situated in the Indian Ocean off the northwest coast of Australia, came under Australian administration in 1934. In 1938 the islands were annexed to the Northern Territory. On the attainment of self-government by the Northern Territory in 1978, the islands which are uninhabited were retained as Commonwealth Territory.

**The Australian Antarctic Territory** (2,360,000 sq

mi.; 6,112,400 sq km), comprises all the islands and territories, other than Adélie Land, situated south of lat. 60° S and lying between long. 160° to 45° E. It came under Australian administration in 1936.

**Heard Island and the McDonald Islands** (158 sq mi.; 409.2 sq km), lying in the sub-Antarctic, were placed under Australian administration in 1947. The islands are uninhabited.

**Christmas Island** (52 sq mi.; 134.7 sq km) is situated in the Indian Ocean. It came under Australian administration in 1958. Population in 1983 was 3,214.

**Coral Sea Islands** (400,000 sq mi.; 1,036,000 sq km, but only a few sq mi. of land) became a territory of Australia in 1969. There is no permanent population on the islands.

# AUSTRIA

**Republic of Austria**
**President:** Kurt Waldheim (1986)
**Chancellor:** Franz Vranitzki (1986)
**Area:** 32,375 sq mi. (83,851 sq km)
**Population (est. mid-1986):** 7,600,000 (average annual growth rate: 0.0%)
**Density per square mile:** 234.7
**Capital:** Vienna
**Largest cities (est. 1983):** Vienna, 1,550,000; Graz, 240,000; Linz, 200,000; Salzburg, 135,000; Innsbruck, 115,000; Klagenfurt, 85,000
**Monetary unit:** Schilling
**Language:** German
**Religion:** Roman Catholic, 89%
**Literacy rate:** 98%
**National name:** Republik Österreich
**Economic summary:** Gross national product (1984): $64.21 billion. Average annual growth rate (1984): 2.2%. Per capita income (1984): $8,500. Land used for agriculture: 20%; labor force: 18%; principal products: livestock, forest products, grains, sugar beets, potatoes. Labor force in industry: 49%; principal products: iron and steel, chemicals, machinery, paper and pulp. Natural resources: iron ore, petroleum, timber, magnesite, aluminum, coal, lignite, cement, copper. Exports: iron and steel products, timber, paper, textiles, electrotechnical machines, chemical products. Imports: machinery, chemicals, foodstuffs, textiles and clothing, petroleum. Major trading partners: West Germany, Italy, Switzerland, U.S., Eastern Europe.

**Geography.** Slightly smaller than Maine, Austria includes much of the mountainous territory of the eastern Alps (about 75% of the area). The country contains many snowfields, glaciers, and snow-capped peaks, the highest being the Grossglockner (12,530 ft; 3,819 m). The Danube is the principal river. Forests and woodlands cover about 40% of the land area.

Almost at the heart of Europe, Austria has as its neighbors Italy, Switzerland, West Germany, Czechoslovakia, Hungary, Yugoslavia, and Liechtenstein.

**Government.** Austria is a federal republic composed of nine provinces (Bundesländer), including Vienna. The President is elected by the people for a term of six years. The bicameral legislature consists of the Bundesrat, with 58 members chosen by the provincial assemblies, and the Nationalrat,

with 183 members popularly elected for four years. Presidency of the Bundesrat revolves every six months, going to the provinces in alphabetical order.

The major political parties are the Social Democratic Party (90 of 183 seats in Nationalrat), led by Chancellor Franz Vranitzki; People's Party (81 seats); Freiheitliche Partei (12 seats).

**History.** Settled in prehistoric times, the Central European land that is now Austria was overrun in pre-Roman times by various tribes, including the Celts. Charlemagne conquered the area in 788 and encouraged colonization and Christianity. In 1252, Ottokar, King of Bohemia, gained possession, only to lose the territories to Rudolf of Hapsburg in 1278. Thereafter, until World War I, Austria's history was largely that of its ruling house, the Hapsburgs.

Austria emerged from the Congress of Vienna in 1815 as the Continent's dominant power. The *Ausgleich* of 1867 provided for a dual sovereignty, the empire of Austria and the kingdom of Hungary, under Francis Joseph I, who ruled until his death on Nov. 21, 1916. He was succeeded by his grandnephew, Charles I.

During World War I, Austria-Hungary was one of the Central Powers with Germany, Bulgaria, and Turkey, and the conflict left the country in political chaos and economic ruin. Austria, shorn of Hungary, was proclaimed a republic in 1918, and the monarchy was dissolved in 1919.

A parliamentary democracy was set up by the Constitution of Nov. 10, 1920. On March 12, 1938, German troops occupied the country, and Hitler proclaimed its *Anschluss* (union) with Germany, annexing it to the Third Reich.

After World War II, the U.S. and Britain declared the Austrians a "liberated" people. But the Russians prolonged the occupation. Finally Austria concluded a state treaty with the U.S.S.R. and the other occupying powers and regained its independence on May 15, 1955. The second Austrian republic, established Dec. 19, 1945, on the basis of the 1920 Constitution (amended in 1929), was declared by the federal parliament to be permanently neutral.

Vienna has since become a headquarters for several international organizations such as OPEC.

On June 8, 1986, former UN Secretary-General Kurt Waldheim was elected to the ceremonial office of President in a campaign marked by controversy over his alleged links to Nazi war-crimes in Yugoslavia.

# BAHAMAS

**Commonwealth of the Bahamas**
**Sovereign:** Queen Elizabeth II
**Governor-General:** Sir Gerald Cash (1979)
**Prime Minister:** Lynden O. Pindling (1967)
**Area:** 5,380 sq mi. (13,939 sq km)
**Population (est. mid-1986):** 200,000 (average annual growth rate: 1.9%)
**Density per square mile:** 37.2
**Capital and largest city (est. 1984 for metropolitan area):** Nassau, 139,000
**Monetary unit:** Bahamian dollar
**Language:** English
**Religions:** Baptist, 29%; Anglican, 23%; Roman Catholic, 23%; Methodist, 7%

Literacy rate: 89%
Member of Commonwealth of Nations
Economic summary: Gross national product (1984):
$1,800 million. Average annual growth rate (1970–82):
4.1%. Per capita income (1984): $7,950. Principal
agricultural products: fruits, vegetables. Major industrial
products: fish, petroleum, pharmaceutical products;
tourism. Natural resources: salt, aragonite. Exports:
lobster, fish, pharmaceuticals, cement, rum. Imports:
foodstuffs, manufactured goods, fuels. Major trading
partners: U.S., U.K., Nigeria, Canada.

**Geography.** The Bahamas are an archipelago of
about 700 islands and 2,400 uninhabited islets and
cays lying 50 miles off the east coast of Florida.
They extend from northwest to southeast for about
760 miles (1,223 km). Only 22 of the islands are inhabited; the most important is New Providence (80
sq mi.; 207 sq km), on which Nassau is situated.
Other islands include Grand Bahama, Abaco, Eleu-
thera, Andros, Cat Island, San Salvador (or Wat-
ling's Island), Exuma, Long Island, Crooked Island,
Acklins Island, Mayaguana, and Inagua.

The islands are mainly flat, few rising above 200
feet (61 m). There are no fresh water streams.
There are several large brackish lakes on several
islands including Inagua and New Providence.

**Government.** The Bahamas moved toward greater
autonomy in 1968 after the overwhelming victory
in general elections of the Progressive Liberal
Party, led by Prime Minister Lynden O. Pindling.
The black leader's party won 29 seats in the House
of Assembly to only 7 for the predominantly white
United Bahamians, who had controlled the islands
for decades before Pindling became Premier in
1967.

With its new mandate from the 85%-black population, Pindling's government negotiated a new
Constitution with Britain under which the colony
became the Commonwealth of the Bahama Islands
in 1969. On July 10, 1973, The Bahamas became
an independent nation as the Commonwealth of
the Bahamas.

In the 1982 election, Pindling's Progressive Liberal Party won 32 of 43 seats in Parliament; the
Free National Movement, 11.

**History.** The islands were reached by Columbus in
October 1492, and were a favorite pirate area in
the early 18th century. The Bahamas were a crown
colony from 1717 until they were granted internal
self-government in 1964.

# BAHRAIN

State of Bahrain
Amir: Sheik Isa bin-Sulman al-Khalifa (1961)
Prime Minister: Sheik Khalifa bin Sulman al-Khalifa (1970)
Area: 254 sq mi. (659 sq km)
Population (est. mid-1986): 400,000 (average annual
growth rate: 2.8%)
Density per square mile: 1,562.5
Capital (est. 1982): Manama, 150,000
Monetary unit: Bahrain dinar
Languages: Arabic (official), English, French
Religion: Islam
Literacy rate : 40%
Economic summary: Gross national product (1982): $3.7

billion. Average annual growth rate (1973–82): 10.7%.
Per capita income (1980): $5,560. Land used for
agriculture: 5%; labor force: 5%; principal products:
eggs, vegetables, fruits. Labor force in industry: 90%;
major products: oil, aluminum, fish. Natural resources: oil,
fish. Exports: oil, aluminum, fish. Imports: machinery, oil-
industry equipment, motor vehicles, foodstuffs. Major
trading partners: Saudi Arabia, U.S., U.K., Japan, Italy.

**Geography.** Bahrain is an archipelago in the Persian Gulf off the coast of Saudi Arabia. The islands
for the most part are level expanses of sand and
rock.

**Government.** A new Constitution was approved in
1973. It created the first elected parliament in the
country's history. Called the National Council, it
consisted of 30 members elected by male citizens
for four-year terms, plus up to 16 Cabinet ministers
as ex-officio members. In August 1975, the Amir
dissolved the National Council.

**History.** A sheikdom that passed from the Persians
to the al-Khalifa family from Arabia in 1782, Bahrain became, by treaty, a British protectorate in
1820. It has become a major Middle Eastern oil
center and, through use of oil revenues, is one of
the most developed of the Persian Gulf sheikdoms.
The Amir, Sheik Isa bin-Sulman al-Khalifa, who
succeeded to the post in 1961, is a member of the
original ruling family. Bahrain announced its independence on Aug. 14, 1971.

# BANGLADESH

People's Republic of Bangladesh
President: Lieut. Gen. H. M. Ershad (1983)
Area: 55,598 sq mi. (143,998 sq km)
Population (est. mid-1986): 104,100,000 (average annual
growth rate: 2.7%)
Density per square mile: 1,872.3
Capital and largest city (est 1982): Dacca, 3,500,000
Monetary unit: Taka
Principal languages: Bengali (official), English
Religions: Islam, 83%; Hindu, 16%
Literacy rate: 25%
Member of Commonwealth of Nations
Economic summary: Gross national product (1983): $11.6
billion. Average annual growth rate (1970–79): 0.8%.
Per capita income (1985): $130. Land used for
agriculture: 66%; labor force, 75%; principal products:
rice, jute, tea, sugar, wheat. Labor force in industry, 11%;
major products: jute goods, textiles, leather, sugar,
fertilizer, paper, pharmaceuticals. Natural resources:
natural gas. Exports: jute goods, jute, tea, leather.
Imports: food grains, fuels, raw cotton, manufactured
goods. Major trading partners: U.S., Japan, Mozambique,
Singapore.

**Geography.** Bangladesh, on the northern coast of
the Bay of Bengal, is surrounded by India, with a
small common border with Burma in the southeast.
It is approximately the size of Wisconsin. The country is low-lying riverine land traversed by the many
branches and tributaries of the Ganges and Brahmaputra rivers. Elevations averages less than 600
feet (183 m) above sea level. Tropical monsoons
and frequent floods and cyclones inflict heavy damage in the delta region.

**Government.** On March 24, 1982, Gen. Hossain

Mohammed Ershad ousted President Abdus Sattar, ending three years of civilian rule. He suspended the Constitution and declared himself Martial Law Administrator, appointing former Chief Justice A. F. N. Ahsanuddin Chowdhury as ceremonial President.

**History.** The former East Pakistan was part of imperial British India until Britain withdrew in 1947. The two Pakistans were united by religion (Islam), but their peoples were separated by culture, physical features, and 1,000 miles of Indian territory. Bangladesh consists primarily of East Bengal (West Bengal is part of India) and its people are primarily Hindu) plus the Sylhet district of the Indian state of Assam. For almost 25 years after independence from Britain, its history was as part of Pakistan (*see* Pakistan).

The East Pakistanis unsuccessfully sought greater autonomy from West Pakistan. The first general elections in Pakistani history, in December 1970, saw virtually all 171 seats of the region (out of 300 for both East and West Pakistan) go to Sheik Mujibur Rahman's Awami League.

Attempts to write an all-Pakistan Constitution to replace the military regime of Gen. Yahya Khan failed. Yahya put down a revolt in March 1971. An estimated one million Bengalis were killed in the fighting or later slaughtered. Ten million more took refuge in India.

In December 1971, India invaded East Pakistan, routed the West Pakistani occupation forces, and created Bangladesh. In February 1974, Pakistan agreed to recognize the independence of Bangladesh.

On Aug. 15, 1975, Mujibur, his wife, and several relatives were assassinated in a coup led by young Army officers. They installed Khondakar Mushtaque Ahmed, a founder of the Awami League, as President.

A military coup forced Ahmed from power Nov. 6, 1975, and Abu Sadat Mohammed Sayem became President and "chief martial law administrator." On April 21, 1977, Gen. Ziaur Rahman, Army Chief of Staff, became president following Sayem's resignation.

On May 30, 1981, Ziaur was killed by a group of army officers in an attempted coup. Vice President Abdus Sattar assumed power and was elected President Nov. 15. On March 24, 1982, Gen. Hossain Mohammad Ershad, army chief of staff, took control in a bloodless coup. Ershad assumed the office of President in 1983.

# BARBADOS

**Sovereign:** Queen Elizabeth II
**Governor-General:** Sir Hugh Springer (1984)
**Prime Minister:** E.W. Barrow (1986)
**Area:** 166 sq. mi. (431 sq km)
**Population (est. mid-1986):** 300,000 (average annual growth rate: 0.9%)
**Density per square mile:** 1,807.2
**Capital and largest city (est. 1982):** Bridgetown, 8,000
**Monetary unit:** Barbados dollar
**Language:** English
**Religions:** Anglican, 70%; Methodist, 9%; Roman Catholic, 4%
**Literacy rate:** 99%
**Member of Commonwealth of Nations**
**Economic summary:** Gross national product (1985): $1,121 million. Average annual growth rate (1970–79): 2.1%. Per capita income (1985): $4,430. Land used for

agriculture: 60%; principal products: sugar cane, subsistence foods. Major industrial products: light manufactures, sugar milling, tourism. Exports: sugar and sugar cane byproducts, clothing. Imports: foodstuffs, machinery, manufactured goods. Major trading partners: U.S., Caribbean nations, U.K., Canada.

**Geography.** An island in the Atlantic about 300 miles (483 km) north of Venezuela, Barbados is only 21 miles long (34 km) and 14 miles across (23 km) at its widest point. It is circled by fine beaches and narrow coastal plains. The highest point is Mount Hillaby (1,105 ft; 337 m) in the north central area.

**Government.** The Barbados legislature dates from 1627. It is bicameral, with a Senate of 21 appointed members and an Assembly of 27 elected members.

The major political parties are the Democratic Labor Party (24 seats in Assembly), led by Prime Minister Errol Barrow; Barbados Labor Party (3 seats), led by H. Bernard St. John.

**History.** Barbados, with a population 90% black, was settled by the British in 1627. It became a crown colony in 1885. It was a member of the Federation of the West Indies from 1958 to 1962. Britain granted the colony independence on Nov. 30, 1966, and it became a parliamentary democracy.

While retaining membership in the Commonwealth of Nations and economic ties with Britain, Barbados seeks broader economic and political relations with Western Hemisphere countries. Diplomatic ties with Cuba were established in 1972.

# BELGIUM

**Kingdom of Belgium**
**Sovereign:** King Baudouin I (1951)
**Premier:** Wilfried Martens (1981)
**Area:** 11,781 sq mi. (30,513 sq km)
**Population (est. mid-1985):** 9,900,000 (average annual growth rate: 0.1%)
**Density per square mile:** 835.14
**Capital:** Brussels
**Largest cities (est. 1984):** Brussels, 982,434; Ghent, 235,401; Charleroi, 213,041; Liège, 203,065; Antwerp, 488,425; Bruges, 118,146
**Monetary Unit:** Belgian franc
**Languages:** Dutch, 57%; French, 32%; bilingual (Brussels), 10%; German, 0.7%.
**Religion:** Roman Catholic, 97%
**National name:** Royaume de Belgique—Koninkrijk van België
**Literacy rate:** 98%
**Economic summary:** Gross national product (1984): $76.3 billion. Annual growth rate (1984): 2.2%. Per capita income (1984): $7,801. Land used for agriculture: 46%; labor force: 25%; principal products: livestock, poultry, grain, sugar beets, flax, tobacco, potatoes, vegetables, fruits. Labor force in industry: 27%; major products: fabricated metal, iron and steel, coal, textiles, chemicals. Exports: iron and steel products, precious stones, textile products. Imports: nonelectrical machinery, motor vehicles, textiles, chemicals, fuels. Major trading partners: West Germany, France, Netherlands, U.K., U.S., Italy.

**Geography.** A neighbor of France, West Germany, the Netherlands, and Luxembourg, Belgium has about 40 miles of seacoast on the North Sea at the Strait of Dover. In area, it is approximately the size of Maryland. The northern third of the country is a plain extending eastward from the seacoast. North of the Sambre and Meuse Rivers is a low plateau; to the south lies the heavily wooded Ardennes plateau, attaining an elevation of about 2,300 feet (700 m).

The Schelde River, which rises in France and flows through Belgium, emptying into the Schelde estuaries, enables Antwerp to be an ocean port.

**Government.** Belgium, a parliamentary democracy under a constitutional monarch, consists of nine provinces. Its bicameral legislature has a Senate, with its 181 members elected for four years—106 by general election, 50 by provincial councillors and 25 by the Senate itself. The 212-member Chamber of Representatives is directly elected for four years by proportional representation. There is universal suffrage, and those who do not vote are fined.

Belgium joined the North Atlantic Alliance in 1949 and is a member of the European Community. NATO and the European Community have their headquarters in Brussels.

The sovereign, Baudouin I, was born Sept. 7, 1930, the son of King Leopold III and Queen Astrid. He became King on July 17, 1951, after the abdication of his father. He married Doña Fabiola de Mora y Aragón on Dec. 15, 1960. Since he has no children, his brother, Prince Albert, is heir to the throne.

The major political parties are the Flemish-speaking Social Christian Party (40 Senators, 49 Representatives); French-speaking Social Christian Party (16 Senators, 20 Representatives); Flemish-speaking Socialist Party (31 Senators, 35 Representatives); French-speaking Socialist Party (21 Senators, 32 Representatives); Flemish-speaking Liberal Party (23 Senators, 22 Representatives); Flemish People's Party (17 Senators, 26 Representatives); French-speaking Liberal Party (20 Senators, 24 Representatives).

**History.** Belgium occupies part of the Roman province of Belgica, named after the Belgae, a people of ancient Gaul. The area was conquered by Julius Caesar in 57–50 B.C., then was overrun by the Franks in the 5th century. It was part of Charlemagne's empire in the 8th century, then in the next century was absorbed into Lotharingia and later into the Duchy of Lower Lorraine. In the 12th century it was partitioned into the Duchies of Brabant and Luxembourg, the Bishopric of Liège, and the domain of the Count of Hainaut, which included Flanders.

In the 16th century, Belgium, with most of the area of the Low Countries, passed to the Duchy of Burgundy and was the marriage portion of Archduke Maximilian of Hapsburg and the inheritance of his grandson, Charles V, who incorporated it into his empire. Then, in 1555, they were united with Spain.

By the treaty of Utrecht in 1713, the country's sovereignty passed to Austria. During the wars that followed the French Revolution, Belgium was occupied and later annexed to France. But with the downfall of Napoleon, the Congress of Vienna in 1815 gave the country to the Netherlands. The Belgians revolted in 1830 and declared their independence.

Germany's invasion of Belgium in 1914 set off World War I. The Treaty of Versailles (1919) gave the areas of Eupen, Malmédy, and Moresnet to Belgium. Leopold III succeeded Albert, King during World War I, in 1934. In World War II, Belgium

was overwhelmed by Nazi Germany, and Leopold III was made prisoner. When he attempted to return in 1950, Socialists and Liberals revolted. He abdicated July 16, 1951, and his son, Baudouin, became King the next day.

Despite the increasingly strong divisions between the French- and Flemish-speaking communities, a Christian Democrat-Liberal coalition that took office in December 1981 came close to setting a record for longevity among the 32 governments that had ruled Belgium since World War II. Headed by Prime Minister Wilfried Martens—the fifth government he had led since 1979—it survived several serious political challenges, including the implementation of an unpopular economic austerity program in 1983 and the deployment of NATO cruise missiles in March 1985. But a riot in a soccer stadium set off a chain of events that threatened its continued existence later that year.

Before the start of the European Soccer Cup final in Brussels on May 29, 1985, 38 people, mostly fans of the Juventus team of Italy, were killed when supporters of the British Liverpool team went on a rampage. Most of the deaths occurred when a stadium wall collapsed. A parliamentary inquiry primarily blamed the English fans for the violence but also faulted Interior Minister Charles Ferdinand Nothomb for security lapses. When he refused to resign, the French-speaking Liberals withdrew from Martens' coalition. Martens thereupon, on July 16, submitted the government's resignation to King Baudouin. The king, who plays a key mediating role during the country's frequent leadership crises, refused the resignation and the coalition remained in office until September, when early elections increased Martens' coalition majority.

# BELIZE

**Sovereign:** Queen Elizabeth II
**Governor-General:** Minita Gordon (1981)
**Prime Minister:** Manuel Esquivel
**Area:** 8,867 sq mi. (22,965 sq km)
**Population (est. mid-1986):** 200,000 (average annual growth rate: 2.5%)
**Density per sq mi.:** 22.6
**Capital (est. 1985):** Belmopan, 5,000
**Largest city (est. 1985):** Belize City, 47,000
**Monetary unit:** Belize dollar
**Languages:** English (official) and Spanish
**Religions:** Roman Catholic, 62%; Anglican, 12%; Methodist, 6%; Baha'i, 2.5%
**Literacy rate:** 90%
**Member of Commonwealth of Nations**
**Economic summary:** Gross national product (1983): $170 million. Average annual growth rate (1984): 1.3%. Per capita income (1983 est. $1,140). Land used for agriculture: 35%; labor force: 30%; principal products: sugar cane, citrus fruits, corn, molasses, rice, bananas, livestock. Labor force in industry: 20%; major products: timber, processed foods, furniture, rum, soap. Natural resource: timber. Exports: sugar, molasses, clothing, lumber, citrus fruits, fish. Imports: fuels, transportation equipment, foodstuffs, textiles, machinery. Major trading partners: U.S., U.K., Trinidad and Tobago, Canada.

**Geography.** Belize (formerly British Honduras) is situated on the Caribbean Sea south of Mexico and east and north of Guatemala. In area, it is about the size of New Hampshire. Most of the country is heavily forested with cedar. Mangrove swamps and cays along the coast give way to hills and mountains in the interior. The highest point is Victoria Peak, 3,681 feet (11,220 m).

**Government.** Formerly the colony of British Honduras, Belize became a fully independent commonwealth on Sept. 21, 1981, after having been self-governing since 1964. Executive power is nominally wielded by Queen Elizabeth II through an appointed Governor-General but effective power is held by the Prime Minister, who is responsible to a 28-member parliament elected by universal suffrage. The major parties are the United Democratic Party (21 of 28 seats), led by Prime Minister Manuel Esquivel; and the People's United Party (7 seats), led by former Prime Minister George Price.

**History.** Once a part of the Mayan empire, the area was deserted until British timber cutters began exploiting valuable hardwoods in the 17th century. Efforts by Spain to dislodge British settlers, including a major naval attack in 1798, were defeated. The territory was formally named a British colony in 1862 but administered by the Governor of Jamaica until 1884.

Guatemala has long made claims to the territory and refused to recognize Britain's efforts to grant independence to Belize. Fear of Guatemala caused many inhabitants to oppose independence until a tentative agreement was reached between Britain, Belize, and Guatemala in March 1981 that would offer access to the Caribbean through Belizean territory for Guatemala. The agreement broke down, however, and 1,600 British troops remained to protect the new state after the flag-raising ceremony on Sept. 21, 1981.

# BENIN

**People's Republic of Benin**
**President:** General Mathieu Kerekou (1972)
**Area:** 43,483 sq mi. (112,622 sq km)
**Population (est. mid-1986):** 4,100,000 (average annual growth rate: 3.0%)
**Density per square mile:** 94.3
**Capital (est. 1984):** Porto-Novo, 208,000
**Largest city (est. 1982):** Cotonou, 490,000
**Monetary unit:** Franc CFA
**Ethnic groups:** Fons and Adjas, Baribas, Yorubas, Mahis
**Languages:** French, African languages
**Religions:** Animist, 70%; Christian, 15%; Islam, 15%
**National name:** Republique Populaire du Benin
**Literacy rate (1981):** 20%
**Economic summary:** Gross national product (1984 est.): $974 million. Average annual growth rate (1970–79): 0.6%. Per capita income (1983): $270. Labor force in agriculture: 70%; principal products: oil palms, peanuts, cotton, coffee, tobacco, corn, rice, livestock, fish. Major industrial products: processed palm oil, palm kernel oil. Natural resources: low-grade iron ore, limestone, some offshore oil. Exports: palm and agricultural products. Imports: clothing, consumer goods, lumber, fuels, foodstuffs, machinery, transportation equipment. Major trading partners: France and other Western European countries.

**Geography.** This West African nation on the Gulf of Guinea, between Togo on the west and Nigeria on the east, is about the size of Tennessee. It is bounded also by Upper Volta and Niger on the north. The land consists of a narrow coastal strip that rises to a swampy, forested plateau and then to highlands in the north. A hot and humid climate blankets the entire country.

**Government.** The change in name from Dahomey to Benin was announced by President Mathieu Kerekou in November 1975. Benin commemorates an African kingdom that flourished in the 17th century. At the same time, Kerekou announced the formation of a political organization, the Party of the People's Revolution of Benin, to mark the first anniversary of his declaration of a "new society" guided by Marxist-Leninist principles.

**History.** One of the smallest and most densely populated states in Africa, Benin was annexed by the French in 1893. The area was incorporated into French West Africa in 1904. It became an autonomous republic within the French Community in 1958, and on Aug. 1, 1960, was granted its independence within the Community.

Gen. Christophe Soglo deposed the first president, Hubert Maga, in an army coup in 1963. He dismissed the civilian government in 1965, proclaiming himself chief of state. A group of young army officers seized power in December 1967, deposing Soglo. They promulgated a new Constitution in 1968.

In December 1969, Benin had its fifth coup of the decade, with the army again taking power. In May 1970, a three-man presidential commission was created to take over the government. The commission had a six-year term; each member serves as president for two years. Maga turned over power as scheduled to Justin Ahomadegbe in May 1972, but six months later yet another army coup ousted the triumvirate and installed Lt. Col. Mathieu Kerekou as President.

# BHUTAN

**Kingdom of Bhutan**
**Ruler:** King Jigme Singye Wangchuk (1972)
**Area:** 18,000 sq mi. (46,620 sq km)
**Population (est. mid-1986):** 1,400,000 (average annual growth rate: 2.0%)
**Density per square mile:** 77.8
**Capital (est. 1984):** Thimphu, 30,000
**Monetary unit:** Ngultrum
**Language:** Dzongkha
**Religions:** Buddhist, 70%; Hindu, 25%; Islam, 5%
**National name:** Druk-yul
**Literacy rate:** 12%
**Economic summary:** Gross national product (est. 1984): $169 million. Average annual growth rate (1982/83): 1.4%. Per capita income (1984): $140. Labor force in agriculture: 95%; principal products: rice, barley, wheat, potatoes, fruit. Major industrial product: cement. Natural resources: timber, hydroelectric power. Exports: fruits and vegetables, timber, coal, cement. Imports: fuels, machinery, vehicles. Major trading partner: India.

**Geography.** Mountainous Bhutan, half the size of Indiana, is situated on the southeast slope of the Himalayas, bordered on the north and east by Tibet and on the south and west by India. The landscape consists of a succession of lofty and rugged mountains running generally from north to south and separated by deep valleys. In the north, towering peaks reach a height of 24,000 feet (7,315 m).

**Government.** Bhutan is a constitutional monarchy. The King rules with a Council of Ministers and a Royal Advisory Council. There is a National Assembly (Parliament), which meets semiannually, but no political parties.

**History.** British troops invaded the country in 1865 and negotiated an agreement under which Britain undertook to pay an annual allowance to Bhutan on condition of good behavior. A treaty with India in 1949 increased this subsidy and placed Bhutan's foreign affairs under Indian control.

In the 1960s, Bhutan undertook modernization, abolishing slavery and the caste system, emancipating women and enacting land reform. In 1985, Bhutan made its first diplomatic links with non-Asian countries.

# BOLIVIA

**Republic of Bolivia**
**President:** Victor Paz Estensoro (1985)
**Area:** 424,162 sq mi. (1,098,581 sq km)
**Population (est. mid-1986):** 6,400,000 (average annual growth rate, 2.8%) (Indian, 53%; mestizo, 32%; white, 15%)
**Density per square mile:** 15.1
**Judicial capital (est. 1973):** Sucre, 85,000
**Administrative capital (est. 1983):** La Paz, 954,000
**Largest cities (est. 1982):** Santa Cruz, 419,000; Cochabamba, 305,000; Oruro, 173,000
**Monetary unit:** Peso boliviano
**Languages:** Spanish, Quechua, Aymara
**Religion:** Roman Catholic, 94%; Baha'i, 3%
**National name:** República de Bolivia
**Literacy rate est.** 75%
**Economic summary:** Gross national product (est. 1985): $4.0 billion. Average annual growth rate (1984): −4%. Per capita income (1985 est.): $400. Labor force in agriculture: 47%; principal products: potatoes, corn, rice, sugar cane, bananas. Labor force in industry: 19%; major products: refined petroleum, processed foods, tin, textiles, clothing. Natural resources: petroleum, natural gas, tin, lead, zinc, copper, tungsten, bismuth, antimony, gold, sulfur, silver, iron ore. Exports: tin, lead, zinc, silver, antimony, coffee, sugar, cotton, natural gas. Imports: foodstuffs, chemicals, capital goods, pharmaceuticals, transport equipment. Major trading partners: Western European and Latin American countries, U.S., Japan.

**Geography.** Landlocked Bolivia, equal in size to California and Texas combined, lies to the west of Brazil. Its other neighbors are Peru and Chile on the west and Argentina and Paraguay on the south.

The country is a low alluvial plain throughout 60% of its area toward the east, drained by the Amazon and Plata river systems. The western part, enclosed by two chains of the Andes, is a great plateau—the Altiplano, with an average altitude of 12,000 feet (3,658 m). More than 80% of the population lives on the plateau, which also contains La Paz. At an altitude of 11,910 feet (3,630 m), it is the highest capital city in the world.

Lake Titicaca, half the size of Lake Ontario, is one of the highest large lakes in the world, at an altitude of 12,507 feet (3,812 m). Islands in the lake hold ruins of the ancient Incas.

**Government.** President Victor Paz Estensoro was inaugurated on Aug. 7, 1985, after the Congress, at a raucous session, chose him over Hugo Banzer, the candidate who had received the most votes in a popular election on July 14. Banzer won 28.6%

of the 1.7 million votes tallied and Paz won 26.4%. Under the Constitution, if no Presidential candidate receives 50% of the vote, Congress chooses between the top two vote-getters. Paz's National Revolutionary Movement won 59 of the 157 congressional seats in the 1985 election, against 51 for Banzer's Nationalist Democratic Action Party. Several smaller parties split the remainder.

**History.** Famous since Spanish colonial days for its mineral wealth, modern Bolivia was once a part of the ancient Incan Empire. After the Spaniards defeated the Incas in the 16th century, Bolivia's predominantly Indian population was reduced to slavery. The country won its independence in 1825 and was named after Simón Bolívar, the famed liberator.

Since 1825 Bolivia has had more than 60 revolutions, 70 Presidents, and 11 Constitutions.

Harassed by internal strife, Bolivia lost great slices of territory to three neighbor nations. Several thousand square miles and its outlet to the Pacific were taken by Chile after the War of the Pacific (1879–84). In 1903 a piece of Bolivia's Acre province, rich in rubber, was ceded to Brazil. And in 1938, after a war with Paraguay, Bolivia gave up claim to nearly 100,000 square miles of the Gran Chaco.

In 1965 a guerrilla movement mounted from Cuba and headed by Maj. Ernesto (Ché) Guevara began a revolutionary war. With the aid of U.S. military advisers, the Bolivian army, helped by the peasants, smashed the guerrilla movement, wounding and capturing Guevara on Oct. 8, 1967, and shooting him to death the next day.

Faltering steps toward restoration of civilian government were halted abruptly on July 17, 1980, when Gen. Luis Garcia Meza Tejada seized power. A series of military leaders followed before the military moved, in 1982, to return the government to civilian rule. Hernán Siles Zuazo was inaugurated President on Oct. 10, 1982.

Under Siles' left-of-center government, the country was regularly shut down by work stoppages, the bulk of Bolivia's natural resources—natural gas, gold, lithium, potassium and tungsten—were either sold on the black market or left in the ground, the country had the lowest per-capita income in South America, and inflation approached 3,000 percent. In 1985, the 73-year-old Siles decided he was unable to carry on and quit a year early.

No candidate won a majority in the elections in 1985 and Victor Paz Estensoro, 77, was picked by Congress to become President. During his administration, inflation has continued to rise and the currency has collapsed. Drastic economic measures were taken toward the end of the year, including a wage freeze and a cutback of government price subsidies, which have lowered the inflation rate to 20%.

# BOPHUTHATSWANA

**See South Africa**

# BOTSWANA

**Republic of Botswana**
**President:** Quett K. Masire (1980)
**Area:** 222,000 sq mi. (576,000 sq km)
**Population (est. mid-1986):** 1,100,000 (average annual growth rate: 3.3%)

**Density per square mile:** 4.95
**Capital and largest city (est. 1984):** Gaborone, 79,000
**Monetary unit:** Pula
**Languages:** English, Setswana
**Religions:** Christian, 48%; Animist, 49%
**Member of Commonwealth of Nations**
**Literacy rate:** 54%
**Economic summary:** Gross national product (1983): $920 million. Average annual growth rate (1970–79): 12.0%. Per capita income (1980): $910. Land used for agriculture: 1%; principal products: livestock, sorghum, corn, millet, cowpeas, beans. Major industrial products: diamonds, copper, nickel, salt, soda ash, potash, coal, frozen beef; tourism. Natural resources: diamonds, copper, nickel, salt, soda ash, potash, coal. Exports: diamonds, cattle, animal products, copper, nickel. Imports: foodstuffs, vehicles, textiles, petroleum products. Major trading partners: South Africa, U.K., U.S.

**Geography.** Twice the size of Arizona, Botswana is in south central Africa, bounded by South-West Africa, Zambia, Zimbabwe, and South Africa. Most of the country is near-desert, with the Kalahari occupying the western part of the country. The eastern part is hilly, with salt lakes in the north.

**Government.** The Botswana Constitution provides, in addition to the unicameral National Assembly, for a House of Chiefs, which has a voice on bills affecting tribal affairs. There is universal suffrage.

The major political parties are the Democratic Party (28 of 34 elective seats in 36-man Legislative Assembly), led by President Quett Masire; National Front (5 seats), led by Kenneth Koma; People's Party (1 seat), led by Kenneth Nkhwa.

**History.** Botswana is the land of the Batawana tribes, which, when threatened by the Boers in Transvaal, asked Britain in 1885 to establish a protectorate over the country, then known as Bechuanaland. In 1961, Britain granted a Constitution to the country. Self-government began in 1965, and on Sept. 30, 1966, the country became independent. Since 1975, it has been an associate member of the European Common Market.

# BRAZIL

**Federative Republic of Brazil**
**President:** José Sarney (1985)
**Area:** 3,286,470 sq mi. (8,511,957 sq km)
**Population (est. mid-1986):** 143,300,000 (average annual growth rate, 2.3%) (approx.: white, 60%; mestizo, 26%; black, 11%)
**Density per square mile:** 43.6
**Capital (1980 census):** Brasilia, 1,470,300
**Largest cities (1980 census):** São Paulo, 12,600,000; Rio de Janeiro, 9,000,000; Salvador, 1,800,000; Belo Horizonte, 2,500,000; Recife, 2,300,000; Porto Alegre, 2,200,000
**Monetary unit:** Cruzado
**Language:** Portuguese
**Religion:** Roman Catholic, 88%; Protestant, 6%
**National name:** Brasil
**Literacy rate:** 74%
**Economic summary:** Gross national product (1985): $321.4 billion. Average annual growth rate (est. 1985): 8.3%. Per capita income (1984): $1,610. Land used for agriculture; 4%; labor force: 27%; principal products: coffee, rice, beef, corn, milk, sugar cane, soybeans, cocoa. Labor force in industry: 24%; major products: steel, chemicals, petrochemicals, machinery, motor vehicles, cement, lumber. Natural resources: iron ore, manganese, bauxite, nickel, other industrial metals. Exports: coffee, iron ore, soybeans, sugar, beef, transport equipment, footwear. Imports: wheat, copper, aluminum, petroleum, machinery, chemicals, pharmaceuticals. Major trading partners: U.S., West Germany, Japan, Saudi Arabia.

**Geography.** Brazil covers nearly half of South America, extends 2,965 miles (4,772 km) north-south, 2,691 miles (4,331 km), east-west, and borders every nation on the continent except Chile and Ecuador. It is the fifth largest country in the world, ranking after the U.S.S.R., Canada, China, and the U.S.

More than a third of Brazil is drained by the Amazon and its more than 200 tributaries. The Amazon is navigable for ocean steamers to Iquitos, Peru, 2,300 miles (3,700 km) upstream. Southern Brazil is drained by the Plata system—the Paraguay, Uruguay, and Paraná Rivers. The most important stream entirely within Brazil is the Sao Francisco, navigable for 1,000 miles (1,903 km), but broken near its mouth by the 275-foot (84 m) Paulo Afonso Falls.

**Government.** Under the Constitution, Brazil is a union of 22 states, 4 territories, and 1 federal district. The President is elected for a six-year term by an electoral college made up of members of the National Congress. The National Congress is composed of two houses—the Senate, whose members serve eight-year terms, and the Chamber of Deputies, elected for four-year terms. Members of Congress are elected by equal, direct, compulsory, and secret suffrage under proportional representation.

The military took control in 1964, ousting the last elected civilian President and installing a series of military men (with the Congress ratifying the junta's choice). Election of a civilian President by the 686-member electoral college took place in January 1985.

Opposition Democratic Movement candidate Tancredo Neves was chosen overwhelmingly to head the first civilian government in 21 years, defeating the governing Democratic Social Party's candidate, Paulo Salim Maluf, by 480 votes to 180 votes, with 17 college delegates abstaining and nine absent. But Neves died of complications following intestinal surgery before taking office, and his Vice Presidential running mate, José Sarney, became President.

**History.** Brazil is the only Latin American nation deriving its language and culture from Portugal. Adm. Pedro Alvares Cabral claimed the territory for the Portuguese in 1500. He brought to Portugal a cargo of wood, pau-brasil, from which the land received its name. Portugal began colonization in 1532 and made the area a royal colony in 1549.

During the Napoleonic wars, King João VI, then Prince Regent, fled the country in 1807 in advance of the French armies and in 1808 set up his court in Rio de Janeiro. João was drawn home in 1820 by a revolution, leaving his son as Regent. When Portugal sought to reduce Brazil again to colonial status, the prince declared Brazil's independence on Sept. 7, 1822, and became Pedro I, Emperor of Brazil.

Harassed by his parliament, Pedro I abdicated in 1831 in favor of his five-year-old son, who became Emperor in 1840 as Pedro II. The son was a popular monarch, but discontent built up and, in 1889, following a military revolt, he had to abdicate. Although a republic was proclaimed, Brazil was under two military dictatorships during the next four years. A revolt permitted a gradual return to stability under civilian Presidents.

The President during World War I, Wenceslau Braz, cooperated with the Allies and declared war on Germany.

In World War II, Brazil cooperated with the Western Allies, welcoming Allied air bases, patrolling the South Atlantic, and joining the invasion of Italy after declaring war on the Axis.

Gen. João Baptista de Oliveira Figueiredo, became President in 1979 and pledged a return to democracy in 1985.

The electoral college's choice of Tancredo Neves on Jan. 15, 1985, as the first civilian President since 1964 brought a nationwide wave of optimism, but the 75-year-old President-elect was hospitalized and underwent a series of intestinal operations. The civilian government was inaugurated on schedule on March 15, but only Neves' Vice Presidential running mate, José Sarney, was sworn in, and he was widely distrusted because he had previously been a member of the governing military regime's political party. When Neves died on April 21, Sarney became President.

Economically, Brazil's $93-billion foreign debt was the Third World's largest, and inflation reached a staggering 229% annual rate in 1984, almost double the 115% rate in 1983. But tough austerity measures imposed by the International Monetary Fund appeared to be taking hold and, by mid-1984, Brazilian economists said the country's recession had ended and Brazil was on the road to recovery.

In 1985 the GNP increased by 8.3% and in February 1986, President Sarney announced an across-the-board price and wage freeze that has brought inflation down to double-digit levels.

# BRUNEI

**State of Brunei**
**Sultan:** Sir Mudo Hassanal Bolkiah (1968)
**Area:** 2,226 sq mi. (5,765 sq km)
**Population (est. mid-1986):** 200,000 (average annual growth rate: 2.6%)
**Density per square mile:** 98
**Capital and largest city (est. 1981):** Bandar Seri Begawan, 64,000
**Monetary unit:** Brunei dollar
**Ethnic groups:** Malay, 65%; Chinese, 24%; other, 11%
**Languages:** Malay and English official; Chinese
**Religions:** Islam, 66%; Christian, 10%; Buddhist, 14%; other, 10%
**Literacy rate:** 45%
**Member of Commonwealth of Nations**
**Economic summary:** Gross national product (1983): $4.4 billion. Average annual growth rate (1970–79): 4.6%. Per capita income (1983): $21,140. Land used for agriculture: 3%; labor force: 5%; principle agricultural products: fruit, rice, pepper. Labor force in industry: 22%; major industrial products: crude petroleum, liquified natural gas. Natural resources: petroleum, natural gas. Exports: crude petroleum, liquified natural gas. Imports: machinery, transport equipment, manufactured goods, foodstuffs. Major trading partners: Japan, U.S., U.K., Singapore, South Korea.

**Geography.** About the size of Delaware, Brunei is an independent sultanate on the northwest coast of the island of Borneo in the South China Sea, wedged between the Malaysian states of Sabah and Sarawak. Three quarters of the thinly populated country is covered with tropical rain forest; there are rich oil and gas deposits.

**Government.** Sultan Hassanal Bolkiah is ruler of the state, a former British protectorate which became fully sovereign and independent on New Year's Day, 1984, presiding over a Privy Council and Council of Ministers appointed by himself. The Constitution provides for a three-tiered system of indirect elections, but the last elections were held in 1965. The only known opposition leader is in exile. In 1985, the Brunei National Democratic Party (BDNP) was formed. The sole political party, it supports an "Islamic monarchy."

**History.** Brunei (pronounced broon-eye) was a powerful state from the 16th to the 19th century, ruling over the northern part of Borneo and adjacent island chains. But it fell into decay and lost Sarawak in 1841, becoming a British protectorate in 1888 and a British dependency in 1905.

The Sultan regained control over internal affairs in 1959, but Britain retained responsibility for the state's defense and foreign affairs until the end of 1983, when the sultanate became fully independent.

Sultain Bolkiah was crowned in 1968 at the age of 22, succeeding his father, Sir Omar Ali Saifuddin, who had abdicated. During his reign, exploitation of the rich Seria oilfield has made the sultanate wealthy. The majority of the population lives in and around the capital, situated on the Brunei River nine miles from its mouth.

# BULGARIA

**People's Republic of Bulgaria**
**Chairman of the State Council:** Todor Zhivkov (1971)
**Prime Minister (Chairman of Council of Ministers):** Georgy Atansov (1986)
**Area:** 42,823 sq mi. (110,912 sq km)
**Population (est. mid-1986):** 9,000,000 (average annual growth rate: 0.2%)
**Density per square mile:** 210.2
**Capital:** Sofia
**Largest cities (est. 1982):** Sofia, 1,094,000; Plovdiv, 367,000; Varna, 295,000; Ruse, 179,000; Burgas, 175,000; Stara Zagora, 165,000
**Monetary unit:** Lev
**Language:** Bulgarian
**Religions:** Reliable figures not available
**National name:** Narodna Republika Bulgariya
**Literacy rate:** 95%
**Economic summary:** Gross national product (1984): $56.4 billion. Annual growth rate (1984): 3.1%. Per capita income (1984): $6,295. Labor force in agriculture: 23%; principal products: grains, tobacco, fruits, vegetables. Labor force in industry: 35%; major products: processed agricultural products, machinery, textiles, clothing. Natural resources: metals, minerals, lumber. Exports: machinery and transport equipment, fuels, minerals, raw materials, agricultural products. Imports: machinery and transportation equipment, fuels, raw materials, metals, agricultural raw materials. Major trading partners: U.S. S.R., Soviet bloc countries.

**Geography.** Two mountain ranges and two great valleys mark the topography of Bulgaria, a country the size of Tennessee. Situated on the Black Sea in the eastern part of the Balkan peninsula, it shares borders with Yugoslavia, Romania, Greece, and

Turkey. The Balkan belt crosses the center of the country, almost due east-west, rising to a height of 7,800 feet (2,377 m). The Rhodope range breaks off from the Balkans in the west, curves, and then straightens out to run nearly parallel along the southern border. Between the two ranges, is the valley of the Maritsa, Bulgaria's principal river. Between the Balkan range and the Danube, which forms most of the northern boundary with Romania, is the Danubian tableland.

Southern Dobruja, a fertile region of 2,900 square miles (7,511 sq km), below the Danube delta, is an area of low hills, fens, and sandy steppes.

**Government.** The present Constitution has been in effect since May 18, 1971. The National Assembly, consisting of 400 members elected for five-year terms, is the governing body. It elects the State Council and the Council of Ministers.

The Communist Party is led by the chairman of the State Council, Todor Zhivkov.

**History.** The first Bulgarians, a tribe of wild horsemen akin to the Huns, crossed the Danube from the north in A.D. 679 and subjugated the Slavic population of Moesia. They adopted a Slav dialect and Slavic customs and twice conquered most of the Balkan peninsula between 893 and 1280. After the Serbs subjected their kingdom in 1330, the Bulgars gradually fell prey to the Turks, and from 1396 to 1878 Bulgaria was a Turkish province. In 1878, Russia forced Turkey to give the country its independence; but the European powers, fearing that Bulgaria might become a Russian dependency, intervened. By the Treaty of Berlin in 1878, Bulgaria became autonomous under Turkish sovereignty.

In 1887, Prince Ferdinand of Saxe-Coburg-Gotha was elected ruler of Bulgaria; on Oct. 5, 1908, he declared the country independent and took the title of Tsar.

Bulgaria joined Germany in World War I and lost. On Oct. 3, 1918, Tsar Ferdinand abdicated in favor of his son, Tsar Boris III. Boris assumed dictatorial powers in 1934–35. When Hitler awarded Bulgaria southern Dobruja, taken from Romania in 1940, Boris joined the Nazis in war the next year and occupied parts of Yugoslavia and Greece. Later the Germans tried to force Boris to send his troops against the Russians. Boris resisted and died under mysterious circumstances on Aug. 28, 1943.

Simeon II, infant son of Boris, became nominal ruler under a regency. Russia declared war on Bulgaria on Sept. 5, 1944. An armistice was agreed to three days later, after Bulgaria had declared war on Germany. Russian troops streamed in the next day.

A Soviet-style people's republic was established in 1947. Since then, Bulgaria acquired the reputation of being the most slavishly loyal to Moscow of all the East European Communist countries. An Italian prosecutor's report in 1984 charged that Bulgaria, possibly with Soviet support, masterminded the 1981 attempt by Turkish gunman Mehmet Ali Agca to assassinate Pope John Paul II.

# BURKINA FASO

**President of National Council of the Revolution:** Capt. Thomas Sankara (1983)
**Area:** 105,870 sq mi. (274,200 sq km)
**Population (est. mid-1986):** 7,100,000 (average annual growth rate, 2.6%)

**Density per square mile:** 67.1
**Capital and largest city (est. 1985):** Ouagadougou, 360,-000
**Monetary unit:** Franc CFA
**Ethnic groups:** Mossis, Bobos, Lobis, Fulanis
**Languages:** French, African languages
**Religions:** Animist, 65%; Islam, 25%; Roman Catholic, 10%
**National name:** Burkina Faso
**Literacy rate:** 10%
**Economic summary:** Gross national product (1983): $1.2 billion. Average annual growth rate (1970–79): —1.2%. Per capita income (1984): $160. Labor force in agriculture: 90%; principal products: millet, sorghum, corn, rice, livestock, peanuts, sugar cane, cotton. Major industrial products: processed agricultural products, light industrial items, brick, brewed products. Natural resources: manganese, limestone, marble, gold, uranium, bauxite, copper. Exports: livestock, peanuts, cotton. Imports: textiles, food and consumer goods, transport equipment, machinery, fuels. Major trading partners: Ivory Coast, France, Ghana, Western European nations, Taiwan.

**Geography.** Slightly larger than Colorado, Burkina Faso, formerly known as Upper Volta, is a landlocked country in West Africa. Its neighbors are Ivory Coast, Mali, Niger, Benin, Togo, and Ghana. The country consists of extensive plains, low hills, high savannas, and a desert area in the north.

**Government.** The former French colony has been governed by a series of military leaders since a coup in November 1980 overthrew the last elected president. All political parties were banned and the political process suspended following the coup.

**History.** The country, called Upper Volta by the French, consists chiefly of the lands of the Mossi Empire, where France established a protectorate over the Kingdom of Ouagadougou in 1897. Upper Volta became a separate colony in 1919, was partitioned among Niger, the Sudan, and the Ivory Coast in 1933 and was reconstituted in 1947. An autonomous republic within the French Community, it became independent on Aug. 5, 1960.

President Maurice Yameogo was deposed on Jan. 3, 1966, by a military coup led by Col. Sangoulé Lamizana, who dissolved the National Assembly and suspended the Constitution. A new Constitution was adopted later that year and a new Assembly was elected. However, dissension within the Volta Democratic Union, the major party, led to renewed military rule. Constitutional rule returned in 1978 with the election of an Assembly and a presidential vote in June in which Gen. Lamizana won by a narrow margin over three other candidates.

On Nov. 25, 1980, there was a bloodless coup which placed Gen. Lamizana under house arrest. Col. Sayé Zerbo took charge as the President of the Military Committee of Reform for National Progress. Maj. Jean-Baptiste Ouedraogo toppled Zerbo in another coup on Nov. 7, 1982. Captain Thomas Sankara, in turn, deposed Ouedraogo a year later. His government changed the country's name on Aug. 3, 1984, to Burkina Faso (the "land of upright men") to sever ties with its colonial past.

# BURMA

**Socialist Republic of the Union of Burma**
**President:** U San Yu (1981)
**Prime Minister:** U Maung Maung Kha (1977)

**Area:** 261,789 sq mi. (678,036 sq km)
**Population (est. mid-1986):** 37,700,000 (average annual growth rate: 2.0%)
**Density per square mile:** 144
**Capital:** Rangoon
**Largest cities (est. 1983):** Rangoon, 2,250,000; (est. 1977 for metropolitan area by U.N.): Mandalay, 533,-000; Moulmein, 220,000; Bassein, 144,000; Pegu, 151,000
**Monetary unit:** Kyat
**Language:** Burmese
**Religions:** Buddhist, 87%; Christian, Islam
**National name:** Pyidaungsu Socialist Thammada Myanma Naingngandau
**Literacy rate:** 78%
**Economic summary:** Gross national product (1983): $6.5 billion. Average annual growth rate (1973–82): 6.0%. Per capita income (1983): $180. Labor force in agriculture: 66%; principal products: sugar cane, corn, rice, peanuts. Labor force in industry: 9%; major products: textiles, footwear, processed agricultural products, wood and wood products, refined petroleum. Natural resources: timber, nickel, cobalt, copper, gold, rubies, sapphires, jade. Exports: rice, teak. Imports: machinery, transportation and construction equipment, manufactured goods. Major trading partners: Singapore, West Germany, U.K., Japan, Indonesia.

**Geography.** Burma occupies the northwest portion of the Indochinese peninsula. India lies to the northwest and China to the northeast. Bangladesh, Laos, and Thailand are also neighbors. The Bay of Bengal touches the southwestern coast.

Slightly smaller than Texas, the country is divided into three natural regions: the Arakan Yoma, a long, narrow mountain range forming the barrier between Burma and India; the Shan Plateau in the east, extending southward into Tenasserim; and the Central Basin, running down to the flat fertile delta of the Irrawaddy in the south. This delta contains a network of intercommunicating canals and nine principal river mouths.

**Government.** On March 2, 1962, the government of U Nu was overthrown and replaced by a Revolutionary Council, which assumed all power in the state. Gen. U Ne Win, as chairman of the Revolutionary Council, became the chief executive.

A new Constitution was approved in 1973 and took effect Jan. 4, 1974. Under it, Burma is a Socialist Democratic Republic with a 475-seat unicameral legislature called the People's Congress. In 1972, Ne Win and his colleagues resigned their military titles and thereafter ruled as "civilians." In 1974, Ne Win dissolved the Revolutionary Council and became President under the new Constitution. He voluntarily relinquished the presidency on Nov. 9, 1981, but retained leadership of the Burmese Socialist Program Party, the only legal party. U Sun Yu was elected President by the People's Congress.

**History.** In 1612, the British East India Company sent agents to Burma, but the Burmese long resisted efforts of British traders, and Dutch and Portuguese as well, to establish posts on the Bay of Bengal. By the Anglo-Burmese War in 1824–26 and two following wars, the British East India Company expanded to the whole of Burma by 1886. Burma was annexed to India. It became a separate colony in 1937.

During World War II, Burma was a key battle-ground; the 800-mile Burma Road was the Allies' vital supply line to China. The Japanese invaded the country in December 1941, and by May 1942 had occupied most of it, cutting the Burma Road. After one of the most difficult campaigns of the war, Allied forces liberated most of Burma prior to the Japanese surrender in August 1945.

Burma became independent on Jan. 4, 1948. In 1951 and 1952 the Socialists achieved power, and Burma became the first Asian country to introduce social legislation.

In 1968, after the government had made headway against the Communist and separatist rebels, the military regime adopted a policy of strict nonalignment and followed "the Burmese Way" to socialism. But the insurgents, reportedly numbering several thousand, continued active.

# BURUNDI

**Republic of Burundi**
**Head of Government:** Col. Jean-Baptiste Bagaza (1976)
**Area:** 10,747 sq mi. (27,834 sq km)
**Population (est. mid-1986):** 4,900,000 (average annual growth rate: 3.0%)
**Density per square mile:** 445.9
**Capital and largest city (1982):** Bujumbura, 175,000
**Monetary unit:** Burundi franc
**Languages:** Kirundi (official), French
**Religions:** Roman Catholic, 78%; Protestant, 5%
**National name:** Republika Y'Uburundi
**Literacy rate:** 23%
**Economic summary:** Gross national product (1983): $1.05 billion. Average annual growth rate (1970–79): 1.5%. Per capita income (1983): $240. Principal agricultural products: coffee, tea, cotton, bananas, sorghum. Major industrial products: light consumer goods. Natural resources: nickel, kaolin, gold, unexploited copper and platinum deposits. Exports: coffee, tea, cotton. Imports: textiles, food, transport equipment, petroleum products. Major trading partners: U.S., Belgium, West Germany, France.

**Geography.** Wedged among Tanzania, Zaire, and Rwanda in east central Africa, Burundi occupies a high plateau divided by several deep valleys. It is equal in size to Maryland.

**Government.** Legislative and executive power is vested in the president.

Burundi's first Constitution, approved July 11, 1974, placed UPRONA (Unity and National Progress), the only political party, in control of national policy.

**History.** Burundi was once part of German East Africa. An integrated society developed among the Watusi, a tall, warlike people and nomad cattle raisers, and the Bahutu, a Bantu people, who were subject farmers. Belgium won a League of Nations mandate in 1923, and subsequently Burundi, with Rwanda, was transferred to the status of a United Nations trust territory.

In 1962, Burundi gained independence and became a kingdom under Mwami Mwambutsa IV, with his son, Louis Rwangasore, as premier.

Premier Micombero overthrew the Mwami, in

1966, installing himself as president.

One of Africa's worst tribal wars, which became genocide, occurred in Burundi in April 1972, following the return of Ntare V. He was given a safe-conduct promise in writing by President Micombero but was "judged and immediately executed" by the Burundi leader. His return was apparently attended by an invasion of exiles of Burundi's Hutu tribe. Whether Hutus living in Burundi joined the invasion is unclear, but after it failed, the victorious Tutsis proceeded to massacre some 100,000 persons in six weeks, with possibly 100,000 more slain by summer.

On Nov. 1, 1976, a military coup led by Lt. Col. Jean-Baptiste Bagaza ousted Micombero, who was serving his second term. Bagaza assumed the presidency Nov. 3, suspended the Constitution, and announced that a 30-member Supreme Revolutionary Council would be the governing body.

Bagaza was elected head of the only legal political party in 1979 and re-elected to a second five-year term as party chieftain in 1984.

# CAMBODIA

**People's Republic of Kampuchea**
**President:** Heng Samrin (1979)
**Prime Minister:** Hun Sen (1985)
**Area:** 69,884 sq mi. (181,000 sq km)
**Population (est. mid-1986):** 6,400,000 (average annual growth rate: 2.3%)
**Density per square mile:** 91.6
**Capital and largest city (est. 1980 for metropolitan area):** Phnom Penh, 500,000
**Monetary unit:** Riel
**Ethnic groups:** Khmer, 90%; Chinese, 5%; other minorities 5%
**Languages:** Khmer (official), French, Vietnamese, Chinese
**Religion:** Theravada Buddhist
**Literacy rate:** 48%
**Economic summary:** Gross national product (1971): $500 million. Principal agricultural products: rice, rubber, corn. Major industrial products: fish, wood and wood products, milled rice. Natural resources: timber, gemstones, iron ore, manganese, phosphate. Exports: natural rubber, rice, pepper, wood. Imports: foodstuffs, fuel, machinery. Major trading partners: China, North Korea, Vietnam, U.S.S.R.

**Geography.** Situated on the Indochinese peninsula, Cambodia is bordered by Thailand and Laos on the north and Vietnam on the east and south. The Gulf of Siam is off the western coast. The country, the size of Missouri, consists chiefly of a large alluvial plain ringed in by mountains and on the east by the Mekong River. The plain is centered on Lake Tonle Sap, which is a natural storage basin of the Mekong.

**Government.** A bloodless coup toppled Prince Sihanouk in 1970. It was led by Lon Nol and Prince Sisowath Sirik Matak, Sihanouk's cousin. Sihanouk moved to Peking to head a government-in-exile. On Oct. 9, 1970, Lon Nol proclaimed himself President.

The Lon Nol regime was overthrown in April 1975 by Pol Pot, a leader of the Communist Khmer Rouge forces, who instituted a xenophobic reign of terror. Pol Pot was in turn ousted on Jan. 8, 1979, by Heng Samrin, a dissident backed by strong Vietnamese forces.

**History.** Cambodia came under Khmer rule about A.D. 600. Under the Khmers, magnificent temples were built at Angkor. The Khmer kingdom once ruled over most of Southeast Asia, but attacks by the Thai and the Vietnamese almost annihilated the empire until the French joined Cambodia, Laos, and Vietnam into French Indochina.

Under Norodom Sihanouk, enthroned in 1941, and particularly under Japanese occupation during World War II, nationalism revived. After the ouster of the Japanese, the Cambodians sought independence, but the French returned in 1946, granting the country a Constitution in 1947 and independence within the French Union in 1949. Sihanouk won full military control during the French-Indochinese War in 1953. He abdicated in 1955 in favor of his parents, remaining head of the government, and when his father died in 1960, became chief of state without returning to the throne. In 1963, he sought a guarantee of Cambodia's neutrality from all parties to the Vietnam War.

On March 18, 1970, while Sihanouk was abroad trying to get North Vietnamese and the Vietcong out of border sanctuaries near Vietnam, anti-Vietnamese riots occurred, and Sihanouk was overthrown.

North Vietnamese and Vietcong units in border sanctuaries began moving deeper into Cambodia, threatening rapid overthrow of the new regime headed by Lon Nol. President Nixon sent South Vietnamese and U.S. troops across the border on April 30. U.S. ground forces, limited to 30-kilometer penetration, withdrew by June 30.

The Vietnam peace agreement of 1973 stipulated withdrawal of foreign forces from Cambodia, but fighting continued between Hanoi-backed insurgents and U.S.-supplied government troops. U.S. air support for the government forces was ended by Congress on Aug. 15, 1973.

Fighting continued and reached a quick climax early in 1975.

As government troops fell back in bitter fighting, Lon Nol fled by air April 1, leaving the government under the interim control of Premier Long Boret. On April 16, the government's capitulation ended the five-year war, but not the travails of war-ravaged Cambodia.

A new Constitution was proclaimed in December 1975, establishing a 250-member People's Assembly, a State Presidium headed by Pol Pot, and a Supreme Judicial Tribunal. Samphan replaced Sihanouk as head of state in April 1976, and the former monarch became a virtual prisoner until freed by Pol Pot in 1979.

In the next two years, from 2 million to 4 million Cambodians are estimated to have died under the brutality of the Pol Pot regime. Border clashes with Vietnam developed into a Vietnamese invasion and by the end of 1978 the Pol Pot government appeared to be collapsing.

Despite the capture of Phnom Penh on Jan. 8 by Heng Samrin, a dissident Khmer Rouge backed by Vietnamese troops, fighting continued in isolated areas. Retreating Pol Pot forces and refugees totaling 40,000 were driven into Thailand by May.

At a meeting in Kuala Lumpur, Malaysia, on June 22, 1982, Sihanouk formed an alliance with Son Sann, his former prime minister, and Khieu Samphan, Pol Pot's representative, to oppose the Heng Samrin regime installed in Phnom Pehn by the Vietnamese.

While Sihanouk remained in exile in North Korea, about 9,000 noncommunist troops loyal to him and another 15,000 under Son Sann joined about 35,000 communist Pol Pot forces fighting the 170,000 Vietnamese troops supporting the Heng Samrin government. According to Washington sources, the Central Intelligence Agency covertly aided the noncommunist resistance groups, funnelling assistance through Thailand. The Cambodian insurgents suffered a major defeat in March 1985 when Vietnamese forces overran their camps in Cambodia and forced them into Thailand. When the Vietnamese spilled over the border, Thai and insurgent forces fought battles with them more than a mile inside Thailand.

# CAMEROON

**Republic of Cameroon**
**President:** Paul Biya (1982)
**Area:** 183,569 sq mi. (475,442 sq km)
**Population (est. mid-1986):** 10,000,000 (average annual growth rate: 2.7%)
**Density per square mile:** 54.5
**Capital:** Yaoundé
**Largest cities (est. 1983):** Douala, 708,000; Yaoundé, 485,000
**Monetary unit:** Franc CFA
**Languages:** French and English (both official); Foulbé, Bamiléke, Ewondo, Donala, Mungaka, Bassa
**Religions:** Roman Catholic, 35%; Animist, 12%; Islam, 35%; Protestant, 18%
**National name:** République Unie du Cameroun
**Literacy rate:** 65%
**Economic summary:** Gross national product (1983): $7.6 billion. Annual growth rate (1983): 5%. Per capita income (1983): $834. Land used for agriculture: 15%; labor force: 73%; principal products: coffee, cocoa, corn, peanuts. Labor force in industry: 5%. Major products: small manufacturing, consumer goods, aluminum. Natural resources: timber, some oil, bauxite. Exports: cocoa, coffee, timber, aluminum, petroleum. Imports: consumer goods, machinery, food, beverages, tobacco, fuel. Major trading partners: France, U.S., Western European nations.

**Geography.** Cameroon is a West African nation on the Gulf of Guinea, bordered by Nigeria, Chad, the Central African Republic, the Congo, Equatorial Guinea, and Gabon. It is nearly twice the size of Oregon.

The interior consists of a high plateau, rising to 4,500 feet (1,372 m), with the land descending to a lower, densely wooded plateau and then to swamps and plains along the coast. Mount Cameroon (13,350 ft.; 4,069 m), near the coast, is the highest elevation in the country. The main rivers are the Benue, Nyong, and Sanaga.

**Government.** After a 1972 plebiscite, a unitary nation was formed out of East and West Cameroon to replace the former Federal Republic. A Constitution was adopted, providing for election of a president every five years and of a 150-seat National Assembly, whose nominal five-year term can be extended or shortened by the president. The Cameroon National Union is the only political party.

**History.** The Republic of Cameroon is inhabited by Hamitic and Semitic peoples in the north, where

Islam is the principal religion, and by Bantu peoples in the central and southern regions, where native animism prevails. The tribes were conquered by many invaders.

The land escaped colonial rule until 1884, when treaties with tribal chiefs brought the area under German domination. After World War I, the League of Nations gave the French a mandate over 80% of the area, and the British 20% adjacent to Nigeria. After World War II, when the country came under a U.N. trusteeship in 1946, self-government was granted, and the Cameroun People's Union emerged as the dominant party by campaigning for reunification of French and British Cameroon and for independence. Accused of being under Communist control, it waged a campaign of revolutionary terror from 1955 to 1958, when it was crushed. In British Cameroon, unification was pressed also by the leading party, the Kamerun National Democratic Party, led by John Foncha.

France set up Cameroun as an autonomous state in 1957, and the next year its legislative assembly voted for independence by 1960. In 1959 a fully autonomous government of Cameroun was formed under Ahmadou Ahidjo. Cameroun became an independent republic on Jan. 1, 1960, adopted a Constitution in a referendum in February, and chose a National Assembly in April. The Assembly elected Ahidjo president. A federal Constitution was approved in 1961, and the Federal Republic of Cameroon came into being in October, headed by Ahidjo and Foncha.

# CANADA

**Sovereign:** Queen Elizabeth II
**Governor General:** Jeanne Sauvé (1984)
**Prime Minister:** Brian Mulroney (1984)
**Area:** 3,851,809 sq mi. (9,976,186 sq km)
**Population (est. mid-1986):** 25,600,000 (British, 44.6%; French, 28.7%; other European, 23%) (growth rate, 1979–80, 0.8%)
**Density per square mile:** 6.5
**Capital:** Ottawa, Ont.
**Largest cities (1981 census; metropolitan areas):** Toronto, 2,998,947; Montreal, 2,828,349; Vancouver, 1,268,-183; Ottawa, 717,978; Edmonton, 657,057; Calgary, 592,743; Winnipeg, 584,842; Quebec, 576,075; Hamilton, 542,095; St. Catherines-Niagara, 304,353; Kitchener, 287,801; London, 283,668; Halifax, 277,727
**Monetary Unit:** Canadian dollar
**Languages:** English, French
**Religions:** Roman Catholic, 47.3%; Protestant, 41.2%; no religion, 7.4%; Eastern Orthodox, 1.5%; Jewish, 1.2%; other, 1.3%
**Literacy rate:** 98%
**Economic Summary:** Gross national product: CA$453,724,-000. Average annual growth rate (1985): 7.8%. Per capita income: (1985): $13,541. Land use for agriculture: 7%; labor force: 4%; Principal products; wheat, barley, oats, livestock. Labor force in industry: 18%. Major products; transportation equipment, petroleum, chemicals, wood products. Exports: wheat, petroleum, lumber and wood products, motor vehicles. Imports: electronic equipment, chemicals. Major trading partners: U.S., Japan, U.K., U.S.S.R.

**Geography.** Covering most of the northern part of the North American continent and with an area larger than that of the United States, Canada has

# Canadian Governors General and Prime Ministers Since 1867

| Term of office | Governor General | Term | Prime Minister | Party |
|---|---|---|---|---|
| 1867–1868 | Viscount Monck[1] | 1867–1873 | Sir John A. MacDonald | Conservative |
| 1869–1872 | Baron Lisgar | 1873–1878 | Alexander Mackenzie | Liberal |
| 1872–1878 | Earl of Dufferin | 1878–1891 | Sir John A. MacDonald | Conservative |
| 1878–1883 | Marquess of Lorne | 1891–1892 | Sir John J. C. Abbott | Conservative |
| 1883–1888 | Marquess of Lansdowne | 1892–1894 | Sir John S. D. Thompson | Conservative |
| 1888–1893 | Baron Stanley of Preston | 1894–1896 | Sir Mackenzie Bowell | Conservative |
| 1893–1898 | Earl of Aberdeen | 1896 | Sir Charles Tupper | Conservative |
| 1898–1904 | Earl of Minto | 1896–1911 | Sir Wilfrid Laurier | Liberal |
| 1904–1911 | Earl Grey | 1911–1917 | Sir Robert L. Borden | Conservative |
| 1911–1916 | Duke of Connaught | 1917–1920 | Sir Robert L. Borden | Unionist |
| 1916–1921 | Duke of Devonshire | 1920–1921 | Arthur Meighen | Unionist |
| 1921–1926 | Baron Byng of Vinny | 1921–1926 | W. L. Mackenzie King | Liberal |
| 1926–1931 | Viscount Willingdon | 1926 | Arthur Meighen | Conservative |
| 1931–1935 | Earl of Bessborough | 1926–1930 | W. L. Mackenzie King | Liberal |
| 1935–1940 | Baron Tweedsmuir | 1930–1935 | Richard B. Bennett | Conservative |
| 1940–1946 | Earl of Athlone | 1935–1948 | W. L. Mackenzie King | Liberal |
| 1946–1952 | Viscount Alexander | 1948–1957 | Louis S. St. Laurent | Liberal |
| 1952–1959 | Vincent Massey | 1957–1963 | John G. Diefenbaker | Conservative |
| 1959–1967 | George P. Vanier | 1963–1968 | Lester B. Pearson | Liberal |
| 1967–1973 | Roland Michener | 1968–1979 | Pierre Elliott Trudeau | Liberal |
| 1974–1979 | Jules Léger | 1979–1980 | Charles Joseph Clark | Conservative |
| 1979–1984 | Edward R. Schreyer | 1980–1984 | Pierre Elliott Trudeau | Liberal |
| 1984– | Jeanne Sauvé | 1984–1984 | John Turner | Liberal |
| | | 1984– | Brian Mulroney | Conservative |

1. Became Governor General of British North America in 1861.

an extremely varied topography. In the east the mountainous maritime provinces have an irregular coast line on the Gulf of St. Lawrence and the Atlantic. The St. Lawrence plain, covering most of southern Quebec and Ontario, and the interior continental plain, covering southern Manitoba and Saskatchewan and most of Alberta, are the principal cultivable areas. They are separated by a forested plateau rising from lakes Superior and Huron.

Westward toward the Pacific, most of British Columbia, Yukon, and part of western Alberta are covered by parallel mountain ranges including the Rockies. The Pacific border of the coast range is ragged with fiords and channels. The highest point in Canada is Mount Logan (19,850 ft; 6,050 m), which is in the Yukon.

Canada has an abundance of large and small lakes. In addition to the Great Lakes on the U.S. border, there are 9 others that are more than 100 miles long (161 km) and 35 that are more than 50 miles long (80 km).

The two principal river systems are the Mackenzie and the St. Lawrence. The St. Lawrence, with its tributaries, is navigable for over 1,900 miles (3,058 km).

**Government.** Canada, a self-governing member of the Commonwealth of Nations, is a federation of 10 provinces (Alberta, British Columbia, Manitoba, New Brunswick, Newfoundland, Nova Scotia, Ontario, Prince Edward Island, Quebec, and Saskatchewan) and two territories (Northwest Territories and Yukon) whose powers were spelled out in the British North America Act of 1867. With the passing of the Constitution Act of 1981, the act and the Constitutional amending power were transferred from the British government to Canada so that the Canadian Constitution is now entirely in the hands of the Canadians.

Actually the Governor General acts only with the advice of the Canadian Prime Minister and the Cabinet, who also sit in the federal Parliament. The Parliament has two houses: a Senate of 104 members appointed for life, and a House of Commons of 282 members apportioned according to provincial population. Elections are held at least every five years or whenever the party in power is voted down in the House of Commons or considers it expedient to appeal to the people. The Prime Minister is the leader of the majority party in the House of Commons—or, if no single party holds a majority, the leader of the party able to command the support of a majority of members of the House. Laws must be passed by both houses of Parliament and signed by the Governor General in the Queen's name.

The 10 provincial governments are nominally headed by Lieutenant Governors appointed by the federal government, but the executive power in each actually is vested in a Cabinet headed by a Premier, who is leader of the majority party. The provincial legislatures are composed of one-house assemblies whose members are elected for four-year terms. They are known as Legislative Assemblies, except in Newfoundland, where it is the House of Assembly, and in Quebec, where it is the National Assembly.

The judicial system consists of a Supreme Court in Ottawa (established in 1875), with appellate jurisdiction, and a Supreme Court in each province, as well as county courts with limited jurisdiction in most of the provinces. The Governor General in Council appoints these judges.

The major political parties are the Progressive Conservative Party (211 of 282 seats in House of Commons), led by Prime Minister Brian Mulroney; Liberal Party (40 seats), led by John T. Turner; and New Democratic Party (30 seats), led by John Edward Broadbent. One Independent holds a seat.

**History.** The Norse explorer Leif Ericson probably reached the shores of Canada (Labrador or Nova Scotia) in A.D. 1000, but the history of the white

## Population by Provinces and Territories

| Province | 1981 (Census) | 1983 (June Estimate) |
|---|---|---|
| Alberta | 2,237,724 | 2,352,300 |
| British Columbia | 2,744,467 | 2,825,000 |
| Manitoba | 1,026,241 | 1,046,300 |
| New Brunswick | 696,403 | 706,600 |
| Newfoundland | 567,681 | 576,200 |
| Nova Scotia | 847,442 | 859,300 |
| Ontario | 8,625,107 | 8,816,000 |
| Prince Edward Island | 122,506 | 123,900 |
| Quebec | 6,438,403 | 6,514,900 |
| Saskatchewan | 968,313 | 992,000 |
| Northwest Territories | 45,741 | 48,600 |
| Yukon Territory | 23,153 | 22,200 |
| **Total** | **24,343,181** | **24,883,400** |

*Source:* Statistics Canada.

man in the country actually began in 1497, when John Cabot, an Italian in the service of Henry VII of England, reached Newfoundland or Nova Scotia. Canada was taken for France in 1534 by Jacques Cartier. The actual settlement of New France, as it was then called, began in 1604 at Port Royal in what is now Nova Scotia; in 1608, Quebec was founded. France's colonization efforts were not very successful, but French explorers by the end of the 17th century had penetrated beyond the Great Lakes to the western prairies and south along the Mississippi to the Gulf of Mexico. Meanwhile, the English Hudson's Bay Company had been established in 1670. Because of the valuable fisheries and fur trade, a conflict developed between the French and English; in 1713, Newfoundland, Hudson Bay, and Nova Scotia (Acadia) were lost to England.

During the Seven Years' War (1756–63), England extended its conquest, and the British Maj. Gen. James Wolfe won his famous victory over Gen. Louis Montcalm outside Quebec on Sept. 13, 1759. The Treaty of Paris in 1763 gave England control.

At that time the population of Canada was almost entirely French, but in the next few decades, thousands of British colonists emigrated to Canada from the British Isles and from the American colonies. In 1849, the right of Canada to self-government was recognized. By the British North America Act of 1867, the Dominion of Canada was created through the confederation of Upper and Lower Canada, Nova Scotia, and New Brunswick. Prince Edward Island joined the Dominion in 1873.

In 1869 Canada purchased from the Hudson's Bay Company the vast middle west (Rupert's Land) from which the provinces of Manitoba (1870), Alberta, and Saskatchewan (1905) were later formed. In 1871, British Columbia joined the Dominion. The country was linked from coast to coast in 1885 by the Canadian Pacific Railway.

During the formative years between 1866 and 1896, the Conservative Party, led by Sir John A. MacDonald, governed the country, except during the years 1873–78. In 1896, the Liberal Party took over and, under Sir Wilfrid Laurier, an eminent French Canadian, ruled until 1911.

By the Statute of Westminster in 1931 the British Dominions, including Canada, were formally declared to be partner nations with Britain, "equal in status, in no way subordinate to each other," and bound together only by allegiance to a common Crown.

Newfoundland became Canada's 10th province on March 31, 1949, following a plebiscite. Canada includes two territories—the Yukon Territory, the area north of British Columbia and east of Alaska, and the Northwest Territories, including all of Canada north of 60° north latitude except Yukon and the northernmost sections of Quebec and Newfoundland. This area includes all of the Arctic north of the mainland, Norway having recognized Canadian sovereignty over the Svendrup Islands in the Arctic in 1931.

The Liberal Party, led by William Lyon Mackenzie King, dominated Canadian politics from 1921 until 1957, when it was succeeded by the Progressive Conservatives. The Liberals, under the leadership of Lester B. Pearson, returned to power in 1963. Pearson remained Prime Minister until 1968, when he retired and was replaced by a former law professor, Pierre Elliott Trudeau. Trudeau maintained Canada's defensive alliance with the United States, but began moving toward a more independent policy in world affairs.

Trudeau set about creating what he termed a "just society," stressing domestic reforms. His election was considered in part a response to the most serious problem confronting the country, the division between French- and English-speaking Canadians, which had led to a separatist movement in the predominantly French province of Quebec. Trudeau, himself a French Canadian, supported programs for bilingualism and an increased measure of provincial autonomy, although he would not tolerate the idea of separatism. In 1974, the provincial government voted to make French the official language of Quebec.

Conflicts over the law establishing French as the dominant language in Quebec, particularly in schooling, kept separatism as a national issue, but by-elections in 1977 produced easy victories for Trudeau's ruling Liberals in four Quebec seats in the national legislature, and polls showed a decline in separatist support both in the province and elsewhere in Canada.

Economic problems appeared to take precedence over politics in 1978, as the Sun Life Assurance Company of Canada, the nation's largest insurance firm, announced that it would move its headquarters from Montreal to Toronto. Many businesses had left the province earlier, but Sun Life was the first to cite the language law as the reason for its departure.

Despite Trudeau's removal of price and wage controls in 1978, continuing inflation and a high rate of unemployment caused him to delay elections until May 22, 1979, the first time since 1935 that a Canadian government had retained office for the allowable five-year term. The delay gave Trudeau no advantage—the Progressive Conservatives under Charles Joseph Clark defeated the Liberals everywhere except in Quebec, New Brunswick, and Newfoundland.

Clark took office as the head of Canada's fifth minority government in the last 20 years, needing the support of 26 New Democratic Party members and six Social Credit members to obtain an absolute majority in the 282-seat House.

Clark's government collapsed after only six months when a motion to defeat the Tory budget carried by 139-133 on Dec. 13, 1979. On the same day, the Quebec law making French the exclusive official language of the province—an issue which had been expected to provide Clark's first major internal test—was voided by the Canadian Supreme Court.

In national elections Feb. 18, 1980, the resurgent Liberals under Trudeau scored an unexpectedly big victory, winning 146 seats (147 when a vacancy was filled a month later), while the Conservatives fell from 136 to 103 and the New Democrats won 32 seats.

Resolving a dispute that had occupied Trudeau since the beginning of his tenure, Queen Elizabeth II, in Ottawa on April 17, 1982, signed the Constitution Act, cutting the last legal tie between Canada and Britain. Since 1867, the British North America Act required British Parliament approval for any Canadian constitutional change.

The new charter was approved by the federal House of Commons, 246–24, on Dec. 2, 1981, and by a 59–23 vote of the Senate six days later. The Constitution retains Queen Elizabeth as Queen of Canada and keeps Canada's membership in the Commonwealth.

Ending an era, Trudeau retired on June 30, 1984, after 16 years as prime minister, except for the nine-month interruption in 1979–80.

His successor as Liberal Party leader and Prime Minister, John N. Turner, called an early election for a new Parliament after polls showed the Liberals had made a big comeback from the last months of Trudeau's term, despite Canada's continuing recession and 11.2% unemployment, the highest in 40 years.

In the national election on Sept. 4, 1984, the Progressive Conservative Party scored an overwhelming victory, fundamentally changing the country's political landscape. The Conservatives, led by Brian Mulroney, a 45-year-old corporate lawyer, won 211 of the 282 seats in the House of Commons, the highest political majority in Canadian history. Turner's Liberals won only 40 seats while the socialist New Democratic party won 30. An independent, who was expected to join the Conservatives, also was elected. Mulroney was sworn in as Canada's 18th Prime Minister on Sept. 17.

## CAPE VERDE

**Republic of Cape Verde**
**President:** Aristides Pereira (1975)
**Premier:** Maj. Pedro Pires (1975)
**Area:** 1,557 sq mi. (4,033 sq km)
**Population (est. mid-1986):** 300,000 (average annual growth rate: 2.4%)
**Density per square mile:** 192.7
**Capital (est. 1982):** Praia, 37,676
**Largest city (est. 1982):** Mindelo, 50,000
**Monetary unit:** Cape Verde escudo
**Language:** Portuguese
**Religion:** Roman Catholic, 98%
**National name:** República de Cabo Verde
**Literacy rate:** 37%
**Economic summary:** Gross national product (1982 prov.): $106 million. Average annual growth rate (1970–79): 4.8%. Per capita income (1982): $355. Principal agricultural products: bananas, corn, sugar cane, coconuts. Major industry: fishing, salt mining. Natural resources: salt, siliceous rock. Exports: fish and shellfish, bananas, salt. Imports: machinery, textiles, petroleum products. Major trading partners: Portugal, Netherlands, Algeria, neighboring African states.

**Geography:** Cape Verde, only slightly larger than Rhode Island, is an archipelago in the Atlantic 385 miles (620 km) west of Dakar, Senegal.

The islands are divided into two groups: Barlavento in the north, comprising Santo Antão (291 sq mi.; 754 sq km), Boa Vista (240 sq mi.; 622 sq km), São Nicolau (132 sq mi.; 342 sq km), São Vicente (88 sq mi.; 246 sq km), Sal (83 sq mi.; 298 sq km), and Santa Luzia (13 sq mi.; 34 sq km); and Sotavento in the south, consisting of São Tiago (383 sq mi.; 992 sq km), Fogo (184 sq mi.; 477 sq km), Maio (103 sq mi.; 267 sq km), and Brava (25 sq mi.; 65 sq km). The islands are mostly mountainous, with the land deeply scarred by erosion. There is an active volcano on Fogo.

**Government.** The islands became independent on July 5, 1975, under an agreement negotiated with Portugal in 1974. The 56-member National Assembly chose Aristides Pereira as President and Maj. Pedro Pires as Premier. All members of the Assembly belong to the African Party for the Independence of Portuguese Guinea and Cape Verde, then the only party that entered candidates in the election. It is committed to union with Guinea-Bissau, another former Portuguese colony.

**History.** Uninhabited upon their discovery in 1456, the Cape Verde islands became part of the Portuguese empire in 1495. A majority of their modern inhabitants are of mixed Portuguese and African ancestry. A coaling station developed during the 19th century on the island of São Vicente has grown in recent years to an oil and gasoline storage depot for ships and aircraft.

## CENTRAL AFRICAN REPUBLIC

**Head of Government:** Gen. André Kolingba (1981)
**Area:** 241,313 sq mi. (625,000 sq km)
**Population (est. mid-1986):** 2,700,000 (average annual growth rate, 2.8%)
**Density per square mile:** 11.2
**Capital and largest city (est. 1984):** Bangui, 473,800
**Monetary unit:** Franc CFA
**Ethnic groups:** Mandja-Baya, Banda, Mbaka, Azande, Yakoma
**Languages:** French (official) and Sango
**Religions:** Protestant, 50%; Roman Catholic, 33%; Animist, 12%, Islam, 3%
**National name:** République Centrafricaine
**Member of French Community**
**Literacy rate:** 33%
**Economic summary:** Gross national product (1983): $690 million. Average annual growth rate (1970–79): 0.9%. Per capita income (1983): $280. Land used for agriculture: 15%; labor force: 88%; principal products: cotton, coffee, peanuts, food crops, livestock. Major industrial products: timber, textiles, soap, cigarettes, processed food. Natural resources: diamonds, timber. Exports: diamonds, cotton, timber, coffee. Imports: machinery and electrical equipment, petroleum products, textiles. Major trading partners: France, Yugoslavia, Japan, U.S., Belgium-Luxembourg.

**Geography.** Situated about 500 miles north (805 km) of the equator, the Central African Republic is a landlocked nation bordered by Cameroon, Chad, the Sudan, Zaire, and the Congo. Twice the size of New Mexico, it is covered by tropical forests in the south and semidesert land in the east. The Ubangi and Shari are the largest of many rivers.

**Government.** On Dec. 4, 1976, the Central African Republic became the Central African Empire. Marshal Jean-Bédel Bokassa, who had ruled the republic since he took power in a military coup Dec.

31, 1965, was declared Emperor Bokassa I. He was overthrown in a coup on Sept. 20, 1979. Former President David Dacko, returned to power and changed the country's name back to the Central African Republic. An army coup on Sept. 1, 1981, deposed Dacko and suspended the Constitution and all political parties. A Military Committee of National Redress was set up to run the country.

**History.** As the colony of Ubangi-Shari, what is now the Central African Republic was united with Chad in 1905 and joined with Gabon and the Middle Congo in French Equatorial Africa in 1910. After World War II a rebellion in 1946 forced the French to grant self-government. In 1958 the territory voted to become an autonomous republic within the French Community, but on Aug. 13, 1960, President David Dacko proclaimed the republic's independence from France.

Dacko undertook to move the country into Peking's orbit, but was overthrown in a coup on Dec. 31, 1965, by the then Col. Jean-Bédel Bokassa, Army Chief of Staff. In August 1977, the U.S. State Department protested the Emperor's jailing of American and British newsmen.

Bokassa staged an elaborate coronation ceremony on the first anniversary of the Empire, inviting 3,500 guests to see him place a diamond-studded crown on his head and sit on a 2.5-ton gilded bronze throne in the shape of an eagle. The cost of the ceremony was one fourth of the annual foreign-exchange earnings of the country, one of the 25 poorest in the world.

# CHAD

**Republic of Chad**
**President:** Hissen Habré (1982)
**Area:** 495,752 sq mi. (1,284,000 sq km)
**Population (est. mid-1986):** 5,200,000 (average annual growth rate, 2.0%)
**Density per square mile:** 10.5
**Capital and largest city (est. 1982):** N'djamena, 325,000
**Monetary unit:** Franc CFA
**Ethnic groups:** Baguirmiens, Kanembous, Saras, Massas, Arabs, Toubous, Goranes
**Languages:** French and Arabic (official), Sara, Kanembou, Ouddai, Massa, Gorane
**Religions:** Islam, 44%; Christian, 33%; Animist, 23%
**National name:** République du Tchad
**Literacy rate:** about 20%
**Economic summary:** Gross national product (1983): $282 million. Average annual growth rate (1970–81): 0.6%. Per capita income (1985): $80. Land used for agriculture: 17%; labor force: 85%; principal products: cotton, cattle, sugar, subsistence crops. Labor force in industry: 4%; major products: livestock and livestock products, beer, food processing, textiles, cigarettes. Natural resources: petroleum, unexploited uranium, kaolin. Exports: cotton, livestock and animal products. Imports: food, motor vehicles and parts, petroleum products, machinery, cement, textiles. Major trading partners: France, Nigeria, and central African countries.

**Geography.** A landlocked country in north central Africa, Chad is about 85% the size of Alaska. Its neighbors are Niger, Libya, the Sudan, the Central African Empire, Cameroon, and Nigeria.

Lake Chad, from which the country gets its name, lies on the western border with Niger and Nigeria. In the north is a desert that runs into the Sahara.

**Government.** Hissen Habré became president of Chad on June 7, 1982, by overthrowing Goukouni Oueddi.

**History.** Chad was absorbed into the colony of French Equatorial Africa, as part of Ubangi-Shari, in 1910. France began the country's development after 1920, when it became a separate colony. In 1946, French Equatorial Africa was admitted to the French Union. By referendum in 1958 the Chad territory became an autonomous republic within the French Union.

An independence movement led by the first Premier and President, François (later Ngarta) Tombalbaye, achieved complete independence on Aug. 11, 1960.

Tombalbaye was killed in the 1975 coup and was succeeded by Gen. Félix Malloum, who faced a Libyan-financed rebel movement, the Chadian National Liberation Front (Frolinat), throughout his tenure in office. A ceasefire backed by Libya, Niger, and the Sudan early in 1978 failed to end the fighting, and French military aid, both troops and supplies, was increased.

Nine rival groups meeting in Lagos, Nigeria, in March 1979 agreed to form a provisional government headed by Goukouni Oueddi, a former Frolinat leader. Fighting broke out again in Chad in March 1980, when Defense Minister Hissen Habré challenged Goukouni and seized the capital. By the year's end, Libyan troops supporting Goukouni recaptured N'djamena, and Libyan President Muammar el-Qaddafi, in January 1981, proposed a merger of Chad with Libya.

The Libyan merger proposal was rejected and Libyan troops withdrew from Chad under pressure from other African countries, but in 1983 poured back into the barren northern part of the country in support of Goukouni. France, in turn, sent troops to the southern part of Chad in support of Habré, resulting in defacto division of the country.

# CHILE

**Republic of Chile**
**President:** Gen. Augusto Pinochet (1973)
**Area:** 292,132 sq mi. (756,622 sq km)
**Population (est. mid-1986):** 12,300,000 (average annual growth rate: 1.6%)
**Density per square mile:** 42.1
**Capital:** Santiago
**Largest cities (est. 1985):** Santiago, 4,231,500; Valparaiso, 266,900; Concepción, 215,800; Antofagasta, 174,100
**Monetary unit:** Peso
**Language:** Spanish
**Religion:** Roman Catholic
**National name:** República de Chile
**Literacy rate:** 96%
**Economic summary:** Gross national product (1984): $17.5 billion. Average annual growth rate (1973–82): 0.8%. Per capita income (1983): $1,870. Land used for agriculture: 7%; labor force 16%; principal products: wheat, corn, sugar beets, vegetables, wine, livestock. Labor force in industry: 15%; major products: processed fish, transportation equipment, iron and steel, pulp, paper. Natural resources: copper, timber, iron ore, nitrates. Exports: copper, iron ore, paper and wood products, fruits. Imports: vehicles, petroleum, capital goods. Major trading partners: U.S., Japan, West Germany, Brazil, Argentina.

**Geography.** Situated south of Peru and west of Bolivia and Argentina, Chile fills a narrow 1,800-mile (2,897 km) strip between the Andes and the Pacific. Its area is nearly twice that of Montana.

One third of Chile is covered by the towering ranges of the Andes. In the north is the mineral-rich Atacama Desert, between the coastal mountains and the Andes. In the center is a 700-mile-long (1,127 km) valley, thickly populated, between the Andes and the coastal plateau. In the south, the Andes border on the ocean.

At the southern tip of Chile's mainland is Punta Arenas, the southernmost city in the world, and beyond that lies the Strait of Magellan and Tierra del Fuego, an island divided between Chile and Argentina. The southernmost point of South America is Cape Horn, a 1,390-foot (424-m) rock on Horn Island in the Wollaston group, which belongs to Chile.

The Juan Fernández Islands, in the South Pacific about 400 miles (644 km) west of the mainland, and Easter Island, about 2,000 miles (3,219 km) west, are Chilean possessions.

**Government.** Under the pre-coup Constitution, the nation elected a President every six years, a Senate of 50 members every eight years (one-half renewable every four years), and a Chamber of Deputies of 150 members every four years.

Leftist parties were abolished immediately after the 1973 military coup that ousted President Salvador Allende Gossens. Other parties were placed "in recess," and on March 12, 1977, the government officially dissolved them.

**History.** Chile was originally under the control of the Incas in the north and the fierce Araucanian people in the south. In 1541, a Spaniard, Pedro de Valdivia, founded Santiago. Chile won its independence from Spain in 1818 under Bernardo O'Higgins and an Argentinian, José de San Martin. O'Higgins, dictator until 1823, laid the foundations of the modern state with a two-party system and a centralized government.

The dictator from 1830 to 1837, Diego Portales, fought a war with Peru in 1836–39 that expanded Chilean territory. The Conservatives were in power from 1831 to 1861. Then the Liberals, winning a share of power for the next 30 years, disestablished the church and limited presidential power. Chile fought the War of the Pacific with Peru and Bolivia from 1879 to 1883, winning Antofagasta, Bolivia's only outlet to the sea, and extensive areas from Peru. A revolt in 1890 led by Jorge Montt overthrew, in 1891, José Balmaceda and established a parliamentary dictatorship that existed until a new Constitution was adopted in 1925. Industrialization began before World War I and led to the formation of Marxist groups.

Juan Antonio Ríos, President during World War II, was originally pro-Nazi but in 1944 led his country into the war on the side of the U.S.

A small abortive army uprising in 1969 raised fear of military intervention to prevent a Marxist, Salvador Allende Gossens, from taking office after his election to the presidency on Sept. 4, 1970, with 36.3% of the vote in a three-way battle. Dr. Allende was the first President in a non-Communist country freely elected on a Marxist-Leninist program.

Allende quickly established relations with Cuba and the People's Republic of China and nationalized several American companies.

Allende's overthrow and death in an army as-sault on the presidential palace in September 1973 ended a 46-year era of constitutional government in Chile, which had boasted the longest such record in Latin America.

The takeover was led by a four-man junta headed by Army Chief of Staff Augusto Pinochet Ugarte, who assumed the office of President.

Committed to "exterminate Marxism," the junta embarked on a right-wing dictatorship. It suspended parliament, banned political activity, and broke relations with Cuba.

The Human Rights Commission of the Organization of American States charged the junta with "most grave violations" of basic liberties. In July, Chile denied entry to a U.N. investigatory panel. On June 9, 1978, the government reversed that policy to permit the U.N. Human Rights Commission to send an investigative mission to Chile.

In 1977, Pinochet, in a speech marking his fourth year in power, promised elections by 1985 if conditions warranted. Earlier, he had abolished DINA, the secret police, and decreed an amnesty for political prisoners, an action Amnesty International said might affect only 200–400 of some 1,500 political prisoners.

Pinochet was inaugurated on March 11, 1981, for an eight-year term as President, at the end of which, according to the Constitution adopted six months earlier, the junta would nominate a civilian as successor, although in July 1986, in the face of increasing protests, Pinochet announced that he might serve another eight-year term.

# CHINA

**People's Republic of China**
**President:** Li Xiannian (1983)
**Premier:** Zhao Ziyang (1980)
**Area:** 3,691,521 sq mi. (9,561,000 sq km)[1]
**Population (est. mid-1986):** 1,050,000,000 (average annual growth rate, 1.0%)
**Density per square mile:** 284.4
**Capital:** Beijing
**Largest cities (est. 1983):** Shanghai, 11,940,000; Beijing (Peking) 9,330,000; Tianjin (Tientsin) 7,850,000; Canton, 6,840,000; Wuhan, 5,940,000; Shenyang (Mukden), 5,210,000; Nanjing (Nanking), 4,560,000; Chongqing (Chungking), 3,890,000; Harbin; 3,730,000
**Monetary unit:** Yuan
**Languages:** Chinese, (Mandarin, Cantonese, and local dialects)
**Religions:** Taoist, Confucuanist, Buddhist, Muslim, atheist
**National name:** Zhonghua Renmin Gongheguo
**Literacy rate:** 76.5%
**Economic summary:** Gross national product (1985 est.); $343 billion. Average annual growth rate (1979–83): 8.2%. Per capita income (1985): $330. Land used for agriculture: 11%; labor force: 75%; principal products: rice, wheat, grains, cotton. Major industrial products: iron and steel, textiles, armaments, petroleum. Natural resources: coal, natural gas, limestone, marble. Exports: agricultural products, oil, minerals, metals, manufactured goods. Imports: grains, chemical fertilizer, steel, industrial raw materials, machinery and equipment. Major trading partners: Japan, Hong Kong, U.S., West Germany, Jordan, Australia, Romania, Canada, Thailand.

1. Including Manchuria and Tibet.

**Geography.** China, which occupies the eastern part of Asia, is slightly larger in area than the U.S. Its coastline is roughly a semicircle. The greater part of the country is mountainous, and only in the

## Provinces and Regions of China

| Name | Area (sq mi.) | Area (sq km) | Capital |
|---|---|---|---|
| Provinces | | | |
| Anhui (Anhwei) | 54,015 | 139,900 | Hefei (Hofei) |
| Fujian (Fukien) | 47,529 | 123,100 | Fuzhou (Fukien) |
| Gansu (Kansu) | 137,104 | 355,100 | Lanzhou (Lanchow) |
| Guangdong (Kwangtung) | 89,344 | 231,400 | Canton |
| Guizhou (Kweichow) | 67,181 | 174,000 | Guiyang (Kweiyang) |
| Hebei (Hopei) | 81,479 | 211,030 | Shijiazhuang (Shitikiachwang) |
| Heilongjiang (Heilungkiang)[1] | 178,996 | 463,600 | Harbin |
| Henan (Honan) | 64,479 | 167,000 | Zhengzhou (Chengchow) |
| Hubei (Hupeh) | 72,394 | 187,500 | Wuhan |
| Hunan | 81,274 | 210,500 | Changsha |
| Jiangsu (Kiangsu) | 40,927 | 106,000 | Nanjing (Nanking) |
| Jiangxi (Kiangsi) | 63,629 | 164,800 | Nanchang |
| Jilin (Kirin)[1] | 72,201 | 187,000 | Changchun |
| Liaoning[1] | 53,301 | 138,050 | Shenyang |
| Quinghai (Chinghai) | 278,378 | 721,000 | Xining (Sining) |
| Shaanxi (Shensi) | 75,598 | 195,800 | Xian (Sian) |
| Shandong (Shantung) | 59,189 | 153,300 | Jinan (Tsinan) |
| Shanxi (Shansi) | 60,656 | 157,100 | Taiyuan |
| Sichuan (Szechwan) | 219,691 | 569,000 | Chengdu (Chengtu) |
| Yunnan | 168,417 | 436,200 | Kunming |
| Zhejiang (Chekiang) | 39,305 | 101,800 | Hangzhou (Hangchow) |
| Autonomous Region | | | |
| Guangxi Zhuang (Kwangsi Chuang) | 85,096 | 220,400 | Nanning |
| Nei Monggol (Inner Mongolia)[1] | 454,633 | 1,177,500 | Hohhot (Huhehot) |
| Ningxia Hui | 30,039 | 77,800 | Yinchuan (Yinchwan) |
| Xinjiang Uygur (Sinkiang Uighur)[1] | 635,829 | 1,646,800 | Urumqi (Urumchi) |
| Xizang (Tibet) | 471,660 | 1,221,600 | Lhasa |

1. Together constitute (with Taiwan) what has been traditionally known as Outer China, the remaining territory forming the historical China Proper. NOTE: Names are in Pinyin, with conventional spelling in parentheses.

lower reaches of the Yellow and Yangtze Rivers are there extensive low plains.

The principal mountain ranges are the Tien Shan, to the northwest; the Kunlun chain, running south of the Taklimakan and Gobi Deserts; and the Trans-Himalaya, connecting the Kunlun with the borders of China and Tibet. Manchuria is largely an undulating plain connected with the north China plain by a narrow lowland corridor. Inner Mongolia contains the relatively fertile southern and eastern portions of the Gobi. The large island of Hainan (13,500 sq mi.; 34,380 sq km) lies off the southern coast.

Hydrographically, China proper consists of three great river systems. The northern part of the country is drained by the Yellow River (Huang Ho), 2,109 miles long (5,464 km) and mostly unnavigable. The central part is drained by the Chang Jiang (Yangtze Kiang), the third longest river in the world 2,432 miles (6,300 km). The Zhujiang (Si Kiang) in the south is 848 miles long (2,197 km) and navigable for a considerable distance. In addition, the Amur (1,144 sq mi.; 2,965 km) forms part of the northeastern boundary.

**Government.** With 2,978 deputies, elected for four-year terms by universal suffrage, the National People's Congress is the chief legislative organ. A State Council has the executive authority. The Congress elects the Premier and Deputy Premiers. All ministries are under the State Council, headed by the Premier.

The Communist Party controls the government.

**History.** By 2000 B.C.; the Chinese were living in the Huang Ho basin, and they had achieved an ad-

vanced stage of civilization by 1200 B.C. The great philosophers Lao-tse, Confucius Mo Ti, and Mencius lived during the Chou dynasty (1122–249 B.C.). The warring feudal states were first united under Emperor Ch'in Shih Huang Ti, during whose reign (246–210 B.C.) work was begun on the Great Wall. Under the Han dynasty (206 B.C.–A.D. 220), China prospered and traded with the West.

In the T'ang dynasty (618–907), often called the golden age of Chinese history, painting, sculpture, and poetry flourished, and printing made its earliest known appearance.

The Mings, last of the native rulers (1368–1644), overthrew the Mongol, or Yuan, dynasty (1280–1368) established by Kublai Khan. The Mings in turn were overthrown in 1644 by invaders from the north, the Manchus.

China closely restricted foreign activities, and by the end of the 18th century only Canton and the Portuguese port of Macao were open to European merchants. Following the Anglo-Chinese War of 1839–42, however, several treaty ports were opened, and Hong Kong was ceded to Britain. Treaties signed after further hostilities (1856–60) weakened Chinese sovereignty and removed foreigners from Chinese jurisdiction. The disastrous Chinese-Japanese War of 1894–95 was followed by a scramble for Chinese concessions by European powers, leading to the Boxer Rebellion (1900), suppressed by an international force.

The death of the Empress Dowager Tzu Hsi in 1908 and the accession of the infant Emperor Hsüan T'ung (Pu-Yi) were followed by a nationwide rebellion led by Dr. Sun Yat-sen, who became first President of the Provisional Chinese Republic in 1911. The Manchus abdicated on Feb. 12, 1912. Dr. Sun resigned in favor of Yuan Shih-k'ai, who suppressed the republicans but was forced by a serious rising in 1915–16 to abandon his intention of declaring himself Emperor. Yuan's death in June 1916 was followed by years of civil war between rival militarists and Dr. Sun's republicans.

Nationalist forces, led by Gen. Chiang Kai-shek and with the advice of Communist experts, soon occupied most of China, setting up a Kuomintang regime in 1928. Internal strife continued, however, and Chiang broke with the Communists.

An alleged explosion on the South Manchurian Railway on Sept. 18, 1931, brought invasion of Manchuria by Japanese forces, who installed the last Manchu Emperor, Henry Pu-Yi, as nominal ruler of the puppet state of "Manchukuo." Japanese efforts to take China's northern provinces in July 1937 were resisted by Chiang, who meanwhile had succeeded in uniting most of China behind him. Within two years, however, Japan seized most of the ports and railways. The Kuomintang government retreated first to Hankow and then to Chungking, while the Japanese set up a puppet government at Nanking headed by Wang Jingwei.

Japan's surrender in 1945 touched off civil war between Nationalist forces under Chiang and Communist forces led by Mao Zedong, the party chairman. Despite U. S. aid, the Chiang forces were overcome by the Maoists, backed by the Soviet bloc, and were expelled from the mainland. The Mao regime, established in Peking as the new capital, proclaimed the People's Republic of China on Oct. 1, 1949, with Zhou Enlai as Premier.

After the Korean War began in June 1950, China led the Communist bloc in supporting North Korea, and on Nov. 26, 1950, the Mao regime intervened openly.

In 1958, Mao undertook the "Great Leap Forward" campaign, which combined the establishment of rural communes with a crash program of village industrialization. These efforts also failed, causing Mao to lose influence to Liu Shaoqi, who became President in 1959, to Premier Zhou, and to Party Secretary Deng Xiaoping.

China exploded its first atomic (fission) bomb in 1964 and produced a fusion bomb in 1967.

Mao moved to Shanghai, and from that base he and his supporters waged what they called a Cultural Revolution. In the spring of 1966 the Mao group formed Red Guard units dominated by youths and students, closing the schools to free the students for agitation.

The Red Guards campaigned against "old ideas, old culture, old habits, and old customs." Often they were no more than uncontrolled mobs, and brutality was frequent. Early in 1967 efforts were made to restore control. The Red Guards were urged to return home. Schools started opening.

Persistent overtures by the Nixon Administration resulted in the dramatic announcement in July that Henry Kissinger, President Richard M. Nixon's national security adviser, had secretly visited Peking and reached agreement on a visit by the President to China.

The movement toward reconciliation, which signaled the end of the U.S. containment policy toward China, provided irresistible momentum for Chinese admission to the U.N. Despite U.S. opposition to expelling Taiwan (Nationalist China), the world body overwhelmingly ousted Chiang in seating Peking.

President Nixon went to Peking for a week early in 1972, meeting Mao as well as Zhou. The summit ended with a historic communiqué on February 28, in which both nations promised to work toward improved relations.

In 1973, the U.S. and China agreed to set up "liaison offices" in each other's capitals, which constituted de facto diplomatic relations. Full diplomatic relations were barred by China as long as the U.S. continued to recognize Nationalist China.

On Jan. 8, 1976, Zhou died. His successor, Vice Premier Deng Xiaoping was supplanted within a month by Hua Guofeng, former Minister of Public Security. Hua became permanent Premier in April. In October he was named successor to Mao as Chairman of the Communist Party.

After Mao died on Sept. 10, a campaign against his widow, Jiang Qing, and three of her "radical" colleagues began. The "Gang of Four" was denounced for having undermined the party, the government, and the economy.

Jiang was brought to trial in 1980 and sentenced on Jan. 25, 1981, to die within two years unless she showed repentance, in which case she would be imprisoned for life.

At the Central Committee meeting of 1977, Deng was reinstated as Deputy Premier, Chief of Staff of the Army, and member of the Central Committee of the Politburo.

At the same time, Jiang Qing, Wang Hongwen, Zhang Chunqiao, and Yao Wenyuan—the notorious "Gang of Four"—were removed from all official posts and banished from the party.

In May 1978, expulsion of ethnic Chinese by Vietnam produced an open rupture. Peking sided with Cambodia in the border fighting that flared between Vietnam and Cambodia, charging Hanoi with aggression.

On Aug. 12, 1978, China and Japan signed a treaty of peace and friendship. Peking and Washington then announced that they would open full diplomatic relations on Jan. 1, 1979. Over Congressional objections, the Carter Administration abrogated the Taiwan defense treaty. Deputy Premier Deng sealed the agreement with a visit to the United States that coincided with the opening of embassies in both capitals on March 1.

On Deng's return from the U.S. 200,000 to 300,000 Chinese troops invaded Vietnam to avenge alleged violations of Chinese territory. The action was seen as a reaction to Vietnam's invasion of Cambodia.

The first People's Congress in five years confirmed Zhao Ziyang, an economic planner, as Premier replacing Hua Guofeng, who had held the post since 1976.

After the Central Committee meeting of June 27–29, 1981, Hu Yaobang, a Deng protégé, was elevated to the party chairmanship, replacing Hua Guofeng. Deng became chairman of the military commission of the central committee, giving him control over the army. The committee's 215 members concluded the session with a statement holding Mao Zedong responsible for the "grave blunder" of the Cultural Revolution.

On June 18, 1983, the Chinese Parliament elected Li Xiannian, an economics and financial specialist, as the first national president since 1969. Previously an outspoken critic of the United States, he was the official host when President Ronald Reagan visited China in April 1984.

Under Deng Xiaoping's leadership, meanwhile, China's Communist idealogy was almost totally reinterpreted and sweeping economic changes were set in motion in the early 1980s. The Chinese scrapped the personality cult that idolized Mao Ze-dong, muted Mao's old call for class struggle and exportation of the Communist revolution, and imported Western technology and management techniques to replace the Marxist tenets that retarded modernization. In the countryside, commune production brigades were disbanded in favor of family-style sharecropping. In the cities, small-scale private enterprise was encouraged.

Also under Deng's leadership, the Chinese Communists worked out an arrangement with Britain for the future of Hong Kong after Britain's lease on most of the British Crown Colony expires in 1997. The flag of the People's Republic of China will be raised but the territory will retain its present social, economic and legal system.

# CHINA (TAIWAN)

**Republic of China**
**President:** Chiang Ching-kuo (1978)
**Premier:** Sun Yun-hsuan (1978)
**Area:** 13,895 sq mi. (35,988 sq km)[1]
**Population (est. mid-1986):** 19,600,000 (average annual growth rate: 1.5%)
**Density per square mile:** 1,410.6
**Capital:** Taipei
**Largest cities (est. 1984):** Taipei, 2,449,702; Kaohsiung, 1,299,082; Taichung, 595,000; Tainan, 585,000; Chilung (Keelung), 350,000
**Monetary unit:** New Taiwan dollar
**Languages:** Chinese (Mandarin) and various dialects
**Religions:** Confucianist, Buddhist, Christian, Taoist
**Literacy rate:** about 89.7%
**Economic summary:** Gross national product (1985 est.): $60 billion. Real growth rate (1985): 4.7%. Per capita income (1983): $3,142. Land used for agriculture: 24%; labor force: 59%; principal products: rice, yams, sugar cane, bananas, pineapples, citrus fruits. Labor force in industry: 42%; major products: textiles, clothing, chemicals, processed foods, electronic equipment, cement, ships, plywood. Natural resources: timber, camphor. Exports: textiles, electrical machinery, plywood. Imports: machinery, basic metals, crude oil, chemicals. Major trading partners: U.S., Japan, Saudi Arabia.

1. Excluding Quemoy and Matsu.

**Geography.** The Republic of China today consists of the island of Taiwan, an island 100 miles (161 km) off the Asian mainland in the Pacific; two offshore islands, Quemoy and Matsu; and the nearby islets of the Pescadores chain. It is slightly larger than the combined areas of Massachusetts and Connecticut.

Taiwan is divided by a central mountain range that runs from north to south, rising sharply on the east coast and descending gradually to a broad western plain, where cultivation is concentrated.

**Government.** The President and the Vice President are elected by the National Assembly for a term of six years. There are five major governing bodies called Yuans: Executive, Legislative, Judicial, Control, and Examination. Taiwan's internal affairs are administered by the Taiwan Provincial Government under the supervision of the Provincial Assembly, which is popularly elected.

The majority and ruling party is the Kuomintang (Nationalist Party) led by President Chiang Ching-kuo. There are also two minority parties: the China Democratic Socialist Party and the Young China Party.

**History.** Taiwan was inhabited by aborigines of Malayan descent when Chinese from the areas now designated as Fukien and Kwangtung began settling it beginning in the 7th century, becoming the majority.

The Portuguese explored the area in 1590, naming it The Beautiful (Formosa). In 1624 the Dutch set up forts in the south, the Spanish in the North. The Dutch threw out the Spanish in 1641 and controlled the island until 1661, when the Chinese General Koxinga took it over, established an independent kingdom, and expelled the Dutch. The Manchus seized the island in 1683 and held it until 1895, when it passed to Japan after the first Sino-Japanese War. Japan developed and exploited it, and it was heavily bombed by American planes during World War II, after which it was restored to China.

After the defeat of its armies on the mainland, the Nationalist Government of Generalissimo Chiang Kai-shek retreated to Taiwan in December 1949. With only 15% of the population consisting of the 1949 immigrants, Chiang dominated the island, maintaining a 600,000-man army in the hope of eventually recovering the mainland. Japan renounced its claim to the island by the San Francisco Peace Treaty of 1951.

By stationing a fleet in the Strait of Formosa the U.S. prevented a mainland invasion in 1953.

The "China seat" in the U.N., which the Nationalists held with U.S. help for over two decades was lost in October 1971, when the People's Republic of China was admitted and Taiwan ousted by the world body.

Chiang died at 87 of a heart attack on April 5, 1975. His son, Chiang Ching-kuo, continued as Premier and dominant power in the Taipei regime. He assumed the presidency in 1978, and Sun Yun-hsuan became Premier.

President Carter's announcement that the U.S. would recognize only the People's Republic of China after Jan. 1, 1979, and that the U.S. defense treaty with the Nationalists would end aroused protests in Taiwan and in the U.S. Congress. Against Carter's wishes, Congress, in a bill governing future relations with Taiwan, guaranteed U.S. action in the event of an attack on the island. The legislation also provided for the continuation of trade and other relations through an American Institute in Taipei, housed in the former American Embassy.

Although the U.S. had assured Taiwan of continuing arms aid, a communiqué on Aug. 17, 1982, signed by Washington and Peking and promising a gradual reduction of such aid, cast a shadow over Taiwan. The Nationalist government protested that the communiqué contradicted the "letter and the spirit" of the Taiwan Relations Act by which the U.S. Congress sought to assure Taiwan's defense.

# COLOMBIA

**Republic of Colombia**
**President:** Virgilio Barco Vargas (1986)
**Area:** 455,355 sq mi. (1,179,369 sq km)
**Population (est. mid-1986):** 30,000,000 (average annual growth rate, 2.1%) (mestizo, 68%; white, 20%; Indian, 7%; black, 5%)
**Density per square mile:** 65.9
**Capital:** Bogotá
**Largest cities (est. 1982):** Bogotá, 4,483,300; Medellín,

1,664,000; Cali, 1,450,000; Baranquilla, 924,000; Cartagena, 470,000; Bucaramanga, 400,000
**Monetary unit:** Peso
**Language:** Spanish
**Religion:** Roman Catholic
**National name:** República de Colombia
**Literacy rate (1985):** 81%
**Economic summary:** Gross national product (est. 1985): $29.0 billion. Average annual growth rate (1970–79): 3.7%. Per capita income (est. 1984): $1,430. Land used for agriculture: 5%; labor force: 29%; principal products: coffee, bananas, rice, corn, sugar cane, cotton, tobacco, sorghum. Labor force in industry: 13%; major products: textiles, processed food, beverages, chemicals, cement. Natural resources: petroleum, natural gas, coal, iron ore, nickel, gold, silver. Exports: coffee, fuel oil, cotton, bananas. Imports: machinery, electrical equipment, chemical products, metals and metal products, transportation equipment. Major trading partners: U.S., West Germany, Japan, Venezuela, Netherlands, Ecuador, Peru.

**Geography.** Colombia, in the northwestern part of South America, is the only country on that continent that borders on both the Atlantic and Pacific Oceans. It is nearly equal to the combined areas of California and Texas.

Through the western half of the country, three Andean ranges run north and south, merging into one at the Ecuadorean border. The eastern half is a low, jungle-covered plain, drained by spurs of the Amazon and Orinoco, inhabited mostly by isolated, tropical-forest Indian tribes. The fertile plateau and valley of the eastern range are the most densely populated parts of the country.

**Government.** Colombia's President, who appoints his own Cabinet, serves for a four-year term. The Senate, the upper house of Congress, has 114 members elected for four years by direct vote. The House of Representatives of 199 members is directly elected for four years.

The major political parties are the Liberal Party (60 of 114 seats in Senate, 114 of 199 seats in House), Conservative Party (51 seats in Senate, 84 seats in House), and a leftist coalition (1 seat in Senate, 1 seat in House).

**History.** Spaniards in 1510 founded Darien, the first permanent European settlement on the American mainland. In 1538 the Spaniards established the colony of New Granada, the area's name until 1861. After a 14-year struggle, in which Simón Bolívar's Venezuelan troops won the battle of Boyacá in Colombia on Aug. 7, 1819, independence was attained in 1824. Bolívar united Colombia, Venezuela, Panama, and Ecuador in the Republic of Greater Colombia (1819–30), but lost Venezuela and Ecuador to separatists. Bolívar's Vice President, Francisco de Paula Santander, founded the Liberal Party as the Federalists while Bolívar established the Conservatives as the Centralists.

Santander's presidency (1832–36) re-established order, but later periods of Liberal dominance (1849–57 and 1861–80), when the Liberals sought to disestablish the Roman Catholic Church, were marked by insurrection and even civil war. Rafael Nuñez, in a 15-year-presidency, restored the power of the central government and the church, which led in 1899 to a bloody civil war and the loss in 1903 of Panama over ratification of a lease to the U.S. of the Canal Zone. For 21 years, until 1930,

the Conservatives held power as revolutionary pressures built up.

The Liberal administrations of Enrique Olaya Herrera and Alfonso López (1930–38) were marked by social reforms that failed to solve the country's problems, and in 1946, insurrection and banditry broke out, claiming hundreds of thousands of lives by 1958. Laureano Gómez (1950–53); the Army Chief of Staff, Gen. Gustavo Rojas Pinilla (1953–56), and a military junta (1956–57) sought to curb disorder by repression.

Julio César Turbay Ayala, Liberal Party candidate in 1978, won a narrow victory—approximately 140,000 of a total of nearly 2.5 million votes—over the Conservative Party candidate. The Liberals also retained control of both the Senate and House.

Government efforts to stamp out the Movement of April 19 (M-19), an urban guerrilla organization, intensified in 1981 with the capture of some of the leaders. In 1986 three of its founders were killed in separate gun battles. The Liberals won a solid majority in 1982, but a party split enabled Belisario Betancur Cuartas, the Conservative candidate, to win the presidency on May 31. After his inauguration, he ended the state of siege that had existed almost continuously for 34 years and renewed the general amnesty of 1981.

On May 25, the liberal Virgilio Barco Vargas was elected by a record-breaking margin.

# COMOROS

**Federal and Islamic Republic of the Comoros**
**President:** Ahmed Abdallah Abderemane (1978)
**Premier:** Ali Mroudjae (1982)
**Area:** 719 sq mi. (1,862 sq km)
**Population (est. 1985):** 469,000 (average annual growth rate: 2.9%)
**Density per square mile:** 652.3
**Capital and largest city (est. 1980):** Moroni (on Grande Comoro), 20,000
**Monetary unit:** Franc CFA
**Language:** French
**Religions:** Islam
**National name:** État Comorien
**Literacy rate (1981):** 15%
**Economic summary:** Gross national product (1984 est.): $92 million. Annual growth rate (1984): 3.1%. Per capita income (1984 est.): $250. Principal agricultural products: perfume essences, copra, coconuts, cloves, vanilla, cinnamon, yams; major industrial products: perfume distillations. Exports: perfume essences, vanilla, copra, cloves. Imports: foodstuffs, fuels, chemicals, cotton textiles, cement. Major trading partners: France, Madagascar, Kenya, Pakistan.

**Geography.** The Comoros Islands—Grande Comoro, Anjouan, Mohéli, and Mayotte (which retains ties to France)—are an archipelago of volcanic origin in the Indian Ocean between Mozambique and Madagascar.

**Government.** A coup by foreign mercenaries on May 13, 1978, deposed President Ali Soilih, who had held power since 1975. A "political and military directorate" headed by Ahmed Abdallah Abderemane and Mohammed Ahmed governed until the adoption of a constitution on Oct. 1 ushered in a republic. With the resignation of Ahmed two days later, Abdallah became president.

**History.** Under French rule since 1886, the Comoros declared themselves independent July 6, 1975. However, Mayotte, with a Christian majority, voted against joining the other, mainly Islamic, islands, in the move to independence and remains French.

A month after independence, Justice Minister Ali Soilih staged a coup with the help of mercenaries, overthrowing the new nation's first president, Ahmed Abdallah. Soilih lowered the voting age to 14, destroyed all records and killed many Comorans. He was overthrown on May 13, 1978, when a small boatload of French mercenaries, some of whom had aided him three years earlier, seized government headquarters.

# CONGO

**People's Republic of the Congo**
**President:** Col. Denis Sassou-Nguessou (1979)
**Prime Minister:** Ange Edouard Poungui (1984)
**Area:** 132,046 sq mi. (342,000 sq km)
**Population (est. mid-1986):** 1,800,000 (average annual growth rate, 2.6%)
**Density per sq mile:** 13.6
**Capital and largest city (est. 1982):** Brazzaville, 450,000
**Monetary unit:** Franc CFA
**Ethnic groups:** Kongo, Teke, Bukongui
**Languages:** French, Lingala, Kokongo
**Religions:** Animist, 48%; Christian, 47%; Muslim, 2%
**National name:** République Populaire du Congo
**Literacy rate:** 56%
**Economic summary:** Gross national product (1983): $2.18 billion. Annual growth rate (1984): 3.1%. Per capita income (1983): $1,320. Principal agricultural products: sugar cane, bananas, coffee, cocoa, peanuts. Labor force in industry: 20%; major products: refined oil, cigarettes, cement, beverages, milled sugar. Natural resources: wood, potash, petroleum, natural gas. Exports: oil, lumber, tobacco, veneer and plywood. Imports: machinery, transportation equipment, manufactured consumer goods, iron and steel, foodstuffs. Major trading partners: France, U.S., Italy, Spain, Brazil.

**Geography.** The Congo is situated in west Central Africa astride the Equator. It borders on Gabon, Cameroon, the Central African Republic, Zaire, and the Angola exclave of Cabinda, with a short stretch of coast on the South Atlantic. Its area is nearly three times that of Pennsylvania.

Most of the inland is tropical rain forest, drained by tributaries of the Zaire (Congo) River, which flows south along the eastern border with Zaire to Stanley Pool. The narrow coastal plain rises to highlands separated from the inland plateaus by the 200-mile-wide Niari River Valley, which gives passage to the coast.

**Government.** Since the coup of September 1968 the country has been governed by a military regime. The Congolese Labor Party is the only party.

**History.** The inhabitants of the former French Congo, mainly Bantu peoples with Pygmies in the north, were subjects of several kingdoms in earlier times.

The Frenchman Pierre Savorgnan de Brazza signed a treaty with Makoko, ruler of the Bateke people, in 1880, which established French control. The area, with Gabon and Ubangi-Shari, was con-

stituted the colony of French Equatorial Africa in 1910. It joined Chad in supporting the Free French cause in World War II. The Congo proclaimed its independence without leaving the French Community in 1960.

Maj. Marien Ngouabi, head of the National Council of the Revolution, took power as president on Jan. 1, 1969. He was sworn in for a second five-year term in 1975. A visit to Moscow by Ngouabi in March ended with the signing of a Soviet-Congolese economic and technical aid pact.

A four-man commando squad assassinated Ngouabi in Brazzaville on March 18, 1977. Five days later the assassination of Émile Cardinal Biayenda, Archbishop of Brazzaville, was announced. Former President Alphonse Massamba-Débat, accused of plotting both deaths, was executed.

Col. Joachim Yhombi-Opango, Army Chief of Staff, assumed the presidency on April 4. In June, the new government agreed to resume diplomatic relations with the U.S., ending a 12-year rift. Yombhi-Opango resigned on Feb. 4, 1979, and was replaced by Col. Denis Sassou-Neguessou.

# COSTA RICA

**Republic of Costa Rica**
**President:** Oscar Arias Sanchez (1986)
**Area:** 19,652 sq mi. (50,898 sq km)
**Population (est. mid-1986):** 2,700,000 (average annual growth rate, 2.6%)
**Density per square mile:** 137.4
**Capital and largest city (est. 1984):** San José, 278,500
**Monetary unit:** Colón
**Language:** Spanish
**Religion:** Roman Catholic
**National name:** República de Costa Rica
**Literacy rate (1984):** 93%
**Economic summary:** Gross national product (1983): $3.5 billion. Average annual growth rate (1981–83): 3.5%. Per capita income (1984): $1,400. Land used for agriculture: 13%; labor force: 27%; principal products: bananas, coffee, sugar cane, rice, corn, livestock. Labor force in industry: 21%; major products: processed foods, textiles and clothing, construction materials, fertilizer. Natural resource: timber. Exports: coffee, bananas, beef, sugar. Imports: manufactured products, machinery, chemicals, foodstuffs, fuels, fertilizer. Major trading partners: U.S., Central American countries, West Germany, Japan.

**Geography.** This Central American country lies between Nicaragua to the north and Panama to the south. Its area slightly exceeds that of Vermont and New Hampshire combined.

Most of Costa Rica is tableland, from 3,000 to 6,000 feet (914 to 1,829 m) above sea level. Cocos Island (10 sq mi.; 26 sq km), about 300 miles (483 km) off the Pacific Coast, is under Costa Rican sovereignty.

**Government.** Under the 1949 Constitution, the president and the one-house Legislative Assembly of 57 members are elected for terms of four years.

The army was abolished in 1949. There is a civil guard of 5,000 and a rural guard of 2,000.

The major political parties are the National Liberation Party (33 of 57 seats in the Legislative Assembly), led by Guillermo Vargas; Unity Party (18 seats), led by Oscar Aguilar; Communist Party (4 seats); Pueblo Unido Party (1 seat); Movimiento Nacional Party (1 seat).

**History.** Costa Rica was inhabited by 25,000 Indians when Columbus discovered it and probably named it in 1502. Few of the Indians survived the Spanish conquest, which began in 1563. The region was administered as a Spanish province. Costa Rica achieved independence in 1821 but was absorbed for two years by Agustín de Iturbide in his Mexican Empire. It was established as a republic in 1848.

Except for the military dictatorship of Tomás Guardia from 1870 to 1882, Costa Rica has enjoyed one of the most democratic governments in Latin America.

Rodrigo Carazo Odio, leader of a four-party coalition called the Unity Party, won the presidency in February 1978. His tenure was marked by a disastrous decline in the economy, which forced postponement of foreign debt payments at the end of 1981. Luis Alberto Monge Álvarez, a former union organizer and cofounder of the National Liberation Party, swept to victory in the Feb. 7, 1982, national elections.

On Feb. 2, 1986, Oscar Arias Sanchez won the national elections on a neutralist platform, defeating Rafael Angel Calderon, who was a stronger supporter of U.S. policies in Central America.

# CUBA

**Republic of Cuba**
**President:** Fidel Castro Ruz (1976)
**Area:** 44,218 sq mi. (114,524 sq km)
**Population (est. mid-1986):** 10,200,000 (average annual growth rate, 1.1%)
**Density per square mile:** 230.7
**Capital:** Havana
**Largest cities (est. 1983):** Havana, 1,972,000; Santiago de Cuba, 348,900; Santa Clara, 173,700; Camagüey, 251,000; Holguin, 189,600
**Monetary unit:** Peso
**Language:** Spanish
**Religion:** Roman Catholic
**National name:** República de Cuba
**Literacy rate:** 96%
**Economic summary:** Gross national product (est. 1982): $14.9 billion in 1974 dollars. Average annual growth rate (1982 est.): 1.4%. Land used for agriculture: 29%; labor force: 22%; principal products: sugar, tobacco, coffee, rice, fruits. Labor force in industry: 21%; major products: refined oil products, textiles, chemicals, processed food, metals, light consumer products. Natural resources: metals, primarily nickel. Exports: sugar, nickel, shellfish, tobacco. Imports: capital goods, industrial raw materials, petroleum, foodstuffs. Major trading partners: U.S.S.R., other Communist bloc countries, Spain

**Geography.** The largest island of the West Indies group (equal in area to Pennsylvania), Cuba is also the westernmost—just west of Hispaniola (Haiti and the Dominican Republic), and 90 miles (145 km) south of Key West, Fla., at the entrance to the Gulf of Mexico.

The island is mountainous in the southeast and south central area (Sierra Maestra). Elsewhere it is flat or rolling.

**Government.** Since 1976, elections have been held every five years to elect the National Assembly, which in turn elects the 31-member Council of States, its President, First Vice-President, five Vice-Presidents, and Secretary. Fidel Castro is President of the Council of State and of the government and First Secretary of the Communist Party of Cuba, the only political party.

**History.** Arawak Indians inhabiting Cuba when Columbus discovered the island in 1492 died off from diseases brought by sailors and settlers. By 1511, Spaniards under Diego Velásquez were founding settlements that served as bases for Spanish exploration. Cuba soon after served as an assembly point for treasure looted by the conquistadores, attracting French and English pirates.

Black slaves and free laborers were imported to work sugar and tobacco plantations, and waves of chiefly Spanish immigrants maintained a European character in the island's culture. Early slave rebellions and conflicts between colonials and Spanish rulers laid the foundation for an independence movement that turned into open warfare from 1867 to 1878. The poet, José Marti, in 1895 led the struggle that finally ended Spanish rule, thanks largely to U.S. intervention in 1898 after the sinking of the battleship *Maine* in Havana harbor.

A treaty in 1899 made Cuba an independent republic under U.S. protection. The U.S. occupation, which ended in 1902, suppressed yellow fever and brought large American investment. From 1906 to 1909, Washington invoked the Platt Amendment to the treaty, which gave it the right to intervene in order to suppress any revolt. U.S. troops came back in 1912 and again in 1917 to restore order. The Platt Amendment was abrogated in 1934.

Fulgencio Batista, an army sergeant, led a revolt in 1934 that overthrew the regime of President Gerado Machado.

Batista's Cuba was a police state. Corrupt officials took payoffs from American gamblers who operated casinos, demanded bribes from Cubans for various public services and enriched themselves with raids on the public treasury. Dissenters were murdered and their bodies dumped in gutters.

Fidel Castro Ruz, a hulking, bearded attorney in his 30s, landed in Cuba on Christmas Day 1956 with a band of 12 fellow revolutionaries, evaded Batista's soldiers, and set up headquarters in the jungled hills of the Sierra Maestra range. By 1958 his force had grown to about 2,000 guerrillas, for the most part young and middle class. Castro's brother, Raul, and Ernesto (Che) Guevara, an Argentine physician, were his top lieutenants. Businessmen and landowners who opposed the Batista regime gave financial support to the rebels. The United States, meanwhile, cut off arms shipments to Batista's army.

The beginning of the end for Batista came when the rebels routed 3,000 government troops and captured Santa Clara, capital of Las Villas province 150 miles from Havana, and a trainload of Batista reinforcements refused to get out of their railroad cars. On New Year's Day 1959, Batista flew to exile in the Dominican Republic and Castro took over the government. Crowds cheered the revolutionaries on their seven-day march to the capital.

The United States initially welcomed what looked like the prospect for a democratic Cuba, but a rude awakening came within a few months when Castro established military tribunals for political opponents, jailed hundreds, and began to veer leftward. Castro disavowed Cuba's 1952 military pact with the United States. He confiscated U.S. investments in banks and industries and seized large U.S.

landholdings, turning them first into collective farms and then into Soviet-type state farms. The United States broke relations with Cuba on Jan. 3, 1961. Castro thereupon forged an alliance with the Soviet Union.

From the ranks of the Cuban exiles who had fled to the United States, the Central Intelligence Agency recruited and trained an expeditionary force, numbering less than 2,000 men, to invade Cuba, with the expectation that the invasion would spark an uprising of the Cuban populace against Castro. The invasion was planned under the Eisenhower administration and President John F. Kennedy gave the go-ahead for it in the first months of his administration, but rejected a CIA proposal for U.S. planes to provide air support. The landing at the Bay of Pigs on April 17, 1961, was a fiasco. Not only did the invaders fail to receive any support from the populace, but Castro's tanks and artillery made short work of the small force.

A Soviet attempt to change the global power balance by installing in Cuba medium-range missiles—capable of striking targets in the United States with nuclear warheads—provoked a crisis between the superpowers in 1962 that had the potential of touching off World War III. After a visit to Moscow by Cuba's war minister, Raul Castro, work began secretly on the missile launching sites. Denouncing the Soviets for "deliberate deception," President Kennedy on Oct. 22 announced that the U.S. navy would enforce a "quarantine" of shipping to Cuba and search Soviet bloc ships to prevent the missiles themselves from reaching the island. After six days of tough public statements on both sides and secret diplomacy, Soviet Premier Nikita Khrushchev on Oct. 28 ordered the missile sites dismantled, crated and shipped back to the Soviet Union, in return for a U.S. pledge not to attack Cuba.

Emigration increased dramatically after April 1, 1980, when Castro, irritated by the granting of asylum to would-be refugees by the Peruvian embassy in Havana, removed guards and allowed 10,000 Cubans to swarm into the embassy grounds.

As an airlift began taking the refugees to Costa Rica, Castro insisted they must go directly to their final destination. At the same time he opened the port of Mariel to a "freedom flotilla" of ships and yachts from the United States, many of them owned or chartered by Cuban-Americans to bring out relatives. More than 125,000 Cubans poured out of Mariel in a mass exodus. It wasn't until after they had reached the United States that it was discovered that the regime had opened prisons and mental hospitals to permit criminals, homosexuals and others unwanted in Cuba to join the refugees.

For most of President Ronald Reagan's first term, U.S.-Cuban relations were frozen, with Secretary of State Alexander Haig calling Havana the "source" of troubles in Central America. But late in 1984, an agreement was reached between the two countries. Cuba would take back more than 2,700 Cubans who had come to the United States in the Mariel exodus but were not eligible to stay in the country under U.S. immigration law because of criminal or psychiatric disqualification. The United States, in exchange, would reinstitute regular immigration for Cubans to the United States.

As the first step in the accord, 23 Cuban aliens who had committed serious crimes either in Cuba or the United States were moved from Atlanta Federal Penitentiary on Feb. 21, 1985, and put aboard a chartered airliner that flew them to Havana.

After a machinegun attack by leftist rebels in June 1985 killed 13 diners—including six Americans—at an outdoor cafe in El Salvador, President Reagan listed Cuba with Iran, Libya, North Korea and Nicaragua in what he called "a confederation of terrorist states" that carried out "outright acts of war" against the United States. He said Cuba had "openly armed, trained and directed terrorists operating on at least three continents." In Havana, Castro ridiculed the charge and said, "This Reagan is a madman, an imbecile, a bum."

# CYPRUS

**Republic of Cyprus**
**President:** Spyros Kyprianou (1977)
**Area:** 3,572 sq mi (9,251 sq km)
**Population (est. mid-1986):** 700,000 (average annual growth rate: 1.3%) (Greek, 80%; Turkish, 18%)
**Density per square mile:** 196
**Capital and largest city (est. 1982):** Nicosia, 123,298
**Monetary unit:** Cyprus pound
**Languages:** Greek, Turkish, English
**Religions:** Greek Orthodox, 76%; Islam, 19%
**National name:** Kypriaki Dimokratia—Kibris Cumhuriyeti
**Member of Commonwealth of Nations**
**Literacy rate (1981):** 89%
**Economic summary:** Gross national product (1985): $3.7 billion. Average annual growth rate (1970–78): 1.4%. Per capita income (1983): $3,270. Land used for agriculture: 47%; labor force: 20%; principal products: vine products, citrus, potatoes, other vegetables. Labor force in industry: 30%; major products: beverages, footwear, clothing, cement, asbestos mining. Natural resources: copper, asbestos, gypsum, building stone, marble, clay, salt. Exports: clothing, machinery. Imports: manufactured goods, machinery and transportation equipment, petroleum products, foodstuffs. Major trading partners: U.K., Lebanon, Italy

**Geography.** The third largest island in the Mediterranean (one and one half times the size of Delaware), Cyprus lies off the southern coast of Turkey and the western shore of Syria. Most of the country consists of a wide plain lying between two mountain ranges that cross the island. The highest peak is Mount Olympus at 6,406 feet (1,953 m).

**Government.** Under the republic's Constitution, for the protection of the Turkish minority the vice president as well as three of the 10 Cabinet ministers must be from the Turkish community, while the House of Representatives is elected by each community separately, 70% Greek Cypriote and 30% Turkish Cypriote representatives.

The Greek and Turkish communities are self-governing in questions of religion, education, and culture. Other governmental matters are under the jurisdiction of the central government. Each community is entitled to a Communal Chamber.

The Greek Communal Chamber, which had 23 members, was abolished in 1965 and its function was absorbed by the Ministry of Education. The Turkish Communal Chamber, however, has continued to function.

The following is a breakdown of the 56 seats held by Greeks: Democratic Front of Spyros Kyprianou (16); AKEL Progressive Party of the Working People (15); Democratic Rally (19); Socialist Party of Dr. Vassos Lyssarides (6). The 24 Turkish members have not attended sessions of the House since 1964.

**History.** Cyprus was the site of early Phoenician and Greek colonies. For centuries its rule passed through many hands. It fell to the Turks in 1571, and a large Turkish colony settled on the island.

In World War I, on the outbreak of hostilities with Turkey, Britain annexed the island. It was declared a crown colony in 1925.

For centuries the Greek population, regarding Greece as its mother country, has sought self-determination and reunion with it *(enosis)*. The resulting quarrel with Turkey threatened NATO. Cyprus became an independent nation on Aug. 16, 1960, with Britain, Greece, and Turkey as guarantor powers.

Archbishop Makarios, president since 1959, was overthrown July 15, 1974, by a military coup led by the Cypriot National Guard. The new regime named Nikos Giorgiades Sampson as president and Bishop Gennadios as head of the Cypriot Church to replace Makarios. The rebels were led by rightist Greek officers who supported *enosis*.

Diplomacy failed to resolve the crisis. Turkey invaded Cyprus by sea and air July 20, 1974, asserting its right to protect the Turkish Cypriote minority.

Geneva talks involving Greece, Turkey, Britain, and the two Cypriote factions failed in mid-August, and the Turks subsequently gained control of 40% of the island. Greece made no armed response to the superior Turkish force, but bitterly suspended military participation in the NATO alliance.

The tension continued after Makarios returned to become President on Dec. 7, 1974. He offered self-government to the Turkish minority, but rejected any solution "involving transfer of populations and amounting to partition of Cyprus."

Turkish Cypriots proclaimed a separate state in the northern part of the island and proposed a "biregional federation."

Makarios died on Aug. 3, 1977, and Spyros Kyprianou was elected to serve the remaining five months of his term. Kyprianou, running unopposed, won a full five-year term in 1978. In February 1983, President Kyprianou was re-elected for another five-year term, polling 57% of the vote.

Kyprianou's victory in the legislative elections on December 8, 1985, was seen as a vote of support for his hard-line approach to reunification talks.

# CZECHOSLOVAKIA

**Czechoslovak Socialist Republic**
**President:** Gustav Husak (1975)
**Premier:** Lubomir Strougal (1970)
**Area:** 49,374 sq mi. (127,896 sq km)
**Population (est. mid-1986):** 15,500,000 (average annual growth rate: 0.3%) (Czech, 64%; Slovak, 30%)
**Density per square mile:** 313.9
**Capital:** Prague
**Largest cities (est. 1982):** Prague, 1,185,000; Bratislava, 395,000; Brno, 375,000; Ostrova, 325,000; Kosice, 210,000; Plzěn, 173,000
**Monetary unit:** Koruna
**Languages:** Czech, Slovak, Hungarian
**Religions:** Roman Catholic, 77%; Czechoslovak Church, 8%; Protestant, 2%; Greek Orthodox, 19%
**National name:** Ceskoslovenská Socialistická Republika
**Literacy rate (1981):** 100%
**Economic summary:** Gross national product (1985); $166 billion. Average annual growth rate (1985); 3.3%. Per

capita income (1985): $5,914. Labor force in agriculture: 16.8%; principal products: wheat, rye, oats, corn, barley, potatoes, sugar beets, hogs, cattle, horses. Labor force in industry: 51.4%; major products: iron and steel, machinery and equipment, cement, textiles, motor vehicles, armaments, chemicals, ceramics. Natural resources: coal/coke, timber, lignite, uranium, magnesite. Exports: machinery, fuels and raw materials, consumer goods. Imports: machinery, equipment, fuels, raw materials, food, consumer goods. Major trading partners: U.S.S.R. and Soviet bloc, West Germany, Austria

**Geography.** Czechoslovakia lies in central Europe, a neighbor of East and West Germany, Poland, the U.S.S.R., Hungary, and Austria. It is equal in size to New York State. The principal rivers—the Elbe, Danube, Oder, and Moldau—are vital commercially to this landlocked country, for both waterborne commerce and agriculture, which flourishes in fertile valleys irrigated by these rivers and their tributaries.

**Government.** Since 1969 the supreme organ of the state has been the Federal Assembly, which has two equal chambers: the Chamber of People, with 200 deputies, and the Chamber of Nations, with 150 deputies (75 from the Czech Socialist Republic and 75 from the Slovak Socialist Republic). The chief executive is the President, who is elected by the Federal Assembly for a five-year term. The Premier and his Cabinet are appointed by the President but are responsible to the Federal Assembly.

The major political parties are the Communist Party, led by General Secretary Gustav Husak in both republics; Socialist Party; People's Party in the Czech Socialist Republic; Slovak Freedom Party and Slovak Reconstruction Party in the Slovak Socialist Republic. Together with trade unions, youth organizations, and other organizations, they form the National Front.

**History.** Probably about the 5th century A.D., Slavic tribes from the Vistula basin settled in the region of modern Czechoslovakia. Slovakia came under Magyar domination. The Czechs founded the kingdom of Bohemia, the Premyslide dynasty, which ruled Bohemia and Moravia from the 10th to the 16th century. One of the Bohemian kings, Charles IV, Holy Roman Emperor, made Prague an imperial capital and a center of Latin scholarship. The Hussite movement founded by Jan Hus (1369?–1415) linked the Slavs to the Reformation and revived Czech nationalism, previously under German domination. A Hapsburg, Ferdinand I, ascended the throne in 1526. The Czechs rebelled in 1618. Defeated in 1620, they were ruled for the next 300 years as part of the Austrian Empire.

In World War I, Czech and Slovak patriots, notably Thomas G. Masaryk and Milan Stefanik, promoted Czech-Slovak independence from abroad while their followers fought against the Central Powers. On Oct. 28, 1918, Czechoslovakia proclaimed itself a republic. Shortly thereafter Masaryk was unanimously elected first President.

Hitler provoked the country's German minority in the Sudetenland to agitate for autonomy. At the Munich Conference on Sept. 30, 1938, France and the U.K., seeking to avoid World War II, agreed that the Nazis could take the Sudetenland Dr. Eduard Beneš, who had succeeded Masaryk, resigned on Oct. 5, 1938, and fled to London. Czechoslovakia became a state within the German orbit and was known as Czecho-Slovakia. In March 1939, the Nazis occupied the country.

Soon after Czechoslovakia was liberated in World War II and the government returned in April 1945, it was obliged to cede Ruthenia to the U.S.S.R. In 1946, a Communist, Klement Gottwald, formed a six-party coalition Cabinet. Pressure from Moscow increased until Feb. 23–25, 1948, when the Communists seized complete control in a coup. Following constituent assembly elections in which the Communists and their allies were unopposed, a new Constitution was adopted.

The "people's democracy" was converted into a "socialist" state by a new Constitution adopted June 11, 1960.

After the death of Stalin and the relaxing of Soviet controls, Czechoslovakia witnessed a nationalist awakening. In 1968 conservative Stalinists were driven from power and replaced by more liberal, reform-minded Communists.

Soviet military maneuvers on Czechoslovak soil in May 1968 were followed in July by a meeting of the U.S.S.R. with Poland, Bulgaria, East Germany, and Hungary in Warsaw that demanded an accounting, which Prague refused. Czechoslovak-Soviet talks on Czechoslovak territory, at Cierna, in late July led to an accord. But the Russians charged that the Czechoslovaks had reneged on pledges to modify their policies, and on Aug. 20–21, troops of the five powers, estimated at 600,000, executed a lightning invasion and occupation.

Soviet secret police seized the top Czechoslovak leadership and detained it for several days in Moscow. But Soviet efforts to establish a puppet regime failed. President Ludvik Svoboda negotiated an accord providing for a gradual troop withdrawal in return for "normalization" of political policy.

Czechoslovakia signed a new friendship treaty with the U.S.S.R. that codified the "Brezhnev doctrine," under which Russia can invade any Eastern European socialist nation that threatens to leave the satellite camp.

One of the most vigorous of the Eastern European groups formed to support human rights in the wake of the 1975 Helsinki Conference on Security and Cooperation in Europe was the Czech "Charter 77," an association of 240 intellectuals who signed a New Year manifesto protesting the suppression of freedom. Detentions of the signers began immediately, and a second manifesto appeared on January 8 with 300 signatures condemning the official reaction to the first. On Jan. 28, the government offered to let five of the dissidents leave the country, but they refused.

Charter 77 adherents marked their first anniversary with a manifesto Jan. 1, 1978, calling for open debate on the observance of human rights in Czechoslovakia. Enough of the group remained in May 1981 for the government to jail 36 persons in the biggest roundup of dissidents since 1971, as part of the precautions against any show of sympathy for Polish workers. The Czech Communist Party was among the most severe of the Eastern European states in condemning what Husak called an attempted "counterrevolutionary coup" in Poland.

# DENMARK

**Kingdom of Denmark**
**Sovereign:** Queen Margrethe II (1972)
**Premier:** Poul Schlüter (1982)
**Area:** 16,631 sq mi. (43,075 sq km)[1]

**Population (est. mid-1986):** 5,100,000 (average annual growth rate: −0.1%)
**Density per square mile:** 306.7
**Capital:** Copenhagen
**Largest cities (est. 1984):** Copenhagen, 1,365,760; Aarhus, 250,404; Odense, 170,961; Alborn, 154,840
**Monetary unit:** Krone
**Language:** Danish
**Religion:** Lutheran (established)
**National name:** Kongeriget Danmark
**Literacy rate:** 100%
**Economic summary:** Gross national product (1985): $72.2 billion. Average annual growth rate (1982–85): 3.1%. Per capita income (1982): $10,973. Labor force in agriculture: 6.9%; principal products: meat, dairy products, fish, grains. Labor force in industry: 31.2%; major products; industrial and construction equipment, electronics, chemicals, textiles. Natural resources: oil, zinc, lead, coal, molybdenum, cryolite, uranium. Exports: meat and dairy products, industrial machinery, textiles and clothing, chemical products, transportation equipment. Imports: industrial raw materials, fuel, machinery and equipment, transport equipment, petroleum, chemicals. Major trading partners: West Germany, Sweden, U.K., U.S.

1. Excluding Faeroe Islands and Greenland. 2. Includes Greenland.

**Geography.** Smallest of the Scandinavian countries (half the size of Maine), Denmark occupies the Jutland peninsula, which extends north from Germany between the tips of Norway and Sweden. To the west is the North Sea and to the east the Baltic.

The country also consists of several Baltic islands; the two largest are Sjaelland, the site of Copenhagen, and Fyn. The narrow waters off the north coast are called the Skagerrak and those off the east, the Kattegat.

**Government.** Denmark has been a constitutional monarchy since 1849. Legislative power is held jointly by the Sovereign and parliament. The Constitution of 1953 provides for a unicameral parliament called the Folketing, consisting of 179 popularly elected members who serve for four years. The Cabinet is presided over by the Sovereign, who appoints the Prime Minister.

The Sovereign, Queen Margrethe II, was born April 16, 1940, and became Queen—the first in Denmark's history—Jan. 15, 1972, the day after her father, King Frederik IX, died at 72 in the 25th year of his reign. Margrethe was the eldest of his three daughters (by Princess Ingrid of Sweden). The nation's Constitution was amended in 1953 to permit her to succeed her father in the absence of a male heir to the throne. (Denmark was ruled six centuries ago by Margrethe I, but she was never crowned Queen since there was no female right of succession.) Margrethe's sisters are Benedikte (born 1944) and Anne Marie (born 1946), now the former Queen of Greece.

The major political parties are the Social Democratic Party (56 seats in the Folketing), led by former Premier Anker Jørgensen; Conservative People's Party (42 seats), led by Premier Poul Schlüter; Socialist People's Party (21 seats), led by Gert Petersen; Liberal Party (22 seats), led by Henning Christophersen; Radical Liberal Party (10 seats); Center Democrats (8 seats); Progress Party (6 seats), Christian People's Party (5 seats); Leftwing Socialists (5 seats).

**History.** Denmark emerged with establishment of the Norwegian dynasty of the Ynglinger in Jutland at the end of the 8th century. Danish mariners played a major role in the raids of the Vikings, or Norsemen, on Western Europe and particularly England. The country was Christianized by St. Ansgar and Harald Blaatand (Bluetooth)—the first Christian king—in the 10th century. Harald's son, Sweyn, conquered England in 1013. His son, Canute the Great, who reigned from 1014 to 1035, united Denmark, England, and Norway under his rule; the southern part of Sweden was part of Denmark until the 17th century. On Canute's death, civil war tore the country until Waldemar I (1157–82) re-established Danish hegemony over the north.

In 1282, the nobles won the Great Charter, and Eric V was forced to share power with parliament and a Council of Nobles. Waldemar IV (1340–75) restored Danish power, checked only by the Hanseatic League of north German cities allied with ports from Holland to Poland. His daughter, Margrethe, in 1397 united under her rule Denmark, Norway, and Sweden. But Sweden later achieved autonomy and in 1523, under Gustavus I, independence.

Denmark supported Napoleon, for which it was punished at the Congress of Vienna in 1815 by the loss of Norway to Sweden. In 1864, Bismarck, together with the Austrians, made war on the little country as an initial step in the unification of Germany. Denmark was neutral in World War I. In 1939, Denmark signed a 10-year pact with Hitler, but less than a year later it was invaded by the Nazis. King Christian X reluctantly cautioned his countrymen to accept the occupation, but there was widespread resistance against the Nazis. In 1944, Iceland declared its independence from Denmark, ending a union that had existed since 1380.

Liberated by British troops in May 1945, the country staged a fast recovery in both agriculture and manufacturing and was a leader in liberalizing trade. It joined the United Nations in 1945 and NATO in 1949.

The Social Democrats largely ran Denmark after the war but were ousted in 1973 when, in an election dominated by protests against high taxes, all established parties lost heavily. The big winner was the new Progress Party. A minority government was formed by the Liberal Democrats, with their leader, Poul Hartling, as Premier. After losing a vote of confidence in January 1975, Hartling resigned and was succeeded by Anker Jørgensen, a Social Democrat who was Premier in 1972–73.

## Outlying Territories of Denmark

### FAEROE ISLANDS

**Status:** Autonomous part of Denmark
**Lagmand (President):** Pauli Ellefsen (1981)
**Area:** 540 sq mi. (1,399 sq km)
**Population (est. 1985):** 46,000 (average annual growth rate: 1.0%)
**Density per square mile:** 79.9
**Capital (est. 1982):** Thorshavn, 12,750
**Monetary unit:** Faeroese krone
**Literacy rate:** 99%
**Economic summary:** Gross national product (1980): $440 million. Average annual growth rate (1970–79): 5.6 %. Per capita income (1980): $10,620. Principal agricultural products: sheep and cattle. Major industrial product: fish. Exports: fish and fish products. Imports: machinery and transport equipment, foodstuffs, petroleum and petroleum products. Major trading partners: Denmark, U.S., U.K., West Germany

This group of 21 islands, lying in the North Atlantic about 200 miles (322 km) northwest of the Shetland Islands, joined Denmark in 1386 and has since been part of the Danish kingdom. The islands were occupied by British troops during World War II, after the German occupation of Denmark.

The Faeroes have home rule under a bill enacted in 1948; they also have two representatives in the Danish Folketing.

### GREENLAND

**Status:** Autonomous part of Denmark
**Premier:** Jonathan Motzfeldt (1983)
**Area:** 840,000 sq mi. (incl. 708,069 sq mi. covered by icecap) (2,175,600 sq km)
**Population (est. 1985):** 54,000 (average annual growth rate: 1.2%)
**Capital (est. 1982):** Godthaab, 10,000
**Monetary unit:** Krone
**Literacy rate:** 99%
**Economic summary:** Gross national product (1980): $430 million. Average annual growth rate (1970–79): 4.4%. Per capita income (1980): $8,290. Principal agricultural products: hay, sheep, garden produce. Major industries: mining, slaughtering, fishing, sealing. Natural resource: cryolite. Exports: fish and fish products, metalic ores and concentrates. Imports: petroleum and petroleum products, machinery and transport equipment, foodstuffs. Major trading partners: Denmark, U.S., Finland, West Germany, U.K.

Greenland, the world's largest island, was colonized in 985–86 by Eric the Red. Danish sovereignty, which covered only the west coast, was extended over the whole island in 1917. In 1941 the U.S. signed an agreement with the Danish minister in Washington, placing it under U.S. protection during World War II but maintaining Danish sovereignty. A definitive agreement for the joint defense of Greenland within the framework of NATO was signed in 1951. A large U.S. air base at Thule in the far north was completed in 1953.

Under 1953 amendments to the Danish Constitution, Greenland became part of Denmark, with two representatives in the Danish Folketing. On May 1, 1979, Greenland gained home rule, with its own local parliament (Landsting), replacing the Greenland Provincial Council.

In February 1982, Greenlanders voted to withdraw from the European Community, which they had joined as part of Denmark in 1973. Danish Premier Anker Jørgensen said he would support the request, but with reluctance.

Greenland is the world's only source of natural cryolite, important in making aluminum.

### DJIBOUTI

**Republic of Djibouti**
**President:** Hassan Gouled Aptidon (1977)
**Prime Minister:** Gourad Hamadou Barkat (1978)
**Area:** 8,996 sq mi. (23,300 sq km)
**Population (est. mid-1986):** 300,000 (average annual growth rate: 2.5%)

**Density per square mile:** 33.3
**Capital (est. 1980):** Djibouti, 200,000
**Monetary unit:** Djibouti franc
**Languages:** Arabic, French, Afar, Somali
**Religions:** Islam, 94%; Christian, 6%
**National name:** Jumhouriyya Djibouti
**Literacy rate:** 20%
**Economic summary:** Gross national product (1984): $308 million. Average annual growth rate (1970–79): −4.9%. Per capita income (1984): $270. Principal agricultural products: goats, sheep, camels. Industries: port and maritime support, construction. Exports: hides, cattle, coffee (in transit from Ethiopia). Imports: machinery, transport equipment, foodstuffs. Major trading partners: France, Ethiopia, Japan, Belgium, U.K., Saudi Arabia, Yemen

**Geography.** Djibouti lies in northeastern Africa on the Gulf of Aden at the southern entrance to the Red Sea. It borders on Ethiopia and Somalia. The country, the size of Massachusetts, is mainly a stony desert, with scattered plateaus and highlands.

**Government.** On May 8, 1977, the population of the French Territory of the Afars and Issas voted by more than 98% for independence. Voters also approved a 65-member interim Constituent Assembly. France transferred sovereignty to the new nation of Djibouti on June 27. Later in the year it became a member of the Organization of African Unity and the Arab League. The People's Progress Assembly is the only legal political party.

**History.** The territory that is now Djibouti was acquired by France between 1843 and 1886 by treaties with the Somali sultans. Small, arid, and sparsely populated, Djibouti is important chiefly because of the capital city's port, the terminal of the Djibouti-Addis Ababa railway that carries 60% of Ethiopia's foreign trade.

Originally known as French Somaliland, the colony voted in 1958 and 1967 to remain under French rule. It was renamed the Territory of the Afars and Issas in 1967 and took the name of its capital city on attaining independence.

Somali rebels in Ethiopia's Ogaden Province cut the railway to Djibouti in June 1977 and there was fear that the new nation might be absorbed by Somalia. In July 1980, Djibouti granted base rights to United States ships and planes in exchange for undisclosed amounts of aid.

# DOMINICA

**Commonwealth of Dominica**
**President:** Sir Clarence Seignoret (1985)
**Prime Minister:** Mary Eugenia Charles (1980)
**Area:** 290 sq mi. (751 sq km)
**Population: (est. mid-1986):** 100,000 (average annual growth rate: 1.7%)
**Density per square mile:** 344.8
**Capital and largest city (est. 1981):** Roseau, 20,000
**Monetary unit:** East Caribbean dollar
**Languages:** English and French patois
**Religions:** Roman Catholic, Anglican, Methodist
**Member of Commonwealth of Nations**
**Literacy rate:** 80%
**Economic summary:** Gross national product (1983): $79.4 million. Average annual growth rate (1981): 8%. Per capita income (1983): $762. Labor force in agriculture: 40%; principal products: bananas, citrus fruits, coconuts,

cocoa. Major industries: agricultural processing; tourism. Exports: bananas, lime juice, cocoa, coconut oil. Imports: machinery and equipment, foodstuffs, manufactured goods, chemicals. Major trading partners: U.K., Caribbean countries, U.S.

**Geography.** Dominica is an island of the Lesser Antilles in the Caribbean south of Guadeloupe and north of Martinique.

**Government.** Dominica is a republic, with a president elected by the House of Assembly as head of state and a prime minister appointed by the president on the advice of the Assembly. The Freedom Party (16 of 21 seats in the Assembly) is led by Prime Minister Mary Eugenia Charles. The Opposition Democratic Labor Party holds four seats and the United Dominica Labor Party one.

**History.** Discovered by Columbus in 1493, Dominica was claimed by Britain and France until 1815, when Britain asserted sovereignty. Dominica, along with other Windward Isles, became a self-governing member of the West Indies Associated States in free association with Britain in 1967.

Full independence was granted on Nov. 3, 1978, and the first Prime Minister, Patrick R. John, declared a socialist course for the new republic.

Dissatisfaction over the slow pace of reconstruction after Hurricane David struck the island in September 1979 brought a landslide victory for the opposition Freedom Party in July 1980. The vote gave the prime ministership to Mary Eugenia Charles, a strong advocate of free enterprise. The Freedom Party won again in 1985 elections, giving Miss Charles a second five-year term as prime minister.

# DOMINICAN REPUBLIC

**President:** Joaquin Bologuer (1986)
**Area:** 18,704 sq mi. (48,442 sq km)
**Population (est. mid-1986):** 6,400,000 (average annual growth rate: 2.5%) (approx.): mestizo, 75%; white, 15%; Negro, 10%
**Density per square mile:** 342.2
**Capital:** Santo Domingo
**Largest cities (est. 1982):** Santo Domingo, 1,313,170; Santiago de los Caballeros, 278,640
**Monetary unit:** Peso
**Language:** Spanish
**Religion:** Roman Catholic
**National name:** República Dominicana
**Literacy rate:** 68%
**Economic summary:** Gross national product (1984 est.): $11.0 billion. Average annual growth rate (1971–82): 4.5%. Per capital income (1983): $1,371. Land used for agriculture: 14%; labor force: 47%; principal products: sugar cane, coffee, cocoa, tobacco, bananas. Labor force in industry: 20%; major products: processed sugar, textiles, nickel, silver, and gold mining. Natural resources: nickel, gold, silver. Exports: sugar, nickel, coffee, tobacco, cocoa. Imports: foodstuffs, petroleum, industrial raw materials, capital equipment. Major trading partners: U.S., Venezuela

**Geography.** The Dominican Republic in the West Indies, occupies the eastern two thirds of the island of Hispaniola, which it shares with Haiti. Its area equals that of Vermont and New Hampshire combined.

Crossed from northwest to southeast by a mountain range with elevations exceeding 10,000 feet (3,048 m), the country has fertile, well-watered land in the north and east, where nearly two thirds of the population lives. The southwest part is arid and has poor soil, except around Santo Domingo.

**Government.** The president is elected by direct vote every four years. Legislative powers rest with a Senate and a Chamber of Deputies, both elected by direct vote, also for four years. All citizens must vote when they reach 18 years of age, or even earlier if they are married.

The major political parties are the Dominican Revolutionary Party, the party of the Administration, led by Dr. José Francisco Peña Gomez; the Reformist Party, led by former President Joaquín Balaguer; Dominican Liberation Party, led by Juan Bosch; Partido Quisquellano Demócrata, led by Elías Wessin y Wessin; Movimiento de Integración Democrática Anti-Releccionista, led by Augusto Lora.

**History.** The Dominican Republic was discovered by Columbus in 1492. He named it La Española, and his son, Diego, was its first viceroy. The capital, Santo Domingo, founded in 1496, is the oldest European settlement in the Western Hemisphere. Spain ceded the colony to France in 1795, and Haitian blacks under Toussaint L'Ouverture conquered it in 1801.

In 1808 the people revolted and the next year captured Santo Domingo, setting up the first republic. Spain regained title to the colony in 1814. In 1821 the people overthrew Spanish rule, but in 1822 they were reconquered by the Haitians. They revolted again in 1844, threw out the Haitians, and established the Dominican Republic, headed by Pedro Santana. Uprisings and Haitian attacks led Santana to make the country a province of Spain from 1861 to 1865. The U.S. Senate refused to ratify a treaty of annexation. Disorder continued until the dictatorship of Ulíses Heureaux; in 1916, when disorder broke out again, the U.S. sent in a contingent of marines, who remained until 1934.

A sergeant in the Dominican army trained by the marines, Rafaél Leonides Trujillo Molina, overthrew Horacio Vásquez in 1930 and established a dictatorship that lasted until his assassination 31 years later.

A new Constitution was adopted in 1962, and the first free elections since 1924 put Juan Bosch, a leftist leader, in office. A planned program of reforms with U.S. support was cut off by a right-wing military coup that replaced Bosch with a civilian triumvirate.

Leftists rebelled April 24, 1965, and President Lyndon Johnson sent in marines and troops. After an OAS ceasefire request May 6, a compromise installed Hector Garcia-Godoy as provisional president. Joaquin Balaguer won in free elections in 1966 against Bosch, and a peacekeeping force of 9,000 U.S. troops and 2,000 from other countries withdrew. Balaguer restored political and economic stability program.

Balaguer's longtime support for free elections faltered in May 1978, when the army suspended the counting of ballots as he trailed in a fourth-term bid. After a warning from President Jimmy Carter, however, Balaguer accepted the victory of Antonio Guzmán of the opposition Dominican Revolutionary Party.

Salvador Jorge Blanco of the Dominican Revolutionary Party was elected President on May 16, 1982, defeating Balaguer and Bosch. Austerity measures imposed by the International Monetary Fund, including sharply higher prices for food and gasoline, provoked rioting in the spring of 1984 that left more than 50 dead.

Saying he feared they would provoke "some kind of revolution," Blanco dragged his feet about putting into effect further IMF demands for higher prices and taxes and devaluation of the peso, and came within weeks of defaulting on several big loans.

The root of the economic difficulties was the country's dependence on earnings from exports of sugar, gold and silver, all of which were selling at depressed prices.

# ECUADOR

**Republic of Ecuador**
**President:** León Febres Cordero (1984)
**Area:** 109,484 sq mi. (270,670 sq km)
**Population (est. mid-1986):** 9,600,000 (average annual growth rate: 2.8%)
**Density per square mile:** 87.7
**Capital:** Quito
**Largest cities (est. 1983):** Guayaquil, 1,750,000; Quito, 880,000; Cuenca, 155,000
**Monetary unit:** Sucre
**Languages:** Spanish, Quéchua, Jibaro
**Religion:** Roman Catholic
**National name:** República del Ecuador
**Literacy rate:** 84%
**Economic summary:** Gross national product (1984). $9.9 billion. Annual growth rate (1983) 3%. Per capita income (1984): $1,165. Land used for agriculture: 11%; labor force: 52%; principal products: bananas, cocoa, sugar cane, fruits, corn, potatoes, rice. Labor force in industry: 13%; major products: processed foods, textiles, fish, petroleum. Natural resources: petroleum, fish, silver, gold. Exports: petroleum, bananas, coffee, cocoa, fish products. Imports: agricultural and industrial machinery, industrial raw materials, foodstuffs, chemical products, transportation and communication equipment. Major trading partners: U.S., Latin American and Western European countries, Japan.

**Geography.** Ecuador, equal in area to Nevada, is in the northwest part of South America fronting on the Pacific. To the north is Colombia and to the east and south is Peru. Two high and parallel ranges of the Andes, traversing the country from north to south, are topped by tall volcanic peaks. The highest is Chimborazo at 20,577 feet (6,272 m).

The Galápagos Islands (or Colón Archipelago) (3,029 sq mi.; 7,845 sq km) in the Pacific Ocean about 600 miles (966 km) west of the South American mainland, became part of Ecuador in 1832.

**Government.** A 1978 Constitution returned Ecuador to civilian government after eight years of military rule. Under its terms, the President is elected by universal suffrage to a term of four years and a House of Representatives of 69 members popularly elected for the same period.

**History.** The tribes in the northern highlands of Ecuador formed the Kingdom of Quito around A.D. 1000 It was absorbed, by conquest and marriage, into the Inca Empire. Pizarro conquered the land in 1532, and through the 17th century a thriving colony was built by exploitation of the Indians. The first revolt against Spain occurred in 1809. Ecuador then joined Venezuela, Colombia, and Panama in a confederacy known as Greater Colombia.

On the collapse of this union in 1830, Ecuador became independent. Subsequent history was one of revolts and dictatorships; it had 48 presidents during the first 131 years of the republic. Conservatives ruled until the Revolution of 1895 ushered in nearly a half century of Radical Liberal rule, during which the church was disestablished and freedom of worship, speech, and press was introduced.

A three-man military junta headed by Vice Adm. Alfredo Poveda, which had taken power in a 1976 coup, agreed to a free presidential election on July 16, 1978. Jaime Roldós Aguilera won the runoff on April 29, 1979, backed by a "center leftist" coalition, the Concentration of Popular Forces.

The 40-year-old President, his wife and Ecuador's minister of defense died in the crash of a small plane May 24, 1981. Vice President Osvaldo Hurtado Larrea became President. León Febres Cordero, leader of the National Reconstruction Front, narrowly won two rounds of voting in 1984 elections and was installed President in August. Combined opposition parties won a majority in the 71-member Congress large enough to block significant action until May 1985 when seven representatives defected to the ruling coalition.

# EGYPT

## Arab Republic of Egypt

**President:** Hosni Mubarak (1981)
**Premier:** Ali Lutfi (1985)
**Area:** 386,900 sq. mi. (1,002,000 sq km)
**Population (est. mid-1986):** 50,500,000 (average annual growth rate: 2.6%)
**Density per square mile:** 130.5
**Capital:** Cairo
**Largest cities (est. 1984):** Cairo, 12,000,000; **(1976 census):** Alexandria, 2,317,705; Giza, 1,246,713; Shubra el Khema, 393,700; El Mahalla el Kubra, 292,-853; Tanta, 284,636; Port Said, 262,620; Mansura, 257,866
**Monetary unit:** Egyptian pound
**Language:** Arabic
**Religions:** Islam, 93%; Christian (mostly Copt), 7%
**Literacy rate:** 40%
**Economic summary:** Gross national product (1983): $20.0 billion. Average annual growth rate (1982): 6%. Per capita income (1985): $500. Land used for agriculture: 3%; labor force: 36%; principal products: cotton, wheat, rice, corn. Labor force in industry: 13%; major products: textiles, processed foods, chemicals, fertilizer, petroleum and petroleum products. Natural resources: iron ore, phosphates, petroleum, gypsum. Exports: cotton, rice, petroleum, cement. Imports: foodstuffs, machinery, fertilizers, woods. Major trading partners: West Germany, Italy, France, U.S, Israel

**Geography.** Egypt, at the northeast corner of Africa on the Mediterranean Sea, is bordered on the west by Libya, on the south by the Sudan, and on the east by the Red Sea and Israel. It is nearly one and one half times the size of Texas.

The historic Nile flows through the eastern third of the country. On either side of the Nile valley are desert plateaus, spotted with oases. In the north,

toward the Mediterranean, plateaus are low, while south of Cairo they rise to a maximum of 1,015 feet (309 m) above sea level. At the head of the Red Sea is the Sinai Peninsula, between the Suez Canal and Israel.

Navigable throughout its course in Egypt, the Nile is used largely as a means of cheap transport for heavy goods. The principal port is Alexandria.

The Nile delta starts 100 miles (161 km) south of the Mediterranean and fans out to a sea front of 155 miles between the cities of Alexandria and Port Said. From Cairo north, the Nile branches into many streams, the principal ones being the Damietta and the Rosetta.

Except for a narrow belt along the Mediterranean, Egypt lies in an almost rainless area, in which high daytime temperatures fall quickly at night.

**Government.** Executive power is held by the President, who can appoint one or more Vice Presidents.

The National Democratic Party, led by President Hosni Mubarak, is the dominant political party. As expected, it won a huge majority (391 of the 448 contested seats) in the new Parliament chosen May 27, 1984, in Egypt's first free, multiparty election since 1952. The New Wafd, a rebirth of Egypt's oldest and most respected political party, ran second (57 seats).

**History.** Egyptian history dates back to about 4000 B.C., when the kingdoms of upper and lower Egypt, already highly civilized, were united. Egypt's "Golden Age" coincided with the 18th and 19th dynasties (16th to 13th centuries B.C.), during which the empire was established. Persia conquered Egypt in 525 B.C.; Alexander the Great subdued it in 332 B.C.; and then the dynasty of the Ptolemies ruled the land until 30 B.C., when Cleopatra, last of the line, committed suicide and Egypt became a Roman province. From 641 to 1517 the Arab caliphs ruled Egypt, and then the Turks took it for their Ottoman Empire.

Napoleon's armies occupied the country from 1798 to 1801. In 1805, Mohammed Ali, leader of a band of Albanian soldiers, became Pasha of Egypt. After completion of the Suez Canal in 1869, the French and British took increasing interest in Egypt.

British troops occupied Egypt in 1882, and British resident agents became its actual administrators, though it remained under nominal Turkish sovereignty. In 1914, this fiction was ended, and Egypt became a protectorate of Britain.

Egyptian nationalism forced Britain to declare Egypt an independent, sovereign state on Feb. 28, 1922, although the British reserved rights for the protection of the Suez Canal and the defense of Egypt. In 1936, by an Anglo-Egyptian treaty of alliance, all British troops and officials were to be withdrawn, except from the Suez Canal Zone. When World War II started, Egypt remained neutral. British imperial troops finally ended the Nazi threat to Suez in 1942 in the battle of El Alamein, west of Alexandria.

In 1951, Egypt abrogated the 1936 treaty and the 1899 Anglo-Egyptian condominium of the Sudan (*See* Sudan). Rioting and attacks on British troops in the Suez Canal Zone followed, reaching a climax in January 1952. The army, led by Gen. Mohammed Naguib, seized power on July 23, 1952. Three days later, King Farouk abdicated in favor of his infant son. The monarchy was abolished and a republic proclaimed on June 18, 1953, with Naguib holding the posts of Provisional President and Premier. He relinquished the latter in 1954 to Gamal Abdel Nasser, leader of the ruling military junta. Naguib was deposed seven months later and Nasser confirmed as President in a referendum on June 23, 1956.

Nasser's policies embroiled his country in continual conflict. In 1956, the U.S. and Britain withdrew their pledges of financial aid for the building of the Aswan High Dam. In reply, Nasser nationalized the Suez Canal and expelled British oil and embassy officials. Israel, barred from the Canal and exasperated by terrorist raids, invaded the Gaza Strip and the Sinai Peninsula. Britain and France, after demanding Egyptian evacuation of the Canal Zone, attacked Egypt on Oct. 31, 1956. Worldwide pressure forced Britain, France, and Israel to halt the hostilities. A U.N. emergency force occupied the Canal Zone, and all troops were evacuated in the spring of 1957.

On Feb. 1, 1958, Egypt and Syria formed the United Arab Republic, which was joined by Yemen in an association known as the United Arab States. However, Syria withdrew from the United Arab Republic in 1961 and Egypt dissolved its ties with Yemen in the United Arab States.

On June 5, 1967, Israel invaded the Sinai Peninsula, the East Bank of the Jordan River, and the zone around the Gulf of Aqaba. A U.N. ceasefire on June 10 saved the Arabs from complete rout.

Nasser declared the 1967 cease-fire void along the Canal in April 1969 and began a war of attrition. The U.S. peace plan of June 19, 1970, resulted in Egypt's agreement to reinstate the cease-fire for at least three months, (from August) and to accept Israel's existence within "recognized and secure" frontiers that might emerge from U.N.-mediated talks. In return, Israel accepted the principle of withdrawing from occupied territories.

Then, on Sept. 28, 1970, Nasser died, at 52, of a heart attack. The new President was Anwar el-Sadat, an associate of Nasser and a former newspaper editor.

The Aswan High Dam, whose financing by the U.S.S.R. was its first step into Egypt, was completed and dedicated in January 1971.

In July 1972, Sadat ordered the expulsion of Soviet "advisors and experts" from Egypt because the Russians had not provided the sophisticated weapons he felt were needed to retake territory lost to Israel in 1967.

The fourth Arab-Israeli war broke out Oct. 6, 1973, while Israelis were commemorating Yom Kippur, the Jewish high holy day. Egypt swept deep into the Sinai, while Syria strove to throw Israel off the Golan Heights.

A U.N.-sponsored truce was accepted on October 22. In January 1974, both sides agreed to a settlement negotiated by U.S. Secretary of State Henry A. Kissinger that gave Egypt a narrow strip along the entire Sinai bank of the Suez Canal. In June, President Nixon made the first visit by a U.S. President to Egypt and full diplomatic relations were established. The Suez Canal was cleared and reopened on June 5, 1975.

Kissinger pursued "shuttle diplomacy" between Cairo and Jerusalem to extend areas of agreement. Israel yielded on three points—the possession of the Mitla and Giddi passes in the Sinai and the Abu Rudeis oil field in the peninsula—and both sides committed themselves to annual renewal of the U.N. peacekeeping force in the Sinai.

In the most audacious act of his career, Sadat flew to Jerusalem at the invitation of Prime Minister Menachem Begin and pleaded before Israel's Knesset on Nov. 20, 1977, for a permanent peace settlement. The Arab world reacted with fury—only Morocco, Tunisia, Sudan, and Oman approved.

Egypt and Israel signed a formal peace treaty on March 26, 1979. The pact ended 30 years of war and established diplomatic and commercial relations.

Egyptian and Israeli officials met in the Sinai desert on April 26, 1979, to implement the peace treaty calling for the phased withdrawal of occupation forces from the peninsula. By mid-1980, two thirds of the Sinai was transferred, but progress here was not matched—the negotiation of Arab autonomy in the Gaza Strip and the West Bank.

Sadat halted further talks in August 1980 because of continued Israeli settlement of the West Bank. On October 6 1981, Sadat was assassinated by extremist Muslim soldiers at a parade in Cairo. Vice President Hosni Mubarak, a former Air Force chief of staff, was confirmed by the parliament as president the next day.

Although feared unrest in Egypt did not occur in the wake of the assassination, and Israel completed the return of the Sinai to Egyptian control on April 25, 1982, Mubarak was unable to revive the autonomy talks. Israel's invasion of Lebanon in June imposed a new strain on him, and brought a marked cooling in Egyptian-Israeli relations, but not a disavowal of the peace treaty.

During 1985, pressures by Moslem fundamentalists to implement Islamic law in Egypt increased. In response, the government began putting all mosques under control of the minister for religious endowments. In July, authorities arrested at least 45 fundamentalists including Sheik Hafez Salama, the fundamentalist cleric spearheading the campaign for immediate application of *sharia*, the Islamic legal code dating back 1,300 years.

In February 1986, a riot by the security forces had to be quelled by the army; an incident that underscored Mubarak's dependence on the army in the face of increasing discontent with the failing economy and growing Islamic fundamentalism.

**Suez Canal.** The Suez Canal, in Egyptian territory between the Arabian Desert and the Sinai Peninsula, is an artificial waterway about 100 miles (161 km) long between Port Said on the Mediterranean and Suez on the Red Sea. Construction work, directed by the French engineer Ferdinand de Lesseps, was begun April 25, 1859, and the Canal was opened Nov. 17, 1869. The cost was 432,807,882 francs. The concession was held by an Egyptian joint stock company, *Compagnie Universelle du Canal Maritime de Suez*, in which the British government held 353,504 out of a total of 800,000 shares. The concession was to expire Nov. 17, 1968, but the company was nationalized July 26, 1956, by unilateral action of the Egyptian government.

The Canal was closed in June 1967 after the Arab-Israeli conflict. With the help of the U.S. Navy, work was begun on clearing the Canal in 1974, after the cease-fire ending the Arab-Israeli war. It was reopened to traffic June 5, 1975.

# EL SALVADOR

**Republic of El Salvador**
**President:** José Napoleón Duarte (1984)
**Area:** 8,260 sq mi. (21,393 sq km)
**Population (est. mid-1986):** 5,100,000 (average annual growth rate: 2.4%)
**Density per square mile:** 617.5
**Capital:** San Salvador
**Largest cities (est. 1982):** San Salvador, 430,000; Santa Miguel, 316,280; Santa Ana, 175,000
**Monetary unit:** Colón
**Language:** Spanish
**Religion:** Roman Catholic
**National name:** República de El Salvador
**Literacy rate:** 65%
**Economic summary:** Gross national product (1983): $3.7 billion. Average annual growth rate (1973–82): 0.6%. Per capita income (1983): $710. Land used for agriculture: 35%; labor force: 40%; principal products: coffee, cotton, corn, sugar, rice, sorghum. Labor force in industry: 16%; major products: processed foods, clothing and textiles, petroleum products. Natural resources: timber, balsam. Exports: coffee, cotton, sugar. Imports: machinery, automotive vehicles, petroleum, foodstuffs, fertilizer. Major trading partners: U.S., Guatemala, Japan, West Germany, Mexico.

**Geography.** Situated on the Pacific coast of Central America, El Salvador has Guatemala to the west and Honduras to the north and east. It is the smallest of the Central American countries, its area equal to that of Massachusetts, and the only one without an Atlantic coastline.

Most of the country is a fertile volcanic plateau about 2,000 feet (607 m) high. There are some active volcanoes and many scenic crater lakes.

**Government.** A new Constitution enacted in 1983 vests executive power in a President elected for a nonrenewable, five-year term, and legislative power in a 60-member National Assembly elected by universal suffrage and proportional representation. Judicial power is vested in a Supreme Court, composed of a President and nine magistrates elected by the Assembly, and subordinate courts.

José Napoleón Duarte, a Christian Democrat regarded as a moderate, was elected President in 1984. In national legislative and municipal elections in 1985, Duarte's Christian Democratic Party won almost 54% of the vote and the majority it was seeking in the National Assembly, badly splintering the previously dominant rightist parties.

**History.** Pedro de Alvarado, a lieutenant of Cortés, conquered El Salvador in 1525. El Salvador, with the other countries of Central America, declared its independence from Spain on Sept. 15, 1821, and was part of a federation of Central American states until that union was dissolved in 1838. Its independent career for decades thereafter was marked by numerous revolutions and wars against other Central American republics.

On Oct. 15, 1979, a junta deposed the President, Gen. Carlos Humberto Romero, seeking to halt increasingly violent clashes between leftist and rightist forces.

On Dec. 4, 1980, three American nuns and an American lay worker were killed in an ambush near San Salvador, causing the Carter Administration to suspend all aid pending an investigation. The naming of José Napoleón Duarte, a moderate civilian, as head of the governing junta brought a

resumption of U.S. aid.

Defying guerrilla threats, voters on March 28, 1982, elected a rightist majority to a constituent assembly that dismissed Duarte and replaced him with a centrist physician, Dr. Alvaro Alfredo Magaña. The rightist majority repealed the laws permitting expropriation of land, and critics charged that the land-reform program begun under Duarte was dead. Even though fighting continued, with reports of government violations of human rights, the Reagan Administration asked certification of El Salvador's eligibility for resumed foreign aid, and this was approved by Congress.

In an election closely monitored by American and other foreign observers, Duarte was elected President in May 1984.

Duarte's Christian Democratic Party scored an unexpected electoral triumph in national legislative and municipal elections held in March 1985, winning almost 54% of the vote and the majority it was seeking in the new National Assembly. The rightist parties that had been dominant in the previous Constituent Assembly demanded that the vote be nullified, but the army high command rejected their assertion the voting had been fraudulent. The army's refusal to support the rightists was interpreted as a turning point in El Salvador's struggle for political stability.

At the same time, U.S. officials said that while the rebels still were far from being defeated, there had been marked improvement in the effectiveness of government troops in the civil war against antigovernment guerrillas that has been waged mainly in the countryside. The rebels responded by initiating a campaign of urban terror; killing and kidnapping town mayors and other pro-government figures. In mid-1986, Duarte called for a new round of talks with the rebels. This was seen as an attempt to revive a popularity that was falling due to his perceived failure to improve the economy, implement promised social programs or end the war.

# EQUATORIAL GUINEA

**Republic of Equatorial Guinea**
**Head of junta:** Lieut. Col. Teodoro Obiang Nguema Mbasogo (1979)
**Area:** 10,830 sq mi. (28,051 sq km)
**Population (est. mid-1986):** 400,000 (average annual growth rate: 2.3%)
**Density per square mile:** 36.9
**Capital and largest city (est. 1983):** Malabo, 37,500
**Monetary unit:** Ekuele
**Languages:** Spanish, Fang, Bubi
**Religions:** Roman Catholic, Protestant, Animist
**National name:** República de Guinea Ecuatorial
**Literacy rate:** 55%
**Economic summary:** Gross national product (1983): $75 million. Per capita income (1985): $172. Land used for agriculture: 8%; labor force: 73%; principal products: cocoa, wood, coffee. Natural resource: wood. Exports: cocoa, wood, coffee. Imports: foodstuffs, textiles, machinery. Major trading partners: Spain, France, China, Netherlands

**Geography.** Equatorial Guinea, formerly Spanish Guinea, consists of Rio Muni (10,045 sq mi.; 26,117 sq km), on the western coast of Africa, and several islands in the Gulf of Guinea, the largest of which is Bioko (formerly Fernando Po) (785 sq mi.; 2,033 sq km). The other islands are Pagalu (formerly Annobón), Corisco, Elobey Grande, and Elobey Chico. The total area is twice that of Connecticut.

**Government.** The Constitution of 1973 was suspended after a coup on Aug. 3, 1979. A Supreme Military Council, headed by the president, exercises all power. Political parties are banned.

**History.** Fernando Po and Annobón came under Spanish control in 1778. From 1827 to 1844, with Spanish consent, Britain administered Fernando Po, but in the latter year Spain reclaimed the island. Río Muni was given to Spain in 1885 by the Treaty of Berlin.

Negotiations with Spain led to independence on Oct. 12, 1968.

In 1969, anti-Spanish incidents in Río Muni, including the tearing down of a Spanish flag by national troops, caused 5,000 Spanish residents to flee for their safety, and diplomatic relations between the two nations became strained. A month later, President Masie Nguema Biyogo Negue Ndong charged that a coup had been attempted against him. He seized dictatorial powers and arrested 80 opposition politicians and even several of his Cabinet ministers and the secretary of the National Assembly.

A coup on Aug. 3, 1979, deposed Masie, and a junta led by Lieut. Col. Teodoro Obiang Nguema Mbasogo took over the government. Obiang expelled Soviet technicians and reinstated cooperation with Spain.

# ETHIOPIA

**Head of State:** Mengistu Haile Mariam (1977)
**Area:** 472,432 sq mi. (1,223,600 sq km)
**Population (est. mid-1986):** 43,900,000 (average annual growth rate: 2.1%)
**Density per square mile:** 92.9
**Capital:** Addis Ababa
**Largest cities (est. 1980):** Addis Ababa, 1,275,000; Asmara, 425,000
**Monetary unit:** Birr
**Languages:** Amharic (official), Galligna, Tigrigna
**Religions:** Ethiopian Orthodox, 49%; Islam, 31%; Animist, 11%
**Literacy rate:** 15%
**Economic summary:** Gross national product (1984): $4.9 billion. Average annual growth rate (1973–82): 2.6%. Per capita income (1984): $115. Land used for agriculture: 13%; labor force: 77%; principal products: coffee, barley, wheat, corn, sugar cane, cotton, oilseeds, livestock. Labor force in industry: 10%; Major industrial products: cement, cotton textiles, refined sugar, processed foods, refined oil. Natural resources: potash, salt, gold, platinum. Exports: coffee, hides and skins, oilseeds. Imports: petroleum, foodstuffs. Major trading partners: Saudi Arabia, Japan, Italy, U.K., France, U.S., U.S.S.R., Djibouti.

**Geography.** Ethiopia is in east central Africa, bordered on the west by the Sudan, the east by Somalia and Djibouti, the south by Kenya, and the north by the Red Sea. It is nearly three times the size of California.

Over its main plateau land, Ethiopia has several high mountains, the highest of which is Ras Dashan at 15,158 feet (4,620 m). The Blue Nile, or Abbai, rises in the northwest and flows in a great semicircle east, south, and northwest before entering the

Sudan. Its chief reservoir, Lake Tana, lies in the northwestern part of the plateau.

**Government.** A provisional military government headed by a 120-member officers' committee (the Dirgue) deposed Ethiopia's traditional monarchy in 1974, suspended parliament, and ruled by decree. It proclaimed Ethiopia a socialist state.

**History.** Black Africa's oldest state, Ethiopia can trace 2,000 years of recorded history. Its now deposed royal line claimed descent from King Menelik I, traditionally believed to have been the son of the Queen of Sheba and King Solomon. The present nation is a consolidation of smaller kingdoms that owed feudal allegiance to the Ethiopian Emperor.

Hamitic peoples migrated to Ethiopia from Asia Minor in prehistoric times. Semitic traders from Arabia penetrated the region in the 7th century B.C. Its Red Sea ports were important to the Roman and Byzantine Empires. Coptic Christianity came to the country in A.D. 341, and a variant of that communion became Ethiopia's state religion.

Ancient Ethiopia reached its peak in the 5th century, then was isolated by the rise of Islam and weakened by feudal wars. Modern Ethiopia emerged under Emperor Menelik II, who established its independence by routing an Italian invasion in 1896. He expanded Ethiopia by conquest.

Disorders that followed Menelik's death brought his daughter to the throne in 1917, with his cousin, Tafari Makonnen, as Regent, heir presumptive, and strongman. When the Empress died in 1930, Tafari was crowned Emperor Haile Selassie I.

As Regent, Haile Selassie outlawed slavery. As Emperor, he worked for centralization of his diffuse realm, in which 70 languages are spoken, and for moderate reform. In 1931, he granted a Constitution, revised in 1955, that created a parliament with an appointed Senate and an elected Chamber of Deputies, and a system of courts. But basic power remained with the Emperor.

Bent on colonial empire, fascist Italy invaded Ethiopia on Oct. 3, 1935, forcing Haile Selassie into exile in May 1936. Ethiopia was annexed to Eritrea, then an Italian colony, and Italian Somaliland to form Italian East Africa, losing its independence for the first time in recorded history. In 1941, British troops routed the Italians, and Haile Selassie returned to Addis Ababa.

Deep discontent erupted in the fall of 1973. A long drought had caused famine that killed 100,000 peasants and drove thousands of others to cities, where food was scarce and inflation was rampant. Charges of mismanagement of drought relief sparked riots in Addis Ababa in 1974, and unpaid troops in Asmara, capital of Eritrea, mutinied to protest conditions.

In August 1974, the Armed Forces Committee nationalized Haile Selassie's palace and estates and directed him not to leave Addis Ababa. On Sept. 12, 1974, he was deposed after nearly 58 years as Regent and Emperor. The 82-year-old "Lion of Judah" was placed under guard. Parliament was dissolved and the Constitution suspended.

On Aug. 27, 1975, Haile Selassie died in a small apartment in his former Addis Ababa palace where he had been treated as a state prisoner. He was 83.

Lt. Col. Mengistu Haile Mariam was named head of state Feb. 2, 1977, to replace Brig. Gen. Teferi Benti, who was killed in a factional fight of the Dirgue after having ruled since 1974. The government was losing its fight to hold Eritrea and in the southeastern region of Ogaden, Somali guerrillas backed by Somali regular forces threatened the ancient city of Harar. In October, the U.S.S.R. announced it would end military aid to Somalia and henceforth back its new ally, Ethiopia. This, together with the intervention of Cuban troops in Ogaden, turned the tide for Mengistu. By March 1978, the badly beaten Somalis had retreated to their homeland. This brought an end to large-scale fighting with Somalia, but border skirmishing continued intermittently through 1986.

The Marxist government still had not quelled the Eritrean secessionists in the north by 1986. In addition, a secessionist struggle was going on in Tigre, the province adjoining Eritrea.

A Communist regime was formally proclaimed on Sept. 10, 1984, with Mengistu as party leader. After enduring years of drought, the country in 1986 was in the throes of the worst famine in more than a decade, with tens—perhaps hundreds—of thousands of Ethiopians reported dying of starvation and related diseases and 6 million in dire need of food.

# FIJI

**Sovereign:** Queen Elizabeth II
**Governor General:** Ratu Sir Penaia K. Gamibu (1983)
**Prime Minister:** Ratu Sir Kamisese Mara (1970)
**Area:** 7,078 sq mi. (18,333 sq km)
**Population (est. mid-1986):** 700,000 (average annual growth rate: 2.4%)
**Density per square mile:** 98.9
**Capital (1982):** Suva (on Viti Levu), 71,000
**Monetary unit:** Fijian dollar
**Languages:** Fijian, Hindustani, English
**Religions:** Christian, 50%; Hindu, 41%; Islam, 8%
**Member of Commonwealth of Nations**
**Literacy rate (1981):** 80%
**Economic summary:** Gross national product (1982): $1.2 billion. Average annual growth rate (1980–85): 2%. Per capita income (1983): $1,735. Rate of inflation (1984): 4.4%. Labor force in agriculture: 44%; principal products: sugar, copra, rice, ginger. Labor force in industry: 16%; major industrial products: refined sugar, gold, lumber. Natural resources: timber, fish, gold, silver. Exports: sugar, copra. Imports: foodstuffs, machinery, manufactured goods, fuels, chemicals. Major trading partners: U.K., Australia, Japan

**Geography.** Fiji consists of more than 500 islands in the southwestern Pacific Ocean about 1,960 miles (3,152 km) from Sydney, Australia. The two largest islands are Viti Levu (4,109 sq mi.; 10,642 sq km) and Vanua Levu (2,242 sq mi.; 5,807 sq km). The island of Rotuma (18 sq mi.; 47 sq km), about 400 miles (644 km) to the north, is a dependency of Fiji. Overall, Fiji is nearly as large as New Jersey.

The largest islands in the group are mountainous and volcanic, with the tallest peak being Mount Victoria (4,341 ft; 1,323 m) on Viti Levu. The islands in the south have dense forests on the windward side and grasslands on the leeward.

**Government.** Executive authority is vested in the Cabinet and legislative authority in a bicameral 74-member Parliament. The major political parties are the Alliance Party, led by Prime Minister Sir Kamisese Mara; National Federation Party, led by Siddiq Koya, and Fijian Nationalist Party, led by Sakeasi Butadroka.

**History.** In 1874, an offer of cession by the Fijian chiefs was accepted, and Fiji was proclaimed a possession and dependency of the British Crown.

During World War II, the archipelago was an important air and naval station on the route from the U.S. and Hawaii to Australia and New Zealand.

Fiji became independent on Oct. 10, 1970. The next year it joined the five-island South Pacific Forum, which intends to become a permanent regional group to promote collective diplomacy of the newly independent members. The Forum also includes Western Samoa, Tonga, Nauru, and the self-governing segments of the Cook Islands.

# FINLAND

**Republic of Finland**
**President:** Mauno H. Koivisto (1982)
**Premier:** Kalevi Sorsa (1982)
**Area:** 130,119 sq mi. (337,009 sq km)
**Population (est. mid-1986):** 4,900,000 (average annual growth rate: 0.4%) (Finnish, 93%; Swedish, 6%)
**Density per square mile:** 37.7
**Capital:** Helsinki
**Largest cities (est. 1983):** Helsinki, 484,471; Tampere, 167,344; Turku, 163,002
**Monetary unit:** Markka
**Languages:** Finnish, Swedish
**Religions:** Lutheran, 90%; Orthodox, 1%
**National name:** Suomen Tasavalta—Republiken Finland
**Literacy rate:** almost 100%
**Economic summary:** Gross national product (1984): $50.1 billion. Average annual growth rate (1973–84): 3.5%. Per capita income (1983): $10,440. Land used for agriculture: 8%; labor force: 12%; principal products: dairy products, cereals, sugar beets, potatoes. Labor force in industry: 33%; major products: metal manufactures, forestry and wood products, refined copper, ships. Natural resource: timber. Exports: timber, paper and pulp, ships, machinery, iron and steel, clothing, footwear. Imports: petroleum and petroleum products, chemicals, transportation equipment, machinery, textile yarns. Major trading partners: Norway, U.S.S.R., Sweden, West Germany, U.K., Japan, U.S..

**Geography.** Finland stretches 700 miles (1,127 km) from the Gulf of Finland on the south to Soviet Petsamo, north of the Arctic Circle. The U.S.S.R. extends along the entire eastern frontier. In area, Finland is three times the size of Ohio.

Off the southwest coast are the Aland Islands, controlling the entrance to the Gulf of Bothnia. Finland has more than 60,000 lakes. Of the few rivers, only the Oulu (Ulea) is navigable to any important extent.

The Swedish-populated Aland Islands (581 sq mi.; 1,505 sq km) have an autonomous status under a law passed in 1951.

**Government.** The president, chosen for six years by the popularly elected Electoral College of 301 members, appoints the Cabinet. The one-chamber Diet, the Eduskunta, consists of 200 members elected for four-year terms by proportional representation.

The major political parties are the Social Democratic Party (57 seats in the Eduskunta), led by Premier Kalevi Sorsa; National Coalition Party (44 seats); Center Party (38 seats); People's Democratic League (Communist) (27 seats); Finnish Rural Party (17 seats); Swedish People's Party (11 seats);

Christian League (3 seats). Premier Sorsa leads a coalition of Social Democratic, Center, Swedish People's Party, and Finnish Rural Party members totaling 106 seats.

**History.** At the end of the 7th century, the Finns came to Finland from their Volga settlements, taking the country from the Lapps, who retreated northward. The Finns' repeated raids on the Scandinavian coast impelled Eric IX, the Swedish King, to conquer the country in 1157 and bring it into contact with Western Christendom. By 1809 the whole of Finland was conquered by Alexander I of Russia, who set up Finland as a Grand Duchy.

The first period of Russification (1809–1905) resulted in a lessening of the powers of the Finnish Diet. The Russian language was made official, and the Finnish military system was superseded by the Russian. The pace of Russification was intensified from 1908 to 1914. When Russian control was weakened as a consequence of the March Revolution of 1917, the Diet on July 20, 1917, proclaimed Finland's independence, which became complete on Dec. 6, 1917.

Finland rejected Soviet territorial demands, and the U.S.S.R. attacked on Nov. 30, 1939. The Finns made an amazing stand of three months and finally capitulated, ceding 16,000 square miles (41,440 sq km) to the U.S.S.R. Under German pressure, the Finns joined the Nazis against Russia in 1941, but were defeated again and ceded the Petsamo area to the U.S.S.R. In 1948, a 20-year treaty of friendship and mutual assistance was signed by the two nations and renewed for another 20 years in 1970.

After 25 years in office, President Urho K. Kekkonen resigned in October 1981 because of ill health. Premier Mauno Koivisto, leader of the Social Democratic Party, was elected President on Jan. 26, 1982, and was sworn in the next day. Radio Moscow hailed Koivisto's victory as a "clear shift to the left" because he won decisively over a conservative rival with support from Finnish Communists. On Feb. 17, Kalevi Sorsa, a Social Democrat, took office as Premier, heading the same center-left coalition Koivisto had led.

# FRANCE

**French Republic**
**President:** François Mitterrand (1981)
**Premier:** Jacques Chirac (1986)
**Area:** 211,208 sq mi. (547,026 sq km)
**Population (est. mid-1986):** 55,400,000 (average annual growth rate: 0.4%)
**Density per square mile:** 262.3
**Capital:** Paris
**Largest cities (est. 1983):** Paris, 2,150,000; **(1982 est.):** Marseilles, 868,435; Lyons, 410,455; Toulouse, 344, 917; Nice, 331,165; Nantes, 237,789; Strasbourg, 247, 068; Bordeaux, 201,965
**Monetary unit:** Franc
**Religion (est.):** Roman Catholic, 90%; Protestant, Jewish, Islam, and others, 10%
**National name:** République Française
**Literacy rate (1981):** 97%
**Economic summary:** Gross national product (1983): $569 billion. Average annual growth rate (1972–83): 2.3%. Per capita income (1983): $10,400. Land used for agriculture, 34%; labor force: 8%; principal products: cereals, feed grains, livestock and dairy products, wine, fruits, vegetables. Labor force in industry: 30%; major

products: chemicals, automobiles, processed foods, iron and steel, aircraft, textiles, clothing. Natural resources: coal, iron ore, bauxite, fish, forests. Exports: textiles and clothing, chemicals, machinery and transport equipment, agricultural products. Imports: machinery, crude petroleum, chemicals, agricultural products. Major trading partners: West Germany, Italy, U.S., Belgium-Luxembourg, U.K., Netherlands.

**Geography.** France (80% the size of Texas) is second in size to the U.S.S.R. among Europe's nations. In the Alps near the Italian and Swiss borders is Europe's highest point—Mont Blanc (15,781 ft; 4,810 m). The forest-covered Vosges Mountains are in the northeast, and the Pyrenees are along the Spanish border.

Except for extreme northern France, which is part of the Flanders plain, the country may be described as four river basins and a plateau. Three of the streams flow west—the Seine into the English Channel, the Loire into the Atlantic, and the Garonne into the Bay of Biscay. The Rhône flows south into the Mediterranean. For about 100 miles (161 km), the Rhine is France's eastern border.

West of the Rhône and northeast of the Garonne lies the central plateau, covering about 15% of France's area and rising to a maximum elevation of 6,188 feet (1,886 m). In the Mediterranean, about 115 miles (185 km) east-southeast of Nice, is Corsica (3,367 sq mi.; 8,721 sq km).

**Government.** The president is elected for seven years by universal suffrage. He appoints the premier, and the Cabinet is responsible to Parliament. The president has the right to dissolve the National Assembly or to ask Parliament for reconsideration of a law. The Parliament consists of two houses: the National Assembly and the Senate.

The major political parties are the Socialists (206 of 577 seats in the National Assembly), led by Pierre Joxe; Rally for the Republic (77 seats), led by Claude Labbe; Union for French Democracy (53 seats), led by Jean-Claude Gaudin; Joint RFR-UFD (147 seats); National Front (35 seats), led by Jean-Marie le Pen, and Communist (29 seats), led by Georges Marchais. The rest are unaffiliated.

**History.** The history of France, as distinct from ancient Gaul, begins with the Treaty of Verdun (843), dividing the territories corresponding roughly to France, Germany, and Italy among the three grandsons of Charlemagne. Julius Caesar had conquered part of Gaul in 57–52 B.C., and it remained Roman until Franks invaded it in the 5th century.

Charles the Bald, inheritor of *Francia Occidentalis*, founded the Carolingian dynasty, which ruled over a kingdom increasingly feudalized. By 987, the crown passed to Hugh Capet, a princeling who controlled only the Ile-de-France, the region surrounding Paris. For 350 years, an unbroken Capetian line added to its domain and consolidated royal authority until the accession in 1328 of Philip VI, first of the Valois line. France was then the most powerful nation in Europe, with a population of 15 million.

The missing pieces in Philip's domain were the French provinces still held by the Plantagenet kings of England, who also claimed the French crown. Beginning in 1338, the Hundred Years' War eventually settled the contest. English longbows defeated French armored knights at Crécy

# Rulers of France

| Name | Born | Ruled[1] |
|---|---|---|
| **CAROLINGIAN DYNASTY** | | |
| Pepin the Short | c. 714 | 751–768 |
| Charlemagne[2] | 742 | 768–814 |
| Louis I the Debonair[3] | 778 | 814–840 |
| Charles I the Bald[4] | 823 | 840–877 |
| Louis II the Stammerer | 846 | 877–879 |
| Louis III[5] | c. 863 | 879–882 |
| Carloman[5] | ? | 879–884 |
| Charles II the Fat[6] | 839 | 884–887 |
| Eudes (Odo), Count of Paris | ? | 888–898 |
| Charles III the Simple[8] | 879 | 893–923[9] |
| Robert I[10] | c. 865 | 922–923 |
| Rudolf (Raoul), Duke of Burgundy | ? | 923–936 |
| Louis IV d'Outremer | c. 921 | 936–954 |
| Lothair | 941 | 954–986 |
| Louis V the Sluggard | c. 967 | 986–987 |
| **CAPETIAN DYNASTY** | | |
| Hugh Capet | c. 940 | 987–996 |
| Robert II the Pious[11] | c. 970 | 996–1031 |
| Henry I | 1008 | 1031–1060 |
| Philip I | 1052 | 1060–1108 |
| Louis VI the Fat | 1081 | 1108–1137 |
| Louis VII the Young | c.1121 | 1137–1180 |
| Philip II (Philip Augustus) | 1165 | 1180–1223 |
| Louis VIII the Lion | 1187 | 1223–1226 |
| Louis IX (St. Louis) | 1214 | 1226–1270 |
| Philip III the Bold | 1245 | 1270–1285 |
| Philip IV the Fair | 1268 | 1285–1314 |
| Louis X the Quarreler | 1289 | 1314–1316 |
| John I[12] | 1316 | 1316 |
| Philip V the Tall | 1294 | 1316–1322 |
| Charles IV the Fair | 1294 | 1322–1328 |
| **HOUSE OF VALOIS** | | |
| Philip VI | 1293 | 1328–1350 |
| John II the Good | 1319 | 1350–1364 |
| Charles V the Wise | 1337 | 1364–1380 |
| Charles VI the Well-Beloved | 1368 | 1380–1422 |
| Charles VII | 1403 | 1422–1461 |
| Louis XI | 1423 | 1461–1483 |
| Charles VIII | 1470 | 1483–1498 |
| Louis XII the Father of the People | 1462 | 1498–1515 |
| Francis I | 1494 | 1515–1547 |
| Henry II | 1519 | 1547–1559 |
| Francis II | 1544 | 1559–1560 |
| Charles IX | 1550 | 1560–1574 |
| Henry III | 1551 | 1574–1589 |
| **HOUSE OF BOURBON** | | |
| Henry IV of Navarre | 1553 | 1589–1610 |
| Louis XIII | 1601 | 1610–1643 |
| Louis XIV the Great | 1638 | 1643–1715 |
| Louis XV the Well-Beloved | 1710 | 1715–1774 |
| Louis XVI | 1754 | 1774–1792[13] |
| Louis XVII (Louis Charles de France)[14] | 1785 | 1793–1795 |

| Name | Born | Ruled[1] |
|---|---|---|
| **FIRST REPUBLIC** | | |
| National Convention | — | 1792–1795 |
| Directory (Directoire) | — | 1795–1799 |
| **CONSULATE** | | |
| Napoleon Bonaparte[15] | 1769 | 1799–1804 |
| **FIRST EMPIRE** | | |
| Napoleon I | 1769 | 1804–1815[16] |
| **RESTORATION OF HOUSE OF BOURBON** | | |
| Louis XVIII le Désiré | 1755 | 1814–1824 |
| Charles X | 1757 | 1824–1830[17] |
| **BOURBON-ORLEANS LINE** | | |
| Louis Philippe ("Citizen King") | 1773 | 1830–1848[18] |
| **SECOND REPUBLIC** | | |
| Louis Napoleon[19] | 1808 | 1848–1852 |
| **SECOND EMPIRE** | | |
| Napoleon III (Louis Napoleon) | 1808 | 1852–1870[20] |
| **THIRD REPUBLIC (PRESIDENTS)** | | |
| Louis Adolphe Thiers | 1797 | 1871–1873 |
| Marie E. P. M. de MacMahon | 1808 | 1873–1879 |
| François P. J. Grévy | 1807 | 1879–1887 |
| Sadi Carnot | 1837 | 1887–1894 |
| Jean Casimir-Périer | 1847 | 1894–1895 |
| François Félix Faure | 1841 | 1895–1899 |
| Émile Loubet | 1838 | 1899–1906 |
| Clement Armand Fallières | 1841 | 1906–1913 |
| Raymond Poincaré | 1860 | 1913–1920 |
| Paul E. L. Deschanel | 1856 | 1920–1920 |
| Alexandre Millerand | 1859 | 1920–1924 |
| Gaston Doumergue | 1863 | 1924–1931 |
| Paul Doumer | 1857 | 1931–1932 |
| Albert Lebrun | 1871 | 1932–1940 |
| **VICHY GOVERNMENT (CHIEF OF STATE)** | | |
| Henri Philippe Pétain | 1856 | 1940–1944 |
| **PROVISIONAL GOVERNMENT (PRESIDENTS)** | | |
| Charles de Gaulle | 1890 | 1944–1946 |
| Félix Gouin | 1884 | 1946–1946 |
| Georges Bidault | 1899 | 1946–1947 |
| **FOURTH REPUBLIC (PRESIDENTS)** | | |
| Vincent Auriol | 1884 | 1947–1954 |
| René Coty | 1882 | 1954–1959 |
| **FIFTH REPUBLIC (PRESIDENTS)** | | |
| Charles de Gaulle | 1890 | 1959–1969 |
| Georges Pompidou | 1911 | 1969–1974 |
| Valéry Giscard d'Estaing | 1926 | 1974–1981 |
| François Mitterrand | 1916 | 1981– |

1. For Kings and Emperors through the Second Empire, year of end of rule is also that of death, unless otherwise indicated. 2. Crowned Emperor of the West in 800. His brother, Carloman, ruled as King of the Eastern Franks from 768 until his death in 771. 3. Holy Roman Emperor 814–840. 4. Holy Roman Emperor 875–877 as Charles II. 5. Ruled jointly 879–882. 6. Holy Roman Emperor 881–887 as Charles III. 7. Died 888. 8. King 893–898 in opposition to Eudes. 9. Died 929. 10. Not counted in regular line of Kings of France by some authorities. Elected by nobles but killed in Battle of Soissons. 11. Sometimes called Robert I. 12. Posthumous son of Louis X; lived for only five days. 13. Executed 1793. 14. Titular King only. He died in prison according to official reports, but many pretenders appeared during the Bourbon restoration. 15. As First Consul, Napoleon held the power of government. In 1804, he became Emperor. 16. Abdicated first time June 1814. Re-entered Paris March 1815, after escape from Elba; Louis XVIII fled to Ghent. Abdicated second time June 1815. He named as his successor his son, Napoleon II, who was not acceptable to the Allies. He died 1821. 17. Died 1836. 18. Died 1850. 19. President; became Emperor in 1852. 20. Died 1873.

(1346) and the English also won the second landmark battle at Agincourt (1415), but the final victory went to the French at Castillon (1453).

Absolute monarchy reached its apogee in the reign of Louis XIV (1643–1715), the Sun King, whose brilliant court was the center of the Western world.

Revolution plunged France into a blood bath beginning in 1789 and ending with a new authoritarianism under Napoleon Bonaparte, who had successfully defended the infant republic from foreign attack and then made himself First Consul in 1799 and Emperor in 1804.

The Congress of Vienna (1815) sought to restore the pre-Napoleonic order in the person of Louis XVIII, but industrialization and the middle class, both fostered under Napoleon, built pressure for change, and a revolution in 1848 drove Louis Phillipe, last of the Bourbons, into exile.

A second republic elected as its president Prince Louis Napoleon, a nephew of Napoleon I, who declared the Second Empire in 1852 and took the throne as Napoleon III. His opposition to the rising power of Prussia ignited the Franco-Prussian War (1870–71), ending in his defeat and abdication.

A new France emerged from World War I as the continent's dominant power. But four years of hostile occupation had reduced northeast France to ruins. The postwar Third Republic was plagued by political instability and economic chaos.

From 1919, French foreign policy aimed at keeping Germany weak through a system of alliances, but it failed to halt the rise of Adolf Hitler and the Nazi war machine. On May 10, 1940, mechanized Nazi troops attacked, and, as they approached Paris, Italy joined with Germany. The Germans marched into an undefended Paris and Marshal Henri Philippe Pétain signed an armistice June 22. France was split into an occupied north and an unoccupied south, the latter becoming a totalitarian state with Pétain as its chief.

Allied armies liberated France in August 1944. The French Committee of National Liberation, formed in Algiers in 1943, established a provisional government in Paris headed by Gen. Charles de Gaulle. The Fourth Republic was born Dec. 24, 1946.

The Empire became the French Union; the National Assembly was strengthened and the presidency weakened; and France joined the North Atlantic Treaty Organization. A war against communist insurgents in Indochina was abandoned after the defeat at Dien Bien Phu. A new rebellion in Algeria (*see* Algeria) threatened a military coup, and on June 1, 1958, the Assembly invited de Gaulle to return as premier with extraordinary powers. He drafted a new Constitution for a Fifth Republic, adopted Sept. 28, which strengthened the presidency and reduced legislative power. He was elected president Dec. 21.

De Gaulle took France out of the NATO military command in 1967 and expelled all foreign-controlled troops from the country. He later went on to attempt to achieve a long-cherished plan of regional reform. This, however, aroused wide opposition. He decided to stake his fate on a referendum. At the voting in April 1969, the electorate defeated the plan. He was succeeded by Georges Pompidou. His successor Georges Pompidou continued the de Gaulle policies of seeking to expand France's influence in the Mideast and Africa, selling arms to South Africa (despite the U.N. embargo), to Libya, and to Greece, and in 1971 he endorsed British entry into the Common Market.

Pompidou died of cancer in April 1974 and the special election to choose a successor was won by Valéry Giscard d'Estaing.

Socialist François Mitterand's stunning victory in the May 10, 1981, Presidential election over the Gaullist alliance that had held power since 1958 was attributed to the challenger's skill in maintaining the Communists' support while holding them at arm's length and Giscard's failure to hold Gaullist support.

The victors immediately moved to carry out campaign pledges to nationalize major industries, halt nuclear testing, suspend nuclear power plant construction, and impose new taxes on the rich. On Feb. 11, 1982, the nationalization bills became law.

The Socialists' policies during Mitterand's first two years created a 12% inflation rate, a huge trade deficit, and devaluations of the franc. In early 1983, Mitterand, embarked on an austerity program to control inflation and reduce the trade deficit. He increased taxes and slashed government spending. A halt in economic growth, declining purchasing power for the average Frenchman, and an increase in unemployment to 10% followed. Mitterand sank lower and lower in the opinion polls.

In mid-1984, Mitterand moved toward the political center. He appointed a new Premier, Laurent Fabius who appointed a new Cabinet of all Socialists, ending the Socialist-Communist coalition. He proposed cuts that would reduce the French worker's income and social security taxes by 5 to 8%. Mitterand promised further tax cuts.

On March 16, 1986, a centrist-Gaullist coalition led by Jacques Chirac won a slim majority in legislative elections. Chirac became Premier initiating a period of "co-habitation" between him and the Socialist President, Mitterand, a cooperation marked by sparring over Chirac's plan to denationalize major industries and effect a harder line on security issues.

## Overseas Departments and Territories of France

### FRENCH GUIANA (including ININI)

**Status:** Overseas Department
**Prefect:** Bernard Courtois (1984)
**Area:** 35,126 sq mi. (90,976 sq km)
**Population (est. 1985):** 78,336 (average annual growth rate: 2.9%)
**Capital (est. 1982):** Cayenne, 37,097
**Monetary unit:** Franc
**Language:** Creole
**Religion:** Roman Catholic
**Literacy rate:** 82%
**Economic summary:** Gross national product (1982): $210 million. Average annual growth rate (1970–79): 0.4%. Per capita income (1982): $3,230. Labor force in agriculture: 14%; principal agricultural products: rice, corn, manioc, cocoa, bananas, sugar cane. Labor force in industry: 12%; major industrial products: timber, rum, rosewood essence, gold mining. Natural resources: bauxite, timber, cinnabar, low-grade iron ore. Exports: shrimp, timber, rum, rosewood essence. Imports: food, consumer and producer goods, petroleum. Major trading partners: U.S., France, Martinique, Japan.

French Guiana, lying north of Brazil and east of

Suriname on the northeast coast of South America, was first settled in 1604. Penal settlements, embracing the area around the mouth of the Maroni River and the Iles du Salut (including Devil's Island), were founded in 1852; they have since been abolished.

During World War II, French Guiana at first adhered to the Vichy government, but the Free French took over in 1943. French Guiana accepted in 1958 the new Constitution of the French Fifth Republic and remained an Overseas Department of the French Republic.

## FRENCH POLYNESIA

**Status:** Overseas Territory
**High Commissioner:** Alain Ohae (1984)
**Area:** 1,544 sq mi. (4,000 sq km)
**Population (est. mid-1986):** 200,000 (average annual growth rate: 2.6%)
**Monetary unit:** Pacific financial community franc
**Language:** French
**Religions:** Protestant, 47%; Roman Catholic, 40%
**Capital (est. 1983):** Papeete (on Tahiti), 23,496
**Economic summary:** Gross national product (1983): $1.3 billion. Average annual growth rate (1970–78): 2.8%. Per capita income (1983): $7,620. Principal agricultural product: copra. Major industries: tourism, maintenance of French nuclear test base. Exports: coconut products, mother of pearl, vanilla. Imports: fuels, foodstuffs, equipment. Major trading partners: France, U.S.

The term French Polynesia is applied to the scattered French possessions in the South Pacific—Mangareva (Gambier), Makatea, the Marquesas Islands, Rapa, Rurutu, Rimatara, the Society Islands, the Tuamotu Archipelago, Tubuai, Raivavae, and the island of Clipperton—which were organized into a single colony in 1903. There are 120 islands, of which 25 are uninhabited.

The High Commissioner is assisted by a Council of Government and a popularly elected Territorial Assembly. The principal and most populous island—Tahiti, in the Society group—was claimed as French in 1768. In 1958, French Polynesia voted in favor of the new Constitution of the French Fifth Republic and remained an Overseas Territory of the French Republic. The natives are mostly Maoris.

The Pacific Nuclear Test Center on the atoll of Mururoa, 744 miles (1,200 km) from Tahiti, was completed in 1966.

## GUADELOUPE

**Status:** Overseas Department
**Prefect:** Claude Saborin (1984)
**Area:** 687 sq mi. (1,779 sq km)
**Population (est. mid-1986):** 300,000 (average annual growth rate: 1.4%)
**Capital (est. 1983):** Basse-Terre, 35,000
**Largest city (est. 1982):** Pointe-à-Pitre, 50,000
**Monetary unit:** Franc
**Language:** French, Creole patois
**Religions:** Roman Catholic
**Literacy rate:** over 70%
**Economic summary:** Gross national product (1982): $1.37 billion. Average annual growth rate (1970–79): 5.1%. Per capita income (1982): $4,170. Land used for agriculture: 22%; labor force: 11%; principal agricultural products: sugar cane, bananas, rum, tobacco. Major industries: construction, public works. Exports: sugar,

fruits and vegetables, bananas. Imports: foodstuffs, clothing, consumer goods, petroleum. Major trading partner: France.

Guadeloupe, in the West Indies about 300 miles (483 km) southeast of Puerto Rico, was discovered by Columbus in 1493. It consists of the twin islands of Basse-Terre and Grande-Terre and five dependencies—Marie-Galante, Les Saintes, La Désirade, St. Barthélemy, and the northern half of St. Martin. The volcano Soufrière (4,813 ft; 1,467 m), also called La Grande Soufrière, is the highest point on Guadeloupe. Violent activity in 1976 and 1977 caused thousands to flee their homes.

French colonization began in 1635. In 1958, Guadeloupe voted in favor of the new Constitution of the French Fifth Republic and remained an Overseas Department of the French Republic.

## MAYOTTE

**Status:** Territorial collectivity
**Prefect:** François Bonnelle (1984)
**Area:** 146 sq mi. (378 sq km)
**Population (est. 1985):** 47,246
**Capital (est. 1985):** Dzaoudzi, 5,675
**Principal products:** vanilla, essential oils, copra

The most populous of the Comoro Islands in the Indian Ocean, with a Christian majority, Mayotte voted in 1974 and 1976 against joining the other, predominantly Moslem islands, in declaring themselves independent. It continues to retain its ties to France.

## MARTINIQUE

**Status:** Overseas Department
**Prefect:** Jean Chevance (1981)
**Area:** 431 sq mi. (1,116 sq km)
**Population (est. mid-1986):** 300,000 (average annual growth rate: 1.1%)
**Capital (est. 1984):** Fort-de-France, 97,814
**Monetary unit:** Franc
**Languages:** French, Creole patois
**Religion:** Roman Catholic
**Literacy rate (1981):** 70%
**Economic summary:** Gross national product (1983): $1.33 billion. Average annual growth rate (1970–79): 4.3%. Per capita income (1983): $4,040. Land used for agriculture: 18%; labor force: 8%; principal agricultural products: sugar cane, bananas, rum, pineapples. Labor force in industry: 5%; major industries: sugar, rum, refined oil, cement, tourism. Natural resource: fish. Exports: bananas, refined petroleum products, rum, sugar, pineapples. Imports: foodstuffs, clothing and other consumer goods, petroleum products. Major trading partners: France, U.S.

Martinique, lying in the Lesser Antilles about 300 miles (483 km) northeast of Venezuela, was probably discovered by Columbus in 1502 and was taken for France in 1635. Following the Franco-German armistice of 1940, it had a semiautonomous status until 1943, when authority was relinquished to the Free French. The area, administered by a Prefect assisted by an elected council, is represented in the French Parliament. In 1958, Martinique voted in favor of the new Constitution of the French Fifth Republic and remained an Overseas Department of the French Republic.

# NEW CALEDONIA AND DEPENDENCIES

**Status:** Overseas Territory
**High Commissioner:** Jacques Roynette (1982)
**Area:** 7,374 sq mi. (19,103 sq km)[1]
**Population (est. mid-1986):** 200,000 (average annual growth rate: 0.8%)
**Capital (est. 1983):** Nouméa, 60,112
**Monetary unit:** Pacific financial community franc
**Languages:** Melanesian and Polynesian dialects
**Religion:** Christian
**Literacy rate:** Not known
**Economic summary:** Gross national product (1983): $1.14 billion. Average annual growth rate (1970–78): −4.9%. Per capita income (1983): $7,820. Principal agricultural products: coffee, copra. Major industrial product: nickel. Natural resources: nickel, chromite, iron ore. Exports: nickel, chrome. Imports: mineral fuels, machinery, transport equipment, foodstuffs. Major trading partners: France, Japan, U.S., Australia.

1. Including dependencies.

New Caledonia (6,466 sq mi.; 16,747 sq km), about 1,070 miles (1,722 km) northeast of Sydney, Australia, was discovered by Capt. James Cook in 1774 and annexed by France in 1853. The government also administers the Isle of Pines, the Loyalty Islands (Uvéa, Lifu, and Maré), the Belep Islands, the Huon Island group, and the Chesterfield Islands.

The natives are Melanesians; about one third of the population is white and one fifth Indochinese and Javanese. The French National Assembly on July 31, 1984, voted a bill into law that granted internal autonomy to New Caledonia and opened the way to possible eventual independence. This touched off ethnic tensions and violence between the natives and the European settlers, with the natives demanding full independence and sovereignty while the settlers wanted to remain part of France. Between November 1984 and February 1985, more than 20 people were killed.

# RÉUNION

**Status:** Overseas Department
**Prefect:** Michel Blangy (1984)
**Area:** 970 sq mi. (2,510 sq km)
**Population (est. mid-1986):** 500,000 (average annual growth rate, 1.8%)
**Capital (est. 1982):** Saint-Denis, 126,323
**Monetary unit:** Franc
**Languages:** French, Creole
**Religion:** Roman Catholic
**Economic summary:** Gross national product (1983): $2.06 billion. Average annual growth rate (1970–79): −0.9%. Principal agricultural products: sugar cane, vanilla, bananas, perfume plants. Major industrial products: rum, cigarettes, processed sugar. Exports: sugar, perfume essences, rum, molasses. Imports: manufactured goods, foodstuffs, beverages, machinery and transportation equipment, petroleum products. Major trading partners: France, Mauritius.

Discovered by Portuguese navigators in the 16th century, the island of Réunion, then uninhabited, was taken as a French possession in 1642. It is located about 450 miles (724 km) east of Madagascar, in the Indian Ocean. In 1958, Réunion approved the Constitution of the Fifth French Republic and remained an Overseas Department of the French Republic.

# ST. PIERRE AND MIQUELON

**Status:** Overseas Territory
**Prefect:** Gerard Lefebvre (1984)
**Area:** 93 sq mi. (242 sq km)
**Population (est. 1983):** 6,000
**Capital (est. 1981):** Saint Pierre, 5,800
**Economic summary:** Major industries: fishing, canneries. Exports: petroleum products, cattle, fish. Major trading partners: Canada, France, U.S.

The sole remnant of the French colonial empire in North America, these islands were first occupied by the French in 1604. Their only importance arises from proximity to the Grand Banks, located 10 miles south of Newfoundland, making them the center of the French Atlantic cod fisheries. On July 19, 1976, the islands became an Overseas Department of the French Republic.

# SOUTHERN AND ANTARCTIC LANDS

**Status:** Overseas Territory
**Administrator:** Claude Pieri
**Area:** 169,614 sq mi. (439,300 sq km)
**Capital:** Port-au-Français

This territory is uninhabited except for the personnel of scientific bases. It consists of Adélie Land (166,752 sq mi.; 431,888 sq km) on the Antarctic mainland and the following islands in the southern Indian Ocean: the Kerguelen and Crozet archipelagos and the islands of Saint-Paul and New Amsterdam.

# WALLIS AND FUTUNA ISLANDS

**Status:** Overseas Territory
**Administrator Superior:** Michel Kuhnmunch (1984)
**Area:** 77 sq mi. (200 sq km)
**Population (est. 1985):** 12,391
**Capital (1980):** Wallis (on Uvea), 600

The two islands groups in the South Pacific between Fiji and Samoa were settled by French missionaries at the beginning of the 19th century. A protectorate was established in the 1880s. Following a referendum by the Polynesian inhabitants, the status was changed to that of an Overseas Territory in 1961.

# GABON

**Gabonese Republic**
**President:** Omar Bongo (1967)
**Premier:** Léon Mébiame (1975)
**Area:** 103,346 sq mi. (267,667 sq km)
**Population (est. mid-1986):** 1,200,000 (average annual growth rate: 1.6%)
**Density per square mile:** 11.6
**Capital and largest city (est. 1983):** Libreville, 257,000
**Monetary unit:** Franc CFA
**Ethnic groups:** Bateke, Obamba, Bakota, Shake, Pongwés, Adumas, Chiras, Punu, and Lumbu
**Languages:** French (official) and Bantu dialects
**Religions:** Roman Catholic, 63.8%, Protestant, 18.4%
**National name:** République Gabonaise
**Member of French Community**
**Literacy rate:** 65%
**Economic summary:** Gross national product (1983): $3.1

billion. Average annual growth rate (1970–79): 5.2%. Per capita income (1983): $3,962. Labor force in agriculture: 65%; principal products: sugar cane, wood, palm, rice, bananas, peanuts. Labor force in industry: 30%; major products: petroleum, natural gas, processed wood, manganese, uranium. Natural resources: wood, petroleum, iron ore, manganese, uranium. Exports: crude petroleum, wood and wood products, minerals. Imports: mining and road-building machinery, electrical equipment, foodstuffs, textiles, transport vehicles. Major trading partners: France, U.S., Brazil, U.K.

**Geography.** This West African land with the Atlantic as its western border is also bounded by Equatorial Guinea, Cameroon, and the Congo. Its area is slightly less than Kentucky's.

From mangrove swamps on the coast, the land becomes divided plateaus in the north and east and mountains in the north. Most of the country is covered by a dense tropical forest.

**Government.** The president is elected for a seven-year term. Legislative powers are exercised by a National Assembly, which is elected for a seven-year term. After his conversion to Islam in 1973, President Bongo changed his given name, Albert Bernard, to Omar. The Parti Démocratique Gabonais (all National Assembly seats) is led by President Bongo. He was re-elected without opposition in 1973 and in 1980.

**History.** Little is known of Gabon's history, even in oral tradition, but Pygmies are believed to be the original inhabitants. Now there are many tribal groups in the country, the largest being the Fang people who constitute a third of the population.

Gabon was first visited by the Portuguese navigator Diego Cam in the 15th century. In 1839, the French founded their first settlement on the left bank of the Gabon Estuary and gradually occupied the hinterland during the second half of the 19th century. It was organized as a French territory in 1888 and became an autonomous republic within the French Union after World War II and an independent republic on Aug. 17, 1960.

Immense resources in oil, uranium, manganese, and iron help give Gabon's inhabitants a per capita annual income of $3,962, the highest in black Africa. To speed exploitation of a billion-ton iron ore reserve in the Belinga-Mekambo region, the government began work in 1969 on a 350-mile railroad leading from the coast into the area. The project was initiated by President León Mba, who died in 1967, and has been continued by his hand-picked successor, Omar Bongo.

In 1974, Bongo negotiated 60% control of an iron-ore venture half-owned by the Bethlehem Steel Corp. In October of that year, he visited Peking and concluded an economic and technical agreement with China.

# GAMBIA

**Republic of the Gambia**
**President:** Sir Dawda K. Jawara (1970)
**Area:** 4,093 sq mi. (10,600 sq km)
**Population (est. mid-1986):** 800,000 (average annual growth rate: 2.0%)
**Density per square mile:** 195.5
**Capital and largest city (est. 1980):** Banjul, 48,000
**Monetary unit:** Dalasi

**Languages:** Native tongues, English (official)
**Religions:** Islam, 85%, Christian, 2%, Animist, 11%
**Member of Commonwealth of Nations**
**Literacy rate:** 20%
**Economic summary:** Gross national product (1983): $200 million. Average annual growth rate (1970–79): 0.4%. Per capita income (1983): $290. Land used for agriculture: 16%; labor force: 76%; principal products: peanuts, rice, palm kernels. Major industrial products: processed peanuts. Natural resources: fish. Exports: peanuts and peanut products, fish. Imports: textiles, foodstuffs, tobacco, machinery, petroleum products. Major trading partners: Western European countries, China, U.K.

**Geography.** Situated on the Atlantic coast in westernmost Africa and surrounded on three sides by Senegal, Gambia is twice the size of Delaware. The Gambia River flows for 200 miles (322 km) through Gambia on its way to the Atlantic. The country, the smallest on the continent, averages only 20 miles (32 km) in width.

**Government.** The president's five-year term is linked to the 35-member unicameral House of Representatives, from which he appoints his Cabinet members and the vice president.

The major political party is the People's Progressive Party (29 seats in House of Representatives), led by President Jawara.

**History.** During the 17th century, Gambia was settled by various companies of English merchants. Slavery was the chief source of revenue until it was abolished in 1807. Gambia became a crown colony in 1843 and an independent nation within the Commonwealth of Nations on Feb. 18, 1965.

Full independence was approved in a 1970 referendum, and on April 24 of that year Gambia proclaimed itself a republic.

President Dawda K. Jawara won overwhelming re-election to his fifth term on May 5, 1982, in a vote that was also seen as an endorsement of his proposal for a confederation with Senegal.

# GERMANY, EAST

**German Democratic Republic**
**Chairman of Council of State:** Erich Honecker (1976)
**Chairman of Council of Ministers:** Willi Stoph (1976)
**Area:** 41,767 sq mi. (108,177 sq km)[1]
**Population (est. mid-1986):** 16,700,000 (average annual growth rate: 0.0%)
**Density per square mile:** 154
**Capital:** Berlin (eastern sector)
**Largest cities (est. 1984):** East Berlin, 1,189,353; Leipzig, 557,129; Dresden, 519,607; Karl-Marx Stadt, 317,460; Magdeburg, 288,949; Halle, 236,870; Rostock, 241,254; Erfurt, 214,552
**Monetary unit:** Mark of the Deutsche Demokratische Republik
**Language:** German
**Religions:** Protestant, 53%; Roman Catholic, 8%
**National name:** Deutsche Demokratische Republik
**Literacy rate:** 99%
**Economic summary:** Gross national product (1984): $163.7 billion. Annual growth rate (1970–79): 2.0%. Per capita income (1984): $9,800. Land used for agriculture: 47%; labor force: 11%; principal products: grains, potatoes, sugar beets, meat and dairy products. Labor force in industry: 38%; major products: steel, chemicals, machinery, electrical and precision engineer-

ing products. Natural resources: brown coal, potash, bauxite. Exports: machinery and equipment, chemical products, textiles, clothing. Imports: raw materials, fuels, agricultural products, machinery and equipment. Major trading partners: U.S.S.R., Soviet bloc, West Germany.

1. Including East Berlin (156 square miles), which has been incorporated into the German Democratic Republic.

**Geography.** East Germany lies on the Baltic Sea with Poland to the east and Czechoslovakia to the south. The border with West Germany is roughly a line running south from Lübeck for about 250 miles. The main river is the Elbe, which flows from Dresden in the southeast to the North Sea in the northwest. The Oder and Neisse Rivers form the border with Poland. Most of the country, which is the size of Tennessee, is situated in the north German plain.

**Government.** The People's Chamber, composed of 500 deputies elected for five-year terms, chooses the chairman and Council of State and the chairman and Council of Ministers, which carries on executive functions.

The major political party is the Socialist Unity (Communist) Party, led by Secretary General Erich Honecker. Others are Christian Democratic Union, Liberal Democratic Party, Democratic Farmers' Party, National Democratic Party.

**History.** (For history before 1945, *see* Germany, West.) The area now occupied by East Germany, as well as adjacent areas in Eastern Europe, consists of Mecklenburg, Brandenburg, Lusatia, Saxony, and Thuringia. Soviet armies conquered the five territories by 1945. In the division of 1945 they were allotted to the U.S.S.R. Soviet forces created a State controlled by the secret police with a single party, the Socialist Unity (Communist) Party. The Russians appropriated East German plants to restore their war-ravaged industry.

When the Federal Republic of Germany was established in West Germany, the East German states adopted a more centralized constitution for the Democratic Republic of Germany, and it was put into effect on Oct. 7, 1949. The U.S.S.R. thereupon dissolved its occupation zone, but Soviet troops remained. The Western Allies declared that the East German Republic was a Soviet creation undertaken without self-determination and refused to recognize it. It was recognized only within the Soviet bloc.

Talks between the two German states on normalization began in 1970, with the East seeking recognition of its existence and the West wanting easing of pressure on Berlin, and rapprochement between the two Germanys accelerated with agreement on a variety of issues (for details, *see* Germany, West). By 1973, normal relations were established, and the two states entered the United Nations.

The 25-year diplomatic hiatus between East Germany and the U.S. ended Sept. 4, 1974, with the establishment of formal relations.

The East German government has repeatedly challenged the Western powers' right of access to Berlin, most recently at the time of President Carter's July 15, 1978, visit to West Berlin. Autobahn traffic between the city and West Germany was deliberately slowed and, as in a similar 1977 case, the

U.S., U.K., and France protested to the U.S.S.R. and the East Germans that such action was illegal under the 1971 Four Power Agreement.

Chairman of the Council of State Erich Honecker gave strong backing to the Soviet Union's stern policy toward Poland as the workers' demand for democratic rights advanced in 1980 and 1981. On Oct. 28, 1980, he closed the border, which had been open between the two states for 10 years, permitting only certified relatives or invited friends to visit. Five million Poles had visited East Germany in the previous year, largely to find cheaper and more abundant consumer goods.

In February 1981, Honecker, in a surprise gesture, declared at his party's 16th Congress that German reunification might eventually be possible, something the Communist regime had ruled out 10 years earlier. He also eased border restrictions on exchanges with West Germany imposed a few months before, but in September 1984 was pressured by the Soviet Union to cancel a planned milestone visit to West Germany.

# GERMANY, WEST

**Federal Republic of Germany**
**President:** Richard von Weizsäcker (1984)
**Chancellor:** Helmut Kohl (1982)
**Area:** 96,010 sq mi. (248,667 sq km)[1]
**Population (est. mid-1986):** 60,700,000, includes West Berlin. (average annual growth rate: −0.2%)
**Density per square mile:** 632.2
**Capital (est. 1984):** Bonn, 291,700
**Largest cities (1984):** Hamburg, 1,600,300; Munich, 1,277,000; Cologne, 932,400; Essen, 628,800; Frankfurt, 604,600; Dortmund, 584,800; Dusseldorf, 570,700; Stuttgart, 563,200; Bremen, 535,800; Hannover, 517,900
**Monetary unit:** Deutsche Mark
**Language:** German
**Religions:** Protestant, 47%; Roman Catholic, 44%
**National name:** Bundesrepublik Deutschland
**Literacy rate:** 99%
**Economic summary:** Gross national product (1984): $616.1 billion. Average annual growth rate (1980–82) 0.2%. Per capita income (1983): $10,672. Land used for agriculture: 33%; labor force: 5%; principal products: grains, potatoes, sugar beets. Labor force in industry: 43%; major products: steel, coal, cement, chemicals, machinery, ships, vehicles. Natural resources: timber, iron, lead. Exports: machines and machine tools, chemicals, motor vehicles, iron and steel products. Imports: manufactured and agricultural products, raw materials, fuels. Major trading partners: France, Netherlands, Belgium-Luxembourg, Italy, U.S., U.K.

1. Excluding West Berlin (184 square miles with 1984 population of 1,860,900).

**Geography.** The Federal Republic of Germany occupies the western half of the central European area historically regarded as German. This was the part of Germany occupied by the United States, Britain, and France after World War II, when the eastern half of prewar Germany was split roughly between a Soviet-occupied zone, which became the present German Democratic Republic, and an area annexed by Poland.

West Germany's neighbors are France, Belgium, Luxembourg, and the Netherlands on the west, Switzerland and Austria on the south, Czechoslova-

# Rulers of Germany and Prussia

| Name | Born | Ruled[1] | Name | Born | Ruled[1] |
|------|------|----------|------|------|----------|
| **KINGS OF PRUSSIA** | | | Karl Doenitz[6] | 1891 | 1945–1945 |
| Frederick I[2] | 1657 | 1701–1713 | | | |
| Frederick William I | 1688 | 1713–1740 | **GERMAN FEDERAL REPUBLIC** | | |
| Frederick II the Great | 1712 | 1740–1786 | **(WEST) (PRESIDENTS)** | | |
| Frederick William II | 1744 | 1786–1797 | Theodor Heuss | 1884 | 1949–1959[9] |
| Frederick William III | 1770 | 1797–1840 | Heinrich Luebke | 1895 | 1959–1969[8] |
| Frederick William IV | 1795 | 1840–1861 | Gustav Heinemann[10] | 1899 | 1969–1974 |
| William I | 1797 | 1861–1871[3] | Walter Scheel | 1919 | 1974–1979 |
| | | | Karl Carstens | 1914 | 1979–1984 |
| **EMPERORS OF GERMANY** | | | Richard von Weizsäcker | 1920 | 1984– |
| William I | 1797 | 1871–1888 | | | |
| Frederick III | 1831 | 1888–1888 | **GERMAN DEMOCRATIC REPUBLIC** | | |
| William II | 1859 | 1888–1918[4] | **(EAST)** | | |
| | | | Wilhelm Pieck[5] | 1876 | 1949–1960 |
| **HEADS OF THE REICH** | | | Walter Ulbricht[11] | 1893 | 1960–1973 |
| Friedrich Ebert[5] | 1871 | 1919–1925 | Willi Stoph[12] | 1914 | 1973–1976 |
| Paul von Hindenburg[5] | 1847 | 1925–1934 | Erich Honecker[12] | 1912 | 1976– |
| Adolf Hitler[6][7] | 1889 | 1934–1945 | | | |

1. Year of end of rule is also that of death, unless otherwise indicated. 2. Was Elector of Brandenburg (1688–1701) as Frederick III. 3. Became Emperor of Germany in 1871. 4. Died 1941. 5. President. 6. Führer. 7. Named Chancellor by President Hindenburg in 1933. 8. Died 1972. 9. Died 1963. 10. Died 1976. 11. Chairman of Council of State. Died 1973. 12. Chairman of Council of State.

kia and East Germany on the east, and Denmark on the north.

The northern plain, the central hill country, and the southern mountain district constitute the main physical divisions of West Germany, which is slightly smaller than Oregon. The Bavarian plateau in the southwest averages 1,600 feet (488 m) above sea level, but it reaches 9,721 feet (2,963 m) in the Zugspitze Mountains, the highest point in the country.

Important navigable rivers are the Danube, rising in the Black Forest and flowing east across Bavaria into Austria, and the Rhine, which rises in Switzerland and flows across the Netherlands in two channels to the North Sea and is navigable by ocean-going and coastal vessels as far as Cologne. The Elbe, which also empties into the North Sea, is navigable within Germany for smaller vessels. The Weser, flowing into the North Sea, and the Main and Mosel (Moselle), both tributaries of the Rhine, are also important.

**Government.** Under the Constitution of May 23, 1949, the Federal Republic was established as a parliamentary democracy. The Parliament consists of the Bundesrat, an upper chamber representing and appointed by the 10 Länder, or states (plus West Berlin), and the Bundestag, a lower house elected for four years by universal suffrage. Each house has non-voting representatives from West Berlin. The entire legislature elects the President of the Republic for a five-year term; the Bundestag alone chooses the Chancellor, or Prime Minister. Each of the Länder and West Berlin have a legislature popularly elected for a four-year or five-year term.

The major political parties are the Christian Democratic Union-Christian Social Union (244 of 498 seats in the Bundestag), led by Chancellor Helmut Kohl; Social Democratic Party (193 seats) led by former Chancellor Willy Brandt; and the Free Democratic Party (34 seats), led by Martin Bange Mann; the Greens (27 seats). Kohl's government is a coalition with the Free Democrats.

**History.** Immediately before the Christian era, when the Roman Empire had pushed its frontier to the Rhine, what is now Germany was inhabited by several tribes believed to have migrated from Central Asia between the 6th and 4th centuries B.C. One of these tribes, the Franks, attained supremacy in western Europe under Charlemagne, who was crowned Holy Roman Emperor A.D. 800. By the Treaty of Verdun (843), Charlemagne's lands east of the Rhine were ceded to the German Prince Louis. Additional territory acquired by the Treaty of Mersen (870) gave Germany approximately the area it maintained throughout the Middle Ages. For several centuries after Otto the Great was crowned King in 936, the German rulers were also usually heads of the Holy Roman Empire.

Relations between state and church were changed by the Reformation, which began with Martin Luther's 95 theses, and came to a head in 1547, when Charles V scattered the forces of the Protestant League at Mühlberg. Freedom of worship was guaranteed by the Peace of Augsburg (1555), but a Counter Reformation took place later, and a dispute over the succession to the Bohemian throne brought on the Thirty Years' War (1618–48), which devastated Germany and left the empire divided into hundreds of small principalities virtually independent of the Emperor.

Meanwhile, Prussia was developing into a state of considerable strength. Frederick the Great (1740–86) reorganized the Prussian army and defeated Maria Theresa of Austria in a struggle over Silesia. After the defeat of Napoleon at Waterloo (1815), the struggle between Austria and Prussia for supremacy in Germany continued, reaching its climax in the defeat of Austria in the Seven Weeks' War (1866) and the formation of the Prussian-dominated North German Confederation (1867).

The architect of German unity was Otto von Bismarck, a conservative, monarchist, and militaristic Prussian Junker who had no use for "empty phrasemaking and constitutions." From 1862 until his retirement in 1890 he dominated not only the German but also the entire European scene. He unified all Germany in a series of three wars against Denmark (1864), Austria (1866), and France (1870–71), which many historians believe were instigated and promoted by Bismarck in his zeal to build a nation through "blood and iron."

On Jan. 18, 1871, King Wilhelm I of Prussia was proclaimed German Emperor in the Hall of Mirrors at Versailles. The North German Confederation, created in 1867, was abolished, and the Second German Reich, consisting of the North and South German states, was born. With a powerful army, an efficient bureaucracy, and a loyal bourgeoisie, Chancellor Bismarck consolidated a powerful centralized state.

Wilhelm II dismissed Bismarck in 1890 and embarked upon a "New Course," stressing an intensified colonialism and a powerful navy. His chaotic foreign policy culminated in the diplomatic isolation of Germany and the disastrous defeat in World War I (1914–18).

The Second German Empire collapsed following the defeat of the German armies in 1918, the naval mutiny at Kiel, and the flight of the Kaiser to the Netherlands on November 10. The Social Democrats, led by Friedrich Ebert and Philipp Scheidemann, crushed the Communists and established a moderate republic with Ebert as President.

The Weimar Constitution of 1919 provided for a President to be elected for seven years by universal suffrage and a bicameral legislature, consisting of the Reichsrat, representing the states, and the Reichstag, representing the people. It contained a model Bill of Rights. It was weakened, however, by a provision that enabled the President to rule by decree.

President Ebert died Feb. 28, 1925, and on April 26, Field Marshal Paul von Hindenburg was elected president.

The mass of Germans regarded the Weimar Republic as a child of defeat, imposed upon a Germany whose legitimate aspirations to world leadership had been thwarted by a world conspiracy. Added to this were a crippling currency debacle, a tremendous burden of reparations, and acute economic distress.

Adolf Hitler, an Austrian war veteran and a fanatical nationalist, fanned discontent by promising a Greater Germany, abrogation of the Treaty of Versailles, restoration of Germany's lost colonies, and destruction of the Jews. When the Social Democrats and the Communists refused to combine against the Nazi threat, President Hindenburg made Hitler chancellor on Jan. 30, 1933.

With the death of Hindenburg on Aug. 2, 1934, Hitler repudiated the Treaty of Versailles and began full-scale rearmament. In 1935 he withdrew Germany from the League of Nations, and the next year he reoccupied the Rhineland and signed the anti-Comintern pact with Japan, at the same time strengthening relations with Italy. Austria was annexed in March 1938. By the Munich agreement in September 1938 he gained the Czech Sudetenland, and in violation of this agreement he completed the dismemberment of Czechoslovakia in March 1939. But his invasion of Poland on Sept. 1, 1939, precipitated World War II.

On May 8, 1945, Germany surrendered unconditionally to Allied and Soviet military commanders, and on June 5 the four-nation Allied Control Council became the *de facto* government of Germany. (For details of World War II, *see* Headline History.)

At the Berlin (or Potsdam) Conference (July 17–Aug. 2, 1945) President Truman, Premier Stalin,

and Prime Minister Clement Attlee of Britain set forth the guiding principles of the Allied Control Council. They were Germany's complete disarmament and demilitarization, destruction of its war potential, rigid control of industry, and decentralization of the political and economic structure. Pending final determination of territorial questions at a peace conference, the three victors agreed in principle to the ultimate transfer of the city of Königsberg (now Kaliningrad) and its adjacent area to the U.S.S.R. and to the administration by Poland of former German territories lying generally east of the Oder-Neisse Line.

For purposes of control Germany was divided in 1945 into four national occupation zones, each headed by a Military Governor.

The Western powers were unable to agree with the U.S.S.R. on any fundamental issue. Work of the Allied Control Council was hamstrung by repeated Soviet vetoes; and finally, on March 20, 1948, Russia walked out of the Council. Meanwhile, the U.S. and Britain had taken steps to merge their zones economically (Bizone); and on May 31, 1948, the U.S., Britain, France, and the Benelux countries agreed to set up a German state comprising the three Western Zones.

The U.S.S.R. reacted by clamping a blockade on all ground communications between the Western Zones and Berlin, an enclave in the Soviet Zone. The Western Allies countered by organizing a gigantic airlift to fly supplies into the beleaguered city, assigning 60,000 men to it. The U.S.S.R. was finally forced to lift the blockade on May 12, 1949.

The Federal Republic of Germany was proclaimed on May 23, 1949, with its capital at Bonn. In free elections, West German voters gave a majority in the Constituent Assembly to the Christian Democrats, with the Social Democrats largely making up the opposition. Konrad Adenauer became chancellor, and Theodor Heuss of the Free Democrats was elected first president.

Agreements in Paris in 1954 giving the Federal Republic full independence and complete sovereignty came into force on May 5, 1955. Under it, West Germany and Italy became members of the Brussels treaty organization created in 1948 and renamed the Western European Union. West Germany also became a member of NATO. In 1955 the U.S.S.R. recognized the Federal Republic. The Saar territory, under an agreement between France and West Germany, held a plebiscite and despite economic links to France voted to rejoin West Germany. It became a state of West Germany on Jan. 1, 1957.

In 1963, Chancellor Adenauer concluded a treaty of mutual cooperation and friendship with France and then retired. He was succeeded by his chief inner-party critic, Ludwig Erhard, who was followed in 1966 by Kurt Georg Kiesinger. He, in turn, was succeeded in 1969 by Willy Brandt, former mayor of West Berlin.

The division between West Germany and East Germany was intensified when the Communists erected the Berlin Wall in 1961. In 1968, the East German Communist leader, Walter Ulbricht, imposed restrictions on West German movements into West Berlin. The Soviet-bloc invasion of Czechoslovakia in August 1968 added to the tension.

A treaty with the U.S.S.R. was signed in Moscow in August 1970 in which force was renounced and respect for the "territorial integrity" of present European states declared.

Three months later, West Germany signed a sim-

ilar treaty with Poland, renouncing force and setting Poland's western border as the Oder-Neisse
Line. It subsequently resumed formal relations
with Czechoslovakia in a pact that "voided" the
Munich treaty that gave Nazi Germany the Sudetenland.

Both German states were admitted to the United
Nations in 1973.

Brandt, winner of a Nobel Peace Prize for his foreign policies, was forced to resign in 1974 when an
East German spy was discovered to be one of his
top staff members. Succeeding him was a moderate
Social Democrat, Helmut Schmidt.

Helmut Schmidt, Brandt's successor as chancellor, staunchly backed U.S. military strategy in Europe nevertheless, staking his political fate on the
strategy of placing U.S. nuclear missiles in Germany unless the Soviet Union reduced its arsenal
of intermediate missiles.

The chancellor also strongly opposed nuclear
freeze proposals and won 2-1 support for his stand
at the convention of Social Democrats in April. But
the nuclear issue, as well as economic problems,
contributed to a Social Democratic defeat in Schmidt's hometown bastion, Hamburg, in which state
elections in June put the opposition Christian
Democrats in first place. The anti-nuclear
"Greens" ran third and the Free Democrats, partners in Schmidt's federal coalition, lost many of
their seats. The Free Democrats then deserted the
Socialists and joined with the Christian Democrats
to unseat Schmidt and install Helmut Kohl as chancellor in 1982.

## BERLIN

**Status:** West Berlin: State of West Germany; East Berlin:
capital of East Germany
**Governing Mayor, West Berlin:** Eberhard Diepgen (1984)
**Mayor, East Berlin:** Erhard Krack
**Area:** 340 square miles (West Berlin, 184; East Berlin, 156
**Population (est. 1983):** 3,033,900 (West Berlin, 1,860,-
900; East Berlin, 1,173,000)

Berlin, the capital of prewar Germany, lies entirely within the borders of East Germany. After
the war, the city was occupied by the forces of the
U.S., Britain, France, and the U.S.S.R. The three
western sectors, now known as West Berlin, contain 55% of the area and two thirds of the population.

West Berlin is a state of the Federal Republic of
Germany, but supreme authority remains in the
hands of the three Western powers in accordance
with postwar agreements. The government is composed of the governing mayor, the 11-member
Senate (his Cabinet), and the House of Representatives, a popularly elected legislative body that
elects the governing mayor and the Senate.

East Berlin is governed by a City Assembly
elected by Communist Party members, and a Magistrate (City Council) chosen by the Assembly and
headed by the mayor. In violation of the Four
Power Agreements, the Soviet Sector has been incorporated into the German Democratic Republic
and is now the capital of that country.

Major anti-Communist riots broke out in East
Berlin in June 1953 and, since Aug. 13, 1961, the
Soviet Sector has been virtually sealed off by a
Communist-built wall, 26 1/2 miles (43 km) long,
running through the city. It was built to stem the
flood of refugees seeking freedom in the West, 200,-
000 having fled in 1961 before the wall was
erected.

# GHANA

**Republic of Ghana**
**Chairman of Provisional National Defense Council:** Flight
Lt. Jerry Rawlings (1981)
**Area:** 92,100 sq mi. (238,537 sq km)
**Population (est. mid-1986):** 13,600,000 (average annual
growth rate: 3.4%)
**Density per square mile:** 147.7
**Capital:** Accra
**Largest cities (est. 1983):** Accra, 1,500,000; Kumasi,
500,000; Sekondi-Takoradi, 350,000
**Monetary unit:** Cedi
**Languages:** Native tongues (Twi, Fanti, Ga, Ewe, Dagbani);
English
**Religions:** Christian, 63%; Animist, 21%; Islam, 16%
**Literacy rate:** 45% (in English)
**Member of Commonwealth of Nations**
**Economic summary:** Gross national product (1983): $3.98
billion. Average annual growth rate (1973–82): −1.1%.
Per capita income (1983): $320. Land used for
agriculture: 12%; labor force: 50%; principal products:
cocoa, coconuts, cassava, yams, rice, rubber. Labor force
in industry: 19%; major products: mining products, cocoa
products, aluminum. Natural resources: gold, diamonds,
bauxite, manganese, fish. Exports: cocoa beans and
products, gold, timber, manganese ore. Imports: textiles
and manufactured goods, food, fuels, transport
equipment. Major trading partners: U.K., Western
European countries, U.S., Nigeria, U.S.S.R.

**Geography.** A West African country bordering on
the Gulf of Guinea, Ghana has the Ivory Coast to
the west, Burkina Faso to the north, and Togo to
the east. It compares in size to Oregon.

The coastal belt, extending about 270 miles (435
km), is sandy, marshy, and generally exposed. Behind it is a gradually widening grass strip. The forested plateau region to the north is broken by
ridges and hills. The largest river is the Volta.

**Government.** Ghana returned to military rule after
two years of constitutional government when
Flight Lt. Jerry Rawlings, who led a coup in 1979
and stepped down voluntarily, seized power on
Dec. 31, 1981. Rawlings heads a Provisional National Defense Council, which exercises all power.

**History.** Created an independent country on
March 6, 1957, Ghana is the former British colony
of the Gold Coast. The area was first seen by Portuguese traders in 1470. They were followed by the
English (1553), the Dutch (1595), and the Swedes
(1640). British rule over the Gold Coast began in
1820, but it was not until after quelling the severe
resistance of the Ashanti in 1901 that it was firmly
established. British Togoland, formerly a colony of
Germany, was incorporated into Ghana by referendum in 1956. As the result of a plebiscite, Ghana
became a republic on July 1, 1960.

Premier Kwame Nkrumah attempted to take
leadership of the Pan-African Movement, holding
the All-African People's Congress in his capital,
Accra, in 1958 and organizing the Union of African
States with Guinea and Mali in 1961. But he oriented his country toward the Soviet Union and
China and built an autocratic rule over all aspects
of Ghanaian life.

In February 1966, while Nkrumah was visiting
Peking and Hanoi, he was deposed by a military
coup led by Gen. Emmanuel K. Kotoka.

A series of military coups followed and on
June 4, 1979, Flight Lieutenant Jerry

Rawlings overthrew Lt. Gen. Frederick Akuffo's military rule on June 4, 1979. Rawlings permitted the election of a civilian president to go ahead as scheduled the following month, and Hilla Limann, candidate of the People's National Party, took office. Charging the civilian government with corruption and repression, Rawlings staged another coup on Dec. 31, 1981. As chairman of the Provisional National Defense Council, Rawlings instituted an austerity program and reduced budget deficits.

On July 11, 1985, a relative of Rawlings, Michael Agbotui Soussoudis, 39, and Sharon M. Scranage, 29, who had been a low-level clerk in the Central Intelligence Agency station in the West African country, were arrested in the United States on espionage charges. Reagan Administration officials said the American woman had given Soussoudis, her Ghanian lover, information about the agency's operations in Ghana and that as a result, at least one CIA informant had been murdered and the CIA feared reprisals would be taken by the Rawlings government against as many as 10 others.

# GREECE

**Hellenic Republic**
**President:** Christos Sartzetakis (1985)
**Premier:** Andreas Papandreou (1981)
**Area:** 50,961 sq mi. (131,990 sq km)
**Population (est. mid-1986):** 10,000,000 (average annual growth rate: 0.4%)
**Density per square mile:** 196.2
**Capital:** Athens
**Largest cities (1981 census):** Athens, 3,027,000; Salonika, 706,000; Patras, 150,000; Larissa, 102,000; Heraklion, 111,000
**Monetary unit:** Drachma
**Language:** Greek
**Religion:** Greek Orthodox
**National name:** Elliniki Dimokratia
**Literacy rate:** 95%
**Economic summary:** Gross national product (1984): $33.5 billion. Annual growth rate (1984): 2.9%. Per capita income (1984): $3,380. Land used for agriculture: 30%; labor force: 28%; principal products: grains, fruits, vegetables, olives, olive oil, tobacco, cotton, livestock, dairy products. Labor force in industry: 29%; major products: textiles, chemicals, food processing. Natural resources: bauxite, iron, forests. Exports: fruits, textiles, tobacco. Imports: machinery and automotive equipment, petroleum, consumer goods, chemicals, foodstuffs. Major trading partners: West Germany, Italy, France, Saudi Arabia, U.S.A.

**Geography.** Greece, on the Mediterranean Sea, is the southernmost country on the Balkan Peninsula in Eastern Europe. It is bordered on the north by Albania, Yugoslavia, and Bulgaria; on the west by the Ionian Sea; and on the east by the Aegean Sea and Turkey. It is slightly smaller than Alabama.

North central Greece, Epirus, and western Macedonia all are mountainous. The main chain of the Pindus Mountains rises to 9,000 feet (2,743 m) in places, separating Epirus from the plains of Thessaly. Mt. Olympus, rising to 9,570 feet (2,909 m) in the north near the Aegean Sea, is the highest point in the country. Greek Thrace is mostly a lowland region separated from European Turkey by the lower Evros River.

Among the many islands are the Ionian group off the west coast; the Cyclades group to the southeast; other islands in the eastern Aegean, including the Dodecanese Islands, Euboea, Lesbos, Samos, and Chios; and Crete, the fourth largest Mediterranean island.

**Government.** A referendum in December 1974, five months after the collapse of a military dictatorship, ended the Greek monarchy and established a republic. Ceremonial executive power is held by the president; the Premier heads the government and is responsible to a 300-member unicameral Parliament.

The major political parties are the Panhellenic Socialist Movement (157 of 300 seats in Parliament), led by Premier Andreas Papandreou; New Democracy Party (111 seats), led by Constantine Mitsotakis; Communist Party (10 seats), led by Harilaos Florakis, Democratic Renewal (10 seats); led by Constantine Stefanopoulos and the Communist Party of the Interior (one seat), led by Leonidas Kyrkos.

**History.** Greece, with a recorded history going back to 766 B.C., reached the peak of its glory in the 5th century B.C., and by the middle of the 2nd century B.C., it had declined to the status of a Roman province. It remained within the Eastern Roman Empire until Constantinople fell to the Crusaders in 1204.

In 1453, the Turks took Constantinople, and by 1460 Greece was a Turkish province. The insurrection made famous by the poet Lord Byron broke out in 1821, and in 1827 Greece won independence with sovereignty guaranteed by Britain, France, and Russia.

The protecting powers chose Prince Otto of Bavaria as the first king of modern Greece in 1832 to reign over an area only slightly larger than the Peloponnese Peninsula. Chiefly under the next king, George I, chosen by the protecting powers in 1863, Greece acquired much of its present territory. During his 57-year reign, a period in which he encouraged parliamentary democracy, Thessaly, Epirus, Macedonia, Crete, and most of the Aegean islands were added from the disintegrating Turkish empire. An unsuccessful war against Turkey after World War I brought down the monarchy, to be replaced by a republic in 1923.

Two military dictatorships and a financial crisis brought George II back from exile, but only until 1941, when Italian and German invaders defeated tough Greek resistance. After British and Greek troops liberated the country in October 1944, Communist guerrillas staged a long campaign in which the government received U.S. aid under the Truman Doctrine, the predecessor of the Marshall Plan.

A military junta seized power in April 1967, sending young King Constantine II into exile December 14. Col. George Papadopoulos, as premier, converted the government to republican form in 1973 and as President ended martial law. He was moving to restore democracy when he was ousted in November of that year by his military colleagues. The regime of the "colonels," which had tortured its opponents and scoffed at human rights, resigned July 23, 1974, after having bungled an attempt to seize Cyprus.

Former Premier Karamanlis returned from exile to become premier of Greece's first civilian government since 1967.

On Jan. 1, 1981, Greece became the 10th member of the European Community. On Oct. 18, the first Socialist government in Greek history won power, and Andreas Papandreou became the new Premier.

The Socialists won parliamentary elections on June 1, 1985, by a comfortable margin, giving Papandreou a license to continue on the leftist course he had set four years previously. Later the same month, a TWA airliner was hijacked by Lebanese Shiite extremists as it left Athens, bringing the Greek government under sharp criticism for what international aviation authorities said was its failure to take adequate security measures at its airports.

# GRENADA

**State of Grenada**
**Sovereign:** Queen Elizabeth II
**Governor General:** Paul Scoon (1978)
**Prime Minister:** Herbert A. Blaize (1984)
**Area:** 133 sq mi. (344 sq km)
**Population (est. mid-1986):** 100,000 (black, 84%; mixed, 11%) (average annual growth rate, 1.8%)
**Density per square mile:** 751.9
**Capital and largest city (est. 1980):** St. George's, 32,000
**Monetary unit:** East Caribbean dollar
**Ethnic groups:** Caribs and Indians
**Language:** English
**Religions:** Roman Catholic, 64%; Anglican, 21%
**Member of Commonwealth of Nations**
**Literacy rate:** 85%
**Economic summary:** Gross national product (1983): $110 million. Annual growth rate (1983): 2.6%. Per capita income (1983): $1,220. Land used for agriculture: 41%; labor force: 24%; principal products: spices, cocoa, bananas. Exports: nutmeg, cocoa beans, bananas, mace. Imports: foodstuffs, machinery, building materials. Major trading partners: U.K., West Indies countries, West Germany, U.S., Belgium

**Geography.** Grenada (the first "a" is pronounced as in "gray") is the most southerly of the Windward Islands, about 100 miles (161 km) from the South American coast. It is a volcanic island traversed by a mountain range, the highest peak of which is Mount St. Catherine (2,756 ft.; 840 m).

**History.** Grenada was discovered by Columbus in 1498. After more than 200 years of British rule, most recently as part of the West Indies Associated States, it became independent Feb. 7, 1974, with Eric M. Gairy as Prime Minister.

The government of Prime Minister Gairy was ousted March 13, 1979, by the New Jewel Movement of Maurice Bishop. Bishop, a protégé of Cuban President Fidel Castro, invited Cuban military advisers to Grenada and on June 20, 1980, called on Grenadians to join a "people's militia" to fight a "people's war" against imperialism.

Bishop was killed in a military coup on Oct. 19, 1983. At the request of five members of the Organization of Eastern Caribbean States, President Reagan ordered an invasion of Grenada on Oct. 25 involving over 1,900 U.S. troops and a small military force from Barbados, Dominica, Jamaica, St. Lucia, and St. Vincent. The troops met strong resistance from Cuban military personnel on the island. Reagan said he ordered the invasion to protect some 1,000 American citizens on the island, and to help restore democratic institutions in that country. A centrist coalition led by Herbert A. Blaize, a 66-

year-old lawyer, won 14 of the 15 seats in Parliament in an election in December 1984, and Blaize became Prime Minister.

# GUATEMALA

**Republic of Guatemala**
**President:** Mario Vinicio Cerezo (1986)
**Area:** 42,042 sq mi. (108,889 sq km)
**Population (est. mid-1986):** 8,600,000 (average annual growth rate: 3.1%)
**Density per square mile:** 204.6
**Capital and largest city (est. 1982):** Guatemala City, 1,250,000
**Monetary unit:** Quetzal
**Languages:** Spanish, Indian dialects
**Religion:** Roman Catholic, Protestant demoninations.
**National name:** República de Guatemala
**Literacy rate (1983):** 51%
**Economic summary:** Gross national product (1983): $8.89 billion. Average annual growth rate (1975–80) 5.7%. Per capita income (1983) $1,120. Land used for agriculture: 14%; labor force. 58%; principal products: corn, beans, coffee, cotton, cattle, sugar, bananas, essential oils, timber. Labor force in industry: 14%; principal products: prepared foods, textiles, construction materials, tires, pharmaceuticals. Natural resources: nickel, timber, shrimp. Exports: coffee, cotton, sugar, petroleum, bananas. Imports: manufactured products, machinery, transportation equipment, chemicals, fuels. Major trading partners: U.S., Central American nations, West Germany, Mexico.

**Geography.** The northernmost of the Central American nations, Guatemala is the size of Tennessee. Its neighbors are Mexico on the north, west, and east and Belize, Honduras, and El Salvador on the east. The country consists of two main regions—the cool highlands with the heaviest population and the tropical area along the Pacific and Caribbean coasts. The principal mountain range rises to the highest elevation in Central America and contains many volcanic peaks. Volcanic eruptions are frequent.

The Petén region in the north contains important resources and archaeological sites of the Mayan civilization.

**Government.** On December 8, 1986, Mario Vinicio Cerezo, a left-of-center Christian Democrat, won in elections that were generally free from military interference. A 100-seat Congress was also elected.

Both the President and the Congress are elected for five-year terms and the President may not be re-elected.

**History.** Once the site of the ancient Mayan civilization, Guatemala, conquered by Spain in 1524, set itself up as a republic in 1839. From 1898 to 1920, the dictator Manuel Estrada Cabrera ran the country, and from 1931 to 1944, Gen. Jorge Ubico Castaneda was the strongman. In 1944 the National Assembly elected Gen. Federico Ponce president, but he was overthrown in October. In December, Dr. Juan José Arévalo was elected as the head of a leftist regime that continued to press its reform program. Jacobo Arbenz Guzmán, administration candidate with pro-Communist leanings, won the 1950 elections.

Arbenz expropriated the large estates, including

plantations of the United Fruit Company. With covert U.S. backing, a revolt was led by Col. Carlos Castillo Armas, and Arbenz took refuge in Mexico. Castillo Armas became president but was assassinated in 1957. Constitutional government was restored in 1958, and Gen. Miguel Ydigoras Fuentes was elected president.

A wave of terrorism, by left and right, began in 1967, and in August 1968 U.S. Ambassador John Gordon Mein was killed when he resisted kidnappers. Fear of anarchy led to the election in 1970 of Army Chief of Staff Carlos Araña Osorio, who had put down a rural guerrilla movement at the cost of nearly 3,000 lives. Araña, surprisingly, pledged social reforms when he took office. Another military candidate, Gen. Kjell Laugerud, won the presidency in 1974 amid renewed political violence.

The administration of Gen. Romeo Lucas Garcia, elected president in 1978, ended in a coup by a three-man military junta on March 23, 1982. Lucas Garcia was charged by Amnesty International with responsibility for at least 5,000 political murders in a reign of brutality and corruption that brought a cutoff of U.S. military aid in 1978. Hopes for improvement under the junta faded when Gen. José Efraín Ríos Montt took sole power in June.

President Oscar Mejía Victores, another general, seized power from Rios Montt in an August 1983 coup and pledged to turn over power to an elected civilian President in 1985. A constituent assembly was elected on July 1, 1984, to write a new Constitution.

**Government.** Military government headed by President Lansana Conté, who promoted himself from colonel to brigadier general after a 1984 coup.

**History.** Previously part of French West Africa, Guinea achieved independence by rejecting the new French Constitution, and on Oct. 2, 1958, became an independent state with Sékou Touré as president. Touré led the country into being the first avowedly Marxist state in Africa. Diplomatic relations with France were suspended in 1965, with the Soviet Union replacing France as the country's chief source of economic and technical assistance.

In 1966, when a Ghanaian military coup deposed Kwame Nkrumah as President, Touré welcomed him to Guinea and declared him joint president and party leader. The titles proved to be only honorary.

Prosperity came in 1960 after the start of exploitation of bauxite deposits. Touré was re-elected to a seven-year term in 1974 and again in 1981.

After 26 years as President, Touré died in the United States in March 1984, following surgery. A week later, a military regime headed by Col. Lansana Conté took power with a promise not to shed any more blood after Touré's harsh rule. Conté became President and his co-conspirator in the coup, Col. Diara Traoré, became Prime Minister, but Conté later demoted Traoré to Education Minister. Traoré tried to seize power on July 4, 1985, while Conté was out of the country, but his attempted coup was crushed by troops loyal to Conté, and Conté announced that Traoré would be shot by firing squad without delay.

# GUINEA

**Republic of Guinea**
**President:** Brig. Gen. Lansana Conté (1984)
**Area:** 94,925 sq mi. (245,857 sq km)
**Population (est. mid-1986):** 6,200,000 (average annual growth rate: 2.3%)
**Density per square mile:** 65.3
**Capital and largest city (est. 1983):** Conakry, 656,000
**Monetary unit:** Syli
**Languages:** French (official), native tongues (Malinké, Susu, Fulani)
**Religions:** Islam, 69%; Animist, 30%
**National name:** République de Guinée
**Literacy rate:** 20%
**Economic summary:** Gross national product (1983): $1.74 billion. Annual growth rate (1984): 1.4%. Per capita income (1983): $300. Principal agricultural products: rice, cassava, millet, corn, coffee, bananas, pineapples. Major industrial products: bauxite, alumina, light manufactured and processed goods. Natural resources: bauxite, iron ore, diamonds, gold, water power. Exports: bauxite, alumina, pineapples, bananas, coffee. Imports: petroleum, machinery, transport equipment, foodstuffs, textiles. Major trading partners: U.S., France, W. Germany, U.K.

**Geography.** Guinea, in West Africa on the Atlantic, is also bordered by Guinea-Bissau, Senegal, Mali, the Ivory Coast, Liberia, and Sierra Leone. Slightly smaller than Oregon, the country consists of a coastal plain, a mountainous region, a savanna interior, and a forest area in the Guinea Highlands. The highest peak is Mount Nimba at about 6,000 feet (1,829 m).

# GUINEA-BISSAU

**Republic of Guinea-Bissau**
**President of Revolutionary Council:** João Bernardo Vieira (1980)
**Area:** 13,948 sq mi. (36,125 sq km)
**Population (est. mid-1986):** 900,000 (average annual growth rate: 1.9%)
**Density per square mile:** 64.5
**Capital and largest city (est. 1980):** Bissau, 110,000
**Monetary unit:** Guinea-Bissau peso
**Language:** Portugese
**Religions:** Animist, 65%; Islam, 30%; Christian, 5%
**National name:** Guiné Bissau
**Literacy rate:** 9%
**Economic summary:** Gross national product (1983): $150 million. Annual growth rate (1983): −5.1%. Per capita income (1983): $180. Labor force in agriculture: 90%; principal products: palm oil, root crops, rice, coconuts, peanuts. Natural resources: potential bauxite deposits. Exports: peanuts, coconuts, shrimp, fish, wood. Imports: foodstuffs, manufactured goods, fuels, transportation equipment. Major trading partner: Portugal.

**Geography.** A neighbor of Senegal and Guinea in West Africa, on the Atlantic coast, Guinea-Bissau is about half the size of South Carolina.

The country is a low-lying coastal region of swamps, rain forests, and mangrove-covered wetlands, with about 25 islands off the coast. The Bijagos archipelago extends 30 miles (48 km) out to sea. Internal communications depend mainly on deep estuaries and meandering rivers, since there are no railroads. Bissau, the capital, is the main port.

**Government.** After the overthrow of Louis Cabral in November 1980, the nine-member Council of the Revolution formed an interm government. In 1982, they formed a new government consisting of the President, the Prime Minister, 13 ministers, 2 vice-ministers, and 5 state secretaries.

**History.** Guinea-Bissau was discovered in 1446 by the Portuguese Nuno Tristao, and colonists in the Cape Verde Islands obtained trading rights in the territory. In 1879 the connection with the Cape Verde Islands was broken. Early in the 1900s the Portuguese managed to pacify some tribesmen, although resistance to colonial rule remained.

The African Party for the Independence of Guinea-Bissau and Cape Verde was founded in 1956 and several years later began guerrilla warfare that grew increasingly effective. By 1974 the rebels controlled most of the countryside, where they formed a government that was soon recognized by scores of countries. The military coup in Portugal in April 1974 brightened the prospects for freedom, and in August the Lisbon government signed an agreement granting independence to the province as of Sept. 10. The new republic took the name Guinea-Bissau. Its government was immediately recognized by the United States.

In November 1980, Prémier João Bernardo Vieira headed a coup that deposed Luis Cabral, President since 1974. A Revolutionary Council assumed the powers of government, with Vieira as its head.

# GUYANA

**Cooperative Republic of Guyana**
**President:** Desmond Hoyte (1985)
**Area:** 83,000 sq mi. (214,969 sq km)
**Population (est. mid-1986):** 800,000 (average annual growth rate: 2.2%) (East Indian, 51%; African, 30%; mixed 10%; Amerindian, 5%)
**Density per square mile:** 9.6
**Capital and largest city (est. 1981):** Georgetown, 200,000
**Monetary unit:** Guyana dollar
**Languages:** English (official), Hindi, Urdu
**Religions:** Hindu, 34%; Protestant, 18%; Islam, 9%; Roman Catholic, 18%; Anglican, 16%
**Member of Commonwealth of Nations**
**Literacy rate:** 86%
**Economic summary:** Gross national product (1983): $410 million. Average annual growth rate (1982): −10%. Per capita income (1983): $465. Labor force in agriculture: 34%; principal products: sugar, rice. Labor force in industry: 22%; major products: bauxite, alumina. Natural resources: bauxite, gold, diamonds, hardwood timber, shrimp. Exports: sugar, bauxite, alumina, rice, timber. Imports: fuels, machinery. Major trading partners: U.K., U.S., Trinidad, Venezuela.

**Geography.** Guyana is situated on the northern coast of South America east of Venezuela, west of Suriname, and north of Brazil. The country consists of a low coastal area and the Guiana Highlands in the south. There is an extensive north-south network of rivers. Guyana is the size of Idaho.

**Government.** Guyana, formerly British Guiana, proclaimed itself a republic on Feb. 23, 1970, ending its tie with Britain while remaining in the Commonwealth.

Guyana has a unicameral legislature, the National Assembly, with 53 members directly elected for five-year terms and 12 elected by local councils. A 24-member Cabinet is headed by the President.

The major political parties are the People's National Congress (41 of 53 seats in National Assembly), led by President Desmond Hoyte; People's Progressive Party (10 seats), led by Dr. Cheddi B. Jagan.

**History.** British Guiana won internal self-government in 1952. The next year the People's Progressive Party, headed by Cheddi B. Jagan, an East Indian dentist, won the elections and Jagan became Prime Minister. British authorities deposed him for alleged Communist connections. A coalition ousted Jagan in 1964, installing a moderate Socialist, Forbes Burnham, a black, as Prime Minister. On May 26, 1966, the country became an independent member of the Commonwealth and resumed its traditional name, Guyana.

After ruling Guyana for 21 years, Burnham died on Aug. 6 1985, in a Guyana hospital after a throat operation. Desmond Hoyte, the country's Prime Minister succeeded him under the Guyanese constitution.

# HAITI

**Republic of Haiti**
**Council President:** Lt. Gen. Henri Namphry (1986)
**Area:** 10,714 sq mi. (27,750 sq km)
**Population (est. mid-1986):** 5,900,000 (average annual growth rate: 2.3%)
**Density per square mile:** 579.9
**Capital and largest city (est. 1980):** Port-au-Prince, 790,000
**Monetary unit:** Gourde
**Languages:** French, Creole
**Religion:** Roman Catholic
**National name:** République d'Haïti
**Literacy rate:** 23%
**Economic summary:** Gross national product (1984): $1.8 billion. Annual growth rate (1984): 2.0%. Per capita income (1983): $333. Land used for agriculture: 31%; labor force: 79%; principal products: coffee, sugar cane, corn, sorghum. Labor force in industry: 7%; major products: refined sugar, textiles, flour, cement, light assembly products. Natural resource: bauxite. Exports: coffee, light industrial products, sugar, cocoa, sisal. Imports: consumer goods, foodstuffs, industrial equipment, petroleum products. Major trading partner: U.S.

**Geography.** Haiti, in the West Indies, occupies the western third of the island of Hispaniola, which it shares with the Dominican Republic. About the size of Maryland, Haiti is two thirds mountainous, with the rest of the country marked by great valleys, extensive plateaus, and small plains. The most densely populated region is the Cul-de-Sac plain near Port-au-Prince.

**Government.** In the face of public protests that began November, 1985, and increased in intensity, Duvalier fled the country on February 7 to an uneasy exile in France. The army chief of staff, Lt. Gen. Henri Namphry, established a governing council with himself as head.

**History.** Discovered by Columbus, who landed at Môle Saint Nicolas on Dec. 6, 1492, Haiti in 1697 became a French possession known as Saint Domingue. An insurrection among a slave population of 500,000 in 1791 ended with a declaration of independence by Pierre-Dominique Toussaint l'Ouverture in 1801. Napoleon Bonaparte suppressed the independence movement, but it eventually triumphed in 1804 under Jean-Jacques Dessalines, who gave the new nation the aboriginal name Haiti.

Its prosperity dissipated in internal strife as well as disputes with neighboring Santo Domingo during a succession of 19th-century dictatorships, a bankrupt Haiti accepted a U.S. customs receivership from 1905 to 1941. Direct U.S. rule from 1915 to 1934 brought a measure of stability and a population growth that made Haiti the most densely populated nation in the hemisphere.

In 1949, after four years of democratic rule by President Dumarsais Estimé, dictatorship returned under Gen. Paul Magloire, who was succeeded by François Duvalier in 1957.

Duvalier established a dictatorship based on secret police, known as the "Ton-ton Macoutes," who gunned down opponents of the regime. Duvalier's son, Jean-Claude, or "Baby Doc," succeeded his father in 1971 as ruler of the poorest nation in the Western Hemisphere.

The ruling council that took power upon the exile of Duvalier has been plagued by protests against the inclusion of former Duvalier aides in the council and by the slow pace of reform.

# HONDURAS

**Republic of Honduras**
**President:** José Azeona H. (1986)
**Area:** 43,277 sq mi. (112,088 sq km)
**Population (est. mid-1986):** 4,600,000 (average annual growth rate: 3.2%) (60% mestizo)
**Density per square mile:** 106.3
**Capital and largest city (1984):** Tegucigalpa, 539,600
**Monetary unit:** Lempira
**Languages:** Spanish, some Indian dialects, English in Bay Islands Department
**Religion:** Roman Catholic
**National name:** República de Honduras
**Literacy rate:** 56%
**Economic summary:** Gross national product (1984): $2.9 billion. Growth rate (1984): 2.4%. Per capita income (1984): $815. Labor force in agriculture: 59%; principal products: bananas, coffee, corn, beans, cotton, sugar cane, tobacco. Labor force in industry: 14%; major products: processed agricultural products, textiles and clothing, wood products. Natural resources: timber, gold, silver, lead, zinc, antimony. Exports: bananas, coffee, lumber, meat, petroleum products, tobacco, sugar, shrimp and lobster. Imports: manufactured goods, machinery, transportation equipment, chemicals, petroleum. Major trading partners: U.S., Caribbean countries, West Germany, Venezuela, Japan, Spain, Netherlands.

**Geography.** Honduras, in the north central part of Central America, has a 400-mile (644-km) Caribbean coastline and a 40-mile (64-km) Pacific frontage. Its neighbors are Guatemala to the west, El Salvador to the south, and Nicaragua to the east. Honduras is slightly larger than Tennessee.

Generally mountainous, the country is marked by fertile plateaus, river valleys, and narrow coastal plains.

**Government.** José Azcona was elected to succeed Roberto Suazo Córdova. He was inaugurated on January 27, 1986.

**History.** Columbus discovered Honduras on his last voyage in 1502. Honduras, with four other countries of Central America, declared its independence from Spain in 1821 and was part of a federation of Central American states until 1838. In that year it seceded from the federation and became a completely independent country.

U.S. Marines intervened in 1903 and 1923. In 1931, 1932, and 1937, major revolutions were crushed by force.

In July 1969, El Salvador invaded Honduras after Honduran landowners had deported several thousand Salvadorans. The fighting left 1,000 dead and tens of thousands homeless. By threatening economic sanctions and military intervention, the OAS induced El Salvador to withdraw.

Although parliamentary democracy returned with the election of Roberto Suazo Córdova as President in 1982 after a decade of military rule, Honduras faced severe economic problems and tensions along its border with Nicaragua. An estimated 12,000 "contra" rebels, waging a guerrilla war against the Sandinista regime in Nicaragua, used Honduras as a training and staging area. At the same time, the United States used Honduras as a site for military exercises and built bases to train both Honduran and Salvadoran troops. Honduras received $125 million in U.S. economic and military aid in 1984.

# HUNGARY

**Hungarian People's Republic**
**President:** Pál Losonczi (1967)
**Premier:** Gyorgy Lazar (1975)
**Area:** 35,919 sq mi. (93,030 sq km)
**Population (est. mid-1986):** 10,600,000 (average annual growth rate: -0.2%)
**Density per square mile:** 295.1
**Capital:** Budapest
**Largest cities (est. 1982):** Budapest, 2,100,000; Miskolc, 225,000; Debrecen, 215,000; Szeged, 200,000; Pécs, 195,000; Györ, 150,000
**Monetary unit:** Forint
**Language:** Magyar
**Religions:** Roman Catholic, 54%; Protestant, 22%; atheist, 7%
**National name:** Magyar Népköztársaság
**Literacy rate:** 98%
**Economic summary:** Gross national product (1984): $77 billion. Annual growth rate (1984): 1.3%. Per capita income (1984): $7,200. Land used for agriculture: 57%; labor force: 21%; principal products: corn, wheat, potatoes, sugar beets, vegetables, wine grapes, fruits. Labor force in industry: 32%; major products: steel, chemicals, pharmaceuticals, textiles, transport equipment. Natural resources: some bauxite and iron. Exports: machinery and tools, industrial and consumer goods, raw materials. Imports: machinery, raw materials. Major trading partners: U.S.S.R., Warsaw Pact countries, West Germany, Yugoslavia, Austria, and Italy.

**Geography.** This central European country the size

of Indiana is bordered by Austria to the west, Czechoslovakia to the north, the U.S.S.R. and Romania to the east, and Yugoslavia to the south.

Most of Hungary is a fertile, rolling plain lying east of the Danube River and drained by the Danube and Tisza rivers. In the extreme northwest is the Little Hungarian Plain. South of that area is Lake Balaton (250 sq mi.; 648 sq km).

**Government.** Hungary is a People's Republic with legislative power vested in the unicameral National Assembly, whose 352 members are elected directly for four-year terms. The supreme body of state power is the 21-member Presidential Council elected by the National Assembly. The supreme administrative body is the Council of Ministers, headed by the Premier.

The Hungarian Socialist Workers (Communist) Party, led by János Kádár, is the only political party.

**History.** About 2,000 years ago, Hungary was part of the Roman provinces of Pannonia and Dacia. In A.D. 896 it was invaded by the Magyars, who founded a kingdom. Christianity was accepted during the reign of Stephen I (St. Stephen) (997–1038).

The peak of Hungary's great period of medieval power came during the reign of Louis I the Great (1342–82), whose dominions touched the Baltic, Black, and Mediterranean seas.

War with the Turks broke out in 1389, and for more than 100 years the Turks advanced through the Balkans. When the Turks smashed a Hungarian army in 1526, western and northern Hungary accepted Hapsburg rule to escape Turkish occupation. Transylvania became independent under Hungarian princes. Intermittent war with the Turks was waged until a peace treaty was signed in 1699.

After the suppression of the 1848 revolt against Hapsburg rule, led by Louis Kossuth, the dual monarchy of Austria-Hungary was set up in 1867.

The dual monarchy was defeated with the other Central Powers in World War I. After a short-lived republic in 1918, the chaotic Communist rule of 1919 under Béla Kun ended with the Romanians occupying Budapest on Aug. 4, 1919. When the Romanians left, Adm. Nicholas Horthy entered the capital with a national army. The Treaty of Trianon of June 4, 1920, cost Hungary 68% of its land and 58% of its population. Meanwhile, the National Assembly had restored the legal continuity of the old monarchy; and, on March 1, 1920, Horthy was elected Regent.

Following the German invasion of Russia on June 22, 1941, Hungary joined the attack against the Soviet Union, but the war was not popular and Hungarian troops were almost entirely withdrawn from the eastern front by May 1943. German occupation troops set up a puppet government after Horthy's appeal for an armistice with advancing Soviet troops on Oct. 15, 1944, had resulted in his overthrow. The German regime soon fled the capital, however, and on December 23 a provisional government was formed in Soviet-occupied eastern Hungary. On Jan. 20, 1945, it signed an armistice in Moscow. Early the next year, the National Assembly approved a constitutional law abolishing the thousand-year-old monarchy and establishing a republic.

By the Treaty of Paris (1947), Hungary had to give up all territory it had acquired since 1937 and to pay $300 million reparations to the U.S.S.R., Czechoslovakia, and Yugoslavia. In 1948 the Communist Party, with the support of Soviet troops

seized control. Hungary was proclaimed a People's Republic and one-party state in 1949. Industry was nationalized, the land collectivized into state farms, and the opposition terrorized by the secret police.

The terror, modeled after that of the U.S.S.R., reached its height with the trial of Jozsef Cardinal Mindszenty, Roman Catholic primate. He confessed to fantastic charges under duress of drugs or brainwashing and was sentenced to life imprisonment in 1949. Protests were voiced in all parts of the world.

On Oct. 23, 1956, anti-Communist revolution broke out in Budapest. To cope with it, the Communists set up a coalition government and called former Premier Imre Nagy back to head it. But he and most of his ministers were swept by the logic of events into the anti-Communist opposition, and he declared Hungary a neutral power, withdrawing from the Warsaw Treaty and appealing to the United Nations for help.

One of his ministers, János Kádár, established a counter-regime and asked the U.S.S.R. to send in military power. Soviet troops and tanks suppressed the revolution in bloody fighting after 190,000 people had fled the country and Mindszenty, freed from jail, had taken refuge in the U.S. Embassy.

Kádár was succeeded as Premier, but not party secretary, by Gyula Kallai in 1965. Continuing his program of national reconciliation, Kádár emptied prisons, reformed the secret police, and eased travel restrictions.

Hungary developed the reputation of being the freest East European state.

After 15 years' asylum in the U.S. Embassy, Mindszenty, under an agreement between the Vatican and the Hungarian regime, was allowed to travel into exile to Rome in 1971. In a move applauded by Kádár, Pope Paul VI removed Mindszenty from his honorary post as Primate of Hungary in 1974. The Cardinal died in Vienna in 1975.

Relations with the U.S. improved in 1972 when World War II debt claims between the two nations were settled. On Jan. 6, 1978, the U.S. returned to Hungary, over anti-Communist protests, the 977-year-old crown of St. Stephen, held at Fort Knox since World War II.

# ICELAND

**Republic of Iceland**

**President:** Vigdis Finnbogadottir (1980)
**Prime Minister:** Steingrimur Hermannsson (1983)
**Area:** 39,709 sq mi. (102,846 sq km)
**Population (est. mid-1986):** 200,000 (average annual growth rate: 1.0%)
**Density per square mile:** 5.04
**Capital and largest city (est. 1983):** Reykjavik, 87,100
**Monetary unit:** New króna
**Language:** Icelandic
**Religion:** Evangelical Lutheran
**National name:** Lydveldid Island
**Literacy rate:** 99.9%
**Economic summary:** Gross national product (1984): $2.1 billion. Annual growth rate (1985): 1.5%. Per capita income (1984): $9,153. Labor force in agriculture: 9%; fishing and fish processing: 13.4%; principal agricultural products: livestock, hay, fodder, cheese. Labor force in industry: 17%; major products: processed aluminum, fish. Natural resources: fish, diatomite, hydroelectric and

geothermal power. Exports: fish, animal products, aluminum. Imports: petroleum products, machinery and transportation equipment, food, textiles. Major trading partners: U.S., U.S.S.R., Western European countries.

1. Including some offshore islands.

**Geography.** Iceland, an island about the size of Kentucky, lies in the north Atlantic Ocean east of Greenland and just touches the Arctic Circle. It is one of the most volcanic regions in the world.

Small fresh-water lakes are to be found throughout the island, and there are many natural phenomena, including hot springs, geysers, sulfur beds, canyons, waterfalls, and swift rivers. More than 13% of the area is covered by snowfields and glaciers, and most of the people live in the 7% of the island comprising fertile coastlands.

**Government.** The president is elected for four years by popular vote. Executive power resides in the prime minister and his Cabinet. The Althing (Parliament) is composed of 60 members in two houses. They elect 20 of themselves to constitute the Upper House, the remaining 40 representing the Lower House.

The major political parties are the Independence Party (23 of 60 seats in the Althing), led by Thorsteinn Pálsson; Progressive Party (14 seats), led by Steingrimur Hermannsson; People's Alliance (10 seats), led by Svavar Gestsson; Social Democratic Party (6 seats), led by Jon B. Hannibalsson; Social Democratic Alliance (4 seats), and the Women's League (3 seats). Prime Minister Steingrimur Hermannsson of the Progressives leads a coalition of his party and the Independence Party.

**History.** Iceland was first settled shortly before 900, mainly by Norse. A Constitution drawn up about 930 created a form of democracy and provided for an Althing, or General Assembly.

In 1262–64, Iceland came under Norwegian rule and passed to ultimate Danish control through the formation of the Union of Kalmar in 1483. In 1874, Icelanders obtained their own Constitution. In 1918, Denmark recognized Iceland as a separate state with unlimited sovereignty but still nominally under the Danish king.

On June 17, 1944, after a popular referendum, the Althing proclaimed Iceland an independent republic.

The British occupied Iceland in 1940, immediately after the German invasion of Denmark. In 1942, the U.S. took over the burden of protection. Iceland refused to abandon its neutrality in World War II and thus forfeited charter membership in the United Nations, but it cooperated with the Allies throughout the conflict. Iceland joined the North Atlantic Treaty Organization in 1949.

Iceland unilaterally extended its territorial waters from 12 to 50 nautical miles in 1972, precipitating a running dispute with Britain known as the "cod war." Icelandic warships harassed British trawlers, which then received aid from British gunboats; some trawlers were shelled, and Icelandic and British warships collided in 1973. The World Court ruled in 1974 and that the 50-mile limit could not be applied unilaterally, but Iceland rejected the ruling.

An agreement calling for registration of all British trawlers fishing within 200 miles of Iceland and a 24-hour time limit on incursions was finally reached in 1976.

# INDIA
**Republic of India**
**President:** Giani Zail Singh (1982)
**Prime Minister:** Rajiv Gandhi (1984)
**Area:** 1,229,737 sq mi. (3,185,019 sq km)
**Population (est. mid-1986):** 785,000,000 (average annual growth rate: 2.3%)
**Density per square mile:** 638.3
**Capital (1980 census):** New Delhi, 619,417
**Largest cities (1981 est.):** Calcutta, 9,194,018; Greater Bombay, 8,243,405; Delhi, 5,729,283; Madras, 4,289,347; Bangalore, 2,921,751; Ahmedabad, 2,548,-057; Kanpur, 1,639,064
**Monetary unit:** Rupee
**Principal languages:** Hindi (official), Bengali, Sindhi, Gujarati, Kannarese, Kashmiri, Malayalam, Marathi, Oriya, Punjabi, Tamil, Telugu, Urdu, Kannada, Assamese (all recognized by the Constitution)
**Religions:** Hindu, 83%; Islam, 11%; Christian, 3%; Sikh, 2%
**National name:** Bharat
**Literacy rate:** 36%
**Member of Commonwealth of Nations**
**Economic summary:** Gross national product (1984): $193 billion. Average annual growth rate (1983–84): 8.0%. Per capita income (1984): $240. Land used for agriculture: 57%; labor force: 63%; principal products: rice, wheat, oilseeds, cotton, tea. Major industrial products: jute, processed food, steel, machinery, transport machinery, cement. Natural resources: iron ore, coal, manganese, mica, bauxite, limestone. Exports: diamonds, iron goods, textiles and clothing, tea. Imports: machinery and transport equipment, petroleum, edible oils, fertilizers. Major trading partners: U.S., U.S.S.R., Japan, Saudi Arabia.

**Geography.** One third the area of the United States, the Republic of India occupies most of the subcontinent of India in south Asia. It borders on China in the northeast. Other neighbors are Pakistan on the west, Nepal and Bhutan on the north, and Burma and Bangladesh on the east.

The country contains a large part of the great Indo-Gangetic plain, which extends from the Bay of Bengal on the east to the Afghan frontier on the Arabian Sea on the west. This plain is the richest and most densely settled part of the subcontinent. Another distinct natural region is the Deccan, a plateau of 2,000 to 3,000 feet (610 to 914 m) in elevation, occupying the southern portion of the subcontinent.

Forming a part of the republic are several groups of islands—the Laccadives (14 islands) in the Arabian Sea and the Andamans (204 islands) and the Nicobars (19 islands) in the Bay of Bengal.

India's three great river systems, all rising in the Himalayas, have extensive deltas. The Ganges flows south and then east for 1,540 miles (2,478 km) across the northern plain to the Bay of Bengal; part of its delta, which begins 220 miles (354 km) from the sea, is within the republic. The Indus, starting in Tibet, flows northwest for several hundred miles in the Kashmir before turning southwest toward the Arabian Sea; it is important for irrigation in Pakistan. The Brahmaputra, also rising in Tibet, flows eastward, first through India and then south into Bangladesh and the Bay of Bengal.

**Government.** India is a federal republic. It is also a member of the Commonwealth of Nations, a status defined at the 1949 London Conference of Prime Ministers, by which India recognizes

Queen as head of the Commonwealth. Under the Constitution effective Jan. 26, 1950, India has a parliamentary type of government.

The constitutional head of the state is the President, who is elected every five years. He is advised by the Prime Minister and a Cabinet based on a majority of the bicameral Parliament, which consists of a Council of States (Rajya Sabha), representing the constituent units of the republic and a House of the People (Lok Sabha), elected every five years by universal suffrage.

The major political parties are Congress Party I (351 of 542 seats in the Lok Sabha), led by Prime Minister Rajiv Gandhi; Lok Dal (secular Janata) Party (41 seats), led by former Prime Minister Charan Singh; Congress II (anti-Gandhi) Party (13 seats); Communist (Marxist independent) Party (35 seats); Communist (pro-Soviet) Party of India (10 seats).

**History.** The Aryans, or Hindus, who invaded India between 2400 and 1500 B.C. from the northwest found a land already well civilized. Buddhism was founded in the 6th century B.C. and spread through northern India. The earliest exact date in Indian history is 327 B.C., when Alexander the Great invaded India.

In 1526, Moslem invaders founded the great Mogul empire, centered on Delhi, which lasted, at least in name, until 1857. Akbar the Great (1542–1605) strengthened this empire and became the ruler of a greater portion of India than had ever before acknowledged the suzerainty of one man. The long reign of his great-grandson, Aurangzeb (1658–1707), represents both the culmination of Mogul power and the beginning of its decay.

Vasco da Gama, the Portuguese explorer, visited India first in 1498, and for the next 100 years the Portuguese had a virtual monopoly on trade with the subcontinent. Meanwhile, the English founded the East India Company, which set up its first factory at Surat in 1612 and began expanding its influence, fighting the Indian rulers and the French, Dutch, and Portuguese traders simultaneously.

Bombay, taken from the Portuguese, became the seat of English rule in 1687. The defeat of French and Islamic armies by Lord Clive in the decade ending in 1760 laid the foundation of the British Empire in India. From then until 1858, when the administration of India was formally transferred to the British Crown following the Sepoy Mutiny of native troops in 1857, the East India Company suppressed native uprisings and extended British rule.

After World War I, in which the Indian states sent more than 6 million troops to fight beside the Allies, Indian nationalist unrest rose to new heights under the leadership of a little Hindu lawyer, Mohandas K. Gandhi, called Mahatma Gandhi. His tactics called for nonviolent revolts against British authority. He soon became the leading spirit of the All-India Congress Party, which was the spearhead of revolt. In 1919 the British gave added responsibility to Indian officials, and in 1935 India was given a federal form of government and a measure of self-rule.

In 1942, with the Japanese pressing hard on the eastern borders of India, the British War Cabinet tried and failed to reach a political settlement with nationalist leaders. The Congress Party took the position that the British must quit India. In 1942, fearing mass civil disobedience, the government of India carried out widespread arrests of Congress leaders, including Gandhi.

Gandhi was released in 1944 and negotiations for a settlement were resumed. Finally, in February 1947, the Labor government announced its determination to transfer power to "responsible Indian hands" by June 1948 even if a Constitution had not been worked out.

Lord Mountbatten as Viceroy, by June 1947, achieved agreement on the partitioning of India along religious lines and on the splitting of the provinces of Bengal and the Punjab, which the Moslems had claimed.

The Indian Independence Act, passed quickly by the British Parliament, received royal assent on July 18, 1947, and on August 15 the Indian Empire passed into history.

Jawaharlal Nehru, leader of the Congress Party, was made Prime Minister. Before an exchange of populations could be arranged, bloody riots occurred among the communal groups, and armed conflict broke out over rival claims to the princely state of Jammu and Kashmir. Peace was restored only with the greatest difficulty. In 1949 a Constitution, along the lines of the U.S. Constitution, was approved making India a sovereign republic. Under a federal structure the states were organized on linguistic lines.

The dominance of the Congress Party contributed to stability. In 1956 the republic absorbed the former French settlements. Five years later, it forcibly annexed the Portuguese enclaves of Goa, Damao, and Diu.

Nehru died in 1964. His successor, Lal Bahadur Shastri, died on Jan. 10, 1966. Nehru's daughter, Indira Gandhi, became Prime Minister, and she continued his policy of nonalignment.

In 1971 the Pakistani Army moved in to quash the independence movement in East Pakistan that was supported by clandestine aid from India, and some 10 million Bengali refugees poured across the border into India, creating social, economic, and health problems. After numerous border incidents, India invaded East Pakistan and in two weeks forced the surrender of the Pakistani army. East Pakistan was established as an independent state and renamed Bangladesh.

In the summer of 1975, the world's largest democracy veered suddenly toward authoritarianism when a judge in Allahabad, Mrs. Gandhi's home constituency, found her landslide victory in the 1971 elections invalid because civil servants had illegally aided her campaign. Amid demands for her resignation, Mrs. Gandhi decreed a state of emergency on June 26 and ordered mass arrests of her critics, including all opposition party leaders except the Communists.

In 1976, India and Pakistan formally renewed diplomatic relations.

Despite strong opposition to her repressive measures and particularly the resentment against compulsory birth control programs, Mrs. Gandhi in 1977 announced parliamentary elections for March. At the same time, she freed most political prisoners.

The landslide victory of Morarji R. Desai unseated Mrs. Gandhi and also defeated a bid for office by her son, Sanjay.

Mrs. Gandhi staged a spectacular comeback in the elections of January 1980.

In 1984, Mrs. Gandhi ordered the Indian Army to root out a band of Sikh holy men and gunmen who were using the holiest shrine of the Sikh religion, the Golden Temple in Amritsar, as a base for terrorist raids in a violent campaign for greater political autonomy in the strategic Punjab border state. As many as 1,000 people were reported killed in the June 5–6 battle, including Jarnall Singh Bhindranwale, the Khomeini-like militant leader, and 93 soldiers. The perceived sacrilege to the Golden Temple kindled outrage among many of India's 14 million Sikhs and brought a spasm of mutinies and desertions by Sikh officers and soldiers in the army.

On Oct. 31, 1984, Mrs. Gandhi was assassinated by two men identified by police as Sikh members of her bodyguard. The ruling Congress I Party chose her second son, Rajiv Gandhi, to succeed her as Prime Minister.

On July 24, Rajiv Gandhi and moderate Sikh leaders agreed on a package of steps to ease Sikh hostility toward the government and end the turmoil in the state of Punjab. A key element called for a change in the Punjab boundaries to increase the Sikh population within the state and give it greater political influence. Prime Minister Gandhi also yielded to demands for more lenient treatment of Sikhs arrested in riots over the last three years. However, it was uncertain whether the settlement would be accepted by the most militant Sikhs.

**Native States.** Most of the 560-odd native states and subdivisions of pre-1947 India acceded to the new nation, and the central government pursued a vigorous policy of integration. This took three forms: merger into adjacent provinces, conversion into centrally administered areas, and grouping into unions of states. Finally, under a controversial reorganization plan effective Nov. 1, 1956, the unions of states were abolished and merged into adjacent states, and India became a union of 15 states and 8 centrally administered areas. A 16th state was added in 1962, and in 1966, the Punjab was partitioned into two states.

Resolution of the territorial dispute over Kashmir grew out of peace negotiations following the two-week India-Pakistan war of 1971. After sporadic skirmishing, an accord reached July 3, 1972, committed both powers to withdraw troops from a temporary cease-fire line after the border was fixed. Agreement on the border was reached Dec. 7, 1972.

In April 1975, the Indian Parliament voted to make the 300-year-old kingdom of Sikkim a full-fledged Indian state, and the annexation took effect May 16.

Situated in the Himalayas, Sikkim was a virtual dependency of Tibet until the early 19th century. Under an 1890 treaty between China and Great Britain, it became a British protectorate, and was made an Indian protectorate after Britain quit the subcontinent.

# INDONESIA

**Republic of Indonesia**
**President:** Suharto (1969)[1]
**Area:** 735,268 sq mi. (1,904,344 sq km)[2]
**Population (est. mid-1986):** 168,400,000 (average annual growth rate: 2.1%)
**Density per square mile:** 229
**Capital:** Jakarta
**Largest cities (est. 1983):** Jakarta, 7,636,000; Surabaja,

2,289,000; Bandung, 1,602,000; Medan, 1,966,000; Semarang, 1,269,000
**Monetary unit:** Rupiah
**Languages:** Bahasa Indonesia (official), Dutch, English, and more than 60 regional languages
**Religions:** Islam, 88%; Christian, 9%; Hindu, Buddhist
**National name:** Republik Indonesia
**Literacy rate:** 64%
**Economic summary:** Gross national product (1985): $90.3 billion. Average annual growth rate (1980–84): 5.9%. Per capita income (1985 est.): $540. Land used for agriculture: 9%; labor force: 66%; principal products: rice, cassava, sugarcane, rubber, coffee. Labor force in industry: 9%; major products: textiles, food and beverages, light manufactures, cement, fertilizer. Natural resources: oil, timber, nickel, natural gas, tin, bauxite, copper. Exports: petroleum and liquid natural gas, timber, rubber, coffee, tin. Imports: rice, wheat, textiles, chemicals, iron and steel. Major trading partners: Japan, U.S., Singapore.

---

1. General Suharto served as Acting President of Indonesia from 1967 to 1969. 2. Includes West Irian (former Netherlands New Guinea), renamed Irian Jaya in March 1973 (159,355 sq mi.; 412,731 sq km), and former Portuguese Timor (5,763 sq mi.; 14,925 sq km), annexed in 1976.

---

**Geography.** Indonesia is part of the Malay archipelago in Southeast Asia with an area nearly three times that of Texas. It consists of the islands of Sumatra, Java, Madura, Borneo (except Sarawak in the north), the Celebes, the Moluccas, and about 30 smaller archipelagos, totaling 13,677 islands, of which about 6,000 are inhabited. Its neighbor to the north is Malaysia and to the east Papua New Guinea.

A backbone of mountain ranges extends throughout the main islands of the archipelago. Earthquakes are frequent, and there are many active volcanoes.

**Government.** The President is elected by the People's Consultative Assembly, whose 920 members include the functioning legislative arm, the 464-member House of Representatives. Meeting at least once every five years, the Assembly has broad policy functions. The House, 100 of whose members are appointed by the President, meets at least once annually. General Suharto was elected unopposed to a fourth five-year term in 1983.

The major political parties are Sekber Golkar, 246 of 464 contested seats in the House; Islamic United Development Party, 94 seats; Democratic Party, 24 seats.

**History.** Indonesia is inhabited by Malayan and Papuan peoples ranging from the more advanced Javanese and Balinese to the more primitive Dyaks of Borneo. Invasions from China and India contributed Chinese and Indian admixtures.

During the first few centuries of the Christian era, most of the islands came under the influence of Hindu priests and traders, who spread their culture and religion. Moslem invasions began in the 13th century, and most of the area was Moslem by the 15th. Portuguese traders arrived early in the 16th century but were ousted by the Dutch about 1595. After Napoleon subjugated the Netherlands homeland in 1811, the British seized the islands but returned them to the Dutch in 1816. In 1922 the islands were made an integral part of the Netherlands kingdom.

During World War II, Indonesia was under Japanese military occupation with nominal native self-government. When the Japanese surrendered to the Allies, President Sukarno and Mohammed Hatta, his Vice President, proclaimed Indonesian independence from the Dutch on Aug. 17, 1945. Allied troops—mostly British Indian troops—fought the nationalists until the arrival of Dutch troops. In November 1946, the Dutch and the Indonesians reached a draft agreement contemplating formation of a Netherlands-Indonesian Union, but differences in interpretation resulted in more fighting between Dutch and Indonesian forces.

On Nov. 2, 1949, Dutch and Indonesian leaders agreed upon the terms of union. The transfer of sovereignty took place at Amsterdam on Dec. 27, 1949. In February 1956 Indonesia abrogated the Union with the Netherlands and in August 1956 repudiated its debt to the Netherlands. In 1963, Netherlands New Guinea was transferred to Indonesia and renamed West Irian. In 1973 it became Irian Jaya.

Hatta and Sukarno, the co-fathers of Indonesian independence, split after it was achieved over Sukarno's concept of "guided democracy." Under Sukarno, the country's leading political figure for almost a half century, the Indonesian Communist Party gradually gained increasing influence.

After an attempted coup was put down by General Suharto, the army chief of staff, and officers loyal to him, thousands of Communist suspects were sought out and killed all over the country. Suharto took over the reins of government, gradually eased Sukarno out of office, and took full power in 1967. Under President Suharto, Indonesia has been strongly anticommunist. It also has been politically stable and has made progress in economic development.

Indonesia invaded the former Portuguese half of the island of Timor in 1975, and annexed the territory in 1976. On a visit to Jakarta in July 1984, Secretary of State George P. Shultz expressed concern about reports of human rights abuses being carried out by Indonesian forces in East Timor. More than 100,000 Timorese, a sixth of the mostly Catholic population, was reported to have died from famine, disease, and fighting since the annexation.

# IRAN

**Islamic Republic of Iran**
**President:** Hojatolislam Sayed Ali Khamenei (1981)
**Prime Minister:** Mir Hussein Moussavi (1981)
**Area:** 636,293 sq mi. (1,648,000 sq km)
**Population (est. mid-1986):** 46,600,000 (average annual growth rate: 2.9%) (Iranian, Kurdish)
**Density per square mile:** 73.2
**Capital:** Teheran
**Largest cities (est. 1982):** Teheran, 6,000,000; Isfahan, 725,000; Mashed, 725,000; Tabriz, 650,000
**Monetary unit:** Rial
**Languages:** Farsi (Persian), Kurdish, Arabic
**Religions:** Shi'ite Moslem, 93%; Sunni Moslem, 5%
**Literacy rate:** 48%
**Economic summary:** Gross national product (1984): $80.4 billion. Per capita income (1982): $1,621. Land used for agriculture: 12%; Labor force: 33%; principal products: wheat, barley, rice, sugar beets, cotton, dates, raisins, sheep, goats. Labor force in industry: 21%; major products: crude and refined oil, textiles, cement, processed foods, steel and copper fabrication. Natural resources: oil, gas, iron, copper. Exports: petroleum. Imports: machinery, military supplies, foodstuffs,

pharmaceuticals. Major trading partners: Japan, West Germany, U.K., Italy, U.S.S.R., Switzerland, Austria

**Geography.** Iran, a Middle Eastern country south of the Caspian Sea and north of the Persian Gulf, is three times the size of Arizona. It shares borders with Iraq, Turkey, the U.S.S.R., Afghanistan, and Pakistan.

In general, the country is a plateau averaging 4,000 feet (1,219 m) in elevation. There are also maritime lowlands along the Persian Gulf and the Caspian Sea. The Elburz Mountains in the north rise to 18,603 feet (5,670 m) at Mt. Damavend. From northwest to southeast, the country is crossed by a desert 800 miles (1,287 km) long.

**Government.** The Pahlavi dynasty was overthrown on Feb. 11, 1979, by followers of the Ayatollah Ruhollah Khomeini. After a referendum endorsed the establishment of a republic, Khomeini drafted a Constitution calling for a President to be popularly elected every four years, an appointed Prime Minister, and a unicameral National Consultative Assembly, popularly elected every four years.

Khomeini also instituted a Revolutionary Council to insure the adherence to Islamic principles in all phases of Iranian life. The Council formally handed over its powers to the Assembly after the organization of the legislature in July 1980, but continued to exercise power as a sort of shadow government.

**History.** Oil-rich Iran was called Persia before 1935. Its key location blocks the lower land gate to Asia and also stands in the way of traditional Russian ambitions for access to the Indian Ocean. After periods of Assyrian, Median, and Achaemenidian rule, Persia became a powerful empire under Cyrus the Great, reaching from the Indus to the Nile at its zenith in 525 B.C. It fell to Alexander in 331–30 B.C. and to the Seleucids in 312–02 B.C., and a native Persian regime arose about 130 B.C. Another Persian regime arose about A.D. 224, but it fell to the Arabs in 637. In the 12th century, the Mongols took their turn ruling Persia, and in the early part of the 18th century, the Turks occupied the country.

An Anglo-Russian convention of 1907 divided Persia into two spheres of influence. British attempts to impose a protectorate over the entire country were defeated in 1919. Two years later, Gen. Reza Pahlavi seized the government and was elected hereditary Shah in 1925. Subsequently he did much to modernize the country and abolished all foreign extraterritorial rights.

Increased pro-Axis activity led to Anglo-Russian occupation of Iran in 1941 and deposition of the Shah in favor of his son, Mohammed Reza Pahlavi.

Ali Razmara became premier in 1950 and pledged to restore efficient and honest government, but he was assassinated after less than nine months in office and Mohammed Mossadegh took over. Mossadegh was ousted in August 1953, by Fazollah Zahedi, whom the Shah had named premier.

Opposition to the Shah spread, despite the imposition of martial law in September 1978, and massive demonstrations demanded the return of the exiled Ayatollah Ruhollah Khomeini. Riots and strikes continued despite the appointment of an opposition leader, Shahpur Bakhtiar, as premier on Dec. 29. The Shah and his family left Iran on Jan. 16, 1979, for a "vacation," leaving power in the hands of a regency council.

Khomeini returned on Feb. 1 to a nation in turmoil as military units loyal to the Shah continued to support Bakhtiar and clashed with revolutionaries. Khomeini appointed Mehdi Bazargan as premier of the provisional government and in two days of fighting, revolutionaries forced the military to capitulate on Feb. 11.

The new government began a program of nationalization of insurance companies, banks, and industries both locally and foreign-owned. Oil production fell amid the political confusion.

Khomeini, ignoring opposition, proceeded with his plans for revitalizing Islamic traditions. He urged women to return to the veil, or chador; banned alcohol and mixed bathing, and prohibited music from radio and television broadcasting, declaring it to be "no different from opium."

Revolutionary militants invaded the U.S. Embassy in Teheran on Nov. 4, 1979, seized staff members as hostages, and precipitated an international crisis.

Khomeini refused all appeals, even a unanimous vote by the U.N. Security Council demanding immediate release of the hostages.

Iranian hostility toward Washington was reinforced by the Carter administration's economic boycott and deportation order against Iranian students in the U.S., the break in diplomatic relations and ultimately an aborted U.S. raid in April aimed at rescuing the hostages.

Even the death of the deposed Shah Mohammed Reza Pahlavi on July 17 had no effect. As the first anniversary of the embassy seizure neared, Khomeini and his followers insisted on their original conditions: guarantee by the U.S. not to interfere in Iran's affairs, cancellation of U.S. damage claims against Iran, release of $8 billion in frozen Iranian assets, an apology, and the return of the assets held by the former imperial family.

These conditions were largely met in an agreement signed by Deputy Secretary of State Warren Christopher on Jan. 19 and the 52 American hostages were released the following day, ending 444 days in captivity.

From the release of the hostages onward, President Bani-Sadr and the conservative clerics of the dominant Islamic Republican Party clashed with growing frequency. He was stripped of his command of the armed forces by Khomeini on June 6 and ousted as President on June 22. On July 24, Prime Minister Mohammed Ali Rajai was elected overwhelmingly to the Presidency.

Rajai and Prime Minister Mohammed Javad Bahonar were killed on Aug. 30 by a bomb in Bahonar's office.

Hojatolislam Mohammed Ali Khamenei, a clergyman, leader of the Islamic Republican Party and spokesman for Khomeini, was elected President on Oct. 2, 1981.

The sporadic war with Iraq regained momentum in 1982, as Iran launched an offensive in March and regained much of the border area occupied by Iraq in late 1980. Khomeini rejected Iraqi bids for a truce, insisting that Iraq's President Saddam Hussein must leave office first.

Iran continued to be at war with Iraq well into 1985. Although Iraq expressed its willingness to cease fighting, Iran stated that it would not stop the war until Iraq agreed to make payment for war damages to Iran, and punish the Iraqi government leaders involved in the conflict. The fighting spread into the Persian Gulf in 1984, with Iraq using French-made Exocet air-to-surface missiles to attack tankers loading at Iran's Kharg Island, and Iran striking back at tankers calling at Saudi Arabia and the smaller, oil-rich Arab Gulf states.

On June 23, 1985, Iran signed an agreement with Libya, its only ally, to increase mutual cooperation.

# IRAQ

**Republic of Iraq**
**President:** Saddam Hussein (1979)
**Area:** 169,284 sq mi. (438,446 sq km)
**Population (est. mid-1986):** 16,000,000 (average annual growth rate: 3.3%) (Arab, 77%; Kurds, 19%)
**Density per square mile:** 94.5
**Capital:** Baghdad
**Largest cities (est. 1982):** Baghdad, 3,300,000; Basra, 375,000; Mosul, 350,000; Kirkuk, 250,000; An Najaf, 225,000
**Monetary unit:** Iraqi dinar
**Languages:** Arabic and Kurdish
**Religions:** Islam, 96%; Christian, 4%
**National name:** Al Jumhouriya Al Iraqia
**Literacy rate:** about 50%
**Economic summary:** Gross national product (1984 est.): $27 billion. Average annual growth rate (1970–79): 9.3%. Per capita income (1981): $2,300. Average rate of inflation (1976–78): 10%. Land used for agriculture, 13%; labor force, 40%; principal products: livestock, wheat, barley, sugarcane, rice. Labor force in industry: 27%; major products: petroleum, cement, textiles. Natural resources: oil, natural gas, gypsum, sulfur. Exports: petroleum, foodstuffs. Imports: manufactured goods, food grains, machinery, chemicals, livestock. Major trading partners: France, Italy, Japan, West Germany, Brazil, U.K., U.S., Pakistan

**Geography.** Iraq, a triangle of mountains, desert, and fertile river valley, is bounded on the east by Iran, on the north by Turkey, the west by Syria and Jordan, and the south by Saudi Arabia and Kuwait. It is twice the size of Idaho.

The country has arid desertland west of the Euphrates, a broad central valley between the Euphrates and Tigris, and mountains in the northeast. The fertile lower valley is formed by the delta of the two rivers, which join about 120 miles (193 km) from the head of the Persian Gulf. The gulf coastline is 26 miles (42 km) long. The only port for seagoing vessels is Basra, which is on the Shatt-al-Arab River near the head of the Persian Gulf.

**Government.** Since the coup d'etat of July 1968, Iraq has been governed by the Arab Ba'ath Socialist Party through a Council of Command of the Revolution headed by the President. There is also a Council of Ministers headed by the President.

**History.** From earliest times Iraq was known as Mesopotamia—the land between the rivers—for it embraces a large part of the alluvial plains of the Tigris and Euphrates.

An advanced civilization existed by 4000 B.C. Sometime after 2000 B.C. the land became the center of the ancient Babylonian and Assyrian empires. It was conquered by Cyrus the Great of Persia in 538 B.C., and by Alexander in 331 B.C. After an Arab conquest in A.D. 637–40, Baghdad became capital of the ruling caliphate. The country was cruelly pillaged by the Mongols in 1258, and during the 16th, 17th, and 18th centuries was the object of repeated Turkish-Persian competition.

Nominal Turkish suzerainty imposed in 1638

was replaced by direct Turkish rule in 1831. In World War I, an Anglo-Indian force occupied most of the country, and Britain was given a mandate over the area in 1920. The British recognized Iraq as a kingdom in 1922 and terminated the mandate in 1932 when Iraq was admitted to the League of Nations. In World War II, Iraq generally adhered to its 1930 treaty of alliance with Britain, but in 1941, British troops were compelled to put down a pro-Axis revolt led by Premier Rashid Ali.

Iraq became a charter member of the Arab League in 1945, and Iraqi troops took part in the Arab invasion of Palestine in 1948.

Faisal II, born on May 2, 1935, succeeded his father, Ghazi I, who was killed in an automobile accident on April 4, 1939. Faisal and his uncle, Crown Prince Abdul-Ilah, were assassinated in August 1958 in a swift revolutionary coup that brought to power a military junta headed by Abdul Karem Kassim. Kassim, in turn, was overthrown and killed in a coup staged March 8, 1963, by the Ba'ath Socialist Party.

Abdel Salam Arif, a leader in the 1958 coup, staged another coup in November 1963, driving the Ba'ath members of the revolutionary council from power. He adopted a new constitution in 1964. In 1966, he, two Cabinet members, and other supporters died in a helicopter crash. His brother, Gen. Abdel Rahman Arif, assumed the presidency, crushed the opposition, and won an indefinite extension of his term in 1967. His regime was ousted in July 1968 by a junta led by Maj. Gen. Ahmed Hassan al-Bakr.

A long-standing dispute over control of the Shatt al-Arab waterway between Iraq and Iran broke into full-scale war on Sept. 20, 1980. Iraqi planes attacked Iranian airfields and the Abadan refinery, and Iraqi ground forces moved into Iran.

Despite the smaller size of its armed forces, Iraq took and held the initiative by seizing Abadan and Khurramshahr together with substantial Iranian territory by December and beating back Iranian counterattacks in January. Peace efforts by the Islamic nations, the nonaligned, and the United Nations failed as 1981 wore on and the war stagnated.

The Iraqis fell back to their own country and dug themselves in behind sandbagged defensive fortifications. With massive firepower, they turned back wave after wave of attacking Iranian troops and revolutionary guards, many of them in their teens. From the beginning of the war in September 1980 to September 1984, foreign military analysts estimated that more than 100,000 Iranians and perhaps 50,000 Iraqis had been killed.

The Iraqis clearly wanted to end the war, but the Iranians refused. In March of 1985, Iraq apparently won the largest battle of the long war, crushing a major Iranian offensive in the southern marshes in a week of heavy fighting that killed an estimated 30,000 Iranians and perhaps 10,000 Iraqis.

In February 1986, Iranian forces broke through on two fronts; on the Fao peninsula in the south and in the northern mountains, signaling a possible decay in the Iraqi military position.

# IRELAND

**President:** Patrick J. Hiliery (1976)
**Taoiseach (Prime Minister):** Garret FitzGerald (1982)
**Area:** 26,600 sq mi. (68,394 sq km)
**Population (est. mid-1986):** 3,600,000 (average annual growth rate, 0.9%)
**Density per square mile:** 135.3
**Capital:** Dublin
**Largest cities (est. 1982):** Dublin, 550,000; Cork, 140,000; Limerick, 60,000
**Monetary unit:** Irish pound (punt)
**Languages:** Irish, English
**Religions:** Roman Catholic, 94%; Protestant, 5%
**National name:** Eire
**Literacy rate:** 99%
**Economic summary:** Gross national product (1984): $16.0 billion. Average annual growth rate (1973–83): 2.2%; Per capita income (1984): $4,440. Land used for agriculture, 70%; labor force in agriculture and fishing: 17%; principal products: cattle and dairy products, pigs, poultry and eggs, sheep and wool, horses, barley, sugar beets. Labor force in industry: 30%; major products: processed foods, metals and engineering, electronics, beverages and tobacco, chemicals. Natural resources: zinc, lead, natural gas, barite, copper, gypsum, limestone, dolomite, peat, silver. Exports: livestock, dairy products, machinery, chemicals, processed foods, manufactured goods, raw materials and minerals. Imports: grains, petroleum products, machinery, chemicals, textile yarn, cereals. Major trading partners: U.K., Western European countries, U.S., Canada.

**Geography.** Ireland is situated in the Atlantic Ocean and separated from Britain by the Irish Sea. Half the size of Arkansas, it occupies the entire island except for the six northern counties of Ulster.

Ireland resembles a basin—a central plain rimmed with mountains, except in the Dublin region. The mountains are low, with the highest peak, Carrantuohill in County Kerry, rising to 3,415 feet (1,041 m).

The principal river is the Shannon, which begins in the north central area, flows south and southwest for about 240 miles (386 km), and empties into the Atlantic.

**Government.** Ireland is a parliamentary democracy. The National Parliament (Oireachtas) consists of the president and two Houses, the House of Representatives (Dáil Éireann) and the Senate (Seanad Éireann), whose members serve for a maximum term of five years. The House of Representatives has 166 members elected by proportional representation; the Senate has 60 members of whom 11 are nominated by the prime minister, 6 by the universities and the remaining 43 from five vocational panels. The prime minister (Taoiseach), who is the head of government, is appointed by the president on the nomination of the House of Representatives, to which he is responsible.

The major political parties are Fianna Fáil (72 of 166 seats in the Dáil), led by former Prime Minister Charles J. Haughey; Fine Gael (69 seats), led by Prime Minister Garret FitzGerald; Labor Party (16 seats), led by Dick Spring; Progressive Democrats (5), led by Desmond O'Malley; Workers Party (2 seats) led by Thomas MacGiolla; Independents (2 seats). The government is a coalition of the Fine Gael and Labor Parties.

**History.** In the Stone and Bronze Ages, Ireland was inhabited by Picts in the north and a people called the Erainn in the south, the same stock, apparently, as in all the isles before the Anglo-Saxon invasion of Britain. About the fourth century B.C., tall, red-haired Celts arrived from Gaul or Galicia. They subdued and assimilated the inhabitants and established a Gaelic civilization.

By the beginning of the Christian Era, Ireland was divided into five kingdoms—Ulster, Connacht, Leinster, Meath, and Munster. St. Patrick introduced Christianity in 432 and the country developed into a center of Gaelic and Latin learning. Irish monasteries, the equivalent of universities, attracted intellectuals as well as the pious and sent out missionaries to many parts of Europe and, some believe, to North America.

Norse depredations along the coasts, starting in 795, ended in 1014 with Norse defeat at the Battle of Clontarf by forces under Brian Borv. In the the 12th century, the Pope gave all Ireland to the English Crown as a papal fief. In 1171, Henry II of England was acknowledged "Lord of Ireland," but local sectional rule continued for centuries, and English control over the whole island was not reasonably absolute until the 17th century. By the Act of Union (1800), England and Ireland became the "United Kingdom of Great Britain and Ireland."

A steady decline in the Irish economy followed in the next decades. The population had reached 8.25 million when the great potato famine of 1846–48 took many lives and drove millions to emigrate to America. By 1921 it was down to 4.3 million.

In the meantime, anti-British agitation continued along with demands for Irish home rule. The advent of World War I delayed the institution of home rule and resulted in the Easter Rebellion in Dublin (April 24–29, 1916), in which Irish nationalists unsuccessfully attempted to throw off British rule. Guerrilla warfare against British forces followed proclamation of a republic by the rebels in 1919.

The Irish Free State was established as a dominion on Dec. 6, 1921, with the six northern counties as part of the United Kingdom. Ireland was neutral in World War II.

In 1948, Éamon de Valera, American-born leader of the Sinn Fein, who had won establishment of the Free State in 1921 in negotiations with Britain's David Lloyd George, was defeated by John A. Costello, who demanded final independence from Britain. The Republic of Ireland was proclaimed on April 18, 1949. It withdrew from the Commonwealth but in 1955 entered the United Nations. Since 1949 the prime concern of successive governments has been economic development.

Through the 1960s, two antagonistic currents dominated Irish politics. One sought to bind the wounds of the rebellion and civil war. The other was the effort of the outlawed extremist Irish Republican Army to bring Northern Ireland into the republic. Despite public sympathy for unification of Ireland, the Dublin government dealt rigorously with IRA guerrillas caught inside the republic's borders.

In the elections of June 11, 1981, Garret M. D. FitzGerald, leader of the Fine Gael, was elected Prime Minister by 81 to 78 with the support of 15 Labor Party members and one independent Socialist added to his own party's 65 members. Other independents abstained, among them Kieran Doherty, a prisoner in Northern Ireland's Maze Prison, who with another prisoner had won election to the Southern Parliament (the Republic's Constitution extends citizenship to anyone born in Northern Ireland). Doherty died after a hunger strike on Aug. 3, one of nine Maze prisoners to do so.

FitzGerald resigned Jan. 27, 1982, after his presentation of an austerity budget aroused the opposition of independents who had backed him previously. Former Prime Minister Haughey was sworn in on March 9 and presented a budget with nearly a $1 billion deficit, with additional public spending aimed at stimulating the lagging economy. FitzGerald was re-elected Prime Minister on Dec. 14, 1982. He called for "strenous efforts and great sacrifices" to be made by the country in order to mitigate the problems of unemployment and its effects on the nation.

# ISRAEL

**State of Israel**
**President:** Chaim Herzog (1983)
**Prime Minister:** Yitzhak Shamir (1986)
**Area:** 7,992 sq mi. (20,699 sq km)
**Population (est. mid-1986):** 4,200,000[2] (average annual growth rate: 1.6%)
**Density per square mile:** 525.5
**Capital:** Jerusalem
**Largest cities (est. 1983):** Jerusalem, 431,800[1]; Tel Aviv, 330,400; Haifa, 227,900; Holon, 133,900; Bat Yam, 129,700
**Monetary unit:** Shekel
**Languages:** Hebrew, Arabic, English
**Religions:** Jewish, 83%, Islam 13.1%, Christian 2.3%, Druze and others, 1.6%
**National name:** Medinat Yisra'el
**Literacy rate:** Jews 94%, non-Jews 83.2%
**Economic summary:** Gross national product (1985): $25.9 Annual growth rate (1985): 2.0%. Per capita income (1984): $6,093. Land used for agriculture: 22%; labor force: 6%; principal products: citrus and other fruits, vegetables, beef, dairy and poultry products. Labor force in industry: 23%; major products: processed foods, cut diamonds, clothing and textiles, chemicals, metal products, transport and electrical equipment, plastics. Natural resources: sulfur, rock salt, phosphates, potash, bromine. Exports: polished diamonds, citrus and other fruits, clothing and textiles, processed foods, high technology products, computerized medical equipment, military hardware, fertilizer and chemical products. Imports: rough diamonds, chemicals, oil, machinery, iron and steel, cereals, textiles, vehicles, ships. Major trading partners: U.S., West Germany, U.K., Switzerland, France, Italy.

1. Includes East Jerusalem. 2. Excludes West Bank, Gaza Strip, East Jerusalem

**Geography.** Israel, slightly smaller than Massachusetts, lies at the eastern end of the Mediterranean Sea. It is bordered by Egypt on the west, Syria and Jordan on the east, and Lebanon on the north.

Northern Israel is largely a plateau traversed from north to south by mountains and broken by great depressions, also running from north to south.

The maritime plain of Israel is remarkably fertile. The southern Negev region, which comprises almost half the total area, is largely a wide desert steppe area. The National Water Project irrigation scheme is now transforming it into fertile land. The Jordan, the only important river, flows from the north through Lake Hule (Waters of Merom) and Lake Kinneret (Sea of Galilee or Sea of Tiberias), finally entering the Dead Sea, 1,290 feet (393 m) below sea level. This "sea," which is actually a salt lake (394 sq mi.; 1,020 sq km), has no outlet, its water balance being maintained by evaporation.

**Government.** Israel, which does not have a written constitution, has a republican form of government headed by a president elected for a five-year term by the Knesset. He may serve no more than two terms. The Knesset has 120 members elected by universal suffrage under proportional representation for four years. The government is administered by the Cabinet, which is headed by the prime minister.

The Knesset decided in June 1950 that Israel would acquire a constitution gradually through the years by the enactment of fundamental laws. Israel grants automatic citizenship to every Jew who desires to settle within its borders, subject to control of the Knesset.

The major political parties are Labor Alignment (44 of 120 seats in the Knesset), led by Prime Minister Shimon Peres; Likud (41 seats), led by Deputy Prime Minister Yitzhak Shamir; Tehiya-Tzomet (5 seats); National Religious Party (4 seats); Democratic Movement for Peace and Equality (Communist) (4 seats); Sephardi Torah Guardians (4 seats); Shinui (3 seats); Movement for Citizens Rights and Peace (3 seats); Yahad (3 seats); other parties (9 seats).

**History.** Palestine, cradle of two great religions and homeland of the modern state of Israel, was known to the ancient Hebrews as the "Land of Canaan." Palestine's name derives from the Philistines, a people who occupied the southern coastal part of the country in the 12th century B.C.

A Hebrew kingdom established in 1000 B.C. was later split into the kingdoms of Judah and Israel; they were subsequently invaded by Assyrians, Babylonians, Egyptians, Persians, Macedonians, Romans, and Byzantines. The Arabs took Palestine from the Byzantine Empire A.D. 634–40. With the exception of a Frankish Crusader kingdom from 1099 to 1187, Palestine remained under Moslem rule until the 20th century (Turkish rule from 1516), when British forces under Gen. Sir Edmund Allenby defeated the Turks and captured Jerusalem Dec. 9, 1917. The League of Nations granted Britain a mandate to govern Palestine, effective in 1923.

Jewish colonies—Jews from Russia established one as early as 1882—multiplied after Theodor Herzl's 1897 call for a Jewish state. The Zionist movement received official approval with the publication of a letter Nov. 2, 1917, from Arthur Balfour, British Foreign Secretary, to Lord Rothschild, a British Jewish leader. Balfour promised support for the establishment of a Jewish homeland in Palestine on the understanding that the civil and religious rights of non-Jewish Palestinians would be safeguarded.

A 1937 British proposal called for an Arab and a Jewish state separated by a mandated area incorporating Jerusalem and Nazareth. Arabs opposed this, demanding a single state with minority rights for Jews, and a 1939 British White Paper retreated, offering instead a single state with further Jewish immigration to be limited to 75,000. Although the White Paper satisfied neither side, further discussion ended on the outbreak of World War II, when the Jewish population stood at nearly 500,000, or 30% of the total. Illegal and legal immigration during the war brought the Jewish population to 678,000 in 1946, compared with 1,269,000 Arabs. Unable to reach a compromise, Britain turned the problem over to the United Nations in 1947, which on November 29 voted for partition—despite strong Arab opposition.

Britain did not help implement the U.N. decision and withdrew on expiration of its mandate May 14, 1948. Zionists had already seized control of areas designated as Jewish, and, on the day of British departure, the Jewish National Council proclaimed the State of Israel.

U.S. recognition came within hours. The next day, Jordanian and Egyptian forces invaded the new nation. At the cease-fire Jan. 7, 1949, Israel increased its original territory by 50%, taking western Galilee, a broad corridor through central Palestine to Jerusalem, and part of modern Jerusalem. (In April 1950, Jordan annexed areas of eastern and central Palestine that had been designated for an Arab state, together with the old city of Jerusalem.)

Chaim Weizmann and David Ben-Gurion became Israel's first president and prime minister. The new government was admitted to the U.N. May 11, 1949.

The next clash with Arab neighbors came when Egypt nationalized the Suez Canal in 1956 and barred Israeli shipping. Coordinating with an Anglo-French force, Israeli troops seized the Gaza Strip and drove through the Sinai to the east bank of the Suez Canal, but withdrew under U.S. and U.N. pressure. In 1967, Israel threatened retaliation against Syrian border raids, and Syria asked Egyptian aid. Egypt demanded the removal of U.N. peace-keeping forces from Suez, staged a national mobilization, closed the Gulf of Aqaba, and moved troops into the Sinai. Starting with simultaneous air attacks against Syrian, Jordanian, and Egyptian air bases on June 5, Israel during a six-day war totally defeated its Arab enemies. Expanding its territory by 200%, Israel at the cease-fire held the Golan Heights, the West Bank of the Jordan River, the Old City, and all of the Sinai and the east bank of the Suez Canal.

Israel insisted that Jerusalem remain a unified city and that peace negotiations be conducted directly, something the Arab states had refused to do because it would constitute a recognition of their Jewish neighbor.

Egypt's President Gamal Abdel Nasser renounced the 1967 cease-fire in 1969 and began a "war of attrition" against Israel, firing Soviet artillery at Israeli forces on the east bank of the canal. Nasser died of a heart attack on Sept. 28, 1970, and was succeeded by Anwar el-Sadat.

In the face of Israeli reluctance even to discuss the return of occupied territories, the fourth Mideast war erupted Oct. 6, 1973, with a surprise Egyptian and Syrian assault on the Jewish holy day of Yom Kippur. Initial Arab gains were reversed when a cease-fire took effect two weeks later, but Israel suffered heavy losses in manpower.

U.S. Secretary of State Henry A. Kissinger arranged a disengagement of forces on both the Egyptian and Syrian fronts. Geneva talks, aimed at a lasting peace, foundered, however, when Israel balked at inclusion of the Palestine Liberation Organization, a group increasingly active in terrorism directed against Israel.

A second-stage Sinai withdrawal signed by Israel and Egypt in September 1975 required Israel to give up the strategic Mitla and Gidi passes and to return the captured Abu Rudeis oil fields. Egypt guaranteed passage of Israeli cargoes through the reopened Suez Canal, and both sides renounced force in the settlement of disputes. Two hundred U.S. civilian technicians were stationed in a widened U.N. buffer zone to monitor and warn either side of truce violations.

A dramatic breakthrough in the tortuous history of Mideast peace efforts occurred Nov. 9, 1977, when Egypt's President Sadat declared his willingness to go anywhere to talk peace. Prime Minister Menachem Begin on Nov. 15 extended an invitation to the Egyptian leader to address the Knesset. Sadat's arrival in Israel four days later raised worldwide hopes. But optimism ebbed even before Begin was invited to Ismailia by Sadat, December 25-26.

An Israeli peace plan unveiled by Begin on his return, and approved by the Knesset, offered to end military administration in the West Bank and the Gaza Strip, with a degree of Arab self-rule but no relinquishment of sovereignty by Israel. Sadat severed talks on Jan. 18 and, despite U.S. condemnation, Begin approved new West Bank settlements by Israelis.

A PLO raid on Israel's coast on March 11, 1978, killed 30 civilians and provoked a full-scale invasion of southern Lebanon by Israel three days later to attack PLO bases. Israel withdrew three months later, turning over strongpoints to Lebanese Christian militia wherever possible rather than to a U.N. peacekeeping force installed in the area.

On March 14, 1979, after a visit by Carter, the Knesset approved a final peace treaty, and 12 days later Begin and Sadat signed the document, together with Carter, in a White House ceremony. Israel began its withdrawal from the Sinai on May 25 by handing over the coastal town of El Arish and the two countries opened their border on May 29.

One of the most difficult periods in Israel's history began with a confrontation with Syria over the placing by Syria of Soviet surface-to-air missiles in the Bekaa Valley of Lebanon in April 1981. President Reagan dispatched Philip C. Habib to prevent a clash. While Habib was seeking a settlement, Begin ordered a bombing raid against an Iraqi nuclear reactor on June 7, invoking the theory of preemptive self-defense because he said Iraq was planning to make nuclear weapons to attack Israel.

Although Israel withdrew its last settlers from the Sinai in April 1982 and agreed to a Sinai "peace patrol" composed of troops from four West European nations, the fragile peace engineered by Habib in Lebanon was shattered on June 9 by a massive Israeli assault on southern Lebanon. The attack was in retaliation for what Israel charged was a PLO attack that critically wounded the Israeli ambassador to London six days earlier.

Israeli armor swept through UNIFIL lines in southern Lebanon, destroyed PLO strongholds in Tyre and Sidon, and reached the suburbs of Beirut on June 10. As Israeli troops ringed Moslem East Beirut, where 5,000 PLO guerrillas were believed trapped, Habib sought to negotiate a safe exit for them. The Arab world loudly protested the entire action, estimated by Lebanon to have cost the lives of 10,000 civilians by mid-July.

A U.S.-mediated accord between Lebanon and Israel, signed on May 17, 1983, provided for Israeli withdrawal from Lebanon. Israeli withdrawal was conditioned on withdrawal of Syrian troops from the Bekaa Valley, however, and the Syrians refused to leave. Israel eventually withdrew its troops from the Beirut area, but kept them in southern Lebanon. Lebanon, under pressure from Syria, canceled the accord in March 1984.

Prime Minister Begin resigned on Sept. 15, 1983. On Oct. 10, Likud Party stalwart Yitzhak Shamir was elected Prime Minister.

After a close election, the two major parties worked out a carefully balanced power-sharing agreement and the Knesset, on Sept. 14, 1985 approved a national unity government including both the Labor Alignment and the Likud bloc. Under the terms, Labor leader Peres was to serve as Prime Minister for the first half of a 50-month term and Shamir, the Likud leader, was to be Deputy Prime Minister and Foreign Minister. For the second half of the term, the two men were to reverse roles.

By the anniversary of the invasion of Lebanon in June of 1985, Israel had withdrawn most—but not all—of its troops from the country. Israeli combat units left, but military advisers remained in a security zone along Israel's northern frontier. In addition to Israel's failure to meet its goals in Lebanon, several other developments during 1985 threatened the tenuous Labor-Likud coalition.

The Peres government decided in May to exchange 1,150 Palestinian prisoners—including terrorists—for three Israeli soldiers who had been held since the Lebanon war by the Popular Front for the Liberation of Palestine, and the subsequent pressure in June for Israel to release more than 700 detained Lebanese Shiites as demanded by Shiites who hijacked a TWA airliner and held 39 Americans hostage. Another development dividing Israelis was the verdict by a three-judge court on July 10 convicting three Jewish settlers of murder and 12 others of different violent crimes against Arabs.

In one hopeful development, the coalition government declared an economic emergency on July 1 and imposed sweeping austerity measures intended to break the country's 260% inflation. Key elements were an 18.8% devaluation of the shekel, price increases in such government-subsidized products as gasoline, dismissal of 9,000 government employees, government spending cuts and a wage and price freeze.

In June 1986, a scandal over the deaths of two terrorists while in the custody of Israeli security, and a dispute over both Shamir's alleged involvement and whether an investigation was appropriate, threatened the government.

# ITALY

**Italian Republic**

**President:** Francesco Cossiga (1985)
**Premier:** Bettino Craxi (1983)
**Area:** 116,500 sq mi. (301,278 sq km)
**Population (est. mid-1986):** 57,200,000 (average annual growth rate: 0.1%)
**Density per square mile:** 485.8
**Capital:** Rome
**Largest cities (1984):** Rome, 2,826,733; Milan, 1,535,-722; Naples, 1,206,955; Turin, 1,049,997; Genoa, 738,099; Palermo, 716,149; Bologna, 442,307; Florence, 435,698; Catania, 377,707; Bari, 368,216.
**Monetary unit:** Lira
**Language:** Italian
**Religion:** Roman Catholic
**National name:** Repubblica Italiana
**Literacy rate:** 97%
**Economic summary:** Gross national product (1985): $408.1 billion. Average annual growth rate (1982–85): 1.1%. Per capita income (1985): $7,151. Land used for agriculture: 40%; labor force: 10%; principal products:

208  *Countries of the World—Italy-Jamaica*

grapes, olives, citrus fruits, vegetables, wheat, corn. Labor force in industry: 30%; major products: machinery, autos, textiles, shoes, chemicals. Natural resources: fish, gas, marble. Exports: Engineering, chemicals, textiles, metals, shoes, food. Imports: engineering, chemicals, food, metals. Major trading partners: West Germany, France, United States, United Kingdom.

**Geography.** Italy is a long peninsula shaped like a boot bounded on the west by the Tyrrhenian Sea and on the east by the Adriatic. Slightly larger than Arizona, it has for neighbors France, Switzerland, Austria, and Yugoslavia.

Approximately 600 of Italy's 708 miles (1,139 km) of length are in the long peninsula that projects into the Mediterranean from the fertile basin of the Po River. The Apennine Mountains, branching off from the Alps between Nice and Genoa, form the peninsula's backbone, and rise to a maximum height of 9,560 feet (2,912 m) at the Gran Sasso d'Italia (Corno). The Alps form Italy's northern boundary.

Several islands form part of Italy. Sicily (9,926 sq mi.; 25,708 sq km) lies off the toe of the boot, across the Strait of Messina, with a steep and rockbound northern coast and gentler slopes to the sea in the west and south. Mount Etna, an active volcano, rises to 10,741 feet (3,274 m), and most of Sicily is more than 500 feet (3,274 m) in elevation. Sixty-two miles (100 km) southwest of Sicily lies Pantelleria (45 sq mi.; 117 sq km), and south of that are Lampedusa and Linosa. Sardinia (9,301 sq mi.; 24,-090 sq km), which is just south of Corsica and about 125 miles (200 km) west of the mainland, is mountainous, stony, and unproductive.

Italy has many northern lakes, lying below the snow-covered peaks of the Alps. The largest are Garda (143 sq mi.; 370 sq km), Maggiore (83 sq mi.; 215 sq km), and Como (55 sq mi.; 142 sq km).

The Po, the principal river, flows from the Alps on Italy's western border and crosses the Lombard plain to the Adriatic.

**Government.** The president is elected for a term of seven years by Parliament in joint session with regional representatives. The president nominates the premier and, upon the premier's recommendations, the members of the Cabinet. Parliament is composed of two houses: a Senate with 315 elective members and a Chamber of Deputies of 630 members elected by the people for a five-year term.

The major political parties are: Christian Democratic Party (225 seats of 630 in Chamber of Deputies), led by Ciriaco De Mita; Communist Party (198 seats), led by Alessandro Natta; Socialist Party (73 seats), led by Premier Bettino Craxi; Italian Social Movement (42 seats), led by Giorgio Almirante; Republican Party (29 seats), led by Giovanni Spadolini; Social Democratic Party (23 seats), led by Franco Nicolazzi; Liberal Party (16 seats), led by Alfredo Biondi; Radical Party (11 seats), led by Giovanni Negri; Proletarian Democracy (7 seats), led by Mario Capanna; South Tyrol Popular Party (3 seats), led by Silvius Magnago; and other groups (3 seats).

**History.** Until A.D. 476, when the German Odoacer became head of the Roman Empire in the west, the history of Italy was largely the history of Rome. From A.D. 800 on, the Holy Roman Emperors, Popes, Normans, and Saracens all vied for control over various segments of the Italian peninsula. Nu-

merous city states, such as Venice and Genoa, and many small principalities flourished in the late Middle Ages.

In 1713, after the War of the Spanish Succession, Milan, Naples, and Sardinia were handed over to Austria, which lost some of its Italian territories in 1735. After 1800, Italy was unified by Napoleon, who crowned himself King of Italy in 1805; but with the Congress of Vienna in 1815, Austria once again became the dominant power in Italy.

Austrian armies crushed Italian uprisings in 1820, 1821, and 1831. In the 1830s Giuseppe Mazzini, brilliant liberal nationalist, organized the Risorgimento (Resurrection), which laid the foundation for Italian unity.

Disappointed Italian patriots looked to the House of Savoy for leadership. Count Camille di Cavour (1810–61), Premier of Sardinia in 1852 and the architect of a united Italy, joined England and France in the Crimean War (1853–56), and in 1859, helped France in a war against Austria, thereby obtaining Lombardy. By plebiscite in 1860, Modena, Parma, Tuscany, and the Romagna voted to join Sardinia. In 1860, Giuseppe Garibaldi conquered Sicily and Naples and turned them over to Sardinia. Victor Emmanuel II, King of Sardinia, was proclaimed King of Italy in 1861.

Allied with Germany and Austria-Hungary in the Triple Alliance of 1882, Italy declared its neutrality upon the outbreak of World War I on the ground that Germany had embarked upon an offensive war. In 1915, Italy entered the war on the side of the Allies.

Benito (Il Duce) Mussolini, a former Socialist, organized discontented Italians in 1919 into the Fascist Party to "rescue Italy from Bolshevism." He led his Black Shirts in a march on Rome and, on Oct. 28, 1922, became premier. He transformed Italy into a dictatorship, embarking on an expansionist foreign policy with the invasion and annexation of Ethiopia in 1935 and allying himself with Adolf Hitler in the Rome-Berlin Axis in 1936. He was executed by Partisans on April 28, 1945 at Dongo on Lake Como.

Following the overthrow of Mussolini's dictatorship and the armistice with the Allies (Sept. 3, 1943), Italy joined the war against Germany as a co-belligerent. King Victor Emmanuel III abdicated May 9, 1946, and left the country after having installed his son as King Humbert II. A plebiscite rejected monarchy, however, and on June 13, King Humbert followed his father into exile.

The peace treaty of Sept. 15, 1947, required Italian renunciation of all claims in Ethiopia and Greece and the cession of the Dodecanese to Greece and of five small Alpine areas to France. Much of the Istrian Peninsula, including Fiume and Pola, went to Yugoslavia.

The Trieste area west of the new Yugoslav territory was made a free territory (until 1954, when the city and a 90-square-mile zone were transferred to Italy and the rest to Yugoslavia).

Scandal brought the long reign of the Christian Democrats to an end when Italy's 40th premier since World War II, Arnaldo Forlani, was forced to resign in the wake of disclosure that many high-ranking Christian Democrats and civil servants belonged to a secret Masonic lodge known as "P-2."

When the Socialists deserted the coalition, Forlani was forced to resign on May 26, 1981, leaving to Giovanni Spadolini of the small Republican Party the task of forming a new government. He was succeeded by Amintore Fanfani, a Christian Democrat, the following year. Bettino Craxi, a Socialist, became Premier in 1983.

On October 14, 1985, the Craxi government nearly fell over a controversy involving the release of a suspected PLO ringleader, Abu Abbas, but he was able to heal the rift with his coalition allies.

This success was short-lived as Craxi was forced to resign on June 27, 1986 following the loss of a key secret-ballot vote in Parliament.

After a month of political wrangling, Craxi was able to form a new government similar to his old one on condition that his term end in March 1987.

## IVORY COAST

**Republic of Ivory Coast**
**President:** Félix Houphouët-Boigny (1960)
**Area:** 124,502 sq mi. (322,462 sq km)
**Population (est. mid-1986):** 10,500,000 (average annual growth rate: 3.0%)
**Density per square mile:** 84.3
**Capital and largest city (est. 1983):** Abidjan, 1,800,000
**Monetary unit:** Franc CFA
**Ethnic groups:** Agnis, Baoulés, Senoufos, Kroumen, Mandes, Dan-Gouros, Akié
**Languages:** French and African languages (Diaula esp.)
**Religions:** Animist, 44%; Christian, 32%; Islam, 24%
**National name:** République de la Côte d'Ivoire
**Literacy rate:** 35%
**Economic summary:** Gross national product (1983): $6.7 billion. Annual growth rate (1982): 1.8%. Per capita income (1983): $720. Labor force in agriculture: 79%; principal products: coffee, cocoa, timber, sugar, corn, cotton. Major industrial products: food, cement. Natural resources: diamonds, iron ore. Exports: coffee, cocoa, tropical woods. Imports: raw materials, consumer goods, fuels. Major trading partners: France, U.S., Western European countries, Nigeria.

**Geography.** The Ivory Coast, in western Africa on the Gulf of Guinea, is a little larger than New Mexico. Its neighbors are Liberia, Guinea, Mali, Upper Volta, and Ghana.

The country consists of a coastal strip in the south, dense forests in the interior, and savannas in the north. Rainfall is heavy, especially along the coast.

**Government.** The government is headed by a President who is elected every five years by popular vote, together with a National Assembly of 175 members.

The Parti Démocratique de la Côte d'Ivoire, a member of the Rassemblement Démocratique Africain, is the only political party.

**History.** The Ivory Coast attracted both French and Portuguese merchants in the 15th century. French traders set up establishments early in the 19th century, and in 1842, the French obtained territorial concessions from local tribes, gradually extending their influence along the coast and inland. The area was organized as a territory in 1893, became an autonomous republic in the French Union after World War II, and achieved independence on Aug. 7, 1960.

The Ivory Coast formed a customs union in 1959 with Dahomey (Benin), Niger, and Upper Volta.

The country is one of the most prosperous and stable in West Africa.

## JAMAICA

**Sovereign:** Queen Elizabeth II
**Governor-General:** Sir Florizel Glasspole (1973)
**Prime Minister:** Edward P. G. Seaga (1980)
**Area:** 4,411 sq mi. (11,424 sq km)
**Population (est. mid-1986):** 2,300,000 (average annual growth rate: 1.8%)
**Density per square mile:** 521.4
**Capital and largest city (est. 1981):** Kingston, 200,000
**Monetary unit:** Jamaican dollar
**Language:** English
**Religions:** Anglican, Baptist, Roman Catholic
**Member of Commonwealth of Nations**
**Literacy rate:** 76%
**Economic summary:** Gross national product (1984): $2.0 billion. Average annual growth rate (1984): −0.1%. Per capita income (1983): $1,245. Land used for agriculture: 25%; labor force: 33% (includes fishing and mining); principal products: sugar cane, citrus fruits, bananas, spices, coconuts, coffee, cocoa. Labor force in industry: 13%; major products: bauxite, textiles, processed foods, light manufactures. Natural resources: bauxite, gypsum. Exports: alumina, bauxite, sugar, clothing, citrus fruits, rum, cocoa. Imports: fuels, machinery, transport and electrical equipment, food, fertilizer. Major trading partners: U.S., U.K., Venezuela.

**Geography.** Jamaica is an island in the West Indies, 90 miles (145 km) south of Cuba and 100 miles (161 km) west of Haiti. It is a little smaller than Connecticut.

The island is made up of a plateau and the Blue Mountains, a group of volcanic hills, in the east. Blue Mountain (7,402 ft.; 2,256 m) is the tallest peak.

**Government.** The legislature is a 60-member House of Representatives elected by universal suffrage and an appointed Senate of 21 members. The Prime Minister is appointed by the Governor-General and must, in the Governor-General's opinion, be the person best able to command the confidence of a majority of the members of the House of Representatives.

The major political parties are the Jamaica Labor Party (all 60 seats in the House of Representatives), led by Prime Minister Edward P. G. Seaga; and the People's National Party (no seats), led by former Prime Minister Michael Manley.

**History.** Jamaica was inhabited by Arawak Indians when Columbus discovered it in 1494 and named it St. Iago. It remained under Spanish rule until 1655, then became a British possession. The island prospered from wealth brought by buccaneers to their base, Port Royal, the capital, until the city disappeared in the sea in 1692 after an earthquake. The Arawaks died off from disease and exploitation, and slaves, mostly black, were imported to work sugar plantations. Abolition of the slave trade (1807), emancipation of the slaves (1833), and a gradual drop in sugar prices led to depressed economic conditions that resulted in an uprising in 1865.

The following year Jamaica's status was changed to that of a colony, and conditions improved considerably. Introduction of banana cultivation made the island less dependent on the sugar crop for its well-being. Overpopulation and problems inherited from the colonial era, such as illiteracy, produced chronic substantial unemployment, leading to much emigration to the Caribbean countries and to the U.S.

On May 5, 1953, Jamaica attained internal autonomy, and in 1958 it led in organizing the West Indies Federation. This effort at Caribbean unification failed. A nationalist labor leader, Sir Alexander Bustamente, led a campaign for withdrawal from the Federation. As the result of a popular referendum in 1961, Jamaica became independent on Aug. 6, 1962.

Michael Manley became Prime Minister in 1972 and initiated a socialist program and in 1977, the government bought 51% of the Kaiser and Reynolds bauxite operations.

The Labor Party defeated Manley's People's National Party in 1980 and its capitalist-oriented leader, Edward P.G. Seaga, became Prime Minister. He instituted measures to encourage private investment. Manley's party boycotted the next election in 1983, leading to a Labor Party sweep of all 60 seats in the House of Representatives.

Like other Caribbean countries, Jamaica was hard-hit by the 1981–82 recession. By 1984, austerity measures that Seaga instituted in the hope of bringing the economy back into balance included elimination of government subsidies and dismissal of many government employees. Devaluation of the Jamaican dollar made Jamaican products more competitive on the world market and Jamaica achieved record growth in tourism and agriculture. Manufacturing also grew. But at the same time, the cost of many foods went up 50% to 75% and thousands of Jamaicans fell deeper into poverty. An increase in fuel prices ignited rioting in January 1985 in which four were killed and 23 were injured.

# JAPAN

**Emperor:** Hirohito (1926)
**Prime Minister:** Yasuhiro Nakasone (1982)
**Area:** 143,574 sq mi. (371,857 sq km)
**Population (est. mid-1986):** 121,500,000 (average annual growth rate: 0.7%)
**Density per square mile:** 846.3
**Capital:** Tokyo
**Largest cities (est. 1985):** Tokyo, 8,425,000; Yokohama, 2,984,000; Osaka, 2,634,000; Nagoya, 2,118,200; Sapporo, 1,543,000; Kyoto, 1,480,000; Kobe, 1,413,000; Fukuoka, 1,162,000; Kitakyusho, 1,054,000; Kawasaki, 1,079,000
**Monetary unit:** Yen
**Language:** Japanese
**Religions:** Shintoist, Buddhist, Christian
**National name:** Nippon
**Literacy rate (1981):** 99%
**Economic summary:** Gross national product (1984): $1,233 billion. Average annual growth rate (1980–84): 4.3%. Per capita income (1984): $10,200. Land used for agriculture, 13%; labor force, including fishing, 9%; principal products: rice, vegetables, fruits, sugar. Labor force in industry: 33%; major products: machinery and equipment, metals and metal products, textiles, autos, chemicals, electrical and electronic equipment. Natural resource: fish. Exports: machinery and equipment, automobiles, metals and metal products, textiles. Imports: fossil fuels, metal ore, raw materials, foodstuffs, machinery and equipment. Major trading partners: U.S.,

Saudi Arabia, Indonesia, UAE, China, Australia, Canada, South Korea

1. Except for Tokyo, figures refer to *shi,* a minor division that may include some scattered or rural population as well as an urban center.

**Geography.** An archipelago extending more than 1,744 miles (2,790 km) from northeast to southwest in the Pacific, Japan is separated from the east coast of Asia by the Sea of Japan. It is approximately the size of Montana.

Japan's four main islands are Honshu, Hokkaido, Kyushu, and Shikoku. The Ryukyu chain to the southwest was U.S.-occupied and the Kuriles to the northeast are Russian-occupied. The surface of the main islands consists largely of mountains separated by narrow valleys. There are about 60 more or less active volcanoes, of which the best-known is Mount Aso. Mount Fuji, seen on postcards, is not active.

**Government.** Japan's Constitution, promulgated on Nov. 3, 1946, replaced the Meiji Constitution of 1889. The 1946 Constitution, sponsored by the U.S. during its occupation of Japan, brought fundamental changes to the Japanese political system, including the abandonment of the Emperor's divine rights. The Diet (Parliament) consists of a House of Representatives of 512 members, elected for four years, and a House of Councilors of 252 members, half of whom are elected every three years for six-year terms. Executive power is vested in the Cabinet, which is headed by a Prime Minister, nominated by the Diet from its members.

Emperor Hirohito, who was born April 29, 1901, succeeded his father, Yoshihito, on Dec. 25, 1926. He was married on Jan. 26, 1924, to Princess Nagako, born in 1903. They have two sons—Crown Prince Akihito (born Dec. 23, 1933) and Prince Hitachi (born Nov. 28, 1935)—and four daughters. Succession to the Japanese throne is in the male line only.

The major political parties are the Liberal Democratic Party (306 of 511 seats in the House of Representatives), led by Prime Minister Yasuhiro Nakason; Socialist Party (84 seats), led by Masatsugu Ishibashi; Clean Government (Komeito) Party (57 seats), led by Yoshikatsu Takeiri; Communist Party (27 seats), led by Kenji Miyamoto; Democratic Socialist Party (26 seats), led by Riyosaku Sasaki; New Liberal Club (6 seats).

**History.** A series of legends attributes creation of Japan to the sun goddess, from whom the later emperors were allegedly descended. The first of them was Jimmu Tenno, supposed to have ascended the throne in 660 B.C.

Recorded Japanese history begins with the first contact with China in the 5th century A.D. Japan was then divided into strong feudal states, all nominally under the Emperor, but with real power often held by a court minister or clan. In 1185, Yoritomo, chief of the Minamoto clan, was designated Shogun (Generalissimo) with the administration of the islands under his control. A dual government system—Shogun and Emperor—continued until 1867.

First contact with the West came about 1542, when a Portuguese ship off course arrived in Japanese waters. Portuguese, traders, Jesuit missionaries, and Spanish, Dutch, and English traders followed. Suspicious of Christianity and of Portuguese support of a local Japanese revolt, the shoguns prohibited all trade with foreign countries; only a Dutch trading post at Nagasaki was permitted. Western attempts to renew trading relations failed until 1853, when Commodore Matthew Perry sailed an American fleet into Tokyo Bay.

Japan now quickly made the transition from a medieval to a modern power. Feudalism was abolished and industrialization was speeded. An imperial army was established with conscription. The shogun system was abolished in 1868 by Emperor Meiji, and parliamentary government was established in 1889. After a brief war with China in 1894–95, Japan acquired Formosa (Taiwan), the Pescadores Islands, and part of southern Manchuria. China also recognized the independence of Korea (Chosen), which Japan later annexed (1910).

In 1904–05, Japan defeated Russia in the Russo-Japanese War, gaining the territory of southern Sakhalin (Karafuto) and Russia's port and rail rights in Manchuria. In World War I Japan seized Germany's Pacific islands and leased areas in China. The Treaty of Versailles then awarded it a mandate over the islands.

At the Washington Conference of 1921–22, Japan agreed to respect Chinese national integrity. The series of Japanese aggressions that was to lead to the nation's downfall began in 1931 with the invasion of Manchuria. The following year, Japan set up this area as a puppet state, "Manchukuo," under Emperor Henry Pu-Yi, last of China's Manchu dynasty. On Nov. 25, 1936, Japan joined the Axis by signing the anti-Comintern pact. The invasion of China came the next year and the Pearl Harbor attack on the U.S. on Dec. 7, 1941.

(For details of World War II (1939–45), see Headline History.)

Japan surrendered formally on Sept. 2, 1945, aboard the battleship *Missouri* in Tokyo Bay after atomic bombs had hit Hiroshima and Nagasaki. Southern Sakhalin and the Kurile Islands reverted to the U.S.S.R., and Formosa (Taiwan) and Manchuria to China. The Pacific islands remained under U.S. occupation. General of the Army Douglas MacArthur was appointed Supreme Commander for the Allied Powers on Aug. 14, 1945.

A new Japanese Constitution went into effect in 1947. In 1949, many of the responsibilities of government were returned to the Japanese. Full sovereignty was granted to Japan by the Japanese Peace Treaty in 1951.

The treaty took effect on April 28, 1952, when Japan returned to full status as a nation. It was admitted into the United Nations in 1958.

Following the visit of Prime Minister Eisaku Sato to Washington in 1969, the U.S. agreed to return Okinawa and other Ryukyu Islands to Japan in 1972, and both nations renewed the security treaty in 1970.

When President Nixon opened a dialogue with Peking in 1972, Prime Minister Kakuei Tanaka, who succeeded Sato in 1972, quickly established diplomatic relations with the mainland Chinese and severed ties with Formosa.

Masayoshi Ohira, Prime Minister since November 1978, died on June 12, 1980, and in national elections held June 22, the ruling Liberal Democrats reversed an eight-year decline in public support, winning a firm parliamentary majority. The party chose Zenko Suzuki, a little-known 66-year-old follower of Ohira, as the new Prime Minister.

Announcement on June 19, 1981 that Japan's gross national product grew at a rate of nearly 5% for the fiscal year ending March 31 brought new demands for increased imports of manufactured goods by Japan, which international trade experts charged was still creating barriers against trade despite repeated promises by Tokyo to relax such restrictions.

The same figure was agreed to by Japan for the following year, and for the first time, Japanese automobile exports declined for the 12-month period ending March 31, 1982. In an effort to remove nontariff trade barriers, which U.S. businessmen held responsible for their inability to increase sales in Japan, the Suzuki government appointed a special ombudsman with authority to cut red tape.

Under continued U.S. prodding, Tokyo announced a $707-million increase in defense spending for fiscal 1982 and $745 million for fiscal 1983, still below the target figure of 1% of the gross national product.

Suzuki was defeated in 1982 by Yasuhiro Nakasone who is considered pro-Western and better relations with the United States have ensued.

Nakasone initiated policies aimed at making the Japanese economy less export-intensive. Despite some opposition to this and his pro-Western policies in general, his Liberal Democratic party won decisively in the elections of July 7, 1986.

# JORDAN

## The Hashemite Kingdom of Jordan
**Ruler:** King Hussein I (1952)
**Prime Minister:** Zeid Rifa'i (1985)
**Area:** 37,297 sq mi. (96,599 sq km)[1]
**Population (est. mid-1986):** 3,700,000[1] (average annual growth rate: 3.7%)
**Density per square mile:** 99.2
**Capital:** Amman
**Largest cities (est. 1981):** Amman, 750,000; Zarka, 265,500; Irbid, 136,200
**Monetary unit:** Jordanian dinar
**Language:** Arabic
**Religions:** Islam, 93%; Christian, 5%
**National name:** Al Mamlaka al Urduniya al Hashemiyah
**Literacy rate:** est. 70%
**Economic summary:** Gross national product (1985): $5.0 billion. Annual growth rate (1984): 2.0%. Per capita income (1985): $1,650. Land used for agriculture: 5%; labor force: 10%; principal products: barley, fruits, vegetables, olive oil. Labor force in industry: 21.5%; major products: phosphate, refined petroleum products, cement. Natural resources: phosphate, potash. Exports: foodstuffs, cement, phosphate. Imports: petroleum products, textiles, capital goods, motor vehicles, foodstuffs. Major trading partners: U.S., Japan, Saudi Arabia, Iraq.

1. Includes territory occupied by Israel in 1967 war.

**Geography.** The Middle East kingdom of Jordan is bordered on the west by Israel and the Dead Sea, on the north by Syria, on the east by Iraq, and on the south Saudi Arabia. It is comparable in size to Indiana.

Arid hills and mountains make up most of the country. The southern section of the Jordan River flows through the country.

**Government.** Jordan is a constitutional monarchy with a bicameral parliament. Its Chamber of Deputies of 60 members is elected for four years by the people, and the 30 members of the Senate are appointed by the King.

All political parties were banned in 1957.

**History.** In biblical times, the country that is now Jordan contained the lands of Edom, Moab, Ammon, and Bashan. In A.D. 106 it became part of the Roman province of Arabia and in 633–36 was conquered by the Arabs.

Taken from the Turks by the British in World War I, Jordan (formerly known as Transjordan) was separated from the Palestine mandate in 1920, and in 1921, placed under the rule of Abdullah ibn Hussein.

In 1923, Britain recognized Jordan's independence, subject to the mandate. In 1946, grateful for Jordan's loyalty in World War II, Britain abolished the mandate. That part of Palestine occupied by Jordanian troops was formally incorporated by action of the Jordanian Parliament in 1950.

King Abdullah was assassinated in 1951. His son Talal was deposed as mentally ill the next year. Talal's son Hussein, born Nov. 14, 1935, succeeded him.

From the beginning of his reign, Hussein had to steer a careful course between his powerful neighbor to the west, Israel, and rising Arab nationalism, frequently a direct threat to this throne. Riots erupted when he joined the Central Treaty Organization (the Baghdad Pact) in 1955, and he incurred further unpopularity when Britain, France, and Israel attacked the Suez Canal in 1956, forcing him to place his army under nominal command of the United Arab Republic of Egypt and Syria.

The 1961 breakup of the UAR eased Arab national pressure on Hussein, who was the first to recognize Syria after it reclaimed its independence. Jordan was swept into the 1967 Arab-Israeli war, however, and lost the old city of Jerusalem and all of its territory west of the Jordan river, the West Bank. Embittered Palestinian guerrilla forces virtually took over sections of Jordan in the aftermath of defeat, and open warfare broke out between the Palestinians and government forces in 1970.

Despite intervention of Syrian tanks, Hussein's Bedouin army defeated the Palestinians, suffering heavy casualties. A U.S. military alert and Israeli armor massed on the Golan Heights contributed psychological weight, but the Jordanians alone drove out the Syrians and invited the departure of 12,000 Iraqi troops who had been in the country since the 1967 war.

In October 1974, Hussein concurred in an Arab summit resolution calling for an independent Palestinian state and endorsing the Palestine Liberation Organization as the "sole legitimate representative of the Palestinian people." This apparent reversal of policy changed with the growing disillusion of Arab states with the P.L.O., however, and by 1977 Hussein referred again to the unity of people on both banks of the Jordan.

As Egypt and Israel neared final agreement on a peace treaty early in 1979, Hussein met with Yassir Arafat, the PLO leader, on March 17 and issued a joint statement of opposition. Although the U.S. pressed Jordan to break Arab ranks on the issue, Hussein elected to side with the great majority, cutting ties with Cairo and joining the boycott against Egypt.

In September 1980, Jordan declared itself with Iraq in its conflict with Iran and, despite threats from Syria, opened ports to war shipments for Iraq.

In April 1983, Jordan rejected the American-sponsored Palestine peace plan.

An attempt to enlist Arafat in a new peace process collapsed in early 1986. Hussein then began a rapproachment with President Assad of Syria.

## KAMPUCHEA

### See Cambodia

# KENYA

**Republic of Kenya**
**President:** Daniel Arap Moi (1978)
**Area:** 224,960 sq mi. (582,646 sq km)
**Population (est. mid-1986):** 21,000,000 (average annual growth rate: 4.2%)
**Density per square mile:** 78.2
**Capital:** Nairobi
**Largest cities (est. 1985):** Nairobi, 1,000,000; Mombasa, 700,000
**Monetary unit:** Kenyan shilling
**Languages:** Swahili (official), Bantu, Kikuyu, English
**Religions:** Protestant, 27%; Roman Catholic, 26%; Animist, 19%; Islam, 6%; Protestent, 19%
**Literacy rate:** 47%
**Member of Commonwealth of Nations**
**Economic summary:** Gross national product (1982): $7.0 billion. Average annual growth rate (1973–82): 5.0%. Per capita income (1980): $420. Land used for agriculture: 20%; labor force in agriculture: 17%; principal products: coffee, sisal, tea, pyrethrum, cotton, livestock. Labor force in industry: 14%; major products: textiles, processed foods, consumer goods, refined oil. Natural resources: wildlife. Exports: coffee, tea, foodstuffs. Imports: machinery, transport equipment, crude oil, paper, iron and steel products. Major trading partners: Western European countries, Japan, U.S., Uganda, U.K. UAE, Saudi Arabia.

**Geography.** Kenya lies on the equator in east central Africa on the coast of the Indian Ocean. It is twice the size of Nevada. Kenya's neighbors are Tanzania, Uganda, the Sudan, Ethiopia, and Somalia.

In the north, the land is arid; the southwestern corner is in the fertile Lake Victoria Basin; and a length of the eastern depression of Great Rift Valley separates western highlands from those that rise from the lowland coastal strip. Large game reserves have been developed.

**Government.** Under its Constitution of 1963, amended in 1964, Kenya has a one-house National Assembly of 171 members, elected for five years by universal suffrage. Since 1969, the president has been chosen by a general election.

The Kenya African National Union, led by the president, is the only political party.

President Jomo Kenyatta died in his sleep on Aug. 22, 1978. Vice President Daniel Arap Moi was elected to succeed him on Oct. 10.

**History.** Kenya, formerly a British colony and protectorate, was made a crown colony in 1920. The whites' domination of the rich plateau area, the White Highlands, long regarded by the Kikiyu people as their territory, was a factor leading to native terrorism, called the Mau Mau movement, in 1952. In 1954 the British began preparing the territory for African rule and independence. In 1961 Jomo Kenyatta was freed from banishment to become leader of the Kenya African National Union.

Internal self-government was granted in 1963; Kenya became independent on Dec. 12, 1963, with Kenyatta the first president. Kenya obtained economic and technical assistance from Communist China beginning in 1964 and later a World Bank loan.

# KIRIBATI

**Republic of Kiribati**
**Sovereign:** Queen Elizabeth II
**Governor General:** Reginald J. Wallace (1980)
**President:** Ieremia Tabai (1979)
**Area:** 264 sq mi. (683 sq km)
**Population (est. 1985):** 62,000 (average annual growth rate: 1.6%)
**Density per square mile:** 234.8
**Capital (est. 1974):** Bairiki (on Tarawa Atoll), 17,100
**Monetary unit:** Australian dollar
**Language:** English
**Religions:** Roman Catholic, 50%; Protestant, 44%
**Member of Commonwealth of Nations**
**Literacy rate:** 90%
**Economic summary:** Gross national product (1983): $30 million. Per capita income (1983): $492. Principal agricultural products: copra, vegetables. Exports: fish, copra. Imports: foodstuffs, fuel, transportation equipment. Major trading partners: New Zealand, Australia, South Korea

**Geography.** Kiribati, formerly the Gilbert Islands, consists of three widely separated main groups of Southwest Pacific islands, the Gilberts on the equator, the Phoenix Islands to the east, and the Line Islands further east. Ocean Island, producer of phosphates, which constitute 99% of the new nation's annual income of $18 million, is also included in the two million square miles of ocean, which will give Kiribati an important fishery resource.

**Government.** The president holds executive power. The legislature consists of a House Assembly with 37 members.

**History.** A British protectorate since 1892, the Gilbert and Ellice Islands became a colony in 1915-16. The two island groups were separated in 1975 and given internal self-government.

Tarawa and others of the Gilbert group were occupied by Japan during World War II. Tarawa was the site of one of the bloodiest battles in U.S. Marine Corps history when Marines landed in November 1943 to dislodge the Japanese defenders.

Princess Anne, representing Queen Elizabeth II, presented the independence documents to the new government on July 12, 1979.

# KOREA, NORTH

**Democratic People's Republic of Korea**
**President:** Marshal Kim Il Sung (1972)
**Premier:** Yi Chong Ok (1977)
**Area:** 46,768 sq mi. (121,129 sq km)
**Population (est. mid-1986):** 20,500,000 (average annual growth rate: 2.3%)
**Density per square mile:** 438.8

**Capital and largest city (est. 1982):** Pyongyang, 1,500,-000
**Monetary unit:** Won
**Language:** Korean
**Religions:** None
**National name:** Democratic People's Republic of Korea
**Literacy rate:** 95% (est.)
**Economic summary:** Gross national product (1984): $23.0 billion. Average annual growth rate (1970–79): 3.8%. Per capita income (1984): $1,170. Land used for agriculture: 19%; labor force, 44%; principal products: corn, rice, vegetables. Major industrial products: machines, electric power, chemicals, textiles, fertilizers, metallurgical products. Natural resources: coal, iron ore. Exports: minerals, chemical and metallurgical products. Imports: machinery and equipment, petroleum, foodstuffs, coking coal. Major trading partners: U.S.S.R., China, Japan.

**Geography.** Korea is a 600-mile (966 km) peninsula jutting from Manchuria and China (and a small portion of the U.S.S.R.) into the Sea of Japan and the Yellow Sea off eastern Asia. North Korea occupies an area slightly smaller than Pennsylvania north of the 38th parallel.

The country is almost completely covered by a series of north-south mountain ranges separated by narrow valleys. The Yalu River forms part of the northern border with Manchuria.

**Government.** The elected Supreme People's Assembly, as the chief organ of government, chooses a Presidium and a Cabinet. The Cabinet, which exercises executive authority, is subject to approval by the Assembly and the Presidium.

The Korean Workers (Communist) Party, led by President Kim Il Sung, is the only political party.

**History.** According to myth, Korea was founded in 2333 B.C. by Tangun. In the 17th century, it became a vassal of China and was isolated from all but Chinese influence and contact until 1876, when Japan forced Korea to negotiate a commercial treaty, opening the land to the U. S. and Europe. Japan achieved control as the result of its war with China (1894–95) and with Russia (1904–05) and annexed Korea in 1910. Japan developed the country but never won over the Korean nationalists.

After the Japanese surrender in 1945, the country was divided into two occupation zones, the U.S.S.R. north of and the U.S. south of the 38th parallel. When the cold war developed between the U.S. and U.S.S.R., trade between the zones was cut off. In 1948, the division between the zones was made permanent with the establishment of separate regimes in the north and south. By mid-1949, the U.S. and U.S.S.R. withdrew all troops. The Democratic People's Republic of Korea (North Korea) was established on May 1, 1948. The Communist Party, headed by Kim Il Sung, was established in power.

On June 25, 1950, the North Korean army launched a surprise attack on South Korea. On June 26, the U.N. Security Council condemned the invasion as aggression and ordered withdrawal of the invading forces. On June 27, President Harry S. Truman ordered air and naval units into action to enforce the U.N. order. The British government did the same, and soon a multinational U.N. command was set up to aid the South Koreans. The North Korean invaders took Seoul and pushed the South Koreans into the southeast corner of their country.

Gen. Douglas MacArthur, U.N. commander, made an amphibious landing at Inchon on September 15 behind the North Korean lines, which resulted in the complete rout of the North Korean army. The U.N. forces drove north across the 38th parallel, approaching the Yalu River. Then Communist China entered the war, forcing the U.N. forces into headlong retreat. Seoul was lost again, then regained; ultimately the war stabilized near the 38th parallel but dragged on for two years while the belligerents negotiated. An armistice was agreed to on July 27, 1953.

President Carter, visiting Seoul from June 29 to July 1, 1979, proposed that the U.S., North Korea, and South Korea meet "to promote dialogue and reduce tensions in the area," possibly leading to reunification of the two Koreas. Pyongyang's official party newspaper rejected the proposal, saying the North favors reunification talks but without the "alien interference" of the U.S.

Kim again rejected as a "foolish burlesque" an invitation on Jan. 12, 1981, by South Korea's military chief, Chun Doo Hwan, to hold reunification talks in Seoul. Kim refused again when Chun repeated the invitation on March 3 during his inauguration as President of the Southern republic.

# KOREA, SOUTH

**Republic of Korea**
**President:** Chun Doo Hwan (1980)
**Premier:** Lho Shin Yong (1985)
**Area:** 38,031 sq mi. (98,500 sq km)
**Population (est. mid-1986):** 43,300,000 (average annual growth rate: 1.6%)
**Density per square mile:** 1,138.5
**Capital:** Seoul
**Largest cities (est. 1985):** Seoul, 9,600,000; Pusan, 3,500,000; Taegu, 2,000,000; Inchon, 1,300,000
**Monetary unit:** Won
**Language:** Korean
**Religions:** Buddhist, 37%; Protestant, 26%; Roman Catholic, 5%; Confucian, 1.8%
**National name:** Dae Han Min Kook
**Literary rate:** 93%
**Economic summary:** Gross national product (1985): $83.1 billion. Average annual growth rate (1976–85): 7.52%. Per capita income (1985): $2,032. Land used for agriculture: 21%; labor force, including fishing, 22.16%; principal products: rice, barley. Labor force in industry: 25.35%; major products: clothing and textiles, processed foods, chemical fertilizers, chemicals, plywood, steel, electronics equipment. Natural resources: iron and copper ore, tungsten, graphite, limestone, coal, gold, silver. Exports: Textiles, electric and electronics, ships, and steel. Imports: oil, grains, chemicals, machinery, electronics. Major trading partners: U.S., Japan.

**Geography.** Slightly larger than Indiana, South Korea lies below the 38th parallel on the Korean peninsula. It is mountainous in the east; in the west and south are many harbors on the mainland and offshore islands.

**Government.** A national referendum in October 1980 approved a new Constitution that provides for election of the President by an electoral college chosen by popular vote. The term of office is for

seven years, limited to one term. A unicameral National Assembly has 276 members, 184 elected directly by popular vote, the remainder appointed in proportion to party strength in the selection.

Major parties are the Democratic Justice Party (148 of 276 National Assembly seats), led by President Chun Doo Hwan, and the opposition New Korea Democratic Party (68 seats), led by Kim Dae Jung and Kim Yong Sam, with the remaining seats held by splinter parties and independents.

**History.** South Korea came into being in the aftermath of World War II as the result of a 1945 agreement making the 38th parallel the boundary between a northern zone occupied by the U.S.S.R. and a southern zone occupied by U.S. forces. (For details, *see* North Korea.)

Elections were held in the U.S. zone in 1948 for a national assembly, which adopted a republican Constitution and elected Syngman Rhee president. The new republic was proclaimed on August 15 and was recognized as the legal government of Korea by the U.N. on Dec. 12, 1948.

On June 25, 1950, South Korea was attacked by North Korean Communist forces. U.S. armed intervention was ordered on June 27 by President Harry S. Truman, and on the same day the U.N. invoked military sanctions against North Korea. Gen. Douglas MacArthur was named commander of the U.N. forces. U.S. and South Korean troops fought a heroic holding action but, by the first week of August, they had been forced back to a 4,000-square-mile beachhead in southeast Korea.

There they stood off superior North Korean forces until September 15, when a major U.N. amphibious attack was launched far behind the Communist lines at Inchon, port of Seoul. By September 30, U.N. forces were in complete control of South Korea. They then invaded North Korea and were nearing the Manchurian and Siberian borders when several hundred thousand Chinese Communist troops entered the conflict in late October. U.N. forces were then forced to retreat below the 38th parallel.

On May 24, 1951, U.N. forces recrossed the parallel and had made important new inroads into North Korea when truce negotiations began on July 10. An armistice was finally signed at Panmunjom on July 27, 1953, leaving a devastated Korea in need of large-scale rehabilitation.

The U.S. and South Korea signed a mutual-defense treaty on Oct. 1, 1953.

Rhee, president since 1948, resigned in 1960 in the face of rising disorders. PoSun Yun was elected to succeed him, but political instability continued. In 1961, Gen. Park Chung Hee took power and subsequently built up the country. The U.S. stepped up military aid, building up South Korea's armed forces to 600,000 men. The South Koreans sent 50,000 troops to Vietnam, at U.S. expense.

Park's assassination on Oct. 26, 1979, by Kim Jae Kyu, head of the Korean Central Intelligence Agency, brought a liberalizing trend as Choi Kyu Hah, the new President, freed imprisoned dissidents. The release of opposition leader Kim Dae Jung in February 1980 generated anti-government demonstrations that turned into riots by May. Choi resigned on Aug. 16. Chun Doo Wha, head of a military Special Committee for National Security Measures, was the sole candidate as the electoral college confirmed him as President on Aug. 27. On Sept. 17, Kim Dae Jung was sentenced to death by a military court on charges of high treason. Chun commuted the sentence on Jan. 23, 1981, and lifted martial law the next day.

Elected to a full seven-year term on Feb. 11, Chun had visited Washington on Feb. 2 to receive President Reagan's assurance that U.S. troops would remain in South Korea and that the sale of U.S. F-16 jet aircraft would be authorized to modernize the Republic's air force. General elections on March 25 gave the ruling Democratic Justice Party a solid majority of the National Assembly.

Chun marked his first anniversary in March 1982 by freeing 2,863 political prisoners, but renewed political unrest in Pusan two weeks later brought a government crackdown. On February 8, 1985, Kim Dae Jung returned to South Korea but was still banned from political activities until April when the unexpected success of his party in the National Assembly elections forced Chun to lift it.

# KUWAIT

**State of Kuwait**
**Emir:** Sheik Jaber al-Ahmad al-Sabah (1977)
**Prime Minister:** Sheik Sa'ad Abdullah al-Salem (1978)
**Area:** 7,780 sq mi. (20,150 sq km)
**Population (est. mid-1986):** 1,800,000 (average annual growth rate: 3.2%)
**Density per square mile:** 231.4
**Capital (est. 1982):** Kuwait, 182,000
**Largest city (est. 1980):** Hawalli, 752,000
**Monetary unit:** Kuwaiti dinar
**Languages:** Arabic and English
**Religions:** Islam, 92%; Christian 6%
**National name:** Dowlat al Kuwait
**Literacy rate:** about 71%
**Economic summary:** Gross national product (1983): $30.3 billion. Average annual growth rate (1973–82): 10.3%. Per capita income (1983): $18,180. Land used for agriculture: 1%. Labor force in industry: 22%; major products: crude and refined oil, fertilizer, chemicals, building materials, shrimp. Natural resources: petroleum, fish, shrimp. Exports: crude and refined petroleum, shrimp. Imports: foodstuffs, automobiles, building materials, machinery, textiles. Major trading partners: U.S., Japan, Italy, Singapore, Japan.

**Geography.** Kuwait is situated northeast of Saudi Arabia at the northern end of the Persian Gulf, south of Iraq. It is slightly larger than Hawaii. The low-lying land is mainly sandy and barren.

**Government.** Sheik Jaber al-Ahmad al-Sabah rules as Emir of Kuwait and appoints the Prime Minister, who appoints his Cabinet (Council of Ministers). The National Assembly consists of 50 members elected by adult males. There are no political parties in Kuwait.

**History.** Kuwait obtained British protection in 1897 when the Sheik feared that the Turks would take over the area. In 1961, Britain ended the protectorate, giving Kuwait independence, but agreed to give military aid on request. Iraq immediately threatened to occupy the area and Sheik Sabah al-Salem al-Sabah called in British troops in 1961. Soon afterward the Arab League sent in troops, replacing the British. The prize was oil.

Oil was discovered in the 1930s. Kuwait proved to have 20% of the world's known oil resources. It has been a major producer since 1946, the world's

second largest oil exporter. The Sheik, who gets half the profits, devotes most of them to the education, welfare, and modernization of his kingdom. In 1966, Sheik Sabah designated a relative, Jaber al-Ahmad al-Sabah, as his successor.

By 1968, the sheikdom had established a model welfare state, and it sought to establish dominance among the sheikdoms and emirates of the Persian Gulf.

A worldwide decline in the price of oil reduced Kuwait's oil income from $18.4 billion in 1980 to only $9 billion in 1984. During the same period Kuwait's support for Iraq in its war with Iran sparked terrorist attacks in Kuwait by radical Shiite Moslem supporters of Iran's Ayatollah Khomeini.

In May 1985, a suicide bomber drove into the motorcade of Sheik Jaber al-Achmad al-Sabah, the ruler. The Sheik escaped with minor cuts and bruises but five people, including the suicide bomber, were killed. In July, bombs exploded in two popular cafes, killing nine people and wounding 56.

# LAOS

**Lao People's Democratic Republic**
**President:** Souphanouvong (1975)
**Premier:** Kaysone Phomvihane (1975)
**Area:** 91,429 sq mi. (236,800 sq km)
**Population (est. mid-1986):** 3,700,000 (average annual growth rate: 2.3%)
**Density per square mile:** 40.5
**Capital and largest city (est. 1980):** Vientiane, 250,000
**Monetary unit:** Kip
**Languages:** Lao (official), French, English
**Religions:** Buddhist, 58%; tribal, 34%
**Literacy rate:** 28%
**Economic summary:** Gross national product (1984): $765 million. Per capita income (1984): $220. Land used for agriculture, 49%; labor force, 75%; principal products: rice, corn, vegetables. Major industrial products: tin, timber, tobacco, textiles, electric power. Natural resources: tin, timber, hydroelectric power. Exports: electric power, forest products, tin concentrates, coffee. Imports: rice, foodstuffs, petroleum products, machinery, transport equipment. Major trading partners: Thailand, Singapore, China, Japan

**Geography.** A landlocked nation in Southeast Asia occupying the northwestern portion of the Indochinese peninsula, Laos is surrounded by China, Vietnam, Cambodia, Thailand, and Burma. It is twice the size of Pennsylvania.

Laos is a mountainous country, especially in the north, where peaks rise above 8,000 feet (2,438 m). Dense forests cover the northern and eastern areas. The Mekong River, which forms the boundary with Burma and Thailand, flows entirely through the country for 300 miles (483 km) of its course.

**Government.** Laos is a people's democratic republic with executive power in the hands of the premier. The monarchy was abolished Dec. 2, 1975, when the Pathet Lao ousted a coalition government and King Sisavang Vatthana abdicated. The King was appointed "Supreme Adviser" to the President, the former Prince Souphanouvong. Former Prince Souvanna Phouma, Premier since 1962, was made an "adviser" to the government.

The Lao People's Revolutionary Party (Pathet Lao), led by Premier Kaysone Phomvihane, is the only political party.

**History.** Laos became a French protectorate in 1893, and the territory was incorporated into the union of Indochina. A strong nationalist movement developed during World War II, but France reestablished control in 1946 and made the King of Luang Prabang constitutional monarch of all Laos. France granted semiautonomy in 1949 and then, spurred by the Viet Minh rebellion in Vietnam, full independence within the French Union in 1950. In 1951, Prince Souphanouvong organized the Pathet Lao, a Communist independence movement, in North Vietnam. The Viet Minh in 1953 established the Pathet Lao in power at Samneua. Viet Minh and Pathet Lao forces invaded central Laos, and civil war resulted.

By the Geneva agreements of 1954 and an armistice of 1955, two northern provinces were given the Pathet Lao, the royal regime the rest. Full sovereignty was given the kingdom by the Paris agreements of Dec. 29, 1954. In 1957, Prince Souvanna Phouma, the royal Premier, and the Pathet Lao leader, Prince Souphanouvong, the Premier's half-brother, agreed to reestablishment of a unified government, with Pathet Lao participation and integration of Pathet Lao forces into the royal army. The agreement broke down in 1959, and armed conflict broke out again.

In 1960, the struggle became three-way as Gen. Phoumi Nosavan, controlling the bulk of the royal army, set up in the south a pro-Western revolutionary government headed by Prince Boun Gum. General Phoumi took Vientiane in December, driving Souvanna Phouma into exile in Cambodia. The Soviet bloc supported Souvanna Phouma. In 1961, a cease-fire was arranged and the three princes agreed to a coalition government headed by Souvanna Phouma.

But North Vietnam, the U.S. (in the form of Central Intelligence Agency personnel), and China remained active in Laos after the settlement. North Vietnam used a supply line (Ho Chi Minh trail) running down the mountain valleys of eastern Laos into Cambodia and South Vietnam, particularly after the U.S.-South Vietnamese incursion into Cambodia in 1970 stopped supplies via Cambodian seaports.

An agreement, reached in 1973 revived coalition government. The Communist Pathet Lao seized complete power in 1975, installing Souphanouvong as president and Kaysone Phomvihane as premier. Since then other parties and political groups have been moribund and most of their leaders have fled the country.

In July 1985, Laos agreed to help the United States search for U.S. servicemen missing since the Indochina war.

In 1985, border clashes between Laos and Thailand intensified, with over 120 skirmishes reported in 1984 and 1985.

# LEBANON

**Republic of Lebanon**
**President:** Amin Gemayel (1982)
**Premier:** Rashid Karami (1984)
**Area:** 4,015 sq mi. (10,400 sq km)
**Population (est. mid-1986):** 2,700,000 (average annual growth rate: 2.1%)
**Density per square mile:** 672.5

**Capital:** Beirut
**Largest cities (est. 1981):** Beirut, 750,000; Tripoli, 200,000
**Monetary unit:** Lebanese pound
**Languages:** Arabic (official), French, English
**Religions:** Christian and Islam
**National name:** Al-Joumhouriya al-Lubnaniya
**Literacy rate:** 75%
**Economic summary:** Gross national product (1983 est.): $5.0 billion. Per capita income: n.a. Land used for agriculture: 27%; labor force: 17%; principal products: fruits, wheat, corn, barley, potatoes, tobacco, olives, onions. Labor force in industry: 19%; major products: processed foods, textiles, cement, chemicals, refined oil. Exports: fruits, vegetables, textiles. Imports: metals, machinery, foodstuffs. Major trading partners: U.S., Western European and Arab countries.

**Geography.** Lebanon lies at the eastern end of the Mediterranean Sea north of Israel and west of Syria. It is four fifths the size of Connecticut.

The Lebanon Mountains, which parallel the coast on the west, cover most of the country, while on the eastern border is the Anti-Lebanon range. Between the two lies the Bekaa Valley, the principal agricultural area.

**Government.** Lebanon is governed by a President, elected by Parliament for a six-year term, and a Cabinet of Ministers appointed by the President but responsible to Parliament.

Parliament has 99 members elected for a four-year term by universal suffrage and chosen by proportional division of religious groups.

**History.** After World War I, France was given a League of Nations mandate over Lebanon and its neighbor Syria, which together had previously been a single political unit in the Ottoman Empire. France divided them in 1920 into separate colonial administrations, drawing a border that separated predominantly Moslem Syria from the kaleidoscope of religious communities in Lebanon in which Maronite Christians were then dominant. After 20 years of the French mandate regime, Lebanon's independence was proclaimed on Nov. 26, 1941, but full independence came in stages. Under an agreement between representatives of Lebanon and the French National Committee of Liberation, most of the powers exercised by France were transferred to the Lebanese government on Jan. 1, 1944. The evacuation of French troops was completed in 1946.

Civil war broke out in 1958, with Moslem factions led by Kamal Jumblat and Saeb Salam rising in insurrection against the Lebanese government headed by President Camille Chamoun, a Maronite Christian. At Chamoun's request, President Eisenhower on July 15 sent U.S. troops to reestablish the government's authority.

Clan warfare between various factions in Lebanon goes back centuries. The hodgepodge includes Maronite Christians, who since independence have dominated the government; Sunni Moslems, who have prospered in business and shared political power; the Druse, a secretive Islamic splinter group; and at the bottom of the heap until recently, Shiite Moslems.

A new—and bloodier—Lebanese civil war that broke out in 1975 resulted in the addition of still another ingredient in the brew—the Syrians. In the fighting between Lebanese factions, 40,000

Lebanese were estimated to have been killed and 100,000 wounded between March 1975 and November 1976. At that point, a Syrian-dominated Arab Deterrent Force intervened and brought large-scale fighting to a halt.

Palestinian guerrillas staging raids on Israel from Lebanese territory drew punitive Israeli raids on Lebanon, and two large-scale Israeli invasions. The first invasion, in retaliation for a PLO terrorist raid on Israel, began on March 14, 1979, and was limited in scope. Chief targets were PLO bases in southern Lebanon. The Israelis withdrew in June after the U.N. Security Council created a 6,000-man peacekeeping force for the area, called UNIFIL. As they departed, the Israelis turned their strongpoints over to a Christian militia that they had organized, instead of to the United Nations force.

The second Israeli invasion came on June 6, 1982, and this time it was a total one. It was in response to an assassination attempt by Palestinian terrorists on the Israeli ambassador in London.

A U.S. special envoy, Philip C. Habib, negotiated the dispersal of most of the PLO to other Arab nations and Israel pulled back some of its forces. The violence seemed to have come to an end when, on Sept. 14, Bashir Gemayel, the 34-year-old President-elect, was killed by a bomb that destroyed the headquarters of his Christian Phalangist Party.

The day after Gemayel's assassination, Israeli troops moved into west Beirut in force. On Sept. 17 it was revealed that Christian militiamen had massacred hundreds of Palestinians in two refugee camps. Israel denied responsibility although its troops had permitted the militiamen to enter the camps.

On Sept. 20, Amin Gemayel, older brother of Bashir Gemayel, was elected President by the parliament.

The massacre in the refugee camps prompted the return of a multinational peacekeeping force composed of U.S. Marines and British, French, and Italian soldiers. Their mandate was to support the central Lebanese government, but they soon found themselves drawn into the struggle for power between different Lebanese factions. During their stay in Lebanon, 260 U.S. Marines and about 60 French soldiers were killed, most of them in suicide bombings of the Marine and French Army compounds on Oct. 23, 1983. The multinational force left in the spring of 1984.

During 1984, Israeli troops remained in southern Lebanon and Syrian troops remained in the Bekaa Valley. By the third anniversary of the invasion, June 6, 1985, all Israeli troops had withdrawn except for several hundred "advisers" to a Christian militia trained and armed by the Israelis.

During 1985, the long-deprived Shiites shouldered aside the traditional urban upper class of Sunni oligarchs as the dominant Moslem faction in west Beirut. The more extremist Shiite factions such as Hizbullah (Party of God), inspired by Iran's Ayatollah Ruhollah Khomeini, wanted to establish an Iranian-style religious state in Lebanon and were virulently anti-Israel and anti-U.S. Fanatic youngsters recruited by Hizbullah drove explosive-laden cars in suicide missions against the Christian militia and its Israeli advisers in southern Lebanon.

Shiite extremists organized the hijacking of a TWA jetliner on June 14, 1985, and murdered one passenger, a to drive home their demand for Israel to release 700 Lebanese—mainly Shiites—detained by Israel. Seventeen days later, after flights back and forth from Beirut to Algiers and the re-

lease of many of the passengers, delicate negotiations involving Syrian President Hafez al-Assad and Nabih Berri, a relatively moderate Shiite leader, and others, brought release of the remaining 39 American hostages who had been moved from the plane to Shiite neighborhoods in Beirut.

In July 1986, Syrian troops took position in Beirut to monitor a peacekeeping agreement that involved a cease-fire and the closing of the militia offices. An earlier accord failed when the Christian militia leader, Elios Hobeika, was defeated by troops loyal to Gemayel, who opposed the agreement.

# LESOTHO

**Kingdom of Lesotho**
**Sovereign:** King Moshoeshoe II (1966)
**Chairman, Military Council:** Maj. Gen. Justin Lekhanya (1986)
**Area:** 11,720 sq mi. (30,355 sq km)
**Population (est. mid-1986):** 1,600,000 (average annual growth rate: 2.5%)
**Density per square mile:** 136.5
**Capital and largest city (est. 1983):** Maseru, 70,000
**Monetary unit:** Loti
**Languages:** English and Sesotho (official)
**Religions:** Roman Catholic, 44%; Lesotho Evangelical Church, 30%; Anglican, 12%
**Member of Commonwealth of Nations**
**Literacy rate:** 55%
**Economic summary:** Gross national product (1983): $670 million. Average annual growth rate (1973–82): 6.5%. Per capita income (1983): $470. Land used for agriculture: 15%; labor force: 87%; principal products: corn, wheat, sorghum, barley. Labor force in industry: 2%. Natural resources: diamonds. Exports: wool, mohair, wheat, cattle, diamonds, hides and skins. Imports: corn, building materials, clothing, vehicles, machinery. Major trading partner: South Africa.

**Geography.** Mountainous Lesotho, the size of Maryland, is surrounded by the Republic of South Africa in the east central part of that country except for short borders on the east and south with two discontinuous units of the Republic of Transkei. The Drakensberg Mountains in the east are Lesotho's principal chain. Elsewhere the region consists of rocky tableland.

**Government.** In January 1986, following an economic crisis caused by a South African blockade, the military overthrew Chief Johnathan and established a Military Council that would exercise a policy less tolerant of anti-apartheid activists within its borders.

The King has also been given greater powers.

**History.** Lesotho (formerly Basutoland) was constituted a native state under British protection by a treaty signed with the native chief Moshesh in 1843. It was annexed to Cape Colony in 1871, but in 1884 it was restored to direct control by the Crown.

The colony of Basutoland became the independent nation of Lesotho on Oct. 4, 1966.

In the 1970 elections, Ntsu Mokhehle, head of the Basutoland Congress Party, claimed a victory, but Jonathan declared a state of emergency, suspended the Constitution, and arrested Mokhehle. The major issue in the election was relations with South Africa, with Jonathan for close ties to the surrounding white nation, while Mokhehle was for a more independent policy. Jonathan jailed 45 opposition politicians, declared the King had "technically abdicated" by siding with the opposition party, exiled him to the Netherlands, and named his Queen and her seven-year-old son as Regent.

The King returned after a compromise with Jonathan in which the new Constitution would name him head of state but forbid his participation in politics.

# LIBERIA

**Republic of Liberia**
**President:** Gen. Samuel K. Doe (1980)
**Area:** 43,000 sq mi. (111,370 sq km)
**Population (est. mid-1986):** 2,300,000 (average annual growth rate: 3.1%)
**Density per square mile:** 53.5
**Capital and largest city (est. 1981):** Monrovia, 245,000
**Monetary unit:** Liberian dollar
**Languages:** English (official) and tribal dialects
**Religions:** Animist, 75%; Christian, 10%; Islam, 15%
**Literacy rate:** 24%
**Economic summary:** Gross national product (1983): $990 million. Average annual growth rate (1973–82): 2.5%. Per capita income (1980): $520. Land used for agriculture: 20%; labor force: 71%; principal products: rubber, rice, palm oil, cassava, coffee, cocoa. Labor force in industry: 5%; major products: iron ore, diamonds, processed rubber, processed food, construction materials. Natural resources: iron ore, rubber, timber, diamonds. Exports: iron ore, rubber, timber, diamonds. Imports: machinery, petroleum products, transport equipment, foodstuffs. Major trading partners: U.S., West Germany, Netherlands, Italy, Belgium.

**Geography.** Lying on the Atlantic in the southern part of West Africa, Liberia is bordered by Sierra Leone, Guinea, and the Ivory Coast. It is comparable in size to Tennessee.

Most of the country is a plateau covered by dense tropical forests, which thrive under an annual rainfall of about 160 inches a year.

**Government.** Since April 25, 1980, Liberia had been under military rule by the 17-member People's Redemptive Council, which suspended the Constitution after overthrowing the civilian government. On July 22, 1984, the Council was replaced with an interim, appointed National Assembly in a step toward return of civilian rule.

**History.** Liberia was founded in 1822 as a result of the efforts of the American Colonization Society to settle freed American slaves in West Africa. In 1847, it became the Free and Independent Republic of Liberia.

The government of Africa's first republic was modeled after that of the United States, and Joseph J. Roberts of Virginia was elected the first president. He laid the foundations of a modern state and initiated efforts, never too successful but pursued for more than a century, to bring the aboriginal inhabitants of the territory to the level of the emigrants. The English-speaking descendants of U.S. blacks, known as Americo-Liberians, were the intellectual and ruling class. The indigenous inhabitants, divided, constitute 99% of the population. After 1920, considerable progress was made toward opening up the interior, a process that was

spurred in 1951 by the establishment of a 43-mile (69-km) railroad to the Bomi Hills from Monrovia.

In July 1971, while serving his sixth term as president, William V. S. Tubman died following surgery and was succeeded by his long-time associate, Vice President William R. Tolbert, Jr.

Tolbert was ousted in a military coup carried out April 12, 1980, by army enlisted men led by Master Sgt. Samuel K. Doe. Tolbert and 27 other high officials were executed. Doe and his colleagues based their action on the grievances of "native" Liberians against corruption and misrule by the Americo-Liberians who had ruled the country since its founding.

In November 1985, an attempted coup against Doe following a disputed re-election, was bloodily put down and the coup leader, a former associate of Doe's, was executed.

# LIBYA

**Socialist People's Libyan Arab Jamahiriya**
**Head of State:** Col. Muammar el-Qaddafi (1969)
**Secretary-General of the General People's Congress:** Muhammad al-Zarruq Rajah (1981)
**Premier:** Jadallah Azzuz et Talhi (1979)
**Area:** 679,536 sq mi. (1,759,998 sq km)
**Population (est. mid-1986):** 3,900,000 (average annual growth rate: 3.3%)
**Density per square mile:** 5.7
**Capital:** Tripoli
**Largest cities (est. 1980):** Tripoli, 1,000,000; Benghazi, 400,000
**Monetary unit:** Libyan dinar
**Language:** Arabic
**Religion:** Islam
**National name:** Al-Jumhuria al-Arabia al-Libya
**Literacy rate:** 50%
**Economic summary:** Gross national product (1983): $25.1 billion. Average annual growth rate (1970–79): −1.6%. Per capita income (1983): $7,500. Land used for agriculture: 6%; labor force: 17%; principal products: wheat, barley, olives, dates, citrus fruits, peanuts. Labor force in industry: 10%; major products: petroleum, processed foods, textiles, handicrafts. Natural resources: petroleum, natural gas. Export: petroleum. Imports: machinery, foodstuffs, manufactured goods. Major trading partners: Italy, West Germany, U.K., France, Spain.

**Geography.** Libya stretches along the northeastern coast of Africa between Tunisia and Algeria on the west and Egypt on the east; to the south are the Sudan, Chad, and Niger. It is one sixth larger than Alaska.

A greater part of the country lies within the Sahara. Along the Mediterranean coast and farther inland is arable plateau land.

**Government.** In a bloodless coup d'etat on Sept. 1, 1969, the military seized power in Libya. King Idris I, who had ruled since 1951, was deposed and the Libyan Arab Republic proclaimed. The official name was changed in 1977 to the Socialist People's Libyan Arab Jamahiriya. The Revolutionary Council that had governed since the coup was renamed the General Secretariat of the General People's Congress. The Arab Socialist Union Organization is the only political party.

**History.** Libya was a part of the Turkish dominions from the 16th century until 1911. Following the outbreak of hostilities between Italy and Turkey in that year, Italian troops occupied Tripoli; Italian sovereignty was recognized in 1912.

Libya was the scene of much desert fighting during World War II. After the fall of Tripoli on Jan. 23, 1943, it came under Allied administration. In 1949, the U.N. voted that Libya should become independent by 1952.

Discovery of oil in the Libyan Desert promised financial stability and funds for economic development.

The Reagan Administration, accusing Libya of supporting international terrorism, closed the Libyan embassy in Washington on May 6, 1981. After talks with Libyan officials in July, the U.S. concluded that no improvement in relations was possible, although U.S. oil companies remained active in Libya and 2,000 U.S. citizens continued to work there.

On Aug. 19, 1981, two U.S. Navy F-14's shot down two Soviet-made SU-22's of the Libyan air force that had attacked them in air space above the Gulf of Sidra, claimed by Libya but held to be international by the U.S. In December, Washington asserted that Libyan "hit squads" had been dispatched to the U.S. and security was drastically tightened around President Reagan and other officials. Reagan requested remaining American citizens to leave Libya and nearly all did by Dec. 15. When the Mobil Oil Company abandoned its operations in April 1982, only four U.S. firms were still in Libya, using Libyan or third-country personnel.

Qaddafi's troops also supported rebels in Chad.

In December 1985, Qaddafi lauded as "heroic" a terrorist attack on Rome and Vienna airports that killed 20 people.

On March 24, 1986, U.S. and Libyan forces skirmished in the Gulf of Sidra, with two Libyan patrol boats being sunk.

On April 14, after a Libyan-backed attack on a West Berlin disco in which two people, including an American serviceman, were killed, Reagan order an air raid on Libyan military installations in which Qaddafi was nearly killed.

# LIECHTENSTEIN

**Principality of Liechtenstein**
**Ruler:** Prince Franz Josef II (1938)
**Prime Minister:** Hans Brunhart (1978)
**Area:** 61 sq mi. (157 sq km)
**Population (est. 1985):** 28,000 (average annual growth rate: 1.8%)
**Density per square mile:** 459.0
**Capital and largest city (est. 1985):** Vaduz, 4,872
**Monetary unit:** Swiss franc
**Language:** German (Alemannish dialect)
**Religions:** Roman Catholic, 86%; Protestant, 9%
**Literacy rate:** 100%
**Economic summary:** Per capita income (1984 est.): $15,000. Labor force in agriculture: 3%; principal products: livestock, vegetables, corn, wheat, potatoes, grapes. Labor force in industry: 43%; major products: high-technology products, building equipment, food products, machinery, industrial goods. Natural resources: timber, hydroelectric power, salt. Exports: manufactured metal products, machines and instruments, chemical products. Imports: raw materials, machinery, processed foods and goods. Major trading partners: Switzerland and other Western European countries.

**Geography.** Tiny Liechtenstein, not quite as large as Washington, D.C., lies on the east bank of the Rhine River south of Lake Constance between Austria and Switzerland. It consists of low valley land and Alpine peaks. Falknis (8,401 ft; 2,561 m) and Naatkopf (8,432 ft; 2,570 m) are the tallest.

**Government.** The Constitution of 1921, amended in 1972, provides for a legislature, the Landtag, of 15 members elected by direct male suffrage.

Prince Hans Adam has been defacto ruler since 1984, when his father, Prince Franz Josef II, relinquished his responsibilities but not his title to the throne.

The major political parties are the Homeland Union (8 of 15 seats in the Landtag) and the Progressive Citizens Party (7 seats).

**History.** Founded in 1719, Liechtenstein was a member of the German Confederation from 1815 to 1866, when it became an independent principality. It abolished its army in 1868 and has managed to stay neutral and undamaged in all European wars since then. In a referendum on July 1, 1984, male voters granted women the right to vote, a victory for Prince Hans Adam.

# LUXEMBOURG

**Grand Duchy of Luxembourg**
**Ruler:** Grand Duke Jean (1964)
**Premier:** Jacques Santer (1984)
**Area:** 999 sq mi. (2,586 sq km)
**Population (est. mid-1986):** 400,000 (Luxembourgian, French, German) (average annual growth rate: 0.0%)
**Density per square mile:** 400.4
**Capital and largest city (est. 1982):** Luxembourg, 80,000
**Monetary unit:** Luxembourg franc
**Languages:** Letzeburgesch, French, German, English
**Religion:** Mainly Roman Catholic
**National name:** Grand-Duché de Luxembourg
**Literacy rate:** 100%
**Economic summary:** Gross national product (1983): $4.7 billion. Average annual growth rate (1984): 4%. Per capita income (1983): $13,988. Land used for agriculture: 21%; labor force: 1%; principal products: livestock, dairy products, wine. Labor force in industry: 39%; major products: steel, plastics, synthetic fibers. Natural resource: Iron ore. Export: steel. Imports: machinery, chemicals, transport equipment. Major trading partners: European Common Market countries.

**Geography.** Luxembourg is a neighbor of Belgium on the west, West Germany on the east, and France on the south. The Ardennes Mountains extend from Belgium into the northern section of Luxembourg.

**Government.** Luxembourg's unicameral legislature, the Chamber of Deputies, consists of 59 members elected for five years.

The major political parties are the Christian Social Party (25 of 64 seats in Chamber of Deputies), led by Prime Minister Jacques Santer; Socialist-Labor (21 seats), led by Robert Krieps; Democratic Party (14 seats), led by Colette Flesch; Communist Party (2 seats); Green Party (2 seats).

**History.** Sigefroi, Count of Ardennes, an offspring of Charlemagne, was Luxembourg's first sovereign ruler. In 1060, the country came under the rule of the House of Luxembourg. From the 15th to the 18th century, Spain, France, and Austria held it in turn. The Congress of Vienna in 1815 made it a Grand Duchy and gave it to William I, King of the Netherlands. In 1839 the Treaty of London ceded the western part of Luxembourg to Belgium.

The eastern part, continuing in personal union with the Netherlands and a member of the German Confederation, became autonomous in 1848 and a neutral territory by decision of the London Conference of 1867, governed by its Grand Duke. Germany occupied the duchy in World Wars I and II. Allied troops liberated the enclave in 1944.

In 1961, Prince Jean, son and heir of Grand Duchess Charlotte, was made head of state, acting for his mother. She abdicated in 1964, and Prince Jean became Grand Duke. Grand Duchess Charlotte died in 1985.

By a customs union between Belgium and Luxembourg, which came into force on May 1, 1922, to last for 50 years, customs frontiers between the two countries were abolished. On Jan. 1, 1948, a customs union with Belgium and the Netherlands (Benelux) came into existence. On Feb. 3, 1958, it became an economic union.

# MADAGASCAR

**Democratic Republic of Madagascar**
**President and Head of State:** Comdr. Didier Ratsiraka (1975)
**Prime Minister:** Lt. Col. Desiré Rakotoarijaona (1977)
**Area:** 230,035 sq mi. (595,791 sq km)
**Population (est. mid-1986):** 10,300,000 (average annual growth rate: 2.8%)
**Density per square mile:** 44.8
**Capital and largest city (est. 1983):** Antananarivo, 700,-000
**Monetary unit:** Malagasy franc
**Languages:** Malagasy, French
**Ethnic groups:** Merina (or Hova), Betsimisaraka, Betsileo, Tsimihety, Antaisaka, Sakalava, Antandroy
**Religions:** Animist, 47%; Roman Catholic, 26%; Protestant, 23%; Islam, 2%
**National language:** Repoblika Demokratika Malagasy
**Literacy rate:** 53%
**Economic summary:** Gross national product (1983): $3 billion. Annual growth rate (1984): 1.6%. Per capita income (1983): $290. Land used for agriculture: 63%; labor force: 75%; principal products: rice, livestock, coffee, vanilla, sugar, cloves, cotton, sisal, peanuts, tobacco. Labor force in industry: 15%; major products: processed food, textiles, assembled automobiles, soap, mining products. Natural resources: graphite, chromium, ilmenite, tar sands, semiprecious stones. Exports: coffee, cloves, vanilla, chromium, graphite, cotton products. Imports: consumer goods, foodstuffs, crude petroleum, rice. Major trading partners: France, U.S.

**Geography.** Madagascar lies in the Indian Ocean off the southeast coast of Africa opposite Mozambique. The world's fourth-largest island, it is twice the size of Arizona. The country's low-lying coastal area gives way to a central plateau. The once densely wooded interior has largely been cut down.

**Government.** The Constitution of Dec. 30, 1975, approved by referendum following a military coup, provides for direct election by universal suffrage of a president for a seven-year term, a Supreme Council of the Revolution as a policy-making body, a unicameral People's National Assembly of 137 members (elected for five-year terms), and a military Committee for Development. The new constitution followed a period of martial rule that began with the suspension of the republic's original bicameral legislature in 1972.

**History.** The present population is of black and Malay stock, with perhaps some Polynesian, called Malagasy. The French took over a protectorate in 1885, and then in 1894–95 ended the monarchy, exiling Queen Rànavàlona III to Algiers. A colonial administration was set up, to which the Comoro Islands were attached in 1908, and other territories later. In World War II, the British occupied Madagascar, which retained ties to Vichy France.

An autonomous republic within the French Community since 1958, Madagascar became an independent member of the Community in 1960. In May 1973, an army coup led by Maj. Gen. Gabriel Ramanantsoa ousted Philibert Tsiranana, president since 1959.

With unemployment and inflation both high, Ramanantsoa resigned Feb. 5, 1975. His leftist-leaning successor, Interior Minister Richard Ratsimandrava, an Army lieutenant colonel, was killed six days later by a machine-gun ambush in Antananarivo, the capital.

On June 15, 1975, Comdr. Didier Ratsiraka was named President. He announced that he would follow a socialist course and, after nationalizing banks and insurance companies, declared all mineral resources nationalized.

# MALAWI

**Republic of Malawi**
**Life President:** Hastings Kamuzu Banda (1966)
**Area:** 45,747 sq mi. (118,484 sq km)
**Population (est. mid-1986):** 7,300,000 (average annual growth rate: 3.2%)
**Density per square mile:** 159.6
**Capital (est. 1983):** Lilongwe, 158,000
**Largest city (est. 1982):** Blantyre, 258,000
**Monetary unit:** Kwacha
**Languages:** English (official) and Chichewa (National)
**Religions:** Christian, 57%; Animist, 19%; Islam, 16%
**Member of Commonwealth of Nations**
**Literacy rate:** 25%
**Economic summary:** Gross national product (1983): $1.4 billion. Average annual growth rate (1979–82): 2.5%. Per capita income (1982): $222. Average rate of inflation (1974–78): 10%. Land used for agriculture: 25%; labor force: 52%; principal products: tobacco, tea, sugar, corn, peanuts. Labor force in industry: 16%; major products: food, beverages, tobacco, textiles, footwear, cement. Natural resource: limestone. Exports: tobacco, sugar, tea. Imports: machinery, transport equipment, building and construction materials, fuel. Major trading partners: U.K., U.S., Zimbabwe, Netherlands, Japan, West Germany, South Africa.

**Geography.** Malawi is a landlocked country the size of Pennsylvania in southeastern Africa, surrounded by Mozambique, Zambia, and Tanzania. Lake Malawi, formerly Lake Nyasa, occupies most of the country's eastern border. The north-south Rift Valley is flanked by mountain ranges and high plateau areas.

**Government.** Under a Constitution that came into effect on July 6, 1966, the president is the sole head of state; there is neither a prime minister nor a vice president. The National Assembly has 107 members.

There is only one national party—the Malawi Congress Party led by President Hastings K. Banda.

**History.** The first European to make extensive explorations in the area was David Livingstone in the 1850s and 1860s. In 1884, Cecil Rhodes's British South African Company received a charter to develop the country. The company came into conflict with the Arab slavers in 1887–89. After Britain annexed the Nyasaland territory in 1891, making it a protectorate in 1892, Sir Harry Johnstone, the first high commissioner, using Royal Navy gunboats, wiped out the slavers.

Nyasaland became the independent nation of Malawi on July 6, 1964. Two years later, it became a republic within the Commonwealth of Nations.

Dr. Hastings K. Banda, Malawi's first Prime Minister, became its first President. He pledged to follow a policy of "discretionary nonalignment." Banda alienated much of Black Africa by maintaining good relations with such white-ruled nations as South Africa and Rhodesia. He argued that his landlocked country had to rely on white-ruled countries for access to the sea and trade.

# MALAYSIA

**Paramount Ruler:** Sultan Iskandar Alhaj D.K., Sultan of Johore (1984)
**Prime Minister:** Mahathir Bin Mohamed (1981)
**Area:** 128,328 sq mi. (332,370 sq km)
**Population (est. mid-1986):** 15,800,000 (average annual growth rate: 2.4%)
**Density per square mile:** 123.1
**Capital:** Kuala Lumpur
**Largest cities (est. 1980 by U.N.):** Kuala Lumpur, 1,000,-000; George Town (Pinang), 300,000; Ipoh, 275,000
**Monetary unit:** Ringgit
**Languages:** Malay (official), Chinese, Tamil, English
**Religions:** Islam, (official), Buddhist, Hindu, Christian, Confucian, Taoist
**Member of Commonwealth of Nations**
**Literacy rate:** 75%
**Economic summary:** Gross national product (1984): $28.4 billion. Average annual growth rate (1973–82): 7.4%. Per capita income (1985): $1,976. Labor force: 12%; principal products: natural rubber, palm oil, tin, petroleum, rice, timber. Major industrial products: processed rubber, timber, and palm oil, tin, petroleum, light manufactures, electronics equipment. Natural resources: tin, oil, copper, timber. Exports: natural rubber, palm oil, tin, timber, petroleum. Imports: machinery, transport equipment, chemicals. Major trading partners: Japan, Singapore, U.S., Western European countries.

**Geography.** Malaysia is at the southern end of the Malay Peninsula in southeast Asia. The nation also includes Sabah and Sarawak on the island of Borneo to the southeast. Its area slightly exceeds that of New Mexico.

Most of Malaysia is covered by dense jungle and swamps, with a mountain range running the length of the peninsula. Extensive forests provide ebony, sandalwood, teak, and other woods.

**Government.** Malaysia is a sovereign constitutional monarchy within the Commonwealth of Nations. The Paramount Ruler is elected for a five-year term by the hereditary rulers of the states from among themselves. He is advised by the prime minister and his cabinet. There is a bicameral legislature. The Senate, whose role is comparable more to that of the British House of Lords than to the U.S. Senate, has 68 members, partly appointed by the Paramount Ruler to represent minority and special interests, and partly elected by the legislative assemblies of the various states.

The House of Representatives, is made up of 180 members, who are elected for five-year terms.

The major political parties are the National Front, a coalition of 10 parties (148 of 177 seats in the House of Representatives); Democratic Action Party (24 seats); Islamic Party (1 seat); Independents (4 seats).

**History.** Malaysia came into existence on Sept. 16, 1963, as a federation of Malaya, Singapore, Sabah (North Borneo), and Sarawak. In 1965, Singapore withdrew from the federation. Since 1966, the 11 states of former Malaya have been known as West Malaysia, and Sabah and Sarawak have been known as East Malaysia.

The Union of Malaya was established April 1, 1946, being formed from the Federated Malay States of Negri Sembilan, Pahang, Perak, and Selangor; the Unfederated Malay States of Johore, Kedah, Kelantan, Perlis, and Trengganu; and two of the Straits Settlements—Malacca and Penang. The Malay states had been brought under British administration during the late 19th and early 20th centuries.

It became the Federation of Malaya on Feb. 1, 1948, and the Federation attained full independence within the Commonwealth of Nations in 1957.

Sabah, constituting the extreme northern portion of the island of Borneo, was a British protectorate administered under charter by the British North Borneo Company from 1881 to 1946, when it assumed the status of a colony. It was occupied by Japanese troops from 1942 to 1945.

Sarawak extends along the northwestern coast of Borneo for about 500 miles (805 km). In 1841, part of the present territory was granted by the Sultan of Brunei to Sir James Brooke. Sarawak continued to be ruled by members of the Brooke family until the Japanese occupation.

From 1963, when Malaysia became independent, it was the target of guerrilla infiltration from Indonesia, but beat off invasion attempts. In 1966, when Sukarno fell and the Communist Party was liquidated in Indonesia, hostilities ended.

In the late 1960s, the country was torn by communal rioting directed against Chinese and Indians, who controlled a disproportionate share of the country's wealth. Beginning in 1968, the government moved to achieve greater economic balance through a rural development program.

Malaysia felt the impact of the "boat people" fleeing Vietnam early in 1978. Because the refugees were mostly ethnic Chinese, the government was apprehensive about any increase of a minority that previously had been the source of internal conflict in the country. In November, authorities banned landings and reversed the order only after several hundred refugees drowned when their fragile boats were towed offshore by Malaysian police.

# MALDIVES

**Republic of Maldives**
**President:** Maumoon Abdul Gayoom (1978)
**Area:** 115 sq mi. (298 sq km)
**Population (est. mid-1986):** 200,000 (average annual growth rate: 3.1%)
**Density per square mile:** 1739.1
**Capital and largest city (est. 1985):** Malé, 46,344
**Monetary unit:** Maldivian rupee
**Language:** Divehi
**Religion:** Islam
**Literacy rate:** 36%
**Economic summary:** Gross national product (1983 est.): $56.0 million. Average annual growth rate (1970–79): −0.7%. Per capita income (est. 1983): $334. Principal agricultural products: coconuts, millet. Labor force in industry: 26%, major products: fish, processed coconuts. Natural resource: fish, coconuts. Export: fish, clothing, ambergris. Imports: rice, foodstuffs. Major trading partners: Japan, Sri Lanka, Singapore, U.S.

**Geography.** The Republic of Maldives is a group of atolls in the Indian Ocean about 417 miles (671 km) southwest of Sri Lanka. Its 1,300 coral islets stretch over an area of 35,200 square miles (90,000 sq km).

**Government.** The 9-member Cabinet is headed by the president. The Majlis (Parliament) is a unicameral legislature consisting of 48 members. Eight of these are appointed by the president. The others are elected for five-year terms, 2 from the capital island of Malé and 2 from each of the 19 administrative atolls.

There are no political parties in the Maldives.

**History.** The Maldives (formerly called the Maldive Islands) are inhabited by an Islamic seafaring people. Originally the islands were under the suzerainty of Ceylon. They came under British protection in 1887 and were a dependency of the then colony of Ceylon until 1948. The independence agreement with Britain was signed July 26, 1965.

For centuries a sultanate, the islands adopted a republican form of government in 1952, but the sultanate was restored in 1954. In 1968, however, as the result of a referendum, a republic was again established in the islands.

Ibrahim Nasir, president since 1968, was removed from office by the Majlis in November 1978 and replaced by Maumoon Abdul Cayoom. A national referendum confirmed the new leader.

# MALI

**Republic of Mali**
**President of the Republic:** Gen. Moussa Traoré
**Area:** 478,819 sq mi. (1,240,142 sq km)
**Population (est. mid-1986):** 7,900,000 (average annual growth rate, 2.8%)
**Density per square mile:** 16.5
**Capital and largest city (est. 1981):** Bamako, 750,000
**Monetary unit:** Franc CFA
**Ethnic groups:** Bambara, Peul, Soninke, Malinke, Songhai, Dogon, Senoufo, Minianka, Berbers, and Moors
**Languages:** French (official), African languages
**Religions:** Islam, 90%; Animist, 9%; Christian, 1%

**National name:** République de Mali
**Literacy rate:** 10%
**Economic summary:** Gross national product (1983): $1.1 billion. Average annual growth rate (1973–82): 4.8%. Per capita income (1983): $150. Principal agricultural products: millet, sorghum, corn, rice, sugar, cotton, peanuts, livestock. Major industrial products: processed foods, textiles. Natural resources: bauxite, iron ore, maganese, phosphate, goats, salt, limestone, gold. Exports: livestock, peanuts, dried fish, cotton, skins. Imports: textiles, vehicles, petroleum products, machinery, sugar. Major trading partners: Western European countries, U.S.S.R., China.

**Geography.** Most of Mali, in West Africa, lies in the Sahara. A landlocked country four fifths the size of Alaska, it is bordered by Guinea, Senegal, Mauritania, Algeria, Niger, Burkina Faso, and the Ivory Coast.

The only fertile area is in the south, where the Niger and Senegal Rivers provide irrigation.

**Government.** The army overthrew the government on Nov. 19, 1968, and formed a provisional government. The Military Committee of National Liberation consists of 14 members and forms the decision-making body.

In late 1969 an attempted coup was foiled, and Lt. Moussa Traoré, president of the Military Committee took over as chief of state and later as head of government, ousting Capt. Yoro Diakité as Premier.

The Malian People's Democratic Union, established in 1976, is the only political party.

**History.** Subjugated by France by the end of the 19th century, this area became a colony in 1904 (named French Sudan in 1920) and in 1946 became part of the French Union. On June 20, 1960, it became independent and, under the name of Sudanese Republic, was federated with the Republic of Senegal in the Mali Federation. However, Senegal seceded from the Federation on Aug. 20, 1960, and the Sudanese Republic then changed its name to the Republic of Mali on September 22.

In the 1960s, Mali concentrated on economic development, continuing to accept aid from both Soviet bloc and Western nations, as well as international agencies. In the late 1960s, it began retreating from close ties with China. But a purge of conservative opponents brought greater power to President Modibo Keita, and in 1968 the influence of the Chinese and their Malian sympathizers increased. By a treaty signed in Peking in 1968, China agreed to help build a railroad from Mali to Guinea, providing Mali with vital access to the sea.

Mali, with Mauritania, the Ivory Coast, Senegal, Dahomey (Benin), Niger, and Burkina Faso signed a treaty establishing the Economic Community for West Africa.

A six-year sub-Sahara drought devastated Mali before disastrously heavy rains began in 1974. Emergency shipments from a dozen nations and international organizations helped alleviate a famine that affected 1.8 million Malians and killed thousands.

Mali and Burkina Faso fought a brief border war from December 25 to 29, 1985.

# MALTA

**Republic of Malta**
**President:** Agatha Barbara (1982)
**Prime Minister:** Carmelo Mifsud Bonnici (1984)
**Area:** 122 sq mi. (316 sq km)
**Population (est. mid-1986):** 400,000 (average annual growth rate: 0.8%)
**Density per square mile:** 3,278.7
**Capital (est. 1982):** Valetta, 15,000
**Largest city (est. 1982):** Sliema, 20,500
**Monetary unit:** Maltese lira
**Languages:** Maltese and English
**Religion:** Roman Catholic
**National name:** Repubblika Ta Malta
**Member of Commonwealth of Nations, Council of Europe**
**Literacy rate:** 83%
**Economic summary:** Gross national product (1983): $1.3 billion. Average annual growth rate (1973–82): 1.5%. Per capita income (1983): $4,000. Land used for agriculture, 45%; labor force: 6%; principal products: fodder crops, potatoes, onions, fruits and vegetables. Labor force in industry: 27%; major products: textiles, wine, beer, processed foods, plastics, electronic equipment. Natural resources: limestone, salt. Exports: textiles, yarns, manufactured goods, ships. Imports: manufactured goods, machinery, transport equipment. Major trading partners: West Germany, U.K., Italy.

**Geography.** The five Maltese islands—with a combined land area smaller than Philadelphia—are in the Mediterranean about 60 miles (97 km) south of the southeastern tip of Sicily.

**Government.** The government is headed by a Prime Minister, responsible to a 65-member House of Representatives elected by universal suffrage.

The major political parties are Malta Labor Party (34 of 65 seats in House of Representatives), led by Prime Minister Carmelo Mifsud Bonnici; Nationalist Party (31 seats), led by Edward Fenech Adami.

**History.** The strategic importance of Malta was recognized by the Phoenicians, who occupied it, as did in their turn the Greeks, Carthaginians, and Romans. The apostle Paul was shipwrecked there in A.D. 58.

The Knights of St. John (Malta), who obtained the three habitable Maltese islands of Malta, Gozo, and Comino from Charles V in 1530, reached their highest fame when they withstood an attack by superior Turkish forces in 1565.

Napoleon seized Malta in 1798, but the French forces were ousted by British troops the next year, and British rule was confirmed by the Treaty of Paris in 1814.

Malta was heavily attacked by German and Italian aircraft during World War II, but was never invaded by the Axis.

Malta became an independent nation on Sept. 21, 1964, and a republic Dec. 13, 1974, but remained in the British Commonwealth. The Governor-General, Sir Anthony Mamo, was sworn in as first president and Dom Mintoff remained prime minister.

After 13 years in office, Mintoff resigned as Prime Minister on Dec. 22, 1984, giving way to chosen successor, Carmelo Mifsud Bonnici, who had been Senior Deputy Prime Minister.

# MAURITANIA

**Islamic Republic of Mauritania**
**Chief of State and Head of Government:** Col. Maaouye Ould Sidi Ahmed Taya (1984)
**Area:** 397,953 sq mi. (1,030,700 sq km)
**Population (est. mid-1986):** 1,900,000 (average annual growth rate: 2.9%)
**Density per square mile:** 4.8
**Capital and largest city (est. 1981):** Nouakchott, 175,000
**Monetary unit:** Ouguyia
**Ethnic groups:** Moors; a black minority (Poulars, Soninkes, and Wolofs)
**Languages:** Arabic and French
**Religion:** Islam
**National name:** République Islamique de Mauritanie
**Literacy rate:** 17%
**Economic summary:** Gross national product (1983): $720 million. Average annual growth rate (1973–82): 3.0%. Per capita income (1983): $450. Principal agricultural products: livestock, millet, maize, wheat, dates, rice. Major industrial products: iron ore, processed fish. Natural resources: copper, iron ore, gypsum, fish. Exports: iron ore, fish, copper. Imports: foodstuffs, petroleum, capital goods. Major trading partners: France, Spain, U.S., U.K., Italy, Japan.

**Geography.** Mauritania, three times the size of Arizona, is situated in northwest Africa with about 350 miles (592 km) of coastline on the Atlantic Ocean. It is bordered by Morocco on the north, Algeria and Mali on the east, and Senegal on the south.

The country is mostly desert, with the exception of the fertile Senegal River valley in the south and grazing land in the north.

**Government.** An Army coup on July 10, 1978, deposed Moktar Ould Daddah, who had been President since Mauritania's independence in 1960. President Mohammed Khouna Ould Haldala, who seized power in the 1978 coup, was in turn deposed in a Dec. 12, 1984, coup by army chief of staff Maaouye Ould Sidi Ahmed Taya, who assumed the title of President.

**History.** Mauritania was first explored by the Portuguese. The French organized the area as a territory in 1904.

Mauritania became an independent nation on Nov. 28, 1960, and was admitted to the United Nations in 1961 over the strenuous opposition of Morocco, which claimed the territory. With Moors, Arabs, Berbers, and blacks frequently in conflict, the government in the late 1960s sought to make Arab culture dominant to unify the land.

Mauritania acquired administrative control of the southern part of the former Spanish Sahara when the colonial administration withdrew in 1975, under an agreement with Morocco and Spain. Mauritanian troops moved into the territory but encountered resistance from the Polisario Front, a Saharan independence movement backed by Algeria. The task of trying to pacify the area proved a heavy burden. Mauritania signed a peace agreement with the Polisario insurgents in August 1979, withdrew from the territory and renounced territorial claims.

Increased military spending and rising casulaties in Western Sahara contributed to the discontent that brought down the civilian government of Ould Daddah in 1978. A succession of military rulers has followed.

# MAURITIUS

**Sovereign:** Queen Elizabeth II
**Governor-General:** Sir Veerosomy Ringadoo (1986)
**Prime Minister:** Aneerood Jugnauth (1982)
**Area:** 787 sq mi. (2,040 sq km)
**Population (est. mid-1986):** 1,000,000 (average annual growth rate: 1.5%) (Indian, 51%; Creole, 33%)
**Density per square mile:** 1,270.7
**Capital and largest city (est. 1980):** Port Louis, 155,000
**Monetary unit:** Mauritian rupee
**Languages:** English (official), French, Creole, Hindi, Urdu, Chinese
**Religions:** Hindu, 46%, Christian (mainly Roman Catholic), 33%; Islam, 16%
**Member of Commonwealth of Nations**
**Literacy rate:** 61%
**Economic summary:** Gross national product (1983): $1.25 billion. Average annual growth rate (1973–82): 3.9%. Per capita income (1983): $1,000. Land used for agriculture: 50%; labor force: 29%; principal products: sugar cane. Labor force in industry: 22%; major products: processed sugar and tea, molasses, rum, textiles. Natural resources: fish. Exports: sugar, tea, molasses. Imports: foodstuffs, manufactured goods. Major trading partners: Western European countries, U.S., U.K.

**Geography.** Mauritius is a mountainous island in the Indian Ocean east of Madagascar.

**Government.** Mauritius is a member of the British Commonwealth, with Queen Elizabeth II as head of state. She is represented by a governor-general, who chooses the prime minister from the unicameral Legislative Assembly. The Legislative Assembly has 70 members, 62 of whom are elected by direct suffrage. The remaining 8 are chosen from among the unsuccessful candidates.

The major parties are the governing Alliance Party coalition, composed of the Mouvement Socialiste Mauricien, the Parti Mauricien Social Democrate, the Labor Party, and the Organisation du Peuple Rodriguais (48 of 70 seats in the Legislative Assembly, led by Prime Minister Aneerood Jugnauth, and the opposition Mouvement Militant Mauricien, led by Paul Berenger.

**History.** Mauritius was seized from France by British troops in 1810 and ceded to Britain by the Treaty of Paris in 1814. Until 1903, Mauritius and the Seychelles were administered as a single colony. The colony of Mauritius became an independent nation on March 12, 1968.

The nation has an Indian majority, descendants of laborers imported from India to work the sugar plantations after the abolition of slavery in 1834. The native blacks speak French and are Roman Catholics.

The Labor Party government of Sir Seewoosagur Ramgoolam, who had ruled Mauritius since independence, was toppled in a 1982 election by the Movement Militant Mauricien, which had campaigned for recovery of Diego Garcia island, separated from Mauritius during the colonial period and leased by Britain to the United States for a naval base. But an Alliance Party coalition, including the Labor Party, regained power at the end of 1983 and brought back Ramgoolam as Prime Minister. He was succeeded by Aneerood Jugnauth of his party in 1982.

# MEXICO

**United Mexican States**
**President:** Miguel de la Madrid Hurtado (1982)
**Area:** 761,600 sq mi. (1,972,547 sq km)
**Population (est. mid-1986):** 81,700,000 (average annual growth rate: 2.6%) (60% mestizo; 30% Indian)
**Density per square mile:** 107.3
**Capital:** Mexico City
**Largest cities (1980 census):** Mexico City, 12,900,000; Guadalajara, 3,000,000; Monterrey, 2,700,000; Ciudad Juarez, 1,120,000; Puebla de Zaragoza, 1,100,000; Leon, 1,000,000
**Monetary unit:** Peso
**Languages:** Spanish, Indian languages
**Religion:** Mainly Roman Catholic
**Official name:** Estados Unidos Mexicanos
**Literacy rate:** 81%
**Economic summary:** Gross national product (1983): $168 billion. Annual growth rate (1983): −5.3%. Per capita income (1983): $2,240. Land used for agriculture, 12%; labor force: 26%; principal products: corn, cotton, sugar cane, fruits. Labor force in industry: 17%; major products: processed foods, chemicals, basic metals and metal products, petroleum. Natural resources: petroleum, silver, copper, gold, lead, zinc, natural gas, timber. Exports: cotton, sugar, shrimp, cattle and meat, petroleum. Imports: machinery, equipment, industrial vehicles, intermediate goods. Major trading partners: U.S., Japan, Western European countries.

**Geography.** The United States' neighbor to the south, Mexico is about one fifth its size. Baja California in the west, an 800-mile (1,287-km) peninsula, forms the Gulf of California. In the east are the Gulf of Mexico and the Bay of Campeche, which is formed by Mexico's other peninsula, the Yucatán.

The center of Mexico is a great, high plateau, open to the north, with mountain chains on east and west and with ocean-front lowlands lying outside of them.

**Government.** The President, who is popularly elected for six years and is ineligible to succeed himself, governs with a Cabinet of secretaries. Congress has two houses—a 400-member Chamber of Deputies, elected for three years, and a 64-member Senate, elected for six years.

Each of the 31 states has considerable autonomy, with a popularly elected governor, a legislature, and a local judiciary. The President of Mexico appoints the mayor of the Federal District.

The major parties are the Partido Revolucionario Institucional (all 64 seats in the Senate and 289 of 400 seats in the Chamber of Deputies); Partido Acción Nacional (38 of 400 seats in Chamber); Partido Socialista Unificado de Mexico (12 seats); Unified Socialist Party (12 seats); and other parties.

**History.** At least two civilized races—the Mayas and later the Toltecs—preceded the wealthy Aztec empire, conquered in 1519–21 by the Spanish under Hernando Cortés. Spain ruled for the next 300 years until 1810 (the date was Sept. 16 and is now celebrated as Independence Day), when the Mexicans first revolted. They continued the struggle and finally won independence in 1821.

From 1821 to 1877, there were two emperors, several dictators, and enough presidents and provisional executives to make a new government on the average of every nine months. Mexico lost Texas (1836), and after defeat in the war with the

U.S. (1846–48) it lost the area comprising the present states of California, Nevada, and Utah, most of Arizona and New Mexico, and parts of Wyoming and Colorado.

In 1855, the Indian patriot Benito Juárez began a series of liberal reforms, including the disestablishment of the Catholic Church, which had acquired vast property. A subsequent civil war was interrupted by the French invasion of Mexico (1861), the crowning of Maximilian of Austria as Emperor (1864), and then his overthrow and execution by forces under Juárez, who again became President in 1867.

The years after the fall of the dictator Porfirio Diaz (1877–80 and 1884–1911) were marked by bloody political-military strife and trouble with the U.S., culminating in the punitive expedition into northern Mexico (1916–17) in unsuccessful pursuit of the revolutionary Pancho Villa. Since a brief period of civil war in 1920, Mexico has enjoyed a period of gradual agricultural, political, and social reforms. Relations with the U.S. were again disturbed in 1938 when all foreign oil wells were expropriated. Agreement on compensation was finally reached in 1941.

The last year of José López Portillo's presidency was shadowed by economic problems caused by falling oil prices.

Miguel de la Madrid Hurtado, candidate of the ruling Partido Revolucionario Institucional, won the July 4 election for a six-year term.

During 1983 and 1984, Mexico suffered its worst financial crisis in 50 years, leading to critically high unemployment and widespread dissatisfaction with the Institutional Revolutionary Party. Its inability to make payments on its $89.8-billion foreign debt as they came due triggered a worldwide debt crisis.

In an election held on July 7, 1985, the ruling Institutional Party declared it had won all seven contested governorships and an overwhelming majority in the national Chamber of Deputies. Shortly afterward, the government slashed oil prices and lowered the value of the peso and by mid-1986, was considering a moratorium on payments of its debt.

Mexican-American relations were strained when, on May 13, 1986, U.S. officials told the Senate that high officials in the Mexican government were involved in drug trafficking. Mexico angrily denied the charges.

# MONACO

**Principality of Monaco**
**Ruler:** Prince Rainier III (1949)
**Minister of State:** Jean Ausseil (1986)
**Area:** 0.73 sq mi. (465 acres)
**Population (est. 1985):** 28,000 (average annual growth rate: 1.2%)
**Density per square mile:** 38,356.2
**Capital:** Monaco-Ville
**Monetary unit:** French franc
**Languages:** French, Monégasque, Italian
**Religion:** Roman Catholic
**National name:** Principauté de Monaco
**Literacy rate:** 99%

**Geography.** Monaco is a tiny, hilly wedge driven into the French Mediterranean coast nine miles east of Nice.

**Government.** Prince Albert of Monaco gave the principality a Constitution in 1911, creating a National Council of 18 members popularly elected for five years. The head of government is the Minister of State.

Prince Rainier III, born May 31, 1923, succeeded his grandfather, Louis II, on the latter's death, May 9, 1949. Rainier was married April 18, 1956, to Grace Kelly, U.S. actress. A daughter, Princess Caroline Louise Marguerite, was born on Jan. 23, 1957 (married to Philippe Junot June 28, 1978 and divorced in 1980; married to Stefano Casiraghi Dec. 29, 1983, and gave birth to a son, Andrea Albert, June 9, 1984); a son, Prince Albert Louis Pierre, on March 14, 1958; and Princess Stéphanie Marie Elisabeth, on Feb. 1, 1965. Princess Grace died Sept. 14, 1982, of injuries received the day before when the car she was driving went off the road near Monte Carlo. She was 52. Her daughter Stéphanie suffered neck injuries.

The special significance attached to the birth of descendants to Prince Rainier stems from a clause in the Treaty of July 17, 1919, between France and Monaco stipulating that in the event of vacancy of the Crown, the Monégasque territory would become an autonomous state under a French protectorate.

The National and Democratic Union (all 18 seats in National Council), led by Auguste Medecin, is the only political party.

**History.** The Phoenicians, and after them the Greeks, had a temple on the Monacan headland honoring Hercules. From *Monoikos*, the Greek surname for this mythological strong man, the principality took its name. After being independent for 800 years, Monaco was annexed to France in 1793 and was placed under Sardinia's protection in 1815. In 1861, it went under French guardianship but continued to be independent.

By a treaty in 1918, France stipulated that the French government be given a veto over the succession to the throne.

Monaco is a little land of pleasure with a tourist business that runs as high as 1.5 million visitors a year. It had popular gaming tables as early as 1856. Five years later, a 50-year concession to operate the games was granted to François Blanc, of Bad Homburg. This concession passed into the hand of a private company in 1898.

Monaco's practice of providing a tax shelter for French businessmen resulted in a dispute between the countries. When Rainier refused to end the practice, France retaliated with a customs tax. In 1967, Rainier took control of the Société des Bains de Mer, operator of the famous Monte Carlo gambling casino, in a program to increase hotel and convention space. He paid $8 million to Greek shipping magnate Aristotle Onassis for his shares:

# MONGOLIA

**Mongolian People's Republic**
**Chairman of Presidium of the Great People's Khural (President):** Jambyn Batmunkh (1984)
**Chairman of Council of Ministers (Premier):** Dumagiin Sodnom (1984)
**Area:** 604,250 sq mi. (1,565,000 sq km)
**Population (est. mid-1986):** 1,900,000 (average annual growth rate: 2.5%)
**Density per square mile:** 3.1

**Capital and largest city (est. 1984):** Ulan Bator, 470,500
**Monetary unit:** Tugrik
**Language:** Mongolian
**Religion:** Lamaistic Buddhism
**National name:** Bugd Nairamdakh Mongol Ard Uls
**Literacy rate:** about 80%
**Economic summary:** Gross national product (1983): $1.8 billion. Average annual growth rate (1970–81): 3.1%. Per capita income: (1983): $1,000 Principal agricultural products: livestock, wheat, oats, barley. Major industrial products: animal products, building materials, minerals. Natural resources: coal, copper, molybdenum. Exports: livestock, animal products, nonferrous metals. Imports: machinery and equipment, clothing, petroleum. Major trading partners: U.S.S.R. and Soviet bloc countries.

**Geography.** Mongolia lies in eastern Asia between Soviet Siberia on the north and China on the south. It is slightly larger than Alaska.

The productive regions of Mongolia—a tableland ranging from 3,000 to 5,000 feet (914 to 1,524 m) in elevation—are in the north, which is well drained by numerous rivers, including the Hovd, Onon, Selenga, and Tula.

Much of the Gobi Desert falls within Mongolia.

**Government.** The Mongolian People's Republic is a socialist state. The highest organ of state power is the Great People's Khural (Parliament), which is elected for a term of four years and is convened once a year. The Great People's Khural elects the Presidium, which consists of a chairman, two vice chairmen, a secretary, and six members. The Council of Ministers is set up by the Great People's Khural and consists of a chairman, vice chairmen, and ministers.

The Mongolian People's Revolutionary Party, led by President Jambyn Batmunkh, is the only political party.

**History.** The Mongolian People's Republic, formerly known as Outer Mongolia, is a Soviet satellite. It contains the original homeland of the historic Mongols, whose power reached its zenith during the 13th century under Kublai Khan. The area accepted Manchu rule in 1689, but after the Chinese Revolution of 1911 and the fall of the Manchus in 1912, the northern Mongol princes expelled the Chinese officials and declared independence under the Khutukhtu, or "Living Buddha."

In 1921, Soviet troops entered the country and facilitated the establishment of a republic by Mongolian revolutionaries in 1924 after the death of the last Living Buddha. China, meanwhile, continued to claim Outer Mongolia but was unable to back the claim with any strength. Under the 1945 Chinese-Russian Treaty, China agreed to give up Outer Mongolia, which, after a plebiscite, became a nominally independent country.

Allied with the U.S.S.R. in its dispute with China, Mongolia has mobilized troops along its borders since 1968 when the two powers became involved in border clashes on the Kazakh-Sinkiang frontier to the west and on the Amur and Ussuri Rivers. A 20-year treaty of friendship and cooperation, signed in 1966, entitled Mongolia to call upon the U.S.S.R. for military aid in the event of invasion.

# MOROCCO

**Kingdom of Morocco**
**Ruler:** King Hassan II (1961)
**Prime Minister:** Karim Lamrani (1984)
**Area:** 177,116 sq mi. (458,730 sq km)
**Population (est. mid-1986):** 23,700,000 (average annual growth rate: 2.6%)
**Density per square mile:** 133.8
**Capital:** Rabat
**Largest cities (1982):** Casablanca, 2,139,204; Rabat, 518,616; Fez, 448,823; Marrakech, 439,728; Meknes, 319,783
**Monetary unit:** Dirham
**Languages:** Arabic, French, Spanish
**Religions:** Islam
**National name:** al-Mamlaka al-Maghrebia
**Literacy rate:** 28%
**Economic summary:** Gross national product (1985): $17.5 billion. Average annual growth rate (est. 1984): 2.0%. Per capita income (1983): $750. Land used for agriculture; 19%; labor force: 50%; products: barley, wheat, citrus fruits, vegetables, wool. Labor force in industry, 15%; major products: textiles, fish, chemicals. Natural resources: phosphates, lead, manganese, fisheries. Exports: phosphates, citrus fruits, vegetables, canned fruits and vegetables, canned fish, carpets. Imports: capital goods, fuels, food stuffs, iron and steel. Major trading partners: France, West Germany, Italy, Saudi Arabia.

**Geography.** Morocco, about one tenth larger than California, is just south of Spain across the Strait of Gibraltar and looks out on the Atlantic from the northwest shoulder of Africa. Algeria is to the east and Mauritania to the south.

On the Atlantic coast there is a fertile plain. The Mediterranean coast is mountainous. The Atlas Mountains, running northeastward from the south to the Algerian frontier, average 11,000 feet (3,353 m) in elevation.

**Government.** The King, after suspending the 1962 Constitution and dissolving Parliament in 1965, promulgated a new Constitution in 1972. He continued to rule by decree until June 3, 1977, when the first free elections since 1962 took place. The 306-member Chamber of Deputies has 204 elected seats, with the balance chosen by local councils and groups.

A coalition of independents loyal to the King and three right-of-center parties, the Constitutional Union Party (83 seats), the National Rally of Independents (61 seats), and the National Democratic Party (24 seats), constitute the government. Opposition parties include the Popular Movement (47 seats) and Isviglol (43 seats).

**History.** Morocco was once the home of the Berbers, who helped the Arabs invade Spain in A.D. 711 and then revolted against them and gradually won control of large areas of Spain for a time after 739.

The country was ruled successively by various native dynasties and maintained regular commercial relations with Europe, even during the 17th and 18th centuries when it was the headquarters of the famous Salé pirates. In the 19th century, there were frequent clashes with the French and Spanish. Finally, in 1904, France and Spain divided Morocco into zones of French and Spanish influence, and these were established as protectorates in 1912.

Meanwhile, Morocco had become the object of big-power rivalry, which almost led to a European war in 1905 when Germany attempted to gain a foothold in the rich mineral country. By terms of the Algeciras Conference (1906), Morocco was internationalized economically, and France's privileges were limited.

The Tangier Statute, concluded by Britain, France, and Spain in 1923, created an international zone at the port of Tangier, permanently neutralized and demilitarized. In World War II, Spain occupied the zone, ostensibly to ensure order, but was forced to withdraw in 1945.

Sultan Mohammed V was deposed by the French in 1953 and replaced by his uncle, but nationalist agitation forced his return in 1955. On his death on Feb. 26, 1961, his son, Hassan, became King.

France and Spain recognized the independence and sovereignty of Morocco in 1956. Later the same year, the Tangier international zone was abolished.

In 1975, tens of thousands of Moroccans crossed the border into Spanish Sahara to back their government's contention that the northern part of the territory was historically part of Morocco. At the same time, Mauritania occupied the southern half of the territory in defiance of Spanish threats to resist such a takeover. Abandoning its commitment to self-determination for the territory, Spain withdrew, and only Algeria protested.

When Mauritania signed a peace treaty with the Algerian-backed Polisario Front in August 1979, Morocco occupied and assumed administrative control of the southern part of the Western Sahara, in addition to the northern part it already occupied. Under pressure from other African leaders, Hassan agreed in mid-1981 to a cease-fire with a referendum under international supervision to decide the fate of the Sahara territory, but the referendum was never carried out.

King Hassan, startled the Reagan Administration in mid-August 1984 by signing a treaty of union with Col. Muammar el-Qaddafi, the Libyan leader. The Moroccans described the treaty as the culmination of a process in which Libya had withdrawn its support for the Polisario in the Western Sahara, and Morocco had agreed to refrain from sending troops to help the French in Chad. Shortly after the treaty signing, the Polisario guerillas were reported on the verge of being quelled.

King Hassan became the second Arab leader to meet with an Israeli leader when, on July 21, 1986, Israeli Prime Minister Shimon Peres came to Morocco.

## MOZAMBIQUE

**People's Republic of Mozambique**
**President:** Samora Moises Machel (1975)
**Area:** 303,073 sq mi. (799,380 sq. km.)
**Population (est. mid-1986):** 14,000,000 (average annual growth rate: 2.5%)
**Density per square mile:** 46.2
**Capital and largest city (est. mid-1982):** Maputo, 785,500
**Monetary unit:** Metical
**Languages:** Portuguese (official), Bantu languages
**Religions:** Animist, 48%; Christian, 17%; Islam, 17%
**National name:** República Popular de Moçambique
**Literacy rate:** 15% (est.)
**Economic summary:** Gross national product (1983): $2.0 billion. Average annual growth rate (1970–79): –5.3%.

Per capita income (1983): $150. Principal agricultural products: cotton, cashew nuts, sugar, tea, copra, peanuts. Labor force in industry: 6%; major products: processed foods, petroleum products, beverages, textiles, tobacco. Natural resources: bauxite, coal, iron ore, fluorite, tantalite, timber. Exports: cashew nuts, cotton, sugar, petroleum products, tea, copra, prawns, citrus, textiles. Imports: machinery and electrical equipment, cotton textiles, vehicles, petroleum, iron and steel. Major trading partners: Portugal, South Africa, U.S., U.K., West Germany, Iraq.

**Geography.** Mozambique stretches for 1,535 miles (2,470 km) along Africa's southeast coast. It is nearly twice the size of California. Tanzania is to the north; Malawi, Zambia, and Zimbabwe to the west; and South Africa and Swaziland to the south.

The country is generally a low-lying plateau broken up by 25 sizable rivers that flow into the Indian Ocean. The largest is the Zambezi; which provides access to central Africa. The principal ports are Maputo and Beira, which is the port for Zimbabwe.

**Government.** After having been under Portuguese colonial rule for 470 years, Mozambique became independent on June 25, 1975. It is a Marxist state. The first President, Samora Moises Machel, is a former nurse who headed the National Front for the Liberation of Mozambique (FRELIMO) in its 10-year guerrilla war for independence and professes to be a Marxist.

**History.** Mozambique was discovered by Vasco da Gama in 1498, although the Arabs had penetrated into the area as early as the 10th century. It was first colonized in 1505, and by 1510, the Portuguese had control of all the former Arab sultanates on the east African coast.

FRELIMO was organized in 1963. Guerrilla activity had become so extensive by 1973 that Portugal was forced to dispatch 40,000 troops to fight the rebels. A cease-fire was signed in September 1974, when Portugal agreed to grant Mozambique independence.

On Jan. 25, 1985, Mozambique's celebration of a decade of independence from Portugal was not a happy one. The Marxist government headed by President Samora Machel was locked in a five-year-old, stalemated, paralyzing war with anti-government guerrillas, known as the MNR, backed at least until the previous year by the white minority government in South Africa. At the same time, like those in much of eastern Africa, the peasants make up most of the population suffered from the consequences of four years of drought, with thousands reported starving.

## NAMIBIA

**See South Africa**

## NAURU

**Republic of Nauru**
**President and Head Chief:** Hammer DeRoburt (1968)
**Area:** 8.2 sq mi. (21 sq km)
**Population (est. 1985):** 8,000 (average annual growth rate: 1.3%)
**Density per square mile:** 975.6
**Capital:** Yaren
**Monetary unit:** Australian dollar
**Languages:** Nauruan and English
**Religions:** Protestant, 58%; Roman Catholic, 24%;

Confucian and Taoist, 8%
**Special relationship within the Commonwealth of Nations**
**Literacy rate:** 99%
**Economic summary:** Gross national product (1984): over $160 million. Per capita income (1981): $21,400. Major industrial products: phosphates. Natural resources: phosphates. Exports: phosphates. Imports: foodstuffs, fuel. Major trading partners: Australia, New Zealand, U.K., Japan.

**Geography.** Nauru (pronounced NAH oo roo) is an island in the Pacific just south of the equator, about 2,500 miles (4,023 km) southwest of Honolulu.

**Government.** Legislative power is invested in a popularly elected 18-member Parliament, which elects the President from among its members. Executive power rests with the President, who is assisted by a five-member Cabinet.

**History.** Nauru was annexed by Germany in 1888. It was placed under joint Australian, New Zealand, and British mandate after World War I, and in 1947 it became a U.N. trusteeship administered by the same three powers. On Jan. 31, 1968, Nauru became an independent republic.

# NEPAL

**Kingdom of Nepal**
**Ruler:** King Birendra Bir Bikram Shah Dev. (1972)
**Prime Minister:** Lokendra Bahadur Chand (1983)
**Area:** 54,463 sq mi. (141,059 sq km)
**Population (est. mid-1986):** 17,400,000 (average annual growth rate: 2.3%)
**Density per square mile:** 319.5
**Capital and largest city (est. 1980):** Katmandu, 400,000
**Monetary unit:** Nepalese rupee
**Languages:** Nepali (official), Newari, Bhutia
**Religions:** Hindu, 90%; Buddhist, 5%; Islam, 3%
**Literacy rate:** 23%
**Economic summary:** Gross national product (1983): $2.7 billion. Average annual growth rate (1973–82): 3.0%. Per capita income (1983): $170. Labor force in agriculture: 93%; principal products: rice, maize, wheat, millet, jute, sugar cane, oilseed, potatoes. Labor force in industry: 2%; major products: cigarettes, bricks, sugar, lumber, jute, hydroelectric power, cement. Natural resources: water, timber, hydroelectric potential. Exports: rice and food products, and timber. Imports: textiles, manufactured goods, construction materials, fuel. Major trading partners: India, Japan.

**Geography.** A landlocked country the size of Arkansas, lying between India and the Tibetan Autonomous Region of China, Nepal contains Mount Everest (29,028 ft.; 8,848 m), the tallest mountain in the world. Along its southern border, Nepal has a strip of level land that is partly forested, partly cultivated. North of that is the slope of the main section of the Himalayan range, including Everest and many other peaks higher than 20,000 feet (6,096 m).

**Government.** A new Constitution promulgated by King Mahendra in 1962 provided for a unicameral legislature called the National Panchayat. All political parties were banned in 1960.

**History.** The Kingdom of Nepal was unified in 1768 by King Prithwi Narayan Shah. A commercial treaty was signed with Britain in 1792, and in 1816, after more than a year's hostilities, the Nepalese agreed to allow British residents to live in Katmandu, the capital. In 1923, Britain recognized the absolute independence of Nepal. Between 1846 and 1951, the country was ruled by the Rana family, which always held the office of prime minister. In 1951, however, the King took over all power and proclaimed a constitutional monarchy.

Mahendra Bir Bikram Shah became King in 1955. Nepal and China settled their differences in 1956, and thereafter Nepal accepted economic aid from the Chinese. The U.S. and the U.S.S.R. also provide aid.

After Mahendra, who had ruled since 1955, died of a heart attack in 1972, Prince Birendra, at 26, succeeded to the throne.

In the first election in 22 years, on May 2, 1980, voters approved the continued autocratic rule by the King with the advice of a partyless Parliament. The King promised, however, that he would eventually permit the election of a new legislature to which the Prime Minister and Cabinet would be responsible.

# THE NETHERLANDS

**Kingdom of the Netherlands**
**Sovereign:** Queen Beatrix (1980)
**Premier:** Ruud Lubbers (1982)
**Area:** 16,041 sq. mi. (41,548 sq. km.)
**Population (est. mid-1986):** 14,500,000 (average annual growth rate: 0.4%)
**Density per square mile:** 903.9
**Capital:** Amsterdam; seat of government: The Hague
**Largest cities (est. 1983):** Rotterdam, 1,025,466; Amsterdam, 994,062; The Hague, 672,127; Utrecht, 501,357.
**Monetary unit:** Guilder
**Language:** Dutch
**Religions:** Roman Catholic, 36%; Dutch Reformed, 19%; unaffiliated, 27%; Islam, 2%
**National name:** Koninkrijk der Nederlanden
**Literacy rate:** 99%
**Economic summary:** Gross national product (1984): $123.8 billion. Annual growth rate (1984): 1.7%. Per capita income (1983): $8,492. Land used for agriculture: 59%; labor force, 10%; principal products: wheat, barley, sugar beets, potatoes, meat and dairy products. Labor force in industry: 30%; major products: metal fabrication, textiles, chemicals, electronic equipment. Exports: foodstuffs, machinery, natural gas, chemicals, petroleum products, textiles. Imports: machinery, crude petroleum, chemicals, textiles, mineral ores. Major trading partners: West Germany, Belgium, France, U.K.

**Geography.** The Netherlands, on the coast of the North Sea, has West Germany to the east and Belgium to the south. It is twice the size of New Jersey.

Part of the great plain of north and west Europe, the Netherlands has maximum dimensions of 190 by 160 miles (360 by 257 km) and is low and flat except in Limburg in the southeast, where some hills rise to 300 feet (92 m). About half the country's area is below sea level, making the famous Dutch dikes a requisite to the use of much land. Reclamation of land from the sea through dikes has continued through recent times.

All drainage reaches the North Sea, and the principal rivers—Rhine, Maas (Meuse), and Schelde—

have their sources outside the country. The Rhine is the most heavily used waterway in Europe.

**Government.** The Netherlands and its former colony of the Netherlands Antilles form the Kingdom of the Netherlands.

The Netherlands is a constitutional monarchy with a bicameral Parliament. The Upper Chamber has 75 members elected for six years by representative bodies of the provinces, half of the members retiring every three years. The Lower Chamber has 150 members elected by universal suffrage for four years. The two Chambers have the right of investigation and interpellation; the Lower Chamber can initiate legislation and amend bills.

The Sovereign, Queen Beatrix Wilhelmina Armgard, born Jan. 31, 1938, was married on March 11, 1966, to Claus von Amsberg, a former West German diplomat. The marriage drew public criticism because of the bridegroom's service in the German army during World War II. In 1967, Beatrix gave birth to a son, Wilhem-Alexander Claus George Ferdinand, the first male heir to the throne since 1884. She also has two other sons, Johan Friso Bernhard Christian David, born in 1968, and Constantijn Christof Frederik Aschwin, born the next year.

Premier Ruud Lubber heads a coalition of Christian Democrats (54 of 150 seats in the Lower Chamber), and Liberals (27 seats). Other major parties are the opposition Labor Party (52 seats), and Democrats '66 (9 seats).

**History.** Julius Caesar found the low-lying Netherlands inhabited by Germanic tribes—the Nervii, Frisii, and Batavi. The Batavi on the Roman frontier did not submit to Rome's rule until 13 B.C., and then only as allies.

A part of Charlemagne's empire in the 8th and 9th centuries A.D., the area later passed into the hands of Burgundy and the Austrian Hapsburgs, and finally in the 16th century came under Spanish rule.

When Philip II of Spain suppressed political liberties and the growing Protestant movement in the Netherlands, a revolt led by William of Orange broke out in 1568. Under the Union if Utrecht (1579), the seven northern provinces became the Republic of the United Netherlands.

The Dutch East India Company was established in 1602, and by the end of the 17th century Holland was one of the great sea and colonial powers of Europe.

The nation's independence was not completely established until after the Thirty Years' War (1618–48), after which the country's rise as a commercial and maritime power began. In 1814, all the provinces of Holland and Belgium were merged into one kingdom, but in 1830 the southern provinces broke away to form the Kingdom of Belgium. A liberal Constitution was adopted by the Netherlands in 1848.

In spite of its neutrality in World War II, the Netherlands was invaded by the Nazis in May 1940, and the East Indies were later taken by the Japanese. The nation was liberated in May 1945. In 1948, after a reign of 50 years, Queen Wilhelmina resigned and was succeeded by her daughter Juliana.

In 1949, after a four-year war, the Netherlands granted independence to the East Indies, which became the Republic of Indonesia. In 1963, it turned over the western half of New Guinea to the new nation, ending 300 years of Dutch presence in Asia. Attainment of independence by Suriname on Nov. 25, 1975, left the Dutch Antilles as the Netherlands' only overseas territory.

Prime Minister Van Agt lost his narrow majority in elections on May 26, 1981, in which the major issue was the deployment of U.S. cruise missiles on Dutch soil. Public opposition to the missiles forced the Netherlands, along with Belgium, to reverse its position in 1982 despite the Prime Minister's personal support for the NATO decision to deploy the new weapons in Western Europe. Van Agt lost his centrist coalition in May 1982 in a dispute over economic policy, and was succeeded by Ruud Lubber as Premier. Lubber announced on November 1, 1985 to accept the deployment of the U.S. missiles.

## Netherlands Autonomous Country

### NETHERLANDS ANTILLES

**Status:** Part of the Kingdom of the Netherlands
**Governor:** Prof. R. A. Romer (1986)
**Premier:** Domenico F. Martina
**Area:** 383 sq mi. (993 sq km)
**Population (est. mid-1986):** 300,000 (average annual growth rate: 1.2%)
**Capital (est. 1978):** Willemstad, 152,000
**Literacy rate:** 95%
**Economic summary:** Gross national product (1983): $131.6 billion. Average annual growth rate (1970–79): 0.9%. Per capita income: $9,140. Principal agricultural products: pigs, goats. Major industries: oil refining, tourism. Natural resource: phosphate. Export: petroleum. Import: petroleum. Major trading partners: U.S., Venezuela.

**Geography.** The Netherlands Antilles comprise two groups of Caribbean islands 500 miles (805 km) apart: one, about 40 miles (64 km) off the Venezuelan coast, consists of Curaçao (173 sq mi.; 448 sq km), Bonaire (95 sq mi.; 246 sq km), and Aruba (69 sq mi.; 179 sq km); the other, lying to the northeast, consists of three small islands with a total area of 34 square miles (88 sq km). Aruba was given separate status within the kingdom effective Jan. 1, 1986. The Dutch acquired Curaçao from Spain in 1643.

**Government.** There is a constitutional government formed by the Governor and Cabinet and an elected Legislative Council. The area has complete autonomy in domestic affairs.

## NEW ZEALAND

### Dominion of New Zealand

**Sovereign:** Queen Elizabeth II
**Governor-General:** Sir Paul Reeves (1985)
**Prime Minister:** David R. Lange (1984)
**Area:** 103,884 sq mi. (269,062 sq km) (excluding dependencies)
**Population (est. mid-1986):** 3,300,000 (average annual growth rate: 0.8%) (European, 87%; Maori and other Polynesian, 11%)
**Density per square mile:** 31.8
**Capital:** Wellington (133,700)
**Largest cities (est. 1982):** Auckland, 825,000; Wellington, 345,000; Christchurch, 325,000; Hamilton, 170,000; Dunedin, 110,900
**Monetary unit:** New Zealand dollar

**Languages:** English, Maori
**Religions:** Church of England, 26%; Presbyterian, 17%; Roman Catholic, 14%
**Member of Commonwealth of Nations**
**Literacy rate:** 98%
**Economic summary:** Gross domestic product (1985): $18.9 billion. Average annual growth rate (1975–85): 2.0%. Per capita income (1983): $7,410. Labor force in agriculture: 10%; principal products: wool, meat, dairy products, livestock. Labor force in industry: 27%; major products: processed foods, textiles, machinery, transport equipment, wood and paper products. Natural resources: forests, coal, gold. Exports: meat, dairy products, wool. Imports: machinery, minerals, chemicals, consumer goods. Major trading partners: Japan, Australia, U.K., U.S.

**Geography.** New Zealand, about 1,250 miles (2,012 km) east of Australia, consists of two main islands and a number of smaller, outlying islands so scattered that they range from the tropical to the antarctic. The country is the size of Colorado.

New Zealand's two main components are North Island and South Island, separated by Cook Strait, which varies from 16 to 190 miles (26 to 396 km) in width. North Island (44,281 sq mi.; 114,688 sq km) is 515 miles (829 km) long and volcanic in its south-central part. It contains many hot springs and beautiful geysers. South Island (58,093 sq mi.; 150,461 sq km) has the Southern Alps along its west coast, with Mount Cook (12,349 ft; 3,764 m) the highest point.

The largest of the outlying islands are the Auckland Islands (234 sq mi.; 606 sq km), Campbell Island (44 sq mi.; 114 sq km), the Antipodes Islands (24 sq mi.; 62 sq km), and the Kermadec Islands (13 sq mi.; 34 sq km).

**Government.** New Zealand was granted self-government in 1852, a full parliamentary system and ministries in 1856, and dominion status in 1907. The Queen is represented by a Governor-General, and the Cabinet is responsible to a unicameral Parliament of 95 members, who are elected by popular vote for three years.

The major political parties are the Labor Party (56 of 95 seats in the House of Representatives), led by Prime Minister David R. Lange; the National Party (37 seats), led by James Bolger; and the Social Party (2 seats).

**History.** New Zealand was discovered and named in 1642 by Abel Tasman, a Dutch navigator. Captain James Cook explored the islands in 1769. In 1840, Britain formally annexed them.

From the first, the country has been in the forefront in instituting social welfare legislation. It adopted old age pensions (1898); a national child welfare program (1907); social security for the aged, widows, and orphans, along with family benefit payments; minimum wages; a 40-hour week and unemployment and health insurance (1938); and socialized medicine (1941).

The New Zealand Labor Party, headed by David Lange, swept Sir Robert Muldoon's conservative National Party from power in a parliamentary election on July 14, 1984. Lange's campaign promise to ban American nuclear-powered and nuclear-armed naval vessels from New Zealand waters provoked a crisis in the 33-year-old Anzus alliance of the United States, Australia and New Zealand. After New Zealand refused to let a U.S. warship make a port call on the ground it might be carrying nuclear weapons, Secretary of State George P. Shultz on July 17, 1985, accused New Zealand of undermining the U.S. nuclear deterrent and weakening its own security.

## Cook Islands and Overseas Territories

**The Cook Islands** (93 sq mi.; 241 sq km) were placed under New Zealand administration in 1901. They achieved self-governing status in association with New Zealand in 1965. Population in 1978 was about 19,600. The seat of government is on Rarotonga Island.

The island's chief exports are citrus juice, clothing, canned fruit, and pineapple juice. Nearly all of the trade is with New Zealand.

**Niue** (100 sq mi.; 259 sq km) was formerly administered as part of the Cook Islands. It was placed under separate New Zealand administration in 1901 and achieved self-governing status in association with New Zealand in 1974. The capital is Alofi. Population in 1980 was about 3,300.

Niue exports passion fruit, copra, plaited ware, honey, and limes. Its principal trading partner is New Zealand.

**The Ross Dependency** (160,000 sq mi.; 414,400 sq km), an Antarctic region, was placed under New Zealand administration in 1923.

**Tokelau** (4 sq mi.; 10 sq km) was formerly administered as part of the Gilbert and Ellice Islands colony. It was placed under New Zealand administration in 1925. Its population is about 1,600.

# NICARAGUA

**Republic of Nicaragua**
**President:** Daniel Ortega (1985)
**Area:** 50,180 sq mi. (130,000 sq km)
**Population (est. mid-1986):** 3,300,000 (average annual growth rate: 3.4%) (mestizo, 70%; white, 17%; black, 9%; Indian, 4%)
**Density per square mile:** 65.8
**Capital and largest city (est. 1985):** Managua, 1,000,000
**Monetary unit:** Cordoba
**Language:** Spanish
**Religion:** Roman Catholic
**National name:** República de Nicaragua
**Literacy rate:** 87%
**Economic summary:** Gross national product (1984): $2.4 billion. Average annual growth rate (1973–82): −1.6%. Per capita income (1983): $900. Land used for agriculture: 7%; labor force: 43%; principal products: cotton, coffee, sugar cane, rice, corn, beans, cattle. Labor force in industry: 15%; major products: processed foods, chemicals, metal products, clothing and textiles. Natural resources: timber, fisheries. Exports: coffee, chemical products, meat, sugar. Imports: machinery, chemicals and pharmaceuticals, transport equipment, clothing, petroleum. Major trading partners: Mexico, West Germany, Japan, France, Cuba, Costa Rica

**Geography.** Largest but most sparsely populated of the Central American nations, Nicaragua borders on Honduras to the north and Costa Rica to the south. It is slightly larger than New York State.

Nicaragua is mountainous in the west, with fertile valleys. A plateau slopes eastward toward the Caribbean.

Two big lakes—Nicaragua, about 100 miles long (161 km), and Managua, about 38 miles long (61 km)—are connected by the Tipitapa River. The Pacific coast is volcanic and very fertile. The Caribbean coast, swampy and indented, is aptly called the "Mosquito Coast."

**Government.** After an election on Nov. 4, 1984, Daniel Ortega began a six-year term as President on Jan. 10, 1985. The major political parties are the Sandinista National Liberation Front (61 of 96 members of the National Assembly, led by President Ortega; the Democratic Conservative Party (14 seats); Independent Liberal Party (9 seats); Popular Social Christian Party (6 seats) and three small Marxist-Leninist groups with two seats each.

**History.** Nicaragua, which established independence in 1838, was first visited by the Spaniards in 1522. The chief of the country's leading Indian tribe at that time was called Nicaragua, from whom the nation derived its name. A U.S. naval force intervened in 1909 after two American citizens had been executed, and a few U.S. Marines were kept in the country from 1912 to 1925. The Bryan-Chamorro Treaty of 1916 (terminated in 1970) gave the U.S. an option on a canal route through Nicaragua, and naval bases. Disorder after the 1924 elections brought in the marines again.

A guerrilla leader, Gen. César Augusto Sandino, began fighting the occupation force in 1927. He fought the U.S. troops until their withdrawal in 1933. They trained Gen. Anastasio (Tacho) Somoza García to head a National Guard. In 1934, Somoza assassinated Sandino and overthrew the Liberal President Juan Batista Sacassa, establishing a military dictatorship with himself as president. He spurred the economic development of the country, meanwhile enriching his family through estates in the countryside and investments in air and shipping lines. On his assassination in 1956, he was succeeded by his son Luis, who alternated with trusted family friends in the presidency until his death in 1967. Another son, Maj. Gen. Anastasio Somoza Debayle, became President in 1967.

Sandinista guerrillas, leftists who took their name from Gen. Sandino, launched a civil war in May 1979.

After seven weeks of fighting, Somoza fled the country on July 17, 1979. The Sandinistas assumed power on July 19, promising to maintain a mixed economy, a non-aligned foreign policy, and a pluralist political system. However, the prominence of Cuban President Fidel Castro at the celebration of the first anniversary of the revolution and a delay of more than five years in holding elections strengthened debate over the true political color of the Sandinistas.

On Jan. 23, 1981, the Reagan Administration suspended U.S. aid, charging that Nicaragua, with the aid of Cuba and the Soviet Union, was supplying arms to rebels in El Salvador. The Sandinistas denied the charges. Later that year, Nicaraguan guerrillas known as "contras," or counterrevolutionaries, began a war to overthrow the Sandinistas.

The long-promised elections were held as scheduled on Nov. 4, 1984, with Daniel Ortega Saavedra, the Sandinista junta coordinator, winning 63% of the votes cast for President. President Reagan dismissed the voting as a Soviet-style sham election. He began a six-year term on Jan. 10, 1985, with

Castro attending the inauguration.

Meanwhile, the war between the Sandinistas and the U.S.-backed Contras continued. Ortega said the war "could be interminable" because the Reagan Administration seemed determined to continue its support of the rebels.

On Feb. 21, 1985, President Reagan denounced the Sandinista regime and said his objective was to "remove it in the sense of its present structure." On May 1, Reagan ordered an embargo on U.S. trade with Nicaragua, telling Congress that the policies and actions of the Sandinistas constituted a threat to U.S. security. In a diplomatic note delivered to Nicaragua on July 19, the Reagan Administration said Nicaragua "may be directly involved" in plans to attack Americans in neighboring Honduras. It warned the Sandinista government the United States would "react accordingly" if such attacks were carried out.

In October 1985, Nicaragua suspended civil liberties and in June 1986, Congress voted $100 million in aid, military and non-military, to the Contras. Nicaragua condemned the action and used it as a pretext to close down *La Prensa*, the sole opposition newspaper.

# NIGER

**Republic of Niger**
**Chief of State:** Gen. Seyni Kountché (1974)
**Area:** 489,206 sq mi. (1,267,044 sq km)
**Population (est. mid-1986):** 6,700,000 (average annual growth rate: 2.8%)
**Density per square mile:** 11.5
**Capital and largest city (est. 1982):** Niamey, 363,000
**Monetary unit:** Franc CFA
**Ethnic groups:** Hausa, 54%; Djerma and Songhai, 24%; Peul, 11%
**Languages:** French (official); Hausa, Songhai; Arabic
**Religions:** Islam, 90%; Animist and Christian, 10%
**National name:** République du Niger
**Literacy rate:** 6%
**Economic summary:** Gross national product (1983): $1.5 billion. Average annual growth rate (1973–82): 6.1%. Per capita income (1983): $300. Land used for agriculture: 3%; labor force: 90%; principal products: peanuts, cotton, livestock, millet, sorghum, bananas, rice. Major industrial products: uranium, cement, bricks, light industrial products. Natural resources: uranium. Exports: uranium, peanuts, livestock, hides, skins. Imports: fuels, machinery, transport equipment, foodstuffs, consumer goods. Major trading partners: France, Nigeria, Japan, Algeria, Libya

**Geography.** Niger, in West Africa's Sahara region, is four fifths the size of Alaska. It is surrounded by Mali, Algeria, Libya, Chad, Nigeria, Benin, and Burkina Faso.

The Niger River in the southwest flows through the country's only fertile area. Elsewhere the land is semiarid.

**Government.** After a military coup on April 15, 1974, Gen. Seyni Kountché suspended the Constitution and instituted rule by decree. Previously, the President was elected by direct universal suffrage for a five-year term and a National House of Assembly of 50 members was elected for the same term.

The Parti Progressiste Nigérien-Rassemblement Démocratique Africain, the only political party, was dissolved in 1974.

**History.** Niger was incorporated into French West Africa in 1896. There were frequent rebellions, but when order was restored in 1922, the French made the area a colony. In 1958, the voters approved the French Constitution and voted to make the territory an autonomous republic within the French Community. The republic adopted a Constitution in 1959 and the next year withdrew from the Community, proclaiming its independence.

The 1974 army coup ousted President Hamani Diori, who had held office since 1960. He was charged with having mishandled relief for the terrible drought that had devastated Niger and five neighboring sub-Saharan nations for several years. An estimated 2 million people were starving in Niger, but 200,000 tons of imported food, half U.S.-supplied, substantially ended famine conditions by the year's end. The new President, Lt. Col. Seyni Kountché, Chief of Staff of the army, installed a 12-man military government. A predominantly civilian government was formed by Kountché in 1976.

# NIGERIA

**Federal Republic of Nigeria**
**President:** Maj. Gen. Ibrahim Babangida (1985)
**Area:** 356,700 sq mi. (923,853 sq km)
**Population (est. mid-1986):** 105,400,000 (average annual growth rate: 3.0%)
**Density per square mile:** 295.5
**Capital:** Lagos
**Largest cities (est. 1980):** Lagos (metropolitan area): 4,000,000; **(est. 1975 by U.N.):** Ibadan, 847,000; Ogbomosho, 432,000; Kano, 399,000
**Monetary unit:** Naira
**Languages:** English (official) and native tongues
**Religions:** Islam, 47%; Christian, 34%; Animist, 18%
**Member of Commonwealth of Nations**
**Literacy rate:** 25-30%
**Economic summary:** Gross national product (1983): $71.0 billion. Average annual growth rate (1970–79): 5.3%. Per capita income (1983): $777. Land used for agriculture: 13%; labor force: 55%; principal products: peanuts, cotton, cocoa, grains, fish, yams, cassava, livestock. Labor force in industry: 10%; major products: crude oil, natural gas, coal, tin, processed rubber, cotton, petroleum, hides, textiles, cement, chemicals. Natural resources: petroleum, tin, columbite, iron ore, coal, limestone, timber. Exports: oil, cocoa, palm products, rubber, timber, tin. Imports: machinery and transport equipment, manufactured goods, chemicals. Major trading partners: U.K., Western European countries, U.S.

**Geography.** Nigeria, one third larger than Texas and black Africa's most populous nation, is situated on the Gulf of Guinea in West Africa. Its neighbors are Benin, Niger, Cameroon, and Chad.

The lower course of the Niger River flows south through the western part of the country into the Gulf of Guinea. Swamps and mangrove forests border the southern coast; inland are hardwood forests.

**Government.** After 12 years of military rule, a new Constitution re-established democratic government in 1979, but it lasted less than four years. The military again took over from the democratically elected civilian government on Dec. 31, 1983. The arms of the military government include a Supreme Military Council and a National Council of State. The various ministers make up the Federal

Executive Council. There are state military governors.

**History.** Between 1879 and 1914, private colonial developments by the British, with reorganizations of the Crown's interest in the region, resulted in the formation of Nigeria as it exists today. During World War I, native troops of the West African frontier force joined with French forces to defeat the German garrison in the Cameroons.

Nigeria became independent on Oct. 1, 1960.

Organized as a loose federation of self-governing states, the independent nation faced an overwhelming task of unifying a country with 250 ethnic and linguistic groups.

Rioting broke out again in 1966, the military commander was seized, and Col. Yakubu Gowon took power. Also in that year, the Moslem Hausas in the north massacred the predominantly Christian Ibos in the east, many of whom had been driven from the north. Thousands of Ibos took refuge in the Eastern Region. The military government there asked Ibos to return to the region and, in May 1967, the assembly voted to secede from the federation and set up the Republic of Biafra. Civil war broke out.

In January 1970, after 31 months of civil war, Biafra surrendered to the federal government.

Gowon's nine-year rule was ended in 1975 by a bloodless coup that made Army Brigadier Muritala Rufai Mohammed the new chief of state. Mohammed was assassinated the next year 1976 by a group of seven young officers, who failed to seize control of the government.

The return of civilian leadership was established with the election of Alhaji Shehu Shagari, as president in 1979.

A coup on December 31, 1983, restored military rule. The military regime headed by Maj. Gen. Mohammed Buhari was overthrown in a bloodless coup on Aug. 27, 1985, led by Maj. Gen. Ibrahim Babangida, who proclaimed himself president.

# NORWAY

**Kingdom of Norway**
**Sovereign:** King Olav V (1957)
**Prime Minister:** Gro Harlem Bruntland (1986)
**Area:** 125,056 sq mi. (323,895 sq km)
**Population (est. mid-1986):** 4,200,000 (average annual growth rate: 0.2%)
**Density per square mile:** 33.6
**Capital:** Oslo
**Largest cities (est. 1985):** Oslo, 447,000; Bergen, 207,416; Trondheim, 134,000; Stavanger, 94,000
**Monetary unit:** Krone
**Language:** Norwegian
**Religion:** Evangelical Lutheran (state), 88%
**National name:** Kongeriket Norge
**Literacy rate:** 100%
**Economic summary:** Gross national product (1984): $54.8 billion. Average annual growth rate (1978–83): 2.8%. Per capita income (1984): $13,333. Land used for agriculture: 3%; labor force, including fishing: 7%; principal products: dairy products, livestock, grain, potatoes, furs, wool. Labor force in industry: 26%; major products: oil and gas, fish, pulp and paper, ships, aluminum, iron, steel, nickel, fertilizers, transportation equipment, hydroelectric power, petrochemicals. Natural resources: fish, timber, hydroelectric power, ores, oil, gas. Exports: oil, natural gas, ships, fish products,

chemicals, pulp and paper, aluminum. reports: machinery, motor vehicles, foodstuffs, iron and steel, textiles and clothing. Major trading partners: U.K., Sweden, West Germany, U.S., Denmark, Netherlands.

**Geography.** Norway is situated in the western part of the Scandinavian peninsula. It extends about 1,100 miles (1,770 km) from the North Sea along the Norwegian Sea to more than 300 miles (483 km) above the Arctic Circle, the farthest north of any European country. It is slightly larger than New Mexico. Sweden borders on most of the eastern frontier, with Finland and the U.S.S.R. in the northeast.

Nearly 70% of Norway is uninhabitable and covered by mountains, glaciers, moors, and rivers. The hundreds of deep fiords that cut into the coastline give Norway an overall oceanfront of more than 12,000 miles (19,312 km). Nearly 50,000 islands off the coast form a breakwater and make a safe coastal shipping channel.

**Government.** Norway is a constitutional hereditary monarchy. Executive power is vested in the King together with a Cabinet, or Council of State, consisting of a Prime Minister and at least seven other members. The Storting, or Parliament, is composed of 157 members elected by the people under proportional representation. The Storting discusses and votes on political and financial questions, but divides itself into two sections (Lagting and Odelsting) to discuss and pass on legislative matters. The King cannot dissolve the Storting before the expiration of its term.

The sovereign is Olav V, born July 2, 1903, only son of Haakon VII and Princess Maud (1869–1938), third daughter of Edward VII of England. He succeeded to the throne on the death of his father Sept. 20, 1957. He married Princess Märtha of Sweden (1901–1954) on March 21, 1929. Their children are Princess Ragnhild Alexandra (born 1930), Princess Astrid (born 1932), and Crown Prince Harald (born 1937). In 1968, the Crown Prince married Sonja Haraldsen, a commoner.

The major political parties are the Labor Party (71 of 157 seats in the Storting), led by Prime Minister Gro Harlem Brundtland; Conservative Party (50 seats), led by former Prime Minister Kåre Willoch; Christian Democratic Party (16 seats), led by Kjell Magne Bondevik; Center Party (12 seats), led by Johan J. Jakobsen; Socialist Left Party (6 seats), led by Hanna Kvanmo; and Party of Progress (2 seats), led by Carl I. Hagen.

**History.** Norwegians, like the Danes and Swedes, are of Teutonic origin. The Norsemen, also known as Vikings, ravaged the coasts of northwestern Europe from the 8th to the 11th century.

In 1815, Norway fell under the control of Sweden. The union of Norway, inhabited by fishermen, sailors, merchants, and peasants, and Sweden, an aristocratic country of large estates and tenant farmers, was not a happy one, but it lasted for nearly a century. In 1905, the Norwegian Parliament arranged a peaceful separation and invited a Danish prince to the Norwegian throne—King Haakon VII. A treaty with Sweden provided that all disputes be settled by arbitration and that no fortifications be erected on the common frontier.

When World War I broke out, Norway joined with Sweden and Denmark in a decision to remain neutral and to cooperate in the joint interest of the three countries. In World War II, Norway was invaded by the Germans on April 9, 1940. It resisted for two months before the Nazis took over complete control. King Haakon and his government fled to London, where they established a government-in-exile. Maj. Vidkun Quisling, whose name is now synonymous with traitor or fifth columnist, was the most notorious Norwegian collaborator with the Nazis. He was executed by the Norwegians on Oct. 24, 1945.

Despite severe losses in the war, Norway recovered quickly. The country led the world in social experimentation. A neighbor of the U.S.S.R., Norway sought to retain good relations with the Soviet Union without losing its identity with the West. It entered the North Atlantic Treaty Organization in 1949.

Verification of U.S. and Soviet oil strikes in separated areas of Norway's sector of the North Sea bottom led the Storting in 1975 to impose stiff tax and royalty rates on concession holders. Following discovery of a North Sea field expected to produce 900,000 barrels a day by 1984, Parliament in 1976 approved establishment of a national refining and distributing company to market petroleum products at home and abroad.

## Dependencies of Norway

**Svalbard** (24,208 sq mi.; 62,700 sq km), in the Arctic Ocean about 360 miles north of Norway, consists of the Spitsbergen group and several smaller islands, including Bear Island, Hope Island, King Charles Land, and White Island (or Gillis Land). It came under Norwegian administration in 1925. The population in 1985 was 3,480 of which 1,227 were Norwegians.

**Bouvet Island** (23 sq mi.; 60 sq km), in the South Atlantic about 1,600 miles south-southwest of the Cape of Good Hope, came under Norwegian administration in 1928.

**Jan Mayen Island** (147 sq mi.; 380 sq km), in the Arctic Ocean between Norway and Greenland, came under Norwegian administration in 1929.

**Peter I Island** (96 sq mi.; 249 sq km), lying off Antarctica in the Bellinghausen Sea, came under Norwegian administration in 1931.

**Queen Maud Land,** a section of Antarctica, came under Norwegian administration in 1939.

# OMAN

**Sultanate of Oman**
**Sultan:** Qabus Bin Said (1970)
**Area:** 105,000 sq mi. (271,950 sq km)[1]
**Population (est. mid-1986):** 1,300,000 (average annual growth rate: 3.3%)
**Density per square mile:** 12.4
**Capital and largest city (est. 1981):** Muscat, 70,000
**Monetary unit:** Omani rial
**Language:** Arabic
**Religion:** Islam
**National name:** Soltanat of Uman
**Literacy rate:** 20%
**Economic summary:** Gross national product (1984): $7.7 billion. Average annual growth rate (1973–82): 10.4%. Per capita income (1984): $6,300. Principal agricultural products: dates, bananas, cereal, livestock.

Major industries: petroleum drilling, fishing, construction. Natural resources: oil, marble, copper, limestone. Exports: oil. Imports: machinery and transport equipment, food, mineral fuels. Major trading partners: U.K., U.S., China, Japan, UAE, Singapore

1. Excluding the Kuria Muria Islands.

**Geography.** Oman is a 1,000-mile-long (1,700-km) coastal plain at the southeastern tip of the Arabian peninsula lying on the Arabian Sea and the Gulf of Oman. The interior is a plateau. The country is the size of Kansas.

**Government.** The Sultan of Oman (formerly called Muscat and Oman), an absolute monarch, is assisted by a council of ministers, six specialized councils, a consultative council and personal advisers.

There are no political parties.

**History.** Although Oman is an independent state under the rule of the Sultan, it has been under British protection since the early 19th century.

Muscat, the capital of the geographical area known as Oman, was occupied by the Portuguese from 1508 to 1648. Then it fell to Persian princes and later was regained by the Sultan.

The Kuria Muria Islands, formerly part of Aden, were given to Oman by the British in 1967.

In a palace coup on July 23, 1970, the Sultan, Sa'id bin Taimur, who had ruled since 1932, was overthrown by his son, who promised to establish a modern government and use new-found wealth to aid the people of this very isolated state.

# PAKISTAN

**Islamic Republic of Pakistan**
**President:** Gen. Mohammad Zia ul-Haq (1977)
**Prime Minister:** Mohammad Khan Junejo
**Area:** 310,400 sq mi. (803,936 sq km)[1]
**Population (est. mid-1986):** 101,900,000 (average annual growth rate: 2.8%)
**Density per square mile:** 328.3
**Capital (1981 census):** Islamabad, 201,000
**Largest cities (1981 census for metropolitan area):** Karachi, 5,208,100; Lahore, 2,952,700; Faisalabad, (Lyallpur) 1,920,000; Rawalpindi, 920,000; Hyderabad, 795,000
**Monetary unit:** Pakistan rupee
**Principal languages:** Urdu (national), English (official), Punjabi, Sindhi, Pashtu, and Baluchi
**Religions:** Islam, 97%; Hindu, Christian, Buddhist, Parsi
**Literacy rate:** 26%
**Economic summary:** Gross national product (1985): $31.0 billion. Annual growth rate (1985): 8.4%. Per capita income (1985): $300. Land used for agriculture: 24%; labor force: 52%; principal products: wheat, rice, cotton. Labor force in industry: 21%; major products: cotton textiles, processed foods, tobacco, chemicals, natural gas. Natural resources: natural gas, limited petroleum, iron ore. Exports: raw and manufactured cotton, rice, carpets, leather, fish. Imports: food grains, edible oil, crude oil, machinery, chemicals, transport equipment. Major trading partners: U.S., U.K., West Germany, Saudi Arabia, Japan, China, UAE.

1. Excluding Kashmir and Jammu. 2. Does not include about 3 million refugees from Afghanistan.

**Geography.** Pakistan is situated in the western part of the Indian subcontinent, with Afghanistan and Iran on the west, India on the east, and the Arabian Sea on the south.

Nearly twice the size of California, Pakistan consists of towering mountains, including the Hindu Kush in the west, a desert area in the east, the Punjab plains in the north, and an expanse of alluvial plains. The 1,000-mile-long (1,609 km) Indus River flows through the country from the Kashmir to the Arabian Sea.

**Government.** On July 5, 1977, Gen. Mohammad Zia ul-Haq, Army Chief of Staff, ousted the civilian government of Prime Minister Zulfikar Ali Bhutto. Zia declared himself Chief Administrator of Martial Law as head of a four-man council. The national and state assemblies were dissolved and all political parties banned, while the Chief Justices of the four states replaced the governors. Elections for new national and provincial assemblies were held in February 1985 and the new Parliament and Prime Minister took office on March 23.

**History.** Pakistan was one of the two original successor states to British India. For almost 25 years following independence in 1947, it consisted of two separate regions East and West Pakistan, but now comprises only the western sector. It consists of Sind, Baluchistan, the former North-West Frontier Province, western Punjab, the princely state of Bahawalpur, and several other smaller native states.

The British became the dominant power in the region in 1797 following Lord Clive's military victory, but rebellious tribes kept the northwest in turmoil. In the northeast, the formation of the Moslem League in 1906 estranged the Moslems from the Hindus. In 1930, the league, led by Mohammed Ali Jinnah, demanded creation of a Moslem state wherever Moslems were in the majority. He supported Britain during the war. Afterward, the league received almost a unanimous Moslem vote in 1946 and Britain agreed to the formation of Pakistan as a separate dominion.

Pakistan was proclaimed a republic March 23, 1956. Iskander Mirza, then Governor General, was elected Provisional President and H. S. Suhrawardy became the first non-Moslem League Prime Minister.

The election of 1970 set the stage for civil war when Sheik Muuibur told East Pakistanis to stop paying taxes to the central government. West Pakistan troops moved in and fighting began. The independent state of Bangladesh, or Bengali nation, was proclaimed March 26, 1971.

The intervention of Indian troops protected the new state and brought President Yahya Kahn down. Bhutto took over and accepted Bangladesh as an independent entity.

Diplomatically, 1976 saw the resumption of formal relations between India and Pakistan.

Pakistan's first elections under civilian rule took place in March 1977 and provoked bitter opposition protest when Bhutto's party was declared to have won 155 of the 200 elected seats in the 216-member National Assembly. A rising tide of violent protest and political deadlock led to a military takeover on July 5. Gen. Mohammed Zia ul-Haq became Chief Martial Law Administrator.

Bhutto was tried and convicted for the 1974 murder of a political opponent, and despite worldwide protests was executed on April 4, 1979, touching off riots by his supporters. Zia declared himself President on Sept. 16, 1978, a month after Fazel Elahi Chaudhry left office upon the completion of his 5-year term.

A measure of representative government was restored with the election of a new National Assembly in February 1985, although leaders of opposition parties were banned from the election and it was unclear what powers Zia would yield to the legislature.

On December 30, 1985, Zia ended martial law. This was tempered by his stated intent to remain in office until 1990. In April 1986, Benazir Bhutto, daughter of Zulfikar Bhutto, returned from exile. She organized mass demonstrations and called for elections in the fall.

# PANAMA

**Republic of Panama**
**President:** Eric Arturo Delvalle (1985)
**Area:** 29,761 sq mi. (77,082 sq km)
**Population (est. mid-1986):** 2,200,000 (average annual growth rate: 2.1%) (mestizo, 65%; black, 13%; white, 11%; Indian, 10%)
**Density per square mile:** 73.9
**Capital and largest city (est. 1980):** Panama City, 400,-000
**Monetary unit:** Balboa
**Language:** Spanish (official)
**Religions:** Roman Catholic, 89%; Islam, 5%; Protestant, 5%
**National name:** República de Panamá
**Literacy rate:** 90%
**Economic summary:** Gross national product (1984): $4.4 billion. Annual growth rate (1984): −1.0%. Per capita income (1984): $2,159. Land used for agriculture: 24%; labor force: 29%; principal products: bananas, corn, sugar, rice, cattle. Labor force in industry: 16%; major industrial products: refined petroleum, sugar. Natural resources: copper (unexploited). Exports: bananas, refined petroleum, sugar, shrimp. Imports: crude oil, crude petroleum, chemicals, food. Major trading partners: U.S., West Germany, Mexico, Venezuela.

**Geography.** The southernmost of the Central American nations, Panama is south of Costa Rica and north of Colombia. The Panama Canal bisects the isthmus at its narrowest and lowest point, allowing passage from the Caribbean Sea to the Pacific Ocean.

Panama is slightly smaller than South Carolina. It is marked by a chain of volcanic mountains in the west, moderate hills in the interior, and a low range on the east coast. There are extensive forests in the fertile Caribbean area.

**Government.** In 1972, a new Constitution was approved by a new 505-seat National Assembly of Community Representatives (corregidores), which was created in the first election in five years. The Charter provides for indirect election of the President by the Assembly for a six-year term.

**History.** Visited by Columbus in 1502 on his fourth voyage and explored by Balboa in 1513, Panama was the principal transshipment point for Spanish treasure and supplies to and from South and Central America in colonial days. In 1821, when Central America revolted against Spain, Panama joined Colombia, which already had declared its independence. For the next 82 years, Panama attempted unsuccessfully to break away from Colombia. After U. S. proposals for canal rights over the

narrow isthmus had been rejected by Colombia, Panama proclaimed its independence with U.S. backing in 1903.

For canal rights in perpetuity, the U.S. paid Panama $10 million and agreed to pay $250,000 each year, increased to $430,000 after devaluation of the U.S. dollar in 1933 and was further increased under a revised treaty signed in 1955. In exchange, the U.S. got the Canal Zone—a 10-mile-wide strip across the isthmus—and a considerable degree of influence in Panama's affairs.

Panama and the U.S. agreed in 1974 to negotiate the eventual reversion of the canal to Panama, despite strongly expressed opposition in the U.S. Congress. The texts of two treaties—one governing the transfer of the canal and the other guaranteeing its neutrality after transfer—were negotiated by August 1977 and were signed by Pres. Omar Torrijos Herara and President Carter in Washington on September 7. A Panamanian referendum approved the treaties by more than two thirds on October 23, but further changes were insisted upon by the U.S. Senate.

The principal change was a reservation specifying that despite the neutrality treaty's specification that only Panama shall maintain forces in its territory after transfer of the canal Dec. 31, 1999, the U.S. should have the right to use military force to keep the canal operating if it should become obstructed. After lengthy debate, the Senate approved the treaties in March-April, 1978. On June 16, Carter and Torrijos exchanged instruments of ratification in Panama City.

The basic treaty provides an increase from the present $2.3 million a year in royalties to $10 million a year during the transition period, with an additional annual payment of $10 million if it can be obtained from tolls. It also requires the use of more Panamanians as canal employees in the interim and pledges the U.S. not to pursue the development of another canal without the agreement of Panama.

Nicolas Ardito Barletta, Panama's first directly elected President in 16 years, was inaugurated on Oct. 11, 1984, for a five-year term. He lacked the necessary support to solve the country's economic crisis and resigned September 28, 1985. He was replaced by Vice President Eric Arturo Delvalle, a member of the Republican Party.

In June, 1986, reports surfaced in the U.S. media that the behind-the-scenes strongman, Gen. Manuel Noriega, was involved in drug trafficking and the murder of an opposition leader. He denied the charges.

**Panama Canal.** First conceived by the Spaniards in 1534, when King Charles V of Spain ordered a survey of a waterway across the Isthmus, a construction concession was granted by the Colombian government in 1878 to St. Lucien N. B. Wyse, representing a French company. Two years later, the French Canal Company, inspired by Ferdinand de Lesseps, began construction of what was to have been a sea-level canal. The effort ended in bankruptcy nine years later and the United States ultimately paid the French $40 million for their rights and assets.

The U.S. project, built on territory controlled by the United States, and calling for the creation of an interior lake connected to both oceans by locks, got under way in 1904. Completed in 1914, the Canal is 40.27 miles long and lifts ships 85 feet above sea level through a series of three locks on the Pacific and Atlantic sides. Enlarged in later years, each lock now measures 1,000 feet in length, 110 feet in width, and 40 feet in depth of water.

# PAPUA NEW GUINEA

**Sovereign:** Queen Elizabeth II
**Governor General:** Sir Kingsford Dibela (1983)
**Prime Minister:** Paias Wingti (1985)
**Area:** 178,704 sq mi. (462,840 sq km)
**Population (est. mid-1986):** 3,400,000 (average annual growth rate: 2.6%)
**Density per square mile:** 19.0
**Capital and largest city (est. 1985):** Port Moresby, 200,-000
**Monetary unit:** Kina
**Languages:** English, Melanesian pidgin, and 717 distinct native languages
**Religions:** Protestant, 64%; Roman Catholic, 33%
**Member of Commonwealth of Nations**
**Literacy rate:** 32%
**Economic summary:** Gross national product (1984): $2.0 billion. Average annual growth rate (1973–82): 1.4%. Per capita income (1984): $850. Labor force in agriculture, including fishing: 77%; principal products: sweet potatoes, coffee, copra, palm oil, cocoa, tea, coconuts, cattle. Major industrial products: clothing, light fabricated metal products, furniture. Natural resources: copper, gold, silver, timber, tuna. Exports: copper, coffee and cocoa beans, copra, timber. Imports: food, machinery, transport equipment, fuels. Major trading partners: Australia, U.K., Japan, West Germany, Singapore.

**Geography.** Papua New Guinea occupies the eastern half of the island of New Guinea, just north of Australia, and many outlying islands. The Indonesian province of Irian Jaya is to the west. To the north and east are the islands of Manus, New Britain, New Ireland, and Bougainville, all part of Papua New Guinea.

Papua New Guinea is about one tenth larger than California. Its mountainous interior has only recently been explored. The high-plateau climate is temperate, in contrast to the tropical climate of the coastal plains. Two major rivers, the Sepik and the Fly, are navigable for shallow-draft vessels.

**Government.** Papua New Guinea attained independence Sept. 16, 1975, ending a United Nations trusteeship under the administration of Australia. Parliamentary democracy was established by a Constitution that invests power in a 109-member national legislature.

The Pangu Party, People's Progress Party, National Party, and United Party are the largest of half a dozen political parties.

**History.** The eastern half of New Guinea was first visited by Spanish and Portuguese explorers in the 16th century, but a permanent European presence was not established until 1884, when Germany declared a protectorate over the northern coast and Britain took similar action in the south. Both nations formally annexed their protectorates and, in 1901, Britain transferred its rights to a newly independent Australia. Australian troops invaded German New Guinea in World War I and retained control under a League of Nations mandate that eventually became a United Nations trusteeship, incorporating a territorial government in the southern region, known as Papua.

Australia granted limited home rule in 1951 and, in 1964, organized elections for the first House of Assembly. Autonomy in internal affairs came nine years later.

After the elections of June 1982, Sir Julius Chan was chosen prime minister by the new legislature.

# PARAGUAY

**Republic of Paraguay**
**President:** Gen. Alfredo Stroessner (1954)
**Area:** 157,047 sq mi. (406,752 sq km)
**Population (est. mid-1986):** 4,100,000 (average annual growth rate: 2.8%) (mestizo, 95%; white, 3%; Indian, 2%)
**Density per square mile:** 22.1
**Capital and largest city (est. 1980):** Asunción, 530,000
**Monetary unit:** Guaraní
**Languages:** Spanish (official), Guaraní
**Religion:** Roman Catholic (official)
**National name:** República del Paraguay
**Literacy rate:** 84%
**Economic summary:** Gross national product (1983): $4.5 billion. Average annual growth rate (1982–83): −1.5%. Per capita income (1983): $1,983. Labor force in agriculture: 44%; principal products: soybeans, cotton, hides, sweet potatoes, tobacco, corn, rice, sugar cane. Labor force in industry: 19%; major products: packed meats, crushed oilseeds, beverages, textiles, light consumer goods, cement. Natural resource: timber. Exports: cotton, soybeans, meat products, tobacco, timber, coffee, hides. Imports: fuels and lubricants, machinery and motors, motor vehicles, beverages, tobacco, foodstuffs. Major trading partners: Argentina, Brazil, West Germany, U.S., Netherlands, Algeria

**Geography.** California-size Paraguay is surrounded by Brazil, Bolivia, and Argentina in south central South America. Eastern Paraguay, between the Paraná and Paraguay Rivers, is upland country with the thickest population settled on the grassy slope that inclines toward the Paraguay River. The greater part of the Chaco region to the west is covered with marshes, lagoons, dense forests, and jungles.

**Government.** The President is elected by popular vote for five years. The legislature is bicameral, consisting of a Senate of 30 members and a Chamber of Representatives of 60 members. There is also a Council of State, whose members are nominated by the government.

The governing Partido Colorado was further strengthened in 1977 when the Partido Liberal Unido, a merger of the Partido Liberal Radical and Partido Liberal, was declared illegal.

**History.** In 1526 and again in 1529, Sebastian Cabot explored Paraguay when he sailed up the Paraná and Paraguay Rivers. From 1608 until their expulsion from the Spanish dominions in 1767, the Jesuits maintained an extensive establishment in the south and east of Paraguay. In 1811, Paraguay revolted against Spanish rule and became a nominal republic under two Consuls.

Actually, Paraguay was governed by three dictators during the first 60 years of independence. The third, Francisco López, waged war against Brazil and Argentina in 1864–65, a conflict in which the male population was almost wiped out. A new Constitution in 1870, designed to prevent dictatorships and internal strife, failed to do so, and not until

1912 did a period of comparative economic and political stability begin.

After World War II, politics became particularly unstable.

Stroessner ruled under a state of siege until 1965, when the dictatorship was relaxed and exiles returned. The Constitution was revised in 1967 to permit Stroessner to be re-elected, and every five years since, he has been re-elected.

Although oil exploration begun by U.S. companies in the Chaco boreal in 1974 has been fruitless, Paraguay found prosperity in another form of energy when construction started in 1978 on the Itaipu Dam on the Parana River as a joint Paraguayan-Brazilian project. The largest hydroelectric development in the world when completed in 1988, Itaipu will generate 12.6 megawatts of electricity, surpassing the U.S. Grand Coulee Dam. With 40,000 Paraguayans working around the clock building the $12-billion project, unemployment has virtually disappeared.

The Stroessner regime was criticized by the U.S. State Department during the Carter administration as a violator of human rights, but unlike Argentina and Uruguay, Paraguay did not suffer cuts in U.S. military aid. The criticism is credited with having reduced the number of political prisoners to a "few hundred."

# PERU

**Republic of Peru**
**President:** Alan Garcia Pérez (1985)
**Premier:** Luis Alva Castro (1985)
**Area:** 496,222 sq mi. (1,285,216 sq km)
**Population (mid-1986):** 20,200,000 (average annual growth rate: 2.5%) (white and mestizo, 52%; Indian, 46%)
**Density per square mile:** 40.7
**Capital:** Lima
**Largest cities (est. 1981):** Lima, 4,164,000; **(est. 1981):** Arequipa, 447,400; Trujillo, 354,600; Chiclayo, 280,200
**Monetary unit:** Sol
**Languages:** Spanish and Quéchua
**Religion:** Roman Catholic
**National name:** República del Perú
**Literacy rate:** est. 72%
**Economic summary:** Gross national product (1984): $17 billion. Average annual growth rate (1973–82): 2.0%. Per capita income (1984): $980. Land used for agriculture: 2%; labor force: 40%; principal products: corn, sugar, cotton, coffee, wool. Labor force in industry: 15%; major products: processed minerals, fish meal, refined petroleum, textiles. Natural resources: minerals and metals, fish, petroleum, timber. Exports: copper, fish products, cotton, sugar, coffee, lead, silver, zinc, wool, iron ore. Imports: machinery, foodstuffs, chemicals, pharmaceuticals. Major trading partners: U.S., Japan, Western European, and Latin American countries.

**Geography.** Peru, in western South America, extends for nearly 1,500 miles (2,414 km) along the Pacific Ocean. Colombia and Ecuador are to the north, Brazil and Bolivia to the east, and Chile to the south.

Five sixths the size of Alaska, Peru is divided by the Andes Mountains into three sharply differentiated zones. To the west is the coastline, much of it arid, extending 50 to 100 miles (80 to 160 km) inland. The mountain area, with peaks over 20,000 feet (6,096 m), lofty plateaus, and deep valleys, lies centrally. Beyond the mountains to the east is the heavily forested slope leading to the Amazonian plains.

**Government.** The President, elected by universal suffrage for a five-year term, holds executive power. A Senate of 60 members and a Chamber of Deputies of 180 members, both elected for five-year terms, share legislative power.

The American Popular Revolutionary Alliance, led by President Alan Garcia Pérez, won control of both houses in 1985 elections. The next largest voting bloc was the United Left, made up of six Marxist parties. Other parties include the Democratic Convergence Party and the Popular Action Party.

**History.** Peru was once part of the great Incan empire and later the major vice-royalty of Spanish South America. It was conquered in 1531–33 by Francisco Pizarro. On July 28, 1821, Peru proclaimed its independence, but the Spanish were not finally defeated until 1824. For a hundred years thereafter, revolutions were frequent, and a new war was fought with Spain in 1864–66.

Peru emerged from 20 years of dictatorship in 1945 with the inauguration of President José Luis Bustamente y Rivero after the first free election in many decades. But he served for only three years and was succeeded in turn by Gen. Manual A. Odria, Manuel Prado y Ugarteche, and Fernando Belaúnde Terry. On Oct. 3, 1968, Belaúnde was overthrown by Gen. Juan Velasco Alvarado.

In 1975, Velasco was replaced in a bloodless coup by his Premier, Gen. Francisco Morales Bermudez, who promised to restore civilian government. In elections held on May 18, 1980, Belaunde Terry, the last previous civilian President and the candidate of the conservative parties that have traditionally ruled Peru, was elected President again. By the end of his five-year term in 1985, the country was in the midst of acute economic and social crisis.

But Peru's fragile democracy survived this period of stress and when he left office in 1985 Belaunde Terry was the first elected President to turn over power to a constitutionally elected successor since 1945. Alan Garcia Pérez, a 36-year-old Social Democrat, won 53% of the vote in a runoff election and was inaugurated President on July 28, 1985. In his inaugural address, he said Peru would limit payments on its foreign debt to no more than 10% of its export earnings, instead of the terms demanded by the International Monetary Fund and foreign bankers.

# THE PHILIPPINES

**Republic of the Philippines**
**President:** Corazon C. Aquino (1986)
**Vice President:** Salvador H. Laurel (1986)
**Area:** 115,830 sq mi. (300,000 sq km)
**Population (est. mid-1986):** 58,100,000 (average annual growth rate: 2.5%)
**Density per square mile:** 501.6
**Capital:** Manila
**Largest cities (est. 1981):** Manila, 1,750,000[1]; Quezon City, 1,175,000; Davao, 625,000; Cebu, 500,000
**Monetary unit:** Peso
**Languages:** Philipino, English, Spanish; dialects: Tagalog, Visayan, Ilocano

**Religions:** Roman Catholic, 85%; Islam, 4%; Aglipayan
(Independent Philippine Christian), 4%; Protestant, 3%
**National name:** Republika ng Pilipinas
**Literacy rate:** 88%
**Economic summary:** Gross national product (1985): $32
billion. Growth rate (1985): −3.9%. Per capita income
(1985): $594. Land used for agriculture: 37%; labor
force: 50%; principal products: rice, corn, coconuts,
sugar cane, bananas, tobacco. Labor force in industry:
12%; major products: processed agricultural products,
textiles, chemicals and chemical products. Natural
resources: forests, metallic and non-metallic minerals.
Exports: coconut products, sugar, logs and lumber,
copper concentrates, bananas, garments, nickel. Imports:
petroleum, industrial equipment, wheat. Major trading
partners: U.S., Japan.

1. Metropolitan area population is 7,500,000.

**Geography.** The Philippine Islands are an archipelago of over 7,000 islands lying about 500 miles (805
km) off the southeast coast of Asia. The overall land
area is comparable to that of Arizona. The northernmost island, Y'Ami, is 65 miles (105 km) from
Taiwan, while the southernmost, Saluag, is 40 miles
(64 km) east of Borneo.

Only about 7% of the islands are larger than one
square mile, and only one third have names. The
largest are Luzon in the north (40,420 sq mi.; 104,-
687 sq km), Mindanao in the south (36,537 sq mi.;
94,631 sq km), Samar (5,124 sq mi.; 13,271 sq km).

The islands are of volcanic origin, with the larger
ones crossed by mountain ranges. The highest peak
is Mount Apo (9,690 ft; 2,954 m) on Mindanao.

**Government.** President Corazon Aquino, in power
since Feb. 25, 1986, after a nearly bloodless "revolution," declared a "revolutionary" government;
suspending Parliament and giving her the power
to rule by decree. It does however, retain the Bill
of Rights. President Aquino is expected to appoint
a commission which will draft a new constitution,
to be submitted to a plebiscite.

The former ruling party, the pro-Marcos New Society Movement, is the main opposition.

**History.** Fernando Magellan, the Portuguese navigator in the service of Spain, discovered the Philippines in 1521. Twenty-one years later, a Spanish exploration party named the group of islands in
honor of Prince Philip, later Philip II of Spain.
Spain retained possession of the islands for the next
350 years.

The Philippines were ceded to the U.S. in 1899
by the Treaty of Paris after the Spanish-American
War. Meanwhile, the Filipinos, led by Emilio Aguinaldo, had declared their independence. They continued guerrilla warfare against U.S. troops until
the capture of Aguinaldo in 1901. By 1902, peace
was established except among the Moros.

The first U.S. civilian Governor-General was William Howard Taft (1901–04). The Jones Law (1916)
provided for the establishment of a Philippine Legislature composed of an elective Senate and House
of Representatives. The Tydings-McDuffie Act
(1934) provided for a transitional period until 1946,
at which time the Philippines would become completely independent.

Under a Constitution approved by the people of
the Philippines in 1935, the Commonwealth of the
Philippines came into being, with Manuel Quezon
y Molina as president.

On Dec. 8, 1941, the Philippines were invaded
by Japanese troops. Following the fall of Bataan

and Corregidor, Quezon established a government-in-exile, which he headed until his death in
1944. He was succeeded by Vice President Sergio
Osmeña.

U.S. forces led by Gen. Douglas MacArthur rein-
vaded the Philippines in October 1944 and, after
the liberation of Manila in February 1945, Osmeña
re-established the government.

The Philippines achieved full independence on
July 4, 1946. Manual A. Roxas y Acuña was elected
first president. Subsequent presidents have been
Elpidio Quirino (1948–53), Ramón Magsaysay
(1953–57). Carlos P. García (1957–61), Diosdado
Macapagal (1961–65), Ferdinand E. Marcos (1965–
86).

Marcos, who had freed the last of the national
leaders still in detention, former Senator Benigno
S. Aquino, Jr., in 1980 and permitted him to go to
the United States, ended eight years of martial law
on January 17, 1981.

Despite having been warned by First Lady Im-
elda Marcos that he risked being killed if he came
back, opposition leader Aquino returned to the
Philippines from self-exile on Aug. 21, 1983. He
was shot to death as he was being escorted from his
plane by military police at Manila International
Airport. The government contended the assassin
was Rolando Galman, a small-time hoodlum allegedly hired by communists, who was in turn shot
dead by Filipino troops, but there was widespread
suspicion that the Marcos government was somehow involved in the murder.

The assassination sparked huge anti-government
rallies and violent clashes between demonstrators
and police, which continued intermittently
through most of 1984, and helped the fragmented
opposition parties score substantial gains in the
May 14, 1984, elections for a National Assembly
with greater power than a previous interim parliament.

On Jan. 23, 1985, one of Marcos' closest associates, Gen. Fabian C. Ver, the armed forces chief
of staff, and 25 others were charged with the 1983
assassination of Aquino. Their trial dragged on
through most of the year, with defense attorneys
charging the evidence against Ver and the other
defendants was fabricated.

In an attempt to re-secure American support,
Marcos set Presidential elections for Feb. 7, 1986.
After Ver's acquittal, and with the support of the
Catholic church, Corazon Aquino, widow of
Benigno Aquino, declared her candidacy. Marcos
was declared the winner but the vote was widely
considered to be rigged and anti-Marcos protests
continued. The defection of Defense Minister Juan
Enrile and Lt.-Gen. Fidel Ramos signaled an end
of military support for Marcos, who fled into exile
in the U.S. on Feb. 25, 1986.

The growth of the Communist insurgency in the
Philippines remains a matter of increasing concern, both in Manila and Washington.

# POLAND

**Polish People's Republic**
**President of the Council of State:** Henryk Jablonski (1972)
**Premier:** Gen. Wojciech Jaruzelski (1981)
**Area:** 120,727 sq mi. (312,683 sq km)
**Population (est. mid-1986):** 37,500,000 (average annual
growth rate: 0.9%)
**Density per square mile:** 310.6

**Capital:** Warsaw
**Largest cities (est. 1982):** Warsaw, 1,625,000; Lodz, 850,000; Krakow, 725,000; Wroclaw, 625,000; Poznan, 560,000; Gdansk, 460,000; Szczecin, 390,000
**Monetary unit:** Zloty
**Language:** Polish (more than 90%)
**Religions:** Roman Catholic, Greek Orthodox, Protestant, Jewish
**National name:** Polska Rzeczpospolita Ludowa
**Literacy rate:** 98%
**Economic summary:** Gross national product (1984): $228.5 billion. Average annual growth rate (1984): 3.4%. Per capita income (1984): $6,190. Labor force in agriculture: 30%; principal products: grains, sugar beets, potatoes, hogs and other livestock. Labor force in industry: 44%; major products: iron and steel, chemicals, textiles, processed foods, transport equipment. Natural resources: coal, sulfur, copper, natural gas. Exports: coal, machinery and equipment, chemicals, industrial products. Imports: machinery and equipment, fuels, raw materials, agricultural and food products. Major trading partners: Communist bloc countries, U.K., Italy, U.S., West Germany, France.

**Geography.** Poland, a country the size of New Mexico in north central Europe, borders on East Germany to the west, Czechoslovakia to the south, and the U.S.S.R. to the east. In the north is the Baltic Sea.

Most of the country is a plain with no natural boundaries except the Carpathian Mountains in the south and the Oder and Neisse Rivers in the east. Other major rivers, which are important to commerce, are the Vistula, Warta, and Bug.

**Government.** The 1952 Constitution describes Poland as a people's republic. The supreme organ of state authority is the Sejm (Parliament), which is composed of 460 members elected for four years.

The major political parties are the Polish United Workers' (Communist) Party (245 of 460 seats in the Sejm), led by First Secretary Wojciech Jaruzelski; United Peasant Party (106 seats), led by Stefan Malinowski; Democratic Party (35 seats), led by Edward Kowalczyk; non-party members and Catholic organizations (74 seats).

**History.** Little is known about Polish history before the 11th century, when King Boleslaus I (the Brave) ruled over Bohemia, Saxony, and Moravia. Mongol invasions in 1241 and 1259 were repelled. Meanwhile, the Teutonic knights of Prussia conquered part of Poland and barred the latter's access to the Baltic. The knights were defeated by Wladislaus II at Tannenberg in 1410 and became Polish vassals, and Poland regained a Baltic shoreline. Poland reached the peak of power between the 14th and 16th centuries, scoring military successes against the Russians and Turks. In 1683, John III (John Sobieski) turned back the Turkish tide at Vienna.

An elective monarchy failed to produce strong central authority, and Prussia, and Austria were able to carry out a first partition of the country in 1772, a second in 1792, and a third in 1795–96. For more than a century thereafter, there was no Polish state, but the Poles never ceased their efforts to regain their independence.

Poland was formally reconstituted in November 1918, with Marshal Josef Pilsudski as Chief of State. In 1919, Ignace Paderewski, the famous pianist and patriot, became the first premier. In 1926, Pilsudski seized complete power in a coup and ruled dictatorially until his death on May 12, 1935, when he was succeeded by Marshal Edward Smigly-Rydz.

Despite a 10-year nonaggression pact signed in 1934, Hitler attacked Poland on Sept. 1, 1939. Russian troops invaded from the east on September 17, and on September 28 a German-Russian agreement divided Poland between Russia and Germany. Wladyslaw Raczkiewicz formed a government-in-exile in France, which moved to London after France's defeat in 1940.

All of Poland was occupied by Germany after the Nazi attack on the U.S.S.R. in June 1941.

The legal Polish government soon fell out with the Russians, and, in 1944, a Communist-dominated Polish Committee of National Liberation received Soviet recognition. Moving to Lublin after that city's liberation, it proclaimed itself the Provisional Government of Poland. Some former members of the Polish government in London joined with the Lublin government to form the Polish Government of National Unity, which Britain and the U.S. recognized.

On Aug. 2, 1945, in Berlin, President Harry S. Truman, Joseph Stalin and Prime Minister Clement Attlee of Britain established a new *de facto* western frontier for Poland along the Oder and Neisse Rivers. (The border was finally agreed to by West Germany in a nonagression pact signed Dec. 7, 1970.) On Aug. 16, 1945, the U.S.S.R. and Poland signed a treaty delimiting the Soviet-Polish frontier. Under these agreements, Poland was shifted westward. In the east it lost 69,860 square miles (180,934 sq km) with 10,772,000 inhabitants; in the west it gained (subject to final peace-conference approval) 38,986 square miles (100,973 sq km) with a prewar population of 8,621,000.

A New Constitution in 1952 made Poland a "people's democracy" of the Soviet type. In 1955, Poland, which had joined the Council for Economic Mutual Assistance in 1949, became a member of the Warsaw Treaty Organization, and its foreign policy became identical with that of the U.S.S.R. The government undertook persecution of the Roman Catholic Church as a remaining source of opposition and in 1953 arrested the primate, Stefan Cardinal Wyszynski. But in June 1956, worker and student riots in Poznan forced reconsideration of the repression.

Wladyslaw Gomulka was elected leader of the United Workers (Communist) Party in 1956. He denounced the Stalinist terror, ousted many Stalinists, relieved Rokossovsky, freed Wyszynski, and improved relations with the church. Most collective farms were dissolved, and the press became freer.

A strike that began in shipyards and spread to other industries in August 1980 produced a stunning victory for workers when the economically hard-pressed government accepted for the first time in a Marxist state the right of workers to organize in independent unions.

Led by Solidarity, a free union founded by Lech Walesa, workers launched a drive for liberty and improved conditions. A national strike for a five-day week in January 1981 led to the dismissal of Premier Pinkowski and the naming of the fourth Premier in less than a year, Gen. Wojciech Jaruzelski.

Antistrike legislation was approved on Dec. 2 and martial law declared on Dec. 13, when Walesa and other Solidarity leaders were arrested. Ten days later, President Reagan ordered sanctions against the Polish government, stopping food shipments and cutting commercial air traffic.

Despite demands for declaring Poland in default, Congress in February authorized payment of $3.5 million in interest charges to U.S. banks that had given loans to Poland for food purchases.

Martial law was formally ended in 1984 but the government retained emergency powers. On July 21, 1984, the Parliament marked the 40th anniversary of Communist rule in Poland by enacting an amnesty bill authorizing the release of 652 political prisoners—virtually all except for those charged with high treason, espionage, and sabotage—and 35,000 common criminals.

The abduction and murder in October 1984 of a pro-Solidarity, Roman Catholic priest, the Rev. Jerzy Popieluszko, jolted the government as no other event had since the start of the Solidarity movement in 1980. After a 25-day trial before a five-judge tribunal, four state security policemen were convicted on Feb. 7, 1985, and sentenced to prison terms of 14 to 25 years for the murder. During the trial, the prosecution sought to know that the four had acted on their own, without the involvement of higher-ups. "Their action stained the good name of Poland," the presiding judge said in imposing sentence.

In July, the government raised meat prices by as much as 15%, completing a four-month cycle of food price increases.

# PORTUGAL

**Portuguese Republic**
**President:** Mario Soares (1986)
**Premier:** Cavaco Silva (1985)
**Area:** 34,340 sq mi. (88,941 sq km)
**Population (est. mid-1986):** 10,100,000 (average annual growth rate: 0.5%)
**Density per square mile:** 294.1
**Capital:** Lisbon
**Largest cities (est. 1982):** Lisbon, 900,000; Opporto, 400,000
**Monetary unit:** Escudo
**Language:** Portuguese
**Religion:** Roman Catholic
**National name:** República Portuguesa
**Literacy rate:** 80%
**Economic summary:** Gross national product (1984): $19.2 billion. Average annual growth rate (1984): −1.7%. Per capita income (1983): $2,247. Land used for agriculture: 39%; labor force: 23%; principal products: grains, potatoes, olives, wine grapes. Labor force in industry: 35%; major products: textiles, footwear, wood pulp, paper, cork, metal products, refined oil, chemicals, canned fish, wine. Natural resources: fish, cork, tungsten ore. Exports: cotton, textiles, cork and cork products, canned fish, wine, timber and timber products, resin. Imports: petroleum, cotton, industrial machinery, iron and steel, chemicals. Major trading partners: Western European countries, U.S.

**Geography.** Portugal occupies the western part of the Iberian Peninsula, bordering on the Atlantic Ocean to the west and Spain to the north and east. It is slightly smaller than Indiana.

The country is crossed by many small rivers, and also by three large ones that rise in Spain, flow into the Atlantic, and divide the country into three geographic areas. The Minho (Miño in Spain) River, part of the northern boundary, cuts through a mountainous area that extends south to the vicinity of the Douro (Duero) River. South of the Douro,

the mountains slope to the plains about the Tagus (Tejo) River. The remaining division is the southern one of Alentejo.

The Azores, stretching over 340 miles (547 km) in the Atlantic, consist of nine islands divided into three groups, with a total area of 902 square miles (2,335 sq km). The nearest continental land is Cape da Roca, Portugal, about 900 miles (1,448 km) to the east. The Azores are an important station on Atlantic air routes, and Britain and the U.S. established air bases there during World War II.

Madeira, consisting of two inhabited islands, Madeira and Porto Santo, and two groups of uninhabited islands, lies in the Atlantic about 535 miles (861 km) southwest of Lisbon. The Madeiras are 307 square miles (796 sq km) in area.

**Government.** The Constitution of 1976, revised in 1982, provides for popular election of a President for a five-year term and for a legislature, the Assembly of the Republic, for four years.

The major political parties are the Social Democrat Party (88 of 250 seats in the Assembly), led by Prime Minister Cavaco Silva; the Socialists (57 seats) led by President Mario Soares; the Democratic Renewal Party (45 seats), led by Antonio Eanes; The United People Alliance (38 seats), and the Center Social Democrats (22 seats) led by Francisco Lucas Pires.

**History.** Portugal was a part of Spain until it won its independence in the middle of the 12th century. King John I (1385–1433) unified his country at the expense of the Castilians and the Moors of Morocco. The expansion of Portugal was brilliantly coordinated by John's son, Prince Henry the Navigator. In 1488, Bartolomew Diaz reached the Cape of Good Hope, proving that the Far East was accessible by sea. In 1498, Vasco da Gama reached the west coast of India. By the middle of the 16th century, the Portuguese Empire included West and East Africa, Brazil, Persia, Indochina, and Malaya.

In 1581, Philip II of Spain invaded Portugal and held it for 60 years, precipitating a catastrophic decline of Portuguese commerce. Courageous and shrewd explorers, the Portuguese proved to be inefficient and corrupt colonizers. By the time the Portuguese dynasty was restored in 1640, Dutch, English, and French competitors began to seize the lion's share of the world's colonies and commerce. Portugal retained Angola and Mozambique in Africa, and Brazil (until 1822).

The corrupt King Carlos, who ascended the throne in 1889, made Joao Franco the Premier with dictatorial power in 1906. In 1908, Carlos and his heir were shot dead on the streets of Lisbon. The new King, Manoel II, was driven from the throne in the Revolution of 1910 and Portugal became a French-style republic.

Traditionally friendly to Britain, Portugal fought in World War I on the Allied side in Africa as well as on the Western Front. Weak postwar governments and a revolution in 1926 brought Antonio Oliveira Salazar to power. He kept Portugal neutral in World War II but gave the Allies naval and air bases after 1943.

Portugal lost the tiny remnants of its Indian empire—Goa, Daman, and Diu—to Indian military occupation in 1961, the year an insurrection broke out in Angola. For the next 13 years, Salazar, who died in 1970, and his successor, Marcello Caetano, fought independence movements amid growing world criticism. Leftists in the armed forces, weary of a losing battle, launched a successful revolution on April 25, 1974.

In 1980, President General Antonia Ramalho Eanes won a second four-year term with 57% of the popular vote.

In late-1985, a PSP-PSD split ended the Soares coalition government. Cavaco Silva, an advocate of free-market economics, was the Social Decmocratic candidate. His party emerged with a plurality, unseating the Socialists.

In an electoral upset, Mario Soares won the presidential elections, defeating the PSD candidate.

## Portuguese Overseas Territory

After the April 1974 revolution, the military junta moved to grant independence to the territories, beginning with Portuguese Guinea in September 1974, which became the Republic of Guinea-Bissau.

Mozambique and Angola followed, leaving only Portuguese Timor and Macao of the former Empire. Despite Lisbon's objections, Indonesia annexed Timor.

## MACAO

**Status:** Territory
**Governor:** Adm. Vasco Almeida Costa (1981)
**Area:** 6 sq mi. (15.5 sq km)
**Population (est. 1982):** 300,000 (average annual growth rate: 1.7%)
**Capital (1970 census):** Macao, 241,413
**Monetary unit:** Patacá
**Literacy rate (1981):** 99% (excluding Chinese)
**Economic summary:** Gross national product (1980): $550 million. Annual average growth rate (1970–79): 15%. Land used for agriculture: 10%; labor force: 5%; principal products: rice and vegetables; Labor force in industry: 30%; major products: textiles, fireworks, fish products. Exports: textiles and clothing, manufactured goods, foodstuffs. Imports: consumer goods, foodstuffs. Major trading partners: Hong Kong, China, U.S., West Germany, France.

Macao comprises the peninsula of Macao and the two small islands of Taipa and Colôane on the South China coast, about 35 miles (53 km) from Hong Kong. Established by the Portuguese in 1557, it is the oldest European outpost in the China trade, but Portugal's sovereign rights to the port were not recognized by China until 1887, and its boundaries are still not delimited. The port has been eclipsed in importance by Hong Kong, but it is still a busy distribution center and also has an important fishing industry.

## QATAR

**State of Qatar**
**Ruler:** Sheik Khalifa bin Hamad al-Thani (1972)
**Area:** 4,000 sq mi. (11,437 sq km)
**Population (est. mid-1986):** 300,000 (average annual growth rate: 2.9%)
**Density per square mile:** 75.0
**Capital (est. 1981):** Doha, 190,000
**Monetary unit:** Qatari riyal
**Language:** Arabic
**Religion:** Islam
**Literacy rate:** 40%
**Economic summary:** Gross national product (1983): $7.6 billion. Average annual growth rate (1970–79): −1.2%.

Per capita income (1983): $27,000. Major industrial product: oil. Natural resources: oil, gas. Export: oil. Major trading partners: U.K., U.S., France, Japan, West Germany.

**Geography.** Qatar occupies a small peninsula that extends into the Persian Gulf from the east side of the Arabian Peninsula. Saudi Arabia is to the west and the United Arab Emirates to the south. The country is mainly barren.

**Government.** Qatar, one of the Arabian Gulf states, lies between Bahrain and United Arab Emirates. For a long time, it was under Turkish protection, but in 1916, the sultan accepted British protection. After the discovery of oil in the 1940s and its exploitation in the 1950s and 1960s, political unrest spread to the sheikdoms. Qatar declared its independence in 1971. The next year the current Sheik, Khalifa bin Hamad al-Thani, ousted his cousin in a bloodless coup.

## ROMANIA

**Socialist Republic of Romania**
**President:** Nicolae Ceausescu (1974)
**Premier:** Constantin Dascalescu (1982)
**Area:** 91,700 sq mi. (237,500 sq km)
**Population (est. mid-1986):** 22,800,000 (Romanian, 87.1%, Hungarian 7.7%, Germans, 1.5%) (average annual growth rate: 0.4%)
**Density per square mile:** 248.6
**Capital:** Bucharest
**Largest cities (est. 1982):** Bucharest, 1,961,189; Brasov, 334,992; Timisoara, 309,258; Constanta, 318,799; Cluj-Napoca, 299,786; Iasi, 370,158; Galati, 286,110
**Monetary unit:** Leu
**Languages:** Romanian, Hungarian, Serbian, German, Turkish
**Religions:** Romanian Orthodox, 80%; Greek Orthodox, 10%
**National name:** Republica Socialista România
**Literacy rate:** 99%
**Economic summary:** Gross national product (1984): $117.6 billion. Average annual growth rate (1984): 4.3%. Per capita income (1984): $5,200. Land used for agriculture: 46%; labor force: 29%; principal products: corn, wheat, beets, potatoes. Labor force in industry: 38%; major products: steel, cement, metal production and processing, chemicals, food processing, textiles. Natural resources: oil, timber, natural gas, coal. Exports: machinery, minerals and metals, foodstuffs, lumber, fuel, manufactures. Imports: machinery, iron ore, coke and coking coal, minerals. Major trading partners: U.S.S.R., East Germany, West Germany, Iran, Iraq, U.S.A.

**Geography.** A country in southeastern Europe slightly smaller than Oregon, Romania is bordered on the west by Hungary and Yugoslavia, on the north and east by the U.S.S.R., on the east by the Black Sea, and on the south by Bulgaria.

The Carpathian Mountains divide Romania's upper half from north to south and connect near the center of the country with the Transylvanian Alps, running east and west.

North and west of these ranges lies the Transylvanian plateau, and to the south and east are the plains of Moldavia and Walachia. In its last 190 miles (306 km), the Danube River flows through Romania only. It enters the Black Sea in northern Dobruja, just south of the border with the Soviet Union.

**Government.** The supreme body of state power and the sole legislative body is the Grand National Assembly, with 465 members elected for five-year terms. It elects a State Council, which provides for the continuity of state power and settles problems between sessions of the Assembly. The supreme executive and administrative body is the Council of Ministers elected by the Assembly.

The Communist Partry, led by Secretary General Nicolae Ceausescu, is the only political party.

**History.** Most of Romania was the Roman province of Dacia from about A.D. 100 to 275. From the 6th to the 12th century, wave after wave of barbarian conquerors—Vlachs, Bulgars, and others—passed over the area. By the 15th century, the main Romanian principalities of Moldavia and Walachia had become satellites within the Ottoman Empire, although they retained much independence. After the Russo-Turkish War of 1828–29, they became Russian protectorates. In 1848, the Romanians rebelled but were suppressed by the Russians. The nation became a kingdom in 1881 after the Congress of Berlin.

King Ferdinand ascended the throne in 1914. At the start of World War I, Romania proclaimed its neutrality, but later joined the Allied side and in 1916 declared war on the Central Powers. The armistice of Nov. 11, 1918, gave Romania vast territories from Russia and the Austro-Hungarian Empire.

The gains of World War I, making Romania the largest Balkan state, included Bessarabia, Transylvania, and Bukovina. The Banat, a Hungarian area, was divided with Yugoslavia.

In 1925, Crown Prince Carol renounced his rights to the throne, and when King Ferdinand died in 1927, Carol's son, Michael (Mihai) became King under a regency. However, Carol returned from exile in 1930, was crowned King Carol II, and gradually became a powerful political force in the country. In 1938, he abolished the democratic Constitution of 1923.

In 1940, the country was reorganized along Fascist lines, and the Fascist Iron Guard became the nucleus of the new totalitarian party. On June 27, the Soviet Union occupied Bessarabia and northern Bukovina. By the Axis-dictated Vienna Award of 1940, two fifths of Transylvania went to Hungary, after which Carol dissolved Parliament and granted the new premier, Ion Antonescu, full power. He abdicated and again went into exile.

Romania subsequently signed the Axis Pact on Nov. 23, 1940, and the following June joined in Germany's attack on the Soviet Union, reoccupying Bessarabia. Following the invasion of Romania by the Red Army in August 1944, King Michael led a coup that ousted the Antonescu government. An armistice with the Soviet Union was signed in Moscow on Sept. 12, 1944.

A Communist-dominated government bloc won elections in 1946, Michael abdicated on Dec. 30, 1947, and Romania became a "people's republic." In 1955, Romania joined the Warsaw Treaty Organization and the United Nations. A decade later, with the adoption of a new Constitution emphasizing national autonomy, and especially after Nicolae Ceausescu came to power in 1967, Bucharest became an increasingly dissident voice in the Soviet bloc.

Despite his liberal international record, at home Ceausescu has harshly suppressed dissidents calling for freedom of expression in the wake of the Helsinki agreements.

# RWANDA

**Republic of Rwanda**
**President:** Maj. Gen. Juvénal Habyarimana (1973)
**Area:** 10,169 sq mi. (26,338 sq km)
**Population (est. mid-1986):** 6,500,000 (average annual growth rate: 3.8%)
**Density per square mile:** 39.2
**Capital and largest city (est. 1981):** Kigali, 155,000
**Monetary unit:** Rwanda franc
**Languages:** Kinyarwanda and French
**Religions:** Roman Catholic, 56%; Protestant, 12%; Islam, 9%; Animist, 23%
**Literacy rate:** 37%
**Economic summary:** Gross national product (1983): $1.5 billion. Average annual growth rate (1984 est.): 2.9%. Per capita income (1983): $270. Land used for agriculture: 41%; labor force: 88%; principal products: coffee, tea, bananas, yams, beans. Labor force in industry: less than 5%; major products: processed foods, light consumer goods, minerals. Natural resources: cassiterite, wolfram. Exports: coffee, tea, tungsten, tin. Imports: textiles, foodstuffs, machinery, and equipment. Major trading partners: U.S., Belgium, West Germany, Kenya, Uganda.

**Geography.** Rwanda, in east central Africa, is surrounded by Zaire, Uganda, Tanzania, and Burundi. It is slightly smaller than Maryland.

Steep mountains and deep valleys cover most of the country. Lake Kivu in the northwest, at an altitude of 4,829 feet (1,472 m) is the highest lake in Africa. Extending north of it are the Virunga Mountains, which include Volcan Karisimbi (14,-187 ft.; 4,324 m), Rwanda's highest point.

**Government.** Grégoire Kayibanda was President from 1962 until he was overthrown in a bloodless coup on July 5, 1973, by the military led by Gen. Juvénal Habyarimana.

In a plebiscite in December 1978, Habyarimana was elected to a five-year term as president and a new constitution adopted that provides for an elected Assembly and a single official party, the National Revolutionary Development Movement.

**History.** Rwanda, which was part of German East Africa, was first visited by European explorers in 1854. During World War I, it was occupied in 1916 by Belgian troops. After the war, it became a Belgian League of Nations mandate, along with Burundi, under the name of Ruanda-Urundi. The mandate was made a U.N. trust territory in 1946. Until the Belgian Congo achieved independence in 1960, Ruanda-Urundi was administered as part of that colony.

Ruanda became the independent nation of Rwanda on July 1, 1962.

# ST. CHRISTOPHER-NEVIS

**Sovereign:** Queen Elizabeth II
**Governor General:** Sir Clement Athelston Arrindell (1985)
**Prime Minister:** Kennedy Alphonse Simmonds (1980)
**Area:** St. Christopher (Kitts) 65 sq mi. (169 sq km); Nevis 35 sq mi. (93 sq km)
**Total population (est. mid-1986):** 40,000 (average annual growth rate: 1.8%)
**Capital:** Basseterre (on St. Kitts), 14,725
**Largest town on Nevis:** Charlestown, 1,771
**Monetary unit:** East Caribbean dollar

**Economic summary:** St. Christopher-Nevis: Gross national product (1983): $40. Per capita income: $889. Principal agricultural products: sugar, cotton. Major industries: sugar processing, salt extraction. Exports: sugar, molasses. Imports: foodstuffs, manufactured goods. Major trading partners: U.S., U.K., Trinidad.

St. Christopher-Nevis was formerly part of the West Indies Associated States which were established in 1967 and consisted of Antigua and St. Kitts-Nevis-Anguilla of the Leeward Islands, and Dominica, Grenada, St. Lucia, and St. Vincent of the Windward Islands. Statehood for St. Vincent was held up until 1969 because of local political uncertainties. (Grenada, became independent in 1974, Dominica in 1978, St. Lucia and St. Vincent in 1979, and Antigua (known as Antigua and Barbuda) in 1981.) Anguilla's association with St. Christopher-Nevis ended in 1980 and it remains a British dependency.

Two members of the Leeward group—the British Virgin Islands and Montserrat—did not become Associated States.

St. Christopher-Nevis became independent on September 19, 1983.

## ST. LUCIA

**Sovereign:** Queen Elizabeth II
**Governor-General:** Sir Allen Lewis (1982)
**Prime Minister:** John Compton (1975)
**Area:** 238 sq mi. (616 sq km)
**Population (est. mid-1986):** 100,000 (average annual growth rate: 2.5%)
**Density per square mile:** 420.2
**Capital (est. 1972):** Castries, 45,000
**Monetary unit:** East Caribbean dollar
**Languages:** English and patois
**Religions:** Roman Catholic, 91%; Anglican, 3%; Seventh-day Adventist, 2%
**Member of Commonwealth of Nations**
**Literacy rate:** 80%
**Economic summary:** Gross national product (1983): $177.6 million. Average annual growth rate (est. 1982): 3.1%. Per capita income (1980): $1,200. Labor force in agriculture: 44%; principal products: bananas, coconuts, sugar, cocoa, spices. Major industrial products: processed limes. Exports: bananas, clothing. Imports: foodstuffs, machinery and equipment, fertilizers, petroleum products. Major trading partners: U.K., U.S., Caribbean countries.

**Geography.** One of the Windward Isles of the Eastern Caribbean, St. Lucia lies just south of Martinique. It is of volcanic origin. A chain of wooded mountains runs from north to south, and from them flow many streams into fertile valleys.

**Government.** A Governor-General represents the sovereign, Queen Elizabeth II. A Prime Minister is head of government, chosen by a 17-member House of Assembly elected by universal suffrage for a maximum term of five years.

**History.** Discovered by Spain in 1503 and ruled by Spain and then France, St. Lucia became a British territory in 1803. With other Windward Isles, St. Lucia was granted home rule in 1967 as one of the West Indies Associated States. On Feb. 22, 1979, St. Lucia achieved full independence in ceremonies boycotted by the opposition St. Lucia Labor Party, which had advocated a referendum before cutting ties with Britain.

Unrest and a strike by civil servants forced Prime Minister John Compton to hold elections in July, in which his United Workers Party lost its majority for the first time in 15 years.

A Labor Party government was ousted in turn by Compton and his followers, who won 14 of 17 seats in elections in May 1982. Labor seats fell from 12 to 2, with one seat won by the Progressive Labor Party.

Formerly dependent on a single crop, bananas, St. Lucia has sought to lower its chronic unemployment and payments deficit. The government provided tax incentives to a U.S. corporation, Amerada Hess, to facilitate location of a $150-million oil refinery and transshipment terminal on the island.

## ST. VINCENT AND THE GRENADINES

**Sovereign:** Queen Elizabeth II
**Governor-General:** Sir Sydney Gun-Munro (1986)
**Prime Minister:** James Mitchell (1984)
**Area:** 150 sq mi. (389 sq km)
**Population (est. mid-1986):** 100,000 (average annual growth rate: 2.5%)
**Density per square mile:** 666.7
**Capital and largest city (est. 1981):** Kingstown, 30,000
**Monetary unit:** East Caribbean dollar
**Language:** English
**Religions:** Anglican, 47%; Methodist, 28%; Roman Catholic, 13%
**Member of Commonwealth of Nations**
**Literacy rate:** 85%
**Economic summary:** Gross national product (1984): $88.9 million. Average annual growth rate: 3%. Per capita income (1984): $781. Land used for agriculture: 50%; labor force: 29%; principal products: bananas, arrowroot, coconuts. Major industry: food processing. Exports: bananas, arrowroot, copra. Imports: foodstuffs, machinery and equipment, chemicals, fuels, clothing. Major trading partners: U.K., U.S., Canada, Caribbean nations.

**Geography.** St. Vincent, chief island of the chain, is 18 miles (29 km) long and 11 miles (18 km) wide. One of the Windward Islands in the Lesser Antilles, it is 100 miles (161 km) west of Barbados. The island is mountainous and well forested. The Grenadines, a chain of nearly 600 islets with a total area of only 17 square miles (27 sq km), extend for 60 miles (96 km) from northeast to southwest between St. Vincent and Grenada, southernmost of the Windwards.

St. Vincent is dominated by the volcano La Soufrière, part of a volcanic range running north and south, which rises to 4,048 feet (1,234 m). The volcano erupted over a 10-day period in April 1979, causing the evacuation of the northern two thirds of the island. (There is also a volcano of the same name on Basse-Terre, Guadeloupe, which became violently active in 1976 and 1977.)

**Government.** A Governor-General represents the sovereign, Queen Elizabeth II. A Prime Minister, elected by a 13-member unicameral legislature, holds executive power. Major political parties are the New Democrats (10 of the 13 seats), led by Prime Minister James Mitchell; and the Labor Party (3 seats), led by Hudson Tannis.

**History.** Discovered by Columbus in 1498, and alternately claimed by Britain and France, St. Vincent became a British colony by the Treaty of Paris in 1783. The islands won home rule in 1969 as part of the West Indies Associated States and achieved full independence Oct. 26, 1979. Prime Minister Milton Cato's government quelled a brief rebellion Dec. 8, 1979 attributed to economic problems following the eruption of La Soufrière in April, 1979. Unlike a 1902 eruption which killed 2,000, there was no loss of life but widespread losses to agriculture.

## SAN MARINO

**Most Serene Republic of San Marino**
**Co-Regents:** Two selected every six months by Grand and General Council
**Area:** 23.6 sq mi. (62 sq km)
**Population (est. 1985):** 23,000 (mostly Italian) (average annual growth rate: 1.6%)
**Density per square mile:** 974.6
**Capital and largest city (est. 1982 for metropolitan area):** San Marino, 4,500
**Monetary unit:** Italian lira
**Language:** Italian
**Religion:** Roman Catholic
**National name:** Repubblica di San Marino
**Literacy rate:** 98%
**Economic summary:** Land used for agriculture: 74%; principal products: wheat and other grains, grapes, fruits, vegetables. Major industrial products: textiles, paper, leather, cement and other building materials. Exports: building stone, lime, chestnuts, wheat, hides, baked goods. Imports: manufactured consumer goods. Major trading partner: Italy.

**Geography:** One tenth the size of New York City, San Marino is surrounded by Italy. It is situated in the Apennines, a little inland from the Adriatic Sea near Rimini.

**Government.** The country is governed by two co-regents. Executive power is exercised by ten ministers. In 1959, the Grand Council granted women the vote.

The major political parties are the Christian Democratic Party (26 of 60 seats in the Grand and General Council); Communist Party (15 seats); Socialist Party (9 seats); United Socialist Party (8 seats); Democratic Socialist Party (1 seat); and Republican Party (1 seat).

**History.** According to tradition, San Marino was founded about A.D. 350 and had good luck for centuries in staying out of the many wars and feuds on the Italian peninsula. It is the oldest republic in the world.

A person born in San Marino remains a citizen and can vote no matter where he lives.

## SÃO TOMÉ AND PRÍNCIPE

**Democratic Republic of São Tomé and Príncipe**
**President:** Manuel Pinto da Costa (1975)
**Area:** 372 sq mi. (1001 sq km)
**Population (est. mid-1986):** 100,000 (average annual growth rate: 2.9%)
**Density per square mile:** 268.8
**Capital and largest city (est. 1981):** São Tomé, 30,551
**Monetary unit:** Dobra

**Language:** Portuguese
**Religions:** Roman Catholic, Evangelical Protestant, Seventh-Day Adventist
**Literacy rate:** 50%
**Economic summary:** Gross national product (1980): $60 million. Average annual growth rate (1970–79): −0.2%. Per capita income (1980): $490. Principal agricultural products: cocoa, copra, coconuts, palm oil, coffee, bananas. Major industrial products: timber, copra. Exports: cocoa, coffee, copra, palm oil. Imports: foodstuffs, textiles, machinery, electrical equipment, fuels, lubricants. Major trading partners: Netherlands, Portugal, West Germany, East Germany, Rep. China.

**Geography.** The tiny volcanic islands of São Tomé and Príncipe lie in the Gulf of Guinea about 150 miles (240 km) off West Africa. São Tomé (about 330 sq mi.; 859 sq km) is covered by a dense mountainous jungle, out of which have been carved large plantations. Príncipe (about 40 sq. mi.; 142 sq km) consists of jagged mountains. Other islands in the republic are Pedras Tinhosas and Rolas.

**Government.** The Constitution grants supreme power to a People's Assembly composed of members elected for four years. The Assembly chooses the President of the republic from candidates named by the Movement for the Liberation of São Tomé and Príncipe, the only legal party.

**History.** São Tomé and Príncipe were discovered, by Portuguese navigators in 1471 and settled by the end of the century. Intensive cultivation by slave labor made the islands a major producer of sugar during the 17th century but output declined until the introduction of coffee and cacao in the 19th century brought new prosperity. The island of São Tomé was the world's largest producer of cacao in 1908 and the crop is still the most important. An exile liberation movement was formed in 1953 after Portuguese landowners quelled labor riots by killing several hundred African workers.

The Portuguese revolution of 1974 brought the end of the overseas empire and the new Lisbon government transferred power to the liberation movement on July 12, 1975. Most of the 4,000 Portuguese inhabitants departed during the transition period.

## SAUDI ARABIA

**Kingdom of Saudi Arabia**
**Ruler and Prime Minister:** King Fahd bin 'Abdulaziz (1982)
**Area:** 865,000 sq mi. (2,250,070 sq km)
**Population (est. mid-1986):** 11,000,000 (average annual growth rate: 3.0%)
**Density per square mile:** 12.7
**Capital:** Riyadh
**Largest cities (est. 1980):** Riyadh, 1,250,000; Jeddah, 1,000,000; Mecca, 750,000
**Monetary unit:** Riyal
**Language:** Arabic
**Religion:** Islam
**National name:** Al-Mamlaka al-'Arabiya as-Sa'udiya
**Literacy rate:** 52%
**Economic summary:** Gross national product (1984): $108 billion. Average annual non-oil growth rate: 5%. Per capita income (1984): $10,335. Labor force in agriculture: 30%; principal products: dates, grains, livestock. Labor force in industry: 29%; major products: petroleum, cement, plastic products, steel. Natural resource: oil.

Exports: petroleum and petroleum products. Imports: manufactured goods, transport equipment, construction materials, processed food. Major trading partners: U.S., Western European countries, Japan, West Germany.

**Geography.** Saudi Arabia occupies most of the Arabian Peninsula, with the Red Sea and the Gulf of Aqaba to the west, the Arabian Gulf to the east. Neighboring countries are Jordan, Iraq, Kuwait, Qatar, the United Arab Emirates, the Sultanate of Oman, the Yemen Arab Republic, and the People's Democratic Republic of Yemen.

A narrow coastal plain on the Red Sea rims a mountain range that spans the length of the western coastline. These mountains gradually rise in elevation from north to south. East of these mountains is a massive plateau which slopes gently downward toward the Arabian Gulf. Part of this plateau is covered by the world's largest sand desert, the Rub Al-Khali, or Empty Quarter. Saudi Arabia's oil region lies primarily along the Arabian Gulf.

**Government.** Saudi Arabia is a monarchy based on the Sharia (Islamic law), as revealed in the Koran (the holy book) and the Hadith (teachings and sayings of the prophet Mohammed). A Council of Ministers was formed in 1953, which acts as a Cabinet under the leadership of the King. There are 21 Ministries.

Royal and ministerial decrees account for most of the promulgated legislation, treaties, and conventions. There are no political parties.

**History.** Mohammed united the Arabs in the 7th century, and his followers, led by the caliphs, founded a great empire, with its capital at Medina. Later, the caliphate capital was transferred to Damascus and then Baghdad, but Arabia retained its importance because of the holy cities of Mecca and Medina. In the 16th and 17th centuries, the Turks established at least nominal rule over much of Arabia, and in the middle of the 18th century, it was divided into separate principalities.

The Kingdom of Saudi Arabia is almost entirely the creation of King Ibn Saud (1882–1953). A descendant of earlier Wahabi rulers, he seized Riyadh, the capital of Nejd, in 1901 and set himself up as leader of the Arab nationalist movement. By 1906 he had established Wahabi dominance in Nejd. He conquered Hejaz in 1924–25, consolidating it and Nejd into a dual kingdom in 1926. In 1932, Hejaz and Nejd became a single kingdom, which was officially named Saudi Arabia. A year later the region of Asir was incorporated into the kingdom.

Oil was discovered in 1936, and commercial production began during World War II. Saudi Arabia was neutral until nearly the end of the war, but it was permitted to be a charter member of the United Nations. The country joined the Arab League in 1945 and took part in the 1948–49 war against Israel.

On Ibn Saud's death in 1953, his eldest son, Saud, began an 11-year reign marked by an increasing hostility toward the radical Arabism of Egypt's Gamal Abdel Nasser. In 1964, the ailing Saud was deposed and replaced by the Premier, Crown Prince Faisal, who gave vocal support but no military help to Egypt in the 1967 Mideast war.

Faisal's assassination by a deranged kinsman in 1975 shook the Middle East, but failed to alter his kingdom's course. His successor was his brother,

Prince Khalid. Khalid gave influential support to Egypt during negotiations on Israeli withdrawal from the Sinai desert.

King Khalid died of a heart attack June 13, 1982, and was succeeded by his half-brother, Prince Fahd bin 'Abdulaziz, 60, who had exercised the real power throughout Khalid's reign. King Fahd, a pro-Western modernist, chose his 58-year-old half-brother, Abdullah, as Crown Prince.

Saudi Arabia and the smaller, oil-rich Arab states on the Persian Gulf, fearful that they might become Ayatollah Ruhollah Khomeini's next targets if Iran conquered Iraq, made large financial contributions to the Iraqi war effort. They began being dragged into the conflict themselves in the spring of 1984, when Iraq and Iran extended their ground war to attacks on Gulf shipping. First, Iraq attacked tankers loading at Iran's Kharg Island terminal with air-to-ground missiles, then Iran struck back at tankers calling at Saudi Arabia and other Arab countries.

President Reagan ordered the sale, at the end of May, of 400 Stinger antiaircraft missiles to Saudi Arabia. Shortly afterward, Saudi fighter planes shot down two Iranian planes as they approached a foreign tanker over the Gulf. The Saudis were directed to the targets by a U.S. Air Force AWAC plane.

At the same time, cheating by other members of the Organization of Petroleum Exporting Countries, competition from nonmember oil producers, and conservation efforts by consuming nations combined to drive down the world price of oil. Saudi Arabia has one-third of all known oil reserves, but falling demand and rising production outside OPEC combined to reduce its oil revenues from $120 billion in 1980 to $43 billion in 1984 to less the $25 billion in 1985, threatening the country with domestic unrest and undermining its influence in the Gulf area. Oil prices plunged to a post-1973 low of $9 a barrel in 1986, partly due to a Saudi-initiated price war.

# SENEGAL

**Republic of Senegal**
**President:** Abdou Diouf (1981)
**Area:** 75,954 sq mi. (196,722 sq km)
**Population (est. mid-1986):** 6,900,000 (average annual growth rate: 2.9%)
**Density per square mile:** 90.8
**Capital and largest city (est. 1982):** Dakar, 975,000
**Monetary unit:** Franc CFA
**Ethnic groups:** Wolofs, Sereres, Peuls, Tukulers, and others
**Languages:** French (official); Wolof, Serer, other tribal dialects
**Religions:** Islam, 91%; Christian, 6%
**National name:** République du Sénégal
**Literacy rate:** 10%
**Economic summary:** Gross national product (1983): $2.5 billion. Average annual growth rate (1983): −14.3%. Per capita income (1983): $400. Land used for agriculture: 27%; labor force: 70%; principal products: peanuts, millet, corn, rice, sorghum. Labor force in industry: 8%; major products: peanut oil, fertilizer, cement, processed food and fish. Natural resources: fish, phosphate. Exports: peanuts, phosphate rock, canned fish. Imports: foodstuffs, consumer goods, machinery, transport equipment. Major trading partners: France, Western European countries, African neighbors.

**Geography.** The capital of Senegal, Dakar, is the westernmost point in Africa. The country, slighty smaller than South Dakota, surrounds Gambia on three sides and is bordered on the north by Mauritania, on the east by Mali, and on the south by Guinea and Guinea-Bissau.

Senegal is mainly a low-lying country, with a semidesert area in the north and northeast and forests in the southwest. The largest rivers include the Senegal in the north and the Gambia in the central region.

**Government.** There is a National Assembly of 100 members, elected every five years. There is universal suffrage and a constitutional guarantee of equality before the law.

The major political party is the Socialist Party, led by President Abdou Diouf. Legal opposition was reconstituted in 1974 with formation of the Senegalese Democratic Party, headed by Abdoulaye Wade, which urged reduction in French and Western influences. Other opposition parties include the African Independence Party and the Republican Party.

**History.** The Portuguese had some stations on the banks of the Senegal River in the 15th century, and the first French settlement was made at Saint-Louis about 1650. The British took parts of Senegal at various times, but the French gained possession in 1840 and organized the Sudan as a territory in 1904. In 1946, together with other parts of French West Africa, Senegal became part of the French Union. On June 20, 1960, it became an independent republic federated with the Sudanese Republic inthe Mali Federation, from which it withdrew two months later.

On Jan. 1, 1973, Senegal joined with six other states to create the West African Economic Community to promote economic development within the region.

# SEYCHELLES

**Republic of Seychelles**
President: France-Albert René (1977)
Area: 175 sq mi. (453 sq km)
Population (est. mid-1986): 100,000 (average annual growth rate: 1.9%)
Density per square mile: 571.4
Capital: Victoria, 24,000
Monetary unit: Seychelles rupee
Languages: Creole (official), English, French
Religions: Roman Catholic, 90%; Anglican, 8%
Member of Commonwealth of Nations, United Nations, Nonaligned Movement
Literacy rate: 65%
Economic summary: Gross national product (1983): $150 million. Average annual growth rate: −0.2%. Per capita income (1983): $2,310. Land used for agriculture: 37%; labor force: 18%; principal products: vanilla, copra, cinnamon. Labor force in industry: 55%; major products: processed copra and vanilla, coconut oil. Exports: cinnamon, vanilla, copra. Imports: food, tobacco, manufactured goods, machinery, petroleum products, textiles, transport equipment. Major trading partners: U.K., Bahrain, Japan, Pakistan.

**Geography.** Seychelles consists of an archipelago of about 100 islands in the Indian Ocean northeast of

Madagascar. The principal islands are Mahé (55 sq mi.; 142 sq km), Praslin (15 sq mi.; 38 sq km), and La Digue (4 sq mi.; 10 sq km). The Aldabra, Farquhar, and Desroches groups are included in the territory of the republic.

**Government.** Seized from France by Britain in 1810, the Seychelles Islands remained a colony until June 29, 1976. The state is an independent republic within the Commonwealth.

On June 5, 1977, Prime Minister Albert René ousted the islands' first President, James Mancham, suspending the Constitution and the 25-member National Assembly. Mancham, whose "lavish spending" and flamboyance were cited by René in seizing power, charged that Soviet influence was at work. The new president denied this and, while more left than his predecessor, pledged to keep the Seychelles in the nonaligned group of countries.

An unsuccessful attempted coup against René attracted international attention when a group of 50 South African mercenaries posing as rugby players attacked the Victoria airport on Nov. 25, 1981. They caused extensive damage before they hijacked an Air India plane and returned to South Africa, where all but five were freed. Only after widespread international protest did the Pretoria government, which denied any responsibility for the attack, reverse the decision and order all the mercenaries tried as hijackers.

# SIERRA LEONE

**Republic of Sierra Leone**
President: Maj. Gen. Joseph Saidu Momoh (1985)
Area: 27,925 sq mi. (72,326 sq km)
Population (est. mid-1986): 3,700,000 (average annual growth rate: 1.8%)
Density per square mile: 132.5
Capital and largest city (est. 1985): Freetown, 500,000
Monetary unit: Leone
Languages: English (official), Mende, Temne, Creole
Religions: Animist, 52%; Islam, 40%; Christian, 9%
Member of Commonwealth of Nations, United Nations
Literacy rate: 25%
Economic summary: Gross national product (1985): $1 billion. Average annual growth rate (1983–84): 0.5%. Per capita income (1983): $380. Land used for agriculture: 25%; labor force: 75%; principal products: coffee, cocoa, ginger, rice. Labor force in industry: 22%; major products: diamonds, bauxite, rutile, beverages, cigarettes, construction goods. Natural resources: diamonds, bauxite, iron ore, rutile. Exports: diamonds, iron ore, palm kernels, cocoa, coffee. Imports: food, petroleum products, chemicals, machinery. Major trading partners: U.K., U.S., Western European countries, Japan.

**Geography.** Sierra Leone, on the Atlantic Ocean in West Africa, is half the size of Illinois. Guinea, in the north and east, and Liberia, in the south, are its neighbors.

Mangrove swamps lie along the coast, with wooded hills and a plateau in the interior. The eastern region is mountainous.

**Government.** Sierra Leone became an independent nation on April 27, 1961, and declared itself a republic on April 19, 1971.

Sierra Leone became a one party state under the aegis of the All People's Congress Party in April 1978.

**History.** The coastal area of Sierra Leone was ceded to English settlers in 1788 as a home for blacks discharged from the British armed forces and also for runaway slaves who had found asylum in London. The British protectorate over the hinterland was proclaimed in 1896.

After elections in 1967, the British Governor-General replaced Sir Albert Margai, head of SLPP, which had held power since independence, with Dr. Stevens, head of APC, as prime minister. The Army took over the government; then another coup in April 1968 restored civilian rule and put the military leaders in jail.

A coup attempt early in 1971 by the army commander was apparently foiled by loyal army officers, but the then Prime Minister Stevens called in troops of neighboring Guinea's army, under a 1970 mutual defense pact, to guard his residence. After perfunctorily blaming the U.S. for the coup attempt, Stevens switched Governors-General, changed the Constitution, and ended up with a republic, of which he was first president. He was accused of taking "sweeping dictatorial powers," but was re-elected in 1978. Dr. Stevens' picked successor, Major-General Joseph Saidu Momoh was elected unopposed on Oct. 1, 1985.

# SINGAPORE

**Republic of Singapore**
**Prime Minister:** Lee Kuan Yew (1959)
**Area:** 238 sq mi. (616 sq km)
**Population (est. mid-1986):** 2,600,000 (average annual growth rate: 1.1%) (Chinese, 76%; Malay, 15%; Indian, 7%)
**Density per square mile:** 10,924.4
**Capital (est. 1983):** Singapore, 2,500,000
**Monetary unit:** Singapore dollar
**Languages:** Malay, Chinese (Mandarin), Tamil, English
**Religions:** Islam, Christian, Buddhist, Hindu, Confucianist, Taoist
**Member of Commonwealth of Nations**
**Literacy rate:** 85%
**Economic summary:** Gross national product (1984): $17.9 billion. Average annual growth rate (1982–84): 7.5%. Per capita income (1984): $7,100. Land used for agriculture: 10%; labor force: 1%; principal products: poultry, hogs, orchids, vegetables, fruits. Labor force in industry: 29.4%; major industries: petroleum refining, oil exploration, ship repair, rubber processing, electronics and other light industry. Exports: petroleum products, rubber, manufactured goods. Imports: capital equipment, manufactured goods, petroleum. Major trading partners: U.S., Japan, Malaysia, Hong Kong, Saudi Arabia, West Germany, China, Thailand.

**Geography.** The Republic of Singapore consists of the main island of Singapore, off the southern tip of the Malay Peninsula between the South China Sea and the Indian Ocean, and 54 nearby islands.

There are extensive mangrove swamps extending inland from the coast, which is broken by many inlets.

**Government.** There is a Cabinet, headed by the Prime Minister, and a Parliament of 79 members elected by universal suffrage.

The People's Action Party, led by Prime Minister Lee Kuan Yew, is the ruling political party in Parliament, holding all but two seats.

**History.** Singapore, founded in 1819 by Sir Stamford Raffles, became a separate crown colony of Britain in 1946, when the former colony of the Straits Settlements was dissolved. The other two settlements—Penang and Malacca—were transferred to the Union of Malaya, and the small island of Labuan was transferred to North Borneo. The Cocos (or Keeling) Islands were transferred to Australia in 1955 and Christmas Island in 1958.

Singapore attained full internal self-government in 1959. On Sept. 16, 1963, it joined Malaya, Sabah (North Borneo), and Sarawak in the Federation of Malaysia. It withdrew from the Federation on Aug. 9, 1965, and proclaimed itself a republic the next month.

# SOLOMON ISLANDS

**Sovereign:** Queen Elizabeth II
**Governor-General:** Sir Baddeley Devesi (1978)
**Prime Minister:** Sir Peter Kenilorea (1984)
**Area:** 11,500 sq mi. (29,785 sq km)
**Population (est. mid-1986):** 300,000 (average annual growth rate: 3.7%)
**Density per square mile:** 26.1
**Capital and largest city (est. 1981):** Honiara (on Guadalcanal), 21,000
**Monetary unit:** Solomon Islands dollar
**Languages:** English, Melanesian dialects
**Religions:** Anglican, 34%; Roman Catholic, 19%; South Seas Evangelical, 25%; other Protestant, 15%
**Member of British Commonwealth**
**Literacy rate:** 60%
**Economic summary:** Gross national product (1983): $160. million. Average annual growth rate (1970–79): 2.3%. Per capita income (1983): $637. Principal agricultural products: copra, palm oil, rice, cocoa, yams, pigs. Major industrial products: processed fish, timber, jute, soap, canned meat, handicrafts. Natural resources: fish, timber. Exports: fish, timber, copra, palm oil. Imports: machinery and transport equipment, foodstuffs, fuel, manufactured goods. Major trading partners: Japan, Australia, U.K.

**Geography.** Lying east of New Guinea, this island nation consists of the southern islands of the Solomon group: Guadalcanal, Malaita, Santa Isabel, San Cristóbal, Choiseul, New Georgia, and numerous smaller islands.

**Government.** After 85 years of British rule, the Solomons achieved independence July 7, 1978. The Crown is represented by a Governor-General and legislative power is vested in a unicameral legislature of 38 members, led by the Prime Minister.

**History.** Discovered in 1567 by Alvaro de Mendana, the Solomons were not visited again for about 200 years. In 1886, Great Britain and Germany divided the islands between them. In 1914, Australian forces took over the German islands and the Solomons became an Australian mandate in 1920. In World War II, most of the islands were occupied by the Japanese. American forces landed on Guadalcanal on Aug. 7, 1942. The islands were the scene of several important U.S. naval and military victories. They are still largely undeveloped, with only 60 miles of paved road and fewer than 1,000 motor vehicles.

# SOMALIA

**Somali Democratic Republic**
**President:** Maj. Gen. Mohamed Siad Barre (1969)
**Area:** 246,199 sq mi. (637,655 sq km)
**Population (est. mid-1986):** 7,800,000 (average annual growth rate: 2.5%)
**Density per square mile:** 20.9
**Capital and largest city (est. 1982):** Mogadishu, 700,000
**Monetary unit:** Somali shilling
**Language:** Somali (official), Arabic, English
**Religion:** Islam
**National name:** Al Jumhouriya As-Somalya Dimocradia
**Literacy rate:** 60%
**Economic summary:** Gross national product (1983): $1.25 billion. Average annual growth rate: 4.7%. Per capita income (1983): $228. Labor force in agriculture: 30%; principal products: livestock, bananas, sorghum, cereals, sugar cane, maize. Labor force in industry: 3%; major products: flour, meat, fish, canned fruit juices. Natural resources: timber. Exports: livestock, skins and hides, bananas. Imports: textiles, construction materials and equipment, machinery, manufactured goods, transport equipment. Major trading partners: Arab countries, Italy, U.S.

**Geography.** Somalia, situated in the Horn of Africa, lies along the Gulf of Aden and the Indian Ocean. It is bounded by Djibouti in the northwest, Ethiopia in the west, and Kenya in the southwest. In area it is slightly smaller than Texas.

Generally arid and barren, Somalia has two chief rivers, the Shebeli and the Juba.

**Government.** Maj. Gen. Mohamed Siad Barre took power on Oct. 21, 1969, in a coup that established a Supreme Revolutionary Council as the governing body, replacing a parliamentary government. On July 1, 1976, Barre dissolved the Council, naming its members to the Somali Socialist Party, organized that day as the nation's only legal political party. In December 1979, a 171-member People's Assembly was elected under a new Constitution adopted in August. The Assembly confirmed Barre as President for a six-year term.

**History.** From the 7th to the 10th century, Arab and Persian trading posts were established along the coast of present-day Somalia. Nomadic tribes occupied the interior, occasionally pushing into Ethiopian territory. In the 16th century, Turkish rule extended to the northern coast and the Sultans of Zanzibar gained control in the south.

After British occupation of Aden in 1839, the Somali coast became its source of food. The French established a coaling station in 1862 at the site of Djibouti and the Italians planted a settlement in Eritrea. Egypt, which for a time-claimed Turkish rights in the area, was succeeded by Britain. By 1920, a British protectorate and an Italian protectorate occupied what is now Somalia. The British ruled the entire area after 1941, with Italy returning in 1950 to serve as United Nations trustee for its former territory.

In mid-1960, Britain and Italy granted independence to their respective sectors, enabling the two to join as the Republic of Somalia on July 1. Somalia broke diplomatic relations with Britain in 1963 when the British granted the Somali-populated Northern Frontier District of Kenya to the Republic of Kenya.

On Oct. 15, 1969, President Abdi Rashid Ali Shermarke was assassinated and the army seized power, dissolving the legislature and arresting all government leaders. Maj. Gen. Mohamed Siad Barre, as President of a renamed Somali Democratic Republic, leaned heavily toward the U.S.S.R.

In 1977, Somalia openly backed rebels in the westernmost area of Ethiopia, the Ogaden desert, which had been seized by Ethiopia at the turn of the century.

Somalia acknowledged defeat in an eight-month war against the Ethiopians, having lost many of what had become a 32,000-man army and most of its tanks and planes. In March 1978, the U.S. agreed to supply $7 million in food over six months, in addition to $6 million in emergency food relief provided in December. The U.S. refused to consider weapons sales, however, unless Somalia gave up all claims to northern Kenya, the Ogaden, and the Republic of Djibouti, all once claimed as "Greater Somalia." Barre refused to do this.

A U.S. announcement on Jan. 9, 1980, that bases for U.S. ships and planes in the Indian Ocean would be sought in Somalia, Oman, and Kenya, brought a request from Somalia for $1 billion worth of modern arms and an equal amount of economic aid. In August, an agreement was signed giving the U.S. use of military bases in Somalia in return for $25 million in military aid in 1981 and more in subsequent years.

# SOUTH AFRICA

**Republic of South Africa**
**President:** Pieter W. Botha (1984)
**Area:** 437,876 sq mi. (1,134,100 sq km)
**Population (est. mid-1986):** 33,200,000 (average annual growth rate: 2.3%) (black, 68%; white, 18%; colored [mixed], 11%; Asian, 3%)
**Density per square mile:** 75.8[1]
**Administrative capital:** Pretoria
**Legislative capital:** Cape Town
**Judicial capital:** Bloemfontein
**Largest cities (est. 1984):** Johannesburg, 1,700,000; Cape Town, 1,000,000; Durban, 1,000,000; Pretoria, 700,000; Port Elizabeth, 600,000; Bloemfontein, 200,000.
**Monetary unit:** Rand
**Languages:** English, Afrikaans, 9 Bantu languages
**Religions (1984):** Dutch Reformed, 40%; Anglican, 11%; Roman Catholic, 8%; other Christian, 25%
**National name:** Republiek van Suid-Afrika
**Literacy rate:** 99% (whites), 50% (Africans)
**Economic summary:** Gross national product (1983): $77 billion. Average annual growth rate: −3%. Per capita income (1983): $2,500. Labor force in agriculture: 53%; principal products: corn, wool, wheat, sugar cane, tobacco, citrus fruits. Labor force in industry: 17%; major products: assembled automobiles, machinery, textiles, iron and steel, chemicals, fertilizer, fish. Natural resources: gold, diamonds, platinum, uranium, coal, iron ore, asbestos, manganese. Exports: gold, wool, diamonds, corn, uranium, sugar, fruits, hides and skins, asbestos, fish products. Imports: motor vehicles, machinery, metals, petroleum products, chemicals, textiles. Major trading partners: U.S., West Germany, Japan, U.K.

1. Excluding South-West Africa (Namibia).

**Geography.** South Africa, on the continent's southern tip, is washed by the Atlantic Ocean on the west and by the Indian Ocean on the south and east. Its neighbors are South-West Africa (Namibia) in the northwest, Zimbabwe and Botswana in the north, and Mozambique and Swaziland in the northeast. The kingdom of Lesotho forms an enclave within the southeastern part of South Africa. Bophuthatswana, Transkei, Ciskei, and Venda are independent states within South Africa, which occupies an area nearly three times that of California.

The country has a high interior plateau, or veld, nearly half of which averages 4,000 feet (1,219 m) in elevation.

There are no important mountain ranges, although the Great Escarpment, separating the veld from the coastal plain, rises to over 11,000 feet (3,350 m) in the Drakensberg Mountains in the east. The principal river is the Orange, rising in Lesotho and flowing westward for 1,300 miles (2,092 km) to the Atlantic.

The southernmost point of Africa is Cape Agulhas, located in Cape Province about 100 miles (161 km) southeast of the Cape of Good Hope.

**Government.** A new Constitution in 1984 created a new office of Executive State President, with potentially authoritarian powers, in place of the previous parliamentary form of government headed by a Prime Minister. Previously, the Presidency was only ceremonial. Pieter W. Botha, Prime Minister since 1978, was sworn in as President on Sept. 14, 1984.

The new Constitution brought Indian and mixed-race people into a racially divided Parliament made up of three separate chambers for different racial groups. It continued to exclude blacks, who make up 73% of the population. It provides for selection of the President by an Electoral College made up of representatives from the three chambers, with the white chamber controlling the election. It empowers him to veto legislation, declare war, summon Parliament, and dismiss it.

Ten "Bantustans," or black homelands, have unicameral legislatures elected by black voters.

**History.** The Dutch East India Company landed the first settlers on the Cape of Good Hope in 1652, launching a colony that by the end of the 18th century numbered only about 15,000. Known as Boers or Afrikaners, speaking a Dutch dialect known as Afrikaans, the settlers as early as 1795 tried to establish an independent republic.

After occupying the Cape Colony in that year, Britain took permanent possession in 1814 at the end of the Napoleonic wars, bringing in 5,000 settlers. Anglicization of government and the freeing of slaves in 1833 drove about 12,000 Afrikaners to make the "great trek" north and east into African tribal territory, where they established the republics of the Transvaal and the Orange Free State.

The discovery of diamonds in 1867 and gold nine years later brought an influx of "outlanders" into the republics and spurred Cecil Rhodes to plot annexation. Rhodes's scheme of sparking an "outlander" rebellion to which an armed party under Leander Starr Jameson would ride to the rescue misfired in 1895, forcing Rhodes to resign as prime minister of the Cape colony. What British expansionists called the "inevitable" war with the Boers eventually broke out on Oct. 11, 1899.

The defeat of the Boers in 1902 led in 1910 to the Union of South Africa, composed of four provinces, the two former republics and the old Cape and Natal colonies. Louis Botha, a Boer, became the first Prime Minister.

Jan Christiaan Smuts brought the nation into World War II on the Allied side against Nationalist opposition, and South Africa became a charter member of the United Nations in 1945, but refused to sign the Universal Declaration of Human Rights. Apartheid—racial separation—dominated domestic politics as the Nationalists gained power and imposed greater restrictions on Bantus, Coloreds, and Asians.

Afrikaner hostility to Britain triumphed in 1961 with the declaration on May 31 of the Republic of South Africa and the severing of ties with the Commonwealth. Nationalist Prime Minister H. F. Verwoerd's government in 1963 asserted the power to restrict freedom of those who opposed rigid racial laws. Three years later, amid increasing racial tension and criticism from the outside world, Verwoerd was assassinated. His Nationalist successor, Balthazar J. Vorster, launched a campaign of conciliation toward conservative black African states, offering development loans and trade concessions.

A critical issue was South-West Africa, where South African rule was challenged by the United Nations when it asserted responsibility for the territory in 1974 under the name Namibia. African demands for immediate freedom for Namibia led to an attempt to expel South Africa from the U.N. in 1974, a move blocked by a U.S., British, and French veto. The General Assembly barred South Africa from its seat anyway, and the seat has remained empty.

A scandal led to Vorster's resignation on June 4, 1979. Pieter W. Botha succeeded him as Prime Minister, and became President on Sept. 14, 1984, after a new Constitution was promulgated substituting a strong Presidency for the previous parliamentary form of government.

South Africa's policy of apartheid—or racial separation—excluded the country's black majority from participation in the country's government and kept blacks at the bottom rung of the economic ladder. Protests against apartheid by militant blacks, beginning in the latter half of 1984, led to a state of emergency being declared twice, the first on July 20, 1985, covered 36 cities and towns and gave the police powers to make arrests without warrants and to detain people indefinitely. The second, declared on July 12, 1986, covered the whole nation. It gave the police a similar extension of powers and banned "subversive" press reports. Some 4,000 activitst were detained.

In 1985, the civil strife claimed 850 lives.

## BOPHUTHATSWANA

**Republic of Bophuthatswana**
**President:** Chief Lucas Mangope (1977)
**Area:** 15,573 sq mi. (40,333 sq km)
**Population (est. 1986):** 1,736,000 (average annual growth rate: 2.8%)
**Density per square mile:** 111.5
**Capital:** Mmabatho
**Largest city (est. 1981):** Mobopane, 53,000
**Monetary unit:** South African rand
**Languages:** Setswana, English, Afrikaans
**Religions:** Methodist, Lutheran, Anglican, Bantu Christian, Dutch Reformed, Roman Catholic

**Geography.** Bophuthatswana consists of seven discontinuous areas within the boundaries of South Africa, most of them in the northern sector near Botswana.

**Government.** The republic has a 108-member Legislative Assembly, three quarters of whom are elected and the others appointed. President Mangope's Democratic Party is the majority party.

**History.** Bophuthatswana was given independence by South Africa on Dec. 6, 1977, following Transkei as the second "homeland" to be established by Pretoria. The new state and Transkei are recognized only by South Africa and each other.

Mangope, as chief minister in the pre-independence period, sought linkage of the six units into a consolidated area, but was unable to achieve his objective. A second issue, the citizenship of Tswanas in South Africa who wished to remain South African nationals, was settled by enabling them to have citizenship in South African homelands not yet independent.

About two thirds of the population of Bophuthatswana live permanently or as migrants in white areas of South Africa.

**Economy.** Bophuthatswana is richer than many other South African homelands, as it has more than half of the republic's platinum deposits. All foreign trade is included with South Africa's, and it is economically dependent at present on that country.

## CISKEI

**Republic of Ciskei**
**President:** Chief Lennox Leslie Wongama Sebe (1981)
**Area:** 3,282 sq mi. (8,500 sq km)
**Population (est. 1982):** 675,000
**Density per square mile:** 205.7
**Capital (est. 1980):** Zwelitsha, 30,750
**Largest city (est. 1981):** Mdantsane, 159,000
**Monetary unit:** South African rand
**Languages:** Xhosa (official) and English
**Religions:** Methodist, Lutheran, Anglican, and Bantu Christian

**Geography.** Ciskei is surrounded by South Africa on three sides, with the Indian Ocean on the south. From a subtropical coastal strip, the land rises through grasslands to the mountainous escarpment that edges the South African interior plateau.

**Government.** Legislative power is vested in a National Assembly with 22 elected seats. Thirty-three hereditary chiefs complete the membership of the Assembly. The President holds executive power. South Africa's State President retains the power to legislate by proclamation and has veto power over the budget. The Ciskei National Independence Party holds all elective seats in the Assembly.

**History.** Oral tradition ascribes the origin of the Cape Nguni peoples to the central lakes area of Africa. They arrived in what is now Ciskei in the mid-17th century. White settlers from the Cape Colony first entered the territory a century later, but the Dutch East India Colony sought unsuccessfully to discourage white penetration. Nine wars between whites and the inhabitants, by now known as Xhosas, occurred between 1779 and 1878.

A Ciskeian territorial authority was established in 1961, with 84 chiefs and an executive council exercising limited self-government. In 1972, 20 elected members were added to the legislative assembly and a chief minister and six cabinet members elected by the assembly to function as an executive.

A proposed Constitution was approved by referendum on Oct. 30, 1980, and independence ceremonies held on Dec. 4. No government outside South Africa recognized the new state.

**Economy.** A subsistence agricultural economy has been superseded by commuter and migratory labor, which accounted for 64% of national income in 1977. There is some light industry and a potential for exploitation of limestone and other minerals.

## SOUTH-WEST AFRICA (NAMIBIA)

**Status:** Mandate
**Area:** 318,261 sq mi. (824,296 sq km)
**Population (est. 1985):** 1,151,000 (average annual growth rate: 1.25%)
**Density per square mile:** 3.6
**Administrator-General:** Louis Pienaar (1986)
**Capital (est. 1980):** Windhoek, 85,000
**Summer capital (est. 1980):** Swakopmund, 17,500
**Monetary unit:** South African rand
**National name:** Suidwes-Afrika/Namibië; South-West Africa/Namibia
**Literacy rate:** 100% whites/28% non-whites
**Economic summary:** Gross national product (1983): $1.5 billion. Average annual growth rate (1970–85): −0.3%. Land used for agriculture: 30%; labor force: 60%; principal products: corn, millet, sorghum, livestock. Labor force in industry: 4%; major products: canned meat, dairy products, tanned leather, textiles, clothing. Natural resources: diamonds, copper, lead, zinc, uranium, fish. Exports: diamonds, copper, lead, zinc, beef cattle, karakul pelts. Imports: construction materials, fertilizer, grain, foodstuffs. Major trading partner: South Africa.

**Geography.** The mandate, bounded on the north by Angola and Zambia and on the east by Botswana and South Africa, was discovered by the Portuguese explorer Diaz in the late 15th century. It is for the most part a portion of the high plateau of southern Africa with a general elevation of from 3,000 to 4,000 feet.

**History.** The territory became a German colony in 1884 but was taken by South African forces in 1915, becoming a South African mandate by the terms of the Treaty of Versailles.

South Africa's application for incorporation of the territory was rejected by the U.N. General Assembly in 1946 and South Africa was invited to prepare a trusteeship agreement instead. By a law passed in 1949, however, the territory was brought into much closer association with South Africa—including representation in its Parliament.

In 1969, South Africa extended its laws to the mandate over the objection of the U.N., particularly its black African members. When South Africa refused to withdraw them, the Security Council condemned it.

Under a 1974 Security Council resolution, South Africa was required to begin the transfer of power to the Namibians by May 30, 1975, or face U.N. action, but 10 days before the deadline Prime Minister Balthazar J. Vorster rejected U.N. supervision. He said, however, that his government was prepared to negotiate Namibian independence, but not with the South-West African People's Organization, the principal black separatist group. Meanwhile, the all-white legislature of South-West Africa eased several laws on apartheid in public places.

Despite international opposition, the Turnhalle Conference in Windhoek drafted a constitution to organize an interim government based on racial divisions, a proposal overwhelmingly endorsed by white voters in the territory in 1977. At the urging of ambassadors of the five Western members of the Security Council—the U.S., Britain, France, West Germany, and Canada—South Africa on June 11 announced rejection of the Turnhalle constitution and acceptance of the Western proposal to include the South-West Africa People's Organization (SWAPO) in negotiations.

Although negotiations continued between South Africa, the western powers, neighboring black African states, and internal political groups, there was still no agreement on a final independence plan. A new round of talks aimed at resolving the 18-year-old conflict ended in a stalemate on July 25, 1984. Dr. Willie van Niekerk, South Africa's Administrator-General in the territory, met in the remote Cape Verde Islands with leaders of the insurgents, including SWAPO leader Sam Nujoma, to "explore the possibilities of bringing about a cessation of violent and armed activities in South-West Africa." South Africa said the insurgents' "inflexible attitude" made it impossible to reach an agreement on a cease-fire.

As policemen wielding riot sticks charged demonstrators in a black, South-West Africa township, South Africa handed over limited powers to a new, multiracial administration in the former German colony on June 17, 1985. Installation of the new government ended South Africa's direct rule, but South Africa retained an effective veto over the new government's decisions along with responsibility for the territory's defense and foreign policy, and South Africa's efforts to quell the insurgents seeking independence continued.

## TRANSKEI

**Republic of Transkei**
**President:** Paramount Chief Tutor N. Ndaware (1986)
**Prime Minister:** Paramount Chief George Matanzima (1979)
**Area:** 15,831 sq mi. (41,002 sq km)
**Population (est. 1982):** 2,400,000 (growth rate: 2.2%)
**Density per square mile:** 151.6
**Capital (est. 1980):** Umtala, 32,500
**Monetary unit:** South African rand
**Languages:** English, Xhosa, Southern Sotho
**Religions:** Christian, 66%; tribal, 24%
**Economic summary:** Gross domestic product: $150 million. Per capita income: $86. Principal agricultural products: tea, corn, sorghum, dry beans. Major industrial products: timber, textiles. Natural resource: timber. Exports: timber, tea, sacks. Imports: foodstuffs, machines, equipment. Major trading partner: South Africa.

**Geography.** Transkei occupies three discontinuous enclaves within southeast South Africa that add up to twice the size of Massachusetts. It has a 270-mile (435 km) coastline on the Indian Ocean. A port is being developed at Port St. Johns. The capital, Umtala, is connected by rail to the South African port of East London, 100 miles (161 km) to the southwest.

**Government.** Transkei was granted independence by South Africa as of Oct. 26, 1976. A constitution

called for organization of a parliament composed of 75 representative chiefs and 75 elected members, with a ceremonial president and executive power in the hands of a prime minister.

The Organization of African States and the chairman of the United Nations Special Committee Against Apartheid denounced the new state as a sham and urged governments not to recognize it.

**History.** British rule was established over the Transkei region between 1866 and 1894, and the Transkeian Territories were formed in 1903. Under the Native Land Act of 1913, the Territories were reserved for black occupation. In 1963, Transkei was given internal self-government and a legislature that elected Paramount Chief Kaiser Matanzima as Chief Minister, a post he retained in elections in 1968 and 1973.

**Economy.** Some 60% of Transkei is cultivated, producing corn, wheat, beans, and sorghum. Grazing is important. Some light industry has been established.

## VENDA

**Republic of Venda**
**President:** Chief Patrick R. Mphephu (1979)
**Area:** 2,510 sq mi. (6,500 sq km)
**Population (est. 1982):** 400,000 (average annual growth rate: 2.4%)
**Density per square mile:** 214.5
**Capital:** Thohoyandou
**Largest town (est. 1980):** Makearela, 2,500
**Monetary unit:** South African rand
**Languages:** Venda, English, Afrikaans
**Religions:** Christian, tribal
**Economic summary:** Gross domestic product: $156 million. Per capita income: $312. Principal agricultural products: meat, tea, fruit, sisal, corn. Major industrial products: timber, graphite, magnetite.

**Geography.** Venda is composed of two noncontiguous territories in northeast South Africa with a total area of about half that of Connecticut. It is mountainous but fertile, well-watered land, with a climate ranging from tropical to subtropical.

**Government.** The third of South Africa's homelands to be granted independence, Venda became a separate republic on Sept. 13, 1979, unrecognized by any government other than South Africa and its sister homelands, Transkei and Bophuthatswana. The President is popularly elected. An 84-seat legislature is half elected, half appointed.

**History.** The first European reached Venda in 1816, but the isolation of the area prevented its involvement in the wars of the 19th century between blacks and whites and with other tribes. Venda came under South African administration after the Boer War in 1902. Limited home rule was granted in 1962. Chief Patrick R. Mphephu, leader of one of the 27 tribes that historically made up the Venda nation, became Chief Minister of the interim government in 1973 and President upon independence in 1979.

# SOVIET UNION

**Union of Soviet Socialist Republics**
**Chairman of Presidium (President):** Andrei A. Gromyko
(1985)
**Chairman of Council of Ministers (Premier):** Nikolai I.
Ryzhkov (1985)
**Area:** 8,649,489 sq mi. (22,402,200 sq km)
**Population (est. mid-1986):** 280,000,000 (average annual
growth rate: 0.9%) (Russian, 52%; Ukrainian, 17%;
Uzbek, 5%; Byelorussian, 4%; Kazak, 3%; Tatar, 2%)
**Density per square mile:** 32.4
**Capital:** Moscow
**Largest cities (est. 1984):** Moscow, 8,537,000; Leningrad,
4,827,000; Kiev, 2,409,000; Tashkent, 1,986,000;
Baku, 1,661,000; Kharvov, 1,536,000; Minsk, 1,442,-
000; Gorky, 1,392,000; Novosibirsk, 1,384,000;
Sverdlovsk, 1,286,000; Kuibyshev, 1,251,000;
Dnepropetrovsk, 1,140,000; Tbilisi, 1,140,000; Odessa,
1,097,000; Erevan, 1,095,000; Omsk, 1,080,-
000; Chelyabinsk, 1,077,000; Benetsk, 1,055,000
**Monetary unit:** Ruble
**Languages:** *See* Population, above
**Religions:** Russian Orthodox (predominant), Islam, Roman
Catholic, Jewish, Lutheran
**National name:** Soyuz Sovyetskikh Sotsialisticheskikh
Respublik
**Literacy rate:** 99.8%
**Economic summary:** Gross national product (1983):
$1,843.0 billion. Average annual growth rate (1976–83):
2.2%. Per capita income (1983): $6,763. Land used for
agriculture: 10%; labor force: 19%; principal products:
wheat, rye, corn, oats, potatoes, sugar beets, cotton and
flax, cattle, pigs, sheep. Labor force in industry: 42%;
major products: ferrous and nonferrous metals, fuels
andpower, building materials, chemicals, machinery.
Natural resources: fossil fuels, water power, timber,
manganese, lead, zinc, nickel, mercury, potash, phosphate.
Exports: petroleum and petroleum products, natural gas,
machinery and equipment, manufactured goods. Imports:
grain, machinery and equipment, foodstuffs, raw
materials, consumer manufactures. Major trading
partners: Soviet bloc, Western industrialized countries.

## Republics of the U.S.S.R.

| Republic and capital | Area sq mi. | Population est. 1981 (thousands) |
|---|---|---|
| Russian S.F.S.R. (Moscow) | 6,593,391 | 139,150 |
| Ukraine (Kiev) | 233,089 | 50,130 |
| Kazakhstan (Alma-Ata) | 1,064,092 | 15,050 |
| Byelorussia (Minsk) | 80,154 | 9,660 |
| Uzbekistan (Tashkent) | 158,069 | 16,160 |
| Georgia (Tbiksi) | 26,872 | 5,070 |
| Azerbaijan (Baku) | 33,475 | 6,205 |
| Lithuania[1] (Vilnius) | 25,174 | 3,445 |
| Moldavia (Kishinev) | 13,012 | 4,000 |
| Latvia[1] (Riga) | 24,595 | 2,540 |
| Kirghizia (Frunze) | 76,641 | 3,655 |
| Tadzhikistan (Duschambe) | 55,019 | 4,010 |
| Armenia (Erevan) | 11,506 | 3,120 |
| Turkmenistan (Ashkhabad) | 188,417 | 2,900 |
| Estonia[1] (Tallin) | 17,413 | 1,485 |

1. Soviet jurisdiction not recognized by the United States.

**Geography.** The U.S.S.R. is the largest unbroken
political unit in the world unit in the world, occupying more than one seventh of the land surface
of the globe. The greater part of its territory is a
vast plain stretching from eastern Europe to the
Pacific Ocean. This plain, relieved only occasionally by low mountain ranges (notably the Urais),
consists of three zones running east and west: the
frozen marshy tundra of the Arctic; the more temperate forest belt; and the steppes or prairies to the
south, which in southern Soviet Asia become
sandy deserts.

The topography is more varied in the south, particularly in the Caucasus between the Caspian and
Black Seas, and in the Tien-Pamir mountain system
bordering Afghanistan, Sinkiang, and Mongolia.
Mountains (Stanovoi and Kolyma) and great rivers
(Amur, Yenisei, Lena) also break up the sweep of
the plain in Siberia.

In the west, the major rivers are the Volga, Dnie-
per, Don, Kama, and Southern Bug.

**Government.** Legislative authority is vested in the
Supreme Soviet of the U.S.S.R., which consists of
two chambers—the Soviet of the Union, with 767
members, and the Soviet of Nationalities, with 750
members. All members of the Supreme Soviet are
elected for five years by the people.

A Presidium is elected by the Supreme Soviet to
deal with state matters when the latter is not in session. It consists of a chairman, first vice chairman,
15 vice chairmen (one for each union republic), 21
members, and a secretary. The chairman of the
Presidium is sometimes referred to as the President.

Executive authority rests with the Council of
Ministers. It is appointed by the Supreme Soviet
and includes a chairman, a first vice chairman, and
various vice chairmen, chairmen of state committees, ministers, etc. The chairman of the Council
of Ministers is often referred to as the Premier.

Judicial authority is vested in the Supreme Court
of the U.S.S.R. It consists of a chairmen, vice chairman, members, and people's assessors, who are
elected by the Supreme Soviet for five years.

Each of the 15 union republics and the 20 autonomous republics has a Supreme Soviet (with a Presidium), a Council of Ministers, and a Supreme
Court. Each of the eight autonomous regions has
a Soviet of People's Deputies.

The Communist Party of the Soviet Union is the
only party. It is the basic power in the country and
has a membership of 18,500,000.

The supreme organ of the party is the Party Congress, which meets at least once in five years. It
elects a Central Committee, consisting of 320
members and 151 candidate members, to carry on
party work between sessions of the Congress.

Within the Central Committee is a Political Bureau (Politburo), which was called the Presidium
from 1952 to 1966. It functions between sessions
of the Central Committee. Also within the Central
Committee is the Secretariat. The present General
Secretary of the Central Committee, Mikhail S.
Gorbachev, has served since March 10, 1985.

**History.** Tradition says the Viking Rurik came to
Russia in A.D. 862 and founded the first Russian
dynasty in Novgorod. The various tribes were
united by the spread of Christianity in the 10th and
11th centuries; Vladimir "the Saint" was converted
in 988. During the 11th century, the grand dukes
of Kiev held such centralizing power as existed. In
1240, Kiev was destroyed by the Mongols, and the
Russian territory was split into numerous smaller
dukedoms, out of which three large centers

# Rulers of Russia Since 1533

| Name | Born | Ruled[1] | Name | Born | Ruled[1] |
|---|---|---|---|---|---|
| Ivan IV the Terrible | 1530 | 1533–1584 | Alexander II | 1818 | 1855–1881 |
| Theodore I | 1557 | 1584–1598 | Alexander III | 1845 | 1881–1894 |
| Boris Godunov | c.1551 | 1598–1605 | Nicholas II | 1868 | 1894–1917[7] |
| Theodore II | 1589 | 1605–1605 | | | |
| Demetrius I[2] | ? | 1605–1606 | **PROVISIONAL GOVERNMENT** | | |
| Basil IV Shuiski | ? | 1606–1610[3] | **(PREMIERS)** | | |
| "Time of Troubles" | — | 1610–1613 | Prince Georgi Lvov | 1861 | 1917–1917 |
| Michael Romanov | 1596 | 1613–1645 | Alexander Kerensky | 1881 | 1917–1917 |
| Alexis I | 1629 | 1645–1676 | | | |
| Theodore III | 1656 | 1676–1682 | **POLITICAL LEADERS** | | |
| Ivan V[4] | 1666 | 1682–1689[5] | N. Lenin | 1870 | 1917–1924 |
| Peter I the Great[4] | 1672 | 1682–1725 | Aleksei Rykov | 1881 | 1924–1930 |
| Catherine I | c.1684 | 1725–1727 | Vyacheslav Molotov | 1890 | 1930–1941 |
| Peter II | 1715 | 1727–1730 | Joseph Stalin[8] | 1879 | 1941–1953 |
| Anna | 1693 | 1730–1740 | Georgi M. Malenkov | 1902 | 1953–1955 |
| Ivan VI | 1740 | 1740–1741[6] | Nikolai A. Bulganin | 1895 | 1955–1958 |
| Elizabeth | 1709 | 1741–1762 | Nikita S. Khrushchev | 1894 | 1958–1964 |
| Peter III | 1728 | 1762–1762 | Leonid I. Brezhnev | 1906 | 1964–1982 |
| Catherine II the Great | 1729 | 1762–1796 | Yuri V. Andropov | 1914 | 1982–1984 |
| Paul I | 1754 | 1796–1801 | Konstantin U. Chernenko | 1912 | 1984–1985 |
| Alexander I | 1777 | 1801–1825 | Mikhail S. Gorbachev | 1931 | 1985– |
| Nicholas I | 1796 | 1825–1855 | | | |

1. For Tsars through Nicholas II, year of end of rule is also that of death, unless otherwise indicated. 2. Also known as Pseudo-Demetrius. 3. Died 1612. 4. Ruled jointly until 1689, when Ivan was deposed. 5. Died 1696. 6. Died 1764. 7. Killed 1918. 8. General Secretary of Communist Party, 1924–53.

emerged—Galicia, Moscow, and Novgorod. The early dukes of Moscow extended their dominions through their office of tribute collector for the Mongols.

In the late 15th century, Duke Ivan III acquired Novgorod and Tver and threw off the Mongol yoke. Ivan IV, the Terrible (1533–84), first Muscovite Tsar, is considered to have founded the Russian state. He crushed the power of rival princes and boyars (great landowners), but Russia remained largely medieval until the reign of Peter the Great (1682–1725), grandson of the first Romanov Tsar, Michael (1613–45). Peter made extensive reforms aimed at westernization and, through his defeat of Charles XII of Sweden at the Battle of Poltava in 1709, he extended Russia's boundaries to the west.

Catherine the Great (1762–96) continued Peter's westernization program and also expanded Russian territory, acquiring the Crimea and part of Poland. During the reign of Alexander I (1801–25), Napoleon's attempt to subdue Russia was defeated (1812–13), and new territory was gained, including Finland (1809) and Bessarabia (1812). Alexander originated the Holy Alliance, which for a time crushed Europe's rising liberal movement.

Alexander II (1855–81) pushed Russia's borders to the Pacific and into central Asia. Serfdom was abolished in 1861, but heavy restrictions were imposed on the emancipated class. Revolutionary strikes following Russia's defeat in the war with Japan forced Nicholas II (1894–1917) to grant a representative national body (Duma), elected by narrowly limited suffrage. It met for the first time in 1906, little influencing Nicholas in his reactionary course.

World War I demonstrated tsarist corruption and inefficiency and only patriotism held the poorly equipped army together for a time. Disorders broke out in Petrograd (now Leningrad) in March 1917, and defection of the Petrograd garrison launched the revolution. Nicholas II was forced to abdicate on March 15, 1917, and he and his family were killed by revolutionists on July 16, 1918.

A provisional government under the successive premierships of Prince Lvov and a moderate, Alexander Kerensky, lost control to the radical, or Bolshevik, wing of the Socialist Democratic Labor Party. On Nov. 7, 1917, the Bolshevik revolution, engineered by N. Lenin[1] and Leon Trotsky, overthrew the Kerensky government and authority was vested in a Council of People's Commissars, with Lenin as Premier.

The humiliating Treaty of Brest-Litovsk (March 3, 1918) concluded the war with Germany, but civil war and foreign intervention delayed Communist control of all Russia until 1920. A brief war with Poland in 1920 resulted in Russian defeat.

The Union of Soviet Socialist Republics was established as a federation on Dec. 30, 1922.

The death of Lenin on Jan. 21, 1924, precipitated an intraparty struggle between Joseph Stalin, General Secretary of the party, and Trotsky, who favored swifter socialization at home and fomentation of revolution abroad. Trotsky was dismissed as Commissar of War in 1925 and banished from the Soviet Union in 1929. He was murdered in Mexico City on Aug. 21, 1940, by a political agent.

Stalin further consolidated his power by a series of purges in the late 1930s, liquidating prominent party leaders and military officers. Stalin assumed the premiership May 6, 1941.

Soviet foreign policy, at first friendly toward Germany and antagonistic toward Britain and France and then, after Hitler's rise to power in 1933, becoming anti-Fascist and pro-League of Nations, took an abrupt turn on Aug. 24, 1939, with the signing of a nonaggression pact with Nazi Germany. The next month, Moscow joined in the Ger-

1. N. Lenin was the pseudonym taken by Vladimir Ilich Ulyanov. It is sometimes given as Nikolai Lenin or V.

man attack on Poland, seizing territory later incorporated into the Ukrainian and Byelorussian S.S.R.'s. The war with Finland, 1939–40, added territory to the Karelian S.S.R. set up March 31, 1940; the annexation of Bessarabia and Bukovina from Romania became part of the new Moldavian S.S.R. on Aug. 2, 1940; and the annexation of the Baltic republics of Estonia, Latvia, and Lithuania in June 1940 (still unrecognized by the U.S.) created the 14th, 15th, and 16th Soviet Republics. (The number of so-called "Union" republics was reduced to 15 in 1956 when the Karelian S.S.R. became one of the 20 Autonomous Soviet Socialist Republics based on ethnic groups.)

Then, after denouncing a 1941 nonaggression pact with Japan in April 1945, when Allied forces were nearing victory in the Pacific, the Soviet Union declared war on Japan on Aug. 8, 1945, and quickly occupied Manchuria, Karafuto, and the Kurile islands.

The U.S.S.R. built a cordon of Communist states running from Poland in the north to Albania and Bulgaria in the south, including East Germany, Czechoslovakia, Hungary, and Romania, composed of the territories Soviet troops occupied at the war's end. With its Eastern front solidified, the Soviet Union launched a political offensive against the non-Communist West, moving first to block the Western access to Berlin. The Western powers countered with an airlift, completed unification of West Germany, and organized the defense of Western Europe in the North Atlantic Treaty Organization.

Stalin died on March 6, 1953, and was succeeded the next day by G. M. Malenkov as Premier. His chief rivals for power—Lavrenti P. Beria (chief of the secret police), Nikolai A. Bulganin, and Lazar M. Kaganovich—were named first deputies. Beria was purged in July and executed on Dec. 23, 1953.

The new power in the Kremlin was Nikita S. Khrushchev, First Secretary of the party.

Khrushchev formalized the Eastern European system into a Council for Mutual Economic Assistance (Comecon) and a Warsaw Pact Treaty Organization as a counterweight to NATO.

In its technological race with the U.S., the Soviet Union exploded a hydrogen bomb in 1953, developed an intercontinental ballistic missile by 1957, sent the first satellite into space (Sputnik I) in 1957, and put Yuri Gagarin in the first orbital flight around the earth in 1961.

Khrushchev's downfall stemmed from his decision to place Soviet nuclear missiles in Cuba and then, when challenged by the U.S., backing down and removing the weapons. He was also blamed for the ideological break with China after 1963.

Khrushchev was forced into retirement on Oct. 15, 1964, and was replaced by Leonid I. Brezhnev as First Secretary of the Party and Aleksei N. Kosygin as Premier.

President Nixon visited the U.S.S.R. for summit talks in May 1972, concluding agreements on strategic-arms limitation and a declaration of principles on future U.S.-Soviet relations.

Presidents Gerald R. Ford and Brezhnev met in Vladivostok in November 1974 and reached tentative agreements to be incorporated into a treaty at the Geneva SALT talks in 1975. They proposed a ceiling of 2,400 ICBM's for each side, of which no more than 1,320 could have MIRV's.

President Carter, actively pursuing both human rights and disarmament, joined with the Soviet

Union in September 1977 to declare that the SALT I accord, which would have expired Oct. 1 without further action, be maintained in effect while the two sides sought a new agreement (SALT II).

Brezhnev's 1977 election to the presidency followed publication of a new Constitution supplanting the one adopted in 1936. It specified the dominance of the Communist Party, previously unstated.

Carter and the ailing Brezhnev signed the SALT II treaty in Vienna on June 18, 1979, setting ceilings on each nation's arsenal of intercontinental ballistic missiles. Doubts about Senate ratification grew, and became a certainty on Dec. 27, when Soviet troops invaded Afghanistan. Despite protests from the Moslem and Western worlds, Moscow insisted that Afghan President Hafizullah Amin had asked for aid in quelling a rebellion.

In the face of evidence that Amin had been liquidated by Soviet advisers before the troops arrived, the Soviet Union vetoed a Security Council resolution on Jan. 7, 1980, that called for a withdrawal. Carter ordered a freeze on grain exports and high-technology equipment and stated that his "opinion of the Russians has changed more drastically in the last week than even in the previous two-and-a-half years."

On Jan. 20, Carter called for a world boycott of the Summer Olympic Games scheduled for Moscow. The boycott, less than complete, nevertheless marred the first Olympics to be held in Moscow as the United States, Canada, Japan, and to a partial extent all the western allies except France and Italy shunned the event.

While the Soviet Union maintained a stony defense in the face of criticism from Western Europe and the U.S., and a summit meeting of 37 Islamic nations that unanimously condemned the "imperialist invasion" of Afghanistan, the growing crisis in Poland increasingly drew world attention.

In reaction to Soviet repression in Poland in December 1981, Reagan ordered economic sanctions aimed at blocking construction of a gas pipeline between the Soviet Union and Western Europe and Japan. Despite the tension between Moscow and Washington, Strategic Arms Reduction Talks (START) began in Geneva between U.S. and Soviet delegations in mid-1982. Negotiations on intermediate missile reduction also continued in Geneva.

On November 10, 1982, Soviet radio and television announced the death of Leonid Brezhnev. Yuri V. Andropov, who formerly headed the K.G.B., was chosen to succeed Brezhnev as General Secretary. By mid-June 1983, Andropov had assumed all of Brezhnev's three titles.

The Soviet Union broke off both the START talks and the parallel negotiations on European-based missiles in November 1983 in protest against the deployment of medium-range U.S. missiles in Western Europe.

After months of illness, Andropov died in February 1984. Konstantin U. Chernenko, a 72-year-old party stalwart who had been close to Brezhnev, succeeded him as General Secretary and, by mid-April, had also assumed the title of President. In the months following Chernenko's assumption of power, the Kremlin took on a hostile mood toward the West of a kind rarely seen since the height of the cold war 30 years before. Led by Moscow, all the Soviet bloc countries except Romania boycotted the 1984 Summer Olympic Games in Los Angeles—tit-for-tat for the U.S.-led boycott of the

1980 Moscow Games, in the view of most observers.

After 13 months in office, Chernenko died on March 10, 1985. He had been ill much of the time and left only a minor imprint on Soviet history.

Chosen to succeed him as Soviet leader was Mikhail S. Gorbachev, at 54 the youngest man to take charge of the Soviet Union since Stalin. Under Gorbachev (pronounced gore-bah-CHAWFF), the Soviet Union began its long-awaited shift to a new generation of leadership. Unlike his immediate predecessors, Gorbachev did not also assume the title of President but wielded power from the post of party General Secretary. In a surprise move, Gorbachev elevated Andrei Gromyko, 75, for 28 years the Soviet Union's stony-faced Foreign Minister, to the largely ceremonial post of President. He installed a younger man with no experience in foreign affairs, Eduard Shevardnadze, 57, as Foreign Minister.

A new round of U.S. Soviet arms reduction negotiations began in Geneva in March 1985, this time involving three types of weapons systems—strategic, or long-range, missiles and bombers; medium-range systems in Europe, and space-based systems. In the new talks, the two sides differed sharply on how to approach the three-part negotiations, with the United States putting the focus on cuts in land-based weapons while the Soviet Union made curbing space weapons its first priority.

After months of quiet negotiations, Reagan and Gorbachev agreed to meet in Geneva on Nov. 19-20,1985—the 11th postwar meeting between the leaders of the two superpowers and the first since former President Carter's 1979 meeting with Brezhnev in Vienna. Expectations for concrete results were low because the Geneva arms talks appeared to be at an impasse, with both sides repeating old slogans. But after a meeting in Helsinki, Finland, with the new Soviet Foreign Minister, Shevardnadze, Secretary of State George Shultz said that if the session turned out well, the two leaders might hold a rotating series of meetings in each other's capitals.

In advance of the summit, the Soviet Union announced that it would halt nuclear testing from Aug. 6.

The Soviet Union took much criticism in early 1986 over the April 24 meltdown at the Chernobyl nuclear plant and its reluctance to give out any information on the accident.

# SPAIN

**Spanish State**
**Ruler:** King Juan Carlos I (1975)
**Prime Minister:** Felipe González Márquez (1982)
**Area:** 194,885 sq mi. (504,750 km)[1]
**Population (est. mid-1986):** 38,800,000 (average annual growth rate: 0.5%) (Spanish, Basque, Catalan, Galician)
**Density per square mile:** 199.1
**Capital:** Madrid
**Largest cities (est. 1983):** Madrid, 3,175,000; Barcelona, 1,750,000; Valencia, 750,000; Seville, 650,000; Zaragoza, 575,000; Vizcaya (Bilbao), 440,000
**Monetary unit:** Peseta
**Languages:** Spanish, Basque, Catalan, Galician
**Religion:** Roman Catholic

**National name:** Estado Español
**Literacy rate:** 97%
**Economic summary:** Gross national product (1984): $160.4 billion. Average annual growth rate (1984): 2.2%. Per capita income (1983): $4,760. Land used for agriculture: 41%; labor force: 17%; principal products: cereals, vegetables, citrus fruits, wine, olives and olive oil, livestock. Labor force in industry: 35%; major products: processed foods, textiles, footwear, petro-chemicals, steel, automobiles, ships. Natural resources: coal, lignite, water power, uranium, mercury, pyrites, fluorospar, gypsum, iron ore, zinc, lead, tungsten, copper. Exports: fresh fruits, iron and steel products, textiles, footwear, automobiles, fruits and vegetables. Imports: machinery and transportation equipment, chemicals, fuels, automobiles, iron, steel. Major trading partners: Western European nations, U.S., Middle Eastern countries.

1. Including the Balearic and Canary Islands.

**Geography.** Spain occupies 85% of the Iberian Peninsula in southwestern Europe, which it shares with Portugal; France is to the northeast, separated by the Pyrenees. The Bay of Biscay lies to the north, the Atlantic Ocean to the west, and the Mediterranean Sea to the south and east: Africa is less than 10 miles (16 km) south at the Strait of Gibraltar.

A broad central plateau slopes to the south and east, crossed by a series of mountain ranges and river valleys.

Principal rivers are the Ebro in the northeast, the Tajo in the central region, and the Guadalquivir in the south.

Off Spain's east coast in the Mediterranean are the Balearic Islands (1,936 sq mi.; 5,014 sq km), the largest of which is Majorca. Sixty miles (97 km) west of Africa are the Canary Islands (2,808 sq mi.; 7,273 sq km).

**Government.** King Juan Carlos I (born Jan. 5, 1938) succeeded Generalissimo Francisco Franco Bahamonde as Chief of State Nov. 22, 1975.

The Cortes, or Parliament, consists of a Chamber of Deputies of 350 members and a Senate of 208, all elected by universal suffrage. The new Cortes, replacing one that was largely appointed or elected by special constituencies, was organized under a constitution adopted by referendum Dec. 6, 1978.

The major political parties are the Spanish Socialist Workers Party (184 of 350 seats in the Chamber of Deputies, 124 of 208 elected Senate seats), led by Prime Minister Felipe González Márquez; Popular Coalition (105 seats in Chamber, 63 in Senate), led by Manuel Fraga Iribarne; United Left (7 seats in Chamber, none in Senate), led by Gerardo Iglesias; Social and Democratic Center (19 seats in Chamber, 3 in Senate), led by Adolfo Suárez; Convergencia i Unió (Catalonian Party) (18 seats in Chamber, 8 in Senate); Basque Party (6 seats in Chamber, 7 in Senate).

**History.** Spain, originally inhabited by Celts, Iberians and Basques, became a part of the Roman Empire in 201 B.C., when it was conquered by Scipio Africanus. In A.D. 412, the barbarian Visigothic leader Ataulf crossed the Pyrenees and ruled Spain, first in the name of the Roman emperor and then independently. In 711, the Moslems under Tariq entered Spain from Africa and within a few years completed the subjugation of the country. In 732, the Franks, led by Charles Martel, defeated the Moslems near Poitiers, thus preventing the further expansion of Islam in southern Europe. Internal dissension of Spanish Islam invited a steady Christian conquest from the north.

Aragon and Castile were the most important Spanish states from the 13th to the 15th century, consolidated by the marriage of Ferdinand II and Isabella I in 1469. The last Moslem stronghold, Granada, was captured in 1492. Roman Catholicism was established as the official state religion and the Jews (1492) and the Moslems (1502) expelled.

In the era of exploration, discovery, and colonization, Spain amassed tremendous wealth and a vast colonial empire through the conquest of Peru by Pizarro (1532–33) and of Mexico by Cortés (1519–21). The Spanish Hapsburg monarchy became for a time the most powerful in the world.

In 1588, Philip II sent his Invincible Armada to invade England, but its destruction cost Spain its supremacy on the seas and paved the way for England's colonization of America. Spain then sank rapidly to the status of a second-rate power and never again played a major role in European politics. Its colonial empire in the Americas and the Philippines vanished in wars and revolutions during the 18th and 19th centuries.

In World War I, Spain maintained a position of neutrality. In 1923, Gen. Miguel Primo de Rivera became dictator. In 1930, King Alfonso XIII revoked the dictatorship, but a strong antimonarchist and republican movement led to his leaving Spain in 1931.[2] The new Constitution declared Spain a workers' republic, broke up the large estates, separated church and state, and secularized the schools. The elections held in 1936 returned a strong Popular Front majority, with Manuel Azaña as President.

On July 18, 1936, a conservative army officer in Morocco, Francisco Franco Bahamonde, led a mutiny against the government. The civil war that followed lasted three years and cost the lives of nearly a million people. Franco was aided by Fascist Italy and Nazi Germany, while Soviet Russia helped the Loyalist side. Several hundred leftist Americans served in the Abraham Lincoln Brigade on the side of the republic. The war ended when Franco took Madrid on March 28, 1939.

Franco became head of the state, national chief of the Falange Party (the governing party), and Premier and Caudillo (leader). In a referendum in 1947, the Spanish people approved a Franco-drafted succession law declaring Spain a monarchy again. Franco, however, continued as Chief of State.

In 1969, Franco and the Cortes designated Prince Juan Carlos Alfonso Víctor María de Borbón (who married Princess Sophia of Greece on May 14, 1962) to become King of Spain when the provisional government headed by Franco came to an end. He is the grandson of Alfonso XIII and the son of Don Juan, pretender to the throne.

Franco died of a heart attack on Nov. 20, 1975, after more than a year of ill health, and Juan Carlos was proclaimed King two days later.

Over strong rightist opposition, the government legalized the Communist Party in advance of the 1977 elections. Premier Adolfo Suaraz Gonzalez's Union of the Democratic Center, a coalition of a dozen centrist and rightist parties, claimed 34.3% of the popular vote in the election.

Under pressure from Catalonian and Basque nationalists, Suárez granted home rule to these regions in 1979, but centrists backed by him did poorly in the 1980 elections for local assemblies in the two areas. Economic problems persisted, along with new incidents of terrorism, and Suárez resigned on Jan. 29, 1981 and was succeded by Leopoldo Calvo Sotelo.

With the overwhelming election of Prime Minister Felipe González Márquez and his Spanish Socialist Workers Party in the Oct. 20, 1982, parliamentary elections, the Franco past was finally buried. The thrust of Gonzalez, a pragmatic moderate, was to modernize rather than radicalize Spain. As promised, the Socialists did not carry out widespread nationalization of private industry, but did seek to nationalize the high-tension power grid.

A treaty admitting Spain, along with Portugal, to the European Economic Community was to take effect on Jan. 1, 1986. Later that year, in June, Spain voted to remain in NATO, but outside of its military command and Gonzalez's Socialists retained their majority in national elections.

# SRI LANKA

**Democratic Socialist Republic of Sri Lanka**
**President:** J. R. Jayewardene (1978)
**Prime Minister:** Ranasinghe Premadasa (1978)
**Area:** 25,332 sq mi. (65,610 sq km)
**Population (est. mid-1986):** 16,600,000 (average annual growth rate: 2.0%)
**Density per square mile:** 602.0
**Capital:** Sri Jayewardenepura Kotte (Colombo)
**Largest cities (est. 1982):** Colombo, 590,000; Dehiwela, 180,000; Jaffna, 125,000
**Monetary unit:** Sri Lanka rupee
**Languages:** Sinhala, Tamil, English
**Religions:** Buddhist, 69%; Hindu, 15%; Islam, 8%; Christian, 8%
**Member of Commonwealth of Nations**
**Literacy rate:** 87%
**Economic summary:** Gross national product (1983): $4.9 billion. Average annual growth rate (1985): 5.1%. Per capita income (1984): $320. Land used for agriculture: 25%; labor force: 53%; principal products: tea, coconuts, rubber, rice, spices. Labor force in industry: 15%; major products: consumer goods, textiles, chemicals, paper and paper products. Natural resources: limestone, graphite, gems. Exports: tea, rubber, petroleum products. Imports: petroleum, machinery, transport equipment, sugar. Major trading partners: Saudi Arabia, Iran, U.S., U.K., Japan.

**Geography.** An island in the Indian Ocean off the southeast tip of India, Sri Lanka is about half the size of Alabama. Most of the land is flat and rolling; mountains in the south central region rise to over 8,000 feet (2,438 m).

**Government.** After 24 years as a British dominion, Ceylon became an independent republic and reverted to the traditional name Sri Lanka (resplendent island) on May 22, 1972. A new Constitution was adopted, replacing that of 1948.

The new Constitution set up the National State Assembly, a 168-member unicameral legislature that serves for six years unless dissolved earlier.

The major political parties are the United National Party (140 of 168 seats in the National Assembly), led by President J.R. Jayewardene: Tamil United Liberation Front (18 seats); Sri Lanka Freedom Party (8 seats), led by Anura Bandaranaike. A split in the Freedom Party has resulted in the formation of the Sri Lanka Mahajaua Party (SLMP).

**History.** Following Portuguese and Dutch rule, Ceylon became an English crown colony in 1798. The British developed coffee, tea, and rubber plantations and granted six Constitutions between 1798 and 1924. The Constitution of 1931 gave a large measure of self-government.

In 1984, Ceylon became a self-governing dominion of the Commonwealth of Nations in 1948.

Presidential elections were held in December 1982, and won by J.R. Jayewardene.

Tension between the Tamil minority and the Sinhalese majority continued to build and erupted in bloody violence in 1983 that grew worse in 1984 and 1985. There are about 2.6 million Tamils in Sri Lanka, while the Sinhalese make up about three-quarters of the 15-million population. Tamil extremists are fighting for a separate nation. About 400 people, mainly Tamils living in the northern part of Sri Lanka, were killed in the violence in 1983.

During 1985, bombings, killings and arrests spread through the northern and eastern regions of the island nation, and the Tamil problem began to undermine economic development. President Jayewardene announced extraordinary measures to combat the separatists, but at the same time sent representatives to the Himalayan kingdom of Bhutan for talks with Tamil representatives.

# SUDAN

**Republic of the Sudan**
**Prime Minister:** Sadig el-Mahdi (1986)
**Area:** 967,491 sq mi. (2,505,802 sq km)
**Population (est. mid-1986):** 22,900,000 (average annual growth rate: 2.9%)
**Density per square mile:** 23.7
**Capital:** Khartoum
**Largest cities (est. 1981):** Khartoum, 1,250,000; Omdurman, 350,000; Port Sudan, 250,000
**Monetary unit:** Sudanese pound
**Languages:** Arabic, English, tribal dialects
**Religions:** Islam, 73%; Animist, 18%; Christian, 9%
**National name:** Jamhuryat es-Sudan Al Demogratia
**Literacy rate:** 20%
**Economic summary:** Gross national product (1984): $7.31 billion. Average annual growth rate (1970-79): 1.5%. Per capita income (1981): $478. Land used for agriculture: 3%; labor force: 78%; principal products: cotton, peanuts, sesame seeds, gum arabic, sorghum, wheat sugar cane. Labor force in industry: 10%; major products: cement, textiles, pharmaceuticals, shoes, processed foods. Natural resources: some iron ore, copper, chrome, industrial metals. Exports: cotton, peanuts, gum arabic, livestock. Imports: textiles, petroleum products, vehicles, tea, wheat. Major trading partners: U.K., West Germany, Italy, India, China, France, Japan.

**Geography.** The Sudan, in northeast Africa, is the largest country on the continent, measuring about one fourth the size of the United States. Its neighbors are Chad and the Central African Republic on the west, Egypt and Libya on the north, Ethiopia on the east, and Kenya, Uganda, and Zaire on the south. The Red Sea washes about 500 miles of the eastern coast.

The country extends from north to south about 1,200 miles (1,931 km) and west to east about 1,000 miles (1,609 km). The northern region is a continuation of the Libyan Desert. The southern region is fertile, abundantly watered, and, in places, heavily forested. It is traversed from north to south by the Nile, all of whose great tributaries are partly or entirely within its borders.

**Government.** A multi-party democracy was established. The centrist Umma party formed a coalition government after the elections of April 4, 1986.

**History.** The early history of the Sudan (known as the Anglo-Egyptian Sudan between 1898 and 1955) is linked with that of Nubia, where a powerful local kingdom was formed in Roman times with its capital at Dongola. After conversion to Christianity in the 6th century, it joined with Ethiopia and resisted Mohammedanization until the 14th century. Thereafter the area was broken up into many small states until 1820–22, when it was conquered by Mohammed Ali, Pasha of Egypt. Egyptian forces were evacuated during the Mahdist revolt (1881–98), but the Sudan was reconquered by the Anglo-Egyptian expeditions of 1896–98, and in 1899 became an Anglo-Egyptian condominium, which was reaffirmed by the Anglo-Egyptian treaty of 1936.

Egypt and Britain agreed in 1953 to grant self-government to the Sudan under an appointed Governor-General. An all-Sudanese Parliament was elected in November-December 1953, and an all-Sudanese government was formed. In December 1955, the Parliament declared the independence of the Sudan, which, with the approval of Britain and Egypt, was proclaimed on Jan. 1, 1956.

In October 1969, Maj. Gen. Gaafar Mohamed Nimeiri, the president of the Council for the Revolution, took over as prime minister. He was elected the nation's first president in 1971 by a reported 98.6% of the vote in a national referendum.

In 1976, a third attempted coup against Nimeiri left 1,000 rebels and loyal troops dead after a fierce battle in Khartoum. Nimeiri accused President Muammar el Qaddafi of Libya of having instigated the attempt and broke relations with Libya.

On April 6, 1985, while out of the country on visits to the United States and Egypt, Nimeiri lost power on April 6, 1985, in the same way he gained it 16 years previously—by a military coup. The new military regime that took over was headed by Nimeiry's Defense Minister, Gen. Abdel Rahman Siwar el-Dahab.

Among the problems that the new government faced were a debilitating civil war with rebels in the south of the country, other sectarian and tribal conflicts, enormous economic problems, and coping with both the continuing arrival of starving refugees from neighboring, famine-stricken Ethiopia, and the famine that affected more than four million Sudanese.

# SURINAME

**Republic of Suriname**
**President:** L. F. Ramdat Misier (1982)
**Prime Minister:** Wim Udenhout (1984)
**Area:** 63,251 sq mi. (163,820 sq km)
**Population (est. mid-1986):** 400,000 (average annual

growth rate: 2.0%) (Hindi, 37%; Creole, 31%;
Indonesian, 15%; Bush Negro, 10%)
**Density per square mile:** 6.3
**Capital and largest city (est. 1982):** Paramaribo, 100,000
**Monetary unit:** Suriname guilder
**Languages:** Dutch, Surinamese (lingua franca)
**Religions:** Protestant, Roman Catholic, Hindu, Islam
**Literacy rate:** 80%
**Economic summary:** Gross national product (1983): $1.28
billion. Average annual growth rate (1979–83): 8%. Per
capita income (1983): $3,420. Land used for agriculture:
0.3%; labor force: 8%; principal products: rice, citrus
fruits, sugar, coffee. Labor force in industry: 15%; major
products: aluminum, alumina, processed foods, lumber,
bricks, cigarettes. Natural resources: bauxite, iron ore,
timber, fish, shrimp. Exports: bauxite, alumina, aluminum,
rice, shrimp, lumber and wood products. Imports: capital
equipment, petroleum, iron and steel, cotton, flour, meat,
dairy products. Major trading partners: U.S., Western
European countries.

**Geography.** Suriname lies on the northeast coast of
South America, with Guyana to the west, French
Guiana to the east, and Brazil to the south. It is
about one tenth larger than Michigan. The principal rivers are the Corantijn on the Guyana border,
the Marowijne in the east, and the Suriname, on
which the capital city of Paramaribo is situated.
The Tumuc-Humac Mountains are on the border
with Brazil.

**Government.** Suriname, formerly known as Dutch
Guiana, became an independent republic on Nov.
25, 1975. The first prime minister, Henck A. E.
Arron, was ousted by a 16-man military junta on
Feb. 25, 1980, and replaced by Dr. Henk R. Chin
A Sen.
Chin A Sen was elevated to the office of Presi-
dent by the junta on Aug. 14, 1980, and the 39-
member National Assembly was abolished and re-
placed by a military cabinet. In 1982, L.F. Ramdat
Missier replaced Sen as president.

**History.** England established the first European
settlement on the Suriname River in 1650 but
transferred sovereignty to the Dutch in 1667 in the
Treaty of Breda, by which the British acquired
New York. Colonization was confined to a narrow
coastal strip, and until the abolition of slavery in
1863, African slaves furnished the labor for the
plantation economy. After 1870, laborers were imported from British India and the Dutch East Indies.
In 1948, the colony was integrated into the Kingdom of the Netherlands and two years later was
granted full home rule in other than foreign affairs
and defense. After race rioting over unemployment and inflation, the Netherlands offered complete independence in 1973. Henck A. E. Arron,
leader of a coalition of Creole (Surinamese of African descent) parties, advocated independence,
while Jaggernath Lachmon, leader of the Surinamese of East Indian descent, urged delay.
Arron retained power in the first post-
independence elections in 1977 but held only a
one-seat margin over Lachmon's group early in
1980. He had promised early elections when Army
sergeants and a lieutenant staged a coup on Feb.
25 and installed a civilian, Dr. Henk R. Chin A Sen,
as Prime Minister. A subsequent military intervention made Chin A Sen president, abolishing the legislature and instituting a military government.

# SWAZILAND

**Kingdom of Swaziland**
**Ruler:** King Mswiti III (1986)
**Prime Minister:** Prince Bhekimpi Dlamini (1983)
**Area:** 6,704 sq mi. (17,363 sq km)
**Population (est. mid-1986):** 700,000 (average annual
growth rate: 3%)
**Density per square mile:** 104.4
**Capital and largest city (est. 1985):** Mbabane, 45,000
**Monetary unit:** Lilangeni
**Languages:** English and Siswati (official)
**Religions:** Christian, 77%; Animist, 27%
**Member of Commonwealth of Nations**
**Literacy rate (1981):** 65%
**Economic summary:** Gross national product (1984): $478
million. Average annual growth rate (1979–82): 1.7%.
Per capita income (1983): $900. Land used for
agriculture: 8%; labor force: 32%; principal products:
corn, livestock, sugar cane, citrus fruits, cotton, rice,
pineapples. Labor force in industry: 25%; major products:
milled sugar, ginned cotton, processed meat and wood.
Natural resources: asbestos, diamonds. Exports: sugar,
wood products, iron ore, asbestos, citrus fruits, cotton.
Imports: motor vehicles, fuels and lubricants, foodstuffs,
chemicals. Major trading partners: South Africa, U.K., U.S.

**Geography.** Swaziland, 85% the size of New Jersey,
is surrounded by South Africa and Mozambique.
The country consists of a high veld in the west and
a series of plateaus descending from 6,000 feet
(1,829 m) to a low veld of 1,500 feet (457 m).

**Government.** In 1967, a new Constitution established King Sobhuza II as head of state and provided for an Assembly of 24 members elected by
universal suffrage, together with a Senate of 12
members—half appointed by the Assembly and
half by the King. In 1973, the King renounced the
Constitution, suspended political parties, and took
total power for himself. In 1977, he replaced the
Parliament with an assembly of tribal leaders. The
Parliament reconvened in 1979.

**History.** Bantu peoples migrated southwest to the
area of Mozambique in the 16th century. A number of clans broke away from the main body in the
18th century and settled as Swaziland. In the 19th
century they organized as a tribe, partly because
they were in constant conflict with the Zulu. Their
ruler, Mswazi, applied to the British in the 1840s
for help against the Zulu. The British and the
Transvaal governments guaranteed the independence of Swaziland in 1881.
South Africa held Swaziland as a protectorate
from 1894 to 1899, but after the Boer War, in 1902,
Swaziland was transferred to British administration. The Paramount Chief was recognized as the
native authority in 1941.
In 1963, the territory was constituted a protectorate, and on Sept. 6, 1968, it became the independent nation of Swaziland.
King Sobhuza died in August 1982, the world's
longest-reigning monarch.

# SWEDEN

**Kingdom of Sweden**
**Sovereign:** King Carl XVI Gustaf (1973)
**Prime Minister:** Ingvar Carlsson (1986)
**Area:** 173,800 sq mi. (449,964 sq km)

**Population (est. mid-1986):** 8,400,000 (average annual growth rate: 0.2%)
**Density per square mile:** 48.3
**Capital:** Stockholm
**Largest cities (est. 1985):** Stockholm, 1,409,000; Göteborg, 696,000; Malmö, 454,000; Uppsala, 150,000
**Monetary unit:** Krona
**Language:** Swedish
**Religion:** Swedish Lutheran, 95%
**National name:** Konungariket Sverige
**Literacy rate:** 99%
**Economic summary:** Gross national product (1985): $95 billion. Average annual growth rate (1970–1984): 2.2%. Per capita income (1984): $11,363. Principal agricultural products: dairy products, grains, sugar beets, potatoes, wood. Labor force in industry: 31%; major products: machinery, instruments, metal products, automobiles. Natural resources: forests, iron ore, hydroelectric power, unmined uranium. Exports: machinery, motor vehicles, wood pulp, paper products, iron and steel products. Imports: machinery, petroleum, yarns, foodstuffs, iron and steel, chemicals. Major trading partners: Norway, West Germany, U.K., Denmark, Finland, U.S.

**Geography.** Sweden occupies the eastern part of the Scandinavian peninsula, with Norway to the west, Finland and the Gulf of Bothnia to the east, and Denmark and the Baltic Sea in the south. It is one tenth larger than California.

The country slopes eastward and southward from the Kjölen Mountains along the Norwegian border, where the peak elevation is Kebnekaise at 6,965 feet (2,123 m) in Lapland. In the north are mountains and many lakes. To the south and east are central lowlands and south of them are fertile areas of forest, valley, and plain.

Along Sweden's rocky coast, chopped up by bays and inlets, are many islands, the largest of which are Gotland and Oland.

**Government.** Sweden is a constitutional monarchy. Under the 1975 Constitution, the Riksdag is the sole governing body. The prime minister is the political chief executive.

In 1967, agreement was reached on part of a new Constitution after 13 years of work. It provided for a single-house Riksdag of 350 members (later amended to 349 seats) to replace the 104-year old bicameral Riksdag. The members are popularly elected for three years. Ninety-two present members of the Riksdag are women.

The King, Carl XVI Gustaf, was born April 30, 1946, and succeeded to the throne Sept. 19, 1973, on the death at 90 of his grandfather, Gustaf VI Adolf. Carl Gustaf was married on June 19, 1976, to Silvia Sommerlath, a West German commoner. They have three children: Princess Victoria, born July 14, 1977; Prince Carl Philip, born May 13, 1979; and Princess Madeleine, born June 10, 1982. Under the new Act of Succession, effective Jan. 1, 1980, the first child of the reigning monarch, regardless of sex, is heir to the throne.

The major political parties are the Social Democratic Party (166 seats in the Riksdag), led by Prime Minister Ingvar Carlsson; Conservative Party (86 seats), led by Ulf Adelsohn; Center Party (56 seats), led by former Prime Minister Thorbjörn Fälldin; Liberal Party (21 seats), led by Bengt Westerberg; Communist Party (20 seats), led by Lars Werner.

**History.** The earliest historical mention of Sweden is found in Tacitus' *Germania*, where reference is made to the powerful king and strong fleet of the Suiones. Toward the end of the 10th century, Olaf Sköttkonung established a Christian stronghold in Sweden. Around 1400, an attempt was made to unite the northern nations into one kingdom, but this led to bitter strife between the Danes and the Swedes.

In 1520, the Danish King, Christian II, conquered Sweden and in the "Stockholm Bloodbath" put leading Swedish personalities to death. Gustavus Vasa (1523–60) broke away from Denmark and fashioned the modern Swedish state.

Sweden played a leading role in the second phase (1630–35) of the Thirty Years' War (1618–48). By the Treaty of Westphalia (1648), Sweden obtained western Pomerania and some neighboring territory on the Baltic. In 1700, a coalition of Russia, Poland, and Denmark united against Sweden and by the Peace of Nystad (1721) forced it to relinquish Livonia, Ingria, Estonia, and parts of Finland.

Sweden emerged from the Napoleonic Wars with the acquisition of Norway from Denmark and with a new royal dynasty stemming from Marshal Jean Bernadotte of France, who became King Charles XIV (1818–44). The artificial union between Sweden and Norway led to an uneasy relationship, and the union was finally dissolved in 1905.

Sweden maintained a position of neutrality in both World Wars.

An elaborate structure of welfare legislation, imitated by many larger nations, began with the establishment of old-age pensions in 1911. Economic prosperity based on its neutralist policy enabled Sweden, together with Norway, to pioneer in public health, housing, and job security programs.

Forty-four years of Socialist government were ended in 1976 with the election of a conservative coalition headed by Thorbjörn Fälldin, a 50-year-old sheep farmer.

Fälldin resigned on Oct. 5, 1978, when his conservative parties partners demanded less restrictions on nuclear power, and his successor, Ola Ullsten, resigned a year later after failing to achieve a consensus on the issue. Returned to office by his coalition partners, Fälldin said he would follow the course directed by a national referendum. On March 23, 1980, voters backed the development of 12 nuclear plants and use of them for at least 25 years to supply 40% of national energy needs while the search for alternative sources continued.

In February 1986, Prime Minister Palme was killed by an unknown assailant. His death shocked the world.

# SWITZERLAND

**Swiss Confederation**
**President:** Alphons Egli (1986)
**Vice President:** Pierre Duboit (1986)
**Area:** 15,941 sq mi. (41,288 sq km)
**Population (est. mid-1986):** 6,500,000 (average annual growth rate: 0.2%) (Swiss, 85%; Italian, 8%; German, 2%; Spanish, 2%; French, 1%—figures by place of birth)
**Density per square mile:** 419.6
**Capital:** Bern
**Largest cities (est. 1984):** Zurich, 354,500; Basel, 176,200; Geneva, 159,500; Bern, 140,600; Lausanne, 126,200

**Monetary unit:** Swiss franc
**Languages:** German, 65%; French, 18%; Italian, 10%; Romansch, 1%
**Religions:** Roman Catholic, 48%; Protestant, 44%
**National name:** Schweiz/Suisse/Svizzera
**Literacy rate:** 99%
**Economic summary:** Gross national product (1984): $96.1 billion. Average annual growth rate (1970–79): 0.2%. Per capita income (1984): $14,300. Land used for agriculture: 26%; labor force: 7%; principal products: cheese and other dairy products, livestock, fruits, grains, wine. Labor force in industry: 38%; major products: watches and clocks, precision instruments, machinery, chemicals, pharmaceuticals, textiles, generators, turbines. Natural resources: water power, timber, salt. Exports: electrical machinery, chemicals, precision instruments, textiles, foodstuffs, textile yarns, dyestuffs, chemicals. Imports: transport equipment, metals and metal products, foodstuffs, chemicals, textile yarns. Major trading partners: West Germany, France, U.S., Italy, U.K.

**Geography.** Switzerland, in central Europe, is the land of the Alps. Its tallest peak is the Dufourspitze at 15,203 feet (4,634 m) on the Swiss side of the Italian border, one of 10 summits of the Monte Rose massif in the Pennine Alps. The tallest peak in all of the Alps, Mont Blanc (15,771 ft; 4,807 m), is actually in France.

Most of Switzerland comprises a mountainous plateau bordered by the great bulk of the Alps on the south and by the Jura Mountains on the northwest. About one fourth of the total area is covered by mountains and glaciers.

The country's largest lakes—Geneva, Constance (Bodensee), and Maggiore—straddle the French, German-Austrian, and Italian borders, respectively.

The Rhine, navigable from Basel to the North Sea, is the principal inland waterway. Other rivers are the Aare and the Rhône.

Switzerland, twice the size of New Jersey, is surrounded by France, West Germany, Austria, Liechtenstein, and Italy.

**Government.** The Swiss Confederation consists of 23 sovereign cantons, of which three are divided into six half-cantons. Federal authority is vested in a bicameral legislature. The Ständerat, or State Council, consists of 46 members, two from each canton. The lower house, the Nationalrat, or National Council, has 200 deputies, elected for four-year terms.

Executive authority rests with the Bundesrat, or Federal Council, consisting of seven members chosen by parliament. The parliament elects the President, who serves for one year and is succeeded by the Vice President. The federal government regulates foreign policy, railroads, postal service, and the national mint. Each canton reserves for itself important local powers.

A constitutional amendment adopted in 1971 by referendum gave women the vote in federal elections and the right to hold federal office. An equal rights amendment was passed in a national referendum June 14, 1981, barring discrimination against women under canton as well as federal law.

The major political parties are the Social Democratic Party (47 of 200 seats in National Council); Radical Democratic Party (54 seats); Christian-Democratic Party (42 seats); People's Party (23 seats). These four parties constitute the ruling coalition.

**History.** Called Helvetia in ancient times, Switzerland in the Middle Ages was a league of cantons of the Holy Roman Empire. Fashioned around the nucleus of three German forest districts of Schwyz, Uri, and Unterwalden, the Swiss Confederation slowly added new cantons. In 1648 the Treaty of Westphalia gave Switzerland its independence from the Holy Roman Empire.

French revolutionary troops occupied the country in 1798 and named it the Helvetic Republic, but Napoleon in 1803 restored its federal government. By 1815, the French- and Italian-speaking peoples of Switzerland had been granted political equality.

In 1815, the Congress of Vienna guaranteed the neutrality and recognized the independence of Switzerland. In the revolutionary period of 1847, the Catholic cantons seceded and organized a separate union called the *Sonderbund.* In 1848 the new Swiss Constitution established a union modeled upon that of the U.S. The Federal Constitution of 1874 established a strong central government while maintaining large powers of control in each canton.

National unity and political conservatism grew as the country prospered from its neutrality. Its banking system became the world's leading repository for international accounts. Strict neutrality was its policy in World Wars I and II. Geneva was the seat of the League of Nations (later the European headquarters of the United Nations) and of a number of international organizations.

In 1971, the Swiss Supreme Court ruled that Swiss banks must show U.S. tax officials records of U.S. citizens suspected of tax fraud, thus significantly modifying a 1934 law that had seemed to forbid any bank disclosures.

# SYRIA

**Syrian Arab Republic**
**President:** Hafez al-Assad (1971)
**Premier:** Abdel Raouf al-Kasm (1980)
**Area:** 71,498 sq mi. (185,180 sq km)
**Population (est. mid-1986):** 10,500,000 (average annual growth rate: 3.8%)
**Density per square mile:** 146.9
**Capital:** Damascus
**Largest cities (est. 1981):** Damascus, 1,200,000; Aleppo, 1,100,000; Homs, 400,000; Hama, 190,000; Latakia, 222,000
**Monetary unit:** Syrian pound
**Language:** Arabic
**Religions:** Islam, 90%; Christian, 10%
**National name:** Al-Jamhouriya al Arabiya As-Souriya
**Literacy rate:** 50%
**Economic summary:** Gross national product (1983): $16.5 billion. Average annual growth rate (1983): 3%. Per capita income (1983): $1,680. Land used for agriculture: 76%; labor force: 29%; principal products: fruits, wheat, sugar beets, sheep, goats. Labor force in industry: 29%; major products: textiles, cement, petroleum, processed food. Natural resources: chrome, manganese, asphalt, iron ore, rock salt, phosphate, oil, natural gas. Exports: petroleum, textiles, tobacco, fruits and vegetables, cotton. Imports: machinery and metal products, textiles, fuels, foodstuffs. Major trading partners: Italy, Romania, U.S.S.R., U.S., Iran, Libya, France.

**Geography.** Slightly larger than North Dakota,

Syria lies at the eastern end of the Mediterranean Sea. It is bordered by Lebanon and Israel on the west, Turkey on the north, Iraq on the east, and Jordan on the south.

Coastal Syria is a narrow plain, in back of which is a range of coastal mountains, and still farther inland a steppe area. In the east is the Syrian Desert, and in the south is the Jebel Druze Range. The highest point in Syria is Mount Hermon (9,232 ft; 2,814 m) on the Lebanese border.

**Government.** Syria's first permanent Constitution was approved in 1973, replacing a provisional charter that had been in force for 10 years. It provided for an elected People's Council as the legislature.

In the first election in 10 years, in 1973, the Ba'ath Arab Socialist Party of President Hafez al-Assad, running on a unified National Progressive ticket with the Communist and Socialist parties, won 70% of the vote and a commensurate proportion of the seats in the People's Assembly. In 1977 and 1981 elections, the ruling Ba'athists won by similar margins.

**History.** Ancient Syria was conquered by Egypt about 1500 B.C., and after that by Hebrews, Phoenicians, Assyrians, Chaldeans, Persians, and Greeks. From 64 B.C. until the Arab conquest in A.D. 636, it was part of the Roman Empire except during brief periods. The Arabs made it a trade center for their extensive empire, but it suffered severely from the Mongol invasion in 1260 and fell to the Ottoman Turks in 1516. Syria remained a Turkish province until World War I.

A secret Anglo-French pact of 1916 put Syria in the French zone of influence. The League of Nations gave France a mandate over Syria after World War I, but the French were forced to put down several nationalist uprisings. In 1930, France recognized Syria as an independent republic, but still subject to the mandate. After nationalist demonstrations in 1939, the French High Commissioner suspended the Syrian Constitution. In 1941, British and Free French forces invaded Syria to eliminate Vichy control. During the rest of World War II, Syria was an Allied base.

Again in 1945, nationalist demonstrations broke into actual fighting, and British troops had to restore order. Syrian forces met a series of reverses while participating in the Arab invasion of Palestine in 1948. In 1958, Egypt and Syria formed the United Arab Republic, with Gamal Abdel Nasser of Egypt as President. However, Syria became independent again on Sept. 29, 1961, following a revolution.

In the war of 1967, Israel quickly vanquished the Syrian army. Before acceding to the U.N. ceasefire, the Israeli forces took over control of the fortified Golan Heights commanding the Sea of Galilee.

Syria joined Egypt in attacking Israel in October 1973 in the fourth Arab-Israeli war, but was pushed back from initial successes on the Golan Heights to end up losing more land. However, in the settlement worked out by U.S. Secretary of State Henry A. Kissinger in 1974, the Syrians recovered all the territory lost in 1973 and a token amount of territory, including the deserted town of Quneitra, lost in 1967.

Syrian troops, in Lebanon since 1976 as part of an Arab peacekeeping force whose other members subsequently departed, intervened increasingly during 1980 and 1981 on the side of Moslem Lebanese in their clashes with Christian militants supported by Israel. When Israeli jets shot down Syrian helicopters operating in Lebanon in April 1981, Syria moved Soviet-built surface-to-air (SAM 6) missiles into Lebanon's Bekaa Valley. Israel demanded that the missiles be removed because they violated a 1976 understanding between the governments. The demand, backed up by bombing raids, prompted the Reagan Administration to send veteran diplomat Philip C. Habib as a special envoy to avert a new conflict between the nations.

Habib's carefully engineered cease-fire was shattered by a new Israeli invasion in June 1982, when Israeli aircraft bombed Bekaa Valley missile sites, claiming to destroy all of them along with 25 Syrian planes that had sought to defend the sites. On the ground, Syrian army units were driven back by Israeli armor along the Lebanese coast. The Syrians, who were equipped with Soviet weapons, were outfought everywhere by U.S.-equipped Israelis.

Nevertheless, while the Israelis overran most of the rest of Lebanon, the Syrians retained their positions in the Bekaa Valley. Over the next three years, as the Israelis gradually withdrew their forces, the Syrians remained. As the various Lebanese factions fought each other, the Syrians became the dominant force in the country, both militarily and politically.

The extent of Syrian influence in Lebanaon was demonstrated dramatically after Lebanese Shiite extremists hijacked a TWA airliner from Athens to Beirut on June 14, 1985. President al-Assad played the key role in delicate, many-sided negotiations that obtained the release of the 39 American hostages from the plane 17 days later.

# TANZANIA

**United Republic of Tanzania**
**President:** Ali Hassan Mwinyi (1985)
**Prime Minister:** Edward Moringe Sokoine (1983)
**Area:** 364,900 sq mi. (945,087 sq km)[1]
**Population (est. mid-1986):** 22,400,000 (average annual growth rate: 3.5%)
**Density per square mile:** 61.4
**Capital and largest city (est. 1980):** Dar es Salaam, 900,000
**Monetary unit:** Tanzanian shilling
**Languages:** Swahili, Bantu, Arabic, English
**Religions:** Christian, 40%; Islam, 30%; Animist, 30%
**Member of Commonwealth of Nations**
**Literacy rate:** 79%
**Economic summary:** Gross national product (1984): $4.2 billion. Average annual growth rate (1984): 0.6%. Per capita income (1984): $210. Land used for agriculture: 45%; labor force: 90%; Principal products: coconuts, maize, rice, wheat, cotton, coffee, sisal, cashew nuts, pyrethrum, cloves. Major industrial products: textiles, light manufactures, refined oil, processed agricultural products, diamonds, cement, fertilizer. Natural resources: hydroelectric potential, unexploited iron and coal. Exports: coffee, cotton, sisal, diamonds, cloves, cashew nuts. Imports: manufactured goods, textiles, machinery and transport equipment, crude oil, foodstuffs. Major trading partners: U.K., China, India, Hong Kong, Uganda, U.S., Japan.

1. Including Zanzibar.

**Geography.** Tanzania is in East Africa on the Indian Ocean. To the north are Uganda and Kenya; to the west, Burundi, Rwanda, and Zaire; and to the south, Mozambique, Zambia, and Malawi. Its area is three times that of New Mexico.

Tanzania contains three of Africa's best-known lakes—Victoria in the north, Tanganyika in the west, and Nyasa in the south. Mount Kilimanjaro in the north, 19,340 feet (5,895 m), is the highest point on the continent.

**Government.** Under the republican form of government, Tanzania has a President elected by universal suffrage who appoints the Cabinet ministers. The 218-member National Assembly is composed of 96 elected members from the mainland, 10 members appointed by the President (from both Tanganyika and Zanzibar), 35 national members (elected by the National Assembly after nomination by various national institutions), 32 members of the Zanzibar Revolutionary Council, 20 other Zanzibar members appointed by the President in agreement with the President of Zanzibar, and up to 20 other Zanzibar members appointed by the President in agreement with the first Vice President, who represents Zanzibar.

The Tanganyika African National Union, the only authorized party on the mainland, and the Afro-Shirazi Party, the only party in Zanzibar and Pemba, merged in 1977 as the Revolutionary Party (Chama Cha Mapinduzi) and elected Julius K. Nyerere as its head.

**History.** Arab traders first began to colonize the area in A.D. 700. Portuguese explorers reached the coastal regions in 1500 and held some control until the 17th century, when the Sultan of Oman took power. With what are now Burundi and Rwanda, Tanganyika became the colony of German East Africa in 1885. After World War I, it was administered by Britain under a League of Nations mandate and later as a U.N. trust territory.

Although not mentioned in old histories until the 12th century, Zanzibar was believed always to have had connections with southern Arabia. The Portuguese made it one of their tributaries in 1503 and later established a trading post, but they were driven out by Arabs from Oman in 1698. Zanzibar was declared independent of Oman in 1861 and, in 1890, it became a British protectorate.

Tanganyika became independent on Dec. 9, 1961; Zanzibar, on Dec. 10, 1963. On April 26, 1964, the two nations merged into the United Republic of Tanganyika and Zanzibar. The name was changed to Tanzania six months later.

An invasion by Ugandan troops in November 1978 was followed by a counterattack in January 1979, in which 5,000 Tanzanian troops were joined by 3,000 Ugandan exiles opposed to President Idi Amin. Within a month, full-scale war developed.

Nyerere kept troops in Uganda in open support of former Ugandan President Milton Obote, despite protests from opposition groups, until the national elections in December 1980. Although Obote asked that the Tanzanians remain after his victory in order to control guerrilla resistance, Nyerere ordered their withdrawal in May 1981, citing the $1-million-a-month drain on his precarious finances.

In November 1985, Nyerere stepped down as President. Ali Hassan Mwinyi, his Vice-President, succeeded him. Nyerere remained chariman of the party.

# THAILAND

**Kingdom of Thailand**
**Ruler:** King Bhumibol Adulyadej (1946)
**Prime Minister:** Gen. Prem Tinsulanonda (1980)
**Area:** 198,455 sq mi. (514,000 sq km)
**Population (est. mid-1986):** 52,800,000 (average annual growth rate: 2.0%) (incl. 2.5 million of Chinese descent born in Thailand)
**Density per square mile:** 266.1
**Capital and largest city (est. 1984):** Bangkok, 5,174,682
**Monetary unit:** Baht
**Languages:** Thai (Siamese), Chinese, English
**Religions:** Buddhist, 95%; Islam, 4%
**National name:** Prothet Thai
**Literacy rate (1985):** 85.5%
**Economic summary:** Gross national product (1984): $52.4 billion. Average annual growth rate (1979–83): 8.2%. Per capita income (1984): $1,030. Land used for agriculture: 38%; labor force: 68%; principal products: rice, rubber, corn, tapioca, sugar, coconuts. Labor force in industry: 10%; major products: processed food, textiles, wood, cement, tin, tungsten. Natural resources: fish, natural gas, forests, fluorite, tin, tungsten. Exports: rice, tapioca, sugar, rubber, tin, textiles. Imports: machinery and transport equipment, fertilizer, crude oil, fuels and lubricants, base metals, chemicals. Major trading partners: Japan, U.S., Singapore, Malaysia, Netherlands, U.K., Hong Kong.

**Geography.** Thailand occupies the western half of the Indochinese peninsula and the northern two thirds of the Malay peninsula in southeast Asia. Its neighbors are Burma on the north and west, Laos on the north and northeast, Cambodia on the east, and Malaysia on the south. Thailand is about the size of France.

Most of the population is supported in the fertile central alluvial plain, which is drained by the Chao Phnaya River and its tributaries.

**Government.** King Bhumibol Adulyadej, who was born Dec. 5, 1927, second son of Prince Mahidol of Songkhla, succeeded to the throne on June 9, 1946, when his brother, King Ananda Mahidol, died of a gunshot wound. He was married on April 28, 1950, to Queen Sirikit; their son, Vajiralongkorn, born July 28, 1952, is the Crown Prince.

After three years of civilian government ended with a military coup on Oct. 6, 1976, Thailand reverted to military rule. Political parties, banned after the coup, gained limited freedom in 1980. The same year, the National Assembly elected Gen. Prem Tinsulanonda as prime minister. A general election on April 18, 1983, resulted in a new coalition government being formed, with Prem continuing as prime minister.

**History.** The Thais first began moving down into their present homeland from the Asian continent in the 6th century A.D. and by the end of the 13th century ruled most of the western portion. During the next 400 years, the Thais fought sporadically with the Cambodians and the Burmese. The British obtained recognition of paramount interest in Thailand in 1824, and in 1896 an Anglo-French accord guaranteed the independence of Thailand.

A coup in 1932 changed the absolute monarchy into a representative government with universal suffrage. After five hours of token resistance on Dec. 8, 1941, Thailand yielded to Japanese occupation and became one of the springboards in World War II for the Japanese campaign against Malaya.

After the fall of its pro-Japanese puppet government in July 1944, Thailand pursued a policy of passive resistance against the Japanese, and after the Japanese surrender, Thailand repudiated the declaration of war it had been forced to make against Britain and the U.S. in 1942.

Thailand's major problem in the late 1960s was suppressing guerrilla action by Communist invaders in the north.

Although Thailand had received $2 billion in U.S. economic and military aid since 1950 and had sent troops (paid by the U.S.) to Vietnam while permitting U.S. bomber bases on its territory, the collapse of South Vietnam and Cambodia in the spring of 1975 brought rapid changes in the country's diplomatic posture.

At the Thai government's insistence, the U.S. agreed to withdraw all 23,000 U.S. military personnel remaining in Thailand by March 1976. Diplomatic relations with China were established in 1975. Meanwhile, overtures toward an accommodation with the new regime in South Vietnam were initiated.

Refugees from Laos, Cambodia, and Vietnam flooded into Thailand in 1978 and 1979, and despite efforts by the United States and other Western countries to resettle them, a total of 130,000 Laotian and Vietnamese refugees were living in camps along the Cambodian border in mid-1980. A drive by Vietnamese occupation forces on western Cambodian areas loyal to the Pol Pot government, culminating in invasions of Thai territory in late June, drove an estimated 100,000 Cambodians across the line as refugees, adding to the 200,000 of their countrymen already in Thailand. The total of 430,000 were being fed by United-Nations and church relief organizations but the Thai government complained of the burden of their presence.

The Vietnamese incursions, notwithstanding Hanoi's claim that the troops were only seeking guerrillas hidden in the refugee camps, prompted a Thai appeal to Washington for military aid. In July, 35 reconditioned tanks and other weapons were flown to Thailand, and the Carter administration pledged its help in the event of a larger attack.

On April 3, 1981, a military coup against the Prem government failed. Another coup attempt on Sept. 9, 1985, was crushed by loyal troops after 10 hours of fighting in Bangkok. Four persons were killed and about 60 wounded.

# TOGO

**Republic of Togo**
**President:** Gen. Gnassingbé Eyadema (1967)
**Area:** 21,925 sq mi. (56,785 sq km)
**Population (est. mid-1986):** 3,000,000 (average annual growth rate: 3.1%)
**Density per square mile:** 136.8
**Capital and largest city (est. 1982):** Lomé, 285,000
**Monetary unit:** Franc CFA
**Languages:** Ewé, Mina (south), Kabyé, Cotocoli (north), French (official), and many dialects
**Religions:** Animist, 46%; Christian, 37%; Islam, 17%
**National name:** République Togolaise
**Literacy rate:** 18%
**Economic summary:** Gross national product (1985): $950 million. Average annual growth rate (1982): 3.2%. Per capita income (1982): $340. Land used for agriculture: 26%; labor force: 78%; principal products: yams,

manioc, millet, sorghum, cocoa, coffee, peanuts. Labor force in industry: 22%; major products: phosphate, textiles. Natural resources: marble, manganese, phosphate, limestone. Exports: phosphate, cocoa, coffee. Imports: consumer goods, fuels, machinery, foodstuffs. Major trading partners: France, U.K., Japan, Netherlands.

**Geography.** Togo, twice the size of Maryland, is on the south coast of West Africa bordering on Ghana to the west, Upper Volta to the north and Benin to the east.

The Gulf of Guinea coastline, only 32 miles long (51 km), is low and sandy. The only port is at Lomé. The Togo hills traverse the central section.

**Government.** The government of Nicolas Grunitzky was overthrown in a bloodless coup on Jan. 13, 1967, led by Lt. Col. Etienne Eyadema (now Gen. Gnassingbé Eyadema). A National Reconciliation Committee was set up to rule the country. In April, however, Eyadema dissolved the Committee and took over as President. In December 1979, a 67-member National Assembly was voted in by national referendum. The Assembly of the Togolese People is the only political party.

**History.** Brazilians were the first traders to settle in Togo. Established as a German colony (Togoland) in 1884, the area was split between the British and the French as League of Nations mandates after World War I and subsequently administered as U. N. trusteeships. The British portion voted for incorporation with Ghana.

Togo became independent on April 27, 1960. Sylvanus Olympio, its first President, was assassinated in 1963 and succeeded by Nicolas Grunitzky.

# TONGA

**Kingdom of Tonga**
**Sovereign:** King Taufa'ahau Tupou IV (1965)
**Prime Minister:** Prince Fatafehi Tu'ipelehake (1965)
**Area:** 290 sq mi. (751 sq km)
**Population (est. 1985):** 107,000 (average annual growth rate: 1.9%)
**Density per square mile:** 369.0
**Capital (est. 1983):** Nuku'alofa, 21,000
**Monetary unit:** Pa'anga
**Languages:** Tongan, English
**Religions:** Free Wesleyan, 47%; Roman Catholic, 16%; Free Church of Tonga, 14%; Mormon, 9%; Church of Tonga, 9%
**Member of Commonwealth of Nations**
**Literacy rate:** 95%
**Economic summary:** Gross national product (1984): $65 million. Average annual growth rate (1970–78): 1.2%. Per capita income (1984): $580. Land used for agriculture: 80%; labor force: 75%; principal products: yams, taro, papaya, pineapples, coconuts, bananas, copra. Major industrial products: copra, desiccated coconut. Natural resources: fish, timber. Exports: copra, coconut products, bananas. Imports: manufactures, foodstuffs, machinery, petroleum. Major trading partners: New Zealand, Australia, U.S., U.K.

**Geography.** Situated east of the Fiji Islands in the South Pacific, Tonga (also called the Friendly Islands) consists of some 150 islands, of which 36 are inhabited.

Most of the islands contain active volcanic craters; others are coral atolls.

**Government.** Tonga is a constitutional monarchy. Executive authority is vested in the Sovereign, a Privy Council, and a Cabinet headed by the Prime Minister. Legislative authority is vested in the Legislative Assembly.

**History.** The present dynasty of Tonga was founded in 1831 by Taufa'ahau Tupou, who took the name George I. He consolidated the kingdom by conquest and in 1875 granted a Constitution.

In 1900, his great-grandson, George II, signed a treaty of friendship with Britain, and the country became a British protected state. The treaty was revised in 1959.

Queen Salote Tupou reigned from 1918 to 1964 and was succeeded by her son, who became King Taufa'ahau Tupou IV.

Tonga became independent on June 4, 1970.

## TRANSKEI
See South Africa

## TRINIDAD AND TOBAGO

Republic of Trinidad and Tobago
**President:** Ellis Clarke (1976)
**Prime Minister:** George M. Chambers (1981)
**Area:** 1,980 sq mi. (5,128 sq km)
**Population (est. mid-1986):** 1,200,000 (average annual growth rate: 1.8%) (black, 43%; East Indian, 40%; mixed, 14%)
**Density per square mile:** 606.1
**Capital and largest city (est. 1981):** Port-of-Spain, 125,-000
**Monetary unit:** Trinidad and Tobago dollar
**Languages:** English (official); Hindi, French, Spanish
**Religions:** Christian, 64%; Hindu, 25%; Islam, 6%
**Member of Commonwealth of Nations**
**Literacy rate:** 95%
**Economic summary:** Gross national product (1984): $8.6 billion. Average annual growth rate (1984): −7.4%. Per capita income (1984): $7,370. Land used for agriculture: 26%; labor force: 13%; principal products: sugar cane, cocoa, coffee, rice, bananas. Labor force in industry: 33%; major products: petroleum, processed food, cement; tourism. Natural resources: petroleum. Exports: petroleum, ammonia, fertilizer. Imports: chemicals, foodstuffs, machinery and equipment. Major trading partners: U.S., U.K., Japan, EEC.

**Geography.** Trinidad and Tobago lies in the Caribbean Sea off the northeast coast of Venezuela. The area of the two islands is slightly less than that of Delaware.

Trinidad, the larger, is mainly flat and rolling, with mountains in the north that reach a height of 3,085 feet (940 m) at Mount Aripo. Tobago is heavily forested with hardwood trees.

**Government.** The legislature consists of a 24-member Senate and a 36-member House of Representatives.

The major political parties are the People's National Movement, led by Prime Minister George M. Chambers (26 seats in the House of Representatives); United Labor Front (8 seats), led by Basdeo Panday; Democratic Action Congress (2 seats).

**History.** Trinidad was discovered by Columbus in 1498 and remained in Spanish possession, despite raids by other European nations, until it capitulated to the British in 1797 during a war between Britain and Spain.

Trinidad was ceded to Britain in 1802, and in 1899 it was united with Tobago as a colony. From 1958 to 1962, Trinidad and Tobago was a part of the West Indies Federation, and on Aug, 31, 1962, it became independent.

On Aug. 1, 1976, Trinidad and Tobago cut its ties with Britain and became a republic, remaining within the Commonwealth and recognizing Queen Elizabeth II only as head of that organization.

## TUNISIA

Republic of Tunisia
**President:** Habib Bourguiba (1957)
**Prime Minister:** Rachid Sfar (1986)
**Area:** 63,379 sq mi. (164,152 sq km)
**Population (est. mid-1986):** 7,200,000 (average annual growth rate: 2.7%)
**Density per square mile:** 113.6
**Capital and largest city (est. 1981):** Tunis, 600,000
**Monetary unit:** Tunisian dinar
**Languages:** Arabic, French
**Religions:** Predominantly Islam; Roman Catholic, Jewish
**National name:** Al-Joumhouria Attunsia
**Literacy rate:** 64%
**Economic summary:** Gross national product (1985): $9.3 billion. Average annual growth rate (1980–83): 4%. Per capital income (1985): $1,280. Land used for agriculture: 28%; labor force: 40%; principal products: wheat, olives, citrus fruits, grapes, dates. Labor force in industry: 21%; major products: crude oil, olive oil, textiles, and leather, chemical fertilizers, petroleum. Natural resources: oil, phosphates, iron ore, lead, zinc. Exports: petroleum, phosphates, textiles. Imports: machinery and equipment, consumer goods, foodstuffs. Major trading partners: France, West Germany, Italy, Greece, U.S.

**Geography.** Tunisia, at the northernmost bulge of Africa, thrusts out toward Sicily to mark the division between the eastern and western Mediterranean Sea. Twice the size of South Carolina, it is bordered on the west by Algeria and by Libya on the south.

Coastal plains on the east rise to a north-south escarpment which slopes gently to the west. Saharan in the south, Tunisia is more mountainous in the north, where the Atlas range continues from Algeria.

**Government.** Executive power is vested by the Constitution in the president, elected for five years and eligible for re-election to two additional terms. Legislative power is vested in a National Assembly elected by universal suffrage.

In 1975, the National Assembly amended the Constitution to make Habib Bourguiba president for life. At 71, Bourguiba was re-elected to a fourth five-year term when he ran unopposed in 1974. There are four political parties, the Socialist Destourian, led by Bourguiba, the Social Democratic Movement, the Popular Unity Movement and the Communist Party.

**History.** Tunisia was settled by the Phoenicians and Carthaginians in ancient times. Except for an interval of Vandal conquest in A.D. 439–533, it was part of the Roman Empire until the Arab conquest of 648–69. It was ruled by various Arab and Berber dynasties until the Turks took it in 1570–74. French troops occupied the country in 1881, and the Bey signed a treaty acknowledging a French protectorate.

Nationalist agitation forced France to grant internal autonomy to Tunisia in 1955 and to recognize Tunisian independence and sovereignty in 1956. The Constituent Assembly deposed the Bey on July 25, 1957, declared Tunisia a republic, and elected Habib Bourguiba as president.

Bourguiba maintained a pro-Western foreign policy that earned him enemies. Tunisia refused to break relations with the U.S. during the Israeli-Arab war in June 1967, and it cracked down on anti-U.S. demonstrators.

Tunisia ended its traditionally neutral role in the Arab world when it joined with the majority of Arab League members to condemn Egypt for concluding a peace treaty with Israel. The Tunisian capital was offered as the temporary headquarters of the League, following the expulsion of Egypt.

In 1985, Israeli jets bombed a PLO headquarters near Tunis in response to the murder of three Israelis by terrorists. U.S. support for the raid strained U.S.-Tunisian relations.

# TURKEY

### Republic of Turkey
**President:** Kenan Evren (1982)
**Prime Minister:** Turgut Özal (1983)
**Area:** 300,947 sq mi. (incl. 9,121 in Europe) (779,452 sq km)
**Population (est. mid-1986):** 52,300,000 (average annual growth rate: 2.5%)
**Density per square mile:** 173.8
**Capital:** Ankara
**Largest cities (1985 census):** Istanbul, 5,494,916; Ankara, 2,251,533; Izmir, 1,489,817; Adana, 776,000; Bursa, 614,133; Gaziantep, 466,302
**Monetary unit:** Turkish Lira
**Language:** Turkish
**Religion:** Islam (Sunni)
**National name:** Türkiye Cumhuriyeti
**Literacy rate:** 80%
**Economic summary:** Gross national product (1985): $64 billion. Average annual growth rate (1985): 4.0%. Per capita income (est. 1985): $1,250. Land used for agriculture: 35%; labor force: 60%; principal products: cotton, tobacco, cereals, sugar beets, fruits, nuts. Labor force in industry: 16%; major products: textiles, processed foods, steel, petroleum. Natural resources: coal, chromite, copper, boron, oil. Exports: cotton, tobacco, fruits, nuts, livestock products, textiles. Imports: crude oil, machinery, transport equipment, metals, mineral fuels, fertilizer, chemicals. Major trading partners: Iran, West Germany, Iraq, France, Italy, U.S.S.R., U.S.

**Geography.** Turkey is at the northeastern end of the Mediterranean Sea in southeast Europe and southwest Asia. To the north is the Black Sea and to the west the Aegean Sea. Its neighbors are Greece and Bulgaria to the west, the U.S.S.R. to the north, Iran to the east, and Syria and Iraq to the south. Overall, it is more than twice the size of Montana.

The Dardanelles, the Sea of Marmara, and the Bosporus divide the country.

Turkey in Europe comprises an area about equal to the state of Massachusetts. It is hilly country drained by the Maritsa River and its tributaries.

Turkey in Asia, or Anatolia, about the size of Texas, is roughly a rectangle in shape with its short sides on the east and west. Its center is a treeless plateau rimmed by mountains.

**Government.** The President is elected by the Grand National Assembly for a seven-year term and is not eligible for re-election.

In a military coup on Sept. 11, 1980, led by Gen. Kenan Evren, the Army Chief of Staff, Premier Süleyman Demirel was ousted, the Grand National Assembly dissolved and the Constitution suspended. Demirel, former Premier Bülent Ecevit, and some 100 legislators and political figures were detained. Martial law was declared and all political parties were dissolved.

Following the adoption of a new Constitution in 1982, parliamentary elections were held in 1983. Prime Minister Turgut Özal's Motherland Party came to power with a 211-seat majority in the 400-seat Grand National Assembly. In local elections in 1984, the Motherland Party also won a majority of municipal posts with about 42% of the total vote.

**History.** The Ottoman Turks first appeared in the early 13th century in Anatolia, subjugating Turkish and Mongol bands pressing against the eastern borders of Byzantium. They gradually spread through the Near East and Balkans, capturing Constantinople in 1453 and storming the gates of Vienna two centuries later. At its height, the Ottoman Empire stretched from the Persian Gulf to western Algeria.

Defeat of the Turkish navy at Lepanto by the Holy League in 1571 and failure of the siege of Vienna heralded the decline of Turkish power. By the 18th century, Russia was seeking to establish itself as the protector of Christians in Turkey's Baikan territories. Russian ambitions were checked by Britain and France in the Crimean War (1854–56), but the Russo-Turkish War (1877–78) gave Bulgaria virtual independence and Romania and Serbia liberation from their nominal allegiance to the Sultan.

Turkish weakness stimulated a revolt of young liberals known as the Young Turks in 1909. They forced Sultan Abdul Hamid to grant a constitution and install a liberal government. Reforms were no barrier to further defeats, however, in a war with Italy (1911–12) and the Balkan Wars (1912–13). Under the influence of German military advisors, Turkey signed a secret alliance with Germany on Aug. 2, 1914, that led to a declaration of war by the Allied powers and the ultimate humiliation of the occupation of Turkish territory by Greek and other Allied troops.

In 1919, the new Nationalist movement, headed by Mustafa Kemal, was organized to resist the Allied occupation and, in 1920, a National Assembly elected him President of both the Assembly and the government. Under his leadership, the Greeks were driven out of Smyrna, and other Allied forces were withdrawn.

The present Turkish boundaries (with the exception of Alexandretta, ceded to Turkey by France in 1939) were fixed by the Treaty of Lausanne (1923) and later negotiations. The caliphate and sultanate were separated, and the sultanate was abolished in 1922. On Oct. 29, 1923, Turkey formally became a republic, with Mustafa Kemal, who took the name Kemal Atatürk, as its first President.

The caliphate was abolished in 1924, and Atatürk proceeded to carry out an extensive program of reform, modernization, and industrialization.

Gen. Ismet Inönü was elected to succeed Atatürk in 1938 and was re-elected in 1939, 1943, and 1946. Defeated in 1950, he was succeeded by Celâl Bayar. In 1939, a mutual assistance pact was concluded with Britain and France. Neutral during most of World War II Turkey, on Feb. 23, 1945, declared war on Germany and Japan, but took no active part in the conflict.

Turkey became a full member of NATO in 1952.

Turkey invaded Cyprus by sea and air July 20, 1974, following the failure of diplomatic efforts to resolve the crisis caused by the ouster of Archbishop Makarios.

Talks in Geneva involving Greece, Turkey, Britain, and Greek Cypriot and Turkish Cypriot leaders brokers down in mid-August. Turkey unilaterally announced a cease-fire August 16, after having gained control of 40% of the island. Turkish Cypriots established their own state in the north on Feb. 13, 1975.

U.S.-Turkish relations, excellent for a generation, were seriously damaged when Congress voted to end arms sales to Turkey in 1975 because arms the U.S. had supplied for mutual defense had been used in the invasion of Cyprus.

In July 1975, after a 30-day warning, Turkey took over control of all the U.S. installations except the big joint defense base at Incirlik, which it reserved for "NATO tasks alone."

The establishment of military government in September 1980 stopped the slide toward anarchy and brought some improvement in the economy. The military regime was criticized, however, for suppression of human rights.

A Constituent Assembly, consisting of the six-member National Security Council and members appointed by them, drafted a new Constitution that was approved by an overwhelming (91.5%) majority of the voters in a Nov. 6, 1982, referendum. Prime Minister Turgut Özal's Motherland Party came to power in parliamentary elections held in late 1983.

# TUVALU

**Sovereign:** Queen Elizabeth II
**Governor-General:** Sir Fiatau Penitala Teo (1978)
**Prime Minister:** Tomasi Puapua (1981)
**Area:** 10 sq mi. (26 sq km)
**Population (est. 1985):** 8,000 (average annual growth rate: 1.7%)
**Density per square mile:** 700.0
**Capital and largest city (est. 1981):** Funafuti, 2,500
**Monetary unit:** Australian dollar
**Languages:** Tuvaluan, English
**Member of the Commonwealth of Nations**
**Literacy rate:** 50%
**Economic summary:** Gross national product (1984): $4 million. Per capita Income (1984): $450. Principal agricultural products: copra and coconuts. Export: copra. Imports: food and fuels. Major trading partners: Australia, U.K., Fiji, New Zealand

**Geography.** Formerly the Ellice Islands, Tuvalu consists of nine small islands scattered over 500,000 square miles of the western Pacific, just south of the equator.

**Government.** Official executive power is vested in a Governor-General, representing the Queen, who is appointed by her on the recommendation of the Tuvalu government. Actual executive power lies with a Prime Minister, who is responsible to a House of Assembly composed of eight elected members.

**History.** The Ellice Islands became a British protectorate in 1892 and were annexed by Britain in 1915–16 as part of the Gilbert and Ellice Islands Colony. The Ellice Islands were separated in 1975, given home rule, and renamed Tuvalu. Full independence was granted on Sept. 30, 1978.

# UGANDA

**Republic of Uganda**
**President:** H.E. Yoweri Museveni (1986)
**Prime Minister:** Dr. Samson Kiseka (1985)
**Area:** 91,343 sq mi. (236,880 sq km)
**Population (est. mid-1986):** 15,200,000 (average annual growth rate: 3.4%)
**Density per square mile:** 166.4
**Capital and largest city (est. 1980):** Kampala, 500,000
**Monetary unit:** Ugandan shilling
**Languages:** English (official), Swahili, Luganda, Ateso, Luo
**Religions:** Christian, 63%; Islam, 6%
**Member of Commonwealth of Nations**
**Literacy rate:** 52%
**Economic summary:** Gross national product (1984): $6.2 billion. Average annual growth rate (1983): 5.0%. Per capita income (1984): $434. Land used for agriculture: 21%; labor force: 90%; principal products: coffee, tea, cotton, sugar, bananas, corn. Labor force in industry: 3%; major products: processed agricultural products, copper, cement, shoes, fertilizer, sheet iron, beverages. Natural resources: copper, sugar, skins and hides. Exports: coffee, cotton. Imports: petroleum products, machinery, transport equipment, metals, food. Major trading partners: U.S., U.K., Kenya.

**Geography.** Uganda, twice the size of Pennsylvania, is in east Africa. It is bordered on the west by Zaire, on the north by the Sudan, on the east by Kenya, and on the south by Tanzania and Rwanda.

The country, which lies across the Equator, is divided into three main areas—swampy lowlands, a fertile plateau with wooded hills, and a desert region. Lake Victoria forms part of the southern border.

**Government.** The country has been run by the National Reistance Council since January 1986.

**History.** Uganda was first visited by European explorers as well as Arab traders in 1844. An Anglo-German agreement of 1890 declared it to be in the British sphere of influence in Africa, and the Imperial British East Africa Company was chartered to develop the area. The company did not prosper financially, and in 1894 a British protectorate was proclaimed.

Uganda became independent on Oct. 9, 1962.

Sir Edward Mutesa was elected the first President and Milton Obote the first Prime Minister of the newly independent country. With the help of a young army officer, Col. Idi Amin, Prime Minister Obote seized control of the government from President Mutesa four years later.

On Jan. 25, 1971, Col. Amin deposed President Obote. Obote went into exile in Tanzania. Amin expelled Asian residents and launched a reign of terror against Ugandan opponents, torturing and killing tens of thousands. In 1976, he had himself proclaimed President for Life. In 1977, Amnesty International estimated that 300,000 may have died under his rule, including church leaders and recalcitrant cabinet ministers.

After Amin held military exercises on the Tanzanian border, angering Tanzania's President Julius Nyerere, a combined force of Tanzanian troops and Ugandan exiles loyal to former President Obote invaded Uganda and chased Amin into exile.

After a series of interim administrations, President Obote led his People's Congress Party to victory in 1980 elections that opponents charged were rigged.

Obote continued Amin's human rights abuses. The U.S. reported in August 1984 that the abuses—"among the most grave in the world"—included large-scale massacres.

On July, 27, 1985, army troops staged a coup taking over the government. Obote fled into exile. The military regime installed Gen. Tito Okello as chief of state.

The National Resistance Army (NRA), an anti-Obote group led by Yoweri Musevni, kept fighting after being excluded from the new regime. They seized Kampala on January 29, 1986, and Musevni was declared President.

## UNION OF SOVIET SOCIALIST REPUBLICS

See Soviet Union

## UNITED ARAB EMIRATES

**Head of State:** Sheik Zayed Bin Sultan Al-Nahayan (1971)
**Prime Minister:** Sheik Rashid Bin Said al-Maktoum (1979)
**Area:** 32,000 sq mi. (82,880 sq km)
**Population (est. mid-1986):** 1,400,000 (Arab, 42%; South Asian, 50%) (average annual growth rate: 2.3%)
**Density per square mile:** 43.8
**Capital and largest city (est. 1981):** Abu Dhabi, 225,000
**Monetary unit:** Dirham
**Language:** Arabic
**Religion:** Islam
**Literacy rate:** 56%
**Economic summary:** Gross national product (1983): $25.7 billion. Average annual growth rate (1973–82): 11.5%. Per capita income (1985): $22,710. Land used for agriculture: 8%; labor force: 5%; principal products: vegetables, dates, tobacco, fruit. Labor force in industry: 36%; major products: fish, light manufactures, petroleum, construction materials. Natural resources: oil. Exports: petroleum, dates, fish. Imports: consumer goods, food. Major trading partners: U.K., Japan, U.S., France.

**Geography.** The United Arab Emirates, in the eastern part of the Arabian Peninsula, extends along part of the Gulf of Oman and the southern coast of the Persian Gulf. The nation is the size of Maine. Its neighbors are Saudi Arabia in the west and south, Qatar in the north, and Oman in the east. Most of the land is barren and sandy.

**Government.** The United Arab Emirates was formed in 1971 by seven emirates known as the Trucial States—Abu Dhabi (the largest), Dubai, Sharjah, Ajman, Fujairah, Ras al Khaimah and Umm al-Qaiwain.

The loose federation allows joint policies in foreign relations, defense, and development, with each member state keeping its internal local system of government headed by its own ruler. A 40-member legislature consists of eight seats each for Abu Dhabi and Dubai, six seats each for Ras al Khaimah and Sharjah, and four each for the others. It is a member of the Arab League.

**History.** Originally the area was inhabited by a seafaring people who were converted to Islam in the seventh century. Later, a dissident sect, the Carmathians, established a powerful sheikdom, and its army conquered Mecca. After the sheikdom disintegrated, its people became pirates.

Threatening the sultanate of Muscat and Oman early in the 19th century, the pirates provoked the intervention of the British, who in 1820 enforced a partial truce and in 1853 a permanent truce. Thus what had been called the Pirate Coast was renamed the Trucial Coast.

## UNITED KINGDOM

**United Kingdom of Great Britain and Northern Ireland**
**Sovereign:** Queen Elizabeth II (1952)
**Prime Minister:** Margaret Thatcher (1979)
**Area:** 94,247 sq mi. (244,100 sq km)
**Population (est. mid-1986):** 56,600,000 (average annual growth rate: 0.2%) (English, Scottish, Welsh, Northern Irish)
**Density per square mile:** 600.6
**Capital:** London, England
**Largest cities (est. mid-1982):** Greater London, 6,765,-100; Birmingham, 1,017,300; Glasgow, 761,000; Leeds, 716,100; Sheffield, 545,800; Liverpool, 510,700; Bradford 464,700; Manchester, 458,600; Edinburgh, 444,700; Bristol, 399,600
**Monetary unit:** Pound sterling (£)
**Languages:** English, Welsh, Gaelic
**Religions:** Church of England (established church); Church of Wales (disestablished); Church of Scotland (established church—Presbyterian); Church of Ireland (disestablished); Roman Catholic; Methodist; Congregational; Baptist; Jewish
**Literacy rate:** 99%
**Economic summary:** Gross national product (1984): $426.3 billion. Average annual growth rate (1984): 2.0%. Per capita income (1984): $7,640. Land used for agriculture: 29%, principal products: cereals, livestock, and livestock products. Major industrial products: steel, heavy engineering and metal manufactures, textiles, motor vehicles and aircraft, electronics, chemicals. Natural resources: coal, oil, gas. Exports: machinery, transport equipment, chemicals, petroleum. Imports: foodstuffs, petroleum, machinery, chemicals, crude materials. Major trading partners: Western European nations, U.S., West Germany, France.

**Geography.** The United Kingdom, consisting of England, Wales, Scotland, and Northern Ireland, is twice the size of New York State. England, in the southeast part of the British Isles, is separated from Scotland on the north by the granite Cheviot Hills; from them the Pennine chain of uplands extends south through the center of England, reaching its highest point in the Lake District in the northwest. To the west along the border of Wales—a land of steep hills and valleys—are the Cambrian Moun-

# Area and Population of United Kingdom

| Subdivision | Area sq mi | Area sq km | Population (est. mid-1983) |
|---|---|---|---|
| England and Wales | 58,381 | 151,207 | 49,600,000 |
| Scotland | 30,414 | 78,772 | 5,200,000 |
| Northern Ireland | 5,452 | 14,121 | 1,600,000 |
| **Total** | **94,247** | **244,100** | **56,400,000** |

tains, while the Cotswolds, a range of hills in Gloucestershire, extend into the surrounding shires.

The remainder of England is plain land, though not necessarily flat, with the rocky sand-topped moors in the southwest, the rolling downs in the south and southeast, and the reclaimed marshes of the low-lying fens in the east central districts.

Scotland is divided into three physical regions—the Highlands, the Central Lowlands, containing two-thirds of the population, and the Southern Uplands. The western Highland coast is intersected throughout by long, narrow sea-lochs, or fiords. Scotland also includes the Outer and Inner Hebrides and other islands off the west coast and the Orkney and Shetland Islands off the north coast.

Wales is generally hilly; the Snowdon range in the northern part culminates in Mount Snowdon (3,560 ft, 1,085 m), highest in both England and Wales.

Important rivers flowing into the North Sea are the Thames, Humber, Tees, and Tyne. In the west are the Severn and Wye, which empty into the Bristol Channel and are navigable, as are the Mersey and Ribble.

**Government.** The United Kingdom is a constitutional monarchy, with a Queen and a Parliament that has two houses: the House of Lords with about 830 hereditary peers, 26 spiritual peers, about 270 life peers and peeresses, and 9 law-lords, who are hereditary, or life, peers, and the House of Commons, which since 1974 has had 635 popularly elected members. Supreme legislative power is vested in Parliament, which sits for five years unless sooner dissolved.

The executive power of the Crown is exercised by the Cabinet, headed by the Prime Minister. The latter, normally the head of the party commanding a majority in the House of Commons, is appointed by the Sovereign, with whose consent he or she in turn appoints the rest of the Cabinet. All ministers must be members of one or the other house of Parliament; they are individually and collectively responsible to the Crown and Parliament. The Cabinet proposes bills and arranges the business of Parliament, but it depends entirely on the votes in the House of Commons. The Lords cannot hold up "money" bills, but they can delay other bills for a maximum of one year.

By the Act of Union (1707), the Scottish Parliament was assimilated with that of England, and Scotland is now represented in Commons by 71 members. The Secretary of State for Scotland, a member of the Cabinet, is responsible for the administration of Scottish affairs.

The major political parties are the Conservative Party (397 of the 650 seats in the House of Commons), led by Prime Minister Margaret Thatcher;

Labor Party (209 seats), led by Neil Kinnock; Social Democrats (6 seats), led by Roy Jenkins; Liberal Party (17 seats), led by David Steel; Ulster Unionists and other Northern Irish parties (17 seats); Scottish Nationalist Party (2 seats); Welsh Nationalist Party (2 seats). The Speaker and three deputies do not normally vote.

**Ruler.** Queen Elizabeth II, born April 21, 1926, elder daughter of King George VI and Queen Elizabeth, succeeded to the throne on the death of her father on Feb. 6, 1952; married Nov. 20, 1947, to Prince Philip, Duke of Edinburgh, born June 10, 1921; their children are Prince Charles[1] (heir presumptive), born Nov. 14, 1948; Princess Anne, born Aug. 15, 1950; Prince Andrew, born Feb. 19, 1960; and Prince Edward, born March 10, 1964. The Queen's sister is Princess Margaret, born Aug. 21, 1930. Prince William Arthur Philip Louis, son of the Prince and Princess of Wales and second in line to the throne, was born June 21, 1982. A second son, Prince Henry Charles Albert David, was born Sept. 15, 1984, and is third in line.

**History.** Roman invasions of the 1st century B.C. brought Britain into contact with the Continent. When the Roman legions withdrew in the 5th century A.D., Britain fell easy prey to the invading hordes of Angles, Saxons, and Jutes from Scandinavia and the Low Countries. Seven large kingdoms were established, and the original Britons were forced into Wales and Scotland. It was not until the 11th century that the country finally became united under the Danish King Canute. Following the death of Edward the Confessor (1066), a dispute about the succession arose, and William, Duke of Normandy, invaded England, defeating the Saxon King, Harold II, at the Battle of Hastings (1066). The Norman conquest introduced Norman law and feudalism.

The reign of Henry II (1154–89), first of the Plantagenets, saw an increasing centralization of royal power at the expense of the nobles, but in 1215 John (1199–1216) was forced to sign the Magna Carta, which awarded the people, especially the nobles, certain basic rights. Edward I (1272–1307) continued the conquest of Ireland, reduced Wales to subjection and made some gains in Scotland. In 1314, however, English forces led by Edward II were ousted from Scotland after the Battle of Bannockburn. The late 13th and early 14th centuries saw the development of a separate House of Commons with tax-raising powers.

Edward III's claim to the throne of France led to the Hundred Years' War (1338–1453) and the loss of almost all the large English territory in France. In England, the great poverty and discontent caused by the war were intensified by the Black Death, a plague that reduced the population by about one third. The Wars of the Roses (1455–85), a struggle for the throne between the House of York and the House of Lancaster, ended in the victory of Henry Tudor (Henry VII) at Bosworth Field (1485).

During the reign of Henry VIII (1509–47), the Church in England asserted its independence from the Roman Catholic Church. Under Edward VI and Mary, the two extremes of religious fanaticism

1. The title Prince of Wales, which is not inherited, was conferred on Prince Charles by his mother on July 26, 1958. The investiture ceremony took place on July 1, 1969. The previous Prince of Wales was Prince Edward Albert, who held the title from 1911 to 1936 before he became Edward VIII.

# Rulers of England and Great Britain

| Name | Born | Ruled[1] | Name | Born | Ruled[1] |
|---|---|---|---|---|---|
| **SAXONS**[2] | | | **HOUSE OF YORK** | | |
| Egbert[3] | c.775 | 828–839 | Edward IV | 1442 | 1461–1483[5] |
| Ethelwulf | ? | 839–858 | Edward V | 1470 | 1483–1483 |
| Ethelbald | ? | 858–860 | Richard III | 1452 | 1483–1485 |
| Ethelbert | ? | 860–866 | | | |
| Ethelred I | ? | 866–871 | **HOUSE OF TUDOR** | | |
| Alfred the Great | 849 | 871–899 | Henry VII | 1457 | 1485–1509 |
| Edward the Elder | c.870 | 899–924 | Henry VIII | 1491 | 1509–1547 |
| Athelstan | 895 | 924–939 | Edward VI | 1537 | 1547–1553 |
| Edmund I the Deed-doer | 921 | 939–946 | Jane (Lady Jane Grey)[6] | 1537 | 1553–1553 |
| Edred | c.925 | 946–955 | Mary I ("Bloody Mary") | 1516 | 1553–1558 |
| Edwy the Fair | c.943 | 955–959 | Elizabeth I | 1533 | 1558–1603 |
| Edgar the Peaceful | 943 | 959–975 | | | |
| Edward the Martyr | c.962 | 975–979 | **HOUSE OF STUART** | | |
| Ethelred II the Unready | 968 | 979–1016 | James I[7] | 1566 | 1603–1625 |
| Edmund II Ironside | c.993 | 1016–1016 | Charles I | 1600 | 1625–1649 |
| | | | | | |
| **DANES** | | | **COMMONWEALTH** | | |
| Canute | 995 | 1016–1035 | Council of State | — | 1649–1653 |
| Harold I Harefoot | c.1016 | 1035–1040 | Oliver Cromwell[8] | 1599 | 1653–1658 |
| Hardecanute | c.1018 | 1040–1042 | Richard Cromwell[8] | 1626 | 1658–1659[9] |
| | | | | | |
| **SAXONS** | | | **RESTORATION OF HOUSE OF** | | |
| Edward the Confessor | c.1004 | 1042–1066 | **STUART** | | |
| Harold II | c.1020 | 1066–1066 | Charles II | 1630 | 1660–1685 |
| | | | James II | 1633 | 1685–1688[10] |
| **HOUSE OF NORMANDY** | | | William III[11] | 1650 | 1689–1702 |
| William I the Conqueror | 1027 | 1066–1087 | Mary II[11] | 1662 | 1689–1694 |
| William II Rufus | c.1056 | 1087–1100 | Anne | 1665 | 1702–1714 |
| Henry I Beauclerc | 1068 | 1100–1135 | | | |
| Stephen of Blois | c.1100 | 1135–1154 | **HOUSE OF HANOVER** | | |
| | | | George I | 1660 | 1714–1727 |
| **HOUSE OF PLANTAGENET** | | | George II | 1683 | 1727–1760 |
| Henry II | 1133 | 1154–1189 | George III | 1738 | 1760–1820 |
| Richard I Coeur de Lion | 1157 | 1189–1199 | George IV | 1762 | 1820–1830 |
| John Lackland | 1167 | 1199–1216 | William IV | 1765 | 1830–1837 |
| Henry III | 1207 | 1216–1272 | Victoria | 1819 | 1837–1901 |
| Edward I Longshanks | 1239 | 1272–1307 | | | |
| Edward II | 1284 | 1307–1327 | **HOUSE OF SAXE-COBURG**[12] | | |
| Edward III | 1312 | 1327–1377 | Edward VII | 1841 | 1901–1910 |
| Richard II | 1367 | 1377–1399[4] | | | |
| | | | **HOUSE OF WINDSOR**[12] | | |
| **HOUSE OF LANCASTER** | | | George V | 1865 | 1910–1936 |
| Henry IV Bolingbroke | 1367 | 1399–1413 | Edward VIII | 1894 | 1936–1936[13] |
| Henry V | 1387 | 1413–1422 | George VI | 1895 | 1936–1952 |
| Henry VI | 1421 | 1422–1461[5] | Elizabeth II | 1926 | 1952– |

1. Year of end of rule is also that of death, unless otherwise indicated. 2. Dates for Saxon kings are still subject of controversy. 3. Became King of West Saxons in 802; considered (from 828) first King of all England. 4. Died 1400. 5. Henry VI reigned again briefly 1470–71. 6. Nominal Queen for 9 days; not counted as Queen by some authorities. She was beheaded in 1554. 7. Ruled in Scotland as James VI (1567–1625). 8. Lord Protector. 9. Died 1712. 10. Died 1701. 11. Joint rulers (1689–1694). 12. Name changed from Saxe-Coburg to Windsor in 1917. 13. Was known after his abdication as the Duke of Windsor, died 1972.

were reached, and it remained for Henry's daughter, Elizabeth I (1558-1603), to set up the Church of England on a moderate basis. In 1588, the Spanish Armada, a fleet sent out by Catholic King Philip II of Spain, was defeated by the English and destroyed during a storm. During Elizabeth's reign, England became a world power.

Elizabeth's heir was a Stuart—James VI of Scotland—who joined the two crowns as James I (1603–25). The Stuart kings incurred large debts and were forced either to depend on Parliament for taxes or to raise money by illegal means. In 1642, war broke out between Charles I and a large segment of the Parliament; Charles was defeated and executed in 1649, and the monarchy was then abolished. After the death in 1658 of Oliver Cromwell, the Lord Protector, the Puritan Commonwealth fell to pieces and Charles II was placed on the throne in 1660. The struggle between the King and Parliament continued, but Charles II knew when to compromise. His brother, James II (1685-88), possessed none of his ability and was ousted by the Revolution of 1688, which confirmed the primacy of Parliament. James's daughter, Mary, and her husband, William of Orange, were now the rulers.

Queen Anne's reign (1702–14) was marked by the Duke of Marlborough's victories over France at Blenheim, Oudenarde, and Malplaquet in the War of the Spanish Succession. England and Scot-

## British Prime Ministers Since 1770

| Name | Term | Name | Term |
|---|---|---|---|
| Lord North (Tory) | 1770–1782 | Marquis of Salisbury (Conservative) | 1886–1892 |
| Marquis of Rockingham (Whig) | 1782–1782 | William E. Gladstone (Liberal) | 1892–1894 |
| Earl of Shelburne (Whig) | 1782–1783 | Earl of Rosebery (Liberal) | 1894–1895 |
| Duke of Portland (Coalition) | 1783–1783 | Marquis of Salisbury (Conservative) | 1895–1902 |
| William Pitt, the Younger (Tory) | 1783–1801 | Earl Balfour (Conservative) | 1902–1905 |
| Henry Addington (Tory) | 1801–1804 | Sir H. Campbell-Bannerman (Liberal) | 1905–1908 |
| William Pitt, the Younger (Tory) | 1804–1806 | Herbert H. Asquith (Liberal) | 1908–1915 |
| Baron Grenville (Whig) | 1806–1807 | Herbert H. Asquith (Coalition) | 1915–1916 |
| Duke of Portland (Tory) | 1807–1809 | David Lloyd George (Coalition) | 1916–1922 |
| Spencer Perceval (Tory) | 1809–1812 | Andrew Bonar Law (Conservative) | 1922–1923 |
| Earl of Liverpool (Tory) | 1812–1827 | Stanley Baldwin (Conservative) | 1923–1924 |
| George Canning (Tory) | 1827–1827 | James Ramsay MacDonald (Labor) | 1924–1924 |
| Viscount Goderich (Tory) | 1827–1828 | Stanley Baldwin (Conservative) | 1924–1929 |
| Duke of Wellington (Tory) | 1828–1830 | James Ramsay MacDonald (Labor) | 1929–1931 |
| Earl Grey (Whig) | 1830–1834 | James Ramsay MacDonald (Coalition) | 1931–1935 |
| Viscount Melbourne (Whig) | 1834–1834 | Stanley Baldwin (Coalition) | 1935–1937 |
| Sir Robert Peel (Tory) | 1834–1835 | Neville Chamberlain (Coalition) | 1937–1940 |
| Viscount Melbourne (Whig) | 1835–1841 | Winston Churchill (Coalition) | 1940–1945 |
| Sir Robert Peel (Tory) | 1841–1846 | Clement R. Attlee (Labor) | 1945–1951 |
| Earl Russell (Whig) | 1846–1852 | Sir Winston Churchill (Conservative) | 1951–1955 |
| Earl of Derby (Tory) | 1852–1852 | Sir Anthony Eden (Conservative) | 1955–1957 |
| Earl of Aberdeen (Coalition) | 1852–1855 | Harold Macmillan (Conservative) | 1957–1963 |
| Viscount Palmerston (Liberal) | 1855–1858 | Sir Alec Frederick Douglas-Home | |
| Earl of Derby (Conservative) | 1858–1859 | (Conservative) | 1963–1964 |
| Viscount Palmerston (Liberal) | 1859–1865 | Harold Wilson (Labor) | 1964–1970 |
| Earl Russell (Liberal) | 1865–1866 | Edward Heath (Conservative) | 1970–1974 |
| Earl of Derby (Conservative) | 1866–1868 | Harold Wilson (Labor) | 1974–1976 |
| Benjamin Disraeli (Conservative) | 1868–1868 | James Callaghan (Labor) | 1976–1979 |
| William E. Gladstone (Liberal) | 1868–1874 | Margaret Thatcher (Conservative) | 1979– |
| Benjamin Disraeli (Conservative) | 1874–1880 | | |
| William E. Gladstone (Liberal) | 1880–1885 | | |
| Marquis of Salisbury (Conservative) | 1885–1886 | | |
| William E. Gladstone (Liberal) | 1886–1886 | | |

land meanwhile were joined by the Act of Union (1707). Upon the death of Anne, the distant claims of the elector of Hanover were recognized, and he became King of Great Britain and Ireland as George I.

The unwillingness of the Hanoverian kings to rule resulted in the formation by the royal ministers of a Cabinet, headed by a Prime Minister, which directed all public business. Abroad, the constant wars with France expanded the British Empire all over the globe, particularly in North America and India. This imperial growth was checked by the revolt of the American colonies (1775–81).

Struggles with France broke out again in 1793 and, during the Napoleonic Wars, which ended at Waterloo in (1815).

The Victorian era, named after Queen Victoria (1837–1901), saw the growth of a democratic system of government that had begun with the Reform Bill of 1832. The two important wars in Victoria's reign were the Crimean War against Russia (1853–56) and the Boer War (1899–1902), the latter enormously extending Britain's influence in Africa.

Increasing uneasiness at home and abroad marked the reign of Edward VII (1901–10). Within four years after the accession of George V in 1910, Britain entered World War I when Germany invaded Belgium. The nation was led by coalition Cabinets, headed first by Herbert Asquith and then, starting in 1916, by the Welsh statesman David Lloyd George. Postwar labor unrest culminated in the general strike of 1926.

King Edward VIII succeeded to the throne on Jan. 20, 1936, at his father's death, but abdicated on Dec. 11, 1936 (in order to marry an American divorcee, Wallis Warfield Simpson) in favor of his brother, who became George VI.

The efforts of Prime Minister Neville Chamberlain to stem the rising threat of Nazism in Germany failed with the German invasion of Poland on Sept. 1, 1939, which was followed by Britain's entry into World War II on September 3. Allied reverses in the spring of 1940 led to Chamberlain's resignation and the formation of another coalition war Cabinet by the Conservative leader, Winston Churchill, who led Britain through most of World War II. Churchill resigned shortly after V-E Day, May 7, 1945, but then formed a "caretaker" government that remained in office until after the parliamentary elections in July, which the Labor Party won overwhelmingly. The government formed by Clement R. Attlee began a moderate socialist program.

For details of World War II (1939–45), *see* Headline History.

In 1951, Churchill again became Prime Minister at the head of a Conservative government. George VI died Feb. 6, 1952, and was succeeded by his daughter Elizabeth II.

Churchill stepped down in 1955 in favor of Sir Anthony Eden, who resigned on grounds of ill health in 1957, and was succeeded by Harold Macmillan and Sir Alec Douglas-Home. In 1964, Harold Wilson led the Labor Party to victory.

A lagging economy brought the Conservatives

back to power in 1970. Prime Minister Edward Heath won Britain's admission to the European Community.

Margaret Thatcher became Britain's first woman Prime Minister as the Conservatives won 339 seats on May 3, 1979.

An Argentine invasion of the Falkland Islands on April 2, 1982, involved Britain in a war 8,000 miles from the home islands. Although Argentina had long claimed the Falklands, known as the Malvinas in Spanish, negotiations were in progress until a month before the invasion. The Thatcher government responded to the invasion with a 40-ship task force, which sailed from Portsmouth on April 5. U.S. efforts to settle the dispute failed and United Nations efforts collapsed as the Argentine military government ignored Security Council resolutions calling for a withdrawal of its forces.

When more than 11,000 Argentine troops on the Falklands surrendered on June 14, 1982, Mrs. Thatcher declared her intention to garrison the islands indefinitely, together with a naval presence. Although four ships were lost to Argentine air attack during the fighting, they were expected to be replaced.

The military victory bolstered Conservative fortunes at least temporarily, but economic problems continued for the government. Unemployment rose to a record 2.91 million in mid-June and a strike by British Railways workers paralyzed the state-owned system in July.

In the general election of June 9, 1982, Prime Minister Thatcher and her Conservative party won a landslide victory over the Laborites and other opponents. The Tories sized 140-seats in the House of Commons, giving the Labor party its worst defeat since 1922.


## NORTHERN IRELAND

**Status:** Part of United Kingdom
**Secretary of State:** James Prior (1981)
**Area:** 5,452 sq mi. (14,121 sq km)
**Population (est. mid-1982):** 1,567,000
**Density per square mile:** 279.7
**Capital and largest city (est. mid-1982):** Belfast, 324,900
**Monetary unit:** British pound sterling
**Languages:** English, Gaelic
**Religions:** Roman Catholic, 35%; Presbyterian, 29%;
Church of Ireland, 24%; Methodist, 5%

**Geography.** Northern Ireland comprises the counties of Antrim, Armagh, Down, Fermanagh, Londonderry, and Tyrone, which make up predominantly Protestant Ulster and form the northern part of the island of Ireland, westernmost of the British Isles. It is slightly larger than Connecticut.

**Government.** Northern Ireland is an integral part of the United Kingdom (it has 12 representatives in the British House of Commons), but under the terms of the government of Ireland Act in 1920, it had a semiautonomous government. But in 1972, after three years of internal strife which resulted in over 400 dead and thousands injured, Britain suspended the Ulster parliament. The Ulster counties became governed directly from London after an attempt to return certain powers to an elected Assembly in Belfast.

The Northern Ireland Assembly was dissolved in 1975 and a Constitutional Convention was elected to write a Constitution acceptable to Protestants and Catholics. The convention failed to reach agreement and closed down the next year.

The major political parties are the United Ulster Unionist Coalition (Protestant) (46 of 78 delegates to the Constitutional Convention); Social Democratic Labor Party (Catholic) (17 delegates); Alliance Party (8 delegates); New Unionist Party of Northern Ireland (Protestant) (5 delegates).

**History.** Ulster was part of Catholic Ireland until the reign of Elizabeth I (1558–1603) when, after crushing three Irish rebellions, the crown confiscated lands in Ireland and settled in Ulster the Scot Presbyterians who became rooted there. Another rebellion in 1641–51, crushed as brutally by Oliver Cromwell, resulted in the settlement of Anglican Englishmen in Ulster. Subsequent political policy favoring Protestants and disadvantaging Catholics encouraged further settlement in Northern Ireland.

But the North did not separate from the South until William Gladstone presented in 1886 his proposal for home rule in Ireland as a means of settling the Irish Question. The Protestants in the North, although they had grievances like the Catholics in the South, feared domination by the Catholic majority. Industry, moreover, was concentrated in the north and dependent on the British market.

When World War I began, civil war threatened between the regions. Northern Ireland, however, did not become a political entity until the six counties accepted the Home Rule Bill of 1920. This set up a semiautonomous Parliament in Belfast and a Crown-appointed Governor advised by a Cabinet of the Prime Minister and eight ministers, as well as a 12-member representation in the House of Commons in London.

As the Republic of Ireland gained its sovereignty, relations improved between North and South, although the Irish Republican Army, outlawed in recent years, continued the struggle to end the partition of Ireland. In 1966–69, communal rioting and street fighting between Protestants and Catholics occurred in Londonderry, fomented by extremist nationalist Protestants, who feared the Catholics might attain a local majority, and by Catholics demonstrating for civil rights.

Rioting, terrorism, and sniping killed more than 2,200 people from 1969 through 1984 and the religious communities, Catholic and Protestant, became hostile armed camps. British troops were brought in to separate them but themselves became a target of Catholics.

In 1973, a new British charter created a 78-member Assembly elected by proportional representation that gave more weight to Catholic strength. It created a Province Executive with committee chairmen of the Assembly heading all government departments except law enforcement, which remained under London's control. Assembly elections in 1973 produced a majority for the new Constitution that included Catholic assemblymen.

Ulster's leaders agreed in 1973 to create an 11-member Executive Body with six seats assigned to Unionists (Protestants) and four to members of Catholic parties. Unionist leader Brian Faulkner headed the Executive. Also agreed to was a Council of Ireland, with 14 seats evenly divided between Dublin and Belfast, which could act only by unanimous vote.

Although the Council lacked real authority, its creation sparked a general strike by Protestant extremists in 1974. The two-week strike caused Faulkner's resignation from the Executive and resumption of direct rule from London.

In April 1974, London instituted a new program that responded to some Catholic grievances, but assigned more British troops to cut off movement of arms and munitions to Ulster's violence-racked cities.

Violence continued unabated, with new heights reached early in 1976 when the Brtish government announced the end of special privileges for political prisoners in Northern Ireland. British Prime Minister James Callaghan visited Belfast in July and pledged that Ulster would remain part of the United Kingdom unless a clear majority wished to separate.

In October 1977, the 1976 Nobel Prize for Peace was awarded to Mairead Corrigan and Betty Williams for their campaign for peace in Northern Ireland. Intermittent violence continued, however, and on Aug. 27, 1979, an I.R.A. bomb killed Earl Mountbatten as he was sailing off southern Ireland.

New talks aimed at a restoration of home rule in Northern Ireland began and quickly ended in January 1980. In May, Mrs. Thatcher met with the new Prime Minister of the Irish Republic, Charles Haughey, but she insisted that the future of Ulster must be decided only by its people and the British Parliament. Haughey declared that an internal solution "cannot and will not succeed."

Civil disturbances reached new heights in the summer of 1981 as Irish nationalist prisoners went on hunger strikes in Maze Prison to attain their demands for "political" status.

Ten nationalists died before the strike ended in August as families of fasters asked that they be fed.

On November 15, 1985, Mrs. Thatcher signed an agreement with Irish Prime Minister Garrett Fitzgerald giving Ireland a consultative role in Northern Ireland affairs. It was met with intense disapproval by Ulster Unionists.

# Dependencies of the United Kingdom

## ANGUILLA

**Status:** Dependency
**Governor:** A.T. Baille (1985)
**Area:** 35 sq mi. (91 sq km)
**Population (1982):** 7,000
**Monetary unit:** East Caribbean dollar
**Literacy:** 80%

Anguilla was originally part of the West Indies Associated States as a component of St. Kitts-Nevis-Anguilla.

In 1967, Anguilla declared its independence from the St. Kitts-Nevis-Anguilla federation. Britain however, did not recognize this action. In February 1969, Anguilla voted to cut all ties with Britain and become an independent republic. In March, Britain landed troops on the island and, on March 30, a truce was signed. In July 1971, Anguilla became a dependency of Britain and two months later Britain ordered the withdrawal of all its troops.

A new Constitution for Anguilla, effective in February 1976, provides for separate administration and a government of elected representatives. The Associated State of St. Kitts-Nevis-Anguilla ended Dec. 19, 1980.

## BERMUDA

**Status:** Self-governing dependency
**Governor:** Viscount Dunrossil (1983)
**Premier:** John Swan (1982)
**Area:** 20 sq mi. (52 sq km)
**Population (est. 1985):** 58,000 (average annual growth rate: 0.5%)
**Capital (est. 1985):** Hamilton, 1,700
**Monetary unit:** Bermuda dollar
**Literacy rate:** 98%
**Economic summary:** Gross national product (1982): $810 million. Average annual growth rate (1982): 4.4%. Per capita income (1981): $12,910. Land used for agriculture: 8%; labor force: 1%; principal products: bananas, vegetables, citrus fruits, dairy products. Labor force in industry: 6.2%; major products: structural concrete, paints, perfumes, furniture. Natural resource: limestone. Exports: semi-tropical produce, light manufactures. Imports: foodstuffs, fuel, machinery. Major trading partners: U.S., U.K., Canada.

Bermuda is an archipelago of about 360 small islands, 580 miles (934 km) east of North Carolina. The largest is (Great) Bermuda, or Long Island. Discovered by Juan de Bermúdez, a shipwrecked Spaniard, early in the 16th century, the islands were settled in 1612 by an offshoot of the Virginia Company and became a crown colony in 1684.

In 1940, sites on the islands were leased for 99 years to the U.S. for air and navy bases. Bermuda is also the headquarters of the West Indies and Atlantic squadron of the Royal Navy.

In 1968, Bermuda was granted a new Constitution, its first Prime Minister, and autonomy, except for foreign relations, defense, and internal security. The predominantly white United Bermuda Party has retained power in four elections against the opposition—the black-led Progressive Laborites—although Bermuda's population is 60% black. Serious rioting occurred in December 1977 after two blacks were hanged for a series of murders, including the 1973 assassination of the Governor, Sir Richard Sharples, and British troops were summoned to restore order.

## BRITISH ANTARCTIC TERRITORY

**Status:** Dependency
**High Commissioner:** Sir Rex Masterson Hunt (1980)
**Area:** 500,000 sq mi. (1,395,000 sq km)
**Population (1976):** 55

The British Antarctic Territory consists of the South Shetland Islands, South Orkney Islands, and Nearby Graham Land on the Antarctic continent, largely uninhabited. They are dependencies of the British crown colony of the Falkland Islands but received a separate administration in 1962, being governed by a British-appointed High Commissioner who is Governor of the Falklands.

## BRITISH INDIAN OCEAN TERRITORY

**Status:** Dependency
**Commissioner:** P.C.F. Gregory-Hunt
**Administrator:** D.H. Doble
**Administrative headquarters:** Victoria, Seychelles
**Area:** 85 sq mi, (220 sq km)

This dependency, consisting of the Chagos Archipelago and other small island groups, was formed in 1965 by agreement with Mauritius and the Seychelles. There is no permanent civilian population in the territory.

## BRITISH VIRGIN ISLANDS

**Status:** Dependency
**Governor:** D. R. Barwick
**Area:** 59 sq mi. (153 sq km)
**Population (est. 1984):** 12,034
**Capital (est. 1975):** Road Town (on Tortola): 3,500
**Monetary unit:** U.S. dollar

Some 36 islands in the Caribbean Sea northeast of Puerto Rico and west of the Leeward Islands, the British Virgin Islands are economically interdependent with the U.S. Virgin Islands to the south. They were formerly part of the administration of the Leeward Islands. They received a separate administration in 1956 as a crown colony. In 1967 a new Constitution was promulgated that provided for a ministerial system of government headed by the Governor. The principal islands are Tortola, Virgin Gorda, Anegada and Jost Van Dyke.

## CAYMAN ISLANDS

**Status:** Dependency
**Governor:** G. P. Lloyd
**Area:** 100 sq mi. (259 sq km)
**Population (est. 1983):** 18,750
**Capital (est. 1980):** Georgetown (on Grand Cayman), 7,600
**Monetary unit:** Cayman Islands dollar

This dependency consists of three islands— Grand Cayman (76 sq mi; 197 sq km), Cayman Brac (22 sq mi; 57 sq km), and Little Cayman (20 sq mi; 52 sq km)—situated about 180 miles (290 km) northwest of Jamaica. They were dependencies of Jamaica until 1959, when they became a unit territory within the Federation of the West Indies. In 1962, upon the dissolution of the Federation, the Cayman Islands became a British dependency. The islands' chief export is turtle products.

## CHANNEL ISLANDS

**Status:** Crown dependencies
**Lieutenant Governor of Jersey:** Adm. Sir William Pillar (1985)
**Lieutenant Governor of Guernsey:** Sir Alexander Boswell
**Area:** 75 sq mi. (194 sq km)
**Population (est. 1984):** 129,300
**Capital of Jersey:** St. Helier
**Capital of Guernsey:** St. Peter Port
**Monetary units:** Guernsey pound; Jersey pound

This group of islands, lying in the English Channel off the northwest coast of France, is the only portion of the Duchy of Normandy belonging to the English Crown, to which it has been attached since the conquest of 1066. It was the only British possession occupied by Germany during World War II.

For purposes of government, the islands are divided into the Bailiwick of Jersey (45 sq mi.; 117 sq km) and the Bailiwick of Guernsey (30 sq mi.; 78 sq km), including Alderney (3 sq mi.; 7.8 sq km); Sark (2 sq mi.; 5.2 sq km), Herm, Jethou, etc. The islands are administered according to their own laws and customs by local governments. Acts of Parliament in London are not binding on the islands unless they are specifically mentioned. The Queen is represented in each Bailiwick by a Lieutenant Governor.

## FALKLAND ISLANDS AND DEPENDENCIES

**Status:** Dependency
**Civil Commissioner:** Sir Rex Masterson Hunt (1980)
**Area:** 4,700 sq mi. (12,173 sq km)
**Population est. (1985):** 2,000
**Capital (est. 1978):** Stanley (on East Falkland), 1,100
**Monetary unit:** Falkland Island pound

This sparsely inhabited dependency consists of a group of islands in the South Atlantic, about 250 miles (402 km) east of the South American mainland. The largest islands are East Falkland and West Falkland. Dependencies are South Georgia Island (1,450 sq mi.; 3,756 sq km), the South Sandwich Islands, and other islets. Three former dependencies—Graham Land, the South Shetland Islands, and the South Orkney Islands—were established as a new British dependency, the British Antarctic Territory, in 1962.

The chief industry is sheep raising and, apart from the production of wool, hides and skins, and tallow, there are no known resources. The whaling industry is carried on from South Georgia Island. The chief export is wool.

## GIBRALTAR

**Status:** Self-governing dependency
**Governor:** Admiral Sir David Williams
**Chief Minister:** Sir Joshua Hassan
**Area:** 2.25 sq mi. (5.8 sq km)
**Population (est. 1985):** 31,000 (average annual growth rate: 0.9%)
**Monetary unit:** Gibraltar pound
**Literacy rate:** Negligible
**Economic summary:** Gross national product (1980): $150 million. Average annual growth rate (1970–79): 4.6%. Exports: re-exports of tobacco, petroleum, wine. Imports: manufactured goods, fuels, foodstuffs. Major trading partners: U.K., Morocco, Portugal, Netherlands.

Gibraltar, at the south end of the Iberian Peninsula, is a rocky promonotory commanding the western entrance to the Mediterranean. Aside from its strategic importance, it is also a free port, naval base, and coaling station. It was captured by the Arabs crossing from Africa into Spain in A.D. 711. In the 15th century, it passed to the Moorish ruler of Granada and later became Spanish. It was captured by an Anglo-Dutch force in 1704 during the War of the Spanish Succession and passed to Great Britain by the Treaty of Utrecht in 1713. Most of the inhabitants of Gibraltar are of Spanish, Italian, and Maltese descent.

Spanish efforts to recover Gibraltar culminated in a referendum in 1967 in which the residents voted overwhelmingly to retain their link with Britain. Spain sealed Gibraltar's land border in 1969 and did not open communications until April 1980, after the two governments had agreed to solve their dispute in keeping with a United Nations resolution calling for restoration of the "Rock" to Spain.

## HONG KONG

**Status:** Dependency
**Governor:** Sir Edward Youde (1982)
**Area:** 398 sq mi. (1,031 sq km)
**Population (est. mid-1986):** 5,700,000 (average annual growth rate: 1.0%)
**Density per square mile:** 14,321.6
**Capital (1976 census):** Victoria (Hong Kong Island), 501,-700
**Monetary unit:** Hong Kong dollar
**Literacy rate:** 75%
**Economic summary:** Gross national product (1980): $21.5 billion. Average annual growth rate (1970–79): 6.5%. Per capita income (1980): $4,210. Land used for agriculture: 14%. labor force, 3%; principal products: vegetables, rice, dairy products. Labor force in industry: 45%; major industrial products: textiles, clothing, toys, transistor radios, watches, electronic components. Exports: clothing, textiles, toys, watches, transistor radios, electronic components. Imports: raw materials, consumer goods, food. Major trading partners: U.S., U.K., Japan, West Germany, China.

The crown colony of Hong Kong comprises the island of Hong Kong (32 sq mi.; 83 sq km), Stone-cutters' Island, Kowloon Peninsula, and the New Territories on the adjoining mainland. The island of Hong Kong, located at the mouth of the Pearl River about 90 miles (145 km) southeast of Canton, was ceded to the Britain in 1841.

Stonecutters' Island and Kowloon were annexed in 1860, and the New Territories, which are mainly agricultural lands, were leased from China in 1898 for 99 years. Hong Kong was attacked by Japanese troops Dec. 7, 1941, and surrendered the following Christmas. It remained under Japanese occupation until August 1945.

After two years of painstaking negotiation, authorities of Britain and the People's Republic of China agreed in 1984 that Hong Kong would return to Chinese sovereignty on June 30, 1997, when Britain's lease on the New Territories expires. They also agreed that the vibrant capitalist enclave on China's coast would retain its status as a free port and its social, economic, and legal system as a special administrative region of China. Current laws will remain basically unchanged.

Under a unique "One Country, Two Systems" arrangement, the Chinese government promised that Hong Kong's lifestyle would remain unchanged for 50 years, and that freedoms of speech, press, assembly, association, travel, right to strike and religious belief would be guaranteed by law.

Hong Kong will continue to have its own finances and issue its own travel documents, and Peking will not levy taxes.

## ISLE OF MAN

**Status:** Dependency
**Lieutenant Governor:** Rear-Adm. Sir Nigel Cecil (1980)
**Area:** 227 sq mi. (588 sq km)
**Population (est. 1982):** 70,000
**Capital (est. 1976):** Douglas, 20,300
**Monetary unit:** Isle of Man pound

Situated in the Irish Sea, equidistant from Scotland, Ireland, and England, the Isle of Man is administered according to its own laws by a government composed of the Lieutenant Governor, a Legislative Council, and a House of Keys, one of the most ancient legislative assemblies in the world.

The chief exports are beef and lamb, fish, and livestock.

## LEEWARD ISLANDS

**See British Virgin Islands; Montserrat**

## MONTSERRAT

**Status:** Dependency
**Governor:** A. C. Watson (1985)
**Area:** 40 sq mi. (104 sq km)
**Population (est. 1980):** 12,100
**Capital (est. 1982):** Plymouth, 3,500
**Monetary unit:** East Caribbean dollar

The island of Montserrat is in the Lesser Antilles of the West Indies. Until 1956, it was a division of the Leeward Islands. It did not join the West Indies Associated States established in 1967.

The chief exports are cattle, potatoes, cotton, lint, recapped tires, mangoes, tomatoes.

## PITCAIRN ISLAND

**Status:** Dependency
**Governor:** T. D. O'Leary (1985)
**Island Magistrate:** Ivan Christian
**Area:** 1.75 sq mi. (4.5 sq km)
**Population (est. 1980):** 63
**Capital:** Adamstown

Pitcairn Island, in the South Pacific about midway between Australia and South America, consists of the island of Pitcairn and the three uninhabited islands of Henderson, Duicie, and Oeno. The island of Pitcairn was settled in 1790 by British mutineers from the ship *Bounty,* commanded by Capt. William Bligh. It was annexed as a British colony in 1838. Overpopulation forced removal of the settlement to Norfolk Island in 1856, but about 40 persons soon returned.

The colony is governed by a 10-member Council presided over by the Island Magistrate, who is elected for a three-year term.

## ST. HELENA

**Status:** Dependency
**Governor:** F. E. Baker (1985)
**Area:** 47 sq mi. (122 sq km)
**Population (est 1983):** 5,250
**Capital (est. 1982):** Jamestown, 1,500
**Monetary unit:** Pound sterling

St. Helena is a volcanic island in the South Atlantic about 1,100 miles (1,770 km) from the west coast of Africa. It is famous as the place of exile of Napoleon (1815–21).

It was taken for England in 1659 by the East India Company and was brought under the direct government of the Crown in 1834.

St. Helena has two dependencies: Ascension (34 sq mi.; 88 sq km), an island about 700 miles (1,127 km) northwest of St. Helena; and Tristan da Cunha (40 sq mi.; 104 sq km), a group of six islands about 1,500 miles (2,414 km) south-southwest of St. Helena.

## TURKS AND CAICOS ISLANDS

**Status:** Dependency
**Governor:** Christopher Turner
**Area:** 193 sq mi. (500 sq km)
**Population (est. 1983):** 7,500
**Capital (est. 1982):** Grand Turk, 3,150
**Monetary unit:** U.S. dollar

These two groups of islands are situated at the southeast end of the Bahamas. The principal islands in the Turks group are Grand Turk and Salt Cay; the principal ones in the Caicos group are South Caicos, East Caicos, Middle (or Grand) Caicos, North Caicos, Providenciales, and West Caicos.

The Turks and Caicos Islands were dependencies of Jamaica until 1959, when they became a unit territory within the Federation of the West Indies. In 1962, when Jamaica became independent, the Turks and Caicos became a British crown colony. The present Constitution has been in force since 1969.

Chief exports in 1974 were crayfish (73%) and conch (25%).

## VIRGIN ISLANDS

**See British Virgin Islands**

## UNITED STATES

**The United States of America**
**President:** Ronald Reagan (1981)
**Area:** 3,540,939 sq mi. (9,171,032 sq km)
**Population (est. mid-1986):** 241,000,000 (average annual growth rate: .7%)
**Density per square mile:** 68.1
**Capital (1984 est.):** Washington, D.C., 622,823
**Largest cities (1984 est.):** New York, 7,164,742; Los Angeles, 3,096,721; Chicago, 2,992,472; Houston, 1,-705,697; Philadelphia, 1,646,713; Detroit, 1,088,973
**Monetary unit:** Dollar
**Language:** English
**Religions:** Protestant (73.5 million members); Roman Catholic (50.5 million members); Jewish (5.9 million members)
**Literacy rate:** 99.5%[1]
**Economic summary:** Gross national product (1984): $3,-988.5 billion; per capita income (1985): $13,451. Labor force in agriculture: 2.7%; principal products: corn, wheat, barley, oats, sugar, potatoes, soybeans, fruits, beef, veal, pork. Labor force in non-agricultural occupations: 97.3%. Major industrial products: petroleum products, fertilizers, cement, pig iron and steel, plastics and resins, newsprint, motor vehicles, machinery, natural gas, electricity. Natural resources: coal, oil, water power, copper, gold, silver, minerals, timber. Exports: machinery, chemicals, aircrafts, military equipment, cereals, motor vehicles, grains. Imports: crude and partly refined petroleum, machinery, automobiles. Major trading partners: Canada, Japan, United Kingdom, West Germany, Mexico, Saudi Arabia.

1. U.S. Census Bureau figure refers to persons 15 or older.

**Government.** The president is elected for a four-year term and may be re-elected only once. In 1985, the bicameral Congress consisted of the 100-member Senate (47 Democrats, 53 Republicans) and the 435-member House of Representatives (253 Democrats, 182 Republicans) which is elected every two years. The minimum voting age is 18.

## URUGUAY

**Oriental Republic of Uruguay**
**President:** Julio Maria Sanguinetti (1985)
**Area:** 72,172 sq mi. (186,926 sq km)
**Population (est. mid-1986):** 3,000,000 (average annual growth rate: 0.9%)
**Density per square mile:** 41.6
**Capital and largest city (est. 1982):** Montevideo, 1,325,-000
**Monetary unit:** Peso
**Language:** Spanish
**Religion:** Roman Catholic, 60%
**National name:** Republica Oriental del Uruguay
**Literacy rate:** 94%
**Economic summary:** Gross national product (1983): $5.4 billion. Average annual growth rate (1983): −4.7%. Per capita income (1983): $2,491. Land used for agriculture: 85%; labor force: 12%; principal products: livestock, grains. Labor force in industry: 29%; major products: processed meats, wool and hides, textiles, shoes, handbags and leather wearing apparel, cement, refined petroleum. Natural resources: hydroelectric power potential. Exports: meat, hides, wool, textiles. Imports: crude petroleum, transportation equipment, chemicals, machinery, metals. Major trading partners: U.S., Brazil, Argentina, Nigeria.

**Geography.** Uruguay, on the east coast of South America south of Brazil and east of Argentina, is comparable in size to the State of Washington.

The country consists of a low, rolling plain in the south and a low plateau in the north. It has a 120-mile (193 km) Atlantic shore line, a 235-mile (378 km) frontage on the Rio de la Plata, and 270 miles (435 km) on the Uruguay River, its western boundary.

**Government.** After elections in November 1984, Julio Maria Sanguinetti was inaugurated as President on March 1, 1985, ending 12 years of military rule. Under the Constitution, Presidents serve a single five-year term. The bicameral Congress, dissolved by the military in 1973, also was restored in 1985. The three political parties are President Sanguinetti's Colorado Party; the Blanco Party, led by Wilson Ferreira Aldunato; and the left-leaning Broad Front.

**History.** Juan Díaz de Solis, a Spaniard, discovered Uruguay in 1516, but the Portuguese were first to settle it when they founded Colonia in 1680. After a long struggle, Spain wrested the country from Portugal in 1778. Uruguay revolted against Spain in 1811, only to be conquered in 1816–20 by the Portuguese from Brazil. Independence was reasserted with Argentine help in 1825, and the republic was set up in 1830.

Independence, however, did not restore order, and a revolt in 1836 touched off nearly 50 years of factional strife, with occasional armed intervention from Argentina and Brazil.

Uruguay, made prosperous by meat and wool exports, founded a welfare state early in the 20th century. A decline began in the 1950s as successive governments struggled to maintain a large bureaucracy and costly social benefits. Economic stagnation and political frustration followed.

A military coup ousted the civilian government in 1973. The military dictatorship that followed used fear and terror to demobilize the population, taking thousands of political prisoners, probably the highest proportion of citizens jailed for political reasons anywhere in the world.

Under the generals, the country's worst economic crisis in decades produced 66% inflation, 30% unemployment and a foreign debt of $5 billion. Per capita income sank to $1,100.

After ruling for 12 years, the military regime permitted election of a civilian government in November 1984 and relinquished rule in March 1985.

# VANUATU

**Republic of Vanuatu**
**President:** George Sokomanu (1980)
**Prime Minister:** Rev. Walter Lini (1980)
**Area:** 5,700 sq mi. (14,763 sq km)
**Population (est. mid-1986):** 100,000 (average annual growth rate: 3.6%)
**Density per square mile:** 17.5
**Capital (est. 1982):** Vila, 17,500
**Monetary unit:** Vatu
**Religions:** Presbyterian, 37%; Roman Catholic, 15%; Anglican, 15%; other Christian, 10%; Animist, 9%
**Literacy rate:** 10-20%
**Economic Summary:** Gross national product (1980): $60 million. Per Capita Income (1980): $530. Average annual growth rate (1970–78): 1.9%. Principal agricultural products: copra, cocoa, coffee, livestock. Exports: copra, cocoa, coffee, frozen fish. Imports: food. Major trading partners: France, U.S., Japan, Australia, Netherlands.

**Geography.** Formerly known as the New Hebrides, Vanuatu is an archipelago of some 80 islands lying between New Caledonia and Fiji in the South Pacific. Largest of the islands is Espiritu Santo (875 sq mi.; 2,266 sq km); others are Efate, Malekula, Malo, Pentecost, and Tanna. The population is largely Melanesian of mixed blood.

**Government.** The constitution by which Vanuatu achieved independence on July 30, 1980, vests executive authority in a President, elected by an electoral college for a five-year term. A unicameral legislature of 39 members exercises legislative power. The Vanuaaku party, led by Prime Minister Walter Lini, holds 26 seats.

**History.** The islands were discovered by Pedro Fernandes de Queiros of Portugal in 1606 and were charted and named by the British navigator James Cook in 1774. Conflicting British and French interests were resolved by a joint naval commission that administered the islands from 1887. A condominium government was established in 1906.

The islands' plantation economy, based on imported Vietnamese labor, was prosperous until the 1920s, when markets for its products declined. The New Hebrides escaped Japanese occupation in World War II and the French population was among the first to support the Gaullist Free French movement.

A brief rebellion by French settlers and plantation workers on Espiritu Santo led by Jimmy Stevens in May 1980 threatened the scheduled independence of the islands. Britain sent a company of Royal Marines and France a contingent of 50 policemen to quell the revolt, which the new government said was financed by the Phoenix Foundation, a right-wing U.S. group. With the British and French forces replaced by soldiers from Papua New Guinea, independence ceremonies took place on July 30. The next month it was reported that Stevens had been arrested and the revolt quelled.

# VATICAN CITY STATE

**Ruler:** Pope John Paul II (1978)
**Area:** 0.17 sq mi. (0.44 sq km)
**Population (est. 1985):** 1,000 (Italian, 85%; Swiss and others, 15%)
**Density per square mile:** 5,882.4
**Monetary unit:** Lira
**Languages:** Latin and Italian
**Religion:** Roman Catholic
**National name:** Stato della Città del Vaticano

**Geography.** The Vatican City State is situated on the Vatican hill, on the right bank of the Tiber River, within the commune of Rome.

**Government.** The Pope has full legal, executive, and judicial powers. Executive power over the area is in the hands of a Commission of Cardinals appointed by the Pope. The College of Cardinals is the Pope's chief advisory body, and upon his death the cardinals elect his successor for life. The cardinals themselves are created for life by the Pope.

In the Vatican the central administration of the Roman Catholic Church throughout the world is carried on by 11 congregations, three tribunals, three main secretariats, and numerous councils, committees, and commissions. In its diplomatic relations, the Holy See is represented by the Papal Secretary of State.

**History.** The Vatican City State, sovereign and independent, is the survivor of the papal states that in 1859 comprised an area of some 17,000 square miles (44,030 sq km). During the struggle for Italian unification, from 1860 to 1870, most of this area became part of Italy.

By an Italian law of May 13, 1871, the temporal power of the Pope was abrogated, and the territory of the Papacy was confined to the Vatican and Lateran palaces and the villa of Castel Gandolfo. The Popes consistently refused to recognize this arrangement and, by the Lateran Treaty of Feb. 11, 1929, between the Vatican and the Kingdom of Italy, the exclusive dominion and sovereign jurisdiction of the Holy See over the city of the Vatican was again recognized, thus restoring the Pope's temporal authority over the area.

The first session of Ecumenical Council Vatican II was opened by John XXIII on Oct. 11, 1962, to plan and set policies for the modernization of the Roman Catholic Church. Pope Paul VI continued the Council, opening the second session on Sept. 29, 1963.

On Aug. 26, 1978, Cardinal Albino Luciani was chosen by the College of Cardinals to succeed Paul VI, who had died of a heart attack on Aug. 6. The new Pope, who took the name John Paul I, was born on Oct. 17, 1912, at Forno di Canale in Italy.

(For a listing of all the Popes, *see* the Index.)

Only 34 days after his election, John Paul I died of a heart attack, ending the shortest reign in 373 years. On Oct. 16, Cardinal Karol Wojtyla, 58, was chosen Pope and took the name John Paul II.

A visit to the Irish Republic and to the United States in September and October 1979, followed by a 12-nation African tour in May 1980 and a visit in July to Brazil, the most populous Catholic nation, further established John Paul's image as a "people's" Pope. On May 13, 1981, a Turkish terrorist shot the Pope in St. Peter's Square, the first assassination attempt against the Pontiff in modern times. Mehmet Ali Agca was sentenced on July 22 to life imprisonment by an Italian Court.

The Pontiff traveled to Britain and Argentina in 1982. He also made another visit to Poland.

On June 3, 1985, the Vatican and Italy ratified a new church-state treaty, known as a concordat, replacing the Lateran Pact of 1929. The new accord affirmed the independence of Vatican City but ended a number of privileges the Catholic Church had in Italy, including its status as the state religion. The treaty ended Rome's status as a "sacred city."

# VENEZUELA

**Republic of Venezuela**
**President:** Jaime Lusinchi (1984)
**Area:** 352,143 sq mi. (912,050 sq km)
**Population (est. mid-1986):** 17,800,000 (average annual growth rate: 2.7%) (mestizo, 67%; white, 21%; black, 10%; Indian, 2%)
**Density per square mile:** 50.5
**Capital:** Caracas
**Largest cities (est. 1981 for metropolitan area):** Caracas, 3,000,000; Maracaibo, 890,000; Valencia, 616,000; Barquisimoto, 498,000
**Monetary unit:** Bolivar
**Language:** Spanish
**Religion:** Roman Catholic
**National name:** Republica de Venezuela
**Literacy rate:** 85.6%
**Economic summary:** Gross national product (1983): $70.8 billion. Average annual growth rate (1982): −1.7%. Per capita income (1983): $4,110. Land used for agriculture, 4%; labor force, 16%; principal products: rice, coffee, corn, sugar, bananas, dairy and meat products. Labor force in industry, 23%; principal products: refined petroleum products, iron and steel, paper products, cement, textiles, transport equipment. Natural resources: petroleum, natural gas, iron ore, hydroelectric power. Exports: petroleum, iron ore. Imports: industrial machinery and equipment, manufactures, chemicals, foodstuffs. Major trading partners: U.S., Canada, Japan, Netherland Antilles.

**Geography.** Venezuela, a third larger than Texas, occupies most of the northern coast of South America on the Caribbean Sea. It is bordered by Colombia to the west, Guyana to the east, and Brazil to the south.

Mountain systems break Venezuela into four distinct areas: (1) the Maracaibo lowlands; (2) the mountainous region in the north and northwest; (3) the Orinoco basin, with the llanos (vast grass-covered plains) on its northern border and great forest areas in the south and southeast; (4) the Guiana Highlands, south of the Orinoco, accounting for nearly half the national territory. About 80% of Venezuela is drained by the Orinoco and its tributaries.

**Government.** Venezuela is a federal republic consisting of 20 states, the Federal District, two territories and 72 islands in the Caribbean. There is a bicameral Congress, the 52 members of the Senate and the 213 members of the Chamber of Deputies being elected by popular vote to five-year terms. The President is also elected for five years. He must be a Venezuelan by birth and over 30 years old. He is not eligible for re-election until 10 years after the end of his term.

The major political parties are the Democratic Action Party, with 23 of 52 Senate seats and 83 of 213 seats in the Chamber of Deputies; Social Christian Party, with 22 Senate seats and 83 Chamber seats, People's Electoral Movement, Democratic Republican Union.

**History.** Columbus discovered Venezuela on his third voyage in 1498. A subsequent Spanish explorer gave the country its name, meaning "Little Venice." There were no important settlements until Caracas was founded in 1567. Simón Bolívar, who led the liberation of much of the continent from Spain, was born in Caracas in 1783. With Bolívar taking part, Venezuela was one of the first South American colonies to revolt against Spain, in 1810, but it was not until 1821 that independence was won. Federated at first with Colombia and Ecuador, the country set up a republic in 1830 and then sank for many decades into a condition of revolt, dictatorship, and corruption.

From 1908 to 1935, Gen. Juan Vicente Gómez ruled tyrannically, picking satellites to alternate with him in the presidential palace. Thereafter, there was a struggle between democratic forces and those backing a return to strong-man rule. Dr. Rómulo Betancourt and the liberal Acción Democrática Party won a majority of seats in a constituent assembly to draft a new Constitution in 1946. A well-known writer, Rómulo Gallegos, candidate of Betancourt's party, easily won the presidential election of 1947. But, the army ousted Gallegos the next year and instituted a military junta.

The country overthrew the dictatorship in 1958 and thereafter enjoyed democratic government. Rafael Caldera Rodríguez, President from 1969 to 1974, legalized the Communist Party and established diplomatic relations with Moscow. In 1974, President Carlos Andrés Perez took office.

In 1976, Venezuela nationalized 21 oil companies, mostly subsidiaries of U.S. firms, offering compensation of $1.28 billion. Oil income in that year was $9.9 billion, and although production decreased 2.2%, revenue remained at the same level in 1977 because of higher prices, largely financing an ambitious social welfare program.

Despite difficulties at home, Pérez continued to play an active foreign role in extending economic aid to Latin neighbors, in backing the human-rights policy of President Carter, and in supporting Carter's return of the Panama Canal to Panama.

Opposition Christian Democrats capitalized on Pérez's domestic problems to elect Luis Herrera Campíns President in Venezuela's fifth consecutive free election, on Dec. 3, 1978.

Herrera Campins at first supported U.S. policy in Central America, lining up behind the government of El Salva but he later shifted toward a "political solution" that would include the insurgents. In March 1982, he assailed Reagan's policy as "interventionist."

When the Falklands war broke out, Venezuela became one of the most vigorous advocates of the Argentine cause and one of the sharpest critics of the U.S. decision to back Britain.

Jaime Lusinchi of the Democratic Action party won the country's sixth consecutive free election, on Dec. 4, 1983, and was inaugurated President in March 1984. In 1985, he reached a debt-rescheduling agreement with Venezuela's creditors for its $21-billion debt.

# VIETNAM

**Socialist Republic of Vietnam**
**President:** Truong Chinh (1981)
**Premier:** Pham Van Dong (1976)
**Area:** 127,246 sq mi. (329,566 sq km)
**Population (est. mid-1986):** 62,000,000 (average annual growth rate: 2.5%)
**Density per square mile:** 487.2
**Capital:** Hanoi
**Largest cities (est. 1979):** Ho Chi Minh City (Saigon),[1] 3,450,000; Hanoi, 2,600,000; Haiphong, 1,280,000; (est. 1973) Da Nang, 492,200; Nha Trang, 216,200; Qui Nho'n, 213,750; Hué 209,000
**Monetary unit:** Dong
**Language:** Vietnamese
**Religions:** Buddhist, Roman Catholic, Islam, Taoist, Confucian, Animist
**National name:** Công Hòa Xa Hôi Chú Nghia Viêt Nam
**Literacy rate:** 78%
**Economic summary:** Gross national product (1983): $9.8 billion. Per capita income (1983): $170. Land used for agriculture: 23%; labor force: 70%; principal products: rice, rubber, fruits and vegetables, corn, sugar cane, fish. Labor force in industry, 5%; major products: processed foods, textiles, cement, chemical fertilizers, glass, tires. Natural resources: forests, coal. Exports: agricultural products, coal, handicrafts. Imports: petroleum, steel products, railroad equipment, chemicals, medicines, raw cotton, fertilizer, grain. Major trading partners: U.S.S.R., Soviet bloc nations, Japan, India, Hong Kong.

1. Includes suburb of Cholon.

**Geography.** Vietnam occupies the eastern and southern part of the Indochinese peninsula in Southeast Asia, with the South China Sea along its entire coast. China is to the north and Laos and Cambodia to the west. Long and narrow on a north-south axis, Vietnam is about twice the size of Arizona.

The Mekong River delta lies in the south and the Red River delta in the north. Heavily forested mountain and plateau regions make up most of the country.

**Government.** Less than a year after the capitulation of the former Republic of Vietnam (South Vietnam) on April 30, 1975, a joint National Assembly convened with 249 deputies representing the North and 243 representing the South. The Assembly set July 2, 1976, as the official reunification date. Hanoi became the capital, with North Vietnamese President Ton Duc Thang becoming President of the new Socialist Republic of Vietnam and North Vietnamese Premier Pham Van Dong becoming its head of government. By 1981, the National Assembly had increased to 496 members. Truong Chinh succeeded Thang in 1981.

Dang Cong san Vietnam (Communist Party), led by First Secretary Truong Chinh, is the ruling political party. There are also the Socialist Party and the Democratic Party.

**History.** The Vietnamese are descendants of Mongoloid nomads from China and migrants from Indonesia. They recognized Chinese suzerainty until the 15th century, an era of nationalistic expansion, when Cambodians were pushed out of the southern area of what is now Vietnam.

A century later, the Portuguese were the first Europeans to enter the area. France established its influence early in the 19th century and within 80 years conquered the three regions into which the country was then divided—Cochin-China in the south, Annam in the center, and Tonkin in the north.

France first unified Vietnam in 1887, when a single governor-generalship was created, followed by the first physical links between north and south—a rail and road system. Even at the beginning of World War II, however, there were internal differences among the three regions.

Japan took over military bases in Vietnam in 1940 and a pro-Vichy French administration remained until 1945. A veteran Communist leader, Ho Chi Minh, organized an independence movement known as the Vietminh to exploit a confused situation. At the end of the war, Ho's followers seized Hanoi and declared a short-lived republic, which ended with the arrival of French forces in 1946.

Paris proposed a unified government within the French Union under the former Annamite emperor, Bao Dai. Cochin-China and Annam accepted the proposal, and Bao Dai was proclaimed emperor of all Vietnam in 1949. Ho and the Vietminh withheld support, and the revolution in China gave them the outside help needed for a war of resistance against French and Vietnamese troops armed largely by the U.S.

A bitter defeat at Dien Bien Phu in northwest Vietnam on May 5, 1954, broke the French military campaign and brought the division of Vietnam at the conference of Geneva that year.

In the new South, Ngo Dinh Diem, Premier under Bao Dai, deposed the monarch in 1955 and established a republic with himself as President. Diem used strong U.S. backing to create an authoritarian regime that suppressed all opposition but could not eradicate the Northern-supplied Communist Viet Cong.

Skirmishing grew into a full-scale war, with escalating U.S. involvement. A military coup, U.S.-inspired in the view of many, ousted Diem Nov. 1, 1963, and a kaleidoscope of military governments followed. The most savage fighting of the war occurred in early 1968, during the Tet holidays.

Although the Viet Cong failed to overthrow the Saigon government, U.S. public reaction to the apparently endless war forced a limitation of U.S. troops to 550,000 and a new emphasis on shifting the burden of further combat to the South Vietnamese. Ho Chi Minh's death on Sept. 3, 1969, brought a quadrumvirate to replace him but no flagging in Northern will to fight.

U.S. bombing and invasion of Cambodia in the summer of 1970—an effort to destroy Viet Cong bases in the neighboring state—marked the end of major U.S. participation in the fighting. Most American ground troops were withdrawn from combat by mid-1971 as heavy bombing of the Ho Chi Minh trail from North Vietnam appeared to cut the supply of men and matériel to the South.

Secret negotiations for peace by Secretary of State Henry A. Kissinger with North Vietnamese officials during 1972 after heavy bombing of Hanoi and Haiphong brought the two sides near agreement in October. When the Northerners demanded the removal of the South's President Nguyen Van Thieu as their price, President Nixon ordered the "Christmas bombing" of the North. The conference resumed and a peace settlement was signed in Paris on Jan. 27, 1973. It called for release of all U.S. prisoners, withdrawal of U.S. forces, limitation of both sides' forces inside South

Vietnam, and a commitment to peaceful reunification.

Despite Chinese and Soviet endorsement, the agreement foundered. U.S. bombing of Communist-held areas in Cambodia was halted by Congress in August 1973, and in the following year Communist action in South Vietnam increased.

An armored attack across the 17th parallel in January 1975 panicked the South Vietnamese army and brought the invasion within 40 miles of Saigon by April 9. Thieu resigned on April 21 and fled, to be replaced by Vice President Tran Van Huong, who quit a week later, turning over the office to Gen. Duong Van Minh. "Big Minh" surrendered Saigon on April 30, ending a war that took 1.3 million Vietnamese and 56,000 American lives, at the cost of $141 billion in U.S. aid.

On May 3, 1977, the U.S. and Vietnam opened negotiations in Paris to normalize relations. One of the first results was the withdrawal of U.S. opposition to Vietnamese membership in the United Nations, formalized in the Security Council on July 20. Two major issues remained to be settled, however: the return of the bodies of some 2,500 U.S. servicemen missing in the war and the claim by Hanoi that former President Nixon had promised reconstruction aid under the 1973 agreement. Negotiations failed to resolve these issues.

The new year also brought an intensification of border clashes between Vietnam and Cambodia and accusations by China that Chinese residents of Vietnam were being subjected to persecution. Peking cut off all aid and withdrew 800 technicians.

By June, 133,000 ethnic Chinese were reported to have fled Vietnam, and a year later as many as 500,000 of the 1.8 million Vietnamese of Chinese ancestry were believed to have escaped.

Hanoi was undoubtedly preoccupied with a continuing war in Cambodia, where 60,000 Vietnamese troops were aiding the Heng Samrin regime in suppressing the last forces of the pro-Chinese Pol Pot regime. In early 1979, Vietnam was conducting a two-front war, defending its northern border against a Chinese invasion and at the same time supporting its army in Cambodia.

Despite Hanoi's claims of total victory, resistance in Cambodia continued through 1984. Vietnam's second conflict, on its border with China, also flared sporadically.

The Hanoi government agreed in July 1984 to resume technical talks with U.S. officials on the possible whereabouts of the 2,490 Americans still listed as missing, most of them believed dead. In August 1985, the North Vietnamese turned over to an American team 26 numbered crates described as containing the remains of 26 U.S. servicemen.

Economic troubles continued, with the government seeking to reschedule its $1.4-billion foreign hard-currency debt, owed mainly to Japan and the International Monetary Fund. The exodus of the Vietnamese boat people also continued, despite a growing tendency by passing ships not to help the Vietnamese fleeing their country by boat.

Starting in 1984, the Vietnamese government began cracking down on Buddhist and Christian groups in the south, detaining clergymen and establishing government-controlled religious organizations.

(For a Vietnam War chronology, see Headline History, page 123.)

# WESTERN SAMOA

**Independent State of Western Samoa**
**Head of State:** Malietoa Tanumafili II (1962)
**Prime Minister:** Va'ai Kolone (1986)
**Area:** 1,093 sq mi. (2,831 sq km)
**Population (est. mid-1986):** 200,000 (average annual growth rate: 3.0%)
**Density per square mile:** 183
**Capital and largest city (1980):** Apia, 33,400
**Monetary unit:** Tala
**Languages:** Samoan and English
**Religions:** Congregational, 50%; Roman Catholic, 22%; Methodist, 16%
**National name:** Samoa i Sísifo
**Member of Commonwealth of Nations**
**Literacy rate:** 90%
**Economic summary:** Gross national product (1978): $130 million. Per capita income (1978): $770. Land used for agriculture: 50%; labor force: 50%; principal products: copra, cocoa, bananas, timber. Labor force in industry: 10%; major products: timber, light industrial products. Natural resource: timber. Exports: copra, cocoa, bananas, timber. Imports: food, manufactured goods, machinery. Major trading partners: West Germany, New Zealand, Australia, U.S.

**Geography.** Western Samoa, the size of Rhode Island, is in the South Pacific Ocean about 2,200 miles (3,540 km) south of Hawaii midway to Sydney, Australia, and about 800 miles (1,287 km) northeast of Fiji. The larger islands in the Samoan chain are mountainous and of volcanic origin. There is little level land except in the coastal areas, where most cultivation takes place.

**Government.** Western Samoa has a 47-member Legislature, consisting mainly of the titleholders (chiefs) of family groups, with two members elected by universal suffrage to represent those not belonging to such groups. When the present Head of State dies, successors will be elected by the Legislature.

**History.** The Samoan islands were discovered in the 18th century and visited by Dutch and French traders. Toward the end of the 19th century, conflicting interests of the U.S., Britain, and Germany resulted in a treaty signed in 1899. It recognized the paramount interests of the U.S. in those islands east of 171° west longitude (American Samoa) and Germany's interests in the other islands (Western Samoa); the British withdrew in return for recognition of their rights in Tonga and the Solomons.

New Zealand occupied Western Samoa in 1914, and was granted a League of Nations mandate. In 1947, the islands became a U.N. trust territory administered by New Zealand.

Western Samoa became independent on Jan. 1, 1962.

# YEMEN

**People's Democratic Republic of Yemen**
**President:** Haider Abubaker Al-Attas (1986)
**Area:** 111,000 sq mi. (287,490 sq km)[1]
**Population (est. mid-1986):** 2,300,000 (average annual growth rate: 3.0%)
**Density per square mile:** 20.7[1]
**National capital and largest city (est. 1981):** Aden, 365,000
**Administrative capital:** Towahi
**Monetary unit:** Yemen dinar

**Language:** Arabic
**Religion:** Islam (Sunni)
**National name:** Jumhurijah al-Yemen al Dimuqratiyah al
   Sha'abijah
**Literacy rate:** 25%
**Economic summary:** Gross national product (1983): $1,
   020 million. Average annual growth rate (1973–78):
   12.7%. Per capita income (1983): $510. Land used for
   agriculture: 0.6%; labor force: 45%; principal products:
   sorghum, millet, wheat, cotton, goats. Labor force in
   industry: 14%; major products: refined oil products, salt,
   fish meal, cloth. Natural resource: fish. Exports: petroleum
   products, textiles, cotton. Imports: crude oil, foodstuffs,
   manufactured goods. Major trading partners: U.K., Japan,
   Yemen Arab Republic, India, Italy, UAE.

1. Excluding Perim and Kamaran islands.

**Geography.** Formerly known as Southern Yemen,
the People's Democratic Republic of Yemen extends along the southern part of the Arabian Peninsula on the Gulf of Aden and the Indian Ocean. It
is comparable in size to Nevada. The Yemen Arab
Republic is to the northwest, Saudi Arabia to the
north, and Oman to the east.
   A 700-mile (1,130-km) narrow coastal plain gives
way to a mountainous region and then a plateau
area.

**Government.** On June 22, 1969, President Qahtan
Mohammed al Shaabi resigned and was replaced
by a five-man Presidential Council.
   A Constitution published in 1970 changed the
state's name from Southern Yemen and established
a 111-seat legislature, the People's Supreme Council of which al-Attas is chairman, and thus head of
state. The only legal political party is the Yemeni
Socialist Party.

**History.** The People's Republic of Southern Yemen
was established Nov. 30, 1967, when Britain
granted independence to the Federation of South
Arabia. This Federation consisted of the state (once
the colony) of Aden and 16 of the 20 states of the
Protectorate of South Arabia (once the Aden Pro-
tectorate). The four states of the Protectorate that
did not join the Federation later became part of
Southern Yemen.
   Salim Robea Ali, chairman of the Presidential
Council since its establishment in 1969, was ousted
and executed June 26, 1978, two days after the as-
sassination of President Ahmed Hussein al-
Ghashmi of the Yemen Arab Republic. Premier Ali
Nasir Muhammad al-Husani assumed the added
duty of Council head.
   Abdul Fattah Ismail was elected President by the
Supreme Council on Dec. 27, 1978 and reversed
Robea's movement toward reconciliation with the
Yemen Arab Republic and an accommodation with
Saudi Arabia. His sudden resignation on April 21,
1980, was reported to have stemmed from the new
Soviet desire to win friends in the Yemen Arab Re-
public and Saudi Arabia.
   In December 1985, a purge of Ismail's hardline
faction led to a brief civil war in which Ismail was
killed but al-Husani was overthrown by Haider al-
Attas, an Ismail ally.

# YEMEN ARAB REPUBLIC

**President:** Col. Ali Abdullah Saleh (1978)
**Premier:** Abdulaziz Abdulghani (1983)
**Area:** 75,290 sq mi. (195,000 sq km)
**Population (est. mid-1986):** 6,300,000 (average annual
   growth rate: 3.0%)

**Density per square mile:** 83.7
**Capital and largest city (est. 1982):** San'a', 275,000
**Monetary unit:** Rial
**Language:** Arabic
**Religion:** Islam
**National name:** Al Jamhuriya al Arabiya Yamaniya
**Literacy rate:** 15% (est.)
**Economic summary:** Gross national product (1983): $3.9
   billion. Per capita income (1983): $510. Land used for
   agriculture: 20%; labor force: 74%; principal products:
   wheat, sorghum, cattle, sheep, cotton, fruits. Major
   industrial products: consumer goods, construction
   materials. Natural resources: traces of copper, sulfur,
   coal, quartz. Exports: cotton, coffee, hides and skins.
   Imports: textiles and other manufactured consumer goods,
   petroleum and petroleum products, sugar, grain, flour.
   Major trading partners: France, Yemen (Aden), Japan,
   Saudi Arabia, Italy.

**Geography.** The Yemen Arab Republic, also known
as North Yemen, occupies the southwestern tip of
the Arabian Peninsula, with its western coast on
the Red Sea opposite Ethiopia. Its neighbors are
Saudi Arabia to the north and east and the People's
Democratic Republic of Yemen to the south. Its
area is slightly less than that of South Dakota.
   A north-south coastal plain 20–50 miles wide
(32–80 km) lies in the west; eastward, there are the
interior highlands, which attain a height of 12,000
feet (3,660 m), and the expanse of the Rub 'al-Khali
Desert.

**Government.** The country's first permanent Constitution was submitted to the National Assembly in
1971. It provided for a 179-member legislature, the
Consultative Council, 20 of whose members would
be chosen by the President and the rest elected
every four years. A five-man executive Presidential
Council was to be chosen by the Consultative
Council.
   In 1974, the army ousted the government in a
bloodless coup and suspended the Constitution and
its various legislative bodies.

**History.** The history of Yemen dates back to the
Minaean kingdom (1200–650 B.C.). It accepted
Islam in A.D. 628, and in the 10th century came
under the control of the Rassite dynasty of the
Zaidi sect. The Turks occupied the area from 1538
to 1630 and from 1849 to 1918. The sovereign status of Yemen was confirmed by treaties signed with
Saudi Arabia and Britain in 1934.
   Yemen joined the Arab League in 1945 and established diplomatic relations with the U.S. in
1946.
   In 1962, a military revolt of elements favoring
President Gamal Abdel Nasser of Egypt broke out.
A ruling junta proclaimed a republic, and Yemen
became an international battleground, with Egypt
and the U.S.S.R. supporting the revolutionaries,
and King Saud of Saudi Arabia and King Hussein
of Jordan the royalists. The civil war continued
until the war between the Arab states and Israel
broke out in June 1967. Nasser had to pull out
many of his troops and agree to a cease-fire and
withdrawal of foreign forces. The war finally ended
with the defeat of the royalists in mid-1969.
   In 1977, Col. Ibrahim al-Hamidi was assassinated
after three years as head of government and was
succeeded by Lt. Col. Ahmed Hussein al-Ghashmi
as head of the Presidential Council. On June 24,
1978, al-Ghashmi was killed by a bomb as he received the credentials of a new ambassador from

the People's Democratic Republic of Yemen. The People's Council elected Col. Ali Abdullah Saleh as President on July 17.

In 1984, the Hunt Oil Co. of Dallas discovered oil in North Yemen, the first time it had been found in the desolate Arab state, one of the world's poorest nations. The company said it was too early to determine the size of the discovery or when production might start. Middle East analysts found news of the oil strike intriguing, partly because North Yemen lies on the Red Sea, far from the war-troubled Persian Gulf and Straits of Hormuz.

# YUGOSLAVIA

**Socialist Federal Republic of Yugoslavia**
**President:** Sinan Hasani (1986)
**President of Federal Executive Council (Premier):** Branko Mikulić (1986)
**Area:** 98,766 sq mi. (255,804 sq km)
**Population (est. mid-1986):** 23,200,000 (average annual growth rate: 0.7%) (Serbian, 36%; Croatian, 20%; Moslem, 9%; Slovene, 8%; Albanian, 8%; Macedonian, 6%, Montenegrin, 3%)
**Density per square mile:** 234.9
**Capital:** Belgrade
**Largest cities (est. 1982):** Belgrade, 1,250,000; Zagreb, 765,000; Skopje, 505,000; Sarajevo, 450,000; Ljubljana, 255,000; Split, 200,000
**Monetary unit:** Dinar
**Languages:** Serbo-Croatian, Slovene, Macedonian (all official)
**Religions:** Greek Orthodox, 41%; Roman Catholic, 32%; Islam, 12%
**National name:** Socijalisticka Federativna Republika Jugoslavija
**Literacy rate:** 85%
**Economic summary:** Gross national product (1984): $128 billion. Average annual growth rate (1984): 1.7%. Per capita income (1984): $5,600. Land used for agriculture: 33%; labor force: 29%; principal products: corn, wheat, tobacco, sugar beets. Labor force in industry: 28%; major products: wood, processed food, nonferrous metals, machinery, textiles. Natural resources: timber, copper, iron, lead, zinc, bauxite. Exports: leather goods, textiles, machinery. Imports: machinery, chemicals, iron, and steel. Major trading partners: U.S.S.R., West Germany, Italy, U.S., Czechoslovakia.

**Geography.** Yugoslavia fronts on the eastern coast of the Adriatic Sea opposite Italy. Its neighbors are Austria, Italy, and Hungary to the north, Romania and Bulgaria to the east, and Greece and Albania to the south. It is slightly larger than Wyoming.

About half of Yugoslavia is mountainous. In the north, the Dinaric Alps rise abruptly from the sea and progress eastward as a barren limestone plateau called the Karst. Montenegro is a jumbled mass of mountains, containing also some grassy slopes and fertile river valleys. Southern Serbia, too, is mountainous. A rich plain in the north and northeast, drained by the Danube, is the most fertile area of the country.

**Government.** Yugoslavia is a federal republic composed of six socialist republics—Serbia (which includes the provinces of Vojvodina and Kosovo), Croatia, Slovenia, Bosnia-Herzegovina, Macedonia, and Montenegro. Actual administration is carried on by the Federal Executive Council and its secretaries.

The League of Communists and the Socialist Alliance of the Working People are the major political parties.

**History.** Yugoslavia was formed Dec. 1, 1918, from the patchwork of Balkan states and territories where World War I began with the assassination of Archduke Ferdinand of Austria at Sarajevo on June 28, 1914. The new Kingdom of Serbs, Croats, and Slovenes included the former kingdoms of Serbia and Montenegro; Bosnia-Herzegovina, previously administered jointly by Austria and Hungary; Croatia-Slavonia, a semi-autonomous region of Hungary, and Dalmatia, formerly administered by Austria. King Peter I of Serbia became the first monarch, his son acting as Regent until his accession as Alexander I on Aug. 16, 1921.

Croatian demands for a federal state forced Alexander to assume dictatorial powers in 1929 and to change the country's name to Yugoslavia. Serbian dominance continued despite his efforts, amid the resentment of other regions. A Macedonian associated with Croatian dissidents assassinated Alexander in Marseilles, France, on Oct. 9, 1934, and his cousin, Prince Paul, became Regent for the King's son, Prince Peter.

Paul's pro-Axis policy brought Yugoslavia to sign the Axis Pact on March 25, 1941, and opponents overthrew the government two days later. On April 6 the Nazis occupied the country, and the young King and his government fled. Two guerrilla armies—the Chetniks under Draza Mihajlovic supporting the monarchy and the Partisans under Tito (Josip Broz) leaning toward the U.S.S.R.—fought the Nazis for the duration of the war. In 1943, Tito established an Executive National Committee of Liberation to function as a provisional government.

Tito won the election held in the fall of 1945, as monarchists boycotted the vote. A new Assembly abolished the monarchy and proclaimed the Federal People's Republic of Yugoslavia, with Tito as Prime Minister.

Ruthlessly eliminating opposition, the Tito government executed Mihajlovic in 1946. With Soviet aid, Tito annexed the greater part of Italian Istria under the 1947 peace treaty with Italy but failed in his claim to the key port of Trieste. Zone B of the former free territory of Trieste went to Yugoslavia in 1954.

Tito broke with the Soviet bloc in 1948 and Yugoslavia has since followed a middle road, combining orthodox Communist control of politics and general overall economic policy with a varying degree of freedom in the arts, travel, and individual enterprise. Tito, who became President in 1953 and President for life under a revised Constitution adopted in 1963, has played a major part in the creation of a "non-aligned" group of states, the so-called "third world."

The Marshal supported his one-time Soviet mentors in their quarrel with Communist China, but even though he imprisoned the writer Mihajlo Mihajlov and other dissenters at home, he criticized Soviet repression of Czecholovakia in 1968.

Tito's death on May 4, 1980, three days before his 88th birthday, removed from the scene the last World War II leader. A rotating presidency designed to avoid internal dissension was put into effect immediately, and the feared clash of Yugoslavia's multiple nationalities and regions appeared to have been averted. A collective presidency, rotated annually among the six republics and two autonomous provinces of the federal republic, continued to govern according to a constitutional change made in 1974.

In March 1981, the Albanian minority, which

forms 80 per cent of the population of the autonomous province of Kosovo, backed Albanian students demonstrating against conditions at the university. By April, the demonstrations had swelled to riots in which 11 were killed as 100,000 people demanded the status of a separate republic, which would enable Kosovo to secede from the Yugoslav federation. Unrest continued in 1982, with 1,700 ethnic Albanians arrested by midyear for "anti-Yugoslav activities."

# ZAIRE

**Republic of Zaire**
**President:** Mobutu Sese Seko (1965)
**Prime Minister:** Kengo Wa Dondo (1982)
**Area:** 905,365 sq mi. (2,344,885 sq km)
**Population (est. mid-1986):** 31,300,000 (average annual growth rate: 2.8%)
**Density per square mile:** 34.6
**Capital:** Kinshasa
**Largest cities (est. 1982):** Kinshasa, 3,000,000; Kananga, 800,000; Lubumbashi, 525,000; Mbuji-Maji, 425,000
**Monetary unit:** Zaire
**Languages:** French; Bantu dialects, mainly Swahili, Lingala, Ishiluba, and Kikongo
**Religions:** Roman Catholic 48%, Protestant 29%, Islam 10%
**Ethnic groups:** Bantu, Sudanese, Nilotics, Pygmies, Hamites
**National name:** République du Zaïre
**Literacy rate:** 40% male, 15% female
**Economic summary:** Gross national product (1983): $5.1 billion. Average annual growth rate: 3.0%. Per capita income (1983): $160. Land used for agriculture: 3%; labor force: 70%, principal products: coffee, palm oil, rubber, sugar, cotton, cocoa, bananas, plantains, vegetables, fruits. Major industrial products: processed and unprocessed minerals. Natural resources: copper, cobalt, zinc, industrial diamonds, manganese, tin, gold, silver, bauxite, iron, coal, 13% of world hydroelectric potential. Exports: copper, cobalt, diamonds, petroleum, coffee. Imports: consumer goods, foodstuffs, mining and other machinery, transport equipment. Major trading partners: Belgium, France, U.S.

**Geography.** Zaire is situated in west central Africa and is bordered by the Congo, the Central African Empire, the Sudan, Uganda, Rwanda, Burundi, Tanzania, Zambia, Angola, and the Atlantic Ocean. It is one quarter the size of the U.S.

The principal rivers are the Ubangi and Bomu in the north and the Zaire (Congo) in the west, which flows into the Atlantic. The entire length of Lake Tanganyika lies along the eastern border with Tanzania and Burundi.

**Government.** Under the Constitution approved by referendum in 1967 and amended in 1974, the third Constitution since 1960, the president and a unicameral Legislature are elected by universal suffrage for five-year terms.

In 1971, the government proclaimed that the Democratic Republic of the Congo would be known as the Republic of Zaire, since the Congo River's name had been changed to the Zaire. In addition, President Joseph D. Mobutu took the name Mobutu Sese Seko and Katanga Province became Shaba.

There is only one political party: the Popular Movement of the Revolution, led by President Mobutu.

**History.** Formerly the Belgian Congo, this territory was inhabited by ancient Negrito peoples (Pygmies), who were pushed into the mountains by Bantu and Nilotic invaders. The American correspondent Henry M. Stanley navigated the Congo River in 1877 and opened the interior to exploration. Commissioned by King Leopold II of the Belgians, Stanley made treaties with native chiefs that enabled the King to obtain personal title to the territory at the Berlin Conference of 1885.

Criticism of forced labor under royal exploitation prompted Belgium to take over administration of the Congo, which remained a colony until agitation for independence forced Brussels to grant freedom on June 30, 1960. Moise Tshombe, Premier of the then Katanga Province seceded from the new republic on July 11, and another mining province, South Kasai, followed. Belgium sent paratroopers to quell the civil war, and with President Joseph Kasavubu and Premier Patrice Lumumba of the national government in conflict, the United Nations flew in a peacekeeping force.

Kasavubu staged an army coup in 1960 and handed Lumumba over to the Katangan forces. A U.N. investigating commission found that Lumumba had been killed by a Belgian mercenary in the presence of Tshombe. Dag Hammarskjold, U.N. Secretary-General, died in a plane crash en route to a peace conference with Tshombe on Sept. 17, 1961.

U.N. Secretary-General U Thant submitted a national reconciliation plan in 1962 that Tshombe rejected. Tshombe's troops fired on the U.N. force in December, and in the ensuing conflict Tshombe capitulated on Jan. 14, 1963. The peacekeeping force withdrew, and, in a complete about-face, Kasavubu named Tshombe Premier to fight a spreading rebellion. Tshombe used foreign mercenaries and, with the help of Belgian paratroops airlifted by U.S. planes, defeated the most serious opposition, a Communist-backed regime in the northeast.

Kasavubu abruptly dismissed Tshombe in 1965 and was himself ousted by Gen. Joseph-Desiré Mobutu, Army Chief of Staff. The new President nationalized the Union Minière, the Belgian copper mining enterprise that had been a dominant force in the Congo since colonial days. The plane carrying the exiled Tshombe was hijacked in 1967 and he was held prisoner in Algeria until his death from a heart attack was announced June 29, 1969.

Mobutu eliminated opposition to win election in 1970 to a term of seven years, which was renewed in a 1977 election. He invited U.S., South African, and Japanese investment to replace Belgian interests. In 1975, he nationalized much of the economy, barred religious instruction in schools, and decreed the adoption of African names.

On March 8, 1977, invaders from Angola calling themselves the Congolese National Liberation Front pushed into Shaba and threatened the important mining center of Kolwezi. France and Belgium responded to Mobutu's pleas for help with weapons, but the U.S. gave only nonmilitary supplies.

In April, France flew 1,500 Moroccan troops to Shaba to defeat the invaders, who were, Mobutu charged, Soviet-inspired, and Cuban-led. U.S. intelligence sources, however, confirmed Soviet and Cuban denials of any participation and identified the rebels as former Katanga gendarmes who had fled to Angola after their 1963 defeat.

On May 15, 1978, a new assault from Angola resulted in the capture of Kolwezi and the death of

100 whites and 300 blacks. In this second invasion, France and Belgium intervened directly as 1,000 Foreign Legion paratroopers repelled the Katangese and 1,750 Belgian soldiers helped evacuate 2,000 Europeans. The U.S. supplied 18 air transports for both the troop movement and the evacuation. This time President Carter himself backed Mobutu's renewed assertions of Soviet-Cuban participation.

In 1984 and 1985, Zaire and Angola signed bilateral agreements aimed at improved relations, including an agreement not to support rebels in each other's country.

# ZAMBIA

**Republic of Zambia**
**President:** Kenneth D. Kaunda (1964)
**Prime Minister:** Kebby Musokotwane (1985)
**Area:** 290,586 sq mi. (752,618 sq km)
**Population (est. mid-1986):** 7,100,000 (average annual growth rate: 3.3%)
**Density per square mile:** 24.4
**Capital:** Lusaka
**Largest cities (est. 1982):** Lusaka, 650,000; Kitwe, 345,000; Ndola, 325,000; Chingola, 195,000
**Monetary unit:** Kwacha
**Languages:** English and local dialects
**Religions:** Animist, Roman Catholic, Protestant, Hindu, Islam
**Member of Commonwealth of Nations**
**Literacy rate:** 54%
**Economic summary:** Gross national product (1984): $2.6 billion. Average annual growth rate (1981): −1.85%. Per capita income (1984): $397. Land used for agriculture: 5%; labor force: 9%; principal products: corn, tobacco, fruits, sugar cane. Labor force in industry: 15%; major products: copper, cobalt, chemicals, zinc, fertilizers. Natural resources: copper, zinc, lead, cobalt, coal. Exports: copper, zinc, lead, cobalt, tobacco. Imports: manufactured goods, machinery and transport equipment, foodstuffs. Major trading partners: U.K., Japan, South Africa, U.S., W. Germany.

**Geography.** Zambia, a landlocked country in south central Africa, is about one tenth larger than Texas. It is surrounded by Angola, Zaire, Tanzania, Malawi, Mozambique, Zimbabwe, Botswana, and SouthWest Africa (Namibia). The country is mostly a plateau that rises to 8,000 feet (2,434 m) in the east.

**Government.** Zambia (formerly Northern Rhodesia) is governed by a president, elected by universal suffrage, and a Legislative Assembly, consisting of 125 members elected by universal suffrage and up to 10 additional members nominated by the president.

In 1972, the Assembly passed a law making the ruling United National Independence Party, led by President Kenneth D. Kaunda, the only legal political party.

**History.** Empire builder Cecil Rhodes obtained mining concessions in 1889 from King Lewanika of the Barotse and sent settlers to the area soon thereafter. It was ruled by the British South Africa Company, which he established, until 1924, when the British government took over the administration.

From 1953 to 1964, Northern Rhodesia was federated with Southern Rhodesia and Nyasaland in the Federation of Rhodesia and Nyasaland. On Oct. 24, 1964, Northern Rhodesia became the independent nation of Zambia.

Kenneth Kaunda, the first president, kept Zambia within the Commonwealth of Nations. The country's economy, dependent on copper exports, was threatened when Rhodesia declared its independence from British rule in 1965 and defied U.N. sanctions, which Zambia supported, an action that deprived Zambia of its trade route through Rhodesia. The U.S., Britain, and Canada organized an airlift in 1966 to ship gasoline into Zambia. In 1967, Britain agreed to finance new trade routes for Zambia.

Kaunda visited China in 1967, and China later agreed to finance a 1,000-mile railroad from the copper fields to Dar es Salaam in Tanzania. A pipeline was opened in 1968 from Ndola in Zambia's copper belt to the Indian Ocean at Dar es Salaam, ending the three-year oil drought.

In 1969, Kaunda announced the nationalization of the foreign copper-mining industry, with Zambia to take 51% (over $1 billion, estimated), and an agreement was reached with the companies on payment. He then announced a similar takeover of foreign oil producers.

Zambia suffered heavy damage from bombing raids by the former Rhodesian air force on Zimbabwean guerrilla bases and on its transportation links. These actions, combined with falling prices for copper and cobalt, forced Kaunda to declare a state of economic austerity in January 1981.

A strike by copper-belt workers, in 1981, directed partly against cuts in consumer subsidies and partly at UNIP, the regime's single party, brought a quick victory for the workers after they shut down production. In February, Kaunda installed a new Prime Minister and a new party chief, both more acceptable to the powerful copper-belt unions, and in April, UNIP readmitted union leaders who had been expelled at the time of the strike.

# ZIMBABWE

**President:** Rev. Canaan Banana (1980)
**Prime Minister:** Robert Mugabe (1980)
**Area:** 150,699 sq mi. (390,308 sq km)
**Population (est. mid-1986):** 9,000,000 (average annual growth rate: 3.5%) (black, 96%; white, 4%)
**Density per square mile:** 59.7
**Capital:** Harare (Salisbury)
**Largest cities (est. 1982 for metropolitan area):** Harare, 675,000; Bulawayo, 400,000
**Monetary unit:** Zimbabwean dollar
**Languages:** English (official), Sindebele, Shona
**Religions:** Christian, 25%; Animist 24%; Syncretic 50%
**Literacy rate:** 30% (blacks), 99% (whites)
**Economic summary:** Gross national product (1982): $6.6 billion. Average annual growth rate (1980–81): 12%. Per capita income (1982): $870. Land used for agriculture: 6%; labor force: 35%; principal agricultural products: tobacco, corn, sugar, cotton, livestock. Labor force in industry: 25%; major products: steel, textiles, chemicals, vehicles, gold, copper. Natural resources: gold, copper, chrome, nickel, tin, asbestos. Exports: gold, tobacco, asbestos, copper, meat, chrome, nickel, corn, sugar. Imports: machinery, petroleum products, transport equipment. Major trading partners: South Africa, UK

**Geography.** Zimbabwe, a landlocked country in south central Africa, is slightly smaller than California. It is bordered by Botswana on the west, Zambia on the north, Mozambique on the east, and South Africa on the south.

A high veld up to 6,000 feet (1,829 m) crosses the country from northeast to southwest. This is flanked by a somewhat lower veld that contains ranching country. Tropical forests that yield hardwoods lie in the southeast.

In the north, on the border with Zambia, is the 175-mile-long (128-m) Kariba Lake, formed by the Kariba Dam across the Zambezi River. It is the site of one of the world's largest hydroelectric projects.

**Government.** Executive power rests with the 26-member Cabinet, headed by the Prime Minister. The President, elected by a majority of the House of Assembly, exercises formal executive powers. The legislature is composed of a 100-member House of Assembly, 80 of whom are elected by black voters and 20 by whites, and a 40-member Senate. Black House members elect 14 Senators and whites elect 10. Ten tribal chiefs—five from Mashonaland and five from Matabeleland—are elected by their peers and six appointed by the President complete the Senate membership.

Major political parties are the Zimbabwe African National Union (64 seats in the House of Assembly), led by Prime Minister Robert Mugabe; Zimbabwe African People's Union (15 seats), led by Joshua Nkomo. The Conservative Alliance, led by former Prime Minister Ian Smith, holds 15 of the 20 seats reserved for whites.

**History.** Zimbabwe was colonized by Cecil Rhodes's British South Africa Company at the end of the 19th century. In 1923, European settlers voted to become the self-governing British colony of Southern Rhodesia rather than merge with the Union of South Africa. After a brief federation with Northern Rhodesia and Nyasaland in the post-World War II period, Southern Rhodesia chose to remain a colony when its two partners voted for independence in 1963.

On Nov. 11, 1965, the white-minority government of Rhodesia unilaterally declared its independence from Britain.

In 1967, the U.N. imposed mandatory sanctions against Rhodesia. The country moved slowly toward meeting the demands of black Africans. The white-minority regime of Prime Minister Ian Smith withstood British pressure, economic sanctions, guerrilla attacks, and a right-wing assault.

On March 1, 1970, Rhodesia formally proclaimed itself a republic, and within the month nine nations, including the U.S., closed their consulates there.

Heightened guerrilla war and a withdrawal of South African military aid—particularly helicopters—marked the beginning of the collapse of Smith's 11 years of resistance in the spring of 1976. Under pressure from South Africa, Smith agreed with the U.S. that majority rule should come within two years.

In the fall, Smith met with black nationalist leaders in Geneva. The meeting broke up six weeks later when the Rhodesian Premier insisted that whites must retain control of the police and armed forces during the transition to majority rule. A British proposal called for Britons to take over these powers.

Divisions between Rhodesian blacks—Bishop Abel Muzorewa of the African National Congress and Ndabaningi Sithole as moderates versus Robert Mugabe and Joshua Nkomo of the Patriotic Front as advocates of guerrilla force—sharpened in 1977 and no agreement was reached. In July, with white residents leaving in increasing numbers and the economy showing the strain of war, Smith rejected outside mediation and called for general elections in order to work out an "internal solution" of the transfer of power.

On March 3, 1978, Smith, Muzorewa, Sithole, and Chief Jeremiah Chirau signed an agreement to transfer power to the black majority by Dec. 31, 1978. They constituted themselves an Executive Council, with chairmanship rotating but Smith retaining the title of Prime Minister. Blacks were named to each cabinet ministry, serving as co-ministers with the whites already holding these posts. African nations and the Patriotic Front leaders immediately denounced the action, but Western governments were more reserved, although none granted recognition to the new regime.

White voters ratified a new constitution on Jan. 30, 1979, enfranchising all blacks, establishing a black majority Senate and Assembly, and changing the country's name to Zimbabwe Rhodesia. A general election on April 24 gave Muzorewa's party 67.3% of the vote.

Muzorewa agreed to negotiate with Mugabe and Nkomo in British-sponsored talks beginning Sept. 9. By December, all parties accepted a new draft constitution, a cease-fire, and a period of British administration pending a general election.

In voting completed on Feb. 29, 1980, Mugabe's ZANU-Patriotic Front party won 57 of the 80 Assembly seats reserved for blacks. Nkomo's ZAPU-Patriotic Front party won 20 seats and Muzorewa's United African National Council only three. In an earlier vote on Feb. 14, the Rhodesian Front won all 20 seats reserved for whites in the Assembly.

At a ceremony on April 18, Prince Charles of Britain handed to President-elect Rev. Canaan Banana the symbols of independence. Mugabe, a Marxist, had already pledged his support for continuation of the existing free-market economy.

On April 18, 1980, Britain formally recognized the independence of Zimbabwe.

In January 1981, Mugabe dismissed Nkomo as Home Minister and his onetime rival left the government in protest. At the same time, the Prime Minister discharged Edgar Z. Tekere, Manpower and Planning Minister, who had been tried and acquitted of the murder of a white farmer.

Mugabe survived both tests and scored an unprecedented triumph when, in response to his appeal for economic aid, Western nations pledged $1.8 billion for the next three years. The United States promised to give $225 million in grants in addition to $50 million in low-interest loans to replace war-damaged housing.

The 1985 harvest was good in Zimbabwe and the country could feed itself. But political turmoil and civil strife continued. In what Western analysts viewed as a free and fair election, President Mugabe's African National Union increased its sizeable majority in the House of Assembly but Mugabe was frustrated because it did not win the 70 seats he sought to cement one-party rule. After the election, Mugabe cracked down on Nkomo's ZAPU-Patriotic Front party.

**(For late reports, see Current Events of 1985-1986)**

# UNITED NATIONS

## The 159 Members of the United Nations

| Country | Joined U.N.[1] | Country | Joined U.N.[1] | Country | Joined U.N.[1] |
|---|---|---|---|---|---|
| Afghanistan | 1946 | Germany, East | 1973 | Panama | 1945 |
| Albania | 1955 | Germany, West | 1973 | Papua New Guinea | 1975 |
| Algeria | 1962 | Ghana | 1957 | Paraguay | 1945 |
| Angola | 1976 | Greece | 1945 | Peru | 1945 |
| Antigua and Barbuda | 1981 | Grenada | 1974 | Philippines | 1945 |
| Argentina | 1945 | Guatemala | 1945 | Poland | 1945 |
| Australia | 1945 | Guinea | 1958 | Portugal | 1955 |
| Austria | 1955 | Guinea-Bissau | 1974 | Qatar | 1971 |
| Bahamas | 1973 | Guyana | 1966 | Romania | 1955 |
| Bahrain | 1971 | Haiti | 1945 | Rwanda | 1962 |
| Bangladesh | 1974 | Honduras | 1945 | St. Christopher and Nevis | 1983 |
| Barbados | 1966 | Hungary | 1955 | St. Lucia | 1979 |
| Belgium | 1945 | Iceland | 1946 | St. Vincent and the Grenadines | 1980 |
| Belize | 1981 | India | 1945 | São Tomé and Príncipe | 1975 |
| Benin | 1960 | Indonesia | 1950 | Saudi Arabia | 1945 |
| Bhutan | 1971 | Iran | 1945 | Senegal | 1960 |
| Bolivia | 1945 | Iraq | 1945 | Seychelles | 1976 |
| Botswana | 1966 | Ireland | 1955 | Sierra Leone | 1961 |
| Brazil | 1945 | Israel | 1949 | Singapore | 1965 |
| Brunei | 1984 | Italy | 1955 | Solomon Islands | 1978 |
| Bulgaria | 1955 | Ivory Coast | 1960 | Somalia | 1960 |
| Burkina Faso | 1960 | Jamaica | 1962 | South Africa | 1945 |
| Burma | 1948 | Japan | 1956 | Spain | 1955 |
| Burundi | 1962 | Jordan | 1955 | Sri Lanka | 1955 |
| Byelorussian S.S.R. | 1945 | Kenya | 1963 | Sudan | 1956 |
| Cambodia | 1955 | Kuwait | 1963 | Suriname | 1975 |
| Cameroon | 1960 | Laos | 1955 | Swaziland | 1968 |
| Canada | 1945 | Lebanon | 1945 | Sweden | 1946 |
| Cape Verde | 1975 | Lesotho | 1966 | Syria | 1945 |
| Central African Republic | 1960 | Liberia | 1945 | Tanzania | 1961 |
| Chad | 1960 | Libya | 1955 | Thailand | 1946 |
| Chile | 1945 | Luxembourg | 1945 | Togo | 1960 |
| China[2] | 1945 | Madagascar | 1960 | Trinidad and Tobago | 1962 |
| Colombia | 1945 | Malawi | 1964 | Tunisia | 1956 |
| Comoros | 1975 | Malaysia | 1957 | Turkey | 1945 |
| Congo | 1960 | Maldives | 1965 | Uganda | 1962 |
| Costa Rica | 1945 | Mali | 1960 | Ukrainian S.S.R. | 1945 |
| Cuba | 1945 | Malta | 1964 | U.S.S.R. | 1945 |
| Cyprus | 1960 | Mauritania | 1961 | United Arab Emirates | 1971 |
| Czechoslovakia | 1945 | Mauritius | 1968 | United Kingdom | 1945 |
| Denmark | 1945 | Mexico | 1945 | United States | 1945 |
| Djibouti | 1977 | Mongolia | 1961 | Uruguay | 1945 |
| Dominica | 1978 | Morocco | 1956 | Vanuatu | 1981 |
| Dominican Republic | 1945 | Mozambique | 1975 | Venezuela | 1945 |
| Ecuador | 1945 | Nepal | 1955 | Vietnam | 1977 |
| Egypt | 1945 | Netherlands | 1945 | Western Samoa | 1976 |
| El Salvador | 1945 | New Zealand | 1945 | Yemen Arab Republic | 1947 |
| Equatorial Guinea | 1968 | Nicaragua | 1945 | Yemen, People's Dem. | |
| Ethiopia | 1945 | Niger | 1960 | Republic of | 1967 |
| Fiji | 1970 | Nigeria | 1960 | Yugoslavia | 1945 |
| Finland | 1955 | Norway | 1945 | Zaire | 1960 |
| France | 1945 | Oman | 1971 | Zambia | 1964 |
| Gabon | 1960 | Pakistan | 1947 | Zimbabwe | 1980 |
| Gambia | 1965 | | | | |

1. The U.N. officially came into existence on Oct. 24, 1945. 2. On Oct. 25, 1971, the U.N. voted membership to the People's Republic of China, which replaced the Republic of China (Taiwan) in the world body.

## Six Official Languages Used by U.N.

There are six official working languages recognized by the United Nations. They are Chinese, English, French, Russian, and Spanish, which have been in use since the world body was organized, and Arabic, which was added by the General Assembly in 1973 and by the Security Council in 1982.

## Member Countries' Assessments to U.N. Budget, 1986

| Country | Total | Country | Total | Country | Total |
|---|---|---|---|---|---|
| Afghanistan | $70,043 | Gambia | 70,043 | Panama | 140,087 |
| Albania | 70,043 | Germany, East | 9,315,778 | Papua New Guinea | 70,043 |
| Algeria | 980,608 | Germany, West | 57,855,878 | Paraguay | 140,087 |
| Angola | 70,043 | Ghana | 70,043 | Peru | 490,304 |
| Antigua and Barbuda | 70,043 | Greece | 3,081,912 | Philippines | 700,434 |
| Argentina | 4,342,694 | Grenada | 70,043 | Poland | 4,482,781 |
| Australia | 11,627,212 | Guatemala | 140,087 | Portugal | 1,260,781 |
| Austria | 5,183,216 | Guinea | 70,043 | Qatar | 280,174 |
| Bahamas | 70,043 | Guinea-Bissau | 70,043 | Romania | 1,330,826 |
| Bahrain | 140,087 | Guyana | 70,043 | Rwanda | 70,043 |
| Bangladesh | 140,087 | Haiti | 70,043 | Saint Christopher and Nevis | 70,043 |
| Barbados | 70,043 | Honduras | 70,043 | St. Lucia | 70,043 |
| Belgium | 8,265,126 | Hungary | 1,540,957 | St. Vincent and the Grenadines | 70,043 |
| Belize | 70,043 | Iceland | 210,130 | São Tomé and Príncipe | 70,043 |
| Benin | 70,043 | India | 2,451,521 | Saudi Arabia | 6,794,214 |
| Bhutan | 70,043 | Indonesia | 980,608 | Senegal | 70,043 |
| Bolivia | 70,043 | Iran | 4,412,737 | Seychelles | 70,043 |
| Botswana | 70,043 | Iraq | 840,521 | Sierra Leone | 70,043 |
| Brazil | 9,806,082 | Ireland | 1,260,781 | Singapore | 700,434 |
| Brunei Darussalam | 280,174 | Israel | 1,540,957 | Solomon Islands | 70,043 |
| Bulgaria | 1,120,695 | Italy | 26,546,463 | Somalia | 70,043 |
| Burkina Faso | 70,043 | Jamaica | 140,087 | South Africa | 3,081,912 |
| Burma | 70,043 | Japan | 75,927,084 | Spain | 14,218,818 |
| Burundi | 70,043 | Jordan | 70,043 | Sri Lanka | 70,043 |
| Byelorussian SSR | 2,381,477 | Kenya | 70,043 | Sudan | 70,043 |
| Cambodia | 70,043 | Kuwait | 2,031,261 | Suriname | 70,043 |
| Cameroon | 70,043 | Laos | 70,043 | Swaziland | 70,043 |
| Canada | 21,433,292 | Lebanon | 70,043 | Sweden | 8,755,431 |
| Cape Verde | 70,043 | Lesotho | 70,043 | Syria | 280,174 |
| Central African Republic | 70,043 | Liberia | 70,043 | Tanzania | 71,909 |
| Chad | 70,043 | Libya | 1,821,130 | Thailand | 630,390 |
| Chile | 490,304 | Luxembourg | 350,217 | Togo | 70,043 |
| China | 5,533,432 | Madagascar | 70,043 | Trinidad and Tobago | 280,174 |
| Colombia | 910,565 | Malawi | 70,043 | Tunisia | 210,130 |
| Comoros | 70,043 | Malaysia | 700,434 | Turkey | 2,385,563 |
| Congo | 70,043 | Maldives | 70,043 | Uganda | 70,043 |
| Costa Rica | 140,087 | Mali | 70,043 | Ukrainian SSR | 8,965,560 |
| Cote D'Ivoire | 140,087 | Malta | 70,043 | U.S.S.R. | 71,444,305 |
| Cuba | 630,390 | Mauritania | 70,043 | United Arab Emirates | 1,260,781 |
| Cyprus | 140,087 | Mauritius | 70,043 | United Kingdom | 34,041,110 |
| Czechoslovakia | 4,903,041 | Mexico | 6,233,867 | United States | 210,277,200 |
| Denmark | 5,043,128 | Mongolia | 70,043 | Uruguay | 280,174 |
| Djibouti | 70,043 | Morocco | 350,217 | Vanuatu | 70,043 |
| Dominica | 70,043 | Mozambique | 70,043 | Venezuela | 4,202,607 |
| Dominican Republic | 210,130 | Nepal | 70,043 | Vietnam | 70,043 |
| Ecuador | 210,130 | Netherlands | 12,187,559 | Western Samoa | 70,043 |
| Egypt | 490,304 | New Zealand | 1,681,044 | Yemen Arab Republic | 70,043 |
| El Salvador | 70,043 | Nicaragua | 70,043 | Yemen, People's Dem. Republic of | 70,043 |
| Equatorial Guinea | 70,043 | Niger | 70,043 | Yugoslavia | 3,221,999 |
| Ethiopia | 70,043 | Nigeria | 1,330,826 | Zaire | 70,043 |
| Fiji | 70,043 | Norway | 3,782,346 | Zambia | 70,043 |
| Finland | 3,502,173 | Oman | 140,087 | Zimbabwe | 140,087 |
| France | 44,617,669 | Pakistan | 420,261 | **TOTAL** | **735,608,914** |
| Gabon | 210,130 | | | | |

## United Nations Headquarters

The first regular session of the General Assembly held at Central Hall, Westminster, London, voted that interim headquarters of the Organization should be located in New York. From London the U.N. moved to Hunter College in the Bronx. In August 1946, an interim headquarters was set up at Lake Success on Long Island. The New York City building at Flushing Meadows, site of the 1939 World's Fair, was converted for the use of the General Assembly. The search for a permanent home ended in December 1946, when the General Assembly accepted an offer from John D. Rockefeller, Jr., of $8,500,000[1] for the purchase of the present Headquarters site—an 18-acre tract in Manhattan, alongside the East River. The U.S. Government lent the U.N. $65,000,000 interest free, which is being repaid in annual installments.

Architectural plans drawn up by an international Board of Design were approved by the Assembly, and construction began in September 1948. By mid-1950, the 39-story Secretariat Building was ready for occupancy, and in the spring of 1951 "United Nations, New York" became the Organization's permanent address.

1. This amount paid for two-thirds of the land; New York City gave one-third.

# Preamble of the United Nations Charter

The Charter of the United Nations was adopted at the San Francisco Conference of 1945. The complete text may be obtained by writing to the United Nations Sales Section, United Nations, New York, N.Y. 10017, and enclosing $1.

We the peoples of the United Nations determined to save succeeding generations from the scourge of war, which twice in our lifetime has brought untold sorrow to mankind, and

To reaffirm faith in fundamental human rights, in the dignity and worth of the human person, in the equal rights of men and women and of nations large and small, and

To establish conditions under which justice and respect for the obligations arising from treaties and other sources of international law can be maintained, and

To promote social progress and better standards of life in larger freedom, and for these ends

To practice tolerance and live together in peace with one another as good neighbors, and

To unite our strength to maintain international peace and security, and

To insure, by the acceptance of principles and the institution of methods, that armed force shall not be used, save in the common interest, and

To employ international machinery for the promotion of the economic and social advancement of all peoples, have resolved to combine our efforts to accomplish these aims.

Accordingly, our respective Governments, through representatives assembled in the city of San Francisco, who have exhibited their full powers found to be in good and due form, have agreed to the present Charter of the United Nations and do hereby establish an international organization to be known as the United Nations.

# Principal Organs of the United Nations

## Secretariat

This is the directorate on U.N. operations, apart from political decisions. All members contribute to its upkeep. Its staff of over 6,000 specialists is recruited from member nations on the basis of as wide a geographical distribution as possible. The staff works under the Secretary-General, whom it assists and advises.

### Secretaries-General

Javier Pérez de Cuéllar, Peru, Jan. 1, 1982.
Kurt Waldheim, Austria, Jan. 1, 1972, to Dec. 31, 1981.
U Thant, Burma, Nov. 3, 1961, to Dec. 31, 1971.
Dag Hammarskjöld, Sweden, April 11, 1953, to Sept. 17, 1961.
Trygve Lie, Norway, Feb. 1, 1946, to April 10, 1953.

## General Assembly

The General Assembly is the world's forum for discussing matters affecting world peace and security, and for making recommendations concerning them. It has no power of its own to enforce decisions.

The Assembly is composed of the 51 original member nations and those admitted since, a total of 159. Each nation has one vote. On important questions including international peace and security, a two-thirds majority of those present and voting is required. Decisions on other questions are made by a simple majority.

The Assembly's agenda can be as broad as the Charter. It can make recommendations to member nations, the Security Council, or both. Emphasis is given on questions relating to international peace and security brought before it by any member, the Security Council, or nonmembers.

The Assembly also maintains a broad program of international cooperation in economic, social, cultural, educational, and health fields, and for assisting in human rights and freedoms.

Among other duties, the Assembly has functions relating to the trusteeship system, and considers and approves the U.N. Budget. Every member contributes to operating expenses according to its means.

## Security Council

The Security Council is the primary instrument for establishing and maintaining international peace. Its main purpose is to prevent war by settling disputes between nations.

Under the Charter, the Council is permitted to dispatch a U.N. force to stop aggression. All member nations undertake to make available armed forces, assistance, and facilities to maintain international peace and security.

Any member may bring a dispute before the Security Council or the General Assembly. Any nonmember may do so if it accepts the charter obligations of pacific settlement.

The Security Council has 15 members. There are five permanent members: the United States, the Soviet Union, Britain, France, and China; and 10 temporary members elected by the General Assembly for two-year terms, from five different regions of the world.

Voting on procedural matters requires a nine-vote majority to carry. However, on questions of substance, the vote of each of the five permanent members is required.

Current temporary members are (term expires Dec. 31, 1986): Australia, Denmark, Madagascar, Thailand, Trinidad and Tobago. (term expires Dec. 31, 1987): Bulgaria, Congo, Ghana, United Arab Emirates, Venezuela.

## Economic and Social Council

This council is composed of 54 members elected by the General Assembly to 3-year terms. It works closely with the General Assembly as a link with groups formed within the U.N. to help peoples in such fields as education, health, and human rights. It insures that there is no overlapping and sets up commissions to deal with economic conditions and collect facts and figures on conditions over the world. It issues studies and reports and may make recommendations to the Assembly and specialized agencies.

### Functional Commissions

Statistical Commission; Population Commission; Commission for Social Development; Commission on Human Rights; Commission on the Status of Women; Commission on Narcotic Drugs.

## Regional Commissions

Economic Commission for Europe (ECE); Economic and Social Commission for Asia and the Pacific (ESCAP); Economic Commission for Latin America and the Caribbean (ECLAC); Economic Commission for Africa (ECA); Economic and Social Commission for Western Asia (ESCWA).

## Trusteeship Council

This council supervises territories administered by various nations and placed under an international trusteeship system by the United Nations. Each nation is charged with developing the self-government of the territory and preserving and advancing the cultural, political, economic, and other forms of welfare of the people.

The Trusteeship Council is currently composed of 5 members: 1 member—the United States—that administers a trust territory, and 4 members—China, France, the Soviet Union, and the United Kingdom—that are permanent members of the Security Council but do not administer trust territories.

The following countries ceased to be administering members because of the independence of territories they had administered: Italy and France in 1960, Belgium in 1962, New Zealand and the United Kingdom in 1968 and Australia in 1975. France and the U.K. became nonadministering members.

As of December 1985, there was only one trust territory: the Trust Territory of the Pacific Islands (administered by the United States).

## International Court of Justice

The International Court of Justice sits at The Hague, the Netherlands. Its 15-judge bench was established to hear disputes among states, which must agree to accept its verdicts. Its judges, charged with administering justice under international law, deal with cases ranging from disputes over territory to those concerning rights of passage.

Following are the members of the Court and the years in which their terms expire:

President: Nagendra Singh, India (1991)
Vice President: Guy Ladreit de Lacharriere, France (1991)
Jose Sette Camara, Brazil (1988)
Nikolai Tarasov, U.S.S.R. (1988)
Roberto Ago, Italy (1988)
Stephen Schwebel, U.S. (1988)
Mohammed Bedjaoui, Algeria (1988)
Jose Maria Ruda, Argentina (1991)
Robert Y. Jennings, United Kingdom (1991)
Keba Mbaye, Senegal (1991)
Taslim Olawale Elias, Nigeria (1994)
Jens Evensen, Norway (1994)
Ni Zhengyu, China (1994)
Manfred Lachs, Poland (1994)
Shigeru Oda, Japan (1994)

## Agencies of the United Nations

### INTL. ATOMIC ENERGY AGENCY (IAEA)

**Established:** Statute for IAEA, approved on Oct. 26, 1956, at a conference held at U.N. Headquarters, New York, came into force on July 29, 1957. The Agency is under the aegis of the U.N., but unlike the following, it is not a specialized agency.

**Purpose:** To promote the peaceful uses of atomic energy; to ensure that assistance provided by it or at its request or under its supervision or control is not used in such a way as to further any military

purpose.

**Headquarters:** Vienna International Center, P.O. Box 100, A-1400 Vienna, Austria

### FOOD AND AGRICULTURE ORGANIZATION OF THE UNITED NATIONS (FAO)

**Established:** October 16, 1945, when constitution became effective.

**Purpose:** To raise nutrition levels and living standards; to secure improvements in production and distribution of food and agricultural products.

**Headquarters:** Via delle Terme di Caracalla, 00100, Rome, Italy.

### GENERAL AGREEMENT ON TARIFFS AND TRADE (GATT)

**Established:** Jan. 1, 1948.

**Purpose:** An International Trade Organization (ITO) was originally planned. Although this agency has not materialized, some of its objectives have been embodied in an international commercial treaty, the General Agreement on Tariffs and Trade. Its purpose is to sponsor trade negotiations.

**Headquarters:** Centre William Rappard, 154 Rue de Lausanne, 1211, Geneva 21, Switzerland.

### INTERNATIONAL BANK FOR RECONSTRUCTION AND DEVELOPMENT (IBRD) (WORLD BANK)

**Established:** December 27, 1945, when Articles of Agreement drawn up at Bretton Woods Conference in July 1944 came into force. Began operations on June 25, 1946.

**Purpose:** To assist in reconstruction and development of economies of members by facilitating capital investment and by making loans to governments and furnishing technical advice.

**Headquarters:** 1818 H St., N.W., Washington, D.C. 20433.

### INTL. CIVIL AVIATION ORGANIZATION (ICAO)

**Established:** April 4, 1947, after working as a provisional organization since June 1945.

**Purpose:** To study problems of international civil aviation; to establish international standards and regulations; to promote safety measures, uniform regulations for operation, simpler procedures at international borders, and the use of new technical methods and equipment. It has evolved standards for meteorological services, traffic control, communications, radio beacons and ranges, search and rescue organization, and other facilities. It has brought about much simplification of customs, immigration, and public health regulations as they apply to international air transport. It drafts international air law conventions, and is concerned with economic aspects of air travel.

**Headquarters:** International Aviation Square, 1000 Sherbrooke St. West, Montreal, Quebec, H3A 2R2, Canada.

### INTL. DEVELOPMENT ASSOCIATION (IDA)

**Established:** Sept. 24, 1960. An affiliate of the World Bank, IDA has the same officers and staff as the Bank.

**Purpose:** To further economic development of its members by providing finance on terms which bear less heavily on balance of payments of members than those of conventional loans.

**Headquarters:** 1818 H St., N.W., Washington, D.C. 20433.

### INTERNATIONAL FINANCE CORPORATION (IFC)

**Established:** Charter of IFC came into force on July 20, 1956. Although IFC is affiliated with the World Bank, it is a separate legal entity, and its funds are entirely separate from those of the Bank. However, membership in the Corporation is open only to Bank members.

**Purpose:** To further economic development by encouraging the growth of productive private enterprise in its member countries, particularly in the less developed areas; to invest in productive private enterprises in association with private investors, without government guarantee of repayment where sufficient private capital is not available on reasonable terms; to serve as a clearing house to bring together investment opportunities, private capital (both foreign and domestic), and experienced management.

**Headquarters:** 1818 H St., N.W., Washington, D.C. 20433.

## INTERNATIONAL FUND FOR AGRICULTURAL DEVELOPMENT (IFAD)

**Established:** June 18, 1976. Began operations in December 1977.

**Purpose:** To mobilize additional funds for agricultural and rural development in developing countries through projects and programs directly benefiting the poorest rural populations.

**Headquarters:** 107 Via del Serafico, 00142, Rome, Italy.

## INTERNATIONAL LABOR ORGANIZATION (ILO)

**Established:** April 11, 1919, when constitution was adopted as Part XIII of Treaty of Versailles. Became specialized agency of U.N. in 1946.

**Purpose:** To contribute to establishment of lasting peace by promoting social justice; to improve labor conditions and living standards through international action; to promote economic and social stability. The U.S. withdrew from the ILO in 1977 and resumed membership in 1980.

**Headquarters:** 4, route des Morillons, CH-1211 Geneva 22, Switzerland.

## INTERNATIONAL MARITIME ORGANIZATION (IMO)

**Established:** March 17, 1958.

**Purpose:** To give advisory and consultative help to promote international cooperation in maritime navigation and to encourage the highest standards of safety and navigation. Its aim is to bring about a uniform system of measuring ship tonnage; systems now vary widely in different parts of the world. Other activities include cooperation with other U.N. agencies on matters affecting the maritime field.

**Headquarters:** 4 Albert Embankment, London SE 1 7SR England.

## INTERNATIONAL MONETARY FUND (IMF)

**Established:** Dec. 27, 1945, when Articles of Agreement drawn up at Bretton Woods Conference in July 1944 came into force. Fund began operations on March 1, 1947.

**Purpose:** To promote international monetary cooperation and expansion of international trade; to promote exchange stability; to assist in establishment of multilateral system of payments in respect of currency transactions between members.

**Headquarters:** 700 19th St., N.W., Washington, D.C. 20431.

## INTERNATIONAL TELECOMMUNICATION UNION (ITU)

**Established:** 1865. Became specialized agency of U.N. in 1947.

**Purpose:** To extend technical assistance to help members keep up with present day telecommunication needs; to standardize communications equipment and procedures; to lower costs. It also works for orderly sharing of radio frequencies and makes studies and recommendations to benefit its members.

**Headquarters:** Place des Nations, 1211 Geneva 20, Switzerland.

## UNITED NATIONS EDUCATIONAL, SCIENTIFIC, AND CULTURAL ORGANIZATION (UNESCO)

**Established:** Nov. 4, 1946, when twentieth signatory to constitution deposited instrument of acceptance with government of U.K.

**Purpose:** To promote collaboration among nations through education, science, and culture in order to further justice, rule of law, and human rights and freedoms without distinction of race, sex, language, or religion.

**Headquarters:** UNESCO House. Place de Fontenoy, 7e, Paris, France.

## UNITED NATIONS INDUSTRIAL DEVELOPMENT ORGANIZATION (UNIDO)

**Established:** Nov. 17, 1966. Became specialized agency of the U.N. in 1985.

**Purpose:** To promote and accelerate the industrialization of the developing countries.

**Headquarters:** UNIDO, Vienna International Centre, P.O. Box 300, A-1400 Vienna, Austria.

## UNIVERSAL POSTAL UNION (UPU)

**Established:** Oct. 9, 1874. Became specialized agency of U.N. in 1947.

**Purpose:** To facilitate reciprocal exchange of correspondence by uniform procedures by all UPU members; to help governments modernize and speed up mailing procedures.

**Headquarters:** Case Postale 3000 Berne 15, Switzerland.

## WORLD HEALTH ORGANIZATION (WHO)

**Established:** April 7, 1948, when 26 members of the U.N. had accepted its constitution, adopted July 22, 1946, by the International Health Conference in New York City.

**Purpose:** To aid attainment by all people of highest possible level of health.

**Headquarters:** Palais des Nations, 1211 Geneva, Switzerland.

## WORLD INTELLECTUAL PROPERTY ORGANIZATION (WIPO)

**Established:** April 26, 1970, when its Convention came into force. Originated as International Bureau of Paris Union (1883) and Berne Union (1886), later succeeded by United International Bureau for the Protection of Intellectual Property (BIRPI). Became a specialized agency of the U.N. in December 1974.

**Purpose:** To promote legal protection of intellectual property, including artistic and scientific works, artistic performances, sound recordings, broadcasts, inventions, trademarks, industrial designs, and commercial names.

**Headquarters:** 32 Chemin des Colombettes, 1211 Geneva 20, Switzerland.

## WORLD METEOROLOGICAL ORGANIZATION (WMO)

**Established:** March 23, 1950, succeeding the International Meteorological Organization, a nongovernmental organization founded in 1878.

**Purpose:** To promote international exchange of weather reports and maximum standardization of observations; to help developing countries establish weather services for their own economic needs; to fill gaps in observation stations; to promote meteorological investigations affecting jet aircraft, satellites, energy resources, etc.

**Headquarters:** 41 Avenue Giuseppe Motta, Geneva, Switzerland.

# MEDIA

## Leading Magazines: United States and Canada

| Magazine | Circulation[1] | Magazine | Circulation[1] |
|---|---|---|---|
| American Health—Fitness of Body & Mind | 792,851 | 1,001 Home Ideas | 1,545,959 |
| Better Homes and Gardens | 8,060,065 | Outdoor Life | 1,514,375 |
| Better Homes and Gardens—Country Home | 783,498 | Parents | 1,729,853 |
| Bon Appetit | 1,300,834 | Penthouse | 3,172,898 |
| Business Week (North America) | 781,810 | People Weekly | 2,970,920 |
| Car and Driver | 900,951 | Playboy | 4,151,324 |
| Changing Times, The Kiplinger Magazine | 1,414,710 | Popular Mechanics | 1,648,058 |
| Chatelaine | 1,098,580 | Popular Photography | 883,044 |
| Cosmopolitan | 3,022,790 | Popular Science | 1,816,139 |
| Country Living | 1,520,381 | Prevention | 2,875,314 |
| Creative Ideas for Living | 757,657 | Psychology Today | 884,224 |
| Discover | 920,676 | Reader's Digest | 17,657,011 |
| Ebony | 1,751,255 | Reader's Digest (Canadian English Edition) | 1,341,394 |
| Essence | 800,248 | Redbook | 4,094,010 |
| Family Circle | 6,661,956 | Rodale's Organic Gardening | 1,221,850 |
| The Family Handyman | 1,206,908 | Rolling Stone | 1,058,027 |
| Field & Stream | 2,008,350 | Self | 1,077,090 |
| Glamour | 2,300,807 | Seventeen | 1,750,513 |
| Globe | 1,723,777 | Smithsonian | 2,240,910 |
| Golf (Incorporating Golfing) | 811,311 | Southern Living | 2,318,824 |
| Golf Digest | 1,228,428 | Sport | 931,893 |
| Good Housekeeping | 5,157,262 | Sports Illustrated | 2,751,360 |
| Gourmet | 991,026 | Star | 3,539,512 |
| Harper's Bazaar | 769,379 | Sunset, The Magazine of Western Living | 1,407,880 |
| Health | 1,029,909 | 'Teen | 1,076,214 |
| Home Mechanix | 1,332,775 | Time | 4,603,307 |
| Hot Rod | 847,055 | Travel and Leisure | 985,499 |
| House Beautiful | 838,464 | Traveler | 995,103 |
| Jet | 819,874 | True Story | 1,523,268 |
| Ladies' Home Journal | 5,235,044 | TV Guide | 16,898,697 |
| Life | 1,512,660 | TV Guide (Canada) | 802,982 |
| McCall's | 6,312,403 | U.S. News & World Report | 2,083,882 |
| Mademoiselle | 1,236,392 | US | 949,086 |
| Money | 1,691,463 | Vogue | 1,179,339 |
| Motor Trend | 781,262 | Weekly World News | 1,047,629 |
| Nation's Business | 868,436 | Weight Watchers Magazine | 874,741 |
| National Enquirer | 4,552,047 | Woman's Day | 6,194,031 |
| National Examiner | 1,101,622 | The Workbasket | 1,742,798 |
| National Geographic | 10,549,349 | Workbench | 875,837 |
| New Woman | 1,219,098 | Yankee | 1,008,581 |
| Newsweek | 3,057,081 | Young Miss | 788,106 |
| Omni | 860,990 | | |

1. Average total paid circulation for the six-month period ending December 31, 1985. The table lists magazines with combined newsstand and subscription circulation of over 750,000. *Source:* Audit Bureau of Circulations. Publishers' Statements for six-month period ending December 31, 1985.

## Major U.S. Daily Newspapers[1]

| City and newspaper | Net paid circulation | | | |
|---|---|---|---|---|
| | Morning[2] | All-Day[2] | Evening[2] | Sunday |
| Akron, Ohio: *Beacon Journal* | — | | 154,652 | 227,261 |
| Albany, N.Y.: *Times-Union* (M & S); *Knickerbocker News* (E) | 86,707 | | 31,523[3] | 171,287 |
| Albuquerque, N.M.: *Journal* (M & S); *Tribune* (E) | 101,075[4] | | 45,905[4] | 140,635[4] |
| Allentown, Pa.: *Call* (M & S) | 130,724 | | — | 172,442 |
| Amarillo, Tex.: *News* (M); *Globe-Times* (E); *News-Globe* (S) | 44,810 | | 27,472[3] | 77,721 |
| Asbury Park, N.J.: *Press* | — | | 129,839 | 192,887 |
| Atlanta: *Constitution* (M); *Journal* (E); *Journal and Constitution* (S) | 251,042[3] | | 187,816[3] | 614,578 |
| Atlantic City, N.J.: *Press* | 78,222 | | — | 87,197 |
| Augusta, Ga.: *Chronicle* (M); *Herald* (E); *Chronicle—Herald* (S) | 63,032[3] | | 18,309[3] | 85,781 |

290

| City and newspaper | Morning[2] | All-Day[2] | Evening[2] | Sunday |
|---|---|---|---|---|
| Austin, Tex.: *American-Statesman* | — | 165,643[3] | — | 201,391 |
| Bakersfield, Calif.: *Californian* | 81,384[4] | — | — | 88,084[4] |
| Baltimore: *Sun* | 204,774[3] | — | 152,153[3] | 427,785 |
| *News American*[7] | — | — | 100,389[3] | 137,600 |
| Bangor, Me.: *News* | 77,502[3] | — | — | 91,488[5] |
| Baton Rouge, La.: *Advocate* (M & S); *State-Times* (E) | 85,108 | — | 35,495 | 139,246 |
| Bergen County (Hackensack), N.J.: *Record* (E); | | | | |
| *Sunday Record* | — | — | 161,969[3][4] | 227,205[4] |
| Beaumont, Tex.: *Enterprise* | 68,659 | — | — | 77,982 |
| Binghamton, N.Y.: *Press & Sun-Bulletin* (M & S) | 66,524 | — | — | 86,583 |
| Birmingham, Ala.: *Post-Herald* (M); *News* (E & S) | 61,877[3] | — | 169,922[3] | 213,264 |
| Boston: *Globe* | 514,097[3] | — | — | 811,149 |
| *Herald* | 358,725[3] | — | — | 282,357 |
| *Christian Science Monitor* | 156,720[3] | — | — | — |
| Bridgeport, Conn: *Telegram* (M); *Post* (E); *Sunday Post* | 18,460[3][4] | — | 64,352[3][4] | 91,665[4] |
| Buffalo, N.Y.: *News* | — | 317,024[3] | — | 370,748 |
| Camden, N.J.: *Courier-Post* | — | — | 108,360[3][4] | 101,065[4] |
| Canton, Ohio: *Repository* | — | — | 58,103[4] | 77,281[4] |
| Cedar Rapids, Iowa: *Gazette* | 70,256 | — | — | 81,147 |
| Charleston, S.C.: *News & Courier* (M); | | | | |
| *Evening Post; News & Courier Post* (S) | 72,852[3] | — | 38,630[3] | 117,712 |
| Charleston, W. Va.: *Gazette* (M); *Daily Mail* (E); | | | | |
| *Gazette-Mail* (S) | 55,040 | — | 53,450 | 108,747 |
| Charlotte, N.C.: *Observer* (M & S); *News* (E) | 192,977[8] | — | 35,293[3][8] | 263,124 |
| Chattanooga, Tenn.: *Times* (M); *News-Free Press* (E & S) | 46,963[3] | — | 56,546[3] | 108,859 |
| Chicago: *Tribune* | 760,031[3] | — | — | 1,163,083 |
| *Sun-Times* | 631,808[3] | — | — | 663,616 |
| *Daily Herald* (M); *Sunday Herald* | 73,019 | — | — | 72,082 |
| Cincinnati: *Enquirer* (M & S); *Post* (E) | 190,686 | — | 120,252 | 316,543 |
| Cleveland: *Plain Dealer* | 454,042[3] | — | — | 549,580 |
| Cocoa, Fla.: *Today* | 68,342 | — | — | 89,169 |
| Colorado Springs, Colo.: *Gazette Telegraph* | 69,481[3] | — | 37,967[3] | 114,457 |
| Columbia, S.C.: *State* (M & S); *Record* (E) | 117,978 | — | 30,698 | 152,868 |
| Columbus, Ohio: *Citizen-Journal* (M); *Dispatch* (E & S) | 115,167[4] | — | 199,011[4] | 371,530 |
| Corpus Christi, Tex.: *Caller* (M); *Times* (E); *Caller-Times* (S) | 62,647[3][4] | — | 22,853[3][4] | 93,497[4] |
| Dallas: *News* | 390,275 | — | — | 521,727 |
| *Times Herald* | — | 244,629 | — | 348,084 |
| *Wall Street Journal* (Southwest edition) | 224,050[3] | — | — | — |
| Davenport, Iowa: *Quad City Times* | — | 59,752 | — | 83,578 |
| Dayton, Ohio: *Journal Herald* (M); *News* (E & S) | 104,657 | — | 113,661 | 226,980 |
| Daytona Beach, Fla.: *Journal* (M); *News* (E); *News-Journal* (S) | 70,399 | — | 30,336[3] | 95,454 |
| Denver: *Post* | 220,861 | — | — | 412,102 |
| *Rocky Mountain News* | 320,441 | — | — | 378,133 |
| Des Moines, Iowa: *Register* | 227,796 | — | — | 370,558 |
| Detroit: *News* | — | 650,445[3] | — | 832,365 |
| *Free Press* | 645,266[3] | — | — | 744,494 |
| Duluth, Minn.: *News-Tribune & Herald* | 62,440 | — | — | 82,112 |
| Erie, Pa.: *News* (M); *Times* (E); *Times-News* (S) | 28,279[3] | — | 43,813[3] | 102,910 |
| El Paso, Tex.: *Times* (M & S); *Herald-Post* (E) | 56,846[4] | — | 31,761[4] | 88,847[4] |
| Evansville, Ind.: *Courier* (M); *Press* (E); *Courier & Press* (S) | 63,335 | — | 39,559 | 115,135 |
| Flint, Mich.: *Journal* | — | — | 108,611[3] | 120,145 |
| Fort Lauderdale, Fla.: *Sun-Sentinel* (M); *News* (E); | | | | |
| *News & Sun-Sentinel* (S) | 155,197[3] | — | 76,992[3] | 288,916 |
| Fort Myers, Fla.: *News-Press* | 82,400 | — | — | 101,128 |
| Fort Wayne, Ind.: *Journal-Gazette* (M & S); *News-Sentinel* (E) | 58,666[4] | — | 57,254[4] | 131,451[4] |
| Fort Worth: *Star-Telegram* | 125,674[3] | — | 129,533[3] | 303,776 |
| Fresno, Calif.: *Bee* | 139,213[4] | — | — | 166,943[4] |
| Gary, Ind.: *Post-Tribune* | — | — | 72,833 | 88,057 |
| Grand Rapids, Mich.: *Press* | — | — | 139,713 | 183,689 |
| Greensboro, N.C.: *News* (M); *Record* (E); *News & Record* (S) | 93,911[3][10] | — | 18,110[3][10] | 127,543 |
| Greensburg, Pa.: *Tribune-Review* | 52,210 | — | — | 79,911 |
| Greenville, S.C.: *News* (M); *Piedmont* (E); *News & Piedmont* (S) | 86,787[3] | — | 24,950[3] | 126,095 |
| Harrisburg, Pa.: *Patriot* (M); *Evening News;* | | | | |
| *Sunday Patriot News* | 51,123[3] | — | 55,045[3] | 167,646 |
| Hartford, Conn.: *Courant* | 220,718 | — | — | 299,893 |
| Honolulu: *Advertiser* (M); *Star-Bulletin* (E); | | | | |
| *Star-Bulletin & Advertiser* (S) | 86,875 | — | 102,151 | 197,887 |

| City and newspaper | Net paid circulation | | | |
|---|---|---|---|---|
| | Morning[2] | All-Day[2] | Evening[2] | Sunday |
| Houston: *Chronicle* | — | 425,434[3] | — | 528,153 |
| Post | 316,209 | — | — | 373,573 |
| Indianapolis: *Star* (M & S); *News* (E) | 225,759[4] | — | 128,387[4] | 394,643[4] |
| Jackson, Miss.: *Clarion-Ledger* (M); *Daily News* (E); *Clarion Ledger-Daily News* (S) | 69,060[3] | | 33,160[3] | 115,940 |
| Jacksonville, Fla.: *Florida Times-Union* (M); *Journal* (E); *Times-Union & Journal* (S) | 162,105[3] | | 42,693[3] | 224,785 |
| Kalamazoo, Mich.: *Gazette* | — | | 63,798 | 75,919 |
| Kansas City, Mo.: *Times* (M); *Star* (E & S) | 277,051 | | 226,895[3] | 402,261 |
| Knoxville, Tenn.: *Journal* (M); *News-Sentinel* (E & S) | 60,574 | | 93,799 | 164,626 |
| Lakeland, Fla.: *Ledger* | 73,573[4] | | — | 92,368[4] |
| Lancaster, Pa.: *Intelligencer-Journal* (M); *New Era* (E); *News* (S) | 43,921[4] | | 57,206[4] | 97,602[4] |
| Lansing, Mich.: *State-Journal* | 67,170 | | — | 81,838 |
| Las Vegas, Nev.: *Review-Journal* | — | 105,478[3] | — | 122,090 |
| Sun | 62,613 | | — | 80,917 |
| Lexington, Ky.: *Herald-Leader* | 110,411 | | — | 134,468 |
| Lincoln, Neb.: *Star* (M); *Journal* (E); *Journal & Star* (S) | 36,749 | | 43,996 | 79,052 |
| Little Rock, Ark.: *Arkansas Gazette* | 125,383 | | — | 160,493 |
| *Arkansas Democrat* | 83,330 | | — | 155,516 |
| Long Beach, Calif.: *Press-Telegram* | 125,299[3] | | 3,385[3] | 136,748 |
| Long Island (Melville), N.Y.: *Newsday* | — | | 582,388[3] | 647,479 |
| Los Angeles: *Times* | 1,088,155[3] | | — | 1,353,376 |
| *Herald-Examiner* | 245,291[3] | | — | 205,331 |
| *Daily News* | 148,133[3] | | — | 161,142 |
| Louisville, Ky.: *Courier-Journal* (M & S); *Times* (E) | 170,721 | | 125,244 | 323,328 |
| Lubbock, Tex.: *Avalanche-Journal* (M & S); *Journal* (E) | 58,981[3] | | 13,066[3] | 77,538 |
| Macon, Ga.: *Telegraph and News* (M & S) | 71,921 | | — | 96,623 |
| Madison, Wis.: *State Journal* (M & S); *Capital Times* (E) | 77,559[3] | | 28,658[3] | 144,847 |
| Memphis, Tenn.: *Commercial Appeal* | 225,674 | | — | 295,412 |
| Miami, Fla.: *Herald* (M & S); *News* (E) | 458,759 | | 58,387 | 559,758 |
| Middletown, N.Y.: *Times Herald-Record* (M); *Sunday Record* | 77,787 | | — | 88,982 |
| Milwaukee: *Sentinel* (M); *Journal* (E & S) | 188,359 | | 294,502 | 514,549 |
| Minneapolis: *Star & Tribune* (M); *Tribune* (S) | 382,499 | | — | 612,604 |
| Mobile, Ala.: *Register* (M); *Press* (E); *Press-Register* (S) | 53,391[3][4] | | 48,565[3][4] | 107,076[4] |
| Modesto, Calif.: *Bee* | 74,260[4] | | — | 80,980[4] |
| Montgomery, Ala. *Advertiser* (M); *Journal* (E); *Journal & Advertise* (S) | 51,754[3] | | 20,713[3] | 85,569 |
| Naperville, Ill.: *Wall Street Journal* (Midwest edition) | 552,258[3] | — | — | — |
| Nashville, Tenn.: *Tennessean* (M & S); *Banner* (E) | 68,930 | | 120,825 | 255,729 |
| New Brunswick, N.J.: *Home News* | — | | 59,341 | 77,698 |
| New Haven, Conn.: *Journal-Courier* (M); *Register* (E & S) | 37,733[3] | | 90,393 | 140,776 |
| New Orleans: *Times-Picayune/States-Item* | — | 280,889[3][4] | — | 351,575[4] |
| New York: *News* | 1,275,268[3] | | — | 1,676,858 |
| *Times* | 1,035,426[3] | | — | 1,625,649 |
| *Post* | — | 751,798[3] | — | — |
| *Wall Street Journal* (Eastern edition) | 792,550[3] | | — | — |
| National edition | 1,985,559[3] | | — | — |
| *Women's Wear Daily* | 64,278[3] | | — | — |
| Newark, N.J.: *Star-Ledger* | 452,148[3][4] | | — | 682,469[4] |
| Newport News—Hampton, Va.: *Press* (M & S); *Times Herald* (E) | 65,181[3][4] | | 36,734[3][4] | 111,638[4] |
| Norfolk-Portsmouth-Virginia Beach-Chesapeake, Va.: *Virginian-Pilot* (M); *Ledger-Star* (E); *Virginian-Pilot/Ledger-Star* (S) | 143,526[3][4] | | 83,764[3][4] | 227,518[4] |
| Oakland, Calif.: *Tribune* (M & S) | 152,211[3] | | — | 157,169 |
| Oklahoma City: *Oklahoman* (M & S) | 239,404[3] | | — | 328,734 |
| Omaha, Neb.: *World Herald* | 118,752[3] | | 102,128[3] | 284,255 |
| Orange County (Santa Ana), Calif.: *Register* | — | 300,985[3] | — | 340,427 |
| Orlando, Fla.: *Sentinel* | — | 263,865[3] | — | 330,251 |
| Palo Alto, Calif.: *Wall Street Journal* (Western edition) | 416,701[3] | | — | — |
| *Peninsula Times Tribune* | — | | 55,264 | 60,343 |
| Peoria, Ill.: *Journal Star* | — | 100,189 | — | 115,235 |
| Philadelphia: *Inquirer* (M & S); *Daily News* (E) | 492,374[3] | | 251,876[3] | 984,569 |
| Phoenix, Ariz.: *Republic* (M & S); *Gazette* (E) | 331,491[4] | | 112,976[4] | 508,008[4] |
| Pittsburgh: *Post-Gazette* (M); *Press* (E & S) | 173,482[3] | | 239,849[3] | 579,910 |
| Pontiac, Mich.: *Press* (E) | — | | 71,693[3] | 79,062 |
| Portland, Me.: *Press-Herald* (M); *Express* (E) | 59,559 | | 26,697 | — |
| *Maine Sunday Telegram* | — | | — | 134,713 |

| City and newspaper | Net paid circulation | | | |
|---|---|---|---|---|
| | Morning[2] | All-Day[2] | Evening[2] | Sunday |
| Portland, Ore.: *Oregonian* | — | 335,162[3] | — | 407,829 |
| Providence, R.I.: *Journal* (M & S); *Bulletin* (E) | 88,607[3] | | 119,310[3] | 258,081 |
| Quincy, Mass.: *Patriot-Ledger* | — | | 90,865[3,4] | 95,540[4,6] |
| Raleigh, N.C.: *News & Observer* (M & S); *Times* (E) | 137,511[4] | | 35,240[4] | 177,707[4] |
| Reading, Pa.: *Times* (M); *Eagle* (E & S) | 45,949 | | 36,620 | 113,715 |
| Richmond, Va.: *Times-Dispatch* (M & S); *News-Leader* (E) | 139,909 | | 111,156 | 240,182 |
| Riverside, Calif.: *Press-Enterprise* (M & S) | 134,540 | | — | 140,132 |
| Roanoke, Va.: *Times & World-News* | 78,386[3] | | 45,970[3] | 126,766 |
| Rochester, N.Y.: *Democrat & Chronicle* (M & S); *Times-Union* (E) | 127,618[3] | | 99,350[3] | 257,969 |
| Rockford, Ill.: *Register Star* | 70,084 | | | 86,597 |
| Sacramento, Calif.: *Bee* | 235,991 | | — | 273,912 |
|   Union | 94,097 | | — | 92,860 |
| St. Louis: *Post-Dispatch* | 318,587[3] | | — | 519,505 |
|   Globe-Democrat | 134,567[3,9] | | — | 119,471[5,9] |
| St. Paul: *Pioneer Press* (M & S); *Dispatch* (E) | | 186,927[3] | | 244,218 |
| St. Petersburg, Fla.: *Times* (M & S); *Independent* (E) | 315,698[4] | | 39,998[4] | 480,095[4] |
| Salt Lake City, Utah: *Tribune* (M & S); | 112,844 | | — | 137,358 |
|   Deseret News (E & S) | — | | 64,592 | 71,967 |
| San Antonio: *Express News* | | 168,098[3] | — | 229,863 |
|   Light | | 142,050[3] | — | 206,026 |
| San Bernardino, Calif.: *Sun* | 82,229 | | — | 86,169 |
| San Diego, Calif.: *Union* (M & S); *Tribune* (E) | 367,728[4] | | 124,724[4] | 391,100[4] |
| San Francisco: *Chronicle* (M); *Examiner* (E); | | | | |
|   Examiner & Chronicle (S) | 554,611[3] | | 150,017[3] | 711,560 |
| San Gabriel Valley, Calif.: *Tribune* (M); *Tribune-News* (S) | 61,826 | | — | 79,631 |
|   Transcript | 8,210[3,4] | | — | — |
| San Jose, Calif.: *Mercury-News* | | 262,922[3] | — | 310,685 |
| Santa Rosa, Calif.: *Press Democrat* | 76,828 | | — | 86,025 |
| Sarasota, Fla.: *Herald-Tribune* (M & S) | 121,141[4] | | — | 145,326[4] |
| Seattle: *Post-Intelligencer* (M); *Times* (E); combined (S) | 202,305[3] | | 230,509[3] | 490,105 |
| Shreveport, La.: *Times* (M & S); *Journal* (E) | 76,636[4] | | 22,847[4] | 109,647[4] |
| South Bend-Mishawake, Ind.: *Tribune* | — | | 95,496 | 124,438 |
| Spokane, Wash.: *Spokesman-Review* (M & S); *Daily Chronicle* (E) | 80,375[3] | | 38,628[3] | 135,233 |
| Springfield, Mass.: *Union* (M); *News* (E); *Republican* (S) | 68,893 | | 65,514 | 155,147 |
| Springfield, Mo.: *News* (M); *Leader & Press* (E); | | | | |
|   News & Leader (S) | 34,577[3,4] | | 25,736[3,4] | 91,653[4] |
| Staten Island, N.Y.: *Advance* (E&S) | — | | 74,898[3] | 84,927 |
| Syracuse, N.Y.: *Post-Standard* (M); *Herald-Journal* (E); | | | | |
|   Herald-American (S) | 84,877 | | 101,980 | 232,617 |
| Tacoma, Wash.: *News-Tribune* (E); *News-Tribune* (S) | — | | 107,678 | 119,150 |
| Tampa, Fla.: *Tribune* | | 228,708 | — | 307,525 |
| Toledo, Ohio: *Blade* | — | | 161,217 | 219,867 |
| Topeka, Kan.: *Capital-Journal* | 67,079 | | — | 76,905 |
| Trenton, N.J.: *Times* (M&S) | 65,505 | | — | 84,059 |
|   Trentonian (M&S) | 67,938[3] | | | 64,615 |
| Tucson, Ariz.: *Daily Star* (M & S); *Citizen* (E) | 80,356 | | 59,147 | 152,472 |
| Tulsa, Okla.: *World* (M & S); *Tribune* (E) | 136,219[4] | | 78,242[4] | 234,438[4] |
| Walnut Creek, Calif.: *Contra Costa Times* | 83,182 | | — | 88,382 |
| Washington, D.C.: *Post* | 781,371[3] | | — | 1,091,307 |
|   Times | 91,161[3] | | — | — |
|   USA Today | 1,168,222 | | — | — |
| West Covina, Calif.; *San Gabriel Valley Tribune* (M); *Tribune-News* (S) | 61,826 | | — | 79,631 |
| West Palm Beach, Fla.: *Post* (M); *Times* (E); *Post-Times* (S) | 119,162[3] | | 26,392[3] | 187,121 |
| Wichita, Kan.: *Eagle-Beacon* | 125,316 | | — | 193,722 |
| Wilmington, Del.: *News* (M); *Journal* (E); *Sunday News Journal* | 66,130[3,4] | | 54,117[3,4] | 130,072[4] |
| Winston-Salem, N.C.; *Journal* | 91,536 | | — | 100,959 |
| Worcester, Mass.: *Telegram* (M & S); *Gazette* (E) | 56,648[4] | | 82,177[4] | 127,145[4] |
| Youngstown, Ohio: *Vindicator* | — | | 97,348[4] | 152,114[4] |

1. Listing is of cities in which any one edition of a newspaper exceeds an average net paid circulation of 75,000; newspapers of smaller circulation in those cities are also included. 2. Unless otherwise indicated, figures are average Monday-through-Saturday circulation for six month period ending March 31, 1986. 3. Average Monday-through-Friday circulation. 4. Three-month average for period ending March 31, 1986. 5. Weekend edition. 6. Saturday edition. 7. Ceased publication May 27, 1986. 8. Oct. 1, 1985 to Nov. 2, 1985. 9. Two-month average for period ending March 31, 1986. 10. Oct. 1, 1985 to Feb. 9, 1986. *Source:* Audit Bureau of Circulations.

# English Language Daily and Sunday U.S. Newspapers
### (number of newspapers as of Feb. 1, 1986; circulation as reported for Sept. 30, 1985)

| State | Morning papers and circulation | | Evening papers and circulation | | Total M and E and circulation | | Sunday papers and circulation | |
|---|---|---|---|---|---|---|---|---|
| Alabama | 15 | 291,520 | 12 | 454,336 | 27 | 745,856 | 19 | 737,213 |
| Alaska | 2 | 58,654 | 6 | 78,286 | 8 | 136,940 | 4 | 142,267 |
| Arizona | 6 | 412,840 | 13 | 262,811 | 19 | 675,651 | 11 | 693,029 |
| Arkansas[1] | 9 | 301,493 | 25 | 206,588 | 33 | 508,081 | 17 | 525,432 |
| California[1] | 42 | 4,231,013 | 76 | 1,853,581 | 115 | 6,084,594 | 59 | 5,966,327 |
| Colorado | 10 | 742,192 | 19 | 212,293 | 29 | 954,485 | 11 | 1,162,377 |
| Connecticut | 8 | 438,488 | 16 | 460,877 | 24 | 899,365 | 11 | 805,771 |
| Delaware | 2 | 91,048 | 1 | 54,456 | 3 | 145,504 | 2 | 160,673 |
| District of Columbia | 3 | 2,177,466 | 0 | 0 | 3 | 2,177,466 | 1 | 1,050,009 |
| Florida[1] | 25 | 2,125,089 | 27 | 750,408 | 50 | 2,875,497 | 34 | 3,209,658 |
| Georgia | 11 | 519,650 | 25 | 552,510 | 36 | 1,072,160 | 16 | 1,151,701 |
| Hawaii | 2 | 89,980 | 4 | 147,496 | 6 | 237,476 | 5 | 244,956 |
| Idaho | 4 | 107,804 | 8 | 102,368 | 12 | 210,172 | 8 | 216,656 |
| Illinois[1] | 16 | 1,540,115 | 58 | 1,185,602 | 72 | 2,728,717 | 24 | 2,739,459 |
| Indiana | 10 | 508,269 | 64 | 1,062,065 | 74 | 1,570,334 | 19 | 1,257,309 |
| Iowa[1] | 12 | 462,777 | 27 | 315,849 | 38 | 778,626 | 11 | 763,139 |
| Kansas[1] | 7 | 269,154 | 40 | 289,149 | 46 | 558,303 | 18 | 495,700 |
| Kentucky | 5 | 331,826 | 20 | 392,785 | 25 | 724,611 | 13 | 647,954 |
| Louisiana[1] | 11 | 469,654 | 16 | 326,463 | 26 | 796,117 | 18 | 881,272 |
| Maine | 5 | 219,312 | 4 | 67,961 | 9 | 287,273 | 2 | 172,084 |
| Maryland | 8 | 370,331 | 8 | 377,295 | 16 | 747,626 | 5 | 660,722 |
| Massachusetts[1] | 7 | 1,214,431 | 39 | 912,554 | 46 | 2,126,985 | 11 | 1,724,815 |
| Michigan[1] | 11 | 1,067,982 | 42 | 1,426,610 | 52 | 2,494,592 | 15 | 2,467,644 |
| Minnesota | 10 | 641,188 | 16 | 286,040 | 26 | 927,228 | 12 | 1,032,350 |
| Mississippi | 5 | 147,298 | 19 | 256,276 | 23 | 403,574 | 12 | 329,408 |
| Missouri | 10 | 870,102 | 39 | 613,307 | 49 | 1,483,409 | 19 | 1,214,649 |
| Montana | 5 | 146,998 | 6 | 50,840 | 11 | 197,828 | 8 | 197,221 |
| Nebraska | 6 | 187,162 | 15 | 289,877 | 19 | 477,039 | 7 | 435,521 |
| Nevada[1] | 4 | 169,768 | 4 | 65,669 | 7 | 235,437 | 4 | 263,117 |
| New Hampshire | 1 | 69,965 | 8 | 143,838 | 9 | 213,803 | 3 | 107,341 |
| New Jersey | 10 | 841,726 | 16 | 860,123 | 26 | 1,701,849 | 17 | 1,820,104 |
| New Mexico | 4 | 130,479 | 16 | 162,457 | 20 | 292,936 | 13 | 266,529 |
| New York[1] | 22 | 5,694,485 | 53 | 2,145,117 | 73 | 7,839,602 | 32 | 5,687,700 |
| North Carolina | 11 | 699,636 | 43 | 687,369 | 54 | 1,387,005 | 29 | 1,301,366 |
| North Dakota[1] | 3 | 73,543 | 8 | 118,377 | 10 | 191,920 | 6 | 178,732 |
| Ohio[1] | 10 | 1,074,936 | 80 | 1,759,924 | 90 | 2,834,860 | 31 | 2,763,655 |
| Oklahoma | 8 | 457,209 | 44 | 364,938 | 52 | 822,147 | 43 | 903,958 |
| Oregon[1] | 5 | 290,461 | 16 | 346,515 | 20 | 636,976 | 10 | 645,837 |
| Pennsylvania[1] | 34 | 1,714,999 | 61 | 1,683,033 | 94 | 3,398,032 | 22 | 3,518,212 |
| Rhode Island | 1 | 87,762 | 6 | 216,936 | 7 | 304,698 | 3 | 299,076 |
| South Carolina | 8 | 438,623 | 9 | 187,079 | 17 | 625,702 | 9 | 585,405 |
| South Dakota | 4 | 72,239 | 8 | 95,523 | 12 | 167,762 | 4 | 128,967 |
| Tennessee[1] | 9 | 509,099 | 21 | 483,163 | 29 | 992,262 | 16 | 1,047,804 |
| Texas[1] | 33 | 2,133,320 | 84 | 1,491,107 | 112 | 3,624,427 | 97 | 4,318,074 |
| Utah | 1 | 109,318 | 5 | 173,900 | 6 | 283,218 | 6 | 313,445 |
| Vermont | 4 | 92,425 | 4 | 31,279 | 8 | 123,704 | 3 | 86,718 |
| Virginia | 11 | 656,949 | 18 | 535,630 | 29 | 1,192,579 | 15 | 925,735 |
| Washington[1] | 9 | 399,939 | 20 | 736,115 | 28 | 1,136,054 | 17 | 1,107,984 |
| West Virginia | 9 | 244,046 | 14 | 208,776 | 23 | 452,822 | 10 | 398,765 |
| Wisconsin | 6 | 298,218 | 29 | 886,958 | 35 | 1,185,176 | 12 | 996,422 |
| Wyoming | 6 | 68,590 | 4 | 32,162 | 10 | 100,752 | 4 | 75,716 |
| **Total** | **482** | **36,361,561** | **1,220** | **26,404,671** | **1,676** | **62,766,232** | **798** | **58,825,978** |
| | | | | | | | | |
| Total U.S., Sept. 30, 1984 | 458 | 35,424,418 | 1,257 | 27,657,322 | 1,688 | 63,081,740 | 783 | 57,573,979 |
| Total U.S., Sept. 30, 1983 | 446 | 33,842,142 | 1,284 | 28,802,461 | 1,701 | 62,644,603 | 722 | 56,747,436 |
| Total U.S., Sept. 30, 1982 | 434 | 33,174,087 | 1,310 | 29,313,090 | 1,711 | 62,487,177 | 768 | 56,260,764 |
| Total U.S., Sept. 30, 1981 | 408 | 30,552,316 | 1,352 | 30,878,429 | 1,730 | 61,430,745 | 755 | 55,180,004 |
| Total U.S., Sept. 30, 1980 | 387 | 29,414,036 | 1,388 | 32,787,804 | 1,745 | 62,201,840 | 736 | 54,676,173 |
| Total U.S., Sept. 30, 1979 | 382 | 28,574,879 | 1,405 | 33,648,161 | 1,763 | 62,223,040 | 720 | 54,379,923 |
| Total U.S., Sept. 30, 1978 | 355 | 27,656,739 | 1,419 | 34,333,258 | 1,756 | 61,989,997 | 696 | 53,990,033 |
| Total U.S., Sept. 30, 1977 | 352 | 26,742,318 | 1,435 | 34,752,822 | 1,753 | 61,495,140 | 668 | 52,429,234 |
| Total U.S., Sept. 30, 1976 | 346 | 25,858,386 | 1,435 | 35,118,625 | 1,762 | 60,977,011 | 650 | 51,565,334 |
| Total U.S., Sept. 30, 1975 | 339 | 25,490,186 | 1,436 | 35,165,245 | 1,756 | 60,655,431 | 639 | 51,096,323 |

1. "All-day" newspapers are listed in morning and evening columns but only once in the total, and their circulations are divided between morning and evening figures. Adjustments have been made in state and U.S. total figures. *Source: Editor and Publisher International Yearbook, 1986.*

**See** the Entertainment and Culture section for additional Media information.

# MILITARY

## The Doomsday Trigger

### By John Guthrie

When the President of the United States is traveling, he is constantly dogged by a sea of photographers and journalists. Awash in the bright lights and hordes of observers, the President conducts the important business of a public press conference.

Beyond the lights, though, at the edge of the press corps, there are a number of individuals whose vital job must be performed anonymously. A secret service agent speaks softly into a tactical radio, another wary agent glances carefully at the President. Standing far back from the crowd is a lone figure, dressed in a dark military uniform. In his hand, he clutches a black leather bag. This satchel, tied to the wrist of a presidential aide, follows the President wherever he goes. It is code-named "The Football," and it contains the Gold Codes—top secret authorization codes for the release and activation of America's nuclear arsenal.

Everything about "The Football"—including the aides who carry it and the White House Communications Agency that controls it—is top secret. It's actually easier to get the government to release a photograph of a nuclear weapon than one of "The Football," which is America's primary nuclear trigger.

The bag has been a public fixture since 1963, and while photos and descriptions of it can be found in various books, the White House, for the purpose of national security, has done its best to shield information about The Football from the general public.

Until 1962, there was no formal technical mechanism for the President to prevent the military's unauthorized use of nuclear weapons. Since WW II, the stated political policy governing the use of nuclear weapons has emphasized that they are for deterrence and retaliation only. The American military contingencies, on the other hand, have considered all possible uses for nuclear weapons—including pre-emptive first strike!

President Truman, the first president with the authority to use nuclear weapons (a responsibility he called "The Sacred Trust"), presided over an arsenal of some 50 devices in 1948. Most of these were unassembled gravity bombs. Under Eisenhower, the number of warheads increased from 1,000 in 1955 to 18,000 in 1960. Of these, 90 percent were completed weapons—strategic and tactical—in military stockpiles around the world. During this same five-year period, the number of designated Soviet targets increased from 3,000 to 20,000!

With tens of thousands of live weapons deployed, Eisenhower, as early as 1954, was compelled to re-state the official U.S. policy. In a revised Basic National Security Policy, he said, "The United States, and its allies must reject the concept of preventive war or acts intended to provoke war."

Just before leaving office, Eisenhower found that the Air Force and Navy had each identified and targeted the same Soviet cities and military bases! Had a war broken out, one Soviet city the size of Hiroshima was scheduled to be hit four times, with some seven megatons! (Hiroshima was leveled with a 13-kiloton device!). To eliminate this interservice duplication, the Joint Strategic Target Planning Staff (JSTPS) was created in the fall of 1960.

In December 1960, the JSTPS issued the first Single Integrated Operations Plan (SIOP). Updated versions of this plan continue today, so that a multiservice plan of attack can be coordinated in the event of a war with the Soviet Union. The SIOP is so secret that it carries its own classification—Extremely Sensitive Information (ESI).

During the Cuban Missile Crisis, there was very real concern in the Kennedy White House that some Soviet commanders in Cuba might launch their missiles without authorization from Moscow. After the crisis, Kennedy reviewed the American system of political control over military nuclear weapons and subsequently issued the highly classified National Security Action Memorandum. This is the essential plan that created The Football and the entire "team" behind it.

In August 1963, the National Communications System was created to respond to "the Federal Government's needs under all conditions, ranging from a normal situation to national emergencies and international crises including nuclear attack."

The White House Communications Agency was created with personnel from sections of the Defense Communications Agency, composed of units of the Defense Communications Operations Unit (responsible for communications and emergency power engineering) and the Defense Communications Support Unit, which "provides certain specialized classified communications facilities from remote locations."

To work in these units, a candidate must pass a special security investigation, called "Yankee White." The criteria include U.S. citizenship, unquestionable loyalty, and an absolute absence of any foreign influence over the individual, his family, or "persons to whom the individual is closely linked." The aides who carry The Football come from the four military branches and are ranked Lt. Colonel, Naval Commander, or Marine Major. They must be knowledgeable about all aspects of the overall SIOP, as well as the various options available to the President for implementing the plan.

SIOP strategic targeting involves four groups: (1) Soviet nuclear forces; (2) Conventional military forces; (3) Military and political leadership; (4) Economic/Industrial targets. The President's "Black Book" is said to contain 75 pages of options

This article is reprinted with permission from the *International Combat Arms—The Journal of Defense Technology*, Volume 4, Number 4. Copyright © 1986 by Peterson Publishing Company, Los Angeles, California. John Guthrie is a Field Editor for the *International Combat Arms*. The facts expressed herein are the sole responsibility of the author.

## Offensive Nuclear Missiles—U.S. and U.S.S.R.

### (Deployed as of early 1986)

| United States | | | | Soviet Union | | | |
|---|---|---|---|---|---|---|---|
| Land-based (ICBMs)[1] | No. silos deployed | Max. No. warheads | Max. range[7] (km) | Land-based (ICBMs)[1] | No. silos deployed | Max. No. warheads[4] | Max. range[7] (km) |
| Titan 2 | 10 | 1 | 12,000 | SS-11 | 448 | 3 | 13,000 |
| Minuteman 2 | 450 | 1 | 12,500 | SS-13 | 60 | 1 | 9,400 |
| Minuteman 3 | 550 | 3 | 14,000 | SS-16 | —[5] | 1 | 9,000 |
| Peacekeeper (MX)[3] | 0[6] | 10 | 14,000 | SS-17 | 150 | 4 | 10,000 |
| Total: | 1,010 | | | SS-18 | 308 | 10 | 11,000 |
| | | | | SS-19 | 360 | 6 | 10,000 |
| | | | | SS-X-24[3] | 0 | 10 | 10,000 |
| | | | | SS-X-25 | 70 | 1 | 10,500 |
| | | | | Total: | 1,396 | | |
| Sea-based (SLBMs)[2] | | | | Sea-based (SLBMs)[2] | | | |
| Poseidon C-3 | 304 | 10 | 4,000 | SS-N-5 | 39 | 1 | 1,400 |
| Trident 1 (C-4) | 360 | 8 | 7,400 | SS-N-6 | 304 | 2 | 3,000 |
| Total: | 664 | | | SS-N-8 | 292 | 1 | 9,100 |
| | | | | SS-N-17 | 12 | 3 | 3,900 |
| | | | | SS-N-18 | 224 | 7 | 8,000 |
| | | | | SS-N-20 | 80 | 9 | 8,300 |
| | | | | SS-NX-23 | 32 | 10 | 8,300 |
| | | | | Total: | 983 | | |

1. ICBM: Intercontental Ballistic Missile 2. SLBM: Submarine-Launched Ballistic Missile 3. In development 4. Number of warheads varies within different models of same type 5. Nearing deployment 6. Ten are scheduled to become operational by the end of 1986. 7. One kilometer = .6214 miles. *Source:* U.S. Department of Defense.

to be used against these four primary groups. Major Attack Options (MAO's), Selected Attack Options (SAO's), and Limited Attack Options (LAO's) all enable the U.S. to respond according to circumstances.

The SIOP also allows the President to select Regional Nuclear Options (RNO's) for use against enemy forces leading a conventional attack against American forces. These plans also allow the President to execute the SIOP during an attack. He may decide to activate Launch on Warning (LOW) or Launch under Attack (LUA) plans in the event of an actual nuclear assault. If the President is faced with extraordinary circumstances, he may even choose a pre-emptive first strike against the Soviets. Again, this is strictly a military option, not a political or military policy.

We can't be certain of everything contained in the top secret satchel, but we do have a rough idea. There is a radio with an antenna about four or six inches long. This would place the frequency in the UHF band. The encryption methods available for radio transmission are unknown.

Also in the bag are sealed copies of the SIOP target option list, the President's Decision Book, and that particular day's Gold Codes. Another result of the Kennedy Administration's review of nuclear weapons control was the implementation of coded

electronic locks (called Permissive Action Links or PALs), which now exist on virtually all American nuclear weapons, except sub-launched missile warheads. These PALs prevent the unauthorized arming and/or detonation of a nuclear device—unless the proper code has been entered. The Gold Code is the first step that the chain of command must take to release nuclear weapons. The National Security Agency is in charge of distributing the daily Gold Codes to The Football, White House, Pentagon, Strategic Air Command HQ and to the "clacker box" aboard the SAC Airborne Command Post.

Use of the Gold Code and the order to execute and SIOP option by any designated member of the National Command Authority constitutes the declaration of military Defense Condition One—War! The NCA includes the President and his successors—the Vice President, House Speaker, Secretary of Defense, etc., all the way down to the brigadier general commanding Cover All. There are elaborate checks and communications protocols to ensure that anyone issuing the Gold Code has the verifiable authority to do so. Ultimately, of course, the security of our nation rests with the integrity of the men and women who shoulder these awesome responsibilities.

## Army Educational Benefits Top $25,000

These benefits are administered under a program known as the New GI Bill Plus New Army College Fund.

The program requires a soldier to contribute $100 per month for one year, an amount matched by a $9,600 government contribution. For those recruits who enlist to train in areas such as Pershing Missile Crew Member, Food Service Specialist, or Tank Turret Mechanic, supplemental benefits are

paid amounting to $3,000 for a two-year enlistment to $14,400 for a four-year enlistment.

Money is paid to veterans on a monthly basis for 36 academic months. A veteran who served a four-year enlistment and is attending a school full-time will receive $700 per month. The full-time student who had served a two-year enlistment receives $472.22 per month. The benefits may be used for studying in college or vocational schools.

# North Atlantic Treaty Organization (NATO)

Set up April 4, 1949, under a regional defense treaty for the North Atlantic area stating that "an armed attack against one . . . shall be considered an attack against . . . all" and that participating nations will take necessary joint counteraction under the United Nations Charter, including the use of armed force. The founding members were the U.S., Canada, Iceland, Norway, Great Britain, the Netherlands, Denmark, Belgium, Luxembourg, Portugal, France, and Italy. Greece, Turkey, and West Germany were added later. Spain formally became the 16th member on May 30, 1982. NATO marked the first time that the United States pledged to go to war to support allies before the outbreak of hostilities. The member nations are represented on the governing NATO Council. Its organization comprises their top foreign, economic, defense, and financial ministers. Its major military commands are SACEUR for Europe and SACLANT for the Atlantic Ocean area.

France and Spain do not participate in NATO's integrated military structure. In an invasion of Western Europe, France and Spain would defend their sovereignty with their own forces.

# Warsaw Pact

Signed May 14, 1955, by Albania, Bulgaria, Czechoslovakia, East Germany, Hungary, Poland, Romania, and the U.S.S.R. Albania, barred from meetings in 1962, withdrew in 1968 after ideological differences. The pact is the Communist equivalent of NATO, providing that an attack on one shall be regarded as an attack on all.

## Comparing NATO and Warsaw Pact Forces

Many factors contribute to the capability to deter or defend against aggression. These include political and social stability, geography, economic strength, human resources, industrial and technological resources, as well as military capabilities. The military forces possessed by each side are clearly important but are not the only elements in this equation, and in comparing each side's military forces it is important to avoid over-simplification. A complete assessment of the global balance of power would have to take into account forces other than those that are available to NATO and the Warsaw Pact. Even if consideration was to be restricted to NATO and the Warsaw Pact capabilities only, a full assessment would have to take into account not just the conventional forces deployed by each side in Europe but also certain worldwide deployments by a number of NATO countries as well as by the Soviet Union. For instance, both the United States and the Soviet Union maintain substantial forces in Asia and the Pacific.

In addition to quantifiable force differences there are also other elements important to an understanding of the balance. These include, for example, differences in military strategy and structure, political organization and cohesion, the qualitative aspect of forces and the availability of timely reinforcements. Other important considerations are the amount of ammunition, fuel, and other stocks possessed by each side, the quality of their equipment, the quality of their civil and military infrastructure, their organization, their personnel, their leadership and morale, as well as each side's economic, industrial, and technological ability to sustain a military conflict.

Geographic and economic dissimilarities between NATO and the Warsaw Pact directly affect the roles and missions of their armed forces. For example, the Warsaw Pact is one geographic entity in contrast to NATO, which is separated by oceans, seas, and in some regions, particularly in the south, by the territory of nations which are not members of the Alliance. This allows the Warsaw Pact to transfer land and air forces and support between different areas via internal and generally secure lines of communications. It also contributes to enabling the Warsaw Pact to select the time and place in which to concentrate its forces.

NATO, on the other hand, must transfer resources along lengthy and vulnerable air and sea routes to and around Europe. The most powerful partner in NATO, the United States, is separated from its European allies by an ocean 3,728 miles (6,000 km) wide. Moreover, NATO nations, to a far greater extent than those of the Warsaw Pact, depend on shipping for vital economic purposes. Thus, unlike the Warsaw Pact, NATO has a fundamental dependence on shipping during peace and war. This fact requires markedly different missions for Warsaw Pact naval forces on the one hand and NATO naval forces on the other. Additionally, NATO lacks geographical depth in Europe between the possible areas of conflict and the coasts, so rendering its rear areas, headquarters and supplies more vulnerable to enemy attack and more difficult to defend.

The Warsaw Pact nations have a standing force of some 6 million personnel of which some 4 million face NATO in Europe. By comparison, the standing forces of the NATO nations total 4.5 million personnel, of which nearly 2.6 million are stationed in Europe.

## Nuclear Weapons Yield

The most widely used standard for measuring the power of nuclear weapons is "yield," expressed as the quantity of TNT that would produce the same energy release. The first atomic bomb exploded at Hiroshima had a yield of 13 to 15 kilotons, or the explosive power of 13 to 15,000 tons of TNT.

The largest nuclear detonation was set off by the Soviet Union in 1962 and had a yield of 58 megatons—equivalent to 58 million tons of TNT.

# Learning To Fight in a Laser Battlefield

## Fort Irwin: Home of the Army's National Training Center

The age-old problem with training soldiers for combat was in making the battlefield action seem real. Until recently, Army combat training was of the "bang, you're dead, no, I shot you" variety. Only blank ammunition was fired, and it was left up to umpires to estimate the casualities. Unfortunately, what the umpires didn't see didn't count, and what they did see was usually arguable. The dilemma of how to create realism in combat training without the danger of using live ammunition persisted until 1980 when the U.S. Army established the National Training Center at Fort Irwin, California.

## The National Training Center (NTC)

Fourteen times a year, for two weeks at a time, selected Army units from all over the continental United States are sent to the National Training Center to fight mock battles in the world's most realistic simulated combat arena. The soldiers are pitted against the Army's special Opposing Forces (OPFOR) who use Soviet-style tactics and military doctrine. The Opposing Forces are appropriately dressed in uniforms of Warsaw Pact nations and are equipped with Soviet-type weapons ranging from rifles to tanks and helicopters.

The pseudo-Soviet army is made up of the 32nd Guards Motorized Rifle Regiment which consists of two permanently assigned units—the 6th Battalion, 31st Mechanized Infantry, and the 1st Battalion, 73rd Armor.

Opposing Force soldiers are trained at a special OPFOR Academy, also at Fort Irwin, where they are given classes on how the Soviet soldier looks, operates, and what tactics he uses. Serving as an OPFOR soldier is no easy task—they are out in the field 200 days a year and, when they are not acting as Warsaw Pact forces, they have to maintain their regular skills as U.S. soldiers.

## The Laser Battlefield

The National Training Center is unique because it is the only place in the world where soldiers can learn to fight in battalion size formations, and where all weapons used are equipped with special laser "bullets" and corresponding detection equipment that indicates when hits are made.

The weapons are fitted with the Multiple Integrated Laser Engagement System (MILES) and are syncronized to operate when the weapon fires its blank ammunition at a target. MILES operates by using eye-safe laser transmitters attached to the weapons that can shoot coded pulses of infrared energy to simulate the effect of live ammunition.

Special detectors that can receive the coded laser pulses are worn by the individual participating troops and are also attached to all vehicles including tanks and helicopters. The MILES decoder determines whether a target was hit by a weapon which could cause damage and whether the shot was accurate enough to cause a casualty. For example, a rifle bullet couldn't destroy a tank and therefore wouldn't count as a hit.

Thanks to the MILES system, the target vehicles or troops are made instantly aware of shooting accuracy by means of sophisticated audio alarms and visual displays.

If an infantryman is being fired upon by an aggressor using a rifle and the shot is a "near miss," he will hear a series of short tones sounded from an alarm worn near the left ear. If he has been "killed" the alarm will sound a continuous tone that can be stopped only by removing a special key from his rifle transmitter which in turn will disable his rifle from further use and eliminate him from continuing combat.

During the two weeks training, the realistic fighting goes on day and night just as it would in a real combat situation.

## Post-Mortem Review

Situated throughout Fort Irwin's 636,000 acres are 44 solar-powered 'interrogator' relay stations which send the signals from the laser battlefield to a computer station high atop a mountain. Objective data such as the type of weapon used, how many rounds of ammunition were fired, the location of the action, etc., are then transmitted to a base computer at the Operations Center in the heart of Fort Irwin's garrison area.

Up to eight mobile video-camera units are present during a simulated combat exeercise and they send live TV pictures back to the Operations Center for recording. Within three hours after the battle has ceased, specially equipped vans deliver video taped recordings of the action to the battlefield for review by unit commanders and trainers to study and learn from their successes and mistakes.

## The NTC Live Fire Range

The NTS also has a special 30,000-meter (32,808 yards) range to fire live ammunition in. Here, on the range battlefield, over 500 computer-operated targets resembling Soviet-style vehicles and infantrymen are strategically placed to simulate an attack. Some of the special targets can even shoot back with styrofoam missiles. Computers indicate when the targets have been hit.

The National Training Center is an outstanding Army success story. Between 1980 and 1986, over 134,000 soldiers trained there were given the best possible preparation to fight and win in combat.

## Air Force Grants Greater Opportunities to Women

In 1986, more than 800 new positions have been opened to women in the Air Force. They include: forward air control post, the airborne battlefield command and control center mission and some munition sites. In addition, women are no longer restricted from assignment to Minuteman missiles as launch control officers. Now only 5% of Air Force jobs are closed to women because of combat restriction.

## Average Strength of Military Formations—1985

| | Division | | | | |
|---|---|---|---|---|---|
| | **Armored** | | **Mechanized** | | **Airborne** |
| **Country** | **Men** | **Tanks** | **Men** | **Tanks** | **Men** |
| United States | 18,300 | 324 | 18,500 | 216 | 16,800 |
| Soviet Union | 10,500 | 322 [1] | 12,500 | 271 [1] | 7,000 |
| China | 9,200 | 300 | 12,700 [3] | 30 [3] | 9,000 |
| Britain [4] | 8,500 | 122 | — | — | — |
| Germany | 17,000 | 300 | 17,500 | 250 | 8–9,000 |
| India | 15,000 | 200 | 17,500 [3] | — | — |
| Israel | — | — | — | — | — |
| Egypt | 11,000 | 300 | 12,000 | 190 | — |

| | Brigade | | | | Squadron |
|---|---|---|---|---|---|
| | **Armored** | | **Mechanized** | | |
| **Country** | **Men** | **Tanks** | **Men** | **Tanks** | **Fighter aircraft** |
| United States | 4,500 | 108 | 4,800 | 54 | 18–24 |
| Soviet Union | 1,300 [2] | 95 [2] | 2,300 [2] | 40 [2] | 12–15 |
| China | 1,200 [2] | 90 [2] | 2,000 | — | 9–10 |
| Britain [4] | — | — | — | — | 8–15 |
| Germany | 4,500 [5] | 110 | 5,000 [5] | 54 | 15–21 |
| India | 6,000 | 150 | 4,500 | — | 12–20 |
| Israel | 3,500 | 80–100 | 3,500 | 36–40 | 15–20 |
| Egypt | 3,500 | 96 | 3,500 | 36 | 10–12 |

1. These tank strengths are for Soviet divisions in Eastern Europe; other Soviet divisions have fewer. 2. Strength of a regiment, which is the equivalent formation in the Soviet and Chinese command structures. (The term "regiment" may also describe a battalion-size unit, particularly in West European countries. The term "group," often used in Latin American countries, is imprecise and may apply to a reinforced battalion or understrength brigade with armored fighting vehicle(s) and/or artillery.) 3. Infantry division. 4. Britain has reintroduced the brigade organization, but combat formations are battle groups based on an armored regiment or mechanized battalion. Armored division strength will rise to 11,500 on mobilization. 5. Manpower levels currently under review. NOTE: Divisional strengths cover organic units only and exclude support units or services outside the divisional structure. *Source:* International Institute for Strategic Studies.

# History of the Armed Services

*Source:* Department of Defense.

## U.S. Army

On June 14, 1775, the Continental Congress "adopted" the New England Armies—a mixed force of volunteers besieging the British in Boston—appointing a committee to draft "Rules and regulations for the government of the Army" and voting to raise 10 rifle companies as a reinforcement. The next day, it appointed Washington commander-in-chief of the "Continental forces to be raised for the defense of liberty," and he took command at Boston on July 3, 1775. The Continental Army that fought the Revolution was our first national military organization, and hence the Army is the senior service. After the war, the army was radically reduced but enough survived to form a small Regular Army of about 700 men under the Constitution, a nucleus for expansion in the 1790s to successfully meet threats from the Indians and from France. From these humble beginnings, the U.S. Army has developed, normally expanding rapidly by absorbing citizen soldiers in wartime and contracting just as rapidly after each war.

## U.S. Navy

The antecedents of the U.S. Navy go back to September 1775, when Gen. Washington commissioned 7 schooners and brigantines to prey on British supply vessels bound for the Colonies or Canada. On Oct. 13, 1775, a resolve of the Continental Congress called for the purchase of 2 vessels for the purpose of intercepting enemy transports. With its passage a Naval Committee of 7 men was formed, and they rapidly obtained passage of legislation calling for procurement of additional vessels. The Continental Navy was supplemented by privateers and ships operated as state navies, but soon after the British surrender it was disestablished.

In 1794, because of dissatisfaction with the payment of tribute to the Barbary pirates, Congress authorized construction of 6 frigates. The first, *United States*, was launched May 10, 1797, but the Navy still remained under the control of the Secretary of War until April 1798, when the Navy Department was created under the Secretary of the Navy with Cabinet rank.

## U.S. Air Force

Until creation of the National Military Establishment in September 1947, which united the services under one department, military aviation was a part of the U.S. Army. In the Army, aeronautical operations came under the Signal Corps from 1907 to 1918, when the Army Air Service was established. In 1926, the Army Air Corps came into being and remained until 1941, when the Army Air

Forces succeeded it as the Army's air arm. On Sept. 18, 1947, the U.S. Air Force was established as an independent military service under the National Military Establishment. At that time, the name "Army Air Forces" was abolished.

## U.S. Coast Guard

Our country's oldest continuous seagoing service, the U.S. Coast Guard, traces its history back to 1790, when the first Congress authorized the construction of ten vessels for the collection of revenue. Known first as the Revenue Marine, and later as the Revenue Cutter Service, the Coast Guard received its present name in 1915 under an act of Congress combining the Revenue Cutter Service with the Life-Saving Service. In 1939, the Lighthouse Service was also consolidated with this unit. The Bureau of Marine Inspection and Navigation was transferred temporarily to the Coast Guard in 1942, permanently in 1946. Through its antecedents, the Coast Guard is one of the oldest organizations under the federal government and, until the

Navy Department was established in 1798, served as the only U.S. armed force afloat. In times of peace, it operates under the Department of Transportation, serving as the nation's primary agency for promoting marine safety and enforcing federal maritime laws. In times of war, or on direction of the President, it is attached to the Navy Department.

## U.S. Marine Corps

Founded in 1775 and observing its official birthday on Nov. 10, the U.S. Marine Corps was developed to serve on land, on sea, and in the air.

Marines have fought in every U.S. war. From an initial two battalions in the Revolution, the Corps reached a peak strength of six divisions and five aircraft wings in World War II. Its present strength is three active divisions and aircraft wings and a Reserve division/aircraft wing team. In 1947, the National Security Act set Marine Corps strength at not less than three divisions and three aircraft wings.

# Service Academies

## U.S. Military Academy

*Source:* U.S. Military Academy.

Established in 1802 by an act of Congress, the U.S. Military Academy is located on the west bank of the Hudson River some 50 miles north of New York City. To gain admission a candidate must first secure a nomination from an authorized source. These sources, and the number of cadetships allocated to each, are:

### Congressional

| | |
|---|---|
| Representatives | 5 each |
| Senators | 5 each |
| Other: Vice Presidential | 5 |
| District of Columbia | 5 |
| Puerto Rico | 6 |
| Am. Samoa, Guam, Virgin Is. | 1 each |

### Military-Service-Connected Nominations
### (Each Class)

| | |
|---|---|
| Presidential | 100 |
| Enlisted members of Army | 85 |
| Enlisted members of Army Reserve/ National Guard | 85 |
| Sons and daughters of deceased and disabled veterans (approximately) | 10 |
| Honor military, naval schools and ROTC | 20 |
| Sons and daughters of persons awarded the Medal of Honor | (unlimited) |

Any number of applicants can meet the requirements for a *nomination* in these categories. *Appointments* (offers of admission), however, can only be made to the number of applicants shown above.

Candidates may be nominated for vacancies during the year preceding the day of admission, which occurs in early July. The best time to apply is during the junior year in high school.

Candidates must be citizens of the U.S., be unmarried, be at least 17 but not yet 22 years old on July 1 of the year admitted, have a secondary-school education or its equivalent, and be able to meet the academic, medical, and physical aptitude

requirements. Academic qualification is determined by an analysis of entire scholastic record, and performance on either the American College Testing (ACT) Assessment Program Test or the College Entrance Examination Board Scholastic Aptitude Test (SAT). Entrance requirements and procedures for appointment are described in the Admissions Bulletin, available without charge from Admissions, U.S. Military Academy, West Point, N.Y. 10996-1797.

Cadets are members of the Regular Army. As such they receive full scholarships and annual salaries from which they pay for their uniforms, textbooks, and incidental expenses. Upon successful completion of the four-year course, the graduate receives the degree of Bachelor of Science and is commissioned a second lieutenant in the Regular Army with a requirement to serve as an officer for a minimum of five years.

## U.S. Naval Academy

*Source:* U.S. Naval Academy.

The Naval School, established in 1845 at Fort Severn, Annapolis, Md., was renamed the U.S. Naval Academy in 1850. A four-year course was adopted a year later.

The Superintendent is a rear admiral. A civilian academic dean heads the academic program. A captain heads the 4,500-man Brigade of Midshipmen and military, professional, and physical training. The faculty is half military and half civilian.

Graduates are awarded the Bachelor of Science or Bachelor of Science in Engineering and are commissioned as officers in the U.S. Navy or Marine Corps.

Applicants *must* obtain a nomination from an official source in order to be considered by the Naval Academy for an appointment. The principle sources are: U.S. Senators, Representatives, the Vice President, the Mayor of Washington, D. C., and the Resident Commissioner of Puerto Rico may each have 5 midshipmen at the Academy at any one time. Ten candidates may be nominated for each vacancy. Well over half of the more than

1,300 appointments as midshipmen made annually originate from these sources.

The President appoints the 65 best-qualified sons and daughters of deceased or disabled veterans, or sons and daughters of prisoners of war or service-men missing in action, and the 100 best-qualified sons and daughters of officers and enlisted men in the regular Armed Services. He also appoints sons and daughters of Medal of Honor holders.

The Secretary of the Navy awards 170 (85 + 85) appointments to regular and reserve personnel of the Navy or Marine Corps; 150 to congressional alternate nominees, all on a competitive, best-qualified basis; and 20 outstanding graduates of NROTC or Honor Naval and Military Schools. He may also make additional appointments each year, to bring the Brigade up to authorized strength, from among qualified congressional and competitive nominees, again on a best-qualified basis. Three fourths of these additional appointments must, by law, be congressional nominees.

There are also limited numbers of appointments available from the Philippines, Canal Zone, Virgin Islands, Guam, American Samoa, and the American republics.

To have basic eligibility for admission, candidates must be citizens of the U.S., of good moral character, at least 17 and not more than 22 years of age on July 1 of their entering year, in the top 40% of their high school class, and unmarried.

In order to be considered for admission, a candidate must obtain a nomination from one of the sources of appointments listed above. The Admissions Board at the Naval Academy examines the candidate's school record, College Board or ACT scores, recommendations from school officials, extracurricular activities, and evidence from other sources concerning his or her character, leadership potential, academic preparation, and physical fitness. Qualification for admission is based on all of the above factors.

Tuition, board, lodging, and medical and dental care are provided. Midshipmen receive over $460 a month for books, uniforms, and personal needs.

For a catalogue or answers to specific questions, write: Superintendent, U.S. Naval Academy, (Attention: Candidate Guidance), Annapolis, Md. 21402-5018.

## U.S. Air Force Academy

*Source:* U.S. Air Force Academy

The bill establishing the Air Force Academy was signed by President Eisenhower on April 1, 1954. The first class of 306 cadets was sworn in on July 11, 1955, at Lowry Air Force Base, Denver, the Academy's temporary location. The Cadet Wing moved into the Academy's permanent home north of Colorado Springs, Colorado, in 1958.

Cadets receive four years of academic, military, and physical education to prepare them for leadership as officers in the Air Force. The Academy is authorized a total of 4,546 cadets. Each new class averages 1,400. The candidates for the Academy must be at least 17 but less than 22 on July 1 of the year for which they enter the Academy, must be a United States citizen, never married, and be able to meet the mental and physical requirements. A candidate is required to take the following examinations and tests: (1) the Service Academies' Qualifying Medical Examination; (2) either the American College Testing (ACT) Assessment Program test or the College Entrance Examination Board Scholastic Aptitude Test (SAT), and (3) a Physical Aptitude Examination.

Each new cadet must deposit $1,000 at the time of admission to the Academy, otherwise cadets receive their entire education at government expense and, in addition, are paid $480 per month base pay. From this sum, they pay for their uniforms, textbooks, tailoring, laundry, entertainment tickets, etc. Upon completion of the four-year course, leading to a Bachelor of Science degree, a cadet who meets the qualifications is commissioned a second lieutenant in the regular U.S. Air Force. About 70 percent enter pilot or navigator training. For details on admissions, write: Director of Cadet Admissions (RRS), HQ USAF Academy, Colorado Springs, CO 80840-5651.

## U.S. Coast Guard Academy

*Source:* U.S. Coast Guard Academy.

The U.S. Coast Guard Academy, New London, Conn., was founded on July 31, 1876, to serve as the "School of Instruction" for the Revenue Cutter Service, predecessor to the Coast Guard.

The J.C. Dobbin, a converted schooner, housed the first Coast Guard Academy, and was succeeded in 1878 by the barque Chase, a ship built for cadet training. First winter quarters were in a sail loft at New Bedford, Mass. The school was moved in 1900 to Curtis Bay, Md., to provide a more technical education, and in 1910 was moved back to New England to Fort Trumbull, New London, Conn. In 1932 the Academy moved to its present location in New London.

The Academy today offers a four-year curriculum for the professional and academic training of cadets, which leads to a Bachelor of Science degree and a commission as ensign in the Coast Guard.

Cadets receive appointment through nation-wide competition, which includes either the December administration of the College Entrance Examination Board tests, or the American College Testing (ACT) Program tests. Applications must be submitted to the Coast Guard not later than December 15 and to the College Entrance Examination Board, 30 days prior to the tests.

Women were admitted to the Coast Guard Academy for the first time during 1976 as members of the Class of 1980. Candidates must be between 17 and 22 years of age, physically sound, and unmarried. They must agree to remain unmarried until graduation and to serve at least five years on active duty. Cadets receive $5,760 per year to cover their uniform and incidental expenses and are furnished their rations and quarters. Applications may be made to Director of Admissions, U.S. Coast Guard Academy, New London, Conn. 06320.

## U.S. Merchant Marine Academy

*Source:* U.S. Merchant Marine Academy.

The U.S. Merchant Marine Academy, situated at Kings Point, N.Y., on the north shore of Long Island, was dedicated Sept. 30, 1943. It is maintained by the Department of Transportation under direction of the Maritime Administration.

The Academy has a complement of approximately 1,000 men and women representing every state, D.C., the Canal Zone, Puerto Rico, Guam, American Samoa, and the Virgin Islands. It is also authorized to admit up to 12 candidates from the Western Hemisphere and 30 other foreign students at any one time.

Candidates are nominated by Senators and members of the House of Representatives. Nominations to the Academy are governed by a state and territory quota system based on population and the results of the College Entrance Examination Board tests.

A candidate must be a citizen not less than 17 and not yet 22 years of age by July 1 of the year in which admission is sought. Fifteen high school credits, including 3 units in mathematics (from algebra, geometry and/or trigonometry), 1 unit in science (physics or chemistry) and 3 in English are required.

The course is four years and includes one year of practical training aboard a merchant ship. Study includes marine engineering, navigation, satellite navigation and communications, electricity, ship construction, naval science and tactics, economics, business, languages, history, etc.

Upon completion of the course of study, a graduate receives a Bachelor of Science degree, a license as a merchant marine deck or engineering officer, and a commission as an ensign in the Naval Reserve.

# The National Guard

*Source:* Departments of the Army and the Air Force, National Guard Bureau.

The National Guard of the U.S. originated in 1636 with the Old North and East Regiments of the Colonial Militia in Massachusetts. It is the oldest military force in the country. Guardmembers have served this country at home and overseas in every major conflict in which the U.S. has participated.

As of January 31, 1986, the Army and Air National Guard totaled about 547,000 men and women serving in 4,980 Army and Air Guard units in all 50 states, Puerto Rico, Guam, the Virgin Islands, and the District of Columbia. ANG units 633 (current as of June 7, 1985), ARNG units, 4,347.

In peacetime, the National Guard is commanded by the governors of the respective states/territories and may be called to state active duty by the governor to assist in state emergencies, disasters, and civil disturbances. During a war or national emergency, the National Guard may be called to active duty by the President or Congress. The National Guard serves as the primary source of augmentation for the Army and the Air Force.

Budget requests for fiscal 1987 are $5.4 billion for the Army National Guard and $3.1 billion for the Air National Guard. Additional money is appropriated directly for the National Guard by the states. Substantial support is also provided by state, county, and municipal governments in land, police and fire protection, maintenance of roads, and the provision of direct county and municipal fiscal support to local units.

The Army National Guard provides 45% of the Army's divisional combat units. That support consists of 10 combat divisions, 13 separate combat brigades, 5 round-out brigades, 4 armored cavalry regiments, 2 special forces groups, one infantry scout group (arctic recon), 18 major command headquarters, and 1,327 other separate battalions, companies, headquarters, and detachments.

Army National Guard forces are vital to the nation's first-line defenses. For example, the 48th Infantry Brigade in the Georgia National Guard is a round-out brigade for the active Army's 24th Infantry Division. Under the round-out concept, Army Guard units work and train with the active Army combat divisions of which they would become part upon mobilization. Integral to the total force policy, programs for increasing readiness are continually being improved.

National Guard units also participate in rotational training at the Army's National Training Center, Fort Irwin, Calif. This training with the active forces further develops the readiness of both units and individuals.

Additionally, Army and Air National Guard units participate annually in Joint Chiefs of Staff, active Army and Air Force, and major unified and specified command readiness exercises and deployments held worldwide with other active and reserve counterparts.

A program implemented in the National Guard provides opportunities for military personnel to seek full-time active duty careers in various duty positions with the Guard. The Active Guard/Reserve (AGR) program offers both officer and enlisted (male and female) personnel tours of full-time military duty in an AGR status which could eventually lead to a 20-year active duty retirement identical to that authorized active Army or Air Force personnel. Positions are located in all states at both state and local unit level. Duties encompass the areas of training, supply, administration, and maintenance. Applicants must be members of the Army or Air National Guard to be considered for AGR positions, and generally qualified to perform the duties required of the position for which they apply.

The Air National Guard has 91 flying units and 542 mission support units which, upon mobilization, would be gained by one of six major commands of the USAF. The gaining major commands are Tactical Air Command (TAC), Strategic Air Command (SAC), Military Airlift Command (MAC), Air Force Communications Command (AFCC), Pacific Air Forces (PACAF), and Alaskan Air Command (AAC).

Air National Guard flying units support four mission areas: strategic offense, with aerial refuelers supporting tactical fighter, bomber, and airlift aircraft; strategic defense, with fighter interceptors fulfilling a daily alert mission; general purpose forces equipped with tactical fighters for air to ground and air to air missions, tactical reconnaissance for battlefield assessment, electronic warfare and close air support; mobility with tactical airlift; and defense wide with rescue and recovery.

The National Guard is administered by the National Guard Bureau, a joint Army and Air Force office in the Pentagon. Chief of the Bureau is Lt. Gen. Emmett H. Walker, Jr., of Mississippi.

The Army National Guard offers its young men and women a broad spectrum of educational opportunities. These not only include skill training associated with their military assignment, but in many instances embrace civilian occupations as well. The list of skills is not limited to those that are equipment oriented but includes management,

## Defense Budget by Major Categories

### (In billions of dollars)

| Major Missions and Programs | 1985 actual | 1986 estimate | 1987 estimate | 1988 estimate | 1989 estimate |
|---|---|---|---|---|---|
| Strategic forces[1] | 27.4 | 24.8 | 25.4 | 27.4 | 29.7 |
| General purpose forces | 118.4 | 109.8 | 128.6 | 138.0 | 146.5 |
| Intelligence and communications | 25.1 | 25.9 | 29.5 | 30.1 | 32.4 |
| Airlift and sealift | 8.7 | 8.1 | 7.5 | 7.0 | 7.3 |
| Guard and reserve | 15.8 | 15.8 | 17.9 | 19.4 | 21.0 |
| Research and development[2] | 24.4 | 26.2 | 32.5 | 34.4 | 35.8 |
| Central supply and maintenance | 26.7 | 23.3 | 26.4 | 28.6 | 30.6 |
| Training, medical, and other general personnel activities | 33.6 | 36.9 | 37.0 | 40.4 | 42.7 |
| Administration and associated activities | 6.1 | 7.1 | 6.0 | 6.2 | 6.6 |
| Support of other nations | 0.6 | 0.5 | 0.8 | 0.9 | 0.9 |
| Total | 278.6 | 285.4 | 312.3 | 333.2 | 354.3 |

1. Excludes strategic systems development included in the research and development category. 2. Excludes research and development in other program areas on systems approved for production.

medical, and other career fields. Some of these educational opportunities may even be pursued in civilian institutions, specifically that of the Clinical Specialist, which is compatible with a Licensed Practical Nurse or Licensed Vocational Nurse.

Participation in the military education system by Army National Guard personnel is not limited to initial entry skill-level training. There are opportunities available to become a qualified aviator, improve managerial and leadership abilities through attending courses designed for middle managers, and, finally, there are the courses offered at the prestigious Senior Service Colleges that address the needs of personnel at the executive level and positions of greater responsibilities.

If openings exist, men and women between the ages of 17 and 35 may enlist for a period of six years followed by a two-year inactive reserve period during which they are subject to recall, should the need arise. In certain circumstances the period of active participation may be less than six years. Upon enlistment, they serve a minimum of 12 weeks on active duty, training with the U.S. Army or the U.S. Air Force, depending upon which branch of the National Guard they choose. The remainder of their term of enlistment is spent in part-time training with their Guard unit.

A woman between the ages of 17 and 35 who has no previous military experience may also enlist in the National Guard for a period of six years. Women in the Army National Guard will receive basic training at either Fort McClellan, Ala., Fort Dix, N.J., or Fort Jackson, S.C.; women in the Air National Guard train at Lackland Air Force Base, Tex. Advanced training takes place at appropriate training centers.

Guard members receive a full day's pay of their military rank for each unit training assembly attended. Additionally, they receive a day's pay of their military rank for each day of their 15 days of annual training, plus any other days on active duty for training at military schools or special assignments. All such training counts toward retirement eligibility at age 60 with 20 or more years of qualifying service.

## Highest Ranking Officers in the Armed Forces

### ARMY[1]
**Generals:** John A. Wickham, Jr., Chief of Staff; Maxwell R. Thurman, Vice Chief of Staff; Bernard W. Rogers, Supreme Allied Commander, Europe; Richard H. Thompson, Glenn K. Otis, William J. Livsey, John R. Galvin, Fred K. Mahaffey; Jack N. Merritt; Joseph T. Palastra, Jr.; Carl E. Vuono.

### AIR FORCE
**Generals:** Robert W. Bazley, Charles L. Donnelly, Jr., Charles A. Gabriel, Robert T. Herres, Andrew P. Iosue, Richard L. Lawson, Earl T. O'Loughlin, Jerome F. O'Malley, Lawrence A. Skantze, Larry D. Welch, Duane H. Cassidy, John T. Chinn, Jr., John L. Piotrowski, Robert D. Russ.

### NAVY
**Admirals:** James D. Watkins, Chief of Naval Operations; William J. Crowe, Jr., Chairman of the Joint Chiefs of Staff; Kinnaird R. McKee; Ronald J. Hays; Lee Baggett, Jr., James A. Lyons, Jr., Carlisle A. H. Trost, James B. Busey, Arthur S. Moreau, Jr.

### MARINE CORPS
**Generals:** Paul X. Kelley, Commandant of the Marine Corps; Thomas R. Morgan, Assistant Commandant of the Marine Corps.
**Lieutenant Generals:** D'Wayne Gray, Alfred M. Gray, Jr., Keith A. Smith, Ernest C. Cheatham, Jr., Joseph J. Went, John Phillips, Frank E. Petersen, Clyde D. Dean.

### COAST GUARD
**Admiral:** Adm. Paul L. Yost, Jr., Commandant.
**Vice Admirals:** James T. Irwin, Vice Commandant; Donald C. Thompson, Commander Atlantic Area; John D. Costello, Commander, Pacific Area.

1. On March 15, 1978, George Washington, the commander of the Continental Army in the American Revolution and our first President, was promoted posthumously to the newly-created rank of General of the Armies of the United States. Congress authorized this title to make it clear that Washington is the Army's senior general. Source: Department of Defense.

# Veterans' Benefits

Although benefits of various kinds date back to Colonial days, veterans of World War I were the first to receive disability compensation, allotments for dependents, life insurance, medical care, and vocational rehabilitation. In 1940, these benefits were slowly broadened.

The following benefits available to veterans require certain minimum periods of active duty during qualifying periods of service and, except for service personnel, are applicable only to those whose discharges are not dishonorable.

**Unemployment allowances.** Every effort is being made to secure employment for Vietnam veterans. Unemployment benefits are administered by the U.S. Department of Labor.

**Loans.** GI loans are made for a variety of purposes, such as: to buy or build a home; to purchase a mobile home with or without a lot; and to refinance a home presently owned and occupied by the veteran. The VA will guarantee the lender against loss up to 60% of a home loan with a maximum of $27,500. On mobile home loans, the amount of the guaranty is 50% of the loan with a maximum of $20,000. The interest rate may not exceed the maximum rate set by the VA and in effect when the loan is made.

**Compensation and rehabilitation benefits.** These are available to those having some service-connected illness or disability.

**Disability compensation.** The VA pays from $68 to $1,335 per month, and for specific conditions up to $3,812 per month, plus allowances for dependents, where the disability is rated 30% or more.

**Vocational rehabilitation.** Necessary training expenses, special equipment, etc., toward a definite job objective are paid for, plus a monthly allowance of up to $310, with increased amounts for dependents, in addition to compensation. Counseling and job search services are provided to assist veterans in obtaining and maintaining employment.

**Medical and dental care.** This includes care in VA and, in certain instances, in non-VA, or other federal hospitals. It also covers outpatient treatment at a VA field facility or, in some cases, by an approved private physician or dentist. Full domiciliary care is also provided where necessary. Nursing home care may be provided at certain VA medical facilities or in approved community nursing homes. Hospital and other medical care may also be provided for the spouse and child dependents of a veteran who is permanently and totally disabled due to a service-connected disability; or for survivors of a veteran who dies from a service-connected disability; or for survivors of a veteran who at the time of death had a total disability, permanent in nature, resulting from a service-connected disability. These latter benefits are usually provided in nonfederal facilities. Eligibility criteria for these benefits vary, and veterans and/or their dependents or survivors should always apply in advance. Contact the nearest VA medical facility.

**Readjustment Counseling.** The VA provides readjustment counseling to veterans of the Vietnam Era in need of assistance in resolving post-war readjustment problems in the areas of employment, family, education, and personal readjustment including post-traumatic stress disorder. Services are provided at community-based Vet Centers. Services include individual family and group counseling, employment and educational counseling, and assistance in obtaining referrals to various governmental and nongovernmental agencies with an interest in assisting Vietnam Era veterans. All Vietnam 'Era veterans are eligible for services except those with a type of discharge which may limit eligibility for VA services. Certain types of discharges are subject to special adjudication to determine eligibility. Contact the nearest Vet Center or VA facility to determine location of Vet Center.

**Dependents' educational assistance.** The VA pays $376 a month for up to 45 months of schooling to sons and daughters of veterans who died of service-connected causes or who were permanently and totally disabled from service-connected causes or died while permanently and totally disabled or who are missing in action, captured in the line of duty, or forcibly detained or interned in the line of duty by a foreign power for more than 90 days. Students must usually be between 18 and 26.

Spouses of veterans whose deaths are adjudged to be service-connected, and spouses of veterans who are permanently and totally disabled due to service-connected causes or who are prisoners of war or are missing in action are also eligible for this educational benefit.

**Veterans readjustment education.** Veterans who served on active duty for at least 181 days after Jan. 31, 1955, but before Jan. 1, 1977, may receive monthly educational assistance under the GI Bill for post-Korean conflict veterans, varying from $376 for single full-time students to $510 for veterans with two dependents, plus $32 for each additional dependent. Veterans and servicepersons who initially entered the military on or after Jan. 1, 1977, may receive educational assistance under a contributory plan. Individuals contribute $25 to $100 from military pay, up to a maximum of $2,700. This amount is matched by the Federal Government on a 2 for 1 basis. Participants, while on active duty, may make a lump sum contribution. Participants receive monthly payments for the number of months they contributed, or for 36 months, whichever is less. No initial enrollments are permitted during the period July 1, 1985, through June 30, 1986.

**Veterans Educational Assistance Act of 1984.** This Act establishes a program of education benefits for individuals entering military service from July 1, 1985, through June 30, 1988. Servicepersons entering active duty during that period will have their basic pay reduced by $100 a month for the first 12 months of their service, unless they specifically elect not to participate in the program. Servicepersons eligible for post-Korean GI Bill benefits as of December 31, 1989, and who serve 3 years in active duty service after July 1, 1985, are also eligible for the new program, but will not have their basic pay reduced. Servicepersons who, after December 31, 1976, received commissions as officers from service academies or scholarship senior ROTC programs are not eligible for this program.

Active duty for three years (two years, if the initial obligated period of active duty is less than three years), or two years active duty plus four years in the Selected Reserve or National Guard will entitle an individual to $300 a month basic benefits. There is also a targeted, discretionary kicker of up to an additional $400 available. A supplemental benefit of up to an additional $300 with a targeted, discretionary kicker of up to $300 more is also available.

An educational entitlement program is also available for members of the Selected Reserve. Eligibility applies to individuals who, from July 1, 1985, through June 30, 1988, enlist, re-enlist, or extend an enlistment for a six-year period. Benefits may be paid to eligible members of the Selected Reserve who complete their initial period of active duty training and complete 180 days of service in the Selected Reserve. Full-time payments will be $140 a month for 36 months.

**Veterans' Benefits Improvement Act of 1984.** Veterans awarded a VA pension during the period February 1, 1985, through January 31, 1989, for whom vocational training is reasonably feasible may be provided training expenses and special services and equipment toward a definite vocational goal. Veterans who participate in this special vocational training program and subsequently lose entitlement to pension for excessive work or training income may continue to receive VA health care and retain priority for treatment for 3 years after the date pension is terminated.

Veterans awarded 100 percent disability compensation based upon unemployability during the period February 1, 1985, through January 31, 1989, for whom a vocational goal is feasible are required to participate in a rehabilitation program. Necessary training expenses, special equipment, etc., toward a definite job objective are paid for, plus a monthly allowance up to $310, with increased amounts for dependents, in addition to compensation. In addition, all veterans granted an unemployability rating before February 1, 1985, the start of the special program period, may receive special assistance in securing employment under the Vocational Rehabilitation Program. Any veteran with an unemployability rating who secures gainful employment during the special program period will be protected from reduction until such veteran has worked continuously for 12 months.

**Pensions.** Pension benefits are payable for wartime veterans totally disabled from non-service-connected causes. These benefits are based on need. Surviving spouses and orphans of wartime veterans have the same eligibility status.

**Insurance.** The VA life insurance programs have approximately 7.3 million policyholders with total coverage of about $211.5 billion. Detailed information on NSLI (National Service Life Insurance), USGLI (United States Government Life Insurance), and VMLI (Veterans Mortgage Life Insurance) may be obtained at any VA Office. Information regarding SGLI (Servicemen's Group Life Insurance) and VGLI (Veterans Group Life Insurance) may be obtained from the Office of Servicemen's Group Life Insurance, 213 Washington St., Newark, N.J. 07102

**Burial benefits.** Burial is provided in any VA national cemetery with available grave space to any deceased veteran of wartime or peacetime service, other than for training, who was discharged under conditions other than dishonorable. Laws of the Congress extended eligibility for burial in a national cemetery to the veteran's spouse, widow, widower, minor children, and under certain conditions, unmarried adult children.

**Headstone or marker.** A government headstone or marker is furnished for any deceased veteran of wartime or peacetime service, other than for training, who was discharged under conditions other than dishonorable and is interred in a national, state veterans', or private cemetery. VA also will furnish markers to veterans' eligible dependents interred in a national or state veterans' cemetery.

## Budget Outlays for National Defense Functions

| Item | 1985 est. | 1984 | 1983 | 1982 | 1981 | 1980 | 1979 | 1975 | 1970 |
|---|---|---|---|---|---|---|---|---|---|
| Defense Dept., military | 246.3 | 220.8 | 204.4 | 180.7 | 153.8 | 131.0 | 113.7 | 85.9 | 80.2 |
| Military personnel | 67.5 | 64.2 | 60.9 | 55.2 | 47.9 | 40.9 | 37.3 | 32.2 | 29.0 |
| Percent of military | 27.4 | 29.1 | 30.0 | 30.5 | 31.1 | 31.2 | 32.8 | 37.5 | 36.2 |
| Operation, maintenance | 74.6 | 67.4 | 64.9 | 59.7 | 51.9 | 44.8 | 36.4 | 26.3 | 21.6 |
| Procurement | 69.7 | 61.9 | 53.6 | 43.3 | 35.2 | 29.0 | 25.4 | 16.0 | 21.6 |
| Research and development | 27.8 | 23.1 | 20.6 | 17.7 | 15.3 | 13.1 | 11.2 | 8.9 | 7.2 |
| Military construction | 4.2 | 3.7 | 3.5 | 2.9 | 2.5 | 2.5 | 2.1 | 1.5 | 1.2 |
| Family housing | 2.7 | 2.4 | 2.1 | 2.0 | 1.7 | 1.7 | 1.5 | 1.1 | .6 |
| Other[1] | −.2 | −1.8 | 1.2 | .1 | .6 | 1.0 | .2 | .1 | 1.0 |
| Atomic energy activities[2] | 7.0 | 6.1 | 5.2 | 4.3 | 3.4 | 2.9 | 2.5 | 1.5 | 1.4 |
| Defense-related activities[3] | .5 | .5 | .3 | .3 | .3 | .1 | .1 | .8 | .1 |
| Total | 253.8 | 227.4 | 209.9 | 185.3 | 157.5 | 134.0 | 116.3 | 86.5 | 81.7 |

1. Revolving and management funds, trust funds, special foreign currency program, allowances, and offsetting receipts. 2. Defense activities only. 3. Includes civil defense activities. *Source:* Office of Management and Budget.

# U.S. Military Actions Other Than Declared Wars

**Hawaii (1893):** U.S. Marines, ordered to land by U.S. Minister John L. Stevens, aided the revolutionary Committee of Safety in overthrowing the native government. Stevens then proclaimed Hawaii a U.S. protectorate. Annexation, resisted by the Democratic administration in Washington, was not formally accomplished until 1898.

**China (1900):** Boxers (a group of Chinese revolutionists) occupied Peking and laid siege to foreign legations. U.S. troops joined an international expedition which relieved the city.

**Panama (1903):** After Colombia had rejected a proposed agreement for relinquishing sovereignty over the Panama Canal Zone, revolution broke out, aided by promoters of the Panama Canal Co. Two U.S. warships were standing by to protect American privileges. The U.S. recognized the Republic of Panama on November 6.

**Dominican Republic (1904):** When the Dominican Republic failed to meet debts owed to the U.S. and foreign creditors, President Theodore Roosevelt declared the U.S. intention of exercising "international police power" in the Western Hemisphere whenever necessary. The U.S. accordingly administered customs and managed debt payments of the Dominican Republic from 1905 to 1907.

**Nicaragua (1911):** The possibility of foreign control over Nicaragua's canal route led to U.S. intervention and agreement. The U.S. landed Marines in Nicaragua (Aug. 14, 1912) to protect American interests there. A small detachment remained until 1933.

**Mexico (1914):** Mexican dictator Victoriano Huerta, opposed by President Woodrow Wilson, had the support of European governments. An incident involving unarmed U.S. sailors in Tampico led to the landing of U.S. forces on Mexican soil. Veracruz was bombarded by the Navy to prevent the landing of munitions from a German vessel. At the point of war, both powers agreed to mediation by Argentina, Brazil, and Chile. Huerta abdicated, and Venustiano Carranza succeeded to the presidency.

**Haiti (1915):** U.S. Marines imposed a military occupation. Haiti signed a treaty making it a virtual protectorate of the U.S. until troops were withdrawn in 1934.

**Mexico (1916):** Raids by Pancho Villa cost American lives on both sides of the border. President Carranza consented to a punitive expedition led by Gen. John J. Pershing, but antagonism grew in Mexico. Wilson withdrew the U.S. force when war with Germany became imminent.

**Dominican Republic (1916):** Renewed intervention in the Dominican Republic with internal administration by U.S. naval officers lasted until 1924.

**Korea (1950):** In this undeclared war, which terminated with the July 27, 1953, truce at Panmunjom and the establishment of a neutral nations' supervisory commission, the U.S. and 15 member-nations of the U.N. came to the aid of the Republic of South Korea, whose 38th-parallel border was crossed by the invading Russian Communist-controlled North Koreans, who were later joined by the Chinese Communists.

**Lebanon (1958 and 1983):** Fearful of the newly formed U.A.R. abetting the rebels of his politically and economically torn country, President Camille Chamoun appealed to the U.S. for military assistance. U.S. troops landed in Beirut in mid-July and left before the end of the year, after internal and external quiet were restored. In September 1983, President Reagan ordered Marines to join an international peacekeeping force in Beirut. On October 23, 241 were killed in the terrorist bombing of the Marine compound. On February 7, 1984, Reagan ordered the Marine contingent withdrawn. He ended the U.S. role in Beirut on March 30 by releasing the Sixth Fleet from the international force.

**Dominican Republic (1965):** On April 28, when a political coup-turned-civil war endangered the lives of American nationals, President Lyndon B. Johnson rushed 400 marines into Santo Domingo, the beginning of an eventual U.S. peak-commitment of 30,000 troops, constituting the preponderant military strength of the OAS-created Inter-American Peace Force, and 6,500 troops, including 5,000 Americans, remained until after the peaceful inauguration of President Joaquín Balaguer on July 1, 1966, and the entire force left the country on September 20.

**Vietnam:** This longest war in U.S. history began with economic and technical assistance after 1954 Geneva accords ending the Indochinese War. By 1964 it had escalated into a major conflict.

This involvement spanning the administrations of five Presidents led to domestic discontent in the late 1960s. By April 1969, U.S. troop strength reached a peak of 543,400. Peace negotiations began in Paris in 1968 but proved fruitless. Finally, on Jan. 27, 1973, a peace accord was signed in Paris by the U.S., North and South Vietnam, and the Vietcong. Within 60 days, U.S. POWs were returned, and the U.S. withdrew all military forces from South Vietnam.

**Grenada (1983):** A left-wing military coup resulted in the intervention of a 1,900-man United States contingent, supported by token forces from Caribbean allies, which engaged an 800-man Cuban Force and secured the island within a few days. The American combat force was brought home two months later although a small non-combat unit was left behind to assist in peacekeeping functions.

## Insignia and Ranks of the Armed Forces

| Army, Air Force, and Marines | | Navy and Coast Guard | | |
|---|---|---|---|---|
| Insignia | Rank | Insignia | Rank | Stripes[1] |
| Five silver stars | General of the Army, AF | Five silver stars | Fleet Admiral | 1—4—0 |
| Four silver stars | General | Four silver stars | Admiral | 1—3—0 |
| Three silver stars | Lieutenant General | Three silver stars | Vice Admiral | 1—2—0 |
| Two silver stars | Major General | Two silver stars | Rear Admiral[2] | 1—1—0 |
| One silver star | Brigadier General | One silver star | Rear Admiral 0-7[2] | 1—0—0 |
| Silver eagle | Colonel | Silver eagle | Captain | 0—4—0 |
| Silver oak leaf | Lieutenant Colonel | Silver oak leaf | Commander | 0—3—0 |
| Gold oak leaf | Major | Gold oak leaf | Lt. Commander | 0—2—1 |
| Two silver bars | Captain | Two silver bars | Lieutenant | 0—2—0 |
| One silver bar | First Lieutenant | One silver bar | Lieutenant (jg) | 0—1—1 |
| One gold bar | Second Lieutenant | One gold bar | Ensign | 0—1—0 |
| Silver bar with 4 enamel bands[3] | Chief Warrant Officer (W-4) | Silver bar with 3 enamel bands[3] | Chief Warrant Officer (W-4) | 0—1—0[4] |
| Silver bar with 3 enamel bands[3] | Chief Warrant Officer (W-3) | Silver bar with 2 enamel bands[3] | Chief Warrant Officer (W-3) | 0—1—0[5] |
| Silver bar with 2 enamel bands[3] | Chief Warrant Officer (W-2) | Gold bar with 3 enamel bands[3] | Chief Warrant Officer (W-2) | 0—1—0[6] |
| Silver bar with 1 enamel band[3] | Warrant Officer (W-1) | Gold bar with 2 enamel bands[3] | | |

1. Of gold embroidery; first figure is number of 2-in. stripes, second is number of 1/2-inch strips, third is number of 1/4-in. stripes. 2. The Navy and the Coast Guard changed the rank of Commodore to Rear Admiral (lower half), a 0–7 grade, in Fiscal Year 1986. The 0–8 grade will be designated Rear Admiral (upper half). 3. Navy and Marine Corps use same size insignia as Army when worn on shoulder straps, but miniature size on shirt collars. Enamel bands are black for Army, scarlet for Marines, medium blue for Air Force, and blue for Navy and Coast Guard. 4. One break. 5. Two breaks. 6. Three breaks.

## Average Military Strength[1]
### (in thousands)

| Year | Army | Air Force | Navy | Marine Corps | Total |
|---|---|---|---|---|---|
| 1941 | 755 | [2] | 218 | 44 | 1,017 |
| 1942 | 1,992 | [2] | 416 | 89 | 2,498 |
| 1943 | 5,224 | [2] | 1,206 | 232 | 6,662 |
| 1944 | 7,507 | [2] | 2,386 | 398 | 10,290 |
| 1945 | 8,131 | [2] | 3,205 | 473 | 11,809 |
| 1950 | 632 | 415 | 412 | 80 | 1,539 |
| 1951 | 1,090 | 584 | 566 | 153 | 2,394 |
| 1952 | 1,597 | 899 | 789 | 219 | 3,504 |
| 1953 | 1,536 | 971 | 809 | 237 | 3,554 |
| 1954 | 1,477 | 939 | 767 | 242 | 3,425 |
| 1955 | 1,311 | 958 | 692 | 217 | 3,178 |
| 1960 | 871 | 828 | 617 | 173 | 2,489 |
| 1965 | 966 | 844 | 669 | 190 | 2,668 |
| 1970 | 1,432 | 834 | 732 | 295 | 3,293 |
| 1971 | 1,238 | 763 | 656 | 234 | 2,891 |
| 1972 | 955 | 749 | 604 | 202 | 2,510 |
| 1973 | 839 | 706 | 580 | 198 | 2,323 |
| 1975 | 779 | 628 | 545 | 193 | 2,145 |
| 1977 | 779 | 577 | 527 | 190 | 2,073 |
| 1978 | 777 | 570 | 530 | 191 | 2,068 |
| 1979 | 765 | 565 | 527 | 188 | 2,045 |
| 1980 | 762 | 561 | 525 | 185 | 2,033 |
| 1981 | 769 | 561 | 531 | 186 | 2,050 |
| 1982 | 777 | 570 | 540 | 189 | 2,077 |
| 1983 | 778 | 581 | 547 | 192 | 2,098 |
| 1984 | 782 | 597 | 561 | 195 | 2,135 |
| 1985 | 780 | 604 | 570 | 197 | 2,151 |

1. Data represent averages of month-end strengths. 2. Air Force data prior to June 30, 1948 included with Army data. NOTE: Detail may not add to totals due to rounding. *Source:* Department of Defense.

## U.S. Casualties in Major Wars

| War | Branch of service | Numbers engaged | Battle deaths | Other deaths | Total deaths | Wounds not mortal | Total casualties[1] |
|---|---|---|---|---|---|---|---|
| Revolutionary War | Army | n.a. | 4,044 | n.a. | n.a. | 6,004 | n.a. |
| 1775 to 1783 | Navy | n.a. | 342 | n.a. | n.a. | 114 | n.a. |
| | Marines | n.a. | 49 | n.a. | n.a. | 70 | n.a. |
| | Total | n.a. | 4,435 | n.a. | n.a. | 6,188 | n.a. |
| War of 1812 | Army | n.a. | 1,950 | n.a. | n.a. | 4,000 | n.a. |
| 1812 to 1815 | Navy | n.a. | 265 | n.a. | n.a. | 439 | n.a. |
| | Marines | n.a. | 45 | n.a. | n.a. | 66 | n.a. |
| | Total | 286,730 | 2,260 | n.a. | n.a. | 4,505 | n.a. |
| Mexican War | Army | n.a. | 1,721 | 11,550 | 13,271 | 4,102 | 17,373 |
| 1846 to 1848 | Navy | n.a. | 1 | n.a. | n.a. | 3 | n.a. |
| | Marines | n.a. | 11 | n.a. | n.a. | 47 | n.a. |
| | Total | 78,718 | 1,733 | n.a. | n.a. | 4,152 | n.a. |
| Civil War[2] | Army | 2,128,948 | 138,154 | 221,374 | 359,528 | 280,040 | 639,568 |
| 1861 to 1865 | Navy | 84,415 | 2,112 | 2,411 | 4,523 | 1,710 | 6,233 |
| | Marines | | 148 | 312 | 460 | 131 | 591 |
| | Total | 2,213,363 | 140,414 | 224,097 | 364,511 | 281,881 | 646,392 |
| Spanish-American War | Army | 280,564 | 369 | 2,061 | 2,430 | 1,594 | 4,024 |
| 1898 | Navy | 22,875 | 10 | 0 | 10 | 47 | 57 |
| | Marines | 3,321 | 6 | 0 | 6 | 21 | 27 |
| | Total | 306,760 | 385 | 2,061 | 2,446 | 1,662 | 4,108 |
| World War I | Army | 4,057,101 | 50,510 | 55,868 | 106,378 | 193,663 | 300,041 |
| 1917 to 1918 | Navy | 599,051 | 431 | 6,856 | 7,287 | 819 | 8,106 |
| | Marines | 78,839 | 2,461 | 390 | 2,851 | 9,520 | 12,371 |
| | Total | 4,734,991 | 53,402 | 63,114 | 116,516 | 204,002 | 320,518 |
| World War II | Army[3] | 11,260,000 | 234,874 | 83,400 | 318,274 | 565,861 | 884,135 |
| 1941 to 1946 | Navy | 4,183,466 | 36,950 | 25,664 | 62,614 | 37,778 | 100,392 |
| | Marines | 669,100 | 19,733 | 4,778 | 24,511 | 67,207 | 91,718 |
| | Total | 16,112,566 | 291,557 | 113,842 | 405,399 | 670,846 | 1,076,245 |
| Korean War | Army | 2,834,000 | 27,704 | 9,429 | 37,133 | 77,596 | 114,729 |
| 1950 to 1953 | Navy | 1,177,000 | 458 | 4,043 | 4,501 | 1,576 | 6,077 |
| | Marines | 424,000 | 4,267 | 1,261 | 5,528 | 23,744 | 29,272 |
| | Air Force | 1,285,000 | 1,200 | 5,884 | 7,084 | 368 | 7,452 |
| | Total | 5,720,000 | 33,629 | 20,617 | 54,246 | 103,284 | 157,530 |
| War in Southeast Asia[4] | Army | 4,386,000 | 30,867 | 7,252 | 38,119 | 96,802 | 134,921 |
| | Navy[5] | 1,842,000 | 1,605 | 911 | 2,516 | 4,178 | 6,694 |
| | Marines | 794,000 | 13,066 | 1,685 | 14,749 | 51,392 | 66,141 |
| | Air Force | 1,740,000 | 1,715 | 603 | 2,318 | 931 | 3,249 |
| | Total | 8,744,000 | 47,253 | 10,449 | 57,702 | 153,303 | 211,005 |

1. Excludes captured or interned and missing in action who were subsequently returned to military control. 2. Union forces only. Totals should probably be somewhat larger as data or disposition of prisoners are far from complete. Final Confederate deaths, based on incomplete returns, were 133,821, to which should be added 26,000–31,000 personnel who died in Union prisons. 3. Army data include Air Force. 4. As of Sept. 30, 1977. 5. Includes a small number of Coast Guard. NOTE: All data are subject to revision. For wars before World War I, information represents best data from available records. However, due to incomplete records and possible difference in usage of terminology, reporting systems, etc., figures should be considered estimates. n.a. = not available. *Source:* Department of Defense.

## The Kamikazes in World War II

During the 13th century, a great typhoon off the coast of Japan nearly destroyed the ships of an invading Mongol army. This seeming intervention by Providence was considered a "Divine Wind" or Kamikaze by the Japanese people.

In late 1944, the United States was in the process of recapturing the Philippine Islands from Japan. In a desperate act to prevent it, Japanese military leaders authorized the formation of a Special Attack Force whose mission was to destroy American aircraft carriers. Each member of this special unit had volunteered to sacrifice his life by diving a bomb-laden plane into the deck of a U.S. flattop.

The suicide fliers were called the Kamikaze, named after the Divine Wind that had saved their country from invasion in the past.

By the end of the war, over 1,200 Kamikaze pilots had sunk 34 U.S. ships and damaged 288 others. There was never a shortage of volunteers for the suicide missions, only a shortage of planes and fuel for them to make their desperate attacks in.

## Casualties in World War I

| Country | Total mobilized forces | Killed or died[1] | Wounded | Prisoners or missing | Total casualties |
|---|---|---|---|---|---|
| Austria-Hungary | 7,800,000 | 1,200,000 | 3,620,000 | 2,200,000 | 7,020,000 |
| Belgium | 267,000 | 13,716 | 44,686 | 34,659 | 93,061 |
| British Empire[2] | 8,904,467 | 908,371 | 2,090,212 | 191,652 | 3,190,235 |
| Bulgaria | 1,200,000 | 87,500 | 152,390 | 27,029 | 266,919 |
| France[2] | 8,410,000 | 1,357,800 | 4,266,000 | 537,000 | 6,160,800 |
| Germany | 11,000,000 | 1,773,700 | 4,216,058 | 1,152,800 | 7,142,558 |
| Greece | 230,000 | 5,000 | 21,000 | 1,000 | 27,000 |
| Italy | 5,615,000 | 650,000 | 947,000 | 600,000 | 2,197,000 |
| Japan | 800,000 | 300 | 907 | 3 | 1,210 |
| Montenegro | 50,000 | 3,000 | 10,000 | 7,000 | 20,000 |
| Portugal | 100,000 | 7,222 | 13,751 | 12,318 | 33,291 |
| Romania | 750,000 | 335,706 | 120,000 | 80,000 | 535,706 |
| Russia | 12,000,000 | 1,700,000 | 4,950,000 | 2,500,000 | 9,150,000 |
| Serbia | 707,343 | 45,000 | 133,148 | 152,958 | 331,106 |
| Turkey | 2,850,000 | 325,000 | 400,000 | 250,000 | 975,000 |
| United States | 4,734,991 | 116,516 | 204,002 | — | 320,518 |

1. Includes deaths from all causes. 2. Official figures. NOTE: For additional U.S. figures, *see* the table on U.S. Casualties in Major Wars in this section.

## Casualties in World War II

| Country | Men in war | Battle deaths | Wounded |
|---|---|---|---|
| Australia | 1,000,000 | 26,976 | 180,864 |
| Austria | 800,000 | 280,000 | 350,117[1] |
| Belgium | 625,000 | 8,460 | 55,513[1] |
| Brazil[2] | 40,334 | 943 | 4,222 |
| Bulgaria | 339,760 | 6,671 | 21,878 |
| Canada | 1,076,343[7] | 32,714[7] | 53,145 |
| China[3] | 17,250,521 | 1,324,516 | 1,762,006 |
| Czechoslovakia | — | 6,683[4] | 8,017 |
| Denmark | — | 4,339 | — |
| Finland | 500,000 | 79,047 | 50,000 |
| France | — | 201,568 | 400,000 |
| Germany | 20,000,000 | 3,250,000[4] | 7,250,000 |
| Greece | — | 17,024 | 47,290 |
| Hungary | — | 147,435 | 89,313 |
| India | 2,393,891 | 32,121 | 64,354 |
| Italy | 3,100,000 | 149,496[4] | 66,716 |
| Japan | 9,700,000 | 1,270,000 | 140,000 |
| Netherlands | 280,000 | 6,500 | 2,860 |
| New Zealand | 194,000 | 11,625[4] | 17,000 |
| Norway | 75,000 | 2,000 | — |
| Poland | — | 664,000 | 530,000 |
| Romania | 650,000[5] | 350,000[6] | — |
| South Africa | 410,056 | 2,473 | — |
| U.S.S.R. | — | 6,115,000[4] | 14,012,000 |
| United Kingdom | 5,896,000 | 357,116[4] | 369,267 |
| United States | 16,112,566 | 291,557 | 670,846 |
| Yugoslavia | 3,741,000 | 305,000 | 425,000 |

1. Civilians only. 2. Army and Navy figures. 3. Figures cover period July 7, 1937–Sept. 2, 1945, and concern only Chinese regular troops. They do not include casualties suffered by guerrillas and local military corps. 4. Deaths from all causes. 5. Against Soviet Russia; 385,847 against Nazi Germany. 6. Against Soviet Russia; 169,822 against Nazi Germany. 7. National Defense Ctr., Candanian Forces Hq., Director of History. NOTE: The figures in this table are unofficial estimates obtained from various sources.

### Military Pensions Revised

The Military Reform Act of 1986 changed pensions for anyone entering the armed forces after August 1, 1986. Under the old law, those who retired after 20 years of service received a pension equal to half of their base pay in the three highest-paid years. The pension increased 2.5 percent of base pay for each additional year of service up to 30 years when it stopped at 75 percent of base pay.

Under the new law, those who retire after 20 years (and usually go on to a new career) will receive 40 percent of base pay for the three highest years. It rises to 75 percent after 30 years of service.

The bill also provides for annual cost-of-living increases.

Early retirement pensions would be adjusted up to a base of 50 percent at age 62, with a 1 percent penalty added after the cost-of-living adjustment for each year of service less than 30 years.

# TRAVEL

## Choosing a Travel Agent

*By Hal Gieseking*

Would your vacation be better, easier or less expensive if you planned it with a travel agent? Here are some candid answers to the most common questions asked by consumers about travel agents.

### What are the advantages of working with a travel agent?

A travel agent can sift through the enormous number of air fares, tours, and cruise offerings to give you many more vacation options than you could probably come up with on your own. As a result of airline deregulation, airlines can change fares hour to hour, leaving consumers confused and sometimes paying more for air travel than they should. Travel agents use computers which have current pricing and schedule information to identify the lowest fares to their clients' intended destinations.

Full-service travel agents can plan and book your entire trip. They make the reservations for airlines, tours, cruises, rail travel, and package vacations and provide you with the tickets. Agents can arrange for visas and travel insurance as well.

(Note: Many agents who bill themselves as "full service" may not be able to get you bus or train tickets or reservations at certain hotels. In addition, some hotels may not pay travel agency commissions; this tends to dampen an agency's enthusiasm for those hotels.)

Perhaps one of the most valuable services a travel agent can perform is to match travelers with the vacations most suitable for them. A professional agent could help a single traveler avoid a couples-oriented resort and would not book an older couple on a disco-till-dawn singles' cruise without telling them what to expect. A professional agent will attempt to identify the travelers' basic interests and what they would most enjoy doing on their vacations and make recommendations accordingly.

### What do travel agents charge for their services?

The majority of travel agents will charge you nothing beyond the cost of your trip. Airlines, tour companies, and cruise lines pay the agents a commission for each booking.

Some travel agents do charge a fee when planning complex itineraries for individual travelers. In this case, you're tapping the professional expertise of someone who can help arrange the day-by-day connections and reservations that can make your whole trip a lot smoother—so the fee can be a real bargain.

You will usually be billed by the agent for any out-of-pocket expenses made on your behalf, long-distance phone calls, telegrams, visa fees, etc.

### How can I find the best travel agent for my needs?

There's a good chance you'll find one right in your neighborhood.

There has been a tremendous surge in the number of travel agents in recent years. Of the over 27,000 travel agencies now operating in the U.S., some 12,000 have opened in just the last eight years.

Talk with friends who have returned from a well-planned trip and ask them what travel agency they used. Then ask them which *travel counselor* they used.

Even within the same agency, travel counselors vary greatly in their abilities and experience. Many are well-seasoned professional agents who have traveled widely and can knowledgeably discuss many parts of the world. Others are brand new at the job and commit almost unbelievable gaffes.

It's usually a good sign if the agent belongs to the American Society of Travel Agents (ASTA) or the Association of Retail Travel Agents (ARTA). Membership in either organization indicates a certain degree of business stability and means the agent subscribes to a code of ethics. Probably the crème de la crème of travel agents are those with the initials "C.T.C." on their letterheads. This means that the individual is a certified travel counselor with a minimum of five years' experience as a travel agent and has completed a graduate-level two-year course offered by the Institute of Certified Travel Agents in Wellesley, Mass.

Another mark of a good travel agent is one who asks a lot of questions about your interests, your plans, and your budget. Agents traditionally give short-shrift to people they believe are just price-shopping for the lowest fare. But if they sense you really want to work with them to plan a trip, the good ones will gladly spend time with you. When the extent of your contact with a travel agency is a counselor who says, "Go look at the brochures and see if there's anything you like," you should go to another agency.

### Is any money paid to a travel agent protected if the agent or the airline or tour company goes out of business?

The only honest, and not very satisfactory, answer is "sometimes."

It goes back to the legal questions that originated with the travel agency business. Are they agents working for the consumers, the travel companies, or both? The answer seems to be both.

In past cases where the travel agent has gone bankrupt after collecting money from clients for airline tickets, the courts have usually held that the travel agency was the agent for the airline and your

Hal Gieseking is editor, The Travel Advisor, *Travel-Holiday* magazine. Reprinted with permission of Travel-Holiday, Travel Building, Floral Park, New York.

paying for tickets was the same as you paying money directly to the airline. The airline had to provide the transportation for which you had paid, whether or not it ever received the money from the travel agent.

Legal decisions about payments made to travel agents by consumers for tours, cruises, and other travel arrangements have been mixed. Should the agent subsequently declare bankruptcy before paying the travel company, that company may—or may not—honor the tickets issued by the agent.

ASTA has created the Tour Payment Protection Plan, a special fund by which the traveler will be reimbursed if a participating tour operator goes out of business. Some 50 tour operators are currently participating in the program. Any ASTA agent can provide you with their names.

ASTA and ARTA probably won't be able to help if one of their members goes bankrupt. However, they can help if you have a money (or other) problem that you are unable to resolve with one of their member agencies. Document the problem in a letter to ASTA's Consumer Affairs Department, 4400 MacArthur Blvd., N.W., Washington, D.C. 20007 or to ARTA's Grievance Committee, 25 South Riverside Avenue, Croton-on-Hudson, NY 10520. Send a carbon of the letter to the recalcitrant agent. Often this carbon may stir more action than any number of phone calls. You can also contact the local Better Business Bureau in the city where the agent is located.

## Will a travel agent help if I have problems during the trip?

The best agents certainly will. For example, if the hotel claims they have no record of your reservation, you should call the agent who made the reservation for help. Some agents can help you reroute your trip if your plans change during your vacation.

Members of ARTA work with Travel Helpline, a company that it owns jointly with Travel Savers. Travel Helpline is a 24-hour service that travelers can phone when they encounter problems in the middle of their trip, such as dishonored reservations, lost luggage, or airline strikes. ARTA agents can provide their clients with a toll-free number to call in the U.S. and a number to call overseas.

Your choice of travel agents is the key to a good trip. If you find a disinterested dud who simply passes out brochures, the burden of travel planning shifts back to you. If you find an agent who is an eager entrepreneur anxious to help you make your whole trip easier, stick with that agent. And share his or her name and address with your friends. You want that travel agent to be in business for a long time.

# U.S. Passport and Customs Information

*Source:* Department of State, Passport Services and Department of the Treasury, Customs Service.

## Passports

With a few exceptions, a passport is required for all United States citizens to depart from and enter the United States and to enter most foreign countries. A United States citizen is not required by United States laws or regulations to have a valid passport for travel to or in North, South, or Central America, except Cuba. It is, however, recommended that a passport be obtained for travel to Central and South America since many of the countries require that United States citizens be in possession of a valid passport. United States travelers should carry documentary evidence of their United States citizenship and identity to facilitate re-entry into the United States. Travelers should check passport and visa requirements with consular officials of the countries to be visited well in advance of their departure date.

Applications for passport may be made to any Passport Agent; to a clerk of any Federal court or State court of record, or a judge or clerk or any probate court, accepting applications; or at a Post Office selected to accept passport applications. Passport agencies are located in Boston; Chicago; Honolulu; Houston; Los Angeles; Miami; New Orleans; New York; Philadelphia; San Francisco; Seattle; Stamford, Conn.; and Washington, D.C.

All persons are required to obtain individual passports in their own names. Neither spouses nor children may be included in each others' passports. Any applicant who is 13 years of age or older must appear in person before the clerk or agent executing the application. For children under the age of 13, a parent or guardian may execute an application for them.

A first passport must be applied for in person. Applicants must present evidence of citizenship (e.g., a birth certificate), personal identification (e.g., driver's license), two identical photographs taken within six months ($2 \times 2$ inches, with the image size measured from the bottom of the chin to the top of the head [including hair] not less than 1 inch nor more than 1 3/8 inches, signed in the center on the reverse; vending machine photographs not acceptable), plus the application. A fee of $35 plus a $7 execution fee is charged for adults 18 years and older. The fee for children under 18 years of age is $20 for a passport and $7 for the execution of the application. No execution fee is payable when using DSP-82, "Application for Passport by Mail."

You may apply by mail if you have been the bearer of a passport issued within eight years prior to the date of a new application; are able to submit your most recent United States passport with your new application; your previous passport was not issued before your 18th birthday. If you are eligible to apply by mail, include your previous passport, completed and signed Application for Passport by Mail, new signed photographs, and the correct passport fee of $35 as explained above. The $7 execution fee is not required when applying by mail.

If you claim citizenship by naturalization, a Certificate of Naturalization is required.

Passports may be amended to show a married name or legal change of name, to correct descriptive data, or to exclude a person previously included.

Any alterations by the bearer other than change of address and notification data appearing in the passport are forbidden.

A passport is valid for ten years from the date of issue for adults over 18 years old and is valid for five years for children under 18 years of age, unless specifically limited by the Secretary of State to a shorter period of validity.

Loss, theft or destruction of passport should be reported immediately to local police authorities and to Passport Services, Washington, D.C., 20520, or, if overseas, to the nearest American embassy or consulate. Your passport is a valuable citizenship and identity document. It should be carefully safeguarded. Its loss could cause you unnecessary travel complications as well as significant expense.

## Customs

United States residents must declare all articles acquired abroad and in their possession at the time of their return. In addition, articles acquired in the U.S. Virgin Islands, American Samoa, or Guam and not accompanying you must be declared at the time of your return. The wearing or use of an article acquired abroad does *not* exempt it from duty. Customs declaration forms are distributed on vessels and planes, and should be prepared in advance of arrival for presentation to the customs inspectors.

If you have not exceeded the duty-free exemption allowed, you may make an oral declaration to the customs inspector. A written declaration is necessary when (1) total fair retail value of articles exceeds $1,400 ($400 tax-free exemption plus $1,000 dutiable at a flat 10% rate) (keep your sales slips); (2) over 1 liter of liquor, 200 cigarettes, or 100 cigars are included; (3) items are not intended for your personal or household use, or articles brought home for another person; and (4) when a customs duty or internal revenue tax is collectible on any article in your possession.

An exception to the above are regulations applicable to articles purchased in the U.S. Virgin Islands, American Samoa, or Guam where you may receive a customs exemption of $800. Not more than $400 of this exemption may be applied to merchandise obtained elsewhere than in these islands. Five liters of alcoholic beverages and 1000 cigarettes may be included provided not more than one liter and 200 cigarettes were acquired elsewhere than in these islands. Articles acquired in and sent from these islands to the United States may be claimed under your duty-free personal exemption if properly declared at the time of your return.

Articles accompanying you, in excess of your personal exemption, up to $1000 will be assessed at a flat rate of duty of 10% based on fair retail value in country of acquisition. (If articles were acquired in the insular possessions, the flat rate of duty is 5% and these goods may accompany you or be shipped home.) These articles must be for your personal use or for use as gifts and not for sale. This provision may be used every 30 days, excluding the day of your last arrival. Any items which have a "free" duty rate will be excluded before duty is calculated.

Other exemptions include in part: automobiles, boats, planes, or other vehicles taken abroad for noncommercial use. Foreign-made personal articles (e.g., watches, cameras, etc.) taken abroad should be registered with Customs before departure. Gifts of not more than $50 can be shipped back to the United States tax and duty free ($100 if mailed from the Virgin Islands, American Samoa, or Guam). Household effects and tools of trade which you take out of the United States are duty free at time of return.

Prohibited and restricted articles include in part: absinthe, narcotics and dangerous drugs, obscene articles and publications, seditious and treasonable materials, hazardous articles (e.g., fireworks, dangerous toys, toxic and poisonous substances, and switchblade knives), biological materials of public health or veterinary importance, fruit, vegetables and plants, meats, poultry and products thereof, birds, monkeys, and turtles.

If you understate the value of an article you declare, or if you otherwise misrepresent an article in your declaration, you may have to pay a penalty in addition to payment of duty. Under certain circumstances, the article could be seized and forfeited if the penalty is not paid.

If you fail to declare an article acquired abroad, not only is the article subject to seizure and forfeiture, but you will be liable for a personal penalty in an amount equal to the value of the article in the United States. In addition, you may also be liable to criminal prosecution.

If you carry more than $10,000 into or out of the United States in currency (either United States or foreign money), negotiable instruments in bearer form, or travelers checks, a report must be filed with United States Customs at the time you arrive or depart with such amounts.

As U.S. restrictions on travel to Cuba, North Korea, Vietnam, and Cambodia have been eased, the Office of Foreign Assets Control (FAC) issued a general license, effective March 21, 1977, which allows visitors to those countries to purchase a maximum of $100 worth of goods. This amount is based on retail value in the country where acquired. These articles must be for personal use—not for resale—and must accompany the traveler on his entry into the U.S. This allowance may be used only once every 6 months.

## Traveler Warnings on World Danger Areas

The Citizens Emergency Center of the U.S. State Department's Bureau of Consular Affairs maintains a hotline which you can call to obtain the latest information about safety conditions in any part of the world. The number is (202) 647-5225, Mon.–Fri., 8:30 A.M.–10:00 P.M. EST.

U.S. citizens can also use this number to obtain help in emergency situations in any part of the world.

You might also be interested the "World Status Map" published monthly by World Status Map, Box 466, Merrifield, Va. 22166. It reports information on danger areas for travelers, travel warnings and advisories from the U.S. State Department, Medical alerts from the World Health Organization and Center for Disease Control, and includes passport, visa, and vaccination requirements for all world countries.

A single copy is $4.50, a six-month subscription is $24.00, and a one-year subscription is $36.00.

# State and City Tourism Offices

The following is a selected list of state, tourism offices. Where a toll-free 800 number is available, it is given. However, the numbers are subject to change.

**ALABAMA**
Bureau of Tourism & Travel
532 S. Perry St.
Montgomery, AL 36104
205-261-4169 or
1-800-ALABAMA

**ALASKA**
Alaska Division of Tourism
P.O. Box E
Juneau, AK 99811
907-465-2010

**ARIZONA**
Arizona Office of Tourism
Suite 180
1480 E. Bethany Home Rd.
Phoenix, AZ 85014
602-255-3618

**ARKANSAS**
Arkansas Department of Parks
and Tourism
1 Capitol Mall
Little Rock, AR 72201.
501-371-7777 or
1-800-482-8999 or
1-800-643-8383
(Out of state)

**CALIFORNIA**
California Office of Tourism
Department of Commerce
1121 L Street
Suite 103
Sacramento, CA 95814
916-332-1396

**COLORADO**
Office of Tourism
Colorado Tourism Board
5500 S. Syracuse #267
Englewood, CO 80111

**CONNECTICUT**
Tourism Promotion Service
Connecticut Department of Economic Development
210 Washington St.
Hartford, CT 06106
203-566-3385 or
1-800-243-1685

**DELAWARE**
Delaware Tourism Office
Delaware Development Office
99 Kings Highway
P.O. Box 1401
Dover, DE 19903
302-736-4271 or
1-800-441-8846

**DISTRICT OF COLUMBIA**
Washington Convention and
Visitors Association
Suite 250
1575 Eye Street, NW
Washington, D.C. 20005
202-789-7000

**FLORIDA**
Department of Commerce Visitors Inquiry
126 Van Buren St.
Tallahassee, FL 32301
904-487-1462

**GEORGIA**
Tourist Division
P.O. Box 1776
Atlanta, GA 30301
404-656-3590

**HAWAII**
Hawaii Visitors Bureau
2270 Kalakaua Ave., Suite 801
Honolulu, HI 96815
808-923-1811

**IDAHO**
Department of Commerce
Statehouse, Rm. 108
Boise, ID 83720
208-334-2470 or
1-800-635-7820
(Out of state)

**ILLINOIS**
Illinois Department of Commerce and Community Af-
fairs Office of Tourism
620 East Adams Street
Springfield, IL 62701
217-782-7139

**INDIANA**
Indiana Dept. of Commerce
Tourism Division
1 North Capitol, Suite 700
Indianapolis, IN 46204
317-232-8860

**IOWA**
Iowa Development Commission
Visitors and Tourism
600 East Court Ave., Suite A
Des Moines, IA 50309
515-281-3100

**KANSAS**
Travel, Tourism, & Film Services Division
Department of Economic Development
400 W. 8th St., 5th Floor
Topeka, KS 66603
913-296-2009

**KENTUCKY**
Department of Travel Develop-
ment
Capital Plaza Tower
Frankfort, KY 40601
502-564-4930 or
1-800-225-TRIP
(Continental United States and
provinces of Ontario and
Quebec, Canada)

**LOUISIANA**
Office of Tourism
P.O. Box 94291
Baton Rouge, LA 70804-9291
504-925-3860 or
1-800-231-4730

**MAINE**
Maine Publicity Bureau
97 Winthrop St., P.O. Box
2300
Hallowell, ME 04347-2300
207-289-2423

**MARYLAND**
Office of Tourist Development
45 Calvert Street
Annapolis, MD 21401
301-269-3517

**MASSACHUSETTS**
Dept. of Food & Agriculture
Bureau of Markets
100 Cambridge St.
Boston, MA 02202
617-727-3018

**MICHIGAN**
Travel Bureau
Department of Commerce
P.O. Box 30226
Lansing, MI 48909
517-373-1195 or 1-800-
5432-YES
or for latest recorded information on special seasonal activities, 1-800-292-5404 (in-
state) or 1-800-248-5708

**MINNESOTA**
Minnesota Office of Tourism
240 Bremer Bldg., 419 N.
Robert St.
St. Paul, MN 55101
612-296-5029 or
1-800-328-1461

**MISSISSIPPI**
Division of Tourism
Department of Economic Devel-
opment
P.O. Box 849
Jackson, MS 39205
601-359-3414 or
1-800-647-2290

## Average Daily Temperatures (°F) in Tourist Cities

| Location | January High | January Low | April High | April Low | July High | July Low | October High | October Low |
|---|---|---|---|---|---|---|---|---|
| **U.S. CITIES** (See Weather and Climate Section) | | | | | | | | |
| **CANADA** | | | | | | | | |
| Ottawa | 21 | 3 | 51 | 31 | 81 | 58 | 54 | 37 |
| Quebec | 18 | 2 | 45 | 29 | 76 | 57 | 51 | 37 |
| Toronto | 30 | 16 | 50 | 34 | 79 | 59 | 56 | 40 |
| Vancouver | 41 | 32 | 58 | 40 | 74 | 54 | 57 | 44 |
| **MEXICO** | | | | | | | | |
| Acapulco | 85 | 70 | 87 | 71 | 89 | 75 | 88 | 74 |
| Mexico City | 66 | 42 | 78 | 52 | 74 | 54 | 70 | 50 |
| **OVERSEAS** | | | | | | | | |
| Australia (Sydney) | 78 | 65 | 71 | 58 | 60 | 46 | 71 | 56 |
| Austria (Vienna) | 34 | 26 | 57 | 41 | 75 | 59 | 55 | 44 |
| Bahamas (Nassau) | 77 | 65 | 81 | 69 | 88 | 75 | 85 | 73 |
| Bermuda (Hamilton) | 68 | 58 | 71 | 59 | 85 | 73 | 79 | 69 |
| Brazil (Rio de Janeiro) | 84 | 73 | 80 | 69 | 75 | 63 | 77 | 66 |
| Denmark (Copenhagen) | 36 | 29 | 50 | 37 | 72 | 55 | 53 | 42 |
| Egypt (Cairo) | 65 | 47 | 83 | 57 | 96 | 70 | 86 | 65 |
| France (Paris) | 42 | 32 | 60 | 41 | 76 | 55 | 59 | 44 |
| Germany (Berlin) | 35 | 26 | 55 | 38 | 74 | 55 | 55 | 41 |
| Greece (Athens) | 54 | 42 | 67 | 52 | 90 | 72 | 74 | 60 |
| Hong Kong | 64 | 56 | 75 | 67 | 87 | 78 | 81 | 73 |
| India (Calcutta) | 80 | 55 | 97 | 76 | 90 | 79 | 89 | 74 |
| Italy (Rome) | 54 | 39 | 68 | 46 | 88 | 64 | 73 | 53 |
| Israel (Jerusalem) | 55 | 41 | 73 | 50 | 87 | 63 | 81 | 59 |
| Japan (Tokyo) | 47 | 29 | 63 | 46 | 83 | 70 | 69 | 55 |
| Nigeria (Lagos) | 88 | 74 | 89 | 77 | 83 | 74 | 85 | 74 |
| Netherlands (Amsterdam) | 40 | 34 | 52 | 43 | 69 | 59 | 56 | 48 |
| Puerto Rico (San Juan) | 81 | 67 | 84 | 69 | 87 | 74 | 87 | 73 |
| South Africa (Cape Town) | 78 | 60 | 72 | 53 | 63 | 45 | 70 | 52 |
| Spain (Madrid) | 47 | 33 | 64 | 44 | 87 | 62 | 66 | 48 |
| United Kingdom (London) | 44 | 35 | 56 | 40 | 73 | 55 | 58 | 44 |
| United Kingdom (Edinburgh) | 43 | 35 | 50 | 39 | 65 | 52 | 53 | 44 |
| U.S.S.R. (Moscow) | 21 | 9 | 47 | 31 | 76 | 55 | 46 | 34 |
| Venezuela (Caracas) | 75 | 56 | 81 | 60 | 78 | 61 | 79 | 61 |
| Yugoslavia (Belgrade) | 37 | 27 | 64 | 45 | 84 | 61 | 65 | 47 |

**MISSOURI**
Missouri Division of Tourism
Truman State Office Bldg.
301 W. High St.
P.O. Box 1055
Jefferson City, MO 65102
314-751-4133

**MONTANA**
Travel Promotion
Department of Commerce
1424 9th Ave.
Helena, MT 59620
406-444-2654 or
   1-800-548-3390

**NEBRASKA**
Dept. of Economic Development
Division of Travel and Tourism
301 Centennial Mall South
P.O. Box 94666
Lincoln, NE 68509
402-471-3796 or
   1-800-742-7595 or

1-800-228-4307 (Out of
   state)

**NEVADA**
Commission on Tourism
Capitol Complex
Carson City, NV 89710
702-885-4322

**NEW HAMPSHIRE**
Office of Vacation Travel
P.O. Box 856
Concord, NH 03301
603-271-2666
or for recorded weekly events,
   ski conditions, foliage reports
   1-800-258-3608

**NEW JERSEY**
Division of Travel and Tourism
CN-826
Trenton, NJ 08625
609-292-2470

**NEW MEXICO**
Economic Development and
   Tourism Department
Tourism and Travel Division
Bataan Memorial Bldg.
Santa Fe, NM 87503
505-827-6230 or
   1-800-545-2040

**NEW YORK**
Division of Tourism
1 Commerce Plaza
Albany, NY 12245
Toll free from all states from
   MI east & VA north
1-800-225-5697 or
   518-474-4116

**NORTH CAROLINA**
Travel and Tourism Division
Department of Commerce
430 North Salisbury St.
Raleigh, NC 27611
919-733-4171 or 1-800-VISIT
   NC

**NORTH DAKOTA**
North Dakota Tourism
Promotion
Liberty Memorial Building
Capitol Grounds
Bismarck, ND 58505
701-224-2525 or
1-800-437-2077 (out
of state)

**OHIO**
Ohio Office of Travel and
Tourism
P.O. Box 1001
Columbus, OH 43216
614-466-8844 or
1-800-Buckeye

**OKLAHOMA**
Oklahoma Tourism and Recreation Dept.
Literature Distribution Center
215 NE 28th Street
Oklahoma City, OK 73105
405-521-2409

**OREGON**
Tourism Division
Oregon Economic Development
595 Cottage St., NE
Salem, OR 97310
503-378-3451 or
1-800-547-7842 (Out of
state)

**PENNSYLVANIA**
Bureau of Travel Development
416 Forum Building
Harrisburg, PA 17120
717-787-5453

**RHODE ISLAND**
Department of Economic Development, Tourism & Promo-
tion Div.
Tourist Division
7 Jackson Walkway

Providence, RI 02903
401-277-2601 or
1-800-556-2484 (For resi-
dents from Maine to Virginia/
West Virginia and Northern
Ohio)

**SOUTH CAROLINA**
South Carolina Division of
Tourism
Box 71
Columbia, SC 29202
803-758-2279

**SOUTH DAKOTA**
South Dakota Division of
Tourism
Box 1000
Pierre, SD 57501
605-773-3301 or
1-800-843-1930

**TENNESSEE**
Department of Tourist Develop-
ment
P.O. Box 23170
Nashville, TN 37202
615-741-2158

**TEXAS**
Travel Information Services
State Highway Department
P.O. Box 5064
Austin, TX 78763-5064
512-465-7401

**UTAH**
Utah Travel Council
Council Hall, Capitol Hill
Salt Lake City, UT 84114
801-533-5681

**VERMONT**
Agency of Development and
Community Affairs
Travel Division
134 State St.

Montpelier, VT 05602
802-828-3236

**VIRGINIA**
Virginia Division of Tourism
202 North Ninth Street
Suite 500
Richmond, VA 23219
804-786-4484

**WASHINGTON**
Washington State Dept. of
Trade and Economic Develop-
ment
General Administration Bldg.
AX-13
Olympia, WA 98504
206-753-5630 or
1-800-541-9274

**WASHINGTON, D.C.**
*See* District of Columbia

**WEST VIRGINIA**
Travel Development—GOECD
1900 Washington St., East
Charleston, WV 25305
304-348-2286 or
1-800-CALL-WVA

**WISCONSIN**
Department of Development
Division of Tourism
Box 7606
Madison, WI 53707
Toll free in WI and neighbor
states 1-800-escapes
others: 608-266-2161

**WYOMING**
Wyoming Travel Commission
I-25 at College Drive
Cheyenne, WY 82002-0660
307-777-7777 or
1-800-CALL-WYO

## Travel Information Sources

**Birnbaum's** (Houghton Mifflin) 12 guides to U.S.
and foreign countries.
**Michelin Guides** (Michelin Tyre Co.)
**Blue Guides** (W.W. Norton)
**Baedeker's Guides** (Prentice-Hall) feature pull-out
maps
**Mobil Travel Guides** (Mobil Oil Corp. and Rand
McNally)

**Dollarwise Guides** (Frommer/Pasmantier) 20 U.S.
and world guides.
**Fodor's Travel Guides** (David McKay) 101 titles, 81
titles updated annually.
**Let's Go** (Harvard Student Agencies, St. Martins
Press) 10 guides to individual countries.
**Nagel's Guides** (Nagel) 60 guides in English.
**National Park Guide** (Rand McNally)

## Foreign Currency Exchange

Visitors can usually change their U.S. dollars into
the appropriate foreign currency at their point of
departure. Most airports have currency exchange
facilities, generally open 9:00 A.M. to 10:00 P.M.

The Deak-Perera Group, the largest private organization specializing in foreign money exchange,
has offices in some airports. It is generally advisable

for an American traveling to a foreign destination
to have a small amount of the foreign currency on
hand on arrival. Currency can usually be exchanged at foreign entry points.

Visitors to the United States can usually exchange their currency into U.S. dollars at their port
of entry.

## Road Mileages Between U.S. Cities[1]

| Cities | Birmingham | Boston | Buffalo | Chicago | Cleveland | Dallas | Denver |
|---|---|---|---|---|---|---|---|
| Birmingham, Ala. | — | 1,194 | 947 | 657 | 734 | 653 | 1,318 |
| Boston, Mass. | 1,194 | — | 457 | 983 | 639 | 1,815 | 1,991 |
| Buffalo, N.Y. | 947 | 457 | — | 536 | 192 | 1,387 | 1,561 |
| Chicago, Ill. | 657 | 983 | 536 | — | 344 | 931 | 1,050 |
| Cleveland, Ohio | 734 | 639 | 192 | 344 | — | 1,205 | 1,369 |
| Dallas, Tex. | 653 | 1,815 | 1,387 | 931 | 1,205 | — | 801 |
| Denver, Colo | 1,318 | 1,991 | 1,561 | 1,050 | 1,369 | 801 | — |
| Detroit, Mich. | 754 | 702 | 252 | 279 | 175 | 1,167 | 1,301 |
| El Paso, Tex. | 1,278 | 2,358 | 1,928 | 1,439 | 1,746 | 625 | 652 |
| Houston, Tex. | 692 | 1,886 | 1,532 | 1,092 | 1,358 | 242 | 1,032 |
| Indianapolis, Ind. | 492 | 940 | 510 | 189 | 318 | 877 | 1,051 |
| Kansas City, Mo. | 703 | 1,427 | 997 | 503 | 815 | 508 | 616 |
| Los Angeles, Calif. | 2,078 | 3,036 | 2,606 | 2,112 | 2,424 | 1,425 | 1,174 |
| Louisville, Ky. | 378 | 996 | 571 | 305 | 379 | 865 | 1,135 |
| Memphis, Tenn. | 249 | 1,345 | 965 | 546 | 773 | 470 | 1,069 |
| Miami, Fla. | 777 | 1,539 | 1,445 | 1,390 | 1,325 | 1,332 | 2,094 |
| Minneapolis, Minn. | 1,067 | 1,402 | 955 | 411 | 763 | 969 | 867 |
| New Orleans, La. | 347 | 1,541 | 1,294 | 947 | 1,102 | 504 | 1,305 |
| New York, N.Y. | 983 | 213 | 436 | 840 | 514 | 1,604 | 1,780 |
| Omaha, Neb. | 907 | 1,458 | 1,011 | 493 | 819 | 661 | 559 |
| Philadelphia, Pa. | 894 | 304 | 383 | 758 | 432 | 1,515 | 1,698 |
| Phoenix, Ariz. | 1,680 | 2,664 | 2,234 | 1,729 | 2,052 | 1,027 | 836 |
| Pittsburgh, Pa. | 792 | 597 | 219 | 457 | 131 | 1,237 | 1,411 |
| St. Louis, Mo. | 508 | 1,179 | 749 | 293 | 567 | 638 | 871 |
| Salt Lake City, Utah | 1,805 | 2,425 | 1,978 | 1,458 | 1,786 | 1,239 | 512 |
| San Francisco, Calif. | 2,385 | 3,179 | 2,732 | 2,212 | 2,540 | 1,765 | 1,266 |
| Seattle, Wash. | 2,612 | 3,043 | 2,596 | 2,052 | 2,404 | 2,122 | 1,373 |
| Washington, D.C. | 751 | 440 | 386 | 695 | 369 | 1,372 | 1,635 |

| Cities | Detroit | El Paso | Houston | Indianapolis | Kansas City | Los Angeles | Louisville |
|---|---|---|---|---|---|---|---|
| Birmingham, Ala. | 754 | 1,278 | 692 | 492 | 703 | 2,078 | 378 |
| Boston, Mass. | 702 | 2,358 | 1,886 | 940 | 1,427 | 3,036 | 996 |
| Buffalo, N.Y. | 252 | 1,928 | 1,532 | 510 | 997 | 2,606 | 571 |
| Chicago, Ill. | 279 | 1,439 | 1,092 | 189 | 503 | 2,112 | 305 |
| Cleveland, Ohio | 175 | 1,746 | 1,358 | 318 | 815 | 2,424 | 379 |
| Dallas, Tex. | 1,167 | 625 | 242 | 877 | 508 | 1,425 | 865 |
| Denver, Colo. | 1,310 | 652 | 1,032 | 1,051 | 616 | 1,174 | 1,135 |
| Detroit, Mich. | — | 1,696 | 1,312 | 290 | 760 | 2,369 | 378 |
| El Paso, Tex. | 1,696 | — | 756 | 1,418 | 936 | 800 | 1,443 |
| Houston, Tex. | 1,312 | 756 | — | 1,022 | 750 | 1,556 | 981 |
| Indianapolis, Ind. | 290 | 1,418 | 1,022 | — | 487 | 2,096 | 114 |
| Kansas City, Mo. | 760 | 936 | 750 | 487 | — | 1,609 | 519 |
| Los Angeles, Calif. | 2,369 | 800 | 1,556 | 2,096 | 1,609 | — | 2,128 |
| Louisville, Ky. | 378 | 1,443 | 981 | 114 | 519 | 2,128 | — |
| Memphis, Tenn. | 756 | 1,095 | 586 | 466 | 454 | 1,847 | 396 |
| Miami, Fla. | 1,409 | 1,957 | 1,237 | 1,225 | 1,479 | 2,757 | 1,111 |
| Minneapolis, Minn. | 698 | 1,353 | 1,211 | 600 | 466 | 2,041 | 716 |
| New Orleans, La. | 1,101 | 1,121 | 365 | 839 | 839 | 1,921 | 725 |
| New York, N.Y. | 671 | 2,147 | 1,675 | 729 | 1,216 | 2,825 | 785 |
| Omaha, Neb. | 754 | 1,015 | 903 | 590 | 204 | 1,733 | 704 |
| Philadelphia, Pa. | 589 | 2,065 | 1,586 | 647 | 1,134 | 2,743 | 703 |
| Phoenix, Ariz. | 1,986 | 402 | 1,158 | 1,713 | 1,226 | 398 | 1,749 |
| Pittsburgh, Pa. | 288 | 1,778 | 1,395 | 360 | 847 | 2,456 | 416 |
| St. Louis, Mo. | 529 | 1,179 | 799 | 239 | 255 | 1,864 | 264 |
| Salt Lake City, Utah | 1,721 | 877 | 1,465 | 1,545 | 1,128 | 728 | 1,647 |
| San Francisco, Calif. | 2,475 | 1,202 | 1,958 | 2,299 | 1,882 | 403 | 2,401 |
| Seattle, Wash. | 2,339 | 1,760 | 2,348 | 2,241 | 1,909 | 1,150 | 2,355 |
| Washington, D.C. | 526 | 1,997 | 1,443 | 565 | 1,071 | 2,680 | 601 |

1. These figures represent estimates and are subject to change.

## Road Mileages Between U.S. Cities

| Cities | Memphis | Miami | Minne-apolis | New Orleans | New York | Omaha | Phila-delphia |
|---|---|---|---|---|---|---|---|
| Birmingham, Ala. | 249 | 777 | 1,067 | 347 | 983 | 907 | 894 |
| Boston, Mass. | 1,345 | 1,539 | 1,402 | 1,541 | 213 | 1,458 | 304 |
| Buffalo, N.Y. | 965 | 1,445 | 955 | 1,294 | 436 | 1,011 | 383 |
| Chicago, Ill. | 546 | 1,390 | 411 | 947 | 840 | 493 | 758 |
| Cleveland, Ohio | 773 | 1,325 | 763 | 1,102 | 514 | 819 | 432 |
| Dallas, Tex. | 470 | 1,332 | 969 | 504 | 1,604 | 661 | 1,515 |
| Denver, Colo. | 1,069 | 2,094 | 867 | 1,305 | 1,780 | 559 | 1,698 |
| Detroit, Mich. | 756 | 1,409 | 698 | 1,101 | 671 | 754 | 589 |
| El Paso, Tex. | 1,095 | 1,957 | 1,353 | 1,121 | 2,147 | 1,015 | 2,065 |
| Houston, Tex. | 586 | 1,237 | 1,211 | 365 | 1,675 | 903 | 1,586 |
| Indianapolis, Ind. | 466 | 1,225 | 600 | 839 | 729 | 590 | 647 |
| Kansas City, Mo. | 454 | 1,479 | 466 | 839 | 1,216 | 204 | 1,134 |
| Los Angeles, Calif. | 1,847 | 2,757 | 2,041 | 1,921 | 2,825 | 1,733 | 2,743 |
| Louisville, Ky. | 396 | 1,111 | 716 | 725 | 785 | 704 | 703 |
| Memphis, Tenn. | — | 1,025 | 854 | 401 | 1,134 | 658 | 1,045 |
| Miami, Fla. | 1,025 | — | 1,801 | 892 | 1,328 | 1,683 | 1,239 |
| Minneapolis, Minn. | 854 | 1,801 | — | 1,255 | 1,259 | 373 | 1,177 |
| New Orleans, La. | 401 | 892 | 1,255 | — | 1,330 | 1,043 | 1,241 |
| New York, N.Y. | 1,134 | 1,328 | 1,259 | 1,330 | — | 1,315 | 93 |
| Omaha, Neb. | 658 | 1,683 | 373 | 1,043 | 1,315 | — | 1,233 |
| Philadelphia, Pa. | 1,045 | 1,239 | 1,177 | 1,241 | 93 | 1,233 | — |
| Phoenix, Ariz. | 1,464 | 2,359 | 1,644 | 1,523 | 2,442 | 1,305 | 2,360 |
| Pittsburgh, Pa. | 810 | 1,250 | 876 | 1,118 | 386 | 932 | 304 |
| St. Louis, Mo. | 295 | 1,241 | 559 | 696 | 968 | 459 | 886 |
| Salt Lake City, Utah | 1,556 | 2,571 | 1,243 | 1,743 | 2,282 | 967 | 2,200 |
| San Francisco, Calif. | 2,151 | 3,097 | 1,997 | 2,269 | 3,036 | 1,721 | 2,954 |
| Seattle, Wash. | 2,363 | 3,389 | 1,641 | 2,606 | 2,900 | 1,705 | 2,818 |
| Washington, D.C. | 902 | 1,101 | 1,114 | 1,098 | 229 | 1,170 | 140 |

| Cities | Phoenix | Pitts-burgh | St. Louis | Salt Lake City | San Francisco | Seattle | Wash-ington |
|---|---|---|---|---|---|---|---|
| Birmingham, Ala. | 1,680 | 792 | 508 | 1,805 | 2,385 | 2,612 | 751 |
| Boston, Mass. | 2,664 | 597 | 1,179 | 2,425 | 3,179 | 3,043 | 440 |
| Buffalo, N.Y. | 2,234 | 219 | 749 | 1,978 | 2,732 | 2,596 | 386 |
| Chicago, Ill. | 1,729 | 457 | 293 | 1,458 | 2,212 | 2,052 | 695 |
| Cleveland, Ohio | 2,052 | 131 | 567 | 1,786 | 2,540 | 2,404 | 369 |
| Dallas, Tex. | 1,027 | 1,237 | 638 | 1,239 | 1,765 | 2,122 | 1,372 |
| Denver, Colo. | 836 | 1,411 | 871 | 512 | 1,266 | 1,373 | 1,635 |
| Detroit, Mich. | 1,986 | 288 | 529 | 1,721 | 2,475 | 2,339 | 526 |
| El Paso, Tex. | 402 | 1,778 | 1,179 | 877 | 1,202 | 1,760 | 1,997 |
| Houston, Tex. | 1,158 | 1,395 | 799 | 1,465 | 1,958 | 2,348 | 1,443 |
| Indianapolis, Ind. | 1,713 | 360 | 239 | 1,545 | 2,299 | 2,241 | 565 |
| Kansas City, Mo. | 1,226 | 847 | 255 | 1,128 | 1,882 | 1,909 | 1,071 |
| Los Angeles, Calif. | 398 | 2,456 | 1,864 | 728 | 403 | 1,150 | 2,680 |
| Louisville, Ky. | 1,749 | 416 | 264 | 1,647 | 2,401 | 2,355 | 601 |
| Memphis, Tenn. | 1,464 | 810 | 295 | 1,556 | 2,151 | 2,363 | 902 |
| Miami, Fla. | 2,359 | 1,250 | 1,241 | 2,571 | 3,097 | 3,389 | 1,101 |
| Minneapolis, Minn. | 1,644 | 876 | 559 | 1,243 | 1,997 | 1,641 | 1,114 |
| New Orleans, La. | 1,523 | 1,118 | 696 | 1,743 | 2,269 | 2,626 | 1,098 |
| New York, N.Y. | 2,442 | 386 | 968 | 2,282 | 3,036 | 2,900 | 229 |
| Omaha, Neb. | 1,305 | 932 | 459 | 967 | 1,721 | 1,705 | 1,178 |
| Philadelphia, Pa. | 2,360 | 304 | 886 | 2,200 | 2,954 | 2,818 | 140 |
| Phoenix, Ariz. | — | 2,073 | 1,485 | 651 | 800 | 1,482 | 2,278 |
| Pittsburgh, Pa. | 2,073 | — | 599 | 1,899 | 2,653 | 2,517 | 241 |
| St. Louis, Mo. | 1,485 | 599 | — | 1,383 | 2,137 | 2,164 | 836 |
| Salt Lake City, Utah | 651 | 1,899 | 1,383 | — | 754 | 883 | 2,110 |
| San Francisco, Calif. | 800 | 2,653 | 2,137 | 754 | — | 817 | 2,864 |
| Seattle, Wash. | 1,482 | 2,517 | 2,164 | 883 | 817 | — | 2,755 |
| Washington, D.C. | 2,278 | 241 | 836 | 2,110 | 2,864 | 2,755 | — |

# Air Distances Between U.S. Cities in Statute Miles

| Cities | Birming-ham | Boston | Buffalo | Chicago | Cleveland | Dallas | Denver |
|---|---|---|---|---|---|---|---|
| Birmingham, Ala. | — | 1,052 | 776 | 578 | 618 | 581 | 1,095 |
| Boston, Mass. | 1,052 | — | 400 | 851 | 551 | 1,551 | 1,769 |
| Buffalo, N. Y. | 776 | 400 | — | 454 | 173 | 1,198 | 1,370 |
| Chicago, Ill. | 578 | 851 | 454 | — | 308 | 803 | 920 |
| Cleveland, Ohio | 618 | 551 | 173 | 308 | — | 1,025 | 1,227 |
| Dallas, Tex. | 581 | 1,551 | 1,198 | 803 | 1,025 | — | 663 |
| Denver, Colo. | 1,095 | 1,769 | 1,370 | 920 | 1,227 | 663 | — |
| Detroit, Mich. | 641 | 613 | 216 | 238 | 90 | 999 | 1,156 |
| El Paso, Tex. | 1,152 | 2,072 | 1,692 | 1,252 | 1,525 | 572 | 557 |
| Houston, Tex. | 567 | 1,605 | 1,286 | 940 | 1,114 | 225 | 879 |
| Indianapolis, Ind. | 433 | 807 | 435 | 165 | 263 | 763 | 1,000 |
| Kansas City, Mo. | 579 | 1,251 | 861 | 414 | 700 | 451 | 558 |
| Los Angeles, Calif. | 1,802 | 2,596 | 2,198 | 1,745 | 2,049 | 1,240 | 831 |
| Louisville, Ky. | 331 | 826 | 483 | 269 | 311 | 726 | 1,038 |
| Memphis, Tenn. | 217 | 1,137 | 803 | 482 | 630 | 420 | 879 |
| Miami, Fla. | 665 | 1,255 | 1,181 | 1,188 | 1,087 | 1,111 | 1,726 |
| Minneapolis, Minn. | 862 | 1,123 | 731 | 355 | 630 | 862 | 700 |
| New Orleans, La. | 312 | 1,359 | 1,086 | 833 | 924 | 443 | 1,082 |
| New York, N. Y. | 864 | 188 | 292 | 713 | 405 | 1,374 | 1,631 |
| Omaha, Neb. | 732 | 1,282 | 883 | 432 | 739 | 586 | 488 |
| Philadelphia, Pa. | 783 | 271 | 279 | 666 | 360 | 1,299 | 1,579 |
| Phoenix, Ariz. | 1,456 | 2,300 | 1,906 | 1,453 | 1,749 | 887 | 586 |
| Pittsburgh, Pa. | 608 | 483 | 178 | 410 | 115 | 1,070 | 1,320 |
| St. Louis, Mo. | 400 | 1,038 | 662 | 262 | 492 | 547 | 796 |
| Salt Lake City, Utah | 1,466 | 2,099 | 1,699 | 1,260 | 1,568 | 999 | 371 |
| San Francisco, Calif. | 2,013 | 2,699 | 2,300 | 1,858 | 2,166 | 1,483 | 949 |
| Seattle, Wash. | 2,082 | 2,493 | 2,117 | 1,737 | 2,026 | 1,681 | 1,021 |
| Washington, D.C. | 661 | 393 | 292 | 597 | 306 | 1,185 | 1,494 |

| Cities | Detroit | El Paso | Houston | Indian-apolis | Kansas City | Los Angeles | Louisville |
|---|---|---|---|---|---|---|---|
| Birmingham, Ala. | 641 | 1,152 | 567 | 433 | 579 | 1,802 | 331 |
| Boston, Mass. | 613 | 2,072 | 1,605 | 807 | 1,251 | 2,596 | 826 |
| Buffalo, N. Y. | 216 | 1,692 | 1,286 | 435 | 861 | 2,198 | 483 |
| Chicago, Ill. | 238 | 1,252 | 940 | 165 | 414 | 1,745 | 269 |
| Cleveland, Ohio | 90 | 1,525 | 1,114 | 263 | 700 | 2,049 | 311 |
| Dallas, Tex. | 999 | 572 | 225 | 763 | 451 | 1,240 | 726 |
| Denver, Colo. | 1,156 | 557 | 879 | 1,000 | 558 | 831 | 1,038 |
| Detroit, Mich. | — | 1,479 | 1,105 | 240 | 645 | 1,983 | 316 |
| El Paso, Tex. | 1,479 | — | 676 | 1,264 | 839 | 701 | 1,254 |
| Houston, Tex. | 1,105 | 676 | — | 865 | 644 | 1,374 | 803 |
| Indianapolis, Ind. | 240 | 1,264 | 865 | — | 453 | 1,809 | 107 |
| Kansas City, Mo. | 645 | 839 | 644 | 453 | — | 1,356 | 480 |
| Los Angeles, Calif. | 1,983 | 701 | 1,374 | 1,809 | 1,356 | — | 1,829 |
| Louisville, Ky. | 316 | 1,254 | 803 | 107 | 480 | 1,829 | — |
| Memphis, Tenn. | 623 | 976 | 484 | 384 | 369 | 1,603 | 320 |
| Miami, Fla. | 1,152 | 1,643 | 968 | 1,024 | 1,241 | 2,339 | 919 |
| Minneapolis, Minn. | 543 | 1,157 | 1,056 | 511 | 413 | 1,524 | 605 |
| New Orleans, La. | 939 | 983 | 318 | 712 | 680 | 1,673 | 623 |
| New York, N. Y. | 482 | 1,905 | 1,420 | 646 | 1,097 | 2,451 | 652 |
| Omaha, Neb. | 669 | 878 | 794 | 525 | 166 | 1,315 | 580 |
| Philadelphia, Pa. | 443 | 1,836 | 1,341 | 585 | 1,038 | 2,394 | 582 |
| Phoenix, Ariz. | 1,690 | 346 | 1,017 | 1,499 | 1,049 | 357 | 1,508 |
| Pittsburgh, Pa. | 205 | 1,590 | 1,137 | 330 | 781 | 2,136 | 344 |
| St. Louis, Mo. | 455 | 1,034 | 679 | 231 | 238 | 1,589 | 242 |
| Salt Lake City, Utah | 1,492 | 689 | 1,200 | 1,356 | 925 | 579 | 1,402 |
| San Francisco, Calif. | 2,091 | 995 | 1,645 | 1,949 | 1,506 | 347 | 1,986 |
| Seattle, Wash. | 1,938 | 1,376 | 1,891 | 1,872 | 1,506 | 959 | 1,943 |
| Washington, D.C. | 396 | 1,728 | 1,220 | 494 | 945 | 2,300 | 476 |

*Source:* National Geodetic Survey.

# Air Distances Between U.S. Cities in Statute Miles

| Cities | Memphis | Miami | Minne-apolis | New Orleans | New York | Omaha | Phila-delphia |
|---|---|---|---|---|---|---|---|
| Birmingham, Ala. | 217 | 665 | 862 | 312 | 864 | 732 | 783 |
| Boston, Mass. | 1,137 | 1,255 | 1,123 | 1,359 | 188 | 1,282 | 271 |
| Buffalo, N. Y. | 803 | 1,181 | 731 | 1,086 | 292 | 883 | 279 |
| Chicago, Ill. | 482 | 1,188 | 355 | 833 | 713 | 432 | 666 |
| Cleveland, Ohio | 630 | 1,087 | 630 | 924 | 405 | 739 | 360 |
| Dallas, Tex. | 420 | 1,111 | 862 | 443 | 1,374 | 586 | 1,299 |
| Denver, Colo. | 879 | 1,726 | 700 | 1,082 | 1,631 | 488 | 1,579 |
| Detroit, Mich. | 623 | 1,152 | 543 | 939 | 482 | 669 | 443 |
| El Paso, Tex. | 976 | 1,643 | 1,157 | 983 | 1,905 | 878 | 1,836 |
| Houston, Tex. | 484 | 968 | 1,056 | 318 | 1,420 | 794 | 1,341 |
| Indianapolis, Ind. | 384 | 1,024 | 511 | 712 | 646 | 525 | 585 |
| Kansas City, Mo. | 369 | 1,241 | 413 | 680 | 1,097 | 166 | 1,038 |
| Los Angeles, Calif. | 1,603 | 2,339 | 1,524 | 1,673 | 2,451 | 1,315 | 2,394 |
| Louisville, Ky. | 320 | 919 | 605 | 623 | 652 | 580 | 582 |
| Memphis, Tenn. | — | 872 | 699 | 358 | 957 | 529 | 881 |
| Miami, Fla. | 872 | — | 1,511 | 669 | 1,092 | 1,397 | 1,019 |
| Minneapolis, Minn. | 699 | 1,511 | — | 1,051 | 1,018 | 290 | 985 |
| New Orleans, La. | 358 | 669 | 1,051 | — | 1,171 | 847 | 1,089 |
| New York, N. Y. | 957 | 1,092 | 1,018 | 1,171 | — | 1,144 | 83 |
| Omaha, Neb. | 529 | 1,397 | 290 | 847 | 1,144 | — | 1,094 |
| Philadelphia, Pa. | 881 | 1,019 | 985 | 1,089 | 83 | 1,094 | — |
| Phoenix, Ariz. | 1,263 | 1,982 | 1,280 | 1,316 | 2,145 | 1,036 | 2,083 |
| Pittsburgh, Pa. | 660 | 1,010 | 743 | 919 | 317 | 836 | 259 |
| St. Louis, Mo. | 240 | 1,061 | 466 | 598 | 875 | 354 | 811 |
| Salt Lake City, Utah | 1,250 | 2,089 | 987 | 1,434 | 1,972 | 833 | 1,925 |
| San Francisco, Calif. | 1,802 | 2,594 | 1,584 | 1,926 | 2,571 | 1,429 | 2,523 |
| Seattle, Wash. | 1,867 | 2,734 | 1,395 | 2,101 | 2,408 | 1,369 | 2,380 |
| Washington, D.C. | 765 | 923 | 934 | 966 | 205 | 1,014 | 123 |

| Cities | Phoenix | Pitts-burgh | St. Louis | Salt Lake City | San Francisco | Seattle | Wash-ington |
|---|---|---|---|---|---|---|---|
| Birmingham, Ala. | 1,456 | 608 | 400 | 1,466 | 2,013 | 2,082 | 661 |
| Boston, Mass. | 2,300 | 483 | 1,038 | 2,099 | 2,699 | 2,493 | 393 |
| Buffalo, N. Y. | 1,906 | 178 | 662 | 1,699 | 2,300 | 2,117 | 292 |
| Chicago, Ill. | 1,453 | 410 | 262 | 1,260 | 1,858 | 1,737 | 597 |
| Cleveland, Ohio | 1,749 | 115 | 492 | 1,568 | 2,166 | 2,026 | 306 |
| Dallas, Tex. | 887 | 1,070 | 547 | 999 | 1,483 | 1,681 | 1,185 |
| Denver, Colo. | 586 | 1,320 | 796 | 371 | 949 | 1,021 | 1,494 |
| Detroit, Mich. | 1,690 | 205 | 455 | 1,492 | 2,091 | 1,938 | 396 |
| El Paso, Tex. | 346 | 1,590 | 1,034 | 689 | 995 | 1,376 | 1,728 |
| Houston, Tex. | 1,017 | 1,137 | 679 | 1,200 | 1,645 | 1,891 | 1,220 |
| Indianapolis, Ind. | 1,499 | 330 | 231 | 1,356 | 1,949 | 1,872 | 494 |
| Kansas City, Mo. | 1,049 | 781 | 238 | 925 | 1,506 | 1,506 | 945 |
| Los Angeles, Calif. | 357 | 2,136 | 1,589 | 579 | 347 | 959 | 2,300 |
| Louisville, Ky. | 1,508 | 344 | 242 | 1,402 | 1,986 | 1,943 | 476 |
| Memphis, Tenn. | 1,263 | 660 | 240 | 1,250 | 1,802 | 1,867 | 765 |
| Miami, Fla. | 1,982 | 1,010 | 1,061 | 2,089 | 2,594 | 2,734 | 923 |
| Minneapolis, Minn. | 1,280 | 743 | 466 | 987 | 1,584 | 1,395 | 934 |
| New Orleans, La. | 1,316 | 919 | 598 | 1,434 | 1,926 | 2,101 | 966 |
| New York, N. Y. | 2,145 | 317 | 875 | 1,972 | 2,571 | 2,408 | 205 |
| Omaha, Neb. | 1,036 | 836 | 354 | 833 | 1,429 | 1,369 | 1,014 |
| Philadelphia, Pa. | 2,083 | 259 | 811 | 1,925 | 2,523 | 2,380 | 123 |
| Phoenix, Ariz. | — | 1,828 | 1,272 | 504 | 653 | 1,114 | 1,983 |
| Pittsburgh, Pa. | 1,828 | — | 559 | 1,668 | 2,264 | 2,138 | 192 |
| St. Louis, Mo. | 1,272 | 559 | — | 1,162 | 1,744 | 1,724 | 712 |
| Salt Lake City, Utah | 504 | 1,668 | 1,162 | — | 600 | 701 | 1,848 |
| San Francisco, Calif. | 653 | 2,264 | 1,744 | 600 | — | 678 | 2,442 |
| Seattle, Wash. | 1,114 | 2,138 | 1,724 | 701 | 678 | — | 2,329 |
| Washington, D.C. | 1,983 | 192 | 712 | 1,848 | 2,442 | 2,329 | — |

*Source:* National Geodetic Survey.

# Air Distances Between World Cities in Statute Miles

| Cities | Berlin | Buenos Aires | Cairo | Calcutta | Cape Town | Caracas | Chicago |
|---|---|---|---|---|---|---|---|
| Berlin | — | 7,402 | 1,795 | 4,368 | 5,981 | 5,247 | 4,405 |
| Buenos Aires | 7,402 | — | 7,345 | 10,265 | 4,269 | 3,168 | 5,598 |
| Cairo | 1,795 | 7,345 | — | 3,539 | 4,500 | 6,338 | 6,129 |
| Calcutta | 4,368 | 10,265 | 3,539 | — | 6,024 | 9,605 | 7,980 |
| Cape Town, South Africa | 5,981 | 4,269 | 4,500 | 6,024 | — | 6,365 | 8,494 |
| Caracas, Venezuela | 5,247 | 3,168 | 6,338 | 9,605 | 6,365 | — | 2,501 |
| Chicago | 4,405 | 5,598 | 6,129 | 7,980 | 8,494 | 2,501 | — |
| Hong Kong | 5,440 | 11,472 | 5,061 | 1,648 | 7,375 | 10,167 | 7,793 |
| Honolulu, Hawaii | 7,309 | 7,561 | 8,838 | 7,047 | 11,534 | 6,013 | 4,250 |
| Istanbul | 1,078 | 7,611 | 768 | 3,638 | 5,154 | 6,048 | 5,477 |
| Lisbon | 1,436 | 5,956 | 2,363 | 5,638 | 5,325 | 4,041 | 3,990 |
| London | 579 | 6,916 | 2,181 | 4,947 | 6,012 | 4,660 | 3,950 |
| Los Angeles | 5,724 | 6,170 | 7,520 | 8,090 | 9,992 | 3,632 | 1,745 |
| Manila | 6,132 | 11,051 | 5,704 | 2,203 | 7,486 | 10,620 | 8,143 |
| Mexico City | 6,047 | 4,592 | 7,688 | 9,492 | 8,517 | 2,232 | 1,691 |
| Montreal | 3,729 | 5,615 | 5,414 | 7,607 | 7,931 | 2,449 | 744 |
| Moscow | 1,004 | 8,376 | 1,803 | 3,321 | 6,300 | 6,173 | 4,974 |
| New York | 3,965 | 5,297 | 5,602 | 7,918 | 7,764 | 2,132 | 713 |
| Paris | 545 | 6,870 | 1,995 | 4,883 | 5,807 | 4,736 | 4,134 |
| Rio de Janeiro | 6,220 | 1,200 | 6,146 | 9,377 | 3,773 | 2,810 | 5,296 |
| Rome | 734 | 6,929 | 1,320 | 4,482 | 5,249 | 5,196 | 4,808 |
| San Francisco | 5,661 | 6,467 | 7,364 | 7,814 | 10,247 | 3,904 | 1,858 |
| Shanghai, China | 5,218 | 12,201 | 5,183 | 2,117 | 8,061 | 9,501 | 7,061 |
| Stockholm | 504 | 7,808 | 2,111 | 4,195 | 6,444 | 5,420 | 4,278 |
| Sydney, Australia | 10,006 | 7,330 | 8,952 | 5,685 | 6,843 | 9,513 | 9,272 |
| Tokyo | 5,540 | 11,408 | 5,935 | 3,194 | 9,156 | 8,799 | 6,299 |
| Warsaw | 320 | 7,662 | 1,630 | 4,048 | 5,958 | 5,517 | 4,667 |
| Washington, D.C. | 4,169 | 5,218 | 5,800 | 8,084 | 7,901 | 2,059 | 597 |

| Cities | Hong Kong | Honolulu | Istanbul | Lisbon | London | Los Angeles | Manila |
|---|---|---|---|---|---|---|---|
| Berlin | 5,440 | 7,309 | 1,078 | 1,436 | 579 | 5,724 | 6,132 |
| Buenos Aires | 11,472 | 7,561 | 7,611 | 5,956 | 6,916 | 6,170 | 11,051 |
| Cairo | 5,061 | 8,838 | 768 | 2,363 | 2,181 | 7,520 | 5,704 |
| Calcutta | 1,648 | 7,047 | 3,638 | 5,638 | 4,947 | 8,090 | 2,203 |
| Cape Town, South Africa | 7,375 | 11,534 | 5,154 | 5,325 | 6,012 | 9,992 | 7,486 |
| Caracas, Venezuela | 10,167 | 6,013 | 6,048 | 4,041 | 4,660 | 3,632 | 10,620 |
| Chicago | 7,793 | 4,250 | 5,477 | 3,990 | 3,950 | 1,745 | 8,143 |
| Hong Kong | — | 5,549 | 4,984 | 6,853 | 5,982 | 7,195 | 693 |
| Honolulu, Hawaii | 5,549 | — | 8,109 | 7,820 | 7,228 | 2,574 | 5,299 |
| Istanbul | 4,984 | 8,109 | — | 2,012 | 1,552 | 6,783 | 5,664 |
| Lisbon | 6,853 | 7,820 | 2,012 | — | 985 | 5,621 | 7,546 |
| London | 5,982 | 7,228 | 1,552 | 985 | — | 5,382 | 6,672 |
| Los Angeles, Calif. | 7,195 | 2,574 | 6,783 | 5,621 | 5,382 | — | 7,261 |
| Manila | 693 | 5,299 | 5,664 | 7,546 | 6,672 | 7,261 | — |
| Mexico City | 8,782 | 3,779 | 7,110 | 5,390 | 5,550 | 1,589 | 8,835 |
| Montreal | 7,729 | 4,910 | 4,789 | 3,246 | 3,282 | 2,427 | 8,186 |
| Moscow | 4,439 | 7,037 | 1,091 | 2,427 | 1,555 | 6,003 | 5,131 |
| New York | 8,054 | 4,964 | 4,975 | 3,364 | 3,458 | 2,451 | 8,498 |
| Paris | 5,985 | 7,438 | 1,400 | 904 | 213 | 5,588 | 6,677 |
| Rio de Janeiro | 11,021 | 8,285 | 6,389 | 4,796 | 5,766 | 6,331 | 11,259 |
| Rome | 5,768 | 8,022 | 843 | 1,161 | 887 | 6,732 | 6,457 |
| San Francisco | 6,897 | 2,393 | 6,703 | 5,666 | 5,357 | 347 | 6,967 |
| Shanghai, China | 764 | 4,941 | 4,962 | 6,654 | 5,715 | 6,438 | 1,150 |
| Stockholm | 5,113 | 6,862 | 1,348 | 1,856 | 890 | 5,454 | 5,797 |
| Sydney, Australia | 4,584 | 4,943 | 9,294 | 11,302 | 10,564 | 7,530 | 3,944 |
| Tokyo | 1,794 | 3,853 | 5,560 | 6,915 | 5,940 | 5,433 | 1,866 |
| Warsaw | 5,144 | 7,355 | 863 | 1,715 | 899 | 5,922 | 5,837 |
| Washington, D.C. | 8,147 | 4,519 | 5,215 | 3,562 | 3,663 | 2,300 | 8,562 |

*Source: Encyclopaedia Britannica.*

# Air Distances Between World Cities in Statute Miles

| Cities | Mexico City | Montreal | Moscow | New York | Paris | Rio de Janeiro | Rome |
|---|---|---|---|---|---|---|---|
| Berlin | 6,047 | 3,729 | 1,004 | 3,965 | 545 | 6,220 | 734 |
| Buenos Aires | 4,592 | 5,615 | 8,376 | 5,297 | 6,870 | 1,200 | 6,929 |
| Cairo | 7,688 | 5,414 | 1,803 | 5,602 | 1,995 | 6,146 | 1,320 |
| Calcutta | 9,492 | 7,607 | 3,321 | 7,918 | 4,883 | 9,377 | 4,482 |
| Cape Town, South Africa | 8,517 | 7,931 | 6,300 | 7,764 | 5,807 | 3,773 | 5,249 |
| Caracas, Venezuela | 2,232 | 2,449 | 6,173 | 2,132 | 4,736 | 2,810 | 5,196 |
| Chicago | 1,691 | 744 | 4,974 | 713 | 4,134 | 5,296 | 4,808 |
| Hong Kong | 8,782 | 7,729 | 4,439 | 8,054 | 5,985 | 11,021 | 5,768 |
| Honolulu | 3,779 | 4,910 | 7,037 | 4,964 | 7,438 | 8,285 | 8,022 |
| Istanbul | 7,110 | 4,789 | 1,091 | 4,975 | 1,400 | 6,389 | 843 |
| Lisbon | 5,390 | 3,246 | 2,427 | 3,364 | 904 | 4,796 | 1,161 |
| London | 5,550 | 3,282 | 1,555 | 3,458 | 213 | 5,766 | 887 |
| Los Angeles | 1,589 | 2,427 | 6,003 | 2,451 | 5,588 | 6,331 | 6,732 |
| Manila | 8,835 | 8,186 | 5,131 | 8,498 | 6,677 | 11,259 | 6,457 |
| Mexico City | — | 2,318 | 6,663 | 2,094 | 5,716 | 4,771 | 6,366 |
| Montreal | 2,318 | — | 4,386 | 320 | 3,422 | 5,097 | 4,080 |
| Moscow | 6,663 | 4,386 | — | 4,665 | 1,544 | 7,175 | 1,474 |
| New York | 2,094 | 320 | 4,665 | — | 3,624 | 4,817 | 4,281 |
| Paris | 5,716 | 3,422 | 1,544 | 3,624 | — | 5,699 | 697 |
| Rio de Janeiro | 4,771 | 5,097 | 7,175 | 4,817 | 5,699 | — | 5,684 |
| Rome | 6,366 | 4,080 | 1,474 | 4,281 | 697 | 5,684 | — |
| San Francisco | 1,887 | 2,539 | 5,871 | 2,571 | 5,558 | 6,621 | 6,240 |
| Shanghai, China | 8,022 | 7,053 | 4,235 | 7,371 | 5,754 | 11,336 | 5,677 |
| Stockholm | 5,959 | 3,667 | 762 | 3,924 | 958 | 6,651 | 1,234 |
| Sydney, Australia | 8,052 | 9,954 | 9,012 | 9,933 | 10,544 | 8,306 | 10,136 |
| Tokyo | 7,021 | 6,383 | 4,647 | 6,740 | 6,034 | 11,533 | 6,135 |
| Warsaw | 6,365 | 4,009 | 715 | 4,344 | 849 | 6,467 | 817 |
| Washington, D.C. | 1,887 | 488 | 4,858 | 205 | 3,829 | 4,796 | 4,434 |

| Cities | San Francisco | Shanghai | Stockholm | Sydney | Tokyo | Warsaw | Washington |
|---|---|---|---|---|---|---|---|
| Berlin | 5,661 | 5,218 | 504 | 10,006 | 5,540 | 320 | 4,169 |
| Buenos Aires | 6,467 | 12,201 | 7,808 | 7,330 | 11,408 | 7,662 | 5,218 |
| Cairo | 7,364 | 5,183 | 2,111 | 8,952 | 5,935 | 1,630 | 5,800 |
| Calcutta | 7,814 | 2,117 | 4,195 | 5,685 | 3,194 | 4,048 | 8,084 |
| Cape Town, South Africa | 10,247 | 8,061 | 6,444 | 6,843 | 9,156 | 5,958 | 7,901 |
| Caracas, Venezuela | 3,904 | 9,501 | 5,420 | 9,513 | 8,799 | 5,517 | 2,059 |
| Chicago | 1,858 | 7,061 | 4,278 | 9,272 | 6,299 | 4,667 | 597 |
| Hong Kong | 6,897 | 764 | 5,113 | 4,584 | 1,794 | 5,144 | 8,147 |
| Honolulu | 2,393 | 4,941 | 6,862 | 4,943 | 3,853 | 7,355 | 4,519 |
| Istanbul | 6,703 | 4,962 | 1,348 | 9,294 | 5,560 | 863 | 5,215 |
| Lisbon | 5,666 | 6,654 | 1,856 | 11,302 | 6,915 | 1,715 | 3,562 |
| London | 5,357 | 5,715 | 890 | 10,564 | 5,940 | 899 | 3,663 |
| Los Angeles | 347 | 6,438 | 5,454 | 7,530 | 5,433 | 5,922 | 2,300 |
| Manila | 6,967 | 1,150 | 5,797 | 3,944 | 1,866 | 5,837 | 8,562 |
| Mexico City | 1,887 | 8,022 | 5,959 | 8,052 | 7,021 | 6,365 | 1,887 |
| Montreal | 2,539 | 7,053 | 3,667 | 9,954 | 6,383 | 4,009 | 488 |
| Moscow | 5,871 | 4,235 | 762 | 9,012 | 4,647 | 715 | 4,858 |
| New York | 2,571 | 7,371 | 3,924 | 9,933 | 6,740 | 4,344 | 205 |
| Paris | 5,558 | 5,754 | 958 | 10,544 | 6,034 | 849 | 3,829 |
| Rio de Janeiro | 6,621 | 11,336 | 6,651 | 8,306 | 11,533 | 6,467 | 4,796 |
| Rome | 6,240 | 5,677 | 1,234 | 10,136 | 6,135 | 817 | 4,434 |
| San Francisco | — | 6,140 | 5,361 | 7,416 | 5,135 | 5,841 | 2,442 |
| Shanghai, China | 6,140 | — | 4,825 | 4,899 | 1,097 | 4,951 | 7,448 |
| Stockholm | 5,361 | 4,825 | — | 9,696 | 5,051 | 501 | 4,123 |
| Sydney, Australia | 7,416 | 4,899 | 9,696 | — | 4,866 | 9,696 | 9,758 |
| Tokyo | 5,135 | 1,097 | 5,051 | 4,866 | — | 5,249 | 6,772 |
| Warsaw | 5,841 | 4,951 | 501 | 9,696 | 5,249 | — | 4,457 |
| Washington, D.C. | 2,442 | 7,448 | 4,123 | 9,758 | 6,772 | 4,457 | — |

*Source: Encyclopaedia Britannica.*

# CALENDAR & HOLIDAYS

## *1987*

### JANUARY

| S | M | T | W | T | F | S |
|---|---|---|---|---|---|---|
| — | — | — | 1 | 2 | 3 |  |
| 4 | 5 | 6 | 7 | 8 | 9 | 10 |
| 11 | 12 | 13 | 14 | 15 | 16 | 17 |
| 18 | 19 | 20 | 21 | 22 | 23 | 24 |
| 25 | 26 | 27 | 28 | 29 | 30 | 31 |

### FEBRUARY

| S | M | T | W | T | F | S |
|---|---|---|---|---|---|---|
| 1 | 2 | 3 | 4 | 5 | 6 | 7 |
| 8 | 9 | 10 | 11 | 12 | 13 | 14 |
| 15 | 16 | 17 | 18 | 19 | 20 | 21 |
| 22 | 23 | 24 | 25 | 26 | 27 | 28 |

### MARCH

| S | M | T | W | T | F | S |
|---|---|---|---|---|---|---|
| 1 | 2 | 3 | 4 | 5 | 6 | 7 |
| 8 | 9 | 10 | 11 | 12 | 13 | 14 |
| 15 | 16 | 17 | 18 | 19 | 20 | 21 |
| 22 | 23 | 24 | 25 | 26 | 27 | 28 |
| 29 | 30 | 31 |  |  |  |  |

### APRIL

| S | M | T | W | T | F | S |
|---|---|---|---|---|---|---|
| — | — | — | 1 | 2 | 3 | 4 |
| 5 | 6 | 7 | 8 | 9 | 10 | 11 |
| 12 | 13 | 14 | 15 | 16 | 17 | 18 |
| 19 | 20 | 21 | 22 | 23 | 24 | 25 |
| 26 | 27 | 28 | 29 | 30 |  |  |

1—New Year's Day
6—Epiphany
15—Martin Luther King's Birthday

2—Groundhog Day
12—Lincoln's Birthday
14—St. Valentine's Day
16—Washington's Birthday

4—Ash Wednesday
15—Purim
17—St. Patrick's Day

5—Daylight Savings Time begins
12—Palm Sunday
14—1st Day of Passover
17—Good Friday
19—Easter
29—1st Day of Ramadan

### MAY

| S | M | T | W | T | F | S |
|---|---|---|---|---|---|---|
| — | — | — | — | — | 1 | 2 |
| 3 | 4 | 5 | 6 | 7 | 8 | 9 |
| 10 | 11 | 12 | 13 | 14 | 15 | 16 |
| 17 | 18 | 19 | 20 | 21 | 22 | 23 |
| 24 | 25 | 26 | 27 | 28 | 29 | 30 |
| 31 |  |  |  |  |  |  |

### JUNE

| S | M | T | W | T | F | S |
|---|---|---|---|---|---|---|
| — | 1 | 2 | 3 | 4 | 5 | 6 |
| 7 | 8 | 9 | 10 | 11 | 12 | 13 |
| 14 | 15 | 16 | 17 | 18 | 19 | 20 |
| 21 | 22 | 23 | 24 | 25 | 26 | 27 |
| 28 | 29 | 30 |  |  |  |  |

### JULY

| S | M | T | W | T | F | S |
|---|---|---|---|---|---|---|
| — | — | — | 1 | 2 | 3 | 4 |
| 5 | 6 | 7 | 8 | 9 | 10 | 11 |
| 12 | 13 | 14 | 15 | 16 | 17 | 18 |
| 19 | 20 | 21 | 22 | 23 | 24 | 25 |
| 26 | 27 | 28 | 29 | 30 | 31 |  |

### AUGUST

| S | M | T | W | T | F | S |
|---|---|---|---|---|---|---|
| — | — | — | — | — | — | 1 |
| 2 | 3 | 4 | 5 | 6 | 7 | 8 |
| 9 | 10 | 11 | 12 | 13 | 14 | 15 |
| 16 | 17 | 18 | 19 | 20 | 21 | 22 |
| 23 | 24 | 25 | 26 | 27 | 28 | 29 |
| 30 | 31 |  |  |  |  |  |

10—Mother's Day
28—Ascension Day
30—Memorial Day

3—1st. Day of Shavuot
7—Pentecost
14—Flag Day
21—Father's Day

1—Canada Day
4—Independence Day

### SEPTEMBER

| S | M | T | W | T | F | S |
|---|---|---|---|---|---|---|
| — | — | 1 | 2 | 3 | 4 | 5 |
| 6 | 7 | 8 | 9 | 10 | 11 | 12 |
| 13 | 14 | 15 | 16 | 17 | 18 | 19 |
| 20 | 21 | 22 | 23 | 24 | 25 | 26 |
| 27 | 28 | 29 | 30 |  |  |  |

### OCTOBER

| S | M | T | W | T | F | S |
|---|---|---|---|---|---|---|
| — | — | — | — | 1 | 2 | 3 |
| 4 | 5 | 6 | 7 | 8 | 9 | 10 |
| 11 | 12 | 13 | 14 | 15 | 16 | 17 |
| 18 | 19 | 20 | 21 | 22 | 23 | 24 |
| 25 | 26 | 27 | 28 | 29 | 30 | 31 |

### NOVEMBER

| S | M | T | W | T | F | S |
|---|---|---|---|---|---|---|
| 1 | 2 | 3 | 4 | 5 | 6 | 7 |
| 8 | 9 | 10 | 11 | 12 | 13 | 14 |
| 15 | 16 | 17 | 18 | 19 | 20 | 21 |
| 22 | 23 | 24 | 25 | 26 | 27 | 28 |
| 29 | 30 |  |  |  |  |  |

### DECEMBER

| S | M | T | W | T | F | S |
|---|---|---|---|---|---|---|
| — | — | 1 | 2 | 3 | 4 | 5 |
| 6 | 7 | 8 | 9 | 10 | 11 | 12 |
| 13 | 14 | 15 | 16 | 17 | 18 | 19 |
| 20 | 21 | 22 | 23 | 24 | 25 | 26 |
| 27 | 28 | 29 | 30 | 31 |  |  |

1—Labor Day
24—1st Day of Rosh Hashana

3—Yom Kippur
8—1st. Day of Sukkot
12—Columbus Day
12—Thanksgiving Day (Canada)
25—Daylight Savings Time ends
31—Halloween

1—All Saint's Day
3—Election Day
11—Veteran's Day
26—Thanksgiving Day
29—1st Sunday of Advent

16—1st Day of Hanukkah
25—Christmas

## Seasons for the Northern Hemisphere, 1987
### Eastern Standard Time

March 20, 10:52 p.m., sun enters sign of Aries; spring begins

June 21, 5:11 p.m., sun enters sign of Cancer, summer begins

Sept. 23, 8:45 a.m., sun enters sign of Libra; fall begins

Dec. 22, 4:46 a.m., sun enters sign of Capricorn; winter begins

## 1986

### JANUARY
| S | M | T | W | T | F | S |
|---|---|---|---|---|---|---|
| — | — | 1 | 2 | 3 | 4 | — |
| 5 | 6 | 7 | 8 | 9 | 10 | 11 |
| 12 | 13 | 14 | 15 | 16 | 17 | 18 |
| 19 | 20 | 21 | 22 | 23 | 24 | 25 |
| 26 | 27 | 28 | 29 | 30 | 31 | |

### FEBRUARY
| S | M | T | W | T | F | S |
|---|---|---|---|---|---|---|
| — | — | — | — | — | — | 1 |
| 2 | 3 | 4 | 5 | 6 | 7 | 8 |
| 9 | 10 | 11 | 12 | 13 | 14 | 15 |
| 16 | 17 | 18 | 19 | 20 | 21 | 22 |
| 23 | 24 | 25 | 26 | 27 | 28 | |

### MARCH
| S | M | T | W | T | F | S |
|---|---|---|---|---|---|---|
| — | — | — | — | — | — | 1 |
| 2 | 3 | 4 | 5 | 6 | 7 | 8 |
| 9 | 10 | 11 | 12 | 13 | 14 | 15 |
| 16 | 17 | 18 | 19 | 20 | 21 | 22 |
| 23 | 24 | 25 | 26 | 27 | 28 | 29 |
| 30 | 31 | | | | | |

### APRIL
| S | M | T | W | T | F | S |
|---|---|---|---|---|---|---|
| — | — | 1 | 2 | 3 | 4 | 5 |
| 6 | 7 | 8 | 9 | 10 | 11 | 12 |
| 13 | 14 | 15 | 16 | 17 | 18 | 19 |
| 20 | 21 | 22 | 23 | 24 | 25 | 26 |
| 27 | 28 | 29 | 30 | | | |

### MAY
| S | M | T | W | T | F | S |
|---|---|---|---|---|---|---|
| — | — | — | — | 1 | 2 | 3 |
| 4 | 5 | 6 | 7 | 8 | 9 | 10 |
| 11 | 12 | 13 | 14 | 15 | 16 | 17 |
| 18 | 19 | 20 | 21 | 22 | 23 | 24 |
| 25 | 26 | 27 | 28 | 29 | 30 | 31 |

### JUNE
| S | M | T | W | T | F | S |
|---|---|---|---|---|---|---|
| 1 | 2 | 3 | 4 | 5 | 6 | 7 |
| 8 | 9 | 10 | 11 | 12 | 13 | 14 |
| 15 | 16 | 17 | 18 | 19 | 20 | 21 |
| 22 | 23 | 24 | 25 | 26 | 27 | 28 |
| 29 | 30 | | | | | |

### JULY
| S | M | T | W | T | F | S |
|---|---|---|---|---|---|---|
| — | — | 1 | 2 | 3 | 4 | 5 |
| 6 | 7 | 8 | 9 | 10 | 11 | 12 |
| 13 | 14 | 15 | 16 | 17 | 18 | 19 |
| 20 | 21 | 22 | 23 | 24 | 25 | 26 |
| 27 | 28 | 29 | 30 | 31 | | |

### AUGUST
| S | M | T | W | T | F | S |
|---|---|---|---|---|---|---|
| — | — | — | — | — | 1 | 2 |
| 3 | 4 | 5 | 6 | 7 | 8 | 9 |
| 10 | 11 | 12 | 13 | 14 | 15 | 16 |
| 17 | 18 | 19 | 20 | 21 | 22 | 23 |
| 24 | 25 | 26 | 27 | 28 | 29 | 30 |
| 31 | | | | | | |

### SEPTEMBER
| S | M | T | W | T | F | S |
|---|---|---|---|---|---|---|
| — | 1 | 2 | 3 | 4 | 5 | 6 |
| 7 | 8 | 9 | 10 | 11 | 12 | 13 |
| 14 | 15 | 16 | 17 | 18 | 19 | 20 |
| 21 | 22 | 23 | 24 | 25 | 26 | 27 |
| 28 | 29 | 30 | | | | |

### OCTOBER
| S | M | T | W | T | F | S |
|---|---|---|---|---|---|---|
| — | — | — | 1 | 2 | 3 | 4 |
| 5 | 6 | 7 | 8 | 9 | 10 | 11 |
| 12 | 13 | 14 | 15 | 16 | 17 | 18 |
| 19 | 20 | 21 | 22 | 23 | 24 | 25 |
| 26 | 27 | 28 | 29 | 30 | 31 | |

### NOVEMBER
| S | M | T | W | T | F | S |
|---|---|---|---|---|---|---|
| — | — | — | — | — | — | 1 |
| 2 | 3 | 4 | 5 | 6 | 7 | 8 |
| 9 | 10 | 11 | 12 | 13 | 14 | 15 |
| 16 | 17 | 18 | 19 | 20 | 21 | 22 |
| 23 | 24 | 25 | 26 | 27 | 28 | 29 |
| 30 | | | | | | |

### DECEMBER
| S | M | T | W | T | F | S |
|---|---|---|---|---|---|---|
| — | 1 | 2 | 3 | 4 | 5 | 6 |
| 7 | 8 | 9 | 10 | 11 | 12 | 13 |
| 14 | 15 | 16 | 17 | 18 | 19 | 20 |
| 21 | 22 | 23 | 24 | 25 | 26 | 27 |
| 28 | 29 | 30 | 31 | | | |

## 1988

### JANUARY
| S | M | T | W | T | F | S |
|---|---|---|---|---|---|---|
| — | — | — | — | — | 1 | 2 |
| 3 | 4 | 5 | 6 | 7 | 8 | 9 |
| 10 | 11 | 12 | 13 | 14 | 15 | 16 |
| 17 | 18 | 19 | 20 | 21 | 22 | 23 |
| 24 | 25 | 26 | 27 | 28 | 29 | 30 |
| 31 | | | | | | |

### FEBRUARY
| S | M | T | W | T | F | S |
|---|---|---|---|---|---|---|
| — | 1 | 2 | 3 | 4 | 5 | 6 |
| 7 | 8 | 9 | 10 | 11 | 12 | 13 |
| 14 | 15 | 16 | 17 | 18 | 19 | 20 |
| 21 | 22 | 23 | 24 | 25 | 26 | 27 |
| 28 | 29 | | | | | |

### MARCH
| S | M | T | W | T | F | S |
|---|---|---|---|---|---|---|
| — | — | 1 | 2 | 3 | 4 | 5 |
| 6 | 7 | 8 | 9 | 10 | 11 | 12 |
| 13 | 14 | 15 | 16 | 17 | 18 | 19 |
| 20 | 21 | 22 | 23 | 24 | 25 | 26 |
| 27 | 28 | 29 | 30 | 31 | | |

### APRIL
| S | M | T | W | T | F | S |
|---|---|---|---|---|---|---|
| — | — | — | — | — | 1 | 2 |
| 3 | 4 | 5 | 6 | 7 | 8 | 9 |
| 10 | 11 | 12 | 13 | 14 | 15 | 16 |
| 17 | 18 | 19 | 20 | 21 | 22 | 23 |
| 24 | 25 | 26 | 27 | 28 | 29 | 30 |

### MAY
| S | M | T | W | T | F | S |
|---|---|---|---|---|---|---|
| 1 | 2 | 3 | 4 | 5 | 6 | 7 |
| 8 | 9 | 10 | 11 | 12 | 13 | 14 |
| 15 | 16 | 17 | 18 | 19 | 20 | 21 |
| 22 | 23 | 24 | 25 | 26 | 27 | 28 |
| 29 | 30 | 31 | | | | |

### JUNE
| S | M | T | W | T | F | S |
|---|---|---|---|---|---|---|
| — | — | — | 1 | 2 | 3 | 4 |
| 5 | 6 | 7 | 8 | 9 | 10 | 11 |
| 12 | 13 | 14 | 15 | 16 | 17 | 18 |
| 19 | 20 | 21 | 22 | 23 | 24 | 25 |
| 26 | 27 | 28 | 29 | 30 | | |

### JULY
| S | M | T | W | T | F | S |
|---|---|---|---|---|---|---|
| — | — | — | — | — | 1 | 2 |
| 3 | 4 | 5 | 6 | 7 | 8 | 9 |
| 10 | 11 | 12 | 13 | 14 | 15 | 16 |
| 17 | 18 | 19 | 20 | 21 | 22 | 23 |
| 24 | 25 | 26 | 27 | 28 | 29 | 30 |
| 31 | | | | | | |

### AUGUST
| S | M | T | W | T | F | S |
|---|---|---|---|---|---|---|
| — | 1 | 2 | 3 | 4 | 5 | 6 |
| 7 | 8 | 9 | 10 | 11 | 12 | 13 |
| 14 | 15 | 16 | 17 | 18 | 19 | 20 |
| 21 | 22 | 23 | 24 | 25 | 26 | 27 |
| 28 | 29 | 30 | 31 | | | |

### SEPTEMBER
| S | M | T | W | T | F | S |
|---|---|---|---|---|---|---|
| — | — | — | — | 1 | 2 | 3 |
| 4 | 5 | 6 | 7 | 8 | 9 | 10 |
| 11 | 12 | 13 | 14 | 15 | 16 | 17 |
| 18 | 19 | 20 | 21 | 22 | 23 | 24 |
| 25 | 26 | 27 | 28 | 29 | 30 | |

### OCTOBER
| S | M | T | W | T | F | S |
|---|---|---|---|---|---|---|
| — | — | — | — | — | — | 1 |
| 2 | 3 | 4 | 5 | 6 | 7 | 8 |
| 9 | 10 | 11 | 12 | 13 | 14 | 15 |
| 16 | 17 | 18 | 19 | 20 | 21 | 22 |
| 23 | 24 | 25 | 26 | 27 | 28 | 29 |
| 30 | 31 | | | | | |

### NOVEMBER
| S | M | T | W | T | F | S |
|---|---|---|---|---|---|---|
| — | — | 1 | 2 | 3 | 4 | 5 |
| 6 | 7 | 8 | 9 | 10 | 11 | 12 |
| 13 | 14 | 15 | 16 | 17 | 18 | 19 |
| 20 | 21 | 22 | 23 | 24 | 25 | 26 |
| 27 | 28 | 29 | 30 | | | |

### DECEMBER
| S | M | T | W | T | F | S |
|---|---|---|---|---|---|---|
| — | — | — | — | 1 | 2 | 3 |
| 4 | 5 | 6 | 7 | 8 | 9 | 10 |
| 11 | 12 | 13 | 14 | 15 | 16 | 17 |
| 18 | 19 | 20 | 21 | 22 | 23 | 24 |
| 25 | 26 | 27 | 28 | 29 | 30 | 31 |

## Pre-Columbian Calendar Systems

The Mayans and the Aztecs both used two calendars—a sacred or ceremonial calendar of 260 days and a 365-day secular calendar that was divided into 18 months of 20 days each. An additional five days were added to complete the 365-day year.

The Mayans were able to approximate the true length of the tropical year with a greater accuracy than does the Gregorian calendar year we now use.

The tropical year is 365.2422 days. The Mayans determined it to be 365.2420 days, whereas the Gregorian calendar year is 365.2425.

Very little is known about the Inca calendar. Because the Incas did not have a written language, early reports about their calendar cannot be verified.

# PERPETUAL CALENDAR

| | | | | | |
|---|---|---|---|---|---|
| 1800 ..4 | 1844 ..9 | 1888 ..8 | 1932 .13 | 1976 .12 | 2020 .11 |
| 1801 ..5 | 1845 ..4 | 1889 ..3 | 1933 ..1 | 1977 ..7 | 2021 ..6 |
| 1802 ..6 | 1846 ..5 | 1890 ..4 | 1934 ..2 | 1978 ..1 | 2022 ..7 |
| 1803 ..7 | 1847 ..6 | 1891 ..5 | 1935 ..3 | 1979 ..2 | 2023 ..1 |
| 1804 ..8 | 1848 .14 | 1892 .13 | 1936 .11 | 1980 .10 | 2024 ..9 |
| 1805 ..3 | 1849 ..2 | 1893 ..1 | 1937 ..6 | 1981 ..5 | 2025 ..4 |
| 1806 ..4 | 1850 ..3 | 1894 ..2 | 1938 ..7 | 1982 ..6 | 2026 ..5 |
| 1807 ..5 | 1851 ..4 | 1895 ..3 | 1939 ..1 | 1983 ..7 | 2027 ..6 |
| 1808 .13 | 1852 .12 | 1896 .11 | 1940 ..9 | 1984 ..8 | 2028 .14 |
| 1809 ..1 | 1853 ..7 | 1897 ..6 | 1941 ..4 | 1985 ..3 | 2029 ..2 |
| 1810 ..2 | 1854 ..1 | 1898 ..7 | 1942 ..5 | 1986 ..4 | 2030 ..3 |
| 1811 ..3 | 1855 ..2 | 1899 ..1 | 1943 ..6 | 1987 ..5 | 2031 ..4 |
| 1812 .11 | 1856 .10 | 1900 ..2 | 1944 .14 | 1988 .13 | 2032 .12 |
| 1813 ..6 | 1857 ..5 | 1901 ..3 | 1945 ..2 | 1989 ..1 | 2033 ..7 |
| 1814 ..7 | 1858 ..6 | 1902 ..4 | 1946 ..3 | 1990 ..2 | 2034 ..1 |
| 1815 ..1 | 1859 ..7 | 1903 ..5 | 1947 ..4 | 1991 ..3 | 2035 ..2 |
| 1816 ..9 | 1860 ..8 | 1904 .13 | 1948 .12 | 1992 .11 | 2036 .10 |
| 1817 ..4 | 1861 ..3 | 1905 ..1 | 1949 ..7 | 1993 ..6 | 2037 ..5 |
| 1818 ..5 | 1862 ..4 | 1906 ..2 | 1950 ..1 | 1994 ..7 | 2038 ..6 |
| 1819 ..6 | 1863 ..5 | 1907 ..3 | 1951 ..2 | 1995 ..1 | 2039 ..7 |
| 1820 .14 | 1864 .13 | 1908 .11 | 1952 .10 | 1996 ..9 | 2040 ..8 |
| 1821 ..2 | 1865 ..1 | 1909 ..6 | 1953 ..5 | 1997 ..4 | 2041 ..3 |
| 1822 ..3 | 1866 ..2 | 1910 ..7 | 1954 ..6 | 1998 ..5 | 2042 ..4 |
| 1823 ..4 | 1867 ..3 | 1911 ..1 | 1955 ..7 | 1999 ..6 | 2043 ..5 |
| 1824 .12 | 1868 .11 | 1912 ..9 | 1956 ..8 | 2000 .14 | 2044 .13 |
| 1825 ..7 | 1869 ..6 | 1913 ..4 | 1957 ..3 | 2001 ..2 | 2045 ..1 |
| 1826 ..1 | 1870 ..7 | 1914 ..5 | 1958 ..4 | 2002 ..3 | 2046 ..2 |
| 1827 ..2 | 1871 ..1 | 1915 ..6 | 1959 ..5 | 2003 ..4 | 2047 ..3 |
| 1828 .10 | 1872 ..9 | 1916 .14 | 1960 .13 | 2004 .12 | 2048 .11 |
| 1829 ..5 | 1873 ..4 | 1917 ..2 | 1961 ..1 | 2005 ..7 | 2049 ..6 |
| 1830 ..6 | 1874 ..5 | 1918 ..3 | 1962 ..2 | 2006 ..1 | 2050 ..7 |
| 1831 ..7 | 1875 ..6 | 1919 ..4 | 1963 ..3 | 2007 ..2 | 2051 ..1 |
| 1832 ..8 | 1876 .14 | 1920 .12 | 1964 .11 | 2008 .10 | 2052 ..9 |
| 1833 ..3 | 1877 ..2 | 1921 ..7 | 1965 ..6 | 2009 ..5 | 2053 ..4 |
| 1834 ..4 | 1878 ..3 | 1922 ..1 | 1966 ..7 | 2010 ..6 | 2054 ..5 |
| 1835 ..5 | 1879 ..4 | 1923 ..2 | 1967 ..1 | 2011 ..7 | 2055 ..6 |
| 1836 .13 | 1880 .12 | 1924 .10 | 1968 ..9 | 2012 ..8 | 2056 .14 |
| 1837 ..1 | 1881 ..7 | 1925 ..5 | 1969 ..4 | 2013 ..3 | 2057 ..2 |
| 1838 ..2 | 1882 ..1 | 1926 ..6 | 1970 ..5 | 2014 ..4 | 2058 ..3 |
| 1839 ..3 | 1883 ..2 | 1927 ..7 | 1971 ..6 | 2015 ..5 | 2059 ..4 |
| 1840 .11 | 1884 .10 | 1928 ..8 | 1972 .14 | 2016 .13 | 2060 .12 |
| 1841 ..6 | 1885 ..5 | 1929 ..3 | 1973 ..2 | 2017 ..1 | 2061 ..7 |
| 1842 ..7 | 1886 ..6 | 1930 ..4 | 1974 ..3 | 2018 ..2 | 2062 ..1 |
| 1843 ..1 | 1887 ..7 | 1931 ..5 | 1975 ..4 | 2019 ..3 | |

**DIRECTIONS:** The number given with each year in the key above is number of calendar to use for that year

## 1

**JANUARY**
```
S  M  T  W  T  F  S
         1  2  3  4  5  6  7
 8  9 10 11 12 13 14
15 16 17 18 19 20 21
22 23 24 25 26 27 28
29 30 31
```
**FEBRUARY**
```
S  M  T  W  T  F  S
             1  2  3  4
 5  6  7  8  9 10 11
12 13 14 15 16 17 18
19 20 21 22 23 24 25
26 27 28
```
**MARCH**
```
S  M  T  W  T  F  S
             1  2  3  4
 5  6  7  8  9 10 11
12 13 14 15 16 17 18
19 20 21 22 23 24 25
26 27 28 29 30 31
```
**APRIL**
```
S  M  T  W  T  F  S
                      1
 2  3  4  5  6  7  8
 9 10 11 12 13 14 15
16 17 18 19 20 21 22
23 24 25 26 27 28 29
30
```
**MAY**
```
S  M  T  W  T  F  S
       1  2  3  4  5  6
 7  8  9 10 11 12 13
14 15 16 17 18 19 20
21 22 23 24 25 26 27
28 29 30 31
```
**JUNE**
```
S  M  T  W  T  F  S
          1  2  3
 4  5  6  7  8  9 10
11 12 13 14 15 16 17
18 19 20 21 22 23 24
25 26 27 28 29 30
```
**JULY**
```
S  M  T  W  T  F  S
                      1
 2  3  4  5  6  7  8
 9 10 11 12 13 14 15
16 17 18 19 20 21 22
23 24 25 26 27 28 29
30 31
```
**AUGUST**
```
S  M  T  W  T  F  S
          1  2  3  4  5
 6  7  8  9 10 11 12
13 14 15 16 17 18 19
20 21 22 23 24 25 26
27 28 29 30 31
```
**SEPTEMBER**
```
S  M  T  W  T  F  S
                1  2
 3  4  5  6  7  8  9
10 11 12 13 14 15 16
17 18 19 20 21 22 23
24 25 26 27 28 29 30
```
**OCTOBER**
```
S  M  T  W  T  F  S
 1  2  3  4  5  6  7
 8  9 10 11 12 13 14
15 16 17 18 19 20 21
22 23 24 25 26 27 28
29 30 31
```
**NOVEMBER**
```
S  M  T  W  T  F  S
             1  2  3  4
 5  6  7  8  9 10 11
12 13 14 15 16 17 18
19 20 21 22 23 24 25
26 27 28 29 30
```
**DECEMBER**
```
S  M  T  W  T  F  S
                1  2
 3  4  5  6  7  8  9
10 11 12 13 14 15 16
17 18 19 20 21 22 23
24 25 26 27 28 29 30
31
```

## 2

**JANUARY**
```
S  M  T  W  T  F  S
    1  2  3  4  5  6
 7  8  9 10 11 12 13
14 15 16 17 18 19 20
21 22 23 24 25 26 27
28 29 30 31
```
**FEBRUARY**
```
S  M  T  W  T  F  S
                1  2  3
 4  5  6  7  8  9 10
11 12 13 14 15 16 17
18 19 20 21 22 23 24
25 26 27 28
```
**MARCH**
```
S  M  T  W  T  F  S
                1  2  3
 4  5  6  7  8  9 10
11 12 13 14 15 16 17
18 19 20 21 22 23 24
25 26 27 28 29 30 31
```
**APRIL**
```
S  M  T  W  T  F  S
 1  2  3  4  5  6  7
 8  9 10 11 12 13 14
15 16 17 18 19 20 21
22 23 24 25 26 27 28
29 30
```
**MAY**
```
S  M  T  W  T  F  S
          1  2  3  4  5
 6  7  8  9 10 11 12
13 14 15 16 17 18 19
20 21 22 23 24 25 26
27 28 29 30 31
```
**JUNE**
```
S  M  T  W  T  F  S
                   1  2
 3  4  5  6  7  8  9
10 11 12 13 14 15 16
17 18 19 20 21 22 23
24 25 26 27 28 29 30
```
**JULY**
```
S  M  T  W  T  F  S
 1  2  3  4  5  6  7
 8  9 10 11 12 13 14
15 16 17 18 19 20 21
22 23 24 25 26 27 28
29 30 31
```
**AUGUST**
```
S  M  T  W  T  F  S
             1  2  3  4
 5  6  7  8  9 10 11
12 13 14 15 16 17 18
19 20 21 22 23 24 25
26 27 28 29 30 31
```
**SEPTEMBER**
```
S  M  T  W  T  F  S
                      1
 2  3  4  5  6  7  8
 9 10 11 12 13 14 15
16 17 18 19 20 21 22
23 24 25 26 27 28 29
30
```
**OCTOBER**
```
S  M  T  W  T  F  S
    1  2  3  4  5  6
 7  8  9 10 11 12 13
14 15 16 17 18 19 20
21 22 23 24 25 26 27
28 29 30 31
```
**NOVEMBER**
```
S  M  T  W  T  F  S
                1  2  3
 4  5  6  7  8  9 10
11 12 13 14 15 16 17
18 19 20 21 22 23 24
25 26 27 28 29 30
```
**DECEMBER**
```
S  M  T  W  T  F  S
                      1
 2  3  4  5  6  7  8
 9 10 11 12 13 14 15
16 17 18 19 20 21 22
23 24 25 26 27 28 29
30 31
```

## 3

**JANUARY**
```
S  M  T  W  T  F  S
       1  2  3  4  5
 6  7  8  9 10 11 12
13 14 15 16 17 18 19
20 21 22 23 24 25 26
27 28 29 30 31
```
**FEBRUARY**
```
S  M  T  W  T  F  S
                   1  2
 3  4  5  6  7  8  9
10 11 12 13 14 15 16
17 18 19 20 21 22 23
24 25 26 27 28
```
**MARCH**
```
S  M  T  W  T  F  S
                   1  2
 3  4  5  6  7  8  9
10 11 12 13 14 15 16
17 18 19 20 21 22 23
24 25 26 27 28 29 30
31
```
**APRIL**
```
S  M  T  W  T  F  S
    1  2  3  4  5  6
 7  8  9 10 11 12 13
14 15 16 17 18 19 20
21 22 23 24 25 26 27
28 29 30
```
**MAY**
```
S  M  T  W  T  F  S
             1  2  3  4
 5  6  7  8  9 10 11
12 13 14 15 16 17 18
19 20 21 22 23 24 25
26 27 28 29 30 31
```
**JUNE**
```
S  M  T  W  T  F  S
                      1
 2  3  4  5  6  7  8
 9 10 11 12 13 14 15
16 17 18 19 20 21 22
23 24 25 26 27 28 29
30
```
**JULY**
```
S  M  T  W  T  F  S
    1  2  3  4  5  6
 7  8  9 10 11 12 13
14 15 16 17 18 19 20
21 22 23 24 25 26 27
28 29 30 31
```
**AUGUST**
```
S  M  T  W  T  F  S
                1  2  3
 4  5  6  7  8  9 10
11 12 13 14 15 16 17
18 19 20 21 22 23 24
25 26 27 28 29 30 31
```
**SEPTEMBER**
```
S  M  T  W  T  F  S
 1  2  3  4  5  6  7
 8  9 10 11 12 13 14
15 16 17 18 19 20 21
22 23 24 25 26 27 28
29 30
```
**OCTOBER**
```
S  M  T  W  T  F  S
       1  2  3  4  5
 6  7  8  9 10 11 12
13 14 15 16 17 18 19
20 21 22 23 24 25 26
27 28 29 30 31
```
**NOVEMBER**
```
S  M  T  W  T  F  S
                   1  2
 3  4  5  6  7  8  9
10 11 12 13 14 15 16
17 18 19 20 21 22 23
24 25 26 27 28 29 30
```
**DECEMBER**
```
S  M  T  W  T  F  S
 1  2  3  4  5  6  7
 8  9 10 11 12 13 14
15 16 17 18 19 20 21
22 23 24 25 26 27 28
29 30 31
```

## 4

**JANUARY**
```
S  M  T  W  T  F  S
          1  2  3  4
 5  6  7  8  9 10 11
12 13 14 15 16 17 18
19 20 21 22 23 24 25
26 27 28 29 30 31
```
**FEBRUARY**
```
S  M  T  W  T  F  S
                      1
 2  3  4  5  6  7  8
 9 10 11 12 13 14 15
16 17 18 19 20 21 22
23 24 25 26 27 28
```
**MARCH**
```
S  M  T  W  T  F  S
                      1
 2  3  4  5  6  7  8
 9 10 11 12 13 14 15
16 17 18 19 20 21 22
23 24 25 26 27 28 29
30 31
```
**APRIL**
```
S  M  T  W  T  F  S
       1  2  3  4  5
 6  7  8  9 10 11 12
13 14 15 16 17 18 19
20 21 22 23 24 25 26
27 28 29 30
```
**MAY**
```
S  M  T  W  T  F  S
          1  2  3
 4  5  6  7  8  9 10
11 12 13 14 15 16 17
18 19 20 21 22 23 24
25 26 27 28 29 30 31
```
**JUNE**
```
S  M  T  W  T  F  S
 1  2  3  4  5  6  7
 8  9 10 11 12 13 14
15 16 17 18 19 20 21
22 23 24 25 26 27 28
29 30
```
**JULY**
```
S  M  T  W  T  F  S
       1  2  3  4  5
 6  7  8  9 10 11 12
13 14 15 16 17 18 19
20 21 22 23 24 25 26
27 28 29 30 31
```
**AUGUST**
```
S  M  T  W  T  F  S
                   1  2
 3  4  5  6  7  8  9
10 11 12 13 14 15 16
17 18 19 20 21 22 23
24 25 26 27 28 29 30
31
```
**SEPTEMBER**
```
S  M  T  W  T  F  S
    1  2  3  4  5  6
 7  8  9 10 11 12 13
14 15 16 17 18 19 20
21 22 23 24 25 26 27
28 29 30
```
**OCTOBER**
```
S  M  T  W  T  F  S
          1  2  3  4
 5  6  7  8  9 10 11
12 13 14 15 16 17 18
19 20 21 22 23 24 25
26 27 28 29 30 31
```
**NOVEMBER**
```
S  M  T  W  T  F  S
                      1
 2  3  4  5  6  7  8
 9 10 11 12 13 14 15
16 17 18 19 20 21 22
23 24 25 26 27 28 29
30
```
**DECEMBER**
```
S  M  T  W  T  F  S
    1  2  3  4  5  6
 7  8  9 10 11 12 13
14 15 16 17 18 19 20
21 22 23 24 25 26 27
28 29 30 31
```

## 5

**JANUARY**
```
S  M  T  W  T  F  S
             1  2  3
 4  5  6  7  8  9 10
11 12 13 14 15 16 17
18 19 20 21 22 23 24
25 26 27 28 29 30 31
```
**FEBRUARY**
```
S  M  T  W  T  F  S
 1  2  3  4  5  6  7
 8  9 10 11 12 13 14
15 16 17 18 19 20 21
22 23 24 25 26 27 28
```
**MARCH**
```
S  M  T  W  T  F  S
 1  2  3  4  5  6  7
 8  9 10 11 12 13 14
15 16 17 18 19 20 21
22 23 24 25 26 27 28
29 30 31
```
**APRIL**
```
S  M  T  W  T  F  S
          1  2  3  4
 5  6  7  8  9 10 11
12 13 14 15 16 17 18
19 20 21 22 23 24 25
26 27 28 29 30
```
**MAY**
```
S  M  T  W  T  F  S
                   1  2
 3  4  5  6  7  8  9
10 11 12 13 14 15 16
17 18 19 20 21 22 23
24 25 26 27 28 29 30
31
```
**JUNE**
```
S  M  T  W  T  F  S
       1  2  3  4  5  6
 7  8  9 10 11 12 13
14 15 16 17 18 19 20
21 22 23 24 25 26 27
28 29 30
```
**JULY**
```
S  M  T  W  T  F  S
          1  2  3  4
 5  6  7  8  9 10 11
12 13 14 15 16 17 18
19 20 21 22 23 24 25
26 27 28 29 30 31
```
**AUGUST**
```
S  M  T  W  T  F  S
                      1
 2  3  4  5  6  7  8
 9 10 11 12 13 14 15
16 17 18 19 20 21 22
23 24 25 26 27 28 29
30 31
```
**SEPTEMBER**
```
S  M  T  W  T  F  S
       1  2  3  4  5
 6  7  8  9 10 11 12
13 14 15 16 17 18 19
20 21 22 23 24 25 26
27 28 29 30
```
**OCTOBER**
```
S  M  T  W  T  F  S
             1  2  3
 4  5  6  7  8  9 10
11 12 13 14 15 16 17
18 19 20 21 22 23 24
25 26 27 28 29 30 31
```
**NOVEMBER**
```
S  M  T  W  T  F  S
 1  2  3  4  5  6  7
 8  9 10 11 12 13 14
15 16 17 18 19 20 21
22 23 24 25 26 27 28
29 30
```
**DECEMBER**
```
S  M  T  W  T  F  S
       1  2  3  4  5
 6  7  8  9 10 11 12
13 14 15 16 17 18 19
20 21 22 23 24 25 26
27 28 29 30 31
```

## 6

**JANUARY**
```
S  M  T  W  T  F  S
                   1  2
 3  4  5  6  7  8  9
10 11 12 13 14 15 16
17 18 19 20 21 22 23
24 25 26 27 28 29 30
31
```
**FEBRUARY**
```
S  M  T  W  T  F  S
       1  2  3  4  5  6
 7  8  9 10 11 12 13
14 15 16 17 18 19 20
21 22 23 24 25 26 27
28
```
**MARCH**
```
S  M  T  W  T  F  S
       1  2  3  4  5  6
 7  8  9 10 11 12 13
14 15 16 17 18 19 20
21 22 23 24 25 26 27
28 29 30 31
```
**APRIL**
```
S  M  T  W  T  F  S
             1  2  3
 4  5  6  7  8  9 10
11 12 13 14 15 16 17
18 19 20 21 22 23 24
25 26 27 28 29 30
```
**MAY**
```
S  M  T  W  T  F  S
                      1
 2  3  4  5  6  7  8
 9 10 11 12 13 14 15
16 17 18 19 20 21 22
23 24 25 26 27 28 29
30 31
```
**JUNE**
```
S  M  T  W  T  F  S
       1  2  3  4  5
 6  7  8  9 10 11 12
13 14 15 16 17 18 19
20 21 22 23 24 25 26
27 28 29 30
```
**JULY**
```
S  M  T  W  T  F  S
             1  2  3
 4  5  6  7  8  9 10
11 12 13 14 15 16 17
18 19 20 21 22 23 24
25 26 27 28 29 30 31
```
**AUGUST**
```
S  M  T  W  T  F  S
 1  2  3  4  5  6  7
 8  9 10 11 12 13 14
15 16 17 18 19 20 21
22 23 24 25 26 27 28
29 30 31
```
**SEPTEMBER**
```
S  M  T  W  T  F  S
          1  2  3  4
 5  6  7  8  9 10 11
12 13 14 15 16 17 18
19 20 21 22 23 24 25
26 27 28 29 30
```
**OCTOBER**
```
S  M  T  W  T  F  S
                   1  2
 3  4  5  6  7  8  9
10 11 12 13 14 15 16
17 18 19 20 21 22 23
24 25 26 27 28 29 30
31
```
**NOVEMBER**
```
S  M  T  W  T  F  S
    1  2  3  4  5  6
 7  8  9 10 11 12 13
14 15 16 17 18 19 20
21 22 23 24 25 26 27
28 29 30
```
**DECEMBER**
```
S  M  T  W  T  F  S
          1  2  3  4
 5  6  7  8  9 10 11
12 13 14 15 16 17 18
19 20 21 22 23 24 25
26 27 28 29 30 31
```

## 7

```
JANUARY              FEBRUARY             MARCH                APRIL
S M T W T F S        S M T W T F S        S M T W T F S        S M T W T F S
            1         1  2  3  4  5         1  2  3  4  5                  1  2
2  3  4  5  6  7  8   6  7  8  9 10 11 12   6  7  8  9 10 11 12   3  4  5  6  7  8  9
9 10 11 12 13 14 15  13 14 15 16 17 18 19  13 14 15 16 17 18 19  10 11 12 13 14 15 16
16 17 18 19 20 21 22 20 21 22 23 24 25 26  20 21 22 23 24 25 26  17 18 19 20 21 22 23
23 24 25 26 27 28 29 27 28                 27 28 29 30 31        24 25 26 27 28 29 30
30 31

MAY                  JUNE                 JULY                 AUGUST
S M T W T F S        S M T W T F S        S M T W T F S        S M T W T F S
1  2  3  4  5  6  7            1  2  3  4                  1  2   1  2  3  4  5  6
8  9 10 11 12 13 14   5  6  7  8  9 10 11   3  4  5  6  7  8  9   7  8  9 10 11 12 13
15 16 17 18 19 20 21  12 13 14 15 16 17 18  10 11 12 13 14 15 16  14 15 16 17 18 19 20
22 23 24 25 26 27 28  19 20 21 22 23 24 25  17 18 19 20 21 22 23  21 22 23 24 25 26 27
29 30 31              26 27 28 29 30        24 25 26 27 28 29 30  28 29 30 31
                                           31

SEPTEMBER            OCTOBER              NOVEMBER             DECEMBER
S M T W T F S        S M T W T F S        S M T W T F S        S M T W T F S
            1  2  3               1               1  2  3  4  5               1  2  3
4  5  6  7  8  9 10   2  3  4  5  6  7  8   6  7  8  9 10 11 12   4  5  6  7  8  9 10
11 12 13 14 15 16 17  9 10 11 12 13 14 15  13 14 15 16 17 18 19  11 12 13 14 15 16 17
18 19 20 21 22 23 24 16 17 18 19 20 21 22  20 21 22 23 24 25 26  18 19 20 21 22 23 24
25 26 27 28 29 30    23 24 25 26 27 28 29  27 28 29 30           25 26 27 28 29 30 31
                     30 31
```

## 8

```
JANUARY              FEBRUARY             MARCH                APRIL
S M T W T F S        S M T W T F S        S M T W T F S        S M T W T F S
1  2  3  4  5  6  7            1  2  3  4               1  2  3   1  2  3  4  5  6  7
8  9 10 11 12 13 14   5  6  7  8  9 10 11   4  5  6  7  8  9 10   8  9 10 11 12 13 14
15 16 17 18 19 20 21  12 13 14 15 16 17 18  11 12 13 14 15 16 17  15 16 17 18 19 20 21
22 23 24 25 26 27 28  19 20 21 22 23 24 25  18 19 20 21 22 23 24  22 23 24 25 26 27 28
29 30 31              26 27 28 29           25 26 27 28 29 30 31  29 30

MAY                  JUNE                 JULY                 AUGUST
S M T W T F S        S M T W T F S        S M T W T F S        S M T W T F S
      1  2  3  4  5               1  2   1  2  3  4  5  6  7               1  2  3  4
6  7  8  9 10 11 12   3  4  5  6  7  8  9   8  9 10 11 12 13 14   5  6  7  8  9 10 11
13 14 15 16 17 18 19  10 11 12 13 14 15 16  15 16 17 18 19 20 21  12 13 14 15 16 17 18
20 21 22 23 24 25 26  17 18 19 20 21 22 23  22 23 24 25 26 27 28  19 20 21 22 23 24 25
27 28 29 30 31        24 25 26 27 28 29 30  29 30 31              26 27 28 29 30 31

SEPTEMBER            OCTOBER              NOVEMBER             DECEMBER
S M T W T F S        S M T W T F S        S M T W T F S        S M T W T F S
                  1   1  2  3  4  5  6            1  2  3                     1
2  3  4  5  6  7  8   7  8  9 10 11 12 13   4  5  6  7  8  9 10   2  3  4  5  6  7  8
9 10 11 12 13 14 15  14 15 16 17 18 19 20  11 12 13 14 15 16 17   9 10 11 12 13 14 15
16 17 18 19 20 21 22 21 22 23 24 25 26 27  18 19 20 21 22 23 24  16 17 18 19 20 21 22
23 24 25 26 27 28 29 28 29 30 31           25 26 27 28 29 30     23 24 25 26 27 28 29
30                                                               30 31
```

## 9

```
JANUARY              FEBRUARY             MARCH                APRIL
S M T W T F S        S M T W T F S        S M T W T F S        S M T W T F S
      1  2  3  4  5               1  2  3               1  2   1  2  3  4  5  6
7  8  9 10 11 12 13   4  5  6  7  8  9 10   3  4  5  6  7  8  9   8  9 10 11 12 13
14 15 16 17 18 19 20  11 12 13 14 15 16 17  10 11 12 13 14 15 16  15 16 17 18 19 20
21 22 23 24 25 26 27  18 19 20 21 22 23 24  17 18 19 20 21 22 23  22 23 24 25 26 27
28 29 30 31          25 26 27 28 29        24 25 26 27 28 29 30  29 30
                                           31

MAY                  JUNE                 JULY                 AUGUST
S M T W T F S        S M T W T F S        S M T W T F S        S M T W T F S
            1  2  3  4                  1   1  2  3  4  5  6               1  2  3
5  6  7  8  9 10 11   2  3  4  5  6  7  8   7  8  9 10 11 12 13   4  5  6  7  8  9 10
12 13 14 15 16 17 18  9 10 11 12 13 14 15  14 15 16 17 18 19 20  11 12 13 14 15 16 17
19 20 21 22 23 24 25 16 17 18 19 20 21 22  21 22 23 24 25 26 27  18 19 20 21 22 23 24
26 27 28 29 30 31    23 24 25 26 27 28 29  28 29 30 31           25 26 27 28 29 30 31
                     30

SEPTEMBER            OCTOBER              NOVEMBER             DECEMBER
S M T W T F S        S M T W T F S        S M T W T F S        S M T W T F S
1  2  3  4  5  6  7               1  2                  1  2   1  2  3  4  5  6  7
8  9 10 11 12 13 14   6  7  8  9 10 11 12   3  4  5  6  7  8  9   8  9 10 11 12 13 14
15 16 17 18 19 20 21 13 14 15 16 17 18 19  10 11 12 13 14 15 16  15 16 17 18 19 20 21
22 23 24 25 26 27 28 20 21 22 23 24 25 26  17 18 19 20 21 22 23  22 23 24 25 26 27 28
29 30                27 28 29 30 31        24 25 26 27 28 29 30  29 30 31
```

## 10

```
JANUARY              FEBRUARY             MARCH                APRIL
S M T W T F S        S M T W T F S        S M T W T F S        S M T W T F S
      1  2  3  4  5               1  2                  1   1  2  3  4  5
6  7  8  9 10 11 12   3  4  5  6  7  8  9   2  3  4  5  6  7  8   6  7  8  9 10 11 12
13 14 15 16 17 18 19 10 11 12 13 14 15 16   9 10 11 12 13 14 15  13 14 15 16 17 18 19
20 21 22 23 24 25 26 17 18 19 20 21 22 23  16 17 18 19 20 21 22  20 21 22 23 24 25 26
27 28 29 30 31       24 25 26 27 28 29     23 24 25 26 27 28 29  27 28 29 30
                                           30 31

MAY                  JUNE                 JULY                 AUGUST
S M T W T F S        S M T W T F S        S M T W T F S        S M T W T F S
            1  2  3   1  2  3  4  5  6  7               1  2  3                  1  2
4  5  6  7  8  9 10   8  9 10 11 12 13 14   6  7  8  9 10 11 12   3  4  5  6  7  8  9
11 12 13 14 15 16 17 15 16 17 18 19 20 21  13 14 15 16 17 18 19  10 11 12 13 14 15 16
18 19 20 21 22 23 24 22 23 24 25 26 27 28  20 21 22 23 24 25 26  17 18 19 20 21 22 23
25 26 27 28 29 30 31 29 30                 27 28 29 30 31        24 25 26 27 28 29 30
                                                                 31

SEPTEMBER            OCTOBER              NOVEMBER             DECEMBER
S M T W T F S        S M T W T F S        S M T W T F S        S M T W T F S
            1  2  3               1  2  3  4   1  2  3  4  5  6               1  2  3  4
7  8  9 10 11 12 13   5  6  7  8  9 10 11   2  3  4  5  6  7  8   1  2  3  4  5  6
14 15 16 17 18 19 20 12 13 14 15 16 17 18   9 10 11 12 13 14 15   7  8  9 10 11 12 13
21 22 23 24 25 26 27 19 20 21 22 23 24 25  16 17 18 19 20 21 22  14 15 16 17 18 19 20
28 29 30             26 27 28 29 30 31     23 24 25 26 27 28 29  21 22 23 24 25 26 27
                                           30                    28 29 30 31
```

## 11

```
JANUARY              FEBRUARY             MARCH                APRIL
S M T W T F S        S M T W T F S        S M T W T F S        S M T W T F S
            1  2  3  4               1  2   1  2  3  4  5  6  7               1  2  3
5  6  7  8  9 10 11   2  3  4  5  6  7  8   8  9 10 11 12 13 14   5  6  7  8  9 10 11
12 13 14 15 16 17 18  9 10 11 12 13 14 15  15 16 17 18 19 20 21  12 13 14 15 16 17 18
19 20 21 22 23 24 25 16 17 18 19 20 21 22  22 23 24 25 26 27 28  19 20 21 22 23 24 25
26 27 28 29 30 31    23 24 25 26 27 28 29  29 30 31              26 27 28 29 30

MAY                  JUNE                 JULY                 AUGUST
S M T W T F S        S M T W T F S        S M T W T F S        S M T W T F S
            1  2      1  2  3  4  5  6               1  2  3  4                     1
3  4  5  6  7  8  9   7  8  9 10 11 12 13   5  6  7  8  9 10 11   2  3  4  5  6  7  8
10 11 12 13 14 15 16 14 15 16 17 18 19 20  12 13 14 15 16 17 18   9 10 11 12 13 14 15
17 18 19 20 21 22 23 21 22 23 24 25 26 27  19 20 21 22 23 24 25  16 17 18 19 20 21 22
24 25 26 27 28 29 30 28 29 30              26 27 28 29 30 31     23 24 25 26 27 28 29
31                                                               30 31

SEPTEMBER            OCTOBER              NOVEMBER             DECEMBER
S M T W T F S        S M T W T F S        S M T W T F S        S M T W T F S
      1  2  3  4  5               1  2  3   1  2  3  4  5  6  7               1  2  3  4  5
6  7  8  9 10 11 12   4  5  6  7  8  9 10   8  9 10 11 12 13 14   6  7  8  9 10 11 12
13 14 15 16 17 18 19 11 12 13 14 15 16 17  15 16 17 18 19 20 21  13 14 15 16 17 18 19
20 21 22 23 24 25 26 18 19 20 21 22 23 24  22 23 24 25 26 27 28  20 21 22 23 24 25 26
27 28 29 30          25 26 27 28 29 30 31  29 30                 27 28 29 30 31
```

## 12

```
JANUARY              FEBRUARY             MARCH                APRIL
S M T W T F S        S M T W T F S        S M T W T F S        S M T W T F S
            1  2  3   1  2  3  4  5  6  7   1  2  3  4  5  6               1  2  3
4  5  6  7  8  9 10   8  9 10 11 12 13 14   7  8  9 10 11 12 13   4  5  6  7  8  9 10
11 12 13 14 15 16 17 15 16 17 18 19 20 21  14 15 16 17 18 19 20  11 12 13 14 15 16 17
18 19 20 21 22 23 24 22 23 24 25 26 27 28  21 22 23 24 25 26 27  18 19 20 21 22 23 24
25 26 27 28 29 30 31 29                    28 29 30 31           25 26 27 28 29 30

MAY                  JUNE                 JULY                 AUGUST
S M T W T F S        S M T W T F S        S M T W T F S        S M T W T F S
                  1               1  2  3               1  2   1  2  3  4  5  6  7
2  3  4  5  6  7  8   6  7  8  9 10 11 12   4  5  6  7  8  9 10   8  9 10 11 12 13 14
9 10 11 12 13 14 15  13 14 15 16 17 18 19  11 12 13 14 15 16 17  15 16 17 18 19 20 21
16 17 18 19 20 21 22 20 21 22 23 24 25 26  18 19 20 21 22 23 24  22 23 24 25 26 27 28
23 24 25 26 27 28 29 27 28 29 30           25 26 27 28 29 30 31  29 30 31
30 31

SEPTEMBER            OCTOBER              NOVEMBER             DECEMBER
S M T W T F S        S M T W T F S        S M T W T F S        S M T W T F S
            1  2  3  4               1  2   1  2  3  4  5  6               1  2  3  4
5  6  7  8  9 10 11   3  4  5  6  7  8  9   7  8  9 10 11 12 13   5  6  7  8  9 10 11
12 13 14 15 16 17 18 10 11 12 13 14 15 16  14 15 16 17 18 19 20  12 13 14 15 16 17 18
19 20 21 22 23 24 25 17 18 19 20 21 22 23  21 22 23 24 25 26 27  19 20 21 22 23 24 25
26 27 28 29 30       24 25 26 27 28 29 30  28 29 30              26 27 28 29 30 31
                     31
```

## 13

```
JANUARY              FEBRUARY             MARCH                APRIL
S M T W T F S        S M T W T F S        S M T W T F S        S M T W T F S
                  1  2   1  2  3  4  5  6   1  2  3  4  5               1  2
3  4  5  6  7  8  9   7  8  9 10 11 12 13   6  7  8  9 10 11 12   3  4  5  6  7  8  9
10 11 12 13 14 15 16 14 15 16 17 18 19 20  13 14 15 16 17 18 19  10 11 12 13 14 15 16
17 18 19 20 21 22 23 21 22 23 24 25 26 27  20 21 22 23 24 25 26  17 18 19 20 21 22 23
24 25 26 27 28 29 30 28 29                 27 28 29 30 31        24 25 26 27 28 29 30
31

MAY                  JUNE                 JULY                 AUGUST
S M T W T F S        S M T W T F S        S M T W T F S        S M T W T F S
1  2  3  4  5  6  7               1  2               1  2   1  2  3  4  5  6
8  9 10 11 12 13 14   5  6  7  8  9 10 11   3  4  5  6  7  8  9   7  8  9 10 11 12 13
15 16 17 18 19 20 21 12 13 14 15 16 17 18  10 11 12 13 14 15 16  14 15 16 17 18 19 20
22 23 24 25 26 27 28 19 20 21 22 23 24 25  17 18 19 20 21 22 23  21 22 23 24 25 26 27
29 30 31             26 27 28 29 30        24 25 26 27 28 29 30  28 29 30 31
                                           31

SEPTEMBER            OCTOBER              NOVEMBER             DECEMBER
S M T W T F S        S M T W T F S        S M T W T F S        S M T W T F S
            1  2  3               1               1  2  3  4  5               1  2  3
4  5  6  7  8  9 10   2  3  4  5  6  7  8   6  7  8  9 10 11 12   4  5  6  7  8  9 10
11 12 13 14 15 16 17  9 10 11 12 13 14 15  13 14 15 16 17 18 19  11 12 13 14 15 16 17
18 19 20 21 22 23 24 16 17 18 19 20 21 22  20 21 22 23 24 25 26  18 19 20 21 22 23 24
25 26 27 28 29 30    23 24 25 26 27 28 29  27 28 29 30           25 26 27 28 29 30 31
                     30 31
```

## 14

```
JANUARY              FEBRUARY             MARCH                APRIL
S M T W T F S        S M T W T F S        S M T W T F S        S M T W T F S
                  1               1  2  3  4  5               1  2  3  4   1  2  3
2  3  4  5  6  7  8   6  7  8  9 10 11 12   5  6  7  8  9 10 11   3  4  5  6  7
9 10 11 12 13 14 15  13 14 15 16 17 18 19  12 13 14 15 16 17 18   9 10 11 12 13 14
16 17 18 19 20 21 22 20 21 22 23 24 25 26  19 20 21 22 23 24 25  16 17 18 19 20 21 22
23 24 25 26 27 28 29 27 28                 26 27 28 29 30 31     23 24 25 26 27 28 29
30 31                                                            30

MAY                  JUNE                 JULY                 AUGUST
S M T W T F S        S M T W T F S        S M T W T F S        S M T W T F S
1  2  3  4  5  6               1  2  3               1   1  2  3  4  5
7  8  9 10 11 12 13   4  5  6  7  8  9 10   2  3  4  5  6  7  8   6  7  8  9 10 11 12
14 15 16 17 18 19 20 11 12 13 14 15 16 17   9 10 11 12 13 14 15  13 14 15 16 17 18 19
21 22 23 24 25 26 27 18 19 20 21 22 23 24  16 17 18 19 20 21 22  20 21 22 23 24 25 26
28 29 30 31          25 26 27 28 29 30     23 24 25 26 27 28 29  27 28 29 30 31
                                           30 31

SEPTEMBER            OCTOBER              NOVEMBER             DECEMBER
S M T W T F S        S M T W T F S        S M T W T F S        S M T W T F S
            1  2   1  2  3  4  5  6  7               1  2  3  4               1  2
3  4  5  6  7  8  9   8  9 10 11 12 13 14   5  6  7  8  9 10 11   3  4  5  6  7  8  9
10 11 12 13 14 15 16 15 16 17 18 19 20 21  12 13 14 15 16 17 18  10 11 12 13 14 15 16
17 18 19 20 21 22 23 22 23 24 25 26 27 28  19 20 21 22 23 24 25  17 18 19 20 21 22 23
24 25 26 27 28 29 30 29 30 31              26 27 28 29 30        24 25 26 27 28 29 30
                                                                 31
```

# The Calendar

## History of the Calendar

The purpose of a calendar is to reckon time in advance, to show how many days have to elapse until a certain event takes place—the harvest, a religious festival, or whatever. The earliest calendars, naturally, were crude, and they must have been strongly influenced by the geographical location of the people who made them. In the Scandinavian countries, for example, where the seasons are pronounced, the concept of the year was determined by the seasons, specifically by the end of winter. The Norsemen, before becoming Christians, are said to have had a calendar consisting of ten months of 30 days each.

But in warmer countries, where the seasons are less pronounced, the Moon became the basic unit for time reckoning; an old Jewish book actually makes the statement that "the Moon was created for the counting of the days." All the oldest calendars of which we have reliable information were lunar calendars, based on the time interval from one new moon to the next—a so-called "lunation." But even in a warm climate there are annual events that pay no attention to the phases of the Moon. In some areas it was a rainy season; in Egypt it was the annual flooding of the Nile. It was, therefore, necessary to regulate daily life and religious festivals by lunations, but to take care of the annual event in some other manner.

The calendar of the Assyrians was based on the phases of the Moon. The month began with the first appearance of the lunar crescent, and since this can best be observed in the evening, the day began with sunset. They knew that a lunation was 29 1/2 days long, so their lunar year had a duration of 354 days, falling eleven days short of the solar year.[1] After three years such a lunar calendar would be off by 33 days, or more than one lunation. We know that the Assyrians added an extra month from time to time, but we do not know whether they had developed a special rule for doing so or whether the priests proclaimed the necessity for an extra month from observation. If they made every third year a year of 13 lunations, their three-year period would cover 1,091 1/2 days (using their value of 29 1/2 days for one lunation), or just about four days too short. In one century this mistake would add up to 133 days by their reckoning (in reality closer to 134 days), requiring four extra lunations per century.

We now know that an eight-year period, consisting of five years with 12 months and three years with 13 months would lead to a difference of only 20 days per century, but we do not know whether such a calendar was actually used.

The best approximation that was possible in antiquity was a 19-year period, with seven of these 19 years having 13 months. This means that the period contained 235 months. This, still using the old value for a lunation, made a total of 6,932 1/2 days, while 19 solar years added up to 6,939.7 days, a difference of just one week per period and about five weeks per century. Even the 19-year period required constant adjustment, but it was the period that became the basis of the religious calendar of

the Jews. The Arabs used the same calendar at first, but Mohammed forbade shifting from 12 months to 13 months, so that the Islamic religious calendar, even today, has a lunar year of 354 days. As a result the Islamic religious festivals run through all the seasons of the year three times per century.

The Egyptians had a traditional calendar with 12 months of 30 days each. At one time they added five extra days at the end of every year. These turned into a five-day festival because it was thought to be unlucky to work during that time.

When Rome emerged as a world power, the difficulties of making a calendar were well known, but the Romans complicated their lives because of their superstition that even numbers were unlucky. Hence their months were 29 or 31 days long, with the exception of February, which had 28 days. However, four months of 31 days, seven months of 29 days, and one month of 28 days added up to only 355 days. Therefore, the Romans invented an extra month called Mercedonius of 22 or 23 days. It was added every second year.

Even with Mercedonius, the Roman calendar was so far off that Caesar, advised by the astronomer Sosigenes, ordered a sweeping reform in 45 B.C. One year, made 445 days long by imperial decree, brought the calendar back in step with the seasons. Then the solar year (with the value of 365 days and 6 hours) was made the basis of the calendar. The months were 30 or 31 days in length, and to take care of the six hours, every fourth year was made a 366-day year. Moreover, Caesar decreed the year began with the first of January, not with the vernal equinox in late March.

This was the Julian calendar, named after Julius Caesar. It is still the calendar of the Eastern Orthodox churches.

However, the year is 11 1/2 minutes shorter than the figure written into Caesar's calendar by Sosigenes, and after a number of centuries, even 11 1/2 minutes add up. *See* table.

While Caesar could decree that the vernal equinox should not be used as the first day of the new year, the vernal equinox is still a fact of Nature that could not be disregarded. One of the first (as far as we know) to become alarmed about this was Roger Bacon. He sent a memorandum to Pope Clement IV, who apparently was not impressed. But Pope Sixtus IV (reigned 1471 to 1484) decided that another reform was needed and called the German astronomer Regiomontanus to Rome to advise him. Regiomontanus arrived in 1475, but one year later he died in an epidemic, one of the recurrent outbreaks of the plague. The Pope himself survived, but his reform plans died with Regiomontanus.

Less than a hundred years later, in 1545, the Council of Trent authorized the then Pope, Gregory XIII, to reform the calendar once more. Most of the mathematical and astronomical work was done by Father Christopher Clavius, S.J. The immediate correction, advised by Father Clavius and ordered by Pope Gregory XIII, was that Thursday, Oct. 4, 1582, was to be the last day of the Julian calendar. The next day was Friday, with the date of October 15. For long-range accuracy, a formula suggested by the Vatican librarian Aloysius Giglio (latinized into Lilius) was adopted: every fourth year is a leap year *unless* it is a century year like 1700 or 1800. Century years can be leap years *only* when they are divisible by 400 (e.g., 1600).

[1]. The correct figures are: lunation: 29 d, 12 h, 44 min, 2.8 sec (29.530585 d); solar year: 365 d, 5 h, 48 min, 46 sec (365.242216 d); 12 lunations: 354 d, 8 h, 48 min, 34 sec (354.3671 d).

## Drift of the Vernal Equinox in the Julian Calendar

| Date | Julian year | Date | Julian year | Date | Julian year |
|------|-------------|------|-------------|------|-------------|
| March 21 | 325 A.D. | March 17 | 837 A.D. | March 13 | 1349 A.D. |
| March 20 | 453 A.D. | March 16 | 965 A.D. | March 12 | 1477 A.D. |
| March 19 | 581 A.D. | March 15 | 1093 A.D. | March 11 | 1605 A.D. |
| March 18 | 709 A.D. | March 14 | 1221 A.D. | | |

This rule eliminates three leap years in four centuries, making the calendar sufficiently correct for all ordinary purposes.

Unfortunately, all the Protestant princes in 1582 chose to ignore the papal bull; they continued with the Julian calendar. It was not until 1698 that the German professor Erhard Weigel persuaded the Protestant rulers of Germany and of the Netherlands to change to the new calendar. In England the shift took place in 1752, and in Russia it needed the revolution to introduce the Gregorian calendar in 1918.

The average year of the Gregorian calendar, in spite of the leap year rule, is about 26 seconds longer than the earth's orbital period. But this discrepancy will need 3,323 years to build up to a single day.

Modern proposals for calendar reform do not aim at a "better" calendar, but at one that is more convenient to use, especially for commercial purposes. A 365-day year cannot be divided into equal halves or quarters; the number of days per month is haphazard; the months begin or end in the middle of a week; a holiday fixed by date (e.g., the Fourth of July) will wander through a week; a holiday fixed in another manner (e.g., Easter) can fall on thirty-five possible dates. The Gregorian calendar, admittedly, keeps the calendar dates in reasonable unison with astronomical events, but it still is full of minor annoyances. Moreover, you need a calendar every year to look up dates; an ideal calendar should be one that you can memorize for one year and that is valid for all other years, too.

In 1834 an Italian priest, Marco Mastrofini, suggested taking one day out of every year. It would be made a holiday and *not* be given the name of a weekday. That would make every year begin with January 1 as a Sunday. The leap-year day would be treated the same way, so that in leap years there would be two unnamed holidays at the end of the year.

About a decade later the philosopher Auguste Comte also suggested a 364-day calendar with an extra day, which he called Year Day.

Since then there have been other unsuccessful attempts at calendar reform.

### Time and Calendar

The two natural cycles on which time measurements are based are the year and the day. The year is defined as the time required for the Earth to complete one revolution around the Sun, while the day is the time required for the Earth to complete one turn upon its axis. Unfortunately the Earth needs 365 days plus about six hours to go around the Sun once, so that the year does not consist of so and so many days; the fractional day has to be taken care of by an extra day every fourth year.

But because the Earth, while turning upon its axis, also moves around the Sun there are two kinds of days. A day may be defined as the interval between the highest point of the Sun in the sky on two successive days. This, averaged out over the year, produces the customary 24-hour day. But one might also define a day as the time interval between the moments when a certain point in the sky, say a conveniently located star, is directly overhead. This is called:

*Sidereal time.* Astronomers use a point which they call the "vernal equinox" for the actual determination. Such a sidereal day is somewhat shorter than the "solar day," namely by about 3 minutes and 56 seconds of so-called "mean solar time."

*Apparent solar time* is the time based directly on the Sun's position in the sky. In ordinary life the day runs from midnight to midnight. It begins when the Sun is invisible by being 12 hours from its zenith. Astronomers use the so-called "Julian Day," which runs from noon to noon; the concept was invented by the astronomer Joseph Scaliger, who named it after his father Julius. To avoid the problems caused by leap-year days and so forth, Scaliger picked a conveniently remote date in the past and suggested just counting days without regard to weeks, months, and years. The Julian Day 2,446,795.5 is Jan. 1, 1987. The reason for having the Julian Day run from noon to noon is the practical one that astronomical observations usually extend across the midnight hour, which would require a change in date (or in the Julian Day number) if the astronomical day, like the civil day, ran from midnight to midnight.

*Mean solar time,* rather than apparent solar time, is what is actually used most of the time. The mean solar time is based on the position of a fictitious "mean sun." The reason why this fictitious sun has to be introduced is the following: the Earth turns on its axis regularly; it needs the same number of seconds regardless of the season. But the movement of the Earth around the Sun is not regular because the Earth's orbit is an ellipse. This has the result (as explained in the section The Seasons) that the Earth moves faster in January and slower in July. Though it is the Earth that changes velocity, it looks to us as if the Sun did. In January, when the Earth moves faster, the *apparent* movement of the Sun looks faster. The "mean sun" of time measurements, then, is a sun that moves regularly all year round; the real Sun will be either ahead of or behind the "mean sun." The difference between the real Sun and the fictitious mean sun is called the *equation of time.*

When the real Sun is west of the mean sun we have the "sun fast" condition, with the real Sun crossing the meridian ahead of the mean sun. The opposite is the "sun slow" situation when the real Sun crosses the meridian after the mean sun. Of course, what is observed is the real Sun. The equation of time is needed to establish mean solar time, kept by the reference clocks.

But if all clocks were actually set by mean solar time we would be plagued by a welter of time differences that would be "correct" but a major nuisance. A clock on Long Island, correctly showing mean solar time for its location (this would be *local*

328 *Calendar and Holidays*

# The Names of the Days

| Latin | Saxon | English | French | Italian | Spanish | German |
|-------|-------|---------|--------|---------|---------|--------|
| Dies Solis | Sun's Day | Sunday | Dimanche | domenica | domingo | Sonntag |
| Dies Lunae | Moon's Day | Monday | Lundi | lunedi | lunes | Montag |
| Dies Martis | Tiw's Day | Tuesday | Mardi | martedi | martes | Dienstag |
| Dies Mercurii | Woden's Day | Wednesday | Mercredi | mercoledi | miércoles | Mittwoch |
| Dies Jovis | Thor's Day | Thursday | Jeudi | giovedi | jueves | Donnerstag |
| Dies Veneris | Frigg's Day | Friday | Vendredi | venedri | viernes | Freitag |
| Dies Saturni | Seterne's Day | Saturday | Samedi | sabato | sábado | Sonnabend |

NOTE: The Romans gave one day of the week to each planet known, the Sun and Moon being considered planets in this connection. The Saxon names are a kind of translation of the Roman names: Tiw was substituted for Mars, Woden (Wotan) for Mercury, Thor for Jupiter (Jove), Frigg for Venus, and Seterne for Saturn. The English names are adapted Saxon. The Spanish and Italian names, which are normally not capitalized, and the French are derived from the Latin. The German names follow the Saxon pattern with two exceptions: Wednesday is Mittwoch (Middle of the Week), and Saturday is Sonnabend (Sunday's Eve).

civil time), would be slightly ahead of a clock in Newark, N.J. The Newark clock would be slightly ahead of a clock in Trenton, N.J., which, in turn, would be ahead of a clock in Philadelphia. This condition actually prevailed in the past until 1883, when *standard time* was introduced. Standard time is the correct mean solar time for a designated meridian, and this time is used for a certain area to the east and west of this meridian. In the U.S. four meridians have been designated to supply standard times; they are 75°, 90°, 105°, and 120° west of Greenwich. The 75° meridian determines Eastern Standard Time. It happens to run through Camden, N.J., where standard time, therefore, is also mean solar time and local civil time. The 90° meridian (which happens to pass through the western part of Memphis, Tenn.) determines Central Standard Time, the 105° meridian (passing through Denver) determines Mountain Standard Time, and the 120° meridian (which runs through Lake Tahoe) determines Pacific Standard Time.

Canada, extending over more territory from west to east, adds one time zone on either side: Atlantic Standard Time (based on 60° west of Greenwich) for New Brunswick, Nova Scotia, and Quebec, and Yukon Standard Time (determined by the 135° meridian) for its extreme West. Alaska, extending still farther to the west, adds two more time zones, Alaska Standard Time (determined by the 150° meridian that passes through Anchorage) and Nome Standard Time, based on the 165° meridian just east of Nome.

In general the Earth is divided into 24 such time zones, which run one hour apart. For practical purposes the time zones sometimes show indentations, and there are a few "subzones" that differ from the neighboring zone by only half an hour, e.g., Newfoundland.

*The date line.* While the time zones are based on the natural event of the Sun crossing the meridian, the date must be an arbitrary decision. The meridians are traditionally counted from the meridian of the observatory of Greenwich in England, which is called the zero meridian. The logical place for changing the date is 12 hours, or 180° from Greenwich. Fortunately, the 180th meridian runs mostly through the open Pacific. The date line makes a zigzag in the north to incorporate the eastern tip of Siberia into the Siberian time system and then another one to incorporate a number of islands into the Alaska time system. In the south there is a similar zigzag for the purpose of tying a number of British-owned islands to the New Zealand time system. Otherwise the date line is the same as 180° from Greenwich. At points to the east of the date line the calendar is one day earlier than at points to the west of it. A traveller going eastward across the date line from one island to another would not have to re-set his watch because he would stay inside the time zone (provided he does so where the date line does *not* coincide with the 180° meridian), but it would be the same time of the previous day.

## The Seasons

The seasons are caused by the tilt of the Earth's axis (23.4°) and not by the fact that the Earth's orbit around the Sun is an ellipse. The average distance of the Earth from the Sun is 93 million miles; the difference between aphelion (farthest away) and perihelion (closest to the Sun) is 3 million miles, so that perihelion is about 91.4 million miles from the Sun. The Earth goes through the perihelion point a few days after New Year, just when the northern hemisphere has winter. Aphelion is passed during the first days in July. This by itself shows that the

# The Names of the Months

**January:** named after Janus, protector of the gateway to heaven
**February:** named after Februalia, a time period when sacrifices were made to atone for sins
**March:** named after Mars, the god of war, presumably signifying that the campaigns interrupted by the winter could be resumed
**April:** from *aperire*, Latin for "to open" (buds)
**May:** named after Maia, the goddess of growth of

plants
**June:** from *juvenis*, Latin for "youth"
**July:** named after Julius Caesar
**August:** named after Augustus, the first Roman Emperor
**September:** from *septem*, Latin for "seven"
**October:** from *octo*, Latin for "eight"
**November:** from *novem*, Latin for "nine"
**December:** from *decem*, Latin for "ten"

NOTE: The earliest Latin calendar was a 10-month one; thus September was the seventh month, October, the eighth, etc. July was originally called Quintilis, as the fifth month; August was originally called Sextilis, as the sixth month.

distance from the Sun is not important within these limits. What is important is that when the Earth passes through perihelion, the northern end of the Earth's axis happens to tilt away from the Sun, so that the areas beyond the Tropic of Cancer receive only slanting rays from a Sun low in the sky.

The tilt of the Earth's axis is responsible for four lines you find on every globe. When, say, the North Pole is tilted away from the Sun as much as possible, the farthest points in the North which can still be reached by the Sun's rays are 23 1/2° from the pole. This is the Arctic Circle. The Antarctic Circle is the corresponding limit 23.4° from the South Pole; the Sun's rays cannot reach beyond this point when we have mid-summer in the North.

When the Sun is vertically above the equator, the day is of equal length all over the Earth. This happens twice a year, and these are the "equinoxes" in March and in September. After having been over the equator in March, the Sun will seem to move northward. The northernmost point where the Sun can be straight overhead is 23.4° north of the equator. This is the Tropic of Cancer; the Sun can never be vertically overhead to the north of this line. Similarly the Sun cannot be vertically overhead to the south of a line 23.4° south of the equator—the Tropic of Capricorn.

This explains the climatic zones. In the belt (the Greek word *zone* means "belt") between the Tropic of Cancer and the Tropic of Capricorn, the Sun can be straight overhead; this is the tropical zone. The two zones where the Sun cannot be overhead but will be above the horizon every day of the year are the two temperate zones; the two areas where the Sun will not rise at all for varying lengths of time are the two polar areas, Arctic and Antarctic.

# Holidays

## Religious and Secular, 1987

Since 1971, by federal law, Washington's Birthday, Memorial Day, Columbus Day, and Veterans' Day have been celebrated on Mondays to create three-day weekends for federal employees. Many states now observe these holidays on the same Mondays. (*See* page 350). The dates given for the holidays listed below are the traditional ones.

**New Year's Day,** Thursday, Jan. 1. A legal holiday in all states and the District of Columbia, New Year's Day has its origin in Roman Times, when sacrifices were offered to Janus, the two-faced Roman deity who looked back on the past and forward to the future.

**Epiphany,** Tuesday, Jan. 6. Falls the twelfth day after Christmas and commemorates the manifestation of Jesus as the Son of God, as represented by the adoration of the Magi, the baptism of Jesus, and the miracle of the wine at the marriage feast at Cana. Epiphany originally marked the beginning of the carnival season preceding Lent, and the evening (sometimes the eve) is known as Twelfth Night.

**Martin Luther King, Jr.'s Birthday,** Thursday, Jan. 15. Honors the late civil rights leader. Became a legal public holiday in 1986.

**Shrove Tuesday,** March 3. Falls the day before Ash Wednesday and marks the end of the carnival season, which once began on Epiphany but is now usually celebrated the last three days before Lent. In France, the day is known as Mardi Gras (Fat Tuesday), and Mardi Gras celebrations are also held in several American cities, particularly in New Orleans. The day is sometimes called Pancake Tuesday by the English because fats, which were prohibited during Lent, had to be used up.

**Ash Wednesday,** March 4. The first day of the Lenten season, which lasts 40 days. Having its origin sometime before A.D. 1000, it is a day of public penance and is marked in the Roman Catholic Church by the burning of the palms blessed on the previous year's Palm Sunday. With his thumb, the priest then marks a cross upon the forehead of each worshipper. The Anglican Church and a few Protestant groups in the United States also observe the day, but generally without the use of ashes.

**Lincoln's Birthday,** Thursday, Feb. 12. A legal holiday in many states, this day was first formally observed in Washington, D.C., in 1866, when both houses of Congress gathered for a memorial address in tribute to the assassinated President.

**St. Valentine's Day,** Saturday, Feb. 14. This day is the festival of two third-century martyrs, both named St. Valentine. It is not known why this day is associated with lovers. It may derive from an old pagan festival about this time of year, or it may have been inspired by the belief that birds mate on this day.

**Washington's Birthday,** Monday, Feb. 16. The birthday of George Washington is celebrated as a legal holiday in every state of the Union, the District of Columbia, and all territories. The observance began in 1796.

**St. Patrick's Day,** Tuesday, March 17. St. Patrick, patron saint of Ireland, has been honored in America since the first days of the nation. There are many dinners and meetings but perhaps the most notable part of the observance is the annual St. Patrick's Day parade on Fifth Avenue in New York City.

**Palm Sunday,** April 12. Is observed the Sunday before Easter to commemorate the entry of Jesus into Jerusalem. The procession and the ceremonies introducing the benediction of palms probably had their origin in Jerusalem.

**Purim (Feast of Lots),** Sunday, March 15. A day of joy and feasting celebrating deliverance of the Jews from a massacre planned by the Persian Minister Haman. The Jewish Queen Esther interceded with her husband, King Ahasuerus, to spare the life of her uncle, Mordecai, and Haman was hanged on the same gallows he had built for Mordecai. The holiday is marked by the reading of the Book of Esther (megillah), and by the exchange of gifts, donations to the poor, and the presentation of Purim plays.

**Good Friday,** April 17. This day commemorates the Crucifixion, which is retold during services from the Gospel according to St. John. A feature in Roman Catholic churches is the Liturgy of the Passion; there is no Consecration, the Host having been consecrated the previous day. The eating of hot cross buns on this day is said to have started in England.

**Easter Sunday,** April 19. Observed in all Christian churches, Easter commemorates the Resurrection of Jesus. It is celebrated on the first Sunday after the full moon which occurs on or next after March 21 and is therefore celebrated between March 22 and April 25 inclusive. This date was fixed by the Council of Nicaea in A.D. 325. The Orthodox Church celebrates Easter on April 19, 1987.

**First Day of Passover (Pesach),** Tuesday, April 14. The Feast of the Passover, also called the Feast of Unleavened Bread, commemorates the escape of the Jews from Egypt. As the Jews fled they ate unleavened bread, and from that time the Jews have allowed no leavening in the houses during Passover, bread being replaced by matzoh.

**Ascension Day,** Thursday, May 28. Took place in the presence of His apostles 40 days after the Resurrection of Jesus. It is traditionally held to have occurred on Mount Olivet in Bethany.

**Pentecost (Whitsunday),** June 27. This day commemorates the descent of the Holy Ghost upon the apostles 50 days after the Resurrection. The sermon by the Apostle Peter, which led to the baptism of 3,000 who professed belief, originated the ceremonies that have since been followed. "Whitsunday" is believed to have come from "white Sunday" when, among the English, white robes were worn by those baptized on the day.

**Memorial Day,** Monday, May 30. Also known as Decoration Day, Memorial Day is a legal holiday in most of the states and in the territories, and is also observed by the armed forces. In 1868, Gen. John A. Logan, Commander in Chief of the Grand Army of the Republic, issued an order designating the day as one in which the graves of soldiers would be decorated. The holiday was originally devoted to honoring the memory of those who fell in the Civil War, but is now also dedicated to the memory of all war dead.

**First Day of Shavuot (Hebrew Pentecost),** Wednesday, June 3. This festival, sometimes called the Feast of Weeks, or of Harvest, or of the First Fruits, falls 50 days after Passover and originally celebrated the end of the seven-week grain harvesting season. In later tradition, it also celebrated the giving of the Law to Moses on Mount Sinai.

**Flag Day,** Sunday, June 14. This day commemorates the adoption by the Continental Congress on June 14, 1777, of the Stars and Stripes as the U.S. flag. Although it is a legal holiday only in Pennsylvania, President Truman, on Aug. 3, 1949, signed a bill requesting the President to call for its observance each year by proclamation.

**Independence Day,** Saturday, July 4. The day of the adoption of the Declaration of Independence in 1776, celebrated in all states and territories. The observance began the next year in Philadelphia.

**Labor Day,** Monday, Sept. 7. Observed the first Monday in September in all states and territories, Labor Day was first celebrated in New York in 1882 under the sponsorship of the Central Labor Union, following the suggestion of Peter J. McGuire, of the Knights of Labor, that the day be set aside in honor of labor.

**First Day of Rosh Hashana (Jewish New Year),** Thursday, Sept. 24. This day marks the beginning of the Jewish year 5748 and opens the Ten Days of Penitence closing with Yom Kippur.

**Columbus Day,** Monday, Oct. 12. A legal holiday in many states, commemorating the discovery of America by Columbus in 1492. Quite likely the first celebration of Columbus Day was that organized in 1792 by the Society of St. Tammany, or Columbian Order, more widely known as Tammany Hall.

**Yom Kippur (Day of Atonement),** Saturday, Oct. 3. This day marks the end of the Ten Days of Penitence that began with Rosh Hashana. It is described in *Leviticus* as a "Sabbath of rest," and synagogue services begin the preceding sundown, resume the following morning, and continue to sundown.

**First Day of Sukkot (Feast of Tabernacles)** Thursday, Oct. 8. This festival, also known as the Feast of the Ingathering, originally celebrated the fruit harvest, and the name comes from the booths or tabernacles in which the Jews lived during the harvest, although one tradition traces it to the shelters used by the Jews in their wandering through the wilderness. During the festival many Jews build small huts in their back yards or on the roofs of their houses.

**Simhat Torah (Rejoicing of the Law),** Friday, Oct. 6. This joyous holiday falls on the eighth day of Sukkot. It marks the end of the year's reading of the Torah (Five Books of Moses) in the synagogue every Saturday and the beginning of the new cycle of reading.

**Halloween,** Saturday, Oct. 31. Eve of All Saints' Day, formerly called All Hallows and Hallowmass. Halloween is traditionally associated in some countries with old customs such as bonfires, masquerading, and the telling of ghost stories. These are old Celtic practices marking the beginning of winter.

**All Saints' Day,** Sunday, Nov. 1. A Roman Catholic and Anglican holiday celebrating all saints, known and unknown.

**Election Day,** (legal holiday in certain states), Tuesday, Nov. 3. Since 1845, by Act of Congress, the first Tuesday after the first Monday in November is the date for choosing Presidential electors. State elections are also generally held on this day.

**Veterans Day,** Wednesday, Nov. 11. Armistice Day was established in 1926 to commemorate the signing in 1918 of the Armistice ending World War I. On June 1, 1954, the name was changed to Veterans Day to honor all men and women who have served America in its armed forces.

**Thanksgiving,** Thursday, Nov. 26. Observed nationally on the fourth Thursday in November by Act of Congress (1941), the first such national proclamation having been issued by President Lincoln in 1863, on the urging of Mrs. Sarah J. Hale, editor of *Godey's Lady's Book.* Most Americans believe that the holiday dates back to the day of thanks ordered by Governor Bradford of Plymouth Colony in New England in 1621, but scholars point out that days of thanks stem from ancient times.

**First Sunday of Advent,** Nov. 29. Advent is the season in which the faithful must prepare themselves for the advent of the Saviour on Christmas. The four Sundays before Christmas are marked by special church services.

**Christmas (Feast of the Nativity),** Friday, Dec. 25. The most widely celebrated holiday of the Chris-

tian year, Christmas is observed as the anniversary of the birth of Jesus. Christmas customs are centuries old. The mistletoe, for example, comes from the Druids, who, in hanging the mistletoe, hoped for peace and good fortune. Use of such plants as holly comes from the ancient belief that such plants blossomed at Christmas. Comparatively recent is the Christmas tree, first set up in Germany in the 17th century, and the use of candles on trees developed from the belief that candles appeared by miracle on the trees at Christmas. Colonial Manhattan Islanders introduced the name Santa Claus, a corruption of the Dutch name for the 4th-century Asia Minor St. Nicholas.

**First Day of Hanukkah (Festival of Lights),** Wed-

## National Holidays Around the World, 1987

| | | | | | | |
|---|---|---|---|---|---|---|
| Afghanistan | Aug. 19 | Ghana | March 6 | Panama | Nov. 3 |
| Albania | Nov. 29 | Greece | March 25 | Papua New Guinea | Sept. 16 |
| Algeria | Nov. 1 | Grenada | Feb. 7 | Paraguay | May 14 |
| Angola | Nov. 11 | Guatemala | Sept. 15 | Peru | July 28 |
| Antigua and Barbuda | Nov. 1 | Guinea | Oct. 2 | Philippines | June 12 |
| Argentina | May 25 | Guinea-Bissau | Sept. 12 | Poland | July 22 |
| Australia | Jan. 26 | Guyana | Feb. 23 | Portugal | June 10 |
| Austria | Oct. 26 | Haiti | Jan. 1 | Qatar | Sept. 3 |
| Bahamas | July 10 | Honduras | Sept. 15 | Romania | Aug. 23 |
| Bahrain | Dec. 16 | Hungary | April 4 | Rwanda | July 1 |
| Bangladesh | March 26 | Iceland | June 17 | St. Lucia | Dec. 13 |
| Barbados | Nov. 30 | India | Jan. 26 | St. Vincent and | |
| Belgium | July 21 | Indonesia | Aug. 17 | the Grenadines | Oct. 27 |
| Belize | Sept. 20 | Iran | April 1 | Sao Tomé and Príncipe | July 12 |
| Benin | Nov. 30 | Iraq | July 14 | Saudi Arabia | Sept. 23 |
| Bhutan | Dec. 17 | Ireland | March 17 | Senegal | April 4 |
| Bolivia | Aug. 6 | Israel | April 15[1] | Seychelles | June 5 |
| Botswana | Sept. 30 | Italy | June 2 | Sierra Leone | April 19 |
| Bourkina Faso | Dec. 11 | Ivory Coast | Dec. 7 | Singapore | Aug. 9 |
| Brazil | Sept. 7 | Jamaica | Aug. 3[2] | Somalia | Oct. 21 |
| Bulgaria | Sept. 9 | Japan | April 29 | South Africa | May 31 |
| Burma | Jan. 4 | Jordan | May 25 | Spain | Oct. 12 |
| Burundi | July 1 | Kenya | Dec. 12 | Sri Lanka | Feb. 4 |
| Cambodia | April 17 | Kuwait | Feb. 25 | Sudan | Jan. 1 |
| Cameroon | May 20 | Laos | Dec. 2 | Suriname | Nov. 25 |
| Canada | July 1 | Lebanon | Nov. 22 | Swaziland | Sept. 6 |
| Cape Verde | Sept. 12 | Lesotho | Oct. 4 | Sweden | April 30 |
| Central African Republic | Dec. 1 | Liberia | July 26 | Syria | April 17 |
| Chad | April 13 | Libya | Sept. 1 | Tanzania | April 26 |
| Chile | Sept. 18 | Luxembourg | June 23 | Thailand | Dec. 5 |
| China | Oct. 1 | Madagascar | June 26 | Togo | April 27 |
| Colombia | July 20 | Malawi | July 6 | Trinidad and Tobago | Aug. 31 |
| Congo | Aug. 15 | Malaysia | Aug. 31 | Tunisia | June 1 |
| Costa Rica | Sept. 15 | Maldives | July 26 | Turkey | Oct. 29 |
| Cuba | Jan. 1 | Mali | Sept. 22 | Uganda | Oct. 9 |
| Cyprus | Oct. 1 | Malta | March 31 | U.S.S.R. | Nov. 7 |
| Czechoslovakia | May 9 | Mauritania | Nov. 28 | United Arab Emirates | Dec. 2 |
| Denmark | April 16 | Mauritius | March 12 | United States | July 4 |
| Djibouti | June 27 | Mexico | Sept. 16 | Uruguay | Aug. 25 |
| Dominican Republic | Feb. 27 | Mongolia | July 11 | Venezuela | July 5 |
| Ecuador | Aug. 10 | Morocco | March 3 | Vietnam | Sept. 2 |
| Egypt | July 23 | Mozambique | June 25 | Western Samoa | June 1 |
| El Salvador | Sept. 15 | Nepal | Dec. 28 | Yemen, People's Dem. | |
| Equatorial Guinea | March 5 | Netherlands | April 30 | Republic of | Oct. 14 |
| Ethiopia | Sept. 12 | New Zealand | Feb. 6 | Yemen Arab Republic | Sept. 26 |
| Fiji | Oct. 10 | Nicaragua | Sept. 15 | Yugoslavia | Nov. 29 |
| Finland | Dec. 6 | Niger | Dec. 18 | Zaire | June 30 |
| France | July 14 | Nigeria | Oct. 1 | Zambia | Oct. 24 |
| Gabon | Aug. 17 | Norway | May 17 | Zimbabwe | April 18 |
| Gambia | Feb. 18 | Oman | Nov. 18 | | |
| Germany, East | Oct. 7 | Pakistan | March 23 | | |

1. Changes yearly according to Hebrew calendar. 2. Celebrated on first Monday in August. *Source:* United Nations.

nesday, Dec. 16. This festival was instituted by Judas Maccabaeus in 165 B.C. to celebrate the purification of the Temple of Jerusalem, which had been desecrated three years earlier by Antiochus Epiphanes, who set up a pagan altar and offered sacrifices to Zeus Olympius. In Jewish homes, a light is lighted on each night of the eight-day festival.

## Legal Holidays in the 50 States, D.C., and Puerto Rico

### HOLIDAYS WIDELY OBSERVED

**January 1, New Year's Day:** All states, D.C., Puerto Rico.

**February 12, Lincoln's Birthday:** California, Connecticut, Florida, Illinois, Indiana, Iowa, Kansas, Kentucky, Maryland, Michigan, Missouri, Montana, New Jersey, New Mexico, New York, Vermont, Washington, West Virginia.

**February (first Monday), Lincoln's Birthday:** Delaware.

**February (second Monday), Lincoln Day:** Arizona.

**February (third Monday), Washington's Birthday:** All states,[2] D.C., Puerto Rico. Called **Washington Day** in Arizona. Called **Presidents' Day** in Hawaii, Wyoming, Oregon, Utah, Alaska, Nebraska, Ohio, Pennsylvania. Called **Washington-Lincoln Day** in Minnesota, Colorado, South Dakota, Wisconsin.

**May 28, Memorial Day:** Puerto Rico.

**May 30, Memorial Day:** Delaware, Illinois, Maryland, New Hampshire, South Dakota, Vermont, New Mexico.

**May (last Monday), Memorial Day:** All states, D.C., Louisiana[2] except those listed above, and Alabama, Mississippi.

**July 4, Independence Day:** All states, D.C., Puerto Rico.

**September (1st Monday), Labor Day:** All states, D.C., Puerto Rico.

**October 12, Columbus Day:** Maryland.

**October (2nd Monday), Columbus Day:** All states, D.C., Louisiana [2], except Alaska, Arkansas, Iowa, Maryland, Mississippi, Nevada, North Carolina, Oklahoma, Oregon, South Carolina, Texas, Washington, Puerto Rico. Also called **Fraternal Day** in Alabama. Called **Discoverers' Day** in Hawaii, **Farmers' Day** in Florida, **Pioneers' Day** in South Dakota.

**November (4th Thursday), Thanksgiving Day:** All states, D.C., Puerto Rico.

**November, Day after Thanksgiving:** Alabama,[2] Illinois, Nebraska, New Hampshire, Oklahoma, Florida, Vermont[2], South Carolina, Washington.

**November (first Tuesday after the first Monday), Election Day:** California, D.C., Delaware, Florida, Hawaii, Illinois, Indiana, Kentucky,[4] Louisiana, Maryland, Missouri, Montana, New Hampshire, New Jersey, New York, Ohio, Oklahoma, Pennsylvania, Rhode Island, South Carolina, Tennessee, Vermont[5], Virginia, West Virginia, Wisconsin, Puerto Rico.

**November 11, Veterans' Day:** All states, D.C., Puerto Rico. Called **Armistice Day** and **Veterans' Day** in New Mexico.

**December 25, Christmas:** All states, D.C., Puerto Rico.

**December, Day after Christmas:** South Carolina.

### OTHER HOLIDAYS

**January 6, Three Kings' Day:** Puerto Rico.

**January 8, Battle of New Orleans Day:** Louisiana.[2]

**January 11, De Hostos' Birthday:** Puerto Rico.

**January 15, Martin Luther King Day:** Arkansas,[3] California, Delaware, Florida, Illinois, Louisiana,[2] Maryland, Massachusetts, Missouri,[2] New Jersey, Oklahoma, Pennsylvania, Rhode Island, South Carolina,[1] West Virginia, Wisconsin.

**January 19, Robert E. Lee's Birthday:** Arkansas[3] Florida, Kentucky, Louisiana,[2] South Carolina.[1] Called **Confederate Heroes Day** in Texas.

**January (second Sunday) Martin Luther King Day,** New Mexico.

**January (first Monday after January 15), Martin Luther King Day,** Connecticut.

**January (third Monday), Martin Luther King Day:** Colorado, Connecticut, Georgia, Kansas, Minnesota, New York, Ohio, Tennessee, Alabama, Indiana, Kentucky, Maine, Michigan, Nebraska, Oregon, Utah, Washington, D.C.

**January (third Monday), Robert E. Lee's Birthday:** Alabama, Mississippi. **Lee-Jackson-King Day** in Virginia.

**January 30, F. D. Roosevelt's Birthday:** Kentucky.

**February or March (1 day before Ash Wednesday), Mardi Gras (Shrove Tuesday):** Alabama, Louisiana (in some parishes).

**February 15, Susan B. Anthony's Birthday:** Florida, Minnesota.

**February 19, Robert E. Lee Day:** Kentucky.

**March (first Tuesday), Town Meeting Day:** Vermont.

**March 2, Texas Independence Day:** Texas.

**March 17, Evacuation Day:** Massachusetts (in Suffolk Co. only).

**March or April (2 days before Easter), Good Friday:** Connecticut, Delaware, Florida, Hawaii, Indiana, Louisiana, Maryland, New Jersey, North Dakota, Pennsylvania, Tennessee, Wisc. (11 a.m.-3 p.m.).

**March or April (1 day after Easter), Easter Monday:** North Carolina.

**March (first Monday), Casimir Pulaski's Birthday:** Illinois.

**March 20, (First Day of Spring), Youth Day:** Oklahoma.[2]

**March 22, Abolition Day:** Puerto Rico.

**March 25, Maryland Day:** Maryland.

**March 26, Prince Jonah Kuhio Kalanianaole Day:** Hawaii.

**March (last Monday), Seward's Day:** Alaska.

**April 2, Pascua Florida Day:** Florida.

**April 5, Good Friday:** Puerto Rico

**April 13, Thomas Jefferson's Birthday:** Alabama, Oklahoma.

**April 16, De Diego's Birthday:** Puerto Rico.

**April (third Monday), Patriots' Day:** Maine, Mass.

**April 21, San Jacinto Day:** Texas.

**April 22, Arbor Day:** Nebraska.

**April 22, Oklahoma Day:** Oklahoma.

**April 26, Confederate Memorial Day:** Florida, Georgia.

**April (4th Monday), Fast Day:** New Hampshire.

**April (last Monday), Confederate Memorial Day:** Alabama, Mississippi.

**May (1st Tuesday after the first Monday), Primary Election Day:** Indiana.

**May (2nd Tuesday after first Monday), Primary Day:** West Virginia.

**May (2nd Sunday), Mother's Day:** Arizona, Okla.[2]

**May 1, Bird Day:** Oklahoma.

**May 8, Truman Day:** Missouri.

**May 11, Minnesota Day:** Minnesota.

**May 20, Mecklenburg Independence Day:** North

Carolina.

**June (first Monday), Jefferson Davis's Birthday:** Alabama, Mississippi.

**June (second Sunday), Flag Day:** New York.

**June (third Sunday), Father's Day:** Arizona.

**June 3, Jefferson Davis's Birthday:** Forida, South Carolina, also called **Confederate Memorial Day** in Kentucky and Louisiana.[2]

**June 9, Senior Citizens Day:** Oklahoma.

**June 11, King Kamehameha I Day:** Hawaii.

**June 14, Flag Day:** Pennsylvania.

**June 15, Separation Day:** Delaware.

**June 17, Bunker Hill Day:** Massachusetts (in Suffolk Co. only).

**June 19, Emancipation Day:** Texas.

**June 20, West Virginia Day:** West Virginia.

**July 17, Muñoz Rivera's Birthday:** Puerto Rico.

**July 24, Pioneer Day:** Utah.

**July 25, Constitution Day:** Puerto Rico.

**July 27, Barbosa's Birthday:** Puerto Rico.

**August (first Sunday), American Family Day:** Arizona.

**August (first Monday), Colorado Day:** Colo.

**August (second Monday), Victory Day:** Rhode Is.

**August 16, Bennington Battle Day:** Vermont.

**August (third Friday), Admission Day:** Hawaii.

**August 27, Lyndon B. Johnson's Birthday:** Texas.

**August 30, Huey P. Long Day:** Louisiana.[2]

**September (first Tuesday), Primary Election Day:** Wisconsin.

**September 9, Admission Day:** California.

**September 12, Defenders' Day:** Maryland.

**September 16, Cherokee Strip Day:** Oklahoma.[2]

**September (1st Saturday after full moon), Indian Day:** Oklahoma.[2]

**October 10, Leif Erickson Day:** Minnesota.

**October 10, Oklahoma Historical Day:** Oklahoma.[2]

**October 18, Alaska Day:** Alaska.

**October 31, Nevada Day:** Nevada.

**November 1, All Saints' Day:** Louisiana.[2]

**November 4, Will Rogers Day:** Oklahoma.[2]

**November (week of the 16th), Oklahoma Heritage Week:** Oklahoma.[2]

**November 19, Discovery Day:** Puerto Rico.

**December 7, Delaware Day:** Delaware.

1. Optional, two of three allowed. 2. Observed only if proclaimed by governor. 3. Employee has choice of observing King's or Lee's Birthday. 4. Presidential election only. 5. All even years.

# Movable Holidays, 1987–1992
## CHRISTIAN AND SECULAR

| Year | Ash Wednesday | Easter | Pentecost | Labor Day | Election Day | Thanksgiving | 1st Sun. Advent |
|---|---|---|---|---|---|---|---|
| 1987 | March 4 | April 19 | June 7 | Sept. 7 | Nov. 3 | Nov. 26 | Nov. 29 |
| 1988 | Feb. 17 | April 3 | May 22 | Sept. 5 | Nov. 8 | Nov. 24 | Nov. 27 |
| 1989 | Feb. 8 | March 26 | May 14 | Sept. 4 | Nov. 7 | Nov. 23 | Dec. 3 |
| 1990 | Feb. 28 | April 15 | June 3 | Sept. 3 | Nov. 6 | Nov. 22 | Dec. 2 |
| 1991 | Feb. 13 | March 31 | May 19 | Sept. 2 | Nov. 5 | Nov. 28 | Dec. 1 |
| 1992 | March 4 | April 19 | June 7 | Sept. 7 | Nov. 3 | Nov. 26 | Nov. 29 |

Shrove Tuesday: 1 day before Ash Wednesday
Palm Sunday: 7 days before Easter
Maundy Thursday: 3 days before Easter
Good Friday: 2 days before Easter

Holy Saturday: 1 day before Easter
Ascension Day: 10 days before Pentecost
Trinity Sunday: 7 days after Pentecost
Corpus Christi: 11 days after Pentecost

NOTE: Easter is celebrated on April 19, 1987, by the Orthodox Church.

## JEWISH

| Year | Purim[1] | 1st day Passover[2] | 1st day Shavuot[3] | 1st day Rosh Hashana[4] | Yom Kippur[5] | 1st day Sukkot[6] | Simhat Torah[7] | 1st day Hanukkah[8] |
|---|---|---|---|---|---|---|---|---|
| 1987 | March 15 | April 14 | June 3 | Sept. 24 | Oct. 3 | Oct. 8 | Oct. 16 | Dec. 16 |
| 1988 | March 3 | April 2 | May 22 | Sept. 12 | Sept. 21 | Sept. 26 | Oct. 4 | Dec. 4 |
| 1989 | March 21 | April 20 | June 9 | Sept. 30 | Oct. 9 | Oct. 14 | Oct. 22 | Dec. 23 |
| 1990 | March 11 | April 10 | May 30 | Sept. 20 | Sept. 29 | Oct. 4 | Oct. 12 | Dec. 12 |
| 1991 | Feb. 28 | March 30 | May 19 | Sept. 9 | Sept. 18 | Sept. 23 | Oct. 1 | Dec. 2 |
| 1992 | March 14 | April 18 | June 7 | Sept. 28 | Oct. 7 | Oct. 12 | Oct. 20 | Dec. 20 |

1. Feast of Lots. 2. Feast of Unleavened Bread. 3. Hebrew Pentecost; or Feast of Weeks, or of Harvest, or of First Fruits. 4. Jewish New Year. 5. Day of Atonement. 6. Feast of Tabernacles, or of the Ingathering. 7. Rejoicing of the Law. 8. Festival of Lights.

Length of Jewish holidays (O=Orthodox, C=Conservative, R=Reform):

Passover: O & C, 8 days (holy days: first 2 and last 2); R, 7 days (holy days: first and last)
Shavuot: O & C, 2 days; R, 1 day
Rosh Hashana: O & C, 2 days; R, 1 day.
Yom Kippur: All groups, 1 day

Sukkot: All groups, 7 days (holy days: O & C, first 2; R, first only)
O & C observe two additional days: Shemini Atseret (Eighth Day of the Feast) and Simhat Torah. R observes Shemini Atseret but not Simhat Torah
Hanukkah: All groups, 8 days

NOTE: All holidays begin at sundown on the evening before the date given.

## Chinese Calendar

The Chinese lunar year is divided into 12 months of 29 or 30 days. The calendar is adjusted to the length of the solar year by the addition of extra months at regular intervals.

The years are arranged in major cycles of 60 years. Each successive year is named after one of 12 animals. These 12-year cycles are continuously repeated. The Chinese New Year is celebrated at the first new moon after the sun enters Aquarius—sometime between Jan. 21 and Feb. 19.

| Rat | Ox | Tiger | Cat (Rabbit) | Dragon | Snake | Horse | Sheep (Goat) | Monkey | Rooster | Dog | Pig |
|-----|-----|-----|-----|-----|-----|-----|-----|-----|-----|-----|-----|
| 1864 | 1865 | 1866 | 1867 | 1868 | 1869 | 1870 | 1871 | 1872 | 1873 | 1874 | 1875 |
| 1876 | 1877 | 1878 | 1879 | 1880 | 1881 | 1882 | 1883 | 1884 | 1885 | 1886 | 1887 |
| 1888 | 1889 | 1890 | 1891 | 1892 | 1893 | 1894 | 1895 | 1896 | 1897 | 1898 | 1899 |
| 1900 | 1901 | 1902 | 1903 | 1904 | 1905 | 1906 | 1907 | 1908 | 1909 | 1910 | 1911 |
| 1912 | 1913 | 1914 | 1915 | 1916 | 1917 | 1918 | 1919 | 1920 | 1921 | 1922 | 1923 |
| 1924 | 1925 | 1926 | 1927 | 1928 | 1929 | 1930 | 1931 | 1932 | 1933 | 1934 | 1935 |
| 1936 | 1937 | 1938 | 1939 | 1940 | 1941 | 1942 | 1943 | 1944 | 1945 | 1946 | 1947 |
| 1948 | 1949 | 1950 | 1951 | 1952 | 1953 | 1954 | 1955 | 1956 | 1957 | 1958 | 1959 |
| 1960 | 1961 | 1962 | 1963 | 1964 | 1965 | 1966 | 1967 | 1968 | 1969 | 1970 | 1971 |
| 1972 | 1973 | 1974 | 1975 | 1976 | 1977 | 1978 | 1979 | 1980 | 1981 | 1982 | 1983 |
| 1984 | 1985 | 1986 | 1987 | 1988 | 1989 | 1990 | 1991 | 1992 | 1993 | 1994 | 1995 |

## Some Old Ideas About New Calendars

Several clever schemes have been devised to make the calendar easier-to-use. Two of these attempts are presented here for your information only. This is not intended to suggest that *Information Please Almanac* is interested in or advocates calendar reform.

The French philosopher Auguste Comte (1798-1857) suggested a 364-day calendar with an extra day, which he called Year Day. He intended to do away with the uneven months and suggested 13 months of 28 days each. This would result in a scheme valid for every one of the 13 months, as shown in the table.

Another suggestion was the World Calendar proposed around 1900. It also contains the extra holiday, but it does produce a very simple calendar, constructed with a quarter year as the basic unit.

In the World Calendar, each quarter begins the first month with a Sunday and has 31 days. The second and third months have 30 days each and the last day of the third month is a Saturday, so that the next quarter begins with a Sunday again.

The first month of the quarter therefore has five Sundays and the other two months have four each, so that every month, all year round, has 26 weekdays. The total number of days per quarter is 91 and the total number of weeks per quarter is 13.

The 364-day calendar is, of course, incomplete. In order to correct this, it was proposed that a day be added on to the end of the year (as December 31st) and called the Year-End World Holiday. In addition, it was suggested that every four years another day be added on to the end of the first half of the year (as June 31st) and named the Leap-Year Holiday. The calendar would thus be balanced.

In this simplified calendar each date in the year could be compared to the corresponding date in every other year and the calendar could be memorized.

## The 13-Month Calendar of Auguste Comte

| Monday | Tuesday | Wednesday | Thursday | Friday | Saturday | Sunday |
|-----|-----|-----|-----|-----|-----|-----|
| 1 | 2 | 3 | 4 | 5 | 6 | 7 |
| 8 | 9 | 10 | 11 | 12 | 13 | 14 |
| 15 | 16 | 17 | 18 | 19 | 20 | 21 |
| 22 | 23 | 24 | 25 | 26 | 27 | 28 |

## The Basic Unit of the World Calendar

| Days | First month | | | | | Second month | | | | | Third month | | | | |
|-----|-----|-----|-----|-----|-----|-----|-----|-----|-----|-----|-----|-----|-----|-----|-----|
| Sunday | 1 | 8 | 15 | 22 | 29 | — | 5 | 12 | 19 | 26 | — | 3 | 10 | 17 | 24 |
| Monday | 2 | 9 | 16 | 23 | 30 | — | 6 | 13 | 20 | 27 | — | 4 | 11 | 18 | 25 |
| Tuesday | 3 | 10 | 17 | 24 | 31 | — | 7 | 14 | 21 | 28 | — | 5 | 12 | 19 | 26 |
| Wednesday | 4 | 11 | 18 | 25 | — | 1 | 8 | 15 | 22 | 29 | — | 6 | 13 | 20 | 27 |
| Thursday | 5 | 12 | 19 | 26 | — | 2 | 9 | 16 | 23 | 30 | — | 7 | 14 | 21 | 28 |
| Friday | 6 | 13 | 20 | 27 | — | 3 | 10 | 17 | 24 | — | 1 | 8 | 15 | 22 | 29 |
| Saturday | 7 | 14 | 21 | 28 | — | 4 | 11 | 18 | 25 | — | 2 | 9 | 16 | 23 | 30 |

## Encounters With Comet Halley:
## The New View Begins To Emerge

*By J. Eberhart*

The international family of five spacecraft that encountered Comet Halley in March 1986 would "rewrite the textbooks," many researchers said, and May 1986 saw the publication of the first detailed notes for the job. Thirty-eight scientific papers, some with more than 30 authors, appear in the May 15 *NATURE*, summarizing initial results from the most elaborate space "flyby" ever mounted.

Together, the two Soviet, one European, and two Japanese craft photographed the comet, sampled its dust and gases, and measured its electromagnetic properties, revealing, among other findings, that comets are even less understood than had been thought.

The nucleus of Comet Halley, far from being an ordinary ball, is an irregular, "potato-shaped" object, in the words of scientists with the Soviet *Vega* spacecraft team. Its double-lobed shape, resembling a large lump with a smaller lump bulging out of the side, measures about 14 by 7.5 by 7.5 kilometers (8.7 by 4.7 by 4.7 miles), according to the *Vega* analysis. A similar result came from Europe's *Giotto* craft, which took its last pictures of the comet from only 1,703 km (1,058 miles) away. *Giotto* actually got to within about 605 km (376 miles), but an apparent glitch in the spacecraft power system ended its observations about 12 seconds earlier.

The nucleus looked extremely dark, reflecting only about 4 percent of the sunlight striking it. The *Vega* and *Giotto* groups both conclude that the largely icy nucleus—more than 80 percent of the material coming from it is water vapor—is covered with a thin layer of nonvolatile material, through which numerous bright outbursts often emerged. "If the ice were not protected by an insulating crust on the surface," writes the *Giotto* group, "then the total gas and dust production would be about an order of magnitude higher than observed."

The close-up photos show striking details, all of which are hidden from earth-based observers by the glare of reflected light. One "large bundle of jets," for example, is reported by the *Giotto* group to have its origin near the nucleus's northern end, where there are "scalloped features resembling craters, each of which appears to be the source of a narrow jet." Study of some of the images, the team reports, indicates that surface features seen "in profile" appear to have slopes of no more than

about 15 degrees, suggesting a "rough 'crater-type terrain" in which features measuring 1 km or less in extent can be identified.

Determining the comet's composition was a major goal of the encounters, not just for the study of Comet Halley but also because many researchers have long felt that comets may represent samples of some of the most primitive material in the solar system. Most of the dust particles were found to be rich in hydrogen, carbon, nitrogen, and oxygen, for example, "suggesting the validity of models that describe cometary dust as including organic material," according to one *Giotto* report.

Similar material has also been proposed by some researchers to be a major component of a class of meteorites known as carbonaceous chondrites, and may also account for the surface appearance of such dark solar-system objects as the rings of Uranus and the dark portions of Saturn's moon Iapetus. Indeed, one *Vega* team notes, "It is reasonable to assume that all of this material is carbonaceous in composition." On the other hand, says one *Giotto* report, mass spectrometer measurements suggest that the cometary particles are "only roughly similar," to a variety of carbonaceous chondrites known as type Cl, which some scientists think may be the type most likely to represent unaltered, primitive solar-system material.

A new finding about the comet, reported by researchers with Japan's *Sakigake* spacecraft, was the discovery that it seems to be emitting radio waves. First detected as far as 10 million km away, the signals showed their maximum intensity at the craft's closest approach, "indicating that the emissions are intimately related to the comet." Several different emission patterns were detected, collectively termed "cometary kilometric radiation" and ranging from intense, sporadic bursts of broad-band noise to continuously rising and falling tones. Though the mechanisms that produce such emissions will—like virtually every other aspect of the encounters—require much additional study, the *Sakigake* team infers that the signals result from "moving shock or bow waves in the coma region of the comet, due to time-dependent variations in the solar wind."

Vast amounts of study lie ahead for all of the Halley-encounter scientists, ranging from the nature of the solar wind's interaction with the comet (the presence or absence of a conventional "bow shock" may be too easy an answer) to the results of additional computer-processing of the spacecraft photos. NASA hopes, meanwhile, to start developing a visit to another comet, this time for an extended look in the 1990s. Rewriting the textbooks will not be easy.

Jonathan Eberhart is Space Sciences Editor, *SCIENCE NEWS*. Reprinted with permission form *SCIENCE NEWS*, the weekly newsmagazine of science, copyright 1986 by Science Service, Inc.

335

## Astronomical Terms

*Planet* is the term used for a body in orbit around the Sun. Its origin is Greek; even in antiquity it was known that a number of "stars" did not stay in the same relative positions to the others. There were five such restless "stars" known—Mercury, Venus, Mars, Jupiter, and Saturn—and the Greeks referred to them as *planetes,* a word which means "wanderers." That the earth is one of the planets was realized later. The additional planets were discovered after the invention of the telescope.

*Satellite* (or *moon*) is the term for a body in orbit around a planet. As long as our own Moon was the only moon known, there was no need for a general term for the moons of planets. But when Galileo Galilei discovered the four main moons of the planet Jupiter, Johannes Kepler (in a letter to Galileo) suggested "satellite" (from the Latin *satelles,* which means "attendant") as a general term for such bodies. The word is used interchangeably with "moons": astronomers speak and write about the moons of Neptune, Saturn, etc. A satellite may be any size.

*Orbit* is the term for the path traveled by a body in space. It comes from the Latin *orbis,* which means circle, circuit, etc., and *orbita,* which means a rut or a wheel track. Theoretically, four mathematical figures are possible orbits: two are open (hyperbola and parabola) and two are closed (ellipse and circle), but in reality all closed orbits are ellipses. These ellipses can be nearly circular, as are the orbits of most planets, or very elongated, as are the orbits of most comets. In these orbits, the Sun is in one focal point of the ellipse, and the other focal point is empty. In the orbits of satellites, the planet stands in one focal point of the orbit. The *primary* of an orbit is the body in the focal point. For planets, the point of the orbit closest to the Sun is the *perihelion,* and the point farthest from the Sun is the *aphelion.* For orbits around the Earth, the corresponding terms are *perigee* and *apogee;* for orbits around other planets, corresponding terms are coined when necessary.

Two heavenly bodies are in *inferior* or *superior conjunction* when they have the same Right Ascension, or are in the same meridian; that is, when one is due north or south of the other. If the bodies appear near each other as seen from the Earth, they will rise and set at the same time. They are in *opposition* when they are opposite each other in the heavens: when one rises as the other is setting. *Greatest elongation* is the greatest apparent angular distance from the Sun, when a planet is most favorably suited for observation. Mercury can be seen with the naked eye only at about this time. An *occultation* of a planet or star is an eclipse of it by some other body, usually the Moon.

*Stars* are the basic units of population in the universe. Our Sun is the nearest star. Stars are very large (our Sun has a diameter of 865,400 miles—a comparatively small star). Stars are composed of intensely hot gasses, deriving their energy from nuclear reactions going on in their interiors.

*Galaxies* are immense systems containing billions of stars. All that you can see in the sky (with a very few exceptions) belongs to our galaxy—a system of roughly 100 billion stars. The few exceptions are other galaxies. Our own galaxy, the rim of which we see as the "Milky Way," is about 100,000 light-years in diameter and about 10,000 light-years in thickness. Its shape is roughly that of a thick lens; more precisely it is a "spiral nebula," a term first used for other galaxies when they were discovered and before it was realized that these were separate and distant galaxies. The spiral galaxy nearest to ours is in the constellation Andromeda. It is somewhat larger than our own galaxy and is visible to the naked eye.

Recent developments in radio astronomy have revealed additional celestial objects that are still incompletely understood.

*Quasars* ("quasi-stellar" objects), originally thought to be peculiar stars in our own galaxy, are now believed to be the most remote objects in the Universe. Spectral studies of quasars indicate that some are 9 billion light years away and moving away from us at the incredible rate of 150,000 miles per second. Quasars emit tremendous amounts of light and microwave radiation. Although they appear to be far smaller than ordinary

## Astronomical Constants

| | |
|---|---|
| Light-year (distance traveled by light in one year) | 5,880,000,000,000 mi. |
| Parsec (parallax of one second, for stellar distances) | 3.259 light-yrs. |
| Velocity of light | 186,281.7 mi./sec. |
| Astronomical unit (A.U.), or mean distance earth-to-sun | ca. 93,000,000 mi.[1] |
| Mean distance, earth to moon | 238,860 mi. |
| General precession | 50".26 |
| Obliquity of the ecliptic | 23° 27'8".26−0".4684(t−1900)[2] |
| Equatorial radius of the earth | 3963.34 statute mi. |
| Polar radius of the earth | 3949.99 statute mi. |
| Earth's mean radius | 3958.89 statute mi. |
| Oblateness of the earth | 1/297 |
| Equatorial horizontal parallax of the moon | 57' 2".70 |
| Earth's mean velocity in orbit | 18.5 mi./sec. |
| Sidereal year | 365d.2564 |
| Tropical year | 365d.2422 |
| Sidereal month | 27d.3217 |
| Synodic month | 29d.5306 |
| Mean sidereal day | 23h56m4s.091 of mean solar time |
| Mean solar day | 24h3m56s.555 of sidereal time |

1. Actual mean distance derived from radar bounces: 92,935,700 mi. The value of 92,897,400 mi. (based on parallax of 8".80) is used in calculations. 2. *t* refers to the year in question, for example, 1986.

## The Brightest Stars

| Star | Constellation | Mag. | Dist. (l.-y.) | Star | Constellation | Mag. | Dist. (l.-y.) |
|------|---------------|------|---------------|------|---------------|------|---------------|
| Sirius | Canis Major | −1.6 | 8 | Antares | Scorpius | 1.2 | 170 |
| Canopus | Carina | −0.9 | 650 | Fomalhaut | Piscis Austrinus | 1.3 | 27 |
| Alpha Centauri | Centaurus | +0.1 | 4 | Deneb | Cygnus | 1.3 | 465 |
| Vega[1] | Lyra | 0.1 | 23 | Regulus | Leo | 1.3 | 70 |
| Capella | Auriga | 0.2 | 42 | Beta Crucis | Crux | 1.5 | 465 |
| Arcturus | Boötes | 0.2 | 32 | Eta Carinae | Carina | 1-7 | — |
| Rigel | Orion | 0.3 | 545 | Alpha-one Crucis | Crux | 1.6 | 150 |
| Procyon | Canis Minor | 0.5 | 10 | Castor | Gemini | 1.6 | 44 |
| Achernar | Eridanus | 0.6 | 70 | Gamma Crucis | Crux | 1.6 | — |
| Beta Centari | Centaurus | 0.9 | 130 | Epsilon Canis Majoris | Canis Major | 1.6 | 325 |
| Altair | Aquila | 0.9 | 18 | Epsilon Ursae Majoris | Ursa Major | 1.7 | 50 |
| Betelgeuse | Orion | 0.9 | 600 | Bellatrix | Orion | 1.7 | 215 |
| Aldebaran | Taurus | 1.1 | 54 | Lambda Scorpii | Scorpius | 1.7 | 205 |
| Spica | Virgo | 1.2 | 190 | Epsilon Carinae | Carina | 1.7 | 325 |
| Pollux | Gemini | 1.2 | 31 | Mira | Cetus | 2-10 | 250 |

1. In 1984, the discovery of a possible planetary system around Vega was reported.

galaxies, some quasars emit as much as 100 times more energy. Some astronomers believe that quasars are the cores of violently exploding galaxies.

*Pulsars* are believed to be rapidly spinning neutron stars, so crushed by their own gravity that a million tons of their matter would hardly fill a thimble. Pulsars are so named because they emit bursts of radio energy at regular intervals. Some have pulse rates as rapid as 10 per second.

A *black hole* is the theoretical end-product of the total gravitational collapse of a massive star or group of stars. Crushed even smaller than an incredibly dense neutron star, such a body may become so dense that not even light can escape its gravitational field. It has been suggested that black holes may be detectable in proximity to normal stars when they draw matter away from their visible neighbors. Strong sources of X-rays in our galaxy and beyond may also indicate the presence of black holes. One possible black hole now being studied is the invisible companion to a supergiant star in the constellation Cygnus.

## Origin of the Universe

Evidence uncovered in recent years tends to confirm that the universe began its existence about 15 billion years ago as a dense, hot globule of gas expanding rapidly outward. At that time, the universe contained nothing but hydrogen and a small amount of helium. There were no stars and no planets. The first stars probably began to condense out of the primordial hydrogen when the universe was about 100 million years old and continued to form as the universe aged. The Sun arose in this way 4.6 billion years ago. Many stars came into being before the Sun was formed; many others formed after the Sun appeared. This process continues, and through telescopes we can now see stars forming out of compressed pockets of hydrogen in outer space.

## Birth and Death of a Star

When a star begins to form as a dense cloud of gas, the individual hydrogen atoms fall toward the center of the cloud under the force of the star's gravity. As they fall, they pick up speed, and their energy increases. The increase in energy heats the gas. When this process has continued for some mil-lions of years, the temperature reaches about 20 million degrees Fahrenheit. At this temperature, the hydrogen within the star ignites and burns in a continuing series of nuclear reactions in which all the elements in the universe are manufactured from hydrogen and helium. The onset of these reactions marks the birth of a star. When a star begins to exhaust its hydrogen supply, its life nears an end. The first sign of old age is a swelling and reddening of its outer regions. Such an aging, swollen star is called a red giant. The Sun, a middle-aged star, will probably swell to a red giant in 5 billion years, vaporizing the earth and any creatures that may be left on its surface. When all its fuel has been exhausted, a star cannot generate sufficient pressure at its center to balance the crushing force of gravity. The star collapses under the force of its own weight; if it is a small star, it collapses gently and remains collapsed. Such a collapsed star, at its life's end, is called a white dwarf. The Sun will probably end its life in this way. A different fate awaits a large star. Its final collapse generates a violent explosion, blowing the innards of the star out into space. There, the materials of the exploded star mix with the primeval hydrogen of the universe. Later in the history of the galaxy, other stars are formed out of this mixture. The Sun is one of these stars. It contains the debris of countless other stars that exploded before the Sun was born.

## Formation of the Solar System

The Sun, like other stars, seems to have been formed 4.6 billion years ago from a cloud of hydrogen mixed with small amounts of other substances that had been manufactured in the bodies of other stars before the Sun was born. This was the parent cloud of the solar system. The dense hot gas at the center of the cloud gave rise to the Sun; the outer regions of the cloud—cooler and less dense—gave birth to the planets.

Our solar system consists of one star (the Sun), nine planets and all their moons, several thousand minor planets called asteroids or planetoids, and an equally large number of comets.

## The Sun

All the stars, including our Sun, are gigantic balls of superheated gas, kept hot by atomic reactions in their centers. In our Sun, this atomic reaction is hydrogen fusion: four hydrogen atoms are combined to form one helium atom. The temperature at the core of our Sun must be 20 million degrees centigrade, the surface temperature is around 6,000 degrees centigrade, or about 11,000 degrees Fahrenheit. The diameter of the sun is 865,400 miles, and its surface area is approximately 12,000 times that of the Earth. Compared with other stars, our Sun is just a bit below average in size and temperature. Its fuel supply (hydrogen) is estimated to last for another 5 billion years.

Our Sun is not motionless in space; in fact it has two proper motions. One is a seemingly straight-line motion in the direction of the constellation Hercules at the rate of about 12 miles per second. But since the Sun is a part of the Milky Way system and since the whole system rotates slowly around its own center, the Sun also moves at the rate of 175 miles per second as part of the rotating Milky Way system.

In addition to this motion, the Sun rotates on its axis. Observing the motion of sun spots (darkish areas which look like enormous whirling storms) and solar flares, which are usually associated with sun spots, has shown that the rotational period of our Sun is just short of 25 days. But this figure is valid for the Sun's equator only; the sections near the Sun's poles seem to have a rotational period of 34 days. Naturally, since the Sun generates its own heat and light, there is no temperature difference between poles and equator.

What we call the Sun's "surface" is technically known as the photosphere. Since the whole Sun is a ball of very hot gas, there is really no such thing as a surface; it is a question of visual impression. The next layer outside the photosphere is known as the chromosphere, which extends several thousand miles beyond the photosphere. It is in steady motion, and often enormous prominences can be seen to burst from it, extending as much as 100,000 miles into space. Outside the chromosphere is the corona. The corona consists of very tenuous gases (essentially hydrogen) and makes a magnificent sight when the Sun is eclipsed.

## The Moon

Mercury and Venus do not have any moons. Therefore, the Earth is the planet nearest the Sun to be orbited by a moon.

The next planet farther out, Mars, has two very small moons. Jupiter has four major moons and twelve minor ones. Saturn, the ringed planet, has fifteen known moons, of which one (Titan) is larger than the planet Mercury. Uranus has five known moons (four of them large) as well as rings, while Neptune has one large and one small moon. Pluto has one moon, discovered in 1978. Some astronomers still consider Pluto to be a "runaway moon" of Neptune.

Our own Moon, with a diameter of 2,160 miles, is one of the larger moons in our solar system and is especially large when compared with the planet that it orbits. In fact, the common center of gravity of the Earth-Moon system is only about 1,000 miles below the Earth's surface. The closest our Moon can come to us (its perigee) is 221,463 miles; the farthest it can go away (its apogee) is 252,710 miles. The period of rotation of our Moon is equal to its period of revolution around the Earth. Hence from Earth we can see only one hemisphere of the Moon. Both periods are 27 days, 7 hours, 43 minutes and 11.47 seconds. But while the rotation of the Moon is constant, its velocity in its orbit is not, since it moves more slowly in apogee than in perigee. Consequently, some portions near the rim which are not normally visible will appear briefly. This phenomenon is called "libration," and by taking advantage of the librations, astronomers have succeeded in mapping approximately 59% of the lunar surface. The other 41% can never be seen from the earth but has been mapped by American and Russian Moon-orbiting spacecraft.

Though the Moon goes around the Earth in the time mentioned, the interval from new Moon to new Moon is 29 days, 12 hours, 44 minutes and 2.78 seconds. This delay of nearly two days is due to the fact that the Earth is moving around the Sun, so that the Moon needs two extra days to reach a spot in its orbit where no part is illuminated by the Sun, as seen from Earth.

## Data for Sun, Moon, and Planets

| | Mean distance from Sun in millions of miles | Period of revolution around the Sun | Eccentricity of orbit | Inclination to ecliptic ° ' | Diameter (miles) | Period of rotation on axis | Inclination of equator to orbit plane ° | Surface gravity (earth = 1) | Density $H_2O = 1$ | Number of satellites | Mean velocity in orbit (mi./sec.) | Max. stellar mag. |
|---|---|---|---|---|---|---|---|---|---|---|---|---|
| Sun | — | — | — | — | 865,400 | 24d. 64² | 7.2 | 28 | 1.4 | 0 | — | −26.7 |
| Moon | — | (27d. 322)¹ | 0.05 | 5  8 | 2,160 | 27d. 322 | 6.7 | 0.16 | 3.3 | 0 | 0.63 | −12.6 |
| Mercury | 36.00 | 87d. 969 | 0.21 | 7  0 | 3,100 | 58. 66d | 7 | 0.28 | 3.8 | 0 | 30 | −1.2 |
| Venus | 67.27 | 224d. 701 | 0.01 | 3 24 | 7,700 | 243. 2d | — | 0.85 | 5.1 | 0 | 22 | −4.4 |
| Earth | 93.00 | 365d. 256 | 0.02 | 0  0 | 7,927³ | 23h 56m | 23.4 | 1.00 | 5.5 | 1 | 18.5 | — |
| Mars | 141.71 | 1y. 881 | 0.09 | 1 51 | 4,200 | 24h 37m | 25.2 | 0.38 | 4.0 | 2 | 15 | −2.8 |
| Jupiter | 483.88 | 11y. 862 | 0.05 | 1 18 | 88,700³ | 9h 50m² | 3.1 | 2.6 | 1.3 | 16 | 8 | −2.5 |
| Saturn | 887.14 | 29y. 458 | 0.06 | 2 29 | 75,100³ | 16h 39m² | 26.8 | 1.2 | 0.7 | 21+ | 6 | −0.4 |
| Uranus | 1783.98 | 84y. 013 | 0.05 | 0 46 | 32,000 | 16. 8h | 98 | 1.1 | 1.3 | 15 | 4 | +5.7 |
| Neptune | 2795.46 | 164y. 794 | 0.01 | 1 46 | 27,700 | 17h 50m | 29 | 1.4 | 2.2 | 2 | 3 | +7.8 |
| Pluto | 3675.27 | 248y. 430 | 0.25 | 17  9 | 1,500(?) | 6d 8h(?) | — | — | >1.0 | 1 | <3 | +14 |

1. Period of revolution around the earth. 2. Voyager 1 and 2 data. 3. The equatorial diameters of the earth, Jupiter, and Saturn are given; polar diameters are: earth 7,900.0 mi., Jupiter 82,789 mi., Saturn 67,170 mi. OTHER DATA ON THE EARTH: Equatorial circumference, 24,902.4 mi.; total area, 196,949,970 sq. mi.; mass, 6.6 sextillion tons; mean diameter, 7,917.8 mi.

If the plane of the Earth's orbit around the Sun (the ecliptic) and the plane of the Moon's orbit around the Earth were the same, the Moon would be eclipsed by the Earth every time it is full, and the Sun would be eclipsed by the Moon every time the Moon is "new" (it would be better to call it the "black Moon" when it is in this position). But because the two orbits do not coincide, the Moon's shadow normally misses the Earth and the Earth's shadow misses the Moon. The inclination of the two orbital planes to each other is 5 degrees. The tides are, of course, caused by the Moon with the help of the Sun, but in the open ocean they are surprisingly low, amounting to about one yard. The very high tides which can be observed near the shore in some places are due to funnelling effects of the shorelines. At new Moon and at full Moon the tides raised by the Moon are reinforced by the Sun; these are the "spring tides." If the Sun's tidal power acts at right angles to that of the Moon (quarter moons) we get the low "neap tides."

## Our Planet Earth

The Earth, circling the Sun at an average distance of 93 million miles, is the fifth largest planet and the third from the Sun. It orbits the Sun at a speed of 67,000 miles per hour, making one revolution in 365 days, 5 hours, 48 minutes, and 45.51 seconds. The Earth completes one rotation on its axis every 23 hours, 56 minutes, and 4.09 seconds. Actually a bit pear-shaped rather than a true sphere, the Earth has a diameter of 7,927 miles at the Equator and a few miles less at the poles. It has an estimated mass of about 6.6 sextillion tons, with an average density of 5.52 grams per cubic centimeter. The Earth's surface area encompasses 196,949,970 square miles of which about three-fourths is water.

**Origin of the Earth.** The Earth, along with the other planets, is believed to have been born 4.5 billion years ago as a solidified cloud of dust and gases left over from the creation of the Sun. For perhaps 500 million years, the interior of the Earth stayed solid and relatively cool, perhaps 2000° F. The main ingredients, according to the best available evidence, were iron and silicates, with small amounts of other elements, some of them radioactive. As millions of years passed, energy released by radioactive decay—mostly of uranium, thorium, and potassium—gradually heated the Earth, melting some of its consituents. The iron melted before the silicates, and, being heavier, sank toward the center. This forced upward the silicates that it found there. After many years, the iron reached the center, almost 4,000 miles deep, and began to accumulate. No eyes were around at that time to view the turmoil which must have taken place on the face of the Earth—gigantic heaves and bubbling of the surface, exploding volcanoes, and flowing lava covering everything in sight. Finally, the iron in the center accumulated as the core. Around it, a thin but fairly stable crust of solid rock formed as the Earth cooled. Depressions in the crust were natural basins in which water, rising from the interior of the planet through volcanoes and fissures, collected to form the oceans. Slowly the Earth acquired its present appearance.

**The Earth Today.** As a result of radioactive heating over millions of years, the Earth's molten *core* is probably fairly hot today, around 11,000° F. By comparison, lead melts at around 800° F. Most of

the Earth's 2,100-mile-thick core is liquid, but there is evidence that the center of the core is solid. The liquid outer portion, about 95% of the core, is constantly in motion, causing the Earth to have a magnetic field that makes compass needles point north and south. The details are not known, but the latest evidence suggests that planets which have a magnetic field probably have a solid core or a partially liquid one.

Outside the core is the Earth's *mantle*, 1,800 miles thick, and extending nearly to the surface. The mantle is composed of heavy silicate rock, similar to that brought up by volcanic eruptions. It is somewhere between liquid and solid, slightly yielding, and therefore contributing to an active, moving Earth. Most of the Earth's radioactive material is in the thin *crust* which covers the mantle, but some is in the mantle and continues to give off heat. The crust's thickness ranges from 5 to 25 miles.

**Continental Drift.** A great deal of recent evidence confirms the long-disputed theory that the continents of the Earth, made mostly of relatively light granite, float in the slightly yielding mantle, like logs in a pond. For many years it had been noticed that if North and South America could be pushed toward western and southern Europe and western Africa, they would fit like pieces in a jigsaw puzzle. Today, there is little question—the continents have drifted widely and continue to do so.

In 10 million years, the world as we know it may be unrecognizable, with California drifting out to sea, Florida joining South America, and Africa moving farther away from Europe and Asia.

**The Earth's Atmosphere.** The thin blanket of atmosphere that envelops the Earth extends several hundred miles into space. From sea level—the very bottom of the ocean of air—to a height of about 60 miles, the air in the atmosphere is made up of the same gases in the same ratio: about 78% nitrogen, 21% oxygen, and the remaining 1% being a mixture of argon, carbon dioxide, and tiny amounts of neon, helium, krypton, xenon, and other gases. The atmosphere becomes less dense with increasing altitude: more than three-fourths of the Earth's huge envelope is concentrated in the first 5 to 10 miles above the surface. At sea level, a cubic foot of the atmosphere weighs about an ounce and a quarter. The entire atmosphere weighs 5,700,000,000,000,000 tons, and the force with which gravity holds it in place causes it to exert a pressure of nearly 15 pounds per square inch. Going out from the Earth's surface, the atmosphere is divided into five regions. The regions, and the heights to which they extend, are: *Troposphere,* 0 to 7 miles (at middle latitudes); *stratosphere,* 7 to 30 miles; *mesosphere,* 30 to 50 miles; *thermosphere,* 50 to 400 miles; and *exosphere,* above 400 miles. The boundaries between each of the regions are known respectively as the *tropopause, stratopause, mesopause,* and *thermopause.* Alternate terms often used for the layers above the troposphere are *ozonosphere* (for stratosphere) and *ionosphere* for the remaining upper layers.

**The Seasons.** Seasons are caused by the 23.4 degree tilt of the Earth's axis, which alternately turns the North and South Poles toward the Sun. Times when the Sun's apparent path crosses the Equator are known as *equinoxes.* Times when the Sun's apparent path is at the greatest distance from the Equator are known as *solstices.* The lengths of the days are most extreme at each solstice. If the

Earth's axis were perpendicular to the plane of the Earth's orbit around the Sun, there would be no seasons, and the days always would be equal in length. Since the Earth's axis is at an angle, the Sun strikes the Earth directly at the Equator only twice a year: in March (vernal equinox) and September (autumnal equinox). In the Northern Hemisphere, spring begins at the vernal equinox, summer at the summer solstice, fall at the autumnal equinox, and winter at the winter solstice. The situation is reversed in the Southern Hemisphere.

## Mercury

Mercury is the planet nearest the Sun. Appropriately named for the wing-footed Roman messenger of the gods, Mercury whizzes around the Sun at a speed of 30 miles per second, completeing one circuit in 88 days. The planet rotates on its axis over a period of nearly 59 days. Daytime on cratered Mercury is hot, about 800 degrees F., although at night the temperature may fall to room temperature. Mercury has no moons, but it does have a trace of atmosphere and a weak magnetic field, according to findings of Mariner 10. Until this spacecraft flew by Mercury in 1974 and 1975, very little was known about the planet, primarily because of its short angular distance from the Sun as seen from Earth, which puts it too close to the Sun to be easily observed.

● Mercury is a naked eye object at morning or evening twilight when it is at greatest elongation.

## Venus

Although Venus is Earth's nearest neighbor, little is known about this planet because it is permanently covered by thick clouds. In 1962, Soviet and American space probes, coupled with Earth-based radar and infrared spectrosoopy, began slowly unraveling some of the mystery surrounding Venus. According to the latest results, Venus' atmosphere is about 96% carbon dioxide, exerting a pressure at the surface 90.5 times greater than Earth's. Walking on Venus would be as difficult as walking a half-mile beneath the ocean. Because of the thick blanket of carbon dioxide, a "greenhouse effect" exists on Venus: Venus intercepts twice as much of the Sun's light as does the Earth. The light enters freely through carbon dioxide gas and is changed to heat radiation in molecular collisions. But carbon dioxide prevents the heat from escaping. Consequently, the temperature of the surface of Venus is over 800 degrees F., hot enough to melt lead. The atmosphere appears to have five distinct layers and to flash almost continuously with lightning. Radar bounced off the planet recently revealed what appear to be large craters and an immense, 900-mile-long canyon. Venus rotates in retrograde motion for a reason not yet known.

In March 1982, the Soviet *Venera 13* and *14* landing craft made the first actual test samples of the Venusian surface by x-ray fluorescence spectroscopy which gave an element-by-element analysis. The terrestrial samples revealed a terrain of basaltic uplands and lowlands.

The Soviets have announced plans to place two more Venera landers on Venus in 1986.

● Venus is the brightest of all the planets and is often visible in the morning or evening, when it is frequently referred to as the Morning Star or Evening Star. At its brightest, it can sometimes be seen with the naked eye in full daylight, if one knows whcrc to look.

## Mars

Mars, on the other side of the Earth from Venus, is Venus' direct opposite in terms of physical properties. Its atmosphere is cold, thin, and transparent, and readily permits observation of the planet's features. We know more about Mars than any other planet except Earth. Mars is a forbidding, rugged planet with huge volcanoes and deep chasms. The largest volcano, Olympus Mons rises 78,000 feet above the surface, higher than Mount Everest. The plains of Mars are pockmarked by the hits of thousands of meteors over the years. Most of our information about Mars comes from the Mariner 9 spacecraft, which orbited the planet in 1971. Mariner 9, photographing 100% of the planet, uncovered spectacular geological formations, including a Martian Grand Canyon that dwarfs the one on Earth. The spacecraft's cameras also recorded what appeared to be dried riverbeds, suggesting the onetime presence of water on the planet. The latter idea gives encouragement to scientists looking for life on Mars, for where there is water, there may be life. However, by 1979, no evidence of life has been found. Temperatures near the equator range from − 17 degrees F. in the daytime to − 130 degrees F. at night. Mars rotates upon its axis in nearly the same period as Earth—24 hours, 37 minutes—so that a Mars day is almost identical to an Earth day. Mars takes 687 days to make one trip around the Sun. Because of its eccentric orbit Mars' distance from the Sun can vary by about 36 million miles. Its distance from Earth can vary by as much as 200 million miles. The atmosphere of Mars is much thinner than Earth's; atmospheric pressure is about 1% that of our planet. Its gravity is one-third of Earth's. Major constituents are carbon dioxide and nitrogen. Water vapor and oxygen are minor constituents. Mars' polar caps, composed mostly of carbon dioxide, recede and advance according to the Martian seasons. Mars was named for the Roman god of war, because when seen from Earth its distinct red color reminded the ancient people of blood. We know now that the reddish hue reflects the oxidized (rusted) iron in the surface material. The landing of two robot Viking spacecraft on the surface of Mars in 1976 provided more information about Mars in a few months than in all the time that has gone before.

## Jupiter

Jupiter, with an equatorial diameter of 88,000 miles, is the largest of a group of planets which differ markedly from the terrestrial planets. The others in the group are Saturn, Uranus, and Neptune. All are large, with very dense atmospheres, and indeed may be giant balls of gas without any perceptible surfaces. They all whirl rapidly around their axes, but more slowly around the Sun, resulting in short days and long years. They have many moons. Majestic Jupiter, named for the king of the Roman gods, rotates so fast that it is greatly flattened at the poles. According to Pioneers 10 and 11, which flew past Jupiter in 1974 and 1975, this planet is a whirling ball of liquid hydrogen with perhaps an Earth-sized iron core. Other atmospheric constituents are helium, methane, and ammonia. Its clouds are probably ammonia ice crystals, becoming ammonia droplets deeper towards the "surface." Temperatures range from perhaps minus 300 degrees F. at the tops of the cloud decks to 100,000 degrees F. or more deep down at the center. The pressure at the center of the planet is estimated to be a crushing 10 million pounds per square inch. The Great Red Spot, a 13,000-mile-wide storm that may have been raging for thousands of years, was found by Voyagers 1 and 2 in 1979 to be cooler at the top than the surrounding clouds, indicating that the Red Spot may tower high above them. Jupiter has 16 satellites. The four largest moons, called Galilean moons, are Europa, Ganymede, Io, and Callisto. *Voyagers 1 and 2* found them to be very different from each other in terms of surface relief, volcanic activity, and other characteristics.

● Even when nearest the Earth, Jupiter is still almost 400 million miles away. But because of its size, it may rival Venus in brilliance when near. Jupiter's four large moons may be seen through field glasses, moving rapidly around Jupiter and changing their position from night to night.

## Saturn

Saturn, the second largest planet in the solar system, is the least dense. It would float in an ocean if there were one big enough to hold it. Aside from its rings, Saturn is very similar to Jupiter except that it is probably colder, being twice as far from the Sun. Recent radar observations of Saturn's rings indicate that they are no more than 10 miles thick, and probably composed of chunks of rock and ice averaging a meter in size. Saturn's ring system begins about 7000 miles from the planet's disk, and extends out to about 35,000 miles. Recent observations have shown Saturn to have between 21 and 23 moons, more than any other planet. The two *Voyager* probes that examined Jupiter in 1979 flew by Saturn in 1980 and 1981. *Voyager 2* will encounter Uranus in 1986.

● Saturn is the last of the planets visible to the naked eye. Saturn is never an object of overwhelming brilliance, but it looks like a bright star. The rings can be seen with a small telescope.

## Uranus

Uranus is the seventh planet from the sun, twice as far out as Saturn. The axis of Uranus is tilted at 98 degrees, so it goes around the Sun nearly lying on its side. In 1977, American astronomers made the startling discovery that Uranus has rings, like Saturn.

The first *Voyager* to Uranus took extensive readings of the planet in January 1986. The information received drastically altered perceptions of the planet. Readings of the atmosphere confirmed previous theories that under the cloud layer a hot ocean of superheated water exists. The pressure caused by the thick atmosphere keeps the water, with a temperature that reaches thousands of degrees, from boiling away and the heat keeps the pressure from solidifying the water. This discovery suggested that Uranus differs in composition from Jupiter and Saturn and that the planet may have formed from a coalescence of comets, as comets and the atmosphere and ocean of Uranus are similarly constituted. Other discoveries about the planetary atmosphere were that the pole facing the sun was no hotter than the pole facing away from the sun and that four large methane clouds in the atmosphere were being blown around the planet in the same direction as the planet's rotation, exactly opposite the way in which they should have blown, according to calculations made based on observed conditions.

Another observation was that the planet's magnetic field is 60 degrees out of sync with the poles of the planet. Explanations for this unique feature included the possibility that Uranus may be experiencing a shift of north and south magnetic poles or that the churning of the ocean or of the molten core of the planet has generated this peculiar field. There is, however, insufficent information for any definite conclusions to be drawn.

*Voyager 2* also expanded the body of information pertaining to the rings and moons of Uranus. A tenth ring was discovered and the rings were discovered to be formed not of fine particles of ice and dust like Saturn but of chunky objects of rock and large ice "boulders".

In addition to the new ring, ten new moons, smaller in diameter and closer to the planet than the five known moons—Oberon, Titania, Umbriel, Ariel, and Miranda—were discovered.

The *Voyager* craft took the first close-up pictures of Uranus's five largest moons, with surprising results. The pictures of Oberon showed surprising activity going on underneath its icy surface. Titania and Ariel were seen to have large rift-valleys scarring the surface, evidence of some sort of eruption of frozen water from within their surfaces. The surface of Umbriel proved to be inexplicably darker than the other moons with no signs of recent crustal activity. Miranda was the biggest surprise with an unparalleled variety of terrain features that caused scientists to label it as a "bizarre hybrid."

Uranus can—on rare occasions—become bright enough to be seen with the naked eye, if one knows exactly where to look; normally, a good set of field glasses or a small portable telescope is required.

## Neptune

Little is known about the distant giant planet of Neptune, although it is believed to be similar to Jupiter and Saturn. Located 2.8 billion miles from the Sun, it must be a grim, frozen world. Neptune has two known moons. The larger moon, Triton, is, along with Jupiter's Ganymede and Callisto, and Saturn's Titan, one of the four largest moons in the solar system. More information about Neptune should be forthcoming when *Voyager 2* passes by the planet in August 1989.

Although Neptune can occasionally be seen with the naked eye, an aid, usually field glasses or small telescopes, is required.

## Pluto

Pluto, the outermost and smallest planet in the solar system, looks more like a terrestrial planet than a gaseous planet. But so little is known about it, that it is difficult to classify. Appropriately named for the Roman god of the underworld, it must be frozen, dark, and dead.

In 1978, light curve studies gave evidence of a moon revolving around Pluto with the same period as Pluto's rotation. Therefore, it stays over the same point on Pluto's surface. In addition, it keeps the same face toward the planet. The discovery of this moon of 500–600 miles in diameter reduces the previously estimated diameter of Pluto to little more than 1,500 miles, making the pair more like a double planet than any other in the solar system. Previously, the Earth-Moon system held this distinction. The density of Pluto is slightly greater than that of water.

## The First Ten Minor Planets (Asteroids)

| Name | Year of discovery | Mean distance from sun (millions of miles) | Orbital period (years) | Diameter (miles) | Magnitude |
|---|---|---|---|---|---|
| 1. Ceres | 1801 | 257.0 | 4.60 | 485 | 7.4 |
| 2. Pallas | 1802 | 257.4 | 4.61 | 304 | 8.0 |
| 3. Juno | 1804 | 247.8 | 4.36 | 118 | 8.7 |
| 4. Vesta | 1807 | 219.3 | 3.63 | 243 | 6.5 |
| 5. Astraea | 1845 | 239.3 | 4.14 | 50 | 9.9 |
| 6. Hebe | 1847 | 225.2 | 3.78 | 121 | 8.5 |
| 7. Iris | 1847 | 221.4 | 3.68 | 121 | 8.4 |
| 8. Flora | 1847 | 204.4 | 3.27 | 56 | 8.9 |
| 9. Metis | 1848 | 221.7 | 3.69 | 78 | 8.9 |
| 10. Hygeia | 1849 | 292.6 | 5.59 | 40 (?) | 9.5 |

Pluto was predicted by calculation when Percival Lowell noticed irregularities in the orbits of Uranus and Neptune. Clyde Tombaugh discovered the planet in 1930, precisely where Lowell predicted it would be. The name Pluto was chosen because the first two letters represent the initials of Percival Lowell.

• Pluto has the most eccentric orbit in the solar system, bringing it at times closer to the Sun than Neptune. Pluto is now approaching the perihelion of its orbit, and for the rest of this century will be closer to the Sun than Neptune. Even then, it can be seen only with a large telescope.

### The Asteroids

Between the orbits of Mars and Jupiter are an estimated 30,000 pieces of rocky debris, known collectively as the asteroids, or planetoids. The first and, incidentally, the largest was discovered during the New Year's night of 1801 by the Italian astronomer Father Piazzi, and its orbit was calculated by the German mathematician Karl Friedrich Gauss. (Gauss invented a new method of calculating orbits on that occasion.) A German amateur astronomer, the physician Olbers, discovered the second asteroid. The number now known, catalogued, and named is around 1,600; the estimated total is about 20 times that figure. A few asteroids do not move in orbits beyond the orbit of Mars, but in orbits which cross the orbit of Mars. The first of them was named Eros because of this peculiar orbit. It had become the rule to bestow female names on the asteroids, but when it was found that Eros crossed the orbit of a major planet, it received a male name. Since then around two dozen orbit-crossers have been discovered, and they are often referred to as the "male asteroids." A few of them—Albert, Adonis, Apollo, Amor, and Icarus—cross the orbit of the Earth, and two of them may come closer than our Moon; but the crossing is like a bridge crossing a highway, not like two highways intersecting. Hence there is very little danger of collision from these bodies. They are all small, three to five miles in diameter, and therefore very difficult objects to identify, even when quite close. Some scientists believe the asteroids represent the remains of an exploded planet.

### Comets

Comets, according to the noted astronomer, Fred L. Whipple, are enormous "snowballs" of frozen gases (mostly carbon dioxide, methane, and water vapor) and contain very little solid material. The whole behavior of comets can then be explained as the behavior of frozen gas being heated by the Sun. When the comet Kohoutek made its first appearance to man in 1973, its behavior seemed to confirm this Whipple theory of the make-up of comets.

Since comets appear in the sky without any warning, people in classical times and especially during the Middle Ages believed that they had a special meaning, which, of course, was bad. Since a natural catastrophe of some sort of a military conflict occurs every year, it was quite simple to blame the comet that happened to be visible. But even in the past, there were some people who used logical reasoning. When, in Roman times, a comet was blamed for the loss of a battle and hence was called a "bad omen," a Roman writer observed that the victors in the battle probably did not think so.

Up until the middle of the sixteenth century, comets were believed to be phenomena of the upper atmosphere; they were usually "explained" as "burning vapors" which had risen from "distant swamps." That nobody had ever actually seen burning vapors rise from a swamp did not matter.

But a large comet which appeared in 1577 was carefully observed by Tycho Brahe, a Danish astronomer who is often, and with the best of reasons, called "eccentric" but who insisted on precise measurements for everything. It was Tycho Brahe's accumulation of literally thousands of precise measurements which later enable his younger collaborator, Johannes Kepler, to discover the laws of planetary motion. Measuring the motion of the comet of 1577, Tycho Brahe could show that it had been far beyond the atmosphere, even though he could not give figures for the distance. Tycho Brahe's work proved that comets were astronomical and not meteorological phenomena.

In 1682, the second Astronomer Royal of Great Britain, Dr. Edmond Halley, checked the orbit of a bright comet that was in the sky then and compared it with earlier comet orbits which were known in part. Halley found that the comet of 1682 was the third to move through what appeared to be the same orbit. And the three appearances were roughly 76 years apart. Halley concluded that this was the same comet, moving around the Sun in a closed orbit, like the planets. He predicted that it would reappear in 1758 or 1759. Halley himself died in 1742, but a large comet appeared sixteen years after his death as predicted and was immediately referred to as "Halley's comet."

In the Spring of 1973, the discovery of comet Kohoutek, apparently headed for a close-Christmastime rendezvous with the Sun, created worldwide excitement. The comet was a visual disappointment, but turned out to be a treasure trove of information on these little-understood celestial objects. Given an unprecedented advance notice of nine months on the advent of the fiery object, scientists were able to study the comet in visible, ultraviolet and infrared light; with optical telescopes, radio telescopes, and radar. They observed it from the ground, from high-flying aircraft, with instruments aboard unmanned satellites, with sounding rockets, and telescopes and cameras on the Earth-orbiting Skylab space station.

Halley's Comet appeared again in 1986, sparking a worldwide effort to study it up close. Five satellites in all took readings from the comet at various distances. Two Soviet craft, *Vega 1* and *Vega 2*, went in close to provide detailed pictures of the comet, including the first of the comet's core. The European Space Agency's craft, *Giotto*, entered the comet itself, coming to within 450 miles of the comet's center and successfully passing through its tail. In addition, two Japanese craft, the *Suisei* and the *Sakigake*, passed at a longer distance in order to analyze the cloud and tail of the comet and the effect of solar radiation upon it. The United States declined to launch a similar mission, citing budgetary constraints imposed by the shuttle program. A space telescope was to study Halley's Comet but was destroyed in the *Challenger* disaster.

The information gained included measurements of the size of the nucleus, an idea of its configuration and the rate of its rotation. The gas and dust of the comet were analyzed as was the material of the tail. This information is considered important because comets are believed to be debris from the formation of the solar system and to have changed little since then.

Astronomers refer to comets as "periodic" or as "non-periodic" comets, but the latter term does not mean that these comets have no period; it merely means that their period is not known. The actual periods of comets run from 3.3 years (the shortest known) to many thousands of years. Their orbits are elliptical, like those of the planets, but they are very eccentric, long and narrow ellipses. Only comet Schwassmann-Wachmann has an orbit which has such a low eccentricity (for a cometary orbit) that it could be the orbit of a minor planet.

When a comet, coming from deep space, approaches the Sun, it is at first indistinguishable from a minor planet. Somewhere between the orbits of Mars and Jupiter its outline becomes fuzzy; it is said to develop a "coma" (the word used here is the Latin word *coma*, which means "hair," not the phonetically identical Greek word which means "deep sleep"). Then, near the orbit of Mars, the comet develops its tail, which at first trails behind. This grows steadily as the comet comes closer and closer to the Sun. As it rounds the Sun (as first noticed by Girolamo Fracastoro) the tail always points away from the Sun so that the comet, when moving away from the Sun, points its tail ahead like the landing lights of an airplane.

The reason for this behavior is that the tail is pushed in these directions by the radiation pressure of the Sun. It sometimes happens that a comet loses its tail at perihelion; it then grows another one. Although the tail is clearly visible against the black of the sky, it is very tenuous. It has been said that if the tail of Halley's comet could be com-

## 21 Famous Comets

| Year and no. | | Name of comet | Period (years) |
|---|---|---|---|
| 1744 | | De Chéseaux's Comet | — |
| 1806 | | Biela's Comet | 6.7 |
| 1811 | I | Great Comet of 1811 | 3000 |
| 1812 | | Di Vico's Comet | 70.7 |
| 1815 | | Olbers' Comet | 74.0 |
| 1819 | I | Encke's Comet | 3.3 |
| 1819 | | Pons-Winnecke Comet | 6.0 |
| 1835 | III | Halley's Comet | 76.3 |
| 1843 | I | Great Comet of 1843 | 512.4 |
| 1844 | II | Great Comet of 1844 | 102,050 |
| 1858 | VI | Donati's Comet | 2,040(?) |
| 1864 | II | Great Comet of 1864 | 2,800,000 |
| 1871 | III | Tuttle's Comet | 13.8 |
| 1874 | III | Coggia's Comet | 6,000(?) |
| 1879 | | Brorsen's Comet | 5.6 |
| 1881 | II | Tebbutt's Comet | — |
| 1889 | VI | Swift's 2nd Comet | 7.0 |
| 1892 | III | Holmes' Comet | 6.9 |
| 1923 | | d'Arrest's Comet | 6.6 |
| 1925 | II | Comet Schwassmann-Wachmann | 16.2 |
| 1973 | I | Comet Kohoutek | 75,000(?) |

pressed to the density of iron, it would fit into a small suitcase.

Although very low in mass, comets are among the largest members of the solar system. The nucleus of a comet may be up to 10,000 miles in diameter; its coma between 10,000 and 50,000 miles in diameter; and its tail as long as 28 million miles.

## Meteors and Meteorites

The term "meteor" for what is usually called a "shooting star" bears an unfortunate resemblance to the term "meteorology," the science of weather and weather forecasting. This resemblance is due to an ancient misunderstanding which wrongly considered meteors an atmospheric phenomenon. Actually, the streak of light in the sky that scientists call a meteor is essentially an astronomical phenomenon: the entry of a small piece of cosmic matter into our atmosphere.

The distinction between "meteors" and "fireballs" (formerly also called "bolides") is merely one of convenience; a fireball is an unusually bright meteor. Incidentally, it also means that a fireball is larger than a faint meteor.

Bodies which enter our atmosphere become visible when they are about 60 miles above the ground. The fact that they grow hot enough to emit light is not due to the "friction" of the atmosphere, as one can often read. The phenomenon responsible for the heating is one of compression. Unconfined air cannot move faster than the speed of sound. Since the entering meteorite moves with 30 to 60 times the speed of sound, the air simply cannot get out of the way. Therefore, it is compressed like the air in the cylinder of a Diesel engine and is heated by compression. This heat—or part of it—is transferred to the moving body. The details of this process are now fairly well understood as a result of re-entry tests with ballistic-missile nose cones.

The average weight of a body producing a faint "shooting star" is only a small fraction of an ounce. Even a bright fireball may not weigh more than 2

# The 88 Recognized Constellations

In astronomical works, the Latin names of the constellations are used. The letter N or S following the Latin name indicates whether the constellation is located to the north or south of the Zodiac. The letter Z indicates that the constellation is within the Zodiac.

| Latin name | Letter | English version | Latin name | Letter | English version | Latin name | Letter | English version |
|---|---|---|---|---|---|---|---|---|
| Andromeda | N | Andromeda | Delphinus | N | Dolphin | Pavo | S | Peacock |
| Antlia | S | Airpump | Dorado | S | Swordfish | Pegasus | N | Pegasus |
| Apus | S | Bird of Paradise | | | (Goldfish) | Perseus | N | Perseus |
| Aquarius | Z | Water Bearer | Draco | N | Dragon | Phoenix | S | Phoenix |
| Aquila | N | Eagle | Equuleus | N | Filly | Pictor | S | Painter (or his |
| Ara | S | Altar | Eridanus | S | Eridanus (river) | | | Easel) |
| Aries | Z | Ram | Fornax | S | Furnace | Pisces | Z | Fishes |
| Auriga | N | Charioteer | Gemini | Z | Twins | Piscis | | |
| Boötes | N | Herdsmen | Grus | S | Crane | Austrinus | S | Southern Fish |
| Caelum | S | Sculptor's Tool | Hercules | N | Hercules | Puppis | S | Poop (of Argo)[1] |
| Camelopardalis | N | Giraffe | Horologium | S | Clock | Pyxis | S | Mariner's |
| Cancer | Z | Crab | Hydra | N | Sea Serpent | | | Compass |
| Canes Venatici | N | Hunting Dogs | Hydrus | S | Water Snake | Reticulum | S | Net |
| Canis Major | S | Great Dog | Indus | S | Indian | Sagitta | N | Arrow |
| Canis Minor | S | Little Dog | Lacerta | N | Lizard | Sagittarius | Z | Archer |
| Capricornus | Z | Goat (or Sea- | Leo | Z | Lion | Scorpius | S | Scorpion |
| | | Goat) | Leo Minor | N | Little Lion | Sculptor | S | Sculptor |
| Carina | S | Keel (of Argo)[1] | Lepus | S | Hare | Scutum | N | Shield |
| Cassiopeia | N | Cassiopeia | Libra | Z | Scales | Serpens | N | Serpent |
| Centaurus | S | Centaur | Lupus | S | Wolf | Sextans | N | Sextant |
| Cepheus | N | Cepheus | Lynx | N | Lynx | Taurus | Z | Bull |
| Cetus | S | Whale | Lyra | N | Lyre (Harp) | Telescopium | S | Telescope |
| Chameleon | S | Chameleon | Mensa | S | Table | Triangulum | N | Triangle |
| Circinus | S | Compasses | | | (mountain) | Triangulum | S | Southern |
| Columba | S | Dove | Microscopium | S | Microscope | Australe | | Triangle |
| Coma Berenices | N | Berenice's Hair | Monoceros | S | Unicorn | Tucana | S | Toucan |
| Corona Australis | S | Southern Crown | Musca | S | Southern Fly | Ursa Major | N | Big Dipper |
| Corona Borealis | N | Northern Crown | Norma | S | Rule | Ursa Minor | N | Little Dipper |
| Corvus | S | Crow (Raven) | | | (straightedge) | Vela | S | Sail (of Argo)[1] |
| Crater | S | Cup | Octans | S | Octant | Virgo | Z | Virgin |
| Crux | S | Southern Cross | Ophiuchus | N | Serpent-Bearer | Volans | S | Flying Fish |
| Cygnus | N | Swan | Orion | S | Orion | Vulpecula | N | Fox |

1. The original constellation Argo Navis (the Ship Argo) has been divided into Carina, Puppis, and Vela. Normally the brightest star in each constellation is designated by alpha, the first letter of the Greek alphabet, the second brightest by beta, the second letter of the Greek alphabet, and so forth. But the Greek letters run through Carina, Puppis, and Vela as if it were still one constellation.

or 3 pounds. Naturally, the smaller bodies are worn to dust by the passage through the atmosphere; only rather large ones reach the ground. Those that are found are called meteorites. (The "meteor," to repeat, is the term for the light streak in the sky.)

The largest meteorite known is still imbedded in the ground near Grootfontein in SW Africa and is estimated to weight 70 tons. The second largest known is the 34-ton Anighito (on exhibit in the Hayden Planetarium, New York), which was found by Admiral Peary at Cape York in Greenland. The largest meteorite found in the United States is the Willamette meteorite (found in Oregon, weight ca. 15 tons), but large portions of this meteorite weathered away before it was found. Its weight as it struck the ground may have been 20 tons.

All these are iron meteorites (an iron meteorite normally contains about 7% nickel), which form one class of meteorites. The other class consists of the stony meteorites, and between them there are the so-called "stony irons." The so-called "tektites" consist of glass similar to our volcanic glass obsidian, and because of the similarity, there is doubt in a number of cases whether the glass is of terrestrial or of extra-terrestrial origin.

Though no meteorite larger than the Grootfontein is actually known, we do know that the Earth has, on occasion, been struck by much larger bod-

ies. Evidence for such hits are the meteorite craters, of which an especially good example is located near the Cañon Diablo in Arizona. Another meteor crater in the United States is a rather old crater near Odessa, Texas. A large number of others are known, especially in eastern Canada; and for many "probables," meteoric origin has now been proved.

The meteor showers are caused by multitudes of very small bodies travelling in swarms. The Earth travels in its orbit through these swarms like a car driving through falling snow. The point from which the meteors seem to emanate is called the *radiant* and is named for the constellation in that area. The Perseid meteor shower in August is the most spectacular of the year, boasting at peak roughly 60 meteors per hour under good atmospheric conditions. The presence of a bright moon diminishes the number of visible meteors.

## The Constellations

Constellations are groupings of stars which form patterns that can be easily recognized and remembered, for example, Orion and the Big Dipper. Actually, the stars of the majority of all constellations do not "belong together." Usually they are at greatly varying distances from the Earth and just happen to lie more or less in the same line of sight

## Symbols

| | | | | | |
|---|---|---|---|---|---|
| ☉ the sun | ♀ Venus | ♃ Jupiter | ♅ Neptune | ✶ occultation | ☽ first quarter |
| ☾ the moon | ⊕ the earth | ♄ Saturn | ♇ Pluto | ♂ opposition | ○ full moon |
| ☿ Mercury | ♂ Mars | ♅ Uranus | ♂ conjunction | ● new moon | ☾ last quarter |

as seen from our solar system. But in a few cases the stars of a constellation are actually associated; most of the bright stars of the Big Dipper travel together and form what astronomers call an open cluster.

If you observe a planet, say Mars, for one complete revolution, you will see that it passes successively through twelve constellations. All planets (except Pluto at certain times) can be observed only in these twelve constellations, which form the so-called Zodiac, and the Sun also moves through the Zodiacal signs, though the Sun's apparent movement is actually caused by the movement of the Earth.

Although the constellations are due mainly to the optical accident of line of sight and have no real significance, astronomers have retained them as reference areas. It is much easier to speak of a star in Orion than to give its geometrical position in the sky. During the Astronomical Congress of 1928, it was decided to recognize 88 constellations. A description of their agreed-upon boundaries was published at Cambridge, England, in 1930, under the title *Atlas Céleste*.

## The Auroras

The "northern lights" *(Aurora borealis)* as well as the "southern lights" *(Aurora australis)* are upper-atmosphere phenomena of astronomical origin. The auroras center around the magnetic (not the geographical) poles of the Earth, which explains why, in the Western Hemisphere, they have been seen as far to the south as New Orleans and Florida while the equivalent latitude in the Eastern Hemisphere never sees an aurora. The northern magnetic pole happens to be in the Western Hemisphere.

The lower limit of an aurora is at about 50 miles. Upper limits have been estimated to be as high as 400 miles. Since about 1880, a connection between the auroras on Earth and the sun spots has been suspected and has gradually come to be accepted. It was said that the sun spots probably eject "particles" (later the word *electrons* was substituted) which on striking the Earth's atmosphere, cause the auroras. But this explanation suffered from certain difficulties. Sometimes a very large sun spot group on the Sun, with individual spots bigger than the Earth itself, would not cause an aurora. Moreover, even if a sun spot caused an aurora, the time that passed between the appearance of the one and the occurrence of the other was highly unpredictable.

This problem of the time lag is, in all probability, solved by the discovery of the Van Allen layer by artificial satellite *Explorer I*. The Van Allen layer is a double layer of charged sub-atomic particles around the Earth. The inner layer, with its center some 1,500 miles from the ground, reaches from about 40° N. to about 40° S. and does not touch the atmosphere. The outer layer, much larger and with its center several thousand miles from the ground,

does touch the atmosphere in the vicinity of the magnetic poles.

It seems probable that the "leakage" of electrons from the outer Van Allen layer causes the auroras. A new burst of electrons from the Sun seems to be caught in the outer layer first. Under the assumption that all electrons are first caught in the outer layer, the time lag can be understood. There has to be an "overflow" from the outer layer to produce an aurora.

## The Atmosphere

Astronomically speaking, the presence of our atmosphere is deplorable. Though reasonably transparent to visible light, the atmosphere may absorb as much as 60% of the visible and near-visible light. It is opaque to most other wave-lengths, except certain fairly short radio waves. In addition to absorbing much light, our atmosphere bends light rays entering at a slant (for a given observer) so that the true position of a star close to the horizon is not what it seems to be. One effect is that we see the Sun above the horizon before it actually is. And the unsteady movement of the atmosphere causes the "twinkling" of the stars, which may be romantic but is a nuisance when it comes to observing.

The composition of our atmosphere near the ground is 78% nitrogen and 21% oxygen, the remaining 1% consisting of other gases, most of it argon. The composition stays the same to an altitude of at least 70 miles (except that higher up two impurities, carbon dioxide and water vapor, are missing), but the pressure drops very fast. At 18,000 feet, half of the total mass of the atmosphere is below, and at 100,000 feet, 99% of the mass of the atmosphere is below. The upper limit of the atmosphere is usually given as 120 miles; no definitive figure is possible, since there is no boundary line between the incredibly attenuated gases 120 miles up and space.

## Astronomical Telescopes

Optical telescopes used in astronomy are of two basic kinds: refracting and reflecting. In the *refractor telescope*, a lens is used to collect light from a distant object and bring it to a focus. A second lens, the eyepiece, then magnifies the image which may be examined visually or photographed directly. The *reflector telescope* uses a concave mirror instead of a lens, which reflects the light rays back toward the upper end of the telescope where they are magnified and observed or photographed. Most large optical telescopes now being built are reflectors.

*Radio telescopes* are used to study radio waves coming from outside the Earth's atmosphere. The waves are gathered by an antenna or "dish," which is a parabolic reflecting surface made of metal or finely meshed wire. Radio signals have been received from the Sun, Moon, and planets, and from the center of our galaxy and other galaxies. Radio signals are the means by which the distant and mysterious quasars and pulsars were recently discovered.

# Conversion of Universal Time (U. T.) to Civil Time

| U.T. | E.D.T.[1] | E.S.T.[2] | C.S.T.[3] | M.S.T.[4] | P.S.T.[5] | U.T. | E.D.T.[1] | E.S.T.[2] | C.S.T.[3] | M.S.T.[4] | P.S.T.[5] |
|---|---|---|---|---|---|---|---|---|---|---|---|
| 00 | *8P | *7P | *6P | *5P | *4P | 12 | 8A | 7A | 6A | 5A | 4A |
| 01 | *9P | *8P | *7P | *6P | *5P | 13 | 9A | 8A | 7A | 6A | 5A |
| 02 | *10P | *9P | *8P | *7P | *6P | 14 | 10A | 9A | 8A | 7A | 6A |
| 03 | *11P | *10P | *9P | *8P | *7P | 15 | 11A | 10A | 9A | 8A | 7A |
| 04 | M | *11P | *10P | *9P | *8P | 16 | N | 11A | 10A | 9A | 8A |
| 05 | 1A | M | *11P | *10P | *9P | 17 | 1P | N | 11A | 10A | 9A |
| 06 | 2A | 1A | M | *11P | *10P | 18 | 2P | 1P | N | 11A | 10A |
| 07 | 3A | 2A | 1A | M | *11P | 19 | 3P | 2P | 1P | N | 11A |
| 08 | 4A | 3A | 2A | 1A | M | 20 | 4P | 3P | 2P | 1P | N |
| 09 | 5A | 4A | 3A | 2A | 1A | 21 | 5P | 4P | 3P | 2P | 1P |
| 10 | 6A | 5A | 4A | 3A | 2A | 22 | 6P | 5P | 4P | 3P | 2P |
| 11 | 7A | 6A | 5A | 4A | 3A | 23 | 7P | 6P | 5P | 4P | 3P |

1. Eastern Daylight Time. 2. Eastern Standard Time, same as Central Daylight Time. 3. Central Standard Time, same as Mountain Daylight Time. 4. Mountain Standard Time, same as Pacific Daylight Time. 5. Pacific Standard Time. NOTES: *denotes previous day. N = noon. M = midnight.

## Eclipses of the Sun and the Moon, 1987

**March 29: Annular-total eclipse of the Sun:** Visible in southern South America, part of Antarctica, Africa except in northwest, extreme southeastern Europe, and southwest Asia,

**April 14: Penumbral eclipse of the Moon:** Beginning phase visible in eastern North America, South America, Antarctica, Africa, Europe, the eastern half of Asia, the Atlantic Ocean, the western half of the Indian Ocean, and the eastern South Pacific Ocean. The end is visible in North America except Alaska, Central and South America, Antarctica, western Africa, western Europe, southern Greenland, the Atlantic Ocean, and the eastern Pacific Ocean.

**September 22–23: Annular eclipse of the Sun:** Visible in Asia, Philippine Islands, Indonesia except southwest, New Guinea, northeastern Australia, and New Zealand except in extreme south.

**October 7: Penumbral eclipse of the Moon:** The beginning phase is visible in North America except Alaska, Central and South America, Africa, Europe, eastern Asia, Greenland, the Atlantic Ocean, and the eastern half of the South Pacific Ocean. The end is visible in North, Central and South America, Antarctica, toward South America, western North Africa, western Europe, Greenland, the Atlantic Ocean, and the eastern Pacific Ocean.

## Phenomena, 1987

### Configurations of Sun, Moon, and Planets

NOTE: The hour listings are in Universal Time. For conversion to United States time zones, see conversion table above.

**JANUARY**

| d | h | |
|---|---|---|
| 3 | 12 | Juno in conjunction with Sun |
| 4 | 19 | Jupiter 1° 3 N of Moon |
| 4 | 23 | Earth at perihelion |
| 5 | 12 | Mars 1° 4 N of Moon |
| 6 | 23 | FIRST QUARTER |
| 12 | 17 | Mercury in superior conjunction |
| 13 | 05 | Moon at apogee |
| 15 | 03 | FULL MOON |
| 15 | 21 | Venus greatest elong. W (47°) |
| 15 | 21 | Venus 8° N of Antares |
| 22 | 23 | LAST QUARTER |
| 24 | 20 | Venus 1° 8 N of Saturn |
| 25 | 14 | Antares 0° 4 S of Moon |
| 26 | 05 | Saturn 6° N of Moon |
| 26 | 07 | Venus 8° N of Moon |
| 26 | 16 | Uranus 5° N of Moon |
| 27 | 10 | Neptune 6° N of Moon |
| 28 | 11 | Moon at perigee |
| 29 | 14 | NEW MOON |
| 31 | 17 | Venus 3° N of Uranus |

**FEBRUARY**

| 1 | 14 | Jupiter 0° 7 N of Moon |
|---|---|---|
| 3 | 11 | Mars 0° 3 S of Moon |
| 5 | 16 | FIRST QUARTER |

| 9 | 16 | Moon at apogee |
|---|---|---|
| 11 | 13 | Venus 1° 3 N of Neptune |
| 12 | 05 | Mercury greatest elong. E (18°) |
| 13 | 21 | FULL MOON |
| 16 | 11 | Pluto stationary |
| 18 | 02 | Mercury stationary |
| 18 | 12 | Spica 1° 1 S of Moon |
| 21 | 09 | LAST QUARTER |
| 21 | 22 | Antares 0° 2 S of Moon |
| 22 | 16 | Saturn 6° N of Moon |
| 23 | 02 | Uranus 5° N of Moon |
| 23 | 20 | Neptune 6° N of Moon |
| 24 | 19 | Venus 7° N of Moon |
| 25 | 16 | Moon at perigee |
| 27 | 18 | Mercury in inferior conjunction |
| 28 | 01 | NEW MOON |

**MARCH**

| 1 | 12 | Jupiter 0° 005 S of Moon |
|---|---|---|
| 4 | 11 | Mars 1° 9 S of Moon |
| 7 | 12 | FIRST QUARTER |
| 9 | 10 | Moon at apogee |
| 12 | 01 | Mercury stationary |
| 15 | 13 | FULL MOON |
| 17 | 18 | Spica 1° 0 S of Moon |
| 21 | 03 | Antares 0° 1 S of Moon |
| 21 | 04 | Equinox |
| 21 | 23 | Saturn 7° N of Moon |

| 22 | 08 | Uranus 5° N of Moon |
|---|---|---|
| 22 | 16 | LAST QUARTER |
| 23 | 03 | Neptune 6° N of Moon |
| 24 | 19 | Moon at perigee |
| 26 | 12 | Venus 3° N of Moon |
| 26 | 21 | Mercury greatest elong. W (28°) |
| 27 | 01 | Jupiter in conjunction with Sun |
| 27 | 08 | Mercury 1° 6 N of Moon |
| 29 | 13 | NEW MOON (Eclipse) |
| 31 | 06 | Saturn stationary |
| 31 | 11 | Pallas stationary |

**APRIL**

| 1 | 04 | Uranus stationary |
|---|---|---|
| 2 | 09 | Mars 3° S of Moon |
| 6 | 07 | Moon at apogee |
| 6 | 08 | FIRST QUARTER |
| 9 | 23 | Neptune stationary |
| 14 | 02 | Spica 1° 0 S of Moon |
| 14 | 03 | FULL MOON (Penumbral Eclipse) |
| 17 | 09 | Antares 0° 1 S of Moon |
| 18 | 05 | Saturn 7° N of Moon |
| 18 | 14 | Uranus 5° N of Moon |
| 18 | 17 | Moon at perigee |
| 19 | 08 | Neptune 6° N of Moon |

| | | |
|---|---|---|
| 19 | 12 | Mercury 1° 4 S of Jupiter |
| 20 | 22 | LAST QUARTER |
| 21 | 12 | Mars 6° N of Aldebaran |
| 25 | 12 | Venus 1° 0 S of Moon |
| 26 | 06 | Jupiter 1° 4 S of Moon |
| 28 | 02 | NEW MOON |
| 29 | 10 | Pluto at opposition |
| 30 | 17 | Ceres stationary |

**MAY**

| | | |
|---|---|---|
| 1 | 07 | Mars 4° S of Moon |
| 4 | 02 | Moon at apogee |
| 4 | 22 | Venus 0° 6 S of Jupiter |
| 6 | 02 | FIRST QUARTER |
| 7 | 10 | Mercury in superior conjunction |
| 11 | 11 | Spica 1° 0 S of Moon |
| 13 | 03 | Pallas at opposition |
| 13 | 13 | FULL MOON |
| 14 | 17 | Antares 0° 2 S of Moon |
| 15 | 11 | Saturn 6° N of Moon |
| 15 | 20 | Uranus 5° N of Moon |
| 15 | 23 | Moon at perigee |
| 16 | 14 | Neptune 6° N of Moon |
| 18 | 22 | Mercury 7° N of Aldebaran |
| 20 | 04 | LAST QUARTER |
| 24 | 00 | Jupiter 2° S of Moon |
| 25 | 16 | Venus 4° S of Moon |
| 27 | 15 | NEW MOON |
| 28 | 04 | Vesta in conjunction with Sun |
| 29 | 13 | Mercury 3° S of Moon |
| 30 | 02 | Mars 4° S of Moon |
| 31 | 18 | Moon at apogee |

**JUNE**

| | | |
|---|---|---|
| 4 | 19 | FIRST QUARTER |
| 7 | 10 | Mercury at greatest elong. E (24°) |
| 7 | 21 | Spica 0° 9 S of Moon |
| 9 | 05 | Saturn at opposition |
| 11 | 03 | Antares 0° 2 S of Moon |
| 11 | 17 | Saturn 6° N of Moon |
| 11 | 21 | FULL MOON |
| 12 | 04 | Uranus 5° N of Moon |
| 12 | 23 | Neptune 6° N of Moon |
| 13 | 01 | Moon at perigee |
| 16 | 10 | Uranus at opposition |
| 18 | 11 | LAST QUARTER |
| 19 | 16 | Venus 5° N of Aldebaran |
| 20 | 11 | Ceres at opposition |
| 20 | 16 | Jupiter 3° S of Moon |
| 20 | 17 | Mercury stationary |
| 21 | 22 | Solstice |
| 24 | 20 | Venus 5° S of Moon |
| 26 | 06 | NEW MOON |
| 27 | 09 | Mars 6° S of Pollux |
| 27 | 21 | Mars 4° S of Moon |
| 28 | 04 | Moon at apogee |
| 28 | 21 | Neptune at opposition |

**JULY**

| | | |
|---|---|---|
| 4 | 01 | Earth at aphelion |
| 4 | 04 | Mercury in inferior conjunction |
| 4 | 09 | FIRST QUARTER |
| 5 | 06 | Spica 0° 6 S of Moon |
| 8 | 12 | Juno stationary |
| 8 | 14 | Antares 0° 1 S of Moon |
| 9 | 01 | Saturn 6° N of Moon |
| 9 | 13 | Uranus 5° N of Moon |
| 10 | 08 | Neptune 6° N of Moon |

| | | |
|---|---|---|
| 11 | 04 | FULL MOON |
| 11 | 10 | Moon at perigee |
| 12 | 01 | Mercury 5° S of Venus |
| 12 | 19 | Pallas stationary |
| 15 | 06 | Mercury stationary |
| 17 | 20 | LAST QUARTER |
| 18 | 05 | Jupiter 4° S of Moon |
| 24 | 00 | Mercury 8° S of Moon |
| 24 | 04 | Pluto stationary |
| 25 | 08 | Moon at apogee |
| 25 | 10 | Mercury greatest elong. W (20°) |
| 25 | 21 | NEW MOON |

**AUGUST**

| | | |
|---|---|---|
| 1 | 13 | Spica 0° 3 S of Moon |
| 2 | 19 | FIRST QUARTER |
| 3 | 15 | Mercury 7° S of Pollux |
| 4 | 23 | Antares 0° 1 N of Moon |
| 5 | 09 | Saturn 6° N of Moon |
| 5 | 20 | Ceres 0° 7 N of Moon |
| 5 | 22 | Uranus 5° N of Moon |
| 6 | 18 | Neptune 6° N of Moon |
| 8 | 19 | Moon at perigee |
| 9 | 10 | FULL MOON |
| 10 | 14 | Ceres stationary |
| 14 | 16 | Jupiter 4° S of Moon |
| 16 | 08 | LAST QUARTER |
| 19 | 15 | Saturn stationary |
| 20 | 06 | Mercury in superior conjunction |
| 20 | 08 | Jupiter stationary |
| 21 | 14 | Moon at apogee |
| 23 | 06 | Venus in superior conjunction |
| 23 | 19 | Juno at opposition |
| 24 | 12 | NEW MOON |
| 25 | 08 | Mars in conjunction with Sun |
| 28 | 19 | Spica 0° 2 S of Moon |

**SEPTEMBER**

| | | |
|---|---|---|
| 1 | 04 | FIRST QUARTER |
| 1 | 06 | Antares 0° 3 N of Moon |
| 1 | 14 | Uranus stationary |
| 1 | 16 | Saturn 6° N of Moon |
| 2 | 05 | Uranus 5° N of Moon |
| 2 | 06 | Ceres 0° 4 N of Moon |
| 3 | 01 | Neptune 6° N of Moon |
| 6 | 03 | Moon at apogee |
| 7 | 18 | FULL MOON |
| 11 | 00 | Jupiter 4° S of Moon |
| 15 | 00 | LAST QUARTER |
| 17 | 07 | Neptune stationary |
| 18 | 03 | Moon at apogee |
| 23 | 03 | NEW MOON (Eclipse) |
| 23 | 13 | Mercury 0° 5 N of Spica |
| 23 | 14 | Equinox |
| 25 | 01 | Spica 0° 1 S of Moon |
| 25 | 05 | Mercury 0° 3 N of Moon |
| 28 | 12 | Antares 0° 3 N of Moon |
| 29 | 00 | Saturn 6° N of Moon |
| 29 | 12 | Uranus 5° N of Moon |
| 29 | 20 | Ceres 0° 2 N of Moon |
| 30 | 08 | Neptune 6° N of Moon |
| 30 | 11 | FIRST QUARTER |

**OCTOBER**

| | | |
|---|---|---|
| 4 | 01 | Moon at perigee |
| 4 | 10 | Mercury greatest elong. E (26°) |
| 4 | 20 | Venus 3° N of Spica |
| 6 | 05 | Juno stationary |

| | | |
|---|---|---|
| 7 | 04 | FULL MOON (Penumbral Eclipse) |
| 8 | 05 | Jupiter 4° S of Moon |
| 14 | 18 | LAST QUARTER |
| 15 | 21 | Moon at Apogee |
| 16 | 20 | Mercury stationary |
| 18 | 15 | Jupiter at opposition |
| 20 | 01 | Mercury 3° S of Venus |
| 21 | 04 | Mars 1° 7 N of Moon |
| 22 | 17 | NEW MOON |
| 24 | 03 | Venus 4° N of Moon |
| 25 | 18 | Antares 0° 2 N of Moon |
| 26 | 09 | Saturn 6° N of Moon |
| 26 | 19 | Uranus 5° N of Moon |
| 27 | 14 | Neptune 6° N of Moon |
| 27 | 15 | Ceres 0° 06 S of Moon |
| 28 | 08 | Mercury in inferior conjunction |
| 29 | 17 | FIRST QUARTER |
| 30 | 03 | Moon at perigee |

**NOVEMBER**

| | | |
|---|---|---|
| 2 | 21 | Pluto in conjunction with Sun |
| 4 | 07 | Jupiter 4° S of Moon |
| 5 | 17 | FULL MOON |
| 5 | 23 | Mercury stationary |
| 11 | 04 | Venus 4° N of Antares |
| 12 | 16 | Mars 3° N of Spica |
| 12 | 18 | Moon at apogee |
| 13 | 09 | Mercury greatest elong. W (19°) |
| 13 | 15 | LAST QUARTER |
| 18 | 17 | Spica 0° 1 S of Moon |
| 19 | 01 | Mars 3° N of Moon |
| 20 | 01 | Mercury 6° N of Moon |
| 20 | 16 | Venus 2° S of Saturn |
| 21 | 07 | NEW MOON |
| 22 | 21 | Saturn 6° N of Moon |
| 23 | 01 | Venus 4° N of Moon |
| 23 | 04 | Uranus 5° N of Moon |
| 23 | 22 | Neptune 6° N of Moon |
| 24 | 10 | Venus 0° 9 S of Uranus |
| 24 | 13 | Ceres 0° 6 S of Moon |
| 24 | 15 | Moon at perigee |
| 27 | 16 | Juno 1° 0 N of Moon |
| 28 | 01 | FIRST QUARTER |

**DECEMBER**

| | | |
|---|---|---|
| 1 | 10 | Jupiter 4° S of Moon |
| 3 | 10 | Venus 2° S of Neptune |
| 5 | 08 | FULL MOON |
| 7 | 22 | Vesta stationary |
| 10 | 14 | Moon at apogee |
| 13 | 12 | LAST QUARTER |
| 16 | 03 | Jupiter stationary |
| 16 | 03 | Saturn in conjunction with Sun |
| 16 | 03 | Spica 0° 1 N of Moon |
| 17 | 21 | Mars 5° N of Moon |
| 19 | 09 | Uranus in conjunction with Sun |
| 19 | 12 | Antares 0° 2 N of Moon |
| 20 | 18 | NEW MOON |
| 22 | 10 | Solstice |
| 22 | 10 | Moon at perigee |
| 22 | 22 | Venus 2° N of Moon |
| 23 | 08 | Mercury in superior conjunction |
| 27 | 10 | FIRST QUARTER |
| 28 | 15 | Jupiter 4° S of Moon |
| 29 | 06 | Pallas in conjunction with Sun |
| 29 | 23 | Neptune in conjunction with Sun |

# AVIATION

## Famous Firsts in Aviation

**1782 First balloon flight.** Jacques and Joseph Montgolfier of Annonay, France, sent up a small smoke-filled balloon about mid-November.

**1783 First hydrogen-filled balloon flight.** Jacques A. C. Charles, Paris physicist, supervised construction by A. J. and M. N. Robert of a 13-ft diameter balloon that was filled with hydrogen. It got up to about 3,000 ft and traveled about 16 mi. in a 45-min flight (Aug. 27).

**First human balloon flights.** A Frenchman, Jean Pilâtre de Rozier made the first captive-balloon ascension (Oct. 15). With the Marquis d'Arlandes, Pilâtre de Rozier made the first free flight, reaching a peak altitude of about 500 ft, and traveling about 5 1/2 mi. in 20 min (Nov. 21).

**1784 First powered balloon.** Gen. Jean Baptiste Marie Meusnier developed the first propeller-driven and elliptically-shaped balloon—the crew cranking three propellers on a common shaft to give the craft a speed of about 3 mph.

**First woman to fly.** Mme. Thible, a French opera singer (June 4).

**1793 First balloon flight in America.** Jean Pierre Blanchard, a French pilot, made it from Philadelphia to near Woodbury, Gloucester County, N.J., in a little over 45 min (Jan. 9).

**1794 First military use of the balloon.** Jean Marie Coutelle, using a balloon built for the French Army, made two 4-hr observation ascents. The military purpose of the ascents seems to have been to damage the enemy's morale.

**1797 First parachute jump.** André-Jacques Garnerin dropped from about 6,500 ft over Monceau Park in Paris in a 23-ft diameter parachute made of white canvas with a basket attached (Oct. 22).

**1843 First air transport company.** In London, William S. Henson and John Stringfellow filed articles of incorporation for the Aerial Transit Company (March 24). It failed.

**1852 First dirigible.** Henri Giffard, a French engineer, flew in a controllable (more or less) steam-engine powered balloon, 144 ft long and 39 ft in diameter, inflated with 88,000 cu ft of coal gas. It reached 6.7 mph on a flight from Paris to Trappe (Sept. 24).

**1860 First aerial photographers.** Samuel Archer King and William Black made two photos of Boston, still in existence.

**1872 First gas-engine powered dirigible.** Paul Haenlein, a German engineer, flew in a semi-rigid-frame dirigible, powered by a 4-cylinder internal-combustion engine running on coal gas drawn from the supporting bag.

**1873 First transatlantic attempt.** *The New York Daily Graphic* sponsored the attempt with a 400,000 cu ft balloon carrying a lifeboat. A rip in the bag during inflation brought collapse of the balloon and the project.

**1897 First successful metal dirigible.** An all-metal dirigible, designed by David Schwarz, a Hungarian, took off from Berlin's Tempelhof Field and, powered by a 16-hp Daimler engine, got several miles before leaking gas caused it to crash (Nov. 13).

**1900 First Zeppelin flight.** Germany's Count Ferdinand von Zeppelin flew the first of his long series of rigid-frame airships. It attained a speed of 18 mi. per h and got 3 1/2 mi. before its steering gear failed (July 2).

**1903 First successful heavier-than-air machine flight.** Aviation was really born on the sand dunes at Kitty Hawk, N.C., when Orville Wright crawled to his prone position between the wings of the biplane he and his brother Wilbur had built, opened the throttle of their homemade 12-hp engine and took to the air. He covered 120 ft in 12 sec. Later that day, in one of four flights, Wilbur stayed up 59 sec and covered 852 ft (Dec. 17).

**1904 First airplane maneuvers.** Orville Wright made the first turn with an airplane (Sept. 15); 5 days later his brother Wilbur made the first complete circle.

**1905 First airplane flight over half an hour.** Orville Wright kept his craft up 33 min 17 sec (Oct. 4).

**1906 First European airplane flight.** Alberto Santos-Dumont, a Brazilian, flew a heavier-than-air machine at Bagatelle Field, Paris (Sept. 13).

**1908 First airplane fatality.** Lt. Thomas E. Selfridge, U.S. Army Signal Corps, was in a group of officers evaluating the Wright plane at Fort Myer, Va. He was up about 75 ft with Orville Wright when the propeller hit a bracing wire and was broken, throwing the plane out of control, killing Selfridge and seriously injuring Wright (Sept. 17).

**1910 First licensed woman pilot.** Baroness Raymonde de la Roche of France, who learned to fly in 1909, received ticket No. 36 on March 8.

**First flight from shipboard.** Lt. Eugene Ely, USN, took a Curtiss plane off from the deck of cruiser *Birmingham* at Hampton Roads, Va., and flew to Norfolk (Nov. 14). The following January, he reversed the process, flying from Camp Selfridge to the deck of the armored cruiser *Pennsylvania* in San Francisco Bay (Jan. 18).

**1911 First U.S. woman pilot.** Harriet Quimby, a magazine writer, who got ticket No. 37.

**1913 First multi-engined aircraft.** Built and flown by Igor Ivan Sikorsky while still in his native Russia.

**1914 First aerial combat.** In August, Allied and German pilots and observers started shooting at each other with pistols and rifles—with negligible results.

**1915 First air raids on England.** German Zeppelins started dropping bombs on four English communities (Jan. 19).

**1918 First U.S. air squadron.** The U.S. Army Air Corps made its first independent raids over enemy lines, in DH-4 planes (British-designed) powered with 400-hp American-designed Liberty engines (April 8).

**First regular airmail service.** Operated for the Post Office Department by the Army, the first regular service was inaugurated with one round trip a day (except Sunday) between Washington, D.C., and New York City (May 15).

**1919 First transatlantic flight.** The NC-4, one of four Curtiss flying boats commanded by Lt. Comdr. Albert C. Read, reached Lisbon, Portugal, (May 27) after hops from Trepassy Bay, Newfoundland, to Horta, Azores (May 16–17), to Ponta Delgada (May 20). The Liberty-powered craft was piloted by Walter Hinton.

**First nonstop transatlantic flight.** Capt. John Alcock and Lt. Arthur Whitten Brown, British World War I flyers, made the 1,900 mi. from St. John's, Newfoundland, to Clifden, Ireland, in 16 h 12 min in a Vickers-Vimy bomber with two 350-hp Rolls-Royce engines (June 15–16).

**First lighter-than-air transatlantic flight.** The British dirigible R-34, commanded by Maj. George H. Scott, left Firth of Forth, Scotland, (July 2) and touched down at Mineola, L.I., 108 h later. The eastbound trip was made in 75 h (completed July 13).

**First scheduled London-Paris passenger service (using airplanes).** Aircraft Travel and Transport inaugurated London-Paris service (Aug. 25). Later the company started the first trans-channel mail service on the same route (Nov. 10).

**1921 First naval vessel sunk by aircraft.** Two battleships being scrapped by treaty were sunk by bombs dropped from Army planes in demonstration put on by Brig. Gen. William S. Mitchell (July 21).

**First helium balloon.** The C-7, non-rigid Navy dirigible was first to use non-inflammable helium as lifting gas, making a flight from Hampton Roads, Va., to Washington, D.C. (Dec. 1).

**1922 First member of Caterpillar Club.** Lt. (later Maj. Gen.) Harold Harris bailed out of a crippled plane he was testing at McCook Field, Dayton, Ohio (Oct. 20), and became the first man to join the Caterpillar Club—those whose lives have been saved by parachute.

**1923 First nonstop transcontinental flight.** Lts. John A. Macready and Oakley Kelly flew a single-engine Fokker T-2 nonstop from New York to San Diego, a distance of just over 2,500 mi. in 26 h 50 min (May 2–3).

**First autogyro flight.** Juan de la Cierva, a brilliant Spanish mathematician, made the first successful flight in a rotary wing aircraft in Madrid (June 9).

**1924 First round-the-world flight.** Four Douglas Cruiser biplanes of the U.S. Army Air Corps took off from Seattle under command of Maj. Frederick Martin (April 6). 175 days later, two of the planes (Lt. Lowell Smith's and Lt. Erik Nelson's) landed in Seattle after a circuitous route—one source saying 26,345 mi., another saying 27,553 mi.

**1926 First polar flight.** Then-Lt. Cmdr. Richard E. Byrd, acting as navigator, and Floyd Bennett as pilot, flew a trimotor Fokker from Kings Bay, Spitsbergen, over the North Pole and back in 15 1/2 h (May 8–9).

**1927 First solo transatlantic flight.** Charles Augustus Lindbergh lifted his Wright-powered Ryan monoplane, *Spirit of St. Louis*, from Roosevelt Field, L.I., to stay aloft 33 h 39 min and travel 3,600 mi. to Le Bourget Field outside Paris (May 20–21).

**First transatlantic passenger.** Charles A. Levine was piloted by Clarence D. Chamberlin from Roosevelt Field, L.I., to Eisleben, Germany, in a Wright-powered Bellanca (June 4–5).

**1928 First east-west transatlantic crossing.** Baron Guenther von Huenefeld, piloted by German Capt. Hermann Koehl and Irish Capt. James Fitzmaurice, left Dublin for New York City (April 12) in a single-engine all-metal Junkers monoplane. Some 37 h later, they crashed on Greely Island, Labrador. Rescued.

**First U.S.-Australia flight.** Sir Charles Kingsford-Smith and Capt. Charles T. P. Ulm, Australians, and two American navigators, Harry W. Lyon and James Warner, crossed the Pacific from Oakland to Brisbane. They went via Hawaii and the Fiji Islands in a trimotor Fokker (May 31–June 8).

**First transarctic flight.** Sir Hubert Wilkins, an Australian explorer and Carl Ben Eielson, who served as pilot, flew from Point Barrow, Alaska, to Spitsbergen (mid-April).

**1929 First of the endurance records.** With Air Corps Maj. Carl Spaatz in command and Capt. Ira Eaker as chief pilot, an Army Fokker, aided by refueling in the air, remained aloft 150 h 40 min at Los Angeles (Jan. 1–7).

**First blind flight.** James H. Doolittle proved the feasibility of instrument-guided flying when he took off and landed entirely on instruments (Sept. 24).

**First rocket-engine flight.** Fritz von Opel, a German auto maker, stayed aloft in his small rocket-powered craft for 75 sec, covering nearly 2 mi. (Sept. 30).

**First South Pole flight.** Comdr. Richard E. Byrd, with Bernt Balchen as pilot, Harold I. June, radio operator, and Capt. A. C. McKinley, photographer, flew a trimotor Fokker from the Bay of Whales, Little America, over the South Pole and back (Nov. 28–29).

**1930 First Paris–New York nonstop flight.** Dieudonné Coste and Maurice Bellonte, French pilots, flew a Hispano-powered Breguet biplane from Le Bourget Field to Valley Stream, L.I., in 37 h 18 min. (Sept. 2–3).

**1931 First flight into the stratosphere.** Auguste Piccard, a Swiss physicist, and Charles Knipfer, ascended in a balloon from Augsburg, Germany, and reached a height of 51,793 ft in a 17-h flight that terminated on a glacier near Innsbruck, Austria (May 27).

**First nonstop transpacific flight.** Hugh Herndon and Clyde Pangborn took off from Sabishiro Beach, Japan, dropped their landing gear, and flew 4,860 mi. to near Wenatchee, Wash., in 41 h 13 min. (Oct. 4–5).

**1932** **First woman's transatlantic solo.** Amelia Earhart, flying a Pratt & Whitney Wasp-powered Lockheed Vega, flew alone from Harbor Grace, Newfoundland, to Ireland in approximately 15 h (May 20–21).

**First westbound transatlantic solo.** James A. Mollison, a British pilot, took a de Havilland Puss Moth from Portmarnock, Ireland, to Pennfield, N.B. (Aug. 18).

**First woman airline pilot.** Ruth Rowland Nichols, first woman to hold three international records at the same time—speed, distance, altitude—was employed by N.Y.-New England Airways.

**1933** **First round-the-world solo.** Wiley Post took a Lockheed Vega, *Winnie Mae*, 15,596 mi. around the world in 7 d 18 h 49 1/2 min (July 15–22).

**1937** **First successful helicopter.** Hanna Reitsch, a German pilot, flew Dr. Heinrich Focke's FW-61 in free, fully controlled flight at Bremen (July 4).

**1939** **First turbojet flight.** Just before their invasion of Poland, the Germans flew a Heinkel He-178 plane powered by a Heinkel S3B turbojet (Aug. 27).

**1942** **First American jet plane flight.** Robert Stanley, chief pilot for Bell Aircraft Corp., flew the Bell XP-59 *Airacomet* at Muroc Army Base, Calif. (Oct. 1).

**1947** **First piloted supersonic flight in an airplane.** Capt. Charles E. Yeager, U.S. Air Force, flew the X-1 rocket-powered research plane built by Bell Aircraft Corp., faster than the speed of sound at Muroc Air Force Base, California (Oct. 14).

**1949** **First round-the-world nonstop flight.** Capt. James Gallagher and USAF crew of 13 flew a Boeing B-50A Superfortress around the world nonstop from Ft. Worth, returning to same point: 23,452 mi. in 94 h 1 min, with 4 aerial refuelings enroute (Feb. 27–March 2).

**1950** **First nonstop transatlantic jet flight.** Col. David C. Schilling (USAF) flew 3,300 mi. from England to Limestone, Maine, in 10 h 1 min (Sept. 22).

**1951** **First solo across North Pole.** Charles F. Blair, Jr., flew a converted P-51 (May 29).

**1952** **First jetliner service.** De Havilland Comet flight inaugurated by BOAC between London and Johannesburg, South Africa (May 2). Flight, including stops, took 23 h 38 min.

**First transatlantic helicopter flight.** Capt. Vincent H. McGovern and 1st Lt. Harold W. Moore piloted 2 Sikorsky H-19s from Westover, Mass., to Prestwick, Scotland (3,410 mi.). Trip was made in 5 steps, with flying time of 42 h 25 min (July 15–31).

**First transatlantic round trip in same day.** British Canberra twin-jet bomber flew from Aldergrove, Northern Ireland, to Gander, Newfoundland, and back in 7 h 59 min flying time (Aug. 26).

**1955** **First transcontinental round trip in same day.** Lt. John M. Conroy piloted F-86 Sabrejet across U.S. (Los Angeles–New York) and back—5,085 mi.—in 11 h 33 min 27 sec (May 21).

**1957** **First round-the-world, nonstop jet plane flight.** Maj. Gen. Archie J. Old, Jr., USAF, led a flight of 3 Boeing B-52 bombers, powered with 8 10,000-lb. thrust Pratt & Whitney Aircraft J57 engines around the world in 45 h 19 min; distance 24,325 mi.; average speed 525 mph. (Completed Jan. 18.)

**1958** **First transatlantic jet passenger service.** BOAC, New York to London (Oct. 4). Pan American started daily service, N.Y. to Paris (Oct. 26).

**First domestic jet passenger service.** National Airlines inaugurated service between New York and Miami (Dec. 10).

**1976** **First regularly-scheduled commercial supersonic transport (SST) flights begin.** Air France and British Airways inaugurate service (January 21). Air France flies the Paris-Rio de Janeiro route; B.A., the London-Bahrain. Both airlines begin SST service to Washington, D.C. (May 24).

**1977** **First successful man-powered aircraft.** Paul MacCready, an aeronautical engineer from Pasadena, Calif., was awarded the Kremer Prize for creating the world's first successful man-powered aircraft. The *Gossamer Condor* was flown by Bryan Allen over the required 3-mile course on Aug. 23.

**1978** **First successful transatlantic balloon flight.** Three Albuquerque, N.M., men, Ben Abruzzo, Larry Newman, and Maxie Anderson, completed the crossing (Aug. 16. Landed, Aug. 17) in their hot air balloon, *Double Eagle II*.

**1979** **First man-powered aircraft to fly across the English Channel.** The Kremer Prize for the Channel crossing was won by Bryan Allen who flew the *Gossamer Albatross* from Folkestone, England to Cap Gris-Nez, France, in 2 h 55 min (June 12).

**1980** **First successful balloon flight over the North Pole.** Sidney Conn and his wife Eleanor, in hot-air balloon *Joy of Sound* (April 11).

**First nonstop transcontinental balloon flight,** and also record for longest overland voyage in a balloon. Maxie Anderson and his son, Kris, completed four-day flight from Fort Baker, Calif., to successful landing outside Matane, Quebec, on May 12 in their helium-filled balloon, *Kitty Hawk*.

**First long-distance solar-powered flight.** Janice Brown, 98-lb former teacher, flew tiny experimental solar-powered aircraft, *Solar Challenger* six miles in 22-min near Marana, Ariz. (Dec. 3). The craft was powered by a 2.75-hp engine.

**First solar-powered aircraft to fly across the English Channel.** Stephen R. Ptacek flew the 210-lb *Solar Challenger* at the average speed of 30 mph from Cormeilles-en-Vexin near Paris to the Royal Manston Air Force Base on England's southeastern coast in 5 h 30 min (July 7).

**1984** **First solo transatlantic balloon flight.** Joe W. Kittinger landed Sept. 18 near Savona, Italy, in his helium-filled balloon *Rosie O'Grady's Balloon of Peace* after a flight of 3,535 miles from Caribou, Me.

# Official World Airplane Records

*Source:* National Aeronautic Association.

## Speed Over Measured Straightaway Course

| Speed (mph) | Date | Type plane | Pilot | Place |
|---|---|---|---|---|
| 314.32 | Dec. 25, 1934 | Caudron | Raymond Delmotte (France) | Istres, France |
| 352.39 | Sept. 13, 1935 | Hughes Special | Howard Hughes (U.S.) | Santa Ana, Calif. |
| 379.63 | Nov. 11, 1937 | BF-113R | Herman Wurster (Germany) | Augsburg, Germany |
| 469.22 | April 26, 1939 | ME-109R | Fritz Wendel (Germany) | Augsburg, Germany |
| 606.25 | Nov. 7, 1945 | Gloster Meteor IV | Group Capt. H. Wilson (U.K.) | Herne Bay, England |
| 615.78 | Sept. 7, 1946 | Gloster Meteor | Group Capt. E. M. Donalson (U.K.) | Littlehampton, England |
| 650.80 | Aug. 25, 1947 | Douglas D-558 | Maj. Marion Carl, (USMC) | Muroc AFB, Calif. |
| 670.98 | Sept. 15, 1948 | North American F-86A | Maj. R. L. Johnson (USAF) | Muroc AFB, Calif. |
| 698.51 | Nov. 19, 1952 | North American F-86D | Capt. James S. Nash (USAF) | Salton Sea, Calif. |
| 755.14 | Oct. 29, 1953 | North American YF | Lt. Col. F. K. Everest, Jr. (USAF) | Salton Sea, Calif. |
| 822.27 | Aug. 20, 1955 | North American F-100C | Col. Horace A. Hanes (U.S.) | Palmdale, Calif. |
| 1,132.14 | March 10, 1956 | Fairey Delta 2 | L. Peter Twiss, D.S.C. (U.K.) | Ford-Chichester, England |
| 1,207.60 | Dec. 12, 1957 | McDonnell F-101A | Maj. Adrian E. Drew (USAF) | Edwards AFB, Calif. |
| 1,404.09 | May 16, 1958 | Lockheed F104 | Capt. Walter W. Irwin (USAF) | Edwards AFB, Calif. |
| 1,483.85 | Oct. 31, 1959 | Sukhoi S-66 | G. Mossolov (U.S.S.R.) | U.S.S.R. |
| 1,525.96 | Dec. 15, 1959 | F-106A Delta Wing Monoplane | Maj. Joseph W. Rogers (USAF) | Edwards AFB, Calif. |
| 1,606.32 | Nov. 22, 1961 | McDonnell F4H | Lt. Col. R. B. Robinson (USMC) | Edwards AFB, Calif. |
| 1,665.89 | July 7, 1962 | E-166 Jet | G. Mossolov (U.S.S.R.) | U.S.S.R. |
| 2,070.101 | May 1, 1965 | Lockheed YF-12A Jet | Col. R. L. Stephens (USAF) | Edwards AFB, Calif. |
| 2,193.16 | July 28, 1976 | Lockheed SR-71A | Capt. Eldon W. Joersz (USAF) | Beale AFB, Calif. |

Fastest U.S. continental: Capt. Robert G. Sowers (USAF)—Convair B-58 "Hustler"—from Los Angeles, Calif., to Kennedy International Airport, N.Y.—2,458.58 statute miles—2 h 0 min 58.71 sec—average speed, 1,214.65 mph—March 5, 1962.

## Speed Over A Closed Circuit

| Speed (mph) | Date | Type plane | Pilot | Place |
|---|---|---|---|---|
| 2,092 | July 27,1976 | Lockheed SR-71A | Maj. Adolphus H. Bledsoe, Jr. (USAF) | Beale, AFB, Calif. |

## Distance, Straight Line

| Distance (mi.) | Date | Crew | From | To |
|---|---|---|---|---|
| 4,911.93 | Sept. 27–29, 1929 | Costes & Bellonte (France) | Le Bourget, France | Manchuria |
| 5,011.35 | July 28–30, 1931 | Russel N. Boardman, John Polando (U.S.) | New York | Istanbul |
| 5,656.93 | Aug. 5–7, 1933 | Maurice Rossi, Paul Codos (France) | New York | Ryack, Syria |
| 6,305.66 | July 12–14, 1937 | Gromov, Youmachev, Daniline (U.S.S.R.) | Moscow | San Jacinto, Calif. |
| 7,158.44 | Nov. 5-7, 1938 | Sqd. Ldr. R. Kellett (U.K.) | Ismailia, Egypt | Darwin, Australia |
| 7,916.00 | Nov. 19–20, 1945 | Col. C. S. Irvine & Lt. Col. G. R. Stanley (U.S.) | Guam | Washington, D.C. |
| 11,235.60 | Sept. 29–Oct. 1, 1946 | Comdr. Thomas D. Davies, Comdrs. Eugene P. Rankin, Walter S. Reid, Lt. Comdr. Ray A. Tabeling (USN) | Perth, Australia | Columbus, Ohio |
| 12,532.28 | Jan. 11, 1962 | Maj. Clyde P. Evely (USAF) | Kadena, Okinawa | Madrid |

Longest light airplane (3,858–6,614 lb) distance: Maximillian A. Conrad—U.S. Piper Comanche 250, Lycoming 0-540-AIAS (250 hp), from Casablanca, Morocco, to Los Angeles, 7,668.48 mi.—June 2-4, 1959.

## Distance, Closed Circuit

| Distance (mi.) | Date | Crew | Place |
|---|---|---|---|
| 6,587.441 | March 23–26, 1932 | Bossoutrot & Rossi (France) | Oran |
| 7,239.588 | May 13–15, 1938 | Comdr. Fujita & Sgt. Maj. Takahashi (Japan) | Kisarasu, Japan |
| 8,037.899 | July 30–Aug. 1, 1939 | Angelo Tondi, Roberto Dagasso, Ferrucio Vignoli (Italy) | Rome |
| 8,854.308 | Aug. 1-2, 1947 | Lt. Col. O. F. Lassiter (U.S.) Capt. W. J. Valentine (U.S.) | Tampa, Fla. |
| 10,078.84 | Dec. 13–14, 1960 | Lt. Col. J. R. Grissom (USAF) | Edwards AFB, Calif. |
| 11,336.92 | June 6–7, 1962 | Capt. William Stevenson (USAF) | Seymour-Johnson, N.C. |
| 11,593.68 | July 10–15, 1986 | Dick Rutan & Jeanna Yeager (U.S.), (Unofficial World record) | California |

## Altitude

| Height (ft) | Date | Crew | Place |
|---|---|---|---|
| 44,819 | Sept. 28, 1933 | G. Lemoine (France) | Villacoublay, France |
| 47,352 | April 11, 1934 | Comdr. Renato Donati (Italy) | Rome |
| 49,944 | Sept. 28, 1936 | Sqd. Ldr. F. R. D. Swain (U.K.) | South Farnborough, England |
| 53,937 | June 30, 1937 | Fl. Lt. M. J. Adam (U.K.) | Farnborough, England |

| Altitude Height (ft) | Date | Crew | Place |
|---|---|---|---|
| 56,046 | Oct. 22, 1938 | Col. Mario Pezzi (Italy) | Montecelio |
| 59,445 [1] | March 23, 1948 | John Cunningham (U.K.) | Hatfield, England |
| 63,668 [1] | May 4, 1953 | Walter F. Gibb (U.K.) | Bristol, England |
| 65,889 [1] | Aug. 29, 1955 | Walter F. Gibb (U.K.) | Bristol, England |
| 70,308 [1] | Aug. 28, 1957 | Michael Randrup (U.K.) | Luton, England |
| 91,243 [1] | May 7, 1958 | Maj. H. C. Johnson (USAF) | Palmdale, Calif. |
| 103,389 [1] | Nov. 14, 1959 | Capt. Joe B. Jordan (USAF) | Edwards AFB, Calif. |
| 314,750 [2] | July 17, 1962 | Maj. Robert M. White (USAF) | Edwards AFB, Calif. |
| 118,898 | July 25, 1973 | Alexander Fedotov (U.S.S.R.) | U.S.S.R. |
| 85,069 [3] | July 28, 1976 | Capt. Robert C. Helt (USAF) | Beale, AFB, Calif. |
| 123,524 | Aug. 31, 1977 | Alexander Fedotov (U.S.S.R.) | U.S.S.R. |

1. Jet-propelled aircraft. 2. X-15-1-rocket plane. 3. In horizontal flight.

## World's 50 Busiest Airports in 1986

| Airport | Passengers[1] | Airport | Passengers[1] |
|---|---|---|---|
| 1. O'Hare International: Chicago | 49,954,362 | 26. International: Mexico City | 12,088,000 |
| 2. Hartsfield Atlanta International: Atlanta | 42,494,630 | 27. Sky Harbor Airport: Phoenix | 11,596,220 |
| 3. International: Los Angeles | 37,647,983 | 28. Tacoma International: Seattle | 11,466,755 |
| 4. International: Dallas/Ft. Worth | 37,104,026 | 29. Amsterdam Airport Schiphol | 11,385,454 |
| 5. Heathrow Airport: London | 31,289,254 | 30. International: Philadelphia | 11,369,864 |
| 6. Kennedy International: New York | 28,945,228 | 31. International: Minneapolis-St. Paul | 10,943,547 |
| 7. International: Newark | 28,576,586 | 32. McCarran International: Las Vegas | 10,797,722 |
| 8. Stapleton International: Denver | 28,485,927 | 33. Madrid/Barajas Airport: Madrid | 10,647,565 |
| 9. Tokyo International (Haneda): Japan | 27,167,402 | 34. Charlotte/Douglas International | 10,531,524 |
| 10. International: San Francisco | 25,018,395 | 35. International: Orlando | 10,034,065 |
| 11. La Guardia: New York | 20,542,452 | 36. Kingsford Smith Airport: Australia | 9,200,122 |
| 12. International: Boston-Logan | 20,448,424 | 37. Zurich Airport | 9,102,128 |
| 13. International: Lambert-St. Louis | 19,942,401 | 38. Stockholm-Arlanda Airport | 9,088,292 |
| 14. International: Miami | 19,853,352 | 39. International: Salt Lake City | 8,987,235 |
| 15. Frankfurt/Main: West Germany | 19,518,670 | 40. International: Tampa | 8,873,532 |
| 16. Orly Airport: Paris | 17,671,065 | 41. Changi Airport: Singapore | 8,691,709 |
| 17. Osaka International: Japan | 17,452,334 | 42. International: San Diego | 7,937,806 |
| 18. International: Honolulu | 16,638,703 | 43. Dusseldorf Airport | 7,930,482 |
| 19. International: Toronto | 15,800,000 | 44. King Abdulaziz International: Saudi Arabia | 7,867,003 |
| 20. Detroit: (Wayne County) | 15,603,601 | 45. Munich-Riem Airport | 7,650,016 |
| 21. International: Pittsburgh | 15,058,178 | 46. Wm. P. Hobby: Houston | 7,587,845 |
| 22. Gatwick Airport: London | 14,882,674 | 47. International: Kansas City | 7,267,025 |
| 23. Charles De Gaulle: Paris | 14,642,278 | 48. Bombay Airport | 7,205,437 |
| 24. National Airport: Washington, D.C. | 14,441,172 | 49. Memphis International Airport | 7,203,887 |
| 25. Intercontinental: Houston | 14,208,443 | 50. Fort Lauderdale-Hollywood Airport | 6,752,966 |

1. Enplaned, deplaned, and transfer, in millions. *Source:* Airport Operators Council International.

## U.S. Airlines Transport Planes, 1986

| Manufacturer | Type/Series | Number of passengers | Cruise speed | Range | Wingspan, ft | Length, ft |
|---|---|---|---|---|---|---|
| **4-ENGINE JET** | | | | | | |
| Boeing | 707-120B | 100–181 | 615 | 6,325 | 142.4 | 145.1 |
| Boeing | 707-320B | 145 | 615 | 5,750 | 145.8 | 152.9 |
| Boeing | 747-SP | 331 | 564 | 6,730 | 195.7 | 184.8 |
| Boeing | 747 PAX | 452 | 557 | 6,500 | 195.7 | 231.9 |
| Boeing | 747 PAX/FRT | 238 | 600 | 5,500 | 195.7 | 231.9 |
| British Aerospace | 146-100 | 88 | 460 | 1,450 | 86.4 | 85.9 |
| British Aerospace | 146-200 | 100 | 460 | 1,450 | 86.4 | 93.8 |
| McDonnell Douglas | DC8-30,-40,-50 | 116/176 | 544 | 7,010 | 142.2 | 150.3 |
| McDonnell Douglas | DC8-60,-70 | 259 | 580 | 7,150 | 142.2 | 187.4 |
| McDonnell Douglas | DC8 PAX/FRT | 180/259 | 600 | 3,700 | 142.2 | 187.4 |
| | | | | | | |
| **4-ENGINE TURBOPROP** | | | | | | |
| DeHavilland | DHC7 | 50 | 275 | 850 | 93.0 | 80.0 |
| Lockheed | L188 | 66/104 | 405 | 2,750 | 99.0 | 104.5 |
| Lockheed | L382 | Cargo | 380 | 2,750 | 99.0 | 104.5 |

| Manufacturer | Type/Series | Number of passengers | Cruise speed | Range | Wingspan, ft | Length, ft |
|---|---|---|---|---|---|---|
| **4-ENGINE PISTON** | | | | | | |
| DeHavilland | Heron | 14/17 | 195 | 750 | 71.5 | 46.5 |
| Douglas | DC6 | 90/100 | 300 | 3,070 | 117.5 | 106.5 |
| Douglas | DC4 | 44/60 | 230 | 2,750 | 117.6 | 94.0 |
| **3-ENGINE JET** | | | | | | |
| Boeing | 727 All Series | 70/131 | 622 | 3,000 | 108.0 | 133.1 |
| Boeing | 727 PAX/FRT | 96 | 600 | 3,000 | 108.0 | 133.1 |
| Boeing | 727-200 | 145 | 622 | 2,400 | 108.0 | 153.1 |
| Boeing | 727F | Cargo | 620 | 1,400 | 108.0 | 153.1 |
| Lockheed | L1011 | 250/400 | 615 | 3,450 | 155.2 | 177.5 |
| Lockheed | L1011 | 266/330 | 580 | 5,998 | 155.2 | 164.2 |
| McDonnell Douglas | DC10-10 | 250/380 | 608 | 6,350 | 155.2 | 182.2 |
| McDonnell Douglas | DC10-30 | 250/380 | 615 | 6,350 | 165.3 | 181.6 |
| McDonnell Douglas | DC10-40 | 250/350 | 615 | 6,350 | 165.3 | 182.3 |
| **2-ENGINE JET** | | | | | | |
| Airbus Industries | A300/310 | 220-345 | 460 | 2000 | 147.1 | 175.9 |
| Boeing | 737-100 | 105 | 577 | 1,300 | 93.0 | 94.0 |
| Boeing | 737-200 | 115/130 | 573 | 1,800 | 92.0 | 100.1 |
| Boeing | 737-200 | 115/130 | 577 | 2,300 | 93.0 | 100.1 |
| Boeing | 737-300 | 149 | 577 | 2,300 | 93.0 | 100.1 |
| Boeing | 757 | 178/224 | 494 | 2,440 | 124.5 | 155.2 |
| Boeing | 767 | 211/290 | 550 | 3,200 | 156.1 | 159.1 |
| Fokker | F28 | 85 | 523 | 1,055 | 82.2 | 96.2 |
| Gulfstream American | 1159 | 19 | 445 | 4,060 | 77.10 | 83.1 |
| British Aerospace | BAC111 | 74/79 | 550 | 1,430 | 88.5 | 93.5 |
| McDonnell Douglas | DC9-10,-20 | 90 | 593 | 2,200 | 93.2 | 104.4 |
| McDonnell Douglas | DC9-30,-40 | 125 | 593 | 2,700 | 93.2 | 125.5 |
| McDonnell Douglas | DC9-30/40 | 139 | 593 | 2,550 | 93.2 | 133.2 |
| McDonnell Douglas | DC9-80 | 137/172 | 576 | 3,060 | 107.9 | 147.9 |
| Marcel Dassault | Falcon-10 | 4–7 | 600 | 2,000 | 42.9 | 45.5 |
| Marcel Dassault | Falcon-20 | 12–14 | 600 | 3,300 | 53.5 | 56.3 |
| Marcel Dassault | Falcon-50 | 12 | 418 | 3,640 | 61.10 | 60.5 |
| **2-ENGINE TURBOPROP** | | | | | | |
| Beechcraft | B-99 | 15 | 280 | 1,150 | 45.8 | 44.5 |
| Beech | 1900 | 19 | 256 | 791 | 54.5 | 57.8 |
| British Aerospace | Jetstream | 14/18 | 250 | 1,440 | 52.0 | 47.0 |
| British Aerospace | 748 | 48 | 244 | 2,760 | 98.5 | 67.0 |
| CASA | C-212 | 22/28 | 230 | 1,400 | 62.5 | 45.9 |
| Convair | CV-580 | 50 | 350 | 1,100 | 105.2 | 79.1 |
| DeHavilland | DHC-6 | 20 | 209 | 745 | 65.0 | 51.8 |
| DeHavilland | DHC-8 | 35-40 | 230 | 1420 | 85. | 73. |
| Embraer | EMB110 | 19 | 212 | 900 | 50.1 | 49.1 |
| Fairchild | F-27 | 40/56 | 265 | 1,450 | 95.1 | 82.1 |
| Fairchild Hiller | FH-227 | 44/52 | 294 | 1,520 | 95.1 | 83.1 |
| Fokker | FK F27 | 40/56 | 265 | 1,450 | 95.1 | 82.1 |
| Fairchild Swrngn | SA226 | 19 | 294 | 2,139 | 46.2 | 59.2 |
| Fairchild Swrngn | SA227 | 21 | 302 | 2,139 | 46.2 | 59.2 |
| Gulfstream Aerospace | GAG159 | 18/37 | 345 | 2,300 | 78.3 | 75.3 |
| Nihon | YS-11 | 60 | 292 | 1,980 | 105.0 | 86.2 |
| Nord | ND262 | 27 | 240 | 500 | 71.9 | 63.2 |
| Nord | ND STC 262 | 25 | 240 | 500 | 74.1 | 63.2 |
| SAAB/Fairchild | SF340A | 36/39 | 260 | 2400 | 147 | 175 |
| Short Bro-Harland | SH SD3 | 30 | 218 | 1,137 | 94.7 | 58.0 |
| **3-ENGINE PISTON** | | | | | | |
| Britten-Norman | MK3 | 18 | 154 | 820 | 53.0 | 48.2 |
| **2-ENGINE PISTON** | | | | | | |
| Beechcraft | BE18 | 7–9 | 236 | 1,515 | 49.7 | 35.2 |
| Beechcraft | B-58 | 4–6 | 195 | 1150 | 37.8 | 29.8 |
| Britten-Norman | BN2 | 10 | 180 | 425 | 49.0 | 35.7 |
| Cessna | 310 | 4–6 | 210 | 600 | 32.0 | 37.0 |
| Cessna | 402 | 6–10 | 239 | 550 | 36.0 | 40.0 |
| Cessna | 404 | 6–11 | 200 | 1,500 | 40.0 | 46.3 |
| Convair | 440 | 50 | 270 | 1,100 | 105.3 | 79.1 |
| Curtis Wright | CW46 | | | | | |
| Douglas | DC3 | 21 | 207 | 1,330 | 95.0 | 64.5 |

| Manufacturer | Type/Series | Number of passengers | Cruise speed | Range | Wingspan, ft | Length, ft |
|---|---|---|---|---|---|---|
| Grumman | G21 | 10 | 160 | 825 | 49.0 | 38.2 |
| Grumman | G73 | 10 | 180 | 1,245 | 66.6 | 48.2 |
| Piper | PA23 | 6 | 206 | 1,519 | 37.2 | 31.1 |
| Piper | PA31 | 6 | 210 | 925 | 40.8 | 34.5 |
| Piper | PA34 | 6 | 220 | 1,036 | 39.0 | 28.5 |
| Piper | PA44 | 4 | 190 | 1,000 | 38.5 | 27.5 |

NOTE: Aircraft performance statistics represented here are to be considered only as "typical" of an aircraft type. Due to the various series (models) of individual aircraft types and the engine options available, it is not feasible to show all the various combinations of performance statistics. Data show the most used manufacturers type and model aircraft used by air carriers and commercial operators as of April 1985. *Source:* Federal Aviation Administration.

## Important American Aircraft Types (U.S. Air Force)

Abbreviations: GA—Garrett AiResearch; All—Detroit Diesel Allison Div. of General Motors; Con—Continental; GD—General Dynamics; GE—General Electric; Lyc—Lycoming; RI—Rockwell International; P&W—Pratt & Whitney; PWC—Pratt & Whitney Aircraft of Canada, Ltd; Wr—Curtiss Wright; kt—knots.

| Type | Manufacturer | Popular name | Power plant | Crew | Wingspan, ft/in. | Length, ft/in. | Height, ft/in. | Gross weight, lb | Speed, mph |
|---|---|---|---|---|---|---|---|---|---|
| **ATTACK** | | | | | | | | | |
| A-7D/K | LTV Corp. | Corsair II | 1 All TF41-A-1 | 1 | 38/9 | 46/1 | 16/0 | 42,000 | 698 |
| A-10A | Fairchild | Thunderbolt II | 2 GE TF34-GE-100 | 1 | 57/5 | 53/4 | 14/8 | 50,000 | 439 |
| A-37B | Cessna | Dragonfly | 2 GE J85-GE-17A | 1 | 35/8 | 29/3 | 8/9 | 14,000 | 507 |
| **BOMBERS** | | | | | | | | | |
| B-52G | Boeing | Stratofortress | 8 P&W J57-P-43W | 6 | 185/0 | 160/11 | 40/8 | 488,000 | 595 |
| B-52H | Boeing | Stratofortress | 8 P&W TF33-P-3 | 6 | 185/0 | — | 40/8 | 488,000 | 595 |
| FB-111A | GD/Ft. Worth | — | 2 P&W TF30-P-7 | 2 | 70/0[3] | 73/6 | 17/1 | 100,000 | Mach 2+ |
| B-1B | RI/N.Amer./Boeing Mil Airplane/GE Eaton Ail Div. | — | 4GE F101-GE 102 | 4-6 | 136[5] | 147/0 | 34/0 | 477,000 | —[6] |
| **FIGHTERS** | | | | | | | | | |
| F-4D/E | McDonnell Douglas | Phantom II | 2 GEJ79-GE-17A | 2 | 38/7 | 63/0 | 16/5 | 61,795 | Mach 2.0 |
| F-15A/B/C/D | McDonnell Douglas | Eagle | 2 P&W F100-PW-100 | 1/2 | 42/10 | 63/9 | 18/6 | 68,000 | Mach 2.5 |
| F-5E/F | Northrop | Tiger II | 2 J85-GE-21B | 1/2 | 26.8 | 47/2 | 13/2 | 24,722 | Mach 1.6 |
| F-16A/B/C/D | GD | Fighting Falcon | 1 P&W F100-PW-200 /GE F-110-GE-100 | 1 | 32.10 | 49.6 | 16/8 | 35,400 | Mach 2 |
| F-106A | GD/Convair | Delta Dart | 1 P&W J75-P-17 | 1/2 | 38/3 | 70/8 | 20/3 | 42,000 | Mach 2.0 |
| F-111 | GD | — | 2 P&W TF30-P-3/100(F) | 2 | 63/0[4] | 73/6 | 17/1 | 100,000 | Mach 2.5 |
| **RECONNAISSANCE** | | | | | | | | | |
| RF-4C | McDonnell Douglas | Phantom II | 2 GE J79-GE-17 | 2 | 38/7 | 63/0 | 16/5 | 61,795 | Mach 2.0 |
| SR-71 | Lockheed | Blackbird | 2 P&W T11D-20B | 2 | 55/7 | 107/5 | 18/6 | 170,000 | Mach 3+ |
| U-2/TR-1 | Lockheed | — | 1 P &W J75-P-13B | 1 | 103/0 | 63/0 | 16/0 | 40,000 | 430 + |
| **OBSERVATION** | | | | | | | | | |
| 0-2A | Cessna | Skymaster | 2 Con 10-360-C/D | 2 | 38/2 | 29/9 | 9/2 | 5,400 | 199 |
| OV-10A[1] | RI | Bronco | 2 T76-G-416/417 | 2 | 40/0 | 41/7 | 15/2 | 14,444 | 281 |
| OA-37B | Cessna | Dragonfly | 2GE J85-GE-17A | 2 | 35/11 | 28/3 | 8/11 | 14,000 | 507 |
| **EARLY WARNING COMMAND, CONTROL AND COMMUNICATIONS** | | | | | | | | | |
| E-3A | Boeing | Sentry (AWACS) | 4 P&W TF33-P-100/A | 20 | 145/9 | 152/11 | 41.9 | 325,000 | 530 |
| E-4A/B | Boeing | — | 4 GE CF6-50E2 | 5 | 195/7 | 231/4 | 63/5 | 800,000 | — |
| **CARGO/TRANSPORT** | | | | | | | | | |
| C-5A | Lockheed/Georgia | Galaxy | 4 GE TF39-GE-1C | 5 | 222/8 | 247/8 | 65/0 | 769,000 | 571 |
| C-9A | McDonnell Douglas | Nightingale | 2 P&W JT8D-9 | 3-8 | 93/5 | 119/3 | 27/6 | 108,000 | 565 |
| C-12A[2] | Beech | — | 2 PWC PT6A-38 | 2 | 54/6 | 43/9 | 15 | 12,500 | 299 kt |
| C-130E/H | Lockheed/Georgia | Hercules | 4 All T56-A-7/-15(H) | 5 | 132/7 | 97/9 | 38/3 | 175,000 | 374 |
| C-140A | Lockheed/Georgia | Jetstar | 4 P&W J60-P-5A | 5 | 54/5 | 60/5 | 20/5 | 40,920 | 550 |
| C-141A | Lockheed/Georgia | Starlifter | 4 P&W TF33-P-7 | 5 | 159/11 | 168/3 | 39/3 | 343,000 | 566 |
| KC-10A | McDonnell Douglas | Extender | 3 GE CF6-50C2 | 4 | 164.4 | 181/7 | 58.1 | 590,000 | 528 |
| KC-135A | Boeing | Stratotanker | 4 P&W J57-P-59W | 4-5 | 130/10 | 136/3 | 38/4 | 297,000 | 585 |
| C-137C[7] | Boeing | — | 4 P&W JT3D-3 | 4 | 145/9 | 152/11 | 42/5 | 322,000 | 627 |

| Type | Manufacturer | Popular name | Power plant | Crew | Wing-span, ft/in. | Length, ft/in. | Height, ft/in. | Gross weight, lb | Speed, mph |
|---|---|---|---|---|---|---|---|---|---|
| **TRAINERS** | | | | | | | | | |
| CT-39 | RI/General Aviation | Sabreliner | 2 P&W J60-P-3 | 2 | 44/5 | 43/9 | 16/0 | 17,700 | 595 |
| T-33A | Lockheed | Shooting Star | 1 All J33-A-35 | 2 | 38/10 | 37/9 | 11/4 | 15,100 | 543 |
| T-37B | Cessna | Tweet | 2 CON J69-T-25 | 2 | 33/9 | 29/3 | 9/2 | 6,600 | 425 |
| T-38A | Northrop | Talon | 2 GE J85GE5 | 2 | 25/3 | 46/4 | 12/10 | 12,093 | Mach 1.2 |
| T-41C | Cessna | Mescalero | 1 CON 10-360-D | 2 | 35/10 | 26/11 | 8/9 | 2,300 | 139 |
| T-43A | Boeing | — | 2 P&W JT8D-9 | 2 | 93/0 | 100/0 | 37/0 | 115,500 | Mach .7 |

1. Air Force/Marines. 2. Air Force/Army. 3. Wing extended; 34 ft fully swept. 4. Wing extended; 31.11 ft fully swept. 5. Wing extended; 78.2-1/2 ft fully swept. 6. High Subsonic, supersonic at altitude. 7. The President's plane, "Air Force One" is a C-137C. *Source:* Department of the Air Force. NOTE: Aircraft dimensions have been rounded to the nearest inch.

## The First Manned Helicopter Flights

Professor Charles Richet made a successful ascent of about two feet in a tethered aircraft with four biplane rotors at Douai, France, on September 19, 1907. The helicopter, designed by Louis and Jacques Breguet, was named the *Gyroplane*.

Paul Cornu, another French aviator, made a six-foot-high, 20-second free flight in a tandem-rotor helicopter that he built at Lisieux on November 13, 1907.

## Helicopter Records

*Source:* National Aeronautic Association.

**Distance in Straight Line**
International: 2,213.04 mi.; 3,561.55 km.
Robert G. Ferry (U.S.) in Hughes YOH-6A helicopter powered by Allison T-63-A-5 engine; from Culver City, Calif., to Ormond Beach, Fla., April 6–7, 1966.

**Distance, Closed Circuit**
International: 1,739.96 mi.; 2,800.20 km.
Jack Schweibold (U.S.) in Hughes YOH-6A helicopter powered by Allison T-62-A-5 engine; Edwards Air Force Base, Calif., March 26, 1966.

**Altitude**
International: 40,820 ft; 12,442 m.
Jean Boulet (France) in Alouette SA 315-001 "Lama" powered by Artouste IIIB 735 KW engine; Istres, France, June 21, 1972.

**Speed Over a 15/25-Km Course**
International: 228.91 mph; 368.4 kph.
Gourguen Karapetyan (U.S.S.R.) in A-10 helicopter powered by 2 TB-3-117 engines; Podmoskov-noye, U.S.S.R., Sept. 21, 1978.

**Altitude in Horizontal Flight**
International: 36,122 ft; 11,010 m.
CWO James K. Church, (U.S.) in Sikorsky CH-54B helicopter powered by 2 P&W JFTD-12 engines; Stratford, CT., Nov. 4, 1971.

**Speed Over a 3-Km Course**
216,839 mph; 348.971 kph.
Byron Graham (U.S.) at Windsor Locks, CT, Dec. 14, 1970 in Sikorsky S-67 Helicopter powered by 2 GE T-58 turbine engines.

**Speed Around the World**
35.40 mph; 56.97 kph.
H. Ross Perot, Jr., pilot; J.W. Coburn, co-pilot (U.S.) in Bell 206 L-II Long Ranger, powered by one Alli-

son 250-C28B of 435 hp. Elapsed time: 29 days 3 h 8 min 13 sec, Sept. 1–30, 1982.

**Speed for 100 Km (Closed Circuit)**
International: 211.35 mph; 340.15 kph.
Boris Galitsky (U.S.S.R.) in MI-6 helicopter powered by 2 TB-2BM turbine engines; Podmoskovnoye, U.S.S.R., Aug. 26, 1964.

**Speed for 500 Km (Closed Circuit)**
International: 214.84 mph; 345.74 kph.
Thomas Doyle (U.S.) in Sikorsky S-76 helicopter powered by 2 Allison 250-C-30 engines; West Palm Beach, Fla., Feb. 8, 1982.

**Speed for 1,000 Km (Closed Circuit)**
International: 200.48 mph; 322.646 kph.
Galina Rastorgoueva (U.S.S.R.) in A-10 helicopter powered by 2 TV2 117A engines; Aug. 13, 1975.

**Speed for 2,000 Km (Closed Circuit)**
International: 146.09 mph; 235.19 kph.
Inna Kopets (U.S.S.R.) in MI-8 helicopter; Sept. 14, 1967.

## Active Pilot Certificates Held[1]

(as of January 1)

| Year | Total | Airline transport | Commercial | Private |
|---|---|---|---|---|
| 1970 | 720,028 | 31,442 | 176,585 | 299,491 |
| 1975 | 733,728 | 41,002 | 192,425 | 305,848 |
| 1980 | 814,667 | 63,652 | 182,097 | 343,276 |
| 1984 | 718,004 | 75,938 | 159,495 | 318,643 |
| 1985 | 722,376 | 79,192 | 155,929 | 320,086 |
| 1986 | 709,540 | 82,740 | 151,632 | 311,086 |

1. Includes other pilot categories—helicopter, glider and lighter-than-air (17,430), and students (146,652). *Source:* Department of Transportation, Federal Aviation Administration.

## Blue Angels To Fly Hornets

The Navy's famous aerial demonstration team known as The Blue Angels are phasing out their 20-year-old A-4F aircaft with the new McDonnell Douglas F/A-18 Hornet. This change will enable the seven-man flight team and their maintenance personnel to augment combat squadrons in time of war with the new multimission front-line jet aircraft. The first Navy squadron equipped with

F/A-18 Hornets became operational in 1982.

The Blue Angels were organized in 1946. At that time they flew the famous carrier-based propellor-driven F-6F Grumman Hellcat of World War II fame.

The transition to the F/A-18 jet aircraft is scheduled for completion by March 1987, and the first demonstration is scheduled for May 1987.

# SPACE

## Let's Go To Mars

### By Carl Sagan

Mars beckons, a storehouse of scientific information—important in its own right but also for the light it may cast on the environment of our own planet. If Mars once had abundant liquid water, what went wrong? How did an Earthlike world become so parched, frigid, and comparatively airless? Is there something here we should know about our own planet?

We humans have been this way before. Christopher Columbus would have understood the call of Mars. But mere scientific exploration does not require a human presence. We can always send smart robots. They are much cheaper, and you can take more risks with them.

Sending humans to Mars must have more than scientific justification, as with the Apollo program. President John F. Kennedy did not ask to find out the origin of the dark lunar lowlands by the end of the 1960s; he asked for an American to land on the Moon and return safely. It was an American political response to the Bay of Pigs fiasco in Cuba and to the fact that the first person to orbit the Earth was a citizen of the Soviet Union. Kennedy explicitly cast the Apollo program in the context of peaceful competition with the Soviet Union. And, as all the world knows, that race the Americans won.

But imagine a different sort of Apollo program, in which cooperation, not competition, was the objective, because the leaders of the U.S. and the U.S.S.R. had come to their senses. Imagine these leaders deciding to do something not just for their nations but also for their species, something that would capture the imaginations of people everywhere and would lay the groundwork for a major advance in human history—the eventual settlement of another planet.

It can be done. It is technologically feasible. It requires no major "breakthroughs." A project to send people to Mars sounds absurdly expensive. But the advances in technology have been so great that such a mission would cost far less than Star Wars, less than the Apollo program, and not much more than a major strategic weapons system. In a joint mission, the cost to any one nation would be still smaller.

But why a joint mission to Mars? Why not jointly feed the hungry in sub-Saharan Africa, or do water reclamation projects in Bangladesh? The United States and the Soviet Union could, if they chose, together help house, educate, provide medical care for, and make increasingly self-reliant every citizen of the planet. But the U.S. and the U.S.S.R. have no such precedent; they have been obsessed by the pursuit of short-term competitive advantages. The political realities, sadly, are that a joint mission to Mars, like Apollo/Soyuz, is well within the realm of practical possibility, while many worthy and more mundane activities are not. Not yet. But a major cooperative success in space can serve as an inspiration and spearhead for joint enterprises on Earth.

Moreover, space missions have an important subsidiary advantage: They use precisely the same aerospace, electronics, rocket, and even nuclear technologies as does the nuclear arms race. . . . An alternative program using the same industries and some military skills for peaceful purposes might be a very good thing; it is foolish to have powerful vested interests—jobs, careers, profits, dividends—mainly dependent upon a continuing arms race. Expeditions to the planets use the same high technology, and the traditional military virtues of organization and valor, in a humane and benign cause.

With or without the United States, the Soviet Union is going to Mars. Since before Sputnik, the Soviets have declared their long-term intention to go to Mars.

A Soviet manned landing on Mars in the early '90s, say, seems unlikely. It is too soon. But a Soviet mission to carry cosmonauts on a close approach to Mars is much easier and just possibly might be launched by 1992. The date is significant—it is the 75th anniversary of the Russian Revolution.

But 1992 is also the 500th anniversary of Christopher Columbus' discovery of what came, propitiously, to be called the New World. Whatever the original motivations were for the age of exploration that Columbus ushered in, the net result has been, in a painful historical process now nearing completion, the linking of the continents, the unification of the world. What could be more fitting for 1992 than the initiation of an international program for the exploration and eventual settlement of another New World? Perhaps by 1992 the nations would merely begin assembling in low Earth-orbit the components of the spacecraft that will take the first humans to Mars. By 1992, the U.S. Space Station is supposed to be ready.

Decades ago, Mars called to the Soviet spaceflight pioneer Konstantin Tsiolkovsky and to his American counterpart, Robert H. Goddard. The rockets they designed were intended not for the destruction of life on Earth but to take us to the planets and the stars. Is there not some special obligation of the two principal spacefaring nations—the two nations that have burdened our planet with 55,000 nuclear weapons—to put things right, to use this technology for good and not for evil, to blaze, on behalf of every human being, the trail to Mars and beyond?

Dr. Carl Sagan is president of The Planetary Society, a nonprofit organization devoted to planetary exploration and the search for extraterrestrial life.

This article has been excerpted from "Let's Go to Mars" by Carl Sagan, first published in *PARADE*. Copyright © 1986 by Carl Sagan. Reprinted by permission of the author and the author's agents, Scott Meredith Literary Agency, Inc., 845 Third Avenue, New York, New York, 10022.

# Manned Space Flight Projects

**Mercury.** *Project Mercury,* America's first manned space program, was designed to further knowledge about man's capabilities in space. *Mercury 3* put the first American, Alan B. Shepard, into space. *Mercury 9,* with astronaut Gordon L. Cooper, was the longest flight.

**Gemini.** *Gemini* was an extension of *Project Mercury,* to determine the effects of prolonged space flight on man—two weeks or longer. "Walks in space" provided invaluable information for astronauts' later walks on the Moon. The *Gemini* spacecraft, twice as large as the *Mercury* capsule, accommodated two astronauts.

**Apollo.** *Apollo* was the designation for the United States' effort to land a man on the Moon and return him safely to Earth. The goal was successfully accomplished with *Apollo 11* on July 20, 1969, culminating eight years of rehearsal and centuries of dreaming. Astronauts Neil A. Armstrong and Col. Edwin E. Aldrin, Jr., scooped up and brought back the first lunar rocks ever seen on Earth—about 47 pounds. Six *Apollo* flights followed, ending with *Apollo 17* in December, 1972. The last three *Apollos* carried mechanized vehicles called lunar rovers for wide-ranging surface exploration of the Moon by astronauts. The rendezvous and docking of an *Apollo* spacecraft with a Russian *Soyuz* craft in Earth orbit on July 18, 1975, closed out the *Apollo* program.

**Skylab.** America's first Earth-orbiting space station. *Project Skylab* was designed to demonstrate that men can work and live in space for prolonged periods without ill effects. Originally the spent third stage of a Saturn 5 moon rocket, *Skylab* measured 118 feet from stem to stern, and carried the most varied assortment of experimental equipment ever assembled in a single spacecraft. Three three-man crews visited the space stations, spending more than 740 hours observing the Sun and bringing home more than 175,000 solar pictures. These were the first recordings of solar activity above Earth's obscuring atmosphere. *Skylab* also evaluated systems designed to gather information on Earth's resources and environmental conditions. *Skylab* biomedical findings indicated that man adapts well to space for at least a period of three months, provided he has a proper diet and adequately programmed exercise, sleep, work, and recreation periods. *Skylab* orbited Earth at a distance of about 300 miles. Five years after the last *Skylab* mission, the 77-ton space station's orbit began to deteriorate faster than expected, owing to unexpectedly high sunspot activity. On July 11, 1979, the parts of *Skylab* that did not burn up in the atmosphere came crashing down on parts of Australia and the Indian Ocean. No one was hurt.

**Space Shuttle.** The *Space Shuttle* is America's manned space transportation system developed by NASA to reduce the cost of using space for commercial, scientific, and defense needs. The *Shuttle* is a manned rocket which, after depositing its payload in space, can be flown back to Earth like a conventional airplane and be available for re-use. Although most of its cargoes will be unmanned, the *Shuttle* can serve as an inhabited Earth-orbiting laboratory for up to 30 days. The *Space Shuttle Columbia* was successfully launched on April 12, 1981. It made five flights (the first four were test runs), the last completed on November 16, 1982. The second shuttle, *Challenger,* made its maiden flight on April 4, 1983. In April 1984, crew members of the *Challenger* captured, repaired, and returned the Solar Max satellite to orbit, making it the first time a disabled satellite had been repaired in space. The third shuttle, *Discovery,* made its first flight on August 30, 1984. The fourth space shuttle, *Atlantis,* made its maiden flight on Oct. 3, 1985. A tragedy occurred on Jan. 28, 1986, when the shuttle *Challenger* exploded, killing the crew of seven 73 seconds after takeoff. It was the world's worst space flight disaster. The next shuttle flight is not expected to occur before the first quarter of 1988.

## NASA Shuttle Tragedy

The American space program underwent an unprecedented tragedy on January 28, 1986, at 11:39:13 a.m. EST when the space shuttle *Challenger* exploded 73 seconds after its takeoff from the Kennedy Space Center in Florida. The explosion, witnessed by a TV audience of millions, resulted in the deaths of crewmembers Gregory B. Jarvis, mission specialist; Christa McAuliffe (who was to be the first schoolteacher in space); Ronald E. McNair, mission specialist; Lt. Col. Ellison S. Onizuka, mission specialist; Judith Resnik, mission specialist; Francis R. Scobee, shuttle commander, and Cmdr. Michael J. Smith, shuttle pilot. The disaster, by far the worst to befall a NASA operation, brought the shuttle program to a halt after 24 successful launches in the past four years, as an investigation was made into the causes of the explosion.

A presidential commission, which was headed by former Secretary of State William P. Rogers and which included both prominent physicists and astronauts, conducted an inquiry into the explosion. NASA disclosures and testimony before the committe indicated that the most likely cause of the explosion was a rupture in a seal on one of the booster rockets which let a jet of flame escape which ignited the fuel. The commission found out through further inquiry that the weakness in the seal was caused by the cold air temperature (the coldest to date for a shuttle launch) and that warnings from the firm that manufactured the booster rockets, regarding the effects of cold weather on the seals, to NASA officials were not made available to those NASA personnel directly responsible for making the decision to launch.

## Unmanned Planetary and Lunar Programs

**Lunar Orbiter.** Series of spacecraft designed to orbit the Moon, taking pictures and obtaining data in support of the subsequent manned Apollo landings. The U.S. launched five *Lunar Orbiters* between Aug. 10, 1966 and Aug. 2, 1967.

**Mariner.** Designation for a series of spacecraft designed to fly past or orbit the planets, particularly Mercury, Venus, and Mars. *Mariners* provided the early information on Venus and Mars. *Mariner 9,* orbiting Mars in 1971, returned the most startling photographs of that planet to date, and helped pave the way for a *Viking* landing in 1976. *Mariner 10* explored Venus and Mercury in 1973 and was the first probe to use a planet's gravity to whip it toward another.

**Pioneer.** Designation for the United States' first series of sophisticated interplanetary spacecraft. *Pioneers 10* and *11* reached Jupiter in 1973 and 1974 and continued on to explore Saturn and the other outer planets. *Pioneer 11,* renamed *Pioneer Saturn,* examined the Saturn system in September 1979. Significant discoveries were the finding of a small new moon and a narrow new ring. In 1986, *Pioneer 10* was the first man-made object to escape the solar system. *Pioneer Venus 1* and *2* reached Venus in 1978 and provided detailed information about that planet's surface and atmosphere.

**Ranger.** NASA's earliest moon exploration program. Spacecraft were designed for a crash landing on the Moon, taking pictures and returning scientific data up to the moment of impact. Provided the first closeup views of the lunar surface. The *Rangers* provided more than 17,000 closeup pictures, giving us more information about the Moon in a few years than in all the time that had gone before.

**Surveyor.** Series of unmanned spacecraft designed to land gently on the Moon and provide information on the surface in preparation for the manned lunar landings. Their legs were instrumented to return data on the surface hardness of the Moon. *Surveyor* dispelled the fear that Apollo spacecraft might sink several feet or more into the lunar dust.

**Viking.** Designation for two spacecraft designed to conduct detailed scientific examination of the planet Mars, including a search for life. *Viking 1* landed on July 20, 1976; *Viking 2,* Sept. 3, 1976. More was learned about the Red Planet in a few short months than in all the time that had gone before. But the question of life on Mars remains unresolved.

**Voyager.** Designation for two spacecraft designed to explore Jupiter and the other outer planets. *Voyager 1* and *Voyager 2* passed Jupiter in 1979 and sent back startling color TV images of that planet and its moons. They took a total of about 33,000 pictures. *Voyager 1* passed Saturn November 1980. *Voyager 2* passed Saturn August 1981 and Uranus January 1986. It should pass Neptune in 1989.

## Notable Unmanned Lunar and Interplanetary Probes

| Spacecraft | Launch date | Destination | Remarks |
|---|---|---|---|
| Pioneer 1 (U.S.) | Oct. 11, 1958 | Moon | Max. alt.: 71,300 mi. Flight duration: 43 h 17.5 min |
| Pioneer 3 (U.S.) | Dec. 6, 1958 | Moon | Max. alt.: 66,654 mi. Discovered outer Van Allen layer. |
| Lunik 1 (U.S.S.R.) | Sept. 12, 1959 | Moon | Landed in area of Mare Serenitatis. |
| Pioneer 5 (U.S.) | March 11, 1960 | Interplanetary | Orbited sun between Earth & Venus. Radio transmission over record distance of 20 million miles. |
| Mariner 2 (U.S.) | Aug. 27, 1962 | Venus | Venus probe. Successful mid-course correction. Passed 21,648 mi. from Venus Dec. 14, 1962. Reported 800° F. surface temp. Contact lost Jan. 3, 1963 at 54 million mi. |
| Ranger 7 (U.S.) | July 28, 1964 | Moon | Impacted near Crater Guericke 68.5 h after launch. Sent 4,316 pictures during last 15 min of flight as close as 1,000 ft above lunar surface. |
| Mariner 4 (U.S.) | Nov. 28, 1964 | Mars | After mid-course correction, passed behind Mars July 14, 1965, taking 22 pictures from about 6,000 mi. |
| Ranger 8 (U.S.) | Feb. 17, 1965 | Moon | 809 lb. After 64.9 h, crashed into Mare Tranquilitatis, 2.59° N of lunar equator. Sent 7,137 pictures. |
| Ranger 9 (U.S.) | March 21, 1965 | Moon | After 64.5 h, hit Crater Alphonsus. Sent 5,814 pictures. |
| Zond 3 (U.S.S.R.) | July 18, 1965 | Moon | Sent close-ups of 3 million sq mi of Moon. Now in solar orbit. |
| Venera 3 (U.S.S.R.) | Nov. 16, 1965 | Venus | 2,112 lb. Entered Venus atmosphere (March 1, 1966). No data sent. |
| Pioneer 6 (U.S.) | Dec. 16, 1965 | Interplanetary | Successfully orbiting Sun (every 311 days) to check space conditions between Earth & Venus. Perihelion: 75.6 million mi. Aphelion: 90.7 million mi. |
| Luna 9 (U.S.S.R.) | Jan. 31, 1966 | Moon | 3,428 lb. Instrument capsule of 220 lb soft-landed Feb. 3, 1966. Sent back about 30 pictures. |
| Luna 10 (U.S.S.R.) | March 31, 1966 | Moon | 540 lb. Orbit achieved April 2, 1966. |
| Surveyor 1 (U.S.) | May 30, 1966 | Moon | Landed June 2, 1966. Sent almost 10,400 pictures, a number after surviving the 14-day lunar night. |
| Lunar Orbiter 1 (U.S.) | Aug. 10, 1966 | Moon | Orbited Moon Aug. 14. 21 pictures sent. |
| Pioneer 7 (U.S.) | Aug. 17, 1966 | Sun Orbit | Orbiting sun (400 days). Perihelion: 92 million mi. Aphelion: 102 million mi. |
| Luna 11 (U.S.S.R.) | Aug. 24, 1966 | Moon | Moon orbit achieved Aug. 27. |
| Luna 12 (U.S.S.R.) | Oct. 22, 1966 | Moon | Moon orbit achieved Oct. 25 for 3.5 h. Transmission |
| Lunar Orbiter 2 (U.S.) | Nov. 7, 1966 | Moon | Orbit achieved Nov. 10. Sent hundreds of excellent pictures. |

| Spacecraft | Launch date | Destination | Remarks |
|---|---|---|---|
| Luna 13 (U.S.S.R.) | Dec. 21, 1966 | Moon | Soft-landed 80 h after launch. Good pictures. Drove spike into Moon's surface. |
| Lunar Orbiter 3 (U.S.) | Feb. 4, 1967 | Moon | Orbited Moon Feb. 8. Terminated Oct. 9, 1967. Excellent pictures. |
| Surveyor 3 (U.S.) | April 17, 1967 | Moon | Soft-landed 65 h after launch on Oceanus Procellarum. Scooped and tested lunar soil. |
| Lunar Orbiter 4 (U.S.) | May 4, 1967 | Moon | Achieved orbit May 7. Changed orbit on command. |
| Venera 4 (U.S.S.R.) | June 12, 1967 | Venus | Arrived Oct. 17. Instrument capsule sent temperature and chemical data. |
| Mariner 5 (U.S.) | June 14, 1967 | Venus | Fly-by Oct. 19, confirming Mariner 2 and Venera 4 findings |
| Surveyor 4 (U.S.) | July 14, 1967 | Moon | Contact lost 2.5 min before landing |
| Explorer 35 (U.S.) | July 19, 1967 | Moon | Orbit July 22. Perilune: 500 mi.; apolune: 4000 mi. |
| Lunar Orbiter 5 (U.S.) | Aug. 2, 1967 | Moon | Orbited Aug. 5, Perilune: 125 mi.; apolune: 3,760 mi. Time 3 h 50 min. After filming, was crashed on Moon. |
| Surveyor 5 (U.S.) | Sept. 8, 1967 | Moon | Landed near lunar equator Sept. 10. Radiological analysis of lunar soil. Mechanical claw for digging soil. |
| Surveyor 6 (U.S.) | Nov. 7, 1967 | Moon | Landed in Sinus Medii Nov. 10. Jumped 8 ft to photograph original position. Sent back 11,524 pictures. |
| Pioneer 8 (U.S.) | Dec. 12, 1967 | Sun Orbit | Achieved Solar orbit. Stopped functioning April 28, 1968. |
| Pioneer 8 (U.S.) | Dec. 12, 1967 | Sun Orbit | Achieved Solar orbit. Stopped functioning April 28, 1968. |
| Surveyor 7 (U.S.) | Jan. 6, 1968 | Moon | Landed near Crater Tycho Jan. 10. Soil analysis. Sent 3,343 pictures. |
| Zond 4 (U.S.S.R.) | March 2, 1968 | Unknown | Achieved parking orbit but was unable to leave. Re-entered March 3. |
| Zond 5 (U.S.S.R.) | Sept. 14, 1968 | Moon | Circumlunar flight |
| Pioneer 9 (U.S.) | Nov. 8, 1968 | Sun Orbit | Achieved orbit. Six experiments returned solar radiation data. |
| Zond 6 (U.S.S.R.) | Nov. 10, 1968 | Moon | Circumlunar flight |
| Venera 5 (U.S.S.R.) | Jan. 5, 1969 | Venus | Landed May 16, 1969. Returned atmospheric data. |
| Venera 6 (U.S.S.R.) | Jan. 10, 1969 | Venus | Landed May 17, 1969. Sent data as Venera 5. |
| Mariner 6 (U.S.) | Feb. 24, 1969 | Mars | Came within 2000 mi. of Mars July 31, 1969. Sent back data & TV pictures. |
| Mariner 7 (U.S.) | March 27, 1969 | Mars | Came within 2000 mi. of Mars Aug. 5, 1969. Sent back data & TV pictures. |
| Venera 7 (U.S.S.R.) | Aug. 17, 1970 | Venus | Reached Venus Dec. 15, 1970. Sent data, apparently from surface, for 58 min. |
| Luna 16 (U.S.S.R.) | Sept. 12, 1970 | Moon | Soft-landed Sept. 20, scooped up rock, returned to Earth Sept. 24. |
| Luna 17 (U.S.S.R.) | Nov. 10, 1970 | Moon | Soft-landed on Sea of Rains Nov. 17. Lunokhod 1, self-propelled vehicle, used for first time. Sent TV photos, made soil analysis, etc. |
| Mars 2 (U.S.S.R.) | May 19, 1971 | Mars | Reached Mars Nov. 27. Dropped landing capsule on surface. |
| Mars 3 (U.S.S.R.) | May 28, 1971 | Mars | Like Mars 2. Capsule landed Dec. 2. TV transmission cut short. |
| Mariner 9 (U.S.) | May 30, 1971 | Mars | First craft to orbit Mars, Nov. 13. 7,300 pictures, 1st closeups of Mars' moon. Transmission ended Oct. 27, 1972. |
| Luna 19 (U.S.S.R.) | Sept. 28, 1971 | Moon | Orbited Moon, making measurements & taking photos. Soft-landed Feb. 21 in Sea of Fertility. Returned Feb. 25 with rock samples. |
| Pioneer 10 (U.S.) | March 3, 1972 | Jupiter | 620-million-mile flight path through asteroid belt passed Jupiter Dec. 3, 1973, to give man first closeup of planet. In 1986, will become first man-made object to escape solar system. |
| Venera 8 (U.S.S.R.) | March 27, 1972 | Venus | Landed July 22. Sent signals for 50 min. Capsule burned or crushed because of surface heat and pressure. Sent data on atmosphere and surface. |
| Luna 21 (U.S.S.R.) | Jan. 8, 1973 | Moon | Soft-landed Jan. 16. Lunokhod 2 (moon-car) scooped up soil samples, returned them to Earth Jan. 27. |
| Pioneer 11 (U.S.) | April 6, 1973 | Jupiter | Flew by 25,000 mi. from Jupiter Dec. 3, 1974—3 times closer than Pioneer 10. |
| Mars 4 (U.S.S.R.) | July 21, 1973 | Mars | Arrived Feb. 1974, briefly sending back photos |
| Mariner 10 (U.S.) | Nov. 3, 1973 | Venus, Mercury | Passed Venus Feb. 5, 1974. Arrived Mercury March 29, 1974, for man's first closeup look at planet. First time gravity of one planet (Venus) used to whip spacecraft toward another (Mercury). |
| Luna 22 (U.S.S.R.) | May 29, 1974 | Moon | Orbited Moon June 2, 1974 |
| Venera 9 (U.S.S.R.) | June 8, 1975 | Venus | Soft-landed Oct. 25, 1976. Photographed surface of planet. |
| Venera 10 (U.S.S.R.) | June 14, 1975 | Venus | (See Venera 9) |
| Viking 1 (U.S.) | Aug. 20, 1975 | Mars | Carrying life-detection labs. Landed July 20, 1976, for detailed scientific research, including pictures. Designed to work for only 90 days, it operated for almost 6 1/2 years before it went silent in November 1982. |
| Viking 2 (U.S.) | Sept. 9, 1975 | Mars | Like Viking 1. Landed Sept. 3, 1976. Functioned 3 1/2 years. |
| Luna 24 (U.S.S.R.) | Aug. 9, 1976 | Moon | Soft-landed Aug. 18, 1976. Returned soil samples Aug. 22, 1976. |

| Spacecraft | Launch date | Destination | Remarks |
|---|---|---|---|
| Voyager 1 (U.S.) | Sept. 5, 1977 | Jupiter, Saturn, Uranus | Fly-by mission. Reached Jupiter in March 1979; passed Saturn Nov. 1980; to reach Uranus 1986. |
| Voyager 2 (U.S.) | Sept. 20, 1977 | Jupiter, Saturn, Uranus | Like Voyager 1. Encountered Jupiter in July 1979; flew by Saturn Aug. 1981; passed Uranus January 1986; to pass Neptune 1989. |
| Pioneer Venus 1 (U.S.) | May 20, 1978 | Venus | Arrived Dec. 4 and orbited Venus, photographing surface and atmosphere. |
| Pioneer Venus 2 (U.S.) | Aug. 8, 1978 | Venus | Four-part multi-probe, landed Dec. 9. |
| Venera 11 (U.S.S.R.) | Sept. 9, 1978 | Venus | Soft-landed Dec. 25, 1978. Transmitted data for 95 minutes. |
| Venera 12 (U.S.S.R.) | Sept. 14, 1978 | Venus | Like Venera 11. Landed Dec. 21 and transmitted data for 1 hour 50 minutes. |
| Venera 13 (U.S.S.R.) | Oct. 30, 1981 | Venus | Landed March 1, 1982. Took first X-ray fluorescence analysis of the planet's surface. Transmitted data 2 hours 7 minutes. |
| Venera 14 (U.S.S.R.) | Nov. 4, 1981 | Venus | Landed March 5, 1982. Like Venera 13, took X-ray fluorescence analysis of Venusian soil. |
| VEGA 1 (U.S.S.R.) | Deployed on Venus, June 10, 1985 | Encounter with | In flyby over Venus while enroute to encounter with Halley's Comet, VEGA 1 and 2 dropped scientific capsules |
| VEGA 2 (U.S.S.R.) | Deployed on Venus, June 14, 1985 | Halley's comet | onto Venus to study atmosphere and surface material. Encountered Halley's Comet on March 6 and March 9, 1986. Took TV pictures, and studied comet's dust particles. |
| Suisei (Japan) | Encountered Hally's Comet March 8, 1986 | Halley's Comet | Spacecraft made fly-by of comet and studied atmosphere with ultraviolet camera. Observed rotation nucleus. |
| Sakigake (Japan) | Encountered Halley's Comet March 10, 1986 | Halley's Comet | Spacecraft made fly-by to study solar wind and magnetic fields. Detected plasma waves. |
| Giotto (ESA) | Encountered Halley's Comet March 13, 1986 | Halley's Comet | European Space Agency spacecraft made closest approach to comet. Studied atmosphere and magnetic fields. Sent back best pictures of nucleus. |

# Notable Manned Space Flights

| Designation and country | Date | Astronauts | Flight time (h/min) | Remarks |
|---|---|---|---|---|
| Vostok 1 (U.S.S.R.) | April 12, 1961 | Yuri A. Gagarin | 1/48 | First manned orbital flight |
| MR III (U.S.) | May 5, 1961 | Alan B. Shepard, Jr. | 0/15 | Range 486 km (302 mi.), peak 187 km (116.5 mi.); capsule recovered. First American in space. |
| Vostok 2 (U.S.S.R.) | Aug. 6–7, 1961 | Gherman S. Titov | 25/18 | First long-duration flight |
| MA VI (U.S.) | Feb. 20, 1962 | John H. Glenn, Jr. | 4/55 | First American in orbit |
| MA IX (U.S.) | May 15–16, 1963 | L. Gordon Cooper, Jr. | 34/20 | Longest Mercury flight |
| Vostok 6 (U.S.S.R.) | June 16–19, 1963 | Valentina V. Tereshkova | 70/50 | First orbital flight by female cosmonaut |
| Voskhod 1 (U.S.S.R.) | Oct. 12, 1964 | Vladimir M. Komarov; Konstantin P. Feoktistov; Boris G. Yegorov | 24/17 | First 3-man orbital flight; also first flight without space suits |
| Voskhod 2 (U.S.S.R.) | March 18, 1965 | Alexei A. Leonov; Pavel I. Belyayev | 26/2 | First "space walk" (by Leonov), 10 min |
| GT III (U.S.) | March 23, 1965 | Virgil I. Grissom; John W. Young | 4/53 | First manned test of Gemini spacecraft |
| GT IV (U.S.) | June 3–7, 1965 | James A. McDivitt; Edward H. White, 2d | 97/48 | First American "space walk" (by White), lasting slightly over 20 min |
| Apollo 7 (U.S.) | Oct. 11–22, 1968 | Walter M. Schirra, Jr.; Donn F. Eisele; R. Walter Cunningham | 260/9 | First manned test of Apollo command module; first live TV transmissions from orbit |
| Soyuz 3 (U.S.S.R.) | Oct. 26-30, 1968 | Georgi T. Bergevooi | 94/51 | First manned rendezvous and possible docking by Soviet cosmonaut |
| Apollo 8 (U.S.) | Dec. 21-27, 1968 | Frank Borman; James A. Lovell, Jr.; William A. Anders | 147/00 | First spacecraft in circumlunar orbit; TV transmissions from this orbit |
| Apollo 9 (U.S.) | Mar. 3-13, 1969 | James A. McDivitt; David R. Scott; Russell L. Schweikart | 241/1 | First manned flight of Lunar Module |
| Apollo 11 (U.S.) | July 16–24, 1969 | Neil A. Armstrong; Edwin E. Aldrin, Jr.; Michael Collins | 195/18 | First manned landing and EVA on Moon; soil and rock samples collected; experiments left on lunar surface |

| Designation and country | Date | Astronauts | Flight time (h/min) | Remarks |
|---|---|---|---|---|
| Soyuz 6 (U.S.S.R.) | Oct. 11–16, 1969 | Gorgiy Shonin; Valriy Kabasov | 118/42 | Three spacecraft and seven men put into earth orbit simultaneously for first time |
| Apollo 12 (U.S.) | Nov. 14–24, 1969 | Charles Conrad, Jr.; Richard F. Gordon, Jr.; Alan Bean | 244/36 | Manned lunar landing mission; investigated Surveyor 3 spacecraft; collected lunar samples. EVA time: 15 h 30 min |
| Soyuz 9 (U.S.S.R.) | June 1–17, 1970 | Andreiyan Nikolayez; Vitaly Sevastianov | 424/59 | Mission to test man's ability to withstand long periods of weightlessness |
| Apollo 14 (U.S.) | Jan. 31–Feb. 9, 1971 | Alan B. Shepard; Stuart A. Roosa; Edgar D. Mitchell | 216/42 | Third manned lunar landing: returned largest amount of lunar material |
| Soyuz 10 (U.S.S.R.) | April 22–24, 1971 | Vladimir A. Shatalov; Alexei S. Yeliseyev; Nikolai Rukavishnikov | 47/46 | Linked up for 5 1/2 hours with orbiting space station, Salyut 1 |
| Soyuz 11 (U.S.S.R.) | June 6–30, 1971 | Georgiy Tomofeyevich Dobrovolskiy; Vladislav Nikolayevich Volkov; Viktor Ivanovich Patsyev | 569/40 | Linked up with first space station, Salyut 1. Astronauts died just before re-entry due to loss of pressurization in spacecraft |
| Apollo 15 (U.S.) | July 26–Aug. 7, 1971 | David R. Scott; James B. Irwin; Alfred M. Worden | 295/12 | Fourth manned lunar landing; first use of Lunar Rover propelled by Scott and Irwin; first live pictures of LM lift-off from Moon; exploration time: 18 hours |
| Apollo 16 (U.S.) | April 16–27, 1972 | John W. Young; Thomas K. Mattingly; Charles M. Duke, Jr. | 265/51 | Fifth manned lunar landing; second use of Lunar Rover Vehicle, propelled by Young and Duke. Total exploration time on the Moon was 20 h 14 min, setting new record. Mattingly's in-flight "walk in space" was 1 h 23 min. Approximately 213 lb of lunar rock returned |
| Apollo 17 (U.S.) | Dec. 7-19, 1972 | Eugene A. Cernan; Ronald E. Evans; Harrison H. Schmitt | 301/51 | Sixth and last manned lunar landing; third to carry lunar rover. Cernan and Schmitt, during three EVA's, completed total of 22 h 05 min 3 sec. USS Ticonderoga recovered crew and about 250 lbs of lunar samples. |
| Skylab SL-2 (U.S.) | May 25-June 22, 1973 | Charles Conrad, Jr.; Josep P. Kerwin; Paul J. Weitz | 672/50 | First manned Skylab launch. Established Skylab Orbital Assembly and conducted scientific and medical experiments |
| Skylab SL-3 (U.S.) | July 28-Sept. 25, 1973 | Alan L. Bean, Jr.; Jack R. Lousma; Owen K. Garriott | 1427/9 | Second manned Skylab launch. New crew remained in space for 59 days, continuing scientific and medical experiments and earth observations from orbit. |
| Skylab SL-4 (U.S.) | Nov. 16, 1973-Feb. 8, 1974 | Gerald Carr; Edward Gibson; William Pogue | 2017/16 | Third manned Skylab launch; obtained medical data on crew for use in extending the duration of manned space flight; crews "walked in space" 4 times, totaling 44 h 40 min. Longest space mission yet—84 d 1 h 16 min. Splashdown in Pacific, Feb. 9, 1974. |
| Soyuz 17 (U.S.S.R.) | Jan. 11–Feb. 9, 1975 | Col. Aleksey Gubarev; Georgi Grechko | 709/20 | Crew spent 30 days in Salyut 4 space station, which was launched Dec. 26, 1974 and placed in Earth orbit |
| Apollo/Soyuz Test Project (U.S. and U.S.S.R.) | July 15–24, 1975 (U.S.) | U.S.: Brig. Gen. Thomas P. Stafford, Vance D. Brand, Donald K. Slayton | 216/05 | World's first international manned rendezvous and docking in space; aimed at developing a space rescue capability. |
| | July 15–21, 1975 (U.S.S.R) | U.S.S.R.: Col. A. A. Leonov, V. N. Kubasov | 223/35 | Apollo and Soyuz docked and crewmen exchanged visits on July 17, 1975. Mission duration for Soyuz: 142 h 31 min. For Apollo: 217 h, 28 min. |
| Soyuz 21 (U.S.S.R.) | July 6–Aug. 24, 1976 | Col. Boris Volynov; Lt. Col. Vitali Zholobov | 1218/24 | Crew spent 50 days aboard Salyut 5 space station, which was launched June 22 |
| Soyuz 24 (U.S.S.R.) | Feb. 7–25, 1977 | Col. V. Gorbatko; Lt. Col. Yuri Glaszkov | 425/23 | Docked and transferred to Salyut 5 on Feb. 8. Returned Feb. 25 |
| Soyuz 31 (U.S.S.R.) | Aug. 26–Nov. 2, 1978 | Valery Bykovsky; Sigmund Jaehn | 1632/0[1] | Docked with Salyut 6 and Soyuz 29; crew returned in Soyuz 29 on Sept. 3, 1978 |
| Soyuz 33 (U.S.S.R.) | April 11–12, 1979 | N. Rukavishnikov; G. Ivanov | — | Commander veteran of Soyuz 16 |
| Soyuz 35 (U.S.S.R.) | April 9–Oct. 11, 1981 | Valery Ryumin; Leonid Popov | — | Docked with Salyut 6; crew set record of 185 days duration in space. |
| Columbia (U.S.) | April 12–14, 1981 | Capt. Robert L. Crippen; John W. Young | 54/20 | Maiden voyage of *Space Shuttle*, the first spacecraft designed specifically for re-use up to 100 times. |
| Salyut 7 (U.S.S.R.) | Feb. 8, 1984— Oct. 2, 1985 | Leonid Zizim; Vladimir Solovyov; Oleg Atkov | 237 days | Record Russian endurance flight in orbiting space station. |

1. Approximate time. NOTE: The letters MR stand for Mercury (capsule) and Redstone (rocket); MA, for Mercury and Atlas (rocket); GT, for Gemini (capsule) and Titan-II (rocket). The first astronaut listed in the Gemini and Apollo flights is the command pilot. The Mercury capsules had names: MR-III was *Freedom 7*, MR-IV was *Liberty Bell 7*, MA-VI was *Friendship 7*, MA-VII was *Aurora 7*, MA-VIII was *Sigma 7*, and MA-IX was *Faith 7*. The figure 7 referred to the fact that the first group of U.S. astronauts numbered seven men. Only one Gemini capsule had a name: GT-III was called *Molly Brown* (after the Broadway musical *The Unsinkable Molly Brown*); thereafter the practice of naming the capsules was discontinued.

# Major Soviet Space Projects

## Scientific Satellites

**Cosmos.** A designation that began in 1962 for many different kinds of Soviet satellites. *Cosmos 1* studied cosmic rays and other varieties of radiation. *Cosmos 936*, launched Aug. 3, 1977, performed biomedical experiments in cooperation with the U.S., France, and Communist bloc countries.

**Elektron.** Satellites launched in pairs to map radiation belts. Apogee: 40,000 miles; perigee: 4,000 miles. Four *Elektron* satellites were launched in 1964.

**Intercosmos.** Russian scientific satellites carrying experiments from other countries. The announced countries participating are from the Soviet bloc. *Intercosmos I* was launched October 14, 1969. *Intercosmos 17*, measuring charged particles and micrometeorites, was launched Sept. 26, 1977.

**Oreol.** Scientific satellites designed to study the upper atmosphere. Launched jointly with France. *Oreol I* was launched in 1971; *Oreol 2*, 1973.

**Meteor.** Designation for a series of about two dozen weather satellites, beginning with *Meteor I* on March 26, 1969. In 1977, four *Meteors* were put in orbit, the last weighing over 3 tons.

**Molniya.** A communications satellite appearing in a highly elliptical orbit over the same portion of Earth each day on each of its climbs to apogee (the highest point), giving good coverage to the Soviet Union. *Molniya 1* and *2* were launched October 14, 1965. In 1975 and 1976, nine *Molniya* satellites were put in orbit.

**Prognoz.** A solar irradiation and magnetosphere satellite for the study of the solar wind. The last *Prognoz* was launched Dec. 22, 1975.

**Polyot.** Earth satellites incorporating on-board propulsion systems which enable them to change their orbits. Only two have been launched to date, in 1963 and 1964.

**Sputnik.** An early designation for Soviet unmanned spacecraft. *Sputnik 1*, launched October 4, 1957, was the world's first Earth-orbiting satellite, and is considered to have ushered in the Space Age.

## Unmanned Planetary and Lunar Programs

**Luna.** Unmanned spacecraft launched to the Moon. These include lunar orbiters, lunar landers, and lunar lander return missions.

**Mars.** Unmanned spacecraft launched to explore the planet Mars. Three spacecraft, each weighing about 1,940 lb, were launched in 1962, but failed to reach their target. *Mars 4* was launched July 21, 1973, arriving at Mars in February, 1974, and briefly transmitting photographs of the planet back to Earth. *Mars 5, 6,* and *7* were launched between July 25 and August 9, 1974, but missed the planet.

**Venera.** Unmanned spacecraft launched to explore the planet Venus. The program was begun in 1961 but, out of 10 known tries, only four can be termed successful. *Venera 11* and *12* were twinned probes, launched Sept. 9 and Sept. 14, 1978, respectively. They soft-landed in late December and transmitted data to earth for 95 minutes and 110 minutes before failing under the intense heat and pressure of the Venusian atmosphere.

**Zond.** Soviet lunar and planetary probes not otherwise designated. *Zond* spacecraft have been launched to Venus, Mars, and the Moon.

**Vega.** *Vega I and Vega II*, unmanned spacecraft launched to fly-by Venus and subsequently deployed scientific capsules on Venus to study atmosphere and surface material. (*Vega I* deployed capsule on Venus, June 10, 1985, and *Vega II* deployed capsule on the planet on June 14, 1985. The two *Vega* spacecraft later encountered Halley's Comet (*Vega I* on March 6, 1986, and *Vega II* on March 9, 1986). They provided detailed pictures, temperature, and composition of dust particles of the comet.

## Manned Space Flight Programs

**Vostok.** The Soviets' first manned capsule, roughly spherical, used to place the first six cosmonauts in Earth orbit (1961–65).

**Voskhod.** Adaptation of the *Vostok* capsule to accommodate two and three cosmonauts. *Voskhod 1* orbited three persons, and *Voskhod 2* orbited two persons performing the world's first manned extravehicular activity.

**Soyuz.** Late-model manned spacecraft with provisions for three cosmonauts and a "working compartment" accessible through a hatch. Soyuz is the Russian word for "union". Since 1973, all *Soyuz* spacecraft have carried two cosmonauts. *Soyuz 19*, launched July 15, 1975, docked with the American *Apollo* spacecraft. A new model of the spacecraft, *Soyuz-T2*, was launched in 1980.

**Salyut.** Earth-orbiting space station intended for prolonged occupancy and re-visitation by cosmonauts. They are usually launched by Soviet Proton rockets. *Salyut 1* was launched April 19, 1971, and was docked with by *Soyuz 10* and *11*. *Salyut 2*, launched April 3, 1973, malfunctioned in orbit and was never occupied. *Salyut 3*, visited by *Soyuz 14* and *16*, was launched June 25, 1974. *Salyut 4* was launched Dec. 26, 1974, and is still in orbit. It was visited by *Soyuz 17, 18,* and *20* (which was unmanned). *Salyut 5*, launched June 22, 1976, was docked with by *Soyuz 21* and *24*. *Salyut 6* was launched on Sept. 29, 1977. A record breaking Russian endurance flight was set (Feb. 8, 1984-Oct. 2, 1985) when Soviet astronauts spent 237 days in orbit aboard *Salyut-7*. On Feb. 20, 1986, a new Soviet space station *Mir* was launched into orbit and, on March 13, 1986, a *Soyuz T-15* spacecraft with two astronauts aboard was launched to make a rendezvous with *Mir*.

## Future Soviet Space Plans

Soviet engineers are directing their efforts towards building an advanced space shuttle, an orbit space-telescope, and a series of unmanned probes of Venus and Mars. They hope to send a manned mission to Mars by the early part of the next century.

# SCIENCE

## The Indoor Radon Story

### By Anthony V. Nero

The public often focuses on nuclear power and weapons as the major sources of environmental radiation. But the scientific community has recently come to realize that the largest dose of radiation that most of us receive comes from the air in our own homes. Significant amounts of radon—a natural radioactive gas—accumulate in our houses simply because we tend to build them on the largest source of radioactivity around: the ground. The risk from indoor radon is typically thousands of times larger than that from other more notorious environmental pollutants. In fact, millions of Americans are exposed to more radiation in their own homes than underground uranium miners experience.

We knew from the beginning that radon was present everywhere. Radon results from the radio-

Anthony V. Nero is a physicist at the University of California's Lawrence Berkeley Laboratory. As leader of the laboratory's indoor radon group and later co-leader of the program on building ventilation and indoor air quality, he has been an international leader in discovering the dimensions of the radon problem. He is author of *A Guidebook to Nuclear Reactors* and has written or been editor of several other volumes on environmental monitoring and indoor radon.

This article is excerpted from "The Indoor Radon Story" by Anthony V. Nero, and is reprinted with permission from *TECHNOLOGY REVIEW*, M.I.T. Alumni Association, copyright 1986.

active decay of radium, a member of the decay chain that begins with uranium. And, like uranium, radium is present in small amounts throughout the earth's crust, including in the soil and rock that the atmosphere and virtually all buildings come into intimate contact with.

Of all indoor pollutants, radon has drawn so much attention because the level of risk for even average exposures is unusually large. Unlike other indoor pollutants, radon comes primarily from outside, entering homes through their understructures after being generated in the ground. Because it is a noble gas, radon doesn't react chemically with the surrounding material. Thus it can migrate, reaching the water or air to which humans have access. The radonisotope of greatest importance is radon-222, which decays with a half-life of four days to a sequence of isotopes with short half-lives: polonium-218, lead-214, bismuth-214, and polonium-214. These isotopes are more harmful than radon itself because they are chemically active: they can attach to airborne particles, walls, and—if inhaled—the lining of the lung. Once collected in the lung, these isotopes are likely to complete their radioactive decay to the next long-lived isotope, lead-210, irradiating the surrounding tissue in the process. The most damaging radiation dose comes from the alpha particles emitted when the two polonium isotopes decay.

### How Does Radon Enter Houses?

A major source of indoor radon is radium in the soil and rock under and around buildings. Radon moves through soil and rock and can enter a building through cracks or openings (sewer pipe and sump pump openings, cracks in concrete, wall-floor joints, hollow concrete block walls, etc.). The amount of radon from soil that reaches a building depends on several factors, including the amount of radium in the surrounding soil or rock, the rate at which radon gas is released from the soil particles or rock, and the soil permeability.

In some regions, water from underground aquifers or wells contains dissolved radon naturally produced in the rock. The churning of water in washers, showers, toilets, and sinks releases much of the dissolved radon.

*Source:* New York State Department of Health.

The high concentrations of radon and its decay products sometimes found in uranium and other mines have been shown to be the cause of elevated lung-cancer rates among mine workers. Radiation levels in homes and other buildings are typically lower. However, if we make the standard assumption that the incidence of lung cancer is proportional to the level of exposure, we can estimate that average concentrations of radon in U.S. homes cause about 10,000 cases of lung cancer per year.

Scientists have continued to find high concentrations of indoor radon in many parts of the country. High levels have been found in Maine, partly because of the large amounts of the gas in domestic water supplies. Communities in Montana, North Dakota, Colorado, and Washington have also discovered high levels, usually from radon generated in the ground. We now believe that high concentrations may exist in any part of the country, and that the vast majority of the areas at highest risk have not been identified simply because there has been no effort to do so.

Radon is an odd pollutant. None of us is responsible for it and all of us are exposed to it: even average levels of exposure carry risks far above those associated with other environmental pollutants. And high levels are enough to cause grave concern. Handling the problem effectively requires a new way of dealing with environmental concerns, coupling the assistance of governmental agencies with efforts of individuals to make their own homes safer. Those who are affected shouldn't panic: this is a problem we have always lived with. But controlling the most significant radiation dose of our lives will require a sustained national effort to find and fix the houses that need help.

## Suppliers of Home Radon Detectors

The only way you can know if radon is a problem in your home or office is to measure the levels. There are measurements that you can perform or you may wish to seek the advice of professional samplers.

While *Information Please* cannot endorse or recommend a specific radon detector for home use, we have listed three inexpensive sources that offer radon detectors and the necessary processing services to the public on a nationwide basis.

**The University of Pittsburgh Radon Project.** Their principal service is to provide a one-week measurement of the radon level in the home for $12.00, including all postage both ways.

Send a check made out to the University of Pittsburgh to: Radon Project, University of Pittsburgh, Pittsburgh, Pa. 15260. You will receive a radon detection kit with instructions. Within two to three weeks after returning the device, you will receive the results along with information on interpreting it.

Be sure to include your name and address with your order. Before ordering, telephone the Radon Project, at (412) 624–3513 for the latest information and instructions.

**Terradex Corporation Track Etch Detector.** Another device to monitor your home for a longer period of time, is the Track Etch radon detector offered by Terradex Corporation, 460 N. Wiget Lane, Walnut Creek, Calif. 94598. Telephone Terradex at (415) 938–2545 for complete information.

The Track Etch detector measures the average

### Glossary

**Alpha Particles.** Charged particles emitted from the nucleus of an atom during radioactive decay. Alpha particles expend a large amount of energy in a thin layer of tissue, thus resulting in large biological damage compared with similar doses of X-rays.

**Aquifer.** A naturally occurring underground water source used for supplying water to wells.

**Half-life.** The amount of time for one-half of the radioactive atoms of an element to undergo the process of radioactive decay. The half-life of radon-222 is 3.8 days.

**Lifetime Risk.** The probability of a certain biological result occurring within a lifetime, from continuous exposure to a particular substance such as radon, usually expressed as a percentage. For example, a risk of 0.1 percent corresponds to 1 chance in 1,000 that a person will show an effect from a lifetime of exposure.

**Picocurie/liter (pCi/l).** A measure of the radioactive decay of about two atoms per minute in a one liter volume. A liter volume corresponds to about one quart. An average person breathes 20,000 liters of air per day.

**Radioactive Decay.** The process by which certain elements spontaneously emit radiation and are transformed into other elements in the process.

**Soil Permeability.** The ease with which a gas such as radon can move through a particular soil.

**Working Level Month (WLM).** Is derived from occupational exposure to radon and represents 170 hours of occupational exposure to an air concentration of 1 working level (WL), a measure of radioactivity of radon decay products in air. When radon is measured in a home atmosphere, a concentration of 4 pCi/l is normally assumed to correspond to .02 WL.

radon level in your home over a three-month period. The Terradex device is offered to the public for $50.00, and it comes with complete instructions. After the exposure period, you return the device to Terradex for analysis. In about three weeks, you will receive a report of the results and how they compare with published guidlines.

**Air Chek.** A third radon testing service is Air Check, P.O. Box 100, Penrose, N.C. 28776. For $19.95 (standard service), you will receive a radon detection device that provides a four- to six-day measurement of the radon levels in your home.

There are two types of service. Standard is shipped to you by first-class or bulk-rate mail and takes several weeks to process. Delux service for faster processing costs $29.95 and the detector is shipped to you by United Parcel blue label. Those requesting delux service will get their results by telephone within 24 hours of testing completion.

You can order both services by major credit card from Air Check, toll-free (800) CK RADON, or (704) 862–4037 in North Carolina.
NOTE: Prices and services listed for all detectors are subject to change.

# Table of Geological Periods

It is now generally assumed that planets are formed by the accretion of gas and dust in a cosmic cloud, but there is no way of estimating the length of this process. Our earth acquired its present size, more or less, between 4,000 and 5,000 million years ago. Life on earth originated about 2,000 million years ago, but there are no good fossil remains from periods earlier than the Cambrian, which began about 550 million years ago. The largely unknown past before the Cambrian Period is referred to as the Pre-Cambrian and is subdivided into the Lower (or older) and Upper (or younger) Pre-Cambrian—also called the Archaeozoic and Proterozoic Eras.

The known geological history of the earth since the beginning of the Cambrian Period is subdivided into three "eras," each of which comprises a number of "periods." They, in turn, are subdivided into "subperiods." In a subperiod, a certain section may be especially well known because of rich fossil finds. Such a section is called a "formation," and it is usually identified by a place name.

## Paleozoic Era

This era began 550 million years ago and lasted for 355 million years. The name was compounded from Greek *palaios* (old) and *zoön* (animal).

| Period | Duration[1] | Subperiods | Events |
|---|---|---|---|
| Cambrian (from *Cambria*, Latin name for Wales) | 70 | Lower Cambrian<br>Middle Cambrian<br>Upper Cambrian | Invertebrate sea life of many types, proliferating during this and the following period |
| Ordovician (from Latin *Ordovices*, people of early Britain) | 85 | Lower Ordovician<br>Upper Odovician | |
| Silurian (from Latin *Silures*, people of early Wales) | 40 | Lower Silurian<br>Upper Silurian | First known fishes; gigantic sea scorpions |
| Devonian (from Devonshire in England) | 50 | Lower Devonian<br>Upper Devonian | Proliferation of fishes and other forms of sea life, land still largely lifeless |
| Carboniferous (from Latin *carbo* = coal + *fero* = to bear) | 85 | Lower or Mississippian<br>Upper of Pennsylvanian | Period of maximum coal formation in swampy forests; early insects and first known amphibians |
| Permian (from district of Perm in Russia) | 25 | Lower Permian<br>Upper Permian | Early reptiles and mammals; earliest form of turtles |

## Mesozoic Era

This era began 195 million years ago and lasted for 135 million years. The name was compounded from Greek *mesos* (middle) and *zoön* (animal). Popular name: Age of Reptiles.

| Period | Duration[1] | Subperiods | Events |
|---|---|---|---|
| Triassic (from *trias* = triad) | 35 | Lower or Buntsandstein (from German *bunt* = colorful + *Sandstein* = sandstone)<br>Middle or Muschelkalk (from German *Muschel* = clam + *Kalk* = limestone)<br>Upper or Keupér (old miners' term) | Early saurians |
| Jurassic (from Jura Mountains) | 35 | Lower or Black Jurassic, or Lias (from French *liais* = hard stone)<br>Middle or Brown Jurassic, or Dogger (old provincial English for ironstone)<br>Upper or White Jurassic, or Malm (Middle English for sand) | Many sea-going reptiles; early large dinosaurs; somewhat later, flying reptiles (pterosaurs), earliest known birds |
| Cretaceous (from Latin *creta* = chalk) | 65 | Lower Cretaceous<br>Upper Cretaceous | Maximum development of dinosaurs; birds proliferating; oppossum-like mammals |

## Cenozoic Era

This era began 60 million years ago and includes the geological present. The name was compounded from Greek *kainos* (new) and *zoön* (animal). Popular name: Age of Mammals.

| Period | Duration[1] | Subperiods | Events |
|---|---|---|---|
| Tertiary (originally thought to be the third of only three periods) | c. 60 | Paleocene (from Greek *palaios* = old + *kainos* = new)<br>Eocene (from Greek *eos* = dawn + *kainos* = new)<br>Oligocene (from Greek *oligos* = few + *kainos* = new)<br>Miocene (from Greek *meios* = less + *kainos* = new)<br>Pliocene (from Greek *pleios* = more + *kainos* = new) | First mammals other than marsupials<br>Formation of amber; rich insect fauna; early bats<br>Steady increase of large mammals<br><br>Mammals closely resembling present types; protohumans |
| Pleistocene (from Greek *pleistos* = most + *kainos* = new) (popular name: Ice Age) | 1 | Four major glaciations, named Günz, Mindel, Riss, and Würm, originally the names of rivers.<br>Last glaciation ended 10,000 to 15,000 years ago | Various forms of early man |
| Holocene (from Greek *holos* = entire + *kainos* = new) | | The present | The last 3,000 years are called "history" |

1. In millions of years.

## Chemical Elements

| Element | Symbol | Atomic no. | Atomic weight | Specific gravity | Melting point °C | Boiling point °C | Number of isotopes[1] | Discoverer | Year |
|---|---|---|---|---|---|---|---|---|---|
| Actinium | Ac | 89 | 227[2] | 10.07[2] | 1050 | 3200 ±300 | 11 | Debierne | 1899 |
| Aluminum | Al | 13 | 26.9815 | 2.6989 | 660.37 | 2467 | 8 | Wöhler | 1827 |
| Americium | Am | 95 | 243[6] | 13.67 | 994 ±4 | 2607 | 13[3] | Seaborg et al. | 1944 |
| Antimony | Sb | 51 | 121.75 | 6.691 | 630.74 | 1750 | 29 | Early historic times | — |
| Argon | Ar | 18 | 39.948 | 1.7837[4] | −189.2 | −185.7 | 8 | Rayleigh and Ramsay | 1894 |
| Arsenic (gray) | As | 33 | 74.9216 | 5.73 | 817 (28 atm.) | 613[5] | 14 | Albertus Magnus | 1250? |
| Astatine | At | 85 | −210 | — | 302 | 337 | 21 | Corson et al. | 1940 |
| Barium | Ba | 56 | 137.34 | 3.5 | 725 | 1640 | 25 | Davy | 1808 |
| Berkelium | Bk | 97 | 247[6] | 14.00[7] | — | — | 8[3] | Seaborg et al. | 1949 |
| Beryllium | Be | 4 | 9.01218 | 1.848 | 1278 ±5 | 2970 (5 mm.) | 6 | Vauquelin | 1798 |
| Bismuth | Bi | 83 | 208.9806 | 9.747 | 271.3 | 1560 ±5 | 19 | Geoffroy | 1753 |
| Boron | B | 5 | 10.81 | 2.37[8] | 2300 | 2550[5] | 6 | Gay-Lussac and Thénard; Davy | 1808 |
| Bromine | Br | 35 | 79.904 | 3.12[4] | −7.2 | 58.78 | 19 | Balard | 1826 |
| Cadmium | Cd | 48 | 112.40 | 8.65 | 320.9 | 765 | 22 | Stromeyer | 1817 |
| Calcium | Ca | 20 | 40.08 | 1.55 | 839 ±2 | 1484 | 14 | Davy | 1808 |
| Californium | Cf | 98 | 251[6] | — | — | — | 12[3] | Seaborg et al. | 1950 |
| Carbon | C | 6 | 12.011 | 1.8–3.5[9] | −3550 | 4827 | 7 | Prehistoric | — |
| Cerium | Ce | 58 | 140.12 | 6.771 | 798 ±3 | 3257 | 19 | Berzelius and Hisinger; Klaproth | 1803 |
| Cesium | Cs | 55 | 132.9055 | 1.873 | 28.40 | 678.4 | 22 | Bunsen and Kirchhoff | 1860 |
| Chlorine | Cl | 17 | 35.453 | 1.56[4] | −100.98 | −34.6 | 11 | Scheele | 1774 |
| Chromium | Cr | 24 | 51.996 | 7.18–7.20 | 1857 ±20 | 2672 | 9 | Vauquelin | 1797 |
| Cobalt | Co | 27 | 58.9332 | 8.9 | 1495 | 2870 | 14 | Brandt | c.1735 |
| Copper | Cu | 29 | 63.546 | 8.96 | 1083.4±0.2 | 2567 | 11 | Prehistoric | — |
| Curium | Cm | 96 | 247[6] | 13.51[2] | 1340 ±40 | — | 13[3] | Seaborg et al. | 1944 |
| Dysprosium | Dy | 66 | 162.50 | 8.540 | 1409 | 2335 | 21 | Boisbaudran | 1886 |
| Einsteinium | Es | 99 | 254[6] | — | — | — | 12[3] | Ghiorso et al | 1952 |
| Erbium | Er | 68 | 167.26 | 9.045 | 1522 | 2510 | 16 | Mosander | 1843 |
| Europium | Eu | 63 | 151.96 | 5.283 | 822 ±5 | 1597 | 21 | Demarcay | 1896 |
| Fermium | Fm | 100 | 257[6] | — | — | — | 10[3] | Ghiorso et al | 1953 |
| Fluorine | F | 9 | 18.9984 | 1.108[4] | −219.62 | −188.14 | 6 | Moissan | 1886 |
| Francium | Fr | 87 | 223[6] | — | 27[2] | 677[2] | 21 | Perey | 1939 |
| Gadolinium | Gd | 64 | 157.25 | 7.898 | 1311 ±1 | 3233 | 17 | Marignac | 1880 |
| Gallium | Ga | 31 | 69.72 | 5.904 | 29.78 | 2403 | 14 | Boisbaudran | 1875 |
| Germanium | Ge | 32 | 72.59 | 5.323 | 937.4 | 2830 | 17 | Winkler | 1886 |
| Gold | Au | 79 | 196.9665 | 19.32 | 1064.43 | 2807 | 21 | Prehistoric | — |
| Hafnium | Hf | 72 | 178.49 | 13.31 | 2227 ±20 | 4602 | 17 | Coster and von Hevesy | 1923 |
| Helium | He | 2 | 4.00260 | 0.1785[4] | −272.2 (26 atm.) | −268.934 | 5 | Janssen | 1868 |
| Holmium | Ho | 67 | 164.9303 | 8.781 | 1470 | 2720 | 29 | Delafontaine and Soret | 1878 |
| Hydrogen | H | 1 | 1.0080 | 0.070[4] | −259.14 | −252.87 | 3 | Cavendish | 1766 |

| Element | Symbol | Atomic no. | Atomic weight | Specific gravity | Melting point °C | Boiling point °C | Number of isotopes[1] | Discoverer | Year |
|---|---|---|---|---|---|---|---|---|---|
| Indium | In | 49 | 114.82 | 7.31 | 156.61 | 2080 | 34 | Reich and Richter | 1863 |
| Iodine | I | 53 | 126.9045 | 4.93 | 113.5 | 184.35 | 24 | Courtois | 1811 |
| Iridium | Ir | 77 | 192.22 | 22.42 | 2410 | 4130 | 25 | Tennant | 1803 |
| Iron | Fe | 26 | 55.847 | 7.894 | 1535 | 2750 | 10 | Prehistoric | — |
| Krypton | Kr | 36 | 83.80 | 3.733[4] | −156.6 | −152.30±0.10 | 23 | Ramsay and Travers | 1898 |
| Lanthanum | La | 57 | 138.9055 | 6.166 | 920 ±5 | 3454 | 19 | Mosander | 1839 |
| Lawrencium | Lr | 103 | 257[6] | — | — | — | 20[3] | Ghiorso et al. | 1961 |
| Lead | Pb | 82 | 207.2 | 11.35 | 327.502 | 1740 | 29 | Prehistoric | — |
| Lithium | Li | 3 | 6.941 | 0.534 | 180.54 | 1347 | 5 | Arfvedson | 1817 |
| Lutetium | Lu | 71 | 174.97 | 9.835 | 1656 ±5 | 3315 | 22 | Urbain | 1907 |
| Magnesium | Mg | 12 | 24.305 | 1.738 | 648.8±0.5 | 1090 | 8 | Black | 1755 |
| Manganese | Mn | 25 | 54.9380 | 7.21–7.44[10] | 1244 ±3 | 1962 | 11 | Gahn, Scheele, and Bergman | 1774 |
| Mendelevium | Md | 101 | 256[6] | — | — | — | 3[3] | Ghiorso et al. | 1955 |
| Mercury | Hg | 80 | 200.59 | 13.546 | −38.87 | 356.58 | 26 | Prehistoric | — |
| Molybdenum | Mo | 42 | 95.94 | 10.22 | 2617 | 4612 | 20 | Scheele | 1778 |
| Neodymium | Nd | 60 | 144.24 | 6.80 & 7.004[10] | 1010 | 3127 | 16 | von Welsbach | 1885 |
| Neon | Ne | 10 | 20.179 | 0.89990 (g/l 0°C/1 atm) | −248.67 | −246.048 | 8 | Ramsay and Travers | 1898 |
| Neptunium | Np | 93 | 237.0482 | 20.25 | 640 ±1 | 3902 | 15[3] | McMillan and Abelson | 1940 |
| Nickel | Ni | 28 | 58.71 | 8.902 | 1453 | 2732 | 11 | Cronstedt | 1751 |
| Niobium (Columbium) | Nb | 41 | 92.9064 | 8.57 | 2468 ±10 | 4742 | 24 | Hatchett | 1801 |
| Nitrogen | N | 7 | 14.0067 | 0.808[4] | −209.86 | −195.8 | 8 | Rutherford | 1772 |
| Nobelium | No | 102 | 254[6] | — | — | — | 7[3] | Ghiorso et al. | 1957 |
| Osmium | Os | 76 | 190.2 | 22.57 | 3045 ±30 | 5027 ±100 | 19 | Tennant | 1803 |
| Oxygen | O | 8 | 15.9994 | 1.14[4] | −218.4 | −182.962 | 8 | Priestley | 1774 |
| Palladium | Pd | 46 | 106.4 | 12.02 | 1552 | 3140 | 21 | Wollaston | 1803 |
| Phosphorus | P | 15 | 30.9738 | 1.82 (white) | 44.1 | 280 | 7 | Brand | 1669 |
| Platinum | Pt | 78 | 195.09 | 21.45 | 1772 | 3827 ±100 | 32 | Ulloa | 1735 |
| Plutonium | Pu | 94 | 244[6] | 19.84 | 641 | 3232 | 16[3] | Seaborg et al. | 1940 |
| Poionium | Po | 84 | 210[6] | 9.32 | 254 | 962 | 34 | Curie | 1898 |
| Potassium | K | 19 | 39.102 | 0.862 | 63.65 | 774 | 10 | Davy | 1807 |
| Praseodymium | Pr | 59 | 140.9077 | 6.772 | 931 ±4 | 3212 | 15 | von Weisbach | 1885 |
| Promethium | Pm | 61 | 145[6] | — | ≈1080 | 2460? | 14 | Marinsky et al. | 1945 |
| Protactinium | Pa | 91 | 231.0359 | 15.37[2] | <1600 | — | 14 | Hahn and Meitner | 1917 |
| Radium | Ra | 88 | 226.0254 | 5.0? | 700 | 1140 | 14 | P. and M. Curie | 1898 |
| Radon | Rn | 86 | 222[6] | 4.4[4] | −71 | −61.8 | 20 | Dorn | 1900 |
| Rhenium | Re | 75 | 186.2 | 21.02 | 3180 | 5627[7] | 21 | Noddack, Berg, and Tacke | 1925 |
| Rhodium | Rh | 45 | 102.9055 | 12.41 | 1966 ±3 | 3727 ±100 | 20 | Wollaston | 1803 |
| Rubidium | Rb | 37 | 85.4678 | 1.532 | 38.89 | 688 | 20 | Bunsen and Kirchoff | 1861 |
| Ruthenium | Ru | 44 | 101.07 | 12.44 | 2310 | 3900 | 16 | Klaus | 1844 |
| Samarium | Sm | 62 | 150.4 | 7.536 | 1072 ±5 | 1778 | 17 | Boisbaudran | 1879 |
| Scandium | Sc | 21 | 44.9559 | 2.989 | 1539 | 2832 | 15 | Nilson | 1879 |
| Selenium | Se | 34 | 78.96 | 4.79 (gray) | 217 | 684.9±1 | 20 | Berzelius | 1817 |
| Silicon | Si | 14 | 28.086 | 2.33 | 1410 | 2355 | 8 | Berzelius | 1824 |
| Silver | Ag | 47 | 107.868 | 10.50 | 961.93 | 2212 | 27 | Prehistoric | — |
| Sodium | Na | 11 | 22.9898 | 0.971 | 97.81±0.03 | 882.9 | 7 | Davy | 1807 |
| Strontium | Sr | 38 | 87.62 | 2.54 | 769 | 1384 | 18 | Davy | 1808 |
| Sulfur | S | 18 | 32.06 | 2.07[11] | 112.8 | 444.674 | 10 | Prehistoric | — |
| Tantalum | Ta | 73 | 180.9479 | 16.654 | 2996 | 5425 ± 100 | 19 | Ekeberg | 1801 |
| Technetium | Tc | 43 | 98.9062 | 11.50[2] | 2172 | 4877 | 23 | Perrier and Segrè | 1937 |
| Tellurium | Te | 52 | 127.60 | 6.24 | 449.5±0.3 | 989.8±3.8 | 29 | von Reichenstein | 1782 |
| Terbium | Tb | 65 | 158.9254 | 8.234 | 1360 ±4 | 3041 | 24 | Mosander | 1843 |
| Thallium | Tl | 81 | 204.37 | 11.85 | 303.5 | 1457 ±10 | 28 | Crookes | 1861 |
| Thorium | Th | 90 | 232.0381 | 11.72 | 1750 | 4790 | 12 | Berzelius | 1828 |
| Thulium | Tm | 69 | 168.9342 | 9.314 | 1545 ±15 | 1727 | 18 | Cleve | 1879 |
| Tin | Sn | 50 | 118.69 | 7.31 (white) | 231.9681 | 2270 | 28 | Prehistoric | — |
| Titanium | Ti | 22 | 47.90 | 4.55 | 1660 ±10 | 3287 | 9 | Gregor | 1791 |
| Tungsten (Wolfram) | W | 74 | 183.85 | 19.3 | 3410 ±20 | 5660 | 22 | J. and F. d'Elhuyar | 1783 |
| Uranium | U | 92 | 238.029 | −18.95 | 1132.3±0.8 | 3818 | 15 | Peligot | 1841 |
| Vanadium | V | 23 | 50.9414 | 6.11 | 1890 ±10 | 3380 | 9 | del Rio | 1801 |
| Xenon | Xe | 54 | 131.30 | 3.52[4] | −111.9 | −107.1±3 | 31 | Ramsay and Travers | 1898 |
| Ytterbium | Yb | 70 | 173.04 | 6.972 | 824 ±5 | 1193 | 16 | Marignac | 1878 |
| Yttrium | Y | 39 | 88.9059 | 4.457 | 1523 ±8 | 3337 | 21 | Gadolin | 1794 |
| Zinc | Zn | 30 | 65.38 | 7.133 | 419.58 | 907 | 15 | Prehistoric | — |
| Zirconium | Zr | 40 | 91.22 | 6.506[2] | 1852 ±2 | 4377 | 20 | Klaproth | 1789 |

1. Isotopes are different forms of the same element having the same atomic number but different atomic weights. 2. Calculated figure. 3. Artificially produced. 4. Liquid. 5. Sublimation point. 6. Mass number of the isotope of longest known life. 7. Estimated. 8. Amorphous. 9. Depending on whether amorphous, graphite or diamond. 10. Depending on allotropic form. 11. Rhombic. —Is approximately. < Is less than. NOTE: There is a dispute between groups at the Lawrence Berkeley Laboratory of the University of California and at the Dubna Laboratory in the Soviet Union concerning the discovery of elements 104, 105, and 106. The Lawrence Berkeley Laboratory claims that 104 and 105 were discovered in 1969 and 1970, respectively, by Ghiorso et al. and has suggested the names Rutherfordium and Hahnium. The U.S. laboratory claims also that Ghiorso et al. discovered element 106 in 1974. No name has yet been suggested for this element. Names will not be official until the controversy is resolved and they have been approved by the International Union for Pure and Applied Chemistry.

## Scientific Inventions, Discoveries, and Theories

Most inventions are the results of the discoveries, theories, experiments, and improvements of many people. This list tries to suggest the development of certain particularly important ideas. In some instances, it tries to connect the fundamental theory with the ultimate practical invention.

**Abacus:** *See* Calculating machine

**Adding machine:** *See* Calculating machine; Computer

**Adrenaline:** (isolation of) Jokichi Takamine, U.S., 1901

**Air brake:** George Westinghouse, U.S., 1868

**Air conditioning:** Willis Carrier, U.S., 1911

**Airplane:** (first powered, sustained, controlled flight) Orville and Wilbur Wright, U.S., 1903. *See also* Jet propulsion, aircraft

**Airship:** (non-rigid) Henri Giffard, France, 1852; (rigid) Ferdinand von Zeppelin, Germany, 1900

**Aluminum manufacture:** (by electrolytic action) Charles M. Hall, U.S., 1866

**Anesthetic:** (first use of anesthetic—ether—on man) Crawford W. Long, U.S., 1842

**Antibiotics:** (first demonstration of antibiotic effect) Louis Pasteur, Jules-François Joubert, France, 1887; (penicillin, first modern antibiotic) Alexander Fleming, England, 1928

**Antiseptic:** (surgery) Joseph Lister, England, 1867

**Antitoxin, diphtheria:** Emil von Behring, Germany, 1890

**Atomic theory:** (ancient) Leucippus, Democritus, Greece, c.500 B.C.; Lucretius, Rome, c.100 B.C.; (modern) John Dalton, England, 1808

**Automobile:** (first with internal combustion engine, 250 rpm) Karl Benz, Germany, 1885; (first with practical high-speed internal combustion engine, 900 rpm) Gottlieb Daimler, Germany, 1885; (first true automobile, not carriage with motor) René Panhard, Emile Lavassor, France, 1891; (carburetor, spray) Charles E. Duryea, U.S., 1892

**Bacteria:** Anton van Leeuwenhoek, The Netherlands, 1683

**Bakelite:** *See* Plastics

**Balloon, hot-air:** Joseph and Jacques Montgolfier, France, 1783

**Ball-point pen:** *See* Pen

**Barometer:** Evangelista Torricelli, Italy, 1643

**Bicycle:** Karl D. von Sauerbronn, Germany, 1816; (first modern model) James Starley, England, 1884

**Bifocal lens:** *See* Lens, bifocal

**Blood, circulation of:** William Harvey, England, 1628

**Braille:** Louis Braille, France, 1829

**Bullet:** (conical) Claude Minié, France, 1849

**Calculating machine:** (Abacus) China, c.190; (logarithms: made multiplying easier and thus calculators practical) John Napier, Scotland, 1614; (slide rule) William Oughtred, England, 1632; (digital calculator) Blaise Pascal, 1642; (multiplication machine) Gottfried Leibnitz, Germany, 1671; (important 19th-century contributors to modern machine) Frank S. Baldwin, Jay R. Monroe, Dorr E. Felt, W. T. Ohdner, William Burroughs, all U.S.; ("analytical engine" design, included concepts of programming, taping) Charles Babbage, England, 1835. *See also* Computer

**Camera:** (hand-held) George Eastman, U.S., 1888; (Polaroid Land) Edwin Land, U.S., 1948. *See also* Photography

**Carburetor:** *See* Automobile

**Celanese:** *See* Fibers, man-made

**Celluloid:** *See* Plastics

**Classification of plants and animals:** (by genera and species) Carolus Linnaeus, Sweden, 1737–53

**Clock, pendulum:** Christian Huygens, The Netherlands, 1656

**Combustion:** (nature of) Antoine Lavoisier, France, 1777

**Computer:** (differential analyzer, mechanically operated) Vannevar Bush, U.S., 1928; (Mark I, first information-processing digital computer) Howard Aiken, U.S., 1944; (ENIAC, Electronic Numerical Integrator and Calculator, first all-electronic) J. Presper Eckert, John W. Mauchly, U.S., 1946; (stored-program concept) John von Neumann, U.S., 1947

**Conditioned reflex:** Ivan Pavlov, Russia, c.1910

**Converter, Bessemer:** William Kelly, U.S., 1851

**Cosmetics:** Egypt, c.4000 B.C.

**Cotton gin:** Eli Whitney, U.S., 1793

**Crossbow:** China, c.300 B.C.

**Cyclotron:** Ernest O. Lawrence, U.S., 1931

**Deuterium:** (heavy hydrogen) Harold Urey, U.S., 1931

**DNA:** (deoxyribonucleic acid) Friedrich Meischer, Germany, 1869; (determination of double-helical structure) F. H. Crick, England, James D. Watson, U.S., 1953

**Dynamite:** Alfred Nobel, Sweden, 1867

**Electric generator (dynamo):** (laboratory model) Michael Faraday, England, 1832; Joseph Henry, U.S., c.1832; (hand-driven model) Hippolyte Pixii, France, 1833; (alternating-current generator) Nikola Tesla, U.S., 1892

**Electric lamp:** (arc lamp) Sir Humphrey Davy, England, 1801; (fluorescent lamp) A. E. Becquerel, France, 1867; (incandescent lamp) Sir Joseph Swann, England, Thomas A. Edison, U.S., contemporaneously, 1870s; (carbon arc street lamp) Charles F. Brush, U.S., 1879; (first widely marketed incandescent lamp) Thomas A. Edison, U.S., 1879; (mercury vapor lamp) Peter Cooper Hewitt, U.S., 1903; (neon lamp) Georges Claude, France, 1911; (tungsten filament) Irving Langmuir, U.S., 1915

**Electric motor:** *See* Motor

**Electromagnet:** William Sturgeon, England, 1823

**Electron:** Sir Joseph J. Thompson, England, 1897

**Elevator, passenger:** (safety device permitting use by passengers) Elisha G. Otis, U.S., 1852; (elevator utilizing safety device) 1857

**E = mc²:** (equivalence of mass and energy) Albert Einstein, Switzerland, 1907

**Engine, internal combustion:** No single inventor. Fundamental theory established by Sadi Carnot, France, 1824; (two-stroke) Étienne Lenoir, France, 1860; (ideal operating cycle for four-stroke) Alphonse Beau de Rochet, France, 1862; (operating four-stroke) Nikolaus Otto, Germany, 1876; (diesel) Rudolf Diesel, Germany, 1892; (rotary) Felix Wankel, Germany, 1956. *See also* Automobile

**Engine, steam:** *See* Steam engine

**Evolution:** (by natural selection) Charles Darwin, England, 1859

**Falling bodies, law of:** Galileo Galilei, Italy, 1590

**Fermentation:** (micro-organisms as cause of) Louis Pasteur, France, c.1860

**Fibers, man-made:** (nitrocellulose fibers treated to change flammable nitrocellulose to harmless cellulose, precursor of rayon) Sir Joseph Swann, England, 1883; (rayon) Count Hilaire de Chardonnet, France, 1889; (Celanese) Henry and Camille Dreyfuss, U.S., England, 1921; (research on polyesters and polyamides, basis for modern man-made fibers) U.S., England, Germany, 1930s; (nylon) Wallace H. Carothers, U.S., 1935

**Fountain pen:** *See* Pen

**Geometry, elements of:** Euclid, Alexandria, Egypt, c.300 B.C.

**Gravitation, law of:** Sir Isaac Newton, England, c. 1665 (published 1687)

**Gunpowder:** China, c.700

**Gyrocompass:** Elmer A. Sperry, U.S., 1905

**Gyroscope:** Léon Foucault, France, 1852

**Helicopter:** Igor Sikorsky, U.S., 1939

**Helium first observed on sun:** Sir Joseph Lockyer, England, 1868

**Heredity, laws of:** Gregor Mendel, Austria, 1865

**Induction, electric:** Joseph Henry, U.S., 1828

**Insulin:** Sir Frederick G. Banting, J. J. R. MacLeod, Canada, 1922

**Intelligence testing:** Alfred Binet, Theodore Simon, France, 1905

**Isotopes:** (concept of) Frederick Soddy, England, 1912; (stable isotopes) J. J. Thompson, England, 1913; (existence demonstrated by mass spectrography) Francis W. Ashton, 1919

**Jet propulsion, aircraft:** Sir Frank Whittle, England, 1930

**Laser:** (theoretical work on) Charles H. Townes, Arthur L. Schawlow, U.S., N. Basov, A. Prokhorov, U.S.S.R., 1958; (first working model) T. H. Maiman, U.S., 1960

**Lens, bifocal:** Benjamin Franklin, U.S., c.1760

**Light, nature of:** (wave theory) Christian Huygens, Denmark, 1678; (electromagnetic theory) James Clerk Maxwell, England, 1873

**Light, speed of:** (theory that light has finite velocity) Olaus Roemer, Denmark, 1675

**Lightning rod:** Benjamin Franklin, U.S., 1752

**Linotype:** *See* Printing

**Lithography:** *See* Printing

**Locomotive:** (steam-powered) Richard Trevithick, England, 1804; (first practical, due to multiple-fire-tube boiler) George Stephenson, England, 1829; (largest steam-powered) Union Pacific's "Big Boy," U.S., 1941

**Logarithms:** *See* Calculating machine

**Loom:** (horizontal, two-beamed) Egypt, c.4400 B.C.; (Jacquard drawloom, pattern controlled by punch cards) Jacques de Vaucanson, France, 1745, Joseph-Marie Jacquard, 1801; (flying shuttle) John Kay, England, 1733; (power-driven loom) Edmund Cartwright, England, 1785

**Machine gun:** James Puckle, England, 1718; Richard J. Gatling, U.S., 1861

**Match:** (phosphorus) François Derosne, France, 1816; (friction) Charles Sauria, France, 1831; (safety) J. E. Lundstrom, Sweden, 1855

**Mendelian law:** *See* Heredity

**Microscope:** (compound) Zacharias Janssen, The Netherlands, 1590; (electron) Vladimir Zworykin et al., U.S., Canada, Germany, 1932–1939

**Motion pictures:** Thomas A. Edison, U.S., 1893

**Motion pictures, sound:** Product of various inventions. First picture with synchronized musical score: *Don Juan,* 1926; with spoken dialogue: *The Jazz Singer,* 1927; both Warner Bros.

**Motor, electric:** Michael Faraday, England, 1822; (alternating-current) Nikola Tesla, U.S., 1892

**Motor, gasoline:** *See* Engine, internal combustion

**Motorcycle:** (motor tricycle) Edward Butler, England, 1884; (gasoline-engine motorcycle) Gottieb Daimier, Germany, 1885

**Neptunium:** (first transuranic element, synthesis of) Edward M. McMillan, Philip H. Abelson, U.S., 1940

**Neutron:** James Chadwick, England, 1932

**Neutron-induced radiation:** Enrico Fermi et al., Italy, 1934

**Nitroglycerin:** Ascanio Sobrero, Italy, 1846

**Nuclear fission:** Otto Hahn, Fritz Strassmann, Germany, 1938

**Nuclear reactor:** Enrico Fermi et al., U.S., 1942

**Nylon:** *See* Fibers, man-made

**Ohm's law:** (relationship between strength of electric current, electromotive force, and circuit resistance) Georg S. Ohm, Germany, 1827

**Ozone:** Christian Schönbein, Germany, 1839

**Paper:** China, c.100 B.C.

**Parachute:** Louis S. Lenormand, France, 1783

**Pen:** (fountain) Lewis E. Waterman, U.S., 1884; (ball-point, for marking on rough surfaces) John H. Loud, U.S., 1888; (ball-point, for handwriting) Lazlo Biro, Argentina, 1944

**Penicillin:** *See* Antibiotics

**Periodic law:** (that properties of elements are functions of their atomic weights) Dmitri Mendeleev, Russia, 1869

**Periodic table:** (arrangement of chemical elements based on periodic law) Dmitri Mendeleev, Russia, 1869

**Phonograph:** Thomas A. Edison, U.S., 1877

**Photography:** (first paper negative, first photograph, on metal) Joseph Nicéphore Niepce, France, 1816–1827; (discovery of fixative powers of hyposulfite of soda) Sir John Herschel, England, 1819; (first direct positive image on silver plate, the daguerreotype) Louis Daguerre, based on work with Niepce, France, 1839; (first paper negative from which a number of positive prints could be made) William Talbot, England, 1841. Work of these four men, taken together, forms basis for all modern photography. (First color images) Alexandre Becquerel, Claude Niepce de Saint-Victor, France, 1848–60; (commercial color film with three emulsion layers, Kodachrome) U.S., 1935. *See also* Camera

**Plastics:** (first material, nitrocellulose softened by vegetable oil, camphor, precursor to Celluloid) Alexander Parkes, England, 1855; (Celluloid, involving recognition of vital effect of camphor) John W. Hyatt, U.S., 1869; (Bakelite, first completely synthetic plastic) Leo H. Baekeland, U.S., 1910; (theoretical background of macromolecules and process of polymerization on which modern plastics industry rests) Hermann Staudinger, Germany, 1922. *See also* Fibers, man-made

**Plow, forked:** Mesopotamia, before 3000 B.C.

**Plutonium, synthesis of:** Glenn T. Seaborg, Edwin M. McMillan, Arthur C. Wahl, Joseph W. Kennedy, U.S., 1941

**Polaroid Land camera:** *See* Camera

**Polio, vaccine against:** (vaccine made from dead virus strains) Jonas E. Salk, U.S., 1954; (vaccine made from live virus strains) Albert Sabin, U.S., 1960

**Positron:** Carl D. Anderson, U.S., 1932

**Pressure cooker:** (early version) Denis Papin, France, 1679

**Printing:** (block) Japan, c.700; (movable type) Korea, c.1400; Johann Gutenberg, Germany, c. 1450 (lithography, offset) Aloys Senefelder, Germany, 1796; (rotary press) Richard Hoe, U.S., 1844; (linotype) Ottman Mergenthaler, U.S. 1884

**Programming, information:** *See* Calculating machine

**Propeller, screw:** Sir Francis P. Smith, England, 1836; John Ericsson, England, worked independently of and simultaneously with Smith, 1837

**Proton:** Ernest Rutherford, England, 1919

**Psychoanalysis:** Sigmund Freud, Austria, c.1904

**Quantum theory:** Max Planck, Germany, 1901

**Rabies immunization:** Louis Pasteur, France, 1885

**Radar:** (limited to one-mile range) Christian Hulsmeyer, Germany, 1904; (pulse modulation, used for measuring height of ionosphere) Gregory Breit, Merle Tuve, U.S., 1925; (first practical radar—radio detection and ranging) Sir Robert Watson-Watt, England, 1934–35

**Radio:** (electromagnetism, theory of) James Clerk Maxwell, England, 1873; (spark coil, generator of electromagnetic waves) Heinrich Hertz, Germany, 1886; (first practical system of wireless telegraphy) Guglielmo Marconi, Italy, 1895; (vacuum electron tube, basis for radio telephony) Sir John Fleming, England, 1904; (triode amplifying tube) Lee de Forest, U.S., 1906; (regenerative circuit, allowing long-distance sound reception) Edwin H. Armstrong, U.S., 1912; (frequency modulation—FM) Edwin H. Armstrong, U.S., 1933

**Radioactivity:** (X-rays) Wilhelm K. Roentgen, Germany, 1895; (radioactivity of uranium) Henri Becquerel, France, 1896; (radioactive elements, radium and polonium in uranium ore) Marie Sklodowska-Curie, Pierre Curie, France, 1898; (classification of alpha and beta particle radiation) Pierre Curie, France, 1900; (gamma radiation) Paul-Ulrich Villard, France, 1900; (carbon dating) Willard F. Libby et al., U.S., 1955

**Rayon:** *See* Fibers, man-made

**Reaper:** Cyrus McCormick, U.S., 1834

**Relativity:** (special and general theories of) Albert Einstein, Switzerland, Germany, U.S., 1905–53

**Revolver:** Samuel Colt, U.S., 1835

**Rifle:** (muzzle-loaded) Italy, Germany, c.1475; (breech-loaded) England, France, Germany, U.S., c.1866; (bolt-action) Paul von Mauser, Germany, 1889; (automatic) John Browning, U.S., 1918

**Roller bearing:** (wooden for cartwheel) Germany or France, c.100 B.C.

**Rubber:** (vulcanization process) Charles Goodyear, U.S., 1839

**Safety match:** *See* Match

**Solar system, universe:** (sun-centered universe) Nicolaus Copernicus, Warsaw, 1543; (establishment of planetary orbits as elliptical) Johannes Kepler, Germany, 1609; (infinity of universe) Giordano Bruno, Italian monk, 1584

**Spectrum:** (heterogeneity of light) Sir Isaac Newton, England, 1665–66

**Spermatozoa:** Anton van Leeuwenhoek, The Netherlands, 1683

**Spinning:** (spinning wheel) India, introduced to Europe in Middle Ages; (Saxony wheel, continuous spinning of wool or cotton yarn) England, c.1500–1600; (spinning jenny) James Hargreaves, England, 1764; (spinning frame) Sir Richard Arkwright, England, 1769; (spinning mule, completed mechanization of spinning, permitting production of yarn to keep up with demands of modern looms) Samuel Crompton, England, 1779

**Steam engine:** (first commercial version based on principles of French physicist Denis Papin) Thomas Savery, England, 1639; (atmospheric steam engine) Thomas Newcomen, England, 1705; (steam engine for pumping water from collieries) Savery, Newcomen, 1725; (modern condensing, doubleacting) James Watt, England, 1782

**Steam engine, railroad:** *See* Locomotive

**Steamship:** Claude de Jouffroy d'Abbans, France, 1783; James Rumsey, U.S., 1787; John Fitch, U.S., 1790. All preceded Robert Fulton, U.S., 1807, credited with launching first commercially successful steamship

**Sulfa drugs:** (parent compound, para-aminobenzenesulfanomide) Paul Gelmo, Austria, 1908; (antibacterial activity) Gerhard Domagk, Germany, 1935

**Syphilis, test for:** *See* Wassermann test

**Tank, military:** Sir Ernest Swinton, England, 1914

**Telegraph:** Samuel F. B. Morse, U.S., 1837

**Telephone:** Alexander Graham Bell, U.S., 1876

**Telescope:** Hans Lippershey, The Netherlands, 1608

**Television:** (mechanical disk-scanning method) successfully demonstrated by J. L. Baird, England, C. F. Jenkins, U.S., 1926; (electronic scanning method) Vladimir K. Zworykin, U.S., 1928; (color, all-electronic) Zworykin, 1925; (color, mechanical disk) Baird, 1928; (color, compatible with black and white) George Valensi, France, 1938; (color, sequential rotating filter) Peter Goldmark, U.S., first introduced, 1951; (color, compatible with black and white) commercially introduced in U.S., National Television Systems Committee, 1953

**Thermometer:** (open-column) Galileo Galilei, c. 1593; (clinical) Santorio Santorio, Padua, c. 1615; (mercury, also Fahrenheit scale) Gabriel D. Fahrenheit, Germany, 1714; (centigrade scale) Anders Celsius, Sweden, 1742; (absolute-temperature, or Kelvin, scale) William Thompson, Lord Kelvin, England, 1848

**Tire, pneumatic:** Robert W. Thompson, England, 1845; (bicycle tire) John B. Dunlop, Northern Ireland, 1888

**Toilet, flush:** Product of Minoan civilization, Crete, c.2000 B.C. Alleged invention by "Thomas Crapper" is untrue.

**Tractor:** Benjamin Holt, U.S., 1900

**Transformer, electric:** William Stanley, U.S., 1885

**Transistor:** John Bardeen, William Shockley, Walter Brattain, U.S., 1948

**Uncertainty principle:** (that position and velocity of an object cannot both be measured exactly, at the same time) Werner Heisenberg, Germany, 1927

**Vaccination:** Edward Jenner, England, 1796

**Vacuum tube:** *See* Radio

**Van Allen (radiation) Belt:** (around the earth) James Van Allen, U.S., 1958

**Vitamins:** (hypothesis of disease deficiency) Sir F. G. Hopkins, Casimir Funk, England, 1912; (vitamin A) Elmer V. McCollum, M. Davis, U.S., 1912–14; (vitamin B) Elmer V. McCollum, U.S., 1915–16; (thiamin, $B_1$) Casimir Funk, England, 1912; (riboflavin, $B_2$) D. T. Smith, E. G. Hendrick, U.S., 1926; (niacin) Conrad Elvehjem, U.S., 1937; ($B_6$) Paul Gyorgy, U.S., 1934; (vitamin C) C. A. Hoist, T. Froelich, Norway, 1912; (vitamin D) Elmer V. McCollum, U.S., 1922; (folic acid) Lucy Wills, England, 1933

**Wassermann test:** (for syphilis) August von Wassermann, Germany, 1906

**Weaving, cloth:** *See* Loom

**Wheel:** (cart, solid wood) Mesopotamia, c.3800–3600 B.C.

**Windmill:** Persia, c.600

**X-ray:** *See* Radioactivity

**Xerography:** Chester Carlson, U.S., 1938

**Zero:** India, c.600; (absolute zero, cessation of all molecular energy) William Thompson, Lord Kelvin, England, 1848

# WEIGHTS & MEASURES

## Measures and Weights

*Source:* Department of Commerce, National Bureau of Standards.

### The International System (Metric)

The International System of Units is a modernized version of the metric system, established by international agreement, i.e. provides a logical and interconnected framework for all measurements in science, industry, and commerce. The system is built on a foundation of seven basic units, and all other units are derived from them. The system weights and measures was legalized in the United States in 1866, and our customary units of weights and measures are defined in terms of the meter and kilogram.)

**Length.** Meter. The meter is defined as 1,650,-763.73 wavelengths in vacuum of the orange-red line of the spectrum of krypton-86.

**Time.** Second. The second is defined as the duration of 9,192,631,770 cycles of the radiation associated with a specified transition of the cesium 133 atom.

**Mass.** Kilogram. The standard for the kilogram is a cylinder of platinum-iridium alloy kept by the International Bureau of Weights and Measures at Paris. A duplicate at the National Bureau of Standards serves as the mass standard for the United States. The kilogram is the only base unit still defined by a physical object.

**Temperature.** Kelvin. The kelvin is defined as the fraction 1/273.16 of the thermodynamic temperature of the triple point of water; that is, the point at which water forms an interface of solid, liquid and vapor. This is defined as 0.01° C on the Centigrade or Celsius scale and 32.02° F on the Fahrenheit scale. The temperature 0° K is called "absolute zero."

**Electric Current.** Ampere. The ampere is defined as that current that, if maintained in each of two long parallel wires separated by one meter in free space, would produce a force between the two wires (due to their magnetic fields) of $2 \times 10^{-7}$ newton for each meter of length. (A newton is the unit of force which when applied to one kilogram mass would experience an acceleration of one meter per second per second.)

**Luminous Intensity.** Candela. The candela is defined as the luminous intensity of 1/600,000 of a square meter of a cavity at the temperature of freezing platinum (2,042K).

**Amount of Substance.** Mole. The mole is the amount of substance of a system that contains as many elementary entities as there are atoms in 0.012 kilograms of carbon-12.

## Tables of Metric Weights and Measures

### LINEAR MEASURE
10 millimeters (mm) = 1 centimeter (cm)
10 centimeters = 1 decimeter (dm) = 100 millimeters
10 decimeters = 1 meter (m) = 1,000 millimeters
10 meters = 1 dekameter (dam)
10 dekameters = 1 hectometer (hm) = 100 meters
10 hectometers = 1 kilometer (km) = 1,000 meters

### AREA MEASURE
100 square millimeters (mm²) = 1 sq centimeter (cm²)
10,000 square centimeters = 1 sq meter (m²) = 1,000,000 sq millimeters
100 square meters = 1 are (a)
100 ares = 1 hectare (ha) = 10,000 sq meters
100 hectares = 1 sq kilometer (km²) = 1,000,000 sq meters

### VOLUME MEASURE
10 milliliters (ml) = 1 centiliter (cl)
10 centiliters = 1 deciliter (dl) = 100 milliliters

10 deciliters = 1 liter (l) = 1,000 milliliters
10 liters = 1 dekaliter (dal)
10 dekaliters = 1 hectoliter (hl) = 100 liters
10 hectoliters = 1 kiloliter (kl) = 1,000 liters

### CUBIC MEASURE
1,000 cubic millimeters (mm³) = 1 cu centimeter (cm³)
1,000 cubic centimeters = 1 cu decimeter (dm³) = 1,000,000 cu millimeters
1,000 cubic decimeters = 1 cu meter (m³) = 1 stere = 1,000,000 cu centimeters = 1,000,000,000 cu millimeters

### WEIGHT
10 milligrams (mg) = 1 centigram (cg)
10 centigrams = 1 decigram (dg) = 100 milligrams
10 decigrams = 1 gram (g) = 1,000 milligrams
10 grams = 1 dekagram (dag)
10 dekagrams = 1 hectogram (hg) = 100 grams
10 hectograms = 1 kilogram (kg) = 1,000 grams
1,000 kilograms = 1 metric ton (t)

# Tables of Customary U.S. Weights and Measures

## LINEAR MEASURE

12 inches (in.) = 1 foot (ft)
3 feet = 1 yard (yd)
5 1/2 yards = 1 rod (rd), pole, or perch (16 1/2 ft)
40 rods = 1 furlong (fur) = 220 yds = 660 ft
8 furlongs = 1 statute mile (mi.) = 1,760 yds = 5,280 ft
3 land miles = 1 league
5,280 feet = 1 statute or land mile
6,076.11549 feet = 1 international nautical mile

## AREA MEASURE

144 square inches = 1 sq ft
9 square feet = 1 sq yd = 1,296 sq in.
30 1/4 square yards = 1 sq rd = 272 1/4 sq ft
160 square rods = 1 acre = 4,840 sq yds = 43,560 sq ft
640 acres = 1 sq mi.
1 mile square = 1 section (of land)
6 miles square = 1 township = 36 sections = 36 sq mi.

## CUBIC MEASURE

1,728 cubic inches = 1 cu ft
27 cubic feet = 1 cu yd

## LIQUID MEASURE

When necessary to distinguish the liquid pint or quart from the dry pint or quart, the word "liquid" or the abbreviation "liq" should be used in combination with the name or abbreviation of the liquid unit.

4 gills (gi) = 1 pint (pt) (= 28.875 cu in.)
2 pints = 1 quart (qt) (= 57.75 cu in.)
4 quarts = 1 gallon (gal) (= 231 cu in.) = 8 pts = 32 gills

## APOTHECARIES FLUID MEASURE

60 minims (min.) = 1 fluid dram (fl dr) (= 0.2256 cu in.)
8 fluid drams = 1 fluid ounce (fl oz) (= 1.8047 cu in.)
16 fluid ounces = 1 pt (= 28.875 cu in.) = 128 fl drs
2 pints = 1 qt (= 57.75 cu in.) = 32 fl oz = 256 fl drs
4 quarts = 1 gal (= 231 cu in.) = 128 fl oz = 1,024 fl drs

## DRY MEASURE

When necessary to distinguish the dry pint or quart from the liquid pint or quart; the word "dry" should be used in combination with the name or abbreviation of the dry unit.

2 pints = 1 qt (=67.2006 cu in.)
8 quarts = 1 peck (pk) (=537.605 cu in.) = 16 pts
4 pecks = 1 bushel (bu) (= 2,150.42 cu in.) = 32 qts

## AVOIRDUPOIS WEIGHT

When necessary to distinguish the avoirdupois dram from the apothecaries dram, or to distinguish the avoirdupois dram or ounce from the fluid dram or ounce, or to distinguish the avoirdupois ounce or pound from the troy or apothecaries ounce or pound, the word "avoirdupois" or the abbreviation "avdp" should be used in combination with the name or abbreviation of the avoirdupois unit.
(The "grain" is the same in avoirdupois, troy, and apothecaries weights.)

27 11/32 grains = 1 dram (dr)
16 drams = 1 oz = 437 1/2 grains
16 ounces = 1 lb = 256 drams = 7,000 grains
100 pounds = 1 hundredweight (cwt)
20 hundredweights = 1 ton (tn) = 2,000 lbs[1]

In "gross" or "long" measure, the following values are recognized:

112 pounds = 1 gross or long cwt[1]
20 gross or long hundredweights = 1 gross or long ton = 2,240 lbs[1]

1. When the terms "hundredweight" and "ton" are used unmodified, they are commonly understood to mean the 100-pound hundredweight and the 2,000-pound ton, respectively; these units may be designated "net" or "short" when necessary to distinguish them from the corresponding units in gross or long measure.

## UNITS OF CIRCULAR MEASURE

Second (") = —
Minute (') = 60 seconds
Degree (°) = 60 minutes
Right angle = 90 degrees
Straight angle = 180 degrees
Circle = 360 degrees

## TROY WEIGHT

24 grains = 1 pennyweight (dwt)
20 pennyweights = 1 ounce troy (oz t) = 480 grains
12 ounces troy = 1 pound troy (lb t) = 240 pennyweights = 5,760 grains

## APOTHECARIES WEIGHT

20 grains = 1 scruple (s ap)
3 scruples = 1 dram apothecaries (dr ap) = 60 grains
8 drams apothecaries = 1 ounce apothecaries (oz ap) = 24 scruples = 480 grains
12 ounces apothecaries = 1 pound apothecaries (lb ap) = 96 drams apothecaries = 288 scruples = 5,760 grains

## GUNTER'S OR SURVEYOR'S CHAIN MEASURE

7.92 inches = 1 link (li)
100 links = 1 chain (ch) = 4 rods = 66 ft
80 chains = 1 statute mile = 320 rods = 5,280 ft

# Metric and U.S. Equivalents

| | | | |
|---|---|---|---|
| 1 angstrom[1] (light wave measurement) | 0.1 millimicron 0.000 1 micron 0.000 000 1 millimeter 0.000 000 004 inch | 1 decimeter | 3.937 inches |
| | | 1 dekameter | 32.808 feet |
| 1 cable's length | 120 fathoms 720 feet 219.456 meters | 1 fathom | 8 feet 1.8288 meters |
| | | 1 foot | 0.3048 meter |
| 1 centimeter | 0.3937 inch | 1 furlong | 10 chains (surveyor's) 660 feet 220 yards 1/8 statute mile 201.168 meters |
| 1 chain (Gunter's or surveyor's) | 66 feet 20.1168 meters | | |

| | |
|---|---|
| 1 inch | 2.54 centimeters |
| 1 kilometer | 0.621 mile |
| 1 league (land) | 3 statute miles<br>4.828 kilometers |
| 1 link (Gunter's or surveyor's) | 7.92 inches<br>0.201 168 meter |
| 1 meter | 39.37 inches<br>1.094 yards |
| 1 micron | 0.001 millimeter<br>0.000 039 37 inch |
| 1 mil | 0.001 inch<br>0.025 4 millimeter |
| 1 mile (statute or land) | 5,280 feet<br>1.609 kilometers |
| 1 mile (nautical international) | 1.852 kilometers<br>1.151 statute miles<br>0.999 U.S. nautical miles |
| 1 millimeter | 0.03937 inch |
| 1 millimicron (mμ) | 0.001 micron<br>0.000 000 039 37 inch |
| 1 nanometer | 0.001 micrometer or<br>0.000 000 039 37 inch |
| 1 point (typography) | 0.013 837 inch<br>1/72 inch (approximately)<br>0.351 millimeter |
| 1 rod, pole, or perch | 16 1/2 feet<br>5.0292 meters |
| 1 yard | 0.9144 meter |

## AREAS OR SURFACES

| | |
|---|---|
| 1 acre | 43,560 square feet<br>4,840 square yards<br>0.405 hectare |
| 1 are | 119.599 square yards<br>0.025 acre |
| 1 hectare | 2.471 acres |
| 1 square centimeter | 0.155 square inch |
| 1 square decimeter | 15.5 square inches |
| 1 square foot | 929.030 square centimeters |
| 1 square inch | 6.4516 square centimeters |
| 1 square kilometer | 0.386 square mile<br>247.105 acres |
| 1 square meter | 1.196 square yards<br>10.764 square feet |
| 1 square mile | 258.999 hectares |
| 1 square millimeter | 0.002 square inch |
| 1 square rod, square pole or square perch | 25.293 square meters |
| 1 square yard | 0.836 square meters |

## CAPACITIES OR VOLUMES

| | |
|---|---|
| 1 barrel, liquid | 31 to 42 gallons[2] |
| 1 barrel, standard for fruits, vegetables, and other dry commodities except cranberries | 7,056 cubic inches<br>105 dry quarts<br>3.281 bushels, struck measure |
| 1 barrel, standard, cranberry | 5.286 cubic inches<br>86 45/64 dry quarts<br>2.709 bushels, struck measure |
| 1 bushel (U.S.) struck measure | 2,150.42 cubic inches<br>35.238 liters |
| 1 bushel, heaped (U.S.) | 2,747.715 cubic inches<br>1.278 bushels, struck measure[3] |
| 1 cord (firewood) | 128 cubic feet |
| 1 cubic centimeter | 0.061 cubic inches |
| 1 cubic decimeter | 61.024 cubic inches |
| 1 cubic foot | 7.481 gallons<br>28.316 cubic decimeters |
| 1 cubic inch | 0.554 fluid ounce<br>4.433 fluid drams<br>16.387 cubic centimeters |
| 1 cubic meter | 1.308 cubic yards |
| 1 cubic yard | 0.765 cubic meter |
| 1 cup, measuring | 8 fluid ounces<br>1/2 liquid pint |
| 1 dram, fluid or liquid (U.S.) | 1/8 fluid ounces<br>0.226 cubic inch<br>3.697 milliliters<br>1.041 British fluid drachms |
| 1 dekaliter | 2.642 gallons<br>1.135 pecks |
| 1 gallon (U.S.) | 231 cubic inches<br>3.785 liters<br>0.833 British gallon<br>128 U.S. fluid ounces |
| 1 gallon (British Imperial) | 277.42 cubic inches<br>1.201 U.S. gallons<br>4.546 liters<br>160 British fluid ounces |
| 1 gill | 7.219 cubic inches<br>4 fluid ounces<br>0.118 liter |
| 1 hectoliter | 26.418 gallons<br>2.838 bushels |
| 1 liter | 1.057 liquid quarts<br>0.908 dry quart<br>61.024 cubic inches |
| 1 milliliter | 0.271 fluid drams<br>16.231 minims<br>0.061 cubic inch |
| 1 ounce, fluid or liquid (U.S.) | 1.805 cubic inch<br>29.574 milliliters<br>1.041 British fluid ounces |

| | | | |
|---|---|---|---|
| 1 peck | 8.810 liters | 1 hundredweight, net or short | 100 pounds<br>45.359 kilograms |
| 1 pint, dry | 33.600 cubic inches<br>0.551 liter | 1 kilogram | 2.205 pounds |
| 1 pint, liquid | 28.875 cubic inches<br>0.473 liter | 1 microgram [µg (the Greek letter mu in combination with the letter g)] | 0.000 001 gram |
| 1 quart, dry (U.S.) | 67.201 cubic inches<br>1.101 liters<br>0.969 British quart | 1 milligram | 0.015 grain |
| 1 quart, liquid (U.S.) | 57.75 cubic inches<br>0.946 liter<br>0.833 British quart | 1 ounce, avoirdupois | 437.5 grains<br>0.911 troy or apothecaries ounce<br>28.350 grams |
| 1 quart (British) | 69.354 cubic inches<br>1.032 U.S. dry quarts<br>1.201 U.S. liquid quarts | 1 ounce, troy or apothecaries | 480 grains<br>1.097 avoirdupois ounces<br>31.103 grams |
| 1 tablespoon, measuring | 3 teaspoons<br>4 fluid drams<br>1/2 fluid ounce | 1 pennyweight | 1.555 grams |
| 1 teaspoon, measuring | 1/3 tablespoon<br>1 1/3 fluid drams | 1 point | 0.01 carat<br>2 milligrams |
| 1 assay ton[4] | 29.167 grams | 1 pound, avoirdupois | 7,000 grains<br>1.215 troy or apothecaries pounds<br>453.592 37 grams |
| 1 carat | 200 milligrams<br>3.086 grains | | |
| 1 dram, apothecaries | 60 grains<br>3.888 grams | 1 pound, troy or apothecaries | 5,760 grains<br>0.823 avoirdupois pound<br>373.242 grams |
| 1 dram, avoirdupois | 27 11/32 (=27.344) grains<br>1.772 grams | 1 ton, gross or long[5] | 2,240 pounds<br>1.12 net tons<br>1.016 metric tons |
| 1 grain | 64.798 91 milligrams | | |
| 1 gram | 15.432 grains<br>0.035 ounce, avoirdupois | 1 ton, metric | 2,204.623 pounds<br>0.984 gross ton<br>1.102 net tons |
| 1 hundredweight, gross or long[5] | 112 pounds<br>50.802 kilograms | 1 ton, net or short | 2,000 pounds<br>0.893 gross ton<br>0.907 metric ton |

1. The angstrom is basically defined as 10⁻¹⁰ meter. 2. There is a variety of "barrels" established by law or usage. For example, federal taxes on fermented liquors are based on a barrel of 31 gallons; many state laws fix the "barrel for liquids" at 31 1/2 gallons; one state fixes a 36-gallon barrel for cistern measurement; federal law recognizes a 40-gallon barrel for "proof spirits"; by custom, 42 gallons comprise a barrel of crude oil or petroleum products for statistical purposes, and this equivalent is recognized "for liquids" by four states. 3. Frequently recognized as 1 1/4 bushels, struck measure. 4. Used in assaying. The assay ton bears the same relation to the milligram that a ton of 2,000 pounds avoirdupois bears to the ounce troy; hence the weight in milligrams of precious metal obtained from one assay ton of ore gives directly the number of troy ounces to the net ton. 5. The gross or long ton and hundredweight are used commercially in the United States to only a limited extent, usually in restricted industrial fields. These units are the same as the British "ton" and "hundredweight."

## Miscellaneous Units of Measure

**Acre:** An area of 43,560 square feet. Originally, the area a yoke of oxen could plow in one day.

**Agate:** Originally a measurement of type size (5 1/2 points). Now equal to 1/14 inch. Used in printing for measuring column length.

**Ampere:** Unit of electric current. A potential difference of one volt across a resistance of one ohm produces a current of one ampere.

**Astronomical Unit (A.U.):** 93,000,000 miles, the average distance of the earth from the sun. Used in astronomy.

**Bale:** A large bundle of goods. In the U.S., the approximate weight of a bale of cotton is 500 pounds. The weight varies in other countries.

**Board Foot (fbm):** 144 cubic inches (12 in. × 12 in. × 1 in.). Used for lumber.

**Bolt:** 40 yards. Used for measuring cloth.

**Btu:** British thermal unit. Amount of heat needed to increase the temperature of one pound of water by one degree Fahrenheit (252 calories).

**Carat (c):** 200 milligrams or 3.086 grains troy.

Originally the weight of a seed of the carob tree in the Mediterranean region. Used for weighing precious stones. *See also* Karat.

**Chain (ch):** a chain 66 feet or one-tenth of a furlong in length, divided into 100 parts called links. One mile is equal to 80 chains. Used in surveying and sometimes called Gunter's or surveyor's chain.

**Cubit:** 18 inches or 45.72 cm. Derived from distance between elbow and tip of middle finger.

**Decibel:** Unit of relative loudness. One decibel is the smallest amount of change detectable by the human ear.

**Ell, English:** 1 1/4 yards or 1/32 bolt. Used for measuring cloth.

**Freight Ton (also called Measurement Ton):** 40 cubic feet of merchandise. Used for cargo freight.

**Great Gross:** 12 gross or 1728.

**Gross:** 12 dozen or 144.

**Hand:** 4 inches or 10.16 cm. Derived from the width of the hand. Used for measuring the height of horses at withers.

**Hertz:** Modern unit for measurement of electromagnetic wave frequencies (equivalent to "cycles per second").

**Hogshead (hhd):** 2 liquid barrels or 14,653 cubic inches.

**Horsepower:** The power needed to lift 33,000 pounds a distance of one foot in one minute (about 1 1/2 times the power an average horse can exert). Used for measuring power of steam engines, etc.

**Karat (kt):** A measure of the purity of gold, indicating how many parts out of 24 are pure. For example, 18 karat gold is 3/4 pure. Sometimes spelled *carat*.

**Knot:** Not a distance, but the rate of speed of one nautical mile per hour. Used for measuring speed of ships.

**League:** Rather indefinite and varying measure, but usually estimated at 3 miles in English-speaking countries.

**Light-Year:** 5,880,000,000,000 miles, the distance light travels in a year at the rate of 186,281.7 miles per second. (If an astronomical unit were represented by one inch, a light-year would be represented by about one mile.) Used for measurements in interstellar space.

**Magnum:** Two-quart bottle. Used for measuring wine, etc.

**Ohm:** Unit of electrical resistance. A circuit in which a potential difference of one volt produces a current of one ampere has a resistance of one ohm.

**Parsec:** Approximately 3.26 light-years or 19.2 trillion miles. Term is combination of first syllables of *pa*rallax and *sec*ond, and distance is that of imaginary star when lines drawn from it to both earth and sun form a maximum angle or parallax of one second (1/3600 degree). Used for measuring interstellar distances.

**Pi ($\pi$):** 3.14159265+. The ratio of the circumference of a circle to its diameter. For practical purposes, the value is used to four decimal places: 3.1416.

**Pica:** 1/6 inch or 12 points. Used in printing for measuring column width, etc.

**Pipe:** 2 hogsheads. Used for measuring wine and other liquids.

**Point:** .013837 (approximately 1/72) inch or 1/12 pica. Used in printing for measuring type size.

**Quintal:** 100,000 grams or 220.46 pounds avoirdupois.

**Quire:** Used for measuring paper. Sometimes 24 sheets but more often 25. There are 20 quires in a ream.

**Ream:** Used for measuring paper. Sometimes 480 sheets, but more often 500 sheets.

**Roentgen:** Dosage unit of radiation exposure produced by X-rays.

**Score:** 20 units.

**Sound, Speed of:** Usually placed at 1,088 ft per second at 32° F at sea level. It varies at other temperatures and in different media.

**Span:** 9 inches or 22.86 cm. Derived from the distance between the end of the thumb and the end of the little finger when both are outstretched.

**Square:** 100 square feet. Used in building.

**Stone:** Legally 14 pounds avoirdupois in Great Britain.

**Therm:** 100,000 Btu's.

**Township:** U. S. land measurement of almost 36 square miles. The south border is 6 miles long. The east and west borders, also 6 miles long, follow the meridians, making the north border slightly less than 6 miles long. Used in surveying.

**Tun:** 252 gallons, but often larger. Used for measuring wine and other liquids.

**Watt:** Unit of power. The power used by a current of one ampere across a potential difference of one volt equals one watt.

## Kelvin Scale

Absolute zero, −273.16° on the Celsius (Centigrade) scale, is 0° Kelvin. Thus, degrees Kelvin are equivalent to degrees Celsius plus 273.16. The freezing point of water, 0° C. and 32° F., is 273.16° K. The conversion formula is K° = C° + 273.16.

## Conversion of Miles to Kilometers and Kilometers to Miles

| Miles | Kilometers | Miles | Kilometers | Miles | Kilometers | Kilometers | Miles | Kilometers | Miles | Kilometers | Miles |
|---|---|---|---|---|---|---|---|---|---|---|---|
| 1 | 1.6 | 8 | 12.8 | 60 | 96.5 | 1 | 0.6 | 8 | 4.9 | 60 | 37.2 |
| 2 | 3.2 | 9 | 14.4 | 70 | 112.6 | 2 | 1.2 | 9 | 5.5 | 70 | 43.4 |
| 3 | 4.8 | 10 | 16.0 | 80 | 128.7 | 3 | 1.8 | 10 | 6.2 | 80 | 49.7 |
| 4 | 6.4 | 20 | 32.1 | 90 | 144.8 | 4 | 2.4 | 20 | 12.4 | 90 | 55.9 |
| 5 | 8.0 | 30 | 48.2 | 100 | 160.9 | 5 | 3.1 | 30 | 18.6 | 100 | 62.1 |
| 6 | 9.6 | 40 | 64.3 | 1,000 | 1609 | 6 | 3.7 | 40 | 24.8 | 1,000 | 621 |
| 7 | 11.2 | 50 | 80.4 | | | 7 | 4.3 | 50 | 31.0 | | |

## Bolts and Screws: Conversion from Fractions of an Inch to Millimeters

| Inch | mm | Inch | mm | Inch | mm | Inch | mm |
|---|---|---|---|---|---|---|---|
| 1/64 | 0.40 | 17/64 | 6.75 | 33/64 | 13.10 | 49/64 | 19.45 |
| 1/32 | 0/79 | 9/32 | 7.14 | 17/32 | 13.50 | 25/32 | 19.84 |
| 3/64 | 1.19 | 19/64 | 7.54 | 35/64 | 13.90 | 51/64 | 20.24 |
| 1/16 | 1.59 | 5/16 | 7.94 | 9/16 | 14.29 | 13/16 | 20.64 |
| 5/64 | 1.98 | 21/64 | 8.33 | 37/64 | 14.69 | 53/64 | 21.03 |
| 3/32 | 2.38 | 11/32 | 8.73 | 19/32 | 15.08 | 27/32 | 21.43 |
| 7/64 | 2.78 | 23/64 | 9.13 | 39/64 | 15.48 | 55/64 | 21.83 |
| 1/8 | 3.18 | 3/8 | 9.53 | 5/8 | 15.88 | 7/8 | 22.23 |
| 9/64 | 3.57 | 25/64 | 9.92 | 41/64 | 16.27 | 57/64 | 22.62 |
| 5/32 | 3.97 | 13/32 | 10.32 | 21/32 | 16.67 | 29/32 | 23.02 |
| 11/64 | 4.37 | 27/64 | 10.72 | 43/64 | 17.06 | 59/64 | 23.42 |
| 3/16 | 4.76 | 7/16 | 11.11 | 11/64 | 17.46 | 15/16 | 23.81 |
| 13/64 | 5.16 | 29/64 | 11.51 | 45/64 | 17.86 | 61/64 | 24.21 |
| 7/32 | 5.56 | 15/32 | 11.91 | 23/32 | 18.26 | 31/32 | 24.61 |
| 15/64 | 5.95 | 31/64 | 12.30 | 47/64 | 18.65 | 63/64 | 25.00 |
| 1/4 | 6.35 | 1/2 | 12.70 | 3/4 | 19.05 | 1 | 25.40 |

## U.S.—Metric Cooking Conversions

| U.S. customary system | | | | Metric | | | |
|---|---|---|---|---|---|---|---|
| Capacity | | Weight | | Capacity | | Weight | |
| 1/5 teaspoon | 1 milliliter | 1 fluid oz | 30 milliliters | 1 milliliter | 1/5 teaspoon | 1 gram | .035 ounce |
| 1 teaspoon | 5 ml | | 28 grams | 5 ml | 1 teaspoon | 100 grams | 3.5 ounces |
| 1 tablespoon | 15 ml | 1 pound | 454 grams | 15 ml | 1 tablespoon | 500 grams | 1.10 pounds |
| 1/5 cup | 50 ml | | | 34 ml | 1 fluid oz | 1 kilogram | 2.205 pounds |
| 1 cup | 240 ml | | | | | | 35 oz |
| 2 cups (1 pint) | 470 ml | | | 100 ml | 3.4 fluid oz | | |
| 4 cups (1 quart) | .95 liter | | | 240 ml | 1 cup | | |
| 4 quarts (1 gal.) | 3.8 liters | | | 1 liter | 34 fluid oz | | |
| | | | | | 4.2 cups | | |
| | | | | | 2.1 pints | | |
| | | | | | 1.06 quarts | | |
| | | | | | 0.26 gallon | | |

## Cooking Measurement Equivalents

| | |
|---|---|
| 16 tablespoons = 1 cup | 2 tablespoons = 1/8 cup |
| 12 tablespoons = 3/4 cup | 2 tablespoons + 2 teaspoons = 1/6 cup |
| 10 tablespoons + 2 teaspoons = 2/3 cup | 1 tablespoon = 1/16 cup |
| 8 tablespoons = 1/2 cup | 2 cups = 1 pint |
| 6 tablespoons = 3/8 cup | 2 pints = 1 quart |
| 5 tablespoons + 1 teaspoon = 1/3 cup | 3 teaspoons = 1 tablespoon |
| 4 tablespoons = 1/4 cup | 48 teaspoons = 1 cup |

## Prefixes and Multiples

| Prefix | Symbol | Equivalent | Multiple/submultiple | Prefix | Symbol | Equivalent | Multiple/submultiple |
|--------|--------|------------|----------------------|--------|--------|------------|----------------------|
| atto | a | quintillionth part | $10^{-18}$ | deci | d | tenth part | $10^{-1}$ |
| femto | f | quadrillionth part | $10^{-15}$ | deka | da | tenfold | $10$ |
| pico | p | trillionth part | $10^{-12}$ | hecto | h | hundredfold | $10^2$ |
| nano | n | billionth part | $10^{-9}$ | kilo | k | thousandfold | $10^3$ |
| micro | $\mu$ | millionth part | $10^{-6}$ | mega | M | millionfold | $10^6$ |
| milli | m | thousandth part | $10^{-3}$ | giga | G | billionfold | $10^9$ |
| centi | c | hundredth part | $10^{-2}$ | tera | T | trillionfold | $10^{12}$ |

# Common Formulas

## Circumference

**Circle:** $C = \pi d$, in which $\pi$ is 3.1416 and $d$ the diameter.

## Area

**Triangle:** $A = \dfrac{ab}{2}$, in which $a$ is the base and $b$ the height.

**Square:** $A = a^2$, in which $a$ is one of the sides.

**Rectangle:** $A = ab$, in which $a$ is the base and $b$ the height.

**Trapezoid:** $A = \dfrac{h(a+b)}{2}$, in which $h$ is the height, $a$ the longer parallel side, and $b$ the shorter.

**Regular pentagon:** $A = 1.720a^2$, in which $a$ is one of the sides.

**Regular hexagon:** $A = 2.598a^2$, in which $a$ is one of the sides.

**Regular octagon:** $A = 4.828a^2$, in which $a$ is one of the sides.

**Circle:** $A = \pi r^2$, in which $\pi$ is 3.1416 and $r$ the radius.

## Volume

**Cube:** $V = a^3$, in which $a$ is one of the edges.

**Rectangular prism:** $V = abc$, in which $a$ is the length, $b$ the width, and $c$ the depth.

**Pyramid:** $V = \dfrac{Ah}{3}$, in which $A$ is the area of the base and $h$ the height.

**Cylinder:** $V = \pi r^2 h$, in which $\pi$ is 3.1416, $r$ the radius of the base, and $h$ the height.

**Cone:** $V = \dfrac{\pi r^2 h}{3}$, in which $\pi$ is 3.1416, $r$ the radius of the base, and $h$ the height.

**Sphere:** $V = \dfrac{4\pi r^3}{3}$, in which $\pi$ is 3.1416 and $r$ the radius.

## Miscellaneous

**Speed per second acquired by falling body:** $v = 32t$, in which $t$ is the time in seconds.

**Distance in feet traveled by falling body:** $d = 16t^2$, in which $t$ is the time in seconds.

**Speed of sound in feet per second through any given temperature of air:** $V = \dfrac{1087 \sqrt{273+t}}{16.52}$, in which $t$ is the temperature Centigrade.

**Cost in cents of operation of electrical device:** $C = \dfrac{Wtc}{1000}$, in which $W$ is the number of watts, $t$ the time in hours, and $c$ the cost in cents per kilowatt-hour.

**Conversion of matter into energy (Einstein's Theorem):** $E = mc^2$, in which $E$ is the energy in ergs, $m$ the mass of the matter in grams, and $c$ the speed of light in centimeters per second. ($c^2 = 9.10^{20}$).

## Decimal Equivalents of Common Fractions

| | | | | | | | | | | | |
|------|-------|------|-------|------|-------|------|-------|------|-------|-------|-------|
| 1/2 | .5000 | 1/10 | .1000 | 2/7 | .2857 | 3/11 | .2727 | 5/9 | .5556 | 7/11 | .6364 |
| 1/3 | .3333 | 1/11 | .0909 | 2/9 | .2222 | 4/5 | .8000 | 5/11 | .4545 | 7/12 | .5833 |
| 1/4 | .2500 | 1/12 | .0833 | 2/11 | .1818 | 4/7 | .5714 | 5/12 | .4167 | 8/9 | .8889 |
| 1/5 | .2000 | 1/16 | .0625 | 3/4 | .7500 | 4/9 | .4444 | 6/7 | .8571 | 8/11 | .7273 |
| 1/6 | .1667 | 1/32 | .0313 | 3/5 | .6000 | 4/11 | .3636 | 6/11 | .5455 | 9/10 | .9000 |
| 1/7 | .1429 | 1/64 | .0156 | 3/7 | .4286 | 5/6 | .8333 | 7/8 | .8750 | 9/11 | .8182 |
| 1/8 | .1250 | 2/3 | .6667 | 3/8 | .3750 | 5/7 | .7143 | 7/9 | .7778 | 10/11 | .9091 |
| 1/9 | .1111 | 2/5 | .4000 | 3/10 | .3000 | 5/8 | .6250 | 7/10 | .7000 | 11/12 | .9167 |

# Conversion Factors

| To change | To | Multiply by | To change | To | Multiply by |
|---|---|---|---|---|---|
| acres | hectares | .4047 | liters | pints (dry) | 1.8162 |
| acres | square feet | 43,560 | liters | pints (liquid) | 2.1134 |
| acres | square miles | .001562 | liters | quarts (dry) | .9081 |
| atmospheres | cms. of mercury | 76 | liters | quarts (liquid) | 1.0567 |
| BTU | horsepower-hour | .0003931 | meters | feet | 3.2808 |
| BTU | kilowatt-hour | .0002928 | meters | miles | .0006214 |
| BTU/hour | watts | .2931 | meters | yards | 1.0936 |
| bushels | cubic inches | 2150.4 | metric tons | tons (long) | .9842 |
| bushels (U.S.) | hectoliters | .3524 | metric tons | tons (short) | 1.1023 |
| centimeters | inches | .3937 | miles | kilometers | 1.6093 |
| centimeters | feet | .03281 | miles | feet | 5280 |
| circumference | radians | 6.283 | miles (nautical) | miles (statute) | 1.1516 |
| cubic feet | cubic meters | .0283 | miles (statute) | miles (nautical) | .8684 |
| cubic meters | cubic feet | 35.3145 | miles/hour | feet/minute | 88 |
| cubic meters | cubic yards | 1.3079 | millimeters | inches | .0394 |
| cubic yards | cubic meters | .7646 | ounces avdp. | grams | 28.3495 |
| degrees | radians | .01745 | ounces | pounds | .0625 |
| dynes | grams | .00102 | ounces (troy) | ounces (avdp) | 1.09714 |
| fathoms | feet | 6.0 | pecks | liters | 8.8096 |
| feet | meters | .3048 | pints (dry) | liters | .5506 |
| feet | miles (nautical) | .0001645 | pints (liquid) | liters | .4732 |
| feet | miles (statute) | .0001894 | pounds ap or t | kilograms | .3782 |
| feet/second | miles/hour | .6818 | pounds avdp | kilograms | .4536 |
| furlongs | feet | 660.0 | pounds | ounces | 16 |
| furlongs | miles | .125 | quarts (dry) | liters | 1.1012 |
| gallons (U.S.) | liters | 3.7853 | quarts (liquid) | liters | .9463 |
| grains | grams | .0648 | radians | degrees | 57.30 |
| grams | grains | 15.4324 | rods | meters | 5.029 |
| grams | ounces avdp | .0353 | rods | feet | 16.5 |
| grams | pounds | .002205 | square feet | square meters | .0929 |
| hectares | acres | 2.4710 | square kilometers | square miles | .3861 |
| hectoliters | bushels (U.S.) | 2.8378 | square meters | square feet | 10.7639 |
| horsepower | watts | 745.7 | square meters | square yards | 1.1960 |
| hours | days | .04167 | square miles | square kilometers | 2.5900 |
| inches | millimeters | 25.4000 | square yards | square meters | .8361 |
| inches | centimeters | 2.5400 | tons (long) | metric tons | 1.016 |
| kilograms | pounds avdp or t | 2.2046 | tons (short) | metric tons | .9072 |
| kilometers | miles | .6214 | tons (long) | pounds | 2240 |
| kilowatts | horsepower | 1.341 | tons (short) | pounds | 2000 |
| knots | nautical miles/hour | 1.0 | watts | Btu/hour | 3.4129 |
| knots | statute miles/hour | 1.151 | watts | horsepower | .001341 |
| liters | gallons (U.S.) | .2642 | yards | meters | .9144 |
| liters | pecks | .1135 | yards | miles | .0005682 |

# Fahrenheit and Celsius (Centigrade) Scales

Zero on the Fahrenheit scale represents the temperature produced by the mixing of equal weights of snow and common salt.

|  | F | C |
|---|---|---|
| Boiling point of water | 212° | 100° |
| Freezing point of water | 32° | 0° |
| Absolute zero | −459.6° | −273.1° |

Absolute zero is theoretically the lowest possible temperature, the point at which all molecular motion would cease.

To convert Fahrenheit to Celsius (Centigrade), subtract 32 and multiply by 5/9.

To convert Celsius (Centigrade) to Fahrenheit, multiply by 9/5 and add 32.

| °Centigrade | °Fahrenheit | °Centigrade | °Fahrenheit |
|---|---|---|---|
| −273.1 | −459.6 | 30 | 86 |
| −250 | −418 | 35 | 95 |
| −200 | −328 | 40 | 104 |
| −150 | −238 | 45 | 113 |
| −100 | −148 | 50 | 122 |
| −50 | −58 | 55 | 131 |
| −40 | −40 | 60 | 140 |
| −30 | −22 | 65 | 149 |
| −20 | −4 | 70 | 158 |
| −10 | 14 | 75 | 167 |
| 0 | 32 | 80 | 176 |
| 5 | 41 | 85 | 185 |
| 10 | 50 | 90 | 194 |
| 15 | 59 | 95 | 203 |
| 20 | 68 | 100 | 212 |
| 25 | 77 | | |

# Roman Numerals

Roman numerals are expressed by letters of the alphabet and are rarely used today except for formality or variety.

There are three basic principles for reading Roman numerals:

1. A letter repeated once or twice repeats its value that many times. (XXX=30, CC=200, etc.).

2. One or more letters placed after another letter of greater value increases the greater value by the amount of the smaller. (VI=6, LXX=70, MCC=1200, etc.).

3. A letter placed before another letter of greater value decreases the greater value by the amount of the smaller. (IV=4, XC=90, CM=900, etc.).

| Letter | Value | Letter | Value | Letter | Value | Letter | Value | Letter | Value |
|--------|-------|--------|-------|--------|-------|--------|-------|--------|-------|
| I | 1 | VII | 7 | XXX | 30 | LXXX | 80 | $\overline{V}$ | 5,000 |
| II | 2 | VIII | 8 | XL | 40 | XC | 90 | $\overline{X}$ | 10,000 |
| III | 3 | IX | 9 | L | 50 | C | 100 | $\overline{L}$ | 50,000 |
| IV | 4 | X | 10 | LX | 60 | D | 500 | $\overline{C}$ | 100,000 |
| V | 5 | XX | 20 | LXX | 70 | M | 1,000 | $\overline{D}$ | 500,000 |
| VI | 6 | | | | | | | $\overline{M}$ | 1,000,000 |

# Mean and Median

The mean, also called the average, of a series of quantities is obtained by finding the sum of the quantities and dividing it by the number of quantities. In the series 1,3,5,18,19,20,25, the mean or average is 13—i.e., 91 divided by 7.

The median of a series is that point which so divides it that half the quantities are on one side, half on the other. In the above series, the median is 18.

The median often better expresses the common-run, since it is not, as is the mean, affected by an excessively high or low figure. In the series 1,3,4, 7,55, the median of 4 is a truer expression of the common-run than is the mean of 14.

### Prime Numbers Between 1 and 1,000

| | | | | | | | | | |
|---|---|---|---|---|---|---|---|---|---|
| 1 | 2 | 3 | 5 | 7 | 11 | 13 | 17 | 19 | 23 |
| 29 | 31 | 37 | 41 | 43 | 47 | 53 | 59 | 61 | 67 |
| 71 | 73 | 79 | 83 | 89 | 97 | 101 | 103 | 107 | 109 |
| 113 | 127 | 131 | 137 | 139 | 149 | 151 | 157 | 163 | 167 |
| 173 | 179 | 181 | 191 | 193 | 197 | 199 | 211 | 223 | 227 |
| 229 | 233 | 239 | 241 | 251 | 257 | 263 | 269 | 271 | 277 |
| 281 | 283 | 293 | 307 | 311 | 313 | 317 | 331 | 337 | 347 |
| 349 | 353 | 359 | 367 | 373 | 379 | 383 | 389 | 397 | 401 |
| 409 | 419 | 421 | 431 | 433 | 439 | 443 | 449 | 457 | 461 |
| 463 | 467 | 479 | 487 | 491 | 499 | 503 | 509 | 521 | 523 |
| 541 | 547 | 557 | 563 | 569 | 571 | 577 | 587 | 593 | 599 |
| 601 | 607 | 613 | 617 | 619 | 631 | 641 | 643 | 647 | 653 |
| 659 | 661 | 673 | 677 | 683 | 691 | 701 | 709 | 719 | 727 |
| 733 | 739 | 743 | 751 | 757 | 761 | 769 | 773 | 787 | 797 |
| 809 | 811 | 821 | 823 | 827 | 829 | 839 | 853 | 857 | 859 |
| 863 | 877 | 881 | 883 | 887 | 907 | 911 | 919 | 929 | 937 |
| 941 | 947 | 953 | 967 | 971 | 977 | 983 | 991 | 997 | (1009) |

# Definitions of Gold Terminology

The term "fineness" defines a gold content in parts per thousand. For example, a gold nugget containing 885 parts of pure gold, 100 parts of silver, and 15 parts of copper would be considered 885-fine.

The word "karat" indicates the proportion of solid gold in an alloy based on a total of 24 parts. Thus, 14-karat (14K) gold indicates a composition of 14 parts of gold and 10 parts of other metals.

The term "gold-filled" is used to describe articles of jewelry made of base metal which are covered on one or more surfaces with a layer of gold alloy. No article having a gold alloy portion of less than one twentieth by weight may be marked "gold-filled." Articles may be marked "rolled gold plate" provided the proportional fraction and fineness designations are also shown.

Electroplated jewelry items carrying at least 7 millionths of an inch of gold on significant surfaces may be labeled "electroplate." Plate thicknesses less than this may be marked "gold flashed" or "gold washed."

# Portraits and Designs of U.S. Paper Currency[1]

| Currency | Portrait | Design on back | Currency | Portrait | Design on back |
|----------|----------|----------------|----------|----------|----------------|
| $1 | Washington | ONE between obverse and reverse of Great Seal of U.S. | $50 | Grant | U.S. Capitol |
| | | | $100 | Franklin | Independence Hall |
| $2[2] | Jefferson | Monticello | $500 | McKinley | Ornate FIVE HUNDRED |
| $2[3] | Jefferson | "The Signing of the Declaration of Independence" | $1,000 | Cleveland | Ornate ONE THOUSAND |
| | | | $5,000 | Madison | Ornate FIVE THOUSAND |
| $5 | Lincoln | Lincoln Memorial | $10,000 | Chase | Ornate TEN THOUSAND |
| $10 | Hamilton | U.S. Treasury Building | $100,000[4] | Wilson | Ornate ONE HUNDRED THOUSAND |
| $20 | Jackson | White House | | | |

1. Denominations of $500 and higher were discontinued in 1969. 2. Discontinued in 1966. 3. New issue, April 13, 1976. 4. For use only in transactions between Federal Reserve System and Treasury Department.

# ENERGY

## Atomic Energy

Just as the Space Age is said to have started with the orbiting of Sputnik I, the Atomic Age is said to have started with the explosion of a test bomb on July 16, 1945, near Alamogordo, N.M., at 5:30 A.M. local time. The bomb was placed on top of a steel tower, and observers were stationed in bunkers 10,000 yards away. The explosion vaporized the steel tower, produced a mushroom cloud rising to 40,000 feet, and melted the desert sand into glass for distances up to 800 yards from the tower.

The first operational use of an atom bomb took place only three weeks later, when a uranium bomb was exploded over Hiroshima, Japan, on Aug. 6, 1945. The bomb, cylindrical in shape, 10 feet long with a diameter of 2 feet 4 inches, weighed about 9,000 pounds. Its explosive force was equal to 20,000 tons of TNT, hence the term "20-kiloton bomb." Three days later another atomic bomb, this time of plutonium, was exploded over Nagasaki.

Of course, the Atomic Age did not begin with the explosion of the test bomb at Alamogordo, just as the Space Age did not begin with the orbiting of the first artificial satellite. In both cases these visible feats were just experiments that proved the theory that had been built up patiently over decades.

At the turn of the century, scientists began to wonder whether the atoms of the chemical elements might not be composed of smaller particles. This was actually a contradiction in terms, because the Greek word *atomos*, from which the word *atom* was derived, meant "indivisible." But there were some indications of particles smaller than an atom—the electrons. In 1907,* Albert Einstein suggested that matter might just be "condensed energy" and gave the conversion formula $E = mc^2$, in which $E$ represents the energy, $m$ the mass, and $c$ the velocity of light. If this formula was correct, a small piece of matter should represent enormous amounts of energy.

*Einstein's famous formula was first published on May 14, 1907. His special theory of relativity was published in 1905.

## Fission and Fusion

Atomic energy can be released in two ways. One is the *fission* of elements with very heavy atoms,

## Largest Nuclear Power Plants in the United States
### (over a million kilowatts)

| Location | Operating utility | Capacity (kilowatts) | Year operative |
|---|---|---|---|
| Cowans Ford Dam, NC (Unit 2) | Duke Power Company | 1,180,000 | 1984 |
| Cowans Ford Dam, NC (Unit 1) | Duke Power Company | 1,180,000 | 1981 |
| Burlington, Kan. | Kansas Gas & Electric | 1,150,000 | 1985 |
| Daisy, Tenn. (Unit 1) | Tennessee Valley Authority | 1,148,000 | 1980 |
| Daisy, Tenn. (Unit 2) | Tennessee Valley Authority | 1,148,000 | 1982 |
| Lake Wylie, S.C.(Unit 1) | Duke Power | 1,145,000 | 1985 |
| Prescott, Ore. (Unit 1) | Portland General Electric Co. | 1,130,000 | 1976 |
| Byron, Ill. (Unit 1) | Commonwealth Edison | 1,120,000 | 1985 |
| Fulton, Mo. | Union Electric Co. | 1,120,000 | 1984 |
| Taft, La. | Louisiana Power & Light | 1,100,000 | 1985 |
| Richland, WA. (Unit 2) | Washington Public Power | 1,100,000 | 1984 |
| San Clemente, CA (Unit 3) | Southern Cal Edison Co. | 1,100,000 | 1984 |
| San Clemente, Calif. (Unit 2) | Southern Cal. Edison Co. | 1,100,000 | 1983 |
| Bridgman, Mich. (Unit 2) | Indiana & Michigan Electric Co. | 1,100,000 | 1978 |
| Salem, N.J. (Unit 2) | Public Service Electric & Gas, N.J. | 1,100,000 | 1981 |
| Salem, N.J. (Unit 1) | Public Service Electric & Gas, N.J. | 1,090,000 | 1977 |
| Diablo Canyon, Calif. | Pacific Gas & Electric | 1,080,000 | 1985 |
| Seneca Ill. (Unit 2) | Commonwealth Edison Co. | 1,078,000 | 1984 |
| Seneca, Ill. (Unit 1) | Commonwealth Edison Co. | 1,078,000 | 1984 |
| Decatur, Ala. (Unit 1) | Tennessee Valley Authority | 1,065,000 | 1974 |
| Decatur, Ala. (Unit 2) | Tennessee Valley Authority | 1,065,000 | 1975 |
| Decatur, Ala. (Unit 3) | Tennessee Valley Authority | 1,065,000 | 1977 |
| Peach Bottom, Pa. (Unit 2) | Philadelphia Electric Co. | 1,065,000 | 1974 |
| Peach Bottom, Pa. (Unit 3) | Philadelphia Electric Co. | 1,065,000 | 1974 |
| Bridgman, Mich. (Unit 1) | Indiana & Michigan Electric Co. | 1,054,000 | 1975 |
| Berwick, Pa. (Unit 1) | Pennsylvania Power & Light | 1,050,000 | 1983 |
| Zion, Ill. (Unit 1) | Commonwealth Edison Co. | 1,040,000 | 1973 |
| Zion, Ill. (Unit 2) | Commonwealth Edison Co. | 1,040,000 | 1974 |

*Source:* Nuclear Regulatory Commission.

such as uranium and plutonium, which will split when struck by a neutron, a sub-atomic particle. The splitting of the heavy atom releases more neutrons, which are then available to split other atoms—the so-called chain reaction. The other way of obtaining atomic energy is *fusion;* four light atoms (hydrogen) are fused together into the next heavier element (helium). The fusion reaction requires enormous heat and very high pressures. These pressures, coupled with very high temperatures, can most easily be produced by exploding a fission bomb.

From about 1910 to 1930, most physicists believed that the release of atomic energy, if it could be done, would be of no practical value. They asserted that causing the release would require more energy than could be obtained. Most astronomers, on the other hand, were convinced that atomic energy was released in the sun and the other stars, because there was no other way to account for the energy the stars radiated into space. Trying to account for the energy radiated by the stars led to theoretical papers predicting what we now call the fusion reaction. At the time (1930), atomic fission was still unknown; it was discovered first by Enrico Fermi in 1934. But nobody yet knew that the sudden bursts of energy observed in the experiments were due to the fission of the uranium-235 atom. This was established (by way of calculation) by Dr. Lise Meitner. Once it was known what happened, the way to a premeditated release of atomic energy was clear.

But nobody could be quite certain whether the release would take the form of an explosion or whether it would be slow enough to be used to generate power. American scientists proceeded under the assumption that the release would be sudden and violent (and the Alamogordo test proved them right), while Professor Heisenberg in Germany thought the slow release to be more likely, which is the reason why the Germans did not start a large-scale atomic energy project.

## Atoms for Peace

The *peaceful* Atomic Age can be said to have been born in 1954, when the original U.S. Atomic Energy Act was amended to release many so-called "secrets" of nuclear energy so that nuclear power plants could be built and radioactive isotopes be used in medicine. The next year, the first International Conference on the Peaceful Uses of the Atom was convened at Geneva, bringing together scientists from all over the world to discuss what hitherto had been considered to be secret.

Actually there was little that was really secret about nuclear energy. When the results of the 1938 experiments were brought to the United States, scientists from different parts of the world openly stated that the possibility of atomic bombs was inherent in the scientific findings.

Once the veil of "secrecy" had been dispelled by revision of the Atomic Energy Act and the Geneva meeting, construction of plants to produce electricity by controlled fission of uranium atoms got under way in the United States and several other industrialized nations. Electric power was first produced as a result of nuclear fission in December 1951 at the National Reactor Testing Station in Idaho. When a reactor was connected to a generator, the nuclear power plant produced enough electricity for about 50 homes.

## Nuclear Disaster at Chernobyl

The world was given a jarring reminder of the potential hazards of nuclear energy in April 1986 when an accident at a Soviet nuclear reactor at Chernobyl (60 mi. north of Kiev) caused the release of large amounts of radiation into the air. The incident had international repercussions due to the Soviets' reluctance to give information on the accident. The accident also revived the issue of safety at nuclear power plants in the U.S.

Although the accident took place on April 26, the outside world was unaware that anything was wrong until April 28 when nuclear technicians throughout Scandanavia detected abnormally high radiation levels. A study of wind patterns for the previous few days showed that the source of the radioactivity was the Soviet Union; further study determined that the source was at Chernobyl. Swedish queries to the Soviets received no reply. Finally, that evening, a Soviet newscaster announced that "An accident has taken place at the Chernobyl power station, and one of the reactors was damaged."

The following day, a Soviet statement was released saying that the accident had caused only two deaths and that it was under control. Soviet actions over the next few weeks were a mix of trying to cope with the emergency and attempting to play down the accident. Soviet diplomats were asking European experts how to extinguish a graphite fire (the reactor has a graphite core) while at the same time refusing to provide further information on the accident and accusing the Western media of exaggerating the disaster for propaganda purposes. In fact, Soviet reticence contributed to rumors abroad, including one report placing the death toll at 2,000. A number of European countries stopped imports of foodstuffs from the Soviet Union and countries near it and issued instructions on how to avoid exposure to excess radiation. In fact, later tests showed Russian meat and milk as having unsafe amounts of radiation.

Western scientists made the deduction, based on satellite photos of the damaged plant and knowledge of its basic design, that the cooling system malfunctioned. The continuing action of the reactor caused the uranium fuel rods to overheat (an emergency back-up system that should have shut down the reactor failed to operate in time). As the uranium fuel began to melt, it emitted hydrogen gas which mixed with the oxygen and was ignited by the intense heat (9,000° F). This caused an explosion that destroyed the reactor building and ignited the graphite core. As the reactor had no containment dome, a structure used on most Western reactors, the core was exposed to the open air. This intensified the graphite fire which melted the uranium fuel, thus releasing radiation directly into the air.

Beginning in mid-May, more information began to come out of the Soviet Union when a Soviet official held a press conference on the accident. Officials of the International Atomic Energy Agency

(IAEA) were permitted to view Chernobyl by helicopter and foreign reporters were allowed to visit the Kiev region. The IAEA confirmed earlier Soviet reports that the fire had been extinguished a little more than a week after the accident. Reports from Dr. Robert Gale, an American who headed a medical team that went to the Soviet Union to assist radiation victims and from the Soviet press agencies, indicated that as of the end of May, the death toll has risen to 23. In addition, another 80 patients were reported to be in "extreme danger" and that several hundred would suffer an increased cancer risk in the long term.

## Production of Crude Petroleum by Countries

### (in thousands of 42-gallon barrels)

| Area and country | Est. 1986[1] | 1985[1] | Est. percent change | Area and country | Est. 1986[1] | 1985[1] | Est. percent change |
|---|---|---|---|---|---|---|---|
| Western Hemisphere | 5,900,590 | 5,946,215 | −0.8 | Syria | 67,525 | 63,875 | 5.7 |
| Argentina | 162,425 | 163,520 | −0.7 | United Arab Emirates | 491,655 | 401,500 | 22.5 |
| Bolivia | 7,300 | 7,665 | −4.8 | Asia-Pacific | 1,198,660 | 1,159,970 | 3.3 |
| Brazil | 210,605 | 186,880 | 12.7 | Australia | 219,000 | 198,925 | 10.1 |
| Canada | 528,155 | 525,235 | 0.6 | Brunei | 58,400 | 47,085 | 24.0 |
| Chile | 12,045 | 13,140 | −8.3 | Burma | 10,950 | 10,950 | — |
| Colombia | 63,875 | 64,240 | −0.6 | India | 229,220 | 224,475 | 2.1 |
| Ecuador | 109,135 | 99,280 | 9.9 | Indonesia | 455,155 | 475,230 | −4.2 |
| Guatemala | 1,460 | 1,095 | 33.3 | Japan | 4,380 | 3,650 | 20.0 |
| Mexico | 848,990 | 970,535 | −12.5 | Malaysia | 183,230 | 169,725 | 8.0 |
| Peru | 64,605 | 69,350 | −6.8 | New Zealand | 6,935 | 4,745 | 46.2 |
| Trinidad and Tobago | 61,320 | 64,605 | −5.1 | Pakistan | 14,600 | 9,855 | 48.1 |
| United States | 3,263,465 | 3,211,270 | 1.6 | Philippines | 2,920 | 4,015 | −27.3 |
| Venezuela | 567,210 | 569,400 | −0.4 | Taiwan | 730 | 1,095 | −33.3 |
| Western Europe | 1,470,220 | 1,396,855 | 5.3 | Thailand | 13,140 | 10,220 | 28.6 |
| Austria | 8,030 | 8,030 | — | Africa | 1,664,765 | 1,756,380 | −5.2 |
| Denmark | 23,360 | 20,440 | 14.3 | Algeria | 220,095 | 235,060 | −6.4 |
| France | 22,265 | 14,600 | 52.5 | Angola/Cabinda[3] | 94,900 | 76,650 | 23.8 |
| West Germany | 30,295 | 29,930 | 1.2 | Cameroon | 67,525 | 47,085 | 43.4 |
| Greece | 10,220 | 9,855 | 3.7 | Congo | 41,975 | 32,850 | 27.8 |
| Italy | 16,790 | 16,790 | — | Egypt | 269,005 | 317,550 | −15.3 |
| Netherlands | 26,645 | 25,550 | 4.3 | Gabon | 58,400 | 54,750 | 6.7 |
| Norway | 311,710 | 255,500 | 22.0 | Ghana | 365 | 730 | −50.0 |
| Spain | 14,600 | 19,345 | −24.5 | Ivory Coast | 7,300 | 10,220 | −28.6 |
| Turkey | 14,600 | 14,600 | — | Libya | 384,345 | 374,125 | 2.7 |
| United Kingdom | 991,705 | 982,215 | −1.0 | Morocco | 365 | 365 | — |
| Middle East | 4,282,545 | 3,800,745 | 12.7 | Nigeria | 472,675 | 559,545 | −15.5 |
| Bahrain | 14,600 | 14,965 | −2.4 | Tunisia | 39,420 | 38,690 | 1.9 |
| Iran | 707,005 | 759,200 | −6.9 | Zaire | 8,395 | 8,760 | −4.2 |
| Iraq | 647,875 | 457,345 | 41.7 | Communist bloc | 5,470,620 | 5,386,670 | 1.6 |
| Israel | 365 | 365 | — | China | 911,040 | 872,350 | 4.4 |
| Kuwait | 382,155 | 345,655 | 10.6 | Romania | 82,490 | 82,490 | — |
| Neutral Zone[2] | 92,345 | 171,185 | −46.1 | U.S.S.R. | 4,394,235 | 4,348,975 | 1.0 |
| Oman | 182,500 | 156,950 | 16.3 | Other communist | 82,855 | 82,855 | — |
| Qatar | 128,845 | 102,200 | 26.1 | **World total** | **19,987,400** | **19,446,835** | **2.8** |
| Saudi Arabia | 1,567,675 | 1,327,505 | 18.1 | | | | |

1. Based on Jan.–Feb. average. 2. Shared by Kuwait and Saudi Arabia. 3. An enclave in West Africa on Atlantic coast between the Congo and Angola.

## Radiation Doses

Radiation doses were originally measured in *roentgens*, (r), a unit of exposure to X-ray or gamma-ray radiation in the air. Today, the *rad* (ra) is the unit commonly used for measuring the amount of radiation to which the whole body, as contrasted with a single organ, is exposed.

The *millirad* is one-thousandth of a rad. Most scientists believe that a dose of a few millirads is safe, but there is significant controversy over the threshold at which a dose becomes hazardous.

The *rem* (for "roentgen equivalent, man") is a measure of ionizing radiation of the type that produces the same damage to human beings as one roentgen of approximately 200 kilowatts of X-radiation.

*Millirem* is the term used to describe the amount of absorption of radiation by humans. The average American is exposed to 100–200 millirems of radiation per year from man-made and natural sources. A normal chest X-ray exposes one to 20–30 millirems.

## Petroleum Imports by Country of Origin, 1975–1985
### (thousand barrels per day)

| | Organization of Petroleum Exporting Countries (OPEC) | | | | | | | | | |
| Year | Saudi Arabia | Vene- zuela | Indo- nesia | Algeria | Nigeria | Total OPEC[1] | Canada | Mexico | United Kingdom | Virgin Is./ Puerto Rico |
|---|---|---|---|---|---|---|---|---|---|---|
| 1975 | 715 | 702 | 390 | 282 | 762 | 3,601 | 846 | 71 | 14 | 496 |
| 1976 | 1,230 | 700 | 539 | 432 | 1,025 | 5,066 | 599 | 87 | 31 | 510 |
| 1977 | 1,380 | 690 | 541 | 559 | 1,143 | 6,193 | 517 | 179 | 126 | 571 |
| 1978 | 1,144 | 645 | 573 | 649 | 919 | 5,751 | 467 | 318 | 180 | 522 |
| 1979 | 1,356 | 690 | 420 | 636 | 1,080 | 5,637 | 538 | 439 | 202 | 523 |
| 1980 | 1,261 | 481 | 348 | 488 | 857 | 4,300 | 455 | 533 | 176 | 476 |
| 1981 | 1,129 | 406 | 366 | 311 | 620 | 3,323 | 447 | 522 | 375 | 389 |
| 1982 | 552 | 412 | 248 | 170 | 514 | 2,146 | 482 | 685 | 456 | 366 |
| 1984 | 325 | 548 | 343 | 323 | 216 | 2,049 | 630 | 748 | 402 | 336 |
| 1985[2] | 167 | 608 | 306 | 190 | 287 | 1,825 | 768 | 815 | 314 | 275 |

1. Excludes petroleum imported into the U.S. indirectly from OPEC countries, primarily from Caribbean and West European refining areas, as petroleum products which were refined from crude oil produced in OPEC countries. 2. Preliminary. NOTE: Data include imports for Strategic Petroleum Reserve, which began in 1977. Sum of components may not equal total due to independent rounding. *Source:* 1975—U.S. Dept. of the Interior, Bureau of Mines; 1976 through 1985—U.S. Dept. of Energy, Energy Information Administration.

## Exports of Crude Oil and Petroleum Products by Country of Destination, 1975–1985
### (Thousand Barrels per Day)

| Year | Canada | Japan | Mexico | Nether- lands | Belgium[1] | Italy | United Kingdom | France | Brazil | Virgin Is./ Puerto Rico |
|---|---|---|---|---|---|---|---|---|---|---|
| 1975 | 22 | 27 | 42 | 23 | 9 | 10 | 7 | 6 | 6 | 12 |
| 1976 | 28 | 25 | 35 | 22 | 12 | 10 | 13 | 6 | 7 | 6 |
| 1977 | 71 | 25 | 24 | 17 | 16 | 10 | 9 | 9 | 6 | 11 |
| 1978 | 108 | 26 | 27 | 18 | 15 | 10 | 7 | 9 | 8 | 86 |
| 1979 | 100 | 34 | 21 | 28 | 19 | 15 | 7 | 13 | 7 | 170 |
| 1980 | 108 | 32 | 28 | 23 | 20 | 14 | 7 | 11 | 4 | 220 |
| 1981 | 89 | 38 | 26 | 42 | 12 | 22 | 5 | 15 | 1 | 221 |
| 1982 | 85 | 68 | 53 | 85 | 17 | 32 | 14 | 24 | 8 | 211 |
| 1983 | 76 | 104 | 24 | 49 | 22 | 35 | 8 | 23 | 2 | 144 |
| 1984 | 83 | 92 | 35 | 37 | 21 | 39 | 14 | 18 | 1 | 152 |
| 1985[2] | 74 | 108 | 61 | 44 | 26 | 30 | 14 | 11 | 3 | 161 |

1. Including Luxembourg. 2. Preliminary. NOTE: Sum of components may not equal total due to independent rounding. *Source:* 1975—Bureau of Mines, Mineral Industry Surveys, *Petroleum Statement, Annual.* ● 1976 through 1980—Energy Information Administration, Energy Data Reports, *Petroleum Statement, Annual.* ● 1981 through 1984—Energy Information Administration, *Petroleum Supply Annual.* ● 1985—Energy Information Administration, *Petroleum Supply Monthly.*

## U.S. Motor Vehicle Fuel Consumption and Related Data
### (1984 estimate)

| Type of vehicle | Total travel (million vehicle miles) | Number of registered vehicles | Average miles traveled per vehicle | Fuel consumed (thousand gallons) | Average fuel con- sumption per vehicle (gallons) | Average miles per gallon |
|---|---|---|---|---|---|---|
| All passenger vehicles | 1,272,994 | 133,930,393 | 9,505 | 75,422,100 | 563 | 16.68 |
| Total personal passenger vehicles | 1,266,265 | 133,346,722 | 9,496 | 74,281,600 | 557 | 17.05 |
| Cars | 1,254,265 | 127,866,900 | 9,809 | 74,041,600 | 579 | 16.94 |
| Motorcycles | 12,000 | 5,479,822 | 2,190 | 240,000 | 44 | 50.00 |
| All buses | 6,729 | 583,671 | 11,529 | 1,140,500 | 1,954 | 5.90 |
| All cargo vehicles | 443,774 | 38,047,099 | 11,664 | 43,313,697 | 1,138 | 10.25 |
| Single unit trucks | 366,905 | 36,787,599 | 9,974 | 28,587,797 | 777 | 12.83 |
| Combinations | 76,869 | 1,259,500 | 61,031 | 14,725,900 | 11,692 | 5.22 |
| All motor vehicles | 1,716,768 | 171,977,492 | 9,969 | 118,735,797 | 689 | 14.46 |

*Source:* Department of Transportation, Federal Highway Administration.

# WRITER'S GUIDE

## A Concise Guide to Style

From *Webster's II New Riverside University Dictionary.* © 1984 by Houghton Mifflin Company.

This section discusses and illustrates the basic conventions of American capitalization, punctuation, and italicization.

### Capitalization

Capitalize the following: **1.** the first word of a sentence: Some spiders are poisonous; others are not. Are you my new neighbor?
**2.** the first word of a direct quotation, except when the quotation is split: Joyce asked, "Do you think that the lecture was interesting?" "No," I responded, "it was very boring." Tom Paine said, "The sublime and the ridiculous are often so nearly related that it is difficult to class them separately."
**3.** the first word of each line in a poem in traditional verse: Half a league, half a league,/Half a league onward,/All in the valley of Death/Rode the six hundred.—Alfred, Lord Tennyson
**4.** the names of people, of organizations and their members, of councils and congresses, and of historical periods and events: Marie Curie, Benevolent and Protective Order of Elks, an Elk, Protestant Episcopal Church, an Episcopalian, the Democratic Party, a Democrat, the Nuclear Regulatory Commission, the U.S. Senate, the Middle Ages, World War I, the Battle of Britain.
**5.** the names of places and geographic divisions, districts, regions, and locales: Richmond, Vermont, Argentina, Seventh Avenue, London Bridge, Arctic Circle, Eastern Hemisphere, Continental Divide, Middle East, Far North, Gulf States, East Coast, the North, the South Shore.
Do not capitalize words indicating compass points unless a specific region is referred to: Turn north onto Interstate 91.
**6.** the names of rivers, lakes, mountains, and oceans: Ohio River, Lake Como, Rocky Mountains, Atlantic Ocean.
**7.** the names of ships, aircraft, satellites, and space vehicles: U.S.S. *Arizona, Spirit of St. Louis,* the spy satellite Ferret-D, Voyager II, the space shuttle Challenger.
**8.** the names of nationalities, races, tribes, and languages: Spanish, Maori, Bantu, Russian.
**9.** words derived from proper names, except in their extended senses: the Byzantine Empire. *But:* byzantine office politics.
**10.** words indicating family relationships when used with a person's name as a title: Aunt Toni and Uncle Jack. *But:* my aunt and uncle, Toni and Jack Walker.
**11.** a title (i.e., civil, judicial, military, royal and noble, religious, and honorary) when preceding a name: Justice Marshall, General Jackson, Mayor Daley, Queen Victoria, Lord Mountbatten, Pope John Paul II, Professor Jacobson, Senator Byrd.
**12.** all references to the President and Vice President of the United States: The President has entered the hall. The Vice President presides over the Senate.

**13.** all key words in titles of literary, dramatic, artistic, and musical works: the novel *The Old Man and the Sea,* the short story "Notes from Underground," an article entitled "On Passive Verbs," James Dickey's poem "In the Tree House at Night," the play *Cat on a Hot Tin Roof,* Van Gogh's *Wheat Field and Cypress Trees,* Beethoven's *Emperor Concerto.*
**14.** *the* in the title of a newspaper if it is a part of the title: *The Wall Street Journal. But:* the New York *Daily News.*
**15.** the first word in the salutation and in the complimentary close of a letter: My dear Carol, Yours sincerely.
**16.** epithets and substitutes for the names of people and places: Old Hickory, Old Blood and Guts, The Oval Office, the Windy City.
**17.** words used in personifications: When is not Death at watch/Within those secret waters?/What wants he but to catch/Earth's heedless sons and daughters?—Edmund Blunden
**18.** the pronoun *I:* I told them that I had heard the news.
**19.** names for the Deity and sacred works: God, the Almighty, Jesus, Allah, the Supreme Being, the Bible, the Koran, the Talmud.
**20.** days of the week, months of the year, holidays, and holy days: Tuesday, May, Independence Day, Passover, Ramadan, Christmas.
**21.** the names of specific courts: The Supreme Court of the United States, the Massachusetts Appeals Court, the United States Court of Appeals for the First Circuit.
**22.** the names of treaties, accords, pacts, laws, and specific amendments: Panama Canal Treaty, Treaty of Paris, Geneva Accords, Warsaw Pact countries, Sherman Antitrust Law, Labor Management Relations Act, took the Fifth Amendment.
**23.** registered trademarks and service marks: Day-Glo, Comsat.
**24.** the names of geologic eras, periods, epochs, and strata and the names of prehistoric divisions: Paleozoic Era, Precambrian, Pleistocene, Age of Reptiles, Bronze Age, Stone Age.
**25.** the names of constellations, planets, and stars: Milky Way, Southern Crown, Saturn, Jupiter, Uranus, Polaris.
**26.** genus but not species names in binomial nomenclature: *Rana pipiens.*
**27.** New Latin names of classes, families, and all groups higher than genera in botanical and zoological nomenclature: Nematoda.
But do not capitalize derivatives from such names: nematodes.
**28.** many abbreviations and acronyms: Dec., Tues., Lt. Gen., M.F.A., UNESCO, MIRV.

### Italicization

Use italics to:
**1.** indicate titles of books, plays, and epic poems:

*War and Peace, The Importance of Being Earnest, Paradise Lost.*

2. indicate titles of magazines and newspapers: *New York* magazine, *The Wall Street Journal*, the New York *Daily News.*

3. set off the titles of motion pictures and radio and television programs: *Star Wars, All Things Considered, Masterpiece Theater.*

4. indicate titles of major musical compositions: Handel's *Messiah*, Adam's *Giselle.*

5. set off the names of paintings and sculpture: *Mona Lisa, Pietà.*

6. indicate words, letters, or numbers that are referred to: The word *hiss* is onomatopoeic. *Can't* means *won't* in your lexicon. You form your *n*'s like *u*'s. A *6* looks like an inverted *9.*

7. indicate foreign words and phrases not yet assimilated into English: *C'est la vie* was the response to my complaint.

8. indicate the names of plaintiff and defendant in legal citations: *Roe* v. *Doe.*

9. emphasize a word or phrase: When you appear on the national news, you are *somebody.*
Use this device sparingly.

10. distinguish New Latin names of genera, species, subspecies, and varieties in botanical and zoological nomenclature: *Homo sapiens.*

11. set off the names of ships and aircraft but not space vehicles: U.S.S. *Arizona, Spirit of St. Louis,* Voyager II, the space shuttle Challenger, the spy satellite Ferret-D.

## Punctuation

**Apostrophe. 1.** indicates the possessive case of singular and plural nouns, indefinite pronouns, and surnames combined with designations such as *Jr., Sr.,* and *II:* my sister's husband, my three sisters' husbands, anyone's guess, they answer each other's phones, John Smith, Jr.'s car.

2. indicates joint possession when used with the last of two or more nouns in a series: Doe and Roe's report.

3. indicates individual possession or authorship when used with each of two or more nouns in a series: Smith's, Roe's, and Doe's reports.

4. indicates the plurals of words, letters, and figures used as such: 60's and 70's; *x*'s, *y*'s, and *z*'s.

5. indicates omission of letters in contractions: aren't, that's, o'clock.

6. indicates omission of figures in dates: the class of '63.

**Brackets. 1.** enclose words or passages in quoted matter to indicate insertion of material written by someone other than the author: A tough but nervous, tenacious but restless race [the Yankees]; materially ambitious, yet prone to introspection. . . .—Samuel Eliot Morison

2. enclose material inserted within matter already in parentheses: (Vancouver [B.C.] January 1, 19—).

**Colon. 1.** introduces words, phrases, or clauses that explain, amplify, or summarize what has gone before: Suddenly I realized where we were: Rome. There are two cardinal sins from which all the others spring: impatience and laziness.—Franz Kafka

2. introduces a long quotation: In his original draft of the *Declaration of Independence*, Jefferson wrote: "We hold these truths to be sacred and undeniable; that all men are created equal and independent, that from that equal creation they derive

rights inherent and inalienable. . . ."

3. introduces a list: We need the following items: pens, paper, pencils, blotters, and erasers.

4. separates chapter and verse numbers in Biblical references: James 1:4.

5. separates city from publisher in footnotes and bibliographies: Chicago: Riverside Press, 1983.

6. separates hour and minute(s) in time designations: 9:30 a.m., a 9:30 meeting.

7. follows the salutation in a business letter: Gentlemen:

**Comma. 1.** separates the clauses of a compound sentence connected by a coordinating conjunction: A difference exists between the musical works of Handel and Haydn, and it is a difference worth noting.
The comma may be omitted in short compound sentences: I heard what you said and I am furious. I got out of the car and I walked and walked.

2. separates *and* or *or* from the final item in a series of three or more: Red, yellow, and blue may be mixed to produce all colors.

3. separates two or more adjectives modifying the same noun if *and* could be used between them without altering the meaning: a solid, heavy gait. *But:* a polished mahogany dresser.

4. sets off nonrestrictive clauses or phrases (i.e., those that if eliminated would not affect the meaning of the sentences): The burglar, who had entered through the patio, went straight to the silver chest.
The comma should not be used when a clause is restrictive (i.e., essential to the meaning of the sentence): The burglar who had entered through the patio went straight to the silver chest; the other burglar searched for the wall safe.

5. sets off words or phrases in apposition to a noun or noun phrase: Plato, the famous Greek philosopher, was a student of Socrates.
The comma should not be used if such words or phrases precede the noun: The Greek philosopher Plato was a student of Socrates.

6. sets off transitional words and short expressions that require a pause in reading or speaking: Unfortunately, my friend was not well traveled. Did you, after all, find what you were looking for? I live with my family, of course.

7. sets off words used to introduce a sentence: No, I haven't been to Paris. Well, what do you think we should do now?

8. sets off a subordinate clause or a long phrase that precedes a principal clause: By the time we found the restaurant, we were starved. Of all the illustrations in the book, the most striking are those of the tapestries.

9. sets off short quotations and sayings: The candidate said, "Actions speak louder than words." "Talking of axes," said the Duchess, "chop off her head!"—Lewis Carroll

10. indicates omission of a word or words: To err is human; to forgive, divine.

11. sets off the year from the month in full dates: Nicholas II of Russia was shot on July 16, 1918.
But note that when only the month and the year are used, no comma appears: Nicholas II of Russia was shot in July 1918.

12. sets off city and state in geographic names: Atlanta, Georgia, is the transportation center of the South. 34 Beach Drive, Bedford, VA 24523.

13. separates series of four or more figures into thousands, millions, etc.: 67,000; 200,000.

14. sets off words used in direct address: I tell you, folks, all politics is applesauce.—Will Rogers Thank you for your expert assistance, Dolores.

**15.** Separates a tag question from the rest of a sentence: You forgot your keys again, didn't you?

**16.** sets off sentence elements that could be misunderstood if the comma were not used: Some time after, the actual date for the project was set.

**17.** follows the salutation in a personal letter and the complimentary close in a business or personal letter: Dear Jessica, Sincerely yours.

**18.** sets off titles and degrees from surnames and from the rest of a sentence: Walter T. Prescott, Jr.; Gregory A. Rossi, S.J.; Susan P. Green, M.D., presented the case.

**Dash. 1.** indicates a sudden break or abrupt change in continuity: "If—if you'll just let me explain—" the student stammered. And the problem—if there really is one—can then be solved.

**2.** sets apart an explanatory, a defining, or an emphatic phrase: Foods rich in protein—meat, fish, and eggs—should be eaten on a daily basis.

More important than winning the election, is governing the nation. That is the test of a political party—the acid, final test.—Adlai E. Stevenson

**3.** sets apart parenthetical matter: Wolsey, for all his faults—and he had many—was a great statesman, a man of natural dignity with a generous temperament. . . .—Jasper Ridley

**4.** marks an unfinished sentence: "But if my bus is late—" he began.

**5.** sets off a summarizing phrase or clause: The vital measure of a newspaper is not its size but its spirit—that is its responsibility to report the news fully, accurately, and fairly.—Arthur H. Sulzberger

**6.** sets off the name of an author or source, as at the end of a quotation: A poet can survive everything but a misprint.—Oscar Wilde

**Ellipses. 1.** indicate, by three spaced points, omission of words or sentences within quoted matter: Equipped by education to rule in the nineteenth century, . . . he lived and reigned in Russia in the twentieth century.—Robert K. Massie

**2.** indicate, by four spaced points, omission of words at the end of a sentence: The timidity of bureaucrats when it comes to dealing with . . . abuses is easy to explain. . . .—*New York*

**3.** indicate, when extended the length of a line, omission of one or more lines of poetry:

Roll on, thou deep and dark blue ocean—roll!

. . . . . . . . . . . . . . . . . . . . . .

Man marks the earth with ruin—his control

Stops with the shore.—Lord Byron

**4.** are sometimes used as a device, as for example, in advertising copy:

To help you Move and Grow
with the Rigors of
Business in the 1980's . . .
and Beyond.—*Journal of Business Strategy*

**Exclamation Point. 1.** terminates an emphatic or exclamatory sentence: Go home at once! You've got to be kidding!

**2.** terminates an emphatic interjection: Encore!

**Hyphen. 1.** indicates that part of a word of more than one syllable has been carried over from one line to the next:

During the revolution, the nation was beset with problems—looting, fighting, and famine.

**2.** joins the elements of some compounds: greatgrandparent, attorney-at-law, ne'er-do-well.

**3.** joins the elements of compound modifiers preceding nouns: high-school students, a fire-and-brimstone lecture, a two-hour meeting.

**4.** indicates that two or more compounds share

a single base: four- and six-volume sets, eight- and nine-year olds.

**5.** separates the prefix and root in some combinations; check the Dictionary when in doubt about the spelling: anti-Nazi, re-elect, co-author, re-form/reform, re-cover/recover, re-creation/-recreation.

**6.** substitutes for the word *to* between typewritten inclusive words or figures: pp. 145-155, the Boston-New York air shuttle.

**7.** punctuates written-out compound numbers from 21 through 99: forty-six years of age, a person who is forty-six, two hundred fifty-nine dollars.

**Parentheses. 1.** enclose material that is not essential to a sentence and that if not included would not alter its meaning: After a few minutes (some say less) the blaze was extinguished.

**2.** often enclose letters or figures to indicate subdivisions of a series: A movement in sonata form consists of the following elements: (1) the exposition, (2) the development, and (3) the recapitulation.

**3.** enclose figures following and confirming written-out numbers, especially in legal and business documents: The fee for my services will be two thousand dollars ($2,000.00).

**4.** enclose an abbreviation for a term following the written-out term, when used for the first time in a text: The patient is suffering from acquired immune deficiency syndrome (AIDS).

**Period. 1.** terminates a complete declarative or mild imperative sentence: There could be no turning back as war's dark shadow settled irrevocably across the continent of Europe.—W. Bruce Lincoln. Return all the books when you can. Would you kindly affix your signature here.

**2.** terminates sentence fragments: Gray clouds—and what looks like a veil of rain falling behind the East German headland. A pair of ducks. A tired or dying swan, head buried in its back feathers, sits on the sand a few feet from the water's edge.—Anthony Bailey

**3.** follows some abbreviations: Dec., Rev., St., Blvd., pp., Co.

**Question Mark. 1.** punctuates a direct question: Have you seen the new play yet? Who goes there? *But:* I wonder who said "Nothing is easy in war." I asked if they planned to leave.

**2.** indicates uncertainty: Ferdinand Magellan (1480?-1521), Plato (427?-347 B.C.).

**Quotation Marks. 1.** Double quotation marks enclose direct quotations: "What was Paris like in the Twenties?" our daughter asked. "Ladies and Gentlemen," the Chief Usher said, "the President of the United States." Robert Louis Stevenson said that "it is better to be a fool than to be dead." When advised not to become a lawyer because the profession was already overcrowded, Daniel Webster replied, "There is always room at the top."

**2.** Double quotation marks enclose words or phrases to clarify their meaning or use or to indicate that they are being used in a special way: This was the border of what we often call "the West" or "the Free World." "The Windy City" is a name for Chicago.

**3.** Double quotation marks set off the translation of a foreign word or phrase: *die Grenze,* "the border."

**4.** Double quotation marks set off the titles of series of books, of articles or chapters in publications, of essays, of short stories and poems, of individual radio and television programs, and of songs and short musical pieces: "The Horizon Concise History" series; an article entitled "On Reflexive

Verbs in English"; Chapter Nine, "The Prince and the Peasant"; Pushkin's "The Queen of Spades"; Tennyson's "Ode on the Death of the Duke of Wellington"; "The Bob Hope Special"; Schubert's "Death and the Maiden."

**5.** Single quotation marks enclose quotations within quotations: The blurb for the piece proclaimed, "Two years ago at Geneva, South Vietnam was virtually sold down the river to the Communists. Today the spunky little . . . country is back on its own feet, thanks to 'a mandarin in a sharkskin suit who's upsetting the Red timetable.' "—Frances FitzGerald

Put commas and periods inside quotation marks; put semicolons and colons outside. Other punctuation, such as exclamation points and question marks, should be put inside the closing quotation marks only if part of the matter quoted.

**Semicolon. 1.** separates the clauses of a compound sentence having no coordinating conjunction: Do not let us speak of darker days; let us rather speak of sterner days.—Winston Churchill

**2.** separates the clauses of a compound sentence in which the clauses contain internal punctuation, even when the clauses are joined by conjunctions: Skis in hand, we trudged to the lodge, stowed our lunches, and donned our boots; and the rest of our party waited for us at the lifts.

**3.** separates elements of a series in which items already contain commas: Among those at the diplomatic reception were the Secretary of State; the daughter of the Ambassador to the Court of St. James's, formerly of London; and two United Nations delegates.

**4.** separates clauses of a compound sentence joined by a conjunctive adverb, such as *however*, *nonetheless*, or *hence*: We insisted upon a hearing; however, the Grievance Committee refused.

**5.** may be used instead of a comma to signal longer pauses for dramatic effect: But I want you to know that when I cross the river my last conscious thought will be of the Corps; and the Corps; and the Corps.—General Douglas MacArthur

**Virgule. 1.** separates successive divisions in an extended date: fiscal year 1983/84.

**2.** represents *per*: 35 km/hr, 1,800 ft/sec.

**3.** means *or* between the words *and* and *or*: Take water skis and/or fishing equipment when you visit the beach this summer.

**4.** separates two or more lines of poetry that are quoted and run in on successive lines of a text: The student actress had a memory lapse when she came to the lines "Double, double, toil and trouble/Fire burn and cauldron bubble/Eye of newt and toe of frog/Wool of bat and tongue of dog" and had to leave the stage in embarrassment.

## Forms of Address[1]

*Source: Webster's II New Riverside University Dictionary.* Copyright © 1984 by Houghton Mifflin Company.

### Academics

**Dean, college or university.** *Address:* Dean _____. *Salutation:* Dear Dean _____.

**President.** *Address:* President _____. *Salutation:* Dear President _____.

**Professor, college or university.** *Address:* Professor _____. *Salutation:* Dear Professor _____.

### Clerical and Religious Orders

**Abbot.** *Address:* The Right Reverend _____ O.S.B. Abbot of _____. *Salutation:* Right Reverend Abbot or Dear Father Abbot.

**Archbishop, Eastern Orthodox.** *Address:* The Most Reverend Joseph, Archbishop of _____. *Salutation:* Your Eminence.

**Archbishop, Roman Catholic.** The Most Reverend _____ _____, Archbishop of _____. *Salutation:* Your Excellency.

**Archdeacon, Episcopal.** *Address:* The Venerable _____ _____, Archdeacon of _____. *Salutation:* Venerable Sir or Dear Archdeacon _____.

**Bishop, Episcopal.** *Address:* The Right Reverend _____ _____, Bishop of _____. *Salutation:* Right Reverend Sir or Dear Bishop _____.

**Bishop, other Protestant.** *Address:* The Reverend _____ _____. *Salutation:* Dear Bishop _____.

**Bishop, Roman Catholic.** *Address:* The Most Reverend _____ _____, Bishop of _____. *Salutation:* Your Excellency or Dear Bishop _____.

**Brotherhood, Roman Catholic.** *Address:* Brother _____ _____, C.F.C. *Salutation:* Dear Brother or Dear Brother Joseph.

**Brotherhood, superior of.** *Address:* Brother Joseph C.F.C. Superior. *Salutation:* Dear Brother Joseph.

**Cardinal.** *Address:* His Eminence Joseph Cardinal Stone. *Salutation:* Your Eminence.

**Clergyman/woman, Protestant.** *Address:* The Reverend _____ _____ or The Reverend _____ _____, D.D. *Salutation:* Dear Mr./Ms. _____ or

**Dean of a cathedral, Episcopal.** *Address:* The Very Reverend _____, Dean of _____. *Salutation:* Dear Dean _____.

**Monsignor.** *Address:* The Right Reverend Monsignor _____. *Salutation:* Dear Monsignor.

**Patriarch, Greek Orthodox.** *Address:* His All Holiness Patriarch Joseph. *Salutation:* Your All Holiness.

**Patriarch, Russian Orthodox.** *Address:* His Holiness the Patriarch of _____. *Salutation:* Your Holiness.

**Pope.** *Address:* His Holiness The Pope. *Salutation:* Your Holiness or Most Holy Father.

**Priest, Roman Catholic.** *Address:* The Reverend _____ _____, S.J. *Salutation:* Dear Reverend Father or Dear Father.

**Rabbi, man or woman.** *Address:* Rabbi _____ _____ or _____ _____ D.D.. *Salutation:* Dear Rabbi _____ or Dear Dr. _____.

**Sisterhood, Roman Catholic.** *Address:* Sister _____, C.S.J. *Salutation:* Dear Sister or Dear Sister _____.

**Sisterhood, superior of.** *Address:* The Reverend Mother Superior, S.C. *Salutation:* Reverend Mother.

### Diplomats

**Ambassador, U.S.** *Address:* The Honorable _____ _____ The Ambassador of the United States. *Salutation:* Sir/Madam or Dear Mr./Madam Ambassador.

**Ambassador to the U.S.** *Address:* His/Her Excellency _____ _____, The Ambassador of _____. *Salutation:* Excellency or Dear Mr./Madam Ambassador.

**Chargé d'Affaires, U.S.** *Address:* The Honorable _____ _____, United States Chargé d'Affaires. *Salutation:* Dear Mr./Ms. _____.

**Consul, U.S.** *Address:* _____ _____, Esq., United

States Consul. *Salutation:* Dear Mr./Ms. _____.

**Minister, U.S. or to U.S.** *Address:* The Honorable _____ _____, The Minister of _____. *Salutation:* Sir/Madam or Dear Mr./Madame Minister.

**Secretary General, United Nations.** *Address:* His/Her Excellency _____ _____, Secretary General of the United Nations. *Salutation:* Dear Mr./Madam/Madame Secretary General.

**United Nations Representative (Foreign).** *Address:* His/Her Excellency _____ _____ Representative of _____ to the United Nations. *Salutation:* Excellency or My dear Mr./Madame _____.

**United Nations Representative (U.S.)** *Address:* The Honorable _____ _____, United States Representative to the United Nations. *Salutation:* Sir/Madam or Dear Mr./Ms. _____.

### Government Officials

**Assemblyman.** *Address:* The Honorable _____ _____. *Salutation:* Dear Mr./Ms. _____.

**Associate Justice, U.S. Supreme Court.** *Address:* Mr./Madam Justice _____. *Salutation:* Dear Mr./Madam Justice or Sir/Madam.

**Attorney General, U.S.** *Address:* The Honorable _____ _____, Attorney General of the United States. *Salutation:* Dear Mr./Madam or Attorney General.

**Cabinet member:** *Address:* The Honorable _____ _____, Secretary of _____. *Salutation:* Sir/Madam or Dear Mr./Madam Secretary.

**Chief Justice, U.S. Supreme Court.** *Address:* The Chief Justice of the United States. *Salutation:* Dear Mr. Chief Justice.

**Commissioner (federal, state, local).** *Address:* The Honorable _____ _____. *Salutation:* Dear Mr./Ms. _____.

**Governor.** *Address:* The Honorable _____ _____, Governor of _____. *Salutation:* Dear Governor _____.

**Judge, Federal:** *Address:* The Honorable _____ _____, Judge of the United States District Court for the _____ District of _____. *Salutation:* Sir/Madam or Dear Judge _____.

**Judge, state of local.** *Address:* The Honorable _____ _____, Judge of the Court of _____. *Salutation:* Dear Judge _____.

**Lieutenant Governor.** *Address:* The Honorable _____ _____, Lieutenant Governor of _____. *Salutation:* Dear Mr./Ms. _____.

**Mayor.** *Address:* The Honorable _____ _____, Mayor of _____. *Salutation:* Dear Mayor _____.

**President, U.S.** *Address:* The President. *Salutation:* Dear Mr. President.

**President, U.S., former.** *Address:* The Honorable _____ _____. *Salutation:* Dear Mr. _____.

**Representative, state.** *Address:* The Honorable _____ _____. *Salutation:* Dear Mr./Ms. _____.

**Representative, U.S.** *Address:* The Honorable _____ _____, United States House of Representatives. *Salutation:* Dear Mr./Ms. _____.

**Senator, state.** *Address:* The Honorable _____ _____, The State Senate, State Capitol. *Salutation:* Dear Senator _____.

**Senator, U.S.** *Address:* The Honorable _____ _____, United States Senate. *Salutation:* Dear Senator _____.

**Speaker, U.S. House of Representatives.** *Address:* The Honorable _____ _____, Speaker of the House of Representatives. *Salutation:* Dear Mr./Madam Speaker.

**Vice President, U.S.** *Address:* The Vice President of the United States. *Salutation:* Sir or Dear Mr. Vice President.

### Military and Naval Officers

**Rank.** *Address:* Full rank, USN (or USCG, USAF, USA, USMC). *Salutation:* Dear (full rank) _____.

### Professions

**Attorney.** *Address:* Mr./Ms. _____ _____, Attorney at law or _____ _____, Esq. *Salutation:* Dear Mr./Ms. _____.

**Dentist.** *Address:* _____ _____, D.D.S. *Salutation:* Dear Dr. _____.

**Physician.** *Address:* _____ _____, M.D. *Salutation:* Dear Dr. _____.

**Veterinarian.** *Address:* _____ _____, D.V.M. *Salutation:* Dear Dr. _____.

1. Forms of address do not always follow set guidelines; the type of salutation is often determined by the relationship between correspondents or by the purpose and content of the letter. However, a general style applies to most occasions. In highly formal salutations, when the addressee is a woman, "Madam" should be substituted for "Sir." When the salutation is informal, "Ms.," "Miss," or "Mrs." should be substituted for "Mr." If a woman addressee has previously indicated a preference for a particular form of address, that form should be used.

## Foreign Words and Phrases

(The English meanings given are not necessarily literal translations.)

*Source: Webster's II New Riverside University Dictionary.* Copyright © 1984 Houghton Mifflin Company.

**à bientôt** [Fr.]: goodbye; I'll see you later

**à bon marché** [Fr.]: at a bargain price

**ab ovo** [Lat.]: from the very beginning

**à compte** [Fr.]: on account

**à deux** [Fr.]: of or involving two individuals

**ad infinitum** [Lat.]: to infinity

**ad valorem** [Lat.]: according to the value

**advocatus diaboli** [Lat.]: devil's advocate

**aide-toi, le ciel t'aidera** [Fr.]: heaven helps those who help themselves—La Fontaine

**à là bonne heure** [Fr.]: at a good time; splendid; all right

**aloha oe** [Hawaiian]: love to you; greetings; farewell

**amende honorable** [Fr.]: public apology; just restitution

**amicus curiae** [Lat.]: friend of the court

**amor vincit omnia** [Lat.]: love conquers all—Virgil

**ancien regime** [Fr.]: the old order

**à peu près** [Fr.]: almost; approximately

**a priori** [Lat.]: from the former

**arrivederci** [Ital.]: goodbye

**ars est celare artem** [Lat.]: (true) art is to conceal art

**ars gratia artis** [Lat.]: art for art's sake

**ars longa, vita brevis** [Lat.]: art is long, life short

**au contraire** [Fr.]: on the contrary

**au courant** [Fr.]: up-to-date

**au fait** [Fr.]: well-informed

**auf Wiedersehen** [G.]: goodbye

**autres temps, autres moeurs** [Fr.]: other times, other customs

**à votre santé** [Fr.]: to your health

**ben trovato** [Ital.]: ingenious

**bête noir** [Fr.]: one particularly disliked

**bona fide** [Lat.]: in good faith; genuine

**bon appétit** [Fr.]: good appetite

**bon mot** [Fr.]: a clever saying

**bon vivant** [Fr.]: an epicure

**carpe diem** [Lat.]: enjoy today

**carte blanche** [Fr.]: unrestricted power to act on one's own

**causa sine qua non** [Lat.]: indispensable condition or cause

**cause célèbre** [Fr.]: a highly controversial issue

**caveat emptor** [Lat.]: let the buyer beware

**chacun à son goût** [Fr.]: everyone to his own taste

**circa** [Lat.]: in approximately

**comme ci comme ça** [Fr.]: so-so

**corpus delicti** [Lat.]: the material evidence of the fact that a crime has been committed

**coup de grâce** [Fr.]: finishing blow

**cri de coeur** [Fr.]: heartfelt appeal

**cum grano salis** [Lat.]: with a grain of salt

**d'accord** [Fr.]: agreed

**danke (schön)** [G.]: thank you (very much)

**de bonne grâce** [Fr.]: with good grace

**de facto** [Lat.]: in reality or fact

**de gustibus non est disputandum** [Lat.]: there is no arguing in matters of taste

**Deo gratias** [Lat.]: thanks be to God

**Deo volente** [Lat.]: God willing

**de profundis** [Lat.]: from the depths

**dernier cri** [Fr.]: the newest fashion

**deus ex machina** [Lat.]: a contrived device to resolve a situation

**dolce far niente** [Ital.]: pleasant idleness

**dramatis personae** [Lat.]: characters in a play

**ecce homo** [Lat.]: behold the man

**éminence grise** [Fr.]: gray eminence; power behind the throne

**en bloc** [Fr.]: wholesale; as one

**enfin** [Fr.]: in conclusion

**en masse** [Fr.]: all together

**en passant** [Fr.]: in passing

**en rapport** [Fr.]: in sympathy or accord; in touch

**entre nous** [Fr.]: between ourselves; confidentially

**ex animo** [Lat.]: from the heart

**ex gratia** [Lat.]: as a favor

**ex more** [Lat.]: according to custom

**experto credite** [Lat.]: believe one who knows from experience

**fait accompli** [Fr.]: an accomplished fact, presumably irreversible

**faute de mieux** [Fr.]: for lack of anything better

**faux pas** [Fr.]: a social blunder

**feux d'artifice** [Fr.]: fireworks; dazzling display, as of wit

**fiat justitia, ruat caelum** [Lat.]: let justice be done even if the heavens fall

**flagrante delicto** [Lat.]: in the very act

**folie de grandeur** [Fr.]: delusion of grandeur

**force de frappe** [Fr.]: strike force—used esp. of nuclear forces

**frisson** [Fr.]: thrill; shudder

**Gesundheit** [G]: good health

**gnōthi seauton** [Gr.]: know thyself

**gracias** [Sp.]: thank you

**grande dame** [Fr.]: great lady

**guten Tag** [G]: good day; hello

**habeas corpus** [Lat.]: writ to bring a person before a court or judge

**hasta la vista** [Sp.]: see you later

**haut monde** [Fr.]: high society; the fashionable world

**hoi polloi** [Gk.]: the common people

**honi soit qui mal y pense** [Fr.]: shame to him who thinks evil of it—motto of the Order of the Garter

**hors concours** [Fr.]: out of the running

**ich dien** [G.]: I serve—motto of the Prince of Wales

**inshallah** [Ar.]: if Allah wills it; God willing

**in vino veritas** [Lat.]: in wine there in truth

**ipso facto** [Lat.]: by the fact itself

**je ne sais quoi** [Fr.]: I know not what; an elusive quality

**jeu de mots** [Fr.]: play on words

**jeu d'esprit** [Fr.]: play of wit

**jeunesse dorée** [Fr.]: gilded youth

**Kinder, Kirche, Küche** [G.]: children, church, kitchen

**laissez faire** [Fr.]: noninterference

**l'art pour l'art** [Fr.]: art for art's sake

**le coeur a ses raisons que la raison ne connait point** [Fr.]: the heart has its reasons that reason knows nothing of—Pascal

**l'état c'est moi** [Fr.]: I am the state—Attributed to Louis XIV

**mano a mano** [Sp.]: hand in hand; together

**mauvais goût** [Fr.]: bad taste

**mea culpa** [Lat.]: I am to blame

**meden agan** [Gk.]: nothing in excess

**mens sana in corpore sano** [Lat.]: a healthy mind in a healthy body—Juvenal

**mirabile dictu** [Lat.]: wonderful to relate

**modus operandi** [Lat.]: a method of operating

**n'est-ce pas?** [Fr.]: isn't that so?

**nicht wahr?** [G.]: isn't that so?

**n'importe** [Fr.]: no matter

**nom de plume** [Fr.]: pen name

**non compos mentis** [Lat.]: not of sound mind

**non sequitur** [Lat.]: it does not fol-

low

**omnia vincit amor** [Lat.]: love conquers all—Virgil

**O tempora! O mores!** [Lat.]: O times! O morals!; what corrupt times we live in!—Cicero

**per annum** [Lat.]: by the year

**per capita** [Lat.]: per unit of population

**per diem** [Lat.]: by the day

**persona non grata** [Lat.]: unacceptable or unwelcome person

**peu à peu** [Fr.]: little by little

**pièce d'occasion** [Fr.]: musical or literary work composed for a special occasion

**plus ça change, plus c'est le même chose** [Fr.]: the more things change, the more they remain the same

**post mortem** [Lat.]: after death

**prêt-à-porter** [Fr.]: ready to wear

**pro bono publico** [Lat.]: for the public good

**pro patria** [Lat.]: for one's country

**que será será** [Sp.]: what will be will be

**quid pro quo** [Lat.]: something for something; an equal exchange

**repondez s'il vous plaît** [Fr.]: please reply— Used on invitation cards (abbr. R.S.V.P.)

**requiescat in pace** [Lat.]: rest in peace

**salto mortale** [Ital.]: deadly leap

**salud** [Sp.]: health; to your health

**sans peur et sans reproche** [Fr.]: without fear and above reproach; chivalrous

**sans-souci** [Fr.]: carefree pleasure

**savoir faire** [Fr.]: the ability to say and do the correct thing

**se non è vero, è ben trovato** [Ital.]: even if it isn't true, it's a wonderful invention

**shalom** [Heb.]: peace, used as a greeting

**sic transit gloria mundi** [Lat.]: thus passes away the glory of the world

**s'il vous plaît** [Fr.]: if you please

**sine die** [Lat.]: with no day set for a future meeting; indefinitely

**sine qua non** [Lat.]: indispensable

**status (in) quo** [Lat.]: the existing condition

**sui generis** [Lat.]: unique; individual

**tant pis** [Fr.]: so much the worse

**tempus fugit** [Lat.]: time flies

**terra incognita** [Lat.]: unknown territory

**ton** [Fr.]: fashionable society

**tout de suite** [Fr.]: immediately; all at once

**tout le monde** [Fr.]: everybody; everyone of importance

**uomo universale** [Ital.]: universal man; one of broad education and ability

**utile dulci** [Lat.]: the useful with the pleasurable—Horace

**veni, vidi, vici** [Lat.]: I came, I saw,

I conquered—attributed to Julius Caesar

**vis-a-vis** [Fr.]: face to face

**vive la différence** [Fr.]: long live the difference (between the sexes)

**wie geht's?** [G.]: how are things?

**wunderbar** [G.]: wonderful

**Wunderkind** [G.]: child prodigy

## Clichés and Redundant Expressions

*(Source: Webster's II New Riverside Dictionary,* Office Edition, Houghton Mifflin Company 1984.)

### Clichés

*Webster's II* defines the word cliché as "A hackneyed expression or idea." Since most clichés express rather clear meanings, the writer will have to determine whether it is a shade of meaning that is hard to convey by fresher wording. If the process of substitution is too difficult, use of some of the phrases that follow may be advisable. But few on the following list are truly indispensable.

acid test
add insult to injury
all in a day's work
all over but the shouting
all work and no play
apple of one's eye
armed to the teeth
as luck would have it
at a loss for words
at one fell swoop
axe to grind
bag and baggage
bark up the wrong tree
beat a dead horse
beat a hasty retreat
beat around the bush
best foot forward
best-laid plans
bigger (or larger) than life
bite off more than one can chew
bolt from the blue
bone of contention
breathe a sigh of relief
bright and early
bring home the bacon
budding genius
bull in a china shop
burning question
burn the midnight oil
busy as a bee
by leaps and bounds
calm before the storm
can't see the forest for the trees
caught red-handed
checkered career
chip off the old block
cool as a cucumber
crying need
cut a long story short
dead giveaway
diamond in the rough
discreet silence
down in the dumps (or mouth)
down one's alley
drastic action
draw the line
ear to the ground
easier said than done
eat one's hat (or words)
eloquent silence
epic struggle
face the music
fall on deaf ears
far cry
fast and loose
fat's in the fire
feather in one's cap
few and far between

fill the bill
first and foremost
fit as a fiddle
flash in the pan
flesh and blood
food for thought
foot in one's mouth
free as a bird (or the air)
fresh as a daisy
generous to a fault
gentle as a lamb
get down to brass tacks
get one's back (or dander) up
gift of gab
gild the lily
goes without saying
grain of salt
grind to a halt
hale and hearty
handwriting on the wall
hard row to hoe
haul (or rake) over the coals
head over heels
heave a sigh of relief
high and dry
high as a kite
hit the nail on the head
hit the spot
hook, line, and sinker
hook or crook
hue and cry
hungry as a bear (or lion)
in no uncertain terms
in on the ground floor
in the final (or last) analysis
in the long run
in the nick of time
in the twinkling of an eye
in this day and age
irons in the fire
jig is up
just deserts
keep one's chin up
labor of love
land-office business
last but not least
last straw
lean over backward
leaps and bounds
leave in the lurch
leave no stone unturned
lend a helping hand
let one's hair down
let the cat out of the bag
let well enough alone
like a house afire (or on fire)
lock, stock and barrel
mad as a hornet (or wet hen)

mad dash
make a long story short
make ends meet
matter of life and death
meet one's Waterloo
method in one's madness
milk of human kindness
mince words
month of Sundays
moot question (or point)
more than meets the eye
more the merrier
motley crew
naked truth
necessary evil
needle in a haystack
neither here nor there
never a dull moment
never rains but it pours
nip in the bud
none the worse for wear
no sooner said than done
nothing new under the sun
once in a blue moon
on cloud nine
opportunity knocks
other side of the coin
out of the frying pan and into the fire
own worst enemy
paint the town red
part and parcel
penny for one's thoughts
perfect gentleman
pet peeve
pick and choose
pillar of society
play it by ear
point with pride
poor but honest
powers that be
pretty as a picture
pretty kettle of fish
pretty penny
psychological moment
quick as a flash
quiet as a mouse
rack one's brains
rain cats and dogs
raise Cain
read the riot act
red-letter day
reliable source
ring true
ripe old age
rub one the wrong way
sadder but wiser
save for a rainy day
seal one's fate (or doom)

second to none
sell like hot cakes
separate the men from the boys
shot in the arm
show one's hand
sick and tired
sigh of relief
sight for sore eyes
six of one and (a) half dozen of the other
skeleton in one's closet
small world
smell a rat
sour grapes
sow one's wild oats
stick out like a sore thumb
stick to one's guns
stiff upper lip
stir up a hornet's nest
straight from the shoulder
straight and narrow

straw in the wind
straw that broke the camel's back
strong as an ox
stubborn as a mule
sweat of one's brow
take a dim view of
take the bull by the horns
talk through one's hat
this day and age
this point in time
throw caution to the winds
throw in the towel
throw the book at
time immemorial
time of one's life
tip the scales
tired as a dog
tit for tat
too funny for words
too little, too late

too numerous to mention
trials and tribulations
true blue
turn over a new leaf
uncharted seas
untimely end
up the creek without a paddle
vanish into thin air
view with alarm
wash one's hands of
wear and tear
wear two hats
wee (small) hours
when all is said and done
wide-open spaces
wise as an owl
without further ado
wolf in sheep's clothing
word to the wise
worse for wear

## Redundant Expressions

**Redundancy**— the needless repetition of ideas— is one of the principal obstacles to writing clear, precise prose. The elements repeated in the phrases and in the brief definitions are italicized. To eliminate redundancy, delete the italic elements in the phrases.

*old* antique: (= an object having special value because of its *age,* esp. a work of art or handicraft more than 100 years *old*)

**ascend** *upward*: (= to go or move *upward*)

**assemble** *together*: (= to bring or gather *together*)

**pointed** barb: (= a sharp *point* projecting in reverse direction to the main point of a weapon or tool)

*first* beginning: (= the *first* part)

**big** *in size*: (= of considerable *size*)

**bisect** *in two*: (= to cut *into two* equal parts)

**blend** *together*: (= to combine, mix, or go well *together*)

**capitol** *building*: (= a *building* in which a legislative body meets)

**coalesce** *together*: (= to grow or come *together* so as to form a whole)

**collaborate** *together* or *jointly*: (= to work *together*, esp. in a joint effort)

*fellow* colleague: (= a *fellow* member of a profession, staff, or academic faculty)

**congregate** *together*: (= to bring or come *together* in a crowd)

**connect** *together*: (= to join or fasten *together*)

**consensus** *of opinion*: (= collective *opinion*)

**courthouse** *building*: (= a *building* in which judicial courts or county government offices are housed)

*habitual* custom: (= a *habitual* practice)

**descend** *downward*: (= to move,

slope, extend, or incline *downward*)

**endorse (a check)** *on the back*: (= to write one's signature *on the back of*, e.g., a check)

**erupt** *violently*: (= to emerge *violently* or to become *violently* active)

**explode** *violently*: (= to burst *violently* from internal pressure)

*real* fact: (= something with *real*, demonstrable existence)

*passing* fad: (= a *passing* fashion)

**few** *in number*: (= amounting to or made up of a *small number*)

**founder** *and sink*: (= to *sink* beneath the water)

*basic* fundamental: (= a *basic* or essential part)

**fuse** *together*: (= to mix *together* by or as if by melting)

**gather** *together*: (= to come *together* or cause to come *together*)

*free* gift: (= something bestowed voluntarily and *without compensation*)

*past* history: (= a narrative of *past* events; something that took place *in the past*)

**hoist** *up*: (= to raise or to haul *up* with or as if with a mechanical device)

*current* or *present* incumbent: (= one *currently* holding an office)

*new* innovation: (= something *new* or unusual)

**join** *together*: (= to bring or put *together* so as to make continuous or form a unit)

**knots** *per hour*: (= a unit of speed, one nautical mile *per hour*, approx. 1.15 statute miles *per hour*)

**large** *in size*: (= greater than av-

erage *in size*)

**merge** *together*: (= to blend or cause to blend *together* gradually)

*necessary* need: (= something *necessary* or wanted)

*universal* panacea: (= a remedy for *all* diseases, evils, or difficulties)

**continue** *to persist*: (= to *continue* in existence)

*individual* person: (= an *individual* human being)

**chief** or **leading** or **main** protagonist: (= the *leading* character in a Greek drama or other literary form; a *leading* or *principal* figure)

*original* prototype: (= an *original* type, form, or instance that is a model on which later stages are based or judged)

**protrude** *out*: (= to push or thrust *outward*)

**recall** *back*: (= to summon *back* to awareness; to bring *back*)

**recoil** *back*: (= to kick or spring *back*; to shrink *back* in fear or loathing; to fall *back*)

**recur** *again* or *repeatedly*: (= to occur *again* or *repeatedly*)

*temporary* reprieve: (= *temporary* relief, as from danger or pain)

**short** *in length* or *height*: (= having very little *length* or *height*)

**small** *in size*: (= characterized by relatively little *size* or slight *dimensions*)

*completely* unanimous: (= being in *complete* harmony, accord, or agreement)

# Business Letter Styles

## The Block Letter

**Houghton Mifflin Company**

Two Park Street, Boston, Massachusetts 02108    Reference Division
(617) 725-5000    Cable HOUGHTON

January 4, 19--

Mr. Peter C. Cunningham
Vice-president, Operations
CCC Chemicals, Ltd.
321 Park Avenue
City, US 98765

Dear Mr. Cunningham:

Subject: Block Letter Style

This is the Block Letter--a format featuring elements aligned with the left margin.
The date is typed from two to six (or more) lines below the letterhead, depending
on the length of the message. The inside address may be typed from two to four
lines below the date line, also depending on message length. Double spacing is
used between the inside address and the salutation. A subject line, if used, appears
two lines below the salutation and two lines above the first message line. Had an
attention line been used here, it would have been positioned two lines below the
last line of the inside address and two lines above the salutation.

The paragraphs are single-spaced internally with double spacing separating them
from each other. Displayed matter such as enumerations and long quotations are
indented by six character spaces. Units within enumerations and any quoted matter
are single-spaced internally with double spacing setting them off from the rest of
the text.

The heading for a continuation sheet begins six lines from the top edge of the page.
The heading is blocked flush with the left margin:

Page 2
Mr. Peter C. Cunningham
January 4, 19--

Skip two lines from the last line of the message to the complimentary close. Allow
at least four blank lines for the written signature. Block the typed signature
and corporate title under the complimentary close. Insert ancillary notations such
as the typist's initials two spaces below the last line of the signature block.

Sincerely yours,

John M. Swanson

John M. Swanson
Executive Vice-president

JMS:ahs

Enclosures: 4

Atlanta / Dallas / Geneva, Illinois / Hopewell, New Jersey / Palo Alto / London

*Source:* The Professional Secretary's Handbook, Copyright ©, Houghton Mifflin Company.

# Business Letter Styles

The Modified Block Letter

---

## Houghton Mifflin Company

Two Park Street, Boston, Massachusetts 02108
(617) 725-5000   Cable HOUGHTON

Reference Division

January 14, 19--

CERTIFIED MAIL
CONFIDENTIAL

Sarah H. O'Day, Esq.
O'Day, Ryan & Sweeney
One Court Street
City, US 98765

Dear Ms. O'Day:

SUBJECT:  MODIFIED BLOCK LETTER

This is the Modified Block Letter, the features of which are similar to those of the
Block Letter with the exception of the positioning of the date line, the complimentary
close, and the typewritten signature block.  The positioning of the date line determines the placement of the complimentary close and the signature block, both of which
must be vertically aligned with the date.  The date itself may be centered on the
page, placed about five spaces to the right of center as shown here, or set flush
with the right margin.  Any one of these positions is acceptable.

The subject line, typed here in capital letters, is set flush left.  Had an attention line been used it too would have been positioned flush with the left margin.
Note that the special mailing and handling notations appear flush left, two lines
above the first line of the inside address.

The continuation sheet heading, unlike that of the Simplified and Block Letters, is
spread across the top of the page, at least six vertical lines beneath the top edge:

Ms. O'Day                        - 2 -                        January 14, 19--

Notice the centered page number enclosed by spaced hyphens.  Another way of styling
the page number is to enclose it with hyphens set tight to the number.  Either
style is entirely acceptable.

The complimentary close--aligned with the date--appears two lines below the last
message line.  At least four blank lines have been allowed for the written signature.  The typed signature block is then aligned with the complimentary close.

Ancillary notations such as typist's initials, enclosure notations, and lists of
copy recipients are placed two lines below the signature block, flush with the
left margin.

                              Very truly yours,

                              Kathleen N. Lear
                              Kathleen N. Lear
                              Permissions Editor

KNL:ahs

Atlanta  Dallas  Geneva, Illinois  Hopewell, New Jersey  Palo Alto  London

---

## Reference Books And Other Sources

This cannot be a record of all the thousands of available sources of information. Nevertheless, these selected references will enable the reader to locate additional facts about many subjects covered in the *Information Please Almanac*. The editors have chosen sources that they believe will be helpful to the general reader.

### General References

Encyclopedias are a unique category, since they attempt to cover most subjects quite thoroughly. The most valuable multivolume encyclopedias are the **Encyclopaedia Britannica** and the **Encyclopedia Americana**. Useful one-volume encyclopedias are the **New Columbia Encyclopedia** and the **Random House Encyclopedia**.

Dictionaries and similar "word books" are also unique: **The American Heritage Dictionary, Second College Edition**, containing 200,000 definitions and specialized usage guidance; **Webster's Third New International Dictionary, Unabridged**; **Webster's II New Riverside University Dictionary**, containing 200,000 definitions plus hundreds of word history paragraphs; and the multivolume **Oxford English Dictionary**, providing definitions in historical order. **Roget's II The New Thesaurus**, containing thousands of synonyms grouped according to meaning, assists writers in choosing just the right word. The quick reference set—**The Word Book II** (over 40,000 words spelled and divided), **The Right Word II** (a concise thesaurus), and **The Written Word II** (a concise guide to writing, style, and usage)—are based on **The American Heritage Dictionary** and are intended for the busy reader needing information fast. Two excellent books of quotations are **Bartlett's Familiar Quotations** and **The Oxford Dictionary of Quotations**.

There are a number of useful atlases: the **New York Times Atlas of the World**, a number of historical atlases (Penguin Books), **Oxford Economic Atlas of the World**, **Rand McNally Cosmopolitan World Atlas: New Census Edition**, and **Atlas of the Historical Geography of the United States** (Greenwood). Many contemporary road atlases of the United States and foreign countries are also available.

A source of information on virtually all subjects is the United States Government Printing Office (GPO). For information, write: Superintendent of Documents, Washington, D.C. 20402.

For help on any subject, consult: **Subject Guide to Books in Print**, **The New York Times Index**, and the **Reader's Guide to Periodical Literature** in your library.

### Specific References

**Airplanes, A Field Guide to** (Houghton Mifflin)
**Almanac, Places Rated** (Rand McNally)
**America Votes** (Congressional Quarterly, Inc.)
**American Indian, Reference Encyclopedia of the** (B. Klein Publications)
**American Revolution, The** (American Heritage)
**Anatomy, Gray's** (Saunders)
**Antiques and Collectibles Price List, the Kovels'**

(Crown)
**Architecture, Encyclopedia of World** (VanNostrand Reinhold)
**Art, History of** (Prentice-Hall)
**Art, Oxford Companion to** (Oxford University Press)
**Art, Who's Who in American** (R.R. Bowker)
**Art Directory, American** (R.R. Bowker)
**Art Terms, Dictionary of: Architecture, Sculpture, Painting & the Graphic Arts** (Sterling)
**Asian-Americans, Who's Who Among** (Gormezano Reference Publications)
**Associations, Encyclopedia of** (Gale Research Co.)
**Authors, 1000–1900, European** (H.W. Wilson)
**Authors, Twentieth Century** (H.W. Wilson)
**Automobile Facts and Figures** (Kallman)
**Automobile Year Book of Models** (Motorbooks International)
**Ballets, Balanchine's Complete Stories of the Great** (Doubleday)
**Banking and Finance, Encyclopedia of** (Bankers Publishing Co.)
**Baseball Encyclopedia** (Macmillan)
(Baseball) **World Series Record Book** (Sporting News)
**Biographical Dictionary, Chambers** (Littlefield)
**Biography Yearbook, Current** (H.W. Wilson)
**Birds, Field Guide to the,** Peterson Field Guide Series (Houghton Mifflin)
**Black Americans, Who's Who Among** (Who's Who Among Black Americans, Inc.)
**Book Review Digest, 1905–** (H.W. Wilson)
**Business and Investment Almanac, Dow Jones-Irwin** (Dow Jones-Irwin)
**Catholic Encyclopedia, New** (Publishers Guild)
**Chemistry, Encyclopedia of** (VanNostrand Rinehold)
**Chemistry and Physics, Handbook of** (Chemical Rubber Co. Press)
**Christian Church, Oxford Dictionary of the** (Oxford University Press)
**Churches, Yearbook of American and Canadian** (Abingdon Press)
**Citizens Band: Radio Service Rules and Regulations** (Federal Communications Commission, Government Printing Office)
**College Cost Book, 1985-86, The** (The College Board)
**Communist Affairs, Yearbook on International** (Hoover Institution Press)
**Composers, Great 1300–1900** (H.W. Wilson)
**Composers Since 1900** (H.W. Wilson)
**Computer Products for Education, The Yellow Book** (NEA Educational Computer Service)
**Computer Science and Technology, Encyclopedia of** (Dekker)
**Computer Terms, Encyclopedia of** (Barron)
**Condo and Co-op Information Book, Complete** (Houghton Mifflin)
**Congressional Quarterly Almanac** (Congressional Quarterly, Inc.)
**Consumer Reports** (Consumers Union)
**Costume, The Dictionary of** (Scribners)
**Drama, Crowell's Handbook of Classical** (T.Y. Crowell)

**Drama, Crowell's Handbook of Contemporary** (T.Y. Crowell)

**Ecology Information and Organizations, Guide to** (H.W. Wilson)

**Energy Factbook** (McGraw-Hill)

**Environment, Living With Our** (U.S. Department of the Interior, Government Printing Office)

**Environmental Science** (Saunders College Publishing)

**Europa Year Book** (Gale Research Co.)

**Fact Books, The Rand McNally** (Rand)

**Facts, Famous First** (H.W. Wilson)

**Facts on File** (Facts on File, Inc.)

**Film: A Reference Guide** (Greenwood)

**Filmgoer's Companion** (Avon)

**Fishing: An Encyclopedic Guide** (Dutton)

**Food and Drink, Dictionary of American** (Ticknor & Fields)

**Football Made Easy** (Jonathan David)

**Games, Book of** (Jazz Press)

**Gardening, Encyclopedia of** (Houghton Mifflin)

**Gardening for Food and Fun** (U.S. Department of Agriculture, Government Printing Office)

**Geography, Dictionary of** (Penguin Books)

**Government Manual, U.S.** (U.S. Office of the Federal Register, Government Printing Office)

**Handicapped Americans, Who's Who Among** (Gormezano Reference Publications)

**Hispanic or Spanish-surnamed Americans, Who's Who Among** (Gormezano Reference Publications)

**History, Album of American** (Scribner's)

**History, Dictionary of American** (Rowman)

**History, Documents of American** (Prentice-Hall)

**History, Encyclopedia of Latin-American** (Greenwood)

**History, Encyclopedia of World** (Houghton Mifflin)

**Hockey, the Illustrated History: An Official Publication of the National Hockey League** (Doubleday)

**Infomania, The Guide to Essential Electronic Services** (Houghton Mifflin Company)

**Islam, Dictionary of** (Orient Book Distributors)

**Jazz in the Seventies, Encyclopedia of** (Horizon)

**Jewish Concepts, Encyclopedia of** (Hebrew Publishers)

**Job Outlook in Brief, The** (U.S. Bureau of Labor Statistics, Government Printing Office)

**Legal Word Book, The** (Houghton Mifflin)

**Libraries, World Guide to** (K. G. Saur)

**Library Directory, American** (R.R. Bowker)

**Literary Market Place** (R. R. Bowker)

**Literature, Oxford Companion to American** (Oxford University Press)

**Literature, Oxford Companion to Classical** (Oxford University Press)

**Literature, Oxford Companion to English** (Oxford University Press)

**(Literature) Reader's Adviser: A Layman's Guide to Literature** (R.R. Bowker)

**Literature, Reader's Encyclopedia of American** (T.Y. Crowell)

**Medical Adviser, Modern Home** (Doubleday)

**Medical & Health Sciences Word Book, The** (Houghton Mifflin)

**Museums, Directory of World** (Facts on File)

**Music and Musicians, Handbook of American** (Da Capo)

**Music, Concise Oxford Dictionary of** (Oxford University Press)

**Music, Harvard Dictionary of** (Harvard University Press)

**Musical Terms, Dictionary of** (Gordon Press)

**Mystery Writers, Twentieth Century Crime and** (St. Martin's Press)

**Mythology** (Little, Brown and Co.)

**Nations, Handbook of New** (T.Y. Crowell)

**Native Americans, Who's Who Among** (Gormezano Reference Publications)

**Operas, New Milton Cross Complete Stories of the Great** (Doubleday)

**Pain, Coping With Chronic** (Sister Kenney Institute)

**Physicians' Desk Reference** (Medical Economics Company)

**Pocket Data Book, U.S.A.** (U.S. Department of Commerce, Bureau of the Census, Government Printing Office)

**Poetry, Granger's Index to** (Columbia University Press)

**Politics, Almanac of American** (National Journal)

**Politics, Who's Who in American** (R.R. Bowker)

**Pop/Rock, Dictionary of American** (Schirmer Books)

**Private Schools, Handbook of** (Porter Sargent)

**Publications, Ayer Directory of** (Ayer Press)

**Religions, The Facts on File Dictionary of** (Facts on File)

**Robert's Rules of Order Revised** (Morrow & Co.)

**Sailboats, A Field Guide to** (Houghton Mifflin)

**Science, American Men and Women of** (R.R. Bowker)

**Science and Technology, Asimov's Biographical Encyclopedia of** (Doubleday)

**Scientific Encyclopedia, VanNostrand's** (VanNostrand Reinhold)

**Secretary's Handbook, The Professional** (Houghton Mifflin)

**Shakespeare, The Riverside** (Houghton Mifflin)

**Stars and Planets, Field Guide to the** (Houghton Mifflin)

**States, Book of** (Council of State Governments)

**Statesman's Year-Book** (St. Martin's)

**Theater, Oxford Companion to the** (Oxford University Press)

**Theater, Who's Who in the** (Gale Research Co.)

**(Travel) The Birnbaum Guides** (Houghton Mifflin)

**United Nations, Demographic Yearbook** (Unipub)

**United Nations, Statistical Yearbook of the** (Unipub)

**United States, Historical Statistics of the** (U.S. Department of Commerce, Bureau of the Census, Government Printing Office)

**United States, Statistical Abstract of the** (U.S. Department of Commerce, Bureau of the Census, Government Printing Office)

**Washington Information Directory** (Congressional Quarterly, Inc.)

**Weather Book, The American** (Houghton Mifflin)

**Who's Who in America** (Marquis)

**Who's Who in Canada** (International Publications Service)

**Wines, Dictionary of American** (Morrow)

**Women, Notable American** (Harvard University Press)

**World War I** (American Heritage)

**World War II** (American Heritage)

**Writer's Market** (Writers Digest)

**Zip Code and Post Office Directory, National** (U.S. Postal Service, Government Printing Office)

See the full range of publications of Dun & Bradstreet and Standard & Poor's for corporate financial and stockholder information.

For detailed information on American colleges and universities, see the many publications of the **American Council on Education.**

Also see many other specialized **Who's Who** volumes not listed here for biographies of famous people in many fields.

# POSTAL REGULATIONS

## Domestic Mail Service

(As of August 1986. Subject to change)

### First Class

First-class consists of letters and written and sealed matter. The rate is 22¢ for the first oz; 17¢ for each additional oz, or fraction of an oz, up to 12 oz. Pieces over 12 oz are subject to priority-mail (heavy pieces) rates. Single postcards, 14¢; double postcards, 28¢ (14¢ for each half). The post office sells prestamped single and double postal cards. Consult your postmaster for information on business-reply mail and presort rates.

The weight limit for first-class mail is 70 lb.

| Weight | Rates |
|---|---|
| First oz | $ .22 |
| Over 1 oz, but not over 2 | .39 |
| Over 2 oz, but not over 3 | .56 |
| Over 3 oz, but not over 4 | .73 |
| Over 4 oz, but not over 5 | .90 |
| Over 5 oz, but not over 6 | 1.07 |
| Over 6 oz, but not over 7 | 1.24 |
| Over 7 oz, but not over 8 | 1.41 |
| Over 8 oz, but not over 9 | 1.58 |
| Over 9 oz, but not over 10 | 1.75 |
| Over 10 oz, but not over 11 | 1.92 |
| Over 11 oz, but not over 12 | 2.09 |
| Over 12 oz, *see* Priority Mail | |

### Priority Mail (over 12 oz to 70 lb)

The zone rate applies to mailable matter over 12 oz of any class carried by air. Your local post office will supply free official zone tables appropriate to your location.

### Airmail

First-class and priority mail receive airmail service.

### Express Mail

Express Mail Service is available for any mailable article up to 70 lb in weight and 108 in. in combined length and girth. Flat rates: up to 2 lb, $10.75; over 2 lb and up to 5 lb, $12.85; 6 to 70 pound rates vary by weight and distance (zones).

Articles received by 5 p.m. at a postal facility offering Express Mail Service will be delivered by 3 p.m. the next day or, if you prefer, your shipment can be picked up as early as 10 a.m. the next business day. Rates include Insurance, Shipment Receipt, and Record of Delivery at the destination post office.

Consult Postmaster for other Express Mail Services and rates.

The Postal Service will refund, upon application to originating office, the postage for any Express Mail shipments not meeting the service standard except for those delayed by strike or work stoppage.

### Second Class

Second-class mail is used primarily by newspapers, magazines, and other periodicals with second-class mailing privileges. For copies mailed by the public, the rate is the applicable single piece third- or fourth-class rate.

### Third Class (under 16 oz)

Third-class mail is used for circulars, books, printed matter, merchandise, seeds, cuttings, bulbs, roots, scions, and plants, and all other mailable matter not in first or second class. There are two rate structures for this class, a single-piece and a bulk rate.

Many community organizations, as well as businesses, find it economical to use this service. Because of the number of categories of third-class mail, you should consult your postmaster for the one best suited to your needs.

#### Third-Class, Single-Piece Rates

| Weight | Rates | Weight | Rates |
|---|---|---|---|
| 0 to 1 oz | $ .22 | Over 8 to 10 oz | $ 1.08 |
| Over 1 to 2 oz | .39 | Over 10 to 12 oz | 1.18 |
| Over 2 to 3 oz | .56 | Over 12 to 14 oz | 1.28 |
| Over 3 to 4 oz | .73 | Over 14 but less | |
| Over 4 to 6 oz | .88 | than 16 oz | 1.38 |
| Over 6 to 8 oz | .98 | | |

### Fourth Class (Parcel Post— 16 oz and over)

Fourth-class mail is used for merchandise, books, printed matter, and all other mailable matter not in first, second, or third class. Special fourth-class rates apply to books, library books, publications or records for the blind, and certain controlled-circulation publications.

Packages should be taken to your local post office, where the postage will be determined according to the weight of the package and the distance it is being sent. Information on weight and size limits for fourth-class mail may be obtained there.

### Special Services

**Registered Mail.** When you use registered mail service, you are buying security—the safest way to send valuables. The full value of your mailing must be declared when mailed. You receive a receipt and the movement of your mail is controlled throughout the postal system. For an additional fee, a return receipt showing to whom, when, and where delivered may be obtained.

#### Fees for articles (in addition to postage)

| Value | | | with Insurance | without Insurance |
|---|---|---|---|---|
| 0.00 | to | $ 100 | $3.60 | $3.55 |
| 100.01 | to | 500 | 3.90 | 3.80 |
| 500.01 | to | 1,000 | 4.25 | 4.15 |

For higher values, consult your postmaster.

**Certified Mail.** Certified mail service provides for a receipt to the sender and a record of delivery at the post office of address. No record is kept at the post office where mailed. It is handled in the ordinary mails and no insurance coverage is provided.
Fee in addition to postage, 75¢.

**Return Receipts.** Requested at time of mailing:
Showing to whom and date delivered $ .70
Showing to whom, date, and address where delivered .90
Requested after mailing:
Showing to whom and date delivered 4.50

**C.O.D. Mail.** Consult your postmaster for fees and conditions of mailing.

**Insured Mail.** Fees, in addition to postage, for coverage against loss or damage:

| Liability | | Fees |
|---|---|---|
| $ .01 to | $25 | $ .50 |
| $ 25.01 to | $50 | 1.10 |
| $ 50.01 to | $100 | 1.40 |
| $ 100.01 to | $150 | 1.80 |
| $ 150.01 to | $200 | 2.10 |
| $ 200.01 to | $300 | 3.00 |
| $ 300.01 to | $400 | 3.70 |
| $ 400.01 to | 500 | 4.40 |

**Special Delivery.** The payment of the special-delivery fee entitles mail to the most expeditious transportation and delivery. The fee is in addition to the regular postage.

#### Weight/Fees

| Class of mail | Not more than 2 lb | More than 2 lb but not more than 10 lb | More than 10 lb |
|---|---|---|---|
| First-class | $2.95 | $3.15 | $4.00 |
| All other classes | 3.10 | 3.60 | 4.50 |

**Special Handling.** Payment of the special-handling fee entitles third- and fourth-class matter to the most expeditious handling and transportation, but not special delivery. The fee is in addition to the regular postage.

| Weight | Fees |
|---|---|
| Not more than 10 lb | $1.10 |
| More than 10 lb | 1.60 |

**Money Orders.** Money orders are used for the safe transmission of money.

| Amount of money order | | | Fees |
|---|---|---|---|
| $ .01 | to | $25 | $ .75 |
| $ 25.01 | to | $700 | 1.00 |

## Minimum Mail Sizes

All mail must be at least 0.007 in. thick and mail that is 1/4 in. or less in thickness must be at least 3 1/2 in. in height, at least 5 in. long, and rectangular in shape (except keys and identification devices). NOTE: Pieces greater than 1/4 in. thick can be mailed even if they measure less than 3 1/2 by 5 inches.

## Adhesive Stamps Available

| Purpose | Form | Denomination and prices |
|---|---|---|
| Ordinary postage | Single or sheet | 1, 2, 3, 4, 5, 7, 10, 12[1], 13[1], 14, 15[1], 17, 18[1], 19[1], 20[1], 22, 25, 28[1], 29[1], 30, 35[1], 37, 39, 40, and 50¢, $1, $2[1], and $5. |
| | Books | 20 at 22 cents ($4.40), 5 at 22 cents ($1.10), 10 at 22 cents ($2.20), 3 at $10.75 ($32.25), and 3 at $12.85 ($38.55). |
| | Coil of 100 | 17, 20[1], and 22¢ (dispenser and stamp affixer for use with these coils are also available). |
| | Coil of 500 | 1, 2, 3, 4, 5, 6, 10, 12, 13[1], 14, 15[1], 17, 18, 20[1], 22¢, and $1. |
| | Coil of 3000 | 1, 2, 3, 4, 5, 6, 10, 12, 13[1], 14, 15[1], 17, 18, 20[1], 22, and 25¢. |
| International airmail postage | Single or sheet | 33, 39, and 44¢ |

1. Will be discontinued when stock is exhausted.

## Non-Standard Mail

All first-class mail weighing one ounce or less and all single-piece rate third-class mail weighing one ounce or less is nonstandard (and subject to a 10¢ surcharge in addition to the applicable postage and fees) if any of the following dimensions are exceeded: length—11 1/2 inches; height—6 1/8 inches; thickness—1/4 inch, or the piece has a height to length (aspect) ratio which does not fall between 1 to 1.3 and 1 to 2.5 inclusive. (The aspect ratio is found by dividing the length by the height. If the answer is between 1.3 and 2.5 inclusive, the piece has a standard aspect ratio).

# International Mail Service

## Letters and Letter Packages

Items of mail containing personal handwritten or typewritten communications having the character of current correspondence must be sent as letters or letter packages. Unless prohibited by the country of destination, dutiable merchandise may be transmitted in packages prepaid at the letter rate of postage. Weight limit for all countries, 4 pounds. For rates, consult your local post office.

## International Airmail

| Destination | Letters and letter packages[1] | Post-cards[2] | Aero-gramme[3] |
|---|---|---|---|
| Central America Colombia, Venezuela, Caribbean Islands, Bahamas, Bermuda, St. Pierre and Miquelon | 39¢ per half oz through 2 oz | | |
| | 33¢ each additional half oz or fraction | 33¢ | 36¢ |
| All other countries except Canada and Mexico | 44¢ per half oz through 2 oz 39¢ each additional half oz through 32 oz 39¢ each additional oz through 64 oz. | 33¢ | 33¢ |

1. Weight limit, 4 lb. 2. 14¢ each for Canada and Mexico. 3. Aerogrammes, which can be folded into the form of an envelope and sent by air to all countries, are available at all post offices for 36¢. No enclosures are permitted.

For Canada and Mexico, *see* Surface Rates.

## Canada and Mexico—Surface Rates

### Letters and Letter Packages

| Weight not over | | Rate | Weight not over | | Rate |
|---|---|---|---|---|---|
| Lb | Oz | | Lb | Oz | |
| 0 | 1 | $0.22 | 0 | 11 | $2.02 |
| 0 | 2 | 0.40 | 0 | 12 | 2.20 |
| 0 | 3 | 0.58 | 1 | 0 | 2.84 |
| 0 | 4 | 0.76 | 1 | 8 | 3.38 |
| 0 | 5 | 0.94 | 2 | 0 | 3.92 |
| 0 | 6 | 1.12 | 2 | 8 | 4.46 |
| 0 | 7 | 1.30 | 3 | 0 | 5.00 |
| 0 | 8 | 1.48 | 3 | 8 | 5.54 |
| 0 | 9 | 1.66 | 4 | 0 | 6.08 |
| 0 | 10 | 1.84 | | | |

Weight limit—4 pounds. NOTE: Letter class mail to Canada and Mexico receives First Class service in the United States and airmail service in Canada and Mexico.

## Countries Other Than Canada and Mexico—Surface Rates

### Letters and Letter Packages

| Weight not over | | Rate | Weight not over | | Rate |
|---|---|---|---|---|---|
| Lb | Oz | | Lb | Oz | |
| 0 | 1 | $0.37 | 0 | 11 | $3.40 |
| 0 | 2 | 0.57 | 0 | 12 | 3.40 |
| 0 | 3 | 0.77 | 1 | 0 | 3.40 |
| 0 | 4 | 0.97 | 1 | 8 | 4.66 |
| 0 | 5 | 1.17 | 2 | 0 | 5.92 |
| 0 | 6 | 1.37 | 2 | 8 | 6.84 |
| 0 | 7 | 1.57 | 3 | 0 | 7.76 |
| 0 | 8 | 1.77 | 3 | 8 | 8.68 |
| 0 | 9 | 3.40 | 4 | 0 | 9.60 |
| 0 | 10 | 3.40 | | | |

Weight limit—4 pounds.

## International Surface Parcel Post

### Other Than Canada

| Weight through lb | Mexico, Central America, Caribbean Islands, Bahamas, Bermuda, St. Pierre and Miquelon | All other countries |
|---|---|---|
| 2 | $ 3.70 | $ 3.90 |
| 3 | 4.90 | 5.20 |
| | $1.20 each additional lb or fraction | $1.30 each additional lb or fraction |

Consult your postmaster for weight/size limits of individual countries.

For other international services and rates consult your local postmaster.

## Canada Surface Parcel Post

Up to 2lb $3.35, $1.05 for each additional lb up to the maximum weight of 66lb. Minimum weight is 1 lb.

## International Money Order Fees

This service available only to certain countries. Consult post office.

## United Nations Stamps

United Nations stamps are issued in three different currencies, namely, U.S. dollars, Swiss francs, and Austrian schillings. Stamps in all three currencies are available at face value at each of the U.N. Postal Administration offices in New York, Geneva, and Vienna. They may be purchased over the counter, by mail, or by opening a Customer Deposit Account.

Mail orders for mint (unused) stamps and postal stationery may be sent to the U.N. Postal Administration in New York, Geneva, and Vienna. Write to: United Nations Postal Administration, P.O. Box 5900, Grand Central Station, New York, N.Y. 10017.

# Authorized 2-Letter State Abbreviations

When the Post Office instituted the ZIP Code for mail in 1963, it also drew up a list of two-letter abbreviations for the states which would gradually replace the traditional ones in use. Following is the official list, including the District of Columbia, Guam, Puerto Rico, and the Virgin Islands (note that only capital letters are used):

| State | Abbr. | State | Abbr. | State | Abbr. |
|---|---|---|---|---|---|
| Alabama | AL | Kentucky | KY | Ohio | OH |
| Alaska | AK | Louisiana | LA | Oklahoma | OK |
| Arizona | AZ | Maine | ME | Oregon | OR |
| Arkansas | AR | Maryland | MD | Pennsylvania | PA |
| California | CA | Massachusetts | MA | Puerto Rico | PR |
| Colorado | CO | Michigan | MI | Rhode Island | RI |
| Connecticut | CT | Minnesota | MN | South Carolina | SC |
| Delaware | DE | Mississippi | MS | South Dakota | SD |
| Dist. of Columbia | DC | Missouri | MO | Tennessee | TN |
| Florida | FL | Montana | MT | Texas | TX |
| Georgia | GA | Nebraska | NE | Utah | UT |
| Guam | GU | Nevada | NV | Vermont | VT |
| Hawaii | HI | New Hampshire | NH | Virginia | VA |
| Idaho | ID | New Jersey | NJ | Virgin Islands | VI |
| Illinois | IL | New Mexico | NM | Washington | WA |
| Indiana | IN | New York | NY | West Virginia | WV |
| Iowa | IA | North Carolina | NC | Wisconsin | WI |
| Kansas | KS | North Dakota | ND | Wyoming | WY |

# The Mail Order Merchandise Rule

The mail order rule adopted by the Federal Trade Commission in October 1975 provides that when you order by mail:

You must receive the merchandise when the seller says you will.

If you are not promised delivery within a certain time period, the seller must ship the merchandise to you no later than 30 days after your order comes in.

If you don't receive it shortly after that 30-day period, you can cancel your order and get your money back.

### How the Rule Works

The seller must notify you if the promised delivery date (or the 30-day limit) cannot be met. The seller must also tell you what the new shipping date will be and give you the option to cancel the order and receive a full refund or agree to the new shipping date. The seller must also give you a free way to send back your answer, such as a stamped envelope or a postage-paid postcard. *If you don't answer, it means that you agree to the shipping delay.*

The seller must tell you if the shipping delay is going to be more than 30 days. You then can agree to the delay or, if you do not agree, the seller must return your money by the end of the first 30 days of the delay.

If you cancel a prepaid order, the seller must mail you the refund within seven business days. Where there is a credit sale, the seller must adjust your account within one billing cycle.

It would be impossible, however, for one rule to apply uniformly to such a varied field as mail order merchandising. For example, the rule does not apply to mail order photo finishing, magazine subscriptions, and other serial deliveries (except for the initial shipment); to mail order seeds and growing plants; to COD orders; or to credit orders where the buyer's account is not charged prior to shipment of the merchandise.

# How to Complain About a Postal Problem

When you have a problem with your mail service, complete a Consumer Service Card which is available from letter carriers and at post offices. This will help your postmaster respond to your problem. If you wish to telephone a complaint, a postal employee will fill out the card for you.

The Consumer Advocate represents consumers at the top management level in the Postal Service. If your postal problems cannot be solved by your local post office, then write to the Consumer Advocate. His staff stands ready to serve you. Write to: The Consumer Advocate, U.S. Postal Service, Washington, D.C. 20260-6320. Or phone: 1-202-245-4514.

# Pornography

You can stop the mailing of unsolicited sexually oriented advertisements to you by filling out a Form 2201, *Application for Listing Pursuant to 39 USC 3010*, at your local post office. Thirty days after your name has been added to the Postal Service reference listing, any mailer who sends you sexually oriented advertisements is subject to legal action by the United States Government.

You may also stop the mailing of any further advertisements to you which you consider "erotically arousing or sexually provocative." Fill out Form 2150, *Notice for Prohibitory Order Against Sender of Pandering Advertisement in the Mail*, at your post office for this purpose.

# RELIGION

## Major Religions of the World

### Judaism

The determining factors of Judaism are: descendance from Israel, the *Torah*, and Tradition.

The name Israel (Jacob, a patriarch) also signifies his descendants as a people. During the 15th–13th centuries B.C., Israelite tribes, coming from South and East, gradually settled in Palestine, then inhabited by Canaanites. They were held together by Moses, who gave them religious unity in the worship of *Jahweh*, the God who had chosen Israel to be his people.

Under Judges, the 12 tribes at first formed an amphictyonic covenant. Saul established kingship (circa 1050 B.C.), and under David, his successor (1000–960 B.C.), the State of Israel comprised all of Palestine with Jerusalem as religio-political center. A golden era followed under Solomon (965–926 B.C.), who built *Jahweh* a temple.

After Solomon's death, the kingdom separated into Israel in the North and Judah in the South. A period of conflicts ensued, which ended with the conquest of Israel by Assyria in 722 B.C. The Babylonians defeated Judah in 586 B.C., destroying Jerusalem and its temple, and deporting many to Babylon.

The era of the kings is significant also in that the great prophets worked in that time, emphasizing faith in *Jahweh* as both God of Israel and God of the universe, and stressing social justice.

When the Persians permitted the Jews to return from exile (539 B.C.), temple and cult were restored in Jerusalem. The Persian rulers were succeeded by the Seleucides. The Maccabaean revolt against these Hellenistic kings gave independence to the Jews in 128 B.C., which lasted till the Romans occupied the country.

Important groups that exerted influence during these times were the Sadducees, priests in the temple in Jerusalem; the Pharisees, teachers of the Law in the synagogues; Essenes, a religious order (from whom Dead Sea Scrolls, discovered in 1947, came); Apocalyptists, who were expecting the heavenly Messiah; and Zealots, who were prepared to fight for national independence.

When the latter turned against Rome in A.D. 66, Roman armies under Titus suppressed the revolt, destroying Jerusalem and its temple in A.D. 70. The Jews were scattered in the *diaspora* (Dispersion), subject to oppressions until the Age of the Enlightenment (18th century) brought their emancipation, although persecutions did not end entirely.

The fall of the Jerusalem temple was an important event in the religious life of the Jews, which now developed around *Torah* (Law) and synagogue. Around A.D. 100 the Sacred Scriptures were codified. Synagogue worship became central, with readings from *Torah* and prophets. Most important prayers are the *Shema* (Hear) and the Prayer of the 18 Benedictions.

Religious life is guided by the commandments contained in the *Torah:* circumcision and *Sabbath*, as well as other ethical and ceremonial commandments.

The *Talmud*, based on the *Mishnah* and its interpretations, took shape over many centuries in the Babylonian and Palestinian Schools. It was a strong binding force of Judaism in the Dispersion.

## Estimated Membership of the Principal Religions of the World

Statistics of the world's religions are only very rough approximations. Aside from Christianity, few religions, if any, attempt to keep statistical records; and even Protestants and Catholics employ differing methods of counting members. All persons of whatever age who have received baptism in the Catholic Church are counted as members, while in most Protestant Churches only those who "join" the church are numbered. The compiling of statistics is further complicated by the fact that in China one may be at the same time a Confucian, a Taoist, and a Buddhist. In Japan, one may be both a Buddhist and a Shintoist.

| Religion | North America[1] | South America | Europe[2] | Asia | Africa | Oceania[3] | World |
|---|---|---|---|---|---|---|---|
| Total Christian | 262,870,400 | 195,431,000 | 329,380,000 | 106,230,000 | 149,200,200 | 18,600,000 | 1,061,711,600 |
| Roman Catholic | 143,850,000 | 185,100,200 | 177,140,200 | 58,100,200 | 59,700,000 | 5,100,200 | 628,990,900 |
| Eastern Orthodox | 5,320,400 | 330,400 | 43,430,300 | 2,800,000 | 6,700,200 | 370,000 | 58,951,100 |
| Protestant | 113,700,000 | 10,000,400 | 108,809,500 | 45,329,800 | 82,800,100 | 13,129,800 | 373,769,600 |
| Jewish | 7,630,000 | 720,200 | 3,800,100 | 4,480,200 | 227,500 | 74,000 | 16,932,000 |
| Muslim | 1,820,300 | 390,100 | 20,400,000 | 381,700,800 | 150,300,000 | 89,000 | 554,700,200 |
| Zoroastrian | 2,700 | 2,600 | 14,000 | 230,000 | 1,500 | — | 250,800 |
| Shinto | 48,000 | — | — | 32,000,000 | — | — | 32,048,000 |
| Taoist | 30,000 | 11,000 | 12,000 | 20,000,000 | — | 3,000 | 20,056,000 |
| Confucian | 100,000 | 56,000 | 410,000 | 150,400,000 | — | 18,000 | 150,984,000 |
| Buddhist | 350,200 | 248,000 | 210,000 | 246,740,300 | 15,000 | 24,000 | 247,587,500 |
| Hindu | 380,000 | 615,200 | 390,000 | 461,300,000 | 800,000 | 325,000 | 463,815,200 |
| Totals | 273,231,600 | 197,474,100 | 354,616,100 | 1,403,081,300 | 300,544,200 | 19,138,000 | 2,548,085,200 |

1. Includes Central America and West Indies. 2. Includes the U.S.S.R. and other countries with established Marxist ideology where continuing religious adherence is difficult to estimate. 3. Includes Australia and New Zealand, as well as islands of the South Pacific. *Source: Britannica Book of the Year, 1986.*

In the 12th century, Maimonides formulated his "13 Articles of Faith," which carried great authority. Fundamental in this creed are: belief in God and his oneness *(Sherma)*, belief in the changeless *Torah*, in the words of Moses and the prophets, belief in reward and punishment, the coming of the Messiah, and the resurrection of the dead.

Judaism is divided into theological schools, the main divisions of which are Orthodox, Conservative, and Reform.

## Christianity

Christianity is founded upon Jesus Christ, to whose life the New Testament writings testify. Jesus, a Jew, was born in about 7 B.C. and assumed his public life, after his 30th year, in Galilee. The Gospels tell of many extraordinary deeds that accompanied his ministry. He proclaimed the Kingdom of God, a future reality that is at the same time already present. Nationalistic-Jewish expectations of the Messiah he rejected. Rather, he referred to himself as the "Son of Man," the Christ, who has power to forgive sins now and who shall also come as Judge at the end of time. Jesus set forth the religio-ethical demands for participation in the Kingdom of God as change of heart and love of God and neighbor.

At the Last Supper he signified his death as a sacrifice, which would inaugurate the New Covenant, by which many would be saved. Circa A.D. 30 he died on a cross in Jerusalem. The early Church carried on Jesus' proclamation, the apostle Paul emphasizing his death and resurrection.

The person of Jesus is fundamental to the Christian faith since it is believed that in his life, death, and resurrection, God's revelation became historically tangible. He is seen as the turning point in history, and man's relationship to God as determined by his attitude to Jesus.

Historically Christianity thus arose out of Judaism, claiming fulfillment of the promises of the Old Testament in Jesus. The early Church designated itself as "the true Israel," which expected the speedy return of Jesus. The mother church was at Jerusalem, but churches were soon founded in many other places. The apostle Paul was instrumental in founding and extending a Gentile Christianity that was free from Jewish legalism.

The new religion spread rapidly throughout the eastern and western parts of the Roman Empire. In coming to terms with other religious movements within the Empire, Christianity began to take definite shape as an organization in its doctrine, liturgy, and ministry circa A.D. 200. In the 4th century the Catholic Church had taken root in countries stretching from Spain in the West to Persia and India in the East. Christians had been repeatedly subject to persecution by the Roman state, but finally gained tolerance under Constantine the Great (A.D. 313). Since that time, the Church became favored under his successors and in 380 the Emperor Theodosius proclaimed Christianity the State religion. Paganism was suppressed and public life was gradually molded in accordance with Christian ethical demands.

It was in these years also that the Church was able to achieve a certain unity of doctrine. Due to differences of interpretation of basic doctrines concerning Christ, which threatened to divide the Catholic Church, a standard Christian Creed was formulated by bishops at successive Ecumenical Councils, the first of which was held in A.D. 325 (Nicaea). The chief doctrines formulated concerned the doctrine of the Trinity, i.e., that there is one God in three persons: Father, Son, and Holy Spirit (Constantinople, A.D. 381); and the nature of Christ as both divine and human (Chalcedon, A.D. 541).

Through differences and rivalry between East and West the unity of the Church was broken by schism in 1054. In 1517 a separation occurred in the Western Church with the Reformation. From the major Protestant denominations [Lutheran, Presbyterian, Anglican (Episcopalian)], many Free Churches separated themselves in an age of individualism.

In the 20th century, however, the direction is toward unity. The Ecumenical Movement led to the formation of the World Council of Churches in 1948 (Amsterdam), which has since been joined by many Protestant and Orthodox Churches.

Through its missionary activity Christianity has spread to most parts of the globe.

### Eastern Orthodoxy

Eastern Orthodoxy comprises the faith and practice of Churches stemming from ancient Churches in the Eastern part of the Roman Empire. The term covers Orthodox Churches in communion with the See of Constantinople, Uniate Churches in communion with Rome, and Nestorian and Monophysite Churches.

The Orthodox, Catholic, Apostolic Church is the direct descendant of the Byzantine State Church and consists of a series of independent national churches that are united by Doctrine, Liturgy, and Hierarchical organization (deacons and priests, who may either be married or be monks before ordination, and bishops, who must be celibates). The heads of these Churches are patriarchs or metropolitans; the Patriarch of Constantinople is only "first among equals." Rivalry between the Pope of Rome and the Patriarch of Constantinople, aided by differences and misunderstandings that existed for centuries between the Eastern and Western parts of the Empire, led to a schism in 1054. Repeated attempts at reunion have failed in past centuries. The mutual excommunication pronounced in that year was lifted in 1965, however, and because of greater interaction in theology between Orthodox Churches and those in the West, a climate of better understanding has been created in the 20th century. First contacts were with Anglicans and Old Catholics. Orthodox Churches belong to the World Council of Churches.

The Eastern Orthodox Churches recognize only the canons of the seven Ecumenical Councils (325–787) as binding for faith and they reject doctrines that have been added in the West.

The central worship service is called the Liturgy, which is understood as representation of God's acts of salvation. Its center is the celebration of the Eucharist, or Lord's Supper.

In their worship *icons* (sacred pictures) are used that have a sacramental meaning as representation. The Mother of Christ, angels, and saints are highly venerated.

The number of sacraments in the Orthodox Church is the same as in the Western Catholic Church.

Orthodox Churches are found in the Balkans and the Soviet Union also, since the 20th century, in Western Europe and other parts of the world, particularly in America.

Eastern Orthodoxy also includes the Uniate Churches that recognize the authority of the Pope but keep their own traditional liturgies and those Churches dating back to the 5th century that emanicipated themselves from the Byzantine State Church: the Nestorian Church in the Near East and India with approximately half a million members and the Monophysite Churches with some 17 million members (Coptic, Ethiopian, Syrian, Armenian, and the Mar Thoma Church in India).

### Roman Catholicism

Roman Catholicism comprises the belief and practice of the Roman Catholic Church. The Church stands under the authority of the Bishop of Rome, the Pope, and is ruled by him and bishops who are held to be, through ordination, successors of Peter and the Apostles, respectively. Fundamental to the structure of the Church is the juridical aspect: doctrine and sacraments are bound to the power of jurisdiction and consecration of the hierarchy. The Pope, as the head of the hierarchy of archbishops, bishops, priests, and deacons, has full ecclesiastical power, granted him by Christ, through Peter. As successor to Peter, he is the Vicar of Christ. The powers that others in the hierarchy possess are delegated.

Roman Catholics believe their Church to be the one, holy, catholic, and apostolic Church, possessing all the properties of the one, true Church of Christ.

The faith of the Church is understood to be identical with that taught by Christ and his Apostles and contained in Bible and Tradition, i.e. the original deposit of faith, to which nothing new may be added. New definitions of doctrines, such as the Immaculate Conception of Mary (1854) and the bodily Assumption of Mary (1950), have been declared by Popes, however, in accordance with the principle of development (implicit-explicit doctrine).

At Vatican Council I (1870) the Pope was proclaimed "endowed with infallibility, *ex cathedra*, i.e., when exercising the office of Pastor and Teacher of all Christians."

The center of Roman Catholic worship is the celebration of the Mass, the Eucharist, which is the commemoration of Christ's sacrificial death and of his resurrection. Other sacraments are Baptism, Confirmation, Confession, Matrimony, Ordination, and Extreme Unction, seven in all. The Virgin Mary and saints, and their relics, are highly venerated and prayers are made to them to intercede with God, in whose presence they are believed to dwell.

The Roman Catholic Church is the largest Christian organization in the world, found in most countries. Some 8 million belong to the Uniate rites, the vast majority to the Latin rite.

Since Vatican Council II (1962–65), and the effort to "update" the Church, many interesting changes and developments have been taking place.

### Protestantism

Protestantism comprises the Christian churches that separated from Rome during the Reformation in the 16th century, initiated by an Augustinian monk, Martin Luther. "Protestant" was originally applied to followers of Luther, who protested at the Diet of Spires (1529) against the decree which prohibited all further ecclesiastical reforms. Subsequently, Protestantism came to mean rejection of attempts to tie God's revelation to earthly institutions, and a return to the Gospel and the Word of God as sole authority in matters of faith and practice. Central in the biblical message is the justification of the sinner by faith alone. The Church is understood as a fellowship and the priesthood of all

# U. S. Church Membership

| Religious group | Members |
|---|---|
| Protestant bodies and others | 78,701,677 |
| Roman Catholics | 52,286,043 |
| Jewish congregations[1] | 5,817,000 |
| Eastern churches | 4,052,668 |
| Old Catholic, Polish National Catholic, Armenian churches | 1,024,582 |
| Buddhist Churches of America | 100,000 |
| Miscellaneous | 190,168 |
| Total[2] | 142,172,138 |

1. Includes Orthodox, Conservative, and Reform. 2. As reported in the *1986 Yearbook* from statistics furnished by 219 religious bodies in the United States.

believers stressed.

The Augsburg Confession (1530) was the principal statement of Lutheran faith and practice. It became a model for other Confessions of Faith, which in their turn had decisive influence on Church polity. Major Protestant denominations are the Lutheran, Reformed (Calvinist), Presbyterian, and Anglican (Episcopal). Smaller ones are the Mennonite, Schwenkfeldians, and Unitarians. In Great Britain and America there are the Congregationalists, Baptists, Quakers, Methodists, and other free church types of communities. (In regarding themselves as being faithful to original biblical Christianity, these Churches differ from such religious bodies as Unitarians, Mormons, Jehovah's Witnesses, and Christian Scientists, who either teach new doctrines or reject old ones.)

Since the latter part of the 19th century, national councils of churches have been established in many countries, e.g. the Federal Council of Churches of Christ in America in 1908. Denominations across countries joined in federations and world alliances, beginning with the Anglican Lambeth Conference in 1867.

Protestant missionary activity, particularly strong in the last century, resulted in the founding of many younger churches in Asia and Africa. The Ecumenical Movement, which originated with Protestant missions, aims at unity among Christians and churches.

## Islam

Islam is the religion founded in Arabia by Mohammed between 610 and 632. Its more than 600 million adherents are found in countries stretching from Morocco in the West to Indonesia in the East.

Mohammed was born in A.D. 570 at Mecca and belonged to the Quraysh tribe, which was active in caravan trade. At the age of 25 he joined the caravan trade from Mecca to Syria in the employment of a rich widow, Khadiji, whom he married. Critical of the idolatry of the inhabitants of Mecca, he began to lead a contemplative life in the deserts. There he received a series of revelations. Encouraged by Khadiji, he gradually became convinced that he was given a God-appointed task to devote himself to the reform of religion and society. Idolatry was to be abandoned.

The *Hegira (Hijra)* (migration) of Mohammed from Mecca, where he was not honored, to Medina, where he was well received, occurred in 622 and marks the beginning of the Muslim era. In 630 he marched on Mecca and conquered it. He died at Medina in 632. His grave there has since been a place of pilgrimage.

Mohammed's followers, called Moslems, revered him as the prophet of *Allah* (God), beside whom there is no other God. Although he had no close knowledge of Judaism and Christianity, he considered himself succeeding and completing them as the seal of the Prophets. Sources of the Islamic faith are the *Qur'an*, regarded as the uncreated, eternal Word of God, and Tradition *(hadith)* regarding sayings and deeds of the prophet.

Islam means surrender to the will of *Allah*. He is the all-powerful, whose will is supreme and determines man's fate. Good deeds will be rewarded at the Last Judgment in paradise and evil deeds will be punished in hell.

The Five Pillars, primary duties, of Islam are: witness; confessing the oneness of God and of Mohammed, his prophet; prayer, to be performed five times a day; almsgiving to the poor and the mosque (house of worship); fasting during daylight hours in the month of Ramadan; and pilgrimage to Mecca at least once in the Moslem's lifetime.

Islam, upholding the law of brotherhood, succeeded in uniting an Arab world that had disintegrated into tribes and castes. Disagreements concerning the succession of the prophet caused a great division in Islam between *Sunnis* and *Shias.* Among these, other sects arose *(Wahhabi).* Doctrinal issues also led to the rise of different schools of thought in theology. Nevertheless, since Arab armies turned against Syria and Palestine in 635, Islam has expanded successfully under Mohammed's successors. Its rapid conquests in Asia and Africa are unsurpassed in history. Turning against Europe, Moslems conquered Spain in 713. In 1453 Constantinople fell into their hands and in 1529 Moslem armies besieged Vienna. Since then, Islam has lost its foothold in Europe.

In modern times it has made great gains in Africa.

## Hinduism

In India alone there are more than 300 million adherents of Hinduism. In contrast to other religions, it has no founder. Considered the oldest religion in the world, it dates back, perhaps, to prehistoric times.

Hinduism is hard to define, there being no common creed, no one doctrine to bind Hindus together. Intellectually there is complete freedom of belief, and one can be monotheist, polytheist, or atheist. What matters is the social system: a Hindu is one born into a caste.

As a religion, Hinduism is founded on the sacred scriptures, written in Sanskrit and called the *Vedas* (*Veda*-knowledge). There are four Vedic books, among which the *Rig Veda* is the most important. It speaks of many gods and also deals with questions concerning the universe and creation. The dates of these works are unknown (1000 B.C.?).

The *Upanishads* (dated 1000–300 B.C.), commentaries on the Vedic texts, have philosophical speculations on the origin of the universe, the nature of deity, of *atman* (the human soul), and its relationship to *Brahman* (the universal soul).

*Brahman* is the principle and source of the universe who can be indicated only by negatives. As the divine intelligence, he is the ground of the visible world, a presence that pervades all beings. Thus the many Hindu deities came to be understood as manifestations of the one *Brahman* from whom everything proceeds and to whom everything ultimately returns. The religio-social system of Hinduism is based on the concept of reincarnation and transmigration in which all living beings, from plants below to gods above, are caught in a cosmic system that is an everlasting cycle of becoming and perishing.

Life is determined by the law of *karma,* according to which rebirth is dependent on moral behavior in a previous phase of existence. The doctrine of transmigration thus provides a rationale for the caste system. In this view, life on earth is regarded as transient *(maya)* and a burden. The goal of existence is liberation from the cycle of rebirth and redeath and entrance into the indescribable state of what in Buddhism is called *nirvana* (extinction of passion).

Further important sacred writings are the Epics *(puranas)*, which contain legendary stories about gods and men. They are the *Mahabharata* (composed between 200 B.C. and A.D. 200) and the *Ramayana.* The former includes the *Bhagavad-Gita* (Song of the Lord), its most famous part, that tells of devotion to *Krishna* (Lord), who appears as an *avatar* (incarnation) of the god *Vishnu,* and of the duty of obeying caste rules. The work begins with a praise of the *yoga* (discipline) system.

The practice of Hinduism consists of rites and ceremonies, performed within the framework of the caste system and centering on the main socioreligious occasions of birth, marriage, and death. There are many Hindu temples, which are dwelling places of the deities and to which people bring offerings. There are also places of pilgrimages, the chief one being Benares on the Ganges, most sacred among the rivers in India.

In modern times work has been done to reform and revive Hinduism. One of the outstanding reformers was Ramakrishna (1836–86), who inspired many followers, one of whom founded the Ramakrishna mission, which seeks to convert others to its religion. The mission is active both in India and in other countries.

## Buddhism

Founded in the 6th century B.C. in northern India by Gautama Buddha, who was born in southern Nepal as son to a king. His birth is surrounded by many legends, but Western scholars agree that he lived from 563 to 483 B.C. Warned by a sage that his son would become an ascetic or a universal monarch, the king confined him to his home. He was able to escape and began the life of a homeless wanderer in search of peace, passing through many disappointments until he finally came to the Tree of Enlightenment, under which he lived in meditation till enlightenment came to him and he became a Buddha (enlightened one).

Now he understood the origin of suffering, summarized in the *Four Noble Truths,* which constitutes the foundation of Buddhism. The Four are the truth of suffering, which all living beings must endure; of the origin of suffering, which is craving and which leads to rebirth; that it can be destroyed; and of the way that leads to cessation of pain, i.e., the *Noble Eightfold Way,* which is the rule of practical Buddhism: right views, right intention, right speech, right action, right livelihood, right effort, right concentration, and right ecstasy.

*Nirvana* is the goal of all existence, the state of complete redemption, into which the redeemed enters. Buddha's insight can free every man from the law of reincarnation through complete emptying of the self.

The nucleus of Buddha's church or association was originally formed by monks and lay-brothers, whose houses gradually became monasteries used as places for religious instruction. The worship service consisted of a sermon, expounding of Scripture, meditation, and confession. At a later stage pilgrimages to the holy places associated with the Buddha came into being, as well as veneration of relics.

In the 3rd century B.C., King Ashoka made Buddhism the State religion of India but, as centuries-passed, it gradually fell into decay through splits, persecutions, and the hostile Brahmans. Buddhism spread to countries outside India, however.

At the beginning of the Christian era, there occurred a split that gave rise to two main types: *Hinayana* (Little Vehicle), or southern Buddhism, and *Mahayana* (Great Vehicle), or northern Buddhism. The former type, more individualistic, survived in Ceylon and southern Asia. *Hinayana* retained more closely the original teachings of the Buddha, which did not know of a personal god or soul. *Mahayana*, more social, polytheistic, and developing a pluralistic pompous cult, was strong in the Himalayas, Tibet, Mongolia, China, Korea, and Japan.

In the present century, Buddhism has found believers also in the West and Buddhist associations have been established in Europe and the U.S.

## Confucianism

Confucius (K'ung Fu-tzu), born in the state of Lu (northern China), lived from 551 to 479 B.C. Tradition, exaggerating the importance of Confucius in life, has depicted him as a great statesman but, in fact, he seems to have been a private teacher. Anthologies of ancient Chinese classics, along with his own Analects *(Lun Yu)*, became the basis of Confucianism. These Analects were transmitted as a collection of his sayings as recorded by his students, with whom he discussed ethical and social problems. They developed into men of high moral standing, who served the State as administrators.

In his teachings, Confucius emphasized the importance of an old Chinese concept *(li)*, which has the connotation of proper conduct. There is some disagreement as to the religious ideas of Confucius, but he held high the concepts handed down from centuries before him. Thus he believed in Heaven *(T'ien)* and sacrificed to his ancestors. Ancestor worship he indeed encouraged as an expression of filial piety, which he considered the loftiest of virtues.

Piety to Confucius was the foundation of the family as well as the State. The family is the nucleus of the State, and the "five relations," between king and subject, father and son, man and wife, older and younger brother, and friend and friend, are determined by the virtues of love of fellow men, righteousness, and respect.

An extension of ancestor worship may be seen in the worship of Confucius, which became official in the 2nd century B.C. when the emperor, in recognition of Confucius' teachings as supporting the imperial rule, offered sacrifices at his tomb.

Mencius (Meng Tse), who lived around 400 B.C., did much to propagate and elaborate Confucianism in its concern with ordering society. Thus, for two millennia, Confucius' doctrine of State, with its emphasis on ethics and social morality, rooted in ancient Chinese tradition and developed and continued by his disciples, has been standard in China and the Far East.

With the revolution of 1911 in China, however, students, burning Confucius in effigy, called for the removal of "the old curiosity shop."

## Shintoism

Shinto, the Chinese term for the Japanese *Kami no Michi*, i.e., the Way of the Gods, comprises the religious ideas and cult indigenous to Japan. *Kami*, or gods, considered divine forces of nature that are worshipped, may reside in rivers, trees, rocks, mountains, certain animals, or, particularly, in the sun and moon. The worship of ancestors, heroes, and deceased emperors was incorporated later.

After Buddhism had come from Korea, Japan's native religion at first resisted it. Then there followed a period of compromise and amalgamation with Buddhist beliefs and ceremonies, resulting, since the 9th century A.D., in a syncretistic religion, a Twofold Shinto. Buddhist deities came to be regarded as manifestations of Japanese deities and Buddhist priests took over most of the Shinto shrines.

In modern times Shinto regained independence from Buddhism. Under the reign of the Emperor Meiji (1868–1912) it became the official State religion, in which loyalty to the emperor was emphasized. The line of succession of emperors is traced back to the first Emperor Jimmu (660 B.C.) and beyond him to the Sun-goddess *Amaterasuomikami*.

The centers of worship are the shrines and temples in which the deities are believed to dwell and believers approach them through *torii* (gateways). Most important among the shrines is the imperial shrine of the Sun-goddess at Ise, where state ceremonies were once held in June and December. The *Yasukuni* shrine of the war dead in Tokyo is also well known.

Acts of worship consist of prayers, clapping of hands, acts of purification, and offerings. On feast days processions and performances of music and dancing take place and priests read prayers before the gods in the shrines, asking for good harvest, the well-being of people and emperor, etc. In Japanese homes there is a god-shelf, a small wooden shrine that contains the tablets bearing the names of ancestors. Offerings are made and candles lit before it.

After World War II the Allied Command ordered the disestablishment of State Shinto. To be distinguished from State Shinto is Sect Shinto, consisting of 13 recognized sects. These have arisen in modern times. Most important among them is *Tenrikyo* in Tenri City (Nara), in which healing by faith plays a central role.

## Taoism

Taoism, a religion of China, was, according to tradition, founded by Lao Tse, a Chinese philosopher, long considered one of the prominent religious leaders from the 6th century B.C.

Data about him are for the most part legendary, however, and the *Tao Te Ching* (the classic of the Way and of its Power), traditionally ascribed to him, is now believed by many scholars to have originated in the 3rd century B.C. The book is composed in short chapters, written in aphoristic rhymes. Central are the word *Tao*, which means way or path and, in a deeper sense, signifies the principle that underlies the reality of this world and manifests itself in nature and in the lives of men, and the word *Te* (power).

The virtuous man draws power from being absorbed in *Tao*, the ultimate reality within an ever-changing world. By non-action and keeping away from human striving it is possible for man to live in harmony with the principles that underlie and govern the universe. *Tao* cannot be comprehended by reason and knowledge, but only by inward quiet.

Besides the *Tao Te Ching,* dating from approximately the same period, there are two Taoist works, written by Chuang Tse and Lieh Tse.

Theoretical Taoism of this classical philosophical movement of the 4th and 3rd centuries B.C. in China differed from popular Taoism, into which it gradually degenerated. The standard of theoretical Taoism was maintained in the classics, of course,

and among the upper classes it continued to be alive until modern times.

Religious Taoism is a form of religion dealing with deities and spirits, magic and soothsaying. In the 2nd century A.D. it was organized with temples, cult, priests, and monasteries and was able to hold its own in the competition with Buddhism that came up at the same time.

After the 7th century A.D., however, Taoist religion further declined. Split into numerous sects, which often operate like secret societies, it has become a syncretistic folk religion in which some of the old deities and saints live on.

## Roman Catholic Pontiffs

St. Peter, of Bethsaida in Galilee, Prince of the Apostles, was the first Pope. He lived first in Antioch and then in Rome for 25 years. In AD 64 or 67, he was martyred. St. Linus became the second Pope.

| Name | Birthplace | Reigned From | Reigned To | Name | Birthplace | Reigned From | Reigned To |
|---|---|---|---|---|---|---|---|
| St. Linus | Tuscia | 67 | 76 | St. Symmachus | Sardinia | 498 | 514 |
| St. Anacletus (Cletus) | Rome | 76 | 88 | St. Hormisdas | Frosinone | 514 | 523 |
| | | | | St. John I | Tuscany | 523 | 526 |
| St. Clement | Rome | 88 | 97 | St. Felix IV (III) | Samnium | 526 | 530 |
| St. Evaristus | Greece | 97 | 105 | Boniface II | Rome | 530 | 532 |
| St. Alexander I | Rome | 105 | 115 | John II | Rome | 533 | 535 |
| St. Sixtus I | Rome | 115 | 125 | St. Agapitus I | Rome | 535 | 536 |
| St. Telesphorus | Greece | 125 | 136 | St. Silverius | Campania | 536 | 537 |
| St. Hyginus | Greece | 136 | 140 | Vigilius | Rome | 537 | 555 |
| St. Pius I | Aquileia | 140 | 155 | Pelagius I | Rome | 556 | 561 |
| St. Anicetus | Syria | 155 | 166 | John III | Rome | 561 | 574 |
| St. Soter | Campania | 166 | 175 | Benedict I | Rome | 575 | 579 |
| St. Eleutherius | Epirus | 175 | 189 | Pelagius II | Rome | 579 | 590 |
| St. Victor I | Africa | 189 | 199 | St. Gregory I (the Great) | Rome | 590 | 604 |
| St. Zephyrinus | Rome | 199 | 217 | | | | |
| St. Callistus I | Rome | 217 | 222 | Sabinianus | Tuscany | 604 | 606 |
| St. Urban I | Rome | 222 | 230 | Boniface III | Rome | 607 | 607 |
| St. Pontian | Rome | 230 | 235 | St. Boniface IV | Marsi | 608 | 615 |
| St. Anterus | Greece | 235 | 236 | St. Deusdedit (Adeodatus I) | Rome | 615 | 618 |
| St. Fabian | Rome | 236 | 250 | | | | |
| St. Cornelius | Rome | 251 | 253 | Boniface V | Naples | 619 | 625 |
| St. Lucius I | Rome | 253 | 254 | Honorius I | Campania | 625 | 638 |
| St. Stephen I | Rome | 254 | 257 | Severinus | Rome | 640 | 640 |
| St. Sixtus II | Greece | 257 | 258 | John IV | Dalmatia | 640 | 642 |
| St. Dionysius | Unknown | 259 | 268 | Theodore I | Greece | 642 | 649 |
| St. Felix I | Rome | 269 | 274 | St. Martin I | Todi | 649 | 655 |
| St. Eutychian | Luni | 275 | 283 | St. Eugene I[3] | Rome | 654 | 657 |
| St. Caius | Dalmatia | 283 | 296 | St. Vitalian | Segni | 657 | 672 |
| St. Marcellinus | Rome | 296 | 304 | Adeodatus II | Rome | 672 | 676 |
| St. Marcellus I | Rome | 308 | 309 | Donus | Rome | 676 | 678 |
| St. Eusebius | Greece | 309[1] | 309[1] | St. Agatho | Sicily | 678 | 681 |
| St. Meltiades | Africa | 311 | 314 | St. Leo II | Sicily | 682 | 683 |
| St. Sylvester I | Rome | 314 | 335 | St. Benedict II | Rome | 684 | 685 |
| St. Marcus | Rome | 336 | 336 | John V | Syria | 685 | 686 |
| St. Julius I | Rome | 337 | 352 | Conon | Unknown | 686 | 687 |
| Liberius | Rome | 352 | 366 | St. Sergius I | Syria | 687 | 701 |
| St. Damasus I | Spain | 366 | 384 | John VI | Greece | 701 | 705 |
| St. Siricius | Rome | 384 | 399 | John VII | Greece | 705 | 707 |
| St. Anastasius I | Rome | 399 | 401 | Sisinnius | Syria | 708 | 708 |
| St. Innocent I | Albano | 401 | 417 | Constantine | Syria | 708 | 715 |
| St. Zozimus | Greece | 417 | 418 | St. Gregory II | Rome | 715 | 731 |
| St. Boniface I | Rome | 418 | 422 | St. Gregory III | Syria | 731 | 741 |
| St. Celestine I | Campania | 422 | 432 | St. Zachary | Greece | 741 | 752 |
| St. Sixtus III | Rome | 432 | 440 | Stephen II (III)[4] | Rome | 752 | 757 |
| St. Leo I (the Great) | Tuscany | 440 | 461 | St. Paul I | Rome | 757 | 767 |
| | | | | Stephen II (IV) | Sicily | 768 | 772 |
| St. Hilary | Sardinia | 461 | 468 | Adrian I | Rome | 772 | 795 |
| St. Simplicius | Tivoli | 468 | 483 | St. Leo III | Rome | 795 | 816 |
| St. Felix III (II)[2] | Rome | 483 | 492 | Stephen IV (V) | Rome | 816 | 817 |
| St. Gelasius I | Africa | 492 | 496 | St. Paschal I | Rome | 817 | 824 |
| Anastasius II | Rome | 496 | 498 | Eugene II | Rome | 824 | 827 |

| Name | Birthplace | Reigned From | To | Name | Birthplace | Reigned From | To |
|---|---|---|---|---|---|---|---|
| Valentine | Rome | 827 | 827 | Bl. Eugene III | Pisa | 1145 | 1153 |
| Gregory IV | Rome | 827 | 844 | Anastasius IV | Rome | 1153 | 1154 |
| Sergius II | Rome | 844 | 847 | Adrian IV | England | 1154 | 1159 |
| St. Leo IV | Rome | 847 | 855 | Alexander III | Siena | 1159 | 1181 |
| Benedict III | Rome | 855 | 858 | Lucius III | Lucca | 1181 | 1185 |
| St. Nicholas I (the Great) | Rome | 858 | 867 | Urban III | Milan | 1185 | 1187 |
| | | | | Gregory VIII | Benevento | 1187 | 1187 |
| Adrian II | Rome | 867 | 872 | Clement III | Rome | 1187 | 1191 |
| John VIII | Rome | 872 | 882 | Celestine III | Rome | 1191 | 1198 |
| Marinus I | Gallese | 882 | 884 | Innocent III | Anagni | 1198 | 1216 |
| St. Adrian III | Rome | 884 | 885 | Honorius III | Rome | 1216 | 1227 |
| Stephen V (VI) | Rome | 885 | 891 | Gregory IX | Anagni | 1227 | 1241 |
| Formosus | Portus | 891 | 896 | Celestine IV | Milan | 1241 | 1241 |
| Boniface VI | Rome | 896 | 896 | Innocent IV | Genoa | 1243 | 1254 |
| Stephen VI (VII) | Rome | 896 | 897 | Alexander IV | Anagni | 1254 | 1261 |
| Romanus | Gallese | 897 | 897 | Urban IV | Troyes | 1261 | 1264 |
| Theodore II | Rome | 897 | 897 | Clement IV | France | 1265 | 1268 |
| John IX | Tivoli | 898 | 900 | Bl. Gregory X | Piacenza | 1271 | 1276 |
| Benedict IV | Rome | 900 | 903 | Bl. Innocent V | Savoy | 1276 | 1276 |
| Leo V | Ardea | 903 | 903 | Adrian V | Genoa | 1276 | 1276 |
| Sergius III | Rome | 904 | 911 | John XXI[7] | Portugal | 1276 | 1277 |
| Anastasius III | Rome | 911 | 913 | Nicholas III | Rome | 1277 | 1280 |
| Landus | Sabina | 913 | 914 | Martin IV[3] | France | 1281 | 1285 |
| John X | Tossignano | 914 | 928 | Honorius IV | Rome | 1285 | 1287 |
| Leo VI | Rome | 928 | 928 | Nicholas IV | Ascoli | 1288 | 1292 |
| Stephen VII (VIII) | Rome | 928 | 931 | St. Celestine V | Isernia | 1294 | 1294 |
| John XI | Rome | 931 | 935 | Boniface VIII | Anagni | 1294 | 1303 |
| Leo VII | Rome | 936 | 939 | Bl. Benedict XI | Treviso | 1303 | 1304 |
| Stephen VIII (IX) | Rome | 939 | 942 | Clement V | France | 1305 | 1314 |
| Marinus II | Rome | 942 | 946 | John XXII | Cahors | 1316 | 1334 |
| Agapitus II | Rome | 946 | 955 | Benedict XII | France | 1334 | 1342 |
| John XII | Tusculum | 955 | 964 | Clement VI | France | 1342 | 1352 |
| Leo VIII[5] | Rome | 963 | 965 | Innocent VI | France | 1352 | 1362 |
| Benedict V[5] | Rome | 964 | 966 | Bl. Urban V | France | 1362 | 1370 |
| John XIII | Rome | 965 | 972 | Gregory XI | France | 1370 | 1378 |
| Benedict VI | Rome | 973 | 974 | Urban VI | Naples | 1378 | 1389 |
| Benedict VII | Rome | 974 | 983 | Boniface IX | Naples | 1389 | 1404 |
| John XIV | Pavia | 983 | 984 | Innocent VII | Sulmona | 1404 | 1406 |
| John XV | Rome | 985 | 996 | Gregory XII | Venice | 1406 | 1415 |
| Gregory V | Saxony | 996 | 999 | Martin V | Rome | 1417 | 1431 |
| Sylvester II | Auvergne | 999 | 1003 | Eugene IV | Venice | 1431 | 1447 |
| John XVII | Rome | 1003 | 1003 | Nicholas V | Sarzana | 1447 | 1455 |
| John XVIII | Rome | 1004 | 1009 | Callistus III | Jativa | 1455 | 1458 |
| Sergius IV | Rome | 1009 | 1012 | Pius II | Siena | 1458 | 1464 |
| Benedict VIII | Tusculum | 1012 | 1024 | Paul II | Venice | 1464 | 1471 |
| John XIX | Tusculum | 1024 | 1032 | Sixtus IV | Savona | 1471 | 1484 |
| Benedict IX[6] | Tusculum | 1032 | 1044 | Innocent VIII | Genoa | 1484 | 1492 |
| Sylvester III | Rome | 1045 | 1045 | Alexander VI | Jativa | 1492 | 1503 |
| Benedict IX (2nd time) | — | 1045 | 1045 | Pius III | Siena | 1503 | 1503 |
| | | | | Julius II | Savona | 1503 | 1513 |
| Gregory VI | Rome | 1045 | 1046 | Leo X | Florence | 1513 | 1521 |
| Clement II | Saxony | 1046 | 1047 | Adrian VI | Utrecht | 1522 | 1523 |
| Benedict IX (3rd time) | — | 1047 | 1048 | Clement VII | Florence | 1523 | 1534 |
| | | | | Paul III | Rome | 1534 | 1549 |
| Damasus II | Bavaria | 1048 | 1048 | Julius III | Rome | 1550 | 1555 |
| St. Leo IX | Alsace | 1049 | 1054 | Marcellus II | Montepulciano | 1555 | 1555 |
| Victor II | Germany | 1055 | 1057 | Paul IV | Naples | 1555 | 1559 |
| Stephen IX (X) | Lorraine | 1057 | 1058 | Pius IV | Milan | 1559 | 1565 |
| Nicholas II | Burgundy | 1059 | 1061 | St. Pius V | Bosco | 1566 | 1572 |
| Alexander II | Milan | 1061 | 1073 | Gregory XIII | Bologna | 1572 | 1585 |
| St. Gregory VII | Tuscany | 1073 | 1085 | Sixtus V | Grottammare | 1585 | 1590 |
| Bl. Victor III | Benevento | 1086 | 1087 | Urban VII | Rome | 1590 | 1590 |
| Bl. Urban II | France | 1088 | 1099 | Gregory XIV | Cremona | 1590 | 1591 |
| Paschal II | Ravenna | 1099 | 1118 | Innocent IX | Bologna | 1591 | 1591 |
| Gelasius II | Gaeta | 1118 | 1119 | Clement VIII | Florence | 1592 | 1605 |
| Callistus II | Burgundy | 1119 | 1124 | Leo XI | Florence | 1605 | 1605 |
| Honorius II | Flagnano | 1124 | 1130 | Paul V | Rome | 1605 | 1621 |
| Innocent II | Rome | 1130 | 1143 | Gregory XV | Bologna | 1621 | 1623 |
| Celestine II | Città di Castello | 1143 | 1144 | Urban VIII | Florence | 1623 | 1644 |
| | | | | Innocent X | Rome | 1644 | 1655 |
| Lucius II | Bologna | 1144 | 1145 | Alexander VII | Siena | 1655 | 1667 |

| Name | Birthplace | Reigned From | To | Name | Birthplace | Reigned From | To |
|------|-----------|------|-----|------|-----------|------|-----|
| Clement IX | Pistoia | 1667 | 1669 | Leo XII | Genga | 1823 | 1829 |
| Clement X | Rome | 1670 | 1676 | Pius VIII | Cingoli | 1829 | 1830 |
| Bl. Innocent XI | Como | 1676 | 1689 | Gregory XVI | Belluno | 1831 | 1846 |
| Alexander VIII | Venice | 1689 | 1691 | Pius IX | Senegallia | 1846 | 1878 |
| Innocent XII | Spinazzola | 1691 | 1700 | Leo XIII | Carpineto | 1878 | 1903 |
| Clement XI | Urbino | 1700 | 1721 | St. Pius X | Riese | 1903 | 1914 |
| Innocent XIII | Rome | 1721 | 1724 | Benedict XV | Genoa | 1914 | 1922 |
| Benedict XIII | Gravina | 1724 | 1730 | Pius XI | Desio | 1922 | 1939 |
| Clement XII | Florence | 1730 | 1740 | Pius XII | Rome | 1939 | 1958 |
| Benedict XIV | Bologna | 1740 | 1758 | John XXIII | Sotto il Monte | 1958 | 1963 |
| Clement XIII | Venice | 1758 | 1769 | Paul VI | Concesio | 1963 | 1978 |
| Clement XIV | Rimini | 1769 | 1774 | John Paul I | Forno di Canale | 1978 | 1978 |
| Pius VI | Cesena | 1775 | 1799 | John Paul II | Wadowice, Poland | 1978 | |
| Pius VII | Cesena | 1800 | 1823 | | | | |

1. Or 310. 2. He should be called Felix II, and his successors of the same name should be numbered accordingly. The discrepancy was caused by the erroneous insertion in some lists of the name of St. Felix of Rome, Martyr. 3. He was elected during the exile of St. Martin I, who endorsed him as Pope. 4. After St. Zachary died, a Roman priest named Stephen was elected but died before his consecration as Bishop of Rome. His name is not included in all lists for this reason. In view of this historical confusion, the *National Catholic Almanac* lists the true Stephen II as Stephen II (III), the true Stephen III as Stephen III (IV), etc. 5. Confusion exists concerning the legitimacy of claims. If the deposition of John was invalid, Leo was an antipope until after the end of Benedict's reign. If the deposition of John was valid, Leo was the legitimate Pope and Benedict an antipope. 6. If the triple removal of Benedict IX was not valid, Sylvester III, Gregory VI, and Clement II were antipopes. 7. Elimination was made of the name of John XX in an effort to rectify the numerical designation of Popes named John. The error dates back to the time of John XV. 8. The names of Marinus I and Marinus II were construed as Martin. In view of these two pontificates and the earlier reign of St. Martin I, this pontiff was called Martin IV. *Source: National Catholic Almanac, from Annuarto Pontificio.*

# Books of the Bible

## OLD TESTAMENT—STANDARD VERSIONS

Genesis
Exodus
Leviticus
Numbers
Deuteronomy
Joshua
Judges
Ruth
I Samuel
II Samuel
I Kings
II Kings
I Chronicles
II Chronicles
Ezra
Nehemiah
Esther
Job
Psalms
Proverbs
Ecclesiastes
Song of Solomon
Isaiah
Jeremiah
Lamentations
Ezekiel

Daniel
Hosea
Joel
Amos
Obadiah
Jonah
Micah
Nahum
Habakkuk
Zephaniah
Haggai
Zechariah
Malachi

## NEW TESTAMENT—STANDARD VERSIONS

Matthew
Mark
Luke
John
Acts
Romans
Corinthians
Galatians
Ephesians
Philippians
Colossians
Thessalonians
Timothy

Titus
Philemon
Hebrews
James
Peter
John
Jude
Revelation

## OLD TESTAMENT—DOUAY VERSION[1]

Genesis
Exodus
Leviticus
Numbers
Deuteronomy
Josue
Judges
Ruth
I Kings
II Kings
III Kings
IV Kings
I Paralipomenon
II Paralipomenon
I Esdras
II Esdras
Tobias
Judith

Esther
Job
Psalms
Proverbs
Ecclesiastes
Canticle of Canticles
Wisdom
Ecclesiasticus
Isaias
Jeremias
Lamentations
Baruch
Ezechiel
Daniel
Osee
Joel
Amos
Abdias
Jonas
Micheas
Nahum
Habacuc
Sophonias
Aggeus
Zacharias
Malachias
I Machabees
II Machabees

1. In the Douay Version of the Bible, the books of the New Testament are the same as those of the Authorized (King James) Version, except that the Revelation of St. John is called the Apocalypse of St. John in the Douay Version.

# Old Testament Apocrypha

The First Book of Esdras
The Second Book of Esdras
Tobit
Judith
The Rest of the Book of Esther
The Wisdom of Solomon
Ecclesiasticus

Baruch
The Song of the Three Holy Children
The History of Susanna
The History of Bel & The Dragon
The Prayer of Manasses
The First Book of the Maccabees
The Second Book of the Maccabees

# IDEAS AND BELIEFS

## Introduction

THIS section explains many of the ideas and beliefs which people have held at different periods in history. Beliefs may be true or false, meaningful or totally meaningless, regardless of the degree of conviction with which they are held. Since man has been moved to action so often by his beliefs they are worth serious study. The section throws a vivid light on human history.

Man has always felt a deep need for emotional security, a sense of "belonging." This need has found expression in the framing of innumerable religious systems, nearly all of which have been concerned with man's relation to a divine ruling power. In the past, people have been accustomed to think of their own religion as true and of all others as false. Latterly we have come to realize that in man's religious strivings there is common ground, for our need in the world today is a morality whereby human beings may live together in harmony.

There is also to be found in man an irresistible curiosity which demands an explanation of the world in which he finds himself. This urge to make the world intelligible takes him into the realm of science where the unknown is the constant challenge. Science is a creative process, always in the making, since the scientist's conjectures are constantly being submitted to severe critical tests.

# A

**Acupuncture,** a quasi-medical system originating in China and based on the supposedly therapeutic effects of implanting fine gold needles in the spinal cord and other specific parts of the body. The site of needle implantation is decided according to traditional texts. The apparent lack of any logical relationship between the implantation sites and any known physiological or anatomical systems within the body has caused acupuncture to be held in low regard by Western medicine. Indeed it is certainly true that acupuncture and other similar practices tend to flourish in parts of the world where orthodox medicine has made little progress or where doctors and trained staff are scarce.

Recent years however have seen a curious and unexpected revival of interest in acupuncture in Europe and America, prompted in large part by the considerable press publicity which has surrounded a number of major surgical operations performed without anesthesia upon human patients and which have been witnessed by sceptical Western specialists. Considerable controversy still surrounds acupuncture and is likely to continue for many years—possibly because it is hard to envisage a theory to explain its effects which is consistent with orthodox medicine. No doubt the immensely powerful effects of suggestion and hypnosis need to be taken into account. Some recent discoveries on the psychology and physiology of pain which show that severe wound pain may be alleviated by electrical stimulation of the nerve endings in the site of the wound may also have some relevance. It is tempting to take the line that acupuncture is based on some "forgotten" or "hidden" medical system and to assume that it is only because Western scientists are blinkered and hidebound that it is not being incorporated in a big way into European and American hospitals. But there are always two sides to an argument; whereas the first reports from Western specialists visiting China were filled with grudging acceptance and genuine puzzlement, more recent visitors have brought back a subtly different story. One of the world's leading experts on pain, for example, who has himself witnessed acupuncture-based surgery, reports four significant findings: (1) contrary to earlier reports, patients *are* sedated, sometimes heavily so, before surgery; (2) those patients who do go for surgery using acupuncture are only chosen after a fairly rigorous selection procedure to see whether they have complete faith in the method; (3) acupuncture does not appear to work with children; and (4) its use appears to be on the decline in the major hospitals in China. Despite this rather sceptical analysis, it is clear that the full story about acupuncture, its nature and its practical value has not yet been told.

**Adlerian Psychology.** In 1911 the Viennese psychoanalyst Alfred Adler (1870–1937) together with his colleague Carl Gustav Jung broke with their friend Sigmund Freud over disputes concerning the latter's theoretic approach to psychoanalysis. Jung and Adler were themselves shortly also to part company, each to set up and develop his own "school" of psychoanalysis. Adler's system of psychotherapy is based on the idea, not of sex as a driving force as in the case of Freud, but on the concept of "compensation" or a drive for power in an attempt to overcome the "inferiority complex" which he held to be universal in human beings. The child naturally feels inferior to adults, but bullying, making him feel insignificant or guilty or contemptible, even spoiling, which makes him feel important within the family but relatively unimportant outside, increases this feeling. Or the child may have physical defects: he may be small or underweight, have to wear glasses, become lame, be constantly ill, or stupid at school. In these ways he develops a sense of inferiority which for the rest of his life he develops a technique to overcome.

This may be done in several ways: he may try to become capable in the very respects in which he feels incompetent—hence many great orators have originally had speech defects; many painters poor eyesight; many musicians have been partially deaf; like Nietzsche, the weakling, he may write about the superman, or like Sandow, the strong man, be born with poor health.

On the other hand he may overdo his attempt and overcompensate. Hence we have the bully who is really a coward, the small man who is self-assertive to an objectionable degree (Hitler, Napoleon, Stalin, and Mussolini were all small men) or the foreigner who like three of these men wanted to be the hero of his adopted country—Hitler the Austrian, Napoleon the Italian, Stalin the Georgian.

But what about the man who can do none of these things, who continues to fail to compensate? He, says Adler, becomes a neurotic because neurosis is an excuse which means "I could have done so-and-so but . . ." It is the unconscious flight into illness—the desire to be ill. Adler's treatment involves disclosing these subterfuges we play on ourselves so that we can deal with the real situation in a more realistic way. Adlerian psychoanalysis still attracts supporters, but its golden days were when the founder was at the head of the movement in the U.S.A., when his views were considered to provide a more "acceptable" theory of the mind than the enormously controversial theories of Freud with their strong sexual orientation.

**Adventists,** a group of American religious sects, the most familiar being the Seventh-Day Adventist Church, which observes Saturday as the true Sabbath. With more than a million members throughout the world, it shares with other Adventists a belief in the imminent second coming of Christ (a doctrine fairly widespread in the U.S.A. during the early decades of the 19th cent. when the end of the world was predicted by William Miller for 1843, then for 1844). Modern Adventists content themselves with the conviction that the "signs" of the Advent are multiplying, the "blessed event" which will solve the world's ills. Believers will be saved, but the sects differ as to whether the unjust will be tortured in hell, annihilated, or merely remain asleep eternally.

**Agnosticism.** *See* **God and Man.**

**Albigenses,** also known as Cathari. French heretical sect (named after the town of Albi in Provence) which appeared in the 11th cent. to challenge the Catholic Church on the way true Christians should lead their lives. They followed a life of extreme asceticism in contrast to the local clergy and their faith was adopted by the mass of the population, especially in Toulouse. Condemned as heretics by Pope Innocent III, the sect was exterminated in the savage Albigensian Crusade (1208–29), initially led by Simon de Montfort. (In his thoroughness, de Montfort also succeeded in destroying the high culture of the Troubadours.)

**Alchemy,** ancient art associated with magic and astrology in which modern chemistry has its roots. The earliest mention of alchemy comes from ancient Egypt but its later practitioners attributed its origins to such varied sources as the fallen angels of the Bible, to Moses and Aaron, but most commonly to Hermes Trismegistus, often identified with the Egyptian god Thoth, whose knowledge of the divine art was handed down only to the sons of kings (cf. the phrase "hermetically sealed"). Its main object was the transmutation of metals. Egyptian speculation concerning this reached its height during the 6th cent. in the Alexandrian period. Brought to Western Europe by the Moslems,

one of its most famous Arab exponents was Jabir (*c.* 760–*c.* 815), known to the Latins as Geber, who had a laboratory at Kufa on the Tigris. One school of early Greek philosophy held that there was ultimately only one elemental matter of which everything was composed. Such men as Albertus Magnus (1206–80) and Roger Bacon (1214–94) assumed that, by removing impurities, this *materia prima* could be obtained. Although Bacon's ideas were in many ways ahead of his time, he firmly believed in the philosopher's stone, which could turn base metals into gold, and in an elixir of life which would give eternal youth. Modern science has, of course, shown in its researches into radioactivity, the possibility of transmutation of certain elements, but this phenomenon has little bearing on either the methods of the alchemist or the mysteries with which he surrounded them. In line with the current considerable revival of interest in the occult, alchemy appears to be staging a comeback, at least as a literary if not an experimental topic.

**Anabaptists.** *See* **Baptists.**

**Analytical Psychology,** the name given by Carl Gustav Jung (1875–1961) of Zürich to his system of psychology, which, like Adler's (*see* **Adlerian Psychology**), took its origin from Freud's psychoanalysis from which both diverged in 1911. Briefly, Jung differed from Freud: (1) in believing that the latter had laid too much emphasis on the sexual drive as the basic one in man and replacing it with the concept of *libido* or life energy of which sex forms a part; (2) in his theory of types: men are either extrovert or introvert (*i.e.* their interest is turned primarily outwards to the world or inwards to the self), and they apprehend experience in four main ways, one or other of which is predominant in any given individual—sensing, feeling, thinking, or intuiting; (3) in his belief that the individual's unconscious mind contains not only repressed materials which, as Freud maintained, were too unpleasant to be allowed into awareness, but also faculties which had not been allowed to develop—*e.g.,* the emotional side of the too rational man, the feminine side of the too masculine one; (4) in the importance he attaches to the existence of a collective unconscious at a still deeper level which contains traces of ancient ways of thought which mankind has inherited over the centuries. These are the *archetypes* and include primitive notions of magic, spirits and witches, birth and death, gods, virgin mothers, resurrection, etc. In the treatment of the neuroses Jung believed in the importance of *(a)* the present situation which the patient refuses to face; *(b)* the bringing together of conscious and unconscious and integrating them.

In the 1940s and '50s interest in Jung's ideas waned, at least in academic circles, as the emphasis among experimental psychologists shifted closer and closer to the "hard" scientific line. This was also true in the field of psychoanalysis where the Jungian as opposed to the Freudian point of view became progressively less popular. At the present time this trend is beginning to reverse, and while Jung's offbeat views on astrology, telepathy, etc., are still unfashionable, a reappraisal of the significance of his views on the nature of the unconscious is taking place and many psychologists feel that his contribution to our understanding of the nature of human mental processes has been greatly underrated. *See also* **Psychoanalysis.**

**Anarchism,** a political philosophy which holds, in the words of the American anarchist Josiah Warren (1798–1874), an early follower of Robert Owen, that "every man should be his own government, his own law, his own church." The idea that governmental interference or even the mere existence of authority is inherently bad is as old as Zeno, the Greek Stoic philosopher, who believed that compulsion perverts the normal nature of man. William Godwin's *Enquiry Concerning Political Justice* (1793) was the first systematic exposition of the doctrine. Godwin (father-in-law of Shelley) claimed that man is by nature sociable, cooperative, rational, and good when given the choice to act freely; that under such conditions men will form voluntary groups to work in complete social harmony. Such groups or communities would be based on equality of income, no state control, and no property: this state of affairs would be brought about by rational discussion and persuasion rather than by revolution.

The French economist Proudhon (1809–65) was the first to bring anarchism to the status of a mass movement. In his book *What is Property?* he stated bluntly that "property is theft" and "governments are the scourge of God". He urged the formation of cooperative credit banks where money could be had without interest and goods would be exchanged at cost value at a rate representing the hours of work needed to produce each commodity. Like Godwin, he disapproved of violence but, unlike Marx, disapproved of trade unions as representing organized groups.

In communistic anarchism these ideas were combined with a revolutionary philosophy, primarily by the Russians Michael Bakunin (1814–76) and Peter Kropotkin (1842–1921) who favored training workers in the technique of "direct action" to overthrow the state by all possible means, including political assassination. In 1868 anarchists joined the First International which broke up a few years later after a bitter struggle between Bakuninists and Marxists. Subsequently small anarchist groups murdered such political figures as Tsar Alexander II of Russia, King Humbert of Italy, Presidents Carnot of France and McKinley of America, and the Empress Elizabeth of Austria.

Anarchism and communism differ in three main ways: (1) anarchism forms no political party, rejects all relationship with established authority, and regards democratic reform as a setback; (2) communism is against capitalism, anarchism against the state as such; (3) both have the final goal of a classless society, but anarchism rejects the idea of an intermediate period of socialist state control accepted by communism. Philosophical anarchists, such as the American writer Henry David Thoreau (1817–62), were primarily individualists who believed in a return to nature, the non-payment of taxes, and passive resistance to state control; in these respects Thoreau strongly influenced Gandhi as did the Christian anarchist Tolstoy.

Anarchism has traditionally been criticized as being impractical—*e.g.*, in a non-authoritarian society, who is going to look after the sewers or clean the streets?—and there is a good deal of force to this argument. In fact anarchistic ideas became progressively less fashionable in the first half of this century. A curious and probably significant revival of interest has taken place in the past decade, however, probably because of a growing sense of disillusion, particularly on the part of young people, with the progress of orthodox political systems. *See also* **Syndicalism.**

**Animism.** To early man and in primitive societies the distinction between animate and inanimate objects was not always obvious—it is not enough to say that living things move and nonliving things do not, for leaves blow about in the wind and streams flow down a hillside. In the religions of early societies, therefore, we find a tendency to believe that life exists in all objects from rocks and pools to seas and mountains. This belief is technically known as *animatism,* which differs from *animism,* a somewhat more sophisticated view which holds that natural objects have no life in themselves but may be the abode of dead people, spirits, or gods who occasionally give them the appearance of life. The classic example of this, of course, is the assumption that an erupting volcano is an expression of anger on the part of the god who resides in it. Such beliefs may seem absurd today, but it is worth realizing that we are not entirely free of them ourselves when we ascribe "personalities" of a limited kind to motor cars, boats, dolls, or models which incur our pleasure or anger depending upon how well they "behave".

**Anthropomorphism,** the attribution of human form, thoughts or motives to non-human entities or life forms from gods to animals. At one end this can be summed up in the once widespread image of God as a "white-bearded old gentleman sitting on a cloud." At the other end is the very common tendency to invest domestic animals and pets with man-like wishes and personalities. At both extremes the belief could be seriously misleading. Firstly, it could be very unwise to assume that God, if he exists, necessarily thinks as humans do and has human interests at heart. Secondly, we shall learn very little about animal behavior if we look upon them as mere extensions of our own personality, and we do them less than justice if we see them simply as human beings of diminutive intelligence.

**Anthroposophy,** a school of religious and philosophical thought based on the work of the German educationist and mystic Rudolf Steiner (1861–1925). Steiner was originally an adherent of Madame Blavatsky's theosophical movement (*cf* Theosophy) but in 1913 broke away to form his own splinter group, the Anthroposophical Society, following ideological disputes over the alleged "divinity" of the Indian boy Krishnamurtl. Steiner was much influenced by the German poet and scientist, Goethe, and believed that an appreciation and love for art was one of the keys to spiritual development. One of the first tasks of his new movement was the construction of a vast temple of arts and sciences, known as the Goetheanum, to act as the headquarters of the society. This structure, which was of striking and revolutionary architectural style, was unfortunately burnt down in 1922 to be replaced by an even more imaginative one which today is one of the most interesting buildings of its kind in the world. Anthroposophy, which ceased to expand greatly following its founder's death, is nevertheless well-established in various parts of the world with specialized, and often very well equipped, schools and clinics which propagate the educational and therapeutic theories of the movement. These, which include the allegedly beneficial powers of music, colored lights, etc., have made little impact on modern educational ideas, but the schools have acquired a reputation for success in the training of mentally handicapped children, though one suspects that these successes are due to the patience and tolerance exercised in these establishments rather than to the curative value of color or music "therapy" itself. Despite its apparent eccentricities, anthroposophy has made its mark on art and architecture, the outstanding modern painter Kandinsky, for example, being particularly influenced by Steiner's ideas and teachings.

**Anticlericalism,** resentment of priestly powers and privileges, traceable in England to Wyclif's insistence in the 14th cent. on the right of all men to have access to the Scriptures. The translation of the Bible into the common tongue was a great landmark in the history of the Bible and the English language. Wyclif's principles were condemned by the Roman Church of his time but were readily accepted during the Reformation. Tudor anticlericalism arose from motives ranging from a greedy desire to plunder the riches of the Church to a genuine dislike of the powers of the priesthood whose spiritual courts still had the right to decide on points of doctrine or morals in an age when the layman felt he was well able to decide for himself. In innumerable ways the Church was permitted to extort money from the laity. It is generally agreed, says Trevelyan, that the final submission of church to state in England was motivated quite as much by anticlericalism as by Protestantism. The rise of the Reformed churches in England satisfied the people generally and anticlericalism never became the fixed principle of permanent parties as happened in France and Italy from the time of Voltaire onwards.

**Antisemitism,** a term first applied about the middle of the last century to those who were anti-Jewish in their outlook. Although this attitude was prevalent for religious reasons throughout the Middle Ages, modern antisemitism differed *(a)* in being largely motivated by economic or political conditions, and *(b)* in being doctrinaire with a pseudo-scientific rationale presented by such men as Gobineau (1816–82) and Houston Stewart Chamberlain (1855–1927), and later by the Nazi and Fascist "philosophers". Beginning in Russia and Hungary with the pogroms of 1882 it gradually spread south and westwards where, in France, the Dreyfus case provided an unsavory example in 1894. Thousands of Jews from Eastern Europe fled to Britain and America during this period; for in these countries antisemitism has rarely been more than a personal eccentricity. During the last war the murder of six million Jews by the Nazis and their accomplices led to a further exodus to various parts of the world and finally to the creation of the state of Israel.

The individual Jew-hater makes unconscious use of the psychological processes of projection and displacement: his greed or sexual guilt is projected on to the Jew (or Negro or Catholic) because he cannot bear to accept them as his own emotions, and his sense of failure in life is blamed on his chosen scapegoat rather than on his own inadequacy.

But there are social causes too and politicians in some lands are well versed in the technique of blaming unsatisfactory conditions (which they themselves may have in part produced) upon minority groups and persuading others to do the same. Historically, the Jew is ideally suited for this role of scapegoat: (1) in the Middle Ages when usury was forbidden to Christians but not to Jews, the latter often became moneylenders incurring the opprobrium generally associated with this trade (*e.g.,* to the simple-minded Russian peasant the Jew often represented, not only the "Christ-killer", but also the moneylender or small shopkeeper to whom he owed money); (2) many trades being closed to Jews, it was natural that they concentrated in others, thus arousing suspicions of "influence" (*i.e.* Jews are felt to occupy a place in certain trades and professions which far exceeds their numerical proportion to the population as a whole); (3) even with the ending of ghetto life, Jews often occupy *en masse* some parts of cities rather than others and this may lead to resentment on the part of the original inhabitants who begin to feel themselves dispossessed; (4) Jews tend to form a closed society and incur the suspicions attached to all closed societies within which social contacts are largely limited to members; marriage outside the group is forbidden or strongly disapproved of, and the preservation, among the orthodox, of cultural and religious barriers tends to isolate them from their fellow citizens. Discrimination, hateful as it is, does not come from one side only and it is such barriers as these that help to maintain an old and cruel folly. *See* **Zionism.**

**Aquarius,** one of the twelve "signs of the Zodiac". This has recently achieved special significance in the mythology of our time because of the pronouncements of astrologers that the world is shifting out of the 2000-years-old cycle of the Age of Pisces, the fish, into that of Aquarius the water-carrier. The exact date of the transition is a matter of astrological controversy, but the consensus is that it began in 1960 and will be completed sometime in the 24th century. The Aquarian Age is predicted to be one of peace and harmony, replacing the era of strife which, ironically, has marked the dominance of the Christian symbol of the fish. Such speculations are totally without scientific backing and are mentioned here only to draw attention to the grip which astrological and other mythical concepts still have on human thinking. One of the first spaceships to carry man to the moon, for example, was named Aquarius by its crew. *See also* **Astrology.**

**Arianism,** formed the subject of the first great controversy within the Christian Church over the doctrine of Arius of Alexandria (d. 336) who denied the divinity of Christ. The doctrine, although at first influential, was condemned at the Council of Nicaea (325), called by the Emperor Constantine, at which Arius was opposed by Athanasius, also of Alexandria, who maintained the now orthodox view that the Son is of one substance with the Father. Arius was banished but the heresy persisted until the 7th cent., especially among the barbarians, the Goths, Vandals and Lombards. Disbelief in the divinity of Christ has formed part of the doctrine of many minor sects since, notably in **Unitarianism** *(q.v.).*

**Assassins,** a sect of Moslem Shi'ites, founded by the Persian Hasan i Sabbath (*c.* 1090), which for more than two centuries established a rule of terror all over Persia and Syria. The coming of the Mongols in 1256 destroyed them in Persia and the Syrian branch suffered a similar fate at the hands of the then Mamluk sultan of Egypt, *c.* 1270. It was a secret order, ruled over by a grand master, under whom the members were strictly organized into classes, according to the degree of initiation into the secrets of the order. The devotees, belonging to one of the lower groups, carried out the actual assassinations under strict laws of obedience, and total ignorance of the objects and ritual of the society. It is believed that the latter were given ecstatic visions under the influence of hashish, whence the term *hashshashin*, which became corrupted to "assassin".

**Associationism.** In psychology, the Associationist school of the 19th cent. accepted the association of ideas as the fundamental principle in mental life. It was represented in Britain by the two Mills and Herbert Spencer, in Germany by J. F. Herbart (1776–1841). To these, mental activity was nothing but the association of "ideas" conceived of as units of both thought and feeling—the emotion of anger or the perception of a chair were both "ideas"—and apart from them the self did not exist. Personality was simply a series of these units coming and going, adding to or cancelling each other out, in accordance with rigid and mechanistic scientific laws.

**Astrology** was once the best available theory for explaining the course of human life and bears much the same historical relationship to astronomy as alchemy does to chemistry. Originally it was divided into the two branches of Natural Astrology which dealt with the movements of the heavenly bodies and their calculations, and Judicial Astrology which studied the alleged influence of the stars and the planets on human life and fate. It was the former that developed into modern astronomy; the latter was, and remains, a primitive myth.

Astrology owes most to the early Babylonians (or Chaldeans) who, being largely nomadic in an environment which permitted an unobstructed view of the sky, readily accepted the idea that divine energy is manifested in the movements of the sun and planets. Gradually this concept became enlarged and the relative positions of the planets both in relation to each other and to the fixed stars became important together with the idea of omens—that, if a particular event occurred while the planets were in a particular position, the recurrence of that position heralded a recurrence of the same sort of event. Soon the planets became associated with almost every aspect of human life. They were bound up with the emotions, with parts of the body, so that astrology played quite a large part in medicine up to late medieval times. Not only was the position of the planet to be considered but also the particular sign of the zodiac (or house of heaven) it was occupying, and it was believed possible to foretell the destiny of an individual by calculating which star was in the ascendant (*i.e.* the sign of the zodiac nearest the eastern horizon and the star which arose at that precise moment) at the time of his birth. Astrology was popular among the Egyptians, the Romans (whose authorities found the Chaldean astrologers a nuisance and expelled them from time to time), and during the Middle Ages when astrologers were often highly respected.

Despite the apparent absurdity of astrological beliefs—for example, how could the pattern of light from stars billions of miles away possibly influence the temperament of single individuals on earth—a substantial number of intelligent and well-educated people take its study in all seriousness. The most interesting "convert" was the psychologist and philosopher, Carl Jung, who conducted a complex experiment in which he compared the "birth signs" of happily married and divorced couples and claimed to find that those most favorably matched in astrological terms were also those more likely to have permanent wedded bliss. Jung's findings were subsequently shown to have been based on a simple statistical fallacy, which did not prevent the brilliant but eccentric psychologist from offering them up as evidence in support of his own theory of "synchronicity" *(q.v.),* an involved and vaguely metaphysical notion which suggests that events in the universe may be significantly related in a "non-causal" fashion. To add fuel to the controversy however, the French mathematician, Michel Gauquelin, has recently offered up fresh data which apparently supports the general astrological view. In a carefully controlled study he noticed statistically significant correspondences between certain astrological signs and the professions of a large number of Frenchmen whose birth time and date were accurately recorded. Gauquelin claims to have repeated his study on a second large sample of his fellow countrymen, though he has been unable to use English people as the exact times of birth are not recorded on their birth certificates! This apparent shot in the arm for astrology is still a matter of great scientific controversy, though Gauquelin's work has been given support from the distinguished British psychologist, H. J. Eysenck, who has pronounced his statistical data to to be incontrovertible. Both scientists, however, carefully refrain from discussing the implications of these curious findings, and the controversy will no doubt increase rather than decrease in the near future.

**Atheism.** *See* **God and Man.**

**Atlantis,** a mythical continent supposed to have lain somewhere between Europe and America and a center of advanced civilization before it was inundated by some great natural catastrophe in pre-Christian times. There is little, if any, serious historical or archaeological evidence for its existence, but the legend of the Golden Land destroyed when the waters of the Atlantic closed over it has remarkable staying power and is believed by large numbers of people. Plato wrote convincingly about the wonders of Atlantis in his dialogues *Timaeus* and *Critias,* while other writers have suggested that the biblical story of the Flood is based on fragmentary accounts of the Atlantean deluge. The lost continent is also of occult significance, largely as the result of the writings of W. Scott-Elliott whose book, *The Story of Atlantis* (recently republished by the Theosophical Society), alleged that by clairvoyance he had been able to contact the spirits of Atlanteans who had been destroyed because of their addiction to black magic. There even exists in Britain today a minor but ardent religious group, the "Atlanteans", who hold that Atlantis still exists today, but on a different metaphysical plane, and that it is possible to communicate with it via individuals with supposedly mediumistic powers (*see* **Spiritualism**). Members of the Atlanteans meet regularly to hear "trance addresses" by one of the high priests of Atlantis, Helio-Arconaphus. Such beliefs are essentially harmless and merely reflect the great variety of religious attitudes which human beings enjoy.

**Atomism.** In philosophy, the atomists were a group of early Greek thinkers, the most important of whom were Leucippus (fl. *c.* 440 B.C.) and his younger contemporary Democritus (*c.* 460–370 B.C.). Prior to these men, although it had been agreed that matter must be composed of tiny ultimate particles and that change must be due to the manner in which these mingled or separated from each other, it was supposed that there existed different types of particle for each material—*e.g.* for flesh, wood, hair, bone. The atomists taught that atoms were all made of a single substance and differed only in the connections (pictured as hooks, grooves, points, etc.) which enabled them to join each other in characteristic ways. Theirs was the first move towards modern atomic theory and a predecessor of the modern concept of chemical linkages.

**Authoritarianism,** a dictatorial form of government as contrasted with a democratic one based on popular sovereignty. Its alleged advantages are the avoidance of the delays and inefficiency said to be characteristic of the latter.

**Automatism,** the production of material, written or spoken in "automatic" fashion—*i.e.,* apparently not under the conscious or volitional control of the individual. This psychologically perplexing phenomenon has occurred from time to time throughout the history of literature and art, and while it has occasionally produced work of great merit (much of William Blake's poetry, Coleridge's "Kubla Khan", etc.) the bulk of it is indifferent and often simply rubbish. Spiritualists claim that the work is produced under the direct guidances of the spirit world, and their argument has attracted considerable attention through the compositions of the pianist Rosemary Brown who, with little or no academic background in musical theory, has produced a number of "original" piano pieces allegedly composed by Beethoven, Mozart, etc., from the astral plane. While few music critics doubt Mrs. Brown's honesty and integrity, most consider her work to be clever pastiche and barely comparable in quality to the masterworks of the dead composers. Nevertheless automatism wants some explaining, and most psychologists today defer judgment, taking the view that it serves to remind us of the fund of material which lies in the unconscious mind, and which is prone to pop up from time to time without warning. Rather similar is the case of Matthew Manning, a young English student who produced clever and artistically intriguing drawings and sketches, allegedly guided by the hands of famous dead artists.

# B

**Baconian Method,** the use of the inductive (as opposed to the deductive or Aristotelian) method of reasoning as proposed by Francis Bacon in the 17th cent. and J. S. Mill in the 19th cent. Deduction argues from supposedly certain first principles (such as the existence of God or Descartes's "I think, therefore I am") what the nature of the universe and its laws *must* be, whereas the only means of obtaining true knowledge of the universe, in Bacon's view, was by the amassing of facts and observations so that when enough were obtained the certain truth would be known in the same way that a child's numbered dots in a playbook joined together by a pencilled line create a picture. However, this is not the way science progresses in practice. Bacon underrated the importance of hypothesis and theory and overrated the reliability of the senses. In discussing the scientific tradition, Sir Karl Popper in his book, *Conjecture*

*and Refutations,* says: "The most important function of observation and reasoning, and even of intuition and imagination, is to help us in the critical examination of those bold conjectures which are the means by which we probe into the unknown." Two of the greatest men who clearly saw that there was no such thing as an inductive procedure were Galileo and Einstein.

**Bahá'i Faith,** a faith which teaches the unity of all religions and the unity of mankind. It arose in Iran from the teachings of the Bab (Mirza Ali Mohammed, 1820–50) and the Bahá'u'lláh (Mirza Husain Ali, 1817–92), thought to be manifestations of God, who in his essence is unknowable. Emphasis is laid on service to others. It has communities in many states and is surprisingly strong in England with a substantial following among university students. Its aims—universal peace, love, fellowship, sexual equality, etc.—are so laudable that it is hard to disagree with anything in the movement. Since the ruling Ayatollah Khomeini's fundamentalist Islamic regime came to power in Iran in 1979 members of the faith have been persecuted and a number of women who refused to recant were executed in 1983. The movement is now guided and administered by an elected order, "The Universal House of Justice".

**Baptists,** a Christian denomination whose distinctive doctrines are that members can only be received by baptism "upon the confession of their faith and sins" and that "baptism is no wise appertaineth to infants." Baptism is therefore by total immersion of adults. Modern Baptists base their doctrines upon the teaching of the Apostles and some hold that the Albigenses *(q.v.)* maintained the true belief through what they regarded as the corruption of the Roman Church in medieval times. On the other hand any connection with the Anabaptist movement during the Reformation is rejected and the beginning of the modern Church is traced to John Smyth, a minister of the Church of England who in Amsterdam came under the influence of the Arminians *(q.v.)* and Mennonites. Smyth died in 1612 when the first Baptist church in England was built at Newgate. This, the "General" Baptist Church, rejected Calvinistic beliefs and held the Arminian doctrine of redemption open to all, but some years later a split occurred with the formation of the "Particular" Baptist Church which was Calvinist in doctrine. In 1891 the two bodies were united in the Baptist Union and today the sect is spread throughout the world, notably in the United States.

The Anabaptist movements of Germany, Switzerland, and Holland also practiced adult baptism in addition to a primitive communism and demanded social reforms. Persecuted by both Catholics and Protestants, their leader, Thomas Münzer, and many others were burned at the stake (1525). However, this sect was noted for its violence under a religious guise, and its taking over of the state of Münster in 1533 was characterized by wild licentiousness, since, as Antinomians, they believed that the "elect" could do no wrong. A revival begun by Menno Simons (d. 1561), a Dutch religious reformer, led to the formation of the Mennonite sect which, while rejecting infant baptism, gave up the objectionable features of the Anabaptists. This reformed sect still exists as small agricultural groups in the original strongholds of the movement and in the United States.

**Beat Generation,** a term first used by the American

writer Jack Kerouac (d. 1969), author of *The Town and the City* and *On the Road,* to define various groups spread across the face of the country, but notably in New York and San Francisco, who, belonging to the post-war generation, represented a complex of attitudes. Briefly, these were: rejection of the values of the past and lack of conviction in the possibility of a future for humanity—hence an acceptance of nothing but the immediate present in terms of experience and sensations; rebellion against organized authority, not out of any political conviction (as in the case of anarchism), but rather from lack of any interest or desire to control events, nature, or people; contempt for the "Square"—the orthodox individual who, stuck firmly in his rut, "plays it safe" and remains confident of the rightness and decency of his moral values.

The Beat Generation of the 1940s and '50s gave way to the Love generation or Flower people, with their flowers, beads, and cowbells. Their social philosophy was the same—living in the present, unconventionally, seeking personal freedom, believing drugs to be essential, claiming to be acting against the rat race, dissociating themselves from politics, taking a superficial interest in the religions of the East, borrowing much of their language, music, and ideas on dress from the American hippy, yet believing in the creation of a new and gentler society based on different forms and values.

Both the Beat and Love generations were forerunners in America of an increasing and certainly welcome social awareness on the part of American students. This led in turn to the "campus revolutions" which were disruptive in their early stages but were also influential as part of the wave of public protest against the American involvement in Vietnam.

**Behaviorism,** a school of psychology founded in 1914 by J. B. Watson (1878–1958), an animal psychologist at Johns Hopkins University, Baltimore. Its main tenet was that the method of introspection and the study of mental states were unscientific and should be replaced by the study of behavior. When animals or human beings were exposed to specific stimuli and their responses objectively recorded, or when the development of a child, as seen in its changing behavior, was noted, these alone were methods which were truly scientific. Watson contributed an important idea to psychology and did a great deal towards ridding it of the largely philosophical speculations of the past. But he also went to absurd extremes, as in his view that thought was nothing but subvocal speech, consisting of almost imperceptible movements of the tongue, throat, and larynx (*i.e.,* when we think, we are really talking to ourselves), and his further opinion that heredity is, except in grossly abnormal cases, of no importance. He claimed that by "conditioning", the ordinary individual could be made into any desired type, regardless of his or her inheritance.

The work of Ivan Pavlov had begun about 1901, but was unknown in America until about ten years later, and it was through another Russian, Vladimir Bekhterev, that the concept of "conditioning" was introduced into the country. Bekhterev's book *Objective Psychology,* describing his new science of "reflexology", was translated in 1913 and played a great part in the development of Behaviorist ideas. The conditioned reflex became central to Watson's theory of learning and habit, formation (*e.g.,* he showed that a year-old child, at first unafraid of white rats, became afraid of them when they came to be associated with a loud noise behind the head). Finally all behavior, including abnormal behavior, came to be explained in terms of conditioned responses; these were built up by association on the infant's three innate emotions of fear, rage, and love, of which the original stimuli were, for the first, loud noises and the fear of falling; for the second, interference with freedom of movement; and for the third, patting and stroking.

Because of its considerable theoretical simplicity and its implicit suggestion that human behavior could be easily described (and even modified or controlled), Pavlovian psychology appeared very attractive to the Communist regime in Russia, and before long it became the "official" dogma in universities and research laboratories. Whereas in America and Western Europe its severe limitations became gradually apparent, in Russia these were ignored or disguised for ideological reasons with the inevitable outcome that Soviet psychology failed to evolve and, at one stage, seemed to be no more than a pallid offshoot of physiology. The recent liberalization which has been taking place throughout Soviet society has led to a considerable broadening of scientific horizons and Pavlovian ideas are no longer looked upon with such unquestioning reverence. In non-Communist countries simple Watsonian behaviorism has evolved into more sophisticated studies of animal learning, largely pioneered by the Harvard psychologist, Skinner. These techniques, which have shown that animals, from monkeys to rats, may be taught to solve a remarkable range of physical problems (such as pressing complex sequences of buttons or levers to escape from a cage) have themselves turned out to be rather disappointing in terms of advancing our general understanding of the workings of the human and animal brain. There is a growing feeling among psychologists that the real keys to the understanding of mankind will only be found through the study of man himself, and not his simpler animal cousins. *See also* **Gestalt Psychology**

**Benthamism.** *See* **Utilitarianism.**

**Bolshevism,** an alternative name for **Communism** *(q.v.),* usually used in the West in a derogatory sense. When the Russian Social Democratic Party at a conference held in London in 1903 split over the issue of radicalism or moderation, it was the radical faction headed by Lenin (who subsequently led the 1917 Revolution and became first Head of State of the Soviet Union) which polled the majority of votes. The Russian for majority is *bolshinstro* and for minority *menshinstro;* hence the radicals became known as Bolsheviki and the moderates as Mensheviki, anglicized as Bolsheviks and Mensheviks. *See* **Communism, Marxism.**

**Bushido,** the traditional code of honour of the Samurai or Japanese military caste corresponding to the European concept of knighthood and chivalry from which it took its separate origin in the 12th cent. Even today it is a potent influence among the upper classes, being based on the principles of simplicity, honesty, courage, and justice which together form a man's idea of personal honour.

# C

**Cabala,** originally a collection of Jewish doctrines about the nature of the Universe, supposedly handed down by Moses to the Rabbis, which evolved into a kind of mystical interpretation of the Old Testament. Students of the history of religious belief have found its origins to be in fact extremely obscure, and some aspects appear to have been lifted from ancient Egyptian sources. Skilled Cabalists hold that the system contains a key to biblical interpretation based on the numerical values of the words and letters of the Scriptures which reveal hidden depths of meaning behind the allegorical Old Testament stories.

**Calvinism,** the branch of Protestantism founded basically (although preceded by Zwingli and others) by Jean Chauvin (1509–64), who was born in Noyon in Picardy. John Calvin, as he is usually called, from the Latin form of his name, Calvinius, provided in his *Institutions of the Christian Religion* the first logical definition and justification of Protestantism, thus becoming the intellectual leader of the Reformation as the older Martin Luther was its emotional instigator. The distinctive doctrine of Calvinism is its dogma of predestination which states that God has unalterably destined some souls to salvation to whom "efficacious grace and the gift of perseverance" is granted and others to eternal damnation. Calvinism, as defined in the Westminster Confession, is established in the Reformed or Presbyterian churches of France, Holland, Scotland, etc., as contrasted with the Lutheran churches, and its harsh but logical beliefs inspired the French Huguenots, the Dutch in their fight against Spanish Catholic domination, and the English Puritans. The rule set up under Calvin's influence in Geneva was marred by the burning at the stake of the anatomist Servetus for the heresy of "pantheism", or, as we should say, Unitarianism.

Perhaps its greatest single influence outside the Church was the result of Calvinist belief that to labor industriously was one of God's commands. This changed the medieval notions of the blessedness of poverty and the wickedness of usury, proclaimed that men should shun luxury and be thrifty, yet implied that financial success was a mark of God's favor. In this way it was related to the rise of capitalism either as cause or effect. Max Weber, the German sociologist, believed that Calvinism was a powerful incentive to, or even cause of, the rise of **capitalism** *(q.v.):* Marx, Sombart, and in England, Tawney, have asserted the reverse view—that Calvinism was a result of developing capitalism, being its ideological justification.

**Capitalism** is an economic system under which the means of production and distribution are owned by a relatively small section of society which runs them at its own discretion for private profit. There exists, on the other hand, a propertyless class of those who exist by the sale of their labor power. Capitalism arose towards the end of the 18th cent. in England where the early factory owners working with small-scale units naturally approved of free enterprise and free trade. But free enterprise has no necessary connection with capitalism; by the beginning of this century monopolies were developing and state protection against foreign competition was demanded. Capitalism is opposed by those who believe in socialism, first, for the moral reasons that it leads to economic inequality and the exploitation of labour and the consuming public, and that public welfare rather than private profit should motivate the economic system; secondly, for the practical reason that capitalism leads to recurrent economic crises. The recent world economic crisis has led to great hopes on the part of Marxists and Communists that capitalism is now involved in its final death throes. It is worth commenting however, that the European war of the 1940s, the great depression of the 30s, the first world war and the Russian Revolution were also, in their turn, confidently held up by Communists as heralding capitalism's imminent collapse.

**Cartomancy,** the art of fortunes or predicting the future by playing cards or by the Tarot pack. The elegant Tarot cards number 78 in all and are probably medieval in origin. They are rich in symbolism and include trump cards depicting the devil, the pope, death, the moon, the wheel of fortune, etc., and are an interesting part of our cultural mythology. There is no evidence whatsoever that they can be used in any objective way to divine the future, and professional fortune tellers and clairvoyants who use them almost certainly rely on a little native, basic psychology to achieve their results.

**Characterology,** the attempt made over many centuries to classify people into personality types on the basis of physical or psychological characteristics. The first attempt was made by Hippocrates in the 5th cent. B.C. who classified temperaments into the *sanguine* (or optimistic), the *melancholic,* the *choleric* (or aggressive), and the *phlegmatic* (or placid); these were supposed to result from the predominance of the following "humors" in the body: red blood, black bile, yellow bile, or phlegm respectively. Theophrastus, a pupil of Aristotle, described, with examples, thirty extreme types of personality (*e.g.* the talkative, the boorish, the miserly, etc.); these were basically literary and imaginative but about the same time "physiognomy" arose which attempted to interpret character from the face. Physiognomy became of importance again during the Renaissance and there are still those today who believe in it in spite of the fact that, broadly speaking, there is no connection whatever between facial features and personality (i.e. although it may be possible to tell from the features that a man is an idiot or some extreme abnormal type and some idea of character may be obtained from an individual's characteristic facial expressions, it is not possible to tell (as Johann Lavater, the best-known physiognomist of the late 18th cent. believed) from the shape of the nose, height of the brow, or dominance of the lower jaw, whether anyone is weak, intellectual or determined). The contention of the 19th cent. Italian criminologist Cesare Lombroso that criminals show typical facial characteristics—prominent cheekbones and jaw, slanting eyes, receding brow, large ears of a particular shape—was disproved by Karl Pearson early this century when he found that 3,000 criminals showed no significant differences of features, carefully measured from a similar number of students at Oxford and Cambridge.

It has, however, been noted that people in general tend to be intellectual or emotional, inward- or outward-looking, and this observation is reflected in the classification of the Scottish psychologist, Alexander Bain (d. 1903), into intellectual, artistic, and practical; Nietzsche's Apollonian and

Dionysian types; William James's "tender" and "toughminded"; and C. G. Jung's introvert and extrovert. Careful experiments have shown that these are not clear-cut and that most individuals fall in between the extremes.

Some connection has been found between temperament and body-build. The German psychiatrist Ernst Kretschmer (b. 1888) showed that manic-depressive patients and normal people who are extroverted and tend to alternate in mood (as do manic-depressives to an exaggerated degree) were usually short and stout or thick-set in build; schizophrenics and normal people, who both show shyness, serious or introverted reactions, were usually tall and slender. The former of "pyknic" body-build are "cyclothyme" in temperament, the latter with "schizothyme" temperament are of two bodily types—the tall and thin or "asthenic" and the muscularly well-proportioned or "athletic". The American Sheldon has confirmed these observations on the whole and gone into further details. According to him the basic body types are: (1) *endomorphic* (rounded build), corresponding to Kretschmer's pyknic, normally associated with the *viscerotonic* temperament (relaxed, sociable); (2) *mesomorphic* (squarish, athletic build), normally associated with the *somatotonic* temperament (energetic, assertive); and (3) *ectomorphic* (linear build) normally associated with the *cerebrotonic* temperament (anxious, submissive, restless). Glandular and metabolic factors have considerable effect on human personality and also, to some extent, on physique. It is not too surprising, therefore, to find an association between body build (or "somatotype" as Sheldon termed it) and general mood. However, Sheldon's original clear-cut and oversimplified categories of body-type are no longer looked upon as reliable indicators of personality.

**Chauvinism,** a term applied to any excessive devotion to cause, particularly a patriotic or military one. The word is derived from Nicholas Chauvin whose excessive devotion to Napoleon made him a laughing-stock.

**Chirognomy,** the attempt to read character from the lines in the hand (as contrasted with chiromancy or palmistry, in which an attempt is made to tell the future in the same way) is an ancient practice which, like astrology *(q.v.)* has no discernible scientific basis but a very considerable popular following. As with astrology, where it is hard to see what kind of link could exist between the constellations and human behavior, so it is equally hard to see how the configuration of lines on the hand could be paralleled by psychological attributes. This argument might be thought of as irrelevant if palmistry, etc. actually had predictive power, but the plain fact is that when put to a scientific test, practitioners of these arts turn out to show no abilities beyond those with which a normally perceptive individual is equipped.

**Christadelphians,** a religious denomination formed in the U.S.A. in the late 1840s by John Thomas, an Englishman from London. They claim to represent the simple apostolic faith of the 1st cent., and, in common with many other sects, hold that they alone interpret the Scriptures truly. They believe that Christ will return soon to set up the Kingdom of God with Jerusalem as its capital. In social life Christadelphians keep to themselves and hold aloof from organizational activities, though they do take an interest in political events if only from the point of view of their belief in biblical prophecy.

**Christian Science,** a religious denomination founded by Mary Baker Eddy (1821–1910), an American lady who sought to organize a church which would reinstate primitive Christianity and its lost element of healing. The sacred books of the movement are the Bible and *Science and Health with Key to the Scriptures* (1891), a revision of *Science and Health,* first published by Mrs. Eddy in 1875. Its main tenets (quoting from an official Christian Science source) are "that nothing is real save God and His spiritual creation, including man in His image and likeness; that man's essential nature is spiritual and wholly good; that matter, evil, disease and sickness are unreal—illusions existing only through ignorance of God. Therefore Christian Scientists renounce for themselves medicine, surgery and drugs and rely on healing through prayer."

The name of the movement seems misleading since it has nothing to do with any of the natural sciences of which Mrs. Eddy had no first-hand knowledge. In using the word, Mrs. Eddy meant that the teaching and acts of Jesus were rooted in unchanging divine law. Mrs. Eddy was at first interested in Spiritualism and afterwards, having been a patient of a faith-healer named Quimby, claimed to have been divinely healed.

There is a good deal of controversy about the efficacy of the Christian Science methods. In principle believers argue that if one has total, unquestioning faith in the healing power of Christ, then all sickness will be revealed as illusion and vanish. The trouble of course is that total faith is almost impossible to achieve, and hence even Christian Scientists inevitably fall ill and die. This makes the Church's argument irrefutable, but there is some evidence that the argument is convincing fewer individuals than it once did. On the other hand the growth of interest in "divine healing" within the more orthodox churches had led to a softening of barriers between Mrs. Eddy's splinter group and the hard-core Christian religions. Christian Science may well fade away after handing over to orthodoxy its single key concept.

**Church of England.** There is some evidence of possible continuity with the Christianity of Roman Britain, but in the main the Church derives from the fusion of the ancient Celtic church with the missionary church of St. Augustine, who founded the See of Canterbury in A.D. 597. To archbishop Theodore in 673 is ascribed its organization in dioceses with settled boundaries, and in parishes. St. Augustine's church was in communion with Rome from the first, but the Church of England was not brought within papal jurisdiction until after the Norman conquest, and was at no time under the complete domination of Rome. It remains the Catholic Church of England without break of continuity, but during the Reformation the royal supremacy was accepted and that of the pope repudiated. Its traditional forms of worship are embodied in the Book of Common Prayer, but the Alternative Service Book of 1980 is now widely used. In 1978, Easter communicants numbered 1,736,000.

The **Anglican Communion** comprises the churches in all parts of the world which are in communion with the Church of England (In the U.S. it is the Episcopal Church). All the bishops of the Anglican Communion meet every ten years in the Lambeth Conference (first held in 1867), over which the Archbishop of Canterbury by custom presides as *primus inter pares.* At the 1968 Conference observers and laymen were admitted for the first time. The last Conference was held in 1978. The next will meet in 1988.

**Clairvoyance.** *See* **Telepathy.**

**Communism,** ideally refers to the type of society in which all property belongs to the community and social life is based on the principle "from each according to his ability, to each according to his needs." There would be public ownership of all enterprises and all goods would be free. Since no such society as yet exists, the word in practice refers to the attempt to achieve such a society by initially overthrowing the capitalist system and establishing a dictatorship of the proletariat (Marx identified the dictatorship with a democratic constitution). Communists believe that their first task is the establishment of socialism under which there remain class distinctions, private property to some extent, and differences between manual and brain workers. The state is regulated on the basis "from each according to his ability, to each according to his work". Lenin applied Marx's analysis to the new conditions which had arisen in 20th-cent. capitalist society. Marxism-Leninism develops continuously with practice since failure to apply its basic principles to changed circumstances and times would result in errors of dogmatism. Mao Tse-tung worked out the techniques of revolutionary action appropriate to China; Che Guevara the guerrilla tactics appropriate to the peasants of Latin America. His counsel "It is not necessary to wait until conditions for making revolution exist; the insurrection can create them", was the opposite of Mao Tse-tung's "Engage in no battle you are not sure of winning", and Lenin's "Never play with insurrection". Two fundamental principles of communism are (1) peaceful coexistence between countries of different social systems, and (2) the class struggle between oppressed and oppressing classes and between oppressed and oppressor nations. Maoism, for example, holds that it is a mistake to lay one-sided stress on peaceful transition towards socialism otherwise the revolutionary will of the proletariat becomes passive and unprepared politically and organizationally for the tasks ahead.

In Russia the civil war developed *after* the revolution; in China the communists fought their civil war *before* they seized power: the Yugoslav partisans won their own guerrilla war *during* their stand against the fascist powers—differences which had important political consequences. Russia suffered three decades of isolationism and totalitarian suppression ("an isolated and besieged fortress") before the death of Stalin. Then came a marked, if zigzagging shift towards "liberalization." Mao Tse-tung held to the orthodox Leninist view about capitalism and communism, regarded détente as a dangerous illusion, and compromise and "revisionism" as a fatal error. The ideological dispute between these two great communist powers which lasted from the '60s to the '80s is ending with the improvement in inter-party relations and today a movement towards détente is taking place. Communist parties in some countries, *e.g.,* Italy, are taking the democratic road to socialism and believe that a communist government should be installed by the ballot box. *See also,* **Marxism, Trotskyism.**

**Congregationalists,** the oldest sect of Nonconformists who hold that each church should be independent of external ecclesiastical authority. They took their origin from the Brownists of Elizabeth's days. Robert Browne (*c.* 1550–*c.* 1633), an Anglican clergyman, who had come to reject bishops, was forced with his followers to seek refuge, first in Holland and then in Scotland where he was imprisoned by the Kirk. In later life he changed his views and is disowned by Congregationalists because of his reversion to Anglicanism. His former views were spread by Henry Barrow and John Greenwood who, under an Act passed in 1592 "for the punishment of persons obstinately refusing to come to church" (and largely designed for the suppression of this sect), were hanged at Tyburn. They had preached *(a)* that the only head of the church is Jesus Christ; *(b)* that, contrary to Elizabethan doctrine, the church had no relationship to the state; *(c)* that the only statute-book was the Bible whereas the Articles of Religion and Book of Common Prayer were mere Acts of Parliament; *(d)* that each congregation of believers was independent and had the power of choosing its own ministers. The body fled once more to Holland and were among the Pilgrims who set sail in the *Mayflower* for America in 1620 while those who remained were joined by Puritans fleeing from Charles I. They became free once more to live in England under the Commonwealth only to be repressed again under Charles II. Finally full liberty of worship was granted under William III. In 1833 the Congregational Union of England and Wales was formed which had no legislative power. It had issued a Declaration of Faith by which no minister was bound; he was responsible to his own church and to nobody else. The sect is widespread both in Britain and the U.S.A. where it is held in special honor because of its connection with the Pilgrim Fathers. In 1972 the Congregational Church in England and Wales and the Presbyterian Church of England decided to unite to form the United Reformed Church. The majority of members who did not join comprise the Congregational Federation.

**Coptic Church,** the sect of Egyptian Christians who, holding "Monophysite" opinions (*i.e.,* refusing to grant the two natures, God and Man, of Christ), were declared heretical by the Council of Chalcedon in 451. They practice circumcision and have dietary laws. Their language is a direct descendant of ancient Egyptian. Like the Armenians, they are regarded as an heretical branch of Eastern Christianity. Their religious head is the patriarch of Alexandria.

**Cynics,** a school of philosophy founded in the time of Alexander the Great by Diogenes. Choosing to live like a dog by rejecting all conventions of religion, manners, or decency, and allegedly living in a tub, Diogenes unwittingly brought on his school the title "Cynic", meaning not "cynical", as the word is understood today, but "canine". His teacher, Antisthenes, who had been a disciple of Socrates, decided, after the latter's death, that all philosophy was useless quibbling and man's sole aim should be simple goodness. He believed in a return to nature, despised luxury, wanted no government, no private property, and associated with working men and slaves. Far from being cynics in the modern sense, Diogenes and Antisthenes were virtuous anarchists rather like old Tolstoy (except that in the practice of their beliefs they were more consistent).

# D

**Deism.** *See* **God and Man.**

**Demonism, Demons, and the Devil.** Demons are ethereal beings of various degrees of significance and power which are believed to be implicated in men's good, but especially evil, fortune. They are common to most cultures. From the anthropological point of view the demon arose as a widespread concept in the following ways: (1) as a psychological projection into the outer world of man's own good or evil emotions and thoughts; (2) as a survival of primitive animism *(q.v.)*, thus spirits are believed to haunt places, trees, stones, and other natural objects; (3) when by warlike invasion the gods of the vanquished become the devils of the conquerors (as when the Jews occupied Canaan); (4) as a primitive belief that spirits of the dead continue after death to hover near their former habitation, and not always entirely welcome to the living; (5) the conception of a supreme source of evil (the Devil or Satan) which took shape among the Jews during their sojourn in Babylon under the influence of Zoroastrianism *(q.v.)*, a religion in which the struggle between the two spirits, Good and Evil, reached its height in the imagination of the ancient world. The Satan of the Old Testament was first regarded as one of God's servants (in the Book of Job he goes up and down the earth to see whether God's commands are obeyed), but when the Jews returned from their captivity he had become identified with Ahriman, the spirit of evil, who was in continual conflict with Ahursa Mazda, the spirit of good. As Dr. Margaret Murray has pointed out, the primitive mind ascribed both good and evil to one power alone; the division into God and the Devil, priest and witch, belongs to a higher stage of civilization. The worship of evil itself, or of its personification in Satan, is a curious practice which seems to have developed hand-in-hand with Christianity and to have received steady support from a small but measurable minority. Many of the ceremonies involved in Satanism or in the so-called Black Mass appear to have been no more than opportunities for sexual excesses of one kind or another—such indulgences being traditionally barred to devout Christians. The alleged power of sex as a form of magic was propagated by the talented but rather mad poet, Aleister Crowley (1875–1947), who scandalized pre-war Europe with his very well-publicized dabblings into Satanism. The self-styled "wickedest man in the world", Crowley was a pathetic rather than shocking figure and died a drug addict. He can hardly be said to have significantly advanced the cause of Demonology, though it has to be admitted that he tried very hard.

**Determinism and Free Will.** The question of whether man is, or is not, free to mold his own destiny is one which has exercised the minds of philosophers since Greek mythology conceived of the Fates as weaving a web of destiny from which no man can free himself. Socrates emphasized that man could through knowledge influence his destiny while ignorance made him the plaything of fate; Plato went further in pointing out that man can, and does, defeat the purposes of the universe and its divine Creator. It is our duty to live a good life, but we can live a foolish and wicked one if we chose. Aristotle wrote "Virtue is a disposition or habit involving deliberate purpose or choice". If this were not so morality would be a sham.

*The Problem for Theology.* The last of the great philosophers of Antiquity and one of the great influences in molding Catholic theology was Plotinus (*c.* 204–70). Soul, he taught, is free, but once enmeshed in the body loses its freedom in the life of sense. Nevertheless, man is free to turn away from sensuality and towards God who is perfect freedom; for even when incarnated in matter the soul does not entirely lose the ability to rescue itself. This conception was carried over into the beliefs of the early Christian Apologists because it appeared to be in line with the teaching of Jesus that He had come to save man from sin. Sin implies guilt, and guilt implies the freedom to act otherwise; furthermore an all-good God cannot be responsible for the sin in the world which must be man's responsibility and this again implies freedom. Pelagius (*c.* 355–*c.* 425), a Welsh priest, not only believed in free will but questioning the doctrine of original sin, said that when men act righteously it is through their own moral effort, and God rewards them for their virtues in heaven. This belief became fairly widespread and was declared a heresy by the Church, being attacked notably by St. Augustine (354–430), a contemporary of Pelagius, who believed in predestination—that, since the sin of Adam, God had chosen who in all future history would be saved and who damned. This represents one tradition in Christianity: the determinism which leads to Calvinism *(q.v.)*. St. Thomas Aquinas (1227–74), the greatest figure of scholasticism and one of the principal saints in the Roman Catholic Church, compromised between the two positions in the sense that, believing man to be free, he yet held that Adam's sin was transmitted to all mankind and only divine grace can bring salvation. But even when God wishes to bestow this salvation, the human will must cooperate. God foresees that some will not accept the offer of grace and predestines them to eternal punishment.

*The Problem for Philosophy.* With the Renaissance, thinkers began to free themselves from the domination of the Church and so study the world objectively and freely without preconceptions. But the more man turned to science, the more he discovered that the world was ruled by apparently inexorable laws and, since the scientist must believe that every event has a cause, he was led back to determinism. Man as part of the universe was subject to law too and all that existed was a vast machine. Francis Bacon (1561–1626) separated the fields of religion and science but left man subject completely to the will of God. Thomas Hobbes (1588–1679) was a rigid determinist and materialist although, having had trouble with the Church in France whence, as a royalist, he had fled, he took care to announce that the Christian God is the Prime Mover.

Modern philosophy begins with René Descartes (1596–1650), a Frenchman who tried to reconcile the mechanical scientific universe of his time with the spiritual need for freedom. He did this by separating completely mind and body; the former, he said, is free, the latter completely determined. But, by admitting that the will can produce states of body, he was left with the problem of how this could happen—a problem which the so-called Occasionists solved to their own satisfaction by stating that the will is free and God so arranges the universe that what a person wills happens. Baruch Spinoza (1632–77), a Dutch Jew whose independence of thought had led to his excommunication from the Amsterdam Synagogue in 1656, was a complete determinist. He asserted that God and Nature are one, everything that happens is a manifestation of God's inscrutable nature, and it is logically impossible that things could be other than they are. Thus both Hobbes and Spinoza were determinists for entirely opposed reasons. The former as a materialist, the latter because he believed in the absolute perfection and universality of God. Yet the great religious mystic and mathematician Blaise Pascal (1623–62) held that, no matter what reason and cold logic may indicate we *know* from direct religious experience that we are free. John Calvin (1509–64) and Martin Luther (1483–1546) were both determinists. *See* **Calvinism.**

To the more practical British philosophers, John Locke (1632–1704) and David Hume (1711–76), free will was related to personality. Locke believed that God had implanted in each individual certain desires and these determine the will; the desires are already there, but we use our will to satisfy them. Hume argued that a man's behavior is the necessary result of his character and if he had a different character he would act otherwise. Accordingly, when a man's actions arise from his own nature and desires he is free. He is not free when external events compel him to act otherwise (*e.g.,* if he strikes another because his own nature is such he is free as he is not if he is compelled to do so against his desire). Leibnitz (1646–1716), although as a German metaphysical philosopher holding very different general views, said much the same thing—that choice is simply selecting the desire that is strongest. But most of the 18th cent. thinkers after Voltaire, with the great exceptions of Rousseau and the later German philosophers Kant, Fichte, Schopenhauer, and Hegel, who were initially influenced by him, accepted determinism. Rousseau (1712–78) began to stem the tide by his declaration that man is a free soul striving to remain free and only prevented from being so by society and the cold science which stifles his feeling heart. Once again the will became important as Kant (1724–1804) asserted that belief in freedom is a moral necessity although it cannot be proved by reason; the moral nature of man shows that there is a "transcendental" world beyond the senses where freedom applies. Fichte and Schelling found freedom in the Absolute ego or God, of whom each individual was part and thus also free. Hegel (1770–1831) saw the whole universe as evolving towards self-awareness and freedom in man although this could only be fully realized in a society that makes for freedom. Even God himself only attains full consciousness and self-realization through the minds of such individuals as are free. This is the goal of the dialectical process. (*See* **Dialectical Materialism.**)

*The Scientist's View.* For the scientist the law of cause and effect is a useful hypothesis since, by and large, it is necessary for him to assume that all events are caused. Nevertheless the modern tendency is to think in terms of statistical probability rather than relentless mechanistic causality, and, although the free will problem does not concern the scientist as such, it is clear that freedom and determinism (assuming the terms to have any meaning at all) are not necessarily opposed. In sociology, for example, we *know* that certain actions will produce certain results upon the behavior of people in general, *e.g.,* that raising the bank rate will discourage business expansion. But this does not mean that Mr. Brown who decides in the circumstances not to add a new wing to his factory is not using his free will. Even in the case of atoms, as Dr. Bronowski has pointed out, the observed results of allowing gas under pressure in a cylinder to rush out occur because most of the atoms are "obeying" the scientific "law" relating to such situations. But this does not mean that some atoms are not busy rushing across the stream or even against it—they are, but the general tendency is outwards and that is what we note. Lastly, the modern philosophical school of Logical Analysis would probably ask, not whether Freewill or Determinism is the true belief, but whether the question has any meaning. For what scientific experiment could we set up to prove one or the other true? The reader will note that some of the philosophers mentioned above are using the words to mean quite different concepts.

**Dialectical Materialism,** the combination of Hegel's dialectic method with a materialist philosophy produced by Karl Marx (1818–83) and his friend Friedrich Engels (1820–95). It is the philosophical basis of **Marxism** *(q.v.)* and **Communism** *(q.v.)* "Dialectic" to the ancient Greek philosophers meant a kind of dialogue or conversation, as used particularly by Socrates, in which philosophical disputes were resolved by a series of successive contradictions: a thesis is put forward and the opposing side holds its contradiction or antithesis until in the course of argument a synthesis is reached in which the conflicting ideas are resolved.

*From Thesis through Antithesis to Synthesis.* Hegel in the 19th century put forward the view that this process applies to the course of nature and history as they strive towards the perfect state. But to him, as to the Greeks, the conflict was in the field of ideas. The "universal reason" behind events works through the ideas held by a particular society until they are challenged by those of another which supersedes them and in turn, usually by war, becomes the agent of universal reason until the arrival of a new challenger. Hegel therefore regarded war as an instrument of progress and his Prussian compatriots found no difficulty in identifying their own state as the new agent of progress by universal conquest. Feuerbach, Lassalle, and other early socialists were impressed by some of Hegel's ideas: *e.g.,* that societies evolved (with the assumption that finally their own ideal society would be achieved) and that truth, morals, and concepts were relative so that a type of society that was "good" at one time was not necessarily so at another. But Marx and Engels in effect turned Hegel upside-down, accepted his dialectic but rejected his belief that ideas were the motive force. On the contrary, they said, ideas are determined by social and economic change as a result of materialistic forces. (*See* **Calvinism,** where it is pointed out that the Marxist view is not that Calvin changed men's economic ideas but rather that a developing capitalism unconsciously changed his.) The historical materialism of Marxism purports to show that the inexorable dialectic determines that feudalism is displaced by capitalism and capitalism by creating a proletariat (its antithesis) inevitably leads to socialism and a classless society. The state, as a tool of the dominant class, withers away. Dialectical materialism is applied in all

spheres. As a philosophy there is little to be said
for it save that it has shown us the close dependence of man's thoughts upon current material
and social conditions. But as a battle cry or a ratio-
nalization of Marxism it wields immense power
over the minds of men. *See* **Marxism.**

**Dianetics.** *See* **Scientology.**

**Doukhobors,** a religious sect of Russian origin,
founded by a Prussian sergeant at Kharkov in the
middle of the 18th century, and now mainly settled in Canada. Like many other sects they belong
to that type of Christianity which seeks direct communication with God and such bodies tend to have
certain traits in common, such as belief in the
"inner light", opposition to war and authority in
general, and often ecstasies which show themselves in physical ways such as shaking, speaking
in strange tongues (glossolalia), and other forms
of what to the unbeliever seem mass hysteria. Liturgy, ritual, or ceremony is non-existent. The Doukhobors were persecuted in Tsarist Russia, but in
1898 Tolstoy used his influence to have them removed to Canada where the government granted
them uninhabited land in what is now Saskatchewan and seven or eight thousand settled down in
peace which they enjoyed for many years. Recently, however, their practices have caused difficulties once more; for even the most tolerant government which is prepared to accept pacifism,
total dependence on communally-owned agriculture, refusal to engage in commerce, non-payment
of taxes, rejection of the marriage ceremony and
separation "when love ceases", finds it difficult to
tolerate, as civilization advances ever closer to
Doukhobor communities, their proneness to "put
off these troublesome disguises which we wear"—
*i.e.,* to walk about naked in the communities of
their more orthodox neighbors. What the future of
the Doukhobors in their various sects (for even
they have their differences) will be it is impossible
to say, but it is difficult to believe that these simple
people can long resist the pressure of modern civilization.

**Dowsing.** *See* **Radiesthesia.**

**Druidism,** the religion of Celtic Britain and Gaul of
which Druids were the priesthood. They were finally wiped out by the Roman general Suetonius
Paulinus about A.D. 58 in their last stronghold, the
island of Anglesey. There are two sources of our
present beliefs in Druidism: (1) the brief and factual records of the Romans, notably Pliny and Julius Caesar, which tell us that they worshipped in
sacred oak groves and presumably practiced a religion doing reverence to the powers of nature
which must have had its roots in early stone age
times and had many cruel rites, *e.g.,* human sacrifice; (2) the beliefs put forward by William Stuke-
ley, an amateur antiquarian who from 1718 did
valuable work by his studies of the stone circles
at Stonehenge and Avebury. However, influenced
by the Romantic movement, he later put forward
the most extravagant theories which unfortunately
are those popularly accepted by those without archaeological knowledge today. Stonehenge and
Avebury were depicted as the temples of the
"white-haired Druid bard sublime" and an attempt
was made to tie up Druidism with early Christianity, above all with the concept of the Trinity. In fact,
these circles have no connection with the Druids.
They may have made ceremonial use of them but
recent evidence suggests that the megalithic
stones at Stonehenge belong to a Bronze Age cul-

ture (2100–1600 B.C.). Nor have Druidism and
Christianity any relationship. Almost nothing is
known of the religion. Yet such were its romantic
associations that, even today, one hears of "Druidic" ceremonies practiced at the appropriate time
of year on Primrose Hill in the heart of London
(though whether seriously or with tongue in cheek,
one does not know). In Wales the name Druid survives as the title for the semi-religious leaders of
the annual festivals of Celtic poetry, drama, and
music known as Eisteddfods. Lingering, but now
tenuous, druidic connections are to be found in all
Celtic parts including Cornwall and Brittany where
Eisteddfods are also held.

**Dualism,** any philosophical or theological theory
which implies that the universe has a double nature, notably Plato's distinction between appearance and reality, soul and body, ideas and material
objects, reason and the evidence of the senses,
which infers that behind the world as we perceive
it there lies an "ideal" world which is more "real"
than that of mere appearance. In religions such as
Zoroastrianism or the Gnostic and Manichaeism
heresies, it was believed that the universe was
ruled by good and evil "principles"—in effect that
there was a good god and a bad one. In psychology, dualism refers to the philosophical theories
which believe mind and body to be separate entities. The opposite of dualism is monism which asserts the essential unity of the substance of the
universe.

An essential problem in the dualistic view lies in
the question as to how and where the two separate
and distinct properties of the universe interact.
Where, for example, does the "mind" actually
mesh with the physical mechanics of the brain and
body—where does the ghost sit in his machine?
Descartes decided that mind and body must interact somewhere and he selected the pineal gland
(an apparently functionless part of the brain) as
the spot. But this did nothing to explain how two
*totally different* aspects of nature can possibly influence each other, and today most philosophers
and psychologists reject dualistic views of life and
personality as posing more problems than they
solve. *See also* **Psychology, Occam's Razor.**

# E

**Education.** Education was no great problem to primitive man, but as societies became more complex
people began to ask themselves such questions
as: *What* should young people be taught? *How*
should they be taught? Should the aim of their education be to bring out their individual qualities or
rather to make them good servants of the state?

The first teachers were priests who knew most
about the traditions, customs, and lore of their societies and thus the first schools were in religious
meeting places. This was notably true of the Jews
who learned from the rabbis in the synagogue.

*The Greeks.* We begin, as always, with the
Greeks whose city-states, based on slavery, educated men (not women) for the sort of life described in Plato's *Dialogues*—the leisured life of
gentlemen arguing the problems of the universe
at their banquets or in the market-place. This
made it necessary to learn debate and oratory (or
rhetoric) especially for those who proposed to
take up politics. The Sophist philosophy taught the

need to build up convincing arguments in a persuasive manner, to learn the rules of logic and master the laws and customs of the Athenians, and to know the literature of the past so that illustrations might be drawn from it. These strolling philosophers who taught for a fee were individualists showing the student how to advance himself at all costs within his community.

Socrates had a more ethical approach, believing that education was good in itself, made a man happier and a better citizen, and emphasized his position as a member of a group. His method of teaching, the dialectic or "Socratic" method, involved argument and discussion rather than overwhelming others by rhetoric and is briefly mentioned under **Dialectical Materialism** *(q.v.)*. Today this method is increasingly used in adult education where a lecture is followed by a period of discussion in which both lecturer and audience participate; for psychologists have shown that people accept ideas more readily when conviction arises through their own arguments than when they are passively thrust down their throats.

Socrates' pupil Plato produced in his book *The Republic* one of the first comprehensive systems of education and vocational selection. Believing that essentially men have very different and unequal abilities he considered that in an idealistic or utopian society they should be put into social classes corresponding to these differences, and suggested the following method: (1) For the first 18 years of a boy's life he should be taught gymnastics and sports, playing and singing music, reading and writing, a knowledge of literature, and if he passed this course sent on to the next stage; those who failed were to become tradesmen and merchants. (2) From 18–20 those successful in the first course were to be given two years of cadet training, the ones thought incapable of further education being placed in the military class as soldiers. (3) The remainder, who were to become the leaders of society, proceeded with advanced studies in philosophy, mathematics, science, and art. Such education was to be a state concern, state supported and controlled, selecting men and training them for service in the state according to their abilities.

Plato's pupil Aristotle even suggested that the state should determine shortly after birth which children should be allowed to live and destroy the physically or mentally handicapped; that marriage should be state-controlled to ensure desirable offspring. However, in their time the leisured and individualistic Sophists held the field and few accepted the educational views of Plato or his pupil.

*Rome.* The Romans were not philosophers and most of their culture came from Greece. Administration was their chief aptitude and Quintilian (A.D. *c.* 35–*c.* 95) based his higher education on the earlier classical tuition in public speaking, but he is important for emphasizing the training of character and for his humanistic approach to the method of teaching that caused his *Institutio oratoria* to be influential for centuries later—indeed one might almost say up to the time of the great Dr. Arnold of Rugby. Education, he believed, should begin early but one must "take care that the child not old enough to love his studies does not come to hate them" by premature forcing; studies must be made pleasant and interesting and students encouraged by praise rather than discouraged when they sometimes fail; play is to be approved of as a sign of a lively disposition and

because gloomy, depressed children are not likely to be good students; corporal punishment should never be used because "it is an insult as you will realize if you imagine it yourself". The world became interested not in *what* he taught but *how* he taught it: he was the pioneer of humanistic education and character-training from Vittorino d. Feltre (1378–1446) of Mantua, through Milton and Pope who commended his works to the modern educationists who have studied their pupils as well as their books.

*The Middle Ages: The Religious View.* With the development of Christianity education once more became a religious problem. The earliest converts had to be taught Christian doctrine and were given instruction in "catechumenal" schools before admission to the group, but as the religion came increasingly into contact with other religions or heresies a more serious training was necessary, and from these newer "catechetical" schools, where the method used was the catechism (*i.e.,* question and answer as known to all Presbyterian children today), the Apologists arose among whom were Clement of Alexandria and the great Origen. From this time education became an instrument of the church and in 529 the Emperor Justinian ordered all pagan schools to be closed.

As typical of the best in medieval education while the lamp of civilization burned low during the Dark Ages, after the fall of Roman power, and survived only in the monasteries, we may mention St. Benedict (*c.* 480–*c.* 547) of Monte Cassino. There, in southern Italy, a rule was established which became a part of monastic life in general. Monastic schools were originally intended for the training of would-be monks, but later others were admitted who simply wanted some education; thus two types of schools developed: one for the *interni* and the other for *externi* or external pupils. Originally studies were merely reading in order to study the Bible, writing to copy the sacred books, and sufficient calculation to be able to work out the advent of holy days or festivals. But by the end of the 6th century the "seven liberal arts" (grammar, rhetoric, dialectic, arithmetic, geometry, music, and astronomy) were added.

*The Renaissance.* The close of the Middle Ages saw the development of two types of secular school. One came with the rise of the new merchant class and the skilled trader whose "guilds" or early trade unions established schools to train young men for their trades but ultimately gave rise to burgher or town schools; the other was the court school founded and supported by the wealthy rulers of the Italian cities—Vittorio da Feltre (mentioned above) presided over the most famous at Mantua.

These Renaissance developments are paralleled in northern Europe by the Protestant reformers who, having with Martin Luther held that everyone should know how to read his Bible in order to interpret it in his own way, were logically committed to popular education, compulsory and universal. In theory this was intended for biblical study, but writing, arithmetic, and other elementary subjects were taught and Luther said that, even if heaven and hell did not exist, education was important. Universal education is a Protestant conception.

*Views of Philosophers.* From this period onwards people were free to put forward any ideas about education, foolish or otherwise, and to create their own types of school. Of English philosophers who theorized about, but did not practice, education we may mention the rationalist Francis Bacon (1561–1626) who saw learning as the dissipation of all prejudices and the collection of concrete facts; the materialist and totalitarian Hobbes (1588–1679) who, as a royalist, believed that the right to determine the kind of education fit for his subjects is one of the absolute rights of the sovereign power or ruler; the gentlemanly Locke (1632–1704) whose ideal was a sound mind in a sound body to be attained by hard physical exercise, wide experience of the world, and enough knowledge to meet the requirements of the pupil's environment. The end result would be one able to get on with his fellows, pious but wise in the ways of the world, independent and able to look after himself, informed but reticent about his knowledge. Classics and religious study were not to be carried to excess, since Locke held that these subjects had been overrated in the past. Locke's pupil was the well-to-do, civilized young man of the 17th century who knew how to behave in society.

Jean-Jacques Rousseau (1712–78), a forerunner of the Romantic movement *(q.v.)*, which despised society and its institutions, put emotion at a higher level than reason. His book *Emile* describes the education of a boy which is natural and spontaneous. Society, he holds, warps the growing mind and therefore the child should be protected from its influences until his development in accordance with his own nature is so complete that he cannot be harmed by it. During the first 4 years the body should be developed by physical training; from 5 to 12 the child would live in a state of nature such that he could develop his powers of observation and his senses; from 13, books would be used and intellectual training introduced, although only in line with the child's own interests, and he would be given instruction only as he came to ask for it. Moral training and contact with his fellows to learn the principles of sympathy, kindness, and helpfulness to mankind would be given between 15 and 20. Girls, however, should be educated to serve men in a spirit of modesty and restraint. His own five children he deposited in a foundling hospital.

*Summary.* Broadly speaking, then, there have been four main attitudes to education: (1) religious, with a view to a life beyond death; (2) state-controlled education, with a view to uniform subservience to authority; (3) "gentlemanly" education, with a view to social graces and easy congress in company; (4) the "child-centered" education, which attempts to follow the pupil's inner nature. It is unnecessary to mention the ordinary method of attempting to instill facts without any considerable degree of cooperation between pupil and teacher in order that the former may, with or without interest, follow some occupation in adult life; for this the philosophers did not consider. Today there remain the two fundamental principles: education for the advantage of the state and its ideology or education for individual development and freedom.

Four educationists of the modern period who have influenced us in the direction of freedom were Johann Pestalozzi of Switzerland (1746–1827) who, by trying to understand children, taught the "natural, progressive, and harmonious development of all the powers and capacities of the human being"; Friedrich Froebel (1782–1852) of Germany, the founder of the Kindergarten who, like Pestalozzi, was influenced by Rousseau but realized the need to combine complete personal development with social adjustment; Maria Montessori (1869–1952) whose free methods have revolutionized infant teaching; John Dewey (1859–1952) who held that the best interests of the group are served when the individual develops his own particular talents and nature.

**Eleatics,** the philosophers of Elea in ancient Greece who, at the time when Heraclitus (*c.* 535–475 B.C.) was teaching that change is all that exists and nothing is permanent, were asserting that change is an illusion. Of the three leaders of this school, Xenophanes asserted that the universe was a solid immovable mass forever the same; Parmenides explained away change as an inconceivable process, its appearance being due to the fact that what we see is unreal; and Zeno (the best-known today) illustrated the same thesis with his famous argument of the arrow which, at any given moment of its flight, must be where it is since it cannot be where it is not. But if it is where it is, it cannot move, this is based, of course, on the delusion that motion is discontinuous. The Eleatics were contemporaries of Socrates.

**Empiricism.** While not a single school of philosophy, empiricism is an approach to knowledge which holds that if a man wants to know what the universe is like the only correct way to do so is to go and look for himself, to collect facts which come to him through his senses. It is, in essence, the method of science as contrasted with rationalism *(q.v.)* which in philosophy implies that thinking or reasoning without necessarily referring to external observations can arrive at truth. Empiricism is typically an English attitude, for among the greatest empirical philosophers were John Locke, George Berkeley, and David Hume. *See* Rationalism.

**Epicureanism.** The two great schools of the Hellenistic period (*i.e.* the late Greek period beginning with the empire of Alexander the Great) were the Stoics and Epicureans, the former founded by Zeno of Citium (not to be confused with Zeno the Eleatic) *(q.v.),* the latter by Epicurus, born in Samos in 342 B.C. Both schools settled in Athens, where Epicurus taught that "pleasure is the beginning and end of a happy life." However, he was no sensualist and emphasized the importance of moderation in all things because excesses would lead to pain instead of pleasure and the best of all pleasures were mental ones. Pleasures could be active or passive but the former contain an element of pain since they are the process of satisfying desire not yet satiated. The latter involving the absence of desire are the more pleasant. In fact, Epicurus in his personal life was more stoical than many Stoics and wrote "when I live on bread and water I spit on luxurious pleasures." He disapproved of sexual enjoyment and thought friendship one of the highest of all joys. A materialist who accepted the atomic theory of Democritus, he was not a determinist, and if he did not disbelieve in the gods he regarded religion and the fear of death as the two primary sources of unhappiness.

**Epiphenomenalism.** *See* Mind and Matter.

**Erastianism,** the theory that the state has the right to decide the religion of its members, wrongly attributed to Erastus of Switzerland (1524–83) who was believed to have held this doctrine. The term has usually been made use of in a derogatory sense—*e.g.,* by the Scottish churches which held that the "call" of the congregation was the only way to elect ministers at a time when, about the turn of the 17th and 18th century, they felt that

Episcopalianism was being foisted on them. "Episcopalianism" (*i.e.* Anglicanism) with its state church, ecclesiastical hierarchy, and system of livings presented by patrons was to them "Erastian" in addition to its other "unscriptural practices."

**Essenes,** a Jewish sect which, during the oppressive rule of Herod (d. 4 B.C.), set up monastic communities in the region of the Dead Sea. They refused to be bound by the scriptural interpretations of the Pharisees and adhered rigorously to the letter of Holy Writ, although with additions of their own which cause them by orthodox Jews today to be regarded as a break-away from Judaism. Among their practices and beliefs were purification through baptism, renunciation of sexual pleasures, scrupulous cleanliness, strict observance of the Mosaic law, communal possession, asceticism. Akin in spirit, although not necessarily identical with them, were the writers of Apocalyptic literature preaching that the evils of the present would shortly be terminated by a new supernatural order heralded by a Messiah who would reign over a restored Israel. The casting out of demons and spiritual healing formed part of these general beliefs which were in the air at that time. The sect has an importance far beyond its size or what has been known about it in the past since the discovery from 1947 onwards of the Dead Sea Scrolls of the Qumran community occupying a monastery in the same area as the Essenes and holding the same type of belief. These scrolls with their references to a "Teacher of Righteousness" preceding the Messiah have obvious relevance to the sources of early Christianity and have given rise to speculations as to whether Jesus might have been influenced by views which, like His own, were unacceptable to orthodox Jews but in line with those of the Dead Sea communities. They seem to show that early Christianity was not a sudden development but a gradual one which had its predecessors.

**Eugenics,** a 19th century movement largely instigated by the British scientist and mathematician, Sir Francis Galton. Galton argued that many of the most satisfactory attributes of mankind—intelligence, physical strength, resistance to disease, etc.—were genetically determined and thus handed down in the normal process of inheritance. From this he reasoned that selective mating of physically "superior" individuals, and its converse, the controlled limitation on the breeding of criminals or the insane, would lead inevitably to a progressive improvement in the overall standards of the human race. In their simplest form these proposals are incontestable, though they do of course introduce marked restrictions on the choice of the individual for marriage and procreation. Worse yet is the way in which the argument can be misapplied or elaborated—as it was in Nazi Germany—to include the sterilization of alcoholics, confirmed criminals and even epileptics. Nevertheless there remains the feeling that there are some aspects of eugenics which intuitively at any rate make good sense and of course the widespread application of birth control is itself an enactment of eugenic principles.

**Evangelicalism,** the belief of those Protestant sects which hold that the essence of the Gospel consists in the doctrine of salvation by faith in the atoning death of Christ and not by good works or the sacraments; that worship should be "free" rather than liturgical through established forms; that ritual is unacceptable and superstitious. Evangelicals are Low Churchmen.

**Evangelism,** the preaching of the Gospel, emphasising the necessity for a new birth or conversion. The evangelistic fervor of John Wesley and George Whitefield (*see* Methodism) aroused the great missionary spirit of the late 18th and 19th century. George Fox, founder of the Society of Friends (*q.v.*), was also an evangelist. Evangelists can be Low, High, or Middle Churchmen.

**Existentialism,** a highly subjective philosophy which many people connect with such names as Jean-Paul Sartre (1905–80) or Albert Camus (1913–60) and assume to be a post-war movement associated with disillusion and a sordid view of life. However, existentialism stems from Sören Kierkegaard (1813–55), the Danish "religious writer"—his own description of himself—in such works as *Either/Or, Fear and Trembling,* and *Concluding Unscientific Postscript.* Between the two wars translations of Kierkegaard into German influenced Martin Heidegger's great work *Being and Time* and the other great existentialist Karl Jaspers; it has strongly influenced modern Protestant theology notably in Karl Barth, Reinhold Niebuhr, and Paul Tillich and beyond that field the French philosopher Gabriel Marcel, the Spanish writer Unamuno in his well-known *The Tragic Sense of Life,* and Martin Buber of Israel in his *I and Thou.* We have it on Heidegger's authority that "Sartre is no philosopher" even if it is to his works that modern existentialists often turn.

Existentialism is extremely difficult for the non-metaphysically-minded to understand. It deals, not with the nature of the universe of what are ordinarily thought of as philosophical problems but describes an attitude to life or God held by the individual. Briefly, its main essentials are: (1) it distinguishes between *essence, i.e.,* that aspect of an entity which can be observed and known—and its *existence*—the fact of its having a place in a changing and dangerous world which is what really matters; (2) existence being basic, each self-aware individual can grasp his own existence on reflection in his own immediate experience of himself and his situation as a free being in the world; what he finds is not merely a knowing self but a self that fears, hopes, believes, wills, and is aware of its need to find a purpose, plan, and destiny in life; (3) but we cannot grasp our existence by thought alone; thus the fact "all men must die" relates to the essence of man but it is necessary to be involved, to draw the conclusion as a person that "I too must die" and experience its impact on our own individual existence; (4) because of the preceding, it is necessary to abandon our attitude of objectivity and theoretical detachment when faced by the problems relating to the ultimate purpose of our own life and the basis of our own conduct; life remains closed to those who take no part in it because it can have no significance; (5) it follows that the existentialist cannot be rationalist in his outlook for this is merely an escape into thought from the serious problems of existence; none of the important aspects of life—failure, evil, sin, folly—nor (in the view of Kierkegaard) even the existence of God or the truth of Christianity—can be proved by reason. "God does not exist; He is eternal," was how he expressed it; (6) life is short and limited in space and time, therefore it is foolish to discuss in a leisurely fashion matters of life and death as if there were all eternity to argue them in. It is necessary to make a leap into the unknown, *e.g.,* accepting Christ (in the case of the Christian existentialist) by faith in the sense of giving and risking the self utterly. This means complete commitment, not a dependence on arguments as to whether certain historical events did, or did not, happen.

To summarize: existentialism of whatever type seems to the outsider to be an attitude to life concerning itself with the individual's ultimate problems (mine, not yours); to be anti-rationalist and anti-idealist (in the sense of being, as it seems to the believer, practical)—in effect it seems to say "life is too short to fool about with argument, you must dive in and become committed" to something. Sartre who called himself an "atheist existentialist" was apparently committed to the belief that "hell is other people," but for most critics the main argument against existentialist philosophy is that it often rests on a highly specialized personal experience and, as such, is incommunicable.

**Existential Psychology,** a new if rather diffuse movement in modern psychology with no specific founder but with a number of figures who have, perhaps against their will, acquired leader status. One of the key figures is the British psychiatrist, R. D. Laing, whose radical views on psychotherapy are counted as being heretical by the vast majority of his medical colleagues. Laing holds that many so-called neurotic and psychotic conditions are essentially not "abnormal" and merely represent extreme strategies by which an individual may adjust to environmental and personal stress. Instead of attempting to suppress or eliminate the psychosis in the traditional manner, one should lead the patient through it thus allowing the individual's "unconscious plan" for his own adjustment to be fulfilled.

**Exorcism,** the removal or ejection of an evil spirit by a ritual or prayer. It is easy to forget that the concept of insanity as representing a disorder of the brain, analogous to physical sickness of the body, is fairly recent in origin. Barely two centuries ago it was considered to be appropriate treatment to put lunatics into chains and beat them daily in the hope that the malevolent beings inhabiting them might be persuaded to depart. Tragically, many of the symptoms of severe forms of mental disorder induce such an apparent change in the personality of the individual as to suggest that an alien individual has indeed taken over their body, and this belief is still common in many parts of the world. Most religious systems have developed some ritual or set of rituals for expelling these demons, and while, not surprisingly, the practice of exorcism by the clergy has declined dramatically in the past century, it is still brought into play now and again in such circumstances as alleged hauntings, poltergeist phenomena, etc. From a scientific point of view, exorcism must be counted as a superstitious rite, but its suggestive power in cases of hysteria, and perhaps even more serious mental illnesses, cannot be completely ruled out. General interest in the topic has been stimulated in part by the resurgence of the practice of Black Magic and witchcraft, largely in the form of experimental dabbling by young people, who no doubt become disillusioned when it fails to live up to its promise. Testimony to the pulling-power of this remnant of our superstitious past is the fact that a sensational and terrifying novel, *The Exorcist,* which its author claimed was based on fact, topped the best-seller lists in 1972; and the even more horrific movie-version became one of the most successful (in box office terms) films of all time. The Church of England, incidentally, takes anything but a dismissive line on the matter, and in fact employs a number of ordained priests as "licensed exorcists". These services are apparently much in demand.

# F

**Fabian Society.** In 1848 (the year of *The Communist Manifesto* by Marx and Engels) Europe was in revolt. In most countries the workers and intellectuals started bloody revolutions against the feudal ruling classes which were no less violently suppressed; hence on the continent socialism took on a Marxist tinge which to some extent it still retains. But at the same time England was undergoing a slow but nonviolent transition in her political and industrial life which led the workers in general to look forward to progress through evolution. Marxism never became an important movement in England even though it took its origin there. There were many reasons for this: the agitation of the Chartists *(q.v.);* the writings of Mill, Ruskin, and Carlyle; the reforms of Robert Owen; the religious movement led by the Wesleys; the cooperative societies; the Christian socialists. Furthermore legislation stimulated by these bodies had led to an extension of the franchise to include a considerable number of wage-earners, remedial measures to correct some of the worst abuses of the factory system, recognition of the trade unions, etc.

This was the background against which the Fabian Society was founded in 1884 with the conviction that social change could be brought about by gradual parliamentary means. (The name is derived from Quintus Fabius Maximus, the Roman general nicknamed "Cunctator," the delayer, who achieved his successes in defending Rome against Hannibal by refusing to give direct battle.) It was a movement of brilliant intellectuals, chief among whom were Sidney and Beatrice Webb, H. G. Wells, G. B. Shaw, Graham Wallas, Sidney Olivier, and Edward Pease. The Society itself was basically a research institution which furnished the intellectual information for social reform and supported all contributing to the gradual attainment by parliamentary means of socialism.

The Webbs's analysis of society emphasized that individualist enterprise in capitalism was a hang-over from early days and was bound to defeat itself since socialism is the inevitable accompaniment of modern industrialism; the necessary result of popular government is control of their economic system by the people themselves. Utopian schemes had been doomed to failure because they were based on the fallacy that society is static and that islands of utopias could be formed in the midst of an unchanging and antagonistic environment. On the contrary, it was pointed out, society develops: "The new becomes old, often before it is consciously regarded as new." Social reorganization cannot usefully be hastened by violent means but only through methods consonant with this natural historical progression—gradual, peaceful, and democratic. The Fabians were convinced that men are rational enough to accept in their common interest developments which can be demonstrated as necessary; thus public opinion will come to see that socialization of the land and industries is essential in the same way that they came to accept the already-existing acts in respect of housing, insurance, medical care, and conditions of work.

The Society collaborated first in the formation of the Independent Labour Party and then with the more moderate Labour Party and the trade unions and Cooperative movement. But in general it disapproved of independent trade union action since change should come from the government and take political form. The class war of Marx was rejected and so too was the idea of the exclusive role of the working class—reform must come from the enlightened cooperation of all classes—not from their opposition.

**Faith Healing,** the belief and practice of curing physical and mental ills by faith in some supernatural power, either allegedly latent in the individual (as with Christian Science) or drawn in some way from God. It is a characteristic of faith healing that it is supposed to be publicly demonstrable—*i.e.,* a "healer" will hold public meetings and invite sick people to come up to be cured on the platform. In the emotionally charged atmosphere which the healer generates, it is not unusual for people to show immediate and striking improvement in their illness, but the almost invariable rule is for relapses to occur within days or hours after the event. When remission is more permanent, the illness is generally hysterical in origin and will often return to the individual in some other form. Spiritualists claim that the healing in such cases is done not by "faith" but by direct intervention of the spirits of doctors, etc., who have died and passed on to another world. Perhaps the world's most famous faith healer in recent years was Harry Edwards (d. 1976), who had literally millions of letters from all parts of the world asking for the healing attention of his spirit guides. Many doctors, while remaining immensely sceptical about the origins and extent of this kind of therapy, are inclined to admit that it might have benefits when the sickness is mildly hysterical in origin. The real danger, of course, comes when patients seek unorthodox therapy before consulting their doctor.

**Fascism.** From the end of medieval times with the opening up of the world, the liberation of the mind and the release of business enterprise, a new spirit arose in Europe exemplified in such movements as the Renaissance, the Reformation, the struggle for democracy, the rise of capitalism, and the Industrial Revolution. With these movements there developed a certain tradition, which, in spite of hindrances and disagreement or failures, was universally held by both right- and left-wing parties however strongly they might fail to agree on the best means of attaining what was felt to be a universal ideal. The hard core of this tradition involved: belief in reason and the possibility of human progress; the essential sanctity and dignity of human life; tolerance of widely different religious and political views; reliance on popular government and the responsibility of the rulers to the ruled; freedom of thought and criticism; the necessity of universal education; impartial justice and the rule of law; the desirability of universal peace. Fascism was the negation of every aspect of this tradition and took pride in being so. Emotion took the place of reason, the "immutable, beneficial, and fruitful inequality of classes" and the right of a self-constituted élite to rule them replaced universal suffrage because absolute authority "quick, sure, unanimous" led to action rather than talk. Contrary opinions are not allowed and justice is in the service of the state; war is desirable to advance the power of the state; and racial inequality made a dogma. Those who belong to the "wrong"

religion, political party, or race are outside the law.

The attacks on liberalism and exaltation of the state derive largely from Hegel and his German followers; the mystical irrationalism from such 19th century philosophers as Schopenhauer, Nietzsche, and Bergson; from Sorel (*see* **Syndicalism**) came the idea of the "myth", and an image which would have the power to arouse the emotions of the masses and from Sorel also the rationale of violence and justification of force. But these philosophical justifications of fascism do not explain why it arose at all and why it arose where it did—in Italy, Germany, and Spain. These countries had one thing in common—disillusionment. Germany had lost the 1914–18 war, Italy had been on the winning side but was resentful about her small gains. Spain had sunk to the level of a third-rate power, and people were becoming increasingly restive under the reactionary powers of the Catholic Church, the landed aristocracy, and the army. In Marxist theory, fascism is the last fling of the ruling class and the bourgeoisie in their attempt to hold down the workers.

*Italian Fascism.* The corporate state set up by Benito Mussolini in Italy claimed to be neither capitalist nor socialist, and after its inception in 1922 the Fascist Party became the only recognized one. Its members wore black shirts, were organized in military formations, used the Roman greeting of the outstretched arm, and adopted as their slogan "Mussolini is always right". Membership of the Party was not allowed to exceed a number thought to be suited to the optimum size of a governing class and new candidates were drawn, after strict examinations, from the youth organizations. The Blackshirts, a Fascist militia, existed separately from the army and were ruled by Fascist headquarters.

At the head of government was Mussolini, "Il Duce" himself, a cabinet of fourteen ministers selected by him and approved by the King to supervise the various functions of government, and the Grand Council or directorate of the Fascist Party, all the members of which were chosen by the Duce. Parliament, which was not allowed to initiate legislation but only to approve decrees from above, consisted of a Senate with life membership and a Chamber of Fasel and Corporations composed of nominated members of the Party, the National Council of Corporations, and selected representatives of the employers' and employees' confederations. Private enterprise was encouraged and protected but rigidly controlled; strikes were forbidden, but a Charter of Labour enforced the collaboration of workers and employers whose disputes were settled in labor courts presided over by the Party. All decisions relating to industry were government-controlled (*e.g.,* wages, prices, conditions of employment and dismissal, the expansion or limitation of production), and some industries such as mining, shipping, and armaments were largely state-owned.

Italian Fascism served as a model in other countries, notably for the German National Socialist Party, in Spain and Japan, and most European nations between the wars had their small fascist parties, the British version led by Sir Oswald Mosley being known as the British Union which relied on "strong-arm tactics", marches and violence. The Public Order Act of 1936 was passed to deal with it. Although fascism in all countries has certain recognizable characteristics, it would be wrong to think of it as an international movement taking fixed forms and with a clearly thought-out rationale as in the case of communism. While there have been minor revivals of interest in Fascism in Italy—presumably as a counter move against the considerable inroads being made by the Communist Party in that country—fascism's final remaining bastion in Europe—Spain—began to crumble with the death of its dictator, General Franco, in 1975. *See* **Nazism**.

**Fatalism.** *See* **Determinism**.

**Fetichism,** originally a practice of the natives of West Africa and elsewhere of attributing magical properties to an object which was used as an amulet, for putting spells on others, or regarded as possessing dangerous powers. In psychology the term refers to a sexual perversion in which objects such as shoes, brassières, hair, etc., arouse sexual excitement.

**Feudalism.** The feudal system took its origins from Saxon times and broadly speaking lasted until the end of the 13th cent. It was a military and political organization based on land tenure, for, of course, society throughout this period was based almost entirely on agriculture. The activities of men divided them into three classes or estates. The First Estate was the clergy, responsible for man's spiritual needs; the Second was the nobility, including kings and emperor as well as the lesser nobles; the Third was composed of all those who had to do with the economic and mainly agricultural life of Europe. The praying men, the fighting men and administrators, and the toilers were all held to be dependent on each other in a web of mutual responsibilities.

The theory of feudalism, although it by no means always worked out in practice, was as follows: the earth was God's and therefore no man owned land in the modern sense of the word. God had given the Pope spiritual charge of men, and secular power over them to the emperor from whom kings held their kingdoms, and in turn the dukes and counts received the land over which they held sway from the king. Members of the second estate held their lands on the condition of fulfilling certain obligations to their overlord and to the people living under them, so when a noble received a fief or piece of land he became the vassal of the man who bestowed it. To him he owed military service for a specified period of the year, attendance at court, and giving his lord counsel. He undertook to ransom his lord when he fell into enemy hands and to contribute to his daughter's dowry and at the knighting of his son. In return the lord offered his vassal protection and justice, received the vassal's sons into his household and educated them for knighthood.

The system was complicated by the fact that large fiefs might be subdivided and abbots often governed church lands held in fief from nobles. The serf or toiling man dwelt on the land of a feudal noble or churchman where he rendered service by tilling the soil or carrying out his craft for his manorial lord in return for protection, justice, and the security of his life and land. He was given a share in the common lands or pastures from which he provided for his own needs. In the modern sense he was not free (although at a later stage he could buy his freedom) since he was attached to the soil and could not leave without the lord's permission. On the other hand he could neither be deprived of his land nor lose his livelihood. Feudal tenures were abolished in England by statute in 1660, although they had for long been inopera-

tive. In Japan a feudal system existed up to 1871, in Russia until 1917, and many relics of it still linger on (*e.g.* the *mezzadria* system of land tenure in parts of Italy).

**Flying Saucers.** In June 1947 an American private pilot, Kenneth Arnold, saw a series of wingless objects flying through the air at a speed which he estimated at thousands of miles an hour. He later told the press that the objects "flew as a saucer would if you skipped it across the water," and the phrase "flying saucers" was erroneously born. What Arnold actually saw has never been satisfactorily explained—it was probably a flight of jet fighters reflecting the sun's rays in a way that made them appear as discs—but since that date literally hundreds of thousands of people all over the world have reported the sighting of strange objects in the sky, coming in a bewildering range of shapes and sizes. Initially the American Air Force launched an official enquiry—Project Bluebook— to attempt to solve the mystery of these "unidentified flying objects" or "U.F.O.s," which finally folded in 1969 after concluding that the bulk of the sightings were probably misinterpretations of natural phenomena and that there was no evidence for the commonly held view that earth was being visited by spacecraft from some other planetary system. A rather similar conclusion was arrived at by the famous University of Colorado project—the Condon Committee—which published its findings in 1968. Despite this clear-cut official attitude, belief in the existence of flying saucers and their origin as alien space vehicles is exceedingly widespread and is held very strongly by people in all walks of life. In 1959 this striking social phenomenon attracted the attention of the psychologist C. G. Jung. He noticed that the press were inclined to report statements that saucers existed when made by prominent people and not publish contrary statements made by equally prominent people. He concluded that flying saucers were in some way welcome phenomena and in his brilliant little book. *Flying Saucers—A Modern Myth,* he hypothesized that the U.F.O.s were the modern equivalent of "signs in the skies." It was Jung's contention that the saucers were looked upon as the harbingers of advanced alien civilizations who had come to save the world from its descent into nuclear catastrophe—archangels in modern dress in fact.

Whatever the validity of this imaginative view of U.F.O.s, it is undeniably true that they exercise a great fascination for millions of people, some of whom invest them with definite religious significance. The best example of the open incorporation of flying saucers into a religious belief system is to be found in the Aetherius Society, an international organization with headquarters in Los Angeles but founded by a former London clerk, George King. Mr. King, who claims to be the mediumistic link between earth and the largely benevolent beings from outer space, regularly relays messages—notably from a Venusian known as Aetherius—to enthusiastic congregations at religious meetings. The sect, which is entirely sincere and dedicated in its beliefs, also makes pilgrimages to the tops of various mountains which have been "spiritually charged" with the aid of the spacebeings in their flying saucers.

Odd though such ideas may seem to most people, they can be readily understood within the context of the very marked decline in orthodox religious belief which we have seen in the past two decades. To an increasing number of people, many of whom feel a desperate need for spiritual guidance and enlightenment, the concepts of the traditionally Western religions seem somehow unsatisfactory. Many therefore turn to cults and splinter groups which use ideas and terminology which to them seem more at home in the twentieth century than those that sprung to life thousands of years ago. To members of the Aetherius Society, for example, the idea that Jesus Christ lives on Venus and rides around in a flying saucer is neither blasphemous nor ludicrous. As long as empty churches testify to the growing, if perhaps only temporary loss of contact between orthodox religions and the man-in-the-street, then one can expect such offbeat ideas as the cults surrounding flying saucers, and the science-fiction-like cult of Scientology *(q.v.)* to expand and flourish.

**Freemasonry,** a widespread, influential secret organization of English origin. Although it can be traced back to the Middle Ages when itinerant working masons in England and Scotland were organized in lodges with secret signs for the recognition of fellow-members, modern freemasonry first arose in England in the early decades of the 18th century. The first Grand Lodge was founded in London in 1716 and Freemasons' Hall was opened in 1776. With its clubs for discussion and social enjoyment (women were excluded) it met a need and became a well-known feature of English life. The movement quickly spread abroad to places which had direct trade links with England. The graded lodge structure, the social prestige conferred by membership, the symbolism, ritual and ceremony, and the emphasis on mutual help have had a lasting appeal. Interest in the occult had more appeal on the Continent than in England. Until a decade or so ago, membership conferred definite business and social advantages, particularly in small communities where the leading middle-class figures were generally members. Recently this advantage has markedly declined and freemason lodges nowadays tend to be little more than worthy charitable organizations. Fear of secret societies has given freemasonry many opponents; it was condemned by the Roman Catholic Church, banned by fascist dictators, and denounced by the Comintern. A statement from the congregation for the doctrine of the faith in 1981 reminded Catholics that under Article 2335 of the Code of Canon Law they are forbidden under pain of excommunication from joining masonic or similar associations.

**Freudian theory.** *See* **Psychoanalysis.**

**Friends, The Society of.** *See* **Quakers.**

**Fundamentalism** is a term covering a number of religious movements which adhere with the utmost rigidity to orthodox tenets; for example the Old Testament statement that the earth was created by God in six days and six nights would be held to be factual rather than allegorical or symbolic. Although the holding of rigid beliefs in the literal truth of the Bible might seem to be frequently contrary to modern scientific findings, the fundamentalists at least do not have the problems of compromise and interpretation to face, and to some people this is no doubt a great attraction. A factor influencing the present troubles in Northern Ireland is the narrow and intolerant form of fundamentalism represented by the extreme brand of Presbyterianism practiced there.

# G

**Gestalt Psychology.** In the latter half of the 19th cent. it became evident to psychologists that in principle there was no good reason why "mental" events should not be just as measurable and manageable as "physical" ones. Intensive studies of learning, memory, perception, and so on were therefore undertaken and the beginnings of an empirical science of psychology were underway. In the early part of the 20th cent. the experiments of Pavlov *(see* **Behaviorism**) and his co-workers suggested that the behavior of an animal, or even men, might ultimately be reduced to a descriptive account of the activities of nervous reflex loops— the so-called conditioned reflexes. With the publication of Watson's important book on Behaviorism in 1914 it looked as though the transfer of psychological studies from the field of philosophy to that of science could now take place. Actually the over-simplified picture of cerebral and mental pictures which Behaviorism offered was rather comparable to the billiard ball view of the universe so fashionable in Victorian science. Just as Behaviorism implied that there was a fundamental building block (the conditioned reflex) from which all mental events could be constructed, so Victorian physics assumed that the entire universe could be described in terms of a vast collection of atoms pushing each other around like billiard balls. The development of nuclear physics was to shatter the latter dream and at the same time a challenge to the naïve "reflex psychology" came from the Gestalt experimental school.

The founders of this school were Max Wertheimer, Kurt Koffka and Wolfgang Köhler, three young psychologists who in 1912 were conducting experiments—notably in vision—which seemed to expose the inadequacies of the behaviorist position. The Pavlov-Watson view, as we have said, implied that complex sensory events were no more than a numerical sum of individual nervous impulses. Wertheimer's group proposed that certain facts of perceptual experiences (ruled out of court as subjective and therefore unreliable by Watson) implied that the whole *(Gestalt)* was something more than simply the sum of its parts. For example, the presentation of a number of photographs, each slightly different, in rapid series gives rise to cinematographic motion. In basic terms, the eye has received a number of discrete, "still" photographs, and yet "motion" is perceived. What, they asked, was the sensory input corresponding to this motion? Some processes within the brain clearly *added* something to the total input as defined in behaviorist terms. An obvious alternative—in a different sense modality—is that of the arrangement of musical notes. A cluster of notes played one way might be called a tune; played backwards they may form another tune, or may be meaningless. Yet in all cases the constituent parts are the same, and yet their relationship to one another is evidently vital. Once again the whole is something more than the simple sum of the parts.

The implications of all this appeared to be that the brain was equipped with the capacity to organize sensory input in certain well-defined ways, and that far from being misleading and scientifically unjustifiable, human subjective studies of visual experience might reveal the very principles of organization which the brain employs. Take a field of dots, more or less randomly distributed; inspection of the field will soon reveal certain patterns or clusters standing out—the constellations in the night sky are a good illustration. There are many other examples, and Wertheimer and his colleagues in a famous series of experiments made some effort to catalogue them and reduce them to a finite number of "Laws of Perceptual Organization" which are still much quoted today.

**Ghosts,** belief in ghosts is one of the most common features of supernatural and mystical philosophy. At its roots it is based on the assumption that Man is essentially an individual created of two separate and distinct substances, mind and body. Most religious systems hold to this dualistic view (*see* **Dualism**), arguing that whereas the body is transient and destructible, the mind or spirit is permanent and survives the death of its physical host. The discarnate spirit is normally assumed to progress to some other realm ("Heaven," "Nirvana," "The Spirit World," etc.) whereupon it loses contact with the mortal world. Occasionally, however, for one reason or another, the spirits may not progress and may become trapped and unable to escape the material world. Traditionally this is supposed to occur when the death of the individual is precipitated by some great tragedy—murder, suicide, etc.—when the site of the tragedy is supposed to be haunted by the earthbound spirit. Although the library of the Society for Psychical Research is crammed with supposedly authentic accounts of hauntings of this kind, scientific interest in ghosts has been waning rapidly in recent years. At one time, in particular in the latter part of the 19th cent., with the upsurge of scientific interest in Spiritualism *(q.v.)*, there were even attempts to call up ghosts in the laboratory. These led to spectacular opportunities for fraud on the part of Spiritualist mediums and the like, but in the long run added little to the cause of science. As we have said, belief in ghosts is largely dependent upon a parallel belief that the mind or soul of man is something essentially separate from the body. With the decline in belief of this notion (it is now almost totally dismissed by most scientists and philosophers) has come an inevitable decline in belief in ghosts.

**Gnosticism.** Among the many heresies of early Christianity, especially during its first two centuries, was a group which came under the heading of Gnosticism. This was a system or set of systems which attempted to combine Christian beliefs with others derived from Oriental and Greek sources, especially those which were of a mystical and metaphysical nature, such as the doctrines of Plato and Pythagoras. There were many Gnostic sects, the most celebrated being the Alexandrian school of Valentius (fl. *c.* 136–*c.* 160). "Gnosis" was understood not as meaning "knowledge" or "understanding" as we understand these words, but "revelation." As in other mystical religions, the ultimate object was individual salvation; sacraments took the most varied forms. Many who professed themselves Christians accepted Gnostic doctrines and even orthodox Christianity contains some elements of Gnostic mysticism. It was left to the bishops and theologians to decide at what point Gnosticism ceased to be orthodox and a difficult task this proved to be. Two of the greatest, Clement of Alexandria and his pupil Origen, unwittingly slipped into heresy when they tried to show that such men as Socrates and Plato, who were in quest of truth, were Christian in intention, and by their lives and works had prepared the way for

Christ. Thus they contradicted Church doctrine which specifically said *Extra ecclesiam nulla salus*—outside the Church there is no salvation.

**God and Man.** The idea of gods came before the idea of God and even earlier in the evolution of religious thought there existed belief in spirits (*see* **Animism**). It was only as a result of a long period of development that the notion of a universal "God" arose, a development particularly well documented in the Old Testament. Here we are concerned only with the views of philosophers, the views of specific religious bodies being given under the appropriate headings. First, however, some definitions.

**Atheism** is the positive disbelief in the existence of a God. **Agnosticism** (a term coined by T. H. Huxley, the 19th cent. biologist and contemporary of Darwin) signifies that one cannot know whether God exists or not. **Deism** is the acceptance of the existence of God, not through revelation, but as a hypothesis required by reason. **Theism** also accepts the existence of God, but, unlike Deism, does not reject the evidence of revelation (*e.g.,* in the Bible or in the lives of the saints). **Pantheism** is the identification of God with all that exists (*i.e.,* with the whole universe). **Monotheism** is the belief in one God, **polytheism** the belief in many (*see also* **Dualism**).

*Early Greek Views.* Among the early Greek philosophers, Thales (*c.* 624–565 B.C.) of Miletus, in Asia Minor, Anaximander (611–547 B.C.), his pupil, and Anaximenes (b. *c.* 570 B.C.), another Miletan, were men of scientific curiosity and their speculations about the origin of the universe were untouched by religious thought. They founded the scientific tradition of critical discussion. Heraclitus of Ephesus (*c.* 540–475 B.C.), was concerned with the problem of change. How does a thing change and yet remain itself? For him all things are flames—processes. "Everything is in flux, and nothing is at rest." Empedocles of Agrigentum in Sicily (*c.* 500–*c.* 430 B.C.) introduced the idea of opposition and affinity. All matter is composed of the so-called four elements—*earth, water, air,* and *fire*—which are in opposition or alliance with each other. All these were materialist philosophers who sought to explain the working of the universe without recourse to the gods.

*Socrates, Plato, and Aristotle.* Socrates (470–899 B.C.) was primarily concerned with ethical matters and conduct rather than the nature of the universe. For him goodness and virtue come from knowledge. He obeyed an "inner voice" and suffered death rather than give up his philosophy. He believed in the persistence of life after death and was essentially a monotheist. Plato (427–347 B.C.) was chiefly concerned with the nature of reality and thought in terms of absolute truths which were unchanging, logical, and mathematical. (*See* **Mind and Matter.**) Aristotle (384–322 B.C.) took his views of matter not from Democritus (atomic view) but from Empedocles (doctrine of four elements), a view which came to fit in well with orthodox medieval theology. Matter is conceived of as potentially alive and striving to attain its particular form, being moved by divine spirit or mind *(nous)*. (An acorn, for example, is matter which contains the form "oak-tree" towards which it strives.) Thus there is a whole series from the simplest level of matter to the perfect living individual. But there must be a supreme source of all movement upon which the whole of Nature depends, a Being that Aristotle describes as the "Unmoved Mover", the ultimate cause of all becoming in the universe. This Being is pure intelligence, a philosopher's God, not a personal one. Unlike Plato, Aristotle did not believe in survival after death, holding that the divine, that is the immortal element in man, is mind.

Among the later Greek thinkers the Epicureans were polytheists whose gods, however, were denied supernatural powers. The Stoics built up a materialistic theory of the universe, based on the Aristotelian model. To them God was an all-pervading force, related to the world as the soul is related to the body, but they conceived of it as material. They developed the mystical side of Plato's idealism and were much attracted by the astrology coming from Babylonia. They were pantheists. The Sceptics were agnostics.

From *Pagan to Christian Thought.* Philo, "the Jew of Alexandria," who was about 20 years older than Jesus, tried to show that the Jewish scriptures were in line with the best in Greek thought. He introduced the *Logos* as a bridge between the two systems. Philo's God is remote from the world, above and beyond all thought and being, and as His perfection does not permit direct contact with matter the divine *Logos* acts as intermediary between God and man. Plotinus (204–70), a Roman, and the founder of Neoplatonism, was the last of the great pagan philosophers. Like Philo, he believed that God had created the world indirectly through emanations—beings coming from Him but not of Him. The world needs God but God does not need the world. Creation is a fall from God, especially the human soul when enmeshed in the body and the world of the senses, yet (*see* **Determinism**) man has the ability to free himself from sense domination and turn towards God. Neoplatonism was the final stage of Greek thought drawing inspiration from the mystical side of Plato's idealism and its ethics from Stoicism.

*Christianity: The Fathers and the Schoolmen.* It was mainly through St. Augustine (354–430), Bishop of Hippo in North Africa, that certain of the doctrines of Neoplatonism found their way into Christianity. Augustine also emphasized the concept of God as all good, all wise, all knowing, transcendent, the Creator of the universe out of nothing. But, he added, since God knows everything, everything is determined by Him forever. This is the doctrine of predestination and its subsequent history is discussed under **Determinism**.

In the early centuries of Christianity, as we have seen, some found it difficult to reconcile God's perfection with His creation of the universe and introduced the concept of the *Logos* which many identified with Christ. Further, it came to be held that a power of divine origin permeated the universe, namely the Holy Spirit or Holy Ghost. Some theory had to be worked out to explain the relationships of these three entities whence arose the conception of the Trinity. God is One; but He is also Three: Father, Son (the *Logos* or Christ), and Holy Ghost.

This doctrine was argued by the Apologists and the Modalists. The former maintained that the *Logos* and the Holy Spirit were emanations from God and that Jesus was the *Logos* in the form of a man. The Modalists held that all three Persons of the Trinity were God in three forms or modes; the *Logos* is God creating, the Holy Spirit God reasoning, and God is God being. This led to a long discussion as to whether the *Logos* was an emanation from God or God in another form: was the

*Logos* of like *nature* with God or of the same *substance?* This was resolved at the Council of Nicaea (325) when Athanasius formulated the orthodox doctrine against Arius *(q.v.):* that the one God is a Trinity of the same substance, three Persons of the same nature—Father, Son, and Holy Ghost.

St. Thomas Aquinas (1227–74), influenced greatly by Aristotle's doctrines, set the pattern for all subsequent Catholic belief even to the present time. He produced rational arguments for God's existence: *e.g.,* Aristotle's argument that, since movement exists, there must be a prime mover, the Unmoved Mover or God; further, we can see that things in the universe are related in a scale from the less to the more complex, from the less to the more perfect, and this leads us to suppose that at the peak there must be a Being with absolute perfection. God is the first and final cause of the universe, absolutely perfect, the Creator of everything out of nothing. He reveals Himself in his Creation and rules the universe through His perfect will. How Aquinas dealt with the problem of predestination is told under **Determinism.**

*Break with Medieval Thought.* Renaissance thinkers, free to think for themselves, doubted the validity of the arguments of the Schoolmen but most were unwilling to give up the idea of God (nor would it have been safe to do so). Mystics (*see* **Mysticism**) or near-mystics such as Nicholas of Cusa (*c.* 1401–64) and Jacob Boehme (1575–1624) taught that God was not to be found by reason but was a fact of the immediate intuition of the mystical experience. Giordano Bruno held that God was immanent in the infinite universe. He is the unity of all opposites, a unity without opposites, which the human mind cannot grasp. Bruno was burned at the stake in 1600 at the instigation of the Inquisition (a body which, so we are told, never caused pain to anyone since it was the civil power, not the Inquisition, that carried out the unpleasant sentences) for his heresy.

Francis Bacon, who died in 1626, separated, as was the tendency of that time, science from religion. The latter he divided into the two categories of natural and revealed theology. The former, through the study of nature, may give convincing proof of the existence of a God but nothing more. Of revealed theology he said: "We must quit the small vessel of human reason . . . as we are obliged to obey the divine law, though our will murmurs against it, so we are obliged to believe in the word of God, though our reason is shocked at it." Hobbes (d. 1679) was a complete materialist and one feels that his obeisance to the notion was politic rather than from conviction. However, he does mention God as starting the universe in motion; infers that God is corporeal but denies that His nature can be known.

*From Descartes Onwards.* Descartes (1596–1650) separated mind and body as different entities but believed that the existence of God could be deduced by the fact that the idea of him existed in the mind. Whatever God puts into man, including his ideas, must be real. God is self-caused, omniscient, omnipotent, eternal, all goodness and truth. But Descartes neglected to explain how mind separate from body can influence body, or God separate from the world can influence matter.

Spinoza (1632–77) declared that all existence is embraced in one substance—God, the all-in-all. He was a pantheist and as such was rejected by his Jewish brethren. But Spinoza's God has neither personality nor consciousness, intelligence nor purpose, although all things follow in strict law from His nature. All the thoughts of everyone in the world, make up God's thoughts.

Bishop Berkeley (1685–1753) took the view that things exist only when they are perceived, and this naturally implies that a tree, for example, ceases to exist when nobody is looking at it. This problem was solved to his own satisfaction by assuming that God, seeing everything, prevented objects from disappearing when we were not present. The world is a creation of God but it is a spiritual or mental world, not a material one.

Hume (1711–76), who was a sceptic, held that human reason cannot demonstrate the existence of God and all past arguments to show that it could were fallacious. Yet we must believe in God since the basis of all hope, morality, and society is based upon the belief. Kant (1724–1804) held a theory similar to that of Hume. We cannot know by reason that God exists, nor can we prove on the basis of argument anything about God. But we can form an idea of the whole of the universe, the one Absolute Whole, and personify it. We need the idea of God on which to base our moral life, although this idea of God is transcendent, *i.e.,* goes beyond experience.

William James (1842–1910), the American philosopher (*see* **Pragmatism**), held much the same view: God cannot be proved to exist, but we have a will to believe which must be satisfied, and the idea works in practice. Hegel (1770–1831) thought of God as a developing process, beginning with "the Absolute" or First Cause and finding its highest expression in man's mind, or reason. It is in man that God most clearly becomes aware of Himself. Finally Comte (1798–1857), the positivist, held that religion belongs to a more primitive state of society and, like many modern philosophers, turned the problem over to believers as being none of the business of science.

**Golden Dawn, Order of,** a strange but intellectually influential secret society founded in 1887 by three former Rosicrucians *(q.v.).* The Society, which was but one of the large number of occult organizations which flourished in the latter half of the 19th cent., was particularly interesting because it attracted so many scholarly eccentrics to its ranks. These included the poet W. B. Yeats, the actress Florence Farr, the writers Arthur Machen and Algernon Blackwood and the poetess Dion Fortune. A member with a less savory reputation was the notorious Aleister Crowley who was ultimately expelled from the order for practising Black Magic. Essentially the movement, like others of its kind, professed to offer important secrets of occult knowledge, and taught its followers the basic principles of White, as opposed to Black Magic. Mainly harmless in their aims and activities, societies such as this served largely as pastimes for individuals of intellectual and academic standing who found the concepts and rituals of the Established Church too dull for their inquisitive minds. Most members of the Order of the Golden Dawn, either became disillusioned when the white magic, which they had so arduously studied, failed to provide any genuine supernatural results and gave up in disgust, or broke away to form their own rival groups. Though these often had equally glamorous names and rituals, they tended to be no more successful and themselves vanished into the mists of obscurity. Today so-called White Magic has become fashionable with many young people, no doubt as the result of the almost total collapse

of the authority of orthodox religion, but it is noticeable that such interest is generally to be found among the less well-educated and intelligent. White Magic had its intellectual heyday in the 19th century and it is unlikely ever to attract such sustained academic interest again.

**Good and Evil.**

*Early Philosophers' Views.* The early Greek philosophers were chiefly concerned with the laws of the universe, consequently it was common belief that knowledge of these laws, and living according to them, constituted the supreme good. Heraclitus, for example, who taught that all things carried with them their opposites, held that good and evil were like two notes in a harmony, necessary to each other. "It is the opposite which is good for us". Democritus, like Epicurus *(q.v.),* held that the main goal of life is happiness, but happiness in moderation. The good man is not merely the one who *does* good but who always *wants* to do so: "You can tell the good man not by his deeds alone but by his desires." Such goodness brings happiness, the ultimate goal. On the other hand, many of the wandering Sophist teachers taught that good was merely social convention, that there are no absolute principles of right and wrong, that each man should live according to his desires and make his own moral code. To Socrates knowledge was the highest good because doing wrong is the result of ignorance: "no man is voluntarily bad." Plato and Aristotle, differing in many other respects, drew attention to the fact that man is composed of three parts: his desires and appetites, his will, and his reason. A man whose reason rules his will and appetites is not only a good but a happy man; for happiness is not an aim in itself but a by-product of the good life. Aristotle, however, emphasized the goal of self-realization, and thought that if the goal of life is (as Plato had said) a rational attitude towards the feelings and desires, it needs to be further defined. Aristotle defined it as the "Golden Mean"—the good man is one who does not go to extremes but balances one extreme against another. Thus courage is a mean between cowardice and foolhardiness. The later philosophers Philo and Plotinus held that evil was in the very nature of the body and its senses. Goodness could only be achieved by giving up the life of the senses and, freed from the domination of the body, turning to God, the source of goodness.

*Christian Views.* St. Augustine taught that everything in the universe is good. Even those things which appear evil are good in that they fit with the harmony of the universe like shadows in a painting. Man should turn his back on the pleasures of the world and turn to the love of God. Peter Abelard (1079–1142) made the more sophisticated distinction when he suggested that the wrongness of an act lies not in the act itself, but in the intention of the doer: "God considers not what is done but in what spirit it is done; and the merit or praise of the agent lies not in the deed but in the intention." If we do what we believe to be right, we may err, but we do not sin. The only sinful man is he who deliberately sets out to do what he knows to be wrong. St. Thomas Aquinas agreed with Aristotle in that he believed the highest good to be realization of self as God has ordained, and he also agreed with Abelard that intention is important. Even a good act is not good unless the doer intended it to have good consequences. Intention will not make a bad act good, but it is the only thing that will make a good act genuinely good.

In general, Christianity has had difficulties in solving the problem of the existence of evil; for even when one accepts that the evil men do is somehow tied up with the body, it is still difficult to answer the question: how could an all-good God create evil? This is answered in one of two ways: *(a)* that Adam was given free will and chose to sin (an answer which still does not explain how sin could exist anywhere in the universe of a God who created everything); *(b)* by denying the reality of evil as some Christians have chosen to do (*e.g.,* Christian Science *q.v.*). The Eastern religions, on the other hand (*see* **Zoroastrianism**), solved the problem in a more realistic way by a dualism which denied that their gods were the creators of the whole universe and allowed the existence of at least two gods, one good and one evil. In Christianity there is, of course, a Devil, but it is not explained from where his evil nature came.

*Later Philosophic Views.* Hobbes equated good with pleasure, evil with pain. They are relative to the individual man in the sense that "one man's meat is another man's poison." Descartes believed that the power to distinguish between good and evil given by God to man is not complete, so that man does evil through ignorance. We act with insufficient knowledge and on inadequate evidence. Locke, believing that at birth the mind is a blank slate, held that men get their opinions of right and wrong from their parents. By and large, happiness is good and pain is evil. But men do not always agree over what is pleasurable and what not. Hence laws exist and these fall into three categories: (1) the divine law; (2) civil laws; (3) matters of opinion or reputation which are enforced by the fact that men do not like to incur the disapproval of their friends. We learn by experience that evil brings pain and good acts bring pleasure and, basically, one is good because not to be so would bring discomfort.

Kant (*see* **God and Man**) found moral beliefs to be inherent in man whether or not they can be proved by reason. There is a categorical imperative which makes us realize the validity of two universal laws: (1) "always act in such a way that the maxim determining your conduct might well become a universal law; act so that you can will that everybody shall follow the principle of your action; (2) "always act so as to treat humanity, whether in thine own person or in that of another, in every case as an end and never as a means."

Schopenhauer (1788–1860) was influenced by Buddhism and saw the will as a blind, impelling striving, and desire as the cause of all suffering. The remedy is to regard sympathy and pity as the basis of all morality and to deny one's individual will. This is made easier if we realise that everyone is part of the Universal Will and therefore the one against whom we are struggling is part of the same whole as ourselves.

John Stuart Mill and Jeremy Bentham were both representatives of the Utilitarian school, believing that good is the greatest good (happiness) of the greatest number (*see* **Utilitarianism**). Lastly, there is the view held mostly by political thinkers that good is what is good for the state or society in general.

**Graphology,** the study of the analysis of human handwriting. There are two approaches to this topic and it is important to separate them clearly. The first involves the attempt on the part of an expert to decide from looking at a signature *(a)* to whom it belongs, and *(b)* whether or not it is forgery. This art is a legitimate, though tricky area of study, and graphologists have been called in as expert witnesses in courts of law. The second approach involves attempts to detect such tenuous variables as character from a study of an individual's handwriting, and the facts here are altogether less clear. Psychologists find it difficult enough to assess character or personality in a face-to-face interview and even when they are equipped with a range of special tests. The general opinion here would seem to be that some slight information might be revealed by a careful study of handwriting, but that the overall effect would be too unreliable for this kind of graphology to be of practical value.

**Gurdjieff,** Russian-Greek mystic who set up an occult commune near Paris in the 1930s, to which were attracted a host of the intellectual and literary avant-garde of the time. His teachings, which are immensely obscure, are presented in allegorical form in a lengthy philosophical novel, *All and Everything,* which has the peculiar sub-title "Beelzebub's Tales to his Grandson." Opinions as to the merits of Gurdjieff's ideas are strikingly varied: some commentators hold that he was one of the century's leading philosophers, others that he was a brazen confidence trickster with a vivid personality and the gift of making trivial observations sound pregnant with meaning. The truth probably lies somewhere in between the two extremes and, despite the fact that a number of highly intelligent individuals still espouse his cause two decades after his death, most people continue to find his books largely unreadable and his philosophy muddled and pretentious.

# H

**Homoeopathy,** a branch of fringe medicine whose motto *Similia Similibus Curantur* (like cures like) sums up its controversial approach to therapy. In essence the homoeopathists claim that a disease can be treated by administering quite minute doses of a substance which produce symptoms (in the healthy person) similar to those induced by the disease itself. The founder and popularizer of this unusual approach to medicine was the German Samuel Hahnemann who was born in 1775, a friend of the physician Mesmer who propagated hypnotherapy. Hahnemann lived to see his ideas spread across the civilized world and despite the grave theoretical difficulties implicit in the question of how the very minute dosages actually achieve any result at all, it remained a respectable approach of medicine until the latter half of the last century. Even today a number of qualified doctors still employ homeopathic ideas within the framework of the national health service, and the late King George V was treated by the eminent homoeopathist, Sir John Weir, but it seems nevertheless to be in slow but steady decline. This is probably due not to any revealed deficiencies in homoeopathy itself, but rather to the extraordinary advances which have been made in orthodox medicine in the last few decades.

**Humanism,** the term applied to (1) a system of education based on the Greek and Latin classics; and (2) the vigorous attitudes that accompanied the end of the Middle Ages and were represented at different periods by the Renaissance, the Reformation, the Industrial Revolution, and the struggle for democracy. These include: release from ecclesiastical authority, the liberation of the intellect, faith in progress, the belief that man himself can improve his own conditions without supernatural help and, indeed has a duty to do so. "Man is the measure of all things" is the keynote of humanism. The humanist has faith in man's intellectual and spiritual resources not only to bring knowledge and understanding of the world but to solve the moral problems of how to use that knowledge. That man should show respect to man irrespective of class, race or creed is fundamental to the humanist attitude to life. Among the fundamental moral principles he would count those of freedom, justice, tolerance and happiness.

**I Ching,** the Chinese "Book of Changes" which is supposed to provide a practical demonstration of the truths of ancient Chinese philosophy. The method consists of casting forty-nine sticks into two random heaps, or more simply, of tossing three coins to see if there is a preponderance of heads or tails. The coins are cast six times whereupon the head-tail sequence achieved is referred to a coded series of phrases in the book, which are supposed to relate in some way to the question held in the mind when the sticks or coins are being cast. The phrases are without exception vague, and platitudinous remarks such as "Evil people do not further the perseverance of the superior man," etc., abound. Consequently it is not difficult to read into such amorphous stuff a suitable "interpretation" or answer to one's unspoken question. The I Ching might well be looked upon as an entertaining parlor game, but it is currently a great fad in Europe and America and is taken with great seriousness by an astonishing number of people.

**Idealism,** in a philosophical sense, the belief that there is no matter in the universe, that all that exists is mind or spirit. *See* **Mind and Matter** and **Realism.**

**Illuminati,** a secret society founded in 1776 by Adam Weishaupt, a Bavarian professor of canon law at Ingolstadt, in an attempt to combat superstition and ignorance by founding an association for rational enlightenment and the regeneration of the world. "He tried to give the social ideals of the Enlightenment realization by conspiratorial means" (J. M. Roberts, *The Mythology of the Secret Societies,* 1972). Under conditions of secrecy it sought to penetrate and control the Masonic lodges for subversive purposes. Among its members were Goethe and Schiller. The order spread to Austria, Italy and Hungary but was condemned by the Roman Catholic Church and dissolved in 1785 by the Bavarian government.

**Immortality.** The belief in a life after death has been widely held since the earliest times. It has certainly not been universal, nor has it always taken a form which everyone would find satisfying. In the early stages of human history or prehistory everything contained a spirit (*see* **Animism**) and it is obvious from the objects left in early graves that the dead were expected to exist in some form after death. The experience of dreams, too, seemed to suggest to the unsophisticated that there was a part of man which could leave his body and wander elsewhere during sleep. In order to save space, it will be helpful to classify the various types of belief

which have existed in philosophical thought regarding this problem: (1) There is the idea that, although *something* survives bodily death, it is not necessarily eternal. Thus most primitive peoples were prepared to believe that man's spirit haunted the place around his grave and that food and drink should be set out for it, but that this spirit did not go on forever and gradually faded away. (2) The ancient Greeks and Hebrews believed for the most part that the souls of the dead went to a place of shades there to pine for the world of men. Their whining ghosts spent eternity in a dark, uninviting region in misery and remorse. (3) Other people, and there were many more of these, believed in the transmigration of souls with the former life of the individual determining whether his next life would be at a higher or lower level. Sometimes this process seems to have been thought of as simply going on and on, by others (*e.g.,* in Hinduism and Buddhism) as terminating in either non-sentience or union with God but in any case in annihilation of the self as self. Believers in this theory were the Greek philosophers Pythagoras, Empedocles, Plato (who believed that soul comes from God and strives to return to God, according to his own rather confused notions of the deity. If it fails to free itself completely from the body it will sink lower and lower from one body to another.) Plotinus held similar views to Plato, and many other religious sects in addition to those mentioned have believed in transmigration. (4) The belief of Plato and Aristotle that if souls continue to exist after death there is no reason why they should not have existed before birth (this in part is covered by (3)), but some have pointed out that eternity does not mean "from now on," but the whole of the time before and after "now"—nobody, however, so far as one knows, held that *individual* souls so exist. (5) The theory that the soul does not exist at all and therefore immortality is meaningless: this was held by Anaximenes in early Greek times; by Leucippus, Democritus, and the other Greek atomists; by the Epicureans from the Greek Epicurus to the Roman Lucretius; by the British Hobbes and Hume; by Comte of France; and William James and John Dewey of America. (6) The thesis, held notably by Locke and Kant, that although we cannot prove the reality of soul and immortality by pure reason, belief in them should be held for moral ends. (For the orthodox Christian view *see* **God and Man, Determinism and Free-will.**) From this summary we can see that many philosophies and religions (with the important exceptions of Islam and Christianity) without denying a future life do deny the permanence of the individual soul in anything resembling its earthly form (*see* **Spiritualism, Psychic Research**).

**Jainism.** The Jains are a small Indian sect, largely in commerce and finance, numbering about 2 million. Their movement founded by Vardhamana, called Mahavira (the great hero), in the 6th cent. B.C. arose rather earlier than Buddhism in revolt against the ritualism and impersonality of **Hinduism** *(q.v.).* It rejects the authority of the early Hindu Vedas and does away with many of the Hindu deities whose place is largely taken by Jainism's twenty-four immortal saints; it despises caste distinctions and modifies the two great

Hindu doctrines of *karma* and transmigration. Jain philosophy is based on *ahimsa,* the sacredness of all life, regarding even plants as the brethren of mankind, and refusing to kill even the smallest insect.

**Jehovah's Witnesses,** a religious body who consider themselves to be the present-day representatives of a religious movement which has existed since Abel "offered unto God a more excellent sacrifice than Cain, by which he obtained witness that he was righteous." Abel was the first "witness," and amongst others were Enoch, Noah, Abraham, Moses, Jeremiah, and John the Baptist. Preeminent among witnesses, of course, was Jesus Christ who is described in the Book of Revelation as "the faithful and true witness." Thus they see themselves as "the Lord's organization," in the long line of those who through the ages have preserved on earth the true and pure worship of God or, as the Witnesses prefer to call Him, "Jehovah-God."

So far as other people are aware, the movement was founded by Charles Taze Russell (Pastor Russell) of Allegany, Pittsburgh, in 1881 under the name, adopted in 1896, of the Watch Tower Bible and Tract Society, which has continued as the controlling organization of Jehovah's Witnesses. Its magazine, *The Watch Tower Announcing Jehovah's Kingdom,* first published in 1879, and other publications are distributed by the zealous members who carry out the house-to-house canvassing. The movement has a strong leadership.

Their teaching centers upon the early establishment of God's new world on earth, preceded by the second coming of Christ. Witnesses believe this has already happened and that Armageddon "will come as soon as the Witness is completed." The millenial period will give sinners a second chance of salvation and "millions now living will never die" (the title of one of their pamphlets).

The dead will progressively be raised to the new earth until all the vacant places left after Armageddon are filled. There is, however, some doubt about the "goatish souls" who have made themselves unpleasant to the Witnesses, those who have accepted (or permitted to be accepted) a blood-transfusion contrary to the Scriptures, and others who have committed grave sins.

Every belief held by the movement, it is asserted, can be upheld, chapter and verse, by reference to the Scriptures. Witnesses regard the doctrine of the Trinity as devised by Satan. In both wars Witnesses have been in trouble for their refusal to take part in war, and it is only fair to add that six thousand suffered for the same reason in German concentration camps.

**Jensenism,** name given to the minority group of psychologists and educationalists who, in general, support the view of the American professor, Arthur Jensen. The latter's studies of individual variation in learning and of the genetic factor in mental ability has led him to argue that heredity is more crucial in determining intellectual ability than environment. By implication this has put him and his colleagues at the center of a divisive "race and intelligence" controversy which has acquired some political overtones. In 1978 Professor H. J. Eysenck was physically assaulted by students at a university lecture because he was reputed to be supporting the Jensenist position.

# L

**Lamaism,** the religion of Tibet. Its beliefs and worship derive from the Mahayana form of Buddhism which was introduced into Tibet in 749. The emphasis laid by its founder on the necessity for self-discipline and conversion through meditation and the study of philosophy deteriorated into formal monasticism and ritualism. The Dalai Lama, as the reincarnated Buddha, was both king and high priest, a sort of pope and emperor rolled into one. Under him was a hierarchy of officials in which the lowest order was that of the monks who became as numerous as one man in every six or seven of the population. The main work carried out by this vast church-state was the collection of taxes to maintain the monasteries and other religious offices. Second in power to the Dalai Lama was the Panchen or Tashi Lama believed to be a reincarnation of Amitabha, another Buddha. The last Dalai Lama fled to India in 1959 when the Chinese entered his country. For a brief period following his departure, the Panchen Lama surprised the Western world by publicly welcoming the Communist invasion, but he later renounced the regime and the suppression of Lamaism in Tibet continued unchecked.

**Logical Positivism,** a school of philosophy founded in Vienna in the 1920s by a group known as "the Vienna circle". Their work was based on that of Ernst Mach, but dates in essentials as far back as Hume. Of the leaders of the group, Schlick was murdered by a student; Wittgenstein came to Britain, and Carnap went to America following the entry of the Nazis. Briefly the philosophy differs from all others in that, while most people have believed that a statement might be *(a)* true, or *(b)* false, logical positivists consider there to be a third category; a statement may be meaningless. There are only two types of statement which can be said to have meaning: (1) those which are tautological, *i.e.,* those in which the statement is merely a definition of the subject, such as "a triangle is a three-sided plane figure" ("triangle" and "three-sided plane figure" are the same thing); and (2) those which can be tested by sense experience. This definition of meaningfulness excludes a great deal of what has previously been thought to be the field of philosophy; in particular it excludes the possibility of metaphysics. Thus the question as to whether there is a God or whether free will exists is strictly meaningless for it is neither a tautological statement nor can it be tested by sense experience.

**Luddites,** a group of peasants and working men who deliberately destroyed spinning and farm machinery in England in the early part of the century, fearing that such devices would destroy their livelihood. Their name was taken from the eccentric Ned Lud who had done the same in a less organized way two or three decades earlier. The Luddites' worst fears were of course not realized, for far from putting human beings out of work the Industrial Revolution created jobs for a vastly increased population. Luddism, dormant for over a century, is beginning to appear again, if in muted form. Public anxiety about the rapid growth in computer technology is manifesting itself in the form of such groups as the Society for the Abolition of Data Processing Machines, which while not of course dedicated to the physical destruction of computers, urge for social and even governmental checks on the development of such things as "data banks." These are vast computer memory stores listing comprehensive records concerning all the people living in a city or country and able to cross-reference them in a way that has never previously been possible. The arguments for and against such data banks and other developments in computer technology are beyond the scope of this section, but the rise of this 20th-century Luddism is of considerable historical and social significance.

**Lycanthropy,** the belief that men may, by the exercise of magical powers or because of some inherited affliction, occasionally transform into wolves. The so-called werewolf is an important feature of mid-European folklore and much the same can be said of the were-tigers and were-bears of Africa and the Far East. There is, needless to say, no such thing as a genuine werewolf known to biology, but it is not hard to see how legends of their existence could arise. There are a number of mental illnesses in which men may deliberately or unconsciously mimic the actions of animals and there are a number of endocrinological disorders which may cause gross changes in the features of the individuals, including the excessive growth of hair. In times when the physiological bases of such afflictions were not properly understood, sufferers from such complaints could easily be persuaded, either by themselves or others, that they were in fact wolfmen. Once the mythology of lycanthropy is established in a society, then of course it will be used by unscrupulous individuals for their own ends—for example revenge killings by people dressed as animals—thus helping to perpetuate the legend.

# M

**Magic,** a form of belief originating in very early days and based on the primitive's inability to distinguish between similarity and identity. The simplest example would perhaps be the fertility rites in which it is believed that a ceremony involving sexual relations between men and women will bring about fertility in the harvest. Or the idea that sticking pins in an image of an individual will bring about harm or even death to the real person. Magic is regarded by some as a form of early science in that man in his efforts to control Nature had recourse to magical practices when the only methods he knew had failed to bring the desired results. It filled a gap. By others magic is regarded as an elementary stage in the evolution of religion. It can be said to have served a purpose there too. Yet magic differs from religion, however closely at times it may come to be related with it in this important respect: religion depends upon a power *outside and beyond* human beings, whereas magic depends upon nothing but the casting of a spell or the performance of a ceremony—the result follows automatically.

The idea that "like produces like" is at the roots of imitative magic, and it is interesting to note that in some languages (*e.g.,* Hebrew and Arabic) there is no word for "resembles" or "similar to." Hence one says "All thy garments are myrrh" instead of "are *like* myrrh." It follows that an event can be compelled by imitating it. One engages in swinging, not for pleasure, but to produce a wind as the swing does; ball games are played to get rainy weather because the black ball represents dark

rainclouds; other ball games, in which one attempts to catch the ball in a cup or hit it with a stick, represent the sexual act (as some gentlemen at Lords (cricket grounds, London) may be distressed to hear) and bring about fertility; in medicine until a few centuries ago herbs were chosen to cure a disease because in some respects their leaves or other parts looked like the part of the body affected (*e.g.,* the common wildflower still known as "eyebright" was used in bathing the eyes because the flower looks like a tiny eye). *See* **Witchcraft, Demonism.**

**Malthusianism,** the theory about population growth put forward by the Rev. Thomas Malthus (1766–1834) in *An Essay on Population* (1798). His three main propositions were (1) "Population is necessarily limited by means of subsistence." (2) "Population invariably increases where means of subsistence increase unless prevented by some very powerful and obvious checks." (3) "These checks, and the checks which repress the superior power of population, and keep its effects on a level with the means of subsistence, are all resolvable into moral restraint, vice and misery." In other words, no matter how great the food supply may become, human reproductive power will always adjust itself so that food will always be scarce in relation to population; the only means to deal with this is by "moral restraint" (*i.e.,* chastity or not marrying), "vice" (*i.e.,* birth-control methods), or misery (*i.e.,* starvation). More specifically, Malthus claimed that while food increases by arithmetical progression, population increases by geometrical progression. It is true that these gloomy predictions did not take place in Malthus's time largely owing to the opening up of new areas of land outside Europe, the development of new techniques in agriculture, the growth of international trade to poorer areas, the increased knowledge of birth-control, and developments in medical science which reduced the misery he had predicted. Furthermore, we now know that as a society becomes industrialized its birth-rate tends to fall. Growth in the world's population has increased from about 465 million in 1650 to over 4,500 million in 1982.

**Manichaeism,** an Asiatic religion which developed from Zoroastrianism *(q.v.)* and shows the influence of Buddhism *(q.v.)* and Gnosticism *(q.v.),* being founded by Mani, a Persian who was born in Babylonia, *c.* 216 A.D. Mani presented himself to Shapur I as the founder of a new religion which was to be to Babylonia what Buddhism was to India or Christianity to the West. His aspiration was to convert the East and he himself made no attempt to interfere directly with Christianity although he represented himself as the Paraclete (the Holy Ghost or "Comforter") and, like Jesus, had twelve disciples. His success in Persia aroused the fury of the Zoroastrian priests who objected to his reforming zeal towards their religion and in 276 Mani was taken prisoner and crucified.

Of Mani's complicated system little can be said here, save that it is based on the struggle of two eternal conflicting principles. God and matter, or light and darkness. Although its founder had no intention of interfering with the West, after his death his followers soon spread the religion from Persia and Mesopotamia to India and China. (Manichaeism flourished in China until the 11th cent.) It reached as far as Spain and Gaul and influenced many of the bishops in Alexandria and in Carthage where for a time St. Augustine accepted Manichaeism. Soon the toleration accorded it under Constantine ended and it was treated as a heresy and violently suppressed. Yet it later influenced many heresies, and even had some influence on orthodox Catholicism which had a genius for picking up elements in other religions which had been shown to appeal to worshippers provided they did not conflict unduly with fundamental beliefs.

**Marxism.** The sociological theories founded by Karl Marx and Friedrich Engels on which modern communist thought is based. Marx and Engels lived in a period of unrestrained capitalism when exploitation and misery were the lot of the industrial working classes, and it was their humanitarianism and concern for social justice which inspired their work. Marx wrote his *Communist Manifesto* in Brussels in 1848 and in his great work. *Das Kapital* (1867), he worked out a new theory of society. Marx showed that all social systems are economically motivated and change as a result of technical and economic changes in methods of production. The driving force of social change Marx found to be in the struggle which the oppressed classes wage to secure a better future. Thus in his celebrated theory of historical materialism he interpreted history in terms of economics and explained the evolution of society in terms of class struggle. (*See* **Dialectical Materialism.**) "In the social production of their means of existence," he wrote, "men enter into definite and unavoidable relations which are independent of their will. These productive relationships correspond to the particular stage in the development of their material productive forces." Marx's theory of historical materialism implies that history is propelled by class struggle with communism and the classless society as the final stage when man will have emancipated himself from the productive process. Marx was the first to put socialism on a rational and scientific basis, and he foretold that socialism would inevitably replace capitalism. His prophecy, however, came to realization not in the advanced countries as he had envisaged but in backward Russia and China. *See also* **Communism.**

**Mesmerism,** a rapidly vanishing name to denote the practice of hypnosis, which owes its popularity, though not its discovery, to the Austrian physician, Anton Mesmer (1733–1815). Mesmer's contribution was the realization that a large number of what we would today call psychosomatic or hysterical conditions could be cured (or at least temporarily alleviated) by one or another form of suggestion. Mesmer himself relied on the idea of what he called "animal magnetism," a supposedly potent therapeutic force emanating from the living body which could be controlled by the trained individual. Mesmer used wands and impressive gadgetry to dispense the marvellous force and he effected a remarkable number of cures of complaints, hitherto looked upon as incurable or totally mysterious in origin—the most typical of these being hysterical blindness, paralysis or deafness, nervous skin conditions, and so on. Hypnosis, which is a valid if very poorly understood psychological phenomenon even today, would probably have been developed much further had not efficient general anaesthetics such as ether, nitrous oxide, etc., been discovered, thus greatly diminishing its role as a pain reliever in surgery. Mesmer, who was three parts charlatan, never really troubled to think deeply about the cause of his undoubted success.

The first man to treat hysteria as a formal class of illness and who made a scientific attempt to treat it with hypnosis was Ambrose Liébeault (1823–1904). He and his colleague Hippolyte Bernheim (1840–1919) believed: *(a)* that hysteria was produced by suggestion, and particularly by autosuggestion on the part of the patient, and *(b)* that suggestion was a normal trait found in varying degrees in everyone. These conclusions are true, but as Freud showed later are far from being the whole truth.

**Messianism.** Most varieties of religious belief rely on the assumption that the deity is a supernatural being either permeating the universe or dwelling in some other sphere, and normally inaccessible to man. Where divine intervention is necessary, the deity is traditionally believed to nominate a human being—in the case of Christianity, for example, Jesus is believed to be the actual son of God. Messianic cults introduce a novel variant on the traditional theme. In these a human being is held to be God himself. He may either nominate himself for this role, relying on his own personality or native talent to acquire the necessary following, or for one reason or another large numbers of people may alight on one individual and declare him the Messiah. While it might seem that beliefs of this kind would be confined to earlier epochs in man's recorded history, this is in fact not the case. In the past century, and even within recent decades, a number of individuals have been held by groups to be actually divine. Among these were the Dutchman Lourens van Voorthuizen, a former fisherman who declared himself to be God in 1950 and got large numbers to accept his claim; the Anglican priest Henry James Prince, who did much the same thing in 1850; and of course the famous Negro George Baker, who convinced hundreds of thousands of other Negroes that he was "Father Divine." To simple people the idea that God is to be found on earth and that one may even be personally introduced to him, is an obviously attractive one. The trouble is that all self-styled gods to this present date have sooner or later seriously disappointed their supporters by performing that most human of acts—dying.

**Metapsychology.** Not to be confused with parapsychology *(q.v.).* The branch or off-shoot of psychology which goes beyond empirical and experimental studies to consider such philosophical matters as the nature of mind, the reality of free will and the mind/body problem. It was originally used by Freud as a blanket descriptive term denoting all mental processes, but this usage is now obsolete.

**Methodism,** the religious movement founded by John Wesley in 1738, at a time when the Anglican Church was in one of its periodic phases of spiritual torpor, with the simple aim of spreading "scriptural holiness" throughout the land. Up to that time Wesley had been a High Churchman but on a visit to Georgia in the United States he was much impressed by the group known as Moravians *(q.v.),* and on his return to England was introduced by his brother Charles, who had already become an adherent, to Peter Böhler, a Moravian minister in England. Passing through a period of spiritual commotion following the meeting, he first saw the light at a small service in Aldersgate in May 1738 "where one was reading Luther's preface to the Epistle to the Romans" and from this time forth all Wesley's energies were devoted to the single object of saving souls.

Soon Whitefield, a follower with Calvinist views, was preaching throughout the country and Charles

Wesley was composing his well-known hymns; John's abilities at this time were taken up in organizing the movement described as "People called Methodists." They were to be arranged in "societies" which were united into "circuits" under a minister, the circuits into "districts" and all knit together into a single body under a conference of ministers which has met annually since 1744. Local lay preachers were also employed and to maintain interest the ministers were moved from circuit to circuit each year.

The class-meeting was the unit of the organization where members met regularly under a chosen leader to tell their "experiences" upon which they were often subjected to severe cross-examination.

Methodism, especially after Wesley's death in 1791, began, like other movements, to develop schisms. These were the long-standing differences which the Baptist movement *(q.v.)* had shown too between Arminian and Calvinist sections—*i.e.*, between those who did and those who did not accept the doctrine of predestination. In the case of the Methodists, this led to a complete break in 1811. Then there were differences associated with the status of the laity, or the relationship of the movement with the Anglican Church. The "Methodist New Connection" of 1797 differed only in giving the laity equal representation with the ministers but the more important break of the Primitive Methodists in 1810 gave still more power to the laity and reintroduced the "camp-meeting" type of service. Finally in 1932, at a conference in the Albert Hall in London, the Wesleyan Methodists, the Primitive Methodists, and the United Methodists became one Church, the Methodist Church.

**Mind and Matter.**

*Early Greek Views: Idealism and Dualism.* Primitive peoples could see that there is a distinction between those things which move and do things by themselves and others, such as stones, which do not. Following the early state of **Animism** *(q.v.),* in which spirits were believed to have their abode in everything, they began to differentiate between matter or substance and a force which seems to move it and shape it into objects and things. Thus to the Greek Parmenides (fl. *c.* 475 B.C.), who was a philosopher of pure reason, thought or mind was the creator of what we observe and in some way not quite clear to himself it seemed that mind was the cause of everything. This is perhaps the first expression of the movement known as Idealism which says, in effect, that the whole universe is mental—a creation either of our own minds or the mind of God. But from Anaxagorus (488–428 B.C.) we have the clearer statement that mind or *nous* causes all movement but is distinct from the substance it moves. He does not, however, think in terms of individual minds but rather of a kind of generalized mind throughout the universe which can be used as an explanation of anything which cannot be explained otherwise. This is the position known as Dualism *(q.v.)* which holds that both mind and matter exist and interact but are separate entities.

Most people in practice are dualists since, rightly or wrongly, mind and body are thought of as two different things: it is the "common-sense" (although not necessarily the true) point of view. Plato in a much more complex way was also a dualist although he held that the world of matter we observe is in some sense not the genuine world. The real world is the world of ideas and the tree we see is not real but simply matter upon which

mind or soul has imprinted the idea of a tree. Everything that exists has its corresponding form in the world of ideas and imprints its pattern upon matter. Mind has always existed and, having become entangled with matter, is constantly seeking to free itself and return to God.

Plato's pupil Aristotle had a much more scientific outlook and held that, although it was mind which gave matter its form, mind is not *outside* matter, as Plato had thought, but *inside* it as its formative principle. Therefore there could be no mind without matter and no matter without mind; for even the lowest forms of matter have some degree of mind which increases in quantity and quality as we move up the scale to more complex things.

So far, nobody had explained how two such different substances as matter and mind could influence each other in any way, and this remains, in spite of attempts to be mentioned later, a basic problem in philosophy.

Two later ideas, one of them rather foolish and the other simply refusing to answer the question, are typified by the Stoics and some members of the Sceptic school. The first is that only matter exists and what we call mind is merely matter of a finer texture, a view which as an explanation is unlikely to satisfy anyone; the other, that of some Sceptics, is that we can know nothing except the fleeting images or thoughts that flicker through our consciousness. Of either mind or matter we know nothing.

*Renaissance Attitude.* Christian doctrines have already been dealt with (*see* **God and Man, Determinism and Free-will**), and the past and future of the soul is dealt with under **Immortality.** Nor need we mention the Renaissance philosophers who were really much more concerned about how to use mind than about its nature. When they did consider the subject they usually dealt with it, as did Francis Bacon, by separating the sphere of science from that of religion and giving the orthodox view of the latter because there were still good reasons for not wishing to annoy the Church.

*17th-cent. Views: Hobbes, Descartes, Guelincx, Spinoza, Locke, Berkeley.* Thomas Hobbes in the 17th cent. was really one of the first to attempt a modern explanation of mind and matter even if his attempt was crude. As a materialist he held that all that exists is matter and hence our thoughts, ideas, images, and actions are really a form of motion taking place within the brain and nerves. This is the materialist theory which states that mind does not exist.

Thus there are three basic theories of the nature of mind and body: idealism, dualism, and materialism, and we may accept any one of the three. But, if we accept dualism, we shall have to explain precisely the relationship between body and mind. In some of his later writings Hobbes seems to suggest that mental processes are the effects of motion rather than motion itself; *i.e.*, they exist, but only as a result of physical processes just as a flame does on a candle. This theory of the relationship is known as *epiphenomenalism.*

Descartes, the great French contemporary of Hobbes, was a dualist who believed that mind and matter both exist and are entirely different entities; therefore he had to ask himself how, for example, the desire to walk leads to the physical motion of walking. His unsatisfactory answer was that, although animals are pure automatons, man is different in that he has a soul which resides in the pineal gland (a tiny structure in the brain which today we know to be a relic of evolution with no present function whatever). In this gland the mind comes in contact with the "vital spirits" of the body and thus there is interaction between the two. This theory is known as *interactionism*, and since we do not accept its basis in the function of the pineal gland, we are simply left with the notion of interaction but without the explanation of how it takes place.

One of Descartes's successors, Arnold Guelinex, produced the even more improbable theory of *psychophysical parallelism* sometimes known as the theory of the "two clocks". Imagine you have two clocks, each keeping perfect time, then supposing you saw one and heard the other, every time one points to the hour the other will strike, giving the impression that the first event causes the second, although in fact they are quite unrelated. So it is with the body and mind in Guelinex's view, each is "wound up" by God in the beginning in such a way as to keep time with the other so that when I have the desire to walk, purely unrelated physical events in my legs cause them to move at the same time. A variety of this theory is *occasionism*, which says that whenever something happens in the physical world, God affects us so that we *think* we are being affected by the happening.

The trouble about all these theories is *(a)* that they really explain nothing, and *(b)* that they give us a very peculiar view of God as a celestial showman treating us as puppets when it would surely have been easier to create a world in which mind and matter simply interacted by their very nature. Spinoza, too, believed in a sort of psychophysical parallelism in that he did not think that mind and body interacted. But since in his theory everything is God, mind and matter are simply two sides of the same penny.

John Locke, another contemporary, thought of the mind as a blank slate upon which the world writes in the form of sensations, for we have no innate or inborn ideas and mind and matter do interact although he does not tell us how. All we know are sensations—*i.e.,* sense impressions. Bishop Berkeley carried this idea to its logical conclusion: if we know nothing but sensations, we have no reason to suppose that matter exists at all. He was, therefore, an idealist.

*18th cent. Views: Hume, Kant.* David Hume went further still and pointed out that, if all we know are sensations, we cannot prove the existence of matter but we cannot prove the existence of mind either. All we can ever know is that ideas, impressions, thoughts, follow each other. We do not even experience a self or personality because every time we look into our "minds" all we really experience are thoughts and impressions. Hume was quick to point out that this was not the same as saying that the self did not exist; it only proved that we cannot know that it does.

Kant made it clear that, although there is a world outside ourselves, we can never know what it is really like. The mind receives impressions and forms them into patterns which conform not to the thing-in-itself but to the nature of mind. Space and time, for example, are not realities but only the form into which our mind fits its sensations. In other words our mind shapes impressions which are no more like the thing in itself than the map of a battlefield with pins showing the position of various army groups at any given moment is like the battlefield. This, of course, is true. From physics and physiol-ogy we know that the sounds we hear are "really" waves in the air, the sights we see "really" electromagnetic waves. What guarantee do we have that the source is "really" like the impression received in our brain? Kant was the leader of the great German Idealist movement of the 18th cent. which in effect said: "why bother about matter when all we can ever know is mental?"

*19th and 20th cent. Views.* The Englishman Bradley, and the Frenchman Henri Bergson in the 19th and early 20th cent. both held in one form or another the belief that mind in some way creates matter and were, therefore, idealists, whereas Comte, the positivist *(q.v.),* and the Americans William James and John Dewey, held that mind is a form of behavior. Certain acts (*e.g.,* reflexes) are "mindless" because they are deliberate; others which are intended may be described for the sake of convenience as "minded" (*i.e.,* purposeful). But like the majority of modern psychologists—insofar as they take any interest in the subject—they regarded mind as a process going on in the living body. Is there any reason, many now ask, why we should think of mind as being any different in nature from digestion? Both are processes going on in the body, the one in the brain the other in the stomach and intestines. Why should we regard them as "things"?

**Mithraism,** a sun-religion which originated in Persia with the worship of the mythical Mithra, the god of light and of truth. It was for two centuries one of early Christianity's most formidable rivals, particularly in the West since the more philosophical Hellenic Christianity of the East had little to fear from it. (Arnold Toynbee has described Mithraism as "a pre-Zoroastrian Iranian paganism—in a Hellenic dress"; Manichaeism as "Zoroastrianism—in a Christian dress".) Mithraism was a mystery-faith with secret rites known only to devotees. It appealed to the soldiers of the Roman Army which explains its spread to the farthest limits of the Roman empire and its decline as the Romans retreated. The religion resembled Zoroastrianism *(q.v.)* in that it laid stress on the constant struggle between good and evil and there are a number of parallels with Christianity. *e.g.,* a miraculous birth, death, and a glorious resurrection, a belief in heaven and hell and the immortality of the soul, a last judgment. Both religions held Sunday as the holy day of the week, celebrated 25 December (date of the pagan winter solstice festival) as the birthday of the founder; both celebrated Easter, and in their ceremonies made use of bell, holy water, and the candle. Mithraism reached its height about 275 A.D. and afterwards declined both for the reason given above and, perhaps, because it excluded women, was emotional rather than philosophical, and had no general organization to direct its course. Yet even today, from the Euphrates to the Tyne, traces of the religion remain and antiquarians are familiar with the image of the sun-god and the inscription *Deo Soli Mithrae, Invicto, Seculari* (dedicated to the sungod of Mithra, the unconquered). Mithraism enjoyed a brief revival of popular interest in the mid-1950s when workers excavating the foundations of the skyscraper, Bucklersbury House in the City of London, found the well-preserved remains of a Roman Mithraic temple. A campaign to save the temple as a national monument resulted in its now being on open display on a site in front of the skyscraper.

**Monasticism.** When in the 4th cent. A.D. Constantine

in effect united state and church there were naturally many who hastened to become Christians for the worldly benefits they expected it to bring in view of the new situation. But there were others who, in their efforts to escape from wordly involvement, went into the deserts of North Africa and Syria to live as hermits and so in these regions there grew up large communities of monks whose lives of renunciation made a considerable impression on the Christian world. They were men of all types but the two main groups were those who preferred to live alone and those who preferred a community life. Among the first must be included St. Anthony, the earliest of the hermits, who was born in Egypt *c.* 250 and who lived alone in a hut near his home for fifteen years and then in the desert for a further twenty. As his fame spread Anthony came forth to teach and advocate a life of extreme austerity, until by the end of his life the Thebaid (the desert around Thebes) was full of hermits following his example. (Not unnaturally, he was constantly assailed by lustful visions which he thoughtfully attributed to Satan.) In the Syrian desert St. Simeon Stylites and others were stimulated to even greater austerities and Simeon himself spent many years on the top of a pillar in a space so small that it was only possible to sit or stand. With some of these men it is obvious that ascetic discipline had become perverted into an unpleasant form of exhibitionism.

The first monastery was founded by Pachomius of Egypt *c.* 315 and here the monks had a common life with communal meals, worship, and work mainly of an agricultural type. In the Eastern part of the Empire St. Basil (*c.* 360) tried to check the growth of the extreme and spectacular practices of the hermits by organizing monasteries in which the ascetic disciplines of fasting, meditation, and prayer, would be balanced by useful and healthy activities. His monasteries had orphanages and schools for boys—not only those who were intended for a monkish life. But the Eastern Church in general continued to favor the hermitic life and ascetic extremes. Originally a spontaneous movement, the monastic life was introduced to the West by St. Athanasius in 339 who obtained its recognition from the Church of Rome and St. Augustine introduced it into North Africa beyond Egypt. The movement was promoted also by St. Jerome, St. Martin of Tours, who introduced it into France, and St. Patrick into Ireland. The monastery of Iona was founded by St. Colomba in 566. But it must be remembered that the Celtic Church had a life of its own which owed more to the Egyptian tradition than to Rome. Unlike the more elaborate monasteries of the Continent those of the early Celtic Church were often little more than a cluster of stone beehive huts, an oratory, and a stone cross. It had its own religious ceremonies and its own art (notably its beautifully carved crosses and the illuminated manuscripts such as the Lindisfarne Gospel (*c.* 700) and the Irish Book of Kells dating from about the same time). The Scottish St. Ninian played a major part in introducing Egyptian texts and art to Britain where, mixed with Byzantine influences and the art of the Vikings, it produced a typical culture of its own. Strangely enough, it was the relatively primitive Celts who played almost as large a part in preserving civilization in Europe during the Dark Ages as the Italians have since. It was St. Columbanus (*c.* 540–615) who founded the great monasteries of Annegray, Luxeuil, and Fontaine in the Vosges country, St. Gall in Switzer-

land, and Bobbio in the Apennines. So, too, it was the Anglo-Saxon Alcuin (*c.* 735–804) who was called from York by Charlemagne to set up a system of education throughout his empire; the most famous of the monastic schools he founded was at Tours. Among those influenced by him was the philosopher John Scotus Erigena.

Meanwhile from the south, as the disintegrating Roman empire became increasingly corrupt, St. Benedict of Nursia (*c.* 480–*c.* 543) fled the pleasures of Rome to lead a hermit's life near Subiaco. Here he founded some small monasteries, but *c.* 520 made a new settlement, the great monastery of Monte Cassino in southern Italy, where he established a "Rule" for the government of monks. This included both study and work and emphasized that education was necessary for the continuance of Christianity. As his influence spread his Rule was adopted by other monasteries, and schools became part of monastic life. It is not possible to describe the many different orders of monks and nuns formed since, nor the mendicant orders of friars (*e.g.,* Franciscans, Dominicans, Carmelites, Augustinians). Outside the Roman Catholic Church, both Eastern Orthodox and Anglican Christians owe much to the monastic movement. Monasticism, of course, is not peculiar to Christianity and forms a major aspect of Buddhism, especially in the form of Lamaism in Tibet (*q.v.*).

**Monophysitism,** a heresy of the 5th cent. which grew out of a reaction against Nestorianism (*q.v.*). The majority of Egyptian Christians were Monophysites (Mono-physite = one nature)—*i.e.* they declared Christ's human and divine nature to be one and the same. This view was condemned at the Council of Chalcedon (A.D. 451) which pronounced that Jesus Christ, true God and true man, has two natures, at once perfectly distinct and inseparably joined in one person and partaking of the one divine substance. However, many continued to hold Monophysite opinions, including the Coptic Church (*q.v.*), declaring the Council to be unoecumenical (*i.e.* not holding the views of the true and universal Christian Church).

**Mormons,** or **Latter-day Saints,** one of the very numerous American religious sects; founded in 1830 by Joseph Smith, the son of a Vermont farmer, who, as a youth, had been influenced by a local religious revival though confused by the conflicting beliefs of the various denominations. He said that while praying for guidance he had been confronted by two heavenly messengers who forbade him to join any existing church but prepare to become the prophet of a new one. Soon, in a series of visions, he was told of a revelation written on golden plates concealed in a nearby hillside. These he unearthed in 1827 and with the help of "Urim and Thummin" translated the "reformed Egyptian" characters into English. Described as the *Book of Mormon,* this was published in 1830 and at the same time a little church of those few who accepted his testimony was founded in Fayette, N.Y. In addition the first of Joseph Smith's "miracles"—the casting out of a devil—was performed. The *Book of Mormon* purports to be a record of early American history and religion, the American Indians being identified as the ten Lost Tribes of Israel, whose fate has never failed to attract the attention of those who prefer myth to fact (cf. British Israelites). Jesus Christ is alleged to have appeared in America after His ascension. Yet Smith's eloquence was able to influence quite educated people, including Sidney Rigdon with whom he went into business for a time. *Doctrine and Covenants* is the title of another book dealing with the revelations Smith claimed to have received. Soon the sect was in trouble with the community both because its members insisted on describing themselves as the Chosen People and others as Gentiles and because they took part in politics, voting as Smith ordered them to. Smith was constantly in trouble with the police. Therefore they were turned out from one city after another until they found themselves a dwelling-place at Nauvoo, Illinois, on the Mississippi.

That would probably have been the end of the story had not Smith been murdered in 1844 and thereby made to appear a martyr, and had there not appeared Brigham Young, a quite extraordinary leader, who stamped out warring factions and drove out the recalcitrant. While persecutions continued Brigham Young announced that it had been revealed that he must lead the faithful to Salt Lake, then outside the area of the United States. There followed the famous trek of more than a thousand miles across desert country in which he led the way, reaching his journey's end in the forbidding valley of the Great Salt Lake on 24 July 1847. By 1851 30,000 Mormons had reached the Promised Land. Here they held their own in a hostile environment and under the practical genius of their leader carried through a vast irrigation scheme and built Salt Lake City which still serves as the headquarters of their sect. In 1850 their pioneer settlement was made Utah Territory, and in 1896 incorporated in the Union. The church was strictly ruled by its leader who also looked after affairs of state for thirty years until his death in 1877.

Polygamy, although opposed by some Mormons, and only sanctioned by Brigham Young when Salt Lake City had been built, is the best-known of Mormon doctrines. It brought the sect into much disrepute and was renounced in 1880. Mormons are millenarians, believing that some time Christ will appear and rule for a thousand years.

Members of the Church of Jesus Christ of Latter-day Saints now number over three million in congregations throughout the world.

The Reorganized Church of Jesus Christ of Latter-day Saints with its headquarters at Independence, Missouri, has been separate and distinct since 1852.

**Mysticism,** a religious attitude which concerns itself with direct relationship with God, "reality" as contrasted with appearance or the "ultimate" in one form or another. All the higher religions have had their mystics who have not always been regarded without suspicion by their more orthodox members, and, as Bertrand Russell points out, there has been a remarkable unity of opinion among mystics which almost transcends their religious differences. Thus, characteristic of the mystical experience in general, have been the following features; (1) a belief in insight as opposed to analytical knowledge which is accompanied in the actual experience by the sense of a mystery unveiled, a hidden wisdom become certain beyond the possibility of doubt: this is often preceded by a period of utter hopelessness and isolation described as "the dark night of the soul"; (2) a belief in unity and a refusal to admit opposition or division anywhere; this sometimes appears in the form of what seem to be contradictory statements: "the way up

and the way down is one and the same" (Heraclitus). There is no distinction between subject and object, the act of perception and the thing perceived; (3) a denial of the reality of time, since if all is one the distinction of past and future must be illusory; (4) a denial of the reality of evil (which does not maintain, *e.g.,* that cruelty is good but that it does not exist in the world of reality as opposed to the world of phantoms from which we are liberated by the insight of the vision). Among the great mystics have been Meister Eckhart and Jakob Boehme, the German religious mystics of the 13th and 16th cent. respectively, Acharya Sankara of India, and St. Theresa and St. John of the Cross of Spain. Mystical movements within the great religions have been: the Zen *(q.v.)* movement within Buddhism; Taoism in China; the Cabalists and Hasidim in Judaism; the Sufis within Islam; some of the Quakers within Christianity.

**Mystery Religions.** *See* **Orphism.**

---

# N

**Natural Law,** the specifically Roman Catholic doctrine that there is a natural moral law, irrespective of time and place, which man can know through his own reason. Originally a product of early rational philosophy, the Christian form of the doctrine is basically due to St. Thomas Aquinas who defined natural law in relation to eternal law, holding that the eternal law is God's reason which governs the relations of all things in the universe to each other. The natural law is that part of the eternal law which relates to man's behavior. Catholic natural law assumes that the human reason is capable of deriving ultimate rules for right behavior, since there are in man and his institutions certain stable structures produced by God's reason which man's reason can know to be correct and true. Thus, the basis of marriage, property, the state, and the contents of justice are held to be available to man's natural reason. The rules of positive morality and civil law are held to be valid only insofar as they conform to the natural law, which man is not only capable of knowing but also of obeying.

Protestant theologians criticize this notion. Thus Karl Barth and many others hold that sinful and fallen man cannot have any direct knowledge of God or His reason or will without the aid of revelation. Another theologian, Reinhold Niebuhr, points out that the principles of the doctrines are too inflexible and that although they are the product of a particular time and circumstance, they are regarded as if they were absolute and eternal. In fact, as most social scientists would also agree, there is no law which can be regarded as "natural" for all men at all times. Nor does it seem sensible to suppose that all or even many men possess either the reason to discern natural law or the ability to obey it; whether or not we accept man's free will (and all Protestant sects do not), we know as a fact of science that people are not always fully responsible for their actions and some not at all.

**Nazism,** the term commonly used for the political and social ideology of the German National Socialist Party inspired and led by Hitler. The term *Nazi* was an abbreviation of *Nazional-socialistische Deutsche Arbeiterpartei.* Those in the Federal Republic today sympathetic to National Socialist aims are known as neo-Nazis. *See* **Fascism.**

**Neoplatonism.** *See* **Determinism and Free Will** and **God and Man.**

**Nestorian Heresy.** The 5th cent. of the Christian Church saw a battle of personalities and opinions waged with fanatical fury between St. Cyril, the patriarch of Alexandria, and Nestorius, patriarch of Constantinople. Nestorius maintained that Mary should not be called the mother of God, as she was only the mother of the human and not of the divine nature of Jesus. This view was contradicted by Cyril (one of the most unpleasant saints who ever lived) who held the orthodox view. In addition to his utter destruction of Nestorius by stealthy and unremitting animosity Cyril was also responsible for the lynching of Hypatia, a distinguished mathematician and saintly woman, head of the Neoplatonist school at Alexandria. She was dragged from her chariot, stripped naked, butchered and torn to pieces in the church, and her remains burned. As if this were not enough Cyril took pains to stir up pogroms against the very large Jewish colony of Alexandria. At the Council of Ephesus (A.D. 431) the Western Bishops quickly decided for Cyril. This Council (reinforced by the Council of Chalcedon in 451) clarified orthodox Catholic doctrine (*see* **Monophysitism**). Nestorius became a heretic, was banished to Antioch where he had a short respite of peace, but later, and in spite of his weakness and age, was dragged about from one place to another on the borders of Egypt. We are assured that his tongue was eaten by worms in punishment for the wicked words he had spoken, but later the Nestorian church flourished in Syria and Persia under the protection of the rulers of Persia and missions were sent to India and China.

**Nihilism,** the name commonly given to the earliest Russian form of revolutionary anarchism. It originated in the early years of Tsar Alexander II (1818–81), the liberator of the serfs, who, during his attempts to bring about a constitutional monarchy, was killed by a bomb. The term "nihilist", however, was first used in 1862 by Turgenev in his novel *Fathers and Children. See* **Anarchism.**

**Nominalism.** Early medieval thinkers were divided into two schools, those who regarded "universals" or abstract concepts as mere names without any corresponding realities (Nominalists), and those who held the opposite doctrine **(Realism)** that general concepts have an existence independent of individual things. The relation between universals and particulars was a subject of philosophical dispute all through the Middle Ages.

The first person to hold the nominalist doctrine was probably Roscelin or Roscellinus in the late 11th cent., but very little is known of him and none of his works remains except for a single letter to Peter Abelard who was his pupil. Roscelin was born in France, accused twice of heresy but recanted and fled to England where he attacked the views of Anselm, according to whom Roscelin used the phrase that universals were a *flatus voci* or breath of the voice. The most important nominalist was the Englishman William of Occam in the 13th cent. who, once and for all, separated the two schools by saying in effect that science is about things (the nominalist view) whereas logic, philosophy, and religion are about terms or concepts (the Platonic tradition). Both are justified, but we must distinguish between them. The proposition "man is a species" is not a proposition of logic or philosophy but a scientific statement since we cannot say whether it is true or false without knowing about man. If we fail to realize that words are conventional signs and that it is important to decide whether or not they have a meaning and refer to something, then we shall fall into logical fallacies of the type: "Man is a species, Socrates is a man, therefore Socrates is a species." This, in effect, is the beginning of the modern philosophy of logical analysis which, to oversimplify, tells us that a statement is not just true or untrue, it may also be meaningless. Therefore, in all the philosophical problems we have discussed elsewhere there is the third possibility that the problem we are discussing has no meaning because the words refer to nothing and we must ask ourselves before going any further "what do we mean by God", and has the word "free will" any definite meaning?

# O

**Occam's Razor,** the philosophical maxim by which William of Occam, the 14th cent. Franciscan has become best-known. This states in the form which is most familiar: "Entities are not to be multiplied without necessity" and as such does not appear in his works. He did, however, say something much to the same effect: "It is vain to do with more what can be done with fewer." In other words, if everything in some science can be interpreted without assuming this or that hypothetical entity, there is no ground for assuming it. This is Bertrand Russell's version and he adds: "I have myself found this a most fruitful principle in logical analysis."

**Occultism.** *see,* **Alchemy, Astrology,** and **Theosophy.**

**Orgonomy,** a pseudo-psychological theory advanced by the German psychiatrist Wilhelm Reich (1897–1957), a pupil of Freud, who was expelled from Germany for attacking the Nazis and who started life afresh in the U.S.A. like so many of his colleagues. Moving quickly away from orthodox psychoanalytic theories, Reich became increasingly obsessed with the view that all living things were permeated with a unique force or energy which he termed "orgone" and which he believed could be photographed and measured with a geiger counter. The key to the successful flow of orgone throughout the body was sexual intercourse and the resulting orgasm (hence "orgone"). Reich achieved a substantial following for his increasingly bizarre views and when he was sentenced to two-years' imprisonment in 1956 for alleged medical malpractice a "civil rights" controversy developed which has not died down to this date. His unfortunate and rather tragic death in prison has fanned the emotional issues and granted him the important role of martyr to his cause. There is currently a strong revival of interest in Reich and orgonomy, partly in tune with the general occult revival. A recent witty, but not totally unsympathetic film about his work "W R—Mysteries of the Organism" has drawn the attention of a large new audience to his teachings.

**Orphism.** The Greeks in general thought very little of their gods, regarding them as similar human beings with human failings and virtues although on a larger scale. But there was another aspect of Greek religion which was passionate, ecstatic, and secret, dealing with the worship of various figures among whom were Bacchus or Dionysus, Orpheus, and Demeter and Persephone of the Eleusinian Mysteries. Dionysus (or Bacchus) was originally a god from Thrace where the people were primitive farmers naturally interested in fertility cults. Dionysus was the god of fertility who only later came to be associated with wine and the divine madness it produces. He assumed the form of a man or a bull and his worship by the time it arrived in Greece became associated with women (as was the case in most of the Mystery Religions) who spent nights on the hills dancing and possibly drinking wine in order to stimulate ecstasy; an unpleasant aspect of the cult was the tearing to pieces of wild animals whose flesh was eaten raw. Although the cult was disapproved of by the orthodox and, needless to say, by husbands, it existed for a long time.

This primitive and savage religion in time was modified by that attributed to Orpheus whose cult was more spiritualized, ascetic, and substituted mental for physical intoxication. Orpheus may have been a real person or a legendary hero and he, too, is supposed to have come from Thrace, but his name indicates that he, or the movement associated with him, came from Crete and originally from Egypt, which seems to have been the source of many of its doctrines. Crete, it must be remembered, was the island through which Egypt influenced Greece in other respects. Orpheus is said to have been a reformer who was torn to pieces by the Maenad worshippers of Dionysus. The Orphics believed in the transmigration of souls and that the soul after death might obtain either eternal bliss or temporary or permanent torment according to its way of life upon earth. They held ceremonies of purification and the more orthodox abstained from animal food except on special occasions when it was eaten ritually. Man is partly earthly, partly heavenly, and a good life increases the heavenly part so that, in the end, he may become one with Bacchus and be called a "Bacchus".

The religion had an elaborate theology. As the Bacchic rites were reformed by Orpheus, so the Orphic rites were reformed by Pythagoras (c. 582 –c. 507 B.C.) who introduced the mystical element into Greek philosophy, which reached its heights in Plato. Other elements entered Greek life from Orphism. One of these was feminism which was notably lacking in Greek civilization outside the Mystery Religions. The other was the drama which arose from the rites of Dionysus. The mysteries of Eleusis formed the most sacred part of the Athenian state religion, and it is clear that they had to do with fertility rites also, for they were in honour of Demeter and Persephone and all the myths speak of them as being associated with the supply of corn to the country. Without being provocative, it is accepted by most anthropologists and many theologians that Christianity, just as it accepted elements of Gnossticism and Mithraism, accepted elements from the Mystery Religions as they in turn must have done from earlier cults. The miraculous birth, the death and resurrection the sacramental feast of bread and wine, symbolizing the eating of the flesh and drinking of the blood of the god, all these are common elements in early religions and not just in one. None of this means that what we are told about Jesus is not true, but it surely does mean: (a) that Christianity was not a sudden development; (b) that the early Church absorbed many of the elements of other religions; (c) that perhaps Jesus Himself made use of certain symbols which He knew had a timeless significance for man and invested them with new meaning.

# P

**Pantheism.** *See* **God and Man.**

**Papal Infallibility.** The basis of papal infallibility is *(a)* that every question of morals and faith is not dealt with in the Bible so it is necessary that there should be a sure court of appeal in case of doubt, and this was provided by Christ when he established the Church as His Teaching Authority upon earth; *(b)* ultimately this idea of the teaching function of the Church shapes the idea of papal infallibility which asserts that the Pope, when speaking officially on matters of faith or morals, is protected by God against the possibility of error. The doctrine was proclaimed in July 1870.

Infallibility is a strictly limited gift which does not mean that the Pope has extraordinary intelligence, that God helps him to find the answer to every conceivable question, or that Catholics have to accept the Pope's views on politics. He can make mistakes or fall into sin, his scientific or historical opinions may be quite wrong, he may write books that are full of errors. Only in two limited spheres is he infallible and in these only when he speaks officially as the supreme teacher and lawgiver of the Church, defining a doctrine that must be accepted by all its members. When, after studying a problem of faith or morals as carefully as possible, and with all available help from expert consultants, he emerges with the Church's answer—on these occasions it is not strictly an answer, it is *the* answer.

Historically speaking, the Roman Catholic Church of the early 19th century was at its lowest ebb of power. Pope Pius IX, in fear of Italian nationalism, revealed his reactionary attitude by the feverish declaration of new dogmas, the canonization of new saints, the denunciation of all modern ideals in the Syllabus of Errors, and the unqualified defence of his temporal power against the threat of Garibaldi. It is not too much to say that everything regarded as important by freedom-loving and democratic people was opposed by the papacy at that time. In 1870, after a long and sordid struggle, the Vatican Council, convened by Pius IX, pronounced the definition of his infallibility. Döllinger, a German priest and famous historian of the Church, was excommunicated because, like many others, he refused to accept the new dogma. It is difficult not to doubt that there was some connection between the pronouncement of the Pope's infallibility and his simultaneous loss of temporal power.

After the humanism of the Second Vatican Council (1962–5) Pope Paul's encyclical *Humanae Vitae* (1968), condemning birth control, came as a great disappointment to the many people (including theologians, priests, and laymen) who had expected there would be a change in the Church's teaching. The Church's moral guidance on this controversial issue, however, does not involve the doctrine of infallibility. (The Roman Catholic Church teaches that papal pronouncements are infallible only when they are specifically defined as such.) That there is unlikely to be any immediate softening of the Church's line on infallibility was made clear in July 1973 when the Vatican's Sacred Congregation for the Doctrine of the Faith published a document strongly reaffirming papal infallibility. The document also reminded Catholics of their obligation to accept the Catholic Church's unique claims to authenticity.

**Parapsychology,** the name given to the study of psychical research *(q.v.)* as an academic discipline, and chosen to denote the topic's supposed status as a branch of psychology. The impetus behind parapsychology came from the psychologist William MacDougall who persuaded Duke University in North Carolina to found a department of parapsychology under J. B. Rhine. Throughout the 1930s and '40s the work of Rhine and his colleagues, who claimed to have produced scientific evidence for the existence of ESP, attracted worldwide attention. Increasing reservations about the interpretation of Rhine's results and an apparent lack of any readily repeatable experiments, however, gradually eroded scientific confidence in the topic. The academic status of parapsychology is at the present time exceedingly uncertain. Rhine retired from university life in 1965 and the world-famous parapsychology laboratory at Duke University was closed. On the other hand the American Association for the Advancement of Science recently admitted the Parapsychology Association (the leading organization for professional parapsychologists) as an affiliated member society. An American government body, the National Institute of Mental Health, has also officially supported some medical research into alleged telepathic dreams, the first "official" grant support of this kind. In Britain a poll of readers in the weekly journal, *New Scientist,* revealed a very high interest in the subject matter of parapsychology, and active research is currently going on at the Dept. of Psychology at Cambridge. Stories of intensive parapsychological research in Soviet Russia are however without foundation and are not supported by Western parapsychologists who have visited Russia.

**Parsees.** *See* **Zoroastrianism.**

**Pavlovian theory.** *See* **Behaviorism.**

**Pentecostalism,** a religious movement within the Protestant churches, holding the belief that an essential feature of true Christianity is a vigorous and profound spiritual or mystical experience which occurs after, and seemingly reinforces the initial conversion. The origins of modern Pentecostalism appear to lie in the occasion on 1 January 1901 when a member of a Bible College in Topeka, Kansas, one Agnes N. Ozman, spontaneously began to speak in an apparently unknown language at one of the college's religious meetings. This "speaking in tongues" was assumed to be evidence of her conversion and "spirit baptism", and became a feature of most Pentecostal meetings in due course. The movement spread rapidly across America, particularly in rural communities, and also was a strong feature of Welsh religious life in the early part of the century. Pentecostal services are enthusiastic and rousing with a strong emphasis on music and participation on the part of the congregation. Pentecostalism is evangelistic in nature and seems to be gaining in strength at the present time, at the expense of more orthodox and staid versions of Christianity. The fiery character Aimee Semple McPherson was one of its most prominent evangelists.

**Phrenology,** a psychological "school" founded in 1800 by two Germans, Franz Josef Gall and Johann Gaspar Spurzheim. Gall was an anatomist who believed there to be some correspondence between mental faculties and the shape of the head.

He tested these ideas in prisons and mental hospitals and began to lecture on his findings, arousing a great deal of interest throughout both Europe and America, where his doctrines were widely accepted. Phrenology became fashionable, and people would go to "have their bumps read" as later men and women of fashion have gone to be psychoanalyzed. Roughly speaking, Gall divided the mind into thirty-seven faculties such as destructiveness, suavity, self-esteem, conscientiousness, and so on, and claimed that each of these was located in a definite area of the brain. He further claimed that the areas in the brain corresponded to "bumps" on the skull which could be read by the expert, thus giving a complete account of the character of the subject. In fact, *(a)* no such faculties are located in the brain anywhere, for this is simply not the way the brain works; *(b)* the faculties described by Gall are not pure traits which cannot be further analysed and are based on a long outdated psychology; *(c)* the shape of the brain bears no specific relationship to the shape of the skull. Phrenology is a pseudo-science; there is no truth in it whatever. But, even so, like astrology, it still has its practitioners.

**Physiocrats.** A French school of economic thought during the 18th cent., known at the time as *Les Economistes* but in later years named physiocrats by Du Pont de Nemours, a member of the School. Other members were Quesnay, Mirabeau, and the great financier Turgot. The physiocrats held the view, common to the 18th cent., and deriving ultimately from Rousseau, of the goodness and bounty of nature and the goodness of man "as he came from the bosom of nature". The aim of governments, therefore, should be to conform to nature; and so long as men do not interfere with each other's liberty and do not combine among themselves, governments should leave them free to find their own salvation. Criminals, madmen, and monopolists should be eliminated. Otherwise the duty of government is *laissez-faire, laissez passer.* From this follows the doctrine of free trade between nations on grounds of both justice and economy; for the greater the competition the more will each one strive to economize the cost of his labour to the general advantage. Adam Smith, although not sharing their confidence in human nature, learned much from the physiocrats, eliminated their errors, and greatly developed their teaching.

**Physiognomy.** *See* **Characterology.**

**Plymouth Brethren,** a religious sect founded by John Nelson Darby, a minister of the Protestant Church of Ireland, and Edward Cronin a former Roman Catholic, in 1827. Both were dissatisfied with the lack of spirituality in their own and other churches and joined together in small meetings in Dublin every Sunday for "the breaking of bread". Soon the movement began to spread through Darby's travels and writings and he finally settled in Plymouth, giving the popular name to the "Brethren". Beginning as a movement open to all who felt the need to "keep the unity of the Spirit", it soon exercized the right to exclude all who had unorthodox views and split up into smaller groups. Among these the main ones were the "Exclusives", the Kellyites, the Newtonites, and "Bethesda" whose main differences were over problems of church government or prophetical powers. Some of these are further split among themselves. Readers of *Father and Son* by Sir Edmund Gosse, which describes life with his father, the eminent naturalist Philip Gosse, who belonged to the Brethren, will recall how this basically kind, honest, and learned man was led through their teachings to acts of unkindness (*e.g.,* in refusing to allow his son and other members of his household to celebrate Christmas and throwing out the small tokens they had secretly bought), and lack of scientific rigor (*e.g.,* in refusing for religious reasons alone to accept Darwinism when all his evidence pointed towards it).

Today, the majority of Brethren belong to the "Open Brethren" assemblies and, unlike the "Exclusives" hold that the Lord's Supper (a commemorative act of "breaking the bread" observed once a week) is for all Christians who care to join them. Baptism is required and Brethren believe in the personal premillennial second coming of Christ.

**Poltergeist,** allegedly a noisy type of spirit which specializes in throwing things about, making loud thumpings and bangings, and occasionally bringing in "apports", *i.e.,* objects from elsewhere. Most so-called poltergeist activities are plain frauds, but the others are almost invariably associated with the presence in the house of someone (often, but not always a child) who is suffering from an adolescent malaise or an epileptic condition. The inference is that those activities which are not simply fraudulent are either due to some unknown influence exuded by such mentally disturbed people, or that they are actually carried out by ordinary physical means by such people when in an hysterical state—*i.e.,* unconsciously. The second hypothesis is much the more probable. *See* **Psychic Research.**

**Polytheism.** *See* **God and Man.**

**Positivism,** also known as the **Religion of Humanity,** was founded by Auguste Comte (1798–1857), a famous mathematician and philosopher born in Montpellier, France. His views up to the end of the century attracted many and it would have been impossible throughout that time to read a book on philosophy or sociology that did not mention them, but today his significance is purely of historical interest. In his *Cours de Philosophie Positive* (1830) he put forward the thesis that mankind had seen three great stages in human thought: (1) the theological, during which man seeks for supernatural causes to explain nature and invents gods and devils; (2) the metaphysical, through which he thinks in terms of philosophical and metaphysical abstractions; (3) the last positive or scientific stage when he will proceed by experimental and objective observation to reach in time "positive truth".

Broadly speaking, there is little to complain of in this analysis; for there does seem to have been some sort of general direction along these lines. However, Comte was not satisfied with having reached this point and felt that his system demanded a religion and, of course, one that was "scientific". This religion was to be the worship of Humanity in place of the personal Deity of earlier times, and for it he supplied not only a Positive Catechism but a treatise on Sociology in which he declared himself the High Priest of the cult. Since, as it stood, the religion was likely to appear somewhat abstract to many, Comte drew up a list of historical characters whom he regarded as worthy of the same sort of adoration as Catholics accord to their saints. The new Church attracted few members, even among those who had a high regard for Comte's scientific work, and its only significant adherents were a small group of Oxford scholars and some in his own country. Frederic Harrison was the best-known English adherent and throughout his life continued to preach Comtist doctrines in London to diminishing audiences.

**Pragmatism,** a typically American school of philosophy which comes under the heading of what Bertrand Russell describes as a "practical" as opposed to a "theoretical" philosophy. Whereas the latter, to which most of the great philosophical systems belong, seeks disinterested knowledge for its own sake, the former *(a)* regards action as the supreme good, *(b)* considers happiness an effect and knowledge a mere instrument of successful activity.

The originator of pragmatism is usually considered to have been the psychologist William James (1842–1910) although he himself attributed its basic principles to his life-long friend, the American philosopher, Charles Sanders Peirce (1839–1914). The other famous pragmatist is John Dewey, best-known in Europe for his works on education (for although American text-books on philosophy express opinions to the contrary, few educated people in Europe have taken the slightest interest in pragmatism and generally regard it as an eccentricity peculiar to Americans). James in his book *The Will to Believe* (1896) points out that we are often compelled to take a decision where no adequate theoretical grounds for a decision exist; for even to do nothing is to decide. Thus in religion we have a right to adopt a believing attitude although not intellectually fully convinced. We should believe truth and shun error, but the failing of the sceptical philosopher is that he adheres only to the latter rule and thus fails to believe various truths which a less cautious man will accept. If believing truth and avoiding error are equally important, then it is a good idea when we are presented with an alternative to believe one of the possibilities at will, since we then have an even chance of being right, whereas we have none if we suspend judgment. The function of philosophy, according to James, is to find out what difference it makes to the individual if a particular philosophy or world-system is true: "An idea is 'true' so long as to believe it is profitable to our lives" and, he adds, the truth is only the expedient in our way of thinking . . . in the long run and on the whole of course". Thus "if the hypothesis of God works satisfactorily in the widest sense of the word, it is true". Bertrand Russell's reply to this assertion is: "I have always found that the hypothesis of Santa Claus 'works satisfactorily in the widest sense of the word'; therefore 'Santa Claus exists' is true, although Santa Claus does not exist." Russell adds that James's concept of truth simply omits as unimportant the question whether God really *is* in His heaven; if He is a useful hypothesis that is enough. "God the Architect of the Cosmos is forgotten; all that is remembered is belief in God, and its effects upon the creatures inhabiting our petty planet. No wonder the Pope condemned the pragmatic defence of religion."

**Predestination.** *See* **Calvinism.**

**Presbyterianism,** a system of ecclesiastical government of the Protestant churches which look back to John Calvin as their Reformation leader. The ministry consists of presbyters who are all of equal rank. Its doctrinal standards are contained in the *Westminster Confession of Faith* (1647) which is, in general, accepted by English, Scottish, and American Presbyterians as the most thorough and logical statement in existence of the Calvinist creed.

The Presbyterian tradition includes uncompromising stress upon the Word of God contained in the Scriptures of the Old and New Testaments as the supreme rule of faith and life, and upon the value of a highly trained ministry, which has given the Church of Scotland a high reputation for scholarship and has in turn influenced the standard of education in Scotland. The unity of the Church is guaranteed by providing for democratic representation in a hierarchy of courts (unlike the Anglican Church, which is a hierarchy of persons). The local kirk session consists of the minister and popularly elected elders (laymen). Ministers, elected by their flocks, are ordained by presbyters (ministers already ordained). Above the kirk session is the court of the presbytery which has jurisdiction over a specified area; above that the court of synod which rules over many presbyteries; and finally the General Assembly which is the Supreme Court of the Church with both judicial and legislative powers, and over which the Moderator of the General Assembly presides. The function of the elders is to help the minister in the work and government of the kirk. The episcopacy set up by James VI and I, and maintained by Charles I was brought to an end by the Glasgow Assembly (1638), but General Assemblies were abolished by Oliver Cromwell and at the Restoration Charles II re-established episcopacy. The Covenanters who resisted were hunted down, imprisoned, transported, or executed over a period of nearly thirty years before William of Orange came to the throne and Presbyterianism was re-established (1690). Today Presbyterians no less than other Christian communities are looking at Christianity as a common world religion in the sense that the principles which unite them are greater than those which divide them. A small but significant step in the direction of international Christian unity was made in 1972 when the Presbyterian and Congregationalist Churches in England were merged to form the United Reformed Church. *See* **Calvinism.**

**Psychic Research** is a general term for the various approaches to the scientific investigation of the paranormal, in particular supposed extrasensory powers of the mind, but also manifestations such as ghosts, poltergeists, spiritualistic phenomena, etc. In recent years the word parapsychology has also come into use, particularly for the investigation of ESP in a laboratory setting, but it is really part of psychic research as the subject's fascinating history reveals.

For all recorded history, and no doubt very much earlier, man has been puzzled at his apparent ability to perceive features of the universe without the use of the normal senses—mind-to-mind contact, dreams about the future which come true, etc. He has also been intrigued by the notion that in addition to the natural world of people and things, there exists in parallel, a *supernatural* world of ghosts, spirits and other similar strange manifestations. Belief in such oddities has been tremendously widespread and still forms one of the major casual conversational topics raised when people see each other socially today. Of course, until the 19th cent. or thereabouts such phenomena, while bizarre, unpredictable and possibly frightening, were not at odds with man's view of himself and his world as revealed through basic religious beliefs. Man was supposed to be in essence a supernatural being with eternal life, and the world was seen as the happy hunting ground of dynamic evil forces which could intervene directly in the lives of humans. The rise of material science in the 19th cent. however began to shake the orthodox religious framework, and as a result in due course scientists began to question the basis of all supernatural powers and manifestations, putting forward the reasonable argument: "if such things *are* real then they should be demonstrable in scientific terms—just as all other aspects of the universe are."

Once having advanced this argument, the next step was to carry it to its conclusion and set about the systematic investigation of the phenomena to see whether they *did* conform in any way to the immensely successful framework of 19th cent. science, and from this step psychic research was born. In fact one can date its origins rather precisely—to 1882 when a group of scholars formed the Society for Psychical Research in London—an organization which still exists today. The first experiments in this slightly eccentric field of science were haphazard and tended to be confined to spiritualistic phenomena such as table tapping, mediumistic messages, ectoplasmic manifestations, etc., which were having a great wave of popularity among the general public at the time. In fact what one might term as the first phase of psychic research—it has gone through three phases in its history—was really heavily tied up with Spiritualism. Before ridiculing it for this, it is only fair to point out that many of the most eminent figures of the time—the great physicists Sir Oliver Lodge and Sir William Crookes, Alfred Russell Wallace, co-discoverer with Darwin of the theory of evolution by natural selection, the brilliant author and creator of Sherlock Holmes, Sir Arthur Conan Doyle, and many others—became convinced Spiritualists as the result of their early experiments. Nevertheless, despite the ardent support of such intellectual giants, medium after medium was in due course detected in fraud sometimes of the most blatant kind—and the majority of scientists gradually became more critical and less likely to be taken in by even the subtlest of trickery. As a result, interest slowly shifted from the séance room to a different realm, and as it did so the first phase of psychic research drew to a close.

The second phase was, broadly speaking, the era of the ghost hunter. With the idea of spirits materializing in laboratories seeming intrinsically less and less credible, scientists began to study what struck them at the time to be basically more "plausible" matters—haunted houses, poltergeist phenomena and so on. For some reason the idea of a house dominated by a psychic presence as the result of some tragic history seemed (at the turn of the century) *somehow* scientifically and philosophically more acceptable than did the old Spiritualist notions about direct communication with the spirit world. The key figure in the "ghost hunting" era was Mr. Harry Price, an amateur magician who became the scourge of fraudulent mediums, but who staked his name and credibility on the authenticity of the alleged poltergeist phenomena at Borley Rectory in Suffolk, which became world famous through his book, *The Most Haunted House in England.* The ancient rectory's catalogue of ghosts and marvels allegedly witnessed by numerous "reliable witnesses" seemed irrefutable. Unfortunately investigations by the Society for Psychical Research some years after Price's death now make it seem certain that Price was responsible for faking some of the Borley phenomena himself, and with these disclosures scientifically "respectable" ghost hunting took a nasty tumble. Thus, with an increasingly critical attitude developing among scientists, haunted houses and poltergeists gradually began to shift out of favor to usher in the third phase of psychic research.

The date of the commencement of this phase can be identified as 1927 when the Parapsychology Laboratory at Duke University in North Carolina was formed by Dr. J. B. Rhine. Here the emphasis was on laboratory studies along the traditional lines of experimental psychology; spirit forms and poltergeists were ignored in favor of the routine testing of literally thousands of people for telepathy, precognition (the ability to see into the future), etc., almost always involving card tests which could be rigidly controlled and the results statistically analysed. By the 1940s Rhine was claiming irrefutable evidence of telepathy achieved by these means, but once again critical forces began to gather and it was pointed out that results obtained in Rhine's laboratory rarely seemed to be replicable in other scientists' laboratories in different parts of the world. In fact the failure of ESP experiments of this kind to be easily repeatable has turned out to be crucial and has led to a growing scepticism on the part of uncommitted scientists who now question whether psychic research and parapsychology have really advanced our understanding of the world of the paranormal in any way. At the present time the topic is in a highly controversial phase.

Although Rhine's university parapsychology laboratory closed with his retirement in 1965 research in the field has continued ever since, especially with the work of Dr. Helmut Schmidt who has made important contributions. In recent years a new Chair and research laboratory has been introduced at the University of Utrecht in the Netherlands.

To sum up the topic one could say that in a curious way, while the third phase of psychic research is now drawing to a close, the evidence suggests that a fourth phase is appearing, and that this may well feature a return to the study of the more sensational and dramatic phenomena reminiscent of the Victorian séance room. If this is so, a century after its foundation the wheel will have turned full circle and psychic research will be back where it started, without in the opinion of most scientists, having solved any of the basic questions which it had set out to answer. *See* **Parapsychology, Poltergeist, Telepathy, Spiritualism.**

**Psychoanalysis,** an approach to the study of human personality involving the rigorous probing, with the assistance of a specially trained practitioner, of an individual's personal problems, motives, goals and attitudes to life in general. Often, and quite understandably, confused with psychology (of which it is merely a part), psychoanalysis has an interesting historical background and has attracted the interest of philosophers, scientists and medical experts since it emerged as a radical and controversial form of mental therapy at the turn of the century. The traditionally accepted founder is the great Austrian Sigmund Freud, but he never failed to acknowledge the impetus that had been given to his own ideas by his talented friend, the physiologist Joseph Breuer, who for most of his working life had been interested in the curious phenomena associated with hypnosis. Breuer had successfully cured the hysterical paralysis of a young woman patient and had noticed that under hypnosis the girl seemed to be recalling emotional experiences, hitherto forgotten, which bore some relationship to the symptoms of her illness. Developing this with other patients Breuer then found that the mere recalling and discussing of the emotional events under hypnosis seemed to produce a dramatic alleviation of the symptoms—a phenomenon which came to be known as *catharsis*. Breuer also noticed another curious side-effect, that his women patients fell embarrassingly and violently in love with him, and he gradually dropped the practice of "mental catharsis", possibly feeling that it was a bit too dangerous to handle. This left the field clear for Freud, whose brilliant mind began to search beyond the therapeutic aspects of the topic to see what light might be thrown on the nature of human personality and psychological mechanisms in general. The most important question concerned the "forgotten" emotional material which turned up, apparently out of the blue, during the hypnotic session. Freud rightly saw that this posed problems for the current theories of memory, for how could something once forgotten *(a)* continue to have an effect on the individual without his being aware of it, and (b) ultimately be brought back to conscious memory again. It must be remembered that at this time memory was considered to be a fairly simple process—information was stored in the brain and was gradually eroded or destroyed with the passage of time and the decay of brain cells. Once lost, it was believed, memories were gone for ever, or at best only partially and inaccurately reproducible. Furthermore, human beings were supposed to be rational (if frequently wilful) creatures who never did anything without thinking about it (if only briefly) beforehand and without being well aware of their reasons for so doing. It was within this framework that Freud had his great insight, one which many people believe to be one of the most important ideas given to mankind. This was simply the realization that the human mind was not a simple entity controlling the brain and body more or less at will, but a complex system made up of a number of integrated parts with at least two major subdivisions—the conscious and the unconscious. The former concerned itself with the normal round of human behavior, including the larger part of rational thought, conversation, etc., and large areas of memory. The latter was principally devoted to the automatic control of bodily functions, such as respiration, cardiac activity, various types of emotional behavior not subject to much conscious modification and a large storehouse of relevant "memories" again not normally accessible to the conscious mind. Occasionally, Freud proposed, an exceedingly unpleasant emotional or otherwise painful event might be so troublesome if held in the conscious mind's store, that it would get shoved down into the unconscious or "repressed" where it would cease to trouble the individual in his normal life. The advantages of this mechanism are obvious, but they also brought with them hazards. With certain kinds of memory, particularly those involving psychological rather than physical pain—as for example a severe sexual conflict or marital problem—repression might be used as a device to save the individual from facing his problem in the "real" world, where he might be able ultimately to solve it, by merely hiding it away in the unconscious and thus pretending it did not exist. Unfortunately, Freud believed, conflicts of this kind were not snuffed out when consigned to the basements of the mind, but rather tended to smolder on, affecting the individual in various ways which he could not understand. Repressed marital conflicts might give rise to impotence, for example, or even to homosexual behavior. Guilt at improper social actions similarly repressed might provoke nervous ties, local paralysis, etc. etc. Following this line of reasoning, Freud argued that if the unwisely repressed material could be dredged up and the individual forced to face the crisis instead of denying it, then dramatic alleviations of symptoms and full recovery should follow.

To the great psychologist and his growing band of followers the stage seemed to be set for a dramatic breakthrough not only in mental therapy but also in a general understanding of the nature of human personality. To his pleasure—for various reasons he was never too happy about hypnosis—Freud discovered that with due patience, skill and guidance an individual could be led to resurrect the material repressed in his unconscious mind in the normal, as opposed to the hypnotic state. This technique, involving long sessions consisting of intimate discussions between patient and therapist became known as psychoanalysis, and it has steadily evolved from its experimental beginnings in the medical schools and universities of Vienna to being a major system of psychotherapy with a worldwide following and important theoretical connotations. Psychoanalysis, as practiced today, consists of a number of meetings between doctor and patient in which the latter is slowly taught to approach and enter the *territory* of his subconscious mind, and examine the strange and "forgotten" material within. A successful analysis, it is claimed, gives the individual greater insight into his own personality and a fuller understanding of the potent unconscious forces which are at work within him and in part dictating his goals.

Freud's initial ideas were of course tentative, and meant to be so. He was however a didactic and forceful personality himself, unwilling to compromise on many points which became controversial as the technique and practice of psychoanalysis developed. The outcome was that some of his early followers, notably the equally brilliant Carl Jung and Alfred Adler, broke away to found their own "schools" or versions of psychoanalysis, with varying degrees of success. Today, psychoanalysis is coming under increasingly critical scrutiny, and its claims are being treated with a good deal of reservation. Notable antagonists include the English psychologist Professor H. J. Eysenck who points out that there is little if any solid experimental data indicating that psychoanalysis is a valid method of treating or curing mental illness. Analysists respond by saying that their system is closer to an art than a craft and not amenable to routine scientific experiment. The controversy will no doubt continue for some time to come, but whatever its validity as therapy, the basic ideas behind psychoanalysis—notably the reality and power of the unconscious mind—are beyond question and have given human beings definite and major insights into the greatest enigma of all—the workings of the human mind.

**Psychometry,** the supposed talent or faculty of divining something about the history and previous owners of an object by holding it in the hand. A common feature of modern Spiritualistic practice, and to a certain extent synonymous with clairvoyance, psychometry is based on an ancient magical assumption that objects somehow take on traces or "memories" of their surroundings which are detectable by specially sensitive individuals. Controlled scientific tests on people claiming to have this power have however proved totally negative. *See also* **Psychic Research.**

**Pyramidology,** a curious belief that the dimensions of the Great Pyramid at Giza, if studied carefully, reveal principles of fundamental historical and religious significance. The perpetrator of this was a Victorian publisher, John Taylor, who discovered that if you divide the height of the pyramid into twice the side of its base you get a number very similar to *pi*—a number of considerable mathematical importance. Later discoveries in the same vein include the finding that the base of the pyramid (when divided by the width of a single casing stone) equals exactly 365—number of days in the year. Many books have been written on the interpretation of the dimensions of the pyramid, none of which has any scientific or archaeological validity. Pyramidology is simply a classic example of the well-known fact that hunting through even a random array of numbers will turn up sequences which appear to be "significant"—always provided that one carefully selects the numbers one wants and turns a blind eye to those that one doesn't! A peculiar variant of pyramidology has recently arisen through the publication of a claim that razor blades kept beneath a cardboard model of a pyramid never lose their cutting edge! Scientific tests have shown that this is not so, but the belief persists—implicit testimony to the mystical power of certain common emblems and symbols.

**Pyrrhonism,** a sceptical philosophy which doubts everything.

# Q

**Quakers,** a religious body founded in England in the 17th cent. by George Fox (1624–91). The essence of their faith is that every individual who believes has the power of direct communication with God who will guide him into the ways of truth. This power comes from the "inner light" of his own heart, the light of Christ, Quakers meet for worship avoiding all ritual, without ordained ministers or prepared sermons; there is complete silence until someone is moved by the Holy Spirit to utter his message.

In the early days Quakers gave vent to violent outbursts and disturbed church services. Friends had the habit of preaching at anyone who happened to be nearby, their denunciation of "steeple-houses" and references to the "inner light," their addressing everyone as "thee" and "thou," their refusal to go beyond "yea" and "nay" in making an assertion and refusing to go further in taking an oath, must have played some part in bringing about the savage persecutions they were forced to endure. Many emigrated to Pennsylvania, founded by William Penn in 1682, and missionaries were sent to many parts of the world. The former violence gave way to gentleness. Friends not only refused to take part in war but even refused to resist personal violence. They took the lead in abolishing slavery, worked for prison reform and better education. As we know them today Quakers are quiet, sincere, undemonstrative people, given to a somewhat serious turn of mind. The former peculiarities of custom and dress have been dropped and interpretation of the Scriptures is more liberal. Although Quakers refuse to take part in warfare, they are always ready to help the victims of war, by organizing relief, helping refugees in distress, or sending their ambulance units into the heat of battle.

**Quietism,** a doctrine of extreme asceticism and contemplative devotion, embodied in the works of Michael Molinos, a 17th century Spanish priest, and condemned by Rome. It taught that the chief duty of man is to be occupied in the continual contemplation of God, so as to become totally independent of outward circumstances and the influence of the senses. Quietists taught that when this stage of perfection is reached the soul has no further need for prayer and other external devotional practices. Similar doctrines have been taught in the Moslem and Hindu religions. *See* **Yoga.**

# R

**Radiesthesia,** the detection, either by some "psychic" faculty or with special equipment, of radiations alleged to be given off by all living things and natural substances such as water, oil, metal, etc. The word radiesthesia is in fact a fancy modern name for the ancient practice of "dowsing," whereby an individual is supposed to be able to detect the presence of hidden underground water by following the movements of a hazel twig held in his hands. Dowsers, or water diviners, as they are sometimes called, claim also to be able to detect the presence of minerals and, hard though it may seem to believe, have actually been hired by major oil companies to prospect for desert wells—though without any notable success. The theory of dowsing is that all things give off a unique radiation signal which the trained individual (via his twig, pendulum, or whatever) can "tune in" to, a theory which, while not backed up by any data known to orthodox sciences, is at least not too fantastically far-fetched. It is when radiesthesists claim to be able to detect the presence of oil, water, or precious metals by holding their pendulum *over a map* of the territory and declare that it is not necessary for them to visit the area in person to find the required spot that the topic moves from the remotely possible to the absurdly improbable. Some practitioners of this art state that they are able to perform even more marvellous feats such as determining the sex of chickens while still in the egg, or diagnosing illness by studying the movements of a pendulum held over a blood sample from the sick individual. Such claims when put to simple scientific test have almost invariably turned out as fiascos. Yet belief in dowsing, water-divining, and the like is still very widespread.

There is an important link between radiesthesia and the pseudo-science of *radionics,* which holds that the twig or pendulum can be superseded by complicated equipment built vaguely according to electronic principles. A typical radionic device consists of a box covered with knobs, dials, etc., by which the practitioner "tunes in" to the "vibration" given off by an object, such as a blood spot, a piece of hair, or even a signature. By the proper interpretation of the readings from the equipment the illness, or even the mental state, of the individual whose blood, hair, or signature is being tested, may be ascertained. The originator of radionics seems to have been a Dr. Albert Abrams who engaged in medical practice using radionic devices in America in the 1920s and '30s. The principal exponent in this country was the late George de la Warr who manufactured radionic boxes for diagnosis and treatment of illnesses, and even a "camera" which he believed to be capable of photographing thought. In a sensational court case in 1960 a woman who had purchased one of the diagnostic devices sued de la Warr for fraud. After a long trial the case was dismissed, the Judge commenting that while he had no good evidence that the device worked as claimed, he felt that de la Warr seriously believed in its validity and thus was not guilty of fraud or misrepresentation.

**Ranters,** a fanatical antinomian (the doctrine that Christians are not bound to keep the law of God) and pantheistic sect in Commonwealth England. The name was also applied to the Primitive Methodists because of their noisy preaching.

**Rationalism** is defined as "the treating of reason as the ultimate authority in religion and the rejection of doctrines not consonant with reason." In practice, rationalism had a double significance: (1) the doctrine was defined above, and (2) a 19th cent. movement which was given to what was then known as "free-thought," "secularism," or agnosticism—*i.e.,* it was in the positive sense antireligious and was represented by various bodies such as the Secular Society, the National Secular Society, and the Rationalist Press Association (founded in 1899).

In the first sense, which implies a particular philosophical attitude to the universe and life, rationalism is not easy to pin down although, at first sight, it would appear that nothing could be simpler. Does it mean the use of pure reason and logic or does it mean, on the other hand, the use of what is generally called the "scientific method" based on a critical attitude to existing beliefs? If we are thinking in terms of the use of pure reason and logic then the Roman Catholic Church throughout most of its history has maintained, not that the whole truth about religion can be discovered by reason, but as St. Thomas Aquinas held, the basis of religion—*e.g.* the existence of God—can be rationally demonstrated. Nobody could have made more use of logic than the schoolmen of the Middle Ages, yet not many people today would accept their conclusions, nor would many non-Catholics accept St. Thomas's proofs of the existence of God even when they themselves are religious. The arguments of a First Cause or Prime Mover or the argument from Design on the whole leave us unmoved, partly because they do not lead up to the idea of a *personal God,* partly because we rightly distrust logic and pure reason divorced from facts and know that, if we begin from the wrong assumptions or premises, we can arrive at some very strange answers. If the existence of a Deity can be proved by reason, then one can also by the use of reason come to the conclusions, or rather paradoxes, such as the following: God is by definition all good, all knowing, all powerful—yet evil exists (because if it does not exist then it cannot be wrong to say "there is no God"). But if evil exists, then it must do so either because of God (in which case He is not all good) or in spite of God (in which case He is not all powerful).

Arguments of this sort do not appeal to the modern mind for two historical reasons: (1) many of us have been brought up in the Protestant tradition which—at least in one of its aspects—insists that we must believe in God by faith rather than by logic and in its extreme form insists on God as revealed by the "inner light"; (2) our increasing trust in the scientific method of observation, experiment and argument. Thus, no matter what Aristotle or St. Thomas may say about a Prime Mover or a First Cause, we remain unconvinced since at least one scientific theory suggests that the universe did not have a beginning and if scientific investigation proved this to be so, then we should be entirely indifferent to what formal logic had to say.

The secularist and rationalist movements of the 19th cent. were anti-religious—and quite rightly so—because at that time there were serious disabilities imposed even in Britain by the Established Church on atheism or agnosticism and freedom of thought. They are of little significance now because very little is left, largely thanks to their efforts, of these disabilities.

Finally, although most people are likely to accept the scientific method as the main means of discovering truth, there are other factors which equally make us doubt the value of "pure" logic and reason unaided by observation. The first of these is the influence of Freud which shows that much of our reasoning is mere rationalizing—*e.g.,* we are more likely to become atheists because we hated our father than because we can prove that there is no God. The second is the influence of a movement in philosophy which, in the form of logical positivism or logical analysis, makes us doubt whether metaphysical systems have any meaning at all. Today, instead of asking ourselves whether Plato was right or wrong, we are much more likely to ask whether he did anything but make for the most part meaningless noises. Religion is in a sense much safer today than it ever was in the 19th cent. when it made foolish statements over matters of science that could be *proved* wrong; now we tend to see it as an emotional attitude to the universe or God (a "feeling of being at home in the universe," as William James put it; which can no more be proved or disproved than being in love.

**Realism** is a word which has so many meanings, and such contradictory ones, in various spheres, that it is difficult to define. We shall limit ourselves to its significance in philosophy. In philosophy, "realism" has two different meanings, diametrically opposed. (1) The most usual meaning is the one we should least expect from the everyday sense of the word—*i.e.,* it refers to all those philosophies from Plato onwards which maintained that the world of appearance is illusory and that ideas, forms, or universals are the only true realities, belonging to the world beyond matter and appearance—the world of God or mind. In early medieval times St. Thomas Aquinas was the chief exponent of this doctrine which was held by the scholastics as opposed to the Nominalists *(q.v.).* (2) In its modern everyday meaning "realism" is the belief that the universe is real and not a creation of mind, that there is a reality that causes the appearance, the "thing-in-itself" as Kant described it. Material things may not really be what they appear to be

(*e.g.* a noise is not the "bang" we experience but a series of shock-waves passing through the atmosphere), yet, for all that, we can be sure that matter exists and it is very possible (some might add) that mind does not.

**Reformation,** the great religious movement of the 16th century, which resulted in the establishment of Protestantism. John Wyclif (d. 1384), John Hus (d. 1415) and others had sounded the warning note, and when later on Luther took up the cause in Germany, and Zwingli in Switzerland, adherents soon became numerous. The wholesale vending of indulgences by the papal agents had incensed the people, and when Luther denounced these things he spoke to willing ears. After much controversy, the reformers boldly prepounded the principles of the new doctrine, and the struggle for religious supremacy grew bitter. They claimed justification (salvation) by faith, and the use as well as the authority of the Scriptures, rejecting the doctrine of transubstantiation, the adoration of the Virgin and Saints, and the headship of the Pope. Luther was excommunicated. But the Reformation principles spread and ultimately a great part of Germany, as well as Switzerland, the Low Countries, Scandinavia, England, and Scotland were won over to the new faith. In England Henry VIII readily espoused the cause of the Reformation, his own personal quarrel with the Pope acting as an incentive. Under Mary there was a brief and sanguinary reaction, but Elizabeth gave completeness to the work which her father had initiated. *See* **Calvinism, Presbyterianism, Baptists, Methodism.**

**Renaissance** is defined in the *Oxford English Dictionary* as: "The revival of art and letters, under the influence of classical models, which began in Italy in the 14th century." It is a term which must be used with care for the following reasons: (1) Although it was first used in the form *rinascita* (rebirth) by Vasari in 1550 and people living at that time certainly were aware that something new was happening, the word had no wide currency until used by the Swiss historian Jacob Burchardt in his classic *The Civilization of the Renaissance in Italy* (1860). (2) The term as used today refers not only to art in its widest sense but to a total change in man's outlook on life which extended into philosophical, scientific, economic, and technical fields. (3) Spreading from Italy there were Renaissance movements in France, Spain, Germany, and northern Europe, all widely different with varying delays in time. As the historian Edith Sichel says: "Out of the Italian Renaissance there issued a new-born art; out of the Northern Renaissance there came forth a new-born religion. There came forth also a great school of poetry, and a drama the greatest that the world had seen since the days of Greece. The religion was the offspring of Germany and the poetry that of England."

The real cause of the Renaissance was not the fall of Constantinople, the invention of printing, or the discovery of America, though these were phases in the process; it was, quite simply, money. The birth of a new merchant class gave rise to individualist attitudes in economic affairs which prepared the way for individualism and humanism. The new wealthy class in time became patrons of the arts whereas previously the Church had been the sole patron and controller. Thus the artist became more free to express himself, more respected, and being more well-to-do could afford to ignore the Church and even, in time, the views of his patrons.

It is true that art continued to serve to a considerable extent the purposes of faith, but it was judged from the standpoint of art. Medieval art was meant to elevate and teach man: Renaissance art to delight his senses and enrich his life. From this free and questing spirit acquired from economic individualism came the rise of modern science and technology; here Italy learned much from the Arab scholars who had translated and commented upon the philosophical, medical, and mathematical texts of antiquity, while denying themselves any interest in Greek art and literature. Arabic-Latin versions of Aristotle were in use well into the 16th cent. The Byzantine culture, though it had preserved the Greek tradition and gave supremacy to Plato, had made no move forward. But the Greek scholars who fled to Italy after the fall of Constantinople brought with them an immense cargo of classical manuscripts. The recovery of these Greek masterpieces, their translation into the vernaculars, and the invention of printing, made possible a completer understanding of the Greek spirit. It was the bringing together of the two heritages, Greek science, and Greek literature, that gave birth to a new vision. But it was not only Aristotle and Plato who were being studied but Ovid, Catullus, Horace, Pliny and Lucretius. What interested Renaissance man was the humanism of the Latin writers, their attitude to science, their scepticism.

The period *c.* 1400–1500 is known as the **Early Renaissance.** During this time such painters as Masaccio, Uccello, Piero della Francesca, Botticelli, and Giovanni Bellini were laying the foundations of drawing and painting for all subsequent periods including our own. They concerned themselves with such problems as anatomy, composition, perspective, and representation of space, creating in effect a grammar or textbook of visual expression. The term **High Renaissance** is reserved for a very brief period when a pure, balanced, classical harmony was achieved and artists were in complete control of the techniques learned earlier. The High Renaissance lasted only from *c.* 1500 to 1527 (the date of the sack of Rome), yet that interval included the earlier works of Michelangelo, most of Leonardo's, and all the Roman works of Raphael.

**Romantic Movement or Romanticism** is the name given not so much to an individual way of thinking but to the gradual but radical transformation of basic human values that occurred in the Western world round about the latter part of the 18th cent. It was a great breakthrough in European consciousness and arose through the writings of certain men living during the half-century or more following, say, 1760. It arose then because both time and place were propitious for the birth of these new ideas. There was a revolution in basic values—in art, morals, politics, religion, etc. The new view was of a world transcending the old one, infinitely larger and more varied.

To understand the Romantic movement it is necessary first to take note of the climate of thought preceding the great change; then to account for its beginning in Germany where it did during the latter part of the 18th century, and finally to appraise the writings of those men whose ideas fermented the new awakening. Briefly, the shift was away from French classicism and from belief in the all-pervasive power of human reason (the Enlightenment) towards the unfettered freedom that the new consciousness was able to engender. What mattered was to live a passionate

and vigorous life, to dedicate oneself to an ideal, no matter what the cost (*e.g.,* Byron).

The ideas of the Enlightenment (*e.g.,* Fontenelle, Voltaire, Montesquieu) had been attacked by the Germans Hamann and Herder and by the ideas of the English philosopher Hume, but Kant, Schiller, and Fichte, Goethe's novel *Wilhelm Meister,* and the French Revolution all had profound effects on the aesthetic, moral, social, and political thought of the time. Friedrich Schlegel (1772–1829) said: "There is in man a terrible unsatisfied desire to soar into infinity; a feverish longing to break through the narrow bonds of individuality." Romanticism undermined the notion that in matters of value there are objective criteria which operate between men. Henceforth there was to be a resurgence of the human spirit, deep and profound, that is still going on.

**Rosicrucians,** an ancient mystical society founded in the 16th cent. by Christian Rosenkreuz which attempted to forge a theoretical link between the great Egyptian religions and the Church of Rome, drawing rituals and philosophy from both camps. The Society did not long survive the death of its founder (he managed to reach the age of 106 incidentally) but has been revived in succeeding centuries by a series of rivalling factions. Perhaps the most famous of these is the Rosicrucian Order (A.M.O.R.C) which has become well-known in the Western world as a result of its heavy advertising in the popular press. Founded by the American H. Spencer Lewis, this offers a simple and good-natured doctrine preaching the Brotherhood of Man, the reincarnation of the soul and the immense latent potential of the human mind. As with many American-based organizations of this kind, the boundary between business and religion is hard to define. It is probably best summed up as a modern secret society which serves an important function in the lives of many people of mystical inclinations.

# S

**Salvation Army.** The religious movement which in 1878 became known by this name arose from the Christian Mission meetings which the Rev. William Booth and his devoted wife had held in the East End of London for the previous thirteen years. Its primary aim was, and still is, to preach the gospel of Jesus Christ to men and women untouched by ordinary religious efforts. The founder devoted his life to the salvation of the submerged classes whose conditions at that time were unspeakably dreadful. Originally his aim had been to convert people and then send them on to the churches, but he soon found that few religious bodies would accept these "low-class" men and women. So it was that social work became part of their effort. Practical help like the provision of soup kitchens, accompanied spiritual ministration. Soon, in the interests of more effective "warfare" against social evils, a military form of organization, with uniforms, brass bands, and religious songs, was introduced. Its magazine *The War Cry* gave as its aim "to carry the Blood of Christ and the Fire of the Holy Ghost into every part of the world.'

General Booth saw with blinding clarity that conversion must be accompanied by an improvement of external conditions. Various books had earlier described the terrible conditions of the slums, but in 1890 he produced a monumental survey entitled *In Darkest England and The Way Out*. From that time forward the Army was accepted and its facilities made use of by the authorities. Today the Army's spiritual and social activities have spread to countries all over the world; every one, no matter what class, color, or creed he belongs to is a "brother for whom Christ died."

**Sceptics.** From Thales of Miletus (*c.* 624–565 B.C.) to the Stoics in the 4th cent. B.C. philosophers had been trying to explain the nature of the universe; each one produced a different theory and each could, apparently, prove that he was right. This diversity of views convinced the Sceptic school founded by Pyrrho (*c.* 360–270 B.C.) that man is unable to know the real nature of the world or how it came into being. In place of a futile search for what must be forever unknowable, the Sceptics recommended that men should be practical, follow custom, and accept the evidence of their senses.

**Schoolmen.** From the time of Augustine to the middle of the 9th cent. philosophy, like science, was dead or merely a repetition of what had gone before. But about that time there arose a new interest in the subject, although (since by then Western Europe was entirely under the authority of the Catholic Church) the main form it took was an attempt to justify Church teaching in the light of Greek philosophy. Those who made this attempt to reconcile Christian beliefs with the best in Plato and Aristotle were known as "schoolmen" and the philosophies which they developed were known as "scholasticism." Among the most famous schoolmen must be counted John Scotus Erigena (*c.* 800 –*c.* 877), born in Ireland and probably the earliest; St. Anselm, archbishop of Canterbury (1033–1109); the great Peter Abelard whose school was in Paris (1079–1142); Bernard of Chartres, his contemporary; and the best-known of all, St. Thomas Aquinas of Naples (1225–74), who was given the name of the "Angelic Doctor."

The philosophies of these men are discussed under various headings **(God and Man, Determinism and Free Will)**, but being severely limited by the Church their doctrines differed from each other much less than those of later philosophical schools. However, one of the great arguments was between the orthodox Realists *(q.v.)* and the Nominalists *(q.v.)* and a second was between the Thomists (or followers of St. Thomas Aquinas) and the Scotists (followers of John Duns Scotus—not to be confused with John Scotus Erigena). The two latter schools were known as the Ancients, while the followers of William of Occam, the Nominalist, were known as the Terminalists. All became reconciled in 1482 in face of the threat from humanism of which the great exponent was Erasmus of Rotterdam (1466–1536).

**Scientology,** an unusual quasi-philosophical system started by the American science-fiction writer L. Ron Hubbard, which claims to be able to effect dramatic improvement in the mental and physical well-being of its adherents. Originally developed in the United States as "Dianetics, the modern science of mental health," it was hailed in Hubbard's first book to be "a milestone for Man comparable to his discovery of fire and superior to his inventions of the wheel and the arch." Such extravagant statements exemplify the literature of the movement, which in the late 1950s began to expand in England when its founder came to live in East Grinstead. Followers of Dianetics and Scientology advance within the cult through a series of levels or grades, most reached by undertaking courses of training and tuition, payment for which may amount to hundreds and, in total, even thousands of pounds. These courses consist largely of mental exercises known as "processing" and "auditing" (now called "pastoral counselling" since more emphasis has recently been laid on the religious aspect). One of the principal goals of a Scientologist is the attainment of the state known as "Clear" (roughly speaking, one "cleared" of certain mental and physical handicaps) when it is believed he (she) will be a literally superior being, equipped with a higher intelligence and a greater command over the pattern of his (her) own life. The Scientologists' claims that their movement is a genuine religion have generally been met with resistance from establishment bodies. In 1967 the Home Office announced that its centers would no longer be recognized as educational establishments and foreigners arriving for its courses would not be granted student status. In 1980 the Home Office lifted this ban. The international headquarters have been moved from East Grinstead to Los Angeles.

**Shakers,** members of a revivalist group, styled by themselves "The United Society of Believers in Christ's Second Appearing," who seceded from Quakerism in 1747 though adhering to many of the Quaker tenets. The community was joined in 1758 by Ann Lee, a young convert from Manchester, who had "revelations" that she was the female Christ; "Mother Ann" was accepted as their leader. Under the influence of her prophetic visions she set out with nine followers for "Immanuel's land" in America and the community settled near Albany, capital of New York state. They were known as the "Shakers" in ridicule because they were given to involuntary movements in moments of religious ecstasy. Central to their faith was the belief in the dual role of God through the male and female Christ: the male principle came to earth in Jesus; the female principle, in "Mother Ann." The sexes were equal and women preached as often as men at their meetings which sometimes included sacred dances—nevertheless the two sexes, even in dancing, kept apart. Their communistic way of living brought them economic prosperity, the Shakers becoming known as good agriculturists and craftsmen, noted for their furniture and textiles. After 1860, however, the movement began to decline and few, if any, are active today.

**Shamans,** the medicine men found in all primitive societies who used their magical arts to work cures, and protect the group from evil influences. The *shaman* was a man apart and wore special garments to show his authority. Shamanism with its magical practices, incantations, trances, exhausting dances, and self-torture is practiced even today by tribes that have survived in a primitive state of culture.

**Shiites or Shia,** a heretical Moslem sect in Persia, opposed by the orthodox Sunnites. The dispute, which came almost immediately after the death of the Prophet and led to bitter feuding, had little to do with matters of doctrine as such but with the succession. After Mohammed's death, there were three possible claimants: Ali, the husband of his daughter Fatima, and two others, one of whom gave up his claim in favor of the other, Omar. The orthodox selected Omar, who was shortly assassinated, and the same happened to his successor as Ali was passed over again. The Shiites are those who maintain that Ali was the true vicar of the Prophet, and that the three orthodox predecessors were usurpers.

**Sikhism.** The Sikh community of the Punjab, which has played a significant part in the history of modern India, came into being during a period of religious revival in India in the 15th and 16th cent. It was originally founded as a religious sect by Guru (teacher) Nanak (1469–1538) who emphasized the fundamental truth of all religions, and whose mission was to put an end to religious conflict. He condemned the formalism both of Hinduism and Islam, preaching the gospel of universal toleration, and the unity of the Godhead, whether He be called Allah, Vishnu, or God. His ideas were welcomed by the great Mogul Emperor Akbar (1542–1605). Thus a succession of Gurus were able to live in peace after Nanak's death; they established the great Sikh center at Amritsar, compiled the sacred writings known as the *Adi Granth,* and improved their organization as a sect. But the peace did not last long, for an emperor arose who was a fanatical Moslem, in face of whom the last Guru, Govind Singh (1666–1708), whose father was put to death for refusal to embrace Islam, had to make himself a warrior and instil into the Sikhs a more aggressive spirit. A number of ceremonies were instituted by Govind Singh; admission to the fraternity was by special rite; caste distinctions were abolished; hair was worn long; the word singh, meaning lion, was added to the original name. They were able to organize themselves into 12 *misls* or confederacies but divisions appeared with the disappearance of a common enemy and it was not until the rise of Ranjit Singh (1780–1839) that a single powerful Sikh kingdom was established, its influence only being checked by the English, with whom a treaty of friendship was made. After the death of Ranjit Singh two Anglo-Sikh wars followed, in 1845–46, and 1848–49, which resulted in British annexation of the Punjab and the end of Sikh independence. In the two world wars the Sikhs proved among the most loyal of Britain's Indian subjects. The partitioning of the continent of India in 1947 into two states, one predominantly Hindu and the other predominantly Moslem, presented a considerable problem in the Punjab, which was divided in such a way as to leave 2 million Sikhs in Pakistan, and a considerable number of Moslems in the Indian Punjab. Although numbering less than 2 per cent. of the population (*c.* 8 million) the Sikhs are a continuing factor in Indian political life. In 1966 the Punjab was divided on a linguistic basis—Punjabi-speaking Punjab and Hindi-speaking Hariana.

**Spiritualism** is a religion which requires to be distinguished from psychical research *(q.v.)* which is a scientific attempt carried on by both believers and non-believers to investigate psychic phenomena including those not necessarily connected with "spirits"—*e.g.,* telepathy or clairvoyance and precognition. As a religion (although for that matter the whole of history is filled with attempts to get in touch with the "spirit world") Spiritualism begins with the American Andrew Jackson Davis who in 1847 published *Nature's Divine Revelations,* a book which is still widely read. In this Davis states that on the death of the physical body, the human spirit remains alive and moves on to one or another of a considerable range of worlds or "spheres" where it commences yet another stage of existence. Since the spirit has not died, but exists with full (and possibly even expanded) consciousness, there should be no reason, Davis argues, why it should not make its presence known to the beings it has temporarily left behind on earth. In 1847, the year of the publication of Davis's book, two young girls, Margaret and Kate Fox, living in a farmhouse at Hydesville, New York, began apparently to act as unwitting mediums for attempts at such between-worlds communication. The girls were the focus for strange rappings and bangs which it was alleged defied normal explanation and which spelt out, in the form of a simple alphabetical code, messages from the spirits of "the dead." The Fox sisters were later to confess that they had produced the raps by trickery, but by that time the fashion had spread across the world and before long "mediums" in all lands were issuing spirit communications (often in much more spectacular form). In the late 19th cent. Spiritualism went into a phase of great expansion and for various reasons attracted the attention of many scientists. Among these were Sir William Crookes, Sir Oliver Lodge, Professor Charles Richet, Alfred Russell Wallace, to say nothing of the brilliant and shrewd creator of Sherlock Holmes, Sir Arthur Conan Doyle. Today many people find it astonishing that people of such brilliance should find the phenomena of the séance room of more than passing interest, but the commitment of the Victorian scientists is understandable if we realize that Spiritualists, after all, claim to do no more than demonstrate as fact what all Christians are called on to believe—that the human personality survives bodily death. Furthermore, at the time of the late 19th cent. peak of Spiritualism, much less was known about human psychology and about the great limitations of sensory perception in typical séance conditions, when lights are dimmed or extinguished and an emotionally charged atmosphere generated. Today the most striking phenomena of the séance room—the alleged materialization of spirit people and the production of such half-spiritual, half-physical substances as ectoplasm—are rarely if ever produced at Spiritualist meetings. Some say that the most probable explanation for this is that too many fraudulent mediums have been caught out and publicly exposed for the profession to be worth the risks. The movement today, which still has a large and often articulate following, now concentrates on the less controversial areas of "mental mediumship," clairvoyance and the like, or on the very widespread practice of "spirit healing." Where people are not deliberately deluded by bogus mediums acting for monetary reward (a practice which largely died out with the "death" of ectoplasm) Spiritualism probably has an important role to play in the life of many people whose happiness has been removed by the death of a much loved relative or spouse. It does not deserve the violent attacks that are often made on it by orthodox clergy who allege that Spiritualists are communicating not with the souls of the departed but with the devil or his emissaries.

**Stoics,** the followers of Zeno, a Greek philosopher in the 4th century B.C., who received their name from the fact that they were taught in the Stoa Poikile or Painted Porch of Athens. They believed that since the world is the creation of divine wisdom and is governed by divine law, it is man's duty to accept his fate. Zeno conceived virtue to be the highest good and condemned the passions. (*See* **God and Man, Determinism and Free Will** for a more detailed account of their beliefs.)

**Swedenborgianism.** The Church of the New Jerusalem, based on the writings of Emanuel Swedenborg (1688–1772), was founded by his followers eleven years after his death. The New Church is regarded by its members not as a sect but as a new dispensation bearing the same relationship to Christianity as Christianity does to Judaism.

**Synchronicity,** an attempt by the psychologist, Carl Gustav Jung, to explain the apparently significant relationship between certain events in the physical universe which seem to have no obvious "causal" link. This rather involved concept is easily understood if one realizes that almost all scientific and philosophical beliefs are based on the notion that the continuous process of change which is taking place in ourselves and in the universe around us is dependent upon a principle known as causality. We can express this another way by saying that an object moves because it has been pushed or pulled by another. We see because light strikes the retina and signals pass up the nervous system to the brain. A stone falls to the ground because the earth's gravity is pulling it towards its center, etc., etc. For all practical purposes every event can be looked upon as being "caused" by some other prior event and this is obviously one of the most important principles of the operation of the universe. Jung, however, felt that there is a sufficiently large body of evidence to suggest that events may be linked in a significant (*i.e.,* nonchance) way without there being any true causal relationship between them. The classic example he held to be the supposed predictive power of astrology by which there appears to be a relationship between the stellar configurations and the personality and life-pattern of individuals on earth. Jung was scientist enough to realize that there could be no causal connection between the aspect of the stars and the lives of people billions of miles from them, yet felt that the evidence for astrology was strong enough to demand an alternative noncausal explanation. The trouble with synchronicity, which has not made much impact on the world of physics or of psychology, is that it is not really an explanation at all but merely a convenient word to describe some puzzling correspondences. The real question, of course, is whether there really are events occurring which are significantly but not *causally* linked, and most scientists today would hold that there were probably not. Still it was typical of the bold and imaginative mind of Jung to tackle head-on one of the principal mysteries of existence and come up with a hypothesis to attempt to meet it.

**Syndicalism,** a form of socialist doctrine which aims at the ownership and control of all industries by the workers, contrasted with the more conventional type of socialism which advocates ownership and control by the state. Since syndicalists have preferred to improve the conditions of the workers by direct action, *e.g.,* strikes and working to rule, rather than through the usual parliamentary procedures, they have been closely related to anarchists *(q.v.)* and are sometimes described as anarcho-syndicalists. Under syndicalism there would be no state; for the state would be replaced by a federation of units based on functional economic organization rather than on geographical representation. The movement had bodies in the United Kingdom, where guild socialism *(q.v.)* was strongly influenced by its doctrines, in France, Germany, Italy, Spain, Argentina, and Mexico, but these gradually declined after the first world war losing many members to the communists. Fascism *(q.v.)* was also strongly influenced by the revolutionary syndicalism of Georges Sorel in making use of his concept of the "myth of the general strike" as an emotional image or ideal goal to spur on the workers; with Mussolini the "myth" became that of the state. Mussolini was also influenced by Sorel's doctrine of violence and the justification of force. Syndicalism had a certain influence in the Labour Party in its early days, but was crushed by men like Ernest Bevin who began to fear that by involving the workers in direct responsibility for their industries, it would put them at a disadvantage when bargaining for wages.

# T

**Telepathy and Clairvoyance.** Telepathy is the alleged communication between one mind and another other than through the ordinary sense channels. Clairvoyance is the supposed faculty of "seeing" objects or events which, by reason of space and time or other causes, are not discernible through the ordinary sense of vision. Such claims have been made from time immemorial but it was not until this century that the phenomena were investigated scientifically. The first studies were undertaken by the Society for Psychical Research, which was founded in 1882 with Professor Henry Sidgwick as its first president. Since then it has carried out a scholarly programme of research without—in accordance with its constitution—coming to any corporate conclusions. In America the center of this research was the Parapsychology Laboratory at Duke University (*see* **Parapsychology**) where at one time it was claimed clear scientific evidence for extra-sensory perception (ESP) had been obtained. These claims have been treated with great reservation by the majority of scientists but despite the belief that the study of ESP was going into eclipse, there remains a small but measurable residue of interest in scientific research in this area. It would be odd if some scientists were not interested in ESP because of the enormous weight of anecdotal evidence which has built up over centuries to support it. The weakness of the scientific as opposed to the casual evidence is however exemplified by the failure of ESP researchers to produce a reliable "repeatable" experiment.

**Theism.** *See* **God and Man.**

**Theosophy** (Sanskrit *Brahma Vidya* = divine wisdom), a system of thought that draws on the mystical teachings of those who assert the spiritual nature of the universe, and the divine nature of man. It insists that man is capable of intuitive insight into the nature of God. The way to wisdom, or self-knowledge, is through the practice of **Yoga** *(q.v.).* Theosophy has close connections with Indian thought through Vedic, Buddhist, and Brahmanist literature. The modern Theosophical Society was founded by Mme H. P. Blavatsky and others in 1875, and popularized by Mrs. Annie Besant.

**Transcendental Meditation,** popularized in the West by the Maharishi Mahesh Yogi, who achieved sensational worldwide publicity by his "conversion" of the Beatles a few years ago. This is a simple meditational system which it is claimed is an aid to relaxation and the reduction of psychological and physical stress. It is reported that the technique can be taught in under five minutes provided that someone trained by the Maharishi is the teacher. The pupil or would-be meditator is given a mantra—a meaningless word which acts as a focal point for the imagination—letting his thoughts flow freely while sitting in a comfortable position. Extraordinary claims are made on behalf of the system. As with most cults, religious and occult systems, there is an initial psychological benefit to anyone who becomes deeply involved. Nevertheless, apart from this simple "participation-effect", there is some evidence that the body's autonomic functions (heart rate, respiratory cycle, brain waves, etc.) can be modified by certain individuals including yogis. Whether it is ultimately beneficial to be able to modify these autonomic functions or not is another matter. The latest evidence from laboratory studies in fact shows that subjects in the most relaxed phase of TM are in fact in a (quite normal) stage of light sleep. The TM movement in Britain is based at Mentmore Towers in Buckinghamshire.

**Transmigration of Souls.** *See* **Immortality.**

**Transubstantiation,** the conversion in the Eucharist of the bread and wine into the body and blood of Christ—a doctrine of the Roman Catholic Church.

**Trotskyism,** a form of communism supporting the views of Leon Trotsky, the assumed name of Lev Bronstein (1879–1940) who, in 1924, was ousted from power by Stalin and later exiled and assassinated in Mexico. Trotsky held that excessive Russian nationalism was incompatible with genuine international communism and that Stalin was concentrating on the economic development of the Soviet Union to an extent which could only lead to a bureaucratic state with a purely nationalist outlook. After the Hungarian uprising in 1956, which was ruthlessly suppressed by the Soviet Armed Forces, a wave of resignations from Western Communist parties took place, many of the dissidents joining the Trotskyist movement.

# U

**Ufology,** cultish interest in the study of strange and unexplained aerial phenomena (unidentified flying objects, hence UFOs). *See* **Flying Saucers.**

**Unitarianism** has no special doctrines, although clearly, as the name indicates, belief is in the single personality of God, *i.e.,* anti-trinitarian. This general statement, however, can be interpreted with varying degrees of subtlety. Thus Unitarian belief may range from a sort of Arianism which accepts that, although Christ was not of divine nature, divine powers had been delegated to him by the Father, to the simple belief that Christ was a man like anyone else, and his goodness was of the same nature as that of many other great and good men. Indeed, today many Unitarians deny belief in a personal God and interpret their religion in purely moral terms, putting their faith in the value of love and the brotherhood of man. The Toleration Act (1689) excluded Unitarians but from 1813 they were legally tolerated in England. Nevertheless attempts were made to turn them out of their chapels on the ground that the preachers did not hold the views of the original founders of the endowments. But this ended with the Dissenting Chapels Act of 1845. In America no such difficulties existed, and in the Boston of the 19th cent. many of the great literary figures were openly Unitarian in both belief and name: *e.g.,* Emerson, Longfellow, Lowell, and Oliver Wendell Holmes.

**Utilitarianism,** a school of moral philosophy of which the main proponents were J. S. Mill (1806–73) and Jeremy Bentham (1748–1832). Bentham based his ethical theory upon the utilitarian principle that the greatest happiness of the greatest number is the criterion of morality. What is good is pleasure or happiness; what is bad is pain. If we act on this basis of self-interest (pursuing what we believe to be our own happiness), then what we do will automatically be for the general good. The serious failing of this thesis is (1) that it makes no distinction between the quality of one pleasure and another, and (2) that Bentham failed to see that the law might not be framed and administered by men as benevolent as himself. J. S. Mill accepted Bentham's position in general but seeing its failings emphasized (1) that self-interest was an inadequate basis for utilitarianism and suggested that we should take as the real criterion of good the social consequences of the act; (2) that some pleasures rank higher than others and held that those of the intellect are superior to those of the senses. Not only is the social factor emphasized, but emphasis is also placed on the nature of the act.

**Utopias.** The name "utopia" is taken from a Greek word meaning "nowhere" and was first used in 1516 by Sir Thomas More (1478–1535) as the title of his book referring to a mythical island in the south Pacific where he sited his ideal society. Since then it has been used of any ideal or fanciful society, and here a few will be mentioned. (The reader may recall that Samuel Butler's 19th century novel, describing an imaginary society in New Zealand where criminals were treated and the sick punished, was entitled *Erewhon* which is the word "nowhere" in reverse.) It should be noted that not all utopias were entirely fanciful—*e.g.,* Robert Owen's and Françis Fourier's beliefs, although found to be impractical, were, in fact, tried out.

*Sir Thomas More.* More wrote at a time when the rise of the wool-growing trade had resulted in farming land being turned over to pasture and there was a great wave of unemployment and a rise in crime among the dispossessed. More began to think in terms of the medieval ideal of small cooperative communities in which class interests and personal gain played a decreasing part, a society which would have the welfare of the people at heart both from the physical and intellectual points of view. His utopia was one in which there was no private property, because the desire for acquisition and private possessions lay at the root of human misery. There was, therefore, only common ownership of land and resources. Each class of worker was equipped to carry out its proper function in the economic scheme and each was fairly rewarded for its share in production so that there was neither wealth nor poverty to inspire conflict. Nobody was allowed to idle, until the time came for him to retire when he became free to enjoy whatever cultural pleasures he wished, but since the system was devoid of the waste associated with competition, the working day would be only six hours. There was to be compulsory schooling and free medical care for everybody, full religious toleration, complete equality of the sexes, and a modern system of dealing with crime which was free from vindictiveness and cruelty. Government was to be simple and direct by democratically elected officials whose powers would be strictly limited and the public expenditure kept under close scrutiny. It will be seen that More was far in advance of his age, and to most democratically minded people in advance of an earlier utopia, Plato's *Republic,* which is described under the heading of Education.

*James Harrington.* James Harrington published his book *The Commonwealth of Oceana* in 1656 and offered it to Oliver Cromwell for his consideration but without tangible results. Better than any other man of his time Harrington understood the nature of the economic revolution which was then taking place, and, like More, saw the private ownership of land as the main cause of conflict. He put forward the theory that the control of property, particularly in the shape of land, determines the character of the political structure of the state; if property were universally distributed among the people the sentiment for its protection would naturally result in a republican form of government. The Commonwealth of Oceana was a society "of laws and not of men"—*i.e.,* it was to be legally based and structured so as to be independent of the good or ill will of any individuals controlling it. Thus there must be a written constitution, a two-house legislature, frequent elections with a secret ballot, and separation of powers between legislature and executive—all today familiar features of parliamentary democracy, but unique in his time.

*Saint-Simon.* The utopias of the late 18th and 19th century come, of course, into the period of the Industrial Revolution and of laissez-faire capitalism. Individual enterprise and complete freedom of competition formed the outlook of the ruling class. Naturally the utopias of this period tended to have a strongly socialist tinge since such theories are obviously produced by those who are not satisfied with existing conditions. Saint-Simon's *New Christianity* (1825) is one such, and by many, Claude Henri, Comte de Saint-Simon (1760–1825) is regarded as the founder of French socialism. His book urged a dedication of society to the principle of human brotherhood and a community which would be led by men of science motivated by wholly spiritual aims. Production property was to be nationalized (or "socialized" as he describes the process) and employed to serve the public good rather than private gain; the worker was to produce according to his capacity and to be rewarded on the basis of individual merit; the principle of inheritance was to be abolished since it denied the principle of reward for accomplishment on which the society was to be founded. Saint-Simon's proposals were not directed towards the poorer classes alone, but to the conscience and intellect of all. He was deeply impressed with the productive power of the new machines and his scheme was, first and foremost, intended as a method of directing that power to the betterment of humanity as a whole.

*Fourier.* Françis Marie Charles Fourier (1772–1837), although by conviction a philosophical anarchist who held that human beings are naturally good if allowed to follow their natural desires, was the originator of what, on the face of it, one would suppose to be the most regimented of the utopias. It consisted of a system of "phalanxes" or cooperative communities each composed of a group of workers and technicians assured of a minimum income and sharing the surplus on an equitable basis. Agriculture was to be the chief occupation of each phalanx and industrial employment planned and so carefully assigned that work would become pleasant and creative rather than burdensome. One of his ideas was that necessary work should receive the highest pay, useful work the next, and pleasant work the least pay. The land was to be scientifically cultivated and natural resources carefully conserved. Most of the members' property was to be privately owned, but the ownership of each phalanx was to be widely diffused among members by the sale of shares. Such "parasitic and unproductive" occupations as stockbroker, soldier, economist, middleman and philosopher would be eliminated and the education of children carried out along vocational lines to train them for their future employment.

The strange thing was that Fourier's suggestions appealed to many in both Europe and the United States and such men (admittedly no economic or technical experts) as Emerson, Thoreau, James Russell Lowell, and Nathaniel Hawthorne strongly supported them. An American Fourier colony known as Brook Farm was established and carried on for eight years when it was dissolved after a serious fire had destroyed most of its property.

*Robert Owen.* Robert Owen (1771–1858), a wealthy textile manufacturer and philanthropist, established communities founded on a kind of utopian socialism in Lanarkshire, Hampshire, and in America. Of his New Lanark community an American observer wrote: "There is not, I apprehend, to be found in any part of the world, a manufacturing community in which so much order, good government, tranquillity, and rational happiness reign." The workers in Lanark were given better housing and education for their children, and it was administered as a cooperative self-supporting community in Scotland. Later in life Owen returned to sponsoring legislation that would remove some of the worst evils of industrial life in those days: reduction of the working day to twelve hours, prohibition of labor for children under the age of ten, public schools for elementary education, and so on. But he lived to see few of his reforms adopted. He also promoted the creation of cooperative societies, the formation of trade unions, labor banks, and exchanges, the workers' educational movement, and even an Anglo-American federation. There can be no doubt that, if he saw little result himself, he left the imprint of his convictions to benefit future communities who may not even know his name.

# V

**Vitalism,** the philosophical doctrine that the behavior of the living organism is, at least in part, due to a vital principle which cannot possibly be explained wholly in terms of physics and chemistry. This belief was held by the rationalist thinker C. E. M. Joad (1891–1953) and is implicit in Henri Bergson's (1859–1941) theory of creative evolution. It was maintained by Bergson that evolution, like the work of an artist, is creative and therefore unpredictable; that a vague need exists beforehand within the animal or plant before the means of satisfying the need develops. Thus we might assume that sightless animals developed the need to become aware of objects before they were in physical contact with them and that this ultimately led to the origins of organs of sight. Earlier this century a form of vitalism described as "emergent evolution" was put forward. This theory maintains that when two or more simple entities come together there may arise a new property which none of them previously possessed. Today biologists would say that it is the *arrangement* of atoms that counts, different arrangements exhibiting different properties, and that biological organization is an essentially dynamic affair, involving the lapse of time.

# W

**Witchcraft.** There are various interpretations and definitions of witchcraft from that of Pennethorne Hughes who states that "witchcraft, as it emerges into European history and literature, represents the old paleolithic fertility cult, plus the magical idea, plus various parodies of contemporary religions" to that of the fanatical Father Montague Summers who says that Spiritualism and witchcraft are the same thing. A leading authority on witchcraft, however, the late Dr. Margaret Murray, distinguishes between Operative Witchcraft (which is really Magic *(q.v.)* and Ritual Witchcraft which, she says, "embraces the religious beliefs and ritual of the people known in late medieval times as 'witches.' " That there were such people we know from history and we know, too, that many of them—the great majority of them women—were tortured or executed or both. Many innocent people perished, especially after the promulgation of the bull *Summis desiderantes* by Pope Innocent VIII in 1484. Himself "a man of scandalous life," according to a Catholic historian, he wrote to "his dear sons," the German professors of theology, Johann Sprenger and Heinrich Kraemer, "witches are hindering men from performing the sexual act and women from conceiving . . ." and delegated them as Inquisitors "of these heretical pravities." In 1494 they codified in the *Malleus Maleficarum* (Hammer of Witches) the ecclesiastical rules for detecting acts of witchcraft. Dr. Murray points out that there have ordinarily been two theories about witchcraft: (1) that there were such things as witches, that they possessed supernatural powers and that the evidence given at their trials was substantially correct; (2) that the witches were simply poor silly creatures who either deluded themselves into believing that they had certain powers or, more frequently, were tortured into admitting things that they did not do. She herself accepts a third theory: that there were such beings as witches, that they really did what they admitted to doing, but that they did not possess supernatural powers. They were in fact believers in the old religion of pre-Christian times and the Church took centuries to root them out. That there existed "covens" of witches who carried out peculiar rites Dr. Murray has no doubt whatever. The first to show that witchcraft was a superstition and that the majority of so-called witches were people suffering from mental illness was the physician Johann Weyer of Cleves (1515–88). His views were denounced by the Catholic Church. Few people realize how deeply the notion of witchcraft is implanted in our minds and how seriously its power is still taken. For example, the Witchcraft Act was not repealed in England until the 1950s. Furthermore, as recently as 1944, when the allied armies were invading Europe, the Spiritualist medium Mrs. Helen Duncan was charged with witchcraft and actually sent to prison—a prosecution which brought forth caustic comments from the then prime minister, Winston Churchill. *See also* **Demonism.**

# Y

**Yoga,** a Hindu discipline which teaches a technique for freeing the mind from attachment to the senses, so that once freed the soul may become fused with the universal spirit (*atman* or Brahman), which is its natural goal. This is the sole function of the psychological and physical exercises which the Yogi undertakes, although few ever reach the final stage of *Samadhi* or union with Brahman which is said to take place in eight levels of attainment. These are: (1) *Yama,* which involves the extinction of desire and egotism and their replacement by charity and unselfishness; (2) *Niyama,* during which certain rules of conduct must be adopted, such as cleanliness, the pursuit of devotional studies, and the carrying out of rituals of purification; (3) *Asana,* or the attainment of correct posture and the reduction to a minimum of all bodily movement (the usual posture of the concentrating Yogi is the "lotus position" familiar from pictures); (4) *Pranayama,* the right control of the life-force or breath in which there are two stages at which the practitioner hopes to arrive, the first being complete absorption in the act of breathing which empties the mind of any other thought, the second being the ability almost to cease to breathe which allegedly enables him to achieve marvellous feats of endurance; (5) *Pratyahara* or abstraction which means the mind's complete withdrawal from the world of sense; (6) *Dharana* in which an attempt is made to think of one thing only which finally becomes a repetition of the sacred syllable OM; (7) *dhyana,* meditation, which finally leads to (8) *Samadhi* the trance state which is a sign of the complete unity of soul with reality.

Yoga is very old, and when the sage Patanjali (*c.* 300 B.C.) composed the book containing these instructions, the *Yoga Sutras,* he was probably collecting from many ancient traditions. Some of the claims made by Yogis seem, to the Western mind, frankly incredible; but in the West and especially in recent years Yoga methods have been used at the lower levels in order to gain improved self-control, better posture, and improved health. Whether it achieves these ends is another matter, but the genuine Yogi regards this as a perversion of the nature and purpose of the discipline.

# Z

**Zen Buddhism,** a Buddhist sect which is believed to have arisen in 6th cent. China but has flourished chiefly in Japan; for some reason it has of recent years begun to attract attention in the West thanks to the voluminous writings of Dr. D. T. Suzuki and the less numerous but doubtless much-read books of Mr. Christmas Humphreys. But the fact that these writings exist does not explain their being read, nor why of all possible Eastern sects this particular one should be chosen in our times. What is Zen's attraction and why should anyone take the trouble to read about something (the word "something" is used for reasons that will become evident) that is not a religion, has no doctrine, knows no God and no afterlife, no good and no evil, and possesses no scriptures but has to be taught by parables which seem to be purposely meaningless? One of the heroes of Zen is the fierce-looking Indian monk Boddhidharma (fl. *c.* 516–34) who brought Buddhism to China, of whom it is recounted that when the Emperor asked him how much merit he had acquired by supporting the new creed, the monk shouted at him: "None whatever!" The emperor then wished to know what was the sacred doctrine of the creed and again the monk shouted: "It is empty—there is nothing sacred!" Dr. Suzuki, having affirmed that there is no God in Zen, goes on to state that this does not mean that Zen denies the existence of God because "neither denial nor affirmation concerns Zen." The most concrete statement he is prepared to make is that the basic idea of Zen is to come in touch with the inner workings of our being, and to do this in the most direct way possible without resorting to anything external or superadded. Therefore anything that has the semblance of an external authority is rejected by Zen. Absolute faith is placed in a man's own inner being. Apparently the intention is that, so far from indulging in inward meditations or such practices as the Yogi uses, the student must learn to act spontaneously, without thinking, and without self-consciousness or hesitation. This is the main purpose of the *koan*, the logically insoluble riddle which the pupil must try to solve. One such is the question put by master to pupil: "A girl is walking down the street, is she the younger or the older sister?" The correct answer, it seems, is to say nothing but put on a mincing gait, to *become* the girl, thus showing that what matters is the experience of being and not its verbal description. Another *koan*: "What is the Buddha?" "Three pounds of flax" is attributed to T'ungshan in the 9th cent. and a later authority's comment is that "none can excel it as regards its irrationality which cuts off all passages to speculation." Zen, in effect, teaches the uselessness of trying to use words to discuss the Absolute.

Zen came to Japan in the 13th cent., more than five centuries after Confucianism or the orthodox forms of Buddhism, and immediately gained acceptance while becoming typically Japanese in the process. One of the reasons why it appealed must have been that its spontaneity and insistence on action without thought, its emphasis on the uselessness of mere words, and such categories as logical opposites, had an inevitable attraction for a people given to seriousness, formality, and logic to a degree which was almost stifling. Zen must have been to the Japanese what nonsense rhymes and nonsense books, like those of Edward Lear and Lewis Carroll, were to the English intellectuals. Lear's limericks, like some of the *koans*, end up with a line which, just at the time when one expects a point to be made, has no particular point at all, and *Alice in Wonderland* is the perfect example of a world, not without logic, but with a crazy logic of its own which has no relationship with that of everyday life. Therefore Zen began to impregnate every aspect of life in Japan, and one of the results of its emphasis on spontaneous action rather than reason was its acceptance by the Samurai, the ferocious warrior class, in such activities as swordsmanship, archery, Japanese wrestling, and later Judo and the Kamikaze dive-bombers. But much of Japanese art, especially landscape gardening and flower-arrangement, was influenced similarly, and Zen is even used in Japanese psychiatry. The very strict life of the Zen monks is based largely on doing things, learning through experience; the periods of meditation in the Zendo hall are punctuated by sharp slaps on the face administered by the abbot to those who are unsatisfactory pupils. Dr. Suzuki denies that Zen is nihilistic, but it is probably its appearance of nihilism and its appeal to the irrational and spontaneous which attracts the Western world at a time when to many the world seems without meaning and life over-

regimented. However, it has influenced such various aspects of Western life as philosophy (Heidegger), psychiatry (Erich Fromm and Hubert Benoit), writing (Aldous Huxley), and painting (Die Zen Gruppe in Germany).

**Zionism,** a belief in the need to establish an autonomous Jewish home in Palestine which, in its modern form, began with Theodor Herzl (1860–1904), a Hungarian journalist working in Vienna. Although Herzl was a more or less assimilated Jew, he was forced by the Dreyfus case and the pogroms in Eastern Europe to conclude that there was no real safety for the Jewish people until they had a state of their own. The Jews, of course, had always in a religious sense thought of Palestine as a spiritual homeland and prayed "next year in Jerusalem," but the religious had thought of this in a philosophical way as affirming old loyalties, not as recommending the formation of an actual state. Therefore Herzl was opposed both by many of the religious Jews and, at the other extreme, by those who felt themselves to be assimilated and in many cases without religious faith. Even after the Balfour Declaration of 1917, there was not a considerable flow of Jews to Palestine, which at that time was populated mainly by Arabs. But the persecutions of Hitler changed all this and, after bitter struggles, the Jewish state was proclaimed in 1948. Today Zionism is supported by the vast majority of the Jewish communities everywhere (although strongly disapproved of in the Soviet Union as "Western imperialism") and Zionism is now an active international force concerned with protecting the welfare and extending the influence of Israel.

**Zoroastrianism,** at one time one of the great world religions, competing in the 2nd cent. A.D. on almost equal terms from its Persian home with Hellenism and the Roman Imperial Government. Under the Achaemenidae (*c.* 550–330 B.C.) Zoroastrianism was the state religion of Persia. Alexander's conquest in 331 B.C. brought disruption but the religion flourished again under the Sassanian dynasty (A.D. *c.* 226–640). With the advance of the Mohammedan Arabs in the 7th cent. Zoroastrianism finally gave way to Islam. A number of devotees fled to India there to become the Parsees. In Persia itself a few scattered societies remain.

The name Zoroaster is the Greek rendering of Zarathustra, the prophet who came to purify the ancient religion of Persia. It is thought that he lived at the beginning of the 6th cent. B.C. He never claimed for himself divine powers but was given them by his followers. The basis of Zoroastrianism is the age-long war between good and evil, Ahura Mazda heading the good spirits and Ahriman the evil ones. Morality is very important since by doing right the worshipper is supporting Ahura Mazda against Ahriman, and the evil-doers will be punished in the last days when Ahura Mazda wins his inevitable victory.

The sacred book of this religion is the *Avesta*. If Zoroastrianism has little authority today, it had a very considerable influence in the past. Its doctrines penetrated into Judaism *(q.v.)* and, through Gnosticism, Christianity. The worship of Mithra by the Romans was an impure version of Zoroastrianism. Manichaeism *(q.v.)* was a Zoroastrian heresy and the Albigensianism of medieval times was the last relic of a belief which had impressed itself deeply in the minds of men.

# GEOGRAPHY

## World Geography
### Explorations and Discoveries
(All years are A.D. unless B.C. is specified.)

| Country or place | Event | Explorer or discoverer | Date |
|---|---|---|---|
| **AFRICA** | | | |
| Sierra Leone | Visited | Hanno, Carthaginian seaman | c. 520 B.C. |
| Congo River | Mouth discovered | Diogo Cão, Portuguese | c. 1484 |
| Cape of Good Hope | Rounded | Bartolomeu Diaz, Portuguese | 1488 |
| Gambia River | Explored | Mungo Park, Scottish explorer | 1795 |
| Sahara | Crossed | Dixon Denham and Hugh Clapperton, English explorers | 1822–23 |
| Zambezi River | Discovered | David Livingstone, Scottish explorer | 1851 |
| Sudan | Explored | Heinrich Barth, German explorer | 1852–55 |
| Victoria Falls | Discovered | Livingstone | 1855 |
| Lake Tanganyika | Discovered | Richard Burton and John Speke, British explorers | 1858 |
| Congo River | Traced | Sir Henry M. Stanley, British explorer | 1877 |
| **ASIA** | | | |
| Punjab (India) | Visited | Alexander the Great | 327 B.C. |
| China | Visited | Marco Polo, Italian traveler | c. 1272 |
| Tibet | Visited | Odoric of Pordenone, Italian monk | c. 1325 |
| Southern China | Explored | Niccolò dei Conti, Venetian traveler | c. 1440 |
| India | Visited (Cape route) | Vasco da Gama, Portuguese navigator | 1498 |
| Japan | Visited | St. Francis Xavier of Spain | 1549 |
| Arabia | Explored | Carsten Niebuhr, German explorer | 1762 |
| China | Explored | Ferdinand Richthofen, German scientist | 1868 |
| Mongolia | Explored | Nikolai M. Przhevalsky, Russian explorer | 1870–73 |
| Central Asia | Explored | Sven Hedin, Swedish scientist | 1890–1908 |
| **EUROPE** | | | |
| Shetland Islands | Visited | Pytheas of Massilia (Marseille) | c. 325 B.C. |
| North Cape | Rounded | Ottar, Norwegian explorer | c. 870 |
| Iceland | Colonized | Norwegian noblemen | c. 890–900 |
| **NORTH AMERICA** | | | |
| Greenland | Colonized | Eric the Red, Norwegian | c. 985 |
| Labrador; Nova Scotia (?) | Discovered | Leif Ericson, Norse explorer | 1000 |
| West Indies | Discovered | Christopher Columbus, Italian | 1492 |
| North America | Coast discovered | Giovanni Caboto (John Cabot), for British | 1497 |
| Pacific Ocean | Discovered | Vasco Núñez de Balboa, Spanish explorer | 1513 |
| Florida | Explored | Ponce de León, Spanish explorer | 1513 |
| Mexico | Conquered | Hernando Cortés, Spanish adventurer | 1519–21 |
| St. Lawrence River | Discovered | Jacques Cartier, French navigator | 1534 |
| Southwest U. S. | Explored | Francisco Coronado, Spanish explorer | 1540–42 |
| Colorado River | Discovered | Hernando de Alarcón, Spanish explorer | 1540 |
| Mississippi River | Discovered | Hernando de Soto, Spanish explorer | 1541 |
| Frobisher Bay | Discovered | Martin Frobisher, English seaman | 1576 |

457

| Country or place | Event | Explorer or discover | Date |
|---|---|---|---|
| Maine Coast | Explored | Samuel de Champlain, French explorer | 1604 |
| Jamestown, Va. | Settled | John Smith, English colonist | 1607 |
| Hudson River | Explored | Henry Hudson, English navigator | 1609 |
| Hudson Bay (Canada) | Discovered | Henry Hudson | 1610 |
| Baffin Bay | Discovered | William Baffin, English navigator | 1616 |
| Lake Michigan | Navigated | Jean Nicolet, French explorer | 1634 |
| Arkansas River | Discovered | Jacques Marquette and Louis Jolliet, French explorers | 1673 |
| Mississippi River | Explored | Sieur de La Salle, French explorer | 1682 |
| Bering Strait | Discovered | Vitus Bering, Danish explorer | 1728 |
| Alaska | Discovered | Vitus Bering | 1741 |
| Mackenzie River (Canada) | Discovered | Sir Alexander Mackenzie, Scottish-Canadian explorer | 1789 |
| Northwest U. S. | Explored | Meriwether Lewis and William Clark | 1804–06 |
| Northeast Passage (Arctic Ocean) | Navigated | Nils Nordenskjöld, Swedish explorer | 1879 |
| Greenland | Explored | Robert Peary, American explorer | 1892 |
| Northwest Passage | Navigated | Roald Amundsen, Norwegian explorer | 1906 |
| **SOUTH AMERICA** | | | |
| Continent | Visited | Columbus, Italian | 1498 |
| Brazil | Discovered | Pedro Alvarez Cabral, Portuguese | 1500 |
| Peru | Conquered | Francisco Pizarro, Spanish explorer | 1532–33 |
| Amazon River | Explored | Francisco Orellana, Spanish explorer | 1541 |
| Cape Horn | Discovered | Willem C. Schouten, Dutch navigator | 1615 |
| **OCEANIA** | | | |
| Papua New Guinea | Visited | Jorge de Menezes, Portuguese explorer | 1526 |
| Australia | Visited | Abel Janszoon Tasman, Dutch navigator | 1642 |
| Tasmania | Discovered | | |
| Australia | Explored | John McDouall Stuart, English explorer | 1828 |
| Australia | Explored | Robert Burke and William Wills, Australian explorers | 1861 |
| New Zealand | Sighted (and named) | Abel Janszoon Tasman | 1642 |
| New Zealand | Visited | James Cook, English navigator | 1769 |
| **ARCTIC, ANTARCTIC, AND MISCELLANEOUS** | | | |
| Ocean exploration | Expedition | Magellan's ships circled globe | 1519–22 |
| Galápagos Islands | Visited | Diego de Rivadeneira, Spanish captain | 1535 |
| Spitsbergen | Visited | Willem Barents, Dutch navigator | 1596 |
| Antarctic Circle | Crossed | James Cook, English navigator | 1773 |
| Antarctica | Discovered | Nathaniel Palmer, U. S. whaler (archipelago) and Fabian Gottlieb von Bellingshausen, Russian admiral (mainland) | 1820–21 |
| Antarctica | Explored | Charles Wilkes, American explorer | 1840 |
| North Pole | Reached | Robert E. Peary, American explorer | 1909 |
| South Pole | Reached | Roald Amundsen, Norwegian explorer | 1911 |

# The Continents

A continent is defined as a large unbroken land mass completely surrounded by water, although in some cases continents are (or were in part) connected by land bridges.

The hypothesis first suggested late in the 19th century was that the continents consist of lighter rocks that rest on heavier crustal material in about the same manner that icebergs float on water. That the rocks forming the continents are lighter than the material below them and under the ocean bot-toms is now established. As a consequence of this fact, Alfred Wegener (for the first time in 1912) suggested that the continents are slowly moving, at a rate of about one yard per century, so that their relative positions are not rigidly fixed. Many geologists that were originally skeptical have come to accept this theory of Continental Drift.

When describing a continent, it is important to remember that there is a fundamental difference between a deep ocean, like the Atlantic, and shallow seas, like the Baltic and most of the North Sea, which are merely flooded portions of a continent. Another and entirely different point to remember is that political considerations have often overridden geographical facts when it came to naming continents.

Geographically speaking, Europe, including the British Isles, is a large western peninsula of the continent of Asia; and many geographers, when referring to Europe and Asia, speak of the Eurasian Continent. But traditionally, Europe is counted as a separate continent, with the Ural and the Caucasus mountains forming the line of demarcation between Europe and Asia.

To the south of Europe, Asia has an odd-shaped peninsula jutting westward, which has a large number of political subdivisions. The northern section is taken up by Turkey; to the south of Turkey there are Syria, Iraq, Israel, Jordan, Saudi Arabia, and a number of smaller Arab countries. All this is part of Asia. Traditionally, the island of Cyprus in the Mediterranean is also considered to be part of Asia, while the island of Crete is counted as European.

The large islands of Java, Borneo, and Sumatra and the smaller islands near them are counted as part of "tropical Asia," while New Guinea is counted as related to Australia. In the case of the Americas, the problem arises as to whether they should be considered one or two continents. There are good arguments on both sides, but since there is now a land bridge between North and South America (in the past it was often flooded) and since no part of the sea east of the land bridge is deep ocean, it is more logical to consider the Americas as one continent.

Politically, based mainly on history, the Americas are divided into North America (from the Arctic to the Mexican border), Central America (from Mexico to Panama, with the Caribbean islands), and South America. Greenland is considered a section of North America, while Iceland is traditionally counted as a European island because of its political ties with the Scandinavian countries.

The island groups in the Pacific are often called "Oceania," but this name does *not* imply that scientists consider them the remains of a continent.

# Volcanoes of the World

About 500 volcanoes have had recorded eruptions within historical times. Almost two thirds of these are in the Northern Hemisphere. Most volcanoes occur at the boundaries of the earth's crustal plates, such as the famous "Ring of Fire" that surrounds the Pacific Ocean plate. Of the world's active volcanoes, about 60% are along the perimeter of the Pacific, about 17% on mid-oceanic islands, about 14% in an arc along the south of the Indonesian islands, and about 9% in the Mediterranean area, Africa, and Asia Minor. Many of the world's volcanoes are submarine and have unrecorded eruptions.

## Pacific "Ring of Fire"

### NORTHWEST
**Japan:** At least 33 active vents.

Aso (5,223 ft; 1,592 m), on Kyushu, has one of the largest craters in the world.

Asama (over 8,300 ft; 2,530 m), on Honshu, is continuously active; violent eruption in 1783.

Azuma (nearly 7,700 ft; 2,347 m), on Honshu, erupted in 1900.

Chokai (7,300 ft; 2,225 m), on Honshu, erupted in 1974 after having been quiescent since 1861.

Fujiyama (Fujisan) (12,385 ft; 3,775 m), on Honshu, southwest of Tokyo. Symmetrical in outline, snow-covered. Regarded as a sacred mountain.

On-take (3,668 ft; 1,118 m), on peninsula of Kyushu. Strong smoke emissions and explosions began November 1973 and continued through 1974.

**U.S.S.R.:** Kamchatka peninsula, 14–18 active volcanoes. Klyuchevskaya (Kluchev) (15,500 ft; 4,724 m) reported active in 1974.

Kurile Islands: At least 13 active volcanoes and several submarine outbreaks.

### SOUTHWEST
**New Zealand:** Mount Tarawera (3,645 ft; 1,112 m), on North Island, had a severe eruption in 1886 that destroyed the famous Pink and White sinter terraces of Rotomahana, a hot lake.

Ngauruhoe (7,515 ft; 2,291 m), on North Island, emits steam and vapor constantly. Erupted 1974.

**Papua New Guinea:** Karkar Island (4,920 ft; 1,500 m). Mild eruptions 1974.

**Philippine Islands:** About 100 eruptive centers; Hibok Hibok, on Camiguin, erupted September 1950 and again in December 1951, when about 750 were reported killed or missing; eruptions continued during 1952–53.

Taal (4,752 ft; 1,448 m), on Luzon. Major eruption in 1965 killed 190; erupted again, 1968.

**Volcano Islands:** Mount Suribachi (546 ft; 166 m), on Iwo Jima. A sulfurous steaming volcano. Raising of U.S. flag over Mount Suribachi was one of the dramatic episodes of World War II.

### NORTHEAST
**Alaska:** Mount Wrangell (14,163 ft; 4,317 m) and Mount Katmai (about 6,700 ft; 2,042 m). On June 6, 1912, a violent eruption (Nova Rupta) of Mount Katmai occurred, during which the "Valley of Ten Thousand Smokes" was formed.

**Aleutian Islands:** There are 32 active vents known and numerous inactive cones. Akutan Island (over 4,000 ft; 1,220 m) erupted in 1974, with ash and debris rising over 300 ft.

Great Sitkin (5,741 ft; 1,750 m). Explosive activity February–September 1974, accompanied by earthquake originating at volcano that registered 2.3 on Richter scale.

**Augustine Island:** Augustine volcano (4,000 ft; 1,220 m) erupted March 27, 1986. It last erupted in 1976.

**California, Oregon, Washington:** Lassen Peak (10,453 ft; 3,186 m) in California is one of two observed active volcanoes in the U.S. outside Alaska and Hawaii. The last period of activity was 1914–17. Mt. St. Helens (9,677 ft; 2,950 m) in the Cascade Range of southwest Washington became active on March 27, 1980, and erupted on May 18 after being inactive since 1857. From April 15 through May 1, 1986, weak activity began for the first time in two years. Other mountains of volcanic origin include Mount Shasta (California), Mount Hood (Oregon), Mount Mazama (Oregon)—the mountain containing Crater Lake, Mount Rainier (Washington), and Mount Baker (Washington), which has been steaming since October 1975, but gives no sign of an impending eruption.

## SOUTHEAST

**Chile and Argentina:** About 25 active or potentially active.

**Colombia:** Huila (nearly 18,900 ft; 5,760 m), a vapor-emitting volcano, and Tolima (nearly 18,500 ft; 5,640 m). Eruption of Puracé (15,600 ft; 4,755 m) in 1949 killed 17 people. Nevado del Ruiz (16,200 ft; 4,938 m.), erupted Nov. 13, 1985, sending torrential floods of mud and water engulfing the town of Armero and killing more than 22,000 people.

**Ecuador:** Cayambe (nearly 19,000 ft; 5,791 m). Almost on the equator.

Cotopaxi (19,344 ft; 5,896 m). Perhaps highest active volcano in the world. Possesses a beautifully formed cone.

Reventador (11,434 ft; 3,485 m). Observed in active state in late 1973.

**El Salvador:** Izalco ("beacon of Central America") (7,830 ft; 2,387 m) first appeared in 1770 and is still growing (erupted in 1950, 1956; last erupted in October–November 1966). San Salvador (6,187 ft; 1,886 m) had a violent eruption in 1923. Conchagua (about 4100 ft; 1,250 m) erupted with considerable damage early in 1947.

**Guatemala:** Santa Maria Quezaltenango (12,361 ft; 3,768 m). Frequent activity between 1902–08 and 1922–28 after centuries of quiescence. Most dangerously active vent of Central America. Other volcanoes include Tajumulco (13,814 ft; 4,211 m) and Atitlán (11,633 ft; 3,546 m).

**Mexico:** Boquerón ("Big Mouth"), on San Benedicto, about 250 mi. south of Lower California. Newest volcano in Western Hemisphere, discovered September 1952.

Colima (about 14,000 ft; 4,270 m), in group that has had frequent eruptions.

Orizaba (Citlaltépetl) (18,701 ft; 5,700 m).

Parícutin (7,450 ft; 2,270 m). First appeared in February 1943. In less than a week, a cone over 140 ft high developed with a crater one quarter mile in circumference. Cone grew more than 1,500 ft (457 m) in 1943. Erupted 1952.

Popocatépetl (17,887 ft; 5,452 m). Large, deep, bell-shaped crater. Not entirely extinct; steam still escapes.

El Chinchonal (7,300 ft; 1,005.6 m) about 15 miles from Pichucalco. Long inactive, it erupted in March 1982.

**Nicaragua:** Volcanoes include Telica, Coseguina, and Momotombo. Between Momotombo on the west shore of Lake Managua and Coseguina overlooking the Gulf of Fonseca, there is a string of more than 20 cones, many still active. One of these, Cerro Negro, erupted in July 1947, with considerable damage and loss of life, and again in 1971.

Concepción (5,100 ft; 1,555 m). Ash eruptions 1973–74.

## Mid-oceanic Islands

**Canary Islands:** Pico de Teide (12,192 ft; 3,716 m), on Tenerife.

**Cape Verde Islands:** Fogo (nearly 9,300 ft; 2,835 m). Severe eruption in 1857; quiescent until 1951.

**Caribbean:** La Soufrière (4,813 ft; 1,467 m), on Basse-Terre, Guadeloupe. Also called La Grande Soufrière. Violent activity in July–August 1976 caused evacuation of 73,000 people; renewed ac-

tivity in April 1977 again caused thousands to flee their homes.

La Soufrière (4,048 ft; 1,234 m), on St. Vincent. Major eruption in 1902 killed over 1,000 people. Eruptions over 10-day period in April 1979 caused evacuation of northern two thirds of island.

**Comoros:** One volcano, Karthala (nearly 8,000 ft; 2,440 m), is visible for over 100 miles. Last erupted in 1904.

**Hawaii:** Mauna Loa ("Long Mountain") (13,680 ft; 4,170 m), on Hawaii, discharges from its high side vents more lava than any other volcano. Largest volcanic mountain in the world in cubic content. Area of crater is 3.7 sq mi. Violent eruption in June 1950, with lava pouring 25 miles into the ocean. Last major eruption in July 1975.

Mauna Kea (13,796 ft; 4,205 m), on Hawaii. Highest mountain in state.

Kilauea (4,090 ft; 1,247 m) is a vent in the side of Mauna Loa, but its eruptions are apparently independent. One of the most spectacular and active craters. Crater has an area of 4.14 sq mi. Earthquake in July 1975 caused major eruption. Eruptions began in September 1977 and reached a height of 980 ft (300 m). Activity ended Oct. 1. Became active again in January 1983, exploding in earnest in March 1983 forming the volcanic cone Pu'u O which has erupted periodically ever since.

**Iceland:** At least 25 volcanoes active in historical times. Very similar to Hawaiian volcanoes. Askja (over 4,700 ft; 1,433 m) is the largest.

**Lesser Antilles (West Indian Islands):** Mount Pelée (over 4,500 ft; 1,370 m), northwestern Martinique. Eruption in 1902 destroyed town of St. Pierre and killed approximately 40,000 people.

**Réunion Island (east of Madagascar):** Piton de la Fournaise (Le Volcan) (8,610 ft; 2,624 m). Large lava flows. Last erupted in 1972.

**Samoan archipelago:** Savai'i Island had an eruption in 1905 that caused considerable damage. Niuafoo (Tin Can), in the Tonga Islands, has a crater that extends 6,000 feet below and 600 feet above water.

## Indonesia

**Sumatra:** Ninety volcanoes have been discovered; 12 are now active. The most famous, Krakatau, is a small volcanic island in the Sunda Strait. Numerous volcanic discharges occurred in 1883. One extremely violent explosion caused the disappearance of the highest peak and the northern part of the island. Fine dust was carried around the world in the upper atmosphere. Over 36,000 persons lost their lives in resultant tidal waves that were felt as far away as Cape Horn. Active in 1972.

## Mediterranean Area

**Italy:** Mount Etna (10,902 ft; 3,323 m), eastern Sicily. Two new craters formed in eruptions of February–March 1947. Worst eruption in 50 years occurred November 1950–January 1951. Erupted again in 1974, 1975, 1977, 1978, 1979, and 1983.

Stromboli (about 3,000 ft; 914 m), Lipari Islands (north of Sicily). Called "Lighthouse of the Mediterranean." Reported active in 1971.

Mount Vesuvius (4,200 ft; 1,280 m), southeast of Naples. Only active volcano on European mainland. Pompeii buried by an eruption, A.D. 79.

## Antarctica

The discovery of two small active volcanoes in 1982 brings to five the total number known on Antarctica. The new ones, 30 miles apart, are on the Weddell Sea side of the Antarctic Peninsula. The largest, Mount Erebus (13,000 ft; 3,962 m), rises from McMurdo Sound. Mount Melbourne (9,000 ft; 2,743 m) is in Victoria Land. The fifth, off the northern tip of the Antarctic Peninsula, is a crater known as Deception Island.

# Principal Types of Volcanoes

(*Source:* U.S. Dept. of Interior, Geological Survey.)

The word "volcano" comes from the little island of Vulcano in the Mediterranean Sea off Sicily. Centuries ago, the people living in this area believed that Vulcano was the chimney of the forge of Vulcan—the blacksmith of the Roman gods. They thought that the hot lava fragments and clouds of dust erupting from Vulcano came from Vulcan's forge. Today, we know that volcanic eruptions are not supernatural but can be studied and interpreted by scientists.

Geologists generally group volcanoes into four main kinds—cinder cones, composite volcanoes, shield volcanoes, and lava domes.

## Cinder Cones

Cinder cones are the simplest type of volcano. They are built from particles and blobs of congealed lava ejected from a single vent. As the gas-charged lava is blown violently into the air, it breaks into small fragments that solidify and fall as cinders around the vent to form a circular or oval cone. Most cinder cones have a bowl-shaped crater at the summit and rarely rise more than a thousand feet or so above their surroundings. Cinder cones are numerous in western North America as well as throughout other volcanic terrains of the world.

## Composite Volcanoes

Some of the Earth's grandest mountains are composite volcanoes—sometimes called *stratovolcanoes.* They are typically steep-sided, symmetrical cones of large dimension built of alternating layers of lava flows, volcanic ash, cinders, blocks, and bombs and may rise as much as 8,000 feet above their bases. Some of the most conspicuous and beautiful mountains in the world are composite volcanoes, including Mount Fuji in Japan, Mount Cotopaxi in Ecuador, Mount Shasta in California, Mount Hood in Oregon, and Mount St. Helens and Mount Rainier in Washington.

Most composite volcanoes have a crater at the summit which contains a central vent or a clustered group of vents. Lavas either flow through breaks in the crater wall or issue from fissures on the flanks of the cone. Lava, solidified within the fissures, forms *dikes* that act as ribs which greatly strengthen the cone.

The essential feature of a composite volcano is a conduit system through which magma from a reservoir deep in the Earth's crust rises to the surface. The volcano is built up by the accumulation of material erupted through the conduit and increases in size as lava, cinders, ash, etc., are added to its slopes.

## Shield Volcanoes

Shield volcanoes, the third type of volcano, are built almost entirely of fluid lava flows. Flow after flow pours out in all directions from a central summit vent, or group of vents, building a broad, gently sloping cone of flat, domical shape, with a profile much like that of a warrior's shield. They are built up slowly by the accretion of thousands of flows of highly fluid basaltic (from *basalt,* a hard, dense dark volcanic rock) lava that spread widely over great distances, and then cool as thin, gently dipping sheets. Lavas also commonly erupt from vents along fractures (rift zones) that develop on the flanks of the cone. Some of the largest volcanoes in the world are shield volcanoes. In northern California and Oregon, many shield volcanoes have diameters of 3 or 4 miles and heights of 1,500 to 2,000 feet. The Hawaiian Islands are composed of linear chains of these volcanoes, including Kilauea and Mauna Loa on the island of Hawaii.

In some shield-volcano eruptions, basaltic lava pours out quietly from long fissures instead of central vents and floods the surrounding countryside with lava flow upon lava flow, forming broad plateaus. Lava plateaus of this type can be seen in Iceland, southeastern Washington, eastern Oregon, and southern Idaho.

## Lava Domes

Volcanic or lava domes are formed by relatively small, bulbous masses of lava too viscous to flow any great distance; consequently, on extrusion, the lava piles over and around its vent. A dome grows largely by expansion from within. As it grows its outer surface cools and hardens, then shatters, spilling loose fragments down its sides. Some domes form craggy knobs or spines over the volcanic vent, whereas others form short, steep-sided lava flows known as "coulees." Volcanic domes commonly occur within the craters or on the flanks of large composite volcanoes. The nearly circular Novarupta Dome that formed during the 1912 eruption of Katmai Volcano, Alaska, measures 800 feet across and 200 feet high. The internal structure of this dome—defined by layering of lava fanning upward and outward from the center—indicates that it grew largely by expansion from within. Mount Pelée in Martinique, West Indies, and Lassen Peak and Mono domes in California, are examples of lava domes.

## Submarine Volcanoes

Submarine volcanoes and volcanic vents are common features on certain zones of the ocean floor. Some are active at the present time and, in shallow water, disclose their presence by blasting steam and rock-debris high above the surface of the sea. Many others lie at such great depths that the tremendous weight of the water above them results in high, confining pressure and prevents the formation and release of steam and gases. Even very large, deepwater eruptions may not disturb the ocean floor.

The famous black sand beaches of Hawaii were created virtually instantaneously by the violent interaction between hot lava and sea water.

## The Pacific Ocean "Ring of Fire"

## Volcanic Activity in the Solar System

(*Source:* U.S. Dept. of Interior, Geological Survey.)

From the 1976-1979 *Viking* mission, scientists have been able to study the volcanoes on Mars, and their studies are very revealing when compared with those of volcanoes on Earth. For example, Martian and Hawaiian volcanoes have gently sloping flanks, large multiple-collapse pits at their centers, and appear to be built of fluid lavas that have left their numerous flow features on their flanks. The most obvious difference between the two is size. The Martian shields are enormous. They can grow to over 17 miles in height and more than 350 miles across, in contrast to a maximum height of about 6 miles and width of 74 miles for the Hawaiian shields.

Source: U.S. Department of the Interior, U.S. Geological Survey.

Surtsey — Hekla
Mt. Katmai
hishaldin
Mt. St. Helens — Mt. Rainier
Mt. Shasta — Mt. Adams
Lassen Peak
Fayal
Mauna Loa
La Palma
Kilauea
Parícutin
Fogo
Cerro Negro — Mt. Pelée
Irazú
Cotopaxi
El Misti
Azul
Tarawera
Burney

60°
40°
0°
40°
60°
0°    120°    60°    0°

## Earth's Volcanic Origin

In July 1979, *Voyager-2* spacecraft images taken of Io, a moon of Jupiter, captured volcanoes in the actual process of eruption. The volcanic plumes photographed rose to some 60 to 100 miles above the surface of the moon. Thus active volcanism is taking place, at present, on at least one planetary body in addition to our Earth.

More than 80 percent of the Earth's surface—above and below sea level—is of volcanic origin. Gaseous emissions from volcanic vents over hundreds of millions of years formed the Earth's earliest oceans and atmosphere. Over geologic eons, countless volcanic eruptions have produced mountains, plateaus, and plains which erosion and weathering have transformed into fertile soils.

## Plate-Tectonics Theory—The Lithosphere Plates of the Earth

*Source:* U.S. Department of the Interior, U.S. Geological Survey.

## World Population, Land Areas, and Elevations

| Area | Estimated population, mid-1986 | Approximate Land area sq mi. | Percent of total land area | Population density per sq mi. | Elevation, feet | |
|---|---|---|---|---|---|---|
| | | | | | Highest | Lowest |
| WORLD | 4,942,000,000 | 58,433,000 | 100.0 | 84.6[1] | Mt. Everest, Asia, 29,028 | Dead Sea, Asia, 1,290 below sea level |
| ASIA, incl. Philippines, Indonesia, and European and Asiatic Turkey; excl. Asiatic U.S.S.R. | 2,876,000,000 | 10,644,000 | 18.2 | 270.2 | Mt. Everest, Tibet-Nepal, 29,028 | Dead Sea, Israel-Jordan, 1,290 below sea level |
| AFRICA | 583,000,000 | 11,707,000 | 20.0 | 49.8 | Mt. Kilimanjaro, Tanzania, 19,340 | Lake Assal, Djibouti, 571 below sea level |
| NORTH AMERICA, including Hawaii, Central America, and Caribbean region | 406,000,000 | 9,360,000 | 16.0 | 43.4 | Mt. McKinley; Alaska, 20,320 | Death Valley, Calif., 282 below sea level |
| SOUTH AMERICA | 270,000,000 | 6,883,000 | 11.8 | 40.5 | Mt. Aconcagua, Arg.-Chile, 23,034 | Valdes Peninsula, 131 below sea level |
| ANTARCTICA | — | 6,000,000 | 10.3 | — | Vinson Massif, Sentinel Range, 16,863 | Sea level |
| EUROPE, incl. Iceland; excl. European U.S.S.R. and European Turkey | 493,000,000 | 1,905,000 | 3.3 | 258.8 | Mont Blanc, France, 15,781 | Sea level |
| OCEANIA, incl. Australia, New Zealand, Melanesia, Micronesia, and Polynesia[2] | 25,000,000 | 3,284,000 | 5.6 | 7.6 | Mauna Kea, Hawaii, 13,796 | Lake Eyre, Australia, 38 below sea level |
| U.S.S.R., both European and Asiatic | 280,000,000 | 8,647,000 | 14.8 | 32.4 | Communism Peak, Pamir, 24,547 | Caspian Sea, 96 below sea level |

1. In computing density per square mile, the area of Antarctica is omitted. 2. Although Hawaii is geographically part of Oceania, its population is included in the population figure for North America. *Source:* Population Reference Bureau, Inc.

## Plate-Tectonics Theory

(*Source:* U.S. Dept. of the Interior, Geological Survey.)

According to the generally accepted "plate-tectonics" theory, scientists believe that the Earth's surface is broken into a number of shifting slabs or plates, which average about 50 miles in thickness. These plates move relative to one another above a hotter, deeper, more mobile zone at average rates as great as a few inches per year. Most of the world's active volcanoes are located along or near the boundaries between shifting plates and are called "plate-boundary" volcanoes. However, some active volcanoes are not associated with plate boundaries, and many of these so-called "intra-plate" volcanoes form roughly linear chains in the interior of some oceanic plates. The Hawaiian Islands provide perhaps the best example of an "intra-plate" volcanic chain, developed by the northwest-moving Pacific plate passing over an inferred "hot spot" that initiates the magma-generation and volcano-formation process. The peripheral areas of the Pacific Ocean Basin, containing the boundaries of several plates, are dotted by many active volcanoes that form the so-called "Ring of Fire." The "Ring" provides excellent examples of "plate-boundary" volcanoes, including Mount St. Helens.

The accompanying figure on page 464 shows the boundaries of lithosphere plates that are active at present. The double lines indicate zones of spreading from which plates are moving apart. The lines with barbs show zones of underthrusting (subduction), where one plate is sliding beneath another. The barbs on the lines indicate the overriding plate. The single line defines a strike-slip fault along which plates are sliding horizontally past one another. The stippled areas indicate a part of a continent, exclusive of that along a plate boundary, which is undergoing active extensional, compressional, or strike-slip faulting.

# The Severity of an Earthquake

(Source: U.S. Dept. of the Interior, Geological Survey.)

## The Richter Magnitude Scale

The Richter magnitude scale was developed in 1935 by Charles F. Richter of the California Institute of Technology as a mathematical device to compare the size of earthquakes. The magnitude of an earthquake is determined from the logarithm of the amplitude of waves recorded by seismographs. Adjustments are included in the magnitude formula to compensate for the variation in the distance between the various seismographs and the epicenter of the earthquakes. On the Richter Scale, magnitude is expressed in whole numbers and decimal fractions. For example, a magnitude of 5.3 might be computed for a moderate earthquake, and a strong earthquake might be rated as magnitude 6.3.

Because of the logarithmic basis of the scale, each whole-number increase in magnitude represents a tenfold increase in measured amplitude; as an estimate of energy, each whole number step in the magnitude scale corresponds to the release of about 31 times more energy than the amount associated with the preceding whole number value.

Earthquakes with magnitudes of about 2.0 or less are usually called microearthquakes; they are not commonly felt by people and are generally recorded only on local seismographs. Events with magnitudes of about 4.5 or greater—there are several thousand such shocks annually—are strong enough to be recorded by sensitive seismographs all over the world.

Great earthquakes, such as the 1906 Good Friday earthquake in Alaska, have magnitudes of 8.0 or higher. On the average, one earthquake of such size occurs somewhere in the world each year. Although the Richter Scale has no upper limit, the largest known shocks have had magnitudes in the 8.8 to 8.9 range.

The Richter Scale is not used to express damage. An earthquake in a densely populated area which results in many deaths and considerable damage may have the same magnitude as a shock in a remote area that does nothing more than frighten the wildlife. Large-magnitude earthquakes that occur beneath the oceans may not even be felt by humans.

## The Modified Mercalli Intensity Scale

The effect of an earthquake on the Earth's surface is called the intensity. The intensity scale consists of a series of certain key responses such as people awakening, movement of furniture, damage to chimneys, and finally—total destruction. Although numerous *intensity scales* have been developed over the last several hundred years to evaluate the effects of earthquakes, the one currently used in the United States is the Modified Mercalli (MM) Intensity Scale. It was developed in 1931 by the American seismologists Harry Wood and Frank Neumann. This scale, composed of 12 increasing levels of intensity that range from imperceptible shaking to catastrophic destruction, is designated by Roman numerals. It does not have a mathematical basis; instead it is an arbitrary ranking based on observed effects.

The Modified Mercalli Intensity value assigned to a specific site after an earthquake has a more meaningful measure of severity to the nonscientist than the magnitude because intensity refers to the effects actually experienced at that place. After the occurrence of widely-felt earthquakes, the Geological Survey mails questionnaires to postmasters in the disturbed area requesting the information so that intensity values can be assigned. The results of this postal canvass and information furnished by other sources are used to assign an intensity value, and to compile isoseismal maps that show the extent of various levels of intensity within the felt area. The maximum observed intensity generally occurs near the epicenter.

The *lower* numbers of the intensity scale generally deal with the manner in which the earthquake is felt by people. The *higher* numbers of the scale are based on observed structural damage. Structural engineers usually contribute information for assigning intensity values of VIII or above.

The Mexico City earthquake on September 19, 1985, was assigned an intensity of IX on the Mercalli Scale.

*The following* is an abbreviated description of the 12 levels of Modified Mercalli intensity.

**I.** Not felt except by a very few under especially favorable conditions.

**II.** Felt only by a few persons at rest, especially on upper floors of buildings. Delicately suspended objects may swing.

**III.** Felt quite noticeably by persons indoors, especially on upper floors of buildings. Many people do not recognize it as an earthquake. Standing motor cars may rock slightly. Vibration similar to the passing of a truck. Duration estimated.

**IV.** Felt indoors by many, outdoors by few during the day. At night, some awakened. Dishes, windows, doors disturbed; walls make cracking sound. Sensation like heavy truck striking building. Standing motor cars rocked noticeably.

**V.** Felt by nearly everyone; many awakened. Some dishes, windows broken. Unstable objects overturned. Pendulum clocks may stop.

**VI.** Felt by all, many frightened. Some heavy furniture moved; a few instances of fallen plaster. Damage slight.

**VII.** Damage negligible in buildings of good design and construction; slight to moderate in well-built ordinary structures; considerable damage in poorly built or badly designed structures; some chimneys broken.

**VIII.** Damage slight in specially designed structures; considerable damage in ordinary substantial buildings with partial collapse. Damage great in poorly built structures. Fall of chimneys, factory stacks, columns, monuments, walls. Heavy furniture overturned.

**IX.** Damage considerable in specially designed structures; well-designed frame structures thrown out of plumb. Damage great in substantial buildings, with partial collapse. Buildings shifted off foundations.

**X.** Some well-built wooden structures destroyed; most masonry and frame structures destroyed with foundations. Rails bent.

**XI.** Few, if any (masonry) structures remain standing. Bridges destroyed. Rails bent greatly.

**XII.** Damage total. Lines of sight and level are distorted. Objects thrown into the air.

# Longitude and Latitude of World Cities
### (and time corresponding to 12:00 noon, eastern standard time)

| City | Long. ° ′ | Lat. ° ′ | Time |
|---|---|---|---|
| Aberdeen, Scotland | 2 9 w | 57 9 n | 5:00 p.m. |
| Adelaide, Australia | 138 36 e | 34 55 s | 2:30 a.m.[1] |
| Algiers | 3 0 e | 36 50 n | 6:00 p.m. |
| Amsterdam | 4 53 e | 52 22 n | 6:00 p.m. |
| Ankara, Turkey | 32 55 e | 39 55 n | 7:00 p.m. |
| Asunción, Paraguay | 57 40 w | 25 15 s | 1:00 p.m. |
| Athens | 23 43 e | 37 58 n | 7:00 p.m. |
| Auckland, New Zealand | 174 45 e | 36 52 s | 5:00 a.m.[1] |
| Bangkok, Thailand | 100 30 e | 13 45 n | midnight[1] |
| Barcelona | 2 9 e | 41 23 n | 6:00 p.m. |
| Belém, Brazil | 48 29 w | 1 28 s | 2:00 p.m. |
| Belfast, Northern Ireland | 5 56 w | 54 37 n | 5:00 p.m. |
| Belgrade, Yugoslavia | 20 32 e | 44 52 n | 6:00 p.m. |
| Berlin | 13 25 e | 52 30 n | 6:00 p.m. |
| Birmingham, England | 1 55 w | 52 25 n | 5:00 p.m. |
| Bogotá, Colombia | 74 15 w | 4 32 n | 12:00 noon |
| Bombay | 72 48 e | 19 0 n | 10:30 p.m. |
| Bordeaux, France | 0 31 w | 44 50 n | 6:00 p.m. |
| Bremen, W. Germany | 8 49 e | 53 5 n | 6:00 p.m. |
| Brisbane, Australia | 153 8 e | 27 29 s | 3:00 a.m.[1] |
| Bristol, England | 2 35 w | 51 28 n | 5:00 p.m. |
| Brussels | 4 22 e | 50 52 n | 6:00 p.m. |
| Bucharest | 26 7 e | 44 25 n | 7:00 p.m. |
| Budapest | 19 5 e | 47 30 n | 6:00 p.m. |
| Buenos Aires | 58 22 w | 34 35 s | 2:00 p.m. |
| Cairo | 31 21 e | 30 2 n | 7:00 p.m. |
| Calcutta | 88 24 e | 22 34 n | 10:30 p.m. |
| Canton, China | 113 15 e | 23 7 n | 1:00 a.m.[1] |
| Cape Town, South Africa | 18 22 e | 33 55 s | 7:00 p.m. |
| Caracas, Venezuela | 67 2 w | 10 28 n | 1:00 p.m. |
| Cayenne, French Guiana | 52 18 w | 4 49 n | 1:00 p.m. |
| Chihuahua, Mexico | 106 5 w | 28 37 n | 11:00 a.m. |
| Chongqing, China | 106 34 e | 29 46 n | 1:00 a.m.[1] |
| Copenhagen | 12 34 e | 55 40 n | 6:00 p.m. |
| Córdoba, Argentina | 64 10 w | 31 28 s | 2:00 p.m. |
| Dakar, Senegal | 17 28 w | 14 40 n | 5:00 p.m. |
| Darwin, Australia | 130 51 e | 12 28 s | 2:30 a.m.[1] |
| Djibouti | 43 3 e | 11 30 n | 8:00 p.m. |
| Dublin | 6 15 w | 53 20 n | 5:00 p.m. |
| Durban, South Africa | 30 53 e | 29 53 s | 7:00 p.m. |
| Edinburgh, Scotland | 3 10 w | 55 55 n | 5:00 p.m. |
| Frankfurt | 8 41 e | 50 7 n | 6:00 p.m. |
| Georgetown, Guyana | 58 15 w | 6 45 n | 1:15 p.m. |
| Glasgow, Scotland | 4 15 w | 55 50 n | 5:00 p.m. |
| Guatemala City, Guatemala | 90 31 w | 14 37 n | 11:00 a.m. |
| Guayaquil, Ecuador | 79 56 w | 2 10 s | 12:00 noon |
| Hamburg | 10 2 e | 53 33 n | 6:00 p.m. |
| Hammerfest, Norway | 23 38 e | 70 38 n | 6:00 p.m. |
| Havana | 82 23 w | 23 8 n | 12:00 noon |
| Helsinki, Finland | 25 0 e | 60 10 n | 7:00 p.m. |
| Hobart, Tasmania | 147 19 e | 42 52 s | 3:00 a.m.[1] |
| Iquique, Chile | 70 7 w | 20 10 s | 1:00 p.m. |
| Irkutsk, U.S.S.R. | 104 20 e | 52 30 n | 1:00 a.m. |
| Jakarta, Indonesia | 106 48 e | 6 16 s | 0:30 a.m.[1] |
| Johannesburg, South Africa | 28 4 e | 26 12 s | 7:00 p.m. |
| Kingston, Jamaica | 76 49 w | 17 59 n | 12:00 noon |
| Kinshasa, Zaire | 15 17 e | 4 18 s | 6:00 p.m. |
| La Paz, Bolivia | 68 22 w | 16 27 s | 1:00 p.m. |
| Leeds, England | 1 30 w | 53 45 n | 5:00 p.m. |
| Leningrad | 30 18 e | 59 56 n | 8:00 p.m. |
| Lima, Peru | 77 2 w | 12 0 s | 12:00 noon |
| Lisbon | 9 9 w | 38 44 n | 5:00 p.m. |
| Liverpool, England | 3 0 w | 53 25 n | 5:00 p.m. |
| London | 0 5 w | 51 32 n | 5:00 p.m. |
| Lyons, France | 4 50 e | 45 45 n | 6:00 p.m. |
| Madrid | 3 42 w | 40 26 n | 6:00 p.m. |
| Manchester, England | 2 15 w | 53 30 n | 5:00 p.m. |
| Manila | 120 57 e | 14 35 n | 1:00 a.m.[1] |
| Marseilles, France | 5 20 e | 43 20 n | 6:00 p.m. |
| Mazatlán, Mexico | 106 25 w | 23 12 n | 10:00 a.m. |
| Mecca, Saudi Arabia | 39 45 e | 21 29 n | 8:00 p.m. |
| Melbourne | 144 58 e | 37 47 s | 3:00 a.m.[1] |
| Mexico City | 99 7 w | 19 26 n | 11:00 a.m. |
| Milan, Italy | 9 10 e | 45 27 n | 6:00 p.m. |
| Montevideo, Uruguay | 56 10 w | 34 53 s | 2:00 p.m. |
| Moscow | 37 36 e | 55 45 n | 8:00 p.m. |
| Munich, Germany | 11 35 e | 48 8 n | 6:00 p.m. |
| Nagasaki, Japan | 129 57 e | 32 48 n | 2:00 a.m.[1] |
| Nagoya, Japan | 136 56 e | 35 7 n | 2:00 a.m.[1] |
| Nairobi, Kenya | 36 55 e | 1 25 s | 8:00 p.m. |
| Nanjing (Nanking), China | 118 53 e | 32 3 n | 1:00 a.m.[1] |
| Naples, Italy | 14 15 e | 40 50 n | 6:00 p.m. |
| Newcastle-on-Tyne, Eng. | 1 37 w | 54 58 n | 5:00 p.m. |
| Odessa, U.S.S.R. | 30 48 e | 46 27 n | 8:00 p.m. |
| Osaka, Japan | 135 30 e | 34 32 n | 2:00 a.m.[1] |
| Oslo | 10 42 e | 59 57 n | 6:00 p.m. |
| Panama City, Panama | 79 32 w | 8 58 n | 12:00 noon |
| Paramaribo, Surinam | 55 15 w | 5 45 n | 1:30 p.m. |
| Paris | 2 20 e | 48 48 n | 6:00 p.m. |
| Peking | 116 25 e | 39 55 n | 1:00 a.m.[1] |
| Perth, Australia | 115 52 e | 31 57 s | 1:00 a.m.[1] |
| Plymouth, England | 4 5 w | 50 25 n | 5:00 p.m. |
| Port Moresby, Papua New Guinea | 147 8 e | 9 25 s | 3:00 a.m.[1] |
| Prague | 14 26 e | 50 5 n | 6:00 p.m. |
| Rangoon, Burma | 96 0 e | 16 50 n | 11:30 p.m. |
| Reykjavik, Iceland | 21 58 w | 64 4 n | 4:00 p.m. |
| Rio de Janeiro | 43 12 w | 22 57 s | 2:00 p.m. |
| Rome | 12 27 e | 41 54 n | 6:00 p.m. |
| Salvador, Brazil | 38 27 w | 12 56 s | 2:00 p.m. |
| Santiago, Chile | 70 45 w | 33 28 s | 1:00 p.m. |
| Sao Paulo, Brazil | 46 31 w | 23 31 s | 2:00 p.m. |
| Shanghai, China | 121 28 e | 31 10 n | 1:00 a.m.[1] |
| Singapore | 103 55 e | 1 14 n | 0:30 a.m.[1] |
| Sofia, Bulgaria | 23 20 e | 42 40 n | 7:00 p.m. |
| Stockholm | 18 3 e | 59 17 n | 6:00 p.m. |
| Sydney, Australia | 151 0 e | 34 0 s | 3:00 a.m.[1] |
| Tananarive, Madagascar | 47 33 e | 18 50 s | 8:00 p.m. |
| Teheran, Iran | 51 45 e | 35 45 n | 8:30 p.m. |
| Tokyo | 139 45 e | 35 40 n | 2:00 a.m.[1] |
| Tripoli, Libya | 13 12 e | 32 57 n | 7:00 p.m. |
| Venice | 12 20 e | 45 26 n | 6:00 p.m. |
| Veracruz, Mexico | 96 10 w | 19 10 n | 11:00 a.m. |
| Vienna | 16 20 e | 48 14 n | 6:00 p.m. |
| Vladivostok, U.S.S.R. | 132 0 e | 43 10 n | 3:00 a.m.[1] |
| Warsaw | 21 0 e | 52 14 n | 6:00 p.m. |
| Wellington, New Zealand | 174 47 e | 41 17 s | 5:00 a.m.[1] |
| Zürich | 8 31 e | 47 21 n | 6:00 p.m. |

1. On the following day.

468 *Geography*

# Highest Mountain Peaks of the World
### (For U.S. peaks, see Index)

| Mountain peak | Range | Location | Height feet | meters |
|---|---|---|---|---|
| Everest[1] | Himalayas | Nepal-Tibet | 29,028 | 8,848 |
| Godwin Austen (K-2) | Karakoram | Kashmir | 28,250 | 8,610 |
| Kanchenjunga | Himalayas | Nepal-Sikkim | 28,208 | 8,598 |
| Lhotse | Himalayas | Nepal-Tibet | 27,890 | 8,501 |
| Makalu | Himalayas | Tibet-Nepal | 27,790 | 8,470 |
| Dhaulagiri I | Himalayas | Nepal | 26,810 | 8,172 |
| Manaslu | Himalayas | Nepal | 26,760 | 8,156 |
| Cho Oyu | Himalayas | Nepal | 26,750 | 8,153 |
| Nanga Parbat | Himalayas | Kashmir | 26,660 | 8,126 |
| Annapurna I | Himalayas | Nepal | 26,504 | 8,078 |
| Gasherbrum I | Karakoram | Kashmir | 26,470 | 8,068 |
| Broad Peak | Karakoram | Kashmir | 26,400 | 8,047 |
| Gasherbrum II | Karakoram | Kashmir | 26,360 | 8,033 |
| Gosainthan | Himalayas | Tibet | 26,291 | 8,013 |
| Gasherbrum III | Karakoram | Kashmir | 26,090 | 7,952 |
| Annapurna II | Himalayas | Nepal | 26,041 | 7,937 |
| Gasherbrum IV | Karakoram | India | 26,000 | 7,925 |
| Kangbachen | Himalayas | Nepal | 25,925 | 7,902 |
| Gyachung Kang | Himalayas | Nepal | 25,910 | 7,897 |
| Himal Chuli | Himalayas | Nepal | 25,895 | 7,893 |
| Disteghil Sar | Karakoram | Kashmir | 25,868 | 7,885 |
| Nuptse | Himalayas | Nepal | 25,850 | 7,829 |
| Kunyang Kish | Karakoram | Kashmir | 25,760 | 7,852 |
| Dakum (Peak 29) | Himalayas | Nepal | 25,760 | 7,852 |
| Masherbrum | Karakoram | Kashmir | 25,660 | 7,821 |
| Nanda Devi | Himalayas | India | 25,645 | 7,817 |
| Chomolonzo | Himalayas | Nepal-Tibet | 25,640 | 7,815 |
| Rakaposhi | Karakoram | Kashmir | 25,550 | 7,788 |
| Batura | Karakoram | Kashmir | 25,540 | 7,785 |
| Kanjut Sar | Karakoram | Kashmir | 25,460 | 7,760 |
| Kamet | Himalayas | India-Tibet | 25,447 | 7,756 |
| Namche Barwa | Himalayas | Tibet | 25,445 | 7,756 |
| Dhaulagiri II | Himalayas | Nepal | 25,427 | 7,750 |
| Saltoro Kangri | Karakoram | India | 25,400 | 7,742 |
| Gurla Mandhata | Himalayas | Tibet | 25,355 | 7,728 |
| Ulugh Muztagh | Kunlun | Tibet | 25,341 | 7,724 |
| Trivor | Karakoram | Kashmir | 25,330 | 7,721 |
| Jannu | Himalayas | Nepal | 25,294 | 7,710 |
| Tirich Mir | Hindu Kush | Pakistan | 25,230 | 7,690 |
| Saser Kangri | Karakoram | India | 25,170 | 7,672 |
| Makalu II | Himalayas | Nepal | 25,130 | 7,660 |
| Chogolisa | Karakoram | India | 25,110 | 7,654 |
| Dhaulagiri IV | Himalayas | Nepal | 25,064 | 7,639 |
| Fang | Himalayas | Nepal | 25,013 | 7,624 |
| Kula Kangri | Himalayas | Bhutan | 24,783 | 7,554 |
| Changtse | Himalayas | Tibet | 24,780 | 7,553 |
| Muztagh Ata | Muztagh Ata | China | 24,757 | 7,546 |
| Skyang Kangri | Himalayas | Kashmir | 24,750 | 7,544 |
| Communism Peak | Pamir | U.S.S.R. | 24,590 | 7,495 |
| Victory Peak | Pamir | U.S.S.R. | 24,406 | 7,439 |
| Sia Kangri | Himalayas | Kashmir | 24,340 | 7,419 |
| Chamlang | Himalayas | Nepal | 24,012 | 7,319 |
| Alung Gangri | Himalayas | Tibet | 23,999 | 7,315 |
| Chomo Lhari | Himalayas | Tibet-Bhutan | 23,996 | 7,314 |
| Muztagh (K-5) | Kunlun | China | 23,891 | 7,282 |
| Amne Machin | Kunlun | China | 23,490 | 7,160 |
| Gaurisankar | Himalayas | Nepal-Tibet | 23,440 | 7,145 |
| Lenin Peak | Pamir | U.S.S.R. | 23,405 | 7,134 |
| Korzhenevski Peak | Pamir | U.S.S.R. | 23,310 | 7,105 |
| Kangto | Himalayas | Tibet | 23,260 | 7,090 |
| Dunagiri | Himalayas | India | 23,184 | 7,066 |
| Pauhunri | Himalayas | India-Tibet | 23,180 | 7,065 |
| Aconcagua | Andes | Argentina-Chile | 23,034 | 7,021 |
| Revolution Peak | Pamir | U.S.S.R. | 22,880 | 6,974 |
| Kangchenjhan | Himalayas | India | 22,700 | 6,919 |
| Siniolchu | Himalayas | India | 22,620 | 6,895 |

| Mountain peak | Range | Location | Height feet | meters |
|---|---|---|---|---|
| Ojos des Salado | Andes | Argentina-Chile | 22,588 | 6,885 |
| Bonete | Andes | Argentina-Chile | 22,546 | 6,872 |
| Simvuo | Himalayas | India | 22,346 | 6,811 |
| Tup | Andes | Argentina | 22,309 | 6,800 |
| Kungpu | Himalayas | Bhutan | 22,300 | 6,797 |
| Falso-Azufre | Andes | Argentina-Chile | 22,277 | 6,790 |
| Moscow Peak | Pamir | U.S.S.R. | 22,260 | 6,785 |
| Veladero | Andes | Argentina | 22,244 | 6,780 |
| Pissis | Andes | Argentina | 22,241 | 6,779 |
| Mercedario | Andes | Argentina-Chile | 22,211 | 6,770 |
| Huascarán | Andes | Peru | 22,198 | 6,766 |
| Tocorpuri | Andes | Bolivia-Chile | 22,162 | 6,755 |
| Karl Marx Peak | Pamir | U.S.S.R. | 22,067 | 6,726 |
| Llullaillaco | Andes | Argentina-Chile | 22,057 | 6,723 |
| Libertador | Andes | Argentina | 22,047 | 6,720 |
| Kailas | Himalayas | Tibet | 22,027 | 6,714 |
| Lingtren | Himalayas | Nepal-Tibet | 21,972 | 6,697 |
| Incahuasi | Andes | Argentina-Chile | 21,719 | 6,620 |
| Carnicero | Andes | Peru | 21,689 | 6,611 |
| Kurumda | Pamir | U.S.S.R. | 21,686 | 6,610 |
| Garmo Peak | Pamir | U.S.S.R. | 21,637 | 6,595 |
| Sajama | Andes | Bolivia | 21,555 | 6,570 |
| Ancohuma | Andes | Bolivia | 21,490 | 6,550 |
| El Muerto | Andes | Argentina-Chile | 21,456 | 6,540 |
| Nacimiento | Andes | Argentina | 21,302 | 6,493 |
| Illimani | Andes | Bolivia | 21,184 | 6,457 |
| Antofalla | Andes | Argentina-Chile | 21,129 | 6,440 |
| Coropuña | Andes | Peru | 21,079 | 6,425 |
| Cuzco (Ausangate) | Andes | Peru | 20,995 | 6,399 |
| Toro | Andes | Argentina-Chile | 20,932 | 6,380 |
| Parinacota | Andes | Bolivia-Chile | 20,768 | 6,330 |
| Chimboraso | Andes | Ecuador | 20,702 | 6,310 |
| Salcantay | Andes | Peru | 20,575 | 6,271 |
| General Manuel Belgrano | Andes | Argentina | 20,505 | 6,250 |
| Chañi | Andes | Argentina | 20,341 | 6,200 |
| Caca Aca | Andes | Bolivia | 20,328 | 6,196 |
| McKinley | Alaska | Alaska | 20,320 | 6,194 |
| Vudor Peak | Pamir | U.S.S.R. | 20,118 | 6,132 |
| Condoriri | Andes | Bolivia | 20,095 | 6,125 |
| Solimana | Andes | Peru | 20,069 | 6,117 |
| Nevada | Andes | Argentina | 20,023 | 6,103 |

1. The U. S. Air Force Planning Charts list the height of Mt. Everest as 29,141 ft.

## Oceans and Seas

| Name | Area sq mi. | sq km | Average depth feet | meters | Greatest known depth feet | meters | Place greatest known depth |
|---|---|---|---|---|---|---|---|
| Pacific Ocean | 64,000,000 | 165,760,000 | 13,215 | 4,028 | 35,820 | 10,918 | Mindanao Deep |
| Atlantic Ocean | 31,815,000 | 82,400,000 | 12,880 | 3,926 | 30,246 | 9,219 | Puerto Rico Trough |
| Indian Ocean | 25,300,000 | 65,526,700 | 13,002 | 3,963 | 24,460 | 7,455 | Sunda Trench |
| Arctic Ocean | 5,440,200 | 14,090,000 | 3,953 | 1,205 | 18,456 | 5,625 | 77° 45' N; 175° W |
| Mediterranean Sea[1] | 1,145,100 | 2,965,800 | 4,688 | 1,429 | 15,197 | 4,632 | Off Cape Matapan, Greece |
| Caribbean Sea | 1,049,500 | 2,718,200 | 8,685 | 2,647 | 22,788 | 6,946 | Off Cayman Islands |
| South China Sea | 895,400 | 2,319,000 | 5,419 | 1,652 | 16,456 | 5,016 | West of Luzon |
| Bering Sea | 884,900 | 2,291,900 | 5,075 | 1,547 | 15,659 | 4,773 | Off Buldir Island |
| Gulf of Mexico | 615,000 | 1,592,800 | 4,874 | 1,486 | 12,425 | 3,787 | Sigsbee Deep |
| Okhotsk Sea | 613,800 | 1,589,700 | 2,749 | 838 | 12,001 | 3,658 | 146° 10' E; 46° 50' N |
| East China Sea | 482,300 | 1,249,200 | 617 | 188 | 9,126 | 2,782 | 25° 16' N; 125° E |
| Hudson Bay | 475,800 | 1,232,300 | 420 | 128 | 600 | 183 | Near entrance |
| Japan Sea | 389,100 | 1,007,800 | 4,429 | 1,350 | 12,276 | 3,742 | Central Basin |
| Andaman Sea | 308,100 | 797,700 | 2,854 | 870 | 12,392 | 3,777 | Off Car Nicobar Island |
| North Sea | 222,100 | 575,200 | 308 | 94 | 2,165 | 660 | Skagerrak |
| Red Sea | 169,100 | 438,000 | 1,611 | 491 | 7,254 | 2,211 | Off Port Sudan |
| Baltic Sea | 163,000 | 422,200 | 180 | 55 | 1,380 | 421 | Off Gotland |

1. Includes Black Sea and Sea of Azov. NOTE: For Caspian Sea, *see* Large Lakes of World elsewhere in this section.

# World's Greatest Man-Made Lakes[1]

| Name of dam | Location | Millions of cubic meters | Thousands of acre-feet | Year completed |
|---|---|---|---|---|
| Owen Falls | Uganda | 204,800 | 166,000 | 1954 |
| Kariba | Zimbabwe | 181,592 | 147,218 | 1959 |
| Bratsk | U.S.S.R. | 169,270 | 137,220 | 1964 |
| High Aswan (Sadd-el-Aali) | Egypt | 168,000 | 136,200 | 1970 |
| Akosombo | Ghana | 148,000 | 120,000 | 1965 |
| Daniel Johnson | Canada | 141,852 | 115,000 | 1968 |
| Guri (Raul Leoni) | Venezuela | 136,000 | 110,256 | 1986 |
| Krasnoyarsk | U.S.S.R. | 73,300 | 59,425 | 1967 |
| Bennett W.A.C. | Canada | 70,309 | 57,006 | 1967 |
| Zeya | U.S.S.R. | 68,400 | 55,452 | 1978 |
| Cabora Bassa | Mozambique | 63,000 | 51,075 | 1974 |
| LaGrande 2 | Canada | 61,720 | 50,037 | 1982 |
| LaGrande 3 | Canada | 60,020 | 48,659 | 1982 |
| Ust'—Ilimsk | U.S.S.R. | 59,300 | 48,075 | 1980 |
| Volga—V.I. Lenin | U.S.S.R. | 58,000 | 47,020 | 1955 |
| Caniapiscau | Canada | 53,790 | 43,608 | 1981 |
| Pati (Chapetón) | Argentina | 53,700 | 43,535 | UC |
| Upper Wainganga | India | 50,700 | 41,103 | UC |
| São Felix | Brazil | 50,600 | 41,022 | UC |
| Bukhtarma | U.S.S.R. | 49,740 | 40,325 | 1960 |
| Atatürk (Karababa) | Turkey | 48,700 | 39,482 | UC |
| Cerros Colorados | Argentina | 48,000 | 38,914 | 1973 |
| Irkutsk | U.S.S.R. | 46,000 | 37,290 | 1956 |
| Tucuruí | Brazil | 36,375 | 29,489 | 1984 |
| Vilyuy | U.S.S.R. | 35,900 | 29,104 | 1967 |
| Sanmenxia | China | 35,400 | 28,700 | 1960 |
| Hoover | Nevada/Arizona | 35,154 | 28,500 | 1936 |
| Sobridinho | Brazil | 34,200 | 27,726 | 1981 |
| Glen Canyon | Arizona | 33,304 | 27,000 | 1964 |
| Jenpeg | Canada | 31,790 | 25,772 | 1975 |

1. Formed by construction of dams. NOTE: UC = under construction. *Source:* Department of the Interior, Bureau of Reclamation and *International Water Power and Dam Construction.*

# Large Lakes of the World

| Name and location | Area | | Length | | Maximum depth | |
|---|---|---|---|---|---|---|
| | sq mi. | sq km | mi. | km | feet | meters |
| Caspian Sea, U.S.S.R.-Iran[1] | 152,239 | 394,299 | 745 | 1,199 | 3,104 | 946 |
| Superior, U.S.-Canada | 31,820 | 82,414 | 383 | 616 | 1,333 | 406 |
| Victoria, Tanzania—Uganda | 26,828 | 69,485 | 200 | 322 | 270 | 82 |
| Aral, U.S.S.R. | 25,659 | 66,457 | 266 | 428 | 223 | 68 |
| Huron, U.S.-Canada | 23,010 | 59,596 | 247 | 397 | 750 | 229 |
| Michigan, U.S. | 22,400 | 58,016 | 321 | 517 | 923 | 281 |
| Tanganyika, Tanzania-Zaire | 12,700 | 32,893 | 420 | 676 | 4,708 | 1,435 |
| Baikal, U.S.S.R. | 12,162 | 31,500 | 395 | 636 | 5,712 | 1,741 |
| Great Bear, Canada | 12,000 | 31,080 | 232 | 373 | 270 | 82 |
| Nyasa, Malawi-Mozambique-Tanzania | 11,600 | 30,044 | 360 | 579 | 2,316 | 706 |
| Great Slave, Canada | 11,170 | 28,930 | 298 | 480 | 2,015 | 614 |
| Chad,[2] Chad-Niger-Nigeria | 9,946 | 25,760 | — | — | 23 | 7 |
| Erie, U.S.-Canada | 9,930 | 25,719 | 241 | 388 | 210 | 64 |
| Winnipeg, Canada | 9,094 | 23,553 | 264 | 425 | 204 | 62 |
| Ontario, U.S.-Canada | 7,520 | 19,477 | 193 | 311 | 778 | 237 |
| Balkash, U.S.S.R. | 7,115 | 18,428 | 376 | 605 | 87 | 27 |
| Ladoga, U.S.S.R. | 7,000 | 18,130 | 124 | 200 | 738 | 225 |
| Onega, U.S.S.R. | 3,819 | 9,891 | 154 | 248 | 361 | 110 |
| Titicaca, Bolivia-Peru | 3,141 | 8,135 | 110 | 177 | 1,214 | 370 |
| Nicaragua, Nicaragua | 3,089 | 8,001 | 110 | 177 | 230 | 70 |
| Athabaska, Canada | 3,058 | 7,920 | 208 | 335 | 407 | 124 |
| Rudolf, Kenya | 2,473 | 6,405 | 154 | 248 | — | — |
| Reindeer, Canada | 2,444 | 6,330 | 152 | 245 | — | — |
| Eyre, South Australia | 2,400[3] | 6,216 | 130 | 209 | varies | varies |
| Issyk-Kul, U.S.S.R. | 2,394 | 6,200 | 113 | 182 | 2,297 | 700 |
| Urmia,[2] Iran | 2,317 | 6,001 | 81 | 130 | 49 | 15 |
| Torrens, South Australia | 2,200 | 5,698 | 130 | 209 | — | — |
| Vänern, Sweden | 2,141 | 5,545 | 87 | 140 | 322 | 98 |

| Name and location | Area | | Length | | Maximum depth | |
|---|---|---|---|---|---|---|
| | sq mi. | sq km | mi. | km | feet | meters |
| Winnipegosis, Canada | 2,086 | 5,403 | 152 | 245 | 59 | 18 |
| Mobutu Sese Seko, Uganda | 2,046 | 5,299 | 100 | 161 | 180 | 55 |
| Nettilling, Baffin Island, Canada | 1,950 | 5,051 | 70 | 113 | — | — |
| Nipigon, Canada | 1,870 | 4,843 | 72 | 116 | — | — |
| Manitoba, Canada | 1,817 | 4,706 | 140 | 225 | 22 | 7 |
| Great Salt, U.S. | 1,800 | 4,662 | 75 | 121 | 15/25 | 5/8 |
| Kioga, Uganda | 1,700 | 4,403 | 50 | 80 | about 30 | 9 |
| Koko-Nor, China | 1,630 | 4,222 | 66 | 106 | — | — |

1. The Caspian Sea is called "sea" because the Romans, finding it salty, named it *Mare Caspium*. Many geographers, however, consider it a lake because it is land-locked. 2. Figures represent high-water data. 3. Varies with the rainfall of the wet season. It has been reported to dry up almost completely on occasion.

## Principal Rivers of the World

### (For other U.S. rivers, see Index)

| River | Source | Outflow | Approx. length | |
|---|---|---|---|---|
| | | | miles | km |
| Nile | Tributaries of Lake Victoria, Africa | Mediterranean Sea | 4,180 | 6,690 |
| Amazon | Glacier-fed lakes, Peru | Atlantic Ocean | 3,912 | 6,296 |
| Mississippi-Missouri-Red Rock | Source of Red Rock, Montana | Gulf of Mexico | 3,741 | 6,020 |
| Yangtze Kiang | Tibetan plateau, China | China Sea | 3,602 | 5,797 |
| Ob | Altai Mts., U.S.S.R. | Gulf of Ob | 3,459 | 5,567 |
| Yellow (Huang Ho) | Eastern part of Kunlan Mts., west China | Gulf of Chihli | 2,900 | 4,667 |
| Yenisei | Tannu-Ola Mts., western Tuva, U.S.S.R. | Arctic Ocean | 2,800 | 4,506 |
| Paraná | Confluence of Paranaiba and Grande rivers | Río de la Plata | 2,795 | 4,498 |
| Irtish | Altai Mts., U.S.S.R. | Ob River | 2,758 | 4,438 |
| Congo | Confluence of Lualaba and Luapula rivers, Zaire | Atlantic Ocean | 2,716 | 4,371 |
| Amur | Confluence of Shilka (U.S.S.R.) and Argun (Manchuria) rivers | Tatar Strait | 2,704 | 4,352 |
| Lena | Baikal Mts., U.S.S.R. | Arctic Ocean | 2,652 | 4,268 |
| Mackenzie | Head of Finlay River, British Columbia, Canada | Beaufort Sea (Arctic Ocean) | 2,635 | 4,241 |
| Niger | Guinea | Gulf of Guinea | 2,600 | 4,184 |
| Mekong | Tibetan highlands | South China Sea | 2,500 | 4,023 |
| Mississippi | Lake Itasca, Minnesota | Gulf of Mexico | 2,348 | 3,779 |
| Missouri | Confluence of Jefferson, Gallatin, and Madison rivers, Montana | Mississippi River | 2,315 | 3,726 |
| Volga | Valdai plateau, U.S.S.R. | Caspian Sea | 2,291 | 3,687 |
| Madeira | Confluence of Beni and Maumoré rivers, Bolivia-Brazil boundary | Amazon River | 2,012 | 3,238 |
| Purus | Peruvian Andes | Amazon River | 1,993 | 3,207 |
| São Francisco | Southwest Minas Gerais, Brazil | Atlantic Ocean | 1,987 | 3,198 |
| St. Lawrence | Lake Ontario | Gulf of St. Lawrence | 1,900 | 3,058 |
| Yukon | Junction of Lewes and Pelly rivers, Yukon Territory, Canada | Bering Sea | 1,900 | 3,058 |
| Rio Grande | San Juan Mts., Colorado | Gulf of Mexico | 1,885 | 3,034 |
| Brahmaputra | Himalayas | Ganges River | 1,800 | 2,897 |
| Indus | Himalayas | Arabian Sea | 1,800 | 2,897 |
| Danube | Black Forest, W. Germany | Black Sea | 1,766 | 2,842 |

| River | Source | Outflow | Approx. length | |
|-------|--------|---------|:------:|:----:|
| | | | miles | km |
| Euphrates | Confluence of Murat Nehri and Kara Su rivers, Turkey | Shatt-al-Arab | 1,739 | 2,799 |
| Darling | Central part of Eastern Highlands, Australia | Murray River | 1,702 | 2,739 |
| Zambezi | 11°21'S, 24°22'E, Zambia | Mozambique Channel | 1,700 | 2,736 |
| Tocantins | Goiás, Brazil | Pará River | 1,677 | 2,699 |
| Murray | Australian Alps, New South Wales | Indian Ocean | 1,609 | 2,589 |
| Nelson | Head of Bow River, western Alberta, Canada | Hudson Bay | 1,600 | 2,575 |
| Paraguay | Mato Grosso, Brazil | Paraná River | 1,584 | 2,549 |
| Ural | Southern Ural Mts., U.S.S.R. | Caspian Sea | 1,574 | 2,533 |
| Ganges | Himalayas | Bay of Bengal | 1,557 | 2,506 |
| Amu Darya (Oxus) | Nicholas Range, Pamir Mts., U.S.S.R. | Aral Sea | 1,500 | 2,414 |
| Japurá | Andes, Colombia | Amazon River | 1,500 | 2,414 |
| Salween | Tibet, south of Kunlun Mts. | Gulf of Martaban | 1,500 | 2,414 |
| Arkansas | Central Colorado | Mississippi River | 1,450 | 2,333 |
| Colorado | Grand County, Colorado | Gulf of California | 1,450 | 2,333 |
| Dnieper | Valdai Hills, U.S.S.R. | Black Sea | 1,419 | 2,284 |
| Ohio-Allegheny | Potter County, Pennsylvania | Mississippi River | 1,306 | 2,102 |
| Irrawaddy | Confluence of Nmai and Mali rivers, northeast Burma | Bay of Bengal | 1,300 | 2,092 |
| Orange | Lesotho | Atlantic Ocean | 1,300 | 2,092 |
| Orinoco | Serra Parima Mts., Venezuela | Atlantic Ocean | 1,281 | 2,062 |
| Pilcomayo | Andes Mts., Bolivia | Paraguay River | 1,242 | 1,999 |
| Xi Jiang (Si Kiang) | Eastern Yunnan Province, China | China Sea | 1,236 | 1,989 |
| Columbia | Columbia Lake, British Columbia, Canada | Pacific Ocean | 1,232 | 1,983 |
| Don | Tula, R.S.F.S.R., U.S.S.R. | Sea of Azov | 1,223 | 1,968 |
| Sungari | China-North Korea boundary | Amur River | 1,215 | 1,955 |
| Saskatchewan | Canadian Rocky Mts. | Lake Winnipeg | 1,205 | 1,939 |
| Peace | Stikine Mts., British Columbia, Canada | Great Slave River | 1,195 | 1,923 |
| Tigris | Taurus Mts., Turkey | Shatt-al-Arab | 1,180 | 1,899 |

## Highest Waterfalls of the World

| Waterfall | Location | River | Height | |
|-----------|----------|-------|:----:|:------:|
| | | | feet | meters |
| Angel | Venezuela | Tributary of Caroni | 3,281 | 1,000 |
| Tugela | Natal, South Africa | Tugela | 3,000 | 914 |
| Cuquenán | Venezuela | Cuquenán | 2,000 | 610 |
| Sutherland | South Island, N.Z. | Arthur | 1,904 | 580 |
| Takkakaw | British Columbia | Tributary of Yoho | 1,650 | 503 |
| Ribbon (Yosemite) | California | Creek flowing into Yosemite | 1,612 | 491 |
| Upper Yosemite | California | Yosemite Creek, tributary of Merced | 1,430 | 436 |
| Gavarnie | Southwest France | Gave de Pau | 1,384 | 422 |
| Vettisfoss | Norway | Mörkedola | 1,200 | 366 |
| Widows' Tears (Yosemite) | California | Tributary of Merced | 1,170 | 357 |
| Staubbach | Switzerland | Staubbach (Lauterbrunnen Valley) | 984 | 300 |

| Waterfall | Location | River | Height feet | Height meters |
|-----------|----------|-------|-------------|---------------|
| Middle Cascade (Yosemite) | California | Yosemite Creek, tributary of Merced | 909 | 277 |
| King Edward VIII | Guyana | Courantyne | 850 | 259 |
| Gersoppa | India | Sharavati | 829 | 253 |
| Kaieteur | Guyana | Potaro | 822 | 251 |
| Skykje | Norway | In Skykjedal (valley of Inner Hardinger Fjord) | 820 | 250 |
| Kalambo | Tanzania-Zambia | — | 720 | 219 |
| Fairy (Mount Rainier Park) | Washington | Stevens Creek | 700 | 213 |
| Trummelbach | Switzerland | Trummelbach (Lauterbrunnen Valley) | 700 | 213 |
| Aniene (Teverone) | Italy | Tiber | 680 | 207 |
| Cascata delle Marmore | Italy | Velino, tributary of Nera | 650 | 198 |
| Maradalsfos | Norway | Stream flowing into Ejkisdalsvand (lake) | 643 | 196 |
| Feather | California | Fall River | 640 | 195 |
| Maletsunyane | Lesotho | Maletsunyane | 630 | 192 |
| Bridalveil (Yosemite) | California | Yosemite Creek | 620 | 189 |
| Multnomah | Oregon | Multnomah Creek, tributary of Columbia | 620 | 189 |
| Vøringsfos | Norway | Bjoreia | 597 | 182 |
| Nevada (Yosemite) | California | Merced | 594 | 181 |
| Skjeggedal | Norway | Tysso | 525 | 160 |
| Marina | Guyana | Tributary of Kuribrong, tributary of Potaro | 500 | 152 |
| Tequendama | Colombia | Funza, tributary of Magdalena | 425 | 130 |
| King George's | Cape of Good Hope, South Africa | Orange | 400 | 122 |
| Illilouette (Yosemite) | California | Illilouette Creek, tributary of Merced | 370 | 113 |
| Victoria | Rhodesia-Zambia boundary | Zambezi | 355 | 108 |
| Handöl | Sweden | Handöl Creek | 345 | 105 |
| Lower Yosemite | California | Yosemite | 320 | 98 |
| Comet (Mount Rainier Park) | Washington | Van Trump Creek | 320 | 98 |
| Vernal (Yosemite) | California | Merced | 317 | 97 |
| Virginia | Northwest Territories, Canada | South Nahanni, tributary of Mackenzie | 315 | 96 |
| Lower Yellowstone | Wyoming | Yellowstone | 310 | 94 |

NOTE: Niagara Falls (New York-Ontario), though of great volume, has parallel drops of only 158 and 167 feet.

## Large Islands of the World

| Island | Location and status | Area sq mi. | Area sq km |
|--------|---------------------|-------------|------------|
| Greenland | North Atlantic (Danish) | 839,999 | 2,175,597 |
| New Guinea | Southwest Pacific (Irian Jaya, Indonesian, west part; Papua New Guinea, east part) | 316,615 | 820,033 |
| Borneo | West mid-Pacific (Indonesian, south part; British protectorate, and Malaysian, north part) | 286,914 | 743,107 |
| Madagascar | Indian Ocean (Malagasy Republic) | 226,657 | 587,042 |
| Baffin | North Atlantic (Canadian) | 183,810 | 476,068 |
| Sumatra | Northeast Indian Ocean (Indonesian) | 182,859 | 473,605 |
| Honshu | Sea of Japan-Pacific (Japanese) | 88,925 | 230,316 |
| Great Britain | Off coast of NW Europe (England, Scotland, and Wales) | 88,758 | 229,883 |
| Ellesmere | Arctic Ocean (Canadian) | 82,119 | 212,688 |
| Victoria | Arctic Ocean (Canadian) | 81,930 | 212,199 |
| Celebes | West mid-Pacific (Indonesian) | 72,986 | 189,034 |
| South Island | South Pacific (New Zealand) | 58,093 | 150,461 |
| Java | Indian Ocean (Indonesian) | 48,990 | 126,884 |
| North Island | South Pacific (New Zealand) | 44,281 | 114,688 |

| Island | Location and status | Area sq. mi. | Area sq. km |
|---|---|---|---|
| Cuba | Caribbean Sea (republic) | 44,218 | 114,525 |
| Newfoundland | North Atlantic (Canadian) | 42,734 | 110,681 |
| Luzon | West mid-Pacific (Philippines) | 40,420 | 104,688 |
| Iceland | North Atlantic (republic) | 39,768 | 102,999 |
| Mindanao | West mid-Pacific (Philippines) | 36,537 | 94,631 |
| Ireland | West of Great Britain (republic, south part; United Kingdom, north part) | 32,597 | 84,426 |
| Hokkaido | Sea of Japan—Pacific (Japanese) | 30,372 | 78,663 |
| Hispaniola | Caribbean Sea (Dominican Republic, east part; Haiti, west part) | 29,355 | 76,029 |
| Tasmania | South of Australia (Australian) | 26,215 | 67,897 |
| Sri Lanka (Ceylon) | Indian Ocean (republic) | 25,332 | 65,610 |
| Sakhalin (Karafuto) | North of Japan (U.S.S.R.) | 24,560 | 63,610 |
| Banks | Arctic Ocean (Canadian) | 23,230 | 60,166 |
| Devon | Arctic Ocean (Canadian) | 20,861 | 54,030 |
| Tierra del Fuego | Southern tip of South America (Argentinian, east part; Chilean, west part) | 18,605 | 48,187 |
| Kyushu | Sea of Japan—Pacific (Japanese) | 16,223 | 42,018 |
| Melville | Arctic Ocean (Canadian) | 16,141 | 41,805 |
| Axel Heiberg | Arctic Ocean (Canadian) | 15,779 | 40,868 |
| Southampton | Hudson Bay (Canadian) | 15,700 | 40,663 |

## Principal Deserts of the World

| Desert | Location | Approximate size | Approx. elevation, ft |
|---|---|---|---|
| Atacama | North Chile | 400 mi. long | 7,000–13,500 |
| Black Rock | Northwest Nevada | About 1,000 sq mi. | 2,000–8,500 |
| Colorado | Southeast California from San Gorgonio Pass to Gulf of California | 200 mi. long and a maximum width of 50 mi. | Few feet above to 250 below sea level |
| Dasht-e-Kavir | Southeast of Caspian Sea, Iran | — | 2,000 |
| Dasht-e-Lut | Northeast of Kerman, Iran | — | 1,000 |
| Gobi (Shamo) | Covers most of Mongolia | 500,000 sq mi. | 3,000–5,000 |
| Great Arabian | Most of Arabia | 1,500 mi. long | — |
| An Nafud (Red Desert) | South of Jauf | 400 mi. by avg of 140 mi. | 3,000 |
| Dahna | Northeast of Nejd | 400 mi. by 30 mi. | — |
| Rub' al-Khali | South portion of Nejd | Over 200,000 sq. mi. | — |
| Syrian (Al-Hamad) | North of lat. 30° N | — | 1,850 |
| Great Australian | Western portion of Australia | About one half the continent | 600–1,000 |
| Great Salt Lake | West of Great Salt Lake to Nevada—Utah boundary | About 110 mi. by 50 mi. | 4,500 |
| Kalahari | South Africa—South-West Africa | About 120,000 sq mi. | Over 3,000 |
| Kara Kum (Desert of Kiva) | Southwest Turkmen, U.S.S.R. | 115,000 sq mi. | — |
| Kyzyl Kum | Uzbek and Kazakh, U.S.S.R. | Over 100,000 sq. mi. | 160 near Lake Aral to 2,000 in southeast |
| Libyan | Libya, Egypt, Sudan | Over 500,000 sq mi. | — |
| Mojave | North of Colorado Desert and south of Death Valley, southeast California | 15,000 sq mi. | 2,000 |
| Nubian | From Red Sea to great west bend of the Nile, Sudan | — | 2,500 |
| Painted Desert | Northeast Arizona | Over 7,000 sq mi. | High plateau, 5,000 |
| Sahara | North Africa to about lat. 15° N and from Red Sea to Atlantic Ocean | 3,200 mi. greatest length along lat. 20° N; area over 3,500,000 sq mi. | 440 below sea level to 11,000 above; avg elevation, 1,400–1,600 |
| Takla Makan | South central Sinkiang, China | Over 100,000 sq mi. | — |
| Thar (Indian) | Pakistan-India | Nearly 100,000 sq mi. | Over 1,000 |

## Interesting Caves and Caverns of the World

**Aggtelek.** In village of same name, northern Hungary. Large stalactitic cavern about 5 miles long.

**Altamira Cave.** Near Santander, Spain. Contains animal paintings (Old Stone Age art) on roof and walls.

**Antiparos.** On island of same name in the Grecian Archipelago. Some stalactites are 20 ft long. Brilliant colors and fantastic shapes.

**Blue Grotto.** On island of Capri, Italy. Cavern hollowed out in limestone by constant wave action. Now half filled with water because of sinking coast. Name derived from unusual blue light permeating the cave. Source of light is a submerged opening, light passing through the water.

**Carlsbad Caverns.** Southeast New Mexico. Largest underground labyrinth yet discovered. Three levels: 754, 900, and 1,320 ft below the surface.

**Fingal's Cave.** On island of Staffa off coast of western Scotland. Penetrates about 200 ft inland. Contains basaltic columns almost 40 ft high.

**Ice Cave.** Near Dobsina, Czechoslovakia. Noted for its beautiful crystal effects.

**Jenolan Caves.** In Blue Mountain plateau, New South Wales, Australia. Beautiful stalactitic formations.

**Kent's Cavern.** Near Torquay, England. Source of much information on Paleolithic man.

**Luray Cavern.** Near Luray, Va. Has large stalactitic and stalagmitic columns of many colors.

**Mammoth Cave.** Limestone cavern in central Kentucky. Cave area is about 10 miles in diameter but has at least 150 miles of irregular subterranean passageways at various levels. Temperature remains fairly constant at 54° F.

**Peak Cavern or Devil's Hole.** Derbyshire, England. About 2,250 ft into a mountain. Lowest part is about 600 ft below the surface.

**Postojna (Postumia) Grotto.** Near Postumia in Julian Alps, about 25 miles northeast of Trieste. Stalactitic cavern, largest in Europe. Piuca (Pivka) River flows through part of it. Caves have numerous beautiful stalactites.

**Singing Cave.** Iceland. A lava cave; name derived from echoes of people singing in it.

**Wind Cave.** In Black Hills of South Dakota. Limestone caverns with stalactites and stalagmites almost entirely missing. Variety of crystal formations called "boxwork."

**Wyandotte Cave.** In Crawford County, southern Indiana. A limestone cavern with five levels of passages; one of the largest in North America. "Monumental Mountain," approximately 135 ft high, is believed to be one of the world's largest underground "mountains."

# U.S. Geography

## Miscellaneous Data for the United States

*Source:* Department of the Interior, U.S. Geological Survey.

| | |
|---|---:|
| Highest point: Mount McKinley, Alaska | 20,320 ft (6,193 m) |
| Lowest point: Death Valley, Calif. | 282 ft (86 m) below sea level |
| Approximate mean altitude | 2,500 ft (762 m) |
| Points farthest apart (50 states): | |
| Log Point, Elliot Key, Fla., and Kure Island, Hawaii | 5,852 mi. (9,418 km) |
| Geographic center (50 states): | |
| In Butte County, S.D. (west of Castle Rock) | 44° 58′ N. lat.  103° 46′ W. long. |
| Geographic center (48 conterminous states): | |
| In Smith County, Kan. (near Lebanon) | 39° 50′ N. lat.  98° 35′ W. long. |
| Boundaries: | |
| Between Alaska and Canada | 1,538 mi. (2,475 km) |
| Between the 48 conterminous states and Canada (incl. Great Lakes) | 3,987 mi. (6,416 km) |
| Between the United States and Mexico | 1,933 mi. (3,111 km) |

## Extreme Points of the United States (50 States)

| | | | Distance[1] | |
|---|---|---|---|---|
| **Extreme point** | **Latitude** | **Longitude** | **mi.** | **km** |
| Northernmost point: Point Barrow, Alaska | 71°23′ N | 156°29′ W | 2,502 | 4,027 |
| Easternmost point: West Quoddy Head, Me. | 44°49′ N | 66°57′ W | 1,785 | 2,873 |
| Southernmost point: Ka Lae (South Cape), Hawaii | 18°56′ N | 155°41′ W | 3,456 | 5,562 |
| Westernmost point: Cape Wrangell, Alaska (Attu Island) | 52°55′ N | 172°27′ E | 3,620 | 5,826 |

1. From geographic center of United States (incl. Alaska and Hawaii), west of Castle Rock, S.D., 44°58′ N. lat., 103°46′ W long.

## Highest, Lowest, and Mean Altitudes in the United States

| State | Altitude, ft[1] | Highest point | Altitude, ft | Lowest point | Altitude, ft |
|---|---|---|---|---|---|
| Alabama | 500 | Cheaha Mountain | 2,407 | Gulf of Mexico | Sea level |
| Alaska | 1,900 | Mount McKinley | 20,320 | Pacific Ocean | Sea level |
| Arizona | 4,100 | Humphreys Peak | 12,633 | Colorado River | 70 |
| Arkansas | 650 | Magazine Mountain | 2,753 | Ouachita River | 55 |
| California | 2,900 | Mount Whitney | 14,494 | Death Valley | 282[2] |
| Colorado | 6,800 | Mount Elbert | 14,433 | Arkansas River | 3,350 |
| Connecticut | 500 | Mount Frissell, on south slope | 2,380 | Long Island Sound | Sea level |
| Delaware | 60 | On Ebright Road | 442 | Atlantic Ocean | Sea level |
| D.C. | 150 | Tenleytown, northwest part | 410 | Potomac River | 1 |
| Florida | 100 | Sec. 30, T6N, R20W[3] | 345 | Atlantic Ocean | Sea level |
| Georgia | 600 | Brasstown Bald | 4,784 | Atlantic Ocean | Sea level |
| Hawaii | 3,030 | Mauna Kea | 13,796 | Pacific Ocean | Sea level |
| Idaho | 5,000 | Borah Peak | 12,662 | Snake River | 710 |
| Illinois | 600 | Charles Mound | 1,235 | Mississippi River | 279 |
| Indiana | 700 | Franklin Township, Wayne County | 1,257 | Ohio River | 320 |
| Iowa | 1,100 | Sec. 29, T100N, R41W[4] | 1,670 | Mississippi River | 480 |
| Kansas | 2,000 | Mount Sunflower | 4,039 | Verdigris River | 680 |
| Kentucky | 750 | Black Mountain | 4,145 | Mississippi River | 257 |
| Louisiana | 100 | Driskill Mountain | 535 | New Orleans | 5[2] |
| Maine | 600 | Mount Katahdin | 5,268 | Atlantic Ocean | Sea level |
| Maryland | 350 | Backbone Mountain | 3,360 | Atlantic Ocean | Sea level |
| Massachusetts | 500 | Mount Greylock | 3,491 | Atlantic Ocean | Sea level |
| Michigan | 900 | Mount Arvon | 1,979 | Lake Erie | 572 |
| Minnesota | 1,200 | Eagle Mountain | 2,301 | Lake Superior | 602 |
| Mississippi | 300 | Woodall Mountain | 806 | Gulf of Mexico | Sea level |
| Missouri | 800 | Taum Sauk Mountain | 1,772 | St. Francis River | 230 |
| Montana | 3,400 | Granite Peak | 12,799 | Kootenai River | 1,800 |
| Nebraska | 2,600 | Johnson Township, Kimball County | 5,426 | Southeast corner of state | 840 |
| Nevada | 5,500 | Boundary Peak | 13,143 | Colorado River | 470 |
| New Hampshire | 1,000 | Mount Washington | 6,288 | Atlantic Ocean | Sea level |
| New Jersey | 250 | High Point | 1,803 | Atlantic Ocean | Sea level |
| New Mexico | 5,700 | Wheeler Peak | 13,161 | Red Bluff Reservoir | 2,817 |
| New York | 1,000 | Mount Marcy | 5,344 | Atlantic Ocean | Sea level |
| North Carolina | 700 | Mount Mitchell | 6,684 | Atlantic Ocean | Sea level |
| North Dakota | 1,900 | White Butte | 3,506 | Red River | 750 |
| Ohio | 850 | Campbell Hill | 1,550 | Ohio River | 433 |
| Oklahoma | 1,300 | Black Mesa | 4,973 | Little River | 287 |
| Oregon | 3,300 | Mount Hood | 11,239 | Pacific Ocean | Sea level |
| Pennsylvania | 1,100 | Mount Davis | 3,213 | Delaware River | Sea level |
| Rhode Island | 200 | Jerimoth Hill | 812 | Atlantic Ocean | Sea level |
| South Carolina | 350 | Sassafras Mountain | 3,560 | Atlantic Ocean | Sea level |
| South Dakota | 2,200 | Harney Peak | 7,242 | Big Stone Lake | 962 |
| Tennessee | 900 | Clingmans Dome | 6,643 | Mississippi River | 182 |
| Texas | 1,700 | Guadalupe Peak | 8,749 | Gulf of Mexico | Sea level |
| Utah | 6,100 | Kings Peak | 13,528 | Beaverdam Creek | 2,000 |
| Vermont | 1,000 | Mount Mansfield | 4,393 | Lake Champlain | 95 |
| Virginia | 950 | Mount Rogers | 5,729 | Atlantic Ocean | Sea level |
| Washington | 1,700 | Mount Rainier | 14,410 | Pacific Ocean | Sea level |
| West Virginia | 1,500 | Spruce Knob | 4,863 | Potomac River | 240 |
| Wisconsin | 1,050 | Timms Hill | 1,451 | Lake Michigan | 581 |
| Wyoming | 6,700 | Gannett Peak | 13,804 | Belle Fourche River | 3,100 |
| United States | 2,500 | Mount McKinley (Alaska) | 20,320 | Death Valley (California) | 282[2] |

1. Approximate mean altitude. 2. Below sea level. 3. Walton County. 4. Osceola County. *Source:* Department of the Interior, U.S. Geological Survey.

## Mason and Dixon's Line

Mason and Dixon's Line (often called the Mason-Dixon Line) is the boundary between Pennsylvania and Maryland, running at a north latitude of 39°43'19.11". The greater part of it was surveyed from 1763–67 by Charles Mason and Jeremiah Dixon, English astronomers who had been appointed to settle a dispute between the colonies. As the line was partly the boundary between the free and the slave states, it has come to signify the division between the North and the South.

# Named Summits in the U.S. Over 14,000 Feet Above Sea Level

| Name | State | Height | Name | State | Height | Name | State | Height |
|---|---|---|---|---|---|---|---|---|
| Mt. McKinley | Alaska | 20,320 | Mt. Antero | Colo. | 14,269 | Windom Peak | Colo. | 14,087 |
| Mt. St. Elias | Alaska | 18,008 | Torreys Peak | Colo. | 14,267 | Mt. Russell | Calif. | 14,086 |
| Mt. Foraker | Alaska | 17,400 | Castle Peak | Colo. | 14,265 | Mt. Eolus | Colo. | 14,084 |
| Mt. Bona | Alaska | 16,421 | Quandary Peak | Colo. | 14,265 | Mt. Columbia | Colo. | 14,073 |
| Mt. Blackburn | Alaska | 16,390 | Mt. Evans | Colo. | 14,264 | Mt. Augusta | Alaska | 14,070 |
| Mt. Sanford | Alaska | 16,237 | Longs Peak | Colo. | 14,255 | Missouri Mtn. | Colo. | 14,067 |
| South Buttress | Alaska | 15,885 | Mt. Wilson | Colo. | 14,246 | Humboldt Peak | Colo. | 14,064 |
| Mt. Vancouver | Alaska | 15,700 | White Mtn. Peak | Calif. | 14,246 | Mt. Bierstadt | Colo. | 14,060 |
| Mt. Churchill | Alaska | 15,638 | North Palisade | Calif. | 14,242 | Sunlight Peak | Colo. | 14,059 |
| Mt. Fairweather | Alaska | 15,300 | Shavano Peak | Colo. | 14,229 | Split Mtn. | Calif. | 14,058 |
| Mt. Hubbard | Alaska | 15,015 | Crestone Needle | Colo. | 14,197 | Handies Peak | Colo. | 14,048 |
| Mt. Bear | Alaska | 14,831 | Mt. Belford | Colo. | 14,197 | Culebra Peak | Colo. | 14,047 |
| East Buttress | Alaska | 14,730 | Mt. Princeton | Colo. | 14,197 | Mt. Lindsey | Colo. | 14,042 |
| Mt. Hunter | Alaska | 14,573 | Mt. Yale | Colo. | 14,196 | Middle Palisade | Calif. | 14,040 |
| Mt. Alverstone | Alaska | 14,565 | Mt. Bross | Colo. | 14,172 | Little Bear Peak | Colo. | 14,037 |
| Browne Tower | Alaska | 14,530 | Kit Carson Mtn. | Colo. | 14,165 | Mt. Sherman | Colo. | 14,036 |
| Mt. Whitney | Calif. | 14,494 | Mt. Wrangell | Alaska | 14,163 | Redcloud Peak | Colo. | 14,034 |
| Mt. Elbert | Colo. | 14,433 | Mt. Shasta | Calif. | 14,162 | Mt. Langley | Calif. | 14,027 |
| Mt. Massive | Colo. | 14,421 | Mt. Sill | Calif. | 14,162 | Mt. Tyndall | Calif. | 14,018 |
| Mt. Harvard | Colo. | 14,420 | El Diente Peak | Colo. | 14,159 | Pyramid Peak | Colo. | 14,018 |
| Mt. Rainier | Wash. | 14,410 | Maroon Peak | Colo. | 14,156 | Wilson Peak | Colo. | 14,017 |
| Mt. Williamson | Calif. | 14,375 | Tabeguache Mtn. | Colo. | 14,155 | Mt. Muir | Calif. | 14,015 |
| Blanca Peak | Colo. | 14,345 | Mt. Oxford | Colo. | 14,153 | Wetterhorn Peak | Colo. | 14,015 |
| La Plata Peak | Colo. | 14,336 | Mt. Sneffels | Colo. | 14,150 | No. Maroon Pk. | Colo. | 14,014 |
| Uncompahgre Pk. | Colo. | 14,309 | Mt. Democrat | Colo. | 14,148 | San Luis Peak | Colo. | 14,014 |
| Crestone Peak | Colo. | 14,294 | Capitol Peak | Colo. | 14,130 | Huron Peak | Colo. | 14,005 |
| Mt. Lincoln | Colo. | 14,286 | Pikes Peak | Colo. | 14,110 | Mt. of the Holy Cross | Colo. | 14,005 |
| Grays Peak | Colo. | 14,270 | Snowmass Mtn. | Colo. | 14,092 | Sunshine Peak | Colo. | 14,001 |

Source: Department of the Interior, U.S. Geological Survey.

## Post-Eruption Map of Mount St. Helens for Sale

A post-eruption map of Mount St. Helens and vicinity that includes color photographs of the major eruption and aftereffects has been published by the U.S. Geological Survey.

The 30- × 40-inch topographical map shows how the area appears in the wake of the violent eruption of May 18, 1980. Presented at a scale of 1:100,000 (one inch equals about 1.68 miles), the map denotes land managed by federal and state agencies and includes numerical designations for roads within the Gifford Pinchot National Forest, viewpoints, campgrounds, picnic areas, visitor centers and points of interest.

On the reverse side of the map, the Forest Service has prepared a text and color photographs providing a narrative of recent Mount St. Helens volcanic activities.

The map, "Mount St. Helens and Vicinity, March 1981," may be purchased by mail for $2.20 each, from the Branch of Distribution, U.S. Geological Survey, Box 25286, Federal Center, Denver, Colo. 80225. Map orders *must* specify the correct title given here, and a check or money order made payable to the U.S. Geological Survey must be included with your order.

## Rivers of the United States

### (350 or more miles long)

**Alabama** (735 mi.; 1,183 km): From junction of Tallapoosa R. and Coosa R. in Alabama to Mobile R.

**Altamaha-Ocmulgee** (392 mi.; 631 km): From junction of Yellow R. and South R., Newton Co. in Georgia to Atlantic Ocean.

**Apalachicola-Chattahoochee** (524 mi.; 843 km): From Towns Co. in Georgia to Gulf of Mexico in Florida.

**Arkansas** (1,459 mi.; 2,348 km): From Lake Co. in Colorado to Mississippi R. in Arkansas.

**Brazos** (870 mi.; 1,400 km): From junction of Salt Fork and Double Mountain Fork in Texas to Gulf of Mexico.

**Canadian** (906 mi.; 1,458 km): From Las Animas Co. in Colorado to Arkansas R. in Oklahoma.

**Cimarron** (600 mi.; 966 km): From Colfax Co. in New Mexico to Arkansas R. in Oklahoma.

**Clark Fork-Pend Oreille** (505 mi.; 813 km): From Silver Bow Co. in Montana to Columbia R. in British Columbia.

**Colorado** (1,450 mi.; 2,333 km): From Rocky Mountain National Park in Colorado to Gulf of California in Mexico.

**Colorado** (862 mi.; 1,387 km): From Dawson Co. in Texas to Matagorda Bay.

**Columbia** (1,243 mi.; 2,000 km): From Columbia Lake in British Columbia to Pacific Ocean (entering between Oregon and Washington).

**Colville** (350 mi.; 563 km): From Brooks Range in Alaska to Beaufort Sea.

**Connecticut** (407 mi.; 655 km): From Third Connecticut Lake in New Hampshire to Long Island Sound in Connecticut.

**Cumberland** (720 mi.; 1,159 km): From junction of Poor and Clover Forks in Harlan Co. in Kentucky to Ohio R.

**Delaware** (390 mi.; 628 km): From Schoharie Co. in New York to Liston Point, Delaware Bay.

**Gila** (630 mi.; 1,014 km): From Catron Co. in New Mexico to Colorado R. in Arizona.

**Green** (360 mi.; 579 km): From Lincoln Co. in Kentucky to Ohio R. in Kentucky.

**Green** (730 mi.; 1,175 km): From Sublette Co. in Wyoming to Colorado R. in Utah.

**Illinois** (420 mi.; 676 km): From St. Joseph Co. in Indiana to Mississippi R. at Grafton in Illinois.

**James** (sometimes called *Dakota*) (710 mi.; 1,143 km): From Wells Co. in North Dakota to Missouri R. in South Dakota.

**Kanawha-New** (352 mi.; 566 km): From junction of North and South Forks of New R. in North Carolina, through Virginia and West Virginia (New River becoming Kanawha River), to Ohio River.

**Koyukuk** (470 mi.; 756 km): From Brooks Range in Alaska to Yukon R.

**Kuskokwim** (724 mi.; 1,165 km): From Alaska Range in Alaska to Kuskokwim Bay.

**Licking** (350 mi.; 563 km): From Magoffin Co. in Kentucky to Ohio R. at Cincinnati in Ohio.

**Little Missouri** (560 mi.; 901 km): From Crook Co. in Wyoming to Missouri R. in North Dakota.

**Milk** (625 mi.; 1,006 km): From junction of forks in Alberta Province to Missouri R.

**Mississippi** (2,348 mi.; 3,779 km): From Lake Itasca in Minnesota to mouth of Southwest Pass in La.

**Mississippi-Missouri-Red Rock** (3,880 mi.; 6,240 km): From source of Red Rock R. in Montana to mouth of Southwest Pass in Louisiana.

**Missouri** (2,315 mi.; 3,726 km): From junction of Jefferson R., Gallatin R., and Madison R. in Montana to Mississippi R. near St. Louis.

**Missouri-Red Rock** (2,700 mi.; 4,340 km): From source of Red Rock R. in Montana to Mississippi R. near St. Louis.

**Mobile-Alabama-Coosa** (780 mi.; 1,255 km): From junction of Etowah R. and Oostanaula R. in Georgia to Mobile Bay.

**Neosho** (460 mi.; 740 km): From Morris Co. in Kansas to Arkansas R. in Oklahoma.

**Niobrara** (431 mi.; 694 km): From Niobrara Co. in Wyoming to Missouri R. in Nebraska.

**Noatak** (350 mi.; 563 km): From Brooks Range in Alaska to Kotzebue Sound.

**North Canadian** (784 mi.; 1,261 km): From Union Co. in New Mexico to Canadian R. in Oklahoma.

**North Platte** (618 mi.; 995 km): From Jackson Co. in Colorado to junction with So. Platte R. in Nebraska to form Platte R.

**Ohio** (981 mi.; 1,579 km): From junction of Allegheny R. and Monongahela R. at Pittsburgh to Mississippi R. between Illinois and Kentucky.

**Ohio-Allegheny** (1,306 mi.; 2,102 km): From Potter Co. in Pennsylvania to Mississippi R. at Cairo in Illinois.

**Osage** (500 mi.; 805 km): From east-central Kansas to Missouri R. near Jefferson City in Missouri.

**Ouachita** (605 mi.; 974 km): From Polk Co. in Arkansas to Red R. in Louisiana.

**Pearl** (411 mi.; 661 km): From Neshoba County in Mississippi to Gulf of Mexico (Mississippi-Louisiana).

**Pecos** (926 mi.; 1,490 km): From Mora Co. in New Mexico to Rio Grande in Texas.

**Pee Dee-Yadkin** (435 mi.; 700 km): From Watauga Co. in North Carolina to Winyah Bay in South Carolina.

**Pend Oreille** (490 mi.; 789 km): Near Butte in Montana to Columbia R. on Washington-Canada border.

**Porcupine** (569 mi.; 916 km): From Yukon Territory, Canada, to Yukon R. in Alaska.

**Potomac** (383 mi.; 616 km): From Garrett Co. in Md. to Chesapeake Bay at Point Lookout in Md.

**Powder** (375 mi.; 603 km): From junction of forks in Johnson Co. in Wyoming to Yellowstone R. in Montana.

**Red** (1,270 mi.; 2,044 km): From junction of forks in Harmon Co. in Oklahoma to Mississippi R. in Louisiana.

**Red** (officially called *Red River of the North*) (545 mi.; 877 km): From junction of Otter Tail R. and Bois de Sioux R. in Minnesota to Lake Winnipeg in Manitoba.

**Republican** (445 mi.; 716 km): From junction of North Fork and Arikaree R. in Nebraska to junction with Smoky Hill R. in Kansas to form the Kansas R.

**Rio Grande** (1,885 mi.; 3,034 km): From San Juan Co. in Colorado to Gulf of Mexico.

**Roanoke** (380 mi.; 612 km): From junction of forks in Montgomery Co. in Virginia to Albemarle Sound in North Carolina.

**Sabine** (380 mi.; 612 km): From junction of forks in Hunt Co. in Texas to Sabine Lake between Texas and Louisiana.

**Sacramento** (377 mi.; 607 km): From Siskiyou Co. in California to Suisun Bay.

**Saint Francis** (425 mi.; 684 km): From Iron Co. in Missouri to Mississippi R. in Arkansas.

**Salmon** (420 mi.; 676 km): From Custer Co. in Idaho to Snake R.

**San Joaquin** (350 mi.; 563 km): From junction of forks in Madera Co. in California to Suisun Bay.

**San Juan** (360 mi.; 579 km): From Archuleta Co. in Colorado to Colorado R. in Utah.

**Santee-Wateree-Catawba** (538 mi.; 866 km): From McDowell Co. in North Carolina to Atlantic Ocean in South Carolina.

**Smoky Hill** (540 mi.; 869 km): From Cheyenne Co. in Colorado to junction with Republican R. in Kansas to form Kansas R.

**Snake** (1,038 mi.; 1,670 km): From Ocean Plateau in Wyoming to Columbia R. in Washington.

**South Platte** (424 mi.; 682 km): From Park Co. in Colorado to junction with North Platte R. in Nebraska to form Platte R.

**Susquehanna** (444 mi.; 715 km): From Otsego Lake in New York to Chesapeake Bay in Maryland.

**Tanana** (659 mi.; 1,060 km): From Wrangell Mts. in Yukon Territory, Canada, to Yukon R. in Alaska.

**Tennessee** (652 mi.; 1,049 km): From junction of Holston R. and French Broad R. in Tennessee to Ohio R. in Kentucky.

**Tennessee-French Broad** (900 mi.; 1,448 km): From Bland Co. in Virginia to Ohio R. at Paducah in Kentucky.

**Tombigbee** (525 mi.; 845 km): From junction of forks in Itawamba Co. in Mississippi to Mobile R. in Alabama.

**Trinity** (360 mi.; 579 km): From junction of forks in Dallas Co. in Texas to Galveston Bay.

**Wabash** (529 mi.; 851 km): From Darke Co. in Ohio to Ohio R. between Illinois and Indiana.

**Washita** (500 mi.; 805 km): From Hemphill Co. in Texas to Red R. in Oklahoma.

**White** (720 mi.; 1,159 km): From Madison Co. in Arkansas to Mississippi R.

**Wisconsin** (430 mi.; 692 km): From Vilas Co. in Wisconsin to Mississippi R.

**Yellowstone** (671 mi.; 1,080 km): From Park Co. in Wyoming to Missouri R. in North Dakota.

**Yukon** (1,979 mi.; 3,185 km): From junction of Lewes R. and Pelly R. in Yukon Territory, Canada, to Bering Sea in Alaska.

# Longitude and Latitude of U.S. and Canadian Cities

### (and time corresponding to 12:00 noon, eastern standard time)

| City | Long. w ° | ' | Lat. n ° | ' | Time | City | Long. w ° | ' | Lat. n ° | ' | Time |
|---|---|---|---|---|---|---|---|---|---|---|---|
| Albany, N.Y. | 73 | 45 | 42 | 40 | 12:00 noon | Memphis, Tenn | 90 | 3 | 35 | 9 | 11:00 a.m. |
| Amarillo, Tex. | 101 | 50 | 35 | 11 | 11:00 a.m. | Miami, Fla. | 80 | 12 | 25 | 46 | 12:00 noon |
| Anchorage, Alaska | 149 | 54 | 61 | 13 | 7:00 a.m. | Milwaukee | 87 | 55 | 43 | 2 | 11:00 a.m. |
| Atlanta | 84 | 23 | 33 | 45 | 12:00 noon | Minneapolis | 93 | 14 | 44 | 59 | 11:00 a.m. |
| Atlantic City, N.J. | 74 | 25 | 39 | 22 | 12:00 noon | Mobile, Ala. | 88 | 3 | 30 | 42 | 11:00 a.m. |
| Austin, Nev. | 117 | 4 | 39 | 29 | 9:00 a.m. | Montgomery, Ala. | 86 | 18 | 32 | 21 | 11:00 a.m. |
| Baker, Ore. | 117 | 50 | 44 | 47 | 9:00 a.m. | Montpelier, Vt. | 72 | 32 | 44 | 15 | 12:00 noon |
| Baltimore | 76 | 38 | 39 | 18 | 12:00 noon | Montreal, Que. | 73 | 35 | 45 | 30 | 12:00 noon |
| Bangor, Me. | 68 | 47 | 44 | 48 | 12:00 noon | Moose Jaw, Sask. | 105 | 31 | 50 | 37 | 10:00 a.m. |
| Birmingham, Ala. | 86 | 50 | 33 | 30 | 11:00 a.m. | Nashville, Tenn. | 86 | 47 | 36 | 10 | 11:00 a.m. |
| Bismarck, N.D. | 100 | 47 | 46 | 48 | 11:00 a.m. | Needles, Calif. | 114 | 36 | 34 | 50 | 9:00 a.m. |
| Boise, Idaho | 116 | 13 | 43 | 36 | 10:00 a.m. | Nelson, B.C. | 117 | 17 | 49 | 30 | 9:00 a.m. |
| Boston | 71 | 5 | 42 | 21 | 12:00 noon | New Haven, Conn. | 72 | 55 | 41 | 19 | 12:00 noon |
| Buffalo, N.Y. | 78 | 50 | 42 | 55 | 12:00 noon | New Orleans | 90 | 4 | 29 | 57 | 11:00 a.m. |
| Calgary, Alberta | 114 | 1 | 51 | 1 | 10:00 a.m. | New York | 73 | 58 | 40 | 47 | 12:00 noon |
| Carlsbad, N.M. | 104 | 15 | 32 | 26 | 10:00 a.m. | Nogales, Ariz. | 110 | 56 | 31 | 21 | 10:00 a.m. |
| Charleston, S.C. | 79 | 56 | 32 | 47 | 12:00 noon | Nome, Alaska | 165 | 30 | 64 | 25 | 6:00 a.m. |
| Charleston, W.Va. | 81 | 38 | 38 | 21 | 12:00 noon | North Platte, Neb. | 100 | 46 | 41 | 8 | 11:00 a.m. |
| Charlotte, N.C. | 80 | 50 | 35 | 14 | 12:00 noon | Oklahoma City | 97 | 28 | 35 | 26 | 11:00 a.m. |
| Cheyenne, Wyo. | 104 | 52 | 41 | 9 | 10:00 a.m. | Ottawa, Ont. | 75 | 43 | 45 | 24 | 12:00 noon |
| Chicago | 87 | 37 | 41 | 50 | 11:00 a.m. | Philadelphia | 75 | 10 | 39 | 57 | 12:00 noon |
| Cincinnati | 84 | 30 | 39 | 8 | 12:00 noon | Phoenix, Ariz. | 112 | 4 | 33 | 29 | 10:00 a.m. |
| Cleveland | 81 | 37 | 41 | 28 | 12:00 noon | Pierre, S.D. | 100 | 21 | 44 | 22 | 11:00 a.m. |
| Columbia, S.C. | 81 | 2 | 34 | 0 | 12:00 noon | Pittsburgh | 79 | 57 | 40 | 27 | 12:00 noon |
| Columbus, Ohio | 83 | 1 | 40 | 0 | 12:00 noon | Port Arthur, Ont. | 89 | 17 | 48 | 30 | 12:00 noon |
| Dallas | 96 | 46 | 32 | 46 | 11:00 a.m. | Portland, Me. | 70 | 15 | 43 | 40 | 12:00 noon |
| Denver | 105 | 0 | 39 | 45 | 10:00 a.m. | Portland, Ore. | 122 | 41 | 45 | 31 | 9:00 a.m. |
| Des Moines, Iowa | 93 | 37 | 41 | 35 | 11:00 a.m. | Providence, R.I. | 71 | 24 | 41 | 50 | 12:00 noon |
| Detroit | 83 | 3 | 42 | 20 | 12:00 noon | Quebec, Que. | 71 | 11 | 46 | 49 | 12:00 noon |
| Dubuque, Iowa | 90 | 40 | 42 | 31 | 11:00 a.m. | Raleigh, N.C. | 78 | 39 | 35 | 46 | 12:00 noon |
| Duluth, Minn. | 92 | 5 | 46 | 49 | 11:00 a.m. | Reno, Nev. | 119 | 49 | 39 | 30 | 9:00 a.m. |
| Eastport, Me. | 67 | 0 | 44 | 54 | 12:00 noon | Richfield, Utah | 112 | 5 | 38 | 46 | 10:00 a.m. |
| El Centro, Calif. | 115 | 33 | 32 | 38 | 9:00 a.m. | Richmond, Va. | 77 | 29 | 37 | 33 | 12:00 noon |
| El Paso | 106 | 29 | 31 | 46 | 10:00 a.m. | Roanoke, Va. | 79 | 57 | 37 | 17 | 12:00 noon |
| Eugene, Ore. | 123 | 5 | 44 | 3 | 9:00 a.m. | Sacramento, Calif. | 121 | 30 | 38 | 35 | 9:00 a.m. |
| Fargo, N.D. | 96 | 48 | 46 | 52 | 11:00 a.m. | St. John, N.B. | 66 | 10 | 45 | 18 | 1:00 p.m. |
| Flagstaff, Ariz. | 111 | 41 | 35 | 13 | 10:00 a.m. | St. Louis | 90 | 12 | 38 | 35 | 11:00 a.m. |
| Fresno, Calif. | 119 | 48 | 36 | 44 | 9:00 a.m. | Salmon, Idaho | 113 | 54 | 45 | 11 | 10:00 a.m. |
| Garden City, Kan. | 100 | 53 | 37 | 58 | 10:00 a.m. | Salt Lake City, Utah | 111 | 54 | 40 | 46 | 10:00 a.m. |
| Grand Junction, Colo. | 108 | 33 | 39 | 5 | 10:00 a.m. | San Antonio | 98 | 33 | 29 | 23 | 11:00 a.m. |
| Grand Rapids, Mich. | 85 | 40 | 42 | 58 | 12:00 noon | San Diego, Calif. | 117 | 10 | 32 | 42 | 9:00 a.m. |
| Havre, Mont. | 109 | 43 | 48 | 33 | 10:00 a.m. | San Francisco | 122 | 26 | 37 | 47 | 9:00 a.m. |
| Helena, Mont. | 112 | 2 | 46 | 35 | 10:00 a.m. | San Juan, P.R. | 66 | 10 | 18 | 30 | 1:00 p.m. |
| Honolulu | 157 | 50 | 21 | 18 | 7:00 a.m. | Santa Fe, N.M. | 105 | 57 | 35 | 41 | 10:00 a.m. |
| Hoquiam, Wash. | 123 | 54 | 46 | 59 | 9:00 a.m. | Sault Ste. Marie, Mich. | 84 | 21 | 46 | 30 | 11:00 a.m. |
| Hot Springs, Ark. | 93 | 3 | 34 | 31 | 11:00 a.m. | Savannah, Ga. | 81 | 5 | 32 | 5 | 12:00 noon |
| Idaho Falls, Idaho | 112 | 1 | 43 | 30 | 10:00 a.m. | Scranton, Pa. | 75 | 39 | 41 | 24 | 12:00 noon |
| Indianapolis | 86 | 10 | 39 | 46 | 12:00 noon | Seattle | 122 | 20 | 47 | 37 | 9:00 a.m. |
| Jackson, Miss. | 90 | 12 | 32 | 20 | 11:00 a.m. | Shreveport, La. | 93 | 42 | 32 | 28 | 11:00 a.m. |
| Jacksonville, Fla. | 81 | 40 | 30 | 22 | 12:00 noon | Sioux Falls, S.D. | 96 | 44 | 43 | 33 | 11:00 a.m. |
| Juneau, Alaska | 134 | 24 | 58 | 18 | 9:00 a.m. | Sitka, Alaska | 135 | 15 | 57 | 10 | 9:00 a.m. |
| Kansas City, Mo. | 94 | 35 | 39 | 6 | 11:00 a.m. | Spokane, Wash. | 117 | 26 | 47 | 40 | 9:00 a.m. |
| Key West, Fla. | 81 | 48 | 24 | 33 | 12:00 noon | Springfield, Ill. | 89 | 38 | 39 | 48 | 11:00 a.m. |
| Kingston, Ont. | 76 | 30 | 44 | 15 | 12:00 noon | Springfield, Mass. | 72 | 34 | 42 | 6 | 12:00 noon |
| Klamath Falls, Ore. | 121 | 44 | 42 | 10 | 9:00 a.m. | Springfield, Mo. | 93 | 17 | 37 | 13 | 11:00 a.m. |
| Knoxville, Tenn. | 83 | 56 | 35 | 57 | 12:00 noon | Syracuse, N.Y. | 76 | 8 | 43 | 2 | 12:00 noon |
| Lander, Wyo. | 108 | 40 | 42 | 50 | 10:00 a.m. | Tampa, Fla. | 82 | 27 | 27 | 57 | 12:00 noon |
| Las Vegas, Nev. | 115 | 12 | 36 | 10 | 9:00 a.m. | Toronto, Ont. | 79 | 24 | 43 | 40 | 12:00 noon |
| Lewiston, Idaho | 117 | 2 | 46 | 24 | 9:00 a.m. | Trinidad, Colo. | 104 | 30 | 37 | 10 | 10:00 a.m. |
| Lincoln, Neb. | 96 | 40 | 40 | 50 | 11:00 a.m. | Victoria, B.C. | 123 | 21 | 48 | 25 | 9:00 a.m. |
| London, Ont. | 81 | 34 | 43 | 2 | 12:00 noon | Watertown, N.Y. | 75 | 55 | 43 | 58 | 12:00 noon |
| Los Angeles | 118 | 15 | 34 | 3 | 9:00 a.m. | Wichita, Kan. | 97 | 17 | 37 | 43 | 11:00 a.m. |
| Louisville, Ky. | 85 | 46 | 38 | 15 | 12:00 noon | Wilmington, N.C. | 77 | 57 | 34 | 14 | 12:00 noon |
| Manchester, N.H. | 71 | 30 | 43 | 0 | 12:00 noon | Winnipeg, Man. | 97 | 7 | 49 | 54 | 11:00 a.m. |

# Coastline of the United States

| State | Lengths, statute miles | | State | Lengths, statute miles | |
|---|---|---|---|---|---|
| | General coastline[1] | Tidal shoreline[2] | | General coastline[1] | Tidal shoreline[2] |
| Atlantic Coast: | | | Gulf Coast: | | |
| Maine | 228 | 3,478 | Florida (Gulf) | 770 | 5,095 |
| New Hampshire | 13 | 131 | Alabama | 53 | 607 |
| Massachusetts | 192 | 1,519 | Mississippi | 44 | 359 |
| Rhode Island | 40 | 384 | Louisiana | 397 | 7,721 |
| Connecticut | — | 618 | Texas | 367 | 3,359 |
| New York | 127 | 1,850 | Total Gulf coast | 1,631 | 17,141 |
| New Jersey | 130 | 1,792 | Pacific Coast: | | |
| Pennsylvania | — | 89 | California | 840 | 3,427 |
| Delaware | 28 | 381 | Oregon | 296 | 1,410 |
| Maryland | 31 | 3,190 | Washington | 157 | 3,026 |
| Virginia | 112 | 3,315 | Hawaii | 750 | 1,052 |
| North Carolina | 301 | 3,375 | Alaska (Pacific) | 5,580 | 31,383 |
| South Carolina | 187 | 2,876 | Total Pacific coast | 7,623 | 40,298 |
| Georgia | 100 | 2,344 | Arctic Coast: | | |
| Florida (Atlantic) | 580 | 3,331 | Alaska (Arctic) | 1,060 | 2,521 |
| Total Atlantic coast | 2,069 | 28,673 | Total Arctic coast | 1,060 | 2,521 |
| | | | States Total | 12,383 | 88,633 |

1. Figures are lengths of general outline of seacoast. Measurements made with unit measure of 30 minutes of latitude on charts as near scale of 1:1,200,000 as possible. Coastline of bays and sounds is included to point where they narrow to width of unit measure, and distance across at such point is included. 2. Figures obtained in 1939–40 with recording instrument on largest-scale maps and charts then available. Shoreline of outer coast, offshore islands, sounds, bays, rivers, and creeks is included to head of tidewater, or to point where tidal waters narrow to width of 100 feet. *Source:* Department of Commerce, National Oceanic and Atmospheric Administration, National Ocean Service.

## The Continental Divide

The Continental Divide is a ridge of high ground which runs irregularly north and south through the Rocky Mountains and separates eastward-flowing from westward-flowing streams. The waters which flow eastward empty into the Atlantic Ocean, chiefly by way of the Gulf of Mexico; those which flow westward empty into the Pacific.

## Geographic Illiterates

Our schools, since the absorption of "geography" into "social studies" would appear to be turning out a generation of geographic illiterates. Geographers, concerned about this, are once again attempting to bring to the attention of the public the extent of this ignorance and the need for more geography to be taught at all levels in our schools.

Chairmen of Departments of Geography in the North Carolina university system joined in this mission. One of their approaches was to administer an exam dealing with geographic facts to introductory college classes at the start of the 1984 fall semester. Results confirmed their fears. Almost three quarters of the students scored less than 50% and there is no reason to believe that North Carolina students are unique in their lack of geographic knowledge. Among the more amazing bits of (mis)information were: Dublin is in Ohio, Vladivostok is in Germany, Lima is in Italy, the Ganges is in Brazil, and the Amazon is in Egypt.

As to knowledge of U.S. geography, less than 50% of the students knew that Alaska and Texas are the two largest states, and 88% could not name all of the Great Lakes.

The test, which employed completion questions instead of multiple-choice, was patterned on, and where practical utilized questions from, an exam sponsored by the *New York Times* in 1950. The reason for adopting this exam was for comparison purposes. Are today's students more or less geographically sophisticated than those of 1950? Not surprisingly, in almost every instance where the same question was used, the showing of the 1984 group was lower, usually considerably lower—as much as 50% or more in some instances. The one question on which the current group scored appreciably better (15% more answered correctly) was "When it is noon in Raleigh what time is it in London?"

In addition to testing the students' geographic knowledge, the exam also asked for background information on the students. They were asked how many geographic courses they had had that were not listed as social studies. In elementary school 71.2% had had no geography courses; in junior high 65%; and in senior high 72.6%. Maybe it's time geography joined the three Rs in the classroom.

How about you? Can you name the states through which you would pass in traveling by automobile on the most direct route between Duluth and Seattle? If not, you have an advantage over the students, you can check it out on the map of the United States in this section. (Based on a report, *GEOGRAPHY: No "Where" in North Carolina 1984*, by Richard J. Kopec, University of North Carolina, Chapel Hill.)

# NORTH AMERICA

LAMBERT AZIMUTHAL EQUAL-AREA
PROJECTION

SCALE OF MILES

0 200 400 600 800 1000

SCALE OF KILOMETERS

0 200 400 600 800 1000

Capitals of Countries ............ ⊙
International Boundaries .... _._._.
Canals ............................

Copyright by C.S. HAMMOND & Co., N.Y.

# UNITED STATES

POLYCONIC PROJECTION

SCALE OF MILES

0  50  100      200      300      400

SCALE OF KILOMETERS

0  100  200      300      400

Capitals of Countries ..................... ☆
State Capitals ...................... △
International Boundaries ............ 
Railroads ........................ 

® Copyright HAMMOND INCORPORATED, Maplewood, N.J.

## CANADA

CONIC PROJECTION

SCALE OF MILES
0 100 200 300 400 500

SCALE OF KILOMETERS
0 100 200 300 400 500

Capitals of Countries ............ ⊕
Provincial & Territorial
Capitals ........................... ◉
Administrative Centers ........ ---

ATLANTIC OCEAN

GREENLAND (KALAALLIT NUNAAT) (Den.)

BAFFIN BAY

DAVIS STRAIT

BAFFIN ISLAND

NEWFOUNDLAND

QUEBEC

NEW BRUNSWICK

NOVA SCOTIA
Halifax

HUDSON BAY

JAMES BAY

NORTHWEST TERRITORIES

KEEWATIN REGION

KITIKMEOT REGION

FORT SMITH REGION

INUVIK REGION

BEAUFORT SEA

YUKON

ROCKY MOUNTAINS

BRITISH COLUMBIA

ALBERTA

SASKATCHEWAN

MANITOBA

ONTARIO

UNITED STATES

ALASKA

COAST MOUNTAINS

Vancouver

Seattle

Portland

GALAPAGOS ISLANDS
(ARCHIPIÉLAGO DE COLON)
(To Ecuador)

SCALE OF MILES
0    50   100   150

PACIFIC OCEAN

I. Pinta
Marchena
Española
Sta. Cruz
San Cristóbal
Santiago
I. Marchena
Fernandina
Isla Isabela
I. Sta. María

OCEAN

ATLANTIC

CARIBBEAN SEA

WEST INDIES

ST. LUCIA
ST. VINC. & GRENS.
BARBADOS
Bridgetown
GRENADA
TRINIDAD & TOBAGO
Port of Spain
Trinidad

PANAMA

COLOMBIA

VENEZUELA

GUYANA

SURINAME

FR. GUIANA
Cayenne

Georgetown
Paramaribo

ECUADOR

Quito

Guayaquil

PERU

Lima

Callao

BOLIVIA

La Paz

Sucre

BRAZIL

Brasília

Recife

Fortaleza

Salvador

Belém

Manaus

Amazon

# SOUTH AMERICA

LAMBERT AZIMUTHAL EQUAL-AREA PROJECTION

SCALE OF MILES

| 0 | 100 | 200 | 400 | 600 |

SCALE OF KILOMETERS

| 0 | 100 200 | 400 | 600 |

Capitals of Countries ☆

International Boundaries

Canals

Copyright by C. S. HAMMOND & CO., N.Y.

40°　A　30°　B　20°　C　10°　D　0°　E　10°　F

70°

Jan Mayen
(Nor.)

60°

N O R W E G I A N

Húnaflói
Breidhafjördhur
Hornn
Akureyri
ICELAND
Reykjavík
Reydharfjördhur
Hofsjökull
Hornafjördhur

Arctic Circle

S E A

Trondheimsfjorden

Senja
Vesterålen
Lofoten

Vestfjorden

Namsos

3

Faeroe Is.
(Den.)　Tórshavn

Shetland Is.
Lerwick

Sognefjorden
Bergen
Hardangerfjorden
Haugesund
Stavanger

Kristiansund
Ålesund

Trondheim

Lillehammer

Drammen
Fredrikstad
Larvik
Arendal
Kristiansand

Oslo

Östersund

Sundsvall

Söderhamn
Falun

Uppsala
Västerås

Örebro
Göteborg
Borås
Jönköping

N
O
R
R
K
E

Norrköping
Linköping

Rockall
(U.K.)

Orkney Is.
Kirkwall
Pentland Firth

Lindesnes
Skagerrak

Ålborg
Ålborg

Halsingborg
Malmö

Helsingborg

Ölan

B
A
L
T
I
C

50°

Hebrides
BRITISH
NO. IRELAND
IRELAND
Dundee
Donegal Bay
Belfast
Dundalk
Dublin
Galway
Limerick
(Luimneach)
Waterford
Cork
Cobh
C. Clear

Moray Firth
Inverness
SCOTLAND
Glasgow
Aberdeen
Edinburgh
Dundee
UNITED
Carlisle
Newcastle
upon Tyne
Manchester
Leeds
IRISH SEA
Liverpool
Sheffield
Hull
KINGDOM

NORTH

SEA

DENMARK

Esbjerg

Kattegat

Copenhagen
Flensburg
Kiel

Stralsund
Rostock
Lübeck

Bornholm

Slupsk

Kolobrzeg
Szczecin
(Stettin)

Byd

Pozn

PO

St. George's Channel
Land's End

WALES
Swansea
Cardiff
Bristol
ENGLAND
Birmingham
LONDON
Southampton
Portsmouth

The Wash
Norwich

Amsterdam
The Hague
Rotterdam

Helgoland
Bremen
Hamburg
Hannover
Bremen
Münster

EAST
BERLIN

Magdeburg
GERMANY
Leipzig
Dresden

Wroclaw
(Brest)

Warta

Czestochowa
Zabrze

O

CZECHOSLO

Plymouth

English Channel
Channel Is.
(Br.)
Cherbourg
Le Havre
Boulogne
Calais
Ghent
Lille
Brussels
BELGIUM
Liège
Antwerp
Rouen
NETH.
Bonn
LUX.
Essen
Dortmund
Cologne
Bonn
Düsseldorf
Wiesbaden
Kassel
Halle
Erfurt
Frankfurt
Plauen
Karl-Marx-
Stadt

Prague
(Praha)
Pilzen
Ostrava

4

40°

Ushant I.
Brest
Rennes
Belle Isle
St-Nazaire
Angers

Seine
Versailles
PARIS
Reims
Marne
Nancy
Metz
Saarbrücken
Mainz
Mannheim
Karlsruhe
Stuttgart
Nuremberg
Regensburg
Danube

Munich

Linz

VIENNA
(Wien)
Salzburg
Bratisl

La Rochelle
I. d'Oléron
Nantes
Loire
Tours
Limoges
Vichy

FRANCE
Orléans
Dijon
Mulhouse
Freiburg
Basel
Zürich
Bern
SWITZ.
Geneva
Mt. Blanc
Innsbruck

AUSTRIA

Graz

Sopron

Ljubljana

Maribor

Balaton
Pécs

Y
U
G
O

Bay of Biscay

El Ferrol
La Coruña
C. Finisterre
Vigo
Miño
Braga
Oviedo
Gijón
Santander
San Sebastián
Biarritz
Bayonne
Pyrenees
Bordeaux
Garonne
Montauban
Toulouse
Clermont-Ferrand
St-Étienne
Dordogne
Lyon
Rhône
Grenoble
Nîmes
Montpellier
G. of Lions
Marseille
Toulon
Turin
(Torino)
Milan
Verona
Trento
Bolzano
Brescia
Venice
(Venezia)
Trieste
Rijeka
Zagreb

Banja Luka

Zadar

Drava

Sava

Sarajevo

Braga
Oporto
Porto
Douro
Coimbra
Valladolid
León
Burgos
Saragossa
(Duero)
Salamanca
Sa. de Guadarrama

Genoa
Parma
Modena
La Spezia
Leghorn
(Livorno)
Florence
Bologna
Ferrara
Nice
MONACO
Ancona
Perugia

Split

Adriatic Sea

PORTUGAL
Lisbon
(Lisboa)
Setúbal
Évora
Guadiana
Tagus
(Tejo)
Badajoz
Toledo
SPAIN
MADRID
ANDORRA

Corsica
(Corse)
Ajaccio
Elba
SAN
MARINO
VATICAN
CITY
ROME
Sardinia
(Sardegna)

ITALY

Foggia

Bari

Cetinje

Mo

5

C. St. Vincent
Guadiana
Sierra Morena
Córdoba
Guadalquivir
Seville
Jerez
G. of Cádiz
Cádiz
Str. of Gibraltar
Tangier

Albacete
Sierra Nevada
Granada
Lorca
Murcia
Alicante
Almería
Cartagena

Valencia
Balearics
Minorca
Ibiza
Palma
Majorca

MEDITER

Iglesias
Cagliari

Olbia
Sassari

Naples
(Napoli)
Vesuvius

Taranto

G. of
Taranto

IONI

Palermo
Messina
Reggio di
Calabria
Syracuse
Catania

MALTA
Valletta

40°

Casablanca
Rabat
Meknès
Fès (Fez)
Marrakech
MOROCCO

Melilla
Oran
Algiers
Constantine
Annaba

Skikda

Bizerte
C. Bon
Tunis
TUNISIA
Pantelleria

Sicily
(Sicilia)

TYRRHENIAN

SEA

R
R
A
N

Catanzaro

ALGERIA

Biskra

Sousse

BARENTS SEA

WHITE SEA

FINLAND

L. Inari

KOLA PEN.

Bay of Mezen'

Gulf of Bothnia

L. Ladoga

LENINGRAD

L. Il'men

Helsinki

Tallinn

ESTONIAN S.S.R.

L. Peipus

LATVIAN S.S.R.

Riga

G. of Riga

LITHUANIAN S.S.R.

Kaunas

Kaliningrad

Vilna

WHITE RUSSIAN S.S.R.

Minsk

MOSCOW (Moskva)

UNION OF SOVIET FEDERATED SOCIALIST REPUBLICS

Volga

Gor'kiy

Kazan'

Kuybyshev

Ul'yanovsk

Saratov

Volgograd (Stalingrad)

Astrakhan'

CASPIAN SEA

WARSAW

POLAND

UKRAINIAN S.S.R.

Kiev

Khar'kov

Dnepropetrovsk

Donets

Donetsk

Rostov

Sea of Azov

CRIMEA

Odessa

ROMANIA

Bucharest

Danube

BULGARIA

Sofia

Plovdiv

ISTANBUL

BLACK SEA

Ankara

TURKEY

Athens

GEORGIAN S.S.R.

Tbilisi

ARMENIAN S.S.R.

Erivan

AZERBAIDZHAN S.S.R.

Baku

Caucasus

Groznyy

IRAN

SYRIA

CYPRUS

Nicosia

## EUROPE

LAMBERT AZIMUTHAL EQUAL AREA PROJECTION

SCALE OF MILES

0    100    200    300    400    500

SCALE OF KILOMETERS

0    100    200    300    400    500

Capitals of Countries ............ ☆

International Boundaries ..........

Canals ..........

Copyright by C.S. HAMMOND & CO., N.Y.

ASIA

LAMBERT AZIMUTHAL EQUAL-AREA PROJECTION

SCALE OF MILES
0    150    300    600    900    1200

SCALE OF KILOMETERS
0    300    600    900    1200

Capitals of Countries ......... ☆
International Boundaries .........
Canals .........

© Copyright HAMMOND INCORPORATED, Maplewood, N.J.

TIME ZONES OF THE WORLD

NOTE: Standard time zones in the U.S.S.R. are always advanced one hour.

Areas not using zone system.

Areas using half hour deviations.

STANDARD TIME ZONES

INTERNATIONAL DATE LINE

NEAR and
MIDDLE EAST
CONIC PROJECTION

SCALE OF MILES
0  100  200  300  400
MILES
0  100  200  300  400
KILOMETERS

Capitals of Countries ⊛
International Boundaries
Other Boundaries

## THE WORLD

MERCATOR PROJECTION

Capitals of Countries............ ●

# ENVIRONMENT

## 1986 Environmental Quality Index

*Source:* Copyright 1986 by the National Wildlife Federation.

Reprinted from the February-March issue of *National Wildlife Magazine*.

*National Wildlife's* annual Environmental Quality Index is a subjective analysis of the state of the nation's natural resources. The information included in each section is based on personal interviews, news reports, and the most recent scientific studies. The judgments on resource trends represent the collective thinking of the editors and the National Wildlife Federation staff, based on consultation with government experts, private specialists, and academic researchers.

**Wildlife: Same.** While some species get help, waterfowl numbers plummet. The bald eagle gained added protection when a federal judge ordered the U.S. Fish and Wildlife Service to ban lead shot in parts of five states where the bird is endangered. The Interior Department placed curbs on duck hunting in 1985 as many populations dropped nearly a third from 1984. Fish and Wildlife Service authorities say the outlook for waterfowl won't improve much because alarming amounts of wetland habitat continue to be drained. Late in 1985 the House of Representatives passed "swampbuster" legislation that, if it becomes law, will end taxpayer subsidies to farmers who destroy wetland. A recent study shows that four-fifths of the 550,000 acres of wetlands lost each year are converted to cropland. Harnessing of the nation's waterways for irrigation, electricity, and flood control also contributes to wetland losses. Another area of concern is the fact that more than a fourth of our 428 National Wildlife Refuges now contain water contaminated by toxic substances. One reason: farm runoff remains uncontrolled.

**Air: Same.** Though significant clean-up progress has been made in recent years—carbon monoxide emissions have been cut by two-thirds since 1975, levels of particulate matter are down by one-fifth, and the amount of lead in the air has been reduced by two-thirds—the scope of the country's air pollution problems clearly is broader than envisioned in 1970. Experts are particularly concerned about problems caused by fossil fuel combustion and toxic chemicals. They feared continuing expansion of coal use will almost certainly lead to an increase of sulfur dioxide and nitrogen dioxide emissions, key factors in the formation of acid rain and sulfate haze. The administration, however, remained reluctant to impose additional control on sulfur emissions. Other areas of concern were ozone—cars, trucks, and power plants are the biggest contributors; toxic air pollutants from chemical plants, hazardous waste sites, gasoline pumps, and other nonindustrial sources; and indoor air pollution.

**Water: Same.** In the 13 years since the Clean Water Act was enacted, industrial wastewater pollution has been reduced by more than a third. However, the overall trend in the nation's water quality is down; a major reason is the country's continuing inability to control nonpoint-source pollution. While it is up to the states to develop plans to control nonpoint pollution, Congress added provisions to the Clean Water Act to provide grants to help fund state efforts and added similar provisions to the Safe Drinking Water Act to assist state groundwater protection plans. More than half of all Americans rely on underground supplies for drinking water and a fair amount of it is contaminated. In the West there is the problem of groundwater depletion. In the last 30 years aquifer use has more than doubled. In the Southwest groundwater withdrawals exceed natural recharge by some 21 billion gallons per day.

**Energy: Same.** (Replaces Minerals). Despite a recent increase, total U.S. energy consumption is still lower today than in 1973. The reason: Americans continue to use energy more efficiently. At the same time renewable energy sources began to make significant contributions to the nation's energy supply. On the other hand the Department of Transportation rolled back its automobile fuel economy standard for 1986 models, and the Department of Energy continued to resist setting efficiency standards for household appliances. Meanwhile, the long-term outlook for domestic oil supplies worsened dramatically. The Interior Department slashed its estimate of oil reserves on the Outer Continental Shelf by more than half. Then, in its haste to find more oil, it unveiled a new five-year plan that would increase the number of offshore lease sales. Under its "Withdrawal Review Program" it also revoked protection on about 180 million acres of public land, opening more than 20 million acres to mining and mineral leasing.

**Forests: Same.** In 1985 Americans grew about twice as much timber as they harvested, as private forests in the eastern and north-central states continued to recover from decades of logging. The biggest and most valuable trees, however, are found in the national forests. Throughout 1985 conservationists were concerned about how they are being managed and how air pollution may be threatening them. To give access to timber, the Forest Service continued to open up more federal woodlands. Unfortunately some of these newly developed areas were being operated at a loss to the U.S. Treasury. Logging roads and other expenses exceed sale prices. Conservationists have shown that new roads cause more than financial damage. They threaten fish and wildlife population and habitat. Meanwhile new studies show that more forests may be at risk from air pollution (acid rain) than researchers had estimated previously.

**Soil: Same.** The nation's farmers suffered through another year of mounting debt and low crop and livestock prices. As they put financial survival ahead of soil conservation, the land continued to deteriorate in many areas. In Wyoming, Montana, and other prairie states, for example, "sodbusters" seeking to take advantage of tax incentives, crop-support programs, and real estate markets have plowed up millions of acres of fragile grasslands. In October 1985 the House of Representatives passed a farm bill that would significantly reduce soil loss if it becomes law. Provisions include taking up to 30 million acres of highly erodible land out of production for ten years and replant them to grass and trees and take federal farm benefits away from farmers who plow fragile prairie and steep hillsides that are not included in the reserve.

**Quality of Life: Same.** Many Americans think environmental quality is slipping. In a cross-section survey of some 1,500 readers of *National Wildlife*, 53 percent of the respondents thought that the environment would be less livable in five years than it is today. When asked "What do you see as the greatest threat to your environment?" readers ranked concerns as: water pollution, air pollution, hazardous wastes, overpopulation in world, acid rain, soil erosion, nuclear power plants, and pollutants in the home in that order. In a sense, the perception that environmental problems are spinning out of control stems from more and better information. Hazards that lay unrecognized for years are now surfacing in distressing numbers.

## Some Endangered and Threatened Species of the World[1]

| Common name | Scientific name | Range |
| --- | --- | --- |
| **MAMMALS** | | |
| Bear, brown | *Ursus arctos pruinosus* | China (Tibet) |
| Bear, brown or grizzly[2] | *Ursus arctos horribilis* | Canada, Western U.S. |
| Cat, leopard | *Felis bengalensis bengalensis* | Eastern Asia |
| Cat, tiger | *Felis tigrinus* | Costa Rica to northern Argentina |
| Cheetah | *Acinonyx jubatus* | Africa to India |
| Chimpanzee[2] | *Pan troglodytes* | Western and Central Africa |
| Chinchilla | *Chinchilla brevicaudata boliviana* | Bolivia |
| Deer, Columbian white-tailed | *Odocoileus virginianus leucurus* | U.S. (Ore., Wash.) |
| Deer, marsh | *Blastocerus dichotomus* | Argentina, Uruguay, Bolivia Paraguay, Brazil |
| Deer, musk | *Moschus moschiferus moschiferus* | Central and East Asia |
| Elephant, Asian | *Elephas maximus* | Southcentral and Southeast Asia |
| Gazelle, Clark's (Dibatag) | *Ammodorcas clarkei* | Somalia, Ethiopia |
| Gazelle, slender-horned (Rhim) | *Gazella leptoceros* | Sudan, Algeria, Egypt, Libya |
| Gorilla | *Gorilla gorilla* | Central and western Africa |
| Ibex, Walia | *Capra walie* | Ethiopia |
| Jaguar | *Panthera onca* | Central and South America, and U.S. (Texas, N.M., Ariz.) |
| Kangaroo, red[2] | *Macropus (=Megaleia) rufus* | Australia |
| Leopard | *Panthera pardus* | Africa and Asia |
| Leopard, snow | *Panthera uncia* | Central Asia |
| Lion, Asiatic | *Panthera leo persica* | Turkey to India |
| Mandrill | *Papio sphinx* | Equatorial West Africa |
| Monkey, black howler[2] | *Alouatta pigra* | Mexico, Guatemala, Belize |
| Ocelot | *Felis pardalis* | Central and South America, Ariz., Texas |
| Orangutan | *Pongo pygmaeus* | Borneo, Sumatra |
| Otter, southern sea[2] | *Enhydra lutris nereis* | West coast U.S. (Wash., Ore., Calif.), south to Mexico (Baja Calif.) |
| Panther, Florida | *Felis concolor coryi* | U.S. (La. and Ark., east to S.C. and Fla.) |
| Prairie dog, Utah | *Cynomys parvidens* | U.S. (Utah) |
| Pronghorn, Sonoran | *Antilocapra americana sonoriensis* | U.S. (Ariz.), Mexico |
| Rat, Morro Bay kangaroo | *Dipodomys heermanni morroensis* | U.S. (Calif.) |
| Rhinoceros, great Indian | *Rhinoceros unicornis* | India, Nepal |
| Sloth, Brazilian three-toed | *Bradypus torquatus* | Brazil |
| Tiger | *Panthera tigris* | Temperate and tropical Asia |
| Whale, humpback | *Megaptera novaeangliae* | Oceanic |
| Wolf, gray | *Canis lupus* | U.S. (48 conterminous other than Minn.[2]), Mexico |
| Zebra, mountain | *Equus zebra zebra* | South Africa |

---

| Common name | Scientific name | Range |
| --- | --- | --- |
| **BIRDS** | | |
| Albatross, short-tailed | *Diomedea albatrus* | North Pacific Ocean: Japan, U.S.S.R U.S. (Alas., Calif., Hawaii, Ore., Wash.) |
| Condor, Andean | *Vultur gryphus* | Colombia to Chile and Argentina |
| Eagle, bald | *Haliaeetus leucocephalus* | Conterminous U.S. (except Wash., Ore., Minn., Wis., Mich.[2]) |
| Falcon, Eurasian peregrine | *Falco peregrinus peregrinus* | Europe, Eurasia south to Africa and Mideast |
| Parakeet, paradise (=beautiful) | *Psephotus pulcherrimus* | Australia |
| Pelican, brown | *Pelecanus occidentalis* | U.S. (Carolinas, Texas, Calif.), West Indies, Central and South America, coastal |
| Penguin, Galápagos | *Spheniscus mendiculus* | Ecuador (Galápagos Islands) |
| Stork, oriental white | *Ciconia ciconia boyciana* | China, Japan, Korea, U.S.S.R. |
| **REPTILES** | | |
| Alligator, American | *Alligator mississippiensis* | Southeastern U.S. (except La., Texas, Fla., certain areas of S.C., Ga.[2] |
| Crocodile, American | *Crocodylus acutus* | U.S. (Fla.), Mexico, South America, Central America, Caribbean |
| Iguana, Anegada ground | *Cyclura pinguis* | West Indies, British Virgin Is. (Anegada Is.) |
| Python, Indian | *Python molurus molurus* | Sri Lanka, India |
| Snake, Atlantic salt marsh[2] | *Nerodia fasciata taeniata* | U.S. (Fla.) |
| **AMPHIBIANS** | | |
| Frog, Israel painted | *Discoglossus nigriventer* | Israel |
| Toad, African viviparous | *Nectophrynoides* spp. | Tanzania, Guinea, Ivory Coast, Cameroon, Liberia, Ethiopia |
| **FISH** | | |
| Catfish, giant | *Pangasianodon gigas* | Thailand |
| Trout, greenback cutthroat[2] | *Salmo clarki stomias* | U.S. (Colo.) |

1. Due to space limitations, does not include all mammals, birds, reptiles, amphibians, and fish or any clams, crustaceans, snails, insects, and plants. 2. Threatened. *Source:* Department of the Interior, Fish and Wildlife Service.

## Sources of Information

*Source:* Brooklyn Botanic Garden, *Handbook on The Environment and The Home Gardener.*

Advice on various aspects of conservation programs and problems is available from national, state, and local organizations. Dr. Richard H. Pough, of the Natural Area Council, has compiled a list of membership organizations that are happy to help smaller groups get started on worthwhile projects in conservation.

**America the Beautiful Fund, Inc.,** 806 15th St. N.W., Room 219, Washington, D.C. 20005
**American Forestry Association,** 1319 18th St., N.W., Washington, D.C. 20036
**Defenders of Wildlife,** 1244 19th St., N.W., Washington, D.C. 20036
**Environmental Defense Fund, Inc.,** 444 Park Ave. South, New York, N.Y. 10016
**Friends of the Earth,** 208 W. 13th St., New York, N.Y. 10011
**Izaak Walton League of America,** 1701 North Fort Myer Dr., Arlington, VA 22209

**National Audubon Society,** 950 Third Ave., New York, N.Y. 10022
**National Park and Conservation Association,** 1701 18th St., N.W., Washington, D.C. 20009
**National Trust for Historic Preservation,** 1785 Massachusetts Ave., N.W., Washington, D.C. 20036
**National Wildlife Federation,** 1412 16th St., N.W., Washington, D.C. 20036
**Natural Science for Youth Foundation,** 763 Silvermine Rd., New Canaan, Conn. 06840
**The Nature Conservancy,** 1800 N. Kent St., Suite 800, Arlington, Va. 22209
**Open Space Institute, Inc.,** Room 1901, 122 East 42nd St., New York, N.Y. 10168
**Sierra Club,** 530 Bush St., San Francisco, Calif. 94108
**The Wilderness Society,** 1901 Pennsylvania Ave., N.W., Washington, D.C. 20006
**World Wildlife Fund,** 1601 Connecticut Ave., N.W., Washington, D.C. 20009

## Don't Eat the Flowers

There are more than 700 species of plants that grow in the United States that have been identified as dangerous if eaten. Among them are some that are commonly favored by gardeners—buttercups, daffodils, lily of the valley, sweet peas, oleander, azalea, bleeding heart, delphinium, and rhododen-

dron. According to a survey of the nation's poison control centers, next to medicines, plants are the leading cause of poisoning in children under five years of age. A threefold increase in plant poisoning, from 1971 levels, is attributed to the house plant explosion and back-to-nature dining.

# Water Supply of the World[1]

The Antarctic Icecap is the largest supply of fresh water, nearly 2 percent of the world's total of fresh and salt water. As can be seen from the table below, the amount of water in our atmosphere is over ten times as large as the water in all the rivers taken together. The fresh water actually available for human use in lakes and rivers and the accessible ground water amounts to only about one third of one percent of the world's total water supply.

| | Surface area (square miles) | Volume (cubic miles) | Percentage of total |
|---|---|---|---|
| Salt Water | | | |
| The oceans | 139,500,000 | 317,000,000 | 97.2 |
| Inland seas and saline lakes | 270,000 | 25,000 | 0.008 |
| Fresh Water | | | |
| Freshwater lakes | 330,000 | 30,000 | 0.009 |
| All rivers (average level) | — | 300 | 0.0001 |
| Antarctic Icecap | 6,000,000 | 6,300,000 | 1.9 |
| Arctic Icecap and glaciers | 900,000 | 680,000 | 0.21 |
| Water in the atmosphere | 197,000,000 | 3,100 | 0.001 |
| Ground water within half a mile from surface | — | 1,000,000 | 0.31 |
| Deep-lying ground water | — | 1,000,000 | 0.31 |
| Total (rounded) | — | 326,000,000 | 100.00 |

1. All figures are estimated. *Source:* Department of the Interior, Geological Survey.

# Speed of Animals

Most of the following measurements are for maximum speeds over approximate quarter-mile distances. Exceptions—which are included to give a wide range of animals—are the lion and elephant, whose speeds were clocked in the act of charging; the whippet, which was timed over a 200-yard course; the cheetah over a 100-yard distance; man for a 15-yard segment of a 100-yard run; and the black mamba, six-lined race runner, spider, giant tortoise, three-toed sloth, and garden snail, which were measured over various small distances.

| Animal | Speed mph | Animal | Speed mph | Animal | Speed mph |
|---|---|---|---|---|---|
| Cheetah | 70 | Mongolian wild ass | 40 | Man | 27.89 |
| Pronghorn antelope | 61 | Greyhound | 39.35 | Elephant | 25 |
| Wildebeest | 50 | Whippet | 35.5 | Black mamba snake | 20 |
| Lion | 50 | Rabbit (domestic) | 35 | Six-lined race runner | 18 |
| Thomson's gazelle | 50 | Mule deer | 35 | Squirrel | 12 |
| Quarter horse | 47.5 | Jackal | 35 | Pig (domestic) | 11 |
| Elk | 45 | Reindeer | 32 | Chicken | 9 |
| Cape hunting dog | 45 | Giraffe | 32 | Spider (Tegenearia atrica) | 1.17 |
| Coyote | 43 | White-tailed deer | 30 | Giant Tortoise | 0.17 |
| Gray fox | 42 | Wart hog | 30 | Three-toed sloth | 0.15 |
| Hyena | 40 | Grizzly bear | 30 | Garden snail | 0.03 |
| Zebra | 40 | Cat (domestic) | 30 | | |

*Source: Natural History* Magazine, March 1974, copyright 1974. The American Museum of Natural History; and James Doherty, Curator of Mammals, N.Y. Zoological Society.

# Animal Names: Male, Female, and Young

| Animal | Male | Female | Young | Animal | Male | Female | Young | Animal | Male | Female | Young |
|---|---|---|---|---|---|---|---|---|---|---|---|
| Ass | Jack | Jenny | Foal | Duck | Drake | Duck | Duckling | Sheep | Ram | Ewe | Lamb |
| Bear | Boar | Sow | Cub | Elephant | Bull | Cow | Calf | Swan | Cob | Pen | Cygnet |
| Cat | Tom | Queen | Kitten | Fox | Dog | Vixen | Cub | Swine | Boar | Sow | Piglet |
| Cattle | Bull | Cow | Calf | Goose | Gander | Goose | Gosling | Tiger | Tiger | Tigress | Cub |
| Chicken | Rooster | Hen | Chick | Horse | Stallion | Mare | Foal | Whale | Bull | Cow | Calf |
| Deer | Buck | Doe | Fawn | Lion | Lion | Lioness | Cub | Wolf | Dog | Bitch | Pup |
| Dog | Dog | Bitch | Pup | Rabbit | Buck | Doe | Bunny | | | | |

*Source:* James Doherty, Curator of Mammals, N.Y. Zoological Society.

# Volunteers Aid Public Land Programs

Some 3,500 volunteers chalked up approximately 150 work-years in a year's service to Bureau of Land Management programs. In monetary terms their contribution represented $1.9 million and expanded the agency's work force by about 1.5 percent. While performing a public service, the volunteers furthered their educational goals and improved their skills through on-job training.

# Animal Group Terminology

Source: James Doherty, Curator of Mammals, N.Y. Zoological Society, and *Information Please* data.

**ants:** colony
**bears:** sleuth, sloth
**bees:** grist, hive, swarm
**birds:** flight, volery
**cattle:** drove
**cats:** clutter, clowder
**chicks:** brood, clutch
**clams:** bed
**cranes:** sedge, seige
**crows:** murder
**doves:** dule
**ducks:** brace, team
**elephants:** herd
**elks:** gang
**finches:** charm
**fish:** school, shoal, draught
**foxes:** leash, skulk
**geese:** flock, gaggle, skein
**gnats:** cloud, horde
**goats:** trip

**gorillas:** band
**hares:** down, husk
**hawks:** cast
**hens:** brood
**hogs:** drift
**horses:** pair, team
**hounds:** cry, mute, pack
**kangaroos:** troop
**kittens:** kindle, litter
**larks:** exaltation
**lions:** pride
**locusts:** plague
**magpies:** tidings
**mules:** span
**nightingales:** watch
**oxen:** yoke
**oysters:** bed
**parrots:** company
**partridges:** covey

**peacocks:** muster, ostentation
**pheasants:** nest, bouquet
**pigs:** litter
**ponies:** string
**quail:** bevy, covey
**rabbits:** nest
**seals:** pod
**sheep:** drove, flock
**sparrows:** host
**storks:** mustering
**swans:** bevy, wedge
**swine:** sounder
**toads:** knot
**turkeys:** rafter
**turtles:** bale
**vipers:** nest
**whales:** gam, pod
**wolves:** pack, route
**woodcocks:** fall

# Gestation, Incubation, and Longevity of Certain Animals

| Animal | Gestation or incubation, in days & (average) | Longevity, in years & (record exceptions) | Animal | Gestation or incubation, in days & (average) | Longevity, in years & (record exceptions) |
|---|---|---|---|---|---|
| Ass | 365 | 18–20 (63) | Horse | 329–345 (336) | 20–25 (50+) |
| Bear | 180–240 [1] | 15–30 (47) | Kangaroo | 32–39 [1] | 4–6 (23) |
| Cat | 52–69 (63) | 10–12 (26+) | Lion | 105–113 (108) | 10 (29) |
| Chicken | 22 | 7–8 (14) | Man | 253–303 | [2] |
| Cow | c. 280 | 9–12 (39) | Monkey | 139–270 [1] | 12–15[1](29) |
| Deer | 197–300 [1] | 10–15 (26) | Mouse | 19–31 [1] | 1–3 (4) |
| Dog | 53–71 (63) | 10–12 (24) | Parakeet (Budgerigar) | 17–20 (18) | 8 (12+) |
| Duck | 21–35[1](28) | 10 (15) | Pig | 101–130 (115) | 10 (22) |
| Elephant | 510–730 (624) [1] | 30–40 (71) | Pigeon | 11–19 | 10–12 (39) |
| Fox | 51–63 [1] | 8–10 (14) | Rabbit | 30–35 (31) | 6–8 (15) |
| Goat | 136–160 (151) | 12 (17) | Rat | 21 | 3 (5) |
| Groundhog | 31–32 | 4–9 | Sheep | 144–152 (151) [1] | 12 (16) |
| Guinea pig | 58–75 (68) | 3 (6) | Squirrel | 44 | 8–9 (15) |
| Hamster, golden | 15–17 | 2 (8) | Whale | 365–547 [1] | — |
| Hippopotamus | 220–255 (240) | 30 (49+) | Wolf | 60–63 | 10–12 (16) |

1. Depending on kind. 2. For life expectancy charts, *see* Index. Source: James Doherty, Curator of Mammals, N.Y. Zoological Society.

# Zoological Gardens

North America abounds in zoos from Canada to Mexico. The Metro Toronto Zoo, opened in 1974, is one of the largest in the world. Its six pavilions simulate the animals' natural habitats. So does the Calgary Zoo which also has a children's zoo. Mexico City's Chapultepec Park includes a large zoo featuring one of the few pairs of pandas outside of Red China, and a children's zoo.

The first zoological garden in the United States was established in Philadelphia in 1874. Since that time nearly every large city in the country has acquired a zoo. Among the largest are San Diego's on the West Coast; Chicago's Brookfield Zoo and those of St. Louis and Kansas City in the Middle West; New Orleans' Audubon Park and Zoological Garden in the South; and in the East the New York Zoological Society's park in the Bronx. The National Zoological Park in Washington, D.C., in a beautiful setting of hills, woods, and streams, was established in 1890 by an act of Congress. The major U.S. zoos now have created large natural-habitat areas for their collections.

In Europe, zoological gardens have long been popular public institutions. The modern concept of zoo keeping may be dated from 1752 with the founding of the Imperial Menagerie at the Schönbrunn Palace in Vienna. It was opened to the public in 1765 and is still in operation. In 1793 the zoological collection of the Jardin des Plantes was established in Paris in the Bois de Boulogne. At Antwerp the Royal Zoological Society founded a large menagerie in 1843. Now its aviary is noted for the principle of lighted and darkened spaces for confining the birds. Germany's famous Tiergarten zoo, in West Berlin, was founded in 1841 and officially opened in 1844. East Berlin has founded its own zoo.

In the British Isles, the Zoological Society of London established its collection in Regent's Park in 1828. It was also responsible for the establishment of the prototype of the open-range zoo, Whipsnade Park, in 1932. Edinburgh's zoo is famous for its collection of penguins, the largest colony in captivity. Dublin Zoo, in Phoenix Park, holds several records for lion breeding.

Other European zoos include the Hellabrunn

Zoo in Munich which specializes in species threatened with extinction and the zoo at Rome that has
part of its collection confined in barless pits.

# Zoos and Aquariums

*Source:* The facilities listed are members of, and accredited by, the American Association of Zoological Parks and Aquariums to ensure that they are maintaining professional standards.

**Abilene Zoological Park,** Texas
**Alaska Zoo,** Anchorage
**Arizona-Sonora Desert Museum,** Tucson
**Audubon Park and Zoological Garden,** New Orleans
**John Ball Zoological Gardens,** Grand Rapids, Mich.
**Baltimore Zoo,** Md.
**Belle Isle Zoo and Aquarium,** Detroit
**Binder Park Zoo,** Battle Creek, Mich.
**Birmingham Zoo,** Ala.
**Brandywine Zoo,** Wilmington, Del.
**Brookgreen Gardens,** Murrells Inlet, S.C.
**Buffalo Zoological Gardens,** N.Y.
**Busch Gardens,** Tampa, Fla.
**Caldwell Zoo,** Texas
**Calgary Zoo,** Alberta, Canada
**Central Florida Zoological Park,** Lake Monroe, Fla.
**Cheyenne Mountain Zoological Park,** Colorado Springs
**Chicago Zoological Park,** Brookfield, Ill.
**Cincinnati Zoo,** Ohio
**Cleveland Metroparks Zoo,** Ohio
**Columbus Zoological Gardens,** Ohio
**Dallas Aquarium,** Texas
**Dallas Zoo,** Texas
**Denver Zoological Gardens,** Colo.
**Detroit Zoological Park,** Mich.
**Discovery Island,** Buena Vista, Fla.
**Duluth Zoological Gardens,** Minn.
**Henry Doorly Zoo,** Omaha, Neb.
**El Paso Zoological Park,** Texas
**Emporia Zoo,** Kan.
**Erie Zoo,** Pa.
**Florida Cypress Gardens, Inc.,** Fla.
**Fort Wayne Children's Zoo,** Ind.
**Fort Worth Zoological Park,** Texas
**Fresno Zoo,** Calif.
**Glen Oak Zoo,** Ill.
**Greater Baton Rouge Zoo,** La.
**Hogle Zoological Gardens,** Salt Lake City, Utah
**Houston Zoological Gardens,** Texas
**Indianapolis Zoo,** Ind.
**Kansas City Zoological Gardens,** Mo.
**Knoxville Zoological Park,** Tenn.
**Little Rock Zoological Gardens,** Ark.
**Lincoln Park Zoological Gardens,** Chicago
**Living Desert Reserve,** Palm Desert, Calif.
**Los Angeles Zoo,** Calif.
**Louisville Zoological Garden,** Ky.
**Marine World Africa USA,** Redwood City, Calif.
**Marineland Amusements, Inc.,** Rancho Palos Verdes, Calif.
**Memphis Zoological Gardens and Aquarium,** Tenn.
**Mesker Park Zoo,** Evansville, Ind.
**Metropolitan Toronto Zoo,** Canada
**Miami Metrozoo,** Fla.

**Miller Park Zoo,** Bloomington, Ill.
**Milwaukee County Zoological Gardens,** Wis.
**Minnesota Zoological Garden,** Apple Valley, Minn.
**Mystic Marinelife Aquarium,** Mystic, Conn.
**National Aquarium in Baltimore,** Md.
**National Zoological Park,** Washington, D.C.
**New England Aquarium,** Boston
**New York Aquarium,** Brooklyn, N.Y.
**New York Zoological Park,** Bronx, N.Y.
**North Carolina Zoological Park,** Asheboro, N.C.
**Northwest Trek Wildlife Park,** Eatonville, Wash.
**Oglebay's Good Children's Zoo,** Wheeling, W.Va.
**Oklahoma City Zoo,** Okla.
**Philadelphia Zoological Garden,** Pa.
**Phoenix Zoo,** Ariz.
**Pittsburgh Aviary,** Pa.
**Point Defiance Zoo and Aquarium,** Tacoma, Wash.
**Gladys Porter Zoo,** Brownsville, Texas
**Potter Park Zoo,** Lansing, Mich.
**Gene Reid Zoological Park,** Tucson, Ariz.
**Lee Richardson Zoo,** Garden City, Kan.
**Rio Grande Zoological Park,** Albuquerque, N.M.
**Riverbanks Zoological Park,** Columbia, S.C.
**Sacramento Zoo,** Calif.
**St. Louis Zoological Park,** Mo.
**Salisbury Zoological Park,** Md.
**San Antonio Zoological Gardens and Aquarium,** Texas
**San Diego Wild Animal Park,** Calif.
**San Diego Zoo,** Calif.
**San Francisco Zoological Gardens,** Calif.
**Santa Ana Zoo,** Calif.
**Santa Barbara Zoological Gardens,** Calif.
**Sea Life Park,** Waimanalo, Hawaii
**Sea World, Inc.,** San Diego, Calif.
**Sea World of Florida,** Orlando
**Sea World of Ohio,** Aurora
**The Seattle Aquarium,** Wash.
**Sedgwick County Zoo,** Wichita, Kan.
**Seneca Park Zoo,** Rochester, N.Y.
**John G. Shedd Aquarium,** Chicago
**Toledo Zoological Gardens,** Ohio
**Topeka Zoological Park,** Kan.
**Ellen Trout Zoo,** Lufkin, Texas
**Tulsa Zoological Park,** Okla.
**Vancouver Public Aquarium,** British Columbia
**Henry Vilas Park Zoo,** Madison, Wis.
**Waikiki Aquarium,** Hawaii
**Washington Park Zoo,** Portland, Ore.
**Wild Animal Park,** Kings Island, Ohio
**Wildlife Safari, Inc.** Winston, Ore.
**Woodland Park Zoological Gardens,** Seattle
**Zooamerica at Hersheypark,** Hershey, Pa.

# The National Park System

*Source:* Department of the Interior, National Park Service.

The National Park System of the United States is administered by the National Park Service, a bureau of the Department of the Interior. Started with the establishment of Yellowstone National Park in 1872, the system includes not only the most extraordinary and spectacular scenic exhibits in the United States but also a large number of sites distinguished either for their historic or prehistoric importance or scientific interest, or for their superior recreational assets. The number and extent of the various types of areas that make up the system follow.

| Type of area | Number | Total acreage[1] | Type of area | Number | Total acreage[1] |
|---|---|---|---|---|---|
| International Historic Site | 1 | 35 | National Battlefield Site | 1 | 1 |
| National Parks | 48 | 47,157,330 | National Historic Parks | 26 | 150,856 |
| National Monuments | 77 | 150,856 | National Recreation Areas | 17 | 3,687,317 |
| National Preserves | 12 | 21,930,133 | National Parkways | 4 | 163,230 |
| National Lakeshores | 4 | 224,786 | National Scenic Rivers & Riverways[4] | 12 | 553,868 |
| National Seashores | 10 | 597,025 | Other Parks[2] | 11 | 32,129 |
| National Historic Sites | 62 | 17,931 | National Capital Parks[3] | 1 | 6,469 |
| National Memorials | 23 | 7,949 | White House | 1 | 18 |
| National Military Parks | 10 | 34,014 | National Mall | 1 | 146 |
| National Battlefield Parks | 3 | 8,169 | Affiliated Areas* | 30 | 51,300 |
| National Battlefields | 10 | 12,722 | **Total** | **337** | **79,455,894** |

1. Acreage as of December 31, 1985. 2. Parks without national designation. 3. Comprised of 346 units within the District of Columbia, Maryland, and Virginia. 4. National Park System Units and components of the Wild & Scenic Rivers System. *Not included in 337 total.

## National Parks

| Name, location, and year authorized | Acreage | Outstanding characteristics |
|---|---|---|
| Acadia (Maine), 1919 | 39,707.00 | Rugged seashore on Mt. Desert Island and adjacent mainland |
| Arches (Utah), 1971 | 73,378.98 | Unusual stone arches, windows, pedestals caused by erosion |
| Badlands (S.D.), 1978 | 243,302.33 | Arid land of fossils, prairie, bison, deer, bighorn, antelope |
| Big Bend (Tex.), 1935 | 741,118.40 | Mountains and desert bordering the Rio Grande |
| Biscayne (Fla.), 1980 | 173,274.00 | Aquatic, coral reef park south of Miami was a national monument, 1968–80 |
| Bryce Canyon (Utah), 1924 | 35,835.08 | Area of grotesque eroded rocks brilliantly colored |
| Canyonlands (Utah), 1964 | 337,570.43 | Colorful wilderness with impressive red-rock canyons, spires, arches |
| Capitol Reef (Utah), 1971 | 241,904.26 | Highly colored sedimentary rock formations in high, narrow gorges |
| Carlsbad Caverns (N.M.), 1930 | 46,755.33 | The world's largest known caves |
| Channel Islands (Calif.) 1980 | 249,353.77 | Area is rich in marine mammals, sea birds, endangered species and archeology |
| Crater Lake (Ore.), 1902 | 183,227.00 | Deep blue lake in heart of inactive volcano |
| Denali (Alaska), 1917 | 4,700,000.00 | Mt. McKinley National Park was renamed and enlarged by Act of Dec. 2, 1980. Contains Mt. McKinley, N. America's highest mountain (20,320 ft) |
| Everglades (Fla.), 1934 | 1,398,937.00 | Subtropical area with abundant bird and animal life |
| Gates of the Arctic (Alaska), 1980 | 7,500,000.00 | Diverse north central wilderness contains part of Brooks Range |
| Glacier (Mont.), 1910 | 1,013,594.67 | Rocky Mountain scenery with many glaciers and lakes |
| Glacier Bay (Alaska), 1980 | 3,225,198.00 | Park was a national monument (1925–1980) popular for wildlife, whale-watching, glacier-calving, and scenery |
| Grand Canyon (Ariz.), 1919 | 1,218,375.24 | Mile-deep gorge, 4 to 18 miles wide, 217 miles long |
| Grand Teton (Wyo.), 1929 | 310,528.00 | Picturesque range of high mountain peaks |
| Great Smoky Mts. (N.C.-Tenn), 1926 | 520,269.44 | Highest mountain range east of Black Hills; luxuriant plant life |
| Guadalupe Mountains (Tex.), 1966 | 76,293.06 | Contains highest point in Texas: Guadalupe Peak (8,751 ft) |
| Haleakala (Hawaii), 1960 | 28,655.25 | World-famous 10,023-ft. Haleakala volcano (dormant) |
| Hawaii Volcanoes (Hawaii), 1916 | 229,177.03 | Spectacular volcanic area; luxuriant vegetation at lower levels |
| Hot Springs (Ark.), 1921 | 5,823.54 | 47 mineral hot springs said to have therapeutic value |
| Isle Royale (Mich.), 1931 | 571,790.11 | Largest wilderness island in Lake Superior; moose, wolves, lakes |
| Katmai (Alaska), 1980 | 3,716,000.00 | Expansion may assure brown bear's preservation. Park was national monument 1918–80; is known for fishing, 1912 eruption, bears |
| Kenai Fjords (Alaska), 1980 | 670,000.00 | Mountain goats, marine mammals, birdlife are features at this seacoast park near Seward |
| Kings Canyon (Calif.), 1940 | 461,636.00 | Huge canyons; high mountains; giant sequoias |
| Kobuk Valley (Alaska), 1980 | 1,750,000.00 | Native culture and anthropology center around the broad Kobuk River in northwest Alaska |
| Lake Clark (Alaska), 1980 | 2,874,000.00 | Park provides scenic and wilderness recreation across Cook Inlet from Anchorage |
| Lassen Volcanic (Calif.), 1916 | 106,372.36 | Exhibits of impressive volcanic phenomena |
| Mammoth Cave (Ky.), 1926 | 52,369.60 | Vast limestone labyrinth with underground river |
| Mesa Verde (Colo.), 1906 | 52,085.14 | Best-preserved prehistoric cliff dwellings in United States |
| Mount Rainier (Wash.), 1899 | 235,404.00 | Single-peak glacial system; dense forests, flowered meadows |

| Name, location, and year authorized | Acreage | Outstanding characteristics |
|---|---|---|
| North Cascades (Wash.), 1968 | 504,780.94 | Roadless Alpine landscape; jagged peaks; mountain lakes; glaciers |
| Olympic (Wash.), 1938 | 914,576.00 | Finest Pacific Northwest rain forest; scenic mountain park |
| Petrified Forest (Ariz.), 1962 | 93,492.57 | Extensive natural exhibit of petrified wood |
| Redwood (Calif.), 1968 | 110,123.00 | Coastal redwood forests; contains world's tallest known tree (369.2 ft) |
| Rocky Mountain (Colo.), 1915 | 265,192.86 | Section of the Rocky Mountains; 107 named peaks over 10,000 ft |
| Sequoia (Calif.), 1890 | 402,487.83 | Giant sequoias; magnificent High Sierra scenery, including Mt. Whitney |
| Shenandoah (Va.), 1926 | 195,072.00 | Tree-covered mountains; scenic Skyline Drive |
| Theodore Roosevelt (N.D.), 1978 | 70,416.39 | Scenic valley of Little Missouri River; T.R. Ranch; Wildlife |
| Virgin Islands (U.S. V.I.), 1956 | 14,695.85 | Beaches; lush hills; prehistoric Carib Indian relics |
| Voyageurs (Minn.), 1971 | 217,892.01 | Wildlife, canoeing, fishing, and hiking |
| Wind Cave (S.D.), 1903 | 28,292.08 | Limestone caverns in Black Hills; buffalo herd |
| Wrangell-St. Elias (Alaska), 1980 | 8,945,000.00 | Largest Park System area has abundant wildlife, second highest peak in U.S. (Mt. St. Elias); adjoins Canadian park |
| Yellowstone (Wyo.-Mont.-Idaho), 1872 | 2,219,822.70 | World's greatest geyser area; abundant falls, wildlife, and canyons |
| Yosemite (Calif.), 1890 | 761,110.00 | Mountains; inspiring gorges and waterfalls; giant sequoias |
| Zion (Utah), 1919 | 146,551.10 | Multicolored gorge in heart of southern Utah desert |

## NATIONAL HISTORICAL PARKS

| Name and location | Total acreage |
|---|---|
| Appomattox Court House (Va.) | 1,325.08 |
| Boston (Mass.) | 41.03 |
| Chaco Culture (N.M.) | 33,977.82 |
| Chesapeake and Ohio Canal (Md.-W.Va.-D.C.) | 20,781.00 |
| Colonial (Va.) | 9,315.39 |
| Cumberland Gap (Ky.-Tenn.-Va.) | 20,274.00 |
| George Rogers Clark (Ind.) | 24.30 |
| Harpers Ferry (W.Va.-Md.) | 2,238.37 |
| Independence (Pa.) | 44.85 |
| Jean Lafitte (La.) | 20,000.00 |
| Kalaupapa (Hawaii) | 10,902.10 |
| Klondike Goldrush (Alaska) | 13,272.38 |
| Kaioko-Honokohau (Hawaii) | 1,160.91 |
| Lowell (Mass.) | 137.08 |
| Lyndon B. Johnson (Tex.) | 1,477.78 |
| Minute Man (Mass.) | 748.00 |
| Morristown (N.J.) | 1,677.65 |
| Nez Perce (Idaho) | 2,108.89 |
| Puuhonua o Honaunau (Hawaii) | 181.80 |
| San Antonio Missions (Tex.) | 477.41 |
| San Juan Island (Wash.) | 1,751.99 |
| Saratoga (N.Y.) | 3,415.00 |
| Sitka (Alaska) | 106.83 |
| Valley Forge (Pa.) | 3,464.70 |
| War in the Pacific (Guam) | 1,958.00 |
| Women's Rights (N.Y.) | 5.00 |

## NATIONAL MONUMENTS

| Name and location | Total acreage |
|---|---|
| Agate Fossil Beds (Neb.) | 3,055.22 |
| Alibates Flint Quarries (Tex.) | 1,370.97 |
| Aniakchak (Alaska) | 139,500.00 |
| Aztec Ruins (N.M.) | 27.14 |
| Bandelier (N.M.) | 36,916.89 |
| Black Canyon (Colo.) | 20,763.00 |
| Booker T. Washington (Va.) | 223.92 |
| Buck Island Reef (U.S. V.I.) | 880.00 |
| Cabrillo (Calif.) | 143.94 |
| Canyon de Chelly (Ariz.) | 83,840.00 |
| Cape Krusenstern (Alaska) | 660,000.00 |
| Capulin Mountain (N.M.) | 775.38 |
| Casa Grande (Ariz.) | 472.50 |
| Castillo de San Marcos (Fla.) | 20.48 |
| Castle Clinton (N.Y.) | 1.00 |
| Cedar Breaks (Utah) | 6,154.60 |
| Chiricahua (Ariz.) | 11,134.80 |
| Colorado (Colo.) | 20,453.95 |

| Name and location | Total acreage |
|---|---|
| Congaree Swamp (S.C.) | 15,138.25 |
| Craters of the Moon (Idaho) | 53,545.05 |
| Custer Battlefield (Mont.) | 765.34 |
| Death Valley (Calif.-Nev.) | 2,067,627.68 |
| Devils Postpile (Calif.) | 798.46 |
| Devils Tower (Wyo.) | 1,346.91 |
| Dinosaur (Utah-Colo.) | 211,272.00 |
| Effigy Mounds (Iowa) | 1,474.63 |
| El Morro (N.M.) | 1,278.72 |
| Florissant Fossil Beds (Colo.) | 5,998.09 |
| Fort Frederica (Ga.) | 213.72 |
| Fort Jefferson (Fla.) | 64,700.00 |
| Fort Matanzas (Fla.) | 298.51 |
| Fort McHenry (Md.) | 43.26 |
| Fort Pulaski (Ga.) | 5,623.10 |
| Fort Stanwix (N.Y.) | 15.52 |
| Fort Sumter (S.C.) | 66.77 |
| Fort Union (N.M.) | 720.60 |
| Fossil Butte (Wyo.) | 8,198.00 |
| George Washington Birthplace (Va.) | 538.23 |
| George Washington Carver (Mo.) | 210.00 |
| Gila Cliff Dwellings (N.M.) | 533.13 |
| Grand Portage (Minn.) | 709.97 |
| Great Sand Dunes (Colo.) | 38,662.18 |
| Hohokam Pima (Ariz.) | 1,690.00 |
| Homestead (Neb.) | 194.57 |
| Hovenweep (Utah-Colo.) | 785.43 |
| Jewel Cave (S.D.) | 1,273.51 |
| John Day Fossil Beds (Ore.) | 14,011.90 |
| Joshua Tree (Calif.) | 559,959.50 |
| Lava Beds (Calif.) | 46,559.87 |
| Lehman Caves (Nev.) | 640.00 |
| Montezuma Castle (Ariz.) | 857.69 |
| Mound City Group (Ohio) | 217.50 |
| Muir Woods (Calif.) | 553.55 |
| Natural Bridges (Utah) | 7,791.00 |
| Navajo (Ariz.) | 360.00 |
| Ocmulgee (Ga.) | 683.48 |
| Oregon Caves (Ore.) | 487.98 |
| Organ Pipe Cactus (Ariz.) | 330,688.86 |
| Pecos (N.M.) | 364.80 |
| Pinnacles (Calif.) | 16,221.77 |
| Pipe Spring (Ariz.) | 40.00 |
| Pipestone (Minn.) | 281.78 |
| Rainbow Bridge (Utah) | 160.00 |
| Russell Cave (Ala.) | 310.45 |
| Saguaro (Ariz.) | 83,573.88 |
| St. Croix Island (Me.) | 35.39 |

| Name and location | Total acreage |
|---|---|
| Salinas (N.M.) | 1,080.00 |
| Scotts Bluff (Neb.) | 2,997.08 |
| Statue of Liberty (N.Y.-N.J.) | 58.38 |
| Sunset Crater (Ariz.) | 3,040.00 |
| Timpanogos Cave (Utah) | 250.00 |
| Tonto (Ariz.) | 1,120.00 |
| Tumacacori (Ariz.) | 16.52 |
| Tuzigoot (Ariz.) | 809.30 |
| Walnut Canyon (Ariz.) | 2,249.46 |
| White Sands (N.M.) | 144,458.24 |
| Wupatki (Ariz.) | 35,253.24 |
| Yucca House (Colo.) | 10.00 |

## NATIONAL PRESERVES

| | |
|---|---|
| Aniakchak (Alaska) | 475,500.00 |
| Bering Land Bridge (Alaska) | 2,770,000.00 |
| Big Cypress (Fla.) | 570,000.00 |
| Big Thicket (Tex.) | 85,850.00 |
| Denali (Alaska) | 1,330,000.00 |
| Gates of the Arctic (Alaska) | 940,000.00 |
| Glacier Bay (Alaska) | 55,000.00 |
| Katmai (Alaska) | 374,000.00 |
| Lake Clark (Alaska) | 1,171,000.00 |
| Noatak (Alaska) | 6,560,000.00 |
| Wrangell-St. Elias (Alaska) | 4,255,000.00 |
| Yukon-Charley (Alaska) | 2,520,000.00 |

## NATIONAL MILITARY PARKS

| | |
|---|---|
| Chickamauga and Chattanooga (Ga.-Tenn.) | 8,102.54 |
| Fort Donelson (Tenn.) | 536.66 |
| Fredericksburg and Spotsylvania (Va.) | 5,908.64 |
| Gettysburg (Pa.) | 3,865.00 |
| Guilford Courthouse (N.C.) | 220.25 |
| Horseshoe Bend (Ala.) | 2,040.00 |
| Kings Mountain (S.C.) | 3,945.29 |
| Pea Ridge (Ark.) | 4,300.35 |
| Shiloh (Tenn.) | 3,837.50 |
| Vicksburg (Miss.) | 1,620.00 |

## NATIONAL BATTLEFIELDS

| | |
|---|---|
| Antietam (Md.) | 3,246.44 |
| Big Hole (Mont.) | 655.61 |
| Cowpens (S.C.) | 841.56 |
| Fort Necessity (Pa.) | 902.80 |
| Monocacy (Md.) | 1,659.04 |
| Moores Creek (N.C.) | 86.52 |
| Petersburg (Va.) | 2,735.00 |
| Stones River (Tenn.) | 330.86 |
| Tupelo (Miss.) | 1.00 |
| Wilson's Creek (Mo.) | 1,749.91 |

## NATIONAL BATTLEFIELD PARKS

| | |
|---|---|
| Kennesaw Mountain (Ga.) | 2,884.38 |
| Manassas (Va.) | 4,513.29 |
| Richmond (Va.) | 771.41 |

## NATIONAL BATTLEFIELD SITE

| | |
|---|---|
| Brices Crossroads (Miss.) | 1.00 |

## NATIONAL HISTORIC SITES

| | |
|---|---|
| Abraham Lincoln Birthplace (Ky.) | 116.50 |
| Adams (Mass.) | 10.00 |
| Allegheny Portage Railroad (Pa.) | 1,134.91 |
| Andersonville (Ga.) | 475.72 |
| Andrew Johnson (Tenn.) | 16.68 |
| Bent's Old Fort (Colo.) | 800.00 |
| Carl Sandburg Home (N.C.) | 263.52 |
| Christiansted (V.I.) | 27.15 |
| Clara Barton (Md.) | 8.59 |
| Edgar Allan Poe (Pa.) | 1.00 |
| Edison (N.J.) | 21.25 |
| Eisenhower (Pa.) | 690.46 |
| Eleanor Roosevelt (N.Y.) | 180.50 |

| Name and location | Total acreage |
|---|---|
| Eugene O'Neill (Calif.) | 13.00 |
| Ford's Theatre (Lincoln Museum) (D.C.) | 0.29 |
| Fort Bowie (Ariz.) | 1,000.00 |
| Fort Davis (Tex.) | 460.00 |
| Fort Laramie (Wyo.) | 832.45 |
| Fort Larned (Kan.) | 718.39 |
| Fort Point (Calif.) | 29.00 |
| Fort Raleigh (N.C.) | 157.27 |
| Fort Scott (Kan.) | 16.69 |
| Fort Smith (Ark.-Okla.) | 743.00 |
| Fort Union Trading Post (N.D.-Mont.) | 434.00 |
| Fort Vancouver (Wash.) | 208.89 |
| Frederick Law Olmsted (Mass.) | 2.00 |
| Friendship Hill (Pa.) | 674.56 |
| Golden Spike (Utah) | 2,735.28 |
| Grant-Kohrs Ranch (Mont.) | 1,498.82 |
| Hampton (Md.) | 59.44 |
| Harry S. Truman (Mo.) | 0.78 |
| Herbert Hoover (Iowa) | 186.80 |
| Home of F. D. Roosevelt (N.Y.) | 290.00 |
| Hopewell Village (Pa.) | 848.06 |
| Hubbell Trading Post (Ariz.) | 160.09 |
| James A. Garfield (Ohio) | 7.82 |
| Jefferson National Expansion Memorial (Mo.) | 90.96 |
| John F. Kennedy (Mass.) | 0.09 |
| John Muir (Calif.) | 8.90 |
| Knife River Indian Villages (N.D.) | 1,293.35 |
| Lincoln Home (Ill.) | 12.28 |
| Longfellow (Mass.) | 1.98 |
| Maggie L. Walker (Va.) | 1.29 |
| Martin Luther King, Jr. (Ga.) | 23.16 |
| Martin Van Buren (N.Y.) | 39.58 |
| Ninety Six (S.C.) | 989.14 |
| Palo Alto Battlefield (Tex.) | 50.00 |
| Puukohola Heiau (Hawaii) | 78.00 |
| Sagamore Hill (N.Y.) | 78.00 |
| Saint-Gaudens (N.H.) | 148.33 |
| Salem Maritime (Mass.) | 9.10 |
| San Juan (P.R.) | 75.00 |
| Saugus Iron Works (Mass.) | 8.51 |
| Sewall-Belmont House (D.C.) | 0.35 |
| Springfield Armory (Mass.) | 54.93 |
| Theodore Roosevelt Birthplace (N.Y.) | 0.11 |
| Theodore Roosevelt Inaugural (N.Y.) | 1.03 |
| Thomas Stone (Md.) | 328.25 |
| Tuskegee Institute (Ala.) | 74.39 |
| Vanderbilt Mansion (N.Y.) | 211.65 |
| Whitman Mission (Wash.) | 98.15 |
| William Howard Taft (Ohio) | 3.07 |

## NATIONAL MEMORIALS

| | |
|---|---|
| Arkansas Post (Ark.) | 389.18 |
| Arlington House, the Robert E. Lee Memorial (Va.) | 27.91 |
| Chamizal (Tex.) | 54.90 |
| Coronado (Ariz.) | 4,750.00 |
| Desoto (Fla.) | 26.84 |
| Federal Hall (N.Y.) | 0.45 |
| Fort Caroline (Fla.) | 138.39 |
| Fort Clatsop (Ore.) | 125.20 |
| General Grant (N.Y.) | 0.76 |
| Hamilton Grange (N.Y.) | 0.71 |
| John F. Kennedy Center for Performing Arts (D.C.) | 17.50 |
| Johnstown Flood (Pa.) | 163.47 |
| Lincoln Boyhood (Ind.) | 192.00 |
| Lincoln Memorial (D.C.) | 163.63 |
| Lyndon Baines Johnson Memorial Grove on the Potomac (D.C.) | 17.00 |
| Mount Rushmore (S.D.) | 1,278.45 |
| Roger Williams (R.I.) | 4.56 |
| Thaddeus Kosciuszko (Pa.) | 0.02 |
| Theodore Roosevelt Island (D.C.) | 88.50 |

| Name and location | Total acreage |
|---|---|
| Thomas Jefferson Memorial (D.C.) | 18.36 |
| USS Arizona Memorial (Hawaii) | 0.00 |
| Washington Monument (D.C.) | 106.01 |
| Wright Brothers (N.C.) | 431.40 |

## NATIONAL CEMETERIES[1]

| | |
|---|---|
| Antietam (Md.) | 11.36 |
| Battleground (D.C.) | 1.03 |
| Fort Donelson (Tenn.) | 15.34 |
| Fredericksburg (Va.) | 12.00 |
| Gettysburg (Pa.) | 20.58 |
| Poplar Grove (Va.) | 8.72 |
| Shiloh (Tenn.) | 10.05 |
| Stones River (Tenn.) | 20.09 |
| Vicksburg (Miss.) | 116.28 |
| Yorktown (Va.) | 2.91 |

## NATIONAL SEASHORES

| | |
|---|---|
| Assateague Island (Md.-Va.) | 39,630.93 |
| Canaveral (Fla.) | 57,627.07 |
| Cape Cod (Mass.) | 43,526.00 |
| Cape Hatteras (N.C.) | 30,319.43 |
| Cape Lookout (N.C.) | 28,414.74 |
| Cumberland Island (Ga.) | 36,410.28 |
| Fire Island (N.Y.) | 19,578.55 |
| Gulf Islands (Fla.-Miss.) | 139,775.46 |
| Padre Island (Tex.) | 130,696.83 |
| Point Reyes (Calif.) | 71,046.07 |

## NATIONAL PARKWAYS

| | |
|---|---|
| Blue Ridge (Va.-N.C.) | 82,117.37 |
| George Washington Memorial (Va.-Md.) | 7,141.63 |
| John D. Rockefeller, Jr.. Memorial (Wyo.) | 23,777.22 |
| Natchez Trace (Miss.-Tenn.-Ala.) | 50,189.33 |

## NATIONAL LAKESHORES

| | |
|---|---|
| Apostle Islands (Wis.) | 67,884.84 |
| Indiana Dunes (Ind.) | 12,870.00 |
| Pictured Rocks (Mich) | 72,898.86 |
| Sleeping Bear Dunes (Mich.) | 71,020.06 |

## NATIONAL SCENIC RIVERS AND RIVERWAYS

| | |
|---|---|
| Alagnak Wild River (Alaska) | 24,038.00 |
| Big South Fork National River & Recreation Area (Ky.-Tenn.) | 122,960.00 |
| Buffalo (Ark.) | 94,221.08 |
| Delaware (N.Y.-N.J.-Pa.) | 1,973.33 |
| Lower St. Croix (Minn.-Wis.) | 9,365.00 |
| Missouri National Recreational River (Neb.) | 59.00 |
| New River Gorge (W. Va.) | 62,024.00 |
| Obed Wild & Scenic River (Tenn.) | 5,101.00 |
| Ozark (Mo.) | 80,698.00 |
| Rio Grande Wild & Scenic (Tex.) | 9,600.00 |
| St. Croix (Minn.-Wis.) | 68,793.28 |
| Upper Delaware (N.Y., N.J.-Pa.) | 75,000.00 |

## NATIONAL CAPITAL PARKS

| | |
|---|---|
| National Capital Parks (D.C.-Va.-Md.) | 6,465.85 |

## WHITE HOUSE

| | |
|---|---|
| White House (D.C.) | 18.07 |

## OTHER PARKS

| | |
|---|---|
| Catoctin Mountain (Md.) | 5,770.22 |
| Constitution Gardens, (D.C.) | 40.00 |
| Fort Washington Park (Md.) | 341.00 |
| Frederick Douglass Home (D.C.) | 8.08 |
| Greenbelt Park (Md.) | 1,175.99 |
| Perry's Victory and International Peace Memorial (Ohio) | 25.38 |

1. The National Cemeteries are not independent areas of the National Park System; each is part of a military park, battlefield, etc., except Battleground. Their acreage is kept separately. Arlington National Cemetery is under the Department of the Army. *See* Index.

| Name and location | Total acreage |
|---|---|
| Piscataway (Md.) | 4,251.00 |
| Prince William Forest (Va.) | 18,571.55 |
| Rock Creek Park (D.C.) | 1,754.37 |
| Vietnam Veterans Memorial (D.C.) | 2.00 |
| Wolf Trap Farm Park for the Performing Arts (Va.) | 130.28 |

## NATIONAL RECREATION AREAS

| | |
|---|---|
| Amistad (Tex.) | 57,272.00 |
| Bighorn Canyon (Wyo.-Mont.) | 120,277.86 |
| Chattahoochee River (Ga.) | 8,699.00 |
| Chickasaw (Okla.) | 9,522.00 |
| Coulee Dam (Wash.) | 100,059.00 |
| Curecanti (Colo.) | 42,114.47 |
| Cuyahoga Valley (Ohio) | 32,460.19 |
| Delaware Water Gap (Pa.-N.J.) | 66,696.79 |
| Gateway (N.Y.-N.J.) | 26,310.93 |
| Glen Canyon (Ariz.-Utah) | 1,236,880.00 |
| Golden Gate (Calif.) | 72,815.04 |
| Lake Chelan (Wash.) | 61,890.07 |
| Lake Mead (Ariz.-Nev.) | 1,496,600.52 |
| Lake Meredith (Tex.) | 44,977.63 |
| Ross Lake (Wash.) | 117,574.09 |
| Santa Monica Mountains (Calif.) | 150,000.00 |
| Whiskeytown-Shasta-Trinity (Calif.) | 42,503.43 |

## NATIONAL SCENIC TRAIL

| | |
|---|---|
| Appalachian (Maine, N.H., Vt., Mass., Conn., N.Y., N.J., Pa., Md., W.Va., Va., N.C., Tenn., Ga.) | 115,969.09 |
| Natchez Trace (Ga.-Ala.-Tenn.) | 694.00 |
| Potomac Heritage (D.C.-Md.-Va.-Pa.) | 704.00 |

## NATIONAL MALL

| | |
|---|---|
| National Mall (D.C.) | 146.35 |

## AFFILIATED AREAS

(National Historic Sites unless otherwise noted.)

| | |
|---|---|
| Afro-American History and Culture (Ohio) | 0.00 |
| American Memorial Park (N. Mariana Is.) | 0.00 |
| Benjamin Franklin (Pa.)[1] | 0.00 |
| Boston African American (Mass.) | 0.00 |
| Cherokee Strip Living Museum (Kan.) | 6.00 |
| Chicago Portage (Ill.) | 91.20 |
| Chimney Rock (Neb.) | 83.36 |
| David Berger (Ohio)[1] | 0.00 |
| Ebey's Landing (Wash.) | 8,000.00 |
| Father Marquette (Mich.) | 52.00 |
| Green Springs Historic District (Va.) | 5,491.00 |
| Gloria Dei Church (Pa.) | 3.71 |
| Historic Camden (S.C.) | 0.00 |
| Ice Age Scenic Trail (Wisc.) | 0.00 |
| Ice Age (Wis.)[2] | 32,500.00 |
| Iditarod National Historic Trail (Alaska) | 0.00 |
| International Peace Garden (N.D.) | 2,330.30 |
| Jamestown (Va.) | 20.63 |
| Lewis & Clark Natl. Historic Trail (Ill., Mo., Kan., Neb., Iowa, Idaho, S.D., N.D., Mont., Ore., Wash.) | 0.00 |
| M. McLeod Bethune Council House (D.C.) | 0.00 |
| McLoughlin House (Ore.) | 0.63 |
| Mormon Pioneer Natl. Historic Trail (Ill., Iowa, Neb., Wyo., Utah) | 0.00 |
| North Country Nat'l Scenic Trail (N.Y., Pa., Ohio, Mich., Wis., Minn., N.D.) | 0.00 |
| Oregon Natl. Historic Trail (Mo., Kan., Neb., Wyo., Idaho, Ore., Wash.) | 0.00 |
| Overmountain Victory Trail (Mo. to Ore.) | 0.00 |
| Pennsylvania Avenue (D.C.) | 0.00 |
| Pinelands Natl. Reserve (N.J.) | 0.00 |
| Roosevelt-Campobello International Park (Canada) | 2,721.50 |
| St. Paul's Church (N.Y.) | 6.12 |
| Touro Synagogue (R.I.) | 0.23 |

1. National Memorial. 2. National Scientific Reserve.

# GENERAL INFORMATION

## A

**Abacus,** a device for making arithmetical calculations, consisting of parallel bars on which are strung movable colored beads. The earliest form of this instrument was used in Mesopotamia about 3000 B.C., and its use spread westward throughout the Graeco-Roman world and eastward to China. An efficient form of the abacus is still used today in parts of Asia.

**Aberration,** in astronomy, is the apparent displacement of a star due to the speed of the observer with the earth (*see* **Parallax**). In optics (i) spherical aberration is when there is blurring of the image and fringes of color at its edges, due to failure of lens to bring light to a single focus; (ii) chromatic aberration is due to the refractive index of glass being different for light of different colors. For instance, violet light is bent more than red.

**Abiogenesis,** or spontaneous generation; the origination of living from non-living matter. The term is applied to such discredited ideas as that frogs could be generated spontaneously by the action of sunlight on mud, or maggots arise spontaneously in dead meat without any eggs from which the maggots hatch being present. Spallanzani (1729–1799) upset the hypothesis of spontaneous generation; Pasteur dealt it a death blow.

**Aborigines,** a term first applied to an ancient mythical people of central Italy, derives from the Latin *ab origine* = from the beginning. It now signifies the original inhabitants of any country, in particular the aboriginal tribes of Australia. In contrast to their highly complex social and religious customs, the material culture of Australian aboriginals is very low and ill adapted to stand up to contact with European civilization. Originally estimated at 300,000, their number has dropped in the last 200 years to some 80,000. They have no legal title to their ancient tribal lands, unlike the native people of the USA, Canada, and New Zealand.

**Absolute Temperature, Absolute Zero.** This is a refined notion requiring some study of thermodynamics for its full understanding. For setting up an absolute temperature scale one must first assign a numerical value to one fixed temperature. For this, the triple point of water has been chosen, *i.e.,* the temperature at which solid, liquid, and gaseous water are all in equilibrium. The triple point is defined to be 273·16 K where K is read for kelvin (after Lord Kelvin). This temperature is 0·01° C on the Celsius scale (*q.v.*) and is thus very close to the melting point of ice. Suppose the pressure and volume of a mass of gas are measured (i) at the triple point of water, giving $(pV)$tr as the product of the pressure and volume; and (ii) at any unknown temperature $T$ K, giving $(pV)$ as the product. Then the absolute temperature, $T$ K, is defined by

$$T\,K = 273\cdot16\,\frac{(pV)}{(pV)\text{tr}}$$

It is to be understood that the gas pressure is very low. The nature of the gas is immaterial. More subtly, it can be shown that the temperature so defined is identical with that derived in a rather abstract way in the science of thermodynamics. The absolute scale is therefore also called the thermodynamic scale. Absolute temperatures can be obtained from Celsius temperatures by adding 273·15; thus the absolute temperature of melting ice is 273·15 K. Conversely, absolute zero is a temperature 273·15 K below the temperature of melting ice, *i.e.,* −273·15° C. Theory shows that absolute zero is unattainable, but it has been approached to within about 1 millionth of a degree. Within ten or so degrees of absolute zero, matter develops some remarkable properties. *See* **Cryogenics, Superconductor, Helium.**

**Acetic Acid,** an organic acid produced when ordinary (ethyl) alcohol is fermented by the organism called *Acetobacter aceti.* The same oxidation process yields vinegar: this is a weak and crude solution of acetic acid obtained by trickling dilute alcoholic liquor over beechwood shavings at 35° C (95° F). The souring of wine is due to the same process. Acetic acid is used as a food preservative and flavouring material, and in the manufacture of cellulose acetate and white lead.

**Acid Rain** is the name given to rain, snow, or sleet contaminated with acid substances so that its acidity is greater than the limit expected by normal concentrations of carbon dioxide dissolving in the rain to give carbonic acid (*p*H 5.5–5.6). The *p*H of acid rain therefore is less than about 5.5. The increased acidity is caused by larger concentrations of a number of contaminants, principally the strong acids, nitric and sulfuric, which arise from industrial effluents containing oxides of nitrogen and sulfur. The European emission of sulfur dioxide doubled between 1940 and 1980. In some European and North American areas such contamination can give a rain *p*H as low as 3 (which is 100 times more acid than *p*H 5). The acid rain can mark fruit and leaves, and adversely affect soil but its main effect is on the aquatic ecosystems especially in regions which cannot naturally buffer acidic inputs such as those with thin soils and granite rocks. It is likely that the disappearance of fish from many Scandinavian lakes has been the result of pollution by acid rain.

**Acids,** substances having a tendency to lose a positive ion (a proton). This general definition overcomes difficulties of earlier views which merely described their properties and asserted that they are chemically opposite to bases. As a whole acids contain ionizable hydrogen, replaceable by a metal, to form a salt. Inorganic acids are compounds of non-metals or metalloids, *e.g.,* sulfuric phosphoric acid. Carboxylic acids contain the group —COOH. *See* **F25.**

**Actinides,** the fourteen metallic elements from thorium (no. 90) to lawrencium (no. 103). All known isotopes of these elements are radioactive and those with atomic number greater than 92 (uranium) have been produced only in significant quantities artificially. Plutonium (no. 94) is obtained from uranium during the course of nuclear reactor operation and the higher transuranic elements can be made from it by the successive capture of neutrons or nuclei of light atoms. The availability of only minute quantities of short-lived isotopes makes the determination of the physical and chemical properties of the higher actinides very difficult. Claims for the discovery of new elements can therefore be controversial and since the discoverers cán name the elements their naming is also controversial. There were three different reports for Nobelium (no. 102). Lawrentium (no. 103) is called Jolistium by Russian authors. Element no. 104 was reported in 1964 by a Russian group and called Kurchatovium but is called Rutherfordium (Rf) in the West. Element no. 105 has been named Hahnium (Hn).

**Aerodynamics,** the science of gases (especially air) in motion, particularly in relation to aircraft (aeronautics). The idea of imitating the birds by the use of wings is of ancient origin. Leonardo da Vinci first carried out experiments in a scientific manner. The invention of the balloon in 1783 and the researches of scientists and engineers in the 19th cent. ultimately led to the development of the airplane.

**Aerolites,** the name given to the class of meteorites composed chiefly of heavy silicates. The other two main classes are *siderolites* (nickel iron and silicates) and *siderites* (nickel iron).

**Agave,** the American aloe or Century Plant which sometimes does not attain to flowering maturity under sixty or seventy years, and then dies. The flower spray may reach a height of 6m (20 ft) and in its development the rush of sap is so great that the Mexicans collect for brewing the strong spirit called mescal. 1,000 liters (264 gal) of sap can be obtained from a single plant. Some species of agave yield sisal used for making cord and rope.

**Air Glow** is the general name given to a large number of relatively weak optical emissions from the earth's upper atmosphere in the height range 70 to 400 km; 44 to 249 mi (approx.). It is distinct from the aurora polaris *(q.v.)* which is usually much brighter and normally only observable at high latitudes. Air glow is produced by a combination of photochemical reactions in the upper atmosphere, excitation by photoelectrons, or by solar ultra-violet light. In the latter case it is more correctly called "dayglow." These emissions occur in the ultra-violet and infra-red spectral regions as well as in visible light.

**Alabaster,** a soft crystalline form of sulphate of lime, or granulated gypsum, easily worked for statuary and other ornamental articles, and capable of being highly polished. Volterra, in Tuscany, yields the finest; that in highest ancient repute came from Alabastron in Egypt, near to the modern Antinoë.

**Alcohols.** A class of organic compounds of general formula R-OH, where R is an aliphatic radical. "Alcohol" is the name used for ethyl alcohol (ethanol); this is produced by distilling fermented liquors, and synthetically from ethylene, a product of pe-

troleum cracking. Industrially ethyl alcohol is used in the manufacture of chloroform, ether, perfumes, etc. Diluted with wood alcohol or other denaturants ethyl alcohol is called "methylated spirits"; the denaturants are varied according to the industrial purposes for which it is required, the methylated spirits then being largely exempt from duty. Wood alcohol (methyl alcohol or methanol) can be obtained by distilling wood or synthetically from water gas.

**Aldehyde,** the generic term for a class of chemical compounds of general formula R-CHO, where R is an organic radical. Except for formaldehyde, which is a gas, aldehydes are volatile liquids. They are produced by oxidation of primary alcohols. Most important aldehyde is formaldehyde (methanol) used in making the plastics described as formaldehyde resins. Formalin (formaldehyde solution in water) is much used for preserving zoological specimens.

**Aldine Editions** are the beautiful books printed in Venice by the Renaissance printer Aldo Pio Manuzio and his family between 1490 and 1597. Italics were first introduced in these books.

**Algebra,** a branch of mathematics in which symbols are used in place of numbers. Sir Isaac Newton styled it the "universal arithmetic". The Chinese were able to solve the quadratic equation before the Christian era but it was Al-Khowarizmi, an Arab mathematician of the early 9th century, who introduced algebra to Europe.

**Alkali,** the general name given to a number of chemicals which are bases *(q.v.).* The term should be limited to the hydroxides of metals in the first and second group of the periodic table and of ammonia, *e.g.,* NaOH, KOH. They are used commercially in the manufacture of paper, glass, soap, and artificial silk. The word comes from the Arabic *al-kali* meaning calcined wood ashes. Alkalis are extremely soluble in water and neutralise acids to form salts and water.

**Alkaloids,** a large group of natural products which contain nitrogen; they are usually basic. Isolated from plants and animals, they include some hormones, vitamins, and drugs. Examples are nicotine, adrenalin, and cocaine. Many alkaloids are made synthetically for medicinal use, *e.g.,* morphine, quinine. Their function in plants is not well understood.

**Allotropy.** Depending on the temperature, pressure or method of preparation, an element may exist in one of several forms, each having different physical properties (crystal structure, electrical conductivity, melting point, etc.). This is known as allotropy and the different forms of the element are called allotropes. Many elements exhibit allotropy, *e.g.,* sulfur, phosphorus, oxygen, tin and carbon, the most well-known allotropes of carbon being diamond and graphite.

**Alloys** are combinations of metals made for their valuable special properties, *e.g.,* durability, strength, lightness, magnetism, rust-resistance, etc. Some well-known ones are brass (zinc + copper), coinage bronze (copper + zinc + tin), steels (iron + carbon + various other materials), soft solder (tin + lead), dental fillings (mercury + various ingredients).

**Alluvium,** river transported deposits of sand, mud and gravel which accumulate to form distinctive features such as levées, flood plains and deltas. The frequent renewal of alluvium by flooding causes riverine lands to be some of the most fertile. In Asia alluvial lands support high densities of population, *e.g.,* The Hwang-ho plains and the Ganges delta.

**Almond,** the fruit of the *Amygdalus communis* originally indigenous to Persia, Asia Minor and N. Africa, now cultivated in Italy, Spain, France, the USA and Australia. It yields both bitter and sweet oil. Bitter almond oil is obtained by macerating and distilling the ripe seeds; it is used for flavoring and scenting purposes, its fragrant odor being due to the presence of benzaldehyde and hydrogen cyanide. When the seeds are pressed sweet almond oil results: this is used in perfumery, and also as a lubricant for very delicate machinery.

**Alpha Particle,** *or* **alpha-ray,** fast-moving helium nucleus ejected by some radioactive atoms, *e.g.,* polonium. It is a combination of 2 neutrons and 2 protons.

**Alphabet** (so called from the first two letters of the Greek alphabet—alpha, beta) is the term applied to the collection of letters from which the words of a language are made up. It grew out of the knowledge that all words can be expressed by a limited number of sounds arranged in various combinations. The Phoenicians were the first to make use of an alphabetic script derived from an earlier Semitic alphabet (earliest known inscriptions *c.* 1500–950 B.C.) from which all other alphabets have sprung. The stages in the development of the alphabet were mnemonic (memory aids), pictorial (actual pictures), ideographic (symbols), and lastly phonetic. All the ideographic systems died out, with the exception of that of the Chinese.

**Altimeter,** an instrument used in aircraft to estimate altitude; its usual essential feature is an aneroid barometer which registers the decrease of pressure with height. Roughly 1 millibar corresponds to 9 m (30 ft). To read an aircraft altimeter correct for its destination, the zero setting must be adjusted for difference of ground height and difference of surface pressure, especially when pressure is falling or when flying towards low pressure.

**Alum** is a compound salt used in various industrial processes, especially dyeing, its constituents being the sulfate of one univalent metal or radical (*e.g.,* potassium, sodium, ammonium, rubidium, caesium, silver, thallium) and the sulfate of a tervalent metal (*e.g.,* aluminum, iron, chromium, manganese), and water of crystallisation.

**Alumina** is the oxide of aluminum. Very valuable as a refractory material. The ruby is almost 100 percent alumina; so also are the emerald, oriental amethyst, etc. An hydrated aluminum oxide is bauxite, chief ore of aluminum from which the metal is extracted electrolytically.

**Aluminum,** element no. 13, symbol Al, is a light metal which conducts electricity well. Its specific gravity at 20° C (68° F) is 2·705. Melting point of aluminium is 660.2° C (1220.4° F). It is made commercially by electrolyzing bauxite dissolved in cryolite (double fluoride of aluminum and sodium). Aluminium alloys because of their strength and lightness are being increasingly used for construction purposes.

**Amalgam** is the term applied to any alloy of which mercury forms a part.

**Amber,** a brittle resinous substance; in origin, fossilised resin. Obtained mostly from the Baltic coasts, and used for ornaments, pipe mouthpieces, etc.

**Amblyopsis,** a species of fish, practically sightless, and with inoperative organs of hearing and feeling, that inhabit the Mammoth Cave of Kentucky. A remarkable illustration of the failure of senses not brought into use.

**Amethyst,** the violet variety of quartz, used as a precious stone, containing traces of manganese, titanium and iron. The finest colored specimens come from Brazil and the Urals.

**Amino acids,** organic compounds containing an amine group and a carboxylic acid group. They are the "building bricks" of proteins *(q.v.).*

**Ammeter,** an instrument for measuring the current flowing in an electric circuit. A contraction of ampere-meter.

**Ammonia,** a colorless gaseous compound comprising three atoms of hydrogen to one of nitrogen. Formerly it was made by heating the horns and hoofs of deer, acquiring the name of spirits of hartshorn. The ammonia of commerce is now procured by coal decomposition in the course of gas-making and by direct synthesis. In the very important Haber process of ammonia production by fixation of atmospheric nitrogen, the nitrogen is made to combine with hydrogen and the ammonia so prepared is converted into nitric acid, ammonium nitrate or ammonium sulfate. The Haber process made Germany self-sufficient in nitrates in the first world war, and was afterwards exploited all over the world.

**Ammonites,** extinct animals related to the Nautilus. The enambered shell is coiled, usually in a plane spiral, and they are confined to Mesozoic rocks.

**Ammonium,** the basic radical of ammonium salts, Composed of one atom of nitrogen and four of hydrogen, it behaves chemically like an ion of a monovalent alkali metal. Ammonium chloride is known as "sal ammoniac". "Sal volatile" is ammonium carbonate.

**Amorphous,** a term used to indicate the absence of crystalline form in any body or substance.

**Anemometer,** an instrument for measuring the strength of the wind. In the most widely used pattern the rotation, about a vertical axis, of a group of hemispherical or conical cups gives a measure of the total flow of air past the cups, various registering devices being employed. The Dines anemograph provides a continuous record of the variation in both velocity and direction; changes of pressure produced in a horizontal tube, kept pointing into the wind by a vane, cause a float, to which a pen is attached, to rise and fall in sympathy with the gusts and lulls. The recently devised hot-wire anemometer, depending upon the change of electrical resistance experienced by a heated wire when cooled, enables very gentle air currents to be investigated.

**Aneroid** is the kind of barometer which does not depend upon atmospheric support of a mercury (or other liquid) column. It consists of a metallic box, partially exhausted of air, with a corrugated lid which moves with atmospheric changes. A lever system magnifies the lid movements about 200 times and atmospheric pressure is read from a dial. The construction of the vacuum chamber provides automatic compensation for temperature changes. An aneroid barometer is the basic component of an altimeter.

**Aniline,** a simple aromatic compound ($C_6H_5NH_2$) related to benzene and ammonia. It is obtained from coal-tar. The name recalls the fact that it was first prepared by distilling indigo (*anil* is Portuguese for indigo). In 1856 W. H. Perkin (1838–1907) discovered the first aniline or coal-tar dye, mauve, and thus founded the modern dyestuff industry.

**Anise,** an umbelliferous plant *(Pimpinella anisum)* found in Egypt and the Levant, and valued for its fruit, aniseed, possessing certain medicinal properties and yielding an aromatic, volatile oil, Also used in cooking. The anise of the Bible is *Anethum graveolens, i.e.,* dill.

**Ant.** There are about 6,000 species of ants, which belong to the same order (Hymenoptera) as the bees, wasps and ichneumon flies. They are social in habit, living in communities of varying size and development. There are three basic castes in ants—the females or *queens,* the *males,* and the *workers* (the last-named being neuter), although specialized forms of workers are sometimes found, *e.g.,* the *soldiers* of the harvesting ants. In the communities of those species of ants which evolved most recently there is a highly complex social life and well-developed division of labor. Some species of these ants make slaves of other species, stealing the cocoons before the adult forms emerge. Many ants "milk" green-flies, which they protect for their honey-like secretion, and most ants' nests contain many "guests", such as beetles and silver fish. Some ants harvest grains of corn, and others, from S. America, live on fungi which they cultivate in underground "mushroom beds".

**Antarctic Exploration.** In earlier centuries it was thought that a great continent must exist in the southern hemisphere, around the South Pole, to balance the known land masses in the north. Its supposed extent was greatly reduced in the 18th century, particularly when Capt. Cook sailed for the first time south of the Antarctic Circle and reached the edge of the icepack. A portion of the ice-covered continent—the coast of Graham Land—was first sighted by Lieut. Edward Bransfield in 1820. Explorers of several other nations sighted portions of the coast-line in other quarters, but the first extensive exploration was made by Capt. James Clarke Ross, who with the *Erebus* and *Terror* penetrated into the Ross Sea in 1841, and discovered the great Ross Ice Barrier in 78° South lat. Interest in the Antarctic did not revive until after 1890, when an international scheme of research was drawn up. A Norwegian, C. E. Borchgrevink, in 1898–1900, was the first to winter in the Antarctic and to travel on the ice barrier. The British share in this work was carried out by Capt. R. F. Scott's expedition in the *Discovery,* 1901–4. Scott's party sledged across the barrier to 82° 17′ South, then a record "farthest south". A little later, Ernest Shackleton beat this by travelling to within 160 km of the South Pole. The Scottish polar explorer William Spiers Bruce led the Scottish national Antarctic Expedition of 1902 in the *Scotia* and discovered Coats Land and founded a meteorological observatory on the South Orkneys. In 1910 Scott organized his second expedition in *Terra Nova,* and became engaged against his will in a "race for the Pole" when, after his departure, the Norwegian Arctic explorer, Roald Amundsen, suddenly announced that he was sailing for the Antarctic. Amundsen set up his base at the eastern end of the Barrier, and, relying on dog teams for hauling his sledges, reached the Pole on 14 December 1911. Meanwhile Scott and his party, their start delayed by adverse weather, were marching southwards, man-hauling their sledges, for Scott was against the use of dogs. After an arduous journey they reached the Pole one month after Amundsen. The return was a struggle against the weather and increasing weakness, probably due to scurvy, until at last they perished within a few kilometers of their base. After the first world war the development of the whaling industry greatly stimulated further exploration. Outstanding expeditions included that of Admiral R. E.

Byrd, 1929, when he flew over the South Pole; the British Graham Land expedition, 1934, which carried out the first extensive mapping of any part of the Antarctic continent; and the US Navy's Antarctic Expedition of 1940, when the whole continent was circumnavigated and great areas photographed from the air. In recent years valuable work has been done by the first International expedition, the Norwegian-British-Swedish Expedition to Queen Maud Land, and by the French in Adélie Land. The Falkland Island Dependencies Survey, set up during the war, has continued the scientific exploration of Graham Land. The Antarctic was the scene of high adventure during the International Geophysical Year (1957–58), when scientists from many countries participated in the explorations. The Commonwealth Trans-Antarctic Expedition set out from opposite sides of the continent and met at the South Pole, the UK party, led by Sir Vivian Fuchs, from the Falklands, and Sir Edmund Hillary and his party from New Zealand. The UK party accomplished the first crossing of the White Continent in 99 days. Their scientific work included the marking of seismic and complementary gravimetric studies at frequent intervals along the 3,510 km (2,200 mi) traverse. Since the Antarctic is becoming important for many reasons, in weather forecasting, in the whaling industry, and as a possible centre for world air routes, the tempo of exploration and research will become even faster in the future.

**Anthracite** is a black coal with a brilliant luster. It contains 92 per cent and over of carbon and burns slowly, without smoke or flame.

**Anthropoid,** meaning "resembling man", a suborder of the primate mammals including man and also the gibbon, chimpanzee, orangutan, and gorilla.

**Anticyclone,** a region where barometric pressure is greater than that of its surroundings. Such a system is distinguished on weather charts by a pattern of isobars, usually circular or oval-shaped, enclosing the center of high pressure where the air is calm. In the remaining areas light or moderately strong winds blow spirally outwards in a clockwise direction in the Northern Hemisphere (and in the reverse direction in the Southern Hemisphere), in accordance with Buys Ballot's law (an observer with back to wind in Northern Hemisphere has lower pressure to left; in Southern to right). Over the British Isles anticyclonic weather is generally quiet and settled, being fair, warm, and sunny in summer and either very cold and often foggy or overcast and gloomy in winter. These systems move slowly and sometimes remain practically stationary for days at a time, that over Siberia being particularly well defined. Extensive belts of almost permanent anticyclones occur in latitudes 30° N and 30° S.

**Antimony.** Metal element, no. 51, symbol Sb. In group 5 of the periodic table. Exists in various forms, the stable form being a grey metal with a layer structure. The other forms are nonconductors. On being burned, it gives off dense fumes of oxide of antimony. By itself it is not of special utility; but as an alloy for hardening other metals, it is much used. As an alloy with lead for type-metal, and with tin and copper or zinc for Britannia-metal, it is of great value. Most important antimony ore is stibnite (antimony sulfide).

**Anti-proton,** the "negative proton", an atomic particle created in high energy collisions of nuclear particles. Its existence was confirmed in Oct. 1955.

**Aphids,** green-flies or plant lice, a numerous species

of destructive insects living on young shoots and foliage, some on roots. Reproduction is by parthenogenesis (virgin birth).

**Apocrypha** (hidden writings), the books which were included in the Septuagint (Greek) and Vulgate (Latin) versions of the Old Testament but excluded from the sacred canon at the Reformation by the Protestants on the grounds that they were not originally written in Hebrew nor regarded as genuine by the Jews. The books include: 1 and 2 Esdras, Tobit, Judith, additions to Esther, Wisdom of Solomon, Ecclesiasticus, Baruch, Song of the Three Holy Children, History of Susannah, Bel and the Dragon, Prayer of Manasses, 1 and 2 Maccabees. The term is usually applied to the additions to the Old Testament, but there are also numerous Christian writings of the same character. *The New English Bible*, which contains the Apocrypha, was published in 1970.

**Appian Way,** the oldest and finest of the Roman roads originally laid by Appius Claudius (312 B.C.) from Rome to Capua and then to Brundisium (Brindisi).

**Arabian Nights Entertainment** *or* **Book of a Thousand and One Nights,** a collection of fascinating tales of the Orient, of mixed Indian, Persian, Arabic, and Egyptian origination, and first made known in Europe by Antoine Galland's French translation (1704–17) from Arabian texts. The "master" tale tells how the princess Shahrazad so beguiles the king through the telling of the tales over one thousand and one nights that her life was spared. English translators include E. W. Lane (1840), Sir Richard Burton (1885–8), John Payne (1882–4).

**Arabic Numerals.** The modern system of numbering, 0, 1, 2, 3, 4, 5, 6, 7, 8, 9, in which the digits depend on their position for their value is called the Arabic numerical notation. The method is, in fact, of Indian origin. By the 9th cent. Hindu science was available in Arabic, and the Persian mathematician Al-Kwarizimi (*c.* 830) in his *Arithmetic* used the so-called "Arabic" system of numbering. Gradually the method spread to Europe, taking the place of the Roman system which was useless for calculation. The West is indebted to the Arabs for the zero symbol, the lack of which had been a serious drawback to Greek mathematics. It made the invention of decimal fractions possible.

**Aramaic Languages,** the Semitic dialects current in Mesopotamia and the regions extending southwest from the Euphrates to Palestine from about the 12th century B.C. until after the rise of Islam, when Aramaic was superseded by Arabic. Both Aramaic and Greek were spoken in Palestine during the time of Christ.

**Archaeopteryx,** a fossil bird providing a connecting link between reptiles and birds. It had feathers, jaws with teeth, no bill, reptilian bones and skull, a long tail, and it probably used its fore-limbs for gliding flight. The first specimen, found in 1861, in the Solenhofen limestone of Bavaria, is in London's Natural History Museum.

**Archimedes' Principle.** When a body is weighed in air and then in any fluid, the apparent loss in weight is equal to the weight of fluid displaced. This scientific fact was noted by the Syracusan philosopher Archimedes (287–212 B.C.) and is frequently used as a basis for density measurements.

**Architecture,** the art and science of building. The provision of shelter for mankind by the orderly arrangement of materials in a manner which expresses man's attitude to living. The forms which buildings take are the outcome of the function for which they are to be used, of the architect's aesthetic sensibility and the structural method adopted. Until the last hundred years structural methods were limited to timber frames, and columns, lintels, load-bearing walls, arches, vaults, and domes in brick or stone. From these few basic elements have evolved the great variety of historic styles of building to be found throughout the world. To give but one example, the Greeks created those systems of decorated columns and beams, known as the Orders, which were adapted by the Romans, revived decoratively rather than structurally during the Renaissance and are still used in debased form on the more presumptuous type of modern building. In recent years, however, architecture has taken on a new meaning. Once confined to the rich, in the form of Church, State or Commerce, it is now, with the coming of democracy, recognized as an essential social service for all. This, and the development of new structural techniques and materials (steel, aluminium, sheet glass, reinforced concrete, plastics and plywoods, to name a few), have made the interest in historic styles, the mainstay of the older architect, of secondary importance. Modern architecture is the creation of buildings with the highest possible standards of functional performance in terms of efficient planning and structure, good artificial and natural lighting, adequate heating or cooling, and proper acoustic conditions consistent with the price the client can afford to pay. At the same time the architect's task is to design a structure and the spaces the structure delimits, internally and externally which are aesthetically stimulating and satisfying, and well related to the land and buildings around.

**Arctic Exploration.** Modern exploration of the Arctic begins in the 16th century when men sought to reach the East Indies by sailing through the Arctic to the Pacific Ocean. The Northeast Passage, via the shores of northern Asia, was the first attempted. In 1553 and 1554 the English navigators Sir Richard Chancellor and Stephen Burrough sailed into the White Sea, but were prevented by storms and ice from advancing farther eastwards. The project was later revived by the Dutch; Barents in 1594 discovered Spitsbergen, but also failed to get beyond Novaya Zemlya. It was not, in fact, until 1879 that the Swede, A. E. Nordenskjöld, in the *Vega,* succeeded in reaching the Pacific. The attempts to find a North-west Passage were more numerous and determined. In 1585 John Davis penetrated Davis Strait and coasted along Baffin Island. Hopes ran high when Henry Hudson discovered Hudson Bay in 1610, but a practicable passage continued to elude explorers. The problem was to find a navigable route through the maze of channels in the short summer season, and to avoid being frozen in with supplies exhausted. After the Napoleonic Wars the Admiralty sent out many naval expeditions which culminated in John Franklin's expedition with the *Erebus* and *Terror* in 1845. The ships were beset by ice in Victoria Channel and, after Franklin's death, were abandoned by their crews, who perished from scurvy and starvation on their march southwards. To ascertain their fate, several further expeditions were despatched, and the crew of the *Investigator,* commanded by R. J. M'Clure, sailing eastwards from Bering Strait, were the first to make the Passage, though in doing so they were obliged to abandon their ship. It was thirty years before the Norwegian, Roald Amundsen, succeeded in sailing the *Gjoa* from the east to west.

In the meantime, the North Pole had become the goal of explorers. Nansen, in 1893, put the *Fram* into the ice-pack to drift across the Polar basin, and himself made an unsuccessful attempt on the Pole across the pack. This was eventually achieved by the American explorer Robert E. Peary, who after several expeditions in the North Greenland region, sledged to the Pole with Eskimo companions in 1909. The next phase was the employment of airships and aeroplanes in Arctic exploration. In 1926 Admiral Byrd made the first flight over the Pole, and in the same year Amundsen and Lincoln Ellsworth flew the airship *Norge* from Spitsbergen to Point Barrow Alaska. Two years later, the *Italia*, commanded by the Italian, Nobile, was wrecked on a return flight from the Pole, and Amundsen lost his life in an attempt to rescue the survivors. With modern developments in aircraft and navigation, flights over the Polar basin are almost a routine matter. The first voyage under the North Pole was made in August 1958 by the American nuclear-powered submarine *Nautilus*.

**Arenaceous Rocks,** the rocks composed of grains of sand, chiefly sandstones; quartz is the most abundant mineral in these rocks.

**Argillaceous Rocks** are a sedimentary group, including the shales and clays.

**Argon,** chemical element no. 18, symbol A. This was the first of the inert gases to be isolated from air by Rayleigh and Ramsay in 1894. Argon is used for filling gas-filled metal filament electric lamps. In gas discharge tube it gives a blue glow.

**Arithmetic Progression,** a sequence of numbers in which the successor of each number is obtained by adding or subtracting a fixed number, for example 2, 5, 8, 11, . . . or 100, 95, 90, 85. . . .

**Armillary Sphere,** an early form of astronomical apparatus with a number of circles representing equator, meridian, ecliptic, etc. Used by Hipparchus and Ptolemy and up to the time of Tycho Brahe for determining the position of the stars.

**Arsenic,** a metalloid element, no. 33, symbol As in group 5 of the periodic table usually met with as a constituent of other minerals, sometimes by itself. Its compounds are very poisonous. Lead arsenate is a powerful insecticide used for spraying fruit trees. The more stable allotropic form (grey) has a layer structure, and conducts electricity.

**Artesian Wells** take their name from Artois in France, where the first wells of this kind were constructed in 1126. They are to be found only when a water-bearing bed is sandwiched between two impervious beds. When a boring is made to the lower part of the bed, the pressure of water is sufficient to cause the water to overflow at the surface. Artesian wells were known to ancient Egypt and China, and have existed in the Sahara since the earliest times. The fountains in Trafalgar Square were once fed by artesian wells sunk through the London clay into the chalk about 250 m (820 ft).

**Aryans,** nomadic peoples who made their way in successive waves from the Eurasian steppes to the Indus and the Nile during the first half of the 2nd millennium B.C. They crossed the Hindu Kush into N.W. India and settled in the valleys of the Indus and Ganges, where an earlier Indus civilisation had flourished, *c.* 3240–2750 B.C. Their religious ideas are reflected in the Veda (oldest Hindu scriptures, written down many centuries later in Vedic, parent language of Sanskrit). Those who made their way to Syria and Egypt founded the Hyksos empire (*c.* 1720–1550 B.C.). The Aryans introduced the horse-drawn chariot and spoke a language from which the great Indo-European family of languages is derived, with one group in India and Iran, and another in Europe. Because of the misuse of the term by the Nazis, Aryan is now referred to as proto-Indo-European.

**Ash,** a familiar deciduous tree of the genus *Fraxinus,* of over 60 species, native to North temperate regions. The ash held an important place in Norse mythology, as it was supposed to support the heavens with its roots in Hell. The species native to Britain, and to Europe, is *F. excelsior,* a tall tree with compound leaves, greenish flowers, winged seeds, and black buds in winter. It is a valuable timber tree, tough and elastic, and largely used for wheels and handles. The rowan, or mountain ash, *Sorbus aucuparia,* with similar leaves and orange berries, belongs to a different family. *F. pendula* or weeping ash is a strain which makes an ideal natural summer house.

**Astrolabe,** a medieval scientific instrument for taking altitudes, observing the sun by day and the stars by night, and used for telling the time and finding the latitude. Used by the ancient Greeks, later by the Arabs and Persians, and introduced into Europe by way of Spain in the 14th cent. Chaucer is said to have sent his son Lois, a ten-year-old student at Oxford, an astrolabe with a treatise on its use in 1391.

**Astronomy.** The Pythagoreans believed the stars and planets moved with uniform circular velocity in crystalline spheres, centered round the earth (the "harmony of the spheres"). Hipparchus (190–120 B.C.) made the first star catalogue, discovered the precession of the equinoxes and introduced the idea of epicyclic motion. His planetary system, in the form it was presented by Ptolemy 200 years later, held until the Renaissance when Copernicus revived the heretical view first put forward by Aristarchus of Samos (310–230 B.C.) that the sun and not the earth was at the center. Galileo, accurate observer and experimenter, went beyond Copernicus; helped by the contributions of Tycho Brahe, Giordano Bruno, Kepler and others, he was able to overthrow the Ptolemaic system of the heavenly spheres and Aristotelian philosophy and pave the way for Newton and modern astronomy. To Galileo we owe the conception of acceleration; to Newton the theory of universal gravitation; they showed that the same laws govern both celestial and terrestrial physics. Three landmarks in more recent times were the discovery of Uranus by Herschel in 1781 which extended the solar system as then recognized; the estimation by Hubble in 1924 of the distance of Andromeda, which showed that our Galaxy was just one of many; and Einstein's theory of relativity which improved on Newton's theory of the solar system by bringing gravitation into the domain of space-time. Today radio-telescopes and space probes are advancing astronomical knowledge and making it possible to explore regions beyond the scope of optical telescopes.

**Athanasian Creed,** one of the three ancient creeds of the Christian Church, often referred to as the *Quicunque Vult,* is a statement of the doctrine of the Trinity and the Incarnation, and though named after St. Athanasius, it is thought to be the work of St. Ambrose (339–97).

**Atmospherics** are electrical impulses which are believed to originate in atmospheric electrical discharges such as lightning. They give rise to crashing background noises in the loudspeakers of radio sets, interfering with reception at distances of up to 6,400 km (3,970 mi) from the center of the disturbance. The location of atmospherics with the aid of radio direction-finding methods gives warning of the approach of thunderstorms.

**Atomic Pile,** an apparatus containing a fissionable element and a moderator, such as heavy water or graphite, in which a self-sustaining fission process proceeds at a controllable rate. The first atomic pile, constructed on a squash court at Chicago, was operated for the first time on 2 December 1942, under the direction of Enrico Fermi. The pile contained 12,400 lb (5,580 kg) of uranium.

**Aurora Polaris.** This wonderful phenomenon of the night sky is a common sight at high northern and southern latitudes, where it is called the aurora borealis and the aurora australis, respectively. It is visible less often at temperate latitudes, and only rarely in the tropics. The auroral ovals, or zones of maximum frequency of aurora, surround both of the earth's geomagnetic poles, and the northern auroral oval includes the northern parts of Scandinavia, Canada, and Alaska. The aurora is the visible manifestation of complex plasma processes occurring within the earth's magnetosphere (*q.v.*), whereby streams of high-energy electrons and protons (mainly) are accelerated and dumped via the earth's magnetic field lines into the upper atmosphere. This mechanism produces the light emission of the aurora. The brightest aurora, which may also extend to lower latitudes, occurs during geomagnetic storms, which are complex and large-scale plasma instabilities within the magnetosphere triggered by fluctuations in the solar wind (*q.v.*)—usually ascribed to "M" regions on the sun associated with coronal holes, flares, and active sunspot groups. Auroral displays may take several forms—a faint glow, a diffuse ribbon of light crossing the heavens, great folded waving curtains or draperies, or the entire sky may be flooded with a rapidly varying brilliant panoply of light. Specially instrumented spacecraft which can directly explore the magnetosphere and high-latitude ionosphere have provided a great deal of our knowledge about this fascinating and complex phenomenon. The aurora is a kind of light essentially different from that of the rainbow which is a partly subjective phenomenon. Each beholder sees his own rainbow, whose light is sunlight refracted and reflected by many raindrops. The raindrops that produce his rainbow depend on his position as well as on the direction of the sun. The aurora, on the contrary, is a light as objective as that of a candle, though produced differently. It is a self-luminescence of the air in particular regions of the atmosphere that lie far above the clouds.

**Average** is a single number designed to give a typical example of a set of numbers, *e.g.,* a cricketer's batting average for a season gives an idea of his typical score. There are several kinds of average and their uses are studied in the science of statistics. A statement that "so and so is the average value" can be misleading if one does not know which average is meant. Three common averages are: the arithmetic average (or mean), the mode, and the median. The arithmetic average of *n* numbers is found by adding them together and dividing by *n*; this is a very common method of averaging. The mode of *n* numbers is the most frequently occurring number. The median is the middle number, *i.e.,* the number which is smaller than just as many of the other numbers as it exceeds. Of the numbers 1, 2, 2, 2, 2, 3, 4, 5, 6, 8, 9, the arithmetic means is 4, the mode is 2, the median is 3.

**Avogadro's Hypothesis.** This is a fundamental concept of chemistry. Equal volumes of all gases under the same conditions of temperature and pressure contain the same number of molecules. This law was instrumental in assigning the formula of molecules. The hypothesis was put forward in 1811, but was not generally accepted until 1860.

# B

**Bacteriophage (Phage),** literally "bacteria eater", *i.e.,* a virus which specifically infects bacteria. In common with viruses which attack animal or plant cells, isolated phages are inert, and can only reproduce by making use of the chemical apparatus of a more sophisticated host cell (in this case a bacterium). However phages may be of two types, virulent or temperate. Virulent phages completely disrupt the normal functioning of the infected bacterium and adapt its reproductive mechanism to produce more phage. This eventually kills the bacterium and the newly assembled phages are released. Temperate phages on the other hand may enter into a remarkable symbiotic relationship with the bacterium, known as lysogeny. The phage genetic material is incorporated into that of the bacterium and is reproduced each time the still functioning bacterium subsequently divides. Furthermore the bacterium is immune from attack by potentially virulent phages of the same type. When such lysogenic bacteria die, phage particles may again be released. Phages carried in lysogenic bacteria are in a state known as prophage and it is often difficult to obtain pure, prophage-free strains of bacteria. Because of their relatively simple structure, phages have been extensively used in research on genetics and molecular biology.

**Baleen** *or* "whalebone" the name given to a series of horny plates growing from the roof of the mouth in those whales classified as Whalebone or Baleen Whales *(Mystacoceti)*. There are 300–400 or so plates on each side, and their inner edges are frayed, the whole system constituting a filter for collecting minute organisms used for food. The Baleen Whales include the Right-Whales, the Pacific Grey-Whale and the Rorquals.

**Ballet** is a combination of four arts; dancing, music, painting, and drama, each of which is ideally of equal importance. The movement of the individual dancers and the "orchestration" of the whole group is in the hands of the choreographer. The dancer's training follows certain basic rules but save in classical ballet there is considerable freedom of movement. Ballet as we know it today developed professionally at the Court of King Louis XIV of France, though it owes its origins to Italy and in the earliest times to Greece and Rome. Its movements were made up from the dances of courtiers, country folk and tumblers. Technique grew more complex as costume became modified, the body gaining complete freedom with the invention of tights. A succession of great dancers—French, Italian and latterly Russian left their imprint on the art. Contemporary ballet reflects the aesthetics of the Russian, Sergei Diaghilêv.

**Balloon,** the modern balloon consists of a bag of plastic material inflated with a gas lighter than air. The first ascent by man in a hot-air ballon was made on 21 November 1783, and in a hydrogen balloon on December 1, 1783. The most famous of the early scientific flights by manned balloons were those of the Englishmen Coxwell and Glaisher, in 1862, when a height of 11 km (6,8 miles) was reached. The first aerial crossing of the English Channel by Blanchard and Jeffries was made on January 7, 1785. Piccard's ascent to 16 km (9.9 miles) in 1931 marked the conquest of the stratosphere. Four years later the American balloon *Explorer 11*, inflated with nearly 112,000 m³ of helium, carried a team of scientists with their floating laboratory to an altitude of 23 km (14.3 miles). In 1957 a pressurized balloon carrying an American doctor rose 31 km (19.3 miles) above the Earth. Meteorologists send their instruments up in balloons to collect data about the upper atmosphere, and of recent years physicists have learned much about cosmic radiation from the study of photographic plates sent to the upper regions in balloons.

**Balsam,** a big genus (140 species) of flowering plants. Many species are cultivated for their showy flowers, *e.g., Impatiens noli-me-tangere,* the yellow balsam or "touch-me-not", so called because the fruit explodes when touched, slinging out the seeds. Balsam fir is a conifer *(Abies balsamea)* from which Canada balsam gum is obtained.

**Bamboo,** a genus of strong grasses, some species growing to over 36 m (118 ft.) in height; much used by oriental peoples for all kinds of purposes. The young shoots of some species are tender and esculent.

**Barbary Ape,** a large monkey belonging to the genus *Macoca.* It is the only monkey living in relative freedom in Europe, a small colony being found on the Rock of Gibraltar. It has no tail.

**Barium,** metal element, no. 56, symbol Ba. In group 2 of the periodic table. The metal is soft and easily cut. It occurs as the sulfate and carbonate in nature. It was first prepared by Sir Humphry Davy in 1808, as an amalgam, by electrolysis of barium chloride. The pure metal was not isolated until 1901.

**Barometer** is an instrument for measuring atmospheric pressure, invented at Florence by Torricelli, pupil of Galileo, in 1644. The standard method consists of balancing the air column against a column of mercury, used on account of its high density. The mercury is contained in a long glass tube, closed at one end, and inverted in a cistern also containing mercury. The height of the mercury column, supporting the air column, is taken as the pressure at the time, and can be read off very accurately by means of a vernier scale. Present-day tendency is to express the readings in units of pressure instead of length, the millibar being adopted (1 mb = 1,000 dynes per sq. cm.; 1,000 mb = of mercury approx.). The standard instrument is correct for pressures at 0° C (32° F) in Lat. 45°, so that corrections have to be applied for temperatures and latitudes other than these. Also a correction has to be made for reducing the pressure to mean sea level.

**Baryons,** the group of heavier subatomic particles which includes the proton, neutron, lambda and omega-minus particles (and their corresponding anti-particles, called anti-baryons). Baryons interact by means of all the known forces of nature (strong, weak, electromagnetic and gravitational). However, in any closed system the total baryon number (*i.e.,* the number of baryons minus the number of anti-baryons) is constant. This means that the proton, being the lightest known baryon, must be stable against spontaneous decay. Unlike the lighter leptons *(q.v.),* baryons are now thought to have internal structure reflecting the fact that they are composed of quarks.

**Basalt Rocks** are fine-grained, dark coloured, of igneous origin and occur either as lava flows as in Mull and Staffa, or as intrusive sheets, like the Edinburgh Castle Rock and Salisbury Crags. One of the most noted examples of columnar basalt is that of the Giant's Causeway in Ireland.

**Base,** a substance having a tendency to accept a proton (H·). This is a wide definition and covers unconventional types of compounds. In aqueous solution bases dissolve with formation of hydroxyl ions, and will neutralise an acid to form a salt. In non-aqueous solvents, like liquid ammonia or hydrogen fluoride, compounds classically regarded as salts can be bases, *e.g.,* sodium fluoride is a base in hydrogen fluoride solution.

**Bas-Relief** ("low relief"), a term used in sculpture to denote a class of sculptures the figures of which are only slightly raised from the surface of the stone or clay upon which the design is wrought.

**Bauhaus,** a German institution for the training of architects, artists and industrial designers founded in 1919 at Weimar by Walter Gropius, (d. 1969). It was closed by Hitler in 1933 and re-opened at Chicago. The Bauhaus doctrine held that there should be no separation between architecture and the fine and applied arts; that art, science and technology should cooperate to create "the compositely inseparable work of art, the great building". Thus it was an organization with a social purpose. The original institution, at the instigation of Gropius, included on its teaching staff not only architects and technicians but also such noted artists as Paul Klee and Wassily Kandinsky.

**Bauxite,** the chief ore of aluminum. Chemically it is aluminum oxide. Aluminum metal is made industrially by electrolyzing purified bauxite dissolved in fused cryolite. Chief producing areas; Jamaica, Australia, Surinam, USSR, Guyana, France, Greece, Guinea, USA, Hungary, Yugoslavia.

**Bears** belong to the Ursidae family of the Carnivora. They are plantigrade mammals, walking (like man) on the soles of their feet. Found in most parts of the world except Australia. The common Brown Bear was once spread over the whole of Europe: it became extinct in England about the 11th century; 2·2·5 m (6·5·8 ft) in length, and stands 1 m (3 ft) or more at the shoulder. The Grizzly Bear of N. America is larger, and the coat is shorter and greyer. The Polar Bear is remarkable in having a white coat all the year round; it spends much time in water, and unlike other bears is entirely carnivorous.

**Beeswax,** the secretion of the bee, used for the formation of the cells or honey comb of the hive; when melted it is what is commercially known as yellow wax, white wax being made by bleaching. Being impervious to water, it acts as a good resistant and is an article of much utility.

**Beetles** (Coleoptera) constitute one of the biggest orders of insects, numbering over 200,000 species. There are two pairs of wings; the hind pair are used for flight, while the front pair are hardened to form a pair of protective covers (clytra). Some beetles have lost the power of flight and then the elytra are joined together.

**Bell, Book and Candle.** To curse by "bell, book, and candle" was a form of excommunication in the Roman Church ending with the words: "Close the book, quench the candle, ring the bell".

**Beryl,** a mineral, of which the emerald is a grass-green variety. Composed of beryllium and aluminum silicates. The pure mineral is colorless; the color of most beryl comes from traces of impurities, notably iron and chromium. Otherwise it is yellowish, greenish-yellow, or blue, and is found in veins which traverse granite or gneiss, or embedded in granite, and sometimes in alluvial soil formed from such rocks.

**Beryllium.** Metallic element, no. 4, symbol Be. Very similar to aluminum, it is stronger than steel and only one-quarter its weight. It is not very abundant, its main source is the mineral, beryl. Copper containing 2 percent beryllium is used for making springs. Because of its special properties the metal is used as a component in spacecraft, missiles and nuclear reactors. This accounts for its recent development on a technical scale. The metal powder is toxic.

**Binary Notation,** for numbers, is a way of representing numbers using only two digits, 0 and 1. Electronic digital computers handle numbers in this form and many people these days are having to learn it. Many school children find it both easy and fascinating as did the great philosopher and mathematician Leibniz. The ordinary, or decimal numbers, 0, 1, 2, 3, 4, 5, 6, 7, 8, 9, 10 are written in binary notation as follows: 0, 1, 10, 11, 100, 101, 110, 111, 1000, 1001, 1010. The reader might divine the rules from this. The point is you "carry 1", *i.e.,* move the digit 1 a place to the left, when you reach 2. In decimal notation you move 1 a place left when you reach 10. In other words, instead of columns for units, tens, hundreds, thousands, etc., the columns are for units, twos, fours, eights, etc. In binary notation: "$1 + 1 = 0$ with 1 to carry". Since every digit in binary notation is either 0 or 1 it requires one bit of information to specify a binary digit.

**Biological Clock.** All living organisms undergo cyclical changes in activity of some sort. These are linked to the changes in their environment which are produced by the alternation of night and day, the phases of the moon and the tides, and the cycle of the seasons. These cycles of activity frequently persist if the organism is put into a constant environment in which there appear to be no external clues as to what time or what season it is. A squirrel, for example, wakes up at about the same time each evening even when it is put into constant darkness. It is usual to refer to these activity patterns as being driven by a biological clock inside the organism. But very little is known about how these biological clocks work.

**Biological Warfare,** is the use for warlike purposes of bacteria, viruses, fungi, or other biological agents. These can be used to spread distress, incapacity, disease or death among the enemy's people or livestock. One of the strange uses to which mankind puts its science is to make naturally infective organisms even more virulent for military use. This sort of research can be done in many countries; it is much cheaper and easier to hide than nuclear weapons development. Secret attack by biological agents is supposed to be easy and it may affect the populations without damaging buildings or bridges. In 1975 the Biological Weapons Convention, 1972, signed by Britain, the United States and Russia, came into force outlawing germ warfare. Any nation suspecting violation may lodge a complaint with the UN Security Council.

**Bismuth,** metallic element, no. 83, symbol Bl, in group 5 of the periodic table. Like antimony, the stable form is a grey, brittle, layer structure; electrical conductor. It is readily fusible, melting at 264°C (507°F) and boiling at about 1420°C (2590°F). Wood's metal, an alloy with one of the lowest melting points (under 65°C (150°F), so that a spoon made of it will melt when placed in a cup of hot tea), contains four parts bismuth, two parts lead, one part tin, one part cadmium.

**Bit,** formerly the word often referred to the metal piece in the mouth of a bridled horse, now more likely to be a technical expression in the mouth of a computer expert. A bit is a unit of information; it is the information that can be conveyed by indicating which of two possibilities obtains. Any object that can be either of two states can therefore store one bit of information. In a technical device, the two states could be the presence or the absence of a magnetic field, or of an electric voltage. Since all numbers can be represented in the binary system (*see* **Binary Notation**) by a row of digits which are *either* 0 *or* 1, it takes one bit of information to specify a binary digit. Bit is short for binary digit.

**Bivalves,** shell-fish whose shell consists of two hinged valves, lying one on each side of the body, such as mussels, oysters and cockles.

**Black Death,** the plague which swept across Europe in the years 1348–50, beginning in the ports of Italy, brought in by merchant ships from Black Sea ports. It was the worst scourge man has ever known; at least a quarter of the European population was wiped out in the first epidemic of 1348. It reached England in the winter of that year. The disease was transmitted to man by fleas from black rats, though this was not known at the time, the specific organism being *Bacillus pestis.* The disease continued to ravage Europe in recurrent outbreaks up to the late 17th cent. The epidemic which raged in England in 1665 wiped out whole villages and one-tenth of London's population of 460,000. Samuel Pepys wrote a grim account of it in his *Diary.*

**Boa,** a term applied to a family of snakes of large size, some attaining a length of 9 m. They are not poisonous, but kill their prey by crushing—constriction—hence the name "boa constrictor". They occur both in the Old World and the New, but are more abundant in the latter. Most Boas retain the eggs within the body until young are fully developed, whereas the Pythons almost all lay leather-shelled eggs.

**Bode's Law,** a numerical relationship formulated by Bode in 1772 (though pointed out earlier by J. D. Titius of Wittenberg), which states that the relative mean distances of the planets from the sun are found by adding 4 to each of the terms 0, 3, 6, 12, 24, 48, 96, and dividing each number by 10. The gap between Mars and Jupiter caused Bode to predict the existence of a planet there, which was later confirmed by the discovery of Ceres and other minor planets. The law breaks down however, for Neptune and Pluto.

**Boiling-point** is the temperature at which a liquid boils. At that point the pressure of the vapor is equal to the pressure of the atmosphere. Under increased pressure the b.p. rises and under less pressure, as on the top of a mountain, it is lower. At standard atmospheric pressure (760 mm of mercury) the b.p. of water is 100°C (212°F); alcohol 784°C (173.1°F; ether 35.6°C (96.1°F).

**Borax** (Sodium Pyroborate) is a white, soluble, crystalline salt. It is widely and diversely used, *e.g.,* as a mild antiseptic, in glazing pottery, in soldering, in the making of pyrex glass, as a cleansing agent and sometimes as a food preservative. Borax occurs naturally in the salt lakes of Tibet, where it is called tincal, in California (Borax Lake, Death Valley), and elsewhere.

**Boron.** A metalloid element, no. 5, symbol B. There are two forms, one crystalline, the other amorphous. It is not very abundant in nature but occurs in concentrated deposits. It is best known in boric acid, which is used as a mild antiseptic (called boracic acid) and borax *(q.v.).* Boron compounds are essential to some plants, *e.g.,* beans. Used in the preparation of various special-purpose alloys, such as impact resistant steel. Compounds of boron and hydrogen are used as rocket fuels.

**Brass,** an exceedingly useful alloy of copper and zinc. Much brass is about two-thirds copper but different proportions give different properties. It is harder than copper and easily worked. Brass in the Bible (Matt. x, 9) probably refers to bronze.

**Breeder Reactor,** a kind of nuclear reactor which besides producing energy by the fission process also produces ("breeds") more nuclear fuel at the same time. A typical reaction is: a neutron induces fission of a U-235 nucleus which breaks up into two medium-sized nuclei and some neutrons; one of the latter then enters a U-238 nucleus turning it into U-239 which then decays radioactively *via* neptunium into plutonium which is useful fuel. There are technical problems in breeder reactors which have delayed their practical use but the "breeding" principle is so valuable that experiments have gone on for many years in, *e.g.,* Scotland and Idaho, and breeder reactors will no doubt increase in importance the more the supply of natural nuclear fuel appears to become depleted.

**Bromine.** A non-metal element, no. 35, symbol Br. member of the halogen family *(q.v.).* It is a red, evil-smelling liquid (Greek *bromos,* a stink). It is an abundant element. In the USA bromide is extracted from sea-water on a large scale. It unites readily with many other elements, the products being termed bromides. Its derivatives with organic compounds are used in synthetic chemistry. Bromoform is a liquid resembling chloroform. Bromides are used in medicine to calm excitement.

**Bronze** is primarily an alloy of copper and tin, and was one of the earliest alloys known, the Bronze Age (began c. 4,000 B.C. in Middle East) in the evolution of tool-using man coming before the Iron Age (c. 2,000 B.C.) Some modern bronzes contain zinc or lead also, and a trace of phosphorus is present in "Phosphor-bronze".

**Bubble Chamber.** An instrument used by physicists to reveal the tracks of fast fundamental particles (*e.g.,* those produced in large accelerating machines) in a form suitable for photography; closely related to the Wilson cloud chamber, but the particles leave trails of small bubbles in a superheated liquid (often liquid hydrogen) instead of droplets of liquid in a supersaturated gas; invented in 1952 by the American physicist, Dr. D. Glaser, Nobel Prizeman, 1960, and developed by Prof. L. W. Alvarez, Univ. of California, Nobel Prizeman, 1968.

**Byzantine Art** developed in the eastern part of the Roman empire after Constantine founded the city of Constantinople (A.D. 330). It has many sources—Greek, Syrian, Egyptian and Islamic—and reached its zenith in the reign of Justinian (527–65). The major art form was ecclesiastical architecture, the basic plan of which was Roman—either basilican (symmetrical about an axis) or centralized (symmetrical about a point). Arched construction was developed, and the dome became the most typical feature, although, unlike the Roman dome which was placed on a round apartment, the Byzantine dome was placed on a square one on independent pendentives. Frequently small domes were clustered round a large one as in the case of the great church of Santa Sophia (537), the climax of Byzantine architecture. Usually the churches were small and include those of SS. Sergius and Bacchus, Sta. Irene (in Constantinople), S. Vitale in Ravenna, and the much later and larger St. Mark's in Venice. Byzantine art also took the form of miniatures, enamels, jewels, and textiles, but mosaics, frescos, and icons *(q.v.)* are its greatest treasures.

# C

**Cactus,** a family of flowering plants numbering about a thousand species adapted to living in very dry situations. The stem is usually fleshy, being composed of succulent tissue, remarkably retentive of water; commonly equipped with sharp thorns which deter animals from eating them. The roots are generally very long, tapping soil water over a large area; a "prickly pear" cactus may have roots covering a circular area 7 m (23 ft.) or more in diameter. The leaves are commonly insignificant or absent, and the stem takes over the photosynthetic leaf function and becomes accordingly flattened to expose greater area to sunlight and air. In some kinds of cactus *(e.g., Echinocactus)* the stem is shaped almost like a sea-urchin.

**Cadmium.** A metallic element, no. 48, symbol Cd, chemically similar to zinc and mercury. Used in alloys to lower the melting point, as in Wood's metal with bismuth and tin. Alloyed with copper to make electric cables. Like zinc, it is a protective metal and is used in electroplating. The cadmium-vapor lamp gives a characteristic frequency used in measuring wavelength.

**Caesium,** also spelt **Cesium,** is an alkali metal element, no. 55, symbol Cs, in first group of the periodic table. It resembles rubidium and potassium and was discovered by Bunsen and Kirchoff in 1860. It was the first element whose existence was discovered spectroscopically. The caesium atom consists of a heavy nucleus surrounded by 55 electrons, 54 of which are arranged in stable orbits, and one of which, known as the valency electron, is in a less stable orbit surrounding them. Used in the construction of photo-electric cells and as an accurate time standard (atomic clock).

**Calcium,** a silvery-white metallic element, no. 20, symbol Ca. It melts at 810° C (1490° F) and is very reactive. It was discovered by Sir Humphry Davy in 1808, but not until 1898 was it obtained pure, by Moissan. Does not occur as metal in nature, but calcium compounds make up a large part of the earth's crust. Most important calcium sources are marble, limestone, chalk (all three are, chemically, calcium carbonate); dolomite, which is the double carbonate of calcium and magnesium; gypsum, a hydrated calcium sulfate; calcium phosphate and calcium fluoride. Igneous rocks contain much calcium silicate. Calcium compounds are essential to plants and are used in fertilizers. Animals require calcium and phosphorus for bone and teeth formation; deficiency is treated by administration of calcium phosphate. Strontium is chemically similar to calcium, and the radioactive strontium 90 from atomic "fall-out" is therefore easily assimilated by the body.

**Carbon,** a non-metallic chemical element no. 6, symbol C, which occurs in crystalline form as diamonds and graphite; amorphous forms of carbon include charcoal and soot, while coke consists mainly of elementary carbon. The biochemistry of plants and animals largely hinges upon carbon compounds. The study of carbon compounds is called Organic Chemistry. **Carbon 14.** A radioactive isotope of carbon, with a half-life *c.* 6,000 years, used in following the path of compounds and their assimilation in the body. Also used in determination of the age of carbon-containing materials such as trees, fossils and very old documents.

**Carbon dioxide.** Commonest of the oxides of carbon. It is formed when carbon and its compounds are burnt with abundant supply of air, and when carbon compounds are oxidized in the respiration process of animals. The atmosphere contains carbon dioxide to the extent of about 325 ppm and is increasing by about 1 ppm per year, principally because of the burning of fossil fuels and possibly because of deforestation which not only leaves more oxidisible material but lowers the amount of carbon dioxide removed by photosynthesis.

**Carbon monoxide** is a colorless gas with no taste or smell. It is formed when coal and coke are burnt with a restricted supply of air; the blue flame to be seen in a coke brazier, for instance, is the flame of carbon monoxide. This gas is very poisonous, forming with the haemoglobin of the blood a compound which is useless for respiration and cherry red in color, which gives a visible sympton of poisoning by carbon monoxide. With nickel it forms a volatile compound, called nickel carbonyl, and this reaction is the basis of the Mond process for extracting nickel.

**Cardinal Virtues,** according to Plato these were justice, prudence, temperance, fortitude—*natural* virtues as distinct from the *theological* virtues of the Roman Catholic Church, faith, hope, charity. The phrase "seven cardinal virtues", combining the two, figures in mediaeval literature. *See* **Sins, Seven Deadly.**

**Cat,** the general name for all members of the class *Felidae* of the carnivorous order, from the lion down to the domestic cat. The latter is believed to be descended from the European and African wild cats. Egypt is credited with having been the first country in which the cat was domesticated.

**Ceramics,** are substances in which a combination of one or more metals with oxygen confers special and valuable properties. These include hardness, and resistance to heat and chemicals. Ceramic comes from the Greek word for pottery, and pottery materials of mud and clay were probably the first man-made ceramics. Nowadays the range is enormous and growing; apart from all the pottery materials, there are firebricks, gems, glasses, concretes, nuclear reactor fuel elements, special materials for electronic devices, colored pigments, electrical insulators, abrasives, and many other things. The scientific study of ceramics is part of materials science. The need to design ceramic objects has inspired great art, and the production of ceramics has become a major industry.

**Cerium,** a scarce metallic element, no. 58, symbol Ce, discovered by Berzelius in 1803. A mixture of cerium and thorium nitrates is used in the manufacture of gas mantles, which owe their incandescent property to the deposit of cerium and thorium oxide with which they are coated.

**Chalcedony,** a mixture of crystalline silica and amorphous hydrated silica, *i.e.,* of quartz and opal. It has a waxy lustre, and is much used by jewellers for necklaces, bracelets, etc. Commonly it is white or creamy. Its bright orange-red variety is called carnelian; its brown variety, sard. Chrysoprase, plasma, bloodstone are varieties which are respectively pale apple-green, dark leek-green, green with red spots.

**Chemical Warfare.** This term is usually restricted to mean the use in war of anti-personnel gases, aerosols and smokes, although explosives, napalm, herbicides and defoliants are also chemical agents that are used in war. Antipersonnel chemical weapons may be classified as *(a)* vesicants

(agents which produce skin blisters, *e.g.,* mustard gas); *(b)* lacrimators (*e.g.,* the original tear gas, CN, and its British-developed successor CS now preferred for riot control); *(c)* sternutators (sneeze and vomiting agents, usually arsenic compounds, *e.g.,* Adamsite DM); *(d)* nerve gases (extremely lethal agents which incapacitate the nervous system, *e.g.,* the G-agents developed during the second world war and the more powerful **V**-agents developed subsequently); *(e)* lung irritants *e.g.,* phosgene and chlorine). Most of these chemicals can be lethal at sufficiently high concentrations and for this reason it is doubtful whether there exists the "humane" chemical agent which instantly incapacitates but leaves no long-term side effects.

The first occasion when poison gas was used on a large scale was in the first world war; more than 100,000 fatalities resulted from the use of principally chlorine, phosgene and mustard gas. World-wide revulsion at the hideous effects of chemical weapons and their potential as indiscriminate weapons of mass destruction resulted in the Geneva Protocol of 1925 which prohibited the use of both chemical and bacteriological weapons. It has now been ratified by over 90 nations including all the major powers (although Japan and America are only recent signatories). The Protocol has been generally well observed although notable violations have been by the Italians in Abyssinia (1935–6), the Japanese in China during the second world war and the Americans in South East Asia in the 1960s. It has however failed to prevent the continual development and stock-piling of lethal chemical agents by many nations, although recently there have been moves towards chemical weapons disarmament. *See also* **Biological Warfare.**

**Chestnut,** the fruit of trees of the genus *Castanea,* members of the family *Fagaceae. C. sativa* is the sweet or Spanish chestnut, C. *dentata* the American chestnut and C. *crenata* the Japanese chestnut. The nut is edible. The wood is used in carpentry and fencing.

**Chivalry** an international brotherhood of knights formed primarily during the 13th century to fight against the infidels in the Crusades. For the French the major battle was against the Moslems in the Holy Land and North Africa, the Spaniards fought the same enemy in their own country, and the Germans were concerned with the heathen of Baltic lands, but Chaucer's "very perfect gentle knight" had fought in all these areas. One did not easily become a knight who had to be of noble birth and then pass through a period of probation, beginning as a boy page in the castle of some great lord, serving his elders and betters humbly while he was taught good manners, singing, playing musical instruments, and the composition of verse. Probably he learned Latin, but he certainly learned French, which was the international language of knights as Latin was of scholars. At fourteen he became a squire and learned to fight with sword, battle-axe and lance, and to endure conditions of hard living while carrying out his duties of waiting on his lord, looking after his horses, and in time accompanying him in battle. Only if he showed himself suitable was he finally knighted by a stroke of the hand or sword on the shoulder from the king or lord. Knighthood was an international order and had its special code of behavior; to honor one's sworn word, to protect the weak, to respect women, and defend the Faith. To some extent it had a civilizing effect on the conduct of war (*e.g.* knights of opposing sides might slaughter each other in battle but feast together after), but, since war was regarded as the supreme form of sport, it cannot be said to have contributed to peace.

**Chlorine,** a gaseous element, no. 17, symbol Cl, of the halogen family, first isolated in 1774 by Scheele by the action of manganese dioxide in hydrochloric acid. It unites easily with many other elements, the compounds resulting being termed chlorides. The gaseous element is greenish-yellow, with a pungent odour. It is a suffocating gas, injuring the lungs at a concentration as low as 1 part in 50,000, and was used during the first world war as a poison gas. Has a powerful bleaching action, usually being used in form of bleaching powder, made by combining lime and chlorine. Also a valuable disinfectant; used, for instance, in rendering water of swimming baths sterile.

**Christmas** means "mass of Christ" from the old English *Cristes maesse,* which is celebrated by the Western church on 25 December. The actual day on which Christ was born is not known and there is some uncertainty about the year, 25 December as the day of Nativity was not generally observed until the 5th century A.D., though, as the winter solstice, it had long been observed as a pagan festival of *sol invictus* (unconquered sun). The first Christmas card dates from about 1843 and the Christmas tree, of pagan origin, was introduced into England from Germany where it had been a tradition since the Middle Ages. Santa Claus is a corruption of Santa Nikolaus (St. Nicholas) patron saint of children, whose feast day properly falls on 6 December.

**Chromium,** a very hard, bluish-white metal element, no. 24, symbol Cr, melting at very high temperature (above $1,900°$ C ($3,450°$ F). Its chief ore is chromite or chrome iron-ore (ferrous chromite). "Ferrochrome" is produced by heating chromite and anthracite in an electric furnace, and chrome steels are prepared by adding the pre-calculated amount of ferrochrome to melted steel. Best known chrome steel is stainless steel first made by Brearley in 1912 and since then developed greatly at Sheffield. A typical formula is 18 percent, chromium, 8 percent, nickel, 74 percent, iron. Equally important are Stellite alloys, containing chromium, cobalt, tungsten (or molybdenum), which have made possible modern high-speed cutting tools. Dies used in manufacture of plastics are commonly of chrome steel. The elementary metal finds little use alone except in chromium-plating for motor cars, etc.

**Chromosomes,** the structures contained within the nucleus of every animal and plant cell by which genetic information is transmitted. The chromosome number in somatic (body) cells is constant for each species of plant and animal, *e.g.,* man (46), cat (38), mouse (40) honey bee (16), fruit fly *Drosophila* (8), potato (48). Chromosomes are long molecules composed of deoxyribonucleoproteins (*i.e.,* proteins and DNA). Human chromosomes have been the subject of much recent research since it has been found that certain disorders are associated with chromosomal aberration, e.g., in Mongolism an extra chromosome is present. *See also* **Genes.**

**Clouds** are formed by the cooling of moist air, the type depending on the way the air cools and the height at which condensation occurs. There are three main classes: (1) high cloud (about 6,100 m; 20,013 ft)—cirrus (delicate and fibrous) cirrostratus (thin white veil), and cirrocumulus (delicately rippled) consisting of ice crystals; (2) medium cloud (above 2,100 m; 6,890 ft)—

altostratus (dense, greyish veil) and altocumulus (broken flattened cloudlets)—chiefly water particles, often supercooled; (3) low cloud (from near ground to 2,100 m)—cumulus (fair weather, broken, dome-topped), cumulominbus (heavy, towering to great heights), stratocumulus (layer of globular masses or rolls), stratus (like fog but off the ground), nimbostratus (low, rainy cloud). The highest clouds of all, and the rarest, are the noctiluccent, seen only on summer nights in high latitudes. They form at about 80 km (50 mi) above the earth and consist of ice-coated dust from meteors.

**Coat of Arms,** in heraldry, a device containing a family's armorial bearings. In medieval times an actual coat upon which such device was embroidered.

**Cobalt,** element no. 24, symbol Cr, a white metal melting at $1,490°$ C ($2714°$ F). Two main ores are *cobalt glance* (in which the element is combined with arsenic and sulphur) and *smaltite* (cobalt arsenide). The principal sources are Ontario and Zaïre. Various cobalt alloys are important, *e.g.,* stellite, ferrocobalt and carboloy. Its monoxide is an important coloring medium, and is used for coloring glass and porcelain blue.

**Coca,** a S. American shrub, *Erythroxylon coca,* also cultivated in Java. The leaves yield cocaine, classified as a dangerous drug. When the natives chew the leaves they are enabled to withstand hunger and fatigue, as cocaine acts both as a mental stimulant and as an anaesthetic on the mucous lining of the stomach.

**Composite Materials,** or more simply composites, are materials which derive useful properties by combining the virtues of two or more components. Combining clay with straw to make tougher bricks is an ancient example in which fibers (straw) are embedded in a matrix or body (the clay). A modern example is fiberglass in which glass fibers are embedded in a plastic matrix. Nature also uses composites as in bamboo in which a lignin matrix binds together the fibers of cellulose to make a light strong structure. Composites may contain flakes or particles embedded in the matrix instead of fibers—it depends on the application. Although the idea is not new composite technology has made rapid strides in the last few decades guided by scientific insight into the nature of solids and the origin of their strengths and weaknesses. The motivation had been that scientifically designed composites offer materials with exceptional strength/weight ratio, desirable magnetic properties and other technological advantages which meet the extreme demands of a variety of industries. For example, composite aluminum containing boron fibers or resin containing graphite fibers can have strength/weight ratios over twice that of high strength solid aluminum. Composites of many kinds are now widespread in industrial use and are attracting much research and development.

**Computer,** a technical device for accepting an input of information, processing this information according to some prescribed program of operations and supplying an output of processed information. Many types of operation can be performed on many types of information and computers are now indispensable in science, business, warfare, government and other activities. Early thinkers in this field were Pascal (17th century), Babbage (19th century) and Turing (1930s), but electronic computers as we know them appeared during the second world war and the first commercial machine was on sale in 1950. Computers are millions of times faster than human beings at computing; and the introduction of computers into an organization does more than just speed up the calculations, it tends to transform the whole nature of the organization. The possibilities for future developments seem enormous. Analog computers and digital computers are two different kinds stemming from the difference between *measuring* and *counting*. Analog types handle data that is repeated by physical quantities of continuously variable size such as voltages or lengths. These quantities can be made to vary like the quantities in a problem which the computer is set to solve; the problem is thus solved by analogy. A slide rule is a rudimentary analog computer in which numbers are represented by lengths of rule. Digital computers handle actual numbers expressed in digits and the quantities in the problem are represented by discrete numbers. These can all be expressed in binary form and thus stored or handled in bits. *See* **Bit, Binary Notation.**

**Continental Drift.** The hypothesis of drifting continents is due to F. B. Taylor, an American geologist who published his theory in 1908, and to the Austrian meteorologist Alfred Wegener in 1910. The latter was impressed by the matching coasts of South America, and Africa, which seemed to him to fit together like the pieces of a jigsaw puzzle. Since then many other people have taken up and developed the idea. According to Wegener, at one time there were two primary super-continents. Laurasia and Gondwanaland. The one in the northern hemisphere consisted of North America, Europe, and the northern part of Asia. Its southern counterpart included Antarctica, Australia, India, Africa and South America. These super-continents broke up, and their various bits moved apart. In particular, the southern hemisphere continents drifted radially northwards away from the south pole, and the two Americas shifted westwards from Europe and Africa. What would have been the leading edges of the land masses on this hypothesis, are now heavily buckled up into mountain belts, such as the Cordillera and the Alpine-Himalayan chain. The resistance afforded to drifting by the strong ocean floors may well have been the cause of such structures. Despite the wealth of geological facts which have a bearing on the problem of continental drift, none of these has been able to decide the issue in a conclusive manner. Further studies of rock magnetism *(q.v.)* and of fossil climates should ultimately establish the concept of continental drift on a firm basis.

**Copper,** one of the most familiar of metals, element no. 29, symbol Cu, used in ancient times as an alloy with tin in producing bronze, and preceding iron as an industrial material. Copper ores are most abundant in the USA, Chile, Canada, Zambia and Zaïre. All copper compounds are poisonous.

**Coral,** an order of small marine animals closely related to the sea-anemone, but differing from it in their ability to develop a limy skeleton. They multiply sexually and by budding. The structure of the coral secretions assumes a variety of forms, fan-like, tree-like, mushroom shape, and so forth. Red coral (the skeleton of *Corallium rubrum*) is mainly obtained from the Mediterranean. The coral reefs of the Pacific and Indian Oceans are often many miles in extent. Living corals occur only in warm seas at about 23° C (73° F).

**Corona** *or* **Solar Corona,** the outer atmosphere of the sun. This glows by virtue of light emitted by the sun and scattered by electrons and dust particles at various heights in the sun's atmosphere and also by light emitted from ionised atoms in the corona itself. Corona light is much fainter than the bright disc of the sun and is invisible against the normal blue of the sky. During total solar eclipses, the corona can be seen by the human eye as a faint glow extending irregularly outwards a few solar diameters from the sun. The sun's atmosphere extends much further than this but is invisible to the eye at large distances from the sun. The corona gases are thought to be very hot (millions of degrees) and in complex violent motion; the gross structure of the corona is connected with the sunspot cycle.

**Crusades** were military expeditions undertaken by some of the Christian nations of Europe with the object of ensuring the safety of pilgrims visiting the Holy Sepulchre and to retain in Christian hands the Holy Places. For two centuries nine crusades were undertaken: First,. 1095–99, under Godfrey of Bouillon, which succeeded in capturing Jerusalem; Second, 1147–49, led by Louis VII of France, a dismal failure, which ended with the fall of Jerusalem; Third, 1180–92, in which Richard I of England took part, making a truce with Saladin; Fourth, 1202–4, led by French and Flemish nobles, a shameful expedition, resulting in the founding of a Latin empire in Constantinople; Fifth, 1217–21, led by John of Brienne; Sixth, 1228–29, under the Emperor Frederick II; Seventh, 1248–54, under St. Louis of France; Eighth, 1270, under the same leadership, but cut short by his death on an ill-judged expedition to Tunis; Ninth, 1271–72, led by Prince Edward of England, which accomplished nothing. Millions of lives and an enormous amount of treasure were sacrificed in these enterprises and Jerusalem remained in the possession of the "infidels". The chief material beneficiaries were the Italian maritime cities; the chief spiritual beneficiary was the Pope; but in literature and the arts both Europe and the Levant benefited enormously from the bringing together of the different cultures.

**Cryogenics** (Greek roots: productive of cold) is the science dealing with the production of very low temperatures and the study of their physical and technological consequences. "Very low" is often taken to mean below about $-150°$ C ($-300°$ F). The growth of cryogenics (essentially a 20th-cent. science) is connected with the discovery of how to liquefy all gases including even helium which resisted liquefaction until 1908. Scientifically, cryogenics is important partly because special phenomena (*e.g.,* superconductivity appear at lower temperatures and partly because more can be learned about ordinary properties by studying them in the absence of heat. Technologically, cryogenics is becoming more and more significant, for example, liquefied gases are rocket propellants, superconductors make valuable magnets, tissue-freezing techniques (using very cold liquids) have been introduced into surgery. *See* **Absolute Temperature.**

**Cuneiform,** (Latin = *wedge-shaped*), an ancient method of writing by impressing wedge-like strokes into tablets of damp clay which when dried and hardened formed a permanent script, form writing developed from its original pictographic form into a phonetic writing and can be traced back to the non-Semitic Sumerians of ancient Mesopotamia, the earliest civilization known to us. It passed to the Semitic Accadians of Babylonia in the 3rd millennium B.C. who adapted it to their own language. Decipherment by Sir Henry Rawlinson, 1835.

# D

**Dactylopterus,** a fish of the gurnard family, with wing-like pectoral fins; sometimes known as the flying fish, though that appellation is more generally given to *Exocaetus exiliens.*

**Daguerreotype,** the first practical photographic process, invented in Paris by M. Daguerre during the years 1824–39. The light-sensitive plate was prepared by bringing iodine in contact with a plate of silver. After exposure a positive image came by development of the plate in mercury vapour. Even for open-air scenes the first daguerreotypes involved exposure of 5–10 minutes. The picture came in one copy and the process was therefore of limited use. The wet collodion process (1851) rendered the technique obsolete.

**Dead Sea Scrolls,** a group of ancient Jewish documents, consisting of scrolls and fragments which have been recovered since 1947 in the vicinity of Qumran near the Dead Sea and which represent one of the most important finds ever made in the field of biblical archaeology and Christian origins. The scrolls written in Hebrew or Aramaic, were found in caves, the first by chance by an Arab shepherd in 1947. These consisted of biblical texts older by a thousand years than the earliest Hebrew manuscript of the Old Testament (A.D. 895). Many fragments have since been discovered, comprising the whole of the Old Testament with the exception of Esther. In addition there are commentaries and other non-biblical writings, including one called "The War of the Sons of Light with the Sons of Darkness". The writing on the scrolls indicates that they were written over a period of two centuries, the greater proportion before the birth of Christ. A nearby ruin is believed to have been the home of a religious sect called the Essenes, to whom the scrolls belonged. By the aid of the latest scientific techniques, including radiocarbon tests, the age of the scrolls is being accurately determined. An account of the scrolls and their implications is given in Edmund Wilson's *The Dead Sea Scrolls: 1947–1969.*

**Deciduous Trees** are such as shed their leaves at certain seasons as distinguished from evergreens or permanent foliaged trees or shrubs.

**Deserts,** vast, barren, stone or sandy wastes where there is almost no rainfall and little or no vegetation. These regions are found in the interior of the continents Africa, Asia and America between 20° and 30° north and south of the equator. Europe is the only continent without deserts. The most famous are the Sahara, the largest in the world, the Gobi desert of central Asia, the Kalahari desert of southwest Africa and the great Australian desert. The marginal extension of deserts (desertification) is a topic of considerable debate. The increasing size of deserts is thought to result from either climate change or the interference by man.

**Deuterium** or "heavy hydrogen". The second isotope of hydrogen; the third is called tritium. Deuterium atoms have in their nuclei a neutron as well as a proton; tritium nuclei have two neutrons and one proton. In ordinary hydrogen gas about one out of every 5,000 atoms is a deuterium atom. Deuterium was discovered in 1932 by Professor Harold Urey. The oxide of deuterium corresponding to water is called "heavy water". The nucleus of the deuterium atom is called a deuteron. An antideuteron consisting of anti-proton and anti-neutron was produced at Brookhaven in 1965, the first compound anti-nucleus ever to be produced.

**Diamond,** a mineral, one of the two crystalline forms of the element carbon (the other is graphite), the hardest known substance, used as a gem and in industry. India was the first country to mine diamonds (the Koh-i-noor, which means "mountain of light", known since 1304, came from Golconda near Hyderabad and came into British possession when the Punjab was annexed in 1849). The celebrated diamond mines of South Africa were discovered in the 1870s. Other important diamond producing countries are Zaïre, USSR, Congo, Ghana, Sierra Leone, Namibia, Angola, Tanzania. The world's biggest diamond is the 3,106-carat Cullinan, discovered near Pretoria, South Africa, in 1905. Diamonds can be made artificially by subjecting carbon to very high temperatures and pressures; many industrial diamonds are made this way. Antwerp is the main diamond centre of the world, London the main marketing centre, Amsterdam the main diamond cutting centre.

**Diatoms.** One-celled algae, comon in fresh and salt water. Distinctive feature is the siliceous wall which is in two halves, one fitting over the other like the lid of a box. These walls are often very finely and beautifully sculptured. The diatoms constitute a class of the plant kingdom known as the Bacillariophyta. *Diatom ooze* is a deep-sea deposit made up of diatom shells. *Diatomite* or *diatomaceous earth* is the mineral form that such diatom oozes assume (sometimes known as kieselguhr which mixed with nitroglycerine yields dynamite).

**Dinosaur,** the name given to a group of extinct reptiles of the Mesozoic period, some of which were of immense size—much larger than crocodiles. *See* **Diplodocus.**

**Diplodocus,** one of the best known of the extinct mammoth dinosaurs. Fossil remains have been discovered in the Jurassic rocks of the United States. Some reached a length of over 24 m.

**Diptych** was a folding two-leaved tablet of wood, ivory, or metal, with polished inner surfaces, utilised for writing with the style by the ancient Greeks and Romans. The same term was applied to the tablets on which the names of the persons to be commemorated were inscribed in the early Church. In art any pair of pictures hinged together is styled a diptych, a set of three, a triptych.

**DNA (Deoxyribonucleic acid),** a polymer molecule in the form of a double-strand helix containing many thousands of sub-units. Contains the genetic information coded in sequences of sub units called bases. The Nobel Prize for medicine was awarded in 1962 for the discovery of the structure of DNA: that for 1968 for interpreting the genetic code and its function in protein synthesis. *See* **Nucleic Acids.**

**Doldrums,** a nautical term applied to those areas of the Atlantic and Pacific within a few degrees of the Equator towards which the trade winds blow and where the weather is calm, hot and sultry. Pressure is low and the air often rises to produce heavy tropical rainfall and squalls, rendering navigation difficult.

# E

**Ebony,** a name applied to various hard black woods, the best of which are grown in Mauritius and Sri Lanka. There are also Indian and American varieties. Only the inner portions, the heartwood, of the trees are of the necessary hardness and blackness. Ebony is largely used in ornamental cabinet work, for piano keys, canes, etc.

**Edda,** the name given to two important collections of early Icelandic literature—*the Elder or Poetic Edda,* poems handed down from the 9th and 10th cent., probably Norwegian in origin, and the *Younger* or *Prose Edda* of Snorri Sturluson compiled about 1230. They treat of mythical and religious legends of an early Scandinavian civilisation.

**Electron Microscope.** A microscope in which beams of electrons are focused by magnetic lenses in a manner analogous to the focusing of light beams in the ordinary optical microscope. Modern electron microscopes have very high resolving power and can magnify up to 1,500,000 times, making it possible to explore the cell and the virus. A development of the electron microscope is the scanning electron microscope (stereoscan), developed at Cambridge, which can examine an essentially thick object, giving a very large depth of focus.

**Elementary Particle,** one of the basic constituents of the material universe. The idea that matter consists of tiny particles goes back to classical times but the modern concept of the atom grew out of the chemistry and physics of the 19th cent. With the discovery of the electron in 1897 and the rise of nuclear physics in the 20th cent., the chemical atom was understood to be a structure built of even more fundamental particles—the electron, the proton and the neutron. In the last few decades, many more particles have been discovered, especially in the study of cosmic rays and by the use of large accelerating machines like those at CERN (Geneva) and Brookhaven National Laboratory (Long Island, New York). Among the later discoveries are the neutrino, the positron, the antiproton, the muon, the pion. These differ in electric charge and mass and other intrinsic properties and many have only a very short lifetime before they change into something else. Whether there is a small number of really elementary particles out of which all the others can be constructed is an unanswered question at the frontier of contemporary physics.

**Elements.** In chemistry, substances which cannot be separated into two or more simpler chemical substances. 91 elements are found naturally on the earth, some are observed spectroscopically in the stars and planets, and a further fourteen have been made artificially. Between them these elements can appear in some 1,200 different isotopes, of which 317 occur in Nature. (There are 274 stable isotopes among 81 stable elements.)

**Emerald.** The rich green variety of beryl (beryllium aluminum silicate). The color is due to the presence of chromium oxide.

**Equator,** the imaginary great circle of the earth, every point of which is 90 degrees from the earth's poles, and dividing the northern from the southern hemisphere. It is from this circle that the latitude of places north and south is reckoned. The celestial equator is the circle in which the plane of the earth's equator meets the celestial sphere (the imaginary sphere, in which the observer is at the centre, used for representing the apparent positions of the heavenly bodies).

**Erbium,** belongs to the group of rare-earth metals discovered by Mosander in 1842. Element no. 68, symbol Fr.

**Ether,** in chemistry, is a volatile inflammable liquid composed of carbon, hydrogen and oxygen. It is a valuable anesthetic obtained by heating alcohol with sulfuric acid. In physics, in the 19th century, all space was supposed to be filled with a substance called ether, the chief property of which was to carry light waves, *i.e.,* light was supposed to be waves in this all-pervading medium known as the ether. Speculation and experiment concerned with the ether were very fruitful in advancing physics. Ultimately the attempts by Michelson and Morley to detect the motion of the earth through the ether were unsuccessful in this respect but profoundly successful in stimulating the theory of relativity. The ether concept has now been abandoned.

**Etruscans,** people believed to have come from Asia Minor who colonised Italy about 900 b.c., settled in what is now Tuscany and part of Umbria, reached the height of their civilization about 500 b.c., and were ultimately absorbed by the Romans. They were skilled technicians in bronze, silver and goldwork, and excelled in the art of granular decoration.

**Eucalyptus.** This genus includes 300 species of evergreen, leathery-leaved trees native to Australia. The oils yielded by different species vary a great deal in their scent and other properties and are chiefly used in pharmacy and perfumery; about 30 species produce oils suitable for medicinal purposes. Various species produce timber.

# F

**Fallout.** Radioactive material produced by nuclear explosions which may cause bodily and genetic damage. (1) *Local fallout,* due to the return to earth of larger particles, occurs locally, and within a few hours after the explosion; (2) *Tropospheric fallout,* due to particles which remain in the troposphere and come down within a month or so, possibly all over the world, but within the altitude in which the explosion occurred; (3) *Stratospheric fallout,* which comes from fragments taken up into the stratosphere and then deposited, in the course of many years, uniformly all over the globe. The two radioactive materials which have given rise to the greatest concern for the health of the individual are strontium-90 and iodine-131. Both these materials are liable to become concentrated in certain parts of the human body, strontium-90 in bone and iodine-131 in the thyroid gland. Radiation exposure may produce genetic effects, that is effects which may show up in succeeding generations. An extensive survey was carried out by scientists of the US Atomic Energy Commission on the islands of Bikini atoll, site of some 23 nuclear tests, 1946–58. Their records, published in 1969, revealed that the intensity of radioactivity underneath the point of explosion was still exceedingly high. Most of the radiation remaining was due to the radioactive isotope caesium-137. The variation in intensity from one place to another seemed to be correlated with the variations of vegetation: where there was little vegetation weathering had been rapid. (The nuclear test ban treaty, 1963, applies to all nuclear tests except those held underground.)

**Fault,** a term designating a breakage coupled with displacement of geological strata.

**Ferrites** are compounds containing iron, oxygen, and one or two of a certain range of other possible metallic elements. Ferrites have recently become very important technically because, unlike ordinary magnetic materials, they combine strong magnetism with electrical insulating properties. Ferriterod aerials are now common in portable radios, and ferrite devices are used in radar.

**Fission, Nuclear.** A nuclear reaction in which the nucleus of an atom (*e.g.*, uranium 235, plutonium) captures a neutron, and the unstable nucleus so produced breaks into two nearly equal fragments and throws out several neutrons as well. In biology the term fission is applied to reproduction by fragmentation of a single-cell organism, as in amoeba.

**Fleas.** Fleas are small parasitic insects belonging to the order *Aphaniptera* (so called because these creatures have no wings). They obtain their food by sucking blood from their host. They are laterally compressed, which immediately distinguishes them from lice. The human flea *(Pulex irritans)* is able to jump vertically a distance of over 18 cm.

**Fluorine,** chemical element, no. 9, member of the halogen family, symbol F, it is found in combination with calcium in fluorspar, and occurs in minute quantities in certain other minerals. Discovered by Scheele in 1771, it was first obtained by Moissan in 1886. A pale yellow gas, it is very reactive and combines with most elements except oxygen. Its acid, hydrogen fluoride, etches glass, the fluorine combining with the silicon to form volatile silicon fluoride. Organic fluorine compounds have found use as very stable polymers which resist a wide variety of chemical actions.

**Fluorspar,** a mineral; chemically calcium fluoride. Can be colorless, green or yellow, but is most common purple. Blue fluorspar under the name of Derbyshire "blue John" has been used for ornamental purposes.

**Frankincense** is of two kinds, one being used as incense in certain religious services and obtained from olibanum, an Eastern shrub, the other is a resinous exudation derived from firs and pines, and largely used in pharmacy.

**Fresco,** a painting executed upon plaster walls or ceilings, a technique which has remained unchanged since it was practised by the great Renaissance artists.

**Frost** occurs when the temperature falls to, or below, 0° C (32° F), which is freezing point. Hoar frost is applied to the needles or feather-like crystals of the ice deposited on the ground, in the same manner as dew. Glazed frost is the clear icy coating which may be formed as a result of rain falling on objects whose temperatures are below the freezing point. These layers of ice, often rendering roads impassable for traffic, damaging overhead power and communication systems and endangering aircraft, can also be caused by condensation from warm, damp winds coming into contact with very cold air and freezing surfaces.

**Functionalism,** in architecture, a movement originated by Le Corbusier, Swiss-born French architect and town-planner, who applied the austere principles of the Purist movement in painting to his own art. From about 1924 he designed in concrete, steel and glass, buildings in which every part had a significance in terms of function on the theory that objects created to carry out their particular function to perfection cannot help being beautiful. "A house is a machine for living in." The style was in vogue between the two wars, and although its severity became somewhat modified, it is still the basis of most modern architecture.

**Futurism,** an Italian school of art and literature initiated by Marinetti, an Italian writer and mountebank friend of Mussolini at a later period. Its origin took the form of a manifesto published in Paris in 1909 in which Marinetti glorified violence, war and the machine age. In its aggression it favored the growth of fascism. One of the distinctive features of Futurist art was the use of the principle of "simultaneity" in which the same figure (*e.g.*, a woman descending a flight of stairs) is represented in successive positions like film "stills" superimposed on each other. In spite of two further manifestoes it was not until 1911 that the first examples of Futurist painting and sculpture appeared by the artists Severini, Balla and Boccioni. Apart from the principle of simultaneity, Futurism derived from Cubist and Post-impressionist techniques. The movement faded out early in the first world war.

# G

**Gallium,** metallic element, no. 31, symbol Ga. related to aluminum, but which can be cut with a knife. It was discovered spectroscopically by L. de Boisbaudran in 1875. Long before Mendeleyev had predicted that an element with its properties would be found to fill the then existing gap in the Periodic Table; this gap came immediately below aluminium, so he suggested the name "eka aluminium" for it.

**Gargoyle,** a projecting spout for carrying off water from the roof gutter of a building. Gargoyles are found only in old structures, modern waterpipe systems having rendered them unnecessary. In Gothic architecture they were turned to architectural account and made to take all kinds of grotesque forms—grinning goblins, hideous monsters, dragons and so forth.

**Garnet,** a group of minerals; chemically they are orthosilicates of the metals calcium, magnesium, titanium, iron, aluminium. Garnets can be colored yellow, brown, black, green or red; the blood-red garnet is an important gemstone.

**Gas** is an elastic fluid substance, the molecules of which are in constant rapid motion, and exerting pressure. The technique whereby gases are liquefied depends on increasing pressure and diminishing temperature. Each gas has a critical point; unless the temperature is brought down to this point no amount of pressure will bring about liquefaction. Last gas to be liquefied was helium (1908) which boils at 209° C (408° F)

**Genes,** the elementary units of heredity. They exist as highly differentiated regions arranged along the length of the chromosomes which the nuclei of cells carry. A chromosome may carry hundreds or even thousands of genes, each with its own particular structure and specific properties. The position of a particular gene on a chromosome is called its locus. The material of the gene is DNA *(q.v.)*.

**Genetic Code.** The elucidation of the structure of DNA *(q.v.)* for which Crick, Wilkins and Watson were jointly awarded the 1962 Nobel Prize for medicine, revealed the code or chemical dictionary out of which messages serving as blueprints for living structures can be made.

**Genetic Engineering** is the name given to the introduction of human choice and design criteria into the construction and combination of genes. This refers not to breeding by selection, a traditional process, but to the biochemical alteration of the actual DNA in cells so as to produce novel self-reproducing organisms. Such manipulations became possible when techniques were recently discovered for severing and rejoining DNA molecules and inserting sections into them. Many people regard this development as fraught with enormous significance. Like nuclear power, it can lead to good, to evil, and to accidental hazards, not all of which can be foreseen. Thus when biologists realised they could create new lifeforms, *e.g.*, bacteria, with novel genes, they appreciated that, as well as medically beneficial strains, new virulent forms might by accident be produced and escape into the world. Ultimately, not imminently, men may be able to design the genes of higher animals and even of man himself and thus consciously influence biological evolution. Many scientists have been brought by these possibilities up against an old problem: is science going too far too fast?

**Geneva Convention,** an agreement made by the European Powers at Geneva in 1864, establishing humane regulations regarding the treatment of the sick and wounded in war and the status of those who minister to them. All persons, hospitals, hospital ships are required to display the Geneva cross—a red cross on a white ground. A second conference held at Geneva in 1868 drew up a supplementary agreement. An important result of this Convention was the establishment of the Red Cross Society in 1870.

**Geothermal Energy.** Some of the heavy elements within the earth's crust are radioactive and this gives rise to a temperature rise towards the centre of the earth. The practical exploitation of this geothermal energy comes about when there are hot springs or geysers. It is believed that these are caused by rainwater slowly percolating down to the hot rocks and blowing out as steam. The homes of people living in Reykjavik are heated by geothermal steam and there are a number of small power stations in various parts of the world. Although the costs in the few cases where geothermal power has actually been exploited are remarkably low, the expense of drilling, etc., required when attempting to exploit the heat in the rocks where surface manifestations do not occur, is likely to limit the use of this source of power.

**Germanium.** A grey, hard, brittle chemical element, no. 32, symbol Ge, chemically related to silicon and tin. Discovered by Winkler in 1886. Its richest ore is germanite containing 6% of the metal. Coal is also a relatively rich source. Since 1948 it has assumed great importance as a semi-conducting material for making transistors. Because of this it has been so intensively studied that more is known about its physical properties than about those of any other element.

**Glaciers** form in the higher Alpine ranges, and are immense consolidated masses of snow, which are gradually impelled by their force down the mountain-sides until they reach a point where the temperature causes them to melt, and they run off in streams. From such glaciers the five great rivers, the Rhine, the Po, the Rhône, the Inn and the Adige, have their source. The longest of the Swiss glaciers is the Gross Aletsch, which sometimes extends over 16 km. Some of the glaciers of the Himalayas are four times as long. The Muir in Alaska is of enormous magnitude, and that of Justedals Brae in Norway is the largest in Europe.

**Gladiators** were professional athletes and combatants in ancient Rome, contesting with each other or with wild beasts. At first they were drawn from the slave and prisoner classes exclusively, but so much were the successful gladiators held in esteem that men came to make a profession of athletics, and gladiatorial training schools were established. When a gladiator was vanquished without being killed in combat, it was left with the spectators to decide his fate, death being voted by holding the hands out with the thumb turned inward, and life by putting forth the hands with the thumb extended. Gladiatorial shows were the chief public displays in Rome from the 3rd to the 4th century A.D.

**Glass** is an amorphous, man-made substance, fluid when hot, solid, though fragile, when cooled. It is made of sand mixed with an alkaline flux, usually soda or potash. While hot, glass can be formed into almost any shape by molding, blowing or, since the early 19th century, by machine pressing. Unrefined glass normally has a greenish tinge, due to the iron content of most sands, but it is transparent or at least translucent. To make truly colorless glass is a difficult and expensive process, and such glass resembling the natural mineral, rock crystal, is given the name crystal. Glass can be tinted by the addition of various metallic oxides, cobalt producing blue, manganese mauve, etc. Because it is at once solid and transparent, glass is the perfect material for windows for which it has been used since Roman times. And since it can be made cheaply and is easy to clean, it has been used for containers in homes, shops and pharmacies, again since Roman days. Glass can also be made into things of beauty, by the use of colored glass and by cutting, engraving, painting and gilding. The earliest vessels of glass so far found come from Egypt and date back to *c.* 1500 B.C. With the invention of glass-blowing in the 1st century A.D., the use of glass spread throughout the Roman empire. Many varieties were made, including superb art glass like the Portland vase. The Arabs were great glassmakers from the 7th to 15th century. During the Renaissance the Venetians created luxurious art glass, rich in color and often manipulated into fantastic forms. Bohemia's 17th-century glass is wonderfully engraved with pictures and cut into glittering facets. During the 1670s in England George Ravenscroft invented a new, heavy, water-clear crystal, with an addition of lead as the magic ingredient, and English lead glass is still the basis for all modern crystals.

**Gueiss,** a metamorphic rock usually containing quartz, felspar and mica. It is banded, the light-coloured minerals being concentrated apart from the dark minerals.

**Gold.** Metallic element, no. 79, symbol Au (Latin *Aurum*) related to silver and copper, the coinage metals. The greatest amount of gold is obtained by treating gold-bearing quartz by the cyanide process. The gold is dissolved out by cyanide solution, which is then run into long boxes filled with zinc shavings when the gold is precipitated as a black slime. This is melted with an oxidizing agent which removes the zinc.

**Golden Number,** the number of any year in the metonic cycle of 19 years, deriving its name from the fact that in the old calendars it was always printed in gold. It is found by adding 1 to the number of the year A.D. and dividing by 19, the remainder being the Golden Number; or, if no remainder, the Golden Number is 19. The only use to which the Golden Number is put now is in making ecclesiastical calculations for determining movable feasts.

**Gothic,** the predominant style of architecture in northern Europe from 12th–15th century. Its most striking characteristic is the extensive use of the pointed arch, but this is really a mere external reflection of the important structural invention of the 12th century, that of the rib vault, whereby the whole pressure of the stone vaulting is supported on slim ribs which cross each other at a rising center. On the outside of the building, the pressure from the vaults is caught up and supported by flying buttresses. A complete Gothic construction gives a marvellous effect of airy lightness, also of something striving upwards, towards the heavens, and this is further accentuated when the churches are crowned by lofty towers and spires. The vital structural elements of Gothic architecture were first put into use in the abbey church of St. Denis in Paris *c.* 1140. The style was further developed in a glorious sequence of cathedrals in northern France: Notre Dame in Paris, Rheims, Amiens, Beauvais and others. When, as in Chartres, the windows are filled with stained glass of glowing colours and the doorways flanked with magnificently carved life-size figures of saints and apostles, the whole effect is one of unsurpassed solemnity and grandeur. From France the style spread to other lands in each of which it developed its own characteristics; thus the English churches tended to have massive towers and delicate spires and, as at Salisbury, were often set in open grounds surrounded by lawns; Flemish and Dutch churches were sometimes built of brick as were those in north Germany and Scandinavia; in Spain the Flamboyant style was followed. The main Gothic cathedral in Italy, that of Milan, although begun in 1386 was not completed until the early 19th century. Late English Gothic is seen, for example, at King's College Chapel, Cambridge, Henry's Chapel at Westminster and St. George's Chapel at Windsor (all *c.* 1500). Gothic is also found in secular buildings, *e.g.,* Little Wenham Hall in Suffolk, the castle at Ghent, the town halls of Louvain and Middelburg and the streets of Gothic houses in Bruges still in use today. Virtually Gothic as a style (excluding the "Gothic revival" of 19th century England) ended at the close of the 15th century. Gothic art is best seen in the illuminated manuscripts of the 13th and 14th century and in the church sculpture. Its characteristic is a complete departure from the cool, perfectionist realism of classical times with distortion to produce emotional effects. The human figures are not ideal forms but recognizable as people we might meet in the street: yet there was also the element of wild imagination, intricate design and a wealth of feeling which might be grotesque, humorous, macabre, or even obscene. Gothic style also found expression in the decorative arts, retaining its architectural character even in small-scale works like caskets, chalices and the like in metalwork and ivory.

**Gravitation.** One of the four, possibly five, types of force known to physics. The others are electromagnetic, nuclear (two types) and color forces. Gravitational forces are an attraction that one piece of matter has for another; they dominate astronomical phenomena, but inside the atom they are negligible compared with the other types of force. Einstein's General Theory of Relativity is the only theory at present extant which attempts to interpret gravitational forces in terms of more fundamental concepts.

**Gresham's Law** states that if money, *i.e.,* money with the higher intrinsic value, and bad money are in circulation together, the bad money will tend to drive out the good money from circulation. For instance, the good money is more likely to be melted down or demanded in payment by foreign creditors.

**Gunpowder,** also called "black powder", the oldest of explosive mixtures, consists of saltpeter, sulfur and charcoal, intimately mixed, the proportions being varied for different intended uses.

**Gypsum,** a whitish mineral consisting of hydrated sulfate of calcium. The finest gypsum is alabaster. When heated gypsum is converted into the powder called Plaster of Paris; the water it loses can be taken up when the plaster is wetted, and the reconversion of Plaster of Paris into gypsum accounts for the way in which the former sets hard. The name "Plaster of Paris" came from the location of important gypsum quarries in the Montmartre district of Paris. It was found after the flood disasters of January 1953 that gypsum could undo the effect of sea-water. By spreading it for the rain to wash into the soil, thousands of acres of farmland in Holland and Britain were made productive again.

**Gyroscope** is a symmetrical rapidly rotating object, typically wheel-like, which because of its mass and rotation possesses a lot of the dynamical property known as angular momentum. Basic dynamical laws tell us that angular momentum is conserved and a consequence of this is that the axis of rotation tends to stay pointing in the same direction. Disturbing influences make a gyroscope's motion complicated but the general effect of the presence of a gyroscope attached to any body is to help to stabilise the body's motion. This is made use of in reducing the rocking of ships and in compasses and control systems in aircraft, torpedoes and missiles.

# H

**Haematite,** ferric oxide, one of the principal iron ores, containing about 70% of the metal. It is usually found in kidney-shaped masses, and is specular, red or brown, in thin fragments but greyish in bulk.

**Haemoglobin,** the pigment containing iron which gives red blood corpuscles their color. It is a respiratory pigment, having the property of picking up oxygen when the blood passes through the lungs to produce the compound known as oxyhaemoglobin. In other parts of the body the oxyhaemoglobin breaks down, liberating oxygen, which is used in the oxidation process (respiration) that the body tissues carry on.

**Hafnium,** a metallic element, no. 72, symbol Hf, discovered by Coster and Hevesy in 1922 and important in the atomic-energy field. It occurs in most zirconium minerals to the extent of about 5 percent.

**Halogens,** the group name for the four non-metallic elements fluorine, chlorine, bromine and iodine. The term "halogen" means "salt-producer".

**Harmonic Motion,** regular periodic motion of the kind exemplified by a ball bobbing up and down at the end of a spring, and by the piston in a steam engine. It may be simple (simple harmonic motion) or composed of two or more simple harmonic motions. In simple harmonic motion the acceleration is proportional to the distance of the moving body from its original rest position.

**Heat,** after prolonged controversy over whether or not heat is a "substance" (formerly called "caloric"), it was established in the 19th century that heat is a form of energy; it is in fact the combined kinetic and potential energy of the atoms of which a body is composed. Heat can be turned into other forms of energy, *e.g.,* a red hot body loses heat by radiating it in the form of electromagnetic waves ("radiant heat"—chiefly infra-red rays). Heat may also be transferred from one place to another by conduction and, in fluids, by convection. All three processes occur when a glowing fire heats a room. A unit quantity of heat is the calorie, which is the amount of heat sufficient to raise the temperature of 1 g of water by 1° C. In general, adding heat to a body raises its temperature. The number of calories required per gram of material to raise the temperature 1° C is called the *specific heat* of the material. However, adding heat may not raise the temperature—but may instead cause a change of state, *e.g.,* from solid to liquid (melting) or liquid to gas (evaporation). The amount of heat required to melt 1 gram of a solid is called the latent heat of melting. Similarly, there is a latent heat of evaporation. Strictly speaking, the specific and latent heats of a substance depend on how much its pressure and volume are allowed to vary during the measurements. Water has a high specific heat, and this makes the oceans a vast heat reservoir, a factor of great meteorological significance. The science of heat is called thermodynamics, and is of great importance in physics and chemistry.

**Helium,** a gaseous element, no. 2, symbol He, first discovered by means of the spectroscope in the sun's atmosphere. This discovery, made in 1868 by the astronomer Sir Norman Lockyer, was followed in 1895 by Sir William Ramsay's proof that the element existed on earth. He found it in the uranium ore, elevite. Later it was established that helium is formed by the radioactive decay of many elements which emit *a*-particles (nuclei of helium atoms) and is contained in all radioactive minerals. The largest source of helium is natural gas, the richest in helium being the gas from certain wells in Utah, USA. Next to hydrogen, helium is the lightest gas known, has a lifting power equal to 92% of hydrogen and the advantage that it is inert and non-inflammable. It is used for inflating airships. Ordinary air contains 1 part in 200,000 of helium. It was the last gaseous element to be liquefied, this being achieved by Onnes in 1908 in Leyden. Liquid helium has many remarkable properties only imperfectly understood. As well as being scientifically fascinating it is indispensable in cryogenics *(q.v.)* as a medium for cooling other substances to temperatures near absolute zero. Hydrogen fusion in the "H bomb" produces helium.

**Hellenic Art.** The art of ancient Greece may be roughly divided into three periods: the prehistoric period (*c.* 1500–1000 B.C.) of the bronze age Mycenaeans; the archaic period (*c.* 600–500 B.C.); and the classical period (*c.* 500–300 B.C.). Of the first period centered on Mycenae in Peloponnesus but extending to the coasts of Asia and the city of Troy we can mention only the massive stone gateways and the shaft graves of Mycenae, where the archaeologist Schllemann discovered painted vases, gold cups, bronze swords and ornaments of what had once been a great, if primitive, civilization. During the archaic period sculpture was the principal form of art expression. The magnificent male and female figures are reminiscent of Egyptian art, but are distinctive in liveliness of facial expression. The vase-paintings of this period became more elaborate, depicting scenes from mythology or ceremonial events. Typical of classical Greek art is the representation of the beautiful and healthy human body deliberately posed and often carrying out heroic or athletic acts. The vast majority of these statues are known to us only through Roman copies. The *Hermes* of Praxiteles

(born *c.* 385 B.C.) is possibly the only existing statue which can be assigned with any degree of certainty to an individual artist. Almost the whole of the Greek genius in architecture was expended on temples which are all basically similar in design—a rectangle with a low-pitched gabled roof resting on side walls. The three orders Doric, Corinthian and Ionic mainly referred to the type of column used, but naturally the whole building was influenced thereby. Some of the main buildings are on the Acropolis, a hill outside Athens, on which stand the Parthenon (from the outer frieze of which the Elgin marbles, now mostly in the British Museum, were taken), the Erechtheum, famous for its Porch of Maidens, and the gateway known as the Propylaca with its broad flight of marble steps. Apart from that on vases, no Greek painting has come down to us, although Greek painters existed and were noted in their time. All we have are copies in mosaic and fresco made by the Romans, at Naples and Pompeii. Of Greek literature in prose, verse and the drama little can be said here. To the early period (*i.e.,* the archaic age) belong Homer's *Iliad* and *Odyssey.* Hesiod's long poem *Work and Days* and Sappho's love poems, and Pindar's Odes. The period of Pericles in the 5th cent. B.C. produced more great literature than any comparable period in history: the philosophical writings of Plato and Aristotle, the tragedies of Aeschylus, Euripides and Sophocles, the comedies of Aristophanes—all these are still part of the European tradition, and together with Greek architecture played a major part in the Renaissance.

**Hellenistic Art,** the age of the period of Greek civilization which began with the conquests of Alexander the Great (356–323 B.C.) and lasted until his former empire (which encompassed most of the Middle East and part of North Africa) was conquered by the Romans in 146 B.C. Culturally it was an important period because it spread Greek culture far beyond its original boundaries—even as far as the north of India, and its centers spread from Athens to the cities of Alexandria in Egypt, Antioch in Syria and Pergamum in Asia Minor. But equally Eastern culture spread to the West: democracy was replaced by absolute monarchy, cosmopolitanism took the place of the Greek tendency to believe that all who were not Greeks were barbarians, and mystical philosophies took the place of Greek rationalism. This was a sensuous, secular, pleasure-loving, rootless society, and these tendencies were reflected in its art. Hellenistic sculpture was sensual, effeminate and violently emotional, depicting individuals and not always noble or beautiful ones. (Classical Greek sculpture was idealistic, showed types rather than individuals and appealed to the intellect rather than the emotions.) Some of the best examples came from the school at Pergamum and later from the island of Rhodes, and the titles themselves speak of their nature: *The Dying Gaul, Gaul Slaying his Wife and Himself* and the famous *Laocoön* (representing Laocoön and his two sons being crushed by two enormous serpents). All these date from about 240 to 50 B.C.—for the culture did not immediately end with the Roman conquest. The enormous frieze of the altar of the temple in Pergamum depicts a battle between gods and giants with tremendous realism and brutal violence far removed from the serene art of classical times. Portrait sculpture is typical of Hellenistic art, where it may almost be said to have been invented, since such ventures in the past had been idealistic rather than realistic. The great Hellenistic cities were geometrically planned and fine public buildings made their appearance in which the slender and graceful Ionic of the ornate Corinthian columns took the place of the more austere and heavy classical ones. Alexandria was celebrated for its vast libraries and was the center of a brilliant intellectual life (the Septuagint or Greek translation of the Bible was prepared here). Here too worked the mathematicians Euclid and Archimedes, the physicians Erasistratus and Herophilus, and the geographer Pytheas. But Hellenistic literature was a pale reflection of the glories of the past and we mention only the comedies of Menander and the pastoral verse of Theocritus of Syracuse.

**Hickory,** several species of American tree of the walnut family, remarkable for its very hard, solid, heavy white wood, and bearing an edible, four-lobed nut.

**Hieroglyphics** are the earliest form of pictured symbolic expression, and are supposed to have been introduced by the ancient Egyptians. They consist of rude depictions of animals, plants, signs and objects, and in their later examples express, in abridged form, ideas and records from which significant historical information has been gleaned. The deciphering of Egyptian hieroglyphics long formed an ardent study, but gradually the key to the riddle was discovered, and most of the ancient records can now be understood. Besides the Egyptian there are also Hittite, Minoan and Mayan hieroglyphic scripts.

**Hittites,** an ancient race (often mentioned in the Old Testament) who inhabited Cappadocia (region of Eastern Asia Minor) from the third to the first millennium B.C. Excavations have revealed that they attained a high level of civilization round about 1350 B.C. The Hittites were rivals of Egypt, disputing with the Pharaohs the mastery of the Middle East. They were the first to smelt iron successfully.

**Holly,** a hardy evergreen shrub, largely grown in England. Its bright dark green prickly curved leaves and clusters of red berries are familiar in all parts of the country, and used as house decoration between Christmas Eve and Twelfth Night, probably a relic from Roman and Teutonic customs. Its wood is white and hard, valued for carved work, while its bark yields a gummy substance which is converted into birdlime.

**Hologram,** a photographic record, taken under special optical conditions, of light reflected from a scene or object. The hologram is typically a piece of film. However it is nothing like a photographic negative of the ordinary kind; for one thing it will show an unintelligible pattern of light and dark patches. Nevertheless if it is illuminated (again under special optical conditions) the light coming through it will form a *three dimensional* image of the original object. Another radical difference between a hologram and an ordinary film is that if the hologram is cut up, each fragment can be used to construct the entire image. Holography, as a method of recording and reproducing photographic information, was conceived by Gabor in 1947 but was only fully realised in practice after the invention of the laser *(q.v.),* which made available powerful sources of coherent light. The use of laser light is one of the "special conditions" referred to above. Technical applications are being explored in many laboratories. Gabor received the 1971 Nobel prize for his discovery and invention.

**Horizon,** the limit of vision, the apparent line where sea and sky, or land and sky meet. This is termed the visible horizon. An ordinary person at the height of at 1.5 m (5 ft.) can see 4.8 km (3 mi.) at 6 m (20 ft.) can see 9.6 km (6 mi.) at 15 m (49 ft.) can see 14.8 km (9.2 mi.) and at 305 m (1000 ft.) can see 67.5 km (42 mi.). The figures are approximate.

**Hornblende,** the commonest member of the amphibole group of minerals, a silicate of calcium, magnesium, iron and aluminum, of a dark green color. It is a constituent of numerous rocks, including diorite, syenite and hornblende schist.

**Hospitallers, Knights,** were of the order of St. John of Jerusalem, at first devoted to the aid of the sick, but afterwards military monks, who became prominent figures in the Crusades of the 12th century. They adopted the Benedictine black habit with the eight-pointed cross worn by the modern St. John's Ambulance Brigade. In 1309 they took Rhodes, but were expelled by the Ottomans in 1522. In 1530 the emperor Charles V gave them the island of Malta, which as Knights of Malta, they held until 1798, when they were dislodged by Napoleon. The Knights still survive as a sovereign order, with headquarters in Rome. *See* **Templars**

**Hydrocarbons** are compounds of carbon and hydrogen. They include the *paraffins,* which are saturated compounds (*e.g.,* methane); the ethylene, acetylene and other series which are unsaturated; compounds with ring structures, *e.g.,* benzene, naphthalene and anthracene. Petroleum is composed almost entirely of hydrocarbons.

**Hydrochloric Acid,** a solution of hydrogen chloride gas in water, and resulting in considerable quantities as a by-product of the soda-ash or salt-cake manufacture. Its solution forms the common hydrochloric or muriatic acid of commerce. It is present to the extent of nearly half a per cent. in the digestive juice secreted by the stomach.

**Hydrocyanic Acid,** cyanide of hydrogen or prussic acid; very poisonous, and of the odor of bitter almonds. It is formed by the action of acids on sodium or potassium cyanide. Used to kill wasps (and in the gas chamber in the USA). It is a very important chemical on account of the reactions of its derivatives in many synthetic fluids. Discovered by Scheele in 1789.

**Hydrogen,** symbol H, the simplest element, atomic number of 1, colorless, and the lightest of all substances. Cavendish in 1766 was the first to recognize that it was an element. It is 14·4 times as light as air, and is found in a free state in volcanic regions. It can be obtained by the action of metals on acids, and forms an explosive mixture with air, burning with oxygen to form water. Commercially it is used to produce the very hot flame of the oxy-hydrogen blowpipe for cutting metals; to fill balloons and airships; to harden certain oils and render them suitable for margarine- and soap-production. The gas can be liquefied, and the presence of the isotope deuterium was detected by Urey in 1931 in the residue of the evaporated liquid. The third isotope, tritium, is very rare. *See also* **Deuterium, Tritium.**

**Hydroponics,** or soilless growth, is the craft and science of growing plants in liquid nutrients instead of soil. Originally a laboratory technique, hydroponics has become since the 1930s a practical method of vegetable, fruit and flower production on both small and large scale. Basically, the growing plants have their roots in troughs of nutrient solution, either in or out of doors. Advantages include: much higher crop yields; the close control of weeds and diseases; quicker growth; and, very important, the possibilities of growing food in places where ordinary agriculture would be impracticable, *e.g.,* deserts and stony land, city roofs, in houses and in remote situations like Antarctic stations. Hydroponics is widely practised and contributes usefully to agriculture and horticulture in many countries, including the USA, Britain, India and France. Its value in spaceships and planetary colonies has often been pointed out by technological prophets.

# I

**Ibis,** belongs to a family of birds related to the stork. The sacred ibis of ancient Egypt is now extinct in Egypt but is found in the lakes and swamps of the Sudan near the Upper Nile. It has white and black plumage and a long curved beak. Other species are found elsewhere, the Glossy Ibis (black plumage glossed with purple and green) occasionally visiting England.

**Ice Ages.** Periods during which the continents were partly or largely covered by ice-sheets and glaciers. The present-day ice-sheets of Greenland and Antarctica are relics of the most recent ice age (one of the eight major ones during the past 700,000 years), which began in the Pleistocene and ended about 10,000 years ago. During this last great glaciation ice sheets covered the northern part of Europe, Asia and North America. There is strong evidence that periodic changes in the earth's orbit around the sun caused the ice ages. The earth is now in one of its warm periods though there are signs that a moderate cooling trend has begun.

**Ichthyosaurus** was a gigantic marine reptile of the Mesozoic age. The fossils are mostly found in the lias formation. Some were over 9 m (29.5 ft).

**Igneous Rocks** are such as have been molten under conditions of great heat at some stage in their history: *e.g.,* granite, basalt.

**Iguanodon,** a genus of extinct dinosaurs, whose fossils are found in the Jurassic and Cretaceous rocks. Iguanodons were 4.5–7.6 m (15–25 ft) long, and walked on their hind legs, the front legs being small and adapted for grasping the branches of trees on the leaves of which they fed.

**Iliad,** the great epic poem of ancient Greece attributed to Homer (*c.* 700 B.C.). It consists of ancient folk tale and saga, welded into an artistic unity, having as plot the carrying off of Helen by Paris to Troy and the subsequent siege of Troy.

**Indium,** a scarce lead-colored metallic element, no. 49, symbol In, found in zinc blende in Saxony and certain other ores. Discovered in 1863 by Reich and Richter. It is an important material in the manufacture of transistors.

**Industrial Revolution.** The name, first given by Engels in 1844, to describe the radical changes that took place in Britain during *c.* 1730–1850 to transform a mainly agricultural country into one predominantly industrial. It began with the mechanization of the textile industry (Hargreave's spinning jenny, 1764, Arkwright's water-frame, 1769, Crompton's mule, 1770, and Watt's steam-engine, 1785), with subsequent major developments in mining, transport and industrial organi-

zation. It was based on Britain's rich mineral resources, particularly coal and iron ore. With the use of the steam-engine as power, industry became concentrated round the coalfields and the great new industrial towns developed—Birmingham, Manchester, Newcastle and Glasgow. Britain became supreme in constructional ironwork (Telford, George and Robert Stephenson). Canals, bridges, railways and ships were built, and great advances were made in the practical application of scientific principles. Aided by colonial exploitation Britain became the most prosperous country in the world. The new industrial capitalists began to replace the country squires as ruling class. But the great accumulation of wealth at one pole of society was matched at the other by poverty and misery, for child labor, long working hours, low wages and slums were features of the industrial revolution in its infancy. As with all great technological developments, the industrial revolution produced related changes in all fields of social life—in politics, art, religion, literature and morals, and with the rise of democracy, social reforms.

**Infra-red Rays** *or* **Radiation.** This is the range of rays which come between the visible red rays and the ultra-short Hertzian radiation. The wavelengths involved range between 0·75 micron (0·75 $\times$ 10 $^{-6}$m) and 100 micron (1 millimeter). Infra-red rays penetrate haze; hence landscapes obscured by haze or cloud can be photographed using plates sensitive to infra-red. Many substances strongly absorb these rays and thereby become hot; this happens in toasting bread. Many industries use infra-red lamps for drying paints and lacquers. Very important to chemists, as a tool in the investigation of the structure of compounds, since various groups of elements absorb infra-red radiation at a characteristic frequency. Infra-red astronomy has developed in recent years.

**Insects.** This huge class of invertebrate animals includes about 100,000 species. Insects are ubiquitous except in the sea, only a very few species being adapted to marine existence. Characteristic features are: the body is divided into three parts, head, thorax and abdomen: the head carries a pair of antennae, the thorax three pairs of legs and usually two pairs of wings. The most primitive insects constituting the sub-class *Apterygota* are wingless. The other sub-class, *Pterygota*, is divided into the *Exopterygota (Hemimetabola),* which have a simple metamorphosis, *e.g.,* cockroach, and the *Endopterygota (Holometabola),* with a complex metamorphosis, *e.g.,* butterfly, bee. Although many are parasitic on man, animals and plants, innumerable animals and some plants use them as food, and many flowering plants are dependent on a variety of insects for pollination leading to the development of seeds and fruits.

**Instruments, Musical.** Musical instruments may be classified in a number of ways, but in general they fall into one of the three main classes, String, Wind and Percussion, according to how the sound in produced. **Stringed Instruments** are those which produce the sound by the vibration of a string: *(a)* by plucking, as in Harp, Lyre, Psaltery, Zither, Lute, Guitar, Balalaika, Ukelele, Harpsichord; *(b)* by friction (bowed), as in Crwth, Rebec, Viol, Violin, Marine Trumpet, Hurdy-Gurdy; *(c)* by striking (hammered), as in Dulcimer, Pianoforte, Clavichord; *(d)* by wind (blown), as in the Aeolian Harp. **Wind Instruments** are those in which the air in the instruments is set in vibration: *(a)* by blowing into a tube (flue-voiced), as in Recorder, Pandean Pipe,

Flute, Organ; *(b)* by means of reeds (reed-voiced), as in Oboe, Clarinet, Saxophone, Bagpipe, Cor Anglais, Bassoon, Organ reed-stops; *(c)* those in which the sound is produced by the vibration of the player's lips against the mouthpiece (lip-voiced), as in Bugle, Horn, Trumpet, Tuba, Trombone, Saxhorn, Flügelhorn, Cornet. In a modern orchestra these are known as the *Brass:* instruments of the flute, oboe and clarinet families as the *Woodwinds.* Then there are the **Percussion Instruments,** which include the Drums, Cymbals, Tambourines, Castenets.

**Insulin** is a hormone which controls the supply of sugar from the blood to muscles. The breakdown of sugar provides energy. In diabetes there is a lack of insulin, causing a build-up of blood sugar which can be released by the injection of insulin. It is secreted by the islet tissue of the pancreas, from which it was isolated in 1922 by Banting and Best. Dr. F. Sanger of Cambridge won the 1958 Nobel Prize in Chemistry for isolating and identifying its amino acid components. Prof. Dorothy Hodgkin and her team at the Dept. of Molecular Biophysics at Oxford succeeded in determining the structure of insulin, a task which would not have been possible without the electronic computer. In 1980 insulin became the first product of genetic engineering techniques to reach clinical trials.

**Intelligence.** Intelligence has been variously defined as the innate potential of a person to learn and understand; to make appropriate judgments; to see the relationships between things; to profit from experience; or to meet adequately new problems and conditions in life. There are many lines of evidence to show that intellectual capacity is closely related to heredity and influenced by environmental factors. The idea of intelligence testing was first devised by the French psychologist Binet at the beginning of this century. He was asked by the French government to invent a test which would weed out backward children in state schools, and thus save public money and avoid holding back the work of the class by teaching children who were incapable of learning at a given standard. Briefly, a series of problems are given to a large number of children and it is thus found out which series can be solved by the average child of a given age-group; if a child of 7 can only pass the tests suitable to the average child of 6, then his mental age is 6. The intelligence quotient or I.Q. is discovered by dividing his mental age by his chronological age and multiplying by 100. A gifted child can usually be spotted at an early age. Although I.Q. tests are the standard method of estimating intelligence, they are not universally accepted as a criterion; a teacher's general judgment may be the best assessment. High intelligence may be inherited, but fail to develop to the full because facilities for education are not available. Recent research suggests that the growth of the brain may be permanently affected by under-nutrition at the time of its fastest growth (the last weeks before birth, and, to a lesser extent, the first weeks after birth). At this vulnerable period even quite minor deprivation can affect the rate and ultimate extent of growth of the brain. This has significance not only for the severely under-nourished babies in the poor parts of the world, but for babies of low birth weight in our own communities.

**Interferon,** identified in 1957 as a defense protein produced in animal cells, is also produced in human immune systems. Its use as a possible anti-cancer agent as well as for other complaints has been limited by extraction problems. Modern production is likely to be by genetic engineering. In 1980 the amino acid sequence was determined for the 150 residues in human interferon.

**Iodine,** a non-metal element, no. 53, symbol I, member of the halogen family *(q.v.),* a substance formerly exclusively obtained from the ribbon-wrack seaweeds. These were burnt and the ashes (kelp) extracted with water. After concentrating the iodides, these were distilled with manganese dioxide and sulfuric acid to yield iodine vapor which was condensed in stoneware bottles. Nearly all iodine now in use is derived from the iodine salt present in Chile saltpeter (natural sodium nitrate). Iodine is used in photography, as an antiseptic solution in alcohol or potassium iodide (tincture of iodine), and in medicine. Discovered by Courtois in 1812.

**Ions,** electrically charged atoms, or groups of atoms. Atoms of the metals lose electrons to become positively charged ions, *e.g.,* the sodium ion ($Na^+$) has one electron less than the atom. The non-metal ions are negatively charged, *e.g.,* the chloride ion ($Cl^-$) has one electron more than the atom. Similarly, a group like the sulfate ion ($SO_4^{2-}$) has more electrons than the constituent atoms. Thus, the hydrogen atom without its electron is a hydrogen ion or *proton* and the helium atom without its two electrons is a helium ion or *alpha-particle.* When an electric force is applied to certain solutions, the ions into which molecules of the dissolved substance are broken up are attracted to the oppositely charged electrodes, their movements constituting an electric current through the solution. In the same way gases, including air, conduct electricity by virtue of free ions. Combustion, radioactivity and ultra-violet and cosmic radiations produce ionisation.

**Iridium,** a white and very hard metallic element, no. 77, symbol Ir, discovered by Tennant in 1804. It occurs naturally as an alloy with platinum or osmium; tips for fountain-pen nibs have been made from the former native alloy. The former standard meter was composed of platinum-iridium alloy as are parts of scientific apparatus and surgical tools that must be non-corrodible.

**Iron** is a metallic element, no. 53, symbol Fe (Latin *ferrum*), occurring widely in nature in such ores as haematite, loadstone (magnetic iron oxide), spathic ore and iron pyrites. It is extracted by a process known as smelting, with coke and limestone in a furnace. Its many uses are familiar, the most important being in the manufacture of cast- and wrought-iron products and of steels, which are alloys mainly of iron with added carbon and various metals. Iron rust is formed by the action of oxygen and water, and is a coating of iron oxide.

**Isotopes.** When one talks of an element, say, uranium or lead, the name of the element is a generic name for a collection of uranium species and lead species. The different species are called isotopes. For any particular element, the number and arrangement of electrons around the nucleus are the same in all the isotopes, so all the isotopes have the same chemical properties. Soddy has described isotopes as "elements, the atoms of which have similar outsides but different insides". For example, in the nucleus of the uranium isotopes, U 235, U 238 and U 239, there are respectively 143, 146 and 147 neutrons, but all have 92 protons. The isotopes have different atomic weights, in this instance respectively 235, 238 and 239. But all have the same chemical properties.

# J

**Jacobins,** a French revolutionary club or party, formed in 1789, and accustomed to meet at a Jacobin convent, hence the name. It became a controlling force in the Revolution, especially in the movement which led to the Terror. Robespierre was its chief spokesman.

**Jade,** an exquisite kind of hardstone, ranging in color from a whitish green to a deep mauvish brown. It can be translucent or opaque and sometimes it is veined. Jade is the common name for two minerals—the rarer *jadeite* (found in Burma, Tibet and China), a sodium-aluminum-silicate, and *nephrite* (found in New Zealand, China, Turkestan and Siberia), a calcium-magnesium silicate. The presence of small quantities of other chemicals accounts for the wide range of shades. In China jade has for centuries been looked upon with great veneration, magical powers have been ascribed to it, and it has been fashioned into ritual objects, also into miniature sculptures of animals or even whole landscapes, charming to look at and incredibly skilfully made. The Chinese word for jade is *yü,* used as a symbol for all that is noble, beautiful and pure.

**Janissaries,** an élite band of Ottoman foot soldiers who acted as the Sultan's bodyguard. They were conscripts, raised by the "tribute of children" from conquered Christian countries, mainly Serbia and Albania. First recruited under Murad I (14th century). They were not allowed to marry. They gained great power under the Ottoman Empire. In 1826 the Sultan Mahmud II had them massacred.

**Jasper,** a precious stone of the chalcedony variety, opaque, and colored red, brown, yellow and sometimes green. It was greatly esteemed by the ancients, the Bible having numerous allusions to it.

**Jelly-fish.** The jelly-fishes, which have gelatinous, translucent bodies fringed at the margin with delicate tentacles, constitute the coelenterate order *Seyphozoa*. The mouth, with a squarish opening, is seen on the underside, and there are four horseshoe-shaped sex organs.

**Jet Stream,** a meteorological term coined in 1946 to describe the relatively narrow belt of strong winds (160–320 km/h; 99–199 mph) at levels in the atmosphere from 5–11 km (3–7 mi). These winds are important in forecasting weather, and can be a valuable aid to aircraft. From the ground, where there may be little wind, the jet stream can sometimes be seen as high cirrus cloud moving across the sky at high speed.

# K

**Kinetic Energy,** the energy possessed by a particle or body in virtue of its motion. If the motion is destroyed, *e.g.,* by the impact of the body with an obstacle, the kinetic energy vanishes, being turned into some other form of energy such as heat and sound. If the body has mass $m$ and speed $v$ its kinetic energy (leaving out corrections due to relativity) is $1/2mv^2$.

**Koto,** a musical instrument in general use in Japan consisting of a series of 13 silken strings stretched across a curved wooden surface, and played with the fingers. Each string is 1.5 m (69 in.) long, and has a separate bridge so fixed as to give the vibration necessary for the note it has to produce. It is a sort of horizontal harp, and in the hands of an expert player is capable of giving forth excellent music.

**Krypton,** one of the rare gas elements, no. 36, symbol Kr, occurring in the air to the extent of 1 part in 20 million. It was discovered in 1898 by Ramsay and Travers. It is used in gas-filled electric lamps.

# L

**Labradorite,** a felspar rich in calcium and of a pearly lustre on cleavage, found in masses in igneous rocks, the best samples of which come from Labrador.

**Labyrinth,** *or* **Maze,** a combination of roads and passages so constructed as to render it difficult for anyone ignorant of the clue to trace the way to the central part. The Egyptian labyrinth near Lake Moeris had 3,000 rooms, half of them subterranean and the remainder above ground. The labyrinth in Crete, according to Greek myth, was built by Daedalus to house the Minotaur. There was one at Lemnos, renowned for its stalactite columns; and another at Clusium constructed by Porsenna, King of Etruria, about 520 B.C. The labyrinth in which Fair Rosamond was concealed was at Woodstock. Hampton Court maze dates from the 16th cent.

**Labyrinthodonts,** gigantic fossil amphibians which get their name from the curious labyrinthine structure of their teeth, probably an evolutionary link between fishes and reptiles. They occur in the Carboniferous, Permian and Triassic formations, and remains have been found in Britain and other parts of Europe. Their heads were long, and their footprints, by which they were discovered, closely resemble the prints of the human hand.

**Lake Dwelling,** the name given to certain prehistoric habitations which were thought to have stood on platforms over lakes, like villages in certain Pacific islands. Recent excavations at the Lake of Burgäschi in Switzerland show that the prehistoric Swiss pile dwellings probably stood on the shores of lakes, not on platforms over the water. Also found at Mere and Glastonbury, Somerset.

**Lamellibranchs (Pelecypods),** the class of aquatic, bi-valve mollusks to which the oysters, cockles, mussels, clams and scallops belong. In these animals the body, which is compressed laterally, is enclosed in two hinged shells held together by muscular action. The gills are thin plates hence the name "lamellibranchs".

**Lapis Lazuli,** an azure-blue mineral, being a silicate of aluminum and sodium. The pigment ultramarine is made by grinding it, though artificial ultramarine has largely superseded it. The mineral (also called *lazurite*) has been used as a gemstone since ancient times.

**Laser.** A remarkable kind of light source that was discovered in 1960. With the laser it is possible to probe the behavior of matter under the influence of enormous energy densities, range and survey vast distances to microscopic accuracy and send millions of telephone and television messages between any two points that can see each other with telescopes. Laser light, in contrast to natural light, is coherent and can be expressed as a regular progression of waves carrying energy along a particular path. Thus the essential difference is that laser light is an orderly sort of wave motion in contrast to ordinary light which is inherently unsteady and therefore an inefficient carrier of information in time. The name *maser,* which is the microwave parent of the laser, derives from the expression *"m*icrowave *a*mplification by the *s* timulated *e*mission of *r*adiation". Upon application to light wavelengths the microwave part of the name lost its meaning and the term maser became generally descriptive of any device in which stimulated emission dominates.

**Laser Fusion** is a method by which it has been proposed that thermonuclear reactions may be controlled and exploited as a source of energy. The idea is to irradiate a millimeter-sized pellet of a mixture of frozen deuterium and tritium with a short ($\sim 10^{-9}$ s) but very intense pulse of energy in the form of laser light. This has the effect of both compressing the pellet by a factor of at least a thousand and heating it to about $10^{8\circ}$ C. Under these conditions, thermonuclear reactions (principally $^2D + {}^2T \rightarrow {}^4He + {}^1n$) proceed sufficiently fast that a net output of energy is obtained before the pellet explosively separates. Formidable technical problems need to be solved before laser fusion can become a practical proposition. These include the development of efficient high-powered lasers and the design of a suitable reactor that can withstand up to 100 micro-hydrogen bomb explosions per second. It is still not clear whether this method of controlling nuclear fusion is more practical than the more conventional approach involving the magnetic confinement of plasmas.

**Latent Heat** is the quantity of heat required to convert 1 gram of a substance from one form into another. For example, when a solid changes into a liquid or a liquid into a gas, the addition of heat to bring about the change produces no rise in temperature, the energy being absorbed in the form of latent heat. An equal amount is released when the process is reversed. The latent heat of fusion of ice is about 79·6 calories per gram, that of the vaporization of water about 539 calories per gram.

**Lateran Councils** were the religious conventions held in the Lateran basilica at Rome for deciding important questions of Church doctrine. The most brilliant was that of 1215 which pronounced in favor of a Crusade.

**Laterite** refers to any tropical soil or soil horizon rich in hydrated ferric and aluminum oxides which harden when exposed to the atmosphere. It is difficult to cultivate and is commonly used for bricks and road metal. Laterite buildings have been known to withstand the weathering for many centuries and a number of fine examples are found in India and S.E. Asia.

**Latitude** of a point on the earth's surface is its angular distance from the equator, measured on the surface of the earth in degrees, minutes and seconds. Thus the equator is $0°$ Lat. and the poles $90°$ Lat. (N. or S.). First determined by Hipparchus of Nicaea about 160 B.C. Latitude introduces zones of climate, *e.g.,* tropical rain, subtropical steppe and desert, temperate rain and polar.

**Lead,** a soft malleable metallic element, no. 82, symbol Pb (Latin *plumbum*), occurring in numerous ores, which are easily smelted. Its most important source is the mineral galena which consists chiefly of lead sulfide; rarely is it found free. Lead is largely used in plumbing on account of its pliability, and in nuclear reactors as a shield against radiation because of its very high density. As an alloy element it combines in the formation of type metal, stereo metal, shot metal, pewter and many other compounds. Oxides of lead are used in some types of glass and in the manufacture of paints (red lead). All lead compounds are poisonous. Leading producers of lead are the United States (Missouri), Australia (Broken Hill) and the Soviet Union.

**Leather** was made in ancient Egypt, Greece and Rome, and has through succeeding centuries played an important part in the service of man. It consists of the dressed hides or skins of animals after the process of tanning has been gone through. Untanned skins are known as pelts. Leather is classed either according to the skins from which it is made or the system of preparation employed. The best-known kinds are morocco, kid, Russian, chamois, Cordovan, grained, patent, russet, tan, calf, Hungarian.

**Lemur,** almost the most primitive member of the primate order of mammals (to which man, apes and monkeys also belong). They are noted for having strong pliant toes enabling them to use their feet as hands, and also well-developed thumbs on the hands. They have long squirrel-like tails, fox-shaped heads and large staring eyes. True lemurs are confined to the Malagasy Rep.; closely related are the "bush-babies" of S. Africa.

**Lenses,** pieces of transparent material designed to focus an image of an illuminated object. Usually of glass, but plastic lenses are common, and quartz, etc. are used for special purposes. The surfaces of the simplest lenses are parts of spheres. Lenses which are thickest, or thinnest, at the center are called convex and concave respectively. Lenses of complex shape are often used in microscopes, etc. Electron lenses are arrangements of electric or magnetic fields which focus beams of electrons, *e.g.,* on to T.V. screens.

**Lepidoptera,** the order of insects with scaly wings and bodies, to which the 90,000 butterflies and moths belong.

**Leptons.** A group of particles which include electrons, neutrinos and muons. All are much lighter than protons or any baryons *(q.v.).*

**Libretto** (It. booklet), the literary text of an opera or oratorio. Usually the composer and the librettist collaborate in the writing of an opera, but several composers (*e.g.,* Wagner) wrote their own librettos. Boito, librettist to Verdi for *Otello* and *Falstaff,* himself composed two operas *Mefistofele* and *Nerone.* Most famous of Italian opera librettists was the poet and dramatist Metastasio (1698–1782). His librettos were set to music by many composers, including Gluck, Handel, Mozart, Rossini.

**Lichens.** In every lichen, two plants are associated, one being an alga and the other a fungus. The fungus derives its food from the alga; probably the alga gains too from the association, being protected against desiccation by the fungus (an example of symbiosis). Lichens are the first plants to colonize bare rocks.

**Light,** a particular kind of electromagnetic disturbance capable of travelling through space, and

Doctor Smith

some kinds of matter, and of affecting our eyes to cause vision. Its finite speed was first demonstrated by O. Römer, using observations of the eclipses of Jupiter's satellites in 1675. In 1860 Maxwell showed that light waves are electromagnetic. Since Einstein's theory of relativity (1905) it has been generally realized that the speed of light is a fundamental natural constant. Visible light with wavelengths between about 4 and $7 \times 10^{-5}$ cm is only a small part of the electromagnetic spectrum. The speed of light in vacuum is about $2\cdot997925 \times 10^8$ m/s.

**Lightning,** the flash of a discharge of electricity between two clouds, or between a cloud and the earth, when the strength of the electric fields becomes so great as to break down the resistance of the intervening air. With "forked" lightning the actual path, often branched, is visible, while with "sheet" lightning the flash is hidden by the clouds which themselves are illuminated. "Ball" lightning or fireballs is the name given to the luminous balls which have been seen floating in the air during a thunderstorm. The Boys camera has provided much information regarding the sequence of events in a lightning discharge. It is found that a flash consists of a number of separate strokes, usually four or five, and that the discharge of electricity to earth begins with a faintly luminous "leader" moving downwards and branching at intervals. As the ground is approached a much brighter luminosity travels back along the conducting channels, lighting up with several branches. The multiple strokes which follow in fractions of a second have the same "return" nature and are rarely branched. Lightning flashes to earth damage structures, cause loss of life and endanger overhead power systems, often interrupting electricity supply. Such storms generally affect radio transmissions and present hazards to aircraft. Thunderclouds may develop energy far exceeding the capacity of our largest power generating stations.

**Limestones,** sedimentary rocks composed wholly or largely of calcium carbonate and formed by two main processes, (1) organic (skeletal remains of organisms), e.g., chalk and (2) chemical (precipitation of calcium carbonate), e.g., oolite. Marble is limestone that will polish after cutting.

**Liquid Crystals** form a special class of substance and are true liquids in that they flow easily and can be poured. However, unlike ordinary liquids, liquid crystals have their molecules arranged with geometrical regularity in one or two dimensions, so that they have a certain internal structure similar to that of solid crystals. They are fairly complicated chemicals with somewhat elongated molecules. Liquid crystals are of interest to biologists as well as to chemists and physicists, and not just because they account for the iridescence of beetles. Some body fluids are in fact liquid crystals. There are also technological applications because of their unique electrical and optical properties. They are receiving increasing attention for these reasons.

**Lithium,** a soft metallic element, no. 3, symbol Li, similar to sodium. It is very reactive and is stored under paraffin oil. It is the lightest metal element.

**Lizard,** the name given to a diversified order of reptiles, of which there are about 1,600 species. Included among the lizards are the geckos, chameleons, glass snakes, skinks and blind worms.

**Loadstone** *or* **Lodestone,** an oxide of iron, found chiefly in Sweden and Norway. Its scientific name is magnetite. It has the power of attracting pieces of iron and served as the first magnets used in compasses. One of the class of nonmetallic magnetic materials nowadays known as "ferrites" *(q.v.).*

**Locust,** insects of the grasshopper family, but much more powerful. They are inhabitants of hot countries, and often make their appearance in untold millions, like clouds, devastating all the vegetation that comes within their course. The locust-tree *(Ceratonia siliqua)* is supposed to have furnished food to St. John the Baptist in the wilderness, and its "beans" have accordingly been styled "St. John's Bread".

**Longitude** of a point on the earth's surface is the angle which the meridian through the poles and that point makes with some standard meridian. The meridian through Greenwich is usually accepted as the standard meridian and the longitude is measured east or west of that line. As the earth revolves through 360° in 24 h, 15° longitude represent 1 hour's difference in apparent time.

**LSD** (d-lysergic acid diethylamide). This hallucinogenic drug has achieved wide notoriety because of its use by certain people to give themselves abnormal mental experiences. Doctors have frequently warned against the dangers of its use. It is active in extremely small quantities and a dose as small as a fifty-millionth part of a gram can cause marked disturbances of the mental function in man. LSD has been used in the study of mental disease because it produces symptoms very similar to mental disorders such as schizophrenia.

**Lutecium,** element (no.71) of the rare-earth metal group discovered in 1907 by Urbain. Symbol Lu.

# M

**Mach Number.** Unit of flight speed. The ratio of speed of flight to speed of sound under same conditions of pressure and density. Speed of sound at sea-level is 762 mile/h (1,226 km/h), so flight speed of 381 mile/h (613 km/h) is equivalent to a Mach Number of 1/2. At supersonic speeds the Mach Number is greater than 1; subsonic speeds, less than 1.

**Macromolecules** are very large molecules about 10,000 times or more as heavy as ordinary small molecules like hydrogen. Most are built up from a large number of simple sub-units, *i.e.,* are polymers. The term macromolecule is often used in biology, e.g., starch and cellulose are biological macromolecules, both built from glucose sub-units. Other important ones are proteins and nucleic acids. The properties of macromolecules depend on the sub-units of which they are composed.

**Maelstrom,** a great whirlpool. The most famous is that off the coast of Norway, between the islands of Moskenes and Mosken, of the Lofoten group the power of which has been much exaggerated.

**Magellan, Clouds of,** the name given to a pair of small galaxies, satellite systems of our own galaxy, visible only from the southern hemisphere. On account of their relative nearness to the earth (186,000 light-years), they are receiving much attention from astronomers.

**Magenta,** a blue-red aniline dye discovered in 1859 by Sir W. H. Perkin, and named after the great battle of that year between the French and Austrians.

**Magma,** molten rock material rich in volatile constituents prior to its eruption at the surface. With the loss of volatiles it becomes lava.

**Magnesium,** a metallic element, no. 12, symbol Mg, first isolated in 1808 by Sir Humphry Davy, who prepared it by electrolyzing the chloride. Its chief ores are magnesite and dolomite. Industrially it is obtained by electrolysis. Many important light alloys contain magnesium. The metal burns with a very bright light, and for this reason it is used in photographers' flash bulbs and also in firework manufacture.

**Magnetic Storms.** These are the effects of magnetospheric storms observed world wide at ground level as fluctuations of as much as 5% in the earth's magnetic field. The largest effects are observed at high latitudes, in the auroral ovals, and are due to electric currents flowing in the ionosphere and between the ionosphere and the magnetosphere. There may be concurrent disruption of radio communications.

**Magnetism,** originally the name given to the quality of attraction for iron possessed by lodestone *(q.v.)*. Now known to be a phenomenon inseparably connected with electricity. Strong magnetic attraction is possessed by a comparatively small class of substances; iron, nickel and cobalt are the most common elements, but there are several less well known, *e.g.,* gadolinium. Many alloys have valuable magnetic properties which make possible numberless technical devices. New magnetic substances are always being developed (*see* **Ferrites**). The earth acts like a huge magnet with its axis inclined at about 11° to the axis of rotation, the magnetic poles being on the Boothia Peninsula (North Canada) and South Victoria Land (Antarctica). The magnetic field at the surface consists of the regular field of a magnetized sphere with an irregular field superimposed upon it. Variation in the magnetic forces occurs from place to place and from time to time, and maps showing the distribution over the globe of points of the same declination (*i.e.,* the angle which the magnetic meridian makes with the geographical one) are of the utmost importance in navigation. Little is known regarding the origin of the main (regular) field of the earth, but it is believed that the irregularities are due to the presence of intense electric currents in the upper atmosphere and local magnetization of rock strata. In 1967 the discovery was claimed of isolated magnetic poles, *i.e.,* north and south magnetic poles existing separately, just as positive and negative electrical charges exist separately. If this is confirmed it will probably rank as one of the most important experimental results of the 20th century, because of its significance for the theory of electromagnetism and fundamental particles. Magnetic field strengths are measured in gauss (e.g.s.) or tesla (S.I.) units.

**Magnetosphere.** The magnetic field of the earth prevents the plasma of the solar wind from directly impinging on the earth's upper atmosphere and ionosphere. The cavity thus maintained within the solar wind is known as the magnetosphere. The tenuous plasma within this cavity is partly of solar and partly of terrestrial origin, from the solar wind and the ionosphere respectively. These plasmas are subject to large perturbations, known as magnetospheric storms, triggered by fluctuations within the solar wind. These storms generate intense auroral displays, magnetic field fluctuations at ground level, and often major disturbances of the upper atmosphere and ionosphere which may result in disruption of radio communications. The inner parts of the magnetosphere contain the Van Allen radiation belts *(q.v.)*. On the sunward side the magnetosphere extends to between 12 and 20 earth radii. However, on the side of the earth away from the sun it extends, like a comet tail, for many millions of km. Jupiter's large magnetic field produces a large magnetosphere, one of the largest features in our planetary system being as large as the sun itself.

**Magnitude** in astronomy is a measure of the apparent brightness of a star, which is inversely proportional to the square of its distance. A low number indicates a bright star, and a high one a faint star. The *absolute magnitude* is a measure of *real* brightness, *i.e.,* the brightness a star would have at a standard distance away of 10 parsecs (32·6 light years). The distance can be calculated if the apparent and absolute magnitudes are known.

**Mammoth,** extinct elephants of gigantic size. In 1799 the first perfectly preserved specimen was found in Siberia in a block of ice. It was in prehistoric times an inhabitant of Britain and other parts of Europe, as well as of Asia and America.

**Manatee,** an aquatic mammal of the sea cow (Sirenia) order of mammals, averaging when full grown from 3–3.6 m (10–12 ft) in length, with shovel-shaped tail, and forelimbs and nails which almost give the appearance of arms and hands. Gentle and trusting they are under threat from man. Protected in Florida. In spite of their ungainly aspect, they are believed to have given rise to the legend of mermaids.

**Mandarin,** the name given to a powerful Chinese official, civil or military, under the old regime, whose rank was shown by the wearing of a button on the cap. Mandarin is the major language of N. China.

**Manganese,** a metallic element, no. 25, symbol Mn, discovered by Scheele, 1774. It is silver-white, not very hard (it forms a hard alloy with carbon), brittle, and tarnishes when exposed to air. Its chief ore is pyrolusite (manganese dioxide). Steels containing manganese are very tough, used for making machine parts.

**Manna,** a tree of the ash genus, *Fraxinus ornus,* growing in the South of Europe and in the East and exuding a sweet substance which is gathered, boiled and eaten.

**Mantis.** Large insects belonging to the same order as the locusts and grasshoppers. The manner in which the forelegs are held, as though in suppliance, has gained for these insects the common name of "praying mantis". They are distributed throughout the warmer countries of the world.

**Maple,** trees native to the northern hemisphere. There are over 100 species. The sycamore is the best-known species growing in Britain. The sugar maple abounds in Canada and the eastern parts of the United States. The sugar is tapped by boring holes in the tree in February and March, and the juice that escapes is collected and evaporated. The maple-leaf is the Canadian national emblem.

**Marble** is limestone in its hardest and most crystalline form. There are many varieties—33 were used in the building of the Paris Opera House—but white is the purest and rarest. White marble was used by the ancient Greeks for their temples and statues. Among the famous marbles of Italy are the Carrara and Siena marbles, which were used by Renaissance sculptors. Devonshire and Derbyshire yield some beautiful marbles and Connemara furnishes a serpentine-marble.

**Marionettes** are puppets moved by strings. They originated in the *Fantoccini* of the 15th century which had such a vogue in Italy and elsewhere on the Continent. The English *Punch and Judy* is a version of Punchinello.

**Marseillaise,** the French national hymn, written and composed by Rouget de L'Isle, a French engineer officer, who was inspired to write it in 1792 to encourage the Strasburg conscripts. It immediately became popular, and received its name from the fact that it was sung by the Marseillaise troops while marching into Paris.

**Marsupials,** members of the order of pouched mammals. Except for the opossums of America, all marsupials occur in Australasia, and include the kangaroos, wallabies and wombats.

**Mastodon,** an extinct order of quadruped closely resembling the elephant in structure, but is larger.

**Megalith,** a prehistoric monument, consisting of a large single stone or a group of such stones, in a circle as at Stonehenge or in burial chambers as at New Grange, Ireland. Megalithic monuments have been constructed by different peoples in different parts of the world since the third millennium B.C.

**Mercator's Projection,** a method of indicating meridians and parallels of latitudes on maps, introduced by Mercator in the 16th century, and still universally used in navigators' charts.

**Mercury** *or* **Quicksilver,** element no. 80, symbol Hg (Latin *hydrargyrum*) is one of the oldest-known metals, whose chief ore is the sulfide, cinnabar, found in certain parts of Spain, China, Japan and South America. It is liquid at ordinary temperature and is used in the construction of barometers and thermometers. Alloys of mercury are called amalgams. It is also of great value in medicine. The metal is used in the mercury-vapor (or "sunlight") lamp, since the vapor gives a bright yellow-white glow in an electric discharge.

**Meridian,** an imaginary circle extending through the North and South Poles and any given place. When the sun is at its midday height at any place it is "on the meridian"; hence the terms ante-meridian (a.m.) and post-meridian (p.m.).

**Mesons** (from Greek *meso*—middle), a family of unstable particles of mass between that of an electron and that of a proton. Some are positive, some negative, some neutral. No stable meson is known, the longest-lived particle having a lifetime of only two-millionths of a second. The first of these particles was discovered in cosmic radiation in 1937 and called the mu-meson or *muon*. In 1947 a heavier type was discovered called the pi-meson or *pion* which behaved like the meson predicted on theoretical grounds by Yukawa in 1935. The pion is connected with the theory of nuclear forces.

**Metamorphic Rocks** are such geological deposits as have undergone alterations of structure and mineral reorganization. The most active agents in producing these metamorphic changes are heat, water and pressure.

**Methane.** The simplest hydrocarbon, compounded of one carbon atom and four hydrogen atoms. This gas occurs over marshes and swamps, where it is liberated in the decay of vegetable matter. It is the main constituent of natural gas, and also occurs in coal-mines, where it is called "fire-damp" because of the explosive character of its mixture with air. Formerly this natural gas was removed from the coal seams and ran to waste; now in many countries (including Britain) it is being used for commercial purposes.

**Microbe,** a term proposed by Sédillot in 1878 to denote any microscopic organism, vegetable or animal, or found on the borderland between the two great natural kingdoms. The term is commonly used, but not by scientists.

**Middle Ages** (*c.* A.D. 400–1500), usually considered to be the period between the decline and fall of the Western Roman Empire and the fall of Constantinople to the Turks. The period covers *(a)* an earlier part ending with the 12th century (sometimes called the Dark Ages) when science was dead, when theology was the main preoccupation, and when the language of the learned West was Latin; and *(b)* a later age of Arabian influence when alchemy and astrology (at that time indistinguishable from astronomy) were central interests, technology was advancing, and Greek learning was transmitted by Arab scholars. Characteristic features of the mediaeval scene were monasticism the Crusades *(q.v.),* Gothic art *(q.v.),* feudalism, and the supremacy of Islam in the field of learning. The period came to an end with the general decline of Christendom and the ushering in of the Renaissance. The term "Middle Ages" was coined by the 17th-century German historian Christoph Keller.

**Millennium,** a period of a thousand years. The term is specifically used of the period of a thousand years during which, according to Rev. xx. 1–5, Christ will reign in person on earth. The Millenarians are a sect that interprets the "Millennium" as beginning with the commencement of the 6001st year from the Creation, which, according to Archbishop Ussher (1581–1650), was in 4004 B.C.

**Minnesingers** were minstrel poets of Germany who, during the 12th and 13th centuries, composed and sang verses of heroism and love. They were of knightly rank, the counterpart of the French troubadours.

**Minstrels** were originally specially appointed instrumentalists and singers—pipers, harpers and gleemen—engaged by barons and manorial lords to amuse their tenants. Later, minstrels assumed nomadic habits, made their way into the houses of the great and were generally welcome. By Elizabeth's time, however, they were too numerous, and were classed as "rogues and vagabonds", along with actors.

**Mirage,** an optical illusion caused by unequal temperatures in different layers of the atmosphere near the earth's surface. These temperature variations alter the refracting power of the air and cause light rays to be curved, making the air act as a huge distorting lens. This can happen at sea, in deserts and elsewhere and various types of mirage are known. A common kind in deserts curves light from the sky so that it appears to come from the ground, deceiving the observer into thinking that the sky is reflected in a lake of water. Inverted images of hills, trees, etc. also look as if reflected in the non-existent lake.

**Mistletoe,** a parasitic evergreen with white berries used as a decoration at Christmas-time. The familiar mistletoe of Europe is the *Viscum album,* which grows on the boughs of lime, willow, apple, poplar, maple, ash, hawthorn but seldom on oak-trees. It was sacred to the Druids, and in Norse mythology it was a mistletoe dart that killed the god Baldur.

**Mitosis,** cell division whereby each daughter cell receives the same number of chromosomes as the parent cell. When the gametes (sex cells) are formed a special type of division occurs (meiosis) in which the number of chromosomes is halved.

**Moabite Stone,** a stone of the 9th century B.C. containing the earliest known inscription in Phoenician characters, and discovered in the highlands of Moab in 1868. It is now in the Louvre, Paris. It records the campaign between Moab and Israel (*c.* 850 B.C.), an account of which is given in the Old Testament (2 Kings 3:27).

**Mohole Project,** a scheme to bore through the earth's crust to take samples of the mantle rocks beneath. Drilling trials, led by an American team of geophysicists, began in 1961 near the island of Guadalupe off the Mexican coast in the Pacific. The project, however, was cancelled in 1966 on account of the escalating cost. Russian geophysicists started on a similar experiment, boring through land rocks where the digging is much deeper and higher temperatures are met with. The name "Anti-Cosmos" was given to the project. The boundary between the earth's crustal and mantle rocks is known as the Mohorovicic Discontinuity, or, more simply, as the Moho. The technology of deep sea drilling came from this project.

**Molecule.** A group of atoms held together by chemical forces.

**Molybdenum,** element no. 42, symbol Mo, a fairly hard white metal with properties resembling those of chromium. Its commonest ore is the sulfide, molybdenite. The chief use of the metals is in the manufacture of alloy steels.

**Monitor,** a family of lizards most resembling dragons. There are about 30 species widely distributed over the tropical parts of Asia, Australia and Africa.

**Monsoons,** regular persistent winds which blow at certain seasons in middle latitudes, mainly in South and East Asia. Their occurrence is related to the great changes of pressure which take place between summer and winter over the land mass. In India the south-west monsoon (June–October) is moisture-laden from its long passage over the sea and in the higher regions, especially, there is heavy rainfall. Sudden reversal of the wind results in the cold north-east monsoon (October–March) which is dry on account of the shelter afforded by the mountain ranges to the north. Frequently the term "monsoon" is applied to denote the associated rainfall without reference to the actual winds.

**Moths,** of the insect order, *Lepidoptera,* differing from butterflies which have clubbed antennae, in having feathery, sometimes thin, pointed antennae, rarely clubbed. Most are nocturnal, and the pupae are usually brown and enclosed in a cocoon unlike those of the butterfly, which are usually naked. *See also* **Lepidoptera.**

**Motion, Laws of.** According to Newton: (1) A body continues in its state of rest or uniform motion in a straight line except in so far as it is compelled by external forces to change that state. (2) Rate of change of momentum is proportional to the applied force, and takes place in the direction in which the force acts. (3) To every action there is an equal and opposite reaction. These laws are the basis of almost all engineering and everyday mechanics. Corrections to them have been made by relativity and the quantum theory.

**Myrrh,** a resinous substance obtained from a tree of the natural order *Amyridaceae,* growing plentifully in Ethiopia and Arabia. Its use for embalming, medical and aromatic purposes may be traced back to the most remote times.

# N

**Nadir,** one of the two poles of the horizon, the other being the zenith. The nadir is the pole vertically below the observer's feet.

**Narcotic,** a medical dictionary definition is that a narcotic is a drug that produces stupor; complete insanity or sleep. In terms of drug addiction, a narcotic has been defined as altering and distorting the user's perception of himself and of the external world, being taken primarily for that purpose.

**Nationalization** is the taking over by the State of the ownership and operation of an industry or service —*e.g.,* coal-mining, railway, transport, gas and electricity. Where this is done without revolution, compensation is usually paid to the previous owners at what is regarded as a fair market price; the compensation is sometimes paid in cash, but more often in fixed-interest-bearing bonds issued either by the State or by the administration of the nationalized service, which is usually a publicly appointed Board or Corporation acting, with greater or lesser autonomy, under the direction of a Minister responsible to Parliament. In some cases the State becomes a partner with private investors in the ownership of a particular enterprise, *e.g.,* oil companies, such as the former Anglo-Iranian and some recent French examples. Nationalization is usually brought about by a separate Act of Parliament relating to each industry or service taken over. These Acts, in Great Britain, include provision for joint consultation at all levels between the administering boards and the workers employed and their Trade Unions. When, as in the Soviet Union, nationalization occurs as an outcome of social revolution no compensation is paid to the dispossessed owners.

**Neanderthal,** the name of the valley lying between Düsseldorf and Wuppertal, where in a limestone cave a now famous skull of a very early species of prehistoric man was discovered in 1856. Fossils of Neanderthal man have been found over a wide area, and from archaeological evidence he began to disappear from Europe during the last Ice Age, about 40,000 B.C.

**Nekton,** term used to differentiate actively swimming aquatic organisms (*e.g.,* fishes) from the "drifters" or plankton.

**Neodymium,** element no. 60, symbol Nd, belonging to the rare earth metal group. Discovered by Welsbach, 1885.

**Neptunium,** element no. 93, symbol Np, one of the four new elements discovered during the progress of the atomic bomb project in the second world war, Neptunium is formed when a neutron enters nucleus of Uranium 238, and it decays radioactively to yield plutonium.

**Neutrino,** a neutral particle which carries energy and spin and although possessing little or no mass plays an important part in the interaction of other fundamental particles. The discovery that there are in fact two distinct neutrinos, each with its counterpart, was discovered in 1962 as a result of an experiment made with the 30,000 million-electronvolt proton accelerator at Brookhaven.

**Neutron,** a neutral particle present in all atomic nuclei except the hydrogen nucleus which is a single proton. In the development of nuclear science and technology the neutron has played a most important role and neutrons produce the radioisotopes now widely used in medicine, agriculture and industry. Neutrons and protons are termed nucleons.

**Neutron Bomb,** a thermonuclear fusion weapon which produces increased lethal radiation while the destructive blast and fallout are significantly less than for a fission weapon of equivalent yield; it kills organic life while sparing property, except within a small radius. In 1978 President Carter reserved his decision on production; in 1981 the new Reagan administration decided to go ahead and stockpile the weapon.

**Nickel,** silver-colored metallic element, no. 28, symbol Ni, fairly soft though harder than iron. Chief source of the metal is the nickel sulfide in iron-copper pyrites deposits in Ontario. Chief uses are: in electroplating, in coins, as an element in alloy steels. A novel method of making pure nickel (by treating the metal with carbon monoxide and heating the resulting liquid, nickel carbonyl) was developed in 1890 by Mond. This discovery led to many technical advances in industrial chemistry, one of which is the production of catalysts.

**Niobium** is a metal element, no. 41, symbol Nb, related to vanadium. Technical development has been slow because of its rare occurrence, although niobium is now used in ferrous alloys to increase resistance to corrosion and produce steel which can be used at high temperatures.

**Nitrogen,** a non-combustible gaseous element, no. 7, symbol N, devoid of taste or smell, and constituting nearly four-fifths of the atmospheric air. Nitrogen compounds are essential to plants and animals, and are used in fertilizers.

**Nitro-Glycerine,** an explosive yellow fluid produced by mixing small quantities of glycerine with a combination of one part of nitric acid and two parts of sulfuric acid. By itself it is a dangerously explosive substance to handle. In 1867, Nobel produced dynamite, a safe explosive made by absorbing nitro-glycerine in kieselguhr.

**Nucleic Acids.** Living matter is built up of cells each of which has a nucleus surrounded by cytoplasm. Cell nuclei are composed chiefly of substances called nucleoproteins, which consist of a protein attached to a nucleic acid (this original name is still used, although nucleic acids are found in the cytoplasm as well as the nucleus). Nucleic acids are complex organic structures made up of chains of compounds called nucleotides. Nucleotide molecules have a sugar group attached to a nitrogenous base and a phosphate group. Only two sugar groups are found in the nucleotides, ribose, giving rise to ribonucleic acids (RNAs, found mainly in the cytoplasm) and deoxyribose, which forms deoxyribonucleic acids (DNAs, found mainly in cell nuclei). Seven different nitrogenous bases have been isolated, so that a number of different nucleotides are possible. A repeating, regular pattern of nucleotides is linked by the phosphate groups, forming nucleic acids. The functions of nucleic acids are of fundamental importance. They are concerned in the process of transmission of inherited qualities in reproduction and in building up body proteins.

**Nylon,** a generic term for any long-chain synthetic polymeric amide which has recurring amide groups as an integral part of the main polymer chain, and which is capable of being formed into a filament in which the structural elements are orientated in the direction of the axis. The first nylon of commercial interest was made in 1935, and the world's first nylon factory—in the United States—began production in 1940.

# O

**Odyssey,** Homer's epic setting forth the incidents of the wanderings of Odysseus on his way back to Ithaca after the Siege of Troy.

**Ohm's Law,** propounded by G. S. Ohm in 1826, is expressed in the equation: electromotive force (in volts) = current (in amperes) × resistance (in ohms). The ohm is the unit of electrical resistance in the metre-kilogram-second system.

**Onyx** *or* **Sardonyx,** a variety of chalcedony built up of different-colored layers, which are parallel and straight (not curved as in agate).

**Opal,** a mineral consisting of hydrous silica, occurring in numerous varieties and colors. Opals have been prized as gems since at least 400 B.C. but the secret of their unique internal "fire" or opalescence has only recently been learned. It is a result of the diffraction of light by a regular array of tiny silica spheres, about 100 nm in diameter, of which gem opals are now known to be composed. Opal miners are called gougers. Chief source—the Andanooka and Coober Pedy fields of South Australia.

**Opium** was known to the ancients, and used by them as a medicine. It is obtained from the poppy *(Papaver somniferum),* the unripe "head" or seed capsule of that flower yielding a juice which when dried becomes the opium of commerce. The poppy is cultivated in India, Iran, Turkey, Macedonia and China for the sake of this juice, which yields various alkaloids, such as morphine, narcotine, codeine, etc. These days the drug is rarely used medicinally.

**Optics,** the branch of physics which investigates the nature and properties of light and the phenomena of colour. Burning lenses were known to the ancient Greeks and Ptolemy wrote a treatise on optics A.D. 150. Lenses as visual aids were known in ancient China but eyeglasses were not in use until the 13th century. Spectacles were in more general use after the invention of printing in the 15th century. The camera obscura was invented in the 16th century and the telescope and microscope at the beginning of the 17th century.

**Orchestra,** a group of instruments and instrumentalists whose playing is under the direction of a conductor. The composition of a typical symphony orchestra is as follows: STRINGS: 1st Violin (16), 2nd Violin (16), Viola (12), Violoncello (12), Double Bass (8). WOODWIND: Flute (3–4), Piccolo (1), Oboe (3), Cor Anglais (1), Bass Oboe (1), Clarinet (3), Bass Clarinet (1), Bassoon (3), Contra-bassoon (1). BRASS: Horn (6), Trumpet (5), Trombone (3–4), Tuba (2). PERCUSSION: Timpani (3–6), Side Drum (1), Bass Drum (1), Cymbals (1), Harp (2).

**Organ** is a musical wind instrument of ancient origin whose tones are produced by the vibrations of air in pipes of varying length. Basically, an organ consists of a number of pipes grouped in rows or ranks according to their special tone-character. The air is fed by bellows or, in modern organs, by a rotary fan electrically driven. Each rank is controlled by a slider, and the knob that controls the slider is called a stop. The organist pulls out the stops to give the tones he wants, the other pipes being kept out of action by the slider. When a particular note on the keyboard is depressed the player may hear, by pulling out the appropriate stop, not only the normal pitch but the note in several octaves. A stop of which the notes are of normal pitch is called an 8-foot stop, a 16-foot stop would give an octave lower, a 4-foot stop an octave higher and a 2-foot stop two octaves higher. The hand keyboard is called a manual, and the foot keyboard the pedal board. The basic tone of an organ is its diapason tone, and is normally of 8-foot length and pitch. Most large organs have four manual keyboards and one pedal board. The most important manual is the great organ which comprises the majority of basic stops. The next in importance is the swell organ, so called because the pipes are enclosed in a box fitted with movable shutters operated by a swell-pedal. The effect provides a controlled crescendo or diminuendo. The tone of a typical English swell has a reedy character. The third manual controls the choir organ—a collection of stops suitable for vocal accompaniment. The fourth manual controls the solo organ—a group of stops which, singly or in combination, may provide a solo melody which the remainder of the organ accompanies. The pedal keyboard controls most of the bass stops. In some very large organs there is a fifth manual controlling the echo organ. This is a small group of stops usually set high in the roof of the building to give the effect of distant music. Most church organs have two or three manuals. Modern cinema organs may have some normal stops but rely chiefly on a number of effects unknown to the straight organ.

**Orion,** a famous constellation of the heavens, comprising nearly a hundred stars, all visible to the naked eye. It contains three stars of the second magnitude in a line, and these are called "Orion's Belt".

**Osmium,** a very hard, bluish-white metallic element, no. 76, symbol Os, of the platinum group and one of the heaviest of known metals. It is obtained from certain sands of South America, California, Australia and Russia. The alloy of osmium and iridium (osmiridium) provides tips for gold fountain-pen nibs.

**Osmosis,** the process by which absorption of liquids through semi-permeable membranes takes place. A solution exerts osmotic pressure (O.P.) or suction in proportion to concentration but also depending on kind of dissolved substance. The roots of the higher plants are covered with fine root-hairs, within the cell-walls of which the sap is normally of a higher concentration than the dissolved matter in the surrounding soil. The root-hairs, therefore, draw into themselves these weaker salt-solutions. (The explanation of water and salt exchanges is complicated by the selective ability of some cells (*e.g.,* roots) to accept or reject particular dissolved substances along with the water. The absorption of salts by a plant is selective, each plant selecting through the semi-permeable membranes of its root-hairs those substances which are most suited to itself.)

**Oxygen** is the most abundant of all terrestrial elements, no. 8, symbol O. In combination, this gaseous element forms about 46% of the earth's crust; one-fifth of the atmosphere; eight-ninths by weight of all water. Discovered independently by Scheele (*c.* 1773) and Priestley (1774). It is col-

orless, tasteless and odorless, and forms the chief life-supporting element of animal and vegetable life.

**Ozone,** a modified form of oxygen, containing three atoms of oxygen per molecule instead of two. It is prepared by passing oxygen through a silent electric discharge. When present in air to the extent of 1 part in 4 million parts of air it kills bacteria, and has been used for this purpose in ventilating systems, *e.g.,* that of underground railways. It is present in extremely small quantities in the lower atmosphere but is comparatively plentiful at heights between 12 and 50 km. As ozone absorbs ultraviolet light of certain wavelengths spectroscopic methods, involving the analysis of sunlight, are chiefly used in ozone determination.

# P

**Palladium,** a scarce metallic element, no. 46, symbol Pd, similar to platinum, with which it is usually found. It is an expensive metal, with desirable properties as a catalyst in reactions involving hydrogen, since it has a remarkable capacity for absorbing this gas; for example, coal gas and air will inflame in the presence of palladium at room temperature. It forms a silver-white alloy with gold, and this is used in some kinds of jewellery. It is used in expensive watches to make non-magnetic springs.

**Paper** has been known in one form or another from very early times. The papyrus reeds of the Nile swamps served the ancient Egyptians for sheets upon which to inscribe their records. The Chinese and Japanese, centuries later, were using something more akin to modern paper in substance, an Asiatic paper-mulberry, yielding a smooth fibrous material, being utilized. With the spread of learning in Western Europe the necessity of a readier medium made itself felt and paper began to be manufactured from pulped rags and other substances. The first known English paper-mill was Sele mill near Stevenage, built about 1490, which produced the paper for an edition of Chaucer in 1498. Other mills were set up under Elizabeth, using linen and cotton as raw material. Other papermaking staples were later introduced, such as surat, esparto grass and wood-pulp. The chief raw material in the world paper industry is wood-pulp, the main exporters being the timber-growing countries of Canada, Sweden and Finland. Canada is the world's chief producer of newsprint and supplies a large proportion of US requirements.

**Papyrus,** the earliest known paper made in Egypt at a very remote period from a large species of reed, *Cyperus papyrus.* This plant is to be found all over tropical Africa, especially in the "sudd" region of the White Nile.

**Parallax,** the change in direction of a body caused by a change in position of the observer. If the parallax is measured (in degrees of angle) and the distance between the two observation points is known the distance of the observed body can be calculated. The distance of heavenly bodies has been found this way. The first stellar distances were so obtained in 1838 by Henderson, Struve and Bessel. Stellar distances are so great that even when the two observations are made at opposite points of the earth's orbit round the sun, the parallax is always less than 1·0" of arc.

**Parchment,** made chiefly from the skins of animals,

usually of goats and sheep, was employed in olden times before printing was invented and superseded papyrus as writing material. Vegetable parchment, invented by W. E. Gaine in 1853, though not equal in strength and durability to skin parchment, is about five times stronger than ordinary paper. Vellum is parchment made from the skins of young calves or lambs.

**Pearl** is produced by certain shelled mollusks, chiefly the oyster. The inner surface of the shells of the pearl oyster yield "mother-of-pearl", and distinct pearls are believed to be morbid secretions, caused by some external irritation. Many fine pearls are found in the actual body of the oyster. The Persian Gulf, Sri Lanka, the north-west coast of Western Australia, many Pacific islands and the Gulf of Mexico are among the most productive pearl-fishing grounds. In ancient times Britain was renowned for its pearl fisheries, the pearls being obtained from a species of freshwater mussel. Western Australia has produced a 40-grain pearl, the finest the world has seen. The largest pearl ever found was the "Beresford-Hope Pearl", which weighed 1,800 grains, over six times as much as the oyster that produced it.

**Perfumes** are essences or odors obtained from floral and other substances. The chief flower perfumes are those obtained from rose, jasmine, orange flower, violet and acacia. Heliotrope perfume is largely obtained from vanilla and almonds. Among the aromatic herbs which yield attractive perfumes are the rosemary, thyme, geranium, lavender, etc., while orange peel, citron peel, musk, sandalwood, patchouli and other vegetable products are largely drawn upon. In recent times chemistry has been called into play in aid of the perfumer, and many of the popular perfumes of today are chemically prepared in simulation of the scents of the flowers or other natural substances the names of which they bear.

*pH* **Value.** Introduced in 1909 by the Danish chemist Sorensen to indicate hydrogen-ion concentration on the basis of electrical conductivity and a view of ionisation since discarded; is now taken as a logarithmic scale of acidity or alkalinity of aqueous solutions: acidity 0–7, neutrality at 7–0, alkalinity 7–14. The *pH* of blood is about 7–6 (faintly alkaline).

**Phalanx,** a name applied by the ancient Greeks to a body of pike-men drawn up in close array, with overlapping shields, and eight, ten or more rows deep. The Macedonians stood sixteen rows deep. As many as 500 men could be in the front row.

**Phosphorus** is a non-metal element, no. 15, symbol P. Most familiar as a waxy, yellow solid which is spontaneously inflammable in air. It has chemical similarities to arsenic, like which it is very poisonous. It was discovered by Brandt in urine in 1669. It is found in most animal and vegetable tissues. It is an essential element of all plants and of the bones of animals. In combination with various metals it forms different phosphates, which are largely utilised as manures. The chief commercial use of phosphorus is in the preparation of matches.

**Photon.** When light behaves like a stream of discrete particles and not like waves, the particles are called photons.

**Pitchblende** *or* **Uraninite,** a relatively scarce mineral. It is nearly all uranium oxide, but lead, thorium, etc., are also present. Pitchblende from Joachimstal in Czechoslovakia was the material in which radium was discovered by the Curies. Other major sources are the Great Lakes region of Canada and Zaïre.

**Plasma Physics** is the physics of wholly ionized gases, *i.e.,* gases in which the atoms initially present have lost practically the whole of the electrons that usually surround their nuclei, so that the gas consists of a mixture of two components, positively charged ions and negatively charged electrons. The physical properties of a *plasma* are very different from those of an unionized gas. In particular, a plasma has a high electrical conductivity and can carry large currents.

**Plastics,** a broad term covering those substances which become plastic when subjected to increased temperatures or pressures. The Plastics Industry is based on synthetic organic examples of this group. There are two classes of plastics: the *thermoplastic,* which become plastic every time they are heated (*e.g.* cellulosic plastics) and *thermosetting,* which undergo chemical change when heated, so that once set they cannot be rendered plastic again (*e.g.,* Bakelite). Plastics are composed of longchained molecules, *e.g.,* polyethylene.

**Platinum,** a metallic element, no. 78, symbol Pt. It is a scarce white metal generally allied with iridium, osmium, ruthenium and palladium. It can only be melted in an oxyhydrogen or electric furnace, but can be rolled out into a film-like sheet, or drawn out to the finest wire; being resistant to acids it is termed a noble metal.

**Pleiades,** famous cluster of stars in the constellation of Taurus. Of the seven principal stars in the group, one is rather faint, and many myths have sprung up about this "lost Pleiad".

**Plutonium,** a chemical element, no. 94, symbol Pu, capable of nuclear fission in the same way as Uranium 235. Not until after it had been synthesised in atomic piles during the second world war was it shown to occur in infinitesimally small traces in nature. Its synthesis in the atomic pile depends on the capture by Uranium 238 nuclei of neutrons; immediate product of this reaction is the element neptunium, but this undergoes rapid radioactive disintegration to plutonium.

**Pogrom.** Russian word meaning "destruction". First used to describe the Czarist attacks on the Jews in 1881 in Russia. In 1938 Hitler ordered a general pogrom in Germany: all synagogues were destroyed and nearly all Jewish shops and homes, Jewish hospitals and children's homes suffered. During the subsequent war Jews of central Europe were systematically exterminated in cold blood by the Nazis.

**Pole-Star** is of the second magnitude, and the last in the tail of the Little Bear constellation. Being near the North pole of the heavens—never more than about one degree from due north—it always remains visible in the Northern hemisphere; hence its use as a guide to seamen.

**Polonium,** a radioactive element, no. 84, symbol Po, discovered by Madame Curie in 1898, and named after her native land of Poland.

**Porcelain.** The word is thought to be derived from the Italian *porcellana,* indicating the texture of a piglet. The majority of porcelain made on the continent was of "hard-paste", or true porcelain, similar to that discovered by the Chinese as early as the T'ang Dynasty (A.D. 618 907). It was composed of *kaolin* (china-clay) and *petuntse* (chinastone) which when fired in a kiln at a temperature of *c.* 1300° C (2370° F) became an extremely hard and translucent material. The recipe of "hard-paste" porcelain remained a secret of the Chinese until 1709, when it was re-discovered in

Europe by Johann Böttger of the Meissen factory (popularly known as Dresden). Aided by disloyal Meissen workmen, factories were later established at Vienna, Venice and in many parts of Germany. Plymouth and Bristol were the only English factories to produce this type of porcelain, from 1768 to 1781. Elsewhere, both in England and France, the material manufactured was known as "soft-paste" or artificial porcelain which was made by blending varying white-firing clays with the ingredients of glass. The French factory of Sèvres began to make some hard-paste porcelain by 1768 and by the 19th century such porcelain was the only type being made throughout the whole of the continent. In England Josiah Spode is credited with the introduction of "bone-china" about 1794. This hybrid-paste was quickly adopted by many other factories and today remains the most popular type of English porcelain.

**Porphyry,** a form of crystalline rock of many varieties that in ancient Egypt was quarried and used for the decorative portions of buildings and vessels. The term is applied generally to the eruptive rocks in which large well-formed crystals of one mineral are set in a matrix of other minerals.

**Positron,** the "positive electron", an atomic particle having the same mass but an electric charge equal but opposite to that of an electron. It was discovered in 1932.

**Potassium,** a metal, no. 19, symbol K (German, *Kalium*). It is similar to sodium, reacting violently with water. It was discovered by Sir Humphry Davy in 1807, and is now generally obtained by the electrolysis of fused potassium hydroxide or chloride/fluoride mixture. Its principal minerals are caranallite and kainite, and it is relatively common in rocks, accounting for about 2 1/2% of the earth's crust. An essential element for healthy plant growth; the ashes of plants are relatively rich in potassium.

**Proteins** are the main chemical substances of living matter; they are a part of every living cell and are found in all animals and plants. All proteins are basically constructed of carbon hydrogen, oxygen and nitrogen, and some contain sulfur, phosphorus (nucleoproteins) and iron (haemoglobin). Proteins are built up of very long chains of amino-acids connected by amide linkages (the synthetic polymers such as "nylon" and casein plastics (from milk) are built up of the same linkages). The structure of protein molecules allows a variety of function. Enzymes, which bring about chemical reactions in living cells, are proteins having specific properties.

**Proton,** a basic constituent of the atomic nucleus, positively charged, having a mass about 1836 times that of the electron. It is a positive hydrogen ion.

**Prout's hypothesis.** The English chemist William Prout (1785–1850) advanced the idea that all atoms are made of hydrogen, and their weights are exact multiples of the weight of a hydrogen atom. With the modification that neutrons as well as protons occur in the nucleus, Prout's belief, though rejected for many years, has been substantially vindicated.

**Psalms, Book of,** for many years attributed to David, but present-day scholars are of opinion that the psalms were written by a series of authors at different times and for different purposes, and that few, if any, were written by David. The Holy Scriptures contain 150.

# Q

**Quartz** is a common and usually colorless mineral, occurring both crystallized and massive. In the first form it is in hexagonal prisms, terminating in pyramids. When pure its specific gravity is 2.66. It is one of the constituents of granite, gneiss, etc. Among the quartz varieties are *rock crystal* (colorless), *smoky quartz* (yellow or brown), *amethyst* (purple), *rose quartz* (pink) and *milky quartz* (white). Quartz veins in metamorphic rocks may yield rich deposits of gold. Mining for gold in the rock is termed quartz-mining.

# R

**Radar.** The basic principle of radar is very similar to that of sight. We switch on a light in the dark, and we *see* an object because the light waves are reflected from it and return to our eye, which is able to detect them. Similarly, the radar station *sees* an object because the invisible radio waves sent out from the transmitter are reflected from it and return to the receiver, which is able to detect them. Thus radar is the use of radio signals that man broadcasts.

The utilization of radio waves for the detection of reflecting surfaces began with the classical experiment of the late Sir Edward Appleton in 1925, which he conducted in order to demonstrate the existence of the Heaviside layer in the upper atmosphere. During the course of the last war developments took place which tremendously improved the methods and instruments used. As in the case of so many of the inventions primarily developed for the purpose of waging war, many useful applications have been found for radar in times of peace, and, in particular, it has proved of great service as an aid to aerial and marine navigation, and in meteorology and astronomy. Radar astronomy investigates the solar system with the echoes of signals sent out from the Earth.

**Radiation,** energy emitted in the form of a beam of rays or waves, *e.g.,* acoustic (sound) radiation from a loudspeaker, radiant heat from a fire, $\beta$-radiation from a radioactive substance. The radiation of electromagnetic waves from a body depends on its temperature, the amount of energy radiated per second being proportional to the fourth power of the absolute temperature. The hotter the body, the shorter the wavelengths of the radiation; thus the color of a glowing body depends on its temperature. Of paramount importance to us is radiation from the sun. Amongst other radiations, the sun sends ultra-violet, visible and infra-red (heat) waves. The principal gases of the atmosphere are transparent to practically all of the solar and sky radiation and also that which the earth re-transmits to space. Carbon dioxide and water vapor, however, strongly absorb certain types, the latter, as clouds, playing an important rôle in regulating the temperature of the globe. The cooling of the ground on a clear night is a result of the outgoing long-wave radiation exceeding that coming down from the sky; at sunrise cooling ceases as the incoming radiation becomes sufficient to compensate for the loss of heat.

**Radioactivity** is the spontaneous transformation of atomic nuclei, accompanied by the emission of ionising radiations. It was discovered in 1896 by Becquerel, who noticed that salts containing uranium sent off radiations which, like X-rays, can blacken a photographic plate. Two years later Marie and Pierre Curie discovered several new chemical elements which possessed the same property, but many times more intense than uranium: the most important of these was radium. Shortly afterwards it was established, mainly by Rutherford, that three types of radiations called $\alpha$-, $\beta$- and $\chi$-rays, are emitted from radioactive substances. It was also Rutherford who, jointly with Soddy, deduced that the emission of the radiations is associated with the spontaneous disintegration of atoms which result in the transformation of one radioactive substance into another. A series of such transformations ends when a stable element is produced. All of the heavy radioactive elements can be arranged in three radioactive series, called, the uranium, thorium and actinium series. Initially, radioactivity was thought to be a property confined only to a few elements occurring in nature. In 1934, however, Irene and Frederick Joliot-Curie discovered that ordinary elements can be transformed into radioactive forms by subjecting them to bombardment with $\alpha$-particles. Following this, it was found that beams of other fast particles produced in accelerators can also render ordinary substances radioactive. Nowadays it is known that radioactivity is a general property of matter; any chemical element can be produced in one or more radioactive forms, or isotopes.

**Radiocarbon Dating** is a method of dating the origin of organic materials or objects by observing their radioactivity. It is of great importance to archaeology because it enables prehistoric dates back to about 50,000 B.C. to be established for animal and vegetable remains. It works because cosmic rays entering the atmosphere create neutrons which convert nitrogen in the air to radioactive carbon. This forms radioactive carbon dioxide and gets incorporated into animals and vegetables throughout the world along with ordinary carbon dioxide in a definite ratio, approximately 1 radio carbon atom to $0.8 \times 10^{13}$ ordinary carbon atoms. When the tissue dies it stops interchanging its carbon with the atmosphere, *e.g.,* by breathing, and the radioactive carbon in it gradually turns into nitrogen emitting a $\beta$-particle. The radiocarbon content decreases by about 1% in 88 years. By measuring the proportion of radioactive carbon left in, say, dead wood, and comparing it with living wood, the age of the dead sample can be calculated. This needs careful laboratory experiments. It is now believed that the proportion of radioactive carbon in the atmosphere varied from time to time in the past because changes in the earth's magnetic field affected the cosmic rays. This has to be allowed for in calculating the radiocarbon date. One use of radiocarbon dating has been to trace the spread of agriculture through the world from its origin in the Near East *c.* 7000 B.C.

**Radium,** a radioactive metallic element, no. 88, symbol Ra, discovered by Marie and Pierre Curie in 1898. Atomic weight 226. Radiotherapy (use of X-rays from radium) is used in the treatment of cancer.

**Redwood** *or* **Sequoia.** This genus of coniferous tree comprises two species of Redwoods occuring in N.W. America. Specimens of one species, the Giant Redwood, reach a height of over 90 m (295 ft.) and a thickness of 11 m (36 ft.) The age of the largest, the General Sherman tree, is put at 3,500 years.

**Refraction.** The change of direction which light rays undergo when passing from one medium to another. The phenomenon is due to the fact that in different media light (and other forms of radiation) has different speeds.

**Refractory,** a substance capable of standing high temperatures and therefore useful for making furnaces and allied apparatus. Some insulating refractories are fire-clay, alumina, porcelain, carborundum, graphite and silica. Some refractory metals are platinum, molybdenum, tungsten, tantalum and the alloys nichrome, chromel, alumel.

**Rhodium,** a metallic element, no. 45, symbol Rh, discovered by Wollaston in 1804. It is found in platinum ores in small amounts, generally less than 2 per cent. With platinum it gives a very hard and durable alloy. It is also used, instead of silver, in putting the reflecting layer on a mirror.

**Rock Magnetism.** The study of naturally occurring magnetism in rocks is a subject which has gained considerable importance in recent years. There are two principal reasons for this. One is that this so-called "fossillized magnetism" may be able to tell us more about the past history of the earth's magnetic field. The other is that after many years of heated dispute between geologists rock magnetism promises to settle once and for all the controversy as to whether or not the continents have changed their relative positions in past times (continental drift theory *(q.v.)*). This branch of geophysical research, in addition to its academic interest, may well have important economic consequences. It might, for instance, become possible to locate mineral deposits once accumulated under special conditions at certain latitudes but now drifted to other places. Salt and similar deposits formed by the continuous evaporation of solutions in hot countries are one example; oil may well be another. There has been a *steady* change in rock magnetization direction with geological time. It is now known with some accuracy that the most recent reversal took place 700,000 years ago. It has been found that the older the rock, the farther removed is its fossil magnetization from the present field.

**Romanesque Architecture,** prevailed throughout Europe from the mid-10th to the 13th century and implies an art which developed from that of the Romans. Notable in Romanesque style were the rounded arch and masonry vaulting. Romanesque led to the graceful and more complex Gothic *(q.v.)*. The Italians never regarded Gothic highly and Romanesque churches, generally based on the basilican plan (oblong with double colonnades and a semi-circular apse at the end), continued to be built there until the beginning of the 15th century. Some of the best examples can be seen at Pisa (11th century), Florence (San Miniato, 1013), Lucca (12th century) and Milan (the 12th century San Ambrogio, most famous of all). In Germany Romanesque architure flourished longer than in France or England; the most famous churches are in the valley of the Rhine, at Cologne (completely destroyed during the second world war), Mainz and Speyer. In France Romanesque churches are found in Burgundy, Provence and Normandy.

**Rosetta Stone,** discovered in 1799 by the French at Rosetta in Egypt, and deposited in the British Museum. It is a piece of black basalt about 91 cm (36 in.) long, and contains a decree of the Egyptian priests of Ptolemy V Epiphanes (205–181 B.C.) in (1) hieroglyphics, (2) demotic and (3) Greek characters. It was the three different inscriptions on the same stone that enabled hiero-glyphic writing to be deciphered.

**Rubber,** substance obtained from the milky juice (latex) exuded by certain tropical trees and shrubs after tapping. Demand spread so rapidly in the 19th century that plantations were established wherever the tree would grow. Seeds of the Para rubber tree *(Hevea brasiliensis)* native to the Amazon basin were obtained by Kew, the young plants shipped to Ceylon and it was from these cultivated trees that the vast plantations of Malaysia and Indonesia developed. Recent years have seen great advances in the production of synthetic rubber.

**Rubidium,** a metallic element, no. 37, symbol Rb, most closely resembling potassium. It is silver-white and very soft, and was discovered in 1861 by Bunsen and Kirchhoff, using the spectroscope. It is rare, occurring in small amounts in the mica called lepidolite and in potash salts of the Stass-furt deposits in Germany.

**Ruby** is a deep red variety of Corundum (aluminum oxide); one of the most valued of precious stones. Burma yields some of the finest, and rubies of inferior color are found in Thailand, Sri Lanka, South Africa and Brazil.

**Runes,** certain characters of an alphabet found in inscriptions in the Germanic languages, found cut into buildings and implements of stone or wood in many parts of northern Europe, including Britain. The runic alphabet originally had 24 letters. Scholars agree that some of the runes derive from Greek and others from Latin.

**Ruthenium,** a greyish-white metallic element, no. 44, symbol Ru, discovered by Claus in 1845. It is harder and more brittle than platinum, in whose ores it occurs.

**Rutile,** mineral titanium dioxide. It is found in many igneous rocks, and in gneisses and schists. Its commonest colour is reddish-brown.

# S

**Saccharin,** a white crystalline solid manufactured from toluene, 550 times as sweet as cane sugar. It is used as a sweetening agent; as a substitute for sugar when sugar is forbidden, as in certain diseases, or when there is a shortage. It has no value as a food.

**St. Elmo's Fire,** a glowing brush-like discharge of electricity which takes place from sharp-pointed objects on mountains or the masts of ships exposed to the intense electric fields of thunderclouds.

**Sanskrit** is the language of ancient India, spoken by the Brahmins, and existing in early Oriental literature. It was the language of literature and government and is now confined to temples and places of learning. Its relationship to the modern Indian languages is rather like that of Latin and Greek to modern European languages.

**Sapphire,** a valuable deep blue variety of Corundum (aluminum oxide) found mostly in India, Sri Lanka and Northern Italy. Synthetic sapphire is often used for gramophone styli.

**Scandium,** a metallic element, no. 21, symbol Sc. It was discovered in 1879 by Nilson, and occurs in small quantities in certain rarer minerals such as wolframite.

**Schist,** the geological name of certain metamorphic rocks composed for the most part of mineral with thin plate-like crystals *(e.g., mica)* so that the layers of a schist are closely parallel. Quartz occurs in schists, and where it preponderates the term "quartz schist" is applied.

**Scythians,** nomadic conquerors and skilled horsemen of ancient times (9th–3rd century B.C.) who inhabited much of Southern Europe and Asiatic Russia.

**Sea Anemones** *or* **Actinaria,** an order of marine animals of the coelenterate class *Antozia.* They form a large and varied group of about 1,100 species and occur in many beautiful colors, flower-like in form.

**Sea Cucumbers** *or* **Holothurians.** These animals constitute the class of echinoderms called *Holothuroidea.* They are elongated and wormlike, with a ring of about twenty tentacles round the mouth. There are about 500 species.

**Sea Elephant** *or* **Elephant Seal,** a curious genus of seal, the males of which possess a proboscis of *c.* 30 cm (11.8 in.) in length that suggests an elephant's trunk. They are found on the coast of California and in certain parts of the Southern Ocean; their blubber has a commercial value.

**Sea Gravimeter,** an instrument to determine the density of the earth's crust beneath the oceans of the world. Designed by Dr. A. Graf of Munich and Dr. J. Lamar Worzel of Columbia University, it can detect changes of one-millionth of the value of gravity at the earth's surface and was used in the oceanographical research programe of the IGY.

**Sea Horse,** sea-fish *(Hippocampus),* very numerous in the tropics and comprising some twenty species. Their bodies are ringed and they have prehensile tails. Their heads are horse-shaped, and they swim in a vertical position.

**Sea Urchin,** species forming the class *Echinoidae.* The body is globular and covered with spines which may be used for both defence and locomotion. The main organs of locomotion are, however, the tube feet, as in starfishes. Much has been learnt of recent years by marine biologists from experiments with the purple sea urchin *Arbacia.*

**Selenium,** a non-metallic element, no. 34, symbol Se; related to sulfur. It is a dark red color, and solid, found associated with sulfur, iron, pyrites, etc., though only in small quantities. It is a semi-conductor *(q.v.)* and its special electrical properties have led to its use in photoelectric cells and rectifiers. Selenium is widely used in the chemical industry as a catalyst in producing aromatic hydrocarbons from less useful hydrocarbons. Also used in making some types of glass.

**Semiconductors,** substances with numerous special and useful electrical properties a few of which are:
(i) they conduct electricity much better than do insulators, but much less well than metals (hence their name);
(ii) their power to conduct depends strongly on their temperatures—which makes them useful for temperature sensitive devices;
(iii) they are sensitive to light—hence their use in photoelectric cells and solar batteries;
(iv) when in contact with metals, or with other suitable semiconductors, they form a boundary layer which conducts electricity much better one way than the other—this is the basis of many rectifiers some of which, called crystal diodes, are an important component in radios and electronic devices;

(v) their electrical properties can be greatly influenced by putting in minute amounts of impurity, this enables semiconductor devices, especially transistors, to be made with carefully selected properties.

Semiconductors were known to Faraday, but the semiconductor age really arrived with the invention of the transistor in 1947. The ubiquitous transistor is only one of very many semiconductor devices which perform a variety of functions in technical apparatus of all kinds. Semiconductors used in technology are usually small crystals, frequently of germanium or silicon, and their robustness and small power consumption often make them superior to other devices, such as thermionic valves, which they often replace. Other semiconducting materials are cadmium sulfide, selenium lead telluride, indium antimonide.

**Serpentine,** a mineral: chemically a hydrous silicate of magnesium. Green serpentine is used as an ornament stone. Fibrous serpentine is called asbestos.

**Silicon,** an important non-metallic element, no. 14, symbol Si, it is related to carbon. Next to oxygen, it is the most abundant constituent of the earth's crust (27% by weight). It occurs in many rocks, and its oxide occurs in many forms (*e.g.* quartz, sand, flint, agate, chalcedony, opal, etc.). Principally used as a semiconducting material for making transistors and similar devices. The circuitry of the computer is etched on a chip of silicon.

**Silk,** the name given to a soft glossy fabric manufactured from the fine thread produced by the silkworm. It was known to, and highly prized by the ancients, being at one time paid for, weight for weight, with gold. The manufacture of silk was carried on in Sicily in the 12th century, later spreading to Italy, Spain and France, where Lyons has been the great center of production from 1450 to this day. It was not manufactured in England before 1604; but when certain French refugees established themselves at Spitalfields in 1688, the industry was developed and became of importance. In the 18th century the Lombes of Derby achieved great success in this industry. Japan, China, Italy, Korea and the Soviet Union are the chief silk-producing countries.

**Silkworm,** the larva of a species of moth, *Bombux mori.* It is native to China, and has been cultivated with success in India, Iran, Turkey and Italy. The silkworm of commerce feeds on mulberry leaves and produces a cocoon of silk varying in color from white to orange. The cocoon is the silken habitation constructed by the worm for its entrance upon the pupal condition, and to obtain the silk the pupa is killed by immersing in hot water.

**Silver,** a white precious metallic element, no. 47, symbol Ag (Latin *argentum*) found in a free state, also in certain combinations, and in a variety of ores. The chief silver-producing regions are the Andes and Cordilleras. Peru, Bolivia and Mexico have yielded vast supplies of the metal since the 16th century, and Colorado and Nevada in the United States have also been very prolific in silver yield.

**Sins, The Seven Deadly or Capital sins** are pride, avarice, lust, anger, gluttony, envy, sloth.

**Sirius,** the dog-star, so called because of its situation in the mouth of the Dog (Canis Major): it is the brightest star in the sky, and is also one of the nearest to us.

**Snake.** The snakes constitute the important reptilian order *Ophidia.* Snakes have a scaly, cylindrical, limbless body, lidless eyes, forked tongue, and the upper and lower jaws joined by an elastic ligament. All snakes have teeth used for seizing prey, and the poisonous varieties are furnished with poison fangs in the upper jaw. These fangs are hollow modified teeth and the venom passes into them from a special gland situated behind the angle of the mouth. Some 2,500 species of snakes are known, divided into 13 families. There are 3 British species—the grass-snake, smooth-snake, and adder.

**Sodium,** a metallic element, no. 11, symbol Na (Latin *Natrium*), first obtained by Sir Humphry Davy in 1807 from caustic soda by means of the electric battery. Its chloride is *common salt;* the deposits of salt (*e.g.,* in Cheshire and at Stassfurt) have come into existence through the drying up of inland seas. Salt occurs in sea-water to the extent of about 3 percent; the Dead Sea contains about 22 percent. The blood of animals is maintained at a level of about 0–6% sodium chloride. That there is sodium in the sun's atmosphere was confirmed in 1859 by Kirchhoff from his spectroscopic observations. Liquid sodium metal has properties which make it suitable as a coolant in some nuclear reactors; a technique of handling this very reactive liquid has had to be developed.

**Solar Wind,** a continuous stream of electrically charged particles blowing outwards from the sun, supplemented from time to time by intense outbursts from particular regions of the sun's surface. These streams of protons and electrons on encountering the earth's magnetic field distort it and cause magnetic storms *(q.v.)* and aurorae *(q.v.).*

**Southern Cross,** popular name of *Crux,* a constellation of the Southern hemisphere, consisting of four bright stars in the form of a Latin cross. It has been called the pole-star of the south and is indispensable to seafarers.

**Specific Gravity,** defined as the ratio of the mass of a particular volume of a substance to the mass of an equal volume of water at 4°C (39°F).

**Spectroscopy.** Newton's arrangement with the prism was the first spectroscope; its function was to separate out the color components of a source of light. Two hundred years elapsed before this apparatus was developed into a precise scientific instrument, capable of measuring both the wavelength and intensity of each color component. In this form it is called a spectrometer. All atoms and molecules have well defined characteristic spectra which can be uesd to recognize them. In order to produce emission spectra it is necessary to energize the material under investigation by some means, such as by heating in a flame. The resulting radiation then consists largely of sharp bright lines, characteristic of the material. Absorption spectra are produced by interposing the experimental material between a white light source and the spectrometer. Then dark lines are seen, corresponding to absorptions of energy, in exactly the same places as the bright lines are observed in the emission spectra. Spectroscopic techniques have now been developed to such an extent that accurate measurements of wavelength and intensity are possible not only in the visible region, but over almost the whole of the electromagnetic spectrum. Two of the most useful types for the chemist are infrared spectroscopy which reveals absorption characteristic of the type of chemical bonds because of their different bond vibration frequencies and nuclear magnetic resonance spectroscopy which operates in the radiofrequency region. It reveals the structure environments of atoms containing particular nuclei. Not only does spectroscopy play an important role in probing the structure of matter, but it can be applied in the field of astronomy. The use of radio wave spectroscopy has led to the discovery of several new types of stellar object, and this data is now producing a complete reappraisal of our understanding of the universe.

**Stalactites** are deposits of calcium carbonate formed on the roofs and sides of limestone caves, and in tunnels, under bridges, and other places where the carbonic acid of rain-water percolates through and partly dissolves the limestone, resulting in the growth of icicle-like forms that often assume groupings. The water that drops from these may deposit further calcium carbonate, which accumulates and hardens into sharp mounds or hillocks called stalagmites.

**Steel,** an alloy of iron and carbon, with varying proportions of other minerals. The famous blades of Damascus and steels of Toledo were made by the cementation and crucible method. The metal produced by the "Bessemer process" *(q.v.)* is of the highest value for structural purposes, rails, etc. In recent years the technique known as continuous casting has been developed which bypasses some major steps in the conventional process of steelmaking.

**Steroids.** A class of structurally related compounds, based on a system of condensed rings of carbon and hydrogen, which are widely distributed in animals and plants. Included in the steroid family are sterols, found in all animal cells, vitamin D, sex hormones, bile acids and cortisone, a drug used in the treatment of rheumatic fever.

**Stoma** (pl. **stomata**), microscopic pores on the surfaces of leaves through which gaseous exchanges take place and water is lost. It has been estimated that a single maize plant bears 200 million stomata, usually closed at night.

**Stonehenge,** a remarkable collection of Bronze Age monuments on Salisbury Plain. The site which contains ditches, earthwork-banks and megaliths (large stones) has long been recognised for its architectural innovations (the trilithon or freestanding arch and the circle of dressed and lintelled stone blocks) and for its astronomical, numerical and geometrical properties. The building and rebuilding, according to modern archaeological research, lasted from about 2100 to 1600 B.C.

**Strontium.** This silver-white metallic element, no. 38, was discovered by Hope and Klaproth in 1793, and isolated by Sir Humphry Davy in 1808. The chief strontium minerals are celestite (sulfate) and strontianite (carbonate). Compounds of strontium give a brilliant color to fireworks and signal flares. Radioactive isotopes of strontium (strontium-90) are formed as fission products in nuclear explosions and tend to collect in bone on account of the chemical similarity of strontium and calcium *(q.v.)*. This hazard is a cause of great alarm. *See* **Fallout.**

**Sublimation,** when a solid substance is heated and then turns into vapor without passing through the liquid stage and then condenses as a solid on a cold surface, it is said to "sublime" and the process is called "sublimation". Iodine behaves in this way, and sublimation is used as a method of purifying it.

**Sulfur,** element no. 16, is a brittle, crystalline solid, symbol S, abounding in the vicinity of volcanoes. It is yellow in color. It occurs in combination with other elements, as sulfates and sulfides, and allied with oxygen, hydrogen, chlorine, etc., is of great commercial utility. Used in its pure state it constitutes the inflammable element in gunpowder; it is also used for matches and for making sulfuric acid.

**Sulfuric Acid,** a compound of great commercial importance, used in a variety of manufactures, and composed of sulfur, oxygen and hydrogen. Extremely corrosive, and is present in acid rain *(q.v.)*.

**Superconductor,** a metal in a state in which its electrical resistance has entirely vanished so that electric currents can flow indefinitely without generating heat or decreasing in strength. The superconducting state of metals was first discovered in mercury by Onnes in Leiden in 1911. There are many magnetic and thermal properties associated with superconductivity and the phenomenon as a whole has proved to be of great scientific interest: it resisted explanation till about 1957. In the meantime many metals and alloys were found to show the property but only at very low temperatures—below $c. -260°$ C $(-500°$ F$)$. There is a growing number of practical applications, *e.g.,* coils of superconducting wire (kept very cold by liquid helium) can be made to carry enough electric current to produce strong magnetic fields. Such fields are very constant and do not require the large supply of electrical power that ordinary electromagnets need.

**Supersonic Speed,** a speed greater than the speed of sound (in air at sea-level sound waves travel at about 1223 km/h; 759.97 mph). When a body travels at a speed which is greater than the speed at which disturbances themselves can travel, a mechanism exists for the generation of waves of enhanced intensity. Thus aircraft traveling at supersonic speeds produce shock waves in the air somewhat analogous to the bow waves of fast-moving ships. These shock waves are regions of intensely disturbed air which produce the sonic boom effect so distressing to people living near supersonic routes. *Supersonic* is not to be confused with *ultrasonic (q.v.)*.

**Symbiosis.** When two organisms live together and both derive mutual benefit from the association, the partnership is known as symbiosis. An example is the symbiosis of an alga and a fungus in lichens; another is the ordinary pea plant and the bacteria which live in the nodules on the pea's roots.

**Synapse** is the point of association between one nerve cell and another. The nervous impulse traveling along one nerve has to be transmitted to the next across a minute gap. This is the synaptic gap. The mode of transmission is chemical though it was at first thought to be electrical. The impulse arriving at the synapse releases a chemical transmitter which diffuses across the gap and stimulates an impulse in the adjacent nerve cell.

# T

**Tantalum,** a scarce bluish metallic element, no. 73, symbol Ta, discovered by Ekeburg in 1802. Chemically related to vanadium and niobium, it is usually associated with the latter in nature. For several purposes it can be used in place of platinum, and it finds application in the making of surgical instruments. Tantalum is very hard, and resistant to acids (other than hydrofluoric acid); it is used in alloys.

**Telescope,** an optical instrument for viewing objects at a distance, "the astronomer's intelligencer". Lippershey is credited with construction of the first in 1608; Galileo constructed several from 1609 and Newton was the first to construct a reflecting telescope. The ordinary telescope consists of an object-glass and an eye-lens, with two intermediates to bring the object into an erect position. A lens brings it near to us, and the magnifier enlarges it for inspection. A refracting telescope gathers the rays together near the eyepiece and is necessarily limited as to size, but the reflecting telescope collects the rays on a larger mirror, and these are thrown back to the eyepiece. The world's largest reflectors are at Mount Pastukhov, Caucasus (6 m; 19.7 ft), Mount Palomar, California (200 in), Mount Wilson, California (100 in), the McDonald Observatory at Mount Locke, Texas (82 in), and the Victoria B.C. Observatory (183 cm; 72.05 in). The *Hale* 200 in telescope at Mount Palomar has revealed objects never before photographed; it is able to probe space and photograph remote galaxies out to a limiting distance of 2,000 million light years. The *Schmidt* telescope at Mount Palomar has been used to make a huge photographic map of the universe. The 98 in *Isaac Newton* telescope has been moved from the Royal Observatory at Herstmonceux, Sussex, to La Palma, Canary Is. The giant steerable radio telescope built by Manchester University at Jodrell Bank, Cheshire, has a 250 ft reflector. The largest single radio dish in the world is the non-steerable 300 m (984.25 in.) instrument at Arecibo in Puerto Rico. Another instrument of radio astronomy is the interferometer which consists of spaced aerials. The biggest of these is in New Mexico, the array consisting of 27 steerable parabolic dishes 82 ft in diameter. Recently the technique of linking radio telescopes on different continents has been developed for fine observation.

**Tellurium,** a relatively scarce element, no. 52, symbol Te, discovered in 1782 by von Reichenstein. Chemically it behaves rather like sulfur; its salts are known as tellurides. It occurs chiefly combined with metals in ores of gold, silver, copper and lead. It is a semiconductor, and some of its compounds (also semiconductors) are coming into use in technical devices.

**Templars** were soldier knights organized in the 12th century for the purpose of protecting pilgrims in their journeyings to and from Jerusalem, and obtained their name from having had granted to them by Baldwin II a temple for their accommodation. At first they were nonmilitary, and wore neither crests nor helmets, but a long wide mantle and a red cross on the left shoulder. They were established in England about 1180. During the crusades they rendered valuable service, showing great bravery and devotion. In the 12th century they founded numerous religious houses in various parts of Europe and became possessed of considerable wealth. It was this that caused their downfall. Kings and Popes alike grew jealous of their influence, and they were subjected to much persecution, and Pope Clement V abolished the Order in 1312. Edward II in 1308 seized all the property of the English Templars. The English possessions of the Order were transferred to the Hospitallers of St. John, afterwards called the Knights of Malta.

**Terbium,** an element, no. 65, symbol Tb, discovered in 1842 by Mosander, belonging to the group of rare-earth metals.

**Teredo,** the scientific name of the ship-worm, a peculiar bivalve mollusk, which lodges itself when young on the bottoms of wooden ships and bores its way inwards, causing much injury.

**Termites,** also known as *White Ants*, though they are not related to the true ants and are placed in an entirely different insect order *(Isoptera)*. They abound in the tropics and also occur in temperate countries, though only two species are common in Europe. There is no British species. They live in colonies and their nests take the form of mounds of earth and wood, cemented together with saliva, and up to 6 m; 19.69 ft). in height. Five separate castes are recognised, three of them being capable of reproduction, and the other two are sterile.

**Thallium,** a blue-grey metallic element, no. 81, symbol Tl, discovered by Crookes in 1861. It is obtained from the flue dust resulting from the burning of pyrites for sulfuric acid manufacture.

**Thorium,** a scarce, dark grey, metal element, no. 90, symbol Th, discovered by Berzelius in 1828. All substances containing thorium are radioactive. Chief source of thorium is monazite sand, big deposits of which occur in Travancore (India), Brazil and the USA. Considered important as a potential source of atomic energy since the discovery that it can be transmuted into $U^{233}$, which is capable of fission like $U^{235}$.

**Tides,** the periodical rise and fall of the waters of the ocean and its arms, are due to the gravitational effect of the moon and sun. Newton was the first to give a general explanation of the phenomenon of the tides. He supposed the ocean to cover the whole earth and to assume at each instant a figure of equilibrium, under the combined gravitational influence of earth, sun and moon, thus making and controlling the tides. At most places there are two tides a day, and the times of high- and low-water vary according to the positions of the sun and moon relative to the earth. When earth, moon and sun are in line (at full moon and new moon) the gravitational pull is greatest and we get "spring" tides. When sun and moon are at right angles (first and third quarters of the moon's phases) we get the smaller "neap" tides.

**Tin** is a white, metal element, no. 50, symbol Sn (Latin *Stannum*), whose commonest ore is cassiterite (tin oxide), which occurs in Malaya, Indonesia, Bolivia, Zaïre, Nigeria and Cornwall. It protects iron from rusting, and the tin coating on tinplate is applied by dipping the thin steel sheet in molten tin or by electrolysis. Tin alloys of importance include solder, bronze, pewter and Britannia metal.

**Titanium,** a scarce metallic element, no. 22, symbol Ti, difficult to extract from ores, found in association with oxygen in rutile, anatase and brookite, as well as with certain magnetic iron ores. It combines with nitrogen at a high temperature. Discovered by the Rev. William Gregor in 1791. Titanium alloys, being very resistant to stress and corrosion, and combining strength with lightness, and finding wide application not only in marine and chemical engineering but in the building of aircraft, rockets, and the nuclear-energy field. Titanium dioxide is now widely used in making paints.

**TNT (Trinitrotoluene).** A high explosive formed by the action of a mixture of nitric and sulfuric acids on toluene. Not highly sensitive to shock, it can be used in shells without danger, and is exploded by a time, or detonator, fuse. Apart from wartime applications, it is used in blasting in quarries and mines.

**Topaz,** a transparent mineral gem, being a silicate and fluoride of aluminum and generally found in granite rocks. Its color is yellow, but it also occurs in pink and blue shades. The best kinds come from Brazil.

**Trade Winds** form part of the circulation of air round the great permanent anticyclones of the tropics and blow inwards from north-east (Northern Hemisphere) and south-east (Southern Hemisphere) towards the equatorial region of low pressure. Atlantic trades are more regular than those of the Pacific. The belts may extend over 2,400 km; 1,491 mi) of latitude and, together with the Doldrums, move north and south in sympathy with the seasonal changes in the sun's declination, the average annual range being about 5 degrees of latitude.

**Tree Rings as Natural Calendar.** The approximate relationship between radiocarbon dating *(q.v.)* and true calendar age for the past 7,000 years has been established from measurements on tree-rings. Because one tree-ring is formed annually and its thickness is characteristic of the climatic conditions during its growth, it is possible, by comparing distinctive groups of rings, to date a series of trees. By using the long-lived Bristle Cone pines, tree-rings dating back to 500 B.C. have been obtained. It has been found that the radiocarbon age around, say, 3000 B.C. is too young by *c.* 600 years and because of short-term fluctuations near, say, 2000 B.C., a particular radiocarbon age can correspond to more than one true calendar age. These corrections are far less than those proved necessary after the publication of the first radiocarbon dates. Tree-rings (based on the measurement of deuterium in wood) can also show the pattern of temperature fluctuations over hundreds of years and thus make it possible to trace climatic changes before written records began. The term for tree-ring dating is dendrochronology.

**Trilobites,** extinct marine arthropods, most abundant in the Cambrian and Ordovician systems. Their appearance may be roughly described as resembling that of a woodhouse, and like that animal the trilobites were capable of rolling their bodies up into a ball.

**Trireme,** an ancient vessel with three rows of oars of great effectuality in early naval warfare. Mentioned by Thucydides. It was a long, narrow vessel propelled by 170 rowers. The Romans copied it from the Greeks.

**Tritium,** a radioactive isotope of hydrogen which has three times the weight of the ordinary hydrogen atom. It is produced by bombarding an isotope of lithium with neutrons and has a half-life of 121 years, decaying with the emission of $\beta$-particles (electrons).

**Troubadours,** lyric poets who flourished from the 12th to the end of the 13th century, chiefly in Provence and the north of Italy. They were often knightly amateurs, and cultivated a lyrical poetry intricate in metre and rhyme and usually of a romantic amatory strain, written in the *langue d'oc.* They did much to cultivate the romantic sentiment in days when society was somewhat barbaric and

helped considerably in the formation of those unwritten codes of honor which served to mitigate the rudeness of medieval days.

**Tsunami,** a seismic sea wave originating from any one of several submarine geological phenomena such as volcanic explosions, landslides of earth movements. Tsunamis are extremely long wavelength waves which travel in the open ocean at speeds up to 640 km/h (398 mph). In deep water their height is only barely perceptible, but on reaching shallow coastal water they may attain heights of up to 30 m (98 ft) and can cause devastation to low-lying areas. The Pacific Ocean, whose rim is a seismically active area, is particularly susceptible to tsunamis. Following the damage caused by a tsunami which struck the volcanic islands of Hawaii on 1 April 1946, an early-warning system has been in operation. Tsunamis are often incorrectly referred to as tidal waves.

**Tuatara** *or* **Sphenodon,** a reptile of great antiquity, the sole surviving species of the *Rhynchocephalia,* found in New Zealand. It has a rudimentary third eye on the top of the head; this is called the pineal eye and corresponds to tissue which in mammals forms the pineal gland.

**Tundra,** the vast treeless plains lying in northern N. America and northern USSR where long severe winters and permanently frozen subsoils (permafrost) have resulted in specially adapted plant communities. The summer thaw and impervious permafrost cause waterlogging of lowland areas and marsh plants occur on these sites. In summer the ground cover of lichens and mosses with some flowering plants is distinctive. Stunted willows and birches occur in certain sites.

**Tungsten,** a hard, brittle metallic element, no. 74, symbol W (it was formerly called wolfram), silver to grey in color. Its chief ores are wolframite (iron and manganese tungstate) and scheelite (calcium tungstate). Tungsten is alloyed in steel for the manufacture of cutting tools; also in the nonferrous alloy stellite. Electric lamp filaments are made from tungsten. Tungsten carbide is one of the hardest substances known and is used for tipping tools.

**Turquoise,** formerly called Turkey-Stone, is a blue or greenish-blue precious stone, the earliest and best specimens of which came from Persia. It is composed of a phosphate of aluminum, with small proportions of copper and iron. India, Tibet, and Silesia yield turquoises, and a variety is found in New Mexico and Nevada. It derives its name from the fact that the first specimens were imported through Turkey.

# U

**Ultrasonics,** sound waves of frequency so high as to be inaudible to humans, *i.e.,* above 15,000 Hz (Hz is SI unit for cycle per sec.). Ultrasonic waves are commonly produced by causing a solid object to vibrate with a suitable high frequency and to impart its vibrations to the air or other fluid. The object may be a quartz or other crystal in which vibrations are excited electrically, or a nickel component which is magnetically energised. There are numerous technical applications, *e.g.* submarine echo soundings, flaw detection in castings, drilling glass and ceramics, emulsification. Ultrasonic waves are an important tool of research in physics. Bats produce very loud sounds when they are flying, but at ultrasonic frequencies (20,000 to 150,000 Hz), so that we cannot ourselves hear them.

**Ultra-Violet Rays.** These are invisible electromagnetic rays whose wavelengths are less than 3900 A. (Angstrom = one hundred-millionth of a centimetre.) The sun's radiation is rich in ultra-violet light, but much of it never reaches the earth, being absorbed by molecules of atmospheric gases (in particular, ozone) as well as by soot and smoke particles. One beneficial effect of ultra-violet light on human beings is that it brings about synthesis of vitamin-I) from certain fatty substances (called sterols) in the skin. The wavelengths which effect this vitamin synthesis also cause sun tan and sun burn. Ultra-violet lamps (which are mercury-vapor discharge lamps) are also used for sterilising the air inside buildings, their rays being lethal to bacteria. Many substances fluoresce under ultra-violet light; for instance, zinc silicate glows green, while cadmium borate throws out red light. This phenomenon is applied practically in fluorescent lamps, the light of requisite hue being secured by judicious mixture of the fluorescent materials which coat the lamp.

**Uranium,** a metallic element, no. 92, symbol U, discovered by Klaproth in 1789 in pitchblende. It is a white metal which tarnishes readily in air. Great developments have followed the discovery that the nucleus of the uranium isotope $U^{235}$ undergoes fission, and uranium minerals have become very important since it was found that atomic energy could be released controllably by taking advantage of fission. Before atomic energy work began to take the major part of the world's output of uranium minerals, the chief users of uranium compounds were the ceramics and textile industries.

**Ursa Major** and **Ursa Minor** ("Greater Bear" and "Lesser Bear"), two celebrated constellations, each of seven stars, in the northern celestial hemisphere, familiar since ancient times. Ursa Major has also been called "the Plough", "Charles's (Charlemagne's) Wain" or "the Wagon". The "Pointers" in this group of bright stars point to the brightest star in Ursa Minor, the Pole Star. Called the Big Dipper and the Little Dipper in the USA.

# V

**Valency.** A term used by chemists is describe the combining ability of an element with respect to hydrogen. Thus oxygen, which forms water, $H_2O$, with hydrogen is said to have a valency of two, nitrogen (forms ammonia, $NH_3$) three, and carbon (forms methane, $CH_4$) four. Chlorine forms hydrogen chloride, HCl, and is said to be monovalent. This empirical approach cannot account for valency in such compounds as carbon monoxide, CO, which appears to require both elements to have the same valency. With the discovery of the electron it was realised that the concept of valency and chemical bonds is intimately concerned with the electronic structure of atoms, and theories have been advanced to explain why the same element can have different valencies in different compounds. Iron, for example, can have a valency of two ($FeCl_2$, ferrous chloride) or three ($FeCl_3$, ferric chloride).

**Vanadium,** a scarce metallic element, no. 23, symbol V, whose chief ores are carnotite and patronite. Some iron ores contain it. Most of the vanadium commercially produced finds its way into vanadium steels, which are used for tools and parts of vehicles, being hard, tough and very resistant to shocks. The oxide is used as a catalyst in industry, especially in making sulfuric acid.

**Van Allen Belts.** One of the most remarkable discoveries made during the IGY, 1957–58, was that the earth is surrounded by a great belt of radiation. Evidence came from *Sputnik II* (which carried the dog Laika) and from the American satellites, *Explorers I* and *III*. The American scientist, J. A. van Allen, was able to explain the puzzling data collected from these satellites. Subsequent observations with deep space-probes showed that there are in fact two zones of high intensity particle radiation surrounding the earth, one concentrated at a distance of about 1,600 km (994 mi), the other at about 24,000 km (14,913 mi). A close relation exists between the shapes of the zones and the earth's magnetic field. Recent evidence suggests that Jupiter also is surrounded by a dense belt of trapped high-energy particles.

**Venus Fly-trap,** a well-known insectivorous plant *(Dionaea muscipula)* occurring in Carolina in damp mossy places. It is related to the Sundew. The leaf is the organ that catches the insects. The leaf blade is in two halves, hinged along the centre line. Each half bears three sensitive hairs called "trigger hairs". When an insect touches a trigger, the two halves of the leaf clap together, trapping the insect between them, when it is digested by a secretion (digestive enzymes) from the leaf, which afterwards absorbs the soluble products.

**Vitamins,** name of a group of organic substances found in relatively minute amounts in certain foodstuffs, essential for growth and the maintenance of normal bodily structure and function. The Hungarian biochemist Szent-Györgyi, who first isolated vitamin C or ascorbic acid, defined the vitamin as "a substance that makes you ill if you don't eat it!"

# W

**Walrus,** a very large marine mammal, related to the seals having in the upper jaw two large curved tusks, which average in length from 38 to 60 cm (15 to 24 in). It lives on bi-valve mollusks, and inhabits the Arctic seas. An adult walrus can exceed 4 m (13 ft) in length and weigh over a ton.

**Water** is the simplest compound of hydrogen and oxygen. It is formed when an electric spark is passed through a mixture of the gases, and is a product of combustion of all hydrogen-containing compounds, *e.g.,* petrol, coal, coal gas and wood. Water is essential to living matter, and is the medium which carries food to animals and plants. Salts in hard water may be removed by distillation of the water or by a process known as ion-exchange (water softening). Pure water freezes at 0° C (32° F) and boils at 100° C (212° F) and is used as a standard of temperature on this scale. It has a maximum density at 4° C (39° F). Heating water above 100° C (212° F) converts it into steam, which is used under pressure to convert heat energy into useful work, as in electrical power stations and steam engines. Water gas is a mixture mainly of carbon monoxide and hydrogen formed by blowing steam and oxygen through red-hot coke: it is used as a fuel. Water is one of the very few compounds which freezes from the surface down rather than from the bulk of the liquid up.

This property has important consequences on the preservation of life in rivers and lakes when they are frozen.

**Whale,** a completely aquatic mammal; the fore-limbs are modified to form fin-like paddles and there is virtually no external trace of the hind-limbs. There are two major groups of whales—the *Toothed Whales,* including the Sperm-whale (Cachalot), Dolphin, Killer-whales and Porpoises; and the *Whalebone Whales.* In the latter a series of whale-bone plates grow down from the roof of the mouth, and, being frayed at their edges into a hairy fringe, together constitute a filtering mechanism. The animal takes in sea water containing minute organisms on which it feeds; the mouth is then closed and the tongue raised when the water is forced out through the filter, on which is left the food. As the tongue is lowered, the whalebone plates straighten up, flicking the food on to the tongue, which transfers it to the gut. Most whale oil is obtained from the thick layer of fat under the skin (blubber), but in the Sperm-whale there is a large reserve of oil in the head. One of the major users of sperm oil is the leather industry. Ambergris used in perfumery comes from the intestine of whales. The number of whales that may be killed in a season is limited by International Convention. The three main whaling nations are Japan, Norway and the Soviet Union.

**Willow,** a water-side-loving tree of the genus *Salix,* to which the osiers belong. The best cricket-bat blades are made from a white willow, *S. alba* var. *caerulea,* a fine tree with bluish-green leaves, mostly found in Essex. Willow is also used for polo balls. Weeping willow, *S. babylonica,* is native to China and is the willow seen on Old China willow-pattern plates.

**Wind,** air set in motion by special atmospheric conditions, is of various degrees, from a slight rustling breeze to a hurricane. Winds are *constant,* as in trade winds or anti-trade winds; *periodic,* as in monsoons and other wind-visitations occurring according to influences of season; *cyclonic* and *anti-cyclonic,* when their motion is spiral: *whirlwinds, hurricanes,* and *tornados,* when high temperature and great density induce extreme agitation. Ordinarily, a wind is named from the point of the compass from which it blows, or it may be expressed in degrees from true north. The *sirocco,* the *mistral,* and the *simoom* are local forms of winds of great velocity. A *blizzard* is a biting blast of icy temperature.

# X

**Xenon** a rare gaseous element, no.54, symbol Xe, occurring in minute quantities in the atmosphere, discovered by Sir William Ramsay and M. W. Travers in 1898.

**X-Rays** were discovered in 1895 by Professor Röntgen, of Wurzburg, while experimenting with a Crookes vacuum tube, when a photographic plate enclosed in a dark box was noticed to have become fogged. X-rays are now commonly used to examine the internal structure of many opaque objects. In medicine, industry and for security, examination may be conducted without physical invasion. X-rays may also be used to probe the structure of matter, for example the atomic structure of crystals. The discovery in the 1960s that cosmic objects emitted intense X-rays has led to many important new astronomical phenomena being discovered.

**Xylem,** the woody tissue of higher plants whose function is to conduct water and mineral salts upwards, and to provide mechanical support.

# Y

**Yak,** a curious, long-haired ox, found in Tibet used as a beast of burden, and also kept for milk and meat.

**Ytterbium,** a chemical, no.70, symbol Yb, element discovered by Urbain in 1907; one of the group of rare earth metals.

**Yttrium,** a chemical element, no.39, symbol Y, discovered by Mosander in 1842. It is found in a few rare minerals such as gadolinite, xenotine, fergusonite and euxenite. One of the group of rare earth metals.

# Z

**Zero,** the cipher signifying nothing originally came from China. The West is indebted to the Arabs for it, who themselves obtained it from India and passed it to European mathematicians towards the end of the Middle Ages. The zero has also been found in Babylonian cuneiform. The Greeks had no such symbol, which hindered the development of their mathematics. The use of zero led to the invention of decimal fractions and to the later developments in astronomy, physics and chemistry. For absolute zero on the temperature scale *see* **Absolute Temperature.**

**Zinc,** a familiar metallic element, no.30, symbol Zn, known to the ancients, and used by them in the making of brass. It occurs as the sulfide carbonate, etc. The ores of zinc are crushed, roasted and reduced with coal. In combination with copper it constitutes the familiar alloy called brass, and zinc itself is much used for roofing and other protective purposes. Zinc ores are mined in Canada, the USA, Mexico, Poland, Australia, Russia, Italy, Spain and many other parts of the world. Zinc smelting is carried on in most industrial countries, including Great Britain.

**Zirconium,** metallic element, no.40, symbol Zr, was discovered by Klaproth in the sand of the rivers of Sri Lanka in 1789. The crystalline metal is white, soft and ductile; in its amorphous condition it is a blue-black powder. Zirconium is used in atomic reactors as containers for fuel elements, since it does not absorb neutrons.

**Zodiacal Light,** a faint cone of light occasionally seen stretching along the zodiac from the western horizon after evening twilight or the eastern horizon before morning twilight. It is believed to be due to the scattering of the sun's light by dust particles in orbit round the sun and extending beyond the earth. Recent observations at the high altitudes station at Chacaltaya in the Andes suggest that the dust is travelling round the sun in regular planetary orbits.

**Zonda,** a warm moist wind in Argentina of great velocity blowing from the north or northwest, and, like the Sirocco in Southern Europe, causes much discomfort. It happens when a depression is moving across the pampas, bringing with it a mass of air from the humid tropics. It is followed by a refreshing wind from the south east.

## First Aid to Crossword Puzzlers

We cannot begin to list all the odd words you will meet with in your daily and Sunday crossword puzzles, for such words run into many thousands. But we have tried to include those that turn up most frequently, as well as many others that should be of help to you when you are unable to go any further.

Also, we do not guarantee that the definitions in your puzzle will be exactly the same as ours, although we have checked every word with a standard dictionary and have followed its definition.

In nearly every case, we have used as the key word the principal noun of the definition, rather than any adjective, adjective phrase, or noun used as an adjective. And, to simplify your searching, we have grouped the words according to the number of spaces you have to fill.

For a list of Foreign Phrases, *see* Index. For Rulers of England and Great Britain, France, Germany and Prussia, and Russia, *see* Countries of the World.

## Words of Two Letters

Ambary, DA
And (French, Latin), ET
Article (Arabic), AL
  (French), LA, LE, UN
  (Spanish), EL, LA, UN
At the (French), AU
  (Spanish), AL
Behold, LO
Bird: Hawaiian, OO
Birthplace: Abraham's, UR
Bone, OS
Buddha, FO
Butterfly: Peacock, IO
Champagne, AY
Chaos, NU
Chief: Burmese, BO
Coin: Roman, AS
  Siamese, AT
Concerning, RE
Dialect: Chinese, WU
Double (Egy. relig.), KA
Drama: Japanese, NO
Egg (comb. form), OO
Esker, OS
Eye (Scotch), EE
Factor: Amplification, MU
Fifty (Greek), NU
Fish: Carplike, ID
Force, OD
Forty (Greek), MU
From (French, Latin, Spanish), DE

(Latin prefix), AB
From the (French), DU
God: Babylonian, EA, ZU
  Egyptian sun, RA
  Hindu unknown, KA
  Semitic, EL
Goddess: Babylonian, AI
  Greek earth, GE
Gold (heraldry), OR
Gulf: Arctic, OB
Heart (Egy. relig.), AB
Indian: South American, GE
King: Of Bashan, OG
Language: Artificial, RO
  Assamese, AO
Lava: Hawaiian, AA
Letter: Greek, MU, NU, PI, XI
  Hebrew, HE, PE
Lily: Palm, TI
Measure: Annamese, LY
  Chinese, HO, HU, KO, LI, MU, PU, TO, TU
  Japanese, GO, JO, MO, RI, SE, TO
  Metric land, AR
  Netherlands, EL
  Portuguese, PE
  Siamese, WA
  Swedish, AM
  Type, EM, EN
Monk: Buddhist, BO
Month: Jewish, AB

Mouth, OS
Mulberry: Indian, AL
Native: Burmese, WA
Note: Of Scale, DO, FA, MI, LA, RE, TI
Of (French, Latin, Spanish), DE
Of the (French), DU
One (Scotch), AE
Pagoda: Chinese, TA
Plant: East Indian fiber, DA
Ridge: Sandy, AS, OS
River: Russian, OB
Sloth: Three-toed, AI
Soul (Egy. relig.), BA
Sound: Hindu mystic, OM
Suffix: Comparative, ER
The. *See* Article
To the: French, AU
  Spanish, AL
Tree: Buddhist sacred, BO
Tribe: Assamese, AO
Type: Jumbled, PI
Weight: Annamese, TA
  Chinese, LI
  Danish, ES
  Japanese, MO
  Roman, AS
Whirlwind: Faeroe Is., OE
Yes (German), JA
  (Italian, Spanish), SI
  (Russian), DA

## Words of Three Letters

**Adherent:** IST
Again, BIS
Age, ERA
Antelope: African, GNU, KOB
Apricot: Japanese, UME
Article (German), DAS, DEM, DEN, DER, DES, DIE, EIN
  (French), LES, UNE
  (Spanish), LAS, LOS, UNA
**Banana:** Polynesian, FEI
Barge, HOY
Bass: African, IYO
Beak, NEB, NIB
Beard: Grain, AWN
Beetle: June, DOR
Being, ENS
Berry: Hawthorn, HAW
Beverage: Hawaiian, AVA
Bird: Australian, EMU
  Crowlike, JAY
  Extinct, MOA

Fabulous, ROC
Frigate, IWA
Parson, POE, TUE, TUI
Sea, AUK
Blackbird, ANI, ANO
Born, NEE
Bronze: Roman, AES
Bugle: Yellow, IVA
By way of, VIA
**Canton:** Swiss, URI
Cap: Turkish, FEZ
Catnip, NEP
Character: In "Faerie Queene," UNA
Coin: Afghan, PUL
  Albanian, LEK
  British Guiana, BIT
  Bulgarian, LEV, LEW
  French, ECU, SOU
  Indian, PIE
  Japanese, SEN, YEN
  Korean, WON

Lithuanian, LIT
Macao, Timor, AVO
Palestinian, MIL
Persian, PUL
Peruvian, SOL
Rumanian, BAN, LEU, LEY
Scandinavian, ORE
Siamese, ATT
  *See also* Money of account
Collection: Facts, ANA
Commune: Belgian, ANS, ATH
  Netherlands, EDE, EPE
Community: Russian, MIR
Constellation: Southern, ARA
Contraction: Poetic, EEN, EER, OER
Covering: Apex of roof, EPI
Crab: Fiddler, UCA
Crag: Rocky, TOR
Cry: Crow, rook, raven, CAW
Cup: Wine, AMA
Cymbal, Oriental, TAL, ZEL

**Disease:** Silkworm, UJI
**Division:** Danish territorial, AMT
  Geologic, EON
Doctrine, ISM
Dowry, DOT
Dry (French), SEC
**Dynasty:** Chinese, CHI, HAN, SUI, WEI,
  YIN
**Eagle:** Sea, ERN
Earth (comb. form), GEO
Egg: Louse, NIT
Eggs: Fish, ROE
Emmet, ANT
Enzyme, ASE
Equal (comb. form), ISO
Extension: building, ELL
**Far** (comb. form), TEL
Farewell, AVE
Fiber: Palm, TAL
Finial, EPI
Fish: Carplike, IDE
  Pikelike, GAR
Flatfish, DAB
Fleur-de-lis, LIS, LYS
Food: Hawaiian, POI
Formerly, NEE
Friend (French), AMI
**Game:** Card, LOO
Garment: Camel-hair, ABA
Gateway, DAR
Gazelle: Tibetan, GOA
Genus: Ducks, AIX
  Grasses, POA
  Grasses (maize), ZEA
  Herbs or shrubs, IVA
  Lizards, UTA
  Rodents (incl. house mice), MUS
  Ruminants (incl. cattle), BOS
  Swine, SUS
Gibbon: Malay, LAR
God: Assyrian, SIN
  Babylonian, ABU, ANU, BEL, HEA,
    SIN, UTU
  Irish sea, LER
  Phrygian, MEN
  Polynesian, ORO
Goddess: Babylonian, AYA
  Etruscan, UNI
  Hindu, SRI, UMA, VAC
  Teutonic, RAN
Governor: Algerian, DEY
  Turkish, BEY
Grampus, ORC
Grape, UVA
Grass: Meadow, POA
Gypsy, ROM
**Hail,** AVE
Hare: Female, DOE
Hawthorn, HAW
Hay: Spread for drying, TED
Herb: Japanese, UDO
  Perennial, PIA
  Used for blue dye, WAD
Herd: Whales, GAM, POD
Hero: Spanish, CID
High (music), ALT
Honey (pharm.), MEL
Humorist: American, ADE
**I** (Latin), EGO
I love (Latin), AMO
Indian: Algonquian, FOX, SAC, WEA
  Chimakuan, HOH
  Keresan, SIA
  Mayan, MAM
  Shoshonean, UTE
  Siouan, KAW, OTO
  South American, ITE, ONA, URO,
    URU, YAO
  Tierra del Fuego, ONA
  Wakashan, AHT
Ingot, PIG
Inlet: Narrow, RIA
Island: Cyclades, IOS
  Dodecanese, COS, KOS
  (French), ILE
  River, AIT

**Jackdaw,** DAW
John (Gaelic), IAN
**Keelbill,** ANI, ANO
Kiln, OST
King: British legendary LUD
Kobold, NIS
**Lace:** To make, TAT
Lamprey, EEL
Language: Artificial, IDO
  Bantu, ILA
  Siamese, LAO, TAI
Leaf: Palm, OLA, OLE
Leaving, ORT
Left: Cause to turn, HAW
Letter: Greek, CHI, ETA, PHI, PSI, RHO,
    TAU
  Hebrew, MEM, NUN, SIN, TAV, VAU
Lettuce, COS
Life (comb. form), BIO
Lily: Palm, TOI
Lizard, EFT
Louse: Young, NIT
Love (Anglo-Irish), GRA
Lute: Oriental, TAR
**Macaw:** Bralizian, ARA
Marble, TAW
Match: Shooting (French), TIR
Meadow, LEA
Measure: Abyssinian, TAT
  Algerian, PIK
  Annamese, GON, MAU, NGU, VUO,
    SAO, TAO, TAT
  Arabian, DEN, SAA
  Belgian, VAT
  Bulgarian, OKA, OKE
  Chinese, FEN, TOU, YIN
  Cloth, ELL
  Cyprus, OKA, OKE, PIK
  Czech, LAN, SAH
  Danish, FOD, MIL, POT
  Dominican Republic, ONA
  Dutch, old, AAM
  East Indian, KIT
  Egyptian, APT, HEN, PIK, ROB
  Electric, MHO, OHM
  Energy, ERG
  English, PIN
  Estonian, TUN
  French, POT
  German, AAM
  Greek, PIK
  Hebrew, CAB, HIN, KOR, LOG
  Hungarian, AKO
  Icelandic, FET
  Indian, GAZ, GUZ, JOW, KOS
  Japanese, BOO, CHO, KEN, RIN,
    SHO, SUN, TAN
  Malabar, ADY
  Metric land, ARE
  Netherlands, KAN, KOP, MUD, VAT,
    ZAK
  Norwegian, FOT, POT
  Persian, GAZ, GUZ, MOU, ZAR, ZER
  Polish, CAL
  Rangoon, DHA, LAN
  Roman, PES, URN
  Russian, FUT, LOF
  Scotch, COP
  Siamese, KEN, NIU, RAI, SAT, SEN,
    SOK, WAH, YOT
  Somaliland, TOP
  Spanish, PIE
  Straits Settlements, PAU, TUN
  Swedish, ALN, FOT, MIL, REF, TUM
  Swiss, POT
  Tunisian, SAA
  Turkish, OKA, OKE, PIK
  Wire, MIL
  Württemberg, IMI
  Yarn, LEA
  Yugoslavian, OKA, RIF
Milk, LAC
Milkfish, AWA
Moccasin, PAC
Money: Yap stone, FEI
Money of Account: Anglo-Saxon, ORA,

ORE
  French, SOU
  Indian, LAC
  Japanese, RIN
  Oman, GAJ
  Virgin Islands, BIT
  *See also* Coin
Monkey: Capuchin, SAI
Morsel, ORT
Mother: Peer Gynt's, ASE
Mountain: Asia Minor, IDA
Mulberry: Indian, AAL, ACH, AWL
Muttonbird: New Zealand, OII
**Nahoor,** SNA
Native: Mindanao, ATA
Neckpiece, BOA
Newt, EFT
No (Scotch), NAE
Note: Guido's highest, ELA
  Of scale, SOL
Nursemaid: Oriental, AMA, IYA
**Ocher:** Yellow, SIL
One (Scotch), YIN
Ornament: Pagoda, TEE
Oven: Polynesian, UMU
Ox: Tibetan, YAK
**Pagoda:** Chinese, TAA
Parrot: Hawk, HIA
  New Zealand, KEA
Part: Footlike, PES
Particle: Electrified, ION
Pasha, DEY
Pass: Mountain, COL
Paste: Rice, AME
Pea: Indian split, DAL
Peasant: Philippine, TAO
Penpoint, NEB, NIB
Piece out, EKE
Pigeon, NUN
Pine: Textile screw, ARA
Pistol (slang), GAT
Pit: Baking, IMU
Plant: Pepper, AVA
Play: By Capek, RUR
Poem: Old French, DIT
Porgy: Japanese, TAI
Priest: Biblical high, ELI
Prince Ethiopian, RAS
Pseudonym: Dickens', BOZ
**Queen:** Fairy, MAB
Quince: Bengal, BEL
**Record:** Ship's, LOG
Refuse: Flax (Scotch), PAB, POB
Resin, LAC
Resort, SPA
Revolver (slang), GAT
Right: Cause to turn, GEE
River: Scotch or English, DEE
  (Spanish), RIO
  Swiss, AAR
Room: Harem, ODA
Rootstock: Fern, ROI
Rose (Persian), GUL
Ruff: Female, REE
Rule: Indian, RAJ
**Sailor,** GOB, TAR
Saint: Female (abbr.), STE
  Mohammedan, PIR
Salt, SAL
Sash: Japanese, OBI
Scrap, ORT
Seed: Poppy, MAW
  Small, PIP
Self, EGO
Serpent: Vedic sky, AHI
Sesame, TIL
Sheep: Female, EWE
  Indian, SHA
  Male, RAM
Sheepfold (Scotch), REE
Shelter, LEE
Shield, ECU
Shooting match (French), TIR
Shrew: European, ERD
Shrub: Evergreen, YEW
Silkworm, ERI

Snake, ASP, BOA
Soak, RET
Son-in-law: Mohammed's, ALI
Sorrel: Wood, OCA
Spade: Long, narrow, LOY
Spirit: Malignant, KER
Spot: Playing-card, PIP
Spread for drying, TED
Spring: Mineral, SPA
Sprite: Water, NIX
Statesman: Japanese, ITO
Stern: Toward, AFT
Stomach: Bird's, MAW
Street (French), RUE
Summer (French), ETE
Sun, SOL
Swamp, BOG, FEN
Swan: Male, COB
**Tea:** Chinese, CHA
Temple: Shinto, SHA
The. *See* Article
Thing (law), RES
Title: Etruscan, LAR
  Monk's, FRA
  Portuguese, DOM
  Spanish, DON
  Turkish, AGA, BEY
Tool: Cutting, ADZ, AXE
  Mining, GAD
  Piercing, AWL
Tree: Candlenut, AMA
  Central American, EBO
  East Indian, SAJ, SAL

Evergreen, YEW
Hawaiian, KOA, KOU
Indian, BEL, DAR
Linden, LIN
New Zealand, AKE
Philippine, DAO, TUA, TUI
Rubber, ULE
  South American, APA
Tribe: New Zealand, ATI
Turmeric, REA
Twice, BIS
Twin: Siamese, ENG
**Uncle** (dialect), EAM, EME
**Veil:** Chalice, AER, AIR
Vessel: Wine, AMA
Vestment: Ecclesiastical, ALB
Vetch: Bitter, ERS
Victorfish, AKU
Vine: New Zealand, AKA
  Philippine, IYO
**Wallaba,** APA
Wapiti, ELK
Water (French), EAU
Waterfall, LIN
Watering place: Prussian, EMS
Weave: Designating plain, UNI
Weight: Annamese, CAN
  Bulgarian, OKA, OKE
  Burmese, MOO, VIS
  Chinese, FEN, HAO, KIN, SSU, TAN, YIN
  Cyprus, OKA, OKE
  Danish, LOD, ORT, VOG

East Indian, TJI
Egyptian, KAT, OKA, OKE
English, for wool, TOD
German, LOT
Greek, MNA, OKA, OKE
Indian, SER
Japanese, FUN, KIN, RIN, SHI
Korean, KON
Malacca, KIP
Mongolian, LAN
Netherlands, ONS
Norwegian, LOD
Polish, LUT
Rangoon, PAI
Roman, BES
Russian, LOT
Siamese, BAT, HAP, PAI
Swedish, ASS, ORT
Turkish, OKA, OKE
Yugoslavian, OKA, OKE
Whales: Herd, GAM, POD
Wildebeest, GNU
Wing, ALA
Witticism, MOT
Wolframite, CAL
Worm: African, LOA
Wreath: Hawaiian, LEI
**Yale,** ELI
Yam: Hawaiian, HOI
Yes (French), OUI
Young: Bring forth, EAN
**Z** (letter), ZED

# Words of Four Letters

**Aborigine:** Borneo, DYAK
Agave, ALOE
Animal: Footless, APOD
Ant: White, ANAI, ANAY
Antelope: African, ASSE, BISA, GUIB, KOBA, KUDU, ORYX, POKU, PUKU, TOPI, TORA
Apoplexy: Plant, ESCA
Apple, POME
Apricot, ANSU
Ardor, ELAN
Armadillo, APAR, PEBA, PEVA, TATU
Ascetic: Mohammedan, SUFI
Association: Chinese, TONG
Astronomer: Persian, OMAR
Avatar: Of Vishnu, RAMA
Axillary, ALAR
**Band:** Horizontal (heraldry), FESS
Barracuda, SPET
Bark: Mulberry, TAPA
Base: Column, DADO
Bearing (heraldry), ORLE
Beer: Russian, KVAS
Beige, ECRU
Being, ESSE
Beverage: Japanese rice, SAKE
Bird: Asian, MINA, MYNA
  Egyptian sacred, IBIS
  Extinct, DODO, MAMO
  Flightless, KIWI
  Gull-like, TERN
  Hawaiian, IIWI, MAMO
  Parson, KOKO
  Unfledged, EYAS
Birds: As class, AVES
Black, EBON
  (French), NOIR
Blackbird: European, MERL
Boat: Flat-bottomed, DORY
Bone: Forearm, ULNA
Bones, OSSA
Box, Japanese, INRO
Bravo (rare), EUGE
Buffalo: Indian wild, ARNA
Bull (Spanish), TORO
Burden, ONUS
**Cabbage:** Sliced, SLAW

Caliph: Mohammedan, OMAR
Canoe: Malay, PRAU, PROA
Cap: Military, KEPI
Cape, NESS
Capital: Ancient Irish, TARA
Case: Article, ETUI
Cat: Wild, BALU, EYRA
Chalcedony, SARD
Chamber: Indian ceremonial, KIVA
Channel: Brain, ITER
Cheese: Dutch, EDAM
Chest: Sepulchral stone, CIST
Chieftain: Arab, EMIR
Church: Part of, APSE, NAVE
  (Scotch), KIRK
Claim (law), LIEN
Cluster: Flower, CYME
Coin: Chinese, TAEL, YUAN
  German, MARK
  Indian, ANNA
  Iranian, RIAL
  Italian, LIRA
  Moroccan, OKIA
  Siamese, BAHT
  South American, PESO
  Spanish, DURO, PESO
  Turkish, PARA
Commune: Belgian, AATH
Composition: Musical, OPUS
Compound: Chemical, DIOL
Constellation: Southern, PAVO
Council: Russian, DUMA
Counsel, REDE
Covering: Seed, ARIL
Cross: Egyptian, ANKH
Cry: Bacchanalian, EVOE
Cup (Scotch), TASS
Cupbearer, SAKI
**Dagger,** DIRK
  Malay, KRIS
Dam: River, WEIR
Dash, ELAN
Date: Roman, IDES
Dawn: Pertaining to, EOAN
Dean: English, INGE
Decay: In fruit, BLET
Deer: Sambar, MAHA

Disease: Skin, ACNE
Disk: Solar, ATEN
Dog: Hunting, ALAN
Drink: Hindu intoxicating, SOMA
Duck, SMEE, SMEW, TEAL
Dynasty: Chinese, CHEN, CHIN, CHOU, CHOW, HSIA, MING, SUNG, TANG, TSIN
  Mongol, YUAN
**Eagle:** Biblical, GIER
  Sea, ERNE
Egyptian: Christian, COPT
Ear: Pertaining to, OTIC
Entrance: Mine, ADIT
Esau, EDOM
Escutcheon: Voided, ORLE
Eskers, OSAR
Evergreen: New Zealand, TAWA
**Fairy:** Persian, PERI
Family: Italian, ESTE
Far (comb. form), TELE
Farewell, VALE
Father (French), PERE
Fennel: Philippine, ANIS
Fever: Malarial, AGUE
Fiber: East Indian, JUTE
Firn, NEVE
Fish: Carplike, DACE
  Hawaiian, ULUA
  Herringlike, SHAD
  Mackerellike, CERO
  Marine, HAKE
  Sea, LING, MERO, OPAH
  Spiny-finned, GOBY
Food: Tropical, TARO
Foot: Metric, IAMB
Formerly, ERST
Founder: Of Carthage, DIDO
France: Southern, MIDI
Furze, ULEX
**Gaelic,** ERSE
Gaiter, SPAT
Game: Card, FARO, SKAT
Garlic: European wild, MOLY
Garment: Hindu, SARI
  Roman, TOGA
Gazelle, CORA

Gem, JADE, ONYX, OPAL, RUBY
Genus: Amphibians (incl. frogs), RANA
 Amphibians (incl. tree toads), HYLA
 Antelopes, ORYX
 Auks, ALCA, URIA
 Bees, APIS
 Birds (American ostriches), RHEA
 Birds (cranes), CRUS
 Birds (magpies), PICA
 Birds (peacocks), PAVO
 Cetaceans, INIA
 Ducks (incl. mallards), ANAS
 Fishes (burbots), LOTA
 Fishes (incl. bowfins), AMIA
 Geese (snow geese), CHEN
 Gulls, XEMA
 Herbs, ARUM, GEUM
 Insects (water scorpions), NEPA
 Lilies, ALOE
 Mammals (mankind), HOMO
 Orchids, DISA
 Owls, ASIO, BUBO, OTUS
 Palms, NIPA
 Sea birds, SULA
 Sheep, OVIS
 Shrubs, Eurasian, ULEX
 Shrubs (hollies), ILEX
 Shrubs (incl. Virginia Willow), ITEA
 Shrubs, tropical, EVEA
 Snakes (sand snakes), ERYX
 Swans, OLOR
 Trees, chocolate, COLA
 Trees (ebony family), MABA
 Trees (incl. maples), ACER
 Trees (olives), OLEA
 Trees, tropical, EVEA
 Turtles, EMYS
Goat: Wild, IBEX, KRAS, TAHR, TAIR, THAR
God: Assyrian, ASUR
 Babylonian, ADAD, ADDU, ENKI, ENZU, IRRA, NABU, NEBO, UTUG
 Celtic, LLEU, LLEW
 Hindu, AGNI, CIVA, DEVA, DEWA, KAMA, RAMA, SIVA, VAYU
 Phrygian, ATYS
 Semitic, BAAL
 Teutonic, HLER
Goddess: Babylonian, ERUA, GULA
 Hawaiian, PELE
 Hindu, DEVI, KALI, SHRI, VACH
Gooseberry: Hawaiian, POHA
Gourd, PEPO
Grafted (heraldry), ENTE
Grandfather (obsolete), AIEL
Grandparents: Pertaining to, AVAL
Grass: Hawaiian, HILO
Gray (French), GRIS
Green (heraldry), VERT
Groom: Indian, SYCE
Half (prefix), DEMI, HEMI, SEMI
Hamlet, DORP
Hammer-head: Part of, PEEN
Handle, ANSA
Harp: Japanese, KOTO
Hartebeest, ASSE, TORA
Hautboy, OBOE
Hawk: Taken from nest (falconry), EYAS
Hearing (law), OYER
Heater: For liquids, ETNA
Herb: Aromatic, ANET, DILL
 Fabulous, MOLY
 Perennial, GEUM, SEGO
 Pot, WORT
 Used for blue dye, WADE, WOAD
Hill: Flat-topped, MESA
 Sand, DENE, DUNE
Hoarfrost, RIME
Hog: Immature female, GILT
Holly, ILEX
House: Cow, BYRE
 (Spanish), CASA
Ice: Floating, FLOE
Image, ICON, IKON
Incarnation: Of Vishnu, RAMA

Indian: Algonquian, CREE, SAUK
 Central American, MAYA
 Iroquoian, ERIE
 Mexican, CORA
 Peruvian, CANA, INCA, MORO
 Shoshonean, HOPI
 Siouan, OTOE
 Southwestern, HOPI, PIMA, YUMA, ZUNI
Insect: Immature, PUPA
Instrument: Stringed, LUTE, LYRE
Ireland, EIRE, ERIN
Jacket: English, ETON
Jail (British), GAOL
Jar, OLLA
Judge: Mohammedan, CADI
Juniper: European, CADE
Kiln, OAST, OVEN
King: British legendary, LUDD, NUDD
Kiss, BUSS
Knife: Philippine, BOLO
Koran: Section of, SURA
Laborer: Spanish American, PEON
Lake: Mountain, TARN
 (Scotch), LOCH
Lamp: Miner's, DAVY
Landing place: Indian, GHAT
Language: Buddhist, PALI
 Japanese, AINU
Latvian, LETT
Layer: Of iris, UVEA
Leaf: Palm, OLAY, OLLA
Legislature: Ukrainian, RADA
Lemur, LORI
Leopard, PARD
Let it stand, STET
Letter: Greek, BETA, IOTA, ZETA
 Hebrew, AYIN, BETH, CAPH, KOPH, RESH, SHIN, TETH, YODH
 Papal, BULL
Lily, ALOE
Literature: Hindu sacred, VEDA
Lizard, GILA
 Monitor, URAN
Loquat, BIWA
Magistrate: Genoese or Venetian, DOGE
Man (Latin), HOMO
Mark: Omission, DELE
 armoset: South American, MICO
Meadow: Fertile, VEGA
Measure: Electric, VOLT, WATT
 Force, DYNE
 Hebrew, OMER
 Printing, PICA
 Spanish or Portuguese, VARA
 Swiss land, IMMI
Medley, OLIO
Merganser, SMEW
Milk (French), LAIT
Molding, GULA
 Curved, OGEE
Mongoose: Crab-eating, URVA
Monk: Tibetan, LAMA
Monkey: African, MONA, WAAG
 Ceylonese, MAHA
 Cochin-China, DOUC
 South American, SAKI, TITI
Monkshood, ATIS
Month: Jewish, ADAR, ELUL, IYAR
Mother (French), MERE
Mountain: Thessaly, OSSA
Mouse: Meadow, VOLE
Mythology: Norse, EDDA
Nail (French), CLOU
Native: Philippine, MORO
Nest: Of pheasants, NIDE
Network, RETE
No (German), NEIN
Noble: Mohammedan, AMIR
Notice: Death, OBIT
Novel: By Zola, NANA
Nursemaid: Oriental AMAH, AYAH, EYAH
Nut: Philippine, PILI
Oak: Holm, ILEX
Oil (comb. form), OLEO

Ostrich: American, RHEA
Oven, KILN, OAST
Owl: Barn, LULU
Ox: Celebes wild, ANOE
 Extinct wild, URUS
Palm, ATAP, NIPA, SAGO
Parliament, DIET
Parrot: New Zealand, KAKA
Pass: Indian mountain, GHAT
Passage: Closing (music), CODA
Peach: Clingstone, PAVY
Peasant: Indian, RYOT
 Old English, CARL
Pepper: Australasian, KAVA
Perfume, ATAR
Persia, IRAN
Person: Extraordinary, ONER
Pickerel or pike, ESOX
Pitcher, EWER
Plant: Aromatic, NARD
 Century, ALOE
 Indigo, ANIL
 Pepper, KAVA
Platform: Raised, DAIS
Plum: Wild, SLOE
Pods: Vegetable, OKRA, OKRO
Poem: Epic, EPOS
Poet: Persian, OMAR
 Roman, OVID
Poison, BANE
 Arrow, INEE
Porkfish, SISI
Portico: Greek, STOA
Premium, AGIO
Priest: Mohammedan, IMAM
Prima donna, DIVA
Prong: Fork, TINE
Pseudonym: Lamb's, ELIA
Queen: Carthaginian, DIDO
 Hindu, RANI
Rabbit, CONY
Race: Of Japan, AINU
Rail: Ducklike, COOT
 North American, SORA
Redshank, CLEE
Refuse: After pressing, MARC
Regiment: Turkish, ALAI
Reliquary, ARCA
Resort: Italian, LIDO
Ridges: Sandy, ASAR, OSAR
River: German, ELBE, ODER
 Italian, ADDA
 Siberian, LENA
Road: Roman, ITER
Rockfish: California, RENA
Rodent: Mouselike, VOLE
 South American, PACA
Rootstock, TARO
Salamander, NEWT
Salmon: Silver, COHO
 Young, PARR
Same (Greek), HOMO
 (Latin), IDEM
Sauce: Fish, ALEC
School: English, ETON
Seaweed, AGAR, ALGA, KELP
Secular, LAIC
Sediment, SILT
Seed: Dill, ANET
 Of vetch, TARE
Serf, ILOT
Sesame, TEEL
Settlement: Eskimo, ETAH
Shark: Atlantic, GATA
 European, TOPE
Sheep: Wild, UDAD
Sheltered, ALEE
Shield, EGIS
Ship: Jason's, ARGO
 Left side of, PORT
 Two-masted, BRIG
Shrine: Buddhist, TOPE
Shrub: New Zealand, TUTU
Sign: Magic, RUNE
Silkworm, ERIA
Skin: Beaver, PLEW

Skink: Egyptian, ADDA
Slave, ESNE
Sloth: Two-toed, UNAU
Smooth, LENE
Snow: Glacial, NEVE
Soapstone, TALC
Society: African secret, EGBO, PORO
Son: Of Seth, ENOS
Song (German), LIED
  Unaccompanied, GLEE
Sound: Lung, RALE
Sour, ACID
Sow: Young, GILT
Spike: Brad-shaped, BROB
Spirit: Buddhist evil, MARA
Stake: Poker, ANTE
Star: Temporary, NOVA
Starch: East Indian, SAGO
Stone: Precious, OPAL
Strap: Bridle, REIN
Strewn (heraldry), SEME
Sweetsop, ATES, ATTA
Sword: Fencing, EPEE, FOIL
**Tambourine:** African, TAAR
Tapir: Brazilian, ANTA
Tax, CESS
Tea: South American, MATE
Therefore (Latin), ERGO
Thing: Extraordinary, ONER
Three (dice, cards, etc.), TREY
Thrush: Hawaiian, OMAO
Tide, NEAP
Tipster: Racing, TOUT

Tissue, TELA
Title: Etruscan, LARS
  Hindu, BABU
  Indian, RAJA
  Mohammedan, EMIR, IMAM
  Persian, BABA
  Spanish, DONA
  Turkish, AGHA, BABA
Toad: Largest-known, AGUA
  Tree, HYLA
Tool: Cutting, ADZE
Track: Deer, SLOT
Tract: Sandy, DENE
Tree: Apple, SORB
  Central American, EBOE
  East Indian, TEAK
  Eucalyptus, YATE
  Guiana and Trinidad, MORA
  Javanese, UPAS
  Linden, LIME, LINN, TEIL, TILL
  Sandarac, ARAR
  Sassafras, AGUE
  Tamarisk salt, ATLE
Tribe: Moro, SULU
Trout, CHAR
**Urchin:** Street, ARAB
**Vessel:** Arab, DHOW
Vestment: Ecclesiastical, COPE
Vetch, TARE
Vine: East Indian, SOMA
Violinist: Famous, AUER
Vortex, EDDY
**Wampum,** PEAG

Wapiti, STAG
Waste: Allowance for, TRET
Watchman: Indian, MINA
Water (Spanish), AGUA
Waterfall, LINN
Wavy (heraldry), ONDE, UNDE
Wax, CERE
  Chinese, PELA
Weed: Biblical, TARE
Weight: Ancient, MINA
  Danish (pl.), ESER
  East Asian, TAEL
  Greek, MINA
  Siamese, BAHT
Well done (rare), EUGE
Whale, CETE
  Killer, ORCA
  White, HUSE, HUSO
Whirlpool, EDDY
Wife: Of Geraint, ENID
Willow: Virginia, ITEA
Wine, PORT
Winged, ALAR
  (Heraldry), AILE
Wings, ALAE
Withered, SERE
Without (French), SANS
Wool: To comb, CARD
Work, OPUS
Wrong: Civil, TORT
**Young:** Bring forth, YEAN

# Words of Five Letters

**Abode of dead:** Babylonian, ARALU
Aborigine: Borneo DAYAK
Aftersong, EPODE
Aloe, AGAVE
Animal: Footless, APODE
Ant, EMMET
Antelope: African, ADDAX, BEISA, CAAMA, ELAND, GUIBA,
  ORIBI, TIANG
  Goat, GORAL, SEROW
  Indian, SASIN
  Siberian, SAIGA
Arch: Pointed, OGIVE
Armadillo, APARA, POYOU, TATOU
Arrowroot, ARARU
Artery: Trunk, AORTA
Association: Russian, ARTEL
  Secret, CABAL
Author: English, READE
Automaton, GOLEM, ROBOT
Award: Motion-picture, OSCAR
**Basket:** Fishing, CREEL
Beer: Russian, KVASS
Bible: Mohammedan, KORAN
Bird: Asian, MINAH, MYNAH
  Indian, SHAMA
  Larklike, PIPIT
  Loonlike, GREBE
  Oscine, VIREO
  South American, AGAMI
  Swimming, GREBE
Black: (French), NOIRE
  (Heraldry), SABLE
Blackbird: European, MERLE, OUSEL, OUZEL
Block: Glacial, SERAC
Blue (heraldry), AZURE
Boat: Eskimo, BIDAR, UMIAK
Bobwhite, COLIN, QUAIL
Bone (comb. form), OSTEO
  Leg, TIBIA
  Thigh, FEMUR
Broom: Twig, BESOM
Brother (French), FRERE
  Moses, AARON
**Canoe:** Eskimo, BIDAR, KAYAK
Cape: Papal, FANON, ORALE
Caravansary, SERAI

Card: Old playing, TAROT
Caterpillar: New Zealand, AWETO
Catkin, AMENT
Cavity: Stone, GEODE
Cephalopod, SQUID
Cetacean, WHALE
Chariot, ESSED
Cheek: Pertaining to, MALAR
Chieftain: Arab, EMEER
Child (Scotch), BAIRN
Cigar, CLARO
Coating: Seed, TESTA
Cockatoo: Palm, ARARA
Coin: Costa Rican, COLON
  Danish, KRONE
  Ecuadorian, SUCRE
  English, GROAT, PENCE
  French, FRANC
  German, KRONE, TALER
  Hungarian, PENGO
  Icelandic, KRONA
  Indian, RUPEE
  Iraqi, DINAR
  Norwegian, KRONE
  Polish, ZLOTY
  Russian, COPEC, KOPEK, RUBLE
  Swedish, KRONA
  Turkish, ASPER
  Yugoslav, DINAR
Collar: Papal, FANON, ORALE
  Roman, RABAT
Commune: Italian, TREIA
Composition: Choral, MOTET
Compound: Chemical, ESTER
Conceal (law), ELOIN
Council: Ecclesiastical, SYNOD
Court: Anglo-Saxon, GEMOT
  Inner, PATIO
Crest: Mountain, ARETE
Crown: Papal, TIARA
Cuttlefish, SEPIA
**Date:** Roman, NONES
Decree: Mohammedan, IRADE
  Russian, UKASE
Deposit: Loam, LOESS
Desert: Gobi, SHAMO

Devilfish, MANTA
Disease: Cereals, ERGOT
Disk, PATEN
Dog: Wild, DHOLE, DINGO
Dormouse, LEROT
Drum, TABOR
Duck: Sea, EIDER
Dynasty: Chinese, CHING, LIANG, SHANG
**Earthquake,** SEISM
Eel, ELVER, MORAY
Ermine: European, STOAT
Ether: Crystalline, APIOL
**Fabric:** Velvetlike, PANNE
Fabulist, AESOP
Family: Italian, CENCI
Fiber: West Indian, SISAL
Fig: Smyrna, ELEME, ELEMI
Figure: Of speech, TROPE
Finch: European, SERIN
Fish: American small, KILLY
Flower: Garden, ASTER
Friend (Spanish), AMIGO
Fruit: Tropical, MANGO
Fungus: Rye, ERGOT
Furze, GORSE
**Gateway,** TORAN, TORII
Gem, AGATE, BERYL, PEARL, TOPAZ
Genus: Barnacles, LEPAS
  Bears, URSUS
  Birds (loons), GAVIA
  Birds (nuthatches), SITTA
  Cats, FELIS
  Dogs, CANIS
  Fishes (chiros), ELOPS
  Fishes (perch), PERCA
  Geese, ANSER
  Grasses, STIPA
  Grasses (incl. oats), AVENA
  Gulls, LARUS
  Hares, rabbits, LEPUS
  Hawks, BUTEO
  Herbs, old world, INULA
  Herbs, trailing or climbing, APIOS
  Herbs, tropical, TACCA, URENA
  Horses, EQUUS
  Insects (olive flies), DACUS
  Lice, plant, APHIS
  Lichens, USNEA
  Lizards, AGAMA
  Moles, TALPA
  Mollusks, OLIVA
  Monkeys, CEBUS
  Palms, ARECA
  Pigeons, GOURA
  Plants (amaryllis family), AGAVE
  Ruminants (goats), CAPRA
  Shrubs, Asiatic, SABIA
  Shrubs (heath), ERICA
  Shrubs (incl. raspberry), RUBUS
  Shrubs, tropical, IXORA, TREMA, URENA
  Ticks, ARGAS
  Trees (of elm family), TREMA, ULMUS
  Trees, tropical, IXORA, TREMA
Goat: Bezoar, PASAN
God: Assyrian, ASHIR, ASHUR, ASSUR
  Babylonian, DAGAN, SIRIS
  Gaelic, DAGDA
  Hindu, BHAGA, INDRA, SHIVA
  Japanese, EBISU
  Philistine, DAGON
  Phrygian, ATTIS
  Teutonic, AEGIR, GYMIR
  Welsh, DYLAN
Goddess: Babylonian, ISTAR, NANAI
  Hindu, DURGA, GAURI, SHREE
Group: Of six, HEXAD
Grove: Sacred to Diana, NEMUS
Growing out, ENATE
Guitar: Hindu, SITAR
Gull: PEWEE, PEWIT
**Hartebeest,** CAAMA
Headdress: Jewish or Persian, TIARA
  Liturgical, MITER, MITRE
Heath, ERICA
Herb: Grasslike marsh, SEDGE
Heron, EGRET

Hog: Young, SHOAT, SHOTE
**Image,** EIKON
Indian: Cariban, ARARA
  Iroquoian, HURON
  Mexican, AZTEC, OPATA, OTOMI
  Muskhogean, CREEK
  Siouan, OSAGE, TETON
  Spanish American, ARARA, CARIB
Inflorescence: Racemose, AMENT
Insect: Immature, LARVA
Intrigue, CABAL
Iris: Yellow, SEDGE
**Juniper,** GORSE, RETEM
**Kidneys:** Pertaining to, RENAL
King: British legendary, LLUDD
Kite: European, GLEDE
Kobold, NISSE
**Land:** Cultivated, ARADA, ARADO
Landholder (Scotch), LAIRD, THANE
Language: Dravidian, TAMIL
Lariat, LASSO, REATA
Laughing, RIANT
Lawgiver: Athenian, DRACO, SOLON
Leaf: Calyx, SEPAL
  Fern, FROND
Lemur, LORIS
Letter: English, AITCH
  Greek, ALPHA, DELTA, GAMMA, KAPPA, OMEGA,
    SIGMA, THETA
  Hebrew, ALEPH, CHETH, GIMEL, SADHE, ZAYIN
Lichen, USNEA
Lighthouse, PHARE
Lizard: Old World, AGAMA
Loincloth, DHOTI
Louse: Plant, APHID
**Macaw:** Brazilian, ARARA
Mahogany: Philippine, ALMON
Mammal: Badgerlike, RATEL
  Civetlike, GENET
  Giraffelike, OKAPI
  Raccoonlike, COATI
Man (French), HOMME
Marble, AGATE
Mark: Insertion, CARET
Market place: Greek, AGORA
Marsupial: Australian, KOALA
Measure: Electric, FARAD, HENRY
  Energy, JOULE
  Metric, LITER, STERE
  Printing, AGATE
  Russian, VERST
Mixture: Smelting, MATTE
Mohicans: Last of, UNCAS
Molding: Convex, OVOLO, TORUS
Mole, TALPA
Monkey: African, PATAS
  Capuchin, SAJOU
  Howling, ARABA
Monkshood, ATEES
Month: Jewish, NISAN, SIVAN, TEBET
Museum (French), MUSEE
Musketeer, ATHOS
**Native:** Aleutian, ALEUT
  New Zealand, MAORI
Neckpiece: Ecclesiastical, AMICE
Nerve (comb. form), NEURO
Nest: Eagle's or hawk's, AERIE
  Insect's, NIDUS
Net: Fishing, SEINE
Newsstand, KIOSK
Nitrogen, AZOTE
Noble: Mohammedan, AMEER
Nodule: Stone, GEODE
Nostrils, NARES
Notched irregularly, EROSE
Nymph: Mohammedan, HOURI
**Official:** Roman, EDILE
Oleoresin, ELEMI
Opening: Mouthlike, STOMA
Oration: Funeral, ELOGE
Ostiole, STOMA
**Page:** Left-hand, VERSO
  Right-hand, RECTO
Palm, ARECA, BETEL
Park: Colorado, ESTES
Perfume, ATTAR

Philosopher: Greek, PLATO
Pillar: Stone, STELA, STELE
Pinnacle: Glacial, SERAC
Plain, LLANO
Plant: Century, AGAVE
 Climbing, LIANA
 Dwarf, CUMIN
 East Asian perennial, RAMIE
 Medicinal, SENNA
 Mustard family, CRESS
Plate: Communion, PATEN
Poem: Lyric, EPODE
Point: Lowest, NADIR
Poplar, ABELE, ALAMO, ASPEN
Porridge: Spanish American, ATOLE
Post: Stair, NEWEL
Priest: Mohammedan, IMAUM
Protozoan, AMEBA
**Queen:** (French), REINE
 Hindu, RANEE
**Rabbit,** CONEY
Rail, CRAKE
Red (heraldry), GULES
Religion: Moslem, ISLAM
Resin, ELEMI
Revoke (law), ADEEM
Rich man, MIDAS, NABOB
Ridge: Sandy, ESKAR, ESKER
River: French, LOIRE, SEINE
Rockfish: California, REINA
Rootstock: Fragrant, ORRIS
Ruff: Female, REEVE
**Sack:** Pack, KYACK
Salt: Ethereal, ESTER
Saltpeter, NITER, NITRE
Salutation: Eastern, SALAM
Sandpiper: Old World, TEREK
Scented, OLENT
School: Fish, SHOAL
 French public, LYCEE
Scriptures: Mohammedan, KORAN
Seaweeds, ALGAE
Seed: Aromatic, ANISE
Seraglio, HAREM, SERAI
Serf, HELOT
Sheep: Wild, AUDAD
Sheeplike, OVINE
Shield, AEGIS
Shoe: Wooden, SABOT
Shoots: Pickled bamboo, ACHAR
Shot: Billiard, CAROM, MASSE
Shrine: Buddhist, STUPA
Shrub: Burning bush, WAHOO
 Ornamental evergreen, TOYON
 Used in tanning, SUMAC
Silk: Watered, MOIRE
Sister (French), SOEUR
 (Latin), SOROR
Six: Group of, HEXAD
Skeleton: Marine, CORAL

Slave, HELOT
Snake, ABOMA, ADDER, COBRA, RACER
Soldier: French, POILU
 Indian, SEPOY
Sour, ACERB
Spirit: Air, ARIEL
Staff: Shepherd's, CROOK
Starwort, ASTER
Steel (German), STAHL
Stockade: Russian, ETAPE
Stop (nautical), AVAST
Storehouse, ETAPE
Subway: Parisian, METRO
**Tapestry,** ARRAS
Tea: Paraguayan, YERBA
Temple: Hawaiian, HEIAU
Terminal: Positive, ANODE
Theater: Greek, ODEON, ODEUM
Then (French), ALORS
Thread: Surgical, SETON
Thrush: Wilson's, VEERY
Title: Hindu, BABOO
 Indian, RAJAH, SAHEB, SAHIB
 Mohammedan, EMEER, IMAUM
Tree: Buddhist sacred, PIPAL
 East Indian cotton, SIMAL
 Hickory, PECAN
 Light-wooded, BALSA
 Malayan, TERAP
 Mediterranean, CAROB
 Mexican, ABETO
 Mexican pine, OCOTE
 New Zealand, MAIRE
 Philippine, ALMON
 Rain, SAMAN
 South American, UMBRA
 Tamarack, LARCH
 Tamarisk salt, ATLEE
 West Indian, ACANA
Trout, CHARR
Troy, ILION, ILIUM
Twin: Siamese, CHANG
**Vestment:** Ecclesiastical, STOLE
Violin: Famous, AMATI, STRAD
Volcano: Mud, SALSE
**Wampum,** PEAGE
War cry: Greek, ALALA
Wavy (heraldry), UNDEE
Weight: Jewish, GERAH
Wen, TALPA
Wheat, SPELT
Wheel: Persian water, NORIA
Whitefish, CISCO
Willow, OSIER
Window: Bay, ORIEL
Wine, MEDOC, RHINE, TINTA, TOKAY
Winged, ALATE
Woman (French), FEMME
**Year:** Excess of solar over lunar, EPACT
**Zoroastrian,** PARSI

## Words of Six or More Letters

**Agave,** MAGUEY
Alkaloid: Crystalline, ESERIN, ESERINE
Alligator, CAYMAN
Amphibole, EDENITE, URALITE
Ant: White, TERMITE
Antelope: African, DIKDIK, DUIKER, GEMSBOK, IMPALA, KOODOO
 European, CHAMOIS
 Indian, NILGAI, NILGAU, NILGHAI, NILGHAU
Ape: Asian or East Indian, GIBBON
Appendage: Leaf, STIPEL, STIPULE
Armadillo, PELUDO, TATOUAY
Arrowroot, ARARAO
Ascetic: Jewish, ESSENE
Ass: Asian wild, ONAGER
Avatar: Of Vishnu, KRISHNA
**Babylonian,** ELAMITE
Badge: Shoulder, EPAULET
Baldness, ALOPECIA

Barracuda, SENNET
Bark: Aromatic, SINTOC
Bearlike, URSINE
Beetle, ELATER
Bible: Zoroastrian, AVESTA
Bird: Sea, PETREL
 South American, SERIEMA
 Wading, AVOCET, AVOSET
Bone: Leg, FIBULA
Branched, RAMATE
Brother (Latin), FRATER
Bunting: European, ORTOLAN
**Call:** Trumpet, SENNET
Canoe: Eskimo, BAIDAR, OOMIAK
Caravansary, IMARET
Cat: Asian or African, CHEETAH
 Leopardlike, OCELOT
Cenobite: Jewish, ESSENE
Centerpiece: Table, EPERGNE

Cetacean, DOLPHIN, PORPOISE
Chariot, ESSEDA, ESSEDE
Chief: Seminole, OSCEOLA
Claim: Release as (law), REMISE
Clock: Water, CLEPSYDRA
Cloud, CUMULUS, NIMBUS
Coach: French hackney, FIACRE
Coin: Czech, KORUNA
 Ethiopian, TALARI
 Finnish, MARKKA
 German, THALER
 Greek, DRACHMA
 Haitian, GOURDE
 Honduran, LEMPIRA
 Hungarian, FORINT
 Indo-Chinese, PIASTER
 Netherlands, GUILDER
 Panamanian, BALBOA
 Paraguayan, GUARANI
 Portuguese, ESCUDO
 Russian, COPECK, KOPECK, ROUBLE
 Spanish, PESETA
 Venezuelan, BOLIVAR
Communion: Last holy, VIATICUM
Conceal (law), ELOIGN
Confection, PRALINE
Construction: Sentence, SYNTAX
Convexity: Shaft of column, ENTASIS
Court: Anglo-Saxon, GEMOTE
Cow: Sea, DUGONG, MANATEE
Cylindrical, TERETE
**Dagger,** STILETTO
 Malay, CREESE, KREESE
Date: Roman, CALENDS, KALENDS
Deer, CARIBOU, WAPITI
Disease: Plant, ERINOSE
Doorkeeper, OSTIARY
Dragonflies: Order of, ODANATA
Drink: Of gods, NECTAR
Drum: TABOUR
 Moorish, ATABAL, ATTABAL
Duck: Fish-eating, MERGANSER
 Sea, SCOTER
Dynasty: Chinese, MANCHU
**Eel,** CONGER
Edit, REDACT
Envelope: Flower, PERIANTH
Eskimo, AMERIND
Ether: Crystalline, APIOLE
Excuse (law), ESSOIN
Eyespots, OCELLI
**Fabric,** ESTAMENE, ESTAMIN, ETAMINE
Falcon: European, KESTREL
Figure: Used as column, CARYATID, TELAMON
Fine: For punishment, AMERCE
Fish: Asian fresh-water, GOURAMI
 Pikelike, BARRACUDA
Five: Group of, PENTAD
Fly: African, TSETSE
Foot: Metric, ANAPEST, IAMBUS
Foxlike, VULPINE
Frying pan, SPIDER
Fur, KARAKUL
**Galley:** Greek or Roman, BIREME, TRIREME
Game: Card, ECARTE
Garment: Greek, CHLAMYS
Gateway, GOPURA, TORANA
Genus: Birds (ravens, crows), CORVUS
 Eels, CONGER
 Fishes, ANABAS
 Foxes, VULPES
 Herbs, ANEMONE
 Insects, CICADA
 Lemurs, GALAGO
 Mints (incl. catnip), NEPETA
 Mollusks, ANOMIA, ASTARTE, TEREDO
 Mollusks (incl. oysters), OSTREA
 Monkeys (spider monkeys), ATELES
 Thrushes (incl. robins), TURDUS
 Trees (of elm family), CELTIS
 Trees (inc. dogwood), CORNUS
 Trees, tropical American, SAPOTA
 Wrens, NANNUS
Gibbon, SIAMANG, WOUWOU
Gland: Salivary, RACEMOSE
Goat: Bezoar, PASANG

Goatlike, CAPRINE
God: Assyrian, ASHSHUR, ASSHUR
 Babylonian, BABBAR, MARDUK, MERODACH, NANNAR,
  NERGAL, SHAMASH
 Hindu, BRAHMA, KRISHNA, VISHNU
 Tahitian, TAAROA
Goddess: Babylonian, ISHTAR
 Hindu, CHANDI, HAIMAVATI, LAKSHMI, PARVATI,
  SARASVATI, SARASWATI
Government, POLITY
Governor: Persian, SATRAP
Grandson (Scotch), NEPOTE
Group: Of five, PENTAD
 Of nine, ENNEAD
 Of seven, HEPTAD
**Hare:** in first year, LEVERET
Harpsichord, SPINET
Herb: Alpine, EDELWEISS
 Chinese, GINSENG
 South African, FREESIA
Hermit, EREMITE
Hero: Legendary, PALADIN
Heron, BITTERN
Horselike, EQUINE
Hound: Short-legged, BEAGLE
House (French), MAISON
**Idiot,** CRETIN
Implement: Stone, NEOLITH
Incarnation: Hindu, AVATAR
Indian, APACHE, COMANCHE, PAIUTE, SENECA
Inn: Turkish, IMARET
Insects: Order of, DIPTERA
Instrument: Japanese banjolike, SAMISEN
 Musical, CLAVIER, SPINET
Interstice, AREOLA
Ironwood, COLIMA
**Juniper:** Old Testament, RAETAM
**Kettledrum,** ATABAL
King: Fairy, OBERON
Kneecap, PATELLA
Knife, MACHETE
**Langur:** Sumatran, SIMPAI
Legislature: Spanish, CORTES
Lemur: African, GALAGO
 Madagascar, AYEAYE
Letter: Greek, EPSILON, LAMBDA, OMICRON, UPSILON
 Hebrew, DALETH, LAMEDH, SAMEKH
Lighthouse, PHAROS
Lizard, IGUANA
Llama, ALPACA
Lockjaw, TETANUS
Locust, CICADA, CICALA
**Macaw:** Brazilian, MARACAN
Maid: Of Astolat, ELAINE
Mammal: Madagascar, TENDRAC, TENREC
Man (Spanish), HOMBRE
Marmoset: South American, TAMARIN
Marsupial, BANDICOOT, WOMBAT
Massacre, POGROM
Mayor: Spanish, ALCALDE
Measure: Electric, AMPERE, COULOMB, KILOWATT
Medicine: Quack, NOSTRUM
Member: Religious order, CENOBITE
Molasses, TREACLE
Monkey: African, GRIVET, NISNAS
 Asian, LANGUR
 Philippine, MACHIN
 South American, PINCHE, SAIMIRI, SAMIRI, SAPAJOU
Monster, CHIMERA, GORGON
 (Comb. form), TERATO
 Cretan, MINOTAUR
Month: Jewish, HESHVAN, KISLEV, SHEBAT, TAMMUZ,
 TISHRI, VEADAR
Mountain: Asia Minor, ARARAT
Mulct, AMERCE
Musketeer, ARAMIS, PORTHOS
**Nearsighted,** MYOPIC
Net, TRAMMEL
New York City, GOTHAM
Nine: Group of, ENNEAD
Nobleman: Spanish, GRANDEE
**Official:** Roman, AEDILE
Onyx: Mexican, TECALI
Order: Dragonflies, ODANATA
 Insects, DIPTERA
Organ: Plant, PISTIL

Ornament: Shoulder, EPAULET
Overcoat: Military, CAPOTE
Ox: Wild, BANTENG
Oxidation: Bronze or copper, PATINA
**Paralysis:** Incomplete, PARESIS
Pear: Alligator, AVOCADO
Persimmon: Mexican, CHAPOTE
Pipe: Peace, CALUMET
Plaid (Scotch), TARTAN
Plain, PAMPAS, STEPPE, TUNDRA
Plant: Buttercup family, ANEMONE
   Century, MAGUEY
   On rocks, LICHEN
Plowing: Fit for, ARABLE
Poem: Heroic, EPOPEE
   Six-lined, SESTET
Point: Highest, ZENITH
Potion: Love, PHILTER, PHILTRE
Protozoan, AMOEBA
Punish, AMERCE
Purple (heraldry), PURPURE
**Queen:** Fairy, TITANIA
**Race:** Skiing, SLALOM
Rat, BANDICOOT, LEMMING
Retort, RIPOST, RIPOSTE
Ring: Harness, TERRET
   Little, ANNULET
Rodent: Jumping, JERBOA
   Spanish American, AGOUTI, AGOUTY
**Sailor:** East Indian, LASCAR
Salmon: Young, GRILSE
Salutation: Eastern, SALAAM
Sandpiper, PLOVER
Sandy, ARENOSE
Sapodilla, SAPOTA, SAPOTE
Saw: Surgical, TREPAN
Seven: Group of, HEPTAD
Sexes: Common to both, EPICENE
Shawl: Mexican, SERAPE
Sheathing: Flower, SPATHE
Sheep: Wild, AOUDAD, ARGALI
Shipworm, TEREDO
Shoes: Mercury's winged, TALARIA
Shortening: Syllable, SYSTOLE
Shrub, SPIRAEA
Sickle-shaped, FALCATE

Silver (heraldry), ARGENT
Snake, ANACONDA
Speech: Loss of, APHASIA
Spiral, HELICAL
Staff: Bishop's, CROSIER, CROZIER
Stalk: Plant, PETIOLE
State: Swiss, CANTON
Studio, ATELIER
Swan: Young, CYGNET
Swimming, NATANT
Sword-shaped, ENSATE
**Terminal:** Negative, CATHODE
Third (music), TIERCE
Thrust: Fencing, RIPOST, RIPOSTE
Tile: Pertaining to, TEGULAR
Tomb: Empty, CENOTAPH
Tooth (comb. form), ODONTO
Tower: Mohammedan, MINARET
Tree: African timber, BAOBAB
   Black gum, TUPELO
   East Indian, MARGOSA
   Locust, ACACIA
   Malayan, SINTOC
   Marmalade, SAPOTE
**Urn:** Tea, SAMOVAR
**Vehicle,** LANDAU, TROIKA
Verbose, PROLIX
Viceroy: Egyptian, KHEDIVE
Vulture: American, CONDOR
**Warehouse** (French), ENTREPOT
Whale: White, BELUGA
Whirlpool, VORTEX
Will: Addition to, CODICIL
   Having left, TESTATE
Wind, CHINOOK, MONSOON, SIMOOM, SIMOON, SI-
   ROCCO
Window: In roof, DORMER
Wine, BARBERA, BURGUNDY, CABERNET, CHABLIS, CHI-
   ANTI, CLARET, MUSCATEL, RIESLING, SAUTERNE,
   SHERRY, ZINFANDEL
Wolfish, LUPINE
Woman: Boisterous, TERMAGANT
Woolly, LANATE
Workshop, ATELIER
Zoroastrian, PARSEE

## Old-Testament Names

**(We do not pretend that this list is all-inclusive. We include only those names which in our opinion one meets most often in crossword puzzles.)**

**Aaron:** First high priest of Jews; son of Amram; brother of Miriam and Moses; father of Abihu, Eleazer, Ithamar, and Nadab.

**Abel:** Son of Adam; slain by Cain.

**Abigail:** Wife of Nabal; later, wife of David.

**Abihu:** Son of Aaron.

**Abimelech:** King of Gerar.

**Abner:** Commander of army of Saul and Ishbosheth; slain by Joab.

**Abraham (or Abram):** Patriarch; forefather of the Jews; son of Terah; husband of Sarah; father of Isaac and Ishmael.

**Absalom:** Son of David and Maacah; revolted against David; slain by Joab.

**Achish:** King of Gath; gave refuge to David.

**Achsa (or Achsah):** Daughter of Caleb; wife of Othniel.

**Adah:** Wife of Lamech.

**Adam:** First man; husband of Eve; father of Cain, Abel, and Seth.

**Adonijah:** Son of David and Haggith.

**Agag:** King of Amalek; spared by Saul; slain by Samuel.

**Ahasuerus:** King of Persia; husband of Vashti and, later, Esther; sometimes identified with Xerxes the Great.

**Ahijah:** Prophet; foretold accession of Jeroboam.

**Ahinoam:** Wife of David.

**Amasa:** Commander of army of David; slain by Joab.

**Amnon:** Son of David and Ahinoam; ravished Tamar; slain by Absalom.

**Amram:** Husband of Jochebed; father of Aaron, Miriam and Moses.

**Asenath:** Wife of Joseph.

**Asher:** Son of Jacob and Zilpah.

**Balaam:** Prophet; rebuked by his donkey for cursing God.

**Barak:** Jewish captain; associated with Deborah.

**Baruch:** Secretary to Jeremiah.

**Bathsheba:** Wife of Uriah; later, wife of David.

**Belshazzar:** Crown prince of Babylon.

**Benaiah:** Warrior of David; proclaimed Solomon King.

**Ben-Hadad:** Name of several kings of Damascus.

**Benjamin:** Son of Jacob and Rachel.

**Bezaleel:** Chief architect of tabernacle.

**Bilbah:** Servant of Rachel; mistress of Jacob.

**Bildad:** Comforter of Job.

**Boaz:** Husband of Ruth; father of Obed.

**Cain:** Son of Adam and Eve; slayer of Abel; father of Enoch.

**Cainan:** Son of Enos.

**Caleb:** Spy sent out by Moses to visit Canaan; father of Achsa.

**Canaan:** Son of Ham.

**Chilion:** Son of Elimelech; husband of Orpah.

**Cush:** Son of Ham; father of Nimrod.

**Dan:** Son of Jacob and Bilhah.

**Daniel:** Prophet; saved from lions by God.

**Deborah:** Hebrew prophetess; helped Israelites conquer Canaanites.

**Delilah:** Mistress and betrayer of Samson.

**Elam:** Son of Shem.

**Eleazar:** Son of Aaron; succeeded him as high priest.

**Eli:** High priest and judge; teacher of Samuel; father of Hophni and Phinehas.

**Eliakim:** Chief minister of Hezekiah.

**Eliezer:** Servant of Abraham.

**Elihu:** Comforter of Job.

**Elijah (or Elias):** Prophet; went to heaven in chariot of fire.

**Elimelech:** Husband of Naomi; father of Chilion and Mahlon.

**Eliphaz:** Comforter of Job.

**Elisha (or Eliseus):** Prophet; successor of Elijah.

**Elkanah:** Husband of Hannah; father of Samuel.

**Enoch:** Son of Cain.

**Enoch:** Father of Methuselah.

**Enos:** Son of Seth; father of Cainan.

**Ephraim:** Son of Joseph.

**Esau:** Son of Isaac and Rebecca; sold his birthright to his brother Jacob.

**Esther:** Jewish wife of Ahasuerus; saved Jews from Haman's plotting.

**Eve:** First woman; created from rib of Adam.

**Ezra (or Esdras):** Hebrew scribe and priest.

**Gad:** Son of Jacob and Zilpah.

**Gehazi:** Servant of Elisha.

**Gideon:** Israelite hero; defeated Midianites.

**Goliath:** Philistine giant; slain by David.

**Hagar:** Handmaid of Sarah; concubine of Abraham; mother of Ishmael.

**Haggith:** Mother of Adonijah.

**Ham:** Son of Noah; father of Cush, Mizraim, Phut, and Canaan.

**Haman:** Chief minister of Ahasuerus; hanged on gallows prepared for Mordecai.

**Hannah:** Wife of Elkanah; mother of Samuel.

**Hanun:** King of Ammonites.

**Haran:** Brother of Abraham; father of Lot.

**Hazael:** King of Damascus.

**Hephzi-Bah:** Wife of Hezekiah; mother of Mannaseh.

**Hiram:** King of Tyre.

**Holofernes:** General of Nebuchadnezzar; slain by Judith.

**Hophni:** Son of Eli.

**Isaac:** Hebrew patriarch; son of Abraham and Sarah; half brother of Ishmael; husband of Rebecca; father of Esau and Jacob.

**Ishmael:** Son of Abraham and Hagar; half brother of Isaac.

**Issachar:** Son of Jacob and Leah.

**Ithamar:** Son of Aaron.

**Jabal:** Son of Lamech and Adah.

**Jabin:** King of Hazor.

**Jacob:** Hebrew patriarch, founder of Israel; son of Isaac and Rebecca; husband of Leah and Rachel; father of Asher, Benjamin, Dan, Gad, Issachar, Joseph, Judah, Levi, Naphtali, Reuben, Simeon, and Zebulun.

**Jael:** Slayer of Sisera.

**Japheth:** Son of Noah.

**Jehoiada:** High priest; husband of Jehoshabeath; revolted against Athaliah and made Joash King of Judah.

**Jehoshabeath (or Jehosheba):** Daughter of Jehoram of Judah; wife of Jehoiada.

**Jephthah:** Judge in Israel; sacrificed his only daughter because of vow.

**Jesse:** Son of Obed; father of David.

**Jethro:** Midianite priest; father of Zipporah.

**Jezebel:** Phoenician princess; wife of Ahab; mother of Ahaziah, Athaliah, and Jehoram.

**Joab:** Commander in chief under David; slayer of Abner, Absalom, and Amasa.

**Job:** Patriarch; underwent many afflictions; comforted by Bildad, Elihu, Eliphaz and Zophar.

**Jochebed:** Wife of Amram.

**Jonah:** Prophet; cast into sea and swallowed by great fish.

**Jonathan:** Son of Saul; friend of David.

**Joseph:** Son of Jacob and Rachel; sold into slavery by his brothers; husband of Asenath; father of Ephraim and Manassah.

**Joshua:** Successor of Moses; son of Nun.

**Jubal:** Son of Lamech and Adah.

**Judah:** Son of Jacob and Leah.

**Judith:** Slayer of Holofernes.

**Kish:** Father of Saul.

**Laban:** Father of Leah and Rachel.

**Lamech:** Son of Methuselah; father of Noah.

**Lamech:** Husband of Adah and Zillah; father of Jabal, Jubal, and Tubal-Cain.

**Leah:** Daughter of Laban; wife of Jacob.

**Levi:** Son of Jacob and Leah.

**Lot:** Son of Haran; escaped destruction of Sodom.

**Maacah:** Mother of Absalom and Tamar.

**Mahlon:** Son of Elimelech; first husband of Ruth.

**Manasseh:** Son of Joseph.

**Melchizedek:** King of Salem.

**Methuselah:** Patriarch; son of Enoch; father of Lamech.

**Michal:** Daughter of Saul; wife of David.

**Miriam:** Prophetess; daughter of Amram; sister of Aaron and Moses.

**Mizraim:** Son of Ham.

**Mordecai:** Uncle of Esther; with her aid, saved Jews from Haman's plotting.

**Moses:** Prophet and lawgiver; son of Amram; brother of Aaron and Miriam; husband of Zipporah.

**Naaman:** Syrian captain; cured of leprosy by Elisha.

**Nabal:** Husband of Abigail.

**Naboth:** Owner of vineyard; stoned to death because he would not sell it to Ahab.

**Nadab:** Son of Aaron.

**Nahor:** Father of Terah.

**Naomi:** Wife of Elimelech; mother-in-law of Ruth.

**Naphtali:** Son of Jacob and Bilhah.

**Nathan:** Prophet; reproved David for causing Uriah's death.

**Nebuchadnezzar (or Nebuchadrezzar):** King of Babylon; destroyer of Jerusalem.

**Nehemiah:** Jewish leader; empowered by Artaxerxes to rebuild Jerusalem.

**Nimrod:** Mighty hunter; son of Cush.

**Noah:** Patriarch; Son of Lamech; escaped Deluge by building Ark; father of Ham, Japheth and Shem.

**Nun (or Non):** Father of Joshua.

**Obed:** Son of Boaz; father of Jesse.

**Og:** King of Bashan.

**Orpah:** Wife of Chilion.

**Othniel:** Kenezite; judge of Israel; husband of Achsa.

**Phinehas:** Son of Eleazer.

**Phinehas:** Son of Eli.

**Phut (or Put):** Son of Ham.

**Potiphar:** Egyptian official; bought Joseph.

**Rachel:** Wife of Jacob.

**Rebecca (or Rebekah):** Wife of Isaac.

**Reuben:** Son of Jacob and Leah.

**Ruth:** Wife of Mahlon, later of Boaz; daughter-in-law of Naomi.

**Samson:** Judge of Israel; famed for strength; betrayed by Delilah.

**Samuel:** Hebrew judge and prophet; son of Elkanah.

**Sarah (or Sara, Sarai):** Wife of Abraham.

**Sennacherib:** King of Assyria.

**Seth:** Son of Adam; father of Enos.

**Shem:** Son of Noah; father of Elam.

**Simeon:** Son of Jacob and Leah.

**Sisera:** Canaanite captain; slain by Jael.

**Tamar:** Daughter of David and Maachah; ravished by Amnon.

**Terah:** Son of Nahor; father of Abraham.

**Tubal-Cain:** Son of Lamech and Zillah.

**Uriah:** Husband of Bathsheba; sent to death in battle by David.

**Vashti:** Wife of Ahasuerus; set aside by him.

**Zadok:** High priest during David's reign.

**Zebulun (or Zabulon):** Son of Jacob and Leah.

**Zillah:** Wife of Lamech.

**Zilpah:** Servant of Leah; mistress of Jacob.

**Zipporah:** Daughter of Jethro; wife of Moses.

**Zophar:** Comforter of Job.

# Kings of Judah and Israel

## Kings Before Division of Kingdom

**Saul:** First King of Israel; son of Kish; father of Ish-Bosheth, Jonathan and Michal.

**Ish-Bosheth (or Eshbaal):** King of Israel; son of Saul.

**David:** King of Judah; later of Israel; son of Jesse; husband of Abigail, Ahinoam, Bathsheba, Michal, etc.; father of Absalom, Adonijah, Amnon, Solomon, Tamar, etc.

**Solomon:** King of Israel and Judah; son of David; father of Rehoboam.

**Rehoboam:** Son of Solomon; during his reign the kingdom was divided into Judah and Israel.

## Kings of Judah (Southern Kingdom)

**Rehoboam:** First King.

**Abijah (or Abijam or Abia):** Son of Rehoboam.

**Asa:** Probably son of Abijah.

**Jehoshaphat:** Son of Asa.

**Jehoram (or Joram):** Son of Jehoshaphat; husband of Athaliah.

**Ahaziah:** Son of Jehoram and Athaliah.

**Athaliah:** Daughter of King Ahab of Israel and Jezebel; wife of Jehoram.

**Joash (or Jehoash):** Son of Ahaziah.

**Amaziah:** Son of Joash.

**Uzziah (or Azariah):** Son of Amaziah.

**Jotham:** Regent, later King; son of Uzziah.

**Ahaz:** Son of Jotham.

**Hezekiah:** Son of Ahaz; husband of Hephzi-Bah.

**Manasseh:** Son of Hezekiah and Hephzi-Bah.

**Amon:** Son of Manasseh.

**Josiah (or Josias):** Son of Amon.

**Jehoahaz (or Joahaz):** Son of Josiah.

**Jehoiachin:** Son of Jehoiakim.

**Jehoiakim:** Son of Josiah.

**Zedekiah:** Son of Josiah; kingdom overthrown by Babylonians under Nebuchadnezzar.

## Kings of Israel (Northern Kingdom)

**Jeroboam I:** Led secession of Israel.

**Nadab:** Son of Jeroboam I.

**Baasha:** Overthrew Nadab.

**Elah:** Son of Baasha.

**Zimri:** Overthrew Elah.

**Omri:** Overthrew Zimri.

**Ahab:** Son of Omri; husband of Jezebel.

**Ahaziah:** Son of Ahab.

**Jehoram (or Joram):** Son of Ahab.

**Jehu:** Overthrew Jehoram.

**Jehoahaz (or Joahaz):** Son of Jehu.

**Jehoash (or Joash):** Son of Jehoahaz.

**Jeroboam II:** Son of Jehoash.

**Zechariah:** Son of Jeroboam II.

**Shallum:** Overthrew Zechariah.

**Menahem:** Overthrew Shallum.

**Pekahiah:** Son of Menahem.

**Pekah:** Overthrew Pekahiah.

**Hoshea:** Overthrew Pekah; kingdom overthrown by Assyrians under Sargon II.

# Prophets

**Major.—**Isaiah, Jeremiah, Ezekiel, Daniel.

**Minor.—**Hosea, Obadiah, Nahum, Haggai, Joel, Jonah, Habakkuk, Zechariah, Amos, Micah, Zephaniah, Malachi.

# Greek and Roman Mythology

(Most of the Greek deities were adopted by the Romans, although in many cases there was a change of name. In the list below, information is given under the Greek name; the name in parentheses is the Latin equivalent. However, all Latin names are listed with cross references to the Greek ones. In addition, there are several deities which were exclusively Roman.)

**Acheron:** *See* Rivers.

**Achilles:** Greek warrior; slew Hector at Troy; slain by Paris, who wounded him in his vulnerable heel.

**Actaeon:** Hunter; surprised Artemis bathing; changed by her to stag and killed by his dogs.

**Admetus:** King of Thessaly; his wife, Alcestis, offered to die in his place.

**Adonis:** Beautiful youth loved by Aphrodite.

**Aeacus:** One of three judges of dead in Hades; son of Zeus.

**Aeëtes:** King of Colchis; father of Medea; keeper of Golden Fleece.

**Aegeus:** Father of Theseus; believing Theseus killed in Crete, he drowned himself, Aegean Sea named for him.

**Aegisthus:** Son of Thyestes; slew Atreus; with Clytemnestra, his paramour, slew Agamemnon; slain by Orestes.

**Aegyptus:** Brother of Danaus; his sons, except Lynceus, slain by Danaides.

**Aeneas:** Trojan; son of Anchises and Aphrodite; after fall of Troy, led his followers eventually to Italy; loved and deserted Dido.

**Aeolus:** *See* Winds.

**Aesculapius:** *See* Asclepius.

**Aeson:** King of Ioclus; father of Jason; overthrown by his brother Pelias; restored to youth by Medea.

**Aether:** Personification of sky.

**Aethra:** Mother of Theseus.

**Agamemnon:** King of Mycenae; son of Atreus; brother of Menelaus; leader of Greeks against Troy; slain on his return home by Clytemnestra and Aegisthus.

**Agiaia:** *See* Graces.

**Ajax:** Greek warrior; killed himself at Troy because Achilles'

armor was awarded to Odysseus.

**Alcestis:** Wife of Admetus; offered to die in his place but saved from death by Hercules.

**Alcmene:** Wife of Amphitryon; mother by Zeus of Hercules.

**Alcyone:** *See* Pleiades.

**Alecto:** *See* Furies.

**Alectryon:** Youth changed by Ares into cock.

**Althaea:** Wife of Oeneus; mother of Meleager.

**Amazons:** Female warriors in Asia Minor; supported Troy against Greeks.

**Amor:** *See* Eros.

**Amphion:** Musician; husband of Niobe; charmed stones to build fortifications for Thebes.

**Amphitrite:** Sea goddess; wife of Poseidon.

**Amphitryon:** Husband of Alcmene.

**Anchises:** Father of Aeneas.

**Ancile:** Sacred shield that fell from heavens; palladium of Rome.

**Andraemon:** Husband of Dryope.

**Andromache:** Wife of Hector.

**Andromeda:** Daughter of Cepheus; chained to cliff for monster to devour; rescued by Perseus.

**Anteia:** Wife of Proetus; tried to induce Bellerophon to elope with her.

**Anteros:** God who avenged unrequited love.

**Antigone:** Daughter of Oedipus; accompanied him to Colonus; performed burial rite for Polynices and hanged herself.

**Antinoüs:** Leader of suitors of Penelope; slain by Odysseus.

**Aphrodite (Venus):** Goddess of love and beauty; daughter

of Zeus; mother of Eros.

**Apollo:** God of beauty, poetry, music; later identified with Helios as Phoebus Apollo; son of Zeus and Leto.

**Aquilo:** *See* Winds.

**Arachne:** Maiden who challenged Athena to weaving contest; changed to spider.

**Ares (Mars):** God of war; son of Zeus and Hera.

**Argo:** Ship in which Jason and followers sailed to Colchis for Golden Fleece.

**Argus:** Monster with hundred eyes; slain by Hermes; his eyes placed by Hera into peacock's tail.

**Ariadne:** Daughter of Minos; aided Theseus in slaying Minotaur; deserted by him on island of Naxos and married to Dionysus.

**Arion:** Musician; thrown overboard by pirates but saved by dolphin.

**Artemis (Diana):** Goddess of moon; huntress; twin sister of Apollo.

**Asclepius (Aesculapius):** Mortal son of Apollo; slain by Zeus for raising dead; later deified as god of medicine. Also known as Asklepios.

**Astarte:** Phoenician goddess of love; variously identified with Aphrodite, Selene, and Artemis.

**Astraea:** Goddess of Justice; daughter of Zeus and Themis.

**Atalanta:** Princess who challenged her suitors to a foot race; Hippomenes won race and married her.

**Athena (Minerva):** Goddess of wisdom; known poetically as Pallas Athena; sprang fully armed from head of Zeus.

**Atlas:** Titan; held world on his shoulders as punishment for warring against Zeus; son of Iapetus.

**Atreus:** King of Mycenae; father of Menelaus and Agamemnon; brother of Thyestes, three of whose sons he slew and served to him at banquet; slain by Aegisthus.

**Atropos:** *See* Fates.

**Aurora:** *See* Eos.

**Auster:** *See* Winds.

**Avernus:** Infernal regions; name derived from small vaporous lake near Vesuvius which was fabled to kill birds and vegetation.

**Bacchus:** *See* Dionysus.

**Bellerophon:** Corinthian hero; killed Chimera with aid of Pegasus; tried to reach Olympus on Pegasus and was thrown to his death.

**Bellona:** Roman goddess of war.

**Boreas:** *See* Winds.

**Briareus:** Monster of hundred hands; son of Uranus and Gaea.

**Briseis:** Captive maiden given to Achilles; taken by Agamemnon in exchange for loss of Chryseis, which caused Achilles to cease fighting, until death of Patroclus.

**Cadmus:** Brother of Europa; planter of dragon seeds from which first Thebans sprang.

**Calliope:** *See* Muses.

**Calypso:** Sea nymph; kept Odysseus on her island Ogygia for seven years.

**Cassandra:** Daughter of Priam; prophetess who was never believed; slain with Agamemnon.

**Castor:** *See* Dioscuri.

**Celaeno:** *See* Pleiades.

**Centaurs:** Beings half man and half horse; lived in mountains of Thessaly.

**Cephalus:** Hunter; accidentally killed his wife Procris with his spear.

**Cepheus:** King of Ethiopia; father of Andromeda.

**Cerberus:** Three-headed dog guarding entrance to Hades.

**Ceres:** *See* Demeter.

**Chaos:** Formless void; personified as first of gods.

**Charon:** Boatman on Styx who carried souls of dead to Hades; son of Erebus.

**Charybdis:** Female monster; personification of whirlpool.

**Chimera:** Female monster with head of lion, body of goat, tail of serpent; killed by Bellerophon.

**Chiron:** Most famous of centaurs.

**Chronos:** Personification of time.

**Chryseis:** Captive maiden given to Agamemnon; his refusal to accept ransom from her father Chryses caused Apollo to send plague on Greeks besieging Troy.

**Circe:** Sorceress; daughter of Helios; changed Odysseus' men into swine.

**Clio:** *See* Muses.

**Clotho:** *See* Fates.

**Clytemnestra:** Wife of Agamemnon, whom she slew with aid of her paramour, Aegisthus; slain by her son Orestes.

**Cocytus:** *See* Rivers.

**Creon:** Father of Jocasta; forbade burial of Polynices; ordered burial alive of Antigone.

**Creüsa:** Princess of Corinth, for whom Jason deserted Medea; slain by Medea, who sent her poisoned robe; also known as Glaüke.

**Creusa:** Wife of Aeneas; died fleeing Troy.

**Cronus (Saturn):** Titan; god of harvests; son of Uranus and Gaea; dethroned by his son Zeus.

**Cupid:** *See* Eros.

**Cybele:** Anatolian nature goddess; adopted by Greeks and identified with Rhea.

**Cyclopes:** Race of one-eyed giants (singular: Cyclops).

**Daedalus:** Athenian artificer; father of Icarus; builder of Labyrinth in Crete; devised wings attached with wax for him and Icarus to escape Crete.

**Danae:** Princess of Argos; mother of Perseus by Zeus, who appeared to her in form of golden shower.

**Danaïdes:** Daughters of Danaüs; at his command, all except Hypermnestra slew their husbands, the sons of Aegyptus.

**Danaüs:** Brother of Aegyptus; father of Danaïdes; slain by Lynceus.

**Daphne:** Nymph; pursued by Apollo; changed to laurel tree.

**Decuma:** *See* Fates.

**Deino:** *See* Graeae.

**Demeter (Ceres):** Goddess of agriculture; mother of Persephone.

**Diana:** *See* Artemis.

**Dido:** Founder and queen of Carthage; stabbed herself when deserted by Aeneas.

**Diomedes:** Greek hero; with Odysseus, entered Troy and carried off Palladium, sacred statue of Athena.

**Diomedes:** Owner of man-eating horses, which Hercules, as ninth labor, carried off.

**Dione:** Titan goddess; mother by Zeus of Aphrodite.

**Dionysus (Bacchus):** God of wine; son of Zeus and Semele.

**Dioscuri:** Twins Castor and Pollux; sons of Leda by Zeus.

**Dis:** *See* Hades.

**Dryads:** Wood nymphs.

**Dryope:** Maiden changed to Hamadryad.

**Echo:** Nymph who fell hopelessly in love with Narcissus; faded away except for her voice.

**Electra:** Daughter of Agamemnon and Clytemnestra; sister of Orestes; urged Orestes to slay Clytemnestra and Aegisthus.

**Electra:** *See* Pleiades.

**Elysium:** Abode of blessed dead.

**Endymion:** Mortal loved by Selene.

**Enyo:** *See* Graeae.

**Eos (Aurora):** Goddess of dawn.

**Epimetheus:** Brother of Prometheus; husband of Pandora.

**Erato:** *See* Muses.

**Erebus:** Spirit of darkness; son of Chaos.

**Erinyes:** *See* Furies.

**Eris:** Goddess of discord.

**Eros (Amor or Cupid):** God of love; son of Aphrodite.

**Eteocles:** Son of Oedipus, whom he succeeded to rule alternately with Polynices; refused to give up throne at end of year; he and Polynices slew each other.

**Eumenides:** *See* Furies.

**Euphrosyne:** *See* Graces.

**Europa:** Mortal loved by Zeus, who, in form of white bull, carried her off to Crete.

**Eurus:** *See* Winds.

**Euryale:** *See* Gorgons.

**Eurydice:** Nymph; wife of Orpheus.

**Eurystheus:** King of Argos; imposed twelve labors on Hercules.

**Euterpe:** *See* Muses.

**Fates:** Goddesses of destiny; Clotho (Spinner of thread of life), Lachesis (Determiner of length), and Atropos (Cutter of thread); also called Moirae. Identified by Romans with their goddesses of fate; Nona, Decuma, and Morta; called Parcae.

**Fauns:** Roman deities of woods and groves.

**Faunus:** *See* Pan.

**Favonius:** *See* Winds.

**Flora:** Roman goddess of flowers.

**Fortuna:** Roman goddess of fortune.

**Furies:** Avenging spirits; Alecto, Megaera, and Tisiphone; known also as Erinyes or Eumenides.

**Gaea:** Goddess of earth; daughter of Chaos; mother of Titans; known also as Ge, Gea, Gaia, etc.

**Galatea:** Statue of maiden carved from ivory by Pygmalion; given life by Aphrodite.

**Galatea:** Sea nymph; loved by Polyphemus.

**Ganymede:** Beautiful boy; successor to Hebe as cupbearer of gods.

**Glaucus:** Mortal who became sea divinity by eating magic grass.

**Glauke:** *See* Creüsa.

**Golden Fleece:** Fleece from ram that flew Phrixos to Colchis; Aeëtes placed it under guard of dragon; carried off by Jason.

**Gorgons:** Female monsters; Euryale, Medusa, and Stheno; had snakes for hair; their glances turned mortals to stone. *See* Medusa.

**Graces:** Beautiful goddesses: Aglaia (Brilliance), Euphrosyne (Joy), and Thalia (Bloom); daughters of Zeus.

**Graeae:** Sentinels for Gorgons; Deino, Enyo, and Pephredo; had one eye among them, which passed from one to another.

**Hades (Dis):** Name sometimes given Pluto; also, abode of dead, ruled by Pluto.

**Haemon:** Son of Creon; promised husband of Antigone; killed himself in her tomb.

**Hamadryads:** Tree nymphs.

**Harpies:** Monsters with heads of women and bodies of birds.

**Hebe (Juventas):** Goddess of youth; cupbearer of gods before Ganymede; daughter of Zeus and Hera.

**Hecate:** Goddess of sorcery and witchcraft.

**Hector:** Son of Priam; slayer of Patroclus; slain by Achilles.

**Hecuba:** Wife of Priam.

**Helen:** Fairest woman in world; daughter of Zeus and Leda; wife of Menelaus; carried to Troy by Paris, causing Trojan War.

**Heliades:** Daughters of Helios; mourned for Phaëthon and were changed to poplar trees.

**Helios (Sol):** God of sun; later identified with Apollo.

**Helle:** Sister of Phrixos; fell from ram of Golden Fleece; water where she fell named Hellespont.

**Hephaestus (Vulcan):** God of fire; celestial blacksmith; son of Zeus and Hera; husband of Aphrodite.

**Hera (Juno):** Queen of heaven; wife of Zeus.

**Hercules:** Hero and strong man; son of Zeus and Alcmene; performed twelve labors or deeds to be free from bondage under Eurystheus; after death, his mortal share was destroyed, and he became immortal. Also known as Herakles or Heracles. Labors: (1) killing Nemean lion; (2) killing Lernaean Hydra; (3) capturing Erymanthian boar; (4) capturing Ceryneian hind; (5) killing man-eating Stymphalian birds; (6) procuring girdle of Hippolyte; (7) cleaning Augean stables; (8) capturing Cretan bull; (9) capturing man-eating horses of Diomedes; (10) capturing cattle of Geryon; (11) procuring golden apples of Hesperides; (12) bringing Cerberus up from Hades.

**Hermes (Mercury):** God of physicians and thieves; messenger of gods; son of Zeus and Maia.

**Hero:** Priestess of Aphrodite; Leander swam Hellespont nightly to see her; drowned herself at his death.

**Hesperus:** Evening star.

**Hestia (Vesta):** Goddess of hearth; sister of Zeus.

**Hippolyte:** Queen of Amazons; wife of Theseus.

**Hippolytus:** Son of Theseus and Hippolyte; falsely accused by Phaedra of trying to kidnap her; slain by Poseidon at request of Theseus.

**Hippomenes:** Husband of Atalanta, whom he beat in race by dropping golden apples, which she stopped to pick up.

**Hyacinthus:** Beautiful youth accidentally killed by Apollo, who caused flower to spring up from his blood.

**Hydra:** Nine-headed monster in marsh of Lerna; slain by Hercules.

**Hygeia:** Personification of health.

**Hyman:** God of marriage.

**Hyperion:** Titan; early sun god; father of Helios.

**Hypermnestra:** Daughter of Danaüs; refused to kill her husband Lynceus.

**Hypnos (Somnus):** God of sleep.

**Iapetus:** Titan; father of Atlas, Epimetheus, and Prometheus.

**Icarus:** Son of Daedalus; flew too near sun with wax-attached wings and fell into sea and was drowned.

**Io:** Mortal maiden loved by Zeus; changed by Hera into heifer.

**Iobates:** King of Lycia; sent Bellerophon to slay Chimera.

**Iphigenia:** Daughter of Agamemnon; offered as sacrifice to Artemis at Aulis; carried by Artemis to Tauris where she became priestess; escaped from there with Orestes.

**Iris:** Goddess of rainbow; messenger of Zeus and Hera.

**Ismene:** Daughter of Oedipus; sister of Antigone.

**Iulus:** Son of Aeneas.

**Ixion:** King of Lapithae; for making love to Hera he was bound to endlessly revolving wheel in Tartarus.

**Janus:** Roman god of gates and doors; represented with two opposite faces.

**Jason:** Son of Aeson; to gain throne of Ioclus from Pelias, went to Colchis and brought back Golden Fleece; married Medea; deserted her for Creüsa.

**Jocasta:** Wife of Laius; mother of Oedipus; unwittingly became wife of Oedipus; hanged herself when relationship was discovered.

**Juno:** *See* Hera.

**Jupiter:** *See* Zeus.

**Juventas:** *See* Hebe.

**Lachesis:** *See* Fates.

**Laius:** Father of Oedipus, by whom he was slain.

**Laocoön:** Priest of Apollo at Troy; warned against bringing wooden horse into Troy; destroyed with his two sons by serpents sent by Athena.

**Lares:** Roman ancestral spirits protecting descendants and homes.

**Lavinia:** Wife of Aeneas after defeat of Turnus.

**Leander:** Swam Hellespont nightly to see Hero; drowned in storm.

**Leda:** Mortal loved by Zeus in form of Swan; mother of Helen, Clytemnestra, Dioscuri.

**Lethe:** *See* Rivers.

**Leto (Latona):** Mother by Zeus of Artemis and Apollo.

**Lucina:** Roman goddess of childbirth; identified with Juno.

**Lynceus:** Son of Aegyptus; husband of Hypermnestra; slew Danaüs.

**Maia:** Daughter of Atlas; mother of Hermes.

**Maia:** *See* Pleiades.

**Manes:** Souls of dead Romans, particularly of ancestors.

**Mars:** *See* Ares.

**Marsyas:** Shepherd; challenged Apollo to music contest and lost; flayed alive by Apollo.

**Medea:** Sorceress; daughter of Aeëtes; helped Jason obtain Golden Fleece; when deserted by him for Creüsa, killed her children and Creüsa.

**Medusa:** Gorgon; slain by Perseus, who cut off her head.

**Megaera:** *See* Furies.

**Meleager:** Son of Althaea; his life would last as long as brand burning at his birth; Althaea quenched and saved it but destroyed it when Meleager slew his uncles.

**Melpomene:** *See* Muses.

**Memnon:** Ethiopian king; made immortal by Zeus; son of Tithonus and Eos.

**Menelaus:** King of Sparta; son of Atreus; brother of Agamemnon; husband of Helen.

**Mercury:** *See* Hermes.

**Merope:** *See* Pleiades.

**Mezentius:** Cruel Etruscan king; ally of Turnus against Aeneas; slain by Aeneas.

**Midas:** King of Phrygia; given gift of turning to gold all he touched.

**Minerva:** *See* Athena.

**Minos:** King of Crete; after death, one of three judges of dead in Hades; son of Zeus and Europa.

**Minotaur:** Monster, half man and half beast, kept in Labyrinth in Crete; slain by Theseus.

**Mnemosyne:** Goddess of memory; mother by Zeus of Muses.

**Moirae:** *See* Fates.

**Momus:** God of ridicule.

**Morpheus:** God of dreams.

**Mors:** *See* Thanatos.

**Morta:** *See* Fates.

**Muses:** Goddesses presiding over arts and sciences: Calliope (epic poetry), Clio (history), Erato (lyric and love poetry), Euterpe (music), Melpomene (tragedy), Polymnia or Polyhymnia (sacred poetry), Terpsichore (choral dance and song), Thalia (comedy and bucolic poetry), Urania (astronomy); daughters of Zeus and Mnemosyne.

**Naiads:** Nymphs of waters, streams, and fountains.

**Napaeae:** Wood nymphs.

**Narcissus:** Beautiful youth loved by Echo; in punishment for not returning her love, he was made to fall in love with his image reflected in pool; pined away and became flower.

**Nemesis:** Goddess of retribution.

**Neoptolemus:** Son of Achilles; slew Priam; also known as Pyrrhus.

**Neptune:** *See* Poseidon.

**Nereids:** Sea nymphs; attendants on Poseidon.

**Nestor:** King of Pylos; noted for wise counsel in expedition against Troy.

**Nike:** Goddess of victory.

**Niobe:** Daughter of Tantalus; wife of Amphion; her children slain by Apollo and Artemis; changed to stone but continued to weep her loss.

**Nona:** *See* Fates.

**Notus:** *See* Winds.

**Nox:** *See* Nyx.

**Nymphs:** Beautiful maidens; inferior deities of nature.

**Nyx (Nox):** Goddess of night.

**Oceanids:** Ocean nymphs; daughters of Oceanus.

**Oceanus:** Eldest of Titans; god of waters.

**Odysseus (Ulysses):** King of Ithaca; husband of Penelope; wandered ten years after fall of Troy before arriving home.

**Oedipus:** King of Thebes; son of Laius and Jocasta; unwittingly murdered Laius and married Jocasta; tore his eyes out when relationship was discovered.

**Oenone:** Nymph of Mount Ida; wife of Paris, who abandoned her; refused to cure him when he was poisoned by arrow of Philoctetes at Troy.

**Ops:** *See* Rhea.

**Oreads:** Mountain nymphs.

**Orestes:** Son of Agamemnon and Clytemnestra; brother of Electra; slew Clytemnestra and Aegisthus; pursued by Furies until his purification by Apollo.

**Orion:** Hunter; slain by Artemis and made heavenly constellation.

**Orpheus:** Famed musician; son of Apollo and Muse Calliope; husband of Eurydice.

**Pales:** Roman goddess of shepherds and herdsmen.

**Palinurus:** Aeneas' pilot; fell overboard in his sleep and was drowned.

**Pan (Faunus):** God of woods and fields; part goat; son of Hermes.

**Pandora:** Opener of box containing human ills; mortal wife of Epimetheus.

**Parcae:** *See* Fates.

**Paris:** Son of Priam; gave apple of discord to Aphrodite, for which she enabled him to carry off Helen; slew Achilles at Troy; slain by Philoctetes.

**Patroclus:** Great friend of Achilles; wore Achilles' armor and was slain by Hector.

**Pegasus:** Winged horse that sprang from Medusa's body at her death; ridden by Bellerophon when he slew Chimera.

**Pelias:** King of Ioclus; seized throne from his brother Aeson; sent Jason for Golden Fleece; slain unwittingly by his daughters at instigation of Medea.

**Pelops:** Son of Tantalus; his father cooked and served him to gods; restored to life; Peloponnesus named for him.

**Penates:** Roman household gods.

**Penelope:** Wife of Odysseus; waited faithfully for him for ten years while putting off numerous suitors.

**Pephredo:** *See* Graeae.

**Periphetes:** Giant; son of Hephaestus; slain by Theseus.

**Persephone (Proserpine):** Queen of infernal regions; daughter of Zeus and Demeter; wife of Pluto.

**Perseus:** Son of Zeus and Danaë; slew Medusa; rescued Andromeda from monster and married her.

**Phaedra:** Daughter of Minos; wife of Theseus; caused the death of her stepson, Hippolytus.

**Phaethon:** Son of Helios; drove his father's sun chariot and was struck down by Zeus before he set world on fire.

**Philoctetes:** Greek warrior who possessed Hercules' bow and arrows; slew Paris at Troy with poisoned arrow.

**Phineus:** Betrothed of Andromeda; tried to slay Perseus but turned to stone by Medusa's head.

**Phlegethon:** *See* Rivers.

**Phosphor:** Morning star.

**Phrixos:** Brother of Helle; carried by ram of Golden Fleece to Colchis.

**Pirithous:** Son of Ixion; friend of Theseus; tried to carry off Persephone from Hades; bound to enchanted rock by Pluto.

**Pleiades:** Alcyone, Celaeno, Electra, Maia, Merope, Sterope or Asterope, Taygeta; seven daughters of Atlas; transformed into heavenly constellation, of which six stars are visible (Merope is said to have hidden in shame for loving a mortal).

**Pluto (Dis):** God of Hades; brother of Zeus.

**Plutus:** God of wealth.

**Pollux:** *See* Dioscuri.

**Polymnia:** *See* Muses.

**Polynices:** Son of Oedipus; he and his brother Eteocles killed each other; burial rite, forbidden by Creon, performed by his sister Antigone.

**Polyphemus:** Cyclops; devoured six of Odysseus' men; blinded by Odysseus.

**Polyxena:** Daughter of Priam; betrothed to Achilles, whom Paris slew at their betrothal; sacrificed to shade of Achilles.

**Pomona:** Roman goddess of fruits.

**Pontus:** Sea god; son of Gaea.

**Poseidon (Neptune):** God of sea; brother of Zeus.

**Priam:** King of Troy; husband of Hecuba; ransomed Hector's body from Achilles; slain by Neoptolemus.

**Priapus:** God of regeneration.

**Procris:** Wife of Cephalus, who accidentally slew her.

**Procrustes:** Giant; stretched or cut off legs of victims to make them fit iron bed; slain by Theseus.

**Proetus:** Husband of Anteia; sent Bellerophon to Iobates to be put to death.

**Prometheus:** Titan; stole fire from heaven for man. Zeus punished him by chaining him to rock in Caucasus where vultures devoured his liver daily.

**Proteus:** Sea god; assumed various shapes when called on to prophesy.

**Psyche:** Beloved of Eros; punished by jealous Aphrodite; made immortal and united with Eros.

**Pygmalion:** King of Cyprus; carved ivory statue of maiden which Aphrodite gave life as Galatea.

**Pyramus:** Babylonian youth; made love to Thisbe through hole in wall; thinking Thisbe slain by lion, killed himself.

**Pyrrhus:** *See* Neoptolemus.

**Python:** Serpent born from slime left by Deluge; slain by Apollo.

**Quirinus:** Roman war god.

**Remus:** Brother of Romulus; slain by him.

**Rhadamanthus:** One of three judges of dead in Hades; son of Zeus and Europa.

**Rhea (Ops):** Daughter of Uranus and Gaea; wife of Cronus; mother of Zeus; identified with Cybele.

**Rivers of Underworld:** Acheron (woe), Cocytus (wailing), Lethe (forgetfulness), Phlegethon (fire), Styx (across which souls of dead were ferried by Charon).

**Romulus:** Founder of Rome; he and Remus suckled in infancy by she-wolf; slew Remus; deified by Romans.

**Sarpedon:** King of Lycia; son of Zeus and Europa; slain by Patroclus at Troy.

**Saturn:** *See* Cronus.

**Satyrs:** Hoofed demigods of woods and fields; companions of Dionysus.

**Sciron:** Robber; forced strangers to wash his feet, then hurled them into sea where tortoise devoured them; slain by Theseus.

**Scylla:** Female monster inhabiting rock opposite Charybdis; menaced passing sailors.

**Selene:** Goddess of moon.

**Semele:** Daughter of Cadmus; mother by Zeus of Dionysus; demanded Zeus appear before her in all his splendor and was destroyed by his lightnings.

**Sibyis:** Various prophetesses; most famous, Cumaean sibyl, accompanied Aeneas into Hades.

**Sileni:** Minor woodland deities similar to satyrs (singular: silenus). Sometimes Silenus refers to eldest of satyrs, son of Hermes or of Pan.

**Silvanus:** Roman god of woods and fields.

**Sinis:** Giant; bent pines, by which he hurled victims against side of mountain; slain by Theseus.

**Sirens:** Minor deities who lured sailors to destruction with their singing.

**Sisyphus:** King of Corinth; condemned in Tartarus to roll huge stone to top of hill; it always rolled back down again.

**Sol:** *See* Helios.

**Somnus:** *See* Hypnos.

**Sphinx:** Monster of Thebes; killed those who could not answer her riddle; slain by Oedipus. Name also refers to other monsters having body of lion, wings, and head and bust of woman.

**Sterope:** *See* Pleiades.

**Stheno:** *See* Gorgons.

**Styx:** *See* Rivers.

**Symplegades:** Clashing rocks at entrance to Black Sea; Argo passed through, causing them to become forever fixed.

**Syrinx:** Nymph pursued by Pan; changed to reeds, from which he made his pipes.

**Tantalus:** Cruel king; father of Pelops and Niobe; condemned in Tartarus to stand chin-deep in lake surrounded by fruit branches; as he tried to eat or drink, water or fruit always receded.

**Tartarus:** Underworld below Hades; often refers to Hades.

**Taygeta:** *See* Pleiades.

**Telemachus:** Son of Odysseus; made unsuccessful journey to find his father.

**Tellus:** Roman goddess of earth.

**Terminus:** Roman god of boundaries and landmarks.

**Terpsichore:** *See* Muses.

**Terra:** Roman earth goddess.

**Thalia:** *See* Graces; Muses.

**Thanatos (Mors):** God of death.

**Themis:** Titan goddess of laws of physical phenomena; daughter of Uranus; mother of Prometheus.

**Theseus:** Son of Aegeus; slew Minotaur; married and deserted Ariadne; later married Phaedra.

**Thisbe:** Beloved of Pyramus; killed herself at his death.

**Thyestes:** Brother of Atreus; Atreus killed three of his sons and served them to him at banquet.

**Tiresias:** Blind soothsayer of Thebes.

**Tisiphone:** *See* Furies.

**Titans:** Early gods from which Olympian gods were derived; children of Uranus and Gaea.

**Tithonus:** Mortal loved by Eos; changed into grasshopper.

**Triton:** Demigod of sea; son of Poseidon.

**Turnus:** King of Rutuli in Italy; betrothed to Lavinia; slain by Aeneas.

**Ulysses:** *See* Odysseus.

**Urania:** *See* Muses.

**Uranus:** Personification of Heaven; husband of Gaea; father of Titans; dethroned by his son Cronus.

**Venus:** *See* Aphrodite.

**Vertumnus:** Roman god of fruits and vegetables; husband of Pomona.

**Vesta:** *See* Hestia.

**Vulcan:** *See* Hephaestus.

**Winds:** Aeolus (keeper of winds), Boreas (Aquilo) (north wind), Eurus (east wind), Notus (Auster) (south wind), Zephyrus (Favonius) (west wind).

**Zephyrus:** *See* Winds.

**Zeus (Jupiter):** Chief of Olympian gods; son of Cronus and Rhea; husband of Hera.

## Norse Mythology

**Aesir:** Chief gods of Asgard.

**Andvari:** Dwarf; robbed of gold and magic ring by Loki.

**Angerbotha (Angrbotha):** Giantess; mother by Loki of Fenrir, Hel, and Midgard serpent.

**Asgard (Asgarth):** Abode of gods.

**Ask (Aske, Askr):** First man; created by Odin, Hoenir, and Lothur.

**Asynjur:** Goddesses of Asgard.

**Atli:** Second husband of Gudrun; invited Gunnar and Hogni to his court, where they were slain; slain by Gudrun.

**Audhumia (Audhumbla):** Cow that nourished Ymir, created Buri by licking ice cliff.

**Balder (Baldr, Baldur):** God of light, spring, peace, joy; son of Odin; slain by Hoth at instigation of Loki.

**Bifrost:** Rainbow bridge connecting Midgard and Asgard.

**Bragi (Brage):** God of poetry; husband of Ithunn.

**Branstock:** Great oak in hall of Volsungs; into it, Odin thrust Gram, which only Sigmund could draw forth.

**Brynhild:** Valkyrie; wakened from magic sleep by Sigurd; married Gunnar; instigated death of Sigurd; killed herself and was burned on pyre beside Sigurd.

**Bur (Bor):** Son of Buri; father of Odin, Hoenir, and Lothur.

**Buri (Bori):** Progenitor of gods; father of Bur; created by Audhumla.

**Embla:** First woman; created by Odin, Hoenir, and Lothur.

**Fafnir:** Son of Rodmar, whom he slew for gold in Otter's skin; in form of dragon, guarded gold; slain by Sigurd.

**Fenrir:** Wolf; offspring of Loki; swallows Odin at Ragnarok and is slain by Vitharr.

**Forseti:** Son of Balder.

**Frey (Freyr):** God of fertility and crops; son of Njorth; originally one of Vanir.

**Freya (Freyja):** Goddess of love and beauty; sister of Frey; originally one of Vanir.

**Frigg (Frigga):** Goddess of sky; wife of Odin.

**Garm:** Watchdog of Hel; slays, and is slain by, Tyr at Ragnarok.

**Gimle:** Home of blessed after Ragnarok.

**Giuki:** King of Nibelungs; father of Gunnar, Hogni, Guttorm, and Gudrun.

**Glathsehim (Gladsheim):** Hall of gods in Asgard.

**Gram (meaning "Angry"):** Sigmund's sword; rewelded by Regin; used by Sigurd to slay Fafnir.

**Greyfell:** Sigmund's horse; descended from Sleipnir.

**Grimhild:** Mother of Gudrun; administered magic potion to Sigurd which made him forget Brynhild.

**Gudrun:** Daughter of Giuki; wife of Sigurd; later wife of Atli and Jonakr.

**Gunnar:** Son of Giuki; in his semblance Sigurd won Brynhild for him; slain at hall of Atli.

**Guttorm:** Son of Giuki; slew Sigurd at Brynhild's request.

**Heimdall (Heimdallr):** Guardian of Asgard.

**Hel:** Goddess of dead and queen of underworld; daughter of Loki.

**Hiordis:** Wife of Sigmund; mother of Sigurd.

**Hoenir:** One of creators of Ask and Embla; son of Bur.

**Hogni:** Son of Giuki; slain at hall of Atli.

**Hoth (Hoder, Hodur):** Blind god of night and darkness; slayer of Balder at instigation of Loki.

**Ithunn (Ithun, Iduna):** Keeper of golden apples of youth; wife of Bragi.

**Jonakr:** Third husband of Gudrun.

**Jormunrek:** Slayer of Swanhild; slain by sons of Gudrun.

**Jotunnheim (Jotunheim):** Abode of giants.

**Lif and Lifthrasir:** First man and woman after Ragnarok.

**Loki:** God of evil and mischief; instigator of Balder's death.

**Lothur (Lodur):** One of creators of Ask and Embla.

**Midgard (Midgarth):** Abode of mankind; the earth.

**Midgard Serpent:** Sea monster; offspring of Loki; slays, and is slain by, Thor at Ragnarok.

**Mimir:** Giant; guardian of well in Jotunnheim at root of Yggdrasil; knower of past and future.

**Mjollnir:** Magic hammer of Thor.

**Nagifar:** Ship to be used by giants in attacking Asgard at

Ragnarok; built from nails of dead men.

**Nanna:** Wife of Balder.

**Nibelungs:** Dwellers in northern kingdom ruled by Giuki.

**Niflheim (Nifelheim):** Outer region of cold and darkness; abode of Hel.

**Njorth:** Father of Frey and Freya; originally one of Vanir.

**Norns:** Demigoddesses of fate: Urth (Urdur) (Past), Verthandi (Verdandi) (Present), Skuld (Future).

**Odin (Othin):** Head of Aesir; creator of world with Vili and Ve; equivalent to Woden (Wodan, Wotan) in Teutonic mythology.

**Otter:** Son of Rodmar; slain by Loki; his skin filled with gold hoard of Andvari to appease Rodmar.

**Ragnarok:** Final destruction of present world in battle between gods and giants; some minor gods will survive, and Lif and Lifthrasir will repeople world.

**Regin:** Blacksmith; son of Rodmar; foster-father of Sigurd.

**Rerir:** King of Huns; son of Sigi.

**Rodmar:** Father of Regin, Otter, and Fafnir; demanded Otter's skin be filled with gold; slain by Fafnir, who stole gold.

**Sif:** Wife of Thor.

**Siggeir:** King of Goths; husband of Signy; he and his sons slew Volsung and his sons, except Sigmund; slain by Sigmund and Sinflotli.

**Sigi:** King of Huns; son of Odin.

**Sigmund:** Son of Volsung; brother of Signy, who bore him Sinflotli; husband of Hiordis, who bore him Sigurd.

**Signy:** Daughter of Volsung; sister of Sigmund; wife of Siggeir; mother by Sigmund of Sinflotli.

**Sigurd:** Son of Sigmund and Hiordis; wakened Brynhild from magic sleep; married Gudrun; slain by Guttorm at instigation of Brynhild.

**Sigyn:** Wife of Loki.

**Sinflotli:** Son of Sigmund and Signy.

**Skuld:** *See* Norns.

**Sleipnir (Sleipner):** Eight-legged horse of Odin.

**Surt (Surtr):** Fire demon; slays Frey at Ragnarok.

**Svartalfaheim:** Abode of dwarfs.

**Swanhild:** Daughter of Sigurd and Gudrun; slain by Jormunrek.

**Thor:** God of thunder; oldest son of Odin; equivalent to Germanic deity Donar.

**Tyr:** God of war; son of Odin; equivalent to Tiu in Teutonic mythology.

**Ull (Ullr):** Son of Sif; stepson of Thor.

**Urth:** *See* Norns.

**Valhalla (Valhall):** Great hall in Asgard where Odin received souls of heroes killed in battle.

**Vali:** Odin's son; Ragnarok survivor.

**Valkyries:** Virgins, messengers of Odin, who selected heroes to die in battle and took them to Valhalla; generally considered as nine in number.

**Vanir:** Early race of gods; three survivors, Njorth, Frey, and Freya, are associated with Aesir.

**Ve:** Brother of Odin; one of creators of world.

**Verthandi:** *See* Norns.

**Vili:** Brother of Odin; one of creators of world.

**Vingolf:** Abode of goddesses in Asgard.

**Vitharr (Vithar):** Son of Odin; survivor of Ragnarok.

**Volsung:** Descendant of Odin, and father of Signy, Sigmund; his descendants were called Volsungs.

**Yggdrasill:** Giant ash tree springing from body of Ymir and supporting universe; its roots extended to Asgard, Jotunnheim, and Niffheim.

**Ymir (Ymer):** Primeval frost giant killed by Odin, Vili, and Ve; world created from his body; also, from his body sprang Yggdrasill.

## Egyptian Mythology

**Aaru:** Abode of the blessed dead.

**Amen (Amon, Ammdn):** One of chief Theban deities; united with sun god under form of Amen-Ra.

**Amenti:** Region of dead where souls were judged by Osiris.

**Anubis:** Guide of souls to Amenti; son of Osiris; jackalheaded.

**Apis:** Sacred bull, an embodiment of Ptah; identified with Osiris as Osiris-Apis or Serapis.

**Geb (Keb, Seb):** Earth god; father of Osiris; represented with goose on head.

**Hathor (Athor):** Goddess of love and mirth; cow-headed.

**Horus:** God of day; son of Osiris and Isis; hawk-headed.

**Isis:** Goddess of motherhood and fertility; sister and wife of Osiris.

**Khepera:** God of morning sun.

**Khnemu (Khnum, Chnuphis, Chnemu, Chnum):** Ramheaded god.

**Khonsu (Khensu, Khuns):** Son of Amen and Mut.

**Mentu (Ment):** Solar deity, sometimes considered god of war; falcon-headed.

**Min (Khem, Chem):** Principle of physical life.

**Mut (Maut):** Wife of Amen.

**Nephthys:** Goddess of the dead; sister and wife of Set.

**Nu:** Chaos from which world was created, personified as a god.

**Nut:** Goddess of heavens; consort of Geb.

**Osiris:** God of underworld and judge of dead; son of Geb and Nut.

**Ptah (Phtha):** Chief deity of Memphis.

**Ra:** God of the Sun, the supreme god; son of Nut; Pharaohs claimed descent from him; represented as lion, cat, or falcon.

**Serapis:** God uniting attributes of Osiris and Apis.

**Set (Seth):** God of darkness or evil; brother and enemy of Osiris.

**Shu:** Solar deity; son of Ra and Hathor.

**Tem (Atmu, Atum, Tum):** Solar deity.

**Thoth (Dhouti):** God of wisdom and magic; scribe of gods; ibis-headed.

## Modern Wedding Anniversary Gift List

| Anniversary | Gift | Anniversary | Gift | Anniversary | Gift |
| --- | --- | --- | --- | --- | --- |
| 1st | Clocks | 10th | Diamond jewelry | 19th | Bronze |
| 2nd | China | 11th | Fashion jewelry and | 20th | Platinum |
| 3rd | Crystal, glass | | accessories | 25th | Sterling Silver Jubilee |
| 4th | Electrical Appliances | 12th | Pearls or colored gems | 30th | Diamond |
| 5th | Silverware | 13th | Textiles, furs | 35th | Jade |
| 6th | Wood | 14th | Gold jewelry | 40th | Ruby |
| 7th | Desk sets, pen and pencil | 15th | Watches | 45th | Sapphire |
| | sets | 16th | Silver holloware | 50th | Golden Jubilee |
| 8th | Linens, laces | 17th | Furniture | 55th | Emerald |
| 9th | Leather | 18th | Porcelain | 60th | Diamond Jubilee |

*Source:* Jewelry Industry Council.

# CONSUMER'S RESOURCE GUIDE

## How to Establish a Credit Rating

### By Sylvia Porter

The ease with which Americans can open a charge account, get a new credit card, or take out a bank loan is directly dependent on the voluminous dossiers in the files of 2,500 credit bureaus throughout the United States and of large numbers of local merchants' associations on virtually every borrower. The bureaus freely exchange this information. They sell it to retailers, banks, other lenders, credit card companies, corporations, etc.—and a credit report almost surely will be obtained on you when you apply for a job or insurance or credit.

Credit bureaus do not "rate" how good or bad a credit risk you are. They simply collect, from merchants with whom you have credit, public records, other sources of information on you which can be used in turn by banks, merchants, etc., to decide whether to grant you credit. The information ranges from your name, address, occupation, employer, and earnings to your former employment and earning record, your marital history, your moving habits, your repayment patterns on previous loans, and records of any court proceedings against you.

The lenders then decide, on the basis of information provided by the credit bureau, whether or not you are a good credit risk. The guidelines vary from lender to lender, of course. A department store may be satisfied if you are in the habit of repaying charges within thirty to sixty days, while a bank may demand that, with very few exceptions, you repay bank loan installments on the due dates.

Or lenders may summarize their policies by telling you they are rating your application in terms of the "Three C's" of Credit. These Three C's are your:

*Character:* your personal characteristics, revealed through factual records, which indicate how you are likely to perform as a borrower. These would include your honesty, sense of responsibility, soundness of judgment, your trustworthiness.

*Capacity:* your financial ability to repay the loan. Your capacity would be judged on the basis of the job you hold, the amount of money you earn, the length of time you have held this or a previous job, your prospects in this or another job.

*Capital:* your assets which can serve as banking—collateral—for your loan. These assets would include your home, bank accounts, stocks and bonds, a car or cars, jewelry, valuable paintings, other tangible property.

These three qualities of Character, Capacity, and Capital form the foundation of any credit rating for you, as an individual or as a family.

To get even more specific, here are points that every lending officer will tick off when considering your application for a loan and your rating as a credit risk.

*Your Employment Record:* How long have you worked for the same company—although not necessarily in the same office or plant of the company? A prime consideration is the stability of your employment. It is up to you to prove your trustworthiness by showing you have not been a job-hopper who might once again leave for a job far away from your present one when, say, less than half your loan payments have been made.

*Your Previous Loans:* Have you ever paid off a loan before? The theory is that, if you have repaid a loan on time before this one, you will repay this loan, too. If you have defaulted on any previous loan, the danger is you'll default again. You'll almost certainly have a poor credit rating if you have any record of defaults or of repossession of items you have bought because you didn't maintain your payments or of suits for being delinquent in payments.

*Your Home:* Do you own your own home? Or have you lived in the apartment in which you now live for some time? If the answer is yes to either question, it's a sign that you probably are trustworthy.

*Your Charge Accounts:* Have you a record of paying your charge accounts regularly? If so, this will be a plus mark for you because it will indicate your sense of responsibility and your ability to repay.

*Your Checking or Savings Accounts:* Do you have either? If so, and particularly if they are at the bank to which you may be applying for a loan, this will be a great help.

Now here are six potential black marks on your credit rating:

(1) If you can't identify yourself. Surely you will have one or more of these: a driver's license, birth certificate, Social Security card, draft card, union card.

(2) If you have a "floating" address. This might be a furnished room in a rooming house or a transient hotel, a post office box number, a mail address in care of a friend. You might offset this, however, if previously you had lived in one place for a long time.

(3) If your employment is in an exceedingly unstable industry or profession and your own job is also basically volatile. If you're a ballet dancer . . . have a strictly seasonal job . . . are in a very restricted field. . . .

(4) If, in some states, you are under twenty-one or eighteen and have no adult to co-sign for you. However, many stores do extend credit to teens without a co-signer anyway, for as a group they have turned out to be good credit risks.

(5) If you apply for a loan at a bank or small loan company or another financial source far from your residence or if you have a record of dealing extensively with numerous small loan companies.

(6) If you are planning to go into the armed services before your loan is repaid. Under these circumstances, the lender almost surely will demand that a co-signer guarantee your loan repayment.

But some lending organizations are engaging in other practices that can restrict credit. For example, banks—and some insurance companies—are turning down loans (and policies) simply because you have the wrong zip code, live in a particular neighborhood. And living *habits* are being used as criteria for establishing "character." If you are offending the "traditional" mores of society (using drugs, for example, keeping late, loud hours, or sharing your apartment with a member of the opposite sex), your lifestyle could be a factor in whether you are granted, or denied, a loan.

# The Fair Credit Reporting Act

*Source:* Federal Deposit Insurance Corporation and Federal Trade Commission.

The Fair Credit Reporting Act became law on April 25, 1971. This Act was passed by Congress to protect consumers against the circulation of inaccurate or obsolete information and to ensure that Consumer Reporting Agencies adopt fair and equitable procedures for obtaining, maintaining, and giving out information about consumers.

Under this law you can take steps to protect yourself if you have been denied credit, insurance, or employment, or if you believe you have had difficulties because of an inaccurate or an unfair Consumer Report.

## You Have the Right

1. To be told the name and address of the Consumer Reporting Agency responsible for preparing a Consumer Report that was used to deny you credit, insurance, or employment or to increase the cost of credit or insurance.

2. To be told by a Consumer Reporting Agency the nature, substance, and sources (except investigative-type sources) of the information (except medical) collected about you.

3. To take anyone of your choice with you when you visit the Consumer Reporting Agency to check on your file.

4. To obtain free of charge all information to which you are entitled if the request is made within 30 days after receipt of a notification that you have been denied credit, insurance, or employment because of information contained in a Consumer Report. Otherwise, the Consumer Reporting Agency is permitted to charge a reasonable fee for giving you the information.

5. To be told who has received a Consumer Report on you within the preceding 6 months or within the preceding 2 years if the report was furnished for employment purposes.

6. To have incomplete or incorrect information reinvestigated unless the Consumer Reporting Agency has reasonable grounds to believe that the dispute is frivolous or irrelevant. If the information is investigated and found to be inaccurate or if the information cannot be verified, you have the right to have such information removed from your file.

7. To have the Agency notify those you name (at no cost to you), who have previously received the incorrect or incomplete information, that this information has been deleted from your file.

8. When a dispute between you and the Reporting Agency about information in your file cannot be resolved, you have the right to have your version of such dispute placed in the file and included in future Consumer Reports.

9. To request the Reporting Agency to send your version of the dispute to certain businesses without charge, if requested within 30 days of the adverse action.

10. To have a Consumer Report withheld from anyone who under the law does not have a legitimate business need for the information.

11. To sue a Reporting Agency for damages if the Agency willfully or negligently violates the law; and, if you are successful, to collect attorney's fees and court costs.

12. Not to have adverse information reported after seven years. One major exception is bankruptcy, which may be reported for 10 years.

13. To be notified by a business that it is seeking information about you which would constitute an Investigative Consumer Report.

14. To request from the business that ordered an Investigative Consumer Report more information about the nature and scope of the investigation.

15. To discover the nature and substance (but not the sources) of the information that was collected for an Investigative Consumer Report.

## The Act Does Not

1. Give you the right to request a Report on yourself from the Consumer Reporting Agency.

2. Give you the right, when you visit the Agency, to receive a copy of your file, although some Agencies will voluntarily give you a copy.

3. Compel anyone to do business with an individual consumer.

4. Apply when you request commercial (as distinguished from consumer) credit or business insurance.

5. Authorize any Federal agency to intervene on behalf of an individual consumer.

## How to Deal With Reporting Agencies

If you want to know what information a Consumer Reporting Agency has collected about you, either arrange for a personal interview at the Agency's office during normal business hours or call in advance for an interview by telephone. Some Agencies will voluntarily make disclosure by mail.

The Consumer Reporting Agencies in your community can be located by consulting the *"Yellow Pages"* of your telephone book under such headings as "Credit" or "Credit Rating or Reporting Agencies.".

If you decide to visit a Consumer Reporting Agency to check on your file, the following check list may be of help.

For instance, in checking your credit file DID YOU:

1. Learn the nature and substance of all the information in your file?

2. Find out the name of each of the businesses (or other sources) that supplied information on you to the Reporting Agency?

3. Learn the name of everyone who received re-

ports on you within the past six months (or the last two years if the Reports were for employment purposes)?

**4.** Request the Agency to reinvestigate and correct or delete information that was found to be inaccurate, incomplete, or obsolete?

**5.** Follow up to determine the results of the reinvestigation?

**6.** Ask the Agency, at no cost to you, to notify those you name who received Reports within the past six months (two years if for employment purposes) that certain information was deleted?

**7.** Follow up to make sure that those named by you did in fact receive notices from the Consumer Reporting Agency?

**8.** Demand that your version of the facts be placed in your file if the reinvestigation did not settle the dispute?

**9.** Request the Agency (if you are willing to pay a reasonable fee) to send your statement of the dispute to those you name who received Reports containing the disputed information within the past six months (two years if received for employment purposes)?

# How to Write a Complaint Letter

## A Few Basic Tips

*Source:* Office of Special Advisor to the President for Consumer Affairs and the Consumer Information Center, Pueblo, CO 81009.

● Include your name, address, and home and work phone numbers.

● Type your letter if possible. If it is handwritten, make sure it is neat and easy to read.

● Make your letter brief and to the point. Include all important facts about your purchase, including the date and place where you made the purchase and any information you can give about the product or service such as serial or model numbers or specific type of service.

● State exactly what you want done about the problem and how long you are willing to wait to get it resolved. Be reasonable.

● Include all documents regarding your problem. Be sure to send COPIES, not originals.

● Avoid writing an angry, sarcastic, or threatening letter. The person reading your letter probably was not responsible for your problem, but may be very helpful in resolving it.

● Keep a copy of the letter for your records.

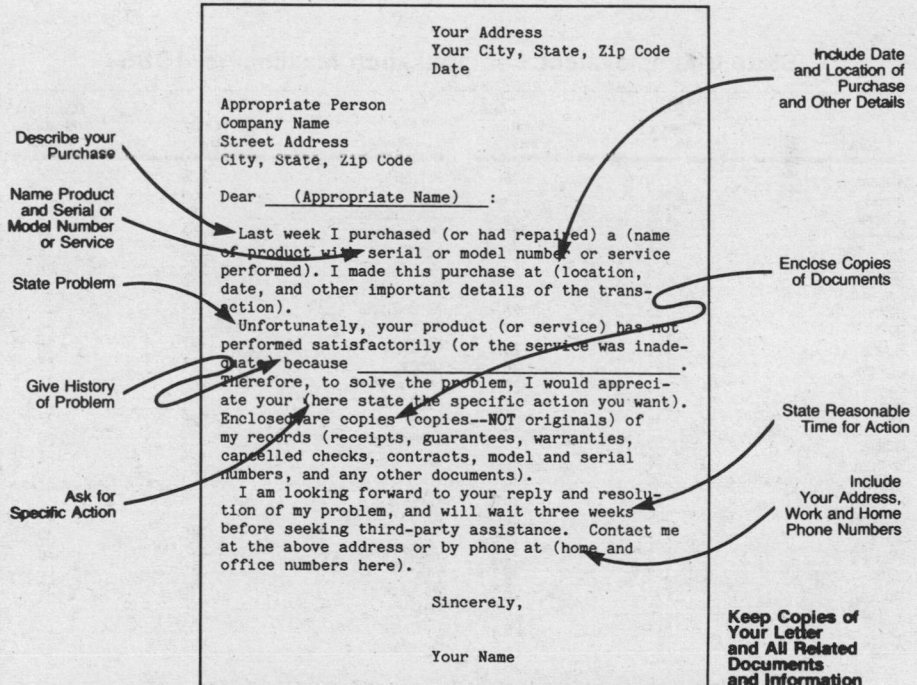

# Unemployment Insurance

Unemployment insurance is managed jointly by the states and the federal government. Most states began paying benefits in 1938 and 1939.

## Under What Conditions Can the Worker Collect?

The laws vary from state to state. In general, a waiting period of one week is required after a claim is filed before collecting unemployment insurance; the worker must be able to work, must not have quit without good cause or have been discharged for misconduct; he must not be involved in a labor dispute; above all, he must be ready and willing to work. He may be disqualified if he refuses, without good cause, to accept a job which is suitable for him in terms of his qualifications and experience, unless the wages, hours and working conditions offered are substantially less favorable than those prevailing for similar jobs in the community.

The unemployed worker must go to the local state employment security office and register for work. If that office has a suitable opening available, he must accept it or lose his unemployment payments, unless he has good cause for the refusal. If a worker moves out of his own state, he can still collect at his new residence; the state in which he is now located will act as agent for the other state, which will pay his benefits.

Benefits are paid only to unemployed workers who have had at least a certain amount of recent past employment or earnings in a job covered by the state law. The amount of employment or earnings, and the period used to measure them, vary from state to state, but the intent of the various laws is to limit benefits to workers whose recent records indicate that they are members of the labor force. The amount of benefits an unemployed worker may receive for any week is also determined by application to his past wages of a formula specified in the law. The general objective is to provide a weekly benefit which is about half the worker's customary weekly wages, up to a maximum set by the law (see table). In a majority of states, the total benefits a worker may receive in a 12-month period is limited to a fraction of his total wages in a prior 12-month period, as well as to a stated number of weeks. Thus, not all workers in a state are entitled to benefits for the number of weeks shown in the table.

## Who Pays for the Insurance?

The total cost is borne by the employer in all but four states. Each state has a sliding scale of rates. The standard rate is set at 5.4% of taxable payroll in most states. But employers with records of less unemployment (that is, with fewer unemployment benefits paid to their former workers) are rewarded with rates lower than the standard 5.4%. The estimated average rate for employers in 1985 was 2.9% of taxable wages or 1.3% of total wages.

## State Unemployment Compensation Maximums, 1986

| State | Weekly benefit[1] | Maximum duration, weeks | State | Weekly benefit[1] | Maximum duration, weeks |
|---|---|---|---|---|---|
| Alabama | 120 | 26 | Nebraska | 126 | 26 |
| Alaska | 188–260 | 26 | Nevada | 166 | 26 |
| Arizona | 125 | 26 | New Hampshire | 150 | 26 |
| Arkansas | 189 | 26 | New Jersey | 214 | 26 |
| California | 166 | 26 | New Mexico | 154 | 26 |
| Colorado | 213 | 26 | New York | 180 | 26 |
| Connecticut | 192–242 | 26 | North Carolina | 175 | 26 |
| Delaware | 195 | 26 | North Dakota | 194 | 26 |
| D. C. | 250 | 26 | Ohio | 147–233 | 26 |
| Florida | 175 | 26 | Oklahoma | 197 | 26 |
| Georgia | 135 | 26 | Oregon | 211 | 26 |
| Hawaii | 200 | 26 | Pennsylvania | 232–240 | 26 |
| Idaho | 179 | 26 | Puerto Rico | 95 | 20 |
| Illinois | 161–209 | 26 | Rhode Island | 183–228 | 26 |
| Indiana | 90–151 | 26 | South Carolina | 125 | 26 |
| Iowa | 158–194 | 26 | South Dakota | 129 | 26 |
| Kansas | 190 | 26 | Tennessee | 120 | 26 |
| Kentucky | 140 | 26 | Texas | 189 | 26 |
| Louisiana | 205 | 26 | Utah | 193 | 26 |
| Maine | 146–219 | 26 | Vermont | 146 | 26 |
| Maryland | 175 | 26 | Virgin Islands | 136 | 26 |
| Massachusetts | 207–310 | 30 | Virginia | 159 | 26 |
| Michigan | 197 | 26 | Washington | 190 | 30 |
| Minnesota | 228 | 26 | West Virginia | 225 | 26 |
| Mississippi | 115 | 26 | Wisconsin | 196 | 26 |
| Missouri | 125 | 26 | Wyoming | 192 | 26 |
| Montana | 171 | 26 | | | |

1. Maximum amounts. When two amounts are shown, higher includes dependents' allowances. *Source:* Department of Labor, Employment and Training Administration.

Contributions for 1986 are required on wages up to $7,000 in all states except Conn., $7,100; Ark., Ga., $7,500; Ala., Colo., D.C., Kans., Ky., Mo., Ohio, Pa., Vt., W. Va., $8,000; Del., $8,250; Ill., $8,500; Okla., $8,900; N.C., $9,200; Mich., $9,500; Wyo., $9,900; N. Mex., $10,300; Wisc., $10,500; Minn., N.J., $10,700; N. Dak., $10,800; R.I., $11,000; Nev., $11,400; Wash., $11,500; Iowa, $12,000; Mont., $12,200; Utah, $12,600; Oreg., V.I., $14,000; Hawaii, Idaho, $15,600; Alaska, $21,600. Employees as well as employers pay a tax in Alaska ranging from 0.5% to 1.0% in accordance with their employer's tax; in N.J., employees pay 1.0% for unemployment insurance. In Ala., employees pay contributions of 1.0% only when the fund is below a specified amount. In Pa., employees pay contributions of 0.1% of all wages paid for employment.

Employers pay an additional unemployment tax to the federal government—0.8% of the first $7,000 paid to each employee. This money is used for the federal and state costs of administering the employment security program, including both unemployment insurance and the employment service. Any amount over these costs, up to the greater of $550 million or 0.125% of total wages subject to contributions under the state unemployment compensation laws for the calendar year, is put in a special fund on which the states draw when the benefit payment funds are low. Any remaining excess is distributed to the states in proportion to their taxable payrolls. These excess funds may be used for benefit payments, or may be used for administrative expenses if so appropriated by the state legislature.

Requirements vary from state to state, but all states cover firms having at least one employee for 20 weeks or a quarterly payroll of $1,500 in the current or preceding calendar year. In some states, firms with one employee at any time are covered. Certain classes of workers are specifically excluded under some or all state laws—members of the employer's family, insurance agents on commission, student nurses, interns, casual labor, and the self-employed.

During periods of high unemployment on either a state or national level, federal-state extended benefits are available to workers who have exhausted their regular benefits. An unemployed worker may receive benefits equal to the weekly benefit he received under the state program for one half the weeks of his basic entitlement to benefits up to a maximum (including regular benefits) of 39 weeks.

## Federal Unemployment Insurance Programs

Amendments to the Social Security Act provided unemployment insurance for Federal civilian employees (1954) and for ex-servicemen (1958). Benefits under these programs are paid by state employment security agencies as agents of the federal government under agreements with the Secretary of Labor. Eligibility for benefits and the amount of benefits paid are determined according to the terms and conditions of the applicable state unemployment insurance law. Thus, federal civilian employees and ex-servicemen are subject to the same eligibility, disqualification, and benefit payment provisions as are claimants for benefits under the state unemployment insurance system.

# Copyrights

*Source:* Library of Congress, Copyright Office.

The copyright law (Title 17 of the United States Code) was amended by the enactment of a statute for its general revision, Public Law 94–553 (90 Stat. 2541), which was signed by the President on October 19, 1976. The new law superseded the copyright act of 1909, as amended, which remained effective until the new enactment took effect on January 1, 1978.

Under the new law, all copyrightable works, whether published or unpublished, are subject to a single system of statutory protection which gives a copyright owner the exclusive right to reproduce the copyrighted work in copies or phonorecords and distribute them to the public by sale, rental, lease, or lending. Among the other rights given to the owner of a copyright are the exclusive rights to prepare derivative works based upon the copyrighted work, to perform the work publicly if it be literary, musical, dramatic, choreographic, a pantomime, motion picture, or other audiovisual work, and in the case of literary, musical, dramatic, and choreographic works, pantomimes, and pictorial, graphic, or sculptural works, including the individual images of a motion picture or other audiovisual work, to display the copyrighted work publicly. All of these rights are subject to certain exceptions, including the principle of "fair use" which the new statute specifically recognizes.

Special provisions are included which permit compulsory licensing for the recording of musical compositions, noncommercial transmissions by public broadcasters of published musical and graphic works, performances of copyrighted music by jukeboxes, and the secondary transmission of copyrighted works on cable television systems.

Copyright protection under the new law extends to original works of authorship fixed in any tangible medium of expression, now known or later developed, from which they can be perceived, reproduced, or otherwise communicated, either directly or with the aid of a machine or device. Works of authorship include books, periodicals and other literary works, musical compositions with accompanying lyrics, dramas and dramatico-musical compositions, pantomimes and choreographic works, motion pictures and other audiovisual works, and sound recordings.

As a mandatory condition of copyright protection under the law in effect before 1978, all published copies of a work were required to bear a copyright notice. The 1976 Act provides for a notice on published copies, but omission or errors will not immediately result in forfeiture of the copyright, and can be corrected within certain time limits. Innocent infringers misled by the omission or error will be shielded from liability.

Registration in the Copyright Office is not a condition of copyright protection but will be a prerequisite to bringing an action in a court of law for infringement. With certain exceptions, the remedies of statutory damages and attorney's fees will not be available for infringements occurring before registration. Copies or phonorecords published in the United States with notice of copyright are required to be deposited for the collections of the Library of Congress, not as a condition of copyright protection, but under provisions of the law subjecting the copyright owner to certain penalties for failure to deposit after a demand by the Register of Copyrights. Registration is permissive, but may be made either at the time the depository requirements are satisfied or at any other time during the subsistence of the copyright.

For works already under statutory protection, the new law retains the present term of copyright of 28 years from first publication (or from registration in some cases), renewable by certain persons for a second period of protection, but it increases the length of the second period to 47 years. Copyrights in their first term on January 1, 1978, must still be renewed during the last (28th) year of the original copyright term to receive the maximum statutory term of 75 years (a first term of 28 years plus a renewal term of 47 years).

Copyrights in their second term on January 1, 1978, are automatically extended up to a maximum of 75 years, without the need for further renewal. Unpublished works that are already in existence on January 1, 1978, but are not protected by statutory copyright and have not yet gone into the public domain, will generally obtain automatic Federal copyright protection for the author's life, plus an additional 50 years after the author's death, but in any event, for a minimal term of 25 years (that is, until December 31, 2002), and if the work is published before that date, then for an additional term of 25 years, through the end of 2027.

For works created on or after January 1, 1978, the new law provides a term lasting for the author's life, plus an additional 50 years after the author's death. For works made for hire, and for anonymous and pseudonymous works (unless the author's identity is revealed in Copyright Office records), the new term will be 75 years from publication or 100 years from creation, whichever is shorter. The new law provides that all terms of copyright will run through the end of the calendar year in which they would otherwise expire. This will not only affect the duration of copyrights, but also the time-limits for renewal registrations.

Works already in the public domain cannot be protected under the new law. The 1976 Act provides no procedure for restoring protection to works in which copyright has been lost for any reason. In general, works published before January 1, 1912, are not under copyright protection in the United States, at least insofar as any version published before that date is concerned.

The new law requires that all visually perceptible copies published in the United States or elsewhere bear a notice of copyright affixed in such manner and location as to give reasonable notice of the claim of copyright. The notice consists of the symbol © (the letter C in a circle), the word "Copyright," or the abbreviation "Copr.," and the year of first publication of the work, and the name of the owner of copyright in the work. EXAMPLE: © *1987 John Doe.*

The notice of copyright prescribed for sound recordings consists of the symbol ℗ (the letter P in a circle), the year of first publication of the sound recording, and the name of the owner of copyright in the sound recording, placed on the surface of the phonorecord, or on the phonorecord label or container, in such manner and location as to give reasonable notice of the claim of copyright EXAMPLE: ℗ *1987 Doe Records, Inc.*

A work by a U.S. citizen may obtain copyright protection in all countries that are members of the Universal Copyright Convention (UCC), provided the copyright notice appearing on all copies from the date of first publication includes the symbol ©, together with the name of the copyright owner and the year date of publication. EXAMPLE: © *John Doe 1987.*

Further information and application forms may be obtained free of charge upon request from the Copyright Office, Library of Congress, Washington, D.C. 20559.

# Patents

*Source:* Department of Commerce, Patent and Trademark Office.

A patent, in the most general sense, is a document issued by a government, conferring some special right or privilege. The term is now restricted mainly to patents for inventions; occasionally, land patents.

The grant of a patent for an invention gives the inventor the privilege, for a limited period of time, of excluding others from making, using, or selling a certain article. However, it does not give him the right to make, use, or sell his own invention if it is an improvement on some unexpired patent whose claims are infringed thereby.

In the U.S., the law provides that a patent may be granted, for a term of 17 years, to any person who has invented or discovered any new and useful art, machine, manufacture, or composition of matter, as well as any new and useful improvements thereof. A patent may also be granted to a person who has invented or discovered and asexually reproduced a new and distinct variety of plant (other than a tuber-propagated one) or has invented a new, original and ornamental design for an article of manufacture.

A patent is granted only upon a regularly filed application, complete in all respects; upon payment of the fees; and upon determination that the disclosure is complete and that the invention is new, useful, and, in view of the prior art, unobvious to one skilled in the art. The disclosure must be of such nature as to enable others to reproduce the invention.

A complete application, which must be addressed to the Commissioner of Patents and Trademarks, Washington, D.C. 20231, consists of a specification with one or more claims; oath or declaration; drawing (whenever the nature of the case admits of it); and a basic filing fee of $170.00[1] The filing fee is not returned to the applicant if the patent is refused. If the patent is allowed, another fee of $280.00[1] is required before the patent is issued. The fee for design patent application is $70.00[1]; the issue fee is $100.00[1]. Maintenance fees are required on utility patents at stipulated intervals.

Applications are ordinarily considered in the order in which they are received. Patents are not granted for printed matter, for methods of doing business, or for devices for which claims contrary to natural laws are made. Applications for a perpetual-motion machine have been made from time to time, but until a working model is presented that actually fulfills the claim, no patent will be issued.

1. Fees quoted are for small entities. Fees are double for corporations.

# Trademarks

*Source:* Department of Commerce, Patent and Trademark Office.

A trademark may be defined as a word, letter, device, or symbol, as well as some combination of these, which is used in connection with merchandise and which points distinctly to the origin of the goods.

Certificates of registration of trademarks are issued under the seal of the Patent and Trademark Office and may be registered by the owner if he is engaged in interstate or foreign commerce, since any Federal jurisdiction over trademarks arises under the commerce clause of the Constitution. Trademarks may be registered by foreign owners who comply with our law, as well as by citizens of foreign countries with which the U.S. has treaties relating to trademarks. American citizens may register trademarks in foreign countries by complying with the laws of those countries. The right to registration and protection of trademarks in many foreign countries is guaranteed by treaties.

General jurisdiction in trademark cases involving Federal Registrations is given to Federal courts. Adverse decisions of examiners on applications for registration are appealable to the Trademark Trial and Appeal Board, whose affirmances, and decisions in *inter partes* proceedings, are subject to court review. Before adopting a trademark, a person should make a search of prior marks to avoid infringing unwittingly upon them.

The duration of a trademark registration is 20 years, but it may be renewed indefinitely for 20-year periods, provided the trademark is still in use at the time of expiration.

The application fee is $175.

## Beware of Illegal Patent Services

It is illegal under patent law (35 USC 33) for anyone to hold himself out as qualified to prepare and prosecute patent applications unless he is registered with the Patent Office. Also, Patent Office regulations forbid registered practitioners advertising for patent business. Some inventors, unaware of this, enter into binding contracts with persons and firms which advertise their assistance in making patent searches, preparing drawings, specifications, and patent applications, only to discover much later that their applications require the services of fully qualified agents or attorneys.

## Birthstones

| Month | Stone | Month | Stone |
|---|---|---|---|
| January | Garnet | July | Ruby or Star Ruby |
| February | Amethyst | August | Peridot or Sardonyx |
| March | Aquamarine or Bloodstone | September | Sapphire or Star Sapphire |
| April | Diamond | October | Opal or Tourmaline |
| May | Emerald | November | Topaz |
| June | Pearl or Alexandrite | December | Turquoise or Zircon |

*Source:* Jewelry Industry Council.

## Additional Consumer Sources

Consult the following special sections of *Information Please Almanac* for specific consumer information

# Directory of Federal Information Centers

If you have questions about any service or agency in the Federal Government, you may want to call the Federal Information Center (FIC) nearest you for a free call or minimum long-distance charge. FICs are prepared to help consumers find needed information or locate the right agency for help with problems. NOTE: Telephone numbers are subject to change.

**Alabama**
Birmingham (205) 322-8591
Mobile (205) 438-1421

**Alaska**
Anchorage (907) 271-3650

**Arizona**
Phoenix (602) 261-3313

**Arkansas**
Little Rock (501) 378-6177

**California**
Los Angeles (213) 894-3800
Sacramento (916) 551-2380
San Diego (619) 293-6030
San Francisco (415) 556-6600
Santa Ana (714) 836-2386

**Colorado**
Colorado Springs (303) 471-9491
Denver (303) 236-7181
Pueblo (303) 544-9523

**Connecticut**
Hartford (203) 527-2617
New Haven (203) 624-4720

**Florida**
Ft. Lauderdale (305) 522-8531
Jacksonville (904) 354-4756
Miami (305) 350-4155
Orlando (305) 422-1800
St. Petersburg (813) 893-3495
Tampa (813) 229-7911
West Palm Beach (305) 833-7566

**Georgia**
Atlanta (404) 221-6891

**Hawaii**
Honolulu (808) 546-8620

**Illinois**
Chicago (312) 353-4242

**Indiana**
Gary (219) 883-4110
Indianapolis (317) 269-7373

**Iowa**
From any Iowa location
800-532-1556 (toll free)

**Kansas**
From any Kansas location
800-432-2934 (toll free)

**Kentucky**
Louisville (502) 582-6261

**Louisiana**
New Orleans (504) 589-6696

**Maryland**
Baltimore (301) 962-4980

**Massachusetts**
Boston (617) 223-7121

**Michigan**
Detroit (313) 226-7016
Grand Rapids (616) 451-2628

**Minnesota**
Minneapolis (612) 349-5333

**Missouri**
St. Louis (314) 425-4106
From other Missouri locations
800-392-7711 (toll free)

**Nebraska**
Omaha (402) 221-3353
From other Nebraska locations
800-642-8383 (toll free)

**New Jersey**
Newark (201) 645-3600
Trenton (609) 396-4400

**New Mexico**
Albuquerque (505) 766-3091

**New York**
Albany (518) 463-4421
Buffalo (716) 846-4010
New York (212) 264-4464
Rochester (716) 546-5075
Syracuse (315) 476-8545

**North Carolina**
Charlotte (704) 376-3600

**Ohio**
Akron (216) 375-5638
Cincinnati (513) 684-2801
Cleveland (216) 522-4040
Columbus (614) 221-1014
Dayton (513) 223-7377
Toledo (419) 241-3223

**Oklahoma**
Oklahoma City (405) 231-4868
Tulsa (918) 584-4193

**Oregon**
Portland (503) 221-2222

**Pennsylvania**
Philadelphia (215) 597-7042
Pittsburgh (412) 644-3456

**Rhode Island**
Providence (401) 331-5565

**Tennessee**
Chattanooga (615) 265-8231
Memphis (901) 521-3285
Nashville (615) 242-5056

**Texas**
Austin (512) 472-5494
Dallas (214) 767-8585
Fort Worth (817) 334-3624
Houston (713) 229-2552
San Antonio (512) 224-4471

**Utah**
Salt Lake City (801) 524-5353

**Virginia**
Norfolk (804) 441-3101
Richmond (804) 643-4928
Roanoke (703) 982-8591

**Washington**
Seattle (206) 442-0570
Tacoma (206) 383-5230

**Wisconsin**
Milwaukee (414) 271-2273

## Shopping for a Bank Credit Card

According to the "Bank Credit Card Observer," a monthly consumer newsletter published by New World Decisions, Inc., 120 Wood Avenue South, Iselin, N.J. 08830, you should ask the following questions when shopping for a bank credit card:

Are there any minimum transaction fees (service charges) for purchases and/or cash advances?

Is there a grace period for cash advances?

What is the annual fee?

Are free credit cards issued to customers who have certain kinds of accounts at the bank?

Is a fee charged for exceeding the credit limit?

Is there a fee for late payments?

Too many customers may assume they need a relationship with banks in their own states to qualify for a bank credit card, but in fact they can apply for cards through the mail from other states. Applicants should shop widely for such cards before making their selection.

There are thousands of toll-free numbers available to consumers. However, very few of them can be used in all states. Most toll-free numbers are for local use only and are listed in your telephone directory.

The following comprises only those "800" numbers known to *Information Please Almanac* that can be used by readers throughout the United States.

## AIDS
**AIDS Hotline**
U.S. Public Health Service
1-800-342-AIDS
1-404-329-1290 (Atlanta, Georgia)
Hours: 24 hours, 7 days

A recording provides the latest information to the public about Acquired Immune Deficiency Syndrome (AIDS).

## ALZHEIMER'S DISEASE
**Alzheimer's Disease and Related Disorders Association, Inc.**
1-800-621-0379
1-800-572-6037 (Illinois)
Hours: 24 hours, 7 days

Information and referral service. Provides support for patients and their families, aids research efforts, etc.

## AUTOMOBILE
**Auto Safety Hotline**
National Highway Traffic Safety Administration
202-426-0123 (Washington, D.C.)
1-800-424-9393 (Elsewhere)
Hours: 8:00–4:00, EST Mon.–Fri.
Answering service after hours.

Handles complaints on safety-related defects, and receives reports of vehicle safety problems. Provides information and in some cases literature on:
- motor vehicle safety recalls
- car seats
- automobile equipment
- tires
- motor homes
- drunk driving
- gas mileage

## BANKING
**Federal Deposit Insurance Corporation**
202-898-3536 (Washington, D.C.)
1-800-424-5488 (Elsewhere)
Hours: 9:00–4:00, EST Mon.–Fri.

Provides general banking information on consumer banking laws. Will refer consumer to proper regulatory agency that supervises institution complaint is being filed against.

**Federal Home Loan Bank Board**
202-377-6988 (Washington, D.C.)
1-800-424-5405 (Elsewhere)
Hours: 24-hour recording

Provides information on federal adjustable mortgage rates.

## BOATING SAFETY HOTLINE
**U.S. Coast Guard**
1-800-368-5647
1-202-472-2385 (Washington, D.C.)
Hours: 8:00—4:00 EST Mon.-Fri.

Provides information on boats and associated equipment involved in safety defect (recall) campaigns for past five model years. Takes complaints about possible safety defects. Cannot resolve nonsafety problems between consumer and manufacturer and cannot recommend or endorse specific boats or products.

## BLIND
**National Federation of the Blind**
1-800-638-7518, 8-5 EST, Mon.-Fri.
1-301-659-9314 (Maryland)

Provides job information. Concerned about the rights of the blind.

## CHEMICALS
**Chemical Referral Center**
1-800-262-8200
1-202-887-1315, collect (Alaska)
In Washington, D.C. call locally.
Hours: 8:00-9:00, EST, Mon.-Fri.

Answers questions regarding the toxicity of chemicals and how to dispose of toxic chemicals. A Chemical Manufacturers Association referral service giving information: Name and phone number of manufacturer's safety liaison.

## CHILD ABUSE
**Parents Anonymous**
1-800-352-0386 (California)
1-800-421-0353 (Elsewhere)
Hours: 9:00–5:00 Mon.–Fri., PST however, there is a 24-hour hotline on answering service.

## COCAINE ABUSE
**National Cocaine Hotline**
1-800-COCAINE
1-201-522-7005 (Alaska and Hawaii)
Hours: 24 hours—7days

Provides information on cocaine and help for cocaine abusers and drug-related problems.

## CIVIL RIGHTS HOTLINE
**Office of Civil Rights**
1-202-863-0100 (Washington, D.C.)
1-800-368-1019 (Elsewhere)
Hours: 9:00—8:00, EST Mon.-Fri. Answering machine after 8:00 p.m., including weekends.

Accepts complaints regarding discrimination on the basis of race, color, national origin, handicap, or age occurring in Health and Human Services programs, i.e. in admission to hospitals, nursing homes, day care centers, or federally funded state health care assistance.

## DEPARTMENT OF DEFENSE
1-800-424-9098 (Washington, D.C.)
223-5080 (Autovon Line)
693-5080 (FTS)
Hours: 8:00–5:00, EST

Operated for citizens to report suspected cases of fraud and waste involving the Department of Defense. The anonymity of callers will be respected.

## DRUG ABUSE
### National Institute on Drug Abuse
### Prevention Branch
1-800-638-2045
1-301-443-2450 (Alaska, Hawaii, and Maryland)
Hours: 8:00—5:00, EST Mon.-Fri.

Gives technical assistance service to individuals, schools, and organizations planning prevention programs for youth and their communities. NOTE: Does not accept crisis calls or provide medical information.

## ELECTIONS
### Federal Election Commission
Clearinghouse on Election Administration
1-800-424-9530
202-376-3120 (Wash. D.C., Alaska, and Hawaii)
Hours: 8:30—5:00, EST Mon.-Fri.

Provides information on Federal elections.

## ENERGY
### Conservation and Renewable Energy
### Inquiry and Referral Service
1-800-462-4983 (Pennsylvania)
1-800-233-3071 (Alaska and Hawaii)
1-800-523-2929 (Elsewhere)
Hours: 9:00–5:00, EST Mon.–Fri.

Provides non-technical information on solar, wind, and other energy heating and cooling technologies, energy conservation, and alcohol fuels.

## ENVIRONMENT
### Hazardous Waste
### RCRA Superfund Hotline
Environmental Protection Agency
202-382-3000 (Washington, D.C.)
1-800-424-9346 (Elsewhere)
Hours: 8:30–4:30, EST Mon.–Fri.

Provides information and interpretation of federal hazardous waste regulations. Will provide referrals regarding other hazardous waste matters.

### Pesticide Hotline
National Pesticide Telecommunications Network
1-800-858-7378
Hours: 24 hours—7 days

Provides information on health hazards of pesticides. Will refer callers to human and animal poison control centers in their states.

### Toxic Substances Control Act Hotline (TSCA)
### Environmental Protection Agency
1-800-424-9065
1-202-544-1404 (Washington, D.C., Alaska, and Hawaii)
Hours: 8:30—5:00, EST Mon.-Fri.

Answers questions and provides technical information on the four toxic substances regulated under the Toxic Substances Control Act: PCBs, CFCs, asbestos, and dioxin. The TSCA Assistance Office also arranges meetings and seminars.

## GAY-LESBIAN HOTLINE
National Gay/Lesbian Crisisline (NGLC)
1-800-221-7044
1-212-529-1604 (New York, Alaska and Hawaii)
Hours: 3:00—9:00 p.m., EST, Mon.-Fri.

Gives assistance to victims of anti-gay/lesbian violence and law enforcement agencies. Offers phone crisis-counseling and referrals, community mobilization, and incident documentation. Provides AIDS information and referrals. The NGLC is an all-purpose, gay-lesbian crisis line.

## HANDICAPPED
### Library of Congress
202-287-5100 (Washington, D.C.)
1-800-424-8567 (Elsewhere)
Hours: 8:00–4:30, EST Mon.–Fri.
Answering service after hours.

Provides information on programs and books for the blind and physically handicapped.

## HEALTH CARE
### Cancer Information Service
National Cancer Institute
National Institutes of Health
Department of Health & Human Services
202-636-5700 (Washington, D.C., and suburbs in Maryland and Virginia)
808-524-1234 (Hawaii) (neighboring islands call collect)
1-800-638-6070 (Alaska)
1-800-422-6237 (National Cancer Institute)
1-800-4-Cancer (Elsewhere)
Hours: 9:00–5:00, Mon.–Fri.

Provides information on cancer, prevention, treatment and ongoing research; fills requests for pamphlets and other literature on cancer.

### National Health Information Center
Department of Health & Human Services
202-429-9091 (Washington, D.C., Virginia, Alaska, and Hawaii)
1-800-336-4797 (Elsewhere)
Hours: 9:00–5:00 Mon.–Fri.

Provides referrals to sources of information on health-related issues.

### Second Surgical Opinion Hotline for Non-Emergency Surgery
Sponsored by Health Care Financing Administration
Department of Health and Human Services
1-800-638-6833
1-800-492-6603 (Maryland)
Hours: 8:00—12:00, 7 days

Callers will be given a free referral to an agency that maintains listing of physicians in their area who will give a second opinion before an operation is performed.

## HOUSING
### Fair Housing Discrimination Hotline
Fair Housing and Equal Opportunity
Department of Housing and Urban Development
202-426-3500 (Washington, D.C.)
1-800-424-8590 (Elsewhere)
Hours: 8:00–4:00 EST, Mon.–Fri.
Answering service after hours.

Receives housing discrimination complaints due to race, color, religion, sex or national origin.

## HOUSEHOLD APPLIANCES
### Major Appliance Consumer Action Panel (MACAP)
1-800-621-0477
1-312-984-5858 (Illinois)
Hours: 8:30—4:30, CST Mon.-Fri.

An independent mediation group that offers to help users of major household appliances resolve complaints if they have been unsuccessful in getting satisfaction from the manufacturer. The Panel's recommendations are not binding to either party.

## INSURANCE
### Federal Crime Insurance
Federal Emergency Management Administration
202-652-2637 (Washington, D.C. and Maryland—will accept collect calls from MD)
1-800-638-8780 (Elsewhere)
Hours: 8:30–7:00, EST Mon.–Fri.
Answering service after hours.

Provides information on federal crime insurance for both homes and businesses.

### Federal Flood Insurance
Federal Emergency Management Admin.
202-564-5200 (Washington, D.C.)
1-800-492-6605 (Maryland)
1-800-638-6831 (Alaska, Hawaii, Puerto Rico, Virgin Islands, Guam)
1-800-638-6620 (Elsewhere)
Hours: 8:00–8:00, EST Mon.–Fri.

Provides information on community participation in the flood program (emergency or regular). If the community does not have a program, it is not eligible for government-subsidized insurance relief. Complaints are referred to the proper office within the agency.

## NUCLEAR TESTING HEALTH RESEARCH
### Nuclear Test Personnel Review (NTPR)
Defense Nuclear Agency
1-800-336-3068
703-285-5610 (Alaska, Hawaii, Puerto Rico, and Virginia. Call collect if necessary)
Hours: 8:30—5:00, EST Mon.-Fri. Recorded message after hours.

Concerned with the health status of Department of Defense personnel, military, and civilians who participated in atmospheric nuclear tests in Nevada or the Pacific Ocean and those who participated in the U.S. post-war occupation of Hiroshima and Nagasaki, Japan. Seeks to make personal contact with those individuals involved.

## ORGAN DONOR INFORMATION
### The Living Bank
1-800-528-2971
1-713-528-2971 (TX call)
Hours: 8:00—5:00, CST Mon.-Fri. Has 24 hour answering service.

The Living Bank International is a nonprofit service organization dedicated to helping those who, after death, wish to donate part or all of their bodies for transplantation, therapy, medical research, or anatomical studies. It provides information and donor registration material. NOTE: The Bank does not receive donated organs and bodies and is not a storage facility for them.

### The American Liver Foundation
1-800-223-0179
Hours: 8:30-4:30, EST, Mon.-Fri.
201-857-2626 (New Jersey)
Hours: 24 hour recording

Answers questions and keeps list of liver transplant centers.

## PARENTS WITHOUT PARTNERS, INC.
1-800-638-8078
Hours: 8:30-5:00, EST Mon.-Fri.

Nonprofit organization for all single parents in U.S. and Canada with over 1,000 chapters nationwide. Helps single parents with raising children, has social and educational programs, and sponsors family activities.

## PRODUCT SAFETY
### Consumer Product Safety Commission
1-800-638-2772
Hours: 8:30–5:00, EST Mon.–Fri.

Provides information on the safety of consumer products. Receives reports of product-related deaths, illnesses, and injuries. Products are not rated or recommended.

## RUNAWAYS
1-800-231-6946 (U.S.A. except Texas)
1-800-392-3352 (Texas)
Hours: 24 hours—7 days

Helps runaways by referring them to shelters, clinics, local hotlines. Will relay messages from parents to the runaway.

## SOCIAL SECURITY AND MEDICARE FRAUD
### Inspector General Hotline
Department of Health and Human Services
1-800-368-5779
Hours: 8:30—5:00, EST Mon.-Fri.

Takes calls on fraud in Social Security payments or abuse, Medicaid and Medicare fraud and other HHS programs. Recording machine after hours.

## SPORTS
### Women's Sports Foundation
1-800-227-3988
Hours: 9:00-5:00, EST Mon.-Fri.

A nonprofit, educational organization founded to encourage all women to be involved in sports. Some of the foundation's services include: information about women's sports and fitness topics, training, coaching, camps, scholarships, internships, etc. Maintains a speaker's bureau referral service of experts on women's sports.

## VIETNAM VETERANS
### Vietnam Veterans of America
1-800-424-7275
202-332-2700 (Washington, D.C.)
Hours: 24 hours, 7 days
8:00-6:30, EST. Mon.-Fri. (202 number)

Answering machine takes messages for information and help. Provides information on Agent Orange. Will answer questions on direct line.

## International Dialing: Codes and Time Differences
## for Many Countries

*Source:* The Professional Secretary's Handbook, Copyright ©, Houghton Mifflin Company.

**To Determine the time in the countries listed below, add the number of hours shown under your own time zone to your local time (or subtract, if preceded by a minus sign). Time differences are based on Standard Time, observed in the U.S. (in most states) from the last Sunday in October until the first Sunday in April. This may vary in some countries. Several countries have more than one time zone. The time differences for these countries are based in the following cities: Sydney, Australia; Rio de Janeiro, Brazil; Jakarta, Indonesia; Kuala Lumpur, Malaysia; and Moscow, U.S.S.R.**

| Country Codes | | City Codes | Time Difference U.S. Time Zones | | | |
|---|---|---|---|---|---|---|
| | | | EST | CST | MST | PST |
| Andorra | 33 | All Points 078 | 6 | 7 | 8 | 9 |
| Argentina | 54 | Buenos Aires 1, Cordoba 51, Rosario 41 | 2 | 3 | 4 | 5 |
| Australia | 61 | Canberra 62, Melbourne 3, Sydney 2 | 16 | 17 | 18 | 19 |
| Austria | 43 | Graz 316, Linz 732, Vienna 222 | 6 | 7 | 8 | 9 |
| Bahrain | 973 | * | 8 | 9 | 10 | 11 |
| Belgium | 32 | Antwerp 31, Brussels 2, Ghent 91, Liege 41 | 6 | 7 | 8 | 9 |
| Belize | 501 | Belize City*, Belmopan 08, Corozal Town 04 | −1 | 0 | 1 | 2 |
| Bolivia | 591 | Cochabamba 42, La Paz 2, Santa Cruz 33 | 1 | 2 | 3 | 4 |
| Brazil | 55 | Belo Horizonte 31, Brasilia 61, Sao Paulo 11 | 2 | 3 | 4 | 5 |
| Chile | 56 | Concepcion 42, Santiago 2, Valparaiso 31 | 2 | 3 | 4 | 5 |
| Colombia | 57 | Bogota*, Cali 3, Medellin 4 | 0 | 1 | 2 | 3 |
| Costa Rica | 506 | * | −1 | 0 | 1 | 2 |
| Cyprus | 357 | Limassol 51, Nicosia 21, Paphos 61 | 7 | 8 | 9 | 10 |
| Denmark | 45 | Aarhus 6, Copenhagen 1 or 2, Odense 9 | 6 | 7 | 8 | 9 |
| East Germany | 37 | Berlin 2, Dresden 51, Leipzig 41 | 6 | 7 | 8 | 9 |
| Ecuador | 593 | Ambato 2, Cuenca 4, Guayaquil 4, Quito 2 | 0 | 1 | 2 | 3 |
| El Salvador | 503 | * | −1 | 0 | 1 | 2 |
| Fiji | 679 | * | 17 | 18 | 19 | 20 |
| Finland | 358 | Helsinki 0, Tampere 31, Turku-Abo 21 | 7 | 8 | 9 | 10 |
| France | 33 | Bordeaux 56, Lille 20, Lyon 7, Marseille 91, Nice 93, Paris 1, Strasbourg 88, Toulouse 61 | 6 | 7 | 8 | 9 |
| Great Britain | 44 | Belfast 232, Birmingham 21, Cardiff 222, Edinburgh 31, Glasgow 41, Leeds 532, Liverpool 51, London 1, Sheffield 742 | 5 | 6 | 7 | 8 |
| Greece | 30 | Athens 1, Iraklion 81, Kavala 51, Larissa 41, Patrai 61, Piraeus 1, Thessaloniki 31, Volos 421 | 7 | 8 | 9 | 10 |
| Guadeloupe | 596 | * | 1 | 2 | 3 | 4 |
| Guatemala | 502 | Guatemala City 2, Quezaltenango* | −1 | 0 | 1 | 2 |
| Guyana | 592 | Bartica 05, Georgetown 02 | 2 | 3 | 4 | 5 |
| Haiti | 509 | Cap Hatien 3, Gonaive 2, Port Au Prince 1 | 0 | 1 | 2 | 3 |
| Honduras | 504 | * | −1 | 0 | 1 | 2 |
| Hong Kong | 852 | Hong Kong 5, Kowloon 3, Sha Tin 0 | 13 | 14 | 15 | 16 |
| Indonesia | 62 | Jakarta 21, Medan 61, Semarang 24 | 12 | 13 | 14 | 15 |
| Iran | 98 | Esfahan 31, Mashad 51, Tabriz 41, Teheran 21 | 8 ½ | 9 ½ | 10 ½ | 11 ½ |
| Iraq | 964 | Baghdad 1, Basra 40, Hilla 30, Mosul 60 | 8 | 9 | 10 | 11 |
| Ireland | 353 | Cork 21, Dublin 1, Galway 91, Limerick 61 | 5 | 6 | 7 | 8 |
| Israel | 972 | Haifa , Jerusalem 2, Ramat Gan 3, Tel Aviv 3 | 7 | 8 | 9 | 10 |

| Country Codes | | City Codes | Time Difference U.S. Time Zones | | | |
|---|---|---|---|---|---|---|
| | | | EST | CST | MST | PST |
| Italy | 39 | Bari 80, Bologna 51, Florence 55, Genoa 10, Milan 2, Naples 81, Palermo 91, Rome 6, Turin 11 | 6 | 7 | 8 | 9 |
| Ivory Coast | 225 | * | 5 | 6 | 7 | 8 |
| Japan | 81 | Kitakyushu 93, Kobe 78, Kyoto 75, Nagoya 52, Osaka 6, Sapporo 11, Tokyo 3, Yokohama 45 | 14 | 15 | 16 | 17 |
| Kenya | 254 | Mombasa 11, Nairobi 2, Nakuru 37 | 8 | 9 | 10 | 11 |
| Kuwait | 965 | * | 8 | 9 | 10 | 11 |
| Liberia | 231 | * | 5 | 6 | 7 | 8 |
| Libya | 218 | Benghazi 61, Misuratha 51, Tripoli 21 | 7 | 8 | 9 | 10 |
| Liechtenstein | 41 | All points 75 | 6 | 7 | 8 | 9 |
| Luxembourg | 352 | * | 6 | 7 | 8 | 9 |
| Malaysia | 60 | Ipoh 5, Kelang 3, Kuala Lumpur 3 | 12 ½ | 13 ½ | 14 ½ | 15 ½ |
| Martinique | 596 | * | 1 | 2 | 3 | 4 |
| Monaco | 33 | All points 93 | 6 | 7 | 8 | 9 |
| Netherlands | 31 | Amsterdam 20, Rotterdam 10 | 6 | 7 | 8 | 9 |
| Netherlands Antilles | 599 | Aruba 8, Curacoa 9 | 1 | 2 | 3 | 4 |
| New Zealand | 64 | Auckland 9, Wellington 4 | 18 | 19 | 20 | 21 |
| Nicaragua | 505 | Chinandega 341, Leon 31, Managua 2 | −1 | 0 | 1 | 2 |
| Nigeria | 234 | Ibadan 22, Kano 64, Lagos 1 | 6 | 7 | 8 | 9 |
| Norway | 47 | Bergen 5, Oslo 2, Trondheim 75 | 6 | 7 | 8 | 9 |
| Panama | 507 | * | 0 | 1 | 2 | 3 |
| Papua New Guinea | 675 | * | 15 | 16 | 17 | 18 |
| Paraguay | 595 | Asuncion 21, Concepcion 31 | 2 | 3 | 4 | 5 |
| Peru | 51 | Arequipa 54, Callao 14, Lima 14, Trujillo 44 | 0 | 1 | 2 | 3 |
| Philippines | 63 | Cebu 32, Davao 35, Iloilo 33, Manila 2 | 13 | 14 | 15 | 16 |
| Portugal | 351 | Coimbra 39, Lisbon 19, Porto 29 | 5 | 6 | 7 | 8 |
| Qatar | 974 | * | 8 | 9 | 10 | 11 |
| Rumania | 40 | Bucharest 0, Cluj 51, Constanta 16 | 7 | 8 | 9 | 10 |
| San Marino | 39 | All points 541 | 6 | 7 | 8 | 9 |
| Saudi Arabia | 966 | Jeddah 2, Mecca 2, Riyadh 1 | 8 | 9 | 10 | 11 |
| Senegal | 221 | * | 5 | 6 | 7 | 8 |
| Singapore | 65 | * | 12 ½ | 13 ½ | 14 ½ | 15 ½ |
| South Africa | 27 | Cape Town 21, Johannesburg 11 | 7 | 8 | 9 | 10 |
| South Korea | 82 | Pusan 51, Seoul 2, Taegu 53 | 14 | 15 | 16 | 17 |
| Soviet Union | 7 | Kiev 044, Leningrad 812, Minsk 017, Moscow 095, Tallinn 0142 | 8 | 9 | 10 | 11 |
| Spain | 34 | Barcelona 3, Madrid 1, Seville 54, Valencia 6 | 6 | 7 | 8 | 9 |
| Sri Lanka | 94 | Colombo 1, Kandy 8, Moratuwa 72 | 10 ½ | 11 ½ | 12 ½ | 13 ½ |
| Surinam | 597 | * | 1 ½ | 2 ½ | 3 ½ | 4 ½ |
| Sweden | 46 | Goteborg 31, Malmo 40, Stockholm 8 | 6 | 7 | 8 | 9 |
| Switzerland | 41 | Basel 61, Berne 31, Geneva 22, St. Moritz 82, Zurich 1 | 6 | 7 | 8 | 9 |
| Tahiti | 689 | * | −5 | −4 | −3 | −2 |
| Taiwan | 886 | Kaohsiung 7, Tainan 62, Taipei 2 | 13 | 14 | 15 | 16 |
| Thailand | 66 | Bangkok 2 | 12 | 13 | 14 | 15 |
| Tunisia | 216 | Menzel Bourguiba 2, Tunis 1 | 6 | 7 | 8 | 9 |
| Turkey | 90 | Adana 711, Ankara 41, Istanbul 11, Izmir 51 | 7 | 8 | 9 | 10 |
| United Arab Emirates | 971 | Abu Dhabi 2, Ajman 6 | 9 | 10 | 11 | 12 |
| Uruguay | 598 | Canelones 332, Mercedes 532, Montevideo 2 | 2 | 3 | 4 | 5 |
| Vatican City | 39 | All points 6 | 6 | 7 | 8 | 9 |
| Venezuela | 58 | Caracas 2, Maracaibo 61, Valencia 41 | 1 | 2 | 3 | 4 |
| West Germany | 49 | Berlin 30, Bonn 228, Essen 201, Frankfurt 611, Hamburg 40, Munich 89 | 6 | 7 | 8 | 9 |
| Yugoslavia | 38 | Belgrade 11, Skoplje 91, Zagreb 41 | 6 | 7 | 8 | 9 |

For city codes not listed dial "0" (operator). *City Codes not required.

# STRUCTURES

## The Seven Wonders of the World

(Not all classical writers list the same items as the Seven Wonders, but most of them agree on the following.)

**The Pyramids of Egypt.** A group of three pyramids, *Khufu, Khafra,* and *Menkaura* at Giza, outside modern Cairo, is often called the first wonder of the world. The largest pyramid, built by Khufu (Cheops), a king of the fourth Dynasty, had an original estimated height of 482 ft (now approximately 450 ft). The base has sides 755 ft long. It contains 2,300,000 blocks; the average weight of each is 2.5 tons. Estimated date of construction is 2800 B.C. Of all the Seven Wonders, the pyramids alone survive.

**Hanging Gardens of Babylon.** Often listed as the second wonder, these gardens were supposedly built by Nebuchadnezzar about 600 B.C. to please his queen, Amuhia. They are also associated with the mythical Assyrian Queen, Semiramis. Archeologists surmise that the gardens were laid out atop a vaulted building, with provisions for raising water. The terraces were said to rise from 75 to 300 ft.

The Walls of Babylon, also built by Nebuchadnezzar, are sometimes referred to as the second (or the seventh) wonder instead of the Hanging Gardens.

**Statue of Zeus (Jupiter) at Olympia.** The work of Phidias (5th century B.C.), this colossal figure in gold and ivory was reputedly 40 ft high. All trace of it is lost, except for reproductions on coins.

**Temple of Artemis (Diana) at Ephesus.** A beautiful structure, begun about 350 B.C. in honor of a non-Hellenic goddess who later became identified with the Greek goddess of the same name. The temple, with Ionic columns 60 ft high, was destroyed by invading Goths in A.D. 262.

**Mausoleum at Halicarnassus.** This famous monument was erected by Queen Artemisia in memory of her husband, King Mausolus of Caria in Asia Minor, who died in 353 B.C. Some remains of the structure are in the British Museum. This shrine is the source of the modern word "mausoleum."

**Colossus at Rhodes.** This bronze statue of Helios (Apollo), about 105 ft high, was the work of the sculptor Chares, who reputedly labored for 12 years before completing it in 280 B.C. It was destroyed during an earthquake in 224 B.C.

**Pharos of Alexandria.** The seventh wonder was the Pharos (lighthouse) of Alexandria, built by Sostratus of Cnidus during the 3rd century B.C. on the island of Pharos off the coast of Egypt. It was destroyed by an earthquake in the 13th century.

## Famous Structures

### Ancient

The *Great Sphinx of Egypt,* one of the wonders of ancient Egyptian architecture, adjoins the pyramids of Giza and has a length of 240 ft. It was built in the 4th dynasty.

Other Egyptian buildings of note include the *Temples of Karnak* and *Edfu* and the *Tombs at Beni Hassan.*

The *Parthenon of Greece,* built on the Acropolis in Athens, was the chief temple to the goddess Athena. It was believed to have been completed by 438 B.C. The present temple remained intact until the 5th century A.D. Today, though the Parthenon is in ruins, its majestic proportions are still discernible.

Other great structures of ancient Greece were the *Temples at Paestum* (about 540 and 420 B.C.); the *Temple of Poseidon* (about 460 B.C.); the *Temple of Apollo* at Corinth (about 540 B.C.); the *Temple of Apollo* at Bassae (about 450–420 B.C.); the famous *Erechtheum* atop the Acropolis (about 421–405 B.C.); the *Temple of Athena Niké* at Athens (about 426 B.C.); the *Olympieum* at Athens (174 B.C.–A.D. 131); the *Athenian Treasury* at Delphi (about 515 B.C.); the *Propylaea* of the Acropolis at Athens (437–432 B.C.); the *Theater of Dionysus* at Athens (about 350–325 B.C.); the *House of Cleopatra* at Delos (138 B.C.) and the *Theater* at Epidaurus (about 325 B.C.).

The *Colosseum (Flavian Amphitheater)* of Rome, the largest and most famous of the Roman amphitheaters, was opened for use A.D. 80. Elliptical in shape, it consisted of three stories and an upper gallery, rebuilt in stone in its present form in the third century A.D. Its seats rise in tiers, which in turn are buttressed by concrete vaults and stone piers. It could seat between 40,000 and 50,000 spectators. It was principally used for gladiatorial combat.

The *Pantheon* at Rome, begun by Agrippa in 27 B.C. as a temple, was rebuilt in its present circular form by Hadrian (A.D. 110–25). Literally the Pantheon was intended as a temple of "all the gods." It is remarkable for its perfect preservation today, and it has served continuously for 20 centuries as a place of worship.

Famous Roman arches include the *Arch of Constantine* (about A.D. 315) and the *Arch of Titus* (about A.D. 80).

### Later European

*St. Mark's Cathedral* in Venice (1063–67), one of the great examples of Byzantine architecture, was begun in the 9th century. Partly destroyed by fire in 976, it was later rebuilt as a Byzantine edifice.

Other famous Byzantine examples of architecture are *St. Sophia* in Istanbul (A.D. 532–37); *San Vitale* in Ravenna (542); *St. Paul's Outside the Walls,* Rome (5th century); the *Kremlin* baptism and marriage church, Moscow (begun in 1397); and *St. Lorenzo Outside the Walls,* Rome, begun in 588.

The *Cathedral Group* at Pisa (1067–1173), one of the most celebrated groups of structures built in Romanesque-style, consists of the cathedral, the cathedral's baptistery, and the *Leaning Tower.* This trio forms a group by itself in the northwest corner of the city. The cathedral and baptistery are built in varicolored marble. The campanile *(Leaning Tower)* is 179 ft. high and leans more than 16 ft out of the perpendicular. There is little reason to believe that the architects intended to have the tower lean.

Other examples of Romanesque architecture include the *Vézelay Abbey* in France (1130); the *Church of Notre-Dame-du-Port* at Clermont-Ferrand in France (1100); the *Church of San Zeno* (begun in 1138) at Verona, and *Durham Cathedral* in England.

The *Alhambra* (1248–1354), located in Granada, Spain, is universally esteemed as one of the greatest masterpieces of Moslem architecture. Designed as a palace and fortress for the Moorish monarchs of Granada, it is surrounded by a heavily fortified wall more than a mile in perimeter. The location of the Alhambra in the Sierra Nevada provides a magnificent setting for this jewel of Moorish Spain.

The *Tower of London* is a group of buildings and towers covering 13 acres along the north bank of the Thames. The central *White Tower,* begun in 1078 during the reign of William the Conqueror, was originally a fortress and royal residence, but was later used as a prison. The *Bloody Tower* is associated with Anne Boleyn and other notables.

*Westminster Abbey,* in London, was begun in 1045 and completed in 1065. It was rebuilt and enlarged in 1245–50.

*Notre-Dame de Paris* (begun in 1163), one of the great examples of Gothic architecture, is a twin-towered church with a steeple over the crossing and immense flying buttresses supporting the masonry at the rear of the church.

Other famous Gothic structures are *Chartres Cathedral* (12th century); *Sainte Chapelle,* Paris (1246–48); *Laon Cathedral,* France (1160–1205); *Reims Cathedral* (about 1210–50; rebuilt after its almost complete destruction in World War I); *Rouen Cathedral* (13th–16th centuries); *Amiens Cathedral* (1218–69); *Beauvais Cathedral* (begun 1247); *Salisbury Cathedral* (1220–60); *York Minster* or the *Cathedral of St. Peter* (begun in the 7th century); *Milan Cathedral* (begun 1386); and *Cologne Cathedral* (13th–19th centuries); badly damaged in World War II.

The *Duomo* (cathedral) in Florence was founded in 1298, completed by Brunelleschi and consecrated in 1436. The oval-shaped dome dominates the entire structure.

The *Vatican* is a group of buildings in Rome comprising the official residence of the Pope. The *Basilica of St. Peter,* the largest church in the Christian world, was begun in 1450. The *Sistine Chapel,* begun in 1473, is noted for the art masterpieces of Michelangelo, Botticelli, and others. The *Basilica of the Savior* (known as *St. John Lateran*) is the first-ranking Catholic Church in the world, for it is the cathedral of the Pope.

Other examples of Renaissance architecture are the *Palazzo Riccardi,* the *Palazzo Pitti* and the *Palazzo Strozzi* in Florence; the *Farnese Palace* in Rome; *Palazzo Grimani* (completed about 1550) in Venice; the *Escorial* (1563–93) near Madrid; the *Town Hall* of Seville (1527–32); the *Louvre,* Paris;

the *Château* at Blois, France; *St. Paul's Cathedral,* London (1675–1710; badly damaged in World War II); the *École Militaire,* Paris (1752); the *Pazzi Chapel,* Florence, designed by Brunelleschi (1429); the Palace of *Fontainebleau* and the *Château de Chambord* in France.

The *Palace of Versailles,* containing the famous Hall of Mirrors, was built during the reign of Louis XIV and served as the royal palace until 1793.

Outstanding European buildings of the 18th and 19th centuries are the *Superga* at Turin, the *Hôtel-Dieu* in Lyons, the *Belvedere Palace* at Vienna, the *Royal Palace* of Stockholm, the *Opera House* of Paris (1863–75); the *Bank of England,* the *British Museum,* the *University of London,* and the *Houses of Parliament,* all in London; the *Panthéon,* the *Church of the Madeleine,* the *Bourse,* and the *Palais de Justice* in Paris.

The *Eiffel Tower,* in Paris, was built for the Exposition of 1889 by Alexandre Eiffel. It is 984 ft high.[1]

1. 1,056 ft, including the television tower.

## Asiatic and African

The *Taj Mahal* (1632–50), at Agra, India, built by Shah Jahan as a tomb for his wife, is considered by some as the most perfect example of the Mogul style and by others as the most beautiful building in the world. Four slim white minarets flank the building, which is topped by a white dome; the entire structure is of marble.

Other examples of Indian architecture are the temples at Benares and Tanjore.

Among famed Moslem edifices are the *Dome of the Rock* or *Mosque of Omar,* Jerusalem (A.D. 691); the *Citadel* (1166), and the *Tombs of the Mamelukes* (15th century), in Cairo; the *Tomb of Humayun* in Delhi; the *Blue Mosque* (1468) at Tabriz, and the *Tamerlane Mausoleum* at Samarkand.

*Angkor Wat,* outside the city of Angkor Thom, Cambodia, is one of the most beautiful examples of Cambodian or Khmer architecture. The sanctuary was built during the 12th century.

*Great Wall of China* (228 B.C.?), designed specifically as a defense against nomadic tribes, has large watch towers which could be called buildings. It was erected by Emperor Ch'in Shih Huang Ti and is 1,400 miles long. Built mainly of earth and stone, it varies in height between 18 and 30 ft.

Typical of Chinese architecture are the pagodas or temple towers. Among some of the better-known pagodas are the *Great Pagoda of the Wild Geese* at Sian (founded in 652); *Nan t'a* (11th century) at Fang Shan; the *Pagoda of Sung Yueh Ssu* (A.D. 523) at Sung Shan, Honan.

Other well-known Chinese buildings are the *Drum Tower* (1273), the *Three Great Halls* in the Purple Forbidden City (1627), *Buddha's Perfume Tower* (19th century), the *Porcelain Pagoda,* and the *Summer Palace,* all at Peking.

## United States

*Rockefeller Center,* in New York City, extends from 5th Ave. to the Avenue of the Americas between 48th and 52nd Sts. (and halfway to 7th Ave. between 47th and 51st Sts.). It occupies more than 22 acres and has 19 buildings.

*The Cathedral of St. John the Divine,* at 112th St. and Amsterdam Ave. in New York City, was begun in 1892 and is now in the final stages of completion. When completed, it will be the largest cathedral in the world: 601 ft long, 146 ft wide at the nave, 320 ft wide at the transept. The east end is designed in Romanesque-Byzantine style, and the nave and west end are Gothic.

*St. Patrick's Cathedral,* at Fifth Ave. and 50th St. in New York City, has a seating capacity of 2,500. The nave was opened in 1877, and the cathedral was dedicated in 1879.

*Louisiana Superdome,* in New Orleans, is the largest arena in the history of mankind. The main area can accommodate up to 95,000 people. It is the world's largest steel-constructed room. Unobstructed by posts, it covers 13 acres and reaches 27 stories at its peak.

*World Trade Center,* in New York City, was dedicated in 1973. Its twin towers are 110 stories high (1,350 ft), and the complex contains over 9 million sq ft of office space. A restaurant is on the 107th floor of the North Tower.

## World's Highest Dams

| Name | River, Country or State | Structural height feet | Structural height meters | Gross reservoir capacity thousands of acre feet | Gross reservoir capacity millions of cubic meters | Year completed |
|------|------------------------|------|--------|------------------|------------------|-----------|
| Rogun | Vakhsh, U.S.S.R. | 1066 | 325 | 9,404 | 11,600 | 1985 |
| Nurek | Vakhsh, U.S.S.R. | 984 | 300 | 8,512 | 10,500 | 1980 |
| Grande Dixence | Dixence, Switzerland | 935 | 285 | 324 | 400 | 1962 |
| Inguri | Inguri, U.S.S.R. | 892 | 272 | 801 | 1,100 | 1984 |
| Chicoasén | Grijalva, Mexico | 869 | 265 | 1,346 | 1,660 | 1981 |
| Vaiont | Vaiont, Italy | 869 | 265 | 137 | 169 | 1961 |
| Tehri | Bhagirathi, India | 856 | 261 | 2,869 | 3,540 | UC |
| Kinshau | Tons, India | 830 | 253 | 1,946 | 2,400 | 1985 |
| Guavio | Orinoco, Colombia | 820 | 250 | 811 | 1,000 | UC |
| Mica | Columbia, Canada | 794 | 242 | 20,000 | 24,670 | 1972 |
| Sayano-Shushensk | Yenisei, U.S.S.R. | 794 | 242 | 25,353 | 31,300 | 1980 |
| Mihoesti | Aries, Romania | 794 | 242 | 5 | 6 | 1983 |
| Chivor | Batá, Colombia | 778 | 237 | 661 | 815 | 1975 |
| Mauvoisin | Drance de Bagnes, Switzerland | 777 | 237 | 146 | 180 | 1957 |
| Oroville | Feather, California | 770 | 235 | 3,538 | 4,299 | 1968 |
| Chirkey | Sulak, U.S.S.R. | 764 | 233 | 2,252 | 2,780 | 1977 |
| Bhakra | Sutlej, India | 741 | 226 | 8,002 | 9,870 | 1963 |
| El Cajón | Humuya, Honduras | 741 | 226 | 4,580 | 5,650 | 1984 |
| Hoover | Colorado, Arizona/Nevada | 726 | 221 | 28,500 | 35,154 | 1936 |
| Contra | Verzasca, Switzerland | 722 | 220 | 70 | 86 | 1965 |
| Dabaklamm | Dorferbach, Austria | 722 | 220 | 191 | 235 | UC |
| Mratinje | Piva, Yugoslavia | 722 | 220 | 713 | 880 | 1973 |
| Dworshak | N. Fk. Clearwater, Idaho | 717 | 219 | 3,453 | 4,259 | 1974 |
| Glen Canyon | Colorado, Arizona | 710 | 216 | 27,000 | 33,304 | 1964 |
| Toktogul | Naryn, U.S.S.R. | 705 | 215 | 15,800 | 19,500 | 1978 |
| Daniel Johnson | Manicouagan, Canada | 703 | 214 | 115,000 | 141,852 | 1968 |
| San Rogue | Agno, Philippines | 689 | 210 | 803 | 990 | UC |
| Luzzone | Brenno di Luzzone, Switzerland | 682 | 208 | 71 | 87 | 1963 |
| Keban | Firat, Turkey | 679 | 207 | 25,110 | 31,000 | 1974 |
| Dez | Dez, Abi, Iran | 666 | 203 | 2,707 | 3,340 | 1963 |
| Almendra | Tormes, Spain | 662 | 202 | 2,148 | 2,649 | 1970 |
| Kölnbrein | Malta, Austria | 656 | 200 | 166 | 205 | 1977 |
| Karun | Karun, Iran | 656 | 200 | 2,351 | 2,900 | 1976 |
| Altinkaya | Kizil Irmak, Turkey | 640 | 195 | 4,672 | 5,763 | 1986 |
| New Bullards Bar | No. Yuba, California | 637 | 194 | 960 | 1,184 | 1968 |
| Lakhwar | Yamuna, India | 630 | 192 | 470 | 580 | 1985 |
| New Melones | Stanislaus, California | 625 | 191 | 2,400 | 2,960 | 1979 |
| Itaipu | Paraná, Brazil/Paraguay | 623 | 190 | 23,510 | 29,000 | 1982 |
| Kurobe 4 | Kurobe, Japan | 610 | 186 | 162 | 199 | 1964 |
| Swift | Lewis, Washington | 610 | 186 | 756 | 932 | 1958 |
| Mossyrock | Cowlitz, Washington | 607 | 185 | 1,300 | 1,603 | 1968 |
| Oymopinar | Manavgat, Turkey | 607 | 185 | 251 | 310 | 1983 |
| Atatürk | Firat, Turkey | 604 | 184 | 39,482 | 48,700 | 1986 |
| Shasta | Sacramento, California | 602 | 183 | 4,550 | 5,612 | 1945 |
| Bennett WAC | Peace, Canada | 600 | 183 | 57,006 | 70,309 | 1967 |
| Karakaya | Firat, Turkey | 591 | 180 | 7,767 | 9,580 | UC |
| Tignes | Isère, France | 591 | 180 | 186 | 230 | 1952 |
| Amir Kabir (Karad) | Karadj, Iran | 591 | 180 | 166 | 205 | 1962 |
| Tachien | Tachia, Taiwan | 591 | 180 | 188 | 232 | 1974 |
| Dartmouth | Mitta-Mitta, Australia | 591 | 180 | 3,243 | 4,000 | 1978 |
| Özköy | Gediz, Turkey | 591 | 180 | 762 | 940 | 1983 |
| Emosson | Barberine, Switzerland | 590 | 180 | 184 | 225 | 1974 |
| Zillergründl | Ziller, Austria | 590 | 180 | 73 | 90 | 1986 |
| Los Leones | Los Leones, Chile | 587 | 179 | 86 | 106 | 1986 |
| New Don Pedro | Tuolumne, California | 585 | 178 | 2,030 | 2,504 | 1971 |
| Alpa-Gera | Cormor, Italy | 584 | 178 | 53 | 65 | 1965 |

| Name | River, country, or state | Structural height (feet) | Structural height (meters) | Gross reservoir capacity (Thousands of acre feet) | Gross reservoir capacity (millions of cubic meters) | Year completed |
|---|---|---|---|---|---|---|
| Kopperston Tailings 3 | Jones Branch, West Virginia | 580 | 177 | — | — | 1963 |
| Takase | Takase, Japan | 577 | 176 | 62 | 76 | 1979 |
| Nader Shah | Marun, Iran | 574 | 175 | 1,313 | 1,620 | 1978 |
| Hasan Ugurlu | Yesil Irmak, Turkey | 574 | 175 | 874 | 1,078 | 1980 |
| Pauti-Mazar | Mazar, Ecuador | 540 | 165 | 405 | 500 | 1984 |
| Hungry Horse | S.Fk., Flathead, Montana | 564 | 172 | 3,470 | 4,280 | 1953 |
| Longyangxia | Huanghe, China | 564 | 172 | 20,025 | 24,700 | 1983 |
| Cabora Bassa | Zambezi, Mozambique | 561 | 171 | 51,075 | 63,000 | 1974 |
| Maqarin | Yarmuk, Jordan | 561 | 171 | 259 | 320 | UC |
| Amaluza | Paute, Ecuador | 558 | 170 | 81 | 100 | 1982 |
| Idikki | Periyar, India | 554 | 169 | 1,618 | 1,996 | 1974 |
| Charvak | Chirchik, U.S.S.R. | 552 | 168 | 1,620 | 2,000 | 1970 |
| Gura Apelor Retezat | Riul Mare, Romania | 552 | 168 | 182 | 225 | 1980 |
| Grand Coulee | Columbia, Washington | 550 | 168 | 9,390 | 11,582 | 1942 |
| Boruca | Terraba, Costa Rica | 548 | 167 | 12,128 | 14,960 | UC |
| Vidraru | Arges, Romania | 545 | 166 | 380 | 465 | 1965 |
| Kremasta (King Paul) | Achelöus, Greece | 541 | 165 | 3,850 | 4,750 | 1965 |

NOTE: UC = under construction. *Source:* Department of the Interior, Bureau of Reclamation and *International Water Power and Dam Construction.*

## World's Largest Dams

| Dam | Location | Volume (thousands) Cubic meters | Volume (thousands) Cubic yards | Year completed |
|---|---|---|---|---|
| New Cornelia Tailings | Arizona | 209,500 | 274,015 | 1973 |
| Pati (Chapetón) | Argentina | 200,000 | 261,590 | UC |
| Tarbela | Pakistan | 121,720 | 159,203 | 1976 |
| Fort Peck | Montana | 96,049 | 125,628 | 1940 |
| Atatürk | Turkey | 84,500 | 110,522 | UC |
| Yacyretá-Apipe | Paraguay/Argentina | 81,000 | 105,944 | UC |
| Guri (Raul Leoni) | Venezuela | 78,000 | 102,014 | 1986 |
| Rogun | U.S.S.R. | 75,500 | 98,750 | 1985 |
| Oahe | South Dakota | 70,339 | 92,000 | 1963 |
| Mangla | Pakistan | 65,651 | 85,872 | 1967 |
| Gardiner | Canada | 65,440 | 85,592 | 1968 |
| Afsluitdijk | Netherlands | 63,400 | 82,927 | 1932 |
| Oroville | California | 59,639 | 78,008 | 1968 |
| San Luis | California | 59,405 | 77,700 | 1967 |
| Nurek | U.S.S.R. | 58,000 | 75,861 | 1980 |
| Garrison | North Dakota | 50,843 | 66,500 | 1956 |
| Cochiti | New Mexico | 48,052 | 62,850 | 1975 |
| Tabka (Thawra) | Syria | 46,000 | 60,168 | 1976 |
| Bennett W.A.C. | Canada | 43,733 | 57,201 | 1967 |
| Tucuruí | Brazil | 43,000 | 56,242 | 1984 |
| Boruca | Costa Rica | 43,000 | 56,242 | UC |
| High Aswan (Sadd-el-Aali) | Egypt | 43,000 | 56,242 | 1970 |
| San Rogue | Philippines | 43,000 | 56,242 | UC |
| Kiev | U.S.S.R. | 42,841 | 56,034 | 1964 |
| Dantiwada Left Embankment | India | 41,040 | 53,680 | 1965 |
| Saratov | U.S.S.R. | 40,400 | 52,843 | 1967 |
| Mission Tailings 2 | Arizona | 40,088 | 52,435 | 1973 |
| Fort Randall | South Dakota | 38,227 | 50,000 | 1953 |
| Kanev | U.S.S.R. | 37,860 | 49,520 | 1976 |
| Mosul | Iraq | 36,000 | 47,086 | 1982 |
| Kakhovka | U.S.S.R. | 35,640 | 46,617 | 1955 |
| Itumbiara | Brazil | 35,600 | 46,563 | 1980 |
| Lauwerszee | Netherlands | 35,575 | 46,532 | 1969 |
| Beas | India | 35,418 | 46,325 | 1974 |
| Oosterschelde | Netherlands | 35,000 | 45,778 | 1986 |

NOTE: UC = under construction. *Source:* Department of the Interior, Bureau of Reclamation and *International Water Power and Dam Construction.*

## World's Largest Hydroelectric Plants

| Name of dam | Location | Rated capacity (MW) | | Year of initial operation |
|---|---|---|---|---|
| | | Present | Ultimate | |
| Itaipu | Brazil/Paraguay | 1,400 | 12,600 | 1984 |
| Grand Coulee | Washington | 6,480 | 10,080 | 1942 |
| Guri (Raul Leoni) | Venezuela | 2,800 | 10,060 | 1968 |
| Tucuruí | Brazil | — | 7,500 | 1985 |
| Sayano-Shushensk | U.S.S.R. | — | 6,400 | 1980 |
| Krasnoyarsk | U.S.S.R. | 6,096 | 6,096 | 1968 |
| Corpus-Posadas | Argentina/Paraguay | — | 6,000 | UC |
| LaGrande 2 | Canada | 5,328 | 5,328 | 1982 |
| Churchill Falls | Canada | 5,225 | 5,225 | 1971 |
| Bratsk | U.S.S.R. | 4,100 | 4,600 | 1964 |
| Ust'—Ilimsk | U.S.S.R. | 3,675 | 4,500 | 1974 |
| Cabora Bassa | Mozambique | 2,075 | 4,150 | 1974 |
| Yacyretá-Apipe | Argentina/Paraguay | — | 4,050 | UC |
| Rogun | U.S.S.R. | — | 3,600 | 1985 |
| Paulo Afonso | Brazil | 3,409 | 3,409 | 1954 |
| Salto Santiago | Brazil | 1,332 | 3,333 | 1980 |
| Pati (Chapetón) | Argentina | — | 3,300 | UC |
| Brumley Gap | Virginia | 3,200 | 3,200 | 1973 |
| Ilha Solteira | Brazil | 3,200 | 3,200 | 1973 |
| Inga I | Zaire | 360 | 2,820 | 1974 |
| Gezhouba | China | 965 | 2,715 | 1981 |
| John Day | Oregon/Washington | 2,160 | 2,700 | 1969 |
| Nurek | U.S.S.R. | 900 | 2,700 | 1976 |
| Revelstoke | Canada | 900 | 2,700 | 1984 |
| Sáo Simao | Brazil | 2,680 | 2,680 | 1979 |
| LaGrande 4 | Canada | 2,637 | 2,637 | 1984 |
| Mica | Canada | 1,736 | 2,610 | 1976 |
| Volgograd—22nd Congress | U.S.S.R. | 2,560 | 2,560 | 1958 |
| Fos do Areia | Brazil | 2,511 | 2,511 | 1983 |
| Itaparica | Brazil | — | 2,500 | 1985 |
| Bennett W.A.C. | Canada | 2,116 | 2,416 | 1969 |
| Chicoasén | Mexico | — | 2,400 | 1980 |
| Atatürk | Turkey | — | 2,400 | UC |
| LaGrande 3 | Canada | 2,310 | 2,310 | 1982 |
| Volga—V.I. Lenin | U.S.S.R. | 2,300 | 2,300 | 1955 |
| Iron Gates I | Romania/Yugoslavia | 2,300 | 2,300 | 1970 |
| Iron Gates II | Romania/Yugoslavia | 270 | 2,160 | 1983 |
| Bath County | Virginia | — | 2,100 | 1985 |
| High Aswan (Saad-el-Aali) | Egypt | 2,100 | 2,100 | 1967 |
| Tarbela | Pakistan | 1,400 | 2,100 | 1977 |
| Piedra del Aquila | Argentina | — | 2,100 | UC |
| Itumbiara | Brazil | 2,080 | 2,080 | 1980 |
| Chief Joseph | Washington | 2,069 | 2,069 | 1956 |
| McNary | Oregon | 980 | 2,030 | 1954 |
| Green River | North Carolina | — | 2,000 | 1980 |
| Tehri | India | — | 2,000 | UC |
| Cornwall | New York | — | 2,000 | 1978 |
| Ludington | Michigan | 1,979 | 1,979 | 1973 |
| Robert Moses—Niagara | New York | 1,950 | 1,950 | 1961 |
| Salto Grande | Argentina/Uruguay | — | 1,890 | 1979 |

Note: MW = Megawatts, UC = under construction. *Source:* Department of the Interior, Bureau of Reclamation and *International Water Power and Dam Construction.*

## The First Skyscraper

A ten-story building isn't anyone's idea of a skyscraper today, but it was in fact the first skyscraper. It was not its height that gave it that distinction but its construction. It was the first building in the world to employ steel skeleton construction and thus became the prototype for the skyscraper.

Designed by William Le Baron Jenny for the Home Insurance Company of New York, it was erected at the corner of La Salle and Adams streets in Chicago. Construction began on May 1, 1884, and was completed in the fall of 1885. It was built of marble and flanked by four columns of polished granite supporting a marble balcony. A steel frame supported the weight of the walls, rather than the walls themselves bearing the weight. Two additional stories were added later.

Four years after completion of the Home Insurance Company Building, the steel-framed skyscraper had totally evolved in Chicago earning it the distinction of being its birth place.

## United States Tallest Buildings

| City | Building | Stories | Height ft | Height m | City | Building | Stories | Height ft | Height m |
|------|----------|---------|-----------|----------|------|----------|---------|-----------|----------|
| Chicago | Sears Tower | 110 | 1,454 | 443 | Boston | John Hancock Tower | 60 | 790 | 241 |
| New York | World Trade Center | 110 | 1,377 | 419 | San Francisco | Bank of America | 52 | 779 | 237 |
| New York | Empire State | 102 | 1,250 | 381 | Minneapolis | IDS Tower | 57 | 775 | 236 |
| Chicago | Standard Oil (Indiana) | 80 | 1,136 | 346 | New York | One Liberty Plaza | 54 | 775 | 236 |
| Chicago | John Hancock Center | 100 | 1,127 | 343 | New York | One Penn Plaza | 57 | 774 | 236 |
| New York | Chrysler | 77 | 1,046 | 319 | Atlanta | Peachtree Plaza | 73 | 754 | 230 |
| Houston | Texas | 75 | 1,002 | 305 | New York | Exxon | 54 | 750 | 229 |
| Houston | Allied Bank | 71 | 985 | 300 | Boston | Prudéntial Tower | 52 | 750 | 229 |
| New York | American International | 66 | 952 | 290 | Detroit | Detroit Plaza Hotel | 73 | 747 | 228 |
| New York | Citicorp Center | 59 | 915 | 279 | Dallas | First International | 55 | 744 | 227 |
| New York | 40 Wall Tower | 71 | 900 | 274 | Los Angeles | Security Pacific Plaza | 55 | 743 | 226 |
| Chicago | Water Tower Place | 74 | 859 | 262 | New York | One Astor Plaza | 54 | 730 | 222 |
| Los Angeles | United California Bank | 62 | 858 | 261 | Houston | Gulf Tower | 52 | 725 | 221 |
| San Francisco | Transamerica Pyramid | 61 | 853 | 260 | New York | Marine Midland | 52 | 724 | 221 |
| Chicago | First National Bank | 60 | 851 | 259 | Houston | One Shell Plaza | 50 | 714 | 218 |
| New York | RCA | 70 | 850 | 259 | Dallas | First International | 56 | 710 | 216 |
| Pittsburgh | U.S. Steel Headquarters | 64 | 841 | 256 | Cleveland | Terminal Tower | 52 | 708 | 216 |
| New York | Chase Manhattan | 60 | 813 | 248 | New York | Union Carbide | 52 | 707 | 215 |
| New York | Pan Am | 59 | 808 | 246 | New York | General Motors | 50 | 705 | 215 |
| New York | Woolworth | 55 | 792 | 241 | New York | Metropolitan Life | 50 | 700 | 213 |

NOTE: Does not include buildings under construction and not completed in 1982. Height does not include TV towers and antennas. *Source: Information Please* questionnaires to building managements.

## Notable Tunnels

| Name | Location | Length mi. | Length km | Year completed |
|------|----------|-----------|-----------|----------------|
| **Railroad, excluding subways** | | | | |
| Seikan | Tsugara Strait, Japan | 33.1 | 53.3 | 1983 |
| Simplon (I and II) | Alps, Switzerland-Italy | 12.3 | 19.8 | 1906 & 1922 |
| Apennine | Genoa, Italy | 11.5 | 18.5 | 1934 |
| St. Gotthard | Swiss Alps | 9.3 | 14.9 | 1881 |
| Lötschberg | Swiss Alps | 9.1 | 14.6 | 1911 |
| Mont Cénis | French Alps | 8.5[1] | 13.7 | 1871 |
| New Cascade | Cascade Mountains, Washington | 7.8 | 12.6 | 1929 |
| Vosges | Vosges, France | 7.0 | 11.3 | 1940 |
| Arlberg | Austrian Alps | 6.3 | 10.1 | 1884 |
| Moffat | Rocky Mountains, Colorado | 6.2 | 9.9 | 1928 |
| Shimuzu | Shimuzu, Japan | 6.1 | 9.8 | 1931 |
| Rimutaka | Wairarapa, New Zealand | 5.5 | 8.9 | 1955 |
| **Vehicular** | | | | |
| St. Gotthard | Alps, Switzerland | 10.2 | 16.4 | 1980 |
| Mt. Blanc | Alps, France-Italy | 7.5 | 12.1 | 1965 |
| Mt. Ena | Japan Alps, Japan | 5.3 | 8.5 | 1976[2] |
| Great St. Bernard | Alps, Switzerland-Italy | 3.4 | 5.5 | 1964 |
| Mount Royal | Montreal, Canada | 3.2 | 5.1 | 1918 |
| Lincoln | Hudson River, New York-New Jersey | 2.5 | 4.0 | 1937 |
| Queensway Road | Mersey River, Liverpool, England | 2.2 | 3.5 | 1934 |
| Brooklyn-Battery | East River, New York City | 2.1 | 3.4 | 1950 |
| Holland | Hudson River, New York-New Jersey | 1.7 | 2.7 | 1927 |
| Hampton Roads | Norfolk, Virginia | 1.4 | 2.3 | 1957 |
| Queens-Midtown | East River, New York City | 1.3 | 2.1 | 1940 |
| Liberty Tubes | Pittsburgh, Pennsylvania | 1.2 | 1.9 | 1923 |
| Baltimore Harbor | Baltimore, Maryland | 1.2 | 1.9 | 1957 |
| Allegheny Tunnels | Pennsylvania Turnpike | 1.2 | 1.9 | 1940[3] |

1. Lengthened to its present 8.5 miles in 1881. 2. Parallel tunnel begun in 1976. 3. Parallel tunnel built in 1965, twin tunnel in 1966. NOTE: UC = under construction. *Source:* American Society of Civil Engineers and International Bridge, Tunnel & Turnpike Association.

# Notable Modern Bridges

| Name | Location | Length of main span, | | Year completed |
|---|---|---|---|---|
| | | ft | m | |
| **Suspension** | | | | |
| Humber | Hull, Britain | 4,626 | 1,410 | 1981 |
| Verrazano-Narrows | Lower New York Bay | 4,260 | 1,298 | 1964 |
| Golden Gate | San Francisco Bay | 4,200 | 1,280 | 1937 |
| Mackinac Straits | Michigan | 3,800 | 1,158 | 1957 |
| Bosporus | Istanbul | 3,524 | 1,074 | 1973 |
| George Washington | Hudson River at New York City | 3,500 | 1,067 | 1931 |
| Ponte 25 de Abril | Tagus River at Lisbon | 3,323 | 1,013 | 1966 |
| Forth Road | Queensferry, Scotland | 3,300 | 1,006 | 1964 |
| Severn | Severn River at Beachley, England | 3,240 | 988 | 1966 |
| Tacoma Narrows | Puget Sound at Tacoma, Wash. | 2,800 | 853 | 1950 |
| Kanmon Strait | Kyushu-Honshu, Japan | 2,336 | 712 | 1973 |
| Angostura | Orinoco River at Ciudad Bolivar, Venezuela | 2,336 | 712 | 1967 |
| Transbay (twin spans) | San Francisco Bay | 2,310 | 704 | 1936 |
| Bronx-Whitestone | East River, New York City | 2,300 | 701 | 1939 |
| Pierre Laporte | St. Lawrence River at Quebec, Canada | 2,190 | 668 | 1970 |
| Delaware Memorial (twin bridges) | Delaware River near Wilmington, Del. | 2,150 | 655 | 1951, 1968 |
| Seaway Skyway | St. Lawrence River at Ogdensburg, N.Y. | 2,150 | 655 | 1960 |
| Gas Pipe Line | Atchafalaya River, Louisiana | 2,000 | 610 | 1951 |
| Walt Whitman | Delaware River at Philadelphia | 2,000 | 610 | 1957 |
| Tancarville | Seine River at Tancarville, France | 1,995 | 608 | 1959 |
| Lillebaelt | Lillebaelt Strait, Denmark | 1,969 | 600 | 1970 |
| Ambassador International | Detroit River at Detroit | 1,850 | 564 | 1929 |
| Throgs Neck | East River, New York City | 1,800 | 549 | 1961 |
| Benjamin Franklin | Delaware River at Philadelphia | 1,750 | 533 | 1926 |
| Skjomen | Narvik, Norway | 1,722 | 525 | 1972 |
| Kvalsund | Hammerfest, Norway | 1,722 | 525 | 1977 |
| Kleve-Emmerich | Rhine River at Emmerich, West Germany | 1,640 | 500 | 1965 |
| Bear Mountain | Hudson River at Peekskill, N.Y. | 1,632 | 497 | 1924 |
| Wm. Preston Lane, Jr., Memorial (twin bridges) | Near Annapolis, Md. | 1,600 | 488 | 1952, 1973 |
| Williamsburg | East River, New York City | 1,600 | 488 | 1903 |
| Newport | Narragansett Bay at Newport, R.I. | 1,600 | 488 | 1969 |
| Brooklyn | East River, New York City | 1,595 | 486 | 1883 |
| **Cantilever** | | | | |
| Quebec Railway | St. Lawrence River at Quebec, Canada | 1,800 | 549 | 1917 |
| Forth Railway (twin spans) | Queensferry, Scotland | 1,710 | 521 | 1890 |
| Minato Ohashi | Osaka, Japan | 1,673 | 510 | 1974 |
| Commodore John Barry | Chester, Pa. | 1,644 | 501 | 1974 |
| Greater New Orleans | Mississippi River, Louisiana | 1,576 | 480 | 1958 |
| Howrah | Hooghly River at Calcutta | 1,500 | 457 | 1943 |
| Transbay Bridge | San Francisco Bay | 1,400 | 427 | 1936 |
| Baton Rouge | Mississippi River, Louisiana | 1,235 | 376 | 1968 |
| Tappan Zee | Hudson River at Tarrytown, N.Y. | 1,212 | 369 | 1955 |
| Longview | Columbia River at Longview, Wash. | 1,200 | 366 | 1930 |
| Patapsco River | Baltimore Outer Harbor Crossing | 1,200 | 366 | 1976 |
| Queensboro | East River, New York City | 1,182 | 360 | 1909 |
| **Steel Arch** | | | | |
| New River Gorge | Fayetteville, W. Va. | 1,700 | 518 | 1977 |
| Bayonne | Kill Van Kull at Bayonne, N.J. | 1,675 | 510 | 1931 |
| Sydney Harbor | Sydney, Australia | 1,670 | 509 | 1932 |
| Fremont | Portland, Ore. | 1,255 | 383 | 1973 |
| Zdákov | Vltava River, Czechoslovakia | 1,244 | 380 | 1967 |
| Port Mann | Fraser River at Vancouver, British Columbia | 1,200 | 366 | 1964 |
| Thatcher Ferry | Panama Canal, Panama | 1,128 | 344 | 1962 |
| Laviolette | St. Lawrence River, Trois Rivieres, Quebec | 1,100 | 335 | 1967 |
| Runcorn-Widnes | Mersey River, England | 1,082 | 330 | 1961 |
| Birchenough | Sabi River at Fort Victoria, Rhodesia | 1,080 | 329 | 1935 |

| Name | Location | Length of main span, ft | Length of main span, m | Year completed |
|------|----------|------------------------:|------------------------:|:--------------:|
| **Cable-Stayed** | | | | |
| Annacis | Vancouver, B.C., Canada | 1525 | 465 | 1986 |
| Yokohama-ko-odan | Kanagawa, Japan | 1509 | 460 | UC |
| Second Hooghly | Calcutta, India | 1500 | 457 | UC |
| Chao Phya | Thailand | 1476 | 450 | 1986 |
| Barrios de Luna | Spain | 1444 | 440 | 1983 |
| Iwaguroshima | Kagawa, Japan | 1378 | 420 | UC |
| Shizakuishishima | Kagawa, Japan | 1378 | 420 | UC |
| Meiko Nishi | Aichi, Japan | 1329 | 405 | 1985 |
| St. Nazaire | Loire River, St. Nazaire, France | 1325 | 404 | 1975 |
| Rande | Rande, Spain | 1312 | 400 | 1977 |
| Dame Point | Jacksonville, Florida, U.S.A. | 1300 | 396 | UC |
| Hale Boggs Memorial | Luling, Louisiana, U.S.A. | 1222 | 373 | 1983 |
| Dusseldorf Flehe | West Germany | 1207 | 368 | 1979 |
| Tjörn | Sweden | 1200 | 366 | 1981 |
| Sunshine Skyway | Tampa, Florida, U.S.A. | 1200 | 366 | UC |
| **Continuous Truss** | | | | |
| Astoria | Columbia River at Astoria, Oregon | 1,232 | 376 | 1966 |
| Oshima | Oshima Island, Japan | 1,066 | 325 | 1976 |
| Croton Reservoir | Croton, N.Y. | 1,052 | 321 | 1970 |
| Tenmon | Kumamoto, Japan | 984 | 300 | 1966 |
| Kuronoseto | Nagashima-Kyushu, Japan | 984 | 300 | 1974 |
| Ravenswood | Ohio River, Ravenswood, W. Va. | 902 | 275 | 1981 |
| Dubuque | Mississippi River at Dubuque, Iowa | 845 | 258 | 1943 |
| Braga Memorial | Taunton River at Somerset, Mass. | 840 | 256 | 1966 |
| Graf Spee | Germany | 839 | 256 | 1936 |
| **Concrete Arch** | | | | |
| Jesse H. Jones Memorial | Houston Ship Channel, Texas | 1,500 | 455 | 1982 |
| KRK | Zagreb, Yugoslavia | 1,280 | 390 | 1979 |
| Gladesville | Parramatta River at Sydney, Australia | 1,000 | 305 | 1964 |
| Amizade | Paraná River at Foz do Iguassu, Brazil | 951 | 290 | 1964 |
| Arrábida | Porto, Portugal | 886 | 270 | 1963 |
| Sandö | Angerman River at Kramfors, Sweden | 866 | 264 | 1943 |
| Shibenik | Krka River, Yugoslavia | 808 | 246 | 1966 |
| Fiumarella | Catanzaro, Italy | 758 | 231 | 1961 |
| Zaporozhe | Old Dnepr River, U.S.S.R. | 748 | 228 | 1952 |
| Novi Sad | Danube River, Yugoslavia | 692 | 211 | 1961 |

1. Concrete bridge. NOTE: UC = under construction. *Source: Encyclopaedia Britannica,* American Society of Civil Engineers, and Bridge Division, Federal Highway Administration.

## Famous Ship Canals

| Name | Location | Length (miles)[1] | Width (feet) | Depth (feet) | Locks | Year opened |
|------|----------|------------------:|-------------:|-------------:|:-----:|:-----------:|
| Albert | Belgium | 80.0 | 53.0 | 16.5 | 6 | 1939 |
| Amsterdam-Rhine | Netherlands | 45.0 | 164.0 | 41.0 | 3 | 1952 |
| Beaumont-Port Arthur | United States | 40.0 | 200.0 | 34.0 | — | 1916 |
| Chesapeake and Delaware | United States | 19.0 | 250.0 | 27.0 | — | 1927 |
| Houston | United States | 43.0 | 300.0 | 34.0 | — | 1914 |
| Kiel (Nord-Ostsee Kanal) | Germany | 61.3 | 144.0 | 36.0 | 4 | 1895 |
| Panama | Canal Zone | 50.7 | 110.0 | 41.0 | 12 | 1914 |
| St. Lawrence Seaway | U.S. and Canada | 2,400.0 [2] | (3) | — | — | 1959 |
|   Montreal to Prescott | U.S. and Canada | 11.5 | 80.0 | 30.0 | 7 | 1959 |
|   Welland | Canada | 27.5 | 80.0 | 27.0 | 8 | 1931 |
|   Sault Ste. Marie | Canada | 1.2 | 60.0 | 16.8 | 1 | 1895 |
|   Sault Ste. Marie | United States | 1.6 | 80.0 | 25.0 | 4 | 1915 |
| Suez | Egypt | 100.6 [4] | 197.0 | 36.0 | — | 1869 |

1. Statute miles. 2. From Montreal to Duluth. 3. 442–550 feet; there are 11.5 miles of locks, 80 feet wide and 30 feet deep.
4. From Port Said lighthouse to entrance channel in Suez roads. *Source:* American Society of Civil Engineers.

## THE DECLARATION OF INDEPENDENCE

### In Congress, July 4, 1776

#### The unanimous Declaration of the thirteen united States of America.

When in the Course of human events it becomes necessary for one people to dissolve the political bands which have connected them with another, and to assume among the powers of the earth, the separate and equal station to which the Laws of Nature and of Nature's God entitle them, a decent respect to the opinions of mankind requires that they should declare the causes which impel them to the separation.

We hold these truths to be self-evident, that all men are created equal, that they are endowed by their Creator with certain unalienable Rights, that among these are Life, Liberty and the pursuit of Happiness.—That to secure these rights, Governments are instituted among Men, deriving their just powers from the consent of the governed,— That whenever any Form of Government becomes destructive of these ends, it is the Right of the People to alter or to abolish it, and to institute new Government, laying its foundation on such principles and organizing its powers in such form, as to them shall seem most likely to effect their Safety and Happiness. Prudence, indeed, will dictate that Governments long established should not be changed for light and transient causes; and accordingly all experience hath shewn that mankind are more disposed to suffer, while evils are sufferable, than to right themselves by abolishing the forms to which they are accustomed. But when a long train of abuses and usurpations, pursuing invariably the same Object evinces a design to reduce them under absolute Despotism, it is their right, it is their duty, to throw off such Government, and to provide new Guards for their future security.— Such has been the patient sufferance of these Colonies; and such is now the necessity which constrains them to alter their former Systems of Government. The history of the present King of Great Britain is a history of repeated injuries and usurpations, all having in direct object the establishment of an absolute Tyranny over these States. To prove this, let Facts be submitted to a candid world.

He has refused his Assent to Laws, the most wholesome and necessary for the public good.

He has forbidden his Governors to pass Laws of immediate and pressing importance, unless suspended in their operation till his Assent should be obtained; and when so suspended, he has utterly neglected to attend to them.

He has refused to pass other Laws for the accommodation of large districts of people, unless those people would relinquish the right of Representation in the Legislature, a right inestimable to them and formidable to tyrants only.

He has called together legislative bodies at places unusual, uncomfortable, and distant from the depository of their Public Records, for the sole purpose of fatiguing them into compliance with his measures.

He has dissolved Representative Houses repeatedly, for opposing with manly firmness his invasions on the rights of the people.

He has refused for a long time, after such dissolutions, to cause others to be elected; whereby the Legislative Powers, incapable of Annihilation, have returned to the People at large for their exercise; the State remaining in the mean time exposed to all the dangers of invasion from without, and convulsions within.

He has endeavoured to prevent the population of these States; for that purpose obstructing the Laws for Naturalization of Foreigners; refusing to pass others to encourage their migrations hither, and raising the conditions of new Appropriations of Lands.

He has obstructed the Administration of Justice, by refusing his Assent to Laws for establishing Judiciary Powers.

He has made Judges dependent on his Will alone, for the tenure of their offices, and the amount and payment of their salaries.

He has erected a multitude of New Offices, and sent hither swarms of Officers to harass our people, and eat out their substance.

He has kept among us, in times of peace, Standing Armies without the Consent of our legislatures.

He has affected to render the Military independent of and superior to the Civil Power.

He has combined with others to subject us to a jurisdiction foreign to our constitution, and unacknowledged by our laws; giving his Assent to their Acts of pretended Legislation:

For quartering large bodies of armed troops among us:

For protecting them, by a mock Trial, from punishment for any Murders which they should commit on the Inhabitants of these States:

For cutting off our Trade with all parts of the

---

NOTE: On April 12, 1776, the legislature of North Carolina authorized its delegates to the Continental Congress to join with others in a declaration of separation from Great Britain; the first colony to instruct its delegates to take the actual initiative was Virginia on May 15. On June 7, 1776, Richard Henry Lee of Virginia offered a resolution to the Congress to the effect "that these United Colonies are, and of right ought to be, free and independent States. . . ." A committee, consisting of Thomas Jefferson, John Adams, Benjamin Franklin, Robert R. Livingston, and Roger Sherman was organized to "prepare a declaration to the effect of the said first resolution." The Declaration of Independence was adopted on July 4, 1776.

Most delegates signed the Declaration August 2, but George Wythe (Va.) signed August 27; Richard Henry Lee (Va.), Elbridge Gerry (Mass.), and Oliver Wolcott (Conn.) in September; Matthew Thornton (N.H.), not a delegate until September, in November; and Thomas McKean (Del.), although present on July 4, not until 1781 by special permission, having served in the army in the interim.

world:

For imposing Taxes on us without our Consent:

For depriving us in many cases, of the benefits of Trial by Jury:

For transporting us beyond Seas to be tried for pretended offences:

For abolishing the free System of English Laws in a neighbouring Province, establishing therein an Arbitrary government, and enlarging its Boundaries so as to render it at once an example and fit instrument for introducing the same absolute rule into these Colonies:

For taking away our Charters, abolishing our most valuable Laws and altering fundamentally the Forms of our Governments:

For suspending our own Legislatures, and declaring themselves invested with power to legislate for us in all cases whatsoever.

He has abdicated Government here, by declaring us out of his Protection and waging War against us.

He has plundered our seas, ravaged our Coasts, burnt our towns, and destroyed the lives of our people.

He is at this time transporting large Armies of foreign Mercenaries to compleat the works of death, desolation, and tyranny, already begun with circumstances of Cruelty & Perfidy scarcely paralleled in the most barbarous ages, and totally unworthy the Head of a civilized nation.

He has constrained our fellow Citizens taken Captive on the high Seas to bear Arms against their Country, to become the executioners of their friends and Brethren, or to fall themselves by their Hands.

He has excited domestic insurrections amongst us, and has endeavoured to bring on the inhabitants of our frontiers, the merciless Indian Savages, whose known rule of warfare, is an undistinguished destruction of all ages, sexes and conditions.

In every stage of these Oppressions We have Petitioned for Redress in the most humble terms: Our repeated Petitions have been answered only by repeated injury. A Prince, whose character is thus marked by every act which may define a Tyrant, is unfit to be the ruler of a free people.

Nor have We been wanting in attentions to our Brittish brethren. We have warned them from time to time of attempts by their legislature to extend an unwarrantable jurisdiction over us. We have reminded them of the circumstances of our emigration and settlement here. We have appealed to their native justice and magnanimity, and we have conjured them by the ties of our common kindred to disavow these usurpations, which would inevitably interrupt our connections and correspondence. They too have been deaf to the voice of justice and of consanguinity. We must, therefore, acquiesce in the necessity, which denounces our Separation, and hold them, as we hold the rest of mankind, Enemies in War, in Peace Friends.

We, therefore, the Representatives of the United States of America, in General Congress, Assembled, appealing to the Supreme Judge of the world for the rectitude of our intentions, do, in the Name, and by Authority of the good People of these Colonies, solemnly publish and declare, That these United Colonies are, and of Right ought to be Free and Independent States; that they are Absolved from all Allegiance to the British Crown, and that all political connection between them and the State of Great Britain, is and ought to be totally dissolved; and that as Free and Independent States, they have full Power to levy War, conclude Peace, contract Alliances, establish Commerce, and to do all other Acts and Things which Independent States may of right do.—And for the support of this Declaration, with a firm reliance on the protection of Divine Providence, we mutually pledge to each other our Lives, our Fortunes and our sacred Honor.

—John Hancock

*New Hampshire*
Josiah Bartlett
Wm. Whipple
Matthew Thornton

*Rhode Island*
Step. Hopkins
William Ellery

*Connecticut*
Roger Sherman
Sam'el Huntington
Wm. Williams
Oliver Wolcott

*New York*
Wm. Floyd
Phil. Livingston
Frans. Lewis
Lewis Morris

*New Jersey*
Richd. Stockton
Jno. Witherspoon
Fras. Hopkinson
John Hart
Abra. Clark

*Pennsylvania*
Robt. Morris
Benjamin Rush
Benj. Franklin
John Morton
Geo. Clymer
Jas. Smith
Geo. Taylor
James Wilson
Geo. Ross

*Massachusetts-Bay*
Saml. Adams
John Adams
Robt. Treat Paine
Elbridge Gerry

*Delaware*
Caesar Rodney
Geo. Read
Tho. M'Kean

*Maryland*
Samuel Chase
Wm. Paca
Thos. Stone
Charles Carroll of Carrollton

*Virginia*
George Wythe
Richard Henry Lee
Th. Jefferson
Benj. Harrison
Ths. Nelson, Jr.
Francis Lightfoot Lee
Carter Braxton

*North Carolina*
Wm. Hooper
Joseph Hewes
John Penn

*South Carolina*
Edward Rutledge
Thos. Heyward, Junr.
Thomas Lynch, Junr.
Arthur Middleton

*Georgia*
Button Gwinnett
Lyman Hall
Geo. Walton

# Constitution of the United States of America

(Historical text has been edited to conform to contemporary American usage.
The bracketed words are designations for your convenience; they are not part of the Constitution.)

*The oldest federal constitution in existence was framed by a convention of delegates from twelve of the thirteen original states in Philadelphia in May, 1787, Rhode Island failing to send a delegate. George Washington presided over the session, which lasted until September 17, 1787. The draft (originally a preamble and seven Articles) was submitted to all thirteen states and was to become effective when ratified by nine states. It went into effect on the first Wednesday in March, 1789, having been ratified by New Hampshire, the ninth state to approve, on June 21, 1788. The states ratified the Constitution in the following order:*

| | | | |
|---|---|---|---|
| Delaware | December 7, 1787 | South Carolina | May 23, 1788 |
| Pennsylvania | December 12, 1787 | New Hampshire | June 21, 1788 |
| New Jersey | December 18, 1787 | Virginia | June 25, 1788 |
| Georgia | January 2, 1788 | New York | July 26, 1788 |
| Connecticut | January 9, 1788 | North Carolina | November 21, 1789 |
| Massachusetts | February 6, 1788 | Rhode Island | May 29, 1790 |
| Maryland | April 28, 1788 | | |

## [Preamble]

We the people of the United States, in order to form a more perfect Union, establish justice, insure domestic tranquility, provide for the common defence, promote the general welfare, and secure the blessings of liberty to ourselves and our posterity, do ordain and establish this Constitution for the United States of America.

## Article I

### Section 1

[Legislative powers vested in Congress.] All legislative powers herein granted shall be vested in a Congress of the United States, which shall consist of a Senate and House of Representatives.

### Section 2

[Composition of the House of Representatives.—1.] The House of Representatives shall be composed of members chosen every second year by the people of the several States, and the electors in each State shall have the qualifications requisite for electors of the most numerous branch of the State Legislature.

[Qualifications of Representatives.—2.] No Person shall be a Representative who shall not have attained to the age of twenty-five years, and been seven years a citizen of the United States, and who shall not, when elected, be an inhabitant of that State in which he shall be chosen.

[Apportionment of Representatives and direct taxes—census.[1]—3.] (Representatives and direct taxes shall be apportioned among the several States which may be included within this Union, according to their respective numbers, which shall be determined by adding to the whole number of free persons, including those bound to service for a term of years, and excluding Indians not taxed, three fifths of all other persons.) The actual enumeration shall be made within three years after the first meeting of the Congress of the United States, and within every subsequent term of ten years, in such manner as they shall by law direct. The number of Representatives shall not exceed one for every thirty thousand, but each State shall have at least one Representative; and until such enumeration shall be made, the State of New Hampshire shall be entitled to choose three, Massachusetts

eight, Rhode-Island and Providence Plantations one, Connecticut five, New York six, New Jersey four, Pennsylvania eight, Delaware one, Maryland six, Virginia ten, North Carolina five, South Carolina five, and Georgia three.

[Filling of vacancies in representation.—4.] When vacancies happen in the representation from any State, the Executive Authority thereof shall issue writs of election to fill such vacancies.

[Selection of officers; power of impeachment.—5.] The House of Representatives shall choose their Speaker and other officers; and shall have the sole power of impeachment.

### Section 3[2]

[The Senate.—1.] The Senate of the United States shall be composed of two Senators from each State, chosen by the Legislature thereof, for six years; and each Senator shall have one vote.

[Classification of Senators; filling of vacancies.—2.] Immediately after they shall be assembled in consequence of the first election, they shall be divided as equally as may be into three classes. The seats of the Senators of the first class shall be vacated at the expiration of the second year, of the second class at the expiration of the fourth year, and of the third class at the expiration of the sixth year, so that one-third may be chosen every second year; and if vacancies happen by resignation, or otherwise, during the recess of the Legislature of any State, the Executive thereof may make temporary appointments (until the next meeting of the Legislature, which shall then fill such vacancies).

[Qualification of Senators.—3.] No person shall be a Senator who shall not have attained to the age of thirty years, and been nine years a citizen of the United States, and who shall not, when elected, be an inhabitant of that State for which he shall be chosen.

[Vice President to be President of Senate.—4.] The Vice President of the United States shall be President of the Senate, but shall have no vote, unless they be equally divided.

[Selection of Senate officers; President pro tempore.—5.] The Senate shall choose their other officers, and also a President pro tempore, in the absence of the Vice President, or when he shall exercise the office of President of the United States.

[Senate to try impeachments.—6.] The Senate

shall have the sole power to try all impeachments. When sitting for that purpose, they shall be on oath or affirmation. When the President of the United States is tried, the Chief Justice shall preside: and no person shall be convicted without the concurrence of two thirds of the members present.

[**Judgment in cases of Impeachment.—7.**] Judgment in cases of impeachment shall not extend further than to removal from office, and disqualification to hold and enjoy any office of honor, trust, or profit under the United States: but the party convicted shall nevertheless be liable and subject to indictment, trial, judgment and punishment, according to Law.

## Section 4

[**Control of congressional elections.—1.**] The times, places, and manner of holding elections for Senators and Representatives, shall be prescribed in each State by the Legislature thereof; but the Congress may at any time by law make or alter such regulations, except as to the places of choosing Senators.

[**Time for assembling of Congress.[3]—2.**] The Congress shall assemble at least once in every year, and such meeting shall be on the first Monday in December, unless they shall by law appoint a different day.

## Section 5

[**Each house to be the judge of the election and qualifications of its members; regulations as to quorum.—1.**] Each House shall be the judge of the elections, returns, and qualifications of its own members, and a majority of each shall constitute a quorum to do business; but a smaller number may adjourn from day to day, and may be authorized to compel the attendance of absent members, in such manner, and under such penalties as each House may provide.

[**Each house to determine its own rules.—2.**] Each House may determine the rules of its proceedings, punish its members for disorderly behavior, and, with the concurrence of two thirds, expel a member.

[**Journals and yeas and nays.—3.**] Each House shall keep a journal of its proceedings, and from time to time publish the same, excepting such parts as may in their judgment require secrecy; and the yeas and nays of the members of either House on any question shall, at the desire of one fifth of those present, be entered on the journal.

[**Adjournment.—4.**] Neither House, during the session of Congress, shall, without the consent of the other, adjourn for more than three days, nor to any other place than that in which the two Houses shall be sitting.

## Section 6

[**Compensation and privileges of members of Congress.—1.**] The Senators and Representatives shall receive a compensation for their services, to be ascertained by law, and paid out of the Treasury of the United States. They shall in all cases, except treason, felony, and breach of the peace, be privileged from arrest during their attendance at the session of their respective Houses, and in going to and returning from the same; and for any speech or debate in either House, they shall not be questioned in any other place.

[**Incompatible offices; exclusions.—2.**] No Senator or Representative shall, during the time for which he was elected, be appointed to any civil office under the authority of the United States, which shall have been created, or the emoluments whereof shall have been increased during such time; and no person holding any office under the United States shall be a member of either House during his continuance in office.

## Section 7

[**Revenue bills to originate in House.—1.**] All bills for raising revenue shall originate in the House of Representatives; but the Senate may propose or concur with amendments as on other bills.

[**Manner of passing bills; veto power of President.—2.**] Every bill which shall have passed the House of Representatives and the Senate, shall, before it becomes a law, be presented to the President of the United States; if he approve he shall sign it, but if not he shall return it, with his objections to that House in which it shall have originated, who shall enter the objections at large on their journal, and proceed to reconsider it. If after such reconsideration two thirds of that House shall agree to pass the bill, it shall be sent, together with the objections, to the other House, by which it shall likewise be reconsidered, and if approved by two thirds of that House, it shall become a law. But in all such cases the votes of both Houses shall be determined by yeas and nays, and the names of the persons voting for and against the bill shall be entered on the journal of each house, respectively. If any bill shall not be returned by the President within ten days (Sundays excepted) after it shall have been presented to him, the same shall be a law, in like manner as if he had signed it, unless the Congress by their adjournment prevent its return, in which case it shall not be a law.

[**Concurrent orders or resolutions, to be passed by President.—3.**] Every order, resolution, or vote to which the concurrence of the Senate and House of Representatives may be necessary (except on a question of adjournment) shall be presented to the President of the United States; and before the same shall take effect, shall be approved by him, or being disapproved by him, shall be repassed by two thirds of the Senate and House of Representatives, according to the rules and limitations prescribed in the case of a bill.

## Section 8

[**General powers of Congress.[4]**]
[**Taxes, duties, imposts, and excises.—1.**] The Congress shall have power to lay and collect taxes, duties, imposts and excises, to pay the debts and provide for the common defense and general welfare of the United States; but all duties, imposts and excises shall be uniform throughout the United States;

[**Borrowing of money.—2.**] To borrow money on the credit of the United States;

[**Regulation of commerce.—3.**] To regulate commerce with foreign nations, and among the several States, and with the Indian tribes;

[**Naturalization and bankruptcy.—4.**] To establish a uniform rule of naturalization, and uniform laws on the subject of bankruptcies throughout the United States;

[**Money, weights and measures.—5.**] To coin money, regulate the value thereof, and of foreign coin, and fix the standard of weights and measures;

[**Counterfeiting.—6.**] To provide for the punishment of counterfeiting the securities and current coin of the United States;

[**Post offices.—7.**] To establish post offices and post roads;

[**Patents and copyrights.—8.**] To promote the

progress of science and useful arts, by securing for limited times to authors and inventors the exclusive right to their respective writings and discoveries;

[Inferior courts.—9.] To constitute tribunals inferior to the Supreme Court;

[Piracies and felonies.—10.] To define and punish piracies and felonies committed on the high seas, and offences against the law of nations;

[War; marque and reprisal.—11.] To declare war, grant letters of marque and reprisal, and make rules concerning captures on land and water;

[Armies.—12.] To raise and support armies, but no appropriation of money to that use shall be for a longer term than two years;

[Navy.—13.] To provide and maintain a navy;

[Land and naval forces.—14.] To make rules for the government and regulation of the land and naval forces;

[Calling out militia.—15.] To provide for calling forth the militia to execute the laws of the Union, suppress insurrections, and repel invasions.

[Organizing, arming, and disciplining militia.—16.] To provide for organizing, arming, and disciplining, the militia, and for governing such part of them as may be employed in the service of the United States, reserving to the States, respectively, the appointment of the officers, and the authority of training the militia according to the discipline prescribed by Congress;

[Exclusive legislation over District of Columbia.—17.] To exercise exclusive legislation in all cases whatsoever, over such district (not exceeding ten miles square) as may, by cession of particular States, and the acceptance of Congress, become the seat of the Government of the United States, and to exercise like authority over all places purchased by the consent of the Legislature of the State in which the same shall be, for the erection of forts, magazines, arsenals, dock-yards, and other needful buildings;—And

[To enact laws necessary to enforce Constitution.—18.] To make all laws which shall be necessary and proper for carrying into execution the foregoing powers, and all other powers vested by this Constitution in the Government of the United States, or in any department or officer thereof.

## Section 9

[Migration or importation of certain persons not to be prohibited before 1808.—1.] The migration or importation of such persons as any of the States now existing shall think proper to admit, shall not be prohibited by the Congress prior to the year one thousand eight hundred and eight, but a tax or duty may be imposed on such importation, not exceeding ten dollars for each person.

[Writ of habeas corpus not to be suspended; exception.—2.] The privilege of the writ of habeas corpus shall not be suspended, unless when in cases of rebellion or invasion the public safety may require it.

[Bills of attainder and ex post facto laws prohibited.—3.] No bill of attainder or ex post facto law shall be passed.

[Capitation and other direct taxes.—4.] No capitation, or other direct, tax shall be laid, unless in proportion to the census or enumeration herein before directed to be taken.[5]

[Exports not to be taxed.—5.] No tax or duty shall be laid on articles exported from any State.

[No preference to be given to ports of any States; interstate shipping.—6.] No preference shall be given by any regulation of commerce or revenue to the ports of one State over those of another: nor shall vessels bound to, or from, one State, be obliged to enter, clear, or pay duties in another.

[Money, how drawn from treasury; financial statements to be published.—7.] No money shall be drawn from the Treasury, but in consequence of appropriations made by law; and a regular statement and account of the receipts and expenditures of all public money shall be published from time to time.

[Titles of nobility not to be granted; acceptance by government officers of favors from foreign powers.—8.] No title of nobility shall be granted by the United States: and no person holding any office of profit or trust under them, shall, without the consent of the Congress, accept of any present, emolument, office, or title, of any kind whatever, from any king, prince, or foreign state.

## Section 10

[Limitations of the powers of the several States.—1.] No State shall enter into any treaty, alliance, or confederation; grant letters of marque and reprisal; coin money; emit bills of credit; make any thing but gold and silver coin a tender in payment of debts; pass any bill of attainder, ex post facto law, or law impairing the obligation of contracts, or grant any title of nobility.

[State imposts and duties.—2.] No State shall, without the consent of the Congress, lay any imposts or duties on imports or exports, except what may be absolutely necessary for executing its inspection laws; and the net produce of all duties and imposts, laid by any State on imports or exports, shall be for the use of the Treasury of the United States; and all such laws shall be subject to the revision and control of the Congress.

[Further restrictions on powers of States.—3.] No State shall, without the consent of Congress, lay any duty of tonnage, keep troops, or ships of war in time of peace, enter into any agreement or compact with another state, or with a foreign power, or engage in war, unless actually invaded, or in such imminent danger as will not admit of delay.

# Article II

## Section 1

[The President; the executive power.—1.] The executive power shall be vested in a President of the United States of America. He shall hold his office during the term of four years, and, together with the Vice President, chosen for the same term, be elected, as follows

[Appointment and qualifications of presidential electors.—2.] Each State shall appoint, in such manner as the Legislature thereof may direct, a number of electors, equal to the whole number of Senators and Representatives to which the State may be entitled in the Congress: but no Senator or Representative, or person holding an office of trust or profit under the United States, shall be appointed an elector.

[Original method of electing the President and Vice President.[6]] (The electors shall meet in their respective States, and vote by ballot for two persons, of whom one at least shall not be an inhabitant of the same State with themselves. And they shall make a list of all the persons voted for, and of the number of votes for each; which list they shall sign and certify, and transmit sealed to the seat of the Government of the United States, directed to the

President of the Senate. The President of the Senate shall, in the presence of the Senate and House of Representatives, open all the certificates, and the votes shall then be counted. The person having the greatest number of votes shall be the President, if such number be a majority of the whole number of electors appointed; and if there be more than one who have such majority, and have an equal number of votes, then the House of Representatives shall immediately choose by ballot one of them for President; and if no person have a majority, then from the five highest on the list the said House shall in like manner choose the President. But in choosing the President, the votes shall be taken by States, the representation from each State having one vote; A quorum for this purpose shall consist of a member or members from two thirds of the States, and a majority of all the states shall be necessary to a choice. In every case, after the choice of the President, the person having the greatest number of votes of the electors shall be the Vice President. But if there should remain two or more who have equal votes, the Senate should choose from them by ballot the Vice President.)

[**Congress may determine time of choosing electors and day for casting their votes.—3.**] The Congress may determine the time of choosing the electors, and the day on which they shall give their votes; which day shall be the same throughout the United States.

[**Qualifications for the office of President.**[7]**—4.**] No person except a natural born citizen, or a citizen of the United States, at the time of the adoption of this Constitution, shall be eligible to the office of President; neither shall any person be eligible to that office who shall not have attained to the age of thirty-five years, and been fourteen years a resident within the United States.

[**Filling vacancy in the office of President.**[8]**—5.**] In case of the removal of the President from office, or of his death, resignation, or inability to discharge the powers and duties of the said office, the same shall devolve on the Vice President, and the Congress may by law provide for the case of removal, death, resignation or inability, both of the President and Vice President, declaring what officer shall then act as President, and such officer shall act accordingly, until the disability be removed, or a President shall be elected.

[**Compensation of the President.—6.**] The President shall, at stated times, receive for his services, a compensation, which shall neither be increased nor diminished during the period for which he shall have been elected, and he shall not receive within that period any other emolument from the United States, or any of them.

[**Oath to be taken by the President.—7.**] Before he enter on the execution of his office, he shall take the following oath or affirmation:—"I do solemnly swear (or affirm) that I will faithfully execute the office of President of the United States, and will to the best of my ability, preserve, protect, and defend the Constitution of the United States."

### Section 2

[**The President to be commander in chief of army and navy and head of executive departments; may grant reprieves and pardons.—1.**] The President shall be Commander in Chief of the Army and Navy of the United States, and of the militia of the several States, when called into the actual service of the United States; he may require the opinion, in writing, of the principal officer in each of the executive departments, upon any subject relating to

the duties of their respective offices, and he shall have power to grant reprieves and pardons for offences against the United States, except in cases of impeachment.

[**President may, with concurrence of Senate, make treaties, appoint ambassadors, etc.; appointment of inferior officers, authority of Congress over.—2.**] He shall have power, by and with the advice and consent of the Senate, to make treaties, provided two thirds of the Senators present concur; and he shall nominate, and by and with the advice and consent of the Senate, shall appoint ambassadors, other public ministers and consuls, judges of the Supreme Court, and all other officers of the United States, whose appointments are not herein otherwise provided for, and which shall be established by law: but the Congress may by law vest the appointment of such inferior officers, as they think proper, in the President alone, in the courts of law, or in the heads of departments.

[**President may fill vacancies in office during recess of Senate.—3.**] The President shall have power to fill up all vacancies that may happen during the recess of the Senate, by granting commissions which shall expire at the end of their session.

### Section 3

[**President to give advice to Congress; may convene or adjourn it on certain occasions; to receive ambassadors, etc.; have laws executed and commission all officers.**] He shall from time to time give to the Congress information of the state of the Union, and recommend to their consideration such measures as he shall judge necessary and expedient; he may, on extraordinary occasions, convene both Houses, or either of them, and in case of disagreement between them, with respect to the time of adjournment, he may adjourn them to such time as he shall think proper; he shall receive ambassadors and other public ministers: he shall take care that the laws be faithfully executed, and shall commission all the officers of the United States.

### Section 4

[**All civil officers removable by impeachment.**] The President, Vice President, and all civil officers of the United States shall be removed from office on impeachment for, and conviction of, treason, bribery, or other high crimes and misdemeanors.

# Article III

### Section 1

[**Judicial powers; how vested; term of office and compensation of judges.**] The judicial Power of the United States, shall be vested in one Supreme Court, and in such inferior courts as the Congress may from time to time ordain and establish. The judges, both of the supreme and inferior courts, shall hold their offices during good behavior, and shall, at stated times, receive for their services, a compensation, which shall not be diminished during their continuance in office.

### Section 2

[**Jurisdiction of Federal courts.**[9]**—1.**] The judicial power shall extend to all cases, in law and equity, arising under this Constitution, the laws of the United States, and treaties made, or which shall be made, under their authority; to all cases affecting ambassadors, other public ministers and consuls; to all cases of admiralty and maritime jurisdiction; to controversies to which the United States, shall be a party; to controversies between two or more States; between a State and citizens of another State; between citizens of different States; between citizens of the same State claiming lands under grants of different states, and between a State, or the citizens thereof, and foreign states, citizens, or subjects.

[**Original and appellate jurisdiction of Supreme Court.—2.**] In all cases affecting ambassadors, other public ministers and consuls, and those in which a State shall be party, the Supreme Court shall have original jurisdiction. In all the other cases before mentioned, the Supreme Court shall have appellate jurisdiction, both as to law and fact, with such exceptions, and under such regulations, as the Congress shall make.

[**Trial of all crimes, except impeachment, to be by jury.—3.**] The trial of all crimes, except in cases of impeachment, shall be by jury; and such trial shall be held in the State where the said crimes shall have been committed; but when not committed within any State, the trial shall be at such place or places as the Congress may by law have directed.

### Section 3

[**Treason defined; conviction of.—1.**] Treason against the United States, shall consist only in levying war against them, or, in adhering to their enemies, giving them aid and comfort. No person shall be convicted of treason unless on the testimony of two witnesses to the same overt act, or on confession in open court.

[**Congress to declare punishment for treason; proviso.—2.**] The Congress shall have power to declare the punishment of treason, but no attainder of treason shall work corruption of blood, or forfeiture except during the life of the person attained.

## Article IV

### Section 1

[**Each State to give full faith and credit to the public acts and records of other States.**] Full faith and credit shall be given in each State to the public acts, records, and judicial proceedings of every other State. And the Congress may by general laws prescribe the manner in which such acts, records, and proceedings shall be proved, and the effect thereof.

### Section 2

[**Privileges of citizens.—1.**] The citizens of each State shall be entitled to all privileges and immunities of citizens in the several States.

[**Extradition between the several States.—2.**] A person charged in any State with treason, felony, or other crime, who shall flee from justice, and be found in another State, shall on demand of the Executive authority of the State from which he fled, be delivered up, to be removed to the State having jurisdiction of the crime.

[**Persons held to labor or service in one State, fleeing to another, to be returned.—3.**] No person held to service or labor in one State, under the laws thereof, escaping into another, shall, in conse-

quence of any law or regulation therein, be discharged from such service or labor, but shall be delivered up on claim of the party to whom such service or labor may be due.

### Section 3

[**New States.—1.**] New States may be admitted by the Congress into this Union; but no new State shall be formed or erected within the jurisdiction of any other State; nor any State be formed by the junction of two or more States, or parts of States, without the consent of the Legislatures of the States concerned as well as of the Congress.

[**Regulations concerning territory.—2.**] The Congress shall have power to dispose of and make all needful rules and regulations respecting the territory or other property belonging to the United States; and nothing in this Constitution shall be so construed as to prejudice any claims of the United States, or of any particular State.

### Section 4

[**Republican form of government and protection guaranteed the several States.**] The United States shall guarantee to every State in this Union a Republican form of government, and shall protect each of them against invasion; and on application of the Legislature, or of the Executive (when the Legislature cannot be convened) against domestic violence.

## Article V

[**Ways in which the Constitution can be amended.**] The Congress, whenever two thirds of both Houses shall deem it necessary, shall propose amendments to this Constitution, or, on the application of the Legislatures of two thirds of the several States shall call a convention for proposing amendments, which, in either case, shall be valid to all intents and purposes, as part of this Constitution, when ratified by the Legislatures of three fourths of the several States, or by conventions in three fourths thereof, as the one or the other mode of ratification may be proposed by the Congress; provided that no amendment which may be made prior to the year one thousand eight hundred and eight shall in any manner affect the first and fourth clauses in the ninth Section of the first Article; and that no State, without its consent, shall be deprived of its equal suffrage in the Senate.

## Article VI

[**Debts contracted under the confederation secured.—1.**] All debts contracted and engagements entered into, before the adoption of this Constitution, shall be as valid against the United States under this Constitution, as under the Confederation.

[**Constitution, laws, and treaties of the United States to be supreme.—2.**] This Constitution, and the laws of the United States which shall be made in pursuance thereof; and all treaties made, or which shall be made, under the authority of the United States, shall be the supreme law of the land; and the judges in every State shall be bound thereby, any thing in the Constitution or laws of

1. The clause included in parentheses is amended by the 14th Amendment, Section 2. 2. The first paragraph of this section and the part of the second paragraph included in parentheses are amended by the 17th Amendment. 3. Amended by the 20th Amendment, Section 2. 4. By the 16th Amendment, Congress is given the power to lay and collect taxes on income. 5. See the 16th Amendment. 6. This clause has been superseded by the 12th Amendment. 7. For qualifications of the Vice President, see 12th Amendment. 8. Amended by the 20th Amendment, Sections 3 and 4. 9. This section is abridged by the 11th Amendment. 10. See the 13th Amendment.

any State to the contrary notwithstanding.

**[Who shall take constitutional oath; no religious test as to official qualification.—3.]** The Senators and Representatives before mentioned, and the members of the several State Legislatures, and all executive and judicial officers, both of the United States and of the several States, shall be bound by oath or affirmation, to support this Constitution; but no religious test shall ever be required as a qualification to any office or public trust under the United States.

## Article VII

**[Constitution to be considered adopted when ratified by nine States.]** The ratification of the conventions of nine States shall be sufficient for the establishment of this Constitution between the States so ratifying the same.

Done in convention by the unanimous consent of the States present the seventeenth day of September in the year of our Lord one thousand seven hundred and eighty seven and of the independence of the United States of America the Twelfth. In witness whereof we have hereunto subscribed our names.

GEORGE WASHINGTON
*President and Deputy from Virginia*

**NEW HAMPSHIRE**

| | |
|---|---|
| John Langdon | Nicholas Gilman |

**MASSACHUSETTS**

| | |
|---|---|
| Nathaniel Gorham | Rufus King |

**CONNECTICUT**

| | |
|---|---|
| Wm. Saml. Johnson | Roger Sherman |

**NEW YORK**

Alexander Hamilton

**NEW JERSEY**

| | |
|---|---|
| Wil. Livingston | Wm. Paterson |
| David Brearley | Jona. Dayton |

**PENNSYLVANIA**

| | |
|---|---|
| B. Franklin | Thomas Mifflin |
| Robt. Morris | Geo. Clymer |
| Thos. FitzSimons | Jared Ingersoll |
| James Wilson | Gouv. Morris |

**DELAWARE**

| | |
|---|---|
| Geo. Read | Gunning Bedford Jun. |
| John Dickinson | Richard Bassett |
| Jaco. Broom | |

**MARYLAND**

| | |
|---|---|
| James McHenry | Dan. of St. Thos. Jenifer |
| Danl. Carroll | |

**VIRGINIA**

| | |
|---|---|
| John Blair | James Madison, Jr. |

**NORTH CAROLINA**

| | |
|---|---|
| Wm. Blount | Richd Dobbs Spaight |
| Hu. Williamson | |

**SOUTH CAROLINA**

| | |
|---|---|
| J. Rutledge | Charles Cotesworth |
| Charles Pinckney | Pinckney |
| | Pierce Butler |

**GEORGIA**

| | |
|---|---|
| William Few | Abr. Baldwin |

Attest: William Jackson, Secretary

# Amendments to the Constitution of the United States

(Amendments I to X inclusive, popularly known as the Bill of Rights, were proposed and sent to the states by the first session of the First Congress. They were ratified Dec. 15, 1791.)

## Article I

**[Freedom of religion, speech, of the press, and right of petition.]** Congress shall make no law respecting an establishment of religion, or prohibiting the free exercise thereof; or abridging the freedom of speech, or of the press; or the right of the people peaceably to assemble, and to petition the Government for a redress of grievances.

## Article II

**[Right of people to bear arms not to be infringed.]** A well regulated militia, being necessary to the security of a free State, the right of the people to keep and bear arms, shall not be infringed.

## Article III

**[Quartering of troops.]** No soldier shall, in time of peace be quartered in any house, without the consent of the owner, nor in time of war, but in a manner to be prescribed by law.

## Article IV

**[Persons and houses to be secure from unreasonable searches and seizures.]** The right of the people to be secure in their persons, houses, papers, and effects, against unreasonable searches and seizures, shall not be violated, and no warrants shall issue, but upon probable cause, supported by oath or affirmation, and particularly describing the place to be searched, and the persons or things to be seized.

## Article V

**[Trials for crimes; just compensation for private property taken for public use.]** No person shall be held to answer for a capital, or otherwise infamous crime, unless on a presentment or indictment of a Grand Jury, except in cases arising in the land or naval forces, or in the militia, when in actual service in time of war or public danger; nor shall any person be subject for the same offence to be twice put in jeopardy of life or limb; nor shall be compelled in any criminal case to be a witness, against himself, nor be deprived of life, liberty, or property, without due process of law; nor shall private property be taken for public use, without just compensation.

# 592 *U.S. Constitution*

## Article VI

[Civil rights in trials for crimes enumerated.] In all criminal prosecutions, the accused shall enjoy the right to a speedy and public trial, by an impartial jury of the State and district wherein the crime shall have been committed, which district shall have been previously ascertained by law, and to be informed of the nature and cause of the accusation; to be confronted with the witnesses against him; to have compulsory process for obtaining witnesses in his favor, and to have the assistance of counsel for his defense.

## Article VII

[Civil rights in civil suits.] In suits at common law, where the value in controversy shall exceed twenty dollars, the right of trial by jury shall be preserved, and no fact tried by a jury, shall be otherwise re-examined in any court of the United States, than according to the rules of the common law.

## Article VIII

[Excessive bail, fines, and punishments prohibited.] Excessive bail shall not be required, nor excessive fines imposed, nor cruel and unusual punishments inflicted.

## Article IX

[Reserved rights of people.] The enumeration in the Constitution, of certain rights, shall not be construed to deny or disparage others retained by the people.

## Article X

[Powers not delegated, reserved to states and people respectively.] The powers not delegated to the United States by the Constitution, nor prohibited by it to the States, are reserved to the States, respectively, or to the people.

## Article XI

(The proposed amendment was sent to the states Mar. 5, 1794, by the Third Congress. It was ratified Feb. 7, 1795.)

[Judicial power of United States not to extend to suits against a State.] The judicial power of the United States shall not be construed to extend to any suit in law or equity, commenced or prosecuted against one of the United States by citizens of another State, or by citizens or subjects of any foreign state.

## Article XII

(The proposed amendment was sent to the states Dec. 12, 1803, by the Eighth Congress. It was ratified July 27, 1804.)

[Present mode of electing President and Vice-President by electors.[1]] The electors shall meet in their respective states, and vote by ballot for President and Vice President, one of whom, at least, shall not be an inhabitant of the same state with themselves; they shall name in their ballots the person voted for as President, and in distinct ballots the person voted for as Vice President, and they shall make distinct lists of all persons voted for as President, and of all persons voted for as Vice President, and of the number of votes for each, which lists they shall sign and certify, and transmit sealed to the seat of the government of the United States, directed to the President of the Senate; the President of the Senate shall, in the presence of the Senate and House of Representatives, open all the certificates and the votes shall then be counted; the person having the greatest number of votes for President, shall be the President, if such number be a majority of the whole number of electors appointed; and if no person have such majority, then from the persons having the highest numbers not exceeding three on the list of those voted for as President, the House of Representatives shall choose immediately, by ballot, the President. But in choosing the President, the votes shall be taken by states, the representation from each State having one vote; a quorum for this purpose shall consist of a member or members from two thirds of the states, and a majority of all the states shall be necessary to a choice. And if the House of Representatives shall not choose a President whenever the right of choice shall devolve upon them, before the fourth day of March next following, then the Vice President shall act as President, as in the case of the death or other constitutional disability of the President. The person having the greatest number of votes as Vice President, shall be the Vice President, if such number be a majority of the whole number of electors appointed, and if no person have a majority, then from the two highest numbers on the list, the Senate shall choose the Vice President; a quorum for the purpose shall consist of two thirds of the whole number of Senators, and a majority of the whole number shall be necessary to a choice. But no person constitutionally ineligible to the office of President shall be eligible to that of Vice President of the United States.

## Article XIII

(The proposed amendment was sent to the states Feb. 1, 1865, by the Thirty-eighth Congress. It was ratified Dec. 6, 1865.)

### Section 1

[Slavery prohibited.] Neither slavery nor involuntary servitude, except as a punishment for crime whereof the party shall have been duly convicted, shall exist within the United States, or any place subject to their jurisdiction.

### Section 2

[Congress given power to enforce this article.] Congress shall have power to enforce this article by appropriate legislation.

## Article XIV

(The proposed amendment was sent to the states June 16, 1866, by the Thirty-ninth Congress. It was ratified July 9, 1868.)

### Section 1

[Citizenship defined; privileges of citizens.] All persons born or naturalized in the United States, and subject to the jurisdiction thereof, are citizens of the United States and of the State wherein they reside. No State shall make or enforce any law which shall abridge the privileges or immunities of citizens of the United States; nor shall any State deprive any person of life, liberty, or property, without due process of law; nor deny to any person within its jurisdiction the equal protection of the laws.

## Section 2

[Apportionment of Representatives.] Representatives shall be apportioned among the several States according to their respective numbers, counting the whole number of persons in each State, excluding Indians not taxed. But when the right to vote at any election for the choice of electors for President and Vice President of the United States, Representatives in Congress, the executive and judicial officers of a State, or the members of the Legislature thereof, is denied to any of the male inhabitants of such State, being twenty-one years of age, and citizens of the United States, or in any way abridged, except for participation in rebellion, or other crime, the basis of representation therein shall be reduced in the proportion which the number of such male citizens shall bear to the whole number of male citizens twenty-one years of age in such State.

## Section 3

[Disqualification for office; removal of disability.] No person shall be a Senator or Representative in Congress, or elector of President and Vice President, or hold any office, civil or military, under the United States, or under any State, who, having previously taken an oath, as a member of Congress, or as an officer of the United States, or as a member of any State Legislature, or as an executive or judicial officer of any State, to support the Constitution of the United States, shall have engaged in insurrection or rebellion against the same, or given aid or comfort to the enemies thereof. But Congress may be a vote of two thirds of each House, remove such disability.

## Section 4

[Public debt not to be questioned; payment of debts and claims incurred in aid of rebellion forbidden.] The validity of the public debt of the United States, authorized by law, including debts incurred for payment of pensions and bounties for services in suppressing insurrection or rebellion, shall not be questioned. But neither the United States nor any State shall assume or pay any debt or obligation incurred in aid of insurrection or rebellion against the United States, or any claim for the loss or emancipation of any slave; but all such debts, obligations, and claims shall be held illegal and void.

## Section 5

[Congress given power to enforce this article.] The Congress shall have power to enforce, by appropriate legislation, the provisions of this article.

# Article XV

(The proposed amendment was sent to the states Feb. 27, 1869, by the Fortieth Congress. It was ratified Feb. 3, 1870.)

## Section 1

[Right of certain citizens to vote established.] The right of citizens of the United States to vote shall not be denied or abridged by the United States or by any State on account of race, color, or previous condition of servitude.

## Section 2

[Congress given power to enforce this article.] The Congress shall have power to enforce this article by appropriate legislation.

# Article XVI

(The proposed amendment was sent to the states July 12, 1909, by the Sixty-first Congress. It was ratified Feb. 3, 1913.)

[Taxes on income; Congress given power to lay and collect.] The Congress shall have power to lay and collect taxes on incomes, from whatever source derived, without apportionment among the several States, and without regard to any census or enumeration.

# Article XVII

(The proposed amendment was sent to the states May 16, 1912, by the Sixty-second Congress. It was ratified April 8, 1913.)

[Election of United States Senators; filling of vacancies; qualifications of electors.]

The Senate of the United States shall be composed of two Senators from each State, elected by the people thereof, for six years; and each Senator shall have one vote. The electors in each State shall have the qualifications requisite for electors of the most numerous branch of the State Legislatures.

When vacancies happen in the representation of any State in the Senate, the executive authority of such State shall issue writs of election to fill such vacancies: Provided, that the legislature of any State may empower the executive thereof to make temporary appointment until the people fill the vacancies by election as the legislature may direct.

This amendment shall not be so construed as to affect the election or term of any Senator chosen before it becomes valid as part of the Constitution.

# Article XVIII[2]

(The proposed amendment was sent to the states Dec. 18, 1917, by the Sixty-fifth Congress. It was ratified by three quarters of the states by Jan. 16, 1919, and became effective Jan. 16, 1920.)

## Section 1

[Manufacture, sale, or transportation of intoxicating liquors, for beverage purposes, prohibited.] After one year from the ratification of this article the manufacture, sale, or transportation of intoxicating liquors within, the importation thereof into, or the exportation thereof from the United States and all territory subject to the jurisdiction thereof for beverage purposes is hereby prohibited.

## Section 2

[Congress and the several States given concurrent power to pass appropriate legislation to enforce this article.] The Congress and the several States shall have concurrent power to enforce this article by appropriate legislation.

## Section 3

[Provisions of article to become operative, when adopted by three fourths of the States.] This article shall be inoperative unless it shall have been ratified as an amendment to the Constitution by the legislatures of the several States, as provided in the Constitution, within seven years from the date of the submission hereof to the States by Congress.

# Article XIX

(The proposed amendment was sent to the states June 4, 1919, by the Sixty-sixth Congress. It was ratified Aug. 18, 1920.)

[**The right of citizens to vote shall not be denied because of sex.**] The right of citizens of the United States to vote shall not be denied or abridged by the United States or by any State on account of sex.

[**Congress given power to enforce this article.**] Congress shall have power to enforce this article by appropriate legislation.

## Article XX

(The proposed amendment, sometimes called the "Lame Duck Amendment," was sent to the states Mar. 3, 1932, by the Seventy-second Congress. It was ratified Jan. 23, 1933; but, in accordance with Section 5, Sections 1 and 2 did not go into effect until Oct. 15, 1933.)

### Section 1

[**Terms of President, Vice President, Senators, and Representatives.**] The terms of the President and Vice President shall end at noon on the twentieth day of January, and the terms of Senators and Representatives at noon on the third day of January, of the years in which such terms would have ended if this article had not been ratified; and the terms of their successors shall then begin.

### Section 2

[**Time of assembling Congress.**] The Congress shall assemble at least once in every year, and such meeting shall begin at noon on the third day of January, unless they shall by law appoint a different day.

### Section 3

[**Filling vacancy in office of President.**] If, at the time fixed for the beginning of the term of the President, the President-elect shall have died, the Vice President-elect shall become President. If a President shall not have been chosen before the time fixed for the beginning of his term, or if the President-elect shall have failed to qualify, then the Vice President shall have qualified; and the Congress may by law provide for the case wherein neither a President-elect nor a Vice President-elect shall have qualified, declaring who shall then act as President, or the manner in which one who is to act shall be selected, and such person shall act accordingly until a President or Vice President shall have qualified.

### Section 4

[**Power of Congress in Presidential succession.**] The Congress may by law provide for the case of the death of any of the persons from whom the House of Representatives may choose a President whenever the right of choice shall have devolved upon them, and for the case of the death of any of the persons from whom the Senate may choose a Vice President whenever the right of choice shall have devolved upon them.

### Section 5

[**Time of taking effect.**] Sections 1 and 2 shall take effect on the 15th day of October following the ratification of this article.

### Section 6

[**Ratification.**] This article shall be inoperative unless it shall have been ratified as an amendment to the Constitution by the legislatures of three fourths of the several States within seven years from the date of its submission.

## Article XXI

(The proposed amendment was sent to the states Feb. 20, 1933, by the Seventy-second Congress. It was ratified Dec. 5, 1933.)

### Section 1

[**Repeal of Prohibition Amendment.**] The eighteenth article of amendment to the Constitution of the United States is hereby repealed.

### Section 2

[**Transportation of intoxicating liquors.**] The transportation or importation into any State, territory, or possession of the United States for delivery or use therein of intoxicating liquors, in violation of the laws thereof, is hereby prohibited.

### Section 3

[**Ratification.**] This article shall be inoperative unless it shall have been ratified as an amendment to the Constitution by convention in the several States, as provided in the Constitution, within seven years from the date of the submission thereof to the States by the Congress.

## Article XXII

(The proposed amendment was sent to the states Mar. 21, 1947, by the Eightieth Congress. It was ratified Feb. 27, 1951.)

### Section 1

[**Limit to number of terms a President may serve.**] No person shall be elected to the office of the President more than twice, and no person who has held the office of President, or acted as President, for more than two years of a term to which some other person was elected President shall be elected to the office of the President more than once. But this article shall not apply to any person holding the office of President when this article was proposed by the Congress, and shall not prevent any person who may be holding the office of President, or acting as President, during the term within which this article becomes operative from holding the office of President or acting as President during the remainder of such term.

### Section 2

[**Ratification.**] This article shall be inoperative unless it shall have been ratified as an amendment to the Constitution by the legislatures of three fourths of the several States within seven years from the date of its submission to the States by the Congress.

## Article XXIII

(The proposed amendment was sent to the states June 16, 1960, by the Eighty-sixth Congress. It was ratified March 29, 1961.)

### Section 1

[**Electors for the District of Columbia.**] The District constituting the seat of Government of the United States shall appoint in such manner as the Congress may direct:

A number of electors of President and Vice President equal to the whole number of Senators and Representatives in Congress to which the District would be entitled if it were a State, but in no event more than the least populous State; they shall be in addition to those appointed by the States, but they shall be considered, for the purposes of the election of President and Vice President, to be electors appointed by a State; and they shall meet in the District and perform such duties as provided by the twelfth article of amendment.

### Section 2

[Congress given power to enforce this article.] The Congress shall have the power to enforce this article by appropriate legislation.

## Article XXIV

(The proposed amendment was sent to the states Aug. 27, 1962, by the Eighty-seventh Congress. It was ratified Jan. 23, 1964.)

### Section 1

[Payment of poll tax or other taxes not to be prerequisite for voting in federal elections.] The right of citizens of the United States to vote in any primary or other election for President or Vice President, for electors for President or Vice President, or for Senator or Representative in Congress, shall not be denied or abridged by the United States or any State by reasons of failure to pay any poll tax or other tax.

### Section 2

[Congress given power to enforce this article.] The Congress shall have the power to enforce this article by appropriate legislation.

## Article XXV

(The proposed amendment was sent to the states July 6, 1965, by the Eighty-ninth Congress. It was ratified Feb. 10, 1967.)

### Section 1

[Succession of Vice President to Presidency.] In case of the removal of the President from office or of his death or resignation, the Vice President shall become President.

### Section 2

[Vacancy in office of Vice President.] Whenever there is a vacancy in the office of the Vice President, the President shall nominate a Vice President who shall take office upon confirmation by a majority vote of both Houses of Congress.

### Section 3

[Vice President as Acting President.] Whenever the President transmits to the President pro tempore of the Senate and the Speaker of the House of Representatives his written declaration that he is unable to discharge the powers and duties of his office, and until he transmits to them a written declaration to the contrary, such powers and duties shall be discharged by the Vice President as Acting President.

### Section 4

[Vice President as Acting President.] Whenever the Vice President and a majority of either the principal officers of the executive departments or of such other body as Congress may by law provide, transmit to the President pro tempore of the Senate and the Speaker of the House of Representatives their written declaration that the President is unable to discharge the powers and duties of his office, the Vice President shall immediately assume the powers and duties of the office as Acting President.

. Thereafter, when the President transmits to the President pro tempore of the Senate and the Speaker of the House of Representatives his written declaration that no inability exists, he shall resume the powers and duties of his office unless the Vice President and a majority of either the principal officers of the executive department or of such other body as Congress may by law provide, transmit within four days to the President pro tempore of the Senate and the Speaker of the House of Representatives their written declaration that the President is unable to discharge the powers and duties of his office. Thereupon Congress shall decide the issue, assembling within forty-eight hours for that purpose if not in session. If the Congress, within twenty-one days after receipt of the latter written declaration, or, if Congress is not in session, within twenty-one days after Congress is required to assemble, determines by two thirds vote of both Houses that the President is unable to discharge the powers and duties of his office, the Vice President shall continue to discharge the same as Acting President; otherwise, the President shall resume the powers and duties of his office.

## Article XXVI

(The proposed amendment was sent to the states Mar. 23, 1971, by the Ninety-second Congress. It was ratified July 1, 1971.)

### Section 1

[Voting for 18-year-olds.] The right of citizens of the United States, who are 18 years of age or older, to vote shall not be denied or abridged by the United States or by any state on account of age.

### Section 2

[Congress given power to enforce this article.] The Congress shall have power to enforce this article by appropriate legislation.

1. Amended by the 20th Amendment, Sections 3 and 4. 2. Repealed by the 21st Amendment.

# The White House

*Source:* Department of the Interior, U.S. National Park Service.

The White House, the official residence of the President, is at 1600 Pennsylvania Avenue in Washington, D.C. The site, covering about 18 acres, was selected by President Washington and Pierre Charles L'Enfant, and the architect was James Hoban. The design of the residence is said to have been suggested by the Duke of Leinster's house in Ireland. The cornerstone was laid Oct. 13, 1792, and the first residents were President and Mrs. John Adams in November 1800. The building was fired by the British in 1814.

From December 1948 to March 1952, the interior of the White House was rebuilt, and the outer walls were strengthened.

The rooms for public functions are on the first floor; the second and third floors are used as the residence of the President and First Family. The most celebrated public room is the East Room, where formal receptions take place. Other public rooms are the Red Room, the Green Room, and the Blue Room. The State Dining Room is used for formal dinners. There are 132 rooms.

# The Mayflower Compact

On Sept. 6, 1620, the _Mayflower,_ a sailing vessel of about 180 tons, started her memorable voyage from Plymouth, England, with about 100[1] pilgrims aboard, bound for Virginia to establish a private permanent colony in North America. Arriving at what is now Provincetown, Mass., on Nov. 11 (Nov. 21, new style calendar), 41 of the passengers signed the famous "Mayflower Compact" as the boat lay at anchor in that Cape Cod harbor. A small detail of the pilgrims, led by William Bradford, assigned to select a place for permanent settlement landed at what is now Plymouth, Mass., on Dec. 21 (n.s.).

The text of the compact follows:

In the name of God, Amen. We, whose names are underwritten, the Loyal Subjects of our dread Sovereign Lord, King _James,_ by the Grace of God, of _Great Britain, France and Ireland,_ King, _Defender of the Faith, &_
Having undertaken for the Glory of God, and Advancement of the Christian Faith, and the Honour of our King and Country, a voyage to plant the first colony in the northern Parts of Virginia; do by these Presents, solemnly and mutually in the Presence of God and one of another, covenant and combine ourselves together into a civil Body Politick, for our better Ordering and Preservation, and Furtherance of the Ends aforesaid; And by Virtue hereof to enact, constitute, and frame, such just and equal Laws, Ordinances, Acts, Constitutions and Offices, from time to time, as shall be thought most meet and convenient for the General good of the Colony; unto which we promise all due Submission and Obedience.
In Witness whereof we have hereunto subscribed our names at _Cape Cod_ the eleventh of _November,_ in the Reign of our Sovereign Lord, King _James_ of _England, France_ and _Ireland,_ the eighteenth, and of _Scotland_ the fifty-fourth. _Anno Domini,_ 1620

| | | | |
|---|---|---|---|
| John Carver | William Mullins | John Billington | Peter Brown |
| Digery Priest | Thomas English | Thomas Tinker | John Turner |
| William Brewster | John Howland | Samuel Fuller | Edward Tilly |
| Edmund Margesson | Stephen Hopkins | Richard Clark | John Craxton |
| John Alden | Edward Winslow | John Allerton | Thomas Rogers |
| George Soule | Gilbert Winslow | Richard Warren | John Goodman |
| James Chilton | Miles Standish | Edward Liester | Edward Fuller |
| Francis Cooke | Richard Bitteridge | William Bradford | Richard Gardiner |
| Moses Fletcher | Francis Eaton | Thomas Williams | William White |
| John Ridgate | John Tilly | Isaac Allerton | Edward Doten |
| Christopher Martin | | | |

1. Historians differ as to whether 100, 101, or 102 passengers were aboard.

# The Monroe Doctrine

The Monroe Doctrine was announced in President James Monroe's message to Congress, during his second term on Dec. 2, 1823, in part as follows:

"In the discussions to which this interest has given rise, and in the arrangements by which they may terminate, the occasion has been deemed proper for asserting as a principle in which rights and interests of the United States are involved, that the American continents, by the free and independent condition which they have assumed and maintain, are henceforth not to be considered as subjects for future colonization by any European power. . . . We owe it, therefore, to candor and to the amicable relations existing between the United States and those powers to declare that we should consider any attempt on their part to extend their system to any portion of this hemisphere as dangerous to our peace and safety. With the existing colonies or dependencies of any European power we have not interfered and shall not interfere. But with the governments who have declared their independence and maintain it, and whose independence we have, on great consideration and on just principles, acknowledged, we could not view any interposition for the purpose of oppressing them or controlling in any other manner their destiny by any European power in any other light than as the manifestation of an unfriendly disposition toward the United States."

# Order of Presidential Succession

1. The Vice President
2. Speaker of the House
3. President pro tempore of the Senate
4. Secretary of State
5. Secretary of the Treasury
6. Secretary of Defense
7. Attorney General
8. Secretary of the Interior
9. Secretary of Agriculture
10. Secretary of Commerce
11. Secretary of Labor
12. Secretary of Health and Human Services
13. Secretary of Housing and Urban Development
14. Secretary of Transportation
15. Secretary of Energy
16. Secretary of Education

NOTE: An official cannot succeed to the Presidency unless that person meets the Constitutional requirements.

# The Star-Spangled Banner

*Francis Scott Key, 1814*

O say, can you see, by the dawn's early light,
What so proudly we hail'd at the twilight's last gleaming?
Whose broad stripes and bright stars, thro' the perilous fight,
O'er the ramparts we watch'd, were so gallantly streaming?
And the rockets' red glare, the bombs bursting in air,
Gave proof thro' the night that our flag was still there.
O say, does that star-spangled banner yet wave
O'er the land of the free and the home of the brave?

On the shore dimly seen thro' the mists of the deep,
Where the foe's haughty host in dread silence reposes,
What is that which the breeze, o'er the towering steep,
As it fitfully blows, half conceals, half discloses?
Now it catches the gleam of the morning's first beam,
In full glory reflected, now shines on the stream:
'T is the star-spangled banner: O, long may it wave
O'er the land of the free and the home of the brave!

And where is that band who so vauntingly swore
That the havoc of war and the battle's confusion,
A home and a country should leave us no more?
Their blood has wash'd out their foul footsteps' pollution.
No refuge could save the hireling and slave
From the terror of flight or the gloom of the grave:
And the star-spangled banner in triumph doth wave
O'er the land of the free and the home of the brave.

O thus be it ever when free-men shall stand
Between their lov'd home and the war's desolation;
Blest with vict'ry and peace, may the heav'n-rescued land
Praise the Pow'r that hath made and preserv'd us a nation!
Then conquer we must, when our cause it is just,
And this be our motto: "In God is our trust!"
And the star-spangled banner in triumph shall wave
O'er the land of the free and the home of the brave!

On Sept. 13, 1814, Francis Scott Key visited the British fleet in Chesapeake Bay to secure the release of Dr. William Beanes, who had been captured after the burning of Washington, D.C. The release was secured, but Key was detained on ship overnight during the shelling of Fort McHenry, one of the forts defending Baltimore. In the morning, he was so delighted to see the American flag still flying over the fort that he began a poem to commemorate the occasion. First published under the title "Defense of Fort M'Henry," and later as "The Star-Spangled Banner," the poem soon attained wide popularity as sung to the tune "To Anacreon in Heaven." The origin of this tune is obscure, but it may have been written by John Stafford Smith, a British composer born in 1750. "The Star-Spangled Banner" was officially made the National Anthem by Congress in 1931, although it had been already adopted as such by the Army and the Navy.

# The Emancipation Proclamation

## January 1, 1863

By the President of the United States of America:

A Proclamation.
Whereas on the 22d day of September, A.D. 1862, a proclamation was issued by the President of the United States, containing, among other things, the following, to wit:
"That on the 1st day of January, A.D. 1863, all persons held as slaves within any State or designated part of a State the people whereof shall then be in rebellion against the United States shall be then, thenceforward, and forever free; and the executive government of the United States, including the military and naval authority thereof, will recognize and maintain the freedom of such persons, or will do not act or acts to repress such persons, or

any of them, in any efforts they may make for their actual freedom.
"That the executive will on the 1st day of January aforesaid, by proclamation, designate the States and parts of States, if any, in which the people thereof, respectively, shall then be in rebellion against the United States; and the fact that any State or the people thereof shall on that day be in good faith represented in the Congress of the United States by members chosen thereto at elections wherein a majority of the qualified voters of such States shall have participated shall, in the absence of strong countervailing testimony, be deemed conclusive evidence that such State and the people thereof are not then in rebellion against the United States."
Now, therefore, I, Abraham Lincoln, President

of the United States, by virtue of the power in me vested as Commander-in-Chief of the Army and Navy of the United States in time of actual armed rebellion against the authority and government of the United States, and as a fit and necessary war measure for suppressing said rebellion, do, on this 1st day of January, A.D. 1863, and in accordance with my purpose so to do, publicly proclaimed for the full period of one hundred days from the first day above mentioned, order and designate as the States and parts of States wherein the people thereof, respectively, are this day in rebellion against the United States the following, to wit:

Arkansas, Texas, Louisiana (except the parishes of St. Bernard, Plaquemines, Jefferson, St. John, St. Charles, St. James, Ascension, Assumption, Terrebonne, Lafourche, St. Mary, St. Martin, and Orleans, including the city of New Orleans), Mississippi, Alabama, Florida, Georgia, South Carolina, North Carolina, and Virginia (except the forty-eight counties designated as West Virginia, and also the counties of Berkeley, Accomac, Northhampton, Elizabeth City, York, Princess Anne, and Norfolk, including the cities of Norfolk and Portsmouth), and which excepted parts are for the present left precisely as if this proclamation were not issued.

And by virtue of the power and for the purpose aforesaid, I do order and declare that all persons held as slaves within said designated States and parts of States are, and henceforward shall be, free; and that the Executive Government of the United States, including the military and naval authorities thereof, will recognize and maintain the freedom of said persons.

And I hereby enjoin upon the people so declared to be free to abstain from all violence, unless in necessary self-defense; and I recommend to them that, in all cases when allowed, they labor faithfully for reasonable wages.

And I further declare and make known that such persons of suitable condition will be received into the armed service of the United States to garrison forts, positions, stations, and other places, and to man vessels of all sorts in said service.

And upon this act, sincerely believed to be an act of justice, warranted by the Constitution upon military necessity, I invoke the considerate judgment of mankind and the gracious favor of Almighty God.

## The Confederate States of America

| State | Seceded from Union | Readmitted to Union[1] | State | Seceded from Union | Readmitted to Union[1] |
|---|---|---|---|---|---|
| 1. South Carolina | Dec. 20, 1860 | July 9, 1868 | 7. Texas | March 2, 1861 | March 30, 1870 |
| 2. Mississippi | Jan. 9, 1861 | Feb. 23, 1870 | 8. Virginia | April 17, 1861 | Jan. 26, 1870 |
| 3. Florida | Jan. 10, 1861 | June 25, 1868 | 9. Arkansas | May 6, 1861 | June 22, 1868 |
| 4. Alabama | Jan. 11, 1861 | July 13, 1868 | 10. North Carolina | May 20, 1861 | July 4, 1868 |
| 5. Georgia | Jan. 19, 1861 | July 15, 1870[2] | 11. Tennessee | June 8, 1861 | July 24, 1866 |
| 6. Louisiana | Jan. 26, 1861 | July 9, 1868 | | | |

1. Date of readmission to representation in U.S. House of Representatives. 2. Second readmission date. First date was July 21, 1868, but the representatives were unseated March 5, 1869. NOTE: Four other slave states—Delaware, Kentucky, Maryland, and Missouri—remained in the Union.

## Lincoln's Gettysburg Address

The Battle of Gettysburg, one of the most noted battles of the Civil War, was fought on July 1, 2, and 3, 1863. On Nov. 19, 1863, the field was dedicated as a national cemetery by President Lincoln in a two-minute speech that was to become immortal. At the time of its delivery the speech was relegated to the inside pages of the papers, while a two-hour address by Edward Everett, the leading orator of the time, caught the headlines.

The following is the text of the address revised by President Lincoln from his own notes:

Fourscore and seven years ago our fathers brought forth on this continent a new nation conceived in liberty and dedicated to the proposition that all men are created equal. Now we are engaged in a great civil war testing whether that nation, or any nation so conceived and so dedicated, can long endure. We are met on a great battlefield of that war. We have come to dedicate a portion of that field as a final resting-place for those who here gave their lives that that nation might live. It is altogether fitting and proper that we should do this. But, in a larger sense, we cannot dedicate, we cannot consecrate, we cannot hallow this ground. The brave men, living and dead, who struggled here have consecrated it far above our poor power to add or detract. The world will little note nor long remember what we say here, but it can never forget what they did here. It is for us the living rather to be dedicated here to the unfinished work which they who fought here have thus far so nobly advanced. It is rather for us to be here dedicated to the great task remaining before us—that from these honored dead we take increased devotion to that cause for which they gave the last full measure of devotion—that we here highly resolve that these dead shall not have died in vain, that this nation under God shall have a new birth of freedom, and that government of the people, by the people, for the people shall not perish from the earth.

# The Early Congresses

At the urging of Massachusetts and Virginia, the First Continental Congress met in Philadelphia on Sept. 5, 1774, and was attended by representatives of all the colonies except Georgia. Patrick Henry of Virginia declared: "The distinctions between Pennsylvanians, New Yorkers and New Englanders are no more. I am not a Virginian but an American." This Congress, which adjourned Oct. 26, 1774, passed intercolonial resolutions calling for extensive boycott by the colonies against British trade.

The following year, most of the delegates from the colonies were chosen by popular election to attend the Second Continental Congress, which assembled in Philadelphia on May 10. As war had already begun between the colonies and England, the chief problems before the Congress were the procuring of military supplies, the establishment of an army and proper defenses, the issuing of continental bills of credit, etc. On June 15, 1775, George Washington was elected to command the Continental army. Congress adjourned Dec. 12, 1776.

Other Continental Congresses were held in Baltimore (1776–77), Philadelphia (1777), Lancaster, Pa. (1777), York, Pa. (1777–78), and Philadelphia (1778–81).

In 1781, the Articles of Confederation, although establishing a league of the thirteen states rather than a strong central government, provided for the continuance of Congress. Known thereafter as the Congress of the Confederation, it held sessions in Philadelphia (1781–83), Princeton, N.J. (1783), Annapolis, Md. (1783–84), and Trenton, N.J. (1784). Five sessions were held in New York City between the years 1785 and 1789.

The Congress of the United States, established by the ratification of the Constitution, held its first meeting on March 4, 1789, in New York City. Several sessions of Congress were held in Philadelphia, and the first meeting in Washington, D.C., was on Nov. 17, 1800.

## Presidents of the Continental Congresses

| Name | Elected | Born | Died |
|---|---|---|---|
| Peyton Randolph, Va. | Sept. 5, 1774 | c.1721 | 1775 |
| Henry Middleton, S.C. | Oct. 22, 1774 | 1717 | 1784 |
| Peyton Randolph, Va. | May 10, 1775 | c.1721 | 1775 |
| John Hancock, Mass. | May 24, 1775 | 1737 | 1793 |
| Henry Laurens, S.C. | Nov. 1, 1777 | 1724 | 1792 |
| John Jay, N.Y. | Dec. 10, 1778 | 1745 | 1829 |
| Samuel Huntington, Conn. | Sept. 28, 1779 | 1731 | 1796 |
| Thomas McKean, Del. | July 10, 1781 | 1734 | 1817 |
| John Hanson, Md. | Nov. 5, 1781 | 1715 | 1783 |
| Elias Boudinot, N.J. | Nov. 4, 1782 | 1740 | 1821 |
| Thomas Mifflin, Pa. | Nov. 3, 1783 | 1744 | 1800 |
| Richard Henry Lee, Va. | Nov. 30, 1784 | 1732 | 1794 |
| John Hancock, Mass.[1] | Nov. 23, 1785 | 1737 | 1793 |
| Nathaniel Gorham, Mass. | June 6, 1786 | 1738 | 1796 |
| Arthur St. Clair, Pa. | Feb. 2, 1787 | 1734 | 1818 |
| Cyrus Griffin, Va. | Jan. 22, 1788 | 1748 | 1810 |

1. Resigned May 29, 1786, never having served, because of continued illness.

## The Great Seal of the U.S.

On July 4, 1776, the Continental Congress appointed a committee consisting of Benjamin Franklin, John Adams, and Thomas Jefferson "to bring in a device for a seal of the United States of America." After many delays, a verbal description of a design by William Barton was finally approved by Congress on June 20, 1782. The seal shows an American bald eagle with a ribbon in its mouth bearing the device *E pluribus unum* (One out of many). In its talons are the arrows of war and an olive branch of peace. On the reverse side it shows an unfinished pyramid with an eye (the eye of Providence) above it.

## The American's Creed

### *William Tyler Page*

"I believe in the United States of America as a government of the people, by the people, for the people; whose just powers are derived from the consent of the governed; a democracy in a republic; a sovereign Nation of many sovereign States; a perfect union, one and inseparable; established upon those principles of freedom, equality, justice, and humanity for which American patriots sacrificed their lives and fortunes.

"I therefore believe it is my duty to my country to love it, to support its Constitution, to obey its laws, to respect its flag, and to defend it against all enemies."

NOTE: William Tyler Page, Clerk of the U.S. House of Representatives, wrote "The American's Creed" in 1917. It was accepted by the House on behalf of the American people on April 3, 1918.

## U.S. Capitol

When the French architect and engineer Maj. Pierre L'Enfant first began to lay out the plans for a new Federal city (now Washington, D.C.), he noted that Jenkins' Hill, overlooking the area, seemed to be "a pedestal waiting for a monument." It was here that the U.S. Capitol would be built. The basic structure as we know it today evolved over a period of more than 150 years. In 1792 a competition was held for the design of a capitol building. Dr. William Thornton, a physician and amateur architect, submitted the winning plan, a simple, low-lying structure of classical proportions with a shallow dome. Later, internal modifications were made by Benjamin Henry Latrobe. After the building was burned by the British in 1814, Latrobe and architect Charles Bulfinch were responsible for its reconstruction. Finally, under Thomas Walter, who was Architect of the Capitol from 1851 to 1865, the House and Senate wings and the imposing cast iron dome topped with the Statue of Freedom were added, and the Capitol assumed the form we see today. It was in the old Senate chamber that Daniel Webster cried out, "Liberty and Union, now and forever, one and inseparable!" In Statuary Hall, which used to be the old House chamber, a small disk on the floor marks the spot where John Quincy Adams was fatally stricken after more than 50 years of service to his country. A whisper from one side of this room can be heard across the vast space of the hall. Visitors can see the original Supreme Court chamber a floor below the Rotunda.

In addition to its historical association, the Capitol Building is also a vast artistic treasure house. The works of such famous artists as Gilbert Stuart, Rembrandt Peale, and John Trumbull are displayed on the walls. The Great Rotunda, with its 180-foot- (54.9-m-) high dome, is decorated with a massive fresco by Constantino Brumidi, which extends some 300 feet (90 m) in circumference. Throughout the building are many paintings of events in U.S. history and sculptures of outstanding Americans. The Capitol itself is situated on a 68-acre (27.5-ha) park designed by the 19th-century landscape architect Frederick Law Olmsted. There are free guided tours of the Capitol, which include admission to the House and Senate galleries. Those who wish to visit the visitors' gallery in either wing without taking the tour may obtain passes from their Senators or Congressmen. Visitors may ride on the monorail subway that joins the House and Senate wings of the Capitol with the Congressional office buildings.

## Washington Monument

Construction of this magnificent Washington, D.C., monument, which draws some two million visitors a year, took nearly a century of planning, building, and controversy. Provision for a large equestrian statue of George Washington was made in the original city plan, but the project was soon dropped. After Washington's death it was taken up again, and a number of false starts and changes of design were made. Finally, in 1848, work was begun on the monument that stands today. The design, by architect Robert Mills, then featured an ornate base. In 1854, however, political squabbling and a lack of money brought construction to a halt. Work was resumed in 1880, and the monument was completed in 1884 and opened to the public in 1888. The tapered shaft, faced with white marble and rising from walls 15 feet thick (4.6 m) at the base was modeled after the obelisks of ancient Egypt. The monument, one of the tallest masonry constructions in the world, stands just over 555 feet (169 m). Memorial stones from the 50 States, foreign countries, and organizations line the interior walls. The top, reached only by elevator, commands a panoramic view of the city.

## The Liberty Bell

The Liberty Bell was cast in England in 1752 for the Pennsylvania Statehouse (now named Independence Hall) in Philadelphia. It was recast in Philadelphia in 1753. It is inscribed with the words, "Proclaim liberty throughout all the land unto all the inhabitants thereof" (Lev. 25:10). The bell was rung on July 8, 1776, for the first public reading of the Declaration of Independence. Hidden in Allentown during the British occupation of Philadelphia, it was replaced in Independence Hall in 1778. The bell cracked on July 8, 1835, while tolling the death of Chief Justice John Marshall. In 1976 the Liberty Bell was moved to a special exhibition building near Independence Hall.

## Arlington National Cemetery

Arlington National Cemetery occupies 612 acres in Virginia on the Potomac River, directly opposite Washington. This land was part of the estate of John Parke Custis, Martha Washington's son. His son, George Washington Parke Custis, built the mansion which later became the home of Robert E. Lee. In 1864, Arlington became a military cemetery. More than 200,000 servicemembers and their dependents are buried there. Expansion of the cemetery began in 1966, using a 180-acre tract of land directly east of the present site.

In 1921, an Unknown American Soldier of World War I was buried in the cemetery; the monument at the Tomb was opened to the public without ceremony in 1932. Two additional Unknowns, one from World War II and one from the Korean War, were buried May 30, 1958. The Unknown Serviceman of Vietnam was buried on May 28, 1984. The inscription carved on the Tomb of the Unknowns reads:

HERE RESTS IN
HONORED GLORY
AN AMERICAN
SOLDIER
KNOWN BUT TO GOD

# History of the Flag

*Source: Encyclopaedia Britannica.*

The first official American flag, the Continental or Grand Union flag, was displayed on Prospect Hill, Jan. 1, 1776, in the American lines besieging Boston. It had 13 alternate red and white stripes, with the British Union Jack in the upper left corner.

On June 14, 1777, the Continental Congress adopted the design for a new flag, which actually was the Continental flag with the red cross of St. George and the white cross of St. Andrew replaced on the blue field by 13 stars, one for each state. No rule was made as to the arrangement of the stars, and while they were usually shown in a circle, there were various other designs. It is uncertain when the new flag was first flown, but its first official announcement is believed to have been on Sept. 3, 1777.

The first public assertion that Betsy Ross made the first Stars and Stripes appeared in a paper read before the Historical Society of Pennsylvania on March 14, 1870, by William J. Canby, a grandson. However, Mr. Canby on later investigation found no official documents of any action by Congress on the flag before June 14, 1777. Betsy Ross's own story, according to her daughter, was that Washington, Robert Morris, and George Ross, as representatives of Congress, visited her in Philadelphia in June 1776, showing her a rough draft of the flag and asking her if she could make one. However, the only actual record of the manufacture of flags by Betsy Ross is a voucher in Harrisburg, Pa., for 14 pounds and some shillings for flags for the Pennsylvania navy.

On Jan. 13, 1794, Congress voted to add two stars and two stripes to the flag in recognition of the admission of Vermont and Kentucky to the Union. By 1818, there were 20 states in the Union, and as it was obvious that the flag would soon become unwieldly, Congress voted April 18 to return to the original 13 stripes and to indicate the admission of a new state simply by the addition of a star the following July 4. The 49th star, for Alaska, was added July 4, 1959; and the 50th star, for Hawaii, was added July 4, 1960.

The first Confederate flag, adopted in 1861 by the Confederate convention in Montgomery, Ala., was called the Stars and Bars; but because of its similarity in colors to the American flag, there was much confusion in the Battle of Bull Run. To remedy this situation, Gen. G. T. Beauregard suggested a battle flag, which was used by the Southern armies throughout the war. The flag consisted of a red field on which was placed a blue cross of St. Andrew separated from the field by a white fillet and adorned with 13[1] white stars for the Confederate states. In May 1863, at Richmond, an official flag was adopted by the Confederate Congress. This flag was white and twice as long as wide; the union, two-thirds the width of the flag, contained the battle flag designed for Gen. Beauregard. A broad transverse stripe of red was added Feb. 4, 1865, so that the flag might not be mistaken for a signal of truce.

1. 11 states formally seceded, and unofficial groups in Kentucky and Missouri adopted ordinances of secession. On this basis, these two states were admitted to the Confederacy, although the official state governments remained in the Union.

## The Pledge of Allegiance[1] to the Flag

"I pledge allegiance to the Flag of the United States of America, and to the Republic for which it stands, one Nation under God,[2] indivisible, with liberty and justice for all."
1. The original pledge was published in the Sept. 8, 1892, issue of *The Youth's Companion* in Boston. For years, the authorship was in dispute between James B. Upham and Francis Bellamy of the magazine's staff. In 1939, after a study of the controversy, the United States Flag Association decided that authorship be credited to Bellamy. 2. The phrase "under God" was added to the pledge on June 14, 1954.

## The Statue of Liberty

The Statue of Liberty ("Liberty Enlightening the World") is a 225-ton, steel-reinforced copper female figure, 152 ft in height, facing the ocean from Liberty[1] Island in New York Harbor. The right hand holds aloft a torch, and the left hand carries a tablet upon which is inscribed: "July IV MDCCLXXVI."

The statue was designed by Frédéric Auguste Bartholdi of Alsace as a gift to the United States from the people of France to memorialize the alliance of the two countries in the American Revolution and their abiding friendship. The French people contributed the $250,000 cost.

The 150-foot pedestal was designed by Richard M. Hunt and built by Gen. Charles P. Stone, both Americans. It contains steel underpinnings designed by Alexander Eiffel of France to support the statue. The $270,000 cost was borne by popular subscription in this country. President Grover Cleveland accepted the statue for the United States on Oct. 28, 1886.

On Sept. 26, 1972, President Richard M. Nixon dedicated the American Museum of Immigration, housed in structural additions to the base of the statue. In 1984 scaffolding went up for a major restoration and the torch was extinguished on July 4. It was relit with much ceremony July 4, 1986 to mark its centennial.

On a tablet inside the pedestal is engraved the following sonnet, written by Emma Lazarus (1849–1887):

### The New Colossus

Not like the brazen giant of Greek fame.
With conquering limbs astride from land to land;
Here at our sea-washed, sunset gates shall stand
A mighty woman with a torch, whose flame
Is the imprisoned lightning, and her name
Mother of Exiles. From her beacon-hand
Glows world-wide welcome; her mild eyes command
The air-bridged harbor that twin cities frame.
"Keep, ancient lands, your storied pomp!" cries she
With silent lips. "Give me your tired, your poor,
Your huddled masses yearning to breathe free,
The wretched refuse of your teeming shore.
Send these, the homeless, tempest-tost to me,
I lift my lamp beside the golden door!"

1. Called Bedloe's Island prior to 1956.

# Presidents

| Name and (party)[1] | Term | State of birth | Born | Died | Religion | Age at inaug. | Age at death |
|---|---|---|---|---|---|---|---|
| 1. Washington (F)[2] | 1789–1797 | Va. | 2/22/1732 | 12/14/1799 | Episcopalian | 57 | 67 |
| 2. J. Adams (F) | 1797–1801 | Mass. | 10/30/1735 | 7/4/1826 | Unitarian | 61 | 90 |
| 3. Jefferson (DR) | 1801–1809 | Va. | 4/13/1743 | 7/4/1826 | Deist | 57 | 83 |
| 4. Madison (DR) | 1809–1817 | Va. | 3/16/1751 | 6/28/1836 | Episcopalian | 57 | 85 |
| 5. Monroe (DR) | 1817–1825 | Va. | 4/28/1758 | 7/4/1831 | Episcopalian | 58 | 73 |
| 6. J. Q. Adams (DR) | 1825–1829 | Mass. | 7/11/1767 | 2/23/1848 | Unitarian | 57 | 80 |
| 7. Jackson (D) | 1829–1837 | S.C. | 3/15/1767 | 6/8/1845 | Presbyterian | 61 | 78 |
| 8. Van Buren (D) | 1837–1841 | N.Y. | 12/5/1782 | 7/24/1862 | Reformed Dutch | 54 | 79 |
| 9. W. H. Harrison (W)[3] | 1841 | Va. | 2/9/1773 | 4/4/1841 | Episcopalian | 68 | 68 |
| 10. Tyler (W) | 1841–1845 | Va. | 3/29/1790 | 1/18/1862 | Episcopalian | 51 | 71 |
| 11. Polk (D) | 1845–1849 | N.C. | 11/2/1795 | 6/15/1849 | Methodist | 49 | 53 |
| 12. Taylor (W)[3] | 1849–1850 | Va. | 11/24/1784 | 7/9/1850 | Episcopalian | 64 | 65 |
| 13. Fillmore (W) | 1850–1853 | N.Y. | 1/7/1800 | 3/8/1874 | Unitarian | 50 | 74 |
| 14. Pierce (D) | 1853–1857 | N.H. | 11/23/1804 | 10/8/1869 | Episcopalian | 48 | 64 |
| 15. Buchanan (D) | 1857–1861 | Pa. | 4/23/1791 | 6/1/1868 | Presbyterian | 65 | 77 |
| 16. Lincoln (R)[4] | 1861–1865 | Ky. | 2/12/1809 | 4/15/1865 | Liberal | 52 | 56 |
| 17. A. Johnson (U)[5] | 1865–1869 | N.C. | 12/29/1808 | 7/31/1875 | ([6]) | 56 | 66 |
| 18. Grant (R) | 1869–1877 | Ohio | 4/27/1822 | 7/23/1885 | Methodist | 46 | 63 |
| 19. Hayes (R) | 1877–1881 | Ohio | 10/4/1822 | 1/17/1893 | Methodist | 54 | 70 |
| 20. Garfield (R)[4] | 1881 | Ohio | 11/19/1831 | 9/19/1881 | Disciples of Christ | 49 | 49 |
| 21. Arthur (R) | 1881–1885 | Vt. | 10/5/1830 | 11/18/1886 | Episcopalian | 50 | 56 |
| 22. Cleveland (D) | 1885–1889 | N.J. | 3/18/1837 | 6/24/1908 | Presbyterian | 47 | 71 |
| 23. B. Harrison (R) | 1889–1893 | Ohio | 8/20/1833 | 3/13/1901 | Presbyterian | 55 | 67 |
| 24. Cleveland (D)[7] | 1893–1897 | — | — | — | — | 55 | — |
| 25. McKinley (R)[4] | 1897–1901 | Ohio | 1/29/1843 | 9/14/1901 | Methodist | 54 | 58 |
| 26. T. Roosevelt (R) | 1901–1909 | N.Y. | 10/27/1858 | 1/6/1919 | Reformed Dutch | 42 | 60 |
| 27. Taft (R) | 1909–1913 | Ohio | 9/15/1857 | 3/8/1930 | Unitarian | 51 | 72 |
| 28. Wilson (D) | 1913–1921 | Va. | 12/28/1856 | 2/3/1924 | Presbyterian | 56 | 67 |
| 29. Harding (R)[3] | 1921–1923 | Ohio | 11/2/1865 | 8/2/1923 | Baptist | 55 | 57 |
| 30. Coolidge (R) | 1923–1929 | Vt. | 7/4/1872 | 1/5/1933 | Congregationalist | 51 | 60 |
| 31. Hoover (R) | 1929–1933 | Iowa | 8/10/1874 | 10/20/1964 | Quaker | 54 | 90 |
| 32. F. D. Roosevelt (D)[3] | 1933–1945 | N.Y. | 1/30/1882 | 4/12/1945 | Episcopalian | 51 | 63 |
| 33. Truman (D) | 1945–1953 | Mo. | 5/8/1884 | 12/26/1972 | Baptist | 60 | 88 |
| 34. Eisenhower (R) | 1953–1961 | Tex. | 10/14/1890 | 3/28/1969 | Presbyterian | 62 | 78 |
| 35. Kennedy (D)[4] | 1961–1963 | Mass. | 5/29/1917 | 11/22/1963 | Roman Catholic | 43 | 46 |
| 36. L. B. Johnson (D) | 1963–1969 | Tex. | 8/27/1908 | 1/22/1973 | Disciples of Christ | 55 | 64 |
| 37. Nixon (R)[8] | 1969–1974 | Calif. | 1/9/1913 | — | Quaker | 56 | — |
| 38. Ford (R) | 1974–1977 | Neb. | 7/14/1913 | — | Episcopalian | 61 | — |
| 39. Carter (D) | 1977–1981 | Ga. | 10/1/1924 | — | Southern Baptist | 52 | — |
| 40. Reagan (R) | 1981– | Ill. | 2/6/1911 | — | Disciples of Christ | 69 | — |

1. F—Federalist; DR—Democratic-Republican; D—Democratic; W—Whig; R—Republican; U—Union. 2. No party for first election. The party system in the U.S. made its appearance during Washington's first term. 3. Died in office. 4. Assassinated in office. 5. The Republican National Convention of 1864 adopted the name Union Party. It renominated Lincoln for President; for Vice President it nominated Johnson, a War Democrat. Although frequently listed as a Republican Vice President and President, Johnson undoubtedly considered himself strictly a member of the Union Party. When that party broke apart after 1868, he returned to the Democratic Party. 6. Johnson was not a professed church member; however, he admired the Baptist principles of church government. 7. Second nonconsecutive term. 8. Resigned Aug. 9, 1974.

# Vice Presidents

| Name and (party)[1] | Term | State of birth | Birth and death dates | President served under |
|---|---|---|---|---|
| 1. John Adams (F)[2] | 1789–1797 | Massachusetts | 1735–1826 | Washington |
| 2. Thomas Jefferson (DR) | 1797–1801 | Virginia | 1743–1826 | J. Adams |
| 3. Aaron Burr (DR) | 1801–1805 | New Jersey | 1756–1836 | Jefferson |
| 4. George Clinton (DR)[3] | 1805–1812 | New York | 1739–1812 | Jefferson and Madison |
| 5. Elbridge Gerry (DR)[3] | 1813–1814 | Massachusetts | 1744–1814 | Madison |
| 6. Daniel D. Tompkins (DR) | 1817–1825 | New York | 1774–1825 | Monroe |
| 7. John C. Calhoun[4] | 1825–1832 | South Carolina | 1782–1850 | J. Q. Adams and Jackson |
| 8. Martin Van Buren (D) | 1833–1837 | New York | 1782–1862 | Jackson |
| 9. Richard M. Johnson (D) | 1837–1841 | Kentucky | 1780–1850 | Van Buren |
| 10. John Tyler (W)[5] | 1841 | Virginia | 1790–1862 | W. H. Harrison |
| 11. George M. Dallas (D) | 1845–1849 | Pennsylvania | 1792–1864 | Polk |
| 12. Millard Fillmore (W)[5] | 1849–1850 | New York | 1800–1874 | Taylor |
| 13. William R. King (D)[3] | 1853 | North Carolina | 1786–1853 | Pierce |
| 14. John C. Breckinridge (D) | 1857–1861 | Kentucky | 1821–1875 | Buchanan |

| Name and (party)[1] | Term | State of birth | Birth and death dates | President served under |
|---|---|---|---|---|
| 15. Hannibal Hamlin (R) | 1861–1865 | Maine | 1809–1891 | Lincoln |
| 16. Andrew Johnson (U)[5] | 1865 | North Carolina | 1808–1875 | Lincoln |
| 17. Schuyler Colfax (R) | 1869–1873 | New York | 1823–1885 | Grant |
| 18. Henry Wilson (R)[3] | 1873–1875 | New Hampshire | 1812–1875 | Grant |
| 19. William A. Wheeler (R) | 1877–1881 | New York | 1819–1887 | Hayes |
| 20. Chester A. Arthur (R)[5] | 1881 | Vermont | 1830–1886 | Garfield |
| 21. Thomas A. Hendricks (D)[3] | 1885 | Ohio | 1819–1885 | Cleveland |
| 22. Levi P. Morton (R) | 1889–1893 | Vermont | 1824–1920 | B. Harrison |
| 23. Adlai E. Stevenson (D) | 1893–1897 | Kentucky | 1835–1914 | Cleveland |
| 24. Garrett A. Hobart (R)[3] | 1897–1899 | New Jersey | 1844–1899 | McKinley |
| 25. Theodore Roosevelt (R)[5] | 1901 | New York | 1858–1919 | McKinley |
| 26. Charles W. Fairbanks (R) | 1905–1909 | Ohio | 1852–1918 | T. Roosevelt |
| 27. James S. Sherman (R)[3] | 1909–1912 | New York | 1855–1912 | Taft |
| 28. Thomas R. Marshall (D) | 1913–1921 | Indiana | 1854–1925 | Wilson |
| 29. Calvin Coolidge (R)[5] | 1921–1923 | Vermont | 1872–1933 | Harding |
| 30. Charles G. Dawes (R) | 1925–1929 | Ohio | 1865–1951 | Coolidge |
| 31. Charles Curtis (R) | 1929–1933 | Kansas | 1860–1936 | Hoover |
| 32. John N. Garner (D) | 1933–1941 | Texas | 1868–1967 | F. D. Roosevelt |
| 33. Henry A. Wallace (D) | 1941–1945 | Iowa | 1888–1965 | F. D. Roosevelt |
| 34. Harry S. Truman (D)[5] | 1945 | Missouri | 1884–1972 | F. D. Roosevelt |
| 35. Alben W. Barkley (D) | 1949–1953 | Kentucky | 1877–1956 | Truman |
| 36. Richard M. Nixon (R) | 1953–1961 | California | 1913– | Eisenhower |
| 37. Lyndon B. Johnson (D)[5] | 1961–1963 | Texas | 1908–1973 | Kennedy |
| 38. Hubert H. Humphrey (D) | 1965–1969 | South Dakota | 1911–1978 | Johnson |
| 39. Spiro T. Agnew (R)[6] | 1969–1973 | Maryland | 1918– | Nixon |
| 40. Gerald R. Ford (R)[7] | 1973–1974 | Nebraska | 1913– | Nixon |
| 41. Nelson A. Rockefeller (R)[8] | 1974–1977 | Maine | 1908–1979 | Ford |
| 42. Walter F. Mondale (D) | 1977–1981 | Minnesota | 1928– | Carter |
| 43. George Bush (R) | 1981– | Massachusetts | 1924– | Reagan |

1. F—Federalist; DR—Democratic-Republican; D—Democratic; W—Whig; R—Republican; U—Union. 2. No party for first election. The party system in the U.S. made its appearance during Washington's first term as President. 3. Died in office. 4. Democratic-Republican with J. Q. Adams; Democratic with Jackson. Calhoun resigned in 1832 to become a U.S. Senator. 5. Succeeded to presidency on death of President. 6. Resigned Oct. 10, 1973, after pleading no contest to Federal income tax evasion charges. 7. Nominated by Nixon on Oct. 12, 1973, under provisions of 25th Amendment. Confirmed by Congress on Dec. 6, 1973, and was sworn in same day. He became President Aug. 9, 1974, upon Nixon's resignation. 8. Nominated by Ford Aug. 20, 1974; confirmed by Congress on Dec. 19, 1974, and was sworn in same day.

## Burial Places of the Presidents

| President | Burial place | President | Burial place |
|---|---|---|---|
| Washington | Mt. Vernon, Va. | Grant | New York City |
| J. Adams | Quincy, Mass. | Hayes | Fremont, Ohio |
| Jefferson | Charlottesville, Va. | Garfield | Cleveland, Ohio |
| Madison | Montpelier Station, Va. | Arthur | Albany, N.Y. |
| Monroe | Richmond, Va. | Cleveland | Princeton, N.J. |
| J. Q. Adams | Quincy, Mass. | B. Harrison | Indianapolis |
| Jackson | The Hermitage, nr. Nashville, Tenn. | McKinley | Canton, Ohio |
| | | T. Roosevelt | Oyster Bay, N.Y. |
| Van Buren | Kinderhook, N.Y. | Taft | Arlington National Cemetery |
| W. H. Harrison | North Bend, Ohio | Wilson | Washington National Cathedral |
| Tyler | Richmond, Va. | Harding | Marion, Ohio |
| Polk | Nashville, Tenn. | Coolidge | Plymouth, Vt. |
| Taylor | Louisville, Ky. | Hoover | West Branch, Iowa |
| Fillmore | Buffalo, N.Y. | F. D. Roosevelt | Hyde Park, N.Y. |
| Pierce | Concord, N.H. | Truman | Independence, Mo. |
| Buchanan | Lancaster, Pa. | Eisenhower | Abilene, Kan. |
| Lincoln | Springfield, Ill. | Kennedy | Arlington National Cemetery |
| A. Johnson | Greeneville, Tenn. | L. B. Johnson | Stonewall, Tex. |

## "In God We Trust"

"In God We Trust" first appeared on U.S. coins after April 22, 1864, when Congress passed an act authorizing the coinage of a 2-cent piece bearing this motto. Thereafter, Congress extended its use to other coins. On July 30, 1956, it became the national motto.

# Wives and Children of the Presidents

| President | Wife's name | Year and place of wife's birth | Married | Wife died | Children of President[1] Sons | Daughters |
|---|---|---|---|---|---|---|
| Washington | Mrs. Martha Dandridge Custis | 1732, Va. | 1759 | 1802 | — | — |
| John Adams | Abigail Smith | 1744, Mass. | 1764 | 1818 | 3 | 2 |
| Jefferson | Mrs. Martha Wayles Skelton | 1748, Va. | 1772 | 1782 | 1 | 5 |
| Madison | Mrs. Dorothy "Dolley" Payne Todd | 1768, N.C. | 1794 | 1849 | — | — |
| Monroe | Elizabeth "Eliza" Kortright | 1768, N.Y. | 1786 | 1830 | — | 2 |
| J. Q. Adams | Louisa Catherine Johnson | 1775, England | 1797 | 1852 | 3 | 1 |
| Jackson | Mrs. Rachel Donelson Robards | 1767, Va. | 1791 | 1828 | — | — |
| Van Buren | Hannah Hoes | 1788, N.Y. | 1807 | 1819 | 4 | — |
| W. H. Harrison | Anna Symmes | 1775, N.J. | 1795 | 1864 | 6 | 4 |
| Tyler | Letitia Christian | 1790, Va. | 1813 | 1842 | 3 | 4 |
|  | Julia Gardiner | 1820, N.Y. | 1844 | 1889 | 5 | 2 |
| Polk | Sarah Childress | 1803, Tenn. | 1824 | 1891 | — | — |
| Taylor | Margaret Smith | 1788, Md. | 1810 | 1852 | 1 | 5 |
| Fillmore | Abigail Powers | 1798, N.Y. | 1826 | 1853 | 1 | 1 |
|  | Mrs. Caroline Carmichael McIntosh | 1813, N.J. | 1858 | 1881 | — | — |
| Pierce | Jane Means Appleton | 1806, N.H. | 1834 | 1863 | 3 | — |
| Buchanan | (Unmarried) | — | — | — | — | — |
| Lincoln | Mary Todd | 1818, Ky. | 1842 | 1882 | 4 | — |
| A. Johnson | Eliza McCardle | 1810, Tenn. | 1827 | 1876 | 3 | 2 |
| Grant | Julia Dent | 1826, Mo. | 1848 | 1902 | 3 | 1 |
| Hayes | Lucy Ware Webb | 1831, Ohio | 1852 | 1889 | 7 | 1 |
| Garfield | Lucretia Rudolph | 1832, Ohio | 1858 | 1918 | 5 | 2 |
| Arthur | Ellen Lewis Herndon | 1837, Va. | 1859 | 1880 | 2 | 1 |
| Cleveland | Frances Folsom | 1864, N.Y. | 1886 | 1947 | 2 | 3 |
| B. Harrison | Caroline Lavinia Scott | 1832, Ohio | 1853 | 1892 | 1 | 1 |
|  | Mrs. Mary Scott Lord Dimmick | 1858, Pa. | 1896 | 1948 | — | 1 |
| McKinley | Ida Saxton | 1847, Ohio | 1871 | 1907 | — | 2 |
| T. Roosevelt | Alice Hathaway Lee | 1861, Mass. | 1880 | 1884 | — | 1 |
|  | Edith Kermit Carow | 1861, Conn. | 1886 | 1948 | 4 | 1 |
| Taft | Helen Herron | 1861, Ohio | 1886 | 1943 | 2 | 1 |
| Wilson | Ellen Louise Axson | 1860, Ga. | 1885 | 1914 | — | 3 |
|  | Mrs. Edith Bolling Galt | 1872, Va. | 1915 | 1961 | — | — |
| Harding | Mrs. Florence Kling DeWolfe | 1860, Ohio | 1891 | 1924 | — | — |
| Coolidge | Grace Anna Goodhue | 1879, Vt. | 1905 | 1957 | 2 | — |
| Hoover | Lou Henry | 1875, Iowa | 1899 | 1944 | 2 | — |
| F. D. Roosevelt | Anna Eleanor Roosevelt | 1884, N.Y. | 1905 | 1962 | 5 | 1 |
| Truman | Bess Wallace | 1885, Mo. | 1919 | 1982 | — | 1 |
| Eisenhower | Mamie Geneva Doud | 1896, Iowa | 1916 | 1979 | 2 | — |
| Kennedy | Jacqueline Lee Bouvier | 1929, N.Y. | 1953 | — | 2 | 1 |
| L. B. Johnson | Claudia Alta "Lady Bird" Taylor | 1912, Tex. | 1934 | — | — | 2 |
| Nixon | Thelma Catherine "Pat" Ryan | 1912, Nev. | 1940 | — | — | 2 |
| Ford | Mrs. Elizabeth "Betty" Bloomer Warren | 1918, Ill. | 1948 | — | 3 | 1 |
| Carter | Rosalynn Smith | 1928, Ga. | 1946 | — | 3 | 1 |
| Reagan | Jane Wyman | 1914, Mo. | 1940[2] | — | 1[3] | 1 |
|  | Nancy Davis | 1923, N.Y. | 1952 | — | 1 | 1 |

1. Includes children who died in infancy. 2. Divorced in 1948. 3. Adopted.

# Elections

## How a President Is Nominated and Elected

The National Conventions of both major parties are held during the summer of a presidential-election year. Earlier, each party selects delegates by primaries, conventions, committees, etc.

For their 1984 National Convention, the Republicans allowed each state a base of 6 delegates at large; the District of Columbia, 14; Puerto Rico, 14; Guam and the Virgin Islands, 4 each. In addition, each state received 3 district delegates for each of its Representatives in the House. This did not apply to the District of Columbia, Puerto Rico, Guam and the Virgin Islands.

Each state was awarded additional delegates at large on the basis of having supported the Republican candidate for President in 1980 and electing Republican candidates for Senator, Governor, and U.S. Representative in the 1980 and 1982 elections.

The number of delegates at the 1984 convention, held in Dallas starting August 20, was 2,234. Following was the apportionment of delegates:

| | | | | | | | | | | | |
|---|---|---|---|---|---|---|---|---|---|---|---|
| Alabama | 38 | Florida | 82 | Kentucky | 37 | Montana | 20 | Ohio | 89 | Texas | 109 |
| Alaska | 18 | Georgia | 37 | Louisiana | 41 | Nebraska | 24 | Oklahoma | 35 | Utah | 26 |
| Arizona | 32 | Guam | 4 | Maine | 20 | Nevada | 22 | Oregon | 32 | Vermont | 19 |
| Arkansas | 29 | Hawaii | 14 | Maryland | 31 | N.H. | 22 | Pa. | 98 | V.I. | 4 |
| California | 176 | Idaho | 21 | Mass. | 52 | N. Jersey | 64 | P.R. | 14 | Virginia | 50 |
| Colorado | 35 | Illinois | 93 | Michigan | 77 | New Mexico | 24 | R.I. | 14 | Washington | 43 |
| Connecticut | 35 | Indiana | 52 | Minnesota | 32 | New York | 136 | S.C. | 35 | W. Va. | 19 |
| Delaware | 19 | Iowa | 37 | Mississippi | 30 | N.C. | 53 | S.D. | 19 | Wisconsin | 46 |
| D.C. | 14 | Kansas | 32 | Missouri | 47 | N.D. | 18 | Tennessee | 46 | Wyoming | 18 |

The Democrats also based the number of delegates on a state's showing in the 1980 and 1982 elections. At the 1984 convention, held in San Francisco starting July 16, there were 3,923[1] delegates casting votes. Following is the apportionment by states:

| | | | | | | | | | | | |
|---|---|---|---|---|---|---|---|---|---|---|---|
| Alabama | 62 | Florida | 143 | Kentucky | 63 | Montana | 25 | Ohio | 175 | Texas | 200 |
| Alaska | 14 | Georgia | 82 | Louisiana | 68 | Nebraska | 30 | Oklahoma | 53 | Utah | 27 |
| Arizona | 39 | Guam | 7 | Maine | 27 | Nevada | 20 | Oregon | 50 | Vermont | 17 |
| Arkansas | 42 | Hawaii | 27 | Maryland | 74 | N. H. | 22 | Pa. | 195 | V.I. | 6 |
| California | 345 | Idaho | 22 | Mass. | 116 | New Jersey | 122 | P.R. | 53 | Virginia | 78 |
| Colorado | 51 | Illinois | 194 | Michigan | 155 | New Mexico | 28 | R.I. | 27 | Washington | 70 |
| Connecticut | 60 | Indiana | 88 | Minnesota | 86 | New York | 285 | S.C. | 48 | W. Va. | 44 |
| Delaware | 18 | Iowa | 58 | Mississippi | 43 | N.C. | 88 | S.D. | 19 | Wisconsin | 89 |
| D. C. | 19 | Kansas | 44 | Missouri | 86 | N.D. | 18 | Tennessee | 76 | Wyoming | 15 |

1. Includes five votes for Democrats abroad and five for the Latin America Regional Democratic Party.

## The Conventions

At each convention, a temporary chairman is chosen. After a credentials committee seats the delegates, a permanent chairman is elected. The convention then votes on a platform, drawn up by the platform committee.

By the third or fourth day, presidential nominations begin. The chairman calls the roll of states alphabetically. A state may place a candidate in nomination or yield to another state.

Voting, again alphabetically by roll call of states, begins after all nominations have been made and seconded. A simple majority is required in each party, although this may require many ballots.

Finally, the vice-presidential candidate is selected. Although there is no law saying that the candidates *must* come from different states, it is, practically, necessary for this to be the case. Otherwise, according to the Constitution (*see* Amendment XII), electors from that state could vote for only one of the candidates and would have to cast their other vote for some person of another state. This could result in a presidential candidate's receiving a majority electoral vote and his running mate's failing to.

## The Electoral College

The next step in the process is the nomination of electors in each state, according to its laws. These electors must not be Federal office holders. In the November election, the voters cast their votes for electors, not for President. In some states, the ballots include only the names of the presidential and vice-presidential candidates; in others, they include only names of the electors. Nowadays, it is rare for electors to be split between parties. The last such occurrence was in North Carolina in 1968[1]; the last before that, in Tennessee in 1948. On three occasions (1824, 1876, and 1888), the presidential candidate with the largest popular vote failed to obtain an electoral-vote majority.

Each state has as many electors as it has Senators and Representatives. For the 1984 election, the total electors were 538, based on 100 Senators, 435 Representatives, plus 3 electoral votes from the District of Columbia as a result of the 23rd Amendment to the Constitution.

On the first Monday after the second Wednesday in December, the electors cast their votes in their respective state capitols. Constitutionally they may vote for someone other than the party candidate but usually they do not since they are pledged to one party and its candidate on the ballot. Should the presidential or vice-presidential candidate die between the November election and the December meetings, the electors pledged to vote for him could vote for whomever they pleased. However, it seems certain that the national committee would attempt to get an agreement among the state party leaders for a replacement candidate.

The votes of the electors, certified by the states, are sent to Congress, where the president of the Senate opens the certificates and has them counted in the presence of both Houses on January 6. The new President is inaugurated at noon on January 20.

Should no candidate receive a majority of the electoral vote for President, the House of Representatives chooses a President from among the three highest candidates, voting, not as individuals, but as states, with a majority (now 26) needed to elect. Should no vice-presidential candidate obtain the majority, the Senate, voting as individuals, chooses from the highest two.

1. In 1956, 1 of Alabama's 11 electoral votes was cast for Walter B. Jones. In 1960, 6 of Alabama's 11 electoral votes and 1 of Oklahoma's 8 electoral votes were cast for Harry Flood Byrd. (Byrd also received all 8 of Mississippi's electoral votes.)

## National Political Conventions Since 1856

| Opening date | Party | Where held | Opening date | Party | Where held |
|---|---|---|---|---|---|
| June 17, 1856 | Republican | Philadelphia | June 10, 1924 | Republican | Cleveland |
| June 2, 1856 | Democratic | Cincinnati | June 24, 1924[2] | Democratic | New York City |
| May 16, 1860 | Republican | Chicago | June 12, 1928 | Republican | Kansas City |
| April 23, 1860 | Democratic | Charleston and Baltimore | June 26, 1928 | Democratic | Houston |
| | | | June 14, 1932 | Republican | Chicago |
| June 7, 1864 | Republican[1] | Baltimore | June 27, 1932 | Democratic | Chicago |
| Aug. 29, 1864 | Democratic | Chicago | June 9, 1936 | Republican | Cleveland |
| May 20, 1868 | Republican | Chicago | June 23, 1936 | Democratic | Philadelphia |
| July 4, 1868 | Democratic | New York City | June 24, 1940 | Republican | Philadelphia |
| June 5, 1872 | Republican | Philadelphia | July 15, 1940 | Democratic | Chicago |
| June 9, 1872 | Democratic | Baltimore | June 26, 1944 | Republican | Chicago |
| June 14, 1876 | Republican | Cincinnati | July 19, 1944 | Democratic | Chicago |
| June 28, 1876 | Democratic | St. Louis | June 21, 1948 | Republican | Philadelphia |
| June 2, 1880 | Republican | Chicago | July 12, 1948 | Democratic | Philadelphia |
| June 23, 1880 | Democratic | Cincinnati | July 17, 1948 | (3) | Birmingham |
| June 3, 1884 | Republican | Chicago | July 22, 1948 | Progressive | Philadelphia |
| July 11, 1884 | Democratic | Chicago | July 7, 1952 | Republican | Chicago |
| June 19, 1888 | Republican | Chicago | July 21, 1952 | Democratic | Chicago |
| June 6, 1888 | Democratic | St. Louis | Aug. 20, 1956 | Republican | San Francisco |
| June 7, 1892 | Republican | Minneapolis | Aug. 13, 1956 | Democratic | Chicago |
| June 21, 1892 | Democratic | Chicago | July 25, 1960 | Republican | Chicago |
| June 16, 1896 | Republican | St. Louis | July 11, 1960 | Democratic | Los Angeles |
| July 7, 1896 | Democratic | Chicago | July 13, 1964 | Republican | San Francisco |
| June 19, 1900 | Republican | Philadelphia | Aug. 24, 1964 | Democratic | Atlantic City |
| July 4, 1900 | Democratic | Kansas City | Aug. 5, 1968 | Republican | Miami Beach |
| June 21, 1904 | Republican | Chicago | Aug. 26, 1968 | Democratic | Chicago |
| July 6, 1904 | Democratic | St. Louis | July 10, 1972 | Democratic | Miami Beach |
| June 16, 1908 | Republican | Chicago | Aug. 21, 1972 | Republican | Miami Beach |
| July 7, 1908 | Democratic | Denver | July 12, 1976 | Democratic | New York City |
| June 18, 1912 | Republican | Chicago | Aug. 16, 1976 | Republican | Kansas City, Mo. |
| June 25, 1912 | Democratic | Baltimore | Aug. 11, 1980 | Democratic | New York City |
| June 7, 1916 | Republican | Chicago | July 14, 1980 | Republican | Detroit |
| June 14, 1916 | Democratic | St. Louis | Aug. 20, 1984 | Republican | Dallas |
| June 8, 1920 | Republican | Chicago | July 16, 1984 | Democratic | San Francisco |
| June 28, 1920 | Democratic | San Francisco | | | |

1. The Convention adopted name Union party to attract War Democrats and others favoring prosecution of war. 2. In session until July 10, 1924. 3. States' Rights delegates from 13 Southern states.

## National Committee Chairmen Since 1944

| Chairman and (state) | Term | Chairman and (state) | Term |
|---|---|---|---|
| **REPUBLICAN** | | **DEMOCRATIC** | |
| Herbert Brownell, Jr. (N.Y.) | 1944–46 | Robert E. Hannegan (Mo.) | 1944–47 |
| Carroll Reece (Tenn.) | 1946–48 | J. Howard McGrath (R.I.) | 1947–49 |
| Hugh D. Scott, Jr. (Pa.) | 1948–49 | William M. Boyle, Jr. (Mo.) | 1949–51 |
| Guy G. Gabrielson (N.J.) | 1949–52 | Frank E. McKinney (Ind.) | 1951–52 |
| Arthur E. Summerfield (Mich.) | 1952–53 | Stephen A. Mitchell (Ill.) | 1952–54 |
| Wesley Roberts (Kan.) | 1953– | Paul M. Butler (Ind.) | 1955–60 |
| Leonard W. Hall (N.Y.) | 1953–57 | Henry M. Jackson (Wash.) | 1960–61 |
| Meade Alcorn (Conn.) | 1957–59 | John M. Bailey (Conn.) | 1961–68 |
| Thruston B. Morton (Ky.) | 1959–61 | Lawrence F. O'Brien (Mass.) | 1968–69 |
| William E. Miller (N.Y.) | 1961–64 | Fred R. Harris (Okla.) | 1969–70 |
| Dean Burch (Ariz.) | 1964–65 | Lawrence F. O'Brien (Mass.) | 1970–72 |
| Ray C. Bliss (Ohio) | 1965–69 | Jean Westwood (Utah) | 1972– |
| Rogers C. B. Morton (Md.) | 1969–71 | Robert S. Strauss (Tex.) | 1972–77 |
| Robert Dole (Kan.) | 1971–73 | Kenneth M. Curtis (Me.) | 1977– |
| George H. Bush (Tex.) | 1973–74 | John C. White (Tex.) | 1977–81 |
| Mary Louise Smith (Iowa) | 1974–77 | Charles T. Manatt (Calif.) | 1981–85 |
| William E. Brock III (Tenn.) | 1977–81 | Paul G. Kirk, Jr. (Mass.) | 1985– |
| Richard Richards (Utah) | 1981–83 | | |
| Frank J. Fahrenkopf, Jr. (Nevada) | 1983– | | |

*Republican National Committee:* 310 First St., S.E., Washington, D. C. 20003.
*Democratic National Committee:* 430 South Capitol St., S.E., Washington, D.C. 20003.

# Presidential Elections, 1789 to 1984

For the original method of electing the President and the Vice President (elections of 1789, 1792, 1796, and 1800), see Article II, Section 1, of the Constitution. The election of 1804 was the first one in which the electors voted for President and Vice President on separate ballots. (See Amendment XII to the Constitution.)

| Year | Presidential candidates | Party | Electoral vote | Year | Presidential candidates | Party | Electoral vote |
|------|------------------------|-------|----------------|------|------------------------|-------|----------------|
| 1789[1] | George Washington | (no party) | 69 | 1796 | John Adams | Federalist | 71 |
| | John Adams | (no party) | 34 | | Thomas Jefferson | Dem.-Rep. | 68 |
| | Scattering | (no party) | 35 | | Thomas Pinckney | Federalist | 59 |
| | Votes not cast | | 8 | | Aaron Burr | Dem.-Rep. | 30 |
| | | | | | Scattering | | 48 |
| 1792 | George Washington | Federalist | 132 | | | | |
| | John Adams | Federalist | 77 | 1800[2] | Thomas Jefferson | Dem.-Rep. | 73 |
| | George Clinton | Anti-Federalist | 50 | | Aaron Burr | Dem.-Rep. | 73 |
| | Thomas Jefferson | Anti-Federalist | 4 | | John Adams | Federalist | 65 |
| | Aaron Burr | Anti-Federalist | 1 | | Charles C. Pinckney | Federalist | 64 |
| | Votes not cast | | 6 | | John Jay | Federalist | 1 |

| Year | Presidential candidates | Party | Electoral vote | Vice-presidential candidates | Party | Electoral vote |
|------|------------------------|-------|----------------|------------------------------|-------|----------------|
| 1804 | Thomas Jefferson | Dem.-Rep. | 162 | George Clinton | Dem.-Rep. | 162 |
| | Charles C. Pinckney | Federalist | 14 | Rufus King | Federalist | 14 |
| 1808 | James Madison | Dem.-Rep. | 122 | George Clinton | Dem.-Rep. | 113 |
| | Charles C. Pinckney | Federalist | 47 | Rufus King | Federalist | 47 |
| | George Clinton | Dem.-Rep. | 6 | John Langdon | Ind. (no party) | 9 |
| | Votes not cast | | 1 | James Madison | Dem.-Rep. | 3 |
| | | | | James Monroe | Dem.-Rep. | 3 |
| | | | | Votes not cast | | 1 |
| 1812 | James Madison | Dem.-Rep. | 128 | Elbridge Gerry | Dem.-Rep. | 131 |
| | De Witt Clinton | Federalist | 89 | Jared Ingersoll | Federalist | 86 |
| | Votes not cast | | 1 | Votes not cast | | 1 |
| 1816 | James Monroe | Dem.-Rep. | 183 | Daniel D. Tompkins | Dem.-Rep. | 183 |
| | Rufus King | Federalist | 34 | John E. Howard | Federalist | 22 |
| | Votes not cast | | 4 | James Ross | Ind. (no party) | 5 |
| | | | | John Marshall | Federalist | 4 |
| | | | | Robert G. Harper | Ind. (no party) | 3 |
| | | | | Votes not cast | | 4 |
| 1820 | James Monroe | Dem-Rep | 231 | Daniel D. Tompkins | Dem.-Rep. | 218 |
| | John Quincy Adams | Ind. (no party) | 1 | Richard Stockton | Ind. (no party) | 8 |
| | Votes not cast | | 3 | Daniel Rodney | Ind. (no party) | 4 |
| | | | | Richard Rush | Ind. (no party) | 1 |
| | | | | Robert G. Harper | Ind. (no party) | 1 |
| | | | | Votes not cast | | 3 |
| 1824[3] | John Quincy Adams | (no party) | 84 | John C. Calhoun | (no party) | 182 |
| | Andrew Jackson | (no party) | 99 | Nathan Sanford | (no party) | 30 |
| | William H. Crawford | (no party) | 41 | Nathaniel Macon | (no party) | 24 |
| | Henry Clay | (no party) | 37 | Andrew Jackson | (no party) | 13 |
| | | | | Martin Van Buren | (no party) | 9 |
| | | | | Henry Clay | (no party) | 2 |
| | | | | Votes not cast | | 1 |
| 1828 | Andrew Jackson | Democratic | 178 | John C. Calhoun | Democratic | 171 |
| | John Quincy Adams | Natl. Rep. | 83 | Richard Rush | Natl. Rep. | 83 |
| | | | | William Smith | Democratic | 7 |
| 1832 | Andrew Jackson | Democratic | 219 | Martin Van Buren | Democratic | 189 |
| | Henry Clay | Natl. Rep. | 49 | John Sergeant | Natl. Rep. | 49 |
| | John Floyd | Ind. (no party) | 11 | Henry Lee | Ind. (no party) | 11 |
| | William Wirt | Antimasonic[4] | 7 | Amos Ellmaker | Antimasonic | 7 |
| | Votes not cast | | 2 | William Wilkins | Ind. (no party) | 30 |
| | | | | Votes not cast | | 2 |

| Year | Presidential candidates | Party | Electoral vote | Vice-presidential candidates | Party | Electoral vote |
|---|---|---|---|---|---|---|
| 1836 | Martin Van Buren | Democratic | 170 | Richard M. Johnson[5] | Democratic | 147 |
| | William H. Harrison | Whig | 73 | Francis Granger | Whig | 77 |
| | Hugh L. White | Whig | 26 | John Tyler | Whig | 47 |
| | Daniel Webster | Whig | 14 | William Smith | Ind. (no party) | 23 |
| | W. P. Mangum | Ind. (no party) | 11 | | | |
| 1840 | William H. Harrison[6] | Whig | 234 | John Tyler | Whig | 234 |
| | Martin Van Buren | Democratic | 60 | Richard M. Johnson | Democratic | 48 |
| | | | | L. W. Tazewell | Ind. (no party) | 11 |
| | | | | James K. Polk | Democratic | 1 |
| 1844 | James K. Polk | Democratic | 170 | George M. Dallas | Democratic | 170 |
| | Henry Clay | Whig | 105 | Theo. Frelinghuysen | Whig | 105 |
| 1848 | Zachary Taylor[7] | Whig | 163 | Millard Fillmore | Whig | 163 |
| | Lewis Cass | Democratic | 127 | William O. Butler | Democratic | 127 |
| 1852 | Franklin Pierce | Democratic | 254 | William R. King | Democratic | 254 |
| | Winfield Scott | Whig | 42 | William A. Graham | Whig | 42 |
| 1856 | James Buchanan | Democratic | 174 | John C. Breckinridge | Democratic | 174 |
| | John C. Fremont | Republican | 114 | William L. Dayton | Republican | 114 |
| | Millard Fillmore | American[8] | 8 | A. J. Donelson | American[8] | 8 |
| 1860 | Abraham Lincoln | Republican | 180 | Hannibal Hamlin | Republican | 180 |
| | John C. Breckinridge | Democratic | 72 | Joseph Lane | Democratic | 72 |
| | John Bell | Const. Union | 39 | Edward Everett | Const. Union | 39 |
| | Stephen A. Douglas | Democratic | 12 | H. V. Johnson | Democratic | 12 |
| 1864 | Abraham Lincoln[9] | Union[10] | 212 | Andrew Johnson | Union[15] | 212 |
| | George B. McClellan | Democratic | 21 | G. H. Pendleton | Democratic | 21 |
| 1868 | Ulysses S. Grant | Republican | 214 | Schuyler Colfax | Republican | 214 |
| | Horatio Seymour | Democratic | 80 | Francis P. Blair, Jr. | Democratic | 80 |
| | Votes not counted[11] | | 23 | Votes not counted[11] | | 23 |

| Year | Presidential candidates | Party | Electoral vote | Popular vote | Vice-presidential candidates and party |
|---|---|---|---|---|---|
| 1872 | Ulysses S. Grant | Republican | 286 | 3,597,132 | Henry Wilson—R |
| | Horace Greeley | Dem., Liberal Rep. | ([12]) | 2,834,125 | B. Gratz Brown—D, LR—(47) |
| | Thomas A. Hendricks | Democratic | 42 | | Scattering—(19) |
| | B. Gratz Brown | Dem., Liberal Rep. | 18 | | Votes not counted—(14) |
| | Charles J. Jenkins | Democratic | 2 | | |
| | David Davis | Democratic | 1 | | |
| | Votes not counted | | 17 | | |
| 1876[13] | Rutherford B. Hayes | Republican | 185 | 4,033,768 | William A. Wheeler—R |
| | Samuel J. Tilden | Democratic | 184 | 4,285,992 | Thomas A. Hendricks—D |
| | Peter Cooper | Greenback | 0 | 81,737 | Samuel F. Cary—G |
| 1880 | James A. Garfield[14] | Republican | 214 | 4,449,053 | Chester A. Arthur—R |
| | Winfield S. Hancock | Democratic | 155 | 4,442,035 | William H. English—D |
| | James B. Weaver | Greenback | 0 | 308,578 | B. J. Chambers—G |
| 1884 | Grover Cleveland | Democratic | 219 | 4,911,017 | Thomas A. Hendricks—D |
| | James G. Blaine | Republican | 182 | 4,848,334 | John A. Logan—R |
| | Benjamin F. Butler | Greenback | 0 | 175,370 | A. M. West—G |
| | John P. St. John | Prohibition | 0 | 150,369 | William Daniel—P |
| 1888 | Benjamin Harrison | Republican | 233 | 5,440,216 | Levi P. Morton—R |
| | Grover Cleveland | Democratic | 168 | 5,538,233 | A. G. Thurman—D |
| | Clinton B. Fisk | Prohibition | 0 | 249,506 | John A. Brooks—P |
| | Alson J. Streeter | Union Labor | 0 | 146,935 | Charles E. Cunningham—UL |
| 1892 | Grover Cleveland | Democratic | 277 | 5,556,918 | Adlai E. Stevenson—D |
| | Benjamin Harrison | Republican | 145 | 5,176,108 | Whitelaw Reid—R |
| | James B. Weaver | People's[15] | 22 | 1,041,028 | James G. Field—Peo |
| | John Bidwell | Prohibition | 0 | 264,133 | James B. Cranfill—P |

| Year | Presidential candidates | Party | Electoral vote | Popular vote | Vice-presidential candidates and party |
|------|------------------------|-------|----------------|--------------|----------------------------------------|
| 1896 | William McKinley | Republican | 271 | 7,035,638 | Garret A. Hobart—R |
| | William J. Bryan | Dem., People's[15] | 176 | 6,467,946 | Arthur Sewall—D—(149) |
| | | | | | Thomas E. Watson—Peo—(27) |
| | John M. Palmer | Natl. Dem. | 0 | 133,148 | Simon B. Buckner—ND |
| | Joshua Levering | Prohibition | 0 | 132,007 | Hale Johnson—P |
| 1900 | William McKinley[16] | Republican | 292 | 7,219,530 | Theodore Roosevelt—R |
| | William J. Bryan | Dem., People's[15] | 155 | 6,358,071 | Adlai E. Stevenson—D, Peo |
| | Eugene V. Debs | Social Democratic | 0 | 94,768 | Job Harriman—SD |
| 1904 | Theodore Roosevelt | Republican | 336 | 7,628,834 | Charles W. Fairbanks—R |
| | Alton B. Parker | Democratic | 140 | 5,084,491 | Henry G. Davis—D |
| | Eugene V. Debs | Socialist | 0 | 402,400 | Benjamin Hanford—S |
| 1908 | William H. Taft | Republican | 321 | 7,679,006 | James S. Sherman—R |
| | William J. Bryan | Democratic | 162 | 6,409,106 | John W. Kern—D |
| | Eugene V. Debs | Socialist | 0 | 402,820 | Benjamin Hanford—S |
| 1912 | Woodrow Wilson | Democratic | 435 | 6,286,214 | Thomas R. Marshall—D |
| | Theodore Roosevelt | Progressive | 88 | 4,126,020 | Hiram Johnson—Prog |
| | William H. Taft | Republican | 8 | 3,483,922 | Nicholas M. Butler—R[17] |
| | Eugene V. Debs | Socialist | 0 | 897,011 | Emil Seidel—S |
| 1916 | Woodrow Wilson | Democratic | 277 | 9,129,606 | Thomas R. Marshall—D |
| | Charles E. Hughes | Republican | 254 | 8,538,221 | Charles W. Fairbanks—R |
| | A. L. Benson | Socialist | 0 | 585,113 | G. R. Kirkpatrick—S |
| 1920 | Warren G. Harding[18] | Republican | 404 | 16,152,200 | Calvin Coolidge—R |
| | James M. Cox | Democratic | 127 | 9,147,353 | Franklin D. Roosevelt—D |
| | Eugene V. Debs | Socialist | 0 | 917,799 | Seymour Stedman—S |
| 1924 | Calvin Coolidge | Republican | 382 | 15,725,016 | Charles G. Dawes—R |
| | John W. Davis | Democratic | 136 | 8,385,586 | Charles W. Bryan—D |
| | Robert M. LaFollette | Progressive, Socialist | 13 | 4,822,856 | Burton K. Wheeler—Prog S |
| 1928 | Herbert Hoover | Republican | 444 | 21,392,190 | Charles Curtis—R |
| | Alfred E. Smith | Democratic | 87 | 15,016,443 | Joseph T. Robinson—D |
| | Norman Thomas | Socialist | 0 | 267,420 | James H. Maurer—S |
| 1932 | Franklin D. Roosevelt | Democratic | 472 | 22,821,857 | John N. Garner—D |
| | Herbert Hoover | Republican | 59 | 15,761,841 | Charles Curtis—R |
| | Norman Thomas | Socialist | 0 | 884,781 | James H. Maurer—S |
| 1936 | Franklin D. Roosevelt | Democratic | 523 | 27,751,597 | John N. Garner—D |
| | Alfred M. Landon | Republican | 8 | 16,679,583 | Frank Knox—R |
| | Norman Thomas | Socialist | 0 | 187,720 | George Nelson—S |
| 1940 | Franklin D. Roosevelt | Democratic | 449 | 27,244,160 | Henry A. Wallace—D |
| | Wendell L. Willkie | Republican | 82 | 22,305,198 | Charles L. McNary—R |
| | Norman Thomas | Socialist | 0 | 99,557 | Maynard C. Krueger—S |
| 1944 | Franklin D. Roosevelt[19] | Democratic | 432 | 25,602,504 | Harry S. Truman—D |
| | Thomas E. Dewey | Republican | 99 | 22,006,285 | John W. Bricker—R |
| | Norman Thomas | Socialist | 0 | 80,518 | Darlington Hoopes—S |
| 1948 | Harry S. Truman | Democratic | 303 | 24,179,345 | Alben W. Barkley—D |
| | Thomas E. Dewey | Republican | 189 | 21,991,291 | Earl Warren—R |
| | J. Strom Thurmond | States' Rights Dem. | 39 | 1,176,125 | Fielding L. Wright—SR |
| | Henry A. Wallace | Progressive | 0 | 1,157,326 | Glen Taylor—Prog |
| | Norman Thomas | Socialist | 0 | 139,572 | Tucker P. Smith—S |
| 1952 | Dwight D. Eisenhower | Republican | 442 | 33,936,234 | Richard M. Nixon—R |
| | Adlai E. Stevenson | Democratic | 89 | 27,314,992 | John J. Sparkman—D |
| 1956 | Dwight D. Eisenhower | Republican | 457 | 35,590,472 | Richard M. Nixon—R |
| | Adlai E. Stevenson | Democratic | 73[20] | 26,022,752 | Estes Kefauver—D |
| 1960 | John F. Kennedy[22] | Democratic | 303 | 34,226,731 | Lyndon B. Johnson—D |
| | Richard M. Nixon | Republican | 219[21] | 34,108,157 | Henry Cabot Lodge—R |

| Year | Presidential candidates | Party | Electoral vote | Popular vote | Vice-presidential candidates and party |
|------|------------------------|-------|---------------|--------------|----------------------------------------|
| 1964 | Lyndon B. Johnson | Democratic | 486 | 43,129,484 | Hubert H. Humphrey—D |
|      | Barry M. Goldwater | Republican | 52 | 27,178,188 | William E. Miller—R |
| 1968 | Richard M. Nixon | Republican | 301 | 31,785,480 | Spiro T. Agnew—R |
|      | Hubert H. Humphrey | Democratic | 191 | 31,275,166 | Edmund S. Muskie—D |
|      | George C. Wallace | American Independent | 46 | 9,906,473 | Curtis F. LeMay—AI |
| 1972 | Richard M. Nixon[23] | Republican | 520[24] | 47,169,911 | Spiro T. Agnew—R |
|      | George McGovern | Democratic | 17 | 29,170,383 | Sargent Shriver—D |
|      | John G. Schmitz | American | 0 | 1,099,482 | Thomas J. Anderson—A |
| 1976 | Jimmy Carter | Democratic | 297 | 40,830,763 | Walter F. Mondale—D |
|      | Gerald R. Ford | Republican | 240[25] | 39,147,973 | Robert J. Dole—R |
|      | Eugene J. McCarthy | Independent | 0 | 756,631 | None |
| 1980 | Ronald Reagan | Republican | 489 | 43,899,248 | George Bush—R |
|      | Jimmy Carter | Democratic | 49 | 36,481,435 | Walter F. Mondale—D |
|      | John B. Anderson | Independent | 0 | 5,719,437 | Patrick J. Lucey—I |
| 1984 | Ronald Reagan | Republican | 525 | 54,455,075 | George Bush—R |
|      | Walter F. Mondale | Democratic | 13 | 37,577,185 | Geraldine A. Ferraro—D |

1. Only 10 states participated in the election. The New York legislature chose no electors, and North Carolina and Rhode Island had not yet ratified the Constitution. 2. As Jefferson and Burr were tied, the House of Representatives chose the President. In a vote by states, 10 votes were cast for Jefferson, 4 for Burr; 2 votes were not cast. 3. As no candidate had an electoral-vote majority, the House of Representatives chose the President from the first three. In a vote by states, 13 votes were cast for Adams, 7 for Jackson, and 4 for Crawford. 4. The Antimasonic Party on Sept. 26, 1831, was the first party to hold a nominating convention to choose candidates for President and Vice-President. 5. As Johnson did not have an electoral-vote majority, the Senate chose him 33–14 over Granger, the others being legally out of the race. 6. Harrison died April 4, 1841, and Tyler succeeded him April 6. 7. Taylor died July 9, 1850, and Fillmore succeeded him July 10. 8. Also known as the Know-Nothing Party. 9. Lincoln died April 15, 1865, and Johnson succeeded him the same day. 10. Name adopted by the Republican National Convention of 1864. Johnson was a War Democrat. 11. 23 Southern electoral votes were excluded. 12. See Election of 1872 in *Unusual Voting Results* under Elections, Presidential, in Index. 13. See Election of 1876 in *Unusual Voting Results* under Elections, Presidential, in Index. 14. Garfield died Sept. 19, 1881, and Arthur succeeded him Sept. 20. 15. Members of People's Party were called Populists. 16. McKinley died Sept. 14, 1901, and Roosevelt succeeded him the same day. 17. James S. Sherman, Republican candidate for Vice President, died Oct. 30, 1912, and the Republican electoral votes were cast for Butler. 18. Harding died Aug. 2, 1923, and Coolidge succeeded him Aug. 3. 19. Roosevelt died April 12, 1945, and Truman succeeded him the same day. 20. One electoral vote from Alabama was cast for Walter B. Jones. 21. Sen. Harry F. Byrd received 15 electoral votes. 22. Kennedy died Nov. 22, 1963, and Johnson succeeded him the same day. 23. Nixon resigned Aug. 9, 1974, and Gerald R. Ford succeeded him the same day. 24. One electoral vote from Virginia was cast for John Hospers, Libertarian Party. 25. One electoral vote from Washington was cast for Ronald Reagan.

## Characteristics of Voters in 1984 Presidential Election

### (in thousands)

| Characteristic | Persons of voting age | Persons reporting they voted Total | Persons reporting they voted Percent | Persons reporting they did not vote | Characteristic | Persons of voting age | Persons reporting they voted Total | Persons reporting they voted Percent | Persons reporting they did not vote |
|----------------|----------------------|-------|---------|----------------|----------------|----------------------|-------|---------|----------------|
| Male | 80,327 | 47,354 | 59.0 | 32,973 | North and West | 112,376 | 69,223 | 61.6 | 43,153 |
| Female | 89,636 | 54,524 | 60.8 | 35,112 | South | 57,587 | 32,709 | 56.8 | 24,878 |
| White | 146,761 | 90,152 | 61.4 | 56,610 | Education | | | | |
| Black | 18,432 | 10,293 | 55.8 | 8,139 | 8 years or less | 20,580 | 8,828 | 42.9 | 11,752 |
| Spanish origin[1] | 9,471 | 3,092 | 32.6 | 6,379 | 9-11 years | 22,068 | 9,798 | 44.4 | 12,270 |
| Age: 18-20 | 11,249 | 4,131 | 36.7 | 7,118 | 12 years | 67,807 | 39,802 | 58.7 | 28,005 |
| 21-24 | 16,727 | 7,276 | 43.5 | 9,451 | 13-15 years | 30,915 | 20,867 | 67.5 | 10,048 |
| 25-34 | 40,292 | 21,978 | 54.5 | 18,313 | 16 or more | 28,593 | 22,617 | 79.1 | 5,976 |
| 35-44 | 30,731 | 19,514 | 63.5 | 11,217 | Employed | 104,173 | 64,170 | 61.6 | 40,003 |
| 45-54 | 22,257 | 15,035 | 67.5 | 7,222 | Unemployed | 7,389 | 3,251 | 44.0 | 4,138 |
| 55-64 | 22,050 | 15,889 | 72.1 | 6,160 | Not in labor force | 58,401 | 34,398 | 58.9 | 24,003 |
| 65-74 | 16,382 | 11,761 | 71.8 | 4,621 | **Total** | **169,963** | **101,878** | **59.9** | **68,085** |
| 75 and over | 10,276 | 6,294 | 61.2 | 3,982 | | | | | |

NOTE: Persons of Spanish origin may be of any race. *Source:* Department of Commerce, Bureau of the Census.

# Qualifications for Voting

The Supreme Court decision of March 21, 1972, declared lengthy requirements for voting in state and local elections unconstitutional and suggested that 30 days was an ample period. Most of the states have changed or eliminated their durational residency requirements to comply with the ruling, as shown.

## NO DURATIONAL RESIDENCY REQUIREMENT

Alabama,[6] Arkansas, Connecticut,[13] Delaware,[12] District of Columbia,[16] Florida,[5] Georgia,[2] Hawaii,[2] Iowa,[6] Louisiana, Maine, Maryland, Massachusetts,[3] Missouri,[4] Nebraska,[9] New Hampshire,[17] New Mexico,[7] North Carolina, Oklahoma, South Carolina,[2] South Dakota,[10] Tennessee, Texas, Virginia, West Virginia,[2] Wyoming[2]

## 30-DAY RESIDENCY REQUIREMENT

Alaska,[18] Arizona,[11] Idaho, Illinois, Indiana, Kentucky,[2] Michigan, Mississippi, Montana, Nevada, New Jersey, New York, North Dakota,[3] Ohio, Pennsylvania, Rhode Island, Utah, Washington

## OTHER

California,[19] Colorado,[1] Kansas, Minnesota[15] and Oregon,[8] 20 days; Vermont, 17 days;[14] Wisconsin, 10 days

1. 29 days for voters residing overseas, 32 days for all other voters. 2. 30-day registration requirement. 3. 10-day for Presidential elections. 4. Must be registered 28 days prior to vote. 5. 30-day registration requirement for national elections; 30-day for state elections. 6. 10-day registration requirement. 7. 42-day registration requirement. 8. Permits registration up to 5 p.m. of day before election with approved ID. 9. Registration requirement, 2nd Friday prior to elections. 10. 15-day registration requirement. 11. Residency in the state 50 days next preceding the election except 30 days for presidential election. 12. Must reside in Delaware and register by the last day that the books are open for registration. 13. Registration deadline 21st day before election; registration and party enrollment deadline the day before primary. 14. Administrative cut-off date for processing applications. 15. Permits registration and voting on election day with approved ID. 16. D.C. must process within 18 days. Registration stops 30 days before any election and until 15 days after. Voters must inform Board of Elections of change of address within 30 days of moving. 17. Registration requirement, 2nd Saturday prior to elections. 18. If otherwise qualified but has not been a resident of the election district for at least 30 days preceding the date of a presidential election, is entitled to register and vote for presidential and vice–presidential candidates. 19. 29 days before an election. *Source: Information Please* questionnaires to the states.

# Unusual Voting Results

## Election of 1872

The presidential and vice-presidential candidates of the Liberal Republicans and the northern Democrats in 1872 were Horace Greeley and B. Gratz Brown. Greeley died Nov. 29, 1872, before his 66 electors voted. In the electoral balloting for President, 63 of Greeley's votes were scattered among four other men, including Brown.

## Election of 1876

In the election of 1876 Samuel J. Tilden, the Democratic candidate, received a popular majority but lacked one undisputed electoral vote to carry a clear majority of the electoral college. The crux of the problem was in the 22 electoral votes which were in dispute because Florida, Louisiana, South Carolina, and Oregon each sent in two sets of election returns. In the three southern states, Republican election boards threw out enough Democratic votes to certify the Republican candidate, Hayes. In Oregon, the Democratic governor disqualified a Republican elector, replacing him with a Democrat. Since the Senate was Republican and the House of Representatives Democratic, it seemed useless to refer the disputed returns to the two houses for solution. Instead Congress appointed an Electoral Commission with five representatives each from the Senate, the House, and the Supreme Court. All but one Justice was named, giving the Commission seven Republican and seven Democratic members. The naming of the fifth Justice was left to the other four. He was a Republican who first favored Tilden but, under pressure from his party, switched to Hayes, ensuring his election by the Commission voting 8 to 7 on party lines.

## Minority Presidents

Fifteen candidates have become President of the United States with a popular vote less than 50% of the total cast. It should be noted, however, that in elections before 1872, presidential electors were not chosen by popular vote in all states. Adams' election in 1824 was by the House of Representatives, which chose him over Jackson, who had a plurality of both electoral and popular votes, but not a majority in the electoral college.

Besides Jackson in 1824, only two other candidates receiving the largest popular vote have failed to gain a majority in the electoral college—Samuel J. Tilden (D) in 1876 and Grover Cleveland (D) in 1888.

The "minority" Presidents follow:

# Vote Received by Minority Presidents

| Year | President | Electoral vote Percent | Popular vote Percent |
|---|---|---|---|
| 1824 | John Q. Adams | 31.8 | 29.8 |
| 1844 | James K. Polk (D) | 61.8 | 49.3 |
| 1848 | Zachary Taylor (W) | 56.2 | 47.3 |
| 1856 | James Buchanan (D) | 58.7 | 45.3 |
| 1860 | Abraham Lincoln (R) | 59.4 | 39.9 |
| 1876 | Rutherford B. Hayes (R) | 50.1 | 47.9 |
| 1880 | James A. Garfield (R) | 57.9 | 48.3 |
| 1884 | Grover Cleveland (D) | 54.6 | 48.8 |
| 1888 | Benjamin Harrison (R) | 58.1 | 47.8 |
| 1892 | Grover Cleveland (D) | 62.4 | 46.0 |
| 1912 | Woodrow Wilson (D) | 81.9 | 41.8 |
| 1916 | Woodrow Wilson (D) | 52.1 | 49.3 |
| 1948 | Harry S. Truman (D) | 57.1 | 49.5 |
| 1960 | John F. Kennedy (D) | 56.4 | 49.7 |
| 1968 | Richard M. Nixon (R) | 56.1 | 43.4 |

# Government Officials
## Cabinet Members With Dates of Appointment

Although the Constitution made no provision for a President's advisory group, the heads of the three executive departments (State, Treasury, and War) and the Attorney General were organized by Washington into such a group; and by about 1793, the name "Cabinet" was applied to it. With the exception of the Attorney General up to 1870 and the Postmaster General from 1829 to 1872, Cabinet members have been heads of executive departments.

A Cabinet member is appointed by the President, subject to the confirmation of the Senate; and as his term is not fixed, he may be replaced at any time by the President. At a change in Administration, it is customary for him to tender his resignation, but he remains in office until a successor is appointed.

The table of Cabinet members lists only those members who actually served after being duly commissioned.

The dates shown are those of appointment. "Cont." indicates that the term continued from the previous Administration for a substantial amount of time.

With the creation of the Department of Transportation in 1966, the Cabinet consisted of 12 members. This figure was reduced to 11 when the Post Office Department became an independent agency in 1970 but, with the establishment in 1977 of a Department of Energy, became 12 again. Creation of the Department of Education in 1980 raised the number to 13.

**WASHINGTON**

| | |
|---|---|
| Secretary of State | Thomas Jefferson 1789 |
| | Edmund Randolph 1794 |
| | Timothy Pickering 1795 |
| Secretary of the Treasury | Alexander Hamilton 1789 |
| | Oliver Wolcott, Jr. 1795 |
| Secretary of War | Henry Knox 1789 |
| | Timothy Pickering 1795 |
| | James McHenry 1796 |
| Attorney General | Edmund Randolph 1789 |
| | William Bradford 1794 |
| | Charles Lee 1795 |

**J. ADAMS**

| | |
|---|---|
| Secretary of State | Timothy Pickering (Cont.) |
| | John Marshall 1800 |
| Secretary of the Treasury | Oliver Wolcott, Jr. (Cont.) |
| | Samuel Dexter 1801 |
| Secretary of War | James McHenry (Cont.) |
| | Samuel Dexter 1800 |
| Attorney General | Charles Lee (Cont.) |
| Secretary of the Navy | Benjamin Stoddert 1798 |

**JEFFERSON**

| | |
|---|---|
| Secretary of State | James Madison 1801 |
| Secretary of the Treasury | Samuel Dexter (Cont.) |
| | Albert Gallatin 1801 |
| Secretary of War | Henry Dearborn 1801 |
| Attorney General | Levi Lincoln 1801 |
| | Robert Smith 1805 |
| | John Breckinridge 1805 |
| | Caesar A. Rodney 1807 |
| Secretary of the Navy | Benjamin Stoddert (Cont.) |
| | Robert Smith 1801 |

**MADISON**

| | |
|---|---|
| Secretary of State | Robert Smith 1809 |
| | James Monroe 1811 |
| Secretary of the Treasury | Albert Gallatin (Cont.) |
| | George W. Campbell 1814 |
| | Alexander J. Dallas 1814 |
| | William H. Crawford 1816 |
| Secretary of War | William Eustis 1809 |
| | John Armstrong 1813 |
| | James Monroe 1814 |
| | William H. Crawford 1815 |
| Attorney General | Caesar A. Rodney (Cont.) |
| | William Pinckney 1811 |
| | Richard Rush 1814 |
| Secretary of the Navy | Paul Hamilton 1809 |
| | William Jones 1813 |
| | B. W. Crowninshield 1814 |

**MONROE**

| | |
|---|---|
| Secretary of State | John Quincy Adams 1817 |
| Secretary of the Treasury | William H. Crawford (Cont.) |
| Secretary of War | John C. Calhoun 1817 |
| Attorney General | Richard Rush (Cont.) |

| | |
|---|---|
| | William Wirt 1817 |
| Secretary of the Navy | B. W. Crowninshield (Cont.) |
| | Smith Thompson 1818 |
| | Samuel L. Southard 1823 |

**J. Q. ADAMS**

| | |
|---|---|
| Secretary of State | Henry Clay 1825 |
| Secretary of the Treasury | Richard Rush 1825 |
| Secretary of War | James Barbour 1825 |
| | Peter B. Porter 1828 |
| Attorney General | William Wirt (Cont.) |
| Secretary of the Navy | Samuel L. Southard (Cont.) |

**JACKSON**

| | |
|---|---|
| Secretary of State | Martin Van Buren 1829 |
| | Edward Livingston 1831 |
| | Louis McLane 1833 |
| | John Forsyth 1834 |
| Secretary of the Treasury | Samuel D. Ingham 1829 |
| | Louis McLane 1831 |
| | William J. Duane 1833 |
| | Roger B. Taney[3] 1833 |
| | Levi Woodbury 1834 |
| Secretary of War | John H. Eaton 1829 |
| | Lewis Cass 1831 |
| Attorney General | John M. Berrien 1829 |
| | Roger B. Taney 1831 |
| | Benjamin F. Butler 1833 |
| Postmaster General[?] | William T. Barry 1829 |
| | Amos Kendall 1835 |
| Secretary of the Navy | John Branch 1829 |
| | Levi Woodbury 1831 |
| | Mahlon Dickerson 1834 |

**VAN BUREN**

| | |
|---|---|
| Secretary of State | John Forsyth (Cont.) |
| Secretary of the Treasury | Levi Woodbury (Cont.) |
| Secretary of War | Joel R. Poinsett 1837 |
| Attorney General | Benjamin F. Butler (Cont.) |
| | Felix Grundy 1838 |
| | Henry D. Gilpin 1840 |
| Postmaster General | Amos Kendall (Cont.) |
| | John M. Niles 1840 |
| Secretary of the Navy | Mahlon Dickerson (Cont.) |
| | James K. Paulding 1838 |

**W. H. HARRISON**

| | |
|---|---|
| Secretary of State | Daniel Webster 1841 |
| Secretary of the Treasury | Thomas Ewing 1841 |
| Secretary of War | John Bell 1841 |
| Attorney General | John J. Crittenden 1841 |
| Postmaster General | Francis Granger 1841 |
| Secretary of the Navy | George E. Badger 1841 |

**TYLER**

| | |
|---|---|
| Secretary of State | Daniel Webster (Cont.) |
| | Abel P. Upshur 1843 |
| | John C. Calhoun 1844 |
| Secretary of the Treasury | Thomas Ewing (Cont.) |

|  | Walter Forward 1841 |
|---|---|
|  | John C. Spencer[3] 1843 |
|  | George M. Bibb 1844 |
| Secretary of War | John Bell (Cont.) |
|  | John C. Spencer 1841 |
|  | James M. Porter[3] 1843 |
|  | William Wilkins 1844 |
| Attorney General | John J. Crittenden (Cont.) |
|  | Hugh S. Legaré 1841 |
|  | John Nelson 1843 |
| Postmaster General | Francis Granger (Cont.) |
|  | Charles A. Wickliffe 1841 |
| Secretary of the Navy | George E. Badger (Cont.) |
|  | Abel P. Upshur 1841 |
|  | David Henshaw[3] 1843 |
|  | Thomas W. Gilmer 1844 |
|  | John Y. Mason 1844 |

**POLK**

| Secretary of State | James Buchanan 1845 |
|---|---|
| Secretary of the Treasury | Robert J. Walker 1845 |
| Secretary of War | William L. Marcy 1845 |
| Attorney General | John Y. Mason 1845 |
|  | Nathan Clifford 1846 |
|  | Isaac Toucey 1848 |
| Postmaster General | Cave Johnson 1845 |
| Secretary of the Navy | George Bancroft 1845 |
|  | John Y. Mason 1846 |

**TAYLOR**

| Secretary of State | John M. Clayton 1849 |
|---|---|
| Secretary of the Treasury | William M. Meredith 1849 |
| Secretary of War | George W. Crawford 1849 |
| Attorney General | Reverdy Johnson 1849 |
| Postmaster General | Jacob Collamer 1849 |
| Secretary of the Navy | William B. Preston 1849 |
| Secretary of the Interior | Thomas Ewing 1849 |

**FILLMORE**

| Secretary of State | Daniel Webster 1850 |
|---|---|
|  | Edward Everett 1852 |
| Secretary of the Treasury | Thomas Corwin 1850 |
| Secretary of War | Charles M. Conrad 1850 |
| Attorney General | John J. Crittenden 1850 |
| Postmaster General | Nathan K. Hall 1850 |
|  | Samuel D. Hubbard 1852 |
| Secretary of the Navy | William A. Graham 1850 |
|  | John P. Kennedy 1852 |
| Secretary of the Interior | Thos. M. T. McKennan 1850 |
|  | Alex. H. H. Stuart 1850 |

**PIERCE**

| Secretary of State | William L. Marcy 1853 |
|---|---|
| Secretary of the Treasury | James Guthrie 1853 |
| Secretary of War | Jefferson Davis 1853 |
| Attorney General | Caleb Cushing 1853 |
| Postmaster General | James Campbell 1853 |
| Secretary of the Navy | James C. Dobbin 1853 |
| Secretary of the Interior | Robert McClelland 1853 |

**BUCHANAN**

| Secretary of State | Lewis Cass 1857 |
|---|---|
|  | Jeremiah S. Black 1860 |
| Secretary of the Treasury | Howell Cobb 1857 |
|  | Philip F. Thomas 1860 |
|  | John A. Dix 1861 |
| Secretary of War | John B. Floyd 1857 |
|  | Joseph Holt 1861 |
| Attorney General | Jeremiah S. Black 1857 |
|  | Edwin M. Stanton 1860 |
| Postmaster General | Aaron V. Brown 1857 |
|  | Joseph Holt 1859 |
|  | Horatio King 1861 |
| Secretary of the Navy | Isaac Toucey 1857 |
| Secretary of the Interior | Jacob Thompson 1857 |

**LINCOLN**

| Secretary of State | William H. Seward 1861 |
|---|---|
| Secretary of the Treasury | Salmon P. Chase 1861 |
|  | William P. Fessenden 1864 |
|  | Hugh McCulloch 1865 |
| Secretary of War | Simon Cameron 1861 |
|  | Edwin M. Stanton 1862 |

| Attorney General | Edward Bates 1861 |
|---|---|
|  | James Speed 1864 |
| Postmaster General | Montgomery Blair 1861 |
|  | William Dennison 1864 |
| Secretary of the Navy | Gideon Welles 1861 |
| Secretary of the Interior | Caleb B. Smith 1861 |
|  | John P. Usher 1863 |

**A. JOHNSON**

| Secretary of State | William H. Seward (Cont.) |
|---|---|
| Secretary of the Treasury | Hugh McCulloch (Cont.) |
| Secretary of War | Edwin M. Stanton (Cont.) |
|  | John M. Schofield 1868 |
| Attorney General | James Speed (Cont.) |
|  | Henry Stanbery 1866 |
|  | William M. Evarts 1868 |
| Postmaster General | William Dennison (Cont.) |
|  | Alexander W. Randall 1866 |
| Secretary of the Navy | Gideon Welles (Cont.) |
| Secretary of the Interior | John P. Usher (Cont.) |
|  | James Harlan 1865 |
|  | Orville H. Browning 1866 |

**GRANT**

| Secretary of State | Elihu B. Washburne 1869 |
|---|---|
|  | Hamilton Fish 1869 |
| Secretary of the Treasury | George S. Boutwell 1869 |
|  | William A. Richardson 1873 |
|  | Benjamin H. Bristow 1874 |
|  | Lot M. Morrill 1876 |
| Secretary of War | John A. Rawlins 1869 |
|  | William W. Belknap 1869 |
|  | Alphonso Taft 1876 |
|  | James D. Cameron 1876 |
| Attorney General | Ebenezer R. Hoar 1869 |
|  | Amos T. Akerman 1870 |
|  | George H. Williams 1871 |
|  | Edwards Pierrepont 1875 |
|  | Alphonso Taft 1876 |
| Postmaster General | John A. J. Creswell 1869 |
|  | Marshall Jewell 1874 |
|  | James N. Tyner 1876 |
| Secretary of the Navy | Adolph E. Borie 1869 |
|  | George M. Robeson 1869 |
| Secretary of the Interior | Jacob D. Cox 1869 |
|  | Columbus Delano 1870 |
|  | Zachariah Chandler 1875 |

**HAYES**

| Secretary of State | William M. Evarts 1877 |
|---|---|
| Secretary of the Treasury | John Sherman 1877 |
| Secretary of War | George W. McCrary 1877 |
|  | Alexander Ramsey 1879 |
| Attorney General | Charles Devens 1877 |
| Postmaster General | David M. Key 1877 |
|  | Horace Maynard 1880 |
| Secretary of the Navy | Richard W. Thompson 1877 |
|  | Nathan Goff, Jr. 1881 |
| Secretary of the Interior | Carl Schurz 1877 |

**GARFIELD**

| Secretary of State | James G. Blaine 1881 |
|---|---|
| Secretary of the Treasury | William Windom 1881 |
| Secretary of War | Robert T. Lincoln 1881 |
| Attorney General | Wayne MacVeagh 1881 |
| Postmaster General | Thomas L. James 1881 |
| Secretary of the Navy | William H. Hunt 1881 |
| Secretary of the Interior | Samuel J. Kirkwood 1881 |

**ARTHUR**

| Secretary of State | James G. Blaine (Cont.) |
|---|---|
|  | F. T. Frelinghuysen 1881 |
| Secretary of the Treasury | William Windom (Cont.) |
|  | Charles J. Folger 1881 |
|  | Walter Q. Gresham 1884 |
|  | Hugh McCulloch 1884 |
| Secretary of War | Robert T. Lincoln (Cont.) |
| Attorney General | Wayne MacVeagh (Cont.) |
|  | Benjamin H. Brewster 1881 |
| Postmaster General | Thomas L. James (Cont.) |
|  | Timothy O. Howe 1881 |
|  | Walter Q. Gresham 1883 |
|  | Frank Hatton 1884 |
| Secretary of the Navy | William H. Hunt (Cont.) |

| | |
|---|---|
| *Secretary of the Interior* | William E. Chandler 1882 |
| | Samuel J. Kirkwood (Cont.) |
| | Henry M. Teller 1882 |

## CLEVELAND

| | |
|---|---|
| *Secretary of State* | Thomas F. Bayard 1885 |
| *Secretary of the Treasury* | Daniel Manning 1885 |
| | Charles S. Fairchild 1887 |
| *Secretary of War* | William C. Endicott 1885 |
| *Attorney General* | Augustus H. Garland 1885 |
| *Postmaster General* | William F. Vilas 1885 |
| | Don M. Dickinson 1888 |
| *Secretary of the Navy* | William C. Whitney 1885 |
| *Secretary of the Interior* | Lucius Q. C. Lamar 1885 |
| | William F. Vilas 1888 |
| *Secretary of Agriculture* | Norman J. Colman 1889 |

## B. HARRISON

| | |
|---|---|
| *Secretary of State* | James G. Blaine 1889 |
| | John W. Foster 1892 |
| *Secretary of the Treasury* | William Windom 1889 |
| | Charles Foster 1891 |
| *Secretary of War* | Redfield Proctor 1889 |
| | Stephen B. Elkins 1891 |
| *Attorney General* | William H. H. Miller 1889 |
| *Postmaster General* | John Wanamaker 1889 |
| *Secretary of the Navy* | Benjamin F. Tracy 1889 |
| *Secretary of the Interior* | John W. Noble 1889 |
| *Secretary of Agriculture* | Jeremiah M. Rusk 1889 |

## CLEVELAND

| | |
|---|---|
| *Secretary of State* | Walter Q. Gresham 1893 |
| | Richard Olney 1895 |
| *Secretary of the Treasury* | John G. Carlisle 1893 |
| *Secretary of War* | Daniel S. Lamont 1893 |
| *Attorney General* | Richard Olney 1893 |
| | Judson Harmon 1895 |
| *Postmaster General* | Wilson S. Bissell 1893 |
| | William L. Wilson 1895 |
| *Secretary of the Navy* | Hilary A. Herbert 1893 |
| *Secretary of the Interior* | Hoke Smith 1893 |
| | David R. Francis 1896 |
| *Secretary of Agriculture* | Julius Sterling Morton 1893 |

## McKINLEY

| | |
|---|---|
| *Secretary of State* | John Sherman 1897 |
| | William R. Day 1898 |
| | John Hay 1898 |
| *Secretary of the Treasury* | Lyman J. Gage 1897 |
| *Secretary of War* | Russell A. Alger 1897 |
| | Elihu Root 1899 |
| *Attorney General* | Joseph McKenna 1897 |
| | John W. Griggs 1898 |
| | Philander C. Knox 1901 |
| *Postmaster General* | James A. Gary 1897 |
| | Charles E. Smith 1898 |
| *Secretary of the Navy* | John D. Long 1897 |
| *Secretary of the Interior* | Cornelius N. Bliss 1897 |
| | Ethan A. Hitchcock 1898 |
| *Secretary of Agriculture* | James Wilson 1897 |

## T. ROOSEVELT

| | |
|---|---|
| *Secretary of State* | John Hay (Cont.) |
| | Elihu Root 1905 |
| | Robert Bacon 1909 |
| *Secretary of the Treasury* | Lyman J. Gage (Cont.) |
| | Leslie M. Shaw 1902 |
| | George B. Cortelyou 1907 |
| *Secretary of War* | Elihu Root (Cont.) |
| | William H. Taft 1904 |
| | Luke E. Wright 1908 |
| *Attorney General* | Philander C. Knox (Cont.) |
| | William H. Moody 1904 |
| | Charles J. Bonaparte 1906 |
| *Postmaster General* | Charles E. Smith (Cont.) |
| | Henry C. Payne 1902 |
| | Robert J. Wynne 1904 |
| | George B. Cortelyou 1905 |
| | George von L. Meyer 1907 |
| *Secretary of the Navy* | John D. Long (Cont.) |
| | William H. Moody 1902 |
| | Paul Morton 1904 |
| | Charles J. Bonaparte 1905 |
| | Victor H. Metcalf 1906 |

| | |
|---|---|
| *Secretary of the Interior* | Truman H. Newberry 1908 |
| | Ethan A. Hitchcock (Cont.) |
| | James R. Garfield 1907 |
| *Secretary of Agriculture* | James Wilson (Cont.) |
| *Secretary of Commerce and Labor* | George B. Cortelyou 1903 |
| | Victor H. Metcalf 1904 |
| | Oscar S. Straus 1906 |

## TAFT

| | |
|---|---|
| *Secretary of State* | Philander C. Knox 1909 |
| *Secretary of the Treasury* | Franklin MacVeagh 1909 |
| *Secretary of War* | Jacob M. Dickinson 1909 |
| | Henry L. Stimson 1911 |
| *Attorney General* | George W. Wickersham 1909 |
| *Postmaster General* | Frank H. Hitchcock 1909 |
| *Secretary of the Navy* | George von L. Meyer 1909 |
| *Secretary of the Interior* | Richard A. Ballinger 1909 |
| | Walter L. Fisher 1911 |
| *Secretary of Agriculture* | James Wilson (Cont.) |
| *Secretary of Commerce and Labor* | Charles Nagel 1909 |

## WILSON

| | |
|---|---|
| *Secretary of State* | William J. Bryan 1913 |
| | Robert Lansing 1915 |
| | Bainbridge Colby 1920 |
| *Secretary of the Treasury* | William G. McAdoo 1913 |
| | Carter Glass 1918 |
| | David F. Houston 1920 |
| *Secretary of War* | Lindley M. Garrison 1913 |
| | Newton D. Baker 1916 |
| *Attorney General* | James C. McReynolds 1913 |
| | Thomas W. Gregory 1914 |
| | A. Mitchell Palmer 1919 |
| *Postmaster General* | Albert S. Burleson 1913 |
| *Secretary of the Navy* | Josephus Daniels 1913 |
| *Secretary of the Interior* | Franklin K. Lane 1913 |
| | John B. Payne 1920 |
| *Secretary of Agriculture* | David F. Houston 1913 |
| | Edwin T. Meredith 1920 |
| *Secretary of Commerce* | William C. Redfield 1913 |
| | Joshua W. Alexander 1919 |
| *Secretary of Labor* | William B. Wilson 1913 |

## HARDING

| | |
|---|---|
| *Secretary of State* | Charles E. Hughes 1921 |
| *Secretary of the Treasury* | Andrew W. Mellon 1921 |
| *Secretary of War* | John W. Weeks 1921 |
| *Attorney General* | Harry M. Daugherty 1921 |
| *Postmaster General* | Will H. Hays 1921 |
| | Hubert Work 1922 |
| | Harry S. New 1923 |
| *Secretary of the Navy* | Edwin Denby 1921 |
| *Secretary of the Interior* | Albert B. Fall 1921 |
| | Hubert Work 1923 |
| *Secretary of Agriculture* | Henry C. Wallace 1921 |
| *Secretary of Commerce* | Herbert Hoover 1921 |
| *Secretary of Labor* | James J. Davis 1921 |

## COOLIDGE

| | |
|---|---|
| *Secretary of State* | Charles E. Hughes (Cont.) |
| | Frank B. Kellogg 1925 |
| *Secretary of the Treasury* | Andrew W. Mellon (Cont.) |
| *Secretary of War* | John W. Weeks (Cont.) |
| | Dwight F. Davis 1925 |
| *Attorney General* | Harry M. Daughtery (Cont.) |
| | Harlan F. Stone 1924 |
| | John G. Sargent 1925 |
| *Postmaster General* | Harry S. New (Cont.) |
| *Secretary of the Navy* | Edwin Denby (Cont.) |
| | Curtis D. Wilbur 1924 |
| *Secretary of the Interior* | Hubert Work (Cont.) |
| | Roy O. West 1928 |
| *Secretary of Agriculture* | Henry C. Wallace (Cont.) |
| | Howard M. Gore 1924 |
| | William M. Jardine 1925 |
| *Secretary of Commerce* | Herbert Hoover (Cont.) |
| | William F. Whiting 1928 |
| *Secretary of Labor* | James J. Davis (Cont.) |

## HOOVER

| | |
|---|---|
| *Secretary of State* | Frank B. Kellogg (Cont.) |

| Secretary of the Treasury | Henry L. Stimson 1929<br>Andrew W. Mellon (Cont.)<br>Ogden L. Mills 1932 |
|---|---|
| Secretary of War | James W. Good 1929<br>Patrick J. Hurley 1929 |
| Attorney General | William D. Mitchell 1929 |
| Postmaster General | Walter F. Brown 1929 |
| Secretary of the Navy | Charles F. Adams 1929 |
| Secretary of the Interior | Ray Lyman Wilbur 1929 |
| Secretary of Agriculture | Arthur M. Hyde 1929 |
| Secretary of Commerce | Robert P. Lamont 1929<br>Roy D. Chapin 1932 |
| Secretary of Labor | James J. Davis (Cont.)<br>William N. Doak 1930 |

## F. D. ROOSEVELT

| Secretary of State | Cordell Hull 1933<br>E. R. Stettinius, Jr. 1944 |
|---|---|
| Secretary of the Treasury | William H. Woodin 1933<br>Henry Morgenthau, Jr. 1934 |
| Secretary of War | George H. Dern 1933<br>Harry H. Woodring 1936<br>Henry L. Stimson 1940 |
| Attorney General | Homer S. Cummings 1933<br>Frank Murphy 1939<br>Robert H. Jackson 1940<br>Francis Biddle 1941 |
| Postmaster General | James A. Farley 1933<br>Frank C. Walker 1940 |
| Secretary of the Navy | Claude A. Swanson 1933<br>Charles Edison 1940<br>Frank Knox 1940<br>James Forrestal 1944 |
| Secretary of the Interior | Harold L. Ickes 1933 |
| Secretary of Agriculture | Henry A. Wallace 1933<br>Claude R. Wickard 1940 |
| Secretary of Commerce | Daniel C. Roper 1933<br>Harry L. Hopkins 1938<br>Jesse H. Jones 1940<br>Henry A. Wallace 1945 |
| Secretary of Labor | Frances Perkins 1933 |

## TRUMAN

| Secretary of State | E. R. Stettinius, Jr. (Cont.)<br>James F. Byrnes 1945<br>George C. Marshall 1947<br>Dean Acheson 1949 |
|---|---|
| Secretary of the Treasury | Henry Morgenthau, Jr. (Cont.)<br>Frederick M. Vinson 1945<br>John W. Snyder 1946 |
| Secretary of Defense | James Forrestal 1947<br>Louis A. Johnson 1949<br>George C. Marshall 1950<br>Robert A. Lovett 1951 |
| Attorney General | Francis Biddle (Cont.)<br>Tom C. Clark 1945<br>J. Howard McGrath 1949<br>James P. McGranery 1952 |
| Postmaster General | Frank C. Walker (Cont.)<br>Robert E. Hannegan 1945<br>Jesse M. Donaldson 1947 |
| Secretary of the Interior | Harold L. Ickes (Cont.)<br>Julius A. Krug 1946<br>Oscar L. Chapman 1949 |
| Secretary of Agriculture | Claude R. Wickard (Cont.)<br>Clinton P. Anderson 1945<br>Charles F. Brannan 1948 |
| Secretary of Commerce | Henry A. Wallace (Cont.)<br>W. Averell Harriman 1946<br>Charles Sawyer 1948 |
| Secretary of Labor | Frances Perkins (Cont.)<br>Lewis B. Schwellenbach 1945<br>Maurice J. Tobin 1948 |
| Secretary of War[2] | Henry L. Stimson (Cont.)<br>Robert P. Patterson 1945<br>Kenneth C. Royall 1947 |
| Secretary of the Navy[2] | James Forrestal (Cont.) |

## EISENHOWER

| Secretary of State | John Foster Dulles 1953<br>Christian A. Herter 1959 |
|---|---|
| Secretary of the Treasury | George M. Humphrey 1953<br>Robert B. Anderson 1957 |
| Secretary of Defense | Charles E. Wilson 1953 |

|  | Neil H. McElroy 1957<br>Thomas S. Gates, Jr. 1959 |
|---|---|
| Attorney General | Herbert Brownell, Jr. 1953<br>William P. Rogers 1958 |
| Postmaster General | Arthur F. Summerfield 1953 |
| Secretary of the Interior | Douglas McKay 1953<br>Frederick A. Seaton 1956 |
| Secretary of Agriculture | Ezra Taft Benson 1953 |
| Secretary of Commerce | Sinclair Weeks 1953<br>Lewis L. Strauss[3] 1958<br>Frederick H. Mueller 1959 |
| Secretary of Labor | Martin P. Durkin 1953<br>James P. Mitchell 1953 |
| Secretary of Health, Education,<br>and Welfare | Oveta Culp Hobby 1953<br>Marion B. Folsom 1955<br>Arthur S. Flemming 1958 |

## KENNEDY

| Secretary of State | Dean Rusk 1961 |
|---|---|
| Secretary of the Treasury | C. Douglas Dillon 1961 |
| Secretary of Defense | Robert S. McNamara 1961 |
| Attorney General | Robert F. Kennedy 1961 |
| Postmaster General | J. Edward Day 1961<br>John A. Gronouski 1963 |
| Secretary of the Interior | Stewart L. Udall 1961 |
| Secretary of Agriculture | Orville L. Freeman 1961 |
| Secretary of Commerce | Luther H. Hodges 1961 |
| Secretary of Labor | Arthur J. Goldberg 1961<br>W. Willard Wirtz 1962 |
| Secretary of Health, Education,<br>and Welfare | Abraham A. Ribicoff 1961<br>Anthony J. Celebrezze 1962 |

## L. B. JOHNSON

| Secretary of State | Dean Rusk (Cont.) |
|---|---|
| Secretary of the Treasury | C. Douglas Dillon (Cont.)<br>Henry H. Fowler 1965<br>Joseph W. Barr[4] 1968 |
| Secretary of Defense | Robert S. McNamara (Cont.)<br>Clark M. Clifford 1968 |
| Attorney General | Robert F. Kennedy (Cont.)<br>N. de B. Katzenbach 1965<br>Ramsey Clark 1967 |
| Postmaster General | John A. Gronouski (Cont.)<br>Lawrence F. O'Brien 1965<br>W. Marvin Watson 1968 |
| Secretary of the Interior | Stewart L. Udall (Cont.) |
| Secretary of Agriculture | Orville L. Freeman (Cont.) |
| Secretary of Commerce | Luther H. Hodges (Cont.)<br>John T. Connor 1964<br>A. B. Trowbridge 1967<br>C. R. Smith 1968 |
| Secretary of Labor | W. Willard Wirtz (Cont.) |
| Secretary of Health, Education,<br>and Welfare | Anthony J. Celebrezze (Cont.)<br>John W. Gardner 1965<br>Wilbur J. Cohen 1968 |
| Secretary of Housing and Urban<br>Development | Robert C. Weaver 1966<br>Robert C. Wood[4] 1969 |
| Secretary of Transportation | Alan S. Boyd 1966 |

## NIXON

| Secretary of State | William P. Rogers 1969<br>Henry A. Kissinger 1973 |
|---|---|
| Secretary of the Treasury | David M. Kennedy 1969<br>John B. Connally 1971<br>George P. Shultz 1972<br>William E. Simon 1974 |
| Secretary of Defense | Melvin R. Laird 1969<br>Elliot L. Richardson 1973<br>James R. Schlesinger 1973 |
| Attorney General | John N. Mitchell 1969<br>Richard G. Kleindienst 1972<br>Elliot L. Richardson 1973<br>William B. Saxbe 1974 |
| Postmaster General[5] | William M. Blount 1969 |
| Secretary of the Interior | Walter J. Hickel 1969<br>Rogers C. B. Morton 1971 |
| Secretary of Agriculture | Clifford M. Hardin 1969<br>Earl L. Butz 1971 |
| Secretary of Commerce | Maurice H. Stans 1969<br>Peter G. Peterson 1972 |

| | |
|---|---|
| | Frederick B. Dent 1973 |
| *Secretary of Labor* | George P. Shultz 1969 |
| | James D. Hodgson 1970 |
| | Peter J. Brennan 1973 |
| *Secretary of Health, Education, and Welfare* | Robert H. Finch 1969 |
| | Elliot L. Richardson 1970 |
| | Caspar W. Weinberger 1973 |
| *Secretary of Housing and Urban Development* | George Romney 1969 |
| | James T. Lynn 1973 |
| *Secretary of Transportation* | John A. Volpe 1969 |
| | Claude S. Brinegar 1973 |

## FORD

| | |
|---|---|
| *Secretary of State* | Henry A. Kissinger (Cont.) |
| *Secretary of the Treasury* | William E. Simon (Cont.) |
| *Secretary of Defense* | James R. Schlesinger (Cont.) |
| | Donald H. Rumsfeld 1975 |
| *Attorney General* | William B. Saxbe (Cont.) |
| | Edward H. Levi 1975 |
| *Secretary of the Interior* | Rogers C. B. Morton (Cont.) |
| | Stanley K. Hathaway 1975 |
| | Thomas S. Kleppe 1975 |
| *Secretary of Agriculture* | Earl L. Butz (Cont.) |
| | John Knebel 1976 |
| *Secretary of Commerce* | Frederick B. Dent (Cont.) |
| | Rogers C. B. Morton 1975 |
| | Elliot L. Richardson 1976 |
| *Secretary of Labor* | Peter J. Brennan (Cont.) |
| | John T. Dunlop 1975 |
| | William J. Usery, Jr. 1976 |
| *Secretary of Health, Education, and Welfare* | Caspar W. Weinberger (Cont.) |
| | F. David Mathews 1975 |
| *Secretary of Housing and Urban Development* | James T. Lynn (Cont.) |
| | Carla A. Hills 1975 |
| *Secretary of Transportation* | Claude S. Brinegar (Cont.) |
| | William T. Coleman, Jr. 1975 |

## CARTER

| | |
|---|---|
| *Secretary of State* | Cyrus R. Vance 1977 |
| | Edmund S. Muskie 1980 |
| *Secretary of the Treasury* | W. Michael Blumenthal 1977 |
| | G. William Miller 1979 |
| *Secretary of Defense* | Harold Brown 1977 |
| *Attorney General* | Griffin B. Bell 1977 |
| | Benjamin R. Civiletti 1979 |
| *Secretary of the Interior* | Cecil D. Andrus 1977 |
| *Secretary of Agriculture* | Bob S. Bergland 1977 |
| *Secretary of Commerce* | Juanita M. Kreps 1977 |
| | Philip M. Klutznick 1979 |
| *Secretary of Labor* | F. Ray Marshall 1977 |
| *Secretary of Health and Human Services[6]* | Joseph A. Califano, Jr. 1977 |
| | Patricia Roberts Harris 1979 |
| *Secretary of Housing and Urban Development* | Patricia Roberts Harris 1977 |
| | Moon Landrieu 1979 |
| *Secretary of Transportation* | Brock Adams 1977 |
| | Neil E. Goldschmidt 1979 |
| *Secretary of Energy* | James R. Schlesinger 1977 |
| | Charles W. Duncan, Jr. 1979 |
| *Secretary of Education* | Shirley Mount Hufstedler 1979 |

## REAGAN

| | |
|---|---|
| *Secretary of State* | Alexander M. Haig, Jr. 1981 |
| | George P. Shultz 1982 |
| *Secretary of the Treasury* | Donald T. Regan 1981 |
| | James A. Baker 3rd 1985 |
| *Secretary of Defense* | Caspar W. Weinberger 1981 |
| *Attorney General* | William French Smith 1981 |
| | Edwin Meese 3rd 1985 |
| *Secretary of the Interior* | James G. Watt 1981 |
| | William P. Clark 1983 |
| | Donald P. Hodel 1985 |
| *Secretary of Agriculture* | John R. Block 1981 |
| *Secretary of Commerce* | Malcolm Baldrige 1981 |
| *Secretary of Labor* | Raymond J. Donovan 1981 |
| | William E. Brock 1985 |
| *Secretary of Health and Human Services* | Richard S. Schweiker 1981 |
| | Margaret M. Heckler 1983 |
| | Otis R. Bowen 1985 |
| *Secretary of Housing and Urban Development* | Samuel R. Pierce, Jr. 1981 |
| *Secretary of Transportation* | Andrew L. Lewis, Jr. 1981 |
| | Elizabeth H. Dole 1983 |
| *Secretary of Energy* | James B. Edwards 1981 |
| | Donald P. Hodel 1983 |
| | John S. Herrington 1985 |
| *Secretary of Education* | T. H. Bell 1981 |
| | William J. Bennett 1985 |

1. The Postmaster General did not become a Cabinet member until 1829. Earlier Postmasters General were: Samuel Osgood (1789), Timothy Pickering (1791), Joseph Habersham (1795), Gideon Granger (1801), Return J. Meigs, Jr. (1814), and John McLean (1823). 2. On July 26, 1947, the Departments of War and of the Navy were incorporated into the Department of Defense. 3. Not confirmed by the Senate. 4. Recess appointment. 5. The Postmaster General is no longer a Cabinet member. 6. Known as Department of Health, Education, and Welfare until May 1980.

## How a Bill Becomes a Law

When a Senator or a Representative introduces a bill, he sends it to the clerk of his house, who gives it a number and title. This is the *first reading*, and the bill is referred to the proper committee.

The committee may decide the bill is unwise or unnecessary and *table* it, thus killing it at once. Or it may decide the bill is worthwhile and hold hearings to listen to facts and opinions presented by experts and other interested persons. After members of the committee have debated the bill and perhaps offered amendments, a vote is taken; and if the vote is favorable, the bill is sent back to the floor of the house.

The clerk reads the bill sentence by sentence to the house, and this is known as the *second reading*. Members may then debate the bill and offer amendments. In the House of Representatives, the time for debate is limited by a *cloture rule*, but there is no such restriction in the Senate for cloture, where 60 votes are required. This makes possible a *filibuster*, in which one or more opponents hold the floor to defeat the bill.

The *third reading* is by title only, and the bill is put to a vote, which may be by voice or roll call, depending on the circumstances and parliamentary rules. Members who must be absent at the time but who wish to record their vote may be paired if each negative vote has a balancing affirmative one.

The bill then goes to the other house of Congress, where it may be defeated, or passed with or without amendments. If the bill is defeated, it dies. If it is passed with amendments, a joint Congressional committee must be appointed by both houses to iron out the differences.

After its final passage by both houses, the bill is sent to the President. If he approves, he signs it, and the bill becomes a law. However, if he disapproves, he *vetoes* the bill by refusing to sign it and sending it back to the house of origin with his reasons for the veto. The objections are read and debated, and a roll-call vote is taken. If the bill receives less than a two-thirds vote, it is defeated and goes no farther. But if it receives a two-thirds vote or greater, it is sent to the other house for a vote.

If that house also passes it by a two-thirds vote, the President's veto is *overridden*, and the bill becomes a law.

Should the President desire neither to sign nor to veto the bill, he may retain it for ten days, Sun-days excepted, after which time it automatically becomes a law without signature. However, if Congress has adjourned within those ten days, the bill is automatically killed, that process of indirect rejection being known as a *pocket veto*.

## Figures and Legends in American Folklore

**Appleseed, Johnny** (John Chapman, 1774–1847): Massachusetts-born nurseryman; reputed to have spread seeds and seedlings from which rose orchards of the Midwest.

**Billy the Kid** (William H. Bonney, 1859–1881): New York-born desperado; killed his first man before he reached his teens; after short life of crime in Wild West, was gunned down by Sheriff Pat Garrett; symbol of lawless West.

**Boone, Daniel** (1734–1820): Frontiersman and Indian fighter, about whom legends of early America have been built; figured in Byron's *Don Juan.*

**Brodie, Steve** (1863–1901): Reputed to have dived off Brooklyn Bridge on July 23, 1886. (Whether he actually did so has never been proved.)

**Buffalo Bill** (William F. Cody, 1846–1917): Buffalo hunter and Indian scout; much of legend about him and Wild West stems from his own Wild West show, which he operated in late 19th century.

**Bunyan, Paul:** Mythical lumberjack; subject of tall tales throughout timber country (that he dug Grand Canyon, for example).

**Crockett, David** (1786–1836): Frontiersman and member of U.S. Congress, about whom legends have been built of heroic feats; died in defense of Alamo.

**Fritchie (or Frietchie), Barbara:** Symbol of patriotism; in ballad by John Greenleaf Whittier, 90-year-old Barbara Fritchie defiantly waves Stars and Stripes as "Stonewall" Jackson's Confederate troops march through Frederick, Md.

**James, Jesse** (1847–1882): Bank and train robber; folklore has given him quality of American Robin Hood.

**Jones, Casey** (John Luther Jones, 1863–1900): Example of heroic locomotive engineer given to feats of prowess; died in wreck with his hand on brake lever when his Illinois Central "Cannonball" express hit freight train at Vaughan, Miss.

**Ross, Betsy** (1752–1836): Member of Philadelphia flag-making family; reported to have designed and sewn first American flag. (Report is without confirmation.)

**Uncle Sam:** Personification of United States and its people; origin uncertain; may be based on inspector of government supplies in Revolutionary War and War of 1812.

## Assassinations and Attempts in U. S. Since 1865

**Cermak, Anton J. (Mayor of Chicago):** Shot Feb. 15, 1933, in Miami by Giuseppe Zangara, who attempted to assassinate Franklin D. Roosevelt; Cermak died March 6.

**Ford, Gerald R. (President of U.S.):** Escaped assassination attempt Sept. 5, 1975, in Sacramento, Calif., by Lynette Alice (Squeaky) Fromm, who pointed but did not fire .45-caliber pistol. Escaped assassination attempt in San Francisco, Calif., Sept. 22, 1975, by Sara Jane Moore, who fired one shot from a .38-caliber pistol that was deflected.

**Garfield, James A. (President of U.S.):** Shot July 2, 1881, in Washington, D.C., by Charles J. Guiteau; died Sept. 19.

**Jordan, Vernon E., Jr. (civil rights leader):** Shot and critically wounded in assassination attempt May 29, 1980, in Fort Wayne, Ind.

**Kennedy, John F. (President of U.S.):** Shot Nov. 22, 1963, in Dallas, Tex., allegedly by Lee Harvey Oswald; died same day. Injured was Gov. John B. Connally of Texas. Oswald was shot and killed two days later by Jack Ruby.

**Kennedy, Robert F. (U.S. Senator from New York):** Shot June 5, 1968, in Los Angeles by Sirhan Bishara Sirhan; died June 6.

**King, Martin Luther, Jr. (civil rights leader):** Shot April 4, 1968, in Memphis by James Earl Ray; died same day.

**Lincoln, Abraham (President of U.S.):** Shot April 14, 1865, in Washington, D.C., by John Wilkes Booth; died April 15.

**Long, Huey P. (U.S. Senator from Louisiana):** Shot Sept. 8, 1935, in Baton Rouge by Dr. Carl A. Weiss; died Sept. 10.

**McKinley, William (President of U.S.):** Shot Sept. 6, 1901, in Buffalo by Leon Czolgosz; died Sept. 14.

**Reagan, Ronald (President of U.S.):** Shot in left lung in Washington by John W. Hinckley, Jr., on March 30, 1981; three others also wounded.

**Roosevelt, Franklin D. (President-elect of U.S.):** Escaped assassination unhurt Feb. 15, 1933, in Miami. *See* Cermak.

**Roosevelt, Theodore (ex-President of U.S.):** Escaped assassination (though shot) Oct. 14, 1912, in Milwaukee while campaigning for President.

**Seward, William H. (Secretary of State):** Escaped assassination (though injured) April 14, 1865, in Washington, D.C., by Lewis Powell (or Paine), accomplice of John Wilkes Booth.

**Truman, Harry S. (President of U.S.):** Escaped assassination unhurt Nov. 1, 1950, in Washington, D.C., as 2 Puerto Rican nationalists attempted to shoot their way into Blair House.

**Wallace, George C. (Governor of Alabama):** Shot and critically wounded in assassination attempt May 15, 1972, at Laurel, Md., by Arthur Herman Bremer. Wallace paralyzed from waist down.

# Members of the Supreme Court of the United States

| Name; apptd. from | Service | | Birth | | | |
| | Term | Yrs | Place | Date | Died | Religion |
| --- | --- | --- | --- | --- | --- | --- |
| **CHIEF JUSTICES** | | | | | | |
| John Jay, N.Y. | 1789-1795 | 5 | N.Y. | 1745 | 1829 | Episcopal |
| John Rutledge, S.C. | 1795 | 0 | S.C. | 1739 | 1800 | Church of England |
| Oliver Ellsworth, Conn. | 1796-1800 | 4 | Conn. | 1745 | 1807 | Congregational |
| John Marshall, Va. | 1801-1835 | 34 | Va. | 1755 | 1835 | Episcopal |
| Roger B. Taney, Md. | 1836-1864 | 28 | Md. | 1777 | 1864 | Roman Catholic |
| Salmon P. Chase, Ohio | 1864-1873 | 8 | N.H. | 1808 | 1873 | Episcopal |
| Morrison R. Waite, Ohio | 1874-1888 | 14 | Conn. | 1816 | 1888 | Episcopal |
| Melville W. Fuller, Ill. | 1888-1910 | 21 | Me. | 1833 | 1910 | Episcopal |
| Edward D. White, La. | 1910-1921 | 10 | La. | 1845 | 1921 | Roman Catholic |
| William H. Taft, Conn. | 1921-1930 | 8 | Ohio | 1857 | 1930 | Unitarian |
| Charles E. Hughes, N.Y. | 1930-1941 | 11 | N.Y. | 1862 | 1948 | Baptist |
| Harlan F. Stone, N.Y. | 1941-1946 | 4 | N.H. | 1872 | 1946 | Episcopal |
| Frederick M. Vinson, Ky. | 1946-1953 | 7 | Ky. | 1890 | 1953 | Methodist |
| Earl Warren, Calif. | 1953-1969 | 15 | Calif. | 1891 | 1974 | Protestant |
| Warren E. Burger, Va. | 1969-1986 | 17 | Minn. | 1907 | — | Presbyterian |
| William H. Rehnquist, Ariz.* | 1986- | | Wis. | 1924 | — | Lutheran |
| **ASSOCIATE JUSTICES** | | | | | | |
| James Wilson, Pa. | 1789-1798 | 8 | Scotland | 1742 | 1798 | Episcopal |
| John Rutledge, S.C. | 1790-1791 | 1 | S.C. | 1739 | 1800 | Church of England |
| William Cushing, Mass. | 1790-1810 | 20 | Mass. | 1732 | 1810 | Unitarian |
| John Blair, Va. | 1790-1796 | 5 | Va. | 1732 | 1800 | Presbyterian |
| James Iredell, N.C. | 1790-1799 | 9 | England | 1751 | 1799 | Episcopal |
| Thomas Johnson, Md. | 1792-1793 | 0 | Md. | 1732 | 1819 | Episcopal |
| William Paterson, N.J. | 1793-1806 | 13 | Ireland | 1745 | 1806 | Protestant |
| Samuel Chase, Md. | 1796-1811 | 15 | Md. | 1741 | 1811 | Episcopal |
| Bushrod Washington, Va. | 1799-1829 | 30 | Va. | 1762 | 1829 | Episcopal |
| Alfred Moore, N.C. | 1800-1804 | 3 | N.C. | 1755 | 1810 | Episcopal |
| William Johnson, S.C. | 1804-1834 | 30 | S.C. | 1771 | 1834 | Presbyterian |
| Brockholst Livingston, N.Y. | 1807-1823 | 16 | N.Y. | 1757 | 1823 | Presbyterian |
| Thomas Todd, Ky. | 1807-1826 | 18 | Va. | 1765 | 1826 | Presbyterian |
| Gabriel Duval, Md. | 1811-1835 | 23 | Md. | 1752 | 1844 | French Protestant |
| Joseph Story, Mass. | 1812-1845 | 33 | Mass. | 1779 | 1845 | Unitarian |
| Smith Thompson, N.Y. | 1823-1843 | 20 | N.Y. | 1768 | 1843 | Presbyterian |
| Robert Trimble, Ky. | 1826-1828 | 2 | Va. | 1777 | 1828 | Protestant |
| John McLean, Ohio | 1830-1861 | 31 | N.J. | 1785 | 1861 | Methodist-Epis. |
| Henry Baldwin, Pa. | 1830-1844 | 14 | Conn. | 1780 | 1844 | Trinity Church |
| James M. Wayne, Ga. | 1835-1867 | 32 | Ga. | 1790 | 1867 | Protestant |
| Philip P. Barbour, Va. | 1836-1841 | 4 | Va. | 1783 | 1841 | Episcopal |
| John Catron, Tenn. | 1837-1865 | 28 | Pa. | 1786 | 1865 | Presbyterian |
| John McKinley, Ala. | 1837-1852 | 14 | Va. | 1780 | 1852 | Protestant |
| Peter V. Daniel, Va. | 1841-1860 | 18 | Va. | 1784 | 1860 | Episcopal |
| Samuel Nelson, N.Y. | 1845-1872 | 27 | N.Y. | 1792 | 1873 | Protestant |
| Levi Woodbury, N.H. | 1845-1851 | 5 | N.H. | 1789 | 1851 | Protestant |
| Robert C. Grier, Pa. | 1846-1870 | 23 | Pa. | 1794 | 1870 | Presbyterian |
| Benjamin R. Curtis, Mass. | 1851-1857 | 5 | Mass. | 1809 | 1874 | (²) |
| John A. Campbell, Ala. | 1853-1861 | 8 | Ga. | 1811 | 1889 | Episcopal |
| Nathan Clifford, Maine | 1858-1881 | 23 | N.H. | 1803 | 1881 | (¹) |
| Noah H. Swayne, Ohio | 1862-1881 | 18 | Va. | 1804 | 1884 | Quaker |
| Samuel F. Miller, Iowa | 1862-1890 | 28 | Ky. | 1816 | 1890 | Unitarian |
| David Davis, Ill. | 1862-1877 | 14 | Md. | 1815 | 1886 | (⁴) |
| Stephen J. Field, Calif. | 1863-1897 | 34 | Conn. | 1816 | 1899 | Episcopal |
| William Strong, Pa. | 1870-1880 | 10 | Conn. | 1808 | 1895 | Presbyterian |
| Joseph P. Bradley, N.J. | 1870-1892 | 21 | N.Y. | 1813 | 1892 | Presbyterian |
| Ward Hunt, N.Y. | 1872-1882 | 9 | N.Y. | 1810 | 1886 | Episcopal |
| John M. Harlan, Ky. | 1877-1911 | 33 | Ky. | 1833 | 1911 | Presbyterian |
| William B. Woods, Ga. | 1880-1887 | 6 | Ohio | 1824 | 1887 | Protestant |
| Stanley Matthews, Ohio | 1881-1889 | 7 | Ohio | 1824 | 1889 | Presbyterian |
| Horace Gray, Mass. | 1882-1902 | 20 | Mass. | 1828 | 1902 | (³) |
| Samuel Blatchford, N.Y. | 1882-1893 | 11 | N.Y. | 1820 | 1893 | Presbyterian |
| Lucius Q. C. Lamar, Miss. | 1888-1893 | 5 | Ga. | 1825 | 1893 | Methodist |
| David J. Brewer, Kan. | 1889-1910 | 20 | Asia Minor | 1837 | 1910 | Protestant |
| Henry B. Brown, Mich. | 1890-1906 | 15 | Mass. | 1836 | 1913 | Protestant |
| George Shiras, Jr., Pa. | 1892-1903 | 10 | Pa. | 1832 | 1924 | Presbyterian |
| Howell E. Jackson, Tenn. | 1893-1895 | 2 | Tenn. | 1832 | 1895 | Baptist |
| Edward D. White, La. | 1894-1910 | 16 | La. | 1845 | 1921 | Roman Catholic |
| Rufus W. Peckham, N.Y. | 1895-1909 | 13 | N.Y. | 1838 | 1909 | Episcopal |
| Joseph McKenna, Calif. | 1898-1925 | 26 | Pa. | 1843 | 1926 | Roman Catholic |

# Members of the Supreme Court of the United States

| Name; apptd. from | Service Term | Yrs | Birth Place | Date | Died | Religion |
|---|---|---|---|---|---|---|
| Oliver W. Holmes, Mass. | 1902-1932 | 29 | Mass. | 1841 | 1935 | Unitarian |
| William R. Day, Ohio | 1903-1922 | 19 | Ohio | 1849 | 1923 | Protestant |
| William H. Moody, Mass. | 1906-1910 | 3 | Mass. | 1853 | 1917 | Episcopal |
| Horace H. Lurton, Tenn. | 1909-1914 | 4 | Ky. | 1844 | 1914 | Episcopal |
| Charles E. Hughes, N.Y. | 1910-1916 | 5 | N.Y. | 1862 | 1948 | Baptist |
| Willis Van Devanter, Wyo. | 1910-1937 | 26 | Ind. | 1859 | 1941 | Episcopal |
| Joseph R. Lamar, Ga. | 1910-1916 | 4 | Ga. | 1857 | 1916 | Ch. of Disciples |
| Mahlon Pitney, N.J. | 1912-1922 | 10 | N.J. | 1858 | 1924 | Presbyterian |
| James C. McReynolds, Tenn. | 1914-1941 | 26 | Ky. | 1862 | 1946 | Disciples of Christ |
| Louis D. Brandeis, Mass. | 1916-1939 | 22 | Ky. | 1856 | 1941 | Jewish |
| John H. Clarke, Ohio | 1916-1922 | 5 | Ohio | 1857 | 1945 | Protestant |
| George Sutherland, Utah | 1922-1938 | 15 | England | 1862 | 1942 | Episcopal |
| Pierce Butler, Minn. | 1923-1939 | 16 | Minn. | 1866 | 1939 | Roman Catholic |
| Edward T. Sanford, Tenn. | 1923-1930 | 7 | Tenn. | 1865 | 1930 | Episcopal |
| Harlan F. Stone, N.Y. | 1925-1941 | 16 | N.H. | 1872 | 1946 | Episcopal |
| Owen J. Roberts, Pa. | 1930-1945 | 15 | Pa. | 1875 | 1955 | Episcopal |
| Benjamin N. Cardozo, N.Y. | 1932-1938 | 6 | N.Y. | 1870 | 1938 | Jewish |
| Hugo L. Black, Ala. | 1937-1971 | 34 | Ala. | 1886 | 1971 | Baptist |
| Stanley F. Reed, Ky. | 1938-1957 | 19 | Ky. | 1884 | 1980 | Protestant |
| Felix Frankfurter, Mass. | 1939-1962 | 23 | Austria | 1882 | 1965 | Jewish |
| William O. Douglas, Conn. | 1939-1975 | 36 | Minn. | 1898 | 1980 | Presbyterian |
| Frank Murphy, Mich. | 1940-1949 | 9 | Mich. | 1890 | 1949 | Roman Catholic |
| James F. Byrnes, S.C. | 1941-1942 | 1 | S.C. | 1879 | 1972 | Episcopal |
| Robert H. Jackson, Pa. | 1941-1954 | 13 | N.Y. | 1892 | 1954 | Episcopal |
| Wiley B. Rutledge, Iowa | 1943-1949 | 6 | Ky. | 1894 | 1949 | Unitarian |
| Harold H. Burton, Ohio | 1945-1958 | 13 | Mass. | 1888 | 1964 | Unitarian |
| Tom C. Clark, Tex. | 1949-1967 | 17 | Tex. | 1899 | 1977 | Presbyterian |
| Sherman Minton, Ind. | 1949-1956 | 7 | Ind. | 1890 | 1965 | Roman Catholic |
| John M. Harlan, N.Y. | 1955-1971 | 16 | Ill. | 1899 | 1971 | Presbyterian |
| William J. Brennan, Jr., N.J. | 1956- | — | N.J. | 1906 | — | Roman Catholic |
| Charles E. Whittaker, Mo. | 1957-1962 | 5 | Kan. | 1901 | 1973 | Methodist |
| Potter Stewart, Ohio | 1958-1981 | 23 | Mich. | 1915 | — | Episcopal |
| Byron R. White, Colo. | 1962- | — | Colo. | 1917 | — | Episcopal |
| Arthur J. Goldberg, Ill. | 1962-1965 | 2 | Ill. | 1908 | — | Jewish |
| Abe Fortas, Tenn. | 1965-1969 | 3 | Tenn. | 1910 | 1982 | Jewish |
| Thurgood Marshall, N.Y. | 1967- | — | Md. | 1908 | — | Episcopalian |
| Harry A. Blackmun, Minn. | 1970- | — | Ill. | 1908 | — | Methodist |
| Lewis F. Powell, Jr., Va. | 1972- | — | Va. | 1907 | — | Presbyterian |
| William H. Rehnquist, Ariz. | 1972-1986 | 14 | Wis. | 1924 | — | Lutheran |
| John Paul Stevens, Ill. | 1975- | — | Ill. | 1920 | — | Protestant |
| Sandra Day O'Connor, Ariz. | 1981- | — | Tex. | 1930 | — | Episcopal |
| Antonin Scalia, D.C.* | 1986- | — | N.J. | 1936 | — | Roman Catholic |

1. Congregational; later Unitarian. 2. Unitarian; then Episcopal. 3. Unitarian or Congregational. 4. Not a member of any church.
* Unconfirmed as of presstime.

## Impeachments of Federal Officials

Source: Congressional Directory

The procedure for the impeachment of Federal officials is detailed in Article I, Section 3, of the Constitution. See Index.

The Senate has sat as a court of impeachment in the following cases:

**William Blount,** Senator from Tennessee; charges dismissed for want of jurisdiction, January 14, 1799.

**John Pickering,** Judge of the U.S. District Court for New Hampshire; removed from office March 12, 1804.

**Samuel Chase,** Associate Justice of the Supreme Court; acquitted March 1, 1805.

**James H. Peck,** Judge of the U.S. District Court for Missouri; acquitted Jan. 31, 1831.

**West H. Humphreys,** Judge of the U.S. District Court for the middle, eastern, and western districts of Tennessee; removed from office June 26, 1862.

**Andrew Johnson,** President of the United States; acquitted May 26, 1868.

**William W. Belknap,** Secretary of War; acquitted Aug. 1, 1876.

**Charles Swayne,** Judge of the U.S. District Court for the northern district of Florida; acquitted Feb. 27, 1905.

**Robert W. Archbald,** Associate Judge, U.S. Commerce Court; removed Jan. 13, 1913.

**George W. English,** Judge of the U.S. District Court for eastern district of Illinois; resigned Nov. 4, 1926; proceedings dismissed.

**Harold Louderback,** Judge of the U.S. District Court for the northern district of California; acquitted May 24, 1933.

**Halsted L. Ritter,** Judge of the U.S. District Court for the southern district of Florida; removed from office April 17, 1936.

# Executive Departments and Agencies

*Source: U.S. Government Manual, 1985—1986.*

Unless otherwise indicated, addresses shown are in Washington, D.C.

**CENTRAL INTELLIGENCE AGENCY (CIA)**
*Washington, D.C. (20505).*
    **Established:** 1947.
    **Director:** William J. Casey.
**COUNCIL OF ECONOMIC ADVISERS (CEA)**
*Executive Office Bldg. (20500).*
    **Members:** 3.
    **Established:** Feb. 20, 1946.
    **Chairman:** Beryl Sprinkel.
**COUNCIL ON ENVIRONMENTAL QUALITY**
*722 Jackson Pl., N.W. (20006).*
    **Members:** 3.
    **Established:** 1969.
    **Chairman:** A. Alan Hill.
**NATIONAL SECURITY COUNCIL (NSC)**
*Old Executive Office Bldg. (20506).*
    **Members:** 4.
    **Established:** July 26, 1947.
    **Chairman:** The President.
    **Other members:** Vice President; Secretary of State; Secretary of Defense.
**OFFICE OF ADMINISTRATION**
*Old Executive Office Bldg. (20500).*
    **Established:** Dec. 12, 1977.
    **Director:** Christopher Hicks
**OFFICE OF MANAGEMENT AND BUDGET**
*Executive Office Bldg. (20503).*
    **Established:** July 1, 1970.
    **Director:** James C. Miller 3rd.
**OFFICE OF SCIENCE AND TECHNOLOGY POLICY**
*Old Executive Office Building (20506).*
    **Established:** May 11, 1976
    **Director:** Dr. Richard G. Johnson (acting)
**OFFICE OF THE UNITED STATES TRADE REPRESENTATIVE**
*600 17th St., N.W. (20506).*
    **Established:** Jan. 15, 1963.
    **Trade Representative:** Clayton Yuetter
**OFFICE OF POLICY DEVELOPMENT**
*1600 Pennsylvania Ave., N.W. (20500).*
    **Established:** Jan. 21, 1981.
    **Director:** Roger B. Porter.

## Executive Departments

**DEPARTMENT OF STATE**
*2201 C St., N.W. (20520).*
    **Established:** 1781 as Department of Foreign Affairs; reconstituted, 1789, following adoption of Constitution; name changed to Department of State Sept. 15, 1789.
    **Secretary:** George P. Shultz.
    **Deputy Secretary:** Kenneth W. Dam.
    **Chief Delegate to U.N.:** Lt. Gen. Vernon A. Walters.
**DEPARTMENT OF THE TREASURY**
*15th St. & Pennsylvania Ave., N.W. (20220).*
    **Established:** Sept. 2, 1789.
    **Secretary:** James A. Baker, 3rd.
    **Deputy Secretary:** Richard G. Darman.
    **Treasurer of the U.S.:** Katherine D. Ortega.
    **Comptroller of the Currency:** C. T. Conover.
**DEPARTMENT OF DEFENSE**
*The Pentagon (20301).*
    **Established:** July 26, 1947, as National Department Establishment; name changed to Department of Defense on Aug. 10, 1949. Subordinate to Secretary of Defense are Secretaries of Army, Navy, Air Force.
    **Secretary:** Caspar W. Weinberger.
    **Deputy Secretary:** William Howard Taft, 4th.
    **Secretary of Army:** John O. Marsh, Jr.
    **Secretary of Navy:** John F. Lehman, Jr.
    **Secretary of Air Force:** E. C. Aldridge, Jr.
    **Commandant of Marine Corps:** Gen. P. X. Kelley.
    **Joint Chiefs of Staff:**[1] Adm. William J. Crowe, Jr. Chairman; Adm. James D. Watkins, Navy; Gen. Charles A. Gabriel, Air Force: Gen. John A. Wickham, Jr., Army; Gen. P. X. Kelly, Marine Corps.
**DEPARTMENT OF JUSTICE**
*Constitution Ave. between 9th & 10th Sts., N.W. (20530).*
    **Established:** Office of Attorney General was created Sept. 24, 1789. Although he was one of original Cabinet members, he was not executive department head until June 22, 1870, when Department of Justice was established.
    **Attorney General:** Edwin Meese, 3rd.
    **Deputy Attorney General:** Carol E. Dinkins.
    **Solicitor General:** Rex E. Lee.
    **Director of FBI:** William H. Webster.
**DEPARTMENT OF THE INTERIOR**
*C St. between 18th & 19th Sts., N.W. (20240).*
    **Established:** March 3, 1849.
    **Secretary:** Donald P. Hodel.
    **Under Secretary:** Anne Dore McLaughlin.
**DEPARTMENT OF AGRICULTURE**
*Independence Ave. between 12th & 14th Sts., S.W. (20250).*
    **Established:** May 15, 1862. Administered by Commissioner of Agriculture until 1889, when it was made executive department.
    **Secretary:** Richard E. Lyng.
    **Deputy Secretary:** James Meyers (designate)
**DEPARTMENT OF COMMERCE**
*14th St. between Constitution Ave. & E St., N.W. (20230).*
    **Established:** Department of Commerce and Labor was created Feb. 14, 1903. On March 4, 1913, all labor activities were transferred out of Department of Commerce and Labor and it was renamed Department of Commerce.
    **Secretary:** Malcolm Baldrige.
    **Deputy Secretary:** Clarence J. Brown.
**DEPARTMENT OF LABOR**
*200 Constitution Ave., N.W. (20210).*
    **Established:** Bureau of Labor was created in 1884 under Department of the Interior; later became independent department without executive rank. Returned to bureau status in Department of Commerce and Labor, but on March 4, 1913, became independent executive department under its present name.
    **Secretary:** William E. Brock.
    **Under Secretary:** Ford B. Ford.
**DEPARTMENT OF HEALTH AND HUMAN SERVICES**[1]
*200 Independence Ave., S.W. (20201).*
    **Established:** April 11, 1953, replacing Federal Security Agency created in 1939.[1]
    **Secretary:** Otis R. Bowen
    **Under Secretary:** Charles D. Baker.
    **Surgeon General:** Dr. C. Everett Koop.

1. Originally Department of Health, Education and Welfare. Name changed in May 1980 when Department of Education was activated.

## DEPARTMENT OF HOUSING AND URBAN DEVELOPMENT
*451 7th St., S.W. (20410).*
**Established:** 1965, replacing Housing and Home Finance Agency created in 1947.
**Secretary:** Samuel R. Pierce, Jr.
**Under Secretary:** Philip Abrams.

## DEPARTMENT OF TRANSPORTATION
*400 7th St., S.W. (20590).*
**Established:** Oct. 15, 1966, as result of Department of Transportation Act, which became effective April 1, 1967.
**Secretary:** Elizabeth Hanford Dole.
**Deputy Secretary:** James H. Burnley, 4th.

## DEPARTMENT OF ENERGY
*1000 Independence Ave., S.W. (20585).*
**Established:** Aug. 1977
**Secretary:** John S. Herrington.
**Deputy Secretary:** Danny J. Boggs.

## DEPARTMENT OF EDUCATION
*400 Maryland Avenue, S.W. (20202).*
**Established:** Oct. 17, 1979.
**Secretary:** William J. Bennett.
**Under Secretary:** Gary L. Jones.

# Major Independent Agencies

## ACTION
*806 Connecticut Ave., N.W. (20525).*
**Established:** July 1, 1971.
**Director:** Donna M. Alvarado.

## CONSUMER PRODUCT SAFETY COMMISSION
*1111 18th St., N.W. (20207).*
**Members:** 5.
**Established:** Oct. 27, 1972.
**Chairman:** Terrence M. Scanlon.

## ENVIRONMENTAL PROTECTION AGENCY (EPA)
*401 M St., S.W. (20460).*
**Established:** Dec. 2, 1970.
**Administrator:** Lee M. Thomas.

## EQUAL EMPLOYMENT OPPORTUNITY COMMISSION (EEOC)
*2401 E St., N.W. (20506).*
**Members:** 5.
**Established:** July 2, 1965.
**Chairman:** Clarence Thomas.

## FARM CREDIT ADMINISTRATION (FCA)
*490 L'Enfant Plaza East, S.W. (20578).*
**Members:** 13.
**Established:** July 17, 1916.
**Chairman of Federal Farm Credit Board:** William D. Wampler

## FEDERAL COMMUNICATIONS COMMISSION (FCC)
*1919 M St., N.W. (20554).*
**Members:** 7.
**Established:** 1934.
**Chairman:** Mark S. Fowler.

## FEDERAL DEPOSIT INSURANCE CORPORATION (FDIC)
*550 17th St., N.W. (20429).*
**Members:** 3.
**Established:** June 16, 1933.
**Chairman:** William M. Isaac.

## FEDERAL ELECTION COMMISSION (FEC)
*1325 K St., N.W. (20463).*
**Members:** 6.
**Established:** 1974.
**Chairman:** John W. McGarry

## FEDERAL MARITIME COMMISSION
*1100 L St., N.W. (20573).*
**Members:** 5.
**Established:** Aug. 12, 1961.
**Chairman:** Edward V. Hickey

## FEDERAL MEDIATION AND CONCILIATION SERVICE (FMCS)
*2100 K St., N.W. (20427).*
**Established:** 1947.
**Director:** Kay McMurray.

## FEDERAL RESERVE SYSTEM (FRS), BOARD OF GOVERNORS OF
*20th St. & Constitution Ave., N.W. (20551).*
**Members:** 7.
**Established:** Dec. 23, 1913.
**Chairman:** Paul A. Volcker.

## FEDERAL TRADE COMMISSION (FTC)
*Pennsylvania Ave. at 6th St., N.W. (20580).*
**Members:** 5.
**Established:** Sept. 26, 1914.
**Chairman:** Daniel Oliver

## GENERAL SERVICES ADMINISTRATION (GSA)
*18th and F Sts., N.W. (20405).*
**Established:** July 1, 1949.
**Administrator:** Terence C. Golden

## INTERSTATE COMMERCE COMMISSION (ICC)
*12th St. & Constitution Ave., N.W. (20423).*
**Members:** 7.
**Established:** Feb. 4, 1887.
**Chairman:** Reese H. Taylor, Jr.

## NATIONAL AERONAUTICS AND SPACE ADMINISTRATION (NASA)
*400 Maryland Ave., S.W. (20546).*
**Established:** 1958.
**Administrator:** James Fletcher

## NATIONAL FOUNDATION ON THE ARTS AND THE HUMANITIES
*1100 Pennsylvania Ave., N.W., (20506).*
**Established:** 1965.
**Chairmen:** National Endowment for the Arts, Frank Hodsoll; National Endowment for the Humanities, Lynn Cheney

## NATIONAL LABOR RELATIONS BOARD (NLRB)
*1717 Pennsylvania Ave., N.W. (20570).*
**Members:** 5.
**Established:** July 5, 1935.
**Chairman:** Donald L. Dotson.

## NATIONAL MEDIATION BOARD
*1425 K St., N.W. (20572).*
**Members:** 3
**Established:** June 21, 1934.
**Chairman:** Walter C. Wallace

## NATIONAL SCIENCE FOUNDATION (NSF)
*1800 G St., N.W. (20550).*
**Established:** 1950.
**Director:** Roland W. Schmitt

## NATIONAL TRANSPORTATION SAFETY BOARD
*800 Independence Ave., S.W. (20594).*
**Members:** 5
**Established:** April 1, 1975.
**Chairman:** James E. Burnett.

## NUCLEAR REGULATORY COMMISSION (NRC)
*1717 H St., N.W. (20555).*
**Members:** 5.
**Established:** Jan. 19, 1975.
**Chairman:** Nunzio J. Pallidino.

## OFFICE OF PERSONNEL MANAGEMENT (OPM)
*1900 E St., N.W. (20415).*
**Members:** 3
**Established:** Jan. 1, 1979.
**Acting Director:** Loretta Cornelius.

## SECURITIES AND EXCHANGE COMMISSION (SEC)
*450 5th St., N.W. (20549).*

**Members:** 5.
**Established:** July 2, 1934
**Chairman:** John S. R. Shad.
**SELECTIVE SERVICE SYSTEM (SSS)**
*National Headquarters (20435).*
**Established:** Sept. 16, 1940.
**Director:** Thomas K. Turnage.
**SMALL BUSINESS ADMINISTRATION (SBA)**
*1441 L St., N.W. (20416).*
**Established:** July 30, 1953.
**Administrator:** James C. Sanders.
**TENNESSEE VALLEY AUTHORITY (TVA)**
*400 West Summit Hill Drive, Knoxville, Tenn. (37902).*
*Washington office: Capitol Hill Office Bldg., 412 First St., S.E. (20444).*
**Members of Board of Directors:** 3.
**Established:** May 18, 1933.
**Chairman:** C. H. Dean, Jr.
**U.S. ARMS CONTROL AND DISARMAMENT AGENCY**
*320 21st St., N.W., (20451).*
**Established:** Sept. 26, 1961.
**Director:** Kenneth L. Adelman.
**Special Representative for Negotiations:** Edward L. Rowny.
**U.S. COMMISSION ON CIVIL RIGHTS**
*1121 Vermont Avenue, N.W. (20425).*
**Members:** 8.
**Established:** 1957.
**Chairman:** Clarence M. Pendleton, Jr.
**U.S. INFORMATION AGENCY**
*400 C St., S.W. (20547).*
**Established:** April 1, 1978.
**Director:** Charles Z. Wick.
**U.S. INTERNATIONAL DEVELOPMENT COOPERATION AGENCY**
*320 21st St., N.W. (20523).*
**Established:** Oct. 1, 1979.
**Acting Director:** M. Peter McPherson.
**U.S. INTERNATIONAL TRADE COMMISSION**
*701 E St., N.W. (20436).*
**Members:** 6.
**Established:** Sept. 8, 1916.
**Chairman:** Paula Stern
**U.S. POSTAL SERVICE**
*475 L'Enfant Plaza West, S.W. (20260).*
**Postmaster General:** Preston R. Tisch
**Deputy Postmaster General:** Jackie A. Strange.
**Established:** Office of Postmaster General and temporary post office system created in 1789. Act of Feb. 20, 1792, made detailed provisions for Post Office Department. Postmaster General became Cabinet member in 1829, and Department received executive status in 1872. In 1970 became independent agency headed by 11-member board of governors. Postmaster General, no longer Cabinet member, is chosen by nine governors, who, with Postmaster General, choose Deputy Postmaster General.
**VETERANS ADMINISTRATION (VA)**
*810 Vermont Ave., N.W. (20420).*
**Established:** July 21, 1930.
**Administrator:** Harry N. Walters.

## Other Independent Agencies

**Administrative Conference of the United States**—2120 L St., N.W. (20037).
**American Battle Monuments Commission**—5127 Pulaski Bldg. (20314).
**Appalachian Regional Commission**—1666 Connecticut Ave., N.W. (20235).
**Board for International Broadcasting**—Suite 1100,

1201 Connecticut Ave., N.W. (20036).
**Commission of Fine Arts**—708 Jackson Place, N.W. (20006).
**Commodity Futures Trading Commission**—2033 K St., N.W. (20581).
**Export-Import Bank of the United States**—811 Vermont Ave., N.W. (20571).
**Federal Emergency Management Agency**—500 C St., S.W. (20472).
**Federal Home Loan Bank Board**—1700 G St., N.W. (20552).
**Federal Labor Relations Authority**—500 C St., S.W. (20472).
**Inter-American Foundation**—1515 Wilson Blvd., Rosslyn, Va. (22209).
**Merit Systems Protection Board**—1120 Vermont Ave., N.W. (20419).
**National Commission on Libraries and Information Science**—7th & D Sts., S.W. (20024).
**National Credit Union Administration**—1776 G St., N.W. (20456).
**Occupational Safety and Health Review Commission**—1825 K St., N.W. (20006).
**Panama Canal Commission**—425 13th St., N.W. (20004).
**Peace Corps**—806 Connecticut Ave., N.W. (20526).
**Pension Benefit Guaranty Corporation**—2020 K St., N.W. (20006).
**Postal Rate Commission**—2000 L St., N.W. (20268).
**President's Committee on Employment of the Handicapped**—1111 20th St., N.W. (20036).
**President's Council on Physical Fitness and Sports**—450 5th St., S.W. (20001).
**Railroad Retirement Board (RRB)**—844 Rush St., Chicago, Ill. (60611); Washington Liaison Office: Room 630, 425 13th St., N.W. (20004).
**U.S. Parole Commission**—5550 Friendship Blvd., Chevy Chase, Md. (20815).

## Legislative Department

**Architect of the Capitol**—U.S. Capitol Building (20515)
**General Accounting Office (GAO)**—441 G St., N.W. (20548)
**Government Printing Office (GPO)**—North Capitol & H Sts., N.W. (20401)
**Library of Congress**—101 Independence Ave. S.E. (20540)
**Office of Technology Assessment**—600 Pennsylvania Ave., S.E. (20510)
**United States Botanic Garden**—Office of Director, 245 First St., S.W. (20024)

## Quasi-Official Agencies

**American National Red Cross**—17th & D Sts., N.W. (20006).
**Legal Services Corporation**—733 15th St., N.W. (20005).
**National Academy of Sciences, National Academy of Engineering, National Research Council, Institute of Medicine**—2101 Constitution Ave., N.W. (20418).
**National Railroad Passenger Corporation (Amtrak)**—400 N. Capitol St., N.W. (20001).
**Smithsonian Institution**—1000 Jefferson Dr., S.W. (20560).
**U.S. Railway Association**—955 L'Enfant Plaza North, S.W. (20595).
**U.S. Synthetic Fuels Corporation**—2121 K St., N.W. (20586).

# Biographies of the Presidents

**GEORGE WASHINGTON** was born on Feb. 22, 1732 (Feb. 11, 1731/2, old style) in Westmoreland County, Va. While in his teens, he trained as a surveyor, and at the age of 20 he was appointed adjutant in the Virginia militia. For the next three years, he fought in the wars against the French and Indians, serving as Gen. Edward Braddock's aide in the disastrous campaign against Fort Duquesne. In 1759, he resigned from the militia, married Martha Dandridge Custis, a widow, and settled down as a gentleman farmer at Mount Vernon, Va.

As a militiaman, Washington had been exposed to the arrogance of the British officers, and his experience as a planter with British commercial restrictions increased his anti-British sentiment. He opposed the Stamp Act of 1765 and after 1770 became increasingly prominent in organizing resistance. A delegate to the Continental Congress, Washington was selected as commander in chief of the Continental Army and took command at Cambridge, Mass., on July 3, 1775.

Inadequately supported and sometimes covertly sabotaged by the Congress, in charge of troops who were inexperienced, badly equipped, and impatient of discipline, Washington conducted the war on the policy of avoiding major engagements with the British and wearing them down by harrassing tactics. His able generalship, along with the French alliance and the growing weariness within Britain, brought the war to a conclusion with the surrender of Cornwallis at Yorktown, Va., on Oct. 19, 1781.

The chaotic years under the Articles of Confederation led Washington to return to public life in the hope of promoting the formation of a strong central government. He presided over the Constitutional Convention and yielded to the universal demand that he serve as first President. He was inaugurated on April 30, 1789, in New York, the first national capital. In office, he sought to unite the nation and establish the authority of the new government at home and abroad. Greatly distressed by the emergence of the Hamilton-Jefferson rivalry, Washington worked to maintain neutrality but actually sympathized more with Hamilton. Following his unanimous re-election in 1792, his second term was dominated by the Federalists. His Farewell Address on Sept. 17, 1796 (published but never delivered) rebuked party spirit and warned against "permanent alliances" with foreign powers.

He died at Mount Vernon on Dec. 14, 1799.

**JOHN ADAMS** was born on Oct. 30 (Oct. 19, old style), 1735, at Braintree (now Quincy), Mass. A Harvard graduate, he considered teaching and the ministry but finally turned to law and was admitted to the bar in 1758. Six years later, he married Abigail Smith. He opposed the Stamp Act, served as lawyer for patriots indicted by the British, and by the time of the Continental Congresses, was in the vanguard of the movement for independence. In 1778, he went to France as commissioner. Subsequently he helped negotiate the peace treaty with Britain, and in 1785 became envoy to London. Resigning in 1788, he was elected Vice President under Washington and was re-elected in 1792.

Though a Federalist, Adams did not get along with Hamilton, who sought to prevent his election to the presidency in 1796 and thereafter intrigued against his administration. In 1798, Adam's independent policy averted a war with France but completed the break with Hamilton and the right-wing Federalists; at the same time, the enactment of the Alien and Sedition Acts, directed against foreigners and against critics of the government, exasperated the Jeffersonian opposition. The split between Adams and Hamilton resulted in Jefferson's becoming the next President. Adams retired to his home in Quincy. He and Jefferson died on the same day, July 4, 1826, the 50th anniversary of the signing of the Declaration of Independence.

His *Defence of the Constitutions of Government of the United States* (1787) contains original and striking, if conservative, political ideas.

**THOMAS JEFFERSON** was born on April 13 (April 2, old style), 1743, at Shadwell in Goochland (now Albemarle) County, Va. A William and Mary graduate, he studied law, but from the start showed an interest in science and philosophy. His literary skill and political clarity brought him to the forefront of the revolutionary movement in Virginia. As delegate to the Continental Congress, he drafted the Declaration of Independence. In 1776, he entered the Virginia House of Delegates and initiated a comprehensive reform program for the abolition of feudal survivals in land tenure and the separation of church and state.

In 1779, he became governor, but constitutional limitations on his power, combined with his own lack of executive energy, caused an unsatisfactory administration, culminating in Jefferson's virtual abdication when the British invaded Virginia in 1781. He retired to his beautiful home at Monticello, Va., to his family. His wife, Martha Wayles Skelton, whom he married in 1772, died in 1782.

Jefferson's *Notes on Virginia* (1784–85) illustrate his many-faceted interests, his limitless intellectual curiosity, his deep faith in agrarian democracy. Sent to Congress in 1783, he helped lay down the decimal system and drafted basic reports on the organization of the western lands. In 1785 he was appointed minister to France, where the Anglo-Saxon liberalism he had drawn from John Locke, the British philosopher, was stimulated by contact with the thought that would soon ferment in the French Revolution. In 1789, Washington appointed him Secretary of State. While favoring the Constitution and a strengthened central government, Jefferson came to believe that Hamilton contemplated the establishment of a monarchy. Growing differences resulted in Jefferson's resignation on Dec. 31, 1793.

Elected vice president in 1796, Jefferson continued to serve as spiritual leader of the opposition to Federalism, particularly to the repressive Alien and Sedition Acts. He was elected President in 1801 by the House of Representatives as a result of Hamilton's decision to throw the Federalist votes to him rather than to Aaron Burr, who had tied him in electoral votes. He was the first President to be inaugurated in Washington, which he had helped to design.

The purchase of Louisiana from France in 1803, though in violation of Jefferson's earlier constitutional scruples, was the most notable act of his administration. Re-elected in 1804, with the Federalist Charles C. Pinckney opposing him, Jefferson tried desperately to keep the United States out of the Napoleonic Wars in Europe, employing to this end the unpopular embargo policy.

After his retirement to Monticello in 1809, he developed his interest in education, founding the University of Virginia and watching its development with never-flagging interest. He died at Monticello on July 4, 1826. Jefferson had an enormous variety of interests and skills, ranging from education and science to architecture and music.

**JAMES MADISON** was born in Port Conway, Va., on March 16, 1751 (March 5, 1750/1, old style). A Princeton graduate, he joined the struggle for independence on his return to Virginia in 1771. In the 1770s and 1780s he was active in state politics, where he championed the Jefferson reform program, and in the Continental Congress. Madison was influential in the Constitutional Convention as leader of the group favoring a strong central government and as recorder of the debates; and he subsequently wrote, in collaboration with Alexander Hamilton and John Jay, the *Federalist* papers to aid the campaign for the adoption of the Constitution.

Serving in the new Congress, Madison soon emerged as the leader in the House of the men who opposed Hamilton's financial program and his pro-British leanings in foreign policy. Retiring from Congress in 1797, he continued to be active in Virginia and drafted the Virginia Resolution protesting the Alien and Sedition Acts. His intimacy with Jefferson made him the natural choice for Secretary of State in 1801.

In 1809, Madison succeeded Jefferson as President, defeating Charles C. Pinckney. His attractive wife, Dolley Payne Todd, whom he married in 1794, brought a new social sparkle to the executive mansion. In the meantime, increasing tension with Britain culminated in the War of 1812—a war for which the United States was unprepared and for which Madison lacked the executive talent to clear out incompetence and mobilize the nation's energies. Madison was re-elected in 1812, running against the Federalist De Witt Clinton. In 1814, the British actually captured Washington and forced Madison to flee to Virginia.

Madison's domestic program capitulated to the Hamiltonian policies that he had resisted 20 years before and he now signed bills to establish a United States Bank and a higher tariff.

After his presidency, he remained in retirement in Virginia until his death on June 28, 1836.

**JAMES MONROE** was born on April 28, 1758, in Westmoreland County, Va. A William and Mary graduate, he served in the army during the first years of the Revolution and was wounded at Trenton. He then entered Virginia politics and later national politics under the sponsorship of Jefferson. In 1786, he married Elizabeth (Eliza) Kortright.

Fearing centralization, Monroe opposed the adoption of the Constitution and, as senator from Virginia, was highly critical of the Hamiltonian program. In 1794, he was appointed minister to France, where his ardent sympathies with the Revolution exceeded the wishes of the State Department. His troubled diplomatic career ended with his recall in 1796. From 1799 to 1802, he was governor of Virginia. In 1803, Jefferson sent him to France to help negotiate the Louisiana Purchase and for the next few years he was active in various negotiations on the Continent.

In 1808, Monroe flirted with the radical wing of the Republican Party, which opposed Madison's candidacy; but the presidential boom came to naught and, after a brief term as governor of Virginia in 1811, Monroe accepted Madison's offer to become Secretary of State. During the War of 1812, he vainly sought a field command and instead served as Secretary of War from September 1814 to March 1815.

Elected President in 1816 over the Federalist Rufus King, and re-elected without opposition in 1820, Monroe, the last of the Virginia dynasty, pursued the course of systematic tranquilization that won for his administrations the name "the era of good feeling." He continued Madison's surrender to the Hamiltonian domestic program, signed the Missouri Compromise, acquired Florida, and with the able assistance of his Secretary of State, John Quincy Adams, promulgated the Monroe Doctrine in 1823, declaring against foreign colonization or intervention in the Americas. He died in New York City on July 4, 1831, the third president to die on the anniversary of Independence.

**JOHN QUINCY ADAMS** was born on July 11, 1767, at Braintree (now Quincy), Mass., the son of John Adams, the second President. He spent his early years in Europe with his father, graduated from Harvard, and entered law practice. His anti-Jeffersonian newspaper articles won him political attention. In 1794, he became minister to the Netherlands, the first of several diplomatic posts that occupied him until his return to Boston in 1801. In 1797, he married Louisa Catherine Johnson.

In 1803, Adams was elected to the Senate, nominally as a Federalist, but his repeated displays of independence on such issues as the Louisiana Purchase and the embargo caused his party to demand his resignation and ostracize him socially. In 1809, Madison rewarded him for his support of Jefferson by appointing him minister to St. Petersburg. He helped negotiate the Treaty of Ghent in 1814, and in 1815 became minister to London. In 1817 Monroe appointed him Secretary of State where he served with great distinction, gaining Florida from Spain without hostilities and playing an equal part with Monroe in formulating the Monroe Doctrine.

When no presidential candidate received a majority of electoral votes in 1824, Adams, with the support of Henry Clay, was elected by the House in 1825 over Andrew Jackson, who had the original plurality. Adams had ambitious plans of government activity to foster internal improvements and promote the arts and sciences, but congressional obstructionism, combined with his own unwillingness or inability to play the role of a politician, resulted in little being accomplished. After being defeated for re-election by Jackson in 1828, he successfully ran for the House of Representatives in 1830. There though nominally a Whig, he pursued as ever an independent course. He led the fight to force Congress to receive antislavery petitions and fathered the Smithsonian Institution.

Stricken on the floor of the House, he died on Feb. 23, 1848. His long and detailed *Diary* gives a unique picture of the personalities and politics of the times.

**ANDREW JACKSON** was born on March 15, 1767, in what is now generally agreed to be Waxhaw, S.C. After a turbulent boyhood as an orphan and a British prisoner, he moved west to Tennessee, where he soon qualified for law practice but found time for such frontier pleasures as horse racing, cockfighting, and dueling. His marriage to Rachel Donelson Robards in 1791 was complicated by subsequent legal uncertainties about the status of her divorce. During the 1790s, Jackson served in the Tennessee Constitutional Convention, the United States House of Representatives and Senate, and on the Tennessee Supreme Court.

After some years as a country gentleman, living at the Hermitage near Nashville, Jackson in 1812 was given command of Tennessee troops sent against the Creeks. He defeated the Indians at Horseshoe Bend in 1814; subsequently he became a major general and won the Battle of New Orleans over veteran British troops, though after the treaty of peace had been signed at Ghent. In 1818, Jackson invaded Florida, captured Pensacola, and hanged two Englishmen named Arbuthnot and Ambrister, creating an international incident. A presidential boom began for him in 1821, and to foster it, he returned to the Senate (1823–25). Though he won a plurality of electoral votes in 1824, he lost in the House when Clay threw his strength to Adams. Four years later, he easily defeated Adams.

As President, Jackson greatly expanded the power and prestige of the presidential office and carried through an unprecedented program of domestic reform, vetoing the bill to extend the United States Bank, moving toward a hard-money currency policy, and checking the program of federal internal improvements. He also vindicated federal authority against South Carolina with its doctrine of nullification and against France on the question of debts. The support given his policies by the workingmen of the East as well as by the farmers of the East, West, and South resulted in his triumphant re-election in 1832 over Clay.

After watching the inauguration of his handpicked successor, Martin Van Buren, Jackson retired to the Hermitage, where he maintained a lively interest in national affairs until his death on June 8, 1845.

**MARTIN VAN BUREN** was born on Dec. 5, 1782, at Kinderhook, N.Y. After graduating from the village school, he became a law clerk, entered practice in 1803, and soon became active in state politics as state senator and attorney general. In 1820, he was elected to the United States Senate. He threw the support of his efficient political organization, known as the Albany Regency, to William H. Crawford in 1824 and to Jackson in 1828. After leading the opposition to Adams's administration in the Senate, he served briefly as governor of New York (1828–29) and resigned to become Jackson's Secretary of State. He was soon on close personal terms with Jackson and played an important part in the Jacksonian program.

In 1832, Van Buren became vice president; in 1836, President. The Panic of 1837 overshadowed his term. He attributed it to the overexpansion of the credit and favored the establishment of an independent treasury as repository for the federal funds. In 1840, he established a 10-hour day on public works. Defeated by Harrison in 1840, he was the leading contender for the Democratic nomination in 1844 until he publicly opposed immediate annexation of Texas, and was subsequently beaten by the Southern delegations at the Baltimore convention. This incident increased his growing misgivings about the slave power.

After working behind the scenes among the antislavery Democrats, Van Buren joined in the movement that led to the Free-Soil Party and became its candidate for President in 1848. He subsequently returned to the Democratic Party while

continuing to object to its pro-Southern policy. He died in Kinderhook on July 24, 1862. His *Autobiography* throws valuable sidelights on the political history of the times.

His wife, Hannah Hoes, whom he married in 1807, died in 1819.

**WILLIAM HENRY HARRISON** was born in Charles City County, Va., on Feb. 9, 1773. Joining the army in 1791, he was active in Indian fighting in the Northwest, became secretary of the Northwest Territory in 1798 and governor of Indiana in 1800. He married Anna Symmes in 1795. Growing discontent over white encroachments on Indian lands led to the formation of an Indian alliance under Tecumseh to resist further aggressions. In 1811, Harrison won a nominal victory over the Indians at Tippecanoe and in 1813 a more decisive one at the Battle of the Thames, where Tecumseh was killed.

After resigning from the army in 1814, Harrison had an obscure career in politics and diplomacy, ending up 20 years later as a county recorder in Ohio. Nominated for President in 1835 as a military hero whom the conservative politicians hoped to be able to control, he ran surprisingly well against Van Buren in 1836. Four years later, he defeated Van Buren but caught penumonia and died in Washington on April 4, 1841, a month after his inauguration. Harrison was the first president to die in office.

**JOHN TYLER** was born in Charles City County, Va., on March 29, 1790. A William and Mary graduate, he entered law practice and politics, serving in the House of Representatives (1817–21), as governor of Virginia (1825–27), and as senator (1827–36). A strict constructionist, he supported Crawford in 1824 and Jackson in 1828, but broke with Jackson over his United States Bank policy and became a member of the Southern state-rights group that cooperated with the Whigs. In 1836, he resigned from the Senate rather than follow instructions from the Virginia legislature to vote for a resolution expunging censure of Jackson from the Senate record.

Elected vice president on the Whig ticket in 1840, Tyler succeeded to the presidency on Harrison's death. His strict-constructionist views soon caused a split with the Henry Clay wing of the Whig party and a stalemate on domestic questions. Tyler's more considerable achievements were his support of the Webster-Ashburton Treaty with Britain and his success in bringing about the annexation of Texas.

After his presidency he lived in retirement in Virginia until the outbreak of the Civil War, when he emerged briefly as chairman of a peace convention and then as delegate to the provisional Congress of the Confederacy. He died on Jan. 18, 1862. He married Letitia Christian in 1813 and, two years after her death in 1842, Julia Gardiner.

**JAMES KNOX POLK** was born in Mecklenburg County, N.C., on Nov. 2, 1795. A graduate of the University of North Carolina, he moved west to Tennessee, was admitted to the bar, and soon became prominent in state politics. In 1825, he was elected to the House of Representatives, where he opposed Adams and, after 1829, became Jackson's floor leader in the fight against the Bank. In 1835, he became Speaker of the House. Four years later, he was elected governor of Tennessee, but was beaten in tries for re-election in 1841 and 1843.

The supporters of Van Buren for the Democratic

nomination in 1844 counted on Polk as his running mate; but, when Van Buren's stand on Texas alienated Southern support, the convention swung to Polk on the ninth ballot. He was elected over Henry Clay, the Whig candidate. Rapidly disillusioning those who thought that he would not run his own administration, Polk proceeded steadily and precisely to achieve four major objectives—the acquisition of California, the settlement of the Oregon question, the reduction of the tariff, and the establishment of the independent treasury. He also enlarged the Monroe Doctrine to exclude all non-American intervention in American affairs, whether forcible or not, and he forced Mexico into a war that he waged to a successful conclusion.

His wife, Sarah Childress, whom he married in 1824, was a woman of charm and ability. Polk died in Nashville, Tenn., on June 15, 1849.

**ZACHARY TAYLOR** was born at Montebello, Orange County, Va., on Nov. 24, 1784. Embarking on a military career in 1808, Taylor fought in the War of 1812, the Black Hawk War, and the Seminole War, meanwhile holding garrison jobs on the frontier or desk jobs in Washington. A brigadier general as a result of his victory over the Seminoles at Lake Okeechobee (1837), Taylor held a succession of Southwestern commands and in 1846 established a base on the Rio Grande, where his forces engaged in hostilities that precipitated the war with Mexico. He captured Monterrey in September 1846 and, disregarding Polk's orders to stay on the defensive, defeated Santa Anna at Buena Vista in February 1847, ending the war in the northern provinces.

Though Taylor had never cast a vote for president, his party affiliations were Whiggish and his availability was increased by his difficulties with Polk. He was elected president over the Democrat Lewis Cass. During the revival of the slavery controversy, which was to result in the Compromise of 1850, Taylor began to take an increasingly firm stand against appeasing the South; but he died in Washington on July 9, 1850, during the fight over the Compromise. He married Margaret Mackall Smith in 1810. His bluff and simple soldierly qualities won him the name Old Rough and Ready.

**MILLARD FILLMORE** was born at Locke, Cayuga County, N.Y., on Jan. 7, 1800. A lawyer, he entered politics with the Anti-Masonic Party under the sponsorship of Thurlow Weed, editor and party boss, and subsequently followed Weed into the Whig Party. He served in the House of Representatives (1833–35 and 1837–43) and played a leading role in writing the tariff of 1842. Defeated for governor of New York in 1844, he became State comptroller in 1848, was put on the Whig ticket with Taylor as a concession to the Clay wing of the party, and became president upon Taylor's death in 1850.

As president, Fillmore broke with Weed and William H. Seward and associated himself with the pro-Southern Whigs, supporting the Compromise of 1850. Defeated for the Whig nomination in 1852, he ran for president in 1856 as candidate of the American, or Know-Nothing Party, which sought to unite the country against foreigners in the alleged hope of diverting it from the explosive slavery issue. Fillmore opposed Lincoln during the Civil War. He died in Buffalo on March 8, 1874.

He was married in 1826 to Abigail Powers, who died in 1853, and in 1858 to Caroline Carmichael McIntosh.

**FRANKLIN PIERCE** was born at Hillsboro, N.H., on Nov. 23, 1804. A Bowdoin graduate, lawyer, and Jacksonian Democrate, he won rapid political advancement in the party, in part because of the prestige of his father, Gov. Benjamin Pierce. By 1831 he was Speaker of the New Hampshire House of Representatives; from 1833 to 1837, he served in the federal House and from 1837 to 1842 in the Senate. His wife, Jane Means Appleton, whom he married in 1834, disliked Washington and the somewhat dissipated life led by Pierce; in 1842 Pierce resigned from the Senate and began a successful law practice in Concord, N.H. During the Mexican War, he was a brigadier general.

Thereafter Pierce continued to oppose antislavery tendencies within the Democratic Party. As a result, he was the Southern choice to break the deadlock at the Democratic convention of 1852 and was nominated on the 49th ballot. In the election, Pierce overwhelmed Gen. Winfield Scott, the Whig candidate.

As president, Pierce followed a course of appeasing the South at home and of playing with schemes of territorial expansion abroad. The failure of his foreign and domestic policies prevented his renomination; and he died in Concord on Oct. 8, 1869, in relative obscurity.

**JAMES BUCHANAN** was born near Mercersburg, Pa., on April 23, 1791. A Dickinson graduate and a lawyer, he entered Pennsylvania politics as a Federalist. With the disappearance of the Federalist Party, he became a Jacksonian Democrat. He served with ability in the House (1821–31), as minister to St. Petersburg (1832–33), and in the Senate (1834–45), and in 1845 became Polk's Secretary of State. In 1853, Pierce appointed Buchanan minister to Britain, where he participated with other American diplomats in Europe in drafting the expansionist Ostend Manifesto.

He was elected president in 1856, defeating John C. Frémont, the Republican candidate, and former President Millard Fillmore of the American Party. The growing crisis over slavery presented Buchanan with problems he lacked the will to tackle. His appeasement of the South alienated the Stephen Douglas wing of the Democratic Party without reducing Southern militancy on slavery issues. While denying the right of secession, Buchanan also denied that the federal government could do anything about it. He supported the administration during the Civil War and died in Lancaster, Pa., on June 1, 1868.

The only president to remain a bachelor throughout his term, Buchanan used his charming niece, Harriet Lane, as White House hostess.

**ABRAHAM LINCOLN** was born in Hardin (now Larue) County, Ky., on Feb. 12, 1809. His family moved to Indiana and then to Illinois, and Lincoln gained what education he could along the way. While reading law, he worked in a store, managed a mill, surveyed, and split rails. In 1834, he went to the Illinois legislature as a Whig and became the party's floor leader. For the next 20 years he practiced law in Springfield, except for a single term (1847–49) in Congress, where he denounced the Mexican War. In 1855, he was a candidate for senator annd the next year he joined the new Republican Party.

A leading but unsuccessful candidate for the vice-presidential nomination with Frémont, Lincoln gained national attention in 1858 when, as

Republican candidate for senator from Illinois, he engaged in a series of debates with Stephen A. Douglas, the Democratic candidate. He lost the election, but continued to prepare the way for the 1860 Republican convention and was rewarded with the presidential nomination on the third ballot. He won the election over three opponents.

From the start, Lincoln made clear that, unlike Buchanan, he believed the national government had the power to crush the rebellion. Not an abolitionist, he held the slavery issue subordinate to that of preserving the Union, but soon perceived that the war could not be brought to a successful conclusion without freeing the slaves. His administration was hampered by the incompetence of many Union generals, the inexperience of the troops, and the harassing political tactics both of the Republican Radicals, who favored a hard policy toward the South, and the Democratic Copperheads, who desired a negotiated peace. The Gettysburg Address of Nov. 19, 1863, marks the high point in the record of American eloquence. Lincoln's long search for a winning combination finally brought Generals Ulysses S. Grant and William T. Sherman to the top; and their series of victories in 1864 dispelled the mutterings from both Radicals and Peace Democrats that at one time seemed to threaten Lincoln's re-election. He was re-elected in 1864, defeating Gen. George B. McClellan, the Democratic candidate. His inaugural address urged leniency toward the South: "With malice toward none, with charity for all . . . let us strive on to finish the work we are in; to bind up the nation's wounds . . ." This policy aroused growing opposition on the part of the Republican Radicals, but before the matter could be put to the test, Lincoln was shot by the actor John Wilkes Booth at Ford's Theater, Washington, on April 14, 1865. He died the next morning.

Lincoln's marriage to Mary Todd in 1842 was often unhappy and turbulent, in part because of his wife's pronounced instability.

**ANDREW JOHNSON** was born at Raleigh, N.C., on Dec. 29, 1808. Self-educated, he became a tailor in Greeneville, Tenn., but soon went into politics, where he rose steadily. He served in the House of Representatives (1843–54), as governor of Tennessee (1853–57), and as a senator (1857–62). Politically he was a Jacksonian Democrat and his specialty was the fight for a more equitable land policy. Alone among the Southern Senators, he stood by the Union during the Civil War. In 1862, he became war governor of Tennessee and carried out a thankless and difficult job with great courage. Johnson became Lincoln's running mate in 1864 as a result of an attempt to give the ticket a nonpartisan and nonsectional character. Succeeding to the presidency on Lincoln's death, Johnson sought to carry out Lincoln's policy, but without his political skill. The result was a hopeless conflict with the Radical Republicans who dominated Congress, passed measures over Johnson's vetoes, and attempted to limit the power of the executive concerning appointments and removals. The conflict culminated with Johnson's impeachment for attempting to remove his disloyal Secretary of War in defiance of the Tenure of Office Act which required senatorial concurrence for such dismissals. The opposition failed by one vote to get the two thirds necessary for conviction.

After his presidency, Johnson maintained an interest in politics and in 1875 was again elected to the Senate. He died near Carter Station, Tenn., on July 31, 1875. He married Eliza McCardle in 1827.

**ULYSSES SIMPSON GRANT** was born (as Hiram Ulysses Grant) at Point Pleasant, Ohio, on April 27, 1822. He graduated from West Point in 1843 and served without particular distinction in the Mexican War. In 1848 he married Julia Dent. He resigned from the army in 1854, after warnings from his commanding officer about his drinking habits, and for the next six years held a wide variety of jobs in the Middle West. With the outbreak of the Civil War, he sought a command and soon, to his surprise, was made a brigadier general. His continuing successes in the western theaters, culminating in the capture of Vicksburg, Miss., in 1863, brought him national fame and soon the command of all the Union armies. Grant's dogged, implacable policy of concentrating on dividing and destroying the Confederate armies brought the war to an end in 1865. The next year, he was made full general.

In 1868, as Republican candidate for president, Grant was elected over the Democrat, Horatio Seymour. From the start, Grant showed his unfitness for the office. His Cabinet was weak, his domestic policy was confused, many of his intimate associates were corrupt. The notable achievement in foreign affairs was the settlement of controversies with Great Britain in the Treaty of London (1871), negotiated by his able Secretary of State, Hamilton Fish.

Running for re-election in 1872, he defeated Horace Greeley, the Democratic and Liberal Republican candidate. The Panic of 1873 graft scandals close to the presidency created difficulties for his second term.

After retiring from office, Grant toured Europe for two years and returned in time to accede to a third-term boom, but was beaten in the convention of 1880. Illness and bad business judgment darkened his last years, but he worked steadily at the *Personal Memoirs*, which were to be so successful when published after his death at Mount McGregor, near Saratoga, N.Y., on July 23, 1885.

**RUTHERFORD BIRCHARD HAYES** was born in Delaware, Ohio, on Oct. 4, 1822. A graduate of Kenyon College and the Harvard Law School, he practiced law in Lower Sandusky (now Fremont) and then in Cincinnati. In 1852 he married Lucy Webb. A Whig, he joined the Republican party in 1855. During the Civil War he rose to major general. He served in the House of Representatives from 1865 to 1867 and then confirmed a reputation for honesty and efficiency in two terms as Governor of Ohio (1868–72). His election to a third term in 1875 made him the logical candidate for those Republicans who wished to stop James G. Blaine in 1876, and he was nominated.

The result of the election was in doubt for some time and hinged upon disputed returns from South Carolina, Louisiana, Florida, and Oregon. Samuel J. Tilden, the Democrat, had the larger popular vote but was adjudged by the strictly partisan decisions of the Electoral Commission to have one fewer electoral vote, 185 to 184. The national acceptance of this result was due in part to the general understanding that Hayes would pursue a conciliatory policy toward the South. He withdrew the troops from the South, took a conservative position on financial and labor issues, and urged civil service reform.

Hayes served only one term by his own wish and

spent the rest of his life in various humanitarian endeavors. He died in Fremont on Jan. 17, 1893.

**JAMES ABRAM GARFIELD,** the last president to be born in a log cabin, was born in Cuyahoga County, Ohio, on Nov. 19, 1831. A Williams graduate, he taught school for a time and entered Republican politics in Ohio. In 1858, he married Lucretia Rudolph. During the Civil War, he had a promising career, rising to major general of volunteers; but he resigned in 1863, having been elected to the House of Representatives, where he served until 1880. His oratorical and parliamentary abilities soon made him the leading Republican in the House, though his record was marred by his unorthodox acceptance of a fee in the DeGolyer paving contract case and by suspicions of his complicity in the Crédit Mobilier scandal.

In 1880, Garfield was elected to the Senate, but instead became the presidential candidate on the 36th ballot as a result of a deadlock in the Republican convention. In the election, he defeated Gen. Winfield Scott Hancock, the Democratic candidate. Garfield's administration was barely under way when he was shot by Charles J. Guiteau, a disappointed office seeker, in Washington on July 2, 1881. He died in Elberton, N.J., on Sept. 19.

**CHESTER ALAN ARTHUR** was born at Fairfield, Vt., on Oct. 5, 1830. A graduate of Union College, he became a successful New York lawyer. In 1859, he married Ellen Herndon. During the Civil War, he held administrative jobs in the Republican state administration and in 1871 was appointed collector of the Port of New York by Grant. This post gave him control over considerable patronage. Though not personally corrupt, Arthur managed his power in the interests of the New York machine so openly that President Hayes in 1877 called for an investigation and the next year Arthur was suspended.

In 1880 Arthur was nominated for vice president in the hope of conciliating the followers of Grant and the powerful New York machine. As president upon Garfield's death, Arthur, stepping out of his familiar role as spoilsman, backed civil service reform, reorganized the Cabinet, and prosecuted political associates accused of post office graft. Losing machine support and failing to gain the reformers, he was not nominated for a full term in 1884. He died in New York City on Nov. 18, 1886.

**STEPHEN GROVER CLEVELAND** was born at Caldwell, N.J., on March 18, 1837. He was admitted to the bar in Buffalo, N.Y., in 1859 and lived there as a lawyer, with occasional incursions into Democratic politics, for more than 20 years. He did not participate in the Civil War. As mayor of Buffalo in 1881, he carried through a reform program so ably that the Democrats ran him successfully for governor in 1882. In 1884 he won the Democratic nomination for President. The campaign contrasted Cleveland's spotless public career with the uncertain record of James G. Blaine, the Republican candidate, and Cleveland received enough Mugwump (independent Republican) support to win.

As president, Cleveland pushed civil service reform, opposed the pension grab and attacked the high tariff rates. While in the White House, he married Frances Folsom in 1886. Renominated in 1888, Cleveland was defeated by Benjamin Harrison, polling more popular but fewer electoral votes. In 1892, he was elected over Harrison. When the Panic of 1893 burst upon the country, Cleveland's attempts to solve it by sound-money measures alienated the free-silver wing of the party, while his tariff policy alienated the protectionists. In 1894, he sent troops to break the Pullman strike. In foreign affairs, his firmness caused Great Britain to back down in the Venezuela border dispute.

In his last years Cleveland was an active and much-respected public figure. He died in Princeton, N.J., on June 24, 1908.

**BENJAMIN HARRISON** was born in North Bend, Ohio, on Aug. 20, 1833, the grandson of William Henry Harrison, the ninth president. A graduate of Miami University in Ohio, he took up the law in Indiana and became active in Republican politics. In 1853, he married Caroline Lavinia Scott. During the Civil War, he rose to brigadier general. A sound-money Republican, he was elected senator from Indiana in 1880. In 1888, he received the Republican nomination for President on the eighth ballot. Though behind on the popular vote, he won over Grover Cleveland in the electoral college by 233 to 168.

As President, Harrison failed to please either the bosses or the reform element in the party. In foreign affairs he backed Secretary of State Blaine, whose policy foreshadowed later American imperialism. Harrison was renominated in 1892 but lost to Cleveland. His wife died in the White House in 1892 and Harrison married her niece, Mary Scott (Lord) Dimmick, in 1896. After his presidency, he resumed law practice. He died in Indianapolis on March 13, 1901.

**WILLIAM McKINLEY** was born in Niles, Ohio, on Jan. 29, 1843. He taught school, then served in the Civil War, rising from the ranks to become a major. Subsequently he opened a law office in Canton, Ohio, and in 1871 married Ida Saxton. Elected to Congress in 1876, he served there until 1891, except for 1883–85. His faithful advocacy of business interests culminated in the passage of the highly protective McKinley Tariff of 1890. With the support of Mark Hanna, a shrewd Cleveland businessman interested in safeguarding tariff protection, McKinley became governor of Ohio in 1892 and Republican presidential candidate in 1896. The business community, alarmed by the progressivism of William Jennings Bryan, the Democratic candidate, spent considerable money to assure McKinley's victory.

The chief event of McKinley's administration was the war with Spain, which resulted in our acquisition of the Philippines and other islands. With imperialism an issue, McKinley defeated Bryan again in 1900. On Sept. 6, 1901, he was shot at Buffalo, N.Y., by Leon F. Czolgosz, an anarchist, and he died there eight days later.

**THEODORE ROOSEVELT** was born in New York City on Oct. 27, 1858. A Harvard graduate, he was early interested in ranching, in politics, and in writing picturesque historical narratives. He was a Republican member of the New York Assembly in 1882–84, an unsuccessful candidate for mayor of New York in 1886, a U.S. Civil Service Commissioner under Benjamin Harrison, Police Commissioner of New York City in 1895, and Assistant Secretary of the Navy under McKinley in 1897. He resigned in 1898 to help organize a volunteer regiment, the Rough Riders, and take a more direct part in the war with Spain. He was elected governor of New York in 1898 and vice president in 1900, in spite of lack of enthusiasm on the part of the bosses.

Assuming the presidency of the assassinated McKinley in 1901, Roosevelt embarked on a wideranging program of government reform and conservation of natural resources. He ordered antitrust suits against several large corporations, threatened to intervene in the anthracite coal strike of 1902, which prompted the operators to accept arbitration, and, in general, championed the rights of the "little man" and fought the "malefactors of great wealth." He was also responsible for such progressive legislation as the Elkins Act of 1901, which outlawed freight rebates by railroads; the bill establishing the Department of Commerce and Labor; the Hepburn Act, which gave the I.C.C. greater control over the railroads; the Meat Inspection Act; and the Pure Food and Drug Act.

In foreign affairs, Roosevelt pursued a strong policy, permitting the instigation of a revolt in Panama to dispose of Colombian objections to the Panama Canal and helping to maintain the balance of power in the East by bringing the Russo-Japanese War to an end, for which he won the Nobel Peace Prize, the first American to achieve a Nobel prize in any category. In 1904, he decisively defeated Alton B. Parker, his conservative Democratic opponent.

Roosevelt's increasing coldness toward his successor, William Howard Taft, led him to overlook his earlier disclaimer of third-term ambitions and to re-enter politics. Defeated by the machine in the Republican convention of 1912, he organized the Progressive Party (Bull Moose) and polled more votes than Taft, though the split brought about the election of Woodrow Wilson. From 1915 on, Roosevelt strongly favored intervention in the European war. He became deeply embittered at Wilson's refusal to allow him to raise a volunteer division. He died in Oyster Bay, N.Y., on Jan. 6, 1919. He was married twice: in 1880 to Alice Hathaway Lee, who died in 1884, and in 1886 to Edith Kermit Carow.

**WILLIAM HOWARD TAFT** was born in Cincinnati on Sept. 15, 1857. A Yale graduate, he entered Ohio Republican politics in the 1880s. In 1886 he married Helen Herron. From 1887 to 1890, he served on the Ohio Superior Court; 1890–92, as solicitor general of the United States; 1892–1900, on the federal circuit court. In 1900 McKinley appointed him president of the Phhilippine Commission and in 1901 governor general. Taft had great success in pacifying the Filipinos, solving the problem of the church lands, improving economic conditions, and establishing limited self-government. His period as Secretary of War (1904–08) further demonstrated his capacity as administrator and conciliator, and he was Roosevelt's hand-picked successor in 1908. In the election, he polled 321 electoral votes to 162 for William Jennings Bryan, who was running for the presidency for the third time.

Though he carried on many of Roosevelt's policies, Taft got into increasing trouble with the progressive wing of the party and displayed mounting irritability and indecision. After his defeat in 1912, he became professor of constitutional law at Yale. In 1921 he was appointed Chief Justice of the

United States. He died in Washington on March 8, 1930.

**THOMAS WOODROW WILSON** was born in Staunton, Va., on Dec. 28, 1856. A Princeton graduate, he turned from law practice to post-graduate work in political science at Johns Hopkins University, receiving his Ph.D. in 1886. He taught at Bryn Mawr, Wesleyan, and Princeton, and in 1902 was made president of Princeton. After an unsuccessful attempt to democratize the social life of the university, he welcomed an invitation in 1910 to be the Democratic gubernatorial candidate in New Jersey, and was elected. His success in fighting the machine and putting through a reform program attracted national attention.

In 1912, at the Democratic convention in Baltimore, Wilson won the nomination on the 46th ballot and went on to defeat Roosevelt and Taft in the election. Wilson proceeded under the standard of the New Freedom to enact a program of domestic reform, including the Federal Reserve Act, the Clayton Antitrust Act, the establishment of the Federal Trade Commission, and other measures designed to restore competition in the face of the great monopolies. In foreign affairs, while privately sympathetic with the Allies, he strove to maintain neutrality in the European war and warned both sides against encroachments on American interests.

Re-elected in 1916 as a peace candidate, he tried to mediate between the warring nations; but when the Germans resumed unrestricted submarine warfare in 1917, Wilson brought the United States into what he now believed was a war to make the world safe for democracy. He supplied the classic formulations of Allied war aims and the armistice of Nov. 11, 1918 was negotiated on the basis of Wilson's Fourteen Points. In 1919 he strove at Versailles to lay the foundations for enduring peace. He accepted the imperfections of the Versailles Treaty in the expectation that they could be remedied by action within the League of Nations. He probably could have secured ratification of the treaty by the Senate if he had adopted a more conciliatory attitude toward the mild reservationists; but his insistence on all or nothing eventually caused the diehard isolationists and diehard Wilsonites to unite in rejecting a compromise.

In September 1919 Wilson suffered a paralytic stroke that limited his activity. After leaving the presidency he lived on in retirement in Washington, dying on Feb. 3, 1924. He was married twice—in 1885 to Ellen Louise Axson, who died in 1914, and in 1915 to Edith Bolling Galt.

**WARREN GAMALIEL HARDING** was born in Morrow County, Ohio, on Nov. 2, 1865. After attending Ohio Central College, Harding became interested in journalism and in 1884 bought the *Marion* (Ohio) *Star*. In 1891 he married a wealthy widow, Florence Kling De Wolfe. As his paper prospered, he entered Republican politics, serving as state senator (1899–1903) and as lieutenant governor (1904–06). In 1910, he was defeated for governor, but in 1914 was elected to the Senate. His reputation as an orator made him the keynoter at the 1916 Republican convention.

When the 1920 convention was deadlocked between Leonard Wood and Frank O. Lowden, Harding became the dark-horse nominee on his solemn affirmation that there was no reason in his past that he should not be. Straddling the League question, Harding was easily elected over James M. Cox, his Democratic opponent. His Cabinet contained some able men, but also some manifestly unfit for public office. Harding's own intimates were mediocre when they were not corrupt. The impending disclosure of the Teapot Dome scandal in the Interior Department and illegal practices in the Justice Department and Veterans' Bureau, as well as political setbacks, profoundly worried him. On his return from Alaska in 1923, he died unexpectedly in San Francisco on Aug. 2.

**JOHN CALVIN COOLIDGE** was born in Plymouth, Vt., on July 4, 1872. An Amherst graduate, he went into law practice at Northampton, Mass., in 1897. He married Grace Anna Goodhue in 1905. He entered Republican state politics, becoming successively mayor of Northampton, state senator, lieutenant governor and, in 1919, governor. His use of the state militia to end the Boston police strike in 1919 won him a somewhat undeserved reputation for decisive action and brought him the Republican vice-presidential nomination in 1920. After Harding's death Coolidge handled the Washington scandals with care and finally managed to save the Republican Party from public blame for the widespread corruption.

In 1924, Coolidge was elected without difficulty, defeating the Democrat, John W. Davis, and Robert M. La Follette running on the Progressive ticket. His second term, like his first, was characterized by a general satisfaction with the existing economic order. He stated that he did not choose to run in 1928.

After his presidency, Coolidge lived quietly in Northampton, writing an unilluminating *Autobiography* and conducting a syndicated column. He died there on Jan. 5, 1933.

**HERBERT CLARK HOOVER** was born at West Branch, Iowa, on Aug. 10, 1874, the first president to be born west of the Mississippi. A Stanford graduate, he worked from 1895 to 1913 as a mining engineer and consultant throughout the world. In 1899, he married Lou Henry. During World War I, he served with distinction as chairman of the American Relief Committee in London, as chairman of the Commission for Relief in Belgium, and as U.S. Food Administrator. His political affiliations were still too indeterminate for him to be mentioned as a possibility for either the Republican or Democratic nomination in 1920, but after the election he served Harding and Coolidge as Secretary of Commerce.

In the election of 1928, Hoover overwhelmed Gov. Alfred E. Smith of New York, the Democratic candidate and the first Roman Catholic to run for the presidency. He soon faced the worst depression in the nation's history, but his attacks upon it were hampered by his devotion to the theory that the forces that brought the crisis would soon bring the revival and then by his belief that there were too many areas in which the federal government had no power to act. In a succession of vetoes, he struck down measures proposing a national employment system or national relief, he reduced income tax rates, and only at the end of his term did he yield to popular pressure and set up agencies such as the Reconstruction Finance Corporation to make emergency loans to assist business.

After his 1932 defeat, Hoover returned to private business. In 1946, President Truman charged him with various world food missions; and from 1947 to 1949 and 1953 to 1955, he was head of the Commission on Organization of the Executive Branch of the Government. He died in New York City on Oct. 20, 1964.

**FRANKLIN DELANO ROOSEVELT** was born in Hyde Park, N.Y., on Jan. 30, 1882. A Harvard graduate, he attended Columbia Law School and was admitted to the New York bar. In 1910, he was elected to the New York State Senate as a Democrat. Reelected in 1912, he was appointed Assistant Secretary of the Navy by Woodrow Wilson the next year. In 1920, his radiant personality and his war service resulted in his nomination for vice president as James M. Cox's running mate. After his defeat, he returned to law practice in New York. In August 1921, Roosevelt was stricken with infantile paralysis while on vacation at Campobello, New Brunswick. After a long and gallant fight, he recovered partial use of his legs. In 1924 and 1928, he led the fight at the Democratic national conventions for the nomination of Gov. Alfred E. Smith of New York, and in 1928 Roosevelt was himself induced to run for governor of New York. He was elected, and was re-elected in 1930.

In 1932, Roosevelt received the Democratic nomination for president and immediately launched a campaign that brought new spirit to a weary and discouraged nation. He defeated Hoover by a wide margin. His first term was characterized by an unfolding of the New Deal program, with greater benefits for labor, the farmers, and the unemployed, and the progressive estrangement of most of the business community.

At an early stage, Roosevelt became aware of the menace to world peace posed by totalitarian fascism, and from 1937 on he tried to focus public attention on the trend of events in Europe and Asia. As a result, he was widely denounced as a warmonger. He was re-elected in 1936 over Gov. Alfred M. Landon of Kansas by the overwhelming electoral margin of 523 to 8, and the gathering international crisis prompted him to run for an unprecedented third term in 1940. He defeated Wendell L. Willkie.

Roosevelt's program to bring maximum aid to Britain and, after June 1941, to Russia was opposed, until the Japanese attack on Pearl Harbor restored national unity. During the war, Roosevelt shelved the New Deal in the interests of conciliating the business community, both in order to get full production during the war and to prepare the way for a united acceptance of the peace settlements after the war. A series of conferences with Winston Churchill and Joseph Stalin laid down the bases for the postwar world. In 1944 he was elected to a fourth term, running against Gov. Thomas E. Dewey of New York.

On April 12, 1945, Roosevelt died of a cerebral hemorrhage at Warm Springs, Ga., shortly after his return from the Yalta Conference. His wife, Anna Eleanor Roosevelt, whom he married in 1905, was a woman of great ability who made significant contributions to her husband's policies.

**HARRY S. TRUMAN** was born on a farm near Lamar, Mo., on May 8, 1884. During World War I, he served in France as a captain with the 129th Field Artillery. He married Bess Wallace in 1919. After engaging briefly and unsuccessfully in the haberdashery business in Kansas City, Mo., Truman entered local politics. Under the sponsorship of Thomas Pendergast, Democratic boss of Missouri, he held a number of local offices, preserving his personal honesty in the midst of a notoriously corrupt political machine. In 1934, he was elected to the Senate and was re-elected in 1940. During his first term he was a loyal but quiet supporter of the New Deal, but in his second term, an appointment as head of a Senate committee to investigate war production brought out his special qualities of honesty, common sense, and hard work, and he won widespread respect.

Elected vice president in 1944, Truman became president upon Roosevelt's sudden death in April 1945 and was immediately faced with the problems of winding down the war against the Axis and preparing the nation for postwar adjustment.

The years 1947–48 were distinguished by civil-rights proposals, the Truman Doctrine to contain the spread of Communism, and the Marshall Plan to aid in the economic reconstruction of war-ravaged nations. Truman's general record, highlighted by a vigorous Fair Deal campaign, brought about his unexpected election in 1948 over the heavily favored Thomas E. Dewey.

Truman's second term was primarily concerned with the Cold War with the Soviet Union, the implementing of the North Atlantic Pact, the United Nations police action in Korea, and the vast rearmament program with its accompanying problems of economic stabilization.

On March 29, 1952, Truman announced that he would not run again for the presidency. After leaving the White House, he returned to his home in Independence, Mo., to write his memoirs. He further busied himself with the Harry S. Truman Library there. He died in Kansas City, Mo., on Dec. 26, 1972.

**DWIGHT DAVID EISENHOWER** was born in Denison, Tex., on Oct. 14, 1890. His ancestors lived in Germany and emigrated to America, settling in Pennsylvania, early in the 18th century. His father, David, had a general store in Hope, Kan., which failed. After a brief time in Texas, the family moved to Abilene, Kan.

After graduating from Abilene High School in 1909, Eisenhower did odd jobs for almost two years. He won an appointment to the Naval Academy at Annapolis, but was too old for admittance. Then he received an appointment in 1910 to West Point, from which he graduated as a second lieutenant in 1915.

He did not see service in World War I, having been stationed at Fort Sam Houston, Tex. There he met Mamie Geneva Doud, whom he married in Denver on July 1, 1916, and by whom he had two sons: Doud Dwight (died in infancy) and John Sheldon Doud.

Eisenhower served in the Philippines from 1935 to 1939 with Gen. Douglas MacArthur. Afterward, Gen. George C. Marshall, the Army Chief of Staff, brought him into the War Department's General Staff and in 1942 placed him in command of the invasion of North Africa. In 1944, he was made Supreme Allied Commander for the invasion of Europe.

After the war, Eisenhower served as Army Chief of Staff from November 1945 until February 1948, when he was appointed president of Columbia University.

In December 1950, President Truman recalled Eisenhower to active duty to command the North Atlantic Treaty Organization forces in Europe. He held his post until the end of May 1952.

At the Republican convention of 1952 in Chicago, Eisenhower won the presidential nomination on the first ballot in a close race with Senator Robert A. Taft of Ohio. In the election, he defeated Gov. Adlai E. Stevenson of Illinois.

Through two terms, Eisenhower hewed to moderate domestic policies. He sought peace through Free World strength in an era of new nationalisms, nuclear missiles, and space exploration. He fostered alliances pledging the United States to resist Red aggression in Europe, Asia, and Latin America. The Eisenhower Doctrine of 1957 extended commitments to the Middle East.

At home, the popular president lacked Republican Congressional majorities after 1954, but he was re-elected in 1956 by 457 electoral votes to 73 for Stevenson.

While retaining most Fair Deal programs, he stressed "fiscal responsibility" in domestic affairs. A moderate in civil rights, he sent troops to Little Rock, Ark., to enforce court-ordered school integration.

With his wartime rank restored by Congress, Eisenhower returned to private life and the role of elder statesman, with his vigor hardly impaired by a heart attack, an ileitis operation, and a mild stroke suffered while in office. He died in Washington on March 28, 1969.

**JOHN FITZGERALD KENNEDY** was born in Brookline, Mass., on May 29, 1917. His father, Joseph P. Kennedy, was Ambassador to Great Britain from 1937 to 1940.

Kennedy was graduated from Harvard University in 1940 and joined the Navy the next year. He became skipper of a PT boat that was sunk in the Pacific by a Japanese destroyer. Although given up for lost, he swam to a safe island, towing an injured enlisted man.

After recovering from a war-aggravated spinal injury, Kennedy entered politics in 1946 and was elected to Congress. In 1952, he ran against Senator Henry Cabot Lodge, Jr., of Massachusetts, and won.

Kennedy was married on Sept. 12, 1953, to Jacqueline Lee Bouvier, by whom he had three children: Caroline, John Fitzgerald, Jr., and Patrick Bouvier (died in infancy).

In 1957 Kennedy won the Pulitzer Prize for a book he had written earlier, *Profiles in Courage.*

After strenuous primary battles, Kennedy won the Democratic presidential nomination on the first ballot at the 1960 Los Angeles convention. With a plurality of only 118,574 votes, he carried the election over Vice President Richard M. Nixon and became the first Roman Catholic president.

Kennedy brought to the White House the dynamic idea of a "New Frontier" approach in dealing with problems at home, abroad, and in the dimensions of space. Out of his leadership in his first few months in office came the 10-year Alliance for Progress to aid Latin America, the Peace Corps, and accelerated programs that brought the first Americans into orbit in the race in space.

Failure of the U.S.-supported Cuban invasion in April 1961 led to the entrenchment of the Communist-backed Castro regime, only 90 miles from United States soil. When it became known that Soviet offensive missiles were being installed in Cuba in 1962, Kennedy ordered a naval "quarantine" of the island and moved troops into position to eliminate this threat to U.S. security. The world seemed on the brink of a nuclear war until Soviet Premier Khrushchev ordered the removal of the missiles.

A sudden "thaw," or the appearance of one, in the cold war came with the agreement with the Soviet Union on a limited test-ban treaty signed in Moscow on Aug. 6, 1963.

In his domestic policies, Kennedy's proposals for medical care for the aged, expanded area redevelopment, and aid to education were defeated, but on minimum wage, trade legislation, and other measures he won important victories.

Widespread racial disorders and demonstrations led to Kennedy's proposing sweeping civil rights legislation. As his third year in office drew to a close, he also recommended an $11-billion tax cut to bolster the economy. Both measures were pending in Congress when Kennedy, looking forward to a second term, journeyed to Texas for a series of speeches.

While riding in a procession in Dallas on Nov. 22, 1963, he was shot to death by an assassin firing from an upper floor of a building. The alleged assassin, Lee Harvey Oswald, was killed two days later in the Dallas city jail by Jack Ruby, owner of a striptease place.

At 46 years of age, Kennedy became the fourth president to be assassinated and the eighth to die in office.

**LYNDON BAINES JOHNSON** was born in Stonewall, Tex., on Aug. 27, 1908. On both sides of his family he had a political heritage mingled with a Baptist background of preachers and teachers. Both his father and his paternal grandfather served in the Texas House of Representatives.

After his graduation from Southwest Texas State Teachers College, Johnson taught school for two years. He went to Washington in 1932 as secretary to Rep. Richard M. Kleberg. During this time, he married Claudia Alta Taylor, known as "Lady Bird." They had two children: Lynda Bird (Robb) and Luci Baines (Nugent).

In 1935, Johnson became Texas administrator for the National Youth Administration. Two years later, he was elected to Congress as an all-out supporter of Franklin D. Roosevelt, and served until 1949. He was the first member of Congress to enlist in the armed forces after the attack on Pearl Harbor. He served in the Navy in the Pacific and won a Silver Star.

Johnson was elected to the Senate in 1948 after he had captured the Democratic nomination by only 87 votes. He was 40 years old. He became the Senate Democratic leader in 1953. A heart attack in 1955 threatened to end his political career, but he recovered fully and resumed his duties.

At the height of his power as Senate leader, Johnson sought the Democratic nomination for president in 1960. When he lost to John F. Kennedy, he surprised even some of his closest associates by accepting second place on the ticket.

Johnson was riding in another car in the motorcade when Kennedy was assassinated in Dallas on Nov. 22, 1963. He took the oath of office in the presidential jet on the Dallas airfield.

With Johnson's insistent backing, Congress finally adopted a far-reaching civil-rights bill, a voting-rights bill, a Medicare program for the aged, and measures to improve education and conservation. Congress also began what Johnson described as "an all-out war" on poverty.

Amassing a record-breaking majority of nearly 16 million votes, Johnson was elected president in his own right in 1964, defeating Senator Barry Goldwater of Arizona.

The double tragedy of a war in Southeast Asia and urban riots at home marked Johnson's last two years in office. Faced with disunity in the nation and challenges within his own party, Johnson surprised the country on March 31, 1968, with the announcement that he would not be a candidate for re-election. He died of a heart attack suffered at his LBJ Ranch on Jan. 22, 1973.

**RICHARD MILHOUS NIXON** was born in Yorba Linda, Calif., on Jan. 9, 1913, to Midwestern-bred parents, Francis A. and Hannah Milhous Nixon, who raised their five sons as Quakers.

Nixon was a high school debater and was undergraduate president at Whittier College in California, where he was graduated in 1934. As a scholarship student at Duke University Law School in North Carolina, he graduated third in his class in 1937.

After five years as a lawyer, Nixon joined the Navy in August 1942. He was an air transport officer in the South Pacific and a legal officer stateside before his discharge in 1946 as a lieutenant commander.

Running for Congress in California as a Republican in 1946, Nixon defeated Rep. Jerry Voorhis. As a member of the House Un-American Activities Committee, he made a name as an investigator of Alger Hiss, a former high State Department official, who was later jailed for perjury. In 1950, Nixon defeated Rep. Helen Gahagan Douglas, a Democrat, for the Senate. He was criticized for portraying her as a Communist dupe.

Nixon's anti-Communism, his Western base, and his youth figured in his selection in 1952 to run for vice president on the ticket headed by Dwight D. Eisenhower. Demands for Nixon's withdrawal followed disclosure that California businessmen had paid some of his Senate office expenses. He televised rebuttal, known as "the Checkers speech" (named for a cocker spaniel given to the Nixons), brought him support from the public and from Eisenhower. The ticket won easily in 1952 and again in 1956.

Eisenhower gave Nixon substantive assignments, including missions to 56 countries. In Moscow in 1959, Nixon won acclaim for his defense of U.S. interests in an impromptu "kitchen debate" with Soviet Premier Nikita S. Khrushchev.

Nixon lost the 1960 race for the presidency to John F. Kennedy.

In 1962, Nixon failed in a bid for California's governorship and seemed to be finished as a national candidate. He became a Wall Street lawyer, but kept his old party ties and developed new ones through constant travels to speak for Republicans.

Nixon won the 1968 Republican presidential nomination after a shrewd primary campaign, then made Gov. Spiro T. Agnew of Maryland his surprise choice for vice president. In the election, they edged out the Democratic ticket headed by Vice President Hubert H. Humphrey by 510,314 votes out of 73,212,065 cast.

Committed to wind down the U.S. role in the Vietnamese War, Nixon pursued "Vietnamization"—training and equipping South Vietnamese to do their own fighting. American ground combat forces in Vietnam fell steadily from 540,000 when Nixon took office to none in 1973 when the military draft was ended. But there was heavy continuing use of U.S. air power.

Nixon improved relations with Moscow and reopened the long-closed door to mainland China with a good-will trip there in February 1972. In May of that year, he visited Moscow and signed agreements on arms limitation and trade expansion and approved plans for a joint U.S.-Soviet space mission in 1975.

Inflation was a campaign issue for Nixon, but he failed to master it as president. On Aug. 15, 1971, with unemployment edging up, Nixon abruptly announced a new economic policy: a 90-day wage-price freeze, stimulative tax cuts, a temporary 10% tariff, and spending cuts. A second phase, imposing guidelines on wage, price and rent boosts, was announced October 7.

The economy responded in time for the 1972 campaign, in which Nixon played up his foreign-policy achievements. Played down was the burglary on June 17, 1972, of Democratic national headquarters in the Watergate apartment complex in Washington. The Nixon-Agnew re-election campaign cost a record $60 million and swamped the Democratic ticket headed by Senator George McGovern of South Dakota with a plurality of 17,999,528 out of 77,718,554 votes. Only Massachusetts, with 14 electoral votes, and the District of Columbia, with 3, went for McGovern.

In January 1973, hints of a cover-up emerged at the trial of six men found guilty of the Wtergate burglary. With a Senate investigation under way, Nixon announced on April 30 the resignations of his top aides, H. R. Haldeman and John D. Ehrlichman, and the dismissal of White House counsel John Dean III. Dean was the star witness at televised Senate hearings that exposed both a White House cover-up of Watergate and massive illegalities in Republican fund-raising in 1972.

The hearings also disclosed that Nixon had routinely tape-recorded his office meetings and telephone conversations.

On Oct. 10, 1973, Agnew resigned as vice president, then pleaded no-contest to a negotiated federal charge of evading income taxes on alleged bribes. Two days later, Nixon nominated the House minority leader, Rep. Gerald R. Ford of Michigan, as the new vice president. Congress confirmed Ford on Dec. 6, 1973.

In June 1974, Nixon visited Israel and four Arab nations. Then he met in Moscow with Soviet leader Leonid I. Brezhnev and reached preliminary nuclear arms limitation agreements.

But, in the month after his return, Watergate ended the Nixon regime. On July 24 the Supreme Court ordered Nixon to surrender subpoenaed tapes. On July 30, the Judiciary Committee referred three impeachment articles to the full membership. On August 5, Nixon bowed to the Supreme Court and released tapes showing he halted an FBI probe of the Watergate burglary six days after it occurred. It was in effect an admission of obstruction of justice, and impeachment appeared inevitable.

Nixon resigned on Aug. 9, 1974, the first president ever to do so. A month later, President Ford issued an unconditional pardon for any offenses Nixon might have committed as president, thus forestalling possible prosecution.

In 1940, Nixon married Thelma Catherine (Pat) Ryan. They had two daughters, Patricia (Tricia) Cox and Julie, who married Dwight David Eisenhower II, grandson of the former president.

**GERALD RUDOLPH FORD** was born in Omaha, Neb., on July 14, 1913, the only child of Leslie and Dorothy Gardner King. His parents were divorced in 1915. His mother moved to Grand Rapids, Mich., and married Gerald R. Ford. The boy was renamed for his stepfather.

Ford captained his high school football team in Grand Rapids, and a football scholarship took him to the University of Michigan, where he starred as varsity center before his graduation in 1935. A job as assistant football coach at Yale gave him an opportunity to attend Yale Law School, from which he graduated in the top third of his class in 1941.

He returned to Grand Rapids to practice law, but entered the Navy in April 1942. He saw wartime service in the Pacific on the light aircraft carrier *Monterey* and was a lieutenant commander when he returned to Grand Rapids early in 1946 to resume law practice and dabble in politics.

Ford was elected to Congress in 1948 for the first of his 13 terms in the House. He was soon assigned to the influential Appropriations Committee and rose to become the ranking Republican on the subcommittee on Defense Department appropriations and an expert in the field.

As a legislator, Ford described himself as "a moderate on domestic issues, a conservative in fiscal affairs, and a dyed-in-the-wool internationalist." He carried the ball for Pentagon appropriations, was a hawk on the war in Vietnam, and kept a low profile on civil-rights issues.

He was also dependable and hard-working and popular with his colleagues. In 1963, he was elected chairman of the House Republican Conference. He served in 1963–64 as a member of the Warren Commission that investigated the assassination of John F. Kennedy. A revolt by dissatisfied younger Republicans in 1965 made him minority leader.

Ford shelved his hopes for the Speakership on Oct. 12, 1973, when Nixon nominated him to fill the vice presidency left vacant by Agnew's resignation under fire. It was the first use of the procedures for filling vacancies in the vice presidency laid down in the 25th Amendment to the Constitution, which Ford had helped enact.

Congress confirmed Ford as vice president on Dec. 6, 1973. Once in office, he said he did not believe Nixon had been involved in the Watergate scandals, but criticized his stubborn court battle against releasing tape recordings of Watergate-related conversations for use as evidence.

The scandals led to Nixon's unprecedented resignation on Aug. 9, 1974, and Ford was sworn in immediately as the 38th president, the first to enter the White House without winning a national election.

Ford assured the nation when he took office that "our long national nightmare is over" and pledged "openness and candor" in all his actions. He won a warm response from the Democratic 93rd Congress when he said he wanted "a good marriage" rather than a honeymoon with his former colleagues. In December 1974 Congressional majorities backed his choice of former New York Gov. Nelson A. Rockefeller as his successor in the again-vacant vice presidency.

The cordiality was chilled by Ford's announcement on Sept. 8, 1974, that he had granted an unconditional pardon to Nixon for any crimes he might have committed as president. Although no formal charges were pending, Ford said he feared "ugly passions" would be aroused if Nixon were brought to trial. The pardon was widely criticized.

To fight inflation, the new president first proposed fiscal restraints and spending curbs and a 5% tax surcharge that got nowhere in the Senate and House. Congress again rebuffed Ford in the spring of 1975 when he appealed for emergency military aid to help the governments of South Vietnam and Cambodia resist massive Communist offensives.

In November 1974, Ford visited Japan, South Korea, and the Soviet Union, where he and Soviet leader Leonid I. Brezhnev conferred in Vladivostok and reached a tentative agreement to limit the number of strategic offensive nuclear weapons. It was Ford's first meeting as president with Brezhnev, who planned a return visit to Washington in the fall of 1975.

Politically, Ford's fortunes improved steadily in the first half of 1975. Badly divided Democrats in Congress were unable to muster votes to override his vetoes of spending bills that exceeded his budget. He faced some right-wing opposition in his own party, but moved to pre-empt it with an early announcement—on July 8, 1975—of his intention to be a candidate in 1976.

Early state primaries in 1976 suggested an easy victory for Ford despite Ronald Reagan's bitter attacks on administration foreign policy and defense programs. But later Reagan primary successes threatened the President's lead. At the Kansas City convention, Ford was nominated by the narrow margin of 1,187 to 1,070. But Reagan had moved the party to the right, and Ford himself was regarded as a caretaker president lacking in strength and vision. He was defeated in November by Jimmy Carter.

In 1948, Ford married Elizabeth Anne (Betty) Bloomer. They had four children, Michael Gerald, John Gardner, Steven Meigs, and Susan Elizabeth.

**JAMES EARL CARTER, JR.,** was born in the tiny village of Plains, Ga., Oct. 1, 1924, and grew up on the family farm at nearby Archery. Both parents were fifth-generation Georgians. His father, James Earl Carter, was known as a segregationist, but treated his black and white workers equally. Carter's mother, Lillian Gordy, was a matriarchal presence in home and community and opposed the then-prevailing code of racial inequality. The future President was baptized in 1935 in the conservative Southern Baptist Church and spoke often of being a "born again" Christian, although committed to the separation of church and state.

Carter married Rosalynn Smith, a neighbor, in 1946. Their first child, John William, was born a year later in Portsmouth, Va. Their other children are James Earl III, born in Honolulu in 1950; Donnel Jeffrey, born in New London, Conn., in 1952, and Amy Lynn, born in Plains in 1967.

In 1946 Carter was graduated from the U.S. Naval Academy at Annapolis and served in the nuclear-submarine program under Adm. Hyman G. Rickover. In 1954, after his father's death, he resigned from the Navy to take over the family's flourishing warehouse and cotton gin, with several thousand acres for growing seed peanuts.

Carter was elected to the Georgia Senate in 1962. In 1966 he lost the race for Governor, but was elected in 1970. His term brought a state government reorganization, sharply reduced agencies, increased economy and efficiency, and new social programs, all with no general tax increase. In 1972 the peanut farmer-politician set his sights on the Presidency and in 1974 built a base for himself as

he criss-crossed the country as chairman of the Democratic Campaign Committee, appealing for revival and reform. In 1975 his image as a typical Southern white was erased when he won support of most of the old Southern civil-rights coalition after endorsement by Rep. Andrew Young, black Democrat from Atlanta, who had been the closest aide to the Rev. Martin Luther King, Jr. At Carter's 1971 inauguration as Governor he had called for an end to all forms of racial discrimination.

In the 1976 spring primaries, he won 19 out of 31 with a broad appeal to conservatives and liberals, black and white, poor and well-to-do. Throughout his campaigning Carter set forth his policies in his soft Southern voice, and with his electric-blue stare faced down skeptics who joked about "Jimmy Who?" His toothy smile became his trademark. He was nominated on the first roll-call vote of the 1976 Bicentennial Democratic National Convention in New York, and defeated Gerald R. Ford in November. Likewise, in 1980 he was renominated on the first ballot after vanquishing Senator Edward M. Kennedy of Massachusetts in the primaries. At the convention he defeated the Kennedy forces in their attempt to block a party rule that bound a large majority of pledged delegates to vote for Carter. In the election campaign, Carter attacked his rivals, Ronald Reagan and John B. Anderson, independent, with the warning that a Reagan Republican victory would heighten the risk of war and impede civil rights and economic opportunity. In November Carter lost to Reagan, who won 489 Electoral College votes and 51% of the popular tally, to 49 electoral votes and 41% for Carter.

In his one term, Carter fought hard for his programs against resistance from an independent-minded Democratic Congress that frustrated many pet projects although it overrode only two vetoes. Many of his difficulties were traced to his aides' brusqueness in dealing with Capitol Hill and insensitivity to Congressional feelings and tradition. Observers generally viewed public dissatisfaction with the "stagflation" economy as a principal factor in his defeat. Others included his jittery performance in the debate Oct. 28 with Reagan and the final uncertainties in the negotiations for freeing the Iranians' hostages, along with earlier staff problems, friction with Congress, long gasoline lines, and the months-long Iranian crisis, including the abortive sally in April 1980 to free the hostages. The President, however, did deflect criticism resulting from the activities of his brother, Billy. Yet, assessments of his record noted many positive elements. There was, for one thing, peace throughout his term, with no American combat deaths and with a brake on the advocates of force. Regarded as perhaps his greatest personal achievements were the Camp David accords between Israel and Egypt and the resulting treaty—the first between Israel and an Arab neighbor. The treaty with China and the Panama Canal treaties were also major achievements. Carter worked for nuclear-arms control. His concern for international human rights was credited with saving lives and reducing torture, and he supported the British policy that ended internecine warfare in Rhodesia, now Zimbabwe. Domestically, his environmental record was a major accomplishment. His judicial appointments won acclaim; the Southerner who had forsworn racism made 265 choices for the Federal bench that included minority members and women. On energy, he ended by price decontrols the practice of holding U.S. petroleum prices far below world levels. —*A.P.R., Jr.*

**RONALD REAGAN,** actor turned politician, New Dealer turned conservative, came to the films and politics from a thoroughly middle-American background—middle class, Middle West, and small town. He was born in Tampico, Ill., Feb. 6, 1911, the second son of John Edward Reagan and Nelle Wilson Reagan, and the family later moved to Dixon, Ill. The father, of Irish descent, was a shop clerk and merchant with Democratic sympathies. It was an impoverished family; Ronald sold home-made popcorn at high school games and worked as a lifeguard to earn money for his college tuition. When the father got a New Deal WPA job, the future President became an ardent Roosevelt Democrat.

Reagan won his B.A. degree in 1932 from Eureka (Ill.) College, where a photographic memory aided in his studies and in debating and college theatricals. In a Depression year, he was making $100 a week as a sports announcer for radio station WHO in Des Moines, Iowa, from 1932 to 1937. His career as a film and TV actor stretched from 1937 to 1966, and his salary climbed to $3,500 a week. As a World War II captain in an Army film studio, Reagan recoiled from what he saw as the laziness of Civil Service workers and soon moved to the Right. As president of the Screen Actors Guild, he resisted what he considered a Communist plot to subvert the film industry. With advancing age, Reagan was eased out of leading-man roles and became a television spokesman for the General Electric Company at $150,000.

With oratorical skill his trademark, Reagan became an active Republican, and in 1964 made a dramatic speech supporting Senator Barry Goldwater, who became the party's Presidential nominee. At the behest of a small group of conservative Southern California businessmen, he ran for Governor with a pledge to cut spending, and was elected by almost a million votes over the political veteran, Democratic Gov. Edmund G. Brown, father of the later Governor.

In the election battle against Jimmy Carter, Reagan rode a tide of resurgent right-wing sentiment among an electorate battered by the winds of unwanted change, longing for a distant, simpler era. Broadening his appeal by espousing moderate policies, Reagan gained much of his success from crossover votes from disaffected Democrats and blue-collar workers.

The incoming Administration immediately set out to "turn the Government around" with a new economic program. In a few months that program had become reality. Despite strenuous opposition in Congress, Reagan triumphed on the major elements of his "supply side" theory to stimulate production and control inflation through tax cuts and sharp reductions in Government spending. Through adroit and daring maneuvering and the exercise of personal charm in television appeals to the public and direct contacts with Congressmen, he won over the converts needed for massive victories. Thus, he achieved the largest budget and tax cuts in recent United States history; many compared the "Reagan revolution" to the early New Deal of Franklin D. Roosevelt.

The President won high acclaim for his nomination of Sandra Day O'Connor of the Arizona Court of Appeals to be the first woman on the Supreme Court.

Internationally, Reagan confronted numerous problems. In his first term the invasion of Grenada was a success, and he accomplished much on trips to Asia and Europe. But the intervention in Lebanon and the withdrawal of the Marines after a disastrous terrorist attack were regarded as military failures. The President also had to cope with Israel's invasion of Lebanon, the Argentine invasion of the Falklands, and the precipitate resignation of Secretary of State Alexander M. Haig, Jr.

Barely three months in office, Reagan was the target of an assassin's bullet. His courageous comeback won public admiration. In 1982, however, his popularity slipped as the country became mired in the worst recession in 40 years, with persistent high unemployment and interest rates. The initial support for his "supply side" economics faded despite ebbing inflation. Nevertheless, the President won crucial battles in Congress.

After Republican setbacks in the 1982 elections, the economy improved, and in 1984 the nation was prospering, with inflation still under control.

In November of that year, Reagan won re-election in a landslide. Early in his second term he scored what many regarded as a victory over the Soviet leader, Mikhail S. Gorbachev, at the Geneva summit conference in November 1985. The President blunted the Soviet drive against the space-based "Star Wars" missile defense scheme.

But soon the popular President encountered setbacks in Congress on foreign policy as resistance to it grew at home and abroad. Capitol Hill was increasingly reluctant to increase spending for the Nicaraguan "contras" and for the Pentagon and to expand the development of the MX missile.

But even severe critics praised Reagan's restrained but decisive handling of the crisis following the hijacking of an American plane in Beirut by Moslem extremists, with two-score Americans held hostage for 17 days and one killed.

In July 1985 the President underwent major abdominal surgery for removal of an intestinal polyp, which proved to be cancerous but not dangerous.

As the second term stretched into 1986, the President met further resistance in his foreign policy. His attack on Libya in April galvanized the nation but drew scathing disapproval from the NATO Allies and weakened the British government, which had approved the use of its airbases. Soon misgiving arose in the U.S. itself. The Alliance was strained further by Reagan's eqivocal decision to abrogate the unratified but hitherto observed second Strategic Arms Limitation Treaty (SALT II).

Domestically, a drastic tax reform bill that Reagan backed won favor in Congress, but the ominously growing budget deficit remained a constant worry. The President and Congress were increasingly at odds over priorities on spending for defense and domestic programs.

The struggle for the Senate in the autumn elections turned into a test of Reagan policies, with the Democrats seeking power to block his judicial appointments and moderate his aggressive, conservative foreign policy. Yet a Gallup poll in mid-year showed Reagan more popular with the public than any previous President in the second year of his second term since World War II.

Reagan is devoted to his wife, Nancy, whom he married after his divorce from the screen actress Jane Wyman. The Reagans spend much time together at the White House and Camp David and at their California home and ranch when Presidential duties permit. Reagan enjoys horseback riding and is a connoisseur of fine wines. The children of the first marriage are Maureen, his daughter by Miss Wyman, and Michael, an adopted son. In the present marriage, the children are Patricia and Ronald. —*A.P.R., Jr.*

# George Bush

## Vice President

As a busy surrogate for the President, George Bush faithfully carried out his duties as two-term Vice President. And, with them, he pursued his quest for the Presidential nomination in 1988 as Republican candidate to succeed Ronald Reagan.

On January 20, 1986, Vice President Bush met with Bishop Desmond Tutu of South Africa to discuss grave international issues. Three days later, as a Presidential hopeful wooing the conservative vote, he attacked New York's Governor Cuomo in strong language. A few months later he conferred in Saudi Arabia with Arab leaders on the oil-price crisis. And so the pattern continued.

In his subdued way, Bush has been influential in White House decisions, particularly in foreign affairs. He was a key supporter of the 1986 Reagan raid on Libya in reprisal for terrorist attacks, and had had a role in the decision to withdraw American forces from Lebanon after its government collapsed in early 1984.

For a few hours in July 1985 Bush emerged as the nation's leader while President Reagan underwent major surgery. And Bush himself had an operation in May 1986 for the removal of a small facial skin cancer.

Bush traveled as the President's representative on important diplomatic missions. Among these were an inspection of African drought areas and attendance at a Geneva conference on famine relief. He led the U.S. delegation to the Chernenko funeral in Moscow, and at Brazil's inauguration of a civilian President. He visited China to show American support for China's economic reforms.

Politically, public-opinion polls gave him strong support despite intense opposition from right-wing front-runners in the Republican sweepstakes.

The 1984 election had been his fifth, and second successful, bid for the Vice-Presidency. By then, despite his reputation as a relative liberal, he had earned acclaim for devotion to Reagan's conservative policies. And right-wingers could relish his record as a two-term Texas Congressman and his background as a former Director of Central Intelligence and a World War II Navy pilot who had won the Distinguished Flying Cross.

George Bush was born June 12, 1924, in Milton, Mass., to Prescott and Dorothy Bush. The family later moved to Connecticut. Bush attended Phillips Academy at Andover, Mass., and served in the Navy from 1942 to 1945. After the war he earned an economics degree and Phi Beta Kappa key at Yale in 2 1/2 years.

In 1945 he married Barbara Pierce of Rye, N.Y., daughter of a magazine publisher, and in 1948 they left Connecticut for a Texas business career. In 1980 he reported an estimated wealth of some $1.4 million. After Bush's second unsuccessful Senate race, President Nixon appointed him U.S. delegate to the United Nations with the rank of Ambassador, and later he became Republican National Chairman. He served as head of the U.S. liaison office in Peking before becoming Director of Central Intelligence.

The Bushes have lived in 17 cities and 28 homes and have traveled in 26 countries. In her husband's frequent absences, Mrs. Bush has been the "matriarch" of a family of four boys and a girl.

Despite Republican emphasis on his Texas connection, Bush sold his Houston home several years ago and now lives at the Vice President's quarters in Washington and the family estate at Kennebunkport, Me.                    —*A.P.R., Jr.*

## Glossary of Political Terms

**Balanced Ticket**—A party ticket listing candidates chosen to win support from regional, ethnic, minority, and other elements of the population.

**Beauty Contest**—The preferential primary in which voters indicate their preference for a candidate in a nonbinding ballot.

**Bloc**—Group of legislators, usually of both major parties, who vote together for some particular interest.

**Brokered Convention**—Decisions on candidates and major issues made by party leaders rather than by rank-and-file delegates.

**Bullet Vote**—Balloting in which the electorate concentrates on single candidates or issues to the neglect of the rest of the slate.

**Confirmation**—Senate action to validate an appointment, treaty, or other action by the President.

**Dark Horse**—An entrant into a political contest not previously mentioned. A person unexpectedly nominated, especially at a party convention.

**Direct Primary**—A party primary in which its members nominate the candidates by direct vote. Also used to choose convention delegates and party leaders. Primaries can be open to members of all parties, making a "crossover" vote possible, or restricted to members of the one party.

**Equal Time**—The legal right to equivalent time on radio or television to reply to charges in a political campaign made on the same medium.

**Favorite Son**—A state political leader to whom the party organization pledges its Presidential nominating delegates to avoid early pressure from declared candidates and to increase the state's delegation's bargaining power at the nominating convention.

**Gerrymander**—The division of a state, county, or other political unit into election districts so as to give one political party a majority in many districts and to concentrate the other party's voting strength into as few districts as possible. In brief, boundary manipulation for political advantage.

**Machine Politics**—The control of party decisions by the organized group of persons who conduct or direct the activities of a political party or similar organization.

**Protest Vote**—A vote expressing broad disapproval of an official or party policy, stressing negative reaction.

**Slush Fund**—A Congressman's office account—contributions are unlimited—the money is used to help run his office, mailings, etc.

**Stalking Horse**—A candidate used to conceal the candidacy of a more important candidate or to draw votes from a rival.

# GREAT DISASTERS

(For later disasters, see Current Events of 1986)

## Earthquakes and Volcanic Eruptions

**A.D. 79 Aug. 24, Italy:** eruption of Mt. Vesuvius buried cities of Pompeii and Herculaneum, killing thousands.

**1556 Jan. 24, Shaanxi (Shensi) Province, China:** most deadly earthquake in history; 830,000 killed.

**1755 Nov. 1, Portugal:** one of the most severe of recorded earthquakes leveled Lisbon and was felt as far away as southern France and North Africa; 10,000–20,000 killed in Lisbon.

**1883 Aug. 26–28, Netherlands Indies:** eruption of Krakatau; violent explosions destroyed two thirds of island. Sea waves occurred as far away as Cape Horn, and possibly England. Estimated 36,000 dead.

**1902 May 8, Martinique, West Indies:** Mt. Pelée erupted and wiped out city of St. Pierre; 40,000 dead.

**1906 April 18, San Francisco:** earthquake accompanied by fire razed more than 4 sq mi.; more than 500 dead or missing.

**1908 Dec. 28, Messina, Sicily:** about 85,000 killed and city totally destroyed.

**1915 Jan. 13, Avezzano, Italy:** earthquake left 29,980 dead.

**1920 Dec. 16, Gansu (Kansu) Province, China:** earthquake killed 200,000.

**1923 Sept. 1, Japan:** earthquake destroyed third of Tokyo and most of Yokohama; more than 140,000 killed.

**1933 March 10, Long Beach, Calif.:** 117 left dead by earthquake.

**1935 May 31, India:** earthquake at Quetta killed an estimated 50,000.

**1939 Jan. 24, Chile:** earthquake razed 50,000 sq mi.; about 30,000 killed.

**Dec. 27, Northern Turkey:** severe quakes destroyed city of Erzingan; about 100,000 casualties.

**1950 Aug. 15, India:** earthquake affected 30,000 sq mi. in Assam; 20,000–30,000 believed killed.

**1963 July 26, Skoplje, Yugoslavia:** four fifths of city destroyed; 1,011 dead, 3,350 injured.

**1964 March 27, Alaska:** strongest earthquake ever to strike North America hit 80 miles east of Anchorage; followed by seismic wave 50 feet high that traveled 8,445 miles at 450 miles per hour; 117 killed.

**1970 May 31, Peru:** earthquake left 50,000 dead, 17,000 missing.

**1972 April 10, Iran:** 5,000 killed in earthquake 600 miles south of Teheran.

**Dec. 22, Managua, Nicaragua:** earthquake devastated city, leaving up to 6,000 dead.

**1976 Feb. 4, Guatemala:** earthquake left over 23,000 dead.

**July 28, Tangshan, China:** earthquake devastated 20-sq-mi. area of city leaving estimated 242,000 dead.

**Aug. 17, Mindanao, Philippines:** earthquake and tidal wave left up to 8,000 dead or missing.

**1977 March 4, Bucharest:** earthquake razed most of downtown Bucharest; 1,541 reported dead, over 11,000 injured.

**1978 Sept. 16, Tabas, Iran:** earthquake destroyed city

in eastern Iran, leaving 25,000 dead.

**1980 Nov. 23, Naples, Italy:** 2,735 killed when earthquake struck southern Italy.

**1982 Dec. 13, Yemen:** 2,800 reported dead in earthquake.

**1985 Sept. 19–20, Mexico:** earthquake registering 8.1 on Richter scale struck central and southwestern regions, devastating part of Mexico City and three coastal states. An estimated 25,000 killed.

**Nov. 14–16, Colombia:** eruption of Nevada del Ruiz, 85 miles northwest of Bogatá, caused mud slides which buried most of the town of Armero and devastated Chinchiná. An estimated 25,000 were killed.

## Floods, Avalanches, and Tidal Waves

**1228 Holland:** 100,000 persons reputedly drowned by sea flood in Friesland.

**1642 China:** rebels destroyed Kaifeng seawall; 300,000 drowned.

**1889 May 31, Johnstown, Pa.:** more than 2,200 died in flood.

**1896 June 15, Sanriku, Japan:** earthquake and tidal wave killed 27,000.

**1928 March 12, Santa Paula, Calif.:** collapse of St. Francis Dam left 450 dead.

**1953 Northwest Europe:** storm followed by floods devastated North Sea coastal areas. Netherlands was hardest hit with 1,794 dead.

**1959 Dec. 2, Frejus, France:** flood caused by collapse of Malpasset Dam left 412 dead.

**1960 Agadir, Morocco:** 10,000–12,000 dead as earthquake set off tidal wave and fire, destroying most of city.

**1962 Jan. 10, Peru:** avalanche down Huascaran, extinct Andean volcano, killed more than 3,000 persons.

**1963 Oct. 9, Italy:** landslide into the Vaiont Dam; flood killed about 2,000.

**1966 Oct. 21, Aberfan, Wales:** avalanche of coal, waste, mud, and rocks killed 144 persons, including 116 children in school.

**1969 Jan. 18–26, Southern California:** floods and mudslides from heavy rains caused widespread property damage; at least 100 dead. Another downpour (Feb. 23–26) caused further floods and mudslides; at least 18 dead.

**1970 Nov. 13, East Pakistan:** 200,000 killed by cyclone-driven tidal wave from Bay of Bengal. Over 100,000 missing.

**1971 Sept. 29, Orissa State, India:** cyclone and tidal wave off Bay of Bengal killed as many as 10,000.

**1972 Feb. 26, Man, W. Va.:** more than 118 died when slag-pile dam collapsed under pressure of torrential rains and flooded 17-mile valley.

**June 9–10, Rapid City, S.D.:** flash flood caused 237 deaths and $160 million in damage.

**June 20, Eastern Seaboard:** tropical storm Agnes, in 10-day rampage, caused widespread flash floods. Death toll was 129, 115,000 were left homeless, and damage estimated at $3.5 billion.

1976 Aug. 1, Loveland, Colo.: Flash flood along Route 34 in Big Thompson Canyon left 139 dead.
1977 Nov. 19, Andhra Pradesh State, India: cyclone and flood from Bay of Bengal left 7,000–10,000 dead.

## Storms and Weather

(For U.S. tornadoes and hurricanes, see Index)

1864 Oct. 5, India: most of Calcutta denuded by cyclone; 70,000 killed.
1930 Sept. 3, Santo Domingo: hurricane killed about 2,000 and injured 6,000.
1934 Sept. 21, Japan: hurricane killed more than 4,000 on Honshu.
1942 Oct. 16, India: cyclone devastated Bengal; about 40,000 lives lost.
1963 May 28–29, East Pakistan: cyclone killed about 22,000 along coast.
 Oct. 2-7, Caribbean: Hurricane Flora killed up to 7,000 in Haiti and Cuba.
1965 May 11–12 and June 1-2, East Pakistan: cyclones killed about 47,000.
 Dec. 15, Karachi, Pakistan: cyclone killed about 10,000.
1974 Sept. 20, Honduras: Hurricane Fifi struck northern section of country, leaving 8,000 dead, 100,000 homeless.
 Dec. 25, Darwin, Australia: cyclone destroyed nearly the entire city, causing mass evacuation.
1977 Nov. 19, India: cyclone struck state of Andhra Pradesh, killing 10,000.

## Fires and Explosions

1666 Sept. 2, England: "Great Fire of London" destroyed St. Paul's Church, etc. Damage £10 million.
1835 Dec. 16, New York City: 530 buildings destroyed by fire.
1871 Oct. 8, Chicago: the "Chicago Fire" burned 17,450 buildings, killed 250 persons; $196 million damage.
 Oct. 8, Peshtigo, Wis.: 1,152 lives lost; 2 billion trees burned.
1872 Nov. 9, Boston: fire destroyed 800 buildings; $75-million damage.
1876 Dec. 5, New York City: fire in Brooklyn Theater killed more than 300.
1881 Dec. 8, Vienna: at least 620 died in fire at Ring Theatre.
1894 Sept. 1, Minnesota: forest fire over 480-square-mile area destroyed six towns and killed 480 people.
1900 May 1, Scofield, Utah: explosion of blasting powder in coal mine killed 200.
 June 30, Hoboken, N.J.: piers of North German Lloyd Steamship line burned; 326 dead.
1903 Dec. 30, Chicago: Iroquois Theatre fire killed 602.
1906 March 10, France: explosion in coal mine in Courrières killed 1,060.
1907 Dec. 6, Monongha, W. Va.: coal mine explosion killed 361.
 Dec. 19, Jacobs Creek, Pa.: explosion in coal mine left 239 dead.
1909 Nov. 13, Cherry, Ill.: explosion in coal mine killed 259.
1911 March 25, New York City: fire in Triangle Shirtwaist Factory fatal to 145.
1913 Oct. 22, Dawson, N.M.: coal mine explosion left

263 dead.
1917 April 10, Eddystone, Pa.: explosion in munitions plant killed 133.
 Dec. 6, Canada: explosion and fire at Halifax when ammunition ship collided with a vessel; 1,500 dead.
1930 April 21, Columbus, Ohio: fire in Ohio State Penitentiary killed 320 convicts.
1937 March 18, New London, Tex.: explosion destroyed schoolhouse; 294 killed.
1942 April 26, Manchuria: explosion in Honkeiko Colliery killed 1,549.
 Nov. 28, Boston: Cocoanut Grove nightclub fire killed 491.
1944 July 6, Hartford, Conn.: fire and ensuing stampede in main tent of Ringling Brothers Circus killed 168, injured 487.
 July 17, Port Chicago, Calif.: 322 killed as ammunition ships explode.
 Oct. 20, Cleveland: liquid-gas tanks exploded, killing 130.
1946 Dec. 7, Atlanta: fire in Winecoff Hotel killed 119.
1947 April 16-18, Texas City, Tex.: most of city destroyed, 561 dead following explosion on ship.
1949 Sept. 2, China: fire on Chongqing (Chungking) waterfront killed 1,700.
1954 May 26, off Quonset Point, R.I.: explosion and fire aboard aircraft carrier *Bennington* killed 103 crewmen.
1956 Aug. 7, Colombia: about 1,100 reported killed when seven army ammunition trucks exploded at Cali.
 Aug. 8, Belgium: 262 died in coal mine fire at Marcinelle.
1960 Jan. 21, Coalbrook, South Africa: coal mine explosion killed 437.
 Nov. 13, Syria: 152 children killed in moviehouse fire.
1961 Dec. 17, Niteroi, Brazil: circus fire fatal to 323.
1962 Feb. 7, Saarland, West Germany: coal mine gas explosion killed 298.
1963 Nov. 9, Japan: explosion in coal mine at Omuta killed 447.
1965 May 28, India: coal mine fire in state of Bihar killed 375.
 June 1, near Fukuoka, Japan: coal mine explosion killed 236.
1967 May 22, Brussels: fire in L'Innovation, major department store, left 322 dead.
 July 29, off North Vietnam: fire on U.S. carrier *Forrestal* killed 134.
1969 Jan. 14, Pearl Harbor, Hawaii: nuclear aircraft carrier *Enterprise* ripped by explosions; 27 dead, 82 injured.
1970 Nov. 1, Saint-Laurent-du-Pont, France: fire in dance hall killed 146 young people.
1972 May 13, Osaka, Japan: 118 people died in fire in nightclub on top floor of Sennichi department store.
 June 6, Wankie, Rhodesia: explosion in coal mine killed 427.
1973 Nov. 29, Kumamoto, Japan: fire in Taiyo department store killed 101.
1974 Feb. 1, Sao Paulo, Brazil: fire in upper stories of bank building killed 189 persons, many of whom leaped to death.
1975 Dec. 27, Dhanbad, India: explosion in coal mine followed by flooding from nearby reservoir left 372 dead.
1977 May 28, Southgate, Ky.: fire in Beverly Hills Supper Club; 167 dead.
1978 July 11, Tarragona, Spain: 140 killed at coastal

campsite when tank truck carrying liquid gas overturned and exploded.

**Aug. 20, Abadan, Iran:** nearly 400 killed when arsonists set fire to crowded theater.

1979 **Dec. 31, Chapais, Quebec, Canada:** fire at Opemiska Club fatal to 45 New Year's Eve partygoers.

1982 **Dec. 18–21, Caracas, Venezuela:** power-plant fire leaves 128 dead.

## Shipwrecks

1833 **May 11, *Lady of the Lake:*** bound from England to Quebec, struck iceberg; 215 perished.

1853 **Sept. 29 *Annie Jane:*** emigrant vessel off coast of Scotland; 348 died.

1865 **April 27, *Sultana:*** boiler explosion on Mississippi River steamboat near Memphis, 1,547 killed.

1898 **Nov. 26, *City of Portland:*** Loss of 157 off Cape Cod.

1904 **June 15, *General Slocum:*** excursion steamer burned in East River, New York; 1,021 perished.

1912 **March 5, *Principe de Asturias:*** Spanish steamer struck rock off Sebastien Point; 500 drowned.

**April 15, *Titanic:*** sank after colliding with iceberg; 1,513 died.

1914 **May 29, *Empress of Ireland:*** sank after collision in St. Lawrence River; 1,024 perished.

1915 **July 24, *Eastland:*** Great Lakes excursion steamer overturned in Chicago River; 812 died.

1928 **Nov. 12, *Vestris:*** British steamer sank in gale off Virginia; 110 died.

1931 **June 14:** French excursion steamer overturned in gale off St. Nazaire; approximately 450 died.

1934 **Sept. 8, *Morro Castle:*** 134 killed in fire off Asbury Park, N.J.

1939 **May 23, *Squalus:*** submarine with 59 men sank off Hampton Beach, N.H.; 33 saved.

**June 1, Submarine *Thetis:*** sank in Liverpool Bay, England; 99 perished.

1942 **Oct. 2, *Queen Mary:*** rammed and sank a British cruiser; 338 aboard the cruiser died.

1945 **April 9:** U.S. ship, loaded with aerial bombs, exploded at Bari, Italy; at least 360 killed.

1948 **Dec. 3, *Kiangya:*** Chinese refugee ship wrecked in explosion; about 1,000 believed dead.

1949 **Sept. 17, *Noronic:*** Canadian Great Lakes cruise ship burned at Toronto dock; about 130 died.

1952 **April 26, *Hobson:*** minesweeper collided with aircraft carrier *Wasp* and sank during night maneuvers in mid-Atlantic; 176 persons lost.

1953 **Jan. 9, *Chang Tyong-Ho:*** South Korean ferry foundered off Pusan; 249 reported dead.

**Jan. 31, *Princess Victoria:*** British ferry sank in Irish Sea; 133 lost.

1956 **July 25, *Andrea Doria:*** Italian liner collided with Swedish liner *Stockholm* off Nantucket Island, Mass., sinking next day; 52, mostly passengers on Italian ship, dead or unaccounted for; over 1,600 rescued.

1962 **April 8, *Dara,*** British liner, exploded and sank in Persian Gulf; 236 persons dead. Caused by time bomb.

1963 **April 10, *Thresher:*** atomic-powered submarine sank in North Atlantic; 129 dead.

**May 4:** U.A.R. ferry capsized and sank in upper Nile; over 200 died.

1968 **Late May, *Scorpion:*** nuclear submarine sank in Atlantic 400 miles S.W. of Azores; 99 dead. (Located Oct. 31.)

1970 **Dec. 15:** ferry in Korean Strait capsized; 261 lost.

1976 **Oct. 20, Luling, La.: *George Prince,*** Mississippi River ferry, rammed by Norwegian tanker *Frosta;* 77 dead.

1983 **May 25, *10th of Ramadan,*** Nile steamer, caught fire and sank in Lake Nasser, near Aswan, Egypt; 272 dead and 75 missing.

## Aircraft Accidents

1921 **Aug. 24, England:** *AR-2* British dirigible, broke in two on trial trip near Hull; 62 died.

1925 **Sept. 3, Caldwell, Ohio:** U.S. dirigible *Shenandoah* broke apart; 14 dead.

1930 **Oct. 5, Beauvais, France:** British dirigible R 101 crashed, killing 47.

1933 **April 4, New Jersey Coast:** U.S. dirigible *Akron* crashed; 73 died.

1937 **May 6, Lakehurst, N.J.:** German zeppelin *Hindenburg* destroyed by fire at tower mooring; 36 killed.

1945 **July 28, New York City:** U.S. Army bomber crashed into Empire State Building; 13 dead.

1949 **Nov. 1, Washington, D.C.:** fighter plane rammed airliner, killing 55.

1951 **Dec. 16, Elizabeth, N.J.:** nonscheduled airliner crash killed 56.

1952 **Jan. 22, Elizabeth, N.J.:** 29 killed, including former Secretary of War Robert P. Patterson, when airliner hit apartments; seven of dead were on ground.

1953 **June 18, near Tokyo:** crash of U.S. Air Force "Globemaster" killed 129 servicemen.

1960 **Feb. 25, Rio de Janeiro:** U.S. Navy plane, flying Navy musicians to perform at dinner given by visiting President Eisenhower, collided with Brazilian airliner, killing 61.

**Dec. 16, New York City:** United and Trans World planes collided in fog, crashed in two bor-

---

## Nuclear Power Plant Accidents

1952 **Dec. 12, Chalk River, near Ottawa, Canada:** A partial meltdown of the reactor's uranium fuel core resulted after the accidental removal of four control rods. Although millions of gallons of radioactive water accumulated inside the reactor, there were no injuries.

1957 **Oct. 7, Windscale Pile No. 1, north of Liverpool, England:** Fire in a graphite-cooled reactor spewed radiation over the countryside, contaminating a 200 sq mi area.

1979 **March 28, Three Mile Island, near Harrisburg, Pa.:**

One of two reactors lost its coolant, which caused the radioactive fuel to overheat and caused a partial meltdown. Some radioactive material was released.

1986 **April 16, Chernobyl, near Kiev, U.S.S.R.:** Explosion and fire in the graphite core of one of four reactors released radioactive material which spread over part of the Soviet Union, Eastern Europe, Scandinavia, and later Western Europe, in the worst such accident to date.

oughs, killing 134 in air and on ground.

1961 **Feb. 15, near Brussels:** 72 on board and farmer on ground killed in crash of Sabena plane; U.S. figure skating team wiped out.

1962 **March 1, New York City:** American Airlines jetliner crashed into Jamaica Bay, near Idlewild Airport, killing all 95 on board.

**June 3, Paris:** chartered Air France Boeing Jet 707 crashed at Orly Airport; 130 dead.

1965 **Feb. 8, New York City:** Eastern Airlines DC-7B went down in Atlantic shortly after take-off from Kennedy International Airport; 84 dead.

1966 **March 5, Japan:** British airliner caught fire and crashed into Mt. Fuji; 124 dead.

**Dec. 24, Binh Thai, South Vietnam:** crash of military-chartered plane in village killed 129.

1967 **April 20, Nicosia, Cyprus:** crash of chartered Swiss Turboprop killed 126.

1969 **March 16, Maracaibo, Venezuela:** Venezuelan jetliner crashed and exploded; 84 crew members and passengers died and 71 were killed on ground.

**Sept. 9, Shelbyville, Ind.:** Allegheny Airlines jetliner and single-engine plane flown by student pilot collided in air and crashed; 83 dead.

1970 **Feb. 15, Santo Domingo, Dominican Republic:** Dominican Republic jetliner plunged into Caribbean on takeoff; 102 dead.

**July 4, Arbucias, Spain:** British Comet crashed into mountains while coming in for landing at Barcelona; 112 dead.

**July 5, Toronto:** Canadian jetliner crashed on landing approach; 109 dead.

**Aug. 9, Cuzco, Peru:** Peruvian turboprop, with 51 teen-age U.S. students among passengers, crashed shortly after takeoff; 99 dead.

**Nov. 14, Huntington, W. Va.:** chartered plane carrying 43 players and coaches of Marshall University football team crashed; 75 dead.

1971 **July 30, Morioka, Japan:** Japanese Boeing 727 and F-86 figher collided in mid-air; toll was 162.

**Sept. 4, near Juneau, Alaska:** Alaska Airlines Boeing 727 crashed into Chilkoot Mountains; 111 killed.

1972 **June 18, London:** B.E.A. Trident jetliner plunged into field minutes after take-off from Heathrow Airport; all 118 aboard dead.

**Aug. 14, East Berlin, East Germany:** Soviet-built East German Ilyushin plane crashed, killing 156.

**Dec. 3, Santa Cruz de Tenerife, Canary Islands:** Spanish charter jet carrying West German tourists crashed on take-off; all 155 aboard killed.

**Dec. 30, Miami, Fla.:** Eastern Airlines Lockheed 1011 TriStar Jumbo jet crashed into Everglades; 101 killed, 75 survived.

1973 **Jan. 22, Kano, Nigeria:** 171 Nigerian Moslems returning from Mecca and five crewmen died in crash.

**April 10, Hochwald, Switzerland:** British airliner carrying tourists to Swiss fair crashed in blizzard; 106 dead.

**July 11, Paris:** Boeing 707 of Varig Airlines, en route to Rio de Janeiro, crashed near airport, killing 122 of 134 passengers.

**July 31, Boston:** Delta Airlines jet crashed in heavy fog in landing at Logan International Airport killing 88 of 89 aboard.

1974 **Jan. 31, Pago Pago, Samoa:** Pan American 707 crashed while landing; 97 of 101 persons aboard killed.

**March 3, Paris:** Turkish DC-10 jumbo jet crashed in forest shortly after take-off; all 346 passengers and crew killed in worst single-plane disaster to date.

**Dec. 1, Berryville, Va.:** all 92 aboard killed in crash of TWA 727 into wooded area.

**Dec. 4, Colombo, Sri Lanka:** Dutch DC-8 carrying Moslems to Mecca crashed on landing approach, killing all 191 persons aboard.

1975 **April 4, near Saigon, Vietnam:** Air Force Galaxy C-5A crashed after take-off, killing 172, mostly Vietnamese children.

**June 24, New York City:** Eastern Airlines Boeing 727, arriving from New Orleans, crashed at Kennedy International Airport, killing 113.

**Aug. 3, Agadir, Morocco:** Chartered Boeing 707, returning Moroccan workers home after vacation in France, plunged into mountainside; all 188 aboard killed.

**Aug. 20, Damascus, Syria:** Czech airliner crashed while landing, killing 126 of 128 persons aboard.

1976 **Sept. 10, Zagreb, Yugoslavia:** midair collision between British Airways Trident and Yugoslav charter DC-9 fatal to all 176 persons aboard; worst mid-air collision on record.

1977 **March 27, Santa Cruz de Tenerife, Canary Islands:** Pan American and KLM Boeing 747s collided on runway. All 249 on KLM plane and 333 of 394 aboard Pan Am jet killed. Total of 582 is highest for any type of aviation disaster.

1978 **Jan. 1, Bombay:** Air India 747 with 213 aboard exploded and plunged into sea minutes after takeoff.

**Sept. 25, San Diego, Calif.:** Pacific Southwest plane collided in midair with Cessna. All 135 on airliner, 2 in Cessna, and 7 on ground killed for total of 144.

**Nov. 15, Colombo, Sri Lanka:** Chartered Icelandic Airlines DC-8, carrying 249 Moslem pilgrims from Mecca, crashed in thunderstorm during landing approach; 183 killed.

1979 **May 25, Chicago:** American Airlines DC-10 lost left engine upon take-off and crashed seconds later, killing all 272 persons aboard and three on the ground in worst U.S. air disaster.

**Aug. 15, Ukraine, U.S.S.R.:** Two planes collided in mid-air; 150 killed.

**Nov. 26, Jidda, Saudi Arabia:** Pakistan International Airlines 707 carrying pilgrims returning from Mecca crashed on take-off; all 156 aboard killed.

**Nov. 28, Mt. Erebus, Antarctica:** Air New Zealand DC-10 crashed on sightseeing flight; 257 killed.

1980 **Jan. 21, near Laskgarak, Iran:** Iran Air Boeing 727 crashed into mountains, killing all 128 aboard.

**March 14, Warsaw:** LOT Polish Airlines Ilyushin 62 crashed while attempting landing; 22 boxers and officials of a U.S. amateur boxing team killed along with 65 others.

**April 25, Santa Cruz de Tenerife, Canary Islands:** Chartered Boeing 727 carrying 138 British vacationers and crew of 8 crashed into mountain while approaching for landing; all killed.

**Aug. 19, Riyadh, Saudi Arabia:** all 301 aboard Saudi Arabian jet killed when burning plane made safe landing but passengers were unable to escape.

1981 **Dec. 1, Ajaccio, Corsica:** Yugoslav DC-9 Super 80 carrying tourists crashed into mountain on landing approach, killing all 178 aboard.

1982 **July 9, Kenner, La.:** Pan Am 727 crashed minutes after take-off from New Orleans, killing all 145 on board and 9 on ground.

# Space Accidents

1967 **Jan. 27, Apollo 1:** A fire aboard the space capsule on the ground at Cape Kennedy, Fla. killed astronauts Virgil L. Grissom, Edward H. White, and Roger Chaffee.
**April 23-24, Soyuz 1:** Vladimir M. Komarov was killed when his craft crashed after its parachute lines released at 23,000 feet for re-entry, became snarled.

1971 **June 6-30, Soyuz 11:** Three cosmonauts, Georgi T. Dolrovolsky, Vladislav N. Volkov, and Viktor I. Patsayev, found dead in the craft after its automatic landing. Apparently the cause of death was loss of pressurization in the space craft during re-entry into the earth's atmosphere.

1986 **Jan 28, Challenger Space Shuttle:** Exploded 73 seconds after lift off, killing all seven crew members. They were: Christa McAuliffe, Francis R. Scobee, Michael J. Smith, Judith A. Resnick, Ronald E. McNair, Ellison S. Onizuka, and Gregory B. Jarvis. A booster leak ignited the fuel, causing the explosion.

---

1983 **June 28,** near Cuenca, Ecuador, Ecuadorean jetliner crashed in mountains, killing 119.
**Aug. 30,** near island of Sakhalin off Siberia, South Korean civlian jetliner shot shown by Soviet fighter after it strayed off course into Soviet airspace. All 269 people aboard killed.

1985 **June 23:** Air-India Boeing 727 exploded over the Atlantic off the coast of Ireland, all 329 aboard killed.
**Aug. 12,** Japan Air Lines Boeing 747 crashed into a mountain, killing 520 of the 524 aboard.
**Dec. 12,** A chartered Arrow Air DC-8, bringing American soldiers home for Christmas, crashed on takeoff from Gander, Newfoundland. All 256 aboard died.

## Railroad Accidents

1904 **Aug. 7, Eden, Colo.:** Two-train collision killed 96.
1910 **March 1, Wellington, Wash.:** two trains swept into canyon by avalanche; 96 dead.
1915 **May 22, Gretna, Scotland:** Two passenger trains and troop train collided; 227 killed.
1917 **Dec. 12, Modane, France:** nearly 550 killed in derailment of troop train near mouth of Mt. Cenis tunnel.
1918 **Nov. 1, New York City:** derailment of subway train in Malbone St. tunnel in Brooklyn left 92 dead.
1939 **Dec. 22, near Magdeburg, Germany:** more than 125 killed in collision; 99 killed in another wreck near Friedrichshafen.
1943 **Dec. 16, near Rennert, N.C.:** 72 killed in derailment and collision of two Atlantic Coast Line trains.
1944 **March 2, near Salerno, Italy:** 521 suffocated when Italian train stalled in tunnel.
**Dec. 31, near Ogden, Utah:** 48 killed in collision of two sections of Southern Pacific's Pacific Limited.
1949 **Oct. 22, near Nowy Dwor, Poland:** more than 200 reported killed in derailment of Danzig-Warsaw express.
1950 **Feb. 17, Rockville Centre, N.Y.:** head-on crash of two Long Island Rail Road commuter trains killed 30.
**Nov. 22, Richmond Hill, N.Y.:** 79 died when one Long Island Rail Road commuter train crashed into rear of another.
1951 **Feb. 6, Woodbridge, N.J.:** 85 died when Pennsylvania Railroad commuter train plunged through temporary overpass.
1952 **Oct. 8, Harrow-Wealdstone, England:** two express trains crashed into commuter train; 112 dead.

1953 **Dec. 24, near Sakvice, Czechoslovakia:** two trains crashed; over 100 dead.
1957 **Sept. 1, near Kendal, Jamaica:** about 175 killed when train plunged into ravine.
**Sept. 29, near Montgomery, West Pakistan:** express train crashed into standing oil train; nearly 300 killed.
**Dec. 4, St. John's, England:** 92 killed, 187 injured as one commuter train crashed into another in fog.
1958 **Sept. 15, near Bayonne, N.J.:** over 40 killed when Central Railroad of New Jersey train went through open drawbridge.
1960 **Nov. 14, Pardubice, Czechoslovakia:** two trains collided; 110 dead, 106 injured.
1962 **May 3, near Tokyo:** 163 killed and 400 injured when train crashed into wreckage of collision between inbound freight train and outbound commuter train.
1963 **Nov. 9, near Yokohama, Japan:** two passenger trains crashed into derailed freight, killing 162.
1964 **July 26, Custoias, Portugal:** passenger train derailed; 94 dead.
1970 **Feb. 4, near Buenos Aires:** 236 killed when express train crashed into standing commuter train.
1972 **July 21, Seville, Spain:** head-on crash of two passenger trains killed 76.
**Oct. 6, near Saltillo, Mexico:** train carrying religious pilgrims derailed and caught fire, killing 204 and injuring over 1,000.
**Oct. 30, Chicago:** two Illinois Central commuter trains collided during morning rush hour; 45 dead and over 200 injured.
1974 **Aug. 30, Zagreb, Yugoslavia:** train entering station derailed, killing 153 and injuring over 60.
1977 **Feb. 4, Chicago:** 11 killed and over 180 injured when elevated train hit rear of another, sending two cars to street.
1982 **Jan. 26, Algeria:** Derailment on Algeirs—Oran line leaves up to 120 dead.
1982 **July 11, Tepic, Mexico:** Nogales-Guadalajara train plunges down mountain gorge killing 120.

## Miscellaneous

1980 **Jan. 20, Sincelejo, Colombia:** Bleachers at a bullring collapsed, leaving 222 dead.
**March 30, Stavanger, Norway:** Floating hotel in North Sea collapsed, killing 123 oil workers.
1981 **July 18, Kansas City, Mo.:** suspended walkway in Hyatt Regency Hotel collapses; 113 dead, 186 injured.
1984 **Dec. 3, Bhopal, India:** Toxic gas, methyl isocyanate, seeped from Union Carbide insecticide plant, killing more than 2,000; injuring about 150,000.

# WEATHER & CLIMATE

## Predicting Future Weather

*By Joseph Alper*

Throughout the history of weather forecasting, meteorologists have complained that they could not make accurate forecasts because they did not have enough information. Now they are in danger of having too much. By the early 1970s, some meteorologists realized they would soon be overwhelmed by all the data. Already the geostationary and polar-orbiting satellites were generating 300 billion bits of information a day, more than enough to record the name and birthdate of every person in the western hemisphere and Europe. Then there are radar, weather balloons, ground stations, airplanes, and perhaps profilers, Doppler radar, and new satellite-based instruments to come. Forecasters would be drowning in a sea of information, and they would end up ignoring most of it. "Even today, forecasters have a hard time assimilating all the information they have access to," says Harlan Saylor, chief of meteorological operations at the National Meteorological Center. "Without some help, anything more would overload. They'd short-circuit."

This is where the latest in computer technology will once again revolutionize meteorology, as it did when the National Meteorological Center received its first supercomputer in mid-1983. The new computer systems do more than convert incoming data into pretty colored maps; they catalogue the data so they can be assembled into time-loop sequences*. The computers can analyze the data, providing instant comparisons between current and past conditions. They can also compile information from several sources into one easily read map. And since a forecaster cannot view data from all the observing systems at once, the computers can sound an alarm if a potentially dangerous situation develops.

The progenitor of all these new systems is McIDAS, the Man-computer Interactive Data Access System, developed at the University of Wisconsin's Space Science and Engineering Center in Madison. In the early 1970s, engineers there built a computer that could convert satellite images into tele-

vision pictures on which a meteorologist could tinker, draw state boundaries, zoom in on an area, add ground-station reports, and so on. The weather forecasting system being developed for the 1990s will contain a McIDAS offspring, and the National Severe Storms Forecast Center in Kansas City, Missouri, is already using a son-of-McIDAS.

In fact, Frederick Ostby, director of the Kansas City center, credits their advanced system, installed three years ago, with a dramatic increase in their ability to forecast tornadoes. "On March 28, 1984, we had a severe outbreak of tornadoes in the Carolinas, a time and place where this wasn't normally expected," he says. "We were able to issue a watch three hours before the first killer tornado struck, and, although 57 people died, the Federal Disaster Survey team that went in afterwards praised the early alert as having saved many, many lives.

"The forecaster on duty then said the storm developed so fast he would have been very hard pressed to spot it and stay on top of it. In my mind, the system paid for itself right then."

Given this new information, all the new gadgets, the new computers, better communications networks, improved forecaster training—in short, all the items on the National Weather Service's wish list—will weather prediction really improve significantly? According to even the most pessimistic forecasters, the ones who stand in the forecast offices and put their theories to the test every 12 hours, the ones who have to make do with substandard equipment and data and catch the flak when they're wrong, the answer is yes. "I've been at this business for a long time, and I've seen a lot of developments come down the pike, and they never quite do as well as they were supposed to," says Harlan Saylor. "But this time I think it's going to be different, because now we're talking about dramatically improving what we can see in the atmosphere, and we're going to give it to the forecaster in a form that is easier, not harder, to use."

Joseph Alper is a contributing editor to *Science 86*. Excerpted by permission from the January/February issue of *Science 86* Magazine. © 1986 by The American Association for the Advancement of Science.

*A computer display of satellite images taken over several hours and shown one after the other in a five-second sequence played over and over. It shows movement patterns of cloud formations.

## Lightning Caused by Cosmic Rays

Cosmic rays from space probably provide the extra potential that triggers a lightning stroke, according to a report made by Johns Hopkins scientists in the late seventies. Such rays, very high-energy particles moving at almost the speed of light, hit the upper atmosphere as an "air shower." When such a shower passes through a thunderhead, it releases electrons from oxygen and nitrogen atoms through ionization of the air. The free electrons are accelerated by the electric field already existing within the cloud, concentrating enough negative charge at the bottom of the cloud to generate a lightning stroke. The first stroke generated is a preliminary "leader stroke" of low luminosity. It travels the zigzag path of least electrical resistance to the ground. When the leader stroke is about 50 yards above the ground, an electric charge leaps up to meet it. These strokes complete the circuit between the cloud and the ground, clearing the way for the powerful return stroke, usually the first lightning seen. Often other strokes follow so quickly that they may seem to be one single stroke.

# Climate of Selected U.S. Cities

(T = trace)

| Month | Temperature, °F | | | | Precipitation | | | Percentage possible sunshine | Percentage relative humidity, afternoon |
|---|---|---|---|---|---|---|---|---|---|
| | Average daily maximum | Average daily minimum | Record high | Record low | Rainfall, inches | Snowfall, inches | Days with precipitation | | |

**Bakersfield, California (NWS Building, Meadows Field): lat. 35° 26′ N, long. 119° 03′ W; elevation: 496 ft**

| Month | Avg max | Avg min | Rec high | Rec low | Rainfall | Snowfall | Days precip | % sunshine | % humidity |
|---|---|---|---|---|---|---|---|---|---|
| January | 56.5 | 39.6 | 82 | 31 | 0.05 | 0.0 | 3 | n.a. | 66 |
| April | 72.7 | 42.9 | 98 | 34 | 0.50 | 0.0 | 2 | n.a. | 30 |
| July | 99.9 | 70.7 | 108 | 61 | T | 0.0 | 0 | n.a. | 24 |
| October | 73.9 | 49.3 | 90 | 41 | 0.13 | 0.0 | 2 | n.a. | 36 |
| Annual | 77.2 | 51.1 | 108 | 31 | 3.42 | 0.0 | 32 | n.a. | 37 |

**Caribou, Maine (Municipal Airport): lat. 46° 52′ N, long. 68° 01′ W; elevation: 624 ft**

| Month | Avg max | Avg min | Rec high | Rec low | Rainfall | Snowfall | Days precip | % sunshine | % humidity |
|---|---|---|---|---|---|---|---|---|---|
| January | 16.6 | −3.2 | 37 | −27 | 2.10 | 27.3 | 26 | n.a. | 74 |
| April | 49.9 | 29.7 | 76 | 18 | 1.74 | 3.9 | 14 | n.a. | 51 |
| July | 75.6 | 56.0 | 88 | 46 | 4.52 | 0.0 | 17 | n.a. | 60 |
| October | 54.4 | 34.5 | 68 | 24 | 1.81 | 0.8 | 10 | n.a. | 55 |
| Annual | 49.1 | 30.2 | 89 | −27 | 35.60 | 122.2 | 195 | n.a. | 61 |

**Charleston, South Carolina (International Airport): lat. 32° 54′ N, long. 80° 02′ W; elevation: 40 ft**

| Month | Avg max | Avg min | Rec high | Rec low | Rainfall | Snowfall | Days precip | % sunshine | % humidity |
|---|---|---|---|---|---|---|---|---|---|
| January | 55.4 | 36.8 | 69 | 21 | 5.12 | T | 14 | 46 | 62 |
| April | 73.7 | 54.2 | 88 | 43 | 6.30 | 0.0 | 11 | 55 | 55 |
| July | 87.9 | 71.9 | 94 | 68 | 4.87 | 0.0 | 10 | 60 | 64 |
| October | 80.3 | 62.2 | 85 | 47 | 1.67 | 0.0 | 6 | 68 | 60 |
| Annual | 75.3 | 55.9 | 99 | 21 | 46.23 | T | 104 | 64 | 57 |

**Chicago, Illinois (O'Hare International Airport): lat. 41° 59′ N, long. 87° 54′ W; elevation: 658 ft**

| Month | Avg max | Avg min | Rec high | Rec low | Rainfall | Snowfall | Days precip | % sunshine | % humidity |
|---|---|---|---|---|---|---|---|---|---|
| January | 25.4 | 8.8 | 41 | −22 | 1.15 | 17.2 | 16 | 46 | 64 |
| April | 54.6 | 36.9 | 83 | 24 | 4.11 | 2.7 | 14 | 37 | 58 |
| July | 82.7 | 57.9 | 99 | 47 | 3.19 | 0.0 | 8 | 72 | 50 |
| October | 64.8 | 44.6 | 76 | 28 | 3.15 | 0.0 | 15 | 33 | 67 |
| Annual | 58.2 | 38.4 | 99 | −22 | 34.00 | 38.1 | 146 | 53 | 60 |

**Dallas–Ft. Worth, Texas (Regional Airport): lat. 32° 54′ N, long. 97° 02′ W; elevation: 551 ft**

| Month | Avg max | Avg min | Rec high | Rec low | Rainfall | Snowfall | Days precip | % sunshine | % humidity |
|---|---|---|---|---|---|---|---|---|---|
| January | 49.9 | 28.7 | 74 | 10 | 1.07 | 0.0 | 4 | 61 | 58 |
| April | 75.2 | 52.1 | 91 | 40 | 1.41 | 0.0 | 5 | 69 | 45 |
| July | 97.2 | 73.7 | 104 | 64 | 0.43 | 0.0 | 3 | 81 | 39 |
| October | 75.6 | 58.4 | 90 | 42 | 6.50 | 0.0 | 17 | 44 | 69 |
| Annual | 76.4 | 54.9 | 106 | 10 | 33.89 | 0.0 | 76 | 65 | 53 |

**Denver, Colorado (Stapleton International Airport): lat. 39° 46′ N, long. 104° 52′ W; elevation: 5,282 ft**

| Month | Avg max | Avg min | Rec high | Rec low | Rainfall | Snowfall | Days precip | % sunshine | % humidity |
|---|---|---|---|---|---|---|---|---|---|
| January | 39.0 | 15.5 | 58 | −19 | 0.18 | 3.4 | 5 | 70 | 54 |
| April | 53.5 | 31.0 | 75 | 23 | 2.42 | 16.8 | 15 | 61 | 45 |
| July | 89.0 | 60.7 | 97 | 55 | 2.11 | 0.0 | 12 | 71 | 34 |
| October | 55.1 | 34.4 | 76 | 21 | 3.47 | 13.1 | 13 | 55 | 53 |
| Annual | 61.9 | 36.7 | 97 | −19 | 16.49 | 65.7 | 116 | 66 | 43 |

**Duluth, Minnesota (International Airport): lat. 46° 50′ N, long. 92° 11′ W; elevation: 1,428 ft**

| Month | Avg max | Avg min | Rec high | Rec low | Rainfall | Snowfall | Days precip | % sunshine | % humidity |
|---|---|---|---|---|---|---|---|---|---|
| January | 15.7 | −1.6 | 41 | −30 | 0.78 | 20.0 | 21 | 45 | 86 |
| April | 51.9 | 32.9 | 71 | 22 | 2.34 | 3.3 | 8 | 61 | 53 |
| July | 78.8 | 54.4 | 89 | 38 | 1.33 | 0.0 | 10 | 66 | 50 |
| October | 52.9 | 38.5 | 70 | 11 | 5.19 | 3.5 | 15 | 29 | 72 |
| Annual | 48.9 | 30.5 | 92 | −30 | 26.83 | 51.6 | 150 | 52 | 64 |

| | Temperature, °F | | | | Precipitation | | | | |
|---|---|---|---|---|---|---|---|---|---|
| Month | Average daily maximum | Average daily minimum | Record high | Record low | Rainfall, inches | Snowfall, inches | Days with precipitation | Percentage possible sunshine | Percentage relative humidity, afternoon |

**Great Falls, Montana (International Airport): lat. 47° 29′ N, long. 111° 22′ W; elevation: 3,663 ft**

| | | | | | | | | | |
|---|---|---|---|---|---|---|---|---|---|
| January | 37.4 | 21.6 | 59 | −19 | 0.72 | 16.2 | 14 | 60 | 66 |
| April | 56.0 | 32.7 | 82 | 17 | 0.94 | 5.2 | 10 | 52 | 40 |
| July | 86.3 | 53.2 | 100 | 43 | 0.05 | 0.0 | 2 | n.a. | 22 |
| October | 51.9 | 28.5 | 82 | −9 | 1.20 | 10.9 | 13 | 52 | 52 |
| Annual | 56.8 | 33.1 | 104 | −26 | 11.81 | 93.0 | 132 | n.a. | 44 |

**Kansas City, Missouri (International Airport): lat. 39° 19′ N, long. 94° 43′ W; elevation: 973 ft**

| | | | | | | | | | |
|---|---|---|---|---|---|---|---|---|---|
| January | 33.3 | 16.6 | 54 | −7 | 0.14 | 1.3 | 5 | 67 | 68 |
| April | 59.1 | 41.5 | 83 | 30 | 6.82 | 0.0 | 15 | 45 | 62 |
| July | 87.1 | 65.1 | 97 | 56 | 3.91 | 0.0 | 4 | 80 | 47 |
| October | 66.6 | 47.0 | 80 | 30 | 6.04 | 0.0 | 18 | 36 | 70 |
| Annual | 63.5 | 43.6 | 109 | −7 | 38.77 | 17.9 | 117 | 55 | 62 |

**Los Angeles, California (International Airport): lat. 33° 56′ N, long. 118° 24′ W; elevation: 97 ft**

| | | | | | | | | | |
|---|---|---|---|---|---|---|---|---|---|
| January | 67.8 | 48.6 | 79 | 41 | 0.39 | 0.0 | 1 | n.a. | 54 |
| April | 69.0 | 53.8 | 83 | 46 | 1.61 | 0.0 | 4 | n.a. | 55 |
| July | 77.1 | 65.5 | 86 | 62 | 0.00 | 0.0 | 0 | n.a. | 64 |
| October | 72.5 | 58.6 | 79 | 53 | 0.28 | 0.0 | 2 | n.a. | 52 |
| Annual | 71.6 | 57.2 | 96 | 41 | 7.81 | 0.0 | 29 | n.a. | 59 |

**Miami, Florida (General Aviation Center): lat. 25° 49′ N, long. 80° 17′ W; elevation: 7 ft**

| | | | | | | | | | |
|---|---|---|---|---|---|---|---|---|---|
| January | 75.9 | 58.0 | 88 | 44 | 0.18 | 0.0 | 3 | 67 | 57 |
| April | 81.3 | 65.0 | 87 | 55 | 4.51 | 0.0 | 7 | 65 | 54 |
| July | 88.5 | 75.3 | 90 | 71 | 7.38 | 0.0 | 20 | 70 | 64 |
| October | 84.5 | 71.8 | 87 | 65 | 2.35 | 0.0 | 13 | 65 | 58 |
| Annual | 82.6 | 67.6 | 96 | 44 | 60.02 | 0.0 | 137 | 65 | 58 |

**New Orleans, Louisiana (International Airport): lat. 29° 59′ N, long. 90° 15′ W; elevation: 4 ft**

| | | | | | | | | | |
|---|---|---|---|---|---|---|---|---|---|
| January | 55.4 | 37.8 | 70 | 21 | 4.10 | 0.0 | 10 | 45 | 58 |
| April | 77.0 | 57.9 | 86 | 43 | 1.72 | 0.0 | 5 | 74 | 54 |
| July | 87.6 | 70.0 | 92 | 65 | 3.86 | 0.0 | 16 | 65 | 64 |
| October | 82.0 | 64.9 | 87 | 45 | 2.84 | 0.0 | 10 | 58 | 60 |
| Annual | 76.3 | 58.2 | 96 | 21 | 52.07 | 0.0 | 111 | 62 | 60 |

**New York, New York (Central Park): lat. 40° 47′ N, long. 73° 58′ W; elevation: 132 ft**

| | | | | | | | | | |
|---|---|---|---|---|---|---|---|---|---|
| January | 35.1 | 24.6 | 57 | 8 | 1.87 | 11.7 | 14 | n.a. | 60 |
| April | 59.5 | 44.2 | 78 | 35 | 6.62 | 0.0 | 9 | n.a. | 55 |
| July | 81.2 | 68.2 | 91 | 59 | 7.03 | 0.0 | 12 | n.a. | 64 |
| October | 68.5 | 55.1 | 79 | 41 | 3.63 | 0.0 | 11 | n.a. | n.a. |
| Annual | 62.4 | 48.5 | 96 | 8 | 57.03 | 29.3 | 145 | n.a. | n.a. |

**Phoenix, Arizona (Sky Harbor International Airport): lat. 33° 26′ N, long. 112° 01′ W; elevation: 1,110 ft**

| | | | | | | | | | |
|---|---|---|---|---|---|---|---|---|---|
| January | 69.8 | 45.0 | 79 | 36 | 0.31 | 0.0 | 1 | 90 | 29 |
| April | 83.2 | 58.1 | 101 | 46 | 0.91 | 0.0 | 3 | 89 | 21 |
| July | 103.1 | 80.3 | 112 | 68 | 5.15 | 0.0 | 10 | 84 | 10 |
| October | 83.3 | 59.4 | 94 | 50 | 0.31 | 0.0 | 4 | 84 | 27 |
| Annual | 86.4 | 61.8 | 113 | 36 | 14.91 | 0.0 | 45 | 86 | 26 |

**Salt Lake City, Utah (International Airport): lat. 40° 47′ N, long. 111° 57′ W; elevation: 4,221 ft**

| | | | | | | | | | |
|---|---|---|---|---|---|---|---|---|---|
| January | 29.5 | 18.1 | 43 | −6 | 0.50 | 7.6 | 12 | 17 | 77 |
| April | 58.1 | 38.8 | 80 | 30 | 4.43 | 25.1 | 19 | 59 | 48 |

| Month | Temperature, °F | | | | Precipitation | | | Percentage possible sunshine | Percentage relative humidity, afternoon |
|---|---|---|---|---|---|---|---|---|---|
| | Average daily maximum | Average daily minimum | Record high | Record low | Rainfall, inches | Snowfall, inches | Days with precipitation | | |
| July | 91.5 | 65.5 | 100 | 56 | 1.72 | 0.0 | 9 | 81 | 33 |
| October | 59.4 | 39.5 | 80 | 28 | 3.70 | 20.4 | 15 | 59 | 49 |
| Annual | 61.0 | 40.9 | 100 | −6 | 21.55 | 97.8 | 144 | 60 | 50 |

**San Francisco, California (International Airport): lat. 37° 37′ N, long. 122° 23′ W; elevation: 8 ft**

| | | | | | | | | | |
|---|---|---|---|---|---|---|---|---|---|
| January | 58.2 | 44.4 | 69 | 38 | 0.46 | 0.0 | 4 | n.a. | 59 |
| April | 65.2 | 46.7 | 87 | 40 | 0.68 | 0.0 | 4 | n.a. | 54 |
| July | 76.2 | 55.0 | 95 | 50 | T | 0.0 | 0 | n.a. | 53 |
| October | 68.9 | 51.8 | 81 | 45 | 1.96 | 0.0 | 4 | n.a. | 62 |
| Annual | 67.5 | 49.4 | 100 | 34 | 14.13 | 0.0 | 57 | n.a. | 58 |

**Seattle, Washington (Seattle-Tacoma Airport): lat. 47° 27′ N, long. 122° 18′ W; elevation: 400 ft**

| | | | | | | | | | |
|---|---|---|---|---|---|---|---|---|---|
| January | 47.8 | 38.5 | 61 | 21 | 3.62 | T | 17 | 27 | 72 |
| April | 56.4 | 41.0 | 83 | 36 | 2.87 | T | 18 | 43 | 56 |
| July | 75.3 | 54.7 | 91 | 50 | 0.17 | 0.0 | 2 | 74 | 46 |
| October | 56.4 | 42.9 | 74 | 31 | 2.14 | T | 13 | 36 | 66 |
| Annual | 58.6 | 44.3 | 91 | 20 | 36.99 | 2.4 | 166 | 48 | 61 |

**Washington, D.C. (National Airport): lat. 38° 51′ N, long. 77° 02′ W; elevation: 10 ft**

| | | | | | | | | | |
|---|---|---|---|---|---|---|---|---|---|
| January | 39.6 | 24.8 | 59 | 3 | 1.71 | 6.5 | 10 | 45 | 54 |
| April | 64.0 | 45.7 | 80 | 36 | 3.71 | T | 14 | 48 | 51 |
| July | 83.9 | 69.1 | 93 | 58 | 4.09 | 0.0 | 14 | 53 | 61 |
| October | 72.1 | 58.2 | 83 | 46 | 3.18 | 0.0 | 7 | 36 | 66 |
| Annual | 66.0 | 49.6 | 97 | 3 | 37.73 | 8.6 | 122 | 50 | 56 |

NOTE: n.a. = not available. 1983 data. Latest available. *Source:* Department of Commerce, NOAA, Environmental Data Service.

## Tropical Storms and Hurricanes, 1886–1985

| | Jan.–April | May | June | July | Aug. | Sept. | Oct. | Nov. | Dec. | Total |
|---|---|---|---|---|---|---|---|---|---|---|
| Number of tropical storms (incl. hurricanes) | 3 | 14 | 53 | 63 | 199 | 284 | 178 | 39 | 6 | 839 |
| Number of tropical storms that reached hurricane intensity | 1 | 3 | 22 | 33 | 142 | 180 | 88 | 20 | 3 | 492 |

## Summary of North Atlantic Tropical Cyclone Statistics, 1985

| Cyclone Number | Name | Class | Dates | Maximum sustained winds (kn) | Lowest pressure (mb) | U.S. ($ damage) (millions) | Deaths |
|---|---|---|---|---|---|---|---|
| 1 | Ana | T | 7/15-7/19 | 60 | 996 | — | — |
| 2 | Bob | H | 7/21-7/26 | 65 | 1002 | — | — |
| 3 | Claudette | H | 8/09-8/17 | 75 | 980 | — | — |
| 4 | Danny | H | 8/12-8/20 | 80 | 987 | 50 | 1 |
| 5 | Elena | H | 8/28-9/04 | 110 | 951 | 1000 | 4 |
| 6 | Fabian | T | 9/15-9/19 | 55 | 992 | — | — |
| 7 | Gloria | H | 9/16-10/02 | 125 | 919 | 900 | 8 |
| 8 | Henri | T | 9/21-9/25 | 50 | 996 | — | — |
| 9 | Isabel | T | 10/07-10/15 | 60 | 997 | — | — |
| 10 | Juan | H | 10/26-11/01 | 75 | 971 | 1500 | 12 |
| 11 | Kate | H | 11/15-11/23 | 105 | 953 | 300 | 5 |

T=Tropical storm, wind speed 34-63 knots. H=Hurricane, wind speed 64 knots or higher. *Source:* National Oceanic and Atmospheric Administration, National Environmental Satellite, Data, and Information Service, National Climatic Data Center, Asheville, N.C.

# Tornadoes That Caused Outstanding Damage

| Date | Number of tornadoes | Deaths | Property losses | States in which storms occurred |
|---|---|---|---|---|
| 1884, Feb. 19 | 60 | 800 | (¹) | Mississippi, Alabama, North and South Carolina, Tennessee, Kentucky, Indiana |
| 1917, May 26–27 | (¹) | 249 | $5,555,000 | Illinois, Indiana, Arkansas, Kentucky, Tennessee, Alabama, Mississippi |
| 1920, April 20 | 6 | 220 | 3,525,000 | Mississippi, Alabama, Tennessee |
| 1924, April 29–30 | 22 | 115 | 4,372,300 | Oklahoma, Arkansas, Alabama, Georgia, Louisiana, North and South Carolina, Virginia |
| 1924, June 28 | 4 | 96 | 13,050,000 | Ohio and Pennsylvania |
| 1925, March 18 | 8 | 792 | 17,872,000 | Missouri, Illinois, Indiana, Kentucky, Tennessee, Alabama |
| 1927, May 8–9 | 36 | 227 | 7,877,000 | Texas, Louisiana, Missouri, Nebraska, Indiana, Michigan |
| 1932, March 21 | 27 | 321 | 5,514,000 | Alabama, Mississippi, Georgia, Tennessee |
| 1936, April 5–6 | 22 | 498 | 21,800,000 | Arkansas, Alabama, Tennessee, Georgia, South Carolina |
| 1944, June 23 | 4 | 153 | 5,160,000 | Pennsylvania, West Virginia, Maryland |
| 1947, April 9–10 | 8 | 167 | 10,030,750 | Texas, Oklahoma, Kansas |
| 1952, March 21–22 | 31 | 343 | 15,327,100 | Arkansas, Tennessee, Missouri, Mississippi, Alabama, Kentucky |
| 1953, June 7–9 | 12 | 234 | 93,230,840 | Michigan, Ohio, and New England states |
| 1953, May 11 | 1 | 114 | 39,500,000 | Texas |
| 1955, May 25 | 13 | 102 | 11,747,500 | Oklahoma and Kansas |
| 1965, April 11–12 | 47 | 257 | 200,000,000 | Iowa, Illinois, Wisconsin, Michigan, Indiana, Ohio |
| 1968, May 15 | 7 | 63 | 65,000,000 | Arkansas, Iowa, Illinois |
| 1970, May 11 | 1 | 26 | 135,000,000 | Texas |
| 1971, Feb. 21 | (¹) | 117 | 17,000,000 | Louisiana, Mississippi |
| 1973, March 31 | 2 | 9 | 115,000,000 | Georgia, South Carolina |
| 1973, May 26–28 | 96 | 22 | (¹) | Hawaii and 18 states in South, Southwest, Midwest, and East |
| 1974, April 3–4 | 144 | 307 | 500,000,000 + | 13 states in East, South, and Midwest |
| 1975, May 6 | 3 | 3 | 400,000,000 + | Nebraska |
| 1977, April 4 | 7 | 22 | 15,000,000 | Alabama |
| 1978, Dec. 3 | 13 | 4 | 100,000,000 + | Louisiana and Arkansas |
| 1979, April 10 | 10 | 54 | (¹) | Texas and Oklahoma |
| 1979, Oct. 3 | 1 | 3 | 200,000,000 | Connecticut |
| 1980, May 13 | 1 | 5 | 40,000,000 | Michigan |
| 1980, Aug. 9–11 | 29 | 0 | 50,000,000 + | Texas |
| 1981, April 4 | 1 | 3 | 12,900,000 | Wisconsin |
| 1983, July 3 | 22 | 0 | 11,000,000 + | Wisconsin |
| 1984, April 26–27 | 47 | 16 | n.a. | Iowa, Illinois, Kansas, Louisiana, Michigan, Minnesota, Missouri, Oklahoma, South Dakota, Wisconsin |
| 1985, May 31 | 30 | 76 | 102,500,000 + | Ohio, Pennsylvania, New York |

1. Not definitely known; believed to be large. NOTE: Additional storms may be listed in the *Current Events* section. n.a. = not available. *Source:* Department of Commerce, National Oceanic and Atmospheric Administration.

# Weather Glossary

**blizzard:** storm characterized by strong winds, low temperatures, and large amounts of snow.

**cyclone:** circulation of winds rotating counterclockwise in the northern hemisphere and clockwise in the southern hemisphere. Hurricanes and tornadoes are both examples of cyclones.

**flash flood:** dangerous rapid rise of water levels in streams, rivers, or over land area.

**gale warning:** winds in the 33—48 knot (38—55 mph) range forecast.

**heavy snow warnings:** issued when 4 inches or more of snow are expected to fall in a 12-hour period or when 6 inches or more are anticipated in a 24-hour period.

**hurricane:** devastating cyclonic storm; winds over 74 mph near storm center; usually tropical in origin; called cyclone in Indian Ocean, typhoon in the Pacific.

**hurricane warning:** winds in excess of 64 knots (74 mph) in connection with hurricane.

**storm warnings:** winds greater than 48 knots (55 mph) are forecast.

**temperature-humidity index (THI):** measure of personal discomfort based on the combined effects of temperature and humidity. Most people are uncomfortable when the THI is 75. A THI of 80 produces acute discomfort for almost everyone.

**tidal waves:** series of ocean waves caused by earthquakes; can reach speeds of 600 mph; they grow in height as they reach shore and can crest as high as 100 feet.

**tornado:** dangerous whirlwind associated with the cumulonimbus clouds of severe thunderstorms; winds up to 300 mph.

**tornado warning:** tornado has actually been detected by radar or sighted in designated area.

**tornado watch:** potential exists in the watch area for storms that could contain tornadoes.

**tsunami:** *see* tidal waves.

**warning:** the designated condition is imminent.

# Location of Killer Tornadoes—1985

| Date | State | County | Total deaths |
|---|---|---|---|
| March 17 | Florida | Sarasota | 2 |
| April 5 | Illinois | Randolph | 1 |
| April 21 | Texas | Throckmorton | 3 |
| April 28 | Texas | Taylor | 1 |
| May 30 | Iowa | Clayton | 2 |
| May 31 | Ohio* | Trumbull | 10 |
| May 31 | Ohio | Licking | 1 |
| May 31 | Pennsylvania | Lycoming | 2 |
| | | Northumberland | 2 |
| | | Union | 2 |
| May 31 | Pennsylvania | Erie | 12 |
| May 31 | Pennsylvania | Crawford | 1 |
| May 31 | Pennsylvania | Crawford | 9 |
| | | Forest | 7 |
| May 31 | Pennsylvania | Venango | 7 |
| May 31 | Pennsylvania | Crawford | 2 |
| May 31 | Pennsylvania* | Mercer | 8 |
| May 31 | Pennsylvania | Beaver | 3 |
| | | Butler | 6 |
| May 31 | Pennsylvania | McKean | 4 |
| June 8 | Michigan | Menominee | 1 |
| June 8 | Wisconsin | Oneida | 2 |
| August 12 | Wisconsin | Juneau | 2 |
| August 16 | Alabama | Walker | 1 |
| November 18 | Arkansas | Marion | 3 |

*Same tornado crossed state boundary. *Source:* National Oceanic and Atmospheric Administration, National Environmental Satellite Data, and Information Service, National Climatic Data Center.

## Summary of 1985 Tornadoes

A total of 684 tornadoes were reported in the United States during 1985, which was well below the 33-year (1953-1985) national average of 749. Twenty of these storms were responsible for the deaths of 94 people. Twenty-eight of the fatalities occurred in mobile homes. Over 550 mobile homes were either damaged or destroyed. Total property damage was estimated to be in excess of $500 million.

No tornado activity was reported in Alaska, Delaware, Maine, Maryland, Nevada, New Hampshire, Oregon, Utah, and Vermont.

## Wind Chill Factors

| Wind speed (mph) | Thermometer reading (degrees Fahrenheit) | | | | | | | | | | | | | | | | |
|---|---|---|---|---|---|---|---|---|---|---|---|---|---|---|---|---|---|
| | 35 | 30 | 25 | 20 | 15 | 10 | 5 | 0 | −5 | −10 | −15 | −20 | −25 | −30 | −35 | −40 | −45 |
| 5 | 33 | 27 | 21 | 19 | 12 | 7 | 0 | −5 | −10 | −15 | −21 | −26 | −31 | −36 | −42 | −47 | −52 |
| 10 | 22 | 16 | 10 | 3 | −3 | −9 | −15 | −22 | −27 | −34 | −40 | −46 | −52 | −58 | −64 | −71 | −77 |
| 15 | 16 | 9 | 2 | −5 | −11 | −18 | −25 | −31 | −38 | −45 | −51 | −58 | −65 | −72 | −78 | −85 | −92 |
| 20 | 12 | 4 | −3 | −10 | −17 | −24 | −31 | −39 | −46 | −53 | −60 | −67 | −74 | −81 | −88 | −95 | −103 |
| 25 | 8 | 1 | −7 | −15 | −22 | −29 | −36 | −44 | −51 | −59 | −66 | −74 | −81 | −88 | −96 | −103 | −110 |
| 30 | 6 | −2 | −10 | −18 | −25 | −33 | −41 | −49 | −56 | −64 | −71 | −79 | −86 | −93 | −101 | −109 | −116 |
| 35 | 4 | −4 | −12 | −20 | −27 | −35 | −43 | −52 | −58 | −67 | −74 | −82 | −89 | −97 | −105 | −113 | −120 |
| 40 | 3 | −5 | −13 | −21 | −29 | −37 | −45 | −53 | −60 | −69 | −76 | −84 | −92 | −100 | −107 | −115 | −123 |
| 45 | 2 | −6 | −14 | −22 | −30 | −38 | −46 | −54 | −62 | −70 | −78 | −85 | −93 | −102 | −109 | −117 | −125 |

NOTES: This chart gives equivalent temperatures for combinations of wind speed and temperatures. For example, the combination of a temperature of 10° Fahrenheit and a wind blowing at 10 mph has a cooling power equal to −9° F. Wind speeds of higher than 45 mph have little additional cooling effect.

# World and U.S. Extremes of Climate

## Highest recorded temperature

| | Place | Date | Degree Fahrenheit | Degree Centigrade |
|---|---|---|---|---|
| World (Africa) | El Azizia, Libya | Sept. 13, 1922 | 136 | 58 |
| North America (U.S.) | Death Valley, Calif. | July 10, 1913 | 134 | 57 |
| Asia | Tirat Tsvi, Israel | June 21, 1942 | 129 | 54 |
| Australia | Cloncurry, Queensland | Jan. 16, 1889 | 128 | 53 |
| Europe | Seville, Spain | Aug. 4, 1881 | 122 | 50 |
| South America | Rivadavia, Argentina | Dec. 11, 1905 | 120 | 49 |
| Antarctica | Esperanza, Palmer Peninsula | Oct. 20, 1956 | 58 | 14 |

## Lowest recorded temperature

| | Place | Date | Degree Fahrenheit | Degree Centigrade |
|---|---|---|---|---|
| World (Antarctica) | Vostok | Aug. 24, 1960 | −127 | −88 |
| Asia | Verkhoyansk/Oimekon | Feb. 6, 1933 | −90 | −68 |
| Greenland | Northice | Jan. 9, 1954 | −87 | −66 |
| North America (excl. Greenland) | Snag, Yukon, Canada | Feb. 3, 1947 | −81 | −63 |
| Europe | Ust 'Shchugor, U.S.S.R. | n.a. | −67 | −55 |
| South America | Sarmiento, Argentina | Jan. 1, 1907 | −27 | −33 |
| Africa | Ifrane, Morocco | Feb. 11, 1935 | −11 | −24 |
| Australia | Charlotte Pass, N.S.W. | July 22, 1947 | −8 | −22 |
| United States | Prospect Creek, Alaska | Jan. 23, 1971 | −80 | −62 |

## Greatest rainfalls

| | Place | Date | Inches | Centimeters |
|---|---|---|---|---|
| 1 minute (U.S.) | Unionville, Md. | — | 1.23 | 3.1 |
| 20 minutes (Romania) | Curtea-de-Arges | — | 8.1 | 20.6 |
| 42 minutes (U.S.) | Holt, Mo. | — | 12 | 30 |
| 12 hours (Indian Ocean) | Belouve, La Réunion | — | 53 | 135 |
| 24 hours (Indian Ocean) | Cilaos, La Réunion | — | 74 | 188 |
| 5 days (Indian Ocean) | Cilaos, La Réunion | — | 152 | 386 |
| 1 month (India) | Cherrapunji | — | 366 | 930 |
| 1 month (U.S.) | Kukui, Maui, Hawaii | — | 460 | 1,168 |
| 12 months (India) | Cherrapunji | — | 1,042 | 2,647 |

## Greatest snowfalls

| | Place | Date | Inches | Centimeters |
|---|---|---|---|---|
| 1 month (U.S.) | Tamarack, Calif. | Jan. 1911 | 390 | 991 |
| 24 hours (U.S.) | Silver Lake, Colo. | April 14–15, 1921 | 76 | 193 |
| 19 hours (France) | Bessans | — | 68 | 173 |
| 1 storm (U.S.) | Mt. Shasta Ski Bowl, Calif. | — | 189 | 480 |
| 1 season (U.S.) | Paradise Ranger Sta., Wash. | — | 1,122 | 2,850 |

NOTE: n.a. = not available. *Source:* National Oceanic and Atmospheric Administration, Environmental Data Service.

## Other Recorded Extremes

**Highest average annual temperature (World):** Dallol, Ethiopia (1960-66), 94° F (34.4° C). **(U.S.):** Key West, Fla. (30-year normal), 78.2° F (25.7° C).

**Lowest average annual temperature (Antarctica):** Plateau Station −70° F (−56° C). **(U.S.):** Barrow, Alaska (30-year normal), 9.3° F (−12.6° C).

**Greatest average yearly rainfall (U.S.):** Mt. Waialeale, Kauai, Hawaii (1912-58), 460 in. (1,168 cm). **(India):** Cherrapunji (74-year avg), 450 in. (1,143 cm).

**Minimum average yearly rainfall (Chile):** Arica (59-year avg), 0.03 in. (0.08 cm) (no rainfall for 14 consecutive years). **(U.S.):** Death Valley, Calif. (49-year avg), 1.63 in. (4.14 cm). Bagdad, Calif., holds the U.S. record for the longest period with no measurable rain, 767 days, from Oct. 3, 1912 to Nov. 8, 1914).

**Hottest summer avg in Western Hemisphere (U.S.):** Death Valley, Calif., 98° F (36.7° C).

**Longest hot spell (W. Australia):** Marble Bar, 100° F (37.8° C) (or above) for 162 consecutive days.

**Largest hailstone (U.S.):** Potter, Neb., 1 1/2 lb (.68 kg).

**Lowest recorded temperature (Antarctica):** Vostok Station, −127° F (−52.7° C) August 1960.

# Devastating North Atlantic Hurricanes of the 20th Century

The following is a selected list of North Atlantic hurricanes based on casualties, damage, and general public interest. Facts about each storm are taken from Weather records, although in some cases only estimates of wind speed are available. Data given in this list pertain only to U.S. land areas except where indicated otherwise.

| Date | Areas hardest hit | Land stations with highest wind speed | Deaths (U.S. only) | Est. damage (millions) | Remarks |
|---|---|---|---|---|---|
| 1900, Aug. 27–Sept. 15 | Galveston, Tex. | Galveston, Tex. (120[1] mph) | 6,000 | $30 | Damage due to both winds and storm wave. Galveston Is. inundated. |
| 1909, Sept. 10–21 | Louisiana and Mississippi | New Orleans, La. (53 mph) | 350 | 5 | Winds 50–75 mi. W of New Orleans, where deaths occurred, were stronger than 68 mph. |
| 1915, Aug. 5–23 | East Texas and Louisiana | Galveston, Tex. (120 mph) | 275 | 50 | Water 5–6 ft deep in Galveston business district. 90% of homes demolished. Warnings issued well ahead of time. |
| 1915, Sept. 22–Oct. 1 | Mid-Gulf Coast | Burrwood, La. (140 mph) | 275 | 13 | Many casualties due to persons insisting on staying in low-lying areas despite warnings. |
| 1919, Sept. 2–15 | Florida, Louisiana, and Texas | Sand Key, Fla. (84[1] mph) | 287 | 22 | 488 persons drowned at sea. |
| 1926, Sept. 11–22 | Florida and Alabama | Miami, Fla. (138 mph) | 243 | 112 | Most deaths were in Miami area. Said to have been one of most destructive storms of century. |
| 1928, Sept. 6–20 | Southern Florida | Lake Okeechobee, Fla. (75[1] mph) | 1,836 | 25 | 1,870 injured. Nearly all deaths were in Lake Okeechobee area. Winds estimated as high as 160 mph caused Lake to overflow into populated areas. |
| 1935, Aug. 29–Sept. 10 | Southern Florida | Tampa, Fla. (86 mph) | 408 | 6 | Sustained winds over Florida Keys est. 150–200 mph. Remembered as "Labor Day Storm." |
| 1938, Sept. 10–22 | Long Island and Southern New England | Blue Hills Obs., Mass. (183 mph) | 600 | 306 | Unusually destructive. Storm center moved as fast as 56 mph at times. 1,754 injured. |
| 1944, Sept. 9–16 | North Carolina to New England | Cape Henry, Va. (150[1] mph) | 46 | 100 | 344 deaths at sea. Shipping lanes were crowded with war-time activity. |
| 1944, Oct. 12–23 | Florida | Dry Tortugas Is. (120 mph) | 18 | 100 | About 300 were killed in Cuba area before storm reached U.S. Evacuation of thousands from threatened areas in Fla. prevented higher toll. |
| 1947, Sept. 4–21 | Florida and Mid-Gulf Coast | Hillsboro Light, Fla. (155 mph) | 51 | 110 | Wind damage especially heavy along Gulf Coast and Florida east coast. |
| 1954, Aug. 25–31 | North Carolina to New England | Block Island, R.I. (135 mph) | 60 | 461 | "CAROL"—more damage than any other single storm to this date. Water and high waves flooded low-lying areas; 1,000 injuries in Long Island—New England area. |
| 1954, Sept. 2–14 | New Jersey to New England | Block Island, R.I. (87 mph) | 21 | 40 | "EDNA"—New England again heavily hit. Gusts of 120 mph at Martha's Vineyard, Mass. |
| 1954, Oct. 5–18 | South Carolina to New York | New York, N.Y. (113 mph) (See Remarks) | 95 | 252 | "HAZEL"—several N.C. localities had winds of 130–150 mph with unusually heavy wave damage resulting. Est. 400–1,000 casualties in Haiti. In Canada there were 78 deaths, mostly due to flooding. |
| 1955, Aug. 7–21 | North Carolina to New England | Wilmington, N.C. (83 mph) | 184 | 832 | "DIANE"—worst floods in history in Southern New England. 16 in. of rain in Hartford area. |
| 1957, June 25–28 | Texas to Alabama | Sabine/Pass, Tex. (100 mph) | 390 | 150 | "AUDREY"—gave an early start to the hurricane season and wiped out Cameron, La. Two weeks later "BERTHA" struck same area. |

| Date | Areas hardest hit | Land stations with highest wind speed | Deaths (U.S. only) | Est. damage (millions) | Remarks |
|---|---|---|---|---|---|
| 1960, Aug. 29–Sept. 13 | Florida to New England | Ft. Myers, Fla. (92 mph) Block Island, R.I. (130 mph) (See Remarks) | 50 | 500 | "DONNA"—hurricane winds from a single storm swept the entire Atlantic seaboard from Florida to New England for the first time in a 75-year record. Winds estimated near 140 mph with gusts 175–180 mph on Central Keys and lower southwest Florida coast. 115 deaths in Antilles, most from flash floods in Puerto Rico. |
| 1961, Sept. 3–15 | Texas coast | Port Lavaca, Tex. (145 mph) | 46 | 408 | "CARLA"—devastated Texas Gulf Coast Cities with 15-foot tides and 15-inch rains. Gusts to 175 mph at Port Lavaca. |
| 1964, Aug. 20–Sept. 5 | Southern Florida, Eastern Virginia | Miami, Fla. (110 mph) | 3 | 129 | "CLEO"—first hurricane in Miami area since 1950. Killed 214 in Caribbean Islands. |
| 1964, Aug. 28–Sept. 16 | Northeastern Florida, Southern Georgia | St. Augustine, Fla. (125 mph) | 5 | 250 | "DORA"—first storm of full hurricane force on record to move inland from east over northeastern Florida. |
| 1965, Aug. 27–Sept. 12 | Southern Florida and Louisiana | Port Sulphur, La. (136 mph) | 75 | 1,420 | "BETSY"—Damage in Louisiana, $1.2 billion. 27,000 homes destroyed, 17,500 injured or ill, 300,000 evacuated. Gusts of 165 mph at Pine Key, Fla. |
| 1967, Sept. 5–22 | Southern Texas | Brownsville, Texas (109 mph gust) | 15 | 200 | "BEULAH"—main damage was caused by torrential rains. |
| 1969, Aug. 14–22 | Mississippi, Louisiana, Alabama, Virginia, W. Virginia | Oil drilling rig east of Boothville, La. (172 mph) | 256 | 1,420 | "CAMILLE"—68 additional persons missing. One of most destructive killer storms ever to hit U.S. |
| 1970, July 23–Aug. 5 | Texas coast | Corpus Christi, Tex. (130 mph) | 11 | 453.8 | "CELIA"—Gusts of 161 mph recorded. |
| 1972, June 14–23 | Florida to New York | Key West, Fla. (43 mph) | 117 | 3,097 | "AGNES"—Devastating floods with many record-breaking river crests. Pa. hardest hit, with 50 deaths. |
| 1975, Sept. 13–24 | Florida and Southern Alabama | Ozark, Ala. (104 mph) | 21 | 490 | "ELOISE"—Structures destroyed from Panama City Beach, Fla., to Ft. Walton Beach, Fla. Major flooding from rainfall. |
| 1976, Aug. 6–10 | New York, New Jersey, and Southern New England | Bridgeport, Conn. (77 mph gust) | 5 | 100 | "BELLE"—Crop damage in the Northeast. Considerable inland stream and road flooding. |
| 1979, Aug. 25–Sept. 7 | Florida to New England | Fort Pierce, Fla. (95 mph gust) | 5 | 320 | "DAVID"—1200 deaths in the Dominican Republic. Homes 80 percent destroyed in Dominica. |
| 1979, Aug. 29–Sept. 14 | Alabama and Mississippi | Dauphin Island, Alabama (145 mph gust) | 5 | 2300 | "FREDERIC"—highest dollar damage ever in the United States. |
| 1980, Aug. 3–10 | Caribbean Islands to Texas Gulf Coast | Port Mansfield, Texas (120 mph gust.) | 28 | 300 | "ALLEN"—Highest tides in 61 years. Over 200 killed in Caribbean Islands. Extensive crop damage in Caribbean. |
| 1983, Aug. 15–21 | Texas Coast | Hobby Airport (94 mph) | 21 | 2000 | "ALICIA"—Extensive damage in Galveston/Houston area. |
| 1985, Aug. 28–Sept. 4 | Florida to Mississippi | Dauphin Island, Ala. (96 mph) | 4 | 1,000 | "ELENA"—one million persons evacuated. |
| 1985, Sept. 16—27 | North Carolina Outer Banks and Long Island, N.Y. | Chesapeake Bay Bridge (92 mph) | 8 | 1,000 | "GLORIA"—downed trees and power outages across southern New England. |
| 1985, Oct. 26–Nov. 1 | Louisiana | Pensacola, Fla. (63 mph gust) | 12 | 1,500 | "JUAN"—Serious damage to offshore oil rigs. Sustained flooding over SE Louisiana. |

1. Wind-measuring equipment disabled at speed indicated. NOTE: Additional hurricanes may be listed in *Current Events*.
*Source:* Department of Commerce, National Oceanic and Atmospheric Administration.

# Record Highest Temperatures by State

| State | Temp, °F | Date | Station | Elevation, feet |
|---|---|---|---|---|
| Alabama | 112 | Sept. 5, 1925 | Centerville | 345 |
| Alaska | 100 | June 27, 1915 | Fort Yukon | est. 420 |
| Arizona | 127 | July 7, 1905* | Parker | 345 |
| Arkansas | 120 | Aug. 10, 1936 | Ozark | 396 |
| California | 134 | July 10, 1913 | Greenland Ranch | −178 |
| Colorado | 118 | July 11, 1888 | Bennett | 5,484 |
| Connecticut | 105 | July 22, 1926 | Waterbury | 400 |
| Delaware | 110 | July 21, 1930 | Millsboro | 20 |
| Florida | 109 | June 29, 1931 | Monticello | 207 |
| Georgia | 113 | May 27, 1978 | Greenville | 860 |
| Hawaii | 100 | Apr. 27, 1931 | Pahala | 850 |
| Idaho | 118 | July 28, 1934 | Orofino | 1,027 |
| Illinois | 117 | July 14, 1954 | E. St. Louis | 410 |
| Indiana | 116 | July 14, 1936 | Collegeville | 672 |
| Iowa | 118 | July 20, 1934 | Keokuk | 614 |
| Kansas | 121 | July 24, 1936* | Alton (near) | 1,651 |
| Kentucky | 114 | July 28, 1930 | Greensburg | 581 |
| Louisiana | 114 | Aug. 10, 1936 | Plain Dealing | 268 |
| Maine | 105 | July 10, 1911* | North Bridgton | 450 |
| Maryland | 109 | July 10, 1936* | Cumberland & Frederick | 623;325 |
| Massachusetts | 107 | Aug. 2, 1975 | New Bedford & Chester | 120;640 |
| Michigan | 112 | July 13, 1936 | Mio | 963 |
| Minnesota | 114 | July 6, 1936* | Moorhead | 904 |
| Mississippi | 115 | July 29, 1930 | Holly Springs | 600 |
| Missouri | 118 | July 14, 1954* | Warsaw & Union | 687;560 |
| Montana | 117 | July 5, 1937 | Medicine Lake | 1,950 |
| Nebraska | 118 | July 24, 1936* | Minden | 2,169 |
| Nevada | 122 | June 23, 1954* | Overton | 1,240 |
| New Hampshire | 106 | July 4, 1911 | Nashua | 125 |
| New Jersey | 110 | July 10, 1936 | Runyon | 18 |
| New Mexico | 116 | July 14, 1934* | Orogrande | 4,171 |
| New York | 108 | July 22, 1926 | Troy | 35 |
| North Carolina | 109 | Sept. 7, 1954* | Weldon | 81 |
| North Dakota | 121 | July 6, 1936 | Steele | 1,857 |
| Ohio | 113 | July 21, 1934* | Gallipolis (near) | 673 |
| Oklahoma | 120 | July 26, 1943* | Tishomingo | 670 |
| Oregon | 119 | Aug. 10, 1898 | Pendleton | 1,074 |
| Pennsylvania | 111 | July 10, 1936* | Phoenixville | 100 |
| Rhode Island | 104 | Aug. 2, 1975 | Providence | 51 |
| South Carolina | 111 | June 28, 1954* | Camden | 170 |
| South Dakota | 120 | July 5, 1936 | Gannvalley | 1,750 |
| Tennessee | 113 | Aug. 9, 1930* | Perryville | 377 |
| Texas | 120 | Aug. 12, 1936 | Seymour | 1,291 |
| Utah | 116 | June 28, 1892 | Saint George | 2,880 |
| Vermont | 105 | July 4, 1911 | Vernon | 310 |
| Virginia | 110 | July 15, 1954 | Balcony Falls | 725 |
| Washington | 118 | Aug. 5, 1961* | Ice Harbor Dam | 475 |
| West Virginia | 112 | July 10, 1936* | Martinsburg | 435 |
| Wisconsin | 114 | July 13, 1936 | Wisconsin Dells | 900 |
| Wyoming | 114 | July 12, 1900 | Basin | 3,500 |

*Also on earlier dates at the same or other places. *Source:* National Oceanic and Atmospheric Administration, Environmental Data and Information Service, National Climatic Center, Asheville, N.C. NOTE: Records as of 1983.

## HIGHEST TEMPERATURE OF RECORD AND LOCATIONS, BY STATES

*Source:* National Oceanic and Atmospheric Administration.

## LOWEST TEMPERATURES OF RECORD AND LOCATIONS BY STATES

## Record Lowest Temperatures by State

| State | Temp, °F | Date | Station | Elevation, feet |
|---|---|---|---|---|
| Alabama | −27 | Jan. 30, 1966 | New Market | 760 |
| Alaska | −80 | Jan. 23, 1971 | Prospect Creek | 1,100 |
| Arizona | −40 | Jan. 7, 1971 | Hawley Lake | 8,180 |
| Arkansas | −29 | Feb. 13, 1905 | Pond | 1,250 |
| California | −45 | Jan. 20, 1937 | Boca | 5,532 |
| Colorado | −60 | Jan. 1, 1979* | Maybell | 5,920 |
| Connecticut | −32 | Feb. 16, 1943 | Falls Village | 585 |
| Delaware | −17 | Jan. 17, 1893 | Millsboro | 20 |
| Florida | −2 | Feb. 13, 1899 | Tallahassee | 193 |
| Georgia | −17 | Jan. 27, 1940 | CCC Camp F-16 | est. 1,000 |
| Hawaii | 14 | Jan. 2, 1961 | Haleakala, Maui Is | 9,750 |
| Idaho | −60 | Jan. 18, 1943 | Island Park Dam | 6,285 |
| Illinois | −35 | Jan. 22, 1930 | Mount Carroll | 817 |
| Indiana | −35 | Feb. 2, 1951 | Greensburg | 954 |
| Iowa | −47 | Jan. 12, 1912 | Washta | 1,157 |
| Kansas | −40 | Feb. 13, 1905 | Lebanon | 1,812 |
| Kentucky | −34 | Jan. 28, 1963 | Cynthiana | 684 |
| Louisiana | −16 | Feb. 13, 1899 | Minden | 194 |
| Maine | −48 | Jan. 19, 1925 | Van Buren | 510 |
| Maryland | −40 | Jan. 13, 1912 | Oakland | 2,461 |
| Massachusetts | −34 | Jan. 18, 1957 | Birch Hill Dam | 840 |
| Michigan | −51 | Feb. 9, 1934 | Vanderbilt | 785 |
| Minnesota | −59 | Feb. 16, 1903* | Pokegama Dam | 1,280 |
| Mississippi | −19 | Jan. 30, 1966 | Corinth | 420 |
| Missouri | −40 | Feb. 13, 1905 | Warsaw | 700 |
| Montana | −70 | Jan. 20, 1954 | Rogers Pass | 5,470 |
| Nebraska | −47 | Feb. 12, 1899 | Camp Clarke | 3,700 |
| Nevada | −50 | Jan. 8, 1937 | San Jacinto | 5,200 |
| New Hampshire | −46 | Jan. 28, 1925 | Pittsburg | 1,575 |
| New Jersey | −34 | Jan. 5, 1904 | River Vale | 70 |
| New Mexico | −50 | Feb. 1, 1951 | Gavilan | 7,350 |
| New York | −52 | Feb. 18, 1979* | Old Forge | 1,720 |
| North Carolina | −29 | Jan. 30, 1966 | Mt. Mitchell | 6,525 |
| North Dakota | −60 | Feb. 15, 1936 | Parshall | 1,929 |
| Ohio | −39 | Feb. 10, 1899 | Milligan | 800 |
| Oklahoma | −27 | Jan. 18, 1930 | Watts | 958 |
| Oregon | −54 | Feb. 10, 1933* | Seneca | 4,700 |
| Pennsylvania | −42 | Jan. 5, 1904 | Smethport | est. 1,500 |
| Rhode Island | −23 | Jan. 11, 1942 | Kingston | 100 |
| South Carolina | −20 | Jan. 18, 1977 | Caesars Head | 3,100 |
| South Dakota | −58 | Feb. 17, 1936 | McIntosh | 2,277 |
| Tennessee | −32 | Dec. 30, 1917 | Mountain City | 2,471 |
| Texas | −23 | Feb. 8, 1933* | Seminole | 3,275 |
| Utah | −50 | Jan. 5, 1913* | Strawberry Tunnel | 7,650 |
| Vermont | −50 | Dec. 30, 1933 | Bloomfield | 915 |
| Virginia | −29 | Feb. 10, 1899 | Monterey | — |
| Washington | −48 | Dec. 30, 1968 | Mazama & Winthrop | 2,120;1,765 |
| West Virginia | −37 | Dec. 30, 1917 | Lewisburg | 2,200 |
| Wisconsin | −54 | Jan. 24, 1922 | Danbury | 908 |
| Wyoming | −63 | Feb. 9, 1933 | Moran | 6,770 |

*Also on earlier dates at the same or other places. *Source:* National Oceanic and Atmospheric Administration, Environmental Data and Information Service, National Climatic Center, Asheville, N.C. NOTE: Records as of 1983.

# Hailstorms

*Source:* From *The American Weather Book* by David M. Ludlum. Copyright © 1982 by David M. Ludlum. Reprinted by permission of Houghton Mifflin Company.

Precipitation in the form of solid spheres of ice or irregular frozen conglomerates contributes a spectacular feature to the atmospheric antics during the warmer portion of the year. Hail originates in a convective cloud of the cumulonimbus type, which develops in the strong updrafts attending frontal turbulence or a local thunderstorm. The most prolific hailstorms result from the formation of supercells in a thunderstorm whose enormous updrafts permit large hailstones to grow by accretion over periods of many minutes. Over the Great Plains, where hailstorms are frequent, most of the crop damage is caused by only a few supercell storms each season.

Most hailstorms cover only a limited area with a scattering of stones falling, but when fully developed they may loose vast quantities of icy matter over a considerable territory. Often hail falls over long areas from 0.5 to 2.0 mi. (0.8 to 3.2 km) wide and from 5 to 10 mi. (8 to 16 km) or more long as the developing storm cloud moves downwind. These areas, known as hailstreaks, can turn white from the accumulating hailstones and be covered to a considerable depth by an icy mass. Total destruction of crops may result, and injury and even death may come to humans and animals when caught in the open by the bombardment from the sky.

The first instance in National Weather Service records of a hail death occurred on May 13, 1939, near Lubbock, Texas, when a 39-year-old farmer died of injuries after being caught in the open during a severe hailstorm. The country's press have reported other hail fatalities: at Amwell, New Jersey, on June 10, 1742; in St. Charles County, Missouri, on September 11, 1863; in Broome, Quebec, on July 28, 1879; near Uvalde, Texas, on May 17, 1909; at Windsor, North Carolina, on May 10, 1931, and near Toronto, Ontario, on June 13, 1976.

A small infant in its mother's arms was reported to have been killed by hail at Fort Collins, Colorado, on July 30, 1979.

On September 3, 1970, a hailstone measuring 17.5 in. (45 cm) in circumference and weighing 1.671 lb (758 gm) was picked up and photographed at Coffeyville in southeast Kansas. The largest stone previously documented by the National Weather Service in the United States was almost the same size; found at Potter in southwestern Nebraska on July 6, 1928, it had a circumference of 17 in. (43.2 cm) and weighed 1.51 lb (680 gm). The *Monthly Weather Review* reported a comparable stone falling at Dubuque in eastern Iowa on June 16, 1882, which also measured 17 in. (43.2 cm) in circumference and weighed 1.75 lb (794 gm).

## Lightning Deaths and Injuries, 1959-1985

| Location | 1959-1985 | | 1985 | |
|---|---|---|---|---|
| | Deaths | Injuries | Deaths | Injuries |
| Open fields, ball fields, etc. | 727 | 1995 | 25 | 111 |
| Under trees | 425 | 862 | 14 | 37 |
| Boating, fishing, and water related | 342 | 372 | 16 | 10 |
| Tractors, heavy road equipment, etc. | 161 | 186 | 3 | 4 |
| Golf courses | 120 | 318 | 4 | 11 |
| Telephones | 30 | 181 | 1 | 4 |
| Various other and unknown locations | 842 | 2806 | 10 | 71 |

*Source:* National Oceanic and Atmospheric Administration, National Environmental Satellite, Data, and Information Service, National Climatic Data Center

## General Summary of Lightning, 1985

Lightning killed 73 people and injured 248 during 1985. Eighty-six percent of the fatalities occurred between the hours of 10 a.m. and 10 p.m., local standard time. Increases (from the national average) in deaths occurred in the following locations: open fields (34% vs. 27%); boating, fishing, and water related (22% vs. 13%); and under trees (19% vs. 16%).

## Deaths by Lightning on the Golf Course

For the period 1959-1985, an average of five percent of the nation's lightning fatalities and/or injuries occurred on golf courses. One hundred twenty people have been killed and 318 have been injured by lightning on golf courses.

Michigan recorded 10% of all lightning deaths reported on golf courses, followed by Pennsylvania (9%), New York (7%), Ohio (6%), and North Carolina, Tennessee, and Wisconsin each recording five percent. These seven states represent 47% of all lightning fatalities and 41% of the lightning injuries recorded on golf courses in the United States for the past 27 years.

No deaths or injuries have been reported on golf courses in Alaska, California, Delaware, Hawaii, Idaho, Nevada, Oregon and Vermont.

# Temperature Extremes in The United States

*Source:* National Oceanic and Atmospheric Administration, Environmental Data and Information Service, and National Center Climatic Center

## The Highest Temperature Extremes

Greenland Ranch, California, with 134° F (56.67° C) on July 10, 1913, holds the record for the highest temperature ever officially observed in the United States. This station was located in barren Death Valley, 178 feet below sea level. Death Valley is about 140 miles long, four to six miles wide, and oriented north to south in southwestern California. Much of the valley is below sea level and is flanked by towering mountain ranges with Mt. Whitney, the highest landmark in the 48 conterminous states, rising to 14,495 feet above sea level, less than 100 miles to the west. Death Valley has the hottest summers in the Western Hemisphere, and is the only known place in the United States where nightime temperatures sometimes remain above 100° F (37.78° C).

The highest annual normal (1941-70 mean) temperature in the United States, 78.2° F (25.67° C), and the highest summer (June-August) normal temperature, 92.8° F (33.78° C), are for Death Valley, California. The highest winter (December-February) normal temperature is 72.8° F (22.67° C) for Honolulu, Hawaii.

Amazing temperature rises of 40° to 50° F (4.44 to 10° C) in a few minutes occasionally may be brought about by chinook winds.[1]

## Some Outstanding Temperature Rises

**In 12 hours:** 83° F (28.34° C), Granville, N.D., Feb. 21, 1918, from −33° F to 50° F (−36.11 to 10° C) from early morning to late afternoon.

**In 15 minutes:** 42° F (5.56° C), Fort Assiniboine, Mont., Jan. 19, 1892, from −5° F to 37° F (−20.56 to 2.78° C).

**In seven minutes:** 34° F (1.11° C), Kipp, Mont., Dec. 1, 1896. The observer also reported that a total rise of 80° F (26.67° C) occurred in a few hours and that 30 inches of snow disappeared in one-half day.

**In two minutes:** 49° F (9.45° C), Spearfish, S.D., Jan. 22, 1943 from −4° F (20° C) at 7:30 a.m. to 45° F (7.22° C) at 7:32 a.m.

## The Lowest Temperature Extremes

The lowest temperature on record in the United States, −79.8° F −62.1° C), was observed at Pros-

pect Creek Camp in the Endicott Mountains of northern Alaska (latitude 66° 48′N, longitude 150° 40′W) on Jan. 23, 1971. The lowest ever recorded in the conterminous 48 states, −69.7° F (−56.5° C), occurred at Rogers Pass, in Lewis and Clark County, Mont., on Jan. 20, 1954. Rogers Pass is in mountainous and heavily forested terrain about one-half mile east of and 140 feet below the summit of the Continental Divide.

The lowest annual normal (1941-70 mean) temperature in the United States is 9.3° F (−12.68° C) for Barrow, Alaska, which lies on the Arctic coast. Barrow also has the coolest summers (June-August) with a normal temperature of 36.4° F (2.44° C). The lowest winter (December-February) normal temperature, is −15.7° F (−26.5° C) for Barter Island on the arctic coast of northeast Alaska.

In the 48 conterminous states, Mt. Washington, N.H. (elevation 6,262 feet) has the lowest annual normal temperature 26.9° F (−2.72° C) and the lowest normal summer temperature, 46.8° F (8.22° C). A few stations in the northeastern United States and in the upper Rocky Mountains have normal annual temperatures in the 30s; summer normal temperatures at these stations are in the low 50s. Winter normal temperatures are lowest in northeastern North Dakota, 5.6° F (−14.23° C) for Langdon Experiment Farm, and in northwestern Minnesota, 5.3° F (−14.83° C) for Hallock.

## Some Outstanding Temperature Falls

**In 24 hours:** 100° F (37.78° C), Browing, Mont., Jan. 23-24, 1916, from 44° to −56° F (6.67° to −48.9° C).

**In 12 hours:** 84° F (28.89° C), Fairfield, Mont., Dec. 24, 1924, from 63° (17.22° C) at noon to −21° F (−29.45° C) at midnight.

**In 2 hours:** 62° F (16.67° C), Rapid City, S.D., Jan. 12, 1911, from 49° F (9.45° C) at 6:00 a.m. to −13° F (−25° C) at 8:00 a.m.

**In 27 minutes:** 58° F (14.45° C), Spearfish, S.D., Jan. 22, 1943, from 54° F (12.22° C) at 9:00 a.m. to −4° F (−20° C) at 9:27 a.m.

**In 15 minutes:** 47° F (8.33° C), Rapid City, S.D., Jan. 10, 1911, from 55° F (12.78° C) at 7:00 a.m. to 8° F (−13.33° C). at 7:15 a.m.

1. A warm, dry wind that descends from the eastern slopes of the Rocky Mountains, causing a rapid rise in temperature. 2. Horizontal movement of any atmospheric element; for example: air, moisture, or heat.

# Winter Indoor Comfort and Relative Humidity

Compared to summer when the moisture content of the air (relative humidity) is an important factor of body discomfort, air moisture has a lesser effect on the human body during outdoor winter activities. But it is a big factor for winter indoor comfort because it has a direct bearing on health and energy consumption.

The colder the outdoor temperature, the more heat must be added indoors for body comfort.

However, the heat that is added will cause a drying effect and lower the indoor relative humidity, unless an indoor moisture source is present.

While a room temperature between 71° and 77° F may be comfortable for short periods of time under very dry conditions, prolonged exposure to dry air has varying effects on the human body and usually causes discomfort. The moisture content of the air is important, and by increasing the rela-

### Average Indoor Relative Humidity, %, for January

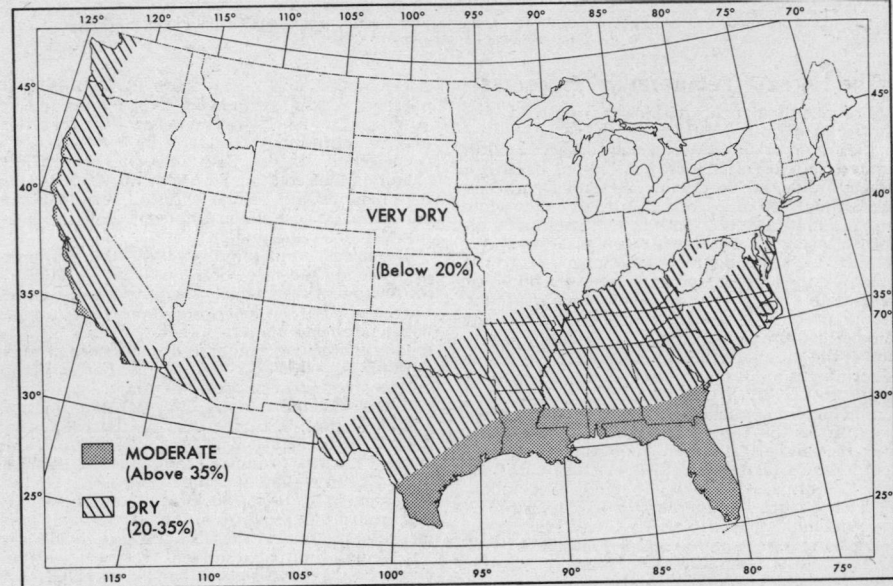

*Source:* National Oceanic and Atmospheric Administration, Environmental Data and Information Service, National Climatic Center.

tive humidity to above 50% within the above temperature range, 80% or more of all average dressed persons would feel comfortable.

## Effects of Dry Air on the Body

Studies have shown that dry air has four main effects on the human body:

1. Breathing dry air is a potential health hazard which can cause such respiratory ailments as asthma, bronchitis, sinusitis, and nosebleeds, or general dehydration since body fluids are depleted during respiration.

2. Skin moisture evaporation can cause skin irritations and eye itching.

3. Irritative effects, such as static electricity which causes mild shocks when metal is touched, are common when the air moisture is low.

4. The "apparent temperature" of the air is lower than what the thermometer indicates, and the body "feels" colder.

These problems can be reduced by simply increasing the indoor relative humidity. This can be done through use of humidifiers, vaporizers, steam generators, sources such as large pans, or water containers made of porous ceramics. Even wet towels or water in a bathtub will be of some help. The lower the room temperature the easier the relative humidity can be brought to its desired level. A relative humidity indicator (hygrometer) may be of assistance in determining the humidity in the house.

Referring to item 4, a more detailed discussion

is necessary. While the indoor temperature as read from a thermometer may be 75° F, the apparent temperature (what it feels like) may be warmer or colder depending on the moisture content of the air. Apparent temperature can vary as much as 8° F within a relative humidity range of 10 to 80 percent (these limits are generally possible in a closed room). Because of evaporation the human body cools when exposed to dry air, and the sense of coldness increases as the humidity decreases. With a room temperature of 70° F, for example, a person will feel colder in a dry room than in a moist room; this is especially noticeable when entering a dry room after bathing.

The table on the following page gives apparent temperatures for various combinations of room temperature and relative humidity. As an example of how to read the table, a room temperature of 70° F combined with a relative humidity of 10% feels like 64° F, but at 80% it feels like 71° F.

Although degrees of comfort vary with age, health, activity, clothing, and body characteristics, the table can be used as a general guideline when raising the apparent temperature and the level of comfort through an increase in room moisture, rather than by an addition of heat to the room. This method of changing the apparent temperature can give the direct benefit of reducing heating costs because comfort can be maintained with a lower thermostat setting if moisture is added. For example, an apparent comfortable temperature can be maintained with a thermostat setting of 75° F with 20% relative humidity or with a 70° F setting with 80 percent humidity. A relative humidity of 20 percent is common for homes without a humidifier during winter in the northern United States.

# Apparent Temperature for Values of Room Temperature and Relative Humidity

**RELATIVE HUMIDITY (%)**

| ROOM TEMPERATURE (°F) | 0 | 10 | 20 | 30 | 40 | 50 | 60 | 70 | 80 | 90 | 100 |
|---|---|---|---|---|---|---|---|---|---|---|---|
| 75 | 68 | 69 | 71 | 72 | 74 | 75 | 76 | 76 | 77 | 78 | 79 |
| 74 | 66 | 68 | 69 | 71 | 72 | 73 | 74 | 75 | 76 | 77 | 78 |
| 73 | 65 | 67 | 68 | 70 | 71 | 72 | 73 | 74 | 75 | 76 | 77 |
| 72 | 64 | 65 | 67 | 68 | 70 | 71 | 72 | 73 | 74 | 75 | 76 |
| 71 | 63 | 64 | 66 | 67 | 68 | 70 | 71 | 72 | 73 | 74 | 75 |
| 70 | 63 | 64 | 65 | 66 | 67 | 68 | 69 | 70 | 71 | 72 | 73 |
| 69 | 62 | 63 | 64 | 65 | 66 | 67 | 68 | 69 | 70 | 71 | 72 |
| 68 | 61 | 62 | 63 | 64 | 65 | 66 | 67 | 68 | 69 | 70 | 71 |
| 67 | 60 | 61 | 62 | 63 | 64 | 65 | 66 | 67 | 68 | 68 | 69 |
| 66 | 59 | 60 | 61 | 62 | 63 | 64 | 65 | 66 | 67 | 67 | 68 |
| 65 | 59 | 60 | 61 | 61 | 62 | 63 | 64 | 65 | 65 | 66 | 67 |
| 64 | 58 | 59 | 60 | 60 | 61 | 62 | 63 | 64 | 64 | 65 | 66 |
| 63 | 57 | 58 | 59 | 59 | 60 | 61 | 62 | 62 | 63 | 64 | 64 |
| 62 | 56 | 57 | 58 | 58 | 59 | 60 | 61 | 61 | 62 | 63 | 63 |
| 61 | 56 | 57 | 57 | 58 | 59 | 59 | 60 | 60 | 61 | 61 | 62 |
| 60 | 55 | 56 | 56 | 57 | 58 | 58 | 59 | 59 | 60 | 60 | 61 |

*Source:* National Oceanic and Atmospheric Administration, Environmental Data and Information Service and National Climatic Center.

# PEOPLE

Many public figures not listed here may be found elsewhere in the *Information Please Almanac*.

| | | | |
|---|---|---|---|
| 48 | Governors | 853 | Sports Personalities |
| 602 | Presidents | 618 | Supreme Court Justices |
| 604 | Presidents' Wives | 602 | Vice Presidents |
| 41 | Senators | | |

A name in parentheses is the original name or form of name. Localities are places of birth. Country name in parenthesis is the present-day name. Dates of birth appear as month/day/year. **Boldface** years in parentheses are dates of **(birth-death)**.
Information has been gathered from many sources, including the individuals themselves. However, the *Information Please Almanac* cannot guarantee the accuracy of every individual item.

## A

**Aalto,** Alvar (architect); Kuortane, Finland **(1898-1976)**
**Abbott,** Bud (William) (comedian); Asbury Park, N.J. **(1898-1974)**
**Abbott,** George (stage producer); Forestville, N.Y., 6/25/1887
**Abel,** Walter (actor); St. Paul, 6/6/1898
**Abelard,** Peter (theologian); nr. Nantes, France **(1079-1142)**
**Abernathy,** Ralph (civil rights leader); Linden, Ala., 3/11/1926
**Acheson,** Dean (statesman); Middletown, Conn. **(1893-1971)**
**Acuff,** Roy Claxton (musician); nr. Maynardsville, Tenn. 9/15/1903
**Adams,** Charles Francis (diplomat); Boston **(1807-1886)**
**Adams,** Don (actor); New York City, 4/19/1927
**Adams,** Edie (Edie Enke) (actress); Kingston, Pa., 4/16/1929
**Adams,** Franklin Pierce (columnist and author); Chicago **(1881-1960)**
**Adams,** Henry Brooks (historian); Boston **(1838-1918)**
**Adams,** Joey (comedian); New York City, 1/6/1911
**Adams,** Maude (Maude Kiskadden) (actress); Salt Lake City, **(1872-1953)**
**Adams,** Samuel (American Revolutionary patriot); Boston **(1722-1803)**
**Adamson,** Joy (naturalist); Troppau, Silesia **(1910-1980)**
**Addams,** Charles (cartoonist); Westfield, N.J., 1/7/1912
**Addams,** Jane (social worker); Cedarville, Ill. **(1860-1935)**
**Adderley,** Julian "Cannonball" (jazz saxophonist); Tampa, Fla. **(1928-1975)**
**Ade,** George (humorist); Kentland, Ind. **(1866-1944)**
**Adenauer,** Konrad (statesman); Cologne, Germany **(1876-1967)**
**Adler,** Alfred (psychoanalyst); Vienna **(1870-1937)**
**Adler,** Larry (musician); Baltimore, 2/10/1914
**Adler,** Richard (songwriter); New York City, 8/3/1921
**Adoree,** Renée (Renée La Fonte) (actress); Lille, France **(1898-1933)**
**Aeschylus** (dramatist); Eleusis (Greece) **(525-456** B.C.)
**Aesop** (fabulist); birthplace unknown **(lived c. 600** B.C.)
**Aherne,** Brian (actor); King's Norton, England **(1902-1986)**
**Aiken,** Conrad (poet); Savannah, Ga. **(1889-1973)**
**Ailey,** Alvin (choreographer); Rogers, Tex., 1/5/1931
**Albanese,** Licia (operatic soprano); Bari, Italy, 7/22/1913
**Albee,** Edward (playwright); Washington, D.C., 3/12/1928
**Albers,** Josef (painter); Bottrop, Germany **(1888-1976)**
**Albert,** Eddie (Edward Albert Heimberger) (actor); Rock Island, Ill., 4/22/1908
**Albertson,** Jack (actor); Malden, Mass. **(1910?-1981)**
**Albright,** Lola (actress); Akron, Ohio, 7/20/1925
**Alcott,** Louisa May (novelist); Germantown, Pa. **(1832-1888)**
**Alda,** Alan (actor); New York City, 1/28/1936
**Alda,** Robert (Alphonso d'Abruzzo) (actor); New York City **(1914-1986)**
**Alden,** John (American Pilgrim); England **(1599?-1687)**
**Alexander the Great** (monarch and conqueror); Pella, Macedonia (Greece) **(356-323** B.C.)
**Alger,** Horatio (author); Revere, Mass. **(1834-1899)**
**Algren,** Nelson (novelist); Detroit **(1909-1981)**
**Allen,** Ethan (American Revolutionary soldier); Litchfield, Conn. **(1738-1789)**
**Allen,** Fred (John Florence Sullivan) (comedian); Cambridge, Mass. **(1894-1956)**
**Allen,** Gracie (Grace Ethel Cecile Rosalie Allen) (comedienne); San Francisco **(1906-1964)**
**Allen,** Mel (Melvin Israel) (sportscaster); Birmingham, Ala., 2/14/1913
**Allen,** Steve (TV entertainer); New York City, 12/26/1921
**Allen,** Woody (Allen Stewart Konigsberg) (actor, writer, and director); Brooklyn, N.Y., 12/1/1935
**Allison,** Fran (actress); LaPorte City, Iowa, 1924(?)
**Allman,** Gregg (singer); Nashville, Tenn., 12/8/1947
**Allyson,** June (Jan Allyson) (actress); New York City, 10/7/1923
**Alonso,** Alicia (ballerina); Havana, 12/21/1921(?)

**Alpert,** Herb (band leader); Los Angeles, 3/31/1935(?)
**Alsop,** Joseph W., Jr. (journalist); Avon, Conn., 10/11/1910
**Alsop,** Stewart (journalist); Avon, Conn. **(1914-1974)**
**Altman,** Robert (film director); Kansas City, Mo., 2/20/1925
**Amati,** Nicola (violin maker); Cremona, Italy **(1596-1684)**
**Ambler,** Eric (suspense writer); London, 6/28/1909
**Ameche,** Don (Dominic Amici) (actor); Kenosha, Wis., 5/31/1908
**Amis,** Kingsley (novelist); London, 4/16/1922
**Amory,** Cleveland (writer and conservationist); Nahant, Mass., 9/2/1917
**Amos** (Freeman F. Gosden) (radio comedian); Richmond, Va., **(1899-1982)**
**Amsterdam,** Morey (actor); Chicago, 12/14/1914
**Andersen,** Hans Christian (author of fairy-tales); Odense, Denmark **(1805-1875)**
**Anderson,** Eddie. *See* Rochester
**Anderson,** Ib (ballet dancer); Copenhagen, 12/14/1954
**Anderson,** Jack (journalist); Long Beach, Calif., 10/19/1922
**Anderson,** Dame Judith (actress); Adelaide, Australia, 2/10/1898
**Anderson,** Lindsay (Gordon) (director); Bangalore, India, 4/17/1923
**Anderson,** Lynn (singer); Grand Forks, N.D., 9/26/1947
**Anderson,** Marian (contralto); Philadelphia, 2/17/1902
**Anderson,** Maxwell (dramatist); Atlantic, Pa. **(1888-1959)**
**Anderson,** Robert (playwright); New York City, 4/28/1917
**Andersson,** Bibi (actress); Stockholm, 11/11/1935
**Andress,** Ursula (actress); Switzerland, 3/19/1938
**Andrews,** Dana (actor); Collins, Miss., 1/1/1909
**Andrews,** Julie (Julia Wells) (actress and singer); Walton-on-Thames, England, 10/1/1935
**Andrews,** La Verne (singer); Minneapolis **(1916-1967)**
**Andrews,** Maxene (singer); Minneapolis, 1/3/1918
**Andrews,** Patti (singer); Minneapolis, 2/16/1920
**Andy** (Charles J. Correll) (radio comedian); Peoria, Ill. **(1890-1972)**
**Angeles,** Victoria de los (Victoria Gamez Cima) (operatic soprano); Barcelona, 11/1/1924
**Anka,** Paul (singer and composer); Ottawa, 7/30/1941
**Ann-Margret** (Ann-Margret Olsson) (actress); Valsjobyn, Sweden, 4/28/1941
**Annabella** (actress); Paris, 1912
**Anouilh,** Jean (playwright); Bordeaux, France, 6/23/1910
**Anthony,** Susan Brownell (woman suffragist); Adams, Mass. **(1820-1906)**
**Antonioni,** Michelangelo (director); Ferrara, Italy, 9/29/1912
**Antony,** Mark (Marcus Antonius) (statesman); Rome **(83?-30** B.C.)
**Anuszkiewicz,** Richard (painter); Erie, Pa., 5/23/1930
**Aquinas,** St. Thomas (philosopher); nr. Aquino (Italy) **(1225?-1274)**
**Arbuckle,** Roscoe "Fatty" (actor and director); San Jose, Calif. **(1887-1933)**
**Archimedes** (physicist and mathematician); Syracuse, Sicily **(287?-212** B.C.)
**Archipenko,** Alexandre (sculptor); Kiev, Russia **(1887-1964)**
**Arden,** Elizabeth (Florence Nightingale Graham) (cosmetics executive); Woodbridge, Canada **(1891-1966)**
**Arden,** Eve (Eunice Quedens) (actress); Mill Valley, Calif., 4/30/1912
**Arendt,** Hannah (historian); Hannover, Germany **(1906-1975)**
**Aristophanes** (dramatist); Athens **448?-380** B.C.)
**Aristotle** (philosopher); Stagirus, Macedonia **(384-322** B.C.)
**Arkin,** Alan (actor and director); New York City, 3/26/1934
**Arledge,** Roone (TV executive); Forest Hills, N.Y., 7/8/1931
**Arlen,** Harold (Hyman Arluck) (composer); Buffalo, N.Y. **(1905-1986)**
**Arlen,** Richard (actor); Charlottesville, Va. **(1900-1976)**
**Arliss,** George (actor); London **(1868-1946)**
**Armstrong,** Louis ("Satchmo") (musician); New Orleans **(1900-1971)**
**Armstrong-Jones,** Anthony. *See* Snowdon, Earl of
**Arnaz,** Desi (Desiderio) (actor and producer); Santiago, Cuba, 3/2/1917

**Arness,** James (James Aurness) (TV actor); Minneapolis, 5/26/1923
**Arno,** Peter (cartoonist); New York City **(1904-1968)**
**Arnold,** Benedict (American Revolutionary War general, charged with treason); Norwich, Conn. **(1741-1801)**
**Arnold,** Eddy (singer); Henderson, Tenn., 5/15/1918
**Arnold,** Edward (actor); New York City **(1890-1956)**
**Arnold,** Matthew (poet and critic); Laleham, England **(1822-1888)**
**Arp,** Jean (sculptor and painter); Strasbourg (France) **(1887-1966)**
**Arquette,** Cliff ("Charley Weaver") (actor); Toledo, Ohio **(1905-1974)**
**Arrau,** Claudio (pianist); Chillán, Chile, 2/6/1903
**Arroyo,** Martina (soprano); New York City, 2/2/1940
**Arthur,** Bea (Bernice Frankel) (actress); New York City, 5/13/1926(?)
**Arthur,** Jean (Gladys Greene) (actress); New York City, 10/17/1905
**Asch,** Sholem (novelist); Kutno, Poland **(1880-1957)**
**Ashkenazy,** Vladimir (concert pianist); Gorki, U.S.S.R., 7/6/1937
**Ashley,** Elizabeth (actress); Ocala, Fla., 8/30/1939
**Ashton,** Sir Frederick William Mallandaine (choreographer); Guayaquil, Ecuador, 9/17/1904
**Asimov,** Isaac (author); Petrovichi, Russia, 1/2/1920
**Asner,** Edward (actor); Kansas City, Mo., 11/15/1929
**Astaire,** Fred (Frederick Austerlitz) (dancer and actor); Omaha, Neb., 5/10/1899
**Astor,** John Jacob (financier); Waldorf (Germany) **(1763-1848)**
**Astor,** Mary (Lucile Langhanke) (actress); Quincy, Ill., 5/3/1906
**Atkins,** Chet (guitarist); nr. Luttrell, Tenn., 6/20/1924
**Atkinson,** Brooks (drama critic); Melrose, Mass. **(1894-1984)**
**Attenborough,** Richard (actor-director) Cambridge, England, 8/29/1923
**Attila** (King of Huns, called "Scourge of God") **(406?-453)**
**Attlee,** Clement Richard (statesman); London **(1883-1967)**
**Auchincloss,** Louis (author); Lawrence, N.Y., 9/27/1917
**Auden,** W(ystan) H(ugh) (poet); York, England **(1907-1973)**
**Audubon,** John James (naturalist and painter); Haiti **(1785-1851)**
**Auer,** Leopold (violinist and teacher); Veszprém, Hungary **(1845-1930)**
**Auer,** Mischa (actor); St. Petersburg, Russia **(1905-1967)**
**Augustine,** Saint (Aurelius Augustinus) (theologian); Tagaste, Numidia (Algeria) **(354-430)**
**Augustus** (Gaius Octavius) (Roman emperor); Rome **(63** B.C.-A.D. **14)**
**Aumont,** Jean-Pierre (actor); Paris, 1/5/1913
**Austen,** Jane (novelist); Steventon, England **(1775-1817)**
**Autry,** Gene (singer and actor); Tioga, Tex., 9/29/1907
**Avalon,** Frankie (singer); Philadelphia, 9/18/1940
**Avedon,** Richard (photographer); New York City, 5/15/1923
**Avery,** Milton (painter); Altmar, N.Y. **(1893-1965)**
**Ax,** Emanuel (pianist); Lvov, U.S.S.R., 6/8/1949
**Axelrod,** George (playwright); New York City, 6/9/1922
**Ayckbourn,** Alan (playwright); London, 4/12/1939
**Ayckroyd,** Dan (actor); Ottawa, Ont., Canada, 7/1/1952
**Ayres,** Lew (actor); Minneapolis, 12/28/1908

# B

**Bacall,** Lauren (Betty Joan Perske) (actress); New York City, 9/16/1924
**Bach,** Johann Sebastian (composer); Eisenach (East Germany) **(1685-1750)**
**Bach,** Karl Phillipp Emanuel (composer); Weimar (East Germany) **(1714-1788)**
**Bacharach,** Burt (songwriter); Kansas City, Mo., 5/12/1929
**Backus,** Jim (actor); Cleveland, 2/25/1913
**Bacon,** Francis (painter); Dublin, 1910
**Bacon,** Francis (philosopher and essayist); London **(1561-1626)**
**Bacon,** Roger (philosopher and scientist); Ilchester, England **(1214?-1294)**
**Baedeker,** Karl (travel-guidebook publisher); Essen (Germany) **(1801-1859)**
**Baez,** Joan (folk singer); Staten Island, N.Y., 1/9/1941
**Bagnold,** Enid (novelist); Rochester, England **(1889-1981)**
**Bailey,** F. Lee (lawyer); Waltham, Mass., 6/10/1933
**Bailey,** Pearl (singer); Newport News, Va., 3/29/1918
**Bainter,** Fay (actress); Los Angeles **(1891-1968)**
**Baird,** Bill (William B.) (puppeteer); Grand Island, Neb., 8/15/1904
**Baker,** Carroll (actress); Johnstown, Pa., 5/28/1931
**Baker,** Josephine (singer and dancer); St. Louis **(1906-1975)**
**Baker,** Kenny (singer and actor); Monrovia, Calif., 9/30/1912
**Baker,** Russell (columnist); Loudoun County, Va., 8/14/1925
**Balanchine,** George (choreographer); St. Petersburg, Russia **(1904-1983)**
**Balboa,** Vasco Nuñez de (explorer); Jerez de los Caballeros (Spain) **(1475-1517)**
**Baldwin,** Faith (novelist); New Rochelle, N.Y. **(1893-1978)**
**Baldwin,** James (novelist); New York City, 8/2/1924
**Balenciaga,** Cristóbal (fashion designer); Guetaria, Spain **(1895-1972)**

**Ball,** Lucille (Dianne Belmont) (actress and producer); Celoron (nr. Jamestown), N.Y., 8/6/1911
**Ballard,** Kaye (Catherine Gloria Balotta) (actress); Cleveland, 11/20/1926
**Balmain,** Pierre (fashion designer); St.-Jean-de-Maurienne, France **(1914-1982)**
**Balsam,** Martin (actor); New York City, 11/4/1919
**Balzac,** Honoré de (novelist); Tours, France **(1799-1850)**
**Bancroft,** Anne (Annemarie Italiano) (actress); New York City, 9/17/1931
**Bancroft,** George (actor); Philadelphia **(1882-1956)**
**Bankhead,** Tallulah (actress); Huntsville, Ala. **(1903-1963)**
**Banneker,** Benjamin (almanacker and mathematician-astronomer on District of Columbia site survey); Ellicott, Md. **(1731-1806)**
**Banting,** Fredrick Grant (physiologist); Alliston, Ont., Canada **(1891-1941)**
**Bara,** Theda (Theodosia Goodman) (actress); Cincinnati **(1890-1955)**
**Barber,** Red (Walter Lanier) (sportscaster); Columbus, Miss., 2/17/1908
**Barber,** Samuel (composer); West Chester, Pa. **(1910-1981)**
**Barca,** Pedro Calderón del al (dramatist); Madrid **(1600-1681)**
**Bardot,** Brigitte (actress); Paris, 1935
**Barenboim,** Daniel (concert pianist and conductor); Buenos Aires, 11/15/1942
**Barnard,** Christiaan N. (heart surgeon); Beauford West, South Africa, 1923
**Barnum,** Phineas Taylor (showman); Bethel, Conn. **(1810-1891)**
**Barrie,** Sir James Matthew (author); Kirriemuir, Scotland **(1860-1937)**
**Barrie,** Wendy (actress); Hong Kong **(1913-1978)**
**Barry,** Gene (Eugene Klass) (actor); New York City, 6/4/1922
**Barry,** John (naval officer); County Wexford, Ireland **(1745-1803)**
**Barrymore,** Diana (actress); New York City **(1921-1960)**
**Barrymore,** Ethel (Ethel Blythe) (actress); Philadelphia **(1879-1959)**
**Barrymore,** Georgiana Drew (actress); Philadelphia **(1856-1893)**
**Barrymore,** John (John Blythe) (actor); Philadelphia **(1882-1942)**
**Barrymore,** Lionel (Lionel Blythe) (actor); Philadelphia **(1878-1954)**
**Barrymore,** Maurice (Herbert Blythe) (actor and playwright); Agra, India **(1847-1905)**
**Bartheime,** Donald (novelist); Philadelphia, 4/7/1931
**Barthelmess,** Richard (actor); New York City **(1897-1963)**
**Bartholomew,** Freddie (actor); London, 3/28/1924
**Bartók,** Béla (composer); Nagyszentmiklos (Romania) **(1881-1945)**
**Barton,** Clara (founder of American Red Cross); Oxford, Mass. **(1821-1912)**
**Baruch,** Bernard Mannes (statesman); Camden, S.C. **(1870-1965)**
**Baryshnikov,** Mikhail Nikolayevich (ballet dancer and artistic director); Riga, Latvia, 1/27/1948
**Basehart,** Richard (actor); Zanesville, Ohio **(1914-1984)**
**Basie,** Count (William) (band leader); Red Bank, N.J. **(1904-1984)**
**Bassey,** Shirley (singer); Cardiff, Wales, 1/8/1937
**Batchelor,** Clarence Daniel (political cartoonist); Osage City, Kan. **(1888-1977)**
**Bates,** Alan (actor); Allestree, England, 2/17/1934
**Battle,** Kathleen (soprano); Portsmouth, Ohio, 8/13/48
**Baudelaire,** Charles Pierre (poet); Paris **(1821-1867)**
**Baudouin** (King); Palace of Laeken, Belgium, 9/7/1930
**Baxter,** Anne (actress); Michigan City, Ind. **(1923-1985)**
**Baxter,** Warner (actor); Columbus, Ohio **(1891-1951)**
**Bean,** Orson (Dallas Frederick Burrows) (actor); Burlington, Vt., 7/22/1928
**Beardsley,** Aubrey Vincent (illustrator); Brighton, England **(1872-1898)**
**Beaton,** Cecil (photographer and designer); London **(1904-1980)**
**Beatty,** Warren (actor and producer); Richmond, Va., 3/30/1937
**Beaumont,** Francis (dramatist); Grace-Dieu, England **(1584-1616)**
**Becket,** Thomas à (Archbishop of Canterbury); London **(1118?-1170)**
**Beckett,** Samuel (playwright); Dublin, 4/13/1906
**Beckmann,** Karl (painter); Leipzig, Germany **(1884-1950)**
**Bede,** Saint ("The Venerable Bede") (scholar); Monkwearmouth, England **(673-735)**
**Beecham,** Sir Thomas (conductor); St. Helens, England **(1879-1961)**
**Beecher,** Henry Ward (clergyman); Litchfield, Conn. **(1813-1887)**
**Beerbohm,** Sir Max (author); London **(1872-1956)**
**Beery,** Noah, Jr. (actor); New York City, 8/10/1916
**Beery,** Wallace (actor); Kansas City, Mo. **(1886-1949)**
**Beethoven,** Ludwig van (composer); Bonn (Germany) **(1770-1827)**
**Begley,** Ed (actor); Hartford, Conn. **(1901-1970)**
**Belafonte,** Harry (singer and actor); New York City, 3/1/1927
**Belasco,** David (dramatist and producer); San Francisco **(1854-1931)**
**Bell,** Alexander Graham (inventor); Edinburgh, Scotland **(1847-1922)**
**Bellamy,** Edward (author); Chicopee Falls, Mass. **(1850-1898)**
**Bellamy,** Ralph (actor); Chicago, 6/17/1904
**Bellini,** Giovanni (painter); Venice **(c.1430-1516)**

Bellow, Saul (novelist); Lachine, Quebec, Canada, 7/10/1915
Bellows, George Wesley (painter and lithographer); Columbus, Ohio (1882-1925)
Belmonde, Jean-Paul (actor); Neuilly-sur-Seine, France, 4/9/1933
Belushi, John (comedian, actor); Chicago (1949-1982)
Benchley, Peter Bradford (novelist); New York City, 5/8/1940
Benchley, Robert Charles (humorist); Worcester, Mass. (1889-1945)
Bendix, William (actor); New York City (1906-1964)
Benes, Eduard (statesman); Kozlany (Czechoslovakia) (1884-1948)
Benét, Stephen Vincent (poet and story writer); Bethlehem, Pa. (1898-1943)
Benét, William Rose (poet and novelist); Ft. Hamilton, Brooklyn, N.Y. (1886-1950)
Ben-Gurion, David (David Green) (statesman); Plónsk (Poland) (1886-1973)
Benjamin, Richard (actor); New York City, 5/22/1938
Bennett, Constance (actress); New York City (1905-1965)
Bennett, Enoch Arnold (novelist and dramatist); Hanley, England (1867-1931)
Bennett, James Gordon (editor); Keith, Scotland (1795-1872)
Bennett, Joan (actress); Palisades, N.J., 2/27/1910
Bennett, Robert Russell (composer); Kansas City, Mo., (1894-1981)
Bennett, Tony (Anthony Benedetto) (singer); Astoria, Queens, N.Y., 8/3/1926
Benny, Jack (Benjamin Kubelsky) (comedian); Chicago (1894-1974)
Bentham, Jeremy Heinrich (economist); London (1748-1832)
Benton, Thomas Hart (painter); Neosho, Mo. (1889-1975)
Berg, Alban (composer); Vienna (1885-1935)
Berg, Gertrude (writer and actress); New York City (1899-1966)
Bergen, Candice (actress); Beverly Hills, Calif., 5/9/1946
Bergen, Edgar (ventriloquist); Chicago, (1903-1978)
Bergen, Polly (actress and singer); Knoxville, Tenn., 7/14/1930
Bergerac, Cyrano de (poet); Paris (1619-1655)
Bergman, Ingmar (film director); Uppsala, Sweden, 7/14/1918
Bergman, Ingrid (actress); Stockholm (1918-1982)
Bergson, Henri (philosopher); Paris (1859-1941)
Berle, Milton (Milton Berlinger) (comedian); New York City, 7/12/1908
Berlin, Irving (Israel Baline) (songwriter); Temum, Russia, 5/11/1888
Berlioz, Louis Hector (composer); La Côte-Saint-André, France (1803-1869)
Berman, Lazar (concert pianist); Leningrad, 1930.
Berman, Shelley (Sheldon) (comedian); Chicago, 2/3/1926
Bernardi, Herschel (actor); New York City (1922-1986)
Bernhardt, Sarah (Rosine Bernard) (actress); Paris (1844-1923)
Bernini, Gian Lorenzo (sculptor and painter); Naples (Italy) (1598-1680)
Bernoulli, Jacques (scientist); Basel, Switzerland (1654-1705)
Bernstein, Leonard (conductor); Lawrence, Mass., 8/25/1918
Berry, Chuck (Charles Edward Berry) (singer); San Jose, Calif., 1/15/1926
Betjeman, Sir John (Poet Laureate); London (1906-1984)
Bickford, Charles (actor); Cambridge, Mass. (1889-1967)
Bierce, Ambrose Gwinnett (journalist); Meigs County, Ohio (1842-1914?)
Bikel, Theodore (actor and folk singer); Vienna, 5/2/1924
Bing, Sir Rudolf (opera manager); Vienna, 1/9/1902
Bingham, George Caleb (painter); Augusta Co., Va. (1811-1879)
Bishop, Joey (Joseph Gottlieb) (comedian); New York City, 2/3/1919
Bismarck-Schönhausen, Prince Otto Eduard Leopold von (statesman); Schönhausen (East Germany) (1815-1898)
Bisset, Jacqueline (actress); Weybridge, England, 9/13/1944
Bixby, Bill (actor); San Francisco, 1/22/1934
Bizet, Georges (Alexandre César Léopold Bizet) (composer); Paris (1838-1875)
Black, Cilla (singer and actress); Liverpool, England, 5/27/1943
Black, Karen (actress); Park Ridge, Ill., 7/1/1942
Black, Shirley Temple (former actress); Santa Monica, Calif., 4/23/1928
Blackmer, Sidney (actor); Salisbury, N.C. (1898-1973)
Blackstone, Sir William (jurist); London (1723-1780)
Blaine, Vivian (actress and singer); Newark, N.J., 11/21/1924
Blair, Janet (actress); Altoona, Pa., 4/23/1921
Blake, Amanda (Beverly Louise Neill) (actress); Buffalo, N.Y., 1931
Blake, Eubie (James Hubert) (pianist); Baltimore, (1883-1983)
Blake, Robert (Michael Gubitosi) (actor); Nutley, N.J., 9/18/1933
Blake, William (poet and artist); London (1757-1827)
Blanc, Mel(vin Jerome) (actor and voice specialist); San Francisco, 5/30/1908
Blass, Bill (fashion designer); Fort Wayne, Ind., 6/22/1922
Bloch, Ernest (composer); Geneva (1880-1959)
Blondell, Joan (actress); New York City (1909-1979)
Bloom, Claire (actress); London, 2/15/1931
Bloomgarden, Kermit (producer); Brooklyn, N.Y. (1904-1976)
Blue, Monte (actor); Indianapolis (1890-1963)
Blyth, Ann (actress); New York City, 8/16/1928

Boccaccio, Giovanni (author); Paris (1313-1375)
Boccherini, Luigi (Rodolfo) (composer); Lucca, Italy (1743-1805)
Boccioni, Umberto (painter and sculptor); Reggio di Calabria, Italy (1882-1916)
Bock, Jerry (composer); New Haven, Conn., 11/23/1928
Bogarde, Dirk (Derek Van den Bogaerde) (film actor and director); London, 3/28/1921
Bogart, Humphrey DeForest (actor); New York City (1899-1957)
Bogdanovich, Peter (producer and director); Kingston, N.Y., 7/30/1939
Bohlen, Charles E. (diplomat); Clayton, N.Y. (1904-1974)
Bbhr, Niels (atomic physicist); Copenhagen (1885-1962)
Bolger, Ray (dancer and actor); Dorchester, Mass., 1/10/1904
Bolivar, Simón (South American liberator); Caracas, Venezuela (1783-1830)
Bologna, Giovanni da (sculptor); Douai (France) (1529-1608)
Bombeck, Erma (author, columnist); Dayton, Ohio 2/21/1927
Bonaparte, Napoleon (Emperor of the French); Ajaccio, Corsica (France) (1769-1821)
Bond, Julian (Georgia legislator); Nashville, Tenn., 1/14/1940
Bondi, Beulah (actress); Chicago (1883-1981)
Bonnard, Pierre (painter); Fontenayaux-Roses, France (1867-1947)
Bono, Sonny (Salvatore) (singer); Detroit, 2/16/1935
Boone, Daniel (frontiersman); nr. Reading, Pa. (1734-1820)
Boone, Pat (Charles) (singer); Jacksonville, Fla., 6/1/1934
Boone, Richard (actor); Los Angeles (1917-1981)
Booth, Edwin Thomas (actor); Bel Air, Md. (1833-1893)
Booth, Evangeline Cory (religious leader); London (1865-1950)
Booth, John Wilkes (actor; assassin of Lincoln); Harford County, Md. (1838-1865)
Booth, Shirley (Thelma Booth Ford) (actress); New York City, 8/30/1907
Bordoni, Irene (actress); Ajaccio (France) (1895-1953)
Borge, Victor (pianist and comedian); Copenhagen, 1/3/1909
Borgia, Cesare (nobleman and soldier); Rome (1475?-1507)
Borgia, Lucrezia (Duchess of Ferrara); Rome (1480-1519)
Borgnine, Ernest (actor); Hamden, Conn., 1/24/1917
Borromini, Francesco (architect); Bissone (Italy) (1599-1667)
Bosch, Hieronymus (Hieronymus van Aeken) (painter); Hertogenbosch (Netherlands) (c.1450-1516)
Bosley, Tom (actor); Chicago, 10/1/1927
Boswell, Connee (singer); New Orleans (1907-1976)
Boswell, James (diarist and biographer); Edinburgh, Scotland (1740-1795)
Botticelli, Sandro (Alessandro di Mariano dei Filipepi) (painter); Florence (Italy) (1444?-1510)
Boulez, Pierre (conductor); Montbrison, France, 3/26/1925
Bourke-White, Margaret (photographer); New York City (1906-1971)
Bow, Clara (actress); Brooklyn, N.Y. (1905-1965)
Bowen, Catherine Drinker (biographer); Haverford, Pa. (1897-1973)
Bowie, David (David Robert Jones) (actor and musician); London, 1/8/1947(?)
Bowie, James (soldier); Burke County, Ga. (1799-1836)
Bowles, Chester (diplomat); Springfield, Mass. (1901-1986)
Boyce, William (composer); London? (1710-1779)
Boyd, Bill (William) ("Hopalong Cassidy") (actor); Cambridge, Ohio (1898-1972)
Boyd, Stephen (Stephen Millar) (actor); Belfast, Northern Ireland (1928-1977)
Boyer, Charles (actor); Figeac, France (1899-1978)
Boy George (George Alan O'Dowd) (singer); London, 1961
Boyle, Robert (scientist); Lismore Castle, Munster, Ireland (1627-1691)
Bracken, Eddie (actor); Astoria, Queens, N.Y., 2/7/1920
Bradbury, Ray Douglas (science-fiction writer); Waukegan, Ill., 8/22/1920
Bradlee, Benjamin C. (editor); Boston, 8/26/1921
Bradley, Omar N. (5-star general); Clark, Mo. (1893-1981)
Bradley, Thomas (Mayor of Los Angeles); Calvert, Tex., 12/29/1917
Brady, Scott (actor); Brooklyn, N.Y., (1924-1985)
Brahe, Tycho (astronomer); Knudstrup, Denmark (1546-1601)
Brahms, Johannes (composer); Hamburg (1833-1897)
Braille, Louis (teacher of blind); Coupvray, France (1809-1862)
Brailowsky, Alexander (pianist); Kiev, Russia (1896-1976)
Bramante, Donato D'Agnolo (architect); Monte Asdrualdo (now Fermignano, Italy) (1444-1514)
Brancusi, Constantin (sculptor); Pestisansi, Romania (1876-1957)
Brando, Marlon (actor); Omaha, Neb., 4/3/1924
Brandt, Willy (Herbert Frahm) (ex-Chancellor); Lübeck, Germany, 12/18/1913
Braque, Georges (painter); Argenteuil, France (1882-1963)
Brazzi, Rossano (actor); Bologna, Italy, 9/18/1916
Brecht, Bertolt (dramatist and poet); Augsburg, Bavaria (1898-1956)
Brel, Jacques (singer and composer); Brussels, (1929-1978)
Brennan, Walter (actor); Lynn, Mass. (1894-1974)
Brent, George (actor); Dublin (1904-1979)

**Breslin,** Jimmy (journalist); Jamaica, Queens, N.Y., 10/17/1930

**Breuer,** Marcel (architect and designer); Pécs, Hungary **(1902-1981)**

**Brewer,** Teresa (singer); Toledo, Ohio, 5/7/1931

**Brewster,** Kingman, Jr. (ex-president of Yale); Longmeadow, Mass., 6/17/1919

**Brezhnev,** Leonid I. (Communist Party Secretary); Dneprodzerzhinsk, Ukraine **(1906-1982)**

**Brice,** Fanny (Fannie Borach) (comedienne); New York City **(1892-1951)**

**Bridges,** Beau (actor); Los Angeles, 12/9/1941

**Bridges,** Lloyd (actor); San Leandro, Calif. 1/15/1913

**Brinkley,** David (TV newscaster); Wilmington, N.C., 7/10/1920

**Britt,** May (Maybritt Wilkins) (actress); Sweden, 3/22/1936

**Britten,** Benjamin (composer); Lowestoft, England **(1913-1976)**

**Britton,** Barbara (actress); Long Beach, Calif. **(1920-1980)**

**Bromfield,** Louis (novelist); Mansfield, Ohio **(1896-1956)**

**Bronson,** Charles (Charles Buchinsky) (actor); Ehrenfield, Pa., 11/3/1922(?)

**Brontë,** Charlotte (novelist); Thornton, England **(1816-1855)**

**Brontë,** Emily Jane (novelist); Thornton, England **(1818-1848)**

**Bronzino,** Agnolo (painter); Monticelli (Italy) **(1503-1572)**

**Brook,** Peter (director); London, 3/21/1925

**Brooke,** Rupert (poet); Rugby, England **(1887-1915)**

**Brooks,** Geraldine (Geraldine Stroock) (actress); New York City **(1925-1977)**

**Brooks,** Gwendolyn (poet); Topeka, Kan., 6/7/1917

**Brooks,** Mel (Melvin Kaminsky) (writer and film director); Brooklyn, N.Y., 1926(?)

**Broun,** Matthew Heywood Campbell (journalist); Brooklyn, N.Y. **(1888-1939)**

**Brown,** Helen Gurley (author); Green Forest, Ark., 2/18/1922

**Brown,** James (singer); Augusta, Ga., 5/3/1934

**Brown,** Joe E. (comedian); Holgate, Ohio **(1892-1973)**

**Brown,** John (abolitionist); Torrington, Conn. **(1800-1859)**

**Brown,** John Mason (critic); Louisville, Ky. **(1900-1969)**

**Brown,** Les (band leader); Reinerton, Pa., 1912

**Brown,** Pamela (actress); London **(1918-1975)**

**Brown,** Vanessa (Smylla Brind) (actress); Vienna, 3/24/1928

**Browne,** Jackson (singer and guitarist); Heidelberg, Germany, 10/9/late 1940s

**Browning,** Elizabeth Barrett (poet); Durham, England **(1806-1861)**

**Browning,** Robert (poet); London **(1812-1889)**

**Brubeck,** Dave (musician); Concord, Calif., 12/6/1920

**Bruce,** Lenny (comedian); Long Island, N.Y. **(1926-1966)**

**Brueghel,** Pieter (painter); nr. Breda, Flanders (Netherlands) **(1520?-1569)**

**Bruhn,** Erik (Belton Evers) (ballet dancer); Copenhagen **(1928-1986)**

**Brunelleschi,** Filippo (architect); Florence (Italy) **(1377-1446)**

**Bruno,** Giordano (philosopher); Nola, Italy **(1548-1600)**

**Brutus,** Marcus Junius (Roman politician); (85?-42 B.C.)

**Bryan,** William Jennings (orator and politician); Salem, Ill. **(1860-1925)**

**Bryant,** Anita (singer); Barnsdall, Okla., 3/25/1940

**Bryant,** William Cullen (poet and editor); Cummington, Mass. **(1794-1878)**

**Brynner,** Yul (Taidje Khan) (actor); Sakhalin Island, Russia **(1920-1985)**

**Brzezinski,** Zbigniew (ex-presidential adviser); Warsaw, 3/28/1928

**Buber,** Martin (philosopher and theologian); Vienna **(1878-1965)**

**Buchanan,** Edgar (actor); Humansville, Mo., **(1903-1979)**

**Buchholz,** Horst (actor); Berlin, 12/4/1933

**Buchwald,** Art (Arthur) (columnist); Mount Vernon, N.Y., 10/20/1925

**Buck,** Pearl S(ydenstricker) (author); Hillsboro, W. Va. **(1892-1973)**

**Buckley,** William F., Jr. (journalist); New York City, 11/24/1925

**Buddha.** *See* Gautama Buddha

**Buffalo Bill** (William Frederick Cody) (scout); Scott County, Iowa **(1846-1917)**

**Bujold,** Genevieve (actress); Montreal, 7/1/1942

**Bujones,** Fernando (ballet dancer); Miami, Fla., 3/9/1955

**Bullins,** Ed (playwright); Philadelphia, 7/2/1935

**Bumbry,** Grace (mezzo-soprano); St. Louis, 1/4/1937

**Bunche,** Ralph J. (statesman); Detroit **(1904-1971)**

**Bundy,** McGeorge (educator); Boston, 3/30/1919

**Bundy,** William Putnam (editor); Washington, D.C., 9/24/1917

**Buñuel,** Luis (film director); Calanda, Spain, **(1900-1983)**

**Bunyan,** John (preacher and author); Elstow, England **(1628-1688)**

**Burbank,** Luther (horticulturist); Lancaster, Mass. **(1849-1926)**

**Burke,** Adm. Arleigh A. (ex-Chief of Naval Operations); Boulder, Colo., 10/19/1901

**Burke,** Billie (comedienne); Washington, D.C. **(1885-1970)**

**Burke,** Edmund (statesman); Dublin **(1729-1797)**

**Burne-Jones,** Edward Coley (painter); Birmingham, England **(1833-1898)**

**Burnett,** Carol (comedienne); San Antonio, 4/26/1936

**Burney,** Fanny (Frances) (writer); King's Lynn, England **(1752-1840)**

**Burns,** George (Nathan Birnbaum) (comedian); New York City, 1/20/1896

**Burns,** Robert (poet); Alloway, Scotland **(1759-1796)**

**Burr,** Aaron (political leader); Newark, N.J. **(1756-1836)**

**Burr,** Raymond (William Stacey Burr) (actor); New Westminster, British Columbia, Canada, 5/21/1917

**Burroughs,** Edgar Rice (novelist); Chicago **(1875-1950)**

**Burrows,** Abe (playwright and director); New York City, **(1910-1985)**

**Burstyn,** Ellen (Edna Rae Gillooly) (actress); Detroit, 12/7/1932

**Burton,** Richard (Richard Jenkins) (actor); Pontrhydfen, Wales **(1925-1984)**

**Bush,** Vannevar (scientist); Everett, Mass. **(1890-1974)**

**Bushman,** Francis X. (actor); Baltimore **(1883-1966)**

**Butler,** Samuel (author); Langar, England **(1835-1902)**

**Buttons,** Red (Aaron Chwatt) (actor); New York City, 2/5/1919

**Buzzi,** Ruth (comedienne); Wequetequock, Conn., 7/24/1936

**Byrd,** Richard Evelyn (polar explorer); Winchester, Va. **(1888-1957)**

**Byron,** George Gordon (6th Baron Byron) (poet); London **(1788-1824)**

# C

**Caan,** James (actor); The Bronx, N.Y., 3/26/1939

**Cabot,** John (Giovanni Caboto) (navigator); Genoa (?) **(1450-1498)**

**Cabot,** Sebastian (navigator); Venice **(1476?-1557)**

**Cadmus,** Paul (painter and etcher); New York City, 12/17/1904

**Caesar,** Gaius Julius (statesman); Rome (100?-44 B.C.)

**Caesar,** Sid (comedian); Yonkers, N.Y., 9/8/1922

**Cagney,** James (actor); New York City **(1899-1986)**

**Cahn,** Sammy (songwriter); New York City, 6/18/1913

**Caine,** Michael (Maurice J. Micklewhite) (actor); London, 3/14/1933

**Calder,** Alexander (sculptor); Lawnton, Pa. **(1898-1976)**

**Caldwell,** Erskine (novelist); White Oak, Ga., 12/17/1903

**Caldwell,** Sarah (opera director and conductor); Maryville, Mo., 1928

**Caldwell,** Taylor (novelist); Manchester, England **(1900-1985)**

**Caldwell,** Zoe (actress); Hawthorn, Australia, 9/14/1933

**Calhern,** Louis (Carl Henry Vogt) (actor); Brooklyn, N.Y. **(1895-1956)**

**Calhoun,** John Caldwell (statesman); nr. Calhoun Mills, S.C. **(1782-1850)**

**Calisher,** Hortense (novelist); New York City, 12/20/1911

**Callas,** Maria (Maria Calogeropoulos) (dramatic soprano); New York City **(1923-1977)**

**Calloway,** Cab (Cabell) (band leader); Rochester, N.Y., 12/25/1907

**Colvet,** Corinne (actress); Paris, 4/30/1926

**Calvin,** John (Jean Chauvin) (religious reformer); Noyon, Picardy **(1509-1564)**

**Cambridge,** Godfrey (comedian); New York City **(1933-1976)**

**Cameron,** Rod (Rod Cox) (actor); Calgary, Alberta, Canada, **(1912-1983)**

**Campbell,** Glen (singer); nr. Delight, Ark., 4/22/1938

**Camus,** Albert (author); Mondovi, Algeria **(1913-1960)**

**Canaletto,** (Giovanni Antonio Canale); (painter) Venice **(1697-1768)**

**Caniff,** Milton (cartoonist); Hillsboro, Ohio, 2/28/1907

**Cannon,** Dyan (actress); Tacoma, Wash., 1/4/1937

**Canova,** Judy (comedienne); Jacksonville, Fla., **(1916-1983)**

**Cantinflas** (Mario Moreno) (comedian); Mexico City, 8/12/1911

**Cantor,** Eddie (Edward Iskowitz) (actor); New York City **(1892-1964)**

**Cantrell,** Lana (singer); Sydney, Australia, 1944

**Capote,** Truman (novelist); New Orleans **(1924-1984)**

**Capp,** Al (Alfred Gerald Caplin) (cartoonist); New Haven, Conn. **(1909-1979)**

**Capra,** Frank (film producer, director); Palermo, Italy, 5/18/1897

**Caravaggio,** Michelangelo Merisi da (painter); Caravaggio (Italy) **(1573-1610)**

**Cardin,** Pierre (fashion designer); nr. Venice, 7/7/1922

**Cardinale,** Claudia (actress); Tunis, Tunisia, 1939

**Carey,** Harry (actor); New York City **(1878-1947)**

**Carey,** Macdonald (actor); Sioux City, Iowa, 3/15/1913

**Carlisle,** Kitty (singer and actress); New Orleans, 9/3/1915

**Carlson,** Richard (actor); Albert Lea, Minn., **(1912-1977)**

**Carlyle,** Thomas (essayist and historian); Ecclefechan, Scotland **(1795-1881)**

**Carmichael,** Hoagy (Hoagland Howard) (songwriter); Bloomington, Ind. **(1899-1981)**

**Carne,** Judy (Joyce Botterill) (singer); Northampton, England, 1939

**Carnegie,** Andrew (industrialist); Dunfermline, Scotland **(1835-1919)**

**Carney,** Art (actor); Mt. Vernon, N.Y., 11/4/1918

**Carnovsky,** Morris (actor); St. Louis, 9/5/1897

**Caron,** Leslie (actress); Paris, 7/1/1931

**Carr,** Vikki (singer); El Paso, 7/19/1942

**Carracci,** Annibale (painter); Bologna (Italy) **(1560-1609)**

**Carracci,** Lodovico (painter); Bologna (Italy) **(1555-1619)**

**Carradine,** David (actor); Hollywood, Calif., 12/8/1936

**Carradine,** John (actor); New York City, 2/5/1906

Carrillo, Leo (actor); Los Angeles **(1881-1961)**
Carroll, Diahann (Carol Diahann Johnson) (singer and actress); Bronx, N.Y., 7/17/1935
Carroll, Leo G. (actor); Weedon, England **(1892-1972)**
Carroll, Lewis (Charles Lutwidge Dodgson) (author and mathematician); Daresbury, England **(1832-1898)**
Carroll, Madeleine (actress); West Bromwich, England, 2/26/1909
Carroll, Pat (comedienne); Shreveport, La., 5/5/1927
Carson, Johnny (TV entertainer); Corning, Iowa, 10/23/1925
Carson, Kit (Christopher) (scout); Madison County, Ky. **(1809-1868)**
Carson, Rachel (biologist and author); Springdale, Pa. **(1907-1964)**
Carter, (Bessie) Lillian (President's mother); Richland, Ga. **(1898-1983)**
Carter, Jack (comedian); New York City, 1923
Cartier, Jacques (explorer); Saint-Malo, Brittany (France) **(1491-1557)**
Cartier-Brisson, Henri (photographer); Chanteloup, France, 8/22/1908
Cartland, Barbara (author); England, 7/9/1901
Caruso, Enrico (Errico) (tenor); Naples, Italy **(1873-1921)**
Carver, George Washington (botanist); Missouri **(1864-1943)**
Cary, Arthur Joyce Lunel (novelist); Londonderry, Ireland **(1888-1957)**
Casals, Pablo (cellist); Vendrell, Spain **(1876-1973)**
Casanova de Seingalt, Giovanni Jacopo (adventurer); Venice **(1725-1798)**
Cash, Johnny (singer); nr. Kingsland, Ark., 2/26/1932
Cass, Peggy (comedienne); Boston, 5/21/1924
Cassatt, Mary (painter); Allegheny, Pa. **(1844-1926)**
Cassavetes, John (actor and director); New York City, 12/9/1929
Cassidy, David (singer); New York City, 4/12/1950
Cassidy, Jack (actor); Richmond Hill, Queens, N.Y. **(1927-1976)**
Cassini, Oleg (Oleg Lolewski-Cassini) (fashion designer); Paris, 4/11/1913
Castagno, Andrea del (painter); San Martino a Corella (Italy) **(c.1421-1457)**
Castellano, Richard (actor); New York City, 9/2/1934
Castle, Irene (Irene Foote) (actress and dancer); New Rochelle, N.Y. **(1893-1969)**
Castle, Vernon Blythe (dancer and aviator); Norwich, England **(1887-1918)**
Castro Ruz, Fidel (Premier); Mayari, Oriente, Cuba, 8/13/1926
Cather, Willa Sibert (novelist); Winchester, Va. **(1876-1947)**
Cato, Marcus Porcius (called Cato the Elder) (statesman); Tusculum (Italy) (234-149 B.C.)
Catt, Carrie Chapman Lane (woman suffragist); Ripon, Wis. **(1859-1947)**
Catton, Bruce (historian); Petoskey, Mich. **(1899-1978)**
Cavaliaro, Carmen (band leader); New York City, 1913
Cavett, Dick (Richard) (TV entertainer); Gibbon, Neb., 11/19/1936
Cellini, Benvenuto (goldsmith and sculptor); Florence (Italy) **(1500-1571)**
Cervantes Saavedra, Miguel de (novelist); Alcalá de Henares, Spain **(1547-1616)**
Cézanne, Paul (painter); Aix-en-Provence, France **(1839-1906)**
Chagall, Marc (painter); Vitebsk, Russia, **(1887-1985)**
Chaliapin, Feodor Ivanovitch (operatic basso); Kazan, Russia **(1873-1938)**
Chamberlain, Arthur Neville (statesman); Edgbaston, England **(1869-1940)**
Chamberlain, Richard (actor); Los Angeles, 3/31/1935(?)
Champion, Gower (choreographer); Geneva, Ill. **(1921-1980)**
Champion, Marge (actress and dancer); Los Angeles, 9/2/1923
Champlain, Samuel de (explorer); nr. Rochefort, France **(1567?-1635)**
Chancellor, John (TV commentator); Chicago, 7/14/1927
Chandler, Raymond (writer); Chicago **(1883-1959)**
Chanel, "Coco" (Gabriel Bonheur) (fashion designer); Issoire France **(1883-1971)**
Chaney, Lon (actor); Colorado Springs, Colo. **(1883-1930)**
Channing, Carol (actress); Seattle, 1/31/1923
Chaplin, Geraldine (actress); Santa Monica, Calif., 7/31/1944
Chaplin, Sir Charles (actor); London **(1889-1977)**
Charisse, Cyd (Tula Finklea) (dancer and actress); Amarillo, Tex., 3/8/1923
Charlemagne (Holy Roman Emperor); birthplace unknown **(742-814)**
Charles, Ray (Ray Charles Robinson) (pianist, singer, and songwriter); Albany Ga., 9/23/1930
Chase, Chevy (Cornelius Crane Chase) (comedian); New York City, 10/8/1943
Chase, Ilka (author and actress); New York City **(1905-1978)**
Chase, Lucia (founder Ballet Theatre [now American Ballet Theatre]); Waterbury, Conn. **(1907-1986)**
Chatterton, Ruth (actress); New York City **(1893-1961)**
Chaucer, Geoffrey (poet); London **(1340?-1400)**
Chávez, Carlos (composer); nr. Mexico City **(1899-1978)**

Chavez, Cesar (labor leader); nr. Yuma, Ariz., 3/31/1927
Chayefsky, Paddy (Sidney) (playwright); New York City, **(1923-1981)**
Checker, Chubby (Ernest Evans) (performer); Philadelphia, 10/3/1941
Cheever, John (novelist); Quincy, Mass. **(1912-1982)**
Chekhov, Anton Pavlovich (dramatist and short-story writer); Taganrog, Russia **(1860-1904)**
Cher (Cherilyn LaPiere) (singer); El Centro, Calif., 5/20/1946
Cherubini, Luigi (composer); Florence **(1760-1842)**
Chesterton, Gilbert Keith (author); Kensington, England **(1874-1936)**
Chevalier, Maurice (entertainer); Paris **(1888-1972)**
Chiang Kai-shek (Chief of State); Feng-hwa, China **(1887-1975)**
Child, Julia (food expert); Pasadena, Calif., 8/15/1912
Chippendale, Thomas (cabinet-maker); Otley, England **(1718?-1779)**
Chirico, Giorgio de (painter); Vólos, Greece, **(1888-1978)**
Chisholm, Shirley (ex-Representative); Brooklyn, N.Y., 11/30/1924
Chopin, Frédéric François (composer); nr. Warsaw **(1810-1849)**
Chou En-lai. *See* Zhou Enlai
Christian, Linda (Blanca Rosa Welter) (actress); Tampico, Mexico, 11/13/1924
Christie, Agatha (mystery writer); Torquay, England, **(1890-1976)**
Christie, Julie (actress); Chukua, India, 4/14/1941
Christopher, Jordon (actor and musician); Youngstown, Ohio, 1941
Christy, June (singer); Springfield, Ill., 1925
Churchill, Sir Winston Leonard Spencer (statesman); Blenheim Palace, Oxfordshire, England **(1874-1965)**
Cicero, Marcus Tullius (orator and statesman); Arpinum (Italy) (106-43 B.C.)
Cid, El (Rodrigo (or Ruy) Díez de Bivar) (Spanish national hero); nr. Burgos, Spain **(1040?-1099)**
Cilento, Diane (actress); Queensland, Australia, 10/5/1933
Cimabue, Giovanni (painter); Florence (Italy) **(c.1240-c.1302)**
Cimino, Michael (film director); New York City, 1943(?)
Clair, René (René Chomette) (film director); Paris **(1898-1981)**
Claire, Ina (Ina Fagan) (actress); Washington, D.C., **(1895-1985)**
Clapton, Eric (singer and guitarist); Ripley, England, 3/30/1945
Clark, Dane (Barney Zanville) (actor); New York City, 2/18/1915
Clark, Dick (TV personality); Mt. Vernon, N.Y., 11/30/1929
Clark, Mark W. (general); Madison Barracks, N.Y. **(1896-1984)**
Clark, Petula (singer); Epsom, England, 11/15/1934
Clark, Roy (country music artist); Meherrin, Va., 4/15/1933
Clark, William (explorer); Caroline County, Va. **(1770-1838)**
Claude Lorrain (Claude Gellée) (painter); Champagne, France **(1600-1682)**
Clausewitz, Karl von (military strategist); Burg (East Germany) **(1780-1831)**
Clay, Henry (statesman); Hanover County, Va. **(1777-1852)**
Clay, Lucius D. (banker, ex-general); Marietta, Ga. **(1897-1978)**
Clayburgh, Jill (actress); New York City, 4/30/1944
Clemenceau, Georges (statesman); Mouilleron-en-Pareds, Vondée, France **(1841-1929)**
Clemens, Samuel L. *See* Mark Twain
Cleopatra (Queen of Egypt); Alexandria, Egypt (69-30 B.C.)
Cliburn, Van (Harvey Lavan Cliburn, Jr.) (concert pianist); Shreveport, La., 7/12/1934
Clifford, Clark M. (ex-Secretary of Defense); Ft. Scott, Kan., 12/25/1906
Clift, Montgomery (actor); Omaha, Neb. **(1920-1966)**
Clooney, Rosemary (singer); Maysville, Ky., 5/23/1928
Close, Glenn (actress); Greenwich, Conn., 3/19/1947
Clurman, Harold (stage producer); New York City **(1901-1980)**
Cobb, Irvin Shrewsbury (humorist); Paducah, Ky. **(1876-1944)**
Cobb, Lee J. (Leo Jacob) (actor); New York City **(1911-1976)**
Coburn, Charles Douville (actor); Savannah, Ga. **(1877-1961)**
Coburn, James (actor); Laurel, Neb., 8/31/1928
Coca, Imogene (comedienne); Philadelphia, 11/18/1908
Cocker, Joe (John Robert Cocker) (singer); Sheffield, England, 5/20/1944
Coco, James (actor); New York City, 3/21/1929
Cocteau, Jean (author); Maison-Lafitte, France **(1891-1963)**
Cody, W. F. *See* Buffalo Bill
Cohan, George Michael (actor and dramatist); Providence, R.I. **(1878-1942)**
Colbert, Claudette (Lily Chauchoin) (actress); Paris, 9/13/1903
Colby, William E. (ex-Director of CIA); St. Paul, 1/4/1920
Cole, Nat "King" (singer); Montgomery, Ala. **(1919-1965)**
Cole, Natalie (singer); Los Angeles, 2/6/1950
Cole, Thomas (painter); Lancashire, England **(1801-1848)**
Coleridge, Samuel Taylor (poet); Ottery St. Mary, England **(1772-1834)**
Colette (Sidonie-Gabrielle Colette) (novelist); St.-Sauveur, France **(c. 1873-1954)**
Collingwood, Charles (TV commentator); Three Rivers, Mich. **(1917-1985)**
Collins, Dorothy (Marjorie Chandler) (singer); Windsor, Ontario, Canada, 11/18/1926

**Collins,** Joan (actress); London 5/23/1933
**Collins,** Judy (singer); Seattle, 5/1/1939
**Colman,** Ronald (actor); Richmond, England **(1891-1958)**
**Colonna,** Jerry (comedian); Boston, 1905
**Columbus,** Christopher (Cristoforo Colombo) (discoverer of America); Genoa (Italy) **(1451-1506)**
**Comden,** Betty (writer); New York City, 5/3/1919
**Comenius,** Johann Amos (educational reformer) Nivnice, Moravia (Czechoslovakia) **(1592-1670)**
**Commager,** Henry Steele (historian); Pittsburgh, 10/25/1902
**Como,** Perry (Pierino) (singer); Canonsburg, Pa., 5/18/1913
**Compton,** Karl Taylor (physicist); Wooster, Ohio **(1887-1954)**
**Comte,** Auguste (philosopher); Montpellier, France **(1798-1857)**
**Conant,** James B. (educator and statesman); Dorchester, Mass. **(1893-1978)**
**Condon,** Eddie (jazz musician); Goodland, Ind. **(1905-1973)**
**Confucius** (K'ung Fu-tzu) (philosopher); Shantung province, China **(c. 551-479 B.C.)**
**Congreve,** William (dramatist); nr. Leeds, England **(1670-1729)**
**Connelly,** Marc (playwright); McKeesport, Pa. **(1890-1980)**
**Connery,** Sean (actor); Edinburgh, Scotland, 8/25/1930
**Conniff,** Ray (band leader); Attleboro, Mass., 11/6/1916
**Connors,** Chuck (actor); Brooklyn, N.Y., 4/10/1921
**Connors,** Mike (Krekor Ohanian) (actor); Fresno, Calif., 8/15/1925
**Conrad,** Joseph (Teodor Jozef Konrad Korzeniowski) (novelist); Berdichev, Ukraine **(1857-1924)**
**Conrad,** Robert (Conrad Robert Falk) (actor); Chicago, 3/1/1935
**Conrad,** William (actor); Louisville, Ky., 9/27/1920
**Conried,** Hans (Frank Foster) (actor); Baltimore **(1915-1982)**
**Constable,** John (painter); East Bergholt, Suffolk, England **(1776-1837)**
**Constantine II** (ex-king); Athens, 6/2/1940
**Conte,** Richard (actor); New York City **(1916-1975)**
**Conti,** Tom (actor); Paisley, Scotland, 11/22/1941
**Converse,** Frank (actor); St. Louis, 1938
**Conway,** Tim (comedian); Chagrin Falls, Ohio, 12/15/1933
**Coogan,** Jackie (actor); Los Angeles **(1914-1984)**
**Cooke,** Alistair (Alfred Alistair); (TV narrator and journalist); Manchester, England, 11/20/1908
**Cooley,** Denton A(rthur) (heart surgeon); Houston, Tex., 8/22/1920
**Coolidge,** Rita (singer); Nashville, Tenn., 1944
**Cooper,** Alice (Vincent Furnier) (rock musician); Detroit, 2/4/1948
**Cooper,** Gary (Frank James Cooper) (actor); Helena, Mont. **(1901-1961)**
**Cooper,** Jackie (actor and director); Los Angeles, 9/15/1922
**Cooper,** James Fenimore (novelist); Burlington, N.J. **(1789-1851)**
**Cooper,** Peter (industrialist and philanthropist); New York City **(1791-1883)**
**Copernicus,** Nicolaus (Mikolaj Kopernik) (astronomer); Thorn, Poland **(1473-1543)**
**Copland,** Aaron (composer); Brooklyn, N.Y., 11/14/1900
**Copley,** John Singleton (painter); Boston, Mass. **(1738-1815)**
**Coppolla,** Francis Ford (film director); Detroit, 4/7/1939
**Corelli,** Arcangelo (composer); Fusignano, Italy **(1653-1713)**
**Corelli,** Franco (operatic tenor); Ancona, Italy, 4/8/1923
**Corneille,** Pierre (dramatist); Rouen, France **(1606-1684)**
**Cornell,** Katharine (actress); Berlin **(1893-1974)**
**Coret,** Jean Baptiste Camille (painter); Paris **(1796-1875)**
**Correggio,** Antonio Allegri da (painter); Correggio (Italy) **(1494-1534)**
**Corsaro,** Frank (opera director); New York harbor, 12/22/1924
**Cortés** (or Cortez), Hernando (explorer); Medellin, Spain **(1485-1547)**
**Cosby,** Bill (actor); Philadelphia, 7/12/1937
**Cosell,** Howard (Howard Cohen) (sportscaster); Winston-Salem, N.C., 3/25/1920
**Costa-Gavras,** Henri (Kostantinos Gavras) (film director); Athens, 1933
**Costello,** Elvis (Declan Patrick McManus) (singer-musician-songwriter); London, 1954
**Costello,** Lou (comedian); Paterson, N.J. **(1908-1959)**
**Cotten,** Joseph (actor); Petersburg, Va., 5/15/1905
**Couperin,** François (composer); Paris **(1668-1733)**
**Courbet,** Gustave (painter); Ornans, France **(1819-1877)**
**Courrèges,** André (fashion designer); Pau, France, 3/9/1923
**Courtenay,** Tom (actor); Hull, England, 2/25/1937
**Cousins,** Norman (publisher); Union Hill, N.J., 6/24/1915
**Cousteau,** Jacques-Yves (marine explorer); St. André-de-Cubzac, France, 6/11/1910
**Coward,** Sir Noel (playwright and actor); Teddington, England **(1899-1973)**
**Cowles,** Gardner, Jr. (newspaper publisher); Algona, Iowa, **(1903-1985)**
**Cowper,** William (poet); Great Berkhamstead, England **(1731-1800)**
**Cozzens,** James Gould (novelist); Chicago **(1903-1978)**
**Crabbe,** Buster (Clarence) (actor); Oakland, Calif. **(1908-1983)**

**Crain,** Jeanne (actress); Barstow, Calif., 5/25/1925
**Cranach,** Lucas, the elder (painter); Kronach (Germany) **(1472-1553)**
**Crane,** Hart (poet); Garrettsville, Ohio **(1899-1932)**
**Crane,** Stephen (novelist and poet); Newark, N.J. **(1871-1900)**
**Cranmer,** Thomas (churchman); Aslacton, England **(1489-1556)**
**Crawford,** Broderick (actor); Philadelphia **(1911-1986)**
**Crawford,** Cheryl (stage producer); Akron, Ohio, 9/24/1902
**Crawford,** Joan (Lucille LeSueur) (actress and business executive); San Antonio **(1908-1977)**
**Crenna,** Richard (actor); Los Angeles, 11/30/1927
**Crespin,** Régine (operatic soprano); Marseilles, France, 2/23/1929
**Crichton,** (John) Michael (novelist); Chicago, 10/23/1942
**Crisp,** Donald (actor); London **(1880-1974)**
**Croce,** Benedetto (philosopher); Peseasseroli, Aquila, Italy **(1866-1952)**
**Croce,** Jim (singer); Philadelphia **(1942-1973)**
**Crockett,** Davy (David) (frontiersman); Greene County, Tenn. **(1786-1836)**
**Cromwell,** Oliver (statesman); Huntingdon, England **(1599-1658)**
**Cronin,** A. J. (Archibald J. Cronin) (novelist); Cardross, Scotland **(1896-1981)**
**Cronkite,** Walter (TV newscaster); St. Joseph, Mo., 11/4/1916
**Cronyn,** Hume (actor); London, Ontario, Canada, 7/18/1911
**Crosby,** Bing (Harry Lillis) (singer, actor); Tacoma, Wash. **(1904-1977)**
**Crosby,** Bob (musician); Spokane, Wash., 8/23/1913
**Cross,** Ben (Bernard) (actor); Paddington, England, 12/16/1947
**Cross,** Milton (opera commentator); New York City **(1897-1975)**
**Crouse,** Russel (playwright); Findlay, Ohio **(1893-1966)**
**Cugat,** Xavier (band leader); Barcelona, Spain, 1/1/1900
**Cukor,** George (film director); New York City **(1899-1983)**
**Cullen,** Bill (William Lawrence Cullen) (radio and TV entertainer); Pittsburgh, 2/18/1920
**Culp,** Robert (actor); Berkeley, Calif., 8/16/1930
**Cummings,** E. E. (Edward Estlin Cummings) (poet); Cambridge, Mass. **(1894-1962)**
**Cummings,** Robert (actor); Joplin, Mo., 6/9/1910
**Curie,** Marie (Marja Sklodowska) (physical chemist); Warsaw **(1867-1934)**
**Curie,** Pierre (physicist) Paris **(1859-1906)**
**Curtin,** Phyllis (soprano); Clarksburg, W.Va., 12/3/1927
**Curtis,** Tony (Bernard Schwartz) (actor); Bronx, N.Y., 6/3/1925
**Curzon,** Clifford (concert pianist); London **(1907-1982)**
**Custer,** George Armstrong (army officer); New Rumley, Ohio **(1839-1876)**

# D

**da Gama,** Vasco (explorer) Sines, Portugal **(1460-1524)**
**Daguerre,** Louis (photographic pioneer); nr. Paris **(1787-1851)**
**Dahl,** Arlene (actress); Minneapolis, 8/11/1928
**Dailey,** Dan (actor and dancer); New York City, **(1917-1978)**
**Daley,** Richard J. (Mayor of Chicago); Chicago **(1902-1976)**
**Dali,** Salvador (painter); Figueras, Spain, 5/11/1904
**Dalton,** John (chemist); nr. Cockermouth, England **(1766-1844)**
**Daly,** James (actor); Wisconsin Rapids, Wis. **(1918-1978)**
**Daly,** John (radio and TV news analyst); Johannesburg, South Africa, 2/20/1914
**d'Amboise,** Jacques (ballet dancer); Dedham, Mass., 7/28/1934
**Damone,** Vic (Vito Farinola) (singer); Brooklyn, N.Y., 6/12/1928
**Damrosch,** Walter Johannes (orchestra conductor); Breslau (Poland) **(1862-1950)**
**Dana,** Charles Anderson (editor); Hinsdale, N.H. **(1819-1897)**
**Dandridge,** Dorothy (actress); Cleveland **(1923-1965)**
**Dangerfield,** Rodney (comedian); Babylon, L.I., N.Y., 1921
**Daniels,** Bebe (Virginia Daniels) (actress); Dallas **(1901-1971)**
**Danilova,** Alexandra (ballerina); Peterhof, Russia, 1/20/1904
**Dannay,** Frederic (novelist, pseudonym Ellery Queen); Brooklyn, N.Y. **(1905-1982)**
**Danner,** Blythe (actress); Philadelphia, 1944(?)
**D'Annunzio,** Gabriele (soldier and author); Francaville at Mare, Pescara, Italy **(1863-1938)**
**Dante** (or Durante) Alighieri (poet); Florence (Italy) **(1265-1321)**
**Danton,** Georges Jacques (French Revolutionary leader); Arcis-sur-Aube, France **(1759-1794)**
**Darnell,** Linda (actress); Dallas **(1921-1965)**
**Darren,** James (actor); Philadelphia, 6/8/1936
**Darrieux,** Danielle (actress); Bordeaux, France, 5/1/1917
**Darrow,** Clarence Seward (lawyer); Kinsman, Ohio **(1857-1938)**
**Darwin,** Charles Robert (naturalist); Shrewsbury, England **(1809-1882)**
**daSilva,** Howard (actor); Cleveland **(1909-1986)**
**Dassin,** Jules (film director); Middletown, Conn., 12/18/1911
**Daumier,** Honoré (caricaturist); Marseilles, France **(1808-1879)**

Dauphin, Claude (actor); Corbeil, France **(1903-1978)**
David, Jacques-Louis (painter); Paris **(1748-1825)**
David (King of Israel and Judah) **(died c. 973 B.C.)**
Davidson, John (singer and actor); Pittsburgh, 12/13/1941
Davies, Marion (Marion Douras) (actress); New York City **(1898?-1961)**
da Vinci, Leonardo (painter and scientist); Vinci, Tuscany (Italy) **(1452-1519)**
Davis, Bette (actress); Lowell, Mass., 4/5/1908
Davis, Elmer Holmes (radio commentator); Aurora, Ind. **(1890-1958)**
Davis, Jefferson (President of the Confederacy); Christian (now Todd) County, Ky. **(1808-1889)**
Davis, Mac (singer); Lubbock, Tex., 1/21/1942
Davis, Miles (jazz trumpeter); Alton, Ill., 5/25/1926
Davis, Ossie (actor and writer); Cogdell, Ga., 12/18/1917
Davis, Sammy, Jr. (actor and singer); New York City, 12/8/1925
Davis, Skeeter (Mary Francis Penick) (singer); Dry Ridge, Ky., 12/30/1931
Davis, Stuart (painter); Philadelphia **(1894-1964)**
Day, Dennis (singer); New York City, 5/21/1917
Day, Doris (Doris von Kappelhoff) (singer and actress); Cincinnati, 4/3/1924
Day, Laraine (La Raine Johnson) (actress); Roosevelt, Utah, 10/13/1920
Dayan, Moshe (ex-Defense Minister of Israel); Dagania, Palestine **(1915-1981)**
Dean, James (actor); Marion, Ind. **(1931-1955)**
Dean, Jimmy (singer); Seth Ward, nr. Plainview, Tex., 8/10/1928
De Bakey, Michael E. (heart surgeon); Lake Charles, La., 9/7/1908
de Beauvoir, Simone (novelist and philosopher); Paris **(1908-1986)**
Debs, Eugene Victor (Socialist leader); Terre Haute, Ind. **(1855-1926)**
Debussy, Claude Achille (composer); St. Germain-en-Laye, France **(1862-1918)**
De Carlo, Yvonne (Peggy Yvonne Middleton) (actress); Vancouver, B.C., Canada, 9/1/1924
de Chirico, Giorgio (painter); Volos, Greece, **(1888-1978)**
Dee, Ruby (Ruby Ann Wallace) (actress); Cleveland, 10/27/1924(?)
Dee, Sandra (Alexandra Zuck) (actress); Bayonne, N.J., 4/23/1942
Defoe, Daniel (novelist); London **(1659?-1731)**
Degas, Hilaire Germain Edgar (painter); Paris **(1834-1917)**
de Gaulle, Charles André Joseph Marie (soldier and statesman); Lille, France **(1890-1970)**
DeHaven, Gloria (actress); Los Angeles, 7/23/1925
de Havilland, Olivia (actress); Tokyo, 7/1/1916
Dekker, Albert (actor); Brooklyn, N.Y. **(1904-1968)**
de Kooning, Willem (painter); Rotterdam, 4/24/1904
Delacroix, Eugène (painter); Charenton-St. Maurice, France **(1798-1863)**
de la Renta, Oscar (fashion designer); Santo Domingo, Dominican Republic, 7/22/1932
Delaunay, Robert (painter); Paris **(1885-1941)**
De Laurentiis, Dino (film producer); Torre Annunziata, Bay of Naples, Italy, 8/8/1919
della Robbia, Andrea (sculptor) Florence **(1435-1525)**
della Robbia, Luca (sculptor); Florence **(1400-1482)**
Delon, Alain (actor); Sceaux, France, 11/8/1935
Del Rio, Dolores (Dolores Ansunsolo) (actress); Durango, Mexico **(1905-1983)**
DeLuise, Dom (comedian); Brooklyn, N.Y., 8/1/1933
Demarest, William (actor); St. Paul **(1892-1983)**
de Mille, Agnes (choreographer); New York City 9/18/1905
De Mille, Cecil Blount (film director); Ashfield, Mass. **(1881-1959)**
Demosthenes (orator); Athens **(385?-322 B.C.)**
Deneuve, Catherine (actress); Paris, 10/22/1943
De Niro, Robert (actor); New York City, 8/17/1943
Dennis, Sandy (actress); Hastings, Neb., 4/27/1937
Denver, John (Henry John Deutschendorf, Jr.) (singer); Roswell, N.M., 12/31/1943
Derain, André (painter); Chatou, Seine-et-Oise, France **(1880-1954)**
Dern, Bruce (actor); Chicago, 6/4/1936
Descartes, René (philosopher and mathematician); La Haye, France **(1596-1650)**
De Seversky, Alexander P. (aviator); Tiflis, Russia **(1894-1974)**
De Sica, Vittorio (film director); Sora, Italy **(1901-1974)**
Desmond, Johnny (composer); Detroit **(1921-1985)**
Desmond, William (actor); Dublin **(1878-1949)**
De Soto, Hernando (explorer); Barcarrota, Spain **(1500?-1542)**
De Valera, Eamon (ex-President of Ireland); New York City **(1882-1975)**
Devine, Andy (actor); Flagstaff, Ariz. **(1905-1977)**
De Vries, Peter (novelist); Chicago, 2/27/1910
Dewey, George (admiral); Montpelier, Vt. **(1837-1917)**
Dewey, John (philosopher and educator); Burlington, Vt. **(1859-1952)**
Dewey, Thomas E. (politician); Owosso, Mich. **(1902-1971)**
Dewhurst, Colleen (actress); Montreal, 1926(?)

Diamond, Neil (singer); Brooklyn, N.Y., 1/24/1941
Diana (Diana Frances Spencer) (Princess of Wales); Sandringham, England, 7/1/61
Dichter, Misha (pianist); Shanghai, 9/27/1945
Dickens, Charles John Huffam (novelist); Portsea, England **(1812-1870)**
Dickey, James (poet); Atlanta, 2/2/1923
Dickinson, Angie (Angeline Brown) (actress); Kulm, N.D., 9/30/1932
Dickinson, Emily Elizabeth (poet); Amherst, Mass. **(1830-1886)**
Diddley, Bo (Elias McDaniel) (guitarist); McComb, Miss., 12/30/1928
Diderot, Denis (encyclopedist); Langres, France **(1713-1784)**
Diefenbaker, John G. (ex-Prime Minister); Grey County, Ontario, Canada **(1895-1979)**
Dietrich, Marlene (Maria Magdalena von Losch) (actress); Berlin, 12/27/1901
Diggs, Dudley (actor); Dublin **(1879-1947)**
Diller, Phyllis (Phyllis Driver) (comedienne); Lima, Ohio, 7/17/1917
Dillman, Bradford (actor); San Francisco, 4/14/1930
Dine, Jim (painter); Cincinnati, 6/16/1935
Diogenes (philosopher); Sinope (Turkey) **(412?-323 B.C.)**
Dion (Dion DiMucci) (singer); Bronx, N.Y., 7/18/1939
Dior, Christian (fashion designer); Granville, France **(1905-1957)**
Disney, Walt(er) Elias (film animator and producer); Chicago **(1901-1966)**
Disraeli, Benjamin (Earl of Beaconsfield) (statesman); London **(1804-1881)**
Dix, Dorothea (civil rights reformer); Hampden, Me. **(1802-1887)**
Dix, Richard (Ernest Carlton Brimmer) (actor); St. Paul **(1894-1949)**
Dixon, Jeane (Jeane Pinckert) (seer); Medford, Wis., 1918
Dobbs, Mattiwilda (soprano); Atlanta, Ga., 7/11/1925
Doctorow, E(dgar) L(aurence) (novelist); New York City, 1/6/1931
Dodgson, C. L. *See* Carroll, Lewis.
Dolin, Anton (dancer); Slinfold, England **(1904-1983)**
Domingo, Placido (tenor); Madrid, 1/21/1941
Domino, Fats (Antoine) (musician); New Orleans, 2/26/1928
Donahue, Phil (television personality); Cleveland, 12/21/1935
Donahue, Troy (Merle Johnson) (actor); New York City, 1/27/1938
Donat, Robert (actor); Withington, England **(1905-1958)**
Donatello (Donato Niccolò di Betto Bardi) (sculptor); Florence **(c. 1386-1466)**
Donne, John (poet); London **(1573-1631)**
Donovan (Donovan Leitch) (singer and songwriter); Glasgow, Scotland, 2/10/1946
Doolittle, James H. (ex-Air Force general); Alameda, Calif., 12/14/1896
Dorati, Antal (orchestra conductor); Budapest, 4/9/1906
Dorsey, Jimmy (band leader); Shenandoah, Pa. **(1904-1957)**
Dorsey, Tommy (band leader); Mahonoy Plains, Pa. **(1905-1956)**
Dos Passos, John (author); Chicago **(1896-1970)**
Dostoevski, Fyodor Mikhailovich (novelist); Moscow **(1821-1881)**
Douglas, Helen Gahagan (ex-Representative); Boonton, N.J. **(1900-1980)**
Douglas, Kirk (Issur Danielovitch) (actor); Amsterdam, N.Y., 12/9/1916
Douglas, Melvyn (Melvyn Hesselberg) (actor); Macon, Ga., **(1901-1981)**
Douglas, Mike (Michael D. Dowd, Jr.) (TV personality); Chicago, 8/11/1925
Douglas, Paul (actor); Philadelphia **(1907-1959)**
Douglas, Stephen Arnold (politician); Brandon, Vt. **(1813-1861)**
Dowling, Eddie (Edward Goucher) (actor and stage producer); Woonsocket, R.I., **(1894-1976)**
Downs, Hugh (TV entertainer); Akron, Ohio, 2/14/1921
Doyle, Sir Arthur Conan (novelist and spiritualist); Edinburgh, Scotland **(1859-1930)**
Drake, Alfred (singer and actor); New York City, 10/7/1914
Drake, Sir Francis (navigator); Tavistock, England **(1545-1596)**
Dreiser, Theodore (writer); Terre Haute, Ind. **(1871-1945)**
Dressler, Marie (Leila Koeber) (actress); Cobourg, Ontario, Canada **(1869-1934)**
Dreyfus, Alfred (French army officer); Mulhouse (France) **(1859-1935)**
Dreyfuss, Richard (actor); Brooklyn, N.Y., 10/29/1947
Drury, Allen (novelist); Houston, 9/2/1918
Dryden, John (poet); Northamptonshire, England **(1631-1700)**
Dubček, Alexander (ex-President of Czechoslovakia); Uhroved (Czechoslovakia), 11/27/1921
Dubinsky, David (David Dobnievski) (labor leader); Brest-Litovsk (U.S.S.R.) **(1892-1982)**
Duchamp, Marcel (painter); Blainville, France **(1887-1968)**
Duchin, Peter (pianist and band leader); New York City, 7/28/1937
Dufay, Guillaume (composer); Cambrai, France **(c. 1400-1474)**
Duff, Howard (actor); Bremerton, Wash., 11/24/1917
Dufy, Raoul (painter); Le Havre, France **(1877-1953)**
Duke, James B. (industrialist); nr. Durham, N.C. **(1856-1925)**
Duke, Patty (Anna Marie Duke) (actress); New York City, 12/14/1946

**Dullea,** Keir (actor); Cleveland, 5/30/1936(?)
**Dulles,** Allen Welsh (ex-Director of CIA); Watertown, N.Y. **(1893-1969)**
**Dulles,** John Foster (statesman); Washington, D.C. **(1888-1959)**
**Dumas,** Alexandre (called Dumas fils) (novelist); Paris **(1824-1895)**
**Dumas,** Alexandre (called Dumas père) (novelist); Villers-Cotterets, France **(1802-1870)**
**Du Maurier,** Daphine (novelist); London, 5/13/1907
**Du Maurier,** George Louis Palmella Busson (novelist); Paris **(1834-1896)**
**Dumont,** Margaret (actress); **(1889-1965)**
**Dunaway,** Faye (actress); Bascom, Fla., 1/14/1941
**Duncan,** Isadora (dancer); San Francisco **(1878-1927)**
**Duncan,** Sandy (actress); Henderson, Tex., 2/20/1946
**Dunn,** James (actor); Santa Monica, Calif. **(1905-1967)**
**Dunne,** Irene (actress); Louisville, Ky., 12/20/1904
**Dunnock,** Mildred (actress); Baltimore, 1/25/1906
**Duns Scotus,** John (theologian); Duns, Scotland **(1265-1303)**
**Du Pont,** Pierre S. (economist); Paris **(1739-1817)**
**Durante,** Jimmy (comedian); New York City **(1893-1980)**
**Durbin,** Deanna (Edna Mae) (actress); Winnipeg, Canada, 12/4/1922
**Dürer,** Albrecht (painter and engraver); Nürnberg (Germany) **(1471-1528)**
**Durrell,** Lawrence George (novelist); Julundur, India, 2/27/1912
**Duse,** Eleonora (actress); Chioggia, Italy **(1859-1924)**
**Duvalier,** Jean-Claude (ex-President; son of "Papa Doc"); Port-au-Prince, Haiti, 7/3/1951
**Duvall,** Robert (actor); San Diego, Calif., 1931
**Dvořák,** Antonin (composer); Nelahozeves (Czechoslovakia) **(1841-1904)**
**Dylan,** Bob (Robert Zimmerman) (folk singer and composer); Duluth, Minn., 5/24/1941

# E

**Eagels,** Joanne (actress); Kansas City, Mo. **(1894-1929)**
**Eakins,** Thomas (painter and sculptor); Philadelphia, **(1844-1916)**
**Earhart,** Amelia (aviator); Atchison, Kan. **(1898-1937)**
**Eastman,** George (inventor); Waterville, N.Y. **(1854-1932)**
**Eastwood,** Clint (actor); San Francisco; 5/31/1931(?)
**Ebsen,** Buddy (Christian Ebsen, Jr.) (actor); Belleville, Ill., 4/2/1908
**Eckstine,** Billy (singer); Pittsburgh, 7/8/1914
**Eddy,** Mary Baker (founder of Christian Science Church); Bow, N.H. **(1821-1910)**
**Eddy,** Nelson (baritone and actor); Providence, R.I. **(1901-1967)**
**Eden,** Sir Anthony (Earl of Avon) (ex-Prime Minister); Durham, England **(1897-1977)**
**Eden,** Barbara (Barbara Huffman) (actress); Tucson, Ariz., 1934
**Edison,** Thomas Alva (inventor); Milan, Ohio **(1847-1931)**
**Edwards,** Blake (film writer-producer); Tulsa, Okla. 7/26/1922
**Edwards,** Jonathan (theologian); East Windsor, Conn. **(1703-1758)**
**Edwards,** Ralph (TV and radio producer); Tulsa, Okla. 7/26/1922
**Edwards,** Vincent (actor); Brooklyn, N.Y., 7/7/1928
**Egan,** Richard (actor); San Francisco, 7/29/1923
**Eggar,** Samantha (actress); London, 5/3/1939
**Eglevsky,** André (ballet dancer); Moscow **(1917-1977)**
**Ehrlich,** Paul (bacteriologist); Strzelin (Poland) **(1854-1915)**
**Einstein,** Albert (physicist); Ulm, Germany **(1879-1955)**
**Eisenhower,** Milton S. (educator); Abilene, Kan., **(1899-1985)**
**Eisenstaedt,** Alfred (photographer and photojournalist); Dirschau (Poland), 12/6/1898
**Ekberg,** Anita (actress); Malmö, Sweden, 9/29/1931
**Eldridge,** Florence (Florence McKechnie) (actress); Brooklyn, N.Y., 9/5/1901
**Elgar,** Sir Edward (composer); Worcester, England **(1857-1934)**
**Elgart,** Larry (band leader); New London, Conn., 3/20/1922
**El Greco** (Domenicos Theotocopoulos) (painter); Candia, Crete (Greece) **(c.1541-1614)**
**Eliot,** George (Mary Ann Evans) (novelist); Chilvers Coton, England **(1819-1880)**
**Eliot,** Thomas Stearns (poet); St. Louis **(1888-1965)**
**Ellington,** Duke (Edward Kennedy) (jazz musician); Washington, D.C. **(1899-1974)**
**Elliot,** "Mama" Cass (Ellen Naomi Cohen) (singer); Baltimore **(1941-1974)**
**Elman,** Mischa (violinist); Stalnoye, Ukraine **(1891-1967)**
**Emerson,** Ralph Waldo (philosopher and poet); Boston **(1803-1882)**
**Enesco,** Georges (composer); Dorohoi, Romania **(1881-1955)**
**Engels,** Friedrich (Socialist writer); Barmen (Germany) **(1820-1895)**
**Entremont,** Philippe (concert pianist); Rheims, France, 6/7/1934
**Epicurus** (philosopher); Samos (Greece) **(341-270** B.C.)
**Epstein,** Sir Jacob (sculptor); New York City **(1880-1959)**
**Erasmus,** Desiderius (Gerhard Gerhards) (scholar); Rotterdam **(1466?-1536)**

**Erhard,** Ludwig (ex-Chancellor); Furth, Germany **(1897-1977)**
**Erickson,** Leif (actor); Alameda, Calif. **(1911-1986)**
**Ericson,** Leif (navigator); **(c. 10th century** A.D.)
**Erikson,** Erik H. (psychoanalyst); Frankfurt, Germany, 6/15/1902
**Ernst,** Max (painter); Bruhl, Germany **(1891-1976)**
**Euclid** (mathematician); Megara (Greece) **(c. 300** B.C.)
**Euler,** Leonhard (mathematician) Basel, Switzerland **(1707-1783)**
**Euripides** (dramatist); Salamis (Greece) **(c.484-407** B.C.)
**Evans,** Dale (Frances Butts) (actress and singer); Uvalde, Tex., 10/31/1912
**Evans,** Dame Edith (actress); London **(1888-1976)**
**Evans,** Maurice (actor); Dorchester, England, 6/3/1901
**Everett,** Chad (actor); (Raymon Lee Cramton) South Bend, Ind., 6/11/1936
**Evers,** Charles (civil rights leader); Decatur, Miss., 9/14/1923(?)
**Evers,** Medgar (civil rights leader); Decatur, Miss. **(1925-1963)**
**Ewell,** Tom (Yewell Tompkins) (actor); Owensboro, Ky., 4/29/1909

# F

**Fabian** (Fabian Anthony Forte) (singer); Philadelphia, 2/6/1943
**Fabray,** Nanette (Nanette Fabarés) (actress); San Diego, Calif., 10/27/1922
**Fadiman,** Clifton (literary critic); Brooklyn, N.Y., 5/15/1904
**Fahrenheit,** Gabriel (German physicist); Danzig (Poland); **(1686-1736)**
**Fairbanks,** Douglas (Douglas Ulman) (actor); Denver **(1883-1939)**
**Fairbanks,** Douglas, Jr. (actor); New York City, 12/9/1909
**Faith,** Percy (conductor); Toronto **(1908-1976)**
**Falk,** Peter (actor); New York City, 9/16/1927
**Falla,** Manuel de (composer); Cadiz, Spain **(1876-1946)**
**Faraday,** Michael (physicist); Newington, England **(1791-1867)**
**Farber,** Barry (radio-TV broadcaster); Baltimore, Md., 1930
**Farentino,** James (actor); Brooklyn, N.Y., 2/24/1938
**Farmer,** James (civil rights leader); Marshall, Tex., 1/12/1920
**Farnum,** William (actor); Boston **(1876-1953)**
**Farrell,** Charles (actor); Onset Bay, Mass., 1901
**Farrell,** Eileen (operatic soprano); Willimantic, Conn., 2/13/1920
**Farrell,** Glenda (actress); Enid, Okla. **(1904-1971)**
**Farrell,** James T. (novelist); Chicago **(1904-1979)**
**Farrell,** Suzanne (Roberta Sue Ficker) (ballerina); Cincinnati, 8/16/1945
**Farrow,** Mia (actress); Los Angeles, 2/9/1946
**Fasanella,** Ralph (painter); New York City, 9/2/1914
**Fassbinder,** Rainer Werner (film and stage director); Bad Wörishofen, West Germany **(1946-1982)**
**Fast,** Howard (novelist); New York City, 11/11/1914
**Faulkner,** William (novelist); New Albany, Miss. **(1897-1962)**
**Fauré,** Gabriel Urbain (composer); Pamiers, France **(1845-1924)**
**Fawcett,** Farrah (actress); Corpus Christi, Tex., 2/2/1947(?)
**Faye,** Alice (Ann Leppert) (actress); New York City, 5/5/1915
**Feiffer,** Jules (cartoonist); New York City, 1/26/1929
**Feininger,** Lyonel (painter); New York City **(1871-1956)**
**Feldon,** Barbara (actress); Pittsburgh, 3/12/1941
**Feliciano,** José (singer); Larez, Puerto Rico, 9/10/1945
**Felker,** Clay S. (editor and publisher); St. Louis, 10/2/1925(?)
**Fellini,** Federico (film director); Rimini, Italy, 1/20/1920
**Fender,** Freddie (Baldemar Huerta) (singer); San Benito, Tex., 1937
**Ferber,** Edna (novelist); Kalamazoo, Mich. **(1885-1968)**
**Ferguson,** Maynard (jazz trumpeter); Verdun, Quebec, Canada, 5/4/1928
**Fermi,** Enrico (atomic physicist); Rome **(1901-1954)**
**Fernandel** (Fernand Joseph Desire Contandin) (actor); Marseilles, France **(1903-1971)**
**Ferrer,** José (actor and director); Santurce, Puerto Rico, 1/8/1912
**Ferrer,** Mel (actor); Elberon, N.J., 8/25/1917
**Fetchit,** Stepin (Lincoln Theodore Perry) (comedian); Key West, Fla. **(1902-1985)**
**Fiedler,** Arthur (conductor); Boston **(1894-1979)**
**Field,** Eugene (poet); St. Louis **(1850-1895)**
**Field,** Marshall (merchant); nr. Conway, Mass. **(1834-1906)**
**Field,** Sally (actress); Pasadena, Calif., 11/6/1946
**Fielding,** Henry (novelist); nr. Glastonbury, England **(1707-1754)**
**Fields,** Gracie (comedienne); Rochdale, England **(1898-1979)**
**Fields,** Totie (comedienne); Hartford, Conn. **(1931-1978)**
**Fields,** W. C. (William Claude Dukenfield) (comedian); Philadelphia **(1880-1946)**
**Fierstein,** Harvey (Forbes) (playwright and actor); Brooklyn, 6/6/1954
**Filene,** Edward A. (merchant); **(1860-1937)**
**Finch,** Peter (actor); Kensington, England **(1916-1977)**
**Finney,** Albert (actor); Salford, England, 5/9/1936
**Firkusny,** Rudolf (pianist); Napajedia (Czechoslovakia), 2/11/1912

Fischer-Dieskau, Dietrich (baritone); Berlin, **5/28/1925**
Fisher, Eddie (Edwin) (singer); Philadelphia, 8/10/1928
Fitzgerald, Barry (William Joseph Shields) (actor); Dublin **(1888-1961)**
Fitzgerald, Edward (radio broadcaster); Troy, N.Y. **(1898(?)-1982)**
Fitzgerald, Ella (singer); Newport News, Va., 4/25/1918
Fitzgerald, F. Scott (Francis Scott Key) (novelist); St. Paul, Minn. **(1896-1940)**
Fitzgerald, Geraldine (actress); Dublin, 11/24/1914
Fitzgerald, Pegeen (radio broadcaster); Norcatur, Kan., 1910
Flack, Roberta (singer); Black Mountain, N.C., 2/10/1940
Flagstad, Kirsten (Wagnerian soprano); Hamar, Norway **(1895-1962)**
Flatt, Lester Raymond (bluegrass musician); Overton County, Tenn. **(1914-1979)**
Flaubert, Gustave (novelist); Rouen, France **(1821-1880)**
Fleming, Sir Alexander (bacteriologist); Lochfield, Scotland **(1881-1955)**
Fleming, Rhonda (Marilyn Louis) (actress); Los Angeles, 8/10/1923
Fletcher, John (dramatist); Rye? England **(1579-1625)**
Flynn, Errol (actor); Hobart, Tasmania **(1909-1959)**
Foch, Nina (actress); Leyden, Netherlands, 4/20/1924
Fodor, Eugene (violinist); Turkey Creek, Colo., 3/5/1950
Fonda, Henry (actor); Grand Island, Neb. **(1905-1982)**
Fonda, Jane (actress); New York City, 12/21/1937
Fonda, Peter (actor); New York City, 2/23/1939
Fontaine, Frank (singer and comedian); Cambridge, Mass. **(1920-1979)**
Fontaine, Joan (Joan de Havilland) (actress); Tokyo, 10/22/1917
Fontanne, Lynn (actress); London, **(1887-1983)**
Fonteyn, Dame Margot (Margaret Hookham) (ballerina); Reigate, England, 5/18/1919
Forbes, Malcolm S(tevenson) (publisher and sportsman); Brooklyn, N.Y., 8/19/1919
Ford, Glenn (Gwyllyn Ford) (actor); Quebec, 5/1/1916
Ford, Harrison (actor); Chicago, 7/13/1942
Ford, Henry (industrialist); Greenfield, Mich. **(1863-1947)**
Ford, Henry, II (auto maker); Detroit, 9/4/1917
Ford, John (film director); Cape Elizabeth, Me. **(1895-1973)**
Ford, Paul (actor); Baltimore **(1901-1976)**
Ford, Tennessee Ernie (Ernie Jennings Ford) (singer); Bristol, Tenn., 2/13/1919
Forrester, Maureen (contralto); Montreal, 7/25/1930
Forsythe, John (actor); Carney's Point, N.J., 1/29/1918
Fosdick, Harry Emerson (clergyman); Buffalo, N.Y. **(1878-1968)**
Fosse, Bob (Robert Louis) (choreographer and director); Chicago, 6/23/1927
Foster, Jodie (Alicia Christian Foster) (actress); Los Angeles, 11/?/1962
Foster, Stephen Collins (composer); nr. Pittsburgh **(1826-1864)**
Foxx, Redd (John Elroy Sanford) (actor and comedian); St. Louis, 12/9/1922
Foy, Eddie, Jr. (dancer and actor); New Rochelle, N.Y. **(1905-1983)**
Fra Angelico (Giovanni da Fiesole) (painter); Vicchio in the Mugello, Tuscany (Italy) **(c.1387-1455)**
Fracci, Carla (ballerina); Milan, Italy, 8/20/1936
Fragonard, Jean Honoré (painter); Grasse, France **(1732-1806)**
Frampton, Peter (rock musician); Beckenham, England, 4/20/1950
France, Anatole (Jacques Anatole François Thibault) (author); Paris **(1844-1924)**
Francescatti, Zino (violinist); Marseilles, France, 8/9/1905
Franciosa, Anthony (Anthony Papaleo) (actor); New York City, 10/25/1928
Francis, Arlene (Arlene Francis Kazanjian) (actress); Boston, 10/20/1908
Francis, Connie (Concetta Franconero) (singer); Newark, N.J., 12/12/1938
Francis, Kay (Katherine Edwina Gibbs) (actress); Oklahoma City **(1903-1968)**
Franciscus, James (actor); Clayton, Mo., 1/31/1934
Francis of Assisi, Saint (Giovanni Francesco Barnardone) (founder of Franciscans); Assisi, Italy **(1182-1226)**
Franck, César Auguste (composer); Liège (Belgium) **(1822-1890)**
Franco Bahamonde, Francisco (Chief of State); El Ferrol, Spain **(1892-1975)**
Franklin, Aretha (singer); Memphis, Tenn., 3/25/1942
Franklin, Benjamin (statesman and scientist); Boston **(1706-1790)**
Frazer, Sir James George (anthropologist); Glasgow, Scotland **(1854-1941)**
Freud, Sigmund (psychoanalyst); Moravia (Czechoslovakia) **(1856-1939)**
Friedan, Betty (Betty Naomi Goldstein) (feminist); Peoria, Ill., 2/4/1921
Fromm, Erich (psychoanalyst); Frankfurt-am-Main, Germany **(1900-1980)**
Frost, David (TV entertainer); Tenterden, England, 4/7/1939
Frost, Robert Lee (poet); San Francisco **(1874-1963)**

Fry, Christopher (playwright); Bristol, England, 12/18/1907
Frye, David (impressionist); Brooklyn, N.Y., 1934
Fuller, R(ichard) Buckminster (Jr.) (architect and educator); Milton, Mass. **(1895-1983)**
Fulton, Robert (inventor); Lancaster County, Pa. **(1765-1815)**
Funt, Allen (TV producer); Brooklyn, N.Y., 9/16/1914
Furness, Betty (Elizabeth) (ex-actress and consumer advocate); New York City, 1/3/1916

# G

Gabel, Martin (actor and producer); Philadelphia **(1912-1986)**
Gabin, Jean (actor); Paris **(1904-1976)**
Gable, (William) Clark (actor); Cadiz, Ohio **(1901-1960)**
Gabo, Naum (sculptor); Briansk, Russia **(1890-1977)**
Gabor, Eva (actress); Budapest, 2/11/1926(?)
Gabor, Zsa Zsa (Sari) (actress); Budapest, 2/6/1923
Gabrieli, Giovanni (composer); Venice **(c.1557-1612)**
Gainsborough, Thomas (painter); Sudbury, Suffolk, England **(1727-1788)**
Galbraith, John Kenneth (economist); Iona Station, Ontario, Canada, 10/15/1908
Galilei, Galileo (astronomer and physicist); Pisa (Italy) **(1564-1642)**
Gallico, Paul (novelist); New York City **(1897-1976)**
Gallup, George H. (poll taker); Jefferson, Iowa **(1901-1984)**
Galsworthy, John (novelist and dramatist); Coombe, England **(1867-1933)**
Galway, James (flutist); Belfast, Northern Ireland, 12/8/1939
Gambling, John A. (radio broadcaster); New York City, 1930
Gandhi, Indira (Indira Nehru) (Prime Minister); Allahabad, India **(1917-1984)**
Gandhi, Mohandas Karamchand (called Mahatma Gandhi) (Hindu leader); Porbandar, India **(1869-1948)**
Gannett, Frank E. (editor and publisher); **(1876-1957)**
Garagiola, Joe (Joseph Henry) (sportscaster); St. Louis, 2/12/1926
Garbo, Greta (Greta Gustafsson) (actress); Stockholm, 9/18/1905
Garcia Lorca, Frederico (author); Fuente Vaqueros, Spain **(1898-1936)**
Gardner, Ava (Lucy Johnson) (actress); Smithfield, N.C., 12/24/1922
Gardner, Erle Stanley (novelist); Malden, Mass. **(1889-1970)**
Garfield, John (Jules Garfinkle) (actor); New York City **(1913-1952)**
Garfunkel, Art (Arthur) (singer); Newark, N.J., 11/5/1941
Gargan, William (actor); Brooklyn, N.Y., **(1905-1979)**
Garibaldi, Giuseppe (Italian nationalist leader); Nice, France **(1807-1882)**
Garland, Judy (Frances Gumm) (actress and singer); Grand Rapids, Minn. **(1922-1969)**
Garner, Erroll (jazz pianist); Pittsburgh **(1921-1977)**
Garner, James (James Bumgarner) (actor); Norman, Okla., 4/7/1928
Garner, Peggy Ann (actress); Canton, Ohio **(1932-1984)**
Garrett, Betty (actress); St. Joseph, Mo., 5/23/1919
Garrick, David (actor); Hereford, England **(1717-1779)**
Garrison, William Lloyd (abolitionist); Newburyport, Mass. **(1805-1879)**
Garroway, Dave (TV host); Schenectady, N.Y. **(1913-1982)**
Garson, Greer (actress); County Down, Northern Ireland, 9/29/1912(?)
Gary, John (singer); Watertown, N.Y., 11/29/1932
Gassman, Vittorio (film actor and director); Genoa, Italy, 9/1/1922
Gaudí, Antonio (architect); Reus, Spain **(1852-1926)**
Gauguin, Eugène Henri Paul (painter); Paris **(1848-1903)**
Gautama Buddha (Prince Siddhartha) (philosopher); Kapilavastu (India) **(563?-?483** B.C.)
Gavin, John (actor, diplomat); Los Angeles, 4/8/1935
Gayle, Crystal (Brenda Gayle Webb) (singer); Paintsville, Ky., 1/9/51
Gaynor, Janet (actress); Philadelphia **(1906-1984)**
Gaynor, Mitzi (Francesca Mitzi Marlene de Czanyi von Gerber) (actress); Chicago, 9/4/1931
Gazzara, Ben (Biago Anthony Gazzara) (actor); New York City, 8/28/1930
Gebel-Williams, Gunther (animal trainer); Schweidnitz (Poland), 1934
Geddes, Barbara Bel (actress); New York City, 10/31/1922
Genet, Jean (playwright); Paris **(1910-1986)**
Genghis Khan (Temujin) (conqueror); nr. Lake Baikal, Russia **(1162-1227)**
Genn, Leo (actor); London **(1905-1978)**
Gentry, Bobbie (Roberta Streeter) (singer); Chickasaw Co., Miss., 7/27/1944
George, David Lloyd (statesman); Manchester, England **(1863-1945)**
Gere, Richard (actor); Philadelphia, 1950
Gericault, Jean Louis (painter); Rouen, France **(1791-1824)**
Gernreich, Rudi (fashion designer); Vienna **(1922-1985)**
Geronimo (Goyathlay) (Apache chieftain); Arizona **(1829-1909)**
Gershwin, George (composer); Brooklyn, N.Y. **(1898-1937)**

Gershwin, Ira (lyricist); New York City, **(1896-1983)**
Getty, J. Paul (oil executive); Minneapolis **(1892-1976)**
Getz, Stan (saxophonist); Philadelphia, 2/2/1927
Ghiberti, Lorenzo (goldsmith and sculptor); Florence **(1378-1455)**
Giacometti, Alberto (sculptor); Switzerland **(1901-1966)**
Giannini, Giancarlo (actor); La Spezia, Italy, 8/1/1942
Gibbon, Edward (historian); Putney, England **(1737-1794)**
Gibson, Charles Dana (illustrator); Roxbury, Mass. **(1867-1944)**
Gibson, Hoot (Edward) (actor); Tememah, Neb. **(1892-1962)**
Gide, André (author); Paris **(1869-1951)**
Gielgud, Sir John (actor); London, 4/14/1904
Gilbert, John (movie actor); Logan, Utah **(1897-1936)**
Gilbert, Sir William Schwenck (librettist); London **(1836-1911)**
Gilels, Emil (concert pianist); Odessa, Ukraine **(1916-1985)**
Gillespie, Dizzy (John Birks Gillespie) (jazz trumpeter); Cheraw, S.C., 10/21/1917
Gimbel, Bernard F. (merchant); Vincennes, Ind. **(1885-1966)**
Gingold, Hermione (actress and comedienne); London, 12/9/1897
Ginsberg, Allen (poet); Newark, N.J., 6/3/1926
Giordano, Luca (painter); Naples, Italy **(1632-1705)**
Giorgione (painter); Castelfranco, (Italy) **(c.1477-1510)**
Giotto di Bondone (painter); Vespignamo (Italy) **(c.1266-1337)**
Giovanni, Nikki (poet); Knoxville, Tenn., 6/7/1943
Giroud, Françoise (French government official); Geneva, 9/21/1916
Gish, Dorothy (actress); Massillon, Ohio **(1898-1968)**
Gish, Lillian (Lillian de Guiche) (actress); Springfield, Ohio, 10/14/1896(?)
Givenchy, Hubert (fashion designer); Beauvais, France, 2/21/1927
Gladstone, William Ewart (statesman); Liverpool, England **(1809-1898)**
Glass, Philip (composer); Baltimore, 1/31/1937
Gleason, Jackie (comedian); Brooklyn, N.Y., 2/26/1916
Gleason, James (actor); New York City **(1886-1959)**
Gluck, Christoph Willibald (composer); Erasbach (Germany) **(1714-1787)**
Gobel, George (comedian); Chicago, 5/20/1920
Godard, Jean Luc (film director); Paris, 12/3/1930
Goddard, Paulette (Marion Levy) (actress); Great Neck, N.Y., 6/3/1911
Godfrey, Arthur (entertainer); New York City **(1903-1983)**
Godunov, Alexander (ballet dancer); Sakhalin, U.S.S.R. 11/28/1949
Goebbels, Joseph Paul (Nazi leader); Rheydt, Germany **(1897-1945)**
Goering, Hermann (Nazi leader); Rosenheim, Germany **(1893-1946)**
Goethals, George Washington (engineer); Brooklyn, N.Y. **(1858-1928)**
Goethe, Johann Wolfgang von (poet); Frankfurt-am-Main, Germany **(1749-1832)**
Gogol, Nikolai Vasilievich (novelist); nr. Mirgorod, Ukraine **(1809-1852)**
Goldberg, Rube (cartoonist); San Francisco **(1883-1970)**
Goldberg, Whoopi (actress); New York City, 1949 (?)
Golden, Harry (Harry Goldhurst) (author); New York City **(1902-1981)**
Goldsmith, Oliver (dramatist and poet); County Longford, Ireland **(1728-1774)**
Goldwyn, Samuel (Samuel Goldfish) (film producer); Warsaw **(1882-1974)**
Golenpaul, Dan (creator of Information Please radio show and editor of almanac of same name); New York City **(1900-1974)**
Gompers, Samuel (labor leader); London **(1850-1924)**
Goodall, Jane (Baroness van Lawick-Goodall) (ethologist); London, 4/3/1934
Goodman, Benny (clarinetist); Chicago **(1909-1986)**
Goodyear, Charles (inventor); New Haven, Conn. **(1800-1860)**
Gordimer, Nadine (novelist and short-story writer); Springs, South Africa, 12/20/1923
Gordon, Max (stage producer); New York City; **(1892-1978)**
Gordon, Ruth (actress); Wollaston, Mass. **(1896-1985)**
Gordy, Berry, Jr. (record company executive); Detroit, 11/28/1929
Gore, Lesley (singer); Tenafly, N.J., 1946
Goren, Charles H. (bridge expert); Philadelphia, 3/4/1901
Gorki, Maxim (Alexei Maximovich Peshkov) (author); Nizhni Novgorod, Russia **(1868-1936)**
Gorky, Arshile (painter); Armenia **(1904-1948)**
Gormé, Eydie (singer); Bronx, N.Y., 8/16/1932
Gorshin, Frank (actor); Pittsburgh, 4/5/1934
Gosden, Freeman F. See Amos
Gould, Chester (cartoonist); Pawnee, Okla. **(1900-1985)**
Gould, Elliott (Elliott Goldstein) (actor); Brooklyn, N.Y., 8/29/1938
Gould, Glenn (concert pianist); Toronto, **(1932-1982)**
Gould, Morton (composer); Richmond Hill, Queens, N.Y., 12/10/1913
Goulet, Robert (singer); Lawrence, Mass., 11/26/1933
Gounod, Charles François (composer); Paris **(1818-1893)**
Goya y Lucientes, Francisco José de (painter); Fuendetodos, Spain **(1746-1828)**

Grable, Betty (actress); St. Louis **(1916-1973)**
Grace, Princess of Monaco (Grace Kelly) (ex-actress); Philadelphia **(1929-1982)**
Graham, Bill (Wolfgang Grajonca) (rock impresario); Berlin, 1931
Graham, Billy (William F.) (evangelist); Charlotte, N.C., 11/7/1918
Graham, Katharine Meyer (newspaper publisher); New York City, 6/16/1917
Graham, Martha (choreographer); Pittsburgh, 5/11/1894(?)
Grahame, Gloria (Gloria Hallwood) (actress); Los Angeles **(1929-1981)**
Grainger, Percy Aldridge (pianist and composer); Melbourne, Australia **(1882-1961)**
Gramm, Donald (Grambach) (bass-baritone); Milwaukee **(1927-1983)**
Granger, Farley (actor); San Jose, Calif., 7/1/1925
Granger, Stewart (James Stewart) (actor); London, 5/6/1913
Grant, Cary (Alexander Archibald Leach) (actor); Bristol, England, 1/18/1904
Grant, Kathryn (actress); Houston, Tex., 1933
Grant, Lee (Lyova Haskell Rosenthal) (actress); New York City, 10/31/1930
Granville, Bonita (actress and producer); New York City, 1923
Grass, Günter (novelist); Danzig (Poland), 10/16/1927
Grauer, Ben (radio and TV announcer); New York City **(1908-1977)**
Graves, Peter (Peter Arness) (actor); Minneapolis, 3/18/1926
Graves, Robert (writer); London **(1895-1985)**
Gray, Barry (Bernard Yaroslaw) (radio interviewer); Atlantic City, N.J., 7/2/1916
Gray, Dolores (singer and actress); Chicago, 6/7/1930
Gray, Thomas (poet); London **(1716-1771)**
Grayson, Kathryn (Zelma Hednick) (singer and actress); Winston-Salem, N.C., 2/9/1923
Greco, Buddy (singer); Philadelphia, 8/14/1926
Greco, José (dancer); Montorio nei Frentani, Itály, 12/23/1918
Greeley, Horace (journalist and politician); Amherst, N.H. **(1811-1872)**
Green, Adolph (actor and lyricist); New York City, 12/2/1915
Green, Al (singer); Forrest City, Ark., 4/13/1946
Greene, Graham (novelist); Berkhamsted, England, 10/2/1904
Greene, Lorne (actor); Ottawa, 2/12/1915
Greene, Martyn (actor); London **(1899-1975)**
Greenstreet, Sydney (actor); Sandwich, England **(1879-1954)**
Greenwood, Joan (actress and director); London, 3/4/1921
Greer, Germaine (feminist); Melbourne, 1/29/1939
Gregory, Cynthia (ballerina); Los Angeles, 7/8/1946
Gregory, Dick (comedian); St. Louis, 1932
Greuze, Jean-Baptiste (painter); Tournus, France **(1725-1805)**
Grey, Joel (Joel Katz) (actor); Cleveland, 4/11/1932
Grey, Zane (author); Zanesville, Ohio **(1875-1939)**
Grieg, Edvard Hagerup (composer); Bergen, Norway **(1843-1907)**
Grier, Roosevelt (entertainer and former athlete); Cuthbert, Ga., 7/14/1932
Griffin, Merv (TV entertainer); San Mateo, Calif., 7/6/1925
Griffith, Andy (actor); Mount Airy, N.C., 6/1/1926
Griffith, David Lewelyn Wark (film producer); La Grange, Ky. **(1875-1948)**
Grigorovich, Yuri (choreographer); Leningrad, 1/1/1927
Grimes, Tammy (actress); Lynn, Mass., 1/30/1934
Grimm, Jacob (author of fairy tales); Hanau (Germany) **(1785-1863)**
Grimm, Wilhelm (author of fairy tales); Hanau (Germany) **(1786-1859)**
Gris, Juan (José Victoriano González) (painter); Madrid **(1887-1927)**
Grizzard, George (actor); Roanoke Rapids, N.C., 4/1/1928
Gromyko, Andrei A. (diplomat); Starye Gromyki, Russia, 7/5/1909
Gropius, Walter (architect); Berlin **(1883-1969)**
Gropper, William (painter, illustrator); New York City **(1897-1977)**
Grosz, George (painter); Germany **(1893-1959)**
Guardino, Harry (actor); New York City, 12/23/1925
Guggenheim, Meyer (capitalist); Langnau, Switzerland **(1828-1905)**
Guinness, Sir Alec (actor); London, 4/2/1914
Guitry, Sacha (Alexandre) (actor and film director); St. Petersburg, Russia **(1885-1957)**
Gumbel, Bryant Charles (TV newscaster); New Orleans, 9/29/1948
Gunther, John (author); Chicago **(1901-1970)**
Gutenberg, Johann (printer); Mainz (Germany) **(1400?-?1468)**
Guthrie, Arlo (singer); New York City, 7/10/1947
Guthrie, Woody (folk singer and composer); Okemah, Okla. **(1912-1967)**
Gwenn, Edmund (actor); London **(1875-1959)**

# H

Hackett, Bobby (trumpeter); Providence, R.I. **(1915-1976)**
Hackett, Buddy (Leonard Hacker) (comedian and actor); Brooklyn,

N.Y., 8/31/1924
Hackman, Gene (actor); San Bernardino, Calif., 1/30/1931
Hagen, Uta (actress); Göttingen, Germany, 6/12/1919
Haggard, Merle (songwriter); Bakersfield, Calif., 4/6/1937
Hagman, Larry (actor); Weatherford, Tex., 1931
Haig, Alexander Meigs, Jr. (ex-Secretary of State and ex-general); Bala-Cynwyd, Pa., 12/2/1924
Haile Selassie (Ras Tafari Makonnen) (ex-Emperor); Ethiopia (1892-1975)
Hailey, Arthur (novelist); Luton, England, 4/5/1920
Halberstam, David (journalist); New York City, 4/10/1934
Hale, Edward Everett (clergyman and author); Boston (1822-1909)
Hale, Nathan (American Revolutionary officer); Coventry, Conn. (1755-1776)
Halevi, Judah (Jewish poet); Toledo, Spain (1085-1140)
Haley, Alex (writer); Ithaca, N.Y., 8/11/1921
Hall, Donald (Andrew, Jr.) (poet) New Haven, Conn., 9/20/1928
Hall, Monty (TV personality); Winnipeg, Canada, 1923
Halley, Edmund (astronomer); London (1656-1742)
Hals, Frans (painter); Antwerp (Netherlands) (1580?-1666)
Halsey, William Frederick, Jr. (naval officer); Elizabeth, N.J. (1882-1959)
Hamill, Pete (journalist); Brooklyn, N.Y., 6/24/1935
Hamilton, Alexander (statesman); Nevis, British West Indies (1757?-1804)
Hamilton, George (actor); Memphis, Tenn., 8/12/1939
Hamilton, Margaret (actress); Cleveland (1902-1985)
Hamlisch, Marvin (composer and pianist); New York City, 6/2/1944
Hammarskjöld, Dag (U.N. Secretary-General); Jönköping, Sweden (1905-1961)
Hammerstein, Oscar, II (librettist and stage producer); New York City (1895-1960)
Hampden, Walter (Walter Hampden Dougherty) (actor); Brooklyn, N.Y. (1879-1955)
Hampton, Lionel (vibraharpist and band leader); Birmingham, Ala., 4/12/1913
Hamsun, Knut (Knut Pedersen) (novelist); Lom, Norway (1859-1952)
Hancock, John (statesman); Braintree, Mass. (1737-1793)
Hand, Learned (jurist); Albany, N.Y. (1872-1961)
Handel, George Frederick (Georg Friedrich Händel) (composer); Halle (East Germany) (1685-1759)
Handy, William Christopher (blues composer); Florence, Ala. (1873-1958)
Hannibal (Carthaginian general); North Africa (247-182 B.C.)
Hanson, Howard (conductor); Wahoo, Neb., (1896-1981)
Harburg, E. Y. "Yip" (songwriter); New York City (1896-1981)
Harding, Ann (actress); San Antonio, Tex. (1902-1981)
Hardwicke, Sir Cedric (actor); Stourbridge, England (1893-1964)
Hardy, Oliver (comedian); Atlanta (1892-1957)
Hardy, Thomas (novelist); Dorsetshire, England (1840-1928)
Harkness, Edward S. (capitalist); Cleveland (1874-1940)
Harlow, Jean (Harlean Carpentier) (actress); Kansas City, Mo. (1911-1937)
Harnick, Sheldon (lyricist); Chicago, 4/30/1924
Harper, Valerie (actress); Suffern, N.Y., 8/22/1940(?)
Harrell, Lynn (cellist); New York City, 1/30/1944
Harriman, W. (William) Averell (ex-Governor of New York); New York City (1891-1986)
Harris, Barbara (actress); Evanston, Ill., 1935
Harris, Emmylou (singer); Birmingham, Ala., 1949
Harris, Julie (actress); Grosse Pointe Park, Mich., 12/2/1925
Harris, Phil (actor and band leader); Linton, Ind., 6/24/1906
Harris, Richard (actor); Limerick, Ireland, 10/1/1933
Harris, Rosemary (actress); Ashby, England, 9/19/1930
Harris, Roy (composer); Lincoln County, Okla. (1898-1979)
Harrison, George (singer and songwriter); Liverpool, England, 2/25/1943
Harrison, Noel (singer and actor); London, 1/29/1936
Harrison, Rex (Reginald Carey) (actor); Huyton, England, 3/5/1908
Hart, Lorenz (lyricist); New York (1895-1943)
Hart, Moss (playwright); New York City (1904-1961)
Hart, William S. (actor); Newburgh, N.Y. (1862-1946)
Harte, Bret (Francis Brett Harte) (author); Albany, N.Y. (1836-1902)
Hartford, Huntington (George Huntington Hartford II) (A.&P. heir); New York City, 4/18/1911
Hartford, John (singer and banjoist); New York City, 12/30/1937
Hartman, David Downs (TV newscaster); Pawtucket, R.I., 5/19/1935
Hartman, Elizabeth (actress); Youngstown, Ohio, 12/23/1941
Harvey, Laurence (Larushka Skikne) (actor); Joniskis, Lithuania (1928-1973)
Harvey, William (physician); Folkestone, England (1578-1657)
Hasso, Signe (actress); Stockholm, 8/15/1915
Havoc, June (June Hovick) (actress); Seattle, 1916
Haver, June (actress); Rock Island, Ill., 6/10/1926
Hawkins, Jack (actor); London (1910-1973)
Hawn, Goldie (actress); Washington, D.C., 11/21/1945

Haworth, Jill (actress); Sussex, England, 1945
Hawthorne, Nathaniel (novelist); Salem, Mass. (1804-1864)
Hay, John Milton (statesman); Salem, Ind. (1838-1905)
Hayakawa, Sessue (actor); Honshu, Japan (1890-1973)
Hayden, Melissa (ballerina); Toronto, 4/25/1923
Hayden, Sterling (Sterling Relyea Walter) (actor and writer); Montclair, N.J. (1916-1986)
Haydn, Franz Joseph (composer); Rohrau (Austria) (1732-1809)
Hayes, Helen (Helen Hayes Brown) (actress); Washington, D.C., 10/10/1900
Hayes, Isaac (composer); Covington, Tenn., 8/20/1942
Hayward, Louis (actor); Johannesburg, South Africa (1909-1985)
Hayward, Susan (Edythe Marrener) (actress); Brooklyn, N.Y. (1919?-1975)
Hayworth, Rita (Margarita Cansino) (actress); New York City, 10/17/1918
Head, Edith (costume designer); Los Angeles (1907-1981)
Hearst, William Randolph (publisher); San Francisco (1863-1951)
Hearst, William Randolph, Jr. (publisher); New York City, 1/27/1908
Heath, Edward (ex-Prime Minister); Broadstairs, England, 7/9/1916
Heatherton, Joey (actress); Rockville Centre, N.Y., 9/14/1944
Hecht, Ben (author); New York City (1894-1964)
Heckart, Eileen (actress); Columbus, Ohio, 3/29/1919
Heflin, Van (Emmet Evan Heflin) (actor); Walters, Okla. (1910-1971)
Hefner, Hugh (publisher); Chicago, 4/9/1926
Hegel, Georg Wilhelm Friedrich (philosopher); Stuttgart (Germany) (1770-1831)
Heifetz, Jascha (concert violinist); Vilna, Russia, 2/2/1901
Heine, Heinrich (Harry) (poet); Düsseldorf (Germany) (1797-1856)
Heinemann, Gustav (ex-President of Germany); Schweim, Germany (1899-1976)
Heisenberg, Werner Karl (physicist); Würzburg, Germany (1901-1976)
Heller, Joseph (novelist); Brooklyn, N.Y., 5/1/1923
Hellman, Lillian (playwright); New Orleans (1905-1984)
Hemingway, Ernest Miller (novelist); Oak Park, Ill. (1899-1961)
Hemmings, David (actor); Guilford, England, 11/2/1941
Henderson, Florence (actress); Dale, Ind., 2/14/1934
Henderson, Skitch (Lyle Russell Cedric) (conductor and pianist); Birmingham, England(?), 1/27/1918
Hendrix, Jimi (James Marshall Hendrix) (guitarist); Seattle (1942-1970)
Henley, Beth (playwright-actress); Jackson, Miss., 5/8/1952
Henning, Doug (magician and actor); Winnipeg, Canada, 1947(?)
Henreid, Paul (actor); Trieste, 1/10/1908
Henri, Robert (painter); Cincinnati (1865-1926)
Henry, O. (William Sydney Porter) (story writer); Greensboro, N.C. (1862-1910)
Henry, Patrick (statesman); Hanover County, Va. (1736-1799)
Henson, Jim (puppeteer); Greenville, Miss., 9/24/1936
Hepburn, Audrey (actress); Brussels, Belgium, 5/4/1929
Hepburn, Katharine (actress); Hartford, Conn., 11/8/1909
Hepplewhite, George (furniture designer); England (?-1786)
Hepworth, Barbara (sculptor); Wakefield, England (1903-1975)
Herachel, William (Frederich Wilhelm) (astronomer); Hanover, Germany (1738-1822)
Herbert, George (poet); Montgomery Castle, Wales (1593-1633)
Herbert, Victor (composer); Dublin (1859-1924)
Herblock (Herbert L. Block) (political cartoonist); Chicago, 10/13/1909
Herman, Woody (Woodrow Charles) (band leader); Milwaukee, 5/16/1913
Herod (Herodes) (called Herod the Great) (King of Judea) (73?-4 B.C.)
Herodotus (historian); Halicarnassus, Asia Minor (Turkey) (c. 484-425 B.C.)
Herrick, Robert (poet); London? (1591-1674)
Hershfield, Harry (humorist and raconteur); Cedar Rapids, Iowa (1885-1974)
Hersholt, Jean (actor); Copenhagen (1886-1956)
Hesburgh, Theodore M. (educator); Syracuse, N.Y., 5/2/1917
Heston, Charlton (actor); Evanston, Ill., 10/4/1924
Heyerdahl, Thor (ethnologist and explorer); Larvik, Norway, 10/6/1914
Hildegarde (Hildegarde Loretta Sell) (singer); Adell, Wis., 2/1/1906
Hill, Arthur (actor); Melfort, Canada, 8/1/1922
Hillary, Sir Edmund (mountain climber); New Zealand, 7/20/1919
Hiller, Wendy (actress); Bramhall, England, 8/15/1912
Hilliard, Harriet. See Nelson, Harriet
Hindemith, Paul (composer); Hanau, Germany (1895-1963)
Hines, Earl "Fatha" (jazz pianist); Duquesne, Pa. (1905-1983)
Hines, Jerome (Jerome Heinz) (basso); Los Angeles, 11/8/1921
Hingle, Pat (actor); Denver, 7/19/1924
Hippocrates (physician); Cos, Greece (c. 460-c. 377 B.C.)
Hirohito (Emperor); Tokyo, 4/29/1901
Hiroshige, Ando (painter); Edo? (Tokyo) (1797-1858)

**Hirsch,** Judd (actor); New York City, 3/15/1935
**Hirschfeld,** Al (Albert) (cartoonist); St. Louis, 6/21/1903
**Hirschhorn,** Joseph Herman (financier, speculator, and art collector); Mitau, Latvia **(1899-1981)**
**Hirt,** Al (trumpeter); New Orleans, 11/7/1922
**Hitchcock,** Alfred J. (film director); London **(1899-1980)**
**Hitler,** Adolf (German dictator); Braunau, Austria **(1889-1945)**
**Hitzig,** William Maxwell (physician); Austria, 12/15/1904
**Hobbes,** Thomas (philosopher); Westport, England **(1588-1679)**
**Hobson,** Laura Z. (Laura K. Zametkin) (novelist); New York City **(1900-1986)**
**Hodges,** Eddie (actor); Hattiesburg, Miss., 3/5/1947
**Hoffa,** James R(iddle) (labor leader); Brazil, Ind., 2/14/1913 (presumed dead, 1977)
**Hoffman,** Dustin (film actor and director); Los Angeles, 8/8/1937
**Hofmann,** Hans (painter); Germany **(1880-1966)**
**Hogarth,** William (painter and engraver); London **(1697-1764)**
**Hokusai,** Katauhika (artist); Yedo, Japan **(1760-1849)**
**Holbein,** Hans (the Elder) (painter); Augsburg (Germany) **(1465?-1524)**
**Holbein,** Hans (the Younger) (painter); Augsburg (Germany) **(1497?-1543)**
**Holbrook,** Hal (actor); Cleveland, 2/17/1925
**Holden,** William (William Franklin Beedle, Jr.) (actor); O'Fallon, Ill. **(1918-1981)**
**Holder,** Geoffrey (dancer); Port-of-Spain, Trinidad, 8/1/1930
**Holiday,** Billie (Eleanora Fagan) (jazz-blues singer); Baltimore **(1915-1959)**
**Holliday,** Judy (Judith Tuvim) (comedienne); New York City **(1922-1965)**
**Holloway,** Stanley (actor); London **(1890-1982)**
**Holloway,** Sterling (actor); Cedartown, Ga., 1905
**Holm,** Celeste (actress); New York City, 4/29/1919
**Holmes,** Oliver Wendell (jurist); Boston **(1841-1935)**
**Holt,** Jack (actor); Winchester, Va. **(1888-1951)**
**Holtz,** Lou (comedian); San Francisco **(1898-1980)**
**Home,** Lord (Alexander Frederick Douglas-Home) (diplomat); London, 7/2/1903
**Homeier,** Skip (George Vincent Homeier) (actor); Chicago, 10/5/1930
**Homer,** Winslow (painter); Boston, Mass. **(1836-1910)**
**Homer** (Greek poet) **(c.850** B.C.?)
**Homolka,** Oscar (actor); Vienna **(1898-1978)**
**Honegger,** Arthur (composer); Le Havre, France **(1892-1955)**
**Hook,** Sidney (philosopher); New York City, 12/20/1902
**Hoover,** J. Edgar (FBI director); Washington, D.C. **(1895-1972)**
**Hope,** Bob (Leslie Townes Hope) (comedian); London, 5/29/1903
**Hopkins,** Anthony (actor); Port Talbot, Wales, 12/31/1937
**Hopkins,** Gerald Manley (poet); Stratford, England **(1844-1899)**
**Hopkins,** Johns (financier); Anne Arundel County, Md. **(1795-1873)**
**Hopkins,** Miriam (actress); Bainbridge, Ga. **(1902-1972)**
**Hopper,** Dennis (actor); Dodge City, Kan., 5/17/1936
**Hopper,** Edward (painter); Nyack, N.Y. **(1882-1967)**
**Horace** (Quintus Horatius Flaccus) (poet); Venosa (Italy) **(65-8** B.C.)
**Horne,** Lena (singer); Brooklyn, N.Y., 6/30/1917
**Horne,** Marilyn (mezzo-soprano); Bradford, Pa., 1/16/1934
**Horowitz,** Vladimir (pianist); Kiev, Russia, 10/1/1904
**Horton,** Edward Everett (comedian); Brooklyn, N.Y. **(1887-1970)**
**Houdini,** Harry (Ehrich Weiss) (magician); Appleton, Wis. **(1874-1926)**
**Houseman,** John (Jacques Haussmann) (producer, director, and actor); Bucharest; 9/22/1902
**Housman,** A(lfred) E(dward) (poet); Fockburg, England **(1859-1936)**
**Houston,** Samuel (political leader); Rockbridge County, Va. **(1793-1863)**
**Howard,** Leslie (Leslie Stainer) (actor); London **(1893-1943)**
**Howard,** Ron (actor-director); Duncan, Okla., 3/1/1954
**Howard,** Trevor (actor); Kent, England, 9/29/1916
**Howe,** Elias (inventor); Spencer, Mass. **(1819-1867)**
**Howe,** Irving (literary critic); New York City, 6/11/1920
**Howe,** Julia Ward (poet and reformer); New York City **(1819-1910)**
**Howes,** Sally Ann (actress); London, 7/20/1934
**Hudson,** Henry (English navigator) **(?-1611)**
**Hudson,** Rock (born Roy Scherer, Jr.; took Roy Fitzgerald as legal name) (actor); Winnetka, Ill., **(1925-1985)**
**Hughes,** Charles Evans (jurist); Glens Falls, N.Y. **(1862-1948)**
**Hughes,** Howard (industrialist and film producer); Houston **(1905-1976)**
**Hughes,** Langston (poet); Joplin, Mo. **(1902-1967)**
**Hugo,** Victor Marie (author); Besançon, France **(1802-1885)**
**Hume,** David (philosopher); Edinburgh, Scotland **(1711-1776)**
**Humperdinck,** Engelbert (Arnold Dorsey) (singer); Madras, India, 5/2/1936
**Humperdinck,** Engelbert (composer); Siegburg (Germany) **(1854-1921)**
**Hunt,** H. L. (industrialist); nr. Vandalia, Ill. **(1889-1974)**

**Hunt,** Marsha (actress); Chicago, 10/17/1917
**Hunter,** Kim (Janet Cole) (actress); Detroit, 11/12/1922
**Hunter,** Tab (Arthur Andrew Gelien) (actor); New York City, 7/11/1931
**Huntley,** Chet (TV newscaster); Cardwell, Mont. **(1911-1974)**
**Hurok,** Sol (Solomon) (impresario); Pogar, Russia **(1884-1974)**
**Hurst,** Fannie (novelist); Hamilton, Ohio **(1889-1968)**
**Hurt,** John (actor); Shirebrook, England, 1/22/1940
**Hus,** Jan (Bohemian religious reformer); Husinetz, nr. Budweis (Czechoslovakia) **(c.1369-1415)**
**Hussein I** (King); Jordan, 11/14/1935
**Huston,** John (film director and writer); Nevada, Mo., 8/5/1906
**Huston,** Walter (Walter Houghston) (actor); Toronto **(1884-1950)**
**Hutchins,** Robert M. (educator); Brooklyn, N.Y. **(1899-1977)**
**Hutton,** Barbara (Woolworth heiress); New York City **(1912-1979)**
**Hutton,** Betty (Betty Thornburg) (actress); Battle Creek, Mich., 2/26/1921
**Hutton,** Lauren (model and actress); Charleston, S.C., 1944
**Hutton,** Timothy (actor); Los Angeles, 8/16/1960
**Huxley,** Aldous (author); Godalming, England **(1894-1963)**
**Huxley,** Sir Julian S. (biologist and author); London **(1887-1975)**
**Huxley,** Thomas Henry (biologist); Ealing, England **(1825-1895)**

# I

**Ian,** Janis (singer); New York City, 5/7/1951
**Ibsen,** Henrik (dramatist); Skien, Norway **(1828-1906)**
**Inge,** William (playwright); Independence, Kan. **(1913-1973)**
**Ingres,** Jean Auguste Dominique (painter); Montauban, France **(1780-1867)**
**Inness,** George (painter); nr. Newburgh, N.Y. **(1825-1894)**
**Ionesco,** Eugene (playwright); Slatina, Romania, 11/26/1912
**Ireland,** John (actor); Vancouver, B.C., Canada, 1/30/1915
**Irons,** Jeremy (actor); Cowes, Isle of Wight, England, 9/19/1948
**Irving,** John (Winslow) (writer); Exeter, N.H., 3/2/1942
**Irving,** Washington (author); New York City **(1783-1859)**
**Isherwood,** Christopher (novelist and playwright); nr. Dilsey and High Lane, England **(1904-1986)**
**Iturbi,** José (concert pianist); Valencia, Spain **(1895-1980)**
**Ives,** Burl (Icle Ivanhoe) (singer); Hunt, Ill., 6/14/1909
**Ives,** Charles E(dward) (composer); Danbury, Conn. **(1874-1954)**

# J

**Jackson,** Anne (actress); Millvale, Pa., 9/3/1926
**Jackson,** Glenda (actress); Hoylake, England, 1937(?)
**Jackson,** Rev. Jesse (civil rights leader); Greenville, S.C., 10/8/1941
**Jackson,** Kate (actress); Birmingham, Ala., 10/29/1949
**Jackson,** Mahalia (gospel singer); New Orleans **(1912-1972)**
**Jackson,** Michael (singer); Gary, Ind., 8/19/1958
**Jackson,** Thomas Jonathan ("Stonewall") (general); Clarksburg, Va. (now W. Va.) **(1824-1863)**
**Jacobi,** Lou (actor); Toronto, 12/28/1913
**Jacobs,** Jane (urbanologist); Scranton, Pa., 5/1/1916
**Jaffe,** Sam (actor); New York City **(1891-1984)**
**Jagger,** Dean (actor); Lima, Ohio, 11/7/1903
**Jagger,** Mick (Michael Phillip) (singer); Dartford, England, 7/26/1944
**James,** Harry (trumpeter); Albany, Ga. **(1916-1983)**
**James,** Henry (novelist); New York City **(1843-1916)**
**James,** Jesse Woodson (outlaw); Clay County, Mo. **(1847-1882)**
**James,** William (psychologist); New York City **(1842-1910)**
**Jameson,** (Margaret) Storm (novelist); Whitby, England, 1897
**Janis,** Byron (pianist); McKeesport, Pa., 3/24/1928
**Jannings,** Emil (actor); Brooklyn, N.Y. **(1886-1950)**
**Janssen,** David (David Meyer) (actor); Naponee, Neb. **(1930-1980)**
**Jay,** John (statesman and jurist); New York City **(1745-1829)**
**Jeanmaire,** Renée (dancer); Paris, 4/29/1924
**Jenner,** Edward (physician); Berkeley, England **(1749-1823)**
**Jennings,** Waylon (singer); Littlefield, Tex., 1937
**Jessel,** George (entertainer); New York City **(1898-1981)**
**Jessup,** Philip C. (diplomat); New York City, 1/5/1897
**Jiang** Qing (political leader); Chucheng, China, 1913 (?)
**Joan of Arc** (Jeanne d'Arc) (saint and patriot); Domremy-la-Pucelle, France **(1412-1431)**
**Joel,** Billy (singer); New York City, 5/9/1949
**Joffrey,** Robert (Abdullah Jaffa Bey Khan) (choreographer); Seattle, 12/24/1930
**John,** Elton (Reginald Kenneth Dwight) (singer and pianist); Pinner, England, 3/25/1947
**Johns,** Glynis (actress); Pretoria, South Africa, 10/5/1923
**Johns,** Jasper (painter and sculptor); Augusta, Ga., 5/15/1930
**Johnson,** James Weldon (author and educator); Jacksonville, Fla.

**(1871-1938)**
**Johnson**, Philip Cortalyou (architect); Cleveland, Ohio, 7/8/1906
**Johnson**, Samuel (lexicographer and author); Lichfield, England **(1709-1784)**
**Johnson**, Van (actor); Newport, R.I., 8/20/1916
**Joliot-Curie**, Frédéric (physicist); Paris **(1900-1958)**
**Joliot-Curie**, Irène (Irène Curie) (physicist); France **(1897-1956)**
**Jolliet** (or Joliet), Louis (explorer); Beaupré, Canada **(1645-1700)**
**Jolson**, Al (Asa Yoelson) (actor and singer); St. Petersburg, Russia **(1886-1950)**
**Jones**, Carolyn (singer and actress); Amarillo, Tex., **(1933-1983)**
**Jones**, Dean (actor); Morgan County, Ala., 1/25/1935
**Jones**, George (singer); Saratoga, Tex., 9/12/1931
**Jones**, Inigo (architect); London **(1573-1652)**
**Jones**, James (novelist); Robinson, Ill. **(1921-1977)**
**Jones**, James Earl (actor); Arkabutla, Miss., 1/17/1931
**Jones**, Jennifer (Phyllis Isley) (actress); Tulsa, Okla., 3/2/1919
**Jones**, John Paul (John Paul) (naval officer); Scotland **(1747-1792)**
**Jones**, Quincy (composer); Chicago, 3/14/1933
**Jones**, Shirley (singer and actress); Smithtown, Pa., 3/31/1934
**Jones**, Tom (Thomas Jones Woodward) (singer); Pontypridd, Wales, 6/7/1940
**Jong**, Erica (writer); New York City, 3/26/1942
**Jonson**, Ben (Benjamin) (poet and dramatist); Westminster, England **(1572-1637)**
**Joplin**, Janis (singer); Port Arthur, Tex. **(1943-1970)**
**Jory**, Victor (actor); Dawson City, Yukon, Canada **(1902-1982)**
**Josquin des Prés** (usually known as Josquin) (composer); Conde-sur-L'Escaut?, Hainaut (France or Belgium) **(c.1445-1521)**
**Jourdan**, Louis (Louis Gendre) (actor); Marseilles, France, 6/19/1920
**Joyce**, James (novelist); Dublin **(1882-1941)**
**Juárez**, Benito Pablo (statesman); Guelatao, Mexico **(1806-1872)**
**Julia**, Raul (Raúl Rafael Carlos Julia y Arcelay) (actor); San Juan, Puerto Rico, 3/9/1940
**Juliana** (Queen); The Hague, Netherlands, 4/30/1909
**Jung**, Carl Gustav (psychoanalyst); Basel, Switzerland **(1875-1961)**
**Jurado**, Katy (actress); Guadalajara, Mexico, 1927

# K

**Kabalevsky**, Dmitri (composer); St. Petersburg, Russia, 12/30/1904
**Kafka**, Franz (author); Prague **(1883-1924)**
**Kádár**, János (Communist Party leader); Hungary, 1912
**Kahn**, Gus (songwriter); Coblenz, Germany **(1886-1941)**
**Kahn**, Louis I. (architect); Oesel Island, Estonia **(1901-1974)**
**Kahn**, Madeline (actress); Boston, 9/29/1942
**Kaminska**, Ida (actress); Odessa, Russia **(1899-1980)**
**Kandinsky**, Wassily (painter); Moscow **(1866-1944)**
**Kanin**, Garson (playwright); Rochester, N.Y., 11/24/1912
**Kant**, Immanuel (philosopher); Königsberg (Kaliningrad, U.S.S.R.) **(1724-1804)**
**Kantor**, MacKinlay (novelist); Webster City, Iowa **(1904-1977)**
**Kaplan**, Gabe (Gabriel) (actor); Brooklyn, N.Y., 3/31/1945
**Karloff**, Boris (William Henry Pratt) (actor); London **(1887-1969)**
**Kaufman**, George S. (playwright); Pittsburgh **(1889-1961)**
**Kaye**, Danny (David Daniel Kominski) (comedian); Brooklyn, N.Y., 1/18/1913
**Kaye**, Sammy (band leader); Cleveland, 3/13/1910
**Kazan**, Elia (director); Constantinople, Turkey, 9/7/1909
**Kazan**, Lainie (Levine) (singer); New York City, 5/15/1940
**Keach**, Stacy (actor); Savannah, Ga., 6/2/1941
**Keaton**, Buster (Joseph Frank Keaton) (comedian); Piqua, Kan. **(1896-1966)**
**Keaton**, Diane (actress); Los Angeles, 1/5/1946
**Keats**, John (poet); London **(1795-1821)**
**Keel**, Howard (singer and actor); Gillespie, Ill., 4/13/1919
**Keeler**, Ruby (Lehy Keeler) (actress and dancer); Halifax, Nova Scotia, Canada, 8/25/1910
**Kefauver**, Estes (legislator); Madisonville, Tenn. **(1903-1963)**
**Keith**, Brian (actor); Bayonne, N.J., 11/14/1921
**Keller**, Helen Adams (author and educator); Tuscumbia, Ala. **(1880-1968)**
**Kellerman**, Sally (actress); Long Beach, Calif., 6/2/1938
**Kelly**, Emmett (clown); Sedan, Kan., **(1898-1979)**
**Kelly**, Gene (dancer and actor); Pittsburgh, 8/23/1912
**Kelly**, Patsy (actress and comedienne); Brooklyn, N.Y. **(1910-1981)**
**Kelly**, Walt (cartoonist); Philadelphia **(1913-1973)**
**Kemal Ataturk** (Mustafa Kemal) (Turkish soldier and statesman); Salonika (Greece) **(1881-1938)**
**Kempis**, Thomas a (mystic); Kempis, Prussia (Germany) **(1380-1471)**
**Kennan**, George F. (diplomat); Milwaukee, 2/16/1904
**Kennedy**, Arthur (actor); Worcester, Mass., 2/17/1914
**Kennedy**, George (actor); New York City, 2/18/1925

**Kennedy**, Jacqueline. *See* Onassis, Jacqueline
**Kennedy**, Joseph P. (financier); Boston **(1888-1969)**
**Kennedy**, Robert Francis (legislator); Brookline, Mass. **(1925-1968)**
**Kennedy**, Rose Fitzgerald (President's mother); Boston, 7/22/1890
**Kent**, Rockwell (painter); Tarrytown Heights, N.Y. **(1882-1971)**
**Kenton**, Stan (Stanley Newcomb) (jazz musician); Wichita, Kan. **(1912-1979)**
**Kepler**, Johannes (astronomer); Weil (Germany) **(1571-1630)**
**Kerensky**, Alexander Fedorovich (statesman); Simbirks, Russia **(1881-1970)**
**Kern**, Jerome David (composer); New York City **(1885-1945)**
**Kerr**, Deborah (actress); Helensburgh, Scotland, 9/30/1921
**Kesey**, Ken (novelist); La Junta, Colo., 9/17/1935
**Kettering**, Charles F. (engineer and inventor); nr. Loudonville, Ohio **(1876-1958)**
**Key**, Francis Scott (lawyer and author of national anthem); Frederick (now Carroll) County, Md. **(1779-1843)**
**Keyes**, Frances Parkinson (novelist); Charlottesville, Va. **(1885-1970)**
**Keynes** (1st Baron of Tilton) (John Maynard Keynes) (economist); Cambridge, England **(1883-1946)**
**Khachaturian**, Aram (composer); Tiflis, Russia **(1903-1978)**
**Khrushchev**, Nikita S. (Soviet leader); Kalinovka, nr. Kursk, Ukraine **(1894-1971)**
**Kibbee**, Guy (actor); El Paso **(1886-1956)**
**Kidd**, Michael (choreographer); Brooklyn, N.Y., 1917
**Kidd**, William (called Captain Kidd) (pirate); Greenock, Scotland **(1645?-1701)**
**Kieran**, John (writer); New York City **(1892-1981)**
**Kierkegaard**, Sören Aalys (philosopher); Copenhagen **(1813-1855)**
**Kiesinger**, Kurt Georg (diplomat); Ebingen, Germany, 4/6/1904
**Kiley**, Richard (actor and singer); Chicago, 3/31/1922
**Kilmer**, Alfred Joyce (poet); New Brunswick, N.J. **(1886-1918)**
**King**, Alan (Irwin Alan Kniberg) (entertainer); Brooklyn, N.Y., 12/26/1927
**King**, B.B. (Riley King) (guitarist); Itta Bena, Miss., 9/16/1925
**King**, Carole (singer and songwriter); Brooklyn, N.Y., 2/9/1941
**King**, Coretta Scott (civil rights leader); Marion, Ala., 4/27/1927
**King**, Martin Luther, Jr. (civil rights leader); Atlanta **(1929-1968)**
**King**, Pee Wee (Frank) (singer); Abrams, Wis., 2/18/1914
**King**, Stephen (writer); Portland, Maine, 9/21/1947
**Kingsley**, Ben (Krishna Bhanji) (actor); Snainton, England, 12/31/1943
**Kingsley**, Sidney (Sidney Kirschner) (playwright); New York City, 10/18/1906
**Kinski**, Nastassja (Nastassja Nakszynski) (actress); West Berlin, 1/24/1961
**Kipling**, Rudyard (author); Bombay **(1865-1936)**
**Kipnis**, Alexander (basso); Ukraine, **(1891-1978)**
**Kirby**, George (comedian); Chicago, **1923(?)**
**Kirk**, Grayson (educator); Jeffersonville, Ohio, 10/12/1903
**Kirk**, Lisa (actress and singer); Charleroi, Pa., 1925
**Kirk**, Phyllis (actress); Plainfield, N.J., 9/18/1930
**Kirkland**, Gelsey (ballerina); Bethlehem, Pa., 12/29/1952
**Kirkpatrick**, Jeane Jordan (educator-public affairs) Duncan, Okla., 11/19/1926
**Kirkpatrick**, Ralph (harpsichordist); Leominster, Mass. **(1911-1984)**
**Kirkwood**, James (actor); Grand Rapids, Mich. **(1883-1963)**
**Kirsten**, Dorothy (soprano); Montclair, N.J., 7/6/1919
**Kissinger**, Henry (Heinz Alfred Kissinger) (ex-Secretary of State); Furth, Germany, 5/27/1923
**Kitt**, Eartha (singer); North, S.C., 1/26/1928
**Klee**, Paul (painter); Münchenbuchsee, nr. Bern, Switzerland **(1879-1940)**
**Klein**, Calvin (fashion designer); Bronx, N.Y., 11/19/1942
**Klein**, Robert (comedian); New York City, 2/8/1942
**Kleist**, Henrich von (poet); Frankfurt an der Oder (East Germany) **(1777-1811)**
**Klemperer**, Otto (conductor); Breslau (Poland) **(1885-1973)**
**Klemperer**, Werner (actor); Cologne, Germany, 3/22/1920
**Klugman**, Jack (actor); Philadelphia, 4/27/1922
**Knievel**, Evel (Robert Craig) (daredevil motorcyclist); Butte, Mont., 10/17/1938
**Knight**, Gladys (singer); Atlanta, 5/28/1944
**Knight**, Ted (Tadeus Wladyslaw Konopka) (actor); Terryville, Conn., **(1923-1986)**
**Knight**, John S. (publisher); Bluefield, W. Va. **(1894-1981)**
**Knopf**, Alfred A. (publisher); New York City **(1892-1984)**
**Knotts**, Don (actor); Morgantown, W.Va., 7/21/1924
**Knox**, John (religious reformer); Haddington, East Lothian, Scotland **(1505-1572)**
**Koch**, Robert (physician); Klausthal (Germany) **(1843-1910)**
**Koestler**, Arthur (novelist); Budapest **(1905-1983)**
**Kokoschka**, Oskar (painter); Pöchlarn Austria **(1886-1980)**
**Kooper**, Al (singer and pianist); Brooklyn, N.Y., 2/5/1944
**Korman**, Harvey (actor); Chicago, 2/15/1927  -
**Kosciusko**, Thaddeus (Tadeusz Andrzej Bonawentura Kosciuszko)

(military officer); Grand Duchy of Lithuania **(1746-1817)**
**Kossuth,** Lajos (patriot); Monok, Hungary **(1802-1894)**
**Kostelanetz,** André (orchestra conductor); St. Petersburg, Russia **(1901-1980)**
**Kosygin,** Aleksei N. (Premier); St. Petersburg, Russia **(1904-1980)**
**Koussevitzky,** Serge (Sergei) Alexandrovitch (orchestra conductor); Vishni Volochek, Tver, Russia **(1874-1951)**
**Kovacs,** Ernie (comedian); Trenton, N.J. **(1919-1962)**
**Kramer,** Stanley E. (film producer and director); New York City, 9/29/1913
**Kràus,** Lili (pianist); Budapest, 3/4/1905(?)
**Kreisler,** Fritz (violinist and composer); Vienna **(1875-1962)**
**Kresge,** S. S. (merchant); Bald Mount, Pa. **(1867-1966)**
**Krips,** Josef (orchestra conductor); Vienna **(1902-1974)**
**Kristofferson,** Kris (singer); Brownsville, Tex., 6/22/1936
**Kruger,** Otto (actor); Toledo, Ohio **(1885-1974)**
**Krupa,** Gene (drummer); Chicago **(1909-1973)**
**Krupp,** Alfred (munitions magnate); Essen; Germany **(1812-1887)**
**Kubelik,** Rafael (conductor); Bychory (Czechoslovakia), 6/29/1914
**Kublai Khan** (Mongol conqueror) **(1216-1294)**
**Kubrick,** Stanley (producer and director); New York City, 7/26/1928
**Kuralt,** Charles (TV journalist); Wilmington, N.C., 9/10/1934
**Kurosawa,** Akira (film director); Tokyo, 3/23/1910
**Kurtz,** Efrem (conductor); St. Petersburg, Russia, 11/7/1900
**Ky,** Nguyen Cao (ex-Vice President of South Vietnam); Son Tay (Vietnam), 9/8/1930

# L

**Ladd,** Alan (actor); Hot Springs, Ark. **(1913-1964)**
**Ladd,** Cheryl (Cheryl Stoppelmoor) (actress); Huron, S.D., 7/12/1951
**Lafayette,** Marquis de (Marie Joseph Paul Yves Roch Gilbert du Motier) (military officer); Auvergne, France **(1757-1834)**
**Lafitte,** Jean (pirate); Bayonne? France **(1780-1826)**
**La Follette,** Robert Marin (politician); Primrose, Wis. **(1855-1925)**
**La Guardia,** Fiorello Henry (Mayor of New York); New York City **(1882-1947)**
**Lahr,** Bert (Irving Lahrheim) (comedian); New York City **(1895-1967)**
**Laine,** Frankie (Frank Paul LoVecchio) (singer); Chicago, 3/30/1913
**Laird,** Melvin (ex-Secretary of Defense); Omaha, Neb., 9/1/1922
**Lamarck,** Chevalier de (Jean Baptiste Pierre Antoine de Monet) (naturalist); Bazantin, France **(1744-1829)**
**Lamarr,** Hedy (Hedwig Kiesler) (actress); Vienna, 1915
**Lamas,** Fernando (actor); Buenos Aires, **(1915-1982)**
**Lamb,** Charles (Elia) (essayist); London **(1775-1834)**
**Lamour,** Dorothy (Dorothy Kaumeyer) (actress); New Orleans, 10/10/1914
**Lancaster,** Burt (actor); New York City, 11/2/1913
**Lanchester,** Elsa (Elsa Sullivan) (actress); London, 10/28/1902
**Landau,** Martin (actor); Brooklyn, N.Y. 1934
**Landers,** Ann (columnist); Sioux City, Iowa, 7/4/1918
**Landon,** Michael (Eugene Maurice Orowitz) (actor); Forest Hills, Queens, N.Y., 10/31/1936(?)
**Lane,** Abbe (singer); New York City, 1933
**Lang,** Fritz (film director); Vienna **(1890-1976)**
**Lang,** Paul Henry (music critic); Budapest, 8/28/1901
**Lange,** Hope (actress); Redding Ridge, Conn., 11/28/1933
**Langella,** Frank (actor); Bayonne, N.J., 1/1/1940
**Langford,** Frances (singer); Lakeland, Fla., 4/4/1913
**Langmuir,** Irving (chemist); Brooklyn, N.Y. **(1881-1957)**
**Langtry,** Lillie (Emily Le Breton) (actress); Island of Jersey **(1852-1929)**
**Lansbury,** Angela (actress); London, 10/16/1925
**Lansing,** Robert (Robert Howell Brown) (actor); San Diego, Calif., 6/5/1928
**Lanza,** Mario (Alfred Arnold Cocozza) (singer and actor); Philadelphia **(1925-1959)**
**Lao-Tzu** (or Lao-Tse) (Li Erh) (philosopher); Honan Province, China (c. 604-531 B.C.)
**Lardner,** Ring (Ringgold Wilmar Lardner) (story writer); Niles, Mich. **(1885-1933)**
**La Rouchefoucauld,** Francois duc de (author); Paris **(1613-1680)**
**La Salle,** Sieur de (Robert Cavelier) (explorer); Rouen, France **(1643-1687)**
**Lasser,** Louise (actress); New York City, 1940(?)
**Lauder,** Sir Harry (Harry MacLennan) (singer); Portobello, Scotland **(1870-1950)**
**Laughton,** Charles (actor); Scarborough, England **(1899-1962)**
**Lauper,** Cyndi (singer); New York City, 6/20/53
**Laurel,** Stan (Arthur Jefferson) (comedian); Ulverston, England **(1890-1965)**
**Laurents,** Arthur (playwright); New York City, 7/14/1918
**Laurie,** Piper (Rosetta Jacobs) (actress); Detroit, 1/22/1932
**Lavoisier,** Antoine-Laurent (chemist); Paris **(1743-1794)**

**Lawford,** Peter (actor); London **(1923-1984)**
**Lawrence,** Carol (Carol Maria Laraia) (dancer and actress); Melrose Park, Ill., 9/5/1932
**Lawrence,** David Herbert (novelist); Nottingham, England **(1885-1930)**
**Lawrence,** Gertrude (Gertrud Klasen) (actress); London **(1900-1952)**
**Lawrence,** Marjorie (singer); Deans Marsh, Australia **(1908-1979)**
**Lawrence,** Steve (Sidney Leibowitz) (singer); Brooklyn, N.Y., 7/8/1935
**Lawrence,** Vicki (Ann) (actress); Inglewood, Calif., 3/26/1949
**Lawrence of Arabia** (Thomas Edward Lawrence, later changed to Shaw) (author and soldier); Tremadoc, Wales **(1888-1935)**
**Leachman,** Cloris (actress); Des Moines, Iowa, 4/30/1926(?)
**Lean,** David (film director); Croydon, England, 3/25/1908
**Lear,** Edward (nonsense poet); London **(1812-1888)**
**le Carré,** John (David John Moore Cornwell) (novelist); Poole, England, 10/19/1931
**Le Corbusier** (Charles Edouard Jeanneret) (architect); La Chaux-de-Fonds, Switzerland **(1887-1965)**
**Lederer,** Francis (actor); Prague, 11/6/1906
**Lee,** Christopher (actor); London, 5/27/1922
**Lee,** Gypsy Rose (Rose Louise Hovick) (entertainer); Seattle **(1919-1970)**
**Lee,** Manfred B. (novelist, pseudonym Ellery Queen); Brooklyn, N.Y. **(1905-1971)**
**Lee,** Peggy (Norma Engstrom) (singer); Jamestown, N.D., 5/26/1920
**Lee,** Robert Edward (Confederate general); Stratford Estate, Va. **(1807-1870)**
**Leeuwenhoek,** Anton van (zoologist) Delft (Netherlands) **(1632-1723)**
**Le Gallienne,** Eva (actress); London, 1/11/1899
**Lehár,** Franz (composer); Komárom (Czechoslovakia) **(1870-1948)**
**Lehman,** Herbert H. (Governor and Senator); New York City **(1878-1963)**
**Lehmann,** Lotte (soprano); Perleberg (Germany) **(1888-1976)**
**Leibniz,** Gottfried W. von (scientist); Leipzig (East Germany) **(1646-1716)**
**Leigh,** Janet (Jeanetta Morrison) (actress); Merced, Calif., 7/6/1927
**Leigh,** Vivien (Vivien Mary Hartley) (actress); Darjeeling, India **(1913-1967)**
**Leighton,** Margaret (actress); nr. Birmingham, England **(1922-1976)**
**Leinsdorf,** Erich (conductor); Vienna, 2/4/1912
**Lemmon,** Jack (actor); Boston, 2/8/1925
**Lenin,** N. (Vladimir Ilich Ulyanov) (Soviet leader); Simbirsk, Russia **(1870-1924)**
**Lennon,** John (singer and songwriter); Liverpool, England **(1940-1980)**
**Lenya,** Lotte (Karoline Blamauer) (singer and actress); Vienna, Austria **(1898-1981)**
**Leonard,** Sheldon (actor and director); New York City, 2/22/1907
**Lerner,** Alan Jay (lyricist); New York City **(1918-1986)**
**Lerner,** Max (columnist); Minsk, Russia, 12/20/1902
**Le Roy,** Mervyn (film producer); San Francisco, 10/15/1900
**Leslie,** Joan (actress); Detroit, 1/26/1925
**Lessing,** Doris (novelist); Kermanshah, Iran, 10/22/1919
**Lester,** Mark (actor); Richmond, England, 1958
**Letterman,** David (TV personality); Indianapolis, 1944
**Levant,** Oscar (pianist); Pittsburgh **(1906-1972)**
**Levene,** Sam (actor); New York City **(1905-1980)**
**Levenson,** Sam (humorist); New York City **(1911-1980)**
**Levi,** Carlo (novelist); Turin, Italy **(1902-1975)**
**Levine,** James (music director, Metropolitan Opera); Cincinnati, 6/23/1943
**Levine,** Joseph E. (film producer); Boston, 9/9/1905
**Lewis,** Jerry (Joseph Levitch) (comedian and film director); Newark, N.J., 3/16/1926
**Lewis,** Jerry Lee (singer); Ferriday, La., 9/29/1935
**Lewis,** John Llewellyn (labor leader); Lucas, Iowa **(1880-1969)**
**Lewis,** Meriwether (explorer); Albemarle Co., Va. **(1774-1809)**
**Lewis,** Shari (Shari Hurwitz) (puppeteer); New York City, 1/17/1934
**Lewis,** Sinclair (novelist); Sauk Centre, Minn. **(1885-1951)**
**Lewis,** Ted (entertainer); Circleville, Ohio **(1891-1971)**
**Ley,** Willy (science writer); Berlin **(1906-1969)**
**Liberace** (Wladziu Liberace) (pianist); West Allis, Wis., 5/16/1919
**Lichtenstein,** Roy (painter); New York City, 10/27/1923
**Lie,** Trygve Halvdan (first U.N. Secretary-General); Oslo **(1896-1968)**
**Lightfoot,** Gordon (singer and songwriter); Orillia, Ontario, Canada, 11/17/1938
**Lillie,** Beatrice (Lady Peel) (actress and comedienne); Toronto, 5/29/1898
**Lin Yutang** (author); Changchow, China **(1895-1976)**
**Lind,** Jenny (Johanna Maria Lind) (soprano); Stockholm **(1820-1887)**
**Lindbergh,** Anne Morrow (author); Englewood, N.J., 6/22/1906
**Lindbergh,** Charles A. (aviator); Detroit **(1902-1974)**
**Linden,** Hal (Harold Lipshitz) (actor); New York City, 3/20/1931
**Lindsay,** Howard (playwright); Waterford, N.Y. **(1889-1968)**

**Lindsay,** John Vliet (ex-Mayor of New York City); New York City, 11/24/1921

**Lindstrom,** Pia (TV newscaster); Stockholm, 11/?/1938

**Linkletter,** Art (radio-TV personality); Moose Jaw, Saskatchewan, Canada, 7/17/1912

**Linnaeus,** Carolus (Carl von Linné) (botanist); Råshult, Sweden **(1707-1778)**

**Lipchitz,** Jacques (sculptor); Druskieniki, Latvia **(1891-1973)**

**Lippi,** Fra Filippo (painter); Florence **(1406-1469)**

**Lippmann,** Walter (columnist, author, and political analyst); New York City **(1889-1974)**

**Lister,** (1st Baron of Lyme Regis) (Joseph Lister) (surgeon); Upton, England **(1827-1912)**

**Liszt,** Franz (composer and pianist); Raiding (Hungary) **(1811-1886)**

**Little,** Cleavon (actor and comedian); Chickasha, Okla., 6/1/1939

**Little,** Rich (impressionist); Ottawa, 11/26/1938

**Livesey,** Roger (actor); Barry, Wales **(1906-1976)**

**Livingstone,** David (missionary and explorer); Lanarkshire, Scotland **(1813-1873)**

**Livingstone,** Mary (Sadye Marks) (comedienne); Seattle **(1909-1983)**

**Llewellyn,** Richard (novelist); St. David's, Wales **(1906-1983)**

**Lloyd,** Harold (comedian); Burchard, Neb. **(1894-1971)**

**Lloyd George,** David (Earl of Dwyfor) (statesman); Manchester, England **(1863-1945)**

**Locke,** John (philosopher); Somersetshire, England **(1632-1704)**

**Lockhart,** Gene (actor); London, Ontario, Canada **(1891-1957)**

**Lockhart,** June (actress); New York City, 6/25/1925

**Lockwood,** Margaret (actress); Karachi (Pakistan), 9/15/1916

**Lodge,** Henry Cabot (legislator); Boston **(1850-1924)**

**Lodge,** Henry Cabot, Jr. (diplomat); Nahant, Mass. **(1902-1985)**

**Loesser,** Frank (composer); New York City **(1910-1969)**

**Loewe,** Frederick (composer); Vienna, 6/10/1904

**Logan,** Joshua (director and producer); Texarkana, Tex., 10/5/1908

**Lollobrigida,** Gina (actress); Subiaco, Italy, 1928

**Lombard,** Carole (Carol Jane Peters) (actress); Ft. Wayne, Ind. **(1908-1942)**

**Lombardo,** Guy (band leader); London, Ontario, Canada **(1902-1977)**

**London,** George (baritone); Montreal **(1920-1985)**

**London,** Jack (John Griffith London) (novelist); San Francisco **(1876-1916)**

**London,** Julie (Julie Peck) (singer and actress); Santa Rosa, Calif., 9/26/1926

**Long,** Huey Pierce (politician); Winnfield, La. **(1893-1935)**

**Longfellow,** Henry Wadsworth (poet); Portland, Me. **(1807-1882)**

**Longworth,** Alice Roosevelt (social figure); New York City **(1884-1980)**

**Loos,** Anita (novelist); Sissons, Calif., **(1888-1981)**

**Lopez,** Trini (Trinidad Lopez III) (singer); Dallas, 5/15/1937

**Lopez,** Vincent (band leader); Brooklyn, N.Y. **(1895-1975)**

**Lord,** Jack (John Joseph Ryan) (actor); New York City, 12/30/1930

**Loren,** Sophia (Sofia Scicolone) (actress); Rome, 9/20/1934

**Lorre,** Peter (Laszlo Löewenstein) (actor); Rosenberg (Czechoslovakia) **(1904-1964)**

**Loudon.** Dorothy (actress, singer); Boston, 9/17/1933

**Louise,** Tina (actress); New York City, 2/11/1937

**Lowell,** Amy (poet); Brookline, Mass. **(1874-1925)**

**Lowell,** James Russell (poet); Cambridge, Mass. **(1819-1891)**

**Lowell,** Robert (poet); Boston **(1917-1977)**

**Loy,** Myrna (Myrna Williams) (actress); nr. Helena, Mont., 8/2/1905

**Loyola,** St. Ignatius of (Iñigo de Oñez y Loyola) (founder of Jesuits); Güipuzcoa Province, Spain **(1491-1556)**

**Lubitsch,** Ernst (film director); Berlin **(1892-1947)**

**Luce,** Clare Boothe (playwright and former Ambassador); New York City, 4/10/1903

**Luce,** Henry Robinson (editor and publisher); Tengchow, China **(1898-1967)**

**Ludlum,** Robert (author); New York City, 5/25/1927

**Lugosi,** Bela (Bela Lugosi Blasko) (actor); Logos, Hungary **(1888-1956)**

**Lukas,** Paul (actor); Budapest **(1895-1971)**

**Lully,** Jean Baptiste (French composer); Florence **(1639-1687)**

**Lumet,** Sidney (film and TV director); Philadelphia, 6/25/1924

**Lunt,** Alfred (actor); Milwaukee **(1892-1977)**

**Lupino,** Ida (actress and director); London, 2/4/1918

**Luther,** Martin (religious reformer); Eisleben (East Germany) **(1483-1546)**

**Lynde,** Paul (comedian); Mt. Vernon, Ohio **(1926-1982)**

**Lynley,** Carol (actress); New York City, 2/13/1942

**Lynn,** Jeffrey (actor); Auburn, Mass., 1909

**Lynn,** Loretta (singer); Butcher's Hollow, Ky., 4/14/1935

# M

**Ma,** Yo-Yo (cellist); Paris, 10/7/1955

**Maazel,** Lorin (conductor); Neuilly, France, 3/5/1930

**MacArthur,** Charles (playwright); Scranton, Pa. **(1895-1956)**

**MacArthur,** Douglas (five-star general); Little Rock Barracks, Ark. **(1880-1964)**

**MacArthur,** James (actor); Los Angeles, 12/8/1937

**Macaulay,** Thomas Babington (author); Rothley Temple, England **(1800-1859)**

**MacDermot,** Galt (composer); Montreal, 12/19/1928

**MacDonald,** James Ramsay (statesman); Lossiemouth, Scotland **(1866-1937)**

**MacDonald,** Jeanette (actress and soprano); Philadelphia **(1907-1965)**

**Macdonald,** Ross (Kenneth Millar) (mystery writer); Los Gatos, Calif. **(1915-1983)**

**MacDowell,** Edward Alexander (composer); New York City **(1861-1908)**

**Macfadden,** Bernarr (physical culturist); nr. Mill Spring, Mo. **(1868-1955)**

**MacGraw,** Ali (actress); New York City, 4/1/1939

**Machaut,** Guillaume de (composer); Marchault, France **(1300-1377)**

**Machiavelli,** Niccolò (political philosopher); Florence (Italy) **(1469-1527)**

**Mack,** Ted (TV personality); Greeley, Colo. **(1904-1976)**

**MacKenzie,** Gisele (Marie Marguerite Louise Gisele LaFleche) (singer and actress); Winnipeg, Manitoba, Canada, 1/10/1927

**MacLaine,** Shirley (Shirley MacLean Beaty) (actress); Richmond, Va., 4/24/1934

**MacLeish,** Archibald (poet); Glencoe, Ill. **(1892-1982)**

**Macmillan,** Harold (ex-Prime Minister); London, 2/10/1894

**MacMurray,** Fred (actor); Kankakee, Ill., 8/30/1908

**MacNeil,** Cornell (baritone); Minneapolis, 1925

**MacRae,** Gordon (singer); East Orange, N.J. **(1921-1986)**

**MacRae,** Sheila (comedienne); London, 9/24/1924

**Madison,** Guy (Robert Moseley) (actor); Bakersfield, Calif., 1/19/1922

**Madonna** (Madonna Louise Ciccone) (singer); Bay City, Mich. 1960

**Maeterlinck,** Count Maurice (author); Ghent, Belgium **(1862-1949)**

**Magellan,** Ferdinand (Fernando de Magalhaes) (navigator); Sabrosa, Portugal **(1480?-1521)**

**Magnani,** Anna (actress); Rome **(1908-1973)**

**Magritte,** René (painter); Belgium **(1898-1967)**

**Magsaysay,** Ramón (statesman); Iba, Luzon, Philippines **(1907-1957)**

**Mahan,** Alfred Thayer (naval historian); West Point, N.Y. **(1840-1914)**

**Mahler,** Gustav (composer and conductor); Kalischt (Czechoslovakia) **(1860-1911)**

**Mailer,** Norman (novelist); Long Branch, N.J., 1/31/1923

**Mailloi,** Aristide (sculptor); Banyuls-sur-Mer, Rousillion, France **(1861-1944)**

**Maimonides,** Moses (Jewish philosopher) Cordoba, Spain **(1135-1204)**

**Main,** Marjorie (Mary Tomlinson Krebs) (actress); Acton, Ind. **(1890-1975)**

**Mainbocher** (Main Rousseau Bocher) (fashion designer); Chicago **(1891-1976)**

**Majors,** Lee (actor); Wyandotte, Mich., 4/23/1940

**Makarova,** Natalia (ballerina); Leningrad, 11/21/1940

**Makeba,** Miriam (singer); Johannesburg, South Africa, 3/4/1932

**Malamud,** Bernard (novelist); Brooklyn, N.Y., **(1914-1986)**

**Malden,** Karl (Miaden Sekulovich) (actor); Chicago, 3/22/1913

**Malone,** Dorothy (actress); Chicago, 1/30/1925

**Malraux,** André (author); Paris **(1901-1976)**

**Malthus,** Thomas Robert (economist); nr. Dorking, England **(1766-1834)**

**Mamet,** David (playwright); Chicago, 11/30/1947

**Manchester,** Melissa (singer); Bronx, N.Y., 2/15/1951

**Manchester,** William (writer); Attleboro, Mass., 4/1/1922

**Mancini,** Henry (composer and conductor); Cleveland, 4/16/1924

**Mandrell,** Barbara (singer); Houston, 12/25/1948

**Manet,** Edouard (painter); Paris **(1832-1883)**

**Mangano,** Silvana (actress); Rome, 4/21/1930

**Mangione,** Chuck (hornist, pianist, and composer); Rochester, N.Y., 11/29/1940

**Manilow,** Barry (singer); Brooklyn, N.Y., 6/17/1946

**Mankiewicz,** Frank F. (columnist); New York City, 5/16/1924

**Mankiewicz,** Joseph L. (film writer and director); Wilkes-Barre, Pa., 2/11/1909

**Mann,** Horace (educator); Franklin, Mass. **(1796-1859)**

**Mann,** Thomas (novelist); Lübeck, Germany **(1875-1955)**

**Mannes,** Marya (writer); New York City, 11/14/1904

**Mansfield,** Jayne (Jayne Palmer) (actress); Bryn Mawr, Pa. **(1932-1967)**

**Mansfield,** Katherine (story writer); Wellington, New Zealand **(1888-1923)**

**Mantovani,** Annunzio (conductor); Venice **(1905-1980)**

**Mao Zedong** (Tse-tung) (Chinese leader); Shao Shan, China **(1893-1976)**

Marat, Jean Paul (French revolutionist); Boudry, Neuchâtei, Switzerland (1743-1793)
Marceau, Marcel (mime); Strasbourg, France, 3/22/1923
March, Fredric (Frederick Bickel) (actor); Racine, Wis. (1897-1975)
Marconi, Guglielmo (inventor); Bologna, Italy (1874-1937)
Marcus Aurelius (Marcus Annius Verus) (Roman emperor); Rome (121-180)
Marcuse, Herbert (philosopher); Berlin, (1898-1979)
Margaret Rose (Princess); Glamis Castle, Angus, Scotland, 8/21/1930
Margrethe II (Queen); Copenhagen, 4/16/1940
Marie Antoinette (Josephe Jeanne Marie Antoinette) (Queen of France); Vienna (1755-1793)
Marisol (sculptor); Venezuela, 1930
Markham, Edwin (poet); Oregon City, Ore. (1852-1940)
Markova, Dame Alicia (Lilian Alice Marks) (ballerina); London, 12/1/1910
Marley, Bob (reggae singer and songwriter); Kingston, Jamaica (1945-1981)
Marlowe, Christopher (dramatist); Canterbury, England (1564-1593)
Marlowe, Julia (Sarah Frances Frost) (actress); Cumberlandshire, England (1866-1950)
Marquand, J(ohn) P(hillips) (novelist); Wilmington, Del. (1893-1960)
Marquette, Jacques (missionary and explorer); Laon, France (1637-1675)
Marriner, Neville (conductor); Lincoln, England, 4/15/1924
Marsh, Jean (actress); Stoke Newington, England, 7/1/1934
Marshall, E.G. (actor); Owatonna, Minn., 6/18/1910
Marshall, George Catlett (general); Uniontown, Pa. (1880-1959)
Marshall, Herbert (actor); London (1890-1968)
Marshall, John (jurist); nr. Germantown, Va. (1755-1835)
Marshall, Penny (actress); New York City, 10/15/1942
Martin, Dean (Dino Crocetti) (singer and actor); Steubenville, Ohio, 6/17/1917
Martin, Dick (actor and comedian); Battle Creek, Mich., 1/30/1922
Martin, Mary (singer and actress); Weatherford, Tex., 12/1/1913
Martin, Steve (comedian); Waco, Tex., 1945(?)
Martin, Tony (Alvin Morris) (singer); San Francisco, 12/25/1913
Martinelli, Giovanni (tenor); Montagnana, Italy (1885-1969)
Martins, Peter (dancer-choreographer); Copenhagen, 10/27/1945
Marvell, Andrew (poet); Winestead, England (1621-1678)
Marvin, Lee (actor); New York City, 2/19/1924
Marx, Chico (Leonard) (comedian); New York City (1891-1961)
Marx, Groucho (Julius) (comedian); New York City (1890-1977)
Marx, Harpo (Arthur) (comedian); New York City (1893-1964)
Marx, Karl (socialist writer); Treves (Germany) (1818-1883)
Marx, Zeppo (Herbert) (comedian); New York City (1901-1979)
Mary Stuart (Queen of Scotland); Linlithgow, Scotland (1542-1587)
Masaryk, Jan Garrigue (statesman); Prague (Czechoslovakia) (1886-1948)
Masaryk, Thomas Garrigue (statesman); Hodonin (Czechoslovakia) (1850-1937)
Masefield, John (poet); Ledbury, England (1878-1967)
Masekela, Hugh (trumpeter); Wilbank, South Africa, 4/4/1939
Mason, James (actor); Huddersfield, England (1909-1984)
Massenet, Jules Emile Frédéric (composer); Montaud, France (1842-1912)
Massey, Raymond (actor); Toronto, (1896-1983)
Massine, Léonide (choreographer); Moscow, (1895-1979)
Masters, Edgar Lee (poet); Garnett, Kan. (1869-1950)
Mastroianni, Marcello (actor); Fontana Liri, Italy, 9/28/1924
Mather, Cotton (clergyman); Boston (1663-1728)
Mathis, Johnny (singer); San Francisco, 9/30/1935
Matisse, Henri (painter); Le Cateau, France (1869-1954)
Matthau, Walter (Walter Matuschanskayasky) (actor); New York City, 10/1/1920
Mature, Victor (actor); Louisville, Ky., 1/19/1916
Maugham, W(illiam) Somerset (author); Paris (1874-1965)
Mauldin, Bill (political cartoonist); Mountain Park, N.M., 10/29/1921
Maupassant, Henri René Albert Guy de (story writer); Normandy, France (1850-1893)
Maurois, André (Emile Herzog) (author); Elbauf, France (1885-1967)
Maximilian (Ferdinand Maximilian Joseph) (Emperor of Mexico); Vienna (1832-1867)
Maxwell, James Clerk (physicist); Edinburgh, Scotland (1831-1879)
May, Elaine (Elaine Berlin) (entertainer-writer); Philadelphia, 4/21/1932
May, Rollo (psychologist); Ada, Ohio, 4/21/1909
Mayall, John (singer and songwriter); Manchester, England, 11/29/1933
Mayo, Charles H. (surgeon); Rochester, Minn. (1865-1939)
Mayo, Charles W. (surgeon); Rochester, Minn. (1898-1968)
Mayo, Virginia (Jones) (actress); St. Louis, 1920
Mayo, William J. (surgeon); Le Sueur, Minn. (1861-1939)
Mazzini, Giuseppe (patriot); Genoa (1805-1872)
McBride, Mary Margaret (radio personality); Paris, Mo. (1899-1976)

McBride, Patricia (ballerina); Teaneck, N.J., 8/23/1942
McCallum, David (actor); Glasgow, Scotland, 9/19/1933
McCambridge, Mercedes (actress); Joliet, Ill., 3/17/1918
McCarthy, Eugene J. (ex-Senator); Watkins. Minn., 3/29/1916
McCarthy, Joseph Raymond (Senator); Grand Chute, Wis. (1908-1957)
McCarthy, Kevin (actor); Seattle, 2/15/1914
McCarthy, Mary (novelist); Seattle, 6/21/1912
McCartney, Paul (singer and songwriter); Liverpool, England, 6/18/1942
McClellan, George Brinton (general); Philadelphia (1826-1885)
McClintock, Barbara (geneticist); Hartford, Conn., 6/16/1902
McCloy, John J. (lawyer and banker); Philadelphia, 3/31/1895
McClure, Doug (actor); Glendale, Calif., 5/11/1938
McCormack, John (tenor); Athlone, Ireland (1884-1945)
McCormack, John W. (ex-Speaker of House); Boston (1891-1980)
McCormack, Patty (actress); New York City, 8/21/1945
McCormick, Cyrus Hall (inventor); Rockbridge County, Va. (1809-1884)
McCoy, Col. Tim (actor); Saginaw, Mich. (1891-1978)
McCracken, James (dramatic tenor); Gary, Ind., 12/16/1926
McCrea, Joel (actor); Los Angeles, 11/5/1905
McCullers, Carson (novelist); Columbus, Ga. (1917-1967)
McDowall, Roddy (actor); London, 9/17/1928
McDowell, Malcolm (actor); Leeds, England, 6/19/1943
McGavin, Darren (actor); San Joaquin, Calif., 5/7/1922
McGinley, Phyllis (poet and writer); Ontario, Ore. (1905-1978)
McGoohan, Patrick (actor); Astoria, Queens, N.Y., 1928
McGuire, Dorothy (actress); Omaha, Neb. 6/14/1919
McKellen, Ian (actor); Burnley, England, 5/25/1939
McKenna, Siobhan (actress); Belfast, Northern Ireland, 5/24/1923
McKuen, Rod (singer and composer); Oakland, Calif., 4/29/1933
McLaglen, Victor (actor); Tunbridge Wells, Kent, England (1886-1959)
McLaughlin, John (guitarist); Yorkshire, England, 1942
McLean, Don (singer and songwriter); New Rochelle, N.Y., 10/2/1945
McLuhan, Marshall (Herbert Marshall) (communications writer); Edmonton, Canada (1911-1980)
McMahon, Ed (TV personality); Detroit, 3/6/1923
McNamara, Robert S. (former president of World Bank); San Francisco, 6/9/1916
McQueen, Steve (Terence Stephen McQueen) (actor); Indianapolis (1930-1980)
Mead, Margaret (anthropologist); Philadelphia, (1901-1978)
Meadows, Audrey (actress); Wu Chang, China, 1922(?)
Meadows, Jayne (actress); Wu Chang, China 9/27/1926
Meany, George (labor leader); New York City (1894-1980)
Meara, Anne (actress); New York City, 1929
Medici, Lorenzo de' (called Lorenzo the Magnificent) (Florentine ruler); Florence (Italy) (1449-1492)
Meeker, Ralph (Ralph Rathgeber) (actor); Minneapolis, 11/21/1920
Mehta, Zubin (conductor); Bombay, 4/29/1936
Meir, Golda (Golda Myerson, nee Mabovitz) (ex-Premier of Israel); Kiev, Russia (1898-1978)
Melanie (Melanie Safka) (singer and songwriter); New York City, 2/3/1947
Melba, Dame Nellie (Helen Porter Mitchell) (soprano); nr. Melbourne (1861-1931)
Melchior, Lauritz (Lebrecht Hommel) (heroic tenor); Copenhagen (1890-1973)
Mellon, Andrew William (financier); Pittsburgh (1855-1937)
Melville, Herman (novelist); New York City (1819-1891)
Mencken, Henry Louis (writer); Baltimore (1880-1956)
Mendel, Gregor Johann (geneticist); Heinzendorf, Austrian Silesia (1822-1884)
Mendeleyev, Dmitri Ivanovich (chemist); Tobolsk, Russia (1834-1907)
Mendelssohn-Bartholdy, Jakob Ludwig Felix (composer); Hamburg (1809-1847)
Mendès-France, Pierre (ex-Premier); Paris (1905-1982)
Menjou, Adolphe (actor); Pittsburgh (1890-1963)
Mennin, Peter (Peter Mennini) (composer); Erie, Pa. (1923-1983)
Menninger, William C. (psychiatrist); Topeka, Kan. (1899-1966)
Menotti, Gian Carlo (composer); Cadegliano, Italy, 7/7/1911
Menuhin, Yehudi (violinist and conductor); New York City, 4/22/1916
Menzies, Robert Gordon (ex-Prime Minister); Jeparit, Australia (1894-1978)
Mercer, Johnny (songwriter); Savannah, Ga. (1909-1976)
Mercer, Mabel (singer); Burton-on-Trent, England (1900-1984)
Mercouri, Melina (actress); Athens, 10/18/1925
Meredith, Burgess (actor); Cleveland, 11/16/1908
Merkel, Una (actress); Covington, Ky. (1903-1986)
Merman, Ethel (Ethel Zimmerman) (singer and actress); Astoria, Queens, N.Y. (1909-1984)
Merrick, David (David Margulois) (stage producer); St. Louis, 11/27/1912

**Merrill,** Dina (actress); New York City, 12/9/1925

**Merrill,** Gary (actor); Hartford, Conn., 8/2/1914

**Merrill,** Robert (baritone); Brooklyn, N.Y., 6/4/1919

**Merton,** Thomas (clergyman and writer); France **(1915-1968)**

**Mesmer,** Franz Anton (physician); Itzmang, nr. Constance (Germany) **(1733-1815)**

**Mesta,** Perle (social figure); Sturgis, Mich. **(1889-1975)**

**Metternich,** Prince Klemens Wenzel Nepomuk Lothar von (statesman); Coblenz (Germany) **(1773-1859)**

**Michelangelo** Buonarreti (painter, sculptor, and architect); Caprese (Italy) **(1475-1564)**

**Michener,** James A. (novelist); New York City, 2/3/1907

**Mickiewicz,** Adam (Polish poet); Zozie, Belorussia (U.S.S.R.) **(1798-1855)**

**Midler,** Bette (singer); Honolulu, 1945

**Mielziner,** Jo (stage designer); Paris **(1901-1976)**

**Mies van der Rohe,** Ludwig (architect and designer); Aachen, Germany **(1886-1969)**

**Mikoyan,** Anastas I. (diplomat); Sanain, Armenia, **(1895-1978)**

**Miles,** Sarah (actress); Essex, England, 12/31/1943

**Miles,** Sylvia (actress); New York City, 9/9/1932

**Miles,** Vera (Vera Ralston) (actress); nr. Boise City, Okla., 8/23/1930

**Milhaud,** Darius (composer); Aix-en-Provence, France **(1892-1974)**

**Mill,** John Stuart (philosopher); London, **(1806-1873)**

**Milland,** Ray (Reginald Truscott-Jones) (actor); Neath, Wales **(1907-1986)**

**Millay,** Edna St. Vincent (poet); Rockland, Me. **(1892-1950)**

**Miller,** Ann (Lucille Ann Collier) (dancer and actress); Cherino, Tex., 4/12/1923

**Miller,** Arthur (playwright); New York City, 10/17/1915

**Miller,** Glenn (band leader); Clarinda, Iowa **(1904-1944)**

**Miller,** Henry (novelist); New York City **(1891-1980)**

**Miller,** Jason (John Miller) (playwright); New York City, 1939(?)

**Miller,** Mitch (Mitchell) (musician); Rochester, N.Y., 7/4/1911

**Miller,** Roger (singer); Fort Worth, 1/2/1936

**Millet,** Jean François (painter); Gruchy, France **(1814-1875)**

**Millett,** Kate (feminist); St. Paul, 9/14/1934

**Millikan,** Robert A. (physicist); Morrison, Ill. **(1869-1953)**

**Mills,** Hayley (actress); London, 4/18/1946

**Mills,** John (actor); Felixstowe, England, 2/22/1908

**Milne,** A(lan) A(lexander) (author); London **(1882-1956)**

**Milstein,** Nathan (concert violinist); Odessa, Russia, 12/31/1904

**Milton,** John (poet); London **(1608-1674)**

**Mimieux,** Yvette (actress); Hollywood, Calif., 1/8/1941

**Mineo,** Sal (actor); New York City **(1939-1976)**

**Minnelli,** Liza (singer and actress); Hollywood, Calif., 3/12/1946

**Minnelli,** Vincente (film director); Chicago **(1913-1986)**

**Minuit,** Peter (Governor of New Amsterdam); Wesel (Germany) **(1580-1638)**

**Miranda,** Carmen (Maria do Carmo da Cunha) (singer and dancer); Lisbon **(1913-1955)**

**Miró,** Joan (painter); Barcelona **(1893-1983)**

**Mitchell,** Cameron (actor); Dallastown, Pa., 4/11/1918

**Mitchell,** Guy (actor); Detroit, 2/27/1927

**Mitchell,** John N. (former Attorney General); Detroit, 9/15/1913

**Mitchell,** Joni (Roberta Joan Anderson) (singer and songwriter); Ft. Macleod, Canada, 11/7/1943

**Mitchell,** Margaret (novelist); Atlanta **(1900-1949)**

**Mitchum,** Robert (actor); Bridgeport, Conn., 8/6/1917

**Mitropoulos,** Dimitri (orchestra conductor); Athens **(1896-1960)**

**Mix,** Tom (actor); Mix Run, Pa. **(1880-1940)**

**Modigliani,** Amedeo (painter); Leghorn, Italy **(1884-1920)**

**Moffo,** Anna (soprano); Wayne, Pa., 6/27/1934

**Mohammed** (prophet); Mecca (Saudi Arabia) **(570-632)**

**Molière** (Jean Baptiste Poquelin) (dramatist); Paris **(1622-1673)**

**Molnar,** Ferenc (dramatist); Budapest **(1878-1952)**

**Molotov,** Vyacheslav M. (V. M. Skryabin) (diplomat); Kukarka, Russia, 3/9/1890

**Mondrian,** Piet (painter); Amersfoort, Netherlands **(1872-1944)**

**Monet,** Claude (painter); Paris **(1840-1926)**

**Monk,** Meredith (choreographer-composer-performing artist); Lima, Peru, 11/20/1942

**Monk,** Thelonious (pianist); Rocky Mount, N.C. **(1918-1982)**

**Monroe,** Marilyn (Norma Jean Mortenson or Baker) (actress); Los Angeles **(1926-1962)**

**Monroe,** Vaughn (Wilton) (band leader); Akron, Ohio **(1912-1973)**

**Monsarrat,** Nicholas (novelist); Liverpool, England, **(1910-1979)**

**Montaigne,** Michel Eyquem de (essayist); nr. Bordeaux, France **(1533-1592)**

**Montalban,** Ricardo (actor); Mexico City, 11/25/1920

**Montand,** Yves (Yvo Montand Livi) (actor and singer); Monsummano, Italy, 10/13/1921

**Montesquieu,** Charles-Louis de Secondat, baron de La Brède and de, (philosopher) nr. Borleaux, France **(1689-1755)**

**Monteverdi,** Claudio (composer); Cremona? Italy **(1567-1643)**

**Montez,** Maria (actress); Dominican Republican **(1918-1951)**

**Montezuma II** (Aztec emperor); Mexico **(1480?-1520)**

**Montgomery,** Elizabeth (actress); Hollywood, Calif., 4/15/1933

**Montgomery,** George (George Montgomery Letz) (actor); Brady, Mont., 8/29/1916

**Montgomery,** Robert (Henry, Jr.) (actor); Beacon, N.Y. **(1904-1981)**

**Montgomery of Alamein,** 1st Viscount of Hindhead (Sir Bernard Law Montgomery) (military leader); London **(1887-1976)**

**Montoya,** Carlos (guitarist); Madrid, 12/13/1903

**Moore,** Clement Clarke (author); New York City **(1779-1863)**

**Moore,** Dudley (actor-writer-musician); Dagenham, England, 4/19/1935

**Moore,** Garry (Thomas Garrison Morfit) (TV personality); Baltimore, 1/31/1915

**Moore,** Grace (soprano); Jellico, Tenn. **(1901-1947)**

**Moore,** Henry (sculptor); Castleford, England, 7/30/1898

**Moore,** Marianne (poet); Kirkwood, Mo. **(1887-1972)**

**Moore,** Mary Tyler (actress); Brooklyn, N.Y., 12/29/1937

**Moore,** Melba (Beatrice) (singer and actress); New York City, 10/27/1945

**Moore,** Roger (actor); London, 10/14/1927(?)

**Moore,** Thomas (poet); Dublin **(1779-1852)**

**Moore,** Victor (actor); Hammonton, N.J. **(1876-1962)**

**Moorehead,** Agnes (actress); Clinton, Mass. **(1906-1974)**

**More,** Henry (philosopher); Grantham, England **(1614-1687)**

**More,** Sir Thomas (statesman and author); London **(1478-1535)**

**Moreau,** Jeanne (actress); Paris, 1/23/1928

**Moreno,** Rita (Rosita Dolores Alverio) (actress); Humacao, Puerto Rico, 12/11/1931

**Morgan,** Dennis (actor); Prentice, Wis., 12/10/1920

**Morgan,** Harry (actor); Detroit, 4/10/1915

**Morgan,** Helen (singer); Danville, Ohio **(1900?-1941)**

**Morgan,** Henry (comedian); New York City, 3/31/1915

**Morgan,** Jane (Florence Currier) (singer); Boston, 1920

**Morgan,** John Pierpont (financier); Hartford, Conn. **(1837-1913)**

**Moriarty,** Michael (actor); Detroit, 4/5/1941

**Morini,** Erica (concert violinist); Vienna, 1/5/1910

**Morison,** Samuel Eliot (historian); Boston **(1887-1976)**

**Morley,** Christopher Darlington (novelist); Haverford, Pa. **(1890-1957)**

**Morley,** Robert (actor); Semley, England, 5/26/1908

**Morrison,** Jim (James Douglas Morrison) (singer and songwriter); Melbourne, Fla. **(1943-1971)**

**Morse,** Marston (mathematician); Waterville, Me. **(1892-1977)**

**Morse,** Robert (actor); Newton, Mass., 5/18/1931

**Morse,** Samuel Finley Breese (painter and inventor); Charlestown, Mass. **(1791-1872)**

**Moses,** Grandma (Mrs. Anna Mary Robertson Moses) (painter); Greenwich, N.Y. **(1860-1961)**

**Moses,** Robert (urban planner); New Haven, Conn., **(1888-1981)**

**Mostel,** Zero (Samuel Joel Mostel) (actor); Brooklyn, N.Y. **(1915-1977)**

**Moussorgsky,** Modest Petrovich (composer); Karev, Russia **(1839-1881)**

**Moyers,** Bill D. (Billy Don) (journalist); Hugo, Okla., 6/5/1934

**Moynihan,** Daniel Patrick (New York Senator); Tulsa, Okla., 3/16/1927

**Mozart,** Wolfgang Amadeus (Johannes Chrysostomus Wolfgangus Theophilus Mozart) (composer); Salzburg (Austria) **(1756-1791)**

**Mudd,** Roger (TV newscaster); Washington, D.C., 2/9/1928

**Muggeridge,** Malcolm (Thomas) (writer); Croydon, England, 3/24/1903

**Muhammad,** Elijah (Elijah Poole) (religious leader); Sandersville, Ga. **(1897-1975)**

**Mulgrew,** Kate (actress); Dubuque, Iowa, 4/?/1929

**Mulhare,** Edward (actor); Ireland, 1923

**Mumford,** Lewis (cultural historian and city planner); Flushing, Queens, N.Y., 10/19/1895

**Munch,** Edvard (painter); Löten, Norway **(1863-1944)**

**Munchhausen,** Karl Friedrick Hieronymus, baron von (anecdotist); Hanover, Germany **(1720-1797)**

**Muni,** Paul (Muni Weisenfreund) (actor); Lemburg (Ukraine) **(1895-1967)**

**Munsel,** Patrice (soprano); Spokane, Wash., 5/14/1925

**Murdoch,** Iris (novelist); Dublin, 7/15/1919

**Murdoch,** Rupert (publisher); Melbourne, 3/11/1931

**Murillo,** Bartolomé Esteban (painter); Seville, Spain **(1617-1682)**

**Murphy,** Audie (actor and war hero); Kingston, Tex. **(1924-1971)**

**Murphy,** Eddie (actor-comedian); Brooklyn, N.Y. 4/3/61

**Murphy,** George (actor, dancer, and ex-Senator); New Haven, Conn., 7/4/1902

**Murray,** Arthur (dance teacher); New York City, 4/4/1895

**Murray,** Bill (actor-comedian); Wilmette, Ill. 9/21/1950

**Murray,** Kathryn (dance teacher); Jersey City, N.J., 1906

**Murray,** Ken (Don Court) (producer); New York City, 7/14/1903

**Murray,** Mae (Marie Adrienne Koenig) (actress); Portsmouth, Va. **(1890-1965)**

**Murrow,** Edward R. (commentator and government official); Greensboro, N.C. **(1908-1965)**
**Mussolini,** Benito (Italian dictator); Dovia, Forli, Italy **(1883-1945)**
**Myerson,** Bess (consumer advocate); Bronx, N.Y., 1924
**Myrdal,** Gunnar (sociologist and economist); Gustaf Parish, Sweden, 12/6/1898

# N

**Nabokov,** Vladimir (novelist); St. Petersburg, Russia **(1899-1977)**
**Nabors,** Jim (actor and singer); Sylacauga, Ala., 6/12/1932
**Nader,** Ralph (consumer advocate); Winsted, Conn., 2/27/1934
**Nagel,** Conrad (actor); Keokuk, Iowa **(1897-1970)**
**Naish,** J. Carrol (actor); New York City **(1900-1973)**
**Naldi,** Nita (Anita Donna Dooley) (actress); New York City **(1899-1961)**
**Napoleon** Bonaparte. *See* Bonaparte, Napoleon
**Nash,** Graham (singer); Blackpool, England, 1942
**Nash,** Ogden (poet); Rye, N.Y. **(1902-1971)**
**Nasser,** Gamal Abdel (statesman); Beni Mor, Egypt **(1918-1970)**
**Nast,** Thomas (cartoonist); Landau (Germany) **(1840-1902)**
**Nation,** Carry Amelia (temperance leader); Garrard County, Ky. **(1846-1911)**
**Natwick,** Mildred (actress); Baltimore, 6/19/1908
**Nazimova,** Alla (actress); Yalta, Crimea, Russia **(1879-1945)**
**Neagle,** Anna (Marjorie Robertson) (actress); London **(1908-1986)**
**Neal,** Patricia (actress); Packard, Ky., 1/20/1926
**Neff,** Hildegarde (actress); Ulm, Germany, 12/28/1925
**Negri,** Pola (Appolina Chapulez) (actress); Bromberg (Poland), c. 1897
**Nehru,** Jawaharlal (first Prime Minister of India); Allahabad, India **(1889-1964)**
**Nelson,** Barry (Neilsen) (actor); San Francisco, 1920
**Nelson,** David (actor); New York City, 10/24/1936
**Nelson,** Harriet Hilliard (Peggy Lou Snyder) (actress); Des Moines, Iowa, 1914
**Nelson,** Ozzie (Oswald) (actor); Jersey City, N.J. **(1907-1975)**
**Nelson,** Ricky (Eric) (singer and actor); Teaneck, N.J. **(1940-1985)**
**Nelson,** Viscount Horatio (naval officer); Burnham Thorpe, England **(1758-1805)**
**Nelson,** Willie (singer); Waco, Texas, 4/30/1933
**Nenni,** Pietro (Socialist leader); Faenza, Italy **(1891-1980)**
**Nero** (Nero Claudius Caesar Drusus Germanicus) (Roman emperor); Antium (Italy) **(37-68)**
**Nero,** Peter (pianist); New York City, 5/22/1934
**Nesbitt,** Cathleen (actress); Cheshire, England **(1889-1982)**
**Nevelson,** Louise (sculptor); Kiev, Russia, 9/23/1900
**Newhart,** Bob (entertainer); Chicago, 9/5/1929
**Newhouse,** Samuel I. (publisher); New York City **(1895-1979)**
**Newley,** Anthony (actor and song writer); London, 9/24/1931
**Newman,** Edwin (news commentator); New York City, 1/25/1919
**Newman,** John Henry (prelate); London **(1801-1890)**
**Newman,** Paul (actor and director); Cleveland, 1/26/1925
**Newman,** Randy (singer); Los Angeles, 11/28/1943
**Newton,** Huey (black activist); New Orleans, 2/17/1942
**Newton,** Sir Isaac (mathematician and scientist); nr. Grantham, England **(1642-1727)**
**Newton,** Wayne (singer); Norfolk, Va., 4/3/1942
**Newton-John,** Olivia (singer); Cambridge, England, 9/26/1948
**Nichols,** Mike (Michael Peschkowsky) (stage and film director); Berlin, 11/6/1931
**Nicholson,** Jack (actor); Neptune, N.J., 4/22/1937
**Nietzsche,** Friedrich Wilhelm (philosopher); nr. Lützen Saxony (East Germany) **(1844-1900)**
**Nightingale,** Florence (nurse); Florence (Italy) **(1820-1910)**
**Nijinsky,** Vaslav (ballet dancer); Warsaw **(1890-1950)**
**Nilsson,** Birgit (soprano); West Karup, Sweden, 5/17/1923
**Nilsson,** Harry (singer and songwriter); Brooklyn, N.Y., 6/15/1941
**Nimitz,** Chester W. (naval officer); Fredericksburg, Tex. **(1885-1966)**
**Nimoy,** Leonard (actor); Boston, 3/26/1931
**Nin,** Anais (author and diarist); Neuilly, France **(1903-1977)**
**Niven,** David (actor); Kirriemuir, Scotland, **(1910-1983)**
**Nizer,** Louis (lawyer and author); London, 2/6/1902
**Nobel,** Alfred Bernhard (industrialist); Stockholm **(1833-1896)**
**Noguchi,** Isamu (sculptor); Los Angeles, 11/7/1904
**Nolan,** Lloyd (actor); San Francisco **(1902-1985)**
**Nolte,** Nick (actor); Omaha, Neb., 1942
**Norell,** Norman (Norman Levinson) (fashion designer); Noblesville, Ind. **(1900-1972)**
**Norman,** Marsha (Marsha Williams) (playwright); Louisville, Ky., 9/21/1947
**Norstad,** Gen. Lauris (ex-commander of NATO forces); Minneapolis,

3/24/1907
**North,** John Ringling (circus director); Baraboo, Wis. **(1903-1985)**
**North,** Sheree (actress); Los Angeles, 1/17/1933
**Norton,** Eleanor Holmes (New York City government official, lawyer); Washington, D.C., 6/13/1937
**Nostradamus** (Michel de Notredame) (astrologer); St. Rémy, France **(1503-1566)**
**Novaes,** Guiomar (pianist); São João de Boa Vista, Brazil **(1895-1979)**
**Novak,** Kim (Marilyn Novak) (actress); Chicago, 2/13/1933
**Novarro,** Ramon (Ramon Samaniegoes) (actor); Durango, Mexico **(1899-1968)**
**Nugent,** Elliott (actor and director); Dover, Ohio, **(1899-1980)**
**Nureyev,** Rudolf (ballet dancer); U.S.S.R., 3/17/1938
**Nuyen,** France (actress); Marseilles, France, 7/31/1939
**Nyro,** Laura (singer and songwriter); Bronx, N.Y., 1947

# O

**Oakie,** Jack (actor); Sedalia, Mo. **(1903-1978)**
**Oates,** Joyce Carol (novelist); Lockport, N.Y., 6/16/1938
**Oberon,** Merle (Estelle Merle O'Brien Thompson) (actress); Tasmania **(1911-1979)**
**O'Brian,** Hugh (Hugh J. Krampe) (actor); Rochester, N.Y., 4/19/1930
**O'Brien,** Edmond (actor); New York City **(1915-1985)**
**O'Brien,** Margaret (Angela Maxine O'Brien) (actress); San Diego, Calif., 1/15/1937
**O'Brien,** Pat (William Joseph O'Brien, Jr.) (actor); Milwaukee, **(1899-1983)**
**O'Casey,** Sean (playwright); Dublin **(1881-1964)**
**Ochs,** Adolph Simon (publisher); Cincinnati **(1858-1935)**
**O'Connor,** Carroll (actor); New York City, 8/2/1924
**O'Connor,** Donald (actor); Chicago, 8/28/1925
**Odets,** Clifford (playwright); Philadelphia **(1906-1963)**
**Odetta** (Odetta Holmes) (folk singer and actress); Birmingham, Ala., 12/31/1930
**Offenbach,** Jacques (composer); Cologne, Germany **(1819-1880)**
**O'Hara,** John (novelist); Pottsville, Pa. **(1905-1970)**
**O'Hara,** Maureen (Maureen FitzSimons) (actress); Dublin, 8/17/1921
**Ohlsson,** Garrick (pianist); Bronxville, N.Y., 4/3/1948
**Ohrbach,** Jerry (actor-singer); Bronx, N.Y., 10/20/1935
**Oistrakh,** David (concert violinist); Odessa, Russia **(1908-1974)**
**O'Keeffe,** Georgia (painter); Sun Prairie, Wis. **(1887-1986)**
**Oland,** Warner (actor); Umea, Sweden **(1880-1938)**
**Olav V** (King of Norway); Sandringham, England, 7/2/1903
**Oldenburg,** Claes (painter); Stockholm, Sweden, 1/28/1929
**Olivier,** Lord (Laurence) (actor); Dorking, England, 5/22/1907
**Olmsted,** Frederick Law (landscape architect); Hartford, Conn. **(1822-1903)**
**Olsen,** Ole (John Sigvard Olsen) (comedian); Peru, Ind. **(1892-1963)**
**Omar Khayyam** (poet and astronomer); Nishapur (Iran) **(died c. 1123)**
**Onassis,** Aristotle (shipping executive); Smyrna, Turkey **(1906-1975)**
**Onassis,** Christina (shipping executive); New York City, 12/11/1950
**Onassis,** Jacqueline Kennedy (Jacqueline Bouvier) (President's widow); Southampton, N.Y., 7/28/1929
**O'Neal,** Ryan (Patrick) (actor); Los Angeles, 4/20/1941
**O'Neal,** Tatum (actress); Los Angeles, Calif., 11/5/1963
**O'Neill,** Eugene Gladstone (playwright); New York City **(1888-1953)**
**O'Neill,** Jennifer (actress); Rio de Janeiro, 2/20/1949
**Oppenheimer,** J. Robert (nuclear physicist); New York City **(1904-1967)**
**Orff,** Carl (composer); Munich, Germany **(1895-1982)**
**Orlando,** Tony (Michael Anthony Orlando Cassavitis) (singer); New York City, 4/3/1944
**Ormandy,** Eugene (conductor); Budapest **(1899-1985)**
**Orozco,** José Clemente (painter); Zapotlán, Jalisco, Mexico **(1883-1949)**
**Orwell,** George (Eric Arthur Blair) (British author); Motihari, India **(1903-1950)**
**Osborn,** Paul (playwright); Evansville, Ind., 9/4/1901
**Osborne,** John (playwright); London, 12/12/1929
**Osler,** Sir William (physician); Bondhead, Ontario, Canada **(1849-1919)**
**Osmond,** Donny (singer); Ogden, Utah, 12/9/1957
**Osmond,** Marie (singer); Ogden, Utah, 1959
**O'Sullivan,** Maureen (actress); County Roscommon, Ireland, 5/17/1911
**Otis,** Elisha (inventor); Halifax, Vt. **(1811-1861)**
**O'Toole,** Peter (actor); Connemara, Ireland, 8/2/1933
**Ovid** (Publius Ovidius Naso) (poet); Sulmona (Italy) **(43 B.C.-?A.D. 17)**
**Owens,** Buck (Alvis Edgar Owens) (singer); Sherman, Tex., 8/12/1929

# P

**Paar,** Jack (TV personality); Canton, Ohio, 5/1/1918
**Pacino,** Al (Alfred) (actor); New York City, 4/25/1940
**Packard,** Vance (author); Granville Summit, Pa., 5/22/1914
**Paderewski,** Ignace Jan (pianist and statesman); Kurylowka, Russian Podolia **(1860-1941)**
**Paganini,** Nicolò (violinist); Genoa (Italy) **(1782-1840)**
**Page,** Geraldine (actress); Kirksville, Mo., 11/22/1924
**Page,** Patti (Clara Ann Fowler) (singer and entertainer); Claremore, Okla., 11/8/1927
**Paige,** Janis (actress); Tacoma, Wash., 9/16/1922
**Paine,** Thomas (political philosopher); Thetford, England **(1737-1809)**
**Palance,** Jack (Walter Palanuik) (actor); Lattimer, Pa., 2/18/1920
**Palestrina,** Giovanni Pierluigi da (composer); Palestrina, Italy **(1526-1594)**
**Paley,** William S. (broadcasting executive); Chicago, 9/28/1901
**Palladio,** Andrea (architect); Padua or Vicenza (Italy) **(1508-1580)**
**Palmer,** Betsy (actress); East Chicago, Ind., 1929
**Palmer,** Lilli (Lilli Peiser) (actress); Posen (Germany) **(1914-1986)**
**Palmerston,** Henry John Templeton (3rd Viscount) (statesman); Broadlands, England **(1784-1865)**
**Papanicolaou,** George N. (physician); Coumi, Greece **(1883-1962)**
**Papas,** Irene (actress); Chiliomodion, Greece, 1929
**Papp,** Joseph (Joseph Papirofsky) (stage producer and director); Brooklyn, N.Y., 6/22/1921
**Paracelaus,** Philippus Aureolus Theophrastus Bombastus von Hohenheim (physican); Einsiedeln, Switzerland **(1493-1541)**
**Park,** Chung Hee (President of South Korea); Sangmo-ri, Korea **(1917-1979)**
**Parker,** Dorothy (Dorothy Rothschild) (author); West End, N.J. **(1893-1967)**
**Parker,** Eleanor (actress); Cedarville, Ohio, 6/26/1922
**Parker,** Fess (actor); Fort Worth, Tex., 1925
**Parker,** Suzy (model and actress); San Antonio, 10/28/1933
**Parkinson,** C(yril) Northcote (historian); Durham, England, 7/30/1909
**Parks,** Bert (Bert Jacobson) (entertainer); Atlanta, 12/30/1914
**Parks,** Gordon (film director); Ft. Scott, Kan., 11/30/1912
**Parnell,** Charles Stewart (statesman); Avondale, Ireland **(1846-1891)**
**Parnis,** Mollie (Mollie Parnis Livingston) (fashion designer); New York City, 3/18/1905
**Parsons,** Estelle (actress); Marblehead, Mass., 11/20/1927
**Parton,** Dolly (singer); Locust Ridge, Tenn. 1/19/1946
**Pascal,** Blaise (philosopher); Clermont, France **(1623-1662)**
**Pasternak,** Boris Leonidovich (author); Moscow **(1890-1960)**
**Pasternak,** Joseph (film producer); Silagy-Somlyo, Romania, 9/19/1901
**Pasteur,** Louis (chemist); Dôle, France **(1822-1895)**
**Paton,** Alan (author): Pietermaritzburg, South Africa, 1/11/1903
**Patton,** George Smith, Jr. (general); San Gabriel, Calif., **(1885-1945)**
**Paul,** Les (Lester William Polfus) (guitarist); Waukesha, Wis., 6/9/1915
**Paul VI** (Giovanni Battista Montini) (Pope); Concesio, nr. Brescia, Italy **(1897-1978)**
**Pauley,** Jane (TV newscaster); Indianapolis, 10/31/1950
**Pauling,** Linus Carl (chemist); Portland, Ore., 2/28/1901
**Pavarotti,** Luciano (tenor); Modena, Italy, 10/12/1935
**Pavlov,** Ivan Petrovich (physiologist); Ryazan district, Russia **(1849-1936)**
**Pavlova,** Anna (ballerina); St. Petersburg, Russia **(1885-1931)**
**Payne,** John (actor); Roanoke, Va., 1912
**Peale,** Norman Vincent (clergyman); Bowersville, Ohio, 5/31/1898
**Pearl,** Minnie (Sarah Ophelia Colley Cannon) (comedienne and singer); Centerville, Tenn., 10/25/1912
**Pears,** Peter (tenor); Farnham, England **(1910-1986)**
**Pearson,** Drew (Andrew Russel Pearson) (columnist); Evanston, Ill. **(1897-1969)**
**Pearson,** Lester B. (statesman); Toronto **(1897-1972)**
**Peary,** Robert Edwin (explorer); Cresson, Pa. **(1856-1920)**
**Peck,** Gregory (actor); La Jolla, Calif., 4/5/1916
**Peckinpah,** Sam (film director); Fresno, Calif. **(1925-1984)**
**Peerce,** Jan (tenor); New York City **(1904-1984)**
**Pegler,** (James) Westbrook (columnist); Minneapolis, **(1894-1969)**
**Pei,** I(eoh) M(ing) (architect); Canton, China, 4/26/1917
**Penn,** Arthur (stage and film director); Philadelphia, 9/27/1922
**Penn,** William (American colonist); London **(1644-1718)**
**Penney,** James C. (merchant); Hamilton, Mo. **(1875-1971)**
**Peppard,** George (actor); Detroit, 10/1/1928
**Pepys,** Samuel (diarist); Bampton, England **(1633-1703)**
**Perelman,** S(idney) J(oseph) (writer); Brooklyn, N.Y. **(1904-1979)**
**Pergolesi,** Giovanni Battista (composer); Jesi, Italy **(1710-1736)**
**Pericles** (statesman); Athens **(died 429** B.C.)
**Perkins,** Osgood (actor); West Newton, Mass. **(1892-1937)**

**Perkins,** Tony (Anthony) (actor); New York City, 4/14/1932
**Perlman,** Itzhak (violinist); Tel Aviv, Israel, 8/31/1945
**Perón, Isabel** (María Estela Martínez Cartas) (former chief of state); La Rioja, Argentina, 2/4/1931
**Perón,** Juan D. (statesman); nr. Lobos, Argentina **(1895-1974)**
**Perón,** Maria Eva Duarte de (political leader); Los Toldos, Argentina **(1919-1952)**
**Perrine,** Valerie (actress and dancer); Galveston, Tex., 9/3/1943
**Pershing,** John Joseph (general); Linn County, Mo. **(1860-1948)**
**Pestalozzi,** Johann (educator); Zurich, Switzerland **(1746-1827)**
**Peters,** Bernadette (Bernadette Lazzara) (actress); New York City, 2/28/1944
**Peters,** Brock (actor-singer); New York City, 7/2/1927
**Peters,** Jean (actress); Canton, Ohio, 10/15/1926
**Peters,** Roberta (Roberta Peterman) (soprano); New York City, 5/4/1930
**Petit,** Roland (choreographer and dancer) Villemombe, France, 1924
**Petrarch** (Francesco Petrarca) (poet); Arezzo (Italy) **(1304-1374)**
**Philip** (Philip Mountbatten) (Duke of Edinburgh); Corfu, Greece, 6/10/1921
**Piaf,** Edith (Edith Gassion) (chanteuse); Paris **(1916-1963)**
**Piatigorsky,** Gregor (cellist); Ekaterinoslav, Russia **(1903-1976)**
**Piazza,** Ben (actor); Little Rock, Ark., 7/30/1934
**Piazza,** Marguerite (soprano); New Orleans, 5/6/1926
**Picasso,** Pablo (painter and sculptor); Málaga, Spain **(1881-1973)**
**Pickford,** Jack (Jack Smith) (actor); Toronto **(1896-1933)**
**Pickford,** Mary (Gladys Mary Smith) (actress); Toronto **(1893-1979)**
**Picon,** Molly (actress); New York City, 6/1/1898
**Pidgeon,** Walter (actor); East St. John, New Brunswick, Canada **(1898-1984)**
**Pinter,** Harold (playwright); London, 10/10/1930
**Pinza,** Ezio (basso); Rome **(1892-1957)**
**Pirandello,** Luigi (dramatist and novelist); nr. Girgenti, Italy **(1867-1936)**
**Piranesi,** Giambattista (artist); Mestre, Italy **(1720-1778)**
**Pissaro,** Camille Jacob (painter); St. Thomas (U.S. Virgin Islands) **(1830-1903)**
**Piston,** Walter (composer); Rockland, Me. **(1894-1976)**
**Pitman,** Sir (Isaac) James (educator and publisher); Bath, England, 8/14/1901
**Pitt,** William ("Younger Pitt") (statesman); nr. Bromley, England **(1759-1806)**
**Pitts,** ZaSu (actress); Parsons, Kan. **(1898-1963)**
**Pius XII** (Eugenio Pacelli) (Pope); Rome **(1876-1958)**
**Pizarro,** Francisco (explorer); Trujillo, Spain **(1470?-1541)**
**Planck,** Max (physicist); Kiel, Germany **(1858-1947)**
**Plato** (Aristocles) (philosopher); Athens (?) **(427?-347** B.C.)
**Pleasence,** Donald (actor); Worksop, England, 10/5/1919
**Pleshette,** Suzanne (actress); New York City, 1/31/1937
**Plimpton,** George (author); New York City, 3/18/1927
**Plisetskaya,** Maya (ballerina); Moscow, 11/20/1925
**Plowright,** Joan (actress); Brigg, England, 10/28/1929
**Plummer,** Christopher (actor); Toronto, 12/13/1929
**Plutarch** (biographer); Chaeronea (Greece) **(46?-?120)**
**Pocahontas** (Matoaka) (American Indian princess); Virginia (?) **(1595?-1617)**
**Podhoretz,** Norman (author); Brooklyn, N.Y., 1/16/1930
**Poe,** Edgar Allan (poet and story writer); Boston, Mass. **(1809-1849)**
**Poitier,** Sidney (film actor and director); Miami, Fla., 2/20/1927
**Polanski,** Roman (film director); Paris, 8/18/1933
**Pollard,** Michael J. (actor); Passaic, N.J., 5/30/1939
**Pollock,** Jackson (painter); Cody, Wyo. **(1912-1956)**
**Polo,** Marco (traveler); Venice **(1254?-?1324)**
**Pompadour,** Mme. de (Jeanne Antoinette Poisson) (courtesan) Versailles **(1721-1764)**
**Pompey** (Gnaeus Pompeius Magnus) (general); Rome (?) **(106-48** B.C.)
**Ponce de León,** Juan (explorer); Servas, Spain **(1460?-1521)**
**Pons,** Lily (coloratura soprano); Cannes, France **(1904-1976)**
**Ponti,** Carlo (director); Milan, Italy, 12/11/1913
**Pope,** Alexander (poet); London **(1688-1744)**
**Porter,** Cole (songwriter); Peru, Ind. **(1892?-1964)**
**Porter,** Katherine Anne (novelist); Indian Creek, Tex. **(1891-1980)**
**Post,** Wiley (aviator); Grand Plain, Tex. **(1900-1935)**
**Poston,** Tom (actor); Columbus, Ohio, 10/17/1927
**Potëmkin,** Grigori Aleksandrovich, Prince (statesman); Khizovo (Khizov, Belorussia, U.S.S.R.) **(1739-1791)**
**Potok,** Chaim (author); New York City, 2/17/1929
**Poulenc,** Francis (composer); Paris **(1899-1963)**
**Pound,** Ezra (poet); Hailey, Idaho **(1885-1972)**
**Poussin,** Nicolas (painter); Villers, France **(1594-1665)**
**Powell,** Adam Clayton, Jr. (Congressman); New Haven, Conn. **(1908-1972)**
**Powell,** Dick (actor); Mt. View, Ark. **(1904-1963)**

**Powell,** Eleanor (actress and tap dancer); Springfield, Mass. **(1912-1982)**

**Powell,** Jane (Suzanne Burce) (actress and singer); Portland, Ore., 4/1/1929

**Powell,** William (actor); Pittsburgh, **(1892-1984)**

**Power,** Tyrone (actor); Cincinnati, Ohio **(1914-1958)**

**Powers,** Stephanie (Taffy Paul) (actress); Hollywood, Calif., 11/12/1942

**Praxiteles** (sculptor); Athens **(c.370-c.330** B.C.**)**

**Preminger,** Otto (film director and producer); Vienna **(1906-1986)**

**Prentiss,** Paula (Paula Ragusa) (actress); San Antonio, 1939

**Presley,** Elvis (singer and actor); Tupelo, Miss. **(1935-1977)**

**Preston,** Robert (Robert Preston Meservey) (actor); Newton Highlands, Mass., 6/8/1918

**Previn,** André (conductor); Berlin, 4/6/1929

**Previn,** Dory (singer); Rahway, N.J., 10/22/1929(?)

**Price,** Leontyne (Mary) (soprano); Laurel, Miss., 2/10/1927

**Price,** Ray (country music artist); Perryville, Tex., 1/12/1926

**Price,** Vincent (actor); St. Louis, 5/27/1911

**Pride,** Charley (singer); Sledge, Miss., 3/18/1938(?)

**Priestley,** J. B. (John B.) (author); Bradford, England **(1894-1984)**

**Priestley,** Joseph (chemist); nr. Leeds, England **(1733-1804)**

**Primrose,** William (violist); Glasgow, Scotland **(1904-1982)**

**Prince** (Prince Roger Nelson) (singer); Minneapolis, 6/7/58

**Prince,** Harold (stage producer); New York City, 1/30/1928

**Prinze,** Freddie (actor); New York City **(1954-1977)**

**Pritchett,** V(ictor) S(awdon) (literary critic); Ipswich, England, 12/16/1900

**Procter,** William (scientist); Cincinnati **(1872-1951)**

**Prokofiev,** Sergei Sergeevich (composer); St. Petersburg, Russia **(1891-1953)**

**Proust,** Marcel (novelist); Paris **(1871-1922)**

**Provine,** Dorothy (actress); Deadwood, S. Dak., 1/20/1937

**Prowse,** Juliet (actress); Bombay, 9/25/1936

**Pryor,** Richard (comedian); Peoria, Ill., 12/1/1940

**Ptolemy** (Claudius Ptolemaeus) (astronomer and geographer); Ptolemais Hermii (Egypt) **(2nd century** A.D.**)**

**Pucci,** Emilio (Marchese di Barsento) (fashion designer); Naples, Italy, 11/20/1914

**Puccini,** Giacomo (composer); Lucca, Italy **(1858-1924)**

**Puente,** Tito (band leader); New York City, 4/20/1923

**Pulaski,** Casimir (military officer); Podolia, Poland **(1748-1779)**

**Pulitzer,** Joseph (publisher); Makó (Hungary) **(1847-1911)**

**Pullman,** George (inventor); Brockton, N.Y. **(1831-1897)**

**Purcell,** Henry (composer); London **(1658-1695)**

**Pusey,** Nathan M. (educator); Council Bluffs, Iowa, 4/4/1907

**Pushkin,** Alexander Sergeevich (poet and dramatist); Moscow **(1799-1837)**

**Puzo,** Mario (novelist); New York City, 10/15/1921

**Pyle,** Ernest Taylor (journalist); Dana, Ind. **(1900-1945)**

**Pythagoras** (mathematician and philosopher); Samos (Greece) **(6th century** B.C.**)**

# Q

**Quayle,** Anthony (actor); Ainsdale, England, 9/7/1913

**Queen,** Ellery: pen name of the late Frederic Dannay and the late Manfred B. Lee

**Queler,** Eve (conductor); New York City, 1/1/1936

**Quennell,** Peter Courtney (biographer); Bromley, England, 3/9/1905

**Quinn,** Anthony (actor); Chihuahua, Mexico, 4/21/1916

# R

**Rabe,** David (playwright); Dubuque, Iowa, 3/10/1940

**Rabelais,** François (satirist); nr. Chinon, France **(1494?-1553)**

**Rabi,** I(sidor) I(saac) (physicist); Rymanow (Poland), 7/29/1898

**Rachmaninoff,** Sergei Wassilievitch (pianist and composer); Oneg Estate, Novgorod, Russia **(1873-1943)**

**Racine,** Jean Baptiste (dramatist); La Ferté-Milon, France **(1639-1699)**

**Radner,** Gilda (comedienne); Detroit, 6/28/1946

**Raft,** George (actor); New York City **(1895-1980)**

**Rainer,** Luise (actress); Vienna, 1912

**Raines,** Ella (actress); Snoqualmie Falls, Wash., 8/6/1921

**Rainier III** (Prince); Monaco, 5/31/1923

**Rains,** Claude (actor); London **(1889-1967)**

**Raitt,** Bonnie (singer); Burbank, Calif., 11/8/1949

**Raleigh,** Sir Walter (courtier and navigator); London **(1552?-1618)**

**Rameau,** Jean-Philippe (composer); Dijon? France **(1683-1764)**

**Randall,** Tony (Leonard Rosenberg) (actor); Tulsa, Okla., 2/26/1920

**Randolph,** A(sa) Philip (labor leader); Crescent City, Fla. **(1889-1979)**

**Raphael** (Raffaello Santi) (painter and architect); Urbino (Italy) **(1483-1520)**

**Rasputin,** Grigori Efimovich (monk); Tobolsk Province, Russia **(1871?-1916)**

**Rathbone,** Basil (actor); Johannesburg, South Africa **(1892-1967)**

**Rather,** Dan (TV newscaster); Wharton, Tex., 10/31/1931

**Ratoff,** Gregory (film director); St. Petersburg, Russia **(1897-1960)**

**Rattigan,** Terence (playwright); London **(1911-1977)**

**Rauschenberg,** Robert (painter); Port Arthur, Tex., 10/22/1925

**Ravel,** Maurice Joseph (composer); Ciboure, France **(1875-1937)**

**Rawls,** Lou (singer); Chicago, 12/1/1935

**Ray,** Man (painter); Philadelphia **(1890-1976)**

**Ray,** Satyajat (film director); Calcutta, 5/2/1922

**Rayburn,** Gene (TV personality); Christopher, Ill., 12/22/1917

**Raye,** Martha (Margie Yvonne Reed) (comedienne and actress); Butte, Mont., 8/27/1916

**Raymond,** Gene (actor); New York City, 8/13/1908

**Reasoner,** Harry (TV commentator); Dakota City, Iowa, 4/17/1923

**Redding,** Otis (singer); Dawson, Ga. **(1941-1967)**

**Reddy,** Helen (singer); Melbourne, 10/25/1941

**Redford,** Robert (Charles Robert Redford, Jr.) (actor); Santa Monica, Calif., 8/18/1937

**Redgrave,** Lynn (actress); London, 3/8/1943

**Redgrave,** Sir Michael (actor); Bristol, England **(1908-1985)**

**Redgrave,** Vanessa (actress); London, 1/30/1937

**Reed,** Donna (actress); Denison, Iowa **(1921-1986)**

**Reed,** Rex (critic); Ft. Worth, 10/2/1940

**Reed,** Walter (army surgeon); Belroi, Va. **(1851-1902)**

**Reese,** Della (Deloreese Patricia Early) (singer); Detroit, 7/6/1932

**Reeves,** Jim (singer); Panola County, Tex. **(1923-1964)**

**Reich,** Steve (composer); New York City, 10/3/1936

**Reid,** Wallace (actor); St. Louis **(1891-1923)**

**Reiner,** Carl (actor); New York City, 3/20/1922

**Reiner,** Fritz (conductor); Budapest **(1888-1963)**

**Reiner,** Robert (actor); Bronx, N.Y., 1945

**Reinhardt,** Max (Max Goldmann) (theater producer); nr. Vienna **(1873-1943)**

**Remarque,** Erich Maria (novelist); Osnabrük, Germany **(1898-1970)**

**Rembrandt** (Rembrandt Harmensz van Rijn) (painter); Leyden (Netherlands) **(1605-1669)**

**Remick,** Lee (Ann) (actress); Boston, 12/14/1935

**Rennert,** Günther (opera director and producer); Essen, Germany, 4/1/1911

**Rennie,** Michael (actor); Bradford, England **(1909-1971)**

**Renoir,** Jean (film director and writer); Paris, **(1894-1979)**

**Renoir,** Pierre Auguste (painter); Limoges, France **(1841-1919)**

**Resnais,** Alain (film director); Vannes, France, 6/3/1922

**Resnik,** Regina (mezzo-soprano); New York City, 8/30/1922

**Respighi,** Ottorino (composer); Bologna, Italy **(1879-1936)**

**Reston,** James (journalist); Clydebank, Scotland, 11/3/1909

**Reuther,** Walter (labor leader); Wheeling, W. Va. **(1907-1970)**

**Revere,** Paul (silversmith and hero of famous ride); Boston **(1735-1818)**

**Revson,** Charles (business executive); Boston **(1906-1975)**

**Reynolds,** Burt (actor); Waycross, Ga., 2/11/1936

**Renolds,** Debbie (Marie Frances Reynolds) (actress); El Paso, 4/1/1932

**Reynolds,** Sir Joshua (painter); nr. Plymouth, England **(1723-1792)**

**Rhodes,** Cecil John (South African statesman); Bishop Stortford, England **(1853-1902)**

**Rice,** Elmer (playwright); New York City **(1892-1967)**

**Rice,** Grantland (sports writer); Murfreesboro, Tenn. **(1880-1954)**

**Rich,** Buddy (Bernard) (drummer); Brooklyn, N.Y., 6/30/1917

**Rich,** Charlie (singer); Colt, Ark., 12/14/1932

**Richardson,** Elliot L. (ex-Cabinet member); Boston, 7/20/1920

**Richardson,** Sir Ralph (actor); Cheltenham, England **(1902-1983)**

**Richardson,** Tony (director); Shipley, England, 6/5/1928

**Richelieu,** Duc de (Armand Jean du Plessis) (cardinal); Paris **(1585-1642)**

**Richie,** Lionel (singer-songwriter); Tuskegee, Ala., 1949 (?)

**Richter,** Charles Francis (seismologist); Hamilton, Canada **(1900-1985)**

**Richter,** Sviatosiav (pianist); Zhitomir, Ukraine, 3/20/1914

**Rickenbacker,** Edward V. (aviator); Columbus, Ohio **(1890-1973)**

**Rickles,** Don (comedian); New York City, 5/8/1926

**Rickover,** Vice Admiral Hyman G. (atomic energy expert); Russia **(1900-1986)**

**Riddle,** Nelson (composer); Hackensack, N.J. **(1921-1985)**

**Ride,** Sally K(risten) (astronaut, astrophysicist); Encino, Calif., 5/26/1951

**Ridgway,** General Matthew B. (ex-Army Chief of Staff); Ft. Monroe, Va., 3/3/1895

**Rigg,** Diana (actress); Doncaster, England, 7/20/1938

**Riley,** James Whitcomb (poet); Greenfield, Ind. **(1849-1916)**

**Rimsky-Korsakov,** Nikolai Andreevich (composer); Tikhvin, Russia **(1844-1908)**

**Rinehart,** Mary (née Roberts) (novelist); Pittsburgh **(1876-1958)**

Ritchard, Cyril (actor and director); Sydney, Australia **(1898-1977)**
Ritter, John (Jonathan) (actor); Burbank, Calif., 9/17/1948
Ritter, Tex (Woodward Maurice Ritter) (singer); Panola County, Tex., **(1905-1973)**
Rivera, Chita (Dolores Conchita Figuero del Rivero) (dancer-actress-singer); Washington, D.C. 1/23/1933
Rivera, Diego (painter); Guanajuato, Mexico **(1886-1957)**
Rivera, Geraldo (Miguel) (TV newscaster); New York City, 7/3/1943
Rivers, Joan (comedienne); Brooklyn, N.Y., 1935(?)
Rivers, Larry (Yitzroch Loiza Grossberg) (painter); New York City, 8/17/1923
Robards, Jason, Jr. (actor); Chicago, 7/26/1922
Robards, Jason, Sr. (actor); Hillsdale, Mich. **(1892-1963)**
Robbins, Harold (Harold Rubin) (novelist); New York City, 5/21/1916
Robbins, Jerome (Jerome Rabinowitz) (choreographer); New York City, 10/11/1918
Robbins, Marty (singer); Glendale, Ariz., **(1925-1982)**
Roberts, (Granville) Oral (evangelist and publisher); nr. Ada, Okla., 1/24/1918
Robertson, Cliff (actor); La Jolla, Calif., 9/9/1925
Robertson, Dale (Dayle) (actor); Oklahoma City, 7/14/1923
Robeson, Paul (singer and actor); Princeton, N.J., **(1898-1976)**
Robespierre, Maximilien François Marie Isidore de (French Revolutionist); Arras, France **(1758-1794)**
Robinson, Bill "Bojangles" (Luther) (dancer); Richmond, Va. **(1878-1949)**
Robinson, Edward G. (Emanuel Goldenberg) (actor); Bucharest **(1893-1973)**
Robinson, Edwin Arlington (poet); Head Tide, Me. **(1869-1935)**
Robson, Dame Flora (actress); South Shields, England **(1902-1984)**
Rochester (Eddie Anderson) (actor); Oakland, Calif. **(1905-1977)**
Rockefeller, David (banker); New York City, 6/12/1915
Rockefeller, John Davison (capitalist); Richford, N.Y. **(1839-1937)**
Rockefeller, John Davison, Jr. (industrialist); Cleveland **(1874-1960)**
Rockefeller, John D., 3rd (philanthropist); New York City **(1906-1978)**
Rockefeller, Laurance S. (conservationist); New York City, 5/26/1910
Rockwell, Norman (painter and illustrator); New York City, **(1894-1978)**
Rodgers, Jimmie (singer); Meridian, Miss. **(1897-1933)**
Rodgers, Richard (composer); New York City **(1902-1979)**
Rodin, François Auguste René (sculptor); Paris **(1840-1917)**
Roentgen, Wilhelm Konrad (physicist); Lennep, Prussia **(1845-1923)**
Rogers, Buddy (Charles) (actor); Olathe, Kan., 8/13/1904
Rogers, Ginger (Virginia McMath) (dancer and actress); Independence, Mo., 7/16/1911
Rogers, Kenny (singer); Houston, 1939(?)
Rogers, Roy (Leonard Slye) (actor); Cincinnati, 11/5/1912
Rogers, Will (William Penn Adair Rogers) (humorist); Oologah, Okla. **(1879-1935)**
Rogers, Will, Jr. (actor); New York City, 10/20/1911
Rogers, William P. (ex-Secretary of State); Norfolk, N.Y., 6/23/1913
Roland, Gilbert (actor); Juarez, Mexico, 12/11/1905
Rolland, Romain (author); Clamecy, France **(1866-1944)**
Rollins, Sonny (saxophonist); New York City, 9/7/1930
Romberg, Sigmund (composer); Szeged (Hungary) **(1887-1951)**
Rome, Harold (composer); Hartford, Conn., 5/27/1908
Romero, Cesar (actor); New York City, 2/15/1907
Romney, George W. (ex-Secretary of HUD); Chihuahua, Mexico, 7/8/1907
Romulo, Carlos P. (diplomat and educator); Manila **(1899-1985)**
Ronsard, Pierre de (poet); La Possonnière nr. Couture (Couture-sur-Loir, France) **(1524-1585)**
Ronstadt, Linda (singer); Tucson, Ariz., 7/30/1946
Rooney, Andy (TV personality); Albany, N.Y., 1/14/1919
Rooney, Mickey (Joe Yule, Jr.) (actor); Brooklyn, N.Y., 9/23/1920
Roosevelt, Anna Eleanor (reformer and humanitarian); New York City **(1884-1962)**
Rorem, Ned (composer); Richmond, Ind., 10/23/23
Rose, Billy (showman); New York City **(1899-1966)**
Rose, Leonard (concert cellist); Washington, D.C. **(1918-1984)**
Ross, Betsy (Betsey Griscom) (flagmaker); Philadelphia **(1752-1836)**
Ross, Diana (singer); Detroit, 3/26/1944
Ross, Katharine (actress); Hollywood, Calif., 1/29/1943
Rossellini, Roberto (film director); Rome **(1906-1977)**
Rossetti, Dante Gabriel (painter and poet); London **(1828-1882)**
Rossini, Gioacchino Antonio (composer); Pesaro (Italy) **(1792-1868)**
Rostand, Edmond (dramatist); Marseilles, France **(1868-1918)**
Rostow, Walt Whitman (economist); New York City, 10/7/1916
Rostropovich, Mstislav (cellist and conductor); Baku, U.S.S.R., 3/12/1927
Roth, Lillian (singer); Boston **(1910-1980)**
Roth, Philip (novelist); Newark, N.J., 3/19/1933
Rothko, Mark (Marcus Rothkovich) (painter); Russia **(1903-1970)**
Rouault, Georges (painter); Paris **(1871-1958)**

Roundtree, Richard (actor); New Rochelle, N.Y., 9/7/1942
Rousseau, Henri (painter); Laval, France **(1844-1910)**
Rousseau, Jean Jacques (philosopher); Geneva **(1712-1778)**
Rovere, Richard H. (journalist); Jersey City, N.J., 5/5/1915
Rowan, Dan (comedian); Beggs, Okla., 7/2/1922
Rowlands, Gena (actress); Cambria, Wis., 6/19/1936(?)
Rubens, Sir Peter Paul (painter); Siegen (Germany) **(1577-1640)**
Rubinstein, Arthur (concert pianist); Lôdz (Poland) **(1887-1982)**
Rubinstein, Helena (cosmetics executive); Krakow (Poland) **(1882?-1965)**
Rudel, Julius (conductor); Vienna, 3/6/1921
Ruggles, Charles (actor); Los Angeles **(1892-1970)**
Rule, Janice (actress); Norwood, Ohio, 8/15/1931
Runcie, Robert (Alexander Kennedy) (Archbishop of Canterbury); Liverpool, England, 10/2/1921
Runyon, (Alfred) Damon (journalist); Manhattan, Kan. **(1884-1945)**
Rusk, Dean (ex-Sec. of State); Cherokee County, Ga., 2/9/1909
Ruskin, John (art critic); London **(1819-1900)**
Russell, Lord Bertrand (Arthur William) (mathematician and philosopher); Trelleck, Wales **(1872-1970)**
Russell, Jane (actress); Bemidji, Minn., 6/21/1921
Russell, Leon (pianist and singer); Lawton, Okla., 4/2/1941
Russell, Lillian (Helen Louise Leonard) (soprano); Clinton, Iowa **(1861-1922)**
Russell, Nipsy (comedian); Atlanta, 1924(?)
Russell, Rosalind (actress); Waterbury, Conn. **(1912-1976)**
Rustin, Bayard (civil rights leader); West Chester, Pa., 1910
Rutherford, Dame Margaret (actress); London **(1892-1972)**
Ryan, Robert (actor); Chicago **(1909-1973)**
Rydell, Bobby (singer); Philadelphia, 1942
Rysanek, Leonie (dramatic soprano); Vienna, 11/14/1928

# S

Saarinen, Eero (architect); Finland **(1910-1961)**
Sabin, Albert B. (polio researcher); Bialystok (Poland), 8/26/1906
Sadat, Anwar el- (President); Egypt **(1918-1981)**
Sade, Marquis de (Donatien Alphonse Francois, Comte de Sade) (libertine and writer); Paris **(1740-1814)**
Safer, Morley (TV newscaster); Toronto, 11/8/1931
Sagan, Françoise (novelist); Cajarc, France, 6/21/1935
Sahl, Mort (Morton Lyon Sahl) (comedian); Montreal, 5/11/1927
Saint, Eva Marie (actress); Newark, N.J., 7/4/1924
Saint-Gaudens, Augustus (sculptor); Dublin **(1848-1907)**
St. James, Susan (Susan Miller) (actress); Los Angeles, 8/14/1946
St. John, Jill (actress); Los Angeles, 8/19/1940
St. Johns, Adela Rogers (journalist and author); Los Angeles, 5/20/1894
Saint-Laurent, Yves (Henri Donat Mathieu) (fashion designer); Oran, Algeria, 8/1/1936
Saint-Saens, Charles Camille (composer); Paris **(1835-1921)**
Sainte-Marie, Buffy (Beverly) (folk singer); Craven, Saskatchewan, Canada, 2/20/1942(?)
Salinger, J(erome) D(avid) (novelist); New York City, 1/1/1919
Salisbury, Harrison E. (journalist); Minneapolis, 11/14/1908
Salk, Jonas (polio researcher); New York City, 10/28/1914
Salk, Leo (psychologist); New York City, 1926
Salomon, Haym (American Revolution financier); Leszno, Poland **(1740-1785)**
Sand, George (Amandine Lucille Aurore Dudevant, née Dupin) (novelist); Paris **(1804-1876)**
Sandburg, Carl (poet and biographer); Galesburg, Ill. **(1878-1967)**
Sanders, George (actor); St. Petersburg, Russia **(1906-1972)**
Sands, Tommy (singer); Chicago, 8/27/1937
Sanger, Margaret (birth control leader); Corning, N.Y. **(1883-1966)**
Santayana, George (philosopher); Madrid **(1863-1952)**
Sappho (poet); Lesbos (Greece) (lived c. 600 B.C.)
Sargent, John Singer (painter); Florence, Italy **(1856-1925)**
Sarnoff, David (radio executive); Minsk, Russia **(1891-1971)**
Saroyan, William (novelist); Fresno, Calif. **(1908-1981)**
Sarrazin, Michael (actor); Quebec, 5/22/1940
Sarto, Andrea del (Andrea Domenico d'Agnolo di Francesco) (painter); Florence (Italy) **(1486-1531)**
Sartre, Jean-Paul (existentialist writer); Paris **(1905-1980)**
Sassoon, Vidal (hair stylist); London, 1/(?)/1928
Saul (King of Israel) **(11th century B.C.)**
Savalas, Telly (Aristoteles) (actor); Garden City, N.Y., 1/21/1924(?)
Savonarola, Girolamo (religious reformer); Ferrara, Italy **(1452-1498)**
Sayão, Bidú (soprano); Rio de Janeiro, 5/11/1902
Scaasi, Arnold (Arnold Isaacs) (fashion designer); Montreal
Scarlatti, Alessandro (composer); Palermo, Italy **(1659-1725)**
Scarlatti, Domenico (composer); Naples, Italy **(1685-1757)**
Scavullo, Francesco (photographer); Staten Island, N.Y. 1/16/1929

Schary, Dore (producer and writer); Newark, N.J. **(1905-1980)**

Schell, Maria (actress); Vienna, 1/15/1926

Schell, Maximilian (actor); Vienna, 12/8/1930

Schiaparelli, Elsa (fashion designer); Rome **(1890?-1973)**

Schiff, Dorothy (newspaper publisher); New York City, 3/11/1903

Schildkraut, Joseph (actor); Vienna **(1896-1964)**

Schiller, Johann Christoph Friedrich von (dramatist and poet); Marbach (Germany) **(1759-1805)**

Schippers, Thomas (conductor); Kalamazoo, Mich. **(1930-1977)**

Schlegel, Friedrich von (philosopher); Hanover? Germany **(1772-1829)**

Schlesinger, Arthur M., Jr. (historian); Columbus, Ohio, 10/15/1917

Schneider, Romy (Rose-Marie Albach) (actress); Vienna **(1938-1982)**

Schoenberg, Arnold (composer); Vienna **(1874-1951)**

Schopenhauer, Arthur (philosopher); Danzig (Poland) **(1788-1860)**

Schubert, Franz Peter (composer); Vienna **(1797-1828)**

Schulberg, Budd (novelist); New York City, 3/27/1914

Schulz, Charles M. (cartoonist); Minneapolis, 11/26/1922

Schuman, Robert (statesman); Luxembourg **(1886-1963)**

Schuman, William (composer); New York City, 8/4/1910

Schumann, Robert Alexander (composer); Zwickau (East Germany) **(1810-1856)**

Schwartz, Arthur (song writer); Brooklyn, N.Y. **(1900-1984)**

Schwartz, Maurice (actor); Russia **(1891-1960)**

Schwarzkopf, Elisabeth (soprano); Jarotschin, Poznán (Poland), 12/9/1915

Schweitzer, Albert (humanitarian); Kaysersburg, Upper Alsace **(1875-1965)**

Scofield, Paul (actor); Hurstpierpoint, England, 1/21/1922

Scorsese, Martin (film director); Flushing, N.Y., 11/17/1942

Scott, George C. (actor); Wise, Va., 10/18/1927

Scott, Lizabeth (Emma Matso) (actress); Scranton, Pa., 1923

Scott, Martha (actress); Jamesport, Mo., 9/22/1914

Scott, Randolph (Randolph Crane) (actor); Orange County, Va., 1/23/1903

Scott, Robert Falcon (explorer); Devonport, England **(1868-1912)**

Scott, Sir Walter (novelist); Edinburgh, Scotland **(1771-1832)**

Scott, Zachary (actor); Austin, Tex. **(1914-1965)**

Scotto, Renata (operatic soprano); Savona, Italy, 2/?/1936?

Scruggs, Earl Eugene (bluegrass musician); Cleveland County, N.C., 1/6/1924

Sebastian, John (composer); New York City, 3/17/1944

Seberg, Jean (actress); Marshalltown, Iowa **(1938-1979)**

Sedaka, Neil (singer); Brooklyn, N.Y., 3/13/1939

Seeger, Pete (folk singer); New York City, 5/3/1919

Segal, Erich (novelist); Brooklyn, N.Y., 6/16/1937

Segal, George (actor); New York City, 2/13/1936

Segovia, Andrés (guitarist); Linares, Spain, 2/21/1893

Selleck, Tom (actor); Detroit, 1/29/1945

Sellars, Peter (theater director); Pittsburgh, Pa., 1958 (?)

Sellers, Peter (actor); Southsea, England **(1925-1980)**

Selznick, David O. (film producer); Pittsburgh **(1902-1965)**

Sendak, Maurice (Bernard) (children's book author and illustrator); Brooklyn, N.Y., 6/10/1928

Sennett, Mack (Michael Sinnott) (film producer); Richmond, Quebec, Canada **(1880-1960)**

Serkin, Peter (pianist); New York City, 7/24/1947

Serkin, Rudolf (pianist); Eger (Hungary), 3/28/1903

Serling, Rod (story writer); Syracuse, N.Y. **(1924-1975)**

Sessions, Roger (composer); Brooklyn, N.Y. **(1896-1985)**

Seurat, Georges (painter); Paris **(1859-1891)**

Seuss, Dr. (Theodor Seuss Geisel) (author and illustrator); Springfield, Mass., 3/2/1904

Sevareid, Eric (TV commentator); Velva, N.D., 11/26/1912

Severinsen, Doc (Carl) (band leader); Arlington, Ore., 7/7/1927

Sexton, Anne (poet); Newton, Mass. **(1928-1974)**

Shahn, Ben(jamin) (painter); Kaunas, Lithuania **(1898-1969)**

Shakespeare, William (dramatist); Stratford on Avon, England **(1564-1616)**

Shankar, Ravi (sitar player); Benares, India, 4/7/1920

Shanker, Albert (labor leader); New York City, 9/14/1928

Sharif, Omar (Michael Shalhoub) (actor); Alexandria, Egypt, 4/10/1932

Shatner, William (actor); Montreal, 3/22/1931

Shaw, Artie (Arthur Arshawsky) (band leader); New York City, 5/23/1910

Shaw, George Bernard (dramatist); Dublin, **(1856-1950)**

Shaw, Irwin (novelist); Brooklyn, N.Y., **(1913-1984)**

Shaw, Robert (actor); Lancashire, England **(1927-1978)**

Shaw, Robert (chorale conductor); Red Bluff, Calif., 4/30/1916

Shearer, Moira (ballerina); Dunfermline, Scotland, 1/17/1926

Shearer, Norma (actress); Montreal, **(1902?-1983)**

Shearing, George (pianist); London, 8/13/1920

Sheen, Fulton J. (Peter Sheen) (Roman Catholic bishop); El Paso, Ill. **(1895-1979)**

Sheen, Martin (Ramon Estevez) (actor); Dayton, Ohio, 8/3/1940

Shelley, Percy Bysshe (poet); nr. Horsham, England **(1792-1822)**

Shepard, Sam (playwright); Ft. Sheridan, Ill. 11/5/1943

Sheraton, Thomas (furniture designer); Stockton-on-Tees, England **(1751-1806)**

Sheridan, Ann (actress); Denton, Tex. **(1915-1967)**

Sheridan, Philip (army officer); Albany, N.Y. **(1831-1888)**

Sheridan, Richard Brinsley (dramatist); Dublin, **(1751-1816)**

Sherman, William Tecumseh (army officer); Lancaster, Ohio **(1820-1891)**

Sherwood, Robert Emmet (playwright); New Rochelle, N.Y. **(1896-1955)**

Shields, Brooke (actress); New York City, 5/31/1965

Shirer, William L. (journalist and historian); Chicago, 2/23/1904

Sholokhov, Mikhail (novelist); Veshenskaya, Russia **(1905-1984)**

Shore, Dinah (Frances Rose Shore) (singer); Winchester, Tenn., 3/1/1917(?)

Short, Bobby (Robert Waltrip Short) (singer and pianist); Danville, Ill., 9/15/1924

Shostakovich, Dmitri (composer); St. Petersburg, Russia **(1906-1975)**

Shriver, Sargent (Robert Sargent Shriver, Jr.) (business executive); Westminster, Md., 11/9/1915

Shulman, Max (novelist); St. Paul, 3/14/1919

Sibelius, Jean (Johann Julius Christian Sibelius) (composer); Tavastehus (Finland) **(1865-1957)**

Sidney, Sylvia (actress); New York City, 8/8/1910

Siepi, Cesare (basso); Milan, Italy, 2/10/1923

Signoret, Simone (Simone Kaminker) (actress); Wiesbaden, Germany **(1921-1985)**

Sikorsky, Igor I. (inventor); Kiev, Russia **(1889-1972)**

Sills, Beverly (Belle Silverman) (soprano, opera director); Brooklyn, N.Y., 5/25/1929

Silone, Ignazio (Secondo Tranquilli) (novelist); Pescina del Marsi, Italy **(1900-1978)**

Silverman, Fred (broadcasting executive); New York City, 9/13/1937

Silvers, Phil (Philip Silversmith) (comedian); Brooklyn, N.Y. **(1912-1985)**

Sim, Alastair (actor); Edinburgh, Scotland **(1900-1976)**

Simenon, Georges (Georges Sim) (mystery writer); Liège, Belgium, 2/13/1903

Simmons, Jean (actress); Crouch Hill, London, 1/31/1929

Simon, Carly (singer and songwriter); New York City, 6/25/1945

Simon, Neil (playwright); Bronx, N.Y., 7/4/1927

Simon, Norton (business executive); Portland, Ore., 2/5/1907

Simon, Paul (singer and songwriter); Newark, N.J., 11/5/1942

Simon, Simone (actress); Marseilles, France, 4/23/1914

Simone, Nina (Eunice Kathleen Waymoa) (singer and pianist); Tryon, N.C., 2/21/1933

Simpson, Adele (Adele Smithline) (fashion designer); New York City, 12/8/1903

Sinatra, Frank (Francis Albert) (singer and actor); Hoboken, N.J., 12/12/1915

Sinclair, Upton Beall (novelist); Baltimore **(1878-1968)**

Singer, Isaac Bashevis (novelist); Radzymin (Poland), 7/14/1904

Siqueiros, David (painter); Chihuahua, Mexico **(1896-1974)**

Sisley, Alfred (painter); Paris **(1839-1899)**

Sitting Bull (Prairie Sioux Indian Chief); on Grand River, S.D. **(c. 1835-1890)**

Skelton, Red (Richard) (comedian); Vincennes, Ind., 7/18/1913

Skinner, B(urrhus) F(rederic) (psychologist); Susquehanna, Pa., 3/20/1904

Skinner, Cornelia Otis (writer and actress); Chicago, **(1901-1979)**

Skinner, Otis (actor); Cambridge, Mass. **(1858-1942)**

Slatkin, Leonard (conductor); Los Angeles, 9/1/1944

Slezak, Walter (actor); Vienna **(1902-1983)**

Sloan, Alfred P., Jr. (industrialist); New Haven, Conn. **(1875-1965)**

Sloan, John (painter); Lock Haven, Pa. **(1871-1951)**

Smetana, Bedrich (composer); Litomysl (Czechoslovakia) **(1824-1884)**

Smith, Adam (economist); Kirkaldy, Scotland **(1723-1790)**

Smith, Alexis (actress); Penticon, Canada, 6/8/1921

Smith, Alfred Emanuel (politician); New York City **(1873-1944)**

Smith, David (sculptor); Decatur, Ind. **(1906-1965)**

Smith, H. Allen (humorist); McLeansboro, Ill. **(1907-1976)**

Smith, Howard K. (TV commentator); Ferriday, La., 5/12/1914

Smith, Jaclyn (actress); Houston, 10/26/(?)

Smith, John (American colonist); Willoughby, Lincolnshire, England **(1580-1631)**

Smith, Joseph (religious leader); Sharon, Vt. **(1805-1844)**

Smith, Kate (Kathryn) (singer); Greenville, Va. **(1909-1986)**

Smith, Maggie (actress); Ilford, England, 12/28/1934

Smith, Red (Walter) (sports-columnist); Green Bay, Wis. **(1905-1982)**

Smollet, Tobias (novelist); Dalquhurn, Scotland **(1721-1771)**

Smothers, Dick (Richard) (comedian); Governors Island, New York City, 11/20/1939

Smothers, Tom (Thomas) (comedian); Governors Island, New York

City, 2/2/1937
**Snow,** Lord (Charles Percy) (author); Leicester, England **(1905-1980)**
**Snowdon,** Earl of (Anthony Armstrong Jones) (photographer); London, 3/7/1930
**Snyder,** Tom (TV personality); Milwaukee, 5/12/1936
**Socrates** (philosopher); Athens **(469-399** B.C.)
**Solomon** (King of Israel); Jerusalem (?) **(died c. 933** B.C.)
**Solon** (lawgiver); Salamis (Greece) **(638?-559** B.C.)
**Solti,** Sir Georg (conductor); Budapest, 10/21/1912
**Solzhenitsyn,** Aleksandr (novelist); Kislovodsk, Russia, 12/11/1918
**Somers,** Suzanne (Suzanne Mahoney) (actress); San Bruno, Calif., 10/16/1946
**Sommer,** Elke (Elke Schletz) (actress); Berlin, 11/5/1942
**Sondheim,** Stephen (composer); New York City, 3/22/1930
**Sontag,** Susan (author and film director); New York City, 1/28/1933
**Sophocles** (dramatist); nr. Athens **(496?-406** B.C.)
**Sothern,** Ann (Harriette Lake) (actress); Valley City, N.D., 1/22/1912
**Soul,** David (David Solberg) (actor); Chicago, 8/28/(?)
**Sousa,** John Philip (composer); Washington, D.C. **(1854-1932)**
**Soyer,** Raphael (painter); Borisoglebsk, Russia, 12/25/1899
**Spaak,** Paul-Henri (statesman); Brussels **(1899-1972)**
**Spacek,** Sissy (Mary Elizabeth) (actress); Quitman, Tex., 12/25/1949
**Spark,** Muriel (novelist); Edinburgh, Scotland, 2/1/1918
**Spector,** Phil (rock producer); Bronx, N.Y., 12/25/1940
**Spencer,** Herbert (philosopher); Derby, England **(1820-1903)**
**Spender,** Stephen (poet); nr. London, 2/28/1909
**Spengler,** Oswald (philosopher); Blankenburg, (East Germany) **(1880-1936)**
**Spenser,** Edmund (poet); London **(1552?-1599)**
**Spewack,** Bella (playwright); Hungary, 3/25/1899
**Spiegel,** Sam (producer); Jaroslaw (Poland) **(1901-1985)**
**Spielberg,** Steven (film director); Cincinnati, 12/18/1947
**Spillane,** Mickey (Frank Spillane) (mystery writer); Brooklyn, N.Y., 3/9/1918
**Spinoza,** Baruch (philosopher); Amsterdam (Netherlands) **(1632-1677)**
**Spivak,** Lawrence (TV producer); Brooklyn, N.Y., 1900
**Spock,** Benjamin (pediatrician); New Haven, Conn., 5/2/1903
**Springsteen,** Bruce (singer and songwriter); Freehold, N.J., 9/23/1949
**Sproul,** Robert G. (educator); San Francisco **(1891-1975)**
**Stack,** Robert (actor); Los Angeles, 1/13/1919
**Stafford,** Jo (singer); Coalinga, Calif., 1918
**Stalin,** Joseph Vissarionovich (Iosif V. Dzhugashvili) (Soviet leader); nr. Tiflis, Russia **(1879-1953)**
**Stalina,** Svetlana Alliluyeva (Stalin's daughter); Moscow, 2/28/1926
**Stallone,** Sylvester (actor and writer); New York City, 7/6/1946
**Stamp,** Terrence (actor); London, 1938
**Stang,** Arnold (comedian); Chelsea, Mass., 1925
**Stanislavski** (Konstantin Sergeevich Alekseev) (stage producer); Moscow **(1863-1938)**
**Stanley,** Sir Henry Morton (John Rowlands) (explorer); Denbigh, Wales **(1841-1904)**
**Stanley,** Kim (Patricia Reid) (actress); Tularosa, N.M., 2/11/1925
**Stans,** Maurice H. (ex-Secretary of Commerce); Shakope, Minn., 3/22/1908
**Stanton,** Frank (broadcasting executive); Muskegon, Mich., 3/20/1908
**Stanwyck,** Barbara (Ruby Stevens) (actress); Brooklyn, N.Y., 7/16/1907
**Stapleton,** Jean (Jeanne Murray) (actress); New York City, 1/19/1923
**Stapleton,** Maureen (actress); Troy, N.Y., 6/21/1925
**Starker,** János (cellist); Budapest 7/5/1926
**Starr,** Kay (Starks) (singer); Dougherty, Okla., 7/21/1922
**Starr,** Ringo (Richard Starkey) (singer and songwriter); Liverpool, England, 7/7/1940
**Stassen,** Harold E. (ex-government official); West St. Paul, Minn., 4/13/1907
**Steegmuller,** Francis (biographer); New Haven, Conn., 7/3/1906
**Steele,** Tommy (singer); London, 12/17/1936
**Stegner,** Wallace (Earle) (novelist and critic); Lake Mills, Iowa, 2/18/1909
**Steichen,** Edward Jean (photographer, artist); Luxembourg **(1879-1973)**
**Steiger,** Rod (Rodney) (actor); Westhampton, N.Y., 4/14/1925
**Stieglitz,** Alfred (photographer); Hoboken, N.J. **(1864-1946)**
**Stein,** Gertrude (author); Allegheny, Pa. **(1874-1946)**
**Steinbeck,** John Ernst (novelist); Salinas, Calif. **(1902-1968)**
**Steinberg,** David (comedian); Winnipeg, Manitoba, Canada, 8/19/1942
**Steinberg,** William (conductor); Cologne, Germany **(1899-1978)**
**Steinem,** Gloria (feminist); Toledo, Ohio, 3/25/1935(?)
**Steinmetz,** Charles (electrical engineer); Breslau (Poland) **(1865-1923)**
**Stendhal** (Marie Henri Beyle) (novelist); Grenoble, France **(1783-1842)**
**Sterling,** Jan (actress); New York City, 4/3/1923
**Stern,** Isaac (concert violinist); Kreminiecz, Russia, 7/21/1920
**Sterne,** Laurence (novelist); Clonmel, Ireland **(1713-1768)**
**Stevens,** Cat (Steven Georgiou) (singer and songwriter); London, 7/?/1947
**Stevens,** Connie (Concetta Ingolia) (singer); Brooklyn, N.Y., 8/8/1938
**Stevens,** George (film director); Oakland, Calif. **(1905-1975)**
**Stevens,** Risë (mezzo-soprano); New York City, 6/11/1913
**Stevens,** Stella (actress); Yazoo City, Miss., 10/1/1936
**Stevenson,** Adlai Ewing (statesman); Los Angeles **(1900-1965)**
**Stevenson,** McLean (actor); Bloomington, Ind., 11/14/1929(?)
**Stevenson,** Robert Louis Balfour (novelist and poet); Edinburgh, Scotland **(1850-1894)**
**Stewart,** James (actor); Indiana, Pa., 5/20/1908
**Stewart,** Rod (Roderick David) (singer); London, 1/10/1945
**Stickney,** Dorothy (actress); Dickinson, N.D. 6/21/1903
**Stills,** Stephen (singer and songwriter); Dallas, 1/3/1945
**Sting** (Gordon Matthew Sumner) (singer and composer); Wallsend, England, 10/2/1951
**Stokes,** Carl (TV newscaster); Cleveland, 6/21/1927
**Stokowski,** Leopold (conductor); London **(1882-1977)**
**Stone,** Edward Durell (architect); Fayetteville, Ark. **(1902-1978)**
**Stone,** Ezra (actor and producer); New Bedford, Mass., 12/2/1917
**Stone,** I(sidor) F(einstein) (journalist); Philadelphia, 12/24/1907
**Stone,** Irving (Irving Tennenbaum) (novelist); San Francisco, 7/14/1903
**Stone,** Lewis (actor); Worcester, Mass. **(1879-1953)**
**Stone,** Lucy (woman suffragist); nr. West Brookfield, Mass. **(1818-1893)**
**Stone,** Sly (Sylvester) (rock musician); 1944
**Storm,** Gale (actress); Bloomington, Tex., 1922
**Stout,** Rex (mystery writer); Noblesville, Ind. **(1886-1975)**
**Stowe,** Harriet Elizabeth Beecher (novelist); Litchfield, Conn. **(1811-1896)**
**Stradivari,** Antonio (violinmaker); Cremona (Italy) **(1644-1737)**
**Strasberg,** Lee (stage director); Budanov, Austria **(1901-1982)**
**Strasberg,** Susan (actress); New York City, 5/22/1938
**Straus,** Oskar (composer); Vienna **(1870-1954)**
**Strauss,** Johann (composer); Vienna **(1825-1899)**
**Strauss,** Lewis L. (naval officer and scientist); Charleston, W. Va. **(1896-1974)**
**Strauss,** Richard (composer); Munich, Germany **(1864-1949)**
**Stravinsky,** Igor (composer); Orlenbaum, Russia **(1882-1971)**
**Streep,** Meryl (Mary Louise) (actress); Summit, N.J., 6/22/1949
**Streisand,** Barbra (singer and actress); Brooklyn, N.Y., 4/24/1942
**Stritch,** Elaine (actress); Detroit, 2/2/1928
**Struthers,** Sally Ann (actress); Portland, Ore., 7/28/1948
**Stuart,** Gilbert Charles (painter); Rhode Island **(1755-1828)**
**Stuart,** James Ewell Brown (known as Jeb) (Confederate army officer); Patrick County, Va. **(1833-1864)**
**Stuyvesant,** Peter (Governor of New Amsterdam); West Friesland (Netherlands) **(1592-1672)**
**Styne,** Jule (Julius Kerwin Stein) (songwriter); London, 12/31/1905
**Styron,** William (William Clark Styron, Jr.) (novelist); Newport News, Va., 6/11/1925
**Sullavan,** Margaret Brooke (actress); Norfolk, Va. **(1911-1960)**
**Sullivan,** Sir Arthur Seymour (composer); London **(1842-1900)**
**Sullivan,** Barry (Patrick Barry) (actor); New York City, 8/29/1912
**Sullivan,** Ed (columnist and TV personality); New York City **(1901-1974)**
**Sullivan,** Francis Loftus (actor); London **(1903-1956)**
**Sullivan,** Frank (Francis John) (humorist); Saratoga Springs, N.Y. **(1892-1976)**
**Sullivan,** Louis Henry (architect); Boston, Mass. **(1856-1924)**
**Sutzberger,** Arthur Ochs (newspaper publisher); New York City, 2/5/1926
**Sumac,** Yma (singer); Ichocan, Peru, 9/10/1927
**Summer,** Donna (La Donna Andrea Gaines) (singer); Boston, 12/31/1948
**Sun Yat-sen** (statesman); nr. Macao **(1866-1925)**
**Susann,** Jacqueline (novelist); Philadelphia **(1926?-1974)**
**Susskind,** David (TV producer); New York City, 12/19/1920
**Sutherland,** Joan (soprano); Sydney, Australia, 11/7/1926
**Suzuki,** Pat (actress); Cressey, Calif., 1931
**Swados,** Elizabeth (composer, playwright); Buffalo, N.Y., 2/5/1951
**Swanson,** Gloria (Gloria May Josephine Svensson) (actress); Chicago, **(1899-1983)**
**Swarthout,** Gladys (soprano); Deepwater, Mo. **(1904-1969)**
**Swayze,** John Cameron (news commentator); Wichita, Kan., 4/4/1906
**Swendenborg,** Emanuel (scientist, philosopher, mystic); Stockholm **(1688-1772)**
**Swift,** Jonathan (satirist); Dublin **(1667-1745)**
**Swinburne,** Algernon Charles (poet); London **(1837-1909)**

**Swope,** Herbert Bayard (journalist); St. Louis **(1882-1958)**
**Sydow,** von, Max (Carl Adolf von Sydow) (actor); Lund, Sweden, 4/10/1929
**Synge,** John Millington (dramatist); nr. Dublin **(1871-1909)**
**Szilard,** Leo (physicist); Budapest **(1898-1964)**

# T

**Taft,** Robert Alphonso (legislator); Cincinnati **(1889-1953)**
**Tagore,** Sir Rabindranath (poet); Calcutta **(1861-1941)**
**Tallchief,** Maria (ballerina); Fairfax, Okla., 1/24/1925
**Talleyrand-Périgord,** Charles Maurice de (statesman); Paris **(1754-1838)**
**Talmadge,** Norma (actress); Niagara Falls, N.Y. **(1897-1957)**
**Talvela,** Martti (basso); Hiitola, Finalnd, 2/4/1935
**Tamerlane** (Timur) (Mongol conqueror); nr. Samarkand (U.S.S.R.) **(1336?-1405)**
**Tandy,** Jessica (actress); London, 6/7/1909
**Tarkington,** (Newton) Booth (novelist); Indianapolis **(1869-1946)**
**Tate,** Allen (John Orley) (poet and critic); Winchester, Ky., **(1899-1979)**
**Tate,** Sharon (actress); Dallas **(1943-1969)**
**Tati,** Jacques (Jacques Tatischeff) (actor); Pecq, France **(1908-1982)**
**Taylor,** Elizabeth (actress); London, 2/27/1932
**Taylor,** Estelle (actress); Wilmington, Del. **(1899-1958)**
**Taylor,** Harold (educator); Toronto, 9/28/1914
**Taylor,** James (singer and songwriter); Boston, 3/12/1948
**Taylor,** (Joseph) Deems (composer); New York City **(1885-1966)**
**Taylor,** Laurette (Laurette Cooney) (actress); New York City **(1884-1946)**
**Taylor,** Gen. Maxwell D. (former Army Chief of Staff); Keytesville, Mo., 8/26/1901
**Taylor,** Robert (Spangler Arlington Brugh) (actor); Filley, Neb. **(1911-1969)**
**Taylor,** Rod (actor); Sydney, Australia, 1/11/1930
**Tchaikovsky,** Peter (Pëtr) Ilich (composer); Votkinsk, Russia **(1840-1893)**
**Teasdale,** Sara (poet); St. Louis **(1884-1933)**
**Tebaldi,** Renata (lyric soprano); Pesaro, Italy, 1/2/1922
**Tecumseh** (Shawnee Indian chief); nr. Springfield, Ohio **(1768?-1813)**
**Telemann,** Georg Philipp (composer); Magdeburg (East Germany) **(1681-1767)**
**Teller,** Edward (atomic physicist); Budapest, 1/15/1908
**Temple,** Shirley. See Black, Shirley Temple
**Tennyson,** Alfred (1st Baron Tennyson) (poet); Somersby, England **(1809-1892)**
**Terhune,** Albert Payson (novelist and journalist); Newark, N.J. **(1872-1942)**
**Terkel,** Studs (writer-interviewer); New York City, 5/16/1912
**Terry,** Ellen Alicia (actress); Coventry, England **(1848-1928)**
**Terry-Thomas** (Thomas Terry Hoar Stevens) (actor); London, 7/14/1911
**Tesla,** Nikola (electrician and inventor); Smiljan (Yugoslavia) **(1856-1943)**
**Thackeray,** William Makepeace (novelist); Calcutta **(1811-1863)**
**Thant,** U (U.N. statesman); Pantanaw (Burma) **(1909-1974)**
**Tharp,** Twyla (dancer and choreographer); Portland, Ind., 7/1/1941(?)
**Thatcher,** Margaret (Prime Minister); Grantham, England, 10/13/1925
**Thaxter,** Phyllis (actress); Portland, Me., 1921
**Thebom,** Blanche (mezzo-soprano); Monessen, Pa., 9/19/1919
**Theodorakis,** Mikis (composer); Chios, Greece, 7/29/1925
**Thieu,** Nguyen Van (ex-President of South Vietnam); Trithuy (Vietnam) 4/5/1923
**Thomas,** Danny (Amos Jacobs) (entertainer and TV producer); Deerfield, Mich., 1/6/1914
**Thomas,** Dylan Marials (poet); Carmarthenshire, Wales **(1914-1953)**
**Thomas,** Lowell (explorer, commentator); Woodington, Ohio **(1892-1981)**
**Thomas,** Marlo (actress); Detroit, 11/21/1943
**Thomas,** Michael Tilson (conductor); Hollywood, Calif., 12/21/1944
**Thomas,** Norman Mattoon (Socialist leader); Marion, Ohio **(1884-1968)**
**Thomas,** Richard (actor); New York City, 6/13/1951
**Thompson,** Dorothy (writer); Lancaster, N.Y. **(1894-1961)**
**Thompson,** Hunter (Stockton) (writer); Louisville, Ky. 7/18/1939
**Thompson,** Sada (actress); Des Moines, Iowa, 9/27/1929
**Thoreau,** Henry David (naturalist and author); Concord, Mass. **(1817-1862)**
**Thorndike,** Dame Sybil (actress); Gainsborough, England **(1882-1976)**
**Thurber,** James Grover (author and cartoonist); Columbus, Ohio **(1894-1961)**
**Tibbett,** Lawrence (baritone); Bakersfield, Calif. **(1896-1960)**
**Tierney,** Gene (actress); Brooklyn, N.Y., 11/20/1920
**Tiffin,** Pamela (actress); Oklahoma City, 10/13/1942
**Tillstrom,** Burr (puppeteer); Chicago **(1917-1985)**
**Tintoretto,** Il (Jacopo Robusti) (painter); Venice **(1518-1594)**
**Tiny Tim** (Herbert Khaury) (entertainer); New York City, 1923(?)
**Tiomkin,** Dmitri (composer); St. Petersburg, Russia **(1894-1979)**
**Titian** (Tiziano Vecelli) (painter); Pieve di Cadore (Italy) **(1477-1576)**
**Tito** (Josip Broz or Brozovich) (President of Yugoslavia); Croatia (Yugoslavia) **(1892-1980)**
**Tocqueville,** Alexis de (writer); Verneuil, France **(1805-1859)**
**Todd,** Thelma (actress); Lawrence, Mass. **(1905-1935)**
**Tolstoi,** Count Leo (Lev) Nikolaevich (novelist); Tula Province, Russia **(1828-1910)**
**Tomlin,** Lily (comedienne); Detroit, 1939(?)
**Tone,** Franchot (actor); Niagara Falls, N.Y. **(1905-1968)**
**Tormé,** Mel (Melvin) (singer); Chicago, 9/13/1925
**Torn,** Rip (Elmore Torn, Jr.) (actor and director); Temple, Tex., 2/6/1931
**Torquemada,** Tomás de (Spanish Inquisitor); Valladolid, Spain **(1420-1498)**
**Toscanini,** Arturo (orchestra conductor); Parma, Italy **(1867-1957)**
**Toulouse-Lautrec** (Henri Marie Raymond de Toulouse-Lautrec Monfa) (painter); Albi, France **(1864-1901)**
**Toynbee,** Arnold J. (historian); London **(1889-1975)**
**Tracy,** Spencer (actor); Milwaukee **(1900-1967)**
**Traubel,** Helen (Wagnerian soprano); St. Louis **(1903-1972)**
**Travolta,** John (actor); Englewood, N.J., 2/18/1954
**Treacher,** Arthur (actor); Brighton, England **(1894-1975)**
**Trevor,** Claire (actress); New York City, 1911
**Trigère,** (Pauline (fashion designer); Paris, 11/4/1912
**Trilling,** Lionel (actor and educator); New York City **(1905-1975)**
**Trotsky,** Leon (Lev Davidovich Bronstein) (statesman); Elisavetgrad, Russia **(1879-1940)**
**Trudeau,** Garry (cartoonist); New York City, 1948
**Trudeau,** Pierre Elliott (former Prime Minister); Montreal, 10/18/1919
**Truffaut,** François (film director); Paris **(1932-1984)**
**Trujillo y Molina,** Rafael Leonidas (Dominican Republic dictator); San Cristóbal, Dominican Republic **(1891-1961)**
**Truman,** Margaret (author); Independence, Mo., 2/17/1924
**Tryon,** Thomas (actor and novelist); Hartford, Conn., 1/14/1926
**Tucker,** Forrest (actor); Plainfield, Ind., 2/12/1919
**Tucker,** Richard (tenor); New York City **(1914-1975)**
**Tucker,** Sophie (Sophie Abuza) (singer); Europe **(1884?-1966)**
**Tudor,** Antony (choreographer); London, 4/4/1909
**Tune,** Tommy (dancer-choreographer); Wichita Falls, Tex., 2/28/1939
**Turgenev,** Ivan Sergeevich (novelist); Orel, Russia **(1818-1883)**
**Turner,** Ike (singer); Clarksdale, Miss., 11/?/1931
**Turner,** Joseph M.W. (painter); London **(1775-1851)**
**Turner,** Kathleen (actress); Springfield, Mo., 1956 (?)
**Turner,** Lana (Julia Jean Mildred Frances Turner) (actress); Wallace, Idaho, 2/8/1920
**Turner,** Nat (civil rights leader); Southampton County, Va. **(1800-1831)**
**Turner,** Tina (Annie Mae Bullock) (singer); Brownsville, Tex., 1939
**Turpin,** Ben (comedian); New Orleans **(1874-1940)**
**Tushingham,** Rita (actress); Liverpool, England, 3/14/1942
**Twain,** Mark (Samuel Langhorne Clemens) (author); Florida, Mo. **(1835-1910)**
**Tweed,** William Marcy (politician); New York City **(1823-1878)**
**Twiggy** (Leslie Hornby) (model); London, 9/19/1949
**Twining,** Gen. Nathan F. (former Air Force Chief of Staff); Monroe, Wis. **(1897-1982)**
**Twitty,** Conway (Harold Lloyd Jenkins) (singer and guitarist); Friars Point, Miss., 9/1/1933
**Tyson,** Cicely (actress); New York City, 12/19/1939(?)

# U

**Udall,** Stewart L. (ex-Secretary of the Interior); St. Johns, Ariz., 1/31/1920
**Uggams,** Leslie (singer and actress); New York City, 5/25/1943
**Ulanova,** Galina (ballerina); St. Petersburg, Russia, 1/10/1910
**Ullmann,** Liv (actress); Tokyo, 12/16/1939
**Ulric,** Lenore (actress); New Ulm, Minn. **(1894-1970)**
**Untermeyer,** Louis (anthologist and poet); New York City **(1885-1977)**
**Updike,** John (novelist); Shillington, Pa., 3/18/1932
**Urey,** Harold C. (physicist); Walkerton, Ind. **(1893-1981)**
**Uris,** Leon (novelist); Baltimore, 8/3/1924
**Ustinov,** Peter (actor and producer); London, 4/16/1921
**Utrillo,** Maurice (painter); Paris **(1883-1955)**

# V

Vaccaro, Brenda (actress); Brooklyn, N.Y., 11/18/1939
Vadim, Roger (Roger Vadim Plemiannikov) (film director); Paris, 1/26/1928
Valentine, Karen (actress); Santa Rosa, Calif., 1947
Valentino, Rudolph (Rodolpho d'Antonguolla) (actor); Castellaneta, Italy **(1895-1926)**
Valentino (Valentino Garavani) (fashion designer); nr. Milan, Italy, 5/11/1932
Vallee, Rudy (Hubert Prior Rudy Vallée) (band leader and singer); Island Pond, Vt. **(1901-1986)**
Valli, Frankie (Frank Castellaccio) (singer); Newark, N.J., 5/3/1937
Van Allen, James Alfred (space physicist); Mt. Pleasant, Iowa, 9/7/1914
Van Buren, Abigail (Mrs. Morton Phillips) (columnist); Sioux City, Iowa, 7/4/1918
Vance, Vivian (actress); Cherryvale, Kan. **(1912-1979)**
Vanderbilt, Alfred G. (sportsman); London, 9/22/1912
Vanderbilt, Cornelius (financier); Port Richmond, N.Y. **(1794-1877)**
Vanderbilt, Gloria (fashion designer) New York City, 2/20/1924
Van Doren, Carl (writer and educator); Hope, Ill. **(1885-1950)**
Van Doren, Mamie (actress); Rowena, S.D., 2/6/1933
Van Dyke, Dick (actor); West Plains, Mo., 12/13/1925
Vandyke (or Van Dyck), Sir Anthony (painter); Antwerp (Belgium) **(1599-1641)**
Van Eyck, Jan (painter); Maeseyck (Belgium) **(c.1390-1441)**
van Gogh, Vincent (painter); Groot Zundert, Brabant **(1853-1890)**
van Hamel, Martine (ballerina); Brussels, 11/16/1945
Van Heusen, Jimmy (Edward Chester Babcock) (songwriter); Syracuse, N.Y., 1/26/1913
Van Peebles, Melvin (playwright); Chicago, 9/21/1932
Vaughan, Sarah (singer); Newark, N.J., 3/27/1924
Vaughan Williams, Ralph (composer); Down Ampney, England **(1872-1958)**
Vaughn, Robert (actor); New York City, 11/22/1932
Velázquez, Diego Rodriguez de Silva y (painter); Seville, Spain **(1599-1660)**
Velez, Lupe (Guadelupe Velez de Villalobos) (actress); San Luis Potosi, Mexico **(1908-1944)**
Venturi, Robert (Charles) (architect); Philadelphia, 6/25/1925
Verdi, Giuseppe (composer); Roncole (Italy) **(1813-1901)**
Verdon, Gwen (actress); Culver City, Calif., 1/13/1925
Vereen, Ben (actor and singer); Miami, Fla., 10/10/1946
Vermeer, Jan (or Jan van der Meer van Delft) (painter); Delft (Netherlands) **(1632-1675)**
Verne, Jules (author); Nantes, France **(1828-1905)**
Veronese, Paolo (Paolo Cagliari); (painter); Vernoa **(1528-1588)**
Verrazano, Giovanni da (navigator); Florence (Italy) **(1485?-1528)**
Verrett, Shirley (mezzo-soprano); New Orleans, 5/31/1933
Vesalius, Andreas (anatomist); Brussels, Belgium **(1515-1564)**
Vespucci, Amerigo (navigator); Florence (Italy) **(1454-1512)**
Vickers, Jon (tenor); Prince Albert, Sask, Canada, 10/29/1926
Vico, Giovanni Battista (philosopher); Naples, Italy **(1668-1744)**
Vidal, Gore (novelist); West Point, N.Y., 10/3/1925
Vidor, King (film director and producer); Galveston, Tex. **(1895-1982)**
Villa, Pancho (Doroteo Arango) (bandit); Rio Grande, Mexico **(1877-1923)**
Villella, Edward (ballet dancer); Bayside, Queens, N.Y., 10/1/1936
Villon, François (François de Montcorbier) (poet); Paris **(1431-1463)**
Vinton, Bobby (singer); Canonsburg, Pa., 4/16/1935(?)
Virgil (or Vergil) (Publius Vergilius Maro) (poet); nr. Mantua (Italy) **(70-19 B.C.)**
Vishnevskaya, Galina (soprano); Leningrad, 10/25/1926
Vivaldi, Antonio (composer); Venice **(1678-1741)**
Vlaminck, Maurice de (painter); Paris **(1876-1958)**
Voight, Jon (actor); Yonkers, N.Y., 12/29/1938
Volta, Alessandro (scientist); Como, Italy **(1745-1827)**
Voltaire (François Marie Arouet) (author); Paris **(1694-1778)**
von Braun, Wernher (rocket scientist); Wirsitz, Germany **(1912-1977)**
von Aroldingen, Karin (Karin Awny Hannelore Reinbold von Aroedingen and Eltzinger) (ballet dancer); Greiz (East Germany) 7/9/1941
von Furstenberg, Betsy (Elizabeth Caroline Maria Agatha Felicitas Therese von Furstenberg-Hedringen) (actress); Nelheim-Heusen, Germany, 8/16/1935
von Fürstenberg, Diane (Diane Simone Michelle Halfin) (fashion designer); Brussels, 12/31/1946
von Hindenburg, Paul (statesman): Posen (Poland) **(1847-1934)**
von Karajan, Herbert (conductor); Salzburg (Austria), 4/5/1908
Vonnegut, Kurt, Jr. (novelist); Indianapolis, 11/11/1922
Von Stroheim, Erich Oswald Hans Carl Maria von Nordenwall (film actor and director); Vienna **(1885-1957)**
Vreeland, Diana (Diana Dalziel) (fashion journalist and museum consultant); Paris, 1903(?)

# W

Wagner, Lindsay (actress); Los Angeles, 6/22/1949
Wagner, Robert (actor); Detroit, 2/10/1930
Wagner, Robert F. (ex-Mayor of New York City); New York City, 4/20/1910
Wagner, Wilhelm Richard (composer); Leipzig (East Germany) **(1813-1883)**
Waldheim, Kurt (U.N. Secretary-General); St. Andrae-Wörden, Austria, 12/21/1918
Walker, Clint (actor); Hartford, Ill., 5/30/1927
Walker, Nancy (Ann Myrtle Swoyer); (actress and comedienne); Philadelphia, 5/10/1922
Wallace, DeWitt (publisher); St. Paul **(1889-1981)**
Wallace, Irving (novelist); Chicago, 3/19/1916
Wallace, Mike (Myron Wallace) (TV interviewer and commentator); Brookline, Mass., 5/9/1918
Wallach, Eli (actor); Brooklyn, N.Y., 12/7/1915
Waller, Thomas "Fats" (pianist); New York City **(1904-1943)**
Wallis, Hal (film producer); Chicago, 9/14/1899
Walpole, Horace (statesman and novelist); London **(1717-1797)**
Waltari, Mika (novelist); Helsinki, Finland, **(1903-1979)**
Walter, Bruno (Bruno Walter Schlesinger) (orchestra conductor); Berlin **(1876-1962)**
Walters, Barbara (TV commentator); Boston, 9/25/1931
Walton, Izaak (author); Stafford, England **(1593-1683)**
Wambaugh, Joseph (author and screenwriter); East Pittsburgh, Pa., 1/22/1937
Wanamaker, John (merchant); Philadelphia **(1838-1922)**
Ward, Barbara (economist); York, England **(1914-1981)**
Warhol, Andy (artist and producer); Cleveland, 8/8/1930(?)
Waring, Fred (band leader); Tyrone, Pa., **(1900-1984)**
Warner, H. B. (Henry Bryan Warner Lickford) (actor); London **(1876-1958)**
Warren, Robert Penn (novelist); Guthrie, Ky., 4/24/1905
Warwick, Dionne (singer); East Orange, N.J., 1941
Washington, Booker Taliaferro (educator); Franklin County, Va. **(1856-1915)**
Waters, Ethel (actress and singer); Chester, Pa. **(1896-1977)**
Waters, Muddy (McKinley Morganfield) (singer and guitarist); Rolling Fork, Miss. **(1915-1983)**
Watson, Thomas John (industrialist); Campbell, N.Y. **(1874-1956)**
Watt, James (inventor); Greenock, Scotland **(1736-1819)**
Watteau, Jean-Antoine (painter); Valanciennes, France **(1684-1721)**
Watts, André (concert pianist); Nuremberg, Germany, 6/20/1946
Waugh, Alec (Alexander Raban Waugh) (novelist); London **(1898-1981)**
Waugh, Evelyn (satirist); London **(1903-1966)**
Wayne, Anthony (military officer); Waynesboro (family farm), nr. Paoli, Pa. **(1745-1796)**
Wayne, David (David McMeekan); (actor); Traverse City, Mich., 1/30/1914
Wayne, John (Marion Michael Morrison) (actor); Winterset, Iowa, **(1907-1979)**
Weaver, Dennis (actor); Joplin, Mo., 6/4/1925
Weaver, Fritz (actor); Pittsburgh, 1/19/1926
Webb, Clifton (Webb Parmelee Hollenbeck) (actor); Indianapolis **(1893-1966)**
Webb, Jack (film actor and producer); Santa Monica, Calif. **(1920-1982)**
Weber, Karl Maria Friedrich Ernst von (composer); nr. Lübeck (Germany) **(1786-1826)**
Webster, Daniel (statesman); Salisbury, N.H. **(1782-1852)**
Webster, Noah (lexicographer); West Hartford, Conn. **(1758-1843)**
Weill, Kurt (composer); Dessau, (East Germany) **(1900-1950)**
Weir, Peter (film director); Sydney, Australia, 8/21/1944
Weizmann, Chaim (statesman); Grodno Province, Russia **(1874-1952)**
Welch, Raquel (Raquel Tejada) (actress); Chicago, 9/5/1942
Weld, Tuesday (Susan) (actress); New York City, 8/27/1943
Welk, Lawrence (band leader); Strasburg, N.D., 3/11/1903
Welles, Orson (actor and producer); Kenosha, Wis. **(1915-1985)**
Wellington, Duke of (Arthur Wellesley) (statesman); Ireland **(1769-1852)**
Wells, H(erbert) G(eorge) (author); Bromley, England **(1866-1946)**
Welty, Eudora (novelist); Jackson, Miss., 4/13/1909
Werfel, Franz (novelist); Prague **(1890-1945)**
Werner, Oskar (Josef Schliessmayer) (film actor and director); Vienna **(1922-1984)**
Wertmuller, Lina (film director); Rome, 1926(?)
Wesley, John (religious leader); Epworth Rectory, Lincolnshire, England **(1703-1791)**
West, Dame Rebecca (Cicily Fairfield); (novelist); County Kerry, Ireland **(1892-1983)**
West, Jessamyn (novelist); nr. North Vernon, Ind. **(1902-1984)**
West, Mae (actress); Brooklyn, N.Y. **(1893-1980)**

**West,** Nathanael (Nathan Weinstein) (novelist); New York City **(1902-1940)**
**Westinghouse,** George (inventor); Central Bridge, N.Y. **(1846-1914)**
**Westmoreland,** William Childs (ex-Army Chief of Staff); Saxon, S.C., 3/26/1914
**Wharton,** Edith Newbold (née Jones) (novelist); New York City **(1862-1937)**
**Wheeler,** Bert (Albert Jerome Wheeler) (comedian); Paterson, N.J. **(1895-1968)**
**Whistler,** James Abbott McNeill (painter and etcher); Lowell, Mass. (1834-1903)
**White,** E(lwyn) B(rooks) (author); Mt. Vernon, N.Y. **(1899-1985)**
**White,** Stanford (architect); New York City **(1853-1906)**
**White,** Theodore H. (historian); Boston **(1915-1986)**
**White,** William Allen (journalist); Emporia, Kan. **(1868-1944)**
**Whitehead,** Alfred North (mathematician and philosopher); Isle of Thanet, England **(1861-1947)**
**Whiteman,** Paul (band leader); Denver **(1891-1967)**
**Whitman,** Walt (Walter) (poet); West Hills, N.Y. **(1819-1892)**
**Whitmore,** James (actor); White Plains, N.Y., 10/1/1921
**Whitney,** Cornelius Vanderbilt (sportsman); New York City, 2/20/1899
**Whitney,** Eli (inventor); Westboro, Mass. **(1765-1825)**
**Whitney,** John Hay (publisher); Ellsworth, Me. **(1904-1982)**
**Whittier,** John Greenleaf (poet); Haverhill, Mass. **(1807-1892)**
**Widmark,** Richard (actor); Sunrise, Minn., 12/26/1914
**Wiesel,** Elie (Eliezer) (author); Signet, Romania, 9/30/1928
**Wilbur,** Richard (poet); New York City, 3/1/1921
**Wilde,** Cornel (film actor and producer); New York City, 10/13/1918
**Wilde,** Oscar Fingal O'Flahertie Wills (author); Dublin **(1854-1900)**
**Wilder,** Billy (film producer and director); Vienna, 6/22/1906
**Wilder,** Gene (Jerome Silberman) (actor); Milwaukee, 6/11/1935(?)
**Wilder,** Thornton (author); Madison, Wis. **(1897-1975)**
**Wilding,** Michael (actor); Westcliff, England **(1912-1979)**
**Wilkins,** Roy (civil rights leader); St. Louis **(1901-1981)**
**Williams,** Andy (singer); Wall Lake, Iowa, 12/3/1930
**Williams,** Billy Dee (actor); New York City, 4/6/1937
**Williams,** Cindy (actress); Van Nuys, Calif., 8/22/(?)
**Williams,** Edward Bennett (lawyer); Hartford, Conn., 5/31/1920
**Williams,** Emlyn (actor and playwright); Mostyn, Wales, 11/26/1905
**Williams,** Esther (actress); Los Angeles, 8/8/1923
**Williams,** Gluyas (cartoonist); San Francisco **(1888-1982)**
**Williams,** Hank, Sr. (Hiram King Williams) (singer); Georgiana, Ala. **(1923-1953)**
**Williams,** Joe (singer); Cordele, Ga., 12/12/1918
**Williams,** Paul (singer, composer, actor); Omaha, Neb., 9/19/1940
**Williams,** Robin (comedian); Chicago, 7/?/1952
**Williams,** Roger (clergyman); London **(1603?-1683)**
**Williams,** Tennessee (Thomas L. Williams) (playwright); Columbus, Miss. **(1911-1983)**
**Williams,** William Carlos (physician and poet); Rutherford, N.J. **(1883-1963)**
**Willkie,** Wendell Lewis (lawyer); Elwood, Ind. **(1892-1944)**
**Willson,** Meredith (composer); Mason City, Iowa **(1902-1984)**
**Wilson,** Don (radio and TV announcer); Lincoln, Neb. **(1900-1982)**
**Wilson,** Edmund (literary critic and author); Red Bank, N.J. **(1895-1972)**
**Wilson,** Flip (Clerow) (comedian); Jersey City, N.J., 12/8/1933
**Wilson,** Harold (ex-Prime Minister); Huddersfield, England, 3/11/1916
**Wilson,** Nancy (singer); Chillicothe, Ohio, 2/20/1937
**Wilson,** Sloan (novelist); Norwalk, Conn., 5/8/1920
**Winchell,** Walter (columnist); New York City **(1897-1972)**
**Windsor,** Duchess of (Bessie Wallis Warfield); Blue Ridge Summit, Pa. **(1896-1986)**
**Windsor,** Duke of (formerly King Edward VIII of England); Richmond Park, England **(1894-1972)**
**Winkler,** Henry (actor); New York City, 10/30/1945
**Winter,** Johnny (guitarist); Leland, Miss., 2/23/1944
**Winters,** Jonathan (comedian); Dayton, Ohio, 11/11/1925
**Winters,** Shelley (Shirley Schrift) (actress); East St. Louis, Ill., 8/18/1922
**Winthrop,** John (first Governor, Massachusetts Bay Colony); Suffolk, England **(1588-1649)**
**Wise,** Stephen Samuel (rabbi); Budapest **(1874-1949)**
**Withers,** Jane (actress); Atlanta, 1927
**Wittgenstein,** Ludwig (Josef Johann) (philosopher); Vienna **(1889-1951)**
**Wodehouse,** P(elham) G(renville) (novelist); Guildford, England **(1881-1975)**
**Wolfe,** Thomas Clayton (novelist); Asheville, N.C. **(1900-1938)**
**Wolfe,** Tom (journalist); Richmond, Va., 3/2/1931
**Wolsey,** Thomas (prelate and statesman); Ipswich, England **(1475?-1530)**
**Wonder,** Stevie (Steveland Judkins, later Steveland Morris) (singer and songwriter); Saginaw, Mich., 5/13/1950

**Wong,** Anna May (Lu Tsong Wong) (actress); Los Angeles **(1907-1961)**
**Wood,** Grant (painter); Anamosa, Iowa **(1892-1942)**
**Wood,** Natalie (Natasha Gurdin) (film actress); San Francisco **(1938-1981)**
**Woodhouse,** Barbara (Blackburn) (dog trainer, author, TV personality): Rathfarnham, Ireland, 5/9/1910
**Woodward,** Joanne (film actress); Thomasville, Ga., 2/27/1930
**Woolf,** Adeline Virginia (née Stephens) (novelist); London **(1882-1941)**
**Woollcott,** Alexander (author-critic); Phalanx, N.J. **(1887-1943)**
**Woolley,** Monty (Edgar Montillion Woolley) (actor); New York City **(1888-1963)**
**Woolworth,** Frank (merchant); Rodman, N.Y. **(1852-1919)**
**Wordsworth,** William (poet); Cockermouth, England **(1770-1850)**
**Worley,** Jo Anne (actress and singer); Lowell, Ind., 9/6/1937
**Wouk,** Herman (novelist); New York City, 5/27/1915
**Wray,** Fay (actress); Alberta, Canada, 1907
**Wren,** Sir Christopher (architect); East Knoyle, England **(1632-1723)**
**Wright,** Frank Lloyd (architect); Richland Center, Wis. **(1869-1959)**
**Wright,** Orville (inventor); Dayton, Ohio **(1871-1948)**
**Wright,** Richard (novelist); nr. Natchez, Miss. **(1908-1960)**
**Wright,** Teresa (actress); New York City, 10/27/1918
**Wright,** Wilbur (inventor); Millville, Ind. **(1867-1912)**
**Wyatt,** Jane (film actress); Campgaw, N.J., 8/12/1912
**Wycliffe,** John (church reformer); Hipswell, England **(1320-1384)**
**Wyeth,** Andrew (painter); Chadds Ford, Pa., 7/12/1917
**Wyler,** William (film director); Mulhouse (France), **(1902-1981)**
**Wyman,** Jane (Sarah Jane Fulks) (actress); St. Joseph, Mo., 1/4/1914
**Wynette,** Tammy (Wynette Pugh) (singer); Tupelo, Miss. 5/5/1942
**Wynn,** Ed (Isaiah Edwin Leopold) (comedian); Philadelphia **(1886-1966)**
**Wynn,** Keenan (actor); New York City, 7/27/1916
**Wynter,** Dana (actress); London, 6/8/1930

# X

**Xavier,** St. Francis (Jesuit missionary); Pamplona, Navarre (Spain) **(1506-1552)**
**Xenophon** (soldier, historian and essayist): Athens, Greece, **(434(?)-355(?) B.C.)**
**Xerxes,** the Great (king): Persian Empire, **(519(?)-465 B.C.)**

# Y

**Yeats,** William Butler (poet); nr. Dublin **(1865-1939)**
**Yevtushenko,** Yevgeny (poet); Zima, U.S.S.R., 7/18/1933
**York,** Alvin Cullun (Sergeant York, World War I hero): Tennessee **(1887-1964)**
**York,** Michael (actor); Fulmer, England, 3/27/1942
**York,** Susannah (Fletcher) (actress); London, 1/9/1942
**Yorty,** Samuel W. (ex-Mayor of Los Angeles); Lincoln, Neb., 10/1/1909
**Young,** Alan (actor); North Shield, England, 11/19/1919
**Young,** Brigham (religious leader); Whitingham, Vt. **(1801-1877)**
**Young,** Gig (Byron Barr) (actor); St. Cloud, Minn. **(1917-1978)**
**Young,** Loretta (Gretchen Young) (actress); Salt Lake City, Utah, 1/6/1913
**Young,** Neil (singer and songwriter); Toronto, 11/12/1945
**Young,** Robert (actor); Chicago, 2/22/1907
**Youngman,** Henny (comedian); England, 1906

# Z

**Zanuck,** Darryl F. (film producer); Wahoo, Neb. **(1902-1979)**
**Zappa,** Frank (Francis Vincent Zappa, Jr.) (singer and songwriter); Baltimore, 12/21/1940
**Zeffirelli,** Franco (director); Florence, Italy, 2/12/1923
**Zenger,** John Peter (printer and journalist): Germany, **(1697-1746)**
**Zhou Enlai** (Premier); Hualyin, China **(1898-1976)**
**Ziegfeld,** Florenz (theatrical producer); Chicago **(1869-1932)**
**Zimbalist,** Efrem (concert violinist); Rostov-on-Don, Russia **(1889-1985)**
**Zimbalist,** Efrem, Jr. (actor); New York City, 11/30/1923
**Zola,** Emile (novelist); Paris **(1840-1902)**
**Zoroaster** (religious leader); Persian Empire **(c. 6th century B.C.)**
**Zukerman,** Pinchas (violinist); Tel Aviv, Israel 7/16/1948
**Zweig,** Stefan (author); Vienna **(1881-1942)**
**Zwingli,** Huldrych (humanist); Wildaus, Switzerland **(1484-1531)**

# AWARDS

## Nobel Prizes

The Nobel prizes are awarded under the will of Alfred Bernhard Nobel, Swedish chemist and engineer, who died in 1896. The interest of the fund is divided annually among the persons who have made the most outstanding contributions in the fields of physics, chemistry, and physiology or medicine, who have produced the most distinguished literary work of an idealist tendency, and who have contributed most toward world peace.

In 1968, a Nobel Prize of economic sciences was established by Riksbank, the Swedish bank, in celebration of its 300th anniversary. The prize was awarded for the first time in 1969.

The prizes for physics and chemistry are awarded by the Swedish Academy of Science in Stockholm, the one for physiology or medicine by the Caroline Medical Institute in Stockholm, that for literature by the academy in Stockholm, and that for peace by a committee of five elected by the Norwegian Storting. The distribution of prizes was begun on December 10, 1901, the anniversary of Nobel's death. The amount of each prize varies with the income from the fund and currently is about $190,000. No Nobel prizes were awarded for 1940, 1941, and 1942; prizes for Literature were not awarded for 1914, 1918, and 1943.

### PEACE

1901 Henri Dunant (Switzerland); Frederick Passy (France)
1902 Elie Ducommun and Albert Gobat (Switzerland)
1903 Sir William R. Cremer (England)
1904 Institut de Droit International (Belgium)
1905 Bertha von Suttner (Austria)
1906 Theodore Roosevelt (U.S.)
1907 Ernesto T. Moneta (Italy) and Louis Renault (France)
1908 Klas P. Arnoldson (Sweden) and Frederik Bajer (Denmark)
1909 Auguste M. F. Beernaert (Belgium) and Baron Paul H. B. B. d'Estournelles de Constant de Rebecque (France)
1910 Bureau International Permanent de la Paix (Switzerland)
1911 Tobias M. C. Asser (Holland) and Alfred H. Fried (Austria)
1912 Elihu Root (U.S.)
1913 Henri La Fontaine (Belgium)
1915 No award
1916 No award
1917 International Red Cross
1919 Woodrow Wilson (U.S.)
1920 Léon Bourgeois (France)
1921 Karl H. Branting (Sweden) and Christian L. Lange (Norway)
1922 Fridtjof Nansen (Norway)
1923 No award
1924 No award
1925 Sir Austen Chamberlain (England) and Charles G. Dawes (U.S.)
1926 Aristide Briand (France) and Gustav Stresemann (Germany)
1927 Ferdinand Buisson (France) and Ludwig Quidde (Germany)
1928 No award
1929 Frank B. Kellogg (U.S.)
1930 Lars O. J. Söderblom (Sweden)
1931 Jane Addams and Nicholas M. Butler (U.S.)
1932 No award
1933 Sir Norman Angell (England)
1934 Arthur Henderson (England)
1935 Karl von Ossietzky (Germany)
1936 Carlos de S. Lamas (Argentina)
1937 Lord Cecil of Chelwood (England)
1938 Office International Nansen pour les Réfugiés (Switzerland)
1939 No award
1944 International Red Cross
1945 Cordell Hull (U.S.)

1946 Emily G. Balch and John R. Mott (U.S.)
1947 American Friends Service Committee (U.S.) and British Society of Friends' Service Council (England)
1948 No award
1949 Lord John Boyd Orr (Scotland)
1950 Ralph J. Bunche (U.S.)
1951 Léon Jouhaux (France)
1952 Albert Schweitzer (French Equatorial Africa)
1953 George C. Marshall (U.S.)
1954 Office of U.N. High Commissioner for Refugees
1955 No award
1956 No award
1957 Lester B. Pearson (Canada)
1958 Rev. Dominique Georges Henri Pire (Belgium)
1959 Philip John Noel-Baker (England)
1960 Albert John Luthuli (South Africa)
1961 Dag Hammarskjöld (Sweden)
1962 Linus Pauling (U.S.)
1963 Intl. Comm. of Red Cross; League of Red Cross Societies (both Geneva)
1964 Rev. Dr. Martin Luther King, Jr. (U.S.)
1965 UNICEF (United Nations Children's Fund)
1966 No award
1967 No award
1968 René Cassin (France)
1969 International Labour Organization
1970 Norman E. Borlaug (U.S.)
1971 Willy Brandt (West Germany)
1972 No award
1973 Henry A. Kissinger (U.S.); Le Duc Tho (North Vietnam)[1]
1974 Eisaku Sato (Japan); Sean MacBride (Ireland)
1975 Andrei D. Sakharov (U.S.S.R.)
1976 Mairead Corrigan and Betty Williams (both Northern Ireland)
1977 Amnesty International
1978 Menachem Begin (Israel) and Anwar el-Sadat (Egypt)
1979 Mother Teresa of Calcutta (India)
1980 Adolfo Pérez Esquivel (Argentina)
1981 Office of the United Nations High Commissioner for Refugees
1982 Alva Myrdal (Sweden) and Alfonso García Robles (Mexico)
1983 Lech Walesa (Poland)
1984 Bishop Desmond Tutu (South Africa)
1985 International Physicians for the Prevention of Nuclear War

1. Le Duc Tho refused prize, charging that peace had not yet been really established in South Vietnam.

## LITERATURE

1901 René F. A. Sully Prudhomme (France)
1902 Theodor Mommsen (Germany)
1903 Björnstjerne Björnson (Norway)
1904 Frédéric Mistral (France) and José Echegaray (Spain)
1905 Henryk Sienkiewicz (Poland)
1906 Giosuè Carducci (Italy)
1907 Rudyard Kipling (England)
1908 Rudolf Eucken (Germany)
1909 Selma Lagerlöf (Sweden)
1910 Paul von Heyse (Germany)
1911 Maurice Maeterlinck (Belgium)
1912 Gerhart Hauptmann (Germany)
1913 Rabindranath Tagore (India)
1915 Romain Rolland (France)
1916 Verner von Heidenstam (Sweden)
1917 Karl Gjellerup (Denmark) and Henrik Pontoppidan (Denmark)
1919 Carl Spitteler (Switzerland)
1920 Knut Hamsun (Norway)
1921 Anatole France (France)
1922 Jacinto Benavente (Spain)
1923 William B. Yeats (Ireland)
1924 Wladyslaw Reymont (Poland)
1925 George Bernard Shaw (England)
1926 Grazia Deledda (Italy)
1927 Henri Bergson (France)
1928 Sigrid Undset (Norway)
1929 Thomas Mann (Germany)
1930 Sinclair Lewis (U.S.)
1931 Erik A. Karlfeldt (Sweden)
1932 John Galsworthy (England)
1933 Ivan G. Bunin (Russia)
1934 Luigi Pirandello (Italy)
1935 No award
1936 Eugene O'Neill (U.S.)
1937 Roger Martin du Gard (France)
1938 Pearl S. Buck (U.S.)
1939 Frans Eemil Sillanpää (Finland)
1944 Johannes V. Jensen (Denmark)
1945 Gabriela Mistral (Chile)
1946 Hermann Hesse (Switzerland)
1947 André Gide (France)
1948 Thomas Stearns Eliot (England)
1949 William Faulkner (U.S.)
1950 Bertrand Russell (England)
1951 Pär Lagerkvist (Sweden)
1952 François Mauriac (France)
1953 Sir Winston Churchill (England)
1954 Ernest Hemingway (U.S.)
1955 Halldór Kiljan Laxness (Iceland)
1956 Juan Ramón Jiménez (Spain)
1957 Albert Camus (France)
1958 Boris Pasternak (U.S.S.R.) (declined)
1959 Salvatore Quasimodo (Italy)
1960 St-John Perse (Alexis St.-Léger Léger) (France)
1961 Ivo Andric (Yugoslavia)
1962 John Steinbeck (U.S.)
1963 Giorgios Seferis (Seferiades) (Greece)
1964 Jean-Paul Sartre (France) (declined)
1965 Mikhail Sholokhov (U.S.S.R.)
1966 Shmuel Yosef Agnon (Israel) and Nelly Sachs (Sweden)
1967 Miguel Angel Asturias (Guatemala)
1968 Yasunari Kawabata (Japan)
1969 Samuel Beckett (France)
1970 Aleksandr Solzhenitsyn (U.S.S.R.)
1971 Pablo Neruda (Chile)
1972 Heinrich Böll (Germany)
1973 Patrick White (Australia)
1974 Eyvind Johnson and Harry Martinson (both Sweden)
1975 Eugenio Montale (Italy)
1976 Saul Bellow (U.S.)
1977 Vicente Aleixandre (Spain)
1978 Isaac Bashevis Singer (U.S.)
1979 Odysseus Elytis (Greece)
1980 Czeslaw Milosz (U.S.)
1981 Elias Canetti (Bulgaria)
1982 Gabriel García Márquez (Colombia)
1983 William Golding (England)
1984 Jaroslav Seifert (Czechoslovakia)
1985 Claude Simon (France)

## PHYSICS

1901 Wilhelm K. Roentgen (Germany), for discovery of Roentgen rays
1902 Hendrik A. Lorentz and Pieter Zeeman (Netherlands), for work on influence of magnetism upon radiation
1903 A. Henri Becquerel (France), for work on spontaneous radioactivity; and Pierre and Marie Curie (France), for study of radiation
1904 John Strutt (Lord Rayleigh) (England), for discovery of argon in investigating gas density
1905 Philipp Lenard (Germany), for work with cathode rays
1906 Sir Joseph Thomson (England), for investigations on passage of electricity through gases
1907 Albert A. Michelson (U.S.), for spectroscopic and metrologic investigations
1908 Gabriel Lippmann (France), for method of reproducing colors by photography
1909 Guglielmo Marconi (Italy) and Ferdinand Braun (Germany), for development of wireless
1910 Johannes D. van der Waals (Netherlands), for work with the equation of state for gases and liquids
1911 Wilhelm Wien (Germany), for his laws governing the radiation of heat
1912 Gustaf Dalén (Sweden), for discovery of automatic regulators used in lighting lighthouses and light buoys
1913 Heike Kamerlingh-Onnes (Netherlands), for work leading to production of liquid helium
1914 Max von Laue (Germany), for discovery of diffraction of Roentgen rays passing through crystals
1915 Sir William Bragg and William L. Bragg (England), for analysis of crystal structure by X rays
1916 No award
1917 Charles G. Barkla (England), for discovery of Roentgen radiation of the elements
1918 Max Planck (Germany), discoveries in connection with quantum theory
1919 Johannes Stark (Germany), discovery of Doppler effect in Canal rays and decomposition of spectrum lines by electric fields
1920 Charles E. Guillaume (Switzerland), for discoveries of anomalies in nickel steel alloys
1921 Albert Einstein (Germany), for discovery of the law of the photoelectric effect
1922 Niels Bohr (Denmark), for investigation of structure of atoms and radiations emanating from them
1923 Robert A. Millikan (U.S.), for work on elementary charge of electricity and photoelectric phenomena
1924 Karl M. G. Siegbahn (Sweden), for investigations in X-ray spectroscopy
1925 James Franck and Gustav Hertz (Germany), for discovery of laws governing impact of electrons upon atoms
1926 Jean B. Perrin (France), for work on discontinuous structure of matter and discovery of the

equilibrium of sedimentation

**1927** Arthur H. Compton (U.S.), for discovery of Compton phenomenon; and Charles T. R. Wilson (England), for method of perceiving paths taken by electrically charged particles

**1928** In 1929, the 1928 prize was awarded to Sir Owen Richardson (England), for work on the phenomenon of thermionics and discovery of the Richardson Law

**1929** Prince Louis Victor de Broglie (France), for discovery of the wave character of electrons

**1930** Sir Chandrasekhara Raman (India), for work on diffusion of light and discovery of the Raman effect

**1931** No award

**1932** In 1933, the prize for 1932 was awarded to Werner Heisenberg (Germany), for creation of the quantum mechanics

**1933** Erwin Schrödinger (Austria) and Paul A. M. Dirac (England), for discovery of new fertile forms of the atomic theory

**1934** No award

**1935** James Chadwick (England), for discovery of the neutron

**1936** Victor F. Hess (Austria), for discovery of cosmic radiation; and Carl D. Anderson (U.S.), for discovery of the positron

**1937** Clinton J. Davisson (U.S.) and George P. Thomson (England), for discovery of diffraction of electrons by crystals

**1938** Enrico Fermi (Italy), for identification of new radioactivity elements and discovery of nuclear reactions effected by slow neutrons

**1939** Ernest Orlando Lawrence (U.S.), for development of the cyclotron

**1943** Otto Stern (U.S.), for detection of magnetic momentum of protons

**1944** Isidor Isaac Rabi (U.S.), for work on magnetic movements of atomic particles

**1945** Wolfgang Pauli (Austria), for work on atomic fissions

**1946** Percy Williams Bridgman (U.S.), for studies and inventions in high-pressure physics

**1947** Sir Edward Appleton (England), for discovery of layer which reflects radio short waves in the ionosphere

**1948** Patrick M. S. Blackett (England), for improvement on Wilson chamber and discoveries in cosmic radiation

**1949** Hideki Yukawa (Japan), for mathematical prediction, in 1935, of the meson

**1950** Cecil Frank Powell (England), for method of photographic study of atom nucleus, and for discoveries about mesons

**1951** Sir John Douglas Cockcroft (England) and Ernest T. S. Walton (Ireland), for work in 1932 on transmutation of atomic nuclei

**1952** Edward Mills Purcell and Felix Bloch (U.S.), for work in measurement of magnetic fields in atomic nuclei

**1953** Fritz Zernike (Netherlands), for development of "phase contrast" microscope

**1954** Max Born (England), for work in quantum mechanics; and Walther Bothe (Germany), for work in cosmic radiation

**1955** Polykarp Kusch and Willis E. Lamb, Jr. (U.S.), for atomic measurements

**1956** William Shockley, Walter H. Brattain, and John Bardeen (U.S.), for developing electronic transistor

**1957** Tsung Dao Lee and Chen Ning Yang (China), for disproving principle of conservation of parity

**1958** Pavel A. Cherenkov, Ilya M. Frank, and Igor E. Tamm (U.S.S.R.), for work resulting in development of cosmic-ray counter

**1959** Emilio Segre and Owen Chamberlain (U.S.), for demonstrating the existence of the anti-proton

**1960** Donald A. Glaser (U.S.), for invention of "bubble chamber" to study subatomic particles

**1961** Robert Hofstadter (U.S.), for determination of shape and size of atomic nucleus; Rudolf Mössbauer (Germany), for method of producing and measuring recoil-free gamma rays

**1962** Lev D. Landau (U.S.S.R.), for his theories about condensed matter

**1963** Eugene Paul Wigner, Maria Goeppert Mayer (both U.S.), and J. Hans D. Jensen (Germany), for research on structure of atom and its nucleus

**1964** Charles Hard Townes (U.S.), Nikolai G. Basov, and Aleksandr M. Prochorov (both U.S.S.R.), for developing maser and laser principle of producing high-intensity radiation

**1965** Richard P. Feynman, Julian S. Schwinger (both U.S.), and Shinichiro Tomonaga (Japan), for research in quantum electrodynamics

**1966** Alfred Kastler (France), for work on energy levels inside atom

**1967** Hans A. Bethe (U.S.), for work on energy production of stars

**1968** Luis Walter Alvarez (U.S.), for study of subatomic particles

**1969** Murray Gell-Mann (U.S.), for study of subatomic particles

**1970** Hannes Alfvén (Sweden), for theories in plasma physics; and Louis Néel (France), for discoveries in antiferromagnetism and ferrimagnetism

**1971** Dennis Gabor (England), for invention of holographic method of three-dimensional imagery

**1972** John Bardeen, Leon N. Cooper, and John Robert Schrieffer (all U.S.), for theory of superconductivity, where electrical resistance in certain metals vanishes above absolute zero temperature

**1973** Ivar Giaever (U.S.), Leo Esaki (Japan), and Brian D. Josephson (U.K.), for theories that have advanced and expanded the field of miniature electronics

**1974** Antony Hewish (England), for discovery of pulsars; Martin Ryle (England), for using radiotelescopes to probe outer space with high degree of precision

**1975** James Rainwater (U.S.) and Ben Mottelson and Aage N. Bohr (both Denmark), for showing that the atomic nucleus is asymmetrical

**1976** Burton Richter and Samuel C. C. Ting (both U.S.), for discovery of subatomic particles known as J and psi

**1977** Philip W. Anderson and John H. Van Vleck (both U.S.), and Nevill F. Mott (U.K.), for work underlying computer memories and electronic devices

**1978** Arno A. Penzias and Robert W. Wilson (both U.S.), for work in cosmic microwave radiation; Piotr L. Kapitsa (U.S.S.R.), for basic inventions and discoveries in low-temperature physics

**1979** Steven Weinberg and Sheldon L. Glashow (both U.S.) and Abdus Salam (Pakistan), for developing theory that electromagnetism and the "weak" force, which causes radioactive decay in some atomic nuclei, are facets of the same phenomenon

**1980** James W. Cronin and Val L. Fitch (both U.S.), for work concerning the assymetry of subatomic particles

**1981** Nicolaas Bloembergen and Arthur L. Schawlow (both U.S.) and Kai M. Siegbahn (Sweden), for developing technologies with lasers and other devices to probe the secrets of complex forms of matter

1982 Kenneth G. Wilson (U.S.), for analysis of changes in matter under pressure and temperature

1983 Subrahmanyam Chandrasekhar and William A. Fowler (both U.S.) for complementary research on processes involved in the evolution of stars

1984 Carlo Rubbia (Italy) and Simon van der Meer (Netherlands), for their role in discovering three subatomic particles, a step toward developing a single theory to account for all natural forces

1985 Klaus von Klitzing (Germany), for developing an exact way of measuring electrical conductivity

## CHEMISTRY

1901 Jacobus H. van't Hoff (Netherlands), for laws of chemical dynamics and osmotic pressure in solutions

1902 Emil Fischer (Germany), for experiments in sugar and purin groups of substances

1903 Svante A. Arrhenius (Sweden), for his electrolytic theory of dissociation

1904 Sir William Ramsay (England), for discovery and determination of place of inert gaseous elements in air

1905 Adolf von Baeyer (Germany), for work on organic dyes and hydroaromatic combinations

1906 Henri Moissan (France), for isolation of fluorine, and introduction of electric furnace

1907 Eduard Buchner (Germany), discovery of cell-less fermentation and investigations in biological chemistry

1908 Sir Ernest Rutherford (England), for investigations into disintegration of elements

1909 Wilhelm Ostwald (Germany), for work on catalysis and investigations into chemical equilibrium and reaction rates

1910 Otto Wallach (Germany), for work in the field of alicyclic compounds

1911 Marie Curie (France), for discovery of elements radium and polonium

1912 Victor Grignard (France), for reagent discovered by him; and Paul Sabatier (France), for methods of hydrogenating organic compounds

1913 Alfred Werner (Switzerland), for linking up atoms within the molecule

1914 Theodore W. Richards (U.S.), for determining atomic weight of many chemical elements

1915 Richard Willstätter (Germany), for research into coloring matter of plants, especially chlorophyll

1916 No award

1917 No award

1918 Fritz Haber (Germany), for synthetic production of ammonia

1919 No award

1920 Walther Nernst (Germany), for work in thermochemistry

1921 Frederick Soddy (England), for investigations into origin and nature of isotopes

1922 Francis W. Aston (England), for discovery of isotopes in nonradioactive elements and for discovery of the whole number rule

1923 Fritz Pregl (Austria), for method of microanalysis of organic substances discovered by him

1924 No award

1925 In 1926, the 1925 prize was awarded to Richard Zsigmondy (Germany), for work on the heterogeneous nature of colloid solutions

1926 Theodor Svedberg (Sweden), for work on disperse systems

1927 In 1928, the 1927 prize was awarded to Heinrich Wieland (Germany), for investigations of bile acids and kindred substances

1928 Adolf Windaus (Germany), for investigations on constitution of the sterols and their connection with vitamins

1929 Sir Arthur Harden (England) and Hans K. A. S. von Euler-Chelpin (Sweden), for research of fermentation of sugars

1930 Hans Fischer (Germany), for work on coloring matter of blood and leaves and for his synthesis of hemin

1931 Karl Bosch and Friedrich Bergius (Germany), for invention and development of chemical high-pressure methods

1932 Irving Langmuir (U.S.), for work in realm of surface chemistry

1933 No award

1934 Harold C. Urey (U.S.), for discovery of heavy hydrogen

1935 Frédéric and Irène Joliot-Curie (France), for synthesis of new radioactive elements

1936 Peter J. W. Debye (Netherlands), for investigations on dipole moments and diffraction of X rays and electrons in gases

1937 Walter N. Haworth (England), for research on carbohydrates and Vitamin C; and Paul Karrer (Switzerland), for work on carotenoids, flavins, and Vitamins A and B

1938 Richard Kuhn (Germany), for carotinoid study and vitamin research (declined)

1939 Adolf Butenandt (Germany), for work on sexual hormones (declined the prize); and Leopold Ruzicka (Switzerland), for work with polymethylenes

1943 Georg Hevesy De Heves (Hungary), for work on use of isotopes as indicators

1944 Otto Hahn (Germany), for work on atomic fission

1945 Artturi Illmari Virtanen (Finland), for research in the field of conservation of fodder

1946 James B. Sumner (U.S.), for crystallizing enzymes; John H. Northrop and Wendell M. Stanley (U.S.), for preparing enzymes and virus proteins in pure form

1947 Sir Robert Robinson (England), for research in plant substances

1948 Arne Tiselius (Sweden), for biochemical discoveries and isolation of mouse paralysis virus

1949 William Francis Giauque (U.S.), for research in thermodynamics, especially effects of low temperature

1950 Otto Diels and Kurt Alder (Germany), for discovery of diene synthesis enabling scientists to study structure of organic matter

1951 Glenn T. Seaborg and Edwin H. McMillan (U.S.), for discovery of plutonium

1952 Archer John Porter Martin and Richard Laurence Millington Synge (England), for development of partition chromatography

1953 Hermann Staudinger (Germany), for research in giant molecules

1954 Linus C. Pauling (U.S.), for study of forces holding together protein and other molecules

1955 Vincent du Vigneaud (U.S.), for work on pituitary hormones

1956 Sir Cyril Hinshelwood (England) and Nikolai N. Semenov (U.S.S.R.), for parallel research on chemical reaction kinetics

1957 Sir Alexander Todd (England), for research with chemical compounds that are factors in heredity
1958 Frederick Sanger (England), for determining molecular structure of insulin
1959 Jaroslav Heyrovsky (Czechoslovakia), for development of polarography, an electrochemical method of analysis
1960 Willard F. Libby (U.S.), for "atomic time clock" to measure age of objects by measuring their radioactivity
1961 Melvin Calvin (U.S.), for establishing chemical steps during photosynthesis
1962 Max F. Perutz and John C. Kendrew (England), for mapping protein molecules with X-rays
1963 Carl Ziegler (Germany) and Giulio Natta (Italy), for work in uniting simple hydrocarbons into large molecule substances
1964 Dorothy Mary Crowfoot Hodgkin (England), for determining structure of compounds needed in combating pernicious anemia
1965 Robert B. Woodward (U.S.), for work in synthesizing complicated organic compounds
1966 Robert Sanderson Mulliken (U.S.), for research on bond holding atoms together in molecule
1967 Manfred Eigen (Germany), Ronald G. W. Norrish, and George Porter (both England), for work in high-speed chemical reactions
1968 Lars Onsager (U.S.), for development of system of equations in thermodynamics
1969 Derek H. R. Barton (England) and Odd Hassel (Norway), for study of organic molecules
1970 Luis F. Leloir (Argentina), for discovery of sugar nucleotides and their role in biosynthesis of carbohydrates
1971 Gerhard Herzberg (Canada), for contributions to knowledge of electronic structure and geometry of molecules, particularly free radicals
1972 Christian Boehmer Anfinsen, Stanford Moore, and William Howard Stein (all U.S.), for pioneering studies in enzymes
1973 Ernst Otto Fischer (W. Germany) and Geoffrey Wilkinson (U.K.), for work that could solve problem of automobile exhaust pollution
1974 Paul J. Flory (U.S.), for developing analytic methods to study properties and molecular structure of long-chain molecules
1975 John W. Cornforth (Australia) and Vladimir Prelog (Switzerland), for research on structure of biological molecules such as antibiotics and cholesterol
1976 William N. Lipscomb, Jr. (U.S.), for work on the structure and bonding mechanisms of boranes
1977 Ilya Prigogine (Belgium), for contributions to nonequilibrium thermodynamics, particularly the theory of dissipative structures
1978 Peter Mitchell (U.K.), for contributions to the understanding of biological energy transfer
1979 Herbert C. Brown (U.S.) and Georg Wittig (West Germany), for developing a group of substances that facilitate very difficult chemical reactions
1980 Paul Berg and Walter Gilbert (both U.S.) and Frederick Sanger (England), for developing methods to map the structure and function of DNA, the substance that controls the activity of the cell
1981 Roald Hoffmann (U.S.) and Kenichi Fukui (Japan), for applying quantum-mechanics theories to predict the course of chemical reactions
1982 Aaron Klug (U.K.), for research in the detailed structures of viruses and components of life

1983 Henry Taube (U.S.), for research on how electrons transfer between molecules in chemical reactions.
1984 R. Bruce Merrifield (U.S.) for research that revolutionized the study of proteins
1985 Herbert A. Hauptman and Jerome Karle (both U.S.) for their outstanding achievements in the development of direct methods for the determination of crystal structures

## PHYSIOLOGY OR MEDICINE

1901 Emil A. von Behring (Germany), for work on serum therapy against diptheria
1902 Sir Ronald Ross (England), for work on malaria
1903 Niels R. Finsen (Denmark), for his treatment of lupus vulgaris with concentrated light rays
1904 Ivan P. Pavlov (U.S.S.R.), for work on the physiology of digestion
1905 Robert Koch (Germany), for work on tuberculosis
1906 Camillo Golgi (Italy) and Santiago Ramón y Cajal (Spain), for work on structure of the nervous system
1907 Charles L. A. Laveran (France), for work with protozoa in the generation of disease
1908 Paul Ehrlich (Germany), and Elie Metchnikoff (U.S.S.R.), for work on immunity
1909 Theodor Kocher (Switzerland), for work on the thyroid gland
1910 Albrecht Kossel (Germany), for achievements in the chemistry of the cell
1911 Allvar Gullstrand (Sweden), for work on the dioptrics of the eye
1912 Alexis Carrel (France), for work on vascular ligature and grafting of blood vessels and organs
1913 Charles Richet (France), for work on anaphylaxy
1914 Robert Bárány (Austria), for work on physiology and pathology of the vestibular system
1915-1918 No award
1919 Jules Bordet (Belgium), for discoveries in connection with immunity
1920 August Krogh (Denmark), for discovery of regulation of capillaries' motor mechanism
1921 No award
1922 In 1923, the 1922 prize was shared by Archibald V. Hill (England), for discovery relating to heat-production in muscles; and Otto Meyerhof (Germany), for correlation between consumption of oxygen and production of lactic acid in muscles
1923 Sir Frederick Banting (Canada) and John J. R. Macleod (Scotland), for discovery of insulin
1924 Willem Einthoven (Netherlands), for discovery of the mechanism of the electrocardiogram
1925 No award
1926 Johannes Fibiger (Denmark), for discovery of the Spiroptera carcinoma
1927 Julius Wagner-Jauregg (Austria), for use of malaria inoculation in treatment of dementia paralytica
1928 Charles Nicolle (France), for work on typhus exanthematicus
1929 Christiaan Eijkman (Netherlands), for discovery of the antineuritic vitamins; and Sir Frederick Hopkins (England), for discovery of growth-promoting vitamins
1930 Karl Landsteiner (U.S.), for discovery of human blood groups
1931 Otto H. Warburg (Germany), for discovery of the character and mode of action of the respiratory ferment

1932 Sir Charles Sherrington (England) and Edgar D. Adrian (U.S.), for discoveries of the function of the neuron

1933 Thomas H. Morgan (U.S.), for discoveries on hereditary function of the chromosomes

1934 George H. Whipple, George R. Minot, and William P. Murphy (U.S.), for discovery of liver therapy against anemias

1935 Hans Spemann (Germany), for discovery of the organizer-effect in embryonic development

1936 Sir Henry Dale (England) and Otto Loewi (Germany), for discoveries on chemical transmission of nerve impulses

1937 Albert Szent-Györgyi von Nagyrapolt (Hungary), for discoveries on biological combustion

1938 Corneille Heymans (Belgium), for determining importance of sinus and aorta mechanisms in the regulation of respiration

1939 Gerhard Domagk (Germany), for antibacterial effect of prontocilate

1943 Henrik Dam (Denmark) and Edward A. Doisy (U.S.), for analysis of Vitamin K

1944 Joseph Erlanger and Herbert Spencer Gasser (U.S.), for work on functions of the nerve threads

1945 Sir Alexander Fleming, Ernst Boris Chain, and Sir Howard Florey (England), for discovery of penicillin

1946 Herman J. Muller (U.S.), for hereditary effects of X-rays on genes

1947 Carl F. and Gerty T. Cori (U.S.), for work on animal starch metabolism; Bernardo A. Houssay (Argentina), for study of pituitary

1948 Paul Mueller (Switzerland), for discovery of insect-killing properties of DDT

1949 Walter Rudolf Hess (Switzerland), for research on brain control of body; and Antonio Caetano de Abreu Freire Egas Moniz (Portugal), for development of brain operation

1950 Philip S. Hench, Edward C. Kendall (both U.S.), and Tadeus Reichstein (Switzerland), for discoveries about hormones of adrenal cortex

1951 Max Theiler (South Africa), for development of anti-yellow-fever vaccine

1952 Selman A. Waksman (U.S.), for co-discovery of streptomycin

1953 Fritz A. Lipmann (Germany-U.S.) and Hans Adolph Krebs (Germany-England), for studies of living cells

1954 John F. Enders, Thomas H. Weller, and Frederick C. Robbins (U.S.), for work with cultivation of polio virus

1955 Hugo Theorell (Sweden), for work on oxidation enzymes

1956 Dickinson W. Richards, Jr., André F. Cournand (both U.S.), and Werner Forssmann (Germany), for new techniques in treating heart disease

1957 Daniel Bovet (Italy), for development of drugs to relieve allergies and relax muscles during surgery

1958 Joshua Lederberg (U.S.), for work with genetic mechanisms; George W. Beadle and Edward L. Tatum (U.S.), for discovering how genes transmit hereditary characteristics

1959 Severo Ochoa and Arthur Kornberg (U.S.), for discoveries related to compounds within chromosomes, which play a vital role in heredity

1960 Sir Macfarlane Burnet (Australia) and Peter Brian Medawar (England), for discovery of acquired immunological tolerance

1961 Georg von Bekesy (U.S.), for discoveries about physical mechanisms of stimulation within cochlea

1962 James D. Watson (U.S.), Maurice H. F. Wilkins, and Francis H. C. Crick (England), for determining structure of deoxyribonucleic acid (DNA)

1963 Alan Lloyd Hodgkin, Andrew Fielding Huxley (both England), and Sir John Carew Eccles (Australia), for research on nerve cells

1964 Konrad E. Bloch (U.S.) and Feodor Lynen (Germany), for research on mechanism and regulation of cholesterol and fatty acid metabolism

1965 François Jacob, André Lwolff, and Jacques Monod (France), for study of regulatory activities in body cells

1966 Charles Brenton Huggins (U.S.), for studies in hormone treatment of cancer of prostate; Francis Peyton Rous (U.S.), for discovery of tumor-producing viruses

1967 Haldan K. Hartline, George Wald, and Ragnar Granit (U.S.), for work on human eye

1968 Robert W. Holley, Har Gobind Khorana, and Marshall W. Nirenberg (U.S.), for studies of genetic code

1969 Max Delbruck, Alfred D. Hershey, and Salvador E. Luria (U.S.), for study of mechanism of virus infection in living cells

1970 Julius Axelrod (U.S.), Ulf S. von Euler (Sweden), and Sir Bernard Katz (England), for studies of how nerve impulses are transmitted within the body

1971 Earl W. Sutherland, Jr. (U.S.), for research on how hormones work

1972 Gerald M. Edelman (U.S.), and Rodney R. Porter (U.K.), for research on the chemical structure and nature of antibodies

1973 Karl von Frisch and Konrad Lorenz (Austria), and Nikolaas Tinbergen (Netherlands), for their studies of individual and social behavior patterns

1974 George E. Palade and Christian de Duve (both U.S.) and Albert Claude (Belgium), for contributions to understanding inner workings of living cells

1975 David Baltimore, Howard M. Temin, and Renato Dulbecco (all U.S.), for work in interaction between tumor viruses and genetic material of the cell

1976 Baruch S. Blumberg and D. Carleton Gajdusek (U.S.), for discoveries concerning new mechanisms for the origin and dissemination of infectious diseases

1977 Rosalyn S. Yalow, Roger C. L. Guillemin, and Andrew V. Schally (all U.S.), for research in role of hormones in chemistry of the body

1978 Daniel Nathans and Hamilton Smith (both U.S.) and Werner Arber (Switzerland), for discovery of restriction enzymes and their application to problems of molecular genetics

1979 Allan McLeod Cormack (U.S.) and Godfrey Newbold Hounsfield (England), for developing computed axial tomography (CAT scan) X-ray technique

1980 Baruj Benacerraf and George D. Snell (both U.S.) and Jean Dausset (France), for discoveries that explain how the structure of cells relates to organ transplants and diseases

1981 Roger W. Sperry and David H. Hubel (both U.S.) and Torsten N. Wiesel (Sweden), for studies vital to understanding the organization and functioning of the brain

1982 Sune Bergstrom and Bengt Samuelsson (Sweden) and John R. Vane (U.K.), for research in prostaglandins, a hormonelike substance involved in a wide range of illnesses

1983 Barbara McClintock (U.S.), for her discovery of mobile genes in the chromosomes of a plant that change the future generations of plants they produce

1984 Cesar Milstein (U.K./Argentina) Georges J.F. Kohler (West Germany), and Niels K. Jerne (U.K./Denmark) for their work in immunology

1985 Michael S. Brown and Joseph L. Goldstein (both U.S.) for their work which has drastically widened our understanding of the cholesterol metabolism and increased our possibilities to prevent and treat atherosclerosis and heart attacks

## ECONOMIC SCIENCE

1969 Ragnar Frisch (Norway) and Jan Tinbergen (Netherlands), for work in econometrics (application of mathematics and statistical methods to economic theories and problems)

1970 Paul A. Samuelson (U.S.), for efforts to raise the level of scientific analysis in economic theory

1971 Simon Kuznets (U.S.), for developing concept of using a country's gross national product to determine its economic growth

1972 Kenneth J. Arrow (U.S.) and Sir John R. Hicks (U.K.), for theories that help to assess business risk and government economic and welfare policies

1973 Wassily Leontief (U.S.), for devising the input-output technique to determine how different sectors of an economy interact

1974 Gunnar Myrdal (Sweden) and Friedrich A. von Hayek (U.K.), for pioneering analysis of the interdependence of economic, social and institutional phenomena

1975 Leonid V. Kantorovich (U.S.S.R.) and Tjalling C. Koopmans (U.S.), for work on the theory of optimum allocation of resources

1976 Milton Friedman (U.S.), for work in consumption analysis and monetary history and theory, and for demonstration of complexity of stabilization policy

1977 Bertil Ohlin (Sweden) and James E. Meade (U.K.), for contributions to theory of international trade and international capital movements

1978 Herbert A. Simon (U.S.), for research into the decision-making process within economic organizations

1979 Sir Arthur Lewis (England) and Theodore Schultz (U.S.), for work on economic problems of developing nations

1980 Lawrence R. Klein (U.S.), for developing models for forecasting economic trends and shaping policies to deal with them

1981 James Tobin (U.S.), for analyses of financial markets and their influence on spending and saving by families and businesses

1982 George J. Stigler (U.S.), for work on government regulation in the economy and the functioning of industry

1983 Gerard Debreu (U.S.), in recognition of his work on the basic economic problem of how prices operate to balance what producers supply with what buyers want.

1984 Sir Richard Stone (U.K.), for his work to develop the systems widely used to measure the performance of national economics

1985 Franco Modigliani (U.S.) for his pioneering work in analyzing the behavior of household savers and the functioning of financial markets

## Enrico Fermi Award

Named in honor of Enrico Fermi, the atomic pioneer, the $100,000 award is given in recognition of "exceptional and altogether outstanding" scientific and technical achievement in atomic energy.

| | | |
|---|---|---|
| 1954 Enrico Fermi | 1968 John A. Wheeler | 1981 W. Bennett Lewis |
| 1956 John von Neumann | 1969 Walter H. Zinn | 1982 Herbert Anderson and Seth |
| 1957 Ernest O. Lawrence | 1970 Norris E. Bradbury |     Neddermeyer |
| 1958 Eugene P. Wigner | 1971 Shields Warren and Stafford | 1983 Alexander Hollaender and |
| 1959 Glenn T. Seaborg |     L. Warren |     John Lawrence |
| 1961 Hans A. Bethe | 1972 Manson Benedict | 1984 Robert R. Wilson and Georges |
| 1962 Edward Teller | 1976 William L. Russell |     Vendryès |
| 1963 J. Robert Oppenheimer | 1978 Harold M. Agnew and Wolfgang | 1985 Norman C. Rasmussen and Marshall |
| 1964 Hyman G. Rickover |     K.H. Panofsky |     N. Rosenblath |
| 1966 Otto Hahn, Lise Meitner, and | 1980 Alvin M. Weinberg and Rudolf | |
|     Fritz Strassman |     E. Peirls | |

## Poets Laureate of England

| | | | | | |
|---|---|---|---|---|---|
| Edmund Spenser | 1591–1599 | Laurence Eusden | 1718-1730 | Alfred Lord Tennyson | 1850-1892 |
| Samuel Daniel | 1599–1619 | Colley Cibber | 1730-1757 | Alfred Austin | 1896-1913 |
| Ben Jonson | 1619–1637 | William Whitehead | 1757-1785 | Robert Bridges | 1913-1930 |
| William Davenant | 1638–1668 | Thomas Warton | 1785-1790 | John Masefield | 1930-1967 |
| John Dryden[1] | 1670–1689 | Henry James Pye | 1790-1813 | C. Day Lewis | 1967-1972 |
| Thomas Shadwell | 1689–1692 | Robert Southey | 1813-1843 | Sir John Betjeman | 1972-1984 |
| Nahum Tate | 1692–1715 | William Wordsworth | 1843-1850 | Ted Hughes | 1984- |
| Nicholas Rowe | 1715-1718 | | | | |

1. First to bear the title officially. *Source: Encyclopaedia Britannica.*

## Poet Laureate of the United States

Robert Penn Warren is the United States' first official Poet Laureate. He was named on February 26, 1986, to the post which was established in 1985.

The law adds the title to that of Consultant in Poetry at the Library of Congress, a position that goes back more than 50 years.

# Motion Picture Academy Awards (Oscars)

## 1928

**Picture:** *Wings,* Paramount
**Director:** Frank Borzage, *Seventh Heaven;* Lewis Milestone, *Two Arabian Nights*
**Actress:** Janet Gaynor, *Seventh Heaven, Street Angel, Sunrise*
**Actor:** Emil Jannings, *The Way of All Flesh, The Last Command*

## 1929

**Picture:** *The Broadway Melody,* M-G-M
**Director:** Frank Lloyd, *The Divine Lady*
**Actress:** Mary Pickford, *Coquette*
**Actor:** Warner Baxter, *In Old Arizona*

## 1930

**Picture:** *All Quiet on the Western Front,* Universal
**Director:** Lewis Milestone, *All Quiet on the Western Front*
**Actress:** Norma Shearer, *The Divorcee*
**Actor:** George Arliss, *Disraeli*

## 1931

**Picture:** *Cimarron:* RKO Radio
**Director:** Norman Taurog, *Skippy*
**Actress:** Marie Dressler, *Min and Bill*
**Actor:** Lionel Barrymore, *A Free Soul*

## 1932

**Picture:** *Grand Hotel,* M-G-M
**Director:** Frank Borzage, *Bad Girl*
**Actress:** Helen Hayes, *The Sin of Madelon Claudet*
**Actor:** Fredric March, *Dr. Jekyll and Mr. Hyde,* and Wallace Beery, *The Champ*

## 1933

**Picture:** *Cavalcade,* Fox
**Director:** Frank Lloyd, *Cavalcade*
**Actress:** Katharine Hepburn, *Morning Glory*
**Actor:** Charles Laughton, *The Private Life of Henry VIII*

## 1934

**Picture:** *It Happened One Night,* Columbia
**Director:** Frank Capra, *It Happened One Night*
**Actress:** Claudette Colbert, *It Happened One Night*
**Actor:** Clark Gable, *It Happened One Night*

## 1935

**Picture:** *Mutiny on the Bounty,* M-G-M
**Director:** John Ford, *The Informer*
**Actress:** Bette Davis, *Dangerous*
**Actor:** Victor McLaglen, *The Informer*

## 1936

**Picture:** *The Great Ziegfeld,* M-G-M
**Director:** Frank Capra, *Mr. Deeds Goes to Town*
**Actress:** Luise Rainer, *The Great Ziegfeld*
**Actor:** Paul Muni, *The Story of Louis Pasteur*
**Supporting Actress:** Gale Sondergaard, *Anthony Adverse*
**Supporting Actor:** Walter Brennan, *Come and Get It*

## 1937

**Picture:** *The Life of Emile Zola,* Warner Bros.
**Director:** Leo McCarey, *The Awful Truth*
**Actress:** Luise Rainer, *The Good Earth*
**Actor:** Spencer Tracy, *Captains Courageous*
**Supporting Actress:** Alice Brady, *In Old Chicago*
**Supporting Actor:** Joseph Schildkraut, *The Life of Emile Zola*

## 1938

**Picture:** *You Can't Take It with You,* Columbia
**Director:** Frank Capra, *You Can't Take It with You*
**Actress:** Bette Davis, *Jezebel*
**Actor:** Spencer Tracy, *Boys Town*
**Supporting Actress:** Fay Bainter, *Jezebel*
**Supporting Actor:** Walter Brennan, *Kentucky*

## 1939

**Picture:** *Gone with the Wind,* Selznick-M-G-M
**Director:** Victor Fleming, *Gone with the Wind*
**Actress:** Vivien Leigh, *Gone with the Wind*
**Actor:** Robert Donat, *Goodbye, Mr. Chips*
**Supporting Actress:** Hattie McDaniel, *Gone with the Wind*
**Supporting Actor:** Thomas Mitchell, *Stagecoach*

## 1940

**Picture:** *Rebecca,* Selznick-UA
**Director:** John Ford, *The Grapes of Wrath*
**Actress:** Ginger Rogers, *Kitty Foyle*
**Actor:** James Stewart, *The Philadelphia Story*
**Supporting Actress:** Jane Darwell, *The Grapes of Wrath*
**Supporting Actor:** Walter Brennan, *The Westerner*

## 1941

**Picture:** *How Green Was My Valley,* 20th Century-Fox
**Director:** John Ford, *How Green Was My Valley*
**Actress:** Joan Fontaine, *Suspicion*
**Actor:** Gary Cooper, *Sergeant York*
**Supporting Actress:** Mary Astor, *The Great Lie*
**Supporting Actor:** Donald Crisp, *How Green Was My Valley*

## 1942

**Picture:** *Mrs. Miniver,* M-G-M
**Director:** William Wyler, *Mrs. Miniver*
**Actress:** Greer Garson, *Mrs. Miniver*
**Actor:** James Cagney, *Yankee Doodle Dandy*
**Supporting Actress:** Teresa Wright, *Mrs. Miniver*
**Supporting Actor:** Van Heflin, *Johnny Eager*

## 1943

**Picture:** *Casablanca,* Warner Bros.
**Director:** Michael Curtiz, *Casablanca*
**Actress:** Jennifer Jones, *The Song of Bernadette*
**Actor:** Paul Lukas, *Watch on the Rhine*
**Supporting Actress:** Katina Paxinou, *For Whom the Bell Tolls*
**Supporting Actor:** Charles Coburn, *The More the Merrier*

## 1944

**Picture:** *Going My Way,* Paramount
**Director:** Leo McCarey, *Going My Way*
**Actress:** Ingrid Bergman, *Gaslight*
**Actor:** Bing Crosby, *Going My Way*
**Supporting Actress:** Ethel Barrymore, *None But the Lonely Heart*
**Supporting Actor:** Barry Fitzgerald, *Going My Way*

## 1945

**Picture:** *The Lost Weekend,* Paramount
**Director:** Billy Wilder, *The Lost Weekend*
**Actress:** Joan Crawford, *Mildred Pierce*
**Actor:** Ray Milland, *The Lost Weekend*
**Supporting Actress:** Anne Revere, *National Velvet*
**Supporting Actor:** James Dunn, *A Tree Grows in Brooklyn*

## 1946

**Picture:** *The Best Years of Our Lives,* Goldwyn-RKO Radio
**Director:** William Wyler, *The Best Years of Our Lives*
**Actress:** Olivia de Havilland, *To Each His Own*
**Actor:** Fredric March, *The Best Years of Our Lives*
**Supporting Actress:** Anne Baxter, *The Razor's Edge*
**Supporting Actor:** Harold Russell, *The Best Years of Our Lives*

## 1947

**Picture:** *Gentleman's Agreement,* 20th Century-Fox
**Director:** Elia Kazan, *Gentleman's Agreement*
**Actress:** Loretta Young, *The Farmer's Daughter*
**Actor:** Ronald Colman, *A Double Life*
**Supporting Actress:** Celeste Holm, *Gentleman's Agreement*
**Supporting Actor:** Edmund Gwenn, *Miracle on 34th Street*

## 1948

**Picture:** *Hamlet,* Rank-Two Cities-U-I
**Director:** John Huston, *Treasure of Sierra Madre*
**Actress:** Jane Wyman, *Johnny Belinda*
**Actor:** Laurence Olivier, *Hamlet*
**Supporting Actress:** Claire Trevor, *Key Largo*
**Supporting Actor:** Walter Huston, *Treasure of Sierra Madre*

## 1949

**Picture:** *All the King's Men,* Rossen-Columbia
**Director:** Joseph L. Mankiewicz, *A Letter to Three Wives*
**Actress:** Olivia de Havilland, *The Heiress*
**Actor:** Broderick Crawford, *All the King's Men*
**Supporting Actress:** Mercedes McCambridge, *All the King's Men*
**Supporting Actor:** Dean Jagger, *Twelve O'Clock High*

## 1950

**Picture:** *All About Eve,* 20th Century-Fox
**Director:** Joseph L. Mankiewicz, *All About Eve*
**Actress:** Judy Holliday, *Born Yesterday*
**Actor:** José Ferrer, *Cyrano de Bergerac*
**Supporting Actress:** Josephine Hull, *Harvey*
**Supporting Actor:** George Sanders, *All About Eve*

## 1951

**Picture:** *An American in Paris,* M-G-M
**Director:** George Stevens, *A Place in the Sun*
**Actress:** Vivien Leigh, *A Streetcar Named Desire*
**Actor:** Humphrey Bogart, *The African Queen*
**Supporting Actress:** Kim Hunter, *A Streetcar Named Desire*
**Supporting Actor:** Karl Malden, *A Streetcar Named Desire*

## 1952

**Picture:** *The Greatest Show on Earth,* DeMille-Paramount
**Director:** John Ford, *The Quiet Man*
**Actress:** Shirley Booth, *Come Back, Little Sheba*
**Actor:** Gary Cooper, *High Noon*
**Supporting Actress:** Gloria Grahame, *The Bad and the Beautiful*
**Supporting Actor:** Anthony Quinn, *Viva Zapata!*

## 1953

**Picture:** *From Here to Eternity,* Columbia
**Director:** Fred Zinnemann, *From Here to Eternity*
**Actress:** Audrey Hepburn, *Roman Holiday*
**Actor:** William Holden, *Stalag 17*
**Supporting Actress:** Donna Reed, *From Here to Eternity*
**Supporting Actor:** Frank Sinatra, *From Here to Eternity*

## 1954

**Picture:** *On the Waterfront,* Horizon-American Corp., Columbia
**Director:** Elia Kazan, *On the Waterfront*
**Actress:** Grace Kelly, *The Country Girl*
**Actor:** Marlon Brando, *On the Waterfront*
**Supporting Actress:** Eva Marie Saint, *On the Waterfront*
**Supporting Actor:** Edmond O'Brien, *The Barefoot Contessa*

## 1955

**Picture:** *Marty,* Hecht and Lancaster, United Artists
**Director:** Delbert Mann, *Marty*
**Actress:** Anna Magnani, *The Rose Tattoo*
**Actor:** Ernest Borgnine, *Marty*
**Supporting Actress:** Jo Van Fleet, *East of Eden*
**Supporting Actor:** Jack Lemmon, *Mister Roberts*

## 1956

**Picture:** *Around the World in 80 Days,* Michael Todd Co., Inc.-U.A.
**Director:** George Stevens, *Giant*
**Actress:** Ingrid Bergman, *Anastasia*
**Actor:** Yul Brynner, *The King and I*
**Supporting Actress:** Dorothy Malone, *Written on the Wind*
**Supporting Actor:** Anthony Quinn, *Lust for Life*

## 1957

**Picture:** *The Bridge on the River Kwai,* Horizon Picture, Columbia
**Director:** David Lean, *The Bridge on the River Kwai*
**Actress:** Joanne Woodward, *The Three Faces of Eve*
**Actor:** Alec Guinness, *The Bridge on the River Kwai*
**Supporting Actress:** Miyoshi Umeki, *Sayonara*
**Supporting Actor:** Red Buttons, *Sayonara*

## 1958

**Picture:** *Gigi,* Arthur Freed Productions, Inc., M-G-M
**Director:** Vincente Minnelli, *Gigi*
**Actress:** Susan Hayward, *I Want to Live!*
**Actor:** David Niven, *Separate Tables*
**Supporting Actress:** Wendy Hiller, *Separate Tables*
**Supporting Actor:** Burl Ives, *The Big Country*

## 1959

**Picture:** *Ben-Hur,* M-G-M
**Director:** William Wyler, *Ben-Hur*
**Actress:** Simone Signoret, *Room at the Top*
**Actor:** Charlton Heston, *Ben-Hur*
**Supporting Actress:** Shelley Winters, *The Diary of Anne Frank*
**Supporting Actor:** Hugh Griffith, *Ben-Hur*

## 1960

**Picture:** *The Apartment,* Mirisch Co., Inc., United Artists
**Director:** Billy Wilder, *The Apartment*
**Actress:** Elizabeth Taylor, *Butterfield 8*
**Actor:** Burt Lancaster, *Elmer Gantry*
**Supporting Actress:** Shirley Jones, *Elmer Gantry*
**Supporting Actor:** Peter Ustinov, *Spartacus*

## 1961

**Picture:** *West Side Story,* Mirisch Pictures, Inc., and B and P Enterprises, Inc., United Artists

**Director:** Robert Wise and Jerome Robbins, *West Side Story*
**Actress:** Sophia Loren, *Two Women*
**Actor:** Maximillian Schell, *Judgment at Nuremberg*
**Supporting Actress:** Rita Moreno, *West Side Story*
**Supporting Actor:** George Chakiris, *West Side Story*

### 1962

**Picture:** *Lawrence of Arabia,* Horizon Pictures, Ltd.-Columbia
**Director:** David Lean, *Lawrence of Arabia*
**Actress:** Anne Bancroft, *The Miracle Worker*
**Actor:** Gregory Peck, *To Kill a Mockingbird*
**Supporting Actress:** Patty Duke, *The Miracle Worker*
**Supporting Actor:** Ed Begley, *Sweet Bird of Youth*

### 1963

**Picture:** *Tom Jones,* A Woodfall Production, UA-Lopert Pictures
**Director:** Tony Richardson, *Tom Jones*
**Actress:** Patricia Neal, *Hud*
**Actor:** Sidney Poitier, *Lilies of the Field*
**Supporting Actress:** Margaret Rutherford, *The V.I.P.s*
**Supporting Actor:** Melvyn Douglas, *Hud*

### 1964

**Picture:** *My Fair Lady,* Warner Bros.
**Director:** George Cukor, *My Fair Lady*
**Actress:** Julie Andrews, *Mary Poppins*
**Actor:** Rex Harrison, *My Fair Lady*
**Supporting Actress:** Lila Kedrova, *Zorba the Greek*
**Supporting Actor:** Peter Ustinov, *Topkapi*

### 1965

**Picture:** *The Sound of Music,* Argyle Enterprises Production, 20th Century-Fox
**Director:** Robert Wise, *The Sound of Music*
**Actress:** Julie Christie, *Darling*
**Actor:** Lee Marvin, *Cat Ballou*
**Supporting Actress:** Shelley Winters, *A Patch of Blue*
**Supporting Actor:** Martin Balsam, *A Thousand Clowns*

### 1966

**Picture:** *A Man for All Seasons,* Highland Films, Ltd., Production, Columbia
**Director:** Fred Zinnemann, *A Man for All Seasons*
**Actress:** Elizabeth Taylor, *Who's Afraid of Virginia Woolf?*
**Actor:** Paul Scofield, *A Man for All Seasons*
**Supporting Actress:** Sandy Dennis, *Who's Afraid of Virginia Woolf?*
**Supporting Actor:** Walter Matthau, *The Fortune Cookie*

### 1967

**Picture:** *In the Heat of the Night,* Mirisch Corp. Productions, United Artists
**Director:** Mike Nichols, *The Graduate*
**Actress:** Katharine Hepburn, *Guess Who's Coming to Dinner*
**Actor:** Rod Steiger, *In the Heat of the Night*
**Supporting Actress:** Estelle Parsons, *Bonnie and Clyde*
**Supporting Actor:** George Kennedy, *Cool Hand Luke*

### 1968

**Picture:** *Oliver!,* Columbia Pictures
**Director:** Sir Carol Reed, *Oliver!*
**Actress:** Katharine Hepburn, *The Lion in Winter* and Barbara Streisand, *Funny Girl*
**Actor:** Cliff Robertson, *Charly*

**Supporting Actress:** Ruth Gordon, *Rosemary's Baby*
**Supporting Actor:** Jack Albertson, *The Subject Was Roses*

### 1969

**Picture:** *Midnight Cowboy,* Jerome Hellman-John Schlesinger Production, United Artists
**Director:** John Schlesinger, *Midnight Cowboy*
**Actress:** Maggie Smith, *The Prime of Miss Jean Brodie*
**Actor:** John Wayne, *True Grit*
**Supporting Actress:** Goldie Hawn, *Cactus Flower*
**Supporting Actor:** Gig Young, *They Shoot Horses Don't They?*

### 1970

**Picture:** *Patton,* Frank McCarthy-Franklin J. Schaffner Production, 20th Century Fox
**Director:** Franklin J. Schaffner, *Patton*
**Actress:** Glenda Jackson, *Women in Love*
**Actor:** George C. Scott, *Patton*
**Supporting Actress:** Helen Hayes, *Airport*
**Supporting Actor:** John Mills, *Ryan's Daughter*

### 1971

**Picture:** *The French Connection,* D'Antoni Productions, 20th Century-Fox
**Director:** William Friedkin, *The French Connection*
**Actress:** Jane Fonda, *Klute*
**Actor:** Gene Hackman, *The French Connection*
**Supporting Actress:** Cloris Leachman, *The Last Picture Show*
**Supporting Actor:** Ben Johnson, *The Last Picture Show*

### 1972

**Picture:** *The Godfather,* Albert S. Ruddy Production, Paramount
**Director:** Bob Fosse, *Cabaret*
**Actress:** Liza Minnelli, *Cabaret*
**Actor:** Marlon Brando, *The Godfather*
**Supporting Actress:** Eileen Heckart, *Butterflies Are Free*
**Supporting Actor:** Joel Gray, *Cabaret*

### 1973

**Picture:** *The Sting,* Universal-Bill-Phillips-George Roy Hill Production, Universal
**Director:** George Roy Hill, *The Sting*
**Actress:** Glenda Jackson, *A Touch of Class*
**Actor:** Jack Lemmon, *Save the Tiger*
**Supporting Actress:** Tatum O'Neal, *Paper Moon*
**Supporting Actor:** John Houseman, *The Paper Chase*

### 1974

**Picture:** *The Godfather, Part II,* Coppola Co. Production, Paramount
**Director:** Francis Ford Coppola, *The Godfather, Part II*
**Actress:** Ellen Burstyn, *Alice Doesn't Live Here Anymore*
**Actor:** Art Carney, *Harry and Tonto*
**Supporting Actress:** Ingrid Bergman, *Murder on the Orient Express*
**Supporting Actor:** Robert De Niro, *The Godfather, Part II*

### 1975

**Picture:** *One Flew Over the Cuckoo's Nest,* Fantasy Films Production, United Artists
**Director:** Milos Forman, *One Flew Over the Cuckoo's Nest*
**Actress:** Louise Fletcher, *One Flew Over the Cuck-*

oo's Nest
**Actor:** Jack Nicholson, *One Flew Over the Cuckoo's Nest*
**Supporting Actress:** Lee Grant, *Shampoo*
**Supporting Actor:** George Burns, *The Sunshine Boys*

### 1976

**Picture:** *Rocky,* Robert Chartoff-Irwin Winkler Production, United Artists
**Director:** John G. Avildsen, *Rocky*
**Actress:** Faye Dunaway, *Network*
**Actor:** Peter Finch, *Network*
**Supporting Actress:** Beatrice Straight, *Network*
**Supporting Actor:** Jason Robards, *All the President's Men*

### 1977

**Picture:** *Annie Hall,* Jack Rollins-Charles H. Joffe Production, United Artists
**Director:** Woody Allen, *Annie Hall*
**Actress:** Diane Keaton, *Annie Hall*
**Actor:** Richard Dreyfuss, *The Goodbye Girl*
**Supporting Actress:** Vanessa Redgrave, *Julia*
**Supporting Actor:** Jason Robards, *Julia*

### 1978

**Picture:** *The Deer Hunter,* Michael Cimino Film Production, Universal
**Director:** Michael Cimino, *The Deer Hunter*
**Actress:** Jane Fonda, *Coming Home*
**Actor:** Jon Voight, *Coming Home*
**Supporting Actress:** Maggie Smith, *California Suite*
**Supporting Actor:** Christopher Walken, *The Deer Hunter*

### 1979

**Picture:** *Kramer vs. Kramer,* Stanley Jaffe Production, Columbia Pictures
**Director:** Robert Benton, *Kramer vs. Kramer*
**Actress:** Sally Field, *Norma Rae*
**Actor:** Dustin Hoffman, *Kramer vs. Kramer*
**Supporting Actress:** Meryl Streep, *Kramer vs. Kramer*
**Supporting Actor:** Melvyn Douglas, *Being There*

### 1980

**Picture:** *Ordinary People,* Wildwood Enterprises Production, Paramount
**Director:** Robert Redford, *Ordinary People*
**Actress:** Sissy Spacek, *Coal Miner's Daughter*

**Actor:** Robert De Niro, *Raging Bull*
**Supporting Actress:** Mary Steenburgen, *Melvin and Howard*
**Supporting Actor:** Timothy Hutton, *Ordinary People*

### 1981

**Picture:** *Chariots of Fire,* Enigma Productions, Ladd Company/Warner Bros.
**Director:** Warren Beatty, *Reds*
**Actress:** Katharine Hepburn, *On Golden Pond*
**Actor:** Henry Fonda, *On Golden Pond*
**Supporting Actress:** Maureen Stapleton, *Reds*
**Supporting Actor:** John Gielgud, *Arthur*

### 1982

**Picture:** *Gandhi,* Indo-British Films Production/Columbia
**Director:** Richard Attenborough, *Gandhi*
**Actress:** Meryl Streep, *Sophie's Choice*
**Actor:** Ben Kingsley, *Gandhi*
**Supporting Actress:** Jessica Lange, *Tootsie*
**Supporting Actor:** Louis Gossett, Jr., *An Officer and a Gentleman*

### 1983

**Picture:** *Terms of Endearment,* Paramount
**Director:** James L. Brooks, *Terms of Endearment*
**Actress:** Shirley MacLaine, *Terms of Endearment*
**Actor:** Robert Duvall, *Tender Mercies*
**Supporting Actress:** Linda Hunt, *The Year of Living Dangerously*
**Supporting Actor:** Jack Nicholson, *Terms of Endearment*

### 1984

**Picture:** *Amadeus,* Orion Pictures
**Director:** Milos Forman, *Amadeus*
**Actress:** Sally Field, *Places in the Heart*
**Actor:** F. Murray Abraham, *Amadeus*
**Supporting Actress:** Dame Peggy Ashcroft, *A Passage to India*
**Supporting Actor:** Haing S. Ngor, *The Killing Fields*

### 1985

**Picture:** *Out of Africa,* Universal
**Director:** Sydney Pollack, *Out of Africa*
**Actress:** Geraldine Page, *The Trip to Bountiful*
**Actor:** William Hurt, *Kiss of the Spider Woman*
**Supporting Actress:** Anjelica Huston, *Prizzi's Honor*
**Supporting Actor:** Don Ameche, *Cocoon*

## Other Academy Awards for 1985

**Art direction:** *Out of Africa,* Stephen Grimes and Josie MacAvin
**Cinematography:** David Watkins, *Out of Africa*
**Costume design:** Emi Wada, *Ran*
**Documentary (feature):** *Broken Rainbow;* **short subject:** *Witness to War: Dr. Charlie Clements*
**Editing:** Thom Noble, *Witness*
**Foreign-language film:** *The Official Story,* Argentina
**Makeup:** Michael Westmore and Zoltan, *Mask*
**Music (original score):** John Barry, *Out of Africa*
**Screenplay (original):** William Kelley, Pamela Wallace and Earl W. Wallace, *Witness;* **adaptation:** Kurt Luedtke, *Out of Africa*

**Short subject (live-action):** *Molly's Pilgrim;* **animated:** *Anna & Bella*
**Song:** "Say You, Say Me," Lionel Richie from *White Nights*
**Sound:** Chris Jenkins, Gary Alexander, Larry Stensvold, and Peter Handford, *Out of Africa*
**Sound-effects editing:** Charles L. Campbell and Robert Rutledge, *Back to the Future*
**Visual effects:** Ken Ralston, Ralph McQuarrie, Scott Farrar, and David Berry, *Cocoon*
**Jean Hersholt Humanitarian Award:** Charles (Buddy) Rogers
**Honorary Award:** Paul Newman and Alex North

## National Society of Film Critics Awards, 1985

**Best Film:** *Ran,* Akira Kurosawa
**Best Documentary:** *Shoah,* Claude Lanzmann
**Best Actress:** Vanessa Redgrave, *Wetherby*

**Best Actor:** Jack Nicholson, *Prizzi's Honor*
**Best Supporting Actress:** Anjelica Huston, *Prizzi's Honor*

**Best Supporting Actor:** John Gielgud, *Plenty* and *The Shooting Party*
**Best Director:** John Huston, *Prizzi's Honor*
**Best Screenplay:** *Lost in America,* Albert Brooks

and Monica Johnson
**Best Cinematography:** *Ran,* Takao Saito and Masa-haru Ueda, with the collaboration of Asakazu Nakai

## George Foster Peabody Awards for Broadcasting, 1985

### Radio

**WHAS, Louisville, Ky.:** *Down and Outside: On the Streets in Louisville*
**Independently produced:** *Liberation Remembered*
**CBS News:** *The Number Man—Bach at Three Hundred*
**Independently produced:** *Breakdown and Back*
**WGBH, Boston,** for its overall programming and its leadership in state-of-the-art broadcasting.

### Television

**WCCO, Minneapolis:** For a five-month investigation by its I-Team, exposing abuses in the home health care industry in Minnesota.
**MacNeil/Lehrer Newshour:** *Apartheid's People*
**NBC News:** *Vietnam Ten Years After*
**CBS News:** *Whose America Is It?*
**CBS Entertainment and Dave Bell Productions:** *Do You Remember Love*
**WBZ, Boston:** *Tender Places*
**NBC,** *An Early Frost*
**KGO, San Francisco:** *The American West: Steinbeck Country*
**Spinning Reels and Home Box Office:** *Braingames*

**WSMV, Nashville, Tenn.:** *A Higher Standard The Final Chapter?*
**Frontline:** *Crisis in Central America*
**The Harvey Milk Film Project, Inc. and WNET/13:** *The Times of Harvey Milk*
**WBBM, Chicago:** *Armed and Dangerous*
**KDKA, Pittsburgh:** *Second Chance*
**KDTV, San Francisco:** During the two major Mexico City earthquakes, demonstrated a commitment to its audience by televising live reports and later raising considerable funds for disaster relief.
**Columbia University Graduate School of Journalism:** *Seminars on Media and Society*
**Central Independent Television and WETA, Washington:** *The Skin Horse*
**Lincoln Center for the Performing Arts, New York:** *Live from Lincoln Center*
**Bob Geldof and Live Aid:** For his personal commitment to helping alleviate hunger throughout the world.
**Lawrence Fraiberg:** In recognition of his outstanding contributions to broadcasting in the United States.
**Johnny Carson:** For almost 25 years of late-night humor on NBC's *Tonight Show with Johnny Carson.*

## American Academy and Institute of Arts and Letters 1986 Awards

### Art

**Academy-Institute Award ($5,000):** Painters: Pat Adams, Gregory Botts, Lois Dodd, and Paul Georges; Sculptor: Lowell Reiland
**Richard and Hinda Rosenthal Foundation Award ($5,000):** Painter, Richard Ryan

### Music

**Academy-Institute Award ($5,000):** Martin Boykan, Martin Brody, Wayne Peterson, and Sheila Silver
**Charles Ives Fellowship ($10,000):** Eric David

Chasalow
**Goddard Lieberson Fellowships ($10,000):** Susan Blaustein and Andrew Mead
**Charles Ives Scholarships ($5,000):** Robert Kyr, James Legg, Glenn Lieberman, Paul Moravec, Martin A. Matalon, and Frank A. Ticheli
**Nathan and Lillian Berliawsky Award ($5,000):** The Composers' Conference and Chamber Music Center, Inc.
**Walter Hinrichson Award (a publication award):** Richard Wilson

## Awards of the Society of Professional Journalists, 1985

(Sigma Delta Chi)

**General reporting:** Jim Stewart, Cox Newspapers (circulation more than 100,000); Art Geiselman, *Albuquerque Journal* (circulation less than 100,000)
**Editorial writing:** Henry B. Bryan, *Dallas Times Herald*
**Washington correspondence:** James O'Shea and Nicholas M. Horrock, *Chicago Tribune*
**Foreign correspondence:** Robert J. Rosenthal, *The Philadelphia Inquirer*
**News photography:** Jay Dickman, *Dallas Times Herald*
**Editorial cartooning:** Doug Marlette, *The Charlotte Observer*
**Public service in newspaper journalism:** *Detroit Free Press* (circulation more than 100,000); *The Arizona Daily Star* (circulation less than 100,000)

**Magazine reporting:** Mark Singer, *The New Yorker*
**Public service in magazine journalism:** *Tropic,* the Sunday magazine of *The Miami Herald*
**Radio reporting:** Tony Hanson, Richard Maloney, and Larry Litwin, KYW-AM, Philadelphia
**Public service in radio journalism:** KGO-AM, San Francisco
**Editorializing on radio:** Nicholas DeLuca and Joan Margalith, KCBS-AM, San Francisco
**Television reporting:** WFAA-TV, Dallas
**Public service in television journalism:** KPRC-TV, Houston (stations in the top 50 markets); KTUL-TV, Tulsa (stations in all other markets)
**Editorializing on television:** Phil Johnson, WWL-TV, New Orleans
**Research about journalism:** Professor Leonard W. Levy of Claremont College, California

# Pulitzer Prize Awards

**(For years not listed, no award was made.)**

*Source:* Columbia University.

## Pulitzer Prizes in Journalism

### MERITORIOUS PUBLIC SERVICE

1918 *New York Times;* also special award to Minna Lewinson and Henry Beetle Hough
1919 *Milwaukee Journal*
1921 *Boston Post*
1922 *New York World*
1923 *Memphis Commercial Appeal*
1924 *New York World*
1926 *Columbus* (Ga.) *Enquirer Sun*
1927 *Canton* (Ohio) *Daily News*
1928 *Indianapolis Times*
1929 *New York Evening World*
1931 *Atlanta Constitution*
1932 *Indianapolis News*
1933 *New York World-Telegram*
1934 *Medford* (Ore.) *Mail Tribune*
1935 *Sacramento Bee*
1936 *Cedar Rapids* (Iowa) *Gazette*
1937 *St. Louis Post-Dispatch*
1938 *Bismarck* (N.D.) *Tribune*
1939 *Miami Daily News*
1940 *Waterbury* (Conn.) *Republican* and *American*
1941 *St. Louis Post-Dispatch*
1942 *Los Angeles Times*
1943 *Omaha World-Herald*
1944 *New York Times*
1945 *Detroit Free Press*
1946 *Scranton* (Pa.) *Times*
1947 *Baltimore Sun*
1948 *St. Louis Post-Dispatch*
1949 *(Lincoln) Nebraska State Journal*
1950 *Chicago Daily News;* and *St. Louis Post-Dispatch*
1951 *Miami Herald;* and *Brooklyn Eagle*
1952 *St. Louis Post-Dispatch*
1953 *Whiteville* (N.C.) *News Reporter;* and *Tabor City* (N.C.) *Tribune*
1954 *Newsday* (Garden City, L.I.)
1955 *Columbus* (Ga.) *Ledger* and *Sunday Ledger-Enquirer*
1956 *Watsonville* (Calif.) *Register-Pajaronian*
1957 *Chicago Daily News*
1958 *(Little Rock) Arkansas Gazette*
1959 *Utica* (N.Y.) *Observer Dispatch* and *Utica Daily Press*
1960 *Los Angeles Times*
1961 *Amarillo* (Tex.) *Globe-Times*
1962 *Panama City* (Fla.) *News-Herald*
1963 *Chicago Daily News*
1964 *St. Petersburg* (Fla.) *Times*
1965 *Hutchinson* (Kan.) *News*
1966 *Boston Globe*
1967 *Louisville Courier-Journal* and *Milwaukee Journal*
1968 *Riverside* (Calif.) *Press-Enterprise*
1969 *Los Angeles Times*
1970 *Newsday* (Garden City, L.I.)
1971 *Winston-Salem* (N.C.) *Journal and Sentinel*
1972 *New York Times*
1973 *Washington Post*
1974 *Newsday* (Garden City, L.I.)
1975 *Boston Globe*
1976 *Anchorage* (Alaska) *Daily News*
1977 *Lufkin* (Tex.) *News*
1978 *Philadelphia Inquirer*

1979 *Point Reyes* (Calif.) *Light*
1980 Gannett News Service
1981 *Charlotte* (N.C.) *Observer*
1982 *Detroit News*
1983 *Jackson* (Miss.) *Clarion-Ledger*
1984 *Los Angeles Times*
1985 *The Fort Worth Star-Telegram*
1986 *Denver Post*

### EDITORIAL

1917 *New York Tribune*
1918 *Louisville Courier-Journal*
1920 Harvey E. Newbranch *(Omaha Evening World-Herald)*
1922 Frank M. O'Brien *(New York Herald)*
1923 William Allen White *(Emporia* [Kan.] *Gazette)*
1924 *Boston Herald* (Frank Buxton); special prize: Frank I. Cobb *(New York World)*
1925 *Charleston* (S.C.) *News and Courier*
1926 *New York Times* (Edward M. Kingsbury)
1927 *Boston Herald* (F. Lauriston Bullard)
1928 Grover Cleveland Hall *(Montgomery* [Ala.] *Advertiser)*
1929 Louis Isaac Jaffe *(Norfolk Virginian-Pilot)*
1931 Charles S. Ryckman *(Fremont* [Neb.] *Tribune)*
1933 *Kansas City* (Mo.) *Star*
1934 E. P. Chase *(Atlantic* [Iowa] *News Telegraph)*
1936 Felix Morley *(Washington Post);* George B. Parker (Scripps-Howard Newspapers)
1937 John W. Owens *(Baltimore Sun)*
1938 W. W. Waymack *(Des Moines Register and Tribune)*
1939 Ronald G. Callvert *(Portland Oregonian)*
1940 Bart Howard *(St. Louis Post-Dispatch)*
1941 Reuben Maury *(New York Daily News)*
1942 Geoffrey Parsons *(New York Herald Tribune)*
1943 Forrest W. Seymour *(Des Moines Register and Tribune)*
1944 *Kansas City* (Mo.) *Star* (Henry J. Haskell)
1945 George W. Potter *(Providence* [R.I.] *Journal-Bulletin)*
1946 Hodding Carter *(*[Greenville, Miss.] *Delta Democrat-Times)*
1947 William H. Grimes *(Wall Street Journal)*
1948 Virginius Dabney *(Richmond Times-Dispatch)*
1949 John H. Crider *(Boston Herald);* Herbert Elliston *(Washington Post)*
1950 Carl M. Saunders *(Jackson* [Mich.] *Citizen Patriot)*
1951 William H. Fitzpatrick *(New Orleans States)*
1952 Louis LaCoss *(St. Louis Globe-Democrat)*
1953 Vermont C. Royster *(Wall Street Journal)*
1954 *Boston Herald* (Don Murray)
1955 *Detroit Free Press* (Royce Howes)
1956 Lauren K. Soth *(Des Moines Register and Tribune)*
1957 Buford Boone *(Tuscaloosa* [Ala.] *News)*
1958 Harry S. Ashmore *(Arkansas Gazette)*
1959 Ralph McGill *(Atlanta Constitution)*
1960 Lenoir Chambers *(Virginian-Pilot)*
1961 William J. Dorvillier *(San Juan* [P.R.] *Star)*
1962 Thomas M. Storke *(Santa Barbara* [Calif.] *News-Press)*

1963 Ira B. Harkey, Jr. *(Pascagoula* [Miss.] *Chronicle)*
1964 Hazel Brannon Smith *(Lexington* [Miss.] *Advertiser)*
1965 John R. Harrison *(Gainesville* [Fla.] *Daily Sun)*
1966 Robert Lasch *(St. Louis Post-Dispatch)*
1967 Eugene Patterson *(Atlanta Constitution)*
1968 John S. Knight (Knight Newspapers)
1969 Paul Greenberg *(Pine Bluff* [Ark.] *Commercial)*
1970 Phillip L. Geyelin *(Washington Post)*
1971 Horance G. Davis, Jr. *(Gainesville* [Fla.] *Sun)*
1972 John Strohmeyer *(Bethlehem* [Pa.] *Globe Times)*
1973 Roger Bourne Linscott *(Berkshire Eagle* [Pittsfield, Mass.])
1974 F. Gilman Spencer *(Trenton* [N.J.] *Trentonian)*
1975 John Daniell Maurice *(Charleston* [W. Va.] *Daily Mail)*
1976 Philip P. Kerby *(Los Angeles Times)*
1977 Warren L. Lerude, Foster Church and Norman F. Cardoza *(Reno* [Nev.] *Gazette* and *Nevada State Journal)*
1978 Meg Greenfield *(Washington Post)*
1979 Edwin M. Yoder, Jr. *(Washington Star)*
1980 Robert L. Bartley *(Wall Street Journal)*
1981 Not awarded
1982 Jack Rosenthal *(New York Times)*
1983 *Miami Herald*
1984 Albert Scardino *(Georgia Gazette)*
1985 Richard Aregood *(Philadelphia Daily News*)
1986 Jack Fuller *(Chicago Tribune)*

## CORRESPONDENCE

1929 Paul Scott Mowrer *(Chicago Daily News)*
1930 Leland Stowe *(New York Herald Tribune)*
1931 H. R. Knickerbocker *(Philadelphia Public Ledger* and *New York Evening Post)*
1932 Walter Duranty *(New York Times);* Charles G. Ross *(St. Louis Post-Dispatch)*
1933 Edgar Ansel Mowrer *(Chicago Daily News)*
1934 Frederick T. Birchall *(New York Times)*
1935 Arthur Krock *(New York Times)*
1936 Wilfred C. Barber *(Chicago Tribune)*
1937 Anne O'Hare McCormick *(New York Times)*
1938 Arthur Krock *(New York Times)*
1939 Louis P. Lochner (Associated Press)
1940 Otto D. Tolischus *(New York Times)*
1941 Group award[1]
1942 Carlos P. Romulo *(Philippines Herald)*
1943 Hanson W. Baldwin *(New York Times)*
1944 Ernie Pyle (Scripps-Howard Newspaper Alliance)
1945 Harold V. (Hal) Boyle (Associated Press)
1946 Arnaldo Cortesi *(New York Times)*
1947 Brooks Atkinson *(New York Times)*
1948 Discontinued

## EDITORIAL CARTOONING

1922 Rollin Kirby *(New York World)*
1924 Jay Norwood Darling *(New York Tribune)*
1925 Rollin Kirby *(New York World)*
1926 D. R. Fitzpatrick *(St. Louis Post-Dispatch)*
1927 Nelson Harding *(Brooklyn Eagle)*
1928 Nelson Harding *(Brooklyn Eagle)*
1929 Rollin Kirby *(New York World)*
1930 Charles R. Macauley *(Brooklyn Eagle)*
1931 Edmund Duffy *(Baltimore Sun)*
1932 John T. McCutcheon *(Chicago Tribune)*
1933 H. M. Talburt *(Washington Daily News)*

1934 Edmund Duffy *(Baltimore Sun)*
1935 Ross A. Lewis *(Milwaukee Journal)*
1937 C. D. Batchelor *(New York Daily News)*
1938 Vaughn Shoemaker *(Chicago Daily News)*
1939 Charles G. Werner *(Daily Oklahoman* [Oklahoma City])
1940 Edmund Duffy *(Baltimore Sun)*
1941 Jacob Burck *(Chicago Times)*
1942 Herbert L. Block (NEA Service)
1943 Jay Norwood Darling *(New York Herald Tribune)*
1944 Clifford K. Berryman *(Washington Evening Star)*
1945 Bill Mauldin (United Features Syndicate)
1946 Bruce Alexander Russell *(Los Angeles Times)*
1947 Vaughn Shoemaker *(Chicago Daily News)*
1948 Reuben L. Goldberg *(New York Sun)*
1949 Lute Pease *(Newark Evening News)*
1950 James T. Berryman *(Washington Evening Star)*
1951 Reg (Reginald W.) Manning *(Arizona Republic* [Phoenix])
1952 Fred L. Packer *(New York Mirror)*
1953 Edward D. Kuekes *(Cleveland Plain Dealer)*
1954 Herbert L. Block *(Washington Post* and *Times-Herald)*
1955 Daniel R. Fitzpatrick *(St. Louis Post-Dispatch)*
1956 Robert York *(Louisville Times)*
1957 Tom Little *(Nashville Tennessean)*
1958 Bruce M. Shanks *(Buffalo Evening News)*
1959 Bill Mauldin *(St. Louis Post-Dispatch)*
1961 Carey Orr *(Chicago Tribune)*
1962 Edmund S. Valtman *(Hartford Times)*
1963 Frank Miller *(Des Moines Register)*
1964 Paul Conrad (formerly of *Denver Post,* later on *Los Angeles Times)*
1966 Don Wright *(Miami News)*
1967 Patrick B. Oliphant *(Denver Post)*
1968 Eugene Gray Payne *(Charlotte* [N.C.] *Observer)*
1969 John Fischetti *(Chicago Daily News)*
1970 Thomas F. Darcy *(Newsday* [Garden City, L.I.])
1971 Paul Conrad *(Los Angeles Times)*
1972 Jeffrey K. MacNelly *(Richmond* [Va.] *News Leader)*
1974 Paul Szep *(Boston Globe)*
1975 Garry Trudeau (Universal Press Syndicate)
1976 Tony Auth *(Philadelphia Inquirer)*
1977 Paul Szep *(Boston Globe)*
1978 Jeffrey K. MacNelly *(Richmond* [Va.] *News Leader)*
1979 Herbert L. Block *(Washington Post)*
1980 Don Wright *(Miami News)*
1981 Mike Peters *(Dayton* [Ohio] *Daily News)*
1982 Ben Sargent *(Austin* [Tex.] *American-Statesman)*
1983 Richard Locher *(Chicago Tribune)*
1984 Paul Conrad *(Los Angeles Times)*
1985 Jeff MacNelly *(Chicago Tribune)*
1986 Jules Feiffer *(Village Voice)*

## NEWS PHOTOGRAPHY

1942 Milton Brooks *(Detroit News)*
1943 Frank Noel (Associated Press)
1944 Frank Filan (Associated Press); Earle L. Bunker *(Omaha World-Herald)*
1945 Joe Rosenthal (Associated Press)
1947 Arnold Hardy
1948 Frank Cushing *(Boston Traveler)*
1949 Nat Fein *(New York Herald Tribune)*
1950 Bill Crouch *(Oakland Tribune)*
1951 Max Desfor (Associated Press)
1952 John Robinson and Don Ultang *(Des Moines Register & Tribune)*
1953 William M. Gallagher *(Flint* [Mich.] *Journal)*
1954 Mrs. Walter M. Schau

1. For the public services and the individual achievements of American news reporters in the war zones.

1955 John L. Gaunt, Jr. *(Los Angeles Times)*
1956 *New York Daily News*
1957 Harry A. Trask *(Boston Traveler)*
1958 William C. Beall *(Washington Daily News)*
1959 William Seaman *(Minneapolis Star)*
1960 Andrew Lopez (United Press International)
1961 Yasushi Nagao (Mainichi Newspapers, Tokyo)
1962 Paul Vathis (Harrisburg [Pa.] bureau of Associated Press)
1963 Hector Rondon (*La Republica,* Caracas, Venezuela)
1964 Robert H. Jackson *(Dallas Times Herald)*
1965 Horst Faas (Associated Press)
1966 Kyoichi Sawada (United Press International)
1967 Jack R. Thornell (Associated Press)
1968 News: Rocco Morabito *(Jacksonville* [Fla.] *Journal);* features: Toshio Sakai (United Press International)
1969 Spot news: Edward T. Adams (Associated Press); features: Moneta Sleet, Jr.
1970 Spot news: Steve Starr (Associated Press); features: Dallas Kinney *(Palm Beach Post)*
1971 Spot news: John Paul Filo (*Valley Daily News and Daily Dispatch* [Tarentum and New Kensington, Pa.]); features: Jack Dykinga *(Chicago Sun-Times)*
1972 Spot news: Horst Faas and Michel Laurent (Associated Press); features: Dave Kennerly (United Press International)
1973 Spot news: Huynh Cong Ut *(Associated Press);* features: Brian Lanker *(Topeka Capital-Journal)*
1974 Spot news: Anthony K. Roberts (Associated Press); features: Slava Veder (Associated Press)
1975 Spot news: Gerald H. Gay *(Seattle Times);* features: Matthew Lewis *(Washington Post)*
1976 Spot news: Stanley J. Forman *(Boston Herald-American);* features: photographic staff of *Louisville Courier-Journal* and *Times*
1977 Spot news: Neal Ulevich (Associated Press) and Stanley J. Forman *(Boston Herald-American);* features: Robin Hood *(Chattanooga News-Free Press)*
1978 Spot news: John Blair, freelance, Evansville, Ind.; features: J. Ross Baughman (Associated Press)
1979 Spot news: Thomas J. Kelly, 3rd *(Pottstown* [Pa.] *Mercury);* features: photographic staff of *Boston Herald-American*
1980 Features: Erwin H. Hagler *(Dallas Times Herald)*
1981 Spot news: Larry C. Price *(Fort Worth Star-Telegram);* features: Taro M. Yamasaki *(Detroit Free Press)*
1982 Spot news: Ron Edmonds (Associated Press); features: John H. White *(Chicago Sun-Times)*
1983 Spot news: Bill Foley (Associated Press); features: James B. Dickman *(Dallas Times Herald)*
1984 Spot news: Stan Grossfeld *(Boston Globe);* features: Anthony Suau *(Denver Post)*
1985 Spot news: photographic staff of *Register,* Santa Ana, Calif.; features: Stan Grossfeld *(Boston Globe)*
1986 Spot news: Michel duCille and Carol Guzy *(Miami Herald);* features: Tom Gralish *(Philadelphia Inquirer)*

### NATIONAL TELEGRAPHIC REPORTING

1942 Louis Stark *(New York Times)*
1944 Dewey L. Fleming *(Baltimore Sun)*
1945 James Reston *(New York Times)*
1946 Edward A. Harris *(St. Louis Post-Dispatch)*

1947 Edward T. Folliard *(Washington Post)*

### NATIONAL REPORTING

1948 Bert Andrews *(New York Herald Tribune);* Nat S. Finney *(Minneapolis Tribune)*
1949 C. P. Trussel *(New York Times)*
1950 Edwin O. Guthman *(Seattle Times)*
1952 Anthony Leviero *(New York Times)*
1953 Don Whitehead (Associated Press)
1954 Richard Wilson (Cowles Newspapers)
1955 Anthony Lewis *(Washington Daily News)*
1956 Charles L. Bartlett *(Chattanooga Times)*
1957 James Reston *(New York Times)*
1958 Relman Morin (Associated Press) and Clark Mollenhoff *(Des Moines Register & Tribune)*
1959 Howard Van Smith *(Miami News)*
1960 Vance Trimble (Scripps-Howard Newspaper Alliance)
1961 Edward R. Cony *(Wall Street Journal)*
1962 Nathan G. Caldwell and Gene S. Graham *(Nashville Tennessean)*
1963 Anthony Lewis *(New York Times)*
1964 Merriman Smith (United Press International)
1965 Louis M. Kohlmeier *(Wall Street Journal)*
1966 Haynes Johnson *(Washington Evening Star)*
1967 Stanley Penn and Monroe Karmin *(Wall Street Journal)*
1968 Howard James *(Christian Science Monitor);* Nathan K. (Nick) Kotz *(Des Moines Register* and *Minneapolis Tribune)*
1969 Robert Cahn *(Christian Science Monitor)*
1970 William J. Eaton *(Chicago Daily News)*
1971 Lucinda Franks and Thomas Powers (United Press International)
1972 Jack Anderson *(United Feature Syndicate)*
1973 Robert Boyd and Clark Hoyt *(Knight Newspapers)*
1974 Jack White *(Providence* [R.I.] *Journal-Bulletin);* and James R. Polk *(Washington Star-News)*
1975 Donald L. Barlett and James B. Steele *(Philadelphia Inquirer)*
1976 James Risser *(Des Moines Register)*
1977 Walter Mears (Associated Press)
1978 Gaylord D. Shaw *(Los Angeles Times)*
1979 James Risser *(Des Moines Register)*
1980 Bette Swenson Orsini and Charles Stafford *(St. Petersburg Times)*
1981 John M. Crewdson *(New York Times)*
1982 Rick Atkinson *(Kansas City* [Mo.] *Times)*
1983 *Boston Globe*
1984 John N. Wilford *(New York Times)*
1985 Thomas J. Knudson *(Des Moines Register)*
1986 Craig Flournoy and George Rodrigue *(Dallas Morning News)* and Arthur Howe *(Philadelphia Inquirer)*

### INTERNATIONAL TELEGRAPHIC REPORTING

1942 Laurence Edmund Allen (Associated Press)
1943 Ira Wolfert (North American Newspaper Alliance, Inc.)
1944 Daniel De Luce (Associated Press)
1945 Mark S. Watson *(Baltimore Sun)*
1946 Homer W. Bigart *(New York Herald Tribune)*
1947 Eddy Gilmore (Associated Press)

### INTERNATIONAL REPORTING

1948 Paul W. Ward *(Baltimore Sun)*
1949 Price Day *(Baltimore Sun)*
1950 Edmund Stevens *(Christian Science Monitor)*
1951 Keyes Beech and Fred Sparks *(Chicago Daily News);* Homer Bigart and Marguerite Higgins

*(New York Herald Tribune);* Relman Morin and Don Whitehead (Associated Press)
1952 John M. Hightower (Associated Press)
1953 Austin C. Wehrwein *(Milwaukee Journal)*
1954 Jim G. Lucas (Scripps-Howard Newspapers)
1955 Harrison E. Salisbury *(New York Times)*
1956 William Randolph Hearst, Jr. and Frank Conniff (Hearst Newspapers) and Kingsbury Smith (INS)
1957 Russell Jones (United Press)
1958 *New York Times*
1959 Joseph Martin and Philip Santora *(New York Daily News)*
1960 A. M. Rosenthal *(New York Times)*
1961 Lynn Heinzerling (Associated Press)
1962 Walter Lippmann (New York Herald Tribune Syndicate)
1963 Hal Hendrix *(Miami News)*
1964 Malcolm W. Browne (Associated Press) and David Halberstam *(New York Times)*
1965 J. A. Livingston *(Philadelphia Bulletin)*
1966 Peter Arnett (Associated Press)
1967 R. John Hughes *(Christian Science Monitor)*
1968 Alfred Friendly *(Washington Post)*
1969 William Tuohy *(Los Angeles Times)*
1970 Seymour M. Hersh (Dispatch News Service)
1971 Jimmie Lee Hoagland *(Washington Post)*
1972 Peter R. Kann *(Wall Street Journal)*
1973 Max Frankel *(New York Times)*
1974 Hedrick Smith *(New York Times)*
1975 William Mullen and Ovie Carter *(Chicago Tribune)*
1976 Sydney H. Schanberg *(New York Times)*
1978 Henry Kamm *(New York Times)*
1979 Richard Ben Cramer *(Philadelphia Inquirer)*
1980 Joel Brinkley and Jay Mather *(Louisville Courier-Journal)*
1981 Shirley Christian *(Miami Herald)*
1982 John Darnton *(New York Times)*
1983 Thomas L. Friedman *(New York Times)*
1984 Karen E. House *(Wall Street Journal)*
1985 Josh Friedman, Dennis Bell, and Ozier Muhammad *(Newsday)*
1986 Lewis M. Simons, Pete Carey, and Katherine Ellison *(San Jose Mercury News)*

## REPORTING

1917 Herbert B. Swope *(New York World)*
1918 Harold A. Littledale *(New York Evening Post)*
1920 John J. Leary, Jr. *(New York World)*
1921 Louis Seibold *(New York World)*
1922 Kirke L. Simpson (Associated Press)
1923 Alva Johnston *(New York Times)*
1924 Magner White *(San Diego Sun)*
1925 James W. Mulroy and Alvin H. Goldstein *(Chicago Daily News)*
1926 William Burke Miller *(Louisville Courier-Journal)*
1927 John T. Rogers *(St. Louis Post-Dispatch)*
1929 Paul Y. Anderson *(St. Louis Post-Dispatch)*
1930 Russell D. Owen *(New York Times);* special award: W. O. Dapping *(Auburn* [N.Y.] *Citizen)*
1931 A. B. MacDonald *(Kansas City* [Mo.] *Star)*
1932 W. C. Richards, D. D. Martin, J. S. Pooler, F. D. Webb, J. N. W. Sloan (all of *Detroit Free Press)*
1933 Francis A. Jamieson (Associated Press)
1934 Royce Brier *(San Francisco Chronicle)*
1935 William H. Taylor *(New York Herald Tribune)*
1936 Lauren D. Lyman *(New York Times)*
1937 John J. O'Neill *(New York Herald Tribune);* William Leonard Laurence *(New York Times);* Howard W. Blakeslee (Associated Press); Gobind Behari Lal (Universal Service); David Dietz (Scripps-Howard Newspapers)

1938 Raymond Sprigle *(Pittsburg Post-Gazette)*
1939 Thomas L. Stokes *(New York World-Telegram)*
1940 S. Burton Heath *(New York World-Telegram)*
1941 Westbrook Pegler *(New York World-Telegram)*
1942 Stanton Delaplane *(San Francisco Chronicle)*
1943 George Weller *(Chicago Daily News)*
1944 Paul Schoenstein and associates *(New York Journal-American)*
1945 Jack S. McDowell *(San Francisco Call-Bulletin)*
1946 William Leonard Laurence *(New York Times)*
1947 Frederick Woltman *(New York World-Telegram)*
1948 George E. Goodwin *(Atlanta Journal)*
1949 Malcolm Johnson *(New York Sun)*
1950 Meyer Berger *(New York Times)*
1951 Edward S. Montgomery *(San Francisco Examiner)*
1952 George de Carvalho *(San Francisco Chronicle)*
1953 Editorial staff *(Providence Journal and Evening Bulletin);*[1] Edward J. Mowery *(New York World-Telegram and Sun)*[2]
1954 *Vicksburg* (Miss.) *Sunday Post-Herald;*[1] Alvin Scott McCoy *(Kansas City* [Mo.] *Star)*[2]
1955 Mrs. Caro Brown *(Alice* [Tex.] *Daily Echo);*[1] Roland Kenneth Towery *(Cuero* [Tex.] *Record)*[2]
1956 Lee Hills *(Detroit Free Press);*[1] Arthur Daley *(New York Times)*[2]
1957 *Salt Lake Tribune;*[1] Wallace Turner and William Lambert *(Portland Oregonian)*[2]
1958 *Fargo* [N.D.] *Forum;*[1] George Beveridge *(Washington* [D.C.] *Evening Star)*[2]
1959 Mary Lou Werner *(Washington* [D.C.] *Evening Star);*[1] John Harold Brislin *(Scranton* [Pa.] *Tribune & Scrantonian)*[2]
1960 Jack Nelson *(Atlanta Constitution);*[1] Miriam Ottenberg *(Washington Evening Star)*[2]
1961 Sanche de Gramont *(New York Herald Tribune);*[1] Edgar May *(Buffalo Evening News)*[2]
1962 Robert D. Mullins *(Deseret News,* Salt Lake City);[1] George Bliss *(Chicago Tribune)*[2]
1963 Sylvan Fox, Anthony Shannon, and William Longgood *(New York World-Telegram and Sun);*[1] Oscar Griffin, Jr. (former editor of *Pecos* [Tex.] *Independent and Enterprise,* now on staff of *Houston Chronicle)*[2]

## GENERAL LOCAL REPORTING

1964 Norman C. Miller *(Wall Street Journal)*
1965 Melvin H. Ruder *(Hungry Horse News,* Columbia Falls, Mont.)
1966 Staff of *Los Angeles Times*
1967 Robert V. Cox *(Chambersburg* [Pa.] *Public Opinion)*
1968 Staff of *Detroit Free Press*
1969 John Fetterman *(Louisville Times* and *Courier-Journal)*
1970 Thomas Fitzpatrick *(Chicago Sun-Times)*
1971 Staff of *Akron* (Ohio) *Beacon*
1972 Richard Cooper and John Machacek *(Rochester* [N.Y.] *Times-Union)*
1973 *Chicago Tribune*
1974 Arthur M. Petacque and Hugh F. Hough *(Chicago Sun-Times)*
1975 *Xenia* (Ohio) *Daily Gazette*
1976 Gene Miller *(Miami Herald)*
1977 Margo Huston *(Milwaukee Journal)*
1978 Richard Whitt *(Louisville Courier-Journal)*
1979 Staff of *San Diego* (Calif.) *Evening Tribune*
1980 Staff of *Philadelphia Inquirer*

1. Reporting under pressure of edition deadlines. 2. Reporting not under pressure of edition deadlines.

1981 *Longview* (Wash.) *Daily News*
1982 *Kansas City* (Mo.) *Star* and *Kansas City* (Mo.) *Times*
1983 *Fort Wayne* (Ind.) *News-Sentinel*
1984 *Newsday*

## GENERAL NEWS REPORTING

1985 Thomas Turcol (*Virginian-Pilot and Ledger-Star*)
1986 Edna Buchanan (*Miami Herald*)

## SPECIAL LOCAL REPORTING

1964 James V. Magee, Albert V. Gaudiosi, and Frederick A. Meyer (*Philadelphia Bulletin*)
1965 Gene Goltz (*Houston Post*)
1966 John A. Frasca (*Tampa Tribune*)
1967 Gene Miller (*Miami Herald*)
1968 J. Anthony Lukas (*New York Times*)
1969 Albert L. Delugach and Denny Walsh (*St. Louis Globe-Democrat*)
1970 Harold Eugene Martin (*Montgomery Advertiser*)
1971 William Hugh Jones (*Chicago Tribune*)
1972 Timothy Leland, Gerard N. O'Neill, Stephen A. Kurkjian, and Ann DeSantis (*Boston Globe*)
1973 Sun Newspapers of Omaha, Neb.
1974 William Sherman (*New York Daily News*)
1975 *Indianapolis Star*
1976 *Chicago Tribune*
1977 Acel Moore and Wendell Rawls, Jr. (*Philadelphia Inquirer*)
1978 Anthony R. Dolan (*Stamford* [Conn.] *Advocate*)
1979 Gilbert M. Gaul and Elliot G. Jaspin (*Pottsville* [Pa.] *Republican*)
1980 Nils J. Bruzelius, Alexander B. Hawes, Jr., Stephen A. Kurkjian, and Joan Vennochi (*Boston Globe*)
1981 Clark Hallas and Robert B. Lowe (*Arizona Daily Star,* Tucson)
1982 Paul Henderson (*Seattle Times*)
1983 Loretta Tofani (*Washington Post*)
1984 *Boston Globe*

## INVESTIGATIVE REPORTING

1985 Lucy Morgan and Jack Reed (*St. Petersburg* [Fla.] *Times*) and William K. Marimow (*Philadelphia Inquirer*)
1986 Jeffrey A. Marx and Michael M. York (*Lexington* [Ky.] *Herald Leader*)

## FEATURE WRITING

1979 Jon D. Franklin (*Baltimore Evening Sun*)
1980 Madeleine Blais (*Miami Herald*)
1981 Teresa Carpenter (*Village Voice,* New York)
1982 Saul Pett (Associated Press)
1983 Nan Robertson (*New York Times*)
1984 Peter M. Rinearson (*Seattle Times*)
1985 Alice Steinbach (*Baltimore Sun*)
1986 John Camp (*St. Paul Pioneer Press and Dispatch*)

## COMMENTARY

1970 Marquis W. Childs (*St. Louis Post-Dispatch*)
1971 William A. Caldwell (*Record* [Hackensack, N.J.])
1972 Mike Royko (*Chicago Daily News*)
1973 David S. Broder (*Washington Post*)
1974 Edwin A. Roberts, Jr. (*National Observer*)
1975 Mary McGrory (*Washington Star*)
1976 Walter W. (Red) Smith (*New York Times*)
1977 George F. Will (*Washington Post* Writers Group)
1978 William Safire (*New York Times*)

1979 Russell Baker (*New York Times*)
1980 Ellen H. Goodman (*Boston Globe*)
1981 Dave Anderson (*New York Times*)
1982 Art Buchwald (*Los Angeles Times* Syndicate)
1983 Claude Sitton (*Raleigh* [N.C.] *News & Observer*)
1984 Vermont Royster (*Wall Street Journal*)
1985 Murray Kempton (*Newsday*)
1986 Jimmy Breslin (*New York Daily News*)

## CRITICISM

1970 Ada Louise Huxtable (*New York Times*)
1971 Harold C. Schonberg (*New York Times*)
1972 Frank Peters, Jr. (*St. Louis Post-Dispatch*)
1973 Ronald Powers (*Chicago Sun-Times*)
1974 Emily Genauer (Newsday Syndicate)
1975 Roger Ebert (*Chicago Sun-Times*)
1976 Alan M. Kriegsman (*Washington Post*)
1977 William McPherson (*Washington Post*)
1978 Walter Kerr (*New York Times*)
1979 Paul Gapp (*Chicago Tribune*)
1980 William A. Henry, 3rd (*Boston Globe*)
1981 Jonathan Yardley (*Washington Star*)
1982 Martin Bernheimer (*Los Angeles Times*)
1983 Manuela Hoelterhoff (*Wall Street Journal*)
1984 Paul Goldberger (*New York Times*)
1985 Howard Rosenberg (*Los Angeles Times*)
1986 Donal Henahan (*New York Times*)

## EXPLANATORY JOURNALISM

1985 Jon Franklin (*Baltimore Evening Sun*)
1986 *New York Times*

## SPECIALIZED REPORTING

1985 Randall Savage and Jackie Crosby (*Macon* [Ga.] *Telegraph and News*)
1986 Andrew Schneider and Mary Pat Flaherty (*Pittsburgh Press*)

## SPECIAL CITATIONS

1938 *Edmonton* (Alberta) *Journal,* special bronze plaque for editorial leadership in defense of freedom of press in Province of Alberta.
1941 *New York Times* for the public educational value of its foreign news report.
1944 Byron Price, Director of the Office of Censorship, for the creation and administration of the newspaper and radio codes. Mrs. William Allen White, for her husband's interest and services during the past seven years as a member of the Advisory Board of the Graduate School of Journalism, Columbia University. Richard Rodgers and Oscar Hammerstein II for their musical *Oklahoma!*
1945 The cartographers of the American press for their war maps.
1947 (Pulitzer centennial year.) Columbia University and the Graduate School of Journalism for their efforts to maintain and advance the high standards governing the Pulitzer Prize awards. The *St. Louis Post-Dispatch* for its unswerving adherence to the public and professional ideals of its founder and its leadership in American journalism.
1948 Dr. Frank D. Fackenthal for his interest and service.
1951 Cyrus L. Sulzberger (*New York Times*) for his exclusive interview with Archbishop Stepinac in a Yugoslav prison.
1952 *Kansas City Star* for coverage of 1951 floods; Max Kase (*New York Journal-American*) for exposures of bribery in college basketball.

1953 *New York Times* for its 17-year publication of "News of the Week in Review"; and Lester Markel, its founder.
1957 Kenneth Roberts for his historical novels.
1958 Walter Lippmann *(New York Herald Tribune)* for his "wisdom, perception and high sense of responsibility" in his commentary on national and international affairs.
1960 Garrett Mattingly, for *The Armada.*
1961 *American Heritage Picture History of the Civil War,* as distinguished example of American book publishing.
1964 Gannett Newspapers, Rochester, N.Y.
1973 James Thomas Flexner for his biography *George Washington.*

1974 Roger Sessions for his "life's work in music."
1976 John Hohenberg for "services for 22 years as administrator of the Pulitzer Prizes"; Scott Joplin for his contributions to American music.
1977 Alex Haley for his novel, *Roots*
1978 E.B. White of *New Yorker* magazine and Richard L. Strout of *Christian Science Monitor*
1982 Milton Babbitt, "for his life's work as a distinguished and seminal American composer."
1984 Theodor Seuss Geisel (Dr. Seuss) for "books full of playful rhymes, nonsense words and strange illustrations."
1985 William H. Schuman for "more than a half century of contribution to American music as a composer and educational leader."

## Pulitzer Prizes in Letters

### FICTION[1]

1918 *His Family.* Ernest Poole
1919 *The Magnificent Ambersons.* Booth Tarkington
1921 *The Age of Innocence.* Edith Wharton
1922 *Alice Adams.* Booth Tarkington
1923 *One of Ours.* Willa Cather
1924 *The Able McLaughlins.* Margaret Wilson
1925 *So Big.* Edna Ferber
1926 *Arrowsmith.* Sinclair Lewis
1927 *Early Autumn.* Louis Bromfield
1928 *The Bridge of San Luis Rey.* Thornton Wilder
1929 *Scarlet Sister Mary.* Julia Peterkin
1930 *Laughing Boy.* Oliver La Farge
1931 *Years of Grace.* Margaret Ayer Barnes
1932 *The Good Earth.* Pearl S. Buck
1933 *The Store.* T. S. Stribling
1934 *Lamb in His Bosom.* Caroline Miller
1935 *Now in November.* Josephine Winslow Johnson
1936 *Honey in the Horn.* Harold L. Davis
1937 *Gone With the Wind.* Margaret Mitchell
1938 *The Late George Apley.* John Phillips Marquand
1939 *The Yearling.* Marjorie Kinnan Rawlings
1940 *The Grapes of Wrath.* John Steinbeck
1942 *In This Our Life.* Ellen Glasgow
1943 *Dragon's Teeth.* Upton Sinclair
1944 *Journey in the Dark.* Martin Flavin
1945 *A Bell for Adano.* John Hersey
1947 *All the King's Men.* Robert Penn Warren
1948 *Tales of the South Pacific.* James A. Michener
1949 *Guard of Honor.* James Gould Cozzens
1950 *The Way West.* A. B. Guthrie, Jr.
1951 *The Town.* Conrad Richter
1952 *The Caine Mutiny.* Herman Wouk
1953 *The Old Man and the Sea.* Ernest Hemingway
1955 *A Fable.* William Faulkner
1956 *Andersonville.* MacKinlay Kantor
1958 *A Death in the Family.* James Agee
1959 *The Travels of Jaimie McPheeters.* Robert Lewis Taylor
1960 *Advise and Consent.* Allen Drury
1961 *To Kill a Mockingbird.* Harper Lee
1962 *The Edge of Sadness.* Edwin O'Connor
1963 *The Reivers.* William Faulkner
1965 *The Keepers of the House.* Shirley Ann Grau
1966 *Collected Stories of Katherine Anne Porter.* Katherine Anne Porter
1967 *The Fixer.* Bernard Malamud
1968 *The Confessions of Nat Turner.* William Styron
1969 *House Made of Dawn.* N. Scott Momaday
1970 *Collected Stories.* Jean Stafford
1972 *Angle of Repose.* Wallace Stegner

1. Before 1948, award was for novels only.

1973 *The Optimist's Daughter.* Eudora Welty
1975 *The Killer Angels.* Michael Shaara
1976 *Humboldt's Gift.* Saul Bellow
1978 *Elbow Room.* James Alan McPherson
1979 *The Stories of John Cheever.* John Cheever
1980 *The Executioner's Song.* Norman Mailer
1981 *A Confederacy of Dunces.* John Kennedy Toole
1982 *Rabbit Is Rich.* John Updike
1983 *The Color Purple.* Alice Walker
1984 *Ironweed.* William Kennedy
1985 *Foreign Affairs,* Alison Lurie
1986 *Lonesome Dove,* Larry McMurtry

### DRAMA

1918 *Why Marry?* Jesse Lynch Williams
1920 *Beyond the Horizon.* Eugene O'Neill
1921 *Miss Lulu Bett.* Zona Gale
1922 *Anna Christie.* Eugene O'Neill
1923 *Icebound.* Owen Davis
1924 *Hell-Bent Fer Heaven.* Hatcher Hughes
1925 *They Knew What They Wanted.* Sidney Howard
1926 *Craig's Wife.* George Kelly
1927 *In Abraham's Bosom.* Paul Green
1928 *Strange Interlude.* Eugene O'Neill
1929 *Street Scene.* Elmer L. Rice
1930 *The Green Pastures.* Marc Connelly
1931 *Alison's House.* Susan Glaspell
1932 *Of Thee I Sing.* George S. Kaufman, Morrie Ryskind, and Ira Gershwin
1933 *Both Your Houses.* Maxwell Anderson
1934 *Men in White.* Sidney Kingsley
1935 *The Old Maid.* Zöe Akins
1936 *Idiot's Delight.* Robert E. Sherwood
1937 *You Can't Take It With You.* Moss Hart and George S. Kaufman
1938 *Our Town.* Thornton Wilder
1939 *Abe Lincoln in Illinois.* Robert E. Sherwood
1940 *The Time of Your Life.* William Saroyan
1941 *There Shall Be No Night.* Robert E. Sherwood
1943 *The Skin of Our Teeth.* Thornton Wilder
1945 *Harvey.* Mary Chase
1946 *State of the Union.* Russel Crouse and Howard Lindsay
1948 *A Streetcar Named Desire.* Tennessee Williams
1949 *Death of a Salesman.* Arthur Miller
1950 *South Pacific.* Richard Rodgers, Oscar Hammerstein II, and Joshua Logan
1952 *The Shrike.* Joseph Kramm
1953 *Picnic.* William Inge
1954 *The Teahouse of the August Moon.* John Patrick
1955 *Cat on a Hot Tin Roof.* Tennessee Williams
1956 *The Diary of Anne Frank.* Frances Goodrich

and Albert Hackett
1957  *Long Day's Journey Into Night.* Eugene O'Neill
1958  *Look Homeward, Angel.* Ketti Frings
1959  *J.B.* Archibald MacLeish
1960  *Fiorello!* George Abbott, Jerome Weidman, Jerry Bock, and Sheldon Harnick
1961  *All the Way Home.* Tad Mosel
1962  *How to Succeed in Business Without Really Trying.* Frank Loesser and Abe Burrows
1965  *The Subject Was Roses.* Frank D. Gilroy
1967  *A Delicate Balance.* Edward Albee
1969  *The Great White Hope.* Howard Sackler
1970  *No Place to Be Somebody.* Charles Gordone
1971  *The Effect of Gamma Rays on Man-in-the-Moon Marigolds.* Paul Zindel
1973  *That Championship Season.* Jason Miller
1975  *Seascape.* Edward Albee
1976  *A Chorus Line.* Conceived by Michael Bennett
1977  *The Shadow Box.* Michael Cristofer
1978  *The Gin Game.* Donald L. Coburn
1979  *Buried Child.* Sam Shepard
1980  *Talley's Folly.* Lanford Wilson
1981  *Crimes of the Heart.* Beth Henley
1982  *A Soldier's Play.* Charles Fuller
1983  *'Night, Mother.* Marsha Norman
1984  *Glengarry Glen Ross.* David Mamet
1985  *Sunday in the Park with George,* Stephen Sondheim and James Lapine

### HISTORY OF UNITED STATES

1917  *With Americans of Past and Present Days.* J. J. Jusserand, Ambassador of France to United States
1918  *A History of the Civil War, 1861–1865.* James Ford Rhodes
1920  *The War With Mexico.* Justin H. Smith
1921  *The Victory at Sea.* William Sowden Sims in collaboration with Burton J. Hendrick
1922  *The Founding of New England.* James Truslow Adams
1923  *The Supreme Court in United States History.* Charles Warren
1924  *The American Revolution—A Constitutional Interpretation.* Charles Howard McIlwain
1925  *A History of the American Frontier.* Frederic L. Paxson
1926  *The History of the United States.* Edward Channing
1927  *Pinckney's Treaty.* Samuel Flagg Bemis
1928  *Main Currents in American Thought.* Vernon Louis Parrington
1929  *The Organization and Administration of the Union Army, 1861–1865.* Fred Albert Shannon
1930  *The War of Independence.* Claude H. Van Tyne
1931  *The Coming of the War: 1914.* Bernadotte E. Schmitt
1932  *My Experiences in the World War.* John J. Pershing
1933  *The Significance of Sections in American History.* Frederick J. Turner
1934  *The People's Choice.* Herbert Agar
1935  *The Colonial Period of American History.* Charles McLean Andrews
1936  *The Constitutional History of the United States.* Andrew C. McLaughlin
1937  *The Flowering of New England.* Van Wyck Brooks
1938  *The Road to Reunion, 1865–1900.* Paul Herman Buck
1939  *A History of American Magazines.* Frank Luther Mott
1940  *Abraham Lincoln: The War Years.* Carl Sandburg

1941  *The Atlantic Migration, 1607–1860.* Marcus Lee Hansen
1942  *Reveille in Washington.* Margaret Leech
1943  *Paul Revere and the World He Lived In.* Esther Forbes
1944  *The Growth of American Thought.* Merle Curti
1945  *Unfinished Business.* Stephen Bonsal
1946  *The Age of Jackson.* Arthur M. Schlesinger, Jr.
1947  *Scientists Against Time.* James Phinney Baxter, 3rd
1948  *Across the Wide Missouri.* Bernard DeVoto
1949  *The Disruption of American Democracy.* Roy Franklin Nichols
1950  *Art and Life in America.* Oliver W. Larkin
1951  *The Old Northwest, Pioneer Period 1815–1840.* R. Carlyle Buley
1952  *The Uprooted.* Oscar Handlin
1953  *The Era of Good Feelings.* George Dangerfield
1954  *A Stillness at Appomattox.* Bruce Catton
1955  *Great River: The Rio Grande in North American History.* Paul Horgan
1956  *The Age of Reform.* Richard Hofstadter
1957  *Russia Leaves the War: Soviet-American Relations, 1917–1920.* George F. Kennan
1958  *Banks and Politics in America: From the Revolution to the Civil War.* Bray Hammond
1959  *The Republican Era: 1869–1901.* Leonard D. White, assisted by Jean Schneider
1960  *In the Days of McKinley.* Margaret Leech
1961  *Between War and Peace: The Potsdam Conference.* Herbert Feis
1962  *The Triumphant Empire, Thunder-Clouds Gather in the West.* Lawrence H. Gipson
1963  *Washington, Village and Capital, 1800–1878.* Constance McLaughlin Green
1964  *Puritan Village: The Formation of a New England Town.* Sumner Chilton Powell
1965  *The Greenback Era.* Irwin Unger
1966  *Life of the Mind in America.* Perry Miller
1967  *Exploration and Empire: The Explorer and Scientist in the Winning of the American West.* William H. Goetzmann
1968  *The Ideological Origins of the American Revolution.* Bernard Bailyn
1969  *Origins of the Fifth Amendment.* Leonard W. Levy
1970  *Present at the Creation: My Years in the State Department.* Dean Acheson
1971  *Roosevelt: The Soldier of Freedom.* James McGregor Burns
1972  *Neither Black Nor White. Slavery and Race Relations in Brazil and the United States.* Carl N. Degler
1973  *People of Paradox: An Inquiry Concerning the Origin of American Civilization.* Michael Kammen
1974  *The Americans: The Democratic Experience, Vol. 3.* Daniel J. Boorstin
1975  *Jefferson and His Time.* Dumas Malone
1976  *Lamy of Santa Fe.* Paul Horgan
1977  *The Impending Crisis: 1841–1861.* David M. Potter (posth)
1978  *The Invisible Hand: The Managerial Revolution in American Business.* Alfred D. Chandler, Jr.
1979  *The Dred Scott Case: Its Significance in Law and Politics.* Don E. Fehrenbacher
1980  *Been in the Storm So Long.* Leon F. Litwack
1981  *American Education: The National Experience; 1783–1876.* Lawrence A. Cremin
1982  *Mary Chestnut's Civil War.* C. Vann Woodward, editor
1983  *The Transformation of Virginia, 1740–1790.* Rhys L. Isaac

1985 *The Prophets of Regulation,* Thomas K. Mc-Craw

1986 *. . . the Heavens and the Earth: A Political History of the Space Age,* Walter A. McDougall

## BIOGRAPHY OR AUTOBIOGRAPHY

1917 *Julia Ward Howe.* Laura E. Richards and Maude Howe Elliott, assisted by Florence Howe Hall

1918 *Benjamin Franklin, Self-Revealed.* William Cabell Bruce

1919 *The Education of Henry Adams.* Henry Adams

1920 *The Life of John Marshall.* Albert J. Beveridge

1921 *The Americanization of Edward Bok.* Edward Bok

1922 *A Daughter of the Middle Border.* Hamlin Garland

1923 *The Life and Letters of Walter H. Page,* Burton J. Hendrick

1924 *From Immigrant to Inventor.* Michael Idvorsky Pupin

1925 *Barrett Wendell and His Letters.* M. A. DeWolfe Howe

1926 *The Life of Sir William Osler.* Harvey Cushing

1927 *Whitman.* Emory Holloway

1928 *The American Orchestra and Theodore Thomas. Charles Edward Russell*

1929 *The Training of an American. The Earlier Life and Letters of Walter H. Page.* Burton J. Hendrick

1930 *The Raven.* Marquis James

1931 *Charles W. Eliot.* Henry James

1932 *Theodore Roosevelt.* Henry F. Pringle

1933 *Grover Cleveland.* Allan Nevins

1934 *John Hay.* Tyler Dennett

1935 *R. E. Lee.* Douglas S. Freeman

1936 *The Thought and Character of William James.* Ralph Barton Perry

1937 *Hamilton Fish.* Allan Nevins

1938 *Pedlar's Progress.* Odell Shepard; *Andrew Jackson.* Marquis James

1939 *Benjamin Franklin.* Carl Van Doren

1940 *Woodrow Wilson. Life and Letters,* Vols. VII and VIII. Ray Stannard Baker

1941 *Jonathan Edwards.* Ola E. Winslow

1942 *Crusader in Crinoline.* Forrest Wilson

1943 *Admiral of the Ocean Sea.* Samuel Eliot Morison

1944 *The American Leonardo: The Life of Samuel F. B. Morse.* Carleton Mabee

1945 *George Bancroft: Brahmin Rebel.* Russel Blaine Nye

1946 *Son of the Wilderness.* Linnie Marsh Wolfe

1947 *The Autobiography of William Allen White*

1948 *Forgotten First Citizen: John Bigelow.* Margaret Clapp

1949 *Roosevelt and Hopkins.* Robert E. Sherwood

1950 *John Quincy Adams and the Foundations of American Foreign Policy.* Samuel Flagg Bemis

1951 *John C. Calhoun: American Portrait.* Margaret Louise Coit

1952 *Charles Evans Hughes.* Merlo J. Pusey

1953 *Edmund Pendleton, 1721–1803.* David J. Mays

1954 *The Spirit of St. Louis.* Charles A. Lindbergh

1955 *The Taft Story.* William S. White

1956 *Benjamin Henry Latrobe.* Talbot F. Hamlin

1957 *Profiles in Courage.* John F. Kennedy

1958 *George Washington.* Douglas Southall Freeman (Vols. 1–6) and John Alexander Carroll and Mary Wells Ashworth (Vol. 7)

1959 *Woodrow Wilson, American Prophet.* Arthur Walworth

1960 *John Paul Jones.* Samuel Eliot Morison

1961 *Charles Sumner and the Coming of the Civil War.* David Donald

1963 *Henry James: Vol. II, The Conquest of London, 1870–1881; Vol. III, The Middle Years, 1881–1895.* Leon Edel

1964 *John Keats.* Walter Jackson Bate

1965 *Henry Adams* (3 Vols.). Ernest Samuels

1966 *A Thousand Days.* Arthur M. Schlesinger, Jr.

1967 *Mr. Clemens and Mark Twain.* Justin Kaplan

1968 *Memoirs, 1925–1950.* George F. Kennan

1969 *The Man From New York.* B. L. Reid

1970 *Huey Long.* T. Harry Williams

1971 *Robert Frost: The Years of Triumph, 1915–1938.* Lawrence Thompson

1972 *Eleanor and Franklin: The Story of Their Relationship Based on Eleanor Roosevelt's Private Papers.* Joseph P. Lash

1973 *Luce and His Empire.* W. A. Swanberg

1974 *O'Neill, Son and Artist.* Louis Sheaffer

1975 *The Power Broker: Robert Moses and the Fall of New York.* Robert A. Caro

1976 *Edith Wharton: A Biography.* Richard W. B. Lewis

1977 *A Prince of Our Disorder.* John E. Mack

1978 *Samuel Johnson.* Walter Jackson Bate

1979 *Days of Sorrow and Pain: Leo Baeck and the Berlin Jews.* Leonard Baker

1980 *The Rise of Theodore Roosevelt.* Edmund Morris

1981 *Peter the Great.* Robert K. Massie

1982 *Grant: A Biography.* William S. McFeely

1983 *Growing Up.* Russell Baker

1984 *Booker T. Washington.* Louis R. Harlan

1985 *The Life and Times of Cotton Mather,* Kenneth Silverman

1986 *Louise Bogan: A Portrait,* Elizabeth Frank

## POETRY[1]

1918 *Love Songs.* Sara Teasdale

1919 *Old Road to Paradise.* Margaret Widdemer; *Corn Huskers.* Carl Sandburg

1922 *Collected Poems.* Edwin Arlington Robinson

1923 *The Ballad of the Harp-Weaver; A Few Figs from Thistles;* eight sonnets in *American Poetry, 1922, A Miscellany.* Edna St. Vincent Millay

1924 *New Hampshire: A Poem With Notes and Grace Notes.* Robert Frost

1925 *The Man Who Died Twice.* Edwin Arlington Robinson

1926 *What's O'Clock.* Amy Lowell

1927 *Fiddler's Farewell.* Leonora Speyer

1928 *Tristram.* Edwin Arlington Robinson

1929 *John Brown's Body.* Stephen Vincent Benét

1930 *Selected Poems.* Conrad Aiken

1931 *Collected Poems.* Robert Frost

1932 *The Flowering Stone.* George Dillon

1933 *Conquistador.* Archibald MacLeish

1934 *Collected Verse.* Robert Hillyer

1935 *Bright Ambush.* Audrey Wurdemann

1936 *Strange Holiness.* Robert P. T. Coffin

1937 *A Further Range.* Robert Frost

1938 *Cold Morning Sky.* Marya Zaturenska

1939 *Selected Poems.* John Gould Fletcher

1940 *Collected Poems.* Mark Van Doren

1941 *Sunderland Capture.* Leonard Bacon

1942 *The Dust Which Is God.* William Rose Benét

1943 *A Witness Tree.* Robert Frost

1944 *Western Star.* Stephen Vincent Benét

1. This prize was established in 1922. The 1918 and 1919 awards were made from gifts provided by the Poetry Society.

1945 *V-Letter and Other Poems.* Karl Shapiro
1947 *Lord Weary's Castle.* Robert Lowell
1948 *The Age of Anxiety.* W. H. Auden
1949 *Terror and Decorum.* Peter Viereck
1950 *Annie Allen.* Gwendolyn Brooks
1951 *Complete Poems.* Carl Sandburg
1952 *Collected Poems.* Marianne Moore
1953 *Collected Poems, 1917–1952.* Archibald MacLeish
1954 *The Waking.* Theodore Roethke
1955 *Collected Poems.* Wallace Stevens
1956 *Poems—North & South.* Elizabeth Bishop
1957 *Things of This World.* Richard Wilbur
1958 *Promises: Poems, 1954–1956.* Robert Penn Warren
1959 *Selected Poems, 1928–1958.* Stanley Kunitz
1960 *Heart's Needle.* William Snodgrass
1961 *Times Three: Selected Verse From Three Decades.* Phyllis McGinley
1962 *Poems.* Alan Dugan
1963 *Pictures From Breughel.* William Carlos Williams
1964 *At the End of the Open Road.* Louis Simpson
1965 *77 Dream Songs.* John Berryman
1966 *Selected Poems.* Richard Eberhart
1967 *Live or Die.* Anne Sexton
1968 *The Hard Hours.* Anthony Hecht
1969 *Of Being Numerous.* George Oppen
1970 *Untitled Subjects.* Richard Howard
1971 *The Carrier of Ladders.* William S. Merwin
1972 *Collected Poems.* James Wright
1973 *Up Country.* Maxine Winokur Kumin
1974 *The Dolphin.* Robert Lowell
1975 *Turtle Island.* Gary Snyder
1976 *Self-Portrait in a Convex Mirror.* John Ashbery
1977 *Divine Comedies.* James Merrill
1978 *Collected Poems.* Howard Nemerov: *Poems, 1976–1978.*
1979 *Now and Then.* Robert Penn Warren.
1980 *Selected Poems.* Donald Rodney Justice
1981 *The Morning of the Poem.* James Schuyler
1982 *The Collected Poems.* Sylvia Plath
1983 *Selected Poems.* Galway Kinnell
1984 *American Primitive.* Mary Oliver
1985 *Yin,* Carolyn Kizer
1986 *The Flying Change,* Henry Taylor

## GENERAL NONFICTION

1962 *The Making of the President, 1960.* Theodore H. White
1963 *The Guns of August.* Barbara W. Tuchman
1964 *Anti-Intellectualism in American Life.* Richard Hofstadter
1965 *O Strange New World.* Howard Mumford Jones
1966 *Wandering Through Winter.* Edwin Way Teale
1967 *The Problem of Slavery in Western Culture.* David Brion Davis
1968 *Rousseau and Revolution.* Will and Ariel Durant
1969 *So Human an Animal.* Rene Jules Dubos; *The Armies of the Night.* Norman Mailer
1970 *Gandhi's Truth.* Erik H. Erikson
1971 *The Rising Sun.* John Toland
1972 *Stilwell and the American Experience in China, 1911–1945.* Barbara W. Tuchman
1973 *Fire in the Lake: The Vietnamese and the Americans in Vietnam.* Frances FitzGerald; and *Children of Crisis* (Vols. 1 and 2). Robert M. Coles
1974 *The Denial of Death.* Ernest Becker
1975 *Pilgrim at Tinker Creek.* Annie Dillard
1976 *Why Survive? Being Old in America.* Robert N. Butler

1977 *Beautiful Swimmers: Watermen, Crabs and the Chesapeake Bay.* William W. Warner
1978 *The Dragons of Eden.* Carl Sagan
1979 *On Human Nature.* Edward O. Wilson
1980 *Gödel, Escher, Bach: An Eternal Golden Braid.* Douglas R. Hofstadter
1981 *Fin-de-Siecle Vienna: Politics and Culture.* Carl E. Schorske
1982 *The Soul of a New Machine.* Tracy Kidder
1983 *Is There No Place on Earth for Me?* Susan Sheehan
1984 *Social Transformation of American Medicine.* Paul Starr
1985 *The Good War: An Oral History of World War II,* Studs Terkel
1986 *Move Your Shadow: South Africa, Black and White,* Joseph Lelyveld

## PULITZER PRIZES IN MUSIC

1943 *Secular Cantata No. 2, A Free Song.* William Schuman
1944 *Symphony No. 4* (Op. 34). Howard Hanson
1945 *Appalachian Spring.* Aaron Copland
1946 *The Canticle of the Sun.* Leo Sowerby
1947 *Symphony No. 3.* Charles Ives
1948 *Symphony No. 3.* Walter Piston
1949 *Louisiana Story* music. Virgil Thomson
1950 *The Consul.* Gian Carlo Menotti
1951 Music for opera *Giants in the Earth.* Douglas Stuart Moore
1952 *Symphony Concertante.* Gail Kubik
1954 *Concerto for Two Pianos and Orchestra.* Quincy Porter
1955 *The Saint of Bleecker Street.* Gian Carlo Menotti
1956 *Symphony No. 3.* Ernst Toch
1957 *Meditations on Ecclesiastes.* Norman Dello Joio
1958 *Vanessa.* Samuel Barber
1959 *Concerto for Piano and Orchestra.* John La Montaine
1960 *Second String Quartet.* Elliott Carter
1961 *Symphony No. 7.* Walter Piston
1962 *The Crucible.* Robert Ward
1963 *Piano Concerto No. 1.* Samuel Barber
1966 *Variations for Orchestra.* Leslie Bassett
1967 *Quartet No. 3.* Leon Kirchner
1968 *Echoes of Time and the River.* George Crumb
1969 *String Quartet No. 3.* Karel Husa
1970 *Time's Encomium.* Charles Wuorinen
1971 *Synchronisms No. 6 for Piano and Electronic Sound.* Mario Davidowsky
1972 *Windows.* Jacob Druckman
1973 *String Quartet No. 3.* Elliott Carter
1974 *Notturno.* Donald Martino
1975 *From the Diary of Virginia Woolf.* Dominick Argento
1976 *Air Music.* Ned Rorem
1977 *Visions of Terror and Wonder.* Richard Wernick
1978 *Déjà Vu for Percussion Quartet and Orchestra.* Michael Colgrass
1979 *Aftertones of Infinity.* Joseph Schwantner
1980 *In Memory of a Summer Day.* David Del Tredici
1981 Not awarded
1982 *Concerto for Orchestra.* Roger Sessions
1983 *Three Movements for Orchestra.* Ellen T. Zwilich
1984 *Canti del Sole.* Bernard Rands
1985 *Symphony RiverRun,* Stephen Albert
1986 *Wind Quintet IV,* George Perle

# New York Drama Critics' Circle Awards

**1935–36**
*Winterset,* Maxwell Anderson
**1936–37**
*High Tor,* Maxwell Anderson
**1937–38**
*Of Mice and Men,* John Steinbeck
*Shadow and Substance,* Paul Vincent Carroll[1]
**1938–39**
(No award) *The White Steed,* Paul Vincent Carroll[1]
**1939–40**
*The Time of Your Life,* William Saroyan
**1940–41**
*Watch on the Rhine,* Lillian Hellman
*The Corn Is Green,* Emlyn Williams[1]
**1941–42**
(No award) *Blithe Spirit,* Noel Coward[1]
**1942–43**
*The Patriots,* Sidney Kingsley
**1943–44**
(No award) *Jacobowsky and the Colonel.* Franz
   Werfel and S. N. Behrman[1]
**1944–45**
*The Glass Menagerie,* Tennessee Williams
**1945–46**
(No award) *Carousel,* Richard Rodgers and Oscar
   Hammerstein II[2]
**1946–47**
*All My Sons,* Arthur Miller
*No Exit,* Jean-Paul Sartre[1]
*Brigadoon,* Alan Jay Lerner and Frederick Loewe[2]
**1947–48**
*A Streetcar Named Desire,* Tennessee Williams
*The Winslow Boy,* Terence Rattigan[1]
**1948–49**
*Death of a Salesman,* Arthur Miller
*The Madwoman of Chaillot,* Jean Giraudoux and
   Maurice Valency[1]
*South Pacific,* Richard Rodgers, Oscar
   Hammerstein II, and Joshua Logan[2]
**1949–50**
*The Member of the Wedding,* Carson McCullers
*The Cocktail Party,* T. S. Eliot[1]
*The Consul,* Gian Carlo Menotti[2]
**1950–51**
*Darkness at Noon,* Sidney Kingsley[3]
*The Lady's Not for Burning,* Christopher Fry[1]
*Guys and Dolls,* Abe Burrows, Jo Swerling, and
   Frank Loesser[2]
**1951–52**
*I Am a Camera,* John Van Druten[4]
*Venus Observed,* Christopher Fry[1]
*Pal Joey,* Richard Rodgers, Lorenz Hart, and John
   O'Hara[2]
*Don Juan in Hell,* George B. Shaw[5]
**1952–53**
*Picnic,* William Inge
*The Love of Four Colonels,* by Peter Ustinov[1]
*Wonderful Town,* Joseph Fields, Jerome Chodorov,
   Betty Comden, Adolph Green, and Leonard
   Bernstein[2]
**1953–54**
*The Teahouse of the August Moon,* John Patrick
*Ondine,* Jean Giraudoux[1]
*The Golden Apple,* John Latouche and Jerome
   Moross[2]
**1954–55**
*Cat on a Hot Tin Roof,* Tennessee Williams
*Witness for the Prosecution,* Agatha Christie[1]
*The Saint of Bleecker Street,* Gian Carlo Menotti[2]
**1955–56**
*The Diary of Anne Frank,* Frances Goodrich and
   Albert Hackett

*Tiger at the Gates,* Jean Giraudoux and
   Christopher Fry[1]
*My Fair Lady,* Frederick Loewe and Alan Jay
   Lerner[2]
**1956–57**
*Long Day's Journey Into Night,* Eugene O'Neill
*Waltz of the Toreadors,* Jean Anouilh[1]
*The Most Happy Fella,* Frank Loesser[2] [6]
**1957–58**
*Look Homeward, Angel,* Ketti Frings[7]
*Look Back in Anger,* John Osborne[1]
*The Music Man,* Meredith Willson[2]
**1958–59**
*A Raisin in the Sun,* Lorraine Hansberry
*The Visit,* Friedrich Duerrenmatt-Maurice Valency[1]
*La Plume de ma Tante,* Robert Dhery and Gerard
   Calvi[2]
**1959–60**
*Toys in the Attic,* Lillian Hellman
*Five Finger Exercise,* Peter Shaffer[1]
*Fiorello!,* Jerome Weidman, George Abbott, Jerry
   Bock, and Sheldon Harnick[2]
**1960–61**
*All the Way Home,* Tad Mosel[3]
*A Taste of Honey,* Shelagh Delaney[1]
*Carnival,* Michael Stewart[2]
**1961–62**
*The Night of the Iguana,* Tennessee Williams
*A Man for All Seasons,* Robert Bolt[1]
*How to Succeed in Business Without Really Trying,*
   Abe Burrows, Jack Weinstock, Willie Gilbert, and
   Frank Loesser[2] [9]
**1962–63**
*Who's Afraid of Virginia Woolf?,* Edward Albee
*Beyond the Fringe,* Alan Bennett, Peter Cook,
   Jonathan Miller, and Dudley Moore[10]
**1963–64**
*Luther,* John Osborne
*Hello, Dolly!,* Michael Stewart and Jerry
   Herman[2] [11]
*The Trojan Women,* Euripides[10] [12]
**1964–65**
*The Subject Was Roses,* Frank D. Gilroy
*Fiddler on the Roof,* Joseph Stein, Jerry Bock, and
   Sheldon Harnick[2] [13]
**1965–66**
*The Persecution and Assassination of Marat as
   Performed by the Inmates of the Asylum of
   Charenton Under the Direction of the Marquis
   de Sade,* Peter Weiss
*The Man of La Mancha,* Dale Wasserman, Mitch
   Leigh, and Joe Darion
**1966–67**
*The Homecoming,* Harold Pinter
*Cabaret,* Joe Masteroff, John Kander, and Fred
   Ebb[2] [14]
**1967–68**
*Rosencrantz and Guildenstern Are Dead,* Tom
   Stoppard
*Your Own Thing,* Donald Driver, Hal Hester, and
   Danny Apolinar[2]
**1968–69**
*The Great White Hope,* Howard Sackler
*1776,* Sherman Edwards and Peter Stone[2]
**1969–70**
*Borstal Boy,* Frank McMahon[15]
*The Effect of Gamma Rays on Man-in-the-Moon
   Marigolds,* Paul Zindel[16]
*Company,* George Furth and Stephen Sondheim[2]
**1970–71**
*Home,* David Storey
*The House of Blue Leaves,* John Guare[16]

*Follies*, James Goldman and Stephen Sondheim[2]
**1971–72**
*That Championship Season*, Jason Miller
*Two Gentlemen of Verona*, adapted by John Guare and Mel Shapiro[2]
*The Screens*, Jean Genet[1]
**1972–73**
*The Changing Room*, David Storey
*The Hot l Baltimore*, by Lanford Wilson[16]
*A Little Night Music*, Hugh Wheeler and Stephen Sondheim[2]
**1973–74**
*The Contractors*, David Storey
*Short Eyes*, Miguel Piñero[16]
*Candide*, Leonard Bernstein, Hugh Wheeler, and Richard Wilbur[2]
**1974–75**
*Equus*, Peter Shaffer
*The Taking of Miss Janie*, Ed Bullins[16]
*A Chorus Line*, James Kirkwood and Nicholas Dante[2]
**1975–76**
*Travesties*, Tom Stoppard
*Streamers*, David Rabe[16]
*Pacific Overtures*, Stephen Sondheim, John Weidman, and Hugh Wheeler[2]
**1976–77**
*Otherwise Engaged*, Simon Gray
*American Buffalo*, David Marmet[16]
*Annie*, Thomas Meehan, Charles Strouse, and Martin Charnin[2]
**1977–78**
*Da*, Hugh Leonard
*Ain't Misbehavin'*, conceived by Richard Maltby, Jr.[2]
**1978–79**
*The Elephant Man*, Bernard Pomerance
*Sweeney Todd*, Hugh Wheeler and Stephen Sondheim[2]
**1979–80**
*Talley's Folly*, Lanford Wilson

*Evita*,[2] Andrew Lloyd Webber and Tim Rice
*Betrayal*, Harold Pinter[1]
**1980–81**
*A Lesson From Aloes*, Athol Fugard
*Crimes of the Heart*, Beth Henley[16]
**1981–82**
*The Life and Adventures of Nicholas Nickleby*, adapted by David Edgar
*A Soldier's Play*, Charles Fuller[16]
**1982–83**
*Brighton Beach Memoirs*, Neil Simon
*Plenty*, David Hare[1]
*Little Shop of Horrors*, Alan Menken and Howard Ashman[2] [17]
**1983–84**
*The Real Thing*, Tom Stoppard
*Glengarry Glen Ross*, David Mamet[16]
*Sunday in the Park with George*, Stephen W Sondheim and James Lapine[2]
**1984-85**
*Ma Rainey's Black Bottom*, August Wilson
(No award for best musical or foreign play)
**1985–86**
*Lie of the Mind*, Sam Shepard
*Benefactors*, Michael Frayn[1]
*The Search for Signs of Intelligent Life in the Universe*, Lily Tomlin and Jane Wagner[18]
(No award for best musical)

1. Citation for best foreign play. 2. Citation for best musical. 3. Based on a novel by Arthur Koestler. 4. Based on Christopher Isherwood's *Berlin Stories*. 5. For "distinguished and original contribution to the theater." 6. Based on Sidney Howard's *They Knew What They Wanted*. 7. Based on a novel by Thomas Wolfe. 8. Based on James Agee's *A Death in the Family*. 9. Based on a book by Shepherd Mead. 10. Special citation. 11. Based on Thornton Wilder's *The Matchmaker*. 12. Translated by Edith Hamilton. 13. Based on Sholem Aleichem's Tevye stories, translated by Arnold Perl. 14. Based on John Van Druten's *I Am a Camera*, which won the award for the best play in 1951–52. 15. Based on Brendan Behan's autobiography. 16. Citation for best American play. 17. Based on a story by Roger Corman. 18. Special citation.

## Antoinette Perry (Tony) Awards, 1986

**Dramatic Play:** *I'm Not Rappaport*, Herb Gardner
**Musical:** *The Mystery of Edwin Drood*
**Actor (play):** Judd Hirsch, *I'm Not Rappaport*
**Actress (play):** Lily Tomlin, *The Search for Signs of Intelligent Life in the Universe*
**Actor, featured (play):** John Mahoney, *The House of Blue Leaves*
**Actress, featured (play):** Swoosie Kurtz, *The House of Blue Leaves*
**Actor (musical):** George Rose, *The Mystery of Edwin Drood*
**Actress (musical):** Bernadette Peters, *Song & Dance*
**Actor, featured (musical):** Michael Rupert, *Sweet Charity*

**Actress, featured (musical):** Bebe Neuwirth, *Sweet Charity*
**Director (play):** Jerry Zaks, *The House of Blue Leaves*
**Director (musical):** Wilford Leach, *The Mystery of Edwin Drood*
**Score:** Rupert Holmes, *The Mystery of Edwin Drood*
**Musical book:** Rupert Holmes, *The Mystery of Edwin Drood*
**Scenic design:** Tony Walton, *The House of Blue Leaves*
**Costumes:** Patricia Zipprodt, *Sweet Charity*
**Lighting:** Pat Collins, *I'm Not Rappaport*
**Choreography:** Bob Fosse, *Big Deal*
**Reproduction of a play or musical:** *Sweet Charity*

## National Book Critics Circle Awards, 1986

**Fiction:** *The Accidental Tourist*, by Anne Tyler (Alfred A. Knopf)
**General nonfiction:** *Common Ground: A Turbulent Decade in the Lives of Three American Families*, by J. Anthony Lukas (Alfred A. Knopf)
**Poetry:** *The Triumph of Achilles*, by Louise Gluck, (Ecco Press)
**Criticism:** *Habitations of the Word*, by William H.

Gass (Simon & Schuster)
**Biography/autobiography:** *Henry James: A Life*, by Leon Edel (Harper & Row)
In addition the Critics Circle awarded a citation for outstanding criticism to Sven Birkerts, a freelance book critic, whose reviews appear in *Parnassus* and other magazines.

# Major Grammy Awards for Recording in 1985

*Source:* National Academy of Recording Arts and Sciences.

**Record:** "We Are the World," USA for Africa (Columbia/CBS)

**Album:** "No Jacket Required," Phil Collins (Atlantic)

**Song:** "We Are the World," Michael Jackson and Lionel Richie

**New Artist:** Sade

**Pop Vocalists:** Whitney Houston, "Saving All My Love for You" (Arista); Phil Collins, "No Jacket Required" (Atlantic)

**Pop Group:** USA for Africa, "We Are the World" (Columbia/CBS)

**Pop Instrumentalist:** Jan Hammer, "Miami Vice Theme" (MCA)

**Rock Vocalists:** Tina Turner, "One of the Living" (Capitol); Don Henley, "The Boys of Summer" (Geffen)

**Rock Group:** Dire Straits, "Money for Nothing" (Warner Bros.)

**Rock Instrumentalist:** Jeff Beck, "Escape" (track from "Flash") (Epic/CBS)

**Rhythm and Blues Vocalists:** Aretha Franklin, "Freeway of Love" (Arista); Stevie Wonder, "In Square Circle" (Tamla/Motown)

**Rhythm and Blues Group:** Commodores, "Nightshift" (Gordy/Motown)

**Rhythm and Blues Instrumentalist:** Ernie Watts, "Musican" (Qwest)

**Rhythm and Blues Song:** "Freeway of Love," Narada Michael Walden and Jeffrey Cohen

**Traditional Blues:** "My Guitar Sings the Blues" (track from "Six Silver Strings") B.B. King (MCA)

**Country Vocalists:** Rosanne Cash, "I Don't Know Why You Don't Want Me" (CBS)

Ronnie Milsap, "Lost in the Fifties Tonight (In the Still of the Night)" (RCA)

**Country Group:** The Judds—Wynonna and Naomi, "Why Not Me" (RCA)

**Country Instrumentalists:** Chet Atkins and Mark Knopfler, "Cosmic Square Dance" (track from Chet Atkins' album "Stay Tuned") (Columbia/CBS)

**Country Song:** "Highwayman," Jimmy L. Webb (Columbia/CBS)

**Jazz Vocalists:** Cleo Laine, "Cleo at Carnegie" (The 10th Anniversary Concert) (DRG); Jon Hendricks and Bobby McFerrin, "Another Night in Tunisia" (track from "Vocalese") (Atlantic)

**Jazz Instrumentalists:** Soloist, Wynton Marsalis, "Black Codes from the Underground" (Columbia/CBS); group, Wynton Marsalis Group, "Black Codes from the Underground" (Columbia/CBS)

**Jazz, Big Band:** John Barry & Bob Wilber, "The Cotton Club/ Original Motion Picture Soundtrack" (Geffen)

**Jazz Fusion:** David Samborn, "Straight to the Heart" (Warner Bros.)

**Gospel Vocalists:** Amy Grant, "Unguarded" (Myrrh/Word); Larnelle Harris, "How Excellent Is Thy Name" (track from "I've Just Seen Jesus") (Benson)

**Gospel Group:** Larnelle Harris and Sandi Patti, "I've Just Seen Jesus" (Impact/Benson)

**Soul Gospel Vocalists:** Shirley Caesar, "Martin" (Rejoice/Word); Marvin Winans, "Bring Back the Days of Yea and Nay" (track from "Tomorrow, the Winans") (Light)

**Soul Gospel Group:** The Winans, "Tomorrow" (Light)

**Inspirational:** Jennifer Holliday, "Come Sunday" (track from "Say You Love Me") (Geffen)

**Ethnic or Traditional:** Rockin' Sidney, "My Toot Toot" (Maison De Soul)

**Reggae:** Jimmy Cliff, "Cliff Hanger" (Columbia/CBS)

**Latin Pop:** Lani Hall, "Es Facil Amar" (A&M)

**Tropical Latin:** Tito Puente and His Latin Ensemble, "Mambo Diablo" (Concord Jazz) and Eddie Palmieri, "Solito" (Musica Latina International)

**Mexican/American:** Vikki Carr, "Simplemente Mujer" (Discos CBS International)

**For Children:** "Follow That Bird" (the original motion picture sound track) Jim Henson's Muppets and the Sesame Street cast (RCA)

**Comedy:** "Whoopi Goldberg" (original Broadway show recording) Whoopi Goldberg (Geffen)

**Spoken Word:** "Ma Rainey's Black Bottom," original Broadway cast (Manhattan)

**Instrumental Composition:** Jan Hammer, "Miami Vice Theme" (MCA)

**Instrumental Arrangement:** Dave Grusin and Lee Ritenour, "Early A.M. Attitude" (track from "Harlequin") (GRP)

**Motion Picture Score:** "Beverly Hills Cop," Sharon Robinson, Jon Gilutin, Bunny Hull, Hawk, Howard Hewett, Micki Free, Sue Sheridan, Howie Rice, Keith Forsey, Harold Faltermeyer, Allee Willis, Dan Sembello, Marc Benno, and Richard Theisen (MCA)

**Cast Show Album:** "West Side Story," John McClure, Album Producer (Deutsche Grammophon)

**Video-Short Form:** "We Are the World," USA for Africa (RCA/Columbia Pictures Home Video)

**Video-Long Form:** "Huey Lewis and the News, The Heart of Rock 'N' Roll," Huey Lewis and the News (Warner Home Video)

**Historical Album:** "100 Singers——100 Years" (RCA/Met)

**Classical Album:** "Berlioz: Requiem," Robert Shaw, conductor, Atlanta Symphony Orchestra and Chorus (Telarc)

**Classical Orchestral Recording:** "Faure: Pelleas et Melisande," Robert Shaw, conductor, Atlanta Symphony Orchestra

**Classical Soloist with Orchestra:** "Elgar, Cello Concerto Op. 85/Walton, Concerto for Cello & Orchestra," Yo-Yo Ma (CBS Masterworks)

**Classical Soloist without Orchestra:** "Ravel: Gaspard de la Nuit, Pavane pour Une Infante Defunte, Valses Nobles et Sentimentales," Vladimir Ashkenazy (London)

**Chamber Music:** "Brahms: Cello and Piano Sonatas in E Minor and F Major," Emanuel Ax and Yo-Yo Ma (RCA)

**Classical Vocal Soloist:** John Aler, "Berlioz: Requiem" (Telarc)

**Classical, Choral:** "Berlioz: Requiem," Robert Shaw, conductor, Atlanta Symphony Chorus and Orchestra (Telarc)

**Opera:** "Schoenberg: Moses und Aron," Sir Georg Solti, conductor, Chicago Symphony Orchestra

**New Classical Artist:** Chicago Pro Musica (Reference)

**Contemporary Composition:** "Requiem," Andrew Lloyd Webber (Angel)

**Producers:** Non-Classical, Phil Collins and Hugh Padgham; Classical, Robert E. Woods

# Presidential Medal of Freedom

The nation's highest civilian award, the Presidential Medal of Freedom, was established in 1963 by President John F. Kennedy to continue and expand Presidential recognition of meritorious service which, since 1945, had been granted as the Medal of Freedom. Kennedy selected the first recipients, but was assassinated before he could make the presentations. They were made by President Johnson. NOTE: An asterisk following a year denotes a posthumous award.

## SELECTED BY PRESIDENT KENNEDY

| | |
|---|---|
| Marian Anderson (contralto) | 1963 |
| Ralph J. Bunche (statesman) | 1963 |
| Ellsworth Bunker (diplomat) | 1963 |
| Pablo Casals (cellist) | 1963 |
| Genevieve Caulfield (educator) | 1963 |
| James B. Conant (educator) | 1963 |
| John F. Enders (bacteriologist) | 1963 |
| Felix Frankfurter (jurist) | 1963 |
| Karl Horton (youth authority) | 1963 |
| Robert J. Kiphuth (athletic director) | 1963 |
| Edwin H. Land (inventor) | 1963 |
| Herbert H. Lehman (statesman) | 1963* |
| Robert A. Lovett (statesman) | 1963 |
| J. Clifford MacDonald (educator) | 1963* |
| John J. McCloy (banker and statesman) | 1963 |
| George Meany (labor leader) | 1963 |
| Alexander Meiklejohn (philosopher) | 1963 |
| Ludwig Mies van der Rohe (architect) | 1963 |
| Jean Monnet (European statesman) | 1963 |
| Luis Muñoz-Marin (Governor of Puerto Rico) | 1963 |
| Clarence B. Randall (industrialist) | 1963 |
| Rudolf Serkin (pianist) | 1963 |
| Edward Steichen (photographer) | 1963 |
| George W. Taylor (educator) | 1963 |
| Alan T. Waterman (scientist) | 1963 |
| Mark S. Watson (journalist) | 1963 |
| Annie D. Wauneka (public health worker) | 1963 |
| E. B. White (author) | 1963 |
| Thornton N. Wilder (author) | 1963 |
| Edmund Wilson (author and critic) | 1963 |
| Andrew Wyeth (artist) | 1963 |

## AWARDED BY PRESIDENT JOHNSON

| | |
|---|---|
| Dean G. Acheson (statesman) | 1964 |
| Eugene R. Black (banker) | 1969 |
| Detlev W. Bronk (neurophysiologist) | 1964 |
| McGeorge Bundy (government service) | 1969 |
| Ellsworth Bunker (diplomat) | 1968 |
| Clark Clifford (statesman) | 1969 |
| Aaron Copland (composer) | 1964 |
| Michael E. DeBakey (surgeon) | 1969 |
| Willem de Kooning (artist) | 1964 |
| Walt Disney (cartoon film producer) | 1964 |
| J. Frank Dobie (author) | 1964 |
| David Dubinsky (labor leader) | 1969 |
| Lena F. Edwards (physician and humanitarian) | 1964 |
| Thomas Stearns Eliot (poet) | 1964 |
| Ralph Ellison (author) | 1969 |
| Lynn Fontanne (actress) | 1964 |
| Henry Ford II (industrialist) | 1969 |
| John W. Gardner (educator) | 1964 |
| W. Averell Harriman (statesman) | 1969 |
| Rev. Theodore M. Hesburgh (educator) | 1964 |
| Bob Hope (comedian) | 1969 |
| John XXIII (Pope) | 1963* |
| Clarence L. Johnson (aircraft engineer) | 1964 |
| Edgar F. Kaiser (industrialist) | 1969 |
| Frederick R. Kappel (telecommunications executive) | 1964 |
| Helen A. Keller (educator) | 1964 |
| John Fitzgerald Kennedy (U.S. President) | 1963* |
| Robert W. Komer (government service) | 1968 |
| Mary Lasker (philanthropist) | 1969 |
| John L. Lewis (labor leader) | 1964 |
| Walter Lippmann (journalist) | 1964 |
| Eugene M. Locke (diplomat) | 1968 |

| | |
|---|---|
| Alfred Lunt (actor) | 1964 |
| John W. Macy, Jr. (government service) | 1969 |
| Ralph McGill (journalist) | 1964 |
| Robert S. McNamara (government service) | 1968 |
| Samuel Eliot Morison (historian) | 1964 |
| Lewis Mumford (urban planner and critic) | 1964 |
| Edward R. Murrow (radio-TV commentator) | 1964 |
| Reinhold Niebuhr (theologian) | 1964 |
| Gregory Peck (actor) | 1969 |
| Leontyne Price (soprano) | 1964 |
| A. Philip Randolph (labor leader) | 1964 |
| Laurance S. Rockefeller (conservationist) | 1969 |
| Walt Whitman Rostow (government service) | 1969 |
| Dean Rusk (statesman) | 1969 |
| Carl Sandburg (poet and biographer) | 1964 |
| Merriman Smith (journalist) | 1969 |
| John Steinbeck (author) | 1964 |
| Helen B. Taussig (pediatrician) | 1964 |
| Cyrus R. Vance (government service) | 1969 |
| Carl Vinson (legislator) | 1964 |
| Thomas J. Watson, Jr. (industrialist) | 1964 |
| James E. Webb (NASA administrator) | 1968 |
| Paul Dudley White (physician) | 1964 |
| William S. White (journalist) | 1969 |
| Roy Wilkins (social welfare executive) | 1969 |
| Whitney M. Young, Jr. (social welfare executive) | 1969 |

## AWARDED BY PRESIDENT NIXON

| | |
|---|---|
| Edwin E. Aldrin (astronaut) | 1969 |
| Apollo 13 Mission Operations Team | 1970 |
| Neil A. Armstrong (astronaut) | 1969 |
| Earl Charles Behrens (journalist) | 1970 |
| Manlio Brosio (NATO secretary general) | 1971 |
| Michael Collins (astronaut) | 1969 |
| Edward K. (Duke) Ellington (musician) | 1969 |
| Edward T. Folliard (journalist) | 1970 |
| John Ford (film director) | 1973 |
| Samuel Goldwyn (film producer) | 1971 |
| Fred Wallace Haise, Jr. (astronaut) | 1970 |
| William M. Henry (journalist) | 1970* |
| Paul G. Hoffman (statesman) | 1974 |
| William J. Hopkins (White House service) | 1971 |
| Arthur Krock (journalist) | 1970 |
| Melvin R. Laird (government service) | 1974 |
| David Lawrence (journalist) | 1970 |
| George Gould Lincoln (journalist) | 1970 |
| James A. Lovell, Jr. (astronaut) | 1970 |
| Dr. Charles L. Lowman (orthopedist) | 1974 |
| Raymond Moley (journalist) | 1970 |
| Eugene Ormandy (conductor) | 1970 |
| William P. Rogers (diplomat) | 1973 |
| Adela Rogers St. Johns (journalist) | 1970 |
| John Leonard Swigert, Jr. (astronaut) | 1970 |
| John Paul Vann (adviser, Vietnam war) | 1972* |
| DeWitt and Lila Wallace (founders, *Reader's Digest*) | 1972 |

## AWARDED BY PRESIDENT FORD

| | |
|---|---|
| I. W. Abel (labor leader) | 1977 |
| John Bardeen (physicist) | 1977 |
| Irving Berlin (composer) | 1977 |
| Norman Borlaug (agricultural scientist) | 1977 |
| Gen. Omar N. Bradley (soldier) | 1977 |
| David K. E. Bruce (diplomat) | 1976 |
| Arleigh Burke (national security) | 1977 |
| Alexander Calder (sculptor) | 1977 |
| Bruce Catton (historian) | 1977 |

| | |
|---|---|
| Joseph P. DiMaggio (baseball star) | 1977 |
| Ariel Durant (author) | 1977 |
| Will Durant (author) | 1977 |
| Arthur Fiedler (conductor) | 1977 |
| Henry J. Friendly (jurist) | 1977 |
| Martha Graham (dancer-choreographer) | 1976 |
| Claudia "Lady Bird" Johnson (service to U.S. scenic beauty) | 1977 |
| Henry A. Kissinger (statesman) | 1977 |
| Archibald MacLeish (poet) | 1977 |
| James A. Michener (author) | 1977 |
| Georgia O'Keeffe (artist) | 1977 |
| Jesse Owens (track champion) | 1976 |
| Nelson A. Rockefeller (government service) | 1977 |
| Norman Rockwell (illustrator) | 1977 |
| Arthur Rubinstein (pianist) | 1976 |
| Donald H. Rumsfeld (government service) | 1977 |
| Katherine Filene Shouse (service to the performing arts) | 1977 |
| Lowell Thomas (radio-TV commentator) | 1977 |
| James D. Watson (biochemist) | 1977 |

**AWARDED BY PRESIDENT CARTER**

| | |
|---|---|
| Ansel Adams (photographer) | 1980 |
| Horace M. Albright (government service) | 1980 |
| Roger Baldwin (civil libertarian) | 1981 |
| Harold Brown (government service) | 1981 |
| Zbigniew Brzezinski (government service) | 1981 |
| Rachel Carson (author) | 1980* |
| Lucia Chase (ballet director) | 1980 |
| Warren M. Christopher (government service) | 1981 |
| Walter Cronkite (TV newscaster) | 1981 |
| Kirk Douglas (actor) | 1981 |
| Arthur J. Goldberg (government service) | 1978 |
| Hubert H. Humphrey (government service) | 1980* |
| Archbishop Iakovos (churchman) | 1980 |
| Lyndon B. Johnson (U.S. President) | 1980* |
| Rev. Dr. Martin Luther King, Jr. (civil rights leader) | 1977* |
| Margaret Craig McNamara (educator) | 1981 |
| Margaret Mead (anthropologist) | 1979* |
| Karl Menninger (psychiatrist) | 1981 |
| Clarence Mitchell, Jr. (civil rights leader) | 1980 |
| Edmund S. Muskie (government service) | 1981 |
| Esther Peterson (government service) | 1981 |
| Roger Tory Peterson (ornithologist) | 1980 |
| Adm. Hyman Rickover (national security) | 1980 |
| Jonas Salk (medical research) | 1977 |
| Beverly Sills (opera singer) | 1980 |
| Gerard C. Smith (government service) | 1981 |
| Robert S. Strauss (government service) | 1981 |
| Elbert Parr Tuttle (government service) | 1981 |
| Earl Warren (government service) | 1981* |
| Robert Penn Warren (author and poet) | 1980 |
| John Wayne (actor) | 1980* |
| Eudora Welty (author) | 1980 |
| Tennessee Williams (playwright) | 1980 |
| Andrew M. Young (government service) | 1981 |

**AWARDED BY PRESIDENT REAGAN**

| | |
|---|---|
| Walter H. Annenberg (publisher and diplomat) | 1986 |
| Howard H. Baker, Jr. (government service) | 1984 |
| George Balanchine (choreographer) | 1983 |
| Count Basie (jazz pianist) | 1985* |
| Earl (Red) Blaik (football coach) | 1986 |
| James H. (Eubie) Blake (composer-pianist) | 1981 |
| Paul W. (Bear) Bryant (football coach) | 1983* |
| James Burnham (editor-historian) | 1983 |
| James Francis Cagney (actor) | 1984 |
| Whittaker Chambers (public servant) | 1984* |
| James Cheek (educator) | 1983 |
| Leo Cherne (economist-humanitarian) | 1984 |
| Terence Cardinal Cooke, His Eminence (theologian) | 1984* |
| Denton Arthur Cooley, M.D. (heart surgeon) | 1984 |
| Jacques-Yves Cousteau (marine explorer) | 1985 |
| Tennessee Ernie Ford (singer) | 1984 |
| R. Buckminster Fuller (architect-geometrician) | 1983 |
| Hector P. Garcia, M.D. (humanitarian) | 1984 |
| Barry Goldwater (government service) | 1986 |
| Gen. Andrew J. Goodpaster (soldier-diplomat) | 1984 |
| Rev. Billy Graham (evangelist) | 1983 |
| Ella T. Grasso (Connecticut governor) | 1981* |
| Philip C. Habib (diplomat) | 1982 |
| Bryce N. Harlow (government service) | 1981 |
| Helen Hayes (actress) | 1986 |
| Eric Hoffer (philosopher-longshoreman) | 1983 |
| Jerome Holland (educator and ambassador) | 1985* |
| Sidney Hook (philosopher-educator) | 1985 |
| Jacob K. Javits (government service) | 1983 |
| Walter H. Judd (government service) | 1981 |
| Jeane J. Kirkpatrick (government service) | 1985 |
| Lincoln Kirstein (ballet director) | 1984 |
| Louis L'Amour (author) | 1984 |
| Morris I. Leibman (lawyer) | 1981 |
| George M. Low (educator and administrator NASA) | 1985* |
| Clare Booth Luce (author-diplomat) | 1983 |
| Dumas Malone (historian) | 1983 |
| Mabel Mercer (jazz singer) | 1983 |
| Norman Vincent Peale (theologian) | 1984 |
| Simon Ramo (industrialist) | 1983 |
| Frank Reynolds (TV anchor) | 1985* |
| Gen. Matthew B. Ridgway (soldier) | 1986 |
| S. Dillon Ripley (cultural and public service) | 1985 |
| Gen. Carlos P. Romulo (Philippino statesman) | 1984 |
| Jack Roosevelt Robinson (baseball player) | 1984* |
| Vermont Royster (journalist) | 1986 |
| Albert B. Sabin (medical research) | 1986 |
| Mohamed Anwar el-Sadat (statesman) | 1984* |
| Eunice Kennedy Shriver (humanitarian) | 1984 |
| Frank Sinatra (entertainer) | 1985 |
| Kate Smith (singer) | 1982 |
| James Stewart (actor) | 1985 |
| Mother Teresa (humanitarian) | 1985 |
| Charles B. Thornton (industrialist) | 1981 |
| Gen. Albert Coady Wedemeyer (national security) | 1985 |
| Charles E. Yeager (public service) | 1985 |

## Winners of Bollingen Prize in Poetry

($5,000 award is given biennially. It is administered by Yale University and the Bollingen Foundation.)

| | | | |
|---|---|---|---|
| 1949 | Ezra Pound | 1962 | John Hall Wheelock and Richard Eberhart |
| 1950 | Wallace Stevens | 1963 | Robert Frost |
| 1951 | John Crowe Ransom | 1965 | Horace Gregory |
| 1952 | Marianne Moore | 1967 | Robert Penn Warren |
| 1953 | Archibald MacLeish and William Carlos Williams | 1969 | John Berryman and Karl Shapiro |
| 1954 | W. H. Auden | 1971 | Richard Wilbur and Mona Van Duyn |
| 1955 | Léonie Adams and Louise Bogan | 1973 | James Merrill |
| 1956 | Conrad Aiken | 1975 | Archie Randolph Ammons |
| 1957 | Allen Tate | 1977 | David Ignatow |
| 1958 | E.E. Cummings | 1979 | W. S. Merwin |
| 1959 | Theodore Roethke | 1981 | Howard Nemerov and May Swenson |
| 1960 | Delmore Schwartz | 1983 | Anthony Hecht and John Hollander |
| 1961 | Yvor Winters | 1985 | John Ashbery and Fred Chappell |

# 1985-86 Obie Award Winners

**Best Performance:** Swoosie Kurtz, *The House of Blue Leaves*
**For Sustained Excellence in Performance:** Edward Herrmann; Kevin Kline
**For Sustained Achievement:** Mabou Mines
**For Distinguished Playwriting:** Wallace Shawn, *Aunt Dan and Lemon*
**Playwriting:** Eric Bogosian, *Drinking in America;* Martha Clarke, *Vienna: Lusthaus;* John Jesurun, *Deep Sleep;* Tadeusz Kantor, *Let the Artist Die;* Lee Nagrin, *Bird/Bear*
**For Performance:** Elisabeth Welch, *Time to Start Living;* Tom Cayler, *A Matter of Life and Death;* Dylan Baker, *Not About Heroes;* Kathryn Pogson, *Aunt Dan and Lemon;* Jill Eikenberry, *Lemon Sky and Life Under Water;* Josef Sommer, *Largo Desolato;* Elizabeth Wilson, *Anteroom;* Farley Granger, *Talley & Son;* Helen Stenborg, *Talley & Son;* Norma Aleandro, *About Love and Other Stories About Love*
**Direction:** Richard Foreman, *Largo Desolato*
**Costume Design:** Rita Ryack
**Lighting Design:** Paul Gallo
**Set Design:** Edward T. Gianfrancesco
**Music:** Genji Ito
**Cash Grants:** P.S. 122, Billie Holiday Theatre, and Mabou Mines

# Recipients of Kennedy Center Honors

The Kennedy Center for the Performing Arts in Washington, D.C., created its Honors awards in 1978 to recognize the achievements of five distinguished contributors to the performing arts. Following are the recipients:

**1978:** Marian Anderson (contralto), Fred Astaire (dancer-actor), Richard Rodgers (Broadway composer), Arthur Rubinstein (pianist), George Balanchine (choreographer).

**1979:** Ella Fitzgerald (jazz singer), Henry Fonda (actor), Martha Graham (dancer-choreographer), Tennessee Williams (playwright), Aaron Copland (composer).

**1980:** James Cagney (actor), Leonard Bernstein (composer-conductor), Agnes de Mille (choreographer), Lynn Fontanne (actress), Leontyne Price (soprano).

**1981:** Count Basie (jazz composer-pianist), Cary Grant (actor), Helen Hayes (actress), Jerome Robbins (choreographer), Rudolf Serkin (pianist).

**1982:** George Abbott (Broadway producer), Lillian Gish (actress), Benny Goodman (jazz clarinetist), Gene Kelly (dancer-actor), Eugene Ormandy (conductor).

**1983:** Katherine Dunham (dancer-choreographer), Elia Kazan (director-author), James Stewart (actor), Virgil Thomson (music critic-composer), Frank Sinatra (singer).

**1984:** Lena Horne (singer), Danny Kaye (comedian-actor), Gian Carlo Menotti (composer), Arthur Miller (playwright), Isaac Stern (violinist).

**1985:** Merce Cunningham (dancer-choreographer), Irene Dunne (actress), Bob Hope (comedian), Alan Jay Lerner (lyricist-playwright), Frederick Loewe (composer), Beverly Sills (soprano and opera administrator).

# 1986 Christopher Awards

## Adult Books

**The City of Joy,** by Dominique Lapierre, translated by Kathryn Spink (Doubleday)
**Healing from the War: Trauma and Transformation After Vietnam,** by Arthur Egendorf (Houghton Mifflin)
**My Quest for Beauty,** by Rollo May (Saybrook Press)
**Pope John XXIII: Shepherd of the Modern World,** by Peter Hebblethwaite (Doubleday)
**Such a Vision of the Street: Mother Teresa—The Spirit and the Work,** by Eileen Egan (Doubleday)

## Children's Books

**The Patchwork Quilt,** by Valerie Flournoy. Illustrated by Jerry Pinkney (Dial)
**Sarah, Plain and Tall,** by Patricia MacLachlan (Harper and Row Junior Books)
**Promise Not to Tell,** by Carolyn Polese. Illustrated by Jennifer Barrett (Human Sciences Press)
**Underdog,** by Marilyn Sachs (Doubleday)

**The Mount Rushmore Story,** by Judith St. George (G.P. Putnam's Sons)

## Television Specials

**ABC News Closeup—The Fire Unleashed** (CBS)
**Do You Remember Love** (CBS)
**The Living Planet—A Portrait of the Earth** (BBC/Time-Life/PBS/WGBH)
**Love Is Never Silent** (NBC)
**A Time to Live** (NBC)
**Out of the Darkness** (CBS)
**Wallenberg—A Hero's Story** (NBC)

## Films

**The Color Purple** (Warner Bros.)
**Marie** (MGM)
**The Official Story** (Almi Pictures, Inc.)
**Shoah** (New Yorker Films)

## Special Christopher Award

**We Are the World** recording

# American Library Association Awards for Children's Books, 1985

**John Newbery Medal for best book:** *Sarah, Plain and Tall*, Patricia MacLachlan (Harper & Row)
**Newbery Honor Books:** *Commodore Perry and the Land of the Shogun*, Rhoda Blumberg (Lothrop, Lee & Shepard); *Dogsong*, Gary Paulsen (Bradbury)
**Randolph Caldecott Medal for best picture book:** *The Polar Express*, written and illustrated by Chris Van Allsburg (Houghton Mifflin)
**Caldecott Honor Books:** *The Relatives Came*, by Cynthia Rylant and illustrated by Stephen Gammell (Bradbury); *King Bidgood's in the Bathtub* by Audrey Wood and illustrated by Don Wood (Harcourt Brace Jovanovich)
**Laura Ingalls Wilder Award for the entire body of an author's work:** Jean Fritz (Putnam)

# American Book Awards, 1985

Established by Association of American Publishers

**Fiction:** *White Noise* by Don Delillo (Elisabeth Sifton Books/Viking)
**First Fiction:** *Easy in the Islands* by Bob Shacochis (Crown Publishers)

**Nonfiction:** *Common Ground: A Turbulent Decade in the Lives of Three American Families* by J. Anthony Lukas (Alfred A. Knopf)

# 1985 World Hunger Media Awards

To encourage, honor, and reward those members of the media who have made significant contributions to bringing public attention to critical issues of world hunger, Kenny and Marianne Rogers created the World Hunger Media Awards.

The judging and distribution of the awards is overseen by World Hunger Year, Inc., the nonprofit organization founded by the late performer/humanitarian Harry Chapin. The awards are made in November at the United Nations.

1985 winners are:
**Best newspaper coverage:** James P. Gannon, *The Des Moines Register*, $7,500; David Willis, *The Christian Science Monitor*, $7,500
**Best periodical coverage:** Barbara Insel, *Foreign Affairs*, $5,000; Joseph Lelyveld, *The New York Times Magazine*, $5,000
**Best television coverage:** Mohamed Amin (Visnews) and Michael Buerk (BBC) for reports on the famine in Ethiopia, $7,500; Marcia Pons, Bob Salter, and James McEnelly, *In the Shadow of Plenty* (KENS), $7,500
**Best radio coverage:** Daniel Zwerdling and John McChesney, *Drought and Famine in Chad* (National Public Radio), $10,000
**Best photojournalism:** Stanley Grossfeld, *The Boston Globe* $10,000
**Best book:** Lloyd Timberlake, *Africa in Crisis* (Earthscan), $10,000
**Best cartoon:** Brian Duffy, "Soil Erosion" and "A Cry . . . I Heard a Cry," *The Des Moines Register*, $10,000

### Special Achievement Award

Each year the panel of judges selects an individual whose efforts deserve special recognition. The recipients of the $20,000 award have been:
**Harry Chapin,** humanitarian/performer (posthumously)
**Shri Vatsa Purushottam,** former Ambassador to the United Nations from India (posthumously)
**Nancy Amidei,** former director of the Food Research Action Center (FRAC) and a leading domestic hunger advocate
**James P. Grant,** UNICEF
The 1985 recipient is:
**Bob Geldof,** Irish rock musician who coordinated the Live Aid rock concerts for African famine relief

# 1986 United Nations Population Award

The Award seeks "to promote the solution of population questions through encouraging the efforts of people in population-related activities and increasing the awareness of population questions." It was established by the General Assembly in 1981 and is presented annually to an individual, to individuals or to an institution for the most outstanding contribution to increasing the awareness of population questions or to their solutions.

The Award consists of a citation, a gold medal and a monetary prize amounting to $25,000 to be shared equally if there is more than one laureate.

Winners to date are:

1983 Indira Gandhi, Prime Minister of India
Qian Xinzhong, Minister in Charge of the State Family Planning Commission and Deputy for the National People's Congress of China

1984 Carmen Miro of Panama, former Director of the Latin American Demographic Center
Sheldon Segal of the United States, Director of the Population Division of The Rockefeller Foundation

1985 International Planned Parenthood Federation, with headquarters in London, England, a federation of national family planning associations in 121 countries

1986 National Population Council of Mexico, an interministerial body responsible for coordinating population planning in Mexico in the context of socio-economic development.

# Medal of Liberty

Irving Berlin, songwriter (Russia)
Franklin Chang-Diaz, astronaut (Costa Rica)
Kenneth Clark, psychologist (Panama)
Hanna Holborn Gray, university president (Germany)
Bob Hope, comedian (England)
Henry A. Kissinger, statesman (Germany)

I.M. Pei, architect (China)
Itzhak Perlman, violinist (Israel)
James B. Reston, journalist (Scotland)
Albert B. Sabin, physician (Poland)
An Wang, industrialist (China)
Elie Wiesel, writer (Romania)

# American Video Awards

Best Female Performance: Aimee Mann, *Voices Carry*
Best Male Performance: Bruce Springsteen, *Glory Days*
Best Group Performance: Wham! *Wham! The Video*
Best New Artist: Sade
Best Pop Video: *Glory Days*, Bruce Springsteen

Urban Contemporary Video: *Party All the Time*, Eddie Murphy
Best Home Video: *Wham! The Video*, Wham!
Cinematography: *I'm On Fire*, Bruce Springsteen
Costume Design: *Material Girl*, Madonna
Choregraphy: *Material Girl*, Madonna

# 1986 National Medal of Arts

Marian Anderson, contralto
Frank Capra, film director
Aaron Copland, composer
Willem de Kooning, artist
Agnes de Mille, choreographer
Eva Le Gallienne, actress and teacher
Alan Lomax, folklorist

Lewis Mumford, philosopher and critic
Eudora Welty, writer
Patrons: Dominique de Menil, a Houston art collector; Seymour H. Knox, founder of the Albright Knox Gallery in Buffalo; Exxon Corporation for support of *Great Performances* on public television

# 1986 MacArthur Foundation Awards

The MacArthur Foundation Fellowships, which range from $164,000 to $300,000 given over a five-year period, are designed to free the recipients from economic pressures, enabling them to devote themselves to research, scholarship, or creative artistic pursuits. The awards are tax-free and there are no strings attached.

Paul R. Adams, professor of neurobiology at the State University of New York, Stony Brook, L.I.
Milton B. Babbitt, composer-theorist and educator, has taught at Princeton University
Christopher I. Beckwith, chairman of the Tibetan Studies Program at Indiana University
Richard M.A. Benson, a specialist in photographic technologies and adjunct associate professor at Yale University
Lester R. Brown, environmentalist and author, founder of the Worldwatch Institute
Caroline W. Bynum, professor of history at the University of Washington.
William A. Christian Jr, a historian, sociologist and author
Nancy Marguerite Farriss, professor of history at the University of Pennsylvania
Benedict H. Gross, professor of mathematics at Harvard University, best known for his work on number theory
Daryl Hine, poet, novelist, playwright
John Robert Horner, curator of paleontology for the Museum of the Rockies at Montana State University
Thomas C. Joe, founder of Center for the Study of

Social Policy and co-author of *By the Few for the Few*
David N. Keightley, professor of history at the University of California at Berkeley
Albert Libchaber, a specialist in nonlinear dynamics and professor at the University of Chicago
David Page, geneticist and Fellow of the Whitehead Institute of the Massachusetts Institute of Technology
George Perle, composer, author, and professor emeritus at the Aaron Copland School of Music at City University of New York
James Randi, professional magician and author of a biography of Houdini and other works
David Rudovsky, professor of law at the University of Pennsylvania, a civil liberties activist; and author
Robert M. Shapley, associate professor of neurophysiology at Rockefeller University
Leo Steinberg, Benjamin Franklin professor of history of art at the University of Pennsylvania, art critic, and author
Richard P. Turco, an expert in atmospheric science and program manager with R & D Associates in Marina del Rey, Calif.
Thomas Whiteside, author and journalist
Allan C. Wilson, professor of biochemistry at the University of California at Berkeley
Jay Wright, poet whose work explores the cultures of Africa and Mexico
Charles Wuorinen, composer-in-residence with the San Francisco Symphony and instructor at the Manhattan School of Music

# ENTERTAINMENT & CULTURE

## Notable Books, 1985

This list has been compiled by the Notable Books Council, Reference and Adult Services, a division of the American Library Association for use by the general reader and by librarians who work with adult readers. The titles were selected for their significant contribution to the expansion of knowledge or for the pleasure they can provide to adult readers. Criteria include wide general appeal and literary merit.

Adams, Ansel and Alinder, Mary Street, **Ansel Adams: An Autobiography,** Little Brown/New York Graphic Society
Allende, Isabel, **The House of the Spirits,** translated by Mayda Bogin, Knopf
Banks, Russell, **Continental Drift,** Harper
Caufield, Catherine, **In the Rainforest,** Knopf
Chute, Carolyn, **The Beans of Egypt, Maine,** Ticknor & Fields
Costantini, Humberto, **The Long Night of Francisco Sanctis,** translated by Norman Thomas di Giovanni, Harper
DeLillo, Don, **White Noise,** Viking/Elisabeth Sifton
Doctorow, E.L., **World's Fair,** Random
Duras, Marguerite, **The Lover,** translated by Barbara Bray, Pantheon
Gordon, Mary, **Men and Angels,** Random
Heaney, Seamus, **Station Island,** Farrar
Hewat, Alan, **Lady's Time,** Harper
Jones, G.C., **Growing Up Hard in Harlan County,** University Press of Kentucky
Kapuscinski, Ryszard, **Shah of Shahs,** translated by William R. Brand and Katarzyna Mroczkowska-Brand, HBJ/Helen and Kurt Wolff
Kidder, Tracy, **House,** Houghton
Kincaid, Jamaica, **Annie John,** Farrar
Lapierre, Dominique, **The City of Joy,** translated by Kathryn Spink, Doubleday
Lelyveld, Joseph, **Move Your Shadow: South Africa, Black and White,** Times Books
Lester, Julius, **Do Lord Remember Me: A Novel,** Holt

Lucie-Smith, Edward, **Art of the 1930's: The Age of Anxiety,** Rizzoli
Lukas, J. Anthony, **Common Ground: A Turbulent Decade in the Lives of Three American Families,** Knopf
McMurtry, Larry, **Lonesome Dove: A Novel,** Simon & Schuster
Maharidge, Dale, **Journey to Nowhere: The Saga of the New Underclass,** photos by Michael Williamson, Doubleday/Dial
Mo, Timothy, **Sour Sweet,** Random/Vintage
Physician Task Force on Hunger in America, **Hunger in America: The Growing Epidemic,** Wesleyan University Press
Reid, T.R., **The Chip: How Two Americans Invented the Microchip and Launched a Revolution,** Simon & Schuster
Robinson, David, **Chaplin: His Life and Art,** McGraw-Hill
Schell, Orville, **To Get Rich Is Glorious: China in the Eighties,** Pantheon
Seagrave, Sterling, **The Soong Dynasty,** Harper
Theroux, Paul, **Sunrise with Seamonsters: Travels and Discoveries, 1964–1984,** Houghton
Tyler, Anne, **The Accidental Tourist,** Knopf
Warren, Robert Penn, **New and Selected Poems, 1923–1985,** Random
Whelan, Richard, **Robert Capa: A Biography,** Knopf
Wilson, Roberta and Wilson, James Q., **Watching Fishes: Life and Behavior on Coral-Reefs,** Harper

*Source:* Reprinted by permission of the American Library Association. Issued as a pamphlet by ALA, 50 E. Huron St., Chicago, Ill. 60611, annually in the spring for the preceding year. © American Library Association 1986.

## Major U.S. Symphony Orchestras and Their Music Directors

*Source:* American Symphony Orchestra League.

**Atlanta Symphony:** Robert Shaw
**Baltimore Symphony:** David Zinman
**Boston Symphony:** Seiji Ozawa
**Buffalo Philharmonic:** Semyon Bychkov
**Chicago Symphony:** Georg Solti
**Cincinnati Symphony:** Jesus Lopez Cobos
**Cleveland Orchestra:** Christoph von Dohnanyi
**Dallas Symphony:** Eduardo Mata
**Denver Symphony:** Philippe Entremont
**Detroit Symphony:** Gunther Herbig
**Houston Symphony:** Sergiu Comissiona[1]
**Indianapolis Symphony:** John Nelson
**Los Angeles Philharmonic:** André Previn
**Milwaukee Symphony:** Lukas Foss
**Minnesota Orchestra:** Edo de Waart
**National Symphony:** (Washington, D.C.): Mstislav

Rostropovich
**New Orleans Symphony Orchestra:** Maxim Shostakovich
**New York Philharmonic:** Zubin Mehta
**Oregon Symphony:** James DePreist
**Philadelphia Orchestra:** Riccardo Muti
**Pittsburgh Symphony:** Lorin Maazel[2]
**Rochester Philharmonic:** Jerzy Semkow[3,4]
**Saint Louis Symphony:** Leonard Slatkin
**Saint Paul Chamber Orchestra:** Pinchas Zukerman
**San Antonio Symphony:** Sixten Ehrling[3]
**San Diego Symphony:** David Atherton
**San Francisco Symphony:** Herbert Blomstedt
**Seattle Symphony:** Gerard Schwarz
**Syracuse Symphony:** Kazuyoshi Akiyama
**Utah Symphony:** Joseph Silverstein

1. Artistic Advisor. 2. Music Consultant and Principal Guest Conductor. 3. Music Advisor. 4. Principal Conductor.

# Major Public Libraries

| City (branches) | Volumes | Circu- lation | Budget (in millions) | City (branches) | Volumes | Circu- lation | Budget (in millions) |
|---|---|---|---|---|---|---|---|
| Akron-Summit County, Ohio (18) | 1,018,400 | 2,324,064 | $9.7 | Louisville, Ky. (20) | 861,549 | 3,055,834 | $6.9 |
| Albuquerque, N.M. (8) | 524,979 | 1,961,969 | 4.1 | Madison, Wis. (7) | 556,738 | 1,853,188 | 4.2 |
| Annapolis, Md. (13) | 1,721,443 | 3,907,253 | 7.5 | Memphis, Tenn. (22) | 3,200,492 | 2,276,417 | 8.0 |
| Atlanta (25) | 1,300,000 | 2,047,744 | 10.2 | Miami-Dade County, Fla. (20) | 2,126,496 | 3,824,000 | 19.8 |
| Austin, Tex. (16) | 1,018,587 | 2,271,227 | 8.8 | Milwaukee (12) | 1,981,481 | 3,505,639 | 12.5 |
| Baltimore (32) | 1,901,964 | 1,794,946 | 11.8 | Minneapolis (14) | 1,727,180 | 2,645,423 | 11.4 |
| Baton Rouge, La. (9) | 514,550 | 1,709,622 | 2.3 | Nashville-Davidson | | | |
| Birmingham, Ala. (19) | 1,100,000 | 2,105,000 | 7.0 | County, Tenn. (15) | 589,737 | 1,863,657 | 5.7 |
| Boston (25) | 5,117,042 | 1,612,287 | 16.4 | Newark, N.J. (11) | 1,300,000 | 1,400,000 | 6.0 |
| Buffalo-Erie County, N.Y. (58) | 3,459,038 | 5,844,768 | 13.0 | New Orleans (11) | 889,050 | 1,144,619 | 4.0 |
| Charleston-Kanawha | | | | New York City (81) | 3,294,960 | 9,557,753 | 58.3 |
| County, W.Va. (11) | 540,518 | 1,015,570 | 2.5 | Research | 8,654,373 | — | 38.8 |
| Charlotte, N.C. (19) | 905,266 | 2,829,997 | 6.7 | Brooklyn (60) | 4,323,457 | 9,120,847 | 29.1 |
| Chicago (87) | 4,536,507 | 7,842,970 | 46.4 | Queens (60) | 5,050,018 | 10,261,806 | 33.8 |
| Cincinnati (40) | 3,531,473 | 6,657,898 | 18.0 | Norfolk, Va. (11) | 769,167 | 905,892 | 3.7 |
| Cleveland (31) | 2,544,778 | 3,805,941 | 21.6 | Oklahoma City-County (10) | 707,842 | 2,413,468 | 7.4 |
| Columbus-Franklin | | | | Omaha, Neb. (9) | 567,961 | 1,783,298 | 3.8 |
| County, Ohio (21) | 1,379,629 | 4,512,232 | 11.7 | Philadelphia (52) | 3,120,806 | 5,373,096 | 34.1 |
| Dallas (18) | 1,788,129 | 4,087,571 | 16.5 | Phoenix, Ariz. (9) | 1,328,000 | 4,374,253 | 10.1 |
| Dayton-Montgomery | | | | Pittsburgh (20) | 1,830,742 | 2,969,022 | 9.9 |
| County Ohio (19) | 1,424,162 | 4,840,728 | 8.3 | Portland-Multnomah | | | |
| Denver (21) | 1,940,125 | 2,586,395 | 11.9 | County, Ore. (14) | 1,182,189 | 3,459,185 | 7.2 |
| Des Moines, Iowa (5) | 979,559 | 1,250,816 | 2.6 | Providence, R.I. (8) | 1,103,421 | 901,053 | 3.5 |
| Detroit (24) | 2,513,529 | 1,332,409 | 19.9 | Richmond, Va. (7) | 702,292 | 961,709 | 2.8 |
| D.C. (26) | 1,404,453 | 1,772,501 | 13.9 | Rochester, N.Y. (11) | 1,286,713 | 1,443,382 | 8.3 |
| El Paso (9) | 1,100,000 | 1,210,000 | 4.1 | Sacramento, Calif. (26) | 1,284,208 | 3,537,099 | 11.4 |
| Erie, Pa. (6) | 420,355 | 1,466,536 | 2.1 | St. Louis (14) | 1,457,314 | 1,120,446 | 6.8 |
| Evansville-Vanderburgh | | | | St. Paul (11) | 1,212,059 | 2,002,954 | 4.8 |
| County Ind. (7) | 589,104 | 1,956,250 | 3.1 | St. Petersburg, Fla. (4)* | n.a. | n.a. | n.a. |
| Fort Wayne-Allen | | | | Salt Lake City-County, Utah (14) | 1,002,081 | 3,193,246 | 8.7 |
| County, Ind. (12) | 1,748,350 | 2,565,740 | 6.1 | San Antonio (15) | 1,541,994 | 2,776,889 | 7.1 |
| Fort Worth (8) | 1,583,131 | 2,935,012 | 5.7 | San Diego, Calif. (30) | 1,631,532 | 4,214,567 | 12.1 |
| Grand Rapids, Mich. (5) | 631,818 | 827,457 | 3.0 | San Francisco (26) | 1,974,896 | 3,043,793 | 15.1 |
| Greenville City-County S.C. (10) | 561,670 | 1,145,962 | 3.4 | San Jose, Calif. (18) | 1,327,600 | 3,100,000 | 11.1 |
| Honolulu (49)1* | n.a. | n.a. | n.a. | Seattle (22) | 1,633,422 | 4,263,754 | 14.0 |
| Houston (32) | 3,147,614 | 6,089,224 | 20.7 | Springfield, Mass. (8) | 650,000 | 1,150,000 | 4.5 |
| Independence, Mo. (26) | 1,350,000 | 3,100,000 | 8.2 | Tampa, Fla. (16) | 1,370,106 | 2,250,000 | 8.5 |
| Indianapolis-Marion | | | | Tucson, Ariz. (15) | 764,000 | 3,930,000 | 7.9 |
| County (23) | 1,520,986 | 4,258,775 | 11.9 | Tulsa City-County, Okla. (20) | 610,230 | 2,119,323 | 6.9 |
| Jackson, Miss. (35) | 876,861 | 1,337,715 | 2.9 | Wichita, Kan. (11) | 800,966 | 1,205,952 | 3.1 |
| Jacksonville, Fla. (11) | 1,471,965 | 1,999,383 | 5.7 | Winston-Salem- | | | |
| Kansas City, Mo. (14) | 2,059,452 | 847,689 | 5.4 | Forsyth County, N.C. (8) | 350,000 | 1,850,000 | 3.7 |
| Knoxville, Tenn. (19) | 628,334 | 1,510,340 | 3.1 | Worcester, Mass. (6) | 605,950 | 684,255 | 2.5 |
| Lincoln, Neb. (7) | 450,770 | 1,341,922 | 2.5 | Youngstown- | | | |
| Long Beach, Calif. (11) | 831,365 | 2,482,233 | 8.7 | Mahoning County, Ohio (23) | 752,899 | 1,541,766 | 4.3 |
| Los Angeles (County) (102) | 4,314,884 | 11,677,635 | 44.3 | | | | |

1. State-wide system. NOTE: n.a. = not available. * Did not reply to questionnaire. *Source: Information Please* questionnaires to the libraries.

# Glossary of Art Movements

**Abstract Expressionism.** American art movement of the 1940s that emphasized form and color within a nonrepresentational framework. Jackson Pollock initiated the revolutionary technique of splattering the paint directly on canvas to achieve the subconscious interpretation of the artist's inner vision of reality.

**Art Deco.** A 1920s style characterized by setbacks, zigzag forms, and the use of chrome and plastic ornamentation. New York's Chrysler Building is an architectural example of the style.

**Art Nouveau.** An 1890s style in architecture, graphic arts, and interior decoration characterized by writhing forms, curving lines, and asymmetrical organization. Some critics regard the style as the first stage of modern architecture.

**Ashcan School.** A group of New York realist artists, formed in 1908, who abandoned decorous subject matter and portrayed the more common as well as the sordid aspects of city life.

**Assemblage (Collage).** Forms of modern sculpture and painting utilizing readymades, found objects, and pasted fragments to form an abstract composition. Louise Nevelson's boxlike enclosures, each with its own composition of assembled objects, illustrate the style in sculpture. Pablo Picasso developed the technique of cutting and pasting natural or manufactured materials to a painted or unpainted surface.

**Barbizon School (Landscape Painting).** A group of painters who, around the middle of the 19th century, reacted against classical landscape and advocated a direct study of nature. They were influenced by English and Dutch landscape masters. Theodore Rousseau, one of the principal figures of the group, led the fight for outdoor painting. In this respect, the school was a forerunner of Impressionism.

**Baroque.** European art and architecture of the 17th and 18th centuries. Giovanni Bernini, a major exponent of the style, believed in the union of the arts of architecture, painting, and sculpture to overwhelm the spectator with ornate and highly dramatized themes. Although the style originated in Rome as the instrument of the Church, it spread throughout Europe in such monumental creations as the Palace of Versailles.

**Beaux Arts.** Elaborate and formal architectural style characterized by symmetry and an abundance of sculptured ornamentation. New York's old Custom House at Bowling Green is an example of the style.

**Black or Afro-American Art.** The work of American artists of African descent produced in various styles characterized by a mood of protest and a search for identity and historical roots.

**Classicism.** A form of art derived from the study of Greek and Roman styles characterized by harmony, balance, and serenity. In contrast, the Romantic Movement gave free rein to the artist's imagination and to the love of the exotic.

**Constructivism.** A form of sculpture using wood, metal, glass, and modern industrial materials expressing the technological society. The mobiles of Alexander Calder are examples of the movement.

**Cubism.** Early 20th-century French movement marked by a revolutionary departure from representational art. Pablo Picasso and Georges Bracque penetrated the surface of objects, stressing basic abstract geometric forms that presented the object from many angles simultaneously.

**Dada.** A product of the turbulent and cynical post-World War I period, this anti-art movement extolled the irrational, the absurd, the nihilistic, and the nonsensical. The reproduction of Mona Lisa adorned with a mustache is a famous example. The movement is regarded as a precursor of Surrealism. Some critics regard HAPPENINGS as a recent development of Dada. This movement incorporates environment and spectators as active and important ingredients in the production of random events.

**Expressionism.** A 20th-century European art movement that stresses the expression of emotion and the inner vision of the artist rather than the exact representation of nature. Distorted lines and shapes and exaggerated colors are used for emotional impact. Vincent Van Gogh is regarded as the precursor of this movement.

**Fauvism.** The name "wild beasts" was given to the group of early 20th-century French painters because their work was characterized by distortion and violent colors. Henri Matisse and Georges Roualt were leaders of this group.

**Futurism.** This early 20th-century movement originating in Italy glorified the machine age and attempted to represent machines and figures in motion. The aesthetics of Futurism affirmed the beauty of technological society.

**Genre.** This French word meaning "type" now refers to paintings that depict scenes of everyday life without any attempt at idealization. Genre paintings can be found in all ages, but the Dutch productions of peasant and tavern scenes are typical.

**Impressionism.** Late 19th-century French school dedicated to defining transitory visual impressions painted directly from nature, with light and color of primary importance. If the atmosphere changed, a totally different picture would emerge. It was not the object or event that counted but the visual impression as caught at a certain time of day under a certain light. Claude Monet and Camille Pissarro were leaders of the movement.

**Mannerism.** A mid-16th century movement, Italian in origin, although El Greco was a major practitioner of the style. The human figure, distorted and elongated, was the most frequent subject.

**Neoclassicism.** An 18th-century reaction to the excesses of Baroque and Rococo, this European art movement tried to recreate the art of Greece and Rome by imitating the ancient classics both in style and subject matter.

**Op Art.** The 1960s movement known as Optical Painting is characterized by geometrical forms that create an optical illusion in which the eye is required to blend the colors at a certain distance.

**Pop Art.** In this return to representational art, the artist returns to the world of tangible objects in a reaction against abstraction. Materials are drawn from the everyday world of popular culture—comic strips, canned goods, and science fiction.

**Rococo.** A French style of interior decoration developed during the reign of Louis XV consisting mainly of asymmetrical arrangements of curves in paneling, porcelain, and gold and silver objects. The characteristics of ornate curves, prettiness, and gaiety can also be found in the painting and sculpture of the period.

**Surrealism.** A further development of Collage, Cubism, and Dada, this 20th-century movement stresses the weird, the fantastic, and the dream-world of the subconscious.

## The Treasure Houses of Britain

The National Gallery of Art in Washington, D.C., reported that just under a million people, 999,000, visited The Treasure Houses of Britain exhibition between Nov. 3, 1985, and April 13, 1986. This topped the number of people, 832,853, who attended the King Tut exhibit there.

Requests for tickets from all over the country were so great that the closing date was moved from March 16 to April 13.

# Twentieth-Century Popular Music

*Source:* © by Pelham Books Ltd. This material first appeared in PEARS CYCLOPAEDIA 1986 published by Pelham Books Ltd., London, England.

## Introduction

"Classical" music of the European tradition has often borrowed the melodies, styles, and instruments of popular songs, and in this century the influence of "low brow" music, in particular jazz, has been considerable. As a musical form of particular identity and technique, jazz deserves serious attention, as do the many other distinct forms of popular music, including rock, since they are an important phenomenon of mass culture.

America, and particularly black America, has dominated 20th-century popular music in the Western World. Jazz is a rhythmic, syncopated style of music, created at the end of the 19th century by black Americans out of their religious and secular (gospel and blues) songs. Its birth place was New Orleans, but jazz was played elsewhere and spread by the 1920s to black communities in the north, and especially Chicago where the best performers assembled and soon began to influence white musicians.

The top American bands—mainly white, but some black—adopted and adapted jazz to bring themselves huge commercial success and immense popularity for their music, which evolved into 1930s' swing. This stamped an indelible impression on all dance music and popular songs.

Music Hall and vaudeville, and the "musicals" of Broadway, London's West End, and Hollywood, now reflected the influence of jazz. Country music, later called country and western, was the only distinctly white American style which flourished through these times, as it does today.

After World War II, jazz and popular music, though inextricably intertwined, went in different directions. Black musicians, tired of swing which watered down their jazz, produced a more sophisticated style called bebop. Then some musicians, black and white, launched a revival of the original New Orleans jazz sounds, and "trad" boomed in American and Britain in the 1950s. This emphasis faced a strong challenge from the performers and fans of a new "modern jazz." By the 1960s, however, this was appreciated only among a minority.

Popular music meets the demands of a mass audience, and since the War has reflected more and more the needs of commerce and a large-scale record industry. Ballad singers and crooners were big business after the War, a time when America's black communities produced rhythm-and-blues. Mixed with aspects of country music, this became rock'n'roll, the 1950s' sensation for the white community.

Here was a watershed: rock in its various forms sprang from rock'n'roll and now dominates the music scene, "pop" is its mass market manifestation, and the divisions between black music and that favored by white audiences have gradually broken down. During the 1960s and 1970s, rock incorporated folk, and, through a blues revival, helped create soul and the modern-day disco phenomenon. It has also expressed in music the "underground," drug culture, the civil rights movement, and anti-war campaigns. The initiative in popular music's development, so long the preserve of Americans, passed briefly to British artists when Beatlemania swept the world after 1963. Since then the music scene has been kaleidoscopic, fash-

ions come and go, but most styles of jazz, rock, or soul have their fans.

The following glossary and biographical notes are intended to help the general reader.

**Acid Rock.** 1960s hyper-amplified music, featuring improvisation and distorted electronic effects, it reflected the "underground" and the craze for drugs, especially LSD, which bring mind expansion. Artists, many based in San Francisco, include Jefferson Airplane and The Grateful Dead.

**Armstrong, (Daniel) Louis (1900–1971).** U.S. jazz trumpeter, singer, and bandleader, called "Satchmo." The great exponent of New Orleans jazz, he became the supreme soloist and showman of jazz.

**Bacharach, Burt (1928–    ).** U.S. singer, pianist, songwriter, arranger, and record producer. His work since the mid-1950s (often with Hal David) includes pop, rock, and soul compositions, and the music for many Broadway shows and films, *e.g.*, *What's New Pussycat* (1964) and *Alfie* (1967).

**Ballads.** Simple narrative or sentimental songs, a form of popular poetry. They were a familiar feature of folk music, and were much loved in music hall. In pop music, the term ballad signifies a slow, down-beat song rather than a rock number.

**Band.** A group of musicians, who feature wind and percussion instruments rather than strings. Military or marching bands have a long tradition, borrowed by the first jazz groups. The jazz line-up varies, but originally had wind instruments playing melody over a rhythm section. Big bands, formed in the 1920s, had sixteen musicians in four sections, usually for dancing. "Modern jazz" bands are much smaller. The rock band consists of electric guitar, bass guitar, and drums with additional singers and features instruments, like keyboards and saxophone.

**Basie, Count (1904–1984).** U.S. jazz musician, big-band leader from 1935, pianist, and composer. A great favorite in the swing era, he remained popular in later years.

**Beach Boys.** U.S. vocal and instrumental pop group of five, originally including Brian, Dennis, and Carl Wilson. America's challenge to the Beatle craze, they pioneered the early 1960s' West Coast surfing beat, with hits like *Surfin' Safari* (1962), *Fun Fun Fun*, *California Girls*, and *Good Vibrations* (1966).

**Beat.** The term signifies the swing of jazz and popular music, not just the number of beats to the bar but the pulse created within and around those bars.

**Beatles.** British vocal and instrumental group, of John Lennon, Paul McCartney, George Harrison, and Ringo Starr (Richard Starkey). The most successful pop group of all time, the Beatles made Liverpool the temporary capital of rock music. Their style was rhythm-and-blues, with attractive harmonies, their songs had simple themes and fresh lyrics. Lennon and McCartney were superb songwriters, and the group's material, performances, records, and films caused Beatlemania across the world. The hits began in 1963 with *Please Please Me* and *She Loves You*, and later featured the more sophisticated, drugs-influenced, *Sergeant Pepper's Lonely Hearts Club Band* (1967). The group disbanded in 1971; John Lennon was murdered in 1980.

**Bebop/Bop.** A style of jazz developed in the late 1940s by Dizzy Gillespie, Charlie Parker, and others to get away from the set arrangements of swing and to feature more subtlety, sophistication, and improvisation. The style borrowed much from European musicology and from Latin America's musical tradition. The balance inside a band's rhythm section changed, so that the bass now provided a constant rhythm and the drums could be used for accentuation or even solos.

**Bee Gees.** Anglo-Australian vocal and instrumental group, featuring brothers Barry, Robin, and Maurice Gibb, who won great popularity in Australia and then Britain in the 1960s with hits like *Massachusetts.* After a temporary break-up, they shot into the superstar league, following the phenomenal success of their music in the disco film, *Saturday Night Fever* (1978).

**Beiderbecke, (Leon) Bix (1903–1931).** U.S. jazz trumpeter and pianist. His roots were in white Dixieland *(q.v.)* and he became one of the most distinguished white performers.

**Berlin, Irving (1888– ).** U.S. composer of over 800 popular songs, such as *Alexander's Ragtime Band* and *White Christmas;* Broadway musicals like *Annie Get Your Gun* (1946) and *Call me Madam* (1950); and film scores.

**Berry, (Charles Ed. Anderson) Chuck (1926– ).** U.S. blues and rock singer and guitarist, this black songwriter composed the best early rock'n'roll and rhythm-and-blues. His 1950s hits, such as *Maybellene* (1955), *Roll Over Beethoven* (1956), and *Sweet Little Sixteen* (1958) were later revived by the Beatles, Rolling Stones, and others.

**Blue Beat.** West Indian pop music style, a forerunner of reggae *(q.v.)* and reaching Britain in the 1960s.

**Blues.** The secular music of black America developed in the 19th century alongside gospel *(q.v.)* when slaves adapted African rhythms and a musical tradition based on a five-note scale to European melodies based on a seven-note scale. The classical blues featured a three-line verse, in which the first line is repeated and rhymes with the third, sung over a twelve-bar sequence (sometimes eight or sixteen bars). "Blue notes" are created by lowering a semitone the third and seventh degrees of the scale.

After emancipation, Afro-Americans continued to express in song their hardship and the injustices they suffered, and the mixture of spirituals (gospel) and worksongs became blues. This music is an emotional release, expressing despondency and tales of loneliness, bad luck or betrayal. Touring "country blues" artists like W. C. Handy were popular before World War I. Later singers like Sonny Boy Williamson added sophistication to the style and female stars of the 1920s and 30s including Ma Rainey and Bessie Smith sang the blues with small jazz groups.

Musicians, such as Louis Armstrong, incorporated the harmonic sequence of the blues as a favorite basis for jazz improvisation. Blues made a similar contribution to popular music, when after World War II urban blacks revived the classic style and created rhythm-and-blues, the forerunner of rock and soul.

**Bolden, Buddy (1868–1931).** U.S. jazz musician and cornet player. He was the original "King" of New Orleans jazz, a legend in his time who left no recordings of his work and who died in a psychiatric hospital.

**Boogie/Boogie Woogie.** The jazz style by which blues was best played on piano. Over a consistently repeated bass motif, a melody is played with great swing to avoid monotony. The music was popular in the 1920s, mainly in bars where the heavy bass, hard and forceful sounds matched the surroundings and atmosphere. The name was coined by pianist and composer Clarence "Pinetop" Smith in his *Pinetop's Boogie Woogie.*

**Bowie, David (1947– ).** British pop singer, born David Jones, who reached 1970s' stardom by fusing "progressive" pop music with sexual ambiguity and bizarre theatricality, as in the creation of *Ziggy Stardust* (1972).

**Brubeck, Dave (1920– ).** U.S. "modern jazz" pianist and composer, born David Warren, who formed the Dave Brubeck Quartet in 1951, winning considerable acclaim and lasting international popularity. His most famous number is *Take Five* but other material includes cantatas and orchestral works.

**Bubble Gum.** Pop music, rock in its most commercialized form, produced from the late 1960s for the subteen audience and record-buying public. Artists and material include the 1910 Fruitgum Company, Ohio Express with *Yummy, Yummy, Yummy,* the Osmonds, the Archies, the Monkees, and David Cassidy. Also called Teenybop music.

**Calypso.** West Indian folk-song style, originally sung by African slaves on the plantations. Highly rhythmic, hypnotic, and with strong lyrics, the traditional calypso is a major ingredient of the present-day reggae style. A watered-down commercial version of the calypso was popular with 1950s' white audiences in Britain.

**Carmichael, Hoagy (1899–1981).** U.S. composer of popular music, often adopted by jazz artists. Songs include *Georgia on My Mind, Lazy River,* and *Riverboat Shuffle.*

**Chicago, Illinois.** The jazz capital moved from New Orleans *(q.v.)* to Chicago, the home of many illustrious musicians between World War I and the Depression. Here jazz evolved and found imitators among white artists such as Bix Beiderbecke, whose music was called the Chicago Style. Black musicians followed their people to northern cities in search of work, and found jobs in "speakeasies" of the prohibition era. Jazz changed to meet the demands of white audiences, stars emerged like King Oliver and Louis Armstrong, and white musicians tried hard to re-create the jazz sound.

In Chicago jazz toughened up, it took in new sounds such as the saxophone, and a new emphasis on the clarinet. The city also saw the 1920s' development of the blues into boogie woogie.

**Clapton, Eric (1945– ).** British rock guitarist, much admired since the late 1960s. He played with Cream (1966–68) and Derek and the Dominoes, and his records include *Wheels of Fire* (1968) and *Layla* (1970).

**Coleman, Ornette (1930– ).** U.S. jazz musician, alto saxophonist, and composer. A great name in "modern jazz," he developed a controversial, original style, ignoring chords to play free melodic lines.

**Coltrane, John William (1926–1967).** U.S. jazz saxophonist. One of the leading innovators in the 1950s and 60s, he was an outstanding musician, played with Coleman, Gillespie, and Davis.

**Country and Western.** Popular music originally associated with rural white "hillbilly" communities in the mountainous areas of southeastern U.S.A. Based on European folk music, this was the music of America's frontier, borrowing from Negro blues and attaining a particular identity in each locality. Popularized nationwide through records and the radio from the 1920s, and by traveling artists like Woody Guthrie, country music absorbed other influences, including the "cowboy" music of America's Southwest. Country and western was thus born, less folksy but still featuring sentimental lyrics and instrumental accompaniment on banjo, guitar, or fiddle. Nashville, Tennessee, is the capital of country and western, which has become a great commercial success.

Rock'n'roll of the mid-1950s derived from a blending of country and western with rhythm-and-blues, and like country the new style appealed mainly to white audiences. Country and western was eclipsed for several years, but a revival in the 1960s brought success to Glen Campbell, Roger Miller, George Hamilton IV, and other artists, many of whom produced a new "uptown" commercialized country and western sound, popular music using country instruments and styles.

**Crooning.** The singing style of male and female popular vocalists in the 1930s and 1940s. Coined in America, the term referred to songs sung in a low, smooth voice. The crooners included Rosemary Clooney, Perry Como, Bing Crosby, Doris Day, Peggy Lee, Dean Martin, and Frank Sinatra, and in Britain Al Bowley before the War, and later Vera Lynn.

**Crosby, (Harry Lillis) Bing (1904–1977).** U.S. pop singer and actor. One of the most successful crooners, with big bands, on records and in films from *c.* 1930. He won an Academy Award (1944) and his *White Christmas* is the world's best-selling record of all time.

**Dance.** Most dances of this century, apart from folk, old time, and classical ballroom routines, are accompanied by jazz-based music, and most rock and popular music is designed for dancing. This reflects the Afro-American tradition where music and dancing are but two facets of the same art.

The cakewalk, performed by southern blacks at the turn of the century, was adapted to produce the Charleston of 1920s, popular with whites as well as blacks and typifying the "Jazz Age." A similar dance was the Black Bottom, demonstrated by Ann Pennington in the film *Scandals of 1926.* These routines were forerunners of the jitterbug,

often called the Lindy Hop by blacks, which involved complex acrobatics, twisting, and whirling. Although anti-social in crowded dance halls, it was the favorite dance of jazz fans in the 1940s and 1950s. A more restrained version adopted by rock'n'rollers was the jive. Ballroom dancers borrowed jazz styles, and had their own fashions for the tango, fox-trot, quick step, etc., which they danced to jazz-influenced popular music and swing. In the 1940s there was a new Latin-American flavor, and a four-four rhythm which were incorporated in the mambo, and for the 1950s, the Cha-Cha.

These styles allowed the dancers to improvise, as did the jive which could be danced in pairs or solo. From the early 1960s solo dancing, "doing one's own thing," became more and more the norm, as fashion passed through the twist, the shuffle, the hustle, and the bump of today's disco dancing.

**Davis, Miles (1926– ).** U.S. jazz trumpeter, who helped develop bebop in the 1940s, and was later known for an introspective style, his fine recordings with small groups, and a blending of rock with jazz. He is considered one of the most influential "modern jazz" musicians.

**Detroit,** *see* **Motown.**

**Disc.** Popular name for the gramophone record, which is a grooved vinyl pressing containing recorded sound. The lateral disc dates from 1887, and the 78 rpm shellac record from 1900, but the music industry was revolutionized by the introduction of 33 rpm vinyl discs in 1948. Stereophonic sound followed in 1956, and quadrophonic about 1970. The record industry is not only the vehicle of popular music, but also the determinant of its trends and fashions.

**Disco.** Discotheques—from the French *disc* (record) and *bibliotheque* (library)—are the late 1970s' entertainment sensation, the venue for a dancing craze unparalleled since the 1920s and 30s. The music is heavy soul on record, a hypnotic, almost computerized sound not easily created live, and the accent is on decor and special effects, mirrors, lasers, films, etc., to create extravagant environments.

The roots go back to youth club dance sessions of the 1960s mod era, then came mobile discos in parties, pubs, and then clubs. The disc jockey emerged as a distinct ingredient in the disco experience, much live rock music became less geared to dancing, and audiences (especially on the Northern Soul scene) rediscovered old recordings of rhythm-&-blues soul, and rock'n'roll. The final boost was given by films like *Thank God It's Friday*, *Car Wash*, and *Saturday Night Fever*. Discos in London and New York are now big business. They range from back room bars to slick, sophisticated establishments like the famous Studio 54 in New York. All depend on high-powered electronic equipment, and the DJ with an endless supply of records—whether soul, reggae, or fashionable novelties like disco arrangements of 1940s swing and Broadway musical numbers. The dance routines change rapidly with fashion, some echo old ballroom classics, others break new ground—*e.g.* disco on roller skates. Whatever the style, the music is a solid wave of pounding sound, with an accent on the melody, simple lyrics, beat, and rhythm.

**Dixieland.** The term refers to the jazz style, born

in New Orleans in the 1900s and made famous across America by the 1920s (*see* Jazz). But the Dixieland label often indicates the white version of New Orleans jazz, as produced by Nick La Rocca's Original Dixieland Jazz Band and others, popular among fashionable whites of the "Jazz Age" and immortalized by Scott Fitzgerald. The first "jazz" to be recorded was in fact white Dixieland played by the Original Dixieland Jazz Band in 1917.

**Domino, (Antoine) Fats (1928– ).** U.S. pianist, composer, and singer of rhythm-and-blues. His record sales of 23 million copies between 1949 and 1960 were exceeded only by Elvis Presley and the Beatles.

**Dorsey, Jimmy (1904–1957) and Tommy (1905–1956).** U.S. musicians and bandleaders. The brothers formed two of the most successful big bands, joining together in 1953 for the Fabulous Dorseys Big Band.

**Dylan, Bob (1941– ).** U.S. singer, guitarist, pianist, and composer, born Robert Zimmerman. Among the most creative and influential rock performers and writers, he helped originate folk rock, with songs like *Blowin' in the Wind* and *Times They are a Changin'*, but his work ranges over a wide field. A cult figure in the 1960s for the generation of civil rights marchers and anti-war protesters, he became a legend in his lifetime. His music also includes *Just Like a Woman, Like a Rolling Stone, Lay Lady Lay*, and the albums *Nashville Skyline* and *John Wesley Harding.*

**Ellington, (Edward Kennedy) Duke (1899–1974).** U.S. jazz pianist, composer, and bandleader from 1918. In the forefront of the jazz scene until his death, as a writer, arranger, and performer. Ellington produced the best in big-band jazz, the finest orchestrations of the blues, as well as classic songs (*e.g. Mood Indigo, I Got it Bad*) and piano suites.

**Fitzgerald, Ella (1918– ).** U.S. jazz singer, famous for a smooth and relaxed style. Her repertoire ranges through jazz, pop, blues, and jazz versions of old masters.

**Folk.** The traditional music of a particular community, ethnic, or national culture, usually songs of uncertain origin, open to variation and improvisation, but expressing usually the history of a people or customs of that people. After World War II, folk became fashionable, as many sought alternatives to materialism and technology. Folk music itself, however, also became big business (*see* **Country and Western**).

Folk has often been incorporated into "classical" compositions, as by Bartók, Britten, Grieg, and Dvořák, and in the 1950s American "country" folk was blended with music of the black folk tradition to produce rock'n'roll. In the 1960s rock composers, such as Bob Dylan, adopted folk and incorporated it into "progressive" rock.

**Folk Rock.** An aspect of the increasingly sophisticated rock music in the 1960s, created by Bob Dylan (*q.v.*) and others out of the then folk revival. A product of white artists, folk rock remixed folk with blues, producing a softer, less strident sound of folk-style melodies and lyrics over a rock beat. Dylan, The Byrds, Peter Paul and Mary, Joan Baez, and Donovan in Britain were practitioners of the style.

**Gershwin, George (1898–1937).** U.S. composer of orchestral works, stage shows such as *Porgy and Bess* (1935) and *Lady Be Good* (1924), and many popular songs, for which his brother Ira wrote lyrics. Among mainstream composers he was one of the first to absorb jazz, as in the immortal *Rhapsody in Blue* (1923), originally for piano and jazz band but later orchestrated. *The Man I Love, I Got Rhythm* (1930), *Let's Call the Whole Thing Off*, and *They Can't Take That Away from Me* are among the most memorable songs.

**Getz, Stan (1927– ).** U.S. jazz saxophonist. He played with Woody Herman in the 1940s, then formed his own group. He managed to win wide popularity while remaining a creative stylist.

**Gillespie, (John Birks) Dizzy (1917– ).** U.S. jazz trumpeter and big-band leader. With Charlie Parker, he created bebop in the 1940s, his arrangements bearing much influence on other musicians.

**Goodman, Benny (1909–1986).** U.S. jazz clarinetist and big-band leader, from 1934. One of the great white jazz artists, he developed swing, achieving enormous commercial success and popularity. A sign of the times, his band of white players got better bookings and greater publicity than the best black bands. Goodman's work relied on arrangements supplied by black musicians such as Fletcher Henderson, and the best was produced in the small jazz groups in which Goodman mixed black and white players.

**Gospel.** Often called "Negro Spirituals," this is Afro-American vocal church music. It draws from the African musical tradition of a five-note scale and retains the "call and response" verse pattern, but gospel evolved when slaves, taught to sing hymns of European style and harmonies, fused the new with their old traditions. Gospel songs reflect not only religious faith but also the protest of black Americans as slaves, *e.g. Go Down Moses*. The Bible provides the symbols for an oppressed people. Gospel continues in black churches, and developed in secular form as blues and soul.

**Guthrie, Woody (1912–1967).** U.S. folk singer, most popular of the white country artists in the 1930s and 40s, and famous for his concert tours as well as records. Songs include the Dust Bowl ballads, and *This Land is My Land*. Bob Dylan is his most illustrious disciple.

**Hampton, Lionel (1913– ).** U.S. jazz vibraphonist, drummer, and bandleader. One of the great black artists who played with Benny Goodman (1936–1940) and later led his own band and small groups.

**Hard Rock.** An element of the sophisticated "progressive" music, developed since the 1960s. This rock music features strongly emphasized beat, hyperamplification, electronic effects, an absence of sweet sounding melodies. Leading performers in this style included Cream and Led Zeppelin.

**Holliday, Billie "Lady Day" (1915–1959).** U.S. jazz and blues singer, well known from the mid-1930s for her work on stage and record with Teddy Wilson, Count Basie, and Artie Shaw. Her tragic life was later immortalized in the film *Lady Sings the Blues* (1972).

**Honky Tonk.** This was the slang name originally given to music of New Orleans' black night spots of the 1900s. Often of ill-repute, they featured piano, dancing, and a back room for girls.

**Hooker, John Lee (1915– ).** U.S. blues singer, well known from 1949 as an exponent of old time blues which he sang while accompanying himself on electric guitar. The style was strongly dramatic, and the swing forceful.

**Jazz.** Jazz is the late 19th-century creation of black Americans, originally the music of African slaves ( *see* **Gospel** and **Blues**), which provided "blue notes" antiphony, emotional strength, and the twelve-bar blues set, synthesized with ragtime *(q.v.)* beat and melody, and using brass instruments as in the traditional marching bands of America's southern blacks. Into this black creation was also mixed aspects of European folk music, and white America's popular songs.

The new sound, spreading from New Orleans *(q.v.)*, was fresh, melodic, rhythmic (usually four beats to the bar), and emotional. Essentially it is first an art of performance, a style of playing or singing rather than a formal composition, though the best jazz comes from accomplished writers like Jelly Roll Morton, Duke Ellington, or Charlie Mingus more recently. They provide a structure, but the style, emphasis, and nuances depend on the performer. Second, jazz relies on improvisation, the spontaneity, and freshness of each performance. Third, the music is melodic. Fourth, jazz adapts vocal techniques to brass and reed instruments, so that they convey the inflexions and contrasts of the human voice. Fifth, jazz provided a musical response to social changes and economic pressures of the day.

New Orleans from the 1890s produced jazz, embracing ragtime, the later work of "classic blues" artists like Ma Rainey and Bessie Smith, and Dixieland *(q.v.)* as the first white spin-off. The music was spread via riverboat and railway by blacks seeking jobs in northern cities. After 1917 Chicago, Kansas City *(qq.v.)*, and New York became centers of a "jazz age," when King Oliver and Louis Armstrong won fame and fortune. As soloists and bandleaders, they represented the best in jazz, imitated and commercialized by others as popular entertainment for a growing and increasingly white audience. More and more white musicians (like Bix Beiderbecke, Artie Shaw, and Benny Goodman) adopted jazz, and in the Depression of the early 1930s many jazz musicians joined dance bands. Popular music thus absorbed jazz, and big bands—black and white—produced swing *(q.v.)*.

By then New York big business had cashed in on jazz, producing a commercial network of records, concerts, films, dance halls, and clubs. White society cashed in on black music, so that white impresarios, bands, and artists got the best bookings and most success. But from Broadway to Harlem, jazz musicians made a living. In the 1940s some blacks including Charlie Parker, Dizzy Gillespie, and Miles Davis, tired of watered down and "arranged" jazz, developed a more sophisticated bebop *(q.v.)* style.

After World War II, jazz divided into two. The revivalist trend originated on America's West Coast, where oldtime New Orleans performers (like Bunk Johnson and George Lewis) were rediscovered, classic recordings reissued, and almost-forgotten numbers recorded. The craze spread even to Britain where the "trad" bands of Humphrey Lyttleton, Chris Barber, and others enjoyed tremendous following until the early 1960s.

"Modern jazz" was the rival trend, developed out of bebop, pioneered by the Miles Davis Group in 1948, using greater improvisation and unorthodox instrumentation (*e.g.* flute, cello, and oboe) and moving the emphasis away from declaration to understatement—from "hot" to "cool." Stan Getz, Stan Kenton, Dave Brubeck, and Gerry Mulligan, mainly West Coasters and many of them white, belonged to this trend. The work of Davis, John Coltrane, and Ornette Coleman, superb in experimentation, stressed consciousness, pride, and the roots of black music. In this jazz linked back to developments in blues, soul, and pop music.

The popularity of jazz, however, decreased in the 1960s, as it became more complex, more expressive, but more an art form than a popular accompaniment for dancing. Nonetheless Jazz is *the* music of the 20th century, an influence on "classical" composers like Ravel on the one hand, and on the other the vital ingredient of popular music and rock, the pre-eminent form and vehicle of big business-orientated mass culture in western society.

**Jesus Rock.** Late 1960s' rock music, adopting Biblical themes. Many songs and full musicals especially *Jesus Christ Superstar* and *Godspell*, attained international success.

**John (Reginald Dwight), Elton (1947– ).** British rock singer, pianist, and composer of numerous songs (lyrics by Bernie Taupin), which won worldwide acclaim and sold millions of records. Albums include *Elton John* (1970), *Goodbye Yellow Brick Road* (1973), *Rock of the Westies* (1975), and *Blue Moves* (1976).

**Jolson, Al (1886–1950).** U.S. singer and comedian in vaudeville and Broadway. He is best known for his blacked-up "minstrel" style, as filmed in *The Jazz Singer* (1927), the first talking movie, and for songs like *Swanee* and *Mammy*.

**Joplin, Scott (1868–1917).** U.S. composer and pianist, principal exponent of ragtime *(q.v.)*. His music became popular again in the 1970s.

**Kansas City, Missouri.** One of the 1920s centers of jazz. This was a time when the city authorities were corrupt; gambling and nightlife thrived, creating a mecca for jazz musicians. The distinctive characteristics of Kansas City jazz were first the continuously repeated "riff" (a one- or two-bar phrase), either backing a soloist or to build up excitement, and second the chase chorus, in which two soloists alternated. Performers included Bennie Moten's Kansas City Orchestra, and Count Basie started here.

**Kenton, (Stanley Newcomb) Stan (1912–1979).** U.S. jazz musician, composer, and bandleader from 1941. Well known for his theme *Artistry in Rhythm* (1945) and for his patronage of other musicians.

**Kern, Jerome (1885–1945).** U.S. songwriter and composer for stage musicals. His work includes *Sally* (1920) and *Showboat* (1927) and songs like *Smoke Gets in Your Eyes* and *Ol' Man River*.

**King, Carole (1941– ).** U.S. songwriter and singer, born Carole Klein. She and her then husband Gerry Goffin wrote some of the best 1960s' pop songs, *e.g. Up on th Roof*, and *It Might as Well Rain Until September*. Her album *Tapestry* (1971) sold more than 10 million copies.

**Liverpool.** *see* Merseybeat.

**Marley, Bob (1946–1981).** Jamaican musician and singer. With his group The Wailers, he is the best-known reggae *(q.v.)* artist. Died of cancer May 1981.

**Memphis, Tennessee.** The base for Stax/Atlantic records which in the 1960s produced a distinctive heavy soul *(q.v.)* sound, *e.g.* records by Otis Reading, Sam and Dave.

**Merseybeat.** A generalization, relating to Liverpool artists, principally The Beatles, who dominated early 1960s' rock. White performers from a British culture created a new hybrid out of black Americans' rhythm-and-blues. Other British musicians, not from Liverpool, like the Rolling Stones, The Animals, and The Who, continued this development.

**Miller, (Alton) Glenn (1904–1944).** U.S. jazz trombonist and leader of the most popular dance band of World War II and of all time. His "swing" sounds were distinctively reedy, and his theme tune *Moonlight Serenade* (1939) is immortal.

**Mingus, Charles (1922–1979).** U.S. jazz composer, bass player, and bandleader from the 1950s. His "modern jazz" experiments with atonal sounds and impressionism produced work like *The Black Saint* and *The Sinner Lady* (1963).

**Minstrel.** A medieval term, referring to itinerant musicians and professional entertainers, it was applied in this century to white singers and banjo players who blacked their faces and mimicked aspects of Afro-American music.

**Mod.** The term refers to an early 1960s' cult among young people in Britain, which involved particular fashions in music as well as clothes, transport, etc. A mod revival in the late 1970s, a reaction against punk *(q.v.)*, brought a new interest in simple rhythm-and-blues.

**Morton, Jelly Roll (1885–1941).** U.S. jazz pianist, composer, and bandleader, born Ferdinand Joseph La Menthe. A pioneer of New Orleans jazz, with Creole origins, he began recording in 1923 with a group called Morton's Red Hot Peppers.

**Motown.** The term refers to Detroit, the base for Tamla Motown records which developed and produced the most successful 1960s soul *(q.v.)*, by Stevie Wonder, The Supremes, The Four Tops, The Temptations, Smokey Robinson and the Miracles.

**Musicals.** The theatrical vehicle for popular music, songs, and dancing, developed in the late 19th century from the best in light opera, review, and music hall. Devised in London's West End and on Broadway, New York, musicals were later adapted or specially written for the cinema. The style dates from London's *In Town* (1892), but the best work came from Broadway, written by George Gershwin, Cole Porter, Jerome Kern, Rodgers and Hart, Rodgers and Hammerstein, Lerner and Lowe, Jule Styne, and Stephen Sondheim.

For Hollywood, Busby Berkeley shared responsibility for classic 1930s' musical films like *Forty Second Street* (1933) and Stanley Donen achieved near perfection with *Singin' in the Rain* (1952).

In Britain, Ivor Novello and Noel Coward were the leading lights. More recent musicals from Britain include Lionel Bart's *Oliver* (1960), and Tim Rice and Andrew Lloyd Webber's *Jesus Christ Superstar* and *Evita*.

In America the recent best includes Leonard Bernstein's *West Side Story* (1957), also *Hair* (1967), *My Fair Lady* (1956), *Fiddler on the Roof* (1964), *Hello Dolly* (1964), and *Grease* (1972).

The musical content of these shows has reflected the fashions of the time. So jazz (in a watered down version) was absorbed in Broadway's heyday, and today's rather different musicals or "rock operas" present some of the best in pop.

**Music Hall.** Known in the United States as vaudeville (or where striptease was involved, as burlesque), this was the theatrical medium for popular music and variety. A late Victorian and Edwardian phenomenon, music hall declined with the advent of the radio and cinema.

**New Orleans, Louisiana.** Commonly acknowledged as the birthplace of jazz, although the same music could be heard elsewhere in the same years of the late 19th century. However, New Orleans as a port had a bustling red light district, Storeyville, with bars and brothels where black musicians worked. The city's culture was also enriched by French influence and its Creole people, and this was reflected in jazz. The legalized brothels were closed down in 1917, and the jazz scene moved north.

**Northern Soul.** A phenomenon of the British pop scene after the late 1960s, its success owing nothing to music industry manipulation but contributing in time to the growth of disco *(q.v.)*. Young people in Northern England wanted to dance, rejected "progressive" rock, and in their clubs and dance halls created big hits out of the most obscure recordings of American rhythm-and-blues and early soul *(qq.v.)*. The dancing craze, skilful, acrobatic, and featuring all-night and all-day marathons, produced new fashions in clothes and music, which the record industry sought to exploit. Eventually the fans drifted back to mainstream soul.

**Oliver, (Joseph) King (1885–1938).** U.S. jazz cornetist, composer, and pioneer jazz-band leader. With his Creole Jazz Band (1922), he launched the career of Louis Armstrong.

**Parker, (Charles Christopher) Charlie "Bird" (1920–1955).** U.S. jazz alto sax player. He recorded with Dizzy Gillespie in the 1940s, and their work in producing bebop *(q.v.)* opened up new harmonic and rhythmic possibilities for musicians.

**Pink Floyd.** British pop group of the 1960s psychedelic era of "underground" *(q.v.)* culture, drug taking, multi-media experiments, and light shows. Starting with rhythm-and-blues, Pink Floyd later produced complex symphonic music using electronic effects.

**Pop Music.** The term coined in the early 1950s indicates a development from popular music to a distinct musical medium for the age of consumerism and "Never Had It So Good," an age of big-business record promotion, radio, television, and advertising, when young people had money to spend. Pop is the music of mass culture, created and marketed to reach most people who are not themselves involved in its creation but merely absorb it.

**Porter, Cole (1892–1964).** U.S. composer and songwriter. His work for stage and film musicals included *Gay Divorcee* (1932), *Anything Goes* (1934), *Kiss Me Kate* (1948), and *High Society* (1956).

**Presley, Elvis (1935–1977).** U.S. pop singer, pre-eminent in rock'n'roll *(q.v.)* from 1953 to 1963, and still "The King" when he died. His music fused blues with country and folk, he had an assured vocal technique, and his records sold over 28 million. The first white artist to reproduce the wildness of black music, he was condemned by the Establishment for his sexy delivery and pelvic gyrations. *Jailhouse Rock, Hound Dog, Heartbreak Hotel,* and *Love Me Tender* were his most successful songs, and of his many films *Flaming Star* (1960) brought out his best performance.

**Punk.** The rebel cult of 1976–78 among young people in Britain, originally whites in deprived urban areas. Musically, punk meant a return to primitive rock, but with more cacophony, obscenities, and angry themes. The Sex Pistols became stars but shocked society.

**Ragtime.** Syncopated piano music, a forerunner of jazz, most popular in the 1890s and 1900s and revived in the 1970s. Outside the mainstream of Afro-American music, ragtime belonged to the tradition of Minstrel shows, "coon" songs, and blacks playing to white audiences. Formal in structure rather than open to improvisation, the best rags were written by Scott Joplin *(q.v.), e.g.* original rags (1899), *Maple Leaf Rag* (1900), and *the Entertainer* (1902).

**Reggae.** West Indian pop music, originally played on makeshift instruments and associated with Jamaica's Rastafarian sect, but increasingly popular in Britain in the 1970s. The music borrows from the calypso and rhythm-and-blues *(qq.v.),* and is related to other West Indian forms like blue beat, ska, and rock steady. Reggae puts a blend of folk and rock against a hypnotically repetitive beat, with a strong bass and a between-beat type of drumming. Since the early successes of Millie Small, Desmond Decker, and Bob Marley, innumerable reggae artists have become prominent, and many performers from other traditions have added reggae flavor to their material.

**Reinhardt, (Jean Baptiste) Django (1910–1953).** Belgian jazz guitarist. Representative of the best of European musicians who took up jazz, this gypsy added folk to jazz and developed guitar improvisation. In the 1930s he formed a jazz quintet with violinist Stephane Grappelli.

**Rhythm-and-Blues.** Pop music developed by America's urban blacks, out of blues and swing *(qq.v.),* after World War II. Its exponents adopted pianos, saxophone, drums, and later electric guitars to supplement traditional instruments, and produced a more insistent rhythm as in jazz. A raw, energetic, but simple music, rhythm-and-blues was the basis of the rock revolution from rock'n'roll, to more sophisticated soul *(qq.v.),* and much in British pop of the 1960s. The best performers from early days included Howlin' Wolf, John Lee Hooker, Ray Charles, Chuck Berry, and Fats Domino, black artists often "covered" on record by white stars.

**Richard, Cliff (1940–  ).** British pop singer, born Harold Webb. Well acclaimed by 1959 with *Living Doll,* a million-selling disc, he remains at the top of his profession, though latterly more of a family entertainer than a wild rock artist.

**Rock'n'Roll/rock.** The dominant pop music trend since 1954. Bill Haley and the Comets' *Rock Around the Clock* (1955) established rock'n'roll as an international sensation appealing to white audiences who found rock's forerunner, black rhythm-and-blues *(q.v.)* too raw and inaccessible. The music belonged to black America, hit songs by whites often originating with black artists, but rock'n'roll incorporated aspects of country music to give it mass appeal. Its image, created in the film *Blackboard Jungle* (1955), was that of rebellion and overt sexuality. Gene Vincent's *Be Bop a Lula* and the Jerry Lee Lewis-Elvis Presley style gave teenagers a chance to let off steam.

The term rock'n'roll, coined by disc jockey Alan Freed, in time became plain rock, still characterized by amplified guitars, driving rhythm, and a vocal lead but taking in new fashions and reflecting social and political concerns.

The early 1960s were dominated by the Beatles and Rolling Stones, with their British-style rhythm-and-blues *(q.v.).* From America came surf sounds, soul, Phil Spector, and most especially folk rock *(qq.v.),* as produced by Bob Dylan, an intelligent rock associated with social consciousness and protest. 1960s material, by the Beatles, Dylan, or others, was often softer and usually more subtle in lyrics and music than the old rock'n'roll. Eric Clapton and Jimi Hendrix revamped the blues *(q.v.).*

Drug taking among artists led to considerable experimentation and a vogue for mind-expanding and psychedelic music *(e.g.* Pink Floyd). This "underground" produced acid rock, hard rock *(qq.v.)* and progressive pop, all of which involved improvisation and proved less and less suitable for dancing. Like folk rock, this music was "intellectual" in its anti-war and anti-Establishment themes.

After Beatlemania, United States trend-setting was no longer assured, and constant interplay between British and American artists has occurred. The 1970s saw a free-for-all of passing fashions and competing fads, but with a basic diet of mindless commercial pop, as a reaction against heavy rock.

**Rock Steady.** West Indian pop music style, a forerunner of reggae *(q.v.).*

**Rodgers, Jimmie (1897–1933).** U.S. country singer, guitarist, and songwriter. He stands first in the Country Music Hall of Fame.

**Rodgers and Hammerstein.** Richard Charles Rodgers (1902–1979) and Oscar Hammerstein II (1895–1960) wrote many successful musicals *(q.v.),* including *Oklahoma* (1943), *Carousel* (1945), *South Pacific* (1949), *The King and I* (1951), and *The Sound of Music* (1959). *Oh, What a Beautiful Morning, Surrey With a Fringe on Top, Some Enchanted Evening, Getting to Know You, Shall We Dance, Edelweiss,* and *My Favourite Things* are among their most memorable songs. Rodgers previously partnered Lorenz Hart.

**Rolling Stones.** British rock group of 1960s and 1970s, originally Mick Jagger, Charlie Watts, Bill Wyman, Keith Richard, and Brian Jones (d. 1969).

Less wholesome in image than the Beatles, the Stones' rhythm-and-blues-based music was loud, angry, sexual, and aggressive, often expressing young people's fantasies and frustrations, *e.g. I Can't Get No Satisfaction* (1965), *Paint it Black* (1966), and *Little Red Rooster* (1963).

**Simon, Paul (1942– ).** U.S. songwriter and singer, famous as part of the Simon and Garfunkel duo (with Art Garfunkel) in the 1960s, who were among the most successful recording artists. Simon's work is mainly smooth, folksy rock but more recently with jazz or reggae flavors. The best material includes *Sounds of Silence* (1966), *Bridge Over Troubled Water* (1970), and *America.*

**Sinatra, (Francis Albert) Frank (1915– ).** U.S. pop singer and film actor. From his work with Tommy Dorsey's big band in the 1940s, Sinatra achieved enormous acclaim, becoming an idol for young people.

**Skiffle.** A form of jazz, originally the music of so-called "spasm bands," in 1920s' America. These were small groups of black musicians in deprived areas, using makeshift instruments and domestic utensils, such as washboards and jugs. A British version evolved after World War II, reaching great popularity 1956–58 in work by Lonnie Donegan, Johnny Duncan, and Ken Colyer.

**Smith, Bessie** (*c.* **1895–1937).** U.S. blues and jazz singer. Starting to record in 1928, she reached peak popularity between 1924 and the Depression. Her mournful style and powerful renderings, mostly about men, money, and drink, became part of jazz history.

**Sondheim, Stephen (1930– ).** U.S. lyricist for musicals, including *West Side Story, Company,* and *A Little Night Music.*

**Songwriters.** *See* Burt Bacharach, Beatles (for John Lennon and Paul McCartney), Irving Berlin, Chuck Berry, David Bowie, Hoagy Carmichael, Bob Dylan, George (and Ira) Gershwin, Woody Guthrie, Elton John, Jerome Kern, Carole King, Musicals, Cole Porter, Paul Simon, Stephen Sondheim.
   The list includes some, but by no means all the best composers of 20th-century popular songs. Many of the great jazz writers and other specialists are excluded, as are notable Britons, *vis.* Ivor Novello (1893–1951), actor, playwright, and composer for *Glamorous Night* (1935), *Careless Rapture* (1936), and *The Dancing Years* (1939); also Lionel Bart (*Oliver*), Rice and Lloyd Webber (*Evita*).
   The list also neglects the early American songwriting teams of Bud de Sylva, Lew Brown and Ray Henderson (*Black Bottom, Birth of the Blues, The Best Things in Life are Free, Together, Sonny Roy,* and *Seventh Heaven,* 1920s); Al Dubin and Harry Warren (*Forty Second Street, We're in the Money, Lullaby of Broadway,* and *September in the Rain,* 1930s); also Sammy Kahn (*Bye Bye Blackbird*).

**Soul.** Black American pop music, derived from gospel blended with rhythm-and-blues (*qq.v.*) in the 1960s. Sophisticated sound depending on multitracking, electronic mixing, etc., soul was mass marketed by Tamia Motown in Detroit and as Memphis Sound by Stax/Atlantic. Its worldwide popularity ensured for black artists a large, lucrative, and vital share in mainstream pop. Soul singers include Ray Charles, James Brown, the Righteous Brothers, the Supremes, and others.

**Spector, Phil (1940– ).** U.S. record company executive, producer, and songwriter. He created the early 1960s multitracked wall of sound for The Crystals (*He's a Rebel* (1962), *Da Doo Ron Ron, And Then I Kissed Him*), The Ronettes (*Baby I Love You, Be My Baby,* 1963), and the Righteous Brothers (*You've Lost That Lovin' Feelin',* 1965).

**Surf Sound.** Rock music of the early 1960s, associated with West Coast surf riding, popularized most by the Beach Boys (*q.v.*) and featuring melodies of traditional ballads (rather than blues) and more complex chord progressions than early rock. Other songs not on surfing themes continued to use the surfing beat.

**Swing.** The popular dance music style of the 1930s and 1940s, the days after prohibition in America when the Depression relaxed and a time of dancing fever. Featuring the four even beats to the bar of New Orleans music and the characteristic riffs of Kansas City (*qq.v.*) jazz, popularized in New York by Count Basie, the music was developed as a new commercialized jazz by the big bands. Benny Goodman's success was followed by that of Artie Shaw, Tommy Dorsey, and others, all white bands. Duke Ellington and Basie, though successful, had nothing like the same popularity or the same financial rewards.

**Tamla Motown,** *see* **Motown.**

**Teeny Bopper.** Like *Bubble Gum* (*q.v.*), pop music produced and marketed for the sub-teen audience. The Monkees (1967) were the first artists created and promoted by TV for this audience.

**Underground.** Pop Music (*e.g.* early Pink Floyd) associated with the counter-culture arts movement in the U.S. and Britain in the 1960s, when many artists, film makers, actors, and writers rejected the conventional structure of artistic success and used their work to advocate such things as revolution, anarchy, and drug taking.

**Waller, (Thomas) Fats (1904–1943).** U.S. jazz and blues pianist and composer. He was a great showman and comedian, but also wrote hit songs like *Honeysuckle Rose* and *Aint Misbehavin'.*

**West Coast Sound.** The soft rock of Crosby, Stills, Nash, and Young, Buffalo Springfield, The Byrds, Joni Mitchell, and the Eagles. Owing much to Bob Dylan but also to the Beach Boys' surfing sounds, the music features close harmony voices, proficient guitar playing, and lyrics which are often about protest, peace, and justice.

**The Who.** British rock group, pre-eminent among "mod" groups in the mid-1960s but consistently popular ever since. Their best work includes *My Generation* (1965), *Substitute* (1966), the rock opera *Tommy* (1968), and *Quadrophenia* (1974).

## Top 10 Videocassettes Sales, 1985

1. **Jane Fonda's Workout** (Karl-Lorimar Home Video)
2. **Prime Time** (Karl-Lorimar Home Video)
3. **Star Trek III-The Search for Spock** (Paramount Home Video)
4. **Purple Rain** (Warner Home Video)
5. **Gone with the Wind** (MGM/UA Home Video)
6. **The Jane Fonda Workout Challenge** (Karl-Lorimar Home Video)
7. **Raiders of the Lost Ark** (Paramount Home Video)
8. **Raquel, Total Beauty and Fitness** (Thorn/EMI Home Video)
9. **We Are the World-The Video Event** (MusicVision)
10. **Wham! The Video** (CBS-Fox Video Music)

*Source: Billboard* © 1985 by Billboard Publications, Inc. Compiled by the Billboard Research Department and reprinted with permission.

## Top 10 Videocassettes Rentals, 1985

1. **The Karate Kid** (RCA/Columbia Home Video)
2. **The Terminator** (Thorn/EMI/HBO Video)
3. **Police Academy** (Warner Home Video)
4. **Romancing the Stone** (CBS-Fox Video)
5. **Revenge of the Nerds** (CBS-Fox Video)
6. **The Natural** (RCA/Columbia Pictures Home Video)
7. **Starman** (RCA/Columbia Pictures Home Video)
8. **The Empire Strikes Back** (CBS-Fox Video)
9. **Bachelor Party** (CBS-Fox Video)
10. **Splash** (Touchstone Home Video)

*Source: Billboard.* © 1985 Billboard Publications, Inc. Compiled by the Billboard Research Department and reprinted with permission.

## Top 10 Music Videocassettes 1985

1. **Madonna** (Warner Music Video)
2. **Wham! The Video** (CBS-Fox Video Music)
3. **Private Dancer** (Sony Video Software)
4. **Dance on Fire** (MCA Distribution Corp.)
5. **All Night Long** (MusicVision)
6. **Prince and The Revolution Live** (Warner Music Video)
7. **We Are the World-The Video Event** (MusicVision)
8. **U2 Live at Red Rocks** (MCA Distribution Corp)
9. **Animalize Live Uncensored** (MusicVision)
10. **Sing Blue Silver** (Thorn/EMI/HBO Home Video)

*Source: Billboard.* © 1985 by Billboard Publications, Inc. Compiled by the Billboard Research Department and reprinted with permission.

## VCR & TV Sales to Retailers, 1985—(53 weeks)

| | |
|---|---:|
| **Television** | |
| Color | 16,995,667 |
| Monochrome | 3,753,860 |
| Total TV[1] | 20,749,527 |
| Projection TV | 265,645 |
| Home VCR | 11,853,118 |
| Color Video Cameras | 394,764 |

1. Excludes projection television.

*Source:* Electronic Industries Association Consumer Electronics Group.

## 10 Top-grossing Concerts
(Nov. 27, 1984—Nov. 30, 1985)

1. **Bruce Springsteen & The E Street Band,** $6,946,380, Giants Stadium, E. Rutherford, N.J., Aug. 18, 19, 21, 22, 31 & Sept. 1, 1985.
2. **Bruce Springsteen & The E Street Band,** $5,688,455, Los Angeles Memorial Coliseum, Los Angeles, Calif., Sept. 27–30 & Oct. 2, 1985.
3. **The Jacksons,** $4,200,000, Dodgers Stadium, Los Angeles, Calif., Nov. 30–Dec. 2, 1984.
4. **Live Aid,** $3,552,800, JFK Stadium, Philadelphia, Pa., July 13, 1985.
5. **The Jacksons,** $3,382,064, Orange Bowl, Miami, Fla. Nov. 2–3, 1984.
6. **Bruce Springsteen & The E Street Band,** $2,771,257 ($3,464,072 Canadian), Exhibition Stadium, Toronto, Ont., Aug. 26–27, 1985.
7. **Bruce Springsteen & The E Street Band,** $2,563,015, Orange Bowl, Miami, Fla., Sept. 9–10, 1985.
8. **Librace, The Rockettes, Dancing Waters,** $2,469,727, Radio City Music Hall, New York, N.Y., April 4–21, 1985.
9. **Bruce Springsteen & The E Street Band,** $2,347,840, Mile High Statium, Denver, Colo., Sept. 23–24, 1985.
10. **Bruce Springsteen & The E Street Band,** $2,194,492, Cotton Bowl, Dallas, Texas, Sept. 13–14, 1985.

*Source:* Copyright 1985 by Amusement Business. Reprinted by permission.

## Top 10 Classical Compact Discs, 1985

1. **Bernstein: West Side Story,** Te Kanawa, Carreras (Bernstein) (DG)
2. **Amadeus Soundtrack,** Neville Marriner (Fantasy)
3. **Time Warp,** Cincinnati Pops (Kunzel) (Telarc)
4. **Tchaikovsky: 1812 Overture,** Cincinnati Pops (Kunzel) (Telarc)
5. **Webber: Requiem, Domingo, Brightman** (Maazel) (Angel)
6. **Star Tracks,** Cincinnati Pops (Kunzel) (Telarc)
7. **Telarc Sampler No. 1.** Various Artists (Telarc)
8. **Copland: Appalachian Spring,** Atlanta Symphony (Telarc)
9. **Haydn/Hummel/L. Mozart: Trumpet Concertos,** Wynton Marsalis, National Philharmonic (CBS)
10. **The Best of Wolfgang Amadeus Mozart,** Neville Marriner (Philips)

*Source: Billboard.* © 1985 by Billboard Publications, Inc. Compiled by the Billboard Research Department and reprinted with permission.

## Top 10 Pop Compact Discs, 1985

1. **No Jacket Required,** Phil Collins (Atlantic)
2. **Born in the U.S.A.,** Bruce Springsteen (Columbia)
3. **Brothers in Arms,** Dire Straits (Warner Bros.)
4. **Songs From the Big Chair,** Tears for Fears (Mercury)
5. **Dark Side of the Moon,** Pink Floyd (Harvest)
6. **Like a Virgin,** Madonna (Sire)
7. **Reckless,** Bryan Adams (A&M)
8. **Dream of the Blue Turtles,** Sting (A&M)
9. **Diamond Life,** Sade (Portrait)
10. **Around the World in a Day,** Prince & The Revolution (Paisley Park)

*Source: Billboard.* © 1985 by Billboard Publications, Inc. Compiled by the Billboard Research Department and reprinted with permission.

## Top 10 Classical Albums, 1985

1. **Amadeus,** Neville Marriner (Fantasy)
2. **Mozart: Requiem,** Academy of Ancient Music (Hogwood) (L'Oiseau-Lyre)
3. **Webber: Requiem** Domingo, Brightman (Maazel) (RCA)
4. **Bernstein: West Side Story,** Te Kanawa, Carreras (Bernstein) (DG)
5. **Haydn/Hummel/L. Mozart: Trumpet Concertos,** Wynton Marsalis, National Philharmonic Orchestra (Leppard) (CBS)
6. **Mamma,** Luciano Pavarotti (Mancini) (London)
7. **Pachelbel: Canon/Fasch: Trumpet Concerto,** Paillard Chamber Orchestra (RCA)
8. **The Best of Wolfgang Amadeus Mozart,** Neville Marriner (Philips)
9. **With a Song in My Heart,** Jessye Norman, Boston Pops (Williams) (Philips)
10. **Gershwin: An American in Paris,** Labeque Sisters (Angel)

*Source: Billboard* © 1985 by Billboard Publications, Inc. Compiled by the Billboard Research Department and reprinted by permission.

## Artists of the Year, 1985

Based on combined singles and albums chart performance—through sales and radio play—during the year.
**Single of the Year:** Careless Whisper, Wham!
**Album of the Year:** Born in the U.S.A., Bruce Springsteen
**Female Artist of the Year:** Madonna
**Male Artist of the Year:** Bruce Springsteen
**Group of the Year:** Prince & The Revolution
**New Artist of the Year:** Whitney Houston
**Country Artist of the Year:** Alabama
**Black Artist of the Year:** Kool & the Gang
**Adult Contemporary Artist of the Year:** Wham!
**Jazz Artist of the Year:** Wynton Marsalis
**Classical Artist of the Year:** Placido Domingo
**Soundtrack of the Year:** Beverly Hills Cop

*Source: Billboard.* © 1985 by Billboard Publications, Inc. Compiled by the Billboard Research Department and reprinted with permission.

## Top 10 Country Single Recordings, 1985

1. **Lost in the Fifties Tonight (In the Still of the Night),** Ronnie Milsap (RCA)
2. **Dixie Road,** Lee Greenwood (MCA)
3. **Real Love,** Dolly Parton with Kenny Rogers (RCA)
4. **Radio Heart,** Charly McClain (Epic)
5. **Highway Man,** Waylon Jennings, Willie Nelson, Johnny Cash, Kris Kristofferson (Columbia)
6. **She's Single Again,** Janie Fricke (Columbia)
7. **I'm for Love,** Hank Williams Jr. (Warner/Curb)
8. **Modern Day Romance,** Nitty Gritty Dirt Band (Warner Bros.)
9. **Fallin' in Love,** Sylvia (RCA)
10. **Forgiving You Was Easy,** Willie Nelson (Columbia)

*Source: Billboard.* © 1985 by Billboard Publications, Inc. Compiled by the Billboard Research Department and reprinted by permission.

## Top 10 Black Single Recordings, 1985

1. **Rock Me Tonight,** Freddie Jackson (Capitol)
2. **You Give Good Love,** Whitney Houston (Arista)
3. **Missing You,** Diana Ross (RCA)
4. **Nightshift,** Commodores (Motown)
5. **Saving All My Love for You,** Whitney Houston (Arista)
6. **In My House,** The Mary Jane Girls (Gordy)
7. **Freeway of Love,** Aretha Franklin (Arista)
8. **Solid,** Ashford & Simpson (Capitol)
9. **Oh, Sheila,** Ready for the World (MCA)
10. **Gotta Get You Home Tonight,** Eugene Wilde (Philly World)

*Source: Billboard.* © 1985 by Billboard Publications, Inc. Compiled by the Billboard Research Department and reprinted with permission.

## Top 10 Pop Single Recordings, 1985

1. **Careless Whisper,** Wham! (Columbia)
2. **Like a Virgin,** Madonna (Sire)
3. **Wake Me Up Before You Go-Go,** Wham! (Columbia)
4. **I Want to Know What Love Is,** Foreigner (Atlantic)
5. **I Feel For You,** Chaka Khan (Warner Bros.)
6. **Out of Touch,** Daryl Hall & John Oates (RCA)
7. **Everybody Wants to Rule the World,** Tears for Fears (Mercury)
8. **Money for Nothing,** Dire Straits (Warner Bros.)
9. **Crazy for You,** Madonna (Sire)
10. **Take On Me,** A-Ha (Warner Bros.)

*Source: Billboard.* © 1985 by Billboard Publications, Inc. Compiled by the Billboard Research Department and reprinted with permission.

## Manufacturers' Dollar Shipments of Phonograph Records

### (in millions)

| | Singles | | Albums[2] | |
|---|---|---|---|---|
| Year | Units | Dollars[1] | Units | Dollars[1] |
| 1979 | 196 | 275 | 318 | 2,136 |
| 1980 | 164 | 269 | 323 | 2,290 |
| 1981 | 155 | 256 | 295 | 2,342 |
| 1982 | 137 | 283 | 244 | 1,925 |
| 1983 | 125 | 269 | 210 | 1,689 |
| 1984 | 131 | 299 | 205 | 1,549 |
| 1985 | 121 | 281 | 167 | 1,281 |

1. List price value. 2. Includes EPs-extended play. *Source:* Recording Industry Association of America, Inc.

## Top 10 Pop Albums, 1985

1. **Born in the U.S.A.,** Bruce Springsteen (Columbia)
2. **Reckless,** Bryan Adams (A&M)
3. **Like a Virgin,** Madonna (Sire)
4. **Make It Big,** Wham! (Columbia)
5. **Private Dancer,** Tina Turner (Capitol)
6. **No Jacket Required,** Phil Collins (Atlantic)
7. **Beverly Hills Cop,** Soundtrack (MCA)
8. **Suddenly,** Billy Ocean (Jive)
9. **Purple Rain,** Prince & The Revolution (Warner Bros.)
10. **Song From the Big City,** Tears for Fears (Mercury)

*Source: Billboard.* © 1985 by Billboard Publications, Inc. Compiled by the Billboard Research Department and reprinted by permission.

## Top 15 Regular Prime Time TV Programs of 1985–86[1]

| Rank | Program name (network) | Total percent of TV households |
|------|------------------------|--------------------------------|
| 1. | Bill Cosby Show (CBS) | 32.3 |
| 2. | Family Ties (NBC) | 29.3 |
| 3. | Murder, She Wrote (CBS) | 26.0 |
| 4. | 60 Minutes (CBS) | 25.7 |
| 5. | Dynasty (ABC) | 23.2 |
| 6. | Cheers (NBC) | 22.9 |
| 7. | Dallas (CBS) | 22.9 |
| 8. | Miami Vice (NBC) | 22.1 |
| 9. | Golden Girls (NBC) | 21.4 |
| 10. | Who's the Boss? (ABC) | 20.7 |
| 11. | Night Court (NBC) | 20.6 |
| 12. | NBC Monday Night Movies | 20.2 |
| 13. | CBS-NFL Football Game 1 | 20.0 |
| 14. | Highway to Heaven (NBC) | 20.0 |
| 15. | Facts of Life (NBC) | 19.9 |
| | **Total U.S. TV households** | **85,900,000** |

1. Oct. 28, 1985, through Nov. 24, 1985. NOTE: Percentages are calculated from average audience viewings, 15 minutes or longer and 2 or more telecasts. *Source:* A. C. Nielsen Company, Nielsen Television Index Audience Estimates.

## Top Evening News Shows 1985–86[1]*

| Rank | Program name (network) | Rating (% of TV households) |
|------|------------------------|------------------------------|
| 1. | CBS Evening News with Dan Rather | 13.3 |
| 2. | NBC Nightly News with Tom Brokaw | 12.1 |
| 3. | World News Tonight with Peter Jennings (ABC) | 11.6 |

1. Sept. 23, 1985, through April 20, 1986.

## Top Morning News Shows 1985–86[1]*

| Rank | Program name (network) | Rating (% of TV households) |
|------|------------------------|------------------------------|
| 1. | Today (NBC) | 5.4 |
| 2. | Good Morning America (ABC) | 5.1 |
| 3. | CBS Morning News | 3.1 |

1. Sept. 23, 1985, through April 20, 1986.

## Top Miniseries 1985–86[1] [2]*

| Rank | Program name (network) | Rating (% of TV households) |
|------|------------------------|------------------------------|
| 1. | North and South (ABC) | 26.0 |
| 2. | Kane & Abel (CBS) | 22.7 |
| 3. | If Tomorrow Comes (CBS) | 22.1 |
| 4. | North and South Book II (ABC) | 21.3 |
| 5. | Sins (CBS) | 20.6 |

1. Sept. 23, 1985, through May 31, 1986. 2. Three or more parts.

## Top 15 Syndicated TV Programs of 1985–86

| Rank | Program | Rating (% U.S.)[1] |
|------|---------|---------------------|
| 1. | Wheel of Fortune | 18.5 |
| 2. | Jeopardy | 11.2 |
| 3. | M.A.S.H. | 9.2 |
| 4. | New Newlywed Game | 8.9 |
| 5. | PM Magazine | 8.8 |
| 6. | Southwest Conference Ftbl. | 8.7 |
| 7. | Three's Company | 8.6 |
| 8. | Entertainment Tonight | 8.4 |
| 9. | Fight Back | 8.0 |
| 10. | People's Court | 7.8 |
| 11. | Price is Right | 7.8 |
| 12. | Honeymooners Season | 7.5 |
| 13. | Small Wonder | 7.4 |
| 14. | Different Strokes | 7.3 |
| 15. | Hee Haw | 7.2 |

1. During November 1985. Ranked on the basis of average 15-minute audience ratings. *Source:* A.C. Nielsen Company, Nielsen Television Index Audience Estimates.

## Top Sports Shows 1985–86[1]*

| Rank | Program name (network) | Rating (% of TV households) |
|------|------------------------|------------------------------|
| 1. | Super Bowl XX (NBC) | 48.3 |
| 2. | 1985 World Series, Game 7 (ABC) | 32.6 |
| 3. | NFC Championship Game (CBS) | 32.5 |
| 4. | AFC Championship Game (NBC) | 32.4 |
| 5. | NFL Football: Chicago at Miami (ABC) | 29.6 |

1. Sept. 23, 1985, through May 31, 1986.

## Top Specials 1985–86[1]*

| Rank | Program name (network) | Rating (% of TV households) |
|------|------------------------|------------------------------|
| 1. | 58th Annual Academy Awards Presentation (ABC) | 27.3 |
| 2. | Bob Hope Christmas Show (NBC) | 24.8 |
| 3. | Bob Hope's High-Flying Birthday! (NBC) | 23.9 |
| 4. | All Star Party for "Dutch" Reagan (CBS) | 21.5 |
| 5. | 10th Annual Circus of Stars (CBS) | 21.1 |
| 6. | 60th Anniversary of the Grand Ole Opry (CBS) | 20.9 |

1. Sept. 23, 1985, through May 31, 1986.

## Top Soap Operas 1985–86[1]*

| Rank | Program name (network) | Rating (% of TV households) |
|------|------------------------|------------------------------|
| 1. | General Hospital (ABC) | 9.3 |
| 2. | The Young and the Restless (CBS) | 8.3 |
| 3. | All My Children (ABC) | 8.1 |
| 4. | One Life to Live (ABC) | 7.9 |
| 5. | Days of Our Lives (NBC) | 7.2 |

1. Sept. 23, 1985, through April 20, 1986.

*Reprinted with permission from *TV Guide.* Copyright © 1986 by Triangle Publication, Inc., Radnor, Pa.

## Weekly TV Viewing by Age
### (in hours and minutes)

| | Time per week | |
|---|---|---|
| | 1985 | 1984 |
| Women 18–34 years old | 32 h 21 min | 31 h 26 min |
| Women 35–54 | 33 h 59 min | 33 h 22 min |
| Women 55 and over | 42 h 15 min | 42 h 07 min |
| Men 18–34 | 26 h 03 min | 25 h 43 min |
| Men 35–54 | 28 h 53 min | 26 h 55 min |
| Men 55 and over | 38 h 01 min | 37 h 11 min |
| Female Teens | 23 h 23 min | 21 h 37 min |
| Male Teens | 23 h 43 min | 23 h 19 min |
| Children 6–11 | 27 h 22 min | 26 h 34 min |
| Children 2–5 | 28 h 15 min | 28 h 20 min |
| **Total Persons** | **31 h 28 min** | **30 h 38 min** |

NOTE: All figures are estimates based on National Audience Demographics Report, November 1985. *Source:* A. C. Nielsen Company, Nielsen Television Index Audience Estimates.

## Television Network Addresses

**American Broadcasting Companies (ABC)**
1330 Avenue of the Americas
New York, N.Y. 10019
**Canadian Broadcasting Corporation (CBC)**
1500 Bronson Avenue
Ottawa, Ontario, Canada K1G 3J5
**Columbia Broadcasting System (CBS)**
51 W. 52nd Street
New York, N.Y. 10019
**Fox Television (WNYW)**
205 E. 67th Street
New York, N.Y. 10021
**National Broadcasting Company (NBC)**
30 Rockefeller Plaza
New York, N.Y. 10020
**Public Broadcasting Service (PBS)**
475 L'Enfant Plaza West, S.W.
Washington, D.C. 20024
**Westinghouse Broadcasting (Group W)**
90 Park Avenue
New York, N.Y. 10016

## Persons Viewing Nightly Prime Time TV[1]
### (in millions)

| | Total persons[2] |
|---|---|
| Monday | 100.2 |
| Tuesday | 99.3 |
| Wednesday | 95.4 |
| Thursday | 98.6 |
| Friday | 94.0 |
| Saturday | 97.5 |
| Sunday | 110.6 |
| **Total average** | **99.3** |

1. Average minute audiences. 2. Based on National Demographics Report (November 1985). NOTE: Prime time is 8–11 p.m. (EST) *Source:* A. C. Nielsen Company, Nielsen Television Index Audience Estimates.

## Average Hours of Household TV Usage
### (in hours and minutes per day)

| | Yearly average | February | July |
|---|---|---|---|
| 1970–71 | 6 h 01 min | 6 h 53 min | 5 h 08 min |
| 1975–76 | 6 h 11 min | 6 h 49 min | 5 h 33 min |
| 1979–80 | 6 h 35 min | 7 h 22 min | 5 h 48 min |
| 1980–81 | 6 h 44 min | 7 h 23 min | 6 h 00 min |
| 1981–82 | 6 h 48 min | 7 h 22 min | 6 h 09 min |
| 1982–83 | 6 h 55 min | 7 h 33 min | 6 h 23 min |
| 1983–84 | 7 h 08 min | 7 h 38 min | 6 h 28 min |
| 1984–85 | 7 h 07 min | 7 h 49 min | 6 h 34 min |

NOTE: Estimates are based on total U.S. TV households, excluding unusual days. *Source:* A. C. Nielsen Company, Nielsen Television Index Audience Estimates.

## Audience Composition of Selected Prime Time Program Types[1]
### (Average Minute Audience)

| | General drama | Suspense and mystery drama | Situation comedy | Adventure | Feature films | All regular network programs 7–11 p.m. |
|---|---|---|---|---|---|---|
| Women (18 and over) | 13,070,000 | 10,480,000 | 13,350,000 | 9,800,000 | 12,660,000 | 11,520,000 |
| Men (18 and over) | 7,680,000 | 8,010,000 | 8,270,000 | 8,260,000 | 9,170,000 | 8,650,000 |
| Teens (12–17) | 1,360,000 | 1,560,000 | 3,010,000 | 1,930,000 | 2,250,000 | 1,910,000 |
| Children (2–11) | 1,820,000 | 1,370,000 | 4,390,000 | 3,950,000 | 2,770,000 | 2,540,000 |
| **Total** | **23,930,000** | **21,420,000** | **29,020,000** | **23,940,000** | **26,850,000** | **24,620,000** |

1. All figures are estimated for the period November 1985. *Source:* A. C. Nielsen Company, Nielsen Television Index Audience Estimates.

## Hours of TV Usage Per Week by Household Income

| | Under $15,000 | $15,000–$19,000 | $20,000–$29,000 | $30,000–39,999 | $40,000+ |
|---|---|---|---|---|---|
| Nov. 1980 | 46 h 03 min | 52 h 38 min | 53 h 40 min | n.a. | n.a. |
| Nov. 1985 | 53 h 55 min | 56 h 10 min | 52 h 04 min | 52 h 57 min | 52 h 19 min |

*Source:* A. C. Nielsen Company, Nielsen Television Index Audience Estimates. NOTE: n.a. = not available.

## Source of Household Viewing—Prime Time
Pay Cable, Basic Cable, and Non-Cable Households

| | Nov. 1985 | | | Nov. 1984 | | | Nov. 1983 | | |
| --- | --- | --- | --- | --- | --- | --- | --- | --- | --- |
| | Pay cable | Basic cable | Non-cable | Pay cable | Basic cable | Non-cable | Pay cable | Basic cable | Non-cable |
| % TV Usage[1] | 71.2 | 68.4 | 61.0 | 67.8 | 63.2 | 58.6 | 71.4 | 63.7 | 60.5 |
| Pay Cable | 12.0 | — | — | 13.0 | — | — | 13.6 | — | — |
| Cable-originated programming | 7.5 | 7.8 | — | 7.3 | 6.3 | — | 6.7 | 5.4 | — |
| Other-on-air stations | 12.7 | 13.6 | 12.4 | 12.2 | 12.8 | 12.4 | 11.5 | 12.9 | 10.3 |
| Network affiliated stations | 46.7 | 50.6 | 52.8 | 43.6 | 46.9 | 49.8 | 48.1 | 48.4 | 53.8 |
| Network share[2] | (66) | (74) | (87) | (64) | (74) | (85) | (67) | (76) | (89) |

1. May be less than sum of reception sources because of simultaneous viewing. 2. Percent Network/Sum of Sources. *Source:* A. C. Nielsen Company, Nielsen Television Index Estimates.

## Major U.S. Fairs and Expositions

**1853** Crystal Palace Exposition, New York City: modeled on similar fair held in London.

**1876** Centennial Exposition, Philadelphia: celebrating 100th year of independence.

**1893** World's Columbian Exposition, Chicago: commemorating 400th anniversary of Columbus' voyage to America.

**1894** Midwinter International Exposition, San Francisco: promoting business revival after Depression of 1893.

**1898** Trans-Mississippi and International Exposition, Omaha, Neb.: exhibiting products, resources, industries, and civilization of states and territories west of the Mississippi River.

**1901** Pan-American Exposition, Buffalo, N.Y.: promoting social and commercial interest of Western Hemisphere nations.

**1904** Louisiana Purchase Exposition, St. Louis: marking 100th anniversary of major land acquisition from France and opening up of the West.

**1905** Lewis and Clark Centennial Exposition, Portland, Ore.: commemorating 100th anniversary of exploration of a land route to the Pacific.

**1907** Jamestown Ter Centennial Exposition, Hampton Roads, Va.: marking 300th anniversary of first permanent English settlement in America.

**1909** Alaska-Yukon-Pacific Exposition, Seattle: celebrating growth of the Puget Sound area.

**1915-16** Panama-Pacific International Exposition, San Francisco: celebrating opening of the Panama Canal.

**1915-16** Panama-California Exposition, San Diego: promoting resources and opportunities for development and commerce of the Western states.

**1926** Sesquicentennial Exposition, Philadelphia: marking 150th year of independence.

**1933-34** Century of Progress International Exposition, Chicago: celebrating 100th anniversary of incorporation of Chicago as a city.

**1935** California Pacific International Exposition, San Diego: marking 400 years of progress since the first Spaniard landed on the West Coast.

**1939-40** New York World's Fair, New York City: "The World of Tomorrow," symbolized by Trylon and Perisphere. Officially commemorating 150th anniversary of inauguration of George Washington as President in New York.

**1939-40** Golden Gate International Exposition, Treasure Island, San Francisco: celebrating new Golden Gate Bridge and Oakland Bay Bridge.

**1962** The Century 21 Exposition, Seattle: "Man in the Space Age," symbolized by 600-foot steel space needle.

**1964-65** New York World's Fair, New York City: "Peace Through Understanding."

**1974** Expo '74, Spokane: "Tomorrow's Fresh, New Environment."

**1982** World's Fair, Knoxville, Tenn.: "Energy Turns the World," symbolized by the bronze-globed Sunsphere.

**1984** Louisiana World Exposition, New Orleans: "The World of Rivers."

## Longest Broadway Runs[1]

| | | | | |
| --- | --- | --- | --- | --- |
| 1. A Chorus Line (M) (1974– ) | 4,552 | | 14. Pippin (M) (1971–77) | 1,994 |
| 2. Oh, Calcutta (M) (1976– ) (revival) | 4,303 | | 15. South Pacific (M) (1949–54) | 1,925 |
| 3. Grease (M) (1972–80) | 3,388 | | 16. Magic Show (M) (1974–78) | 1,920 |
| 4. Fiddler on the Roof (1964–72) | 3,242 | | 17. Deathtrap (1978–82) | 1,792 |
| 5. Life with Father (1939–47) | 3,224 | | 18. Gemini (1977–81) | 1,788 |
| 6. Tobacco Road (1933–41) | 3,182 | | 19. Harvey (1944–49) | 1,775 |
| 7. Hello, Dolly! (M) (1964–71) | 2,844 | | 20. Dancin' (M) (1978–82) | 1,774 |
| 8. My Fair Lady (M) (1956–62) | 2,717 | | 21. Hair (M) (1968–72) | 1,750 |
| 9. 42nd Street (M) (1980– ) | 2,453 | | 22. The Wiz (M) (1975–79) | 1,672 |
| 10. Annie (M) (1977–83) | 2,377 | | 23. Born Yesterday (1946–49) | 1,642 |
| 11. Oklahoma (M) (1943–48) | 2,377 | | 24. Ain't Misbehavin' (M) (1978–82) | 1,604 |
| 12. Man of La Mancha (M) (1965–71) | 2,328 | | 25. The Best Little Whorehouse in | |
| 13. Abie's Irish Rose | 2,327 | | Texas (M) (1976–82) | 1,584 |

1. As of July 13, 1986. M = musical. Years are those of opening and closing.

# Motion Picture Revenues

| Top Money Makers[1] | | Top Rentals 1985[2] | |
|---|---|---|---|
| 1. E.T. The Extra-Terrestrial (Universal, 1982) | $227,960,804 | 1. Back to the Future (Universal) | $94,000,000 |
| 2. Star Wars (20th Century-Fox, 1977) | 193,500,000 | 2. Rambo: First Blood Part II (Tri-Star) | 80,000,000 |
| 3. Return of the Jedi (20th Century-Fox, 1983) | 168,002,414 | 3. Rocky IV (M-G-M/Universal) | 65,000,000 |
| 4. The Empire Strikes Back (20th Century-Fox, 1980) | 141,600,000 | 4. Beverly Hills Cop (Paramount) | 50,000,000 |
| | | 5. Cocoon (20th Century Fox) | 40,000,000 |
| 5. Jaws (Universal, 1975) | 129,961,081 | 6. The Goonies (Warner Brothers) | 29,900,000 |
| 6. Ghostbusters (Columbia) | 128,216,446 | 7. Witness (Paramount) | 28,000,000 |
| 7. Raiders of the Lost Ark (Paramount, 1981) | 115,598,000 | 8. Police Academy 2-Their First Assignment (Warner Brothers) | 27,200,000 |
| 8. Indiana Jones and the Temple of Doom (Paramount, 1984) | 109,000,000 | 9. National Lampoon's European Vacation (Warner Brothers) | 25,600,000 |
| 9. Beverly Hills Cop (Paramount, 1984) | 108,000,000 | 10. A View To A Kill (M-G-M/United Artists) | 25,200,000 |
| 10. Grease (Paramount, 1978) | 96,300,000 | 11. Fletch (Universal) | 23,923,119 |
| 11. Tootsie (Columbia, 1982) | 95,206,129 | 12. Spies Like Us (Warner Brothers) | 23,000,000 |
| 12. Back to the Future (Universal, 1985) | 94,000,000 | 13. Pale Rider (Warner Brothers) | 20,800,000 |
| 13. The Exorcist (Warner Brothers, 1973) | 89,000,000 | 14. The Jewel of the Nile (20th Century Fox) | 20,000,000 |
| 14. The Godfather (Paramount, 1972) | 86,275,000 | 15. Mask (Universal) | 19,869,872 |
| 15. Superman (Warner Brothers, 1978) | 82,800,000 | 16. Brewster's Millions (Universal) | 19,383,923 |
| 16. Close Encounters of the Third Kind (Columbia, 1977/80) | 82,750,000 | 17. Pee-wee's Big Adventure (Warner Brothers) | 18,100,000 |
| | | 18. E. T. The Extra-Terrestrial (Universal) | 17,983,815 |
| 17. Rambo: First Blood Part II (Tri-Star, 1985) | 80,000,000 | 19. Mad Max Beyond Thunderdome (Warner Brothers) | 17,900,000 |
| 18. The Sound of Music (20th Century-Fox, 1965) | 79,748,000 | |  |
| 19. Gremlins (Warner Brothers, 1984) | 79,500,000 | 20. Jagged Edge (Columbia) | 17,500,000 |
| 20. The Sting (Universal, 1973) | 78,198,608 | 21. The Breakfast Club (Universal) | 17,254,081 |
| 21. Gone With the Wind (M-G-M/United Artists, 1939) | 76,700,000 | 22. Commando (20th Century Fox) | 17,000,000 |
| 22. Saturday Night Fever (Paramount, 1977) | 74,100,000 | 23. Silverado (Columbia) | 16,582,358 |
| 23. National Lampoon's Animal House (Universal, 1978) | 70,778,176 | 24. St. Elmo's Fire (Columbia) | 16,343,197 |
| 24. Rocky III (M-G-M/United Artists, 1982) | 65,800,000 | 25. White Nights (Columbia) | 16,000,000 |
| 25. Superman II (Warner Bros., 1981) | 65,100,000 | | |

NOTE: United States and Canada only. 1. Figures are not be confused with gross box-office receipts from sale of tickets. 2. Figures are total rentals collected by film distributors as of Dec. 31, 1984. *Source: Variety.*

# Miss America Winners

1921 Margaret Gorman, Washington, D.C.
1922-23 Mary Campbell, Columbus, Ohio
1924 Ruth Malcolmson, Philadelphia, Pa.
1925 Fay Lamphier, Oakland, Calif.
1926 Norma Smallwood, Tulsa, Okla.
1927 Lois Delaner, Joliet, Ill.
1933 Marion Bergeron, West Haven, Conn.
1935 Henrietta Leaver, Pittsburgh, Pa.
1936 Rose Coyle, Philadelphia, Pa.
1937 Bette Cooper, Bertrand Island, N.J.
1938 Marilyn Meseke, Marion, Ohio
1939 Patricia Donnelly, Detroit, Mich.
1940 Frances Marie Burke, Philadelphia, Pa.
1941 Rosemary LaPlanche, Los Angeles, Calif.
1942 Jo-Caroll Dennison, Tyler, Texas
1943 Jean Bartel, Los Angeles, Calif.
1944 Venus Ramey, Washington, D.C.
1945 Bess Myerson, New York, N.Y.
1946 Marilyn Buferd, Los Angeles, Calif.
1947 Barbara Walker, Memphis, Tenn.
1948 BeBe Shopp, Hopkins, Minn.
1949 Jacque Mercer, Litchfield, Ariz.
1951 Yolande Betbeze, Mobile, Ala.
1952 Coleen Kay Hutchins, Salt Lake City, Utah
1953 Neva Jane Langley, Macon, Ga.
1954 Evelyn Margaret Ay, Ephrata, Pa.
1955 Lee Meriwether, San Francisco, Calif.
1956 Sharon Ritchie, Denver, Colo.
1957 Marian McKnight, Manning, S.C.
1958 Marilyn Van Derbur, Denver, Colo.

1959 Mary Ann Mobley, Brandon, Miss.
1960 Lynda Lee Mead, Natchez, Miss.
1961 Nancy Fleming, Montague, Mich.
1962 Maria Fletcher, Asheville, N.C.
1963 Jacquelyn Mayer, Sandusky, Ohio
1964 Donna Axum, El Dorado, Ark.
1965 Vonda Kay Van Dyke, Phoenix, Ariz.
1966 Deborah Irene Bryant, Overland Park, Kan.
1967 Jane Anne Jayroe, Laverne, Okla.
1968 Debra Dene Barnes, Moran, Kan.
1969 Judith Anne Ford, Belvidere, Ill.
1970 Pamela Anne Eldred, Birmingham, Mich.
1971 Phyllis Ann George, Denton, Texas
1972 Laurie Lea Schaefer, Columbus, Ohio
1973 Terry Anne Meeuwsen, DePere, Wis.
1974 Rebecca Ann King, Denver, Colo.
1975 Shirley Cothran, Fort Worth, Texas
1976 Tawney Elaine Godin, Yonkers, N.Y.
1977 Dorothy Kathleen Benham, Edina, Minn.
1978 Susan Perkins, Columbus, Ohio
1979 Kylene Baker, Galax, Va.
1980 Cheryl Prewitt, Ackerman, Miss.
1981 Susan Powell, Elk City, Okla.
1982 Elizabeth Ward, Russellville, Ark.
1983 Debra Maffett, Anaheim, Calif.
1984 Vanessa Williams, Milwood, N.Y.[1]
     Suzette Charles, Mays Landing, N.J.
1985 Sharlene Wells, Salt Lake City, Utah
1986 Susan Akin, Meridian, Miss.
1987 (*See* Current Events)
1. Resigned July 23, 1984.

## States and Territories

State flower, bird, etc., are official unless otherwise indicated; dates in parentheses are those of adoption. Largest cities include incorporated places only. For secession and readmission dates of the former Confederate states, *see* Index. For lists of Governors, Senators, and Representatives, *see* Index. For additional state information, *see* the sections on "Business and the Economy," "Elections," "Taxes," and "U.S. Statistics."

## ALABAMA

**Capital:** Montgomery
**Governor:** George Corley Wallace, D (to Jan. 1987)
**Lieut. Governor:** William J. Baxley, D (to Jan. 1987)
**Secy. of State:** Don Seigleman, D (to Jan. 1987)
**Comptroller:** Tom Brassell
**Atty. General:** Charles A. Graddick, D (to Jan. 1987)
**Organized as territory:** March 3, 1817
**Entered Union & (rank):** Dec. 14, 1819 (22)
**Present constitution adopted:** 1901
**Motto:** *Audemus jura nostra defendere* (We dare defend our rights)
**State flower:** Camellia (1959)
**State bird:** Yellowhammer (1927)
**State song:** "Alabama" (1931)
**State tree:** Southern pine (longleaf) (1949)
**Nickname:** Yellowhammer State
**Origin of name:** May come from Choctaw meaning "thicket-clearers" or "vegetation-gatherers"
**1980 population (1980 census) & (rank):** 3,893,888 (22)
**1985 est. population (July 1) & (rank):** 4,021,000 (22)
**1984 land area & (rank):** 50,767 sq mi. (131,487 sq km) (28)
**Geographic center:** In Chilton Co., 12 mi. SW of Clanton
**Number of counties:** 67
**Largest cities (1980 census):** Birmingham, 284,413; Mobile, 200,452; Montgomery, 178,157; Huntsville, 142,513; Tuscaloosa, 75,143; Gadsden, 47,565
**State forests:** 8 (14,248.58 ac.)
**State parks:** 22 (45,614 ac.)
**1984 net receipts:** $11,209,764,125
**1984 net disbursements:** $10,731,012,294
**1985 net receipts:** $11,641,948,246
**1985 net disbursements:** $11,986,185,244

Spanish explorers are believed to have arrived at Mobile Bay in 1519, and the territory was visited in 1540 by the explorer Hernando de Soto. The first permanent European settlement in Alabama was founded by the French at Fort Louis in 1702. The British gained control of the area in 1763 by the Treaty of Paris, but had to cede almost all the Alabama region to the U.S. after the American Revolution. The Confederacy was founded at Montgomery in February 1861 and, for a time, the city was the Confederate capital.

During the last part of the 19th century, the economy of the state slowly improved. At Tuskegee Institute, founded in 1881 by Booker T. Washington, Dr. George Washington Carver carried out his famous agricultural research.

In the 1950s and '60s, Alabama was the site of such landmark civil-rights actions as the bus boycott in Montgomery (1955–56) and the "Freedom March" from Selma to Birmingham (1965).

Today, Alabama is the leading heavy-industry state in the South. Textiles, iron, and steel lead its manufacturing, which centers around Birmingham, the "Pittsburgh of the South." Industry is growing rapidly in other areas, including the Tennessee River Valley, with its great Muscle Shoals power plant. Manufacturing also includes cement, feed, fertilizer, chemical, rubber, and aluminum products. The state ranks high in the output of poultry, cotton, cattle, hogs, corn, potatoes, peanuts, and fruit.

Points of interest include the George C. Marshall Space Flight Center at Huntsville, Russell Cave National Monument near Bridgeport, and the White House of the Confederacy in Montgomery.

## ALASKA

**Capital:** Juneau
**Governor:** Bill Sheffield, D (to Dec. 1986)
**Lieut. Governor:** Stephen McAlpine, D (to Dec. 1986)
**Commissioner of Administration:** Eleanor Andrews, D (to Dec. 1986)
**Atty. General:** Hal M. Brown, D (to Dec. 1986)
**Organized as territory:** 1912
**Entered Union & (rank):** Jan. 3, 1959 (49)
**Constitution ratified:** April 24, 1956
**Motto:** North to the Future
**State flower:** Forget-me-not
**State tree:** Sitka spruce
**State bird:** Willow ptarmigan
**State fish:** King salmon
**State song:** "Alaska's Flag"
**Nickname:** The state is commonly called "The Last Frontier" or "Land of the Midnight Sun"
**Origin of name:** Corruption of Aleut word meaning "great land" or "that which the sea breaks against"
**1980 population (1980 census) & (rank):** 401,851 (50)
**1985 est. population (July 1) & (rank):** 521,000 (49)
**1984 land area & (rank):** 570,833 sq mi. (1,478,458 sq km) (1)
**Geographic center:** 60 mi. NW of Mt. McKinley
**Number of boroughs:** 10
**Largest cities (1984 est.):** Anchorage, 227,070; Fairbanks, 26,629; Juneau, 25,964; Ketchikan, 12,712; Sitka, 8,194; Kodiak, 6,030; Bethel, 3,869
**State forests:** None
**State parks:** 5; 59 waysides and areas (3.3 million ac.)
**General revenue (fiscal 1984–85):** $3,776,779
**General expenditures (fiscal 1984–85):** $3,649,440

Vitus Bering, a Dane working for the Russians, and Alexei Chirikov discovered the Alaskan mainland and the Aleutian Islands in 1741. The tremendous land mass of Alaska—equal to one fifth of the continental U.S.—was unexplored in 1867 when Secretary of State William Seward arranged for its purchase from the Russians for $7,200,000. The transfer of the territory took place on Oct. 18, 1867. Despite a price of about two cents an acre, the purchase was widely ridiculed as "Seward's Folly." The first official census (1880) reported a total of 33,426 Alaskans, all but 430 being of aboriginal stock. The Gold Rush of 1898 resulted in a mass influx of more than 30,000 people. Since then, Alaska has returned billions of dollars' worth of products to the U.S.

In 1968, a large oil and gas reservoir near Prudhoe Bay on the Arctic Coast was found. The Prudhoe Bay reservoir, with an estimated recoverable 10 billion barrels of oil and 27 trillion cubic feet of gas, is twice as large as any other oil field in North America. The Trans-Alaska pipeline was completed in 1977 at a cost of $7.7 billion. On June 20, oil started flowing through the 800-mile-long pipeline from Prudhoe Bay to the port of Valdez.

Other industries important to Alaska's economy are fisheries, wood and wood products, and furs.

Denali National Park and Mendenhall Glacier in North Tongass National Forest are of interest, as is the large totem pole collection at Sitka National Historical Park. The Katmai National Park includes the "Valley of Ten Thousand Smokes," an area of active volcanoes.

# ARIZONA

**Capital:** Phoenix
**Governor:** Bruce Babbitt, D (to Jan. 1987)
**Secy. of State:** Rose Mofford, D (to Jan. 1987)
**Atty. General:** Bob Corbin, R (to Jan. 1987)
**State Treasurer:** Ray Rottas, R (to Jan. 1987)
**Organized as territory:** Feb. 24, 1863
**Entered Union & (rank):** Feb. 14, 1912 (48)
**Present constitution adopted:** 1911
**Motto:** *Ditat Deus* (God enriches)
**State flower:** Flower of saguaro cactus (1931)
**State bird:** Cactus wren (1931)
**State colors:** Blue and old gold (1915)
**State song:** "Arizona," a march song (1919)
**State tree:** Paloverde (1957)
**Nickname:** Grand Canyon State
**Origin of name:** From the Indian "Arizonac," meaning "little spring"
**1980 population (1980 census) & (rank):** 2,718,425 (29)
**1985 est. population (July 1) & (rank):** 3,187,000 (27)
**1984 land area & (rank):** 113,508 sq mi. (293,986 sq km) (6)
**Geographic center:** In Yavapai Co., 55 mi. ESE of Prescott
**Number of counties:** 15
**Largest cities (1980 census):** Phoenix, 789,704; Tucson, 330,537; Mesa, 152,453; Tempe, 106,743; Glendale, 97,172; Scottsdale, 86,622; Yuma, 42,481
**State forests:** None
**State parks:** 16
**State revenue (fiscal 1984-85):** $3,664,046,745
**State expenditure (fiscal 1984-85):** $3,820,844,425

Marcos de Niza, a Spanish Franciscan friar, was the first European to explore Arizona. He entered the area in 1539 in search of the mythical Seven Cities of Gold. Although he was followed a year later by another gold seeker, Francisco Vásquez de Coronado, most of the early settlement was for missionary purposes. In 1776 the Spanish established Fort Tucson. In 1848, after the Mexican War, most of the Arizona territory became part of the U.S., and the southern portion of the territory was added by the Gadsden Purchase in 1853.

In 1973 the world's biggest dam, the New Cornelia Tailings, was completed near Ajo.

Arizona history is rich in legends of America's Old West. It was here that the great Indian chiefs Geronimo and Cochise led their people against the frontiersmen. Tombstone, Ariz., was the site of the West's most famous shoot-out—the gunfight at the O.K. Corral. Today, Arizona has the largest U.S. Indian population; more than 14 tribes are represented on 19 reservations.

Manufacturing has become Arizona's most important industry. Principal products include electrical, communications, and aeronautical items. The state produces over half the country's copper. Agriculture is also important to the state's economy.

State attractions include such famous scenery as the Grand Canyon, the Petrified Forest, and the Painted Desert. Hoover Dam, Lake Mead, Fort Apache, and the reconstructed London Bridge at Lake Havasu City are of particular interest.

# ARKANSAS

**Capital:** Little Rock
**Governor:** Bill Clinton, D (to Jan. 1987)
**Lieut. Governor:** Winston Bryant, D (to Jan. 1987)
**Secy. of State:** W. J. McCuen, D (to Jan. 1987)
**Atty. General:** Steve Clark (to Jan. 1987)
**Auditor of State:** Julia Hughes Jones, D (to Jan. 1987)
**Treasurer of State:** Jimmie Lou Fisher, D (to Jan. 1987)
**Land Commissioner:** Charles Daniels, D (to Jan. 1987)
**Organized as territory:** March 2, 1819
**Entered Union & (rank):** June 15, 1836 (25)
**Present constitution adopted:** 1874
**Motto:** *Regnat populus* (The people rule)
**State flower:** Apple Blossom (1901)
**State tree:** Pine (1939)
**State bird:** Mockingbird (1929)
**State insect:** Honeybee
**State song:** "Arkansas" (1963)
**Nickname:** Land of Opportunity
**Origin of name:** From the Quapaw Indians
**1980 population (1980 census) & (rank):** 2,286,435 (33)
**1985 est. population (July 1) & (rank):** 2,359,000 (33)
**1984 land area & (rank):** 52,078 sq mi. (134,883 sq km) (27)
**Geographic center:** In Pulaski Co., 12 mi. NW of Little Rock
**Number of counties:** 75
**Largest cities (1980 census):** Little Rock, 158,461; Fort Smith, 71,626; North Little Rock, 64,288; Pine Bluff, 56,636; Fayetteville, 36,608; Hot Springs, 35,781
**State forests:** None
**State parks:** 44
**State tax receipts (fiscal year 1984-1985):** $1,997,731,342
**Taxes from all sources (fiscal year 1984-1985):** $3,239,400,000
**State general expenditure (fiscal year 1984-1985):** $3,169,900,000

Hernando de Soto, in 1541, was among the early European explorers to visit the territory. It was a Frenchman, Henri de Tonty, who in 1686 founded the first permanent white settlement—the Arkansas Post. In 1803 the area was acquired by the U.S. as part of the Louisiana Purchase.

Food products are the state's largest employing sector, with lumber and wood products a close second. Arkansas is also a leader in the production of cotton, rice, and soybeans. The state produces 97% of the nation's high-grade domestic bauxite ore—the source of aluminum. It also has the country's only active diamond mine; located near Murfreesboro, it is operated as a tourist attraction.

Hot Springs National Park is a major state attraction.

Blanchard Springs Caverns, the Arkansas Territorial Capitol Restoration at Little Rock, and Dogpatch U.S.A. near Harrison are of interest.

# CALIFORNIA

**Capital:** Sacramento
**Governor:** George Deukmejian, R (to Jan. 1987)
**Lieut. Governor:** Leo McCarthy, D (to Jan. 1987)
**Secy. of State:** March Fong Eu, D (to Jan. 1987)
**Controller:** Ken Cory, D (to Jan. 1987)
**Atty. General:** John Van de Kamp, D (to Jan. 1987)
**Treasurer:** Jesse M. Unruh, D (to Jan. 1987)
**Entered Union & (rank):** Sept. 9, 1850 (31)
**Present constitution adopted:** 1879
**Motto:** *Eureka* (I have found it)
**State flower:** Golden poppy (1903)
**State tree:** California redwoods *(Sequoia sempervirens & Sequoia gigantea)* (1937 & 1953)
**State bird:** California valley quail (1931)
**State animal:** California grizzly bear (1953)
**State fish:** California golden trout (1947)
**State colors:** Blue and gold (1951)
**State song:** "I Love You, California" (1951)
**Nickname:** Golden State
**Origin of name:** From a book, *Las Sergas de Esplandián,* by Garcia Ordóñez de Montalvo, c. 1500
**1980 population (1980 census) & (rank):** 23,667,565 (1)
**1985 est. population (July 1) & (rank):** 26,365,000 (1)
**1984 land area & (rank):** 156,299 sq mi. (404,815 sq km) (3)
**Geographic center:** In Madera Co., 35 mi. NE of Madera
**Number of counties:** 58
**Largest cities (1980 census):** Los Angeles, 2,966,850; San Diego, 875,538; San Francisco, 678,974; San Jose, 629,442; Long Beach, 361,334; Oakland, 339,337
**State forests:** 8 (70,283 ac.)
**State parks and beaches:** 180 (723,000 ac.)
**State general revenue (fiscal year 1986–87):** $31,200,000,000
**State general expenditure (fiscal year 1986–87):** $30,600,000,000

Although California was sighted by Spanish navigator Juan Rodríguez Cabrillo in 1542, its first Spanish mission (at San Diego) was not established until 1769. California became a U.S. Territory in 1847 when Mexico surrendered it to John C. Frémont. On Jan. 24, 1848, James W. Marshall discovered gold at Sutter's Mill, starting the California Gold Rush and bringing settlers to the state in large numbers.

In 1964, the U.S. Census Bureau estimated that California had become the most populous state, surpassing New York. California also leads the country in personal income and consumer expenditures.

Leading industries include manufacturing (transportation equipment, machinery, and electronic equipment), agriculture, and tourism. Principal natural resources include petroleum, cement, and natural gas.

The Bank of America National Trust and Savings Association, founded by the Giannini family, ranks first or second in the world.

Death Valley, in the southeast, is 282 feet below sea level, the lowest point in the nation; and Mt. Whitney (14,495 ft) is the highest point in the contiguous 48 states. Lassen Peak is one of two active U.S. volcanos outside of Alaska and Hawaii; its last eruptions were recorded in 1917. The General Sherman Tree in Sequoia National Park is estimated to be about 3,500 years old and a stand of bristlecone pine trees in the White Mountains may be over 4,000 years old.

Other points of interest include Yosemite National Park, Disneyland, Hollywood, the Golden Gate bridge, San Simeon State Park, and Point Reyes National Seashore.

# COLORADO

**Capital:** Denver
**Governor:** Richard D. Lamm, D (to Jan. 1987)
**Lieut. Governor:** Nancy E. Dick, D (to Jan. 1987)
**Secy. of State:** Natalie Meyer, R (to Jan 1987)
**Treasurer:** Roy Romer, D (to Jan. 1987)
**Controller:** James A. Stroup
**Atty. General:** Duane Woodard, R (to Jan. 1987)
**Organized as territory:** Feb. 28, 1861
**Entered Union & (rank):** Aug. 1, 1876 (38)
**Present constitution adopted:** 1876
**Motto:** *Nil sine Numine* (Nothing without Providence)
**State flower:** Rocky Mountain columbine (1899)
**State tree:** Colorado blue spruce (1939)
**State bird:** Lark bunting (1931)
**State animal:** Rocky Mountain bighorn sheep
**State colors:** Blue and white (1911)
**State song:** "Where the Columbines Grow" (1915)
**Nickname:** Centennial State
**Origin of name:** From the Spanish, "ruddy" or "red"
**1980 population (1980 census) & (rank):** 2,889,735 (28)
**1985 est. population (July 1) & rank:** 3,231,000 (26)
**1984 land area & (rank):** 103,595 sq mi. (268,311 sq km) (8)
**Geographic center:** In Park Co., 30 mi. NW of Pikes Peak
**Number of counties:** 63
**Largest cities (1980 census):** Denver, 492,365; Colorado Springs, 214,821; Aurora, 158,588; Lakewood, 113,808; Pueblo, 101,686; Arvada, 84,576; Boulder, 76,685
**State forests:** 1 (71,000 ac.)
**Total state revenue (fiscal 1984–85):** $4,838,000,000
**Total state expenditure (fiscal 1984–85):** $4,498,000,000

First visited by Spanish explorers in the 1500s, the territory was claimed for Spain by Juan de Ulibarri in 1706. The U.S. obtained eastern Colorado as part of the Louisiana Purchase in 1803, the central portion in 1845 with the admission of Texas as a state, and the western part in 1848 as a result of the Mexican War.

Colorado has the highest mean elevation of any state, with more than 1,000 Rocky Mountain peaks over 10,000 feet high and 54 towering above 14,000 feet. Pikes Peak, the most famous of these mountains, was discovered by U.S. Army Lieut. Zebulon M. Pike in 1806.

Gold was first discovered near present-day Denver in 1858 and at Cripple Creek in 1891. Rich silver deposits were also found in 1875.

Once primarily a mining and agricultural state, today Colorado draws the largest segment of its income from manufacturing. Denver is a leader in electronics and space-age industry. Pueblo, the "Pittsburgh of the West," makes iron, steel, brick, tile, and foundry products.

Rich in natural resources, Colorado now produces most of the world's molybdenum. Uranium, vanadium, gold, silver, lead, tin, zinc, and other minerals are also mined. Colorado's highly developed irrigation system promotes farming of wheat, hay, beans, sugar beets, corn, potatoes, barley, and truck vegetables. Cattle and sheep raising is also important.

Tourism has developed into a major industry largely because of Colorado's magnificent scenery. Among the major attractions are Rocky Mountain National Park, Garden of the Gods, Great Sand Dunes and Dinosaur National Monuments, Pikes Peak and Mt. Evans Highway, and Mesa Verde National Park (prehistoric cliff dwellings).

Colorado Springs, with the nearby U.S. Air Force Academy, is probably the most popular tourist center in the Rocky Mountains, while Aspen and Vail have become leading ski resorts.

## CONNECTICUT

**Capital:** Hartford
**Governor:** William A. O'Neill, D (to Jan. 1987)
**Lieut. Governor:** Joseph J. Fauliso, D (to Jan. 1987)
**Secy. of State:** Julia H. Tashjian, D (to Jan. 1987)
**Comptroller:** J. Edward Caldwell, D (to Jan. 1987)
**Treasurer:** Joan R. Kemler, D (to Jan. 1987)
**Atty. General:** Joseph I. Lieberman, D (to Jan. 1987)
**Entered Union & (rank):** Jan. 9, 1788 (5)
**Present constitution adopted:** Dec. 30, 1965
**Motto:** *Qui transtulit sustinet* (He who transplanted still sustains)
**State flower:** Mountain laurel (1907)
**State tree:** White Oak (1947)
**State animal:** Sperm whale (1975)
**State bird:** American robin (1943)
**State Hero:** Nathan Hale (1985)
**State insect:** Praying mantis (1977)
**State mineral:** Garnet (1977)
**State song:** "Yankee Doodle" (1978)
**State ship:** USS Nautilus (SSN571) (1983)
**Official designation:** *Constitution State* (1959)
**Nickname:** Nutmeg State
**Origin of name:** From an Indian word (Quinnehtukqut) meaning "beside the long tidal river"
**1980 population (1980 census) & (rank):** 3,107,576 (25)
**1985 est. population (July 1) & (rank):** 3,174,000 (28)
**1984 land area & (rank):** 4,872 sq mi. (12,618 km) (48)
**Geographic center:** In Hartford Co., at East Berlin
**Number of counties:** 8
**Largest cities (1980 census):** Bridgeport, 142,546; Hartford, 136,392; New Haven, 126,109; Waterbury, 103,266; Stamford, 102,453; Norwalk, 77,767
**State forests:** 30 (138,029 ac.)
**State parks:** 87 (29,214 ac.)
**State general revenue (fiscal 1984–85):** $7,174,000,000
**State general expenditure (fiscal 1984–85):** $6,556,358,658

The Dutch navigator, Adriaen Block, was the first European of record to explore the area, sailing up the Connecticut River in 1614. In 1633, Dutch colonists built a fort and trading post near present-day Hartford, but soon lost control to English Puritans migrating south from the Massachusetts Bay Colony.

English settlements, established in the 1630s at Windsor, Wethersfield, and Hartford, united in 1639 to form the Connecticut Colony and adopted the *Fundamental Orders*, considered the world's first written constitution.

The colony's royal charter of 1662 was exceptionally liberal. When Gov. Edmund Andros tried to seize it in 1687, it was hidden in the Hartford Oak, commemorated in Charter Oak Place.

Connecticut played a prominent role in the Revolutionary War, serving as the Continental Army's major supplier. Sometimes called the "Arsenal of the Nation," the state became one of the most industrialized in the nation.

Today, Connecticut factories produce weapons, sewing machines, jet engines, helicopters, motors, hardware and tools, cutlery, clocks, locks, ball bearings, silverware, and submarines. Hartford, which has the oldest U.S. newspaper still being published—the *Courant*, established 1764—is the insurance capital of the nation.

Poultry, fruit, and dairy products account for the largest portion of farm income, and Connecticut shade-grown tobacco is acknowledged to be the nation's most valuable crop, per acre.

Connecticut is a popular resort area with its 250-mile Long Island Sound shoreline and many inland lakes. Among the major points of interest are the American Shakespeare Theatre in Stratford, Yale University's Gallery of Fine Arts and Peabody Museum. Other famous museums include the P.T. Barnum, Winchester Gun, and American Clock and Watch. The town of Mystic features a recreated 19th-century New England seaport and the Mystic Marinelife Aquarium.

## DELAWARE

**Capital:** Dover
**Governor:** Michael N. Castle, R (to Jan. 1989)
**Lieut. Governor:** S. B. Woo, D (to Jan. 1989)
**Secy. of State:** Michael Harkins, R (Pleasure of Governor)
**State Treasurer:** Janet C. Rzewnicki, R (to Jan. 1987)
**Atty. General:** Charles M. Oberly III, D (to Jan. 1987)
**Entered Union & (rank):** Dec. 7, 1787 (1)
**Present constitution adopted:** 1897
**Motto:** Liberty and independence
**State colors:** Colonial blue and buff
**State flower:** Peach blossom
**State tree:** American holly
**State bird:** Blue Hen chicken
**State insect:** Ladybug
**State song:** "Our Delaware"
**Nicknames:** Diamond State; First State
**Origin of name:** From Delaware River and Bay; named in turn for Sir Thomas West, Lord De La Warr
**1980 population (1980 census) & (rank):** 594,317 (47)
**1985 est. population (July 1) & (rank):** 622,000 (47)
**1984 land area & (rank):** 1,932 sq mi. (5,005 sq km) (49)
**Geographic center:** In Kent Co., 11 mi. S of Dover
**Number of counties:** 3
**Largest cities (1980 census):** Wilmington, 70,195; Newark, 25,247; Dover, 23,512; Elsmere, 6,493; Milford, 5,356; Seaford, 5,256; New Castle, 4,709; Lewes, 2,197
**State forests:** 3 (6,149 ac.)
**State parks:** 10
**State receipts (1985):** $882,039,300[1]
**State disbursements (1985):** $799,095,800[1]

1. General Funds, does not include federal funds.

Henry Hudson, sailing under the Dutch flag, is credited with Delaware's discovery in 1609. The following year, Capt. Samuel Argall of Virginia named Delaware for his colony's governor, Thomas West, Baron De La Warr. An attempted Dutch settlement failed in 1631. Swedish colonization began at Fort Christina (now Wilmington) in 1638, but New Sweden fell to Dutch forces led by New Netherlands' Gov. Peter Stuyvesant in 1655.

England took over the area in 1664 and it was transferred to William Penn as the southern Three Counties in 1682. Semiautonomous after 1704, Delaware fought as a separate state in the American Revolution and became the first state to ratify the constitution in 1787.

During the Civil War, although a slave state, Delaware did not secede from the Union.

In 1802, Éleuthère Irénée du Pont established a gunpowder mill near Wilmington that laid the foundation for Delaware's huge chemical industry. Delaware's manufactured products now also include vulcanized fiber, glazed kid and morocco leathers, textiles, paper, dental supplies, metal products, machinery, machine tools, and automobiles.

Delaware also grows a great variety of fruits and vegetables and is a U.S. pioneer in the food-canning industry. Corn, soybeans, potatoes, and hay are important crops. Delaware's broiler chicken farms supply the big Eastern markets, and fishing is another major industry.

Points of interest include the Fort Christina Monument, Hagley Museum, Holy Trinity Church (erected in 1698, the oldest Protestant church in the United States still in use), and Winterthur Museum, in and near Wilmington; central New Castle, an almost unchanged late 18th-century capital; and the Delaware Museum of Natural History.

Popular recreation areas include Cape Henlopen, Delaware Seashore, Trapp Pond State Park, and Rehoboth Beach.

## DISTRICT OF COLUMBIA

*See* listing at end of *50 Largest Cities of the United States.*

# FLORIDA

**Capital:** Tallahassee
**Governor:** Bob Graham, D (to Jan. 1987)
**Lieut. Governor:** Wayne Mixson, D (to Jan. 1987)
**Secy. of State:** George Firestone, D (to Jan. 1987)
**Comptroller:** Gerald Lewis, D (to Jan. 1987)
**Commissioner of Agriculture:** Doyle Connor, D (to Jan. 1987)
**Atty. General:** Jim Smith, D (to Jan. 1987)
**Organized as territory:** March 30, 1822
**Entered Union & (rank):** March 3, 1845 (27)
**Present constitution adopted:** 1969
**Motto:** In God we trust (1868)
**State flower:** Orange blossom (1909)
**State bird:** Mockingbird (1927)
**State song:** "Suwannee River" (1935)
**Nickname:** Sunshine State (1970)
**Origin of name:** From the Spanish, meaning "feast of flowers" (Easter)
**1980 population (1980 census) & (rank):** 9,746,342 (7)
**1985 est. population (July 1) & (rank):** 11,366,000 (6)
**1984 land area & (rank):** 54,153 sq mi. (140,256 sq km) (26)
**Geographic center:** In Hernando Co., 12 mi. NNW of Brooksville
**Number of counties:** 67
**Largest cities (1984 est.):** Jacksonville, 571,421; Miami, 383,027; Tampa, 275,512; St. Petersburg, 242,115; Fort Lauderdale, 152,053; Hialeah, 157,137
**State forests:** 4 (306,881 ac.)
**State parks:** 88 (215,820 ac.)
**State tax receipts (fiscal 1984–85):** $8,441,948,160
**Other state revenue (fiscal 1984–85):** $19,101,750,909
**State expenditures (fiscal 1984–85):** $27,051,840,585

In 1513, Ponce De Leon, seeking the mythical "Fountain of Youth," discovered and named Florida, claiming it for Spain. Later, Florida would be held at different times by Spain and England until Spain finally sold it to the United States in 1819. (Incidentally, France established a colony named Fort Caroline in 1564 in the state that was to become Florida.)

Florida's early 19th-century history as a U.S. territory was marked by wars with the Seminole Indians that did not end until 1842, although a treaty was actually never signed.

One of the nation's fastest-growing states, Florida's population has gone from 2.8 million in 1950 to more than 11.3 million in 1985.

Florida's economy rests on a solid base of tourism, (the state entertained more than 30.1 million American visitors in 1985) manufacturing, and agriculture.

In recent years, oranges and grapefruit lead Florida's crop list, followed by vegetables, potatoes, melons, strawberries, sugar cane, dairy products, cattle and calves, and forest products.

Major tourist attractions are Miami Beach, Palm Beach, St. Augustine (founded in 1565, thus the oldest permanent city in the U.S.), Daytona Beach, and Fort Lauderdale on the East Coast. West Coast resorts include Sarasota, Tampa, Key West and St. Petersburg. Disney World, located on a 27,000-acre site near Orlando, is a popular attraction.

Also drawing many visitors are the NASA Kennedy Space Center's Spaceport USA, located in the town of Kennedy Space Center, and Everglades National Park.

# GEORGIA

**Capital:** Atlanta
**Governor:** Joe Frank Harris, D (to Jan. 1987)
**Lieut. Governor:** Zell Miller, D (to Jan. 1987)
**Secy. of State:** Max Cleland, D (to Jan. 1987)
**Comptroller General:** Johnnie Caldwell, D (to Jan. 1987)
**Atty. General:** Michael J. Bowers, D (to Jan. 1987)
**Entered Union & (rank):** Jan. 2, 1788 (4)
**Present constitution adopted:** 1977
**Motto:** Wisdom, justice, and moderation
**State flower:** Cherokee rose (1916)
**State tree:** Live oak (1937)
**State bird:** Brown thrasher (1935)
**State song:** "Georgia on my Mind" (1922)
**Nicknames:** Peach State, Empire State of the South
**Origin of name:** In honor of George II of England
**1980 population (1980 census) & (rank):** 5,463,105 (13)
**1985 est. population (July 1) & (rank):** 5,976,000 (11)
**1984 land area & (rank):** 58,056 sq mi. (150,365 sq km) (21)
**Geographic center:** In Twiggs Co., 18 mi. SE of Macon
**Number of counties:** 159
**Largest cities (1980 census):** Atlanta, 425,022; Columbus, 169,441; Savannah, 141,634; Macon, 116,860; Albany, 74,550; Augusta, 47,532; Athens, 42,549; Warner Robins, 39,893
**State forests:** 25,258,000 ac. (67% of total state area)
**State parks:** 53 (42,600 ac.)
**State revenue receipts (fiscal 1984–1985):** $4,607,813,413
**State revenue expenditures (fiscal 1984–85):** $4,348,841,664

Hernando de Soto, the Spanish explorer, first traveled parts of Georgia in 1540. British claims later conflicted with those of Spain. After obtaining a royal charter, Gen. James Oglethorpe established the first permanent settlement in Georgia in 1733 as a refuge for English debtors. In 1742, Oglethorpe defeated Spanish invaders in the Battle of Bloody Marsh.

A Confederate stronghold, Georgia was the scene of extensive military action during the Civil War. Union General William T. Sherman burned Atlanta and destroyed a 60-mile wide path to the coast where he captured Savannah in 1864.

The largest state east of the Mississippi, Georgia is typical of the changing South with an ever-increasing industrial development. Atlanta, largest city in the state, is the communications and transportation center for the Southeast and the area's chief distributor of goods.

Georgia leads the nation in the production of paper and board, tufted textile products, and processed chicken. Other major manufactured products are transportation equipment, food products, apparel, and chemicals.

Important agricultural products are corn, cotton, tobacco, soybeans, eggs, and peaches. Georgia produces twice as many peanuts as the next leading state. From its vast stands of pine come more than half the world's resins and turpentine and 74.4% of the U.S. supply. Georgia is also a leader in the production of marble, kaolin, barite, and bauxite.

Principal tourist attractions in Georgia include the Okefenokee National Wildlife Refuge, Andersonville Prison Park and National Cemetery, Chickamauga and Chattanooga National Military Park, the Little White House at Warm Springs where Pres. Franklin D. Roosevelt died in 1945, Sea Island, the enormous Confederate Memorial at Stone Mountain, Kennesaw Mountain National Battlefield Park, and Cumberland Island National Seashore.

# HAWAII

**Capital:** Honolulu (on Oahu)
**Governor:** George R. Ariyoshi, D (to Dec. 1986)
**Lieut. Governor:** John Waihee, D (to Dec. 1986)
**Comptroller:** Hideo Murakami, (to Dec. 1986)
**Atty. General:** Corinne Watanabe (approval pending)
**Organized as territory:** 1900
**Entered Union & (rank):** Aug. 21, 1959 (50)
**Motto:** *Ua Mau Ke Ea O Ka Aina I Ka Pono* (The life of the land is perpetuated in righteousness)
**State flower:** Hibiscus
**State song:** "Hawaii Ponoi"
**State bird:** Nene (Hawaiian goose)
**Nickname:** Aloha State
**Origin of name:** Uncertain. The islands may have been named by Hawaii Loa, their traditional discoverer. Or they may have been named after Hawaii or Hawaiki, the traditional home of the Polynesians.
**1980 population (1980 census) & (rank):** 964,691 (39)
**1985 est. population (July 1) & (rank):** 1,054,000 (39)
**1984 land area & (rank):** 6,425 sq mi. (16,641 sq km) (47)
**Geographic center:** Between islands of Hawaii and Maui
**Number of counties:** 4 plus one non-functioning county (Kalawao)
**Largest cities (1980 census):** Honolulu, 365,048; Hilo, 37,017[1]
**State parks and historic sites:** 74
**Total state government revenues (fiscal 1983–84):** $2,163,163,000
**Total state government expenditures (fiscal 1983–84):** $2,077,673,000

1. There are no political boundaries to Honolulu or any other place, but statistical boundaries are assigned under state law.

First settled by Polynesians sailing from other Pacific islands in the 6th century, Hawaii was visited in 1778 by British Captain James Cook who

called the group the Sandwich Islands.

Hawaii was a native kingdom throughout most of the 19th century when the expansion of the vital sugar industry (pineapple came after 1898) meant increasing U.S. business and political involvement. In 1893, Queen Liliuokalani was deposed and a year later the Republic of Hawaii was established with Sanford B. Dole as president. Then, following its annexation in 1898, Hawaii became a U.S. Territory in 1900.

The Japanese attack on the naval base at Pearl Harbor on Dec. 7, 1941, was directly responsible for U.S. entry into World War II.

Hawaii, 2,397 miles west-southwest of San Francisco, is a 1,523-mile chain of islets and eight main islands—Hawaii, Kahoolawe, Maui, Lanai, Molokai, Oahu, Kauai, and Niihau. The Northwestern Hawaiian Islands, other than Midway, are administratively part of Hawaii.

The temperature is mild and Hawaii's soil is fertile for tropical fruits and vegetables. Cane sugar and pineapple are the chief products. Hawaii also grows coffee, bananas and nuts. The tourist business is Hawaii's largest source of outside income.

Hawaii's highest peak is Mauna Kea (13,796 ft.). Mauna Loa (13,679 ft.) is the largest volcanic mountain in the world in cubic content.

Among the major points of interest are Hawaii Volcanoes National Park (Hawaii), Haleakala National Park (Maui), Puuhonua o Honaunau National Historical Park (Hawaii), Polynesian Cultural Center (Oahu), the U.S.S. *Arizona* Memorial at Pearl Harbor, and Iolani Palace (the only royal palace in the U.S.), Bishop Museum, and Waikiki Beach (all in Honolulu).

# IDAHO

**Capital:** Boise
**Governor:** John V. Evans, D (to Jan. 1987)
**Lieut. Governor:** David Leroy, R (to Jan. 1987)
**Secy. of State:** Pete T. Cenarrusa, R (to Jan. 1987)
**State Auditor:** Joe R. Williams, D (to Jan. 1987)
**Atty. General:** James Jones, R (to Jan. 1987)
**Treasurer:** Marjorie Ruth Moon, D (to Jan. 1987)
**Organized as territory:** March 3, 1863
**Entered Union & (rank):** July 3, 1890 (43)
**Present constitution adopted:** 1890
**Motto:** *Esto perpetua* (May you last forever)
**State flower:** Syringa (1931)
**State tree:** White pine (1935)
**State bird:** Mountain bluebird (1931)
**State horse:** Appaloosa (1975)
**State gem:** Star garnet (1967)
**State song:** "Here We Have Idaho"
**Nicknames:** Gem State; Spud State; Panhandle State
**Origin of name:** Means "Gem of the Mountains"
**1980 population (1980 census) & (rank):** 944,038 (41)
**1985 est. population (July 1) & (rank):** 1,005,000 (40)
**1984 land area & (rank):** 82,413 sq mi. (213,449 sq km) (11)
**Geographic center:** In Custer Co., at Custer, SW of Challis
**Number of counties:** 44, plus small part of Yellowstone National Park
**Largest cities (1980 census):** Boise, 102,160; Pocatello, 46,340; Idaho Falls, 39,590; Lewiston, 27,986; Twin Falls, 26,209; Nampa, 25,112; Coeur d'Alene, 20,054
**State forests:** 881,000 ac.
**State parks:** 21 (38,487) ac.
**State revenue (1985 total funds):** $1,355,356,100
**State expenditure (1985 total funds):** $1,355,356,100

After its acquisition by the U.S. as part of the

Louisiana Purchase in 1803, the region was explored by Meriwether Lewis and William Clark in 1805–06. Northwest boundary disputes with Great Britain were settled by the Oregon Treaty in 1846 and the first permanent U.S. settlement in Idaho was established by the Mormons at Franklin in 1860.

After gold was discovered on Orofino Creek in 1860, prospectors swarmed into the territory, but left little more than a number of ghost towns.

In the 1870s, growing white occupation of Indian lands led to a series of battles between U.S. forces and the Nez Percé, Bannock, and Sheepeater tribes.

Mining, lumbering, and irrigation farming have been important for years. Idaho produces more than one third of all the silver mined in the U.S. It also ranks high among the states in antimony, lead, cobalt, garnet, phosphate rock, vanadium, zinc, and mercury.

Idaho's most impressive growth began when World War II military needs made processing agricultural products a big industry, particularly the dehydrating and freezing of potatoes. The state produces about one fourth of the nation's potato crop, as well as wheat, apples, corn, barley, sugar beets, and hops. More money is made from livestock in the state than from all agricultural products.

With the growth of winter sports, tourism now outranks mining in dollar revenue. Idaho's many streams and lakes provide fishing, camping, and boating sites. The nation's largest elk herds draw hunters from all over the world and the famed Sun Valley resort attracts thousands of visitors to its swimming and skiing facilities.

Other points of interest are the Craters of the Moon National Monument; Nez Percé National Historic Park, which includes many sites visited by Lewis and Clark; and the State Historical Museum in Boise.

# ILLINOIS

**Capital:** Springfield
**Governor:** James R. Thompson, R (to Jan. 1987)
**Lieut. Governor:** George H. Ryan, R (to Jan. 1987)
**Secy. of State:** Jim Edgar, R (to Jan. 1987)
**Comptroller:** Roland J. Burris, D (to Jan. 1987)
**Atty. General:** Neil F. Hartigan, D (to Jan. 1987)
**Treasurer:** James H. Donnewald, D (to Jan. 1987)
**Organized as territory:** Feb. 3, 1809
**Entered Union & (rank):** Dec. 3, 1818 (21)
**Present constitution adopted:** 1970
**Motto:** State sovereignty, national union
**State flower:** Violet (1908)
**State tree:** White oak (1973)
**State bird:** Cardinal (1929)
**State insect:** Monarch butterfly
**State song:** "Illinois" (1925)
**State mineral:** Fluorite (1965)
**Nickname:** Prairie State
**Origin of name:** From an Indian word and French suffix meaning "tribe of superior men"
**1980 population (1980 census) & (rank):** 11,426,596 (5)
**1985 est. population (July 1) & (rank):** 11,535,000 (5)
**1984 land area & (rank):** 55,645 sq mi. (144,120 sq km) (24)
**Geographic center:** In Logan County 28 mi. NE of Springfield
**Number of counties:** 102
**Largest cities (1984 census):** Chicago, 2,992,472; Rockford, 136,531; Peoria, 117,113; Springfield, 101,-

570; Decatur, 91,851; Aurora, 85,735
**Public use areas:** 187 (275,000 ac.), incl. state parks, memorials, forests and conservation areas
**Total state revenue, all funds, all sources (fiscal 1984–85):** $15,250,000,000
**Total state expenditures, all funds (fiscal 1984–85):** $14,885,000,000

French explorers Marquette and Joliet, in 1673, were the first Europeans of record to visit the region. In 1699 French settlers established the first permanent settlement at Cahokia, near present-day East St. Louis.

Great Britain obtained the region at the end of the French and Indian War in 1763. The area figured prominently in frontier struggles during the Revolutionary War and in Indian wars during the early 19th century.

Significant episodes in the state's early history include the growing migration of Eastern settlers following the opening of the Erie Canal in 1825; the Black Hawk War, which virtually ended the Indian troubles in the area; and the rise of Abraham Lincoln from farm laborer to President-elect.

Today, Illinois stands high in manufacturing, coal mining, agriculture, and oil production. The sprawling Chicago district (including a slice of Indiana) is a great iron and steel producer, meat packer, grain exchange, and railroad center. Chicago is also famous as a busy long-flight airport city and Great Lakes port.

Illinois ranks first in the nation in export of agricultural products and second in hog production. An important dairying state, Illinois is also a leader in corn, oats, wheat, barley, rye, truck vegetables, and the nursery products.

The state manufactures a great variety of industrial and consumer products: railroad cars, clothing, furniture, tractors, liquor, watches, and farm implements are just some of the items made in its factories and plants.

Central Illinois is noted for shrines and memorials associated with the life of Abraham Lincoln. In Springfield are the Lincoln Home, the Lincoln Tomb, and the restored Old State Capitol. Other points of interest are the home of Mormon leader Joseph Smith in Nauvoo and, in Chicago: the Art Institute, Field Museum, Museum of Science and Industry, Shedd Aquarium, Adler Planetarium, Merchandise Mart, and Chicago Portage National Historic Site.

# INDIANA

**Capital:** Indianapolis
**Governor:** Robert D. Orr, R (to Jan. 1989)
**Lieut. Governor:** John M. Mutz, R (to Jan. 1989)
**Secy. of State:** Edwin J. Simcox, R (to Dec. 1986)
**Treasurer:** Julian L. Ridlen, R (to Feb. 1987)
**Atty. General:** Linley E. Pearson, R (to Jan. 1989)
**Auditor:** Otis E. Cox, D (to Dec. 1986)
**Organized as territory:** May 7, 1800
**Entered Union & (rank):** Dec. 11, 1816 (19)
**Present constitution adopted:** 1851
**Motto:** The Crossroads of America
**State flower:** Peony (1957)
**State tree:** Tulip tree (1931)
**State bird:** Cardinal (1933)
**State song:** "On the Banks of the Wabash, Far Away" (1913)
**Nickname:** Hoosier State
**Origin of name:** Meaning "land of Indians"

**1980 population (1980 census) & (rank):** 5,490,260 (12)
**1985 est. population (July 1) & (rank):** 5,499,000 (14)
**1984 land area & (rank):** 35,932 sq mi. (93,064 sq km) (38)
**Geographic center:** In Boone Co., 14 mi. NNW of Indianapolis
**Number of Counties:** 92
**Largest cities (1980 census):** Indianapolis, 700,807; Fort Wayne, 172,028; Gary, 151,953; Evansville, 130,496; South Bend, 109,727; Hammond, 93,714; Muncie, 77,216
**State parks:** 19 (54,126 ac.)
**State memorials:** 16 (941.977 ac.)
**State general revenue (fiscal 1984–85):** $3,672,000,000
**State general expenditure (fiscal 1984–85):** $3,775,000,000

First explored for France by La Salle in 1679–80, the region figured importantly in the Franco-British struggle for North America that culminated with British victory in 1763.

George Rogers Clark led American forces against the British in the area during the Revolutionary War and, prior to becoming a state, Indiana was the scene of frequent Indian uprisings until the victory of Gen. William Henry Harrison at Tippecanoe in 1811.

Indiana's 41-mile Lake Michigan waterfront—one of the world's great industrial centers—turns out iron, steel, and oil products. Products include automobile parts and accessories, mobile homes and recreational vehicles, truck and bus bodies, aircraft engines, farm machinery, and fabricated structural steel. Phonograph records, wood office furniture, and pharmaceuticals are also manufactured.

The state is a leader in agriculture with corn the principal crop. Hogs, soybeans, wheat, oats, rye, tomatoes, onions, and poultry also contribute heavily to Indiana's agricultural output. Much of the building limestone used in the U.S. is quarried in Indiana which is also a large producer of coal.

Wyandotte Cave, one of the largest in the U.S., is located in Crawford County in southern Indiana and West Baden and French Lick are well known for their mineral springs. Other attractions include Indiana Dunes National Lakeshore, Indianapolis Motor Speedway, Lincoln Boyhood National Memorial, and the George Rogers Clark National Historical Park.

# IOWA

**Capital:** Des Moines
**Governor:** Terry E. Branstad, R (to Jan. 1987)
**Lieut. Governor:** Robert T. Anderson, D (to Jan. 1987)
**Secy. of State:** Mary Jane Odell, R (to Jan. 1987)
**Treasurer:** Michael L. Fitzgerald, D (to Jan. 1987)
**Atty. General:** Tom Miller, D (to Jan. 1987)
**Organized as territory:** June 12, 1838
**Entered Union & (rank):** Dec. 28, 1846 (29)
**Present constitution adopted:** 1857
**Motto:** Our liberties we prize and our rights we will maintain
**State flower:** Wild rose (1897)
**State bird:** Eastern goldfinch (1933)
**State colors:** Red, white, and blue (in state flag)
**State song:** "Song of Iowa"
**Nickname:** Hawkeye State
**Origin of name:** Probably from an Indian word meaning "I-o-w-a, this is the place," or "The Beautiful Land"
**1980 population (1980 census) & (rank):** 2,913,808 (27)
**1985 est. population (July 1) & (rank):** 2,884,000 (29)
**1984 land area & (rank):** 55,965 sq mi. (144,950 sq km) (23)

**Geographic center:** In Story Co., 5 mi. NE of Ames
**Number of counties:** 99
**Largest cities (1980 census):** Des Moines, 191,003; Cedar Rapids, 110,243; Davenport, 103,264; Sioux City, 82,003; Waterloo, 75,985; Dubuque, 62,321; Council Bluffs, 56,449; Iowa City, 50,508; Ames, 45,775
**State forests:** 5 (28,000 ac.)
**State parks:** 95 (49,237)
**Total est. revenue fiscal year 1984–85:** $5,915,000,000[1]
**Total est. expenditures fiscal year 1984–1985:** $5,915,000,000[1]

1. From all sources including state university tuition fees.

The first Europeans to visit the area were the French explorers, Father Jacques Marquette and Louis Jolliet in 1673. The U.S. obtained control of the area in 1803 as part of the Louisiana Purchase.

During the first half of the 19th century, there was heavy fighting between white settlers and Indians. Lands were taken from the Indians after the Black Hawk War in 1832 and again in 1836 and 1837.

When Iowa became a state in 1846, its capital was Iowa City; the more centrally located Des Moines became the new capital in 1857. At that time, the state's present boundaries were also drawn.

Although Iowa produces a tenth of the nation's food supply, the value of Iowa's manufactured products is three times that of its agriculture. Major industries are food and associated products, nonelectrical machinery, electrical equipment, printing and publishing, and fabricated products.

Iowa stands in a class by itself as an agricultural state. Its farms sell over $9 billion worth of crops and livestock annually. Iowa leads the nation in all livestock and hog marketings, with about 27% of the pork supply and 9% of the grain-fed cattle. Iowa's forests produce hardwood lumber, particularly walnut, and its mineral products include cement, limestone, sand, gravel, gypsum, and coal.

Tourist attractions include the Herbert Hoover birthplace and library near West Branch; the Amana Colonies; Fort Dodge Historical Museum, Fort, and Stockade; the Iowa State Fair at Des Moines in August; and the Effigy Mounds National Monument at Marquette, a prehistoric Indian burial site.

# KANSAS

**Capital:** Topeka
**Governor:** John W. Carlin, D (to Jan. 1987)
**Lieut. Governor:** Tom Docking, D (to Jan. 1987)
**Secy. of State:** Jack H. Brier, R (to Jan. 1987)
**Treasurer:** Joan Finney, D (to Jan. 1987)
**Atty. General:** Robert T. Stephan, R (to Jan. 1987)
**Organized as territory:** May 30, 1854
**Entered Union & (rank):** Jan. 29, 1861 (34)
**Present constitution adopted:** 1859
**Motto:** *Ad astra per aspera* (To the stars through difficulties)
**State flower:** Sunflower (1903)
**State tree:** Cottonwood (1937)
**State bird:** Western meadow lark (1937)
**State animal:** Buffalo (1955)
**State song:** "Home on the Range" (1947)
**Nicknames:** Sunflower State; Jayhawk State
**Origin of name:** From a Siouan word meaning "people of the south wind"
**1980 population (1980 census) & (rank):** 2,364,236 (32)
**1985 est. population (July 1) & (rank):** 2,450,000 (32)

**1984 land area & (rank):** 81,781 sq mi. (211,814 sq km) (13)
**Geographic center:** In Barton Co., 15 mi. NE of Great Bend
**Number of counties:** 105
**Largest cities (1980 census):** Wichita, 279,835; Kansas City, 161,148; Topeka, 115,266; Overland Park, 81, 784; Lawrence, 52,738; Salina, 41,843; Hutchinson, 40,284
**State parks:** 22 (14,394 ac.)
**State operating revenue (fiscal 1984–85):** $3,661,433,000
**State operating expenditure (fiscal 1984–85):** $3,369,898,000

Spanish explorer Francisco de Coronado, in 1541, is considered the first European to have traveled this region. La Salle's extensive land claims for France (1682) included present-day Kansas. Ceded to Spain by France in 1763, the territory reverted back to France in 1800 and was sold to the U.S. as part of the Louisiana Purchase in 1803.

Lewis and Clark, Zebulon Pike, and Stephen H. Long explored the region between 1803 and 1819. The first permanent settlements in Kansas were outposts—Fort Leavenworth (1827), Fort Scott (1842), and Fort Riley (1853)—established to protect travelers along the Santa Fe and Oregon Trails.

Just before the Civil War, the conflict between the pro- and anti-slavery forces earned the region the grim title "Bleeding Kansas."

Today, wheat fields, oil well derricks, herds of cattle, and grain storage elevators are chief features of the Kansas landscape. A leading wheat-growing state, Kansas also raises corn, sorghums, oats, barley, soy beans, and potatoes. Kansas stands high in petroleum production and mines zinc, coal, salt, and lead. It is also the nation's leading producer of helium.

Wichita is one of the nation's leading aircraft manufacturing centers, ranking first in production of private aircraft. Kansas City is an important transportation, milling, and meat-packing center.

Points of interest include the new Kansas Museum of History at Topeka, the Eisenhower boyhood home and the new Eisenhower Memorial Museum and Presidential Library at Abilene, John Brown's cabin at Osawatomie, recreated Front Street in Dodge City, Fort Larned (once the most important military post on the Santa Fe Trail), and Fort Leavenworth and Fort Riley.

# KENTUCKY

**Capital:** Frankfort
**Governor:** Martha Layne Collins, D (to Dec. 1987)
**Lieut. Governor:** Steven L. Beshear, D (to Dec. 1987)
**Secy. of State:** Drexell R. Davis, D (to Jan. 1988)
**State Treasurer:** Frances Jones Mills, D (to Jan. 1988)
**State Auditor:** Mary Ann Tobin, D (to Jan. 1988)
**Atty. General:** David Armstrong, D (to Jan. 1988)
**Entered Union & (rank):** June 1, 1792 (15)
**Present constitution adopted:** 1891
**Motto:** United we stand, divided we fall
**State tree:** Coffeetree
**State flower:** Goldenrod
**State bird:** Kentucky cardinal
**State song:** "My Old Kentucky Home"
**Nickname:** Bluegrass State
**Origin of name:** From an Iroquoian word "Ken-tah-ten" meaning "land of tomorrow"
**1980 population (1980 census) & (rank):** 3,660,777 (23)
**1985 est. population (July 1) & (rank):** 3,726,000 (23)
**1984 land area & (rank):** 39,669 sq mi. (102,743 sq km) (37)

**Geographic center:** In Marion Co., 3 mi. NNW of Lebanon
**Number of counties:** 120
**Largest cities (1985 proj.):** Louisville, 293,834; Lexington, 214,072; Owensboro, 56,419; Covington, 47,725; Bowling Green, 45,549; Paducah, 29,699; Hopkinsville, 30,406
**State forests:** 9 (44,173 ac.)
**State parks:** 43 (40,574 ac.)
**Total state revenue (1983–84):** $4,752,552,000[1]
**Total state expenditure (1983–84):** $4,258,175,000

1. Operating funds only.

Kentucky was the first region west of the Allegheny Mountains settled by American pioneers. James Harrod established the first permanent settlement at Harrodsburg in 1774; the following year Daniel Boone, who had explored the area in 1767, blazed the Wilderness Trail and founded Boonesboro.

Politically, the Kentucky region was originally part of Virginia, but early statehood was gained in 1792.

During the Civil War, as a slaveholding state with a considerable abolitionist population, Kentucky was caught in the middle of the conflict, supplying both Union and Confederate forces with thousands of troops.

In recent years, manufacturing has shown important gains, but agriculture and mining are still vital to Kentucky's economy. Kentucky prides itself on producing some of the nation's best tobacco, horses, and whiskey. Corn, soybeans, wheat, fruit, hogs, cattle, and dairy farming are also important.

Among the manufactured items produced in the state are furniture, aluminum ware, brooms, shoes, lumber products, machinery, textiles, and iron and steel products. Kentucky also produces significant amounts of petroleum, natural gas, fluorspar, clay, and stone. However, coal accounts for 90% of the total mineral income.

Louisville, the largest city, famed for the Kentucky Derby at Churchill Downs, is also the location of a large state university, whiskey distilleries, and cigarette factories. The Bluegrass country around Lexington is the home of some of the world's finest race horses. Other attractions are Mammoth Cave, the George S. Patton, Jr., Military Museum at Fort Knox, and Old Fort Harrod State Park.

# LOUISIANA

**Capital:** Baton Rouge
**Governor:** Edwin W. Edwards, R (to March 1988)
**Lieut. Governor:** Robert L. Freeman, D (to March 1988)
**Secy. of State:** James H. Brown, Jr., D (to March 1988)
**Treasurer:** Mary Evelyn Parker, D (to March 1988)
**Atty. General:** William J. Guste, Jr., D (to March 1988)
**Organized as territory:** March 26, 1804
**Entered Union & (rank):** April 30, 1812 (18)
**Present constitution adopted:** 1974
**Motto:** Union, justice, and confidence
**State flower:** Magnolia (1900)
**State tree:** Bald cypress
**State bird:** Pelican
**State song:** "Give Me Louisiana," and "You Are My Sunshine"
**Nicknames:** Pelican State; Sportsman's Paradise; Creole State; Sugar State
**Origin of name:** In honor of Louis XIV of France
**1980 population (1980 census) & (rank):** 4,206,312 (19)
**1985 est. population (July 1) & (rank):** 4,481,000 (18)
**1984 land area & (rank):** 44,521 sq mi. (115,310 sq km) (33)

**Geographic center:** In Avoyelles Parish, 3 mi. SE of Marksville
**Number of parishes (counties):** 64
**Largest cities (1980 census):** New Orleans, 557,927; Baton Rouge, 219,419; Shreveport, 205,820; Lafayette, 81,961; Lake Charles, 75,226; Monroe, 57,597; Alexandria, 51,565
**State forests:** 1 (8,000 ac.)
**State parks:** 30 (13,932 ac.)
**State general revenue (fiscal 1985–86):** $7,156,319,089
**Capital outlay: (fiscal 1985–86):** $635,887,528
**State general expenditure, including capital outlay (fiscal 1985–86):** $7,265,260,894

Louisiana has a rich, colorful historical background. Early Spanish explorers were Piñeda, 1519; Cabeza de Vaca, 1528; and de Soto in 1541. La Salle reached the mouth of the Mississippi and claimed the land drained by it and its tributaries for Louis XIV of France in 1682.

Louisiana became a French crown colony in 1731, was ceded to Spain in 1763, returned to France in 1800, and sold by Napoleon to the U.S. as part of the Louisiana Purchase (with large territories to the north and northwest) in 1803.

In 1815, Gen. Andrew Jackson's troops defeated a larger British army in the Battle of New Orleans, neither side aware that the treaty ending the War of 1812 had been signed.

As to total value of its mineral output, Louisiana is a leader in natural gas, salt, petroleum, and sulfur production. Much of the oil and sulfur comes from offshore deposits. The state also produces large crops of sweet potatoes, rice, sugarcane, pecans, soybeans, corn, and cotton.

Leading manufactures include chemicals, processed food, petroleum and coal products, paper, lumber and wood products, transportation equipment, and apparel.

Louisiana marshes supply most of the nation's muskrat fur as well as that of opossum, raccoon, mink, and otter, and large numbers of game birds.

Major points of interest include New Orleans with its French Quarter and Superdome, plantation homes near Natchitoches and New Iberia, Cajun country in the Mississippi delta region, Chalmette National Historical Park, and the state capital at Baton Rouge.

# MAINE

**Capital:** Augusta
**Governor:** Joseph E. Brennan, D (to Jan. 1987)
**Secy. of State:** Rodney F. Quinn, D (to Jan. 1987)
**Controller:** Donald A. Brown (term indefinite)
**Atty. General:** James Tierney, D (to Jan. 1987)
**Entered Union & (rank):** March 15, 1820 (23)
**Present constitution adopted:** 1820
**Motto:** *Dirigo* (I direct)
**State flower:** White pine cone and tassel (1895)
**State tree:** White pine tree (1945)
**State bird:** Chickadee (1927)
**State fish:** Landlocked salmon (1969)
**State mineral:** Tourmaline (1971)
**State song:** "State of Maine Song" (1937)
**Nickname:** Pine Tree State
**Origin of name:** First used to distinguish the mainland from the offshore islands. It has been considered a compliment to Henrietta Maria, Queen of Charles I of England. She was said to have owned the province of Mayne in France.
**1980 population (1980 census) & (rank):** 1,125,027 (38)
**1985 est. population (July 1) & (rank):** 1,164,000 (38)

**1984 land area & (rank):** 30,995 sq mi. (80,277 sq km) (39)
**Geographic center:** In Piscataquis Co., 18 mi. N of Dover-Foxcroft
**Number of counties:** 16
**Largest cities (1980 census):** Portland, 61,572; Lewiston, 40,481; Bangor, 31,643; Auburn, 23,128; South Portland, 22,712; Augusta, 21,819; Biddeford, 19,638
**State forests:** 1 (21,000 ac.)
**State parks:** 26 (247,627 ac.)
**State historic sites:** 18 (403 ac.)
**State total revenue (fiscal 1984):** $1,484,942,056
**State total expenditure (fiscal 1984):** $1,436,652,458

John Cabot and his son, Sebastian, are believed to have visited the Maine coast in 1498. However, the first permanent English settlements were not established until more than a century later, in 1623.

The first naval action of the Revolutionary War occurred in 1775 when colonials captured the British sloop *Margaretta* off Machias on the Maine coast. In that same year, the British burned Falmouth (now Portland).

Long governed by Massachusetts, Maine became the 23rd state as part of the Missouri Compromise in 1820.

Maine produced 26.5 million hundred weight of potatoes or 9.4% of the national production in 1981 and 95% of the nation's low-bush blueberries. Farm income is also derived from apples, sweet corn, peas, and beans, with poultry and eggs the largest items.

The state is one of the world's largest pulp-paper producers. It ranks fifth in boot-and-shoe manufacturing. With more than 90% of its area forested, Maine turns out wood products from boats to toothpicks.

Maine leads the world in the production of the familiar flat tins of sardines, producing more than 100 million of them annually. Lobstermen normally catch 80–90% of the nation's true total of lobsters.

A scenic seacoast, beaches, lakes, mountains, and resorts make Maine a popular vacationland. There are more than 2,500 lakes and 5,000 streams, plus 26 state parks, to attract hunters, fishermen, skiers, and campers.

Major points of interest are: Bar Harbor, Allagash National Wilderness Waterway, the Wadsworth-Longfellow House in Portland, Roosevelt Campobello International Park, and the St. Croix Island National Monument.

# MARYLAND

**Capital:** Annapolis
**Governor:** Harry Hughes, D (to Jan. 1987)
**Lieut. Gov.:** J. Joseph Curran, D (to Jan. 1987)
**Secy. of State:** Lorraine M. Sheehan, D (appointed by governor)
**Comptroller of the Treasury:** Louis L. Goldstein, D (to Jan. 1987)
**Treasurer:** William S. James, D (to Jan. 1987)
**Atty. General:** Stephen H. Sachs, D (to Jan. 1987)
**Entered Union & (rank):** April 28, 1788 (7)
**Present constitution adopted:** 1867
**Motto:** *Fatti maschii, parole femine* (Manly deeds, womanly words)
**State flower:** Black-eyed susan (1918)
**State tree:** White oak (1941)
**State bird:** Baltimore oriole (1947)
**State dog:** Chesapeake Bay retriever (1964)

**State fish:** Rockfish (1965)
**State insect:** Baltimore checkerspot butterfly (1973)
**State sport:** Jousting (1962)
**State song:** "Maryland! My Maryland!" (1939)
**Nicknames:** Free State; Old Line State
**Origin of name:** In honor of Henrietta Maria (Queen of Charles I of England)
**1980 population (1980 census) & (rank):** 4,216,975 (18)
**1985–86 est. population (July 1) & (rank):** 4,392,000 (20)
**1984 land area & (rank):** 9,837 sq mi. (25,477 sq km) (42)
**Geographic center:** In Prince Georges Co., 4 1/2 mi. NW of Davidsonville
**Number of counties:** 23, and 1 independent city
**Largest cities (1980 census):** Baltimore, 786,775; Rockville, 43,811; Hagerstown, 34,132; Bowie, 33,695; Annapolis, 31,740; Frederick, 28,086; Gaithersburg, 26,424
**State forests:** 10 (120,921 ac.)
**State parks:** 42 (70,302 ac.)
**State general revenue (1985 est.):** $3,782,557,000
**State general expenditure (1985 est.):** $3,772,290,433

In 1608, Chesapeake Bay was explored by Capt. John Smith. Charles I granted a royal charter to Cecil Calvert, Lord Baltimore, in 1632 and English Roman Catholics landed on St. Clement's (now Blakistone Island) in 1634. Religious freedom, granted all Christians in the Toleration act passed by the Maryland assembly in 1649, was ended by a Puritan revolt, 1654–58.

In 1814, when the British unsuccessfully tried to capture Baltimore, the bombardment of Fort McHenry inspired Francis Scott Key to write *The Star Spangled Banner.*

Maryland is almost cut in two by the Chesapeake Bay, and the many estuaries and rivers create one of the longest waterfronts of any state. The Bay produces more seafood—oysters, crabs, clams, fin fish—than any comparable body of water. Important agricultural products, in order of cash value, are chickens, dairy products, corn, cattle, tobacco, and vegetables. Maryland is a leader in vegetable canning. Sand, gravel, lime and cement, stone, coal, and clay are the chief mineral products.

Manufacturing industries produce missiles, airplanes, steel, clothing, and chemicals. Baltimore, home of The Johns Hopkins University and Hospital, ranks as the nation's second port in foreign tonnage. Annapolis, site of the U.S. Naval Academy, has one of the earliest state houses (1772–79) still in regular use by a State government.

Among the popular attractions in Maryland are the Fort McHenry National Monument, Harpers Ferry and Chesapeake and Ohio Canal National Historical Parks, St. Marys City restoration near Leonardtown, USS *Constellation* at Baltimore, U.S. Naval Academy in Annapolis, Assateague Island National Seashore, and Catoctin Mountain and Piscataway parks.

# MASSACHUSETTS

**Capital:** Boston
**Governor:** Michael S. Dukakis, D (to Jan. 1987)
**Lieut. Governor:** To be elected
**Secy. of the Commonwealth:** Michael Joseph Connolly, D (to Jan. 1987)
**Treasurer & Receiver-General:** Robert Q. Crane, D (to Jan. 1987)
**Auditor of the Commonwealth:** John J. Finnegan, D (to Jan. 1987)

**Atty. General:** Francis X. Bellotti (to Jan. 1987)
**Entered Union & (rank):** Feb. 6, 1788 (6)
**Motto:** *Ense petit placidam sub libertate quietem* (By the sword we seek peace, but peace only under liberty)
**State flower:** Mayflower (1918)
**State tree:** American elm (1941)
**State bird:** Chickadee (1941)
**State colors:** Blue and gold
**State song:** "All Hail to Massachusetts" (1966)
**State beverage:** Cranberry juice (1970)
**State insect:** Ladybug (1974)
**Nicknames:** Bay State; Old Colony State
**Origin of name:** From two Indian words meaning "Great mountain place"
**1985 est. population (July 1) & (rank):** 5,822,000 (12)
**1984 land area & (rank):** 7,824 sq mi. (20,265 sq km) (45)
**Geographic center:** In Worcester Co., in S part of city of Worcester
**Number of counties:** 14
**Largest cities (1980 census):** Boston, 562,994; Worcester, 161,799; Springfield, 152,319; New Bedford, 98,478; Cambridge, 95,322; Brockton, 95,172; Fall River, 94,574
**State forests and parks:** 129 (242,000 ac.)[1]
**State general revenue (fiscal 1984–85):** $8,367,500,000
**State general expenditure (fiscal 1984–85):** $8,250,700,000

1. The Metropolitan District Commission, an agency of the Commonwealth serving municipalities in the Boston area, has about 14,000 acres of parkways and reservations under its jurisdiction.

Massachusetts has played a significant role in American history since the Pilgrims, seeking religious freedom, founded Plymouth Colony in 1620.

As one of the most important of the 13 colonies, Massachusetts became a leader in resisting British oppression. In 1773, the Boston Tea Party protested unjust taxation. The Minutemen started the American Revolution by battling British troops at Lexington and Concord on April 19, 1775.

During the 19th century, Massachusetts was famous for the vigorous intellectual activity of famous writers and educators and for its expanding commercial fishing, shipping, and manufacturing interests.

Massachusetts pioneered in the manufacture of textiles and shoes. Today, these industries have been replaced in importance by activity in the electronics and communications equipment fields.

The state's cranberry crop is the nation's largest. Also important are dairy and poultry products, nursery and greenhouse produce, vegetables, and fruit.

Tourism has become an important factor in the economy of the state because of its numerous recreational areas and historical landmarks.

Cape Cod has summer theaters, water sports, and an artists' colony at Provincetown. Tanglewood, in the Berkshires, features the summer concerts of the Boston Symphony.

Among the many other points of interest are Old Sturbridge Village, Minute Man National Historical Park between Lexington and Concord, and, in Boston: Old North Church, Old State House, Faneuil Hall, the USS *Constitution* and the John F. Kennedy Library.

# MICHIGAN

**Capital:** Lansing
**Governor:** James J. Blanchard, D (to Jan. 1987)

**Lieut. Governor:** Martha W. Griffiths, D (to Jan. 1987)
**Secy. of State:** Richard H. Austin, D (to Jan. 1987)
**Atty. General:** Frank J. Kelley, D (to Jan. 1987)
**Organized as territory:** Jan. 11, 1805
**Entered Union & (rank):** Jan. 26, 1837 (26)
**Present constitution adopted:** April 1, 1963, (effective Jan. 1, 1964)
**Motto:** *Si quaeris peninsulam amoenam circumspice* (If you seek a pleasant peninsula, look around you)
**State flower:** Apple blossom (1897)
**State bird:** Robin
**State fish:** Brook trout (1965)
**State gem:** Isle Royal Greenstone (Chlorastrolite) (1972)
**State stone:** Petoskey stone (1965)
**Nickname:** Wolverine State
**Origin of name:** From two Indian words meaning "great lake"
**1980 population (1980 census) & (rank):** 9,262,078 (8)
**1985 est. population (July 1) & (rank):** 9,088,000 (8)
**1984 land area & (rank):** 56,954 sq mi. (147,511 sq km) (22)
**Geographic center:** In Wexford Co., 5 mi. NNW of Cadillac
**Number of counties:** 83
**Largest cities (1980 census):** Detroit, 1,203,339; Grand Rapids, 181,843; Warren, 161,134; Flint, 159,611; Lansing, 130,414; Sterling Heights, 108,999; Ann Arbor, 107,966
**State forests:** 33 (3,762,184 ac.)
**State parks and recreation areas:** 92 (216,857 ac.)
**State general revenue (fiscal 1984–85):** $9,842,992,000
**State general expenditure (fiscal 1984–85):** $8,909,511,000

Indian tribes were living in the Michigan region when the first European, Etienne Brulé of France, arrived in 1618. Other French explorers, including Marquette, Jolliet, and La Salle, followed, and the first permanent settlement was established in 1668 at Sault Ste. Marie. France was ousted from the territory by Great Britain in 1763, following the French and Indian War.

After the Revolutionary War, the U.S. acquired most of the region, which remained the scene of constant conflict between the British and U.S. forces and their respective Indian allies through the War of 1812.

Bordering on four of the five Great Lakes, Michigan is divided into Upper and Lower Peninsulas by the Straits of Mackinac, which link Lakes Michigan and Huron. The two parts of the state are connected by the Mackinac Bridge, one of the world's longest suspension bridges. To the north, connecting Lakes Superior and Huron are the busy Sault Ste. Marie Canals.

While Michigan ranks first among the states in production of motor vehicles and parts, it is also a leader in many other manufacturing and processing lines including prepared cereals, machine tools, airplane parts, refrigerators, hardware, steel springs, and furniture.

The state produces important amounts of iron, copper, iodine, gypsum, bromine, salt, lime, gravel, and cement. Michigan's farms grow apples, cherries, pears, grapes, potatoes, and sugar beets and the annual value of its forest products is estimated at $2 billion. With over 36,000 miles of streams, some 11,000 lakes, and a 2,000 mile shoreline, Michigan is a prime area for both commercial and sport fishing.

Points of interest are the automobile plants in Dearborn, Detroit, Flint, Lansing, and Pontiac; Mackinac Island; Pictured Rocks and Sleeping Bear Dunes National Lakeshores, Greenfield Village near Dearborn; and the many summer resorts along both the inland and Great Lakes.

# MINNESOTA

**Capital:** St. Paul
**Governor:** Rudy Perpich, D (to Jan. 1987)
**Lieut. Governor:** Marlene Johnson, D (to Jan. 1987)
**Secy. of State:** Joan Growe (to Jan. 1987)
**State Auditor:** Arne Carlson, R (to Jan. 1987)
**Atty. General:** Hubert H. Humphrey III, D (to Jan. 1987)
**State Treasurer:** Robert Mattson, D (to Jan. 1987)
**Organized as territory:** March 3, 1849
**Entered Union & (rank):** May 11, 1858 (32)
**Present constitution adopted:** 1858
**Motto:** L'Etoile du Nord (The North Star)
**State flower:** Showy lady slipper (1902)
**State tree:** Red (or Norway) pine
**State bird:** Common loon (also called Great Northern Diver)
**State song:** "Hail Minnesota"
**Nicknames:** North Star State; Gopher State; Land of 10,000 Lakes
**Origin of name:** From a Dakota Indian word meaning "sky-tinted water"
**1980 population (1980 census) & (rank):** 4,075,970 (21)
**1985 est. population (July 1) & (rank):** 4,193,000 (21)
**1984 land area & (rank):** 79,548 sq mi. (206,030 sq km) (14)
**Geographic center:** In Crow Wing Co., 10 mi. SW of Brainerd
**Number of counties:** 87
**Largest cities (1980 census):** Minneapolis, 370,951; St. Paul, 270,230; Duluth, 92,811; Bloomington, 81,831; Rochester, 57,890; Edina, 46,073
**State forests:** 55 (2,984,000 ac.)
**State parks:** 92 (202,205 ac.)
**Total revenue (fiscal 1985–86):** $5,583,962,700
**Total expenditures (fiscal 1985–86):** $5,045,418,800

Following the visits of several French explorers, fur traders, and missionaries, including Marquette and Jolliet and La Salle, the region was claimed for Louis XIV by Daniel Greysolon, Sieur Duluth, in 1679.

The U.S. acquired eastern Minnesota from Great Britain after the Revolutionary War and 20 years later bought the western part from France in the Louisiana Purchase of 1803. Much of the region was explored by U.S. Army Lt. Zebulon M. Pike before cession of the northern strip of Minnesota bordering Canada by Britain in 1818.

The state is rich in natural resources. A few square miles of land in the north in the Mesabi, Cuyuna, and Vermillion ranges, produce more than 60% of the nation's iron ore. The state's farms rank high in yields of corn, wheat, rye, alfalfa, and sugar beets. Other leading farm products include butter, eggs, milk, potatoes, green peas, barley, and livestock.

Minnesota's factory production includes nonelectrical machinery, fabricated metals, flour-mill products, plastics, electronic computers, scientific instruments, and processed foods.

Minneapolis is the trade center of the Northwest; St. Paul is the nation's biggest publisher of calendars and law books. These "twin cities" are the nation's third largest trucking center. Duluth has the nation's largest inland harbor and now handles a significant amount of foreign trade. Rochester is the home of the Mayo Clinic, an internationally famous medical center.

Today, tourism is a major revenue producer in Minnesota, with fishing, hunting, water sports, and winter sports bringing in millions of visitors each year.

Among the most popular attractions are the St. Paul Winter Carnival; the Tyrone Guthrie Theatre, the Institute of Arts, Walker Art Center, and Minnehaha Park, in Minneapolis; Voyageurs National Park; North Shore Drive; and the Minnesota Zoological Gardens.

hay. Poultry and eggs are also important.

The state abounds in historical landmarks and is the home of the Vicksburg National Military Park where visitors may see the remains of forts, trenches, and other military relics used in the 1863 Union-army siege of the city. Other National Park Service areas are Brices Cross Roads National Battlefield Site, Tupelo National Battlefield, and part of Natchez Trace National Parkway. Pre-Civil War mansions are the special pride of Natchez, Oxford, Hattiesburg, and Jackson.

# MISSISSIPPI

**Capital:** Jackson
**Governor:** William A. Allain, D (to Jan. 1988)
**Lieut. Governor:** Brad Dye, D (to Jan. 1988)
**Secy. of State:** Dick Molpus, D (to Jan. 1988)
**Treasurer:** Bill Cole, D (to Jan. 1988)
**Atty. General:** Edwin Lloyd Pittman, D (to Jan. 1988)
**Organized as Territory:** April 7, 1798
**Entered Union & (rank):** Dec. 10, 1817 (20)
**Present constitution adopted:** 1890
**Motto:** *Virtute et armis* (By valor and arms)
**State flower:** Flower or bloom of the magnolia or evergreen magnolia (1952)
**State tree:** Magnolia (1938)
**State bird:** Mockingbird (1944)
**State song:** "Go, Mississippi" (1962)
**Nickname:** Magnolia State
**Origin of name:** From an Indian word meaning "Father of Waters"
**1980 population (1980 census) & (rank):** 2,520,638 (31)
**1985 est. population (July 1) & (rank):** 2,613,000 (31)
**1984 land area & (rank):** 47,233 sq mi. (122,333 sq km) (31)
**Geographic center:** In Leake Co., 9 mi. WNW of Carthage
**Number of counties:** 82
**Largest cities (1980 census):** Jackson, 202,895; Biloxi, 49,311; Hattiesburg, 40,829; Greenville, 40,613; Gulfport, 39,676; Pascagoula, 29,318
**State forests:** 1 (1,760 ac.)
**State parks:** 27 (16,763 ac.)
**State general revenue (fiscal 1986 projection):** $1,560,000,000
**State general expenditure (fiscal 1986 projection):** $1,560,000,000

First explored for Spain by Hernando de Soto who discovered the Mississippi River in 1540, the region was later claimed by France. In 1699, a French group under Sieur d'Iberville established the first permanent settlement near present-day Biloxi.

Great Britain took over the area in 1763 after the French and Indian War, ceding it to the U.S. in 1783 after the Revolution. Spain did not relinquish its claims until 1798, and in 1810 the U.S. annexed West Florida from Spain, including what is now southern Mississippi.

Mississippi, the stronghold of the Old South, has until the past decade been one of the least industrialized states, with more than half its population making a living from the soil. However, a recent industrialization program has attracted manufacturing industries such as lumber, furniture, paper, food processing, apparel, chemicals, transportation equipment, and machinery.

Cotton, nevertheless, is still king with the state rahking second to Texas in cotton production, though soybeans have become Mississippi's largest crop. Other important farm products are corn, peanuts, pecans, rice, sugarcane, sweet potatoes, and

# MISSOURI

**Capital:** Jefferson City
**Governor:** John D. Ashcroft, R (to Jan. 1989)
**Lieut. Governor:** Harriett Woods, D (to Jan. 1989)
**Secy. of State:** Roy D. Blunt, R (to Jan. 1989)
**Auditor:** Margaret Kelly, R (to Jan. 1987)
**Treasurer:** Wendell Bailey, R (to Jan. 1989)
**Atty. General:** William L. Webster, R (to Jan. 1989)
**Organized as territory:** June 4, 1812
**Entered Union & (rank):** Aug. 10, 1821 (24)
**Present constitution adopted:** 1945
**Motto:** *Salus populi suprema lex esto* (The welfare of the people shall be the supreme law)
**State flower:** Hawthorn (1923)
**State bird:** Bluebird (1927)
**State colors:** Red, white, and blue (1913)
**State song:** "Missouri Waltz" (1949)
**State rock:** Mozarkite (1967)
**State mineral:** Galena (1967)
**Nickname:** Show-me State
**Origin of name:** Named after a tribe called Missouri Indians. "Missouri" means "town of the large canoes."
**1980 population (1980 census) & (rank):** 4,916,759 (15)
**1985 est. population (July 1) & (rank):** 5,029,000 (15)
**1984 land area & (rank):** 68,945 sq mi. (178,568 sq km) (18)
**Geographic center:** In Miller Co., 20 mi. SW of Jefferson City
**Number of counties:** 114, plus 1 independent city
**Largest cities (1980 census):** St. Louis, 453,085; Kansas City, 448,159; Springfield, 133,116; Independence, 111,806; Columbia, 62,061; Florissant, 55,372
**State forests and Tower sites:** 93 (265,000 ac.)
**State parks:** 71 (97,314 ac.)[1]
**State cash receipts (fiscal 1985):** $5,337,962,742
**State general expenditure (fiscal 1986):** $5,072,846,996

1. Includes 24 historic sites and 1 archaeological site.

De Soto visited the Missouri area in 1541. France's claim to the entire region was based on La Salle's travels in 1682. French fur traders established Ste. Genevieve in 1735 and St. Louis was first settled in 1764.

The U.S. gained Missouri from France as part of the Louisiana Purchase in 1803, and the territory was admitted as a state following the Missouri Compromise of 1820. Throughout the pre-Civil War period and during the war, Missourians were sharply divided in their opinions about slavery and in their allegiances, supplying both Union and Confederate forces with troops. However, the state itself remained in the Union.

Historically, Missouri played a leading role as a gateway to the West, St. Joseph being the eastern starting point of the Pony Express, while the much-traveled Santa Fe and Oregon Trails began in Independence. Now a popular vacationland, Missouri has 11 major lakes and numerous fishing streams, springs, and caves. Bagnell Dam, across the Osage

River in the Ozarks, completed in 1931, created one of the largest man-made lakes in the world, covering 65,000 acres of surface area.

Manufacturing, paced by the aerospace industry, provides more income and jobs than any other segment of the economy. Missouri is also a leading producer of transportation equipment, shoes, lead, and beer. Among the major crops are corn, soybeans, wheat, oats, barley, potatoes, tobacco, and cotton.

Points of interest include Mark Twain's boyhood home and Mark Twain Cave (Hannibal), the Harry S. Truman Library and Museum (Independence), the house where Jesse James was killed in St. Joseph, Jefferson National Expansion Memorial (St. Louis), and the Ozark National Scenic Riverway.

it ranks high among the states in wheat and barley, with rye, oats, flaxseed, sugar beets, and potatoes other important crops. Sheep and cattle raising make significant contributions to the state's economy.

Tourist attractions include hunting, fishing, skiing, and dude ranching. Glacier National Park, on the Continental Divide, is a scenic and vacation wonderland with 60 glaciers, 200 lakes, and many streams with good trout fishing.

Other major points of interest include the Custer Battlefield National Monument, Virginia City, Yellowstone National Park, Museum of the Plains Indians at Browning, and the Fort Union Trading Post and Grant-Kohr's Ranch National Historic Sites.

## MONTANA

**Capital:** Helena
**Governor:** Ted Schwinden, D (to Jan. 1989)
**Lieut. Governor:** George Turman, D (to Jan. 1989)
**Secy. of State:** Jim Waltermire, R (to Jan. 1989)
**Auditor:** Andrea "Andy" Bennett, R (to Jan. 1989)
**Atty. General:** Michael Greely, D (to Jan. 1989)
**Organized as territory:** May 26, 1864
**Entered Union & (rank):** Nov. 8, 1889 (41)
**Present constitution adopted:** 1972
**Motto:** *Oro y plata* (Gold and silver)
**State flower:** Bitterroot (1895)
**State tree:** Ponderosa pine (1949)
**State stones:** Sapphire and agate (1969)
**State bird:** Western meadow lark (1931)
**State song:** "Montana" (1945)
**Nickname:** Treasure State
**Origin of name:** Chosen from Latin dictionary by J. M. Ashley. It is a Latinized Spanish word.
**1985 est. population (July 1) & (rank):** 826,000 (44)
**1984 land area & (rank):** 145,392 sq mi. (376,564 sq km) (4)
**Geographic center:** In Fergus Co., 12 mi. W of Lewistown
**Number of counties:** 56, plus small part of Yellowstone National Park
**Largest cities (1980 census):** Billings, 66,824; Great Falls, 56,725; Butte-Silver Bow, 37,205; Missoula, 33,388; Helena, 23,938; Bozeman, 21,645; Havre, 10,891
**State forests:** 7 (214,000 ac.)
**State parks and recreation areas:** 77 (18,273 ac.)
**State general revenue (fiscal year 1984–85):** $364,521,847
**State general expenditure (fiscal year 1984–85):** $434,579,737

First explored for France by François and Louis-Joseph Verendrye in the early 1740s, much of the region was acquired by the U.S. from France as part of the Louisiana Purchase in 1803. Before western Montana was obtained from Great Britain in the Oregon Treaty of 1846, American trading posts and forts had been established in the territory.

The major Indian wars (1867–1877) included the famous 1876 Battle of the Little Big Horn, better known as "Custer's Last Stand," in which Cheyennes and Sioux killed George A. Custer and more than 200 of his men in southeastern Montana.

Much of Montana's early history was concerned with mining with copper, lead, zinc, silver, coal, and oil as principal products.

Butte, sitting on the "richest hill in the world," is the center of the area that once supplied half of the U.S. copper.

Fields of grain cover much of Montana's plains;

## NEBRASKA

**Capital:** Lincoln
**Governor:** Bob Kerrey, D (to Jan. 1987)
**Lieut. Governor:** Donald L. McGinley, D (to Jan. 1987)
**Secy. of State:** Allen J. Beerman, R (to Jan. 1987)
**Atty. General:** Robert Spire, R (to Jan. 1987)
**Auditor:** Ray A. C. Johnson, R (to Jan. 1987)
**Treasurer:** Kay A. Orr, R (to Jan. 1987)
**Organized as territory:** May 30, 1854
**Entered Union & (rank):** March 1, 1867 (37)
**Present constitution adopted:** Nov. 1, 1875 (extensively amended 1919–20)
**Motto:** Equality before the law
**State flower:** Goldenrod (1895)
**State tree:** Cottonwood (1972)
**State bird:** Western meadow lark (1929)
**State insect:** Honey Bee (1975)
**State gem stone:** Blue agate (1967)
**State rock:** Prairie agate (1967)
**State fossil:** Mammoth (1967)
**State song:** "Beautiful Nebraska" (1967)
**Nicknames:** Cornhusker State; Beef State; Tree Planters State
**Origin of name:** From an Oto Indian word meaning "flat water"
**1980 population (1980 census) & (rank):** 1,570,006 (35)
**1985 est. population (July 1) & (rank):** 1,606,000 (35)
**1984 land area & (rank):** 77,727 sq mi. (198,508 sq km) (15)
**Geographic center:** In Custer Co., 10 mi. NW of Broken Bow
**Number of counties:** 93
**Largest cities (1980 census):** Omaha, 313,911; Lincoln, 171,932; Grand Island, 33,180; North Platte, 24,479; Fremont, 23,979; Hastings, 23,045; Bellevue, 21,813
**State forests:** None
**State parks:** 93 areas, 4 categories, 5 major areas
**State general revenue (fiscal year 1984–85):** $781,000,000
**State general expenditure (fiscal year 1984–85):** $809,000,000

French fur traders first visited Nebraska in the early 1700s. Part of the Louisiana Purchase in 1803, Nebraska was explored by Lewis and Clark in 1804–06.

Robert Stuart pioneered the Oregon Trail across Nebraska in 1812–13 and the first permanent settlement was established at Bellevue in 1823. Western Nebraska was acquired by treaty following the Mexican War in 1848. The Union Pacific began its transcontinental railroad at Omaha in 1865. In 1937, Nebraska became the only state in the Union to have a unicameral (one-house) legislature. Members are elected to it without party designation.

Nebraska is a leading grain-producer with

bumper crops of rye, corn, and wheat. More varieties of grass, valuable for forage, grow in this state than in any other in the nation.

The state's sizable cattle and hog industries make Omaha with its surrounding area the nation's largest meat-packing center and the second-largest cattle market in the world.

Manufacturing has become diversified in Nebraska, strengthening the state's economic base. Firms making electronic components, auto accessories, pharmaceuticals, and mobile homes have joined such older industries as clothing, farm machinery, chemicals, and transportation equipment. Oil was discovered in 1939 and natural gas in 1949.

Among the principal attractions are Agate Fossil Beds, Homestead, and Scotts Bluff National Monuments; Chimney Rock National Historic Site; a recreated pioneer village at Minden; the Union stockyards in Omaha; the Stuhr Museum of the Prairie Pioneer with 57 original 19th-century buildings near Grand Island; and the Sheldon Memorial Art Gallery at the University of Nebraska in Lincoln.

# NEVADA

**Capital:** Carson City
**Governor:** Richard H. Bryan, D (to Jan. 1987)
**Lieut. Governor:** Robert A. Cashell, R (to Jan. 1987)
**Secy. of State:** Wm. D. Swackhamer, D (to Jan. 1987)
**State Treasurer:** Patty D. Cafferata, R (to Jan. 1987)
**Controller:** Darrel R. Daines, R (to Jan. 1987)
**Atty. General:** Brian McKay, R (to Jan. 1987)
**Organized as territory:** March 2, 1861
**Entered Union & (rank):** Oct. 31, 1864 (36)
**Present constitution adopted:** 1864
**Motto:** All for Our Country
**State flower:** Sagebrush (1967)
**State tree:** Single-leaf pinon (1953)
**State bird:** Mountain bluebird (1967)
**State animal:** Desert bighorn sheep (1973)
**State colors:** Silver and blue (unofficial)
**State song:** "Home Means Nevada" (1933)
**Nicknames:** Sagebrush State; Silver State; Battle-born State
**Origin of name:** Spanish: "snowcapped"
**1980 population (1980 census) & (rank):** 800,493 (43)
**1985 est. population (July 1) & (rank):** 936,000 (43)
**1984 land area & (rank):** 109,893 sq mi. (284,624 sq km) (7)
**Geographic center:** In Lander Co., 26 mi. SE of Austin
**Number of counties:** 16, plus 1 independent city
**Largest cities (est. as of July 1, 1985):** Las Vegas, 193,052; Reno, 115,464; North Las Vegas, 45,920; Sparks, 49,612; Carson City, 35,400; Henderson, 37,046; Boulder City, 11,425
**State forests:** None
**State parks:** 20 (150,000 ac., including leased lands)
**General fund revenue (fiscal 1985–86):** $479,168,851
**General fund expenditure (fiscal 1985–86):** $474,168,851

Trappers and traders, including Jedediah Smith, and Peter Skene Ogden, entered the Nevada area in the 1820s. In 1843–45, John C. Fremont and Kit Carson explored the Great Basin and Sierra Nevada.

In 1848 following the Mexican War, the U.S. obtained the region and the first permanent settlement was a Mormon trading post near present-day Genoa.

The driest state in the nation with an average annual rainfall of only 3.73 inches, much of Nevada is uninhabited, sagebrush-covered desert.

Nevada was made famous by the discovery of the fabulous Comstock Lode in 1859 and its mines have produced large quantities of gold, silver, copper, lead, zinc, mercury, barite, and tungsten. Oil was discovered in 1954. Copper now far exceeds all other minerals in value of production.

In 1931, the state created two industries, divorce and gambling. For many years, Reno and Las Vegas were the "divorce capitals of the nation." More liberal divorce laws in many states have ended this distinction, but Nevada is the gambling and entertainment capital of the U.S. State gambling taxes account for 45% of tax revenues. Although Nevada leads the nation in per capita gambling revenue, it ranks only fourth in total gambling revenue.

Near Las Vegas, on the Colorado River, stands Hoover Dam, which impounds the waters of Lake Mead, one of the world's largest artificial lakes.

The state's agricultural crop consists mainly of hay, alfalfa seed, barley, and wheat.

Nevada manufactures gaming devices, chemicals, forest products, suntan lotion, and stone-clay-glass products.

Major resort areas flourish in Lake Tahoe, Reno, and Las Vegas. Recreation areas include those at Pyramid Lake, Lake Tahoe, and Lake Mead and Lake Mohave, both in Lake Mead National Recreation Area. Among the other attractions are Hoover Dam, Virginia City, and Lehman Caves National Monument.

# NEW HAMPSHIRE

**Capital:** Concord
**Governor:** John H. Sununu, R (to Jan. 1987)
**Secy. of State:** William M. Gardner, D (to Dec. 1986)
**Commissioner:** Stephen M. Kennedy
**Atty. General:** Stephen E. Merrill (to July 1989)
**Entered Union & (rank):** June 21, 1788 (9)
**Present constitution adopted:** 1784
**Motto:** Live free or die
**State flower:** Purple lilac (1919)
**State tree:** White birch (1947)
**State bird:** Purple finch (1957)
**State songs:** "Old New Hampshire" (1949) and "New Hampshire, My New Hampshire" (1963)
**Nickname:** Granite State
**Origin of name:** From the English county of Hampshire
**1980 population (1980 census) & (rank):** 920,610 (42)
**1985 est. population (July 1) & (rank):** 998,000 (41)
**1984 land area & (rank):** 8,993 sq mi. (23,292 sq km) (44)
**Geographic center:** In Belknap Co., 3 mi. E of Ashland
**Number of counties:** 10
**Largest cities (1980 census):** Manchester, 90,936; Nashua, 67,865; Concord, 30,400; Portsmouth, 26,254; Dover, 22,377; Rochester, 21,560; Keene, 21,449
**State forests & parks:** 175 (96,975 ac.)
**State revenue (fiscal 1984–85):** $971,407,695
**State expenditure (fiscal 1984–85):** $959,322,772

Under an English land grant, Capt. John Smith sent settlers to establish a fishing colony at the mouth of the Piscataqua River, near present-day Rye and Dover, in 1623. Capt. John Mason, who participated in the founding of Portsmouth in 1630, gave New Hampshire its name.

After a 38-year period of union with Massachusetts, New Hampshire was made a separate royal colony in 1679. As leaders in the revolutionary cause, New Hampshire delegates received the honor of being the first to vote for the Declaration of Independence on July 4, 1776. New Hampshire is the only state that ever played host at the formal conclusion of a foreign war when, in 1905, Portsmouth was the scene of the treaty ending the Russo-Japanese War.

Abundant water power early turned New Hampshire into an industrial state and manufacturing is the principal source of income in the state. The most important industrial products are leather goods, electrical and other machinery, textiles, and pulp and paper products.

Dairy and poultry farming and growing fruit, truck vegetables, corn, potatoes, and hay are the major agricultural pursuits.

Tourism, because of New Hampshire's scenic and recreational resources, now brings over $400 million into the state annually.

Vacation attractions include Lake Winnipesaukee, largest of 1,300 lakes and ponds; the 724,000-acre White Mountain National Forest; Daniel Webster's birthplace near Franklin; Strawberry Banke, restored building of the original settlement at Portsmouth; and the famous "Old Man of the Mountain" granite head profile, the state's official emblem, at Franconia.

Today, New Jersey, an area of wide industrial diversification, is known as the Crossroads of the East. Products from over 15,000 factories can be delivered overnight to almost 60 million people, representing 12 states and the District of Columbia. The greatest single industry is chemicals and New Jersey is one of the foremost research centers in the world. Many large oil refineries are located in northern New Jersey and other important manufactures are pharmaceuticals, instruments, machinery, electrical goods, and apparel.

Of the total land area, 43% is forested and about 24% is devoted to agriculture. The state ranks high in production of almost all garden vegetables. Tomatoes, asparagus, corn, and blueberries are important crops, and poultry farming and dairying make significant contributions to the state's economy.

Tourism is the second largest industry in New Jersey. The state has numerous resort areas on 127 miles of Atlantic coastline. In 1977, New Jersey voters approved legislation allowing legalized casino gambling in Atlantic City. Points of interest include the Walt Whitman House in Camden, the Delaware Water Gap, the Edison National Historic Site in West Orange, and Princeton University.

## NEW JERSEY

**Capital:** Trenton
**Governor:** Thomas H. Kean, R (to Jan. 1990)
**Secy. of State:** Jane Burgio, R (to Jan. 1990)
**Treasurer:** Kenneth Biederman, R (to Jan. 1990)
**Atty. General:** Irwin I. Kimmelman, R (to Jan. 1990)
**Entered Union & (rank):** Dec. 18, 1787 (3)
**Present constitution adopted:** 1947
**Motto:** Liberty and prosperity
**State flower:** Purple violet (1913)
**State bird:** Eastern goldfinch (1935)
**State insect:** Honeybee (1974)
**State tree:** Red oak (1950)
**State animal:** Horse (1977)
**State colors:** Buff and blue (1965)
**Nickname:** Garden State
**Origin of name:** From the Channel Isle of Jersey
**1980 population (1980 census) & (rank):** 7,364,823 (9)
**1985 est. population (July 1) & (rank):** 7,562,000 (9)
**1984 land area & (rank):** 7,468 sq mi. (19,342 sq km) (46)
**Geographic center:** In Mercer Co., 5 mi. SE of Trenton
**Number of counties:** 21
**Largest cities (1980 census):** Newark, 329,248; Jersey City, 223,532; Paterson, 137,970; Elizabeth, 106,201; Trenton, 92,124; Camden, 84,910; Clifton, 77,690
**State forests:** 11
**State parks:** 40 (73,483 ac.)
**State general revenue (fiscal 1985-86):** $6,514,276,000
**State appropriations (fiscal 1985-86):** $6,329,276,000

New Jersey's early colonial history was involved with that of New York (New Netherlands), of which it was a part. One year after the Dutch surrender to England in 1664, New Jersey was organized as an English colony under Gov. Philip Carteret.

In the late 1600s the colony was divided between Carteret and William Penn; later it would be administered by the royal governor of New York. Finally, in 1738, New Jersey was separated from New York under its own royal governor, Lewis Morris.

Because of its key location between New York City and Philadelphia, New Jersey saw much fighting during the American Revolution.

## NEW MEXICO

**Capital:** Santa Fe
**Governor:** Toney Anaya, D (to Jan. 1987)
**Lieut. Governor:** Mike Runnels, D (to Jan. 1987)
**Secy. of State:** Clara Jones, D (to Jan. 1987)
**Atty. General:** Paul Bardacke, D (to Jan. 1987)
**State Auditor:** Albert Romero, D (to Jan. 1987)
**State Treasurer:** James B. Lewis, D (to Jan. 1987)
**Commissioner of Public Lands:** Jim Baco, D (to Jan. 1987)
**Organized as territory:** Sept. 9, 1850
**Entered Union & (rank):** Jan. 6, 1912 (47)
**Present constitution adopted:** 1911
**Motto:** *Crescit eundo* (It grows as it goes)
**State flower:** Yucca (1927)
**State tree:** Pinon (1949)
**State animal:** Black bear (1963)
**State bird:** Roadrunner (1949)
**State fish:** Cutthroat trout (1955)
**State vegetables:** Chile and frijol (1965)
**State gem:** Turquoise (1967)
**State colors:** Red and yellow of old Spain (1925)
**State song:** "O Fair New Mexico" (1917)
**Spanish language state song:** "Asi Es Nuevo Mejico" (1971)
**Nicknames:** Land of Enchantment; Sunshine State
**Origin of name:** From the country of Mexico
**1980 population (1980 census) & (rank):** 1,302,981 (37)
**1985 est. population (July 1) & (rank):** 1,450,000 (37)
**1984 land area & (rank):** 121,335 sq mi. (314,258 sq km) (5)
**Geographic center:** In Torrance Co., 12 mi. SSW of Willard
**Number of counties:** 33
**Largest cities (July 1, 1984 est.):** Albuquerque, 350,575; Santa Fe, 52,274; Las Cruces, 50,275; Roswell, 45,702; Farmington, 37,332; Hobbs, 35,029
**State-owned forested land:** 933,000 ac.
**State parks:** 29 (105,012 ac.)
**State general revenue (fiscal 1984-85):** 2,943,540,000
**State general expenditure (fiscal 1984-85):** 2,671,225,000

Francisco Vásquez de Coronado, Spanish explorer searching for gold, traveled the region that became New Mexico in 1540-42. In 1598 the first

Spanish settlement was established on the Rio Grande River by Juan de Onate and in 1610 Santa Fe was founded and made the capital of New Mexico.

The U.S. acquired most of New Mexico in 1848, as a result of the Mexican War, and the remainder in the 1853 Gadsden Purchase. Union troops captured the territory from the Confederates during the Civil War. With the surrender of Geronimo in 1886, the Apache Wars and most of the Indian troubles in the area were ended.

Since 1945, New Mexico has been a leader in energy research and development with extensive experiments conducted at Los Alamos Scientific Laboratory and Sandia Laboratories in the nuclear, solar, and geothermal areas.

Minerals are the state's richest natural resource and New Mexico leads the U.S. in output of uranium and potassium salts. Petroleum, natural gas, copper, gold, silver, zinc, lead, and molybdenum also contribute heavily to the state's income.

The principal manufacturing industries include food products, chemicals, transportation equipment, lumber, electrical machinery, and stone-clay-glass products. More than two thirds of New Mexico's farm income comes from livestock products, especially sheep. Cotton, pecans, and sorghum are the most important field crops. Corn, peanuts, beans, onions, and lettuce are also grown.

Tourist attractions in New Mexico include the Carlsbad Caverns National Park, Inscription Rock at El Morro National Monument, the ruins at Fort Union, Billy the Kid mementos at Lincoln, and the White Sands and Gila Cliff Dwellings National Monuments.

# NEW YORK

**Capital:** Albany
**Governor:** Mario M. Cuomo, D (to Jan. 1987)
**Lieut. Governor:** vacant
**Secy. of State:** Gail S. Shaffer, D (to Jan. 1987)
**Comptroller:** Edward V. Regan, R (to Jan. 1987)
**Atty. General:** Robert Abrams, D (to Jan. 1987)
**Entered Union & (rank):** July 26, 1788 (11)
**Present constitution adopted:** 1777 (last revised 1938)
**Motto:** *Excelsior* (Ever upward)
**State animal:** Beaver (1975)
**State fish:** Brook trout (1975)
**State gem:** Garnet (1969)
**State flower:** Rose (1955)
**State tree:** Sugar maple (1956)
**State bird:** Bluebird
**State song:** "I Love New York" (1980)
**Nickname:** Empire State
**Origin of name:** In honor of the English Duke of York
**1980 population (1980 census) & (rank):** 17,558,165 (2)
**1985 est. population (July 1) & (rank):** 17,783,000 (2)
**1984 land area & (rank):** 47,377 sq mi. (122,707 sq km) (30)
**Geographic center:** In Madison Co., 12 mi. S of Oneida and 26 mi. SW of Utica
**Number of counties:** 62
**Largest cities (1984 est.):** New York, 7,164,742; Buffalo, 338,982; Rochester, 242,562; Yonkers, 191,234; Syracuse, 164,219; Albany, 99,451; Utica, 72,935
**State forest preserves:** Adirondacks, 2,500,000 ac., Catskills, 250,000 ac.
**State parks:** 150 (250,000 ac.)
**State general fund income (fiscal 1986–87):** $23,047,000,000
**State general fund outgo (fiscal 1986–87):** $22,996,000,000

Giovanni da Verrazano, Italian-born navigator sailing for France, discovered New York Bay in 1524. Henry Hudson, an Englishman employed by the Dutch, reached the bay and sailed up the river now bearing his name in 1609, the same year that northern New York was explored and claimed for France by Samuel de Champlain.

In 1624 the first permanent Dutch settlement was established at Fort Orange (now Albany); one year later Peter Minuit is said to have purchased Manhattan Island from the Indians for trinkets worth about $24 and founded the Dutch colony of New Amsterdam (now New York City), which was surrendered to the English in 1664.

For a short time, New York City was the U.S. capital and George Washington was inaugurated there as first President on April 30, 1789.

New York's extremely rapid commercial growth may be partly attributed to Governor De Witt Clinton, who pushed through the construction of the Erie Canal (Buffalo to Albany), which was opened in 1825. Today, the 559-mile Governor Thomas E. Dewey Thruway connects New York City with Buffalo and with Connecticut, Massachusetts, and Pennsylvania express highways. Two toll-free superhighways, the Adirondack Northway (linking Albany with the Canadian border) and the North-South-Expressway (crossing central New York from the Pennsylvania border to the Thousand Isalnds) have been opened.

New York, with the great metropolis of New York City, is the spectacular nerve center of the nation. It is a leader in manufacturing, foreign trade, commercial and financial transactions, book and magazine publishing, and theatrical production.

New York City is not only a national but an international leader. A leading seaport, its John F. Kennedy International Airport is one of the busiest airports in the world. The largest manufacturing center in the country, in 1982 its manufacturing establishments employed 529,000 persons. The apparel industry is the city's largest manufacturing employer, with printing and publishing second.

Nearly all the rest of the state's manufacturing is done on Long Island, along the Hudson River north to Albany and through the Mohawk Valley, Central New York, and Southern Tier regions to Buffalo. The St. Lawrence seaway and power projects have opened the North Country to industrial expansion and have given the state a second seacoast.

The state ranks second in the nation in manufacturing with 1,383,300 employees in 1983. The principal industries are machinery, printing and publishing, instruments, apparel, and chemicals.

The convention and tourist business is one of the state's most important sources of income.

New York farms are famous for raising cattle and calves, producing corn for grain, poultry, and the raising of vegetables and fruits. The state is a leading wine producer.

Among the major points of interest are Castle Clinton, Fort Stanwix, and Statue of Liberty National Monuments; Niagara Falls; U.S. Military Academy at West Point; National Historic Sites that include homes of Franklin D. Roosevelt at Hyde Park and Theodore Roosevelt in Oyster Bay and New York City; National Memorials, including Grant's Tomb and Federal Hall in New York City; Fort Ticonderoga; the Baseball Hall of Fame in Cooperstown; and the United Nations, skyscrapers, museums, theaters, and parks in New York City.

# NORTH CAROLINA

**Capital:** Raleigh
**Governor:** James G. Martin, R (to Jan. 1989)
**Lieut. Governor:** Robert B. Jordan III, D (to Jan. 1989)
**Secy. of State:** Thad Eure, D (to Jan. 1989)
**Treasurer:** Harlan E. Boyles (to Jan. 1989)
**Auditor:** Edward Renfrow, D (to Jan. 1989)
**Atty. General:** Lacey H. Thornburg, D (to Jan. 1989)
**Entered Union & (rank):** Nov. 21, 1789 (12)
**Present constitution adopted:** 1971
**Motto:** *Esse quam videri* (To be rather than to seem)
**State flower:** Dogwood (1941)
**State tree:** Pine (1963)
**State bird:** Cardinal (1943)
**State mammal:** Gray Squirrel (1969)
**State insect:** Honeybee (1973)
**State Reptile:** Turtle (1979)
**State gem stone:** Emerald (1973)
**State shell:** Scotch bonnet (1965)
**State song:** "The Old North State" (1927)
**State colors:** Red and blue (1945)
**Nickname:** Tar Heel State
**Origin of name:** In honor of Charles I of England
**1980 population (1980 census) & (rank):** 5,881,766 (10)
**1985 est. population (July 1) & (rank):** 6,255,000 (10)
**1984 land area & (rank):** 48,843 sq mi. (126,504 sq km) (29)
**Geographic center:** In Chatham Co., 10 mi. NW of Sanford
**Number of counties:** 100
**Largest cities (est. as of July 1, 1984):** Charlotte, 338,107; Raleigh, 180,559; Greensboro, 159,744; Winston-Salem, 146,886; Durham, 106,115; High Point, 66,380
**State forests:** 1
**State parks:** 28 (120,000 ac.)
**State total general revenue (est. fiscal 1985–86):** $4,927,000,000
**State total general fund expenditures (est. fiscal 1985–86):** $4,977,900,000

---

English colonists, sent by Sir Walter Raleigh, unsuccessfully attempted to settle Roanoke Island in 1585 and 1587. Virginia Dare, born there in 1587, was the first child of English parentage born in America.

In 1653 the first permanent settlements were established by English colonists from Virginia near the Roanoke and Chowan Rivers.

The region was established as an English proprietary colony in 1663–65 and its early history was the scene of Culpepper's Rebellion (1677), the Quaker-led Cary Rebellion of 1708, the Tuscarora Indian War in 1711–13, and many pirate raids.

During the American Revolution, there was relatively little fighting within the state, but many North Carolinians saw action elsewhere. Despite considerable pro-Union, anti-slavery sentiment, North Carolina joined the Confederacy.

North Carolina is the nation's largest furniture, tobacco, brick, and textile producer. It holds second place in the Southeast in population and first place in the value of its industrial and agricultural production. This production is highly diversified, with metalworking, chemicals, and paper constituting enormous industries. Tobacco, corn, cotton, hay, peanuts, and truck and vegetable crops are of major importance. It is the country's leading producer of mica and lithium.

Tourism is also important, with travelers and vacationers spending more than $1 billion annually in North Carolina. Sports include year-round golfing, skiing at mountain resorts, both fresh and salt water fishing, and hunting.

Among the major attractions are the Great Smoky Mountains, the Blue Ridge National Parkway, the Cape Hatteras and Cape Lookout National Seashores, the Wright Brothers National Memorial at Kitty Hawk, Guilford Courthouse and Moores Creek National Military Parks, Carl Sandburg's home near Hendersonville, and the Old Salem Restoration in Winston-Salem.

# NORTH DAKOTA

**Capital:** Bismarck
**Governor:** George A. Sinner, D (to Jan. 1989)
**Lieut. Governor:** Ruth Meiers, D (to Jan. 1989)
**Secy. of State:** Ben Meier, R (to Jan. 1985)
**Auditor:** Robert W. Peterson, R (to Jan. 1989)
**State Treasurer:** Robert Hanson, D (to Jan. 1989)
**Atty. General:** Nicholas Spaeth, D (to Jan. 1989)
**Organized as territory:** March 2, 1861
**Entered Union & (rank):** Nov. 2, 1889 (39)
**Present constitution adopted:** 1889
**Motto:** Liberty and union, now and forever: one and inseparable
**State tree:** American Elm (1947)
**State bird:** Western meadow lark (1947)
**State song:** "North Dakota Hymn" (1947)
**Nickname:** Sioux State; Flickertail State
**Origin of name:** From the Dakotah tribe, meaning "allies"
**1980 population (1980 census) & (rank):** 652,717 (46)
**1985 est. population (July 1) & (rank):** 685,000 (46)
**1984 land area & (rank):** 70,665 sq mi (183,113 sq km) (17)
**Geographic center:** In Sheridan Co., 5 mi. SW of McClusky
**Number of counties:** 53
**Largest cities (1980 census):** Fargo, 61,383; Bismarck, 44,485; Grand Forks, 43,765; Minot, 32,843; Jamestown, 16,280; Dickinson, 15,924; Mandan, 15,513
**State forests:** None
**State parks:** 14 (14,922.6 ac.)
**Total state collections (fiscal 1985):** $1,221,321,198
**Total state disbursements (fiscal 1985):** $1,153,875,207

---

North Dakota was explored in 1738–40 by French Canadians led by Vérendrye. In 1803, the U.S. acquired most of North Dakota from France in the Louisiana Purchase. Lewis and Clark explored the region in 1804–06 and the first settlements were made at Pembina in 1812 by Scottish and Irish families while this area was still in dispute between the U.S. and Great Britain.

In 1818, the U.S. obtained the northeastern part of North Dakota by treaty with Great Britain and took possession of Pembina in 1823.

North Dakota is the most rural of all the states, with farms covering more than 90% of the land. Only Kansas produces more wheat, and the state's coal and oil reserves are plentiful.

Other agricultural products include barley, rye, oats, and flaxseed, sugar beets, and hay; beef cattle, sheep, and hogs are also important to the state's economy.

Recently, manufacturing industries have grown, especially food processing and farm equipment. The state also produces natural gas, lignite, salt, clay, sand, and gravel.

The Garrison Dam on the Missouri River provides extensive irrigation and produces 400,000 kilowatts of electricity for the Missouri Basin areas.

Known for its waterfowl, grouse, and deer hunting and bass, trout, and northern pike fishing, North Dakota has 20 state parks and recreation areas. Points of interest include the International

Peace Garden near Dunseith, Fort Union Trading Post National Historic Site, the State Capitol at Bismarck, the Badlands, and Fort Lincoln, now a state park, from which Gen. George Custer set out on his last campaign in 1876.

# OHIO

**Capital:** Columbus
**Governor:** Richard F. Celeste, D (to Jan. 1987)
**Lieut. Governor:** Vacant since the death of Myrl H. Shoemaker, D
**Secy. of State:** Sherrod Brown, D (to Jan. 1987)
**Auditor:** Thomas E. Ferguson (to Jan. 1987)
**Treasurer:** Mary Ellen Withrow, D (to Jan. 1987)
**Atty. General:** Anthony J. Celebrezze, Jr., D (to Jan. 1987)
**Entered Union & (rank):** March 1, 1803 (17)
**Present constitution adopted:** 1851
**Motto:** With God, all things are possible
**State flower:** Scarlet carnation (1904)
**State tree:** Buckeye (1953)
**State bird:** Cardinal (1933)
**State insect:** Ladybug (1975)
**State gem stone:** Flint (1965)
**State song:** "Beautiful Ohio"
**State drink:** Tomato juice (1965)
**Nickname:** Buckeye State
**Origin of name:** From an Iroquoian word meaning "great river"
**1980 population (1980 census) & (rank):** 10,797,624 (6)
**1985 est. population (July 1) & (rank):** 10,744,000 (7)
**1984 land area & (rank):** 41,004 sq mi. (106,201 sq km) (35)
**Geographic center:** In Delaware Co., 25 mi. NNE of Columbus
**Number of counties:** 88
**Largest cities (1980 census):** Cleveland, 573,822; Columbus, 565,032; Cincinnati, 385,457; Toledo, 354,635; Akron, 237,177; Dayton, 203,371; Youngstown, 115,436
**State forests:** 19 (172,744 ac.)
**State parks:** 71 (198,027 ac.)
**State actual revenue (fiscal year 1984–85):** $14,711,372,000
**State actual expenditure (fiscal year 1984–85):** $14,051,664,000

First explored for France by La Salle in 1669, the Ohio region became British property after the French and Indian War. Ohio was acquired by the U.S. after the Revolutionary War in 1783 and, in 1788, the first permanent settlement was established at Marietta, capital of the Northwest Territory.

The 1790s saw severe fighting with the Indians in Ohio; a major battle was won by Maj. Gen. Anthony Wayne at Fallen Timbers in 1794. In the War of 1812, Commodore Oliver H. Perry defeated the British in the Battle of Lake Erie on Sept. 10, 1813.

Ohio is one of the nation's industrial leaders, ranking third in the value of manufactured products. Important manufacturing centers are located in or near Ohio's major cities. Akron is known for rubber; Canton for roller bearings; Cincinnati for jet engines and machine tools; Cleveland for auto assembly and parts, refining, and steel; Dayton for office machines, refrigeration, and heating and auto equipment; Youngstown and Steubenville for steel; and Toledo for glass and auto parts.

The state's thousands of factories almost overshadow its importance in agriculture and mining. Its fertile soil produces soybeans, corn, oats, grapes, and clover. More than half of Ohio's farm receipts come from dairying and sheep and hog raising. Ohio is the top state in lime production and among the leaders in coal, clay, salt, sand, and gravel. Petroleum, gypsum, cement, and natural gas are also important.

Tourism is a valuable revenue producer, bringing in over $3 billion annually. Attractions include the Indian burial grounds at Mound City Group National Monument, Perry's Victory International Peace Memorial, the Pro Football Hall of Fame at Canton, and the homes of Presidents Grant, Taft, Hayes, Harding, and Garfield.

# OKLAHOMA

**Capital:** Oklahoma City
**Governor:** George P. Nigh, D (to Jan. 1987)
**Lieut. Governor:** Spencer Bernard, D (to Jan. 1987)
**Secy. of State:** Jeannette Edmondson, D (to Jan. 1987)
**Treasurer:** Leo Winters, D (to Jan. 1987)
**Atty. General:** Michael C. Turpen, D (to Jan. 1987)
**Organized as territory:** May 2, 1890
**Entered Union & (rank):** Nov. 16, 1907 (46)
**Present constitution adopted:** 1907
**Motto:** *Labor omnia vincit* (Labor conquers all things)
**State flower:** Mistletoe (1893)
**State tree:** Redbud (1937)
**State bird:** Scissor-tailed flycatcher (1951)
**State animal:** Bison (1972)
**State reptile:** Mountain boomer lizard (1969)
**State stone:** Rose Rock (barite rose) (1968)
**State colors:** Green and white (1915)
**State song:** "Oklahoma" (1953)
**Nickname:** Sooner State
**Origin of name:** From two Choctaw Indian words meaning "red people"
**1980 population (1980 census) & (rank):** 3,025,290 (26)
**1985 est. population (July 1) & (rank):** 3,301,000 (25)
**1984 land area & (rank):** 68,655 sq mi. (177,817 sq km) (19)
**Geographic center:** In Oklahoma Co., 8 mi. N of Oklahoma City
**Number of counties:** 77
**Largest cities (1980 census):** Oklahoma City, 403,213; Tulsa, 360,919; Lawton, 80,054; Norman, 68,020; Enid, 50,363; Midwest City, 49,559; Muskogee, 40,011
**State forests:** None
**State parks:** 36 (57,487 ac.)
**Total state revenue (1985):** $4,491,932,858
**Total state expenditure (1985):** $4,673,529,265

Francisco Vásquez de Coronado first explored the region for Spain in 1541. The U.S. acquired most of Oklahoma in 1803 in the Louisiana Purchase from France; the Western Panhandle region became U.S. territory with the annexation of Texas in 1845.

Set aside as Indian Territory in 1834, the region was divided into Indian Territory and Oklahoma Territory on May 2, 1890. The two were combined to make a new state, Oklahoma, on November 16, 1907.

On April 22, 1899, the first day homesteading was permitted, 50,000 people swarmed into the area. Those who tried to beat the noon starting gun were called "Sooners." Hence the state's nickname.

Oil has made Oklahoma a rich state and Tulsa one of the world's wealthiest cities per capita. Oil refining, meat packing, food processing, and machinery manufacturing (especially construction and oil equipment) are important industries.

Other minerals produced in Oklahoma include natural gas, helium, gypsum, zinc, cement, coal, copper, and silver.

Oklahoma's rich plains produce bumper yields of wheat, as well as large crops of sorghum, corn, cotton, and peanuts. Its beef cattle herd is among the largest in the nation; more than half of Oklahoma's annual farm receipts are contributed by livestock products.

Tourist attractions include the National Cowboy Hall of Fame in Oklahoma City, the Will Rogers Memorial in Claremore, the Cherokee Cultural Center with a restored Cherokee village, the restored Fort Gibson Stockade near Muskogee, and the Lake Texoma recreation area.

# OREGON

**Capital:** Salem
**Governor:** Victor G. Atiyeh, R (to Jan. 1987)
**Secy. of State:** Barbara Roberts, R (to Jan. 1989)
**Treasurer:** Bill Rutherford, R (to Jan. 1989)
**Atty. General:** David B. Frohnmayer, R (to Jan. 1989)
**Organized as territory:** Aug. 14, 1848
**Entered Union & (rank):** Feb. 14, 1859 (33)
**Present constitution adopted:** 1859
**Motto:** The Union (1957)
**State flower:** Oregon grape (1899)
**State tree:** Douglas fir (1939)
**State animal:** Beaver (1969)
**State bird:** Western meadow lark (1927)
**State fish:** Chinook salmon (1961)
**State rock:** Thunderegg (1965)
**State colors:** Navy blue and gold (1959)
**State song:** "Oregon, My Oregon" (1927)
**Nickname:** Beaver State
**Poet Laureate:** William E. Stafford (1974)
**Origin of name:** Unknown. However, it is generally accepted that the name, first used by Jonathan Carver in 1778, was taken from the writings of Maj. Robert Rogers, an English army officer.
**1980 population (1980 census) & (rank):** 2,633,105 (30)
**1985 est. population (July 1) & (rank):** 2,687,000 (30)
**1984 land area & (rank):** 96,184 sq mi. (249,117 sq km) (10)
**Geographic center:** In Crook Co., 25 mi. SSE of Prineville
**Number of counties:** 36
**Largest cities (est. as of July 1, 1985):** Portland, 379,000; Eugene, 106,100; Salem, 94,600; Medford, 41,975; Springfield, 40,690
**State forests:** 820,000 ac.
**State parks:** 240 (93,330 ac.)
**State general revenue (1985–87 est.):** $3,337,425,982
**State general expenditure (1985–87 est.):** $3,264,356,399

Spanish and English sailors are believed to have sighted the Oregon coast in the 1500s and 1600s. Capt. James Cook, seeking the Northwest Passage, charted some of the coastline in 1778. In 1792, Capt. Robert Gray, in the *Columbia*, discovered the river named after his ship and claimed the area for the U.S.

In 1805 the Lewis and Clark expedition explored the area and John Jacob Astor's fur depot, Astoria, was founded in 1811. Disputes for control of Oregon between American settlers and the Hudson Bay Company were finally resolved in the 1846 Oregon Treaty in which Great Britain gave up claims to the region.

Oregon has a five-billion-dollar wood processing industry. Its salmon-fishing industry is one of the world's largest.

In agriculture, the state leads in growing peppermint, winter pears, fresh plums, prunes, blackberries, boysenberries, filberts, Blue Lake beans, and cover seed crops, and also raises strawberries, hops, wheat and other grains, sugar beets, potatoes; green peas, fiber flax, dairy products, livestock and poultry, apples, pears, and cherries. Oregon is the source of all the nickel produced in the U.S.

With the low-cost electric power provided by Bonneville Dam, McNary Dam, and other dams in the Pacific Northwest, Oregon has developed steadily as a manufacturing state. Leading manufactures are lumber and plywood, metalwork, machinery, aluminum, chemicals, paper, food packing, and electronic equipment.

Crater Lake National Park, Mount Hood, and Bonneville Dam on the Columbia are major tourist attractions. Oregon Dunes National Recreation Area has been established near Florence. Other points of interest include the Oregon Caves National Monument, Cape Perpetua in Siuslaw National Forest, Columbia River Gorge between The Dalles and Troutdale, and Hells Canyon.

# PENNSYLVANIA

**Capital:** Harrisburg
**Governor:** Richard L. Thornburgh, R (to Jan. 1987)
**Lieut. Governor:** William W. Scranton III, R (to Jan. 1987)
**Secy. of the Commonwealth:** William R. Davis (to Jan. 1987)
**Auditor General:** Don Bailey, D (to Jan. 1989)
**Atty. General:** Leroy S. Zimmerman, R (to Jan. 1989)
**Entered Union & (rank):** Dec. 12, 1787 (2)
**Present constitution adopted:** 1874
**Motto:** Virtue, liberty, and independence
**State flower:** Mountain laurel (1933)
**State tree:** Hemlock (1931)
**State bird:** Ruffed grouse (1931)
**State dog:** Great Dane (1965)
**State colors:** Blue and gold
**State song:** None
**Nickname:** Keystone State
**Origin of name:** In honor of Adm. Sir. William Penn, father of William Penn. It means "Penn's Woodland."
**1980 population (1980 census) & (rank):** 11,863,895 (4)
**1985 est. population (July 1) & (rank):** 11,853,000 (4)
**1984 land area & (rank):** 44,888 sq mi. (116,260 sq km) (32)
**Geographic center:** In Centre Co., 2 1/2 mi. SW of Bellefonte
**Number of counties:** 67
**Largest cities (1980 census):** Philadelphia, 1,688,210; Pittsburgh, 423,959; Erie, 119,123; Allentown, 103,758; Scranton, 88,117; Reading, 78,686; Bethlehem, 70,419
**State forests:** 1,930,108 ac.
**State parks:** 120 (297,438 ac.)
**Total est. resources subject to general appropriations (fiscal year 1986–87):** $9,699,946,000
**Total est. appropriations (fiscal year 1986–87):** $9,698,896,000

Rich in historic lore, Pennsylvania territory was disputed in the early 1600s among the Dutch, the Swedes, and the English. England acquired the region in 1664 with the capture of New York and in 1681 Pennsylvania was granted to William Penn, a Quaker, by King Charles II.

Philadelphia was the seat of the federal government almost continuously from 1776 to 1800; there the Declaration of Independence was signed in

1776 and the U.S. Constitution drawn up in 1787. Valley Forge, of Revolutionary War fame, and Gettysburg, the turning-point of the Civil War, are both in Pennsylvania. The Liberty Bell is located in a glass pavilion across from Independence Hall in Philadelphia.

Approximately 23% of all American pig iron steel is made in Pennsylvania, which ranks first among the states in steel wire and structural metal production. Other manufactures include machinery, chemicals, storage batteries, motor vehicles and trailers, computers, textiles and apparel, shoes, plastics, and explosives. Pennsylvania produces almost all the nation's anthracite coal. Also important are bituminous coal, cement, stone, petroleum, natural gas, lime, clays, zinc, and iron.

Prosperous farms brought in total receipts of more than $1.3 billion in 1973. The state ranked high in milk cows, chickens, and turkeys. Agricultural products include apples, peaches, potatoes, corn, wheat, barley, buckwheat, and mushrooms.

Tourists now spend approximately $6 billion in Pennsylvania annually. Among the chief attractions: the Gettysburg National Military Park, Valley Forge National Historical Park, Independence National Historical Park in Philadelphia, the Pennsylvania Dutch region, the Eisenhower farm near Gettysburg, and the Delaware Water Gap National Recreation Area.

# RHODE ISLAND

**Capital:** Providence
**Governor:** Edward D. DiPrete, R (to Jan. 1987)
**Lieut. Governor:** Richard A. Licht, D (to Jan. 1987)
**Secy. of State:** Susan Farmer, R (to Jan. 1987)
**Controller:** Edward Casper (civil service)
**Atty. General:** Arlene Violet, R (to Jan. 1987)
**Entered Union & (rank):** May 29, 1790 (13)
**Present constitution adopted:** 1843
**Motto:** Hope
**State flower:** Violet (unofficial)
**State tree:** Red maple (official)
**State bird:** Rhode Island Red (official)
**State colors:** Blue, white, and gold (in state flag)
**State song:** "Rhode Island" (1946)
**Nickname:** The Ocean State
**Origin of name:** From the Greek Island of Rhodes
**1980 population (1980 census) & (rank):** 947,154 (40)
**1985 est. population (July 1) & (rank):** 968,000 (42)
**1984 land area & (rank):** 1,055 sq mi. (2,732 sq km) (50)
**Geographic center:** In Kent Co., 1 mi. SSW of Crompton
**Number of counties:** 5
**Largest cities (1980 census):** Providence, 156,804; Warwick, 87,123; Cranston, 71,992; Pawtucket, 71,204; East Providence, 50,980; Woonsocket, 45,914
**State forests:** 11 (20,900 ac.)
**State parks:** 17 (8,200 ac.)
**State general revenue (fiscal 1984–85):** $1,375,062,130
**State general expenditure (fiscal 1984–85):** $1,341,554,518

From its beginnings, Rhode Island has been distinguished by its support for freedom of conscience and action, started by Roger Williams, who was exiled by the Massachusetts Bay Colony Puritans in 1636, and was the founder of the present state capital, Providence. Williams was followed by other religious exiles who founded Pocasset, now Portsmouth, in 1638 and Newport in 1639.

The first Baptist church in the U.S. was established in Providence in 1638 and Rhode Island pro-

vided a haven for Quakers in 1657 and for Jews from Holland in 1659.

Rhode Island's rebellious, authority-defying nature was further demonstrated by the burnings of the British revenue cutters *Liberty* and *Gaspee* prior to the Revolution, by its early declaration of independence from Great Britain in May 1776, its refusal to participate actively in the War of 1812, and by Dorr's Rebellion of 1842, which protested property requirements for voting.

Rhode Island, smallest of the 50 states, is densely populated and highly industrialized. The state pioneered in the manufacture of jewelry and silverware and still retains first place in the U.S. Other leading industries are primary metal processing, metal products, machinery, rubber and plastics, food processing, chemicals, transportation equipment and electronic equipment.

With more than eight tenths of the population living in urban areas, adjacent areas of the state are involved in dairying and poultry and truck farming. Nursery and greenhouse products, potatoes, corn, apples, oats, and hay lead the crop list.

Newport became famous as the summer capital of society in the mid-19th century. Touro Synagogue (1763) is the oldest in the U.S. Other points of interest include the Roger Williams National Memorial in Providence, Samuel Slater's Mill in Pawtucket, the General Nathaniel Greene Homestead in Coventry and Block Island.

# SOUTH CAROLINA

**Capital:** Columbia
**Governor:** Richard W. Riley, D (to Jan. 1987)
**Lieut. Governor:** Mike Daniel, D (to Jan. 1987)
**Secy. of State:** John T. Campbell, D (to Jan. 1987)
**Comptroller General:** Earl E. Morris, Jr. (to Jan. 1987)
**Atty. General:** T. Travis Medlock, D (to Jan. 1987)
**Entered Union & (rank):** May 23, 1788 (8).
**Present constitution adopted:** 1895
**Mottoes:** *Animis opibusque parati* (Prepared in mind and resources) and *Dum spiro spero* (While I breathe, I hope)
**State flower:** Carolina yellow jessamine (1924)
**State tree:** Palmetto tree (1939)
**State bird:** Carolina wren (1948)
**State song:** "Carolina" (1911)
**Nickname:** Palmetto State
**Origin of name:** In honor of Charles I of England
**1980 population (1980 census) & (rank):** 3,121,833 (24)
**1985 est. population (July 1) & (rank):** 3,347,000 (24)
**1984 land area & (rank):** 30,203 sq mi. (78,227 sq km) (40)
**Geographic center:** In Richland Co., 13 mi. SE of Columbia
**Number of counties:** 46
**Largest cities (1980 census):** Columbia, 100,385; Charleston, 69,510; North Charleston, 62,534; Greenville, 58,242; Spartanburg, 43,826; Rock Hill, 35,344
**State forests:** 4 (124,052 ac.)
**State parks:** 50 (61,726 ac.)
**State general fund revenue (fiscal 1984–85):** $2,393,372,198[1]
**State general expenditures (fiscal 1984–85):** $2,397,054,372[1]

1. Highway Dept. has separate funding and expenditures.

Following exploration of the coast in 1521 by De Gordillo, the Spanish tried unsuccessfully to establish a colony near present-day Georgetown in 1526 and the French also failed to colonize Parris Island near Fort Royal in 1562.

The first English settlement was made in 1670

at Albemarle Point on the Ashley River, but poor conditions drove the settlers to the site of Charleston (originally called Charles Town). South Carolina, officially separated from North Carolina in 1729, was the scene of extensive military action during the Revolution and again during the Civil War. The Civil War began in 1861 as South Carolina troops fired on federal Fort Sumter in Charleston Harbor and the state was the first to secede from the Union.

Once primarily agricultural, South Carolina has built so many large textile and other mills that today its factories produce eight times the output of its farms in cash value. Charleston makes asbestos, wood, pulp, and steel products; chemicals, machinery, and apparel are also important.

Farms have become fewer but larger in recent years. South Carolina grows more peaches than any other state except California; it ranks fourth in tobacco. Other farm products include cotton, peanuts, sweet potatoes, soybeans, corn, and oats. Poultry and dairy products are also important revenue producers.

Points of interest include Fort Sumter National Monument, Fort Moultrie, Fort Johnson, and aircraft carrier USS *Yorktown* in Charleston Harbor; the Middleton, Magnolia, and Cypress Gardens in Charleston; Cowpens National Battlefield; and the Hilton Head resorts.

# SOUTH DAKOTA

**Capital:** Pierre
**Governor:** William J. Janklow, R (to Jan. 1987)
**Lieut. Governor:** Lowell C. Hansen II, R (to Jan. 1987)
**Atty. General:** Mark Meierhenry, R (to Jan. 1987)
**Secy. of State:** Alice Kundert, R (to Jan. 1987)
**State Auditor:** Vern Larson, R (to Jan. 1987)
**State Treasurer:** David L. Volk, R (to Jan. 1987)
**Organized as territory:** March 2, 1861
**Entered Union & (rank):** Nov. 2, 1889 (40)
**Present constitution adopted:** 1889
**Motto:** Under God the people rule
**State flower:** American pasqueflower (1903)
**State grass:** Western wheat grass (1970)
**State tree:** Black Hills spruce (1947)
**State bird:** Ring-necked pheasant (1943)
**State insect:** Honeybee (1978)
**State animal:** Coyote (1949)
**State mineral stone:** Rose quartz (1966)
**State gem stone:** Fairburn agate (1966)
**State colors:** Blue and gold (in state flag)
**State song:** "Hail! South Dakota" (1943)
**State fish:** Walleye (1982)
**Nicknames:** Sunshine State; Coyote State
**Origin of name:** Same as for North Dakota
**1980 population (1980 census) & (rank):** 690,768 (45)
**1985 est. population (July 1) & (rank):** 708,000 (45)
**1984 land area & (rank):** 75,952 sq mi. (196,715 sq km) (16)
**Geographic center:** In Hughes Co., 8 mi. NE of Pierre
**Number of counties:** 67 (64 county governments)
**Largest cities (1980 census):** Sioux Falls, 81,343; Rapid City, 46,492; Aberdeen, 25,851; Watertown, 15,649; Brookings, 14,951; Mitchell, 13,916; Huron, 13,000
**State forests:** None[1]
**State parks:** 13 plus 39 recreational areas (87,269 ac.)[2]
**State general revenue (fiscal 1985):** $318,047,579
**State general expenditure (fiscal 1985):** $318,876,627

1. No designated state forests; about 13,000 ac. of state land is forestland. 2. Acreage includes 39 recreation areas and 80 roadside parks, in addition to 12 state parks.

Exploration of this area began in 1743 when Louis-Joseph and François Verendrye came from France in search of a route to the Pacific.

The U.S. acquired the region as part of the Louisiana Purchase in 1803 and it was explored by Lewis and Clark in 1804–06. Fort Pierre, the first permanent settlement, was established in 1817 and, in 1831, the first Missouri River steamboat reached the fort.

Settlement of South Dakota did not begin in earnest until the arrival of the railroad in 1873 and the discovery of gold in the Black Hills the following year.

Agriculture is South Dakota's basic industry. In 1985, South Dakota ranked first in the U.S. in the production of oats and rye. It also ranked among the top five states in beef cows that have calved, all sheep and lambs, durum wheat, other spring wheat, barley, flaxseed, and sunflower seed. In 1985, the state boasted 3,600,000 cattle, 540,000 sheep, and 1,610,000 hogs.

South Dakota is the nation's second leading producer of gold (Nevada ranks first) and the Homestake Mine is the richest in the U.S. Other minerals produced include berylium, bentonite, granite, silver, petroleum, and uranium.

Processing of foods produced by farms and ranches is the largest South Dakota manufacturing industry, followed by lumber, wood products, and machinery, including farm equipment.

The Black Hills are the highest mountains east of the Rockies. Mt. Rushmore, in this group, is famous for the likenesses of Washington, Jefferson, Lincoln, and Theodore Roosevelt, which were carved in granite by Gutzon Borglum. The Badlands offer scenic masses of bare rock and clay unrelieved by any vegetation. Other points of interest are Deadwood, where Wild Bill Hickok was killed in 1876; the Crazy Horse Memorial near Custer; and the Corn Palace in Mitchell.

# TENNESSEE

**Capital:** Nashville
**Governor:** Lamar Alexander, R (to Jan. 1987)
**Lieut. Governor:** John S. Wilder, D (to Jan. 1985)
**Secy. of State:** Gentry Crowell, D (to Jan. 1985)
**Atty. General:** W. J. Michael Cody, D (to 1993)
**State Treasurer:** Harlan Matthews, D (to Jan. 1985)
**Entered Union & (rank):** June 1, 1796 (16)
**Present constitution adopted:** 1870; amended 1953, 1960, 1966, 1972, 1978
**Motto:** "Tennessee—America at its best!" (1965)
**State flower:** Iris (1933)
**State tree:** Tulip poplar (1947)
**State bird:** Mockingbird (1933)
**State horse:** Tennessee walking horse
**State animal:** Raccoon
**State wild flower:** Passion flower
**State song:** "Tennessee Waltz" (1965)
**Nickname:** Volunteer State
**Origin of name:** Of Cherokee origin; the exact meaning is unknown
**1980 population (1980 census) & (rank):** 4,591,120 (17)
**1985 est. population (July 1) & (rank):** 4,762,000 (17)
**1984 land area & (rank):** 41,155 sq mi. (106,591 sq km) (34)
**Geographic center:** In Rutherford Co., 5 mi. NE of Murfreesboro
**Number of counties:** 95
**Largest cities (1980 census):** Memphis, 646,174; Nashville, 455,651; Knoxville, 175,045; Chattanooga,

169,558; Clarksville, 54,777; Jackson, 49,131
**State forests:** 14 (155,752 ac.)
**State parks:** 21 (130,000 ac.)
**State general revenue (1984):** $5,335,000
**State general expenditure (1984):** $4,830,000

First visited by the Spanish explorer de Soto in 1541, the Tennessee area would later be claimed by both France and England as a result of the 1670s and 1680s explorations of Marquette and Joliet, La Salle, and the Englishmen James Needham and Gabriel Arthur.

Great Britain obtained the region following the French and Indian War in 1763 and it was rapidly occupied by settlers moving in from Virginia and the Carolinas.

During 1784–87, the settlers formed the "state" of Franklin, which was disbanded when the region was allowed to send representatives to the North Carolina legislature. In 1790 Congress organized the territory south of the Ohio River and Tennessee joined the Union in 1796.

Although Tennessee joined the Confederacy during the Civil War, there was much pro-Union sentiment in the state, which was the scene of extensive military action.

The state is now predominantly industrial; in 1970, 58.8% of its population lived in urban areas. Among the most important products are chemicals, textiles, apparel, electrical machinery, furniture, and leather goods. Other lines include food processing, lumber, primary metals, and metal products. The state is known as the U.S. hardwood-flooring center and ranks first in the production of marble, zinc, pyrite, and ball clay.

Tennessee is one of the leading tobacco-producing states in the nation and its farming income is also derived from livestock and dairy products as well as corn, cotton, and soybeans.

With six other states, Tennessee shares the extensive federal reservoir developments on the Tennessee and Cumberland River systems. The Tennessee Valley Authority operates a number of dams and reservoirs in the state.

Among the major points of interest: the Andrew Johnson National Historic Site at Greenville, American Museum of Atomic Energy at Oak Ridge, Great Smoky Mountains National Park, The Hermitage (home of Andrew Jackson near Nashville), Rock City Gardens near Chattanooga, and three National Military Parks.

# TEXAS

**Capital:** Austin
**Governor:** Mark White, D (to Jan. 1987)
**Lieut. Governor:** William P. Hobby, D (to Jan. 1987)
**Secy. of State:** Myra McDaniel, D (to Jan. 1987)
**Comptroller:** Bob Bullock (to Jan. 1987)
**Atty. General:** Jim Mattox, D (to Jan. 1987)
**Entered Union & (rank):** Dec. 29, 1845 (28)
**Present constitution adopted:** 1876
**Motto:** Friendship
**State flower:** Bluebonnet (1901)
**State tree:** Pecan (1919)
**State bird:** Mockingbird (1927)
**State song:** "Texas, Our Texas" (1930)
**Nickname:** Lone Star State
**Origin of name:** From an Indian word meaning "friends"
**1980 population (1980 census) & (rank):** 14,229,288 (3)
**1985 est. population (July 1) & (rank):** 16,370,000 (3)
**1984 land area & (rank):** 262,017 sq mi. (678,623 sq km) (2)

**Geographic center:** In McCulloch Co., 15 mi. NE of Brady
**Number of counties:** 254
**Largest cities (1980 census):** Houston, 1,595,138; Dallas, 904,078; San Antonio, 785,023; El Paso, 425,259; Fort Worth, 385,164; Austin, 345,496
**State forests:** 4 (6,306 ac.)
**State parks:** 83 (64 developed)
**Total net revenue: (fiscal 1984–85):** $17,165,051,133
**Total net expenditures (fiscal 1984–85):** $16,186,691,147

Spanish explorers, including Cabeza de Vaca and Coronado, were the first to visit the region in the 16th and 17th centuries, settling at Ysleta near present-day El Paso in 1682. In 1685, La Salle established a short-lived French colony at Matagorda Bay.

Americans, led by Stephen F. Austin, began to settle along the Brazos River in 1821 when Texas was controlled by Mexico, recently independent from Spain. In 1836, following a brief war between the American settlers in Texas and the Mexican government, and famous for the battles of the Alamo and San Jacinto, the Independent Republic of Texas was proclaimed with Sam Houston as president.

After Texas became the 28th U.S. state in 1845, border disputes led to the Mexican War of 1846–48.

Today, Texas, second only to Alaska in land area, leads all other states in such categories as oil, cattle, sheep, and cotton. Possessing enormous natural resources, Texas is a major agricultural state and an industrial giant.

Sulfur, salt, helium, asphalt, graphite, bromine, natural gas, cement, and clays give Texas first place in mineral production—nearly $8 billion in 1973. Chemicals, oil refining, food processing, machinery, and transportation equipment are among the major Texas manufacturing industries.

Texas ranches and farms produce beef cattle, poultry, rice, pecans, peanuts, sorghum, and an extensive variety of fruits and vegetables.

Millions of tourists spend well over $2 billion annually visiting more than 70 state parks, recreation areas, and points of interest such as the Gulf Coast resort area, the Lyndon B. Johnson Space Center in Houston, the Alamo in San Antonio, the state capital in Austin, and the Big Bend and Guadalupe Mountains National Parks.

# UTAH

**Capital:** Salt Lake City
**Governor:** Norman H. Bangerter, R (to Jan. 1989)
**Lieut. Governor:** W. Val Oveson, R (to Jan. 1989)
**Atty. General:** David Wilkinson, R (to Jan. 1989)
**Organized as territory:** Sept. 9, 1850
**Entered Union & (rank):** Jan. 4, 1896 (45)
**Present constitution adopted:** 1896
**Motto:** Industry
**State flower:** Sego lily (1911)
**State tree:** Blue spruce (1933)
**State bird:** Seagull (1955)
**State emblem:** Beehive
**State song:** "Utah, We Love Thee"
**Nickname:** Beehive State
**Origin of name:** From the Ute tribe, meaning "people of the mountains"
**1970 population & (rank):** 1,059,273 (36)

1980 population (1980 census) & (rank): 1,461,037 (36)
1985 est. population (July 1) & (rank): 1,645,000 (36)
1984 land area & (rank): 82,073 sq mi. (212,569 sq km) (12)
Geographic center: In Sanpete Co., 3 mi. N. of Manti
Number of counties: 29
Largest cities (1980 census): Salt Lake City, 163,697; Provo, 52,210; Ogden, 64,407; Orem, 52,399; Sandy City, 52,210; Bountiful, 32,877; West Jordan, 27,192; Logan, 26,844; Murray, 25,750
State forests: None
State parks: 44 (64,097 ac.)
Total state revenues (fiscal 1985): $2,145,000,000
Total state expenditures (fiscal 1985): $1,977,000,000
Cash balance—Unappropriated general fund balance (fiscal 1985): $18,919,000

The region was first explored for Spain by Franciscan friars, Escalante and Dominguez in 1776. In 1824 the famous American frontiersman Jim Bridger discovered the Great Salt Lake.

Fleeing the religious persecution encountered in eastern and middle-western states, the Mormons reached the Great Salt Lake in 1847 and began to build Salt Lake City. The U.S. acquired the Utah region in the treaty ending the Mexican War in 1848 and the first transcontinental railroad was completed with the driving of a golden spike at Promontory Point in 1869.

Mormon difficulties with the federal government about polygamy did not end until the Mormon Church renounced the practice in 1890, six years before Utah became a state.

In recent years, manufacturing has become Utah's most important industry, ahead of mining, agriculture, and tourism. The state's factories produce transportation equipment, food products, machinery, metal products, and electrical equipment. Utah has also become an important aerospace research and production center and is a leading warehousing and distribution point for much of the western U.S.

Rich in natural resources, Utah has long been a leading producer of copper, gold, silver, lead, zinc, and molybdenum. Oil has also become a major product; with Colorado and Wyoming, Utah shares what have been called the world's richest oil shale deposits.

Ranked eighth among the states in number of sheep in 1973, Utah also produces large crops of apricots and cherries as well as sugar beets, potatoes, onions, alfalfa, winter wheat, and beans. Utah's farmlands and crops require extensive irrigation.

Utah is a great vacationland with 11,000 miles of fishing streams and 147,000 acres of lakes and reservoirs. Among the many tourist attractions are Arches, Bryce Canyon, Canyonlands, Capitol Reef, and Zion National Parks; Dinosaur, Natural Bridges, and Rainbow Bridge National Monuments; the Mormon Tabernacle in Salt Lake City; and Monument Valley.

# VERMONT

Capital: Montpelier
Governor: Madeleine M. Kunin, D (to Jan. 1987)
Lieut. Governor: Peter P. Smith, R (to Jan. 1987)
Secy. of State: James H. Douglas (to Jan. 1987)
Treasurer: Emory A. Hebard, R (to Jan. 1987)
Auditor of Accounts: Alexander V. Acebo (to Jan. 1987)
Atty. General: Jeffrey L. Amestoy, R (to Jan. 1987)
Entered Union & (rank): March 4, 1791 (14)

Present constitution adopted: 1793
Motto: Vermont, Freedom, and Unity
State flower: Red clover (1894)
State tree: Sugar maple (1949)
State bird: Hermit thrush (1941)
State animal: Morgan horse (1961)
State insect: Honeybee (1978)
State song: "Hail, Vermont!" (1938)
Nickname: Green Mountain State
Origin of name: From the French "vert mont," meaning "green mountain"
1980 population (1980 census) & (rank): 511,456 (48)
1985 est. population (July 1) & (rank): 535,000 (48)
1984 land area & (rank): 9,273 sq mi. (24,017 sq km) (43)
Geographic center: In Washington Co., 3 mi. E of Roxbury
Number of counties: 14
Largest cities (1980 census): Burlington, 37,712; Rutland, 18,436; South Burlington, 10,679; Barre, 9,824; Montpelier, 8,241; St. Albans, 7,308; Winooski, 6,318
State forests: 34 (113,953 ac.)
State parks: 45 (31,325 ac.)
State receipts (fiscal 1985): $838,164,179
State disbursements (fiscal 1985): $848,315,756

The Vermont region was explored and claimed for France by Samuel de Champlain in 1609 and the first French settlement was established at Fort Ste. Anne in 1666. The first English settlers moved into the area in 1724 and built Fort Drummer on the site of present-day Brattleboro. England gained control of the area in 1763 after the French and Indian War.

First organized to drive settlers from New York out of Vermont, the Green Mountain Boys, led by Ethan Allen, won fame by capturing Fort Ticonderoga from the British on May 10, 1775, in the early days of the Revolution.

In 1777 Vermont adopted its first constitution abolishing slavery and providing for universal male suffrage without property qualifications. In 1791 Vermont became the first state after the original 13 to join the Union.

Vermont leads the nation in the production of monument granite, marble, and maple syrup. It is also a leader in the production of asbestos and talc.

In ratio to population, Vermont keeps more dairy cows than any other state. Vermont's soil is devoted to dairying, truck farming, and fruit growing because the rugged, rocky terrain discourages extensive farming.

Principal manufactured goods are machine tools, computer components, stone and clay products, lumber, furniture, and paper.

Tourism is a major industry in Vermont. Vermont's many famous ski areas include Stowe, Killington, Mt. Snow, Bromley, Jay Peak, and Sugarbush. Hunting and fishing also attract many visitors to Vermont each year. Among the many points of interest are the Green Mountain National Forest, Bennington Battle Monument, the Calvin Coolidge Homestead at Plymouth, and the Marble Exhibit in Proctor.

# VIRGINIA

Capital: Richmond
Governor: Gerald L. Baliles, D (to Jan. 1990)
Lieut. Governor: L. Douglas Wilder, D (to Jan. 1990)
Secy. of the Commonwealth: Sandra D. Bowen (apptd. by governor)
Comptroller: Edward J. Mazur (apptd. by governor)
Atty. General: Mary Sue Terry, D (to Jan. 1990)

**Entered Union & (rank):** June 25, 1788 (10)
**Present constitution adopted:** 1970
**Motto:** *Sic semper tyrannis* (Thus always to tyrants)
**State flower:** American dogwood (1918)
**State bird:** Cardinal (1950)
**State dog:** American foxhound (1966)
**State shell:** Oyster shell
**State song:** "Carry Me Back to Old Virginia" (1940)
**Nicknames:** The Old Dominion; Mother of Presidents
**Origin of name:** In honor of Elizabeth "Virgin Queen" of England
**1980 population (1980 census) & (rank):** 5,346,818 (14)
**1985 est. population (July 1) & (rank):** 5,706,000 (13)
**1984 land area & (rank):** 39,703 sq mi. (102,832 sq km) (36)
**Geographic center:** In Buckingham Co., 5 mi. SW of Buckingham
**Number of counties:** 95, plus 41 independent cities
**Largest cities (1980 census):** Norfolk, 266,979; Virginia Beach, 262,199; Richmond, 219,214; Newport News, 144,903; Hampton, 122,617; Chesapeake, 114,486
**State forests:** 8 (49,566 ac.)
**State parks and recreational parks:** 22, plus 3 in process of acquisition and/or development (42,722 ac.)[1]
**State revenue (fiscal 1984–85):** $7,750,100,000
**State expenditure (fiscal 1984–85):** $7,535,900,000

1. Does not include portion of Breaks Interstate Park (Va.-Ky., 1,200 ac.) which lies in Virginia.

The history of America is closely tied to that of Virginia, particularly in the Colonial period. Jamestown, founded in 1607, was the first permanent English settlement in North America and slavery was introduced there in 1619. The surrenders ending both the American Revolution (Yorktown) and the Civil War (Appomattox) occurred in Virginia. The state is called the "Mother of Presidents" because eight chief executives of the United States were born there.

Today, Virginia has a large number of diversified manufacturing industries including chemicals, textiles, food products, and clothing. Other important lines are lumber, paper, furniture, cigarettes, electrical machinery, transportation equipment, and stone-glass-clay products.

Agriculture remains an important sector in the Virginia economy and the state ranks among the leaders in the U.S. in tobacco, peanuts, apples, and sweet potatoes. Other crops include corn, vegetables, barley, and peaches. Famous for its turkeys and Smithfield hams, Virginia also has a large dairy industry.

Coal mining accounts for roughly 70% of Virginia's mineral output, and lime, zinc, and stone are also mined.

Points of interest include Mt. Vernon and other places associated with George Washington; Monticello, home of Thomas Jefferson; Stratford, home of the Lees; Richmond, capital of the Confederacy and of Virginia; and Williamsburg, the restored Colonial capital.

The Chesapeake Bay Bridge-Tunnel spans the mouth of Chesapeake Bay, connecting Cape Charles with Norfolk. Consisting of a series of low trestles, two bridges and two mile-long tunnels, the complex is 18 miles (29 km) long. It was opened in 1964.

Other attractions are the Shenandoah National Park, Fredericksburg and Spotsylvania National Military Park, the Booker T. Washington birthplace near Roanoke, Arlington House (the Robert E. Lee Memorial), the Skyline Drive, and the Blue Ridge National Parkway.

# WASHINGTON

**Capital:** Olympia
**Governor:** Booth Gardner, D (to 1989)
**Lieut. Governor:** John A. Cherberg, D (to 1989)
**Secy. of State:** Ralph Munro (to 1989)
**State Treasurer:** Robert S. O'Brien (to 1989)
**Atty. General:** Kenneth O. Eikenberry (to 1989)
**Organized as territory:** March 2, 1853
**Entered Union & (rank):** Nov. 11, 1889 (42)
**Present constitution adopted:** 1889
**Motto:** *Al-Ki* (Indian word meaning "by and by")
**State flower:** Rhododendron (1949)
**State tree:** Western hemlock (1947)
**State bird:** Willow goldfinch (1951)
**State fish:** Steelhead trout (1969)
**State gem:** Petrified wood (1975)
**State colors:** Green and gold (1925)
**State song:** "Washington, My Home" (1959)
**State dance:** Square dance (1979)
**Nicknames:** Evergreen State; Chinook State
**Origin of name:** In honor of George Washington
**1980 population (1980 census) & (rank):** 4,132,180 (20)
**1985 est. population (July 1) & (rank):** 4,409,000 (19)
**1984 land area & (rank):** 66,511 sq mi (172,264 sq km) (20)
**Geographic center:** In Chelan Co., 10 mi. WSW of Wenatchee
**Number of counties:** 39
**Largest cities (1980 census):** Seattle, 493,846; Spokane, 171,300; Tacoma, 158,501; Bellevue, 73,903; Everett, 54,413; Yakima, 49,826; Bellingham, 45,794
**State forest lands:** 1,922,880 ac.
**State parks:** 202 (171,700 ac.)[1]
**State revenue (1983–85 biennium):** $9,965,200,000
**State expenditure (1983–85 biennium):** $9,911,300,000

1. Parks and undeveloped areas administered by Parks and Recreation Dept. Game Dept. administers wildlife and recreation areas totaling 762,895 acres.

As part of the vast Oregon Country, Washington territory was visited by Spanish, American, and British explorers—Bruno Heceta for Spain in 1775, the American Capt. Robert Gray in 1792, and Capt. George Vancouver for Britain in 1792–94. Lewis and Clark explored the Columbia River region and coastal areas for the U.S. in 1805–06.

Rival American and British settlers and conflicting territorial claims threatened war in the early 1840s. However, in 1846 the Oregon Treaty set the boundary at the 49th parallel and war was averted.

Washington is a leading lumber producer. Its rugged surface is rich in stands of Douglas fir, hemlock, ponderosa and white pine, spruce, larch, and cedar. The state holds first place in apples, blueberries, hops, and red raspberries and it ranks high in potatoes, winter wheat, pears, grapes, apricots, and strawberries. Livestock and livestock products make important contributions to total farm revenue and the commercial fishing catch of salmon, halibut, and bottomfish makes a significant contribution to the state's economy.

Manufacturing industries in Washington include aircraft and missiles, shipbuilding and other transportation equipment, lumber, food processing, metals and metal products, chemicals, and machinery.

The Columbia River contains one third of the potential water power in the U.S., harnessed by such dams as the Grand Coulee, one of the greatest power producers in the world. Washington has 90 dams throughout the state built for irrigation, power, flood control, and water storage. Its abundance of electrical power makes Washington the nation's largest producer of refined aluminum.

Among the major points of interest: Mt. Rainier, Olympic; and North Cascades. In 1980, Mount St. Helens, a peak in the Cascade Range in Southwestern Washington erupted on May 18th. Also of interest are National Parks; Whitman Mission and Fort Vancouver National Historic Sites; and the Pacific Science Center and Space Needle in Seattle.

## WEST VIRGINIA

**Capital:** Charleston
**Governor:** Arch A. Moore, Jr., R (to Jan. 1989)
**Secy. of State:** Ken Heckler, D (to Jan. 1989)
**State Auditor:** Glen Gainer (to Jan. 1989)
**Atty. General:** Charlie Brown, D (to Jan. 1989)
**Entered Union & (rank):** June 20, 1863 (35)
**Present constitution adopted:** 1872
**Motto:** *Montani semper liberi* (Mountaineers are always free)
**State flower:** Rhododendron (1903)
**State tree:** Sugar maple (1949)
**State bird:** Cardinal (1949)
**State animal:** Black bear
**State colors:** Blue and gold (unofficial)
**State songs:** "West Virginia, My Home Sweet Home," "The West Virginia Hills," and "This Is My West Virginia" (adopted by Legislature in 1947, 1961 and 1963 as official state songs)
**Nickname:** Mountain State
**Origin of name:** Same as for Virginia
**1980 population (1980 census) & (rank):** 1,950,279 (34)
**1985 est. population (July 1) & (rank):** 1,936,000 (34)
**1984 land area & (rank):** 24,119 sq mi. (62,468 sq km) (41)
**Geographic center:** In Braxton Co., 4 mi. E of Sutton
**Number of counties:** 55
**Largest cities (1980 census):** Charleston, 63,968; Huntington, 63,684; Wheeling, 43,070; Parkersburg, 39,967; Morgantown, 27,605; Weirton, 25,371
**State forests:** 9 (77,000 ac.)
**State parks:** 34 (65,861 ac.)
**Total state revenue (fiscal 1985–86):** $1,546,700,000
**Total state expenditure (fiscal 1985–86):** $1,597,000,000

West Virginia's early history from 1609 until 1863 is largely shared with Virginia, of which it was a part until Virginia seceded from the Union in 1861. Then the delegates of 40 western counties formed their own government, which was granted statehood in 1863.

First permanent settlement dates from 1731 when Morgan Morgan founded Mill Creek. In 1742 coal was discovered on the Coal River, an event that would be of great significance in determining West Virginia's future.

The state usually ranks first in bituminous coal production with about 20% of the U.S. total. It also is a leader in steel, glass, aluminum, and chemical manufactures; natural gas, oil, quarry products, and hardwood lumber.

Poultry, dairy products, cattle, and sheep account for the major portion of farm receipts. Apples, peaches, wheat, corn, and hay are profitable crops. More than 75% of West Virginia is covered with forests.

Tourism is increasingly popular in mountainous West Virginia and visitors spend over $1.4 billion annually. More than a million acres have been set aside in 34 state parks and recreation areas and in 9 state forests.

Major points of interest include Harpers Ferry and Chesapeake and Ohio Canal National Historical Parks, White Sulphur Springs and Berkeley Springs resorts, the scenic railroad at Cass, and the historic homes at Charles Town.

## WISCONSIN

**Capital:** Madison
**Governor:** Anthony S. Earl, D (to Jan. 1987)
**Lieut. Governor:** James T. Flynn, D (to Jan. 1987)
**Secy. of State:** Douglas J. La Follette, D (to Jan. 1987)
**State Treasurer:** Charles P. Smith, D (to Jan. 1987)
**Atty. General:** Bronson C. La Follette, D (to Jan. 1987)
**Superintendent of Public Instruction:** Herbert J. Grover, Nonpartisan (to July 1989)
**Organized as territory:** July 4, 1836
**Entered Union & (rank):** May 29, 1848 (30)
**Present constitution adopted:** 1848
**Motto:** Forward
**State flower:** Wood violet
**State tree:** Sugar maple
**State bird:** Robin
**State animal:** Badger; "wild life" animal: white-tailed deer; "domestic" animal: dairy cow
**State insect:** Honeybee (1977)
**State fish:** Musky (Muskellunge)
**State song:** "On Wisconsin"
**State mineral:** Galena (1971)
**State rock:** Red Granite (1971)
**Nickname:** Badger State
**Origin of name:** French corruption of an Indian word whose meaning is disputed
**1980 population (1980 census) & (rank):** 4,705,521 (16)
**1985 est. population (July 1) & (rank):** 4,775,000 (16)
**1984 land area & (rank):** 54,426 sq mi. (140,964 sq km) (25)
**Geographic center:** In Wood Co., 9 mi. SE of Marshfield
**Number of counties:** 72
**Largest cities (1980 census):** Milwaukee, 636,236; Madison, 170,616; Green Bay, 87,899; Racine, 85,725; Kenosha, 77,685; West Allis, 63,982; Appleton, 58,913
**State forests:** 9 (476,004 ac.)
**State parks & scenic trails:** 48 parks, 9 trails (66,185 ac.)
**State revenue (fiscal 1984–85):** $12,068,755,818
**State expenditure (fiscal 1984–85):** $9,981,002,251

The Wisconsin region was first explored for France by Jean Nicolet, who landed at Green Bay in 1634. In 1660 a French trading post and Roman Catholic mission were established near present-day Ashland.

Great Britain obtained the region in settlement of the French and Indian War in 1763; the U.S. acquired it in 1783 after the Revolutionary War. However, Great Britain retained actual control until after the War of 1812. The region was successively governed as part of the territories of Indiana, Illinois, and Michigan between 1800 and 1836, when it became a separate territory.

Wisconsin leads the nation in milk and cheese production. In 1984 the state ranked first in the number of milk cows (1,828,000) and produced 17% of the nation's total output of milk. Other important farm products are peas, beets, corn, potatoes, cabbage, maple sugar, and cranberries.

The chief industrial products of the state are automobiles, machinery, furniture, paper, beer, and processed foods. Wisconsin ranks second among the 47 paper-producing states.

Wisconsin pioneered in social legislation, providing pensions for the blind (1907), aid to dependent children (1913), and old-age assistance (1925). In labor legislation, the state was the first to enact an unemployment compensation law (1932) and the first in which a workman's compensation law actually took effect. Wisconsin had the first state-wide primary-election law and the first successful income-tax law. In April 1984, Wisconsin became the first state to adopt the Uniform Marital Property Act. The act took effect on January 1, 1986.

The state has over 8,500 lakes, of which Winnebago is the largest. Water sports, ice-boating, and fishing are popular, as are skiing and hunting. Public parks and forests take up one seventh of the land, with 48 state parks, 9 state forests, 9 state trails, 3 recreational areas, and 2 national forests.

Among the many points of interest are the Apostle Islands National Lakeshore; Ice Age National Scientific Reserve; the Circus World Museum at Baraboo; the Wolf, St. Croix, and Lower St. Croix national scenic riverways; and the Wisconsin Dells.

# WYOMING

**Capital:** Cheyenne
**Governor:** Ed Herschler, D (to Jan. 1987)
**Secy. of State:** Thyra G. Thomson, R (to Jan. 1987)
**Auditor:** James B. Griffith, Jr., R (to Jan. 1987)
**Treasurer:** Stan Smith, R (to Jan. 1987)
**Atty. General:** A. G. McClintock, D (apptd. by Governor)
**Organized as territory:** May 19, 1869
**Entered Union & (rank):** July 10, 1890 (44)
**Present constitution adopted:** 1890
**Motto:** Equal rights (1955)
**State flower:** Indian paintbrush (1917)
**State tree:** Cottonwood (1947)
**State bird:** Meadow lark (1927)
**State gemstone:** Jade (1967)
**State insignia:** Bucking horse (unofficial)
**State song:** "Wyoming" (1955)
**Nickname:** Equality State
**Origin of name:** From the Delaware Indian word, meaning "mountains and valleys alternating"; the same as the Wyoming Valley in Pennsylvania
**1980 population (1980 census) & (rank):** 469,557 (49)
**1985 est. population (July 1) & (rank):** 509,000 (50)
**1984 land area & (rank):** 96,989 sq mi. (251,201 sq km) (9)
**Geographic center:** In Fremont Co., 58 mi. ENE of Lander
**Number of counties:** 23, plus Yellowstone National Park

**Largest cities (1980 census):** Casper, 51,016; Cheyenne, 47,283; Laramie, 24,410; Rock Springs, 19,458; Sheridan, 15,146; Green River, 12,807; Gillette, 12,134
**State forests:** None
**State parks:** 9 (44,732 ac.)
**Estimated income (biennium 1987–88):** $2,135,953,198
**Estimated expenditure (biennium 1987–88):** $2,283,095,460

The U.S. acquired the territory from France as part of the Louisiana Purchase in 1803. John Colter, a fur-trapper, is the first white man known to have entered present Wyoming. In 1807 he explored the Yellowstone area and brought back news of its geysers and hot springs.

Robert Stuart pioneered the Oregon Trail across Wyoming in 1812–13 and, in 1834, Fort Laramie, the first permanent trading post in Wyoming, was built. Western Wyoming was obtained by the U.S. in the 1846 Oregon Treaty with Great Britain and as a result of the treaty ending the Mexican War in 1848.

When the Wyoming Territory was organized in 1869 Wyoming women became the first in the nation to obtain the right to vote. In 1925 Mrs. Nellie Tayloe Ross was elected first woman governor in the United States.

Wyoming's towering mountains and vast plains provide spectacular scenery, grazing lands for sheep and cattle, and rich mineral deposits.

Mining, particularly oil and natural gas, is the most important industry. In January 1981, Wyoming led the nation in sodium carbonate (natrona) and bentonite production, and was second in uranium.

Wyoming ranks second among the states in wool production. In January 1981, its sheep numbered 1,110,000, exceeded only by Texas and California; it also had 1,350,000 cattle. Principal crops include wheat, oats, sugar beets, corn, potatoes, barley, and alfalfa.

Second in mean elevation to Colorado, Wyoming has many attractions for the tourist trade, notably Yellowstone National Park. Cheyenne is famous for its annual "Frontier Days" celebration. Flaming Gorge, the Fort Laramie National Historic Site, and Devils Tower and Fossil Butte National Monuments are other National points of interest.

# Self-Governing Areas

## PUERTO RICO

**Capital:** San Juan
**Governor:** Rafael Hernández-Colón, Popular Democratic Party
**Song:** "La Borinqueña"
**1970 population:** 2,712,033
**1980 population:** 3,196,520
**1980 land area: (1980 census):** San Juan, 424,600; Bayamón, 185,087; Ponce, 161,739; Carolina, 147,835; Caguas, 87,214; Mayagüez, 82,968

Puerto Rico is an island about 100 miles long and 35 miles wide at the northeastern end of the Caribbean Sea. It is a self-governing Commonwealth freely and voluntarily associated with the U.S. Under its Constitution, a Governor and a Legislative Assembly are elected by direct vote for a four-year period. The judiciary is vested in a Supreme

Court and lower courts established by law. The people elect a Resident Commissioner to the U.S. House of Representatives, where he has a voice but no vote. The island was formerly an unincorporated territory of the U.S. after being ceded by Spain as a result of the Spanish-American War.

The Commonwealth, established in 1952, has one of the highest standards of living in Latin America. Featuring Puerto Rican economic development is Operation Bootstrap. There are now over 1,600 manufacturing plants which have been created by this program. It has also greatly increased transportation and communications facilities, electric power, housing, and other industries.

The island's chief exports are chemicals, apparel, fish products and electronic products.

Columbus discovered the island on his second voyage to America in 1493.

# GUAM

**Capital:** Agaña
**Governor:** Ricardo J. Bordallo
**1950 population:** 59,498
**1960 population:** 67,044
**1970 population:** 84,996
**1980 population:** 105,979
**1980 land area:** 209 sq mi. (541 sq km)

Guam, the largest of the Mariana Islands, is independent of the trusteeship assigned to the U.S. in 1947. It was acquired by the U.S. from Spain in 1898 (occupied 1899) and was placed under the Navy Department.

In World War II, Guam was seized by the Japanese on Dec. 11, 1941; but on July 21, 1944, it was once more in U.S. hands.

On Aug. 1, 1950, President Truman signed a bill which granted U.S. citizenship to the people of Guam and established self-government. However, the people do not vote in national elections. In 1972 Guam elected its first delegate to the U.S. Congress. The Executive Branch of the Guam government is under the general supervision of the U.S. Secretary of the Interior. In November 1970, Guam elected its first Governor.

Military installations and tourism are important factors in Guam's economy.

# Non-Self-Governing Territories

## AMERICAN SAMOA

**Capital:** Pago Pago
**Governor:** A.P. Lutali
**Lieut. Governor:** Eni F. Hunkin
**1960 population:** 20,051
**1970 population:** 27,159
**1981 population:** 33,000
**1980 land area:** 77 sq mi (199 sq km)

American Samoa, a group of five volcanic islands and two coral atolls located some 2,600 miles south of Hawaii in the South Pacific Ocean, is an unincorporated, unorganized territory of the U.S., administered by the Department of the Interior.

By the Treaty of Berlin, signed Dec. 2, 1899, and ratified Feb. 16, 1900, the U.S. was internationally acknowledged to have rights extending over all the islands of the Samoa group east of longitude 171° west of Greenwich. On April 17, 1900, the chiefs of Tutuila and Aunu'u ceded those islands to the U.S. In 1904, the King and chiefs of Manu'a ceded the islands of Ofu, Olosega and Tau (composing the Manu'a group) to the U.S. Swains Island, some 214 miles north of Samoa, was included as part of the territory by Act of Congress March 4, 1925; and on Feb. 20, 1929, Congress formally accepted sovereignty over the entire group and placed the responsibility for administration in the hands of the President. From 1900 to 1951, by Presidential direction, the Department of the Navy governed the territory. On July 1, 1951, administration was transferred to the Department of the Interior. The first Constitution for the territory was signed on April 27, 1960, and became effective on Oct. 17, 1960. It was revised in 1967.

Congress has provided for a non-voting delegate to sit in the House of Representatives in 1981.

The principal products are canned tuna, pet food, fish meal, mats, and handicrafts.

## BAKER, HOWLAND, AND JARVIS ISLANDS

These Pacific islands were not to play a role in the extraterritorial plans of the U.S. until May 13, 1936. President F. D. Roosevelt, at that time, placed them under the control and jurisdiction of the Secretary of the Interior for administration purposes.

Baker Island is a saucer-shaped atoll with an area of approximately one square mile. It is about 1,650 miles from Hawaii.

Howland Island, 36 miles to the northeast, is approximately one and a half miles long and half a mile wide.

Jarvis Island is several hundred miles to the east and is approximately two miles long by one and an eighth miles wide.

Baker, Howland, and Jarvis have been uninhabited since 1942. In 1974, these islands became part of the National Wildlife Refuge System, administered by the U.S. Fish & Wildlife Service, Department of The Interior.

## CANTON AND ENDERBURY ISLANDS

Canton and Enderbury islands, the largest of the Phoenix group, are jointly administered by the U.S. and Great Britain after an agreement signed April 6, 1939. The status of Canton and Enderbury was the subject of negotiations between the U.S., U.K., and Gilbert Islands Governments in 1979. The negotiations resulted in the signing on September 20, 1979, of a Treaty of Friendship between the U.S. and the Republic of Kiribati, which, once ratified by the U.S. Senate, will formally renounce the U.S. claim to Canton and Enderbury. The Republic of Kiribati declared its independence on July 12, 1979.

Canton is triangular in shape and the largest of the eight islands of this group. It lies about 1,600 miles southwest of Hawaii and was discovered at the turn of the 18th century by U.S. whalers. After World War II it served as an aviation support facility, and later as a missile tracking station. Since 1967, the island has been utilized by the U.S. Air Force Space and Missile Test Center.

Enderbury is rectangular in shape and is 3.5 miles long by 1.5 miles wide. It is unpopulated and lies about 32 miles southeast of Canton.

## JOHNSTON ATOLL

Johnston is a coral atoll about 700 miles southwest of Hawaii. It consists of four small islands— Johnston Island, Sand Island, Hikina Island, and Akau Island—which lie on a reef about 9 miles long in a northeast-southwest direction.

The atoll was discovered by Capt. Charles James Johnston of *H.M.S. Cornwallis* in 1807. In 1858 it was claimed by Hawaii, and later became a U.S. possession.

Johnston Atoll is a Naval Defense Sea Area and Airspace Reservation and is closed to the public.

The administration of Johnston Atoll is under the jurisdiction of the Defense Nuclear Agency, Commander, Johnston Atoll (FCDNA), APO San Francisco, CA 96305.

## KINGMAN REEF

Kingman Reef, located about 1,000 miles south of Hawaii, was discovered by Capt. E. Fanning in 1798, but named for Capt. W. E. Kingman, who rediscovered it in 1853. The reef, drying only on its northeast, east and southeast edges, is of atoll character. The reef is triangular in shape, with its apex northward; it is about 9.5 miles long, east and west, and 5 miles wide, north and south, within the 100-fathom curve.

A United States possession, Kingman Reef is a Defense Sea Area and Airspace Reservation, and is closed to the public. The Airspace Entry Control has been suspended, but is subject to immediate reinstatement without notice. No vessel, except those authorized by the Secretary of the Navy, shall be navigated in the area within the 3-mile limit.

## MIDWAY ISLANDS

Midway Islands, lying about 1,150 miles west-northwest of Hawaii, were discovered by Captain N. C. Brooks of the Hawaiian bark *Gambia* on July 5, 1859, in the name of the United States. The atoll was formally declared a U.S. possession in 1867, and in 1903 Theodore Roosevelt made it a naval reservation.

Midway Islands consist of a circular atoll, 6 miles in diameter, and enclosing two islands. Eastern Island, on its southeast side, is triangular in shape, and about 1.2 miles long. Sand Island on its south side, is about 2 miles long in a northeast-southwest direction.

The Midway Islands are within a naval defensive sea area. The Navy Department maintains an installation and has jurisdiction over the atoll. Permission to enter the Naval Defense Sea Area must be obtained in advance from the Commander Third Fleet (N31), Pearl Harbor, HI 96860.

## U.S. VIRGIN ISLANDS

**Capital:** Charlotte Amalie (on St. Thomas)
**Governor:** Juan Luis
**1970 population:** 62,468
**1985 est. population:** 110,800 (St. Croix, 57,020; St. Thomas, 51,020; St. John, 2,760)
**1980 land area:** 132 sq mi (342 sq km): St. Croix, 80 sq.

mi. (207 sq km), St. Thomas, 32 sq mi (83 sq km), St. John, 20 sq mi. (52 sq km)

The Virgin Islands, consisting of nine main islands and some 75 islets, were discovered by Columbus in 1493. Since 1666, England has held six of the main islands; the other three (St. Croix, St. Thomas, and St. John), as well as about 50 of the islets, were eventually acquired by Denmark, which named them the Danish West Indies. In 1917, these islands were purchased by the U.S. from Denmark for $25 million.

Congress granted U.S. citizenship to Virgin Islanders in 1927; and, in 1931, administration was transferred from the Navy to the Department of the Interior. Universal suffrage was given in 1936 to all persons who could read and write the English language. The Governor was elected by popular vote for the first time in 1970; previously he had been appointed by the President of the U.S. A unicameral 15-man legislature serves the Virgin Islands, and Congressional legislation gave the islands a non-voting Representative in Congress.

The "Constitution" of the Virgin Islands is the Revised Organic Act. of 1954 in which the U.S. Congress defines the three branches of the territorial government, i.e., the Executive Branch, the Legislative Branch, and the Judicial Branch. Residents of the islands substantially enjoy the same rights as those enjoyed by mainlanders with one important exception: citizens of the U.S. who are residents may not vote in presidential elections.

About 80% of the population is black, and there is limited farming, fishing, and cattle raising. Industrial products include rum, watches, costume jewelry, alumina, pharmaceuticals, and petroleum products. Tourism is the principal industry.

## WAKE ISLAND

Wake Island, about halfway between Midway and Guam, is an atoll comprising the three islets of Wilkes, Peale, and Wake. They were discovered by the British in 1796 and annexed by the U.S. in 1899. The entire area comprises 3 square miles and has no native population. In 1938, Pan American Airways established a seaplane base and Wake Island has been used as a commercial base since then. On Dec. 8, 1941, it was attacked by the Japanese, who finally took possession on Dec. 23. It was surrendered by the Japanese on Sept. 4, 1945.

The President, acting pursuant to the Hawaii Omnibus Act, assigned responsibility for Wake to the Secretary of the Interior in 1962. The Department of Transportation exercised civil administration of Wake through an agreement with the Department of the Interior until June 1972.

# Trust Territory of the Pacific Islands (Micronesia)

In 1885, Germany assumed a protectorate over the Marshall Islands; and, in 1899, she purchased the Northern Mariana and Caroline Islands from Spain. These islands were occupied by the Japanese in 1914 and were mandated to Japan by the League of Nations in 1919. On April 2, 1947, the U. N. Security Council approved a trusteeship agreement proposed by the U.S. under which the

Northern Mariana, Caroline, and Marshall Islands became a Strategic Trust Territory under the administration of the U.S. The measure was approved by the President, with the agreement of Congress, on July 18, 1947. Administration was transferred from the Navy to the Department of the Interior on July 1, 1951. However, during 1953, administration of the islands of the Northern Marianas, except

Rota, was transferred back to the Navy. The Department of the Interior again took over administration of these islands in July, 1962. The 1980 population of the Northern Marianas was 16,780.

In February 1975 a covenant was signed by the U.S. and the Marianas Political Status Commission that would make the 14 islands in the Northern Marianas a commonwealth under American sovereignty. The covenant was overwhelmingly ratified by the people of the islands and was approved by President Ford on March 24, 1976.

On April 9, 1978, in Hilo, Hawaii, the heads of the three Micronesian political status commissions and the U.S. negotiator signed a statement of agreed principles which is intended to form the basis of a free association relationship between the U.S. and Micronesia. Compact of Free Association was signed by the U.S. and the respective with a 1980 population of 116,149, Micronesian commissions in 1982. The document now must be approved by the people of the three Micronesian entities, the U.S. Congress, and the United Nations.

The entire group with a 1980 population of 116,149 comprises more than 2,000 islands, but the total land area is only 533 sq mi. (1,381 sq km), many of the islands being only tiny coral reefs. There are six administrative districts: Kosrae, Marshall Islands, Palau, Ponape, Truk, and Yap.

The Micronesians are the main ethnic group; however, the inhabitants of two outlying islands, Kapingamarangi and Nukuoro, are Polynesian. The population of the Trust Territory in 1980 was estimated to be 116,974.

## MARIANA ISLANDS

The Mariana Islands, east of the Philippines and south of Japan, include the islands of Guam, Rota, Saipan, Tinian, Pagan, Guguan, Agrihan, and Aguijan. Guam, the largest, is independent of the trusteeship, having been acquired by the U.S. from Spain in 1898. (For more information, *see* the entry on Guam in this section.) The remaining islands, referred to as the Northern Mariana Islands, will become a commonwealth of the United States, pursuant to P.L. 94-241, upon termination of the trusteeship agreement.

Chief crops are copra and fresh fruits and vegetables.

## CAROLINE ISLANDS

The Caroline Islands, east of the Philippines and south of the Marianas, include the Yap, Truk, and the Palau groups and the islands of Ponape and Kosrae, as well as many coral atolls.

The islands are composed chiefly of volcanic rock, and their peaks rise 2,000 to 3,000 feet above sea level. Chief exports of the islands are copra, fish products, and handicrafts.

## MARSHALL ISLANDS

The Marshall Islands, east of the Carolines, are divided into two chains: the western or Ralik group, including the atolls Kwajalein, Wotho, Bikini, and Enewetak; and the eastern or Ratak group, including the atolls Mili, Majuro, Maloelap, Wotje, and Likiep.

The islands are of the coral-reef type and rise only a few feet above sea level. The chief crop is coconuts; exports include copra, tortoise shell, mother-of-pearl, etc.

Bikini and Enewetak were the scene of several atom-bomb tests after World War II: Enewetak was returned to Trust Territory administration in August 1976. In April 1977, some 55 original inhabitants, the forerunner of 450 returnees, were resettled after an absence of 30 years.

## Tabulated Data on State Governments

| State | Governor | | Legislature[1] | | | | | Highest Court[2] | | |
|---|---|---|---|---|---|---|---|---|---|---|
| | Term, years | Annual salary | Member-ship U[3] | L[4] | Term, yrs. U[3] | L[4] | Salaries of members[5] | | Mem-bers | Term, years | Annual salary[6] |
| Alabama | 4 [10] | 63,839 [16] | 35 | 105 | 4 | 4 | 95 | per diem[22] | 9 | 6 | $63,800 [6 29] |
| Alaska | 4 | 81,648 | 20 | 40 | 4 | 2 | 46,800 | per annum | 5 | ([8]) | 85,278 |
| Arizona | 4 | 62,500 | 30 | 60 | 2 | 2 | 15,000 | per annum | 5 | 6 | 67,500 |
| Arkansas | 2 | 35,000 | 35 | 100 | 4 | 2 | 7,500 | per annum[25] | 7 | 8 | 46,214 |
| California[30] | 4 | 49,100 | 40 | 80 | 4 | 2 | 37,105 [30] | per annum | 7 | 12 | 62,935 [25] |
| Colorado | 4 | 70,000 | 35 | 65 | 4 | 2 | 17,500 | per annum[26] | 7 | 10 | 63,000 |
| Connecticut | 4 | 65,000 | 36 | 151 | 2 | 2 | 26,000 | per biennium | 6 | 8 | 69,103 |
| Delaware | 4 [9] | 70,000 | 21 | 41 | 4 | 2 | 20,900 | per annum | 5 | 12 | 82,600 |
| Florida | 4 [10] | 78,757 | 40 | 120 | 4 | 2 | 18,000 | per annum | 7 | 6 | 78,064 |
| Georgia | 4 [9] | 69,356 | 56 | 180 | 2 | 2 | 7,200 | per annum | 7 | 6 | 70,886 |
| Hawaii | 4 | 59,400 | 25 | 51 | 4 | 2 | 15,600 | per year | 5 | 10 | 56,430 |
| Idaho | 4 | 55,000 | 42 | 84 | 2 | 2 | 8,000 | per annum | 5 | 6 | 59,750 |
| Illinois | 4 | 85,000 | 59 | 118 | 4-2 | 2 | 32,500 | per annum | 7 | 10 | 85,000 |
| Indiana | 4 [10] | 66,000 | 50 | 100 | 4 | 2 | 11,600 | per annum | 5 | ([24]) | 60,000 |
| Iowa | 4 | 64,000 | 50 | 100 | 4 | 2 | 14,600 | per annum | 9 | 8 | 60,900 |
| Kansas | 4 | 65,000 | 40 | 125 | 4 | 2 | 99 | per diem[22] | 7 | 6 | 59,143 [31] |
| Kentucky | 4 [7] | 60,000 | 38 | 100 | 4 | 2 | 100 | per diem[22] | 7 | 8 | 62,506 |
| Louisiana | 4 | 73,440 | 39 | 105 | 4 | 4 | 16,800 | per annum | 7 | 10 | 66,566 |
| Maine | 4 | 70,000 [16] | 33 | 151 | 2 | 2 | 11,500 | per biennium[16] | 7 | 7 | 61,698 |
| Maryland | 4 [10] | 78,000 | 47 | 141 | 4 | 4 | 21,000 | per annum | 7 | 10 | 70,928 |
| Massachusetts | 4 | 75,000 | 40 | 160 | 2 | 2 | 30,000 | per annum | 7 | Life | 65,000 |

| State | Governor Term, years | Governor Annual salary | Legislature[1] Membership U[3] | L[4] | Term, yrs. U[3] | L[4] | Salaries of members[5] | Highest Court[2] Members | Term, years | Annual salary[6] |
|---|---|---|---|---|---|---|---|---|---|---|
| Michigan | 4 | 85,800 | 38 | 110 | 4 | 2 | 36,520 per annum[16] | 7 | 8 | 81,400 |
| Minnesota | 4 | 87,942 | 67 | 134 | 4 | 2 | 22,350 per annum[16] | 9 | 6 | 68,400[6] |
| Mississippi | 4[7] | 63,000 | 52 | 122 | 4 | 4 | 10,000 per session[5] | 9 | 8 | 59,000 |
| Missouri | 4[10] | 81,000 | 34 | 163 | 4 | 2 | 19,530 per annum[5] | 7 | 12 | 78,300 |
| Montana | 4 | 48,923 | 50 | 100 | 4 | 2 | 59.12 per diem[16] | 6 | 8 | 50,452[6] |
| Nebraska | 4[10] | 40,000 | 49[11] | — | 4[11] | — | 4,800 per annum | 7 | 6 | 48,315 |
| Nevada | 4 | 77,500 | 21 | 42 | 4 | 2 | 7,800 per biennium | 5 | 6 | 73,500 |
| New Hampshire | 2 | 62,880 | 24 | ([12]) | 2 | 2 | 200 per biennium | 5 | ([13]) | 59,876 |
| New Jersey | 4[10] | 85,000 | 40 | 80 | 4[14] | 2 | 25,000 per annum | 7 | 7[15] | 78,000 |
| New Mexico | 4[7] | 60,000 | 42 | 70 | 4 | 2 | 75 per diem | 5 | 8 | 57,000 |
| New York | 4 | 100,000 | 61 | 150 | 2 | 2 | 43,000 per annum | 7 | 14 | 92,500[6] |
| North Carolina | 4[9] | 98,196[16] | 50 | 120 | 2 | 2 | 8,400 per annum[16] | 7 | 8 | 69,144[6] |
| North Dakota | 4 | 65,000[16] | 53 | 106 | 4 | 2 | 90 per diem[16][23] | 5 | 10 | 59,140[6] |
| Ohio | 4 | 65,000 | 33 | 99 | 4 | 2 | 33,242 per annum | 7 | 6 | 75,500 |
| Oklahoma | 4 | 70,000 | 48 | 101 | 4 | 2 | 20,000[16] per annum | ([19]) | 6 | 59,136 |
| Oregon | 4[10] | 72,000 | 30 | 60 | 4 | 2 | 850[32] per annum | 7 | 6 | 59,844[6] |
| Pennsylvania | 4[10] | 85,000 | 50 | 203 | 4 | 2 | 35,000 per annum | 7 | 10 | 76,500 |
| Rhode Island | 2 | 49,500 | 50 | 100 | 2 | 2 | 5 per diem[17] | 5 | ([18]) | 71,093 |
| South Carolina | 4[7] | 60,000 | 46 | 124 | 4 | 2 | 10,000 per annum | 5 | 10 | 47,000 |
| South Dakota | 4[10] | 57,325 | 35 | 70 | 2 | 2 | 6,000 per biennium | 5 | 3[28] | 56,975 |
| Tennessee | 4 | 85,000[27] | 33 | 99 | 4 | 2 | 12,500 per annum | 5 | 8 | 67,500 |
| Texas | 4 | 91,600 | 31 | 150 | 4 | 2 | 7,200 per annum | ([20]) | 6 | 76,600 |
| Utah | 4 | 60,000 | 29 | 75 | 4 | 2 | 25 per diem[16] | 5 | 10 | 58,000 |
| Vermont | 2 | 60,000 | 30 | 150 | 2 | 2 | 300 per week[21] | 5 | 6 | 49,000[6] |
| Virginia | 4[7] | 85,000 | 40 | 100 | 4 | 2 | 11,000 per annum | 7 | 12 | 78,463[6] |
| Washington* | 4 | 63,000 | 49 | 98 | 4 | 2 | 12,850 per annum | 9 | 6 | 51,500 |
| West Virginia | 4[10] | 72,000 | 34 | 100 | 4 | 2 | 7,200 per annum | 5 | 12 | 55,000 |
| Wisconsin | 4 | 86,149 | 33 | 99 | 4 | 2 | 29,992 per annum | 7 | 10 | 70,720 |
| Wyoming | 4 | 70,000 | 30 | 62 | 4 | 2 | 75 per diem[16] | 5 | 8 | 63,500 |

1. General Assembly in Ark., Colo., Conn., Del., Ga., Ind., Ky., Md., Mo., N.C., Ohio, Pa., R.I., S.C., Tenn., Vt., Va.; Legislative Assembly in N.D., Ore.; General Court in Mass., N.H.; Legislature in other states. Meets biennially in Calif., Ky., Me., Mont., Nev., N.H., N.J., N.C., N.D., Ore., Pa., Texas, Wash. and Wyo.; meets annually in other states. 2. Court of Appeals in Md., N.Y.; Supreme Court of Virginia in Va., Supreme Judicial Court in Me., Mass.; Supreme Court in other states. 3. Upper house: Senate in all states. 4. Lower house: Assembly in Calif., Nev., N.Y., Wis.; House of Delegates in Md., Va., W.Va.; General Assembly in N.J.; House of Representatives in other states. 5. Does not include additional payments for expenses, mileage, special sessions, etc., or additional per diem payments beyond salary shown. 6. In some states, Chief Justice receives a higher salary. 7. Cannot succeed himself. 8. Appointed for 3 years; thereafter subject to approval or rejection on a nonpartisan ballot for 10-year term. 9. May serve only 2 terms, consecutive or otherwise. 10. May not serve 3rd consecutive term. 11. Unicameral legislature. 12. Constitutional number: 375–400. 13. Until 70 years old. 14. When term begins in Jan. of 2nd year following U.S. census, term shall be 2 years. 15. 2nd term receive tenure, mandatory retirement at 70. 16. Plus additional expenses. 17. For 60 days only. 18. Term of good behavior. 19. 9 members in Supreme Court, highest in civil cases; 3 in Court of Criminal Appeals. 20. 9 members in Supreme Court, highest in civil cases; 9 in Court of Criminal Appeals. 21. To limit of $11,000 per biennium; $2,000 for special session. 22. When in session. 23. Plus $180 per month when not in session. 24. Appointed for 2 years; thereafter elected popularly for 10-year term. 25. To receive cost of living increase not to exceed 10% in the two year period. 26. Plus $2,500 per month when performing official duties. 27. Adjusted annually according to increase in Consumer Price Index. 28. Subsequent terms, 8 years. 29. Plus $600 per month whether legislature is in session or not. 30. As of July 1, 1986. 31. Plus $600 per month when not in session. 32. Plus $400 monthly when not in session and per diem allowance when in session. NOTE: An asterisk (*) indicates that up-to-date information has not been provided. *Source: Information Please* questionnaires to the states.

## Population Growth of States, 1980-2000

More than half the population growth in the United States in the period 1980-2000 will occur in just five states, according to the National Planning Association, a Washington, D.C., economic research organization. Ten states will account for two-thirds of the population growth.

California, Florida, Texas, Arizona, and North Carolina are projected to have the largest population increases, totaling 21.8 million or 54 percent of total population growth from 1980 to 2000. Another 14 percent of U.S. growth is projected for the five states with the next largest increases: Georgia, Washington, Colorado, Virginia, and Tennessee.

The NPA demographic projection shows that 79 percent of the population expansion in the last two decades of this century will occur in the South and the West, continuing the trend of the past decades.

Relatively little growth is projected for most of the other parts of the country. In the Northeast, Massachusetts is projected to have the largest population increase with a 560,000 gain, and in the Great Lakes area Michigan with 549,000. Population is projected to decline in New York, West Virginia, and the District of Columbia.

Most of the differences in population growth among the states can be attributed to the migration of people responding to job opportunities. However, the migration of retired people and the demographic characteristics of the population at the beginning of the period also have significant effects on growth rates. They determine the birth and death rates and age structure of the remaining population.

# 50 Largest Cities of the United States

Data supplied by Bureau of the Census and by the cities in response to *Information Please* questionnaires.

## ALBUQUERQUE, N.M.

**Incorporated as city:** 1891
**Mayor:** Ken Schultz (to Dec. 1989)
**1980 population (1980 census) & (rank):** 331,767 (44)
**1985 est. population:** 370,584
**1984 est. rank:** (44)
**1984 land area:** 95.3 sq mi. (247 sq km)
**Altitude:** 4,958 ft.
**Location:** Central part of state on Rio Grande River
**County:** Bernalillo
**Churches:** 211
**City-owned parks:** 135
**Radio stations:** 30
**Television stations:** 6
**Assessed valuation (1984):** $1,553,000,000
**City tax rate (1984):** $21.223 per $1,000
**Bonded debt (1984):** $115,605,000
**Revenue (Fiscal 1985):** $278,839,594 (est.)
**Expenditures (Fiscal 1985):** $270,490,645 (est.)
**Chamber of Commerce:** Greater Albuquerque Chamber of Commerce, 401 2nd St., N.W., Albuquerque, N.M. 87102. Albuquerque Hispano Chamber of Commerce, 1520 Central Ave., S.E., Albuquerque, N.M. 87106

## ATLANTA, GA.

**Incorporated as city:** 1847
**Mayor:** Andrew Young (to Jan. 1987)
**1980 population (1980 census) & (rank):** 425,022 (30)
**1984 est. population & (rank):** 426,090 (31)
**1984 city land area:** 131.4 sq mi. (340.3 sq km)
**Altitude:** Highest, 1,050 ft; lowest, 940
**Location:** In northwest central part of state, near Chattahoochee River
**Counties:** Fulton and De Kalb
**Churches (18-county area):** 1,500+
**City-owned parks:** 294 (3,178 ac.)
**Radio stations (18-county area):** AM, 24; FM, 17
**Television stations (18-county area):** 7 commercial; 2 PBS
**Gross assessed valuation (1985):** $5,675,276,736
**City tax rate (1985):** $36.81 per $1,000
**Total bonded debt (1985):** $155,910,000
**Revenue (incl. General Fund, Airport Revenues, Water/Sewer Fund) (1985):** $439,901,530
**Expenditures (1985):** $235,800,435
**Chamber of Commerce:** Atlanta Chamber of Commerce, 1300 N Omni International, Atlanta, Ga. 30303
Information is gathered on 2 geographic areas:
**City of Atlanta, and 18 county MSA**

## AUSTIN, TEX.

**Incorporated as city:** 1839
**Mayor:** Frank Cooksey (to 1987)
**1980 population (1980 census) & (rank):** 345,496 (42)
**1984 est. rank:** (39)
**1986 est. population:** 468,000
**1984 land area:** 116.0 sq mi. (300 sq km)
**Altitude:** Highest, 425 ft
**Location:** In south central part of state, on the Colorado River
**County:** Seat of Travis Co.

**Churches:** 353 churches, representing 45 denominations
**City-owned parks and playgrounds:** 157 (10,000 ac.)
**Radio stations:** AM, 6; FM, 12
**Television stations:** 3 commercial; 1 PBS; 1 independent
**Assessed valuation (1985):** $17,027,314,332
**Tax rate (1985):** $1.614 per $100
**Bonded debt (1982–83):** $947,998,663
**Revenue (1984–85):** $206,275,062
**Expenditures (1984–85):** $284,598,965
**Chamber of Commerce:** Austin Chamber of Commerce, 901 W Riverside Dr., Austin, Tex. 78704

## BALTIMORE, MD.

**Incorporated as city:** 1797
**Mayor:** William D. Schaefer (to Dec. 1986)
**1980 population (1980 census) & (rank):** 786,775 (10)
**1984 est. population & (rank):** 763,570 (12)
**1984 land area:** 80.3 sq mi. (208 sq km)
**Altitude:** Highest, 490 ft; lowest, sea level
**Location:** On Patapsco River, about 12 mi. from Chesapeake Bay
**County:** Independent city
**Churches:** Roman Catholic, 72; Jewish, 50; Protestant and others, 344
**City-owned parks:** 347 park areas and tracts (6,314 ac.)
**Radio stations:** AM, 11; FM, 9
**Television stations:** 5
**Assessed valuation (est. 1986):** $5,366,659,000
**City tax rate (1985):** $6.00 per $100.00
**Net bonded debt (July 1985):** $249,551,610
**Revenue (est. 1986):** $1,337,942,106
**Expenditures (1986):** $1,337,942,106
**Chamber of Commerce:** Greater Baltimore Committee, 2 Hopkins Plaza, Baltimore, Md. 21201

## BATON ROUGE, LA.

**Incorporated as a city:** 1817
**Mayor:** Pat Screen (to Dec. 1988)
**1980 population (1980 Census) & (rank:)** 220,394, Rank (63)
**1985 est. population:** 242,581
**1984 est. rank:** (39)
**1985 Land Area:** 74.7 sq mi.
**Altitude:** Highest, 190 ft; lowest, 15 ft
**Location:** In southeastern part of state, on Mississippi River
**County:** Seat of East Baton Rouge Parish
**Churches:** 422
**City Owned Parks:** 128 parks, (3,484 ac.)
**Radio Stations:** AM 7; FM 6
**Television Stations:** 4
**Assessed Valuation (1985):** $830,416,070
**City Tax Rate (1985):** 6.87 ml per $1,000.
**Bonded Debt (1985):** $69,475,402.
**Revenue (1985):** $138,386,357.
**Expenditures (1985):** $129,307,749.
**Chamber of Commerce:** Greater Baton Rouge Chamber of Commerce, P.O. Box 3217, Baton Rouge, La. 70821

## BOSTON, MASS.

**Incorporated as city:** 1822
**Mayor:** Raymond L. Flynn (to Jan. 1988)
**1980 population (1980 census) & (rank):** 562,994 (20)
**1984 est. population & (rank):** 570,719 (20)
**1985 land area:** 47.2 sq mi. (122 sq km)
**Altitude:** Highest, 330 ft; lowest, sea level
**Location:** On Massachusetts Bay, at mouths of Charles and
   Mystic Rivers
**County:** Seat of Suffolk Co.
**Churches:** Protestant, 187; Roman Catholic, 73; Jewish, 28;
   others, 100
**City-owned parks, playgrounds, etc.:** 2,276.36 ac.
**Radio stations:** AM, 9; FM, 8
**Television stations:** 7
**Assessed valuation (est. Fiscal 1986):** $19,000,000,000
**City tax rate (1986):** $13.70 residential, $26.52
   commercial, per $1000
**Gross direct bonded debt (July 1, 1985):** $527,778,000
**Revenue (est. 1986):** $1,040,000,000
**Expenditures (est. 1986):** $1,040,000,000
**Chamber of Commerce:** Boston Chamber of Commerce,
   125 High St., Boston, Mass. 02110

## BUFFALO, N.Y.

**Incorporated as city:** 1832
**Mayor:** James Griffin (to Dec. 1989)
**1980 population (1980 census) & (rank):** 357,870 (39)
**1984 est. population & (rank):** 338,982 (46)
**1984 land area:** 41.8 sq mi. (198 sq km)
**Altitude:** Highest, 698 ft; lowest, 571
**Location:** At east end of Lake Erie, on Niagara River
**County:** Seat of Erie Co.
**Churches:** 60 denominations, with over 1,100 churches
**County-owned parks:** 9 public parks (3,000 ac.)
**Radio stations:** AM, 10; FM, 13
**Television stations:** 5 (plus reception from 4 Canadian
   stations)
**Assessed valuation (1985–86):** $1,015,061,000
**City tax rate (1985–86):** $89.09 per $1,000
**Total funded debt (long-term, June 30, 1985):** $109,055,-
   000
**Revenue (general fund, 1985):** $364,158,000
**Expenditures (Fiscal 1985):** $357,072,000
**Chamber of Commerce:** Buffalo Area Chamber of
   Commerce, 107 Delaware Ave., Buffalo, N.Y. 14202

## CHARLOTTE, N.C.

**Incorporated as city:** 1768
**Mayor:** Harvey Gantt (to Nov. 1987)
**1980 population (1980 census) & (rank):** 314,447 (47)
**1986 est. population:** 353,448
**1984 est. (rank):** (48)
**1986 land area:** 149 sq mi. (372 sq km)
**Altitude:** 765 ft
**Location:** In the southern part of state near the border of
   South Carolina
**County:** Seat of Mecklenburg Co.
**Churches:** Protestant, over 400; Roman Catholic, 8; Jewish,
   3; Greek Orthodox, 1
**City-owned parks and parkways:** 87
**Radio stations:** AM, 8; FM, 4
**Television stations:** 4 commercial; 2 PBS
**Assessed valuation (1985):** $13,491,002,719
**City tax rate (includes county 1986):** $1.3425 per $100
**Bonded debt (April 30, 1986):** $292,010,000

**Revenue (Fiscal 1985):** $235,620,224
**Expenditures (Fiscal 1985):** $210,456,631
**Chamber of Commerce:** Charlotte Chamber, P.O. Box
   32785, Charlotte, N.C., 28232

## CHICAGO, ILL.

**Incorporated as city:** 1837
**Mayor:** Harold Washington (to April 1987)
**1980 population (1980 census) & (rank):** 3,005,072 (2)
**1984 est. population & (rank):** 2,992,472 (3)
**1986 land area:** 228.1 sq mi. (591 sq km)
**Altitude:** Highest, 672 ft; lowest, 578.5
**Location:** On lower west shore of Lake Michigan
**County:** Seat of Cook Co.
**Churches:** Protestant, 850; Roman Catholic, 263; Jewish,
   51
**City-owned parks:** 568
**Radio stations:** AM, 18, FM, 19
**Television stations:** 9
**Assessed valuation (1984):** $15,181,244,926
**Total Chicago tax rate (1984):** $10.160 per $100
**Total gross bonded debt (1985):** $1,446,000,000
**Revenue (est. 1985):** $1,963,490,016
**Expenditures (est. 1985):** $1,963,490,016
**Chamber of Commerce:** Chicago Association of Commerce
   & Industry, 200 N. LaSalle, Chicago, Ill. 60602

## CINCINNATI, OHIO

**Incorporated as city:** 1819
**Mayor:** Charles Luken (to Nov. 1987)
**City Manager:** Scott Johnson
**1980 population (1980 census) & (rank):** 385,457 (32)
**1986 est. population:** 370,000
**1984 est. rank:** (38)
**1986 land area:** 78.1 sq mi. (202 sq km)
**Altitude:** Highest, 960 ft; lowest, 441
**Location:** In southwestern corner of state on Ohio River
**County:** Seat of Hamilton Co.
**Churches:** 850
**City-owned parks:** 96 (4,345 ac.)
**Radio stations:** AM, 9; FM, 15 (Greater Cincinnati)
**Television stations:** 6
**Assessed valuation (1986):** $3,011,536,155
**City tax rate (1986):** $11.40 per $1,000
**Bonded debt (1986):** $166,141,030
**Revenue (general fund, 1986):** $151,705,000
**Expenditures (general fund, 1986):** $160,269,710
**Chamber of Commerce:** Cincinnati Chamber of Commerce,
   120 W Fifth St., Cincinnati, Ohio 45202

## CLEVELAND, OHIO

**Incorporated as city:** 1836
**Mayor:** George V. Voinovich (to Dec. 1989)
**1980 population (1980 census) & (rank):** 573,822 (18)
**1984 est. population & (rank):** 546,543 (23)
**1984 land area:** 79.0 sq mi. (205 sq km)
**Altitude:** Highest, 1048 ft.; lowest, 573
**Location:** On Lake Erie at mouth of Cuyahoga River
**County:** Seat of Cuyahoga Co.
**Churches:** [1] Protestant, 980; Roman Catholic, 187; Jewish,
   31; Eastern Orthodox, 22
**City-owned parks:** 41 (1,930 ac.)
**Radio stations:** AM, 15; FM, 17
**Television stations:** 7
**Assessed valuation (1986):** $3,778,167,338

City tax rate (1985): $77.5 per $1,000
Bonded debt (Dec. 31, 1985): $484,215,000
Revenue (est. 1986): $264,211,000
Expenditures (est. 1986): $268,078,000
Chamber of Commerce: Greater Cleveland Growth Association, 690 Union Commerce Building, Cleveland, Ohio 44115
1. 100-mile area.

## COLUMBUS, OHIO

Incorporated as city: 1834
Mayor: Dana G. Rinehart (to Jan. 1988)
1980 population (1980 census) & (rank): 565,032 (19)
1986 est. population: 583,722
1984 est. rank (19)
1986 land area: 189.03 sq mi. (490 sq km)
Altitude: Highest, 902 ft; lowest, 702
Location: In central part of state, on Scioto River
County: Seat of Franklin Co.
Churches: Protestant, 436; Roman Catholic, 62; Jewish, 5; Other, 8
City-owned parks: 203 (11,638 ac.)
Radio stations: AM, 7; FM, 11
Television stations: 5 commercial, 1 PBS
Assessed valuation (1986): $5,297,945,399
City tax rate (1986): $47.57 per $1,000
Bonded debt (Dec. 31, 1985): $861,665,000
Revenue (1985): $501,289,000
Expenditures (1985): $459,000,000
Chamber of Commerce: Columbus Area Chamber of Commerce, P.O. Box 1527, Columbus, Ohio 43216

## DALLAS, TEX.

Incorporated as city: 1856
Mayor: A. Starke Taylor (to April 1987)
City Manager: Charles Anderson (apptd. Oct. 1981)
1980 population (1980 census) & (rank): 904,078 (7)
1984 est. population & (rank): 974,234 (7)
1984 land area: 333.0 sq mi. (862 sq km)
Altitude: Highest, 750 ft; lowest, 375
Location: In northeastern part of state, on Trinity River
County: Seat of Dallas Co.
Churches: 1,200 (in Dallas Co.)
City-owned parks: 301 (47,533.5 ac.)
Radio stations: AM, 8; FM, 14
Television stations: 5 commercial, 1 PBS
Assessed valuation (1985–86): $38,250,096,000
City tax rate (1985–86): $.4918 per $100
Bonded debt (Sept. 30, 1985): $1,051,455,460[1]
Revenue (1985): $454,124,488
Expenditures (1985–86): $454,121,690
Chamber of Commerce: Dallas Chamber of Commerce. 1507 Pacific, Dallas, Tex. 75201
1. Latest figure available, decreased after date indicated.

## DENVER, COLO.

Incorporated as city: 1861
Mayor: Federico Pena (to July 1987)
1980 population (1980 census) & (rank): 492,365 (24)
1985 est. population: 505,100
1984 est. rank (24)
1984 land area: 110.6 sq mi. (287 sq km)
Altitude: Highest, 5,470 ft; lowest, 5,130
Location: In northeast central part of state, on South Platte River

County: Coextensive with Denver Co.
Churches:[1] Protestant, 815; Roman Catholic, 63; Jewish, 13
City-owned parks: 155 (3,600 ac.)
City-owned mountain parks: 40 (13,448 ac.)
Radio stations: AM, 18; FM, 13[1]
Television stations: 5
Assessed valuation (1985): $2,878,477,400
City tax rate (1984): $28.11 per $1,000[2]
Bonded debt (1984): $290,858,000[2]
Revenue (1984): $724,713,800[2]
Expenditures (1984): $671,650,800[2]
Chamber of Commerce: Denver Chamber of Commerce, 1301 Welton, Denver, Colo. 80204
1. Metropolitan area. 2. Excluding school district.

## DETROIT, MICH.

Incorporated as city: 1815
Mayor: Coleman A. Young (to Jan. 1990)
1980 population (1980 census) & (rank): 1,203,339 (6)
1986 est. population: 1,100,000
1984 est. rank (6)
1984 land area: 143 sq mi. (370 sq km)
Altitude: Highest, 685 ft; lowest, 574
Location: In southeastern part of state, on Detroit River
County: Seat of Wayne Co.
Churches: [1]Protestant, 2,204; Roman Catholic, 333; Jewish, 40
City-owned parks: 52 parks (3,843 ac.); 350 sites (5,838 ac.)
Radio stations: AM, 16; FM, 33 (7-county area)
Television stations: 11 (incl. Windsor, Ontario, Canada)[1]
Assessed valuation (1985): $5,230,620,665
City tax rate (1985–86): $32.321 per $1,000
Net bonded debt (May 1985): General obligations, (net): $234,920,200
Revenue (1985–86): $1,651,177,506[2]
Expenditures (1985–86): $1,651,177,506[2]
Chamber of Commerce: Greater Detroit Chamber of Commerce, 150 Michigan Ave., Detroit, Mich. 48226
1. Six-county metropolitan area. 2. Excludes utilities.

## EL PASO, TEX.

Incorporated as city: 1873
Mayor: Jonathan Rogers (to April 1987)
1980 population (1980 census) & (rank): 425,259 (28)
1985 est. population: 484,568
1984 est. rank (26)
1984 land area: 239.2 sq mi. (620 sq km)
Altitude: 4,000 ft
Location: In far western part of state, on Rio Grande
County: Seat of El Paso Co.
Churches: Protestant, 284; Roman Catholic, 39; Jewish, 3; others, 15
City-owned parks: 114[1] (1,558 ac.)
Radio Stations: AM, 17; FM, 17
Television stations: 5
Assessed valuation (1985): $9,710,359,986
City tax rate (1984): $4.52 per $1,000, city; $6.78, El Paso Independent School District; $7.70, Ysleta Independent School District
Bonded debt (1985): $39,785,000
Revenue (1985): $114,021,614
Expenditures (1985): $111,072,788
Chamber of Commerce: El Paso Chamber of Commerce, 10 Civic Center Plaza, El Paso, Tex. 79944
1. Includes 101 developed and 13 undeveloped parks.

## FORT WORTH, TEX.

**Incorporated as city:** 1873
**Mayor:** Bob Bolen (to April 1987)
**City Manager:** Douglas Harman
**1980 population (1980 census) & (rank):** 385,164 (33)
**1984 est. population & (rank):** 414,562 (32)
**1984 land area:** 240.1 sq mi. (622 sq km)
**Altitude:** Highest, 780 ft; lowest, 520
**Location:** In north central part of state, on Trinity River
**County:** Seat of Tarrant Co.
**Churches:** Protestant, 392; Roman Catholic, 16; Jewish, 2
**City-owned parks:** 136 (8,189 ac.; 3,500 ac. in Nature Center)
**Radio stations:** AM, 6; FM, 8
**Television stations:** 6 (2 local)
**Assessed valuation (1984–85):** $12,355,737,899
**City tax rate (1983–84):** $.7390 per $100
**Bonded debt (1984–85):** $351,126,976
**Revenue (1984–85):** $294,726,780
**Expenditures (1984–85):** $294,726,780
**Chamber of Commerce:** Fort Worth Chamber of Commerce, 700 Throckmorton, Fort Worth, Tex. 76102

## HONOLULU, HAWAII

**Incorporated as city and county:** 1907
**Mayor:** Frank F. Fasi (to Jan. 1989)
**1980 population (1980 census) & (rank):** 365,048 (36)
**1984 est. population & (rank):** 805,000[1] (11)
**1984 land area:** 617 sq. mi (1,600 sq km)[1]
**Altitude:** Highest, 4,025 ft; lowest, sea level
**Location:** The city and county government's jurisdiction includes the entire island of Oahu
**Churches:** Roman Catholic, 33; Buddhist, 32; Jewish, 2; Protestant and others, 328
**City-owned parks:** 5,279 ac.
**Radio stations:** AM, 19; FM, 10
**Television stations:** 8
**Assessed valuation (1983):** $29,935,810,842 (100% of market value.)
**City and county tax rate (1984):** $6.75 per $1,000 (residential); $9.00 per $1,000 (commercial); $10.00 per $1,000 (hotel/resort)
**Bonded debt (June 1985):** $177,447,470
**Net revenue (1984–85):** $449,197,937
**Net expenditures (1984–85):** $411,140,495
**Chamber of Commerce:** Chamber of Commerce of Hawaii, 735 Bishop St., Honolulu, Hawaii 96813
1. City and county area.

## HOUSTON, TEX.

**Incorporated as city:** 1837
**Mayor:** Kathryn J. Whitmire (to Dec. 1987)
**1980 population (1980 census) & (rank):** 1,595,138 (5)
**1984 est. population & (rank):** 1,705,697 (4)
**1984 land area:** 556.4 sq mi. (1,441 sq km)
**Altitude:** Highest, 120 ft; lowest, sea level
**Location:** In southeastern part of state, near Gulf of Mexico
**County:** Seat of Harris Co.
**Churches:** 1,750[2]
**City-owned parks:** 298 (31,671 ac.)
**Radio stations:** AM, 22; FM, 26[1]
**Television stations:** 7 commercial, 1 PBS
**Assessed valuation (1985–86):** $75,963,746,000
**City tax rate (1985):** $.495 per $100
**Bonded debt (1985–86):** $1,192,324,000
**Revenue (1985–86):** $726,589,700
**Expenditures (1985–86):** $726,033,100

**Chamber of Commerce:** Houston Chamber of Commerce, 1100 Milam Building, Houston, Tex. 77002
1. Includes annexations since 1970. 2. Metropolitan area (Harris County).

## INDIANAPOLIS, IND.

**Incorporated as city:** 1832 (reincorporated 1838)
**Mayor:** William H. Hudnut III (to Jan. 1988)
**1980 population (1980 census) & (rank):** 700,807 (12)
**1984 est. population & (rank):** 710,280 (14)
**1984 land area:** 352.0 sq mi. (912 sq km)
**Altitude:** Highest, 840 ft; lowest, 700
**Location:** In central part of the state, on West Fork of White River
**County:** Seat of Marion Co.
**Churches:** 1,200[1]
**City-owned parks:** 188 (10,206 ac.)
**Radio stations:** AM, 9; FM, 18
**Television stations:** 7[1]
**Assessed valuation (1985):** (consolidated city), $3,865,413,030; (Marion County) $4,130,266,450
**City tax rate (Center Township, 1985 payable 1986):** $127.47 per $1,000
**Gross debt (consolidated city, Dec. 31, 1985):** $216,531,000
**Revenue (1985):** $275,284,676
**Expenditures (1985):** $288,275,752
**Chamber of Commerce:** Indianapolis Chamber of Commerce, 320 N Meridian St., Indianapolis, Ind. 46202
1. Marion County.

## JACKSONVILLE, FLA.

**Incorporated as city:** 1822
**Mayor:** Jake M. Godbold (to July 1, 1987)
**1980 population (1980 census) & (rank):** 540,920 (22)
**1985 est. population:** 630,920
**1984 est. rank** (19)
**1984 land area:** 759.6 sq mi. (1,967 sq km)
**Altitude:** Highest, 71 ft; lowest, sea level
**Location:** On St. Johns River, 20 miles from Atlantic Ocean
**County:** Duval
**Churches:** Protestant, 535; Roman Catholic, 20; Jewish, 5; others, 11
**City-owned parks and playgrounds:** 138 (1,522 ac.)
**Radio stations:** AM, 15; FM, 10
**Television stations:** 6 commercial, 1 PBS
**Assessed valuation (1985):** $10,738,000,000
**City tax rate (1982–83):** $19.64 per $1,000 (old county area); $19.97 per $1,000 (old city area)
**Bonded debt (1983):** $76,153,961
**Revenue (1983–84):** $1,228,217,110
**Expenditures (1983–84):** $1,228,217,110
**Chamber of Commerce:** Jacksonville Area Chamber of Commerce, Jacksonville, Fla. 32202

## KANSAS CITY, MO.

**Incorporated as city:** 1850
**Mayor:** Richard L. Berkley (April 10, 1987)
**City Manager:** David H. Olson (apptd. Nov. 1984)
**1980 population (1980 census) & (rank):** 448,159 (27)
**1984 est. population & (rank):** 443,075 (29)
**1984 land area:** 316.3 sq mi. (819 sq km)
**Altitude:** Highest, 1,014 ft; lowest, 722
**Location:** In western part of state, at juncture of Missouri and Kansas Rivers

County: Located in Jackson, Clay, and Platte Co.
Churches: 1,100 churches of all denominations
City-owned parks and playgrounds: 174 (7,600 ac.)
Radio stations: AM, 14; FM, 13[1]
Television stations: 6[1]
Assessed valuation (1984–85): $2,850,867,341
City tax rate (1984–85): $9.86 per $1,000
Bonded debt (1984–85): $48,575,000
Revenue (1984–85): $371,400,001
Expenditures (1984–85): $339,243,266
Budget (gross total, 1984–85): $394,271,895
Chamber of Commerce: Chamber of Commerce of Greater Kansas City, 920 Main St., Kansas City, Mo. 64105
1. Metropolitan area.

## LONG BEACH, CALIF.

Founded: 1881
Mayor: Ernie Kell (to July 1986)
City Manager: John E. Dever (apptd. Jan. 1, 1977)
1980 population (1980 census) & (rank): 361,334 (37)
1986 est. population: 392,251
1984 est. rank: (37)
1985 land area: 49.8 sq mi. (129 sq km)
Altitude: Highest, 170 ft; lowest, sea level
Location: On San Pedro Bay, south of Los Angeles
County: In Los Angeles Co.
Churches: 236
City-owned parks: 42 (1,182 ac.)
Radio stations: AM, 2; FM, 2
Television stations: 1 (cable)
Assessed valuation (1985): $14,091,708,255
City tax rate (1984–85): none; county, $10 per $1,000
Bonded debt (1985–86): $378,305,000
Revenue (1985–86): $1,150,933,666
Expenditures (1985–86): $1,101,174,965
Chamber of Commerce: Long Beach Chamber of Commerce, 50 Oceangate Plaza, Long Beach, Calif. 90802

## LOS ANGELES, CALIF.

Incorporated as city: 1850
Mayor: Tom Bradley (to June 1989)
1980 population (1980 census) & (rank): 2,966,850 (3)
1986 est. population: 3,215,506
1984 est. rank: (2)
1984 land area: 467.2 sq mi. (1,210 sq km)
Altitude: Highest, 5,081 ft; lowest, sea level
Location: In southwestern part of state, on Pacific Ocean
County: Seat of Los Angeles Co.
Churches: 1,963 of all denominations
City-owned parks: 353 (15,045 ac.)
Radio stations: AM, 32; FM, 40
Television stations: 18
Assessed valuation (1985–86): $104,507,422,507
City tax rate (1984–85): $0.0072 per $1,000
Gross debt (June 30, 1986): general obligation bonds, $34,015,000; revenue bonds, $2,437,258,000
Revenue (1984–85): $1,932,802,930
Expenditures (1984–85): $1,802,419,715
Chamber of Commerce: Los Angeles Chamber of Commerce, 404 S Bixel St., Los Angeles, Calif. 90017

## MEMPHIS, TENN.

Incorporated as city: 1826
Mayor: Richard C. Hackett (to Dec. 1987)
1980 population (1980 census) & (rank): 646,356 (15)
1984 est. population & (rank): 648,399 (16)
1984 land area: 290 sq mi. (751.30 sq km)
Altitude: Highest, 331 ft
Location: In southwestern corner of state, on Mississippi River
County: Seat of Shelby Co.
Churches: 800
Parks and playgrounds: 172 (5,572 ac.)
Radio stations: AM, 12; FM, 8
Television stations: 6
Assessed valuation (1984): $3,171,306,134
City tax rate (1983): $31.30 per $1,000
Bonded debt (June 30, 1985): $415,425,361
Revenue (1985): $639,090,163[1]
Expenditures (1985): $641,770,506[1]
Chamber of Commerce: Memphis Area Chamber of Commerce, P.O. Box 224, Memphis, Tenn. 38101
1. Includes all Governmental Fund types and Expendable Trust Funds.

## MIAMI, FLA.

Incorporated as city: 1896
Mayor: Xavier L. Suarez (to Nov. 1987)
City manager: Cesar Odio (apptd. Dec. 1985)
1980 population (1980 census) & (rank): 346,865 (41)
1986 est. population: 380,446
1984 est. rank: (34)
1986 land area: 34.3 sq mi. (89 sq km)
Altitude: Average, 12 ft
Location: In southeastern part of state, on Biscayne Bay
County: Seat of Dade Co.
Churches: Protestant, 592; Roman Catholic, 53; Jewish, 48
City-owned parks: 109
Radio stations: AM, 18; FM, 20
Television stations: 5 commercial, 2 PBS
Assessed valuation (1985–86): $9,315,878,243
City tax rate (1985–86): $9.8571 per $1,000
Bonded debt (1983–84): $131,020,000
Revenue (1985–86): $195,858,316
Expenditures (1985–86): $195,858,316
Chamber of Commerce: Greater Miami Chamber of Commerce, 391 N.E. 15th St., Miami, Fla. 33132

## MILWAUKEE, WIS.

Incorporated as city: 1846
Mayor: Henry W. Maier (to April 1988)
1980 population (1980 census) & (rank): 636,236 (16)
1984 est. population & (rank): 620,811 (18)
1984 land area: 95.8 sq mi. (248 sq km)
Altitude: 580.60 ft
Location: In southeastern part of state, on Lake Michigan
County: Seat of Milwaukee Co.
Churches: 411
County-owned parks: 14,061 ac.
Radio stations: AM, 9; FM, 14
Television stations: 9
Assessed valuation (1985): $11,076,973,939
City tax rate (1985): $32.37 per $1,000
Gross debt (1985): $268,560,000
Revenue (1985): $584,795,815
Expenditures (1985): $591,535,478
Chamber of Commerce: Metropolitan Milwaukee Association of Commerce, 828 N. Broadway, Milwaukee, Wis. 53202

## MINNEAPOLIS, MINN.

**Incorporated as city:** 1867
**Mayor:** Donald M. Fraser (to Jan. 1990)
**1980 population (1980 census) & (rank):** 370,951 (34)
**1984 est. population & (rank):** 358,335 (42)
**1984 land area:** 55.1 sq mi. (143 sq km)
**Altitude:** Highest, 945 ft; lowest, 695
**Location:** In southeast central part of state, on Mississippi River
**County:** Seat of Hennepin Co.
**Churches:** 419
**City-owned parks:** 153
**Radio stations:** AM, 17; FM, 15 (metro area)
**Television stations:** 6 (metro area)
**Assessed valuation (1985):** $2,836,858,452[1]
**City tax rate (1985):** $34.890 per $1,000
**Net debt (Dec. 31, 1985):** $71,165,000
**Revenue (1985):** $359,220,368
**Expenditures (1985):** $350,023,163
**Chamber of Commerce:** Greater Minneapolis Chamber of Commerce, 15 S Fifth Street, Minneapolis, Minn. 55402
1. Assessed valuations on majority of properties now range from 18.5% (homesteads) to 43% (commercial, industrial) of actual market value.

## NASHVILLE, TENN.

**Incorporated as city:** 1806
**Mayor:** Richard H. Fulton (to Sept. 1987)
**1980 population (1980 census) & (rank):** 455,651 (25)
**1984 est. population & (rank):** 462,450 (27)
**1984 land area:** 479.4 sq mi. (1,242 sq km)
**Altitude:** Highest, 1,100 ft; lowest, approx. 400 ft
**Location:** In north central part of state, on Cumberland River
**County:** Davidson
**Churches:** Protestant, 739; Roman Catholic, 16; Jewish, 3
**City-owned parks:** 68 (6,650 ac.)
**Radio stations:** AM, 11; FM, 8
**Television stations:** 5
**Assessed valuation (1985):** $4,711,108,000
**City tax rate (1985):** $39.20 per $1,000
**Bonded debt (March 1986):** $393,491,000
**Revenue (1985):** $399,897,970
**Expenditures (1985):** $384,727,032
**Chamber of Commerce:** Nashville Area Chamber of Commerce, 161 Fourth Ave. North, Nashville, Tenn. 37219

## NEWARK, N.J.

**Incorporated as city:** 1836
**Mayor:** Sharpe James (to June 1990)
**1980 population (1980 census) & (rank):** 329,248 (46)
**1984 est. population & (rank):** 314,387 (49)
**1984 land area:** 24.1 sq mi. (62 sq km)
**Altitude:** Highest, 273.4 ft; lowest, sea level
**Location:** In northeastern part of state, on Passaic River and Newark Bay
**County:** Seat of Essex Co.
**Churches:** Roman Catholic, 32; Jewish, 4; Protestant and others, 250
**City-owned parks:** 40 (and 20 mini parks); (39.3 ac.)
**County-governed parks in city:** 7 (743.97 ac.)
**Radio stations:** AM, 2; FM, 4
**Television stations:** 2
**Assessed valuation (1986):** $1,004,730,400
**City tax rate (1985):** $119.30 per $1,000
**Net bonded debt (1986):** $54,220,980.19

**Revenue (est. 1986):** $342,969,589
**Expenditures (est. 1986):** $342,969,589
**Chamber of Commerce:** Greater Newark Chamber of Commerce, 50 Park Place, Newark, N.J. 07102

## NEW ORLEANS, LA.

**Incorporated as city:** 1805
**Mayor:** Sidney J. Barthelemy (to May 1990)
**1980 population (1980 census) & (rank):** 557,927 (21)
**1985 est. population:** 564,383
**1984 est. population:** (22)
**1984 land area:** 199.4 sq mi. (516 sq km)
**Altitude:** Highest, 15 ft; lowest, −4
**Location:** In southeastern part of state, between Mississippi River and Lake Ponchartrain
**Parish:** Seat of Orleans Parish
**Churches:** 644
**City-owned parks:** 250 (4,460 ac.)
**Radio stations:** AM, 12; FM, 10
**Television stations:** 7
**Assessed valuation (1985):** $1,615,447,954
**City tax rate (1985):** $109.375 per $1,000
**Bonded debt (Dec. 31, 1985):** $301,000,000
**Revenue (est. 1985):** $348,000,000
**Expenditures (est. 1985):** $328,700,000
**Chamber of Commerce:** New Orleans and the River Region Chamber of Commerce, 301 Camp Street, New Orleans, La. 70130

## NEW YORK, N.Y.

**Chartered as "Greater New York":** 1898
**Mayor:** Edward Koch (to Dec. 31, 1989)
**Borough Presidents:** Bronx, Stanley Simon; Brooklyn, Howard Golden; Manhattan, Andrew Stein; Queens, Claire Shulman; Staten Island, Ralph J. Lamperti
**1980 population (1980 census) & (rank):** 7,071,639 (1)[1]
**1984 est. population & (rank):** 7,164,742 (1)[1]
**1984 land area:** 303.7 sq mi. (786 sq km) (Queens, 109; Brooklyn, 72; Staten Island, 55; Bronx, 42.5; Manhattan, 23.0)
**Altitude:** Highest, 410 ft; lowest, sea level
**Location:** In south of state, at mouth of Hudson River (also known as the North River as it passes Manhattan)
**Counties:** Consists of 5 counties: Bronx, Kings (Brooklyn), New York (Manhattan), Queens, Richmond (Staten Island)
**Churches:** Protestant, 1,766; Jewish, 1,256; Roman Catholic, 437; Orthodox, 66
**City-owned parks:** 1,588 (25,434 ac.)
**Radio stations:** AM and FM, 7; AM only, 10; FM only, 12
**Television stations:** 6 commercial, 1 PBS
**Assessed valuation (1985–86):** $52,643,593,088
**City tax rate (1985–86):** $9.323 commercial, $.0910 residential, per $100
**Revenues (1984–85):** 18,802,000
**Expenditures (1984–85):** $18,796,000
**Chamber of Commerce:** New York Chamber of Commerce and Industry, 65 Liberty St., New York, N.Y. 10005
1. For population of boroughs, see Index.

## OAKLAND, CALIF.

**Incorporated as city:** 1854
**Mayor:** Lionel J. Wilson (to June 30, 1989)
**City Manager:** Henry L. Gardner (apptd. June 1981)
**1980 population (1980 census) & (rank):** 339,337 (43)
**1985 est. population:** 352,100
**1984 est. rank** (43)

**1984 land area:** 53.9 sq mi.
**Altitude:** Highest, 1,700 ft; lowest, sea level
**Location:** In west central part of state, on east side of San Francisco Bay
**County:** Seat of Alameda Co.
**Churches:** 374, representing over 78 denominations in the City; over 500 churches in Alameda County
**City-owned parks:** 2,196 ac.
**Radio stations:** AM, 3; FM, 2
**Television stations:** 9 commercial; 3 PBS
**Assessed valuation (1984–85):** $9,821,567,076 (25% of appraised value)
**City tax rate (1984–85):** $1.2725%[1]
**Bonded debt (est. June 1985):** $1,375,600
**Revenue (1984–85 est.):** $215,536,000
**Expenditures (1984–85):** $227,348,000
**Chamber of Commerce:** Oakland Chamber of Commerce, 1939 Harrison St., Suite 400, Oakland, Calif. 94612
1. Code area 17001.

## OKLAHOMA CITY, OKLA.

**Incorporated as city:** 1890
**Mayor:** Andy Coats (to April 1987)
**City Manager:** Don Boun, Acting City Manager
**1980 population (1980 census) & (rank):** 403,213 (31)
**1984 est. population & (rank):** 443,172 (28)
**1984 land area:** 621.5 sq mi. (1,563 sq km)
**Altitude:** Highest, 1,320 ft; lowest, 1,140
**Location:** In central part of state, on North Canadian River
**County:** Seat of Oklahoma Co.
**Churches:** Roman Catholic, 15; Jewish, 2; Protestant and others, 741
**City-owned parks:** 138 (3,944 ac.)
**Television stations:** 8
**Radio stations:** AM, 10; FM, 14
**Assessed valuation (1984–85):** $1,604,822,477
**City tax rate (1985–86):** $12.59 per $1,000
**Bonded debt (1985–86):** $152,705,670
**Revenue (general fund, 1984–85):** $124,600,473
**Expenditures (general fund, 1984–85):** $121,471,303
**Chamber of Commerce:** Oklahoma City Chamber of Commerce, 1 Santa Fe Plaza, Oklahoma City, Okla. 73102

## OMAHA, NEB.

**Incorporated as city:** 1857
**Mayor:** Mike Boyle (to June 1989)
**1980 population (1980 census) & (rank):** 313,911 (48)
**1985 est. population:** 342,795
**1984 est. rank:** (47)
**1984 land area:** 90.9 sq mi. (235 sq km)
**Altitude:** Highest, 1,270 ft
**Location:** In eastern part of state, on Missouri River
**County:** Seat of Douglas Co.
**Churches:** Protestant, 246; Roman Catholic, 44; Jewish, 4
**City-owned parks:** 99 (3,671.6 ac.)
**Radio stations:** AM, 7; FM, 6
**Television stations:** 4
**Assessed valuation (1986):** $8,139,458,830
**City tax rate (1986):** $0.6192 per $1,000
**Bonded debt (1985):** $100,334,641
**Revenue (1985):** $208,023,308
**Expenditures (1985):** $204,029,784
**Chamber of Commerce:** Omaha Chamber of Commerce, 1301 Harway St., Omaha, Neb. 68102

## PHILADELPHIA, PA.

**First charter as city:** 1701
**Mayor:** W. Wilson Goode (to Jan. 1988)
**1980 population (1980 census) & (rank):** 1,688,210 (4)
**1984 est. population & (rank):** 1,646,713 (5)
**1984 land area:** 136.0 sq mi. (352 sq km)
**Altitude:** Highest, 440 ft; lowest, sea level
**Location:** In southeastern part of state, at junction of Schuylkill and Delaware Rivers
**County:** Seat of Philadelphia Co. (coterminous)
**Churches:** Roman Catholic, 139; Jewish, 70; Protestant and others, 830
**City-owned parks:** 630 (10,252 ac.)
**Radio stations:** AM, 20; FM, 22
**Television stations:** 8
**Assessed valuation (1986):** $6,276,000,000
**City and school district tax rate (1985):** $74.75 per $1,000
**Net bonded debt (June 30, 1985):** $2,115,379,000 (incl. revenue bonds of $645,085,000 for water and sewer; $407,130,000 for gas works; $78,846,000 for aviation)
**Revenue (1985):** $1,535,569,000
**Expenditures (1985):** $1,561,440,000
**Chamber of Commerce:** Philadelphia Chamber of Commerce, 1346 Chestnut St., Suite 800, Philadelphia, Pa. 19107

## PHOENIX, ARIZ.

**Incorporated as city:** 1881
**Mayor:** Terry Goddard (to Jan. 1988)
**City Manager:** Marvin A. Andrews (appt. Oct. 1976)
**1980 population (1980 census) & (rank):** 789,704 (9)
**1984 est. population & (rank):** 853,266 (9)
**1983 land area:** 344.4 sq mi.
**Altitude:** Highest, 2,740 ft.; lowest, 1,017
**Location:** In center of state, on Salt River
**County:** Seat of Maricopa Co.
**City-owned parks:** 142 (26,647 ac.)
**Radio stations:** AM, 19; FM, 15
**Television stations:** 8 commercial; 1 PBS
**Assessed valuation (1985–86):** $3,851,711,000
**City tax rate (1985–86):** $16.30 per $1,000
**Bonded debt (May 1986):** $1,111,790,000
**Revenues (est. 1985–86):** $792,616,000
**Expenditures (est. 1985–86):** $701,061,000
**Chamber of Commerce:** Phoenix Chamber of Commerce, 805 N Second St., Phoenix, Ariz. 85004

## PITTSBURGH, PA.

**Incorporated as city:** 1816
**Mayor:** Richard S. Caliguiri (to Jan. 1990)
**1980 population (1980 census) & (rank):** 423,959 (30)
**1984 est. population & (rank):** 402,583 (33)
**1984 land area:** 55.4 sq mi. (144 sq km)
**Altitude:** Highest, 1,240 ft; lowest, 715
**Location:** In southwestern part of state, at beginning of Ohio River
**County:** Seat of Allegheny Co.
**Churches:** Protestant, 348; Roman Catholic, 86; Jewish, 28; Orthodox, 26
**City-owned parks and playgrounds:** 88 (2,471 ac.)
**Radio stations:** AM, 18; FM, 9
**Television stations:** 4
**Assessed valuation (1985):** land, $574,623,513; buildings, $2,082,015,596
**City tax rate (1985):** $27 per $1,000 buildings; $151.50 per $1,000 land

Net bonded debt (Oct. 1984): $221,402,005
Revenue (1985): $277,100,000
Expenditures (1985): $277,100,000
Chamber of Commerce: The Chamber of Commerce of Greater Pittsburgh, 411 Seventh Ave., Pittsburgh, Pa. 15222

## PORTLAND, ORE.

Incorporated as city: 1851
Mayor: John (Bud) Clark (to Dec. 1988)
1980 population (1980 census) & (rank): 366,383 (35)
1986 est. population: 341,415
1984 est. rank: (40)
1986 land area: 125 sq mi. (524 sq km)
Altitude: Highest, 1,073 ft; lowest, sea level
Location: In northwestern part of state, on Willamette River
County: Seat of Multnomah Co.
Churches: Protestant, 332; Roman Catholic, 39; Jewish, 4; Buddhist, 4; Vedanta Society, 1
City-owned parks: 175 (8,000 ac.)
Radio stations: AM, 14; FM, 12
Television stations: 5 commercial, 1 PBS
Assessed valuation (1985–86): $13,494,651,000 (at 100% of cash value)
City tax rate (1985–86): $13.30 per $1,000
Bonded debt (July 1, 1986): $114,000,000
Revenue (est. 1986–87): $736,200,000
Expenditures (est. 1986–87): $736,200,000
Chamber of Commerce: Portland Chamber of Commerce, 221 NW 2nd Ave., Portland, Ore. 97209

## ST. LOUIS, MO.

Incorporated as city: 1822
Mayor: Vincent Schoemehl, Jr. (to April 1989)
1980 population (1980 census) & (rank): 453,085 (26)
1985 est. population: 401,874
1984 est. rank: (30)
1984 land area: 61.4 sq mi. (159 sq km)
Altitude: Highest, 616 ft; lowest, 413
Location: In east central part of state, on Mississippi River
County: Independent city
Churches: 900[1]
City-owned parks: 89 (2,639 ac.)
Radio stations: AM, 18; FM, 20[1]
Television stations: 6 commercial; 1 PBS
Assessed valuation (1984): $1,816,000,000
City tax rate (1983): $61.40 per $1,000
Bonded debt (1984–85): $39,675,000
Revenue (1985–86): $268,880,201
Expenditures (1985–86): $266,218,405
Chamber of Commerce: St. Louis Regional Commerce and Growth Association, 10 Broadway, St. Louis, Mo. 63102
1. Metropolitan area.

## SAN ANTONIO, TEX.

Incorporated as city: 1837
Mayor: Henry Cisneros (to May 1987)
City Manager: Louis J. Fox (apptd. Jan. 1982)
1980 population (1980 census) & (rank): 786,023 (11)
1984 est. population & (rank): 842,779 (10)
1984 land area: 269.10 sq mi. (697 sq km)
Altitude: 700 ft
Location: In south central part of state, on San Antonio River
County: Seat of Bexar Co.
City-owned parks: Approximately 5,881 ac.
Radio stations: AM, 13; FM, 12

Television stations: 5
Assessed valuation (1985): $17,057,304,959
City tax rate (1985): $.4141 per $100
Net funded debt (Sept. 1985): $263,063,203
Revenue (Fiscal 1984–85): $256,183,614
Expenditures (Fiscal 1984–85): $242,724,031
Chamber of Commerce: Greater San Antonio Chamber of Commerce, P.O. Box 1628, 602 E Commerce, San Antonio, Tex. 78296
1. Excludes transfers.

## SAN DIEGO, CALIF.

Incorporated as city: 1850
Mayor: Maureen O'Connor (to June 1990)
City Manager: Sylvester Murray (apptd. Sept. 1985)
1980 population (1980 census) & (rank): 875,538 (8)
1986 est. population: 1,013,400
1984 est. rank: (8)
1986 land area: 403.4 sq mi. (1,045 sq km)
Altitude: Highest, 1,591 ft; lowest, sea level
Location: In southwesternmost part of state, on San Diego Bay
County: Seat of San Diego Co.
Churches: Roman Catholic, 80; Jewish, 8; Protestant 334; Eastern Orthodox, 7; other, 6
City park and recreation facilities: 266 (27,531 ac.)
Radio stations: AM, 13; FM, 20
Television stations: 7
Assessed valuation (1986): $33,807,388,145
City tax rate (1986): $2.20 per $1,000
Bonded debt (1986): $17,380,000
Revenue (est. 1987): $616,203,256
Expenditures (est. 1987): $616,203,256
Chamber of Commerce: San Diego Chamber of Commerce, 110 W. C St., Suite 1600, San Diego, Calif. 92101

## SAN FRANCISCO, CALIF.

Incorporated as city: 1850
Mayor: Dianne Feinstein (to Jan. 1988)
1980 population (1980 census) & (rank): 678,974 (13)
1984 est. population & (rank): 712,753 (13)
1984 land area: 46.4 sq mi. (120 sq km)
Altitude: Highest, 925 ft; lowest, sea level
Location: In northern part of state between Pacific Ocean and San Francisco Bay
County: Coextensive with San Francisco Co.
Churches: 540 of all denominations
City-owned parks and squares: 120
Radio stations: 22
Television stations: 7
Assessed valuation (1986–87): $30,500,000,000 (100% of valuation)
City and county tax rate (1985–86): $1.14 per $100
Bonded debt (1985–86): $843,205,000
Revenue (1986–87): $1,811,173,316
Expenditures (1986–87): $1,884,798,710
Chamber of Commerce: Greater San Francisco Chamber of Commerce, 465 California St., San Francisco, Calif. 94104

## SAN JOSE, CALIF.

Incorporated as city: 1850
Mayor: Thomas McEnery (to Dec. 31, 1986)
City Manager: Gerald E. Newfarmer (apptd. July 1983)
1980 population (1980 census) & (rank): 629,546 (17)

**1986 est. population:** 713,385
**1984 est. rank:** (15)
**1986 land area:** 169.1 sq. mi (438 sq km)
**Altitude:** Highest, 4,372 ft.; lowest, sea level
**Location:** In northern part of state, on south San Francisco Bay, 50 miles from San Francisco
**County:** Seat of Santa Clara County
**Churches:** 403
**City-owned parks and playgrounds:** 143 (2,948 ac.)
**Radio stations:** 14
**Television stations:** 4
**Assessed valuation (1985–86):** $25,397,109,331 (100% of valuation)
**City tax rate (1985–86):** $1.55 per $1,000
**Bonded debt (June 1985):** $16,631,000
**Revenue (1985–86):** $952,184,567
**Expenditures (1985–86):** $952,184,567
**Chamber of Commerce:** San Jose Chamber of Commerce, One Paseo de San Antonio, San Jose, Calif. 95113

# SEATTLE, WASH.

**Incorporated as city:** 1869
**Mayor:** Charles Royer (to Nov. 1989)
**1980 population (1980 census) & (rank):** 493,846 (23)
**1984 est. population & (rank):** 488,474 (25)
**1984 land area:** 144.6 sq mi. (375 sq km)
**Altitude:** Highest, 540 ft; lowest, sea level
**Location:** In west central part of state, on Puget Sound
**County:** Seat of King Co.
**Churches:** Roman Catholic, 36; Jewish, 13; Protestant and others, 535
**City-owned parks, playgrounds, etc.:** 278 (4,773.4 ac.)
**Radio stations:** AM, 22; FM, 26
**Television stations:** 3 commercial; 1 educational
**Assessed valuation (1985):** $22,344,255,000
**City B & O tax rate (1985):** $3.60 per $1,000
**Bonded debt (1985):** $210,505,000
**Revenue (1985):** $882,014,041
**Expenditures (1985):** $853,559,659
**Chamber of Commerce:** Seattle Chamber of Commerce, 1200 One Union Square, Seattle, Wash. 98101

# TOLEDO, OHIO

**Incorporated as city:** 1837
**Mayor:** Donna Owens (to Dec. 1987)
**City Manager:** Phillip Hawkey
**1980 population (1980 census) & (rank):** 354,635 (40)
**1984 est. population & (rank):** 343,939 (45)
**1984 land area:** 84.2 sq mi. (218 sq km)
**Altitude:** 630 ft
**Location:** In northwestern part of state, on Maumee River at Lake Erie
**County:** Seat of Lucas Co.
**Churches:** Protestant, 301; Roman Catholic, 55; Jewish, 4; others, 98
**City-owned parks and playgrounds:** 134 (2,650.90 ac.)
**Radio stations:** AM, 8; FM, 8
**Television stations:** 4
**Assessed valuation (Jan. 1, 1986):** $2,763,049,173
**City tax rate (Jan. 1, 1986):** $63.95 per $1,000
**Bonded debt (Jan. 1, 1986):** $159,658,782
**Revenue (est. 1986):** $283,085,170
**Expenditures (est. 1986):** $261,535,714
**Chamber of Commerce:** Toledo Area Chamber of Commerce, 218 Huron St., Toledo, Ohio 43604

# TUCSON, ARIZ.

**Incorporated as city:** 1877
**Mayor:** Lewis C. Murphy (to Dec. 1987)
**1980 population (1980 census) & (rank):** 330,537 (45)
**1986 est. population:** 384,385
**1894 est. rank** (41)
**1984 land area:** 98.8 sq mi. (256 sq km)
**Altitude:** 2,500 ft
**Location:** In southeastern part of state, on the Santa Cruz River
**County:** Seat of Pima Co.
**Churches:** Protestant, 181; Roman Catholic, 24; other, 136
**City-owned parks and parkways:** (2,001.75 ac.)
**Radio stations:** AM, 14; FM, 9
**Television stations:** 3 commercial; 1 educational; 3 other
**Assessed valuation (1985):** $1,351,873,867
**City tax rate (1985):** $.7566 per $100
**Net bonded debt (1985):** $65,147,141
**Revenue (1985):** $228,287,843
**Expenditures (1985):** $236,141,409
**Chamber of Commerce:** Tucson Chamber of Commerce, P.O. Box 991, Tucson, Ariz. 85702

# TULSA, OKLA.

**Incorporated as city:** 1898
**Mayor:** Dick Crawford (to May 1988)
**1980 population (1980 census) & (rank):** 360,919 (38)
**1985 est. population:** 386,000
**1984 est. rank:** (36)
**1985 land area:** 187.5 sq mi. (486 sq km)
**Altitude:** 674 ft
**Location:** In northeastern part of state, on Arkansas River
**County:** Seat of Tulsa Co.
**Churches:** Protestant, 593; Roman Catholic, 32; Jewish, 2; others, 4
**City parks and playgrounds:** 113 (5,050 ac.)
**Radio stations:** AM, 7; FM, 10
**Television stations:** 5 commercial; 1 PBS; 1 cable
**Assessed valuation (1985–86):** $1,481,692,604
**City tax rate (1985–86):** $80.47 per $1,000
**Bonded debt (July 1985):** $133,228,000
**Revenue (1984–85):** $293,381,000
**Expenditures (1984–85):** $282,240,000
**Chamber of Commerce:** Metropolitan Tulsa Chamber of Commerce, 616 S Boston, Tulsa, Okla. 74119

# VIRGINIA BEACH, VA.

**Incorporated as city:** 1963
**Mayor:** Robert Jones (to June 30, 1988)
**1980 population (1980 census) & (rank):** 262,199 (57)
**1986 est. population:** 343,200
**1984 est. rank:** (50)
**1986 land area:** 258.7 sq mi. (670 sq km)
**Altitude:** 12 ft
**Location:** Southeastern most portion of state, on Atlantic coastline
**County:** None
**Churches:** Protestant, 159; Catholic, 8; Jewish, 4
**City-owned parks:** 108 (1,406 ac.)
**Radio stations:** AM 18, FM 22
**Television stations:** 4 commercial, 1 PBS
**City tax rate (1984–1985):** $.8 per $100
**Bonded debt (1984–1985):** $291,565,000
**Revenue (1984–85):** 315,891,000
**Expenditures (1984–85):** $299,441,000
**Chamber of Commerce:** Virginia Beach Chamber of Commerce, Municipal Center, Virginia Beach, Va., 23456-9002

## WASHINGTON, D.C.

**Land ceded to Congress:** 1788 by Maryland; 1789 by Virginia (retroceded to Virginia Sept. 7, 1846)
**Seat of government transferred to D. C.:** Dec. 1, 1800
**Created municipal corporation:** Feb. 21, 1871
**Mayor:** Marion Barry, Jr. (to Jan. 1987)
**Motto:** *Justitia omnibus* (Justice to all)
**Flower:** American beauty rose
**Tree:** Scarlet oak
**Origin of name:** In honor of Columbus
**1980 population (1980 census) & (rank):** 638,432 (15)
**1984 est. population & (rank):** 622,823 (17)
**1984 land area:** 62.7 sq mi. (162 sq km)
**Geographic center:** Near corner of Fourth and L Sts., NW
**Altitude:** Highest, 420 ft; lowest, sea level
**Location:** Between Virginia and Maryland, on Potomac River
**Churches:** Protestant, 446; Roman Catholic, 23; Jewish, 10; others, 23
**City parks:** 753 (7,725 ac.)
**Radio stations:** AM, 15; FM, 16
**Television stations:** 6 (including 2 UHF stations)
**Assessed valuation (1986):** $24,887,897,678[1]
**City tax rate (1984–85):** $20.30 per $1,000 (hotels); $18.20 per $1,000 (commercial)
**Bonded debt: (Fiscal 1986):** $2,059,489,000
**Revenue (Fiscal 1987, est.):** $2,931,793,000
**Expenditures (Fiscal 1987, est.):** $2,931,793,000
**Chamber of Commerce:** D.C. Chamber of Commerce, 1319 F St., NW, Washington, D.C. 20004

1. On taxable property only. More than 50% of all land in District of Columbia is owned by the Federal government and tax-exempt organizations, and therefore is nontaxable.

The District of Columbia—identical with the City of Washington—is the capital of the United States and the first carefully planned capital in the world.

D.C. history began in 1790 when Congress directed selection of a new capital site, 10 miles square, along the Potomac. When the site was determined, it included 30.75 square miles on the Virginia side of the river. In 1846, however, Congress returned that area to Virginia.

The city was planned and partly laid out by Major Pierre Charles L. 'Enfant, a French engineer. This work was perfected and completed by Major Andrew Ellicott. In 1814, during the War of 1812, a British force fired the capital, and it was from the white paint applied to cover fire damage that the President's home was called the White House.

Until Nov. 3, 1967, the District of Columbia was administered by three commissioners appointed by the President. On that day, a government consisting of a mayor-commissioner and a 9-member Council, all appointed by the President with the approval of the Senate, took office. On May 7, 1974, the citizens of the District of Columbia approved the Home Rule Charter, giving them their first form of elected government in over 100 years. The District also has one non-voting member in the House of Representatives.

On Aug. 22, 1978, the Senate passed a proposed constitutional amendment to give Washington, D.C., voting representation in the Congress. The House had approved the legislation in the spring. The amendment had to be ratified by at least 28 state legislatures within seven years to become effective. As of 1985 it died.

## Population of 50 Largest U.S. Cities by Rank

### (Population estimates for July 1, 1984)

| City | Population | 1984 Rank | 1980 Rank | City | Population | 1984 Rank | 1980 Rank |
|---|---|---|---|---|---|---|---|
| New York, NY | 7,164,742 | 1 | 1 | El Paso, TX | 463,809 | 26 | 29 |
| Los Angeles, CA | 3,096,721 | 2 | 3 | Nashville–Davidson, TN | 462,450 | 27 | 26 |
| Chicago, IL | 2,992,472 | 3 | 2 | Oklahoma City, OK | 443,172 | 28 | 32 |
| Houston, TX | 1,705,697 | 4 | 5 | Kansas City, MO | 443,075 | 29 | 28 |
| Philadelphia, PA | 1,646,713 | 5 | 4 | St. Louis, MO | 429,296 | 30 | 27 |
| Detroit, MI | 1,088,973 | 6 | 6 | Atlanta, GA | 426,090 | 31 | 30 |
| Dallas, TX | 974,234 | 7 | 7 | Fort Worth, TX | 414,562 | 32 | 34 |
| San Diego, CA | 960,452 | 8 | 8 | Pittsburgh, PA | 402,583 | 33 | 31 |
| Phoenix, AZ[1] | 853,266 | 9 | 9 | Austin, TX | 397,001 | 34 | 42 |
| San Antonio, TX | 842,779 | 10 | 11 | Long Beach, CA | 378,752 | 35 | 37 |
| Honolulu, HI[2] | 805,266 | 11 | 12 | Tulsa, OK | 374,535 | 36 | 38 |
| Baltimore, MD | 763,570 | 12 | 10 | Miami, FL | 372,634 | 37 | 41 |
| San Francisco, CA | 712,753 | 13 | 14 | Cincinnati, OH | 370,481 | 38 | 33 |
| Indianapolis, IN | 710,280 | 14 | 13 | Baton Rouge, LA[3] | 368,571 | 39 | 43 |
| San Jose, CA | 686,178 | 15 | 18 | Portland, OR | 365,861 | 40 | 36 |
| Memphis, TN | 648,399 | 16 | 15 | Tucson, AZ[1] | 365,422 | 41 | 45 |
| Washington, DC | 622,823 | 17 | 16 | Minneapolis, MN | 358,335 | 42 | 35 |
| Milwaukee, WI | 620,811 | 18 | 17 | Oakland, CA | 351,898 | 43 | 44 |
| Jacksonville, FL | 577,971 | 19 | 23 | Albuquerque, NM | 350,575 | 44 | 46 |
| Boston, MA | 570,719 | 20 | 21 | Toledo, OH | 343,939 | 45 | 40 |
| Columbus, OH | 566,114 | 21 | 20 | Buffalo, NY | 338,982 | 46 | 39 |
| New Orleans, LA | 559,101 | 22 | 22 | Omaha, NE[1] | 332,237 | 47 | 48 |
| Cleveland, OH | 546,543 | 23 | 19 | Charlotte, NC | 330,838 | 48 | 49 |
| Denver, CO | 504,588 | 24 | 25 | Newark, NJ | 314,387 | 49 | 47 |
| Seattle, WA | 488,474 | 25 | 24 | Virginia Beach, VA | 308,664 | 50 | 57 |

*Source:* U.S. Department of Commerce, Bureau of the Census.

# Tabulated Data on City Governments

| City | Mayor Term, years | Mayor Salary[1] | City manager's salary[2] | Council or Commission Name | Members | Term, years | Salary[3] |
|---|---|---|---|---|---|---|---|
| Albuquerque, N.M. | 4 | $52,600 | 52,500[4] | Council | 9 | 4 | $5,260 |
| Atlanta | 4 | 50,000 | — | Council | 19 | 4 | 12,500 |
| Austin, Tex. | 3 | 26,000 | 100,000 | Council | 6 | 3 | 30,000 |
| Baltimore | 4 | 53,000 | — | Council | 19 | 4 | 23,000 |
| Baton Rouge, La. | 4 | 70,000 | — | Council | 12 | 4 | 3,600 |
| Boston | 4 | 65,000 | — | Council | 13 | 2 | 32,500 |
| Buffalo, N.Y. | 4 | 55,000 | — | Council | 13 | 2[5] | 25,000 |
| Charlotte, N.C. | 2 | 12,000 | 75,000 | Council | 11 | 2 | 6,000 |
| Chicago | 4 | 60,000 | — | Council | 50 | 4 | 27,600 |
| Cincinnati | 2 | 34,135 | 82,500 | Council | 9 | 2 | 30,635 |
| Cleveland | 4 | 62,956 | — | Council | 21 | 4 | 26,664 |
| Columbus, Ohio | 4 | 65,000 | — | Council | 7 | 4 | 15,000 |
| Dallas* | 2 | 50[6] | — | Council | 11 | 2 | 50[6] |
| Denver | 4 | 59,879 | — | Council | 13 | 4 | 21,890[22] |
| Detroit | 4 | 80,291 | — | Council | 9 | 4 | 43,585 |
| El Paso | 2 | 25,000 | — | Council | 7[7] | 2 | 15,000 |
| Fort Worth | 2 | 10[8] | 100,000 | Council | 9 | 2 | 10[8] |
| Honolulu | 4 | 75,000 | 70,305[9] | Council | 9 | 4 | 26,400[3] |
| Houston* | 2 | 81,560 | — | Council | 14 | 2 | 21,750 |
| Indianapolis | 4 | 70,500 | — | Council | 29 | 4 | 7,560[10] |
| Jacksonville, Fla. | 4 | 40,000 | — | Council | 19 | 4 | 18,000 |
| Kansas City, Mo. | 4 | 41,500 | 94,500 | Council | 13[7] | 4 | 14,000 |
| Long Beach, Calif.* | 2 | 1,000[12] | — | Council | 9[13] | 4 | 1,000[12] |
| Los Angeles | 4 | 88,778 | — | Council | 15 | 4 | 53,266 |
| Memphis, Tenn. | 4 | 60,000 | 57,000 | Council | 13 | 4 | 6,000 |
| Miami, Fla. | 2 | 5,000[14] | 92,000 | Commission | 5[7] | 4 | 5,000 |
| Milwaukee | 4 | 74,393 | — | Council | 16 | 4 | 31,391 |
| Minneapolis | 4 | 57,000 | 71,161 | Council | 13 | 4 | 42,000 |
| Nashville, Tenn. | 4 | 50,000 | — | Council | 41 | 4 | 5,400 |
| Newark, N.J. | 4 | 63,814 | 57,881[16] | Council | 9 | 4 | 29,780[24] |
| New Orleans | 4 | 75,905 | 76,404 | Council | 7 | 4 | 42,500 |
| New York | 4 | 110,000 | 85,500[15] | Council | 35 | 4 | 47,500 |
| Oakland, Calif. | 4 | 15,000 | 90,000 | Council | 9[7] | 4 | ([17]) |
| Oklahoma City | 4 | 2,000 | 75,000 | Council | 8 | 4 | 20[18] |
| Omaha, Neb. | 4 | 50,950 | — | Council | 7 | 4 | 13,650[3] |
| Philadelphia | 4 | 70,000 | 59,375[19] | Council | 17 | 4 | 40,000 |
| Phoenix, Ariz. | 2 | 37,500 | 112,000 | Council | 9[7] | 2 | 18,000 |
| Pittsburgh | 4 | 59,280 | — | Council | 9 | 4 | 33,800 |
| Portland, Ore.* | 4 | 60,656 | — | Commission | 4 | 4 | 48,630 |
| St. Louis | 4 | 71,266 | — | Board of Aldermen | 29 | 4 | 12,500 |
| San Antonio | 2 | 3,000[20] | 100,000 | Council | 11[7] | 2 | 20[21] |
| San Diego, Calif. | 4 | 50,000 | 95,000 | Council | 8 | 4 | 35,000 |
| San Francisco | 4 | 107,348 | 106,146 | Board of Supervisors | 11 | 4 | 23,928 |
| San Jose, Calif. | 4 | 35,000 | 95,129 | Council | 10 | 4 | 26,200 |
| Seattle | 4 | 80,762 | — | Council | 9 | 4 | 54,005 |
| Toledo, Ohio | 2 | 36,900 | 80,000 | Council | 9[13] | 2 | 7,800 |
| Tucson, Ariz. | 4 | 25,000 | 72,000 | Council | 7 | 4 | 12,000 |
| Tulsa, Okla. | 2 | 50,000 | — | Commission | 4 | 2 | 38,500 |
| Virginia Beach, Va. | 2 | 17,000 | 85,000[25] | Council | 11 | 4 | 15,000 |
| Washington, D.C. | 4 | 81,830 | 72,300 | Council | 13 | 4 | 47,475[23] |

1. Annual salary unless otherwise indicated. 2. Annual salary. City Manager's term is indefinite and at will of Council (or Mayor). 3. Annual salary unless otherwise indicated. In some cities, President of Council receives a higher salary. 4. City Administrative Officer appointed by Mayor, approved by Council. 5. For 9 District Councilmen; 4 years for 3 Councilmen-at-Large. 6. Per Council meeting; not over $2,600 per year. 7. Including Mayor. 8. Per week and per Council meeting. 9. Managing Director appointed by Mayor; no Council approval required. 10. Plus $40 per meeting for three meetings a month. 11. Chief Administrative Officer appointed by Mayor; not subject to Council confirmation. 12. Per month. 13. Including Mayor and Vice-Mayor. 14. Plus $2,500 expense account. 15. No City Manager; salary is for Deputy Mayor. 16. Business Administrator, appointed by Mayor and confirmed by Council. 17. Flat $500 per month, or $6,000 annually. 18. Per Council meeting; not to exceed 5 meetings a month. 19. Appointed by Mayor, with title of Managing Director. 20. Plus Council pay. 21. Per Council meeting; not over $1,040 per year. 22. Council President receives $28,992. 23. Council Chairman receives $57,475. 24. Annual allowance in lieu of expenses: Council members $10,000; Council President $11,500. 25. Plus $4,000 in travel expenses.
NOTE: An asterisk (*) indicates up-to-date information not provided. *Source: Information Please* questionnaires to the cities.

# U.S. STATISTICS

## Population
### Colonial Population Estimates (in round numbers)

| Year | Population | Year | Population | Year | Population | Year | Population |
|------|-----------|------|-----------|------|-----------|------|-----------|
| 1610 | 350 | 1660 | 75,100 | 1710 | 331,700 | 1760 | 1,593,600 |
| 1620 | 2,300 | 1670 | 111,900 | 1720 | 466,200 | 1770 | 2,148,100 |
| 1630 | 4,600 | 1680 | 151,500 | 1730 | 629,400 | 1780 | 2,780,400 |
| 1640 | 26,600 | 1690 | 210,400 | 1740 | 905,600 | | |
| 1650 | 50,400 | 1700 | 250,900 | 1750 | 1,170,800 | | |

### National Censuses[1]

| Year | Resident population[2] | Land area, sq mi. | Pop. per sq mi. | Year | Resident population[2] | Land area, sq mi. | Pop. per sq mi. |
|------|-----------|------|------|------|-----------|------|------|
| 1790 | 3,929,214 | 864,746 | 4.5 | 1890 | 62,947,714 | 2,969,640 | 21.2 |
| 1800 | 5,308,483 | 864,746 | 6.1 | 1900 | 75,994,575 | 2,969,834 | 25.6 |
| 1810 | 7,239,881 | 1,681,828 | 4.3 | 1910 | 91,972,266 | 2,969,565 | 31.0 |
| 1820 | 9,638,453 | 1,749,462 | 5.5 | 1920 | 105,710,620 | 2,969,451 | 35.6 |
| 1830 | 12,866,020 | 1,749,462 | 7.4 | 1930 | 122,775,046 | 2,977,128 | 41.2 |
| 1840 | 17,069,453 | 1,749,462 | 9.8 | 1940 | 131,669,275 | 2,977,128 | 44.2 |
| 1850 | 23,191,876 | 2,940,042 | 7.9 | 1950 | 150,697,361 | 2,974,726 | 50.7 |
| 1860 | 31,443,321 | 2,969,640 | 10.6 | 1960 | 179,323,175 | 3,540,911 | 50.6 |
| 1870 | 39,818,449 | 2,969,640 | 13.4 | 1970 | 203,302,031 | 3,540,023 | 57.4 |
| 1880 | 50,155,783 | 2,969,640 | 16.9 | 1980 | 226,545,805 | 3,618,770 | 62.6 |

1. Beginning with 1960, figures include Alaska and Hawaii. 2. Excludes armed forces overseas. NOTE: n.a. = not available.
*Source:* Department of Commerce, Bureau of the Census.

## Population Distribution by Age, Race, Nativity, and Sex

| Year | Total | Under 5 | 5–19 | 20–44 | 45–62 | 65 and over | Total | Native born | Foreign born | Black | Other races[1] |
|------|-------|---------|------|-------|-------|-------------|-------|-------------|--------------|-------|----------------|
| | | | Age | | | | White[1] (Race and nativity) | | | | |
| **PERCENT DISTRIBUTION** | | | | | | | | | | | |
| 1860[2] | 100.0 | 15.4 | 35.8 | 35.7 | 10.4 | 2.7 | 85.6 | 72.6 | 13.0 | 14.1 | 0.3 |
| 1870[2] | 100.0 | 14.3 | 35.4 | 35.4 | 11.9 | 3.0 | 87.1 | 72.9 | 14.2 | 12.7 | 0.2 |
| 1880[2] | 100.0 | 13.8 | 34.3 | 35.9 | 12.6 | 3.4 | 86.5 | 73.4 | 13.1 | 13.1 | 0.3 |
| 1890[3] | 100.0 | 12.2 | 33.9 | 36.9 | 13.1 | 3.9 | 87.5 | 73.0 | 14.5 | 11.9 | 0.3 |
| 1900 | 100.0 | 12.1 | 32.3 | 37.7 | 13.7 | 4.1 | 87.9 | 74.5 | 13.4 | 11.6 | 0.5 |
| 1910 | 100.0 | 11.6 | 30.4 | 39.0 | 14.6 | 4.3 | 88.9 | 74.4 | 14.5 | 10.7 | 0.4 |
| 1920 | 100.0 | 10.9 | 29.8 | 38.4 | 16.1 | 4.7 | 89.7 | 76.7 | 13.0 | 9.9 | 0.4 |
| 1930 | 100.0 | 9.3 | 29.5 | 38.3 | 17.4 | 5.4 | 89.8 | 78.4 | 11.4 | 9.7 | 0.5 |
| 1940 | 100.0 | 8.0 | 26.4 | 38.9 | 19.8 | 6.8 | 89.8 | 81.1 | 8.7 | 9.8 | 0.4 |
| 1950 | 100.0 | 10.7 | 23.2 | 37.6 | 20.3 | 8.1 | 89.5 | 82.8 | 6.7 | 10.0 | 0.5 |
| 1960 | 100.0 | 11.3 | 27.1 | 32.2 | 20.1 | 9.2 | 88.6 | 83.4 | 5.2 | 10.5 | 0.9 |
| 1970[2] | 100.0 | 8.4 | 29.5 | 31.7 | 20.6 | 9.8 | 87.6 | 83.4 | 4.3 | 11.1 | 1.4 |
| 1980 | 100.0 | 7.2 | 24.8 | 37.1 | 19.6 | 11.3 | 83.1 | n.a. | n.a. | 11.7 | 5.2 |
| **MALES PER 100 FEMALES** | | | | | | | | | | | |
| 1860[2] | 104.7 | 102.4 | 101.2 | 107.9 | 111.5 | 98.3 | 105.3 | 103.7 | 115.1 | 99.6 | 260.8 |
| 1870[2] | 102.2 | 102.9 | 101.2 | 99.2 | 114.5 | 100.5 | 102.8 | 100.6 | 115.3 | 96.2 | 400.7 |
| 1880[2] | 103.6 | 103.0 | 101.3 | 104.0 | 110.2 | 101.4 | 104.0 | 102.1 | 115.9 | 97.8 | 362.2 |
| 1890[3] | 105.0 | 103.6 | 101.4 | 107.3 | 108.3 | 104.2 | 105.4 | 102.9 | 118.7 | 99.5 | 165.2 |
| 1900 | 104.4 | 102.1 | 100.9 | 105.8 | 110.7 | 102.0 | 104.9 | 102.8 | 117.4 | 98.6 | 185.2 |
| 1910 | 106.0 | 102.5 | 101.3 | 108.1 | 114.4 | 101.1 | 106.6 | 102.7 | 129.2 | 98.9 | 185.6 |
| 1920 | 104.0 | 102.5 | 100.8 | 102.8 | 115.2 | 101.3 | 104.4 | 101.7 | 121.7 | 99.2 | 156.6 |
| 1930 | 102.5 | 103.0 | 101.4 | 100.5 | 109.1 | 100.5 | 102.9 | 101.1 | 115.8 | 97.0 | 150.6 |
| 1940 | 100.7 | 103.2 | 102.0 | 98.1 | 105.2 | 95.5 | 101.2 | 100.1 | 111.1 | 95.0 | 140.5 |

| | | | Age | | | | Race and nativity | | | |
|---|---|---|---|---|---|---|---|---|---|---|
| | | | | | | | White[1] | | | |
| Year | Total | Under 5 | 5–19 | 20–44 | 45–62 | 65 and over | Total | Native born | Foreign born | Black | Other races[1] |
| 1950 | 98.6 | 103.9 | 102.5 | 96.2 | 100.1 | 89.6 | 99.0 | 98.8 | 102.0 | 93.7 | 129.7 |
| 1960 | 97.1 | 103.4 | 102.7 | 95.6 | 95.7 | 82.8 | 97.4 | 97.6 | 94.2 | 93.3 | 109.7 |
| 1970[2] | 94.8 | 104.0 | 103.3 | 95.1 | 91.6 | 72.1 | 95.3 | 95.9 | 83.8 | 90.8 | 100.2 |
| 1980 | 94.5 | 104.7 | 104.0 | 98.1 | 90.7 | 67.6 | 94.8 | n.a. | n.a. | 89.6 | 100.3 |

1. The 1980 census data for white and other races categories are not directly comparable to those shown for the preceding years because of the changes in the way some persons reported their race, as well as changes in 1980 procedures relating to racial classification. 2. Excludes persons for whom age is not available. 3. Excludes persons enumerated in the Indian Territory and on Indian reservations. NOTES: Data exclude Armed Forces overseas. Beginning in 1960, includes Alaska and Hawaii, n.a. = not available. *Source:* Department of Commerce, Bureau of the Census.

## Population and Rank of Large Metropolitan Areas, 1970–1980
### (over 150,000)

| Standard metropolitan statistical area | 1980 Census | | 1970 Census | | Change, 1970–80 | |
|---|---|---|---|---|---|---|
| | Number | Rank | Number | Rank | Number | % |
| Akron, Ohio | 660,328 | 57 | 679,239 | 52 | −18,911 | −2.7 |
| Albany–Schenectady–Troy, N.Y. | 795,019 | 50 | 777,977 | 43 | 17,042 | 2.2 |
| Albuquerque, N.M. | 454,499 | 86 | 333,266 | 102 | 121,233 | 36.4 |
| Alexandria, La. | 151,985 | 205 | 131,749 | 203 | 20,236 | 15.4 |
| Allentown–Bethlehem–Easton, Pa.-N.J. | 636,714 | 62 | 594,382 | 60 | 42,332 | 7.2 |
| Amarillo, Tex. | 173,699 | 188 | 144,396 | 192 | 29,303 | 20.3 |
| Anaheim–Santa Ana–Garden Grove, Calif. | 1,931,570 | 18 | 1,421,233 | 20 | 510,337 | 36.0 |
| Anchorage, Alaska | 173,017 | 191 | 126,385 | 211 | 46,632 | 36.9 |
| Ann Arbor, Mich. | 264,748 | 145 | 234,103 | 141 | 30,645 | 13.1 |
| Appleton–Oshkosh, Wis. | 291,325 | 129 | 276,948 | 121 | 14,377 | 5.2 |
| Asheville, N.C. | 177,761 | 184 | 161,059 | 181 | 16,702 | 10.4 |
| Atlanta | 2,029,618 | 16 | 1,595,517 | 18 | 434,101 | 27.3 |
| Atlantic City, N.J. | 194,119 | 171 | 175,043 | 168 | 19,076 | 10.9 |
| Augusta, Ga.-S.C. | 327,372 | 113 | 275,787 | 122 | 51,585 | 18.8 |
| Austin, Tex. | 536,450 | 70 | 360,463 | 93 | 175,987 | 48.9 |
| Bakersfield, Calif. | 403,089 | 97 | 330,234 | 104 | 72,855 | 22.1 |
| Baltimore | 2,174,023 | 14 | 2,071,016 | 13 | 103,007 | 5.0 |
| Baton Rouge, La. | 493,973 | 80 | 375,628 | 87 | 118,345 | 31.6 |
| Battle Creek, Mich. | 187,338 | 177 | 180,129 | 164 | 7,209 | 4.1 |
| Beaumont–Port Arthur, Tex. | 375,497 | 104 | 347,568 | 97 | 27,929 | 8.1 |
| Biloxi–Gulfport, Miss. | 191,918 | 174 | 160,070 | 183 | 31,848 | 19.9 |
| Binghamton, N.Y.-Pa. | 301,336 | 126 | 302,672 | 111 | −1,336 | −0.4 |
| Birmingham, Ala. | 847,360 | 45 | 767,230 | 44 | 80,130 | 10.5 |
| Boise, Idaho | 173,036 | 190 | 112,230 | 232 | 60,806 | 54.2 |
| Boston | 2,763,357 | 10 | 2,899,101 | 8 | −135,744 | −4.6 |
| Bridgeport, Conn. | 395,455 | 98 | 401,752 | 82 | −6,297 | −1.5 |
| Brockton, Mass. | 169,374 | 196 | 150,416 | 186 | 18,958 | 12.7 |
| Brownsville–Harlingen–San Benito, Tex. | 209,680 | 164 | 140,368 | 194 | 69,312 | 49.4 |
| Buffalo, N.Y. | 1,242,573 | 31 | 1,349,211 | 24 | −106,638 | −7.9 |
| Canton, Ohio | 404,421 | 96 | 393,789 | 83 | 10,632 | 2.7 |
| Cedar Rapids, Iowa | 169,775 | 194 | 163,213 | 179 | 6,562 | 4.1 |
| Champaign–Urbana–Rantoul, Ill. | 168,392 | 197 | 163,281 | 178 | 5,111 | 3.2 |
| Charleston–North Charleston, S.C. | 430,301 | 91 | 336,036 | 100 | 94,265 | 28.1 |
| Charleston, W. Va. | 269,595 | 142 | 257,140 | 133 | 12,455 | 4.9 |
| Charlotte–Gastonia, N.C. | 637,218 | 61 | 557,785 | 62 | 79,433 | 14.3 |
| Chattanooga, Tenn.-Ga. | 426,540 | 92 | 370,857 | 90 | 55,683 | 15.1 |
| Chicago | 7,102,328 | 3 | 6,974,755 | 3 | 127,573 | 1.9 |
| Cincinnati, Ohio-Ky.-Ind. | 1,401,403 | 27 | 1,387,207 | 22 | 14,196 | 1.1 |
| Clarksville–Hopkinsville, Tenn.-Ky. | 150,220 | 209 | 118,945 | 220 | 31,275 | 26.3 |
| Cleveland | 1,898,720 | 19 | 2,063,729 | 14 | −165,009 | −7.9 |
| Colorado Springs, Colo. | 317,458 | 120 | 239,288 | 139 | 78,170 | 32.7 |
| Columbia, S.C. | 408,176 | 95 | 322,880 | 107 | 85,296 | 26.5 |
| Columbus, Ga.-Ala. | 239,196 | 154 | 238,584 | 140 | 612 | 0.3 |
| Columbus, Ohio | 1,093,293 | 35 | 1,017,847 | 33 | 75,446 | 7.5 |
| Corpus Christi, Tex. | 326,228 | 114 | 284,832 | 118 | 41,396 | 14.6 |

| Standard metropolitan statistical area | 1980 Census Number | 1980 Census Rank | 1970 Census Number | 1970 Census Rank | Change, 1970-80 Number | Change, 1970-80 % |
|---|---|---|---|---|---|---|
| Dallas-Fort Worth | 2,974,878 | 8 | 2,377,623 | 12 | 597,255 | 25.2 |
| Davenport-Rock Island-Moline, Iowa-Ill. | 383,958 | 100 | 362,638 | 91 | 21,320 | 5.9 |
| Dayton, Ohio | 830,070 | 47 | 852,531 | 40 | −22,461 | −2.6 |
| Daytona Beach, Fla. | 258,762 | 148 | 169,487 | 174 | 89,275 | 52.7 |
| Denver-Boulder, Colo. | 1,619,921 | 22 | 1,239,545 | 27 | 380,376 | 30.7 |
| Des Moines, Iowa | 338,048 | 111 | 313,562 | 109 | 24,486 | 7.9 |
| Detroit | 4,352,762 | 5 | 4,435,051 | 5 | −82,289 | −1.8 |
| Duluth-Superior, Minn.-Wis. | 266,650 | 143 | 265,350 | 126 | 1,300 | 0.5 |
| El Paso | 479,899 | 82 | 359,291 | 94 | 120,608 | 33.6 |
| Erie, Pa. | 279,780 | 135 | 263,654 | 128 | 16,126 | 6.2 |
| Eugene-Springfield, Ore. | 275,226 | 138 | 215,401 | 151 | 59,825 | 27.8 |
| Evansville, Ind.-Ky. | 309,408 | 123 | 284,959 | 117 | 24,449 | 8.6 |
| Fall River, Mass.-R.I. | 176,831 | 185 | 169,549 | 173 | 7,282 | 4.3 |
| Fayetteville-Springdale, Ark. | 177,850 | 183 | 127,846 | 208 | 50,004 | 39.2 |
| Fayetteville, N.C. | 247,160 | 152 | 212,042 | 152 | 35,118 | 16.6 |
| Flint, Mich. | 521,589 | 77 | 508,664 | 69 | 12,925 | 2.6 |
| Fort Lauderdale-Hollywood, Fla. | 1,014,043 | 37 | 620,100 | 58 | 393,943 | 63.6 |
| Fort Myers-Cape Coral, Fla. | 205,266 | 166 | 105,216 | 238 | 100,050 | 95.1 |
| Fort Smith, Ark.-Okla. | 203,269 | 167 | 160,421 | 182 | 42,848 | 26.8 |
| Fort Wayne, Ind. | 382,961 | 101 | 361,984 | 92 | 20,977 | 5.8 |
| Fresno, Calif. | 515,013 | 78 | 413,329 | 77 | 101,684 | 24.7 |
| Gainesville, Fla. | 151,348 | 208 | 104,764 | 239 | 46,584 | 44.5 |
| Galveston-Texas City, Tex. | 195,940 | 170 | 169,812 | 172 | 26,128 | 15.4 |
| Gary-Hammond-East Chicago, Ind. | 642,781 | 58 | 633,367 | 54 | 9,414 | 1.5 |
| Grand Rapids, Mich. | 601,680 | 64 | 539,225 | 67 | 62,455 | 11.6 |
| Green Bay, Wis. | 175,280 | 187 | 158,244 | 185 | 17,036 | 10.8 |
| Greensboro-Winston-Salem-High Point, N.C. | 827,385 | 48 | 724,129 | 47 | 103,256 | 14.3 |
| Greenville-Spartanburg, S.C. | 568,758 | 68 | 473,454 | 71 | 95,304 | 20.2 |
| Hamilton-Middletown, Ohio | 258,787 | 147 | 226,207 | 145 | 32,580 | 14.5 |
| Harrisburg, Pa. | 446,072 | 88 | 410,505 | 80 | 35,567 | 8.7 |
| Hartford, Conn. | 726,114 | 54 | 720,581 | 48 | 5,533 | 0.8 |
| Honolulu | 762,874 | 52 | 630,528 | 55 | 132,346 | 21.0 |
| Houston | 2,905,350 | 9 | 1,999,316 | 16 | 906,034 | 45.4 |
| Huntington-Ashland, W. Va.-Ky.-Ohio | 311,350 | 122 | 286,935 | 116 | 24,415 | 8.6 |
| Huntsville, Ala. | 308,593 | 124 | 282,450 | 119 | 26,143 | 9.3 |
| Indianapolis | 1,166,929 | 34 | 1,111,352 | 29 | 55,577 | 5.1 |
| Jackson, Mich. | 151,495 | 207 | 143,274 | 193 | 8,221 | 5.8 |
| Jackson, Miss. | 320,425 | 117 | 258,906 | 130 | 61,519 | 23.8 |
| Jacksonville, Fla. | 737,519 | 53 | 621,827 | 57 | 115,692 | 18.7 |
| Jersey City, N.J. | 556,972 | 69 | 607,839 | 59 | −50,867 | −8.3 |
| Johnson City-Kingsport-Bristol, Tenn.-Va. | 433,638 | 90 | 373,591 | 88 | 60,047 | 16.1 |
| Johnstown, Pa. | 264,506 | 146 | 262,822 | 129 | 1,684 | 0.7 |
| Kalamazoo-Portage, Mich. | 279,192 | 137 | 257,723 | 132 | 21,469 | 8.4 |
| Kansas City, Mo.-Kan. | 1,327,020 | 29 | 1,273,926 | 25 | 53,094 | 4.2 |
| Killeen-Temple, Tex. | 214,656 | 162 | 159,794 | 184 | 54,862 | 34.4 |
| Knoxville, Tenn. | 476,517 | 83 | 409,409 | 81 | 67,108 | 16.4 |
| Lafayette, La. | 150,017 | 210 | 111,643 | 233 | 38,374 | 34.4 |
| Lake Charles, La. | 167,048 | 198 | 145,415 | 189 | 21,633 | 14.9 |
| Lakeland-Winter Haven, Fla. | 321,652 | 116 | 228,515 | 143 | 93,137 | 40.8 |
| Lancaster, Pa. | 362,346 | 108 | 320,079 | 108 | 42,267 | 13.3 |
| Lansing-East Lansing, Mich. | 468,482 | 84 | 424,271 | 75 | 44,211 | 10.5 |
| Las Vegas, Nev. | 461,816 | 85 | 273,288 | 123 | 188,528 | 69.0 |
| Lawrence-Haverhill, Mass.-N.H. | 281,981 | 133 | 258,564 | 131 | 23,417 | 9.1 |
| Lexington-Fayette, Ky. | 318,136 | 119 | 266,701 | 125 | 51,435 | 19.3 |
| Lima, Ohio | 218,244 | 160 | 210,074 | 153 | 8,170 | 3.9 |
| Lincoln, Neb. | 192,884 | 173 | 167,972 | 176 | 24,912 | 14.9 |
| Little Rock-North Little Rock, Ark. | 393,494 | 99 | 323,296 | 106 | 70,198 | 21.8 |
| Long Branch-Asbury Park, N.J. | 503,173 | 79 | 461,849 | 72 | 41,324 | 9.0 |
| Longview-Marshall, Tex. | 151,752 | 206 | 120,770 | 217 | 30,982 | 25.7 |
| Lorain-Elyria, Ohio | 274,909 | 139 | 256,843 | 134 | 18,066 | 7.1 |
| Los Angeles-Long Beach, Calif. | 7,477,657 | 2 | 7,041,980 | 2 | 435,677 | 6.2 |
| Louisville, Ky.-Ind. | 906,240 | 43 | 867,330 | 39 | 38,910 | 4.5 |
| Lowell, Mass.-N.H. | 233,410 | 155 | 218,268 | 149 | 15,142 | 7.0 |
| Lubbock, Tex. | 211,651 | 163 | 179,295 | 165 | 32,356 | 18.1 |
| Lynchburg, Va. | 153,260 | 204 | 134,744 | 198 | 18,516 | 13.8 |
| Macon, Ga. | 254,623 | 149 | 226,782 | 144 | 27,841 | 12.3 |
| Madison, Wis. | 323,545 | 115 | 290,272 | 114 | 33,273 | 11.5 |
| Manchester, N.H. | 160,767 | 202 | 132,512 | 201 | 28,255 | 21.4 |
| McAllen-Pharr-Edinburg, Tex. | 283,229 | 132 | 181,535 | 162 | 101,694 | 56.1 |

| Standard metropolitan statistical area | 1980 Census Number | 1980 Census Rank | 1970 Census Number | 1970 Census Rank | Change, 1970–80 Number | Change, 1970–80 % |
|---|---|---|---|---|---|---|
| Melbourne-Titusville-Cocoa, Fla. | 272,959 | 140 | 230,006 | 142 | 42,953 | 18.7 |
| Memphis, Tenn.-Ark.-Miss. | 912,887 | 42 | 834,103 | 41 | 78,784 | 9.5 |
| Miami, Fla. | 1,625,979 | 21 | 1,267,792 | 26 | 358,187 | 28.3 |
| Milwaukee | 1,397,143 | 28 | 1,403,884 | 21 | −6,741 | −0.4 |
| Minneapolis-St. Paul | 2,114,256 | 15 | 1,965,391 | 17 | 148,865 | 7.6 |
| Mobile, Ala. | 442,819 | 89 | 376,690 | 86 | 66,129 | 17.6 |
| Modesto, Calif. | 265,902 | 144 | 194,506 | 158 | 71,396 | 36.8 |
| Montgomery, Ala. | 272,687 | 141 | 225,911 | 146 | 46,776 | 20.8 |
| Muskegon-Norton Shores-Muskegon Heights, Mich. | 179,591 | 182 | 175,410 | 166 | 4,181 | 2.4 |
| Nashville-Davidson, Tenn. | 850,505 | 44 | 699,271 | 50 | 151,234 | 21.7 |
| Nassau-Suffolk, N.Y. | 2,605,813 | 11 | 2,555,868 | 9 | 49,945 | 2.0 |
| Newark, N.J. | 1,965,304 | 17 | 2,057,468 | 15 | −92,164 | −4.4 |
| New Bedford, Mass. | 169,425 | 195 | 161,288 | 180 | 8,137 | 5.1 |
| New Brunswick-Perth Amboy-Sayreville, N.J. | 595,893 | 65 | 583,813 | 61 | 12,080 | 2.1 |
| New Haven-West Haven, Conn. | 417,592 | 93 | 411,287 | 79 | 6,305 | 1.6 |
| New London-Norwich, Conn.-R.I. | 248,554 | 151 | 241,862 | 138 | 6,692 | 2.8 |
| New Orleans | 1,186,725 | 33 | 1,046,470 | 32 | 140,255 | 13.5 |
| Newport News-Hampton, Va. | 364,449 | 107 | 333,140 | 103 | 31,309 | 9.4 |
| New York, N.Y.-N.J. | 9,119,737 | 1 | 9,973,716 | 1 | −853,979 | −8.5 |
| Norfolk-Virginia Beach-Portsmouth, Va.-N.C. | 806,691 | 49 | 732,600 | 46 | 74,091 | 10.2 |
| Northeast Pennsylvania | 640,396 | 60 | 621,882 | 56 | 18,514 | 3.0 |
| Oklahoma City | 834,088 | 46 | 699,092 | 51 | 134,996 | 19.4 |
| Omaha, Neb.-Iowa | 570,399 | 67 | 542,646 | 65 | 27,753 | 5.2 |
| Orlando, Fla. | 700,699 | 55 | 453,270 | 74 | 247,429 | 54.6 |
| Oxnard-Simi Valley-Ventura, Calif. | 529,899 | 75 | 378,497 | 85 | 151,402 | 40.1 |
| Parkersburg-Marietta, W. Va.-Ohio | 162,836 | 201 | 148,132 | 187 | 14,704 | 10.0 |
| Paterson-Clifton-Passaic, N.J. | 447,585 | 87 | 460,782 | 73 | −13,197 | −2.8 |
| Pensacola, Fla. | 289,782 | 131 | 243,075 | 137 | 46,707 | 19.3 |
| Peoria, Ill. | 365,864 | 106 | 341,979 | 98 | 23,885 | 7.0 |
| Philadelphia, Pa.-N.J. | 4,716,818 | 4 | 4,824,110 | 4 | −107,292 | −2.2 |
| Phoenix, Ariz. | 1,508,030 | 26 | 971,228 | 35 | 536,802 | 55.3 |
| Pittsburgh | 2,263,894 | 13 | 2,401,362 | 11 | −137,468 | −5.7 |
| Portland, Me. | 183,625 | 181 | 170,081 | 171 | 13,544 | 8.0 |
| Portland, Ore.-Wash. | 1,242,187 | 32 | 1,007,131 | 34 | 235,057 | 23.4 |
| Poughkeepsie, N.Y. | 245,055 | 153 | 222,295 | 147 | 22,760 | 10.3 |
| Providence-Warwick-Pawtucket, R.I.-Mass. | 919,216 | 41 | 908,887 | 37 | 10,329 | 1.2 |
| Provo-Orem, Utah | 218,106 | 161 | 137,776 | 196 | 80,330 | 58.4 |
| Racine, Wis. | 173,132 | 189 | 170,838 | 170 | 2,294 | 1.4 |
| Raleigh-Durham, N.C. | 530,673 | 73 | 419,254 | 76 | 111,419 | 26.6 |
| Reading, Pa. | 312,509 | 121 | 296,382 | 112 | 16,127 | 5.5 |
| Reno, Nev. | 193,623 | 172 | 121,068 | 216 | 72,555 | 60.0 |
| Richmond, Va. | 632,015 | 63 | 547,542 | 64 | 84,473 | 15.5 |
| Riverside-San Bernardino-Ontario, Calif. | 1,557,080 | 25 | 1,139,149 | 28 | 417,931 | 36.7 |
| Roanoke, Va. | 224,548 | 159 | 203,153 | 157 | 21,395 | 10.6 |
| Rochester, N.Y. | 971,879 | 39 | 961,516 | 36 | 10,363 | 1.1 |
| Rockford, Ill. | 279,514 | 136 | 272,063 | 124 | 7,451 | 2.8 |
| Sacramento, Calif. | 1,014,002 | 38 | 803,793 | 42 | 210,209 | 26.2 |
| Saginaw, Mich. | 228,059 | 158 | 219,743 | 148 | 8,316 | 3.8 |
| St. Cloud, Minn. | 163,256 | 199 | 134,585 | 199 | 28,671 | 21.4 |
| St. Louis, Mo.-Ill. | 2,355,276 | 12 | 2,410,884 | 10 | −55,608 | −2.3 |
| Salem, Ore. | 249,895 | 150 | 186,658 | 160 | 63,237 | 33.9 |
| Salinas-Seaside-Monterey-Calif. | 290,444 | 130 | 247,450 | 136 | 42,994 | 17.4 |
| Salt Lake City-Ogden, Utah | 936,255 | 40 | 705,458 | 49 | 230,797 | 32.8 |
| San Antonio | 1,071,954 | 36 | 888,179 | 38 | 183,775 | 20.7 |
| San Diego, Calif. | 1,861,846 | 20 | 1,357,854 | 23 | 503,992 | 37.2 |
| San Francisco-Oakland, Calif. | 3,252,721 | 6 | 3,109,249 | 6 | 143,472 | 4.7 |
| San Jose, Calif. | 1,295,071 | 30 | 1,065,313 | 31 | 229,758 | 21.6 |
| Santa Barbara-Santa Maria-Lompoc, Calif. | 298,660 | 128 | 264,324 | 127 | 34,336 | 13.0 |
| Santa Cruz, Calif. | 188,141 | 175 | 123,790 | 213 | 64,351 | 52.0 |
| Santa Rosa, Calif. | 299,827 | 127 | 204,885 | 156 | 94,942 | 46.4 |
| Sarasota, Fla. | 202,251 | 168 | 120,413 | 218 | 81,838 | 68.0 |
| Savannah, Ga. | 230,728 | 156 | 207,987 | 154 | 22,741 | 11.0 |
| Seattle-Everett, Wash. | 1,606,765 | 23 | 1,424,605 | 19 | 182,160 | 12.8 |
| Shreveport, La. | 376,646 | 103 | 336,000 | 101 | 40,646 | 12.1 |
| South Bend, Ind. | 280,772 | 134 | 279,813 | 120 | 959 | 0.4 |
| Spokane, Wash. | 341,835 | 110 | 287,487 | 115 | 54,348 | 19.0 |
| Springfield, Ill. | 187,789 | 176 | 171,020 | 169 | 16,769 | 9.9 |

| Standard metropolitan statistical area | 1980 Census Number | Rank | 1970 Census Number | Rank | Change, 1970–80 Number | % |
|---|---|---|---|---|---|---|
| Springfield-Chicopee-Holyoke, Mass.-Conn. | 530,668 | 74 | 541,752 | 66 | −11,084 | −2.0 |
| Springfield, Mo. | 207,704 | 165 | 168,053 | 175 | 39,651 | 23.6 |
| Springfield, Ohio | 183,885 | 180 | 187,606 | 159 | −3,721 | −1.9 |
| Stamford, Conn. | 198,854 | 169 | 206,340 | 155 | −7,486 | −3.6 |
| Steubenville-Weirton, Ohio-W. Va. | 163,099 | 200 | 166,385 | 177 | −3,286 | −1.9 |
| Stockton, Calif. | 347,342 | 109 | 291,073 | 113 | 56,269 | 19.4 |
| Syracuse, N.Y. | 642,375 | 59 | 636,596 | 53 | 5,779 | 1.0 |
| Tacoma, Wash. | 485,643 | 81 | 412,344 | 78 | 73,299 | 17.8 |
| Tallahassee, Fla. | 159,542 | 203 | 109,355 | 235 | 50,187 | 45.9 |
| Tampa-St. Petersburg, Fla. | 1,569,492 | 24 | 1,088,549 | 30 | 480,943 | 44.2 |
| Terre Haute, Ind. | 176,583 | 186 | 175,143 | 167 | 1,440 | 0.9 |
| Toledo, Ohio-Mich. | 791,599 | 51 | 762,658 | 45 | 28,941 | 3.8 |
| Topeka, Kan. | 185,442 | 179 | 180,619 | 163 | 4,823 | 2.7 |
| Trenton, N.J. | 307,863 | 125 | 304,116 | 110 | 3,747 | 1.3 |
| Tucson, Ariz. | 531,263 | 72 | 351,667 | 95 | 179,596 | 51.1 |
| Tulsa, Okla. | 689,628 | 56 | 549,154 | 63 | 140,474 | 25.6 |
| Utica-Rome, N.Y. | 320,180 | 118 | 340,477 | 99 | −20,297 | −5.9 |
| Vallejo-Fairfield-Napa, Calif. | 334,402 | 112 | 251,129 | 135 | 83,273 | 33.2 |
| Waco, Tex. | 170,755 | 193 | 147,553 | 188 | 23,202 | 15.8 |
| Washington, D.C.-Md.-Va. | 3,060,240 | 7 | 2,910,111 | 7 | 150,129 | 5.2 |
| Waterbury, Conn. | 228,178 | 157 | 216,808 | 150 | 11,370 | 5.3 |
| West Palm Beach-Boca Raton, Fla. | 573,125 | 66 | 348,993 | 96 | 224,132 | 64.3 |
| Wheeling, W. Va.-Ohio | 185,566 | 178 | 181,954 | 161 | 3,612 | 2.0 |
| Wichita, Kan. | 411,313 | 94 | 389,352 | 84 | 21,961 | 5.7 |
| Wilmington, Del.-N.J.-Md. | 524,108 | 76 | 499,493 | 70 | 24,615 | 5.0 |
| Worcester, Mass. | 372,940 | 105 | 372,144 | 89 | 796 | 0.3 |
| Yakima, Wash. | 172,508 | 192 | 145,212 | 191 | 27,296 | 18.8 |
| York, Pa. | 381,255 | 102 | 329,540 | 105 | 51,715 | 15.7 |
| Youngstown-Warren, Ohio | 531,350 | 71 | 537,124 | 68 | −5,774 | −1.0 |

NOTE: The general concept of a standard metropolitan statistical area (SMSA) is one of a large population nucleus together with adjacent communities that have a high degree of economic and social integration with that nucleus. *Source:* Department of Commerce, Bureau of the Census.

## Population by Age, Sex, Race, and Spanish Origin, 1980
### (in thousands)

| Age | White Male | Female | Black Male | Female | Spanish origin Male | Female | Other races Male | Female | All persons Male | Female |
|---|---|---|---|---|---|---|---|---|---|---|
| Under 5 | 7,509 | 7,127 | 1,370 | 1,335 | 983 | 940 | 351 | 344 | 9,230 | 8,806 |
| 5-9 | 6,990 | 6,631 | 1,314 | 1,283 | 922 | 886 | 304 | 299 | 8,608 | 8,213 |
| 10-14 | 7,100 | 6,730 | 1,346 | 1,309 | 851 | 821 | 317 | 301 | 8,762 | 8,340 |
| 15-19 | 7,746 | 7,448 | 1,391 | 1,378 | 834 | 805 | 307 | 280 | 9,445 | 9,107 |
| 20-24 | 8,815 | 8,696 | 1,369 | 1,473 | 999 | 913 | 331 | 310 | 10,515 | 10,479 |
| 25-29 | 9,250 | 9,067 | 1,301 | 1,448 | 999 | 900 | 336 | 350 | 10,886 | 10,865 |
| 30-34 | 8,636 | 8,522 | 1,121 | 1,287 | 800 | 759 | 340 | 361 | 10,096 | 10,171 |
| 35-39 | 7,608 | 7,635 | 862 | 1,027 | 609 | 616 | 272 | 304 | 8,741 | 8,967 |
| 40-44 | 6,023 | 6,144 | 653 | 789 | 446 | 469 | 212 | 233 | 6,889 | 7,166 |
| 45-49 | 4,946 | 5,099 | 563 | 692 | 361 | 386 | 169 | 177 | 5,679 | 5,969 |
| 50-54 | 4,637 | 4,872 | 514 | 634 | 306 | 332 | 131 | 154 | 5,281 | 5,660 |
| 55-59 | 4,771 | 5,219 | 500 | 601 | 269 | 301 | 108 | 138 | 5,380 | 5,957 |
| 60-64 | 4,585 | 5,219 | 439 | 543 | 211 | 240 | 95 | 115 | 5,120 | 5,877 |
| 65-69 | 3,821 | 4,615 | 361 | 472 | 137 | 171 | 72 | 90 | 4,254 | 5,176 |
| 70-74 | 2,899 | 3,914 | 258 | 373 | 99 | 140 | 56 | 66 | 3,213 | 4,352 |
| 75-79 | 1,924 | 3,044 | 172 | 270 | n.a. | n.a. | 39 | 46 | 2,135 | 3,360 |
| 80-84 | 1,051 | 2,001 | 84 | 149 | n.a. | n.a. | 18 | 25 | 1,153 | 2,176 |
| 85 and over | 695 | 1,779 | 65 | 140 | n.a. | n.a. | 13 | 19 | 773 | 1,938 |
| All ages | 99,006 | 103,762 | 13,683 | 15,204 | 8,953 | 8,872 | 3,472 | 3,612 | 116,161 | 122,579 |
| 15 and over | 77,407 | 83,274 | 9,653 | 11,277 | 6,196 | 6,226 | 2,500 | 2,668 | 89,560 | 97,219 |
| 20 and over | 69,661 | 75,826 | 8,261 | 9,898 | 5,362 | 5,420 | 2,193 | 2,388 | 80,115 | 88,112 |
| 65 and over | 10,390 | 15,353 | 940 | 1,403 | 364 | 503 | 198 | 246 | 11,529 | 17,002 |
| 75 and over | 3,670 | 6,824 | 321 | 559 | 128 | 191 | 70 | 90 | 4,062 | 7,473 |
| Median age | 31.2 | 33.6 | 25.2 | 27.8 | 24.4 | 25.4 | 26.9 | 28.9 | 30.3 | 32.7 |

NOTE: n.a. = not available. *Source:* Department of Commerce, Bureau of the Census.

## Population by State

| State | 1980 | Percent change, 1970–80 | Pop. per sq. mi., 1980 | Pop. rank, 1980 | 1970 | 1950 | 1900 | 1790 |
|---|---|---|---|---|---|---|---|---|
| Alabama | 3,893,888 | +13.1 | 76.7 | 22 | 3,444,354 | 3,061,743 | 1,828,697 | — |
| Alaska | 401,851 | +32.8 | 0.7 | 50 | 302,583 | 128,643 | 63,592 | — |
| Arizona | 2,718,425 | +53.1 | 23.9 | 29 | 1,775,399 | 749,587 | 122,931 | — |
| Arkansas | 2,286,435 | +18.9 | 43.9 | 33 | 1,923,322 | 1,909,511 | 1,311,564 | — |
| California | 23,667,565 | +18.5 | 151.4 | 1 | 19,971,069 | 10,586,223 | 1,485,053 | — |
| Colorado | 2,889,735 | +30.8 | 27.9 | 28 | 2,209,596 | 1,325,089 | 539,700 | — |
| Connecticut | 3,107,576 | + 2.5 | 637.8 | 25 | 3,032,217 | 2,007,280 | 908,420 | 237,946 |
| Delaware | 594,317 | + 8.4 | 307.6 | 47 | 548,104 | 318,085 | 184,735 | 59,096 |
| D.C. | 638,432 | −15.6 | — | — | 756,668 | 802,178 | 278,718 | — |
| Florida | 9,746,324 | +43.5 | 180.0 | 7 | 6,791,418 | 2,771,305 | 528,542 | — |
| Georgia | 5,463,105 | +19.1 | 94.1 | 13 | 4,587,930 | 3,444,578 | 2,216,331 | 82,548 |
| Hawaii | 964,691 | +25.3 | 150.1 | 39 | 769,913 | 499,794 | 154,001 | — |
| Idaho | 944,038 | +32.4 | 11.5 | 41 | 713,015 | 588,637 | 161,772 | — |
| Illinois | 11,426,518 | + 2.8 | 205.3 | 5 | 11,110,285 | 8,712,176 | 4,821,550 | — |
| Indiana | 5,490,260 | + 5.7 | 152.8 | 12 | 5,195,392 | 3,934,224 | 2,516,462 | — |
| Iowa | 2,913,808 | + 3.1 | 52.1 | 27 | 2,825,368 | 2,621,073 | 2,231,853 | — |
| Kansas | 2,364,236 | + 5.1 | 28.9 | 32 | 2,249,071 | 1,905,299 | 1,470,495 | — |
| Kentucky | 3,660,257 | +13.7 | 92.3 | 23 | 3,220,711 | 2,944,806 | 2,147,174 | 73,677 |
| Louisiana | 4,206,312 | +15.4 | 94.5 | 19 | 3,644,637 | 2,683,516 | 1,381,625 | — |
| Maine | 1,125,027 | +13.2 | 36.3 | 38 | 993,722 | 913,774 | 694,466 | 96,540 |
| Maryland | 4,216,975 | + 7.5 | 428.7 | 18 | 3,923,897 | 2,343,001 | 1,188,044 | 319,728 |
| Massachusetts | 5,737,037 | + 0.8 | 733.3 | 11 | 5,689,170 | 4,690,514 | 2,805,346 | 378,787 |
| Michigan | 9,262,078 | + 4.3 | 162.6 | 8 | 8,881,826 | 6,371,766 | 2,420,982 | — |
| Minnesota | 4,075,970 | + 7.1 | 51.2 | 21 | 3,806,103 | 2,982,483 | 1,751,394 | — |
| Mississippi | 2,520,638 | +13.7 | 53.4 | 31 | 2,216,994 | 2,178,914 | 1,551,270 | — |
| Missouri | 4,916,759 | + 5.1 | 71.3 | 15 | 4,677,623 | 3,954,653 | 3,106,665 | — |
| Montana | 786,690 | +13.3 | 5.4 | 44 | 694,409 | 591,024 | 243,329 | — |
| Nebraska | 1,569,825 | + 5.7 | 20.5 | 35 | 1,485,333 | 1,325,510 | 1,066,300 | — |
| Nevada | 800,493 | +63.8 | 7.3 | 43 | 488,738 | 160,083 | 42,335 | — |
| New Hampshire | 920,610 | +24.8 | 102.4 | 42 | 737,681 | 533,242 | 411,588 | 141,885 |
| New Jersey | 7,364,823 | + 2.7 | 986.2 | 9 | 7,171,112 | 4,835,329 | 1,883,669 | 184,139 |
| New Mexico | 1,302,981 | +28.1 | 10.7 | 37 | 1,017,055 | 681,187 | 195,310 | — |
| New York | 17,558,072 | − 3.7 | 370.6 | 2 | 18,241,391 | 14,830,192 | 7,268,894 | 340,120 |
| North Carolina | 5,881,813 | +15.7 | 120.4 | 10 | 5,084,411 | 4,061,929 | 1,893,810 | 393,751 |
| North Dakota | 652,717 | + 5.7 | 9.4 | 46 | 617,792 | 619,636 | 319,146 | — |
| Ohio | 10,797,624 | + 1.3 | 263.3 | 6 | 10,657,423 | 7,946,627 | 4,157,545 | — |
| Oklahoma | 3,025,290 | +18.2 | 44.1 | 26 | 2,559,463 | 2,233,351 | 790,391[1] | — |
| Oregon | 2,633,149 | +25.9 | 27.4 | 30 | 2,091,533 | 1,521,341 | 413,536 | — |
| Pennsylvania | 11,863,895 | + 0.5 | 264.3 | 4 | 11,800,766 | 10,498,012 | 6,302,115 | 434,373 |
| Rhode Island | 947,154 | − 0.3 | 897.8 | 40 | 949,723 | 791,896 | 428,556 | 68,825 |
| South Carolina | 3,121,833 | +20.5 | 103.4 | 24 | 2,590,713 | 2,117,027 | 1,340,316 | 249,073 |
| South Dakota | 690,768 | + 3.7 | 9.1 | 45 | 666,257 | 652,740 | 401,570 | — |
| Tennessee | 4,591,120 | +16.9 | 111.6 | 17 | 3,926,018 | 3,291,718 | 2,020,616 | 35,691 |
| Texas | 14,229,288 | +27.1 | 54.3 | 3 | 11,198,655 | 7,711,194 | 3,048,710 | — |
| Utah | 1,461,037 | +37.9 | 17.8 | 36 | 1,059,273 | 688,862 | 276,749 | — |
| Vermont | 511,456 | +15.0 | 55.2 | 48 | 444,732 | 377,747 | 343,641 | 85,425 |
| Virginia | 5,346,818 | +14.9 | 134.7 | 14 | 4,651,448 | 3,318,680 | 1,854,184 | 747,610[2] |
| Washington | 4,132,180 | +21.1 | 62.1 | 20 | 3,413,244 | 2,378,963 | 518,103 | — |
| West Virginia | 1,950,279 | +11.8 | 80.8 | 34 | 1,744,237 | 2,005,552 | 958,800 | — |
| Wisconsin | 4,705,521 | + 6.5 | 86.5 | 16 | 4,417,821 | 3,434,575 | 2,069,042 | — |
| Wyoming | 469,557 | +41.3 | 4.8 | 49 | 332,416 | 290,529 | 92,531 | — |
| **Total U.S.** | **226,545,805** | **+11.4** | **62.6** | **—** | **203,302,031** | **151,325,798** | **76,212,168** | **3,929,214** |

1. Includes population of Indian Territory: 1900, 392,960. 2. Until 1863, Virginia included what is now West Virginia. *Source:* Department of Commerce, Bureau of the Census.

## Victims of Crime

The chance of being a violent crime victim is higher than the risk of being affected by divorce, death by cancer, injury or death by fire or being hurt in a traffic accident. Still, a person is much more likely to die from natural causes than as a result of a criminal victimization.

Victims of crime are more often men than women. Younger people are much more likely than the elderly to be victims. But the elderly have a greater fear of crime and may restrict their lives in ways that reduce their chances of being victimized. Blacks are more likely to be victims than whites or other racial groups. Violent crime rates are higher for lower income people. Theft rates are highest for people with low incomes (less than $3,000 per year) and those with high incomes (over $25,000). Young black males have the highest violent crime rates; elderly white females have the lowest rates.

# Incorporated Places Over 25,000 Population

Asterisk denotes more than one ZIP code for a city and refers to Postmaster. To find the ZIP code for a particular address, consult the ZIP code directory available in every post office. For latest population figures of many cities, see listing for individual states in the United States section.

| City and major ZIP code | 1980 census | 1970 census | City and major ZIP code | 1980 census | 1970 census |
|---|---|---|---|---|---|
| Aberdeen, SD (57401) | 25,851 | 26,476 | Bell Gardens, CA (90201) | 34,117 | 29,308 |
| Abilene, TX (79604*) | 98,315 | 89,653 | Bellingham, WA (98225*) | 45,794 | 39,375 |
| Addison, IL (60101) | 29,759 | 24,482 | Beloit, WI (53511) | 35,207 | 35,729 |
| Akron, OH (44309*) | 237,177 | 275,425 | Bergenfield, NJ (07621) | 25,568 | 29,000 |
| Alameda, CA (94501) | 63,852 | 70,968 | Berkeley, CA (94704*) | 103,328 | 114,091 |
| Albany, GA (31706*) | 74,550 | 72,623 | Berwyn, IL (60402) | 46,840 | 52,502 |
| Albany, NY (12212*) | 101,727 | 115,781 | Bessemer, AL (35020*) | 31,729 | 33,428 |
| Albany, OR (97321) | 26,678 | 18,181 | Bethel Park, PA (15102) | 34,755 | 34,758 |
| Albuquerque, NM (87101*) | 331,767 | 244,501 | Bethlehem, PA (18016*) | 70,419 | 72,686 |
| Alexandria, LA (71301*) | 51,565 | 41,811 | Bettendorf, IA (52722) | 27,381 | 22,126 |
| Alexandria, VA (22313*) | 103,217 | 110,927 | Beverly, MA (01915) | 37,655 | 38,348 |
| Alhambra, CA (91802*) | 64,615 | 62,125 | Beverly Hills, CA (90213*) | 32,367 | 33,416 |
| Allen Park, MI (48101) | 34,196 | 40,747 | Billings, MT (59101*) | 66,842 | 61,581 |
| Allentown, PA (18101*) | 103,758 | 109,871 | Biloxi, MS (39530*) | 49,311 | 48,486 |
| Alton, IL (62002) | 34,171 | 39,700 | Binghamton, NY (13902*) | 55,860 | 64,123 |
| Altoona, PA (16603*) | 57,078 | 63,115 | Birmingham, AL (35203*) | 284,413 | 300,910 |
| Amarillo, TX (79120*) | 149,230 | 127,010 | Bismarck, ND (58501) | 44,485 | 34,703 |
| Ames, IA (50010) | 45,775 | 39,505 | Blacksburg, VA (24060) | 30,638 | 9,384 |
| Anaheim, CA (92803*) | 219,311 | 166,408 | Blaine, MN (55433) | 28,558 | 20,573 |
| Anchorage, AK (99502*) | 174,431 | 48,081 | Bloomfield, NJ (07003) | 47,792 | 52,029 |
| Anderson, IN (46018*) | 64,695 | 70,787 | Bloomington, IL (61701) | 44,189 | 39,992 |
| Anderson, SC (29621*) | 27,965 | 27,556 | Bloomington, IN (47401) | 52,044 | 43,262 |
| Annapolis, MD (21401*) | 31,740 | 30,095 | Bloomington, MN (55420*) | 81,831 | 81,970 |
| Ann Arbor, MI (48106*) | 107,966 | 100,035 | Blue Springs, MO (64015) | 25,927 | 6,779 |
| Anniston, AL (36201*) | 29,523 | 31,533 | Boca Raton, FL (33432*) | 49,505 | 28,506 |
| Antioch, CA (94509) | 42,683 | 28,060 | Boise, ID (83708*) | 102,160 | 74,990 |
| Appleton, WI (54911*) | 58,913 | 56,377 | Bolingbrook, IL (60439) | 37,261 | 7,651 |
| Arcadia, CA (91006) | 45,994 | 45,138 | Bossier City, LA (71111*) | 50,817 | 43,769 |
| Arlington, TX (76010*) | 160,113 | 90,229 | Boston, MA (02205*) | 562,994 | 641,071 |
| Arlington Heights, IL (60004*) | 66,116 | 65,058 | Boulder, CO (80302*) | 76,685 | 66,870 |
| Arvada, CO (80001*) | 84,576 | 49,844 | Bountiful, UT (84010) | 32,877 | 27,751 |
| Asheville, NC (28810*) | 53,583 | 57,820 | Bowie, MD (20715*) | 33,695 | 35,028 |
| Ashland, KY (41101) | 27,064 | 29,245 | Bowling Green, KY (42101) | 40,450 | 36,705 |
| Athens, GA (30601*) | 42,549 | 44,342 | Bowling Green, OH (43402) | 25,728 | 14,656 |
| Atlanta, GA (30304*) | 425,022 | 495,039 | Boynton Beach, FL (33435*) | 35,624 | 18,115 |
| Atlantic City, NJ (08401*) | 40,199 | 47,859 | Bradenton, FL (33506*) | 30,170 | 21,040 |
| Attleboro, MA (02703) | 34,196 | 32,907 | Brea, CA (92621) | 27,913 | 18,447 |
| Auburn, AL (36830) | 28,471 | 22,767 | Bremerton, WA (98310*) | 36,208 | 35,307 |
| Auburn, NY (13021) | 32,548 | 34,599 | Bridgeport, CT (06602*) | 142,546 | 156,542 |
| Auburn, WA (98002*) | 26,417 | 21,653 | Bristol, CT (06010) | 57,370 | 55,487 |
| Augusta, GA (30901*) | 47,532 | 59,864 | Brockton, MA (02403*) | 95,172 | 89,040 |
| Aurora, CO (80010*) | 158,588 | 74,974 | Broken Arrow, OK (74012*) | 35,761 | 11,018 |
| Aurora, IL (60507*) | 81,293 | 74,389 | Brookfield, WI (53005) | 34,035 | 31,761 |
| Austin, TX (78710*) | 345,496 | 253,539 | Brooklyn Center, MN (55429*) | 31,230 | 35,173 |
| Azusa, CA (91702) | 29,380 | 25,217 | Brooklyn Park, MN (55007) | 43,332 | 26,230 |
| Bakersfield, CA (93302*) | 105,735 | 69,515 | Brook Park, OH (44142) | 26,195 | 30,774 |
| Baldwin Park, CA (91706) | 50,554 | 47,285 | Brownsville, TX (78520*) | 84,997 | 52,522 |
| Baltimore, MD (21233*) | 786,775 | 905,787 | Brunswick, OH (44212) | 28,104 | 15,852 |
| Bangor, ME (04401) | 31,643 | 33,168 | Bryan, TX (77801*) | 44,337 | 33,719 |
| Barberton, OH (44203) | 29,751 | 33,052 | Buena Park, CA (90622*) | 64,165 | 63,646 |
| Bartlesville, OK (74003*) | 34,568 | 29,683 | Buffalo, NY (14240*) | 357,870 | 462,768 |
| Baton Rouge, LA (70821*) | 219,419 | 165,921 | Burbank, CA (91505*) | 84,625 | 88,871 |
| Battle Creek, MI (49016*) | 35,724 | 38,931 | Burbank, IL (60459) | 28,462 | — |
| Bay City, MI (48706) | 41,593 | 49,449 | Burlingame, CA (94010) | 26,173 | 27,320 |
| Bayonne, NJ (07002) | 65,047 | 72,743 | Burlington, IA (52601) | 29,529 | 32,366 |
| Baytown, TX (77520*) | 56,923 | 43,980 | Burlington, NC (27215) | 37,266 | 35,930 |
| Beaumont, TX (77704*) | 118,102 | 117,548 | Burlington, VT (05401) | 37,712 | 38,633 |
| Beavercreek, OH (45401) | 31,589 | — | Burnsville, MN (55337) | 35,674 | 19,940 |
| Beaverton, OR (97005*) | 30,582 | 18,577 | Burton, MI (48502) | 29,976 | — |
| Bell, CA (90201) | 25,450 | 21,836 | Butte, MT (59701) | 37,205 | 23,368 |
| Belleville, IL (62220*) | 41,580 | 41,223 | Calumet City, IL (60409) | 39,697 | 33,107 |
| Belleville, NJ (07109) | 35,367 | 37,629 | Camarillo, CA (93010) | 37,797 | 19,219 |
| Bellevue, WA (98009*) | 73,903 | 61,196 | Cambridge, MA (02140) | 95,322 | 100,361 |
| Bellflower, CA (90706) | 53,441 | 52,334 | Camden, NJ (08101*) | 84,910 | 102,551 |

| City and major ZIP code | 1980 census | 1970 census | City and major ZIP code | 1980 census | 1970 census |
|---|---|---|---|---|---|
| Campbell, CA (95008) | 27,067 | 23,797 | Cuyahoga Falls, OH (44222*) | 43,890 | 49,815 |
| Canton, OH (44711*) | 93,077 | 110,053 | Cypress, CA (90630) | 40,391 | 31,569 |
| Cape Coral, FL (33910) | 32,103 | — | Dallas, TX (75260*) | 904,078 | 844,401 |
| Cape Girardeau, MO (63701) | 34,361 | 31,282 | Daly City, CA (94015*) | 78,519 | 66,922 |
| Carbondale, IL (62901) | 26,414 | 22,816 | Danbury, CT (06810*) | 60,470 | 50,781 |
| Carlsbad, CA (92008) | 35,490 | 14,944 | Danville, IL (61832) | 38,985 | 42,570 |
| Carlsbad, NM (88220) | 25,496 | 21,297 | Danville, VA (24541*) | 45,642 | 46,391 |
| Carrollton, TX (75006*) | 40,595 | 13,855 | Davenport, IA (52802*) | 103,264 | 98,469 |
| Carson, CA (90749) | 81,221 | 71,150 | Davis, CA (95616) | 36,640 | 23,488 |
| Carson City, NV (89701) | 32,022 | 15,468 | Dayton, OH (45401*) | 193,444 | 243,023 |
| Casper, WY (82601*) | 51,016 | 39,361 | Daytona Beach, FL (32015*) | 54,176 | 45,327 |
| Cedar Falls, IA (50613) | 36,322 | 29,597 | Dearborn, MI (48120*) | 90,660 | 104,199 |
| Cedar Rapids, IA (52401*) | 110,243 | 110,642 | Dearborn Heights, MI (48127) | 67,706 | 80,069 |
| Cerritos, CA (90701) | 53,020 | 15,856 | Decatur, AL (35602*) | 42,002 | 38,044 |
| Champaign, IL (61820*) | 58,133 | 56,837 | Decatur, IL (62521*) | 94,081 | 90,397 |
| Chandler, AZ (85224) | 29,673 | 13,763 | Deerfield Beach, FL (33441) | 39,193 | 16,662 |
| Chapel Hill, NC (27514) | 32,421 | 26,199 | De Kalb, IL (60115) | 33,099 | 32,949 |
| Charleston, SC (29423*) | 69,510 | 66,945 | Del City, OK (73155*) | 28,424 | 27,133 |
| Charleston, WV (25301*) | 63,968 | 71,505 | Delray Beach, FL (33444*) | 34,325 | 19,915 |
| Charlotte, NC (28228*) | 314,447 | 241,420 | Del Rio, TX (78840) | 30,034 | 21,330 |
| Charlottesville, VA (22906*) | 39,916 | 38,880 | Denton, TX (76201*) | 48,063 | 39,874 |
| Chattanooga, TN (37401*) | 169,558 | 119,923 | Denver, CO (80202*) | 492,365 | 514,678 |
| Chelsea, MA (02150) | 25,431 | 30,625 | Des Moines, IA (50318*) | 191,003 | 201,404 |
| Chesapeake, VA (23320*) | 114,486 | 89,580 | Des Plaines, IL (60018*) | 53,568 | 57,239 |
| Chester, PA (19013*) | 45,794 | 56,331 | Detroit, MI (48233*) | 1,203,339 | 1,514,063 |
| Cheyenne, WY (82001*) | 47,283 | 41,254 | Dothan, AL (36303*) | 48,750 | 36,733 |
| Chicago, IL (60607*) | 3,005,072 | 3,369,357 | Downers Grove, IL (60515*) | 42,572 | 32,544 |
| Chicago Heights, IL (60411) | 37,026 | 40,900 | Downey, CA (90241*) | 82,602 | 88,573 |
| Chico, CA (95926) | 26,603 | 19,580 | Dubuque, IA (52001) | 62,321 | 62,309 |
| Chicopee, MA (01021*) | 55,112 | 66,676 | Duluth, MN (55806*) | 92,811 | 100,578 |
| Chino, CA (91710) | 40,165 | 20,411 | Duncanville, TX (75138*) | 27,781 | 14,105 |
| Chula Vista, CA (92010*) | 83,927 | 67,901 | Dunedin, FL (33528) | 30,203 | 17,639 |
| Cicero, IL (60650) | 61,232 | 67,058 | Durham, NC (27701*) | 100,538 | 95,438 |
| Cincinnati, OH (45234*) | 385,457 | 453,514 | East Chicago, IN (46312) | 39,786 | 49,982 |
| Claremont, CA (91711) | 30,950 | 24,776 | East Cleveland, OH (44112) | 36,957 | 39,660 |
| Clarksville, TN (37041*) | 54,777 | 31,719 | East Detroit, MI (48021) | 38,280 | 45,920 |
| Clearwater, FL (33575*) | 85,528 | 52,074 | East Lansing, MI (48823) | 51,392 | 47,540 |
| Cleveland, OH (44101*) | 573,822 | 750,879 | Easton, PA (18042) | 26,027 | 29,450 |
| Cleveland, TN (37311) | 26,415 | 21,446 | East Orange, NJ (07019*) | 77,690 | 75,471 |
| Cleveland Heights, OH (44118) | 56,438 | 60,767 | East Point, GA (30364) | 37,486 | 39,315 |
| Clifton, NJ (07015*) | 74,388 | 82,437 | East Providence, RI (02914) | 50,980 | 48,207 |
| Clinton, IA (52732) | 32,828 | 34,719 | East St. Louis, IL (62201*) | 55,200 | 70,169 |
| Clovis, CA (93612) | 33,021 | 13,856 | Eau Claire, WI (54701*) | 51,509 | 44,619 |
| Clovis, NM (88101) | 31,194 | 28,495 | Edina, MN (55424*) | 46,073 | 44,046 |
| College Station, TX (77840) | 37,272 | 17,676 | Edmond, OK (73034) | 34,637 | 16,633 |
| Colorado Springs, CO (80901*) | 214,821 | 135,517 | Edmonds, WA (98020) | 27,679 | 23,684 |
| Columbia, MO (65201*) | 62,061 | 58,812 | El Cajon, CA (92020*) | 73,892 | 52,273 |
| Columbia, SC (29201*) | 100,385 | 113,542 | El Dorado, AR (71730) | 25,270 | 25,283 |
| Columbia, TN (38401) | 26,571 | 21,471 | Elgin, IL (60120) | 63,798 | 55,691 |
| Columbus, GA (31908*) | 169,441 | 155,028 | Elizabeth, NJ (07207*) | 106,201 | 112,654 |
| Columbus, IN (47201*) | 30,614 | 26,457 | Elk Grove, IL (60007) | 28,907 | 20,346 |
| Columbus, MS (39701*) | 27,383 | 25,795 | Elkhart, IN (46515*) | 41,305 | 43,152 |
| Columbus, OH (43216*) | 565,032 | 540,025 | Elmhurst, IL (60126) | 44,276 | 46,392 |
| Compton, CA (90220*) | 81,286 | 78,547 | Elmira, NY (14901*) | 35,327 | 39,945 |
| Concord, CA (94520*) | 103,255 | 85,164 | El Monte, CA (91734*) | 79,494 | 69,892 |
| Concord, NH (03301*) | 30,400 | 30,022 | El Paso, TX (79910*) | 425,259 | 322,261 |
| Coon Rapids, MN (55433) | 35,826 | 30,505 | Elyria, OH (44035*) | 57,538 | 53,427 |
| Coral Gables, FL (33114) | 43,241 | 42,494 | Emporia, KS (66801) | 25,287 | 23,327 |
| Coral Springs, FL (33065) | 37,349 | 1,489 | Englewood, CO (80110*) | 30,021 | 33,695 |
| Corona, CA (91720) | 37,791 | 27,519 | Enid, OK (73701) | 50,363 | 44,986 |
| Corpus Christi, TX (78408*) | 231,999 | 204,525 | Erie, PA (16515*) | 119,123 | 129,265 |
| Corvallis, OR (97333*) | 40,960 | 35,056 | Escondido, CA (92025*) | 64,355 | 36,792 |
| Costa Mesa, CA (92626*) | 82,562 | 72,660 | Euclid, OH (44117) | 59,999 | 71,552 |
| Council Bluffs, IA (51501) | 56,449 | 60,348 | Eugene, OR (97401*) | 105,624 | 79,028 |
| Covina, CA (91722*) | 33,751 | 30,395 | Evanston, IL (60204*) | 73,706 | 80,113 |
| Covington, KY (41011*) | 49,563 | 52,535 | Evansville, IN (47708*) | 130,496 | 138,764 |
| Cranston, RI (02910*) | 71,992 | 74,287 | Everett, MA (02149) | 37,195 | 42,485 |
| Crystal, MN (55428*) | 25,543 | 30,925 | Everett, WA (98201*) | 54,413 | 53,622 |
| Culver City, CA (90230) | 38,139 | 34,451 | Fairborn, OH (45324) | 29,702 | 32,267 |
| Cumberland, MD (21502*) | 25,933 | 29,724 | Fairfield, CA (94533) | 58,099 | 44,146 |
| Cupertino, CA (95014) | 34,015 | 17,895 | Fairfield, OH (45014) | 30,777 | 14,680 |

| City and major ZIP code | 1980 census | 1970 census | City and major ZIP code | 1980 census | 1970 census |
|---|---|---|---|---|---|
| Fair Lawn, NJ (07410) | 32,229 | 38,040 | Hackensack, NJ (07602*) | 36,039 | 36,008 |
| Fall River, MA (02722*) | 92,574 | 96,898 | Hagerstown, MD (21740) | 34,132 | 35,862 |
| Fargo, ND (58102*) | 61,383 | 53,365 | Hallandale, FL (33009) | 36,517 | 23,849 |
| Farmington, NM (87401) | 31,222 | 21,979 | Haltom City, TX (76117) | 29,014 | 28,127 |
| Farmington Hills, MI (48024) | 58,056 | — | Hamilton, OH (45012*) | 63,189 | 67,865 |
| Fayetteville, AR (72701) | 36,608 | 30,729 | Hammond, IN (46320*) | 93,714 | 107,983 |
| Fayetteville, NC (28302*) | 59,507 | 53,510 | Hampton, VA (23670*) | 122,617 | 120,779 |
| Ferndale, MI (48220) | 26,227 | 30,850 | Hanover Park, IL (60103) | 28,850 | 11,735 |
| Findlay, OH (45840) | 35,594 | 35,800 | Harlingen, TX (78551*) | 43,543 | 33,503 |
| Fitchburg, MA (01420) | 39,580 | 43,343 | Harrisburg, PA (17105*) | 53,264 | 68,061 |
| Flagstaff, AZ (86001) | 34,743 | 26,117 | Hartford, CT (06101*) | 136,392 | 158,017 |
| Flint, MI (48502*) | 159,611 | 193,317 | Harvey, IL (60426) | 35,810 | 34,636 |
| Florence, AL (35631*) | 37,029 | 34,031 | Hattiesburg, MS (39401) | 40,829 | 38,277 |
| Florence, SC (29501) | 29,176 | 25,997 | Haverhill, MA (01830) | 46,865 | 46,120 |
| Florissant, MO (63033*) | 55,372 | 65,908 | Hawthorne, CA (90250) | 56,447 | 53,304 |
| Fond du Lac, WI (54935) | 35,863 | 35,515 | Hayward, CA (94544*) | 94,342 | 93,058 |
| Fontana, CA (92335) | 37,107 | 20,673 | Hazleton, PA (18201) | 27,318 | 30,426 |
| Fort Collins, CO (80521*) | 65,092 | 43,337 | Hempstead, NY (11551*) | 40,404 | 39,411 |
| Fort Dodge, IA (50501) | 29,423 | 31,263 | Hendersonville, TN (37075) | 26,561 | 412 |
| Fort Lauderdale, FL (33310*) | 153,279 | 139,590 | Hialeah, FL (33010*) | 145,254 | 102,452 |
| Fort Lee, NJ (07024) | 32,449 | 30,631 | Highland, IN (46322) | 25,935 | 24,947 |
| Fort Myers, FL (33906*) | 36,638 | 27,351 | Highland Park, IL (60035) | 30,611 | 32,263 |
| Fort Pierce, FL (33450*) | 33,802 | 29,721 | Highland Park, MI (48203) | 27,909 | 35,444 |
| Fort Smith, AR (72901*) | 71,626 | 62,802 | High Point, NC (27260*) | 63,808 | 63,229 |
| Fort Wayne, IN (46802*) | 172,028 | 178,269 | Hillsboro, OR (97123*) | 27,664 | 14,675 |
| Fort Worth, TX (76101*) | 385,164 | 393,455 | Hilo, HI (96720) | 35,269 | 26,353 |
| Fountain Valley, CA (92728) | 55,080 | 31,886 | Hobbs, NM (88240) | 29,153 | 26,025 |
| Frankfort, KY (40601) | 25,973 | 21,902 | Hoboken, NJ (07030) | 42,460 | 45,380 |
| Frederick, MD (21701) | 28,086 | 23,641 | Hoffman Estates, IL (60195) | 37,272 | 22,238 |
| Freeport, IL (61032) | 26,266 | 27,736 | Holland, MI (49423) | 26,281 | 26,479 |
| Freeport, NY (11520) | 38,272 | 40,374 | Hollywood, FL (33022*) | 121,323 | 106,873 |
| Fremont, CA (94538*) | 131,945 | 100,869 | Holyoke, MA (01040) | 44,678 | 50,112 |
| Fresno, CA (93706*) | 218,202 | 165,655 | Honolulu, HI (96820*) | 365,048 | 324,871 |
| Fridley, MN (55432) | 30,228 | 29,233 | Hopkinsville, KY (42240) | 27,318 | 21,395 |
| Fullerton, CA (92631*) | 102,034 | 85,987 | Hot Springs, AR (71901*) | 35,781 | 35,631 |
| Gadsden, AL (35901*) | 47,565 | 53,928 | Houma, LA (70360) | 32,602 | 30,922 |
| Gainesville, FL (32602*) | 81,371 | 64,510 | Houston, TX (77201*) | 1,595,138 | 1,233,535 |
| Gaithersburg, MD (20877*) | 26,424 | 8,344 | Huber Heights, OH (45424) | 35,480 | — |
| Galesburg, IL (61401) | 35,305 | 36,290 | Huntington, WV (25704*) | 63,684 | 74,315 |
| Galveston, TX (77553*) | 61,902 | 61,809 | Huntington Beach, CA (92647*) | 170,505 | 115,960 |
| Gardena, CA (90247*) | 45,165 | 41,021 | Huntington Park, CA (90255) | 46,223 | 33,744 |
| Garden City, MI (48135) | 35,640 | 41,864 | Huntsville, AL (35813*) | 142,513 | 139,282 |
| Garden Grove, CA (92640*) | 123,307 | 121,155 | Hurst, TX (76053) | 31,420 | 27,215 |
| Garfield, NJ (07026) | 26,803 | 30,797 | Hutchinson, KS (67501) | 40,284 | 36,885 |
| Garfield Heights, OH (44125) | 34,938 | 41,417 | Idaho Falls, ID (83401*) | 39,590 | 35,776 |
| Garland, TX (75040*) | 138,857 | 81,437 | Independence, MO (64051*) | 111,806 | 111,630 |
| Gary, IN (46401*) | 151,953 | 175,415 | Indianapolis, IN (46206*) | 700,807 | 736,856 |
| Gastonia, NC (28052) | 47,333 | 47,322 | Inglewood, CA (90311*) | 94,245 | 89,985 |
| Glendale, AZ (85301*) | 97,172 | 36,228 | Inkster, MI (48141) | 35,190 | 38,595 |
| Glendale, CA (91209*) | 139,060 | 132,664 | Iowa City, IA (52240*) | 50,508 | 46,850 |
| Glendora, CA (91740) | 38,500 | 32,143 | Irvine, CA (92713) | 62,134 | — |
| Glenview, IL (60025) | 32,060 | 24,880 | Irving, TX (75061*) | 109,943 | 97,260 |
| Gloucester, MA (01930) | 27,768 | 27,941 | Irvington, NJ (07111) | 61,493 | 59,743 |
| Goldsboro, NC (27530) | 31,871 | 26,960 | Ithaca, NY (14850) | 28,732 | 26,226 |
| Grand Forks, ND (58201) | 43,765 | 39,008 | Jackson, MI (49201*) | 39,739 | 45,484 |
| Grand Island, NE (68801) | 33,180 | 32,358 | Jackson, MS (39205*) | 202,895 | 153,968 |
| Grand Junction, CO (81501*) | 27,956 | 20,170 | Jackson, TN (38301*) | 49,131 | 39,996 |
| Grand Prairie, TX (75051*) | 71,462 | 50,904 | Jacksonville, AR (72076) | 27,589 | 19,832 |
| Grand Rapids, MI (49501*) | 181,843 | 197,649 | Jacksonville, FL (32203*) | 540,920 | 504,265 |
| Granite City, IL (62040) | 36,815 | 40,685 | Jamestown, NY (14701) | 35,775 | 39,795 |
| Great Falls, MT (59403*) | 56,725 | 60,091 | Janesville, WI (53545*) | 51,071 | 46,426 |
| Greeley, CO (80631*) | 53,006 | 38,902 | Jefferson City, MO (65101) | 33,619 | 32,407 |
| Green Bay, WI (54301*) | 87,899 | 87,809 | Jersey City, NJ (07303*) | 223,532 | 260,350 |
| Greenfield, WI (53220) | 31,467 | 24,424 | Johnson City, TN (37601) | 39,753 | 33,770 |
| Greensboro, NC (27420*) | 155,642 | 144,076 | Johnstown, PA (15901*) | 35,496 | 42,476 |
| Greenville, MS (38701*) | 40,613 | 39,648 | Joliet, IL (60436*) | 77,956 | 78,827 |
| Greenville, NC (27834) | 35,740 | 29,063 | Jonesboro, AR (72401) | 31,530 | 27,050 |
| Greenville, SC (29602*) | 58,242 | 61,436 | Joplin, MO (64801) | 39,023 | 39,256 |
| Gresham, OR (97030) | 33,005 | 10,030 | Kalamazoo, MI (49001*) | 79,722 | 85,555 |
| Gulfport, MS (39503*) | 39,676 | 40,791 | Kankakee, IL (60901) | 30,141 | 30,944 |

| City and major ZIP code | 1980 census | 1970 census | City and major ZIP code | 1980 census | 1970 census |
|---|---|---|---|---|---|
| Kansas City, KS (66110*) | 161,148 | 168,213 | Los Altos, CA (94022) | 25,769 | 25,062 |
| Kansas City, MO (64108*) | 448,159 | 507,330 | Los Angeles, CA (90052*) | 2,966,850 | 2,811,801 |
| Kearny, NJ (07032) | 35,735 | 37,585 | Los Gatos, CA (95030) | 26,906 | 22,613 |
| Kenner, LA (70062*) | 66,382 | 29,858 | Louisville, KY (40231*) | 298,840 | 361,706 |
| Kennewick, WA (99336) | 34,397 | 15,212 | Loveland, CO (80537) | 30,244 | 16,220 |
| Kenosha, WI (53141*) | 77,685 | 78,805 | Lowell, MA (01853*) | 92,418 | 94,239 |
| Kent, OH (44240) | 26,164 | 28,183 | Lubbock, TX (79408*) | 173,979 | 149,101 |
| Kentwood, MI (49508) | 30,438 | 20,310 | Lufkin, TX (75901) | 28,562 | 23,049 |
| Kettering, OH (45429) | 61,186 | 71,864 | Lynchburg, VA (24506*) | 66,743 | 54,083 |
| Killeen, TX (76541*) | 46,296 | 35,507 | Lynn, MA (01901*) | 78,471 | 90,294 |
| Kingsport, TN (37662*) | 32,027 | 31,938 | Lynwood, CA (90262) | 48,548 | 43,354 |
| Kingsville, TX (78363) | 28,808 | 28,915 | Macon, GA (31213*) | 116,896 | 122,423 |
| Kinston, NC (28501) | 25,234 | 23,020 | Madisón, WI (53707*) | 170,616 | 171,809 |
| Kirkwood, MO (63122) | 27,987 | 31,679 | Madison Heights, MI (48071) | 35,375 | 38,599 |
| Knoxville, TN (37901*) | 175,045 | 174,587 | Malden, MA (02148) | 53,386 | 56,127 |
| Kokomo, IN (46902*) | 47,808 | 44,042 | Manchester, NH (03103*) | 90,936 | 87,754 |
| La Crosse, WI (54601*) | 48,347 | 50,286 | Manhattan, KS (66502) | 32,644 | 27,575 |
| Lafayette, IN (47901*) | 43,011 | 44,955 | Manhattan Beach, CA (90266) | 31,542 | 35,352 |
| Lafayette, LA (70501*) | 81,961 | 68,908 | Manitowoc, WI (54220) | 32,547 | 33,430 |
| La Habra, CA (90631) | 45,232 | 41,350 | Mankato, MN (56001) | 28,651 | 30,895 |
| Lake Charles, LA (70601*) | 75,226 | 77,998 | Mansfield, OH (44901*) | 53,927 | 55,047 |
| Lakeland, FL (33802*) | 47,406 | 42,803 | Maple Heights, OH (44137) | 29,735 | 34,093 |
| Lakewood, CA (90714*) | 74,654 | 83,025 | Maplewood, MN (55109) | 26,990 | 25,186 |
| Lakewood, CO (80215) | 113,808 | 92,743 | Margate, FL (33063*) | 35,900 | 8,867 |
| Lakewood, OH (44107) | 61,963 | 70,173 | Marietta, GA (30060*) | 30,829 | 27,216 |
| Lake Worth, FL (33461*) | 27,048 | 23,714 | Marion, IN (46952*) | 35,874 | 39,607 |
| La Mesa, CA (92041) | 50,308 | 39,178 | Marion, OH (43302) | 37,040 | 38,646 |
| La Mirada, CA (90638) | 40,986 | 30,808 | Marlborough, MA (01752) | 30,617 | 27,936 |
| Lancaster, CA (93534*) | 48,027 | — | Marshalltown, IA (50158) | 26,938 | 26,219 |
| Lancaster, OH (43130) | 34,953 | 32,911 | Mason City, IA (50401) | 30,144 | 30,279 |
| Lancaster, PA (17604*) | 54,725 | 57,690 | Massillon, OH (44646) | 30,557 | 32,539 |
| Lansing, IL (60438) | 29,039 | 25,805 | Maywood, IL (60153) | 27,998 | 29,019 |
| Lansing, MI (48924*) | 130,414 | 131,403 | McAllen, TX (78501) | 66,281 | 37,636 |
| La Puente, CA (91747*) | 30,882 | 31,092 | McKeesport, PA (15134*) | 31,012 | 37,977 |
| Laredo, TX (78041*) | 91,449 | 69,024 | Medford, MA (02155) | 58,076 | 64,397 |
| Largo, FL (33540*) | 58,977 | 24,230 | Medford, OR (97501) | 39,603 | 28,973 |
| Las Cruces, NM (88001*) | 45,086 | 37,857 | Melbourne, FL (32901*) | 46,536 | 40,236 |
| Las Vegas, NV (89114*) | 164,674 | 125,787 | Melrose, MA (02176) | 30,055 | 33,180 |
| Lauderdale Lakes, FL (33313) | 25,426 | 10,577 | Memphis, TN (38101*) | 646,174 | 623,988 |
| Lauderhill, FL (33313) | 37,271 | 8,465 | Menlo Park, CA (94025) | 26,369 | 26,826 |
| Lawrence, IN (46226) | 25,591 | 16,353 | Menomonee Falls, WI (53051) | 27,845 | 31,697 |
| Lawrence, KS (66044) | 52,738 | 45,698 | Mentor, OH (44060) | 42,065 | 36,912 |
| Lawrence, MA (01842*) | 63,175 | 66,915 | Merced, CA (95340) | 36,499 | 22,670 |
| Lawton, OK (73501*) | 80,054 | 74,470 | Meriden, CT (06450) | 57,118 | 55,959 |
| Leavenworth, KS (66048) | 33,656 | 25,147 | Meridian, MS (39301) | 46,577 | 45,083 |
| Lebanon, PA (17042) | 25,711 | 28,572 | Merrillville, IN (46410) | 27,677 | — |
| Lee's Summit, MO (64063) | 28,741 | 16,230 | Mesa, AZ (85201*) | 152,453 | 63,049 |
| Leominster, MA (01453) | 34,508 | 32,939 | Mesquite, TX (75149*) | 67,053 | 55,131 |
| Lewiston, ID (83501) | 27,986 | 26,068 | Miami, FL (33152*) | 346,865 | 334,859 |
| Lewiston, ME (04240) | 40,481 | 41,779 | Miami Beach, FL (33139) | 96,298 | 87,072 |
| Lexington, KY (40511*) | 204,165 | 108,137 | Michigan City, IN (46360) | 36,850 | 39,369 |
| Lima, OH (45802*) | 47,381 | 53,734 | Middletown, CT (06457) | 39,040 | 36,924 |
| Lincoln, NE (68501*) | 171,932 | 149,518 | Middletown, OH (45042) | 43,719 | 48,767 |
| Lincoln Park, MI (48146) | 45,105 | 52,984 | Midland, MI (48640) | 37,250 | 35,176 |
| Linden, NJ (07036) | 37,836 | 41,409 | Midland, TX (79702*) | 70,525 | 59,463 |
| Lindenhurst, NY (11757) | 26,919 | 28,359 | Midwest City, OK (73140*) | 49,559 | 48,212 |
| Little Rock, AR (72231*) | 158,461 | 132,483 | Milford, CT (06460) | 49,101 | 50,858 |
| Littleton, CO (80120*) | 28,631 | 26,466 | Milpitas, CA (95035) | 37,820 | 26,561 |
| Livermore, CA (94550) | 48,349 | 37,703 | Milwaukee, WI (53201*) | 636,236 | 717,372 |
| Livonia, MI (48150*) | 104,814 | 110,109 | Minneapolis, MN (55401*) | 370,951 | 434,400 |
| Lodi, CA (95240) | 35,221 | 28,691 | Minnetonka, MN (55343) | 38,683 | 35,776 |
| Logan, UT (84321) | 26,844 | 22,333 | Minot, ND (58701) | 32,843 | 32,290 |
| Lombard, IL (60148) | 37,295 | 34,043 | Miramar, FL (33023) | 32,813 | 23,997 |
| Lompoc, CA (93436) | 26,267 | 25,284 | Mishawaka, IN (46544*) | 40,201 | 36,060 |
| Long Beach, CA (90809*) | 361,334 | 358,879 | Missoula, MT (59806*) | 33,388 | 29,497 |
| Long Beach, NY (11561) | 34,073 | 33,127 | Mobile, AL (36601*) | 200,452 | 190,026 |
| Long Branch, NJ (07740) | 29,819 | 31,774 | Modesto, CA (95350*) | 106,602 | 61,712 |
| Longmont, CO (80501) | 42,942 | 23,209 | Moline, IL (61265) | 45,709 | 46,237 |
| Longview, TX (75602*) | 62,762 | 45,547 | Monroe, LA (71203*) | 57,597 | 56,374 |
| Longview, WA (98632) | 31,052 | 28,373 | Monroeville, PA (15146) | 30,977 | 29,011 |
| Lorain, OH (44052*) | 75,416 | 78,185 | Monrovia, CA (91016) | 30,531 | 30,562 |

| City and major ZIP code | 1980 census | 1970 census | City and major ZIP code | 1980 census | 1970 census |
|---|---|---|---|---|---|
| Montclair, NJ (07042*) | 38,321 | 44,043 | Norwood, OH (45212*) | 26,342 | 30,420 |
| Montebello, CA (90640) | 52,929 | 42,807 | Novato, CA (94947) | 43,916 | 31,006 |
| Monterey, CA (93940) | 27,558 | 26,302 | Nutley, NJ (07110) | 28,998 | 31,913 |
| Monterey Park, CA (91754) | 54,338 | 49,166 | Oak Forest, IL (60452) | 26,096 | 19,271 |
| Montgomery, AL (36119*) | 177,857 | 133,386 | Oakland, CA (94615*) | 339,337 | 361,561 |
| Moore, OK (73153*) | 35,063 | 18,761 | Oak Lawn, IL (60454*) | 60,590 | 60,305 |
| Moorhead, MN (56560) | 29,998 | 29,687 | Oak Park, IL (60301*) | 54,887 | 62,511 |
| Morgantown, WV (26505) | 27,605 | 29,431 | Oak Park, MI (48237) | 31,537 | 36,762 |
| Mountain View, CA (94042*) | 58,655 | 54,132 | Oak Ridge, TN (37830) | 27,662 | 28,319 |
| Mount Prospect, IL (60056) | 52,634 | 34,995 | Ocala, FL (32678*) | 37,170 | 22,583 |
| Mount Vernon, NY (10551*) | 66,713 | 72,778 | Oceanside, CA (92054*) | 76,698 | 40,494 |
| Muncie, IN (47302*) | 77,216 | 69,082 | Odessa, TX (79760*) | 90,027 | 78,380 |
| Murfreesboro, TN (37130) | 32,845 | 26,360 | Ogden, UT (84401*) | 64,407 | 69,478 |
| Murray, UT (84107) | 25,750 | 21,206 | Oklahoma City, OK (73125*) | 403,136 | 368,164 |
| Muskegon, MI (49440*) | 40,823 | 44,631 | Olathe, KS (66061*) | 37,258 | 17,917 |
| Muskogee, OK (74401) | 40,011 | 37,331 | Olympia, WA (98501*) | 27,447 | 23,296 |
| Nacogdoches, TX (75961) | 27,149 | 22,544 | Omaha, NE (68108*) | 313,911 | 346,929 |
| Nampa, ID (83651) | 25,112 | 20,768 | Ontario, CA (91761*) | 88,820 | 64,118 |
| Napa, CA (94558*) | 50,879 | 36,103 | Orange, CA (92667*) | 91,788 | 77,365 |
| Naperville, IL (60566*) | 42,330 | 22,794 | Orange, NJ (07051*) | 31,136 | 32,566 |
| Nashua, NH (03061*) | 67,865 | 55,820 | Orem, UT (84057*) | 52,399 | 25,729 |
| Nashville, TN (37202*) | 455,651 | 426,029 | Orlando, FL (32802*) | 128,291 | 99,006 |
| National City, CA (92050) | 48,772 | 43,184 | Oshkosh, WI (54901) | 49,620 | 53,082 |
| Naugatuck, CT (06770) | 26,456 | 23,034 | Ottumwa, IA (52501) | 27,381 | 29,610 |
| New Albany, IN (47150) | 37,103 | 38,402 | Overland Park, KS (66204) | 81,784 | 77,934 |
| Newark, CA (94560) | 32,126 | 27,153 | Owensboro, KY (43201) | 54,450 | 50,329 |
| Newark, DE (19711*) | 25,247 | 21,298 | Oxnard, CA (93030*) | 108,195 | 71,225 |
| Newark, NJ (07102*) | 329,248 | 381,930 | Pacifica, CA (94044) | 36,866 | 36,020 |
| Newark, OH (43055) | 41,200 | 41,836 | Paducah, KY (42001) | 29,315 | 31,627 |
| New Bedford, MA (02741*) | 98,478 | 101,777 | Palatine, IL (60067*) | 32,166 | 26,050 |
| New Berlin, WI (53151) | 30,529 | 26,910 | Palm Springs, CA (92263*) | 32,366 | 20,936 |
| New Britain, CT (06050*) | 73,840 | 83,441 | Palo Alto, CA (94303*) | 55,225 | 56,040 |
| New Brunswick, NJ (08901*) | 41,442 | 41,885 | Panama City, FL (32401*) | 33,346 | 32,096 |
| New Castle, PA (16101*) | 33,621 | 38,559 | Paramount, CA (90723) | 36,407 | 34,734 |
| New Haven, CT (06511*) | 126,109 | 137,707 | Paramus, NJ (07652) | 26,474 | 28,381 |
| New Iberia, LA (70560) | 32,766 | 30,147 | Paris, TX (75460) | 25,498 | 23,441 |
| New London, CT (06320) | 28,842 | 31,630 | Parkersburg, WV (26101*) | 39,967 | 44,208 |
| New Orleans, LA (70113*) | 557,927 | 593,471 | Park Forest, IL (60466) | 26,222 | 30,638 |
| Newport, RI (02840) | 29,259 | 34,562 | Park Ridge, IL (60068) | 38,704 | 42,614 |
| Newport Beach, CA (92660*) | 62,556 | 49,582 | Parma, OH (44129) | 92,548 | 100,216 |
| Newport News, VA (23607*) | 144,903 | 138,177 | Pasadena, CA (91109*) | 118,550 | 112,951 |
| New Rochelle, NY (10802*) | 70,794 | 75,385 | Pasadena, TX (77501*) | 112,560 | 89,957 |
| Newton, MA (02158) | 83,622 | 91,263 | Pascagoula, MS (39567) | 29,318 | 27,264 |
| New York, NY (10001*) | 7,071,639 | 7,895,563 | Passaic, NJ (07055) | 52,463 | 55,124 |
| Bronx borough (10451*) | 1,168,972 | 1,471,701 | Paterson, NJ (07510*) | 137,970 | 144,824 |
| Brooklyn borough (11201*) | 2,230,936 | 2,602,012 | Pawtucket, RI (02860*) | 71,204 | 76,984 |
| Manhattan borough (10001*) | 1,428,285 | 1,539,233 | Peabody, MA (01960) | 45,976 | 48,080 |
| Queens borough[1] | 1,891,325 | 1,987,174 | Pembroke Pines, FL (33024) | 35,776 | 15,496 |
| Staten Island borough (10314*) | 352,121 | 295,443 | Pensacola, FL (32501*) | 57,619 | 59,507 |
| Niagara Falls, NY (14302*) | 71,384 | 85,615 | Peoria, IL (61601*) | 124,160 | 126,963 |
| Niles, IL (60648) | 30,363 | 31,432 | Perth Amboy, NJ (08861*) | 38,951 | 38,798 |
| Norfolk, VA (23501*) | 266,979 | 307,951 | Petaluma, CA (94952) | 33,834 | 24,870 |
| Normal, IL (61761) | 35,672 | 26,396 | Petersburg, VA (23804*) | 41,055 | 36,103 |
| Norman, OK (73070*) | 68,020 | 52,117 | Phenix City, AL (36867) | 26,928 | 25,281 |
| Norristown, PA (19401*) | 34,684 | 38,169 | Philadelphia, PA (19104*) | 1,688,210 | 1,949,996 |
| Northampton, MA (01060) | 29,286 | 29,664 | Phoenix, AZ (85026*) | 789,704 | 584,303 |
| Northbrook, IL (60062) | 30,778 | 25,422 | Pico Rivera, CA (90660) | 53,387 | 54,170 |
| North Charleston, SC (29406) | 62,534 | — | Pine Bluff, AR (71601*) | 56,636 | 57,389 |
| North Chicago, IL (60064) | 38,774 | 47,275 | Pinellas Park, FL (33565) | 32,811 | 22,287 |
| Northglenn, CO (80233) | 29,847 | 27,785 | Pittsburg, CA (94565) | 33,034 | 21,423 |
| North Las Vegas, NV (89030) | 42,739 | 46,067 | Pittsburgh, PA (15219*) | 423,959 | 520,089 |
| North Little Rock, AR (72114*) | 64,288 | 60,040 | Pittsfield, MA (01201) | 51,974 | 57,020 |
| North Miami, FL (33161) | 42,566 | 34,767 | Placentia, CA (92670) | 35,041 | 21,948 |
| North Miami Beach, FL (33160) | 36,553 | 30,544 | Plainfield, NJ (07061*) | 45,555 | 46,862 |
| North Olmsted, OH (44070) | 36,486 | 34,861 | Plano, TX (75074*) | 72,331 | 17,872 |
| North Richland Hills, TX (76118) | 30,592 | 16,514 | Plantation, FL (33318) | 48,653 | 23,523 |
| North Tonawanda, NY (14120) | 35,760 | 36,012 | Pleasant Hill, CA (94523) | 25,124 | 24,610 |
| Norwalk, CA (90650) | 85,286 | 90,164 | Pleasanton, CA (94566) | 35,160 | 18,328 |
| Norwalk, CT (06856*) | 77,767 | 79,288 | Plum, PA (15239) | 25,390 | 21,932 |
| Norwich, CT (06360) | 38,074 | 41,739 | | | |

| City and major ZIP code | 1980 census | 1970 census | City and major ZIP code | 1980 census | 1970 census |
|---|---|---|---|---|---|
| Plymouth, MN (55447*) | 31,615 | 18,077 | St. Paul, MN (55101*) | 270,230 | 309,866 |
| Pocatello, ID (83201) | 46,340 | 40,036 | St. Petersburg, FL (33730*) | 238,647 | 216,159 |
| Pomona, CA (91766*) | 92,742 | 87,384 | Salem, MA (01970) | 38,220 | 40,556 |
| Pompano Beach, FL (33060*) | 52,618 | 38,587 | Salem, OR (97301*) | 89,233 | 68,725 |
| Ponca City, OK (74601*) | 26,238 | 25,940 | Salina, KS (67401) | 41,843 | 37,714 |
| Pontiac, MI (48056*) | 76,715 | 85,279 | Salinas, CA (93907*) | 80,479 | 58,896 |
| Portage, IN (46368) | 27,409 | 19,127 | Salt Lake City, UT (84119*) | 163,697 | 175,885 |
| Portage, MI (49081) | 38,157 | 33,590 | San Angelo, TX (76902*) | 73,240 | 63,884 |
| Port Arthur, TX (77640) | 61,251 | 57,371 | San Antonio, TX (78284*) | 786,023 | 654,153 |
| Port Huron, MI (48060) | 33,981 | 35,794 | San Bernardino, CA (92403*) | 118,794 | 106,869 |
| Portland, ME (04101*) | 61,572 | 65,116 | San Bruno, CA (94066) | 35,417 | 36,254 |
| Portland, OR (97208*) | 366,383 | 379,967 | San Buenaventura (Ventura), CA (93002*) | 74,393 | 57,964 |
| Portsmouth, NH (03801) | 26,254 | 25,717 | San Clemente, CA (92672) | 27,325 | 17,063 |
| Portsmouth, OH (45662) | 25,943 | 27,633 | San Diego, CA (92199*) | 875,538 | 697,471 |
| Portsmouth, VA (23705*) | 104,577 | 110,963 | Sandusky, OH (44870) | 31,360 | 32,674 |
| Poughkeepsie, NY (12601*) | 29,757 | 32,029 | Sandy City, UT (84070*) | 52,210 | 6,438 |
| Prichard, AL (36610*) | 39,541 | 41,578 | San Francisco, CA (94188*) | 678,974 | 715,674 |
| Providence, RI (02940*) | 156,804 | 179,116 | San Gabriel, CA (91776*) | 30,072 | 29,336 |
| Provo, UT (84603*) | 74,108 | 53,131 | San Jose, CA (95101*) | 629,546 | 459,913 |
| Pueblo, CO (81003*) | 101,686 | 97,774 | San Leandro, CA (94577*) | 63,952 | 68,698 |
| Quincy, IL (62301) | 42,554 | 45,288 | San Luis Obispo, CA (93401) | 34,252 | 28,036 |
| Quincy, MA (02269) | 84,743 | 87,966 | San Mateo, CA (94402*) | 77,561 | 78,991 |
| Racine, WI (53401*) | 85,725 | 95,162 | San Rafael, CA (94901*) | 44,700 | 38,977 |
| Rahway, NJ (07065*) | 26,723 | 29,114 | Santa Ana, CA (92711*) | 204,023 | 155,710 |
| Raleigh, NC (27611*) | 150,255 | 122,830 | Santa Barbara, CA (93102*) | 74,414 | 70,215 |
| Rancho Cucamonga, CA (91730) | 55,250 | — | Santa Clara, CA (95050*) | 87,746 | 86,118 |
| Rancho Palos Verdes, CA (90274) | 36,577 | — | Santa Cruz, CA (95060*) | 41,483 | 32,076 |
| Rapid City, SD (57701) | 46,492 | 43,836 | Santa Fe, NM (87501*) | 48,953 | 41,167 |
| Raytown, MO (64133*) | 31,759 | 33,306 | Santa Maria, CA (93456*) | 39,685 | 32,749 |
| Reading, PA (19603*) | 78,686 | 87,643 | Santa Monica, CA (90406*) | 88,314 | 88,289 |
| Redding, CA (96001*) | 41,995 | 16,659 | Santa Rosa, CA (95402*) | 83,320 | 50,006 |
| Redlands, CA (92373) | 43,619 | 36,355 | Sarasota, FL (33578*) | 48,868 | 40,237 |
| Redondo Beach, CA (90277*) | 57,102 | 57,451 | Saratoga, CA (95070) | 29,261 | 26,810 |
| Redwood City, CA (94064*) | 54,951 | 55,686 | Savannah, GA (31401*) | 141,390 | 118,349 |
| Reno, NV (89510*) | 100,756 | 72,863 | Sayreville, NJ (08872) | 29,969 | 32,508 |
| Renton, WA (98057*) | 30,612 | 25,878 | Schaumburg, IL (60194) | 53,305 | 18,531 |
| Revere, MA (02151) | 42,423 | 43,159 | Schenectady, NY (12301*) | 67,972 | 77,958 |
| Rialto, CA (92376) | 37,474 | 28,370 | Scottsdale, AZ (85251*) | 88,622 | 67,823 |
| Richardson, TX (75080*) | 72,496 | 48,405 | Scranton, PA (18505*) | 88,117 | 102,696 |
| Richfield, MN (55423) | 37,851 | 47,231 | Seal Beach, CA (90740) | 25,975 | 24,441 |
| Richland, WA (99352) | 33,578 | 26,290 | Seaside, CA (93955) | 36,567 | 36,883 |
| Richmond, CA (94802*) | 74,676 | 79,043 | Seattle, WA (98109*) | 493,846 | 530,831 |
| Richmond, IN (47374) | 41,349 | 43,999 | Selma, AL (36701) | 26,684 | 27,379 |
| Richmond, VA (23232*) | 219,214 | 249,332 | Shaker Heights, OH (44120) | 32,487 | 36,306 |
| Ridgewood, NJ (07451*) | 25,208 | 27,547 | Shawnee, KS (66202*) | 29,653 | 20,946 |
| Riverside, CA (92507*) | 170,591 | 140,089 | Shawnee, OK (74801) | 26,506 | 25,075 |
| Riviera Beach, FL (33404) | 26,489 | 21,401 | Sheboygan, WI (53081) | 48,085 | 48,484 |
| Roanoke, VA (24022*) | 100,220 | 92,115 | Shelton, CT (06484) | 31,314 | 27,165 |
| Rochester, MN (55901*) | 57,890 | 53,766 | Sherman, TX (75090) | 30,413 | 29,061 |
| Rochester, NY (14692*) | 241,741 | 295,011 | Shreveport, LA (71102*) | 205,820 | 182,064 |
| Rockford, IL (61125*) | 139,712 | 147,370 | Simi Valley, CA (93065*) | 77,500 | 59,832 |
| Rock Hill, SC (29730) | 35,344 | 33,846 | Sioux City, IA (51101*) | 82,003 | 85,925 |
| Rock Island, IL (61201) | 47,036 | 50,166 | Sioux Falls, SD (57101*) | 81,343 | 72,488 |
| Rockville, MD (20850*) | 43,811 | 42,739 | Skokie, IL (60076*) | 60,278 | 68,322 |
| Rockville Centre, NY (11570) | 25,412 | 27,444 | Slidell, LA (70458) | 26,718 | 16,101 |
| Rocky Mount, NC (27801) | 41,283 | 34,284 | Somerville, MA (02143) | 77,372 | 88,779 |
| Rome, GA (30161) | 29,654 | 30,759 | Somerville, NJ (08876) | 29,969 | 32,508 |
| Rome, NY (13440) | 43,826 | 50,148 | South Bend, IN (46624*) | 109,727 | 125,580 |
| Rosemead, CA (91770) | 42,604 | 40,972 | South Euclid, OH (44121) | 25,713 | 29,579 |
| Roseville, MI (48066) | 54,311 | 60,529 | Southfield, MI (48037*) | 75,568 | 69,285 |
| Roseville, MN (55113*) | 35,820 | 34,438 | South Gate, CA (90280) | 66,784 | 56,909 |
| Roswell, NM (88201) | 39,676 | 33,908 | Southgate, MI (48195) | 32,058 | 33,909 |
| Royal Oak, MI (48068*) | 70,893 | 86,238 | South San Francisco, CA (94080) | 49,393 | 46,646 |
| Sacramento, CA (95813*) | 275,741 | 257,105 | Sparks, NV (89431) | 40,780 | 24,187 |
| Saginaw, MI (48605*) | 77,508 | 91,849 | Spartanburg, SC (29301*) | 43,826 | 44,546 |
| St. Charles, MO (63301) | 36,087 | 31,834 | Spokane, WA (99210*) | 171,300 | 170,516 |
| St. Clair Shores, MI (48080*) | 76,210 | 88,093 | Springfield, IL (62703*) | 100,054 | 91,753 |
| St. Cloud, MN (56301) | 42,566 | 39,691 | Springfield, MA (01101*) | 152,319 | 163,905 |
| St. Joseph, MO (64501*) | 76,691 | 72,748 | Springfield, MO (65801*) | 133,116 | 120,096 |
| St. Louis, MO (63155*) | 453,085 | 622,236 | Springfield, OH (45501*) | 72,563 | 81,941 |
| St. Louis Park, MN (55426*) | 42,931 | 48,883 | | | |

| City and major ZIP code | 1980 census | 1970 census |
|---|---|---|
| Springfield, OR (97477*) | 41,621 | 26,874 |
| Stamford, CT (06904*) | 102,453 | 108,798 |
| State College, PA (16801*) | 36,130 | 32,833 |
| Sterling Heights, MI (48077) | 108,999 | 61,365 |
| Steubenville, OH (43952) | 26,400 | 30,771 |
| Stillwater, OK (74074*) | 38,268 | 31,126 |
| Stockton, CA (95208*) | 149,779 | 109,963 |
| Stow, OH (44224) | 25,303 | 20,061 |
| Strongsville, OH (44136) | 28,577 | 15,182 |
| Suffolk, VA (23434*) | 47,621 | 9,858 |
| Sunnyvale, CA (94086*) | 106,618 | 95,976 |
| Sunrise, FL (33338) | 39,681 | 7,403 |
| Superior, WI (54880) | 29,571 | 32,237 |
| Syracuse, NY (13220*) | 170,105 | 197,297 |
| Tacoma, WA (98413*) | 158,501 | 154,407 |
| Tallahassee, FL (32301*) | 81,548 | 72,624 |
| Tamarac, FL (33320) | 29,376 | 5,193 |
| Tampa, FL (33630*) | 271,523 | 277,714 |
| Taunton, MA (02780) | 45,001 | 43,756 |
| Taylor, MI (48180) | 77,568 | 70,020 |
| Tempe, AZ (85282*) | 106,743 | 63,550 |
| Temple, TX (76501*) | 42,354 | 33,431 |
| Temple City, CA (91780) | 28,972 | 31,034 |
| Terre Haute, IN (47808*) | 61,125 | 70,335 |
| Texarkana, TX (75501*) | 31,271 | 30,497 |
| Texas City, TX (77590*) | 41,403 | 38,908 |
| Thornton, CO (80229) | 40,343 | 13,326 |
| Thousand Oaks, CA (91360*) | 77,072 | 35,873 |
| Tinley Park, IL (60477) | 26,171 | 12,572 |
| Titusville, FL (32780) | 31,910 | 30,515 |
| Toledo, OH (43601*) | 354,635 | 383,062 |
| Topeka, KS (66603*) | 115,266 | 125,011 |
| Torrance, CA (90510*) | 129,881 | 134,968 |
| Torrington, CT (06790) | 30,987 | 31,952 |
| Trenton, NJ (08650*) | 92,124 | 104,786 |
| Troy, MI (48099*) | 67,102 | 39,419 |
| Troy, NY (12180*) | 56,638 | 62,918 |
| Tucson, AZ (85726*) | 330,537 | 262,933 |
| Tulsa, OK (74101*) | 360,919 | 330,350 |
| Turlock, CA (95380) | 26,287 | 13,992 |
| Tuscaloosa, AL (35403*) | 75,211 | 65,773 |
| Tustin, CA (92680) | 32,317 | 22,313 |
| Twin Falls, ID (83301) | 26,209 | 21,914 |
| Tyler, TX (75712*) | 70,508 | 57,770 |
| Union City, CA (94587) | 39,406 | 14,724 |
| Union City, NJ (07087) | 55,593 | 57,305 |
| University City, MO (63130) | 42,738 | 47,527 |
| Upland, CA (91786) | 47,647 | 32,551 |
| Upper Arlington, OH (43221) | 35,648 | 38,727 |
| Urbana, IL (61801) | 35,978 | 33,976 |
| Utica, NY (13504*) | 75,632 | 91,373 |
| Vacaville, CA (95688) | 43,367 | 21,690 |
| Valdosta, GA (31601) | 37,596 | 32,303 |
| Vallejo, CA (94590*) | 80,303 | 71,710 |
| Valley Stream, NY (11580*) | 35,769 | 40,413 |
| Vancouver, WA (98661*) | 42,834 | 41,859 |
| Vicksburg, MS (39180) | 25,434 | 25,478 |
| Victoria, TX (77901*) | 50,695 | 41,349 |
| Vineland, NJ (08360) | 53,753 | 47,399 |
| Virginia Beach, VA (23450*) | 262,199 | 172,106 |
| Visalia, CA (93277*) | 49,729 | 27,130 |

| City and major ZIP code | 1980 census | 1970 census |
|---|---|---|
| Vista, CA (92083) | 35,834 | 24,688 |
| Waco, TX (76701*) | 101,261 | 95,326 |
| Walla Walla, WA (99362) | 25,618 | 23,619 |
| Walnut Creek, CA (94596*) | 53,643 | 39,844 |
| Waltham, MA (02154) | 58,200 | 61,582 |
| Warner Robins, GA (31093) | 39,893 | 33,491 |
| Warren, MI (48089*) | 161,134 | 179,260 |
| Warren, OH (44481*) | 56,629 | 63,494 |
| Warwick, RI (02887*) | 87,123 | 83,694 |
| Washington, DC (20013*) | 638,432 | 756,668 |
| Waterbury, CT (06701*) | 103,266 | 108,033 |
| Waterloo, IA (50701*) | 75,985 | 75,533 |
| Watertown, NY (13601) | 27,861 | 30,787 |
| Waukegan, IL (60085*) | 67,653 | 65,134 |
| Waukesha, WI (53186) | 50,365 | 39,695 |
| Wausau, WI (54401) | 32,426 | 32,806 |
| Wauwatosa, WI (53213) | 51,308 | 58,676 |
| Weirton, WV (26062) | 25,371 | 27,131 |
| West Allis, WI (53213) | 63,982 | 71,649 |
| West Covina, CA (91793*) | 80,291 | 68,034 |
| Westfield, MA (01085) | 36,465 | 31,433 |
| Westfield, NJ (07091*) | 30,447 | 33,720 |
| West Haven, CT (06516) | 53,184 | 52,851 |
| West Jordan, UT (84084) | 27,192 | 4,221 |
| Westland, MI (48185) | 84,603 | 86,749 |
| West Memphis, AR (72301) | 28,138 | 26,070 |
| West Mifflin, PA (15122) | 26,279 | 28,070 |
| Westminster, CA (92683) | 71,133 | 60,076 |
| Westminster, CO (80030*) | 50,211 | 19,512 |
| West New York, NJ (07093) | 39,194 | 40,627 |
| West Orange, NJ (07052) | 39,510 | 43,715 |
| West Palm Beach, FL (33401*) | 63,305 | 57,375 |
| Wheaton, IL (60187) | 43,043 | 31,138 |
| Wheat Ridge, CO (80033) | 30,293 | 29,778 |
| Wheeling, WV (26003) | 43,070 | 48,188 |
| White Plains, NY (10602*) | 46,999 | 50,346 |
| Whittier, CA (90605*) | 69,717 | 72,863 |
| Wichita, KS (67276*) | 279,835 | 276,554 |
| Wichita Falls, TX (76307*) | 94,201 | 96,265 |
| Wilkes-Barre, PA (18701*) | 51,551 | 58,856 |
| Williamsport, PA (17701) | 33,401 | 37,918 |
| Wilmette, IL (60091) | 28,229 | 32,134 |
| Wilmington, DE (19850*) | 70,195 | 80,386 |
| Wilmington, NC (28402*) | 44,000 | 46,169 |
| Wilson, NC (27893) | 34,424 | 29,347 |
| Winona, MN (55987) | 25,075 | 26,438 |
| Winston-Salem, NC (27102*) | 131,885 | 133,683 |
| Woburn, MA (01801) | 36,626 | 37,406 |
| Woodland, CA (95695) | 30,235 | 20,677 |
| Woonsocket, RI (02895) | 45,914 | 46,820 |
| Worcester, MA (01613*) | 161,799 | 176,572 |
| Wyandotte, MI (48192) | 34,006 | 41,061 |
| Wyoming, MI (49509) | 59,616 | 56,560 |
| Yakima, WA (98903*) | 49,826 | 45,588 |
| Yonkers, NY (10701*) | 195,351 | 204,297 |
| Yorba Linda, CA (92686) | 28,254 | 11,856 |
| York, PA (17405*) | 44,619 | 50,335 |
| Youngstown, OH (44501*) | 115,436 | 140,909 |
| Yuma, AZ (85364*) | 42,481 | 29,007 |
| Zanesville, OH (43701) | 28,655 | 33,045 |

1. Queens has four major ZIP codes: 11690*—Far Rockaway; 11351*—Flushing; 11431*—Jamaica; 11101*—Long Island City. *Sources:* Department of Commerce, Bureau of the Census; *National ZIP Code & Post Office Directory.*

## Bay Area Outranks Philadelphia

According to the U.S. Census Bureau, the population of California's Bay Area grew by 441,000 since the 1980 census, displacing Philadelphia as the nation's fourth largest metropolitan area. The Bay area of San Francisco-Oakland-San Jose grew to more than 5.8 million people. This compares with Philadelphia's gain of 100,000, to total nearly 5.8 million.

## Territorial Expansion

| Accession | Date | Area[1] |
|---|---|---|
| United States | — | 3,618,770 |
| Territory in 1790 | — | 891,364 |
| Louisiana Purchase | 1803 | 831,321 |
| Florida | 1819 | 69,866 |
| Texas | 1845 | 384,958 |
| Oregon | 1846 | 283,439 |
| Mexican Cession | 1848 | 530,706 |
| Gadsden Purchase | 1853 | 29,640 |
| Alaska | 1867 | 591,004 |
| Hawaii | 1898 | 6,471 |
| Other territory | — | 4,664 |
| Philippines | 1898 | 115,600 [2] |
| Puerto Rico | 1899 | 3,515 |
| Guam | 1899 | 209 |
| American Samoa | 1900 | 77 |
| Canal Zone[3] | 1904 | 553 |
| Virgin Islands of U.S. | 1917 | 132 |
| Trust Territory of Pacific Islands | 1947 | 717 [4] |
| All other | — | 14 |
| **Total, 1980** | — | **3,623,434** |

1. Total land and water area in square miles. 2. Became independent in 1946. 3. Reverted to Panama. 4. Land area only; includes Northern Mariana Islands. *Source:* Department of Commerce, Bureau of the Census.

## Total Population

| Area | 1960 | 1970 | 1980 |
|---|---|---|---|
| 50 states of U.S. | 179,323,175 | 203,302,031 | 226,545,805 |
| 48 coterminous | 178,464,236 | 202,229,535 | 225,179,263 |
| Alaska | 226,167 | 302,583 | 401,851 |
| Hawaii | 632,772 | 769,913 | 964,691 |
| American Samoa | 20,051 | 27,159 | 32,297 |
| Canal Zone | 42,122 | 44,198 | ([1]) |
| Canton Island | 320 | n.a. | — |
| Corn Islands | 1,872 | ([2]) | — |
| Guam | 67,044 | 84,996 | 105,979 |
| Johnston Atoll | 156 | 1,007 | 327 |
| Midway | 2,356 | 2,220 | 453 |
| Puerto Rico | 2,349,544 | 2,712,033 | 3,196,520 |
| Swan Islands | 28 | 22 | n.a. |
| Trust Ter. of Pac. Is. | 70,724 | 90,940 | 132,929 [3] |
| Virgin Is. of U.S. | 32,099 | 62,468 | 96,569 |
| Wake Island | 1,097 | 1,647 | 302 |
| Population abroad | 1,374,421 | 1,737,836 | 995,546 |
| Armed forces | 609,720 | 1,057,776 | 515,408 |
| Other[4] | n.a. | n.a. | n.a. |
| **Total** | **183,285,009** | **208,066,557** | **231,106,727** |

1. Granted independence on Oct. 1, 1979. 2. Returned to Nicaragua April 25, 1971. 3. Includes Northern Mariana Islands. 4. Includes Baker Island, Enderbury Island, Howland Island, and Jarvis Island, all uninhabited. NOTE: n.a. = unavailable. *Source:* Department of Commerce, Bureau of the Census.

## Population by Race, 1980 Census

| State | White | Black | Spanish origin | Other | State | White | Black | Spanish origin | Other |
|---|---|---|---|---|---|---|---|---|---|
| Ala. | 2,869,688 | 995,623 | 33,100 | 24,750 | Mont. | 740,148 | 1,786 | 9,974 | 44,756 |
| Alaska | 308,455 | 13,619 | 9,497 | 78,407 | Neb. | 1,490,569 | 48,389 | 28,020 | 31,048 |
| Ariz. | 2,240,033 | 75,034 | 440,915 | 402,799 | Nev. | 699,377 | 50,791 | 53,786 | 49,016 |
| Ark. | 1,890,002 | 373,192 | 17,873 | 22,319 | N.H. | 910,099 | 3,990 | 5,587 | 6,521 |
| Calif. | 18,031,689 | 1,819,282 | 4,543,770 | 3,817,591 | N.J. | 6,127,090 | 924,786 | 491,867 | 312,282 |
| Colo. | 2,570,596 | 101,702 | 339,300 | 216,517 | N.M. | 976,465 | 24,042 | 476,089 | 299,461 |
| Conn. | 2,799,420 | 217,433 | 124,499 | 90,723 | N.Y. | 13,961,106 | 2,401,842 | 1,659,245 | 1,194,340 |
| Del. | 488,543 | 95,971 | 9,671 | 10,711 | N.C. | 4,453,010 | 1,316,050 | 56,607 | 105,369 |
| D.C. | 171,796 | 488,229 | 17,652 | 17,626 | N.D. | 625,536 | 2,568 | 3,903 | 24,591 |
| Fla. | 8,178,387 | 1,342,478 | 857,898 | 219,127 | Ohio | 9,597,266 | 1,076,734 | 119,880 | 123,419 |
| Ga. | 3,948,007 | 1,465,457 | 61,261 | 50,801 | Okla. | 2,597,783 | 204,658 | 57,413 | 222,825 |
| Hawaii | 318,608 | 17,352 | 71,479 | 629,040 | Ore. | 2,490,192 | 37,059 | 65,833 | 105,412 |
| Idaho | 901,641 | 2,716 | 36,615 | 39,578 | Pa. | 10,654,325 | 1,047,609 | 154,004 | 164,794 |
| Ill. | 9,225,575 | 1,675,229 | 635,525 | 517,657 | R.I. | 896,692 | 27,584 | 19,707 | 22,878 |
| Ind. | 5,004,567 | 414,732 | 87,020 | 70,880 | S.C. | 2,145,122 | 948,146 | 33,414 | 25,940 |
| Iowa | 2,838,805 | 41,700 | 25,536 | 32,882 | S.D. | 638,955 | 2,144 | 4,028 | 49,079 |
| Kan. | 2,167,752 | 126,127 | 63,333 | 69,329 | Tenn. | 3,835,078 | 725,949 | 34,081 | 29,723 |
| Ky. | 3,379,648 | 259,490 | 27,403 | 22,295 | Tex. | 11,197,663 | 1,710,250 | 2,985,643 | 1,320,470 |
| La. | 2,911,243 | 1,237,263 | 99,105 | 55,466 | Utah | 1,382,550 | 9,225 | 60,302 | 69,262 |
| Me. | 1,109,850 | 3,128 | 5,005 | 11,682 | Vt. | 506,736 | 1,135 | 3,304 | 3,585 |
| Md. | 3,158,412 | 958,050 | 64,740 | 99,984 | Va. | 4,229,734 | 1,008,311 | 79,873 | 108,234 |
| Mass. | 5,362,836 | 221,279 | 141,043 | 152,922 | Wash. | 3,777,296 | 105,544 | 119,986 | 247,323 |
| Mich. | 7,868,956 | 1,198,710 | 162,388 | 190,678 | W. Va. | 1,874,751 | 65,051 | 12,707 | 9,842 |
| Minn. | 3,936,948 | 53,342 | 32,124 | 86,858 | Wis. | 4,442,598 | 182,593 | 62,981 | 80,144 |
| Miss. | 1,615,190 | 887,206 | 24,731 | 18,242 | Wyo. | 447,716 | 3,364 | 24,499 | 19,736 |
| Mo. | 4,346,267 | 514,274 | 51,667 | 56,903 | **Total** | **188,340,790** | **26,488,218** | **14,605,883** | **11,675,817** |

*Source:* Department of Commerce, Bureau of the Census.

### Never Married Adults Rate Rising

The percentage of young adults in their twenties and early thirties that have never married has increased. Among men 20 to 24, the percentage that had not married increased to 75 percent. For women in the same age group, the percentage increased to 57 percent. The never married percentage also increased significantly for people 25 to 29 and those 30 to 34.

## Immigration to U.S. by Country of Origin

(Figures are totals, not annual averages, and were tabulated as follows: 1820–67, alien passengers arrived; 1868–91 and 1895–97, immigrant aliens arrived; 1892–94 and 1898 to present, immigrant aliens admitted. Data before 1906 relate to country whence alien came; 1906-80, to country of last permanent residence; 1981 to present data based on country of birth.

| Countries | 1985 | 1820–1985 | 1971-80 | 1961-70 | 1951-60 | 1941-50 | 1931-40 | 1820–1930 |
|---|---|---|---|---|---|---|---|---|
| **Europe:** Albania[1] | 45 | 2,744 | 329 | 98 | 59 | 85 | 2,040 | — |
| Austria[2] | 419 | 4,320,478 | 9,478 | 20,621 | 67,106 | 24,860 | 3,563 | 3,658,978 |
| Belgium | 538 | 206,129 | 5,329 | 9,192 | 18,575 | 12,189 | 4,817 | 153,388 |
| Bulgaria[3] | 249 | 69,148 | 1,188 | 619 | 104 | 375 | 938 | 64,918 |
| Czechoslovakia[1] | 1,222 | 143,713 | 6,023 | 3,273 | 918 | 8,347 | 14,393 | 105,620 |
| Denmark | 478 | 367,514 | 4,439 | 9,201 | 10,984 | 5,393 | 2,559 | 332,466 |
| Estonia[1] | 7 | 1,228 | 91 | 163 | 185 | 212 | 506 | — |
| Finland[1] | 290 | 35,609 | 2,868 | 4,192 | 4,925 | 2,503 | 2,146 | 17,447 |
| France | 2,187 | 765,356 | 25,069 | 45,237 | 51,121 | 38,809 | 12,623 | 582,375 |
| Germany[2] | 7,235 | 7,026,077 | 74,414 | 190,796 | 477,765 | 226,578 | 114,058 | 5,907,893 |
| Great Britain: England | 13,408 | 5,023,150 | 137,374 | 174,452 | 156,171 | 112,252 | 21,756 | 2,619,435 |
| Scotland | — | — | — | 29,849 | 32,854 | 16,131 | 6,887 | 726,887 |
| Wales | — | — | — | 2,052 | 2,589 | 3,209 | 735 | 85,659 |
| Not specified[4] | — | — | — | 3,675 | 3,884 | — | — | 793,741 |
| Greece | 2,579 | 681,801 | 92,369 | 85,969 | 47,608 | 8,973 | 9,119 | 421,489 |
| Hungary[2] | 1,009 | — | 6,550 | 5,401 | 36,637 | 3,469 | 7,861 | 473,373 |
| Ireland | 1,397 | 4,697,526 | 11,490 | 37,461 | 57,332 | 26,967 | 13,167 | 4,578,941 |
| Italy | 3,214 | 5,323,729 | 129,368 | 214,111 | 185,491 | 57,661 | 68,028 | 4,651,195 |
| Latvia[1] | 25 | 2,799 | 207 | 510 | 352 | 361 | 1,192 | — |
| Lithuania[1] | 39 | 4,155 | 248 | 562 | 242 | 683 | 2,201 | — |
| Luxembourg[1] | 17 | 3,041 | 307 | 556 | 684 | 820 | 565 | — |
| Netherlands | 1,217 | 367,657 | 10,492 | 30,606 | 52,277 | 14,860 | 7,150 | 246,609 |
| Norway[5] | 361 | 859,133 | 3,941 | 15,484 | 22,935 | 10,100 | 4,740 | 800,115 |
| Poland[6] | 9,464 | 559,329 | 37,234 | 53,539 | 9,985 | 7,571 | 17,026 | 397,729 |
| Portugal | 3,781 | 481,180 | 101,710 | 76,065 | 19,588 | 7,423 | 3,329 | 252,715 |
| Romania[7] | 5,188 | 190,817 | 12,393 | 2,531 | 1,039 | 1,076 | 3,871 | 153,074 |
| Spain | 1,413 | 272,325 | 34,141 | 44,659 | 7,894 | 2,898 | 3,258 | 166,865 |
| Sweden[5] | 1,076 | 1,278,083 | 6,531 | 17,116 | 21,697 | 10,665 | 3,960 | 1,213,488 |
| Switzerland | 729 | 353,846 | 8,235 | 18,453 | 17,675 | 10,547 | 5,512 | 290,168 |
| U.S.S.R.[8] | 3,521 | 3,425,284 | 38,961 | 2,336 | 584 | 548 | 1,356 | 3,341,991 |
| Yugoslavia[3] | 1,662 | 125,588 | 30,540 | 20,381 | 8,225 | 1,576 | 5,835 | 50,952 |
| Other Europe | 273 | 57,465 | 4,049 | 4,203 | 8,155 | 3,983 | 2,361 | 33,699 |
| Total Europe | 63,043 | 36,659,826 | 800,368 | 1,123,363 | 1,325,640 | 621,124 | 347,552 | 32,121,210 |
| **Asia:** China[9] | 39,682 | 748,414 | 124,326 | 34,764 | 9,657 | 16,709 | 4,928 | 377,245 |
| India | 26,026 | 324,631 | 164,154 | 27,189 | 1,973 | 1,761 | 496 | 9,377 |
| Japan[10] | 4,086 | 435,179 | 49,775 | 39,988 | 46,250 | 1,555 | 1,948 | 275,643 |
| Turkey | 1,691 | 400,471 | 13,399 | 10,142 | 3,519 | 798 | 1,065 | 360,171 |
| Other Asia | 193,206 | 2,740,431 | 1,236,544 | 315,688 | 88,707 | 11,537 | 7,644 | 35,895 |
| Total Asia[11] | 264,691 | 4,649,126 | 1,588,178 | 427,771 | 150,106 | 32,360 | 16,081 | 1,058,331 |
| **America:** Canada and | | | | | | | | |
| Newfoundland[12] | 11,385 | 4,194,190 | 169,939 | 413,310 | 377,952 | 171,718 | 108,527 | 2,897,201 |
| Central America | 26,302 | 474,666 | 134,640 | 101,330 | 44,751 | 21,665 | 5,861 | 43,293 |
| Mexico[13] | 61,077 | 2,567,973 | 640,294 | 453,937 | 299,811 | 60,589 | 22,319 | 755,936 |
| South America | 39,058 | 972,422 | 295,741 | 257,954 | 91,628 | 21,831 | 7,803 | 113,499 |
| West Indies | 85,281 | 2,202,958 | 741,126 | 470,213 | 123,091 | 49,725 | 15,502 | 431,469 |
| Other America[13] | — | 109,896 | 789 | 19,630 | 59,711 | 29,276 | 25 | 31 |
| Total America | 221,103 | 10,521,805 | 1,982,529 | 1,716,374 | 996,944 | 354,804 | 160,037 | 4,241,429 |
| **Africa** | 17,117 | 234,336 | 80,779 | 28,954 | 14,092 | 7,367 | 1,750 | 24,310 |
| **Australia and New Zealand** | 2,041 | 132,972 | 23,788 | 19,562 | 11,506 | 13,805 | 2,231 | 52,301 |
| Pacific Islands[14] | 113 | 25,461 | 1,806 | 1,769 | 4,698 | 5,437 | 780 | 10,365 |
| Countries not specified[15] | 1,901 | 296,832 | 15,866 | 3,884 | 12,493 | 142 | — | 254,066 |
| **Total all countries** | 570,009 | 52,520,358 | 4,493,314 | 3,321,677 | 2,515,479 | 1,035,039 | 528,431 | 37,762,012 |

1. Countries established since beginning of World War I are included with countries to which they belonged. 2. Data for Austria-Hungary not reported until 1861. Austria and Hungary recorded separately after 1905. Austria included with Germany 1938–45. 3. Bulgaria, Serbia, Montenegro first reported in 1899. Bulgaria reported separately since 1920. In 1920, separate enumeration for Kingdom of Serbs, Croats, Slovenes; since 1922, recorded as Yugoslavia. 4. United Kingdom not specified; for 1901–51, included in "Other Europe." 5. Norway included with Sweden 1820–68. 6. Included with Austria-Hungary, Germany, and Russia 1899–1919. 7. No record of immigration until 1880. 8. From 1931–63, the U.S.S.R. was broken down into European U.S.S.R. and Asian U.S.S.R. Since 1964, total U.S.S.R. has been reported in Europe. 9. Beginning in 1957, China includes Taiwan. 10. No record of immigration until 1861. 11. From 1952, Asia included Philippines. From 1934–51, Philippines were included in Pacific Islands; before 1934, total U.S.S.R. has been reported in separate tables as insular travel. 12. Includes all British North American possessions, 1820–98. 13. No record of immigration, 1886–93. 14. Included with "Countries not specified" prior to 1925. 15. Includes 32,897 persons returning in 1906 to their homes in U.S. *Source:* Department of Justice, Immigration and Naturalization Service. NOTE: Data are latest available.

## Immigrant and Nonimmigrant Aliens Admitted to U.S.

| Period[1] | Immigrants | Non-immigrants | Total | Period[1] | Immigrants | Non-immigrants | Total |
|---|---|---|---|---|---|---|---|
| 1901-10 | 8,795,386 | 1,007,909 | 9,803,295 | 1978 | 601,442 | 9,343,710 | 9,945,152 |
| 1911-20 | 5,735,811 | 1,376,271 | 7,112,082 | 1979[2] | 460,348 | 7,060,082 | 7,520,430 |
| 1921-30 | 4,107,209 | 1,774,896 | 5,882,090 | 1980 | 530,639 | n.a. | — |
| 1931-40 | 528,431 | 1,574,071 | 2,102,502 | 1981 | 596,600 | 11,756,903 | 12,353,503 |
| 1941-50 | 1,035,039 | 2,461,359 | 3,496,398 | 1982 | 594,131 | 11,779,359 | 12,373,490 |
| 1951-60 | 2,515,479 | 7,113,023 | 9,628,502 | 1983[3] | 559,763 | 9,849,458 | 10,409,221 |
| 1961-70 | 3,321,677 | 24,107,224 | 27,428,901 | 1984 | 543,903 | 9,426,759 | 9,970,662 |
| 1971-77 | 2,797,209 | 45,236,597 | 48,033,806 | 1985 | 570,009 | n.a. | — |

1. Fiscal year ending June 30 prior to 1977. After 1977 for fiscal year ending Sept. 30, except as noted. 2. Figures for October 1978–June 1979. 3. Figures for calendar year 1983. Nonimmigrant aliens include visitors for business or pleasure, students, foreign government officials, and others temporarily in the U.S. NOTE: n.a. = not available. *Source:* Department of Justice, Immigration and Naturalization Service.

## Persons Naturalized Since 1907

| Period[1] | Civilian | Military | Total | Period[1] | Civilian | Military | Total |
|---|---|---|---|---|---|---|---|
| 1907-30 | 2,713,389 | 300,506 | 3,013,895 | 1979[3] | 158,276 | 5,874 | 164,150 |
| 1931-40 | 1,498,573 | 19,891 | 1,518,464 | 1980 | 153,343 | 4,595 | 157,938 |
| 1941-50 | 1,837,229 | 149,799 | 1,987,028 | 1981 | 162,227 | 4,090 | 166,317 |
| 1951-60 | 1,148,241 | 41,705 | 1,189,946 | 1982 | 170,071 | 3,617 | 173,688 |
| 1961-70 | 1,084,195 | 36,068 | 1,120,263 | 1983 | 175,752 | 3,196 | 178,948 |
| 1971-80 | 1,397,846 | 66,926 | 1,464,772 | 1907-83 | 10,187,523 | 625,798 | 10,813,321 |

1. Fiscal year ending June 30, except as noted. 2. Starting 1977, Fiscal year ending Sept. 30. *Source:* Department of Justice, Immigration and Naturalization Service. NOTE: Data are latest available.

## Population of Largest Indian Reservations, 1985

| | | | | | |
|---|---|---|---|---|---|
| Navajo (Ariz., N.M., Utah) | 166,665 | Rosebud (S.D.) | 11,685 | Yakima (Wash.) | 7,987 |
| Cherokee (Okla.) | 42,992 | Gila River (Ariz.) | 10,556 | Zuni (N.M.) | 7,754 |
| Creek (Okla.) | 42,519 | Turtle Mountain (N.D.) | 9,583 | Northern Pueblos (N.M.) | 7,705 |
| Papago (Ariz.) | 22,501 | Chickasaw (Okla.) | 9,020 | Shawnee (Okla.) | 7,615 |
| Choctaw (Okla.) | 20,054 | Hopi (Ariz.) | 8,952 | Pawnee (Okla.) | 7,335 |
| Pine Ridge (S.D.) | 18,191 | Standing Rock (N.D., S.D.) | 8,443 | Blackfeet (Mont.) | 6,715 |
| South Pueblos (N.M.) | 16,375 | Fort Apache (Ariz.) | 8,311 | Wind River (Wyo.) | 5,254 |

NOTE: The Bureau of Indian Affairs lists 786,019 Indians residing on or near Federal reservations as of January 1985. The total Indian population of the United States, according to the 1980 census, is 1,418,195. *Source:* Department of the Interior, Bureau of Indian Affairs.

## Persons Below Poverty Level
## by Age, Region, Race, and Spanish Origin, 1984

| | Number below poverty level (1,000) | | | | Percent below poverty level | | | |
|---|---|---|---|---|---|---|---|---|
| Age and region | All races[2] | White | Black | Spanish origin[1] | All races[2] | White | Black | Spanish origin[1] |
| Under 15 years | 11,455 | 7,195 | 3,805 | 2,049 | 22.2 | 17.2 | 48.5 | 39.9 |
| 15 to 21 | 4,633 | 3,070 | 1,371 | 714 | 17.6 | 14.2 | 35.9 | 32.1 |
| 22 to 44 | 9,886 | 6,902 | 2,549 | 1,440 | 11.7 | 9.6 | 26.1 | 22.8 |
| 45 to 64 | 4,398 | 3,209 | 1,056 | 427 | 9.9 | 8.2 | 24.0 | 17.7 |
| 65 and older | 3,330 | 2,579 | 710 | 176 | 12.4 | 10.7 | 31.7 | 21.5 |
| Northeast | 6,531 | 4,646 | 1,754 | 1,216 | 13.2 | 10.7 | 33.2 | 38.7 |
| Midwest | 8,303 | 6,004 | 2,112 | 427 | 14.1 | 11.5 | 37.9 | 30.1 |
| South | 12,792 | 7,573 | 5,012 | 1,391 | 16.2 | 12.0 | 33.6 | 26.0 |
| West | 6,074 | 4,732 | 612 | 1,772 | 13.1 | 11.8 | 26.6 | 25.3 |
| Total | 33,700 | 22,955 | 9,490 | 4,806 | 14.4 | 11.5 | 33.8 | 28.4 |

1. Persons of Spanish origin may be any race. 2. Includes races not shown separately. *Source:* U.S. Bureau of the Census.

## Population Projections to 2075[1]
### (in millions)

| Sex, race, age group | 2000 | 2025 | 2050 | 2075 | Sex, race, age group | 2000 | 2025 | 2050 | 2075 |
|---|---|---|---|---|---|---|---|---|---|
| **MALE, WHITE** | 108.8 | 117.3 | 115.1 | 112.7 | **FEMALE, BLACK** | 18.7 | 23.9 | 27.2 | 28.8 |
| Up to 19 years | 30.5 | 28.9 | 27.7 | 26.7 | Up to 19 years | 6.2 | 6.7 | 6.7 | 6.5 |
| 20 to 39 years | 31.2 | 30.5 | 29.3 | 28.2 | 20 to 39 years | 5.5 | 6.5 | 7.0 | 6.8 |
| 40 to 59 years | 30.5 | 29.1 | 28.9 | 28.1 | 40 to 59 years | 4.4 | 5.5 | 6.5 | 6.9 |
| 60 to 79 years | 13.8 | 24.8 | 22.2 | 22.0 | 60 to 79 years | 2.0 | 4.2 | 4.9 | 5.7 |
| 80 and over | 2.8 | 4.0 | 7.0 | 7.6 | 80 and over | 0.6 | 1.0 | 2.2 | 2.9 |
| **FEMALE, WHITE** | 114.0 | 123.4 | 123.0 | 119.9 | **TOTALS**[2] | 268.0 | 301.0 | 308.8 | 310.6 |
| Up to 19 years | 29.0 | 27.5 | 26.3 | 25.3 | Up to 19 years | 74.9 | 73.7 | 72.1 | 70.6 |
| 20 to 39 years | 30.2 | 29.4 | 28.3 | 27.2 | 20 to 39 years | 75.2 | 76.8 | 76.3 | 74.9 |
| 40 to 59 years | 31.1 | 29.1 | 28.7 | 27.9 | 40 to 59 years | 72.4 | 72.4 | 74.9 | 75.3 |
| 60 to 79 years | 17.4 | 28.9 | 25.4 | 24.8 | 60 to 79 years | 35.4 | 63.7 | 59.8 | 61.7 |
| 80 and over | 6.3 | 8.5 | 14.3 | 14.5 | 80 and over | 10.1 | 14.4 | 15.7 | 28.2 |
| **MALE, BLACK** | 17.1 | 22.0 | 25.0 | 26.5 | Males | 130.4 | 146.1 | 148.8 | 149.9 |
| Up to 19 years | 6.4 | 6.9 | 6.8 | 6.6 | Females | 137.6 | 154.9 | 160.1 | 160.7 |
| 20 to 39 years | 5.4 | 6.5 | 7.0 | 6.9 | White | 222.8 | 240.7 | 238.1 | 232.6 |
| 40 to 59 years | 3.8 | 5.2 | 6.2 | 6.7 | Black | 35.7 | 45.9 | 52.1 | 55.3 |
| 60 to 79 years | 1.3 | 3.1 | 4.0 | 4.8 | Median age | 36.3 | 40.0 | 41.6 | 42.6 |
| 80 and over | 0.2 | 0.4 | 1.0 | 1.4 | | | | | |

1. Based on average of 1.9 lifetime births per woman. 2. Includes all races. NOTE: Zero population growth is expected to be reached by 2050. Details may not add because of rounding. *Source:* Department of Commerce, Bureau of the Census.

# Marriage and Divorce

## Marriages and Divorces

| Year | Marriage Number | Marriage Rate[2] | Divorce[1] Number | Divorce[1] Rate[2] | Year | Marriage Number | Marriage Rate[2] | Divorce[1] Number | Divorce[1] Rate[2] |
|---|---|---|---|---|---|---|---|---|---|
| 1900 | 709,000 | 9.3 | 55,751 | .7 | 1962 | 1,577,000 | 8.5 | 413,000 | 2.2 |
| 1905 | 842,000 | 10.0 | 67,976 | .8 | 1963 | 1,654,000 | 8.8 | 428,000 | 2.3 |
| 1910 | 948,166 | 10.3 | 83,045 | .9 | 1964 | 1,725,000 | 9.0 | 450,000 | 2.4 |
| 1915 | 1,007,595 | 10.0 | 104,298 | 1.0 | 1965 | 1,800,000 | 9.3 | 479,000 | 2.5 |
| 1920 | 1,274,476 | 12.0 | 170,505 | 1.6 | 1966 | 1,857,000 | 9.5 | 499,000 | 2.5 |
| 1925 | 1,188,334 | 10.3 | 175,449 | 1.5 | 1967 | 1,927,000 | 9.7 | 523,000 | 2.6 |
| 1930 | 1,126,856 | 9.2 | 195,961 | 1.6 | 1968 | 2,069,258 | 10.4 | 584,000 | 2.9 |
| 1935 | 1,327,000 | 10.4 | 218,000 | 1.7 | 1969 | 2,145,438 | 10.6 | 639,000 | 3.2 |
| 1940 | 1,595,879 | 12.1 | 264,000 | 2.0 | 1970 | 2,158,802 | 10.6 | 708,000 | 3.5 |
| 1945 | 1,612,992 | 12.2 | 485,000 | 3.5 | 1971 | 2,190,481 | 10.6 | 773,000 | 3.7 |
| 1948 | 1,811,155 | 12.4 | 408,000 | 2.8 | 1972 | 2,282,154 | 11.0 | 845,000 | 4.1 |
| 1949 | 1,579,798 | 10.6 | 397,000 | 2.7 | 1973 | 2,284,108 | 10.9 | 915,000 | 4.4 |
| 1950 | 1,667,231 | 11.1 | 385,144 | 2.6 | 1974 | 2,229,667 | 10.5 | 977,000 | 4.6 |
| 1951 | 1,594,694 | 10.4 | 381,000 | 2.5 | 1975 | 2,152,662 | 10.1 | 1,036,000 | 4.9 |
| 1952 | 1,539,318 | 9.9 | 392,000 | 2.5 | 1976 | 2,154,807 | 10.0 | 1,083,000 | 5.0 |
| 1953 | 1,546,000 | 9.8 | 390,000 | 2.5 | 1977 | 2,178,367 | 10.1 | 1,091,000 | 5.0 |
| 1954 | 1,490,000 | 9.2 | 379,000 | 2.4 | 1978 | 2,282,272 | 10.5 | 1,130,000 | 5.2 |
| 1955 | 1,531,000 | 9.3 | 377,000 | 2.3 | 1979 | 2,341,799 | 10.6 | 1,181,000 | 5.4 |
| 1956 | 1,585,000 | 9.5 | 382,000 | 2.3 | 1980 | 2,406,708 | 10.6 | 1,182,000 | 5.2 |
| 1957 | 1,518,000 | 8.9 | 381,000 | 2.2 | 1981 | 2,438,000 | 10.6 | 1,219,000 | 5.3 |
| 1958 | 1,451,000 | 8.4 | 368,000 | 2.1 | 1982 | 2,495,000 | 10.8 | 1,180,000 | 5.1 |
| 1959 | 1,494,000 | 8.5 | 395,000 | 2.2 | 1983 | 2,444,000 | 10.5 | 1,179,000 | 5.0 |
| 1960 | 1,523,000 | 8.5 | 393,000 | 2.2 | 1984 | 2,487,000 | 10.5 | 1,155,000 | 4.9 |
| 1961 | 1,548,000 | 8.5 | 414,000 | 2.3 | 1985[3] | 2,425,000 | 10.2 | 1,187,000 | 5.0 |

1. Includes annulments. 2. Per 1,000 population. Divorce rates for 1941–46 are based on population including armed forces overseas. Marriage rates are based on population excluding armed forces overseas. 3. Provisional. NOTE: Marriage and divorce figures for most years include some estimated data. Alaska is included beginning 1959, Hawaii beginning 1960. *Source:* Department of Health and Human Services, National Center for Health Statistics.

## Percent of Population Ever Married

| Age group, years[1] | 1985 | 1980 | 1970 | 1960 | 1950 | 1940 | 1930 | 1920 | 1910 | 1900 |
|---|---|---|---|---|---|---|---|---|---|---|
| Males: 15 to 19 | 1.3 | 2.7 | 2.6 | 3.3 | 2.9 | 1.5 | 1.5 | 1.8 | 1.0 | 0.9 |
| 20 to 24 | 24.4 | 31.2 | 45.3 | 46.9 | 41.0 | 27.8 | 29.0 | 29.1 | 24.7 | 22.2 |
| 25 to 29 | 61.3 | 67.0 | 80.9 | 79.2 | 76.2 | 64.0 | 63.2 | 60.5 | 57.1 | 54.1 |
| 30 to 34 | 79.2 | 84.1 | 90.6 | 88.1 | 86.8 | 79.3 | 78.8 | 75.8 | 73.9 | 72.3 |
| 35 to 44 | 90.6 | 92.5 | 93.3 | 91.9 | 90.4 | 86.0 | 85.7 | 83.8 | 83.3 | 83.0 |
| 45 to 54 | 93.8 | 93.9 | 92.5 | 92.6 | 91.5 | 88.9 | 88.6 | 88.0 | 88.8 | 89.7 |
| Females: 15 to 19 | 6.6 | 8.8 | 9.7 | 13.5 | 14.4 | 10.0 | 10.9 | 10.8 | 9.8 | 9.4 |
| 20 to 24 | 41.5 | 49.8 | 64.2 | 71.6 | 67.7 | 52.8 | 53.9 | 54.4 | 51.5 | 48.4 |
| 25 to 29 | 73.6 | 79.1 | 89.5 | 89.5 | 86.7 | 77.2 | 78.3 | 76.9 | 75.0 | 72.4 |
| 30 to 34 | 86.5 | 90.5 | 93.8 | 93.1 | 90.7 | 85.3 | 86.8 | 85.1 | 83.8 | 83.4 |
| 35 to 44 | 93.2 | 94.5 | 94.8 | 93.9 | 91.7 | 89.6 | 90.0 | 88.6 | 88.6 | 88.9 |
| 45 to 54 | 95.4 | 95.3 | 95.1 | 93.0 | 92.2 | 91.3 | 90.9 | 90.4 | 91.4 | 92.2 |

1. 1980 and 1984: 15 years and over; previous years: 14 and older. *Source:* Department of Commerce, Bureau of the Census.

## Persons Living Alone, by Sex and Age
### (numbers in thousands)

| Sex and age[1] | 1985 Number | 1985 Percent | 1980 Number | 1980 Percent | 1975 Number | 1975 Percent | 1970 Number | 1970 Percent | 1960 Number | 1960 Percent |
|---|---|---|---|---|---|---|---|---|---|---|
| **BOTH SEXES** | | | | | | | | | | |
| 15 to 24 years | 1,324 | 6.4 | 1,726 | 9.4 | 1,111 | 8.0 | 556 | 5.1 | 234 | 3.3 |
| 25 to 44 years | 6,228 | 30.2 | 4,729 | 25.8 | 2,744 | 19.7 | 1,604 | 14.8 | 1,212 | 17.2 |
| 45 to 64 years | 4,939 | 24.0 | 4,514 | 24.7 | 4,076 | 29.2 | 3,622 | 33.4 | 2,720 | 38.5 |
| 65 years and over | 8,112 | 39.4 | 7,328 | 40.1 | 6,008 | 43.1 | 5,071 | 46.7 | 2,898 | 41.0 |
| **Total, 15 years and over** | **20,602** | **100.0** | **18,296** | **100.0** | **13,939** | **100.0** | **10,851** | **100.0** | **7,063** | **100.0** |
| **MALE** | | | | | | | | | | |
| 15 to 24 years | 750 | 9.5 | 947 | 13.6 | 610 | 4.4 | 274 | 2.5 | 124 | 1.8 |
| 25 to 44 years | 3,713 | 46.9 | 2,920 | 41.9 | 1,689 | 12.1 | 933 | 8.6 | 686 | 9.7 |
| 45 to 64 years | 1,845 | 23.3 | 1,613 | 23.2 | 1,329 | 9.5 | 1,152 | 10.6 | 965 | 13.7 |
| 65 years and over | 1,614 | 20.4 | 1,486 | 21.3 | 1,290 | 9.3 | 1,174 | 10.8 | 853 | 12.1 |
| **Total, 15 years and over** | **7,922** | **100.0** | **6,966** | **100.0** | **4,918** | **35.3** | **3,532** | **32.5** | **2,628** | **37.2** |
| **FEMALE** | | | | | | | | | | |
| 15 to 24 years | 573 | 4.5 | 779 | 6.9 | 501 | 3.6 | 282 | 2.6 | 110 | 1.6 |
| 25 to 44 years | 2,514 | 19.8 | 1,809 | 16.0 | 1,055 | 7.6 | 671 | 6.2 | 526 | 7.4 |
| 45 to 64 years | 3,095 | 24.4 | 2,901 | 25.6 | 2,747 | 19.7 | 2,470 | 22.8 | 1,755 | 24.8 |
| 65 years and over | 6,498 | 51.2 | 5,842 | 51.6 | 4,718 | 33.8 | 3,897 | 35.9 | 2,045 | 29.0 |
| **Total, 15 years and over** | **12,680** | **100.0** | **11,330** | **100.0** | **9,021** | **64.7** | **7,319** | **67.5** | **4,436** | **62.8** |

1. Prior to 1980, data are for persons 14 years and older. *Source:* Department of Commerce, Bureau of the Census.

## Characteristics of Unmarried-Couple Households, 1985
### (number in thousands)

| Characteristics | Number | Percent | Characteristics | Number | Percent |
|---|---|---|---|---|---|
| Unmarried-couple households | 1,983 | 100.0 | Presence of children: | | |
| | | | No children under 15 years | 1,380 | 69.6 |
| Age of Householders: | | | Some children under 15 years | 603 | 30.4 |
| Under 25 years | 425 | 21.4 | | | |
| 25–44 years | 1,203 | 60.7 | Sex of householders: | | |
| 45–64 years | 239 | 12.1 | Male | 1,224 | 61.7 |
| 65 years and over | 116 | 5.8 | Female | 758 | 38.2 |

*Source:* U.S. Bureau of the Census.

## Households, Families, and Married Couples

| Date | Households | | Families | | Married couples |
|---|---|---|---|---|---|
| | Number | Average population per household | Number | Average population per family | Number |
| June 1890 | 12,690,000 | 4.93 | — | — | — |
| April 1930 | 29,905,000 | 4.11 | — | — | 25,174,000 |
| April 1940 | 34,949,000 | 3.67 | 32,166,000 | 3.76 | 28,517,000 |
| April 1950 | 43,554,000 | 3.37 | 39,303,000 | 3.54 | 36,091,000 |
| April 1955 | 47,874,000 | 3.33 | 41,951,000 | 3.59 | 37,556,000 |
| March 1960[1] | 52,799,000 | 3.33 | 45,111,000 | 3.67 | 40,200,000 |
| March 1965 | 57,436,000 | 3.29 | 47,956,000 | 3.70 | 42,478,000 |
| March 1970 | 63,401,000 | 3.14 | 51,586,000 | 3.58 | 45,373,000 |
| March 1975 | 71,120,000 | 2.94 | 55,712,000 | 3.42 | 47,547,000 |
| March 1980 | 80,776,000 | 2.76 | 59,550,000 | 3.29 | 49,714,000 |
| March 1982 | 83,527,000 | 2.72 | 61,019,000 | 3.25 | 50,294,000 |
| March 1983 | 83,918,000 | 2.73 | 61,393,000 | 3.26 | 50,666,000 |
| March 1984 | 85,407,000 | 2.71 | 61,997,000 | 3.24 | 50,864,000 |
| March 1985 | 86,789,000 | 2.69 | 62,706,000 | 3.23 | 51,114,000 |

1. First year in which figures for Alaska and Hawaii are included. *Source:* Department of Commerce, Bureau of the Census.

## Families Maintained by Women, With No Husband Present
### (numbers in thousands)

| | 1985 | | 1980 | | 1975 | | 1970 | | 1960 | |
|---|---|---|---|---|---|---|---|---|---|---|
| | Number | Percent | Number | Percent | Number | Percent | Number | Percent | Number | Percent |
| Age of women: | | | | | | | | | | |
| Under 35 years | 3,395 | 33.5 | 3,015 | 34.6 | 2,356 | 32.5 | 1,364 | 24.4 | 796 | 17.7 |
| 35 to 44 years | 2,545 | 25.1 | 1,916 | 22.0 | 1,510 | 20.9 | 1,074 | 19.2 | 940 | 20.9 |
| 45 to 64 years | 2,736 | 27.0 | 2,514 | 28.9 | 2,266 | 31.3 | 2,021 | 36.1 | 1,731 | 38.5 |
| 65 years and over | 1,454 | 14.4 | 1,260 | 14.5 | 1,108 | 15.3 | 1,131 | 20.2 | 1,027 | 22.9 |
| Median age | 41.4 | — | 41.7 | — | 43.4 | — | 48.5 | — | 50.1 | — |
| Presence of children: | | | | | | | | | | |
| No own children under 18 years | 4,123 | 40.7 | 3,260 | 37.4 | 2,838 | 39.2 | 2,665 | 47.7 | 2,397 | 53.3 |
| With own children under 18 years | 6,006 | 59.3 | 5,445 | 62.6 | 4,404 | 60.8 | 2,926 | 52.3 | 2,097 | 46.7 |
| Total own children under 18 years | 10,731 | — | 10,204 | — | 9,227 | — | 6,694 | — | 4,674 | — |
| Average per family | 1.06 | — | 1.17 | — | 1.27 | — | 1.20 | — | 1.04 | — |
| Average per family with children | 1.79 | — | 1.87 | — | 2.10 | — | 2.29 | — | 2.24 | — |
| Race: | | | | | | | | | | |
| White | 6,941 | 68.5 | 6,052 | 69.5 | 5,212 | 72.0 | 4,165 | 74.5 | 3,547 | 78.9 |
| Black[1] | 2,964 | 29.3 | 2,495 | 28.7 | 1,940 | 26.8 | 1,382 | 24.7 | 947 | 21.1 |
| Other | 224 | 2.2 | 158 | 1.8 | 90 | 1.2 | 44 | 0.8 | n.a. | n.a. |
| Marital status: | | | | | | | | | | |
| Married, husband absent | 1,773 | 17.5 | 1,769 | 20.3 | 1,647 | 22.7 | 1,326 | 23.7 | 1,099 | 24.5 |
| Widowed | 2,671 | 26.4 | 2,570 | 29.5 | 2,559 | 35.3 | 2,396 | 42.9 | 2,325 | 51.7 |
| Divorced | 3,834 | 37.9 | 3,008 | 34.6 | 2,110 | 29.1 | 1,259 | 22.5 | 694 | 15.4 |
| Single | 1,850 | 18.3 | 1,359 | 15.6 | 926 | 12.8 | 610 | 10.9 | 376 | 8.4 |
| **Total families maintained by women** | **10,129** | **100.0** | **8,705** | **100.0** | **7,242** | **100.0** | **5,591** | **100.0** | **4,494** | **100.0** |

1. Includes other races in 1960. NOTE: n.a. = not available. (—) as shown in this table, means "not applicable." *Source:* Department of Commerce, Bureau of the Census.

## Suicide Facts

The American Association of Suicidology, a non-profit organization founded in 1968 to further the understanding and prevention of suicide, reports that:

- An American attempts suicide every minute.
- Suicide claims the lives of at least 30,000 Americans annually.
- Suicide is now the eighth leading cause of death in America.
- Suicide is the third leading cause of death in young people.
- The incidence of suicide in young people has nearly tripled in the past 30 years.
- Suicide victims come from all walks of life, from all economic and educational backgrounds.

## Selected Family Characteristics

| Characteristics | 1984 Number (thousands) | Median income | Characteristics | 1984 Number (thousands) | Median income |
|---|---|---|---|---|---|
| **ALL RACES** | | | Tenure status | | |
| All families | 62,706 | 26,433 | Owner occupied | 45,015 | 30,686 |
| Type of residence | | | Renter occupied | 16,691 | 16,918 |
| Nonfarm | (NA) | (NA) | Occupier paid no cash rent | 1,000 | 14,962 |
| Farm | (NA) | (NA) | Educational attainment of | | |
| Location of residence | | | householder | | |
| Inside metropolitan areas | (NA) | (NA) | Elementary | 8,195 | 14,937 |
| 1,000,000 or more | (NA) | (NA) | High school | 29,117 | 24,677 |
| Inside central cities | (NA) | (NA) | College | 22,268 | 37,298 |
| Outside central cities | (NA) | (NA) | 1 to 3 years | 9,644 | 30,665 |
| Under 1,000,000 | (NA) | (NA) | 4 years or more | 12,624 | 43,169 |
| Inside central cities | (NA) | (NA) | 4 years | 6,847 | 40,724 |
| Outside central cities | (NA) | (NA) | 5 years or more | 5,777 | 46,656 |
| Outside metropolitan areas | (NA) | (NA) | Total, 25 years and over | 59,579 | 27,199 |
| Region | | | | | |
| Northeast | 13,149 | 28,487 | **WHITE** | | |
| North Central | 15,839 | 26,753 | All families | 54,400 | 27,686 |
| South | 21,781 | 24,094 | Type of residence | | |
| West | 11,938 | 28,077 | Nonfarm | (NA) | (NA) |
| Type of family | | | Farm | (NA) | (NA) |
| Married-couple family | 50,350 | 29,612 | Location of residence | | |
| Wife in paid labor force | 26,938 | 34,668 | Inside metropolitan areas | (NA) | (NA) |
| Wife not in paid labor force | 23,412 | 23,582 | 1,000,000 or more | (NA) | (NA) |
| Male householder, no | | | Inside central cities | (NA) | (NA) |
| wife present | 2,228 | 23,325 | Outside central cities | (NA) | (NA) |
| Female householder, no | | | Under 1,000,000 | (NA) | (NA) |
| husband present | 10,129 | 12,803 | Inside central cities | (NA) | (NA) |
| Number of earners[2] | | | Outside central cities | (NA) | (NA) |
| No earners | 9,221 | 11,377 | Outside metropolitan areas | (NA) | (NA) |
| 1 earner | 17,949 | 20,291 | Region | | |
| 2 earners | 26,160 | 31,707 | Northeast | 11,631 | 29,705 |
| 3 earners | 6,029 | 39,828 | North Central | 14,309 | 27,683 |
| 4 earners | 2,570 | 50,278 | South | 17,953 | 26,054 |
| Size of family | | | West | 10,507 | 28,509 |
| 2 persons | 25,349 | 22,070 | Type of family | | |
| 3 persons | 14,804 | 27,781 | Married-couple families | 45,643 | 30,058 |
| 4 persons | 13,259 | 31,097 | Wife in paid labor force | 23,979 | 35,176 |
| 5 persons | 5,894 | 30,777 | Wife not in paid labor | | |
| 6 persons | 2,175 | 28,081 | force | 21,664 | 24,246 |
| 7 persons or more | 1,225 | 25,804 | Male householder, no wife | | |
| Occupation group of longest[4] | | | present | 1,816 | 25,110 |
| job of householder | 47,786 | 30,426 | Female householder, no | | |
| Executives, administrators | | | husband present | 6,941 | 15,134 |
| and managerial | 6,942 | 42,996 | Number of earners[2] | 53,777 | 27,752 |
| Professional specialty | 5,780 | 41,873 | No earners | 7,674 | 12,941 |
| Technical and related | | | 1 earner | 15,219 | 22,050 |
| support | 1,437 | 33,528 | 2 earners | 23,303 | 32,260 |
| Sales | 5,216 | 32,602 | 3 earners | 5,317 | 40,374 |
| Administrative support, | | | 4 earners or more | 2,263 | 51,309 |
| including clerical | 4,115 | 26,718 | | | |
| Precision production, | | | **BLACK** | | |
| craft and repair | 9,170 | 29,853 | All families | 6,778 | 15,432 |
| Machine operators, assem- | | | Type of residence | | |
| blers and inspectors | 3,840 | 25,553 | Nonfarm | (NA) | (NA) |
| Transportation and mater- | | | Farm | (NA) | (NA) |
| ial moving | 3,037 | 27,025 | Location of residence | | |
| Handlers, equipment clean- | | | Inside metropolitan areas | (NA) | (NA) |
| ers, helpers, laborers | 1,721 | 21,178 | 1,000,000 or more | (NA) | (NA) |
| Service workers | 4,538 | 20,027 | Inside central cities | (NA) | (NA) |
| Private household | 218 | 7,807 | Outside central cities | (NA) | (NA) |
| Other | 4,319 | 20,600 | Under 1,000,000 | (NA) | (NA) |
| Farming, forestry and fishing | 1,938 | 16,782 | Inside central cities | (NA) | (NA) |
| | | | Outside central cities | (NA) | (NA) |

| Characteristics | 1984 | | Characteristics | 1984 | |
|---|---|---|---|---|---|
| | Number (thousands) | Median income | | Number (thousands) | Median income |
| Outside metropolitan areas | (NA) | (NA) | Location of residence | | |
| Region | | | Inside metropolitan areas | (NA) | (NA) |
| Northeast | 1,322 | 16,326 | 1,000,000 or more | (NA) | (NA) |
| North Central | 1,345 | 14,367 | Inside central cities | (NA) | (NA) |
| South | 3,561 | 14,863 | Outside central cities | (NA) | (NA) |
| West | 550 | 19,209 | Under 1,000,000 | (NA) | (NA) |
| Type of family | | | Inside central cities | (NA) | (NA) |
| Married-couple families | 3,469 | 23,418 | Outside central cities | (NA) | (NA) |
| Wife in paid labor force | 2,221 | 28,775 | Outside metropolitan areas | (NA) | (NA) |
| Wife not in paid labor force | 1,248 | 14,502 | Region | | |
| Male householder, no wife present | 344 | 15,724 | Northeast | 808 | 14,663 |
| | | | North Central | 313 | 21,126 |
| Female householder, no husband present | 2,964 | 8,648 | South | 1,273 | 19,195 |
| | | | West | 1,545 | 20,244 |
| Number of earners[2] | 6,671 | 15,337 | Type of family | | |
| No earners | 1,376 | 5,277 | Married-couple families | 2,824 | 22,599 |
| 1 earner | 2,312 | 11,809 | Wife in paid labor force | 1,387 | 27,609 |
| 2 earners | 2,237 | 25,334 | Wife not in paid labor force | 1,437 | 17,160 |
| 3 earners | 527 | 32,984 | Male householder, no wife present | 210 | 18,578 |
| 4 earners or more | 218 | 38,143 | | | |
| | | | Female householder, no husband present | 905 | 8,452 |
| **SPANISH ORIGIN OF HOUSEHOLDER[3]** | | | Number of earners[2] | 3,905 | 18,772 |
| All families | 3,939 | 18,833 | No earners | 599 | 5,814 |
| Type of residence | | | 1 earner | 1,290 | 14,479 |
| Nonfarm | (NA) | (NA) | 2 earners | 1,485 | 24,447 |
| Farm | (NA) | (NA) | 3 earners | 370 | 31,715 |
| | | | 4 earners or more | 161 | 44,387 |

1. Family data are as of March 1985. 2. Excludes families with members in the Armed Forces. 3. Persons of Spanish origin may be of any race. 4. Includes persons whose longest job was in the armed forces. *Source:* Department of Commerce, Bureau of the Census. NOTE: Data are the latest available.

# Births

## Live Births and Birth Rates

| Year | Births[1] | Rate[2] | Year | Births[1] | Rate[2] | Year | Births[1] | Rate[2] |
|---|---|---|---|---|---|---|---|---|
| 1910 | 2,777,000 | 30.1 | 1952[3] | 3,913,000 | 25.1 | 1968 | 3,501,564 | 17.5 |
| 1915 | 2,965,000 | 29.5 | 1953[3] | 3,965,000 | 25.1 | 1969 | 3,600,206 | 17.8 |
| 1920 | 2,950,000 | 27.7 | 1954[3] | 4,078,000 | 25.3 | 1970 | 3,731,386 | 18.4 |
| 1925 | 2,909,000 | 25.1 | 1955 | 4,104,000 | 25.0 | 1971 | 3,555,970 | 17.2 |
| 1930 | 2,618,000 | 21.3 | 1956[3] | 4,218,000 | 25.2 | 1972 | 3,258,411 | 15.6 |
| 1935 | 2,377,000 | 18.7 | 1957[3] | 4,308,000 | 25.3 | 1973 | 3,136,965 | 14.9 |
| 1940 | 2,559,000 | 19.4 | 1958[3] | 4,255,000 | 24.5 | 1974 | 3,159,958 | 14.9 |
| 1943 | 3,104,000 | 22.7 | 1959[3] | 4,295,000 | 24.3 | 1975 | 3,144,198 | 14.8 |
| 1944 | 2,939,000 | 21.2 | 1960[3] | 4,257,850 | 23.7 | 1976 | 3,167,788 | 14.8 |
| 1945 | 2,858,000 | 20.4 | 1961[3] | 4,268,326 | 23.3 | 1977 | 3,326,632 | 15.4 |
| 1946 | 3,411,000 | 24.1 | 1962[3] | 4,167,362 | 22.4 | 1978 | 3,333,279 | 15.3 |
| 1947 | 3,817,000 | 26.6 | 1963[3] | 4,098,020 | 21.7 | 1979 | 3,494,398 | 15.9 |
| 1948 | 3,637,000 | 24.9 | 1964[3] | 4,027,490 | 21.0 | 1980 | 3,612,258 | 15.9 |
| 1949 | 3,649,000 | 24.5 | 1965[3] | 3,760,358 | 19.4 | 1982 | 3,680,537 | 15.9 |
| 1950 | 3,632,000 | 24.1 | 1966[3] | 3,606,274 | 18.4 | 1983 | 3,638,933 | 15.5 |
| 1951[3] | 3,823,000 | 24.9 | 1967 | 3,520,959 | 17.8 | 1984[4] | 3,697,000 | 15.7 |
| | | | | | | 1985[4] | 3,749,000 | 15.7 |

1. Figures through 1959 include adjustment for underregistration; beginning 1960, figures represent number registered. For comparison, the 1959 registered count was 4,245,000. 2. Rates are per 1,000 population estimated as of July 1 for each year except 1940, 1950, 1960, 1970, and 1980, which are as of April 1, the census date; for 1942–46 based on population including armed forces overseas. 3. Based on 50% sample of births. 4. Provisional. NOTE: Alaska is included beginning 1959; Hawaii beginning 1960. Since 1972, based on 100% of births in selected states and on 50% sample in all other states. *Sources:* Department of Commerce, Bureau of the Census; and Department of Health and Human Services, National Center for Health Statistics.

## Median Age at First Marriage

| Year | Males | Females | Year | Males | Females | Year | Males | Females | Year | Males | Females |
|------|-------|---------|------|-------|---------|------|-------|---------|------|-------|---------|
| 1900 | 25.9  | 21.9    | 1930 | 24.3  | 21.3    | 1960 | 22.8  | 20.3    | 1983 | 25.4  | 22.8    |
| 1910 | 25.1  | 21.6    | 1940 | 24.3  | 21.5    | 1970 | 23.2  | 20.8    | 1984 | 25.4  | 23.0    |
| 1920 | 24.6  | 21.2    | 1950 | 22.8  | 20.3    | 1980 | 24.7  | 22.0    | 1985 | 25.5  | 23.3    |

*Source:* Department of Commerce, Bureau of the Census.

## Live Births by Age of Mother

| Year[1] and race | Total | \<br>Under 15 yr | \<br>15–19 yr | Age of mother\<br>20–24 yr | \<br>25–29 yr | \<br>30–34 yr | \<br>35–39 yr | \<br>40–44 yr | \<br>45 yr and over |
|---|---|---|---|---|---|---|---|---|---|
| 1940 | 2,558,647 | 3,865 | 332,667 | 799,537 | 693,268 | 431,468 | 222,015 | 68,269 | 7,558 |
| 1945 | 2,858,449 | 4,028 | 298,868 | 832,746 | 785,299 | 554,906 | 296,852 | 78,853 | 6,897 |
| 1950 | 3,631,512 | 5,413 | 432,911 | 1,155,167 | 1,041,360 | 610,816 | 302,780 | 77,743 | 5,322 |
| 1955 | 4,014,112 | 6,181 | 493,770 | 1,290,939 | 1,133,155 | 732,540 | 352,320 | 89,777 | 5,430 |
| 1960 | 4,257,850 | 6,780 | 586,966 | 1,426,912 | 1,092,816 | 687,722 | 359,908 | 91,564 | 5,182 |
| 1965 | 3,760,358 | 7,768 | 590,894 | 1,337,350 | 925,732 | 529,376 | 282,908 | 81,716 | 4,614 |
| 1970 | 3,731,386 | 11,752 | 644,708 | 1,418,874 | 994,904 | 427,806 | 180,244 | 49,952 | 3,146 |
| 1975 | 3,144,198 | 12,642 | 582,238 | 1,093,676 | 936,786 | 375,500 | 115,409 | 26,319 | 1,628 |
| 1979 | 3,494,398 | 10,699 | 549,472 | 1,188,663 | 1,069,246 | 516,999 | 135,096 | 23,018 | 1,205 |
| 1980 | 3,612,258 | 10,169 | 552,161 | 1,226,200 | 1,108,291 | 550,354 | 140,793 | 23,090 | 1,200 |
| 1981 | 3,629,238 | 9,632 | 527,392 | 1,212,000 | 1,128,188 | 581,454 | 146,056 | 23,326 | 1,190 |
| 1982 | 3,680,537 | 9,773 | 513,758 | 1,205,979 | 1,151,934 | 605,273 | 167,920 | 24,664 | 1,236 |
| 1983 | 3,638,933 | 9,752 | 489,286 | 1,160,274 | 1,147,720 | 624,516 | 180,353 | 25,882 | 1,150 |
| White | 2,904,250 | 4,031 | 338,152 | 917,533 | 956,098 | 520,547 | 146,973 | 20,114 | 802 |
| Black | 586,027 | 5,439 | 136,666 | 203,062 | 143,584 | 70,862 | 22,390 | 4,006 | 198 |
| Other | 734,683 | 5,721 | 151,134 | 242,741 | 191,622 | 103,969 | 33,380 | 5,768 | 348 |

1. Data for 1940–55 are adjusted for underregistration. Beginning 1960, registered births only are shown. Data for 1960–70 based on a 50% sample of births. Since 1972, based on 100% of births in selected states and on 50% sample in all other states. Beginning 1960, including Alaska and Hawaii. NOTE: Data refer only to births occurring within the U.S. Figures are shown to the last digit as computed for convenience in summation. They are not assumed to be accurate to the last digit. Figures for age of mother not stated are distributed. *Sources:* Department of Commerce, Bureau of the Census; and Department of Health and Human Services, National Center for Health Statistics. NOTE: Data are latest available.

## Births to Unmarried Women

### (in thousands, except as indicated)

| Age and race | 1983 | 1980 | 1975 | 1970 | 1965 | 1960 | 1955 | 1950 | 1940 |
|---|---|---|---|---|---|---|---|---|---|
| By age of mother: | | | | | | | | | |
| Under 15 years | 8.8 | 9.0 | 11.0 | 9.5 | 6.1 | 4.6 | 3.9 | 3.2 | 2.1 |
| 15–19 years | 261.2 | 262.8 | 222.5 | 190.4 | 123.1 | 87.1 | 56.0 | 56.0 | 40.5 |
| 20–24 years | 265.5 | 237.3 | 134.0 | 126.7 | 90.7 | 68.0 | 55.7 | 43.1 | 27.2 |
| 25–29 years | 126.5 | 99.6 | 50.2 | 40.6 | 36.8 | 32.1 | 28.0 | 20.9 | 10.5 |
| 30–34 years | 53.8 | 41.0 | 19.8 | 19.1 | 19.6 | 18.9 | 16.1 | 10.8 | 5.2 |
| 35–39 years | 18.2 | 13.2 | 8.1 | 9.4 | 11.4 | 10.6 | 8.3 | 6.0 | 3.0 |
| 40 years and over | 3.6 | 2.9 | 2.3 | 3.0 | 3.7 | 3.0 | 2.4 | 1.7 | 1.0 |
| By race: | | | | | | | | | |
| White | 370.8 | 320.1 | 186.4 | 175.1 | 123.7 | 82.5 | 64.2 | 53.5 | 40.3 |
| Black and other | 367.0 | 345.7 | 261.6 | 223.6 | 167.5 | 141.8 | 119.2 | 88.1 | 49.2 |
| **Total of above births** | 737.8 | 665.8 | 447.9 | 398.7 | 291.2 | 224.3 | 183.4 | 141.6 | 89.5 |
| Percent of all births[1] | 20.3 | 18.4 | 14.2 | 10.7 | 7.7 | 5.3 | 4.5 | 3.9 | 3.5 |
| Rate[2] | 30.4 | 29.4 | 24.8 | 26.4 | 23.4 | 21.8 | 19.3 | 14.1 | 7.1 |

1. Through 1955, based on data adjusted for underregistration; thereafter, registered births. 2. Rate per 1,000 unmarried (never married, widowed, and divorced) women, 15–44 years old. *Sources:* Department of Commerce, Bureau of the Census; and Department of Health and Human Services, National Center for Health Statistics. NOTE: Data are latest available.

# 794 *U.S. Statistics*

## Live Births and Birth Rates

| State | 1984[1] number | 1984[1] rate | 1983[1] number | 1983[1] rate | State | 1984[1] number | 1984[1] rate | 1983[1] number | 1983[1] rate |
|---|---|---|---|---|---|---|---|---|---|
| Alabama | 58,604 | 14.7 | 57,685 | 14.6 | Montana | 13,846 | 16.8 | 13,794 | 16.9 |
| Alaska | 12,247 | 24.5 | 11,500 | 24.0 | Nebraska | 26,483 | 16.5 | 26,816 | 16.8 |
| Arizona | 33,440 | 14.2 | 52,659 | 17.8 | Nevada | 15,276 | 16.8 | 14,251 | 16.0 |
| Arkansas | 54,821 | 18.0 | 33,630 | 14.4 | New Hampshire | 12,656 | 13.0 | 13,973 | 14.6 |
| California | 455,075 | 17.8 | 413,915 | 16.4 | New Jersey | 97,488 | 13.0 | 95,406 | 12.8 |
| Colorado | 54,471 | 17.1 | 55,159 | 17.6 | New Mexico | 26,285 | 18.5 | 30,186 | 21.6 |
| Connecticut | 39,237 | 12.4 | 40,380 | 12.9 | New York | 251,062 | 14.2 | 249,618 | 14.1 |
| Delaware | 9,487 | 15.5 | 9,538 | 15.7 | North Carolina | 86,705 | 14.1 | 84,655 | 13.9 |
| D.C. | 19,123 | 30.7 | 18,592 | 29.8 | North Dakota | 12,738 | 18.6 | 13,200 | 19.4 |
| Florida | 155,236 | 14.1 | 148,695 | 13.9 | Ohio | 159,939 | 14.9 | 160,330 | 14.9 |
| Georgia | 91,761 | 15.7 | 91,090 | 15.9 | Oklahoma | 53,425 | 16.2 | 54,085 | 16.4 |
| Hawaii | 18,658 | 18.0 | 19,005 | 18.6 | Oregon | 39,536 | 14.8 | 41,045 | 15.4 |
| Idaho | 17,072 | 17.1 | 18,540 | 18.7 | Pennsylvania | 159,911 | 13.4 | 159,210 | 13.4 |
| Illinois | 175,907 | 15.3 | 175,679 | 15.3 | Rhode Island | 13,219 | 13.7 | 13,061 | 13.7 |
| Indiana | 79,134 | 14.4 | 82,169 | 15.0 | South Carolina | 48,215 | 14.6 | 48,513 | 14.9 |
| Iowa | 42,611 | 14.6 | 43,783 | 15.1 | South Dakota | 12,383 | 17.5 | 12,409 | 17.7 |
| Kansas | 38,570 | 15.8 | 39,498 | 16.3 | Tennessee | 70,407 | 14.9 | 67,739 | 14.5 |
| Kentucky | 51,964 | 14.0 | 55,252 | 14.9 | Texas | 306,192 | 19.2 | 287,044 | 18.3 |
| Louisiana | 83,195 | 18.6 | 80,610 | 18.2 | Utah | 39,677 | 24.0 | 40,752 | 25.2 |
| Maine | 16,513 | 14.3 | 16,323 | 14.2 | Vermont | 7,419 | 14.0 | 7,671 | 14.6 |
| Maryland | 58,790 | 13.5 | 57,857 | 13.4 | Virginia | 79,342 | 14.1 | 77,448 | 14.0 |
| Massachusetts | 79,386 | 13.7 | 78,670 | 13.6 | Washington | 73,605 | 16.9 | 63,729 | 14.8 |
| Michigan | 134,517 | 14.8 | 131,873 | 14.5 | West Virginia | 25,509 | 12.8 | 26,911 | 13.7 |
| Minnesota | 65,788 | 15.8 | 64,698 | 15.6 | Wisconsin | 73,088 | 15.3 | 72,611 | 15.3 |
| Mississippi | 42,695 | 16.4 | 44,025 | 17.0 | Wyoming | 9,026 | 17.7 | 9,515 | 18.5 |
| Missouri | 78,517 | 15.7 | 76,739 | 15.4 | **Total** | **3,697,000** | **15.7** | **3,693,620** | **16.0** |

1. Provisional. NOTE: Based on 100% of births in selected states and 50% sample in others. Rates are per 1,000 population. *Source:* Department of Health and Human Services, National Center for Health Statistics.

## Live Births by Race or National Origin

| Race | 1983 | 1982 | Race | 1983 | 1982 |
|---|---|---|---|---|---|
| White | 2,904,250 | 2,942,054 | Chinese | 14,354 | 13,716 |
| Black | 586,027 | 592,641 | Filipino | 17,676 | 16,640 |
| American Indian[1] | 41,571 | 41,289 | Other[2] | 66,383 | 63,521 |
| Japanese | 8,672 | 8,686 | Total[3] | 3,638,933 | 3,680,537 |

1. Includes Eskimos and Aleuts. 2. Hawaiian, Asian and Pacific Islander. 3. Includes births of other races not shown separately. Data are latest available. *Source:* Department of Health and Human Services, National Center for Health Statistics.

## Live Births by Sex and Sex Ratio[1]

| Year | Total[2] Male | Total[2] Female | Total[2] Males per 1,000 females | White Male | White Female | White Males per 1,000 females | Black Male | Black Female | Black Males per 1,000 females |
|---|---|---|---|---|---|---|---|---|---|
| 1970[3] | 1,915,378 | 1,816,008 | 1,055 | 1,590,140 | 1,501,124 | 1,059 | 290,508 | 281,854 | 1,031 |
| 1975[4] | 1,613,135 | 1,531,063 | 1,054 | 1,312,308 | 1,239,688 | 1,059 | 259,610 | 251,971 | 1,030 |
| 1976[4] | 1,624,436 | 1,543,352 | 1,053 | 1,319,717 | 1,247,897 | 1,058 | 260,661 | 253,818 | 1,027 |
| 1977[4] | 1,705,916 | 1,620,716 | 1,053 | 1,383,440 | 1,307,630 | 1,058 | 275,556 | 268,665 | 1,026 |
| 1978[4] | 1,709,394 | 1,623,885 | 1,053 | 1,378,222 | 1,302,894 | 1,058 | 279,598 | 271,942 | 1,028 |
| 1979[4] | 1,791,267 | 1,703,131 | 1,052 | 1,442,981 | 1,365,439 | 1,057 | 293,013 | 284,842 | 1,029 |
| 1980[4] | 1,852,616 | 1,759,642 | 1,053 | 1,490,140 | 1,408,592 | 1,058 | 299,033 | 290,583 | 1,029 |
| 1981[4] | 1,860,272 | 1,768,966 | 1,052 | 1,494,451 | 1,414,232 | 1,057 | 297,864 | 289,923 | 1,027 |
| 1982[4] | 1,885,676 | 1,794,861 | 1,051 | 1,509,704 | 1,432,350 | 1,054 | 301,121 | 291,520 | 1,033 |
| 1983[4] | 1,865,553 | 1,773,380 | 1,052 | 1,492,385 | 1,411,865 | 1,057 | 297,011 | 289,016 | 1,028 |

1. Excludes births to nonresidents of U.S. 2. Includes races other than white and black. 3. Based on 50% sample of births. 4. Based on 100% of births for selected states and 50% sample in all others. *Source:* Department of Health and Human Services, National Center for Health Statistics. NOTE: Data are latest available.

# Mortality
## Death Rates for Selected Causes

| Cause of death | Death rates per 100,000 | | | | | | | |
|---|---|---|---|---|---|---|---|---|
| | 1984[1] | 1983[1] | 1980 | 1950 | 1945–49 | 1940–44 | 1920–24 | 1900–04 |
| Typhoid fever | n.a. | n.a. | 0.0 | 0.1 | 0.2 | 0.6 | 7.3 | 26.7 |
| Communicable diseases of childhood | n.a. | n.a. | 0.0 | 1.3 | 2.3 | 4.6 | 33.8 | 65.2 |
| Measles | — | — | 0.0 | 0.3 | 0.6 | 1.1 | 7.3 | 10.0 |
| Scarlet fever | n.a. | n.a. | 0.0 | 0.2 | 0.1 | 0.4 | 4.0 | 11.8 |
| Whooping cough | — | — | 0.0 | 0.7 | 1.0 | 2.2 | 8.9 | 10.7 |
| Diphtheria | n.a. | n.a. | 0.0 | 0.3 | 0.7 | 1.0 | 13.7 | 32.7 |
| Pneumonia and influenza | 25.0 | 22.9 | 23.3 | 31.3 | 41.3 | 63.7 | 140.3 | 184.3 |
| Influenza | 0.6 | 0.6 | 1.1 | 4.4 | 5.0 | 13.0 | 34.8 | 22.8 |
| Pneumonia | 24.4 | 22.3 | 22.0 | 26.9 | 37.2 | 50.7 | 105.5 | 161.5 |
| Tuberculosis | 0.8 | 0.8 | 0.8 | 22.5 | 33.3 | 43.4 | 96.7 | 184.7 |
| Cancer | 191.6 | 188.3 | 182.5 | 139.8 | 134.0 | 123.1 | 86.9 | 67.7 |
| Diabetes mellitus | 15.6 | 15.2 | 15.0 | 16.2 | 24.1 | 26.2 | 17.1 | 12.2 |
| Major cardiovascular diseases | 412.9 | 418.1 | 434.5 | 510.8 | 493.1 | 490.4 | 369.9 | 359.5 |
| Diseases of the heart | 324.4 | 327.6 | 335.2 | 356.8 | 325.1 | 303.2 | 169.8 | 153.0 |
| Cerebrovascular diseases | 65.5 | 66.8 | 74.6 | 104.0 | 93.8 | 91.7 | 93.5 | 106.3 |
| Nephritis and nephrosis | 8.5 | 7.9 | 7.6 | 16.4 | 48.4 | 72.1 | 81.5 | 84.3 |
| Syphilis | 0.0 | 0.0 | 0.1 | 5.0 | 8.4 | 12.7 | 17.6 | 12.9 |
| Appendicitis | 0.2 | 0.2 | 0.3 | 2.0 | 3.5 | 7.2 | 14.0 | 9.4 |
| Accidents, all forms | 40.1 | 39.0 | 46.0 | 60.6 | 67.6 | 73.0 | 70.8 | 79.2 |
| Motor vehicle accidents | 19.6 | 18.7 | 23.0 | 23.1 | 22.3 | 22.7 | 12.9 | n.a. |
| Infant mortality[2] | 10.6 | 10.6 | 12.5 | 29.2 | 33.3 | 42.4 | 76.7 | n.a. |
| Neonatal mortality[2] | 6.9 | 7.3 | 8.4 | 20.5 | 22.9 | 26.2 | 39.7 | n.a. |
| Fetal mortality[2] | n.a. | 8.4 | n.a. | 22.9 | 24.3 | 28.5 | 39.2 [3] | n.a. |
| Maternal mortality[2] | n.a. | 0.1 | 0.1 | 0.8 | 1.4 | 2.8 | 6.9 | n.a. |
| All causes | 866.7 | 858.9 | 874.2 | 963.8 | 1,003.3 | 1,062.0 | 1,196.6 | 1,621.6 |

1. Based on a 10% sample of deaths. 2. Rates per 1,000 live births. 3. 1922–24. NOTE: Includes only deaths occurring within the registration areas. Beginning with 1940, area includes the entire United States; beginning with 1960, Alaska and Hawaii are included. Rates per 100,000 population residing in areas, enumerated as of April 1 for 1940, 1950 and 1980 and estimated as of July 1 for all other years. Due to changes in statistical methods, death rates are not strictly comparable. n.a. = not available. *Source:* Department of Health and Human Services, National Center for Health Statistics.

## Accident Rates, 1984

| Class of accident | | One every | Class of accident | | One every |
|---|---|---|---|---|---|
| All accidents | Deaths | 6 minutes | Workers off-job | Deaths | 15 minutes |
| | Injuries | 4 seconds | | Injuries | 13 seconds |
| Motor-vehicle | Deaths | 11 minutes | Home | Deaths | 26 minutes |
| | Injuries | 19 seconds | | Injuries | 11 seconds |
| Work | Deaths | 46 minutes | Public non-motor-vehicle | Deaths | 28 minutes |
| | Injuries | 17 seconds | | Injuries | 14 seconds |

NOTE: Data are latest available. *Source:* National Safety Council.

## Improper Driving as Factor in Accidents, 1984

| Kind of improper driving | Fatal accidents | | | Injury accidents | | | All accidents[1] | | |
|---|---|---|---|---|---|---|---|---|---|
| | Total | Urban | Rural | Total | Urban | Rural | Total | Urban | Rural |
| Improper driving | 56.7 | 57.7 | 56.2 | 73.7 | 74.3 | 73.0 | 72.1 | 74.4 | 68.0 |
| Speed too fast[2] | 23.8 | 23.7 | 23.8 | 18.6 | 15.5 | 22.2 | 16.4 | 14.7 | 19.4 |
| Right of way | 15.7 | 16.8 | 15.2 | 26.2 | 31.8 | 19.3 | 26.4 | 30.4 | 19.2 |
| Drove left of center | 6.6 | 6.3 | 6.7 | 3.4 | 1.9 | 5.3 | 2.8 | 1.9 | 4.3 |
| Improper overtaking | 2.7 | 1.5 | 3.3 | 2.3 | 1.5 | 3.3 | 2.8 | 2.3 | 3.6 |
| Made improper turn | 1.3 | 1.3 | 1.4 | 2.8 | 3.0 | 2.6 | 4.0 | 4.4 | 3.2 |
| Followed too closely | 0.7 | 0.8 | 0.7 | 6.4 | 7.5 | 5.2 | 7.0 | 8.1 | 5.3 |
| Other improper driving | 5.9 | 7.3 | 5.1 | 14.0 | 13.1 | 15.1 | 12.7 | 12.6 | 13.0 |
| No improper driving | 43.3 | 42.3 | 43.8 | 26.3 | 25.7 | 27.0 | 27.9 | 25.6 | 32.0 |
| Total | 100.0% | 100.0% | 100.0% | 100.0% | 100.0% | 100.0% | 100.0% | 100.0% | 100.0% |

1. Principally property-damage accidents, but also includes fatal and injury accidents. 2. Includes "speed too fast for conditions." *Source:* Urban and rural reports from eight state traffic authorities to National Safety Council. NOTE: Figures are latest available.

## Motor-Vehicle Deaths by Type of Accident

| Year | Pedes-trians | Other motor vehicles | Railroad trains | Street cars | Pedalcycles | Animal-drawn vehicle or animal | Fixed objects | Deaths from non-collision accidents | Total deaths[1] |
|---|---|---|---|---|---|---|---|---|---|
| | | | | | | Deaths from collisions with— | | | |
| 1965 | 8,900 | 20,800 | 1,556 | 5 | 680 | 120 | 2,200 | 14,900 | 49,161 |
| 1970 | 9,900 | 23,200 | 1,459 | 3 | 780 | 100 | 3,800 | 15,400 | 54,633 |
| 1975 | 8,400 | 19,550 | 979 | 1 | 1,000 | 100 | 3,130 | 12,700 | 45,853 |
| 1980 | 9,700 | 22,000 | 800 | — | 1,200 | 100 | 4,400 | 15,100 | 53,300 |
| 1982 | 8,600 | 18,900 | 600 | — | 1,100 | 100 | 3,600 | 13,100 | 46,000 |
| 1983 | 8,000 | 19,300 | 600 | — | 1,100 | 100 | 3,000 | 12,500 | 44,600 |
| 1984 | 8,200 | 20,300 | 700 | — | 1,000 | 100 | 3,200 | 12,700 | 46,200 |

1. Totals do not equal sums of various types because totals are estimated; these have been made to nearest 10 deaths for some types and to nearest 50 deaths for others. NOTE: Figures are latest available. *Source:* National Safety Council.

## Accidental Deaths by Principal Types

| Year | Motor vehicle | Falls | Drown-ing | Fire burns | Ingestion of food or object | Fire-arms | Poison (solid, liquid) | Poison by gas |
|---|---|---|---|---|---|---|---|---|
| 1975 | 45,853 | 14,896 | 8,000 | 6,071 | 3,106 | 2,380 | 4,694 | 1,577 |
| 1978 | 52,411 | 13,690 | 7,026 | 6,163 | 3,063 | 1,806 | 3,035 | 1,737 |
| 1979 | 53,524 | 13,216 | 6,872 | 5,991 | 3,243 | 2,004 | 3,165 | 1,472 |
| 1980 | 53,300 | 12,600 | 7,100 | 5,600 | 2,900 | 1,800 | 3,000 | 1,300 |
| 1982 | 46,000 | 11,600 | 6,200 | 5,000 | 2,900 | 1,900 | 3,000 | 1,400 |
| 1983 | 44,600 | 11,700 | 6,600 | 4,600 | 3,200 | 1,900 | 3,000 | 1,300 |
| 1984 | 46,200 | 11,600 | 5,700 | 4,800 | 3,100 | 1,800 | 3,900 | 1,300 |

NOTE: Figures are latest available. *Source:* National Safety Council.

## Deaths and Death Rates

| State | Total deaths[1] 1984 rate | Total deaths[1] 1983 rate | Motor vehicle traffic deaths[2] 1984 rate | Motor vehicle traffic deaths[2] 1983 rate | Motor vehicle traffic deaths[2] 1982 rate | State | Total deaths[1] 1984 rate | Total deaths[1] 1983 rate | Motor vehicle traffic deaths[2] 1984 rate | Motor vehicle traffic deaths[2] 1983 rate | Motor vehicle traffic deaths[2] 1982 rate |
|---|---|---|---|---|---|---|---|---|---|---|---|
| Alabama | 9.4 | 8.8 | 3.1 | 3.2 | 3.0 | Montana | 8.1 | 8.2 | 3.1 | 4.0 | 3.8 |
| Alaska | 4.0 | 4.0 | 2.4 | 3.9 | 2.9 | Nebraska | 9.3 | 9.3 | 2.3 | 2.1 | 2.3 |
| Arizona | 8.0 | 7.8 | 3.3 | 2.6 | 3.7 | Nevada | 8.0 | 7.8 | 3.6 | 3.8 | 4.4 |
| Arkansas | 10.0 | 9.9 | 2.8 | 3.2 | 3.3 | New Hamshire | 7.9 | 8.1 | 2.6 | 2.6 | 2.5 |
| California | 7.6 | 7.5 | 2.9 | 2.6 | 2.7 | New Jersey | 8.8 | 8.9 | 1.6 | 1.7 | 2.0 |
| Colorado | 6.6 | 6.4 | 2.5 | 2.6 | 2.8 | New Mexico | 6.9 | 7.1 | 4.3 | 4.3 | 4.9 |
| Connecticut | 8.8 | 8.1 | 2.2 | 2.1 | 2.7 | New York | 9.5 | 9.6 | 2.4 | 2.5 | 2.7 |
| Delaware | 8.3 | 8.4 | 2.6 | 2.3 | 2.7 | North Carolina | 8.4 | 8.3 | 3.0 | 2.8 | 3.1 |
| D.C. | 13.3 | 13.4 | 2.3 | 1.8 | 1.1 | North Dakota | 8.6 | 8.6 | 1.7 | 2.1 | 2.8 |
| Florida | 10.6 | 10.7 | 3.3 | 3.3 | 3.5 | Ohio | 9.0 | 9.1 | 2.2 | 2.1 | 2.2 |
| Georgia | 8.1 | 8.0 | 2.9 | 3.1 | 2.5 | Oklahoma | 8.9 | 8.6 | 2.8 | 2.7 | 3.5 |
| Hawaii | 5.7 | 5.6 | 1.9 | 2.2 | 2.7 | Oregon | 8.7 | 8.1 | 3.4 | 2.7 | 2.7 |
| Idaho | 6.6 | 7.0 | 2.8 | 3.2 | 3.2 | Pennsylvania | 10.3 | 10.2 | 2.4 | 2.4 | 2.6 |
| Illinois | 8.5 | 8.7 | 2.3 | 2.3 | 2.5 | Rhode Island | 10.0 | 9.9 | 1.3 | 1.6 | 1.9 |
| Indiana | 8.6 | 8.8 | 2.5 | 2.5 | 2.5 | South Carolina | 7.7 | 7.8 | 3.6 | 3.4 | 3.4 |
| Iowa | 9.0 | 9.4 | 2.1 | 2.5 | 2.5 | South Dakota | 9.1 | 9.4 | 2.3 | 2.6 | 2.3 |
| Kansas | 8.9 | 8.8 | 2.7 | 2.2 | 2.8 | Tennessee | 9.7 | 9.0 | 3.0 | 2.9 | 3.1 |
| Kentucky | 9.0 | 9.0 | 2.8 | 3.0 | 3.3 | Texas | 7.5 | 7.3 | 2.9 | 3.0 | 3.4 |
| Louisiana | 8.2 | 8.1 | 3.6 | 4.3 | 3.8 | Utah | 5.6 | 5.5 | 2.7 | 2.5 | 2.7 |
| Maine | 9.3 | 9.8 | 2.5 | 2.8 | 2.2 | Vermont | 8.4 | 9.3 | 2.7 | 2.3 | 2.7 |
| Maryland | 8.0 | 8.0 | 2.1 | 2.1 | 2.3 | Virginia | 7.8 | 7.8 | 2.4 | 2.1 | 2.1 |
| Massachusetts | 10.2 | 9.4 | 1.7 | 1.7 | 1.8 | Washington | 8.1 | 7.2 | 2.2 | 2.2 | 2.4 |
| Michigan | 8.3 | 8.2 | 2.4 | 2.1 | 2.3 | West Virginia | 9.8 | 9.8 | 4.0 | 4.4 | 4.2 |
| Minnesota | 8.1 | 8.2 | 1.8 | 1.8 | 2.0 | Wisconsin | 8.7 | 8.7 | 2.4 | 2.2 | 2.4 |
| Mississippi | 8.6 | 8.9 | 3.8 | 4.1 | 4.2 | Wyoming | 5.9 | 5.8 | 3.2 | 3.2 | 3.8 |
| Missouri | 10.4 | 10.1 | 2.6 | 2.5 | 2.6 | Total U.S. | 8.7 | 8.6 | 2.7 | 2.7 | 2.9 |

1. Provisional rates per 1,000 population, by place of occurrence. 2. Per 100 million vehicle-miles. *Sources:* Department of Health and Human Services, National Center for Health Statistics; National Safety Council.

# Annual Death Rates

| Year | Rate | Year | Rate | Year | Deaths | Rate |
|------|------|------|------|------|--------|------|
| 1900 | 17.2 | 1939 | 10.6 | 1962 | 1,756,720 | 9.5 |
| 1905 | 15.9 | 1940 | 10.8 | 1963 | 1,813,549 | 9.6 |
| 1910 | 14.7 | 1941 | 10.5 | 1964 | 1,798,051 | 9.4 |
| 1915 | 13.2 | 1942 | 10.3 | 1965 | 1,828,136 | 9.4 |
| 1918 | 18.1 [1] | 1943 | 10.9 | 1966 | 1,863,149 | 9.5 |
| 1920 | 13.0 | 1944 | 10.6 | 1967 | 1,851,323 | 9.4 |
| 1923 | 12.1 | 1945 | 10.6 | 1968 | 1,930,082 | 9.7 |
| 1924 | 11.6 | 1946 | 10.0 | 1969 | 1,921,990 | 9.5 |
| 1925 | 11.7 | 1947 | 10.1 | 1970[2] | 1,921,031 | 9.5 |
| 1926 | 12.1 | 1948 | 9.9 | 1971 | 1,927,542 | 9.3 |
| 1927 | 11.3 | 1949 | 9.7 | 1972 | 1,963,944 | 9.4 |
| 1928 | 12.0 | 1950 | 9.6 | 1973 | 1,973,003 | 9.3 |
| 1929 | 11.9 | 1951 | 9.7 | 1974 | 1,934,388 | 9.1 |
| 1930 | 11.3 | 1952 | 9.6 | 1975 | 1,892,879 | 8.8 |
| 1931 | 11.1 | 1953 | 9.6 | 1976 | 1,909,440 | 8.8 |
| 1932 | 10.9 | 1954 | 9.2 | 1977 | 1,899,597 | 8.6 |
| 1933 | 10.7 | 1955 | 9.3 | 1978 | 1,927,788 | 8.7 |
| 1934 | 11.1 | 1956 | 9.4 | 1979 | 1,913,841 | 8.5 |
| 1935 | 10.9 | 1957 | 9.6 | 1980 | 1,989,841 | 8.7 |
| 1936 | 11.6 | 1958 | 9.5 | 1982 | 1,974,797 | 8.5 |
| 1937 | 11.3 | 1959 | 9.4 | 1983 | 2,019,201 | 8.6 |
| 1938 | 10.6 | 1960 | 9.5 | 1984[3] | 2,047,000 | 8.7 |
|      |      |      |     | 1985[3] | 2,084,000 | 8.7 |

1. Year of influenza epidemic. 2. First year for which deaths of nonresidents are excluded. 3. Provisional. NOTE: Includes only deaths occurring within the registration area. Beginning with 1933, area includes entire U.S.; with 1959 includes Alaska, and with 1960 includes Hawaii. Excludes fetal deaths. Rates per 1,000 population residing in area, as of April 1 for 1940, 1950, 1960, 1970, and 1980, and estimated as of July 1 for all other years. *Sources:* Department of Commerce, Bureau of the Census; and Department of Health and Human Services, National Center for Health Statistics.

# Death Rates by Age, Race, and Sex

| Age | 1984[1] | 1983[2] | 1980[2] | 1975[2] | 1970 | 1960 | 1984[1] | 1983[2] | 1980[2] | 1975[2] | 1970[2] | 1960 |
|-----|------|------|------|------|------|------|------|------|------|------|------|------|
| | **White males** | | | | | | **White females** | | | | | |
| Under 1 year | 10.0 | 10.5 | 12.3 | 15.9 | 21.1 | 26.9 | 8.3 | 8.4 | 9.6 | 12.2 | 16.1 | 20.1 |
| 1–4 | 0.5 | 0.6 | 0.7 | 0.7 | 0.8 | 1.0 | 0.4 | 0.4 | 0.5 | 0.6 | 0.8 | 0.9 |
| 5–14 | 0.3 | 0.3 | 0.4 | 0.4 | 0.5 | 0.5 | 0.2 | 0.2 | 0.2 | 0.3 | 0.3 | 0.3 |
| 15–24 | 1.4 | 1.4 | 1.7 | 1.7 | 1.7 | 1.4 | 0.5 | 0.5 | 0.6 | 0.6 | 0.6 | 0.5 |
| 25–34 | 1.6 | 1.5 | 1.7 | 1.7 | 1.8 | 1.6 | 0.6 | 0.6 | 0.7 | 0.7 | 0.8 | 0.9 |
| 35–44 | 2.3 | 2.3 | 2.6 | 3.0 | 3.4 | 3.3 | 1.2 | 1.2 | 1.4 | 1.6 | 1.9 | 1.9 |
| 45–54 | 6.3 | 6.4 | 7.0 | 7.9 | 8.8 | 9.3 | 3.5 | 3.5 | 3.7 | 4.1 | 4.6 | 4.6 |
| 55–64 | 16.2 | 16.4 | 17.3 | 19.5 | 22.0 | 22.3 | 8.7 | 8.7 | 8.8 | 9.4 | 10.1 | 10.8 |
| 65–74 | 37.8 | 38.2 | 40.4 | 43.6 | 48.1 | 48.5 | 20.3 | 20.3 | 20.7 | 21.5 | 24.7 | 27.8 |
| 75–84 | 85.1 | 85.6 | 88.3 | 96.1 | 101.0 | 103.0 | 51.6 | 51.6 | 54.0 | 60.3 | 67.0 | 77.0 |
| 85 and over | 185.1 | 184.4 | 191.0 | 182.6 | 185.5 | 217.5 | 139.1 | 142.8 | 149.8 | 144.9 | 159.8 | 194.8 |
| | **All other males** | | | | | | **All other females** | | | | | |
| Under 1 year | 19.7 | 19.8 | 23.5 | 30.0 | 40.2 | 51.9 | 16.1 | 16.2 | 19.4 | 25.2 | 31.7 | 40.7 |
| 1–4 | 0.8 | 0.9 | 1.0 | 1.1 | 1.4 | 2.1 | 0.6 | 0.7 | 0.8 | 0.9 | 1.2 | 1.7 |
| 5–14 | 0.4 | 0.4 | 0.4 | 0.6 | 0.6 | 0.8 | 0.2 | 0.3 | 0.3 | 0.3 | 0.4 | 0.5 |
| 15–24 | 1.5 | 1.6 | 2.0 | 2.4 | 3.0 | 2.1 | 0.6 | 0.6 | 0.7 | 0.9 | 1.1 | 1.1 |
| 25–34 | 2.9 | 2.9 | 3.6 | 4.5 | 5.0 | 3.9 | 1.1 | 1.2 | 1.4 | 1.6 | 2.2 | 2.6 |
| 35–44 | 5.1 | 5.0 | 5.9 | 7.4 | 8.7 | 7.3 | 2.6 | 2.4 | 2.9 | 3.6 | 4.9 | 5.5 |
| 45–54 | 11.1 | 11.2 | 13.1 | 14.2 | 16.5 | 15.5 | 5.6 | 6.1 | 6.9 | 7.8 | 9.8 | 11.4 |
| 55–64 | 23.8 | 24.3 | 26.1 | 28.1 | 30.5 | 31.5 | 13.6 | 13.6 | 14.2 | 16.4 | 18.9 | 24.1 |
| 65–74 | 45.5 | 45.2 | 47.5 | 49.7 | 54.7 | 56.6 | 26.2 | 26.8 | 28.6 | 31.7 | 36.8 | 39.8 |
| 75–84 | 80.8 | 84.0 | 86.9 | 86.0 | 89.8 | 86.6 | 55.6 | 56.1 | 58.6 | 59.8 | 63.9 | 67.1 |
| 85 and over | 137.8 | 134.8 | 157.7 | 116.9 | 114.1 | 152.4 | 103.3 | 109.4 | 119.2 | 91.8 | 102.9 | 128.7 |

1. Provisional. Based on a 10% sample of deaths. 2. Excludes deaths of nonresidents of U.S. NOTE: Excludes fetal deaths. Rates are per 1,000 population in each group, enumerated as of April 1 for 1960, 1970, and 1980, and estimated as of July 1 for all other years. NOTE: Data are latest available. *Sources:* Department of Commerce, Bureau of the Census; and Department of Health and Human Services, National Center for Health Statistics.

# Expectation of Life

## Expectation of Life in the United States

| Calendar period | Age 0 | 10 | 20 | 30 | 40 | 50 | 60 | 70 | 80 |
|---|---|---|---|---|---|---|---|---|---|
| **WHITE MALES** | | | | | | | | | |
| 1850[1] | 38.3 | 48.0 | 40.1 | 34.0 | 27.9 | 21.6 | 15.6 | 10.2 | 5.9 |
| 1890[1] | 42.50 | 48.45 | 40.66 | 34.05 | 27.37 | 20.72 | 14.73 | 9.35 | 5.40 |
| 1900–1902[2] | 48.23 | 50.59 | 42.19 | 34.88 | 27.74 | 20.76 | 14.35 | 9.03 | 5.10 |
| 1909–1911[2] | 50.23 | 51.32 | 42.71 | 34.87 | 27.43 | 20.39 | 13.98 | 8.83 | 5.09 |
| 1919–1921[3] | 56.34 | 54.15 | 45.60 | 37.65 | 29.86 | 22.22 | 15.25 | 9.51 | 5.47 |
| 1929–1931 | 59.12 | 54.96 | 46.02 | 37.54 | 29.22 | 21.51 | 14.72 | 9.20 | 5.26 |
| 1939–1941 | 62.81 | 57.03 | 47.76 | 38.80 | 30.03 | 21.96 | 15.05 | 9.42 | 5.38 |
| 1949–1951 | 66.31 | 58.98 | 49.52 | 40.29 | 31.17 | 22.83 | 15.76 | 10.07 | 5.88 |
| 1959–1961 | 67.55 | 59.78 | 50.25 | 40.98 | 31.73 | 23.22 | 16.01 | 10.29 | 5.89 |
| 1969–1971 | 67.94 | 59.69 | 50.22 | 41.07 | 31.87 | 23.34 | 16.07 | 10.38 | 6.18 |
| 1979–1981 | 70.82 | 61.98 | 52.45 | 43.31 | 34.04 | 25.26 | 17.56 | 11.35 | 6.76 |
| 1982 | 71.5 | 62.6 | 53.0 | 43.8 | 34.5 | 25.6 | 17.9 | 11.6 | 7.0 |
| 1983 | 71.1 | 62.7 | 53.1 | 43.9 | 34.6 | 25.7 | 17.9 | 11.5 | 6.9 |
| 1984 | 71.8 | 62.7 | 53.1 | 43.9 | 34.6 | 25.7 | 18.0 | 11.6 | 6.8 |
| **WHITE FEMALES** | | | | | | | | | |
| 1850[1] | 40.5 | 47.2 | 40.2 | 35.4 | 29.8 | 23.5 | 17.0 | 11.3 | 6.4 |
| 1890[1] | 44.46 | 49.62 | 42.03 | 35.36 | 28.76 | 22.09 | 15.70 | 10.15 | 5.75 |
| 1900–1902[2] | 51.08 | 52.15 | 43.77 | 36.42 | 29.17 | 21.89 | 15.23 | 9.59 | 5.50 |
| 1909–1911[2] | 53.62 | 53.57 | 44.88 | 36.96 | 29.26 | 21.74 | 14.92 | 9.38 | 5.35 |
| 1919–1921[3] | 58.53 | 55.17 | 46.46 | 38.72 | 30.94 | 23.12 | 15.93 | 9.94 | 5.70 |
| 1929–1931 | 62.67 | 57.65 | 48.52 | 39.99 | 31.52 | 23.41 | 16.05 | 9.98 | 5.63 |
| 1939–1941 | 67.29 | 60.85 | 51.38 | 42.21 | 33.25 | 24.72 | 17.00 | 10.50 | 5.88 |
| 1949–1951 | 72.03 | 64.26 | 54.56 | 45.00 | 35.64 | 26.76 | 18.64 | 11.68 | 6.59 |
| 1959–1961 | 74.19 | 66.05 | 56.29 | 46.63 | 37.13 | 28.08 | 19.69 | 12.38 | 6.67 |
| 1969–1971 | 75.49 | 66.97 | 57.24 | 47.60 | 38.12 | 29.11 | 20.79 | 13.37 | 7.59 |
| 1979–1981 | 78.22 | 69.21 | 59.44 | 49.76 | 40.16 | 30.96 | 22.45 | 14.89 | 8.65 |
| 1982 | 78.8 | 69.7 | 59.9 | 50.2 | 40.6 | 31.3 | 22.8 | 15.3 | 9.0 |
| 1983 | 78.7 | 69.6 | 59.8 | 50.1 | 40.4 | 31.2 | 22.6 | 15.1 | 8.8 |
| 1984 | 78.8 | 69.6 | 59.8 | 50.1 | 40.5 | 31.2 | 22.7 | 15.2 | 9.0 |
| **ALL OTHER MALES[4]** | | | | | | | | | |
| 1900–1902[2] | 32.54 | 41.90 | 35.11 | 29.25 | 23.12 | 17.34 | 12.62 | 8.33 | 5.12 |
| 1909–1911[2] | 34.05 | 40.65 | 33.46 | 27.33 | 21.57 | 16.21 | 11.67 | 8.00 | 5.53 |
| 1919–1921[3] | 47.14 | 45.99 | 38.36 | 32.51 | 26.53 | 20.47 | 14.74 | 9.58 | 5.83 |
| 1929–1931 | 47.55 | 44.27 | 35.95 | 29.45 | 23.36 | 17.92 | 13.15 | 8.78 | 5.42 |
| 1939–1941 | 52.33 | 48.54 | 39.74 | 32.25 | 25.23 | 19.18 | 14.38 | 10.06 | 6.46 |
| 1949–1951 | 58.91 | 52.96 | 43.73 | 35.31 | 27.29 | 20.25 | 14.91 | 10.74 | 7.07 |
| 1959–1961 | 61.48 | 55.19 | 45.78 | 37.05 | 28.72 | 21.28 | 15.29 | 10.81 | 6.87 |
| 1969–1971 | 60.98 | 53.67 | 44.37 | 36.20 | 28.29 | 21.24 | 15.35 | 10.68 | 7.57 |
| 1979–1981 | 65.63 | 57.40 | 47.87 | 39.13 | 30.64 | 22.92 | 16.54 | 11.36 | 7.22 |
| 1982 | 66.8 | 58.4 | 48.8 | 39.9 | 31.3 | 23.4 | 16.8 | 11.7 | 7.5 |
| 1983 | 67.2 | 58.8 | 49.1 | 40.2 | 31.5 | 23.5 | 16.8 | 11.5 | 7.4 |
| 1984 | 67.2 | 58.8 | 49.2 | 40.2 | 31.6 | 23.7 | 16.9 | 11.6 | 7.5 |
| **ALL OTHER FEMALES[4]** | | | | | | | | | |
| 1900–1902[2] | 35.04 | 43.02 | 36.89 | 30.70 | 24.37 | 18.67 | 13.60 | 9.62 | 6.48 |
| 1909–1911[2] | 37.67 | 42.84 | 36.14 | 29.61 | 23.34 | 17.65 | 12.78 | 9.22 | 6.05 |
| 1919–1921[3] | 46.92 | 44.54 | 37.15 | 31.48 | 25.60 | 19.76 | 14.69 | 10.25 | 6.58 |
| 1929–1931 | 49.51 | 45.33 | 37.22 | 30.67 | 24.30 | 18.60 | 14.22 | 10.38 | 6.90 |
| 1939–1941 | 55.51 | 50.83 | 42.14 | 34.52 | 27.31 | 21.04 | 16.14 | 11.81 | 8.00 |
| 1949–1951 | 62.70 | 56.17 | 46.77 | 38.02 | 29.82 | 22.67 | 16.95 | 12.29 | 8.15 |
| 1959–1961 | 66.47 | 59.72 | 50.07 | 40.83 | 32.16 | 24.31 | 17.83 | 12.46 | 7.66 |
| 1969–1971 | 69.05 | 61.49 | 51.85 | 42.61 | 33.87 | 25.97 | 19.02 | 13.30 | 9.01 |
| 1979–1981[5] | 74.00 | 65.64 | 55.88 | 46.39 | 37.16 | 28.59 | 20.49 | 14.44 | 9.17 |
| 1982[5] | 75.0 | 66.5 | 56.8 | 47.2 | 37.9 | 29.2 | 21.5 | 15.0 | 9.5 |
| 1983 | 74.9 | 66.4 | 56.6 | 47.0 | 37.7 | 29.0 | 21.3 | 14.6 | 9.3 |
| 1984 | 75.2 | 66.6 | 56.8 | 47.3 | 38.0 | 29.4 | 21.5 | 14.9 | 9.4 |

1. Massachusetts only; white and nonwhite combined, the latter being about 1% of the total. 2. Original Death Registration States. 3. Death Registration States of 1920. 4. Data for periods 1900–1902 and 1929–1931 relate to blacks only. *Sources:* Department of Health and Human Services, National Center for Health Statistics; Department of Commerce, Bureau of the Census. NOTE: Data are latest available.

# Expectation of Life and Mortality Probabilities, 1982

| Age | Total persons | Expectation of life in years White Male | White Female | All other Male | All other Female | Total persons | Mortality probability per 1,000 White Male | White Female | All other Male | All other Female |
|---|---|---|---|---|---|---|---|---|---|---|
| 0 | 74.6 | 71.7 | 78.7 | 67.2 | 74.9 | 11.2 | 10.8 | 8.6 | 18.3 | 15.2 |
| 1 | 74.5 | 71.5 | 78.4 | 67.4 | 75.1 | .8 | .8 | .6 | 1.1 | .8 |
| 2 | 73.5 | 70.5 | 77.4 | 66.5 | 74.1 | .6 | .6 | .5 | .9 | .7 |
| 3 | 72.6 | 69.6 | 76.4 | 65.5 | 73.2 | .5 | .5 | .4 | .8 | .6 |
| 4 | 71.6 | 68.6 | 75.5 | 64.6 | 72.2 | .4 | .4 | .3 | .6 | .5 |
| 5 | 70.6 | 67.6 | 74.5 | 63.6 | 71.3 | .3 | .4 | .3 | .5 | .4 |
| 6 | 69.7 | 66.6 | 73.5 | 62.7 | 70.3 | .3 | .3 | .2 | .4 | .3 |
| 7 | 68.7 | 65.7 | 72.5 | 61.7 | 69.3 | .3 | .3 | .2 | .4 | .3 |
| 8 | 67.7 | 64.7 | 71.5 | 60.7 | 68.3 | .2 | .3 | .2 | .3 | .2 |
| 9 | 66.7 | 63.7 | 70.6 | 59.7 | 67.4 | .2 | .2 | .2 | .3 | .2 |
| 10 | 65.7 | 62.7 | 69.6 | 58.8 | 66.4 | .2 | .2 | .1 | .3 | .2 |
| 11 | 64.7 | 61.7 | 68.6 | 57.8 | 65.4 | .2 | .2 | .1 | .3 | .2 |
| 12 | 63.7 | 60.7 | 67.6 | 56.8 | 64.4 | .2 | .3 | .2 | .4 | .2 |
| 13 | 62.8 | 59.8 | 66.6 | 55.8 | 63.4 | .3 | .4 | .2 | .5 | .3 |
| 14 | 61.8 | 58.8 | 65.6 | 54.8 | 62.4 | .4 | .6 | .3 | .6 | .3 |
| 15 | 60.8 | 57.8 | 64.6 | 53.9 | 61.4 | .6 | .8 | .4 | .7 | .4 |
| 16 | 59.8 | 56.9 | 63.7 | 52.9 | 60.5 | .7 | 1.0 | .4 | .9 | .4 |
| 17 | 58.9 | 55.9 | 62.7 | 51.9 | 59.5 | .8 | 1.2 | .5 | 1.1 | .5 |
| 18 | 57.9 | 55.0 | 61.7 | 51.0 | 58.5 | .9 | 1.3 | .5 | 1.3 | .5 |
| 19 | 57.0 | 54.1 | 60.7 | 50.1 | 57.5 | 1.0 | 1.4 | .5 | 1.5 | .6 |
| 20 | 56.0 | 53.1 | 59.8 | 49.1 | 56.6 | 1.0 | 1.5 | .5 | 1.7 | .7 |
| 21 | 55.1 | 52.2 | 58.8 | 48.2 | 55.6 | 1.1 | 1.5 | .5 | 1.9 | .7 |
| 22 | 54.2 | 51.3 | 57.8 | 47.3 | 54.7 | 1.1 | 1.6 | .5 | 2.1 | .8 |
| 23 | 53.2 | 50.4 | 56.9 | 46.4 | 53.7 | 1.1 | 1.6 | .5 | 2.2 | .8 |
| 24 | 52.3 | 49.4 | 55.9 | 45.5 | 52.7 | 1.1 | 1.6 | .5 | 2.3 | .9 |
| 25 | 51.3 | 48.5 | 54.9 | 44.6 | 51.8 | 1.1 | 1.6 | .5 | 2.4 | .9 |
| 26 | 50.4 | 47.6 | 54.0 | 43.7 | 50.8 | 1.1 | 1.5 | .5 | 2.5 | 1.0 |
| 27 | 49.4 | 46.7 | 53.0 | 42.8 | 49.9 | 1.1 | 1.5 | .6 | 2.6 | 1.0 |
| 28 | 48.5 | 45.7 | 52.0 | 41.9 | 48.9 | 1.2 | 1.5 | .6 | 2.7 | 1.0 |
| 29 | 47.6 | 44.8 | 51.0 | 41.1 | 48.0 | 1.2 | 1.5 | .6 | 2.9 | 1.1 |
| 30 | 46.6 | 43.9 | 50.1 | 40.2 | 47.0 | 1.2 | 1.5 | .6 | 3.0 | 1.2 |
| 31 | 45.7 | 42.9 | 49.1 | 39.3 | 46.1 | 1.2 | 1.5 | .6 | 3.2 | 1.2 |
| 32 | 44.7 | 42.0 | 48.1 | 38.4 | 45.1 | 1.3 | 1.6 | .7 | 3.3 | 1.3 |
| 33 | 43.8 | 41.1 | 47.2 | 37.5 | 44.2 | 1.3 | 1.6 | .7 | 3.5 | 1.4 |
| 34 | 42.8 | 40.1 | 46.2 | 36.7 | 43.3 | 1.4 | 1.7 | .7 | 3.6 | 1.5 |
| 35 | 41.9 | 39.2 | 45.2 | 35.8 | 42.3 | 1.5 | 1.7 | .8 | 3.8 | 1.7 |
| 36 | 41.0 | 38.3 | 44.3 | 34.9 | 41.4 | 1.5 | 1.8 | .9 | 4.0 | 1.8 |
| 37 | 40.0 | 37.3 | 43.3 | 34.1 | 40.5 | 1.6 | 1.9 | 1.0 | 4.2 | 2.0 |
| 38 | 39.1 | 36.4 | 42.3 | 33.2 | 39.6 | 1.8 | 2.0 | 1.1 | 4.4 | 2.1 |
| 39 | 38.2 | 35.5 | 41.4 | 32.4 | 38.6 | 1.9 | 2.2 | 1.2 | 4.7 | 2.3 |
| 40 | 37.2 | 34.6 | 40.4 | 31.5 | 37.7 | 2.1 | 2.4 | 1.3 | 5.0 | 2.5 |
| 41 | 36.3 | 33.6 | 39.5 | 30.7 | 36.8 | 2.2 | 2.6 | 1.4 | 5.3 | 2.7 |
| 42 | 35.4 | 32.7 | 38.5 | 29.8 | 35.9 | 2.4 | 2.8 | 1.6 | 5.8 | 2.9 |
| 43 | 34.5 | 31.8 | 37.6 | 29.0 | 35.0 | 2.7 | 3.1 | 1.7 | 6.3 | 3.2 |
| 44 | 33.6 | 30.9 | 36.7 | 28.2 | 34.1 | 3.0 | 3.4 | 1.9 | 7.0 | 3.6 |
| 45 | 32.7 | 30.0 | 35.7 | 27.4 | 33.2 | 3.3 | 3.8 | 2.1 | 7.7 | 4.0 |
| 46 | 31.8 | 29.1 | 34.8 | 26.6 | 32.4 | 3.6 | 4.2 | 2.3 | 8.5 | 4.4 |
| 47 | 30.9 | 28.2 | 33.9 | 25.8 | 31.5 | 4.0 | 4.6 | 2.6 | 9.2 | 4.9 |
| 48 | 30.0 | 27.4 | 33.0 | 25.0 | 30.7 | 4.5 | 5.2 | 2.9 | 9.9 | 5.3 |
| 49 | 29.1 | 26.5 | 32.1 | 24.3 | 29.8 | 4.9 | 5.8 | 3.2 | 10.6 | 5.7 |
| 50 | 28.3 | 25.7 | 31.2 | 23.5 | 29.0 | 5.4 | 6.4 | 3.6 | 11.3 | 6.2 |
| 51 | 27.4 | 24.8 | 30.3 | 22.8 | 28.2 | 6.0 | 7.1 | 3.9 | 12.1 | 6.7 |
| 52 | 26.6 | 24.0 | 29.4 | 22.1 | 27.4 | 6.6 | 7.9 | 4.3 | 13.0 | 7.2 |
| 53 | 25.8 | 23.2 | 28.5 | 21.4 | 26.6 | 7.2 | 8.8 | 4.8 | 14.1 | 7.9 |
| 54 | 24.9 | 22.4 | 27.7 | 20.7 | 25.8 | 7.9 | 9.7 | 5.2 | 15.4 | 8.6 |
| 55 | 24.1 | 21.6 | 26.8 | 20.0 | 25.0 | 8.6 | 10.7 | 5.6 | 16.8 | 9.4 |
| 56 | 23.3 | 20.8 | 25.9 | 19.3 | 24.2 | 9.4 | 11.8 | 6.2 | 18.2 | 10.2 |
| 57 | 22.6 | 20.1 | 25.1 | 18.7 | 23.5 | 10.3 | 13.0 | 6.7 | 19.7 | 11.1 |
| 58 | 21.8 | 19.3 | 24.3 | 18.0 | 22.7 | 11.2 | 14.1 | 7.4 | 21.5 | 12.1 |
| 59 | 21.0 | 18.6 | 23.4 | 17.4 | 22.0 | 12.2 | 15.4 | 8.1 | 23.4 | 13.1 |
| 60 | 20.3 | 17.9 | 22.6 | 16.8 | 21.3 | 13.3 | 16.8 | 8.9 | 25.5 | 14.2 |
| 61 | 19.6 | 17.2 | 21.8 | 16.3 | 20.6 | 14.5 | 18.2 | 9.7 | 27.6 | 15.4 |
| 62 | 18.8 | 16.5 | 21.0 | 15.7 | 19.9 | 15.7 | 19.8 | 10.6 | 29.5 | 16.5 |
| 63 | 18.1 | 15.8 | 20.3 | 15.2 | 19.2 | 17.0 | 21.6 | 11.5 | 31.0 | 17.4 |
| 64 | 17.4 | 15.2 | 19.5 | 14.6 | 18.5 | 18.3 | 23.6 | 12.5 | 32.2 | 18.1 |
| 65 | 16.7 | 14.5 | 18.7 | 14.1 | 17.9 | 19.7 | 25.7 | 13.5 | 33.2 | 18.8 |

| Age | Total persons | White Male | White Female | All other Male | All other Female | Total persons | White Male | White Female | All other Male | All other Female |
|---|---|---|---|---|---|---|---|---|---|---|
| | | Expectation of life in years | | | | | Mortality probability per 1,000 | | | |
| 66 | 16.1 | 13.9 | 18.0 | 13.6 | 17.2 | 21.3 | 28.0 | 14.6 | 34.3 | 19.6 |
| 67 | 15.4 | 13.3 | 17.2 | 13.0 | 16.5 | 23.0 | 30.5 | 15.9 | 36.1 | 20.9 |
| 68 | 14.8 | 12.7 | 16.5 | 12.5 | 15.9 | 25.0 | 33.3 | 17.3 | 39.0 | 22.9 |
| 69 | 14.1 | 12.1 | 15.8 | 12.0 | 15.3 | 27.3 | 36.3 | 19.0 | 42.7 | 25.4 |
| 70 | 13.5 | 11.5 | 15.1 | 11.5 | 14.6 | 29.7 | 39.5 | 20.8 | 47.1 | 28.3 |
| 71 | 12.9 | 11.0 | 14.4 | 11.0 | 14.0 | 32.3 | 43.0 | 22.8 | 51.6 | 31.2 |
| 72 | 12.3 | 10.5 | 13.7 | 10.6 | 13.5 | 35.1 | 46.8 | 24.9 | 55.6 | 33.8 |
| 73 | 11.7 | 9.9 | 13.1 | 10.2 | 12.9 | 38.0 | 50.9 | 27.3 | 58.5 | 35.9 |
| 74 | 11.2 | 9.4 | 12.4 | 9.8 | 12.4 | 41.0 | 55.3 | 29.9 | 60.6 | 37.5 |
| 75 | 10.7 | 9.0 | 11.8 | 9.4 | 11.9 | 44.3 | 60.2 | 32.8 | 62.4 | 39.2 |
| 76 | 10.1 | 8.5 | 11.2 | 9.0 | 11.3 | 47.9 | 65.3 | 36.0 | 64.6 | 41.2 |
| 77 | 9.6 | 8.1 | 10.6 | 8.6 | 10.8 | 51.9 | 70.9 | 39.6 | 67.9 | 44.0 |
| 78 | 9.1 | 7.7 | 10.0 | 8.2 | 10.3 | 56.4 | 76.9 | 43.6 | 72.5 | 47.8 |
| 79 | 8.6 | 7.2 | 9.4 | 7.8 | 9.8 | 61.4 | 83.2 | 48.2 | 78.7 | 52.5 |
| 80 | 8.1 | 6.9 | 8.8 | 7.4 | 9.3 | 67.0 | 90.0 | 53.5 | 86.5 | 58.4 |
| 81 | 7.7 | 6.5 | 8.3 | 7.1 | 8.8 | 73.3 | 97.3 | 59.6 | 95.9 | 65.3 |
| 82 | 7.3 | 6.1 | 7.8 | 6.8 | 8.4 | 80.45 | 105.0 | 66.6 | 106.9 | 73.3 |
| 83 | 6.9 | 5.8 | 7.3 | 6.5 | 8.0 | 88.5 | 113.0 | 75.0 | 119.3 | 82.5 |
| 84 | 6.5 | 5.5 | 6.9 | 6.4 | 7.7 | 97.7 | 121.3 | 85.0 | 132.7 | 92.8 |
| 85 | 6.1 | 5.2 | 6.5 | 6.3 | 7.5 | — | — | — | — | — |

*Source:* Department of Health and Human Services, National Center for Health Statistics. NOTE: Data are latest available.

# Law Enforcement and Crime

## Full-Time Law Enforcement Employees, 1985

| City | Officers | Civilians | Total | 1984 Total | City | Officers | Civilians | Total | 1984 Total |
|---|---|---|---|---|---|---|---|---|---|
| Atlanta | 1,278 | 289 | 1,567 | 1,563 | Minneapolis | 677 | 91 | 768 | 760 |
| Baltimore | 2,965 | 520 | 3,485 | 3,541 | New Orleans | 1,378 | 386 | 1,764 | 1,828 |
| Birmingham, Ala. | 619 | 184 | 803 | 809 | New York | 26,073 | 6,255 | 32,328 | 33,014 |
| Boston | 1,829 | 373 | 2,202 | 2,088 | Newark, N.J. | 1,122 | 158 | 1,280 | 1,178 |
| Buffalo, N.Y. | 993 | 113 | 1,106 | 1,132 | Norfolk, Va. | 617 | 65 | 682 | 697 |
| Chicago | 11,871 | 1,915 | 13,786 | 13,845 | Oakland, Calif. | 617 | 298 | 915 | 923 |
| Cincinnati | 883 | 168 | 1,051 | 1,034 | Oklahoma City | 732 | 187 | 919 | 970 |
| Cleveland | 1,742 | 186 | 1,928 | 2,010 | Omaha, Neb. | 574 | 164 | 738 | 741 |
| Columbus, Ohio | 1,223 | 319 | 1,542 | 1,487 | Philadelphia | 6,966 | 798 | 7,764 | 7,894 |
| Dallas | 2,170 | 511 | 2,681 | 2,581 | Phoenix, Ariz. | 1,704 | 656 | 2,360 | 2,279 |
| Denver | 1,349 | 310 | 1,659 | 1,672 | Pittsburgh | 1,210 | 169 | 1,379 | 1,350 |
| Detroit | 4,640 | 645 | 5,285 | 4,465 | Portland, Ore. | 758 | 191 | 949 | 890 |
| El Paso | 686 | 214 | 900 | 846 | Rochester, N.Y. | 570 | 131 | 701 | — |
| Fort Worth | 771 | 236 | 1,007 | 1,022 | St. Louis | 1,627 | 513 | 2,140 | 2,203 |
| Honolulu | 1,639 | 344 | 1,983 | 1,998 | St. Paul | 517 | 125 | 642 | 633 |
| Houston | 4,363 | 1,345 | 5,708 | 5,263 | San Antonio | 1,273 | 286 | 1,559 | 1,498 |
| Indianapolis | 951 | 338 | 1,289 | 1,240 | San Diego, Calif. | 1,407 | 544 | 1,951 | 1,877 |
| Jacksonville, Fla. | 945 | 672 | 1,617 | 1,614 | San Francisco | 1,929 | 824 | 2,753 | 2,757 |
| Kansas City, Mo. | 1,114 | 517 | 1,631 | 1,636 | San Jose, Calif. | 976 | 270 | 1,246 | 1,139 |
| Long Beach, Calif. | 652 | 376 | 1,028 | 893 | Seattle | 1,039 | 375 | 1,414 | 1,385 |
| Los Angeles | 7,051 | 2,584 | 9,635 | 9,364 | Tampa, Fla. | 692 | 204 | 896 | 864 |
| Louisville, Ky. | 650 | 185 | 835 | 851 | Toledo, Ohio | 758 | 52 | 810 | 801 |
| Memphis, Tenn. | 1,154 | 409 | 1,563 | 1,522 | Tucson, Ariz. | 647 | 207 | 854 | 765 |
| Miami, Fla. | 1,040 | 391 | 1,431 | 1,435 | Tulsa, Okla. | 694 | 163 | 857 | 834 |
| Milwaukee | 2,041 | 347 | 2,388 | 2,372 | Washington, D.C. | 3,837 | 504 | 4,341 | 4,376 |

NOTE: As of Oct. 31, 1985. *Source:* Department of Justice, Federal Bureau of Investigation, *Uniform Crime Reports for the United States, 1986.*

## Estimated Arrests, 1985[1]

| | | | |
|---|---:|---|---:|
| Murder and non-negligent manslaughter | 18,330 | Weapons—carrying, possession, etc. | 180,900 |
| Forcible rape | 36,970 | Prostitution and commercial vice | 113,800 |
| Robbery | 136,870 | Sex offenses, except forcible rape | |
| Aggravated assault | 305,390 | and prostitution | 100,600 |
| Burglary | 443,300 | Drug abuse violations | 211,400 |
| Larceny—theft | 1,348,400 | Gambling | 32,100 |
| Motor vehicle theft | 133,900 | Offenses against family and children | 58,800 |
| Arson | 19,500 | Driving under the influence | 1,788,400 |
| Total violent crime | 497,560 | Liquor laws | 548,600 |
| Total property crime | 1,945,100 | Drunkenness | 964,800 |
| Other assaults | 637,600 | Disorderly conduct | 671,700 |
| Forgery and counterfeiting | 87,600 | Vagrancy | 33,800 |
| Fraud | 342,600 | All other offenses, except traffic | 2,489,200 |
| Embezzlement | 11,400 | Curfew and loitering law violations | 12,900 |
| Stolen property—buying, receiving, possessing | 127,100 | Runaways | 161,200 |
| Vandalism | 259,600 | **Total** | **11,945,200** |

1. Arrest totals based on all reporting agencies and estimates for unreported areas. 2. Because of rounding, items may not add to totals. *Source:* Department of Justice, Federal Bureau of Investigation, *Uniform Crime Reports for the United States,* 1986.


## Number of Arrests by Sex and Age

| | Male | | | | Female | | | |
|---|---|---|---|---|---|---|---|---|
| | Total | | Under 18 | | Total | | Under 18 | |
| Offense | 1985 | 1984 | 1985 | 1984 | 1985 | 1984 | 1985 | 1984 |
|---|---:|---:|---:|---:|---:|---:|---:|---:|
| Serious crimes | 1,540,744 | 1,498,019 | 482,653 | 461,896 | 416,585 | 389,987 | 117,719 | 111,884 |
| Murder[1] | 12,904 | 13,030 | 1,124 | 1,028 | 1,815 | 1,975 | 115 | 106 |
| Forcible rape | 28,865 | 28,342 | 4,316 | 4,343 | 303 | 254 | 80 | 56 |
| Robbery | 105,401 | 105,409 | 26,758 | 26,627 | 8,639 | 8,189 | 1,951 | 1,848 |
| Aggravated assault | 211,228 | 212,391 | 28,330 | 26,561 | 32,926 | 33,414 | 5,202 | 5,311 |
| Burglary—breaking or entering | 326,959 | 321,370 | 124,388 | 120,191 | 26,753 | 25,979 | 9,764 | 9,511 |
| Larceny—theft | 744,423 | 715,423 | 255,810 | 246,771 | 334,053 | 309,472 | 95,379 | 90,654 |
| Motor vehicle theft | 97,835 | 88,767 | 36,256 | 30,695 | 10,093 | 8,867 | 4,619 | 3,832 |
| Arson | 13,129 | 12,943 | 5,671 | 5,680 | 2,003 | 1,837 | 609 | 566 |
| All other | | | | | | | | |
| Other assaults | 416,735 | 370,637 | 57,218 | 52,218 | 75,937 | 66,033 | 17,259 | 15,751 |
| Forgery and counterfeiting | 46,286 | 45,526 | 4,962 | 4,723 | 23,181 | 22,869 | 2,302 | 2,148 |
| Fraud | 151,773 | 140,030 | 13,350 | 13,375 | 111,825 | 99,846 | 3,812 | 3,948 |
| Embezzlement | 5,624 | 4,821 | 451 | 330 | 3,184 | 2,692 | 195 | 171 |
| Stolen property—buying, receiving, possessing | 89,619 | 86,461 | 23,032 | 20,775 | 11,890 | 11,334 | 2,386 | 2,246 |
| Vandalism | 181,600 | 173,513 | 81,987 | 78,451 | 20,192 | 19,106 | 7,730 | 7,373 |
| Weapons—carrying, possession, etc. | 134,210 | 129,699 | 22,421 | 19,766 | 10,970 | 10,414 | 1,628 | 1,356 |
| Prostitution and commercialized vice | 29,584 | 29,114 | 708 | 754 | 67,592 | 65,424 | 1,638 | 1,723 |
| Sex offenses, except forcible rape and prostitution | 74,602 | 73,808 | 12,599 | 12,588 | 6,108 | 5,451 | 1,107 | 883 |
| Drug abuse violations | 562,754 | 495,638 | 63,255 | 57,376 | 90,038 | 79,677 | 10,932 | 10,204 |
| Gambling | 21,995 | 24,198 | 666 | 628 | 3,879 | 3,891 | 33 | 67 |
| Offenses against family and children | 35,553 | 34,574 | 1,444 | 974 | 5,086 | 4,712 | 804 | 528 |
| Driving under the influence | 1,208,416 | 1,273,098 | 16,089 | 17,255 | 157,131 | 166,868 | 2,420 | 2,768 |
| Liquor laws | 350,942 | 325,204 | 76,322 | 73,886 | 67,823 | 62,920 | 27,483 | 25,567 |
| Drunkenness | 726,214 | 797,954 | 19,112 | 19,663 | 70,573 | 75,473 | 3,697 | 3,698 |
| Disorderly conduct | 435,198 | 418,211 | 59,944 | 57,793 | 99,252 | 86,449 | 14,291 | 13,291 |
| Vagrancy | 24,592 | 26,207 | 2,016 | 1,666 | 3,001 | 2,989 | 447 | 399 |
| All other offenses, except traffic | 1,671,002 | 1,602,843 | 206,878 | 201,418 | 307,269 | 287,927 | 53,649 | 52,215 |
| Curfew and loitering law violations | 49,258 | 50,347 | 49,258 | 50,347 | 15,985 | 15,603 | 15,985 | 15,603 |
| Runaways | 53,808 | 46,613 | 53,808 | 46,613 | 72,473 | 64,697 | 72,473 | 64,697 |
| **Total** | **7,810,509** | **7,646,515** | **1,248,235** | **1,192,495** | **1,639,974** | **1,544,362** | **357,990** | **336,520** |

1. Includes non-negligent manslaughter. NOTE: 9,596 agencies reporting; 1985 estimated population 183,022,000. *Source:* Department of Justice, Federal Bureau of Investigation, *Uniform Crime Reports for the United States, 1986.*

# Arrests by Race, 1985

## (in thousands)

| Offense | White | Black | Other[1] | Total | Offense | White | Black | Other[1] | Total |
|---|---|---|---|---|---|---|---|---|---|
| **Serious crimes** | | | | | Prostitution and | | | | |
| Murder[2] | 7,817 | 7,562 | 233 | 15,612 | commercial vice | 55,960 | 43,314 | 1,551 | 100,825 |
| Forcible rape | 16,470 | 14,669 | 414 | 31,553 | Sex offenses, except | | | | |
| Robbery | 44,824 | 73,946 | 1,164 | 119,934 | forcible rape and | | | | |
| Aggravated assault | 152,189 | 105,902 | 4,137 | 262,228 | prostitution | 67,922 | 17,501 | 1,274 | 86,697 |
| Burglary | 265,135 | 110,104 | 5,340 | 380,579 | Drug abuse violation[5] | 482,486 | 210,298 | 7,225 | 700,009 |
| Larceny-theft | 790,882 | 360,098 | 25,996 | 1,176,976 | Gambling | 12,452 | 13,684 | 1,394 | 27,530 |
| Motor vehicle theft | 75,596 | 37,239 | 2,097 | 114,932 | Offenses against | | | | |
| Arson | 12,645 | 3,806 | 259 | 16,710 | family and children | 31,036 | 16,594 | 677 | 48,307 |
| **All other** | | | | | Driving under the | | | | |
| Other assaults | 359,307 | 179,496 | 9,167 | 547,970 | influence | 1,316,890 | 143,882 | 25,603 | 1,486,375 |
| Forgery and | | | | | Liquor laws | 391,698 | 59,113 | 14,403 | 465,214 |
| counterfeiting | 50,538 | 23,754 | 846 | 75,138 | Drunkenness | 666,634 | 143,261 | 20,130 | 830,025 |
| Fraud | 192,513 | 91,842 | 2,414 | 286,769 | Disorderly conduct | 395,300 | 175,025 | 9,474 | 579,799 |
| Embezzlement | 6,896 | 2,762 | 136 | 9,794 | Vagrancy | 20,333 | 8,451 | 1,014 | 29,798 |
| Stolen property— | | | | | All other offenses | | | | |
| buying, receiving, | | | | | except traffic | 1,398,119 | 701,839 | 34,303 | 2,134,261 |
| possessing | 68,470 | 40,168 | 1,182 | 109,820 | Suspicion | 5,861 | 5,247 | 109 | 11,217 |
| Vandalism | 176,195 | 43,808 | 3,558 | 223,561 | Curfew and loitering | | | | |
| Weapons—carrying, | | | | | law violations | 53,055 | 15,874 | 1,499 | 71,428 |
| possession, etc. | 101,946 | 52,529 | 2,084 | 156,559 | Runaways | 118,512 | 18,376 | 2,970 | 139,858 |
| | | | | | **Total** | 7,337,681 | 2,721,144 | 180,653 | 10,239,478 |

1. Includes American Indian, Alaskan Native, and Asian or Pacific Islander. 2. Includes non-negligent manslaughter. NOTE: Figures represent arrests reported by 11,231 agencies serving a total 1985 population of 200,277,000 as estimated by FBI. *Source:* Department of Justice, Federal Bureau of Investigation, *Uniform Crime Reports for the United States, 1986.*

# Total Arrests, by Age Groups, 1983

| Age | Arrests | Age | Arrests | Age | Arrests | Age | Arrests | Age | Arrests |
|---|---|---|---|---|---|---|---|---|---|
| Under 15 | 585,745 | 18 | 480,368 | 22 | 471,486 | 30–34 | 1,226,564 | 50–54 | 219,376 |
| 15 | 335,837 | 19 | 493,216 | 23 | 456,093 | 35–39 | 794,079 | 55 and | |
| 16 | 401,239 | 20 | 494,530 | 24 | 446,095 | 40–44 | 487,908 | over | 350,083 |
| 17 | 439,718 | 21 | 492,825 | 25–29 | 1,803,471 | 45–49 | 310,976 | **Total** | **10,289,609** |

NOTE: Based on reports furnished to the FBI by 11,249 agencies covering a 1985 estimated population of 203,035,000. *Source:* Department of Justice, Federal Bureau of Investigation, *Uniform Crime Reports for the United States, 1986.*

# Federal Prosecutions of Public Corruption: 1975 to 1984

(Prosecution of persons who have corrupted public office in violation of Federal Criminal Statutes. As of Dec. 31, 1984)

| Prosecution status | 1984 | 1983 | 1982 | 1981 | 1980 | 1979 | 1978 | 1977 | 1976 | 1975 |
|---|---|---|---|---|---|---|---|---|---|---|
| **Total:[1]** Indicted | 936 | 1,073 | 729 | 878 | 721 | 687 | 557 | 507 | 563 | 255 |
| Convicted | 934 | 972 | 671 | 730 | 552 | 555 | 409 | 440 | 380 | 179 |
| Awaiting trial | 269 | 222 | 186 | 231 | 213 | 187 | 205 | 210 | 199 | 27 |
| **Federal officials:** Indicted | 408 | 460 | 158 | 198 | 123 | 128 | 133 | 129 | 111 | 53 |
| Convicted | 429 | 424 | 147 | 159 | 131 | 115 | 91 | 94 | 101 | 43 |
| Awaiting trial | 77 | 58 | 38 | 23 | 16 | 21 | 42 | 32 | 1 | 5 |
| **State officials:** Indicted | 58 | 81 | 49 | 87 | 72 | 58 | 55 | 50 | 59 | 36 |
| Convicted | 52 | 65 | 43 | 66 | 51 | 32 | 56 | 38 | 35 | 18 |
| Awaiting trial | 21 | 26 | 18 | 36 | 28 | 30 | 20 | 33 | 30 | 5 |
| **Local officials:** Indicted | 203 | 270 | 257 | 244 | 247 | 212 | 171 | 157 | 194 | 139 |
| Convicted | 196 | 226 | 232 | 211 | 168 | 156 | 127 | 164 | 100 | 94 |
| Awaiting trial | 74 | 61 | 58 | 102 | 82 | 67 | 72 | 62 | 98 | 15 |

1. Includes individuals who are neither public officials nor employees, but who were involved with public officials or employees in violating the law, now shown separately. NOTE:—represents zero. *Source:* U.S. Department of Justice, *Federal Prosecutions of Corrupt Public Officials, 1970–1980,* and *Report to Congress on the Activities and Operations of the Public Integrity Section,* annual.

# Crime Rates for Population Groups and Selected Cities, 1984
### (offenses known to the police per 100,000 population, as of July 1)

| Group and city | Murder | Forcible rape | Robbery | Aggravated assault | Total | Burglary—breaking or entering | Larceny—theft | Motor vehicle theft | Total | Total all crimes |
|---|---|---|---|---|---|---|---|---|---|---|
| | | | **Violent crime** | | | | **Property crime** | | | |
| Cities over 250,000 | 18.6 | 74 | 670 | 526 | 1,288 | 2,114 | 4,123 | 1,070 | 7,308 | 8,596 |
| 100,000–249,999 | 10.4 | 53 | 284 | 408 | 756 | 1,893 | 4,277 | 537 | 6,707 | 7,462 |
| 50,000–99,999 | 5.9 | 38 | 185 | 320 | 549 | 1,440 | 3,415 | 494 | 5,349 | 5,898 |
| 25,000–49,999 | 4.4 | 26 | 116 | 242 | 390 | 1,205 | 3,251 | 369 | 4,826 | 5,216 |
| 10,000–24,999 | 3.4 | 19 | 68 | 196 | 287 | 956 | 2,803 | 270 | 4,028 | 4,315 |
| Under 10,000 | 2.9 | 17 | 39 | 192 | 251 | 824 | 2,677 | 194 | 3,695 | 3,946 |
| Total, 7,975 cities | 9.0 | 42 | 285 | 340 | 677 | 1,486 | 3,493 | 565 | 5,544 | 6,220 |
| Suburbs | 10.6 | 55 | 172 | 454 | 993 | 2,089 | 4,322 | 563 | 6,973 | 7,696 |
| Rural areas | 5.2 | 18 | 15 | 122 | 160 | 651 | 987 | 102 | 1,741 | 1,900 |
| Selected cities: | | | | | | | | | | |
| Baltimore | 27.3 | 72 | 1,015 | 862 | 1,976 | 1,755 | 3,871 | 687 | 6,313 | 8,288 |
| Chicago | 24.6 | 75 | 947 | 943 | 1,990 | 1,834 | 3,897 | 1,448 | 7,179 | 9,170 |
| Dallas | 29.8 | 103 | 490 | 603 | 1,226 | 3,033 | 6,388 | 839 | 10,260 | 11,486 |
| Detroit | 45.3 | 134 | 1,619 | 545 | 2,343 | 3,913 | 4,248 | 3,749 | 11,910 | 14,254 |
| Indianapolis | 10.4 | 69 | 391 | 456 | 926 | 1,731 | 2,873 | 641 | 5,245 | 6,171 |
| Los Angeles | 24.1 | 75 | 869 | 668 | 1,636 | 2,185 | 4,088 | 1,543 | 7,816 | 9,452 |
| Memphis | 17.3 | 121 | 728 | 533 | 1,399 | 2,284 | 3,170 | 1,211 | 6,665 | 8,064 |
| New York | 20.2 | 53 | 1,110 | 662 | 1,846 | 1,796 | 3,499 | 1,234 | 6,529 | 8,375 |
| Philadelphia | 15.8 | 56 | 562 | 302 | 936 | 1,099 | 2,116 | 799 | 4,014 | 4,949 |
| Phoenix | 11.6 | 60 | 242 | 418 | 732 | 2,222 | 4,726 | 510 | 7,458 | 8,190 |
| San Antonio | 18.7 | 87 | 310 | 213 | 629 | 2,759 | 4,655 | 809 | 8,223 | 8,852 |
| San Diego | 10.8 | 41 | 275 | 296 | 622 | 1,600 | 3,613 | 919 | 6,132 | 6,755 |
| San Francisco | 10.1 | 69 | 726 | 498 | 1,302 | 1,837 | 4,381 | 804 | 7,022 | 8,324 |
| Washington, D.C. | 28.1 | 59 | 977 | 658 | 1,722 | 1,758 | 4,409 | 702 | 6,870 | 8,591 |

*Source:* U.S. Federal Bureau of Investigation, *Crime in the United States*, annual.

# Percent of Firearms Usage in Selected Crimes, by Region: 1982–1984

| Region | Murder[1] 1984 | 1983 | 1982 | Aggravated assault 1984 | 1983 | 1982 | Robbery 1984 | 1983 | 1982 |
|---|---|---|---|---|---|---|---|---|---|
| Northeast | 51.1 | 50.5 | 52.2 | 13.6 | 14.1 | 14.9 | 29.7 | 30.6 | 33.2 |
| Midwest | 60.5 | 59.0 | 60.6 | 21.8 | 22.2 | 23.1 | 36.8 | 34.7 | 38.9 |
| South | 63.2 | 63.8 | 65.8 | 25.3 | 24.9 | 26.1 | 42.1 | 44.3 | 47.3 |
| West | 54.9 | 53.6 | 55.1 | 20.5 | 20.4 | 22.0 | 35.7 | 37.2 | 41.2 |
| U.S. Total | 58.8 | 58.3 | 60.2 | 21.1 | 21.2 | 22.4 | 35.8 | 36.7 | 39.9 |

1. Murder includes non-negligent manslaughter. *Source:* U.S. Federal Bureau of Investigation, *Crime in the United States*, annual.

# Reported Child Neglect and Abuse Cases: 1981 to 1983

| Division | Percent change 1982-83 | Total number of reports (1,000) 1983 | 1982 | 1981 | Reports per 1,000 population 1983 | 1982 | 1981 |
|---|---|---|---|---|---|---|---|
| New England | +17.2 | 58.5 | 49.9 | 39.0 | 4.7 | 4.0 | 3.1 |
| Middle Atlantic | −4.3 | 101.0 | 105.5 | 101.9 | 2.7 | 4.0 | 2.8 |
| North Central | +9.3 | 235.4 | 222.8 | 196.2 | 8.8 | 8.6 | 7.7 |
| South Atlantic | +25.5 | 228.5 | 182.1 | 174.8 | 5.9 | 4.8 | 4.6 |
| South Central | −9.9 | 165.3 | 171.2 | 154.5 | 8.2 | 8.9 | 8.1 |
| Mountain | +19.3 | 49.5 | 41.5 | 37.3 | 4.0 | 3.6 | 3.2 |
| Pacific | +8.2 | 163.3 | 151.0 | 142.5 | 4.9 | 4.6 | 4.4 |
| U.S. Total | +8.4 | 1,001.4 | 924.1 | 846.2 | 4.3 | 4.0 | 3.7 |

*Source:* American Humane Association, *National Analysis of Official Child Neglect and Abuse Reporting*, annual.

## Prisoners Under Sentence of Death

| Characteristic | 1984 | 1983 | 1982 | Characteristic | 1984 | 1983 | 1982 |
|---|---|---|---|---|---|---|---|
| White | 804 | 690 | 604 | Marital status: | | | |
| Black and other | 601 | 512 | 446 | Never married | 570 | 484 | 413 |
| Under 20 years | 11 | 12 | 18 | Married | 443 | 368 | 317 |
| 20–24 years | 215 | 217 | 195 | Divorced or separated[1] | 392 | 350 | 320 |
| 25–34 years | 702 | 597 | 531 | Time elapsed since sentencing: | | | |
| 35–54 years | 453 | 359 | 294 | 6 months or less | | | |
| 55 years and over | 24 | 17 | 12 | 7–12 months | 279 | 251 | 264 |
| | | | | 13–47 months | 694 | 622 | 525 |
| | | | | 48–71 months | 228 | 186 | 150 |
| Schooling completed: | | | | 72 months and over | 204 | 143 | 111 |
| 7 years or less | 121 | 99 | 81 | Legal status at arrest: | | | |
| 8 years | 137 | 123 | 105 | Not under sentence | 739 | 605 | 556 |
| 9–11 years | 401 | 358 | 318 | On parole or probation | 279 | 225 | 182 |
| 12 years | 385 | 319 | 258 | In prison or escaped | 66 | 58 | 53 |
| More than 12 years | 110 | 88 | 78 | Unknown | 321 | 314 | 259 |
| Unknown | 251 | 215 | 210 | **Total** | **1,405** | **1,202** | **1,050** |

1. Includes widows, widowers, and unknown. NOTE: As of Dec. 31. Excludes prisoners under sentence of death confined in local correctional systems pending appeal or who had not been committed to prison. *Source:* U.S. Bureau of Justice Statistics, *Capital Punishment,* annual.

## Methods of Execution[1]

| State | Method | State | Method |
|---|---|---|---|
| Alabama[2] | Electrocution | Nevada[2] | Lethal injection |
| Alaska | No death penalty | New Hampshire[2] | Hanging |
| Arizona[2] | Lethal gas | New Jersey | Lethal injection |
| Arkansas[2] | Electrocution | New Mexico | Lethal injection |
| California* | Lethal gas | New York | No death penalty |
| Colorado[2] | Lethal gas | North Carolina[2] | Lethal gas or injection |
| Connecticut[2] | Electrocution | North Dakota | No death penalty |
| Delaware | Hanging | Ohio[2] | Electrocution |
| D.C. | No death penalty | Oklahoma | Lethal injection |
| Florida | Electrocution | Oregon[5] | Lethal injection |
| Georgia[2] | Electrocution | Pennsylvania[2,*] | Electrocution |
| Hawaii | No death penalty | Rhode Island | No death penalty([3]) |
| Idaho[2] | Lethal injection or firing squad | South Carolina[2] | Electrocution |
| | | South Dakota | Lethal injection |
| Illinois | Lethal injection | Tennessee[2] | Electrocution |
| Indiana[2] | Electrocution | Texas[2] | Lethal injection |
| Iowa | No death penalty | Utah[2] | Firing squad or lethal injection |
| Kansas | No death penalty | Vermont | Electrocution[7] |
| Kentucky[2] | Electrocution | Virginia | Electrocution |
| Louisiana[2] | Electrocution | Washington[2,*] | Hanging or lethal injection |
| Maine | No death penalty | West Virginia | No death penalty |
| Maryland[2] | Lethal gas | Wisconsin | No death penalty |
| Massachusetts[5] | No death penalty | Wyoming | Lethal injection |
| Michigan | No death penalty | U.S. (Fed. Govt.)* | ([4]) |
| Minnesota | No death penalty | American Samoa | No death penalty |
| Mississippi[2] | Lethal injection | Guam | No death penalty |
| Missouri | Lethal gas | Puerto Rico | No death penalty |
| Montana[2] | Hanging, or lethal injection[6] | Virgin Islands | No death penalty |
| Nebraska[2] | Electrocution | | |

1. On July 1, 1976, by a 7-2 decision, the U.S. Supreme Court upheld the death penalty as not being "cruel or unusual." However, in another ruling the same day, the Court, by a 5-4 vote, stated that states may not impose "mandatory" capital punishment on every person convicted of murder. These decisions left uncertain the fate of condemned persons throughout the U.S. On Oct. 4, the Court refused to reconsider its July ruling, which allows some states to proceed with executions of condemned prisoners. The first execution in this country since 1967 was in Utah on Jan. 17, 1977. Gary Mark Gilmore was executed by shooting. 2. Voted to restore death penalty after June 29, 1972, Supreme Court decision ruling capital punishment unconstitutional. 3. Person shall be executed by gas if he commits murder while serving a prison term. 4. Method shall be that used by state in which sentence is imposed. If state does not have death penalty, federal judge shall prescribe method for carrying out sentence. 5. Death penalty has been passed, but not been used. 6. Defendant may choose between hanging and a lethal injection. *Source: Information Please* questionnaires to the states. 7. Last execution in 1954. NOTE: An asterisk after the name of the state indicates non-reply.

# Motor Vehicle Laws, 1986

| State | Age for license | | Age for driver's license[1] | | | Driver's license duration | Fee | Annual safety inspection required |
|-------|-----------|-------|---------|-----------|-------------|---------------------------|-----|----------------------------------|
| | Motor-cycle | Moped | Regular | Learner's | Restrictive | | | |
| Alabama | 14 | 14 | 16 | 15[5] | 14[11] | 4 yrs. | $15.00 | no[18] |
| Alaska | 14 | 14 | 16 | 14 | 14[11] | 5 | 5.00 | no[18] |
| Arizona | 16 | 16 | 18 | 15 7 mo.[6,8] | 16[6] | 3 or 4 | 5.25/7 | no[19] |
| Arkansas | 16 | | 16 | (5) | 14[6] | 2 or 4 | 6/12.00 | yes |
| California | 18 | 15 1/2 | 18 | 15[4,7] | 16[4] | 4 | 10.00 | no[18] |
| Colorado | 16 | 16 | 21 | 15 1/2[5] | 16[6] | 4 | 6.50 | no[20] |
| Connecticut | 18 | 16 | 18 | | 16[4] | 2 or 4 | 21/32.50 | yes[21,22] |
| Delaware | 18 | 16 | 18 | (5) | 16[4,6] | 4 | 10.00 | yes |
| D. C. | 16 | 16 | 18 | (5) | 16[6] | 4 | 15.00 | yes |
| Florida | 15 | 15 | 16 | (5) | 15[6] | 4 | 15.00 | no |
| Georgia | 16 | 15 | 18 | 15 | 16[6] | 4 | 4.50 | no[20] |
| Hawaii | 15 | 15 | 18 | (5) | 15[6] | 4[14] | 4-12.00 | yes[23] |
| Idaho | 16 | | 16 | (5) | 14[4] | 3 | 10.00 | no |
| Illinois | 18 | 16 | 18 | (5) | 16[4,6] | 3 or 4 | 12.00 | no[24] |
| Indiana | 16 | 15[13] | 18 | 15[8] | 16 1 mo.[4,6] | 4[15] | 6.00 | no |
| Iowa | 18 | 14 | 18 | 14 | 16[4] | 6[16] | 20.00 | (25) |
| Kansas | 14 | 14 | 16 | (5) | 14 | 4 | 7.00 | (18) |
| Kentucky | 16 | 16 | 18 | (5) | 16[6] | 4 | 8.00 | no |
| Louisiana | 15 | 16 | 17 | | 15[2,17] | 4 | 10.00 | yes |
| Maine | 17 | 16 | 17 | (5) | 15[4] | 4 | 16.00 | yes |
| Maryland | 18 | 16 | 18 | (5) | 16[4,6] | 4 | 20.00 | no[26] |
| Massachusetts | 17 | 16 | 18 | (5) | 16 1/2[4,6] | 4 | 25.00 | yes[22] |
| Michigan | 18 | 15 | 18 | (5) | 16[4,6] | 2 or 4 | 3.75/7.50 | no[18] |
| Minnesota | 18 | 15 | 19 | 15[8] | 16[4] | 4 | 10.00 | no[18] |
| Mississippi | 15[13] | | 15 | (5) | | 4 | 13.00 | yes |
| Missouri | 16 | 16 | 16 | | 15[4] | 3 | 7.50 | yes |
| Montana | 16 | 16 | 18 | (5) | 15[4,6] | 4 | 12.00 | no |
| Nebraska | 16 | 14 | 16 | 15[5] | 14 | 4 | 10.00 | no |
| Nevada | 16 | 16 | 16 | 15 1/2[5] | 14[6,10] | 4 | 10.00[17] | no |
| New Hampshire | 18 | 16 | 16[4] | | 16[4] | 4 | 20.00 | 6 mos. |
| New Jersey | 17 | 15 | 17 | | 16 | 4 | 16–17.50 | 2 yrs. |
| New Mexico | 16 | 13 | 16 | 15 | 14[12] | 4 | 10.00 | no |
| New York | 16 | 16 | 17[3] | | 16[6] | 4 | 17.50 | yes |
| North Carolina | 18 | 16 | 18 | | 15[4,6] | 4 | 10.00 | yes |
| North Dakota | 16 | 14 | 16 | (5) | 14[4,6] | 4 | 8.00 | no[18] |
| Ohio | 18 | 14 | 18 | 16[5,6] | 14[3] | 4 | 5.00 | no[18] |
| Oklahoma | 14 | | 16 | | 15 1/2[4] | 2 | 9.00 | yes |
| Oregon | 16 | 16 | 16 | 15[5] | 14 | 4 | 21.00 | no[18] |
| Pennsylvania | 16 | 16 | 18[3] | 17[8] | 16[6] | 4 | 21.50 | yes |
| Rhode Island | 18 | 16 | 18 | (5) | 16[4] | 5 | 20.00 | yes |
| South Carolina | 15 | 12[13] | 16 | 15[9] | 15 | 4 | 10.00 | yes |
| South Dakota | 14 | 14 | 16 | (5) | 14 | 4 | 6.00 | no |
| Tennessee | 16 | 14 | 16 | (5) | 15 | 4 | 13.00 | no |
| Texas | 18 | 15 | 16[4] | 15[7] | 15[3] | 4 | 16.00 | yes |
| Utah | 16 | 16 | 16[4] | (5) | | 4 | 5.00 | yes |
| Vermont | 18 | 16 | 18 | 15[9] | 16[7] | 2 or 4 | 10/16 | yes |
| Virginia | 18 | 16[13] | 18 | 15 8 mo.[5,6] | 16[4,6] | 5 | 12.00 | yes |
| Washington | 18 | 16 | 18 | 15[8] | 16[4] | 2 | 14.00 | no[18] |
| West Virginia | 16 | 16 | 18 | (5) | 16[6] | 4 | 10.00 | yes |
| Wisconsin | 18 | 16 | 18 | (5) | 16[4] | 4 | 9.00 | no |
| Wyoming | 16 | 16 | 16 | 15[6,7] | 14[6,7] | 4 | 5-10.00 | no |

1. Full driving privileges at age given in "Regular" column. A license restricted or qualified in some manner may be obtained at age given in "Restricted" column. 2. 70 or older. 3. Upon proof of hardship. 4. Must have completed approved driver education course. 5. Learner's permit required. 6. Guardian's or parental consent required. 7. Driver with learner's permit must be accompanied by locally licensed operator 18 years or older. 8. Must be enrolled in driver education course. 9. Driver with learner's permit must be accompanied by locally licensed operator 21 years or older. 10. To and from school or transporting handicapped. 11. Restricted to mopeds. 12. For use while enrolled in driver education course. Must be accompanied by instructor. 13. No license required. 14. 2 years if 15-24 or over 65. 15. 3 years if over 75. 16. 2 years if under 18 or over 65. 17. 70 and older, $5.00. 18. State troopers are authorized to inspect at their discretion. 19. Arizona emission inspection fee $5. 20. Annual emissions test in some counties. 21. Used motor vehicles being registered in Connecticut from out-of-state are required to be inspected and approved and Connecticut cars 10 years old and older must be inspected upon being sold or transferred. 22. Annual emissions test. 23. If car is 10 years or older, every 6 months. 24. Trucks and buses only. 25. Prior to first registration and transfers. 26. All used vehicles upon resale or transfer. NOTES: A driver's license is required in every state. The national speed limit is 55 miles per hour. All states have an *implied consent* Chemical Test Law for alcohol. *Source:* American Automobile Association.

## Law Enforcement Officers Killed in Line of Duty
### (beginning 1973, includes federal officers)

| Area | 1984 | 1983 | 1982 | 1981 | 1980 | 1979 | 1978 | 1975 | 1970 | 1965 | 1960 |
|---|---|---|---|---|---|---|---|---|---|---|---|
| New England | 4 | 4 | 5 | 5 | 6 | 2 | 4 | 4 | 2 | 3 | 3 |
| Middle Atlantic | 17 | 16 | 12 | 12 | 25 | 19 | 13 | 24 | 29 | 10 | 7 |
| East North Central | 18 | 20 | 32 | 16 | 14 | 23 | 13 | 32 | 38 | 10 | 9 |
| West North Central | 4 | 6 | 9 | 13 | 9 | 5 | 11 | 8 | 6 | 3 | 3 |
| South Atlantic | 28 | 27 | 29 | 35 | 32 | 36 | 23 | 31 | 23 | 15 | 13 |
| East South Central | 14 | 13 | 13 | 21 | 15 | 22 | 16 | 18 | 5 | 9 | 2 |
| West South Central | 27 | 24 | 33 | 24 | 25 | 19 | 30 | 22 | 15 | 14 | 6 |
| Mountain | 13 | 10 | 11 | 8 | 11 | 14 | 7 | 14 | 4 | 7 | 0 |
| Pacific | 19 | 24 | 16 | 19 | 21 | 18 | 24 | 22 | 24 | 12 | 5 |
| Puerto Rico and Virgin Islands | 3 | 6 | 3 | 3 | 6 | 4 | 4 | 8 | n.a. | n.a. | n.a. |
| **CAUSE** | | | | | | | | | | | |
| By felons | — | 80[2] | 92 | 91 | 104[3] | 106[4] | 93 | 129[1] | 100 | 53 | n.a. |
| In accidents | — | 72 | 72 | 66 | 61 | 58 | 52 | 56 | 46 | 30 | n.a. |
| **Total** | 147 | 152[2] | 164 | 157 | 165[3] | 165[4] | 145 | 185[1] | 146 | 83 | 48 |

1. Includes one officer in Guam. 2. Includes one officer each in Guam and Mariana Islands. 3. Includes one officer killed in Virgin Islands. 4. Includes two officers killed on Guam. NOTE: n.a. = not available. *Source: Statistical Abstract of the United States, 1986.*

## Minimum Legal Age for Purchase of Liquor, Wine, and Beer

| State | Liquor | Wine | Beer | State | Liquor | Wine | Beer |
|---|---|---|---|---|---|---|---|
| Alabama | 21 | 21 | 21 | Montana | 19 | 19 | 19 |
| Alaska | 21 | 21 | 21 | Nebraska | 21 | 21 | 21 |
| Arizona | 21 | 21 | 21 | Nevada | 21 | 21 | 21 |
| Arkansas | 21 | 21 | 21 | New Hampshire | 21 | 21 | 21 |
| California | 21 | 21 | 21 | New Jersey | 21 | 21 | 21 |
| Colorado | 21 | 21 | 21[1] | New Mexico | 21 | 21 | 21 |
| Connecticut | 21 | 21 | 21 | New York | 21 | 21 | 21 |
| Delaware | 21 | 21 | 21 | North Carolina | 21 | 21 | 21 |
| D.C. | 21 | 21[2] | 18 | North Dakota | 21 | 21 | 21 |
| Florida[4] | 21 | 21 | 21 | Ohio | 21 | 21 | 19 |
| Georgia | 21 | 21 | 21 | Oklahoma | 21 | 21 | 21 |
| Hawaii | 18 | 18 | 18 | Oregon | 21 | 21 | 21 |
| Idaho | 19 | 19 | 19 | Pennsylvania | 21 | 21 | 21 |
| Illinois | 21 | 21 | 21 | Rhode Island | 21 | 21 | 21 |
| Indiana | 21 | 21 | 21 | South Carolina | 21 | 21 | 21 |
| Iowa[5] | 21 | 21 | 21 | South Dakota | 21 | 21 | 21[3] |
| Kansas | 21 | 21 | 20[7] | Tennessee[6] | 21 | 21 | 21 |
| Kentucky | 21 | 21 | 21 | Texas | 21 | 21 | 21 |
| Louisiana | 18 | 18 | 18 | Utah | 21 | 21 | 21 |
| Maine | 21 | 21 | 21 | Vermont | 21 | 21 | 21 |
| Maryland | 21 | 21 | 21 | Virginia | 21 | 21 | 21 |
| Massachusetts | 21 | 21 | 21 | Washington | 21 | 21 | 21 |
| Michigan | 21 | 21 | 21 | West Virginia | 21 | 21 | 21 |
| Minnesota | 21 | 21 | 21 | Wisconsin[5] | 21 | 21 | 21 |
| Mississippi | 21 | 21 | 21 | Wyoming | 19 | 19 | 19 |
| Missouri | 21 | 21 | 21 | | | | |

1. 3.2 beer: 18. 2. Table wine: 18. 3. 3.2 beer: 19. 4. Exempts military personnel: 18. 5. Exempts those 19 or older on effective date. 6. Except off-base military personnel, persons consuming alcohol in a religious service, or accompanied by parent or guardian. 7. 21, 7/87. *Source:* Distilled Spirits Council of the United States.

## The Fear of Crime

The fear of crime, in general, is the fear of a random unprovoked attack by a stranger. More than half of all homicides are committed by someone known to the victim. Three of every five other violent crimes are committed by strangers. Almost half of all assaults are by friends or relatives. Robbery is the violent crime most often committed by strangers, and homicide is the least often committed by strangers. It is widely believed that a very large proportion of crimes committed by relatives are not reported to the police and are not revealed to crime survey interviewers.

# U.S. District Courts—Criminal Cases Commenced and Defendants Disposed of, by Nature of Offense: 1983 and 1984

## [For years ending June 30]

| | | DISPOSITION OF DEFENDANTS, 1983 | | | | | | | | 1983 | |
| | 1984 cases com-menced[1] | Not convicted | | Convicted | | | Sentenced | | | | De-fend-ants dis-posed of |
| Nature of offense | | Total | Ac-quitted | Total | Guilty plea | Court or jury | Im-prison-ment | Proba-tion | Fine and other | Cases com-menced[1] | |
|---|---|---|---|---|---|---|---|---|---|---|---|
| General offenses: | | | | | | | | | | | |
| Homicide | 156 | 48 | 15 | 118 | 79 | 39 | 79 | 16 | 23 | 156 | 153 |
| Robbery | 1,329 | 138 | 25 | 1,245 | 1,023 | 223 | 1,146 | 94 | 5 | 1,357 | 1,529 |
| Assault | 525 | 162 | 50 | 410 | 321 | 89 | 262 | 119 | 29 | 552 | 601 |
| Burglary | 155 | 40 | 5 | 159 | 142 | 17 | 127 | 29 | 3 | 184 | 203 |
| Larceny-theft | 3,400 | 712 | 118 | 3,426 | 3,139 | 287 | 1,480 | 1,781 | 165 | 3,409 | 4,199 |
| Embezzlement and fraud | 7,646 | 1,403 | 269 | 7,705 | 6,946 | 759 | 2,864 | 4,591 | 250 | 7,705 | 9,166 |
| Auto theft | 286 | 79 | 9 | 340 | 302 | 38 | 231 | 106 | 3 | 354 | 551 |
| Forgery, counterfeiting | 1,966 | 399 | 53 | 2,027 | 1,853 | 174 | 1,125 | 882 | 20 | 2,324 | 2,752 |
| Sex offenses | 163 | 39 | 13 | 85 | 64 | 21 | 68 | 14 | 3 | 141 | 130 |
| DAPCA[3] | 5,611 | 1,732 | 311 | 7,459 | 5,793 | 1,666 | 5,756 | 1,584 | 119 | 5,088 | 9,164 |
| Misc. general offenses | 14,674 | 3,647 | 507 | 13,130 | 11,800 | 1,330 | 4,572 | 4,664 | 3,894 | 13,658 | 14,881 |
| Total[2] | 35,911 | 8,397 | 1,375 | 36,104 | 31,461 | 4,643 | 17,710 | 13,880 | 4,514 | 34,028 | 43,320 |

1. Excludes transfers. 2. Includes items not shown separately. 3. All marijuana, narcotics, and controlled substances under the Drug, Abuse, Prevention and Control Act. *Source: Statistical Abstract of the United States,* 1986.

# Murder Victims by Weapons Used

| | | Weapons used or cause of death | | | | | | |
| | Murder victims, total | Guns | | Cutting or stabbing | Blunt object[1] | Strangu-lation and hands, fists, feet | Arson[3] | All other[2] |
| Year | | Total | Percent | | | | | |
|---|---|---|---|---|---|---|---|---|
| 1965 | 8,773 | 5,015 | 57.2 | 2,021 | 505 | 894 | 226 | 112 |
| 1968 | 12,503 | 8,105 | 64.8 | 2,317 | 713 | 936 | 294 | 138 |
| 1969 | 13,575 | 8,876 | 65.4 | 2,534 | 613 | 1,039 | 322 | 191 |
| 1970 | 13,649 | 9,039 | 66.2 | 2,424 | 604 | 1,031 | 353 | 198 |
| 1971 | 16,183 | 10,712 | 66.2 | 3,017 | 645 | 1,295 | 314 | 200 |
| 1972 | 15,832 | 10,379 | 65.6 | 2,974 | 672 | 1,291 | 331 | 185 |
| 1973 | 17,123 | 11,249 | 65.7 | 2,985 | 848 | 1,445 | 173 | 423 |
| 1974 | 18,632 | 12,474 | 66.9 | 3,228 | 976 | 1,417 | 153 | 384 |
| 1975 | 18,642 | 12,061 | 64.7 | 3,245 | 1,001 | 1,646 | 193 | 496 |
| 1977 | 18,033 | 11,274 | 62.5 | 3,440 | 849 | 1,431 | 252 | 787 |
| 1978 | 18,714 | 11,910 | 63.6 | 3,526 | 896 | 1,422 | 255 | 705 |
| 1979 | 20,591 | 13,040 | 63.3 | 3,954 | 997 | 1,557 | 276 | 767 |
| 1980 | 21,860 | 13,650 | 62.0 | 4,212 | 1,094 | 1,666 | 291 | 947 |
| 1981 | 20,053 | 12,523 | 62.4 | 3,886 | 1,038 | 1,469 | 258 | 658 |
| 1982 | 19,485 | 11,721 | 60.2 | 4,065 | 957 | 1,657 | 279 | 630 |
| 1983 | 18,673 | 10,895 | 58.0 | 4,075 | 1,062 | 1,656 | 216 | 769 |
| 1984 | 16,689 | 9,819 | 58.8 | 3,540 | 973 | 1,407 | 192 | 758 |
| 1985 | 17,545 | 10,296 | 58.7 | 3,694 | 972 | 1,491 | 243 | 849 |

1. Refers to club, hammer, etc. 2. Includes poison, explosives, unknown, drowning, and not stated. 3. Before 1973, includes drowning. *Source:* Department of Justice, Federal Bureau of Investigation, *Uniform Crime Reports for the United States, 1986.*

# Prisoners on Parole

Within one year after release on parole, about 12% of those released are likely to be back in prison. About half of these are returned for minor violations, but the other half are for new, major convictions. Within three years of release, 72% of parolees are considered to be successful, either being discharged (56%) or continued on parole (16%). The proportion returned to prison (24%) is double the one-year performance; this indicates that half of all parolees who return to prison do so in the first year. Forty-five percent of the returns within three years are for major convictions.

## Firsts in America

This selection is based on our editorial judgment. Other sources may list different firsts.

**Admiral in U.S. Navy:** David Glasgow Farragut, 1866.

**Air-mail route, first transcontinental:** Between New York City and San Francisco, 1920.

**Assembly, representative:** House of Burgesses, founded in Virginia, 1619.

**Bank established:** Bank of North America, Philadelphia, 1781.

**Birth in America to English parents:** Virginia Dare, born Roanoke Island, N.C., 1587.

**Botanic garden:** Established by John Bartram in Philadelphia, 1728. (Oldest still existing was established in Cambridge, Mass., in 1807.)

**Cartoon, colored:** "The Yellow Kid," by Richard Outcault, in *New York World*, 1895.

**College:** Harvard, founded 1636.

**College to confer degrees on women:** Oberlin (Ohio) College, 1841.

**College to establish coeducation:** Oberlin (Ohio) College, 1833.

**Electrocution of a criminal:** William Kemmler in Auburn Prison, Auburn, N.Y., Aug. 6, 1890.

**Five and Ten Cents Store:** Founded by Frank Woolworth, Utica, N.Y., 1879 (moved to Lancaster, Pa., same year).

**Fraternity:** Phi Beta Kappa; founded Dec. 5, 1776, at College of William and Mary.

**Law to be declared unconstitutional by U.S. Supreme Court:** Judiciary Act of 1789. Case: *Marbury v. Madison*, 1803.

**Library, circulating:** Philadelphia, 1731.

**Newspaper, illustrated daily:** *New York Daily Graphic*, 1873.

**Newspaper published daily:** *Pennsylvania Packet and General Advertiser*, Philadelphia, Sept., 1784.

**Newspaper published over a continuous period:** *The Boston News-Letter*, April, 1704.

**Newsreel:** Pathé Frères of Paris, in 1910, circulated a weekly issue of their *Pathé Journal*.

**Oil well, commercial:** Titusville, Pa., 1859.

**Panel quiz show on radio:** *Information Please*, May 17, 1938.

**Postage stamps issued:** 1847.

**Public School:** Boston Latin School, Boston, 1635.

**Railroad, transcontinental:** Central Pacific and Union Pacific railroads, joined at Promontory, Utah, May 10, 1869.

**Savings bank:** The Provident Institute for Savings, Boston, 1816.

**Science museum:** Founded by Charleston (S.C.) Library Society, 1773.

**Skyscraper:** Home Insurance Co., Chicago, 1885 (10 floors, 2 added later).

**Slaves brought into America:** At Jamestown, Va., 1619, from a Dutch ship.

**Sorority:** Kappa Alpha Theta, at De Pauw University, 1870.

**State to abolish capital punishment:** Michigan, 1847.

**State to enter Union after original 13:** Vermont, 1791.

**Steam-heated building:** Eastern Hotel, Boston, 1845.

**Steam railroad (carried passengers and freight):** Baltimore & Ohio, 1830.

**Strike on record by union:** Journeymen Printers, New York City, 1776.

**Subway:** Opened in Boston, 1897.

**"Tabloid" picture newspaper:** *The Illustrated Daily News* (now *The Daily News*), New York City, 1919.

**Vaudeville theater:** Gaiety Museum, Boston, 1883.

**Woman astronaut to ride in space:** Dr. Sally K. Ride, 1983.

**Woman astronaut to walk in space:** Dr. Kathryn D. Sullivan, 1984.

**Woman cabinet member:** Frances Perkins, Secretary of Labor, 1933.

**Woman candidate for President:** Victoria Claflin Woodhull, nominated by National Woman's Suffrage Assn. on ticket of Nation Radical Reformers, 1872.

**Woman candidate for Vice-President:** Geraldine A. Ferraro, nominated by a major party on ticket of the Democratic Party, 1984.

**Woman doctor of medicine:** Elizabeth Blackwell; M.D. from Geneva Medical College of Western New York, 1849.

**Woman elected governor of a state:** Mrs. Nellie Tayloe Ross, Wyoming, 1925.

**Woman elected to U.S. Senate:** Mrs. Hattie Caraway, Arkansas; elected Nov., 1932.

**Woman graduate of law school:** Mrs. Ada H. Kepley, Union College of Law, Chicago, 1870.

**Woman member of U.S. House of Representatives:** Jeannette Rankin; elected Nov., 1916.

**Woman member of U.S. Senate:** Mrs. Rebecca Latimer Felton of Georgia; appointed Oct. 3, 1922.

**Woman member of U.S. Supreme Court:** Mrs. Sandra Day O'Connor; appointed July 1981.

**Woman suffrage granted:** Wyoming Territory, 1869.

**Written constitution:** *Fundamental Orders of Connecticut*, 1639.

*Source: Information Please* questionnaires to organizations. Names are listed alphabetically according to key word in title; figure in parentheses is year of founding; other figure is membership. An asterisk (*) before a name indicates that up-to-date information has not been provided.

**Abortion Federation, National** (1976): 900 Pennsylvania Ave. S.E., Washington, D.C., 20003. 285; Barbara Radford, Executive Director.

**Abortion Rights Action League, National** (1969): 1424 K St. N.W., Washington, D.C. 20005. 145, 000; Kate Michelman, Executive Director.

**Accountants, American Institute of Certified Public** (1887): 1211 Avenue of the Americas, New York, N.Y. 10036. 240,000; Philip B. Chenok, President.

**Accountants, National Association of** (1919): 10 Paragon Dr., P.O. Box 433, Montvale, N.J., 07645. 96,000; Robert L. Shultis, Executive Director.

**ACME, Inc.—The association of management consulting firms** (1929): 230 Park Ave., New York, N.Y. 10169. 60 firms; Joseph J. Brady, President.

**Acoustical Society of America** (1929): 335 E. 45th St., New York, N.Y. 10017. 5,700; Betty H. Goodfriend, Secretary.

**Actors' Equity Association** (1913): 165 W. 46th St., New York, N.Y. 10036. Alan Eisenberg, Executive Secretary.

**Actuaries, Society of** (1949): 500 Park Blvd., Itasca, Ill. 60143. 10,000; John E. O'Connor, Jr., Executive Director.

**Aeronautic Association, National** (1905): 1400 Eye St. N.W., Washington, D.C. 20005. 200,000; Clifton F. von Kann, President.

**Aeronautics and Astronautics, American Institute of** (1932): 1633 Broadway, New York, N.Y. 10019. 38,000; James J. Harford, Executive Director.

**Aerospace Industries Association of America** (1919): 1725 De Sales St. N.W., Washington, D.C. 20036. 50 companies; S. L. Wright, Vice President.

**Aerospace Medical Association** (1929): Washington National Airport, Washington, D.C. 20001-4977. 4,000; Dr. Rufus R. Hessberg, Executive Vice President.

**African-American Institute, The** (1953): 833 United Nations Plaza, New York, N.Y. 10017. Donald B. Easum, President.

**Afro-American Life and History, Association for the Study of** (1915): 1401 14th St. N.W., Washington, D.C. 20005. 2,000; B. J. Gillespie, Executive Director.

**AFS International/Intercultural Programs** (1947): 313 E. 43rd St., New York, N.Y. 10017. 100, 000; William M. Dyal, Jr., President.

**Aging Association, American** (1970): Univ. of Nebraska Medical Center, 42nd and Dewey Ave., Omaha, Neb. 68105. 500; Denham Harman, M.D., Executive Director.

**Agnostics, Society of Evangelical** (1975): Box 515, Auberry, Calif. 93602. 1,075; William Henry Young, Administrator.

**Agricultural Engineers, American Society of** (1907): 2950 Niles Rd., St. Joseph, Mich. 49085. 12,000; J. L. Butt, Executive Vice President.

**Agricultural History Society** (1919): 1301 New York Ave. N.W., Washington, D.C. 20005. 1,400; Wayne D. Rasmussen, Secretary-Treasurer.

**Agronomy, American Society of** (1907): 677 S. Segoe Rd., Madison, Wis. 53711-1086. 13,000; Dale Moss, President.

**Aircraft Association, Experimental** (1953): Wittman Airfield, Oshkosh, Wis. 54903-3086. 105, 000; Paul H. Poberezny, founder and President.

**Aircraft Owners and Pilots Association** (1939): 421 Aviation Way, Frederick, Md. 21701. 265, 000; John L. Baker, President.

**Air Force Association** (1946): 1501 Lee Highway, Arlington, Va., 22209. 228,000; David L. Gray, Executive Director.

**Air Line Pilots Association** (1931): 1625 Massachusetts Ave. N.W., Washington, D.C. 20036 and 535 Herndon Pkwy., Herndon, Va. 22070. 33, 000; Henry A. Duffy, President.

**Air Pollution Control Association** (1907): P.O. Box 2861, Pittsburgh, Pa. 15230. 8,000; G. Steve Hart, Executive Vice President.

**Air Transport Association of America** (1936): 1709 New York Ave. N.W., Washington, D.C. 20006. 31 airlines; William F. Bolger, President.

**Al-Anon Family Group Headquarters, Inc.** (1951): P.O. Box 862, Midtown Station, New York, N.Y. 10018-0862. Susan Handley Brew, Public Information Coordinator.

**Alcoholism, National Council on** (1944): 12 W. 21st St., New York, N.Y. 10010. 200 affiliates; Thomas Seessel, Executive Director.

**Alcohol Problems, American Council on** (1900): 2908 Patricia Dr., Des Moines, Iowa 50322. 3,500; William N. Plymat, Executive Director.

**Alcoholics Anonymous** (1935): P.O. Box 459, Grand Central Station, New York, N.Y. 10163. 1,000,000. Address communications to General Service Office.

**Alexander Graham Bell Association for the Deaf** (1890): 3417 Volta Place N.W., Washington, D.C. 20007. 6,000; Donna Dickman, Ph.D., Executive Director.

**Allergy and Immunology, American Academy of** (1943): 611 E. Wells St., Milwaukee, Wis. 53202. 3,600; Donald L. McNeil, Executive Director.

**Alzheimer's Disease and Related Disorders Association, Inc., The (ADRDA)** (1980): 70 E. Lake St., Chicago, Ill. 60601-5997. 140 Chapters and Affiliates; Jerome H. Stone, President. Toll-free information: 1-800-621-0379.

**America-Mideast Educational and Training Services (AMIDEAST)** (1951): 1100 17th St. N.W., Washington, D.C. 20036. 200; Orin D. Parker, President.

**American Federation of Labor and Congress of Industrial Organizations (AFL-CIO)** (1955): 815 16th St. N.W., Washington, D.C. 20006. 13,100, 000; Murray Seeger, Director of Information.

**American Friends Service Committee** (1917): 1501 Cherry St., Philadelphia, Pa. 19102. Paul E. Brink, Director of Information.

**American Indian Affairs, Association on** (1923): 95 Madison Ave., New York, N.Y. 10016. 50,000.

**American Legion, The** (1919): P.O. Box 1055, Indianapolis, Ind. 46206. 2,730,000; Robert W. Spanogle, National Adjutant.

**American Legion Auxiliary** (1919): 777 N. Meridian St., Indianapolis, Ind. 46204. 950,000; Miriam Junge, National Secretary.

**American Mensa, Ltd.** (1945): 2626 E. 14th St., Brooklyn, N.Y. 11235. 53,000; Amy E. Shaughnessy, Chairman.

**American Montessori Society** (1960): 150 Fifth Ave., New York, N.Y. 10011. 10,000; Bretta Weiss, National Director.

**American Planning Association** (1978): 1313 E. 60th St., Chicago, Ill. 60637. 21,000; Israel Stollman, Executive Director.

**Americans for Democratic Action** (1947): 1411 K St. N.W., Washington, D.C. 20005. 75,000; Ann F. Lewis, National Director.

**American States, Organization of** (1948): General Secretariat, Washington, D.C. 20006. 32 countries; Joyo Clemente Baena Soares, Secretary General.

**American Universities, Association of** (1900): One Dupont Circle N.W., Suite 730, Washington, D.C. 20036. Robert M. Rosenzweig, President.

**Amnesty International/USA** (1961): 322 Eighth Ave., New York, N.Y. 10001. 150,000; John G. Healey, Executive Director.

**AMVETS (American Veterans of World War II, Korea, and Vietnam)** (1944): 4647 Forbes Blvd., Lanham, Md. 20706. 200,000; Morgan S. Ruph, National Executive Director.

**AMVETS Auxiliary National Department** (1946): 4647 Forbes Blvd., Lanham, Md. 20706. 75,000. Dorothy Ruph, Executive Secretary.

**Animal Protection Institute of America** (1968): 6130 Freeport Blvd., Suite 100, Sacramento, Calif. 95822. Belton P. Mouras, President.

**Animals, Fund For** (1967): 200 W. 57th St., New York, N.Y. 10019. 175,000; Cleveland Amory, President.

**Animals, The American Society for the Prevention of Cruelty to (ASPCA)** (1866): 441 E. 92nd St., New York, N.Y. 10128. 210,000; John F. Kullberg, President.

**Animal Welfare Institute** (1951): P.O. Box 3650, Washington, D.C. 20007. 8,600; Christine Stevens, President.

**Anthropological Association, American** (1902): 1703 New Hampshire Ave. N.W., Washington, D.C. 20009. 10,100; Edward J. Lehman, Executive Director.

**Anti-Defamation League of B'nai B'rith** (1913): 823 United Nations Plaza, New York, N.Y. 10017. Nathan Perlmutter, National Director; Kenneth J. Bialkin, National Chairman.

**Antiquarian Society, American** (1812): 185 Salisbury St., Worcester, Mass. 01609. 468; Marcus A. McCorison, Director and Librarian.

**Anti-Vivisection Society, The American** (1883): Suite 204, Noble Plaza, 801 Old York Rd., Jenkintown, Pa. 19046. 15,000; William A. Cave, President.

**Appraisers, American Society of** (1936): P.O. Box 17265, Washington, D.C. 20041. 6,000; Paul L. O'Brien, Executive Director.

**Arbitration Association, American** (1926): 140 W. 51st St., New York, N.Y. 10020. 4,825; E. W. Dippold, Corporate Secretary.

**Arboriculture, International Society of** (1924): 5 Lincoln Square, Urbana, Ill. 61801. 4,500; Erwin C. Bundy, Executive Director.

**Archaeological Institute of America** (1879): P.O. Box 1901, Kenmore Station, Boston, Mass.

02215. 9,000; James. R. Wiseman, President.

**Archaeology, Institute of Nautical** (1973): Texas A&M University, Drawer AU, College Station, Tex. 77840. 750; George F. Bass, President.

**Architects, American Institute of** (1857): 1735 New York Ave. N.W., Washington, D.C. 20006. 50,000; Louis L. Marines, Chief Executive Officer.

**Architectural Historians, Society of** (1940): 1700 Walnut St., Philadelphia, Pa. 19103. 4,200; David Bahlman, Executive Secretary.

**Army, Association of the United States** (1950): 2425 Wilson Blvd., Arlington, Va. 22201. 160,000; Robert F. Cocklin, Executive Vice President.

**Arthritis Foundation** (1948): 1314 Spring St., N.W., Atlanta, Ga. 30309. 72 local chapters/divisions; Clifford M. Clarke, CAE, President.

**Arts, National Endowment for the** (1965): 1100 Pennsylvania Ave. N.W., Washington, D.C. 20506. Francis S. M. Hodssoll, Chairman.

**Arts, The American Federation of** (1909): 41 E. 65th St., New York, N.Y. 10021. 1,400; Wilder Green, Director.

**Arts and Letters, American Academy and Institute of** (1898): 633 W. 155th St., New York, N.Y. 10032. 250; Margaret M. Mills, Executive Director.

**Astronomical Society, American** (1899): Louisiana State University, Box BK, LSU Observatory, Baton Rouge, La. 70803. 4,000; Arlo U. Landolt, Secretary.

**Atheists, American** (1963): P.O. Box 2117, Austin, Tex. 78768. 40,000; Dr. Madalyn O'Hair, President.

**Auctioneers Association, National** (1949): 8880 Ballentine, Overland Park, Kan. 66214. 6,100; Harvey L. McCray, Executive Vice President.

**Audubon Society, National** (1905): 950 Third Ave., New York, N.Y. 10022. 510,000; Barbara Linton, Information Services.

**Authors League of America** (1912): 234 W. 44th St., New York, N.Y. 10036. 14,000; Nancy Weidner, Administrator.

**Autism, National Society for Children and Adults With** (1965): 1234 Massachusetts Ave. N.W., Washington, D.C. 20005. 7,000; Roy Morgan, Executive Director.

**Automobile Association, American** (1902): 8111 Gatehouse Rd., Falls Church, Va. 22047. 26,500,000; J. B. Creal, President.

**Automobile Club, National** (1924): One Market Plaza, San Francisco, Calif. 94105. 427,780; Arthur Hedges, President and CEO.

**Automobile Dealers Association, National** (1917): 8400 Westpark Dr., McLean, Va. 22102. 20,000; Frank E. McCarthy, Executive Vice President.

**Automotive Engineers, Inc., Society of** (1905): 400 Commonwealth Dr., Warrendale, Pa. 15096. 48,000; Max E. Rumbaugh, Jr., Executive Vice President.

**Automotive Hall of Fame** (1939): P.O. Box 1727, Midland, Mich. 48641-1727. Donald N. Richetti, President.

**Bar Association, American** (1898): 750 N. Lake Shore Dr., Chicago, Ill. 60611. 312,333; Thomas H. Gonser, Executive Director and Chief Operating Officer.

**Bar Association, Federal** (1920): 1815 H St. N.W., Washington, D.C. 20006. 14,000; John G. Blanche, Executive Staff Director.

**Barber Shop Quartet Singing in America, Society for the Preservation and Encouragement of** (1938): 6315 Third Ave., Kenosha, Wis., 53140-5199. 38,000; Hugh Ingraham CAE, Executive

Director.

**Bible Society, American** (1816): 1865 Broadway, New York, N.Y. 10023. 600,000; Charles W. Baas, Alice E. Ball, John D. Erickson, General Officers.

**Biblical Literature, Society of** (1880): 2201 S. University Blvd., Denver, Colo. 80210. 5,000; Kent Harold Richards, Executive Secretary-Treasurer.

**Bibliographical Society of America** (1904): P.O. Box 397, Grand Central Station, New York, N.Y. 10163. 1,400; G. Thomas Tanselle, President.

**Bide-A-Wee Home Association** (1903): 410 E. 38th St., New York, N.Y. 10016. 8,600; Ursula Goetz, Executive Director.

**Big Brothers/Big Sisters of America** (1977): 230 N. 13th St., Philadelphia, Pa. 19107. Betty Larkin, Director of Communications.

**Biological Chemists, American Society of** (1906): 9650 Rockville Pike, Bethesda, Md. 20814. 6,600; Charles C. Hancock, Executive Officer.

**Biological Sciences, American Institute of** (1947): 730 11th St. N.W., Washington, D.C. 20001-4584. 12,500; Dr. Charles M. Chambers, Executive Director.

**Blind, American Council of the** (1961): 1010 Vermont Ave. N.W., Suite 1100, Washington, D.C. 20085. 20,000; Oral O. Miller, J.D., National Representative.

**Blind, National Federation of the** (1940): 1800 Johnson St., Baltimore, Md. 21230. 50,000; Kenneth Jernigan, President.

**Blindness, National Society to Prevent** (1908): 79 Madison Ave., New York, N.Y. 10016. 26 affiliates; Michael L. Weamer, Executive Director.

**Blindness, Research to Prevent** (1960): 598 Madison Ave., New York, N.Y. 10022. 3,300; David F. Weeks, President.

**Blue Cross and Blue Shield Association** (1946 and 1948): 676 St. Clair, Chicago, Ill. 60611. 81 Plans; JoAnn B. Malkin, Director, Public Relations.

**B'nai B'rith International** (1843): 1640 Rhode Island Ave. N.W., Washington, D.C. 20036. 500,000; Hank Siegel, Press Officer.

**Booksellers Association, American** (1900): 122 E. 42nd St., New York, N.Y. 10168. 5,557; Bernard E. Rath, Executive Director.

**Botanical Gardens & Arboreta, American Association of** (1971): P.O. Box 206, Swarthmore, Pa. 19081. 1,000; Susan H. Lathrop, Executive Director.

**Boy Scouts of America** (1910): 1325 Walnut Hill Lane, Irving, Tex. 75038-3096. 4,754,479.

**Boys Clubs of America** (1906): 771 First Ave., New York, N.Y. 10017. 1,285,000.

**Bridge, Tunnel, and Turnpike Association, International** (1932): 2120 L St. N.W., Suite 305, Washington, D.C. 20037. 215 agencies; John J. Hassett, Executive Director.

**Broadcasters, National Association of** (1922): 1771 N St. N.W., Washington, D.C. 20036. 5,000; Edward Fritts, President.

**Brookings Institution, The** (1927): 1775 Massachusetts Ave. N.W., Washington, D.C. 20036. Margaret M. Rhoades, Public Affairs Director.

**Brooks Bird Club, Inc., The** (1932): 707 Warwood Ave., Wheeling, W. Va. 26003. 1,000; Helen B. Conrad, Administrator.

**Business Bureaus, Council of Better** (1970): 1515 Wilson Blvd., Arlington, Va. 22209. William H. Pankersley, President.

**Business Clubs, National Association of American** (1922): 3315 No. Main St., High Point, N.C. 27260, 6,800; Paul Skoglund, Executive Secretary.

**Business Education Association, National** (1946): 1914 Association Dr., Reston, Va. 22091. 18,000; O. J. Byrnside, Jr., Executive Director.

**Business Law Association, American** (1923): Dept. of Insurance, Legal Studies, and Real Estate, Univ. of Georgia, Athens, Ga. 30602. 1,100; Jan W. Henkel, Executive Secretary.

**Business Women's Association, American** (1949): 9100 Ward Parkway, P.O. Box 8728, Kansas City, Mo. 64114. 112,000; Carolyn B. Elman, Executive Director.

**Campers & Hikers Association, National** (1949): 7172 Transit Rd., Buffalo, N.Y. 14221. 28,000 families; Fran Opela, National Office Manager.

**Camp Fire, Inc.** (1910): 4601 Madison Ave., Kansas City, Mo. 64112. 400,000; David Bahlmann, National Executive Director.

**Camping Association, The American** (1910): Bradford Woods, Martinsville, Ind. 46151. 6,000; Armand Ball, Executive Vice President.

**Cancer Council, United** (1959): 650 E. Carmel Dr., Suite 340, Carmel, Ind. 46032. 50 agencies; Mary L. Turcotte, Acting Executive Director.

**Cancer Society, American** (1913): 90 Park Ave., New York, N.Y. 10016. 2,443,842 volunteers; G. Robert Gadberry, Executive Vice President.

**CARE, Inc.** (1945): 660 First Ave., New York, N.Y. 10016. 23 agencies plus 19 public members; Philip Johnston, Executive Director.

**Cartoonists Society, National** (1946): 9 Ebony Court, Brooklyn, N.Y. 11229. 450; Marge Devine, Scribe.

**Catholic Bishops, National Conference of** (1966): 1312 Massachusetts Ave. N.W., Washington, D.C. 20005. The Most Rev. James Malone, President.

**Catholic Charities USA** (1910): 1319 F St. N.W., Washington, D.C. 20004. 3,300 individuals, 850 agencies and institutions; Fr. Thomas J. Harvey, Executive Director.

**Catholic Conference, United States** (1966): 1312 Massachusetts Ave. N.W., Washington, D.C. 20005. Rev. Daniel F. Hoye, General Secretary.

**Catholic Daughters of the Americas** (1903): 10 W. 71st St., New York, N.Y. 10023. 165,000; Lorraine McMahon, Executive Secretary.

**Catholic Historical Society, American** (1884): 263 S. Fourth St., Philadelphia, Pa. 19106. 950; The Rev. Msgr. James P. McCoy, President.

**Catholic War Veterans of the U.S.A.** (1935): 2 Massachusetts Ave. N.W., Washington, D.C. 20001. 50,000; Walter Drahan, National Commander.

**Ceramic Society, American** (1899): 65 Ceramic Dr., Columbus, Ohio 43214. 12,926; Paul Holbrook, Executive Director.

**Cerebral Palsy Associations, United** (1949): 66 E. 34th St., New York, N.Y. 10016. 250 affiliates; James E. Introne, Executive Director.

**Chamber of Commerce of the U.S.** (1912): 1615 H St. N.W., Washington, D.C. 20062. 220,486; Richard L. Lesher, President.

**Chaplain's Association, National** (1900): 352 W. Broad St., Groveland, Fla. 32736-2506. 5,452; Gen. Doyle E. Varvel, Commander.

**Chaplains Association of the U.S.A., Military** (1925): P.O. Box 645, Riverdale, Md. 20737. 1,575; William F. Emery, Executive Director.

**Chartered Life Underwriters, American Society of** (1929): 270 Bryn Mawr Ave., Bryn Mawr, Pa. 19010. 32,000; John R. Driskill, CLU, ChFC, Executive Vice President.

**Chemical Engineers, American Institute of** (1908): 345 E. 47th St., New York, N.Y. 10017. 60,000; J. Charles Forman, Executive Director and Secretary.

**Chemical Manufacturers Association, Inc.** (1872): 2501 M St. N.W., Washington, D.C. 20037. 200 companies; Charles W. Van Vlack, Corporate Secretary.

**Chemical Society, American** (1876): 1155 16th St. N.W., Washington, D.C. 20036. 135,000; John K. Crum, Executive Director.

**Chemists, American Institute of** (1923): 7315 Wisconsin Ave., Bethesda, Md. 20814. 5,000; David A. H. Roethel, Executive Director.

**Chemists, American Society of Biological** (1906): 9650 Rockville Pike, Bethesda, Md. 20814. 6,600; Charles C. Hancock, Executive Officer.

**Chemistry, American Association for Clinical** (1948): 1725 K St. N.W., Washington, D.C. 20006. 6,247; Ronald Whorton, Executive Director.

**Chemists and Chemical Engineers, Association of Consulting** (1928): 50 E. 41st St., New York, N.Y. 10017. 125; Roland D. Glenn, Executive Director.

**Chess Federation, United States** (1939): 186 Rt. 9W, New Windsor, N.Y. 12550. 54,000; Gerard J. Dullea, Executive Director.

**Child Labor Committee, National** (1904): 1501 Broadway, Rm. 1111, New York, N.Y. 10036. Jeffrey Newman, Executive Director.

**Children's Aid Society, The** (1853): 105 E. 22nd St., New York, N.Y. 10010. 1,207; Philip Coltoff, Executive Director.

**Children's Book Council** (1945): 67 Irving Place, New York, N.Y. 10003. 65 publishing houses; John Donovan, President.

**Child Welfare League of America** (1920): 67 Irving Pl., New York, N.Y. 10003. David S. Liederman, Executive Director.

**Chiropractic Association, American** (1963): 1916 Wilson Blvd., Arlington, Va. 22201. 21,300; G.M. Brassard, D.C., Executive Vice President.

**Christians and Jews, National Conference of** (1928): 71 Fifth Ave., New York, N.Y. 10003. 200,000; Jacqueline G. Wexler, President.

**Churches of Christ, USA, National Council of** (1950): 475 Riverside Drive, New York, N.Y. 10115. 31 Protestant and Orthodox communions; Arie R. Brouwer, General Secretary.

**Cities, National League of** (1924): 1301 Pennsylvania Ave. N.W., Washington, D.C. 20004. 15,000 cities; Alan Beals, Executive Director.

**Civil Air Patrol** (1941): Maxwell AFB, Ala. 36112-5572. 66,000; Col. John T. Massingale, Jr., Executive Director.

**Civil Engineers, American Society of** (1852): 345 E. 47th St., New York, N.Y. 10017. 102,345; Edward O. Pfrang, Executive Director.

**Civil Liberties Union, American** (1920): 132 W. 43rd St., New York, N.Y. 10036. 200,000; Alan Reitman, Associate Director.

**Clinical Pathologists, American Society of** (1922): 2100 W. Harrison St., Chicago, Ill. 60612. 34,000; Robert A. Dietrich, Chief of Staff.

**Collectors Association, American** (1939): Box 35106, Minneapolis, Minn. 55435. 3,159; John W. Johnson, Executive Vice President.

**College Board, The** (1900): 45 Columbus Ave., New York, N.Y. 10023. 2,550 institutions; George Hanford, President.

**College Placement Council** (1956): 62 E. Highland Ave., Bethlehem, Pa. 18017. 2,500; Jesse M. Smith, Executive Director.

**Colleges, Association of American** (1915): 1818 R St. N.W., Washington, D.C. 20009. 560 institutions; Dr. John W. Chandler, President.

***Colored Women's Clubs, National Association of** (1896): 5808 16th St. N.W., Washington, D.C.

20011. 40,000; Mrs. Otelia E. Champion, National President.

**Common Cause** (1970): 2030 M St. N.W., Washington, D.C. 20036. 250,000; Archibald Cox, Chairman.

**Community and Junior Colleges, American Association of** (1920): One Dupont Circle N.W., Suite 410, Washington, D.C. 20036-1176. 1,221 institutions; Dale Parnell, President and C.E.O.

**Community Cultural Center Association, American** (1978): 19 Foothills Dr., Pompton Plains, N.J. 07444. Milli Janz, Executive Director.

**Composers, Authors, and Publishers, American Society of (ASCAP)** (1914): One Lincoln Plaza, New York, N.Y. 10023. 40,000; Morton Gould, President.

**Composers/USA, National Association of** (1932): P.O. Box 49652, Barrington Station, Los Angeles, Calif. 90049. 550; Marshall Bialosky, President.

**Congress of Racial Equality (CORE)** (1942): 236 W. 116th St., New York, N.Y. 10026. Nationwide network of chapters; Roy Innis, National Chairman.

***Conscientious Objectors, Central Committee for** (1948): 2208 South St., Philadelphia, Pa. 19146.

**Conservation Engineers, Association of** (1961): Missouri Dept. of Conservation, P.O. Box 180, Jefferson City, Mo. 65102. William F. Lueckenhoff, Secretary-Treasurer.

**Consumer Federation of America** (1968): 1424 16th St. N.W., Washington, D.C. 20036. 220 member organizations; Stephen Brobeck, Executive Director.

**Consumer Interests, American Council on** (1953): 240 Stanley Hall, Univ. of Missouri, Columbia, Mo. 65211. 1,800; Barbara Slusher, Executive Director.

**Consumers League, National** (1899): 815 15th St. N.W., Suite 516, Washington, D.C. 20005. Linda F. Golodner, Executive Director.

**Consumers Union** (1936): 256 Washington St., Mt. Vernon, N.Y. 10553. 3,500,000 subscribers to *Consumer Reports;* Rhoda H. Karpatkin, Executive Director.

**Contract Bridge League, American** (1927): P.O. Box 161192, Memphis, Tenn. 38186. 200,000; Ralph Cohen, Executive Director.

**Cooperative Business Association, National (formerly Cooperative League of the U.S.A)** (1916): 1401 New York Ave. N.W., Suite 1100, Washington, D.C. 20005. E. Morgan Williams, President.

**Counselors and Family Therapists, National Academy of** (1972): 225 Jericho Turnpike, Suite 4, Floral Park, N.Y. 11001. 900; Eileen Gallagher, Executive Director.

**Country Music Association** (1958): Box 22299, Nashville, Tenn. 37202. 8,000; Jo Walker-Meador, Executive Director.

**Credit Association, International** (1912): P.O. Box 27357, St. Louis, Mo. 63141. 16,500; William J. Henderson, President.

**Credit Management, National Association of** (1896): 520 Eighth Ave., New York, N.Y. 10018. 44,000; Virginia DuBon, Corporate Secretary.

**Credit Union National Association** (1934): P.O. Box 431, Madison, Wis. 53701. 52 state leagues representing 18,000 credit unions; Jim R. Williams, President.

**Crime and Delinquency, National Council on** (1907): 77 Maiden Lane, San Francisco, Calif. 94108. Nationwide membership; Barry Krisberg, President.

**Criminal Investigators Association, International**

**(ICIA)** (1982): P.O. Box 15350, Chevy Chase, Md. 20815. 1,000; Daniel Meany III, Executive Director.

**Dairy Council, National** (1915): 6300 N. River Rd., Rosement, Ill. 60018. Elwood W. Speckmann, Ph.D., President.

**Daughters of the American Revolution, National Society** (1890): 1776 D St. N.W., Washington, D.C. 20006. 210,000; Mrs. Raymond Franklin Fleck, President General.

**Daughters of the Confederacy, United** (1894): 328 N. Boulevard, Richmond, Va. 23220. 27,000.

**Deaf, National Association of the** (1880): 814 Thayer Ave., Silver Spring, Md. 20910. Gary W. Olsen, Executive Director.

**Defenders of Wildlife** (1947): 1244 19th St. N.W., Washington, D.C. 20036. 80,000; Joyce Kelly, President.

**Defense Preparedness Association, American** (1919): Rosslyn Center, Suite 900, 1700 N. Moore St., Arlington, Va. 22209. 45,000; H.A. Miley, Jr., President.

**Democratic Club, National** (1834): The 60 East Club, 60 E. 42nd St., New York, N.Y. 10165. John G. Treacy, Secretary.

**Dental Association, American** (1859): 211 E. Chicago Ave., Chicago, Ill. 60611. 145,000; Dr. Thomas J. Ginley, Executive Director.

**Diabetes Association, American** (1940): 1660 Duke St., Alexandria, Va. 22314. Robert S. Bolan, Executive Vice President.

**Dietetic Association, The American** (1917): 430 N. Michigan Ave., Chicago, Ill. 60611. 52,000; Julian F. Haynes, Executive Director.

**Dignity** (1969): 1500 Massachusetts Ave. N.W., Suite 11, Washington, D.C. 20005. 5,000; James A. Bussen, President.

**Disabled American Veterans** (1920): 807 Maine Ave. S.W., Washington, D.C. 20024. Thomas K. Keller, National Director of Communications.

**Dowsers, Inc., The American Society of** (1961): Danville, Vt. 05828. 3,500; Dwin Gordon, President.

**Drug, Chemical, and Allied Trades Association** (1890): 42-40 Bell Blvd., Suite 604, Bayside, N.Y. 11361. 504; Joseph D. Madden, Executive Vice President.

**Ducks Unlimited** (1937): One Waterfowl Way, Long Grove, Ill. 60047. 600,000; Dale E. Whitesell, Executive Vice President.

**Eagles, Fraternal Order of** (1898): 2401 W. Wisconsin Ave., Milwaukee, Wis. 53233. 795,000; Robert W. Hansen, Publications Editor.

**Earthwatch** (1970): 680 Mt. Auburn St., Box 403, Watertown, Mass. 02272. 25,000; Brian Rosborough, President.

**Eastern Star, Order of,** (1876): 1618 New Hampshire Ave. N.W., Washington, D.C. 20009. 2,500,000; Helen D. Roquemore Cox, Most Worthy Grand Matron.

**Easter Seal Society, The National** (1921): 2023 W. Ogden Ave., Chicago, Ill. 60612. 50 affiliated state societies and Puerto Rico; John R. Garrison, Executive Director.

**Economic Association, American** (1885): 1313 21st Ave. So., Nashville, Tenn. 37212. 20,000 members, 5,500 inst. subs.; C. Elton Hinshaw, Secretary.

**Economic Development, Committee for** (1942): 477 Madison Ave., New York, N.Y. 10022. 225; Robert C. Holland, President.

**Edison Electric Institute** (1933): 1111 19th St. N.W., Washington, D.C. 20036-3691. 200; Wil-

liam McCollam, Jr., President.

**Education, American Council on** (1918): One Dupont Circle N.W., Washington, D.C. 20036. 1,300 (organizational members); Robert H. Atwell, President.

**Education, Council for Advancement and Support of** (1974): 11 Dupont Circle N.W., Washington, D.C. 20036. 12,000; Gary Quehl, President.

**Educational Exchange, International, Council on** (1947): 205 E. 42nd St., New York, N.Y. 10017. 174; Jack Egle, President-Executive Director.

**Educational Research Association, American** (1906): 1230 17th St. N.W., Washington, D.C. 20036. 14,000; William J. Russell, Executive Officer.

**Education Association, National** (1857): 1201 16th St. N.W., Washington, D.C. 20036. 1,801, 936; Don Cameron, Executive Director.

**Electrochemical Society, The** (1902): 10 S. Main St., Pennington, N.J. 08534. 6,274; Roque J. Calvo, Assistant Executive Secretary.

**Electronic Industries Association** (1924): 2001 Eye St. N.W., Washington, D.C. 20006. 1,000 member companies; Peter F. McCloskey, President.

**Electroplaters and Surface Finishers Society, American** (1909): 12644 Research Pkwy., Orlando, Fla. 32826. 10,000; J. H. Schumacher, Jr., Executive Director.

**Energy Engineers, Association of** (1978): 4025 Pleasantdale Rd., Suite 340, Atlanta, Ga. 30340. 6,000; Albert Thumann, Executive Director.

**Elks of the U.S.A., Benevolent and Protective Order of the** (1868): 2750 Lake View Ave., Chicago, Ill. 60614. 1,600,000; Stanley F. Kocur, Grand Secretary.

**English-Speaking Union of the United States** (1920): 16 E. 69th St., New York, N.Y. 10021. 32,000; John D. Walker, Executive Director.

**Entomological Society of America** (1886): 4603 Calvert Rd., College Park, Md. 20740. 9,000; W. Darryl Hunsin, Executive Director.

**Exceptional Children, The Council for** (1922): 1920 Association Dr., Reston, Va. 22091. 49, 000; Jeptha V. Greer, Executive Director.

**Experimental Test Pilots, The Society of** (1956): 44814 Elm St., Lancaster, Calif. 93534. 1,781; Thomas H. Smith, Executive Director.

**Exploration Geophysicists, Society of** (1930): P.O. Box 702740, Tulsa, Okla. 74170. 19,000; John Hyden, Executive Director.

**Family Physicians, American Academy of** (1947): 1740 W. 92nd St., Kansas City, Mo. 64114. 57, 700; Robert Graham, M.D., Acting Executive Vice President.

**Family Relations, National Council on** (1938): 1910 W. County Rd. B, Suite 147, St. Paul, Minn. 55113. 4,000; Mary Jo Czaplewski, Executive Director.

**Family Service America** (1911): 11700 W. Lake Park Dr., Park Place, Milwaukee, Wis. 53224. 280 member agencies; Geneva B. Johnson, President and Chief Executive Officer.

**Farm Bureau Federation, American** (1919): 225 Touhy Ave., Park Ridge, Ill. 60068. 3.3 million member families; J. Patrick Batts, Director of Information.

**Farmer Cooperatives, National Council of** (1929): 50 F St. N.W., Washington, D.C. 20001. 165; Wayne A. Boutwell, President.

**Federal Employees, National Federation of** (1917): 1016 16th St. N.W., Washington, D.C. 10036. rep. 150,000; James M. Peirce, President.

**Feline and Canine Friends, Inc.** (1973): 505 N.

Bush St., Anaheim, Calif. 92805. 1,000; Rose Hosea, Founder-President.

**Fellowship of Reconciliation** (1915): Box 271, Nyack, N.Y. 10960. 33,000; Verne Cooperrider, Interim Executive Secretary.

**Female Executives, National Association for** (1972): 1041 Third Ave., New York, N.Y. 10021. 175,000; Leslie Smith, Director of Association Services.

**Film Library Association, Educational** (1943): 45 John St., New York, N.Y. 10038. 1,600; Marilyn J. Levin, Executive Director.

**Financial Analysts Federation** (1947): 1633 Broadway, Suite 1402, New York, N.Y. 10019. 15,500; John N. Bailey, Executive Director.

**Fire Protection Association, National** (1896): Batterymarch Park, Quincy, Mass. 02269. 33,400; Robert W. Grant, President.

**Fleet Reserve Association** (1924): 1303 New Hampshire Ave. N.W., Washington, D.C. 20036. 167,000; Robert W. Nolan, National Executive Secretary.

**Flight Test Engineers, Society of** (1968): P.O. Box 4047, Lancaster, Calif. 93539. 1,100; Dianne Van Norman, Executive Director.

**Flying Saucer Clubs of America, Amalgamated** (1959): P.O. Box 39, Yucca Valley, Calif. 92284. 5,600; Gabriel Green, President.

**Foreign Policy Association** (1918): 205 Lexington Ave., New York, N.Y. 10016. Thetis Reavis, Vice President for Public Affairs.

**Foreign Relations, Council on** (1921): 58 E. 68th St., New York, N.Y. 10021. 2,376; Peter Tarnoff, President.

**Foreign Student Affairs, National Association for** (1948): 1860 19th St. N.W., Washington, D.C. 20009. 5,300; John Reichard, Executive Vice President.

**Foreign Study, American Institute for** (1965): 102 Greenwich Ave., Greenwich, Conn. 06830. 300, 000; Henry C. Kahn, President.

*****Foreign Trade Council, Inc., National** (1914): 100 E. 42nd St., New York, N.Y. 10017. Over 650 companies; Richard W. Roberts, President.

**Forensic Sciences, American Academy of** (1948): 225 S. Academy Blvd., Colorado Springs, Colo. 80910. 2,800; Beth Ann Lipskin, Executive Director.

**Forest Council, American** (1932): 1250 Connecticut Ave. N.W., Suite 320, Washington, D.C. 20036. 100; Laurence D. Wiseman, President.

**Foresters, Society of American** (1900): 5400 Grosvenor Lane, Bethesda, Md. 20814. 20,000; Ronald R. Christensen, Executive Vice President.

**Forestry Association, American** (1875): 1319 18th St. N.W., Washington, D.C. 20036. 40,000; R. Neil Sampson, Executive Vice President.

**Fortean Organization, International** (1965): P.O. Box 367, Arlington, Va. 22210-0367. 800; Raymond D. Manners, President and Editor.

**Foster Parents Plan International** (1937). Box 804, East Greenwich, R.I. 02818. George W. Ross, International Executive Director.

**Foundrymen's Society, American** (1896): Golf & Wolf Rds., Des Plaines, Ill. 60016-2277. 14,000; Charles H. Jones, Executive Vice President.

**4-H Program** (early 1900s): Room 3860-S, U.S. Department of Agriculture, Washington, D.C. 20250. 4,300,000; Donald L. Stormer, Deputy Administrator.

**Freedom of Information Center** (1958): Box 858, Univ. of Missouri-Columbia, Columbia, Mo. 65205. Dr. Paul Fisher, Director.

**French-American Chamber of Commerce in the**

**U.S.** (1896): 509 Madison Ave., Suite 1900, New York, N.Y. 10022. Trade Association; Chantal Soichet, General Manager.

**French Institute/Alliance Française** (1911): 22 E. 60th St., New York, N.Y. 10022. 8,500; Jean Vallier, Director.

**Friends of Animals** (1957): One Pine St., Neptune, N.J. 07753. 125,000; Alice Herrington, President and Founder.

**Friends of the Earth** (1969): 530 Seventh St. S.E., Washington, D.C. 20003. 18,000; Geoff Webb, Acting Executive Director.

**Future Farmers of America** (1928): 5632 Mt. Vernon Hgwy., Alexandria, Va. 22309. 430,000; Larry D. Case, National Advisor.

**Future Homemakers of America** (1945): 1910 Association Dr., Reston, Va. 22091. 350,000; Louisa Liddell, Executive Director.

**Gamblers Anonymous Fellowship:** Box 17173, Los Angeles, Calif. 90017. 12,000; Irving S., National Executive Secretary.

**Genealogical Society, National** (1903): 4527 17th St. N., Arlington, Va. 22207. 7,200; Margaret M. Redmond, Executive Director.

**Genetic Association, American** (1903): 818 18th St. N.W., Washington, D.C. 20006. 1,600; Barbara Kuhn, Administrative Secretary.

**Geographers, Association of American** (1904): 1710 16th St. N.W., Washington, D.C. 20009. 5, 300; Robert T. Aangeenbrug, Executive Director.

**Geographical Society, The American** (1851): 156 Fifth Ave., Suite 600, New York, N.Y. 10010. 763; Mary Lynne Bird, Director.

**Geographic Education, National Council for** (1915): Western Illinois Univ., Macomb, Ill. 61455. 3,200; James W. Vining, Executive Director.

**Geographic Society, National** (1888): 17th and M Sts. N.W., Washington, D.C. 20036. 10,500,000; Gilbert M. Grosvenor, President.

**Geological Institute, American** (1948): 4220 King St., Alexandria, Va. 22302. 17 member societies representing 70,000 geoscientists; Marvin E. Kauffman, Executive Director.

**Geological Society of America, Inc.** (1888): 3300 Penrose Pl., P.O. Box 9140, Boulder, Colo. 80301. 16,800; F. Michael Wahl, Executive Director.

**Geriatrics Society, American** (1942): 10 Columbus Circle, Suite 1470, New York, N.Y. 10019. 5, 000; Linda Hiddemen Barondess, Executive Vice President.

**Gideons International, The** (1889): 2900 Lebanon Rd., Nashville, Tenn. 37214. 90,000; M.A. Henderson, Executive Director.

**Gifted, The Association for the** (1958): The Council for Exceptional Children, 1920 Association Dr., Reston, Va. 22091. 2,100; Anne Crabbe, President.

**Girls Clubs of America** (1945): 205 Lexington Ave., New York, N.Y. 10016. 250,000; Margaret Gates, National Executive Director.

**Girl Scouts of the U.S.A.** (1912): 830 Third Ave., New York, N.Y. 10022. 2,900,000; Rhoda Pauley, Communications Services.

**Graphic Artists, Society of American** (1916): 32 Union Square, Rm. 1214, New York, N.Y. 10003. Stephen Gamin, President.

**Graphoanalysis Society, International** (1929): 111 N. Canal St., Chicago, Ill. 60606. 10,000; V. Peter Ferrara, President.

**Group Psychotherapy Association, American** (1942): 25 E. 21st St., 6th Floor, New York, N.Y. 10010. 3,200; Marsha S. Block, Chief Executive

Officer.

Gray Panthers, The National (1970): 311 S. Juniper St., Suite 601, Philadelphia, Pa. 19107. Over 100 chapters.

Guide Dog Foundation for the Blind, Inc. (1946): 371 E. Jericho Turnpike, Smithtown, N.Y. 11787. 710; David Nydick, Executive Director.

Hadassah, The Women's Zionist Organization of America (1912): 50 W. 58th St., New York, N.Y. 10019. 385,000; Zmira Goodman, Executive Director.

Health, Physical Education, Recreation, and Dance, American Alliance for (1885): 1900 Association Dr., Reston, Va. 22091. 50,000; Dr. Jack E. Razor, Executive Vice President.

Hearing and Speech Action, National Association for (1910): 10801 Rockville Pike, Rockville, Md. 20852. 1500.

Heart Association, American (1924): 7320 Greenville Ave., Dallas, Tex. 75231. 200,000 members, 2,000,000 volunteers; Dudley Hafner, Executive Vice President.

Heating, Refrigerating, and Air-Conditioning Engineers, Inc., American Society of (1894): 1791 Tullie Circle N.E., Atlanta, Ga. 30329. 50,000; Frank Coda, Executive Director.

Helicopter Association, International (1948): 1619 Duke St., Alexandria, Va. 22314-3406. 1,200; Frank L. Jensen, Jr., President.

Hemispheric Affairs, Council on (1975): 1612 20th St. N.W., Washington, D.C. 20009. Laurence R. Birns, Director.

Historians, The Organization of American (1907): Indiana Univ., 112 N. Bryan St., Bloomington, Ind. 47401. 8,500; William Leuchtenburg, President.

Historical Association, American (1884): 400 A St. S.E., Washington, D.C. 20003. 15,000; Samuel R. Gammon, Executive Director.

Historic Preservation, National Trust for (1949): 1785 Massachusetts Ave. N.W., Washington, D.C. 20036. 175,000; J. Jackson Walter, President.

Home Economics Association, American (1909): 2010 Massachusetts Ave. N.W., Washington, D.C. 20036. 25,000.

Horse Shows Association, Inc., American (1917): 220 E. 42nd St., New York, N.Y. 10017-5806. 47,000; Richard E. McDevitt, President.

Horticultural Association, National Junior (1935): 5885 104th St., Fremont, Mich. 49412. 12,500; Mr. Clare Harnden, Executive Secretary.

Horticultural Society, American (1922): Box 0105, Mt. Vernon, Va. 22121. 45,000; Charles A. Huckins, Executive Director.

Hospital Association, American (1898): 840 N. Lake Shore Dr., Chicago, Ill. 60611, 6,184 institutions; Carol M. McCarthy, Ph.D., President.

Humane Association, American (1877): 9725 E. Hampden, Denver, Colo. 80231.

Humane Society of the United States (1954): 2100 L St. N.W., Washington, D.C. 20037. 510,000; Patrick B. Parkes, Vice President for Field Services.

Humanities, National Endowment for the (1965): 1100 Pennsylvania Ave. N.W., Washington, D.C. 20506; John Agresto, Acting Chairman.

Hydrogen Energy, International Association for (1975): P.O. Box 248266, Coral Gables, Fla. 33124. 2,500; T. Nejat Veziroglu, President.

Illustrators, Society of (1901): 128 E. 63rd St., New York, N.Y. 10021. 950; Walter Hortens, President.

Indian Rights Association (1882): 1505 Race St., Philadelphia, Pa. 19102. 1,000; Dr. Melanie Beth Oliviero, Executive Director.

Industrial Engineers, Institute of (1948): 25 Technology Park/Atlanta, Norcross, Ga. 30092. 43,000; David L. Belden, Ph.D., P.E., Executive Director.

Intercultural Education, Training, and Research, Society for (1974): 1414 22nd St. N.W., Suite 101, Washington, D.C. 20037. 1,400; Dr. Diane Zeller, Executive Director.

Interfraternity Conference, National (1909): 3901 W. 86th St., Suite 280, Indianapolis, Ind. 46268. 58; Jonathan J. Brant, Executive Director.

Iron and Steel Institute, American (1908): 1000 16th St. N.W., Washington, D.C. 20036. 1,500; Robert B. Peabody, President.

Izaak Walton League of America (1922): 1701 N. Ft. Myer Dr., Suite 1100, Arlington, Va. 22209. 50,000; Jack Lorenz, Executive Director.

Jaycees, The United States (1920): P.O. Box 7, Tulsa, Okla. 74121. 272,000; Gram Hopkins, Executive Vice President.

Jewish Appeal, United (1939): 99 Park Ave., New York, N.Y. 10016. Stanley B. Horowitz, President.

Jewish Committee, American (1906): 165 E. 56th St., New York, N.Y. 10022. 50,000; Morton Yarmon, Director of Public Relations.

Jewish Community Centers, World Confederation of (1946): 12 Hess St., Jerusalem, Israel 94185. Don Scher, Executive Director.

Jewish Congress, American (1918): 15 E. 84th St., New York, N.Y. 10028. 50,000; Henry Siegman, Executive Director.

Jewish Historical Society, American (1892): 2 Thornton Rd., Waltham, Mass. 02154. 3,750; Bernard Wax, Director.

Jewish War Veterans of the U.S.A. (1896): 1811 R St. N.W., Washington, D.C. 20009.

Jewish Women, National Council of (1893): 15 E. 26th St., New York, N.Y. 10010. 100,000; Dadie Perlov, CAE, Executive Director.

*John Birch Society (1958): 395 Concord Ave., Belmont, Mass. 02178. Under 100,000; Charles J. Humphries, Clerk of Corporation.

Journalists, Society of Professional, Sigma Delta Chi (1909): 53 W. Jackson Blvd., Suite 731, Chicago, Ill. 60604. 22,000; Russell C. Tornabene, Executive Officer.

Journalists and Authors, American Society of (1948): 150 Broadway, Suite 1907, New York, N.Y. 10036. 750; Alexandra S.E. Cantor, Executive Secretary.

Judaism, American Council for (1943): 298 Fifth Ave., New York, N.Y. 10001. 10,000; Alan V. Stone, President.

*Junior Achievement (1919): 550 Summer St., Stamford, Conn. 06901. 6,750,000; Glenn V. Gardinier, National Public Relations Director.

Junior Leagues, Inc., Association of (1921): 825 Third Ave., New York, N.Y. 10022. 266 Leagues, 163,000 members.

Junior Statesmen of America (1934): 650 Bair Island Rd., Suite 201, Redwood City, Calif. 94063. 10,000; Richard Prosser, Executive Director.

JWB (1917): 15 E. 26th St., New York, N.Y. 10010-1579. 275 affiliated community centers, YM-YWHAs, and camps; Arthur Rotman, Executive Vice President.

Kennel Club, American (1884): 51 Madison Ave., New York, N.Y. 10010. 444 member clubs; James E. Dearinger, Secretary.

Kiwanis International (1915): 3636 Woodview Trace, Indianapolis, Ind. 46268. 313,000; G. H. "Gil" Zitzelsberger, International Secretary.

Knights of Columbus (1882): One Columbus Plaza, New Haven, Conn. 06507. 1,425,265; Virgil C.

Dechant, Supreme Knight.

**Knights of Pythias, Supreme Lodge** (1864): 35 E. Rose St., Stockton, Calif. 95202. 104,736; Jule O. Pritchard, Supreme Secretary.

**Knights Templar, Grand Encampment of** (1816): 14 E. Jackson Blvd., Suite 1700, Chicago, Ill. 60604. 340,000; Charles R. Neumann, Grand Recorder.

**La Leche League International** (1956): 9616 Minneapolis Ave., Franklin Park, Ill. 60131. 40,000; Betty Wagner, Executive Director.

**Law, American Society of International** (1906): 2223 Massachusetts Ave. N.W., Washington, D.C. 20008. 4,500; John Lawrence Hargrove, Executive Vice President and Executive Director.

**League of Women Voters of the U.S.** (1920): 1730 M St. N.W., Washington, D.C. 20036. 114,000; Grant D. Thompson, Executive Director.

**Legal Aid and Defender Association, National** (1911): 1625 K St. N.W., Suite 800, Washington, D.C. 20006. 5,000; Clinton Lyons, Executive Director.

**Legal Secretaries, National Association of** (1950): 2250 E. 73rd St., Suite 550, Tulsa, Okla. 74136. 18,000; Judi A. Kruse, Executive Administrator.

**Leukemia Society of America** (1949): 733 Third Ave., New York, N.Y. 10017. Lawrence D. Ellis, M.D., President.

**Library Association, American** (1876): 50 E. Huron St., Chicago, Ill. 60611. 42,000; Thomas J. Galvin, Executive Director.

**Life Insurance, American Council of** (1976): 1850 K St. N.W., Washington, D.C. 20006. 625; Richard S. Schweiker, President.

**Life Underwriters, American Society of Chartered** (1928): 270 Bryn Mawr Ave., Bryn Mawr, Pa. 19010. 32,000; John R. Driskill, Executive Vice President.

**Life Underwriters, National Association of** (1890): 1922 F St. N.W., Washington, D.C. 20006. Jack E. Bobo, Executive Vice President.

**Lions Clubs International** (1917): 300 22nd St., Oak Brook, Ill. 60570. 1,348,142. Roy Schaetzel, Executive Administrator.

**Lung Association, American** (1904): 1740 Broadway, New York, N.Y. 10019. 139 affiliated local associations; James A. Swomley, Managing Director.

**Lupus Foundation of America, Inc.,** (1976): 1717 Massachusetts Ave. N.W., Suite 203, Washington, D.C. 20036. 240 chapters and groups; Virginia J. Masters, Executive Secretary, 4434 Covington Hwy., Decatur, Ga., 30035.

**Magazine Editors, American Society of** (1963): 575 Lexington Ave., New York, N.Y. 10022. 550; Robert E. Kenyon, Executive Director.

**Magazine Publishers Association** (1919): 575 Lexington Ave., New York, N.Y. 10022. 251 publishing companies rep. 1,200 magazines; William F. Gorog, President.

**Management Association, American** (1923): 135 W. 50th St., New York, N.Y. 10020. 80,000; Patricia Conway, Corporate Secretary.

**Management Consultants, Institute of** (1968): 19 W. 44th St., Suite 810, New York, N.Y. 10036. 1,700; John F. Hartshorne, Executive Director.

**Manufacturers, National Association of** (1895): 1331 Pennsylvania Ave. N.W., Suite 1500–North Lobby, Washington, D.C. 20004-1703. 13,500; Joni C. Hodgson, Secretary.

**Manufacturers' Agents National Association (MANA)** (1947): 23016 Mill Creek Rd., P.O. Box 3467, Laguna Hills, Calif. 92654. 9,000; James J. Gibbons, President.

**\*March of Dimes Birth Defects Foundation** (1938): 1275 Mamaroneck Ave., White Plains, N.Y. 10605. 300 chapters; Charles L. Massey, President.

**Marine Corps Association** (1913): Box 1775 Marine Corps Base, Quantico, Va. 22134. B.Gen. G.L. Bartlett, U.S.M.C. (Ret.), Secretary-Treasurer.

**Marine Corps League** (1923): 956 N. Monroe St., Arlington, Va. 22201. 30,000; All mail to: Robert N. Forsyth, PNC., National Adjutant Paymaster.

**Marine Technology Society** (1963): 2000 Florida Ave., Suite 500, Washington, D.C. 20009. 2,500; Harold Palmer, Ph.D., Executive Director.

**Masons, Ancient and Accepted Scottish Rite, Northern Masonic Jurisdiction, Supreme Council 33** (1867): 33 Marrett Rd., Lexington, Mass. 02173. 466,159; Lynn J. Sanderson, Grand Secretary General.

**Masons, Ancient and Accepted Scottish Rite, Southern Jurisdiction, Supreme Council** (1801): 1733 16th St. N.W., Washington, D.C. 20009. 641,785; C. Fred Kleinknecht, Sovereign Grand Commander.

**Masons, Royal Arch, General Grand Chapter International** (1797): 1084 New Circle Rd. N.E., Lexington, Ky. 40505. 375,000; Charles K.A. McGaughey, General Grand Secretary.

**Massachusetts Audubon Society** (1896): South Great Rd., Lincoln, Mass. 01773. 33,000 member households; Dr. Gerard A. Bertrand, President.

**Mathematical Association of America** (1915): 1529 18th St. N.W., Washington, D.C. 20036. Dr. Alfred B. Willcox, Executive Director.

**Mathematical Society, American** (1888): P.O. Box 6248, Providence, R.I. 02940. 22,030; William J. LeVeque, Executive Director.

**Mathematical Statistics, Institute of** (1935): 3401 Investment Blvd. #7, Hayward, Calif. 94545. 3,000; Nicholas P. Jewell, Treasurer.

**Mayflower Descendants, General Society of** (1897): 4 Winslow St., P.O. Box 3297, Plymouth, Mass. 02361. 21,000; Mrs. Clayton M. Merrick Jr., Historian General.

**Mayors, U.S. Conference of** (1932): 1620 Eye St. N.W., Washington, D.C. 20006. 7 standing committees; John J. Gunther, Executive Director.

**Mechanical Engineers, American Society of** (1880): 345 E. 47th St., New York, N.Y. 10017. 115,000; Paul F. Allmendinger, Executive Director.

**Mechanics, American Academy of** (1969): Dept. of Civil Engineering, Northwestern Univ., Evanston, Ill. 60201. 1,200; Eli Reshotko, President-Elect.

**\*Medical Association, American** (1847): 535 N. Dearborn St., Chicago, Ill. 60610-4377.

**Medical Library Association** (1898): 919 N. Michigan Ave., Chicago, Ill. 60611. 5,000; Raymond A. Palmer, Executive Director.

**Mental Health Association, National** (1909): 1021 Prince St., Alexandria, Va., 22314-2971. 1,000,000.

**Metals, American Society for** (1920): Metals Park, Ohio 44073. 51,000; Edward L. Langer, Managing Director.

**Meteorological Society, American** (1919): 45 Beacon St., Boston, Mass. 02108. 10,000; Kenneth C. Spengler, Executive Director.

**Mining, Metallurgical and Petroleum Engineers, American Institute of** (1871): 345 E. 47th St., New York, N.Y. 10017. 4 Member Societies: Society of Mining Engineers, 25,740; The Metallurgical Society, 12,132; Iron & Steel Society, 6,359; Society of Petroleum Engineers, 56,509. Robert H. Marcrum, AIME Executive Director.

Mining and Metallurgical Society of America (1910): 275 Madison Ave., Suite 2301, New York, N.Y. 10016. 300; Hans W. Schreiber, President.

Model Aeronautics, Academy of (1936): 1810 Samuel Morse Dr., Reston, Va. 22090. 95,000; John Worth, Executive Director.

Modern Language Association of America (1883): 10 Astor Place, New York, N.Y. 10003. 30,000.

Modern Woodmen of America (1883): Mississippi River at 17th St., Rock Island, Ill. 61201. 550,000; W.B. Foster, President.

Moose, Loyal Order of (1888): Mooseheart, Ill. 60539. 1,775,227; Donald H. Ross, Supreme Secretary.

Motion Picture & Television Engineers, Society of (1916): 595 W. Hartsdale Ave., White Plains, N.Y. 10607. 8,500; Lynette Robinson, Executive Director.

Motion Picture Arts & Sciences, Academy of (1927): 8949 Wilshire Blvd., Beverly Hills, Calif. 90211. James M. Roberts, Executive Director.

Multiple Sclerosis Society, National (1946): 205 E. 42nd St., New York, N.Y. 10017. Thor Hanson, Vice Admiral, USN (Ret.), President and C.E.O.

Muscular Dystrophy Association (1950): 810 Seventh Ave., New York, N.Y. 10019. 1,945,800 volunteers, Jerry Lewis, National Chairman.

Museum of Natural History, American (1869): Central Park West at 79th St., New York, N.Y. 10024. 500,000; Robert G. Goelet, President.

Museums, American Association of (1906): 1055 Thomas Jefferson St. N.W., Washington, D.C. 20007. 9,000; Lawrence Reger, Director.

Music Council, National (1940): 570 Seventh Ave., 20th floor, New York, N.Y. 10018. 65 National Music Organizations; Benjamin S. Dunham, Executive Vice President.

Musicians, American Federation of (1896): 1501 Broadway, Suite 600 Paramount Bldg., New York, N.Y. 10036. 230,000; Victor W. Fuentealba, President.

Music Publishers Association, Inc., National (1917): 205 E. 42nd St., New York, N.Y. 10017. Trade Organization/Harry Fox Agency-Licensing Organization. Edward P. Murphy, President and CEO.

Muzzle Loading Rifle Association, National (1933): P.O. Box 67, Friendship, Ind. 47021. 30,000; Rosetta Smith, Business Manager.

Narcolepsy and Cataplexy Foundation of America (1975): 1410 York Ave., Suite 2D, New York, N.Y. 10021. 3,982; Bruno George Ronty, Ph.D., General Director.

National Association for the Advancement of Colored People (1909): 4805 Mt. Hope Dr., Baltimore, Md. 21215. 450,000; Benjamin L. Hooks, Executive Director and CEO.

National Grange, The (1867): 1616 H St. N.W., Washington, D.C. 20006. 400,000; Edward Andersen, Master.

National PTA (National Congress of Parents and Teachers) (1897): 700 N. Rush St., Chicago, Ill. 60611. 5,840,000; Robert N. Woerner. Executive Administrator.

Natural Science for Youth Foundation (1961): 11 Wildwood Valley, Atlanta, Ga. 30338. 350; John Ripley Forbes, Chairman of the Board.

Nature Conservancy, The (1951): 1800 N. Kent St., Arlington, Va. 22209. 275,000; William D. Blair, Jr., President.

Naval Institute, United States (1873): Annapolis, Md. 21402. 90,000; James A. Barber, Jr., Executive Director.

Naval Architects and Marine Engineers, The Society of (1893): One World Trade Center, Suite 1369, New York, N.Y. 10048. 13,091; Robert G. Mende, Secretary and Executive Director.

Navy League of the United States (1902): 2300 Wilson Blvd., Arlington, Va. 22201. 54,328; William G. Sizemore, Executive Director.

Naval Engineers, American Society of (1888): 1452 Duke St., Alexandria, Va. 22314. 8,000; Capt. James L. McVoy, USN (Ret.), Executive Director.

Navigation, The Institute of (1945): 815 15th St. N.W., Suite 832, Washington, D.C. 20005. 3,000; Frank B. Brady, Executive Director.

Neurofibromatosis Foundation, The National (1978): 141 Fifth Ave., Suite 7S, New York, N.Y. 10010. 15,000; Peter Bellermann, Executive Director.

Newspaper Editors, American Society of (1922): P.O. Box 17004, Washington, D.C. 20041. 920; Lee Stinnett, Executive Director.

Newspaper Publishers Association, American (1887): The Newspaper Center, P.O. Box 17407, Dulles International Airport, Washington, D.C. 20041. 1,395; Jerry W. Friedheim, Executive Vice President and General Manager.

Nuclear Society, American (1954): 555 N. Kensington Ave., La Grange Park, Ill. 60525. 15,000; Octave J. Du Temple, Executive Director.

Numismatic Association, American (1891): 818 N. Cascade Ave., Colorado Springs, Colo. 80903. 37,000; Ruthann Brettell, Executive Director.

Nurses' Association, American (1896): 1101 14th St. N.W. Washington, D.C. 20005. 188,000.

Nutrition, American Institute of (1930): 9650 Rockville Pike, Bethesda, Md. 20814. 2,400; Richard G. Allison, Executive Officer.

Odd Fellows, Sovereign Grand Lodge, Independent Order of (1819): 422 Trade St., Winston-Salem, N.C. 27101. 1,200,000; Robert W. Wepking, Sovereign Grand Secretary.

Olympic Committee, United States (1921): 1750 East Boulder St., Colorado Springs, Colo. 80909. Michael Moran, Director, Public Information/Media Relations.

Optical Society of America (1916): 1816 Jefferson Place N.W., Washington, D.C. 20036. 9,110; Jarus W. Quinn, Executive Director.

Optometric Association, American (1898): 243 N. Lindbergh Blvd., St. Louis, Mo. 63141. 25,000; O. Gordon Banks, Executive Director.

Organization of American States, General Secretariat (1890): 1889 F St. N.W., Washington, D.C. 20006. 32 member nations.

Ornithologists' Union, American (1883): c/o National Museum of Natural History, Smithsonian Institution, Washington, D.C. 20560. 4,000; Frances C. James, President.

ORT Federation, American (1922): 817 Broadway, New York, N.Y. 10003. 160,000; Donald H. Klein, Executive Vice President.

Osteopathic Association, American (1897): 212 E. Ohio St., Chicago, Ill. 60611-3269. 30,000; John Perrin, Executive Director.

Overeaters Anonymous (1960): P.O. Box 92870, Los Angeles, Calif. 90009. 100,000.

Parents Without Partners (1957): 8807 Colesville Rd., Silver Springs, Md. 20910. 209,729; Maurine McKinley, Executive Director.

Parks & Conservation Association, National (1919): 1701 18th St. N.W., Washington, D.C. 20009. 55,000; Paul C. Pritchard, President.

Pathologists, American Association of (1976): 9650 Rockville Pike, Bethesda, Md. 20814.

2,400; Dr. Kenneth M. Endicott, Executive Officer.

**Petroleum Geologists, American Association of** (1917): P.O. Box 979, Tulsa, Okla. 74101-0979. 44,000; Fred A. Dix, Executive Director.

**Pharmaceutical Association, American** (1852): 2215 Constitution Ave. N.W., Washington, D.C. 20037. 50,000; Dr. John F. Schlegel, President.

**Philatelic Society, American** (1886): P.O. Box 8000, State College, Pa. 16803. 53,000; Keith A. Wagner, Executive Director.

**Philosophical Society, American** (1743): 104 S. 5th St., Philadelphia, Pa. 19106. 600; Herman H. Goldstine, Executive Officer.

**Photogrammetry and Remote Sensing, American Society for** (1934): 210 Little Falls St., Falls Church, Va. 22046. 8,000; William D. French, Executive Director and Secretary-Treasurer.

**Photographic Society of America** (1933): 2005 Walnut St., Philadelphia, Pa. 19103. 15,500.

**Photography, International Center of** (1974): 1130 Fifth Ave., New York, N.Y. 10128. Cornell Capa, Director.

**Physical Society, American** (1899): 335 E. 45th St., New York, N.Y. 10017. 37,000; W. W. Havens, Jr., Executive Secretary.

**Physical Therapy Association, American (APTA)** (1921): 1111 N. Fairfax St., Alexandria, Va. 22314. Royce Noland, Executive Director.

**Physics, American Institute of** (1931): 335 E. 45th St., New York, N.Y. 10017. 75,000; H. William Koch, Executive Director.

**Planetary Society, The** (1979): 65 N. Catalina Ave., Pasadena, Calif. 91106. 110,000; Louis Friedman, Executive Director.

**Planned Parenthood Federation of America** (1916): 810 Seventh Ave., New York, N.Y. 10019. 187 affiliates.

**Plastics Engineers, Society of** (1942): 14 Fairfield Dr., Brookfield Center, Conn. 06805. 25,000; Robert D. Forger, Executive Director.

**Police, American Federation of** (1966): Records Center, 1100 N.E. 125th St., North Miami, Fla. 33161. 55,000; Gerald S. Arenberg, Executive Director.

*****Police and Fire Fighters Association** (1961): 1000 Connecticut Ave. N.W., Suite 9, Washington, D.C. 20036.

**Police Hall of Fame, American** (1960): 14600 S. Tamiami Trail, North Port, Fla. 33596. 55,000; Chief Robert Ferguson, President.

**Political and Social Science, American Academy of** (1889): 3937 Chestnut St., Philadelphia, Pa. 19104. Marvin E. Wolfgang, President.

**Political Science, Academy of** (1880): 2852 Broadway, New York, N.Y. 10025. 11,000; C. Lowell Harriss, Executive Director.

**Powder Metallurgy Institute, American** (1958): 105 College Rd. East, Princeton, N.J. 08540. 2,400; Kempton H. Roll, Executive Director.

*****Practical Nurse Education and Service, National Association for** (1941): 10801 Peartree Lane, Suite 151, St. Louis, Mo. 63074.

**Press Club, National** (1908): National Press Bldg., Washington, D.C. 20045. 4,500; Mary Kay Quinlan, President.

**Professional Engineers, National Society of** (1934): 1420 King St., Alexandria, Va. 22314. 75,000; Donald G. Weinert, Executive Director.

**Psychiatric Association, American** (1844): 1400 K St. N.W., Washington, D.C. 20005. 32,270; Robert O. Pasnau, M.D., President.

**Psychoanalytic Association, The American** (1911): 309 E. 49th St., New York, N.Y. 10017. 3,000 analysts; Dr. Edward Joseph, President.

**Psychological Association, American** (1892): 1200 17th St. N.W., Washington, D.C. 20036. 63,000; Leonard D. Goodstein, Ph.D., Executive Officer.

**Public Health Association, American** (1872): 1015 15th St. N.W., Washington, D.C. 20005. 30,201; William H. McBeath, M.D., Executive Director.

**Puppeteers of America** (1937): 5 Cricklewood Path, Pasadena, Calif. 91107. Gayle Schluter, Membership Officer.

**Quality Control, The American Society for** (1946): 230 W. Wells St., Milwaukee, Wis. 53203. 50,000; Sandra J. Edson, Executive Director.

**Railroads, Association of American** (1934): 50 F St. N.W., Washington, D.C. 20001. William H. Dempsey, President.

**Recording Arts and Sciences, National Academy of** (1958): 303 N. Glenoaks Blvd., Suite M-140 Burbank, Calif. 91502. 7,300; C. Michael Greene, National President.

**Red Cross, American** (1881): 17th and D Sts. N.W., Washington, D.C. 20006. Over 2,900 chapters; Richard F. Schubert, President.

**Rehabilitation Association, National** (1925): 633 S. Washington St., Alexandria, Va. 22314. 17,000; David L. Mills, Executive Director.

**Research and Enlightenment, Association for** (1931): 67th St. & Atlantic Ave. (P.O. Box 595), Virginia Beach, Va. 23451. 60,000; Charles Thomas Cayce, President.

**Reserve Officers Association of the United States** (1922): 1 Constitution Ave. N.E., Washington, D.C. 20002. 125,000; MG Evan L. Hultman, AUS (Ret.), National Executive Director.

**Retarded Citizens, Association for** (1950): 2501 Avenue J, Arlington, Tex. 76006. 1,300 units; Alan Abeson, National Executive Director.

**Retired Federal Employees, National Association of** (1921): 1533 New Hampshire Ave. N.W., Washington, D.C. 20036. 495,000; L. J. Andolsek, President.

**Retired Persons, American Association of** (1958): 1909 K St. N.W., Washington, D.C. 20049. 22,000,000; Cyril F. Brickfield, Executive Director.

**Reye's Syndrome Foundation, National** (1974): 426 N. Lewis St., Bryan, Ohio 43506. John E. Freudenberger, President.

**RID-USA (Remove Intoxicated Drivers)** (1978): Box 520, Schenectady, N.Y. 12301. Over 150 chapters; Doris Aiken, President.

**Rifle Association of America, National** (1871): 1600 Rhode Island Ave. N.W., Washington, D.C. 20036. 3,000,000; G. Ray Arnett, Executive Vice President.

**Right to Life, National Committee** (1973): 419 7th St. N.W., Washington, D.C. 20004. Dr. David N. O'Steen, Executive Director.

**Rotary International** (1905): 1600 Ridge Ave., Evanston, Ill. 60201. 1,000,000; Philip H. Lindsey, General Secretary.

**Safety Council, National** (1913): 444 N. Michigan Ave., Chicago, Ill. 60611. Robert W. O'Brien, Director of Public Relations.

**Salvation Army, The** (1865): 799 Bloomfield Ave., Verona, N.J. 07044. 420,971; Col. James Osborne, National Chief Secretary.

**SANE, Committee for a SANE Nuclear Policy** (1957): 711 G St. S.E., Washington, D.C. 20003. 140,000; David Cortright, Executive Director.

**Save Our Shores, Inc.** (1969): P.O. Box 103, North Quincy, Mass. 02171. 50,000; Clara Yeomans, President.

**Save the Children Federation** (1932): P.O. Box

5403, Brady Station, Little Rock, Ark. 72215. 10, 700; Jane Alexander, Administrative Coordinator.

**Save-the-Redwoods League** (1918): 114 Sansome St., San Francisco, Calif. 94104. 40,000; John B. Dewitt, Executive Director.

**\*Savings Institutions, National Council of** (1920): 1101 15th St. N.W., Suite 400, Washington, D.C. 20005.

**Science, American Association for the Advancement of** (1848): 1333 H St. N.W., Washington, D.C. 20005. 136,000; Carol L. Rogers, Communications and Membership.

**Science Fiction Association, American** (1954); Box 9010, Scottsdale, Ariz. 85252. 26,200; James L. Stone, Executive Vice President.

**Science Fiction Society, World** (1939): Box 1270, Kendall Sq. Sta., Cambridge, Mass. 02142. 5, 000; Donald E. Eastlake, Chairman, Standing Committee.

**Science Writers, Inc., National Association of** (1934): P.O. Box 294, Greenlawn, N.Y. 11740. 1,230; Philip M. Boffey, President.

**Scientists, Federation of American (FAS)** (1945): 307 Massachusetts Ave. N.E., Washington, D.C. 20002. 5,000; Jeremy J. Stone, Executive Director.

**Scrabble Crossword Game Players** (1972): 4320 Veterans Memorial Highway, Holbrook, N.Y., 11741. 7,000; James A. Houle, President.

**Screen Actors Guild** (1933): 7065 Hollywood Blvd., Hollywood, Calif. 90028. Patty Duke, President.

**Sculpture Society, National** (1893): 15 E. 26th St., New York, N.Y. 10010. 350; Claire A. Stein, Executive Director.

**Seeing Eye** (1929): P.O. Box 375M, Morristown, N.J. 07960. Stuart Grout, President.

**Senior Citizens, National Alliance of** (1974): 2525 Wilson Blvd., Arlington, Va. 22201. 770,000; C.C. Clinkscales III, National Director.

**Shrine of North America (Shriners Hospitals)** (1872): Box 25356, Tampa, Fla. 33622. 900, 000; Charles G. Cumpstone, Jr., Executive Director.

**Sierra Club** (1892): 730 Polk St., San Francisco, Calif. 94109. 374,000; Douglas Wheeler, Executive Director.

**Small Business Association, National** (1937): 1155 15th St. N.W., Washington, D.C. 20005. 25,000; George A. Abbott, President.

**Social Welfare, National Conference on** (1873): 1730 M St. N.W., Suite 911, Washington, D.C. 20036. 4,000; Joyce M. Black, President.

**Social Work Education, Council on** (1919): 1744 R St. N.W., Washington, D.C. 20009. 5,000; Eunice Shatz, Ph.D., Executive Director.

**Social Workers, National Association of** (1955): 7981 Eastern Ave., Silver Spring, Md. 20910. Mark G. Battle, Executive Director.

**Sociological Association, American** (1905): 1722 N St. N.W., Washington, D.C. 20036. 12,000; William V. D'Antonio, Executive Officer.

**Soil Conservation Society of America** (1945): 7515 N.E. Ankeny Rd., Ankeny, Iowa 50021. 14, 000; Walt Peechatka, Executive Vice President.

**Songwriters Guild of America, The** (1931): 276 Fifth Ave., New York, N.Y. 10001. 4,200; Lewis M. Bachman, Executive Director.

**Sons of Italy in America, Order** (1905): 219 E St. N.E., Washington, D.C. 20002. 100,000; Michal A. Caira, National Executive Director.

**Sons of the American Revolution, National Society of the** (1889): 1000 S. 4th St., Louisville, Ky.

40203. 23,500; Wayne R. Wiedman, Executive Secretary.

**Soroptimist International of the Americas** (1921): 1616 Walnut St., Philadelphia, Pa. 19103. 40, 000; Elaine Halford, Executive Director.

**\*Southern Christian Leadership Conference** (1957): 334 Auburn Ave. N.E., Atlanta, Ga. 30303. 1,000,000; 350 chapters, 260 affiliated organizations; Dr. Joseph E. Lowery, President.

**Space Education Association, U.S.** (1973): 746 Turnpike Rd., Elizabethtown, Pa. 17022-1161. 1, 000; Stephen M. Cobaugh, International President.

**Special Olympics** (1968): 1350 New York Ave. N.W., Suite 500, Washington, D.C., 20005. 1, 000,000; Eunice Kennedy Shriver, Board Chairman.

**Speech-Language-Hearing Association, American** (1925): 10801 Rockville Pike, Rockville, Md. 20852. 46,000; Frederick T. Spahr, Executive Director.

**Sports Car Club of America** (1944): 9033 E. Easter Place, Englewood, Colo. 80112. 34,000; John Clagett, Communications Manager.

**State Garden Clubs, Inc., National Council of** (1929): 4401 Magnolia Ave., St. Louis, Mo. 63110. 308,623; Mrs. John N. Fehrer, President.

**State Governments, The Council of** (1933): P.O. Box 11910, Iron Works Pike, Lexington, Ky. 40578. All state officials, all 50 states; Carl W. Stenberg, Executive Director.

**Statistical Association, American** (1839): 806 15th St. N.W., Washington, D.C. 20005. 15,000; Fred C. Leone, Executive Director.

**\*Student Association, United States** (1978): 1012 14th St. N.W., Washington, D.C. 20005.

**Students Against Drunken Driving (SADD)** (1981): 10812 Ashfield Rd., Adelphi, Md., 20783. 175 local groups; Melissa Kinsley, Chairwoman.

**Surgeons, American College of** (1913): 55 E. Erie, St., Chicago, Ill. 60611. 47,800; C. Rollins Hanlon, Director.

**Surveying and Mapping, American Congress on** (1941): 210 Little Falls St., Falls Church, Va. 22046. 10,700; Marshall W. Davies, Acting Executive Director.

**Symphony Orchestra League, American** (1942): 633 E St. N.W., Washington, D.C. 20004. 4,300; Catherine French, Chief Executive Officer.

**TASH: The Association for Persons with Severe Handicaps** (1973): 7010 Roosevelt Way, N.E., Seattle, Wash. 98115. 5,500; Liz Lindley, Executive Director.

**Tax Foundation, Inc.** (1937): One Thomas Circle N.W., Suite 500, Washington, D.C. 20005. 1,000; Robert C. Brown, President.

**Teachers, American Federation of** (1916): 555 New Jersey Ave. N.W., Washington, D.C., 20001. 630,000; Albert Shanker, President.

**Television Arts and Sciences, National Academy of** (1948): 110 W. 57th St., New York, N.Y., 10019. 15,000; John Cannon, President.

**Testing & Materials, American Society for** (1898): 1916 Race St., Philadelphia, Pa. 19103. 30,000; Joseph J. O'Grady, President.

**Theatre Guild** (1919): 226 W. 47th St., New York, N.Y. 10036. 105,000; Jesse Gross, Managing Director.

**Theosophical Society in America, The** (1875): P.O. Box 270, Wheaton, Ill. 60189-0270. 4,900; Mrs. Dora Kunz, President.

**Toastmasters International** (1924): P.O. Box 10400, 2200 N. Grand Ave., Santa Ana, Calif.,

**92711. 110,000;** Terrence C. McCann, Executive Director.

**Toughlove** (1977): P.O. Box 1069, Doylestown, Pa. 18901. 1200 local groups; Phyllis and David York, Founders.

**Travel Agents, American Society of (ASTA)** (1931): 4400 MacArthur Blvd. N.W., Washington, D.C. 20007. 22,000; Francis H. Goranin, Chairman.

**Travelers Aid Services** (1905/1982); 2 Lafayette St., New York, N.Y. 10007. Lucy N. Friedman, Executive Director. (Result of merger of Travelers Aid Society of New York and Victim Services Agency in 1982).

**UFOs, National Investigations Committee on** (1957): 14617 Victory Blvd., Suite 4, Van Nuys, Calif. 91411. 55 countries; Dr. Frank E. Stranges, Ph.D., President.

**UNICEF, U.S. Committee for** (1947): 331 E. 38th St., New York, N.Y. 10016. 2,500,000 volunteers; Lawrence E. Bruce, Jr., President.

**United Negro College Fund Inc.** (1944): 500 E. 62nd St., New York, N.Y. 10021. Christopher F. Edley, President and C.E.O.

**University Foundation, International** (1973): 1301 S. Noland Rd., Independence, Mo. 64055. 12,000; Dr. John Wayne Johnston, President.

**University Women, American Association of** (1881): 2401 Virginia Ave. N.W., Washington, D.C. 20037. 175,000; Anne L. Bryant, Executive Director.

**Urban League, National** (1910): 500 E. 62nd St., New York, N.Y. 10021. 116; James D. Williams, Director of Communications.

**U.S. Committee Against Nuclear War** (1982): 401 C. St. N.E., Suite 303, Washington, D.C. 20002; William C. Oldaker, Executive Director.

**\*USO (United Service Organizations)** (1941): 601 Indiana Ave. N.W., Washington, D.C. 20036.

**Variety Clubs International** (1927): 1540 Broadway, New York, N.Y. 10036. 15,000; John J. Burlinson, Jr., Executive Director.

**Veterans Committee, American (AVC)** (1944): 1735 DeSales St. N.W., 4th Floor, Washington, D.C. 20036. 25,000; June A. Willenz, Executive Director.

**Veterans of Foreign Wars of the U.S.** (1899): V.F.W. Bldg., 34th and Broadway, Kansas City, Mo. 64111. V.F.W. and Auxiliary, 2,685,000; Howard E. Vander Clute, Jr., Adjutant General.

**Veterinary Medical Association, American** (1863): 930 N. Meacham Rd., Schaumburg, Ill. 60196. 42,000; Dr. A. Freeman, Executive Vice President.

**Visually Handicapped, Division for the** (1952): The Council for Exceptional Children, 1920 Association Dr., Reston, Va. 22091. 1,000; Vincent McVeigh, President.

**War Resisters League** (1923): 339 Lafayette St., New York, N.Y. 10012. 18,000; Linnea Capps, Chairwoman.

**Washington Legal Foundation** (1976): 1705 N St. N.W., Washington, D.C. 20036. 200,000; Daniel J. Popeo, General Counsel.

**\*Water Quality Association** (1974): 4151 Naperville Rd., Lisle, Ill. 60532.

**Water Resources Association, American** (1964): 5410 Grosvenor Lane, Suite 220, Bethesda, Md. 20814. 3,000; Kenneth D. Reid, Executive Director.

**Welding Society, American** (1919): 550 N.W. LeJeune Rd., Miami, Fla. 33126, 32,000; Paul W. Ramsey, Executive Director.

**Whale Protection Fund** (1976): 624 Ninth St. N.W., Washington, D.C., 20001. 450,000; Natasha Atkins, Director.

**Wildlife Federation, National** (1936): 1412 16th St. N.W., Washington, D.C. 20036. 4,500,000; Jay D. Hair, Executive Vice President.

**Wildlife Fund, World** (1961): 1255 23rd St. N.W., Washington, D.C. 20037. 220,000; William Reilly, President.

**Woman's Christian Temperance Union, National** (1874): 1730 Chicago Ave., Evanston, Ill. 60201. 200,000; Martha G. Edgar, President.

**Women, National Organization for (NOW)** (1966): 1401 New York Ave. N.W., Suite 800, Washington, D.C. 20005-2102. 200,000; Eleanor Smeal, President.

**Women's American ORT** (1927): 315 Park Ave. South, New York, N.Y. 10010. 145,000; Dr. Marsha Firestone, Executive Director.

**Women's Clubs, General Federation of** (1890): 1734 N St., N.W., Washington, D.C. 20036. 500,000; Phyllis V. Roberts, International President.

**Women's Educational and Industrial Union** (1877): 356 Boylston St., Boston, Mass. 02116. 2,200; Elizabeth C. Whitman, Executive Director.

**Women's International League for Peace and Freedom** (1915): 1213 Race St., Philadelphia, Pa. 19107. 15,000; Jane Midgley, Executive Director.

**Women Strike for Peace** (1961): 145 S. 13th St., Philadelphia, Pa. 19107. 9,000; Ethel Taylor, National Coordinator.

**World Future Society** (1966): 4916 St. Elmo Ave., Bethesda, Md. 75231. 25,000; Edward Cornish, President.

**World Health, American Association for** (1951): 515 22nd St. N.W., Washington, D.C. 20037. 500; Burl R. Wagenheim, Acting Executive Director.

**World Peace, International Association of Educators for** (1969): P.O. Box 3282, Mastin Lake Station, Huntsville, Ala. 35810. 20,000; Dr. Charles Mercieca, Executive Vice President.

**YMCA of the USA** (1844): 101 N. Wacker Dr., Chicago, Ill. 60606. 13,500,000; Solon B. Cousins, National Executive Director.

**Young Engineers & Scientists of America Foundation, Inc.** (1959): P.O. Box 9066, Phoenix, Ariz. 85068. 250 chapters; Americo Lazzari, P.E., Board Chairman.

**Young Women's Christian Association of the U.S.A.** (1858 in U.S.A., 1855 in England): 726 Broadway, New York, N.Y. 10003. 2,030,922; Jane Pinkerton, Director of Communications/PR.

**Youth Hostels, Inc., American** (1934): P.O. Box 37613, Washington, D.C. 20013-7613. 100,000.

**Zero Population Growth** (1968): 1601 Connecticut Ave. N.W., Washington, D.C. 20009. 15,000; Susan Weber, Executive Director.

**Zionist Organization of America** (1897): ZOA House, 4 E. 34th St., New York, N.Y. 10016. 135,000; Paul I. Flacks, Executive Vice President and National Secretary.

**Zoological Parks and Aquariums, American Association of** (1924): Oglebay Park, Wheeling, W. Va. 26003. 4,350; Robert O. Wagner, Executive Director.

**Zoologists, American Society of** (1890): Box 2739, California Lutheran Univ., Thousand Oaks, Calif. 91360. 4,300; William R. Dawson, President.

# EDUCATION

## How Does a Selective College Use Tests?

### By Edward B. Wall

In June 1980 in Portsmouth, New Hampshire, I attended the annual meeting of a group of admission officers called the "Expendables," which simply means the small colleges in New England which are not members of the so-called "Ivy Group."

The major item on the agenda was the subject of testing, which was only natural considering the present controversy about truth in testing as well as state and federal legislation pending and already in effect. During the course of that particular session one of my counterparts said: *"The problem is not the tests themselves, nor is it the legislation, but rather the use and misuse of tests. I think we should go on record as a group with a public statement on how we use tests in the admission process."* Knowing full well that it would take forever for the group to agree on such a statement, let alone write one, I decided to share with counselors, counterparts, friends, prospective students, and their parents some thoughts on how we used tests in the admission process at Amherst.

I do not think that we *misuse* them—but it is the misuse of tests, and nothing else, that is behind the present flap over testing.

**First,** as we have said so many times before, tests are rarely controlling in our admission decisions. How could they be, considering the fact that we seek the widest possible variety of talents, interests, achievement, socio-economic, racial and ethnic backgrounds, personalities, and career goals in a class of only 375—which is selected from an applicant pool better than ten times that size, where all but a couple of hundred applicants are academically qualified for admission and could do the work of the college if there were room?

**Second,** we have much higher expectations on test results for students who come from educated homes and so-called "advantaged" public schools as well as from some of the better private schools. Tests are always looked at in the light of a student's educational, linguistic, cultural, and socioeconomic background. There is no reason to expect someone from an "uneducated" home, with few or no books or periodicals, from a bilingual home where English may be the applicant's second language or from a home where no English is spoken at all, or from an inferior school with limited facilities or opportunities to do well on these **educationally, linguistically, culturally, and socio-economically biased examinations.**

**Third,** it is our feeling that unless a student has a learning disability (and those who have should be permitted to take the tests untimed) or comes from a bilingual home, these tests separate readers from non-readers, i.e., students who read a lot for fun from those who don't. We concede that there are

This article is reprinted with permission of the author from "Behind the Scenes: An Inside Look at the Selective College Admissions Process" by Edward B. Wall, Independent Educational Counselor and former Dean of Admission, Amherst College.

some students who are slow readers and others who freeze under the pressure of time, but we feel that they are rare. We also feel that test results, particularly those of the SAT and English Composition Achievement Test, may indicate little more about a student than the fact that he or she is good at taking these kinds of tests.

**Fourth,** while SATs do tell us something about a student's ability to read with understanding, to reason with words and numbers, and to understand quantitative relationships, such tests tell us nothing about *"motivation, drive, attitude, imagination, or the other skills and interests that are"* in the words of Fred Glimp, former Dean of Admission at Harvard, *"vital to the academic process."* **Achievement Tests,** however, are different, and, in conjunction with the SAT, we think they tell us many things about a student's personality characteristics, such as drive and motivation (or lack of those qualities), the kind of teaching in his or her school, and his or her adaptability to new pressure situations.

**An Observation:** If students watched less television, read more good books for fun, were forced to read more difficult books in their English classes and to write critically more often and at length about what they have read with immediate feedback on such writing guaranteed, there is no question in our minds that taking these standardized tests would be much less traumatic, and the results more satisfying to the takers themselves. Instead, to quote Fred Glimp again, *"The high school student today often ends up focusing all of his energies on the task of performing well on such examinations to the neglect of those very qualities (understanding, humility, perspective, and a sense of humor) which are generally thought to render an education negotiable in life."*

**Fifth,** we agree with Emery Walker, Dean of Admission Emeritus of Claremont-McKenna and Harvey Mudd College, who, near the end of his career, waged a campaign for a different reporting system for the College Board test results. In a motion presented at the Annual Meeting of the College Board on Tuesday, October 28, 1980, he said: *"The scores take on an importance they don't deserve because of the human need for simple answers"* and goes on to say, *"I think reporting the scores as error-range is the best idea. A 500 should be reported as 470-530. This says, 'Somewhere in there is your score;' it diminishes the impression of precision and, in turn the assumption of validity. Kids will be less elated over small gains in scores and less disappointed over small losses. The simplicity of a single number leads people to think they know exactly what it means and discourages them from trying to find out; an error-range report will send some people to the literature to learn what the 60-point spread means."* We wholeheartedly agree!

I suspect that it is ultimately our fault that all of this has happened, but if all of us published open and honest statistical reports on our entering classes—which only a few of us do—and read carefully the material published by the College Board and Educational Testing Service, the kids themselves, we ourselves, and the tests themselves would not be under the fire they are at the present time. In a way, all of us, except the kids, deserve what has happened, because we have brought this controversy upon ourselves. And when a large segment of the public thinks and feels that it is being victimized, the designers, distributors, and users of the tests must face the music and be held accountable for their sins by the takers of these tests.

It is how tests are used that matters. Quality of program, quality of performance in that program, and how that is corroborated by teachers, counselors, and heads of schools will continue to be the first items we consider in an application.

Tests are important, too, but they will control what we do only if an applicant's academic program is unchallenging and academic performance is poor or mediocre. Even then, tests will always be looked at in the light of his/her educational, linguistic, cultural, and socio-economic background.

In the last analysis, it must always be borne in mind that, no matter what a highly selective college does in its admission process, it will always be forced for lack of room to deny admission to many well-qualified applicants, by whatever measures that quality is determined. If parents and students could only realize that what matters is what a student does wherever he/she goes to college and not *where* he/she goes, there would be little or no controversy over testing.

## State Compulsory School Attendance Laws

| State | Enactment[1] | Age limits | State | Enactment[1] | Age limits |
|---|---|---|---|---|---|
| Alabama | 1915 | 7–16 | Montana | 1883 | 7–16 |
| Alaska | 1929 | 7–16 | Nebraska | 1887 | 7–16 |
| Arizona | 1899 | 8–16 | Nevada | 1873 | 7–17 |
| Arkansas | 1909 | 7–15 | New Hampshire | 1871 | 6–16 |
| California | 1874 | 6–16 | New Jersey | 1875 | 6–16 |
| Colorado | 1889 | 7–16 | New Mexico | 1891 | 8–17 |
| Connecticut | 1872 | 7–16 | New York | 1874 | 6–16 |
| Delaware | 1907 | 6–16 | North Carolina | 1907 | 7–16 |
| D. C. | 1864 | 7–16 | North Dakota | 1883 | 7–16 |
| Florida | 1915 | 7–16 | Ohio | 1877 | 6–18 |
| Georgia | 1916 | 7–16 | Oklahoma | 1907 | 7–16 |
| Hawaii | 1896 | 6–18 | Oregon | 1889 | 7–18 |
| Idaho | 1887 | 7–16 | Pennsylvania | 1895 | 8–17 |
| Illinois | 1883 | 7–16 | Rhode Island | 1883 | 7–16 |
| Indiana | 1897 | 7–16 | South Carolina | 1915 | 7–16 |
| Iowa | 1902 | 7–16 | South Dakota | 1883 | 7–16 |
| Kansas | 1874 | 7–16 | Tennessee | 1905 | 7–16 |
| Kentucky | 1896 | 7–16 | Texas | 1915[2] | 7–17 |
| Louisiana | 1910 | 7–15 | Utah | 1890 | 6–18 |
| Maine | 1875 | 7–17 | Vermont | 1867 | 7–16 |
| Maryland | 1902 | 6–16 | Virginia | 1908 | 6–17 |
| Massachusetts | 1852 | 6–16 | Washington | 1871 | 8–18 |
| Michigan | 1871 | 6–16 | West Virginia | 1897 | 7–16 |
| Minnesota | 1885 | 7–16 | Wisconsin | 1879 | 7–16 |
| Mississippi | 1918 | 6–14 | Wyoming | 1876 | 7–16 |
| Missouri | 1905 | 7–16 | | | |

1. Date of enactment of first compulsory attendance law. 2. A compulsory school attendance law was contained in a law of 1873 establishing free public schools. However, the provision was omitted in superseding legislation passed in 1876. *Source:* Department of Education, National Center for Educational Statistics.

## Persons Not Enrolled in School, October 1985

### (in thousands)

| Age | Population | Total not enrolled | | High school graduate | | Not high school graduate (dropouts)[1] | |
|---|---|---|---|---|---|---|---|
| | | Number | Percent | Number | Percent | Number | Percent |
| 14 and 15 years | 7,505 | 143 | 1.9 | 10 | 0.1 | 132 | 1.8 |
| 16 and 17 years | 7,260 | 606 | 8.3 | 101 | 1.4 | 505 | 7.0 |
| 18 and 19 years | 7,204 | 3,488 | 48.4 | 2,457 | 34.1 | 1,031 | 14.3 |
| 20 and 21 years | 7,679 | 4,971 | 64.7 | 3,907 | 50.9 | 1,064 | 13.9 |
| 22 to 24 years | 12,239 | 10,171 | 83.1 | 8,448 | 69.0 | 1,724 | 14.1 |

1. Persons who are not enrolled in school and who are not high school graduates are considered dropouts. *Source:* Department of Commerce, Bureau of the Census.

## School Enrollment, October 1985
### (in thousands)

| Age | White Enrolled | White Percent | Black Enrolled | Black Percent | Spanish origin[1] Enrolled | Spanish origin[1] Percent | All races Enrolled | All races Percent |
|---|---|---|---|---|---|---|---|---|
| 3 and 4 years | 2,250 | 38.6 | 469 | 42.7 | 213 | 27.0 | 2,801 | 38.9 |
| 5 and 6 years | 5,437 | 96.4 | 1,030 | 95.7 | 662 | 94.5 | 6,697 | 96.1 |
| 7 to 9 years | 7,892 | 99.3 | 1,499 | 98.4 | 1,000 | 98.4 | 9,740 | 99.1 |
| 10 to 13 years | 10,572 | 99.3 | 2,050 | 99.5 | 1,322 | 99.4 | 13,109 | 99.3 |
| 14 and 15 years | 6,007 | 98.1 | 1,106 | 97.9 | 606 | 96.1 | 7,362 | 98.1 |
| 16 and 17 years | 5,449 | 91.6 | 994 | 91.7 | 562 | 84.5 | 6,654 | 91.7 |
| 18 and 19 years | 3,105 | 52.4 | 472 | 44.1 | 238 | 41.8 | 3,716 | 51.6 |
| 20 and 21 years | 2,318 | 36.1 | 298 | 27.7 | 137 | 24.0 | 2,708 | 35.3 |
| 22 to 24 years | 1,744 | 17.0 | 215 | 13.7 | 125 | 11.6 | 2,068 | 16.9 |
| 25 to 29 years | 1,635 | 9.2 | 192 | 7.4 | 120 | 6.6 | 1,942 | 9.2 |
| 30 to 34 years | 1,043 | 6.2 | 119 | 5.1 | 83 | 5.7 | 1,218 | 6.1 |
| Total | 47,452 | 47.8 | 8,444 | 50.9 | 5,070 | 47.7 | 58,013 | 48.3 |

1. Persons of Spanish origin may be of any race. NOTE: Figures include persons enrolled in nursery school, kindergarten, elementary school, high school, and college. *Source:* Department of Commerce, Bureau of the Census.

## School Enrollment by Grade, Control, and Race
### (in thousands)

| Grade level and type of control | White Oct. 1985[3] | White Oct. 1980[4] | White Oct. 1970 | Black Oct. 1985[3] | Black Oct. 1980[4] | Black Oct. 1970 | All races[1] Oct. 1985[3] | All races[1] Oct. 1980[4] | All races[1] Oct. 1970 |
|---|---|---|---|---|---|---|---|---|---|
| Nursery school: Public | 617 | 432 | 198 | 212 | 180 | 129 | 854 | 633 | 333 |
| Private | 1,470 | 1,205 | 695 | 120 | 115 | 49 | 1,637 | 1,354 | 763 |
| Kindergarten: Public | 2,545 | 2,172 | 2,233 | 562 | 440 | 374 | 3,221 | 2,690 | 2,674 |
| Private | 515 | 423 | 473 | 63 | 50 | 53 | 594 | 486 | 536 |
| Grades 1–8: Public | 18,817 | 19,743 | 24,923 | 4,131 | 4,058 | 4,668 | 23,803 | 24,398 | 30,001 |
| Private | 2,776 | 2,768 | 3,715 | 175 | 202 | 200 | 3,063 | 3,051 | 3,949 |
| Grades 9–12: Public | 10,258 | 12,056[2] | 11,599 | 2,068 | 2,200[2] | 1,794 | 12,764 | 14,556[2] | 13,545 |
| Private | 1,120 | — | 1,124 | 63 | — | 41 | 1,215 | — | 1,170 |
| College: Public | 7,131 | 8,875[2] | 5,168 | 860 | 1,007[2] | 422 | 8,379 | 10,180[2] | 5,699 |
| Private | 2,203 | — | 1,591 | 190 | — | 100 | 2,483 | — | 1,714 |
| Total: Public | 39,368 | — | 44,121 | 7,834 | — | 7,387 | 49,021 | — | 52,225 |
| Private | 8,084 | — | 7,598 | 612 | — | 443 | 8,992 | — | 8,132 |
| Grand Total | 47,452 | 47,673 | 51,719 | 8,446 | 8,251 | 7,830 | 58,013 | 57,348 | 60,357 |

1. Includes persons of Spanish origin. 2. Total public and private. Breakdown not available. 3. Estimates controlled to 1980 census base. 4. Estimates controlled to 1970 census base. *Source:* Department of Commerce, Bureau of the Census.

## Federal Funds for Some Major Programs for Education, Fiscal Year 1987[1]

| Program | Amount in thousands | Program | Amount in thousands |
|---|---|---|---|
| Elementary–secondary | | Higher education facilities | 23,000 |
| Educationally disadvantaged | $ 3,688,163 | Aid for institutional development | 19,263 |
| Special programs | 75,000 | Vocational education | 408,122 |
| Bilingual education | 142,951 | Adult basic and secondary education | 104,000 |
| School assistance in federally | | Education for the handicapped | |
| affected areas | 533,000 | State grant program | 1,135,145 |
| Higher education | | Preschool incentive grants | 29,000 |
| Program development | 19,263 | Special populations | 47,430 |
| Student assistance | | Training and information | 57,025 |
| Pell grants | 1,435,200 | All other | 34,500 |
| Work study/grants | — | Indian education | |
| Direct loans to students | 25,000 | Education research and improvement | 70,231 |
| Special programs for the disadvantaged | — | Total | $7,846,293 |

1. Estimated outlay for fiscal year 1986. *Source: Budget of the United States Government,* Fiscal Year 1987.

# High School and College Graduates

| Year of graduation | High School | | | College[1] | | |
|---|---|---|---|---|---|---|
| | Men | Women | Total | Men | Women | Total |
| 1900 | 38,075 | 56,808 | 94,883 | 22,173 | 5,237 | 27,410 |
| 1910 | 63,676 | 92,753 | 156,429 | 28,762 | 8,437 | 37,199 |
| 1920 | 123,684 | 187,582 | 311,266 | 31,980 | 16,642 | 48,622 |
| 1929–30 | 300,376 | 366,528 | 666,904 | 73,615 | 48,869 | 122,484 |
| 1939–40 | 578,718 | 642,757 | 1,221,475 | 109,546 | 76,954 | 186,500 |
| 1949–50 | 570,700 | 629,000 | 1,199,700 | 328,841 | 103,217 | 432,058 |
| 1959–60 | 898,000 | 966,000 | 1,864,000 | 254,063 | 138,377 | 392,440 |
| 1964–65 | 1,314,000 | 1,351,000 | 2,665,000 | 316,286 | 213,717 | 530,003 |
| 1965–66 | 1,308,000 | 1,324,000 | 2,632,000 | 328,853 | 222,194 | 551,047 |
| 1966–67 | 1,332,000 | 1,348,000 | 2,679,000 | 353,349 | 237,198 | 590,547 |
| 1967–68 | 1,341,000 | 1,361,000 | 2,702,000 | 390,507 | 276,203 | 666,710 |
| 1968–69 | 1,402,000 | 1,427,000 | 2,829,000 | 444,380 | 319,805 | 764,185 |
| 1969–70 | 1,433,000 | 1,463,000 | 2,896,000 | 484,174 | 343,060 | 827,234 |
| 1970–71 | 1,456,000 | 1,487,000 | 2,943,000 | 511,138 | 366,538 | 877,676 |
| 1971–72 | 1,490,000 | 1,518,000 | 3,008,000 | 541,313 | 389,371 | 930,684 |
| 1972–73 | 1,501,000 | 1,536,000 | 3,037,000 | 564,680 | 407,700 | 972,380 |
| 1973–74 | 1,515,000 | 1,565,000 | 3,080,000 | 575,843 | 423,749 | 999,592 |
| 1974–75 | 1,541,000 | 1,599,000 | 3,140,000 | 533,797 | 425,052 | 978,849 |
| 1975–76 | 1,554,000 | 1,601,000 | 3,155,000 | 557,817 | 430,578 | 988,395 |
| 1976–77 | 1,548,000 | 1,606,000 | 3,154,000 | 547,919 | 435,989 | 983,908 |
| 1977–78 | 1,535,000 | 1,599,000 | 3,134,000 | 487,000 | 434,000 | 921,000 |
| 1978–79 | 1,531,800 | 1,602,400 | 3,134,200 | 529,996 | 460,242 | 990,238 |
| 1979–80 | 1,500,000 | 1,558,000 | 3,058,000 | 526,327 | 473,221 | 999,548 |
| 1980–81 | 1,483,000 | 1,537,000 | 3,020,000 | 470,000[3] | 465,000[3] | 935,000[3] |
| 1981–82 | 1,474,000 | 1,527,000 | 3,001,000 | 473,000[3] | 480,000[3] | 953,000[3] |
| 1982–83 | 1,438,000[2] | 1,452,000[2] | 2,890,000[2] | 480,000[2][3] | 490,000[2][3] | 970,000[2][3] |

1. Includes bachelor's and first-professional degrees. 2. Preliminary data. 3. Bachelor's degree only. NOTE: Includes graduates from public and private schools. Beginning in 1959–60, figures include Alaska and Hawaii. Because of rounding, details may not add to totals. Most recent data available. *Source:* Department of Education, National Center for Education Statistics.

## Major U.S. College and University Libraries
### (Top 50 based on number of volumes in library)

| Institution | Volumes | Microforms[1] | Institution | Volumes | Microforms[1] |
|---|---|---|---|---|---|
| Harvard | 10,929,899 | 3,728,002 | U of Iowa | 2,661,728 | 2,534,227 |
| Yale | 8,192,144 | 2,144,124 | U of Pittsburgh | 2,583,597 | 1,861,428 |
| U of Illinois | 6,808,048 | 1,991,702 | Pennsylvania State | 2,556,027 | 1,773,368 |
| U of California, Berkeley | 6,610,872 | 3,146,663 | Johns Hopkins | 2,506,132 | 1,441,756 |
| U of Michigan | 5,805,748 | 2,676,077 | U of Kansas | 2,485,748 | 1,568,027 |
| Columbia | 5,459,972 | 3,178,254 | U of Florida | 2,474,542 | 2,743,021 |
| U of Texas | 5,402,357 | 3,403,469 | Rochester | 2,473,305 | 2,524,942 |
| U of California, Los Angeles | 5,365,264 | 3,601,884 | U of Southern California | 2,441,102 | 1,652,813 |
| Stanford | 5,318,153 | 2,920,353 | U of Georgia | 2,415,673 | 3,122,764 |
| Cornell | 4,874,447 | 3,522,702 | SUNY–Buffalo | 2,310,828 | 2,883,232 |
| U of Chicago | 4,660,683 | 1,411,921 | U of Missouri | 2,254,750 | 3,187,381 |
| U of Wisconsin | 4,494,680 | 2,624,474 | Rutgers | 2,218,913 | 2,098,916 |
| U of Washington | 4,416,024 | 4,331,060 | Syracuse | 2,186,470 | 2,592,231 |
| Indiana | 4,365,624 | 1,614,717 | U of Utah | 2,157,104 | 2,076,598 |
| U of Minnesota | 4,229,107 | 2,003,729 | Louisiana State | 2,147,840 | 2,271,965 |
| Ohio State | 3,983,395 | 2,520,652 | U of South Carolina | 2,117,042 | 2,160,360 |
| Princeton | 3,751,967 | 1,845,806 | U of Oklahoma | 2,108,359 | 2,401,278 |
| Duke | 3,458,720 | 1,214,139 | Wayne State | 2,084,110 | 1,554,939 |
| U of Pennsylvania | 3,282,105 | 1,771,609 | U of Massachusetts | 2,068,005 | 1,309,937 |
| North Carolina | 3,184,517 | 2,312,147 | U of Colorado | 2,051,953 | 2,810,799 |
| Northwestern | 3,124,611 | 1,519,982 | Washington U, St. Louis | 2,029,838 | 1,464,768 |
| Michigan State | 3,062,867 | 2,035,637 | U of Hawaii | 2,013,146 | 2,313,410 |
| U of Arizona | 3,049,172 | 2,906,485 | Arizona State | 2,000,762 | 2,075,398 |
| New York | 2,879,338 | 1,823,585 | U of California, Davis | 1,995,437 | 2,105,941 |
| U of Virginia | 2,713,404 | 3,132,566 | MIT | 1,993,922 | 1,500,080 |

1. Includes reels of microfilm and number of microcards, microprint sheets, and microfiches. *Source:* Association of Research Libraries.

# College and University Endowments, 1983-84

## (top 75 in millions of dollars)

| Institution | Endowment (market value) | Voluntary support[1] | Expenditures[2] | Institution | Endowment (market value) | Voluntary support[1] | Expenditures[2] |
|---|---|---|---|---|---|---|---|
| Harvard U | $3,017.6 | $145.6 | $n.a. | U of Minnesota | $181.5 | $66.2 | $669.5 |
| Princeton U | 1,500.0 | 79.4 | 166.5 | Baylor U | 176.0 | 27.0 | 68.8 |
| Yale U | 1,318.6 | 85.4 | 389.0 | Trinity U | 175.8 | 11.1 | 28.7 |
| Stanford U | 1,194.8 | 125.5 | 665.0 | Grinnell C | 174.5 | 11.7 | 18.3 |
| Columbia U | 989.1 | 93.4 | 515.5 | Swarthmore C | 174.4 | 5.0 | 23.5 |
| Massachusetts Inst. of Tech. | 770.2 | 78.3 | 431.0 | George Washington U | 169.8 | 12.1 | 171.0 |
| Washington U | 633.5 | 47.0 | 304.6 | Loyola U of Chicago | 169.0 | 25.4 | 100.9 |
| Rice U | 609.3 | 24.9 | 73.4 | Amherst C | 168.1 | 10.8 | 30.5 |
| U of Rochester | 581.9 | 27.4 | 211.4 | U of Richmond | 163.0 | 11.5 | 26.5 |
| Northwestern U | 578.6 | 46.5 | 295.8 | Baylor C of Medicine | 161.7 | 16.4 | 170.0 |
| Cornell U | 549.4 | 91.9 | 574.2 | Oberlin C | 157.0 | 6.2 | n.a. |
| U of Chicago | 547.6 | 60.3 | 276.2 | U of Kansas | 156.4 | 13.9 | 153.0 |
| Emory U | 535.8 | 21.2 | 159.4 | Texas Christian U | 153.5 | 12.4 | 48.7 |
| New York U | 451.8 | 45.2 | 449.1 | Berea C | 150.3 | 10.3 | 14.7 |
| U of Pennsylvania | 437.1 | 65.9 | 502.2 | Wake Forest U | 145.6 | 12.1 | 115.9 |
| Dartmouth C | 414.1 | 39.9 | 125.3 | Rensselaer Polytechnic Inst. | 144.6 | 19.1 | 99.8 |
| Johns Hopkins U | 393.1 | 57.6 | 399.1 | U of Wisconsin–Madison | 143.3 | 60.7 | 525.4 |
| Rockefeller U | 391.3 | 21.3 | 72.3 | U of Pittsburgh | 142.9 | 13.1 | 322.5 |
| U of Notre Dame | 306.9 | 33.8 | 79.2 | Tulane University | 141.7 | 27.3 | 92.8 |
| Vanderbilt U | 284.4 | 27.5 | 168.9 | Georgetown U | 141.0 | 27.0 | 205.3 |
| U of Southern California | 280.3 | 63.7 | 405.3 | Pomona C | 136.9 | 16.6 | 23.5 |
| California Inst. of Tech. | 275.9 | 38.5 | 115.0 | Lehigh U | 130.1 | 18.3 | 74.0 |
| Duke U | 266.2 | 53.6 | 241.2 | Middlebury C | 128.4 | 4.6 | 27.8 |
| Loyola U, New Orleans | 260.4 | 2.9 | 32.1 | Lafayette C | 117.0 | 9.2 | 25.3 |
| U of Virginia | 256.0 | 35.6 | n.a. | Texas A&M U | 114.1 | 55.9 | 244.4 |
| Case Western Reserve U | 240.6 | 31.3 | 149.9 | U of Nebraska | 112.8 | 21.7 | 288.1 |
| U of Michigan | 237.0 | 55.7 | 575.9 | Boston U | 110.7 | 19.3 | 305.1 |
| Southern Methodist U | 233.7 | 24.3 | 95.6 | Washington State U | 110.3 | 12.5 | n.a. |
| Princeton Theol. Seminary | 233.5 | 2.0 | 11.5 | Thomas Jefferson U | 110.2 | 8.4 | 89.3 |
| Smith C | 222.4 | 19.6 | 39.7 | Brandeis U | 107.2 | 21.7 | 76.1 |
| Wellesley C | 205.1 | 14.9 | 40.4 | U of Washington | 103.9 | 51.2 | 429.6 |
| Brown U | 202.1 | 23.6 | 123.2 | U of Illinois | 103.5 | 70.7 | 786.6 |
| Williams C | 200.0 | 12.9 | 32.5 | U of Cincinnati | 101.0 | 15.3 | 244.9 |
| Carnegie-Mellon U | 193.5 | 29.2 | 136.2 | Syracuse U | 100.8 | 16.9 | 150.0 |
| U of Texas—Austin | 191.8 | 43.0 | 408.4 | Carleton C | 97.0 | 8.4 | 23.7 |
| Wesleyan U | 188.5 | 6.2 | 44.0 | Mount Holyoke C | 96.8 | 8.5 | 29.2 |
| U of Delaware | 186.7 | 10.9 | 136.9 | St. Louis U | 94.9 | 13.8 | 105.8 |

1. Gifts from business, alumni, religious denominations, and others. 2. Figure represents about 80% of typical operating budget. Does not include auxiliary enterprises and capital outlays. NOTE: C = College; U = University; n.a. = not available. *Source:* Council for Financial Aid to Education.

# Institutions of Higher Education—Average Salaries and Fringe Benefits for Faculty Members, 1970-1985[1]

## (in thousands of dollars)

| Control and Academic Rank | 1985 | 1984 | 1983 | 1982 | 1981 | 1980 | 1979 | 1978 | 1977 | 1975 | 1970 |
|---|---|---|---|---|---|---|---|---|---|---|---|
| **Average Salaries** | | | | | | | | | | | |
| Public: All ranks | 31.2 | 29.4 | 28.6 | 26.2 | 23.9 | 22.1 | 20.5 | 19.3 | 18.3 | 16.6 | 13.1 |
| Professor | 39.6 | 37.1 | 36.0 | 33.7 | 31.0 | 28.8 | 26.8 | 25.4 | 24.3 | 21.7 | 17.3 |
| Associate professor | 30.2 | 28.4 | 27.5 | 25.7 | 23.4 | 21.9 | 20.5 | 19.5 | 18.6 | 16.7 | 13.2 |
| Assistant professor | 25.0 | 23.5 | 22.6 | 21.2 | 19.2 | 18.0 | 16.8 | 16.0 | 15.2 | 13.7 | 10.9 |
| Instructor | 19.5 | 19.1 | 17.7 | 16.7 | 15.1 | 14.8 | 13.9 | 13.1 | 12.2 | 11.2 | 9.1 |
| Private: All ranks | 33.0 | 31.1 | 29.2 | 26.8 | 24.4 | 22.1 | 21.2 | 19.4 | 18.4 | 16.6 | 13.1 |
| Professor | 44.1 | 41.5 | 38.8 | 35.8 | 32.7 | 30.1 | 28.1 | 26.2 | 25.1 | 22.4 | 17.8 |
| Associate professor | 30.9 | 29.4 | 27.5 | 25.4 | 23.1 | 21.0 | 19.8 | 18.7 | 17.8 | 16.0 | 12.6 |
| Assistant professor | 25.0 | 23.7 | 22.1 | 20.4 | 18.4 | 17.0 | 16.0 | 15.1 | 14.4 | 13.0 | 10.3 |
| Instructor | 19.0 | 18.4 | 17.6 | 15.9 | 14.4 | 13.3 | 13.2 | 12.1 | 11.6 | 10.9 | 8.6 |
| **Average Fringe Benefits—All Ranks Combined** | | | | | | | | | | | |
| Public | 7.0 | 6.0 | 5.4 | 5.1 | 4.7 | 3.9 | 3.4 | 3.0 | 2.7 | 2.5 | 1.9 |
| Private | 7.2 | 6.4 | 5.7 | 5.4 | 4.9 | 4.1 | 3.6 | 3.3 | 3.0 | 2.8 | 2.2 |

1. Figures are for 9 months teaching for full-time faculty members in four-year colleges and universities. *Source:* U.S. Bureau of the Census, *Statistical Abstract of the United States: 1986.*

# Accredited U.S. Senior Colleges and Universities

*Source:* The Guidance Information System™, a product of Houghton Mifflin Company/TSC® Division.

Schools listed are those that offer at least a Bachelor's degree, and are fully accredited by one of the institutional and professional accrediting associations. Included are accredited colleges outside the U.S.

Tuition, room, and board listed are average annual figures (including fees) subject to fluctuation, usually covering two semesters, two out of three trimesters, or three out of four quarters, depending on school calendar.

For further information, write to the Registrar of the school concerned.

NOTE: n.a. = information not available. — = does not apply. Enrollment figures are approximate. (C) = Coeducational, (M) = primarily for men, (W) = primarily for women.

Abbreviations used for controls:

| | | | |
|---|---|---|---|
| AB | American Baptist | GGF | Grace Gospel Fellowship |
| AC | Advent Christian | ID | Interdenominational |
| AG | Assemblies of God | Ind | Independent |
| AL | American Lutheran | L | Lutheran |
| AME | African Methodist Episcopal | LCA | Lutheran Church of America |
| B | Baptist | LDS | Latter Day Saints |
| Br | Brethren | MB | Mennonite Brethren |
| CB | Church of Brethren | MC | Missionary Church |
| CC | Church of Christ | Men | Mennonite |
| CE | Christian Evangelical | Mor | Moravian |
| CG | Church of God | Naz | Nazarene |
| ChC | Christian Church | ND | Non-denominational |
| CMA | Christian & Missionary Alliance | OBS | Open Bible Standard |
| CME | Christian Methodist Episcopal | P | Private |
| CP | Cumberland Presbyterian | PH | Pentecostal Holiness |
| CR | Christian Reformed | Pub | Public |
| DC | Disciples of Christ | PUS | Presbyterian, U.S. |
| E | Episcopal | RC | Roman Catholic |
| EC | Evangelical Covenant | RCA | Reformed Church in America |
| EFC | Evangelical Free Church | RP | Reformed Presbyterian |
| EL | Evangelical Lutheran | SB | Southern Baptist |
| F | Friends | SDA | Seventh Day Adventist |
| FG | Foursquare Gospel | UCC | United Church of Christ |
| FM | Free Methodist | UM | United Methodist |
| FWB | Free Will Baptist | UP | United Presbyterian |
| | | W | Wesleyan |
| | | WM | Wesleyan Methodist |

| Institution and location | Enrollment | Control | Tuition ($) Res. | Tuition ($) Nonres. | Rm/Bd ($) |
|---|---|---|---|---|---|
| Abilene Christian University; Abilene, Tex. 79699 | 3,956 (C) | P | 3,450 | 3,450 | 2,150 |
| Adams State College; Alamosa, Colo. 81102 | 1,670 (C) | Pub | 1,106 | 2,750 | 2,380 |
| Adelphi University; Garden City, N.Y. 11530 | 6,130 (C) | P | 6,370 | 6,370 | 3,300 |
| Adrian College; Adrian, Mich. 49221 | 1,146 (C) | P/UM | 6,252 | 6,252 | 2,114 |
| Agnes Scott College; Decatur, Ga. 30030 | 540 (W) | P | 7,800 | 7,800 | 3,095 |
| Akron, University of; Akron, Ohio 44325 | 22,550 (C) | Pub | 1,716 | 3,860 | 2,652 |
| Alabama, University of; University, Ala. 35486 | 12,599 (C) | Pub | 1,254 | 2,690 | 2,300 |
| Alabama, University of–Birmingham; Birmingham, Ala. 35294 | 10,200 (C) | Pub | 1,476 | 2,862 | 2,898 |
| Alabama, University of–Huntsville; Huntsville, Ala. 35899 | 6,116 (C) | Pub | 1,200 | 2,400 | 2,990 |
| Alabama A&M University; Normal, Ala. 35762 | 3,128 (C) | S | 800 | 1,532 | 1,650 |
| | 3,128 (C) | Pub | 800 | 1,532 | 1,650 |
| Alabama State University; Montgomery, Ala. 36195 | 3,286 (C) | Pub | 960 | 1,920 | 1,620 |
| Alaska, University of–Anchorage; Anchorage, Alas. 99508 | 4,063 (C) | Pub | 918 | 2,358 | 3,200 |
| Alaska, University of–Fairbanks; Fairbanks, Alas. 99701 | 4,738 (C) | Pub | 959 | 2,399 | 2,450 |
| Alaska, University of–Juneau; Juneau, Alas. 99801 | 2,099 (C) | Pub | 960 | 2,400 | 1,600 |
| Alaska Bible College; Glennallen, Alas. 99588 | 62 (C) | P/ID | 1,650 | 1,650 | 3,000 |
| Alaska Pacific University; Anchorage, Alas. 99508 | 457 (C) | P/UM | 4,200 | 5,200 | 3,680 |
| Albany College of Pharmacy; Albany, N.Y. 12208 | 620 (C) | P | 4,435 | 4,435 | n.a. |
| Albany State College; Albany, Ga. 31705 | 1,758 (C) | Pub | 1,314 | 2,376 | 1,974 |
| Albertus Magnus College; New Haven, Conn. 06511 | 560 (W) | P/RC | 6,570 | 6,570 | 3,630 |
| Albion College; Albion, Mich. 49224 | 1,614 (C) | P/UM | 6,784 | 6,784 | 3,052 |
| Albright College; Reading, Pa. 19603 | 1,347 (C) | P/UM | 8,245 | 8,245 | 2,755 |
| Alcorn State University; Lorman, Miss. 39096 | 2,442 (C) | Pub | 1,350 | 1,950 | 1,550 |
| Alderson–Broaddus College; Philippi, W. Va. 26416 | 750 (C) | P/AB | 5,338 | 5,338 | 1,926 |
| Alfred University; Alfred, N.Y. 14802 | 2,000 (C) | P | 9,089 | 9,089 | 3,020 |
| Alice Lloyd College; Pippa Passes, Ky. 41844 | 546 (C) | P | 2,580 | 2,580 | 1,650 |
| Allegheny College; Meadville, Pa. 16335 | 1,950 (C) | P | 7,815 | 7,815 | 2,550 |
| Allen University; Columbia, S.C. 29204 | 400 | P | 2,810 | 2,810 | 1,900 |

| Institution and location | Enrollment | Control | Tuition ($) | | Rm/Bd ($) |
|---|---|---|---|---|---|
| | | | Res. | Nonres. | |
| Allentown College of St. Francis de Sales; Center Valley, Pa. 18034 | 800 (C) | P/RC | 5,300 | 5,300 | 3,080 |
| Alliance College; Cambridge Springs, Pa. 16403 | 277 (C) | P | 3,300 | 3,300 | 2,350 |
| Alma College; Alma, Mich. 48801 | 1,005 (C) | P | 7,450 | 7,450 | 2,870 |
| Alvernia College; Reading, Pa. 19607 | 787 (C) | P/RC | 3,690 | 3,690 | 2,770 |
| Alverno College; Milwaukee, Wis. 53215 | 1,704 (W) | P | 4,920 | 4,920 | 2,100 |
| Amber University; Garland, Tex. 75041 | 310 (C) | P | 2,400 | 2,400 | n.a. |
| American Baptist College; Nashville, Tenn. 37207 | 138 (C) | P/B | 1,500 | 1,500 | 1,100 |
| American College in Paris; Paris, France 75007 | 900 (C) | P | 6,395 | 6,395 | n.a. |
| American College of Puerto Rico; Bayamon, P.R. 00619 | 3,515 (C) | P | 1,800 | 1,800 | n.a. |
| American College of Switzerland; 1854 Leysin (HM), Switzerland | 325 (C) | P | 11,056 | 11,056 | 2,304 |
| American International College; Springfield, Mass. 01109 | 1,350 (C) | P | 5,250 | 5,250 | 2,581 |
| American Technological University; Killeen, Tex. 76540 | 300 (C) | P | 2,720 | 2,720 | 2,380 |
| American University; Washington, D.C. 20016 | 5,200 (C) | P | 8,934 | 8,934 | 4,250 |
| American University in Cairo; Cairo, Egypt | 1,915 (C) | P | 1,540 | 5,500 | 3,820 |
| Americas, University of the–Puebla; Puebla, Mexico 72820 | 4,250 (C) | P | 1,800 | 1,800 | 900 |
| Amherst College; Amherst, Mass. 01002 | 1,535 (C) | P | 11,141 | 11,141 | 3,500 |
| Anderson College; Anderson, Ind. 46012 | 1,800 (C) | P/CG | 4,900 | 4,900 | 1,920 |
| Andrews University; Berrien Springs, Mich. 49104 | 1,936 (C) | P/SDA | 6,300 | 6,300 | 3,150 |
| Angelo State University; San Angelo, Tex. 76909 | 5,500 (C) | Pub | 1,108 | 4,852 | 4,204 |
| Anna Maria College for Men and Women; Paxton, Mass. 01612 | 550 (C) | P | 5,250 | 5,250 | 3,100 |
| Antillian College; Mayaguez, P.R. 00709 | 867 (C) | P/SDA | 2,122 | 2,122 | 1,440 |
| Antioch College; Yellow Springs, Ohio 45387 | 506 (C) | P | 7,390 | 7,390 | 2,900 |
| Antioch Los Angeles; Venice, Calif. 90291 | 182 | P | 4,950 | 4,950 | n.a. |
| Antioch San Francisco; San Francisco, Calif. 94108 | 108 | P | 4,950 | 4,950 | n.a. |
| Antioch Santa Barbara; Santa Barbara, Calif. 93101 | 13 | P | 4,950 | 4,950 | n.a. |
| Antioch Seattle; Seattle, Wash. 98109 | 66 | P | 4,950 | 4,950 | n.a. |
| Antioch University–Philadelphia; Philadelphia, Pa. 19130 | 419 (C) | P | 3,850 | 3,850 | n.a. |
| Appalachian Bible College; Bradley, W. Va. 25818 | 180 (C) | P/Ind | 2,600 | 2,600 | 2,550 |
| Appalachian State University; Boone, N.C. 28608 | 9,008 (C) | Pub | 835 | 3,680 | 1,650 |
| Aquinas College; Grand Rapids, Mich. 49506 | 2,800 (C) | P/RC | 5,992 | 5,992 | 2,786 |
| Arizona, University of; Tucson, Ariz. 85721 | 23,110 (C) | Pub | 1,136 | 4,260 | 2,972 |
| Arizona College of the Bible; Phoenix, Ariz. 85021 | 200 (C) | P/ID | 3,290 | 3,290 | 2,750 |
| Arizona State University; Tempe, Ariz. 85287 | 30,376 (C) | Pub | 1,136 | 4,260 | 2,500 |
| Arkansas, Univ. of, at Fayetteville; Fayetteville, Ark. 72701 | 11,462 (C) | Pub | 900 | 2,160 | 2,000 |
| Arkansas, Univ. of, at Little Rock; Little Rock, Ark. 72204 | 8,893 (C) | Pub | 1,000 | 2,520 | n.a. |
| Arkansas, Univ. of, at Monticello; Monticello, Ark. 71655 | 1,785 (C) | Pub | 850 | 1,850 | 1,720 |
| Arkansas, Univ. of, at Pine Bluff; Pine Bluff, Ark. 71601 | 2,765 (C) | Pub | 890 | 2,150 | 1,670 |
| Arkansas Baptist College; Little Rock, Ark. 72202 | 210 | P | 1,350 | 1,350 | 1,938 |
| Arkansas College; Batesville, Ark. 72501 | 712 (C) | P/PUS | 4,100 | 4,100 | 2,071 |
| Arkansas State University; State University, Ark. 72467 | 8,446 (C) | Pub | 872 | 2,072 | 1,830 |
| Arkansas Tech. University; Russellville, Ark. 72801 | 3,600 (C) | Pub | 920 | 1,800 | 1,900 |
| Arlington Baptist College; Arlington, Tex. 76012 | 200 (C) | P | 1,500 | 1,500 | 1,800 |
| Armstrong State College; Savannah, Ga. 31419 | 2,750 (C) | Pub | 1,400 | 4,100 | n.a. |
| Armstrong University; Berkeley, Calif. 94704 | 240 (C) | P | 2,808 | 2,808 | n.a. |
| Arnold & Marie Schwartz College of Pharmacy & Health Sciences. See Long Island University Center, Brooklyn Center | | | | | |
| Art Academy of Cincinnati; Cincinnati, Ohio 45202 | 225 (C) | P | 4,370 | 4,370 | n.a. |
| Art Center College of Design; Pasadena, Calif. 91103 | 1,190 (C) | P | 5,690 | 5,690 | n.a. |
| Art Institute of Chicago, School of the; Chicago, Ill. 60603 | 1,120 (C) | P | 7,200 | 7,200 | n.a. |
| Asbury College; Wilmore, Ky. 40390 | 989 (C) | P | 4,554 | 4,554 | 2,613 |
| Ashland College; Ashland, Ohio 44805 | 1,408 (C) | P/Br | 6,950 | 6,950 | 2,910 |
| Assumption College; Worcester, Mass. 01609 | 1,600 (C) | P/RC | 6,400 | 6,400 | 3,450 |
| Athens State College; Athens, Ala. 35611 | 1,392 (C) | Pub | 1,200 | 2,400 | 2,674 |
| Atlanta Christian College; East Point, Ga. 30344 | 147 (C) | P | 2,376 | 2,376 | 2,150 |
| Atlanta College of Art; Atlanta, Ga. 30309 | 245 (C) | P | 5,800 | 5,800 | 2,865 |
| Atlantic, College of the; Bar Harbor, Maine 04609 | 120 (C) | P | 6,975 | 6,975 | 2,650 |
| Atlantic Christian College; Wilson, N.C. 27893 | 1,303 (C) | P/DC | 4,000 | 4,000 | 2,000 |
| Atlantic Union College; South Lancaster, Mass. 01561 | 610 (C) | P/SDA | 6,859 | 6,859 | 2,800 |
| Auburn University; Auburn University, Ala. 36849 | 16,826 (C) | Pub | 1,200 | 2,700 | 2,500 |
| Auburn University at Montgomery; Montgomery, Ala. 36193 | 4,390 (C) | Pub | 1,005 | 2,250 | 1,080 |
| Augsburg College; Minneapolis, Minn. 55454 | 1,700 (C) | P/AL | 6,190 | 6,190 | 2,500 |
| Augusta College; Augusta, Ga. 30910 | 3,591 (C) | Pub | 1,095 | 3,015 | n.a. |
| Augustana College; Rock Island, Ill. 61201 | 2,100 (C) | P/LCA | 6,690 | 6,690 | 2,700 |
| Augustana College; Sioux Falls, S.D. 57197 | 1,866 (C) | P/AL | 6,475 | 6,475 | 2,225 |
| Aurora College; Aurora, Ill. 60506 | 1,305 (C) | P/AC | 5,525 | 5,525 | 2,835 |
| Austin College; Sherman, Tex. 75090 | 1,152 (C) | P/PUS | 5,995 | 5,995 | 2,952 |
| Austin Peay State University; Clarksville, Tenn. 37040 | 4,632 (C) | Pub | 1,029 | 3,177 | 2,500 |
| Averett College; Danville, Va. 24541 | 1,000 (C) | P/SB | 4,550 | 4,550 | 3,150 |
| Avila College; Kansas City, Mo. 64145 | 1,576 (C) | P/RC | 4,780 | 4,780 | 2,200 |
| Azusa Pacific University; Azusa, Calif. 91702 | 1,600 (C) | P/Ind | 5,700 | 5,700 | 3,000 |
| Babson College; Wellesley, Mass. 02157 | 1,435 (C) | P | 8,420 | 8,420 | 4,270 |
| Baker University; Baldwin City, Kan. 66006 | 751 (C) | P/UM | 4,220 | 4,220 | 2,410 |
| Baldwin–Wallace College; Berea, Ohio 44017 | 3,228 (C) | P/UM | 6,843 | 6,843 | 3,050 |

| Institution and location | Enrollment | Control | Tuition ($) Res. | Tuition ($) Nonres. | Rm/Bd ($) |
|---|---|---|---|---|---|
| Ball State University; Muncie, Ind. 47306 | 15,214 (C) | Pub | 1,662 | 3,825 | 2,187 |
| Baltimore, University of; Baltimore, Md. 21201 | 2,268 (C) | Pub | 1,490 | 2,780 | n.a. |
| Baltimore Hebrew College; Baltimore, Md. 21215 | 505 (C) | P | 1,980 | 1,980 | n.a. |
| Baptist Bible College; Springfield, Mo. 65803 | 1,300 (C) | P/B | 1,550 | 1,550 | 1,970 |
| Baptist Bible Institute; Graceville, Fla. 32440 | 350 (C) | P/SB | 1,089 | 1,089 | 2,225 |
| Baptist Bible College of Pennsylvania; Clarks Summit, Pa. 18411 | 646 (C) | P | 4,480 | 4,480 | 2,319 |
| Baptist Christian College; Shreveport, La. 71108 | 300 | P | 1,800 | 1,800 | n.a. |
| Baptist College at Charleston; Charleston, S.C. 29411 | 1,646 (C) | P/SB | 4,140 | 4,140 | 2,484 |
| Barat College; Lake Forest, Ill. 60045 | 628 (C) | P | 5,595 | 5,595 | 2,700 |
| Barber–Scotia College; Concord, N.C. 28025 | 400 (C) | P/UP | 5,417 | 5,417 | 4,300 |
| Bard College; Annandale–on–Hudson, N.Y. 12504 | 750 (C) | P | 11,154 | 11,154 | 3,490 |
| Barnard College of Columbia University; New York, N.Y. 10027 | 2,300 (W) | P | 10,546 | 10,546 | 4,730 |
| Barry University; Miami Shores, Fla. 33161 | 3,069 (C) | P | 5,995 | 5,995 | 3,500 |
| Bartlesville Wesleyan College; Bartlesville, Okla. 74003 | 618 (C) | P/W | 4,200 | 4,200 | 2,200 |
| Bassist College; Portland, Ore. 97201 | 230 | P | 4,750 | 4,750 | n.a. |
| Bates College; Lewiston, Maine 04240 | 1,450 (C) | P | 11,835 | 11,835 | 2,765 |
| Baylor College of Medicine; Houston, Tex. 77025 | 42 (C) | P | 3,750 | 3,750 | n.a. |
| Baylor University; Waco, Tex. 76706 | 9,640 (C) | P/SB | 3,672 | 3,672 | 2,694 |
| Beaver College; Glenside, Pa. 19038 | 1,351 (C) | P | 6,900 | 6,900 | 3,000 |
| Behrend College. See Pennsylvania State University | | | | | |
| Belhaven College; Jackson, Miss. 39202 | 850 (C) | P/PUS | 5,000 | 5,000 | 1,950 |
| Bellarmine College; Louisville, Ky. 40205 | 2,236 (C) | P/RC | 4,200 | 4,200 | 2,110 |
| Bellevue College; Bellevue, Neb. 68005 | 2,675 (C) | P | 1,770 | 1,770 | n.a. |
| Belmont Abbey College; Belmont, N.C. 28012 | 890 (C) | P/RC | 3,817 | 4,767 | 3,770 |
| Belmont College; Nashville, Tenn. 37203 | 2,125 (C) | P/SB | 3,100 | 3,100 | 5,580 |
| Beloit College; Beloit, Wis. 53511 | 1,050 (C) | P | 8,590 | 8,590 | 2,610 |
| Bemidji State University; Bemidji, Minn. 56601 | 3,343 (C) | Pub | 1,691 | 2,581 | 1,785 |
| Benedict College; Columbia, S.C. 29204 | 1,373 (C) | P/Ind | 5,070 | 5,070 | 1,700 |
| Benedictine College; Atchison, Kan. 66002 | 898 (C) | P/RC | 4,875 | 4,875 | 2,485 |
| Benjamin Franklin University; Washington, D.C. 20036 | 300 (C) | P | 3,045 | 3,045 | n.a. |
| Bennett College; Greensboro, N.C. 27401 | 585 (W) | P/UM | 3,600 | 3,600 | 1,550 |
| Bennington College; Bennington, Vt. 05201 | 550 (C) | P | 13,970 | 13,970 | 2,980 |
| Bentley College; Waltham, Mass. 02254 | 3,890 (C) | P | 7,300 | 7,300 | 3,416 |
| Berea College; Berea, Ky. 40404 | 1,550 (C) | P | 125 | 125 | 2,007 |
| Berklee College of Music; Boston, Mass. 02215 | 2,425 (C) | P | 4,390 | 4,390 | 3,650 |
| Berkshire Christian College; Lenox, Mass. 01240 | 100 (C) | P/AC | 1,395 | 1,395 | 2,600 |
| Bernard M. Baruch Coll. See New York, City Univ. of | | | | | |
| Berry College; Mount Berry, Ga. 30149 | 1,188 (C) | P | 4,380 | 4,380 | 2,595 |
| Bethany Bible College; Santa Cruz, Calif. 95066 | 509 (C) | P/AG | 3,502 | 3,502 | 2,386 |
| Bethany College; Bethany, W. Va. 26032 | 785 (C) | P/DC | 7,610 | 7,610 | 2,700 |
| Bethany College; Lindsborg, Kan. 67456 | 760 (C) | P/LCA | 4,610 | 4,610 | 2,585 |
| Bethany Nazarene College; Bethany, Okla. 73008 | 1,163 (C) | P/Naz | 3,400 | 3,400 | 2,318 |
| Bethel College; McKenzie, Tenn. 38201 | 469 (C) | P/CP | 2,850 | 2,850 | 1,815 |
| Bethel College; Mishawaka, Ind. 46545 | 573 (C) | P/MC | 4,671 | 4,671 | 2,160 |
| Bethel College; North Newton, Kan. 67117 | 643 (C) | P/Men | 4,750 | 4,750 | 2,524 |
| Bethel College; St. Paul, Minn. 55112 | 1,791 (C) | P/B | 6,590 | 6,590 | 2,790 |
| Bethune–Cookman College; Daytona Beach, Fla. 32015 | 1,724 (C) | P | 3,337 | 3,337 | 2,270 |
| Biola University; La Mirada, Calif. 90639 | 2,024 (C) | P/Ind | 5,732 | 5,732 | 3,018 |
| Birmingham–Southern College; Birmingham, Ala. 35254 | 1,575 (C) | P/UM | 5,600 | 5,600 | 2,500 |
| Bishop College; Dallas, Tex. 75241 | 987 (C) | P/AB | 3,018 | 3,018 | 2,220 |
| Blackburn College; Carlinville, Ill. 62626 | 500 (C) | P | 5,700 | 5,700 | 2,800 |
| Black Hills State College; Spearfish, S.D. 57783 | 2,100 (C) | Pub | 1,450 | 2,566 | 1,860 |
| Bloomfield College; Bloomfield, N.J. 07003 | 1,254 (C) | P | 5,435 | 5,435 | 2,730 |
| Bloomsburg State Coll. See Bloomsburg Univ. of Pennsylvania | | | | | |
| Bloomsburg University of Pennsylvania; Bloomsburg, Pa. 17815 | 6,052 (C) | Pub | 1,714 | 2,892 | 1,800 |
| Bluefield College; Bluefield, Va. 24605 | 337 (C) | P/SB | 3,460 | 3,460 | 2,520 |
| Bluefield State College; Bluefield, W. Va. 24701 | 2,400 (C) | Pub | 840 | 2,300 | n.a. |
| Blue Mountain College; Blue Mountain, Miss. 38610 | 375 (C) | P/SB | 2,500 | 2,500 | 1,810 |
| Bluffton College; Bluffton, Ohio 45817 | 594 (C) | P/Men | 5,715 | 5,715 | 2,349 |
| Boca Raton, College of; Boca Raton, Fla. 33431 | 900 (C) | P | 6,700 | 6,700 | 3,200 |
| Boise State University; Boise, Idaho 83725 | 9,313 (C) | Pub | 1,058 | 2,958 | 2,415 |
| Boricua College; New York, N.Y. 10032 | 1,000 (C) | P | 3,800 | 3,800 | n.a. |
| Borromeo College of Ohio; Wickliffe, Ohio 44092 | 91 (M) | P/RC | 3,600 | 3,600 | 1,800 |
| Boston College; Chestnut Hill, Mass. 02167 | 10,632 (C) | P/RC | 9,578 | 9,578 | 4,583 |
| Boston Conservatory; Boston, Mass. 02215 | 407 (C) | P | 5,990 | 5,990 | 3,470 |
| Boston University; Boston, Mass. 02215 | 13,880 (C) | P | 11,100 | 11,100 | 4,700 |
| Bowdoin College; Brunswick, Maine 04011 | 1,350 (C) | P | 10,850 | 10,850 | 3,795 |
| Bowie State College; Bowie, Md. 20715 | 1,847 (C) | Pub | 1,678 | 3,023 | 2,817 |
| Bowling Green State University; Bowling Green, Ohio 43403 | 15,168 (C) | Pub | 1,952 | 4,260 | 2,018 |
| Bradford College; Bradford, Mass. 01830 | 400 (C) | P | 7,495 | 7,495 | 3,845 |
| Bradley University; Peoria, Ill. 61625 | 4,950 (C) | P | 6,310 | 6,310 | 2,960 |
| Brandeis University; Waltham, Mass. 02254 | 2,800 (C) | P | 11,275 | 11,275 | 4,760 |
| Brenau: The Women's College; Gainesville, Ga. 30501 | 637 (W) | P | 4,300 | 4,300 | 3,600 |

| Institution and location | Enrollment | Control | Tuition ($) Res. | Tuition ($) Nonres. | Rm/Bd ($) |
|---|---|---|---|---|---|
| Brescia College; Owensboro, Ky. 42301 | 800 (C) | P/RC | 4,000 | 4,000 | 2,100 |
| Brewton–Parker College; Mount Vernon, Ga. 30445 | 1,281 (C) | P | 2,340 | 2,340 | 1,710 |
| Briar Cliff College; Sioux City, Iowa 51104 | 1,300 (C) | P/RC | 4,800 | 4,800 | 2,049 |
| Bridgeport, University of; Bridgeport, Conn. 06601 | 4,083 (C) | P | 7,200 | 7,200 | 3,780 |
| Bridgeport Engineering Institute; Bridgeport, Conn. 06606 | 830 (C) | P | 2,810 | 2,810 | n.a. |
| Bridgewater College; Bridgewater, Va. 22812 | 800 (C) | P | 5,400 | 5,400 | 2,850 |
| Bridgewater State College; Bridgewater, Mass. 02324 | 5,400 (C) | Pub | 1,336 | 3,532 | 2,222 |
| Brigham Young University; Provo, Utah 84602 | 24,612 (C) | P/LDS | 1,550 | 1,550 | 2,500 |
| Hawaii Campus; Laie, Oahu, Hawaii 96762 | 2,000 (C) | P/LDS | 1,250 | 1,250 | 2,000 |
| Bristol College; Bristol, Tenn. 37621 | 700 (C) | P | 3,200 | 3,200 | 1,900 |
| Brooklyn Center. *See* Long Island University Center | | | | | |
| Brooklyn College. *See* New York, City University of | | | | | |
| Brooks Institute of Photography; Santa Barbara, Calif. 93108 | 663 (C) | P | 3,900 | 3,900 | n.a. |
| Brown University; Providence, R.I. 02912 | 5,600 (C) | P | 11,690 | 11,690 | 4,221 |
| Bryan College; Dayton, Tenn. 37321 | 500 (C) | P | 3,900 | 3,900 | 2,880 |
| Bryant College; Smithfield, R.I. 02917 | 3,080 (C) | P | 5,600 | 5,600 | 4,140 |
| Bryn Mawr College; Bryn Mawr, Pa. 19010 | 1,083 (W) | P | 10,450 | 10,450 | 4,425 |
| Bucknell University; Lewisburg, Pa. 17837 | 3,245 (C) | P | 10,650 | 10,650 | 2,800 |
| Buena Vista College; Storm Lake, Iowa 50588 | 950 (C) | P | 6,863 | 6,863 | 2,368 |
| Burlington College; Burlington, Vt. 05401 | 204 (C) | P | 4,650 | 4,650 | n.a. |
| Butler University; Indianapolis, Ind. 46208 | 2,405 (C) | P | 6,864 | 6,864 | 2,820 |
| Cabrini College; Radnor, Pa. 19087 | 730 (W) | P/RC | 5,200 | 5,200 | 3,800 |
| Caldwell College; Caldwell, N.J. 07006 | 750 (W) | P | 5,370 | 5,370 | 3,350 |
| California, University of; Berkeley, Calif. 94720: | | | | | |
| UC, Berkeley; Berkeley, Calif. 94720 | 22,321 (C) | Pub | 1,450 | 5,536 | 7,648 |
| UC, Davis; Davis, Calif. 95616 | 14,600 (C) | Pub | 1,355 | 5,438 | 3,220 |
| UC, Irvine; Irvine, Calif. 92717 | 10,211 (C) | Pub | 1,404 | 5,490 | 4,386 |
| UC, Los Angeles; Los Angeles, Calif. 90024 | 22,901 (C) | Pub | 1,406 | 5,492 | 2,950 |
| UC, Riverside; Riverside, Calif. 92521 | 3,833 (C) | Pub | 1,308 | 5,124 | 3,450 |
| UC, San Diego; La Jolla, Calif. 92093 | 11,700 (C) | Pub | 1,330 | 5,146 | 4,011 |
| UC, Santa Barbara; Santa Barbara, Calif. 93106 | 15,277 (C) | Pub | 1,299 | 4,863 | 2,972 |
| UC, Santa Cruz; Santa Cruz, Calif. 95064 | 6,922 (C) | Pub | 1,389 | 5,205 | 3,864 |
| California Baptist College; Riverside, Calif. 92504 | 561 (C) | P/SB | 4,484 | 4,484 | 2,524 |
| California College of Arts and Crafts; Oakland, Calif. 94618 | 1,054 (C) | P | 6,520 | 6,520 | 3,100 |
| California Institute of Technology; Pasadena, Calif. 91125 | 830 (C) | P | 10,555 | 10,555 | 4,300 |
| California Institute of the Arts; Valencia, Calif. 91355 | 625 (C) | P | 7,800 | 7,800 | 3,600 |
| California Lutheran University; Thousand Oaks, Calif. 91360 | 1,459 (C) | P/AL | 7,640 | 7,640 | 2,900 |
| California Maritime Academy; Vallejo, Calif. 94590 | 450 (C) | Pub | 1,094 | 3,094 | 3,422 |
| California Polytechnic State University; San Luis Obispo, Calif. 93407 | 15,000 (C) | Pub | 875 | 4,655 | 3,115 |
| California State Coll. (Pa.). *See* California Univ. of Pennsylvania | | | | | |
| California State College–Bakersfield; Bakersfield, Calif. 93311 | 2,380 (C) | Pub | 627 | 4,900 | 3,000 |
| California State Polytechnic University–Pomona; Pomona, Calif. 91768 | 15,640 (C) | Pub | 645 | 3,689 | 3,123 |
| California State University–Chico; Chico, Calif. 95929 | 13,000 (C) | Pub | 710 | 4,220 | 2,434 |
| California St. Univ.–Dominguez Hills; Carson, Calif. 90747 | 5,550 (C) | Pub | 652 | 4,308 | 2,752 |
| California State Univ.–Fresno; Fresno, Calif. 93740 | 13,854 (C) | Pub | 716 | 4,496 | 2,721 |
| California State Univ.–Fullerton; Fullerton, Calif. 92634 | 19,689 (C) | Pub | 674 | 3,301 | n.a. |
| California State Univ.–Hayward; Hayward, Calif. 94542 | 9,230 (C) | Pub | 630 | 4,014 | n.a. |
| California State Univ.–Long Beach; Long Beach, Calif. 90840 | 26,398 (C) | Pub | 656 | 4,436 | 3,500 |
| California State Univ.–Los Angeles; Los Angeles, Calif. 90032 | 15,670 (C) | Pub | 924 | 4,176 | 2,000 |
| California State Univ.–Northridge; Northridge, Calif. 91330 | 23,507 (C) | Pub | 700 | 4,520 | 3,180 |
| California State Univ.–Sacramento; Sacramento, Calif. 95819 | 18,200 (C) | Pub | 651 | 4,881 | 3,046 |
| California State Univ.–San Bernardino; San Bernardino, Calif. 92407 | 5,000 (C) | Pub | 696 | 3,936 | 2,402 |
| California State Univ.–Stanislaus; Turlock, Calif. 95380 | 3,087 (C) | Pub | 735 | 4,459 | 2,763 |
| California Univ. of Pennsylvania; California, Pa. 15419 | 4,096 (C) | Pub | 1,600 | 2,876 | 1,950 |
| Calumet College; Whiting, Ind. 46394 | 1,130 (C) | P/RC | 2,700 | 2,700 | n.a. |
| Calvary Bible College; Kansas City, Mo. 64147 | 356 (C) | P/Ind | 2,852 | 2,852 | 2,160 |
| Calvin College; Grand Rapids, Mich. 49506 | 4,003 (C) | P/CR | 5,300 | 5,300 | 2,370 |
| Cameron University; Lawton, Okla. 73505 | 4,799 (C) | Pub | 500 | 1,300 | 1,540 |
| Campbellsville College; Campbellsville, Ky. 42718 | 656 (C) | P/SB | 3,360 | 3,360 | 2,430 |
| Campbell University; Buie's Creek, N.C. 27506 | 1,900 (C) | P/SB | 5,000 | 5,000 | 2,500 |
| Canisius College; Buffalo, N.Y. 14208 | 2,882 (C) | P | 5,700 | 5,700 | 2,970 |
| Capital University; Columbus, Ohio 43209 | 1,695 (C) | P/AL | 7,420 | 7,420 | 2,940 |
| Capitol Institute of Technology; Laurel, Md. 20708 | 1,100 (C) | P | 4,392 | 4,392 | n.a. |
| Cardinal Glennon College; St. Louis, Mo. 63119 | 85 | P/RC | 5,000 | 5,000 | 1,250 |
| Cardinal Stritch College; Milwaukee, Wis. 53217 | 1,383 (C) | P/RC | 4,960 | 4,960 | 2,500 |
| Carleton College; Northfield, Minn. 55057 | 1,864 (C) | P | 10,250 | 10,250 | 2,550 |
| Carlow College; Pittsburgh, Pa. 15213 | 1,208 (W) | P/RC | 6,286 | 6,286 | 3,444 |
| Carnegie–Mellon University; Pittsburgh, Pa. 15213 | 4,348 (C) | P | 10,310 | 10,310 | 3,740 |
| Carroll College; Helena, Mont. 59625 | 1,501 (C) | P/RC | 3,740 | 3,740 | 2,344 |
| Carroll College; Waukesha, Wis. 53186 | 1,190 (C) | P/UP | 6,730 | 6,730 | 2,440 |

| Institution and location | Enrollment | Control | Tuition ($) Res. | Tuition ($) Nonres. | Rm/Bd ($) |
|---|---|---|---|---|---|
| Carson–Newman College; Jefferson City, Tenn. 37760 | 1,731 (C) | P/SB | 4,000 | 4,000 | 2,760 |
| Carthage College; Kenosha, Wis. 53140 | 1,000 (C) | P/LCA | 5,860 | 5,860 | 2,405 |
| Case Western Reserve University; Cleveland, Ohio 44106 | 3,334 (C) | P | 9,100 | 9,100 | 3,810 |
| Castleton State College; Castleton, Vt. 05735 | 1,377 (C) | Pub | 2,167 | 4,548 | 3,042 |
| Catawba College; Salisbury, N.C. 28144 | 1,000 (C) | P/UCC | 4,750 | 4,750 | 2,240 |
| Cathedral College of the Immaculate Conception; Douglaston, N.Y. 11362 | 83 (M) | P/RC | 3,800 | 3,800 | 2,000 |
| Catholic University of America; Washington, D.C. 20064 | 2,524 (C) | P | 7,400 | 7,400 | 3,900 |
| Catholic University of Puerto Rico; Ponce, P.R. 00732 | 11,720 (C) | P/RC | 1,815 | 1,815 | 2,200 |
| Cayey University College. *See* Puerto Rico, University of | | | | | |
| Cedar Crest College; Allentown, Pa. 18104 | 530 (W) | P | 7,610 | 7,610 | 3,360 |
| Cedarville College; Cedarville, Ohio 45314 | 1,817 (C) | P/B | 4,124 | 4,124 | 2,610 |
| Centenary College; Hackettstown, N.J. 07840 | 600 (W) | P | 5,000 | 5,000 | 3,800 |
| Centenary College of Louisiana; Shreveport, La. 71104 | 738 (C) | P/UM | 4,340 | 4,340 | 2,530 |
| Center for Creative Studies; Detroit, Mich. 48202 | 1,124 (C) | P | 6,100 | 6,100 | 3,070 |
| Central Arkansas, University of; Conway, Ark. 72032 | 5,675 (C) | Pub | 900 | 1,670 | 1,870 |
| Central Baptist College; Conway, Ark. 72032 | 232 (C) | P/B | 1,000 | 1,000 | 1,280 |
| Central Bible College; Springfield, Mo. 65803 | 821 (C) | P/AG | 2,184 | 2,184 | 2,180 |
| Central Christian College of the Bible; Moberly, Mo. 65270 | 85 (C) | P/ChC | 1,700 | 1,700 | 1,690 |
| Central College; Pella, Iowa 50219 | 1,550 (C) | P/RCA | 5,939 | 5,939 | 2,378 |
| Central Connecticut State University; New Britain, Conn. 06050 | 10,860 (C) | Pub | 1,277 | 3,237 | 2,717 |
| Central Florida, University of; Orlando, Fla. 32816 | 12,877 (C) | Pub | 1,049 | 3,537 | 2,585 |
| Central Methodist College; Fayette, Mo. 65248 | 659 (C) | P/UM | 4,890 | 4,890 | 2,460 |
| Central Michigan University; Mt. Pleasant, Mich. 48858 | 14,450 (C) | Pub | 1,507 | 3,770 | 2,350 |
| Central Missouri State University; Warrensburg, Mo. 64093 | 7,688 (C) | Pub | 1,254 | 2,342 | 2,070 |
| Central New England College of Technology; Worcester, Mass. 01610 | 2,300 (C) | P | 6,100 | 6,100 | n.a. |
| Central State University; Edmond, Okla. 73034 | 9,000 (C) | Pub | 700 | 1,600 | 1,600 |
| Central State University; Wilberforce, Ohio 45384 | 2,452 (C) | Pub | 1,413 | 2,574 | 2,868 |
| Central Washington University; Ellensburg, Wash. 98926 | 6,111 (C) | Pub | 1,248 | 4,242 | 2,565 |
| Central Wesleyan College; Central, S.C. 29630 | 418 (C) | P/WM | 4,580 | 4,580 | 2,130 |
| Centre College of Kentucky; Danville, Ky. 40422 | 750 (C) | P | 6,650 | 6,650 | 2,775 |
| Chadron State College; Chadron, Neb. 69337 | 1,900 (C) | Pub | 1,031 | 1,646 | 1,836 |
| Chaminade University of Honolulu; Honolulu, Hawaii 96816 | 2,290 (C) | P/RC | 4,210 | 4,210 | 3,000 |
| Chapman College; Orange, Calif. 92666 | 1,578 (C) | P | 8,900 | 8,900 | 3,400 |
| Charleston, College of; Charleston, S.C. 29424 | 4,994 (C) | Pub | 1,636 | 3,036 | 2,390 |
| Charleston, University of; Charleston, W. Va. 25304 | 1,377 (C) | P | 5,300 | 5,300 | 3,100 |
| Charter Oak College; Hartford, Conn. 06106 | 900 (C) | Pub | 150 | 190 | n.a. |
| Chatham College; Pittsburgh, Pa. 15232 | 550 (W) | P | 6,860 | 6,860 | 3,340 |
| Chestnut Hill College; Philadelphia, Pa. 19118 | 820 (W) | P/RC | 5,050 | 5,050 | 2,870 |
| Cheyney University of Pennsylvania; Cheyney, Pa. 19319 | 1,351 (C) | Pub | 1,775 | 3,043 | 2,260 |
| Chicago, University of—The College; Chicago, Ill. 60637 | 3,000 (C) | P | 11,350 | 11,350 | 4,529 |
| Chicago State University; Chicago, Ill. 60628 | 7,327 (C) | Pub | 1,758 | 3,218 | n.a. |
| Christ College–Irvine; Irvine, Calif. 92715 | 385 (C) | P/L | 4,200 | 4,200 | 1,440 |
| Christian Brothers College; Memphis, Tenn. 38104 | 1,564 (C) | P/RC | 4,750 | 4,750 | 2,690 |
| Christian Heritage College; El Cajon, Calif. 92021 | 400 | P/Ind | 3,870 | 3,870 | 2,210 |
| Christopher Newport College; Newport News, Va. 23606 | 4,150 (C) | Pub | 1,650 | 2,800 | n.a. |
| Church College of Hawaii. *See* Brigham Young University— Hawaii Campus | | | | | |
| Cincinnati, University of; Cincinnati, Ohio 45221 | 28,507 (C) | Pub | 2,046 | 4,944 | 3,060 |
| Cincinnati Bible College; Cincinnati, Ohio 45204 | 634 (C) | P/ChC | 2,402 | 2,402 | 2,330 |
| Circleville Bible College; Circleville, Ohio 43113 | 186 (C) | P/CC | 2,450 | 2,450 | 1,850 |
| Citadel–The Military College of South Carolina; Charleston, S.C. 29409 | 2,000 (M) | Pub | 4,506 | 6,604 | 1,650 |
| City College (NYC). *See* New York, City University of | | | | | |
| City University; Bellevue, Wash. 98008 | 1,464 (C) | P | 2,190 | 2,190 | n.a. |
| Claflin College; Orangeburg, S.C. 29115 | 900 (C) | P/UM | 2,752 | 2,752 | 1,695 |
| Claremont McKenna College; Claremont, Calif. 91711 | 825 (C) | P | 10,000 | 10,000 | 3,840 |
| Claremont Men's College. *See* Claremont McKenna College | | | | | |
| Harvey Mudd College; Claremont, Calif. 91711 | 540 (C) | P | 10,100 | 10,100 | 4,350 |
| Pitzer College; Claremont, Calif. 91711 | 740 (C) | P | 10,188 | 10,188 | 3,154 |
| Pomona College; Claremont, Calif. 91711 | 1,325 (C) | P | 10,000 | 10,000 | 4,100 |
| Scripps College; Claremont, Calif. 91711 | 600 (W) | P | 10,074 | 10,074 | 4,626 |
| Clarion State College. *See* Clarion University of Pennsylvania | | | | | |
| Clarion University of Pennsylvania; Clarion, Pa. 16214 | 5,400 (C) | Pub | 1,795 | 3,070 | 2,010 |
| Clark College; Atlanta, Ga. 30314 | 1,966 (C) | P | 4,755 | 4,755 | 1,190 |
| Clarke College; Dubuque, Iowa 52001 | 857 (W) | P/RC | 5,770 | 5,770 | 2,280 |
| Clarkson College of Technology. *See* Clarkson University | | | | | |
| Clarkson University; Potsdam, N.Y. 13676 | 3,814 (C) | P | 8,800 | 8,800 | 3,750 |
| Clark University; Worcester, Mass. 01610 | 2,200 (C) | P | 9,200 | 9,200 | 3,020 |
| Clearwater Christian College; Clearwater, Fla. 33519 | 250 | P | 3,000 | 3,000 | 2,500 |
| Cleary College; Ypsilanti, Mich. 48197 | 881 (C) | P | 3,510 | 3,510 | n.a. |

| Institution and location | Enrollment | Control | Tuition ($) Res. | Tuition ($) Nonres. | Rm/Bd ($) |
|---|---|---|---|---|---|
| Clemson University; Clemson, S.C. 29634 | 10,334 (C) | Pub | 1,682 | 3,910 | 2,150 |
| Cleveland College of Jewish Studies; Beachwood, Ohio 44122 | 325 | P | 900 | 900 | n.a. |
| Cleveland Institute of Art; Cleveland, Ohio 44106 | 496 (C) | P | 5,450 | 5,450 | 3,200 |
| Cleveland Institute of Music; Cleveland, Ohio 44106 | 133 (C) | P | 7,820 | 7,820 | 3,490 |
| Cleveland State University; Cleveland, Ohio 44115 | 13,411 (C) | Pub | 1,713 | 3,426 | 2,350 |
| | | | | | |
| Clinch Valley College. See Virginia, University of | | | | | |
| Coe College; Cedar Rapids, Iowa 52402 | 1,186 (C) | P/UP | 6,620 | 6,620 | 2,370 |
| Cogswell College; Cupertino, Calif. 95014 | 220 (C) | P | 5,000 | 5,000 | n.a. |
| Coker College; Hartsville, S.C. 29550 | 369 (C) | P | 5,660 | 5,660 | 2,855 |
| Colby College; Waterville, Me. 04901 | 1,675 (C) | P | 9,800 | 9,800 | 3,560 |
| Colby-Sawyer College; New London, N.H. 03257 | 450 (W) | P | 8,600 | 8,600 | 3,800 |
| Coleman College; La Mesa, Calif. 92041 | 950 (C) | P | 6,375 | 6,375 | n.a. |
| | | | | | |
| Colgate University; Hamilton, N.Y. 13346 | 2,600 (C) | P | 9,700 | 9,700 | 3,490 |
| College Misericordia; Dallas, Pa. 18612 | 1,200 (W) | P/RC | 4,350 | 4,350 | 2,600 |
| Colorado, University of; Boulder, Colo. 80309: | | | | | |
| U. of Colorado at Boulder; Boulder, Colo. 80309 | 18,568 (C) | Pub | 1,424 | 5,713 | 2,630 |
| U. of Colorado at Colorado Springs; Colorado Springs, Colo. 80933 | 3,917 (C) | Pub | 1,196 | 4,290 | n.a. |
| U. of Colorado at Denver; Denver, Colo. 80202 | 6,378 (C) | Pub | 1,040 | 4,534 | n.a. |
| Colorado Christian College; Lakewood, Colo. 80226 | 355 (C) | P | 4,615 | 4,615 | 1,750 |
| | | | | | |
| Colorado College; Colorado Springs, Colo. 80903 | 1,850 (C) | P | 8,840 | 8,840 | 2,775 |
| Colorado School of Mines; Golden, Colo. 80401 | 2,000 (C) | Pub | 2,880 | 7,680 | 3,000 |
| Colorado State University; Fort Collins, Colo. 80523 | 15,166 (C) | Pub | 1,446 | 4,700 | 2,904 |
| Colorado Technical College; Colorado Springs, Colo. 80907 | 689 (C) | P | 3,750 | 3,750 | n.a. |
| Colorado Women's College. See Denver, Univ. of | | | | | |
| Columbia Bible College; Columbia, S.C. 29230 | 559 (C) | P | 3,420 | 3,420 | 2,280 |
| Columbia Christian College; Portland, Ore. 97216 | 263 (C) | P | 3,825 | 3,825 | 2,295 |
| | | | | | |
| Columbia College; Chicago, Ill. 60605 | 4,715 (C) | P | 3,816 | 3,816 | n.a. |
| Columbia College; Columbia, Mo. 65216 | 682 (C) | P | 5,070 | 5,070 | 2,496 |
| Columbia College; Columbia, S.C. 29203 | 1,050 (W) | P/UM | 5,800 | 5,800 | 2,400 |
| Columbia Union College; Takoma Park, Md. 20912 | 927 (C) | P/SDA | 5,733 | 5,733 | 1,990 |
| Columbia University–Columbia College; New York, N.Y. 10027 | 2,900 (M) | P | 10,390 | 10,390 | 4,387 |
| Columbus College; Columbus, Ga. 31993 | 3,386 (C) | Pub | 1,086 | 3,006 | 2,975 |
| Columbus College of Art and Design; Columbus, Ohio 43215 | 1,000 (C) | P | 5,890 | 5,890 | 3,300 |
| | | | | | |
| Combs College of Music; Philadelphia, Pa. 19118 | 50 (C) | P | 5,225 | 5,225 | 2,860 |
| Conception Seminary College; Conception, Mo. 64433 | 114 | P/RC | 3,860 | 3,860 | 2,520 |
| Concord College; Athens, W. Va. 24712 | 2,355 (C) | Pub | 908 | 2,418 | 2,463 |
| Concordia College; Ann Arbor, Mich. 48105 | 450 (C) | P/L | 4,504 | 4,504 | 2,780 |
| Concordia College; Bronxville, N.Y. 10708 | 560 (C) | P/L | 5,190 | 5,190 | 3,170 |
| Concordia College; Moorhead, Minn. 56560 | 2,481 (C) | P/AL | 6,430 | 6,430 | 2,070 |
| Concordia College; Portland, Ore. 97211 | 414 (C) | P | 5,300 | 5,300 | 3,250 |
| | | | | | |
| Concordia College; River Forest, Ill. 60305 | 1,127 (C) | P/L | 4,560 | 4,560 | 2,586 |
| Concordia College; St. Paul, Minn. 55104 | 746 (C) | P/L | 4,575 | 4,575 | 1,980 |
| Concordia College–Wisconsin; Mequon, Wis. 53092 | 850 (C) | P/L | 4,400 | 4,400 | 2,590 |
| Concordia Lutheran College; Austin, Tex. 78705 | 444 (C) | P/L | 3,600 | 3,600 | 2,750 |
| Concordia Teachers College; Seward, Neb. 68434 | 860 (C) | P/L | 5,200 | 5,200 | 2,100 |
| Connecticut, University of; Storrs, Conn. 06268 | 16,239 (C) | Pub | 1,801 | 4,971 | 2,466 |
| Connecticut College; New London, Conn. 06320 | 1,917 (C) | P | 10,300 | 10,300 | 2,930 |
| | | | | | |
| Conservatory of Music of Puerto Rico; Hato Rey, P.R. 00918 | 251 (C) | Pub | 210 | 210 | n.a. |
| Converse College; Spartanburg, S.C. 29301 | 755 (W) | P | 6,250 | 6,250 | 3,000 |
| Cooper Union; New York, N.Y. 10003 | 1,060 (C) | P | 300 | 300 | n.a. |
| Coppin State College; Baltimore, Md. 21216 | 2,300 (C) | Pub | 1,451 | 2,707 | n.a. |
| Corcoran School of Art; Washington, D.C. 20006 | 220 (C) | P | 5,400 | 5,400 | 3,200 |
| Cornell College; Mt. Vernon, Iowa 52314 | 1,101 (C) | P | 7,624 | 7,624 | 2,798 |
| | | | | | |
| Cornell University; Ithaca, N.Y. 14853 | 12,680 (C) | P | 11,500 | 11,500 | 3,825 |
| Cornish Institute; Seattle, Wash. 98102 | 450 (C) | P | 5,508 | 5,508 | n.a. |
| Corpus Christi State Univ.; Corpus Christi, Tex. 78412 | 1,932 (C) | Pub | 840 | 3,960 | 4,214 |
| Covenant College; Lookout Mountain, Tenn. 37350 | 515 (C) | P/RP | 4,800 | 4,800 | 2,570 |
| Creighton University; Omaha, Neb. 68178 | 4,075 (C) | P | 5,624 | 5,624 | 2,756 |
| | | | | | |
| Culver-Stockton College; Canton, Mo. 63435 | 651 (C) | P | 4,500 | 4,500 | 1,900 |
| Cumberland College; Williamsburg, Ky. 40769 | 2,008 (C) | P/SB | 3,280 | 3,280 | 1,876 |
| Cumberland University of Tennessee; Lebanon, Tenn. 37087 | 700 (C) | P | 3,300 | 3,300 | 2,480 |
| Curry College; Milton, Mass. 02186 | 1,325 (C) | P | 7,850 | 7,850 | 3,925 |
| C. W. Post Center. See Long Island Univ. Center | | | | | |
| | | | | | |
| Daemen College; Amherst, N.Y. 14226 | 1,500 (C) | P | 5,300 | 5,300 | 2,800 |
| Dakota State College; Madison, S.D. 57042 | 919 (C) | Pub | 1,384 | 2,496 | 1,760 |
| Dakota Wesleyan University; Mitchell, S.D. 57301 | 693 (C) | P/UM | 3,890 | 3,890 | 2,300 |
| Dallas, University of; Irving, Tex. 75062 | 1,060 (C) | P/RC | 4,950 | 4,950 | 2,780 |
| Dallas Baptist University; Dallas, Tex. 75211 | 1,627 (C) | P/SB | 3,850 | 3,850 | 2,400 |
| | | | | | |
| Dallas Christian College; Dallas, Tex. 75234 | 135 (C) | P/ChC | 1,888 | 1,888 | 2,160 |
| Dana College; Blair, Neb. 68008 | 418 (C) | P/AL | 5,310 | 5,310 | 2,250 |
| Daniel Webster College; Nashua, N.H. 03063 | 445 (C) | P | 6,750 | 6,750 | 3,090 |
| Dartmouth College; Hanover, N.H. 03755 | 4,200 (C) | P | 11,679 | 11,679 | 4,360 |
| David Lipscomb College; Nashville, Tenn. 37203 | 2,132 (C) | P/CC | 3,485 | 3,485 | 2,310 |

| Institution and location | Enrollment | Control | Tuition ($) | | Rm/Bd ($) |
|---|---|---|---|---|---|
| | | | Res. | Nonres. | |
| Davidson College; Davidson, N.C. 28036 | 1,372 (C) | P/PUS | 8,380 | 8,380 | 2,795 |
| Davis and Elkins College; Elkins, W. Va. 26241 | 900 (C) | P/PUS | 5,351 | 5,351 | 2,925 |
| Dayton, University of; Dayton, Ohio 45469 | 6,300 (C) | P/RC | 5,740 | 5,740 | 2,854 |
| Defiance College; Defiance, Ohio 43512 | 905 (C) | P/UCC | 5,270 | 5,270 | 2,515 |
| Delaware, University of; Newark, Del. 19716 | 13,839 (C) | P | 2,100 | 4,800 | 2,400 |
| Delaware State College; Dover, Del. 19901 | 2,095 (C) | Pub | 810 | 860 | 2,000 |
| Delaware Valley College of Science and Agriculture; Doylestown, Pa. 18901 | 1,250 (C) | P | 6,000 | 6,000 | 2,800 |
| DeLourdes College; Des Plaines, Ill. 60016 | 204 | P/RC | 1,950 | 1,950 | n.a. |
| Delta State University; Cleveland, Miss. 38732 | 3,200 (C) | Pub | 1,000 | 1,182 | 1,440 |
| Denison University; Granville, Ohio 43023 | 2,100 (C) | P | 9,600 | 9,600 | 2,960 |
| Denver, University of; Denver, Colo. 80208 | 3,408 (C) | P | 6,984 | 6,984 | 3,030 |
| Colorado Women's College; Denver, Colo. 80220 | 366 (W) | P | 5,760 | 5,760 | n.a. |
| DePaul University; Chicago, Ill. 60604 | 7,714 (C) | P | 5,850 | 5,850 | 3,279 |
| DePauw University; Greencastle, Ind. 46135 | 2,300 (C) | P/UM | 8,200 | 8,200 | 3,215 |
| Deree College–Division of the American College of Greece; Athens, Greece GR-153 42 | 1,680 (C) | P | 1,800 | 1,800 | n.a. |
| Detroit, University of; Detroit, Mich. 48221 | 3,768 (C) | P/RC | 5,820 | 5,820 | 2,418 |
| Detroit Bible College. *See* William Tyndale College | | | | | |
| Detroit College of Business; Dearborn, Mich. 48126 | 3,216 (C) | P | 3,645 | 3,645 | n.a. |
| DeVry Institute of Technology; Atlanta, Ga. 30341 | 2,904 (C) | P | 3,846 | 3,846 | n.a. |
| DeVry Institute of Technology; Chicago, Ill. 60618 | 3,664 (C) | P | 3,846 | 3,846 | n.a. |
| DeVry Institute of Technology; City of Industry, Calif. 91744 | 2,226 | P | 3,846 | 3,846 | n.a. |
| DeVry Institute of Technology; Columbus, Ohio 43209 | 3,249 (C) | P | 3,846 | 3,846 | n.a. |
| DeVry Institute of Technology; Irving, Tex. 75062 | 2,259 (C) | P | 3,846 | 3,846 | n.a. |
| DeVry Institute of Technology; Kansas City, Mo. 64131 | 1,951 (C) | P | 3,846 | 3,846 | n.a. |
| DeVry Institute of Technology; Lombard, Ill. 60148 | 3,211 | P | 3,846 | 3,846 | n.a. |
| DeVry Institute of Technology; Phoenix, Ariz. 85021 | 3,446 (C) | P | 3,846 | 3,846 | n.a. |
| DeVry Technical Institute; Woodbridge, N.J. 07095 | 2,956 | P | 3,846 | 3,846 | n.a. |
| Dickinson College; Carlisle, Pa. 17013 | 1,867 (C) | P/UM | 10,200 | 10,200 | 3,150 |
| Dickinson State College; Dickinson, N.D. 58601 | 1,249 (C) | Pub | 1,143 | 2,119 | 1,630 |
| Dillard University; New Orleans, La. 70122 | 1,197 (C) | P | 3,900 | 3,900 | 2,600 |
| District of Columbia, Univ. of the; Washington, D.C. 20008 | 12,780 (C) | Pub | 496 | 2,344 | n.a. |
| Divine Word College; Epworth, Iowa 52045 | 72 (M) | P/RC | 3,800 | 3,800 | 1,200 |
| Doane College; Crete, Neb. 68333 | 650 (C) | P/UCC | 5,620 | 5,620 | 2,100 |
| Dr. Martin Luther College; New Ulm, Minn. 56073 | 517 (C) | P/EL | 1,950 | 1,950 | 1,680 |
| Dominican College of Blauvelt; Orangeburg, N.Y. 10962 | 1,654 (C) | P | 3,970 | 3,970 | 3,300 |
| Dominican College of San Rafael; San Rafael, Calif. 94901 | 550 (C) | P/RC | 6,650 | 6,650 | 3,955 |
| Dominican School of Philosophy and Theology; Berkeley, Calif. 94709 | 13 (M) | P/RC | 3,600 | 3,600 | n.a. |
| Don Bosco College; Newton, N.J. 07860 | 66 (M) | P/RC | 3,010 | 3,010 | 1,925 |
| Dordt College; Sioux Center, Iowa 51250 | 1,021 (C) | P/CR | 5,350 | 5,350 | 1,800 |
| Dowling College; Oakdale, N.Y. 11769 | 2,139 (C) | P | 4,675 | 4,675 | 2,848 |
| Drake University; Des Moines, Iowa 50311 | 3,811 (C) | P | 7,130 | 7,130 | 2,970 |
| Drew University–College of Liberal Arts; Madison, N.J. 07940 | 1,500 (C) | P/UM | 9,925 | 9,925 | 3,250 |
| Drexel University; Philadelphia, Pa. 19104 | 7,272 (C) | P | 6,093 | 6,093 | 3,250 |
| Drury College; Springfield, Mo. 65802 | 956 (C) | P/UCC | 5,075 | 5,075 | 2,204 |
| Dubuque, Univ. of–Coll. of Liberal Arts; Dubuque, Iowa 52001 | 986 (C) | P/UP | 5,675 | 5,675 | 2,250 |
| Duke University; Durham, N.C. 27706 | 5,800 (C) | P | 9,180 | 9,180 | 3,463 |
| Duquesne University; Pittsburgh, Pa. 15282 | 4,267 (C) | P/RC | 6,270 | 6,270 | 3,048 |
| Dyke College; Cleveland, Ohio 44115 | 1,380 (C) | P | 3,350 | 3,350 | n.a. |
| D'Youville College; Buffalo, N.Y. 14201 | 1,200 (C) | P | 5,510 | 5,510 | 2,470 |
| Earlham College; Richmond, Ind. 47374 | 1,000 (C) | P/F | 8,820 | 8,820 | 2,850 |
| East Carolina University; Greenville, N.C. 27834 | 11,833 (C) | Pub | 764 | 3,610 | 2,070 |
| East Central University; Ada, Okla. 74820 | 3,577 (C) | Pub | 800 | 1,700 | 2,100 |
| Eastern College; St. Davids, Pa. 19087 | 850 (C) | P/AB | 6,470 | 6,470 | 2,430 |
| Eastern Connecticut State Univ.; Willimantic, Conn. 06226 | 3,631 (C) | Pub | 1,288 | 3,248 | 2,684 |
| Eastern Illinois University; Charleston, Ill. 61920 | 9,926 (C) | Pub | 1,493 | 3,653 | 2,212 |
| Eastern Kentucky University; Richmond, Ky. 40475 | 10,961 (C) | Pub | 954 | 2,724 | 2,036 |
| Eastern Mennonite College; Harrisonburg, Va. 22801 | 848 (C) | P/Men | 5,250 | 5,250 | 2,328 |
| Eastern Michigan University; Ypsilanti, Mich. 48197 | 15,155 (C) | Pub | 1,454 | 3,438 | 2,618 |
| Eastern Montana College; Billings, Mont. 59101 | 4,173 (C) | Pub | 1,053 | 2,481 | 3,375 |
| Eastern Nazarene College; Quincy, Mass. 02170 | 775 (C) | P/Naz | 4,758 | 4,758 | 2,550 |
| Eastern New Mexico University; Portales, N.M. 88130 | 3,732 (C) | Pub | 802 | 2,506 | 1,796 |
| Eastern Oregon State College; La Grande, Ore. 97850 | 1,681 (C) | Pub | 1,422 | 1,422 | 2,505 |
| Eastern Washington University; Cheney, Wash. 99004 | 7,619 (C) | Pub | 1,212 | 4,206 | 2,400 |
| Eastman School of Music; Rochester, N.Y. 14604 | 420 | P | 9,000 | 9,000 | 3,370 |
| East Stroudsburg University of Pennsylvania; East Stroudsburg, Pa. 18301 | 3,859 (C) | Pub | 1,570 | 2,748 | 2,000 |
| East Tennessee State University; Johnson City, Tenn. 37614 | 8,298 (C) | Pub | 948 | 3,096 | 1,940 |
| East Texas Baptist University; Marshall, Tex. 75670 | 699 (C) | P/SB | 3,150 | 3,150 | 2,363 |
| East Texas State University; Commerce, Tex. 75428 | 4,319 (C) | Pub | 750 | 3,990 | 2,362 |
| East–West University; Chicago, Ill. 60605 | 542 | P | 3,630 | 3,630 | n.a. |

| Institution and location | Enrollment | Control | Tuition ($) Res. | Tuition ($) Nonres. | Rm/Bd ($) |
|---|---|---|---|---|---|
| Eckerd College; St. Petersburg, Fla. 33733 | 1,150 (C) | P/PUS | 8,225 | 8,225 | 3,020 |
| Edgewood College; Madison, Wis. 53711 | 800 (C) | P/RC | 4,800 | 4,800 | 2,500 |
| Edinboro University of Pennsylvania; Edinboro, Pa. 16444 | 5,312 (C) | Pub | 1,810 | 3,070 | 1,940 |
| Edward Waters College; Jacksonville, Fla. 32209 | 794 | P/AME | 2,716 | 2,716 | 3,400 |
| Electronic Data Processing College of Puerto Rico; Hato Rey, P.R. 00918 | 2,111 (C) | P | 1,881 | 1,881 | n.a. |
| Elizabeth City State University; Elizabeth City, N.C. 27909 | 1,700 (C) | Pub | 864 | 3,366 | 1,800 |
| Elizabethtown College; Elizabethtown, Pa. 17022 | 1,375 (C) | P/CB | 7,325 | 7,325 | 3,050 |
| Elmhurst College; Elmhurst, Ill. 60126 | 1,800 (C) | P/UCC | 5,550 | 5,550 | 2,630 |
| Elmira College; Elmira, N.Y. 14901 | 1,674 (C) | P | 7,250 | 7,250 | 3,200 |
| Elms College; Chicopee, Mass. 01013 | 600 | P | 6,150 | 6,150 | 3,150 |
| Elon College; Elon College, N.C. 27244 | 2,869 (C) | P/UCC | 3,576 | 3,576 | 2,610 |
| Embry-Riddle Aeronautical Univ.; Daytona Beach, Fla. 32010 | 4,800 (C) | P | 4,025 | 4,025 | 2,500 |
| Prescott Campus; Prescott, Ariz. 86301 | 1,000 (C) | P | 4,025 | 4,025 | 2,500 |
| Emerson College; Boston, Mass. 02116 | 2,089 (C) | P | 8,270 | 8,270 | 5,250 |
| Emmanuel College; Boston, Mass. 02115 | 1,000 (W) | P/RC | 6,200 | 6,200 | 3,300 |
| Emmanuel College School of Christian Ministries; Franklin Springs, Ga. 30639 | 30 (C) | P/PH | 2,430 | 2,430 | 1,935 |
| Emory and Henry College; Emory, Va. 24327 | 780 (C) | P/UM | 5,097 | 5,097 | 2,688 |
| Emory University; Atlanta, Ga. 30322 | 4,177 (C) | P | 9,370 | 9,370 | 3,600 |
| Emporia State University; Emporia, Kan. 66801 | 3,928 (C) | Pub | 1,090 | 2,266 | 2,060 |
| Erskine College; Due West, S.C. 29639 | 460 (C) | P/RP | 6,015 | 6,015 | 2,550 |
| Eugene Bible College; Eugene, Ore. 97405 | 130 (C) | P/OBS | 2,726 | 2,726 | 2,070 |
| Eureka College; Eureka, Ill. 61530 | 530 (C) | P/DC | 4,800 | 4,800 | 2,700 |
| Evangel College; Springfield, Mo. 65802 | 1,780 (C) | P/AG | 3,260 | 3,260 | 2,300 |
| Evansville, University of; Evansville, Ind. 47714 | 3,525 (C) | P/UM | 6,595 | 6,595 | 2,742 |
| Evergreen State College; Olympia, Wash. 98505 | 2,841 (C) | Pub | 1,212 | 4,206 | 2,790 |
| Fairfield University; Fairfield, Conn. 06430 | 2,899 (C) | P/RC | 6,900 | 6,900 | 3,730 |
| Fairhaven College–Western Washington University; Bellingham, Wash. 98225 | 215 (C) | Pub | 1,200 | 4,191 | 2,799 |
| Fairleigh Dickinson Univ.-Madison; Madison, N.J. 07940 | 2,400 (C) | P | 6,048 | 6,048 | 3,692 |
| Fairleigh Dickinson Univ.-Rutherford; Rutherford, N.J. 07070 | 1,600 (C) | P | 6,048 | 6,048 | 3,692 |
| Fairleigh Dickinson Univ.-Teaneck; Teaneck, N.J. 07666 | 3,700 (C) | P | 6,048 | 6,048 | 3,692 |
| Fairmont State College; Fairmont, W. Va. 26554 | 4,800 (C) | Pub | 856 | 2,316 | 2,400 |
| Faith Baptist Bible College; Ankeny, Iowa 50021 | 295 (C) | P/B | 3,170 | 3,170 | 2,310 |
| Faulkner University; Montgomery, Ala. 36193 | 1,600 (C) | P | 3,040 | 3,040 | 2,460 |
| Fayetteville State University; Fayetteville, N.C. 28301 | 2,567 (C) | Pub | 912 | 3,758 | 1,820 |
| Felician College; Lodi, N.J. 07644 | 643 (W) | P/RC | 3,910 | 3,910 | n.a. |
| Ferris State College; Big Rapids, Mich. 49307 | 10,762 (C) | Pub | 1,671 | 3,381 | 2,454 |
| Ferrum College; Ferrum, Va. 24088 | 1,200 (C) | P/UM | 5,200 | 5,200 | 2,750 |
| Findlay College; Findlay, Ohio 45840 | 1,499 (C) | P/CG | 5,430 | 5,430 | 2,500 |
| Fisk University; Nashville, Tenn. 37203 | 737 (C) | P | 4,315 | 4,315 | 2,085 |
| Fitchburg State College; Fitchburg, Mass. 01420 | 5,372 (C) | Pub | 1,184 | 3,380 | 2,130 |
| Flagler College; St. Augustine, Fla. 32085 | 1,040 (C) | P | 3,470 | 3,470 | 2,180 |
| Flaming Rainbow University; Stilwell, Okla. 74960 | 245 | P | 2,710 | 2,710 | n.a. |
| Florida, University of; Gainesville, Fla. 32611 | 28,226 (C) | Pub | 970 | 2,969 | 3,240 |
| Florida A&M University; Tallahassee, Fla. 32307 | 5,101 (C) | Pub | 1,020 | 3,067 | 2,060 |
| Florida Atlantic University; Boca Raton, Fla. 33431 | 8,987 (C) | Pub | 1,066 | 3,600 | 2,700 |
| Florida Christian College; Kissimmee, Fla. 32742 | 130 | P | 2,295 | 2,295 | 2,145 |
| Florida Institute of Technology; Melbourne, Fla. 32901 | 3,900 (C) | P | 5,472 | 5,472 | 2,745 |
| Florida International University; Miami, Fla. 33199 | 15,875 (C) | Pub | 939 | 2,667 | 3,425 |
| Florida Memorial College; Miami, Fla. 33054 | 1,750 (C) | P/AB | 3,050 | 3,050 | 2,250 |
| Florida Southern College; Lakeland, Fla. 33801 | 1,815 (C) | P/UM | 4,490 | 4,490 | 3,000 |
| Florida State University; Tallahassee, Fla. 32306 | 16,147 (C) | Pub | 912 | 2,520 | 2,550 |
| Fontbonne College; St. Louis, Mo. 63105 | 860 (W) | P/RC | 5,565 | 5,565 | 2,850 |
| Fordham University–Lincoln Center; New York, N.Y. 10023 | 2,373 (C) | P | 5,700 | 5,700 | n.a. |
| Fordham Univ.-Rose Hill Campus; New York, N.Y. 10458 | 4,785 (C) | P | 6,850 | 6,850 | 3,500 |
| Forsyth School for Dental Hygienists; Boston, Mass. 02115 | 150 (C) | P | 5,900 | 5,900 | 4,620 |
| Fort Hays State University; Hays, Kan. 67601 | 3,954 (C) | Pub | 1,152 | 2,328 | 1,898 |
| Fort Lauderdale College; Fort Lauderdale, Fla. 33301 | 1,000 (C) | P | 3,300 | 3,300 | n.a. |
| Fort Lewis College; Durango, Colo. 81301 | 3,700 (C) | Pub | 990 | 3,388 | 2,110 |
| Fort Valley State College; Fort Valley, Ga. 31030 | 1,870 (C) | Pub | 1,640 | 2,560 | 2,438 |
| Fort Wayne Bible College; Fort Wayne, Ind. 46807 | 360 (C) | P/MC | 4,174 | 4,174 | 2,390 |
| Framingham State College; Framingham, Mass. 01701 | 3,211 (C) | Pub | 1,398 | 3,594 | 2,070 |
| Francis Marion College; Florence, S.C. 29501 | 3,067 (C) | Pub | 1,100 | 2,200 | 2,700 |
| Franklin and Marshall College; Lancaster, Pa. 17604 | 2,000 (C) | P/UCC | 10,200 | 10,200 | 3,280 |
| Franklin College; Franklin, Ind. 46131 | 715 (C) | P/AB | 6,330 | 6,330 | 2,480 |
| Franklin Pierce College; Rindge, N.H. 03461 | 975 (C) | P | 7,195 | 7,195 | 3,055 |
| Franklin University; Columbus, Ohio 43215 | 4,272 (C) | P | 2,858 | 2,858 | n.a. |
| Freed-Hardeman College; Henderson, Tenn. 38340 | 1,050 (C) | P/CC | 3,040 | 3,040 | 2,260 |
| Free Will Baptist Bible College; Nashville, Tenn. 37205 | 358 (C) | P/FWB | 2,400 | 2,400 | 2,160 |
| Fresno Pacific College; Fresno, Calif. 93702 | 450 (C) | P/MB | 5,390 | 5,390 | 2,600 |
| Friends Bible College; Haviland, Kan. 67059 | 135 (C) | P/F | 4,000 | 4,000 | 1,600 |

| Institution and location | Enrollment | Control | Tuition ($) Res. | Tuition ($) Nonres. | Rm/Bd ($) |
|---|---|---|---|---|---|
| Friends University; Wichita, Kan. 67213 | 804 (C) | P/F | 4,280 | 4,280 | 2,040 |
| Friends World College; Huntington, N.Y. 11743 | 450 | P | 5,700 | 5,700 | 3,900 |
| Frostburg State College; Frostburg, Md. 21532 | 3,225 (C) | Pub | 1,546 | 2,864 | 2,860 |
| Furman University; Greenville, S.C. 29613 | 2,400 (C) | P/SB | 6,656 | 6,656 | 3,048 |
| Gallaudet College; Washington, D.C. 20002 | 1,260 (C) | P | 2,154 | 2,154 | 2,946 |
| Gannon University; Erie, Pa. 16541 | 2,938 (C) | P/RC | 4,800 | 4,800 | 2,300 |
| Gardner–Webb College; Boiling Springs, N.C. 28017 | 1,640 (C) | P/SB | 4,530 | 4,530 | 2,570 |
| General Motors Institute. *See* GMI Engineering and Management Institute | | | | | |
| Geneva College; Beaver Falls, Pa. 15010 | 1,197 (C) | P/RP | 5,360 | 5,360 | 2,710 |
| George Fox College; Newberg, Ore. 97132 | 625 (C) | P/F | 5,770 | 5,770 | 2,595 |
| George Mason University; Fairfax, Va. 22030 | 12,229 (C) | Pub | 1,608 | 3,120 | 3,524 |
| Georgetown College; Georgetown, Ky. 40324 | 1,003 (C) | P/SB | 4,262 | 4,262 | 2,788 |
| Georgetown University; Washington, D.C. 20057 | 5,300 (C) | P/RC | 9,300 | 9,300 | 4,400 |
| George Washington University; Washington, D.C. 20052 | 6,143 (C) | P | 8,245 | 8,245 | 4,520 |
| Georgia, University of; Athens, Ga. 30602 | 19,958 (C) | Pub | 1,632 | 4,302 | 2,340 |
| Georgia College; Milledgeville, Ga. 31061 | 3,226 (C) | Pub | 1,128 | 3,048 | 1,710 |
| Georgia Institute of Technology; Atlanta, Ga. 30332 | 8,806 (C) | Pub | 1,587 | 4,692 | 3,030 |
| Georgian Court College; Lakewood, N.J. 08701 | 1,234 (W) | P/RC | 4,930 | 4,930 | 3,000 |
| Georgia Southern College; Statesboro, Ga. 30458 | 6,001 (C) | Pub | 1,242 | 3,162 | 1,890 |
| Georgia Southwestern College; Americus, Ga. 31709 | 1,930 (C) | Pub | 1,320 | 3,300 | 2,000 |
| Georgia State University; Atlanta, Ga. 30303 | 15,038 (C) | Pub | 1,320 | 4,383 | n.a. |
| Gettysburg College; Gettysburg, Pa. 17325 | 1,850 (C) | P/L | 8,575 | 8,575 | 2,609 |
| Glassboro State College; Glassboro, N.J. 08028 | 5,500 (C) | Pub | 1,450 | 2,168 | 3,250 |
| Glenville State College; Glenville, W. Va. 26351 | 1,800 (C) | Pub | 850 | 2,300 | 2,450 |
| GMI Engineering & Management Institute; Flint, Mich. 48502 | 2,997 (C) | P | 5,264 | 5,264 | 2,100 |
| Goddard College; Plainfield, Vt. 05667 | 180 (C) | P | 6,950 | 6,950 | 2,400 |
| God's Bible School and College; Cincinnati, Ohio 45210 | 300 | P | 1,440 | 1,440 | 2,050 |
| Golden Gate University; San Francisco, Calif. 94105 | 2,552 (C) | P | 3,328 | 3,328 | n.a. |
| Goldey Beacom College; Wilmington, Del. 19808 | 2,025 (C) | P | 3,600 | 3,600 | 2,950 |
| Gonzaga University; Spokane, Wash. 99258 | 2,261 (C) | P | 6,700 | 6,700 | 2,940 |
| Gordon College; Wenham, Mass. 01984 | 1,258 (C) | P | 7,722 | 7,722 | 2,850 |
| Goshen College; Goshen, Ind. 46526 | 951 (C) | P/Men | 5,520 | 5,520 | 2,385 |
| Goucher College; Towson, Md. 21204 | 950 (W) | P | 8,800 | 8,800 | 4,440 |
| Governors State University; University Park, Ill. 60466 | 2,293 (C) | Pub | 1,168 | 3,424 | n.a. |
| Grace Bible College; Grand Rapids, Mich. 49509 | 130 (C) | P/GGF | 2,310 | 2,310 | 2,150 |
| Grace College; Winona Lake, Ind. 46590 | 783 (C) | P | 4,333 | 4,333 | 2,460 |
| Grace College of the Bible; Omaha, Neb. 68108 | 290 (C) | P/Ind | 2,820 | 2,820 | 2,000 |
| Graceland College; Lamoni, Iowa 50140 | 1,000 (C) | P | 5,145 | 5,145 | 1,955 |
| Grambling State University; Grambling, La. 71245 | 4,587 (C) | Pub | 1,094 | 1,774 | 2,062 |
| Grand Canyon College; Phoenix, Ariz. 85017 | 1,515 (C) | P/SB | 2,891 | 2,891 | 2,005 |
| Grand Rapids Baptist College; Grand Rapids, Mich. 49505 | 727 (C) | P/B | 3,730 | 3,730 | 2,628 |
| Grand Valley State College; Allendale, Mich. 49401 | 6,292 (C) | Pub | 1,502 | 3,504 | 2,720 |
| Grand View College; Des Moines, Iowa 50316 | 1,340 (C) | P/LCA | 4,540 | 4,540 | 2,000 |
| Gratz College; Philadelphia, Pa. 19141 | 317 (C) | P | 810 | 810 | n.a. |
| Great Falls, College of; Great Falls, Mont. 59405 | 1,025 (C) | P/RC | 3,400 | 3,400 | 1,800 |
| Great Lakes Bible College; Lansing, Mich. 48901 | 155 (C) | P/CC | 2,490 | 2,490 | 2,703 |
| Green Mountain College; Poultney, Vt. 05764 | 450 (C) | P | 5,737 | 5,737 | 3,408 |
| Greensboro College; Greensboro, N.C. 27401 | 575 (C) | P/UM | 4,500 | 4,500 | 2,300 |
| Greenville College; Greenville, Ill. 62246 | 628 (C) | P/FM | 5,742 | 5,742 | 2,735 |
| Griffin College; Seattle, Wash. 98121 | 1,000 (C) | P | 4,950 | 4,950 | n.a. |
| Grinnell College; Grinnell, Iowa 50112 | 1,207 (C) | P | 8,436 | 8,436 | 2,544 |
| Grove City College; Grove City, Pa. 16127 | 2,162 (C) | P | 3,470 | 3,470 | 1,900 |
| Guam, University of; Mangilao, Guam 96913 | 2,280 (C) | Pub | 731 | 1,211 | 2,200 |
| Guilford College; Greensboro, N.C. 27410 | 1,132 (C) | P/F | 5,480 | 5,480 | 2,660 |
| Gustavus Adolphus College; St. Peter, Minn. 56082 | 2,210 (C) | P/LCA | 7,850 | 7,850 | 2,300 |
| Gwynedd–Mercy College; Gwynedd Valley, Pa. 19437 | 2,000 (W) | P/RC | 4,900 | 4,900 | 2,750 |
| Hahnemann University of Allied Health Professions; Philadelphia, Pa. 19102 | 846 (C) | P | 5,400 | 5,400 | 3,500 |
| Hamilton College; Clinton, N.Y. 13323 | 1,600 (C) | P | 10,900 | 10,900 | 3,450 |
| Hamline University; St. Paul, Minn. 55104 | 1,177 (C) | P/UM | 7,475 | 7,475 | 2,815 |
| Hampden–Sydney College; Hampden–Sydney, Va. 23943 | 775 (M) | P/PUS | 8,195 | 8,195 | 2,680 |
| Hampshire College; Amherst, Mass. 01002 | 950 (C) | P | 11,850 | 11,850 | 3,125 |
| Hampton University; Hampton, Va. 23668 | 3,400 (C) | P | 4,065 | 4,065 | 1,930 |
| Hannibal–LaGrange College; Hannibal, Mo. 63401 | 764 (C) | P/SB | 3,264 | 3,264 | 1,794 |
| Hanover College; Hanover, Ind. 47243 | 1,015 (C) | P/UP | 4,680 | 4,680 | 2,120 |
| Harding University; Searcy, Ark. 72143 | 2,828 (C) | P/CC | 3,408 | 3,408 | 2,400 |
| Hardin–Simmons University; Abilene, Tex. 79698 | 1,817 (C) | P | 3,828 | 3,828 | 2,390 |
| Harris–Stowe State College; St. Louis, Mo. 63103 | 1,340 (C) | Pub | 792 | 1,552 | n.a. |
| Hartford, University of; West Hartford, Conn. 06117 | 5,589 (C) | P | 8,575 | 8,575 | 4,133 |
| Hartwick College; Oneonta, N.Y. 13820 | 1,397 (C) | P | 8,600 | 8,600 | 3,075 |
| Harvard and Radcliffe Colleges; Cambridge, Mass. 02138 | 6,603 | P | 11,390 | 11,390 | 4,755 |

| Institution and location | Enrollment | Control | Tuition ($) Res. | Tuition ($) Nonres. | Rm/Bd ($) |
|---|---|---|---|---|---|
| Harvey Mudd College. *See* Claremont Colleges | | | | | |
| Hastings College; Hastings, Neb. 68901 | 830 (C) | P/UP | 5,550 | 5,550 | 2,220 |
| Haverford College; Haverford, Pa. 19041 | 1,000 (C) | P | 9,990 | 9,990 | 3,700 |
| Hawaii, University of, at Hilo; Hilo, Hawaii 96720 | 1,158 (C) | Pub | 255 | 1,730 | 3,094 |
| Hawaii, University of, at Manoa; Honolulu, Hawaii 96822 | 14,645 (C) | Pub | 1,020 | 3,870 | 2,442 |
| Hawaii, University of–West Oahu College; Pearl City, Hawaii 96782 | 443 (C) | Pub | 680 | 2,340 | n.a. |
| Hawaii Loa College; Kaneohe, Hawaii 96744 | 475 (C) | P | 5,300 | 5,300 | 3,200 |
| Hawaii Pacific College; Honolulu, Hawaii 96813 | 3,707 (C) | P | 3,630 | 3,630 | n.a. |
| Hawthorne College; Antrim, N.H. 03440 | 350 (C) | P | 6,350 | 6,350 | 3,100 |
| Health Sciences, University of–School of Related Health Sciences; North Chicago, Ill. 60064 | 70 (C) | P | 5,599 | 5,599 | n.a. |
| Hebrew College; Brookline, Mass. 02146 | 180 (C) | P | 1,300 | 1,300 | n.a. |
| Hebrew Union College–Jewish Institute of Religion; Los Angeles, Calif. 90007 | 75 | P | 5,100 | 5,100 | n.a. |
| Hebrew Union College–Jewish Institute of Religion; New York, N.Y. 10012 | 16 (M) | P | 4,900 | 4,900 | n.a. |
| Heidelberg College; Tiffin, Ohio 44883 | 1,010 (C) | P | 8,200 | 8,200 | 2,750 |
| Hellenic College; Brookline, Mass. 02146 | 71 | P | 4,060 | 4,060 | 2,570 |
| Henderson State University; Arkadelphia, Ark. 71923 | 2,781 (C) | Pub | 850 | 1,680 | 1,650 |
| Hendrix College; Conway, Ark. 72023 | 975 (C) | P/UM | 4,200 | 4,200 | 1,905 |
| Herbert H. Lehman College. *See* New York, City University of | | | | | |
| Heritage College; Toppenish, Wash. 98948 | 306 | P | 2,640 | 2,640 | n.a. |
| High Point College; High Point, N.C. 27261 | 1,353 (C) | P/UM | 4,530 | 4,530 | 2,000 |
| Hillsdale College; Hillsdale, Mich. 49242 | 1,000 (C) | P | 6,870 | 6,870 | 3,030 |
| Hillsdale Free Will Baptist College; Moore, Okla. 73153 | 142 | P | 2,000 | 2,000 | 2,100 |
| Hiram College; Hiram, Ohio 44234 | 1,100 (C) | P | 8,404 | 8,404 | 2,634 |
| Hobart and William Smith Colleges; Geneva, N.Y. 14456 | 1,800 (C) | P | 9,600 | 9,600 | 3,600 |
| Hofstra University; Hempstead, N.Y. 11550 | 6,500 (C) | P | 6,320 | 6,320 | 3,230 |
| Hollins College; Hollins College, Va. 24020 | 850 (W) | P | 8,250 | 8,250 | 3,650 |
| Holy Apostles College and Seminary; Cromwell, Conn. 06416 | 57 (M) | P/RC | 2,600 | 2,600 | 2,400 |
| Holy Cross, College of the; Worcester, Mass. 01610 | 2,500 (C) | P/RC | 9,200 | 9,200 | 4,100 |
| Holy Family College; Philadelphia, Pa. 19114 | 1,633 (C) | P | 4,400 | 4,400 | n.a. |
| Holy Names College; Oakland, Calif. 94619 | 550 (C) | P/RC | 6,570 | 6,570 | 3,400 |
| Hong Kong Baptist College; Kowloon, Hong Kong | 2,200 | Pub | 550 | 550 | n.a. |
| Hood College; Frederick, Md. 21701 | 1,070 (W) | P | 8,350 | 8,350 | 4,235 |
| Hope College; Holland, Mich. 49423 | 2,522 (C) | P/RCA | 6,780 | 6,780 | 2,916 |
| Hotel and Restaurant Management, School of, of Widener University; Wilmington, Del. 19803 | 450 (C) | P | 5,200 | 5,200 | 3,500 |
| Houghton College; Houghton, N.Y. 14744 | 1,290 (C) | P/W | 5,900 | 5,900 | 2,495 |
| Houghton College–Buffalo Suburban Campus; West Seneca, N.Y. 14225 | 130 (C) | P | 4,400 | 4,400 | 1,860 |
| Houston, Univ. of–Clear Lake; Houston, Tex. 77058 | 3,063 (C) | Pub | 758 | 3,254 | n.a. |
| Houston, Univ. of–Downtown; Houston, Tex. 77002 | 7,213 (C) | Pub | 770 | 4,010 | 2,714 |
| Houston, Univ. of–University Park; Houston, Tex. 77004 | 31,095 (C) | Pub | 742 | 3,240 | 3,200 |
| Houston Baptist University; Houston, Tex. 77074 | 2,775 (C) | P | 3,960 | 3,960 | 2,163 |
| Howard Payne University; Brownwood, Tex. 76801 | 1,000 (C) | P/SB | 2,490 | 2,490 | 2,160 |
| Howard University; Washington, D.C. 20059 | 8,874 (C) | P | 3,365 | 3,365 | 2,950 |
| Human Services, College for; New York, N.Y. 10014 | 630 | P | 5,520 | 5,520 | n.a. |
| Humboldt State University; Arcata, Calif. 95521 | 6,221 (C) | Pub | 760 | 4,230 | 3,100 |
| Hunter College. *See* New York, City University of | | | | | |
| Huntingdon College; Montgomery, Ala. 36194 | 790 (C) | P/UM | 3,790 | 3,790 | 2,760 |
| Huntington College; Huntington, Ind. 46750 | 433 (C) | P/BC | 5,500 | 5,500 | 2,295 |
| Huron College; Huron, S.D. 57350 | 400 (C) | P | 4,240 | 4,240 | 2,375 |
| Husson College; Bangor, Me. 04401 | 1,482 (C) | P | 5,550 | 5,550 | 3,100 |
| Huston–Tillotson College; Austin, Tex. 78702 | 569 (C) | P | 3,000 | 3,000 | 2,377 |
| Idaho, College of; Caldwell, Idaho 83605 | 670 (C) | P | 5,800 | 5,800 | 2,556 |
| Idaho, University of; Moscow, Idaho 83843 | 7,106 (C) | Pub | 1,010 | 3,010 | 2,223 |
| Idaho State University; Pocatello, Idaho 83209 | 5,926 (C) | Pub | 1,040 | 2,940 | 2,292 |
| Illinois, Univ. of, at Chicago; Chicago, Ill. 60680 | 17,081 (C) | Pub | 1,935 | 4,563 | 4,986 |
| Illinois, Univ. of, at Urbana–Champaign; Urbana, Ill. 61801 | 27,232 (C) | Pub | 1,844 | 4,472 | 3,100 |
| Illinois Benedictine College; Lisle, Ill. 60532 | 1,800 (C) | P/RC | 5,286 | 5,286 | 2,690 |
| Illinois College; Jacksonville, Ill. 62650 | 800 (C) | P | 3,900 | 3,900 | 1,985 |
| Illinois Institute of Technology; Chicago, Ill. 60616 | 2,934 (C) | P | 7,970 | 7,970 | 3,477 |
| Illinois State University; Normal, Ill. 61761 | 18,253 (C) | Pub | 1,429 | 3,421 | 2,289 |
| Illinois Wesleyan University; Bloomington, Ill. 61702 | 1,600 (C) | P | 7,290 | 7,290 | 2,880 |
| Immaculata College; Immaculata, Pa. 19345 | 1,800 (W) | P/RC | 4,500 | 4,500 | 3,200 |
| Incarnate Word College; San Antonio, Tex. 78209 | 1,293 (C) | P/RC | 4,768 | 4,768 | 2,174 |
| Indiana Central University; Indianapolis, Ind. 46227 | 2,561 (C) | P/UM | 5,980 | 5,980 | 2,450 |
| Indiana Institute of Technology; Fort Wayne, Ind. 46803 | 800 (C) | P | 4,650 | 4,650 | 2,580 |
| Indiana State University; Terre Haute, Ind. 47809 | 8,962 (C) | Pub | 1,542 | 3,622 | 2,176 |
| Indiana University–Bloomington; Bloomington, Ind. 47405 | 23,000 (C) | Pub | 1,680 | 4,650 | 2,425 |
| Indiana University–East; Richmond, Ind. 47374 | 1,317 (C) | Pub | 1,406 | 3,371 | n.a. |
| Indiana University–Kokomo; Kokomo, Ind. 46902 | 2,292 (C) | Pub | 1,390 | 3,355 | n.a. |
| Indiana University–Northwest; Gary, Ind. 46408 | 3,868 (C) | Pub | 1,386 | 3,351 | n.a. |

| Institution and location | Enrollment | Control | Tuition ($) Res. | Tuition ($) Nonres. | Rm/Bd ($) |
|---|---|---|---|---|---|
| Indiana University of Pennsylvania; Indiana, Pa. 15705 | 11,690 (C) | Pub | 1,978 | 2,956 | 2,074 |
| Indiana University–Purdue University at Columbus; Columbus, Ind. 47201 | 950 (C) | Pub | 1,500 | 3,500 | n.a. |
| Indiana University–Purdue University at Fort Wayne; Fort Wayne, Ind. 46805 | 9,200 (C) | Pub | 1,478 | 3,600 | n.a. |
| Indiana University–Purdue University at Indianapolis; Indianapolis, Ind. 46202 | 15,118 (C) | Pub | 1,116 | 2,952 | 2,500 |
| Indiana University–South Bend; South Bend, Ind. 46634 | 4,324 (C) | Pub | 1,368 | 3,350 | n.a. |
| Indiana University–Southeast; New Albany, Ind. 47150 | 4,200 (C) | Pub | 1,130 | 2,730 | n.a. |
| Insurance, College of; New York, N.Y. 10007 | 940 (C) | P | 4,860 | 4,860 | 5,562 |
| Inter American University–Arecibo Regional College; Arecibo, P.R. 00612 | 3,700 (C) | P | 1,760 | 1,760 | n.a. |
| International Bible College; Florence, Ala. 35630 | 132 | P | 1,500 | 1,500 | 520 |
| International College; Honolulu, Hawaii 96809 | 46 | P | 1,870 | 1,870 | n.a. |
| International Institute of the Americas of World University; Hato Rey, P.R. 00917 | 4,600 (C) | P | 2,280 | 2,280 | n.a. |
| International Training, School for; Brattleboro, Vt. 05301 | 70 (C) | P | 6,300 | 6,300 | 2,700 |
| Iona College; New Rochelle, N.Y. 10801 | 3,536 (C) | P | 5,650 | 5,650 | 3,700 |
| Iowa, University of; Iowa City, Iowa 52242 | 21,586 (C) | Pub. | 1,390 | 4,080 | 2,240 |
| Iowa State University; Ames, Iowa 50011 | 22,795 (C) | Pub | 1,390 | 4,080 | 2,040 |
| Iowa Wesleyan College; Mount Pleasant, Iowa 52641 | 652 (C) | P/UM | 5,600 | 5,600 | 2,270 |
| Ithaca College; Ithaca, N.Y. 14850 | 5,145 (C) | P | 7,046 | 7,046 | 3,140 |
| Jackson College for Women. *See* Tufts University | | | | | |
| Jackson State University; Jackson, Miss. 39217 | 6,500 (C) | Pub | 1,172 | 1,186 | 2,132 |
| Jacksonville State University; Jacksonville, Ala. 36265 | 6,241 (C) | Pub | 800 | 1,050 | 1,600 |
| Jacksonville University; Jacksonville, Fla. 32211 | 2,125 (C) | P | 5,020 | 5,020 | 2,720 |
| James Madison University; Harrisonburg, Va. 22807 | 8,496 (C) | Pub | 2,392 | 4,222 | 2,828 |
| Jamestown College; Jamestown, N.D. 58401 | 550 (C) | P/UP | 5,620 | 5,620 | 1,995 |
| Jarvis Christian College; Hawkins, Tex. 75765 | 590 (C) | P | 3,400 | 3,400 | 1,919 |
| Jersey City State College; Jersey City, N.J. 07305 | 6,334 (C) | Pub | 1,320 | 1,960 | 1,250 |
| Jewish Theological Seminary of America; New York, N.Y. 10027 | 100 | P | 4,125 | 4,125 | 4,300 |
| John Brown University; Siloam Springs, Ark. 72761 | 800 (C) | P | 3,200 | 3,200 | 2,400 |
| John Carroll University; Cleveland, Ohio 44118 | 3,200 (C) | P/RC | 5,824 | 5,824 | 3,375 |
| John F. Kennedy University–Evenings; Orinda, Calif. 94563 | 306 (C) | P | 3,351 | 3,351 | n.a. |
| John Jay Coll. of Criminal Justice. *See* New York, City Univ. of | | | | | |
| Johns Hopkins University; Baltimore, Md. 21218 | 2,400 (C) | P | 9,400 | 9,400 | 3,900 |
| Johnson and Wales College; Providence, R.I. 02903 | 5,100 (C) | P | 5,490 | 5,490 | 3,200 |
| Johnson Bible College; Knoxville, Tenn. 37998 | 397 (C) | P/ChC | 2,150 | 2,150 | 2,125 |
| Johnson C. Smith University; Charlotte, N.C. 28216 | 1,272 (C) | P | 3,552 | 3,552 | 1,806 |
| Johnson State College; Johnson, Vt. 05656 | 1,022 (C) | Pub | 2,260 | 4,688 | 3,194 |
| Johnston College, Calif. *See* Redlands, University of | | | | | |
| John Wesley College; High Point, N.C. 27260 | 80 (C) | P/ID | 2,010 | 2,010 | n.a. |
| Jones College–Jacksonville; Jacksonville, Fla. 32211 | 1,700 (C) | P | 2,147 | 2,147 | n.a. |
| Judson College; Elgin, Ill. 60120 | 485 (C) | P/B | 5,810 | 5,810 | 2,940 |
| Judson College; Marion, Ala. 36756 | 329 (W) | P/SB | 3,105 | 3,105 | 3,080 |
| Juilliard School; New York, N.Y. 10023 | 591 (C) | P | 6,100 | 6,100 | n.a. |
| Juniata College; Huntingdon, Pa. 16652 | 1,200 (C) | P | 8,050 | 8,050 | 2,750 |
| Kalamazoo College; Kalamazoo, Mich. 49007 | 1,115 (C) | P/AB | 8,400 | 8,400 | 2,982 |
| Kansas, University of; Lawrence, Kan. 66045 | 18,155 (C) | Pub | 1,300 | 3,150 | 2,100 |
| Kansas, University of–College of Health Sciences; Kansas City, Kan. 66103 | 551 (C) | Pub | 1,080 | 2,990 | n.a. |
| Kansas City Art Institute; Kansas City, Mo. 64111 | 450 (C) | P | 7,200 | 7,200 | 3,000 |
| Kansas Newman College; Wichita, Kan. 67213 | 901 (C) | P | 4,110 | 4,110 | 2,060 |
| Kansas State University; Manhattan, Kan. 66506 | 13,000 (C) | Pub | 1,301 | 3,212 | 2,020 |
| Kansas Wesleyan University; Salina, Kan. 67401 | 666 (C) | P/UM | 4,077 | 4,077 | 2,499 |
| Kean College of New Jersey; Union, N.J. 07083 | 12,000 (C) | Pub | 1,335 | 1,994 | 2,658 |
| Kearney State College; Kearney, Neb. 68849 | 8,300 (C) | Pub | 1,024 | 1,608 | 1,740 |
| Keene State College; Keene, N.H. 03431 | 2,815 (C) | Pub | 1,878 | 4,278 | 2,254 |
| Kendall College; Evanston, Ill. 60201 | 343 (C) | P | 4,875 | 4,875 | 2,900 |
| Kendall School of Design; Grand Rapids, Mich. 49503 | 680 (C) | P | 4,428 | 4,428 | n.a. |
| Kennesaw College; Marietta, Ga. 30061 | 6,402 (C) | Pub | 1,044 | 2,964 | n.a. |
| Kent State University; Kent, Ohio 44242 | 16,220 (C) | Pub | 2,104 | 3,704 | 2,396 |
| Kentucky, University of; Lexington, Ky. 40506 | 16,002 (C) | Pub | 1,332 | 3,812 | 2,543 |
| Kentucky Christian College; Grayson, Ky. 41143 | 430 (C) | P/ChC | 2,223 | 2,223 | 2,118 |
| Kentucky State University; Frankfort, Ky. 40601 | 2,339 (C) | Pub | 884 | 2,654 | 1,930 |
| Kentucky Wesleyan College; Owensboro, Ky. 42301 | 850 (C) | P/UM | 4,300 | 4,300 | 2,500 |
| Kenyon College; Gambier, Ohio 43022 | 1,460 (C) | P | 10,300 | 10,300 | 2,800 |
| Keuka College; Keuka Park, N.Y. 14478 | 450 (W) | P | 6,300 | 6,300 | 2,580 |
| King College; Bristol, Tenn. 37620 | 585 (C) | P/PUS | 4,050 | 4,050 | 2,700 |
| King's College; Briarcliff Manor, N.Y. 10510 | 647 (C) | P/ND | 5,780 | 5,780 | 2,485 |
| King's College; Wilkes-Barre, Pa. 18711 | 2,271 (C) | P/RC | 5,550 | 5,550 | 2,870 |
| Knox College; Galesburg, Ill. 61401 | 944 (C) | P | 8,565 | 8,565 | 2,730 |

| Institution and location | Enrollment | Control | Tuition ($) Res. | Tuition ($) Nonres. | Rm/Bd ($) |
|---|---|---|---|---|---|
| Knoxville College; Knoxville, Tenn. 37921 | 500 (C) | P | 3,417 | 3,417 | 2,034 |
| Kutztown Univ. of Pennsylvania; Kutztown, Pa. 19530 | 5,724 (C) | Pub | 1,738 | 3,006 | 1,840 |
| | | | | | |
| Laboratory Institute of Merchandising; New York, N.Y. 10022 | 260 | P | 5,895 | 5,895 | 4,000 |
| Lafayette College; Easton, Pa. 18042 | 2,070 (C) | P | 9,950 | 9,950 | 3,525 |
| LaGrange College; LaGrange, Ga. 30240 | 954 (C) | P/UM | 3,090 | 3,090 | 2,010 |
| Lake Erie College; Painesville, Ohio 44077 | 1,000 (W) | P | 6,400 | 6,400 | 3,000 |
| Lake Forest College; Lake Forest, Ill. 60045 | 1,100 (C) | P | 9,140 | 9,140 | 2,430 |
| Lakeland College; Sheboygan, Wis. 53082 | 400 (C) | P/UCC | 5,900 | 5,900 | 2,750 |
| Lake Superior State College; Sault Ste. Marie, Mich. 49783 | 2,651 (C) | Pub | 1,527 | 2,832 | 2,642 |
| | | | | | |
| Lamar University; Beaumont, Tex. 77710 | 14,230 (C) | Pub | 1,285 | 4,405 | 2,450 |
| Lambuth College; Jackson, Tenn. 38301 | 800 (C) | P/UM | 3,900 | 3,900 | 2,080 |
| Lancaster Bible College; Lancaster, Pa. 17601 | 343 (C) | P | 4,330 | 4,330 | 2,240 |
| Lander College; Greenwood, S.C. 29646 | 2,323 (C) | Pub | 1,270 | 1,870 | 1,940 |
| Lane College; Jackson, Tenn. 38301 | 795 (C) | P/CME | 2,700 | 2,700 | 1,810 |
| Langston University; Langston, Okla. 73050 | 2,026 (C) | Pub | 936 | 2,438 | 2,375 |
| Laredo State University; Laredo, Tex. 78040 | 444 (C) | Pub | 585 | 3,825 | 2,600 |
| | | | | | |
| La Roche College; Pittsburgh, Pa. 15237 | 1,607 (C) | P | 4,760 | 4,760 | 2,750 |
| La Salle University; Philadelphia, Pa. 19141 | 4,901 (C) | P/RC | 6,150 | 6,150 | 3,170 |
| La Verne, University of; La Verne, Calif. 91750 | 1,304 (C) | P/Ind | 7,190 | 7,190 | 3,430 |
| Lawrence Institute of Technology; Southfield, Mich. 48075 | 5,444 (C) | P | 2,520 | 2,520 | 3,312 |
| Lawrence University; Appleton, Wis. 54912 | 1,050 (C) | P | 9,252 | 9,252 | 2,574 |
| Lebanon Valley College; Annville, Pa. 17003 | 759 (C) | P/UM | 7,450 | 7,450 | 3,000 |
| Lee College; Cleveland, Tenn. 37311 | 1,204 (C) | P | 2,400 | 2,400 | 2,694 |
| | | | | | |
| Lee College of the University of Judaism; Los Angeles, Calif. 90077 | 111 | P | 4,650 | 4,650 | 3,350 |
| Lehigh University; Bethlehem, Pa. 18015 | 4,465 (C) | P | 10,500 | 10,500 | 3,680 |
| Le Moyne College; Syracuse, N.Y. 13214 | 1,800 (C) | P | 6,235 | 6,235 | 2,630 |
| LeMoyne-Owen College; Memphis, Tenn. 38126 | 955 (C) | P | 5,070 | 5,070 | n.a. |
| Lenoir-Rhyne College; Hickory, N.C. 28603 | 1,434 (C) | P/LCA | 4,831 | 4,831 | 1,850 |
| Lesley College; Cambridge, Mass. 02238 | 500 (C) | P | 7,800 | 7,800 | 4,250 |
| | | | | | |
| LeTourneau College; Longview, Tex. 75607 | 800 (C) | P | 5,554 | 5,554 | 2,940 |
| Lewis and Clark College; Portland, Ore. 97219 | 1,626 (C) | P | 8,740 | 8,740 | 3,553 |
| Lewis-Clark State College; Lewiston, Idaho 83501 | 2,000 (C) | Pub | 1,008 | 2,908 | 2,520 |
| Lewis University; Romeoville, Ill. 60441 | 2,393 (C) | P/RC | 5,668 | 5,668 | 2,690 |
| Liberty University; Lynchburg, Va. 24506 | 6,934 (C) | P/B | 3,210 | 3,210 | 2,900 |
| L.I.F.E. Bible College; Los Angeles, Calif. 90026 | 456 (C) | P/FG | 2,412 | 2,412 | 2,025 |
| Limestone College; Gaffney, S.C. 29340 | 1,500 (C) | P | 5,460 | 5,460 | 2,440 |
| | | | | | |
| Lincoln Christian College; Lincoln, Ill. 62656 | 350 (C) | P/CC | 3,100 | 3,100 | 1,890 |
| Lincoln Memorial University; Harrogate, Tenn. 37752 | 1,314 (C) | P | 3,000 | 3,000 | 2,100 |
| Lincoln University; Jefferson City, Mo. 65101 | 3,321 (C) | Pub | 927 | 1,854 | 2,629 |
| Lincoln University; Lincoln University, Pa. 19352 | 1,050 (C) | Pub | 1,930 | 2,930 | 2,300 |
| Lincoln University; San Francisco, Calif. 94118 | 189 | P | 2,850 | 2,850 | n.a. |
| Lindenwood College; St. Charles, Mo. 63301 | 1,414 (C) | P | 5,200 | 5,200 | 3,200 |
| Linfield College; McMinnville, Ore. 97128 | 1,107 (C) | P | 7,480 | 7,480 | 2,514 |
| | | | | | |
| Livingstone College; Salisbury, N.C. 28144 | 618 (C) | P/AME | 2,800 | 2,800 | 1,996 |
| Livingston University; Livingston, Ala. 35470 | 1,289 (C) | Pub | 1,038 | 1,038 | 1,707 |
| Lock Haven University; Lock Haven, Pa. 17745 | 2,600 (C) | Pub | 1,600 | 2,868 | 1,864 |
| Loma Linda University; Loma Linda, Calif. 92350 | 3,115 (C) | P/SDA | 6,250 | 6,250 | 2,616 |
| Loma Linda University-La Sierra; Riverside, Calif. 92515 | 2,300 (C) | P/SDA | 6,150 | 6,150 | 2,616 |
| Long Island University; Greenvale, N.Y. 11548: | | | | | |
| Arnold & Marie Schwartz College of Pharmacy; Brooklyn, N.Y. 11201 | 1,100 (C) | P | 6,000 | 6,000 | 3,450 |
| Brooklyn Center; Brooklyn, N.Y. 11201 | 4,212 (C) | P | 5,500 | 5,500 | 3,420 |
| C.W. Post Campus; Greenvale, N.Y. 11548 | 6,001 (C) | P | 5,970 | 5,970 | 3,050 |
| Southampton Campus; Southampton, N.Y. 11968 | 1,150 (C) | P | 6,960 | 6,960 | 3,910 |
| Longwood College; Farmville, Va. 23901 | 2,900 (C) | Pub | 2,018 | 3,200 | 2,668 |
| Loras College; Dubuque, Iowa 52001 | 2,000 (C) | P | 5,800 | 5,800 | 2,300 |
| | | | | | |
| Loretto Heights College; Denver, Colo. 80236 | 800 (C) | P | 6,740 | 6,740 | 3,360 |
| Louisiana College; Pineville, La. 71359 | 1,266 (C) | P/SB | 2,486 | 2,486 | 1,884 |
| Louisiana State Univ. and A&M Coll.; Baton Rouge, La. 70803 | 24,098 (C) | Pub | 1,277 | 3,277 | 2,014 |
| LSU-Shreveport; Shreveport, La. 71115 | 4,287 (C) | Pub | 980 | 2,210 | n.a. |
| Louisiana Tech University; Ruston, La. 71272 | 9,411 (C) | Pub | 1,146 | 2,025 | 2,100 |
| | | | | | |
| Louisville, University of; Louisville, Ky. 40292 | 15,436 (C) | Pub | 1,340 | 3,820 | 2,200 |
| Lourdes College; Sylvania, Ohio 43560 | 860 (C) | P/RC | 3,050 | 3,050 | n.a. |
| Lowell, University of; Lowell, Mass. 01854 | 8,626 (C) | Pub | 1,430 | 3,986 | 2,791 |
| Loyola College; Baltimore, Md. 21210 | 2,700 (C) | P/RC | 6,550 | 6,550 | 3,535 |
| Loyola Marymount University; Los Angeles, Calif. 90045 | 4,025 (C) | P/RC | 7,289 | 7,289 | 3,400 |
| Loyola University; New Orleans, La. 70118 | 3,580 (C) | P/RC | 4,828 | 4,828 | 3,466 |
| | | | | | |
| Loyola University of Chicago; Chicago, Ill. 60011 | 6,640 (C) | P | 5,590 | 5,590 | 3,498 |
| Lubbock Christian College; Lubbock, Tex. 79407 | 1,034 (C) | P/CC | 3,800 | 3,800 | 2,044 |
| Lutheran Bible Institute; Issaquah, Wash. 98027 | 210 (C) | P/L | 3,179 | 3,179 | 2,287 |
| Luther College; Decorah, Iowa 52101 | 2,085 (C) | P/AL | 6,880 | 6,880 | 2,220 |
| Lycoming College; Williamsport, Pa. 17701 | 1,250 (C) | P | 7,380 | 7,380 | 2,900 |

| Institution and location | Enrollment | Control | Tuition ($) Res. | Nonres. | Rm/Bd ($) |
|---|---|---|---|---|---|
| Lynchburg College; Lynchburg, Va. 24501 | 1,658 (C) | P | 6,625 | 6,625 | 3,400 |
| Lyndon State College; Lyndonville, Vt. 05851 | 900 (C) | Pub | 2,205 | 4,517 | 3,042 |
| Macalester College; St. Paul, Minn. 55105 | 1,703 (C) | P | 8,080 | 8,080 | 2,800 |
| MacMurray College; Jacksonville, Ill. 62650 | 700 (C) | P/UM | 5,950 | 5,950 | 2,650 |
| Madonna College; Livonia, Mich. 48150 | 3,777 (C) | P | 2,690 | 2,690 | 2,410 |
| Magdalen College; Bedford, N.H. 03102 | 50 | P | 4,000 | 4,000 | 2,500 |
| Maharishi International University; Fairfield, Iowa 52556 | 344 (C) | P | 6,060 | 6,060 | 2,112 |
| Maine, Univ. of–Augusta; Augusta, Me. 04330 | 3,100 (C) | Pub | 1,413 | 3,630 | n.a. |
| Maine, Univ. of–Farmington; Farmington, Me. 04938 | 2,255 (C) | Pub | 1,413 | 3,630 | 2,850 |
| Maine, Univ. of–Fort Kent; Fort Kent, Me. 04743 | 650 (C) | Pub | 1,413 | 3,630 | 2,743 |
| Maine, Univ. of–Machias; Machias, Me. 04654 | 850 (C) | Pub | 1,413 | 3,630 | 2,650 |
| Maine, Univ. of–Orono; Orono, Me. 04469 | 10,084 (C) | Pub | 1,509 | 4,560 | 2,921 |
| Maine, Univ. of–Presque Isle; Presque Isle, Me. 04769 | 1,285 (C) | Pub | 1,413 | 3,630 | 2,692 |
| Maine Maritime Academy; Castine, Me. 04420 | 550 (C) | Pub | 2,390 | 4,510 | 3,150 |
| Mallinckrodt College; Wilmette, Ill. 60091 | 260 (C) | P/RC | 2,730 | 2,730 | n.a. |
| Malone College; Canton, Ohio 44709 | 1,039 (C) | P/F | 5,370 | 5,370 | 2,610 |
| Manchester College; North Manchester, Ind. 46962 | 947 (C) | P/CB | 5,920 | 5,920 | 2,280 |
| Manhattan Christian College; Manhattan, Kan. 66502 | 190 (C) | P/CC | 1,920 | 1,920 | 2,060 |
| Manhattan College; Riverdale, Bronx, N.Y. 10471 | 4,800 (C) | P | 6,100 | 6,100 | 3,800 |
| Manhattan School of Music; New York, N.Y. 10027 | 435 (C) | P | 6,500 | 6,500 | n.a. |
| Manhattanville College; Purchase, N.Y. 10577 | 1,048 (C) | P | 8,400 | 8,400 | 4,190 |
| Mankato State University; Mankato, Minn. 56001 | 12,600 (C) | Pub | 1,628 | 2,452 | 1,712 |
| Mannes College of Music; New York, N.Y. 10024 | 120 (C) | P | 6,100 | 6,100 | 2,500 |
| Mansfield University; Mansfield, Pa. 16933 | 2,701 (C) | Pub | 1,600 | 2,818 | 1,988 |
| Marian College; Indianapolis, Ind. 46222 | 1,100 (C) | P/RC | 4,500 | 4,500 | 2,300 |
| Marian College of Fond du Lac; Fond du Lac, Wis. 54935 | 364 (C) | P/RC | 5,200 | 5,200 | 2,040 |
| Marietta College; Marietta, Ohio 45750 | 1,186 (C) | P | 8,000 | 8,000 | 2,600 |
| Marion College; Marion, Ind. 46953 | 1,050 (C) | P/WM | 5,336 | 5,336 | 2,490 |
| Marist College; Poughkeepsie, N.Y. 12601 | 2,700 (C) | P | 5,904 | 5,904 | 3,560 |
| Marlboro College; Marlboro, Vt. 05344 | 179 (C) | P | 9,725 | 9,725 | 3,620 |
| Marquette University; Milwaukee, Wis. 53233 | 8,793 (C) | P | 6,026 | 6,026 | 3,150 |
| Marshall University; Huntington, W. Va. 25705 | 8,600 (C) | Pub | 960 | 2,600 | 2,778 |
| Mars Hill College; Mars Hill, N.C. 28754 | 1,419 (C) | P/SB | 4,490 | 4,490 | 1,860 |
| Martin Center College; Indianapolis, Ind. 42605 | 200 | P | 2,250 | 2,250 | n.a. |
| Mary, University of; Bismarck, N.D. 58501 | 1,094 | P | 3,900 | 3,900 | 1,890 |
| Mary Baldwin College; Staunton, Va. 24401 | 832 (W) | P/PUS | 6,650 | 6,650 | 4,535 |
| Marycrest College; Davenport, Iowa 52804 | 1,500 (C) | P/RC | 5,670 | 5,670 | 2,050 |
| Marygrove College; Detroit, Mich. 48221 | 1,020 (C) | P/RC | 4,200 | 4,200 | 2,230 |
| Mary Hardin–Baylor, University of; Belton, Tex. 76513 | 1,255 (C) | P/SB | 3,400 | 3,400 | 2,290 |
| Maryland, Univ. of–Baltimore County; Baltimore, Md. 21228 | 7,914 (C) | Pub | 1,626 | 4,502 | 3,035 |
| Maryland, Univ. of–College Park; College Park, Md. 20742 | 28,000 (C) | Pub | 1,496 | 4,202 | 3,620 |
| Maryland, Univ. of–Eastern Shore; Princess Anne, Md. 21853 | 1,230 (C) | Pub | 1,350 | 3,804 | 2,810 |
| Maryland, Univ. of, University College; College Park, Md. 20742 | 11,800 (C) | Pub | 1,824 | 1,824 | n.a. |
| Maryland Institute–College of Art; Baltimore, Md. 21217 | 800 (C) | P | 6,700 | 6,700 | 3,150 |
| Marylhurst Coll. for Lifelong Learning; Marylhurst, Ore. 97036 | 1,400 (C) | P | 5,040 | 5,040 | n.a. |
| Marymount College; Tarrytown, N.Y. 10591 | 936 | P | 6,710 | 6,710 | 4,130 |
| Marymount College of Kansas; Salina, Kan. 67401 | 620 (C) | P/RC | 4,200 | 4,200 | 2,400 |
| Marymount College of Virginia; Arlington, Va. 22207 | 1,332 (W) | P | 5,940 | 5,940 | 3,530 |
| Marymount Manhattan College; New York, N.Y. 10021 | 1,600 (C) | P | 5,450 | 5,450 | n.a. |
| Maryville College; Maryville, Tenn. 37801 | 523 (C) | P | 5,265 | 5,265 | 2,825 |
| Maryville College; St. Louis, Mo. 63141 | 2,043 (C) | P | 5,190 | 5,190 | 2,660 |
| Mary Washington College; Fredericksburg, Va. 22401 | 2,880 (C) | Pub | 1,902 | 3,722 | 3,058 |
| Marywood College; Scranton, Pa. 18509 | 2,000 (W) | P/RC | 4,450 | 4,450 | 2,600 |
| Massachusetts, Univ. of–Amherst; Amherst, Mass. 01003 | 19,500 (C) | Pub | 2,000 | 5,200 | 2,850 |
| Massachusetts, Univ. of–Boston; Boston, Mass. 02125 | 11,500 (C) | Pub | 1,296 | 4,320 | n.a. |
| Massachusetts College of Art; Boston, Mass. 02115 | 1,196 (C) | Pub | 960 | 3,216 | n.a. |
| Massachusetts College of Pharmacy and Allied Health Sciences; Boston, Mass. 02115 | 785 (C) | P | 6,098 | 6,098 | 4,017 |
| Massachusetts Institute of Technology; Cambridge, Mass. 02139 | 4,700 (C) | P | 11,800 | 11,800 | 4,350 |
| Massachusetts Maritime Academy; Buzzards Bay, Mass. 02532 | 850 (C) | Pub | 4,000 | 4,000 | 3,000 |
| Master's College, The; Newhall, Calif. 91322 | 425 | P/B | 4,070 | 4,070 | 2,850 |
| Mayville State College; Mayville, N.D. 58257 | 730 (C) | Pub | 1,137 | 2,205 | 1,713 |
| McKendree College; Lebanon, Ill. 62258 | 1,200 (C) | P/UM | 4,600 | 4,600 | 2,600 |
| McMurry College; Abilene, Tex. 79697 | 1,657 (C) | P/UM | 3,330 | 3,330 | 2,160 |
| McNeese State University; Lake Charles, La. 70609 | 6,650 (C) | Pub | 992 | 1,872 | 1,650 |
| McPherson College; McPherson, Kan. 67460 | 475 (C) | P/CB | 4,340 | 4,340 | 2,350 |
| Medaille College; Buffalo, N.Y. 14214 | 880 (C) | P | 4,530 | 4,530 | n.a. |
| Medical College of Georgia; Augusta, Ga. 30912 | 745 (C) | Pub | 1,443 | 3,987 | 2,873 |
| Medical University of South Carolina; Charleston, S.C. 29425 | 853 (C) | Pub | 1,500 | 3,000 | 2,310 |
| Memphis Academy of Arts; Memphis, Tenn. 38112 | 250 (C) | P | 5,200 | 5,200 | 2,000 |
| Memphis State University; Memphis, Tenn. 38152 | 16,005 (C) | Pub | 1,066 | 3,214 | 2,224 |
| Menlo College; Atherton, Calif. 94025 | 644 (C) | P | 7,670 | 7,670 | 4,320 |

| Institution and location | Enrollment | Control | Tuition ($) Res. | Tuition ($) Nonres. | Rm/Bd ($) |
|---|---|---|---|---|---|
| Mercer University; Macon, Ga. 31207 | 2,400 (C) | P/SB | 5,364[1] | 5,364 | 2,613 |
| Mercer University-Atlanta; Atlanta, Ga. 30341 | 1,466 (C) | P/SB | 4,568 | 4,568 | n.a. |
| Mercer University School of Pharmacy; Atlanta, Ga. 30312 | 400 (C) | P/SB | 6,300 | 6,300 | n.a. |
| Mercy College; Dobbs Ferry, N.Y. 10522 | 8,800 (C) | P | 4,200 | 4,200 | n.a. |
| Mercy College of Detroit; Detroit, Mich. 48219 | 2,235 (C) | P/RC | 3,968 | 3,968 | 1,650 |
| Mercyhurst College; Erie, Pa. 16546 | 1,706 (C) | P/RC | 5,710 | 5,710 | 2,340 |
| Meredith College; Raleigh, N.C. 27607 | 1,507 (C) | P | 3,930 | 3,930 | 1,720 |
| Merrimack College; North Andover, Mass. 01845 | 2,200 (C) | P/RC | 6,800 | 6,800 | 3,750 |
| Mesa College; Grand Junction, Colo. 81502 | 3,500 (C) | Pub | 1,086 | 3,200 | 2,326 |
| Messiah College; Grantham, Pa. 17027 | 1,846 (C) | P | 5,670 | 5,670 | 2,910 |
| Methodist College; Fayetteville, N.C. 28301 | 1,236 (C) | P | 5,200 | 5,200 | 2,600 |
| Metropolitan State College; Denver, Colo. 80204 | 14,559 (C) | Pub | 1,048 | 3,740 | n.a. |
| Metropolitan State University; St. Paul, Minn. 55101 | 3,736 (C) | Pub | 1,332 | 2,436 | n.a. |
| Miami, University of; Coral Gables, Fla. 33124 | 8,800 (C) | P | 8,840 | 8,840 | 3,800 |
| Miami Christian College; Miami, Fla. 33167 | 254 (C) | P/ID | 3,770 | 3,770 | 2,510 |
| Miami University; Oxford, Ohio 45056 | 13,681 (C) | Pub | 2,475 | 2,475 | 2,325 |
| Michigan, Univ. of-Ann Arbor; Ann Arbor, Mich. 48109 | 22,000 (C) | Pub | 2,222 | 7,268 | 2,900 |
| Michigan, Univ. of-Dearborn; Dearborn, Mich. 48128 | 6,500 (C) | Pub | 1,770 | 5,434 | n.a. |
| Michigan, Univ. of-Flint; Flint, Mich. 48502 | 5,380 (C) | Pub | 1,472 | 4,768 | n.a. |
| Michigan Christian College; Rochester, Mich. 48063 | 332 (C) | P/CC | 2,880 | 2,880 | 2,252 |
| Michigan State University; East Lansing, Mich. 48824 | 33,217 (C) | Pub | 1,919 | 4,535 | 2,538 |
| Michigan Technological University; Houghton, Mich. 49931 | 5,749 (C) | Pub | 1,773 | 4,137 | 2,540 |
| Mid-America Bible College; Oklahoma City, Okla. 73170 | 229 | P/CG | 3,382 | 3,382 | 2,076 |
| Mid-America Nazarene College; Olathe, Kan. 66061 | 1,040 (C) | P | 3,863 | 3,863 | 2,566 |
| Middlebury College; Middlebury, Vt. 05753 | 1,900 (C) | P | 14,500 | 14,500 | — |
| Middle Tennessee State Univ.; Murfreesboro, Tenn. 37132 | 11,369 (C) | Pub | 1,000 | 3,200 | 1,596 |
| Midland Lutheran College; Fremont, Neb. 68025 | 801 (C) | P/L | 5,500 | 5,500 | 2,230 |
| Mid-South Bible College; Memphis, Tenn. 38182 | 205 (C) | P | 2,880 | 2,880 | 2,200 |
| Midwest College of Engineering; Lombard, Ill. 60148 | 193 | P | 4,800 | 4,800 | n.a. |
| Midwestern State University; Wichita Falls, Tex. 76308 | 4,012 (C) | Pub | 870 | 3,990 | 2,152 |
| Miles College; Birmingham, Ala. 35208 | 600 (C) | P/CME | 3,000 | 3,000 | 1,850 |
| Millersville University of Pennsylvania; Millersville, Pa. 17551 | 6,151 (C) | Pub | 1,600 | 2,868 | 2,130 |
| Milligan College; Milligan College, Tenn. 37682 | 600 (C) | P | 4,296 | 4,296 | 2,292 |
| Millikin University; Decatur, Ill. 62522 | 1,559 (C) | P | 6,471 | 6,471 | 2,850 |
| Millsaps College; Jackson, Miss. 39210 | 1,228 (C) | P/UM | 6,035 | 6,035 | 2,600 |
| Mills College; Oakland, Calif. 94613 | 739 (C) | P | 8,400 | 8,400 | 4,100 |
| Milwaukee School of Engineering; Milwaukee, Wis. 53202 | 1,771 (C) | P | 6,435 | 6,435 | 2,775 |
| Minneapolis Coll. of Art and Design; Minneapolis, Minn. 55404 | 540 (C) | P | 6,600 | 6,600 | 2,700 |
| Minnesota, Univ. of-Duluth; Duluth, Minn. 55812 | 7,206 (C) | Pub | 1,648 | 4,039 | 2,505 |
| Minnesota, Univ. of-Morris; Morris, Minn. 56267 | 1,682 (C) | Pub | 1,895 | 4,775 | 2,593 |
| Minnesota, Univ. of-Twin Cities; Minneapolis, Minn. 55455 | 46,445 (C) | Pub | 1,830 | 4,510 | 3,060 |
| Minnesota Bible College; Rochester, Minn. 55902 | 84 (C) | P/CC | 2,250 | 2,250 | 3,800 |
| Minot State College; Minot, N.D. 58701 | 2,700 (C) | Pub | 1,008 | 1,896 | 1,470 |
| Mississippi, University of; University, Miss. 38677 | 7,354 (C) | Pub | 1,517 | 2,699 | 2,300 |
| Mississippi, Univ. of, Medical Center; Jackson, Miss. 39216 | 633 (C) | Pub | 1,185 | 2,161 | 2,324 |
| Mississippi College; Clinton, Miss. 39058 | 1,880 (C) | P | 3,556 | 3,556 | 2,400 |
| Mississippi State University; Mississippi State, Miss. 39762 | 9,942 (C) | Pub | 1,492 | 2,674 | 2,200 |
| Mississippi University for Women; Columbus, Miss. 39701 | 2,039 (W) | Pub | 1,075 | 2,257 | 1,760 |
| Mississippi Valley State University; Itta Bena, Miss. 38941 | 2,344 (C) | Pub | 1,140 | 2,334 | 1,535 |
| Missouri, Univ. of-Columbia; Columbia, Mo. 65211 | 17,126 (C) | Pub | 1,488 | 4,308 | 2,192 |
| Missouri, Univ. of-Kansas City; Kansas City, Mo. 64110 | 6,302 (C) | Pub | 1,575 | 4,395 | 5,096 |
| Missouri, Univ. of-Rolla; Rolla, Mo. 65401 | 5,092 (C) | Pub | 1,718 | 4,988 | 2,815 |
| Missouri, Univ. of-St. Louis; St. Louis, Mo. 63121 | 9,473 (C) | Pub | 1,468 | 4,268 | n.a. |
| Missouri Baptist College; St. Louis, Mo. 63141 | 530 (C) | P/SB | 3,800 | 3,800 | 2,000 |
| Missouri Southern State College; Joplin, Mo. 64801 | 4,529 (C) | Pub | 934 | 1,774 | 1,756 |
| Missouri Valley College; Marshall, Mo. 65340 | 564 (C) | P | 5,000 | 5,000 | 3,100 |
| Missouri Western State College; St. Joseph, Mo. 64507 | 3,999 (C) | Pub | 975 | 1,835 | 1,750 |
| Mobile College; Mobile, Ala. 36613 | 804 (C) | P/SB | 3,040 | 3,040 | 2,350 |
| Molloy College; Rockville Centre, N.Y. 11570 | 1,595 (C) | P/RC | 4,300 | 4,300 | n.a. |
| Monmouth College; Monmouth, Ill. 61462 | 700 (C) | P/UP | 7,440 | 7,440 | 2,490 |
| Monmouth College; West Long Branch, N.J. 07764 | 3,691 (C) | P | 6,332 | 6,332 | 3,060 |
| Montana, University of; Missoula, Mont. 59812 | 7,114 (C) | Pub | 1,149 | 2,913 | 2,480 |
| Montana College of Mineral Science and Technology; Butte, Mont. 59701 | 1,958 (C) | Pub | 988 | 2,889 | 2,700 |
| Montana State University; Bozeman, Mont. 59717 | 9,965 (C) | Pub | 1,191 | 3,006 | 2,766 |
| Montclair State College; Upper Montclair, N.J. 07043 | 11,300 (C) | Pub | 1,404 | 2,044 | 3,360 |
| Monterey Institute of Intl. Studies; Monterey, Calif. 93940 | 74 (C) | P | 6,250 | 6,250 | n.a. |
| Montevallo, University of; Montevallo, Ala. 35115 | 2,225 (C) | Pub | 1,142 | 1,954 | 2,060 |
| Moody Bible Institute; Chicago, Ill. 60610 | 1,331 (C) | P/ID | 460 | 460 | 3,200 |
| Moore College of Art; Philadelphia, Pa. 19103 | 600 (W) | P | 6,300 | 6,300 | 3,400 |
| Moorhead State University; Moorhead, Minn. 56560 | 7,234 (C) | Pub | 1,592 | 2,769 | 1,695 |
| Moravian College; Bethlehem, Pa. 18018 | 1,279 (C) | P/Mor | 7,575 | 7,575 | 2,625 |
| Morehead State University; Morehead, Ky. 40351 | 4,780 (C) | Pub | 944 | 2,714 | 2,200 |

| Institution and location | Enrollment | Control | Tuition ($) Res. | Nonres. | Rm/Bd ($) |
|---|---|---|---|---|---|
| Morehouse College; Atlanta, Ga. 30314 | 2,056 (M) | P | 3,950 | 3,950 | 2,750 |
| Morgan State University; Baltimore, Md. 21239 | 3,885 (C) | Pub | 1,498 | 2,946 | 4,568[a] |
| Morningside College; Sioux City, Iowa 51106 | 1,500 (C) | P/UM | 6,336 | 6,336 | 2,150 |
| Morris Brown College; Atlanta, Ga. 30314 | 1,268 (C) | P/AME | 3,500 | 3,500 | 2,090 |
| Morris College; Sumter, S.C. 39150 | 700 (C) | P | 2,882 | 2,882 | 1,890 |
| Mount Angel Seminary; St. Benedict, Ore. 97373 | 34 | P/RC | 2,625 | 2,625 | 2,400 |
| Mount Holyoke College; South Hadley, Mass. 01075 | 1,921 (W) | P | 11,275 | 11,275 | 3,325 |
| Mount Ida College; Newton Centre, Mass. 02159 | 62 (W) | P | 5,383 | 5,383 | 3,710 |
| Mount Marty College; Yankton, S.D. 57078 | 620 (C) | P/RC | 4,570 | 4,570 | 2,120 |
| Mount Mary College; Milwaukee, Wis. 53222 | 1,278 (W) | P/RC | 4,840 | 4,840 | 2,320 |
| Mount Mercy College; Cedar Rapids, Iowa 52402 | 1,287 (C) | P | 5,230 | 5,230 | 2,175 |
| Mount Olive College; Mount Olive, N.C. 28365 | 420 (C) | P | 4,000 | 4,000 | 2,550 |
| Mount Saint Clare College; Clinton, Iowa 52732 | 400 (C) | P | 3,880 | 3,880 | 2,370 |
| Mount St. Joseph on the Ohio, College of; Mount St. Joseph, Ohio 45051 | 2,100 (W) | P/RC | 5,322 | 5,322 | 2,902 |
| Mount Saint Mary College; Newburgh, N.Y. 12550 | 1,130 (C) | P | 4,800 | 4,800 | 2,750 |
| Mount Saint Mary's College; Emmitsburg, Md. 21727 | 1,500 (C) | P/RC | 6,500 | 6,500 | 3,000 |
| Mount St. Mary's College; Los Angeles, Calif. 90049 | 798 (W) | P/RC | 6,660 | 6,660 | 3,848 |
| Mount Saint Vincent, College of; Riverdale, N.Y. 10471 | 1,100 (C) | P | 6,150 | 6,150 | 3,750 |
| Mount Senario College; Ladysmith, Wis. 54848 | 760 (C) | P | 4,200 | 4,200 | 2,200 |
| Mount Union College; Alliance, Ohio 44601 | 1,000 (C) | P | 8,130 | 8,130 | 2,470 |
| Mount Vernon College; Washington, D.C. 20007 | 463 (W) | P | 7,992 | 7,992 | 4,644 |
| Mount Vernon Nazarene College; Mount Vernon, Ohio 43050 | 1,058 (C) | P | 4,126 | 4,126 | 2,284 |
| Muhlenberg College; Allentown, Pa. 18104 | 1,522 (C) | P/L | 9,000 | 9,000 | 2,700 |
| Multnomah School of the Bible; Portland, Ore. 97220 | 597 (C) | P | 3,680 | 3,680 | 2,060 |
| Mundelein College; Chicago, Ill. 60660 | 1,182 (W) | P/RC | 5,970 | 5,970 | 2,775 |
| Murray State University; Murray, Ky. 42071 | 6,175 (C) | Pub | 100 | 2,820 | 1,880 |
| Museum Art School, Portland. *See* Pacific Northwest Coll. of Art | | | | | |
| Muskingum College; New Concord, Ohio 43762 | 1,025 (C) | P/UP | 8,000 | 8,000 | 2,700 |
| NAES College; Chicago, Ill. 60659 | 37 | P | 3,375 | 3,375 | n.a. |
| Naropa Institute; Boulder, Colo. 80302 | 126 | P | 4,015 | 4,015 | n.a. |
| Nathaniel Hawthorne College. *See* Hawthorne College | | | | | |
| National College; Rapid City, S.D. 57709 | 1,054 | P | 4,800 | 4,800 | 2,790 |
| National College–Albuquerque; Albuquerque, N.M. 87108 | 375 | P | 4,080 | 4,080 | n.a. |
| National College, Colorado Springs Extension; Colorado Springs, Colo. 80932 | 375 | P | 3,600 | 3,600 | n.a. |
| National College of Chiropractic; Lombard, Ill. 60148 | 886 (C) | P | 8,280 | 8,280 | 4,500 |
| National College of Education; Evanston, Ill. 60201 | 1,440 (C) | P | 4,950 | 4,950 | 3,105 |
| National University; San Diego, Calif. 92108 | 7,058 (C) | P | 5,580 | 5,580 | n.a. |
| Nazareth College in Kalamazoo; Nazareth, Mich. 49074 | 821 (C) | P | 5,430 | 5,430 | 2,530 |
| Nazareth College of Rochester; Rochester, N.Y. 14610 | 1,300 (C) | P | 5,700 | 5,700 | 3,200 |
| Nebraska, University of–Lincoln; Lincoln, Neb. 68508 | 17,939 (C) | Pub | 1,513 | 3,770 | 2,010 |
| Nebraska, University of–Omaha; Omaha, Neb. 68182 | 11,640 (C) | Pub | 1,421 | 3,679 | n.a. |
| Nebraska Christian College; Norfolk, Neb. 68701 | 156 | P | 1,577 | 1,577 | 1,863 |
| Nebraska Wesleyan University; Lincoln, Neb. 68504 | 1,300 (C) | P/UM | 5,610 | 5,610 | 2,250 |
| Neumann College; Aston, Pa. 19014 | 975 (C) | P | 4,720 | 4,720 | n.a. |
| Nevada, University of–Las Vegas; Las Vegas, Nev. 89154 | 8,672 (C) | Pub | 1,080 | 3,280 | 2,575 |
| Nevada, University of–Reno; Reno, Nev. 89557 | 6,801 (C) | Pub | 1,152 | 3,352 | 2,424 |
| Newberry College; Newberry, S.C. 29108 | 650 (C) | P/LCA | 5,700 | 5,700 | 2,500 |
| New Church, Academy of the; Bryn Athyn, Pa. 19009 | 129 (C) | P | 2,247 | 2,247 | 2,193 |
| New College of California; San Francisco, Calif. 94110 | 400 (C) | P | 3,600 | 3,600 | n.a. |
| New College of the University of South Florida; Sarasota, Fla. 33580 | 420 (C) | Pub | 1,098 | 3,026 | 3,030 |
| Newcomb College of Tulane University; New Orleans, La. 70118 | 1,732 (W) | P | 10,080 | 10,080 | 3,965 |
| New England, University of; Biddeford, Me. 04005 | 550 (C) | P | 5,900 | 5,900 | 3,050 |
| New England Baptist Bible College; South Portland, Me. 04106 | 30 | P | 1,750 | 1,750 | 2,500 |
| New England College; Henniker, N.H. 03242 | 1,125 (C) | P | 7,550 | 7,550 | 3,350 |
| New England College–Arundel Campus; Sussex BN18 ODA, England | 250 | P | 7,110 | 7,110 | 3,250 |
| New England Conservatory of Music; Boston, Mass. 02115 | 407 (C) | P | 8,850 | 8,850 | 4,400 |
| New England Institute of Technology; Providence, R.I. 02907 | 1,500 (C) | P | 4,650 | 4,650 | 2,520 |
| New Hampshire, University of; Durham, N.H. 03824 | 9,046 (C) | Pub | 2,500 | 6,370 | 2,614 |
| New Hampshire College; Manchester, N.H. 03104 | 1,700 (C) | P | 6,738 | 6,738 | 3,704 |
| New Haven, University of; West Haven, Conn. 06516 | 1,775 (C) | P | 6,000 | 6,000 | 3,222 |
| New Jersey Institute of Technology; Newark, N.J. 07102 | 5,034 (C) | Pub | 1,940 | 3,880 | 3,020 |
| New Mexico, University of; Albuquerque, N.M. 87131 | 20,129 (C) | Pub | 888 | 3,048 | 2,086 |
| New Mexico Highlands University; Las Vegas, N.M. 87701 | 1,725 (C) | Pub | 599 | 2,303 | 1,848 |
| New Mexico Inst. of Mining & Technology; Socorro, N.M. 87801 | 966 (C) | Pub | 817 | 2,973 | 2,568 |
| New Mexico State University; Las Cruces, N.M. 88003 | 11,197 (C) | Pub | 1,026 | 3,652 | 1,848 |
| New Orleans, University of; New Orleans, La. 70148 | 13,411 (C) | Pub | 1,224 | 2,900 | 2,638 |
| New Rochelle, College of–School of Arts & Sciences and School of Nursing, New Rochelle, N.Y. 10801 | 950 (C) | P | 5,610 | 5,610 | 3,370 |

| Institution and location | Enrollment | Control | Tuition ($) Res. | Nonres. | Rm/Bd ($) |
|---|---|---|---|---|---|
| New School for Social Research; New York, N.Y. 10011 | 250 (C) | P | 6,750 | 6,750 | 3,980 |
| New School of Music; Philadelphia, Pa. 19103 | 50 (C) | P | 5,800 | 5,800 | n.a. |
| New York, City University of; New York, N.Y. 10021: | | | | | |
| Bernard M. Baruch College; New York, N.Y. 10010 | 12,937 (C) | Pub | 1,284 | 2,584 | n.a. |
| Brooklyn College; Brooklyn, N.Y. 11210 | 11,000 (C) | Pub | 1,250 | 2,550 | n.a. |
| City College; New York, N.Y. 10031 | 10,361 (C) | Pub | 1,321 | 2,621 | n.a. |
| College of Staten Island; Staten Island, N.Y. 10301 | 10,179 (C) | Pub | 1,500 | 2,600 | n.a. |
| Herbert H. Lehman College; Bronx, N.Y. 10468 | 8,600 (C) | Pub | 1,276 | 2,576 | n.a. |
| Hunter College; New York, N.Y. 10021 | 14,462 (C) | Pub | 1,250 | 2,550 | 2,025 |
| John Jay College of Criminal Justice; New York, N.Y. 10019 | 5,858 (C) | Pub | 1,316 | 2,616 | n.a. |
| Medgar Evers College; Brooklyn, N.Y. 11225 | 2,823 (C) | Pub | 1,225 | 2,025 | n.a. |
| New York City Technical Coll.; Brooklyn, N.Y. 11201 | 11,115 (C) | Pub | 1,250 | 2,500 | n.a. |
| Queens College; Flushing, N.Y. 11367 | 14,050 (C) | Pub | 1,250 | 2,500 | n.a. |
| York College; Jamaica, N.Y. 11451 | 4,300 (C) | Pub | 1,250 | 2,500 | n.a. |
| New York, State University of; Albany, N.Y. 12246: | | | | | |
| SUNY–Albany; Albany, N.Y. 12222 | 11,500 (C) | Pub | 1,467 | 3,317 | 2,583 |
| SUNY–Buffalo; Buffalo, N.Y. 14214 | 17,816 (C) | Pub | 1,619 | 3,469 | 3,080 |
| SUNY–Purchase; Purchase, N.Y. 10577 | 3,864 (C) | Pub | 1,350 | 3,200 | 2,500 |
| SUNY–Stony Brook; Stony Brook, N.Y. 11794 | 11,388 (C) | Pub | 1,475 | 3,325 | 2,938 |
| SUNY College at Brockport; Brockport, N.Y. 14420 | 5,810 (C) | Pub | 1,475 | 3,325 | 2,950 |
| SUNY College at Buffalo; Buffalo, N.Y. 14222 | 10,050 (C) | Pub | 1,457 | 3,307 | 2,850 |
| SUNY College at Cortland; Cortland, N.Y. 13045 | 5,225 (C) | Pub | 1,375 | 3,225 | 2,910 |
| SUNY College at Fredonia; Fredonia, N.Y. 14063 | 4,491 (C) | Pub | 1,459 | 3,250 | 2,600 |
| SUNY College at Geneseo; Geneseo, N.Y. 14454 | 4,550 (C) | Pub | 1,350 | 3,200 | 2,500 |
| SUNY College at New Paltz; New Paltz, N.Y. 12561 | 4,712 (C) | Pub | 1,350 | 3,200 | 2,890 |
| SUNY College at Old Westbury; Old Westbury, N.Y. 11568 | 3,755 (C) | Pub | 1,350 | 3,200 | 3,000 |
| SUNY College at Oneonta; Oneonta, N.Y. 13820 | 5,390 (C) | Pub | 1,545 | 3,400 | 2,800 |
| SUNY College at Oswego; Oswego, N.Y. 13126 | 7,211 (C) | Pub | 1,350 | 3,200 | 2,716 |
| SUNY College at Plattsburgh; Plattsburgh, N.Y. 12901 | 5,692 (C) | Pub | 1,468 | 3,318 | 2,964 |
| SUNY College at Potsdam; Potsdam, N.Y. 13676 | 3,848 (C) | Pub | 1,500 | 3,325 | 2,870 |
| College of Agriculture and Life Sciences at Cornell; Ithaca, N.Y. 14853 | 3,000 (C) | Pub | 4,360 | 7,420 | 3,600 |
| SUNY–College of Ceramics at Alfred University; Alfred, N.Y. 14802 | 696 (C) | Pub | 2,700 | 3,900 | 3,020 |
| SUNY College of Environmental Science and Forestry; Syracuse, N.Y. 13210 | 1,000 (C) | Pub | 1,350 | 3,250 | 3,810 |
| SUNY–College of Human Ecology at Cornell; Ithaca, N.Y. 14853 | 1,161 (C) | Pub | 4,360 | 7,420 | 3,600 |
| SUNY–College of Technology; Utica, N.Y. 13504 | 2,341 (C) | Pub | 1,485 | 3,335 | n.a. |
| SUNY–Empire State College; Saratoga Springs, N.Y. 12866 | 5,200 (C) | Pub | 2,081 | 4,856 | n.a. |
| SUNY–Fashion Institute of Technology; New York, N.Y. 10001 | 11,058 (C) | Pub | 1,500 | 2,850 | 3,381 |
| SUNY–Health Science Center at Syracuse; Syracuse, N.Y. 13210 | 235 (C) | Pub | 2,805 | 3,305 | 3,050 |
| SUNY Maritime College; Fort Schuyler, Bronx, N.Y. 10465 | 730 (C) | Pub | 1,425 | 3,250 | 3,014 |
| SUNY–School of Industrial and Labor Relations of Cornell; Ithaca, N.Y. 14853 | 630 (C) | Pub | 4,060 | 6,784 | 3,405 |
| SUNY–University Center at Binghamton; Binghamton, N.Y. 13901 | 9,245 (C) | Pub | 1,501 | 3,351 | 2,900 |
| New York, University of the State of, Regents College Degrees; Albany, N.Y. 12230 | 17,000 (C) | Pub | 225 | 225 | n.a. |
| New York City Technical Coll. See New York, City Univ. of | | | | | |
| New York Institute of Technology; Central Islip, N.Y. 11722 | 340 (C) | P | 4,474 | 4,474 | 3,294 |
| New York Institute of Technology; Old Westbury, N.Y. 11568 | 7,122 (C) | P | 4,474 | 4,474 | n.a. |
| New York Institute of Technology; Metropolitan Center; New York, N.Y. 10023 | 2,810 (C) | P | 4,474 | 4,474 | n.a. |
| New York University; New York, N.Y. 10003 | 15,000 (C) | P | 8,714 | 8,714 | 4,580 |
| Niagara University; Niagara University, N.Y. 14109 | 2,675 (C) | P | 6,000 | 6,000 | 3,130 |
| Nicholls State University; Thibodaux, La. 70310 | 6,063 (C) | Pub | 992 | 1,872 | 1,820 |
| Nichols College; Dudley, Mass. 01570 | 814 (C) | P | 5,345 | 5,345 | 3,080 |
| Norfolk State University; Norfolk, Va. 23504 | 6,875 (C) | Pub | 1,200 | 2,140 | 2,190 |
| North Adams State College; North Adams, Mass. 01247 | 2,100 (C) | Pub | 1,300 | 3,500 | 2,400 |
| North Alabama, University of; Florence, Ala. 35632 | 4,825 (C) | Pub | 940 | 1,340 | 1,896 |
| North Carolina, Univ. of–Asheville; Asheville, N.C. 28804 | 2,686 (C) | Pub | 760 | 3,262 | 2,100 |
| North Carolina, Univ. of–Chapel Hill; Chapel Hill, N.C. 27514 | 13,719 (C) | Pub | 794 | 3,392 | 2,756 |
| North Carolina, Univ. of–Charlotte; Charlotte, N.C. 28223 | 9,355 (C) | Pub | 716 | 3,562 | 2,218 |
| North Carolina, Univ. of–Greensboro; Greensboro, N.C. 27412 | 7,401 (C) | Pub | 888 | 3,808 | 2,340 |
| North Carolina, Univ. of–Wilmington; Wilmington, N.C. 28403 | 5,514 (C) | Pub | 807 | 3,653 | 2,140 |
| North Carolina Agricultural and Technical State University; Greensboro, N.C. 27411 | 4,955 (C) | Pub | 888 | 3,446 | 1,772 |
| North Carolina Central University; Durham, N.C. 27707 | 3,532 (C) | Pub | 834 | 3,800 | 2,003 |
| North Carolina School of the Arts; Winston-Salem, N.C. 27117 | 473 (C) | Pub | 1,248 | 3,807 | 2,288 |
| North Carolina State University–Raleigh; Raleigh, N.C. 27695 | 20,500 (C) | Pub | 839 | 3,759 | 2,576 |
| North Carolina Wesleyan College; Rocky Mount, N.C. 27801 | 1,174 (C) | P/UM | 4,940 | 4,940 | 2,490 |
| North Central Bible College; Minneapolis, Minn. 55404 | 1,095 (C) | P | 3,520 | 3,520 | 2,466 |
| North Central College; Naperville, Ill. 60566 | 1,750 (C) | P | 6,480 | 6,480 | 2,832 |
| North Dakota, University of; Grand Forks, N.D. 58202 | 9,358 (C) | Pub | 1,167 | 2,160 | 1,884 |

| Institution and location | Enrollment | Control | Tuition ($) Res. | Tuition ($) Nonres. | Rm/Bd ($) |
|---|---|---|---|---|---|
| North Dakota State University; Fargo, N.D. 58105 | 8,521 (C) | Pub | 1,194 | 2,388 | 1,878 |
| Northeastern Bible College; Essex Fells, N.J. 07021 | 228 (C) | P | 4,000 | 4,000 | 2,500 |
| Northeastern Illinois University; Chicago, Ill. 60625 | 7,738 (C) | Pub | 1,220 | 3,260 | n.a. |
| Northeastern Oklahoma State Univ.; Tahlequah, Okla. 74464 | 6,500 (C) | Pub | 500 | 1,200 | 2,032 |
| Northeastern University; Boston, Mass. 02115 | 16,934 (C) | P | 7,933 | 7,933 | 4,680 |
| Northeast Louisiana University; Monroe, La. 71209 | 10,000 (C) | Pub | 988 | 1,868 | 1,620 |
| Northeast Missouri State University; Kirksville, Mo. 63501 | 6,320 (C) | Pub | 770 | 1,670 | 1,670 |
| Northern Arizona University; Flagstaff, Ariz. 86011 | 9,852 (C) | Pub | 1,136 | 3,692 | 2,015 |
| Northern Colorado, University of; Greeley, Colo. 80639 | 7,688 (C) | Pub | 1,187 | 3,585 | 2,677 |
| Northern Illinois University; DeKalb, Ill. 60115 | 18,217 (C) | Pub | 1,630 | 3,862 | 2,294 |
| Northern Iowa, University of; Cedar Falls, Iowa 50614 | 10,431 (C) | Pub | 1,242 | 2,998 | 1,902 |
| Northern Kentucky University; Highland Heights, Ky. 41076 | 7,879 (C) | Pub | 1,000 | 2,880 | 1,200 |
| Northern Michigan University; Marquette, Mich. 49855 | 7,489 (C) | Pub | 1,472 | 3,392 | 2,451 |
| Northern Montana College; Havre, Mont. 59501 | 1,811 (C) | Pub | 859 | 2,264 | 2,500 |
| Northern State College; Aberdeen, S.D. 57401 | 2,560 (C) | Pub | 1,262 | 2,305 | 1,550 |
| North Florida, University of; Jacksonville, Fla. 32216 | 6,600 (C) | Pub | 850 | 2,730 | 1,600 |
| North Georgia College; Dahlonega, Ga. 30591 | 1,736 (C) | Pub | 1,143 | 1,920 | 1,710 |
| Northland College; Ashland, Wis. 54806 | 575 (C) | P | 5,395 | 5,395 | 2,700 |
| North Park College; Chicago, Ill. 60625 | 1,000 (C) | P/EC | 6,500 | 6,500 | 2,900 |
| Northrop University; Inglewood, Calif. 90306 | 1,800 (C) | P | 6,960 | 6,960 | 4,768 |
| North Texas State University; Denton, Tex. 76203 | 15,376 (C) | Pub | 782 | 4,002 | 2,942 |
| Northwest Bible College; Minot, N.D. 58701 | 103 (C) | P/CG | 2,670 | 2,670 | 1,900 |
| Northwest Christian College; Eugene, Ore. 97401 | 224 (C) | P/DC | 4,140 | 4,140 | 2,519 |
| Northwest College; Kirkland, Wash. 98083 | 671 (C) | P | 4,003 | 4,003 | 1,941 |
| Northwestern College; Orange City, Iowa 51041 | 860 (C) | P/RCA | 5,550 | 5,550 | 2,200 |
| Northwestern College; Roseville, Minn. 55113 | 972 (C) | P/ID | 5,775 | 5,775 | 2,295 |
| Northwestern Oklahoma State University; Alva, Okla. 73717 | 1,830 (C) | Pub | 602 | 1,648 | 1,416 |
| Northwestern State Univ. of Louisiana; Natchitoches, La. 71497 | 4,450 (C) | Pub | 1,402 | 2,482 | 1,880 |
| Northwestern University; Evanston, Ill. 60201 | 6,900 (C) | P | 11,031 | 11,031 | 3,884 |
| Northwest Missouri State University; Maryville, Mo. 64468 | 4,311 (C) | Pub | 990 | 1,830 | 1,910 |
| Northwest Nazarene College; Nampa, Idaho 83651 | 1,007 (C) | P/Naz | 4,260 | 4,260 | 2,220 |
| Northwood Institute of Florida; West Palm Beach, Fla. 33409 | 350 | P | 5,200 | 5,200 | 3,600 |
| Northwood Institute of Michigan; Midland, Mich. 48640 | 1,950 (C) | P | 4,950 | 4,950 | 2,676 |
| Northwood Institute of Texas; Cedar Hill, Tex. 75104 | 200 | P | 5,034 | 5,034 | 2,676 |
| Norwich University; Northfield, Vt. 05663 | 1,400 (C) | P | 8,600 | 8,600 | 3,200 |
| Notre Dame, College of; Belmont, Calif. 94002 | 650 (C) | P/RC | 6,500 | 6,500 | 3,900 |
| Notre Dame, University of; Notre Dame, Ind. 46556 | 7,500 (C) | P | 7,985 | 7,985 | 2,545 |
| Notre Dame College; Manchester, N.H. 03104 | 685 (W) | P/RC | 4,475 | 4,475 | 3,000 |
| Notre Dame College of Ohio; Cleveland, Ohio 44121 | 765 (W) | P/RC | 4,410 | 4,410 | 2,544 |
| Notre Dame of Maryland, College of; Baltimore, Md. 21210 | 570 (W) | P/RC | 5,500 | 5,500 | 3,300 |
| Nova University; Ft. Lauderdale, Fla. 33314 | 1,525 (C) | P | 3,850 | 3,850 | 4,100 |
| Nyack College; Nyack, N.Y. 10960 | 511 (C) | P/CMA | 5,180 | 5,180 | 2,772 |
| Oakland City College; Oakland City, Ind. 47660 | 616 (C) | P/B | 4,850 | 4,850 | 2,160 |
| Oakland University; Rochester, Mich. 48063 | 10,315 (C) | Pub | 1,585 | 3,957 | 2,755 |
| Oakwood College; Huntsville, Ala. 35896 | 1,465 (C) | P/SDA | 4,290 | 4,290 | 2,295 |
| Oberlin College; Oberlin, Ohio 44074 | 2,757 (C) | P | 10,162 | 10,162 | 3,550 |
| Oblate College; Washington, D.C. 20017 | 32 (M) | P/RC | 2,500 | 2,500 | n.a. |
| Occidental College; Los Angeles, Calif. 90041 | 1,586 (C) | P | 10,219 | 10,219 | 3,965 |
| Oglala Lakota College; Kyle, S.D. 57752 | 800 (C) | Pub | 720 | 720 | n.a. |
| Oglethorpe University; Atlanta, Ga. 30319 | 1,050 (C) | P | 5,430 | 5,430 | 2,980 |
| Ohio Dominican College; Columbus, Ohio 43219 | 1,129 (C) | P/RC | 5,250 | 5,250 | 2,960 |
| Ohio Institute of Technology, Columbus. See DeVry Institute of Technology, Columbus | | | | | |
| Ohio Northern University; Ada, Ohio 45810 | 1,964 (C) | P/UM | 5,925 | 5,925 | 2,385 |
| Ohio State University; Columbus, Ohio 43210 | 40,828 (C) | Pub | 1,704 | 4,416 | 2,814 |
| Ohio State University–Lima; Lima, Ohio 45804 | 1,043 (C) | Pub | 1,653 | 4,365 | n.a. |
| Ohio State University–Mansfield; Mansfield, Ohio 44906 | 1,012 (C) | Pub | 1,653 | 4,365 | n.a. |
| Ohio State University–Marion; Marion, Ohio 43302 | 789 (C) | Pub | 1,653 | 4,365 | n.a. |
| Ohio State University–Newark; Newark, Ohio 43055 | 915 (C) | Pub | 1,653 | 4,365 | n.a. |
| Ohio University; Athens, Ohio 45701 | 12,500 (C) | Pub | 1,990 | 4,000 | 2,760 |
| Ohio University–Lancaster; Lancaster, Ohio 43130 | 1,500 (C) | Pub | 1,605 | 3,606 | n.a. |
| Ohio University–Zanesville; Zanesville, Ohio 43701 | 1,000 (C) | Pub | 1,605 | 3,606 | n.a. |
| Ohio Valley College; Parkersburg, W. Va. 26101 | 225 | P | 3,080 | 3,080 | 2,480 |
| Ohio Wesleyan University; Delaware, Ohio 43015 | 1,304 (C) | P/UM | 8,525 | 8,525 | 3,390 |
| Oklahoma, University of–Health Sciences Center; Oklahoma City, Okla. 73190 | 970 (C) | Pub | 883 | 2,552 | n.a. |
| Oklahoma, University of–Norman; Norman, Okla. 73019 | 15,639 (C) | Pub | 867 | 2,523 | 2,396 |
| Oklahoma Baptist University; Shawnee, Okla. 74801 | 1,604 (C) | P/B | 3,300 | 3,300 | 2,000 |
| Oklahoma Christian College; Oklahoma City, Okla. 73111 | 1,538 (C) | P/CC | 3,130 | 3,130 | 2,100 |
| Oklahoma City University; Oklahoma City, Okla. 73106 | 1,400 (C) | P/M | 3,500 | 3,500 | 2,570 |
| Oklahoma State University; Stillwater, Okla. 74078 | 17,264 (C) | Pub | 662 | 1,961 | 2,244 |
| Old Dominion University; Norfolk, Va. 23508 | 11,670 (C) | Pub | 1,678 | 3,118 | 3,224 |
| Olivet College; Olivet, Mich. 49076 | 683 (C) | P/UCC | 5,080 | 5,080 | 2,350 |

| Institution and location | Enrollment | Control | Tuition ($) Res. | Tuition ($) Nonres. | Rm/Bd ($) |
|---|---|---|---|---|---|
| Olivet Nazarene College; Kankakee, Ill. 60901 | 1,703 (C) | P/Naz | 4,142 | 4,142 | 2,274 |
| Oral Roberts University; Tulsa, Okla. 74171 | 3,787 (C) | P | 4,480 | 4,480 | 2,600 |
| Oregon, University of; Eugene, Ore. 97403 | 12,635 (C) | Pub | 1,487 | 4,190 | 2,277 |
| Oregon Coll. of Education. *See* Western Oregon State Coll. | | | | | |
| Oregon Health Science University; Portland, Ore. 97201 | 2,000 (C) | Pub | 4,724 | 9,554 | 2,924 |
| Oregon Institute of Technology; Klamath Falls, Ore. 97601 | 2,700 (C) | Pub | 1,403 | 4,018 | 2,400 |
| Oregon State University; Corvallis, Ore. 97331 | 13,396 (C) | Pub | 1,449 | 3,552 | 2,443 |
| Orlando College; Orlando, Fla. 32810 | 900 (C) | P | 7,897 | 7,897 | n.a. |
| Otis Art Institute of Parsons School of Design; Los Angeles, Calif. 90057 | 683 (C) | P | 6,490 | 6,490 | 1,825 |
| Ottawa University; Ottawa, Kan. 66067 | 485 (C) | P/AB | 4,344 | 4,344 | 2,378 |
| Ottawa University–Phoenix Center; Phoenix, Ariz. 85021 | 250 | P | 2,280 | 2,280 | n.a. |
| Otterbein College; Westerville, Ohio 43081 | 1,735 (C) | P/UM | 7,155 | 7,155 | 2,889 |
| Ouachita Baptist University; Arkadelphia, Ark. 71923 | 1,414 (C) | P/B | 3,100 | 3,100 | 1,750 |
| Our Lady of Angels College. *See* Neumann College | | | | | |
| Our Lady of Holy Cross College; New Orleans, La. 70114 | 614 (C) | P/RC | 3,350 | 3,350 | n.a. |
| Our Lady of the Lake–University of San Antonio; San Antonio, Tex. 78285 | 1,177 (C) | P/RC | 4,320 | 4,320 | 2,200 |
| Ozark Christian College; Joplin, Mo. 64801 | 460 | P | 2,080 | 2,080 | 1,690 |
| Ozarks, College of the; Clarksville, Ark. 72830 | 634 (C) | P/UP | 2,010 | 2,010 | 1,650 |
| Ozarks, School of the; Point Lookout, Mo. 65726 | 1,200 (C) | P | 4,120 | 4,120 | 3,216 |
| Pace University; New York, N.Y. 10038 | 9,026 (C) | P | 5,968 | 5,968 | 3,606 |
| Pace University–College of White Plains; White Plains, N.Y. 10603 | 1,835 (C) | P | 5,968 | 5,968 | 3,606 |
| Pace University–Pleasantville–Briarcliff; Pleasantville, N.Y. 10570 | 4,343 (C) | P | 5,968 | 5,968 | 3,606 |
| Pacific, University of the; Stockton, Calif. 95211 | 3,502 (C) | P | 10,247 | 10,247 | 3,928 |
| Pacific Christian College; Fullerton, Calif. 92631 | 432 (C) | P/ChC | 3,400 | 3,400 | 2,600 |
| Pacific Lutheran University; Tacoma, Wash. 98447 | 3,082 (C) | P | 7,155 | 7,155 | 3,210 |
| Pacific Northwest College of Art; Portland, Ore. 97205 | 160 (C) | P | 4,300 | 4,300 | n.a. |
| Pacific Oaks College; Pasadena, Calif. 91103 | 50 (C) | P | 6,300 | 6,300 | n.a. |
| Pacific States University; Los Angeles, Calif. 90006 | 680 | P | 2,820 | 2,820 | n.a. |
| Pacific Union College; Angwin, Calif. 94508 | 1,398 (C) | P/SDA | 6,540 | 6,540 | 2,295 |
| Pacific University; Forest Grove, Ore. 97116 | 673 (C) | P/UCC | 6,515 | 6,515 | 2,520 |
| Paier College of Art, Inc.; Hamden, Conn. 06511 | 344 (C) | P | 7,300 | 7,300 | n.a. |
| Paine College; Augusta, Ga. 30910 | 752 (C) | P/UM | 3,500 | 3,500 | 1,950 |
| Palm Beach Atlantic College; West Palm Beach, Fla. 33401 | 1,100 (C) | P/SB | 4,350 | 4,350 | 2,150 |
| Panama Canal College; APO Miami, Fla. 34002 | 300 | Pub | 680 | 3,734 | n.a. |
| Pan American University; Edinburg, Tex. 78539 | 8,691 (C) | Pub | 552 | 3,144 | 2,080 |
| Panhandle State University; Goodwell, Okla. 73939 | 1,320 (C) | Pub | 699 | 1,766 | 1,615 |
| Park College; Parkville, Mo. 64152 | 471 (C) | P/LDS | 4,480 | 4,480 | 2,240 |
| Parks College of St. Louis University; Cahokia, Ill. 62206 | 1,032 (C) | P/RC | 4,367 | 4,367 | 2,590 |
| Parsons School of Design; New York, N.Y. 10011 | 1,700 (C) | P | 7,470 | 7,470 | 3,700 |
| Patten College; Oakland, Calif. 94601 | 200 (C) | P/CE | 2,800 | 2,800 | 2,850 |
| Paul Quinn College; Waco, Tex. 76704 | 500 (C) | P | 2,100 | 2,100 | 2,550 |
| Peabody Conservatory of Music; Baltimore, Md. 21202 | 256 (C) | P | 7,850 | 7,850 | 3,300 |
| Pembroke State University; Pembroke, N.C. 28372 | 1,955 (C) | Pub | 650 | 3,152 | 1,530 |
| Pennsylvania, University of; Philadelphia, Pa. 19104 | 9,200 (C) | P | 11,200 | 11,200 | 4,650 |
| Pennsylvania State University; University Park, Pa. 16802 | 29,504 (C) | Pub | 2,760 | 5,544 | 2,960 |
| Pennsylvania State University–Behrend; Erie, Pa. 16563 | 2,250 (C) | Pub | 2,760 | 5,544 | 2,750 |
| Pennsylvania State University–Berks; Reading, Pa. 19608 | 220 (C) | Pub | 2,494 | 5,544 | n.a. |
| Pennsylvania State University at Harrisburg–The Capital College; Middletown, Pa. 17057 | 1,800 (C) | Pub | 2,700 | 5,544 | 2,750 |
| Pepperdine University; Malibu, Calif. 90265 | 2,695 (C) | P/CC | 9,440 | 9,440 | 3,920 |
| Pepperdine University–Seaver College; Malibu, Calif. 90265 | 2,492 (C) | P | 10,230 | 10,230 | 4,160 |
| Peru State College; Peru, Neb. 68421 | 1,474 (C) | Pub | 826 | 1,380 | 1,896 |
| Pfeiffer College; Misenheimer, N.C. 28109 | 811 (C) | P/UM | 4,380 | 4,380 | 2,160 |
| Pharmacy, School of (Ga.). *See* Mercer Univ. | | | | | |
| Philadelphia College of the Arts; Philadelphia, Pa. 19102 | 1,400 (C) | P | 7,600 | 7,600 | 2,300 |
| Philadelphia College of Bible; Langhorne, Pa. 19047 | 546 (C) | P | 3,980 | 3,980 | 2,530 |
| Philadelphia College of Pharmacy and Science; Philadelphia, Pa. 19104 | 1,183 (C) | P | 6,200 | 6,200 | 2,950 |
| Philadelphia College of Textiles and Science; Philadelphia, Pa. 19144 | 1,600 (C) | P | 5,900 | 5,900 | 3,150 |
| Philadelphia College of the Performing Arts; Philadelphia, Pa. 19102 | 400 (C) | P | 6,600 | 6,600 | 2,100 |
| Philander Smith College; Little Rock, Ark. 72202 | 937 (C) | P/UM | 1,736 | 1,736 | 2,300 |
| Phillips University; Enid, Okla. 73702 | 660 (C) | P | 4,248 | 4,248 | 2,170 |
| Phoenix, University of; Phoenix, Ariz. 85004 | 2,350 (C) | P | 4,160 | 4,160 | n.a. |
| Piedmont Bible College; Winston-Salem, N.C. 27101 | 286 (C) | P | 2,700 | 2,700 | 2,100 |
| Piedmont College; Demorest, Ga. 30535 | 410 (C) | P/Ind | 1,320 | 2,220 | 2,400 |
| Pikeville College; Pikeville, Ky. 41501 | 500 (C) | P/UP | 3,300 | 3,300 | 2,200 |
| Pillsbury Baptist Bible College; Owatonna, Minn. 55060 | 400 | P | 2,400 | 2,400 | 2,246 |
| Pine Manor College; Chestnut Hill, Mass. 02167 | 540 (W) | P | 8,864 | 8,864 | 4,984 |
| Pittsburgh, University of; Pittsburgh, Pa. 15260 | 19,003 (C) | P | 3,010 | 5,900 | 2,836 |
| Pittsburgh, University of–Bradford; Bradford, Pa. 16701 | 1,000 (C) | P | 2,900 | 5,800 | 2,700 |

| Institution and location | Enrollment | Control | Tuition ($) Res. | Tuition ($) Nonres. | Rm/Bd ($) |
|---|---|---|---|---|---|
| Pittsburgh, University of–Greensburg; Greensburg, Pa. 15601 | 1,500 (C) | P | 3,030 | 6,030 | 2,680 |
| Pittsburgh, University of,–Johnstown; Johnstown, Pa. 15904 | 3,258 (C) | P | 2,970 | 5,860 | 2,572 |
| Pittsburg State University; Pittsburg, Kan. 66762 | 3,838 (C) | Pub | 1,102 | 2,352 | 2,152 |
| Pitzer College. *See* Claremont Colleges | | | | | |
| Plymouth State College; Plymouth, N.H. 03264 | 3,200 (C) | Pub | 1,761 | 4,311 | 2,300 |
| Point Loma Nazarene College; San Diego, Calif. 92106 | 1,703 (C) | P/Naz | 4,821 | 4,821 | 2,776 |
| Point Park College; Pittsburgh, Pa. 15222 | 2,644 (C) | P | 5,420 | 5,420 | 2,680 |
| Polytechnic Institute of New York; Brooklyn, N.Y. 11201 | 2,600 (C) | P | 8,400 | 8,400 | 5,000 |
| Pomona College. *See* Claremont Colleges | | | | | |
| Pontifical College Josephinum; Columbus, Ohio 43085 | 104 | P/RC | 2,280 | 2,280 | 1,870 |
| Portland, University of; Portland, Ore. 97203 | 2,234 (C) | P | 5,940 | 5,940 | 2,690 |
| Portland School of Art; Portland, Me. 04101 | 250 (C) | P | 5,850 | 5,850 | 3,100 |
| Portland State University; Portland, Ore. 97207 | 11,534 (C) | Pub | 1,470 | 4,173 | 2,098 |
| Post College; Waterbury, Conn. 06708 | 1,642 (C) | P | 6,050 | 6,050 | 3,410 |
| Potsdam Coll. of Arts & Science. *See* New York, State Univ. of | | | | | |
| Prairie View A&M University; Prairie View, Tex. 77446 | 3,900 | Pub | 878 | 4,118 | 2,700 |
| Pratt Institute; Brooklyn, N.Y. 11205 | 2,724 (C) | P | 7,100 | 7,100 | 3,465 |
| Presbyterian College; Clinton, S.C. 29325 | 930 (C) | P | 5,588 | 5,588 | 2,342 |
| Princeton University; Princeton, N.J. 08544 | 4,600 (C) | P | 11,780 | 11,780 | 4,200 |
| Principia College; Elsah, Ill. 62028 | 700 (C) | P | 7,962 | 7,962 | 3,880 |
| Providence College; Providence, R.I. 02918 | 3,674 (C) | P | 7,003 | 7,003 | 3,700 |
| Puerto Rico, Polytechnic University of; Hato Rey, San Juan, P.R. 00918 | 1,621 | P | 7,500 | 7,500 | n.a. |
| Puerto Rico, University of–Cayey University College; Cayey, P.R. 00633 | 3,520 (C) | Pub | 500 | 1,500 | n.a. |
| Puerto Rico, University of–Humacao University College; Humacao, P.R. 00661 | 3,545 (C) | Pub | 600 | n.a. | n.a. |
| Puerto Rico, University of–Mayaguez Campus; Mayaguez, P.R. 00708 | 9,700 (C) | Pub | 665 | 2,625 | n.a. |
| Puerto Rico, University of–Medical Science; San Juan, P.R. 00936 | 1,700 (C) | Pub | 360 | 3,000 | n.a. |
| Puget Sound, University of; Tacoma, Wash. 98416 | 2,825 (C) | P | 7,850 | 7,850 | 3,240 |
| Puget Sound Christian College; Edmonds, Wash. 98020 | 109 (C) | P | 2,450 | 2,450 | 2,175 |
| Purdue University; West Lafayette, Ind. 47907 | 26,500 (C) | Pub | 1,532 | 4,556 | 2,500 |
| Purdue University–Calumet; Hammond, Ind. 46323 | 6,468 (C) | Pub | 1,531 | 3,782 | n.a. |
| Purdue University–North Central; Westville, Ind. 46391 | 2,611 (C) | Pub | 1,455 | 3,780 | n.a. |
| Queens College; Charlotte, N.C. 28274 | 650 (W) | P/PUS | 5,650 | 5,650 | 3,150 |
| Queens College (NYC). *See* New York, City University of | | | | | |
| Quincy College; Quincy, Ill. 62301 | 1,401 (C) | P/RC | 5,400 | 5,400 | 2,420 |
| Quinnipiac College; Hamden, Conn. 06518 | 2,000 (C) | P | 6,360 | 6,360 | 3,000 |
| Radcliffe College. *See* Harvard and Radcliffe Colleges | | | | | |
| Rabbinical College of America; Morristown, N.J. 07960 | 230 (M) | P | 3,450 | 3,450 | 2,900 |
| Radford University; Radford, Va. 24142 | 6,024 (C) | Pub | 1,796 | 2,546 | 3,050 |
| Ramapo College of New Jersey; Mahwah, N.J. 07430 | 4,000 (C) | Pub | 1,450 | 2,050 | 3,150 |
| Randolph–Macon College; Ashland, Va. 23005 | 992 (C) | P | 7,140 | 7,140 | 3,300 |
| Randolph–Macon Woman's College; Lynchburg, Va. 24503 | 750 (W) | P/UM | 7,600 | 7,600 | 3,500 |
| Redlands, University of; Redlands, Calif. 92374 | 1,200 (C) | P | 8,410 | 8,410 | 3,505 |
| Reed College; Portland, Ore. 97202 | 1,063 (C) | P | 9,960 | 9,960 | 3,190 |
| Reformed Bible College; Grand Rapids, Mich. 49506 | 215 (C) | P | 3,300 | 3,300 | 2,300 |
| Regis College; Denver, Colo. 80221 | 1,050 (C) | P/RC | 6,936 | 6,936 | 3,630 |
| Regis College; Weston, Mass. 02193 | 1,102 (W) | P/RC | 6,800 | 6,800 | 3,600 |
| Reno Business College; Reno, Nev. 89503 | 300 (C) | P | 3,835 | 3,835 | n.a. |
| Rensselaer Polytechnic Institute; Troy, N.Y. 12180 | 4,800 (C) | P | 11,100 | 11,100 | 3,650 |
| Research College of Nursing; Kansas City, Mo. 64132 | 238 | P | 5,340 | 5,340 | 2,375 |
| Rhode Island, University of; Kingston, R.I. 02881 | 8,770 (C) | Pub | 2,125 | 5,811 | 3,528 |
| Rhode Island College; Providence, R.I. 02908 | 8,000 (C) | Pub | 1,234 | 3,614 | 2,996 |
| Rhode Island School of Design; Providence, R.I. 02903 | 1,690 (C) | P | 9,000 | 9,000 | 3,800 |
| Rhodes College; Memphis, Tenn. 38112 | 1,063 | P/PUS | 7,660 | 7,660 | 3,255 |
| Rice University; Houston, Tex. 77251 | 2,600 (C) | P | 4,400 | 4,400 | 3,850 |
| Richmond, University of; Richmond, Va. 23173 | 2,700 (C) | P/B | 7,675 | 7,675 | 2,400 |
| Richmond College, The American International College of London; London, England TW10 6JP | 950 (C) | P | 6,330 | 6,330 | 2,565 |
| Rider College; Lawrenceville, N.J. 08648 | 3,100 (C) | P | 6,850 | 6,850 | 3,210 |
| Ringling School of Art and Design; Sarasota, Fla. 33580 | 400 (C) | P | 5,600 | 5,600 | 3,500 |
| Rio Grande College; Rio Grande, Ohio 45674 | 1,600 (C) | P | 1,170 | 4,170 | 2,700 |
| Ripon College; Ripon, Wis. 54971 | 900 (C) | P | 8,822 | 8,822 | 2,290 |
| Rivier College; Nashua, N.H. 03060 | 650 (W) | P/RC | 5,280 | 5,280 | 2,900 |
| Roanoke Bible College; Elizabeth City, N.C. 27909 | 130 (C) | P | 1,550 | 1,550 | 1,650 |
| Roanoke College; Salem, Va. 24153 | 1,250 (C) | P/LCA | 6,500 | 6,500 | 2,750 |
| Robert Morris College; Coraopolis, Pa. 15108 | 5,288 (C) | P | 3,480 | 3,480 | 2,400 |
| Roberts Wesleyan College; Rochester, N.Y. 14624 | 680 (C) | P/FM | 5,814 | 5,814 | 2,508 |
| Rochester, University of; Rochester, N.Y. 14627 | 4,531 (C) | P | 10,330 | 10,330 | 4,325 |

| Institution and location | Enrollment | Control | Tuition ($) Res. | Tuition ($) Nonres. | Rm/Bd ($) |
|---|---|---|---|---|---|
| Rochester Institute of Technology; Rochester, N.Y. 14623 | 12,000 (C) | P | 7,701 | 7,701 | 3,696 |
| Rockford College; Rockford, Ill. 61108 | 1,150 (C) | P | 5,990 | 5,990 | 2,700 |
| Rockhurst College; Kansas City, Mo. 64110 | 2,132 (C) | P/RC | 5,530 | 5,530 | 2,925 |
| Rocky Mountain College; Billings, Mont. 59102 | 515 (C) | P | 4,030 | 4,030 | 2,470 |
| Roger Williams College; Bristol, R.I. 02809 | 2,300 (C) | P | 6,008 | 6,008 | 3,490 |
| Rollins College; Winter Park, Fla. 32789 | 1,350 (C) | P | 8,842 | 8,842 | 3,134 |
| Roosevelt University; Chicago, Ill. 60605 | 4,129 (C) | P | 5,040 | 5,040 | 3,210 |
| Rosary College; River Forest, Ill. 60305 | 1,000 (C) | P/RC | 5,940 | 5,940 | 2,860 |
| Rose–Hulman Institute of Technology; Terre Haute, Ind. 47803 | 1,310 (M) | P | 7,350 | 7,350 | 2,750 |
| Rosemont College; Rosemont, Pa. 19010 | 600 (W) | P/RC | 6,080 | 6,080 | 3,960 |
| Rush University; Chicago, Ill. 60612 | 262 (C) | P | 5,730 | 5,730 | 3,255 |
| Russell Sage College; Troy, N.Y. 12180 | 1,306 (W) | P | 7,100 | 7,100 | 3,130 |
| Rust College; Holly Springs, Miss. 38635 | 900 (C) | P | 2,250 | 2,250 | 1,276 |
| Rutgers University–Camden College of Arts and Sciences; Camden, N.J. 08102 | 2,669 (C) | Pub | 2,177 | 4,029 | 3,046 |
| Rutgers University–College of Engineering; New Brunswick, N.J. 08903 | 2,727 (C) | Pub | 2,424 | 4,480 | 2,842 |
| Rutgers University–College of Nursing–Newark; Newark, N.J. 07102 | 542 (C) | Pub | 2,147 | 3,999 | n.a. |
| Rutgers University–College of Pharmacy; New Brunswick, N.J. 08903 | 739 (C) | Pub | 2,322 | 4,276 | 2,842 |
| Rutgers University–Cook College; New Brunswick, N.J. 08903 | 3,110 (C) | Pub | 2,360 | 4,314 | 2,842 |
| Rutgers University–Douglass College; New Brunswick, N.J. 08903 | 3,341 (C) | Pub | 2,257 | 4,109 | 2,842 |
| Rutgers University–Livingston College; New Brunswick, N.J. 08903 | 3,476 (C) | Pub | 2,275 | 4,127 | 2,842 |
| Rutgers University–Mason Gross School of the Arts; New Brunswick, N.J. 08903 | 400 (C) | Pub | 2,220 | 4,072 | 2,842 |
| Rutgers University–Newark College of Arts and Sciences; Newark, N.J. 07102 | 3,673 (C) | Pub | 2,154 | 4,006 | n.a. |
| Rutgers University–Rutgers College; New Brunswick, N.J. 08903 | 8,718 (C) | Pub | 2,271 | 4,123 | 2,842 |
| Rutgers University—University College–Camden; Camden, N.J. 08102 | 998 (C) | Pub | (3) | (4) | n.a. |
| Rutgers University—University College–Newark; Newark, N.J. 07102 | 1,705 (C) | Pub | (3) | (4) | n.a. |
| Rutgers University—University College–New Brunswick; New Brunswick, N.J. 08903 | 3,280 (C) | Pub | (3) | (4) | n.a. |
| Sacred Heart, Univ. of the; Santurce, P.R. 00924 | 8,256 (C) | P/RC | 1,904 | 1,904 | 2,700 |
| Sacred Heart College; Belmont, N.C. 28012 | 450 (W) | P/RC | 3,710 | 3,710 | 2,400 |
| Sacred Heart Seminary; Detroit, Mich. 48206 | 265 | P/RC | 2,600 | 2,600 | 1,750 |
| Sacred Heart University; Bridgeport, Conn. 06606 | 4,172 (C) | P | 4,500 | 4,500 | n.a. |
| Saginaw Valley State College; University Center, Mich. 48710 | 4,440 (C) | Pub | 1,628 | 3,317 | 2,530 |
| St. Alphonsus College; Suffield, Conn. 06078 | 43 | P/RC | 4,500 | 4,500 | 2,900 |
| St. Ambrose College; Davenport, Iowa 52803 | 1,800 (C) | P/RC | 5,970 | 5,970 | 2,530 |
| St. Andrews Presbyterian College; Laurinburg, N.C. 28352 | 750 (C) | P/PUS | 4,850 | 5,800 | 2,850 |
| St. Anselm College; Manchester, N.H. 03102 | 1,700 (C) | P | 6,660 | 6,660 | 3,440 |
| St. Augustine's College; Raleigh, N.C. 27611 | 1,716 (C) | P/E | 3,200 | 3,200 | 2,300 |
| St. Benedict, College of; St. Joseph, Minn. 56374 | 1,765 (W) | P/RC | 6,235 | 6,235 | 2,495 |
| St. Bonaventure University; St. Bonaventure, N.Y. 14778 | 2,350 (C) | P | 5,950 | 5,950 | 3,315 |
| St. Catherine, College of; St. Paul, Minn. 55105 | 2,484 (W) | P/RC | 6,425 | 6,425 | 2,590 |
| St. Cloud State University; St. Cloud, Minn. 56301 | 11,263 (C) | Pub | 1,615 | 2,578 | 1,700 |
| St. Edward's University; Austin, Tex. 78704 | 2,100 (C) | P/RC | 4,960 | 4,960 | 2,800 |
| St. Elizabeth, College of; Convent Station, N.J. 07961 | 991 (C) | P | 6,000 | 6,000 | 3,000 |
| St. Francis, College of; Joliet, Ill. 60435 | 1,080 (C) | P/RC | 4,990 | 4,990 | 2,710 |
| St. Francis College; Brooklyn, N.Y. 11201 | 2,436 (C) | P | 4,410 | 4,410 | n.a. |
| St. Francis College; Fort Wayne, Ind. 46808 | 965 (C) | P/RC | 4,160 | 4,160 | 2,500 |
| St. Francis College; Loretto, Pa. 15940 | 1,100 (C) | P/RC | 5,376 | 5,376 | 3,000 |
| St. Hyacinth College and Seminary; Granby, Mass. 01033 | 52 (M) | P/RC | 3,000 | 3,000 | 3,000 |
| St. John Fisher College; Rochester, N.Y. 14618 | 1,600 (C) | P | 5,750 | 5,750 | 3,060 |
| St. John's College; Annapolis, Md. 21404 | 400 (C) | P | 9,720 | 9,720 | 3,300 |
| Saint John's College; Camarillo, Calif. 93010 | 100 (M) | P/RC | 2,900 | 2,900 | 2,900 |
| St. John's College; Santa Fe, N.M. 87501 | 301 (C) | P | 9,720 | 9,720 | 3,300 |
| St. John's Seminary College of Liberal Arts; Brighton, Mass. 02135 | 85 | P/RC | 2,250 | 2,250 | 2,250 |
| Saint John's University; Collegeville, Minn. 56321 | 1,875 (M) | P/RC | 6,175 | 6,175 | 2,760 |
| St. John's University; Jamaica, N.Y. 11439 | 14,413 (C) | P/RC | 4,730 | 4,730 | n.a. |
| St. John Vianney College Seminary; Miami, Fla. 33165 | 66 (M) | P/RC | 2,375 | 2,375 | 2,375 |
| St. Joseph, College of; Rutland, Vt. 05701 | 315 (C) | P/RC | 4,600 | 4,600 | 2,741 |
| St. Joseph College; West Hartford, Conn. 06117 | 719 (W) | P/RC | 6,000 | 6,000 | 3,350 |
| St. Joseph's College; Brooklyn, N.Y. 11205 | 873 (C) | P | 4,200 | 4,200 | n.a. |
| St. Joseph's College; Mountain View, Calif. 94039 | 119 | P/RC | 4,500 | 4,500 | 1,000 |
| St. Joseph's College; North Windham, Me. 04062 | 560 (C) | P/RC | 5,350 | 5,350 | 3,050 |
| St. Joseph's College; Rensselaer, Ind. 47978 | 847 (C) | P/RC | 6,210 | 6,210 | 2,670 |
| St. Joseph's College–Suffolk; Patchogue, N.Y. 11772 | 1,445 (C) | P | 4,130 | 4,130 | n.a. |

| Institution and location | Enrollment | Control | Tuition ($) Res. | Tuition ($) Nonres. | Rm/Bd ($) |
|---|---|---|---|---|---|
| St. Joseph Seminary College; St. Benedict, La. 70457 | 90 (M) | P | 2,500 | 2,500 | 2,800 |
| St. Joseph's University; Philadelphia, Pa. 19131 | 2,350 (C) | P/RC | 5,800 | 5,800 | 3,700 |
| St. Lawrence University; Canton, N.Y. 13617 | 2,200 (C) | P | 10,125 | 10,125 | 3,385 |
| St. Leo College; St. Leo, Fla. 33574 | 1,141 (C) | P/RC | 5,210 | 5,210 | 2,320 |
| St. Louis Christian College; Florissant, Mo. 63033 | 160 (C) | P | 2,016 | 2,016 | 1,450 |
| St. Louis College of Pharmacy; St. Louis, Mo. 63110 | 698 (C) | P | 3,300 | 3,300 | 2,450 |
| St. Louis University; St. Louis, Mo. 63103 | 6,563 (C) | P | 5,720 | 5,720 | 3,000 |
| St. Martin's College; Lacey, Wash. 98503 | 617 (C) | P | 5,996 | 5,996 | 2,860 |
| St. Mary, College of; Omaha, Neb. 68124 | 1,009 (W) | P/RC | 4,920 | 4,920 | 2,400 |
| St. Mary College; Leavenworth, Kan. 66048 | 1,008 (W) | P | 4,840 | 4,840 | 2,760 |
| St. Mary of the Plains College; Dodge City, Kan. 67801 | 644 (C) | P/RC | 4,090 | 4,090 | 2,200 |
| St. Mary-of-the-Woods Coll.; St. Mary-of-the-Woods, Ind. 47876 | 350 (W) | P/RC | 5,835 | 5,835 | 2,700 |
| St. Mary's College; Notre Dame, Ind. 46556 | 1,835 (W) | P/RC | 6,983 | 6,983 | 3,052 |
| St. Mary's College; Orchard Lake, Mich. 48033 | 280 (C) | P | 3,050 | 3,050 | 2,450 |
| St. Mary's College; Winona, Minn. 55987 | 1,200 (C) | P | 6,200 | 6,200 | 2,500 |
| St. Mary's College of California; Moraga, Calif. 94575 | 2,400 (C) | P/RC | 6,398 | 6,398 | 3,382 |
| St. Mary's College of Maryland; St. Mary's City, Md. 20686 | 1,426 (C) | Pub | 2,050 | 3,350 | 3,500 |
| St. Mary's University of San Antonio; San Antonio, Tex. 78284 | 2,066 (C) | P/RC | 4,952 | 4,952 | 2,570 |
| St. Meinrad College; St. Meinrad, Ind. 47577 | 169 (M) | P/RC | 3,050 | 3,058 | 3,492 |
| St. Michael's College; Winooski, Vt. 05404 | 1,650 (C) | P/RC | 6,874 | 6,874 | 2,762 |
| St. Norbert College; De Pere, Wis. 54115 | 1,751 (C) | P/RC | 6,545 | 6,545 | 2,550 |
| St. Olaf College; Northfield, Minn. 55057 | 3,029 (C) | P/AL | 7,725 | 7,725 | 2,425 |
| St. Paul Bible College; Bible College, Minn. 55375 | 658 (C) | P/CMA | 3,884 | 3,884 | 2,500 |
| St. Paul's College; Lawrenceville, Va. 23868 | 697 (C) | P | 3,190 | 3,190 | 2,405 |
| St. Peter's College; Jersey City, N.J. 07306 | 2,100 (C) | P/RC | 5,507 | 5,507 | 4,815 |
| St. Rose, The College of; Albany, N.Y. 12203 | 2,032 (C) | P | 5,670 | 5,670 | 3,210 |
| St. Scholastica, College of; Duluth, Minn. 55811 | 1,440 (C) | P/RC | 6,130 | 6,130 | 2,544 |
| St. Teresa, College of; Winona, Minn. 55987 | 422 (W) | P | 6,200 | 6,200 | 2,300 |
| St. Thomas, College of; St. Paul, Minn. 55105 | 4,271 (C) | P | 5,940 | 5,940 | 2,400 |
| St. Thomas, University of; Houston, Tex. 77006 | 1,548 (C) | P/RC | 3,200 | 3,200 | 2,990 |
| St. Thomas Aquinas College; Sparkill, N.Y. 10968 | 1,800 (C) | P | 4,200 | 4,200 | 2,700 |
| Saint Thomas University; Miami, Fla. 33054 | 2,100 (C) | P/RC | 5,250 | 5,250 | 3,150 |
| Saint Vincent College; Latrobe, Pa. 15650 | 1,163 (C) | P/RC | 5,475 | 5,475 | 2,600 |
| St. Xavier College; Chicago, Ill. 60655 | 2,200 (C) | P/RC | 5,740 | 5,740 | 3,232 |
| Salem College; Salem, W. Va. 26426 | 1,000 (C) | P | 5,157 | 5,157 | 2,640 |
| Salem College; Winston-Salem, N.C. 27108 | 725 (W) | P | 5,790 | 5,790 | 6,100 |
| Salem State College; Salem, Mass. 01970 | 5,287 (C) | Pub | 1,086 | 3,282 | 2,137 |
| Salisbury State College; Salisbury, Md. 21801 | 4,100 (C) | Pub | 1,742 | 3,120 | 2,700 |
| Salve Regina—The Newport College; Newport, R.I. 02840 | 1,500 (C) | P | 6,900 | 6,900 | 3,960 |
| Samford University; Birmingham, Ala. 35229 | 2,738 (C) | P/SB | 3,690 | 3,690 | 2,238 |
| Sam Houston State University; Huntsville, Tex. 77341 | 8,679 (C) | Pub | 880 | 4,000 | 2,690 |
| San Diego, University of; San Diego, Calif. 92110 | 3,400 (C) | P/RC | 7,340 | 7,340 | 4,160 |
| San Diego State University; San Diego, Calif. 92182 | 29,589 (C) | Pub | 630 | 3,756 | 3,104 |
| Imperial Valley Campus; Calexico, Calif. 92231 | 200 (C) | Pub | 718 | 4,227 | n.a. |
| San Francisco, University of; San Francisco, Calif. 94117 | 3,431 (C) | P/RC | 6,450 | 6,450 | 3,490 |
| San Francisco Art Institute; San Francisco, Calif. 94133 | 452 (C) | P | 6,200 | 6,200 | n.a. |
| San Francisco Conservatory of Music, The; San Francisco, Calif. 94122 | 140 (C) | P | 6,695 | 6,695 | n.a. |
| San Francisco State Univ.; San Francisco, Calif. 94132 | 18,000 (C) | Pub | 682 | 4,912 | 3,198 |
| Sangamon State University; Springfield, Ill. 62708 | 1,570 (C) | Pub | 1,098 | 3,126 | 2,210 |
| San Jose Bible College; San Jose, Calif. 95108 | 175 (C) | P/ChC | 3,640 | 3,640 | 2,000 |
| San Jose State University; San Jose, Calif. 95192 | 20,573 (C) | Pub | 630 | 4,860 | 5,000 |
| Santa Clara, University of; Santa Clara, Calif. 95053 | 3,600 (C) | P/RC | 7,263 | 7,263 | 3,909 |
| Santa Fe, College of; Santa Fe, N.M. 87501 | 950 (C) | P/RC | 3,500 | 3,500 | 2,460 |
| Sarah Lawrence College; Bronxville, N.Y. 10708 | 840 (C) | P | 10,779 | 10,779 | 4,506 |
| Savannah College of Art and Design; Savannah, Ga. 31401 | 929 (C) | P | 4,710 | 4,710 | 2,150 |
| Savannah State College; Savannah, Ga. 31404 | 2,300 (C) | Pub | 1,280 | 2,560 | 2,400 |
| Schiller International University; 6900 Heidelberg, W. Ger. | 1,080 | P | 5,700 | 5,700 | 4,000 |
| Schreiner College; Kerrville, Tex. 78028 | 518 (C) | P | 4,775 | 4,775 | 3,240 |
| Science and Arts, University of, of Oklahoma; Chickasha, Okla. 73018 | 1,316 (C) | Pub | 656 | 1,920 | 1,600 |
| Scranton, University of; Scranton, Pa. 18510 | 3,460 (C) | P/RC | 5,280 | 5,280 | 2,910 |
| Scripps College. *See* Claremont Colleges | | | | | |
| Seattle Pacific University; Seattle, Wash. 98119 | 2,800 (C) | P/FM | 5,997 | 5,997 | 3,090 |
| Seattle University; Seattle, Wash. 98122 | 3,262 (C) | P/RC | 6,660 | 6,660 | 3,333 |
| Seaver College. *See* Pepperdine University | | | | | |
| Seton Hall University; South Orange, N.J. 07079 | 4,494 (C) | P/RC | 5,160 | 5,160 | 3,236 |
| Seton Hill College; Greensburg, Pa. 15601 | 854 (W) | P | 6,050 | 6,050 | 2,910 |
| Shaw University; Raleigh, N.C. 27611 | 1,773 (C) | P | 2,570 | 2,570 | 1,444 |
| Sheldon Jackson College; Sitka, Alaska 99835 | 203 (C) | P/UP | 3,976 | 3,976 | 3,600 |
| Shenandoah College and Conservatory of Music; Winchester, Va. 22601 | 932 (C) | P | 6,000 | 6,000 | 2,800 |

| Institution and location | Enrollment | Control | Tuition ($) Res. | Nonres. | Rm/Bd ($) |
|---|---|---|---|---|---|
| Shepherd College; Shepherdstown, W. Va. 25443 | 3,777 (C) | Pub | 840 | 2,300 | 2,433 |
| Shimer College; Waukegan, Ill. 60085 | 100 (C) | P | 4,800 | 4,800 | 1,625 |
| Shippensburg University; Shippensburg, Pa. 17257 | 5,180 (C) | Pub | 1,822 | 3,090 | 1,990 |
| Shorter College; Rome, Ga. 30161 | 771 (C) | P | 3,640 | 3,640 | 2,240 |
| Siena College; Loudonville, N.Y. 12211 | 2,700 (C) | P | 5,565 | 5,565 | 3,360 |
| Siena Heights College; Adrian, Mich. 49221 | 1,380 (C) | P | 4,710 | 4,710 | 2,800 |
| Sierra Nevada College; Incline Village, Nev. 89450 | 225 (C) | P | 2,600 | 2,600 | 3,000 |
| Silver Lake College; Manitowoc, Wis. 54220 | 470 (C) | P/RC | 4,600 | 4,600 | n.a. |
| Simmons College; Boston, Mass. 02115 | 1,642 (W) | P | 8,604 | 8,604 | 3,920 |
| Simon's Rock of Bard College; Great Barrington, Mass. 01230 | 300 (C) | P | 9,330 | 9,330 | 3,170 |
| Simpson College; Indianola, Iowa 50125 | 1,224 (C) | P | 6,100 | 6,100 | 2,195 |
| Simpson College; San Francisco, Calif. 94134 | 277 (C) | P/CMA | 3,770 | 3,770 | 2,100 |
| Sinte Gleska College; Rosebud, S.D. 57570 | 536 (C) | P | 848 | 848 | n.a. |
| Sioux Falls College; Sioux Falls, S.D. 57105 | 870 (C) | P/B | 4,950 | 4,950 | 2,300 |
| Skidmore College; Saratoga Springs, N.Y. 12866 | 2,227 (C) | P | 9,877 | 9,877 | 3,780 |
| Slippery Rock State College. *See* Slippery Rock University of Pennsylvania | | | | | |
| Slippery Rock Univ. of Pennsylvania; Slippery Rock, Pa. 16057 | 5,831 (C) | Pub | 1,838 | 3,106 | 1,922 |
| Smith College; Northampton, Mass. 01063 | 2,550 (W) | P | 10,570 | 10,570 | 4,120 |
| Sojourner–Douglass College; Baltimore, Md. 21205 | 500 (C) | P | 4,125 | 4,125 | n.a. |
| Sonoma State University; Rohnert Park, Calif. 94928 | 4,034 (C) | Pub | 697 | 4,477 | 3,100 |
| South, University of the; Sewanee, Tenn. 37375 | 1,020 (C) | P/E | 9,285 | 9,285 | 2,410 |
| South Alabama, University of; Mobile, Ala. 36688 | 8,110 (C) | Pub | 1,530 | 2,130 | 2,430 |
| Southampton College. *See* Long Island Univ. Center | | | | | |
| South Carolina, University of; Columbia, S.C. 29208 | 15,089 (C) | Pub | 1,608 | 3,288 | 2,500 |
| South Carolina, Univ. of–Aiken; Aiken, S.C. 29801 | 2,071 (C) | Pub | 1,200 | 2,540 | n.a. |
| South Carolina, Univ. of–Coastal Carolina; Conway, S.C. 29526 | 2,923 (C) | Pub | 1,200 | 2,540 | n.a. |
| South Carolina, Univ. of–Spartanburg; Spartanburg, S.C. 29303 | 2,935 (C) | Pub | 1,260 | 2,460 | 2,660 |
| South Carolina State College; Orangeburg, S.C. 29117 | 3,694 (C) | Pub | 1,050 | 2,100 | 1,998 |
| South Dakota, University of; Vermillion, S.D. 57069 | 4,229 (C) | Pub | 1,512 | 2,832 | 1,902 |
| South Dakota School of Mines and Technology; Rapid City, S.D. 57701 | 2,040 (C) | Pub | 1,790 | 3,264 | 1,940 |
| South Dakota State University; Brookings, S.D. 57007 | 5,976 (C) | Pub | 1,469 | 2,789 | 1,572 |
| Southeastern Baptist College; Laurel, Miss. 39440 | 125 | P | 1,200 | 1,200 | 1,330 |
| Southeastern Bible College; Birmingham, Ala. 35256 | 200 (C) | P/ID | 2,920 | 2,920 | 2,070 |
| Southeastern College of the Assemblies of God; Lakeland, Fla. 33801 | 1,000 (C) | P/AG | 1,800 | 1,800 | 1,400 |
| Southeastern Louisiana University; Hammond, La. 70402 | 7,932 (C) | Pub | 1,088 | 1,968 | 1,590 |
| Southeastern Massachusetts University; North Dartmouth, Mass. 02747 | 5,000 (C) | Pub | 1,288 | 3,844 | 3,350 |
| Southeastern Oklahoma State Univ.; Durant, Okla. 74701 | 3,364 (C) | Pub | 720 | 2,000 | 1,980 |
| Southeastern University; Washington, D.C. 20024 | 672 (C) | P | 3,900 | 3,900 | n.a. |
| Southeast Missouri State Univ.; Cape Girardeau, Mo. 63701 | 8,500 (C) | Pub | 1,000 | 2,000 | 1,875 |
| Southern Arkansas University; Magnolia, Ark. 71753 | 2,013 (C) | Pub | 870 | 1,430 | 1,738 |
| Southern California, Univ. of; Los Angeles, Calif. 90089 | 15,888 (C) | P | 9,626 | 9,626 | 3,750 |
| Southern California College; Costa Mesa, Calif. 92626 | 886 (C) | P/AG | 4,888 | 4,888 | 2,900 |
| Southern College of Seventh-Day Adventists; Collegedale, Tenn. 37315 | 1,468 (C) | P/SDA | 5,536 | 5,536 | 2,384 |
| Southern Colorado, University of; Pueblo, Colo. 81001 | 3,881 (C) | Pub | 1,216 | 4,170 | 2,714 |
| Southern Connecticut State Univ.; New Haven, Conn. 06515 | 6,436 (C) | Pub | 1,160 | 3,060 | 2,900 |
| Southern Illinois Univ.–Carbondale; Carbondale, Ill. 62901 | 18,651 (C) | Pub | 1,603 | 3,742 | 2,570 |
| Southern Illinois Univ.–Edwardsville; Edwardsville, Ill. 62026 | 8,184 (C) | Pub | 1,348 | 3,439 | 2,614 |
| Southern Indiana, University of; Evansville, Ind. 47714 | 4,026 | Pub | 1,333 | 3,286 | 2,390 |
| Southern Maine, University of; Gorham, Me. 04038 | 8,700 (C) | Pub | 1,509 | 4,560 | 2,640 |
| Southern Methodist College; Orangeburg, S.C. 29115 | 57 | P | 1,470 | 1,470 | 1,700 |
| Southern Methodist University; Dallas, Tex. 75275 | 5,800 (C) | P/M | 7,879 | 7,879 | 3,990 |
| Southern Missionary College. *See* Southern College of Seventh-Day Adventists | | | | | |
| Southern Mississippi, Univ. of; Hattiesburg, Miss. 39406 | 9,589 (C) | Pub | 1,391 | 2,573 | 2,060 |
| Southern Oregon State College; Ashland, Ore. 97520 | 3,870 (C) | Pub | 1,473 | 3,786 | 2,450 |
| Southern Technical Institute; Marietta, Ga. 30060 | 3,580 (C) | Pub | 1,212 | 3,234 | 2,675 |
| Southern University–Baton Rouge; Baton Rouge, La. 70813 | 9,022 (C) | Pub | 662 | 1,292 | 3,576 |
| Southern University–New Orleans; New Orleans, La. 70126 | 2,709 (C) | Pub | 726 | 1,406 | n.a. |
| Southern Utah State College; Cedar City, Utah 84720 | 2,700 (C) | Pub | 966 | 2,574 | 1,959 |
| Southern Vermont College; Bennington, Vt. 05201 | 600 (C) | P | 3,900 | 3,900 | 2,880 |
| South Florida, University of; Tampa, Fla. 33620 | 19,292 (C) | Pub | 950 | 2,550 | 2,500 |
| Southwest, College of the; Hobbs, N.M. 88240 | 253 (C) | P | 1,226 | 1,226 | 1,440 |
| Southwest Baptist University; Bolivar, Mo. 65613 | 1,947 (C) | P | 3,680 | 3,680 | 1,550 |
| Southwestern Adventist College; Keene, Tex. 76059 | 734 (C) | P | 5,430 | 5,430 | 2,826 |
| Southwestern Assemblies of God College; Waxahachie, Tex. 75165 | 640 (C) | P | 2,100 | 2,100 | 2,500 |
| Southwestern College; Winfield, Kan. 67156 | 585 (C) | P/UM | 3,070 | 3,070 | 2,397 |
| Southwestern Conservative Baptist Bible College; Phoenix, Ariz. 85032 | 138 (C) | P/B | 2,900 | 2,900 | 2,350 |
| Southwestern Louisiana, University of; Lafayette, La. 70504 | 14,611 (C) | Pub | 829 | 1,709 | 1,682 |

| Institution and location | Enrollment | Control | Tuition ($) Res. | Tuition ($) Nonres. | Rm/Bd ($) |
|---|---|---|---|---|---|
| Southwestern Oklahoma State Univ.; Weatherford, Okla. 73096 | 4,300 (C) | Pub | 600 | 1,600 | 1,200 |
| Southwestern University; Georgetown, Tex. 78626 | 1,081 (C) | P/UM | 5,900 | 5,900 | 3,300 |
| Southwest Missouri State Univ.; Springfield, Mo. 65804 | 14,000 (C) | Pub | 1,200 | 2,400 | 2,080 |
| Southwest State University; Marshall, Minn. 56258 | 2,421 (C) | Pub | 1,700 | 3,200 | 1,800 |
| Southwest Texas State Univ.; San Marcos, Tex. 78666 | 17,420 (C) | Pub | 778 | 4,018 | 2,294 |
| Spalding University; Louisville, Ky. 40203 | 950 (C) | P/RC | 4,100 | 4,100 | 2,150 |
| Spelman College; Atlanta, Ga. 30314 | 1,600 (W) | P | 3,500 | 3,500 | 3,000 |
| Spertus College of Judaica; Chicago, Ill. 60605 | 100 (C) | P | 2,880 | 2,880 | n.a. |
| Spring Arbor College; Spring Arbor, Mich. 49283 | 696 (C) | P | 5,690 | 5,690 | 2,308 |
| Springfield College; Springfield, Mass. 01109 | 2,000 (C) | P | 6,210 | 6,210 | 2,860 |
| Spring Garden College; Philadelphia, Pa. 19119 | 1,470 (C) | P | 5,450 | 5,450 | 3,720 |
| Spring Hill College; Mobile, Ala. 36608 | 985 (C) | P/RC | 6,600 | 6,600 | 3,230 |
| Stanford University; Stanford, Calif. 94305 | 6,524 (C) | P | 11,208 | 11,208 | 4,700 |
| Staten Island, Coll. of (NYC). *See* New York, City Univ. of | | | | | |
| Stephen F. Austin State Univ.; Nacogdoches, Tex. 75962 | 11,000 (C) | Pub | 870 | 4,000 | 2,700 |
| Stephens College; Columbia, Mo. 65215 | 987 (W) | P | 7,500 | 7,500 | 3,100 |
| Sterling College; Sterling, Kan. 67579 | 439 (C) | P/PUS | 4,300 | 4,300 | 2,400 |
| Stetson University; Deland, Fla. 32720 | 2,109 (C) | P | 6,200 | 6,200 | 2,500 |
| Steubenville, University of; Steubenville, Ohio 43952 | 840 (C) | P/RC | 5,220 | 5,220 | 2,900 |
| Stevens Institute of Technology; Hoboken, N.J. 07030 | 1,550 (C) | P | 9,600 | 9,600 | 3,590 |
| Stillman College; Tuscaloosa, Ala. 35403 | 699 (C) | P/PUS | 2,430 | 2,430 | 2,040 |
| Stockton State College; Pomona, N.J. 08240 | 4,923 (C) | Pub | 1,425 | 2,025 | 2,917 |
| Stonehill College; North Easton, Mass. 02357 | 1,750 (C) | P/RC | 6,550 | 6,550 | 3,380 |
| Strayer College; Washington, D.C. 20005 | 1,226 (C) | P | 3,240 | 3,240 | n.a. |
| Suffolk University; Boston, Mass. 02108 | 3,411 (C) | P | 5,846 | 5,846 | n.a. |
| Sul Ross State University; Alpine, Tex. 79832 | 1,510 (C) | Pub | 748 | 3,244 | 2,606 |
| Sul Ross State Univ.–Uvalde Study Center; Uvalde, Tex. 78801 | 300 (C) | Pub | 720 | 3,960 | n.a. |
| Susquehanna University; Selinsgrove, Pa. 17870 | 1,400 (C) | P/L | 7,100 | 7,100 | 2,870 |
| Swain School of Design; New Bedford, Mass. 02740 | 200 (C) | P | 6,100 | 6,100 | 3,000 |
| Swarthmore College; Swarthmore, Pa. 19081 | 1,300 (C) | P | 10,220 | 10,220 | 3,880 |
| Sweet Briar College; Sweet Briar, Va. 24595 | 750 (W) | P | 8,400 | 8,400 | 2,900 |
| Syracuse University; Syracuse, N.Y. 13210 | 13,940 (C) | P | 8,140 | 8,140 | 4,220 |
| Tabor College; Hillsboro, Kan. 67063 | 380 (C) | P/MB | 3,990 | 3,990 | 2,190 |
| Talladega College; Talladega, Ala. 35160 | 559 (C) | P | 2,967 | 2,967 | 2,030 |
| Tampa, University of; Tampa, Fla. 33606 | 1,867 (C) | P | 6,876 | 6,876 | 3,034 |
| Tampa College; Tampa, Fla. 33614 | 650 (C) | P | 3,508 | 3,508 | n.a. |
| Tarkio College; Tarkio, Mo. 64491 | 700 (C) | P/UP | 5,070 | 5,070 | 3,100 |
| Tarleton State University; Stephenville, Tex. 76402 | 4,000 (C) | Pub | 786 | 4,026 | 2,224 |
| Taylor University; Upland, Ind. 46989 | 1,424 (C) | P/ID | 6,230 | 6,230 | 2,590 |
| Temple University; Philadelphia, Pa. 19122 | 16,500 (C) | Pub | 3,092 | 5,430 | 3,304 |
| Temple University–Ambler; Ambler, Pa. 19002 | 3,983 (C) | Pub | 3,092 | 5,430 | 3,330 |
| Tennessee, Univ. of–Chattanooga; Chattanooga, Tenn. 37402 | 6,172 (C) | Pub | 1,010 | 3,156 | 1,730 |
| Tennessee, Univ. of–Knoxville; Knoxville, Tenn. 37996 | 19,005 (C) | Pub | 1,125 | 3,279 | 2,625 |
| Tennessee, Univ. of–Martin; Martin, Tenn. 38238 | 5,064 (C) | Pub | 1,038 | 3,192 | 2,040 |
| Tennessee, Univ. of–Memphis, Health Science Center; Memphis, Tenn. 38163 | 406 (C) | Pub | 1,977 | 4,128 | 2,625 |
| Tennessee State University; Nashville, Tenn. 37203 | 6,078 (C) | Pub | 954 | 3,102 | 2,832 |
| Tennessee Technological Univ.; Cookeville, Tenn. 38505 | 6,835 (C) | Pub | 951 | 2,148 | 2,001 |
| Tennessee Temple University; Chattanooga, Tenn. 37404 | 2,019 (C) | P/B | 2,590 | 2,590 | 2,000 |
| Tennessee Wesleyan College; Athens, Tenn. 37303 | 495 (C) | P/UM | 3,624 | 3,624 | 2,610 |
| Texas, University of–Arlington; Arlington, Tex. 76019 | 19,796 (C) | Pub | 874 | 3,994 | 3,500 |
| Texas, University of–Austin; Austin, Tex. 78712 | 36,633 (C) | Pub | 765 | 3,475 | 3,800 |
| Texas, University of–Dallas; Richardson, Tex. 75083 | 4,212 (C) | Pub | 642 | 3,234 | n.a. |
| Texas, University of–El Paso; El Paso, Tex. 79968 | 11,950 (C) | Pub | 810 | 5,130 | 2,600 |
| Texas, University of–Health Science Center at Dallas; Dallas, Tex. 75235 | 304 (C) | Pub | 700 | 3,510 | n.a. |
| Texas, University of–Health Science Center at San Antonio; San Antonio, Tex. 78284 | 700 (C) | Pub | 441 | 3,761 | n.a. |
| Texas, University of, Medical Branch–Galveston; Galveston, Tex. 77550 | 581 (C) | Pub | 2,470 | 13,350 | 2,500 |
| Texas, University of–Permian Basin; Odessa, Tex. 79762 | 1,126 (C) | Pub | 696 | 3,936 | 1,120 |
| Texas, University of–San Antonio; San Antonio, Tex. 78285 | 11,090 (C) | Pub | 840 | 3,975 | 3,380 |
| Texas, University of–Tyler; Tyler, Tex. 75701 | 2,192 (C) | Pub | 720 | 3,960 | n.a. |
| Texas A&I University–Kingsville; Kingsville, Tex. 78363 | 3,927 (C) | Pub | 840 | 4,000 | 2,220 |
| Texas A&M University; College Station, Tex. 77843 | 30,000 (C) | Pub | 870 | 3,600 | 3,990 |
| Texas A&M University at Galveston; Galveston, Tex. 77553 | 650 (C) | Pub | 695 | 3,815 | 2,950 |
| Texas Christian University; Fort Worth, Tex. 76129 | 5,425 (C) | P/DC | 5,100 | 5,100 | 2,500 |
| Texas College; Tyler, Tex. 75702 | 600 (C) | P/CME | 4,980 | 4,980 | 2,150 |
| Texas Lutheran College; Seguin, Tex. 78155 | 1,011 (C) | P | 3,950 | 3,950 | 2,325 |
| Texas Southern University; Houston, Tex. 77004 | 9,002 (C) | Pub | 656 | 3,248 | 2,830 |
| Texas Tech University; Lubbock, Tex. 79409 | 23,000 (C) | Pub | 1,150 | 4,300 | 2,600 |
| Texas Wesleyan College; Fort Worth, Tex. 76105 | 1,490 (C) | P/M | 3,875 | 3,875 | 2,950 |
| Texas Woman's University; Denton, Tex. 76204 | 4,045 (W) | Pub | 732 | 3,972 | 2,420 |
| Thiel College; Greenville, Pa. 16125 | 900 (C) | P/LCA | 6,602 | 6,602 | 3,152 |
| Thomas A. Edison State College; Trenton, N.J. 08625 | 4,300 (C) | Pub | 175 | 250 | n.a. |

| Institution and location | Enrollment | Control | Tuition ($) Res. | Tuition ($) Nonres. | Rm/Bd ($) |
|---|---|---|---|---|---|
| Thomas Aquinas College; Santa Paula, Calif. 93060 | 134 (C) | P/RC | 6,425 | 6,425 | 3,170 |
| Thomas College; Waterville, Me. 04901 | 400 (C) | P | 5,954 | 5,954 | 3,325 |
| Thomas Jefferson University; Philadelphia, Pa. 19107 | 717 (C) | P | 7,800 | 7,800 | 3,400 |
| Thomas More College; Crestview Hills, Ky. 41017 | 1,350 (C) | P | 4,470 | 4,470 | 2,750 |
| Tiffin University; Tiffin, Ohio 44883 | 700 (C) | P | 3,700 | 3,700 | 2,350 |
| Tift College; Forsyth, Ga. 31029 | 300 (W) | P/B | 3,054 | 3,054 | 2,665 |
| Toccoa Falls College; Toccoa Falls, Ga. 30598 | 640 (C) | P | 2,800 | 2,800 | 2,100 |
| Toledo, University of; Toledo, Ohio 43606 | 17,787 (C) | Pub | 1,669 | 3,784 | 2,300 |
| Tougaloo College; Tougaloo, Miss. 39174 | 698 (C) | P | 3,160 | 3,160 | 1,500 |
| Touro College; New York, N.Y. 10036 | 1,594 (C) | P | 5,940 | 5,940 | 4,500 |
| Towson State University; Towson, Md. 21204 | 13,912 (C) | Pub | 1,597 | 2,917 | 3,582 |
| Transylvania University; Lexington, Ky. 40508 | 816 (C) | P/DC | 6,725 | 6,725 | 2,898 |
| Trenton State College; Ewing Township, N.J. 08625 | 7,525 (C) | Pub | 1,450 | 2,090 | 2,950 |
| Trevecca Nazarene College; Nashville, Tenn. 37203 | 866 (C) | P | 3,615 | 3,615 | 2,220 |
| Trinity Bible Institute; Ellendale, N.D. 58436 | 507 (C) | P | 2,818 | 2,818 | 2,384 |
| Trinity Christian College; Palos Heights, Ill. 60463 | 509 (C) | P/CR | 5,420 | 5,420 | 2,405 |
| Trinity College; Burlington, Vt. 05401 | 950 (W) | P/RC | 5,490 | 5,490 | 3,050 |
| Trinity College; Deerfield, Ill. 60015 | 650 (C) | P/EFC | 5,900 | 5,900 | 2,830 |
| Trinity College; Hartford, Conn. 06106 | 1,886 (C) | P | 8,620 | 8,620 | 3,200 |
| Trinity College; Washington, D.C. 20017 | 641 (W) | P/RC | 6,825 | 6,825 | 4,325 |
| Trinity University; San Antonio, Tex. 78284 | 2,334 (C) | P | 6,960 | 6,960 | 3,125 |
| Trinity College of Florida; Dunedin, Fla. 33528 | 100 | P | 1,620 | 1,620 | 1,800 |
| Tri-State University; Angola, Ind. 46703 | 1,013 (C) | P | 5,578 | 5,578 | 2,520 |
| Troy State University; Troy, Ala. 36082 | 3,973 (C) | Pub | 1,086 | 1,629 | 1,890 |
| Troy State University–Montgomery; Montgomery, Ala. 36195 | 1,526 (C) | Pub | 1,080 | 1,080 | n.a. |
| Troy State University–Dothan/Ft. Rucker; Dothan, Ala. 36301 | 1,135 (C) | Pub | 885 | 1,140 | n.a. |
| Tufts University; Medford, Mass. 02155 | 4,378 (C) | P | 10,900 | 10,900 | 4,750 |
| Tulane University; New Orleans, La. 70118 | 6,400 (C) | P | 10,080 | 10,080 | 3,965 |
| Tulsa, University of; Tulsa, Okla. 74104 | 3,650 (C) | P | 5,200 | 5,200 | 2,700 |
| Tusculum College; Greeneville, Tenn. 37743 | 400 (C) | P/UP | 3,900 | 3,900 | 2,674 |
| Tuskegee University; Tuskegee, Ala. 36088 | 3,300 (C) | P | 4,200 | 4,200 | 2,150 |
| Union College; Barbourville, Ky. 40906 | 643 (C) | P | 4,150 | 4,150 | 1,980 |
| Union College; Lincoln, Neb. 68506 | 750 (C) | P/SDA | 6,380 | 6,380 | 2,190 |
| Union College; Schenectady, N.Y. 12308 | 2,020 (C) | P | 10,338 | 10,338 | 3,525 |
| Union for Experimenting Colleges and Universities; Cincinnati, Ohio 45201 | 200 | P | 5,200 | 5,200 | n.a. |
| Union University; Jackson, Tenn. 38305 | 1,511 (C) | P/SB | 3,050 | 3,050 | 1,860 |
| U.S. Air Force Academy; Colorado Springs, Colo. 80840 | 4,661 (C) | Pub | 1,000 | 1,000 | — |
| U.S. Coast Guard Academy; New London, Conn. 06320 | 750 (C) | Pub | 500 | 500 | — |
| U.S. International University; San Diego, Calif. 92131 | 1,500 (C) | P | 6,850 | 6,850 | 3,400 |
| U.S. Merchant Marine Academy; Kings Point, N.Y. 11024 | 1,021 (C) | Pub | 785 | 785 | — |
| U.S. Military Academy; West Point, N.Y. 10996 | 4,500 (C) | Pub | 1,000 | 1,000 | — |
| U.S. Naval Academy; Annapolis, Md. 21402 | 4,500 (C) | Pub | 1,000 | 1,000 | — |
| United Wesleyan College; Allentown, Pa. 18103 | 201 (C) | P | 3,700 | 3,700 | 2,300 |
| Unity College; Unity, Me. 04988 | 275 (C) | P | 4,334 | 5,372 | 3,086 |
| Upper Iowa University; Fayette, Iowa 52142 | 714 (C) | P | 5,280 | 5,280 | 2,460 |
| Upsala College; East Orange, N.J. 07019 | 1,158 (C) | P | 6,800 | 6,800 | 3,170 |
| Urbana College; Urbana, Ohio 43078 | 600 (C) | P | 4,725 | 4,725 | 2,550 |
| Ursinus College; Collegeville, Pa. 19426 | 1,170 (C) | P | 7,250 | 7,250 | 3,300 |
| Ursuline College; Pepper Pike, Ohio 44124 | 1,515 (W) | P/RC | 4,000 | 4,000 | 2,390 |
| Utah, University of; Salt Lake City, Utah 84112 | 19,000 (C) | Pub | 1,258 | 3,596 | 2,650 |
| Utah State University; Logan, Utah 84322 | 9,295 (C) | Pub | 1,224 | 2,500 | 3,600 |
| Utica College of Syracuse University; Utica, N.Y. 13502 | 1,359 (C) | P | 6,405 | 6,405 | 2,760 |
| Valdosta State College; Valdosta, Ga. 31698 | 5,302 (C) | Pub | 1,200 | 3,120 | 1,800 |
| Valley City State College; Valley City, N.D. 58072 | 1,075 (C) | Pub | 1,128 | 2,196 | 1,797 |
| Valley Forge Christian College; Phoenixville, Pa. 19460 | 601 (C) | P/AG | 2,200 | 2,200 | 2,000 |
| Valparaiso University; Valparaiso, Ind. 46383 | 3,200 (C) | P/L | 6,380 | 6,380 | 2,430 |
| Vanderbilt University; Nashville, Tenn. 37212 | 5,300 (C) | P | 9,300 | 9,300 | 3,600 |
| VanderCook College of Music; Chicago, Ill. 60616 | 105 (C) | P | 5,358 | 5,358 | 3,418 |
| Vassar College; Poughkeepsie, N.Y. 12601 | 2,250 (C) | P | 9,680 | 9,680 | 3,900 |
| Vennard College; University Park, Iowa 52595 | 184 (C) | P | 3,099 | 3,099 | 1,886 |
| Vermont, University of; Burlington, Vt. 05401 | 7,447 (C) | Pub | 2,680 | 7,438 | 3,326 |
| Vermont College of Norwich University; Montpelier, Vt. 05602 | 630 (C) | P | 8,600 | 8,600 | 3,200 |
| Villa Julie College; Stevenson, Md. 21153 | 1,079 | P | 3,950 | 3,950 | n.a. |
| Villa Maria College; Erie, Pa. 16505 | 600 (W) | P | 4,950 | 4,950 | 2,600 |
| Villanova University; Villanova, Pa. 19085 | 6,300 (C) | P | 6,400 | 6,400 | 3,800 |
| Virginia, University of; Charlottesville, Va. 22906 | 10,967 (C) | Pub | 2,050 | 2,050 | 3,650 |
| Virginia, University of–Clinch Valley College; Wise, Va. 24293 | 1,266 (C) | Pub | 1,404 | 2,220 | 2,250 |
| Virginia Commonwealth University; Richmond, Va. 23284 | 14,566 (C) | Pub | 1,798 | 4,088 | 2,990 |
| Virginia Intermont College; Bristol, Va. 24201 | 481 (C) | P/B | 4,375 | 4,375 | 2,600 |
| Virginia Military Institute; Lexington, Va. 24450 | 1,300 (M) | Pub | 4,190 | 7,090 | 2,385 |

| Institution and location | Enrollment | Control | Tuition ($) Res. | Tuition ($) Nonres. | Rm/Bd ($) |
|---|---|---|---|---|---|
| Virginia Polytechnic Institute and State University; Blacksburg, Va. 24061 | 18,289 (C) | Pub | 2,019 | 4,029 | 1,758 |
| Virginia State University; Petersburg, Va. 23803 | 3,402 (C) | Pub | 1,800 | 3,100 | 2,200 |
| Virginia Union University; Richmond, Va. 23220 | 1,112 (C) | P/B | 3,754 | 3,754 | 2,350 |
| Virginia Wesleyan College; Norfolk, Va. 23502 | 1,000 (C) | P/UM | 5,700 | 5,700 | 3,250 |
| Virgin Islands, College of the; St. Thomas, V.I. 00802 | 2,500 (C) | Pub | 684 | 1,884 | 2,492 |
| Visual Arts, School of; New York, N.Y. 10010 | 2,300 (C) | P | 6,200 | 6,200 | 3,500 |
| Viterbo College; La Crosse, Wis. 54601 | 1,092 (C) | P/RC | 4,650 | 4,650 | 2,110 |
| Voorhees College; Denmark, S.C. 29042 | 560 (C) | P/E | 2,742 | 2,742 | 2,142 |
| Wabash College; Crawfordsville, Ind. 47933 | 830 (M) | P | 6,900 | 6,900 | 2,875 |
| Wadhams Hall Seminary College; Ogdensburg, N.Y. 13669 | 55 (M) | P | 2,795 | 2,795 | 2,800 |
| Wagner College; Staten Island, N.Y. 10301 | 2,000 (C) | P/L | 6,060 | 6,060 | 3,720 |
| Wake Forest University; Winston–Salem, N.C. 27109 | 3,356 (C) | P/B | 6,600 | 6,600 | 2,580 |
| Walla Walla College; College Place, Wash. 99324 | 1,525 (C) | P/SDA | 6,516 | 6,516 | 2,400 |
| Walsh College; Canton, Ohio 44720 | 1,269 (C) | P/RC | 4,360 | 4,360 | 2,500 |
| Walsh College of Accountancy and Business Administration; Troy, Mich. 48007 | 1,615 (C) | P | 2,520 | 2,520 | n.a. |
| Warner Pacific College; Portland, Ore. 97215 | 400 (C) | P/CG | 5,400 | 5,400 | 2,295 |
| Warner Southern College; Lake Wales, Fla. 33853 | 294 (C) | P/CG | 4,245 | 4,245 | 2,245 |
| Warren Wilson College; Swannanoa, N.C. 28778 | 443 (C) | P | 5,750 | 5,750 | — |
| Wartburg College; Waverly, Iowa 50677 | 1,320 (C) | P/AL | 6,490 | 6,490 | 2,440 |
| Washburn University of Topeka; Topeka, Kan. 66621 | 6,043 (C) | Pub | 1,614 | 2,364 | 2,430 |
| Washington, University of; Seattle, Wash. 98195 | 23,468 (C) | Pub | 1,590 | 4,446 | 3,000 |
| Washington and Jefferson College; Washington, Pa. 15301 | 1,050 (C) | P | 8,210 | 8,210 | 2,590 |
| Washington and Lee University; Lexington, Va. 24450 | 1,370 (M) | P | 7,600 | 7,600 | 3,116 |
| Washington Bible College; Lanham, Md. 20706 | 400 (C) | P | 3,680 | 3,680 | 2,670 |
| Washington College; Chestertown, Md. 21620 | 750 (C) | P | 7,550 | 7,550 | 3,240 |
| Washington State University; Pullman, Wash. 99164 | 14,500 (C) | Pub | 1,606 | 4,462 | 2,550 |
| Washington University; St. Louis, Mo. 63130 | 4,447 (C) | P | 9,200 | 9,200 | 3,781 |
| Wayland Baptist University; Plainview, Tex. 79072 | 1,676 (C) | P | 3,180 | 3,180 | 2,460 |
| Waynesburg College; Waynesburg, Pa. 15370 | 803 (C) | P | 5,790 | 5,790 | 2,530 |
| Wayne State College; Wayne, Neb. 68787 | 2,185 (C) | Pub | 1,052 | 1,637 | 1,854 |
| Wayne State University; Detroit, Mich. 48202 | 19,217 (C) | Pub | 1,760 | 3,860 | 3,100 |
| Webber College; Babson Park, Fla. 33827 | 450 (C) | P | 3,970 | 3,970 | 2,330 |
| Webb Institute of Naval Architecture; Glen Cove, N.Y. 11542 | 84 (C) | P | — | — | 3,150 |
| Weber State College; Ogden, Utah 84408 | 11,000 (C) | Pub | 950 | 2,574 | 2,280 |
| Webster University; St. Louis, Mo. 63119 | 1,854 (C) | P | 4,885 | 4,885 | 2,560 |
| Wellesley College; Wellesley, Mass. 02181 | 2,016 (W) | P | 10,960 | 10,960 | 4,020 |
| Wells College; Aurora, N.Y. 13026 | 500 (W) | P | 9,230 | 9,230 | 3,320 |
| Wentworth Institute of Technology; Boston, Mass. 02115 | 4,046 (C) | P | 5,990 | 5,990 | 3,800 |
| Wesleyan College; Macon, Ga. 31297 | 403 (W) | P/M | 5,425 | 5,425 | 3,075 |
| Wesleyan University; Middletown, Conn. 06457 | 2,600 (C) | P | 10,860 | 10,860 | 4,195 |
| Wesley College; Dover, Del. 19901 | 1,000 (C) | P/UM | 4,822 | 4,822 | 2,978 |
| Wesley College; Florence, Miss. 39073 | 75 (C) | P/M | 1,415 | 1,415 | 1,875 |
| Westbrook College; Portland, Me. 04103 | 1,100 (C) | P | 6,415 | 6,415 | 3,090 |
| West Chester Univ. of Pennsylvania; West Chester, Pa. 19383 | 8,618 (C) | Pub | 1,731 | 2,999 | 2,080 |
| West Coast Christian College; Fresno, Calif. 93710 | 260 (C) | P/CG | 2,280 | 2,280 | 1,998 |
| West Coast University; Los Angeles, Calif. 90020 | 850 (C) | P | 5,022 | 5,022 | n.a. |
| West Coast University; Orange, Calif. 92668 | 260 | P | 5,022 | 5,022 | n.a. |
| Western Baptist College; Salem, Ore. 97301 | 282 (C) | P/B | 4,473 | 4,473 | 2,460 |
| Western Carolina University; Cullowhee, N.C. 28723 | 5,202 (C) | Pub | 851 | 3,693 | 1,810 |
| Western Connecticut State University; Danbury, Conn. 06810 | 6,025 (C) | Pub | 1,265 | 3,025 | 2,500 |
| Western Illinois University; Macomb, Ill. 61455 | 8,912 (C) | Pub | 1,415 | 3,455 | 2,170 |
| Western International University; Phoenix, Ariz. 85021 | 606 | P | 3,420 | 3,420 | n.a. |
| Western Kentucky University; Bowling Green, Ky. 42101 | 9,353 (C) | Pub | 1,030 | 2,910 | 2,290 |
| Western Maryland College; Westminster, Md. 21157 | 1,300 (C) | P | 7,275 | 7,275 | 2,860 |
| Western Michigan University; Kalamazoo, Mich. 49008 | 15,958 (C) | Pub | 1,496 | 3,626 | 2,588 |
| Western Montana College; Dillon, Mont. 59725 | 825 (C) | Pub | 919 | 2,350 | 2,460 |
| Western New England College; Springfield, Mass. 01119 | 3,116 (C) | P | 5,560 | 5,560 | 3,490 |
| Western New Mexico University; Silver City, N.M. 88061 | 1,522 (C) | Pub | 600 | 2,156 | 2,030 |
| Western Oregon State College; Monmouth, Ore. 97361 | 3,032 (C) | Pub | 1,428 | 3,741 | 2,307 |
| Western State College of Colorado; Gunnison, Colo. 81230 | 3,156 (C) | Pub | 1,076 | 3,748 | 1,968 |
| Western Washington University; Bellingham, Wash. 98225 | 8,375 (C) | Pub | 1,236 | 4,224 | 2,450 |
| Westfield State College; Westfield, Mass. 01085 | 3,000 (C) | Pub | 888 | 2,976 | 2,263 |
| West Florida, University of; Pensacola, Fla. 32514 | 5,108 (C) | Pub | 1,099 | 3,400 | 2,769 |
| West Georgia College; Carrollton, Ga. 30118 | 4,800 (C) | Pub | 1,317 | 3,399 | 1,770 |
| West Liberty State College; West Liberty, W. Va. 26074 | 2,487 (C) | Pub | 840 | 2,300 | 2,414 |
| West Los Angeles, Univ. of; Los Angeles, Calif. 90066 | 260 (C) | P | 2,550 | 2,550 | n.a. |
| Westmar College; LeMars, Iowa 51031 | 530 (C) | P/UM | 5,602 | 5,602 | 2,520 |
| Westminster Choir College; Princeton, N.J. 08540 | 280 (C) | P | 6,774 | 6,774 | 3,240 |
| Westminster College; Fulton, Mo. 65251 | 630 (M) | P | 5,600 | 5,600 | 2,650 |
| Westminster College; New Wilmington, Pa. 16142 | 1,200 (C) | P/UP | 6,480 | 6,480 | 2,450 |

| Institution and location | Enrollment | Control | Tuition ($) Res. | Tuition ($) Nonres. | Rm/Bd ($) |
|---|---|---|---|---|---|
| Westminster Coll. of Salt Lake City; Salt Lake City, Utah 84105 | 1,270 (C) | P | 4,930 | 4,930 | 2,950 |
| Westmont College; Santa Barbara, Calif. 93108 | 1,169 (C) | P | 7,470 | 7,470 | 3,710 |
| West Oahu College. *See* Hawaii, University of. | | | | | |
| West Texas State University; Canyon, Tex. 79016 | 4,956 (C) | Pub | 740 | 3,980 | 2,200 |
| West Virginia Institute of Technology; Montgomery, W. Va. 25136 | 2,865 (C) | Pub | 880 | 2,390 | 2,617 |
| West Virginia State College; Institute, W. Va. 25112 | 4,465 (C) | Pub | 840 | 2,300 | 2,271 |
| West Virginia University; Morgantown, W. Va. 26506 | 13,915 (C) | Pub | 1,160 | 3,140 | 2,961 |
| West Virginia Wesleyan College; Buckhannon, W. Va. 26201 | 1,392 (C) | P/UM | 5,450 | 5,450 | 2,820 |
| Wheaton College; Norton, Mass. 02766 | 1,100 (W) | P | 10,750 | 10,750 | 3,910 |
| Wheaton College; Wheaton, Ill. 60187 | 2,199 (C) | P | 6,240 | 6,240 | 2,798 |
| Wheeling College; Wheeling, W. Va. 26003 | 653 (C) | P | 6,000 | 6,000 | 3,235 |
| Wheelock College; Boston, Mass. 02215 | 550 (W) | P | 7,040 | 7,040 | 3,500 |
| White Plains, Coll. of, of Pace Univ. *See* Pace Univ. | | | | | |
| Whitman College; Walla Walla, Wash. 99362 | 1,170 (C) | P | 7,960 | 7,960 | 3,330 |
| Whittier College; Whittier, Calif. 90608 | 1,200 (C) | P | 8,625 | 8,625 | 3,430 |
| Whitworth College; Spokane, Wash. 99251 | 1,231 (C) | P/UP | 7,105 | 7,105 | 2,710 |
| Wichita State University; Wichita, Kan. 67208 | 13,500 (C) | Pub | 1,285 | 3,090 | 2,260 |
| Widener University; Chester, Pa. 19013 | 2,200 (C) | P | 5,940 | 5,940 | 2,860 |
| Wilberforce University; Wilberforce, Ohio 45384 | 797 (C) | P/AME | 4,200 | 4,200 | 2,280 |
| Wiley College; Marshall, Tex. 75670 | 557 (C) | P | 2,982 | 2,982 | 2,050 |
| Wilkes College; Wilkes-Barre, Pa. 18766 | 1,850 (C) | P | 5,750 | 5,750 | 2,760 |
| Willamette University; Salem, Ore. 97301 | 1,250 (C) | P | 7,010 | 7,010 | 2,950 |
| William and Mary, College of; Williamsburg, Va. 23185 | 4,789 (C) | Pub | 2,290 | 6,168 | 3,000 |
| William Carey College; Hattiesburg, Miss. 39401 | 1,473 (C) | P | 3,168 | 3,168 | 2,000 |
| William Jewell College; Liberty, Mo. 64068 | 1,990 (C) | P/B | 4,940 | 4,940 | 2,300 |
| William Paterson College; Wayne, N.J. 07470 | 7,893 (C) | Pub | 1,386 | 1,986 | 3,316 |
| William Penn College; Oskaloosa, Iowa 52577 | 500 (C) | P/F | 6,170 | 6,170 | 2,180 |
| Williams College; Williamstown, Mass. 01267 | 2,030 (C) | P | 10,128 | 10,128 | 3,360 |
| William Smith College. *See* Hobart and William Smith Colleges | | | | | |
| William Tyndale College; Farmington Hills, Mich. 48018 | 335 (C) | P | 2,656 | 2,656 | 2,590 |
| William Woods College; Fulton, Mo. 65251 | 750 (W) | P | 6,130 | 6,130 | 2,370 |
| Wilmington College; New Castle, Del. 19720 | 1,200 (C) | P | 3,360 | 3,360 | 1,260 |
| Wilmington College of Ohio; Wilmington, Ohio 45177 | 832 (C) | P/F | 6,186 | 6,186 | 2,480 |
| Wilson College; Chambersburg, Pa. 17201 | 300 (W) | P/UP | 7,126 | 7,126 | 2,861 |
| Wingate College; Wingate, N.C. 28174 | 1,500 (C) | P/SB | 3,670 | 3,670 | 2,200 |
| Winona State University; Winona, Minn. 55987 | 5,000 (C) | Pub | 1,650 | 2,550 | 1,800 |
| Winston-Salem Bible College; Winston-Salem, N.C. 27102 | 50 | P | 900 | 900 | 2,000 |
| Winston-Salem State University; Winston-Salem, N.C. 27110 | 2,400 (C) | Pub | 845 | 3,095 | 1,925 |
| Winthrop College; Rock Hill, S.C. 29733 | 4,065 (C) | Pub | 1,380 | 2,278 | 2,052 |
| Wisconsin, University of–Eau Claire; Eau Claire, Wis. 54701 | 10,408 (C) | Pub | 1,500 | 4,400 | 2,040 |
| Wisconsin, University of–Green Bay; Green Bay, Wis. 54302 | 4,530 (C) | Pub | 1,370 | 4,170 | 2,385 |
| Wisconsin, University of–La Crosse; La Crosse, Wis. 54601 | 8,769 (C) | Pub | 1,400 | 4,250 | 1,620 |
| Wisconsin, University of–Madison; Madison, Wis. 53706 | 30,900 (C) | Pub | 1,300 | 4,400 | 2,510 |
| Wisconsin, University of–Milwaukee; Milwaukee, Wis. 53201 | 21,721 (C) | Pub | 1,400 | 4,500 | 2,400 |
| Wisconsin, University–Oshkosh; Oshkosh, Wis. 54901 | 9,900 (C) | Pub | 1,420 | 4,420 | 1,880 |
| Wisconsin, University of–Parkside; Kenosha, Wis. 53141 | 5,500 (C) | Pub | 1,144 | 3,632 | n.a. |
| Wisconsin, University of–Platteville; Platteville, Wis. 53818 | 5,105 (C) | Pub | 1,225 | 3,709 | 1,800 |
| Wisconsin, University of–River Falls; River Falls, Wis. 54022 | 5,000 (C) | Pub | 1,302 | 3,936 | 3,198 |
| Wisconsin, University of–Stevens Point; Stevens Point, Wis. 54481 | 8,756 (C) | Pub | 1,334 | 4,080 | 2,350 |
| Wisconsin, University of–Stout; Menomonie, Wis. 54751 | 7,169 (C) | Pub | 1,477 | 4,480 | 1,892 |
| Wisconsin, University of–Superior; Superior, Wis. 54880 | 1,728 (C) | Pub | 1,264 | 3,897 | 2,670 |
| Wisconsin, University of–Whitewater; Whitewater, Wis. 53190 | 9,708 (C) | Pub | 1,300 | 4,000 | 1,800 |
| Wisconsin Lutheran College; Milwaukee, Wis. 53226 | 131 | P | 4,770 | 4,770 | 2,520 |
| Wittenberg University; Springfield, Ohio 45501 | 2,142 (C) | P | 9,100 | 9,100 | 2,980 |
| Wofford College; Spartanburg, S.C. 29301 | 1,106 (C) | P/UM | 5,675 | 5,675 | 3,010 |
| Woodbury University; Los Angeles, Calif. 90017 | 951 (C) | P | 6,060 | 6,060 | n.a. |
| Wooster, College of; Wooster, Ohio 44691 | 1,711 (C) | P | 9,220 | 9,220 | 2,910 |
| Worcester Polytechnic Institute; Worcester, Mass. 01609 | 2,695 (C) | P | 9,820 | 9,820 | 3,695 |
| Worcester State College; Worcester, Mass. 01602 | 3,500 (C) | Pub | 1,173 | 2,269 | 2,125 |
| World College West; Petaluma, Calif. 94952 | 100 (C) | P | 5,600 | 5,600 | 2,900 |
| Wright State University; Dayton, Ohio 45435 | 11,842 (C) | Pub | 1,752 | 3,504 | 2,840 |
| Wyoming, University of; Laramie, Wyo. 82071 | 8,150 (C) | Pub | 778 | 2,442 | 2,670 |
| Xavier University; Cincinnati, Ohio 45207 | 3,973 (C) | P | 5,900 | 5,900 | 2,900 |
| Xavier University of Louisiana; New Orleans, La. 70125 | 1,772 (C) | P | 4,100 | 4,100 | 2,650 |
| Yale University; New Haven, Conn. 06520 | 5,100 (C) | P | 10,520 | 10,520 | 4,500 |
| Yeshiva University; New York, N.Y. 10033 | 1,660 (C) | P | 7,450 | 7,450 | 3,520 |
| York College (NYC). *See* New York, City University of | | | | | |
| York College of Pennsylvania; York, Pa. 17405 | 4,455 (C) | P | 3,232 | 3,232 | 2,122 |
| Youngstown State Univ.; Youngstown, Ohio 44555 | 14,684 (C) | Pub | 1,335 | 2,310 | 2,415 |

1. In-city, $4,185. 2. Out-of-state, $6,016. 3. $61 per credit. 4. $122 per credit.

# Selected Degree Abbreviations

**A.B.** Bachelor of Arts
**AeEng.** Aeronautical Engineer
**A.M.T.** Master of Arts in Teaching
**B.A.** Bachelor of Arts
**B.A.E.** Bachelor of Arts in Education, or Bachelor of Art Education, Aeronautical Engineering, Agricultural Engineering, or Architectural Engineering
**B.Ag.** Bachelor of Agriculture
**B.A.M.** Bachelor of Applied Mathematics
**B.Arch.** Bachelor of Architecture
**B.B.A.** Bachelor of Business Administration
**B.C.E.** Bachelor of Civil Engineering
**B.Ch.E.** Bachelor of Chemical Engineering
**B.C.L.** Bachelor of Canon Law
**B.D.** Bachelor of Divinity
**B.E.** Bachelor of Education or Bachelor of Engineering
**B.E.E.** Bachelor of Electrical Engineering
**B.F.** Bachelor of Forestry
**B.F.A.** Bachelor of Fine Arts
**B.J.** Bachelor of Journalism
**B.L.S.** Bachelor of Liberal Studies or Bachelor of Library Science
**B.Litt.** Bachelor of Literature
**B.M.** Bachelor of Medicine or Bachelor of Music
**B.M.S.** Bachelor of Marine Science
**B.N.** Bachelor of Nursing
**B.Pharm.** Bachelor of Pharmacy
**B.R.E.** Bachelor of Religious Education
**B.S.** Bachelor of Science
**B.S.Ed.** Bachelor of Science in Education
**C.E.** Civil Engineer
**Ch.E.** Chemical Engineer
**D.B.A.** Doctor of Business Administration
**D.D.** Doctor of Divinity[1]
**D.D.S.** Doctor of Dental Surgery or Doctor of Dental Science
**D.L.S.** Doctor of Library Science
**D.M.D.** Doctor of Dental Medicine
**D.O.** Doctor of Osteopathy
**D.M.S.** Doctor of Medical Science
**D.P.A.** Doctor of Public Administration[2]
**D.P.H.** Doctor of Public Health
**D.R.E.** Doctor of Religious Education
**D.S.W.** Doctor of Social Welfare or Doctor of Social Work
**D.Sc.** Doctor of Science[3]
**D.V.M.** Doctor of Veterinary Medicine
**Ed.D.** Doctor of Education[2]
**Ed.S.** Education Specialist
**E.E.** Electrical Engineer

**E.M.** Engineer of Mines
**E.Met.** Engineer of Metallurgy
**I.E.** Industrial Engineer or Industrial Engineering
**J.D.** Doctor of Laws[2]
**J.S.D.** Doctor of Juristic Science
**L.H.D.** Doctor of Humane Letters[3]
**Litt.B.** Bachelor of Letters
**LL.B.** Bachelor of Laws
**LL.D.** Doctor of Laws[3]
**LL.M.** Master of Laws
**M.A.** Master of Arts
**M.Aero.E.** Master of Aeronautical Engineering
**M.B.A.** Master of Business Administration
**M.C.E.** Master of Christian Education or Master of Civil Engineering
**M.C.S.** Master of Computer Science
**M.D.** Doctor of Medicine
**M.Div.** Master of Divinity
**M.E.** Master of Engineering
**M.Ed.** Master of Education
**M.Eng.** Master of Engineering
**M.F.A.** Master of Fine Arts
**M.H.A.** Master of Hospital Administration
**M.L.S.** Master of Library Science
**M.M.** Master of Music
**M.M.E.** Master of Mechanical Engineering or Master of Music Education
**M.Mus.** Master of Music
**M.N.** Master of Nursing
**M.R.E.** Master of Religious Education
**M.S.** Master of Science
**M.S.W.** Master of Social Work
**M.Th.** Master of Theology
**Nuc.E.** Nuclear Engineer
**O.D.** Doctor of Optometry
**Pharm.D.** Doctor of Pharmacy[2]
**Ph.B.** Bachelor of Philosophy
**Ph.D.** Doctor of Philosophy
**S.B.** Bachelor of Science
**Sc.D.** Doctor of Science[3]
**S.J.D.** Doctor of Juridical Science or Doctor of the Science of Law
**S.Sc.D** Doctor of Social Science
**S.T.B.** Bachelor of Sacred Theology
**S.T.D.** Doctor of Sacred Theology
**S.T.M.** Master of Sacred Theology
**Th.B.** Bachelor of Theology
**Th.D.** Doctor of Theology
**Th.M.** Master of Theology

1. Honorary. 2. Earned and honorary. 3. Usually honorary.

## Academic Costume: Colors Associated With Fields

| Field | Color | Field | Color |
|---|---|---|---|
| Agriculture | Maize | Medicine | Green |
| Arts, Letters, Humanities | White | Music | Pink |
| Commerce, Accountancy, Business | Drab | Nursing | Apricot |
| | | Oratory (Speech) | Silver gray |
| Dentistry | Lilac | Pharmacy | Olive Green |
| Economics | Copper | Philosophy | Dark blue |
| Education | Light Blue | Physical Education | Sage Green |
| Engineering | Orange | Public Admin. including Foreign Service | Peacock blue |
| Fine Arts, Architecture | Brown | Public Health | Salmon pink |
| Forestry | Russet | Science | Golden yellow |
| Journalism | Crimson | Social Work | Citron |
| Law | Purple | Theology | Scarlet |
| Library Science | Lemon | Veterinary Science | Gray |

## Major Sports Contents

For sports not listed, see index listing under "Sports"

## Sports Personalities

A name in parentheses is the original name or form of name. Localities are places of birth. Dates of birth appear as month/day/year. **Boldface** years in parentheses are dates of **(birth-death)**.
Information has been gathered from many sources, including the individuals themselves. However, the *Information Please Almanac* cannot guarantee the accuracy of every individual item.

**Aaron,** Hank (Henry) (baseball); Mobile, Ala., 2/5/1934
**Aaron,** Tommie (baseball); Mobile, Ala. **(1939–1984)**
**Abdul-Jabbar,** Kareem (Lewis Ferdinand Alcindor, Jr.) (basketball); New York City, 4/16/1947
**Adderly,** Herbert A. (football); Philadelphia, 6/8/1939
**Affleck, Francis** (auto racing) **(1951-1985)**
**Alcindor,** Lew. *See* Abdul-Jabbar
**Ali,** Muhammad (Cassius Clay) (boxing); Louisville, Ky., 1/18/1942
**Allen,** Dick (Richard Anthony) (baseball); Wampum, Pa., 3/8/1942
**Allison,** Bobby (Robert Arthur) (auto racing); Hueytown, Ala., 12/3/1937
**Alston, Walker** (baseball); Venice, Ohio **(1911-1984)**
**Alworth,** Lance (football); Houston, 8/3/1940
**Anderson,** Donny (Gary Donny) (football); Brooklyn, N.Y., 4/3/1949
**Anderson,** Ken (football); Batavia, Ill., 2/15/1949
**Anderson,** Sparky (George) (baseball); Bridgewater, S.D., 2/22/1934
**Andretti,** Mario (auto racing); Montona, Trieste, Italy, 2/28/1940
**Anthony,** Earl (bowling); Kent, Wash., 4/27/1938
**Appling,** Luke (baseball); High Point, N.C., 4/2/1907
**Arcaro,** Eddie (George Edward) (jockey); Cincinnati, 2/19/1916
**Ashe,** Arthur (tennis); Richmond, Va., 7/10/1943
**Austin,** Tracy (tennis); Rolling Hills, Calif., 12/2/1962
**Averill,** Earl (baseball); Everett, Wash. **(1915–1983)**
**Babashoff,** Shirley (swimming); Whittier, Calif., 1/31/1957
**Baer,** Max (boxer); Omaha, Neb. **(1909-1959)**
**Bakken,** Jim (James Leroy) (football); Madison, Wis., 11/2/1940
**Banks,** Ernie (baseball); Dallas, 1/31/1931
**Bannister,** Roger (runner); Harrow, England, 3/24/1929
**Barry,** Rick (Richard) (basketball); Elizabeth, N.J., 3/28/1944
**Bauer,** Hank (Henry) (baseball); East St. Louis, Ill., 7/31/1922
**Baugh,** Sammy (football); Temple, Tex., 3/17/1914
**Bayi,** Filbert (runner); Karratu, Tanganyika, 6/23/1953
**Baylor,** Elgin (basketball); Washington, D.C., 9/16/1934
**Beamon,** Bob (long jumper); New York City, 8/2/1946
**Bee,** Clair (basketball); Cleveland, Ohio **(1896–1983)**
**Beliveau,** Jean (hockey); Three Rivers, Quebec, Canada, 8/31/1931
**Bell,** Rickey (football); Inglewood, Calif. **(1949-1984)**
**Beman,** Deane (golf); Washington, D.C., 4/22/1938
**Bench,** Johnny (Johnny Lee) (baseball); Oklahoma City, 12/7/1947
**Berg,** Patty (Patricia Jane) (golf); Minneapolis, 2/13/1918
**Berning,** Susie Maxwell (golf); Pasadena, Calif., 7/22/1941

**Berra,** Yogi (Lawrence) (baseball); St. Louis, 5/12/1925
**Biletnikoff,** Frederick (football); Erie, Pa., 2/23/1943
**Bird,** Larry (basketball); French Lick, Ind., 12/7/1956
**Blaik,** Earl H. (football); Detroit, 2/15/1897
**Blanda,** George Frederick (football); Youngwood, Pa., 9/17/1927
**Blue,** Vida (baseball); Mansfield, La., 7/28/1949
**Borg,** Björn (tennis); Stockholm, 6/6/1956
**Boros,** Julius (golf); Fairfield, Conn., 3/3/1920
**Bossy,** Mike (hockey); Montreal, 1/22/1957
**Boston,** Ralph (long jumper); Laurel, Miss., 5/9/1939
**Bradley,** Bill (William Warren) (basketball); Crystal City, Mo., 7/28/1943
**Bradshaw,** Terry (football); Shreveport, La., 9/2/1948
**Brathwaite, Chris** (track); Eugene, Ore. **(1949-1984)**
**Breedlove,** Craig (Norman) (speed driving); Los Angeles, 3/23/1938
**Brett,** George (baseball); Glendale, W. Va., 5/15/1953
**Brock,** Louis Clark (baseball); El Dorado, Ark., 6/18/1939
**Brown,** Jimmy (football); St. Simon Island, Ga., 2/17/1936
**Brown,** Larry (football); Clairton, Pa., 9/19/1947
**Brumel,** Valeri (high jumper); Tolbuzino, Siberia, 4/14/1942
**Bryant,** Paul "Bear" (football); Tuscaloosa, Ala. **(1913–1983)**
**Bryant,** Rosalyn Evette (track); Chicago, 1/7/1956
**Burton,** Michael (swimming); Des Moines, Iowa, 7/3/1947
**Butkus,** Dick (Richard Marvin) (football); Chicago, 12/9/1942
**Campanella,** Roy (baseball); Homestead, Pa., 11/19/1921
**Campbell,** Earl (football); Tyler, Tex., 3/29/1955
**Caponi,** Donna Maria (golf); Detroit, 1/29/1945
**Cappelletti,** Gino (football); Keewatin, Minn., 3/26/1934
**Carew,** Rod (Rodney Cline) (baseball); Gatun, Panama, 10/1/1945
**Carlos,** John (sprinter); New York City, 6/5/1945
**Carlton,** Steven Norman (baseball); Miami, Fla., 12/22/1944
**Carner,** Joanne Gunderson (Mrs. Don) (golf); Kirkland, Wash., 3/4/1939
**Casals,** Rosemary (tennis); San Francisco, 9/16/1948
**Casper,** Billy (golf); San Diego, Calif., 6/24/1931
**Caulkins,** Tracy (swimming); Wimona, Minn., 1/11/63
**Cauthen,** Steve (jockey); Covington, Ky., 5/1/1960
**Chamberlain,** Wilt (Wilton) (basketball); Philadelphia, 8/21/1936
**Chapot,** Frank (equestrian); Camden, N.J., 2/24/1934
**Chinaglia,** Giorgio (soccer); Carrara, Italy, 1/24/1947

Clarke, Bobby (Robert Earle) (hockey); Flin Flon, Manitoba, Canada, 8/13/1949
Clay, Cassius. *See* Ali, Muhammad
Clemente, Roberto Walker (baseball); Carolina, Puerto Rico **(1934-1972)**
Cobb, Tyrus Raymond (Ty) (baseball); Narrows, Ga. **(1886-1961)**
Cochran, Barbara Ann (skiing); Claremont, N.H., 1/4/1951
Cochran, Marilyn (skiing); Burlington, Vt., 2/7/1950
Cochran, Robert (skiing); Claremont, N.H., 12/11/1951
Coe, Sebastian Newbold (track); London, England, 9/29/1956
Colavito, Rocky (Rocco Domenico) (baseball); New York City, 8/10/1933
Comaneci, Nadia (gymnast); Onesti, Romania, 11/12/1961
Connors, Jimmy (James Scott) (tennis); East St. Louis, Ill., 9/2/1952
Cordero, Angel (jockey); Santurce, Puerto Rico, 5/8/1942
Cournoyer, Yvan Serge (hockey); Drummondville, Quebec, Canada, 11/22/1943
Court, Margaret Smith (tennis); Albury, New South Wales, Australia, 7/16/1942
Cousy, Bob (basketball); New York City, 8/9/1928
Crabbe, Buster (swimming); Scottsdale, Ariz. **(1908–1983)**
Crenshaw, Ben (golf); Austin, Tex., 1/11/1952
Cronin, Joe (baseball executive); San Francisco, **(1906–1984)**
Cruyff, Johan (soccer); Amsterdam, Netherlands, 4/25/47
Csonka, Larry (Lawrence Richard) (football); Stow, Ohio, 12/25/1946
Dancer, Stanley (harness racing); New Egypt, N.J., 7/25/1927
Dark, Alvin (baseball); Comanche, Okla., 1/7/1922
Davenport, Willie (track); Troy, Ala., 6/6/1943
Dawson, Leonard Ray (football); Alliance, Ohio, 6/20/1935
Dean, Dizzy (Jay Hanna) (baseball); Lucas, Ark. **(1911-1974)**
DeBusschere, Dave (basketball); Detroit, 10/16/1940
Delvecchio, Alex Peter (hockey); Fort William, Ontario, Canada, 12/4/1931
Demaret, Jim (golf); Houston **(1910-1983)**
Dempsey, Jack (William H.) (boxing); Manassa, Colo. **(1895-1983)**
DeVicenzo, Roberto (golf); Buenos Aires, 4/14/1923
Dibbs, Edward George (tennis); Brooklyn, New York, 2/23/1951
Dietz, James W. (rowing); New York, N.Y., 1/12/1949
DiMaggio, Joe (baseball); Martinez, Calif., 11/25/1914
Dionne, Marcel (hockey); Drummondville, Quebec, Canada, 8/3/1951
Dominguín, Luis Miguel (matador); Madrid, 12/9/1926
Dorsett, Tony (football); Rochester, Pa., 4/7/1954
Dryden, Kenneth (hockey); Hamilton, Ontario, Canada, 8/4/1947
Drysdale, Don (baseball); Van Nuys, Calif., 7/23/1936
Duran, Roberto (boxing); Panama City, 6/16/1951
Durocher, Leo (baseball); West Springfield, Mass., 7/27/1906
Durr, François (tennis); Algiers, Algeria, 12/25/1942
El Cordobés, (Manuel Benítez Pérez) (matador); Palma del Río, Córdoba, Spain, 5/4/1936(?)
Elder, Lee (golf); Dallas, 7/14/1934
Emerson, Roy (tennis); Kingsway, Australia, 11/3/1936
Ender, Kornelia (swimming); Plauen, East Germany, 10/25/1958
Erving, Julius (Dr. J) (basketball); Roosevelt, N.Y., 2/22/1950
Esposito, Phil (Philip Anthony) (hockey); Sault Ste. Marie, Ontario, Canada, 2/20/1942
Evans, Lee (runner); Mandena, Calif., 2/25/1947
Ewbank, Weeb (football); Richmond, Ind., 5/6/1907
Feller, Robert (Bobby) (baseball); Van Meter, Iowa, 11/3/1918
Feuerbach, Allan Dean (track); Preston, Iowa, 1/12/1948
Finley, Charles O. (sportsman); Ensley, Ala., 2/22/1918
Fischer, Bobby (chess); Chicago, 3/9/1943
Fitzsimmons, Bob (Robert Prometheus) (boxer); Cornwall, England **(1862-1917)**
Fleming, Peggy Gale (ice skating); San Jose, Calif., 7/27/1948
Ford, Whitey (Edward) (baseball); New York City, 10/21/1928
Foreman, George (boxing); Marshall, Tex., 1/10/1949
Fosbury, Richard (high jumper); Portland, Ore., 3/6/1947
Fox, Nellie (Jacob Nelson) (baseball); St. Thomas, Pa. **(1927-1975)**
Foxx, James Emory (baseball); Sudlersville, Md., **(1907-1967)**
Foyt, A. J. (auto racing); Houston, 1/16/1935
Francis, Emile (hockey); North Battleford, Sask., 9/13/1926
Fratianne, Linda (figure skating); Los Angeles, 8/2/1960
Frazier, Joe (boxing); Beauford, S.C., 1/17/1944
Frazier, Walt (basketball); Atlanta, 3/29/1945
Frick, Ford C. (baseball); Wawaka, Ind., **(1894-1978)**
Furniss, Bruce (swimming); Fresno, Calif., 5/27/1957
Gable, Dan (wrestling); Waterloo, Iowa, 10/25/1945
Gabriel, Roman (football); Wilmington, N.C., 8/5/1940
Gallagher, Michael Donald (skiing); Yonkers, N.Y., 10/3/1941
Garms, Debs (baseball); Glen Rose, Tex. **(1908-1984)**
Garvey, Steve (baseball); Tampa, Fla., 12/22/1948
Gehrig, Lou (Henry Louis Gehrig) (baseball); New York City **(1903-1941)**
Gehringer, Charlie (baseball); Fowlerville, Mich., 5/11/1903
Geoffrion, Bernie (Boom Boom) (hockey); Montreal, 2/14/1931

Gerulaitis, Vitas (tennis); Brooklyn, N.Y., 7/26/1954
Giacomin, Ed (hockey); Sudbury, Ontario, Canada, 6/6/1939
Gibson, Bob (baseball); Omaha, Neb., 11/9/1935
Gifford, Frank (football); Santa Monica, Calif., 8/16/1930
Gilbert, Rod (Rodrique) (hockey); Montreal, 7/1/1941
Giles, Warren (baseball executive); Tiskilwa, Ill. **(1896–1979)**
Gilmore, Artis (basketball); Chipley, Fla., 9/21/1949
Glance, Harvey (track); Phenix City, Ala., 3/28/1957
Gonzalez, Pancho (tennis); Los Angeles, 5/9/1928
Goodell, Brian Stuart (swimming); Stockton, Calif., 4/2/1959
Goodrich, Gail (basketball); Los Angeles, 4/23/1943
Goolagong Cawley, Evonne (tennis); Griffith, Australia, 7/31/1951
Gossage, Rich "Goose" (baseball); Colorado Springs, Colo., 4/5/1951
Gottfried, Brian (tennis); Baltimore, Md., 1/27/1952
Graham, David (golf); Windson, Australia, 5/23/1946
Graham, Otto Everett (football); Waukegan, Ill., 12/6/1921
Grange, Red (Harold) (football); Forksville, Pa., 6/13/1904
Green, Hubert (golf); Birmingham, Ala., 12/28/1946
Greene, Charles E. (sprinter); Pine Bluff, Ark., 3/21/1945
Gretzky, Wayne (hockey); Brantford, Ont., 1/26/1961
Griese, Bob (Robert Allen) (football); Evansville, Ind., 2/3/1945
Grove, Lefty (Robert Moses) (baseball); Lonaconing, Md., **(1900-1975)**
Groza, Lou (football); Martins Ferry, Ohio, 1/25/1924
Guidry, Ronald Ames (baseball); Lafayette, La., 8/28/1950
Gunter, Nancy Richey (tennis); San Angelo, Tex., 8/23/1942
Halas, George (football); Chicago **(1895-1983)**
Hall, Gary (swimming); Fayetteville, N.C., 8/7/1951
Hamill, Dorothy (figure skater); Chicago, 1956(?)
Hammond, Kathy (runner); Sacramento, Calif., 11/2/1951
Harris, Franco (football); Ft. Dix, N.J., 3/7/1950
Hartack, William, Jr. (jockey); Colver, Pa., 12/9/1932
Haughton, William (harness racing); Gloversville, N.Y. **(1923-1986)**
Havlicek, John (basketball); Martins Ferry, Ohio, 4/8/1940
Hayes, Elvin (basketball); Rayville, La., 11/17/1945
Haynie, Sandra (golf); Fort Worth, 6/4/1943
Heiden, Eric (speed skating); Madison, Wis., 6/14/1958
Hencken, John (swimming); Culver City, Calif., 5/29/1954
Henderson, Rickey (baseball); Chicago, 12/25/1958
Henie, Sonja (ice skater); Oslo **(1912-1969)**
Hernandez, Keith (baseball); San Francisco, 10/20/1953
Hickcox, Charles (swimming); Phoenix, Ariz., 2/6/1947
Hines, James (sprinter); Dumas, Ark., 9/10/1946
Hodges, Gil (baseball); Princeton, Ind. **(1924-1972)**
Hogan, Ben (golf); Dublin, Tex., 8/13/1912
Holmes, Larry (boxing); Cuthert, Ga., 11/3/1949
Hornsby, Rogers (baseball); Winters, Tex. **(1896-1963)**
Hornung, Paul (football); Louisville, Ky., 12/23/1935
Houk, Ralph (baseball); Lawrence, Kan., 8/9/1919
Howard, Elston (baseball); St. Louis **(1929-1980)**
Howe, Gordon (hockey); Floral, Sask., Canada, 3/31/1928
Howell, Jim Lee (football); Lonoke, Ark., 9/27/1914
Hubbell, Carl (baseball); Carthage, Mo., 6/22/1903
Huff, Sam (Robert Lee) (football); Morgantown, W. Va., 10/4/1934
Hull, Bobby (hockey); Point Anne, Ontario, Canada, 1/3/1939
Hunter, Jim (Catfish) (baseball); Hertford, N.C., 4/8/1946
Huntley, Joni (track); McMinnville, Ore., 8/4/1956
Hutson, Donald (football); Pine Bluff, Ark., 1/31/1913
Insko, Del (harness racing); Amboy, Minn., 7/10/1931
Irwin, Hale (golf); Joplin, Mo., 6/3/1945
Jackson, Reggie (baseball); Wyncote, Pa., 5/18/1946
Jeffries, James J. (boxer); Carroll, Ohio **(1875-1953)**
Jenkins, Ferguson Arthur (baseball); Chatham, Ontario, Canada, 12/13/1943
Jenner, (W.) Bruce (track); Mt. Kisco, N.Y., 10/28/1949
Jezek, Linda (swimming); Palo Alto, Calif., 3/10/1960
Johnson, Earvin (Magic) (basketball); E. Lansing, Mich., 8/14/1959
Johnson, Anthony (rowing); Washington, D.C., 11/16/1940
Johnson, Jack (John Arthur Johnson) (boxer); Galveston, Tex. **(1876-1946)**
Johnson, Rafer (decathlon); Hillsboro, Tex., 8/18/1935
Jones, Deacon (David) (football); Eatonville, Fla., 12/9/1938
Juantoreno, Alberto (track); Santiago, Cuba, 12/3/1951
Jurgensen, Sonny (football); Wilmington, N.C., 8/23/1934
Kaat, Jim (baseball); Zeeland, Mich., 11/7/1938
Kaline, Al (Albert) (baseball); Baltimore, 12/19/1934
Keino, Kipchoge (runner); Kapchemoiymo, Kenya, 1/?/1940
Kelly, Leroy (football); Philadelphia, 5/20/1942
Kelly, Red (Leonard Patrick) (hockey); Simcoe, Ontario, Canada, 7/9/1927
Killebrew, Harmon (baseball); Payette, Idaho, 6/29/1936
Killy, Jean-Claude (skiing); Saint-Cloud, France, 8/30/1943
Kilmer, Bill (William Orland) (football); Topeka, Kan., 9/5/1939
King, Billie Jean (Billie Jean Moffitt) (tennis); Long Beach, Calif., 11/22/1943

**Kinsella,** John (swimming); Oak Park, Ill., 8/26/1952
**Kodes,** Jan (tennis); Prague, 3/1/1946
**Kolb,** Claudia (swimming); Hayward, Calif., 12/19/1949
**Koosman,** Jerry Martin (baseball); Appleton, Minn., 12/23/1942
**Korbut,** Olga (gymnast); Grodno, Byelorussia, U.S.S.R., 5/16/1955
**Koufax,** Sandy (Sanford) (baseball); Brooklyn, N.Y., 12/30/1935
**Kramer,** Jack (tennis); Las Vegas, Nev., 8/1/1921
**Kramer,** Jerry (football); Jordan, Mont., 1/23/1936
**Kuhn,** Bowie Kent (baseball); Takoma Park, Md., 10/28/1926
**Kwalik,** Ted (Thaddeus John) (football); McKees Rocks, Pa., 4/15/1947
**Lafleur,** Guy Damien (hockey); Thurson, Quebec, Canada, 8/20/1951
**Laird,** Ronald (walker); Louisville, Ky., 5/31/1935
**Lamonica,** Daryle (football); Fresno, Calif., 7/17/1941
**Landis,** Kenesaw Mountain (1st baseball commissioner); Millville, Ohio **(1866-1944)**
**Landry,** Tom (football); Mission, Tex., 9/11/1924
**Landy,** John (runner); Australia, 4/4/1930
**Larrieu,** Francie (track); Palo Alto, Calif., 11/28/1952
**Lasorda,** Tom (baseball); Norristown, Pa., 9/22/1927
**Laver,** Rod (tennis); Rockhampton, Australia, 8/9/1938
**Lendl,** Ivan (tennis); Prague, 3/7/1960
**Leonard,** Benny (Benjamin Leiner) (boxer); New York City **(1896-1947)**
**Leonard,** Sugar Ray (boxing); Wilmington, N.C., 5/17/1956
**Lewis,** Carl (track); Willingboro, N.J., 7/1/1961
**Linehan,** Kim (swimming); Bronxville, N.Y., 12/11/1962
**Liquori,** Marty (runner); Montclair, N.J., 9/11/1949
**Little,** Floyd Douglas (football); New Haven, Conn., 7/4/1942
**Little,** Lou (football); Leominster, Mass., **(1893-1979)**
**Littler,** Gene (golf); San Diego, Calif., 11/16/1920
**Lloyd,** Chris Evert (Christine Marie) (tennis); Fort Lauderdale, Fla., 12/21/1954
**Lombardi,** Vince (football); Brooklyn, N.Y. **(1913-1970)**
**Longden,** Johnny (horse racing); Wakefield, England, 2/14/1907
**Lopez,** Al (baseball); Tampa, Fla., 8/20/1908
**Lopez,** Nancy (golf); Torrance, Calif., 1/6/1957
**Louis,** Joe (Joe Louis Barrow) (boxing); Lafayette, Ala. **(1914-1981)**
**Lynn,** Frederic Michael (baseball); Chicago, Ill., 2/3/1952
**Lynn,** Janet (figure skating); Rockford, Ill., 4/6/1953
**Mack,** Connie (Cornelius Alexander McGillicuddy) (baseball executive); East Brookfield, Mass. **(1862-1956)**
**Mackey,** John (football); New York City, 9/24/1941
**Mahovlich,** Frank (Francis William) (hockey); Timmins, Ontario, Canada, 1/10/1938
**Mahre,** Phil (skiing); White Pass, Wash., 5/10/1957
**Mann,** Carol (golf); Buffalo, N.Y., 2/3/1941
**Manning,** Madeline (runner); Cleveland, 1/11/1948
**Mantle,** Mickey Charles (baseball); Spavinaw, Okla., 10/20/1931
**Marciano,** Rocky (boxing); Brockton, Mass. **(1923-1969)**
**Marichal,** Juan (baseball); Laguna Verde, Montecristi, Dominican Republic, 10/20/1937
**Maris,** Roger (baseball); Hibbing, Minn. **1934-1985)**
**Martin,** Billy (Alfred Manuel) (baseball); Berkeley, Calif., 5/16/1928
**Martin,** Rick (Richard Lionel) (hockey); Verdun, Quebec, Canada, 7/26/1951
**Mathews,** Ed (Edwin) (baseball); Texarkana, Tex., 10/13/1931
**Matson,** Randy (shot putter); Kilgore, Tex., 3/5/1945
**Mays,** Willie (baseball); Westfield, Ala., 5/6/1931
**McAdoo,** Bob (basketball); Greensboro, N.C., 9/25/1951
**McCarthy,** Joe (Joseph Vincent) (baseball); Philadelphia **(1887-1978)**
**McCovey,** Willie Lee (baseball); Mobile, Ala., 1/10/1938
**McEnroe,** John Patrick, Jr. (tennis); Wiesbaden, Germany, 2/16/1959
**McGraw,** John Joseph (baseball); Truxton, N.Y. **(1873-1934)**
**McLain,** Dennis (baseball); Chicago, 3/24/1944
**McMillan,** Kathy Laverne (track); Raeford, N.C., 11/7/1957
**Merrill,** Janice (track); New London, Conn., 6/18/1962
**Meyer,** Deborah (swimming); Haddonfield, N.J., 8/14/1952
**Middlecoff,** Cary (golf); Halls, Tenn., 1/6/1921
**Mikita,** Stan (hockey); Sokolce, Czechoslovakia, 5/20/1940
**Milburn,** Rodney, Jr. (hurdler); Opelousas, La., 5/18/1950
**Miller,** Johnny (golf); San Francisco, 4/29/1947
**Montgomery,** Jim (swimming); Madison, Wis., 1/24/1955
**Moore,** Archie (boxing); Benoit, Miss., 12/13/1916
**Morgan,** Joe Leonard (baseball); Bonham, Tex., 9/19/1943
**Morrall,** Earl (football); Muskegon, Mich., 5/17/1934
**Morton,** Craig L. (football); Flint, Mich., 2/5/1943
**Mosconi,** Willie (pocket billiards); Philadelphia, 6/27/1913
**Moser,** Annemarie. *See* Proell, Annemarie
**Moses,** Edward Corley (track); Dayton, Ohio, 8/31/1958
**Mungo,** Van Lingo (baseball); Pageland, S.C. **(1911-1985)**
**Munson,** Thurman (baseball); Akron, Ohio, **(1947-1979)**
**Murphy,** Calvin (basketball); Norwalk, Conn., 5/9/1948
**Musial,** Stan (baseball); Donora, Pa., 11/21/1920

**Myers,** Linda (archery); York, Pa., 6/19/1947
**Naber,** John (swimming); Evanston, Ill., 1/20/1956
**Namath,** Joe (Joseph William) (football); Beaver Falls, Pa., 5/31/1943
**Nastase,** Ilie (tennis); Bucharest, 7/19/1946
**Navratilova,** Martina (tennis); Prague, 10/18/1956
**Nehemiah,** Renaldo (track); Newark, N.J., 3/24/1959
**Nelson,** Cindy (skiing); Lutsen, Minn., 8/19/1955
**Newcombe,** John (tennis); Sydney, Australia, 5/23/1943
**Niekro,** Phil (baseball); Lansing, Ohio, 4/1/1939
**Nicklaus,** Jack (golf); Columbus, Ohio, 1/21/1940
**North,** Lowell (yachting); Springfield, Mo., 12/2/1929
**Oerter,** Al (discus thrower); New York City, 9/19/1936
**Okker,** Tom (tennis); Amsterdam, 2/22/1944
**Oldfield,** Barney (racing driver); Fulton County, Ohio **(1878-1946)**
**Oliva,** Tony (Pedro) (baseball); Pinar Del Rio, Cuba, 7/20/1940
**Olsen,** Merlin Jay (football); Logan, Utah, 9/15/1940
**O'Malley,** Walter (baseball executive); New York City **(1903–1979)**
**Orantes,** Manuel (tennis); Granada, Spain, 2/6/1949
**Orr,** Bobby (hockey); Parry Sound, Ontario, Canada, 3/20/1948
**Ovett,** Steve (track); Brighton, England, 10/9/1955
**Owens,** Jesse (track); Decatur, Ala. **(1914-1980)**
**Pace,** Darrell (archery); Cincinnati, 10/23/1956
**Paige,** Satchel (Leroy) (baseball); Mobile, Ala., **(1906-1982)**
**Palmer,** Arnold (golf); Latrobe, Pa., 9/10/1929
**Palmer,** James Alvin (baseball); New York City, 10/15/1945
**Parent,** Bernard Marcel (hockey); Montreal, 4/3/1945
**Park,** Brad (Douglas Bradford) (hockey); Toronto, Ontario, Canada, 7/6/1948
**Parseghian,** Ara (football); Akron, Ohio, 5/21/1923
**Pasarell,** Charles (tennis); San Juan, Puerto Rico, 2/12/1944
**Patterson,** Floyd (boxing); Waco, N.C., 1/4/1935
**Peete,** Calvin (golf); Detroit, Mich., 7/18/1943
**Pelé** (Edson Arantes do Nascimento) (soccer); Tres Coracoes, Brazil, 10/23/1940
**Perry,** Gaylord (baseball); Williamston, N.C., 9/15/1938
**Perry,** Jim (baseball); Williamston, N.C., 9/15/1938
**Pettit,** Bob (basketball); Baton Rouge, La., 12/12/1932
**Petty,** Richard Lee (auto racing); Randleman, N.C., 7/2/1937
**Pincay,** Laffit, Jr. (jockey); Panama City, Panama, 12/29/1946
**Plante,** Jacques (hockey); Shawinigan Falls, Quebec, Canada, 1/17/1929
**Player,** Gary (golf); Johannesburg, South Africa, 11/1/1935
**Plunkett,** Jim (football); San Jose, Calif., 12/5/1947
**Potvin,** Denis Charles (hockey); Hull, Quebec, Canada, 10/29/1953
**Powell,** Boog (John) (baseball); Lakeland, Fla., 8/17/1941
**Prefontaine,** Steve Roland (runner); Coos Bay, Ore. **(1951-1975)**
**Prince,** Bob (baseball announcer); Pittsburgh **(1917-1985)**
**Proell,** Annemarie Moser (Alpine skier); Kleinarl, Austria, 3/27/1953
**Ralston,** Dennis (tennis); Bakersfield, Calif., 7/27/1942
**Rankin,** Judy Torluemke (golf); St. Louis, Mo., 2/18/1945
**Ratelle,** Jean (Joseph Gilbert Yvon Jean) (hockey); St. Jean, Quebec, Canada, 10/29/1953
**Rawls,** Betsy (Elizabeth Earle) (golf); Spartanburg, S.C., 5/4/1928
**Reed,** Willis (basketball); Hico, La., 6/25/1942
**Reese,** Pee Wee (Harold) (baseball); Ekron, Ky., 7/23/1919
**Resch,** Glenn "Chico" (hockey); Moose Jaw, Saskatchewan, Canada, 7/10/1948
**Richard,** Maurice (hockey); Montreal, 8/14/1924
**Riessen,** Martin (tennis); Hinsdale, Ill., 12/4/1941
**Rigney,** William (baseball); Alameda, Calif., 1/29/1918
**Rizzuto,** Phil (baseball); New York City, 9/25/1918
**Roark,** Helen Wills Moody (tennis); Centerville, Calif., 10/6/1906
**Robertson,** Oscar (basketball); Charlotte, Tenn., 11/24/1938
**Robinson,** Arnie (track); San Diego, Calif., 4/7/1948
**Robinson,** Brooks (baseball); Little Rock, Ark., 5/18/1937
**Robinson,** Frank (baseball); Beaumont, Tex., 8/31/1935
**Robinson,** Jackie (baseball); Cairo, Ga. **(1919-1972)**
**Robinson,** Larry Clark (hockey); Marvelville, Ontario, Canada, 6/2/1951
**Robinson,** (Sugar) Ray (boxing); Detroit, 5/3/1920
**Rockne,** Knute Kenneth (football); Voss, Norway **(1888-1931)**
**Rockwell,** Martha (skiing); Providence, R.I., 4/26/1944
**Rono,** Harry (track); Kiptaragon, Kenya, 2/12/1952
**Rose,** Pete (Peter Edward) (baseball); Cincinnati, 4/14/1942
**Rosenbloom,** Maxie (boxing); New York City **(1904-1976)**
**Rosewall,** Ken (tennis); Sydney, Australia, 11/2/1934
**Rote,** Kyle (football); San Antonio, 10/27/1928
**Rozelle,** Pete (Alvin Ray) (commissioner of National Football League); South Gate, Calif., 3/1/1926
**Rudolph,** Wilma Glodean (sprinter); St. Bethlehem, Tenn., 6/23/1940
**Russell,** Bill (basketball); Monroe, La., 2/12/1934
**Ruth,** Babe (George Herman Ruth) (baseball); Baltimore **(1895-1948)**
**Rutherford,** Johnny (auto racing); Fort Worth, 3/12/1938
**Ryan,** Nolan (Lynn Nolan, Jr.) (baseball); Refugio, Tex., 1/31/1947
**Ryon,** Luann (archery); Long Beach, Calif., 1/13/1953

**Ryun,** Jim (runner); Wichita, Kan., 4/29/1947
**Salazar,** Alberto (track); Havana, 8/7/1958
**Samuels, Howard** (horse racing, soccer); New York City **(1920-1984)**
**Santana,** Manuel (Manuel Santana Martinez) (tennis); Chamartin, Spain, 5/10/1938
**Sayers,** Gale (football); Wichita, Kan., 5/30/1943
**Schmidt,** Mike (baseball); Dayton, Ohio, 9/27/1949
**Schoendienst,** Al (Albert) (baseball); Germantown, Ill., 2/2/1923
**Schollander,** Donald (swimming); Charlotte, N.C., 4/30/1946
**Seagren,** Bob (Robert Lloyd) (pole vaulter); Pomona, Calif., 10/17/1946
**Seaver,** Tom (baseball); Fresno, Calif., 11/17/1944
**Seidler,** Maren (track); Brooklyn, N.Y., 6/11/1962
**Selke, Frank** (ice hockey); Canada **(1893-1985)**
**Shepherd,** Lee (auto racing) **(1945-1985)**
**Shoemaker,** Willie (jockey); Fabens, Tex., 8/19/1931
**Shore, Eddie** (ice hockey); Saskatchewan, Canada **(1902-1985)**
**Shorter,** Frank (runner); Munich, Germany, 10/31/1947
**Shriver,** Pam (tennis); Baltimore, 7/4/1962
**Shula,** Don (Donald Francis) (football); Grand River, Ohio, 1/4/1930
**Silvester,** Jay (discus thrower); Tremonton, Utah, 2/27/1937
**Simpson,** O. J. (Orenthal James) (football); San Francisco, 7/9/1947
**Sims,** Billy (football); St. Louis, 9/18/1955
**Smith,** Bubba (Charles Aaron) (football); Orange, Tex., 2/28/1945
**Smith,** Ronnie Ray (sprinter); Los Angeles, 3/28/1949
**Smith,** Stanley Roger (tennis); Pasadena, Calif., 12/14/1946
**Smith,** Tommie (sprinter); Clarksville, Tex., 6/5/1944
**Smoke,** Marcia Jones (canoeing); Oklahoma City, 7/18/1941
**Snead,** Sam (golf); Hot Springs, Va., 5/27/1912
**Sneva,** Tom (auto racing); Spokane, Wash., 6/1/1948
**Snider,** Duke (Edwin) (baseball); Los Angeles, 9/19/1926
**Solomon,** Harold (tennis); Washington, D.C., 9/17/1952
**Spahn,** Warren (baseball); Buffalo, N.Y., 4/23/1921
**Speaker,** Tristram (baseball); Hubbard City, Tex. **(1888-1958)**
**Spinks,** Leon (boxing); St. Louis, 7/11/1953
**Spitz,** Mark (swimming); Modesto, Calif., 2/10/1950
**Stabler,** Kenneth (football); Foley, Ala., 12/25/1945
**Stagg,** Amos Alonzo (football); West Orange, N.J. **(1862-1965)**
**Stargell,** Willie (Wilver Dornell) (baseball); Earlsboro, Okla., 3/6/1941
**Starr,** Bart (football); Montgomery, Ala., 1/9/1934
**Staub,** Daniel "Rusty" (baseball); New Orleans, 4/4/1944
**Staubach,** Roger (football); Cincinnati, 2/5/1942
**Steinkraus,** William C. (equestrian); Cleveland, 10/12/1925
**Stenerud,** Jan (football); Fetsund, Norway, 11/26/1942
**Stengel,** Casey (Charles Dillon) (baseball); Kansas City, Mo. **(1891-1975)**
**Stenmark,** Ingemar (Alpine skier); Tarnaby, Sweden, 3/18/1956
**Stockton,** Richard LaClede (tennis); New York City, 2/18/1951
**Stones,** Dwight Edwin (track); Los Angeles, 12/6/1953
**Strawberry,** Darryl (baseball); Los Angeles, 3/12/1962
**Sullivan,** John Lawrence (boxer); Boston **(1858-1918)**
**Sutton,** Don (Donald Howard) (baseball); Clio, Ala., 4/2/1945
**Swann,** Lynn (football); Alcoa, Tenn., 3/7/1952
**Tanner,** Leonard Roscoe III (tennis); Chattanooga, Tenn., 10/15/1951
**Tarkenton,** Fran (Francis) (football); Richmond, Va., 2/3/1940
**Tebbetts,** Birdie (George R.) (baseball); Nashua, N.H., 11/10/1914
**Thoeni,** Gustavo (Alpine skier); Trafoi, Italy, 2/28/1951
**Thompson,** David (basketball); Shelby, N.C., 7/13/1954

**Thorpe,** Jim (James Francis Thorpe) (all-around athlete); nr. Prague, Okla. **(1888-1953)**
**Tilden,** William Tatem II (tennis); Philadelphia **(1893-1953)**
**Tittle,** Y. A. (Yelberton Abraham) (football); Marshall, Tex., 10/24/1926
**Toomey,** William (decathlon); Philadelphia, 1/10/1939
**Trevino,** Lee (golf); Dallas, 12/1/1939
**Tunney,** Gene (James J.) (boxing); New York City **(1898-1978)**
**Tyus,** Wyomia (runner); Griffin, Ga., 8/29/1945
**Ueberroth,** Peter (baseball); Evanston, Ill., 9/2/1937
**Unitas,** John (football); Pittsburgh, 5/7/1933
**Unser,** Al (auto racing); Albuquerque, N. Mex., 5/29/1939
**Unser,** Bobby (auto racing); Albuquerque N. Mex., 2/20/1934
**Valenzuela,** Fernando (baseball); Sonora, Mexico, 11/1/1960
**Van Brocklin,** Norm (football); Eagle Butte, S. Dak. **(1926-1983)**
**Vilas,** Guillermo (tennis); Mar del Plata, Argentina, 8/17/1952
**Viren,** Lasse (track); Myrskyla, Finland, 7/12/1949
**Wade,** Virginia (tennis); Bournemouth, England, 7/10/1945
**Wagner,** Honus (John Peter Honus) (baseball); Carnegie, Pa. **(1867-1955)**
**Wakefield,** Dick (baseball); Chicago **(1921-1985)**
**Walcott,** Jersey Joe (Arnold Cream) (boxing); Merchantville, N.J., 1/31/1914
**Walsh,** Adam (football) **(1902-1985)**
**Walton,** Bill (basketball); La Mesa, Calif., 11/5/1952
**Waterfield,** Bob (football); Burbank, Calif. **(1921-1983)**
**Watson,** Martha Rae (track); Long Beach, Calif., 8/19/1946
**Watson,** Tom (golf); Kansas City, Mo., 9/4/1949
**Weaver,** Earl (baseball); St. Louis, 8/14/1930
**Webster,** Alex (football); Kearny, N.J., 4/19/1931
**Weiskopf,** Tom (golf); Massillon, Ohio, 11/9/1942
**Weiss,** George (baseball executive); New Haven, Conn. **(1895-1972)**
**Weissmuller,** Johnny (swimmer and actor); Windber, Pa. **(1904-1984)**
**Weld,** Philip (sailing); Cambridge, Mass. **(1915-1984)**
**West,** Jerry (basketball); Cheylan, W. Va., 5/28/1938
**White,** Willye B. (long jumper); Money, Miss., 1/1/1936
**Whitworth,** Kathy (golf); Monahans, Tex., 9/27/1939
**Widing,** Juha (ice hockey); Vancouver, Canada **(1948-1985)**
**Wilkens,** Mac Maurice (track); Eugene, Ore., 11/15/1950
**Wilkins,** Lennie (basketball); 11/25/1937
**Wilkinson,** Bud (football); Minneapolis, 4/23/1916
**Williams, Del** (football); New Orleans **(1945-1984)**
**Williams,** Dick (baseball); St. Louis, 5/7/1929
**Williams,** Ted (baseball); San Diego, Calif., 8/30/1918
**Wills,** Maury (baseball); Washington, D.C., 10/2/1932
**Winfield,** Dave (baseball); St. Paul, Minn., 10/3/1951
**Wohlhuter,** Richard C. (runner); Geneva, Ill. 12/23/1945
**Wood, Joseph "Smokey"** (baseball); Kansas City, Mo. **(1890-1985)**
**Woodhead,** Cynthia (swimming); Riverside, Calif., 2/7/1964
**Wottle,** David James (runner); Canton, Ohio, 8/7/1950
**Wright,** Mickey (Mary Kathryn) (golf); San Diego, Calif., 2/14/1935
**Yarborough,** Cale (William Caleb) (auto racing); Timmonsville, S.C., 3/27/1939
**Yarbrough,** Leeroy (auto racing); Jacksonville, Fla. **(1938-1984)**
**Yastrzemski,** Carl (baseball); Southampton, N.Y., 8/22/1939
**Young,** Cy (Denton True Young) (baseball); Gilmore, Ohio **(1867-1955)**
**Young,** Sheila (speed skater, bicycle racer); Detroit, 10/14/1950

# JIM THORPE'S OLYMPIC MEDALS RETURNED

More than 70 years after he won the pentathlon and decathlon at Stockholm, Sweden, Jim Thorpe's Olympic gold medals were returned posthumously to him by the International Olympic Committee. Thorpe, an Oklahoma Sac and Fox Indian, became one of the greatest all-around athletes ever produced in America. He was an all-American football player at the Carlisle Institute, an Indian trade school in Pennsylvania, and starred in baseball and track and field. After winning the medals in the 1912 Olympics, he was forced to give them up when he admitted he had played two seasons for money as a semipro baseball player in 1909 and 1910. Under the rules, he had lost his amateur status by taking money and thus was theoretically ineligible for the Olympics. In October of 1982, after many years of vigorous efforts by his family and other officials in athletics, the I.O.C. reinstated Thorpe in its archives as a co-winner of the two events. At ceremonies in Los Angeles in January 1983, Antonio Samaranch, president of the I.O.C. presented Thorpe's children with gold medals to replace those he had turned back. Thorpe, who later in his career played major-league baseball and pro football, died at the age of 65 in 1953.

# THE OLYMPIC GAMES

(W)—Site of Winter Games. (S)—Site of Summer Games

| | | | | | | |
|---|---|---|---|---|---|---|
| 1896 | Athens | 1936 | Garmisch-Partenkirchen (W) | 1968 | Mexico City (S) |
| 1900 | Paris | 1936 | Berlin (S) | 1972 | Sapporo, Japan (W) |
| 1904 | St. Louis | 1948 | St. Moritz (W) | 1972 | Munich (S) |
| 1906 | Athens | 1948 | London (S) | 1976 | Innsbruck, Austria (W) |
| 1908 | London | 1952 | Oslo (W) | 1976 | Montreal (S) |
| 1912 | Stockholm | 1952 | Helsinki (S) | 1980 | Lake Placid (W) |
| 1920 | Antwerp | 1956 | Cortina d'Ampezzo, Italy (W) | 1980 | Moscow (S) |
| 1924 | Chamonix (W) | 1956 | Melbourne (S) | 1984 | Sarajevo, Yugoslavia (W) |
| 1924 | Paris (S) | 1960 | Squaw Valley, Calif. (W) | 1984 | Los Angeles (S) |
| 1928 | St. Moritz (W) | 1960 | Rome (S) | 1988 | Calgary, Alberta (W) |
| 1928 | Amsterdam (S) | 1964 | Innsbruck, Austria (W) | 1988 | Seoul, South Korea (S) |
| 1932 | Lake Placid (W) | 1964 | Tokyo (S) | | |
| 1932 | Los Angeles (S) | 1968 | Grenoble, France (W) | | |

The first Olympic Games of which there is record were held in 776 B.C., and consisted of one event, a great foot race of about 200 yards held on a plain by the River Alpheus (now the Ruphia) just outside the little town of Olympia in Greece. It was from that date that the Greeks began to keep their calendar by "Olympiads," the four-year spans between the celebrations of the famous games.

The modern Olympic Games, which started in Athens in 1896, are the result of the devotion of a French educator, Baron Pierre de Coubertin, to the idea that, since young people and athletics have gone together through the ages, education and athletics might go hand-in-hand toward a better international understanding.

The principal organization responsible for the staging of the Games every four years is the International Olympic Committee (IOC). Other important roles are played by the National Olympic Committees in each participating country, international sports federations, and the organizing committee of the host city.

The headquarters of the 89-member International Olympic Committee are in Lausanne, Switzerland. The president of the IOC is Juan Antonio Samaranch of Spain.

The Olympic motto is "Citius, Altius, Fortius,"— "Faster, Higher, Stronger." The Olympic symbol is five interlocking circles colored blue, yellow, black, green, and red, on a white background, representing the five continents. At least one of those colors appears in the national flag of every country.

The ideal of peaceful international athletic competition has been severely tested the past four Olympiads, dating back to the 1972 raid by Arab terrorists on the Olympic village in Munich, Germany. Eleven Israelis, five terrorists, and a German police officer were all killed in the siege.

In 1976, political problems kept one-quarter of the IOC-member nations from competing. The most pressing was the conflict over recognition of Taiwan or Mainland China as the correct representative of that country. An additional 31 nations withdrew over the failure to bar New Zealand, which had a soccer team touring apartheid South Africa.

A total of 66 nations, including the United States, did not participate in 1980, over the Soviet Union's invasion of Afghanistan. Those Summer Games were scheduled for Moscow.

Considering this action, it was almost inevitable that the Soviet Union would take some similar action for the 1984 games, held in Los Angeles. Officially, the Soviet Union, and nearly the entire Soviet-communist bloc, withdrew over dissatisfaction with security measures in Los Angeles.

The 1988 games are scheduled for Seoul, South Korea, and there has been talk of a boycott my several Communist nations if North Korea is not included as a co-sponsor.

## Summer Games

(EVENTS LISTED ARE THOSE CURRENTLY HELD)

### TRACK AND FIELD—MEN

#### 100-Meter Dash

| | | |
|---|---|---|
| 1896 | Thomas Burke, United States | 12s |
| 1900 | Francis W. Jarvis, United States | 10.8s |
| 1904 | Archie Hahn, United States | 11s |
| 1906 | Archie Hahn, United States | 11.2s |
| 1908 | Reginald Walker, South Africa | 10.8s |
| 1912 | Ralph Craig, United States | 10.8s |
| 1920 | Charles Paddock, United States | 10.8s |
| 1924 | Harold Abrahams, Great Britain | 10.6s |
| 1928 | Percy Williams, Canada | 10.8s |
| 1932 | Eddie Tolan, United States | 10.3s |
| 1936 | Jesse Owens, United States | 10.3s[1] |
| 1948 | Harrison Dillard, United States | 10.3s |
| 1952 | Lindy Remigino, United States | 10.4s |
| 1956 | Bobby Morrow, United States | 10.5s |
| 1960 | Armin Hary, Germany | 10.2s |
| 1964 | Robert Hayes, United States | 10s |
| 1968 | James Hines, United States | 9.9s |
| 1972 | Valery Borzov, U.S.S.R. | 10.14s |
| 1976 | Hasely Crawford, Trinidad and Tobago | 10.06s |
| 1980 | Allan Wells, Britain | 10.25s |
| 1984 | Carl Lewis, United States | 9.99s |

1. Wind assisted.

#### 200-Meter Dash

| | | |
|---|---|---|
| 1900 | John Tewksbury, United States | 22.2s |
| 1904 | Archie Hahn, United States | 21.6s |
| 1908 | Robert Kerr, Canada | 22.6s |
| 1912 | Ralph Craig, United States | 21.7s |

| | | |
|---|---|---|
| 1920 | Allan Woodring, United States | 22s |
| 1924 | Jackson Scholz, United States | 21.6s |
| 1928 | Percy Williams, Canada | 21.8s |
| 1932 | Eddie Tolan, United States | 21.2s |
| 1936 | Jesse Owens, United States | 20.7s |
| 1948 | Melvin E. Patton, United States | 21.1s |
| 1952 | Andrew Stanfield, United States | 20.7s |
| 1956 | Bobby Morrow, United States | 20.6s |
| 1960 | Livio Berruti, Italy | 20.5s |
| 1964 | Henry Carr, United States | 20.3s |
| 1968 | Tommie Smith, United States | 19.8s |
| 1972 | Valery Borzov, U.S.S.R. | 20s |
| 1976 | Don Quarrie, Jamaica | 20.23s |
| 1980 | Pietro Mennea, Italy | 20.19s |
| 1984 | Carl Lewis, United States | 19.80s |

## 400-Meter Dash

| | | |
|---|---|---|
| 1896 | Thomas Burke, United States | 54.2s |
| 1900 | Maxwell Long, United States | 49.4s |
| 1904 | Harry Hillman, United States | 49.2s |
| 1906 | Paul Pilgrim, United States | 53.2s |
| 1908 | Wyndham Halswelle, Great Britain (walkover) | 50s |
| 1912 | Charles Reidpath, United States | 48.2s |
| 1920 | Bevil Rudd, South Africa | 49.6s |
| 1924 | Eric Liddell, Great Britain | 47.6s |
| 1928 | Ray Barbuti, United States | 47.8s |
| 1932 | William Carr, United States | 46.2s |
| 1936 | Archie Williams, United States | 46.5s |
| 1948 | Arthur Wint, Jamaica, B.W.I. | 46.2s |
| 1952 | George Rhoden, Jamaica, B.W.I. | 45.9s |
| 1956 | Charles Jenkins, United States | 46.7s |
| 1960 | Otis Davis, United States | 44.9s |
| 1964 | Mike Larrabee, United States | 45.1s |
| 1968 | Lee Evans, United States | 43.8s |
| 1972 | Vincent Matthews, United States | 44.66s |
| 1976 | Alberto Juantorena, Cuba | 44.26s |
| 1980 | Viktor Markin, U.S.S.R. | 44.60s |
| 1984 | Alonzo Babers, United States | 44.27s |

## 800-Meter Run

| | | |
|---|---|---|
| 1896 | Edwin Flack, Australia | 2m11s |
| 1900 | Alfred Tysoe, Great Britain | 2m1.4s |
| 1904 | James Lightbody, United States | 1m56s |
| 1906 | Paul Pilgrim, United States | 2m1.2s |
| 1908 | Mel Sheppard, United States | 1m52.8s |
| 1912 | Ted Meredith, United States | 1m51.9s |
| 1920 | Albert Hill, Great Britain | 1m53.4s |
| 1924 | Douglas Lowe, Great Britain | 1m52.4s |
| 1928 | Douglas Lowe, Great Britain | 1m51.8s |
| 1932 | Thomas Hampson, Great Britain | 1m49.8s |
| 1936 | John Woodruff, United States | 1m52.9s |
| 1948 | Malvin Whitfield, United States | 1m49.2s |
| 1952 | Malvin Whitfield, United States | 1m49.2s |
| 1956 | Tom Courtney, United States | 1m47.7s |
| 1960 | Peter Snell, New Zealand | 1m46.3s |
| 1964 | Peter Snell, New Zealand | 1m45.1s |
| 1968 | Ralph Doubell, Australia | 1m44.3s |
| 1972 | David Wottle, United States | 1m45.9s |
| 1976 | Alberto Juantorena, Cuba | 1m43.5s |
| 1980 | Steve Ovett, Britain | 1m45.4s |
| 1984 | Joaquin Cruz, Brazil | 1m43.0s |

## 1,500-Meter Run

| | | |
|---|---|---|
| 1896 | Edwin Flack, Australia | 4m33.2s |
| 1900 | Charles Bennett, Great Britain | 4m6s |
| 1904 | James Lightbody, United States | 4m5.4s |
| 1906 | James Lightbody, United States | 4m12s |
| 1908 | Mel Sheppard, United States | 4m3.4s |
| 1912 | Arnold Jackson, Great Britain | 3m56.8s |
| 1920 | Albert Hill, Great Britain | 4m1.8s |
| 1924 | Paavo Nurmi, Finland | 3m53.6s |
| 1928 | Harry Larva, Finland | 3m53.2s |

| | | |
|---|---|---|
| 1932 | Luigi Beccali, Italy | 3m51.2s |
| 1936 | Jack Lovelock, New Zealand | 3m47.8s |
| 1948 | Henri Eriksson, Sweden | 3m49.8s |
| 1952 | Joseph Barthel, Luxembourg | 3m45.2s |
| 1956 | Ron Delany, Ireland | 3m41.2s |
| 1960 | Herb Elliott, Australia | 3m35.6s |
| 1964 | Peter Snell, New Zealand | 3m38.1s |
| 1968 | Kipchoge Keino, Kenya | 3m34.9s |
| 1972 | Pekka Vasala, Finland | 3m36.3s |
| 1976 | John Walker, New Zealand | 3m39.17s |
| 1980 | Sebastian Coe, Britain | 3m38.4s |
| 1984 | Sebastian Coe, Britain | 3m32.53s |

## 5,000-Meter Run

| | | |
|---|---|---|
| 1912 | Hannes Kolehmainen, Finland | 14m36.6s |
| 1920 | Joseph Guillemot, France | 14m55.6s |
| 1924 | Paavo Nurmi, Finland | 14m31.2s |
| 1928 | Willie Ritola, Finland | 14m38s |
| 1932 | Lauri Lehtinen, Finland | 14m30s |
| 1936 | Gunnar Hockert, Finland | 14m22.2s |
| 1948 | Gaston Reiff, Belgium | 14m17.6s |
| 1952 | Emil Zatopek, Czechoslovakia | 14m6.6s |
| 1956 | Vladimir Kuts, U.S.S.R. | 13m39.6s |
| 1960 | Murray Halberg, New Zealand | 13m43.4s |
| 1964 | Bob Schul, United States | 13m48.8s |
| 1968 | Mohamed Gammoudi, Tunisia | 14m.05s |
| 1972 | Lasse Viren, Finland | 13m26.4s |
| 1976 | Lasse Viren, Finland | 13m24.76s |
| 1980 | Miruts Yifter, Ethiopia | 13m21s |
| 1984 | Savd Advita, Morocco | 13m5.59s |

## 10,000-Meter Run

| | | |
|---|---|---|
| 1912 | Hannes Kolehmainen, Finland | 31m20.8s |
| 1920 | Paavo Nurmi, Finland | 31m45.8s |
| 1924 | Willie Ritola, Finland | 30m23.2s |
| 1928 | Paavo Nurmi, Finland | 30m18.8s |
| 1932 | Janusz Kusocinski, Poland | 30m11.4s |
| 1936 | Ilmari Salminen, Finland | 30m15.4s |
| 1948 | Emil Zatopek, Czechoslovakia | 29m59.6s |
| 1952 | Emil Zatopek, Czechoslovakia | 29m17s |
| 1956 | Vladimir Kuts, U.S.S.R. | 28m45.6s |
| 1960 | Peter Bolotnikov, U.S.S.R. | 28m32.2s |
| 1964 | Billy Mills, United States | 28m24.4s |
| 1968 | Naftali Temu, Kenya | 29m27.4s |
| 1972 | Lasse Viren, Finland | 27m38.4s |
| 1976 | Lasse Viren, Finland | 27m40.38s |
| 1980 | Miruts Yifter, Ethiopia | 27m42.7s |
| 1984 | Alberto Cova, Italy | 27m47.5s |

## Marathon

| | | |
|---|---|---|
| 1896 | Spiridon Loues, Greece | 2h58m50s |
| 1900 | Michel Teato, France | 2h59m45s |
| 1904 | Thomas Hicks, United States | 3h28m53s |
| 1906 | William J. Sherring, Canada | 2h51m23.65s |
| 1908 | John J. Hayes, United States | 2h55m18.4s |
| 1912 | Kenneth McArthur, South Africa | 2h36m54.8s |
| 1920 | Hannes Kolehmainen, Finland | 2h32m35.8s |
| 1924 | Albin Stenroos, Finland | 2h41m22.6s |
| 1928 | A. B. El Quafi, France | 2h32m57s |
| 1932 | Juan Zabala, Argentina | 2h31m36s |
| 1936 | Kitei Son, Japan | 2h29m19.2s |
| 1948 | Delfo Cabrera, Argentina | 2h34m51.6s |
| 1952 | Emil Zatopek, Czechoslovakia | 2h23m3.2s |
| 1956 | Alain Mimoun, France | 2h25m |
| 1960 | Abebe Bikila, Ethiopia | 2h15m16.2s |
| 1964 | Abebe Bikila, Ethiopia | 2h12m11.2s |
| 1968 | Mamo Wold, Ethiopia | 2h20m26.4s |
| 1972 | Frank Shorter, United States | 2h12m19.8s |
| 1976 | Walter Cierpinski, East Germany | 2h09m55s |
| 1980 | Walter Cierpinski, East Germany | 2h11m3s |
| 1984 | Carlos Lopes, Portugal | 2hr9m.55s |

## 110-Meter Hurdles

| | | |
|---|---|---|
| 1896 | Thomas Curtis, United States | 17.6s |
| 1900 | Alvin Kraenzlein, United States | 15.4s |
| 1904 | Frederick Schule, United States | 16s |
| 1906 | R. G. Leavitt, United States | 16.2s |
| 1908 | Forrest Smithson, United States | 15s |
| 1912 | Frederick Kelly, United States | 15.1s |
| 1920 | Earl Thomson, Canada | 14.8s |
| 1924 | Daniel Kinsey, United States | 15s |
| 1928 | Sydney Atkinson, South Africa | 14.8s |
| 1932 | George Saling, United States | 14.6s |
| 1936 | Forrest Towns, United States | 14.2s |
| 1948 | William Porter, United States | 13.9s |
| 1952 | Harrison Dillard, United States | 13.7s |
| 1956 | Lee Calhoun, United States | 13.5s |
| 1960 | Lee Calhoun, United States | 13.8s |
| 1964 | Hayes Jones, United States | 13.6s |
| 1968 | Willie Davenport, United States | 13.3s |
| 1972 | Rodney Milburn, United States | 13.24s |
| 1976 | Guy Drut, France | 13.30s |
| 1980 | Thomas Munkett, East Germany | 13.39s |
| 1984 | Roger Kingdom, United States | 13.20s |

## 200-Meter Hurdles

| | | |
|---|---|---|
| 1900 | Alvin Kraenzlein, United States | 25.4s |
| 1904 | Harry Hillman, United States | 24.6s |

## 400-Meter Hurdles

| | | |
|---|---|---|
| 1900 | John Tewksbury, United States | 57.6s |
| 1904 | Harry Hillman, United States | 53s |
| 1908 | Charles Bacon, United States | 55s |
| 1920 | Frank Loomis, United States | 54s |
| 1924 | F. Morgan Taylor, United States | 52.6s |
| 1928 | Lord David Burghley, Great Britain | 53.4s |
| 1932 | Robert Tisdall, Ireland | 51.8s[1] |
| 1936 | Glenn Hardin, United States | 52.4s |
| 1948 | Roy Cochran, United States | 51.1s |
| 1952 | Charles Moore, United States | 50.8s |
| 1956 | Glenn Davis, United States | 50.1s |
| 1960 | Glenn Davis, United States | 49.3s |
| 1964 | Rex Cawley, United States | 49.6s |
| 1968 | David Hemery, Great Britain | 48.1s |
| 1972 | John Akii-Bua, Uganda | 47.8s |
| 1976 | Edwin Moses, United States | 47.64s |
| 1980 | Volker Beck, East Germany | 48.70s |
| 1984 | Edwin Moses, United States | 47.75s |

1. Record not allowed.

## 2,500-Meter Steeplechase

| | | |
|---|---|---|
| 1900 | George Orton, United States | 7m34s |
| 1904 | James Lightbody, United States | 7m39.6s |

## 3,000-Meter Steeplechase

| | | |
|---|---|---|
| 1920 | Percy Hodge, Great Britain | 10m0.4s |
| 1924 | Willie Ritola, Finland | 9m33.6s |
| 1928 | Toivo Loukola, Finland | 9m21.8s |
| 1932 | Volmari Iso-Hollo, Finland | 10m33.4s[1] |
| 1936 | Volmari Iso-Hollo, Finland | 9m3.8s |
| 1948 | Thure Sjoestrand, Sweden | 9m4.6s |
| 1952 | Horace Ashenfelter, United States | 8m45.4s |
| 1956 | Chris Brasher, Great Britain | 8m41.2s |
| 1960 | Zdzislaw Krzyskowiak, Poland | 8m34.2s |
| 1964 | Gaston Roelants, Belgium | 8m30.8s |
| 1968 | Amos Biwott, Kenya | 8m51s |
| 1972 | Kipchoge Keino, Kenya | 8m23.6s |
| 1976 | Anders Gardervd, Sweden | 8m08.02s |
| 1980 | Bronislaw Malinowski, Poland | 8m9.7s |
| 1984 | Julius Korir, Kenya | 8m11.80s |

1. About 3,450 meters—extra lap by error.

## 10,000-Meter Walk

| | | |
|---|---|---|
| 1912 | George Goulding, Canada | 46m28.4s |
| 1920 | Ugo Frigerio, Italy | 48m6.2s |
| 1924 | Ugo Frigerio, Italy | 47m49s |
| 1948 | John Mikaelsson, Sweden | 45m13.2s |
| 1952 | John Mikaelsson, Sweden | 45m2.8s |

## 20,000-Meter Walk

| | | |
|---|---|---|
| 1956 | Leonid Spirin, U.S.S.R. | 1h31m27.4s |
| 1960 | Vladimir Golubnichy, U.S.S.R. | 1h34m7.2s |
| 1964 | Ken Mathews, Great Britain | 1h29m34s |
| 1968 | Vladimir Golubnichy, U.S.S.R. | 1h33m58.4s |
| 1972 | Peter Frenkel, East Germany | 1h26m42.4s |
| 1976 | Daniel Bautista, Mexico | 1h24m40.6s |
| 1980 | Maurizio Damiliano, Italy | 1h23m35.5s |
| 1984 | Ernesto Conto, Mexico | 1m23.13s |

## 50,000-Meter Walk

| | | |
|---|---|---|
| 1932 | Thomas W. Green, Great Britain | 4h50m10s |
| 1936 | Harold Whitlock, Great Britain | 4h30m41.1s |
| 1948 | John Ljunggren, Sweden | 4h41m52s |
| 1952 | Giuseppe Dordoni, Italy | 4h28m7.8s |
| 1956 | Norman Read, New Zealand | 4h30m42.8s |
| 1960 | Donald Thompson, Great Britain | 4h25m30s |
| 1964 | Abdon Pamich, Italy | 4h11m12.4s |
| 1968 | Christoph Hohne, East Germany | 4h20m13.6s |
| 1972 | Bern Kannernberg, West Germany | 3h56m11.6s |
| 1980 | Hartwig Gauder, East Germany | 3h49m24s |
| 1984 | Raul Gonzalez, Mexico | 3hr47m26s |

## 400-Meter Relay (4 × 100)

| | | |
|---|---|---|
| 1912 | Great Britain | 42.4s |
| 1920 | United States | 42.2s |
| 1924 | United States | 41s |
| 1928 | United States | 41s |
| 1932 | United States | 40s |
| 1936 | United States | 39.8s |
| 1948 | United States | 40.6s |
| 1952 | United States | 40.1s |
| 1956 | United States | 39.5s |
| 1960 | Germany | 39.5s |
| 1964 | United States | 39s |
| 1968 | United States | 38.2s |
| 1972 | United States | 38.19s |
| 1976 | United States | 38.33s |
| 1980 | U.S.S.R. | 38.26s |
| 1984 | United States | 37.83s |

## 1,600-Meter Relay (4 × 400)

| | | |
|---|---|---|
| 1912 | United States | 3m16.6s |
| 1920 | Great Britain | 3m22.2s |
| 1924 | United States | 3m16s |
| 1928 | United States | 3m14.2s |
| 1932 | United States | 3m8.2s |
| 1936 | Great Britain | 3m9s |
| 1948 | United States | 3m10.4s |
| 1952 | Jamaica, B.W.I. | 3m3.9s |
| 1956 | United States | 3m4.8s |
| 1960 | United States | 3m2.2s |
| 1964 | United States | 3m0.7s |
| 1968 | United States | 2m56.1s |
| 1972 | Kenya | 2m59.8s |
| 1976 | United States | 2m58.65s |
| 1980 | U.S.S.R. | 3m01.1s |
| 1984 | United States | 2m57.91s |

## Team Race

| | | Pts |
|---|---|---|
| 1900 | Great Britain (5,000 meters) | 26 |
| 1904 | United States (4 miles) | 27 |
| 1908 | Great Britain (3 miles) | 6 |
| 1912 | United States (3,000 meters) | 9 |

| 1920 | United States (3,000 meters) | 10 |
| 1924 | Finland (3,000 meters) | 9 |

## Standing High Jump

| 1900 | Ray Ewry, United States | 5 ft 5 in. |
| 1904 | Ray Ewry, United States | 4 ft 11 in. |
| 1906 | Ray Ewry, United States | 5 ft 1 5/8 in. |
| 1908 | Ray Ewry, United States | 5 ft 2 in. |
| 1912 | Platt Adams, United States | 5 ft 4 1/8 in. |

## Running High Jump

| 1896 | Ellery Clark, United States | 5 ft 11 1/4 in. |
| 1900 | Irving Baxter, United States | 6 ft 2 3/4 in. |
| 1904 | Samuel Jones, United States | 5 ft 11 in. |
| 1906 | Con Leahy, Ireland | 5 ft 9 7/8 in. |
| 1908 | Harry Porter, United States | 6 ft 3 in. |
| 1912 | Alma Richards, United States | 6 ft 4 in. |
| 1920 | Richmond Landon, United States | 6 ft 4 1/4 in. |
| 1924 | Harold Osborn, United States | 6 ft 5 15/16 in. |
| 1928 | Robert W. King, United States | 6 ft 4 3/8 in. |
| 1932 | Duncan McNaughton, Canada | 6 ft 5 5/8 in. |
| 1936 | Cornelius Johnson, United States | 6 ft 7 15/16 in. |
| 1948 | John Winter, Australia | 6 ft 6 in. |
| 1952 | Walter Davis, United States | 6 ft 8 5/16 in. |
| 1956 | Charles Dumas, United States | 6 ft 11 1/4 in. |
| 1960 | Robert Shavlakadze, U.S.S.R. | 7 ft 1 in. |
| 1964 | Valeri Brumel, U.S.S.R. | 7 ft 1 3/4 in. |
| 1968 | Dick Fosbury, United States | 7 ft 4 1/4 in. |
| 1972 | Yuri Tarmak, U.S.S.R. | 7 ft 3 3/4 in. |
| 1976 | Jacek Wszola, Poland | (2.25m) 7 ft 4 1/2 in. |
| 1980 | Gerd Wessig, East Germany | 7 ft 8 3/4 in. |
| 1984 | Dietmar Mogenburg, West Germany | 7 ft 8 1/2 in. |

## Long Jump

| 1896 | Ellery Clark, United States | 20 ft 9 3/4 in. |
| 1900 | Alvin Kraenzlein, United States | 23 ft 6 7/8 in. |
| 1904 | Myer Prinstein, United States | 24 ft 1 in. |
| 1906 | Myer Prinstein, United States | 23 ft 7 1/2 in. |
| 1908 | Frank Irons, United States | 24 ft 6 1/2 in. |
| 1912 | Albert Gutterson, United States | 24 ft 11 1/4 in. |
| 1920 | William Pettersson, Sweden | 23 ft 5 1/2 in. |
| 1924 | DeHart Hubbard, United States | 24 ft 5 1/8 in. |
| 1928 | Edward B. Hamm, United States | 25 ft 4 3/4 in. |
| 1932 | Edward Gordon, United States | 25 ft 3/4 in. |
| 1936 | Jesse Owens, United States | 26 ft. 5 5/16 in. |
| 1948 | Willie Steele, United States | 25 ft 8 in. |
| 1952 | Jerome Biffle, United States | 24 ft 10 in. |
| 1956 | Gregory Bell, United States | 25 ft 8 1/4 in. |
| 1960 | Ralph Boston, United States | 26 ft 7 3/4 in. |
| 1964 | Lynn Davies, Great Britain | 26 ft 5 3/4 in. |
| 1968 | Bob Beamon, United States | 29 ft 2 1/2 in. |
| 1972 | Randy Williams, United States | 27 ft 1/2 in. |
| 1976 | Arnie Robinson, United States | (8.35m) 24 ft 7 3/4 in. |
| 1980 | Lutz Dombrowski, E. Germany | 28 ft 1/4 in. |
| 1984 | Carl Lewis, United States | 28 ft 1/4 in. |

## Triple Jump

| 1896 | James B. Connolly, United States | 45 ft |
| 1900 | Myer Prinstein, United States | 47 ft 4 1/4 in. |
| 1904 | Myer Prinstein, United States | 47 ft |
| 1906 | P. G. O'Connor, Ireland | 46 ft 2 in. |
| 1908 | Timothy Ahearne, Great Britain | 48 ft 11 1/4 in. |
| 1912 | Gustaf Lindblom, Sweden | 48 ft 5 1/8 in. |
| 1920 | Vilho Tuulos, Finland | 47 ft 6 7/8 in. |
| 1924 | Archie Winter, Australia | 50 ft 11 1/8 in. |
| 1928 | Mikio Oda, Japan | 49 ft 10 13/16 in. |
| 1932 | Chuhei Nambu, Japan | 51 ft 7 in. |
| 1936 | Naoto Tajima, Japan | 52 ft 5 7/8 in. |
| 1948 | Arne Ahman, Sweden | 50 ft 6 1/4 in. |
| 1952 | Adhemar da Silva, Brazil | 53 ft 2 1/2 in. |
| 1956 | Adhemar da Silva, Brazil | 53 ft 7 1/2 in. |
| 1960 | Jozef Schmidt, Poland | 55 ft 1 3/4 in. |
| 1964 | Jozef Schmidt, Poland | 55 ft 3 1/4 in. |

| 1968 | Viktor Saneyev, U.S.S.R. | 57 ft 3/4 in. |
| 1972 | Viktor Saneyev, U.S.S.R. | 56 ft 11 in. |
| 1976 | Viktor Saneyev, U.S.S.R. | (17.29m) 56 ft 8 3/4 in. |
| 1980 | Jaak Uudmae, U.S.S.R. | 56 ft 11 1/8 in. |
| 1984 | Al Joyner, United States | 56 ft 7 1/2 in. |

## Pole Vault

| 1896 | William Hoyt, United States | 10 ft 9 3/4 in. |
| 1900 | Irving Baxter, United States | 10 ft 9 7/8 in. |
| 1904 | Charles Dvorak, United States | 11 ft 6 in. |
| 1906 | Fernand Gouder, France | 11 ft 6 in. |
| 1908 | Alfred Gilbert, United States, and Edward Cook, United States (tie) | 12 ft 2 in. |
| 1912 | Harry Babcock, United States | 12 ft 11 1/2 in. |
| 1920 | Frank Foss, United States | 13 ft 5 9/16 in. |
| 1924 | Lee Barnes, United States | 12 ft 11 1/2 in. |
| 1928 | Sabin W. Carr, United States | 13 ft 9 3/8 in. |
| 1932 | William Miller, United States | 14 ft 1 7/8 in. |
| 1936 | Earle Meadows, United States | 14 ft 3 1/4 in. |
| 1948 | Guinn Smith, United States | 14 ft 1 1/4 in. |
| 1952 | Robert Richards, United States | 14 ft 11 1/8 in. |
| 1956 | Robert Richards, United States | 14 ft 11 1/2 in. |
| 1960 | Don Bragg, United States | 15 ft 5 1/8 in. |
| 1964 | Fred Hansen, United States | 16 ft 8 3/4 in. |
| 1968 | Bob Seagren, United States | 17 ft 8 1/2 in. |
| 1972 | Wolfgang Nordwig, East Germany | 18 ft 1/2 in. |
| 1976 | Tadeusz Slusarski, Poland | (5.50m) 18 ft 1/2 in. |
| 1980 | Wladyslaw Kozakiewicz, Poland | 18 ft 11 1/2 in. |
| 1984 | Pierre Quinon, France | 18 ft 10 1/4 in. |

## 16-lb Shot-Put

| 1896 | Robert Garrett, United States | 36 ft 9 3/4 in. |
| 1900 | Richard Sheldon, United States | 46 ft 3 1/8 in. |
| 1904 | Ralph Rose, United States | 48 ft 7 in. |
| 1906 | Martin Sheridan, United States | 40 ft 4 4/5 in. |
| 1908 | Ralph Rose, United States | 46 ft 7 1/2 in. |
| 1912 | Pat McDonald, United States | 50 ft 4 in. |
| 1920 | Ville Porhola, Finland | 48 ft 7 1/8 in. |
| 1924 | Clarence Houser, United States | 49 ft 2 1/2 in. |
| 1928 | John Kuck, United States | 52 ft 11 11/16 in. |
| 1932 | Leo Sexton, United States | 52 ft 6 3/16 in. |
| 1936 | Hans Woellke, Germany | 53 ft 1 3/4 in. |
| 1948 | Wilbur Thompson, United States | 56 ft 2 in. |
| 1952 | Parry O'Brien, United States | 57 ft 1 1/2 in. |
| 1956 | Parry O'Brien, United States | 60 ft 11 in. |
| 1960 | Bill Nieder, United States | 64 ft 6 3/4 in. |
| 1964 | Dallas Long, United States | 66 ft 8 1/4 in. |
| 1968 | Randy Matson, United States | 67 ft 4 3/4 in. |
| 1972 | Wladyslaw Komar, Poland | 69 ft 6 in. |
| 1976 | Udo Beyer, East Germany | (21.05m) 69 ft 3/4 in. |
| 1980 | Vladimir Kiselyov, U.S.S.R. | 70 ft 1/2 in. |
| 1984 | Alessandro Andrei, Italy | 69 ft 9 in. |

## Discus Throw

| 1896 | Robert Garrett, United States | 95 ft 7 1/2 in. |
| 1900 | Rudolf Bauer, Hungary | 118 ft 2 7/8 in. |
| 1904 | Martin Sheridan, United States | 128 ft 10 1/2 in. |
| 1906 | Martin Sheridan, United States | 136 ft 1/3 in. |
| 1908 | Martin Sheridan, United States | 134 ft 2 in. |
| 1912 | Armas Taipale, Finland | 145 ft 9/16 in. |
| 1920 | Elmer Niklander, Finland | 146 ft 7 in. |
| 1924 | Clarence Houser, United States | 151 ft 5 1/4 in. |
| 1928 | Clarence Houser, United States | 155 ft 2 4/5 in. |
| 1932 | John Anderson, United States | 162 ft 4 7/8 in. |
| 1936 | Ken Carpenter, United States | 165 ft 7 3/8 in. |
| 1948 | Adolfo Consolini, Italy | 173 ft 2 in. |
| 1952 | Simeon Iness, United States | 180 ft 6 1/2 in. |
| 1956 | Al Oerter, United States | 184 ft 10 1/2 in. |
| 1960 | Al Oerter, United States | 194 ft 2 in. |
| 1964 | Al Oerter, United States | 200 ft 1 1/2 in. |
| 1968 | Al Oerter, United States | 212 ft 6 in. |
| 1972 | Ludvik Danek, Czechoslovakia | 211 ft 3 in. |

| 1976 | Mac Wilkins, United States | (67.5m) 221 ft 5 in. |
| 1980 | Viktor Rashchupkin, U.S.S.R. | 218 ft 8 in. |
| 1984 | Rolf Dannenberg, West Germany | 218 ft 6 in. |

## Javelin Throw

| 1906 | Eric Lemming, Sweden | 175 ft 6 in. |
| 1908 | Eric Lemming, Sweden | 179 ft 10 1/2 in. |
| 1912 | Eric Lemming, Sweden | 198 ft 11 1/4 in. |
| 1920 | Jonni Myyra, Finland | 215 ft 9 3/4 in. |
| 1924 | Jonni Myyra, Finland | 206 ft 6 3/4 in. |
| 1928 | Eric Lundquist, Sweden | 218 ft 6 1/8 in. |
| 1932 | Matti Jarvinen, Finland | 238 ft 7 in. |
| 1936 | Gerhard Stoeck, Germany | 235 ft 8 5/16 in. |
| 1948 | Kaj Rautavaara, Finland | 228 ft 10 1/2 in. |
| 1952 | Cy Young, United States | 242 ft 3/4 in. |
| 1956 | Egil Danielsen, Norway | 281 ft 2 1/4 in. |
| 1960 | Viktor Tsibulenko, U.S.S.R. | 277 ft 8 3/8 in. |
| 1964 | Pauli Nevala, Finland | 271 ft 2 1/4 in. |
| 1968 | Janis Lusis, U.S.S.R. | 295 ft 7 in. |
| 1972 | Klaus Wolfermann, West Germany | 296 ft 10 in. |
| 1976 | Miklos Nemeth, Hungary | (94.58m) 310 ft 4 in. |
| 1980 | Dainis Kula, U.S.S.R. | 299 ft 2 3/8 in. |
| 1984 | Arto Haerkoenen, Finland | 284 ft 8 in. |

## 16-lb Hammer Throw

| 1900 | John Flanagan, United States | 167 ft 4 in. |
| 1904 | John Flanagan, United States | 168 ft 1 in. |
| 1908 | John Flanagan, United States | 170 ft 4 1/4 in. |
| 1912 | Matt McGrath, United States | 179 ft 7 1/8 in. |
| 1920 | Pat Ryan, United States | 173 ft 5 5/8 in. |
| 1924 | Fred Tootell, United States | 174 ft 10 1/4 in. |
| 1928 | Patrick O'Callaghan, Ireland | 168 ft 7 1/2 in. |
| 1932 | Patrick O'Callaghan, Ireland | 176 ft 11 1/8 in. |
| 1936 | Karl Hein, Germany | 185 ft 4 in. |
| 1948 | Imre Nemeth, Hungary | 183 ft 11 1/2 in. |
| 1952 | Jozsef Csermak, Hungary | 197 ft 11 9/16 in. |
| 1956 | Harold Connolly, United States | 207 ft 2 3/4 in. |
| 1960 | Vasily Rudenkov, U.S.S.R. | 220 ft 1 5/8 in. |
| 1964 | Romuald Klim, U.S.S.R. | 228 ft 9 1/2 in. |
| 1968 | Gyula Zsivotzky, Hungary | 240 ft 8 in. |
| 1972 | Anatoly Bondarchuk, U.S.S.R. | 247 ft 8 1/2 in. |
| 1976 | Yuri Sedykh, U.S.S.R. | (77.52m) 254 ft 4 in. |
| 1980 | Yuri Sedykh, U.S.S.R. | (81.80m) 268 ft 4 1/2 in. |
| 1984 | Juha Tiainen, Finland | 256 ft 2 in. |

## Decathlon

| 1912 | Jim Thorpe, United States | — |
| | Hugo Wieslander, Sweden | — |
| 1920 | Helge Lovland, Norway | 6,804.35 pts. |
| 1924 | Harold Osborn, United States | 7,710.775 pts. |
| 1928 | Paavo Yrjola, Finland | 8,053.29 pts. |
| 1932 | James Bausch, United States | 8,462.23 pts. |
| 1936 | Glenn Morris, United States | 7,900 pts.[1] |
| 1948 | Robert B. Mathias, United States | 7,139 pts. |
| 1952 | Robert B. Mathias, United States | 7,887 pts. |
| 1956 | Milton Campbell, United States | 7,937 pts. |
| 1960 | Rafer Johnson, United States | 8,392 pts. |
| 1964 | Willi Holdorf, Germany | 7,887 pts.[1] |
| 1968 | Bill Toomey, United States | 8,193 pts. |
| 1972 | Nikolai Avilov, U.S.S.R. | 8,454 pts. |
| 1976 | Bruce Jenner, United States | 8,618 pts. |
| 1980 | Daley Thompson, Britain | 8,495 pts. |
| 1984 | Daley Thompson, Britain | 8,797 pts. |

1. Point system revised.

# TRACK AND FIELD—WOMEN

## 100-Meter Dash

| 1928 | Elizabeth Robinson, United States | 12.2s |
| 1932 | Stella Walsh, Poland | 11.9s |
| 1936 | Helen Stephens, United States | 11.5s |
| 1948 | Fanny Blankers-Koen, Netherlands | 11.9s |
| 1952 | Marjorie Jackson, Australia | 11.5s |
| 1956 | Betty Cuthbert, Australia | 11.5s |
| 1960 | Wilma Rudolph, United States | 11s |
| 1964 | Wyomia Tyus, United States | 11.4s |
| 1968 | Wyomia Tyus, United States | 11s |
| 1972 | Renate Stecher, East Germany | 11.07s |
| 1976 | Annegret Richter, West Germany | 11.08s |
| 1980 | Lyudmila Kondratyeva, U.S.S.R. | 11.06s |

## 200-Meter Dash

| 1948 | Fanny Blankers-Koen, Netherlands | 24.4s |
| 1952 | Marjorie Jackson, Australia | 23.7s |
| 1956 | Betty Cuthbert, Australia | 23.4s |
| 1960 | Wilma Rudolph, United States | 24s |
| 1964 | Edith McGuire, United States | 23s |
| 1968 | Irena Szewinska, Poland | 22.5s |
| 1972 | Renate Stecher, East Germany | 22.4s |
| 1976 | Baerbel Eckert, East Germany | 22.37s |
| 1980 | Barbara Wockel, East Germany | 22.03s |
| 1984 | Valerie Brisco-Hooks, United States | 21.81s |

## 400-Meter Dash

| 1964 | Betty Cuthbert, Australia | 52s |
| 1968 | Colette Besson, France | 52s |
| 1972 | Monika Zehrt, East Germany | 51.08s |
| 1976 | Irena Szewinska, Poland | 49.29s |
| 1980 | Marita Koch, East Germany | 48.88s |
| 1984 | Valerie Brisco-Hooks, United States | 48.83s |

## 800-Meter Run

| 1928 | Lina Radke, Germany | 2m16.8s |
| 1960 | Ljudmila Shevcova, U.S.S.R. | 2m4.3s |
| 1964 | Ann Packer, Great Britain | 2m1.1s |
| 1968 | Madeline Manning, United States | 2m0.9s |
| 1972 | Hildegard Falck, West Germany | 1m58.6s |
| 1976 | Tatiana Kazankina, U.S.S.R. | 1m54.94s |
| 1980 | Nadezhda Olizarenko, U.S.S.R. | 1m53.5s |
| 1984 | Doina Melinte, Romania | 1m57.60s |

## 1,500-Meter Run

| 1972 | Ludmila Bragina, U.S.S.R. | 4m01.4s |
| 1976 | Tatiana Kazankina, U.S.S.R. | 4m05.48s |

## 3,000-Meter Run

| 1984 | Maricica Puica, Romania | 8m35.96s |

## 80-Meter Hurdles

| 1932 | Mildred Didrikson, United States | 11.7s |
| 1936 | Trebisonda Valla, Italy | 11.7s |
| 1948 | Fanny Blankers-Koen, Netherlands | 11.2s |
| 1952 | Shirley S. de la Hunty, Australia | 10.9s |
| 1956 | Shirley S. de la Hunty, Australia | 10.7s |
| 1960 | Irina Press, U.S.S.R. | 10.8s |
| 1964 | Karin Balzer, Germany | 10.5s[1] |
| 1968 | Maureen Caird, Australia | 10.3s |

1. Wind assisted.

## 100-Meter Hurdles

| 1972 | Annelie Ehrhardt, East Germany | 12.59s |
| 1976 | Johanna Schaller, East Germany | 12.77s |
| 1980 | Vera Komisova, U.S.S.R. | 12.56s |
| 1984 | Benita Fitzgerald-Brown, United States | 12.84s |

## 400-Meter Hurdle

| 1984 | Nawai El Moutawakel, Morocco | 54.61s |

## 400-Meter Relay

| 1928 | Canada | 48.4s |
|------|--------|-------|
| 1932 | United States | 47s |
| 1936 | United States | 46.9s |
| 1948 | Netherlands | 47.5s |
| 1952 | United States | 45.9s |
| 1956 | Australia | 44.5s |
| 1960 | United States | 44.5s |
| 1964 | Poland | 43.6s |
| 1968 | United States | 42.8s |
| 1972 | West Germany | 42.81s |
| 1976 | East Germany | 42.55s |
| 1980 | East Germany | 41.60s |
| 1984 | United States | 41.65s |

## 1,600-Meter Relay

| 1972 | East Germany | 3m23s |
|------|--------------|-------|
| 1976 | East Germany | 3m19.23s |
| 1980 | U.S.S.R. | 3m20.2s |
| 1984 | United States | 3m18.29s |

## Marathon

| 1984 | Joan Benoit, United States | 2 hr 24 m 52s |
|------|----------------------------|---------------|

## Running High Jump

| 1928 | Ethel Catherwood, Canada | 5 ft 3 in. |
|------|--------------------------|------------|
| 1932 | Jean Shiley, United States | 5 ft 5 1/4 in. |
| 1936 | Ibolya Csak, Hungary | 5 ft 3 in. |
| 1948 | Alice Coachman, United States | 5 ft 6 1/8 in. |
| 1952 | Ester Brand, South Africa | 5 ft 5 3/4 in. |
| 1956 | Mildred McDaniel, United States | 5 ft 9 1/4 in. |
| 1960 | Iolanda Balas, Romania | 6 ft 3/4 in. |
| 1964 | Iolanda Balas, U.S.S.R. | 6 ft 2 3/4 in. |
| 1968 | Miloslava Rezkova, Czechoslovakia | 5 ft 11 3/4 in. |
| 1972 | Ulrike Meyfarth, West Germany | 6 ft 3 5/8 in. |
| 1976 | Rosemarie Ackerman, E. Germany | (1.93m) 6 ft 4 in. |
| 1980 | Sara Simeoni, Italy | 6 ft 5 1/2 in. |
| 1984 | Ulrike Meyfarth, West Germany | 6 ft 7 1/2 in. |

## Long Jump

| 1948 | Olga Gyarmati, Hungary | 18 ft 8 1/4 in. |
|------|------------------------|-----------------|
| 1952 | Yvette Williams, New Zealand | 20 ft 5 3/4 in. |
| 1956 | Elzbieta Krzesinska, Poland | 20 ft 9 3/4 in. |
| 1960 | Vera Krepkina, U.S.S.R. | 20 ft 10 3/4 in. |
| 1964 | Mary Rand, Great Britain | 22 ft 2 in. |
| 1968 | Viorica Ciscopoleanu, Romania | 22 ft 4 1/2 in. |
| 1972 | Heidemarie Rosendahl, West Germany | 22 ft 3 in. |
| 1976 | Angela Voigt, East Germany | (6.72m) 22 ft 1/2 in. |
| 1980 | Tatiana Kolpakova, U.S.S.R. | 23 ft 2 in. |
| 1984 | Anisoara Stanciu, Romania | 22 ft 10 in. |

## Shot-Put

| 1948 | Micheline Ostermeyer, France | 45 ft 1 1/2 in. |
|------|------------------------------|-----------------|
| 1952 | Galina Zybina, U.S.S.R. | 50 ft 1 1/2 in. |
| 1956 | Tamara Tishkyevich, U.S.S.R. | 54 ft 5 in. |
| 1960 | Tamara Press, U.S.S.R. | 56 ft 9 7/8 in. |
| 1964 | Tamara Press, U.S.S.R. | 59 ft 6 in. |
| 1968 | Margitta Gummel, East Germany | 64 ft 4 in. |
| 1972 | Nadezhda Chizhova, U.S.S.R. | 69 ft |
| 1976 | Ivanka Christova, Bulgaria | (21.16m) 69 ft 5 in. |
| 1980 | Ilona Sluplanek, East Germany | 73 ft 6 in. |
| 1984 | Claudia Losch, West Germany | 67 ft 2 1/4 in. |

## Discus Throw

| 1928 | Helena Konopacka, Poland | 129 ft 11 7/8 in. |
|------|--------------------------|-------------------|
| 1932 | Lillian Copeland, United States | 133 ft 2 in. |
| 1936 | Gisela Mauermayer, Germany | 156 ft 3 3/16 in. |
| 1948 | Micheline Ostermeyer, France | 137 ft 6 1/2 in. |
| 1952 | Nina Romaschkova, U.S.S.R. | 168 ft 8 7/16 in. |

| 1956 | Olga Fikotova, Czechoslovakia | 176 ft 1 1/2 in. |
|------|-------------------------------|------------------|
| 1960 | Nina Ponomareva, U.S.S.R. | 180 ft 8 1/4 in. |
| 1964 | Tamara Press, U.S.S.R. | 187 ft 10 3/4 in. |
| 1968 | Lia Manoliu, Romania | 191 ft 2 1/2 in. |
| 1972 | Faina Melnik, U.S.S.R. | 218 ft 7 in. |
| 1976 | Evelin Schlaak, East Germany | (69.0m) 226 ft 4 in. |
| 1980 | Evelin Jahl, East Germany | 229 ft 6 1/2 in. |
| 1984 | Ria Stalman, Netherlands | 214 ft 5 in. |

## Javelin Throw

| 1932 | Mildred Didrikson, United States | 143 ft 4 in. |
|------|----------------------------------|--------------|
| 1936 | Tilly Fleischer, Germany | 148 ft 2 3/4 in. |
| 1948 | Herma Bauma, Austria | 149 ft 6 in. |
| 1952 | Dana Zatopek, Czechoslovakia | 165 ft 7 in. |
| 1956 | Inessa Janzeme, U.S.S.R. | 176 ft 8 in. |
| 1960 | Elvira Ozolina, U.S.S.R. | 183 ft 8 in. |
| 1964 | Mihaela Penes, Romania | 198 ft 7 1/2 in. |
| 1968 | Angela Nemeth, Hungary | 198 ft 0 in. |
| 1972 | Ruth Fuchs, East Germany | 209 ft 7 in. |
| 1976 | Ruth Fuchs, East Germany | (65.94m) 216 ft 4 in. |
| 1980 | Maria Colon, Cuba | 224 ft 5 in. |
| 1984 | Tessa Sanderson, Britain | 228 ft 2 in. |

## Pentathlon

| 1964 | Irina Press, U.S.S.R. | 5,246 pts. |
|------|-----------------------|------------|
| 1968 | Ingrid Becker, West Germany | 5,098 pts. |
| 1972 | Mary Peters, Britain | 4,801 pts. |
| 1976 | Siegrun Siegl, East Germany | 4,745 pts. |
| 1980 | Nadyezhda Tkachenko, U.S.S.R. | 5,083 pts. |
| 1984 | Daniele Masala, Italy | 5,469 pts. |

# SWIMMING—MEN

## 100 Meters Freestyle

| 1896 | Alfred Hajos, Hungary | 1m22.2s |
|------|-----------------------|---------|
| 1904 | Zoltan de Halmay, Hungary | 1m2.8s[1] |
| 1906 | Charles Daniels, United States | 1m13s |
| 1908 | Charles Daniels, United States | 1m5.6s |
| 1912 | Duke P. Kahanamoku, United States | 1m3.4s |
| 1920 | Duke P. Kahanamoku, United States | 1m1.4s |
| 1924 | John Weissmuller, United States | 59s |
| 1928 | John Weissmuller, United States | 58.6s |
| 1932 | Yasuji Miyazaki, Japan | 58.2s |
| 1936 | Ferenc Csik, Hungary | 57.6s |
| 1948 | Walter Ris, United States | 57.3s |
| 1952 | Clarke Scholes, United States | 57.4s |
| 1956 | Jon Henricks, Australia | 55.4s |
| 1960 | John Devitt, Australia | 55.2s |
| 1964 | Don Schollander, United States | 53.4s |
| 1968 | Michael Wenden, Australia | 52.2s |
| 1972 | Mark Spitz, United States | 51.22s |
| 1976 | Jim Montgomery, United States | 49.99s |
| 1980 | Jorg Woithe, East Germany | 50.40s |
| 1984 | Rowdy Gaines, United States | 49.80s |

1. 100 yards.

## 200-Meter Freestyle

| 1900 | Frederick Lane, Australia | 2m25.2s |
|------|---------------------------|---------|
| 1904 | Charles Daniels, United States | 2m44.2s[1] |
| 1968 | Michael Wenden, Australia | 1m55.2s |
| 1972 | Mark Spitz, United States | 1m52.78s |
| 1976 | Bruce Furniss, United States | 1m50.29s |
| 1980 | Sergei Kopliakov, U.S.S.R. | 1m49.81s |
| 1984 | Michael Gross, West Germany | 1m47.44s |

1. 220 yards

## 400-Meter Freestyle

| 1896 | Paul Neumann, Austria | 8m12.6s[1] |
|------|-----------------------|-----------|
| 1904 | Charles Daniels, United States | 6m16.2s[2] |
| 1906 | Otto Sheff, Austria | 6m23.8s |
| 1908 | Henry Taylor, Great Britain | 5m36.8s |

| | | |
|---|---|---|
| 1912 | George Hodgson, Canada | 5m24.4s |
| 1920 | Norman Ross, United States | 5m26.8s |
| 1926 | Jonn Weissmuller, United States | 5m4.2s |
| 1928 | Albert Zorilla, Argentina | 5m1.6s |
| 1932 | Clarence Crabbe, United States | 4m48.4s |
| 1936 | Jack Medica, United States | 4m44.5s |
| 1948 | William Smith, United States | 4m41s |
| 1952 | Jean Boiteux, France | 4m30.7s |
| 1956 | Murray Rose, Australia | 4m27.3s |
| 1960 | Murray Rose, Australia | 4m18.3s |
| 1964 | Don Schollander, United States | 4m12.2s |
| 1968 | Mike Burton, United States | 4m9s |
| 1972 | Bradford Cooper, Australia | 4m00.27s[3] |
| 1976 | Brian Goodell, United States | 3m51.93s |
| 1980 | Vladimir Salnikov, U.S.S.R. | 3m51.31s |
| 1984 | George DiCarlo, United States | 3m51.23s |

1. 500 meters. 2. 440 yards. 3. Rick DeMont, United States, won but was disqualified following day for medical reasons.

## 1,500 Meter Freestyle

| | | |
|---|---|---|
| 1904 | Emil Rausch, Germany | 27m18.2s[1] |
| 1906 | Henry Taylor, Great Britain | 28m28s[2] |
| 1908 | Henry Taylor, Great Britain | 22m48.4s |
| 1912 | George Hodgson, Canada | 22m |
| 1920 | Norman Ross, United States | 22m23.2s |
| 1924 | Andrew Charlton, Australia | 20m6.6s |
| 1928 | Arne Borg, Sweden | 19m51.8s |
| 1932 | Kusuo Kitamura, Japan | 19m12.4s |
| 1936 | Noboru Terada, Japan | 19m13.7s |
| 1948 | James McLane, United States | 19m18.5s |
| 1952 | Ford Konno, United States | 18m30s |
| 1956 | Murray Rose, Australia | 17m58.9s |
| 1960 | Jon Konrads, Australia | 17m19.6s |
| 1964 | Robert Windle, Australia | 17m1.7s |
| 1968 | Michael Burton, United States | 16m38.9s |
| 1972 | Michael Burton, United States | 15m52.58s |
| 1976 | Brian Goodell, United States | 15m02.4s |
| 1980 | Vladimir Salnikov, U.S.S.R. | 14m58.27s |
| 1984 | Michael O'Brien, United States | 15m05.2s |

1. One mile. 2. 1,600 meters

## 100-Meter Backstroke

| | | |
|---|---|---|
| 1904 | Walter Brack, Germany | 1m16.8s[1] |
| 1908 | Arno Bieberstein, Germany | 1m24.6s |
| 1912 | Harry Hebner, United States | 1m21.2s |
| 1920 | Warren Kealoha, United States | 1m15.2s |
| 1924 | Warren Kealoha, United States | 1m13.2s |
| 1928 | George Kojac, United States | 1m8.2s |
| 1932 | Masaji Kiyokawa, Japan | 1m8.6s |
| 1936 | Adolph Kiefer, United States | 1m5.9s |
| 1948 | Allen Stack, United States | 1m6.4s |
| 1952 | Yoshinobu Oyakawa, United States | 1m5.4s |
| 1956 | David Thiele, Australia | 1m2.2s |
| 1960 | David Thiele, Australia | 1m1.9s |
| 1968 | Roland Matthes, East Germany | 58.7s |
| 1972 | Roland Matthes, East Germany | 56.58s |
| 1976 | John Naber, United States | 55.49s |
| 1980 | Bengt Baron, Sweden | 56.53s |
| 1984 | Rick Carey, United States | 55.79s |

1. 100 yards

## 200-Meter Backstroke

| | | |
|---|---|---|
| 1900 | Ernst Hoppenberg, Germany | 2m47s |
| 1964 | Jed Graef, United States | 2m10.3s |
| 1968 | Roland Matthes, East Germany | 2m9.6s |
| 1972 | Roland Matthes, East Germany | 2m2.82s |
| 1976 | John Naber, United States | 1m59.19s |
| 1980 | Sandor Wladar, Hungary | 2:01.93s |
| 1984 | Rick Carey, United States | 2m00.23s |

## 100-Meter Breaststroke

| | | |
|---|---|---|
| 1968 | Donald McKenzie, United States | 1m7.7s |

| | | |
|---|---|---|
| 1972 | Nobutaka Taguchi, Japan | 1m4.94s |
| 1976 | John Hencken, United States | 1m03.11s |
| 1980 | Duncan Goodhew, Britain | 1m03.34s |
| 1984 | Steve Lindqvist, United States | 1m01.65s |

## 200-Meter Breaststroke

| | | |
|---|---|---|
| 1908 | Frederick Holman, Great Britain | 3m9.2s |
| 1912 | Walter Bathe, Germany | 3m1.8s |
| 1920 | Haken Malmroth, Sweden | 3m4.4s |
| 1924 | Robert Skelton, United States | 2m56.6s |
| 1928 | Yoshiyuki Tsuruta, Japan | 2m48.8s |
| 1932 | Yoshiyuki Tsuruta, Japan | 2m45.4s |
| 1936 | Tetsuo Hamuro, Japan | 2m41.5s |
| 1948 | Joseph Verdeur, United States | 2m39.3s |
| 1952 | John Davies, Australia | 2m34.4s |
| 1956 | Masaru Furukawa, Japan | 2m34.7s |
| 1960 | Bill Mulliken, United States | 2m37.4s |
| 1964 | Ian O'Brien, Australia | 2m27.8s |
| 1968 | Felipe Munoz, Mexico | 2m28.7s |
| 1972 | John Hencken, United States | 2m21.55s |
| 1976 | David Willkie, Britain | 2m15.11s |
| 1980 | Robertas Zulpa, U.S.S.R. | 2m15.85s |
| 1984 | Victor Davis, Canada | 2m13.34s |

## 100-Meter Butterfly

| | | |
|---|---|---|
| 1968 | Douglas Russell, United States | 55.9s |
| 1972 | Mark Spitz, United States | 54.27s |
| 1976 | Matt Vogel, United States | 54.35s |
| 1980 | Par Arvidsson, Sweden | 54.92s |
| 1984 | Michael Gross, West Germany | 53.08s |

## 200-Meter Butterfly

| | | |
|---|---|---|
| 1956 | Bill Yorzyk, United States | 2m19.3s |
| 1960 | Mike Troy, United States | 2m12.8s |
| 1964 | Kevin Berry, Australia | 2m6.6s |
| 1968 | Carl Robie, United States | 2m8.7s |
| 1972 | Mark Spitz, United States | 2m00.7s |
| 1976 | Mike Bruner, United States | 1m59.23s |
| 1980 | Sergei Fesenko, U.S.S.R. | 1m59.76s |
| 1984 | Jon Sieben, Australia | 1m57.0s |

## 200-Meter Individual Medley

| | | |
|---|---|---|
| 1968 | Charles Hickcox, United States | 2m12s |
| 1972 | Gunnar Larsson, Sweden | 2m7.17s |

## 400-Meter Individual Medley

| | | |
|---|---|---|
| 1964 | Dick Roth, United States | 4m45.4s |
| 1968 | Charles Hickcox, United States | 4m48.4s |
| 1972 | Gunnar Larsson, Sweden | 4m31.98s |
| 1976 | Rod Strachan, United States | 4m23.68s |
| 1980 | Aleksandr Sidorenko, U.S.S.R. | 4m22.8s |
| 1984 | Alex Baumann, Canada | 4m17.41s |

## 400-Meter Freestyle Relay

| | | |
|---|---|---|
| 1964 | United States | 3m32.2s |
| 1968 | United States | 3m31.7s |
| 1972 | United States | 3m26.42s |

## 800-Meter Freestyle Relay

| | | |
|---|---|---|
| 1908 | Great Britain | 10m55.6s |
| 1912 | Australia | 10m11.2s |
| 1920 | United States | 10m4.4s |
| 1924 | United States | 9m53.4s |
| 1928 | United States | 9m36.2s |
| 1932 | Japan | 8m58.4s |
| 1936 | Japan | 8m51.5s |
| 1948 | United States | 8m46s |
| 1952 | United States | 8m31.1s |
| 1956 | Australia | 8m23.6s |
| 1960 | United States | 8m10.2s |
| 1964 | United States | 7m52.1s |

| 1968 | United States | 7m52.3s |
|---|---|---|
| 1972 | United States | 7m35.78s |
| 1976 | United States | 7m23.22s |
| 1980 | U.S.S.R. | 7m23.50s |
| 1984 | United States | 7m16.59s |

## 400-Meter Medley Relay

| 1960 | United States | 4m5.4s |
|---|---|---|
| 1964 | United States | 3m58.4s |
| 1968 | United States | 3m54.9s |
| 1972 | United States | 3m48.16s |
| 1976 | United States | 3m42.22s |
| 1980 | Australia | 3m45.70s |
| 1984 | United States | 3m39.30s |

## Springboard Dive

| | | Points |
|---|---|---|
| 1908 | Albert Zuerner, Germany | 85.5 |
| 1912 | Paul Guenther, Germany | 79.23 |
| 1920 | Louis Kuehn, United States | 675 |
| 1924 | Albert White, United States | 696.4 |
| 1928 | Pete Desjardins, United States | 185.04 |
| 1932 | Michael Galitzen, United States | 161.38 |
| 1936 | Richard Degener, United States | 163.57 |
| 1948 | Bruce Harlan, United States | 163.64 |
| 1952 | David Browning, United States | 205.59 |
| 1956 | Robert Clotworthy, United States | 159.56 |
| 1960 | Gary Tobian, United States | 170.00 |
| 1964 | Ken Sitzberger, United States | 159.90 |
| 1968 | Bernard Wrightson, United States | 170.15 |
| 1972 | Vladimir Vasin, U.S.S.R. | 594.09 |
| 1976 | Phil Boggs, United States | 619.05 |
| 1980 | Alexsandr Portnov, U.S.S.R. | 905.02 |
| 1984 | Greg Louganis, United States | 754.41 |

## Platform Dive

| | | Points |
|---|---|---|
| 1904 | G. E. Sheldon, United States | 12.75 |
| 1906 | Gottlob Walz, Germany | 156 |
| 1908 | Hjalmar Johansson, Sweden | 83.75 |
| 1912 | Erik Adlerz, Sweden | 73.94 |
| 1920 | Clarence Pinkston, United States | 100.67 |
| 1924 | Albert White, United States | 487.3 |
| 1928 | Pete Desjardins, United States | 98.74 |
| 1932 | Harold Smith, United States | 124.80 |
| 1936 | Marshall Wayne, United States | 113.58 |
| 1948 | Samuel Lee, United States | 130.05 |
| 1952 | Samuel Lee, United States | 156.28 |
| 1956 | Joaquin Capilla, Mexico | 152.44 |
| 1960 | Bob Webster, United States | 165.56 |
| 1964 | Bob Webster, United States | 148.58 |
| 1968 | Klaus Dibiasi, Italy | 164.18 |
| 1972 | Klaus Dibiasi, Italy | 504.12 |
| 1976 | Klaus Dibiasi, Italy | 600.51 |
| 1980 | Falk Hoffman, E. Germany | 835.65 |
| 1984 | Greg Louganis, United States | 710.91 |

# SWIMMING—WOMEN

## 100-Meter Freestyle

| 1912 | Fanny Durack, Australia | 1m22.2s |
|---|---|---|
| 1920 | Ethelda Bleibtrey, United States | 1m13.6s |
| 1924 | Ethel Lackie, United States | 1m12.4s |
| 1928 | Albina Osipowich, United States | 1m11s |
| 1932 | Helene Madison, United States | 1m6.8s |
| 1936 | Hendrika Mastenbroek, Netherlands | 1m5.9s |
| 1948 | Greta Andersen, Denmark | 1m6.3s |
| 1952 | Katalin Szoke, Hungary | 1m6.8s |
| 1956 | Dawn Fraser, Australia | 1m2s |
| 1960 | Dawn Fraser, Australia | 1m1.2s |
| 1964 | Dawn Fraser, Australia | 59.5s |

| 1968 | Marge Jan Henne, United States | 1m |
|---|---|---|
| 1972 | Sandra Neilson, United States | 58.59s |
| 1976 | Kornelia Ender, East Germany | 55.65s |
| 1980 | Barbara Krause, East Germany | 54.79s |
| 1984 | Carrie Steinseifer, United States | 55.92s |

## 200-Meter Freestyle

| 1968 | Debbie Meyer, United States | 2m10.5s |
|---|---|---|
| 1972 | Shane Gould, Australia | 2m3.56s |
| 1976 | Kornelia Ender, East Germany | 1m59.26s |
| 1980 | Barbara Krause, East Germany | 1m58.33s |
| 1984 | Mary Wayle, United States | 1m59.23s |

## 400-Meter Freestyle

| 1920 | Ethelda Bleibtrey, United States | 4m34s[1] |
|---|---|---|
| 1924 | Martha Norelius, United States | 6m2.2s |
| 1928 | Martha Norelius, United States | 5m42.8s |
| 1932 | Helene Madison, United States | 5m28.5s |
| 1936 | Hendrika Mastenbroek, Netherlands | 5m26.4s |
| 1948 | Ann Curtis, United States | 5m17.8s |
| 1952 | Valerie Gyenge, Hungary | 5m12.1s |
| 1956 | Lorraine Crapp, Australia | 4m54.6s |
| 1960 | Chris von Saltza, United States | 4m50.6s |
| 1964 | Ginny Duenkel, United States | 4m43.3s |
| 1968 | Debbie Meyer, United States | 4m31.8s |
| 1972 | Shane Gould, Australia | 4m19.04s |
| 1976 | Petra Thumer, East Germany | 4m09.89s |
| 1980 | Ines Diers, East Germany | 4m08.76s |
| 1984 | Tiffany Cohen, United States | 4m07.10s |

1. 300 meters.

## 800-Meter Freestyle

| 1968 | Debbie Meyer, United States | 9m24s |
|---|---|---|
| 1972 | Keena Rothhammer, United States | 8m53.68s |
| 1976 | Petra Thumer, East Germany | 8m37.14s |
| 1980 | Michelle Ford, Australia | 8m28.90s |
| 1984 | Tiffany Cohen, United States | 8m24.95s |

## 100-Meter Backstroke

| 1924 | Sybil Bauer, United States | 1m23.2s |
|---|---|---|
| 1928 | Marie Braun, Netherlands | 1m22s |
| 1932 | Eleanor Holm, United States | 1m19.4s |
| 1936 | Dina Senff, Netherlands | 1m18.9s |
| 1948 | Karen Harup, Denmark | 1m14.4s |
| 1952 | Joan Harrison, South Africa | 1m14.3s |
| 1956 | Judy Grinham, Great Britain | 1m12.9s |
| 1960 | Lynn Burke, United States | 1m9.3s |
| 1964 | Cathy Ferguson, United States | 1m7.7s |
| 1968 | Kaye Hall, United States | 1m6.2s |
| 1972 | Melissa Belote, United States | 1m5.78s |
| 1976 | Ulrike Richter, East Germany | 1m01.83s |
| 1980 | Rica Reinisch, East Germany | 1m00.86s |
| 1984 | Theresa Andrews, United States | 1m02.55s |

## 200-Meter Backstroke

| 1968 | Pokey Watson, United States | 2m24.8s |
|---|---|---|
| 1972 | Melissa Belote, United States | 2m19.19s |
| 1976 | Ulrike Richter, East Germany | 2m13.43s |
| 1980 | Rica Reinisch, East Germany | 2m11.77s |
| 1984 | Jolanda DeRover, Netherlands | 2m12.38s |

## 100-Meter Breaststroke

| 1968 | Djurdjica Bjedov, Yugoslavia | 1m15.8s |
|---|---|---|
| 1972 | Catherine Carr, United States | 1m13.58s |
| 1976 | Hannelore Anke, East Germany | 1m11.16s |
| 1980 | Ute Geweniger, East Germany | 1m10.22s |
| 1984 | Petra Van Staveren, Netherlands | 1m09.88s |

## 200-Meter Breaststroke

| 1924 | Lucy Morton, Great Britain | 3m33.2s |
|---|---|---|
| 1928 | Hilde Schrader, Germany | 3m12.6s |
| 1932 | Clare Dennis, Australia | 3m6.3s |
| 1936 | Hideko Maehata, Japan | 3m6.6s |

| | | |
|---|---|---|
| 1948 | Nel van Vliet, Netherlands | 2m57.2s |
| 1952 | Eva Szekely, Hungary | 2m51.7s |
| 1956 | Ursala Happe, Germany | 2m53.1s |
| 1960 | Anita Lonsbrough, Great Britain | 2m49.5s |
| 1964 | Galina Prozumenschikova, U.S.S.R. | 2m46.4s |
| 1968 | Sharon Wichman, United States | 2m44.4s |
| 1972 | Beverly Whitfield, Australia | 2m41.71s |
| 1976 | Marina Koshevaia, U.S.S.R. | 2m33.35s |
| 1980 | Lina Kachushite, U.S.S.R. | 2m29.54s |
| 1984 | Anne Ottenbrite, Canada | 2m30.38s |

## 100-Meter Butterfly

| | | |
|---|---|---|
| 1956 | Shelley Mann, United States | 1m11s |
| 1960 | Carolyn Schuler, United States | 1m9.5s |
| 1964 | Sharon Stouder, United States | 1m4.7s |
| 1968 | Lynn McClements, Australia | 1m5.5s |
| 1972 | Mayumi Aoki, Japan | 1m3.34s |
| 1976 | Kornelia Ender, East Germany | 1m00.13s |
| 1980 | Caren Metschuck, East Germany | 1m00.42s |
| 1984 | Mary Meagher, United States | 59.26s |

## 200-Meter Butterfly

| | | |
|---|---|---|
| 1968 | Ada Kok, Netherlands | 2m24.7s |
| 1972 | Karen Moe, United States | 2m15.57s |
| 1976 | Andrea Pollack, East Germany | 2m11.41s |
| 1980 | Ines Geissler, East Germany | 2m10.44s |
| 1984 | Mary Meagher, United States | 2m06.90s |

## 200-Meter Individual Medley

| | | |
|---|---|---|
| 1968 | Claudia Kolb, United States | 2m24.7s |
| 1972 | Shane Gould, Australia | 2m23.07s |
| 1984 | Tracy Caulkins, United States | 1m12.64s |

## 400-Meter Individual Medley

| | | |
|---|---|---|
| 1964 | Donna de Varona, United States | 5m18.7s |
| 1968 | Claudia Kolb, United States | 5m8.5s |
| 1972 | Gail Neall, Australia | 5m2.97s |
| 1976 | Ulrike Tauber, East Germany | 4m42.77s |
| 1980 | Petra Schneider, East Germany | 4m36.29s |
| 1984 | Tracy Caulkins, United States | 4m39.21s |

## 400-Meter Freestyle Relay

| | | |
|---|---|---|
| 1912 | Great Britain | 5m52.8s |
| 1920 | United States | 5m11.6s |
| 1924 | United States | 4m58.8s |
| 1928 | United States | 4m47.6s |
| 1932 | United States | 4m38s |
| 1936 | Netherlands | 4m36s |
| 1948 | United States | 4m29.2s |
| 1952 | Hungary | 4m24.4s |
| 1956 | Australia | 4m17.1s |
| 1960 | United States | 4m8.9s |
| 1964 | United States | 4m3.8s |
| 1968 | United States | 4m2.5s |
| 1972 | United States | 3m55.19s |
| 1976 | United States | 3m44.82s |
| 1980 | East Germany | 3m42.71s |
| 1984 | United States | 3m44.43s |

## 400-Meter Medley Relay

| | | |
|---|---|---|
| 1960 | United States | 4m41.1s |
| 1964 | United States | 4m33.9s |
| 1968 | United States | 4m28.3s |
| 1972 | United States | 4m20.75s |
| 1976 | East Germany | 4m07.95s |
| 1980 | East Germany | 4m06.67s |
| 1984 | United States | 4m08.34s |

## Springboard Dive

| | | Points |
|---|---|---|
| 1920 | Aileen Riggin, United States | 539.90 |
| 1924 | Elizabeth Becker, United States | 474.5 |

## DISTRIBUTION OF MEDALS
## 1984 SUMMER GAMES

| Country | Gold | Silver | Bronze | Total |
|---|---|---|---|---|
| United States | 83 | 61 | 30 | 174 |
| West Germany | 17 | 19 | 23 | 59 |
| Rumania | 20 | 16 | 17 | 53 |
| Canada | 10 | 18 | 16 | 44 |
| Britain | 5 | 10 | 22 | 37 |
| China | 15 | 8 | 9 | 32 |
| Italy | 14 | 6 | 12 | 32 |
| Japan | 10 | 8 | 14 | 32 |
| France | 5 | 7 | 15 | 27 |
| Australia | 4 | 8 | 12 | 24 |
| South Korea | 6 | 6 | 7 | 19 |
| Sweden | 2 | 11 | 6 | 19 |
| Yugoslavia | 7 | 4 | 7 | 18 |
| Netherlands | 5 | 2 | 6 | 13 |
| Finland | 4 | 3 | 6 | 13 |
| New Zealand | 8 | 1 | 2 | 11 |
| Brazil | 1 | 5 | 2 | 8 |
| Switzerland | 0 | 4 | 4 | 8 |
| Mexico | 2 | 3 | 1 | 6 |
| Denmark | 0 | 3 | 3 | 6 |
| Spain | 1 | 2 | 2 | 5 |
| Belgium | 1 | 1 | 2 | 4 |
| Austria | 1 | 1 | 1 | 3 |
| Portugal | 1 | 0 | 2 | 3 |
| Jamaica | 0 | 1 | 2 | 3 |
| Norway | 0 | 1 | 2 | 3 |
| Turkey | 0 | 0 | 3 | 3 |
| Venezuela | 0 | 0 | 3 | 3 |
| Morocco | 2 | 0 | 0 | 2 |
| Kenya | 1 | 0 | 1 | 2 |
| Greece | 0 | 1 | 1 | 2 |
| Nigeria | 0 | 1 | 1 | 2 |
| Puerto Rico | 0 | 1 | 1 | 2 |
| Algeria | 0 | 0 | 2 | 2 |
| Pakistan | 1 | 0 | 0 | 1 |
| Colombia | 0 | 1 | 0 | 1 |
| Egypt | 0 | 1 | 0 | 1 |
| Ireland | 0 | 1 | 0 | 1 |
| Ivory Coast | 0 | 1 | 0 | 1 |
| Peru | 0 | 1 | 0 | 1 |
| Syria | 0 | 1 | 0 | 1 |
| Thailand | 0 | 1 | 0 | 1 |
| Cameroon | 0 | 0 | 1 | 1 |
| Dominican Republic | 0 | 0 | 1 | 1 |
| Iceland | 0 | 0 | 1 | 1 |
| Taiwan | 0 | 0 | 1 | 1 |
| Zambia | 0 | 0 | 1 | 1 |

| | | |
|---|---|---|
| 1928 | Helen Meany, United States | 78.62 |
| 1932 | Georgia Coleman, United States | 87.52 |
| 1936 | Marjorie Gestring, United States | 89.27 |
| 1948 | Victoria M. Draves, United States | 108.74 |
| 1952 | Patricia McCormick, United States | 147.30 |
| 1956 | Patricia McCormick, United States | 142.36 |
| 1960 | Ingrid Kramer, Germany | 155.81 |
| 1964 | Ingrid Kramer Engel, Germany | 145.00 |
| 1968 | Sue Gossick, United States | 150.77 |
| 1972 | Micki King, United States | 450.03 |
| 1976 | Jennifer Chandler, United States | 506.19 |
| 1980 | Irina Kalinina, U.S.S.R. | 725.91 |
| 1984 | Sylvie Bernier, Canada | 530.70 |

## Platform Dive

| | | Points |
|---|---|---|
| 1912 | Greta Johansson, Sweden | 39.9 |
| 1920 | Stefani Fryland, Denmark | 34.60 |

| 1924 | Caroline Smith, United States | 166 |
| 1928 | Elizabeth B. Pinkston, United States | 31.60 |
| 1932 | Dorothy Poynton, United States | 40.26 |
| 1936 | Dorothy Poynton Hill, United States | 33.92 |
| 1948 | Victoria M. Draves, United States | 68.87 |
| 1952 | Patricia McCormick, United States | 79.37 |
| 1956 | Patricia McCormick, United States | 84.85 |
| 1960 | Ingrid Kramer, Germany | 91.28 |
| 1964 | Lesley Bush, United States | 99.80 |
| 1968 | Milena Duchkova, Czechoslovakia | 109.59 |
| 1972 | Ulrika Knape, Sweden | 390.00 |
| 1976 | Elena Vaytsekhovskaia, U.S.S.R. | 406.59 |
| 1980 | Martina Jaschke, East Germany | 596.25 |
| 1984 | Zhou Jihong, China | 435.51 |

## BASKETBALL—MEN

| 1904 | United States | 1964 | United States |
| 1936 | United States | 1968 | United States |
| 1948 | United States | 1972 | U.S.S.R. |
| 1952 | United States | 1976 | United States |
| 1956 | United States | 1980 | Yugoslavia |
| 1960 | United States | 1984 | United States |

## BASKETBALL—WOMEN

| 1976 | U.S.S.R. |
| 1980 | U.S.S.R. |
| 1984 | United States |

## BOXING

(U.S. winners only)

(U.S. boycotted Olympics in 1980)

### Flyweight—112 pounds (51 kilograms)

| 1904 | George V. Finnegan | 1952 | Nate Brooks |
| 1920 | Frank De Genaro | 1976 | Leo Randolph |
| 1924 | Fidel La Barba | 1984 | Steve McCrory |

### Bantamweight—119 (54 kg)

| 1904 | O.L. Kirk |

### Featherweight—126 pounds (57 kg)

| 1904 | O.L. Kirk | 1984 | Meldrick Taylor |
| 1924 | Jackie Fields | | |

### Lightweight—132 pounds (60 kg)

| 1904 | H.J. Spanger | 1976 | Howard Davis |
| 1920 | Samuel Mosberg | 1984 | Pernell Whitaker |
| 1968 | Ronnie Harris | | |

### Light Welterweight—140 pounds (63.5 kg)

| 1952 | Charles Adkins | 1976 | Ray Leonard |
| 1972 | Ray Seales | 1984 | Jerry Page |

### Welterweight—148 pounds (67 kg)

| 1904 | Al Young | 1984 | Mark Breland |
| 1932 | Edward Flynn | | |

### Light Middleweight—157 pounds (71 kg)

| 1960 | Wilbert McClure | 1984 | Frank Tate |

### Middleweight—165 pounds (75 kg)

| 1904 | Charles Mayer | 1960 | Eddie Cook |
| 1932 | Carmen Barth | 1976 | Michael Spinks |
| 1952 | Floyd Patterson | | |

### Light Heavyweight—179 pounds (81 kg)

| 1920 | Edward Eagan | 1960 | Cassius Clay |
| 1952 | Norvel Lee | 1976 | Leon Spinks |
| 1956 | James Boyd | | |

### Heavyweight—201 pounds

| 1904 | Sam Berger | 1964 | Joe Frazier |
| 1952 | Edward Sanders | 1968 | George Foreman |
| 1956 | Pete Rademacher | 1984 | Henry Tillman |

### Super Heavyweight (unlimited)

| 1984 | Tyrell Biggs |

# Winter Games

## FIGURE SKATING—MEN

| 1908 | Ulrich Salchow, Sweden |
| 1920 | Gillis Grafstrom, Sweden |
| 1924 | Gillis Grafstrom, Sweden |
| 1928 | Gillis Grafstrom, Sweden |
| 1932 | Karl Schaefer, Austria |
| 1936 | Karl Schaefer, Austria |
| 1948 | Richard Button, United States |
| 1952 | Richard Button, United States |
| 1956 | Hayes Alan Jenkins, United States |
| 1960 | David Jenkins, United States |
| 1964 | Manfred Schnelldorfer, Germany |
| 1968 | Wolfgang Schwartz, Austria |
| 1972 | Ondrej Nepela, Czechoslovakia |
| 1976 | John Curry, Great Britain |
| 1980 | Robin Cousins, Great Britain |
| 1984 | Scott Hamilton, United States |

| 1928 | Sonja Henie, Norway |
| 1932 | Sonja Henie, Norway |
| 1936 | Sonja Henie, Norway |
| 1948 | Barbara Ann Scott, Canada |
| 1952 | Jeannette Altwegg, Great Britain |
| 1956 | Tenley Albright, United States |
| 1960 | Carol Heiss, United States |
| 1964 | Sjoukje Dijkstra, Netherlands |
| 1968 | Peggy Fleming, United States |
| 1972 | Beatrix Schuba, Austria |
| 1976 | Dorothy Hamill, United States |
| 1980 | Anett Poetzsch, East Germany |
| 1984 | Katarina Witt, East Germany |

## SPEED SKATING—MEN

(U.S. winners only)

### 500 Meters

| 1924 | Charles Jewtraw | 44.0 |
| 1932 | John A. Shea | 43.4 |
| 1952 | Kenneth Henry | 43.2 |

## FIGURE SKATING—WOMEN

| 1908 | Madge Syers, Britain |
| 1920 | Magda Julin-Maurey, Sweden |
| 1924 | Herma Szabo-Planck, Austria |

| 1964 | Terrence McDermott | 40.1 |
| 1980 | Eric Heiden | 38.03 |

## 1,000 Meters

| 1976 | Peter Mueller | 1:19.32 |
| 1980 | Eric Heiden | 1:15.18 |

## 1,500 Meters

| 1932 | John A. Shea | 2:57.5 |
| 1980 | Eric Heiden | 1:55.44 |

## 5,000 Meters

| 1932 | Irving Jaffee | 9:40.8 |
| 1980 | Eric Heiden | 7:02.29 |

## 10,000 Meters

| 1932 | Irving Jaffee | 19:13.6 |
| 1980 | Eric Heiden | 14:28.13 |

## SPEED SKATING—WOMEN

### 500 Meters

| 1972 | Anne Henning | 43.33 |
| 1976 | Sheila Young | 42.76 |

### 1,500 Meters

| 1972 | Dianne Holum | 2:20.85 |

## SKIING, ALPINE—MEN

### Downhill

| 1948 | Henri Oreiller, France | 2m55.0s |
| 1952 | Zeno Colo, Italy | 2m30.8s |
| 1956 | Anton Sailer, Austria | 2m52.2s |
| 1960 | Jean Vuarnet, France | 2m06.2s |
| 1964 | Egon Zimmermann, Austria | 2m18.16s |
| 1968 | Jean-Claude Killy, France | 1m59.85s |
| 1972 | Bernhard Russi, Switzerland | 1m51.43s |
| 1976 | Franz Klammer, Austria | 1m45.72s |
| 1980 | Leonhard Stock, Austria | 1m45.50s |
| 1984 | Bill Johnson, United States | 1m45.59s |

### Slalom

| 1948 | Edi Reinalter, Switzerland | 2m10.3s |
| 1952 | Othmar Schneider, Austria | 2m00.0s |
| 1956 | Anton Sailer, Austria | 194.7 pts. |
| 1960 | Ernst Hinterseer, Austria | 2m08.9s |
| 1964 | Josef Stiegler, Austria | 2m10.13 |
| 1968 | Jean-Claude Killy, France | 1m39.73s |
| 1972 | Francisco Fernandez Ochoa, Spain | 1m49.27s |
| 1976 | Piero Gros, Italy | 2m03.29s |
| 1980 | Ingemar Stenmark, Sweden | 1m44.26s |
| 1984 | Phil Mahre, United States | 1m39.41s |

### Giant Slalom

| 1952 | Stein Eriksen, Norway | 2m25.0s |
| 1956 | Anton Sailer, Austria | 3m00.1s |
| 1960 | Roger Staub, Switzerland | 1m48.3s |
| 1964 | François Bonlieu, France | 1m46.71s |
| 1968 | Jean-Claude Killy, France | 3m29.28s |
| 1972 | Gustavo Thoeni, Italy | 3m09.52s |
| 1976 | Heini Hemmi, Switzerland | 3m26.97s |
| 1980 | Ingemar Stenmark, Sweden | 2m40.74s |
| 1984 | Max Julen, Switzerland | 1m20.54s |

## DISTRIBUTION OF MEDALS
## 1984 WINTER GAMES
(Sarajevo, Yugoslavia)

| | Gold | Silver | Bronze | Total |
|---|---|---|---|---|
| Soviet Union | 6 | 10 | 9 | 25 |
| East Germany | 9 | 9 | 6 | 24 |
| Finland | 4 | 3 | 6 | 13 |
| Norway | 3 | 2 | 4 | 9 |
| United States | 4 | 4 | 0 | 8 |
| Sweden | 4 | 2 | 2 | 8 |
| Czechoslovakia | 0 | 2 | 4 | 6 |
| Switzerland | 2 | 2 | 1 | 5 |
| Canada | 2 | 1 | 1 | 4 |
| West Germany | 2 | 1 | 1 | 4 |
| France | 0 | 1 | 2 | 3 |
| Italy | 2 | 0 | 0 | 2 |
| Liechtenstein | 0 | 0 | 2 | 2 |
| Britain | 1 | 0 | 0 | 1 |
| Yugoslavia | 0 | 1 | 0 | 1 |
| Austria | 0 | 0 | 1 | 1 |

## SKIING, ALPINE—WOMEN

### Downhill

| 1948 | Hedi Schlunegger, Switzerland | 2m28.3s |
| 1952 | Trude Jochum-Beiser, Austria | 1m47.1s |
| 1956 | Madeleine Berthod, Switzerland | 1m40.1s |
| 1960 | Heidi Biebl, Germany | 1m37.6s |
| 1964 | Christl Haas, Austria | 1m55.39s |
| 1968 | Olga Pall, Austria | 1m40.87s |
| 1972 | Marie-Therese Nadig, Switzerland | 1m36.68s |
| 1976 | Rosi Mittermeier, West Germany | 1m46.16s |
| 1980 | Annemarie Proell Moser, Austria | 1m37.52s |
| 1984 | Michela Figini, Switzerland | 1m13.36s |

### Slalom

| 1948 | Gretchen Fraser, United States | 1m57.2s |
| 1952 | Andrea Mead Lawrence, United States | 2m10.6s |
| 1956 | Renee Colliard, Switzerland | 112.3 pts. |
| 1960 | Anne Heggtveigt, Canada | 1m49.6s |
| 1964 | Christine Goitschel, France | 1m29.86s |
| 1968 | Marielle Goitschel, France | 1m25.86s |
| 1972 | Barbara Cochran, United States | 1m31.24s |
| 1976 | Rosi Mittermeier, West Germany | 1m30.54s |
| 1980 | Hanni Wenzel, Liechtenstein | 1m25.09s |
| 1984 | Paoletta Magoni, Italy | 1m36.47s |

### Giant Slalom

| 1952 | Andrea M. Lawrence, United States | 2m06.8s |
| 1956 | Ossi Reichert, Germany | 1m56.5s |
| 1960 | Yvonne Ruegg, Switzerland | 1m39.9s |
| 1964 | Marielle Goitschel, France | 1m52.24s |
| 1968 | Nancy Greene, Canada | 1m51.97s |
| 1972 | Marie-Therese Nadig, Switzerland | 1m29.90s |
| 1976 | Kathy Kreiner, Canada | 1m29.13s |
| 1980 | Hanni Wenzel, Liechtenstein | 2m41.66s |
| 1984 | Debbie Armstrong, United States | 2m20.98s |

## ICE HOCKEY

| 1920 | Canada | 1960 | United States |
| 1924 | Canada | 1964 | U.S.S.R. |
| 1928 | Canada | 1968 | U.S.S.R. |
| 1932 | Canada | 1972 | U.S.S.R. |
| 1936 | Great Britain | 1976 | U.S.S.R. |
| 1948 | Canada | 1980 | United States |
| 1952 | Canada | 1984 | U.S.S.R. |
| 1956 | U.S.S.R. | | |

## SKIING, NORDIC, JUMPING

### 90-Meter Hill

| | | Points |
|---|---|---|
| 1924 | Jacob T. Thams, Norway | 227.5 |
| 1928 | Alfred Andersen, Norway | 230.5 |
| 1932 | Birger Ruud, Norway | 228.0 |
| 1936 | Birger Ruud, Norway | 232.0 |
| 1948 | Peter Hugsted, Norway | 228.1 |
| 1952 | A. Bergmann, Norway | 226.0 |
| 1956 | Antti Hyvarinen, Finland | 227.0 |
| 1960 | Helmut Recknagel, Germany | 227.2 |
| 1964 | Toralf Engan, Norway | 230.7 |
| 1968 | Vladimir Beloussov, U.S.S.R. | 231.3 |
| 1972 | Wojciech Fortuna, Poland | 219.9 |
| 1976 | Karl Schnabl, Austria | 234.8 |
| 1980 | Jouko Tormanen, Finland | 271.0 |
| 1984 | Matti Nykaenen, Finland | 231.2 |

### Small Hill (70 meters)

| | | |
|---|---|---|
| 1964 | Veikko Kankkonen, Finland | 229.9 |
| 1968 | Jiri Raska, Czechoslovakia | 216.5 |
| 1972 | Yukio Kasaya, Japan | 244.2 |
| 1976 | Hans-Georg Aschenbach, East Germany | 252.0 |
| 1980 | Anton Innauer, Austria | 266.3 |
| 1984 | Jens Weissflog, East Germany | 215.2 |

## FINAL OVER-ALL 1984 OLYMPIC HOCKEY STANDINGS

### GROUP A

| | W | L | T | Pts | GF | GA |
|---|---|---|---|---|---|---|
| Soviet Union | 7 | 0 | 0 | 14 | 48 | 5 |
| West Germany | 4 | 1 | 0 | 9 | 34 | 21 |
| Sweden | 4 | 2 | 1 | 9 | 33 | 16 |
| Italy | 1 | 4 | 0 | 2 | 15 | 31 |
| Yugoslavia | 1 | 4 | 0 | 2 | 8 | 37 |
| Poland | 1 | 5 | 0 | 2 | 20 | 44 |

### GROUP B

| | | | | | | |
|---|---|---|---|---|---|---|
| Czechoslovakia | 6 | 1 | 0 | 12 | 40 | 9 |
| Canada | 4 | 3 | 0 | 8 | 24 | 16 |
| United States | 2 | 2 | 2 | 6 | 23 | 21 |
| Finland | 2 | 3 | 1 | 5 | 31 | 26 |
| Austria | 1 | 4 | 0 | 2 | 13 | 37 |
| Norway | 0 | 4 | 1 | 1 | 15 | 43 |

**Seventh Place**
United States 7, Poland 4

**Third place**
Sweden 2, Canada 0

**Fifth Place**
West Germany 7, Finland 4

**Championship**
Soviet Union 2, Czechoslovakia 0

**Medal Round**
Czechoslovakia 2, Sweden 0
Soviet Union 4, Canada 0

# Other 1984 Olympic Games Champions

## SUMMER

**Archery**
Men—Darrell Pace, United States
Women—Hyang-Soun Seo, South Korea

**Boxing**
106 lb—Paul Gonzalez, United States
112 lb—Steve McCrory, United States
119 lb—Maurizio Stecca, Italy
126 lb—Meldrick Taylor, United States
132 lb—Pernell Whitaker, United States
139 lb—Jerry Page, United States
148 lb—Mark Breland, United States
157 lb—Frank Tate, United States
165 lb—Joun-Sup Shin, South Korea
179 lb—Anton Josipovic, Yugoslavia
201 lb—Henry Tillman, United States
Over 201—Tyrell Biggs, United States

**Canoeing**
500 m—Larry Cain, Canada
1,000 m—Ulrich Eiche, West Germany
500-m pairs—Yugoslavia (Matija Ljubekt and Mirko Nisovic)
1,000-m pairs—Romania (Ivan Potzaichin and Toma Simionov)
**Kayak—Men**
500 m—Ian Ferguson, New Zealand
1,000 m—Alan Thompson, New Zealand
500-m pairs—New Zealand (Ian Ferguson and Paul MacDonald)
1,000-m pairs—Canada (Hugh Fisher and Alwyn Moris)
1,000-m fours—New Zealand (Grant Bramwell, Ian Ferguson, Paul MacDonald, Alan Thompson)

**Kayak—Women**
500 m—Agneta Andersson, Sweden
500-m pairs—Sweden (Agneta Andersson and Anna Olsson)
500-m fours—Romania (Agafia Constantin, Nastasia Ionescu, Tecia Marinescu, Maria Stefan)

**Cycling—Men**
4,000-m Individual pursuit—Steve Hegg, United States
Individual road race—Alexi Grewal, United States
1,000-m Time trials—Fredy Schmidtke, West Germany
4,000-m Team pursuit—Australia
Sprint—Mark Gorski, United States
Points race—Roger Ilegems, Belgium
100-km road team trials—Italy

**Cycling—Women**
Individual road race—Connie Carpenter, United States

**Equestrian**
Dressage—Dr. Reiner Klimke, West Germany
Dressage team—West Germany
Jumping—Joe Fargia, United States
Jumping, team—United States
Three-day event—Mark Todd, New Zealand
Team three-day event—United States

**Fencing**
Foil—Mauro Numa, Italy
Team foil—Italy
Epee—Philippe Boisse, France
Team epee—West Germany
Sabre—Jean-Francois Lamour, France

Team sabre—Italy
Women's foil—Luan Jujie, China
Women's team foil—West Germany

**Gymnastics—Men**
All-around—Koji Gushiken, Japan
Floor exercises—Li Ning, China
Horizontal bar—Shinji Morisue, Japan
Parallel bars—Bart Conner, United States
Pommel horse—Li Ning, China and Peter Vidmar, United States
Rings—Koji Gushiken, Japan and Li Ning, China
Vault—Lou Yun, China
Team—United States

**Gymnastics—Women**
All-around—Mary Lou Retton, United States
Balance beam—Simona Pauca, Romania, and Ecaterina Szabo, Romania
Floor exercises—Ecaterina Szabo, Romania
Uneven bars—Ma Yanhonjg, China
Vault—Evaterina Szabo, Romania
Team—Romania

**Judo**
Lightweight—Byeong-Keun Ahn, South Korea
Extra lightweight—Shinji Hosokawa, Japan
Half lightweight—Yoshiyuki Matsuoka, Japan
Half middleweight—Frank Wieneke, West Germany
Middleweight—Peter Seisenbacher, Austria
Half heavyweight—Hyoung-Za Ha, South Korea
Heavyweight—Hitoshi Saito, Japan

**Modern Pentathlon**
Individual—Daniele Masala, Italy
Team—Italy

## Rowing—Men

Singles—Pertti Karppinen, Finland
Doubles—United States (Bradley Lewis and Paul Enquist)
Quadruples—West Germany (Albert Hedderich, Raimond Hormann, Dieter Wiedenmann, Michael Dursch)
Pairs—Romania (Petru Iosub, Valer Toma)
Pairs with coxswain—Italy (Carmine Abbaginale, Giuseppe Abbaginale)
Fours—New Zealand (Leslie O'Connell, Conrad Robertson, Shane O'Brien, Keith Trask)
Fours with coxswain—Britain (Martin Cross, Richard Budgett, Andrew Holmes, Steve Redgrave)
Eights—Canada (Pat Turner, Kevin Neufield, Mark Evans, Grant Main, Paul Steele, Mike Evans, Dean Crawford, Blair Horm, Brian McMahon)

## Rowing—Women

Singles—Valeria Racila, Romania
Doubles—Romania
Pairs—Romania
Pairs with coxswain—Romania
Fours with coxswain—Romania
Quadruple sculls—Romania
Eights—United States

## Shooting—Men

Free pistol—Xu Haifeng, China
Rapid-fire pistol—Takeo Kamachi, Japan
Small-bore rifle—Ed Etzel, United States
Small-bore rifle, 3 positions—Malcolm Cooper, Britain
Rifle running game target—Li Yuwei, China
Trap—Luciano Giovanetti, Italy

Skeet—Matthew Dryke, United States
Air rifle—Philippe Heberle, France

## Shooting—Women

Air rifle—Pat Spurgin, United States
Small-bore rifle, 3 positions—Wu Xiaoxuan, China
Sport pistol—Linda Thom, Canada

## Synchronized Swimming

Solo—Tracie Ruiz, United States
Duet—United States (Candy Costie and Tracie Ruiz)

## Weight Lifting

115 lb—Zeng Guoqiang, China
123 lb—Wu Shude, China
132 lb—Chen Weigang, China
149 lb—Yao Jingyuang, China
165 lb—Karl Heinz Radschinsky, West Germany
182 lb—Petre Becheru, Romania
198 lb—Nicu Vlad, Romania
220 lb—Rolf Miller, West Germany
242 lb—Norberto Oberburger, Italy
Over 242—Dinko Lukim, Australia

## Wrestling—Freestyle

106 lb—Bobby Weaver, United States
114.5 lb—Saban Trstena, Yugoslavia
125.5 lb—Hideaki Tomiyama, Japan
136.5 lb—Randy Lewis, United States
149.5 lb—In-Tak You, South Korea
163 lb—David Schultz, United States
181 lb—Mark Schultz, United States
198.5 lb—Ed Banach, United States
220 lb—Lou Banach, United States
Over 220—Bruce Baumgartner, United States

## Wrestling—Greco-Roman

106 lb—Vincenzo Maenza, Italy
114.5 lb—Atsuji Miyahara, Japan
125.5 lb—Pasquale Passarelli, West Germany
136.5 lb—Weon Kee Kim, South Korea
150 lb—Viado Lisjak, Yugoslavia
163 lb—Jouko Salomaki, Finland
181 lb—Ion Draica, Romania
198.5 lb—Steven Fraser, United States
220 lb—Vasile Andrei, Romania
Over 220—Jeff Blatnick, United States

## Yachting

Windglider—Stephan Van Den Berg, Netherlands
Finn—Russell Coutts, New Zealand
Flying Dutchmen—United States (Jonathan McKee, Bill Buchan)
470 Class—Spain
Soling—United States (Robert Haines Jr., Ed Trevelyan, Rod Davis)
Star—United States (William Buchan, Steve Erickson)
Tornado—New Zealand

## Team Champions

Field hockey, men—Pakistan
Field hockey, women—Netherlands
Handball, men—Yugoslavia
Handball, women—Yugoslavia
Soccer—France
Volleyball, men—United States
Volleyball, women—China
Water polo—Yugoslavia

# WINTER

## Biathlon

Individual—Eirik Kvalfoss, Norway (10 km); P. Angerer, West Germany (20 km)
Relay—Soviet Union (Dmitry Vassiliev, Youry Kachkarov, Algulmantas Shalna, Serguey Bouliguin)

## Bobsledding

2-man—East Germany (Wolfgang Hoppe, captain)
4-man—East Germany (Wolfgang Hoppe, Roland Wetzig, Dietmar Schauerhanmer, Andreas Kirchner)

## Figure Skating

Men—Scott Hamilton, United States
Women—Katarina Witt, East Germany
Pairs—Elena Valova and Oleg Vasiliev, Soviet Union
Dance—Jayne Torvill and Christopher Dean, Britain

## Speed Skating—Men

500 m—Sergei Fokicheu, Soviet Union
1,000 m—Gaetan Boucher, Canada
1,500 m—Gaetan Boucher, Canada
5,000 m—Tomas Gustafson, Sweden
10,000 m—Igor Malkov, Soviet Union

## Speed Skating—Women

500 m—Christina Rothernberger, East Germany
1,000 m—Karin Enke, East Germany
1,500 m—Karin Enke, East Germany

3,000 m—Andrea Schoene, East Germany

## Hockey

Team—Soviet Union

## Luge

Men—Paul Hildgartner, Italy
Doubles—Hans Stangassinger and Franz Wembacher, West Germany
Women—Steffi Martin, East Germany

## Skiing, Nordic—Men

Combined—Tom Sandberg, Norway
70-m jump—Jens Weissflog, East Germany
90-m jump—Matti Nykaenen, Finland

## Cross-Country Skiing—Men

15 km—Gunde Svan, Sweden
30 km—Nikolai Zimiatov, Soviet Union
50 km—Thomas Wassberg, Sweden
40-km relay—Sweden (Thomas Wassberg, Benny Kohlberg, Jan Ottoson, Gunde Svan)

## Cross-Country Skiing—Women

5 km—Marja-Liisa Hamalainen, Finland
10 km—Marja-Liisa Hamalainen, Finland
20 km—Marja-Liisa Hamalainen, Finland
20-km relay—Norway (Inger Helene Nybraaten, Anne Jahra, Brit Petersen, Berit Aunli)

# FOOTBALL

The pastime of kicking around a ball goes back beyond the limits of recorded history. Ancient savage tribes played football of a primitive kind. There was a ball-kicking game played by Athenians, Spartans, and Corinthians 2500 years ago, which the Greeks called *Episkuros*. The Romans had a somewhat similar game called *Harpastum* and are supposed to have carried the game with them when they invaded the British Isles in the First Century, B.C.

Undoubtedly the game known in the United States as Football traces directly to the English game of Rugby, though the modifications have been many. Informal football was played on college lawns well over a century ago, and an annual Freshman-Sophomore series of "scrimmages" began at Yale in 1840. The first formal intercollegiate football game was the Princeton-Rutgers contest at New Brunswick, N.J., on Nov. 6, 1869, with Rutgers winning by 6 goals to 4.

In those days, games were played with 25, 20, 15, or 11 men on a side. In 1880, there was a convention at which Walter Camp of Yale persuaded the delegates to agree to a rule calling for 11 players on a side. The game grew so rough that it was attacked as brutal, and some colleges abandoned the sport. Conditions were so bad in 1906 that President Theodore Roosevelt called a meeting of Yale, Harvard, and Princeton representatives at the White House in the hope of reforming and improving the game. The outcome was that the game, with the forward pass introduced and some other modifications of the rules inserted, became faster and cleaner.

The first professional game was played in 1895 at Latrobe, Pa. The National Football League was founded in 1921. The All-American Conference went into action in 1946. At the end of the 1949 season the two circuits merged, retaining the name of the older league. In 1960, the American Football League began operations. In 1970, the leagues merged. The United States Football League played its first season in 1983, from March to July. It suspended spring operation after the 1985 season, and planned a 1986 move to fall.

## College Football

### NATIONAL COLLEGE FOOTBALL CHAMPIONS

The "National Collegiate A. A. Football Guide" recognizes as unofficial national champion the team selected each year by press association polls. Where The Associated Press poll (of writers) does not agree with the United Press International poll (of coaches), the guide lists both teams selected.

| | | | | | | | | | |
|---|---|---|---|---|---|---|---|---|---|
| 1937 | Pittsburgh | 1949 | Notre Dame | 1959 | Syracuse | 1969 | Texas | | So. California |
| 1938 | Texas Christian | 1950 | Oklahoma | 1960 | Minnesota | 1970 | Texas and Nebraska | 1979 | Alabama |
| 1939 | Texas A & M | 1951 | Tennessee | 1961 | Alabama | | | 1980 | Georgia |
| 1940 | Minnesota | 1952 | Michigan State | 1962 | So. California | 1971 | Nebraska | 1981 | Clemson |
| 1941 | Minnesota | 1953 | Maryland | 1963 | Texas | 1972 | So. California | 1982 | Penn State |
| 1942 | Ohio State | 1954 | Ohio State and U.C.L.A. | 1964 | Alabama | 1973 | Notre Dame | 1983 | Miami |
| 1943 | Notre Dame | | | 1965 | Alabama and Michigan State | 1974 | Oklahoma and So. California | 1984 | Brigham Young |
| 1944 | Army | 1955 | Oklahoma | | | 1975 | Oklahoma | 1985 | Oklahoma |
| 1945 | Army | 1956 | Oklahoma | | | 1976 | Pittsburgh | | |
| 1946 | Notre Dame | 1957 | Auburn and Ohio State | 1966 | Notre Dame | 1977 | Notre Dame | | |
| 1947 | Notre Dame | | | 1967 | So. California | 1978 | Alabama and | | |
| 1948 | Michigan | 1958 | Louisiana State | 1968 | Ohio State | | | | |

### RECORD OF ANNUAL MAJOR BOWL COLLEGE FOOTBALL GAMES

**Rose Bowl**
(At Pasadena, Calif.)

| | | | | | |
|---|---|---|---|---|---|
| 1902 | Michigan 49, Stanford 0 | 1931 | Alabama 24, Washington State 0 | 1950 | Ohio State 17, California 14 |
| 1916 | Washington State 14, Brown 0 | 1932 | So. California 21, Tulane 12 | 1951 | Michigan 14, California 6 |
| 1917 | Oregon 14, Pennsylvania 0 | 1933 | So. California 35, Pittsburgh 0 | 1952 | Illinois 40, Stanford 7 |
| 1918 | Mare Island Marines 19, Camp Lewis 7 | 1934 | Columbia 7, Stanford 0 | 1953 | So. California 7, Wisconsin 0 |
| | | 1935 | Alabama 29, Stanford 13 | 1954 | Michigan State 28, U.C.L.A. 20 |
| 1919 | Great Lakes 17, Mare Island Marines 0 | 1936 | Stanford 7, So. Methodist 0 | 1955 | Ohio State 20, So. California 7 |
| | | 1937 | Pittsburgh 21, Washington 0 | 1956 | Michigan State 17, U.C.L.A. 14 |
| 1920 | Harvard 7, Oregon 6 | 1938 | California 13, Alabama 0 | 1957 | Iowa 35, Oregon State 19 |
| 1921 | California 28, Ohio State 0 | 1939 | So. California 7, Duke 3 | 1958 | Ohio State 10, Oregon 7 |
| 1922 | Washington and Jefferson 0, California 0 | 1940 | So. California 14, Tennessee 0 | 1959 | Iowa 38, California 12 |
| | | 1941 | Stanford 21, Nebraska 13 | 1960 | Washington 44, Wisconsin 8 |
| 1923 | So. California 14, Penn State 3 | 1942 | Oregon State 20, Duke 16[1] | 1961 | Washington 17, Minnesota 7 |
| 1924 | Navy 14, Washington 14 | 1943 | Georgia 9, U.C.L.A. 0 | 1962 | Minnesota 21, U.C.L.A. 3 |
| 1925 | Notre Dame 27, Stanford 10 | 1944 | So. California 29, Washington 0 | 1963 | So. California 42, Wisconsin 37 |
| 1926 | Alabama 20, Washington 19 | 1945 | So. California 25, Tennessee 0 | 1964 | Illinois 17, Washington 7 |
| 1927 | Alabama 7, Stanford 7 | 1946 | Alabama 34, So. California 14 | 1965 | Michigan 34, Oregon State 7 |
| 1928 | Stanford 7, Pittsburgh 6 | 1947 | Illinois 45, U.C.L.A. 14 | 1966 | U.C.L.A. 14, Michigan State 12 |
| 1929 | Georgia Tech 8, California 7 | 1948 | Michigan 49, So. California 0 | 1967 | Purdue 14, So. California 13 |
| 1930 | So. California 47, Pittsburgh 14 | 1949 | Northwestern 20, California 14 | 1968 | So. California 14, Indiana 3 |

| | |
|---|---|
| 1969 | Ohio State 27, So. California 16 |
| 1970 | So. California 10, Michigan 3 |
| 1971 | Stanford 27, Ohio State 17 |
| 1972 | Stanford 13, Michigan 12 |
| 1973 | So. California 42, Ohio State 17 |
| 1974 | Ohio State 42, So. California 21 |
| 1975 | So. California 18, Ohio State 17 |
| 1976 | U.C.L.A. 23, Ohio State 10 |
| 1977 | So. California 14, Michigan 6 |
| 1978 | Washington 27, Michigan 20 |
| 1979 | So. California 17, Michigan 10 |
| 1980 | So. California 17, Ohio State 16 |
| 1981 | Michigan 23, Washington 6 |
| 1982 | Washington 28, Iowa 0 |
| 1983 | U.C.L.A. 24, Michigan 14 |
| 1984 | U.C.L.A. 45, Illinois 9 |
| 1985 | USC 20, Ohio St. 17 |
| 1986 | U.C.L.A. 45, Iowa 28 |
| 1. Played at Durham, N.C. | |

## Orange Bowl

(At Miami)

| | |
|---|---|
| 1933 | Miami (Fla.) 7, Manhattan 0 |
| 1934 | Duquesne 33, Miami (Fla.) 7 |
| 1935 | Bucknell 26, Miami (Fla.) 0 |
| 1936 | Catholic 20, Mississippi 19 |
| 1937 | Duquesne 13, Mississippi State 12 |
| 1938 | Auburn 6, Michigan State 0 |
| 1939 | Tennessee 17, Oklahoma 0 |
| 1940 | Georgia Tech 21, Missouri 7 |
| 1941 | Mississippi State 14, Georgetown 7 |
| 1942 | Georgia 40, Texas Christian 26 |
| 1943 | Alabama 37, Boston College 21 |
| 1944 | Louisiana State 19, Texas A&M 14 |
| 1945 | Tulsa 26, Georgia Tech 12 |
| 1946 | Miami (Fla.) 13, Holy Cross 6 |
| 1947 | Rice 8, Tennessee 0 |
| 1948 | Georgia Tech 20, Kansas 14 |
| 1949 | Texas 41, Georgia 28 |
| 1950 | Santa Clara 21, Kentucky 13 |
| 1951 | Clemson 15, Miami (Fla.) 14 |
| 1952 | Georgia Tech 17, Baylor 14 |
| 1953 | Alabama 61, Syracuse 6 |
| 1954 | Oklahoma 7, Maryland 0 |
| 1955 | Duke 34, Nebraska 7 |
| 1956 | Oklahoma 20, Maryland 6 |
| 1957 | Colorado 27, Clemson 21 |
| 1958 | Oklahoma 48, Duke 21 |
| 1959 | Oklahoma 21, Syracuse 6 |
| 1960 | Georgia 14, Missouri 0 |
| 1961 | Missouri 21, Navy 14 |
| 1962 | Louisiana State 25, Colorado 7 |
| 1963 | Alabama 17, Oklahoma 0 |
| 1964 | Nebraska 13, Auburn 7 |
| 1965 | Texas 21, Alabama 17 |
| 1966 | Alabama 39, Nebraska 28 |
| 1967 | Florida 27, Georgia Tech 12 |
| 1968 | Oklahoma 26, Tennessee 24 |
| 1969 | Penn State 15, Kansas 14 |
| 1970 | Penn State 10, Missouri 3 |
| 1971 | Nebraska 17, Louisiana State 12 |
| 1972 | Nebraska 38, Alabama 6 |
| 1973 | Nebraska 40, Notre Dame 6 |
| 1974 | Penn State 16, Louisiana State 9 |
| 1975 | Notre Dame 13, Alabama 11 |
| 1976 | Oklahoma 14, Michigan 6 |
| 1977 | Ohio State 27, Colorado 10 |
| 1978 | Arkansas 31, Oklahoma 6 |
| 1979 | Oklahoma 31, Nebraska 24 |
| 1980 | Oklahoma 24, Florida State 7 |
| 1981 | Oklahoma 18, Florida State 17 |
| 1982 | Clemson 22, Nebraska 15 |
| 1983 | Nebraska 21, Louisiana State 20 |

| | |
|---|---|
| 1984 | Miami 31, Nebraska 30 |
| 1985 | Washington 28, Oklahoma 17 |
| 1986 | Oklahoma 25, Penn St. 10 |

## Sugar Bowl

(At New Orleans)

| | |
|---|---|
| 1935 | Tulane 20, Temple 14 |
| 1936 | Texas Christian 3, Louisiana State 2 |
| 1937 | Santa Clara 21, Louisiana State 14 |
| 1938 | Santa Clara 6, Louisiana State 0 |
| 1939 | Texas Christian 15, Carnegie Tech 7 |
| 1940 | Texas A & M 14, Tulane 13 |
| 1941 | Boston College 19, Tennessee 13 |
| 1942 | Fordham 2, Missouri 0 |
| 1943 | Tennessee 14, Tulsa 7 |
| 1944 | Georgia Tech 20, Tulsa 18 |
| 1945 | Duke 29, Alabama 26 |
| 1946 | Oklahoma A & M 33, St. Mary's (Calif.) 13 |
| 1947 | Georgia 20, North Carolina 10 |
| 1948 | Texas 27, Alabama 7 |
| 1949 | Oklahoma 14, North Carolina 6 |
| 1950 | Oklahoma 35, Louisiana State 0 |
| 1951 | Kentucky 13, Oklahoma 7 |
| 1952 | Maryland 28, Tennessee 13 |
| 1953 | Georgia Tech 24, Mississippi 7 |
| 1954 | Georgia Tech 42, West Virginia 19 |
| 1955 | Navy 21, Mississippi 0 |
| 1956 | Georgia Tech 7, Pittsburgh 0 |
| 1957 | Baylor 13, Tennessee 7 |
| 1958 | Mississippi 39, Texas 7 |
| 1959 | Louisiana State 7, Clemson 0 |
| 1960 | Mississippi 21, Louisiana State 0 |
| 1961 | Mississippi 14, Rice 6 |
| 1962 | Alabama 10, Arkansas 3 |
| 1963 | Mississippi 17, Arkansas 13 |
| 1964 | Alabama 12, Mississippi 7 |
| 1965 | Louisiana State 13, Syracuse 10 |
| 1966 | Missouri 20, Florida 18 |
| 1967 | Alabama 34, Nebraska 7 |
| 1968 | Louisiana State 20, Wyoming 13 |
| 1969 | Arkansas 16, Georgia 2 |
| 1970 | Mississippi 27, Arkansas 22 |
| 1971 | Tennessee 34, Air Force Academy 13 |
| 1972 | Oklahoma 40, Auburn 22 |
| 1973 | Oklahoma 14, Penn State 0 |
| 1974 | Notre Dame 24, Alabama 23 |
| 1975 | Nebraska 13, Florida 10 |
| 1976 | Alabama 13, Penn State 6 |
| 1977 | Pittsburgh 27, Georgia 3 |
| 1978 | Alabama 35, Ohio State 6 |
| 1979 | Alabama 14, Penn State 7 |
| 1980 | Alabama 24, Arkansas 9 |
| 1981 | Georgia 17, Notre Dame 10 |
| 1982 | Pittsburgh 24, Georgia 20 |
| 1983 | Penn State 27, Georgia 23 |
| 1984 | Auburn 9, Michigan 7 |
| 1985 | Nebraska 28, LSU 10 |
| 1986 | Tennessee 35, Miami, Fla. 7 |

## Cotton Bowl

(At Dallas)

| | |
|---|---|
| 1937 | Texas Christian 16, Marquette 6 |
| 1938 | Rice 28, Colorado 14 |
| 1939 | St. Mary's (Calif.) 20, Texas Tech. 13 |
| 1940 | Clemson 6, Boston College 3 |
| 1941 | Texas A & M 13, Fordham 12 |
| 1942 | Alabama 29, Texas A & M 21 |
| 1943 | Texas 14, Georgia Tech 7 |
| 1944 | Randolph Field 7, Texas 7 |
| 1945 | Oklahoma A & M 34, Texas Christian 0 |

| | |
|---|---|
| 1946 | Texas 40, Missouri 27 |
| 1947 | Louisiana State 0, Arkansas 0 |
| 1948 | So. Methodist 13, Penn State 13 |
| 1949 | So. Methodist 21, Oregon 13 |
| 1950 | Rice 27, North Carolina 13 |
| 1951 | Tennessee 20, Texas 14 |
| 1952 | Kentucky 20, Texas Christian 7 |
| 1953 | Texas 16, Tennessee 0 |
| 1954 | Rice 28, Alabama 6 |
| 1955 | Georgia Tech 14, Arkansas 6 |
| 1956 | Mississippi 14, Texas Christian 13 |
| 1957 | Texas Christian 28, Syracuse 27 |
| 1958 | Navy 20, Rice 7 |
| 1959 | Air Force 0, Texas Christian 0 |
| 1960 | Syracuse 23, Texas 14 |
| 1961 | Duke 7, Arkansas 6 |
| 1962 | Texas 12, Mississippi 7 |
| 1963 | Louisiana State 13, Texas 0 |
| 1964 | Texas 28, Navy 6 |
| 1965 | Arkansas 10, Nebraska 7 |
| 1966 | Louisiana State 14, Arkansas 7 |
| 1967 | Georgia 24, So. Methodist 9 |
| 1968 | Texas A & M 20, Alabama 16 |
| 1969 | Texas 36, Tennessee 13 |
| 1970 | Texas 21, Notre Dame 17 |
| 1971 | Notre Dame 24, Texas 11 |
| 1972 | Penn State 30, Texas 6 |
| 1973 | Texas 17, Alabama 13 |
| 1974 | Nebraska 19, Texas 3 |
| 1975 | Penn State 41, Baylor 20 |
| 1976 | Arkansas 31, Georgia 10 |
| 1977 | Houston 30, Maryland 21 |
| 1978 | Notre Dame 38, Texas 10 |
| 1979 | Notre Dame 35, Houston 34 |
| 1980 | Houston 17, Nebraska 14 |
| 1981 | Alabama 30, Baylor 2 |
| 1982 | Texas 14, Alabama 12 |
| 1983 | Southern Methodist 7, Pittsburgh 3 |
| 1984 | Georgia 10, Texas 9 |
| 1985 | Boston College 45, Houston 28 |
| 1986 | Texas A & M 36, Auburn 16 |

## Gator Bowl

(At Jacksonville, Fla. Played on Saturday nearest New Year's Day of year indicated)

| | |
|---|---|
| 1953 | Florida 14, Tulsa 13 |
| 1954 | Texas Tech 35, Auburn 13 |
| 1955 | Auburn 33, Baylor 13 |
| 1956 | Vanderbilt 25, Auburn 13 |
| 1957 | Georgia Tech 21, Pittsburgh 14 |
| 1958 | Tennessee 3, Texas A & M 0 |
| 1959 | Mississippi 7, Florida 3 |
| 1960 | Arkansas 14, Georgia Tech 7 |
| 1961 | Florida 13, Baylor 12 |
| 1962 | Penn State 30, Georgia Tech 15 |
| 1963 | Florida 17, Penn State 7 |
| 1964 | No. Carolina 35, Air Force 0 |
| 1965 | Florida State 36, Oklahoma 19 |
| 1966 | Georgia Tech 31, Texas Tech 21 |
| 1967 | Tennessee 18, Syracuse 12 |
| 1968 | Penn State 17, Florida State 17 |
| 1969 | Missouri 35, Alabama 10 |
| 1970 | Florida 14, Tennessee 13 |
| 1971 | Auburn 35, Mississippi 28 |
| 1972 | Georgia 7, North Carolina 3 |
| 1973 | Auburn 24, Colorado 3 |
| 1974 | Texas Tech 28, Tennessee 19 |
| 1975 | Auburn 27, Texas 3 |
| 1976 | Maryland 13, Florida 0 |
| 1977 | Notre Dame 20, Penn State 9 |
| 1978 | Pittsburgh 34, Clemson 3 |

| | | | | | |
|---|---|---|---|---|---|
| 1979 | Clemson 17, Ohio State 15 | 1982 | North Carolina 31, Arkansas 27 | 1985 | Oklahoma St. 21, South Carolina 14 |
| 1980 | North Carolina 17, Michigan 15 | 1983 | Florida State 31, West Virginia 12 | 1986 | Florida State 34, Oklahoma St. 23 |
| 1981 | Pittsburgh 37, South Carolina 9 | 1984 | Florida 14, Iowa 6 | | |

## RESULTS OF OTHER 1985 SEASON BOWL GAMES

All-American (Birmingham, Ala., Dec. 31)—Georgia Tech 17, Michigan State 14

Aloha (Honolulu, Dec. 28)—Alabama 24, Southern California 3

Bluebonnet (Houston, Dec. 31)—Air Force 24, Texas 16

California (Fresno, Dec. 14)—Fresno State 51, Bowling Green 7

Cherry (Pontiac, Mich., Dec. 21)—Maryland 35, Syracuse 18

Fiesta (Tempre, Ariz., Jan. 1)—Michigan 27, Nebraska 23

Florida Citrus (Orlando, Fla., Dec. 28)—Ohio State 10, Brigham Young 7

Freedom (Anaheim, Calif., Dec. 30)—Washington 20, Colorado 17

Holiday (San Diego, Dec. 22)—Arkansas 18, Arizona State 17

Independence (Shreveport, La., Dec. 21)—Minnesota 20, Clemson 13

Liberty (Memphis, Dec. 27)—Baylor 21, Louisiana State 7

Peach (Atlanta, Dec. 31)—Army 31, Illinois 29

Sun (El Paso, Tex., Dec. 28)—Georgia 13; Arizona 13

## HEISMAN MEMORIAL TROPHY WINNERS

The Heisman Memorial Trophy is presented annually by the Downtown Athletic Club of New York City to the nation's outstanding college football player, as determined by a poll of sportswriters and sportscasters.

| | | | | | |
|---|---|---|---|---|---|
| 1935 | Jay Berwanger, Chicago | 1952 | Billy Vessels, Oklahoma | 1969 | Steve Owens, Oklahoma |
| 1936 | Larry Kelley, Yale | 1953 | Johnny Lattner, Notre Dame | 1970 | Jim Plunkett, Stanford |
| 1937 | Clinton Frank, Yale | 1954 | Alan Ameche, Wisconsin | 1971 | Pat Sullivan, Auburn |
| 1938 | Davey O'Brien, Texas Christian | 1955 | Howard Cassady, Ohio State | 1972 | Johnny Rodgers, Nebraska |
| 1939 | Nile Kinnick, Iowa | 1956 | Paul Hornung, Notre Dame | 1973 | John Cappelletti, Penn State |
| 1940 | Tom Harmon, Michigan | 1957 | John Crow, Texas A & M | 1974-75 | Archie Griffin, Ohio State |
| 1941 | Bruce Smith, Minnesota | 1958 | Pete Dawkins, Army | 1976 | Tony Dorsett, Pittsburgh |
| 1942 | Frank Sinkwich, Georgia | 1959 | Billy Cannon, Louisiana State | 1977 | Earl Campbell, Texas |
| 1943 | Angelo Bertelli, Notre Dame | 1960 | Joe Bellino, Navy | 1978 | Billy Sims, Oklahoma |
| 1944 | Leslie Horvath, Ohio State | 1961 | Ernie Davis, Syracuse | 1979 | Charles White, Southern California |
| 1945 | Felix Blanchard, Army | 1962 | Terry Baker, Oregon State | 1980 | George Rogers, South Carolina |
| 1946 | Glenn Davis, Army | 1963 | Roger Staubach, Navy | 1981 | Marcus Allen, Southern California |
| 1947 | Johnny Lujack, Notre Dame | 1964 | John Huarte, Notre Dame | 1982 | Hershel Walker, Georgia |
| 1948 | Doak Walker, So. Methodist | 1965 | Mike Garrett, Southern California | 1983 | Mike Rozier, Nebraska |
| 1949 | Leon Hart, Notre Dame | 1966 | Steve Spurrier, Florida | 1984 | Doug Flutie, Boston College |
| 1950 | Vic Janowicz, Ohio State | 1967 | Gary Beban, U.C.L.A. | 1985 | Bo Jackson, Auburn |
| 1951 | Dick Kazmaier, Princeton | 1968 | O. J. Simpson, Southern California | | |

## COLLEGE FOOTBALL HALL OF FAME

(Kings Island, Interstate 71, Kings Mills, Ohio)

(Date given is player's last year of competition)

### Players

Abell, Earl—Colgate, 1915
Agase, Alex—Purdue/Illinois, 1946
Agganis, Harry—Boston Univ., 1952
Albert, Frank—Stanford, 1941
Aldrich, Chas. (Ki)—T.C.U., 1938
Aldrich, Malcolm—Yale, 1921
Alexander, John—Syracuse, 1920
Alworth, Lance—Arkansas, 1961
Ameche, Alan (Horse)—Wisconsin, 1954
Amling, Warren—Ohio State, 1946
Anderson, H. (Hunk)—Notre Dame, 1921
Atkins, Doug—Tennessee, 1952
Bacon, C. Everett—Wesleyan, 1912
Bagnell, Francis (Reds)—Penn, 1950
Baker, Hobart (Hobey)—Princeton, 1913
Baker, John—So. Calif., 1931
Baker, Terry—Oregon State, 1962
Ballin, Harold—Princeton, 1914
Banker, Bill—Tulane, 1929
Banonis, Vince—Detroit, 1941
Barnes, Stanley—S. California, 1921
Barrett, Charles—Cornell, 1915
Baston, Bert—Minnesota, 1916
Battles, Cliff—W. Va. Wesleyan, 1931
Baugh, Sammy—Texas Christian U., 1936
Bausch, James—Kansas, 1930
Beagle, Ron—Navy, 1955
Beckett, John—Oregon, 1913
Bednarik, Chuck—Pennsylvania, 1948

Bellini, Joe—Navy, 1960
Benbrook, A.—Michigan, 1911
Bertelli, A.—Notre Dame, 1943
Berry, Charlie—Lafayette, 1924
Berwanger, John (Jay)—Chicago, 1935
Bettencourt, Larry—St. Mary's, 1927
Blanchard, Felix (Doc)—Army, 1946
Bock, Ed—Iowa State, 1938
Bomar, Lynn—Vanderbilt, 1924
Bomeisler, Doug (Bo)—Yale, 1913
Booth, Albie—Yale, 1931
Borries, Fred—Navy, 1934
Bosely, Bruce—West Virginia, 1955
Bottari, Vic—California, 1939
Boynton, Ben—Williams, 1920
Bozis, Al—Georgetown, 1941
Brewer, Charles—Harvard, 1895
Bright, John—Drake, 1951
Brodie, John—Stanford, 1956
Brooke, George—Pennsylvania, 1895
Brown, George—Navy, San Diego St., 1947
Brown, Gordon—Yale, 1900
Brown, John, Jr.—Navy, 1913
Brown, Johnny Mack—Alabama, 1925
Brown, Raymond (Tay)—So. California, 1932
Bunker, Paul—Army, 1902
Butkus, Dick—Illinois, 1964
Butler, Robert—Wisconsin, 1912
Cafego, George—Tennessee, 1939

Cagle, Chris—SW La./Army, 1929
Cain, John—Alabama, 1932
Cameron, Eddie—Wash. & Lee, 1924
Campbell, David C.—Harvard, 1901
Cannon, Billy—L.S.U., 1959
Cannon, Jack—Notre Dame, 1929
Carideo, Frank—Notre Dame, 1930
Caroline, J.C.—Illinois, 1954
Carney, Charles—Illinois, 1921
Carpenter, Bill—Army, 1959
Carpenter, C. Hunter—VPI, 1905
Carroll, Charles—Washington, 1928
Casey, Edward L.—Harvard, 1919
Cassady, Howard—Ohio State, 1955
Chamberlain, Guy—Nebraska, 1915
Chapman, Sam—Cal.-Berkeley, 1938
Christman, Paul—Missouri, 1940
Clark, Earl (Dutch)—Colo. College, 1929
Clevenger, Zora—Indiana, 1903
Cochran, Gary—Princeton, 1895
Cody, Josh—Vanderbilt, 1920
Coleman, Don—Mich. State, 1951
Conerly, Chuck—Mississippi, 1947
Connor, George—Notre Dame, 1947
Corbin, W.—Yale, 1888
Corbus, William—Stanford, 1933
Cowan, Hector—Princeton, 1889
Coy, Edward H. (Tad)—Yale, 1909
Crawford, Fred—Duke, 1933

Peck, Robert—Pittsburgh, 1916
Pennock, Stanley B.—Harvard, 1914
Pfann, George—Cornell, 1923
Phillips, H.D.—U. of South, 1904
Pingel, John—Michigan State, 1938
Pihos, Pete—Indiana, 1945
Pinckert, Ernie—So. California, 1931
Poe, Arthur—Princeton, 1899
Pollard, Fritz—Brown, 1916
Poole, Barney—Miss./Army, 1947
Pregulman, Merv—Michigan, 1943
Price, Eddie—Tulane, 1949
Pund, Henry—Georgia Tech, 1928
Ramsey, Gerrard—Wm. & Mary, 1942
Reeds, Claude—Oklahoma, 1913
Reid, Steve—Northwestern, 1936
Reid, William—Harvard, 1900
Renfro, Mel—Oregon, 1963
Rentner, Ernest—Northwestern, 1932
Reynolds, Robert—Nebraska, 1952
Reynolds, Robert—Stanford, 1935
Richter, Les—California, 1951
Rinehart, Charles—Lafayette, 1897
Rodgers, Ira—West Virginia, 1919
Rogers, Edward L.—Minnesota, 1903
Romig, Joe—Colorado, 1961
Rosenberg, Aaron—So. California, 1934
Rote, Kyle—So. Methodist, 1950
Routt, Joe—Texas A&M, 1937
Salmon, Louis—Notre Dame, 1904
Sauer, George—Nebraska, 1933
Sayers, Gale—Kansas, 1964
Scarbath, Jack—Maryland, 1952
Scarlett, Hunter—Pennsylvania, 1909
Schoonover, Wear—Arkansas, 1929
Schreiner, Dave—Wisconsin, 1942
Schultz, Adolf (Germany)—Mich., 1908
Schwab, Frank—Lafayette, 1922
Schwartz, Marchmont—Notre Dame, 1931
Schwegler, Paul—Washington, 1931
Scott, Clyde—Arkansas, 1949
Scott, Tom—Virginia, 1953
Seibels, Henry—Sewanee, 1899
Shakespeare, Bill—Notre Dame, 1935
Shelton, Murray—Cornell, 1915
Shevlin, Tom—Yale, 1905
Shively, Bernie—Illinois, 1926
Simons, Claude—Tulane, 1934
Simpson, O.J.—So. Calif., 1968
Sington, Fred—Alabama, 1930
Sinkwich, Frank—Georgia, 1942
Sitko, Emil—Notre Dame, 1949
Skladany, Joe—Pittsburgh, 1933
Slater, F.F. (Duke)—Iowa, 1921

Smith, Bruce—Minnesota, 1941
Smith, Ernie—So. California, 1932
Smith, Harry—So. California, 1939
Smith, John (Clipper)—Notre Dame, 1927
Smith, Riley—Alabama, 1935
Smith, Vernon—Georgia, 1931
Snow, Neil—Michigan, 1901
Sparlis, Al—U.C.L.A., 1945
Spears, Clarence W.—Dartmouth, 1915
Spears, W.D.—Vanderbilt, 1927
Sprackling, William—Brown, 1911
Sprague, M. (Bud)—Texas/Army, 1928
Spurrier, Steve—Florida, 1966
Stafford, Harrison—Texas, 1932
Stagg, Amos Alonzo—Yale, 1889
Staubach, Roger—Navy, 1963
Steffen, Walter—Chicago, 1908
Stein, Herbert—Pittsburgh, 1921
Steuber, Robert—Missouri, 1943
Stevens, Mal—Yale, 1923
Stinchcomb, Gaylord—Ohio State, 1920
Stevenson, Vincent—Pennsylvania, 1905
Strom, Brock—Air Force, 1959
Strong, Ken—New York Univ., 1928
Strupper, George—Georgia Tech, 1917
Stuhldreher, Harry—Notre Dame, 1924
Stydahar, Joe—West Virginia, 1935
Suffridge, Robert—Tennessee, 1940
Suhey, Steve—Pennsylvania State, 1947
Sundstrom, Frank—Cornell, 1923
Swanson, Clarence—Nebraska, 1921
Swiacki, Bill—Holy Cross/Colombia, 1947
Swink, Jim—Texas Christian, 1956
Taliafarro, George—Indiana, 1948
Taylor, Charles—Stanford, 1942
Thompson, Joe—Pittsburgh, 1907
Thorne, Samuel B.—Yale, 1906
Thorpe, Jim—Carlisle, 1912
Ticknor, Ben—Harvard, 1930
Tigert, John—Vanderbilt, 1904
Tinsley, Gaynell—La. State U., 1936
Tipton, Eric—Duke, 1938
Tonnemaker, Clayton—Minnesota, 1949
Torrey, Robert—Pennsylvania, 1906
Travis, Ed Tarkio—Missouri, 1920
Trippi, Charles—Georgia, 1946
Tryon, J. Edward—Colgate, 1925
Utay, Joe—Texas A&M, 1907
Van Brocklin, Norm—Oregon, 1948
Van Sickel, Dale—Florida, 1929
Van Surdam, Henderson—Wesleyan, 1905
Very, Dexter—Penn State, 1912
Vessels, Billy—Oklahoma, 1931
Vick, Ernie—Michigan, 1921

Wagner, Huber—Pittsburgh, 1913
Walker, Doak—So. Methodist, 1949
Wallace, Bill—Rice, 1935
Walsh, Adam—Notre Dame, 1924
Warburton, I. (Cotton)—So. Calif., 1934
Ward, Robert (Bob)—Maryland, 1951
Warner, William—Cornell, 1903
Washington, Ken—U.C.L.A., 1939
Wedemeyer, Herman J.—St. Mary's, 1947
Weekes, Harold—Columbia, 1902
Weir, Ed—Nebraska, 1925
Welch, Gus—Carlisle, 1914
Weller, John—Princeton, 1935
Wendell, Percy—Harvard, 1913
West, D. Belford—Colgate, 1919
Weyand, Alex—Army, 1915
Wharton, Charles—Pennsylvania, 1896
Wheeler, Arthur—Princeton, 1894
White, Byron (Whizzer)—Colorado, 1937
Whitmire, Don—Alabama/Navy, 1944
Wickhorst, Frank—Navy, 1926
Widseth, Ed—Minnesota, 1936
Wildung, Richard—Minnesota, 1942
Williams, James—Rice, 1949
Willis, William—Ohio State, 1945
Wilson, George—Washington, 1925
Wilson, Harry—Penn State/Army, 1923
Wistert, Albert A.—Michigan, 1942
Wistert, Al—Michigan, 1949
Wistert, Frank (Whitey)—Mich., 1933
Wood, Barry—Harvard, 1931
Wojciechowicz, Alex—Fordham, 1936
Wyant, Andrew—Bucknell/Chicago, 1894
Wyatt, Bowden—Tennessee, 1938
Wyckoff, Clint—Cornell, 1896
Yoder, Lloyd—Carnegie Tech, 1926
Young, Claude (Buddy)—Illinois, 1946
Young, Harry—Wash. & Lee, 1916
Young, Walter—Oklahoma, 1938
Zarnas, Gus—Ohio State, 1937

## Coaches

Bill Alexander
Dr. Ed Anderson
Ike Armstrong
Matty Bell
Hugo Bezdek
Dana X. Bible
Bernie Bierman
Earl (Red) Blaik
Frank Broyles
Paul "Bear" Bryant
Charles W. Caldwell
Walter Camp
Len Casanova
Frank Cavanaugh
Fritz Crisler
Duffy Daugherty
Bob Devaney
Dan Devine
Gil Dobie
Michael Donohue

Gus Dorais
Bill Edwards
Charles (Rip) Engle
Don Faurot
Jake Gaither
Ernest Godfrey
Andy Gustafson
Jack Harding
Edward K. Hall
Richard Harlow
Jesse Harper
Percy Haughton
Woody Hayes
John W. Heisman
R. A. (Bob) Higgins
Orin E. Hollingberry
William Ingram
Morley Jennings
Howard Jones
L. (Biff) Jones

Thomas (Tad) Jones
Ralph (Shug) Jordan
Andy Kerr
Frank Leahy
George E. Little
Lou Little
El (Slip) Madigan
Charley McClendon
Herbert McCracken
Daniel McGugin
DeOrmond (Tuss) Mc-
Laughry
L. R. (Dutch) Meyer
Bernie Moore
Scrappy Moore
Ray Morrison
George A. Munger
Clarence Munn
Frank Murray
William Murray

Ed (Hooks) Mylin
Earle (Greasy) Neale
Jess Neely
Robert Neyland
Homer Norton
Frank (Buck) O'Neill
Bennie Owen
Ara Parseghian
James Phalea
E. N. Robinson
Knute Rockne
E. L. (Dick) Romney
William W. Roper
Darrell Royal
George F. Sanford
Francis A. Schmidt
Floyd (Ben) Schwartz-
walder
Clark Shaughnessy

Buck Shaw
Andrew L. Smith
Carl Snavely
Amos A. Stagg
Jock Sutherland
James Tatum
Frank W. Thomas
John H. Vaught
Wallace Wade
Lynn Waldorf
Glenn (Pop) Warner
E. E. (Tad) Wieman
John W. Wilce
Bud Wilkinson
Henry L. Williams
George W. Woodruff
Fielding H. Yost
Robert Zuppke

## 1985 N.C.A.A. CHAMPIONSHIP PLAYOFFS

### DIVISION I-AA

**Quarterfinals**

Georgia Southern 28, Middle Tenn. St. 21
Furman 59, Rhode Island 15
Northern Iowa 17, Eastern Washington 14
Nevada–Reno 24, Arkansas St. 23

**Semifinals**

Georgia Southern 40, Northern Iowa 33
Furman 35, Nevada–Reno 12

**Championship**

Georgia Southern 44, Furman 42

### DIVISION II

**Quarterfinals**

South Dakota 13, Central St. (Ohio) 10 (2 OT)
North Alabama 14, Fort Valley St. (Ga.) 7
Bloomsburg (Pa.) 38, Hampton (Va.) 28
North Dakota St. 31, Cal–Davis 12

**Semifinals**

North Alabama 34, Bloomsburg 0
North Dakota St. 16, South Dakota 7

**Championship**

North Dakota State 35, North Alabama 7

### DIVISION III

**Quarterfinals**

Ithaca 50, Montclair St. 28
Gettysburg 22, Salisbury 6
Central Iowa 71, Occidental 0
Augustana (Ill.) 21, Mount Union 14

**Semifinals**

Ithaca 34, Gettysburg 0
Augustana 14, Central Iowa 7

**Championship**

Augustana 20, Ithaca 7

## NATIONAL ASSOCIATION OF INTERCOLLEGIATE ATHLETICS 1985 CHAMPIONSHIPS

### DIVISION I

**Quarterfinals**

Hillsdale 47, Salem (W.Va.) 3
Mesa (Colo.) 39, Western Oregon 32
Henderson St. (Ark.) 18, Central St. (Okla.) 15
Central Arkansas 32, Pittsburg St. (Kan.) 22

**Semifinals**

Hillsdale 24, Mesa 21
Central Arkansas 21, Henderson St. 9

**Championship**

Hillsdale 10, Central Arkansas 10 (tie)

### DIVISION II

**Quarterfinals**

Findlay (Ohio) 7, St. Ambrose (Iowa) 0
Northwestern (Iowa) 32, Benedictine (Kan.) 22
Wisconsin–LaCrosse 24, Carroll (Mont.) 0
Pacific Lutheran (Wash.) 30, Linfield (Ore.) 12

**Semifinals**

Pacific Lutheran 40, Findlay 29
Wisconsin–LaCrosse 35, Northwestern 28

# *Professional Football*

## NATIONAL FOOTBALL LEAGUE FINAL STANDING 1985

**AMERICAN CONFERENCE**
**Eastern Division**

|  | W | L | T | Pct | Pts | OP |
|---|---|---|---|---|---|---|
| Miami | 12 | 4 | 0 | .750 | 428 | 320 |
| New York Jets[1] | 11 | 5 | 0 | .688 | 393 | 264 |
| New England[1] | 11 | 5 | 0 | .688 | 362 | 290 |
| Indianapolis | 5 | 11 | 0 | .312 | 320 | 386 |
| Buffalo | 2 | 14 | 0 | .125 | 200 | 381 |

**Central Division**

| Cleveland | 8 | 8 | 0 | .500 | 287 | 294 |
|---|---|---|---|---|---|---|
| Cincinnati | 7 | 9 | 0 | .438 | 441 | 437 |
| Pittsburgh | 7 | 9 | 0 | .438 | 379 | 355 |
| Houston | 5 | 11 | 0 | .312 | 284 | 412 |

**Western Division**

| Los Angeles Raiders | 12 | 4 | 0 | .750 | 354 | 308 |
|---|---|---|---|---|---|---|
| Denver | 11 | 5 | 0 | .688 | 380 | 329 |
| Seattle | 8 | 8 | 0 | .500 | 349 | 303 |
| San Diego | 8 | 8 | 0 | .500 | 467 | 435 |
| Kansas City | 6 | 10 | 0 | .375 | 317 | 360 |

1. Wild card qualifier for playoffs.

**Playoffs:** New England 26, Jets 14; Miami 24, Cleveland 21; New England 27, Raiders 20
**Conference championship:** New England 31, Miami 14

**NATIONAL CONFERENCE**
**Eastern Division**

|  | W | L | T | Pct | Pts | OP |
|---|---|---|---|---|---|---|
| Dallas | 10 | 6 | 0 | .625 | 357 | 333 |
| New York Giants[1] | 10 | 6 | 0 | .625 | 399 | 283 |
| Washington | 10 | 6 | 0 | .625 | 297 | 212 |
| Philadelphia | 7 | 9 | 0 | .438 | 286 | 310 |
| St. Louis | 5 | 11 | 0 | .313 | 278 | 414 |

**Central Division**

| Chicago | 15 | 1 | 0 | .938 | 456 | 198 |
|---|---|---|---|---|---|---|
| Green Bay | 8 | 8 | 0 | .500 | 337 | 355 |
| Minnesota | 7 | 9 | 0 | .438 | 346 | 359 |
| Detroit | 7 | 9 | 0 | .438 | 307 | 366 |
| Tampa Bay | 2 | 14 | 0 | .125 | 294 | 448 |

**Western Division**

| Los Angeles Rams | 11 | 5 | 0 | .688 | 340 | 277 |
|---|---|---|---|---|---|---|
| San Francisco[1] | 10 | 6 | 0 | .625 | 411 | 263 |
| New Orleans | 5 | 11 | 0 | .313 | 294 | 401 |
| Atlanta | 4 | 12 | 0 | .250 | 282 | 452 |

1. Wild card qualifier for playoffs.

**Playoffs:** Giants 17, San Francisco 3; Rams 20, Dallas 0; Chicago 21, Giants 0
**Conference championship:** Chicago 24, Los Angeles Rams 0

## LEAGUE CHAMPIONSHIP—SUPER BOWL XX

(Jan. 26, 1986, at The Louisiana Superdome, New Orleans, La.; Attendance 73,818)

### Scoring

| | 1st Q | 2nd Q | 3rd Q | 4th Q | Final |
|---|---|---|---|---|---|
| Chicago (NFC) | 13 | 10 | 21 | 2 | 46 |
| New England (AFC) | 3 | 0 | 0 | 7 | 10 |

**Scoring**—Chicago: Touchdowns: Suhey, 11-yard run; McMahon, 2-yard run; McMahon, 1-yard run; Phillips, 28-yard interception return; Perry, 1-yard run. Conversions: Butler, 5 (kicks). Field goals: Butler, 3, 28, 24, and 25 yards. Safety: Waechter (tackle Grogan in end zone). New England: Touchdown: Fryar, 8-yard pass from Grogan. Field goal: Franklin, 36.

### Statistics of the Game

| | Chicago | New England |
|---|---|---|
| First downs | 23 | 12 |
| Yards gained rushing | 167 | 7 |
| Yards gained passing | 241 | 116 |
| Passes completed | 12 | 17 |
| Passes intercepted by | 2 | 0 |
| Punts | 4-43 | 6-44 |
| Fumbles lost | 2 | 4 |
| Yards penalized | 35 | 35 |

## SUPER BOWLS I–XX

| Game | Date | Winner | Loser | Site | Attendance |
|---|---|---|---|---|---|
| XX | Jan. 26, 1986 | Chicago (AFC) 46 | New England (AFC) 10 | Superdome, New Orleans | 73,818 |
| XIX | Jan. 20, 1985 | San Francisco (NFC) 38 | Miami (AFC) 16 | Stanford Stadium, Palo Alto, Calif. | 84,059 |
| XVIII | Jan. 22, 1984 | Los Angeles Raiders (AFC) 38 | Washington 9 | Tampa Stadium, Tampa, Fla | 72,920 |
| XVII | Jan. 30, 1983 | Washington (NFC) 27 | Miami (AFC) 17 | Rose Bowl, Pasadena, Calif. | 103,667 |
| XVI | Jan. 24, 1982 | San Francisco (NFC) 26 | Cincinnati (AFC) 21 | Silverdome, Pontiac, Mich. | 81,270 |
| XV | Jan. 25, 1981 | Oakland (AFC) 27 | Philadelphia (NFC) 10 | Superdome, New Orleans | 75,500 |
| XIV | Jan. 20, 1980 | Pittsburgh (AFC) 31 | Los Angeles (NFC) 19 | Rose Bowl, Pasadena | 103,985 |
| XIII | Jan. 21, 1979 | Pittsburgh (AFC) 35 | Dallas (NFC) 31 | Orange Bowl, Miami | 79,484 |
| XII | Jan. 15, 1978 | Dallas (NFC) 27 | Denver (AFC) 10 | Superdome, New Orleans | 75,583 |
| XI | Jan. 9, 1977 | Oakland (AFC) 32 | Minnesota (NFC) 14 | Rose Bowl, Pasadena | 103,424 |
| X | Jan. 18, 1976 | Pittsburgh (AFC) 21 | Dallas (NFC) 17 | Orange Bowl, Miami | 80,187 |
| IX | Jan. 12, 1975 | Pittsburgh (AFC) 16 | Minnesota (NFC) 6 | Tulane Stadium, New Orleans | 80,997 |
| VIII | Jan. 13, 1974 | Miami (AFC) 24 | Minnesota (NFC) 7 | Rice Stadium, Houston | 71,882 |
| VII | Jan. 14, 1973 | Miami (AFC) 14 | Washington (NFC) 7 | Memorial Coliseum, Los Angeles | 90,182 |
| VI | Jan. 16, 1972 | Dallas (NFC) 24 | Miami (AFC) 3 | Tulane Stadium, New Orleans | 81,591 |
| V | Jan. 17, 1971 | Baltimore (AFC) 16 | Dallas (NFC) 13 | Orange Bowl, Miami | 79,204 |
| IV | Jan. 11, 1970 | Kansas City (AFL) 23 | Minnesota (NFL) 7 | Tulane Stadium, New Orleans | 80,562 |
| III | Jan. 12, 1969 | New York (AFL) 16 | Baltimore (NFL) 7 | Orange Bowl, Miami | 75,389 |
| II | Jan. 14, 1968 | Green Bay (NFL) 33 | Oakland (AFL) 14 | Orange Bowl, Miami | 75,546 |
| I | Jan. 15, 1967 | Green Bay (NFL) 35 | Kansas City (AFL) 10 | Memorial Coliseum, Los Angeles | 61,946 |

1. Super Bowls I to IV were played before the American Football League and National Football League merged into the NFL, which was divided into two conferences, the NFC and AFC.

## NATIONAL LEAGUE CHAMPIONS

| Year | Champion (W-L-T) | Year | Champion (W-L-T) | Year | Champion (W-L-T) |
|---|---|---|---|---|---|
| 1921 | Chicago Bears (Staley's) (10–1–1) | 1925 | Chicago Cardinals (11–2–1) | 1929 | Green Bay Packers (12–0–1) |
| 1922 | Canton Bulldogs (10–0–2) | 1926 | Frankford Yellow Jackets (14–1–1) | 1930 | Green Bay Packers (10–3–1) |
| 1923 | Canton Bulldogs (11–0–1) | 1927 | New York Giants (11–1–1) | 1931 | Green Bay Packers (12–2–0) |
| 1924 | Cleveland Indians (7–1–1) | 1928 | Providence Steamrollers (8–1–2) | 1932 | Chicago Bears (7–1–6) |

| Year | Eastern Conference winners (W-L-T) | Western Conference winners (W-L-T) | League champion playoff results |
|---|---|---|---|
| 1933 | New York Giants (11–3–0) | Chicago Bears (10–2–1) | Chicago Bears 23, New York 21 |
| 1934 | New York Giants (8–5–0) | Chicago Bears (13–0–0) | New York 30, Chicago Bears 13 |
| 1935 | New York Giants (9–3–0) | Detroit Lions (7–3–2) | Detroit 26, New York 7 |
| 1936 | Boston Redskins (7–5–0) | Green Bay Packers (10–1–1) | Green Bay 21, Boston 6 |
| 1937 | Washington Redskins (8–3–0) | Chicago Bears (9–1–1) | Washington 28, Chicago Bears 21 |
| 1938 | New York Giants (8–2–1) | Green Bay Packers (8–3–0) | New York 23, Green Bay 17 |
| 1939 | New York Giants (9–1–1) | Green Bay Packers (9–2–0) | Green Bay 27, New York 0 |
| 1940 | Washington Redskins (9–2–0) | Chicago Bears (8–3–0) | Chicago Bears 73, Washington 0 |
| 1941 | New York Giants (8–3–0) | Chicago Bears (10–1–1)² | Chicago Bears 37, New York 9 |
| 1942 | Washington Redskins (10–1–1) | Chicago Bears (11–0–0) | Washington 14, Chicago Bears 6 |
| 1943 | Washington Redskins (6–3–1)² | Chicago Bears (8–1–1) | Chicago Bears 41, Washington 21 |
| 1944 | New York Giants (8–1–1) | Green Bay Packers (8–2–0) | Green Bay 14, New York 7 |
| 1945 | Washington Redskins (8–2–0) | Cleveland Rams (9–1–0) | Cleveland 15, Washington 14 |
| 1946 | New York Giants (7–3–1) | Chicago Bears (8–2–1) | Chicago Bears 24, New York 14 |
| 1947 | Philadelphia Eagles (8–4–0)² | Chicago Cardinals (9–3–0) | Chicago Cardinals 28, Philadelphia 21 |
| 1948 | Philadelphia Eagles (9–2–1) | Chicago Cardinals (11–1–0) | Philadelphia 7, Chicago Cardinals 0 |
| 1949 | Philadelphia Eagles (11–1–0) | Los Angeles Rams (8–2–2) | Philadelphia 14, Los Angeles 0 |
| 1950¹ | Cleveland Browns (10–2–0)² | Los Angeles Rams (9–3–0)² | Cleveland 30, Los Angeles 28 |
| 1951¹ | Cleveland Browns (11–1–0) | Los Angeles Rams (8–4–0) | Los Angeles 24, Cleveland 17 |
| 1952¹ | Cleveland Browns (8–4–0) | Detroit Lions (9–3–0)² | Detroit 17, Cleveland 7 |

| | | |
|---|---|---|
| 1953 | Cleveland Browns (11-1-0) | Detroit Lions (10-2-0) | Detroit 17, Cleveland 16 |
| 1954 | Cleveland Browns (9-3-0) | Detroit Lions (9-2-1) | Cleveland 56, Detroit 10 |
| 1955 | Cleveland Browns (9-2-1) | Los Angeles Rams (8-3-1) | Cleveland 38, Los Angeles 14 |
| 1956 | New York Giants (8-3-1) | Chicago Bears (9-2-1) | New York 47, Chicago Bears 7 |
| 1957 | Cleveland Browns (9-2-1) | Detroit Lions (8-4-0)[3] | Detroit 59, Cleveland 14 |
| 1958 | New York Giants (9-3-0)[2] | Baltimore Colts (9-3-0) | Baltimore 23, New York 17[3] |
| 1959 | New York Giants (10-2-0) | Baltimore Colts (9-3-0) | Baltimore 31, New York 16 |
| 1960 | Philadelphia Eagles (10-2-0) | Green Bay Packers (8-4-0) | Philadelphia 17, Green Bay 13 |
| 1961 | New York Giants (10-3-1) | Green Bay Packers (11-3-0) | Green Bay 37, New York 0 |
| 1962 | New York Giants (12-2-0) | Green Bay Packers (13-1-0) | Green Bay 16, New York 7 |
| 1963 | New York Giants (11-3-0) | Chicago Bears (11-1-2) | Chicago 14, New York 10 |
| 1964 | Cleveland Browns (10-3-1) | Baltimore Colts (12-2-0) | Cleveland 27, Baltimore 0 |
| 1965 | Cleveland Browns (11-3-0) | Green Bay Packers (11-3-1)[2] | Green Bay 23, Cleveland 12 |
| 1966 | Dallas Cowboys (10-3-1) | Green Bay Packers (12-2-0) | Green Bay 34, Dallas 27 |
| 1967 | Dallas Cowboys (9-5-0)[2] | Green Bay Packers (9-4-1)[2] | Green Bay 21, Dallas 17 |
| 1968 | Cleveland Browns (10-4-0)[2] | Baltimore Colts (13-1-0)[2] | Baltimore 34, Cleveland 0 |
| 1969 | Cleveland Browns (10-3-1)[2] | Minnesota Vikings (12-2-0)[2] | Minnesota 27, Cleveland 7 |

1. League was divided into American and National Conferences, 1950–52 and again in 1970, when leagues merged. 2. Won divisional playoff. 3. Won at 8:15 of sudden death overtime period.

## NATIONAL CONFERENCE CHAMPIONS

| Year | Eastern Division | Central Division | Western Division | Champion |
|---|---|---|---|---|
| 1970 | Dallas Cowboys (10-4-0) | Minnesota Vikings (12-2-0) | San Francisco 49ers (10-3-1) | Dallas |
| 1971 | Dallas Cowboys (11-3-0) | Minnesota Vikings (11-3-0) | San Francisco 49ers (9-5-0) | Dallas |
| 1972 | Washington Redskins (11-3-0) | Green Bay Packers (10-4-0) | San Francisco 49ers (8-5-1) | Washington |
| 1973 | Dallas Cowboys (10-4-0) | Minnesota Vikings (12-2-0) | Los Angeles Rams (12-2-0) | Minnesota |
| 1974 | St. Louis Cardinals (10-4-0) | Minnesota Vikings (10-4-0) | Los Angeles Rams (10-4-0) | Minnesota |
| 1975 | St. Louis Cardinals (11-3-0) | Minnesota Vikings (12-2-0) | Los Angeles Rams (12-2-0) | Dallas |
| 1976 | Dallas Cowboys (11-3-0) | Minnesota Vikings (11-2-1) | Los Angeles Rams (10-3-1) | Minnesota |
| 1977 | Dallas Cowboys (12-2-0) | Minnesota Vikings (9-5-0) | Los Angeles Rams (10-4-0) | Dallas |
| 1978 | Dallas Cowboys (12-4-0) | Minnesota Vikings (8-7-1) | Los Angeles Rams (12-4-0) | Dallas |
| 1979 | Dallas Cowboys (11-5-0) | Tampa Bay Buccaneers (10-6-0) | Los Angeles Rams (9-7-0) | Los Angeles |
| 1980 | Philadelphia Eagles (12-4-0) | Minnesota Vikings (9-7-0) | Atlanta Falcons (12-4-0) | Philadelphia |
| 1981 | Dallas Cowboys (12-4-0) | Tampa Bay Buccaneers (9-7-0) | San Francisco 49ers (13-3-0) | San Francisco |
| 1982* | Washington Redskins won conference title and also had best regular-season record (8-1-0) | | | |
| 1983 | Washington Redskins (14-2-0) | Detroit Lions (8-8-0) | San Francisco 49ers (10-6-0) | Washington |
| 1984 | Washington Redskins (11-5-0) | Chicago Bears (10-6-0) | San Francisco 49ers (15-1) | San Francisco |
| 1985 | Dallas Cowboys (10-6-0) | Chicago Bears (15-1-0) | Los Angeles Rams (11-5-0) | Chicago |

*Schedule reduced to 9 games from usual 16, with no standings kept in Eastern, Central, and Western Divisions, because of 57-day player strike.

## AMERICAN CONFERENCE CHAMPIONS

| Year | Eastern Division | Central Division | Western Division | Champion |
|---|---|---|---|---|
| 1970 | Baltimore Colts (11-2-1) | Cincinnati Bengals (8-6-0) | Oakland Raiders (8-4-2) | Baltimore |
| 1971 | Miami Dolphins (10-3-1) | Cleveland Browns (9-5-0) | Kansas City Chiefs (10-3-1) | Miami |
| 1972 | Miami Dolphins (14-0-0) | Pittsburgh Steelers (11-3-0) | Oakland Raiders (10-3-1) | Miami |
| 1973 | Miami Dolphins (12-2-0) | Cincinnati Bengals (10-4-0) | Oakland Raiders (9-4-1) | Miami |
| 1974 | Miami Dolphins (11-3-0) | Pittsburgh Steelers (10-3-1) | Oakland Raiders (12-2-0) | Pittsburgh |
| 1975 | Baltimore Colts (10-4-0) | Pittsburgh Steelers (12-2-0) | Oakland Raiders (11-3-0) | Pittsburgh |
| 1976 | Baltimore Colts (11-3-0) | Pittsburgh Steelers (10-4-0) | Oakland Raiders (13-1-0) | Oakland |
| 1977 | Baltimore Colts (10-4-0) | Pittsburgh Steelers (9-5-0) | Denver Broncos (12-2-0) | Denver |
| 1978 | New England Patriots (11-5-0) | Pittsburgh Steelers (14-2-0) | Denver Broncos (10-6-0) | Pittsburgh |
| 1979 | Miami Dolphins (10-6-0) | Pittsburgh Steelers (12-4-0) | San Diego Chargers (12-4-0) | Pittsburgh |
| 1980 | Buffalo Bills (11-5-0) | Cleveland Browns (11-5-0) | San Diego Chargers (11-5-0) | Oakland |
| 1981 | Miami Dolphins (11-4-1) | Cincinnati Bengals (12-4-0) | San Diego Chargers (10-6-0) | Cincinnati |
| 1982* | Miami Dolphins won the conference title, but the Los Angeles Raiders had best regular-season record (8-1-0). | | | |
| 1983 | Miami (12-4-0) | Pittsburgh (10-6-0) | Los Angeles Raiders (12-4-0) | Los Angeles Raiders |
| 1984 | Miami (14-2-0) | Pittsburgh (9-7-0) | Denver (13-3-0) | Miami |
| 1985 | Miami (12-4-0) | Cleveland (8-8) | Los Angeles Raiders (12-4-0) | New England |

*Schedule reduced to 9 games from usual 16, with no standings kept in Eastern, Central, and Western Divisions, because of 57-day player strike.

## AMERICAN LEAGUE CHAMPIONS

| Year | Eastern Division (W-L-T) | Western Division (W-L-T) | League champion, playoffs results |
|---|---|---|---|
| 1960 | Houston Oilers (10-4-0) | Los Angeles Chargers (10-4-0) | Houston 24, Los Angeles 16 |
| 1961 | Houston Oilers (10-3-1) | San Diego Chargers (12-2-0) | Houston 10, San Diego 3 |
| 1962 | Houston Oilers (11-3-0) | Dallas Texans (11-3-0) | Dallas 20, Houston 17[1] |
| 1963 | Boston Patriots (8-6-1)[2] | San Diego Chargers (11-3-0) | San Diego 51, Boston 10 |
| 1964 | Buffalo Bills (12-2-0) | San Diego Chargers (8-5-1) | Buffalo 20, San Diego 7 |
| 1965 | Buffalo Bills (10-3-1) | San Diego Chargers (9-2-3) | Buffalo 23, San Diego 0 |

| 1966 | Buffalo Bills (9-4-1) | Kansas City Chiefs (11-2-1) | Kansas City 31, Buffalo 7 |
| 1967 | Houston Oilers (9-4-1) | Oakland Raiders (13-1-0) | Oakland 40, Houston 7 |
| 1968 | New York Jets (11-3-0) | Oakland Raiders (12-2-0)[2] | New York 27, Oakland 23 |
| 1969 | New York Jets (10-4-0) | Oakland Raiders (12-1-1) | Kansas City 17, Oakland 7[3] |

1. Won at 2:45 of second sudden death overtime period. 2. Won divisional playoff. 3. Kansas City defeated New York, 13–6, and Oakland defeated Houston, 56–7, in interdivisional playoffs.

## NATIONAL FOOTBALL LEAGUE GOVERNMENT

**Commissioner's Office:** Pete Rozelle, commissioner; Don Weiss, executive director; Tom Sullivan, treasurer; John Schoemer, comptroller; Jay Moyer, executive vice-president/legal counsel; Jan Van Duser, director of operations; Jim Heffernan, director of public relations; Joe Browne, director of communications; Warren Welsh, director of security; Charles R. Jackson, assistant director of security; Joel Bussert, director of player personnel; Art McNally, supervisor of officials; Joe Rhein, director of administration; Mel Blount, director of player relations; Jim Steeg, director of special events.

**American Conference:** Lamar Hunt, president; Al Ward, assistant to the president; Pete Abitante, director of information.

**National Conference:** Wellington Mara, president; Bill Granholm, assistant to the president; Dick Maxwell, director of information.

## PRO FOOTBALL HALL OF FAME

(National Football Museum, Canton, Ohio)

Teams named are those with which player is best identified; figures in parentheses indicate number of playing seasons.

| | |
|---|---|
| Adderley, Herb, defensive back, Packers, Cowboys (12) | 1961–72 |
| Alworth, Lance, wide receiver, Chargers, Cowboys (11) | 1962–72 |
| Atkins, Doug, defensive end, Browns, Bears, Saints (17) | 1953–69 |
| Badgro, Morris, end, N.Y. Yankees, Giants, Bklyn. Dodgers (8) | 1927, 1930–36 |
| Battles, Cliff, back, Redskins (6) | 1932–37 |
| Baugh, Sammy, quarterback, Redskins (16) | 1937–52 |
| Bednarik, Chuck, center-lineback, Eagles (14) | 1949–62 |
| Bell, Bert, N.F.L. founder, owner Eagles and Steelers, N.F.L. Commissioner | 1946–59 |
| Bell, Bobby, linebacker, Chiefs (12) | 1963–74 |
| Berry, Raymond, end, Colts (13) | 1955–67 |
| Bidwell, Charles W., owner Chicago Cardinals | 1933–47 |
| Blanda, George, quarterback-kicker, Bears, Oilers, Raiders (27) | 1949–75 |
| Brown, Jim, fullback, Browns (9) | 1957–65 |
| Brown, Paul E., coach, Browns (1946–62), Bengals (1968–75) | 1946–75 |
| Brown, Roosevelt, tackle, Giants (13) | 1953–65 |
| Brown, Willie, cornerback, Broncos, Raiders (16) | 1963–78 |
| Butkus, Dick, linebacker, Bears (19) | 1965–73 |
| Canadeo, Tony, back, Packers (11) | 1941–52 |
| Carr, Joe, president N.F.L. (18) | 1921–39 |
| Chamberlin, Guy, end 4 teams (9) | 1919–27 |
| Christiansen, Jack, defensive back, Lions (8) | 1951–58 |
| Clark, Earl (Dutch), Qback, Spartans, Lions (7) | 1931–38 |
| Connor, George, tackle, linebacker, Bears (8) | 1948–55 |
| Conzelman, Jimmy, Qback 5 teams (10), owner | 1921–48 |
| Davis, Willie, defensive end, Packers (10) | 1960–69 |
| Donovan, Art, defensive tackle, Colts (12) | 1950–61 |
| Driscoll, John (Paddy), Qback, Cards, Bears (11) | 1919–29 |
| Dudley, Bill, back, Steelers, Lions, Redskins (9) | 1942–53 |
| Edwards, Albert Glen (Turk), tackle, Redskins (9) | 1932–40 |
| Ewbank, Weeb, coach Colts, Jets (20) | 1954–73 |
| Fears, Tom, end, Rams (9); coach, Saints | 1948–56 |
| Flaherty, Ray, end, Yankees, Giants (9); coach, Redskins, Yankees (14) | 1928–49 |
| Ford, Len, end, def. end, Browns, Packers (11) | 1948–58 |
| Fortmann, Daniel J., guard, Bears (8) | 1936–43 |
| Gatski, Frank, offensive lineman, Browns (12) | 1946–57 |
| George, Bill, linebacker, Bears, Rams (15) | 1952–66 |
| Gifford, Frank, back, Giants (12) | 1952–64 |
| Gillman, Sid, coach, Rams, Chargers, Oilers (18) | 1955–70, 73–74 |
| Graham, Otto, quarterback, Browns (10) | 1946–55 |
| Grange, Harold (Red), back, Bears, Yankees (9) | 1925–34 |
| Gregg, Forrest, tackle, Packers (15) | 1956–71 |
| Groza, Lou, place-kicker, tackle, Browns (21) | 1946–67 |
| Guyon, Joe, back, 6 teams (8) | 1919–27 |
| Halas, George, N.F.L. founder, owner and coach, | |

| | |
|---|---|
| Staleys and Bears, end (11) | 1919–67 |
| Healey, Ed, tackle, Bears (8) | 1920–27 |
| Hein, Mel, center, Giants (15) | 1931–45 |
| Henry, Wilbur (Pete), tackle, Bulldogs, Giants (8) | 1920–28 |
| Herber, Arnie, Qback, Packers, Giants (13) | 1930–45 |
| Hewitt, Bill, end, Bears, Eagles (9) | 1932–43 |
| Hinkle, Clarke, fullback, Packers (10) | 1932–41 |
| Hirsch, Elroy (Crazy Legs), back, end, Rams (12) | 1946–57 |
| Hornung, Paul, running back, Packers (9) | 1957–62 1964–66 |
| Houston, Ken def. back, Oilers, Redskins (14) | 1967–80 |
| Hubbard, R. (Cal), tackle, Giants, Packers (9) | 1927–36 |
| Huff, Sam, linebacker, Giants, Redskins (13) | 1956–67, 1969 |
| Hunt, Lamar, Founder A.F.L., owner Texans, Chiefs | 1959– |
| Hutson, Don, end, Packers (11) | 1935–45 |
| Jones, David (Deacon), defensive end, Rams, Chargers, Redskins (14) | 1961–74 |
| Jurgensen, Sonny, quarterback, Eagles, Redskins (18) | 1957–74 |
| Kiesling, Walt, guard 6 teams (13) | 1926–38 |
| Kinard, Frank (Bruiser), tackle, Dodgers (9) | 1938–47 |
| Lambeau, Earl (Curly), N.F.L. founder, coach, end, back, Packers (11) | 1919–53 |
| Lane, Richard (Night Train), defensive back, Rams, Cardinals, Lions (14) | 1952–65 |
| Lanier, Willie, linebacker, Chiefs (11) | 1967–77 |
| Lary, Yale, defensive back, punter, Lions (11) | 1952–64 |
| Laveill, Dante, end, Browns (11) | 1946–56 |
| Layne, Bobby, Qback, Bears, Lions, Steelers (15) | 1948–62 |
| Leemans, Alphonse (Tuffy), back, Giants (8) | 1936–43 |
| Lilly, Bob, defensive tackle, Cowboys (14) | 1961–74 |
| Lombardi, Vince, coach, Packers, Redskins (11) | 1959–70 |
| Luckman, Sid, quarterback, Bears (12) | 1939–50 |
| Lyman, Roy (Link), tackle, Bulldogs, Bears (11) | 1922–34 |
| Mara, Tim, N.F.L. founder, owner Giants | 1925–59 |
| Marchetti, Gino, defensive end, Colts (14) | 1952–66 |
| Marshall, George P., N.F.L. founder, owner Redskins | 1932–65 |
| Matson, Ollie, back, Cardinals, Rams, Lions, Eagles (14) | 1952–66 |
| McAfee, George, back, Bears (8) | 1940–50 |
| McCormack, Mike, tackle, N.Y. Yankees, Cleveland Browns (10) | 1951–1962 |
| McElhenny, Hugh, back, 49ers, Vikings, Giants (13) | 1952–64 |
| McNally, John (Blood), back, 7 teams (15) | 1925–39 |
| Michalske, August, guard, Yankees, Packers (11) | 1926–37 |
| Millner, Wayne, end, Redskins (7) | 1936–45 |
| Mitchell, Bobby, wide receiver, Browns, Redskins (11) | 1958–68 |
| Mix, Ron, tackle, Chargers (11) | 1960–71 |
| Moore, Lenny, back, Colts (12) | 1956–67 |
| Motley, Marion, fullback, Browns, Steelers (9) | 1946–55 |

Musso, George, guard-tackle, Bears (12) — 1933–44
Nagurski, Bronko, fullback, Bears (9) — 1930–43
Namath, Joe, quarterback, Jets, Rams (13) — 1965–77
Neale, Earle (Greasy), coach, Eagles — 1941–50
Nevers, Ernie, fullback, Chicago Cardinals (5) — 1926–31
Nitschke, Ray, linebacker, Packers (15) — 1958–72
Nomellini, Leo, defensive tackle, 49ers (14) — 1950–63
Olsen, Merlin, defensive tackle, Rams (15) — 1962–76
Otto, Jim, center, Raiders (15) — 1960–74
Owen, Steve, tackle, Giants (9), coach, Giants (13) — 1924–53
Parker, Clarence (Ace), quarterback, Dodgers (7) — 1937–46
Parker, Jim, guard, tackle, Colts (11) — 1957–67
Perry, Joe, fullback, 49ers, Colts (16) — 1948–63
Pihos, Pete, end, Eagles (9) — 1947–55
Ray, Hugh, Shorty, N.F.L. advisor — 1938–52
Reeves, Dan, owner Rams — 1941–71
Ringo, Jim, center, Packers (15) — 1963–67
Robustelli, Andy, def. end, Rams, Giants (14) — 1951–64
Rooney, Art, N.F.L. founder, owner Steelers — 1933–
Rozelle, Pete, commissioner, NFL, — 1960–present
Sayers, Gale, back, Bears (7) — 1965–71
Schmidt, Joe, linebacker, Lions (13) — 1953–65
Simpson, O.J., back, Bills, 49ers (11) — 1969–79
Starr, Bart, quarterback, coach, Packers (16) — 1956–71
Staubach, Roger, quarterback, Cowboys (11) — 1969–79

Stautner, Ernie, defensive tackle, Steelers (14) — 1950–63
Strong, Ken, back, Giants, Yankees (14) — 1929–47
Stydahar, Joe, tackle, Bears (9); coach,
  Rams, Cardinals (5) — 1936–54
Tarkenton, Fran, quarterback, Vikings, Giants (18) — 1961–78
Taylor, Charlie, wide receiver, Redskins (14) — 1964–77
Taylor, Jim, fullback, Packers, Saints (10) — 1958–67
Thorpe, Jim, back, 7 teams (12) — 1915–28
Tittle, Y. A., Qback, Colts, 49ers, Giants (17) — 1948–64
Trafton, George, center, Bears (13) — 1920–32
Trippi, Charley, back, Chicago Cardinals (9) — 1947–55
Tunnell, Emlen, def. back, Giants, Packers (14) — 1948–61
Turner, Clyde (Bulldog), center, Bears (13) — 1940–52
Unitas, John, quarterback, Colts (18) — 1956–73
Van Brocklin, Norm, Qback, Rams, Eagles (12) — 1949–60
Van Buren, Steve, back, Eagles (8) — 1944–51
Walker, Doak, running back, def. back, kicker, Lions (6) — 1950–55
Warfield, Paul, wide receiver, Browns, Dolphins
  (13) — 1964–74, 76–77
Waterfield, Bob, quarterback, Rams (8) — 1945–52
Weinmeister, Arnie, tackle, N.Y. Yankees, Giants (6) — 1948–53
Willis, Bill, Guard, Browns (8) — 1946–53
Wilson, Larry, defensive back, Cardinals (13) — 1960–72
Wojciechowicz, Alex, center, Lions, Eagles (13) — 1938–50

# N.F.L. INDIVIDUAL LIFETIME, SEASON, AND GAME RECORDS

(American Football League records were incorporated into N.F.L. records after merger of the leagues)

## All-Time Leading Touchdown Scorers

| | Yrs | Rush | Pass rec | Returns | TD |
|---|---|---|---|---|---|
| Jim Brown | 9 | 106 | 20 | 0 | 126 |
| John Riggins[1] | 14 | 104 | 12 | 0 | 116 |
| Lenny Moore | 12 | 63 | 48 | 2 | 113 |
| Walter Payton[1] | 11 | 98 | 11 | 0 | 109 |
| Don Hutson | 11 | 3 | 99 | 3 | 105 |
| Franco Harris | 12 | 91 | 9 | 0 | 100 |
| Jim Taylor | 10 | 83 | 10 | 0 | 93 |
| Bobby Mitchell | 11 | 18 | 65 | 8 | 91 |
| Leroy Kelly | 10 | 74 | 13 | 3 | 90 |
| Charley Taylor | 13 | 11 | 79 | 0 | 90 |

1. Still active.

## All-Time Leading Receivers

| | Yrs | Pass rec | Yds | Avg |
|---|---|---|---|---|
| Charley Joiner[1] | 17 | 716 | 11,706 | 16.3 |
| Charley Taylor | 13 | 649 | 9,110 | 14.0 |
| Don Maynard | 15 | 633 | 11,834 | 18.7 |
| Raymond Berry | 13 | 631 | 9,275 | 14.7 |
| Steve Largent[1] | 10 | 624 | 10,059 | 16.1 |
| Harold Carmichael | 14 | 590 | 8,985 | 15.2 |
| Fred Biletnikoff | 14 | 589 | 8,974 | 15.2 |
| Harold Jackson | 16 | 579 | 10,372 | 17.9 |
| Lionel Taylor | 10 | 567 | 7,195 | 12.7 |
| Lance Alworth | 11 | 542 | 10,226 | 18.9 |
| Bobby Mitchell | 11 | 521 | 7,954 | 15.3 |

1. Still active in National Football League.

## All-Time Leading Passers

| | Comp | Pct comp | Yds | TD | Int | Rating |
|---|---|---|---|---|---|---|
| Joe Montana[1] | 1,627 | 63.3 | 19,262 | 133 | 67 | 92.4 |
| Roger Staubach | 1,685 | 57.0 | 22,700 | 153 | 109 | 83.4 |
| Sonny Jurgensen | 2,433 | 57.1 | 32,224 | 255 | 189 | 82.6 |
| Len Dawson | 2,136 | 57.1 | 28,711 | 239 | 183 | 82.6 |
| Neil Lomax[1] | 1,047 | 57.3 | 13,406 | 79 | 55 | 82.3 |
| Danny White[1] | 1,422 | 59.4 | 17,911 | 130 | 107 | 82.3 |
| Ken Anderson | 2,643 | 59.4 | 32,667 | 196 | 158 | 82.0 |
| Dan Fouts[1] | 2,839 | 59.0 | 37,492 | 228 | 205 | 81.8 |
| Bart Starr | 1,808 | 57.4 | 24,718 | 152 | 138 | 80.5 |
| Fran Tarkenton | 3,686 | 57.0 | 47,003 | 342 | 266 | 80.4 |

1. Still active.

## All-Time Leading Rushers

| | Yrs | Att | Yds | Av |
|---|---|---|---|---|
| Walter Payton[1] | 11 | 3,371 | 14,860 | |
| Jim Brown | 9 | 2,359 | 12,312 | |
| Franco Harris | 13 | 2,949 | 12,1 | |
| John Riggins[1] | 14 | 2,916 | 1 | |
| O.J. Simpson | 11 | 2,404 | | |
| Tony Dorsett | 9 | 2,44 | | |
| Joe Perry | 16 | 1, | | |
| Earl Campbell[1] | 8 | | | |
| Jim Taylor | 10 | | | |
| Larry Csonka | 1 | | | |

1. Still active in Natio

The passing ratings are based on performance standards established for the completion percentage, interception percentage, touchdown percentage and average pass gain. Passers are allocated points according to how their marks compare with those standards. This listing is based on 1,500 or more pass attempts. 1. Still active in National Footbal League.

All-Tim

| | | | | |
|---|---|---|---|---|
| Fred Cox | 15 | 0 | 282 | 519 | 1,365 |
| Lou Groza | 17 | 1 | 234 | 641 | 1,349 |
| Mark Moseley[2] | 15 | 0 | 288 | 457 | 1,321 |
| Gino Cappelletti | 11 | 42 | 176 | 350 | 1,130[1] |
| Don Cockroft | 13 | 0 | 216 | 432 | 1,080 |
| Garo Yepremian | 14 | 0 | 210 | 444 | 1,074 |
| Bruce Gossett | 11 | 0 | 219 | 374 | 1,031 |

1. Includes four 2-point conversions. 2. Still active in National Football League.

## Scoring

Most points scored, lifetime—2,002, George Blanda, Chicago Bears, 1949–58; Baltimore, 1950; Houston, 1960–66; Oakland, 1967–75 (9tds, 943 pat, 335 fgs).

Most points, season—176, Paul Hornung, Green Bay, 1960 (15 td, 41 pat, 15 fg).

Most points, game—40, Ernie Nevers, Chicago Cardinals, 1929 (6 td, 4 pat).

Most points, per quarter—29, Don Hutson, Green Bay, 1945 (4 td, 5 pat).

Most touchdowns, lifetime—126, Jim Brown, Cleveland, 1957–65.

Most touchdowns, season—23, O.J. Simpson, Buffalo, 1975.

Most touchdowns, game—6, Ernie Nevers, Chicago Cardinals, 1929; William Jones, Cleveland, 1951; Gale Sayers, Chicago Bears, 1965.

Most points after touchdown, lifetime—943, George Blanda, Chicago Bears, 1949–58; Baltimore, 1950; Houston, 1960–66; Oakland, 1967–75.

Most points after touchdown, game—9, Pat Harder, Chicago Cardinals, 1948; Bob Waterfield, Los Angeles, 1950; Charlie Gogolak, Washington, 1966.

Most consecutive points after touchdown—234, Tommy Davis, San Francisco, 1959–65.

Most points after touchdown, no misses, season—56, Danny Villanueva, Dallas, 1966.

Most field goals, lifetime—373, Jan Stenerud, Kansas City, 1967–79; Green Bay Packers, 1980–8... 1985.

Most field goals, se...

Most f...

Most yards gained, game—554, Norm Van Brocklin, Los Angeles, 1951.

Most touchdown passes, lifetime—342, Fran Tarkenton, Minnesota, 1961–66, 72–78; New York Giants, 1967–71.

Most touchdown passes, season—48, Dan Marino, Miami, 1984.

Most touchdown passes, game—7, Sid Luckman, Chicago Bears, 1943; Adrian Burk, Philadelphia, 1954; George Blanda, Houston 1961; Y.A. Tittle, New York Giants, 1963; Joe Kapp, Minnesota, 1969.

Most consecutive games, touchdown passes—47, John Unitas, Baltimore.

Most consecutive passes attempted, none intercepted—294, Bart Starr, Green Bay, 1964–65.

Longest pass completion—99 yards, Frank Filchock (to Andy Farkas), Washington, 1939; George Izo (to Bob Mitchell), Washington, 1963; Karl Sweetan (to Pat Studstill), Detroit, 1966; Sonny Jurgensen (to Gerry Allen), Washington, 1968, (all for touchdowns).

Most pass receptions, lifetime—716, Charlie Joiner, Houston Oilers, 1969–72, Cincinnati Bengals, 1972–75, San Diego Chargers, 1976–85.

Most pass receptions, season—106, Art Monk, Washington, 1984.

Most pass receptions, game—18, Tom Fears, Los Angeles, 1950.

Most consecutive games, pass receptions—127, Harold Carmichael, Philadelphia, 1972–80.

Most yards gained, pass receptions, lifetime—11,834, Don Maynard, New York Giants, 1958; New York Jets, 1960–72; St. Louis, 1973.

Most yards gained receptions, season—1,746, Charley Hennigan, Houston, 1961.

Most yards gained receptions, game—303, Jim Benton, Cleveland Rams, 1945.

Most touchdown pass receptions, lifetime—99, Don Hutson, Green Bay, 1935–45.

Most touchdown pass receptions, season—17, Don Hutson, Green Bay, 1942; Elroy Hirsch, Los Angeles, 1951; Bill Groman, Houston, 1961.

Most touchdown pass receptions, game—5, Bob Shaw, Chicago Cards, 1950.

Most consecutive games, touchdown pass receptions—11, Elroy Hirsch, Los Angeles, 1950–51; Buddy Dial, Pittsburgh, 1959–60.

Most pass interceptions, lifetime—81, Paul Krause, Washington, 1964–67; Minnesota, 1968–79.

Most pass interceptions, season—14, Richard (Night Train) Lane, Los Angeles, 1952.

Most pass interceptions, game—4, by 15 players.

Longest pass interception return—102 yards, Bob Smith, Chicago Bears, 1949; Erich Barnes, New York Giants, 1961; Gary Barbaro, Kansas City, 1977; Louis Breeden, Cincinnati, 1981.

...ing

...t punt—98 yards, Steve O'Neal, New York Jets, 1969.

...average punting, lifetime—45.10 yards, Sammy Baugh, ...ington, 1937–52.

...unt return—98 yards, Gil LeFebvre, Cincinnati Reds, 1933; ... West, Minnesota, 1968; Dennis Morgan, Dallas, 1974.

...ck-off return—106 yards, Roy Green, St. Louis, 1979; Al ...ael, Green Bay, 1956; Noland Smith, Kansas City, 1967.

| | Yrs | TD | FG | PAT | Pts |
|---|---|---|---|---|---|
| | 4.4 | | | | |
| | 5.2 | | | | 2,002 |
| | 4.1 | | | | 1,669 |
| | 3.9 | | | | 1,439 |
| | 4.5 | | | | 1,380 |
| | 5.0 | | | | |
| | 4.2 | | | | |
| | 4.4 | | | | |
| | 4.3 | | | | |

| ...302 | | | | | |
| 11,236 | | | | | |
| 10,832 | | | | | |
| 9,723 | | | | | |
| 9,407 | | | | | |
| 8,597 | | | | | |
| 8,081 | | | | | |

| | Leading Scorers | | | | | |
|---|---|---|---|---|---|---|
| | George Blanda | 26 | 9 | 335 | 943 | |
| | Jan Stenerud[2] | 19 | 0 | 373 | 550 | |
| | Jim Turner | 16 | 0 | 304 | 521 | |
| | Jim Bakken | 17 | 0 | 282 | 534 | |

...2,187 1,941 1,891

...al Football League.

...nton, Minnesota,

...Miami, 1984.

...New York Jets,

...s, Baltimore,

...Minnesota,

...1984.

## TEAM NICKNAMES AND HOME FIELD CAPACITIES

### AMERICAN CONFERENCE
**Eastern Division**

| | | |
|---|---|---|
| Buffalo Bills | Rich Stadium (AT) | 80,020 |
| Indianapolis Colts[1] | Hoosier Dome (AT) | 61,500 |
| Miami Dolphins | Orange Bowl (G) | 75,059 |
| New England Patriots | Sullivan Stadium (ST) | 61,297 |
| New York Jets[2] | Giants Stadium (AT) | 76,891 |

**Central Division**

| | | |
|---|---|---|
| Cincinnati Bengals | Riverfront Stadium (AT) | 59,754 |
| Cleveland Browns | Municipal Stadium (G) | 80,322 |
| Houston Oilers | Astrodome (AT) | 50,496 |
| Pittsburgh Steelers | Three Rivers Stadium (AT) | 59,000 |

**Western Division**

| | | |
|---|---|---|
| Denver Broncos | Mile High Stadium (G) | 75,103 |
| Kansas City Chiefs | Arrowhead Stadium (TT) | 78,067 |
| Los Angeles Raiders[3] | Memorial Coliseum (G) | 92,498 |
| San Diego Chargers | Jack Murphy Stadium (G) | 53,675 |
| Seattle Seahawks | Kingdome (AT) | 64,757 |

1. Moved franchise from Baltimore prior to 1984 season. 2. Moved to Giants Stadium; East Rutherford, N.J. prior to 1984 season. 3. Moved franchise to Los Angeles for 1982 season. Shift is still being argued in courts, as city of Oakland tries to regain franchise.

### NATIONAL CONFERENCE
**Eastern Division**

| | | |
|---|---|---|
| Dallas Cowboys | Texas Stadium (TT) | 65,101 |
| New York Giants | Giants Stadium (AT)[1] | 76,891 |
| Philadelphia Eagles | Veterans Stadium (AT) | 72,204 |
| St. Louis Cardinals | Busch Memorial Stadium (AT) | 51,392 |
| Washington Redskins | R.F. Kennedy Stadium (G) | 55,045 |

**Central Division**

| | | |
|---|---|---|
| Chicago Bears | Soldier Field (AT) | 65,793 |
| Detroit Lions | Pontiac Silverdome (AT) | 80,638 |
| Green Bay Packers | Lambeau Field (G) | 56,189 |
| | Milwaukee Stadium (G) | 55,958 |
| Minnesota Vikings | Hubert Humphrey Metrodome (ST) | 62,212 |
| Tampa Bay Buccaneers | Tampa Stadium | 72,812 |

**Western Division**

| | | |
|---|---|---|
| Atlanta Falcons | Atlanta-Fulton Stadium | 60,748 |
| Los Angeles Rams | Anaheim Stadium | 69,007 |
| New Orleans Saints | Louisiana Superdome | 71,330 |
| San Francisco 49ers | Candlestick Park | 61,185 |

1. At East Rutherford, N.J. NOTE: Stadium playing surfaces in parentheses: (AT) Astro Turf; (G) Grass; (ST) Super Turf; (TT) Tartan Turf.

## UNITED STATES FOOTBALL LEAGUE

The United States Football League played its inaugural season in the spring and summer of 1983. The league originated with the concept that football was popular enough with television viewers and football ticket buyers to warrant year-round play. The idea, at first, was to play in the spring and summer, so as not to compete directly with the powerful, established National Football League.

Games were scheduled between March and July, and television contracts with ABC-TV and the ESPN cable network helped finance the league at the start by guaranteeing two years of network coverage and paying the U.S.F.L. $12 million annually.

The league, which started with 12 teams, added six more in 1984 and began serious bidding for established N.F.L. players and top college prospects. The New Jersey Generals, owned by the flamboyant Donald Trump, led the way with such big-name signees as running back Hershel Walker and quarterback Doug Flutie.

During the league's third year of operations, a decision was made to move to direct competition in the fall with the N.F.L., starting in September, 1986. Several franchises were in financial trouble, however, and the prospect of sitting idle for more than a year made the league's future questionable. The final spring season was completed in July, 1985, and the next regular season contests were not scheduled until September, 1986.

## UNITED STATES FOOTBALL LEAGUE FINAL STANDINGS—1985

### EASTERN CONFERENCE

| | W | L | T | Pct | Pts | OP |
|---|---|---|---|---|---|---|
| Birmingham | 13 | 5 | 0 | .722 | 436 | 299 |
| New Jersey | 11 | 7 | 0 | .611 | 418 | 377 |
| Memphis | 11 | 7 | 0 | .611 | 428 | 337 |
| Baltimore | 10 | 7 | 1 | .583 | 368 | 260 |
| Tampa Bay | 10 | 8 | 0 | .556 | 404 | 422 |
| Jacksonville | 9 | 9 | 0 | .500 | 407 | 402 |
| Orlando | 5 | 13 | 0 | .278 | 308 | 484 |

### WESTERN CONFERENCE

| | W | L | T | Pct | Pts | OP |
|---|---|---|---|---|---|---|
| Oakland | 13 | 4 | 1 | .750 | 473 | 359 |
| Denver | 11 | 7 | 0 | .611 | 439 | 431 |
| Houston | 10 | 8 | 0 | .556 | 544 | 388 |
| Arizona | 8 | 10 | 0 | .444 | 376 | 405 |
| Portland | 6 | 12 | 0 | .333 | 275 | 422 |

| | W | L | T | Pct | Pts | Op |
|---|---|---|---|---|---|---|
| San Antonio | 5 | 13 | 0 | .278 | 296 | 436 |
| Los Angeles | 3 | 15 | 0 | .167 | 266 | 456 |

### Playoffs

**Quarterfinals**

Birmingham 22, Houston 20
Memphis 48, Denver 7
Oakland 30, Tampa Bay 27
Baltimore 20, New Jersey 17

**Semifinals**

Oakland 28, Memphis 19
Baltimore 28, Oakland 24

**Final**

Baltimore 28, Birmingham 14

# FISHING

## WORLD ALL-TACKLE FISHING RECORDS

### Caught with Rod and Reel in Fresh Water

*Source:* International Game Fish Association

| Species | lb-oz | Where caught | Year | Angler |
|---|---|---|---|---|
| Bass, Largemouth | 22-4 | Montgomery Lake, Ga. | 1932 | George W. Perry |
| Bass, Peacock | 26-8 | Mataveni River, Columbia | 1982 | Rod Neubert |
| Bass, Redeye | 8-3 | Flint River, Ga. | 1977 | David A. Hubbard |
| Bass, Rock | 3-0 | York River, Ontario | 1974 | Peter Gulgin |
| Bass, Smallmouth | 11-15 | Dale Hollow Lake, Ky. | 1955 | David L. Hayes |
| Bass, Spotted | 9-0 | Lake Perris, Calif. | 1984 | Jeffrey L. Mathews |
| Bass, Striped | 78-8 | Atlantic City, N.J. | 1982 | Albert McReynolds |
| Bass, Striped (landlocked) | 59-12 | Colorado River, Ariz. | 1977 | Frank W. Smith |
| Bass, White | 5-9 | Colorado River, Texas | 1977 | David S. Cordill |
| Bass, Whiterock | 20-6 | Savannah River, Ga. | 1978 | Danny Wood |
| Bass, Yellow | 2-4 | Lake Monroe, Ind. | 1977 | Donald L. Stalker |
| Bluegill | 4-12 | Ketona Lake, Ala. | 1950 | T.S. Hudson |
| Bowfin | 21-8 | Florence, S.C. | 1980 | Robert L. Harmon |
| Buffalo, Bigmouth | 70-5 | Bussey Brake, Bastrop, La. | 1980 | Delbert Sisk |
| Buffalo, Smallmouth | 68-8 | Lake Hamilton, Ark. | 1984 | Jerry L. Dolezal |
| Bullhead, Black | 8-0 | Lake Waccabuc, N.Y. | 1951 | Kani Evans |
| Bullhead, Brown | 5-8 | Veal Pond, Ga. | 1975 | Jimmy Andrews |
| Burbot | 18-4 | Pickford, Mich. | 1980 | Tom Courtemanche |
| Carp | 57-13 | Potomac River, Wash., D.C. | 1983 | David Nikolow |
| Catfish, Blue | 97-0 | Missouri River, S.D. | 1959 | Edward B. Elliott |
| Catfish, Channel | 58-0 | Santee–Cooper Res., S.C. | 1964 | W.B. Whaley |
| Catfish, Flathead | 91-4 | Lake Lewisville, Texas | 1982 | Mike Rogers |
| Char, Arctic | 32-9 | Tree River, Canada | 1985 | Peter Goulding |
| Crappie, Black | 4-8 | Kerr Lake, Va. | 1981 | L. Carl Herring, Jr. |
| Crappie, White | 5-3 | Enid Dam, Mississippi | 1957 | Fred L. Bright |
| Dolly Varden | 8-1 | Nakwasina River, Alaska | 1985 | Loyal Johnson |
| Drum, Freshwater | 54-8 | Nickajack Lake, Tenn. | 1972 | Benny E. Hull |
| Gar, Alligator | 279 | Rio Grande River, Tex. | 1951 | Bill Valverde |
| Gar, Longnose | 50-5 | Trinity River, Texas | 1954 | Townsend Miller |
| Gar, Shortnose | 4-9 | Mississippi River, Minnesota | 1984 | Matthew "Dewy" Ocel |
| Inconnu | 38-2 | Kobuk River, Alaska | 1982 | Mark L. Feldman |
| Muskellunge | 69-15 | St. Lawrence River, N.Y. | 1957 | Arthur Lawton |
| Muskellunge, Tiger | 51-3 | Lac-Vieux-Desert, Wisc.-Mich. | 1919 | John A. Knobla |
| Perch, White | 4-12 | Messalonskee Lake, Maine | 1949 | Mrs. Earl Small |
| Perch, Yellow | 4-3 | Bordentown, N.J. | 1865 | Dr. C.C. Abbot |
| Pickerel, Eastern Chain | 9-6 | Homerville, Ga. | 1961 | Baxley McQuaig, Jr. |
| Redhorse, Northern | 3-11 | Missouri River, S.D. | 1977 | Phillip Laumeyer |
| Redhorse, Silver | 11-7 | Plum Creek, Wisconsin | 1985 | Neal D.G. Long |
| Salmon, Atlantic | 79-2 | Tana River, Norway | 1928 | Henrik Henriksen |
| Salmon, Chinook | 97-4 | Kenai River, Alaska | 1985 | Les Anderson |
| Salmon, Chum | 27-3 | Raymond Cove, Alaska | 1977 | Robert A. Jahnke |
| Salmon, Coho | 31-0 | Cowichan Bay, B.C., Canada | 1947 | Mrs. Lee Hallberg |
| Salmon, Landlocked | 22-8 | Sebago Lake, Maine | 1907 | Edward Blakely |
| Salmon, Pink | 12-9 | Moose & Kenai Rivers, Alaska | 1974 | Steven Alan Lee |
| Salmon, Sockeye | 12-8 | Situk River, Yakutat, Alaska | 1983 | Mike Boswell |
| Shad, American | 11-1 | Delaware River, N.J. | 1984 | Charles J. Mower |
| Sturgeon | 468-0 | Benicia, Calif. | 1983 | Joey Pallotta III |
| Sturgeon, White | 380-0 | Snake River, Idaho | 1973 | Del Canty |
| Sunfish, Green | 2-2 | Stockton Lake, Missouri | 1971 | Paul M. Dilley |
| Sunfish, Redbreast | 1-12 | Suwannee River, Fla. | 1984 | Alvin Buchanan |
| Sunfish, Redear | 4-10 | Mill Pond, Fla. | 1985 | C.L. Windham |
| Tigerfish | 61-11 | Lake Tanganyika, Zambia | 1984 | Don Hunter |
| Trout, Brook | 14-8 | Nipigon River, Ontario | 1916 | Dr. W.J. Cook |
| Trout, Brown | 35-15 | Nahuel Huapi, Argentina | 1952 | Eugenio Cavaglia |
| Trout, Bull | 32-0 | Lake Pend Orielle, Idaho | 1949 | N.L. Higgins |
| Trout, Cutthroat | 41-0 | Pyramid Lake, Nev. | 1925 | John Skimmerhorn |
| Trout, Golden | 11-0 | Cook's Lake, Wyoming | 1948 | Charles S. Reed |
| Trout, Lake | 65-0 | Great Bear Lake, N.W.T., Canada | 1970 | Larry Daunis |
| Trout, Rainbow | 42-2 | Bell Island, Alaska | 1970 | David Robert White |
| Trout, Tiger | 20-13 | Lake Michigan, Wisc. | 1978 | Peter M. Friedland |
| Walleye | 25-0 | Old Hickory Lake, Tenn. | 1960 | Mabry Harper |
| Whitefish, Lake | 14-6 | Meaford, Ontario, Canada | 1984 | Dennis M. Laycock |
| Whitefish, Mountain | 5-0 | Athabasca River, Alberta, Canada | 1963 | Orville Welch |
| Whitefish, Round | 6-0 | Putahow River, Manitoba, Canada | 1984 | Allan J. Ristori |

## Caught With Rod and Reel in Salt Water

*Source:* International Game Fish Association

| Species | lb-oz | Where caught | Year | Angler |
|---|---|---|---|---|
| Albacore | 88-2 | Canary Islands | 1977 | Siegfried Dickemann |
| Amberjack | 155-10 | Challenger Bank, Bermuda | 1981 | Joseph Dawson |
| Barracuda | 83 | Lagos, Nigeria | 1952 | K. J. W. Hackett |
| Bass, Black Sea | 9-0 | Montauk, N.Y. | 1983 | Salvatore Vicari |
| Bass, Giant Sea | 563-8 | Anacapa Island, Calif. | 1968 | J. D. McAdam, Jr. |
| Bass, Striped | 78-8 | Atlantic City, N.J. | 1982 | Albert J. McReynolds |
| Blackfish (Tautog) | 21-8 | Wachapreague, Virginia | 1984 | Tommy Wood |
| Bluefish | 31-12 | North Carolina | 1972 | James M. Hussey |
| Bonefish | 19 | Zululand, S. Africa | 1962 | Brian W. Batchelor |
| Bonito, Atlantic | 18-4 | Fayal Island, Azores | 1984 | D. Gama Higgs |
| Bonito, Pacific | 23-8 | Victoria, Mahe | 1975 | Mrs. Anne Cochain |
| Cobia | 135-9 | Shark Bay, Australia | 1985 | Peter Goulding |
| Cod, Atlantic | 98-12 | Isle of Shoals, N.H. | 1969 | Alphonse Bielevich |
| Cod, Pacific | 30-0 | Andrew Bay, Alaska | 1984 | Donald R. Vaughn |
| Conger | 102-8 | Plymouth, Devon, England | 1983 | Raymond Ewart Street |
| Dolphin | 87 | Papagallo Gulf, Costa Rica | 1976 | Manual Salazar |
| Drum, Black | 113-1 | Lewes, Del. | 1975 | G. M. Townsend |
| Drum, Red | 94-2 | Avon, North Carolina | 1984 | David G. Deuel |
| Flounder, Summer | 22-7 | Montauk, N.Y. | 1975 | Charles Nappi |
| Halibut, Atlantic | 250 | Gloucester, Mass. | 1981 | Louis P. Sirard |
| Halibut, California | 45 | Santa Cruz Island, Calif. | 1982 | Jack C. Meserve |
| Hailbut, Pacific | 350 | Homer, Alaska | 1982 | Vern S. Foster |
| Jack, Crevalle | 54-7 | Port Michel, Gabon | 1982 | Thomas F. Gibson, Jr. |
| Jack, Horse-eye | 24-8 | Miami, Fla. | 1982 | Tito Schnau |
| Jack, Pacific Crevalle | 23-14 | Las Arenas, Mexico | 1985 | Ken Mayer |
| Jewfish | 680 | Fernandina Beach, Fla. | 1961 | Lynn Joyner |
| Lingcod | 56-0 | Elfin Cove, Alaska | 1985 | Stephen E. Webb |
| Mackerel, King | 90 | Key West, Florida | 1976 | Norton I. Thomton |
| Mackerel, Spanish | 12-0 | Ft. Pierce, Florida | 1984 | John F. Colligan |
| Marlin, Atlantic Blue | 1282 | St. Thomas, Virgin Islands | 1977 | Larry Martin |
| Marlin, Black | 1560 | Cabo Blanco, Peru | 1953 | A. C. Glassel, Jr. |
| Marlin, Pacific Blue | 1376 | Kaaiwi Point, Kona, Hawaii | 1982 | Jay Wm. deBeaubien |
| Marlin, Striped | 455-4 | Mayor Island, New Zealand | 1982 | Bruce Jenkinson |
| Marlin, White | 181-14 | Victoria, Brazil | 1979 | Evandro Luiz Coser |
| Permit | 51-8 | Lake Worth, Fla. | 1978 | William M. Kenney |
| Pollack | 26-7 | Salcombe, England | 1984 | Robert Perry |
| Pollack (virens) | 46-7 | Brielle, N.J. | 1975 | John T. Holton |
| Pompano, African | 41-8 | Fort Lauderdale, Fla. | 1979 | Wayne Sommers |
| Sailfish, Atlantic | 128-1 | Luanda, Angola, Africa | 1974 | Harm Steyn |
| Sailfish, Pacific | 221 | Santa Cruz Is., Galapagos Is. | 1947 | C. W. Stewart |
| Seabass, White | 83-12 | San Felipe, Mexico | 1953 | L. C. Baumgardner |
| Shark, Blue | 437 | Catherine Bay, Australia | 1976 | Peter Hyde |
| Shark, Hammerhead | 991 | Sarasota, Fla. | 1982 | Allen Ogle |
| Shark, Mako | 1080 | Montauk, N.Y. | 1979 | James L. Melanson |
| Shark, Porbeagle | 465 | Padstow, Cornwall, England | 1976 | Jorge Potier |
| Shark, Thresher | 802 | Tutukaka, New Zealand | 1981 | Dianne North |
| Shark, Tiger | 1780 | Cherry Grove, S.C. | 1964 | Walter Maxwell |
| Shark, White | 2664 | South Australia | 1959 | Alfred Dean |
| Snapper, Cubera | 121-8 | Cameron, La. | 1982 | Mike Hebert |
| Snook | 53-10 | Costa Rica | 1978 | Gilbert Ponzi |
| Spearfish | 90-13 | Madeira Island, Portugal | 1980 | Joseph Larkin |
| Swordfish | 1182 | Iquique, Chile | 1953 | L. E. Marron |
| Tanguigue | 99 | Scottburgh, Natal, South Africa | 1982 | Michael John Wilkinson |
| Tarpon | 283 | Lake Maracalbo, Venezuela | 1956 | M. Salazar |
| Trevally, Bigeye | 15-0 | Isla Coiba, Panama | 1984 | Sally S. Timms |
| Trevally, Giant | 137-9 | McKenzie State Park, Hawaii | 1983 | Roy K. Gushiken |
| Tuna, Atlantic Bigeye | 375-8 | Ocean City, Md. | 1977 | Cecil Browne |
| Tuna, Blackfin | 42 | Bermuda | 1978 | Alan J. Card |
| Tuna, Bluefin | 1496 | Nova Scotia, Canada | 1979 | Ken Fraser |
| Tuna, Dog-tooth | 194 | Kwan-Tall Island, Korea | 1980 | Kim Chul |
| Tuna, Longtail | 79-2 | Montague Island, Australia | 1982 | Tim Simpson |
| Tuna, Pacific Big-Eyed | 435 | Cobo Blanco, Peru | 1957 | R.V. A. Lee |
| Tuna, Skipjack | 41-12 | Black River, Mauritius | 1982 | Bruno de Ravel |
| Tuna, Southern Bluefin | 348-5 | Whakatane, New Zealand | 1981 | Rex Wood |
| Tuna, Yellowfin | 388-12 | Mexico | 1977 | Curt Wiesenmutter |
| Wahoo | 149 | Cat Cay, Bahamas | 1962 | John Pirovano |
| Weakfish | 19-2 | Jones Beach Inlet, N.Y. | 1984 | Dennis Roger Rooney |
| Yellowtail, California | 71-15 | Alijos Rocks, Mexico | 1979 | Michael Carpenter |
| Yellowtail, Southern | 114-10 | Tauranga, New Zealand | 1984 | Mike Godfrey |

# BASKETBALL

Basketball may be the one sport whose exact origin is definitely known. In the winter of 1891–92, Dr. James Naismith, an instructor in the Y.M.C.A. Training College (now Springfield College) at Springfield, Mass., deliberately invented the game of basketball in order to provide indoor exercise and competition for the students between the closing of the football season and the opening of the baseball season. He affixed peach baskets overhead on the walls at opposite ends of the gymnasium and organized teams to play his new game in which the purpose was to toss an association (soccer) ball into one basket and prevent the opponents from tossing the ball into the other basket. The game is fundamentally the same today, though there have been improvements in equipment and some changes in rules.

Because Dr. Naismith had eighteen available players when he invented the game, the first rule was: "There shall be nine players on each side." Later the number of players became optional, depending upon the size of the available court, but the five-player standard was adopted when the game spread over the country. United States soldiers brought basketball to Europe in World War I, and it soon became a world-wide sport.

## College Basketball

### NATIONAL COLLEGIATE A.A. CHAMPIONS

| | | | | | | | |
|---|---|---|---|---|---|---|---|
| 1939 | Oregon | 1950 | C.C.N.Y. | 1961 | Cincinnati | 1978 | Kentucky |
| 1940 | Indiana | 1951 | Kentucky | 1962 | Cincinnati | 1979 | Michigan State |
| 1941 | Wisconsin | 1952 | Kansas | 1963 | Loyola (Chicago) | 1980 | Louisville |
| 1942 | Stanford | 1953 | Indiana | 1964 | U.C.L.A. | 1981 | Indiana |
| 1943 | Wyoming | 1954 | La Salle | 1965 | U.C.L.A. | 1982 | North Carolina |
| 1944 | Utah | 1955 | San Francisco | 1966 | Texas Western | 1983 | North Carolina State |
| 1945 | Oklahoma A & M | 1956 | San Francisco | 1967–73 | U.C.L.A. | 1984 | Georgetown |
| 1946 | Oklahoma A & M | 1957 | North Carolina | 1974 | No. Carolina State | 1985 | Villanova |
| 1947 | Holy Cross | 1958 | Kentucky | 1975 | U.C.L.A. | 1986 | Louisville |
| 1948 | Kentucky | 1959 | California | 1976 | Indiana | | |
| 1949 | Kentucky | 1960 | Ohio State | 1977 | Marquette | | |

### NATIONAL INVITATION TOURNAMENT (NIT) CHAMPIONS

| | | | | | | | |
|---|---|---|---|---|---|---|---|
| 1939 | Long Island U. | 1952 | La Salle | 1964 | Bradley | 1976 | Kentucky |
| 1940 | Colorado | 1953 | Seton Hall | 1965 | St. John's (N.Y.C.) | 1977 | St. Bonaventure |
| 1941 | Long Island U. | 1954 | Holy Cross | 1966 | Brigham Young | 1978 | Texas |
| 1942 | West Virginia | 1955 | Duquesne | 1967 | So. Illinois | 1979 | Indiana |
| 1943–44 | St. John's (N.Y.C.) | 1956 | Louisville | 1968 | Dayton | 1980 | Virginia |
| 1945 | DePaul | 1957 | Bradley | 1969 | Temple | 1981 | Tulsa |
| 1946 | Kentucky | 1958 | Xavier (Cincinnati) | 1970 | Marquette | 1982 | Bradley |
| 1947 | Utah | 1959 | St. John's (N.Y.C.) | 1971 | North Carolina | 1983 | Fresno State |
| 1948 | St. Louis | 1960 | Bradley | 1972 | Maryland | 1984 | Michigan |
| 1949 | San Francisco | 1961 | Providence | 1973 | Virginia Tech | 1985 | U.C.L.A. |
| 1950 | C.C.N.Y. | 1962 | Dayton | 1974 | Purdue | 1986 | Ohio State |
| 1951 | Brigham Young | 1963 | Providence | 1975 | Princeton | | |

### N.C.A.A. MAJOR COLLEGE INDIVIDUAL SCORING RECORDS

**Single Season Averages**

| Player, Team | Year | G | FG [1] | FT | Pts | Avg |
|---|---|---|---|---|---|---|
| Pete Maravich, Louisiana State | 1969–70 | 31 | 522 [1] | 337 | 1381 [1] | 44.5 [1] |
| Pete Maravich | 1968–69 | 26 | 433 | 282 | 1148 | 44.2 |
| Pete Maravich | 1967–68 | 26 | 432 | 274 | 1138 | 43.8 |
| Frank Selvy, Furman | 1953–54 | 29 | 427 | 355 [1] | 1209 | 41.7 |
| Johnny Neumann, Mississippi | 1970–71 | 23 | 366 | 191 | 923 | 40.1 |
| Freeman Williams, Portland State | 1976–77 | 26 | 417 | 176 | 1010 | 38.8 |
| Billy McGill, Utah | 1961–62 | 26 | 394 | 221 | 1009 | 38.8 |
| Calvin Murphy, Niagara | 1967–68 | 24 | 337 | 242 | 916 | 38.2 |
| Austin Carr, Notre Dame | 1969–70 | 29 | 444 | 218 | 1106 | 38.1 |

1. Record.

# N.C.A.A. CAREER SCORING TOTALS

## Division I

| Player, Team | Last year | G | FG | FT | Pts | Avg |
|---|---|---|---|---|---|---|
| Pete Maravich, Louisiana State | 1970 | 83 | 1387[1] | 893[1] | 3667[1] | 44.2[1] |
| Austin Carr, Notre Dame | 1971 | 74 | 1017 | 526 | 2560 | 34.6 |
| Oscar Robertson, Cincinnati | 1960 | 88 | 1052 | 869 | 2973 | 33.8 |
| Calvin Murphy, Niagara | 1970 | 77 | 947 | 654 | 2548 | 33.1 |
| Dwight Lamar[2] | 1973 | 57 | 768 | 326 | 1862 | 32.7 |
| Frank Selvy, Furman | 1954 | 78 | 922 | 694 | 2538 | 32.5 |
| Rick Mount, Purdue | 1970 | 72 | 910 | 503 | 2323 | 32.3 |
| Darrel Floyd, Furman | 1956 | 71 | 868 | 545 | 2281 | 32.1 |
| Nick Werkman, Seton Hall | 1964 | 71 | 812 | 649 | 2273 | 32.0 |

1. Record. 2. Also played two seasons in college division.

## Division II

| Player, Team | Last year | G | FG | FT | Pts | Avg |
|---|---|---|---|---|---|---|
| Travis Grant, Kentucky State | 1972 | 121 | 1760[1] | 525 | 4045[1] | 33.4[1] |
| John Rinka, Kenyon | 1970 | 99 | 1261 | 729 | 3251 | 32.8 |
| Florindo Vieira, Quinnipiac | 1957 | 69 | 761 | 741 | 2263 | 32.8 |
| Willie Shaw, Lane | 1964 | 76 | 960 | 459 | 2379 | 31.3 |
| Mike Davis, Virginia Union | 1969 | 89 | 1014 | 730 | 2758 | 31.0 |
| Henry Logan, Western Carolina | 1968 | 107 | 1263 | 764 | 3290 | 30.7 |
| Willie Scott, Alabama State | 1969 | 103 | 1277 | 601 | 3155 | 30.6 |
| Gregg Northington, Alabama State | 1972 | 75 | 894 | 403 | 2191 | 29.2 |
| Bob Hopkins, Grambling | 1956 | 126 | 1403 | 953 | 3759 | 29.8 |

1. Record.

## TOP SINGLE-GAME SCORING MARKS

| Player, Team (Opponent) | Yr | Pts | Player, Team (Opponent) | Yr | Pts |
|---|---|---|---|---|---|
| Selvy, Furman (Newberry) | 1954 | 100[1] | Floyd, Furman (Morehead) | 1955 | 67 |
| Williams, Portland State (Rocky Mtn.) | 1978 | 81 | Maravich, LSU (Tulane) | 1969 | 66 |
| Mikvy, Temple (Wilkes) | 1951 | 73 | Handlan, W & L (Furman) | 1951 | 66 |
| Williams, Portland State (So. Oregon) | 1977 | 71 | Roberts, Oral Roberts (N.C. A&T) | 1977 | 66 |
| Maravich, LSU (Alabama) | 1970 | 69 | Williams, Portland State (Geo. Fox Coll.) | 1978 | 66 |
| Murphy, Niagara (Syracuse) | 1969 | 68 | Roberts, Oral Roberts (Oregon) | 1977 | 65 |

1. Record.

# MEN'S N.C.A.A. BASKETBALL CHAMPIONSHIPS—1986

## DIVISION I
### First Round—East

Duke 85, Mississippi Valley 78
Old Dominion 72, West Virginia 64
Oklahoma 80, Northeastern 74
DePaul 72, Virginia 68
St. Joseph's 60, Richmond 59
Cleveland State 83, Indiana 79
Navy 87, Tulsa 68
Syracuse 101, Brown 52

Bradley 83, Texas El-Paso 65
Alabama–Birmingham 66, Missouri 64
North Carolina 84, Utah 72
Nevada–Las Vegas 74, Northeast Louisiana 51
Maryland 69, Pepperdine 64
St. John's 83, Montana State 64
Auburn 73, Arizona 63

### First Round—Southeast

Georgia Tech 68, Marist 53
Villanova 71, Virginia Tech 62
Memphis State 95, Ball State 63
Louisiana State 94, Purdue 87 (2 OT)
Illinois 75, Fairfield 51
Alabama 97, Xavier, Ohio 80
Western Kentucky 67, Nebraska 59
Kentucky 75, Davidson 55

### First Round—Midwest

Temple 61, Jacksonville 50 (OT)
Kansas 71, North Carolina A&T 46
Georgetown 70, Texas Tech 64
Michigan State 72, Washington 70
Michigan 70, Akron 64
Iowa State 81, Miami, Ohio 79 (OT)
North Carolina State 66, Iowa 64
Arkansas–Little Rock 90, Notre Dame 83

### First Round—West

Louisville 93, Drexel 73

### Second Round—East

Duke 89, Old Dominion 61
DePaul 74, Oklahoma 69
Navy 97, Syracuse 85
Cleveland State 75, St. Joseph's 69

### Second Round—Southeast

Louisiana State 83, Memphis State 81
Georgia Tech 66, Villanova 61
Alabama 58, Illinois 56
Kentucky 71, Western Kentucky 64

### Second Round—Midwest

Michigan State 80, Georgetown 68
Kansas 65, Temple 43
North Carolina State 80, Arkansas–Little Rock 66 (2 OT)
Iowa State 72, Michigan 69

### Second Round—West

Louisville 82, Bradley 68
North Carolina 77, Alabama–Birmingham 59
Auburn 81, St. John's 65
Nevada–Las Vegas 70, Maryland 64

**Third Round—East**
Navy 71, Cleveland State 70
Duke 74, DePaul 67

**Third Round—Southeast**
Kentucky 68, Alabama 63
Louisiana State 70, Georgia Tech 64

**Third Round—Midwest**
North Carolina State 70, Iowa State 66
Kansas 96, Michigan State 86

**Third Round—West**
Auburn 70, Nevada–Las Vegas 63
Louisville 94, North Carolina 79

**Regional Finals**
East—Duke 71, Navy 50
Southeast—Louisiana State 59, Kentucky 57
Midwest—Kansas 75, North Carolina State 67
West—Louisville 84, Auburn 76

**National Semifinals**
(Dallas, Texas, March 29, 1986)

Louisville 88, Louisiana State 77
Duke 71, Kansas 67

**National Final**
(Dallas, Texas, March 31, 1986)
Louisville 72, Duke 69

**DIVISION II**
**Semifinals**
Southeast Missouri State 90, Cheyney (Pa.) 81
Sacred Heart (Conn.) 86, Florida Southern 80

**Championship**
Sacred Heart 93, Southeast Missouri State 87

**DIVISION III**
**Semifinals**
Potsdam State (N.Y.) 91, Jersey City State 89
LeMoyne-Owen (Tenn.) 86, Nebraska Wesleyan 80

**Championship**
Potsdam State 76, LeMoyne-Owen 73

## WOMEN'S N.C.A.A. BASKETBALL CHAMPIONSHIPS—1986

**DIVISION I**
**First Round—East**
James Madison 55, Providence 53
Villanova 60, LaSalle 55

**First Round—Mideast**
Middle Tennessee State 78, South Carolina 77
Illinois 69, Ohio 68

**First Round—Midwest**
Missouri 66, Arkansas 65
Drake 73, Kentucky 70

**First Round—West**
Montana 58, Utah 46
Washington 69, North Texas State 54

**Second Round—East**
James Madison 71, Virginia 62
Western Kentucky 74, St. Joseph's 65
Penn State 63, North Carolina State 59
Rutgers 85, Villanova 58

**Second Round—Mideast**
Georgia 103, Illinois 64
Ohio State 87, Maryland 71
Tennessee 73, Iowa 68
Louisiana State 78, Middle Tennessee State 65

**Second Round—Midwest**
Auburn 61, Southern Illinois 39
Texas 108, Missouri 67
Mississippi 84, Drake 71
Oklahoma 86, Vanderbilt 67

**Second Round—West**
Southern California 81, Montana 50
North Carolina 82, Nevada–Las Vegas 76
Long Beach State 78, Texas Tech 73
Louisiana Tech 79, Washington 54

**Third Round—East**
Western Kentucky 72, James Madison 51
Rutgers 85, Penn State 72

**Third Round—Mideast**
Louisiana State 81, Ohio State 80
Tennessee 85, Georgia 82

**Third Round—Midwest**
Mississippi 56, Auburn 55 (OT)
Texas 85, Oklahoma 59

**Third Round—West**
Louisiana Tech 71, Long Beach State 69
Southern California 84, North Carolina 70

**Regional Finals**
East—Western Kentucky 89, Rutgers 74
Mideast—Tennessee 67, Louisiana State 65
Midwest—Texas 66, Mississippi 63
West—Southern California 80, Louisiana Tech 64

**National Semifinals**
(March 28, 1986, at Lexington, Ky.)
Texas 90, Western Kentucky 65
Southern California 83, Tennessee 59

**National Championship**
(March 30, 1986, at Lexington, Ky.)
Texas 97, Southern California 81

**DIVISION II**
**Semifinals**
North Dakota State 77, Philadelphia Textile 61
Cal Poly–Pomona 71, Delta State 68

**Championship**
Cal Poly–Pomona 70, North Dakota State 63

**DIVISION III**
**Championship**
Salem State 89, Bishop 85

## LEADING N.C.A.A. SCORERS—1985–1986
**Division I**

|  | FG | FT | Pts | Avg |
|---|---|---|---|---|
| 1. Terrance Bailey, Wagner | 321 | 212 | 854 | 29.4 |
| 2. Scott Skiles, Michigan St. | 331 | 188 | 850 | 27.4 |
| 3. Joe Yezbak, U.S. International | 299 | 157 | 755 | 27.0 |
| 4. Reggie Miller, UCLA | 274 | 202 | 750 | 25.9 |
| 5. Ron Harper, Miami (Ohio) | 312 | 133 | 757 | 24.4 |
| 6. Dell Curry, Virginia Tech | 305 | 112 | 722 | 24.1 |
| 7. Reggie Lewis, Northeastern | 265 | 184 | 714 | 23.8 |

| | | | | |
|---|---|---|---|---|
| 8. Len Bias, Maryland | 267 | 209 | 743 | 23.2 |
| 9. Frank Ross, American | 270 | 105 | 645 | 23.0 |
| 10. Walter Berry, St. John's (N.Y.) | 327 | 174 | 828 | 23.0 |
| 11. Lamont Harris, St. Francis (Pa.) | 247 | 149 | 643 | 23.0 |
| 12. Jim McCaffrey, Holy Cross | 218 | 135 | 571 | 22.8 |
| 13. Gay Elmore, VMI | 232 | 173 | 637 | 22.8 |
| 14. David Robinson, Navy | 294 | 208 | 796 | 22.7 |
| 15. Greg Grant, Utah St. | 250 | 132 | 632 | 22.6 |
| 16. Steve Alford, Indiana | 254 | 122 | 630 | 22.5 |
| 16. Anthony Watson, San Diego St. | 246 | 138 | 630 | 22.5 |
| 18. Dwyane Randall, Nevada-Reno | 240 | 122 | 602 | 22.3 |
| 19. Kevin Houston, Army | 228 | 144 | 600 | 22.2 |
| 20. Tony White, Tennessee | 249 | 124 | 622 | 22.2 |
| 21. Larry Krystkowiak, Montana | 258 | 193 | 709 | 22.2 |
| 22. John Newman, Richmond | 253 | 153 | 659 | 22.0 |
| 23. Byron Larkin, Xavier (Ohio) | 261 | 132 | 654 | 21.8 |
| 24. Don Marbury, Texas A&M | 285 | 127 | 697 | 21.8 |
| 25. Chad Tucker, Butler | 235 | 139 | 609 | 21.8 |
| 25. Norris Coleman, Kansas St. | 254 | 101 | 609 | 21.8 |

## NATIONAL ASSOCIATION OF INTERCOLLEGIATE ATHLETICS—1986

### MEN'S TOURNAMENT
### Round of 16

St. Thomas Aquinas (NY) 77, Atlantic Christian (NC) 71
College of Charleston (S.C.) 59, Cumberland (Ky) 46
Southwestern (Tex) 53, Wisconsin–Eau Claire 47
Southeast Oklahoma 79, Huron (S.D.) 66
Central Washington 59, Birmingham (Ala.) 56
Charleston 55, Drury (Mo.) 51
David Lipscomb (Tenn.) 79, Emporia (Kan) State 76
Arkansas–Monticello 72, Wayland Baptist (Tex) 66
### Semifinals

David Lipscomb 102, St. Thomas Aquinas 91
Arkansas–Monticello 67, Southeast Oklahoma 61
### Third place

Southeast Oklahoma 75, St. Thomas Aquinas 74
### Championship

David Lipscomb 67, Arkansas-Monticello 54
### WOMEN'S TOURNAMENT
### Third place

Louisiana College 85, Georgia Southwestern 78

### Championship

Francis Marion (S.C.) 75, Wayland Baptist (Tex) 65

## NATIONAL INVITATION TOURNAMENT (N.I.T)—1986

### Semifinals

(March 24, 1986, at Madison Square Garden, N.Y.)

Wyoming 67, Florida 58
Ohio State 79, Louisiana Tech 66
### Third place

Louisiana Tech 67, Florida 62
### Championship

(March 26, 1986, at Madison Square Garden, N.Y.)

Ohio State 73, Wyoming 63

## N.C.A.A. LEADING REBOUNDERS— 1985-1986

| | Games | No. | Avg |
|---|---|---|---|
| 1. David Robinson, Navy | 35 | 455 | 13.0 |
| 2. Greg Anderson, Houston | 28 | 360 | 12.9 |
| 3. Brad Sellers, Ohio St. | 33 | 416 | 12.6 |
| 4. Ron Harper, Miami (Ohio) | 31 | 362 | 11.7 |
| 5. Larry Krystkowiak, Montana | 32 | 364 | 11.4 |
| 6. Walter Berry, St. John's (N.Y.) | 36 | 399 | 11.1 |
| 7. Don Hill, Bethune-Cookman | 29 | 317 | 10.9 |
| 8. Kevin Carter, Loyola (Md.) | 28 | 304 | 10.9 |
| 9. David Boone, Marquette | 30 | 319 | 10.6 |
| 10. Horace Grant, Clemson | 34 | 357 | 10.5 |
| 11. Dwyane Randall, Nevada-Reno | 27 | 283 | 10.5 |
| 12. Bob McCann, Morehead St. | 27 | 282 | 10.4 |
| 13. Rickie Winslow, Houston | 27 | 281 | 10.4 |
| 14. Jerry Adams, Oregon | 28 | 289 | 10.3 |
| 15. Harold Pressley, Villanova | 37 | 374 | 10.1 |
| 16. Dan Palombizio, Ball St. | 30 | 302 | 10.1 |
| 17. Melvin Stewart, Texas So. | 25 | 251 | 10.0 |
| 18. Doug Cook, Florida A&M | 28 | 281 | 10.0 |
| 19. Michael Clarke, Ark.-Little Rock | 31 | 309 | 10.0 |
| 20. Andre Moore, Loyola (Ill.) | 27 | 268 | 9.9 |
| 21. Largest Agbejeimisin, Wagner | 28 | 276 | 9.9 |
| 22. Chris Dudley, Yale | 26 | 256 | 9.8 |
| 23. Lamont Harris, St. Francis (Pa.) | 28 | 274 | 9.8 |
| 24. Ronnie Grandison, New Orleans | 28 | 271 | 9.7 |
| 25. Albert Thomas, Centenary | 30 | 289 | 9.6 |

# Professional Basketball

## NATIONAL BASKETBALL ASSOCIATION CHAMPIONS

*Source:* Matt Winick, Director of Media Information, National Basketball Association.

The National Basketball Association was originally the Basketball Association of America. It took its current name in 1949 when it merged with the National Basketball League.

| Season | Eastern Conference (W-L) | Western Conference (W-L) | Playoff Champions[1] |
|---|---|---|---|
| 1946–47 | Washington Capitols (49–11) | Chicago Stags (39–22) | Philadelphia Warriors |
| 1947–48 | Philadelphia Warriors (27–21) | St. Louis Bombers (29–19) | Baltimore Bullets |
| 1948–49 | Washington Capitols (38–22) | Rochester Royals (45–15) | Minneapolis Lakers |
| 1949–50 | Syracuse Nationals (51–13) | Indianapolis Olympians (39–25) | Minneapolis Lakers |
| 1950–51 | Philadelphia Warriors (40–26) | Minneapolis Lakers (44–24) | Rochester Royals |
| 1951–52 | Syracuse Nationals (40–26) | Rochester Royals (41–25) | Minneapolis Lakers |
| 1952–53 | New York Knickerbockers (47–23) | Minneapolis Lakers (48–22) | Minneapolis Lakers |
| 1953–54 | New York Knickerbockers (44–28) | Minneapolis Lakers (46–26) | Minneapolis Lakers |
| 1954–55 | Syracuse Nationals (43–29) | Ft. Wayne Pistons (43–29) | Syracuse Nationals |
| 1955–56 | Philadelphia Warriors (45–27) | Ft. Wayne Pistons (37–35) | Philadelphia Warriors |
| 1956–57 | Boston Celtics (44–28) | St. Louis Hawks (38–34) | Boston Celtics |
| 1957–58 | Boston Celtics (48–23) | St. Louis Hawks (41–31) | St. Louis Hawks |
| 1958–59 | Boston Celtics (52–20) | St. Louis Hawks (49–23) | Boston Celtics |
| 1959–60 | Boston Celtics (59–16) | St. Louis Hawks (46–29) | Boston Celtics |
| 1960–61 | Boston Celtics (57–22) | St. Louis Hawks (51–29) | Boston Celtics |
| 1961–62 | Boston Celtics (60–20) | Los Angeles Lakers (54–26) | Boston Celtics |
| 1962–63 | Boston Celtics (58–22) | Los Angeles Lakers (53–27) | Boston Celtics |
| 1963–64 | Boston Celtics (59–21) | San Francisco Warriors (48–32) | Boston Celtics |
| 1964–65 | Boston Celtics (62–18) | Los Angeles Lakers (49–31) | Boston Celtics |

| Season | Eastern Conference (W-L) | Western Conference (W-L) | Playoff Champions[1] |
|---|---|---|---|
| 1965–66 | Philadelphia 76ers (55–25) | Los Angeles Lakers (45–35) | Boston Celtics |
| 1966–67 | Philadelphia 76ers (68–13) | San Francisco Warriors (44–37) | Philadelphia 76ers |
| 1967–68 | Philadelphia 76ers (62–20) | St. Louis Hawks (56–26) | Boston Celtics |
| 1968–69 | Baltimore Bullets (57–25) | Los Angeles Lakers (55–27) | Boston Celtics |
| 1969–70 | New York Knickerbockers (60–22) | Atlanta Hawks (48–34) | New York Knicks |
| 1970–71 | Baltimore Bullets (42–40) | Milwaukee Bucks (66–16) | Milwaukee Bucks |
| 1971–72 | New York Knickerbockers (48–34) | Los Angeles Lakers (69–13) | Los Angeles Lakers |
| 1972–73 | New York Knickerbockers (57–25) | Los Angeles Lakers (69–22) | New York Knicks |
| 1973–74 | Boston Celtics (56–26) | Milwaukee Bucks (59–23) | Boston Celtics |
| 1974–75 | Washington Bullets (60–22) | Golden State Warriors (48–34) | Golden State Warriors |
| 1975–76 | Boston Celtics (54–28) | Phoenix Suns (42–40) | Boston Celtics |
| 1976–77 | Philadelphia 76ers (50–32) | Portland Trail Blazers (49–33) | Portland Trail Blazers |
| 1977–78 | Washington Bullets (44–38) | Seattle Super Sonics (47–35) | Washington Bullets |
| 1978–79 | Washington Bullets (54–28) | Seattle Super Sonics (52–30) | Seattle Super Sonics |
| 1979–80 | Philadelphia 76ers (59–23) | Los Angeles Lakers (60–22) | Los Angeles Lakers |
| 1980–81 | Boston Celtics (62–20) | Phoenix Suns (57–25) | Boston Celtics |
| 1981–82 | Boston Celtics (63–19) | Los Angeles Lakers (57–25) | Los Angeles Lakers |
| 1982–83 | Philadelphia 76ers (65–17) | Los Angeles Lakers (58–24) | Philadelphia 76ers |
| 1983–84 | Boston Celtics (56–26) | Los Angeles Lakers (58–24) | Boston Celtics |
| 1984–85 | Boston Celtics (63–19) | Los Angeles Lakers (62–20) | Los Angeles Lakers |
| 1985–86 | Boston Celtics (67–15) | Houston Rockets (51–31) | Boston Celtics |

1. Playoffs may involve teams other than conference winners.

## INDIVIDUAL N.B.A. SCORING CHAMPIONS

| Season | Player, Team | G | FG | FT | Pts | Avg |
|---|---|---|---|---|---|---|
| 1953–54 | Neil Johnston, Philadelphia Warriors | 72 | 591 | 577 | 1759 | 24.4 |
| 1954–55 | Neil Johnston, Philadelphia Warriors | 72 | 521 | 589 | 1631 | 22.7 |
| 1955–56 | Bob Pettit, St. Louis Hawks | 72 | 646 | 557 | 1849 | 25.7 |
| 1956–57 | Paul Arizin, Philadelphia Warriors | 71 | 613 | 591 | 1817 | 25.6 |
| 1957–58 | George Yardley, Detroit Pistons | 72 | 673 | 655 | 2001 | 27.8 |
| 1958–59 | Bob Pettit, St. Louis Hawks | 72 | 719 | 667 | 2105 | 29.2 |
| 1959–60 | Wilt Chamberlain, Philadelphia Warriors | 72 | 1065 | 577 | 2707 | 37.6 |
| 1960–61 | Wilt Chamberlain, Philadelphia Warriors | 79 | 1251 | 531 | 3033 | 38.4 |
| 1961–62 | Wilt Chamberlain, Philadelphia Warriors | 80 | 1597 | 835 | 4029 | 50.4 |
| 1962–63 | Wilt Chamberlain, San Francisco Warriors | 80 | 1463 | 660 | 3586 | 44.8 |
| 1963–64 | Wilt Chamberlain, San Francisco Warriors | 80 | 1204 | 540 | 2948 | 36.9 |
| 1964–65 | Wilt Chamberlain, San Francisco Warriors-Phila. 76ers | 73 | 1063 | 408 | 2534 | 34.7 |
| 1965–66 | Wilt Chamberlain, Philadelphia 76ers | 79 | 1074 | 501 | 2649 | 33.5 |
| 1966–67 | Rick Barry, San Francisco Warriors | 78 | 1011 | 753 | 2775 | 35.6 |
| 1967–68 | Dave Bing, Detroit Pistons | 79 | 835 | 472 | 2142 | 27.1 |
| 1968–69 | Elvin Hayes, San Diego Rockets | 82 | 930 | 467 | 2327 | 28.4 |
| 1969–70 | Jerry West, Los Angeles Lakers | 74 | 831 | 647 | 2309 | 31.2 |
| 1970–71 | Lew Alcindor,[1] Milwaukee Bucks | 82 | 1063 | 470 | 2596 | 31.7 |
| 1971–72 | Kareem Abdul-Jabbar, Milwaukee Bucks | 81 | 1159 | 504 | 2822 | 34.8 |
| 1972–73 | Nate Archibald, Kansas City-Omaha Kings | 80 | 1028 | 663 | 2719 | 34.0 |
| 1973–74 | Bob McAdoo, Buffalo Braves | 74 | 901 | 459 | 2261 | 30.8 |
| 1974–75 | Bob McAdoo, Buffalo Braves | 82 | 1095 | 641 | 2831 | 34.5 |
| 1975–76 | Bob McAdoo, Buffalo Braves | 78 | 934 | 559 | 2427 | 31.1 |
| 1976–77 | Pete Maravich, New Orleans Jazz | 73 | 886 | 501 | 2273 | 31.1 |
| 1977–78 | George Gervin, San Antonio Spurs | 82 | 864 | 504 | 2232 | 27.2 |
| 1978–79 | George Gervin, San Antonio | 80 | 947 | 471 | 2365 | 29.6 |
| 1979–80 | George Gervin, San Antonio | 78 | 1024 | 505 | 2585 | 33.1 |
| 1980–81 | Adrian Dantley, Utah Jazz | 80 | 909 | 632 | 2452 | 30.7 |
| 1981–82 | George Gervin, San Antonio | 79 | 993 | 555 | 2551 | 32.3 |
| 1982–83 | Alex English, Denver Nuggets | 82 | 959 | 406 | 2326 | 28.4 |
| 1983–84 | Adrian Dantley, Utah Jazz | 79 | 802 | 813 | 2418 | 30.6 |
| 1984–85 | Bernard King, New York Knicks | 55 | 691 | 426 | 1809 | 32.9 |
| 1985–86 | Dominique Wilkins, Atlanta Hawks | 78 | 888 | 527 | 2366 | 30.3 |

1. (Kareem Abdul-Jabbar).

## N.B.A. LIFETIME LEADERS
(Through 1985–1986 season)

**Scoring**

| | Yrs | FG | FT | Pts |
|---|---|---|---|---|
| (a) Kareem Abdul-Jabbar | 17 | 14,484 | 6,140 | 35,108 |
| Wilt Chamberlain | 14 | 12,681 | 6,057 | 31,419 |
| (a) Julius Erving* | 15 | 11,418 | 6,065 | 29,021 |
| (a) Dan Issel* | 15 | 10,421 | 6,591 | 27,482 |

| | | | | |
|---|---|---|---|---|
| Elvin Hayes | 16 | 10,976 | 5,356 | 27,313 |
| Oscar Robertson | 14 | 9,508 | 7,694 | 26,710 |
| (a) George Gervin* | 14 | 11,362 | 2,737 | 26,595 |
| John Havlicek | 16 | 10,513 | 5,369 | 26,395 |
| Rick Barry* | 14 | 9,695 | 5,713 | 25,279 |
| Jerry West | 14 | 9,016 | 7,160 | 25,192 |
| Elgin Baylor | 14 | 8,693 | 5,763 | 23,149 |

| | | | | |
|---|---|---|---|---|
| Hal Greer | 15 | 8,504 | 4,578 | 21,586 |
| Walt Bellamy | 14 | 7,914 | 5,113 | 20,941 |
| Bob Petit | 11 | 7,349 | 6,182 | 20,880 |

(a) Active player. *Includes statistics compiled in the American Basketball Association.

## Scoring Average
(400 games or 10,000 points minimum)

| | Games | Pts | Avg |
|---|---|---|---|
| Wilt Chamberlain | 1,045 | 31,419 | 30.1 |
| Elgin Baylor | 846 | 23,149 | 27.4 |
| Jerry West | 932 | 25,192 | 27.0 |
| (a) Kareem Abdul-Jabbar | 1,328 | 35,108 | 26.4 |
| Bob Petit | 792 | 20,880 | 26.4 |
| (a) Adrian Dantley | 677 | 17,936 | 26.4 |
| Oscar Robertson | 1,040 | 26,710 | 25.7 |
| (a) George Gervin* | 1,060 | 26,595 | 25.1 |
| (a) Julius Erving* | 1,183 | 29,021 | 24.5 |
| Rick Barry* | 1,020 | 25,279 | 24.8 |
| Pete Maravich | 658 | 15,948 | 24.2 |
| (a) Moses Malone | 768 | 18,336 | 23.8 |

(a) Active player. *Includes statistics compiled in the American Basketball Association.

## Rebounds

| | |
|---|---|
| Wilt Chamberlain | 23,924 |
| Bill Russell | 21,620 |
| Elvin Hayes | 16,279 |
| (a) Kareem Abdul–Jabbar | 16,105 |
| Nate Thurmond | 14,464 |
| Walt Bellamy | 14,241 |
| Wes Unseld | 13,769 |
| Jerry Lucas | 12,942 |
| Bob Pettit | 12,849 |
| Paul Silas | 12,357 |

(a) Active player.

## Free-Throw Percentage
(1,200 free throws made minimum)

| | FTA | FTM | Pct |
|---|---|---|---|
| Rick Barry | 4,243 | 3,818 | .900 |
| Calvin Murphy | 3,864 | 3,445 | .892 |
| Bill Sharman | 3,557 | 3,143 | .884 |
| Mike Newlin | 3,456 | 3,005 | .870 |
| (a) Larry Bird | 2,856 | 2,481 | .869 |
| (a) Kiki Vandeweghe | 2,717 | 2,352 | .866 |
| Fred Brown | 2,211 | 1,896 | .858 |
| Larry Siegfried | 1,945 | 1,662 | .854 |
| James Silas | 1,690 | 1,440 | .852 |
| Flynn Robinson | 1,881 | 1,597 | .849 |
| (a) Junior Bridgeman | 2,196 | 1,859 | .847 |
| (a) Ricky Sobers | 2,695 | 2,272 | .843 |

(a) Active player.

## Field-Goal Percentage
(2,000 field goals minimum)

| | FGA | FGM | Pct |
|---|---|---|---|
| (a) Artis Gilmore | 8,809 | 5,287 | .600 |
| (a) Darryl Dawkins | 6,019 | 3,446 | .573 |
| (a) Kareem Abdul-Jabbar | 25,752 | 14,484 | .562 |
| (a) Bill Cartwright | 4,646 | 2,585 | .556 |
| (a) Kevin McHale | 5,529 | 3,056 | .553 |
| (a) Adrian Dantley | 11,644 | 6,404 | .550 |
| (a) Bobby Jones | 6,199 | 3,412 | .550 |
| (a) Buck Williams | 4,764 | 2,621 | .550 |
| (a) Cedric Maxwell | 5,645 | 3,100 | .549 |
| (a) Ervin Johnson | 6,102 | 3,310 | .542 |

(a) Active player.

## Assists

| | |
|---|---|
| Oscar Robertson | 9,887 |
| Lenny Wilkens | 7,211 |
| Bob Cousy | 6,955 |
| Guy Rodgers | 6,917 |
| Nate Archibald | 6,476 |
| Jerry West | 6,238 |
| John Havlicek | 6,114 |
| (a) Norm Nixon | 6,047 |
| Dave Bing | 5,397 |
| Kevin Porter | 5,314 |

(a) Active player.

## N.B.A. MOST VALUABLE PLAYERS

| | | | | | |
|---|---|---|---|---|---|
| 1956 | Bob Pettit | 1971–72 | Lew Alcindor (Kareem Abdul-Jabbar) | 1980 | Kareem Abdul-Jabbar, Los Angeles |
| 1957 | Bob Cousy | | | | |
| 1958 | Bill Russell | 1973 | Dave Cowens | 1981 | Julius Erving, Philadelphia |
| 1959 | Bob Pettit | 1974 | Kareem Abdul-Jabbar, Milwaukee | 1982 | Moses Malone, Houston |
| 1960 | Wilt Chamberlain | | | 1983 | Moses Malone, Philadelphia |
| 1961–63 | Bill Russell | 1975 | Bob McAdoo, Buffalo | 1984 | Larry Bird, Boston |
| 1964 | Oscar Robertson | 1976–77 | Kareem Abdul-Jabbar, Los Angeles | 1985 | Larry Bird, Boston |
| 1965 | Bill Russell | | | 1986 | Larry Bird, Boston |
| 1966–68 | Wilt Chamberlain | 1978 | Bill Walton, Portland | | |
| 1969 | Wes Unseld | 1979 | Moses Malone, Houston | | |
| 1970 | Willis Reed | | | | |

## N.B.A. TEAM RECORDS

Most points, game—186, Detroit vs. Denver, 3 overtimes, 1983
Most points, quarter—58, Buffalo vs. Boston, 1968
Most points, half—97, Atlanta vs. San Diego, 1970
Most points, overtime period—22, Detroit vs. Cleveland, 1973
Most field goals, game—74, Detroit 1983
Most field goals, quarter—23, Boston, 1959; Buffalo, 1972
Most field goals, half—40, Boston, 1959; Syracuse, 1963; Atlanta, 1979
Most assists, game—53, Milwaukee, 1978
Most rebounds, game—109, Boston 1960
Most points, both teams, game—370 (Detroit 186, Denver 184) 3 overtimes, Denver, December 13, 1983
Most points, both teams, quarter—96 (Boston 52, Minneapolis 44), 1959; (Detroit 53, Cincinnati 43), 1972
Most points, both teams, half—170 (Philadelphia 90, Cincinnati 80), Philadelphia, 1971
Longest winning streak—33, Los Angeles, 1971–72
Longest losing streak—20, Philadelphia, 1973
Longest winning streak at home—36, Philadelphia, 1966–67
Most games won, season—69, Los Angeles, 1971–72
Most games lost, season—73, Philadelphia, 1972–73
Highest average points per game—126.5, Denver, 1981–82

## N.B.A. INDIVIDUAL RECORDS

Most points, game—100, Wilt Chamberlain, Philadelphia vs. New York at Hershey, Pa., 1962
Most points, quarter—33, George Gervin, San Antonio, 1978
Most points, half—59, Wilt Chamberlain, Philadelphia, 1962
Most free throws, game—28, Wilt Chamberlain, Philadelphia, vs. New York at Hershey, Pa. 1962; 28, Adrian Dantley, Utah, vs. Houston, 1984

Most free throws, quarter—14, Rick Barry, San Francisco, 1966
Most free throws, half—19, Oscar Robertson, Cincinnati, 1964
Most field goals, game—36, Wilt Chamberlain, Philadelphia, 1962
Most consecutive field goals, game—18, Wilt Chamberlain, San Francisco, 1963; Wilt Chamberlain, Philadelphia, 1967
Most assists, game—29, Kevin Porter, New Jersey Nets, 1978
Most rebounds, game—55, Wilt Chamberlain, Philadelphia, 1963

## NATIONAL BASKETBALL ASSOCIATION
## FINAL STANDINGS OF THE CLUBS—1985–1986

### EASTERN CONFERENCE
#### Atlantic Division

|  | W | L | Pct | Games behind |
|---|---|---|---|---|
| Boston Celtics | 67 | 15 | .817 | — |
| Philadelphia 76ers | 54 | 28 | .659 | 13 |
| Washington Bullets | 39 | 43 | .476 | 28 |
| New Jersey Nets | 39 | 43 | .476 | 28 |
| New York Knickerbockers | 23 | 59 | .280 | 44 |

#### Central Division

|  | W | L | Pct | Games behind |
|---|---|---|---|---|
| Milwaukee Bucks | 57 | 25 | .695 | — |
| Atlanta Hawks | 50 | 32 | .610 | 7 |
| Detroit Pistons | 46 | 36 | .561 | 11 |
| Chicago Bulls | 30 | 52 | .366 | 27 |
| Cleveland Cavaliers | 29 | 53 | .354 | 28 |
| Indiana Pacers | 26 | 56 | .317 | 31 |

### WESTERN CONFERENCE
#### Midwest Division

|  | W | L | Pct | Games behind |
|---|---|---|---|---|
| Houston Rockets | 51 | 31 | .622 | — |
| Denver Nuggets | 47 | 35 | .573 | 4 |
| Dallas Mavericks | 44 | 38 | .537 | 7 |
| Utah Jazz | 42 | 40 | .512 | 9 |
| Sacramento Kings | 37 | 45 | .451 | 14 |
| San Antonio Spurs | 35 | 47 | .427 | 16 |

#### Pacific Division

|  | W | L | Pct | Games behind |
|---|---|---|---|---|
| Los Angeles Lakers | 62 | 20 | .756 | — |
| Portland Trail Blazers | 40 | 42 | .488 | 22 |
| Los Angeles Clippers | 32 | 50 | .390 | 30 |
| Phoenix Suns | 32 | 50 | .390 | 30 |
| Seattle SuperSonics | 31 | 51 | .378 | 31 |
| Golden State Warriors | 30 | 52 | .366 | 32 |

## N.B.A. PLAYOFFS—1986

### EASTERN CONFERENCE
#### First Round

Boston defeated Chicago, 3 games to 0
Atlanta defeated Detroit, 3 games to 1
Philadelphia defeated Washington, 3 games to 2
Milwaukee defeated New Jersey, 3 games to 0

#### Semifinal Round

Milwaukee defeated Philadelphia, 4 games to 3
Boston defeated Atlanta, 4 games to 1

#### Conference Finals

Boston defeated Milwaukee, 4 games to 0
   May 13—Boston 128, Milwaukee 96
   May 15—Boston 122, Milwaukee 111
   May 17—Boston 111, Milwaukee 107
   May 18—Boston 111, Milwaukee 98

### WESTERN CONFERENCE
#### First Round

Houston defeated Sacramento, 3 games to 0
Los Angeles Lakers defeated San Antonio, 3 games to 0
Denver defeated Portland, 3 games to 1
Dallas defeated Utah, 3 games to 1

#### Semifinal Round

Los Angeles Lakers defeated Dallas, 4 games to 2
Houston defeated Denver, 4 games to 2

#### Conference Finals

Houston defeated Los Angeles Lakers, 4 games to 1
   May 10—Los Angeles 119, Houston 107
   May 13—Houston 112, Los Angeles 102
   May 16—Houston 117, Los Angeles 109
   May 18—Houston 105, Los Angeles 95
   May 21—Houston 114, Los Angeles 112

#### CHAMPIONSHIP

Boston defeated Houston, 4 games to 2
   May 26—Boston 112, Houston 100
   May 29—Boston 117, Houston 95
   June 1—Houston 106, Boston 104
   June 3—Boston 106, Houston 103
   June 5—Houston 111, Boston 96
   June 8—Boston 114, Houston 97

### FIELD-GOAL LEADERS—1985–1986
(Minimum 300 FG made)

|  | FG | Att | Pct |
|---|---|---|---|
| Steve Johnson, San Antonio | 362 | 573 | .632 |
| Artis Gilmore, San Antonio | 423 | 684 | .618 |
| Larry Nance, Phoenix | 582 | 1,001 | .581 |
| James Worthy, Lakers | 629 | 1,086 | .579 |
| Kevin McHale, Boston | 561 | 978 | .574 |
| Charles Barkley, Philadelphia | 595 | 1,041 | .572 |
| Kareem Abdul-Jabbar, Lakers | 755 | 1,338 | .564 |
| Adrian Dantley, Utah | 818 | 1,453 | .563 |
| Alton Lister, Milwaukee | 318 | 557 | .551 |
| Robert Parish, Boston | 530 | 966 | .549 |

### FREE-THROW LEADERS—1985–1986
(Minimum 125 FT made)

|  | FT | Att | Pct |
|---|---|---|---|
| Larry Bird, Boston | 441 | 492 | .896 |
| Chris Mullin, Golden State | 189 | 211 | .896 |
| Mike Gminski, New Jersey | 351 | 393 | .893 |
| Jim Paxson, Portland | 217 | 244 | .889 |
| George Gervin, Chicago | 283 | 322 | .879 |
| Franklin Edwards, Clippers | 132 | 151 | .874 |
| Ervin Johnson, Lakers | 378 | 434 | .871 |
| Kiki Vanderweghe, Portland | 523 | 602 | .869 |
| Brad Davis, Dallas | 198 | 228 | .868 |
| Jeff Malone, Washington | 322 | 371 | .868 |

## REBOUND LEADERS— 1985–1986

(Minimum 70 games or 800 rebounds)

| | G | Off | Def | Total | Avg |
|---|---|---|---|---|---|
| Bill Laimbeer, Detroit | 82 | 305 | 770 | 1075 | 13.1 |
| Charles Barkley, Philadelphia | 80 | 354 | 672 | 1026 | 12.8 |
| Buck Williams, New Jersey | 82 | 329 | 657 | 986 | 12.0 |
| Moses Malone, Philadelphia | 74 | 339 | 533 | 872 | 11.8 |
| Ralph Sampson, Houston | 79 | 258 | 621 | 879 | 11.1 |
| Larry Smith, Golden State | 77 | 384 | 472 | 856 | 11.1 |
| Larry Bird, Boston | 82 | 190 | 615 | 805 | 9.8 |
| LaSalle Thompson, Sacramento | 80 | 252 | 518 | 770 | 9.6 |
| James Donaldson, Dallas | 83 | 171 | 624 | 795 | 9.6 |
| Robert Parish, Boston | 81 | 246 | 524 | 770 | 9.5 |

## 3-POINT FIELD-GOAL LEADERS— 1985–1986

(Minimum 25 made)

| | FG | Att | Pct |
|---|---|---|---|
| Craig Hodges, Milwaukee | 73 | 162 | .451 |
| Trent Tucker, New York | 41 | 91 | .451 |
| Ernie Grunfeld, New York | 26 | 61 | .426 |
| Larry Bird, Boston | 82 | 194 | .423 |
| World B. Free, Cleveland | 71 | 169 | .420 |
| Kyle Macy, Chicago | 58 | 141 | .411 |
| Michael Cooper, Lakers | 63 | 163 | .387 |
| Dale Ellis, Dallas | 63 | 173 | .364 |
| Kevin McKenna, Washington | 27 | 75 | .360 |

## LEADING SCORERS—1985–1986

| | G | FG | FT | Pts | Avg |
|---|---|---|---|---|---|
| Dominique Wilkins, Atlanta | 78 | 888 | 577 | 2,366 | 30.3 |
| Adrian Dantley, Utah | 76 | 818 | 630 | 2267 | 29.8 |
| Alex English, Denver | 81 | 951 | 511 | 2,414 | 29.8 |
| Larry Bird, Boston | 82 | 796 | 441 | 2,115 | 25.8 |
| Purvis Short, Golden State | 64 | 633 | 351 | 1,632 | 25.5 |
| Kiki Vandeweghe, Portland | 79 | 719 | 523 | 1,962 | 24.8 |
| Moses Malone, Philadelphia | 74 | 571 | 617 | 1,759 | 23.8 |
| Akeem Olajuwon, Houston | 68 | 625 | 347 | 1,597 | 23.5 |
| Mike Mitchell, San Antonio | 82 | 802 | 317 | 1,921 | 23.4 |

| | | | | | |
|---|---|---|---|---|---|
| World B. Free, Cleveland | 75 | 652 | 379 | 1,754 | 23.4 |
| Kareem Abdul-Jabbar, Lakers | 79 | 755 | 336 | 1,846 | 23.4 |
| Mark Aguirre, Dallas | 74 | 668 | 318 | 1,670 | 22.6 |
| Jeff Malone, Washington | 80 | 735 | 322 | 1,795 | 22.4 |
| Walter Davis, Phoenix | 70 | 624 | 257 | 1,523 | 21.8 |
| Rolando Blackman, Dallas | 82 | 677 | 404 | 1,762 | 21.5 |
| Kevin McHale, Boston | 68 | 561 | 326 | 1,448 | 21.3 |
| Jo Barry Carroll, Golden State | 79 | 650 | 377 | 1,677 | 21.2 |
| Isiah Thomas, Detroit | 77 | 609 | 365 | 1,609 | 20.9 |
| Orlando Woolridge, Chicago | 70 | 540 | 364 | 1,448 | 20.7 |
| Marques Johnson, Clippers | 75 | 613 | 298 | 1,525 | 20.3 |

## STEALS LEADERS—1985–1986

(Minimum 70 games or 125 steals)

| | GP | No. | Avg |
|---|---|---|---|
| Alvin Robertson, San Antonio | 82 | 301 | 3.67 |
| Michael Ray Richardson, New Jersey | 47 | 125 | 2.66 |
| Clyde Drexler, Portland | 75 | 197 | 2.63 |
| Maurice Cheeks, Philadelphia | 82 | 207 | 2.52 |
| Lafayette Lever, Denver | 78 | 178 | 2.28 |
| Isiah Thomas, Detroit | 77 | 171 | 2.22 |
| Charles Barkley, Philadelphia | 80 | 173 | 2.16 |
| Paul Pressey, Milwaukee | 80 | 168 | 2.10 |
| Larry Bird, Boston | 82 | 166 | 2.02 |
| Darwin Cook, New Jersey | 79 | 156 | 1.97 |

## ASSISTS LEADERS—1985–1986

(Minimum 70 games or 400 assists)

| | G | No. | Avg |
|---|---|---|---|
| Ervin Johnson, Lakers | 72 | 907 | 12.6 |
| Isiah Thomas, Detroit | 77 | 830 | 10.8 |
| Reggie Theus, Sacramento | 82 | 788 | 9.6 |
| John Bagley, Cleveland | 78 | 735 | 9.4 |
| Maurice Cheeks, Philadelphia | 82 | 753 | 9.2 |
| Sleepy Floyd, Golden State | 82 | 746 | 9.1 |
| John Lucas, Houston | 65 | 571 | 8.8 |
| Norm Nixon, Clippers | 67 | 576 | 8.6 |
| Glenn Rivers, Atlanta | 53 | 443 | 8.4 |
| Clyde Drexler, Portland | 75 | 600 | 8.0 |

## BLOCKED-SHOTS LEADERS—1985–1986

(Minimum 70 games or 100 blocked shots)

| | GP | No. | Avg |
|---|---|---|---|
| Manute Bol, Washington | 80 | 397 | 4.96 |
| Mark Eaton, Utah | 80 | 369 | 4.61 |
| Akeem Olajuwon, Houston | 68 | 231 | 3.40 |
| Wayne Cooper, Denver | 78 | 227 | 2.91 |
| Benoit Benjamin, Clippers | 79 | 206 | 2.61 |
| Jawann Oldham, Chicago | 52 | 134 | 2.58 |
| Herb Williams, Indiana | 78 | 184 | 2.36 |
| Tree Rollins, Atlanta | 74 | 167 | 2.26 |
| Patrick Ewing, New York | 50 | 103 | 2.06 |
| Kevin McHale, Boston | 68 | 134 | 1.97 |

# *SHUFFLEBOARD*

## U.S.-INTERNATIONAL PRO WORLD CHAMPIONSHIP

(Lakeland, Fla., Jan. 23-25, 1986)

Men—Bob Pearson and Dick Whitaker, Florida, defeated Glen Peltier, Canada, and Junior Kinney, Florida, 77-64, 79-40, and 76-68, 75-27 in final matches.

Women—Dolores Norman, Canada, and Therese Charbonneau, Massachusetts, defeated Chris Smith and Glenna Pegram, Florida, 45-82, 75-69, 77-50 in final matches.

# HOCKEY

Ice hockey, by birth and upbringing a Canadian game, is an offshoot of field hockey. Some historians say that the first ice hockey game was played in Montreal in December 1879 between two teams composed almost exclusively of McGill University students, but others assert that earlier hockey games took place in Kingston, Ontario, or Halifax, Nova Scotia. In the Montreal game of 1879, there were fifteen players on a side, who used an assortment of crude sticks to keep the puck in motion. Early rules allowed nine men on a side, but the number was reduced to seven in 1886 and later to six.

The first governing body of the sport was the Amateur Hockey Association of Canada, organized in 1887. In the winter of 1894–95, a group of college students from the United States visited Canada and saw hockey played. They became enthused over the game and introduced it as a winter sport when they returned home. The first profes-

sional league was the International Hockey League, which operated in northern Michigan in 1904–06.

Until 1910, professionals and amateurs were allowed to play together on "mixed teams," but this arrangement ended with the formation of the first "big league," the National Hockey Association, in eastern Canada in 1910. The Pacific Coast League was organized in 1911 for western Canadian hockey. The league included Seattle and later other American cities. The National Hockey League replaced the National Hockey Association in 1917. Boston, in 1924, was the first American city to join that circuit. The league expanded to include western cities in 1967. The Stanley Cup was competed for by "mixed teams" from 1894 to 1910, thereafter by professionals. It was awarded to the winner of the N.H.L. playoffs from 1926–67 and now to the league champion. The World Hockey Association was organized in October 1972 and was dissolved after the 1978–79 season when the N.H.L. absorbed four of the teams.

## STANLEY CUP WINNERS

Emblematic of World Professional Championship; N.H.L. Championship after 1967

| | | | | | |
|---|---|---|---|---|---|
| 1894 | Montreal A.A.A. | 1922 | Toronto St. Patricks | 1947–49 | Toronto Maple Leafs |
| 1895 | Montreal Victorias | 1923 | Ottawa Senators | 1950 | Detroit Red Wings |
| 1896 | Winnipeg Victorias | 1924 | Montreal Canadiens | 1951 | Toronto Maple Leafs |
| 1897–99 | Montreal Victorias | 1925 | Victoria Cougars | 1952 | Detroit Red Wings |
| 1900 | Montreal Shamrocks | 1926 | Montreal Maroons | 1953 | Montreal Canadiens |
| 1901 | Winnipeg Victorias | 1927 | Ottawa Senators | 1954–55 | Detroit Red Wings |
| 1902 | Montreal A.A.A. | 1928 | N.Y. Rangers | 1956–60 | Montreal Canadiens |
| 1903–05 | Ottawa Silver Seven | 1929 | Boston Bruins | 1961 | Chicago Black Hawks |
| 1906 | Montreal Wanderers | 1930–31 | Montreal Canadiens | 1962–64 | Toronto Maple Leafs |
| 1907 | Kenora Thistles[1] | 1932 | Toronto Maple Leafs | 1965–66 | Montreal Canadiens |
| 1907 | Mont. Wanderers[2] | 1933 | N.Y. Rangers | 1967 | Toronto Maple Leafs |
| 1908 | Montreal Wanderers | 1934 | Chicago Black Hawks | 1968–69 | Montreal Canadiens |
| 1909 | Ottawa Senators | 1935 | Montreal Maroons | 1970 | Boston Bruins |
| 1910 | Montreal Wanderers | 1936–37 | Detroit Red Wings | 1971 | Montreal Canadiens |
| 1911 | Ottawa Senators | 1938 | Chicago Black Hawks | 1972 | Boston Bruins |
| 1912–13 | Quebec Bulldogs | 1939 | Boston Bruins | 1973 | Montreal Canadiens |
| 1914 | Toronto | 1940 | N.Y. Rangers | 1974–75 | Philadelphia Flyers |
| 1915 | Vancouver Millionaires | 1941 | Boston Bruins | 1976–79 | Montreal Canadiens |
| 1916 | Montreal Canadiens | 1942 | Toronto Maple Leafs | 1980–83 | New York Islanders |
| 1917 | Seattle Metropolitans | 1943 | Detroit Red Wings | 1984 | Edmonton Oilers |
| 1918 | Toronto Arenas | 1944 | Montreal Canadiens | 1985 | Edmonton Oilers |
| 1919 | No champion | 1945 | Toronto Maple Leafs | 1986 | Montreal Canadiens |
| 1920–21 | Ottawa Senators | 1946 | Montreal Canadiens | 1. January. 2. March. | |

## NATIONAL HOCKEY LEAGUE YEARLY TROPHY WINNERS

### The Hart Trophy—Most Valuable Player

| | | | |
|---|---|---|---|
| | | 1944 | Babe Pratt, Toronto |
| | | 1945 | Elmer Lach, Montreal Canadiens |
| 1924 | Frank Nighbor, Ottawa | 1946 | Max Bentley, Chicago |
| 1925 | Billy Burch, Hamilton | 1947 | Maurice Richard, Montreal Canadiens |
| 1926 | Nels Stewart, Montreal Maroons | 1948 | Buddy O'Connor, New York Rangers |
| 1927 | Herb Gardiner, Montreal Canadiens | 1949 | Sid Abel, Detroit |
| 1928 | Howie Morenz, Montreal Canadiens | 1950 | Chuck Rayner, New York Rangers |
| 1929 | Roy Worters, New York Americans | 1951 | Milt Schmidt, Boston |
| 1930 | Nels Stewart, Montreal Maroons | 1952–53 | Gordon Howe, Detroit |
| 1931–32 | Howie Morenz, Montreal Canadiens | 1954 | Al Rollins, Chicago |
| 1933 | Eddie Shore, Boston | 1955 | Ted Kennedy, Toronto |
| 1934 | Aurel Joliat, Montreal Canadiens | 1956 | Jean Belveau, Montreal Canadiens |
| 1935–36 | Eddie Shore, Boston | 1957–58 | Gordon Howe, Detroit |
| 1937 | Babe Siebert, Montreal Canadiens | 1959 | Andy Bathgate, New York Rangers |
| 1938 | Eddie Shore, Boston | 1960 | Gordon Howe, Detroit |
| 1939 | Toe Blake, Montreal Canadiens | 1961 | Bernie Geoffrion, Montreal Canadiens |
| 1940 | Ebbie Goodfellow, Detroit | 1962 | Jacques Plante, Montreal Canadiens |
| 1941 | Bill Cowley, Boston | 1963 | Gordon Howe, Detroit |
| 1942 | Tom Anderson, New York Americans | 1964 | Jean Beliveau, Montreal Canadiens |
| 1943 | Bill Cowley, Boston | 1965–66 | Bobby Hull, Chicago |

| 1967–68 | Stan Mikita, Chicago |
|---|---|
| 1969 | Phil Esposito, Boston |
| 1970–72 | Bobby Orr, Boston |
| 1973 | Bobby Clarke, Philadelphia |
| 1974 | Phil Esposito, Boston |
| 1975–76 | Bobby Clarke, Philadelphia |
| 1977–78 | Guy Lafleur, Montreal |
| 1979 | Bryan Trottier, N.Y. Islanders |
| 1980 | Wayne Gretzky, Edmonton |
| 1981 | Wayne Gretzky, Edmonton |
| 1982 | Wayne Gretzky, Edmonton |
| 1983 | Wayne Gretzky, Edmonton |
| 1984 | Wayne Gretzky, Edmonton |
| 1985 | Wayne Gretzky, Edmonton |
| 1986 | Wayne Gretzky, Edmonton |

## Vezina Trophy—Leading Goalkeeper

| 1956–60 | Jacques Plante, Montreal |
|---|---|
| 1961 | Johnny Bower, Toronto |
| 1962 | Jacques Plante, Montreal |
| 1963 | Glenn Hall, Chicago |
| 1964 | Charlie Hodge, Montreal |
| 1965 | Terry Sawchuk—Johnny Bower, Toronto |
| 1966 | Lorne Worsley—Charlie Hodge, Montreal |
| 1967 | Glenn Hall—Denis DeJordy, Chicago |
| 1968 | Lorne Worsley—Rogatien Vachon, Montreal |
| 1969 | Glenn Hall—Jacques Plante, St. Louis |
| 1970 | Tony Esposito, Chicago |
| 1971 | Ed Giacomin—Gilles Villemure, New York |
| 1972 | Tony Esposito—Gary Smith, Chicago |
| 1973 | Ken Dryden, Montreal |
| 1974 | Bernie Parent, Philadelphia, and Tony Esposito, Chicago |
| 1975 | Bernie Parent, Philadelphia |
| 1976 | Ken Dryden, Montreal |
| 1977–79 | Ken Dryden—Michel Larocque, Montreal |
| 1980 | Bob Sauve—Don Edwards, Buffalo |
| 1981 | Richard Sevigny, Denis Herron and Michel Larocque, Montreal |
| 1982 | Billy Smith, New York Islanders |
| 1983 | Pete Peeters, Boston |
| 1984 | Tom Barrasso, Buffalo |
| 1985 | Pelle Lindbergh, Philadelphia |
| 1986 | John Vanbiesbrouck, New York Rangers |

## James Norris Trophy—Defenseman

| 1954 | Red Kelly, Detroit |
|---|---|
| 1955–58 | Doug Harvey, Montreal |
| 1959 | Tom Johnson, Montreal |
| 1960–62 | Doug Harvey, Montreal, New York (62) |
| 1963–65 | Pierre Pilote, Chicago |
| 1966 | Jacques Laperriere, Montreal |
| 1967 | Harry Howell, New York |
| 1968–75 | Bobby Orr, Boston |
| 1976 | Denis Potvin, N.Y. Islanders |
| 1977 | Larry Robinson, Montreal |
| 1978 | Denis Potvin, N.Y. Islanders |
| 1980 | Larry Robinson, Montreal |
| 1981 | Randy Carlyle, Pittsburgh |
| 1982 | Doug Wilson, Chicago |
| 1983–84 | Rod Langway, Washington |
| 1985 | Paul Coffey, Edmonton |
| 1986 | Paul Coffey, Edmonton |

## Lady Byng Trophy—Sportsmanship

| 1960 | Don McKenney, Boston |
|---|---|
| 1961 | Red Kelly, Detroit |
| 1962–63 | Dave Keon, Toronto |
| 1964 | Ken Wharram, Chicago |
| 1965 | Bobby Hull, Chicago |
| 1966 | Alex Delvecchio, Detroit |
| 1967–68 | Stan Mikita, Chicago |
| 1969 | Alex Delvecchio, Detroit |
| 1970 | Phil Goyette, St. Louis |
| 1971 | John Bucyk, Boston |
| 1972 | Jean Ratelle, New York |
| 1973 | Gil Perreault, Buffalo |

| 1974 | John Buyck, Boston |
|---|---|
| 1975 | Marcel Dionne, Detroit |
| 1976 | Jean Ratelle, N.Y. Rangers–Boston |
| 1977 | Marcel Dionne, Los Angeles |
| 1978 | Butch Goring, Los Angeles |
| 1979 | Bob MacMillan, Atlanta |
| 1980 | Wayne Gretzky, Edmonton |
| 1981 | Rick Kehoe, Pittsburgh |
| 1982 | Rick Middleton, Boston |
| 1983–84 | Mike Bossy, N.Y. Islanders |
| 1985 | Jari Kurri, Edmonton |
| 1986 | Mike Bossy, N.Y. Islanders |

## Calder Trophy—Rookie

| 1962 | Bobby Rousseau, Montreal |
|---|---|
| 1963 | Kent Douglas, Toronto |
| 1964 | Jacques Laperriere, Montreal |
| 1965 | Roger Crozier, Detroit |
| 1966 | Brit Selby, Toronto |
| 1967 | Bobby Orr, Boston |
| 1968 | Derek Sanderson, Boston |
| 1969 | Danny Grant, Minnesota |
| 1970 | Tony Esposito, Chicago |
| 1971 | Gilbert Perreault, Buffalo |
| 1972 | Ken Dryden, Montreal |
| 1973 | Steve Vickers, New York Rangers |
| 1974 | Denis Potvin, N.Y. Islanders |
| 1975 | Eric Vail, Atlanta |
| 1976 | Bryan Trottier, N.Y. Islanders |
| 1977 | Willi Plett, Atlanta |
| 1978 | Mike Bossy, N.Y. Islanders |
| 1979 | Bobby Smith, Minnesota |
| 1980 | Ray Bourque, Boston |
| 1981 | Peter Stastny, Quebec |
| 1982 | Dale Hawerchuk, Winnipeg |
| 1983 | Steve Larmer, Chicago |
| 1984 | Tom Barrasso, Buffalo |
| 1985 | Mario Lemieux, Pittsburgh |
| 1986 | Gary Suter, Calgary |

## Art Ross Trophy—Leading scorer

| 1955 | Bernie Geoffrion, Montreal |
|---|---|
| 1956 | Jean Beliveau, Montreal |
| 1957 | Gordie Howe, Detroit |
| 1958–59 | Dickie Moore, Montreal |
| 1960 | Bobby Hull, Chicago |
| 1961 | Bernie Geoffrion, Montreal |
| 1962 | Bobby Hull, Chicago |
| 1963 | Gordie Howe, Detroit |
| 1964–65 | Stan Mikita, Chicago |
| 1966 | Bobby Hull, Chicago |
| 1967–68 | Stan Mikita, Chicago |
| 1969 | Phil Esposito, Boston |
| 1970 | Bobby Orr, Boston |
| 1971–74 | Phil Esposito, Boston |
| 1975 | Bobby Orr, Boston |
| 1976–78 | Guy Lafleur, Montreal |
| 1979 | Bryan Trottier, N.Y. Islanders |
| 1980 | Marcel Dionne, Los Angeles |
| 1981–86 | Wayne Gretzky, Edmonton |

## N.H.L. CHAMPIONS
## Prince of Wales Trophy

| 1939 | Boston |
|---|---|
| 1940 | Boston |
| 1941 | Boston |
| 1942 | New York |
| 1943 | Detroit |
| 1944–47 | Montreal |
| 1948 | Toronto |
| 1948–55 | Detroit |
| 1956 | Montreal |
| 1957 | Detroit |
| 1958–62 | Montreal |
| 1963 | Toronto |

| 1964 | Montreal |
|---|---|
| 1965 | Detroit |
| 1966 | Montreal |
| 1967 | Chicago |

**Eastern Division**

| 1968–69 | Montreal |
|---|---|
| 1970 | Chicago |
| 1971 | Boston |
| 1972 | Boston |
| 1973 | Montreal |
| 1974 | Boston |

**Prince of Wales Conference**

| 1975 | Buffalo |
|---|---|
| 1976–79 | Montreal |
| 1980 | Buffalo |
| 1981 | Montreal |
| 1982 | New York Islanders |
| 1983 | New York Islanders |
| 1984 | New York Islanders |
| 1985 | Philadelphia |
| 1986 | Montreal |

**CAMPBELL BOWL**
**Western Division**

| 1968 | Philadelphia |
|---|---|
| 1969 | St. Louis |
| 1970 | St. Louis |
| 1971–73 | Chicago |
| 1974 | Philadelphia |

**Clarence Campbell Conference**

| 1975 | Philadelphia |
|---|---|
| 1976–77 | Philadelphia |
| 1978–79 | N.Y. Islanders |
| 1980 | Philadelphia |
| 1981 | New York Islanders |
| 1982 | Edmonton |
| 1983 | Edmonton |
| 1984 | Edmonton |
| 1985 | Edmonton |
| 1986 | Calgary |

## NATIONAL HOCKEY LEAGUE
### Final Standing of the Clubs—1985–86

**PRINCE OF WALES CONFERENCE**
**Patrick Division**

| | W | L | T | GF | GA | Pts |
|---|---|---|---|---|---|---|
| Philadelphia Flyers | 53 | 23 | 4 | 335 | 241 | 110 |
| Washington Capitals | 50 | 23 | 7 | 315 | 272 | 107 |
| New York Islanders | 39 | 29 | 12 | 327 | 284 | 90 |
| New York Rangers | 36 | 38 | 6 | 280 | 276 | 78 |
| Pittsburgh Penguins | 34 | 38 | 8 | 313 | 305 | 76 |
| New Jersey Devils | 28 | 49 | 3 | 301 | 374 | 59 |

**Adams Division**

| | W | L | T | GF | GA | Pts |
|---|---|---|---|---|---|---|
| Quebec Nordiques | 43 | 31 | 6 | 330 | 289 | 92 |
| Montreal Canadiens | 40 | 33 | 7 | 330 | 280 | 87 |
| Boston Bruins | 37 | 31 | 12 | 311 | 288 | 86 |
| Hartford Whalers | 40 | 36 | 4 | 332 | 302 | 84 |
| Buffalo Sabres | 37 | 37 | 6 | 296 | 291 | 80 |

**CLARENCE CAMPBELL CONFERENCE**
**Norris Division**

| | W | L | T | GF | GA | Pts |
|---|---|---|---|---|---|---|
| Chicago Black Hawks | 39 | 33 | 8 | 351 | 350 | 86 |
| Minnesota North Stars | 38 | 33 | 9 | 327 | 305 | 85 |
| St. Louis Blues | 37 | 34 | 9 | 302 | 291 | 83 |
| Toronto Maple Leafs | 25 | 48 | 7 | 311 | 386 | 57 |
| Detroit Red Wings | 17 | 57 | 6 | 266 | 415 | 40 |

**Smythe Division**

| | W | L | T | GF | GA | Pts |
|---|---|---|---|---|---|---|
| Edmonton Oilers | 56 | 17 | 7 | 426 | 310 | 119 |
| Calgary Flames | 40 | 31 | 9 | 354 | 315 | 89 |
| Winnipeg Jets | 26 | 47 | 7 | 295 | 372 | 59 |
| Vancouver Canucks | 23 | 44 | 13 | 282 | 333 | 59 |
| Los Angeles Kings | 23 | 49 | 8 | 284 | 389 | 54 |

## Stanley Cup Playoffs—1986

**Preliminary Round**

Washington Capitals defeated New York Islanders, 3 games to 0
Montreal Canadiens defeated Boston Bruins, 3 games to 0
New York Rangers defeated Philadelphia Flyers, 3 games to 2
Hartford Whalers defeated Quebec Nordiques, 3 games to 0
Toronto Maple Leafs defeated Chicago Black Hawks, 3 games to 0
Edmonton Oilers defeated Vancouver Canucks, 3 games to 0
Calgary Flames defeated Winnipeg Jets, 3 games to 0
St. Louis Blues defeated Minnesota North Stars, 3 games to 2

**Quarterfinal Round**

New York Rangers defeated Washington Capitals, 4 games to 2
Montreal Canadiens defeated Hartford Whalers, 4 games to 3
Calgary Flames defeated Edmonton Oilers, 4 games to 3
St. Louis Blues defeated Toronto Maple Leafs, 4 games to 3

**Semifinal Round**

Montreal Canadiens defeated New York Rangers, 4 games to 1
  May 1—Montreal 2, New York 1[1]
  May 3—Montreal 6, New York 1[1]
  May 5—Montreal 4, New York 3 (OT)
  May 7—New York 2, Montreal 0
  May 9—Montreal 3, New York 1[1]

1. At Montreal.

Calgary defeated St. Louis, 4 games to 3
  May 2—St. Louis 3, Calgary 2[1]
  May 4—Calgary 8, St. Louis 2[1]
  May 6—Calgary 5, St. Louis 3
  May 8—St. Louis 5, Calgary 2
  May 10—Calgary 4, St. Louis 2[1]
  May 12—St. Louis 6, Calgary 5 (OT)
  May 14—Calgary 2, St. Louis 1[1]

1. At Calgary.

**Championship**

Montreal defeated Calgary, 4 games to 1
  May 16—Calgary 5, Montreal 2[1]
  May 18—Montreal 3, Calgary 2 (OT)[1]
  May 20—Montreal 5, Calgary 3

May 22—Montreal 1, Calgary 0
May 24—Montreal 4, Calgary 3

1. At Montreal.

## N.H.L. LEADING SCORERS—1985–86

| | GP | G | A | Pts |
|---|---|---|---|---|
| Wayne Gretzky, Edmonton | 80 | 52 | 163 | 215 |
| Mario Lemieux, Pittsburgh | 79 | 48 | 93 | 141 |
| Paul Coffey, Edmonton | 79 | 48 | 90 | 138 |
| Jari Kurri, Edmonton | 78 | 68 | 63 | 131 |
| Mike Bossy, N.Y. Islanders | 80 | 61 | 62 | 123 |
| Peter Stastny, Quebec | 76 | 41 | 81 | 122 |
| Denis Savard, Chicago | 80 | 47 | 69 | 116 |
| Mats Naslund, Montreal | 80 | 43 | 67 | 110 |
| Dale Hawerchuk, Winnipeg | 80 | 46 | 59 | 105 |
| Neal Broten, Minnesota | 80 | 29 | 76 | 105 |
| Michel Goulet, Quebec | 75 | 53 | 50 | 103 |
| Glenn Anderson, Edmonton | 72 | 54 | 48 | 102 |
| Bernie Federko, St. Louis | 80 | 34 | 68 | 102 |
| Troy Murray, Chicago | 80 | 45 | 54 | 99 |
| Brian Propp, Philadelphia | 72 | 40 | 57 | 97 |
| Bernie Nicholls, Los Angeles | 80 | 36 | 61 | 97 |
| Bryan Trottier, N.Y. Islanders | 78 | 37 | 59 | 96 |
| Marcel Dionne, Los Angeles | 80 | 36 | 58 | 94 |
| Joe Mullen, St. Louis-Calgary | 77 | 44 | 46 | 90 |
| Dino Ciccarelli, Minnesota | 75 | 44 | 45 | 89 |
| Dave Andreychuk, Buffalo | 80 | 36 | 51 | 87 |
| Bobby Smith, Montreal | 79 | 31 | 55 | 86 |
| Tim Kerr, Philadelphia | 76 | 58 | 26 | 84 |
| Keith Crowder, Boston | 78 | 38 | 46 | 84 |
| Mark Messier, Edmonton | 63 | 35 | 49 | 84 |

## OTHER N.H.L. AWARDS—1986

Selke (Best defensive forward)—Troy Murray, Chicago
Smythe (Most valuable in playoffs)—Patrick Roy, Montreal

## N.H.L. LEADING GOALTENDERS—1985–86
### (Minimum 1,400 minutes)

| | G | Min | GA | Avg |
|---|---|---|---|---|
| Bob Froese, Philadelphia | 51 | 2728 | 116 | 2.55 |
| Al Jensen, Washington | 44 | 2437 | 129 | 3.18 |
| Clint Malarchuk, Quebec | 46 | 2657 | 142 | 3.21 |
| Kelly Hrudey, N.Y. Islanders | 45 | 2563 | 137 | 3.21 |
| John Vanbiesbrouck, N.Y. Rangers | 61 | 3326 | 184 | 3.32 |
| Pat Riggin, Boston | 39 | 2272 | 127 | 3.35 |
| Pete Peeters, Washington | 34 | 2021 | 113 | 3.35 |
| Patrick Roy, Montreal | 47 | 2651 | 150 | 3.39 |
| Rick Wamsley, St. Louis | 42 | 2517 | 144 | 3.43 |
| Don Beaupre, Minnesota | 52 | 3073 | 182 | 3.55 |
| Roberto Romano, Pittsburgh | 46 | 2684 | 159 | 3.55 |
| Greg Millen, St. Louis | 36 | 2168 | 129 | 3.57 |
| Gilles Meloche, Pittsburgh | 34 | 1989 | 119 | 3.59 |
| Tom Barrasso, Buffalo | 60 | 3561 | 214 | 3.61 |
| Mike Liut, Hartford | 57 | 3282 | 198 | 3.62 |

## N.H.L. CAREER SCORING LEADERS

(Listed in order of total points scored; figures in parentheses indicate the top 10 in goals scored.)

| | Yrs | Games | G | A | Pts |
|---|---|---|---|---|---|
| Gordie Howe (1) | 26 | 1,767 | 801 | 1,049 | 1,850 |
| Marcel Dionne (3)[1] | 15 | 1,163 | 665 | 934 | 1,599 |
| Phil Esposito (2) | 18 | 1,282 | 717 | 873 | 1,590 |
| Stan Mikita (6) | 22 | 1,394 | 541 | 926 | 1,467 |
| John Bucyk (5) | 23 | 1,540 | 556 | 813 | 1,369 |
| Wayne Gretzky[1] | 7 | 553 | 481 | 856 | 1,337 |
| Gil Perreault (10) | 16 | 1,171 | 503 | 807 | 1,310 |
| Alex Delvecchio | 24 | 1,549 | 456 | 825 | 1,281 |
| Jean Ratelle | 21 | 1,281 | 491 | 776 | 1,267 |
| Guy Lafleur (8) | 14 | 961 | 518 | 728 | 1,246 |
| Norm Ullman | 20 | 1,410 | 490 | 739 | 1,229 |
| Jean Beliveau (9) | 20 | 1,215 | 507 | 712 | 1,219 |
| Bobby Clarke | 15 | 1,144 | 358 | 852 | 1,210 |
| Bobby Hull (4) | 16 | 1,063 | 610 | 560 | 1,170 |
| Darryl Sittler | 15 | 1,096 | 484 | 637 | 1,121 |
| Frank Mahovlich (7) | 18 | 1,181 | 533 | 570 | 1,103 |
| Henri Richard | 20 | 1,256 | 358 | 688 | 1,046 |
| Rod Gilbert | 18 | 1,065 | 406 | 615 | 1,021 |

1. Still active in N.H.L.

# Bowling

## AMERICAN BOWLING CONGRESS CHAMPIONS

| Year | Singles | All-events | Year | Singles | All-events |
|---|---|---|---|---|---|
| 1959 | Ed Lubanski | Ed Lubanski | 1974 | Gene Krause | Bob Hart |
| 1960 | Paul Kulbaga | Vince Lucci | 1975 | Jim Setser | Bobby Meadows |
| 1961 | Lyle Spooner | Luke Karen | 1976 | Mike Putzer | Jim Lindquist |
| 1962 | Andy Renaldo | Billy Young | 1977 | Frank Gadaleto | Bud Debenham |
| 1963 | Fred Delello | Bus Owalt | 1978 | Rich Mersek | Chris Cobus |
| 1964 | Jim Stefanich | Les Zikes, Jr. | 1979 | Rick Peters | Bob Basacchi |
| 1965 | Ken Roeth | Tom Hathaway | 1980 | Mike Eaton | Steve Fehr |
| 1966 | Don Chapman | John Wilcox | 1981 | Rob Vital | Rod Toft |
| 1967 | Frank Perry | Gary Lewis | 1982 | Bruce Bohm | Rich Wonders |
| 1968 | Wayne Kowalski | Vince Mazzanti | 1983 | Rick Kendrick | Tony Cariello |
| 1969 | Greg Campbell | Eddie Jackson | 1984 | Bob Antczak and | Bob Goike |
| 1970 | Jake Yoder | Mike Berlin | | Neal Young (tie) | |
| 1971 | Al Cohn | Al Cohn | 1985 | Glen Harbison | Barry Asher |
| 1972 | Bill Pointer | Mac Lowry | 1986 | Jess Mackey | Ed Marazka |
| 1973 | Ed Thompson | Ron Woolet | | | |

# PROFESSIONAL BOWLERS ASSOCIATION
## National Championship Tournament

| | | | |
|---|---|---|---|
| 1960 Don Carter | 1967 Dave Davis | 1974 Earl Anthony | 1981 Earl Anthony |
| 1961 Dave Soutar | 1968 Wayne Zahn | 1975 Earl Anthony | 1982 Earl Anthony |
| 1962 Carmen Salvino | 1969 Mike McGrath | 1976 Paul Colwell | 1983 Earl Anthony |
| 1963 Billy Hardwick | 1970 Mike McGrath | 1977 Tommy Hudson | 1984 Bob Chamberlain |
| 1964 Bob Strampe | 1971 Mike Lemongello | 1978 Warren Nelson | 1985 Mike Aulby |
| 1965 Dave Davis | 1972 Johnny Guenther | 1979 Mike Aulby | 1986 Tom Crites |
| 1966 Wayne Zahn | 1973 Earl Anthony | 1980 Johnny Petraglia | |

## BOWLING PROPRIETORS' ASSOCIATION OF AMERICA—MEN
### United States Open[1]

| | | | |
|---|---|---|---|
| 1971 Mike Lemongello | 1975 Steve Neff | 1979 Joe Berardi | 1983 Gary Dickinson |
| 1972 Don Johnson | 1976 Paul Moser | 1980 Steve Martin | 1984 Mark Roth |
| 1973 Mike McGrath | 1977 Johnny Petraglia | 1981 Marshall Holman | 1985 Marshall Holman |
| 1974 Larry Laub | 1978 Nelson Burton, Jr. | 1982 Dave Husted | 1986 Steve Cook |

1. Replaced All-Star tournament and is rolled as part of B.P.A. tour.

## WOMEN'S INTERNATIONAL BOWLING CONGRESS CHAMPIONS

| Year | Singles | All-events | Year | Singles | All-events |
|---|---|---|---|---|---|
| 1959 | Mae Bolt | Pat McBride | 1974 | Shirley Garms | Judy C. Soutar |
| 1960 | Marge McDaniels | Judy Roberts | 1975 | Barbara Leicht | Virginia Norton |
| 1961 | Elaine Newton | Evelyn Teal | 1976 | Bev Shonk | Betty Morris |
| 1962 | Martha Hoffman | Flossie Argent | 1977 | Akiko Yamaga | Akiko Yamaga |
| 1963 | Dot Wilkinson | Helen Shablis | 1978 | Mae Bolt | Annese Kelly |
| 1964 | Jean Havlish | Jean Havlish | 1979 | Betty Morris | Betty Morris |
| 1965 | Doris Rudell | Donna Zimmerman | 1980 | Betty Morris | Cheryl Robinson |
| 1966 | Gloria Bouvia | Kate Helbig | 1981 | Virginia Norton | Virginia Norton |
| 1967 | Gloria Paeth | Carol Miller | 1982 | Gracie Freeman | Aleta Rzepecki |
| 1968 | Norma Parks | Susie Reichley | 1983 | Aleta Rzepecki | Virginia Norton |
| 1969 | Joan Bender | Helen Duval | 1984 | Freida Gates | Shinobu Saitoh |
| 1970 | Dorothy Fothergill | Dorothy Fothergill | 1985 | Polly Schwarzel | Aleta Sill |
| 1971 | Mary Scruggs | Lorrie Nichols | 1986 | Dana Stewart | Robin Romeo |
| 1972 | D. D. Jacobson | Mildred Martorella | | | Maria Lewis (tie) |
| 1973 | Bobby Buffaloe | Toni Calvery | | | |

## WIBC QUEENS TOURNAMENT CHAMPIONS

| | | | |
|---|---|---|---|
| 1961 Janet Harman | 1968 Phyllis Massey | 1975 Cindy Powell | 1982 Katsuko Sugimoto |
| 1962 Dorothy Wilkinson | 1969 Ann Feigel | 1976 Pamela Buckner | 1983 Aleta Rzepecki |
| 1963 Irene Monterosso | 1970 Mildred Martorella | 1977 Dana Stewart | 1984 Kazue Inahashi |
| 1964 D.D. Jacobson | 1971 Mildred Martorella | 1978 Loa Boxberger | 1985 Aleta Sill |
| 1965 Betty Kuczynski | 1972 Dorothy Fothergill | 1979 Donna Adamek | 1986 Cora Fiebig |
| 1966 Judy Lee | 1973 Dorothy Fothergill | 1980 Donna Adamek | |
| 1967 Mildred Martorella | 1974 Judy Soutar | 1981 Katsuko Sugimoto | |

## BOWLING PROPRIETORS' ASSOCIATION OF AMERICA—WOMEN
### United States Open[1]

| | | | |
|---|---|---|---|
| 1971 Paula Carter | 1975 Paula Carter | 1979 Diana Silva | 1983 Dana Miller |
| 1972 Lorrie Nichols | 1976 Patty Costello (Pa.) | 1980 Pat Costello (Calif.) | 1984 Karen Ellingsworth |
| 1973 Mildred Martorella | 1977 Betty Morris | 1981 Donna Adamek | 1985 Pat Mercatanti |
| 1974 Pat Costello (Calif.) | 1978 Donna Adamek | 1982 Shinobu Saitoh | 1986 Wendy MacPherson |

## AMERICAN BOWLING CONGRESS TOURNAMENT—1986
### (Las Vegas, Nev., Feb. 8-June 21, 1986)

#### Regular Division

| | |
|---|---|
| Singles—Jeff Mackey, Mexico, Missouri | 774 |
| Doubles—Bob Larson and Donald Cook, Milwaukee, Wis. | 1418 |
| All Events—Ed Marzka, Detroit, Mich. | 2116 |
| Team—Faball Enterprises No. 2, Milwaukee | 3253 |
| Team All-Events—Faball Enterprises No. 1, Milwaukee | 9614 |

#### Booster Division

| | |
|---|---|
| Team—The Breakers, Vancouver, British Columbia, Canada | 2828 |

## PROFESSIONAL BOWLERS ASSOCIATION CHAMPIONSHIP—1986

(Toledo, Ohio, March 29, 1986)

Winner—Tom Crites, Tampa, Fla. (defeated Mike Aulby, Indianapolis, Ind., the defending champion, 190-184 in final).
Third place—Mark Roth, Spring Lake Heights, N.J.
Fourth place—Mike Edward, Tulsa, Okla.
Fifth place—Pete Weber, St. Louis, Mo.

## WIBC QUEENS TOURNAMENT—1986

(Orange County, Calif., May 13-17, 1986)

Winner—Cora Fiebig, Madison Heights, Mich. (defeated Barbara Thorberg, St. Louis, Mo., 223-177 in final).
Third place—Donna Adamek, Duarte, Calif.
Fourth place—Betty Morris-Simon, Simi Valley, Calif.
Fifth place—Cindy Schuble, Louisville, Ky.

## WOMEN'S INTERNATIONAL BOWLING CONGRESS TOURNAMENT—1986

(April 3-June 30, Orange County, Calif.)

### Open Division

| | |
|---|---:|
| Singles—Dana Stewart, Morgan Hill, Calif. | 698 |
| Doubles—Sally Gates, Palmdale, Calif., and Marilyn Frazier, Lancaster, Calif. | 1260 |
| All Events—Tie between Robin Romeo, Van Nuyes, Calif., and Maria Lewis, Manteca, Calif. | 1877 |
| Team—Sillia's Pro Shop, Cleveland, Ohio | 2891 |

### Division I

| | |
|---|---:|
| Singles—Diane Smith, Lake Cowichan, British Columbia, Canada | 688 |
| Doubles—Cindy Brennan, Missoula, Mont., and Joy Eckley, Ronan, Mont. | 1188 |
| All-Events—Nancy Schubert-Baker, Baltimore, Md. | 1780 |
| Team—Royal Buick, Tucson, Ariz. | 2672 |

### Division II

| | |
|---|---:|
| Singles—Kitty Elend, Ontario, Calif. | 656 |
| Doubles—Kitty Elend, Ontario, Calif., and Arlene Magana, St. Chino, Calif. | 1110 |
| All Events—Kitty Elend, Ontario, Calif. | 1819 |
| Team—Caffe Trucky, Wessington Springs, S.D. | 2530 |

---

# SKIING

## ALPINE WORLD CUP OVERALL WINNERS

| Year | Men | Women | Team |
|---|---|---|---|
| 1967 | Jean-Claude Killy, France | Nancy Greene, Canada | France |
| 1968 | Jean-Claude Killy, France | Nancy Greene, Canada | France |
| 1969 | Karl Schranz, Austria | Gertrude Gabl, Austria | Austria |
| 1970 | Karl Schranz, Austria | Michel Jacot, France | France |
| 1971 | Gustavo Thoeni, Italy | Annemarie Proell, Austria | France |
| 1972 | Gustavo Thoeni, Italy | Annemarie Proell, Austria | France |
| 1973 | Gustavo Thoeni, Italy | Annemarie Proell Moser, Austria | Austria |
| 1974 | Piero Gros, Italy | Annemarie Proell Moser, Austria | Austria |
| 1975 | Gustavo Thoeni, Italy | Annemarie Proell Moser, Austria | Austria |
| 1976 | Ingemar Stenmark, Sweden | Rosi Mittermaier, West Germany | Austria |
| 1977 | Ingemar Stenmark, Sweden | Lise-Marie Morerod, Switzerland | Austria |
| 1978 | Ingemar Stenmark, Sweden | Hanni Wenzel, Liechtenstein | Austria |
| 1979 | Peter Luescher, Switzerland | Annemarie Proell Moser, Austria | Austria |
| 1980 | Andreas Wenzel, Liechtenstein | Hanni Wenzel, Liechtenstein | Liechtenstein |
| 1981 | Phil Mahre, United States | Marie-Theres Nadig, Switzerland | Switzerland |
| 1982 | Phil Mahre, United States | Erika Hess, Switzerland | Austria |
| 1983 | Phil Mahre, United States | Tamara McKinney, United States | |
| 1984 | Pirman Zurbriggen, Switzerland | Erika Hess, Switzerland | |
| 1985 | Marc Girardelli, Luxembourg | Michela Figini, Switzerland | Switzerland |
| 1986 | Marc Girardelli, Luxembourg | Maria Walliser, Switzerland | Switzerland |

## UNITED STATES CHAMPIONSHIPS—1986

### ALPINE
#### Men's Events

| | |
|---|---:|
| Downhill—Doug Lewis, Salisbury, Vt. | 1:44.71 |
| Slalom—Henrik Smith-Meyer, Norway | 1:46.29 |
| Giant Slalom—Tiger Shaw, Stowe, Vt. | 2:13.13 |

#### Women's Events

| | |
|---|---:|
| Downhill—Hillary Lindh, Juneau, Alaska | 1:50.29 |
| Slalom—Tamara McKinney, Squaw Valley, Calif. | 1:38.15 |
| Giant Slalom—Beth Madsen, Aspen, Col. | 2:19.09 |

### NORDIC
#### Men's Cross Country

| | |
|---|---:|
| 15 kilometers—George Welk, Seely, Wis. | :41:00.8 |
| 30 kilometers—Audun Endestad, Fairbanks, Alaska | 1:18:32.7 |
| 50 kilometers—Audun Endestad, Fairbanks, Alaska | 2:13:21.4 |

#### Women's Cross Country

| | |
|---|---:|
| 5 kilometers—Cami Thompson, Stowe, Vt. | :14:09.7 |
| 10 kilometers—Nancy Fiddler | :29:16.7 |
| 20 kilometers—Leslie Krichko | 1:05:08.7 |

## NORDIC WORLD CUP—1986

**Overall—Men**      **Pts**
Cross Country

| | Pts |
|---|---|
| 1. Gunde Svan, Sweden | 145 |
| 2. Tor Mogren, Sweden | 101 |
| 3. V. Smirnov, Soviet Union | 28 |
| Best American finish—Audun Endestad | 2 |

Jumping

| | |
|---|---|
| 1. Matt Nykaenen, Finland | 250 |
| 2. Ernst Vettari, Austria | 232 |
| 3. Andreas Felder, Austria | 170 |
| Best American finish—Rick Mewborn | 25 |

**Overall—Women**
Cross Country

| | |
|---|---|
| 1. M. Matikkaenen, Finland | 107 |
| 2. M. Dahlmo, Norway | 106 |
| 3. Brit Pettersen, Norway | 102 |
| Best American finish—none | |

Nordic Men's Combined

| | |
|---|---|
| 1. Hermann Weinbuch, West Germany | 140 |
| 2. Geir Andersen, Norway | 87 |
| 3. Thomas Mueller, West Germany | 86 |
| Best American finish—none | |

### COLLEGIATE

(University of Vermont, Burlington, Vt., March 5-8, 1986)

### Men—N.C.A.A.

| | |
|---|---|
| Slalom—John Skajem, Colorado | 1:19.68 |
| Giant slalom—Miles DeChamps, Dartmouth | 1:57.21 |
| Cross country—Hans-Martin Sjulstad, Utah | :41:55.7 |

Cross country relay—Utah (Asmund Drivenes, Erik Baumann, Hans-Martin Sjulstad)    1:35:15.8

### Women—N.C.A.A.

| | |
|---|---|
| Slalom—Gabriella Hamberg, Vermont | 1:19.98 |
| Giant slalom—Lynda McGehee, Colorado | 2:03.07 |
| Cross country—Hanne Krogstad, Vermont | :32:30.8 |

Cross country relay—Colorado (Ingrid Butts, Jill Anderson, Kristin Petty)    :56:39.1
Team (men & women)—Utah 612; Vermont 602; Wyoming 554.

## ALPINE NATIONS CUP—1985

     **Pts**
Overall

| | Pts |
|---|---|
| 1. Switzerland | 2,677 |
| 2. Austria | 1,315 |
| 3. West Germany | 853 |
| 4. Italy | 852 |
| 5. France | 592 |
| 6. United States | 500 |
| 7. Yugoslavia | 320 |
| 8. Sweden | 286 |
| 9. Liechtenstein | 270 |
| 10. Luxembourg | 262 |

### COLLEGIATE

(Montana State University, March 6–9, 1985)

### Men—N.C.A.A.

Slalom—Jeff Durtschi, Utah
Giant slalom—Tom Foote, Dartmouth
Cross country—John Aalberg, Utah
Cross country relay—Vermont

### Women—N.C.A.A.

Slalom—Ann Melander, Wyoming
Giant slalom—Ann Melander, Wyoming

Cross country—Kristen Petty, Colorado
Cross country relay—Wyoming
Team (men & women)—Wyoming, 764; Utah, 744; Vermont, 721

## WORLD ALPINE CHAMPIONSHIPS—1985

(Held every other year)

### Men's Events

Slalom—Jonas Nilsson, Sweden
Giant slalom—Markus Wasmeier, West Germany
Combined—Pirmin Zurbriggen, Switzerland

### Women's Events

Slalom—Perrine Pelen, France
Giant slalom—Diann Roffe, United States
Combined—Erika Hess, Switzerland

## ALPINE WORLD CUP—1986

| **Overall—Men** | **Pts** |
|---|---|
| Max Girardelli, Luxembourg | 294 |
| Pirmin Zubriggen, Switzerland | 284 |
| Michael Wasmaier, West Germany | 214 |
| Peter Mueller, Switzerland | 204 |
| Ingemar Stenmark, Sweden | 196 |
| Best American finish—Doug Lewis | 43 (39th place) |
| **Overall—Women** | **Pts** |
| Maria Walliser, Switzerland | 287 |
| Erika Hess | 242 |
| Erena Schneider, Switzerland | 216 |
| Olga Chareatova, Czechoslovakia | 199 |
| Brigette Oertli, Switzerland | 181 |
| Best American finish—Pam Fletcher | 66 (23rd place) |
| **Event Leaders—Men** | **Pts** |
| Downhill—Peter Wirnsberger, Austria | 120 |
| 2. Peter Mueller, Switzerland | 115 |
| 3. Michael Mair, Italy | 92 |
| Best American finish—Doug Lewis | 40 |
| Slalom—Rok Petrovic, Yugoslavia | 125 |
| 2. Ingemar Stenmark, Sweden | 100 |
| 2. Peter Frommelt, Liechtenstein | 100 |
| 2. Eojon Krizas, Yugoslavia | 100 |
| Best American finish—Tiger Shaw | 24 |
| Giant Slalom—Joel Gaspoz, Switzerland | 97 |
| 2. Ingemar Stenmark, Sweden | 96 |
| 3. Hubert Strolz, Austria | 90 |
| Best American finish—Tiger Shaw | 4 |
| Combined—Markus Wasmeier, West Germany | 90 |
| 2. Leonard Stock, Austria | 88 |
| 3. Pirmin Zurbriggen, Switzerland | 77 |
| Best American finish—none | |
| **Event Leaders—Women** | |
| Downhill—Maria Walliser, Switzerland | 115 |
| 2. K. Gutensohn, Austria | 110 |
| 3. Laurie Graham, Canada | 105 |
| Best American finish—Pam Fletcher | 46 |
| Slalom—1. R. Steiner, Austria | 110 |
| 1. Erika Hess, Switzerland | 110 (tie) |
| 3. Perrine Pelen, France | 77 |
| Best American finish—Tamara McKinney | 35 |
| Giant slalom—Brena Schneider, Switzerland | 110 |
| 2. Traudl Haecher, West Germany | 88 |
| 3. Mateja Suef, Yugoslavia | 84 |
| Best American finish—Tamara McKinney | 18 |
| Combined—1. Maria Walliser, Switzerland | 85 |
| 2. Erika Hess, Switzerland | 63 |
| 3. Michela Figina, Switzerland | 43 |
| Best American finish—none | |

# SPEED SKATING

## U.S. OUTDOOR CHAMPIONS

**Men**

| | | | | | |
|---|---|---|---|---|---|
| 1959-60 | Ken Bartholomew | 1979 | Erik Henriksen | 1969 | Sally Blatchford |
| 1961 | Ed Rudolph | 1980 | Greg Oly | 1970-71 | Sheila Young |
| 1962 | Floyd Bedbury | 1981 | Tom Grannes | 1972 | Ruth Moore, Nancy Thorne |
| 1963 | Tom Gray | 1982 | Greg Oly | 1973 | Nancy Class |
| 1964 | Neil Blatchford | 1983 | Michael Ralston | 1974 | Kris Garbe |
| 1965-66 | Rich Wurster | 1984 | Michael Ralston | 1975 | Nancy Swider |
| 1967 | Mike Passarella | 1985 | Andy Gabel | 1976 | Connie Carpenter |
| 1968-70 | Peter Cefalu | 1986 | Eric Klein | 1977 | Liz Crowe |
| 1971 | Jack Walters | **Women** | | 1978 | Paula Class, Betsy Davis |
| 1972 | Barth Levy | 1960 | Mary Novak | 1979 | Gretchen Byrnes |
| 1973 | Mike Woods | 1961 | Jean Ashworth | 1980 | Shari Miller |
| 1974 | Leigh Barczewski, Mike Passarella | 1962 | Jean Omelenchuk | 1981 | Lisa Merrifield |
| | | 1963 | Jean Ashworth | 1982 | Lisa Merrifield |
| 1975 | Rich Wurster | 1964 | Diane White | 1983 | Janet Hainstock |
| 1976 | John Wurster | 1965 | Jean Omelenchuk | 1984 | Janet Hainstock |
| 1977 | Jim Chapin | 1966 | Diane White | 1985 | Betsy Davis |
| 1978 | Bill Heinkel | 1967 | Jean Ashworth | 1986 | Deb Perkins |
| | | 1968 | Helen Lutsch | | |

## WORLD SPEED SKATING RECORDS

**Men**

| Distance | Time | Skater | Place | Year |
|---|---|---|---|---|
| 500 m | 0:36.57 | Pavel Pegov | Medeo, U.S.S.R. | 1983 |
| 1,000 m | 1:12.58 | Pavel Pegov | Medeo, U.S.S.R. | 1983 |
| 1,500 m | 1:53.26 | Oleg Bojiev | Medeo, U.S.S.R. | 1984 |
| 3,000 m | 4:03.31 | Andre Hoffman, E. Germany | Devos, Switzerland | 1985 |
| 5,000 m | 6:49.15 | Victor Shasherin | Medeo, U.S.S.R. | 1984 |
| 10,000 m | 14:12.14 | Geir Karistad, | Inzell, West Germany | 1986 |
| All-Around | 160.807 | Victor Shasherin | Medeo, U.S.S.R. | 1984 |

**Women**

| Distance | Time | Skater | Place | Year |
|---|---|---|---|---|
| 500 m | 0:39.69 | Christa Rothenburger, E. Germany | Medeo | 1983 |
| 1,000 m | 1:19.31 | Natalya Petruseva, U.S.S.R. | Medeo | 1983 |
| 1,500 m | 2:03.34 | Andrea Schone, E. Germany | Medeo | 1984 |
| 3,000 m | 4:20.91 | Andrea Schone, E. Germany | Medeo | 1984 |
| 5,000 m | 7:32.82 | Andrea Schone, E. Germany | Sarajevo, Yugoslavia | 1985 |
| All-around | 171.760 | Andrea Schone, E. Germany | Medeo | 1984 |

### U.S. OUTDOOR CHAMPIONS—1986

Men—Eric Klein, St. Louis, Mo.
Women—Deb Perkins, Milwaukee, Wis.
Intermediate Men—Akio Tagawa, Milwaukee, Wis.
Intermediate Women—Michelle Kline, St. Paul, Minn.
Junior boys—Nathanial Mills, Chicago, Ill.
Junior girls—Kristen Talbot, Saratoga Springs, N.Y.

### U.S. INDOOR CHAMPIONS—1986

Men—Brian Arseneau, Chicago, Ill.
Women—Bonnie Blair, Champaigne, Ill.
Intermediate men—Mark Greenwalf, Chicago, Ill.
Intermediate women—More D'Andrea, Saratoga Springs, N.Y.
Junior boys—Nathanial Mills, Chicago, Ill.
Junior girls—Heather Haster, St. Paul, Minn.

### WORLD SPRINT CHAMPIONSHIPS—1986

(Karuizawa, Japan, Feb. 22-23, 1986)

**Men**

| | |
|---|---|
| 500 m—Dan Jensen, United States | :36.84 |
| 1,000 m—Igor Zhelezovski, Soviet Union | 1:14.14 |
| Overall champion—Igor Zhelezovski, Soviet Union | 149:085 pts |

**Women**

| | |
|---|---|
| 500 m—Karin Kania, East Germany | :40.00 |
| 1,000 m—Stahnke, East Germany | 1:20.76 |
| Overall champion—Karin Kania, East Germany | 160.060 pts |

### WORLD CHAMPIONSHIPS—1986

**Men**

(Feb. 15-16, Inzell, West Germany)

| | |
|---|---|
| Overall champion—Hein Vergeer, Netherlands | 161.937 pts |
| 500 m—Oleg Bogiev, Soviet Union | :37.99 |
| 1,500 m—Oleg Bogiev, Soviet Union | 1:54.95 |
| 5,000 m—Hein Vergeer, Netherlands | 6:54.91 |
| 10,000 m—Geir Karistad, Norway | 14:12.14 |

**Women**

(The Hague, Netherlands, Feb. 8-9, 1986)

| | |
|---|---|
| Overall champion—Karin Kania, East Germany | 175.649 pts |
| 500 m—Karin Kania, East Germany | :41.13 seconds |
| 1,500 m—Karin Kania, East Germany | 2:08.34 |
| 3,000 m—Karin Kania, East Germany | 4:27.77 |
| 5,000 m—Andrea Ehrig, East Germany | 7:42.89 |

# SPORTS ORGANIZATIONS AND INFORMATION BUREAUS

(Note: Addresses are subject to change)

**Amateur Athletic Union of the U.S.** 3400 West 86th St., Indianapolis, Ind. 46268

**Amateur Basketball Association.** 1750 East Boulder St., Colorado Springs, Colo. 80909

**Amateur Hockey Association of the U.S.** 2997 Broadmoor Valley Road, Colorado Springs, Colo. 80906

**Amateur Softball Association.** 2801 N.E. 50th St., Oklahoma City, Okla. 73111

**American Amateur Racketball Association.** 815 North Weber St., Suite 101, Colorado Springs, Colo. 80903

**American Association of Professional Baseball Clubs.** P.O. Box 382, Wichita, Kan. 67201

**American Bowling Congress.** 5301 South 76th St., Greendale, Wis. 53129-0500

**American Hockey League.** 218 Memorial Ave., West Springfield, Mass. 01089

**American Horse Shows Association.** 220 E. 42nd St., New York, N.Y. 10017-5806

**American Kennel Club Inc.** 51 Madison Ave., New York, N.Y. 10010

**American League (baseball).** 350 Park Ave., New York, N.Y. 10022

**Athletics Congress/USA, The.** P.O. Box 120, Indianapolis, Ind. 46206

**Baseball Hall of Fame.** Cooperstown, N.Y. 13326

**Football Hall of Fame (college).** Kings Island, Ohio 45034

**Intercollegiate (Big Ten) Conference** (1896). 1111 Plaza Dr., Suite 600, Schaumburg, Ill. 60195-4990

**International Game Fish Association.** 3000 East Las Olas Blvd., Fort Lauderdale, Fla. 33316

**International League (baseball).** Box 608, Grove City, Ohio 43123

**International Olympic Committee.** Chateau de Vidy, 1007 Lausanne, Switzerland

**International Tennis Hall of Fame.** 194 Bellevue Ave., Newport, R.I. 02840

**Ladies Professional Golf Association.** 4675 Sweetwater Blvd., Sugar Land, Texas, 77479

**Little League Baseball.** P.O. Box 3485 Williamsport, Pa. 17701

**National Archery Association.** 1750 E. Boulder St., Colorado Springs, Colo. 80909

**National Association for Stock Car Auto Racing.** P.O. Box K, Daytona Beach, Fla. 32015—9947

**National Association of Intercollegiate Athletics.** 1221 Baltimore St., Kansas City, Mo. 64105

**National Baseball Congress.** P.O. Box 1420, Wichita, Kan. 67201

**National Collegiate Athletic Association.** P.O. Box 1906, Mission, Kan. 66201

**National Duckpin Bowling Congress.** Fairview Ave., Baltimore-Linthicum, Md. 21090

**National Field Archery Association.** Rt. 2, Box 514, Redlands, Calif. 92373

**National Football Foundation.** 1865 Palmer Ave., Larchmont, N.Y. 10538. *See also:* Football Hall of Fame (college)

**National Football League.** 410 Park Ave., New York, N.Y. 10022

**National Hockey League.** 1155 Metcalfe St., Suite 960, Montreal, Que., Canada H3B 2W2

**National Horseshoe Pitchers Association.** Box 810, Circleville, Ohio 43113

**National Hot Rod Association.** P.O. Box 150, North Hollywood, Calif. 91603

**National Junior College Athletic Association.** P.O. Box 7305, Colorado Springs, Colo. 80933—7305

**National Rifle Association of America.** 1600 Rhode Island Ave., N.W., Washington, D.C. 20036

**National Skeet Shooting Association.** P.O. Box 28188, San Antonio, Tex. 78228

**New York Racing Association.** P.O. Box 90, Jamaica, N.Y. 11417

**National Shuffleboard Association.** Box 6343, Trailer Estates, Bradenton, Fla. 33507

**New York State Athletic Commission** (boxing and wrestling). 270 Broadway, New York, N.Y. 10007

**North American Yacht Racing Union.** *See* United States Yacht Racing Union

**North American Soccer League.** 1841 Broadway, Suite 411, New York, N.Y. 10023

**PGA TOUR, Inc.,** 112 TPC Blvd., Sawgrass, Ponte Vecra, Fla. 32082

**Pro Football Hall of Fame,** Canton, Ohio 44708

**Roller Skating Rink Operators Association.** P.O. Box 81846, Lincoln, Neb. 68501

**Thoroughbred Racing Assns. of N. America.** 3000 Marcus Ave., Lake Success, N.Y. 11042

**USA Amateur Boxing Federation,** 1750 East Boulder St., Colorado Springs, Colo. 80909

**United States Amateur Confederation of Roller Skating.** P.O. Box 83067, Lincoln, Neb. 68501

**United States Auto Club.** 4910 West 16th St., Speedway, Ind. 46224

**U.S. Baseball Federation,** 2160 Greenwood Ave., Trenton, N.J. 08609

**U.S. Chess Federation.** 186 Route 9W, New Windsor, N.Y. 12550

**U.S. Cycling Federation.** 1750 East Boulder St., Colorado Springs, Colo. 80909

**U.S. Fencing Assn.,** 1750 E. Boulder St., Colorado Springs, Colo. 80909

**U.S. Figure Skating Association.** 20 First Street, Colorado Springs, Colo. 80906

**U.S. Football League.** 52 Vanderbilt Ave., New York, N.Y. 10017

**U.S. Golf Association.** Golf House, Far Hills, N.J. 07931

**United States Gymnastics Federation** 1099 N. Meridian St., Indianapolis, Ind. 46204

**U.S. Handball Association.** 930 N. Benton Ave., Tucson, Ariz. 85711

**U.S. Olympic Committee.** 1750 East Boulder Street, Colorado Springs, Colo. 80909

**U.S. Polo Association.** 1301 W. 22nd St., Oak Brook, Ill. 60521

**U.S. Rowing Assn.** 251 N. Illinois St., Suite 980, Indianapolis, Ind. 46204

**U.S. Soccer Federation.** 1750 East Boulder St., Colorado Springs, Colo. 80909—5791

**U.S. Tennis Association.** 1212 Avenue of the Americas, New York, N.Y. 10036

**U.S. Trotting Association.** 750 Michigan Ave., Columbus, Ohio 43215

**U.S. Yacht Racing Union.** P.O. Box 209, Goat Island, Newport, R.I. 02840

**Women's International Bowling Congress.** 5301 S. 76th St., Greendale, Wis. 53129

# FIGURE SKATING

## WORLD CHAMPIONS

**Men**

| | | | | | | |
|---|---|---|---|---|---|---|
| 1960 | Alain Giletti, France | 1980 | Jan Hoffman, East Germany | 1973 | Karen Magnusson, Canada |
| 1961 | No competition | 1981 | Scott Hamilton, United States | 1974 | Christine Errath, East Germany |
| 1962 | Donald Jackson, Canada | 1982 | Scott Hamilton, United States | 1975 | Dianne de Leeuw, Netherlands |
| 1963 | Don McPherson, Canada | 1983 | Scott Hamilton, United States | 1976 | Dorothy Hamill, United States |
| 1964 | Manfred Schnelldorfer, West Germany | 1984 | Scott Hamilton, United States | 1977 | Linda Fratianne, United States |
| | | 1985 | Alexandr Fadeev, U.S.S.R. | 1978 | Anett Poetzsch, East Germany |
| 1965 | Alain Calmat, France | 1986 | Brian Boitano, United States | 1979 | Linda Fratianne, United States |
| 1966-68 | Emmerich Danzer, Austria | | | 1980 | Anett Poetzsch, East Germany |
| 1969-70 | Tim Wood, United States | **Women** | | 1981 | Denise Beillmann, Switzerland |
| 1971-73 | Ondrej Nepela, Czechoslovakia | 1956-60 | Carol Heiss, United States | 1982 | Elaine Zavak, United States |
| 1974 | Jan Hoffman, East Germany | 1961 | No competition | 1983 | Rosalynn Sumners, United States |
| 1975 | Sergei Yolkov, U.S.S.R. | 1962-64 | Sjoukje Dijkstra, Netherlands | 1984 | Katarina Witt, East Germany |
| 1976 | John Curry, Britain | 1965 | Petra Burka, Canada | 1985 | Katarina Witt, East Germany |
| 1977 | Vladimir Kovalev, U.S.S.R. | 1966-68 | Peggy Fleming, United States | 1986 | Debi Thomas, United States |
| 1978 | Charles Tickner, United States | 1969-70 | Gabriele Seyfert, East Germany | | |
| 1979 | Vladimir Kovalev, U.S.S.R. | 1971-72 | Beatrix Schuba, Austria | | |

## U.S. CHAMPIONS

**Men**

| | | | | | | |
|---|---|---|---|---|---|---|
| 1946-52 | Richard Button | 1976 | Terry Kubicka | 1957-60 | Carol Heiss |
| 1953-56 | Hayes Jenkins | 1977-80 | Charles Tickner | 1961 | Laurence Owen |
| 1957-60 | David Jenkins | 1981 | Scott Hamilton | 1962 | Barbara Roles Pursley |
| 1961 | Bradley Lord | 1982 | Scott Hamilton | 1963 | Lorraine Hanlon |
| 1962 | Monty Hoyt | 1983 | Scott Hamilton | 1964-68 | Peggy Fleming |
| 1963 | Tommy Liz | 1984 | Scott Hamilton | 1969-73 | Janet Lynn |
| 1964 | Scott Allen | 1985 | Brian Boitano | 1974-76 | Dorothy Hamill |
| 1965 | Gary Visconti | 1986 | Brian Boitano | 1977-80 | Linda Fratianne |
| 1966 | Scott Allen | | | 1981 | Elaine Zayak |
| 1967 | Gary Visconti | **Women** | | 1982 | Rosalynn Sumners |
| 1968-70 | Tim Wood | 1943-48 | Gretchen Merrill | 1983 | Rosalynn Sumners |
| 1971 | John M. Petkevich | 1949-50 | Yvonne Sherman | 1984 | Rosalynn Sumners |
| 1972 | Ken Shelley | 1951 | Sonya Klopfer | 1985 | Tiffany Chin |
| 1973-75 | Gordon McKellen | 1952-56 | Tenley Albright | 1986 | Debi Thomas |

### UNITED STATES CHAMPIONS—1986
(Uniondale, N.Y., Feb. 4-9, 1986)

Men's singles—Brian Boitano, Peninsula Figure Skating Club, San Jose, Calif.
Women's singles—Debi Thomas, Los Angeles Figure Skating Club
Pairs—Gillian Wachsman and Todd Waggoner, Skating Club of Wilmington, Del.
Dance—Renee Roca, Genessee Figure Skating Club, Rochester, N.Y., and Donald Adair, Academy Figure Skating Club, Detroit
Junior men singles—Mark Mitchell, Skating Club of Hartford, Conn.
Junior women singles—Cindy Vortz, Los Angeles Figure Skating Club

Junior pairs—Kristi Yamaguchi and Rudy Galindo, St. Moritz Figure Skating Club, San Francisco
Junior dance—Colette Huber, Los Angeles Figure Skating Club and Ron Kravette, Rim of the World Figure Skating Club, Los Angeles

### WORLD CHAMPIONS—1986
(Geneva, Switzerland, March 17-23, 1986)

Men's single—Brian Boitano, United States
Women's single—Debi Thomas, United States
Pairs—Ekaterina Gordeeva and Sergei Grinkov, Soviet Union
Dance—Natalia Bestemianova and Andrei Bokin, Soviet Union

# VOLLEYBALL

### U.S. VOLLEYBALL ASSOCIATION CHAMPIONSHIPS—1986

**National Champions**

Men—Molten, Torrance, Calif.; Runnerup: Banana Boat
Women—Merrill Lynch, Albuquerque, N.M.; Runnerup: Chrysler
Senior Men—Outrigger Canoe Club, Honolulu, Hawaii; Runnerup: Chuck's/Nick's of San Diego.
Senior Women—The Mavericks, California; Runnerup: Red Sand
Golden Masters—The Legends; Runnerup: Outrigger Canoe Club

### N.C.A.A. CHAMPIONSHIPS

**Men**

(May 2-3, 1986, Penn State University, University Park, Pa.)

Final—Pepperdine University, Malibu, Calif., defeated Southern California, Los Angeles, Calif., 7-15, 15-13, 15-11, 5-15, 16-14

**Women**

DIVISION I—University of the Pacific, Stockton, Calif., champion
DIVISION II—Portland State University, Portland, Ore., champion
DIVISION III—Elmhurst College, Elmhurst, Ill., champion

### N.A.I.A. CHAMPIONSHIPS

**Women**

St. Mary's defeated Biola, 15-11, 15-13, 15-3 in final match.
Semifinals—Biola defeated Wisconsin-Milwaukee, 15-7, 15-12. St. Mary's defeated Hawaii-Hilo, the defending champion,[1] 5-15, 15-8, 15-7.
1. Hawaii-Hilo had won title for four consecutive years.

# SWIMMING

## WORLD RECORDS—MEN

(Through Aug. 23, 1986)
Approved by the International Swimming Federation (F.I.N.A.)
(F.I.N.A. discontinued acceptance of records in yards in 1968)
*Source*: United States Swim Team.

| Distance | Record | Holder | Country | Date |
|---|---|---|---|---|
| **Freestyle** | | | | |
| 50 meters | 0:22.33 | Matt Biondi | United States | June 26, 1986 |
| 100 meters | 0:48.74 | Matt Biondi | United States | June 24, 1986 |
| 200 meters | 1:47.44 | Michael Gross | West Germany | July 29, 1984 |
| 400 meters | 3:47.80 | Michael Gross | West Germany | June 27, 1985 |
| 800 meters | 7:50.64 | Vladimir Salnikov | Soviet Union | July 4, 1986 |
| 1,500 meters | 14:54.76 | Vladimir Salnikov | Soviet Union | Feb. 22, 1983 |
| **Backstroke** | | | | |
| 100 meters | 0:55.19 | Rick Carey | United States | Aug. 21, 1983 |
| 200 meters | 1:58.14 | Igor Poliansky | Soviet Union | March 1, 1985 |
| **Breaststroke** | | | | |
| 100 meters | 1:01.65 | Steve Lundquist | United States | July 29, 1984 |
| 200 meters | 2:13.34 | Victor Davis | Canada | Aug. 2, 1984 |
| **Butterfly** | | | | |
| 100 meters | 0:52.84 | Pablo Morales | United States | June 23, 1986 |
| 200 meters | 1:56.65 | Michael Gross | West Germany | Aug. 10, 1985 |
| **Individual Medley** | | | | |
| 200 meters | 2:01.42 | Alex Baumann | Canada | Aug. 4, 1984 |
| 400 meters | 4:17.41 | Alex Baumann | Canada | July 30, 1984 |
| **Freestyle Relay** | | | | |
| 400 meters | 3:17.08 | United States | National Team | Aug. 10, 1985 |
| 800 meters | 7:15.69 | United States | National Team | July 30, 1984 |
| **Medley Relay** | | | | |
| 400 meters | 3:38.28 | United States | National Team | Aug. 10, 1985 |

## WORLD RECORDS—WOMEN

| Distance | Record | Holder | Country | Date |
|---|---|---|---|---|
| **Freestyle** | | | | |
| 50 Meters | 0:25.28 | Tamara Costache | Romania | Aug. 23, 1986 |
| 100 Meters | 0:54.73 | Kristin Otto | East Germany | Aug. 19, 1986 |
| 200 Meters | 1:57.75 | Kristin Otto | East Germany | May 23, 1984 |
| 400 Meters | 4:06.28 | Tracy Wickham | Australia | Aug. 24, 1978 |
| 800 Meters | 8:24.62 | Tracy Wickham | Australia | Aug. 5, 1978 |
| 1,500 Meters | 16:04.49 | Kim Linehan | United States | Aug.19, 1979 |
| **Backstroke** | | | | |
| 100 Meters | 1:00.59 | Ina Kleber | East Germany | Aug. 24, 1984 |
| 200 Meters | 2:09.91 | Cornelia Sirch | East Germany | Aug. 7, 1982 |
| **Breaststroke** | | | | |
| 100 Meters | 1:08.11 | Sylvia Gerasch | East Germany | Aug. 21, 1986 |
| 200 Meters | 2:27.40 | Silke Hoerner | East Germany | Aug. 18, 1986 |
| **Butterfly** | | | | |
| 100 Meters | 0:57.93 | Mary T. Meagher | United States | Aug. 16, 1982 |
| 200 Meters | 2:05.96 | Mary T. Meagher | United States | Aug. 13, 1982 |
| **Individual Medley** | | | | |
| 200 Meters | 2:11.73 | Ute Geweniger | East Germany | July 4, 1981 |
| 400 Meters | 4:36.10 | Petra Schneider | East Germany | Aug. 1, 1982 |

## Freestyle

| 400 Meters | 3:40.57 | East German National Team | East Germany | Aug. 19, 1986 |
| 800 Meters | 7:59.33 | East German National Team | East Germany | Aug. 17, 1986 |

## Medley Relay

| 400 Meters | 4:03.69 | East German National Team | East Germany | Aug. 24, 1984 |

## U.S. SHORT-COURSE SWIMMING RECORDS

*Source*: United States Swimming Team.

### MEN
#### Freestyle

| 50 yards—Matt Biondi, 1986 | 0:19.22 |
| 100 yards—Matt Biondi, 1985 | 0:41.87 |
| 200 yards—Matt Biondi | 1:33.22 |
| 500 yards—Mike O'Brien, 1985 | 4:13.06 |
| 1,000 yards—Mike O'Brien, 1985 | 8:47.38 |
| 1,650 yards—Jeff Kostoff, 1986 | 14:37.87 |

#### Backstroke

| 100 yards—Rick Carey, 1983 | 0:48.25 |
| 200 yards—Rick Carey, 1983 | 1:44.43 |

#### Breaststroke

| 100 yards—Steve Lundquist, 1983 | 0:52.48 |
| 200 yards—Steve Lundquist, 1981 | 1:55.01 |

#### Butterfly

| 100 yards—Pablo Morales, 1986 | 0:46.26 |
| 200 yards—Pablo Morales, 1985 | 1:42.85 |

#### Individual Medley

| 200 yards—Bill Barrett, 1982 | 1:45.00 |
| 400 yards—Jeff Kostoff, 1985 | 3:46.54 |

#### Relays

| 200-yard freestyle—Mission Viejo, 1981 | 1:18.55 |
| 400-yard freestyle—California, 1986 | 2:53.02 |
| 800-yard freestyle—Florida Aquatic Club, 1979 | 6:25.42 |
| 400-yard medley—S.M.U., 1983 | 3:12.63 |

### WOMEN
#### Freestyle

| 50 yards—Tammy Thomas, 1983 | 0:22.13 |
| 100 yards—Tammy Thomas, 1983 | 0:48.40 |
| 200 yards—Cynthia Woodhead, 1979 | 1:44.10 |
| 500 yards—Tracy Caulkins, 1979 | 4:36.25 |
| 1000 yards—Tiffany Cohen, 1985 | 9:28.32 |
| 1,650 yards—Tiffany Cohen, 1983 | 15:46.54 |

#### Backstroke

| 100 yards—Sue Walsh, 1983 | 0:54.74 |
| 200 yards—Tracy Caulkins, 1981 | 1:57.02 |

#### Breaststroke

| 100 yards—Tracy Caulkins, 1981 | 1:01.13 |
| 200 yards—Tracy Caulkins, 1980 | 2:11.46 |

#### Butterfly

| 100 yards—Jenna Johnson, 1986 | 0:52.69 |
| 200 yards—Mary T. Meagher, 1981 | 1:52.99 |

#### Individual Medley

| 200 yards—Tracy Caulkins, 1984 | 1:57.06 |
| 400 yards—Tracy Caulkins, 1981 | 4:04.63 |

#### Relays

| 200-yard freestyle—Stanford, 1981 | 1:31.12 |
| 400-yard freestyle—Florida, 1984 | 3:18.52 |
| 800-yard freestyle—Florida, 1984 | 7:06.98 |
| 200-yard medley—Stanford, 1986 | 1:40.22 |
| 400-yard medley—Florida, 1982 | 3:40.99 |

## U.S. SHORT COURSE CHAMPIONSHIPS

(Orlando, Fla., March 25-29, 1986)

### Men's Events

| 50-yd freestyle—Siong Ang, The Woodlands Swim Club | :20.07 |
| 100-yd freestyle—Randy Everett, Concord-Hill Pleasant | :43.77 |
| 200-yd freestyle—Troy Dalbey, San Jose Aquatics | 1:35.34 |
| 500-yd freestyle—Troy Dalbey, San Jose Aquatics | 4:17.30 |
| 1,000-yd freestyle—Dan Jorgensen, Irvine Novaquatics | 8:48.68 |
| 1,650-yd freestyle—Dan Jorgensen, Irvine Novaquatics | 14:53.67 |
| 100-yd backstroke—Mark Tewksbury, U. of Calgary | :49.33 |
| 200-yd backstroke—Rick Carey, Badger Swim Club | 1:45.57 |
| 100-yd breaststroke—Tom Genz, Little Rock Racquet | :54.56 |
| 200-yd breaststroke—Jozsef Szabo, Hungary | 1:59.36 |
| 100-yd butterfly—Tom Ponting, U. of Calgary | :47.61 |
| 200-yd butterfly—Benny Nielsen, Mission Bay | 1:45.62 |
| 200-yd individual medley—David Wharton, Foxcatcher | 1:47.11 |
| 400-yd individual medley—Tamas Darnyi, Hungary | 3:46.67[1] |
| 400-yd freestyle relay—San Jose "A" | 2:59.20 |
| 800-yd freestyle relay—San Jose "A" | 6:32.85 |
| 400-yd medley relay—Little Rock Racquet | 3:18.30 |
| All-events team champion—1. Mission Viejo | 348.0 |
| 2. San Jose Aquatics | 347.0 |
| 3. Santa Clara | 220.5 |

[1]. Meet record.

### Women's Events

| 50-yd freestyle—Jeanne Doolan, Texas Aquatics | :22.88 |
| 100-yd freestyle—Conny Van Bentum, Golden Bear | :49.90 |
| 200-yd freestyle—Conny Van Bentum, Golden Bear | 1:46.67 |
| 500-yd freestyle—Debbie Babashoff, Mission Viejo | 4:42.74 |
| 1,000-yd freestyle—Kim Brown, Southern California | 9:33.79 |
| 1,650-yd freestyle—Kim Brown, Southern California | 16:05.18 |
| 100-yd backstroke—Beth Barr, Pensacola Aquatics | :55.73 |
| 200-yd backstroke—Andrea Hayes, Pensacola Junior | 1:57.63 |
| 100-yd breaststroke—Jenny Hau, Mission City | 1:01.88 |
| 200-yd breaststroke—Hiroko Nagasaki, Golden Bear | 2:12.81 |
| 100-yd butterfly—Conny Van Bentum, Golden Bear | :54.01 |
| 200-yd butterfly—Michelle Griglione, Curl Swim Club | 1:56.86 |
| 200-yd individual medley—Michelle Griglione, Curl Swim Club | 1:59.98 |
| 400-yd individual medley—Michelle Griglione, Curl Swim Club | 4:12.95 |
| 400-yd freestyle relay—Curl "A" | 3:21.18 |
| 800-yd freestyle relay—Curl "A" | 7:16.80 |
| 400-yd medley relay—Curl "A" | 3:45.75 |
| All-events team champion—1. Curl Swim Club | 479.0 |
| 2. Foxcatcher | 275.0 |
| 3. Golden Bear | 261.5 |
| Combined team champion—1. Mission Viejo | 603.0 |
| 2. Curl Swim Club | 525.0 |
| 3. Foxcatcher | 408.0 |

## U.S. LONG-COURSE CHAMPIONSHIPS

(August 4-8, 1986, Santa Clara, Calif.)

**Men's Events**

| | |
|---|---|
| 50-m freestyle—Scott McCadam, Mustang | :22.85 |
| 100-m freestyle—Scott McCadam, Mustang | :50.51 |
| 200-m freestyle—Arthur Wojdat, Mission Viejo | 1:51.05 |
| 400-m freestyle—Gary Brinkman, San Jose | 3:54.84 |
| 800-m freestyle—Gary Brinkman, San Jose | 8:02.08 |
| 1,500-m freestyle—Gary Brinkman, San Jose | 15:26.32 |
| 100-m backstroke—Rick Carey, Badger Swim Club | :57.26 |
| 200-m backstroke—Rick Carey, Badger Swim Club | 2:02.06 |
| 100-m breaststroke—Brett Beedle, Los Altos | 1:04.45 |
| 200-m breaststroke—Sam Schwartz, Indian Valley | 2:19.29 |
| 100-m butterfly—Chris O'Neil, Aggie Swim Club | :54.69 |
| 200-m butterfly—Melvin Stewart, Mecklenburg | 2:00.17 |
| 200-m individual medley—Bill Stapleton, Longhorn | 2:02.96 |
| 400-m individual medley—Bill Stapleton, Longhorn | 4:21.69 |
| 400-m freestyle relay—Club Wolverine "A" | 3:24.30 |
| 800-m freestyle relay—Longhorn Aquatics | 7:32.05 |
| 400-m medley relay—Concord-Pleasant Hill "A" | 3:47.97 |
| Team champion—1. San Jose Aquatics | 370.0 |
| 2. Mission Viejo | 228.0 |
| 3. Longhorn Aquatics | 212.0 |

**Women's Events**

| | |
|---|---|
| 50-m freestyle—Grace Cornelius, Suburban | :26.20 |
| 100-m freestyle—Grace Cornelius, Suburban | :57.05 |
| 200-m freestyle—Susan Habermas, Rockville-Montgomery | 2:02.52 |
| 400-m freestyle—Tiffany Cohen, Mission Bay | 4:14.04 |
| 800-m freestyle—Tiffany Cohen, Mission Bay | 8:36.72 |
| 1,500-m freestyle—Leslie Daland, Simi Valley | 16:19.92 |
| 100-m backstroke—Beth Barr, Pensacola | 1:04.00 |
| 200-m backstroke—Andrea Hayes, Pensacola | 2:14.59 |
| 100-m breaststroke—Tracey McFarlane, Palm Springs | 1:12.31 |
| 200-m breaststroke—Amy Shaw, Mission Viejo | 2:33.08 |
| 100-m butterfly—Julia Gorman, North Baltimore | 1:01.42 |
| 200-m butterfly—Tiffany Cohen, Mission Bay | 2:12.66 |
| 200-m individual medley—Whitney Hedgepeth, Virginia | 2:18.47 |
| 400-m individual medley—Whitney Hedgepeth, Virginia | 4:51.57 |
| 400-m freestyle relay—Fort Lauderdale "A" | 3:52.04 |
| 800-m freestyle relay—Mission Bay "A" | 8:15.20 |
| 400-m medley relay—Mission Bay Makos "A" | 4:19.21 |
| Team champion—1. Mission Bay | 588.0 |
| 2. Foxcatcher | 252.0 |
| 3. Fort Lauderdale | 226.0 |
| Combined-team champions—1. Mission Bay | 701.0 |
| 2. San Jose Aquatics | 456.0 |
| 3. Foxcatcher | 428.0 |

## NATIONAL COLLEGIATE ATHLETIC ASSOCIATION MEN'S CHAMPIONSHIP—1986

(Indianapolis, Ind., April 3-5, 1986)

**Division 1**

| | |
|---|---|
| 50-y freestyle—Matt Biondi, California | 0:19.22[1] |
| 100-y freestyle—Matt Biondi, California | 0:42.03 |
| 200-y freestyle—Matt Biondi, California | 1:33.85 |
| 500-y freestyle—Matt Cetlinski, Florida | 4:15.19 |
| 1,650-y freestyle—Jeff Kostoff, Stanford | 14:37.87[1] |
| 100-y backstroke—Mark Rhodenbaugh, Southern Methodist | 0:48.67 |
| 200-y backstroke—Sean Murphy, Stanford | 1:45.90 |
| 100-y breaststroke—G. Minervini, UCLA | 0:53.75 |
| 200-y breaststroke—John Moffett, Stanford | 1:56.91 |
| 100-y butterfly—Pablo Morales, Stanford | :46.26[1] |
| 200-y butterfly—Pablo Morales, Stanford | 1:43.05 |
| 200-y individual medley—Pablo Morales, Stanford | 1:45.43 |
| 400-y individual medley—Richard Prado, Southern Methodist | 3:46.71 |
| 400-y freestyle relay—California | 2:53.02[1] |

| | |
|---|---|
| 800-y freestyle relay—California | 6:21.58 |
| 400-y medley relay—Stanford | 3:12.47 |
| 1-m dive—Doug Shaffer, U.C.L.A. | 560.20 points |
| 3-m dive—Li Hongping, Southern California | 601.90 points |
| Team—1. Stanford | 404 points |
| 2. California | 335 |
| 3. Texas | 325.5 |

1. N.C.A.A. record

## NATIONAL COLLEGIATE ATHLETIC ASSOCIATION WOMEN'S CHAMPIONSHIPS—1986

(Fayetteville, Arkansas, March 20-22, 1986)

| | |
|---|---|
| 50-y freestyle—Jenna Johnson, Stanford | 0:22.46 |
| 100-y freestyle—Jenna Johnson, Stanford | 0:49.03 |
| 200-y freestyle—Conny Van Bentum, California | 1:46.45 |
| 500-y freestyle—Tami Bruce, Florida | 4:40.87 |
| 1,650-y freestyle—Tami Bruce, Florida | 15:56.81 |
| 100-y backstroke—Betsy Mitchell, Texas | 0:55.00 |
| 200-y backstroke—Betsy Mitchell, Texas | 1:57.26 |
| 100-y breaststroke—Cindy Ounpuu, Florida | 1:02.57 |
| 200-y breaststroke—Cindy Ounpuu, Florida | 2:13.25 |
| 100-y butterfly—Jenna Johnson, Stanford | 52.69 |
| 200-y butterfly—Mary T. Meagher, California | 1:54.52 |
| 200-y individual medley—Susan Rapp, Stanford | 2:01.80 |
| 400-y individual medley—Patty Sabbo, Texas | 4:16.58 |
| 200-y freestyle relay—Stanford | 1:31.27 |
| 400-y freestyle relay—Florida | 3:19.07 |
| 800-y freestyle relay—Florida | 7:10.81 |
| 200-y medley relay—Stanford | 1:40.22 |
| 400-y medley relay—Texas | 3:41.99 |
| 1-m dive—Megan Neyer, Florida | 480.20 points |
| 3-m dive—Megan Neyer, Florida | 532.35 points |
| Team—1. Texas | 633.0 points |
| 2. Florida | 586.0 points |
| 3. Stanford | 538.0 points |

## U.S. DIVING CHAMPIONSHIPS—1986

**INDOOR**

(Indianapolis, Ind. April 16-20, 1986)

**Men's Events**

| | |
|---|---|
| 1-meter—Greg Louganis, Boca Raton, Fla. | 625.05 |
| 3-meter—Greg Louganis, Boca Raton, Fla. | 695.22 |
| 10-meter platform—Greg Louganis, Boca Raton, Fla. | 634.50 |
| Team—McDonald's Divers | |

**Women's Events**

| | |
|---|---|
| 1-meter—Megan Neyer, Boca Raton, Florida | 442.89 |
| 3-meter—Michele Mitchell, Scottsdale, Ariz. | 505.65 |
| 10-meter platform—Michele Mitchell, Scottsdale, Ariz. | 432.60 |
| Team—Mission Bay Makos | |

**OUTDOOR**

(Orlando, Fla., Aug. 5-9, 1986)

**Men's Events**

| | |
|---|---|
| 1-meter—Greg Louganis, Boca Raton, Fla. | 606.87 |
| 3-meter—Greg Louganis, Boca Raton, Fla. | 683.70 |
| 10-meter platform—Greg Louganis, Boca Raton, Fla. | 655.20 |

**Women's Events**

| | |
|---|---|
| 1-meter—Megan Neyer, Boca Raton, Fla. | 473.55 |
| 3-meter—Megan Neyer, Boca Raton, Fla. | 547.23 |
| 10-meter platform—Michele Mitchell, Scottsdale, Ariz. | 439.26 |

# BOXING

Whether it be called pugilism, prize fighting or boxing, there is no tracing "the Sweet Science" to any definite source. Tales of rivals exchanging blows for fun, fame or money go back to earliest recorded history and classical legend. There was a mixture of boxing and wrestling called the "pancratium" in the ancient Olympic Games and in such contests the rivals belabored one another with hands fortified with heavy leather wrappings that were sometimes studded with metal. More than one Olympic competitor lost his life at this brutal exercise.

There was little law or order in pugilism until Jack Broughton, one of the early champions of England, drew up a set of rules for the game in 1743. Broughton, called "the father of English box-

ing," also is credited with having invented boxing gloves. However, these gloves—or "mufflers" as they were called—were used only in teaching "the manly art of self-defense" or in training bouts. All professional championship fights were contested with "bare knuckles" until 1892, when John L. Sullivan lost the heavyweight championship of the world to James J. Corbett in New Orleans in a bout in which both contestants wore regulation gloves.

The Broughton rules were superseded by the London Prize Ring Rules of 1838. The 8th Marquis of Queensberry, with the help of John G. Chambers, put forward the "Queensberry Rules" in 1866, a code that called for gloved contests. Amateurs took quickly to the Queensberry Rules, the professionals slowly.

## HISTORY OF WORLD HEAVYWEIGHT CHAMPIONSHIP FIGHTS

(Bouts in which a new champion was crowned)

Source: Nat Fleischer's Ring *Boxing Encyclopedia and Record Book,* published and copyrighted by The Ring Book Shop, Inc., 120 West 31st St., New York, N.Y. 10001.

| Date | Where held | Winner, weight, age | Loser, weight, age | Rounds | Referee |
|---|---|---|---|---|---|
| Sept. 7, 1892 | New Orleans, La. | James J. Corbett, 178 (26) | John L. Sullivan, 212 (33) | 21 | Prof. John Duffy |
| March 17, 1897 | Carson City, Nev. | Bob Fitzsimmons, 167 (34) | James J. Corbett, 183 (30) | KO 14 | George Siler |
| June 9, 1899 | Coney Island, N.Y. | James J. Jeffries, 206 (24)[1] | Bob Fitzsimmons, 167 (37) | KO 11 | George Siler |
| Feb. 23, 1906 | Los Angeles | Tommy Burns, 180 (24)[2] | Marvin Hart, 188 (29) | 20 | James J. Jeffries |
| Dec. 26, 1908 | Sydney, N.S.W. | Jack Johnson, 196 (30) | Tommy Burns, 176 (27) | KO 14 | Hugh McIntosh |
| April 5, 1915 | Havana, Cuba | Jess Willard, 230 (33) | Jack Johnson, 205 1/2 (37) | KO 26 | Jack Welch |
| July 4, 1919 | Toledo, Ohio | Jack Dempsey, 187 (24) | Jess Willard, 245 (37) | KO 3 | Ollie Pecord |
| Sept. 23, 1926 | Philadelphia | Gene Tunney, 189 (28)[3] | Jack Dempsey, 190 (31) | 10 | Pop Reilly |
| June 12, 1930 | New York | Max Schmeling, 188 (24) | Jack Sharkey, 197 (27) | WF 4 | Jim Crowley |
| June 21, 1932 | Long Island City | Jack Sharkey, 205 (29) | Max Schmeling, 188 (26) | 15 | Gunboat Smith |
| June 29, 1933 | Long Island City | Primo Carnera, 260 1/2 (26) | Jack Sharkey, 201 (30) | KO 6 | Arthur Donovan |
| June 14, 1934 | Long Island City | Max Baer, 209 1/2 (25) | Primo Carnera, 263 1/4 (27) | KO 11 | Arthur Donovan |
| June 13, 1935 | Long Island City | Jim Braddock, 193 3/4 (29) | Max Baer, 209 1/2 (26) | 15 | Jack McAvoy |
| June 22, 1937 | Chicago | Joe Louis, 197 1/4 (23) | Jim Braddock, 197 (31) | KO 8 | Tommy Thomas |
| June 22, 1949 | Chicago | Ezzard Charles, 181 3/4 (27)[4] | Joe Walcott, 195 1/2 (35) | 15 | Davey Miller |
| Sept. 27, 1950 | New York | Ezzard Charles, 184 1/2 (29)[5] | Joe Louis, 218 (36) | 15 | Mark Conn |
| July 18, 1951 | Pittsburgh | Joe Walcott, 194 (37) | Ezzard Charles, 182 (30) | KO 7 | Buck McTiernan |
| Sept. 23, 1952 | Philadelphia | Rocky Marciano, 184 (29)[6] | Joe Walcott, 196 (38) | KO 13 | Charley Daggert |
| Nov. 30, 1956 | Chicago | Floyd Patterson, 182 1/4 (21) | Archie Moore, 187 3/4 (42) | KO 5 | Frank Sikora |
| June 26, 1959 | New York | Ingemar Johansson, 196 (26) | Floyd Patterson, 182 (24) | KO 3 | Ruby Goldstein |
| June 20, 1960 | New York | Floyd Patterson, 190 (25) | Ingemar Johansson, 194 3/4 (27) | KO 5 | Arthur Mercante |
| Sept. 25, 1962 | Chicago | Sonny Liston, 214 (28) | Floyd Patterson, 189 (27) | KO 1 | Frank Sikora |
| Feb. 25, 1964 | Miami Beach, Fla. | Cassius Clay, 210 (22)[7] | Sonny Liston, 218 (30) | KO 7 | Barney Felix |
| March 4, 1968 | New York | Joe Frazier, 204 1/2 (24)[8] | Buster Mathis, 243 1/2 (23) | KO 11 | Arthur Mercante |
| April 27, 1968 | Oakland, Calif. | Jimmy Ellis, 197 (28)[9] | Jerry Quarry, 195 (22) | 15 | Elmer Costa |
| Feb. 16, 1970 | New York | Joe Frazier, 205 (26)[10] | Jimmy Ellis, 201 (29) | KO 5 | Tony Perez |
| Jan. 22, 1973 | Kingston, Jamaica | George Foreman, 217 1/2 (24) | Joe Frazier, 214 (29) | KO 2 | Arthur Mercante |
| Oct. 30, 1974 | Kinshasa, Zaire | Muhammad Ali, 216 1/2 (32) | George Foreman, 220 (26) | KO 8 | Zack Clayton |
| Feb. 15, 1978 | Las Vegas, Nev. | Leon Spinks, 197 (25) | Muhammad Ali, 224 1/2 (36) | 15 | Howard Buck |
| June 9, 1978 | Las Vegas, Nev. | Larry Holmes, 212 (28)[11] | Ken Norton, 220 (32) | 15 | Mills Lans |
| Sept. 15, 1978 | New Orleans | Muhammad Ali, 221 (36)[12] | Leon Spinks, 201 (25) | 15 | Lucien Joubert |
| Oct. 20, 1979 | Pretoria, S. Africa | John Tate, 240 (24)[13] | Gerrie Coetzee, 222 (24) | 15 | Carlos Berrocal |
| March 31, 1980 | Knoxville, Tenn. | Mike Weaver, 207 1/2 (27) | John Tate, 232 (25) | KO 15 | Ernesto Magana Ansorena |
| Dec. 10, 1982 | Las Vegas, Nev. | Michael Dokes, 216 (24) | Mike Weaver, 209 1/2 (30) | KO 1 | Joey Curtis |
| Sept. 23, 1983 | Richfield, Ohio | Gerrie Coetzee, 215 (28) | Michael Dokes, 217 (25) | KO 10 | Tony Perez |
| March 9, 1984 | Las Vegas, Nev. | Tim Witherspoon, 220 1/2 (26)[14] | Greg Page, 239 1/2 (25) | 12 | Mills Lane |
| August 31, 1984 | Las Vegas, Nev. | Pinklon Thomas, 216 (26) | Tim Witherspoon, 217 (26) | 12 | Richard Steele |
| Nov. 9, 1984 | Las Vegas, Nev. | Larry Holmes, 221 1/2 (35)[15] | James Smith 227 (31) | KO 12 | Dave Pearl |
| Dec. 1, 1984 | Sun City, S. Africa | Greg Page, 236 (25)[16] | Gerrie Coetzee, 217 (29) | KO 8 | unavailable |
| April 29, 1985 | Buffalo, N.Y. | Tony Tubbs, 229 (26)[16] | Greg Page, 239 1/2 (26) | 15 | unavailable. |
| Sept. 21,1985 | Las Vegas, Nev. | Michael Spinks, 200 (29) | Larry Holmes, 221 (35) | 15 | Carlos Padilla |
| Jan. 17, 1986 | Atlanta, Ga. | Tim Witherspoon, 227 (28) | Tony Tubbs, 229 (27) | 15 | unavailable. |

1. Jeffries retired as champion in March 1905. He named Marvin Hart and Jack Root as leading contenders and agreed to referee their fight in Reno, Nev., on July 3, 1905, with the stipulation that he would term the winner the champion. Hart, 190 (28), knocked out Root, 171 (29), in the 12th round. 2. Burns claimed the title after defeating Hart. 3. Tunney retired as champion after defeating Tom Heeney on July 26, 1928. 4. After Louis announced his retirement as champion on March 1, 1949, Charles won recognition from the National Boxing Association as champion by defeating Walcott. 5. Charles gained

undisputed recognition as champion by defeating Louis, who came out of retirement. 6. Retired as Champion April 27, 1956. 7. The World Boxing Association later withdrew its recognition of Clay as champion and declared the winner of a bout between Ernie Terrell and Eddie Machen would gain its version of the title. Terrell, 199 (25), won a 15-round decision from Machen, 192 (32), in Chicago on March 5, 1965. Clay, 212 1/4 (25) and Terrell, 212 1/2 (27) met in Houston on Feb. 6, 1967, Clay winning a 15-round decision. 8. Winner recognized by New York, Massachusetts, Maine, Illinois, Texas and Pennsylvania to fill vacated title when Clay was stripped of championship for failing to accept U. S. Induction. 9. Bout was final of eight-man tournament to fill Clay's place and is recognized by World Boxing Association. 10. Bout settled controversy over title. 11. Holmes won World Boxing Council title after WBC had withdrawn recognition of Spinks, March 18, 1978, and awarded its title to Norton, WBC, said Spinks had reneged on agreement to fight Norton 12. Ali regained World Boxing Association championship. 13. Tate won WBA title after Ali retired and left it vacant. 14. Tim Witherspoon and Greg Page fought for the WBC heavyweight title vacated by Larry Holmes, who could not come to agreement on a deal to fight Page, the No. 1 contender. Holmes declared he would fight under the banner of the International Boxing Federation. Several dates were set and postponed for fights between Holmes and Gerry Coetzee, the WBA champ, the latest being Nov. 16, 1984.15. First fight under banner of International Boxing Federation. 16. New W.B.A. champion.

## OTHER WORLD BOXING TITLEHOLDERS

(Through Aug. 20, 1984)

### Light Heavyweight

| | | | | | |
|---|---|---|---|---|---|
| 1903 | Jack Root, George Gardner | 1952–61 | Archie Moore[3] | 1979 | Mike Rossman (WBA), Vict |
| 1903–05 | Bob Fitzsimmons | 1961–63 | Harold Johnson | | Galindez (WBA), Marvin |
| 1905–12 | Philadelphia Jack O'Brien[1] | 1963–65 | Willie Pastrano | | Johnson (WBC), Matthew |
| 1912–16 | Jack Dillon | 1965–66 | José Torres | | (Franklin) Saad |
| 1916–20 | Battling Levinsky | 1966–67 | Dick Tiger | | Muhammad (WBC) |
| 1920–22 | Georges Carpentier | 1968 | Dick Tiger, Bob Foster | 1980 | Matthew Saad Muhammad |
| 1923 | Battling Siki | 1969–70 | Bob Foster | | (WBC), Marvin Johnson |
| 1923–25 | Mike McTigue | 1971 | Vicente Rondon (WBA), Bob | | (WBA), Eddie (Gregory) |
| 1925–26 | Paul Berlenbach | | Foster (WBC) | | Mustafa Muhammad |
| 1926–27 | Jack Delaney[2] | 1972–73 | Bob Foster (WBA, WBC) | | (WBA) |
| 1927 | Mike McTigue | 1974 | John Conteh (WBA), Bob | 1981 | Matthew Saad Muhammad |
| 1927–29 | Tommy Loughran | | Foster (WBC)[14] | | (WBC), Eddie Mustafa |
| 1930 | Jimmy Slattery | 1975–76 | Victor Galindez (WBA), John | | Muhammad (WBA), |
| 1930–34 | Maxie Rosenbloom | | Conteh (WBC) | | Michael Spinks (WBA), |
| 1934–35 | Bob Olin | 1977 | Victor Galindez (WBA), John | | Dwight Braxton (WBC) |
| 1935–39 | John Henry Lewis | | Conteh (WBC)[4], Miguel | 1982 | Dwight Braxton (WBC), |
| 1939 | Melio Bettina | | Cuello (WBC) | | Michael Spinks (WBA) |
| 1939–41 | Billy Conn[2] | 1978 | Victor Galindez (WBA), Mike | 1983 | Michael Spinks (undisputed) |
| 1941 | Anton Christoforidis (NBA) | | Rossman (WBA), Miguel | 1984 | Michael Spinks (undisputed) |
| 1941–48 | Gus Lesnevich | | Cuello (WBC), Mate Parlov | 1985 | Michael Spinks (undisputed)[5] |
| 1948–50 | Freddie Mills | | (WBC), Marvin Johnson | 1986 | Marvin Johnson (WBA) |
| 1950–52 | Joey Maxim | | (WBC) | | Dennis Andries (WBC) |

1. Retired. 2. Abandoned title. 3. NBA withdrew recognition in 1961, New York Commission in 1962; recognized thereafter only by California and Europe. 4. WBC withdrew recognition. 5. Spinks relinquished title in 1985 to fight for heavyweight title.

### Middleweight

| | | | | | |
|---|---|---|---|---|---|
| 1867–72 | Tom Chandler | | Ken Overlin, Billy Soose, | 1967 | Nino Benvenuti, Emile Griffith |
| 1872–81 | George Rooke | | Tony Zale[4] | 1968 | Emile Griffith, Nino Benvenuti |
| 1881–82 | Mike Donovan[1] | 1941–47 | Tony Zale | 1969 | Nino Benvenuti |
| 1884–91 | Jack (Nonpareil) Dempsey | 1947–48 | Rocky Graziano | 1970 | Nino Benvenuti, Carlos Mon- |
| 1891–97 | Bob Fitzsimmons[2] | 1948 | Tony Zale | | zon |
| 1908 | Stanley Ketchel, Billy Papke | 1948–49 | Marcel Cerdan | 1971–73 | Carlos Monzon |
| 1908–10 | Stanley Ketchel[3] | 1949–51 | Jake LaMotta | 1974–75 | Carlos Monzon (WBA), |
| 1913 | Frank Klaus | 1952 | Ray Robinson, Randy Turpin | | Rodrigo Valdez (WBC) |
| 1913–14 | George Chip | 1951–52 | Ray Robinson[1] | 1976 | Carlos Monzon (WBA, WBC), |
| 1914–17 | Al McCoy | 1953–55 | Carl Olson | | Rodrigo Valdez (WBC) |
| 1917–20 | Mike O'Dowd | 1955–57 | Ray Robinson[5] | 1977 | Carlos Monzon (WBA, |
| 1920–23 | Johnny Wilson | 1957 | Gene Fullmer, Ray Robinson | | WBC)[1], Rodrigo Valdez |
| 1923–26 | Harry Greb | 1957–58 | Carmen Basilio | | (WBA, WBC) |
| 1926 | Tiger Flowers | 1958–60 | Ray Robinson[6] | 1978 | Rodrigo Valdez, Hugo Corro |
| 1926–31 | Mickey Walker[2] | 1960–61 | Paul Pender[7] | 1979 | Hugo Corro, Vito Antuofermo |
| 1931–41 | Gorilla Jones, Ben Jeby, | 1959–62 | Gene Fullmer (NBA) | 1980 | Vito Antuofermo, Alan |
| | Marcel Thil, Lou Brouillard, | 1961–62 | Terry Downes[1] | | Minter, Marvin Hagler |
| | Vince Dundee, Teddy | 1962 | Paul Pender[1] | 1981 | Marvin Hagler |
| | Yarosz, Babe Risko, | 1962–63 | Dick Tiger | 1982–86 | Marvelous Marvin Hagler |
| | Freddy Steele, Al Hostak, | 1963–65 | Joey Giardello | | (undisputed) |
| | Solly Kreiger, Fred | 1965–66 | Dick Tiger | | |
| | Apostoli, Ceferino Garcia, | 1966 | Emile Griffith | | |

1. Retired. 2. Abandoned title. 3. Died. 4. National Boxing Association and New York Commission disagreed on champions. Those listed were accepted by one or the other until Zale gained world-wide recognition. 5. Ended retirement in 1954. 6. NBA withdrew recognition. 7. Recognized by New York, Massachusetts, and Europe.

## Welterweight

| | | | | | |
|---|---|---|---|---|---|
| 1892–94 | Mysterious Billy Smith | 1933–34 | Jimmy McLarnin, Barney Ross | 1971 | Billy Backus, José Napoles |
| 1894–96 | Tommy Ryan | 1934–35 | Jimmy McLarnin | 1972–74 | José Napoles |
| 1896 | Kid McCoy[2] | 1935–38 | Barney Ross | 1975 | José Napoles (WBA, WBC)[3], |
| 1896– | | 1938–40 | Henry Armstrong | | Angel Espada (WBA), John |
| 1900 | Mysterious Billy Smith | 1940–41 | Fritzie Zivic | | Stracey (WBC) |
| 1900 | Rube Ferns | 1941–46 | Freddie Cochrane | 1976 | Angel Espada (WBA), José |
| 1900–01 | Matty Matthews | 1946 | Marty Servo[1] | | Cuevas (WBA), John Stracey |
| 1901 | Ruby Ferns | 1946–51 | Ray Robinson[2] | | (WBC), Carlos |
| 1901–04 | Joe Walcott | 1951 | Johnny Bratton (NBA) | | Palomino |
| 1904 | Dixie Kid[2] | 1951–54 | Kid Gavilan | 1977–78 | José Cuevas (WBA), Carlos |
| 1904–06 | Joe Walcott | 1954–55 | Johnny Saxton | | Palomino (WBC) |
| 1906–07 | Honey Mellody | 1955 | Tony DeMarco | 1979 | José Cuevas (WBA), Carlos |
| 1907 | Mike (Twin) Sullivan[2] | 1955–56 | Carmen Basilio | | Palomino (WBC), Wilfredo |
| 1915–19 | Ted Lewis | 1956 | Johnny Saxton | | Benitez (WBC) |
| 1919–22 | Jack Britton | 1956–57 | Carmen Basilio[2] | 1980 | José Cuevas (WBA), |
| 1922–26 | Mickey Walker | 1958 | Virgil Akins | | Ray Leonard (WBC), |
| 1926–27 | Pete Latzo | 1959–60 | Don Jordan | | Roberto Duran (WBC), |
| 1927–29 | Joe Dundee | 1960–61 | Benny (Kid) Paret | | Thomas Hearns (WBA) |
| 1929–30 | Jackie Fields | 1961 | Emile Griffith | 1981 | Ray Leonard (WBC), Thomas |
| 1930 | Young Jack Thompson | 1961–62 | Benny (Kid) Paret | | Hearns (WBA), Ray |
| 1930–31 | Tommy Freeman | 1962–63 | Emile Griffith, Luis Rodriguez | | Leonard (WBC, WBA) |
| 1931 | Young Jack Thompson | 1963–66 | Emile Griffith[2] | 1982 | Ray Leonard |
| 1931–32 | Lou Brouillard | 1966–69 | Curtis Cokes | 1983–85 | Donald Curry (WBA) |
| 1932–33 | Jackie Fields | 1969 | Curtis Cokes, José Napoles | 1983–85 | Milton McCrory (WBC) |
| 1933 | Young Corbett 3rd | 1970 | José Napoles, Billy Backus | 1985–86 | Donald Curry (undisputed) |

1. Retired. 2. Abandoned title. 3. WBA withdrew recognition.

## Lightweight

| | | | | | |
|---|---|---|---|---|---|
| 1869–99 | Kid Lavigne | 1954 | Paddy DeMarco | 1977 | Roberto Duran (WBA), Esteban De Jesus (WBC) |
| 1899– | | 1954–55 | James Carter | | |
| 1902 | Frank Erne | 1955–56 | Wallace Smith | 1978 | Roberto Duran (WBA, WBC) |
| 1902–08 | Joe Gans | 1956–62 | Joe Brown | 1979 | Roberto Duran[2], Jim Watt |
| 1908–10 | Battling Nelson | 1962–65 | Carlos Ortiz | | (WBC), Ernesto Espana |
| 1910–12 | Ad Wolgast | 1965 | Ismael Laguna | | (WBA) |
| 1912–14 | Willie Ritchie | 1965–68 | Carlos Ortiz | 1980 | Ernesto Espana (WBA), |
| 1914–17 | Freddy Welsh | 1968 | Teo Cruz | | Hilmer Kenty (WBA), Jim |
| 1917–25 | Benny Leonard[1] | 1969 | Teo Cruz, Mando Ramos | | Watt (WBC) |
| 1925 | Jimmy Goodrich | 1970 | Mando Ramos, Ismael | 1981 | Hilmer Kenty (WBA), Sean |
| 1925–26 | Rocky Kansas | | Laguna, Ken Buchanan | | O'Grady (WBA), James |
| 1926–30 | Sammy Mandell | 1971 | Ken Buchanan (WBA), Mando | | Watt (WBC), Alexis |
| 1930 | Al Singer | | Ramos (WBC), Pedro Car- | | Arguello (WBC), Arturo |
| 1930–33 | Tony Canzoneri | | rasco (WBC) | | Frias (WBA) |
| 1933–35 | Barney Ross[2] | 1972 | Ken Buchanan (WBA), | 1982 | Arturo Frias (WBA), Ray |
| 1935–36 | Tony Canzoneri | | Roberto Duran (WBA), | | Mancini (WBA), Alexis |
| 1936–38 | Lou Ambers | | Pedro Carrasco (WBC), | | Arguello (WBC) |
| 1938–39 | Henry Armstrong | | Mando Ramos (WBC), | 1983 | Edwin Rosario (WBC), |
| 1939–40 | Lou Ambers | | Chango Carmona (WBC), | | Ray Mancini (WBA) |
| 1940–41 | Lew Jenkins | | Rodolfo Gonzalez (WBC) | 1984 | Edwin Rosario (WBC), |
| 1941–42 | Sammy Angott[1] | 1973 | Roberto Duran (WBA), | | Livingstone Bramble (WBA) |
| 1943–47 | Beau Jack (N.Y.), Bob | | Rodolfo Gonzalez (WBC)) | 1985 | Jose Luis Ramirez (WBC), |
| | Montgomery (N.Y.), | 1974 | Roberto Duran (WBA), | | Hector Camacho (WBC), |
| | Sammy Angott (NBA), | | Rodolfo Gonzalez (WBC), | | Livingstone Bramble (WBA) |
| | Juan Zurita (NBA), Ike | | Guts Ishimatsu (WBC) | 1986 | Hector Camacho (WBC), |
| | Williams (NBA) | 1975 | Roberto Duran (WBA), Guts | | Livingstone Bramble (WBA), |
| 1947–51 | Ike Williams | | Ishimatsu (WBC) | | Jim Paul (IBF) |
| 1951–52 | James Carter | 1976 | Roberto Duran (WBA), Guts | | |
| 1952 | Lauro Salas | | Ishimatsu (WBC), Esteban | | |
| 1952–54 | James Carter | | De Jesus (WBC) | | |

1. Retired. 2. Abandoned title.

## Featherweight

| | | | | | |
|---|---|---|---|---|---|
| 1889 | Dal Hawkins[1] | 1923–25 | Johnny Dundee[1] | 1936–37 | Petey Sarron |
| 1890 | Billy Murphy | 1925–27 | Louis (Kid) Kaplan[1] | 1937–38 | Henry Armstrong[1] |
| 1892– | | 1927–28 | Benny Bass | 1938–40 | Joey Archibald |
| 1900 | George Dixon | 1928 | Tony Canzoneri | 1940–41 | Harry Jefra, Joey Archibald |
| 1900–01 | Terry McGovern | 1928–29 | Andre Routis | 1941–42 | Chalky Wright |
| 1901 | Young Corbett[1] | 1929–32 | Battling Battalino[1] | 1942–48 | Willie Pep |
| 1901–12 | Abe Attell | 1932 | Tommy Paul (NBA), Kid | 1948–49 | Sandy Saddler[2] |
| 1912–23 | Johnny Kilbane | | Chocolate (N.Y.) | 1949–50 | Willie Pep |
| 1923 | Eugene Criqui | 1933–36 | Freddie Miller | 1950-57 | Sandy Saddler |

| 1957–59 | Kid Bassey | 1973 | Ernesto Marcel (WBA), José Legra (WBC), Eder Jofre (WBC) | | Lopez (WBC) |
|---|---|---|---|---|---|
| 1959–63 | Davey Moore | | | 1979 | Eusebio Pedroza (WBA), Danny Lopez (WBC) |
| 1963–64 | Sugar Ramos | | | | |
| 1964–67 | Vicente Saldivar[2] | 1974 | Ernesto Marcel (WBA)[2], Ruben Olivares (WBA), Alexis Arguello (WBA), Eder Jofre (WBC), Bobby Chacon (WBC) | 1980 | Eusebio Pedroza (WBA), Danny Lopez (WBC), Salvador Sanchez (WBC) |
| 1968 | Howard Winstone, José Legra,[3] Paul Rojas (WBA), Sho Saijo (WBA) | | | | |
| | | | | 1981 | Eusebio Pedroza (WBA), Salvador Sanchez (WBC) |
| 1969 | Sho Saijo (WBA), Johnny Famechon[3] | 1975 | Alexis Arguello (WBA), Bobby Chacon (WBC), Ruben Olivares (WBC), David Kotey (WBC)[2] | 1982 | Eusebio Pedroza (WBA), Salvador Sanchez (WBC)[4] |
| 1970 | Sho Saijo (WBA), Johnny Famechon,[3] Vicente Salvidar,[3] Kuniaki Shibata[3] | | | 1983 | Juan Laporte (WBC), Eusebio Pedroza (WBA) |
| | | 1976 | Alexis Arguello (WBA),[2] David Kotey (WBC), Danny Lopez (WBC) | 1984 | Wilfred Gomez (WBC), Eusebio Pedroza (WBA) |
| 1971 | Sho Saijo (WBA), Antonio Gomez (WBA), Kuniaki Shibata (WBC) | | | 1985 | Eusebio Pedroza (WBA), Barry McGuigan (WBA), Azumah Nelson (WBC) |
| | | 1977 | Rafael Ortega (WBA), Danny Lopez (WBC) | | |
| 1972 | Antonio Gomez (WBA), Ernesto Marcel (WBA), Kuniaki Shibata (WBC), Clemente Sanchez (WBC), José Legra (WBC) | 1978 | Rafael Ortega (WBA), Cecilio Lastra (WBA), Eusebio Pedroza (WBA), Danny | 1986 | Barry McGuigan (WBA), Stevie Cruz (WBA), Azumah Nelson (WBC) |

1. Abandoned title. 2. Retired. 3. Recognized in Europe, Mexico, and Orient. 4. Killed in auto accident.

## Bantamweight

| 1890–92 | George Dixon[1] | 1948–50 | Manuel Ortiz | 1975 | Soo Hwan Hong (WBA), Alfonso Zamora (WBA), Rodolfo Martinez (WBC) |
|---|---|---|---|---|---|
| 1894–99 | Jimmy Barry[2] | 1950–52 | Vic Towoel | | |
| 1899– 1900 | Terry McGovern[1] | 1952–54 | Jimmy Carruthers[2] | | |
| | | 1954–55 | Robert Cohen | 1976 | Alfonso Zamora (WBA), Rodolfo Martinez (WBC), Carlos Zarate (WBC) |
| 1901 | Harry Harris[1] | 1956 | Robert Cohen, Mario D'Agata, Raul Macias (NBA) | | |
| 1902–03 | Harry Forbes | | | 1977 | Alfonso Zamora (WBA), Jorge Lujan (WBA), Carlos Zarate (WBC) |
| 1903–04 | Frankie Neil | | | | |
| 1904 | Joe Bowker[1] | 1957 | Mario D'Agata, Alphonse Halimi | | |
| 1905–07 | Jimmy Walsh[1] | | | 1978 | Jorge Lujan (WBA), Carlos Zarate (WBC) |
| 1910–14 | Johnny Coulon | 1958–59 | Alphonse Halimi | | |
| 1914–17 | Kid Williams | 1959–60 | Jose Becerra[2] | 1979 | Jorge Lujan (WBA), Carlos Zarate (WBC), Lupe Pinto (WBC) |
| 1917–20 | Pete Herman | 1960–61 | Alphonse Halimi[4] | | |
| 1920 | Joe Lynch | 1961–62 | Johnny Caldwell[4] | | |
| 1920–21 | Joe Lynch, Pete Herman, Johnny Buff | 1961–65 | Eder Jofre | 1980 | Jorge Lujan (WBA), Lupe Pintor (WBC), Julian Solis (WBA), Jeff Chandler (WBA) |
| | | 1965–68 | Masahika (Fighting) Harada | | |
| 1922 | Johnny Buff, Joe Lynch | 1968 | Masahika (Fighting) Harada, Lionel Rose | | |
| 1923 | Joe Lynch | | | 1981 | Lupe Pintor (WBC), Jeff Chandler (WBA) |
| 1924 | Joe Lynch, Abe Goldstein | 1969 | Lionel Rose, Ruben Olivares | | |
| 1924 | Abe Goldstein, Eddie (Cannonball) Martin | 1970 | Ruben Olivares, Chucho Castillo | 1982 | Lupe Pintor (WBC), Jeff Chandler (WBA) |
| 1925 | Eddie (Cannonball) Martin, Charlie (Phil) Rosenberg[3] | 1971 | Chucho Castillo, Ruben Olivares | 1983 | Jeff Chandler (WBA), Albert Dauila (WBC) |
| | | 1972 | Ruben Olivares, Rafael Herrera, Enrique Pinder | | |
| 1927–28 | Bud Taylor (NBA)[1] | | | 1984 | Richie Sandqual (WBA), Albert Dauila (WBC) |
| 1929–34 | Al Brown | 1973 | Enrique Pinder (WBA), Romeo Anaya (WBA), Arnold Taylor (WBC), Rodolfo Martinez (WBC), Rafael Herrera | | |
| 1935 | Al Brown, Baltazar Sangchili | | | 1985 | Richard Sandoval (WBA), Daniel Zaragoza (WBC), Miguel Lora (WBC) |
| 1936 | Baltazar Sangchili, Tony Marino, Sixto Escobar | | | | |
| 1937 | Sixto Escobar, Harry Jeffra | 1974 | Arnold Taylor (WBA), Soo Hwan Hong (WBA), Rafael Herrera (WBC), Rodolfo Martinez (WBC) | 1986 | Richard Sandoval (WBA), Bernardo Pinango (WBA), Jeff Fenech (IBF) |
| 1938 | Harry Jeffra, Sixto Escobar | | | | |
| 1939–40 | Sixto Escobar[2] | | | | |
| 1940–42 | Lou Salica | | | | |
| 1942–46 | Manuel Ortiz | | | | |
| 1947 | Manuel Ortiz, Harold Dade | | | | |

1. Abandoned title. 2. Retired. 3. Deprived of title for failing to make weight. 4. Recognized in Europe.

## Flyweight

| 1916–23 | Jimmy Wilde | 1932–35 | Jackie Brown | 1954–60 | Pascual Perez |
|---|---|---|---|---|---|
| 1923–26 | Pancho Villa[1] | 1935–38 | Bennie Lynch[4] | 1960–62 | Pone Kingpetch |
| 1925 | Frankie Genaro | 1939 | Peter Kane[4] | 1962–63 | Masahika (Fighting) Harada |
| 1925–27 | Fidel La Barba[2] | 1943–47 | Jackie Paterson[1] | 1963–64 | Hiroyuki Ebihara |
| 1927–31 | Corporal Izzy Schwartz, Frankie Genaro, Emile (Spider) Pladner, Midget Wolgast, Young Perez[3] | 1947–50 | Rinty Monaghan[2] | 1964–65 | Pone Kingpetch |
| | | 1950 | Terry Allen | 1965–66 | Salvatore Burrini |
| | | 1950–52 | Dado Marino | 1966 | Walter McGown, Chartchai Chionoi |
| | | 1952–54 | Yoshio Shirai | | |

| | | | | | | |
|---|---|---|---|---|---|---|
| 1966–68 | Charchai Chionoi | 1974 | Chartchai Chionoi (WBA), | | Miguel Canto (WBC), Park | |
| 1969 | Bernabe Villacampa, Efran | | Susumu Hanagata (WBA), | | Chan-Hee (WBC) | |
| | Torres (WBA) | | Betulio Gonzalez (WBC), | 1980 | Luis Ibarra (WBA), Kim Tae | |
| 1970 | Bernabe Villacampa, | | Shoji Oguma (WBC) | | Shik (WBA), Park | |
| | Chartchai Chionoi, Erbito | 1975 | Susumu Hanagata (WBA), | | Chan-Hee (WBC), Shoji | |
| | Salavarria, Berkrerk | | Erbito Salavarria (WBA), | | Oguma (WBC) | |
| | Chartvanchai (WBA), | | Shoji Oguma (WBC), | 1983 | Frank Cedeno (WBC), | |
| | Masao Ohba (WBA) | | Miguel Canto (WBC) | | Santos Lacia (WBA) | |
| 1971 | Masao Ohba (WBA), Erbito | 1976 | Erbito Salavarria (WBA), | 1984 | Koji Kobayashy (WBA), | |
| | Salavarria (WBC) | | Alfonso Lopez (WBA), | | Gabriel Bernal (WBC), | |
| 1972 | Masao Ohba (WBA), Erbito | | Guty Espadas (WBA), | | Santos Laciar (WBA) | |
| | Salavarria (WBC), Betulio | | Miguel Canto (WBC) | 1985 | Sot Chitalasa (WBC) | |
| | Gonzalez (WBC), Venice | 1977 | Guty Espadas (WBA), Miguel | | Santos Laciar (WBA) | |
| | Borkorsor (WBC) | | Canto (WBC) | 1986 | Hilario Zapata (WBA) | |
| 1973 | Masao Ohba (WBA), | 1978 | Guty Espadas (WBA), Betulio | | Julio Cesar-Chevez (WBC) | |
| | Chartchai Chionoi (WBA), | | Gonzalez (WBA), Miguel | | | |
| | Venice Borkorsor (WBC), | | Canto (WBC) | | | |
| | Betulio Gonzalez (WBC) | 1979 | Betulio Gonzalez (WBA), | | | |

1. Died. 2. Retired. 3. Claimants to NBA and New York Commission titles. 4. Abandoned title.

# BOXING—AMATEUR

## WORLD AMATEUR CHAMPIONSHIPS—1986

(May 12-18, 1986, at Reno, Nev.)

106 lb—Juan Torres, Cuba
112 lb—Pedro Reyes, Cuba
119 lb—Moon Sung-Kil, Korea
125 lb—Kelcie Banks, United States
132 lb—Adolfo Horta, Cuba
139 lb—Vasill Shishov, Soviet Union
147 lb—Kenneth Gould, United States
156 lb—Angel Espinosa, Cuba
165 lb—Darin Allen, United States
178 lb—Pablo Romero, Cuba
201—Felix Savon, Cuba
Over 201 lb—Biagio Chianese, Italy

## NATIONAL GOLDEN GLOVES CHAMPIONSHIPS—1986

(Cedar Rapids, Iowa, May 5-10, 1986)

106 lb—Michael Carabajal, Las Vegas, Nev.
112 lb—Anthony Wilson, Washington, D.C.
119 lb—Fernando Rodriguez, Pennsylvania
125 lb—William Little, Knoxville, Tenn.
132 lb—Levell Finger, St. Louis, Mo.

139 lb—Roy Jones, Knoxville, Tenn.
147 lb—Frank Liles, Syracuse, N.Y.
156 lb—Mylon Watkins, Las Vegas, Nev.
165 lb—Richard White, Los Angeles, Calif.
178 lb—Harvey Richards, Springfield, Ill.
201 lb—Orlin Norris, Fort Worth, Texas
Over 201 lb—Tevin George, Louisiana
Team champion: Knoxville, Tenn.

## UNITED STATES CHAMPIONSHIPS—1986

(March 31-April 5, Beaumont, Texas)

106 lb—Brian Lonon, U.S. Army-Fort Hood
112 lb—Arthur Johnson, St. Louis, Mo.
119 lb—Michael Collins, LaPorte, Tex.
125 lb—Kelcie Banks, Chicago, Ill.
132 lb—Vincent Phillips, U.S. Army-Fort Riley
139 lb—Nuck Kakouris, St. Louis, Mo.
147 lb—none
156 lb—Michael Moorer, Monessen, Pa.
165 lb—Anthony Hembrick, U.S. Army-Fort Bragg
178 lb—Loren Ross, U.S. Army-Fort Hood
201 lb—Michael Bent, Cambria Heights, N.Y.
Over 201 lb—Alex Garcia, San Fenando, Calif.

# FENCING

## WORLD CHAMPIONSHIPS—1986

Men's foil—Andre Borella, Italy
Men's epee—Philippe Riboud, France
Men's sabre—Ser Mindirgassob, Soviet Union
Women's foil—Anja Fichtel, West Germany
Men's foil team—Italy
Men's epee team—West Gemany
Men's sabre team—Soviet Union
Women's foil team—Soviet Union

## UNITED STATES CHAMPIONS—1986

### U.S. Fencing Association

(winner, club, region)

Men's foil—Michael Marx, Salle Auriol Fencing Club, Oregon
Men's epee—Lee Shelley, Salle Santelli Fencing Club, New Jersey
Men's sabre—Peter Westbrook, New York Fencers Club, New York City
Women's foil—Caitlin Billodeau, New York Fencers Club, New York City
Women's epee—Vincent Bradford, University of Texas-Austin Fencing Club

Men's foil team—New York Fencers Club
Men's sabre team—New York Fencers Club
Men's epee team—New York Athletic Club
Women's foil team—New York Fencers Club

## WORLD UNIVERSITY GAMES—1985

(Kobe, Japan, Aug. 26-Sept. 5, 1985)

Men's foil—1. A. Robak, Poland; 2. Michael Marx, Portland, Ore.; 3. A. Ibragimob, Soviet Union.
Men's epee—1. A. Mojaev, Soviet Union; 2. R. Manzi, Italy; 3. P. Merenico, Cuba.
Men's sabre—1. S. Mindirgaso, Soviet Union; 2. L. Csongradi, Hungary; 3. V. Etropolski, Bulgaria.
Women's foil—1. Luan Jujie, People's Republic of China; 2. O. Voshakina, Soviet Union; 3. M. Soboleva, Soviet Union.
Men's foil team—Hungary
Men's epee team—Soviet Union
Men's sabre team—Soviet Union
Women's foil team—Italy

# HORSE RACING

Ancient drawings on stone and bone prove that horse racing is at least 3000 years old, but Thoroughbred Racing is a modern development. Practically every thoroughbred in training today traces its registered ancestry back to one or more of three sires that arrived in England about 1728 from the Near East and became known, from the names of their owners, as the Byerly Turk, the Darley Arabian, and the Godolphin Arabian. The Jockey Club (English) was founded at Newmarket in 1750 or 1751 and became the custodian of the Stud Book as well as the court of last resort in deciding turf affairs.

Horse racing took place in this country before the Revolution, but the great lift to the breeding industry came with the importation in 1798, by Col. John Hoomes of Virginia, of Diomed, winner of the Epsom Derby of 1780. Diomed's lineal descendants included such famous stars of the American turf as American Eclipse and Lexington. From 1800 to the time of the Civil War there were race courses and breeding establishments plentifully scattered through Virginia, North Carolina, South Carolina, Tennessee, Kentucky, and Louisiana.

The oldest stake event in North America is the Queen's Plate, a Canadian fixture that was first run in the Province of Quebec in 1836. The oldest stake event in the United States is The Travers, which was first run at Saratoga in 1864. The gambling that goes with horse racing and trickery by jockeys, trainers, owners, and track officials caused attacks on the sport by reformers and a demand among horse racing enthusiasts for an honest and effective control of some kind, but nothing of lasting value to racing came of this until the formation in 1894 of The Jockey Club.

## "TRIPLE CROWN" WINNERS IN THE UNITED STATES[1]
### (Kentucky Derby, Preakness and Belmont Stakes)

| Year | Horse | Owner | Year | Horse | Owner |
|---|---|---|---|---|---|
| 1919 | Sir Barton | J. K. L. Ross | 1946 | Assault | Robert J. Kleberg |
| 1930 | Gallant Fox | William Woodward | 1948 | Citation | Warren Wright |
| 1935 | Omaha | William Woodward | 1973 | Secretariat | Meadow Stable |
| 1937 | War Admiral | Samuel D. Riddle | 1977 | Seattle Slew | Karen Taylor |
| 1941 | Whirlaway | Warren Wright | 1978 | Affirmed | Louis Wolfson |
| 1943 | Count Fleet | Mrs. John Hertz | | | |

1. Statistics relative to thoroughbred racing in this publication are reproduced from the *American Racing Manual*, by special permission of the copyright owners. TRIANGLE PUBLICATIONS, INC. Reproduction prohibited.

## KENTUCKY DERBY
Churchill Downs; 3-year-olds; 1 1/4 miles.

| Year | Winner | Jockey | Wt. | Win val. | Year | Winner | Jockey | Wt. | Win val. |
|---|---|---|---|---|---|---|---|---|---|
| 1875 | Aristides | O. Lewis | 100 | $2,850 | 1909 | Wintergreen | V. Powers | 117 | $4,850 |
| 1876 | Vagrant | R. Swim | 97 | 2,950 | 1910 | Donau | F. Herbert | 117 | 4,850 |
| 1877 | Baden Baden | W. Walker | 100 | 3,300 | 1911 | Meridian | G. Archibald | 117 | 4,850 |
| 1878 | Day Star | J. Carter | 100 | 4,050 | 1912 | Worth | C. H. Shilling | 117 | 4,850 |
| 1879 | Lord Murphy | C. Schauer | 100 | 3,550 | 1913 | Donerail | R. Goose | 117 | 5,475 |
| 1880 | Fonso | G. Lewis | 105 | 3,800 | 1914 | Old Rosebud | J. McCabe | 114 | 9,125 |
| 1881 | Hindoo | J. McLaughlin | 105 | 4,410 | 1915 | Regret | J. Notler | 112 | 11,450 |
| 1882 | Apollo | B. Hurd | 102 | 4,560 | 1916 | George Smith | J. Loftus | 117 | 9,750 |
| 1883 | Leonatus | W. Donohue | 105 | 3,760 | 1917 | Omar Khayyam | C. Borel | 117 | 16,600 |
| 1884 | Buchanan | I. Murphy | 110 | 3,990 | 1918 | Exterminator | W. Knapp | 114 | 14,700 |
| 1885 | Joe Cotton | E. Henderson | 110 | 4,630 | 1919 | Sir Barton | J. Loftus | 112 1/2 | 20,825 |
| 1886 | Ben Ali | P. Duffy | 118 | 4,890 | 1920 | Paul Jones | T. Rice | 126 | 30,375 |
| 1887 | Montrose | I. Lewis | 118 | 4,200 | 1921 | Behave Yourself | C. Thompson | 126 | 38,450 |
| 1888 | Macbeth II | G. Covington | 115 | 4,740 | 1922 | Morvich | A. Johnson | 126 | 46,775 |
| 1889 | Spokane | T. Kiley | 118 | 4,970 | 1923 | Zev | E. Sande | 126 | 53,600 |
| 1890 | Riley | I. Murphy | 118 | 5,460 | 1924 | Black Gold | J. D. Mooney | 126 | 52,775 |
| 1891 | Kingman | I. Murphy | 122 | 4,680 | 1925 | Flying Ebony | E. Sande | 126 | 52,950 |
| 1892 | Azra | A. Clayton | 122 | 4,230 | 1926 | Bubbling Over | A. Johnson | 126 | 50,075 |
| 1893 | Lookout | E. Kunze | 122 | 4,090 | 1927 | Whiskery | L. McAtee | 126 | 51,000 |
| 1894 | Chant | F. Goodale | 122 | 4,020 | 1928 | Reigh Count | C. Lang | 126 | 55,375 |
| 1895 | Halma | J. Perkins | 122 | 2,970 | 1929 | Clyde Van Dusen | L. McAtee | 126 | 53,950 |
| 1896 | Ben Brush | W. Simms | 117 | 4,850 | 1930 | Gallant Fox | E. Sande | 126 | 50,725 |
| 1897 | Typhoon H | F. Garner | 117 | 4,850 | 1931 | Twenty Grand | C. Kurtsinger | 126 | 48,725 |
| 1898 | Plaudit | W. Simms | 117 | 4,850 | 1932 | Burgoo King | E. James | 126 | 52,350 |
| 1899 | Manuel | F. Taral | 117 | 4,850 | 1933 | Brokers Tip | D. Meade | 126 | 48,925 |
| 1900 | Lieut. Gibson | J. Boland | 117 | 4,850 | 1934 | Cavalcade | M. Garner | 126 | 28,175 |
| 1901 | His Eminence | J. Winkfield | 117 | 4,850 | 1935 | Omaha | W. Saunders | 126 | 39,525 |
| 1902 | Alan-a-Dale | J. Winkfield | 117 | 4,850 | 1936 | Bold Venture | I. Hanford | 126 | 37,725 |
| 1903 | Judge Himes | H. Booker | 117 | 4,850 | 1937 | War Admiral | C. Kurtsinger | 126 | 52,050 |
| 1904 | Elwood | F. Prior | 117 | 4,850 | 1938 | Lawrin | E. Arcaro | 126 | 47,050 |
| 1905 | Agile | J. Martin | 122 | 4,850 | 1939 | Johnstown | J. Stout | 126 | 46,350 |
| 1906 | Sir Huon | R. Troxler | 117 | 4,850 | 1940 | Gallahadion | C. Bierman | 126 | 60,150 |
| 1907 | Pink Star | A. Minder | 117 | 4,850 | 1941 | Whirlaway | E. Arcaro | 126 | 61,275 |
| 1908 | Stone Street | A. Pickens | 117 | 4,850 | 1942 | Shut Out | W. D. Wright | 126 | 64,225 |

| Year | Winner | Jockey | Wt. | Win val. | Year | Winner | Jockey | Wt. | Win val. |
|---|---|---|---|---|---|---|---|---|---|
| 1943 | Count Fleet | J. Longden | 126 | $ 60,725 | 1965 | Lucky Debonair | W. Shoemaker | 126 | $112,000 |
| 1944 | Pensive | C. McCreary | 126 | 64,675 | 1966 | Kauai King | D. Brumfield | 126 | 120,500 |
| 1945 | Hoop Jr. | E. Arcaro | 126 | 64,850 | 1967 | Proud Clarion | R. Ussery | 126 | 119,700 |
| 1946 | Assault | W. Mehrtens | 126 | 96,400 | 1968 | Forward Pass[1] | I. Valenzuela | 126 | 122,600 |
| 1947 | Jet Pilot | E. Guerin | 126 | 92,160 | 1969 | Majestic Prince | W. Hartack | 126 | 113,200 |
| 1948 | Citation | E. Arcaro | 126 | 83,400 | 1970 | Dust Commander | M. Manganello | 126 | 127,800 |
| 1949 | Ponder | S. Brooks | 126 | 91,600 | 1971 | Canonero II | G. Avila | 126 | 145,500 |
| 1950 | Middleground | W. Boland | 126 | 92,650 | 1972 | Riva Ridge | R. Turcotte | 126 | 140,300 |
| 1951 | Count Turf | C. McCreary | 126 | 98,050 | 1973 | Secretariat | R. Turcotte | 126 | 155,050 |
| 1952 | Hill Gail | E. Arcaro | 126 | 96,300 | 1974 | Cannonade | A. Cordero, Jr. | 126 | 274,000 |
| 1953 | Dark Star | H. Moreno | 126 | 90,050 | 1975 | Foolish Pleasure | J. Vasquez | 126 | 209,600 |
| 1954 | Determine | R. York | 126 | 102,050 | 1976 | Bold Forbes | A. Cordero, Jr. | 126 | 165,200 |
| 1955 | Swaps | W. Shoemaker | 126 | 108,400 | 1977 | Seattle Slew | J. Cruguet | 126 | 214,700 |
| 1956 | Needles | D. Erb | 126 | 123,450 | 1978 | Affirmed | S. Cauthen | 126 | 186,900 |
| 1957 | Iron Liege | W. Hartack | 126 | 107,950 | 1979 | Spectacular Bid | R. Franklin | 126 | 228,650 |
| 1958 | Tim Tam | I. Valenzuela | 126 | 116,400 | 1980 | Genuine Risk | J. Vasquez | 126 | 250,550 |
| 1959 | Tomy Lee | W. Shoemaker | 126 | 119,650 | 1981 | Pleasant Colony | J. Velasquez | 126 | 317,200 |
| 1960 | Venetian Way | W. Hartack | 126 | 114,850 | 1982 | Gato del Sol | E. Delahoussaye | 126 | 417,600 |
| 1961 | Carry Back | J. Sellers | 126 | 120,500 | 1983 | Sunny's Halo | E. Delahoussaye | 126 | 426,000 |
| 1962 | Decidedly | W. Hartack | 126 | 119,650 | 1984 | Swale | L. Pincay Jr. | 126 | 537,400 |
| 1963 | Chateaugay | B. Baeza | 126 | $108,900 | 1985 | Spend a Buck | A. Cordero, Jr. | 126 | 406,800 |
| 1964 | Northern Dancer | W. Hartack | 126 | 114,300 | 1986 | Ferdinand | W. Shoemaker | 126 | 609,400 |

1. Dancer's Image finished first but was disqualified after traces of drug were found in system.

## PREAKNESS STAKES

Pimlico; 3-year-olds; 1 3/16 miles; first race 1873.

| Year | Winner | Jockey | Wt. | Win Val. | Year | Winner | Jockey | Wt. | Win val. |
|---|---|---|---|---|---|---|---|---|---|
| 1919 | Sir Barton | J. Loftus | 126 | $24,500 | 1958 | Tim Tam | I. Valenzuela | 126 | $97,900 |
| 1930 | Gallant Fox | E. Sande | 126 | 51,925 | 1959 | Royal Orbit | W. Harmatz | 126 | 136,200 |
| 1931 | Mate | G. Ellis | 126 | 48,225 | 1960 | Bally Ache | R. Ussery | 126 | 121,000 |
| 1932 | Burgoo King | E. James | 126 | 50,375 | 1961 | Carry Back | J. Sellers | 126 | 126,200 |
| 1933 | Head Play | C. Kurtsinger | 126 | 26,850 | 1962 | Greek Money | J. Rotz | 126 | 135,800 |
| 1934 | High Quest | R. Jones | 126 | 25,175 | 1963 | Candy Spots | W. Shoemaker | 126 | 127,500 |
| 1935 | Omaha | W. Saunders | 126 | 25,325 | 1964 | Northern Dancer | W. Hartack | 126 | 124,200 |
| 1936 | Bold Venture | G. Woolf | 126 | 27,325 | 1965 | Tom Rolfe | R. Turcotte | 126 | 128,100 |
| 1937 | War Admiral | C. Kurtsinger | 126 | 45,600 | 1966 | Kauai King | D. Brumfield | 126 | 129,000 |
| 1938 | Dauber | M. Peters | 126 | 51,875 | 1967 | Damascus | W. Shoemaker | 126 | 141,500 |
| 1939 | Challedon | G. Seabo | 126 | 53,710 | 1968 | Forward Pass | I. Valenzuela | 126 | 142,700 |
| 1940 | Bimelech | F.A. Smith | 126 | 53,230 | 1969 | Majestic Prince | W. Hartack | 126 | 129,500 |
| 1941 | Whirlaway | E. Arcaro | 126 | 49,365 | 1970 | Personality | E. Belmonte | 126 | 151,300 |
| 1942 | Alsab | B. James | 126 | 58,175 | 1971 | Canonero II | G. Avila | 126 | 137,400 |
| 1943 | Count Fleet | J. Longden | 126 | 43,190 | 1972 | Bee Bee Bee | E. Nelson | 126 | 135,300 |
| 1944 | Pensive | C. McCreary | 126 | 60,075 | 1973 | Secretariat | R. Turcotte | 126 | 129,900 |
| 1945 | Polynesian | W.D. Wright | 126 | 66,170 | 1974 | Little Current | M. Rivera | 126 | 156,000 |
| 1946 | Assault | W. Mehrtens | 126 | 96,620 | 1975 | Master Derby | D. McHargue | 126 | 158,100 |
| 1947 | Faultless | D. Dodson | 126 | 98,005 | 1976 | Elocutionist | J. Lively | 126 | 129,700 |
| 1948 | Citation | E. Arcaro | 126 | 91,870 | 1977 | Seattle Slew | J. Cruguet | 126 | 138,600 |
| 1949 | Capot | T. Atkinson | 126 | 79,985 | 1978 | Affirmed | S. Cauthen | 126 | 136,200 |
| 1950 | Hill Prince | E. Arcaro | 126 | 56,115 | 1979 | Spectacular Bid | R. Franklin | 126 | 165,300 |
| 1951 | Bold | E. Arcaro | 126 | 83,110 | 1980 | Codex | A. Cordero | 126 | 180,600 |
| 1952 | Blue Man | C. McCreary | 126 | 86,135 | 1981 | Pleasant Colony | J. Velasquez | 126 | 270,800 |
| 1953 | Native Dancer | E. Guerin | 126 | 65,200 | 1982 | Aloma's Ruler | J. Kaenel | 126 | 209,900 |
| 1954 | Hasty Road | J. Adams | 126 | 91,600 | 1983 | Deputed Testimony | D. Miller | 126 | 251,200 |
| 1955 | Nashua | E. Arcaro | 126 | 67,550 | 1984 | Gate Dancer | A. Cordero | 126 | 243,600 |
| 1956 | Fabius | W. Hartack | 126 | 84,250 | 1985 | Tank's Prospect | Pat Day | 126 | 423,200 |
| 1957 | Bold Ruler | E. Arcaro | 126 | 65,250 | 1986 | Snow Chief | A. Solis | 126 | 411,900 |

## BELMONT STAKES

Belmont Park; 3-year-olds; 1 1/2 miles.

Run at Jerome Park 1867 to 1890; at Morris Park 1890–94; at Belmont Park 1905–62; at Aqueduct 1963–67. Distance 1 5/8 miles prior to 1874; reduced to 1 1/2 miles, 1874; reduced to 1 1/4 miles, 1890; reduced to 1 1/8 miles, 1893; increased to 1 1/4 miles, 1895; increased to 1 3/8 miles, 1896; reduced to 1 1/4 miles in 1904; increased to 1 1/2 miles, 1926.

| Year | Winner | Jockey | Wt. | Win val. | Year | Winner | Jockey | Wt. | Win val. |
|---|---|---|---|---|---|---|---|---|---|
| 1919 | Sir Barton | J. Loftus | 126 | $11,950 | 1936 | Granville | J. Stout | 126 | 29,800 |
| 1930 | Gallant Fox | E. Sande | 126 | 66,040 | 1937 | War Admiral | C. Kurtsinger | 126 | 38,020 |
| 1931 | Twenty Grand | C. Kurtsinger | 126 | 58,770 | 1938 | Pasteurized | J. Stout | 126 | 34,530 |
| 1932 | Faireno | T. Malley | 126 | 55,120 | 1939 | Johnstown | J. Stout | 126 | 37,020 |
| 1933 | Hurryoff | M. Garner | 126 | 49,490 | 1940 | Bimelech | F.A. Smith | 126 | 35,030 |
| 1934 | Peace Chance | W.D. Wright | 126 | 43,410 | 1941 | Whirlaway | E. Arcaro | 126 | 39,77- |
| 1935 | Omaha | W. Saunders | 126 | 35,480 | 1942 | Shut Out | E. Arcaro | 126 | 44,520 |

| Year | Winner | Jockey | Wt. | Win val. | Year | Winner | Jockey | Wt. | Win val. |
|---|---|---|---|---|---|---|---|---|---|
| 1943 | Count Fleet | J. Longden | 126 | $35,340 | 1965 | Hail to All | J. Sellers | 126 | $104,150 |
| 1944 | Bounding Home | G.L. Smith | 126 | 55,000 | 1966 | Amberoid | W. Boland | 126 | 117,700 |
| 1945 | Pavot | E. Arcaro | 126 | 56,675 | 1967 | Damascus | W. Shoemaker | 126 | 104,950 |
| 1946 | Assault | W. Mehrtens | 126 | 75,400 | 1968 | Stage Door Johnny | H. Gustines | 126 | $117,700 |
| 1947 | Phalanx | R. Donoso | 126 | 78,900 | 1969 | Arts and Letters | B. Baeza | 126 | 104,050 |
| 1948 | Citation | E. Arcaro | 126 | 77,700 | 1970 | High Echelon | J. Rotz | 126 | 115,000 |
| 1949 | Capot | T. Atkinson | 126 | 60,900 | 1971 | Pass Catcher | R. Blum | 126 | 97,710 |
| 1950 | Middleground | W. Boland | 126 | 61,350 | 1972 | Riva Ridge | R. Turcotte | 126 | 93,540 |
| 1951 | Counterpoint | D. Gorman | 126 | $ 82,000 | 1973 | Secretariat | R. Turcotte | 126 | 90,120 |
| 1952 | One Count | E. Arcaro | 126 | 82,400 | 1974 | Little Current | M. Rivera | 126 | 101,970 |
| 1953 | Native Dancer | E. Guerin | 126 | 82,500 | 1975 | Avatar | W. Shoemaker | 126 | 116,160 |
| 1954 | High Gun | E. Guerin | 126 | 89,000 | 1976 | Bold Forbes | A. Cordero, Jr. | 126 | 117,000 |
| 1955 | Nashua | E. Arcaro | 126 | 83,700 | 1977 | Seattle Slew | J. Cruguet | 126 | 109,080 |
| 1956 | Needles | D. Erb | 126 | 83,600 | 1978 | Affirmed | S. Cauthen | 126 | 110,580 |
| 1957 | Gallant Man | W. Shoemaker | 126 | 77,300 | 1979 | Coastal | R. Hernandez | 126 | 161,400 |
| 1958 | Cavan | P. Anderson | 126 | 73,440 | 1980 | Temperence Hill | E. Maple | 126 | 176,220 |
| 1959 | Sword Dancer | W. Shoemaker | 126 | 93,525 | 1981 | Summing | G. Martens | 126 | 170,580 |
| 1960 | Celtic Ash | W. Hartack | 126 | 96,785 | 1982 | Conquistador Cielo | L. Pincay, Jr. | 126 | 159,720 |
| 1961 | Sherluck | B. Baeza | 126 | 104,900 | 1983 | Caveat | L. Pincay, Jr. | 126 | 215,100 |
| 1962 | Jaipur | W. Shoemaker | 126 | 109,550 | 1984 | Swale | L. Pincay, Jr. | 126 | 310,020 |
| 1963 | Chateaugay | B. Baeza | 126 | 101,700 | 1985 | Creme Fraiche | Eddie Maple | 126 | 307,740 |
| 1964 | Quadrangle | M. Ycaza | 126 | 110,850 | 1986 | Danzig Connection | C. McCarron | 126 | 338,640 |

## TRIPLE CROWN RACES—1986

(For 3-year-olds, carrying 126 pounds; jockeys in parenthesis)

**Kentucky Derby** (Churchill Downs, Louisville, Ky., May 3, 1986; gross purse: $784,400; 1 1/4 miles)—1. Ferdinand (Shoemaker); mutual returns: $37.40, 16.20, 8.60. 2. Bold Arrangement (McCarron) 9.40, 6.80. 3. Broad Brush (Bracciale) 9.20. 4. Rampage (Day). 5. Badger Land (Velasquez). 6. Wheatley Hall (Stevens). 7. Fobby Forbes (Romero). 8. Icy Groom (Maple). 9. Wise Times (Allen). 10. Mogambo (Vasquez). 11. Snow Chief (Solis). 12. Zabaleta (McHargue). 13. Southern Appeal (Davidson). 14. Bachelor Beau (Melancon). 15. Vernon Castle (Delahoussaye). 16. Groovy (Pincay, Jr.). Time: 2:02 4/5. Winner's purse: $609,400. Margin of victory: 2 1/4 lengths. Attendance: 123,819.

**Preakness Stakes** (Pimlico, Md., May 17, 1986; gross purse: $534, 400; 1 3/16 miles)—1. Snow Chief (Solis); mutual returns: $7.20, $4.80, $3.60. 2. Ferdinand (Shoemaker), 4.80, 3.20. 3. Broad Brush (McCarron) 3.00. 4. Badger Land (Velasquez). 5. Miracle Wood (Miller, Jr.). 6. Groovy (Perret). 7. Clear Choice (Vasquez). Time: 1:54 4/5. Winner's purse: $411,900. Margin of victory: 4 lengths. Attendance: 87,652.

**Belmont Stakes** (Elmont, N.Y., June 7, 1986; gross purse: $564,400, 1 1/2 miles)—1. Danzig Connection (McCarron); mutual return: $18.00, 8.20, 5.40. 2. Johns Treasure (Pincay, Jr.) 6.40, 4.60. 3. Ferdinand (Shoemaker) 3.80. 4. Personal Flag (Velasquez). 5. Fobby Forbes (Bracciale). 6. Mogambo (Santos). 7. Rampage (Day). 8. Bordeaux Box (Maple). 9. Parade Marshal (Bailey). 10. Imperious

Spirit (Hernandez). Time: 2:29 4/5. Winner's purse: $338,640. Margin of victory: 1 1/2 lengths. Attendance: 43,157.

## ECLIPSE AWARDS—1986

The Eclipse Awards in thoroughbred racing are given on the basis of voting by three groups: The Daily Racing Form, the National Turf Writers Association, and the racing secretaries at tracks who are members of the Thoroughbred Racing Association.

| | |
|---|---|
| Horse of the Year | Spend A Buck |
| 2-year-old colt | Tasso |
| 2-year-old filly | Family Style |
| 3-year-old colt | Spend A Buck |
| 3-year-old filly | Mom's Command |
| Older colt or gelding | Vanlandingham |
| Older filly or mare | Life's Magic |
| Male turf horse | Cozzene |
| Female turf horse | Pebbles |
| Sprinter | Precisionist |
| Steeplechase | Flatterer |
| Owner | Eugene V. and Joyce Klein |
| Trainer | D. Wayne Lukas |
| Jockey | Laffit Pincay, Jr. |
| Apprentice jockey | Art Madrid, Jr. |
| Breeder | Nelson Bunker Hunt |

## When Is a Horse a Horse?

Terms by which a horse is known in racing, as explained by John I. Day of the Thoroughbred Racing Associations: a *foal* is a young horse of either sex and while unweaned is known as a *suckling*. When separated from his *dam*, or maternal parent, he is a *weanling* until Jan. 1 following his birth, when he becomes a *yearling*. He may be a *colt*, if male, and remain so (unless he becomes a *gelding*, or unsexed) until he is 5 years old; or, if female, a *filly* until 5. From 5 on, they are *horses* or *mares* and when they become parents, *sires* or *dams*.

## Origin of Individual Racing Silks

The practice of using individual racing silks to distinguish horses is over 200 years old. They were first introduced in October 1762 at Newmarket, England, when a group of sportsmen conceived the unique idea. In the quaint phraseology of the time, "for the greater convenience of distinguishing horses in the running, as also for the prevention of disputes arising from not knowing the colours worn by riders, seventeen gentlemen came to the decision to register their colours," and the stewards of the Newmarket meeting "hoped" in the name of the Jockey Club that the gentlemen "would take care that their riders be provided with dresses accordingly." Lord Grosvenor, the Lord Derby of that day, chose orange as his color.

# TRACK AND FIELD

Running, jumping, hurdling and throwing weights—track and field sports, in other words—are as natural to young people as eating, drinking and breathing. Unorganized competition in this form of sport goes back beyond the Cave Man era. Organized competition begins with the first recorded Olympic Games in Greece, 776 B.C., when Coroebus of Elis won the only event on the program, a race of approximately 200 yards. The Olympic Games, with an ever-widening program of events, continued until "the glory that was Greece" had faded and "the grandeur that was Rome" was tarnished, and finally were abolished by decree of Emperor Theodosius I of Rome in A.D. 394. The Tailteann Games of Ireland are supposed to have antedated the first Olympic Games by some centuries, but we have no records of the specific events and winners thereof.

Professional contests of speed and strength were popular at all times and in many lands, but the widespread competition of amateur athletes in track and field sports is a comparatively modern development. The first organized amateur athletic meet of record was sponsored by the Royal Military Academy at Woolwich, England, in 1849. Oxford and Cambridge track and field rivalry began in 1864, and the English amateur championships were established in 1866. In the United States such organizations as the New York Athletic Club and the Olympic Club of San Francisco conducted track and field meets in the 1870s, and a few colleges joined to sponsor a meet in 1874. The success of the college meet led to the formation of the Intercollegiate Association of Amateur Athletes of America and the holding of an annual set of championship games beginning in 1876. The Amateur Athletic Union, organized in 1888, has been the ruling body in American amateur athletics since that time. In 1980, The Athletics Congress of the U.S.A. took over the governing of track and field from the A.A.U.

## WORLD RECORDS—MEN

(Through Sept. 8, 1986)
Recognized by the International Athletic Federation.
The I.A.A.F. decided late in 1976 not to recognize records in yards except for the one-mile run.
The I.A.A.F. also requires automatic timing for all records for races of 400 meters or less.

| Event | Record | Holder | Home Country | Where Made | Date |
|---|---|---|---|---|---|
| **Running** | | | | | |
| 100 m | 0:09.93 | Calvin Smith | U.S. | Colorado Springs | July 3, 1983 |
| 200 m | 0:19.72 | Pietro Mennea | Italy | Mexico City | Sept. 17, 1979 |
| 400 m | 0:43.86 | Lee Evans | U.S. | Mexico City | Oct. 18, 1968 |
| 800 m | 1:41.8 | Sebastian Coe | England | Florence, Italy | June 10, 1981 |
| 1,000 m | 2:12.40 | Sebastian Coe | England | Oslo, Norway | July 11, 1981 |
| 1,500 m | 3:29.45 | Said Aouita | Morocco | Berlin | August 23, 1985 |
| 1 mile | 3:46.31 | Steve Cram | Great Britain | Oslo | July 27, 1985 |
| 2,000 m | 4:51.39 | Steve Cram | Great Britain | Budapest | August 4, 1985 |
| 3,000 m | 7:32.1 | Henry Rono | Kenya | Oslo | June 27, 1978 |
| 3,000-m steeplechase | 8:05.1 | Henry Rono | Kenya | Seattle, Wash. | May 13, 1978 |
| 5,000 m | 13:00.40 | Said Aouita | Morocco | Oslo | July 27, 1985 |
| 10,000 m | 27:13.81 | Fernando Mamede | Portugal | Stockholm, Swe. | July 2, 1984 |
| 25,000 m | 1:13:55.8 | Toshihiko Seko | Japan | Christchurch, N.Z. | March 22, 1981 |
| 30,000 m | 1:29:18.8 | Toshihiko Seko | Japan | Christchurch, N.Z. | March 22, 1981 |
| 20,000 m | 57:24.2 | Jos Hermans | Netherlands | Papandal, Neth. | May 1, 1976 |
| 1 hour | 13 mi. 24 yd | Jos Hermans | Netherlands | Papandal, Neth. | May 1, 1976 |
| Marathon | 2:07:11.0 | Carlos Lopes | Portugal | Rotterdam | April 20, 1985 |
| **Walking** | | | | | |
| 20,000 m | 1:18:39.9 | Ernesto Canto | Mexico | Fana, Norway | May 5, 1984 |
| 2 hours | 17 mi. 1,092 yd | Ralph Kowalsky | East Germany | East Berlin | March 28, 1982 |
| 30,000 m walk | 2:06:27.0 | Maurizio Damilano | Italy | Milanese, Italy | May 5, 1985 |
| 50,000 m | 3:41.39 | Raul Gonzales | Mexico | Bergen, Norway | May 25, 1979 |
| **Hurdles** | | | | | |
| 110 m | 0:12.93 | Renaldo Nehemiah | U.S. | Zurich, Switzerland | Aug. 19, 1981 |
| 400 m | 0:47.02 | Edwin Moses | U.S. | Koblenz, W. Ger. | Aug. 31, 1983 |
| **Relay Races** | | | | | |
| 400 m (4×100) | 0:37.83 | Olympic Team | U.S. | Los Angeles, Ca. | Aug. 11, 1984 |
| 800 m (4×200) | 1:20.26 | So. California | U.S. | Tempe, Ariz. | May 27, 1978 |
| | | (Joel Andrews, James Sanford, Billy Mullins, Clancy Edwards) | | | |
| 1,600 m (4×400) | 2:56.16 | National Team | U.S. | Mexico City | Oct. 20, 1968 |
| | | (Vince Matthews, Ron Freeman, Larry James, Lee Evans) | | | |
| 3,200 m (4×800) | 7:03.89 | National Team | Britain | London | Aug. 30, 1982 |
| | | (Peter Elliot, Garry Cook, Steve Cram, Sebastian Coe) | | | |

## Field Events

| | | | | |
|---|---|---|---|---|
| High Jump | 7 ft 10 1/2 in. | Rudolf Povarnitsin | U.S.S.R. | Donetsk | August 11, 1985 |
| Long jump | 29 ft 2 1/2 in. | Bob Beamon | U.S. | Mexico City | Oct. 18, 1968 |
| Triple Jump | 58 ft 11 1/2 in. | Willie Banks | Los Angeles, Calif. | Indianapolis | June 16, 1985 |
| Pole vault | 19 ft 8 1/2 in. | Sergey Bubka | U.S.S.R. | Moscow | July 8, 1986 |
| Shot put | 74 ft 3 1/2 in. | Udo Beyer | E. Germany | Berlin | Aug. 20, 1986 |
| Discus throw | 243 ft 0 in. | Juergen Schult | East Germany | Neubrandenburg | June 6, 1986 |
| Hammer throw | 284 ft 7 in. | Yuriy Syedikh | U.S.S.R. | Stuttgart | Aug. 28, 1986 |
| Javelin throw | 343 ft 10 in. | Uwe Hohn | E. Germany | Oslo, Norway | July 20, 1984 |
| Decathlon | 8,798pts. | Jurgen Hingsen | W. Germany | Mannheim, W. Ger. | June 8-9, 1984 |

## WORLD RECORDS—WOMEN

| Event | Record | Holder | Home Country | Where Made | Date |
|---|---|---|---|---|---|
| **Running** | | | | | |
| 100 m | 0:10.76 | Evelyn Ashford | U.S. | Zurich, Switz. | Aug. 22, 1984 |
| 200 m | 0:21.71 | Heike Drechsler | East Germany | Stuttgart | Aug. 28, 1986 |
| 400 m | 0:47.99 | Jarmila Kratochvilova | Czechoslovakia | Helsinki, Fin. | Aug. 10, 1983 |
| 800 m | 1:53.28 | Jarmila Kratochvilova | Czechoslovakia | Munich, W. Ger. | July 26, 1983 |
| 1,500 m | 3:52.47 | Tatyana Kazankina | U.S.S.R. | Zurich, Switz. | Aug. 13, 1980 |
| 1 mile | 4:16.71 | Mary Decker Slaney | U.S.A. | Zurich | Aug. 21, 1985 |
| 3,000 m | 8:22.62 | Tatyana Kazankina | U.S.S.R. | Moscow | Aug. 26, 1984 |
| 5,000 m | 14:37.33 | Ingrid Kristiansen | Norway | Stockholm | Aug. 5, 1986 |
| 10,000 m | 30:13.74 | Ingrid Kristiansen | Norway | Oslo | July 5, 1986 |
| Marathon | 2:21:06.0 | Ingrid Kristiansen | Norway | London | April 21, 1985 |
| **Hurdles** | | | | | |
| 100 m | 0:12.36 | Yordanka Donkova | Bulgaria | Sofia | Aug. 13, 1986 |
| 400 m | 0:53.33 | Maria Stepanova | U.S.S.R. | Stuttgart | Aug. 28, 1986 |
| **Relay Races** | | | | | |
| 400 m (4×100) | 0:41.53 | East Germany | E. Germany | Berlin, E. Ger. | July 31, 1983 |
| 800 m (4×200) | 1:28.15 | East Germany | E. Germany | Jena, E. Ger. | Aug. 9, 1980 |
| 1,600 m (4×400) | 3:15.92 | East Germany | E. Germany | Erfurt, E. Ger. | June 3, 1984 |
| 3,200 m (4×800) | 7:52.3 | U.S.S.R. | U.S.S.R. | Podolsk, U.S.S.R. | Aug. 16, 1976 |
| **Field Events** | | | | | |
| High jump | 6 ft 9 3/4 in. | Stefka Kostadinova | Bulgaria | Sofia | May 25, 1986 |
| Long jump | 24 ft 5 1/2 in. | Heike Drechsler | East Germany | Dresden | July 3, 1986 |
| Triple jump | 44 ft 6 3/4 in. | Wendy Brown | U.S. | Austin, Tex. | May 30, 1985 |
| Shot put | 73 ft 11 in. | Natalya Lisovskaya | U.S.S.R. | Sochi, U.S.S.R. | May 27, 1984 |
| Discus throw | 254 ft 1 in. | Fatima Whitbread | East Germany | Stuttgart | Aug. 28, 1986 |
| Javelin throw | 247 ft 4 in. | Petra Felke | East Germany | Schwerin, E. Ger. | June 4, 1985 |
| Heptathlon | 7,161 pts | Jackie Joyner | United States | Houston, Tex. | Aug 1-2, 1986 |

## AMERICAN RECORDS—MEN

(Through Sept. 8, 1986)
Officially approved by The Athletics Congress.

| Event | Record | Holder | Where Made | Date |
|---|---|---|---|---|
| **Running** | | | | |
| 100 m | 0:09.93 | Calvin Smith | Colorado Springs, Colo. | July 3, 1983 |
| 200 m | 0:19.75 | Carl Lewis | Indianapolis, Ind. | June 19, 1983 |
| 400 m | 0:43.86 | Lee Evans | Mexico City | Oct. 16, 1968 |
| 800 m | 1:42.69 | Johnny Gray | Koblenz, W. Ger. | Aug. 29, 1985 |
| 1,000 m | 2:13.9 | Richard Wohlhuter | Oslo, Norway | July 30, 1974 |
| 1,500 m | 3:29.77 | Sydney Maree | Cologne, W. Ger. | Aug. 25, 1985 |
| 1 mile | 3:47.69 | Steve Scott | Oslo, Norway | July 7, 1982 |
| 2,000 m | 4:54.71 | Steve Scott | Ingelhelm, W. Ger. | Aug. 31, 1982 |
| 3,000 m | 7:35.84 | Doug Padilla | Oslo, Norway | July 9, 1983 |
| 5,000 m | 13:01.15 | Sydney Maree | Oslo, Norway | July 27, 1985 |
| 10,000 m | 27:20.56 | Mark Nenow | Brussels | Sept. 5, 1986 |
| 20,000 m | 58:15.0 | Bill Rodgers | Boston, Mass. | Aug. 9, 1977 |
| 25,000 m | 1:14:11.8 | Bill Rodgers | Saratoga, Cal. | Feb. 21, 1979 |
| 30,000 m | 1:31.49 | Bill Rodgers | Saratoga, Cal. | Feb. 21, 1979 |
| 1 hour | 12 mi., 1351 yds | Bill Rodgers | Boston, Mass. | Aug. 9, 1977 |
| 3,000-m steeplechase | 8:09.17 | Henry Marsh | Koblenz, W. Ger. | Aug. 29, 1985 |

## Hurdles

| | | | | |
|---|---|---|---|---|
| 110 m | 0:12.93 | Renaldo Nehemiah | Zurich, Switz. | Aug. 19, 1981 |
| 400 m | 0:47.02 | Edwin Moses | Koblenz, W. Ger. | Aug. 31, 1983 |

## Relay Races

| | | | | |
|---|---|---|---|---|
| 400 m (4×100) | 0:37.83 | U.S. Olympic Team | Los Angeles, Cal. | Aug. 11, 1984 |
| 800 m (4×200) | 1:20.26 | Southern California | Tempe, Ariz. | May 27, 1978 |
| 1,600 m (4×400) | 2:56.16 | U.S. Olympic Team | Mexico City | Oct. 20, 1968 |
| 3,200 m (4×800) | 7:06.50 | Santa Monica Track Club | Walnut | Apr. 26, 1986 |

## Field Events

| | | | | |
|---|---|---|---|---|
| High jump | 7 ft 8 1/2 in. | Jim Howard | Houston, Texas | May 25, 1985 |
| Long jump | 29 ft 2 1/2 in. | Bob Beamon | Mexico City | Oct. 18, 1968 |
| Triple jump | 58 ft 11 1/2 in. | Willie Banks | Indianapolis, Ind. | June 16, 1985 |
| Pole vault | 19 ft 4 1/4 in. | Joe Dial | Norman, Okla. | April 25, 1986 |
| Shot put | 72 ft 9 3/4 in. | Brian Oldfield | San Jose, Cal. | May 26, 1984 |
| Discus throw | 237 ft 4 in. | Ben Plucknett | Stockholm, Swe. | July 7, 1981 |
| Javelin throw | 327 ft 2 in. | Tom Petranoff | Los Angeles, Cal. | May 15, 1983 |
| Hammer throw | 265 ft 4 in. | Jud Logan | Walnut | April 27, 1986 |
| Decathlon | 8,617 pts | Bruce Jenner | Montreal, Can. | July 29–30, 1976 |

## AMERICAN RECORDS—WOMEN

| Event | Record | Holder | Where Made | Date |
|---|---|---|---|---|
| **Running** | | | | |
| 100 m | 0:10.76 | Evelyn Ashford | Zurich, Switz. | Aug. 22, 1984 |
| 200 m | 0:21.81 | Valerie Brisco-Hooks | Los Angeles, Cal. | Aug. 9, 1984 |
| 400 m | 0:48.83 | Valerie Brisco-Hooks | Los Angeles, Cal. | Aug. 6, 1984 |
| 800 m | 1:56.90 | Mary Decker Slaney | Bern | Aug. 16, 1985 |
| 1,500 m | 3:57.12 | Mary Decker Slaney | Stockholm, Swe. | July 26, 1983 |
| 1000 m | 2:34.8 | Mary Decker Slaney | Eugene, Ore. | July 4, 1985 |
| 1 mile | 4:16.71 | Mary Decker Slaney | Zurich | Aug. 21, 1985 |
| 3,000 m | 8:29.69 | Mary Decker Slaney | Cologne | Aug. 25, 1985 |
| 5,000 m | 15:06.53 | Mary Decker Slaney | Eugene, Ore. | June 1, 1985 |
| 10,000 m | 31:35.3 | Mary Decker Slaney | Eugene, Ore. | July 16, 1982 |

### Hurdles

| | | | | |
|---|---|---|---|---|
| 100 m | 12.79 | Stephanie Hightower | Karl-Marx-Stadt, E. Ger. | July 10, 1982 |
| 400 m hurdle | :54.66 | Latanya Sheffield | Austin, Tex. | May 31, 1985 |

### Relay Races

| | | | | |
|---|---|---|---|---|
| 400 m (4×100) | 0:41.61 | U.S. National Team | Colorado Springs, Col. | July 3, 1983 |
| 800 m (4×200) | 1:32.6 | U.S. National Team | Bourges, France | June 24, 1979 |
| 1,600 m (4×400) | 3:18.29 | U.S. Olympic Team | Los Angeles, Cal. | Aug. 11, 1984 |

### Field Events

| | | | | |
|---|---|---|---|---|
| High jump | 6 ft 7 in. | Louise Ritter | Rome, Italy | Sept. 1, 1983 |
| Long jump | 23 ft 9 in. | Jackie Joyner | Zurich | Aug. 21, 1985 |
| Triple jump | 44 ft 9 3/4 in. | Terri Turner | Indianapolis, Ind. | June 5–7, 1986 |
| Shot put | 62 ft 9 1/4 in. | Ramona Pagel | Los Angeles, Calif. | May 26, 1985 |
| Discus throw | 216 ft 10 in. | Carol Cady | San Jose, Calif. | May 31, 1986 |
| Javelin throw | 227 ft 5 in. | Kate Schmidt | Furth, W. Ger. | Sept. 10, 1977 |
| Heptathlon | 7,161 pts | Jackie Joyner | Moscow | July 6–7, 1986 |

## HISTORY OF THE RECORD FOR THE MILE RUN

| Time | Athlete | Country | Year | Location |
|---|---|---|---|---|
| 4:36.5 | Richard Webster | England | 1865 | England |
| 4:29.0 | William Chinnery | England | 1868 | England |
| 4:28.8 | Walter Gibbs | England | 1868 | England |
| 4:26.0 | Walter Slade | England | 1874 | England |
| 4:24.5 | Walter Slade | England | 1875 | London |

| 4:23.2 | Walter George | England | 1880 | London |
|---|---|---|---|---|
| 4:21.4 | Walter George | England | 1882 | London |
| 4:18.4 | Walter George | England | 1884 | Birmingham, England |
| 4:18.2 | Fred Bacon | Scotland | 1894 | Edinburgh, Scotland |
| 4:17.0 | Fred Bacon | Scotland | 1895 | London |
| 4:15.6 | Thomas Conneff | United States | 1895 | Travers Island, N.Y. |
| 4:15.4 | John Paul Jones | United States | 1911 | Cambridge, Mass. |
| 4:14.4 | John Paul Jones | United States | 1913 | Cambridge, Mass. |
| 4:12.6 | Norman Taber | United States | 1915 | Cambridge, Mass. |
| 4:10.4 | Paavo Nurmi | Finland | 1923 | Stockholm |
| 4:09.2 | Jules Ladoumegue | France | 1931 | Paris |
| 4:07.6 | Jack Lovelock | New Zealand | 1933 | Princeton, N.J. |
| 4:06.8 | Glenn Cunningham | United States | 1934 | Princeton, N.J. |
| 4:06.4 | Sydney Wooderson | England | 1937 | London |
| 4:06.2 | Gundar Hägg | Sweden | 1942 | Göteborg, Sweden |
| 4:06.2 | Arne Andersson | Sweden | 1942 | Stockholm |
| 4:04.6 | Gunder Hägg | Sweden | 1942 | Stockholm |
| 4:02.6 | Arne Andersson | Sweden | 1943 | Göteborg, Sweden |
| 4:01.6 | Arne Andersson | Sweden | 1944 | Malmö, Sweden |
| 4:01.4 | Gunder Hägg | Sweden | 1945 | Malmö, Sweden |
| 3:59.4 | Roger Bannister | England | 1954 | Oxford, England |
| 3:58.0 | John Landy | Australia | 1954 | Turku, Finland |
| 3:57.2 | Derek Ibbotson | England | 1957 | London |
| 3:54.5 | Herb Elliott | Australia | 1958 | Dublin |
| 3:54.4 | Peter Snell | New Zealand | 1962 | Wanganui, N.Z. |
| 3:54.1 | Peter Snell | New Zealand | 1964 | Auckland, N.Z. |
| 3:53.6 | Michel Jazy | France | 1965 | Rennes, France |
| 3:51.3 | Jim Ryun | United States | 1966 | Berkeley, Calif. |
| 3:51.1 | Jim Ryun | United States | 1967 | Bakersfield, Calif. |
| 3:51.0 | Filbert Bayi | Tanzania | 1975 | Kingston, Jamaica |
| 3:49.4 | John Walker | New Zealand | 1975 | Göteborg, Sweden |
| 3:49.0 | Sebastian Coe | England | 1979 | Oslo |
| 3:48.8 | Steve Ovett | England | 1980 | Oslo |
| 3:48.53 | Sebastian Coe | England | 1981 | Zurich, Switzerland |
| 3:48.40 | Steve Ovett | England | 1981 | Koblenz, W. Ger. |
| 3:47.33 | Sebastian Coe | England | 1981 | Brussels |
| 3:46.31 | Steve Cram | England | 1985 | Oslo |

## TOP TEN WORLD'S FASTEST INDOOR MILES

| Time | Athlete | Country | Date | Location |
|---|---|---|---|---|
| 3:49.78 | Eamonn Coghlan | Ireland | Feb. 27, 1983 | East Rutherford, N.J. |
| 3:50.6 | Eamonn Coghlan | Ireland | Feb. 20, 1981 | San Diego |
| 3:51.2 | Ray Flynn[1] | Ireland | Feb. 27, 1983 | East Rutherford, N.J. |
| 3:51.8 | Steve Scott[1] | United States | Feb. 20, 1981 | San Diego |
| 3:52.28 | Steve Scott[2] | United States | Feb. 27, 1983 | East Rutherford, N.J. |
| 3:52:30 | Frank O'Mara | Ireland | Feb. , 1986 | New York |
| 3:52.37 | Eamonn Coughlan | Ireland | Feb. 9, 1985 | East Rutherford, N.J. |
| 3:52.40 | Sydney Maree | United States | Feb. 9, 1985 | East Rutherford, N.J. |
| 3:52.56 | Jose Abascal[3] | Spain | Feb. 27, 1983 | East Rutherford, N.J. |
| 3:52.6 | Eamonn Coghlan | Ireland | Feb. 16, 1979 | San Diego |
| 3:52.8 | John Walker[2] | New Zealand | Feb. 20, 1981 | San Diego |

1. Finished second. 2. Finished third. 3. Finished fourth. 4. Finished fifth.

## TOP TEN WORLD'S FASTEST OUTDOOR MILES

| Time | Athlete | Country | Date | Location |
|---|---|---|---|---|
| 3:46.31 | Steve Cram | England | July 27, 1985 | Oslo |
| 3:47.33 | Sebastian Coe | England | Aug. 28, 1981 | Brussels |
| 3:47.69 | Steve Scott | United States | July 7, 1982 | Oslo |
| 3:47.79 | Jose Gonzalez | Spain | July 27, 1985 | Oslo |
| 3:48.40 | Steve Ovett | England | Aug. 26, 1981 | Koblenz, W. Ger. |
| 3:48.53 | Sebastian Coe | England | Aug. 19, 1981 | Zurich |
| 3:48.53 | Steve Scott | United States | June 26, 1982 | Oslo |
| 3:48.8 | Steve Ovett | England | July 1, 1980 | Oslo |
| 3:48.83 | Sydney Maree | United States | Sept. 9, 1981 | Rieti, Italy |
| 3:48.85 | Sydney Maree[1] | United States | June 26, 1982 | Oslo |

1. Finished second. NOTE: Professional marks not included.

## TOP TEN POLE VAULT DISTANCES

(Some of early dates are the winning heights of A.A.U. champion for that year, used to show progression from one foot level to the next. Figures from A.A.U. records and *Track & Field News*.)

**Fiberglas Poles**

| | | | | | |
|---|---|---|---|---|---|
| 1986 | Sergey Bubka | 19 ft 8 1/2 in. | 1984 | Sergey Bubka | 19 ft 3 1/2 in. |
| 1985 | Sergey Bubka | 19 ft 8 1/4 in. | 1984 | Sergey Bubka | 19 ft 2 1/4 in. |
| 1984 | Sergey Bubka | 19 ft 5 3/4 in. | 1984 | Sergey Bubka | 19 ft 1 1/2 in. |
| 1984 | Thierry Vigneron | 19 ft 4 3/4 in. | 1983 | Thierry Vigneron | 19 ft 1 1/2 in. |
| 1984 | Sergey Bubka | 19 ft 4 1/4 in. | 1981 | Vladimir Polyokov | 19 ft 3/4 in. |

## THE ATHLETIC CONGRESS NATIONAL CHAMPIONSHIPS INDOOR

(Madison Square Garden, New York, Feb. 28, 1986)

### Men's Events

| | |
|---|---|
| 60 yd—Lee McRae, Pittsburgh | 0:06.06 |
| 440 yd—Antonio McKay, Mazda Track Club | 0:47.60 |
| 600 yd—Elvis Forde, Atlantic Coast Club | 1:08.28 |
| 1,000 yd—Johnny Gray, Santa Monica Track Club | 2:04.52 |
| Mile—Marcus O'Sullivan, New Balance Track Club | 3:57.27 |
| 3-miles—Doug Padilla, Athletics West | 13:05.58 |
| 60 yd hurdles—Mark McKoy, Pacific Coast Club | 0:06.95 |
| 2-mile walk—Jim Heiring, Track America | 12:05.94[1] |
| Sprint Medley relay—Karamu Flyers | 2:01.96 |
| Mile relay—Seton Hall | 3:11.92 |
| 2-mile relay—Westchester Puma Track Club | 7:33.18 |
| High jump—Jim Howard, Pacific Coast Club | 7 ft. 8 in. |
| Pole vault—Sergey Bubka, U.S.S.R. | 19 ft 6 1/4 in.[1] |
| Triple jump—Mike Conley, Tyson International | 56 ft 10 1/4 in. |
| Long jump—Mike Conley, Tyson International | 27 ft 1 3/4 in. |
| Shot put—Greg Tafralis, New York Athletic Club | 68 ft 11 1/4 in. |
| 35-pound weight throw—Jud Logan, New York Athletic Club | 77 ft 1 1/4 in. |
| Team—New York Athletic Club | 18 points |

### Women's Events

| | |
|---|---|
| 60 yd—Jeannette Bolden, World Class Athletic Club | 0:06.57 |
| 220 yd—Marita Koch, East Germany | 0:22.89 |
| 440 yd—Diane Dixon, Atoms Track Club | 0:52.52 |
| 880 yd—Siggun Ludwigs, East Germany | 2:05.93 |
| Mile—Maricica Puica, Romania | 4:35.00 |
| 2-mile—Lynn Jennings, Athletics West | 9:28.15 |
| 60 yd hurdles—Stephania Hightower, Columbus, Ohio | 0:07.44 |
| Mile walk—Teresa Vaill, Pine Plains, N.Y. | 6:53.58 |
| 640 yd relay—Tennessee State | 1:11.59 |
| 880 yd relay—Tennessee State | 1:43.71 |
| Mile relay—Atoms Track Club | 3:44.23 |
| High jump—Debbie Brill, Pacific Coast Club | 6 ft, 5 1/2 inches |
| Long jump—Heike Dreshsler, East Germany | 23 ft, 0 3/4 in. |
| Team—Atoms Track Club | 13 points |

1. World indoor record.

## THE ATHLETICS CONGRESS NATIONAL CHAMPIONSHIPS—1986

(Eugene, Oregon, June 18-21, 1986)

### OUTDOOR

#### Men's Events

| | |
|---|---|
| 100 m—Carl Lewis, Santa Monica T.C. | 0:09.91 |
| 200 m—Floyd Heard, Texas A&M | 0:20.03 |
| 400 m—Darrell Robinson, Mazda T.C. | 0:44.47 |
| 800 m—Johnny Gray, Santa Monica T.C. | 1:44.73 |
| 1,500 m—Steve Scott, Tiger T.C. | 3:42.41 |
| 3000 m—Henry Marsh, Athletics West | 8:19.16 |
| 5,000 m—Doug Padilla, Athletics West | 13:46.69 |
| 10,000 m—Gerry Donakowski, Athletics West | 28:21.11 |
| 110 m hurdles—Greg Foster, World Class A.C. | 0:13.26 |
| 400 m hurdles—Danny Harris, Athletics West | 0:48.90 |
| 20,000 m walk—Tim Lewis, New York A.C. | 1:25:22 |
| High jump—Doug Nordquist, Tiger T.C. | 7 ft 7 3/4 in. |
| Pole Vault—Mike Tully, New York A.C. | 19 ft 0 1/4 in. |
| Long jump—Carl Lewis, Santa Monica T.C. | 28 ft 5 1/2 in. |
| Triple jump—Charlie Simpkins, Team Nike | 58 ft 9 1/4 in. |
| Shot put—John Brenner, Mazda T.C. | 69 ft 2 1/2 in. |
| Discus throw—John Powell, Mazda T.C. | 216 ft 4 in. |
| Hammer throw—Bill Green, Mazda T.C. | 250 ft 0 in. |
| Javelin throw—Tom Petranoff, Athletics West | 250 ft 5 in. |
| Decathlon—Dave Johnson, Puma T.C.—8,203 points | |
| Team—Athletics West | 88 points |

#### Women's Events

| | |
|---|---|
| 100 m—Pam Marshall, Mazda T.C. | 0:10.80 |
| 200 m—Pam Marshall, Mazda T.C. | 0:22.24 |
| 400 m—Diane Dixon, Atoms T.C. | 0:50.41 |
| 800 m—Claudette Groenendaal, Athletics West | 1:59.79 |
| 1,500 m—Linda Detlefsen, Athletics West | 4:08.00 |
| 3,000 m—Mary Knisely, New Balance T.C. | 8:46.18 |
| 5,000 m—Betty Springs, Athletics West | 15:30.99 |
| 10,000 m—Nanette Doak, Athletics West | 32.29.86 |
| 100 m hurdles—Benita Fitzgerald—Brown, Mazda T.C. | 0:12.83 |
| 400 m hurdles—Judi Brown-King, Athletics West | 0:55.46 |
| 10,000 m walk—Debbie Lawrence, Overland Park, Kansas | 50:28.86 |
| 400 yd relay—cancelled | |
| 4 × 440 yd relay—cancelled | |
| 4 × 880 yd relay—Club Northwest | 8:45.9 |
| 800 m sprint relay—Southern California | 1:40.1 |
| High jump—Louise Ritter, Pacific Coast Club | 6 ft 4 in. |
| Long jump—Carol Lewis, Santa Monica T.C. | 22 ft 9 in. |
| Triple jump—Wendy Brown, Puma T.C. | 45 ft 2 1/2 in. |
| Shot put—Ramona Pagel, Mazda T.C. | 61 ft 1 1/2 in. |
| Discus throw—Carol Cady, Stanford T.C. | 205 ft 9 in. |

Javelin throw—Helena Uusitalo, Washington    191 ft 9 in.
Heptathlon—Jane Frederick, Athletics West    6,230 points
Team—Athletics West    85 points

Triple jump—Kenny Harrison, Kansas    56 ft. 0 in.
Discus—Olay Jenssen, Texas-El Paso    198 ft, 2 in.
Shot put—Lars Nelson, Southern Methodist    21.2 meters
Javelin—Dag Wennlund, Texas–Austin    78.86 meters
Hammer throw—Ken Flax, Oregon    257 ft, 0 in.[1]
Decathlon—Mike Ramos, Washington    8,261 points[1]
Team—Southern Methodist
    Washington State

1. Collegiate record.

## N.C.A.A. CHAMPIONSHIPS—1986

### INDOOR

(Oklahoma City, Okla., March 14-15, 1986)

#### Men's Events

| | |
|---|---|
| 55 m—Lee McRae, Pittsburgh | 0:05.99 |
| 55 m hurdles—Tom Wilcher, Michigan | 0:07.22 |
| 500 m—Roddie Haley, Arkansas | 0:59.82 |
| 1,000 m—Freddie Williams | 2:18.74 |
| 3,000 m—Paul Donovan, Arkansas | 7:54.60 |
| Mile—Paul Larkin, Oklahoma State | 4:01.38 |
| 1,600 m relay—Southern Methodist | 3:06.24 |
| 3,200 m relay—Arkansas | 7:20.72 |
| High jump—James Lott, Texas | 7 ft, 5 in. |
| Triple jump—Frank Rutherford, Houston | 55 ft. 9 in. |
| Long jump—Ken Harrison, Kansas State | 8.17 meters |
| Pole vault—Doug Fraley, Fresno St. | 18 ft 3 3/4 in. |
| Shotput—Ronald Backes, Minnesota | 68 ft., 11 1/4 in. |
| Team—Arkansas | 49 points |
|     Villanova | 22 points |
| Division III Team—Frostburg State, Maryland | |

#### Women's Events

| | |
|---|---|
| 55 m—Gwen Torrence, Georgia | 0:06.62 |
| 55 m hurdles—Rosalind Pendergraft-Council, Auburn | 0:07.53 |
| 500 m—Ilrey Oliver, Tennessee | 1:09.68 |
| 1,000 m—Karol Davidson, Texas | 2:42.68 |
| Mile—Elizabeth Lynch, Alabama | 4:37.73 |
| 3,000 m—Stephania Herbst, Wisconsin | 8:54.98 |
| 1,600 m relay—Tennessee-Knoxville | 3:34.19 |
| 3,200 m relay—Florida | 8:31.74 |
| Long jump—Cynthia Henry, Texas-El Paso | 5.56 meter |
| Triple jump—Wendy Brown, Southern California | 44 ft., 3 1/4 in. |
| Shotput—Regina Cavanough, Rice | 17.67 meters |
| Team—Alabama | 41 points |
|     Texas | 31 points |
| Division III Team—University of Massachusettes at Boston | |

### OUTDOOR

(Indianapolis, Ind., June 4-7, 1986)

#### Men's Events

| | |
|---|---|
| 100 m—Lee McRae, Pittsburgh | 0:10.11 |
| 200 m—Floyd Herd, Texas A&M | 0:20.34 |
| 400 m—Gabriel Tiacoh, Washington St. | 0:44.30[1] |
| 800 m—Fred Williams, Abilene Christian | 1:46.61 |
| 1,500 m—Dub Myers, Oregon | 3:41.72 |
| 3,000 m—Julius Korir, Washington St. | 8:21.17 |
| 5,000 m—Terry Brahm, Indiana | 13:56.64 |
| 10,000 m—Keith Hanson, Marquette | 29:02.68 |
| 110 m hurdles—Keith Talley, Alabama | 0:13.36 |
| 1,600 m relay—Southern Methodist | 3:01.62 |
| High jump—James Lott, Texas | 7 ft., 3 in. |
| Long jump—Eric Metcalf, Texas-Austin | 8.24 meters |
| Pole vault—Jeff Pasco, Arkansas | 5.5 meters |

#### Women's Events

| | |
|---|---|
| 100 m—Juliet Cuthbert, Texas | 0:11.27 |
| 200 m—Juliet Cuthbert, Texas | 0:22.71 |
| 400 m—Lillie Leatherwood | 0:51.23 |
| 800 m—Karen Bakewell, Miami–Ohio | 2:00.85 |
| 1,500 m—Alisa Harvey, Tennessee | 4:17.48 |
| 3000 m—Lisa Breizing, Kentucky | 9:11.39 |
| 5,000 m—Stephanie Herbst, Wisconsin | 15:42.36 |
| 100 m hurdles—Rosalind Council, Auburn | 0:13.03 |
| 400 m hurdles—Maria Osifo, Texas Southern | 0:55.16 |
| 400 m relay—Tennessee | 3:29.00 |
| 1,600 m relay—Tennessee | 3:29.35 |
| High jump—Rita Graves, Kansas | 6 ft 2 in. |
| Long jump—Cynthia Henry, Texas-El Paso | 6.54 meters |
| Triple jump—Terri Turner, Texas | 44 ft 9 3/4 in. |
| Shotput—Regina Cavanough, Rice | 17.31 meters |
| Javelin—Helena Uusitalo, Washington | 58.86 meters |
| Discus—Toni Lutiens, UCLA | 183 ft 2 in. |
| Team—Texas | |
|     Alabama | |

## UNITED STATES CROSS COUNTRY CHAMPIONSHIPS—1985

(Raleigh, North Carolina, Nov. 29-30, 1985)

### Men—10,000 meters

| | |
|---|---|
| 1. Pat Porter, Athletics West | 30:33.1 |
| 2. Bruce Bickford, New Balance T.C. | 30:54.4 |
| 3. Ed Eyestone, Reebok R.T. | 31:03.7 |
| 4. Tim Hacker, Wisconsin | 31:12.0 |
| 5. John Esker, Athletics West | 31:13.9 |
| 6. Alan Scharsu, Athletics West | 31:15.7 |
| 7. Brendan Quinn, New Balance T.C. | 31:31.5 |
| 8. Yobes Ondieki, Team Etonic | 31:35.8 |
| 9. Marcus O'Sullivan, New Balance T.C. | 31:36.7 |
| 10. Keith Hanson, Marquette | 31:37.3 |
| Team—Athletics West | |

### Women—5,000 meters

| | |
|---|---|
| 1. Lynn Jennings, Athletics West | 17:27.9 |
| 2. Lesley Welch, Brighton, Mass. | 17:57.6 |
| 3. Christine McMiken, Puma T.C. | 18:07.7 |
| 4. Betty Springs, Athletics West | 18:11.8 |
| 5. Cathy Easker, Athletics West | 18:17.0 |
| 6. Jan Merrill, Age Group AA | 18:24.5 |
| 7. Lisa Welch, Reebok R.C. | 18:26.7 |
| 8. Nan Doak, Athletics West | 18:27.4 |
| 9. Kayla Skelly, Western Michigan | 18:28.6 |
| 10. Patricia Matava, Virginia | 18:29.1 |
| Team—Athletics West | |

# STANDARD MEASUREMENTS IN SPORTS

## BASEBALL

**Home plate to pitcher's box:** 60 feet 6 inches.
**Plate to second base:** 127 feet 3 3/8 inches.
**Distance from base to base (home plate included):** 90 feet.
**Size of bases:** 15 inches by 15 inches.
**Pitcher's plate:** 24 inches by 6 inches.
**Batter's box:** 4 feet by 6 feet.
**Home plate:** 17 inches by 12 inches by 12 inches, cut to a point at rear.
**Home plate to backstop:** Not less than 60 feet (recommended).
**Weight of ball:** Not less than 5 ounces nor more than 5 1/4 ounces.
**Circumference of ball:** Not less than 9 inches nor more than 9 1/4 inches.
**Bat:** Must be round, not over 2 3/4 inches in diameter at thickest part, nor more than 42 inches in length, and of solid wood in one piece or laminated wood.

## BASKETBALL

(National Collegiate A.A. Men's Rules)

**Playing court:** College: 94 feet long by 50 feet wide (ideal dimensions). High School: 84 feet long by 50 feet wide (ideal inside dimensions).
**Baskets:** Rings 18 inches in inside diameter, with white cord 12-mesh nets, 15 to 18 inches in length. Each ring is made of metal, is not more than 5/8 of an inch in diameter, and is bright orange in color.
**Height of basket:** 10 feet (upper edge).
**Weight of ball:** Not less than 20 ounces nor more than 22.
**Circumference of ball:** No greater than 30 inches and not less than 29 1/2.
**Free-throw line:** 15 feet from the face of the backboard, 2 inches wide.

## BOWLING

**Lane dimensions:** Overall length 62 feet 10 3/16 inches, measuring from foul line to pit (not including tail plank), with 1/2 inch tolerance permitted. Foul line to center of No. 1 pinspot 60 feet, with 1/2 inch tolerance permitted. Lane width, 41 1/2 inches with a tolerance of 1/2 inch permitted. Approach, not less than 15 feet. Gutters, 9 5/16 inches wide with 3/16 plus or 5/16 minus tolerances permitted.
**Ball:** Circumference, not more than 27 inches. Weight, 16 pounds maximum.

## BOXING

**Ring:** Professional matches take place in an area not less than 18 nor more than 24 feet square including apron. It is enclosed by four covered ropes, each not less than one inch in diameter. The floor has a 2-inch padding of Ensolite (or equivalent) underneath ring cover that extends at least 6 inches beyond the roped area in the case of elevated rings. For U.S.A./A.B.F. or amateur boxing, not less than 16 nor more than 20 feet square within the ropes. The floor must extend beyond the ring ropes not less than 2 feet. The ring posts shall be connected to the three ring ropes with the extension not shorter than 18 inches and must be properly padded.

**Gloves:** In professional fights, not less than 8-ounce gloves generally are used. U.S.A./A.B.F., 10 ounces for 106 pounds through 156 pounds; 12-ounce for 165 pounds through +201 pounds; for international competition, 8 ounces for lighter classes, 10 ounces for heavier divisions.
**Headguards:** Mandatory in amateur boxing.

## FOOTBALL

(N.C.A.A.)

**Length of field:** 120 yards. (including 10 yards of end zone at each end).
**Width of field:** 53 1/3 yards (160 feet).
**Height of goal posts:** At least 30 feet.
**Height of crossbar:** 10 feet.
**Width of goal posts (above crossbar):** 23 feet 4 inches, inside to inside, and not more than 24 feet, outside to outside.
**Length of ball:** 10 7/8 to 11 7/16 inches (long axis).
**Circumference of ball:** 20 3/4 to 21 1/4 inches (middle); 27 3/4 to 28 1/2 inches (long axis).

## GOLF

**The ball, specifications:** Broadened to require that the ball be designed to perform as if it were spherically symmetrical. The weight of the ball shall not be greater than 1.620 ounces avoirdupois, and the size shall not be less than 1.680 inches in diameter.
**Velocity of ball:** Not greater than 250 feet per second when tested on U.S.G.A. apparatus, with 2 percent tolerance.
**Hole:** 4 1/4 inches in diameter and at least 4 inches deep.
**Clubs:** 14 is the maximum number permitted.
**Overall distance standard:** A brand of ball shall not exceed a distance of 280 yards plus 6% when tested on USGA apparatus under specified conditions, on an outdoor range at USGA Headquarters.

## HOCKEY

**Size of rink:** 200 feet long by 85 feet wide surrounded by a wooden wall not less than 40 inches and not more than 48 inches above level of ice.
**Size of goal:** 6 feet wide by 4 feet in height.
**Puck:** 1 inch thick and 3 inches in diameter, made of vulcanized rubber; weight 5 1/2 to 6 ounces.
**Length of stick:** Not more than 58 inches from heel to end of shaft nor 12 1/2 inches from heel to end of blade. Blade should not be more than 3 inches in width but not less than 2 inches, except goal keeper's stick, which shall not exceed 3 1/2 inches in width except at the heel, where it must not exceed 4 1/2 inches.

## TENNIS

**Size of court:** Rectangle 78 feet long and 27 feet wide (singles); 78 feet long and 36 feet wide (doubles).
**Height of net:** 3 feet in center, gradually rising to reach 3-foot 6-inch posts at a point 3 feet outside each side of court.
**Ball:** Shall be more than 2 1/2 inches and less than 2 5/8 inches in diameter and weigh more than 2 ounces and less than 2 1/16 ounces.
**Service line:** 21 feet from net.

# COLLEGE SOCCER

1985 N.C.A.A. DIVISION I PLAYOFFS

## REGIONAL FINALS

Hartwick 2, Columbia 0
Boston 2, Connecticut 1 (OT)
Penn State 6, Temple 5
South Carolina 1, Clemson 0
American 3, George Mason 1
Evansville 3, Indiana 0
Southern Methodist 2, Air Force 1
U.C.L.A. 1, Nevada–Las Vegas 0

## QUARTERFINALS

American 2, South Carolina 0
Hartwick 1, Boston 0
Evansville 1, Penn State 0
U.C.L.A. 2, Southern Methodist 0

## SEMIFINALS

American 1, Hartwick 0
U.C.L.A. 3, Evansville 1

## CHAMPIONSHIP

(at Seattle, Dec. 14, 1985)
U.C.L.A. 1, American 0 (8 overtimes, NCAA record)

# TENNIS

Lawn tennis is a comparatively modern modification of the ancient game of court tennis. Major Walter Clopton Wingfield thought that something like court tennis might be played outdoors on lawns, and in December, 1873, at Nantclwyd, Wales, he introduced his new game under the name of *Sphairistike* at a lawn party. The game was a success and spread rapidly, but the name was a total failure and almost immediately disappeared when all the players and spectators began to refer to the new game as "lawn tennis." In the early part of 1874, a young lady named Mary Ewing Outerbridge returned from Bermuda to New York, bringing with her the implements and necessary equipment of the new game, which she had obtained from a British Army supply store in Bermuda. Miss Outerbridge and friends played the first game of lawn tennis in the United States on the grounds of the Staten Island Cricket and Baseball Club in the spring of 1874.

For a few years, the new game went along in haphazard fashion until about 1880, when standard measurements for the court and standard equipment within definite limits became the rule. In 1881, the U.S. Lawn Tennis Association (whose name was changed in 1975 to U.S. Tennis Association) was formed and conducted the first national championship at Newport, R.I. The international matches for the Davis Cup began with a series between the British and United States players on the courts of the Longwood Cricket Club, Chestnut Hill, Mass., in 1900, with the home players winning.

Professional tennis, which got its start in 1926 when the French star Suzanne Lenglen was paid $50,000 for a tour, received full recognition in 1968. Staid old Wimbledon, the London home of what are considered the world championships, let the pros compete. This decision ended a long controversy over open tennis and changed the format of the competition. The United States championships were also opened to the pros and the site of the event, long held at Forest Hills, N.Y., was shifted to the National Tennis Center in Flushing Meadows, N.Y., in 1978. Pro tours for men and women became worldwide in play that continued throughout the year.

## DAVIS CUP CHAMPIONSHIPS

No matches in 1901, 1910, 1915–18, and 1940–45.

| | | | |
|---|---|---|---|
| 1900 | United States 3, British Isles 0 | 1931 | France 3, Great Britain 2 |
| 1902 | United States 3, British Isles 2 | 1932 | France 3, United States 2 |
| 1903 | British Isles 4, United States 1 | 1933 | Great Britain 3, France 2 |
| 1904 | British Isles 5, Belgium 0 | 1934 | Great Britain 4, United States 1 |
| 1905 | British Isles 5, United States 0 | 1935 | Great Britain 5, United States 0 |
| 1906 | British Isles 5, United States 0 | 1936 | Great Britain 3, Australia 2 |
| 1907 | Australasia 3, British Isles 2 | 1937 | United States 4, Great Britain 1 |
| 1908 | Australasia 3, United States 2 | 1938 | United States 3, Australia 2 |
| 1909 | Australasia 5, United States 0 | 1939 | Australia 3, United States 2 |
| 1911 | Australasia 5, United States 0 | 1946 | United States 5, Australia 0 |
| 1912 | British Isles 3, Australasia 2 | 1947 | United States 4, Australia 1 |
| 1913 | United States 3, British Isles 2 | 1948 | United States 5, Australia 0 |
| 1914 | Australasia 3, United States 2 | 1949 | United States 4, Australia 1 |
| 1919 | Australasia 4, British Isles 1 | 1950 | Australia 4, United States 1 |
| 1920 | United States 5, Australasia 0 | 1951 | Australia 3, United States 2 |
| 1921 | United States 5, Japan 0 | 1952 | Australia 4, United States 1 |
| 1922 | United States 4, Australasia 1 | 1953 | Australia 3, United States 2 |
| 1923 | United States 4, Australasia 1 | 1954 | United States 3, Australia 2 |
| 1924 | United States 5, Australasia 0 | 1955 | Australia 5, United States 0 |
| 1925 | United States 5, France 0 | 1956 | Australia 5, United States 0 |
| 1926 | United States 4, France 1 | 1957 | Australia 3, United States 2 |
| 1927 | France 3, United States 2 | 1958 | United States 3, Australia 2 |
| 1928 | France 4, United States 1 | 1959 | Australia 3, United States 2 |
| 1929 | France 3, United States 2 | 1960 | Australia 4, Italy 1 |
| 1930 | France 4, United States 1 | 1961 | Australia 5, Italy 0 |

| | |
|---|---|
| 1962 | Australia 5, Mexico 0 |
| 1963 | United States 3, Australia 2 |
| 1964 | Australia 3, United States 2 |
| 1965 | Australia 4, Spain 1 |
| 1966 | Australia 4, India 1 |
| 1967 | Australia 4, Spain 1 |
| 1968 | United States 4, Australia 1 |
| 1969 | United States 5, Romania 0 |
| 1970 | United States 5, West Germany 0 |
| 1971 | United States 3, Romania 2 |
| 1972 | United States 3, Romania 2 |
| 1973 | Australia 5, United States 0 |
| 1974 | South Africa (Default by India) |
| 1975 | Sweden 3, Czechoslovakia 2 |
| 1976 | Italy 4, Chile 1 |
| 1977 | Australia 3, Italy 1 |
| 1978 | United States 4, Britain 1 |
| 1979 | United States 5, Italy 0 |
| 1980 | Czechoslovakia 3, Italy 2 |
| 1981 | United States 3, Argentina 1 |
| 1982 | United States 3, France 0 |
| 1983 | Australia 3, Sweden 2 |
| 1984 | Sweden 4, United States 1 |
| 1985 | Sweden 3, West Germany 2 |

## FEDERATION CUP CHAMPIONSHIPS

World team competition for women conducted by International Lawn Tennis Federation.

| | | | | | |
|---|---|---|---|---|---|
| 1963 | United States 2, Australia 1 | 1971 | Australia 3, Britain 0 | 1979 | United States 3, Australia 0 |
| 1964 | Australia 2, United States 1 | 1972 | South Africa 2, Britain 1 | 1980 | United States 3, Australia 0 |
| 1965 | Australia 2, United States 1 | 1973 | Australia 3, South Africa 0 | 1981 | United States 3, Britain 0 |
| 1966 | United States 3, West Germany 0 | 1974 | Australia 2, United States 1 | 1982 | United States 3, West Germany 0 |
| 1967 | United States 2, Britain 0 | 1975 | Czechoslovakia 3, Australia 0 | 1983 | Czechoslovakia 2, West Germany 1 |
| 1968 | Australia 3, Netherlands 0 | 1976 | United States 2, Australia 1 | 1984 | Czechoslovakia 2, Australia 1 |
| 1969 | United States 2, Australia 1 | 1977 | United States 2, Australia 1 | 1985 | United States 3, Czechoslovakia 0 |
| 1970 | Australia 3, West Germany 0 | 1978 | United States 2, Australia 1 | | |

# U.S. CHAMPIONS
## Singles—Men

**NATIONAL**

| | | | | | | OPEN | |
|---|---|---|---|---|---|---|---|
| 1881–87 | Richard D. Sears | 1917–18 | R. Lindley Murray[2] | 1948–49 | Richard Gonzales | | |
| 1888–89 | Henry Slocum, Jr. | 1919 | William Johnston | 1950 | Arthur Larsen | 1968 | Arthur Ashe |
| 1890–92 | Oliver S. Campbell | 1920–25 | Bill Tilden | 1951–52 | Frank Sedgman | 1969 | Rod Laver |
| 1893–94 | Robert D. Wrenn | 1926–27 | Jean Rene Lacoste | 1953 | Tony Trabert | 1970 | Ken Rosewall |
| 1895 | Fred H. Hovey | 1928 | Henri Cochet | 1954 | Vic Seixas | 1971 | Stan Smith |
| 1896–97 | Robert D. Wrenn | 1929 | Bill Tilden | 1955 | Tony Trabert | 1972 | Ilie Nastase |
| 1898– | | 1930 | John H. Doeg | 1956 | Ken Rosewall | 1973 | John Newcombe |
| 1900 | Malcolm Whitman | 1931–32 | Ellsworth Vines | 1957 | Mal Anderson | 1974 | Jimmy Connors |
| 1901–02 | William A. Larned | 1933–34 | Fred J. Perry | 1958 | Ashley Cooper | 1975 | Manuel Orantes |
| 1903 | Hugh L. Doherty | 1935 | Wilmer L. Allison | 1959–60 | Neale Fraser | 1976 | Jimmy Connors |
| 1904 | Holcombe Ward | 1936 | Fred J. Perry | 1961 | Roy Emerson | 1977 | Guillermo Vilas |
| 1905 | Beals C. Wright | 1937–38 | Don Budge | 1962 | Rod Laver | 1978 | Jimmy Connors |
| 1906 | William J. Clothier | 1939 | Robert L. Riggs | 1963 | Rafael Osuna | 1979 | John McEnroe |
| 1907–11 | William A. Larned | 1940 | Donald McNeill | 1964 | Roy Emerson | 1980–81 | John McEnroe |
| 1912–13 | Maurice McLoughlin | 1941 | Robert L. Riggs | 1965 | Manuel Santana | 1982 | Jimmy Connors |
| | | 1942 | Fred Schroeder | 1966 | Fred Stolle | 1983 | Jimmy Connors |
| 1914 | R. N. Williams II | 1943 | Joseph Hunt | 1967 | John Newcombe | 1984 | John McEnroe |
| 1915 | William Johnston | 1944–45 | Frank Parker | 1968 | Arthur Ashe | 1985–86 | Ivan Lendl |
| 1916 | R. N. William II | 1946–47 | Jack Kramer | 1969 | Rod Laver | | |

## Singles—Women

**NATIONAL**

| | | | | | | OPEN | |
|---|---|---|---|---|---|---|---|
| 1887 | Ellen F. Hansel | 1905 | Elisabeth H. Moore | 1936 | Alice Marble | 1965 | Margaret Smith |
| 1888–89 | Bertha Townsend | 1906 | Helen Homans | 1937 | Anita Lizana | 1966 | Maria Bueno |
| 1890 | Ellen C. Roosevelt | 1907 | Evelyn Sears | 1938–40 | Alice Marble | 1967 | Billie Jean King |
| 1891–92 | Mabel E. Cahill | 1908 | Maud | 1941 | Sarah Palfrey | 1968–69 | Margaret Smith |
| 1893 | Aline M. Terry | | Bargar–Wallach | | Cooke | | Court[3] |
| 1894 | Helen R. Helwig | 1909–11 | Hazel V. | 1942–44 | Pauline Betz | | |
| 1895 | Juliette P. | | Hotchkiss | 1945 | Sarah Cooke | OPEN | |
| | Atkinson | 1912–14 | Mary K. Browne | 1946 | Pauline Betz | 1968 | Virginia Wade |
| 1896 | Elisabeth H. | 1915–18 | Molla Bjurstedt | 1947 | Louise Brough | 1969–70 | Margaret Court |
| | Moore | 1919 | Hazel Hotchkiss | 1948–50 | Margaret Osborne | 1971–72 | Billie Jean King |
| 1897–98 | Juliette P. | | Wightman | | duPont | 1973 | Margaret Court |
| | Atkinson | 1920–22 | Molla Bjurstedt | 1951–53 | Maureen Connolly | 1974 | Billie Jean King |
| 1899 | Marion Jones | | Mallory | 1954–55 | Doris Hart | 1975–78 | Chris Evert |
| 1900 | Myrtle McAteer | 1923–26 | Helen N. Wills | 1956 | Shirley Fry | 1979 | Tracy Austin |
| 1901 | Elisabeth H. | 1926 | Molla B. Mallory | 1957–58 | Althea Gibson | 1980 | Chris Evert-Lloyd |
| | Moore | 1927–29 | Helen N. Wills | 1959 | Maria Bueno | 1981 | Tracy Austin |
| 1902 | Marion Jones | 1930 | Betty Nuthall | 1960–61 | Darlene Hard | 1982 | Chris Evert-Lloyd |
| 1903 | Elisabeth H. Moore | 1931 | Helen Wills Moody | 1962 | Margaret Smith | 1983–84 | Martina Navratilova |
| 1904 | May Sutton | 1932–35 | Helen Jacobs | 1963–64 | Maria Bueno | 1985 | Hana Mandlikova |
| | | | | | | 1986 | Martina Navratilova |

## Doubles—Men

**NATIONAL**

| | | | | | |
|---|---|---|---|---|---|
| 1920 | Bill Johnston–C. J. Griffin | 1938 | Don Budge–Gene Mako | 1954 | Vic Seixas–Tony Trabert |
| 1921–22 | Bill Tilden–Vincent Richards | 1939 | A. K. Quist–J. E. Bromwich | 1955 | Kosei Kamo–Atsushi Miyagi |
| 1923 | Bill Tilden–B. I. C. Norton | 1940–41 | Jack Kramer–F. R. Schroeder | 1956 | Lewis Hoad–Ken Rosewall |
| 1924 | H. O. Kinsey–R. G. Kinsey | 1942 | Gardnar Mulloy–Bill Talbert | 1957 | Ashley Cooper–Neale Fraser |
| 1925–26 | Vincent Richards–R. N. Williams II | 1943 | Jack Kramer–Frank Parker | 1958 | Ham Richardson–Alex Olmedo |
| | | 1944 | Don McNeill–Bob Falkenburg | 1959–60 | Neale Fraser–Roy Emerson |
| 1927 | Bill Tilden–Frank Hunter | 1945 | Gardnar Mulloy–Bill Talbert | 1961 | Chuck McKinley–Dennis Ralston |
| 1928 | G. M. Lott, Jr.–V. Hennessy | 1946 | Gardnar Mulloy–Bill Talbert | 1962 | Rafael Osuna–Antonio Palafox |
| 1929–30 | G. M. Lott, Jr.–J. H. Doeg | 1947 | Jack Kramer–Fred Schroeder | 1963–64 | Chuck McKinley–Dennis Ralston |
| 1931 | W. L. Allison–John Van Ryn | 1948 | Gardnar Mulloy–Bill Talbert | 1965–66 | Fred Stolle–Roy Emerson |
| 1932 | E. H. Vines, Jr.–Keith Gledh | 1949 | John Bromwich–William Sidwell | 1967 | John Newcombe–Tony Roche |
| 1933–34 | G. M. Lott, Jr.–L. R. Stoefen | 1950 | John Bromwich–Frank Sedgman | 1968 | Stan Smith–Bob Lutz[3] |
| 1935 | W. L. Allison–John Van Ryn | 1951 | Frank Sedgman–Ken McGregor | 1969 | Richard Crealy–Allan Stone[3] |
| 1936 | Don Budge–Gene Mako | 1952 | Vic Seixas–Mervyn Rose | | |
| 1937 | G. von Cramm–H. Henkel | 1953 | Mervyn Rose–Rex Hartwig | | |

## OPEN

| | | | | | |
|---|---|---|---|---|---|
| 1968 | Stan Smith–Bob Lutz | 1975 | Jimmy Connors–Ilie Nastase | 1982 | Kevin Curren–Steve Denton |
| 1969 | Fred Stolle–Ken Rosewall | 1976 | Marty Riessen–Tom Okker | 1983 | John McEnroe–Peter Fleming |
| 1970 | Nikki Pilic–Fred Barthes | 1977 | Frew McMillan–Bob Hewitt | 1984 | John Fitzgerald–Tomas Smid |
| 1971 | John Newcombe–Roger Taylor | 1978 | Bob Lutz–Stan Smith | 1985 | Ken Flach–Robert Seguso |
| 1972 | Cliff Drysdale–Roger Taylor | 1979 | John McEnroe–Peter Fleming | 1986 | Andres Gomez–Slobodan Zivo- |
| 1973 | John Newcombe–Owen Davidson | 1980 | Stan Smith–Bob Lutz | | jinovic |
| 1974 | Bob Lutz–Stan Smith | 1981 | John McEnroe–Peter Fleming | | |

1. Challenge round abandoned in 1912. 2. Patriotic Tournament in 1917. 3. With the inaugural of the Open Tournament in 1968, the United States Lawn Tennis Association held a national championship at Longwood, Chestnut Hill, Mass. which barred contract professionals in 1968 and 1969.

## Doubles—Women

### NATIONAL

| | | | |
|---|---|---|---|
| 1924 | G. W. Wightman–Helen Wills | 1948–50 | A. Louise Brough–Margaret O. duPont |
| 1925 | Mary K. Browne–Helen Wills | | |
| 1926 | Elizabeth Ryan–Eleanor Goss | 1951–54 | Doris Hart–Shirley Fry |
| 1927 | L. A. Godfree–Ermyntrude Harvey | 1955–57 | A. Louise Brough–Margaret O. duPont |
| 1928 | Hazel Hotchkiss Wightman–Helen Wills | | |
| | | 1958–59 | Darlene Hard–Jeanne Arth |
| 1929 | Phoebe Watson–L. R. C. Michell | 1960 | Darlene Hard–Maria Bueno |
| 1930 | Betty Nuthall–Sarah Palfrey | 1961 | Darlene Hard–Lesley Turner |
| 1931 | Betty Nuthall–E. B. Wittingstall | 1962 | Darlene Hard–Maria Bueno |
| 1932 | Helen Jacobs–Sarah Palfrey | 1963 | Margaret Smith–Robyn Ebbern |
| 1933 | Betty Nuthall–Freda James | 1964 | Karen Hantze Susman–Billie Jean Moffitt |
| 1934 | Helen Jacobs–Sarah Palfrey | | |
| 1935 | Helen Jacobs–Sarah Palfrey Fabyan | 1965 | Nancy Richey–Carole Caldwell Graebner |
| 1936 | Marjorie G. Van Ryn–Carolin Babcock | 1966 | Nancy Richey–Maria Bueno |
| | | 1967 | Billie Jean King–Rosemary Casals |
| 1937–40 | Sarah Palfrey Fabyan–Alice Marble | 1968 | Margaret Court–Maria Bueno[3] |
| 1941 | Sarah Palfrey Cooke–Margaret Osborne | 1969 | Margaret Court–Virginia Wade[3] |
| 1942–47 | A. Louise Brough–Margaret Osborne | | |

### OPEN

| | |
|---|---|
| 1968 | Maria Bueno–Margaret Court |
| 1969 | Darlene Hard–Francoise Durr |
| 1970 | Margaret Court–Judy Dalton |
| 1971 | Rosemary Casals–Judy Dalton |
| 1972 | Francoise Durr–Betty Stove |
| 1973 | Margaret Court–Virginia Wade |
| 1974 | Billie Jean King–Rosemary Casals |
| 1975 | Margaret Court–Virginia Wade |
| 1976 | Linky Boshoff–Ilana Kloss |
| 1977 | Martina Navratilova–Betty Stove |
| 1978 | Billie Jean King–Martina Navratilova |
| 1979 | Betty Stove–Wendy Turnbull |
| 1980 | Billie Jean King–Martina Navratilova |
| 1981 | Kathy Jordan–Anne Smith |
| 1982 | Rosemary Casals–Wendy Turnbull |
| 1983–84 | Martina Navratilova–Pam Shriver |
| 1985 | Claudia Khode-Kilsch–Helena Sukova |
| 1986 | Martina Navratilova–Pam Shriver |

1. Challenge round abandoned in 1912. 2. Patriotic Tournament in 1917. 3. With the inaugural of the Open Tournament in 1968, the United States Lawn Tennis Association held a national championship at Longwood, Chestnut Hill, Mass. which barred contract professionals in 1968 and 1969.

## U.S. INDOOR CHAMPIONS

### Singles—Men

| | |
|---|---|
| 1964 | Charles McKinley |
| 1965 | Erik Lundquist |
| 1966 | Charles Pasarell |
| 1967 | Charles Pasarell |
| 1968 | Cliff Richey |
| 1969 | Stan Smith |
| 1970 | Ilie Nastase |
| 1971 | Clark Graebner |
| 1972 | Stan Smith |
| 1973–75 | Jimmy Connors |
| 1976 | Ilie Nastase |
| 1977 | Bjorn Borg |
| 1978–79 | Jimmy Connors |
| 1980 | John McEnroe |
| 1981 | Gene Mayer |
| 1982 | Johan Kriek |
| 1983–84 | Jimmy Connors |
| 1985 | Stefan Edberg |
| 1986 | Brad Gilbert |

### Singles—Women

| | |
|---|---|
| 1964 | Mary Ann Eisel |
| 1965 | Nancy Richey |
| 1966 | Billie Jean King |
| 1967 | Billie Jean King |
| 1968 | Billie Jean King |
| 1969 | Mary Ann Eisel |
| 1970 | Mary Ann Curtis |
| 1971 | Billie Jean King |
| 1972 | Not held |
| 1973 | Evonne Goolagong |
| 1974 | Billie Jean King |
| 1975 | Martina Navratilova |
| 1976 | Virginia Wade |
| 1977 | Chris Evert |
| 1978 | Chris Evert |
| 1979 | Evonne Goolagong |
| 1980 | Tracy Austin |
| 1981 | Martina Navratilova |
| 1982 | Barbara Potter |
| 1983 | Kim Shaefer |
| 1984 | Martina Navratilova |
| 1985 | Hana Mandlikova |
| 1986 | Martina Navratilova |

### Doubles—Men

| | |
|---|---|
| 1967 | Arthur Ashe–Charles Pasarell |
| 1968 | Thomas Koch–Tom Okker |
| 1969 | Stan Smith–Bob Lutz |
| 1970 | Arthur Ashe–Stan Smith |
| 1971 | Manuel Orantes–Juan Gisbert |
| 1972 | Manuel Orantes–Andres Gimeno |
| 1973 | Juan Gisbert–Jurgen Fassbender |
| 1974 | Jimmy Connors–Frew McMillan |
| 1975 | Jimmy Connors–Ilie Nastase |
| 1976–77 | Sherwood Stewart–Fred McNair |
| 1978 | Brian Gottfried–Raul Ramirez |
| 1979 | Wojtek Fibak–Tom Okker |
| 1980 | John McEnroe–Brian Gottfried |
| 1981 | Gene Mayer–Sandy Mayer |
| 1982 | Kevin Curren–Steve Denton |
| 1983 | Peter McNamara–Paul McNamee |
| 1984 | Fritz Bushning–Peter Fleming |
| 1985 | Pavel Slozil–Tomas Smid |
| 1986 | Ken Flach–Robert Seguso |

### Doubles—Women

| | |
|---|---|
| 1967 | Carol Aucamp–Mary Ann Eisel |
| 1968 | Rosemary Casals–Billie Jean King |
| 1969 | Mary Ann Eisel–Valerie Ziegenfuss |
| 1970 | Peaches Bartkowicz–Nancy Richey |
| 1971 | Billie Jean King–Rosemary Casals |
| 1972 | Not held |
| 1973 | Olga Morozova–Marina Kroshina |
| 1974 | Not held |
| 1975 | Billie Jean King–Rosemary Casals |
| 1976 | Rosemary Casals–Francoise Durr |
| 1977 | Martina Navratilova–Betty Stove |
| 1978 | Kerry Reid–Wendy Turnbull |
| 1979 | Billie Jean King–Martina Navratilova |
| 1980 | Ann Kiyomura–Candy Reynolds |
| 1981 | Martina Navratilova–Pam Shriver |
| 1982 | Rosemary Casals–Wendy Turnbull |
| 1983 | Billie Jean King–Sharon Walsh |
| 1984–85 | Martina Navratilova–Pam Shriver |
| 1986 | Kathy Jordan–Elizabeth Smylie |

# BRITISH (WIMBLEDON) CHAMPIONS
## (Amateur from inception in 1877 through 1967)

## Singles—Men

| | | | | | | | |
|---|---|---|---|---|---|---|---|
| 1908–09 | Arthur Gore | 1930 | Bill Tilden | 1952 | Frank Sedgman | 1968–69 | Rod Laver |
| 1910–13 | A. F. Wilding | 1931 | S. B. Wood | 1953 | Vic Siexas | 1970–71 | John Newcombe |
| 1914 | N. E. Brookes | 1932 | Ellsworth Vines | 1954 | Jaroslav Drobny | 1972 | Stan Smith |
| 1919 | G. L. Patterson | 1933 | J. H. Crawford | 1955 | Tony Trabert | 1973 | Jan Kodes |
| 1920–21 | Bill Tilden | 1934–36 | Fred Perry | 1956–57 | Lewis Hoad | 1974 | Jimmy Connors |
| 1922 | G. L. Patterson | 1937–38 | Don Budge | 1958 | Ashley Cooper | 1975 | Arthur Ashe |
| 1923 | William Johnston | 1939 | Robert L. Riggs | 1959 | Alex Olmedo | 1976–80 | Bjorn Borg |
| 1924 | Jean Borotra | 1946 | Yvon Petra | 1960 | Neale Fraser | 1981 | John McEnroe |
| 1925 | Rene Lacoste | 1947 | Jack Kramer | 1961–62 | Rod Laver | 1982 | Jimmy Connors |
| 1926 | Jean Borotra | 1948 | R. Falkenburg | 1963 | Chuck McKinley | 1983–84 | John McEnroe |
| 1927 | Henri Cochet | 1949 | Fred Schroeder | 1964–65 | Roy Emerson | 1985–86 | Boris Becker |
| 1928 | Rene Lacoste | 1950 | Budge Patty | 1966 | Manuel Santana | | |
| 1929 | Jean Cochet | 1951 | Richard Savitt | 1967 | John Newcombe | | |

## Singles—Women

| | | | | | | | |
|---|---|---|---|---|---|---|---|
| 1919–23 | Lenglen | 1938 | Helen Wills Moody | 1962 | Karen Susman | 1976 | Chris Evert |
| 1924 | Kathleen McKane | 1939 | Alice Marble | 1963 | Margaret Smith | 1977 | Virginia Wade |
| 1925 | Lenglen | 1946 | Pauline M. Betz | 1964 | Maria Bueno | 1978–79 | Martina Navratilova |
| 1926 | Godfree | 1947 | Margaret Osborne | 1965 | Margaret Smith | 1980 | Evonne Goolagong |
| 1927–29 | Helen Wills | 1948–50 | A. Louise Brough | 1966–67 | Billie Jean King | | Cawley |
| 1930 | Helen Wills Moody | 1951 | Doris Hart | 1968 | Billie Jean King | 1981 | Chris Evert-Lloyd |
| 1931 | Frl. C. Aussen | 1952–54 | Maureen Connolly | 1969 | Ann Jones | 1982–86 | Martina Navratilova |
| 1932–33 | Helen Wills Moody | 1955 | A. Louise Brough | 1970 | Margaret Court | | |
| 1934 | D. E. Round | 1956 | Shirley Fry | 1971 | Evonne Goolagong | | |
| 1935 | Helen Wills Moody | 1957–58 | Althea Gibson | 1972–73 | Billie Jean King | | |
| 1936 | Helen Jacobs | 1959–60 | Maria Bueno | 1974 | Chris Evert | | |
| 1937 | D. E. Round | 1961 | Angela Mortimer | 1975 | Billie Jean King | | |

## Doubles—Men

| | | | | | | |
|---|---|---|---|---|---|---|
| 1953 | K. Rosewall–L. Hoad | 1965 | John Newcombe–Tony Roche | 1979 | Peter Fleming–John McEnroe |
| 1954 | R. Hartwig–M. Rose | 1966 | John Newcombe–Ken Fletcher | 1980 | Peter McNamara–Paul McNamee |
| 1955 | R. Hartwig–L. Hoad | 1967 | Bob Hewitt–Frew McMillan | 1981 | John McEnroe–Peter Fleming |
| 1956 | L. Hoad–K. Rosewall | 1968–70 | John Newcombe–Tony Roche | 1982 | Paul McNamee–Peter McNamara |
| 1957 | Gardnar Mulloy–Budge Patty | 1971 | Rod Laver–Roy Emerson | 1983–84 | John McEnroe–Peter Fleming |
| 1958 | Sven Davidson–Ulf Schmidt | 1972 | Bob Hewitt–Frew McMillan | 1985 | Heinz Gunthardt–Balazs Taroczy |
| 1959 | Roy Emerson–Neale Fraser | 1973 | Jimmy Connors–Ilie Nastase | 1986 | Joakim Nystrom–Mats Wilander |
| 1960 | Dennis Ralston–Rafael Osuna | 1974 | John Newcombe–Tony Roche | | |
| 1961 | Roy Emerson–Neale Fraser | 1975 | Vitas Gerulaitis–Sandy Mayer | | |
| 1962 | Fred Stolle–Bob Hewitt | 1976 | Brian Gottfried–Raul Ramirez | | |
| 1963 | Rafael Osuna–Antonio Palafox | 1977 | Ross Case–Geoff Masters | | |
| 1964 | Fred Stolle–Bob Hewitt | 1978 | Fred McMillan–Bob Hewitt | | |

## Doubles—Women

| | | | | | | |
|---|---|---|---|---|---|---|
| 1956 | Althea Gibson–Angela Buxton | 1966 | Nancy Richey–Maria Bueno | 1979 | Billie Jean King–Martina Navratilova |
| 1957 | Althea Gibson–Darlene Hard | 1967–68 | Billie Jean King–Rosemary Casals | | |
| 1958 | Althea Gibson–Maria Bueno | 1969 | Margaret Court–Judy Tegart | 1980 | Kathy Jordan–Anne Smith |
| 1959 | Darlene Hard–Jeanne Arth | 1970–71 | Billie Jean King–Rosemary Casals | 1981 | Martina Navratilova–Pam Shriver |
| 1960 | Darlene Hard–Maria Bueno | 1972 | Billie Jean King–Betty Stove | 1982–84 | Pam Shriver–Martina Navratilova |
| 1961 | Karen Hantze–Billie Jean Moffitt | 1973 | Billie Jean King–Rosemary Casals | 1985 | Kathy Jordan–Elizabeth Smylie |
| 1962 | Karen Hantze Susman–Billie Jean Moffitt | 1974 | Evonne Goolagong–Peggy Michel | 1986 | Pam Shriver–Martina Navratilova |
| | | 1975 | Ann Kiyomura–Kazuko Sawamatsu | | |
| 1963 | Darlene Hard–Maria Bueno | 1976 | Chris Evert–Martina Navratilova | | |
| 1964 | Margaret Smith–Les Turnerley | 1977 | Helen Cawley–JoAnne Russell | | |
| 1965 | Billie Jean Moffitt–Maria Bueno | 1978 | Wendy Turnbull–Kerry Reid | | |

## UNITED STATES CHAMPIONS—1986

### U.S. Open

(Flushing Meadow, Aug. 25-Sept. 7, 1986)

Men's singles—Final: Ivan Lendl, Czechoslovakia, defeated Miloslav Mecir, Czechoslovakia, 6-4, 6-2, 6-2
Semifinals: Ivan Lendl, Czechoslovakia, defeated Stefan Edberg, Sweden, 7-6 (8-6), 6-2, 6-3; Miloslav Mecir, Czechoslovakia, defeated Boris Becker, West Germany, 4-6, 6-3, 6-4, 3-6, 6-3.
Women's singles—Final—Martina Navratilova, Fort Worth, Texas; defeated Helena Sukova, Czechoslovakia, 6-3, 6-2
Semifinals: Martina Navratilova, Fort Worth, Texas, defeated Steffi Graf; West Germany, 6-1, 6-7 (3-7), 7-6 (10-8); Helena Sukova, Czechoslovakia, defeated Chris Evert-Lloyd, Fort Lauderdale, Fla., 6-2, 6-4.
Men's doubles—Final: Andres Gomez, Ecuador, and Slobodan Zivojinovic, Yugoslavia, defeated Joakim Nystrom and Mats Wilander, Sweden, 4-6, 6-3, 6-3, 4-6, 6-3
Women's doubles—Final: Martina Navratilova, Fort Worth, Texas, and Pam Shriver, Lutherville, Md., defeated Hana Mandlikova, Czechoslovakia, and Wendy Turnbull, Australia, 6-4, 3-6, 6-3
Mixed doubles—Final: Raffaella Reggi, Italy and Sergio Casal, Spain, defeated Martina Navratilova, Fort Worth, Texas and Peter Fleming, Seabrook Island, S.C. 6-4, 6-4

### National Clay Court

(Indianapolis, Ind., April 27-May 4, 1986)

Men's singles final—Andres Gomez, Ecuador, defeated Thierry Tulasne, France, 6-4, 7-6 (7-1).
Women's singles final—Steffi Graf, West Germany, defeated Gabriela Sabatini, Argentina, 2-6, 7-6 (7-5), 6-4.
Men's doubles final—Hans Gildemeister, Chile, and Andres Gomez, Ecuador, defeated John Fitzgerald, Australia and Sherwood Stewart, Woodlands, Texas, 6-4, 6-3.
Women's doubles final—Steffi Graf, West Germany, and Gabriela Sabatini, Argentina, defeated Gigi Fernandez, San Juan, Puerto Rico, and Robin White, Fort Worth, Texas, 6-2, 6-0.

### World Championship Tennis

(Forest Hills, N.Y., May 5-11, 1986)

Singles final—Yannick Noah, France, defeated Guillermo Vilas, Argentina, 7-6 (7-3), 6-0.
Doubles final—Andres Gomez, Ecuador, and Hans Gildemeister, Chile, defeated Boris Becker, West Germany, and Slobodan Zivojinovich, Yugoslavia, 7-6 (8-6), 7-6 (7-4).

### U.S. National Indoor

(Memphis, Tenn., Feb. 3-10, 1986)

Singles final—Brad Gilbert, Piedmont, Calif., defeated Stefan Edberg, Sweden, 7-5, 7-5.
Doubles final—Ken Flach, Sebring, Fla. and Robert Seguso, Prairie Oaks, Fla. defeated Guy Forget, France and Anders Jarryd, Sweden, 6-4, 4-6, 7-6 (7-5).

### U.S. Pro Indoor

(Philadelphia, Jan. 27-Feb. 2, 1986)

Singles final—Ivan Lendl, Czechoslovakia, won by injury default by Tim Mayotte, Bradenton, Fla.
Doubles final—Scot Davis, San Jose, Calif., and David Tate, Las Vegas, Nev., defeated Stefan Edberg, Sweden, and Andes Jarryd, Sweden, 7-6 (7-3), 3-6, 6-3, 7-5.

### U.S. Pro

(Brookline, Mass., July 21-27, 1986)

Singles final—Andres Gomez, Ecuador, defeated Martin Jalte, Argentina 7-5, 6-4. Doubles final—Andres Gomez, Ecuador and Hans Gildemeister, Chile, defeated Dan Cassidy, Hollywood, Fla. and Mel Purcell, Murray, Ky. 4-6, 7-5, 6-0

## OTHER 1986 CHAMPIONS

### Wimbledon Open

Men's singles—Boris Becker, West Germany, defeated Ivan Lendl, Czechoslovakia, 6-4, 6-3, 7-5.
Women's singles—Martina Navratilova, Fort Worth, Tex. defeated Hana Mandlikova, Czecholslovakia, 7-5, 6-3.
Men's doubles—Joakim Nystrom, Sweden, and Mats Wilander, Sweden, defeated Gary Donnelly, Phoenix, Ariz. and Peter Fleming, Chatam, N.J., 7-6, 6-3, 6-3.
Women's doubles—Martina Navratilova, Fort Worth, Texas, and Pam Shriver, Lutherville, Md. defeated Hana Mandlikova, Czechoslovakia, and Wendy Turnbull, Australia, 6-1, 6-3.

### French Open

Men's singles—Ivan Lendl, Czechoslovakia, defeated Mikael Penfors, Sweden, 6-3, 6-2, 6-4.
Women's singles—Chris Evert-Lloyd, Fort Lauderdale, Fla. defeated Martina Navratilova, Fort Worth, Texas, 2-6, 6-3, 6-3.
Men's doubles—Tomas Smid, Czechoslovakia, and John Fitzgerald, Australia, defeated Stefan Edberg, Sweden, and Anders Jarryd, Sweden, 6-3, 4-6, 6-3, 6-7 (7-4), 14-12.
Women's doubles—Martina Navratilova, Fort Worth, Texas, and Andrea Temesvari, Hungary, defeated Steffi Graf, West Germany, and Gabriela Sabatini, Argentina, 6-1, 6-2.
Mixed doubles—Kathy Jordan, King of Prussia, Pa. and Ken Flach, Prairie Oaks, Fla. defeated Rosalyn Fairbank, South Africa, and Mark Edmondson, Australia, 3-6, 7-6 (7-3), 6-3.

### Australian Open

Men's singles—Stefan Edbeg, Sweden, defeated Mats Wilander, Sweden, 6-4, 6-3, 6-3.
Women's singles—Martina Navratilova, Fort Worth, Texas, defeated Chris Evert-Lloyd, Fort Lauderdale, Fla., 6-2, 4-6, 6-2
Men's doubles—Paul Annacone, Southampton, N.Y. and Christo Van Rensberg, South Africa, defeated Mark Edmondson, Australia, and Kim Warwick, Australia, 3-6, 7-6, 6-4, 6-4.
Women's doubles—Martina Navratilova, Fort Worth Texas, and Pam Shriver, Lutherville, Md. defeated Claudia Khode-Kilsch, West Germany, and Helena Sukova, Czechoslovakia, 6-3, 6-4.

## DAVIS CUP RESULTS—1985

### Finals

Sweden 3, West Germany 2 (at Munich, West Germany)
Singles—Mats Wilander, Sweden, defeated Michael Westphal, West Germany, 6-3, 6-4, 10-8; Boris Becker, West Germany, defeated Stefan Edbery, Sweden, 6-3, 3-6, 7-5, 8-6; Stefan Edberg, Sweden, defeated Michael Westphal, West Germany, 3-6, 7-5, 6-4, 6-3. Boris Becker, West Germany, defeated Mats Wilander, Sweden, 6-3, 2-6, 6-3, 6-3.
Doubles—Mats Wilander-Joakim Nystrom, Sweden, defeated Boris Becker-Andreas Maurer, West Germany, 6-4, 6-2, 6-1.

## MEN'S FINAL TENNIS EARNINGS—1985

Player and amount: Ivan Lendl, $1,971,074; John McEnroe, $1,455,611; Mats Wilander, $1,081,697; Stefan Edberg, $731,152; Boris Becker, $625,757; Jimmy Connors, $562,336; Anders Jarryd, $534,822; Yannick Noah, $406,881; Tomas Smid, $404,460; Robert Seguso, $394,908.

## WOMEN'S FINAL TENNIS EARNINGS—1985

Player and amount: Martina Navratilova, $1,328,829; Chris Evert-Lloyd, $972,782; Hana Mandlikova, $579,847; Helena Sukova, $422,387; Pam Shriver, $419,686; Claudia Kohde-Kilsch, $398,120; Zina Garrison, $274,470; Manuela Maleeva, $271,271; Carling Bassett, $197,591; Kathy Rinaldi, $191,750.

# ROWING

Rowing goes back so far in history that there is no possibility of tracing it to any particular aboriginal source. The oldest rowing race still on the calendar is the "Doggett's Coat and Badge" contest among professional watermen of the Thames (England) that began in 1715. The first Oxford-Cambridge race was held at Henley in 1829. Competitive rowing in the United States began with matches between boats rowed by professional oarsmen of the New York water front. They were oarsmen who rowed the small boats that plied as ferries from Manhattan Island to Brooklyn and return, or who rowed salesmen down the harbor to meet ships arriving from Europe. Since the first salesman to meet an incoming ship had some advantage over his rivals, there was keen competition in the bidding for fast boats and the best oarsmen. This gave rise to match races.

Amateur boat clubs sprang up in the United States between 1820 and 1830 and seven students of Yale joined together to purchase a four-oared lap-streak gig in 1843. The first Harvard-Yale race was held Aug. 3, 1852, on Lake Winnepesaukee, N.H. The first time an American college crew went abroad was in 1869 when Harvard challenged Oxford and was defeated on the Thames. There were early college rowing races on Lake Quinsigamond, near Worcester, Mass., and on Saratoga Lake, N.Y., but the Intercollegiate Rowing Association in 1895 settled on the Hudson, at Poughkeepsie, as the setting for the annual "Poughkeepsie Regatta." In 1950 the I.R.A. shifted its classic to Marietta, Ohio, and in 1952 it was moved to Syracuse, N.Y. The National Association of Amateur Oarsmen, organized in 1872, has conducted annual championship regattas since that time.

## INTERCOLLEGIATE ROWING ASSOCIATION REGATTA
(Varsity Eight-Oared Shells)

Rowed at 4 miles, Poughkeepsie, N.Y., 1895–97, 1899–1916, 1925–32, 1934–41. Rowed at 3 miles, Saratoga, N.Y., 1898; Poughkeepsie, 1921–24, 1947–49; Syracuse, N.Y., 1952–1963, 1965–67. Rowed at 2,000 meters, Syracuse, N.Y., 1964 and from 1968 on. Rowed at 2 miles, Ithaca, N.Y., 1920; Marietta, Ohio, 1950–51. Suspended 1917–19, 1933, 1942–46.

| Year | Time | First | Second | Year | Time | First | Second |
|------|------|-------|--------|------|------|-------|--------|
| 1895 | 21:25 | Columbia | Cornell | 1941 | 18:53 3/10 | Washington | California |
| 1896 | 19:59 | Cornell | Harvard | 1947 | 13:59 1/5 | Navy | Cornell |
| 1897 | 20:47 4/5 | Cornell | Columbia | 1948 | 14:06 2/5 | Washington | California |
| 1898 | 15:51 1/2 | Pennsylvania | Cornell | 1949 | 14:42 3/5 | California | Washington |
| 1899 | 20:04 | Pennsylvania | Wisconsin | 1950 | 8:07.5 | Washington | California |
| 1900 | 19:44 3/5 | Pennsylvania | Wisconsin | 1951 | 7:50.5 | Wisconsin | Washington |
| 1901 | 18:53 1/5 | Cornell | Columbia | 1952 | 15:08.1 | Navy | Princeton |
| 1902 | 19:03 3/5 | Cornell | Wisconsin | 1953 | 15:29.6 | Navy | Cornell |
| 1903 | 18:57 | Cornell | Georgetown | 1954 | 16:04.4 | Navy[1] | Cornell |
| 1904 | 20:22 3/5 | Syracuse | Cornell | 1955 | 15:49.9 | Cornell | Pennsylvania |
| 1905 | 20:29 | Cornell | Syracuse | 1956 | 16:22.4 | Cornell | Navy |
| 1906 | 19:36 4/5 | Cornell | Pennsylvania | 1957 | 15:26.6 | Cornell | Pennsylvania |
| 1907 | 20:02 2/5 | Cornell | Columbia | 1958 | 17:12.1 | Cornell | Navy |
| 1908 | 19:24 1/5 | Syracuse | Columbia | 1959 | 18:01.7 | Wisconsin | Syracuse |
| 1909 | 19:02 | Cornell | Columbia | 1960 | 15:57 | California | Navy |
| 1910 | 20:42 1/5 | Cornell | Pennsylvania | 1961 | 16:49.2 | California | Cornell |
| 1911 | 20:10 4/5 | Cornell | Columbia | 1962 | 17:02.9 | Cornell | Washington |
| 1912 | 19:31 2/5 | Cornell | Wisconsin | 1963 | 17:24 | Cornell | Navy |
| 1913 | 19:28 3/5 | Syracuse | Cornell | 1964 | 6:31.1 | California | Washington |
| 1914 | 19:37 4/5 | Columbia | Pennsylvania | 1965 | 16:51.3 | Navy | Cornell |
| 1915 | 19:36 3/5 | Cornell | Stanford | 1966 | 16:03.4 | Wisconsin | Navy |
| 1916 | 20:15 2/5 | Syracuse | Cornell | 1967 | 16:13.9 | Pennsylvania | Wisconsin |
| 1920 | 11:02 3/5 | Syracuse | Cornell | 1968 | 6:15.6 | Pennsylvania | Washington |
| 1921 | 14:07 | Navy | California | 1969 | 6:30.4 | Pennsylvania | Dartmouth |
| 1922 | 13:33 3/5 | Navy | Washington | 1970 | 6:39.3 | Washington | Wisconsin |
| 1923 | 14:03 1/5 | Washington | Navy | 1971 | 6:06 | Cornell | Washington |
| 1924 | 15:02 | Washington | Wisconsin | 1972 | 6:22.6 | Pennsylvania | Brown |
| 1925 | 19:24 4/5 | Navy | Washington | 1973 | 6:21 | Wisconsin | Brown |
| 1926 | 19:28 3/5 | Washington | Navy | 1974 | 6:33 | Wisconsin | Mass. Inst. of Technology |
| 1927 | 20:57 | Columbia | Washington | | | | |
| 1928 | 18:35 4/5 | California | Columbia | 1975 | 6:08.2 | Wisconsin | M.I.T. |
| 1929 | 22:58 | Columbia | Washington | 1976 | 6:31 | California | Princeton |
| 1930 | 21:42 | Cornell | Syracuse | 1977 | 6:32.4 | Cornell | Pennsylvania |
| 1931 | 18:54 1/5 | Navy | Cornell | 1978 | 6:39.5 | Syracuse | Brown |
| 1932 | 19:55 | California | Cornell | 1979 | 6:26.4 | Brown | Wisconsin |
| 1934 | 19:44 | California | Washington | 1980 | 6:46 | Navy | Northeastern |
| 1935 | 18:52 | California | Cornell | 1981 | 5:57.3 | Cornell | Navy |
| 1936 | 19:09 3/5 | Washington | California | 1982 | 5:57.5 | Cornell | Princeton |
| 1937 | 18:33 3/5 | Washington | Navy | 1983 | 6:14.4 | Brown | Navy |
| 1938 | 18:19 | Navy | California | 1984 | 5:54.7 | Navy | Pennsylvania |
| 1939 | 18:12 3/5 | California | Washington | 1985 | 5:49.9 | Princeton | Brown |
| 1940 | 22:42 | Washington | Cornell | 1986 | 5:50.2 | Brown | Pennsylvania |

1. Disqualified.

# HARNESS RACING

Oliver Wendell Holmes, the famous Autocrat of the Breakfast Table, wrote that the running horse was a gambling toy but the trotting horse was useful and, furthermore, "horse-racing is not a republican institution; horse-trotting is." Oliver Wendell Holmes was a born-and-bred New Englander, and New England was the nursery of the harness racing sport in America. Pacers and trotters were matters of local pride and prejudice in Colonial New England, and, shortly after the Revolution, the Messenger and Justin Morgan strains produced many winners in harness racing "matches" along the turnpikes of New York, Connecticut, Rhode Island, Massachusetts, Vermont, and New Hampshire.

There was English thoroughbred blood in Messenger and Justin Morgan, and, many years later, it was blended in Rysdyk's Hambletonian, foaled in 1849. Hambletonian was not particularly fast under harness but his descendants have had almost a monopoly of prizes, titles, and records in the harness racing game. Hambletonian was purchased as a foal with its dam for a total of $124 by William Rysdyk of Goshen, N.Y., and made a modest fortune for the purchaser.

Trotters and pacers often were raced under saddle in the old days, and, in fact, the custom still survives in some places in Europe. Dexter, the great trotter that lowered the mile record from 2:19 3/4 to 2:17 1/4 in 1867, was said to handle just as well under saddle as when pulling a sulky. But as sulkies were lightened in weight and improved in design, trotting under saddle became less common and finally faded out in this country.

## WORLD RECORDS

Established in a Race or Against Time at One Mile
*Source:* Research Specialist, United States Trotting Association

### Trotting on Mile Track

| | Record | Holder | Driver | Where Made | Year |
|---|---|---|---|---|---|
| All Age | 1:53 2/5 | Prakas | Bill O'Donnell | DuQuoin, Illl. | 1985 |
| | 1:54* | Arndon | Del Miller | Lexington, Ky. | 1982 |
| | 1:54 4/5[1] | Lindy's Crown | Howard Beissinger | Du Quoin, Ill. | 1980 |
| 2–year-old | 1:56[1] | TV Yankee | Tom Haughton | Lexington, Ky. | 1982 |
| | 1:55 4/5* | Fancy Crown | George Sholte | Lexington, Ky. | 1983 |
| 3–year-old | 1:53 2/5 | Praka | Bill O'Donnell | DuQuoin, Ill. | 1985 |
| | 1:53 4/5 | Fancy Crown | Bill O'Donnell | Springfield, Ill. | 1984 |
| | 1:54* | Arndon | Del Miller | Lexington, Ky. | 1982 |
| | 1:55[1] | Speedy Somolli | Howard Beissinger | Du Quoin, Ill. | 1978 |
| | 1:55[1] | Florida Pro | George Sholty | Du Quoin, Ill. | 1978 |
| | 1:55[1] | Jazz Cosmos | Mickey McNichol | Lexington, Ky. | 1982 |
| 4–year-old | 1:54 3/5 | Premium Lobell | Dan Shetter | DuQuoin, Ill. | 1984 |
| | 1:54 4/5[1] | Lindy's Crown | Howard Beissinger | DuQuoin, Ill. | 1980 |
| | 1:54 4/5* | Nevele Pride | Stanely Dancer | Indianapolis | 1969 |

### Trotting on Five-Eights Mile Track

| | Record | Holder | Driver | Where Made | Year |
|---|---|---|---|---|---|
| All Age | 1:57 1/5[1] | Lindy's Crown | Howard Beissinger | Wilmington, Del. | 1980 |
| 2–year-old | 1:58 2/5[1] | Mr. Drew | Jan Nordin | Wilmington, Del. | 1982 |
| 3–year-old | 1:57 2 | Baltic Speed | Jan Nordin | Pompano Beach, Fla. | 1984 |
| | 1:57 2/5[1] | Arndon | Del Miller | Montreal, Quebec | 1982 |
| 4–year-old | 1:57 1/5[1] | Lindy's Crown | Howard Beissinger | Wilmington, Del. | 1980 |

### Trotting on Half-Mile Track

| | Record | Holder | Driver | Where Made | Year |
|---|---|---|---|---|---|
| All Age | 1:56 4/5[1] | Nevele Pride | Stanley Dancer | Saratoga Springs, N.Y. | 1969 |
| 2–year-old | 2:00[1] | Incredible Nevele | Glen Garnsey | Delaware, Ohio | 1981 |
| 3–year-old | 1:57.1 | Fancy Crown | Bill O'Donnell | Delaware, Ohio | 1984 |
| 4–year-old | 1:56 4/5[1] | Nevele Pride | Stanley Dancer | Saratoga Springs, N.Y. | 1969 |

### Pacing on Mile Track

| | Record | Holder | Driver | Where Made | Year |
|---|---|---|---|---|---|
| All Age | 1:49 3/5[1] | Nihilator | Bill O'Donnell | East Rutherford, N.J. | 1985 |
| | 1:49 1/5* | Niatross | Clint Galbraith | Lexington, Ky. | 1980 |
| 2–year-old | 1:52.4 | Nihilator | Bill O'Donnell | East Rutherford, N.J. | 1984 |
| 3–year-old | 1:51 3/5[1] | Trenton | Tommy Haughton | Springfield, Ill. | 1982 |
| | 1:49 1/5* | Niatross | Clint Galbraith | Lexington, Ky. | 1980 |
| | 1:49.3 | Nihilator | Bill O'Donnell | East Rutherford, N.J. | 1985 |
| 4–year-old | 1:50 4/5* | Fan Hanover | Glen Garnsey | Lexington, Ky. | 1982 |
| | 1:51 4/5[1] | It's Fritz | Martin Allen | Lexington, Ky. | 1983 |
| | 1:51.4 | On the Road Again | William Gilmour | East Rutherford, N.J. | 1985 |
| | 1:51.4 | Save Fuel | John Campbell | East Rutherford, N.J. | 1985 |

### Pacing on Five-Eighths Mile Track

| | Record | Holder | Driver | Where Made | Year |
|---|---|---|---|---|---|
| All Age | 1:52 1/5[1] | It's Fritz | Martin Allen | Meadow Lands, Pa. | 1983 |
| 2–year-old | 1:54.1 | Dragon's Lair | Jeff Mallet | Meadowlands, Lands, Pa. | 1984 |
| 3–year-old | 1:52.1 | Marauder | Dick Richardson, Jr. | Meadow Lands, Pa. | 1985 |
| 4–year-old | 1:52 1/5[1] | It's Fritz | Martin Allen | Meadow Lands, Pa. | 1983 |

### Pacing on Half-Mile Track

| | Record | Holder | Driver | Where Made | Year |
|---|---|---|---|---|---|
| All Age | 1:53 3/5[1] | It's Fritz | Martin Allen | Louisville, Ky. | 1983 |
| 2–year-old | 1:56.0 | Cervantes Osborne | Donald Irvine, Jr. | Delaware, Ohio | 1984 |
| | 1:56 1/5[1] | Signed N. Sealed | Bill O'Donnell | Louisville, Ky. | 1983 |
| 3–year-old | 1:53.3 | Legal Notice | John Hayes, Jr. | Delaware, Ohio | 1984 |
| 4–year-old | 1:53 3/5[1] | It's Fritz | Martin Allen | Louisville, Ky. | 1983 |

1. Record set in race. *Record set in time trial.

## HARNESS RACING RECORDS FOR THE MILE

| Trotters | | | Pacers | | |
|---|---|---|---|---|---|
| **Time** | **Trotter, age, driver** | **Year** | **Time** | **Pacer, age, driver** | **Year** |
| 2:00 | Lou Dillon, 5, Millard Sanders | 1903 | 2:00 1/2 | John R. Gentry, 7, W.J. Andrews | 1896 |
| 1:58 1/2 | Lou Dillon, 5, Millard Sanders | 1903 | 1:59 1/4 | Star Pointer, 8, D. McClary | 1897 |
| 1:58 | Uhlan, 8, Charles Tanner | 1912 | 1:59 | Dan Patch, 7, M. E. McHenry | 1903 |
| 1:58 | Peter Manning, 5, T. W. Murphy | 1921 | 1:56 1/4 | Dan Patch, 7, M. E. McHenry | 1903 |
| 1:57 3/4 | Peter Manning, 5, T. W. Murphy | 1921 | 1:56 | Dan Patch, 8, H. C. Hersey | 1904 |
| 1:57 | Peter Manning, 6, T. W. Murphy | 1922 | 1:55 | Billy Direct, 4, Vic Fleming | 1938 |
| 1:56 3/4 | Peter Manning, 6, T. W. Murphy | 1922 | 1:55 | Adios Harry, 4, Luther Lyons | 1955 |
| 1:56 3/4 | Greyhound, 5, Sep Palin | 1937 | 1:54 3/5 | Adios Butler, 4, Paige West | 1960 |
| 1:56 | Greyhound, 5, Sep Palin | 1937 | 1:54 | Bret Hanover, 4, Frank Ervin | 1966 |
| 1:55 1/4 | Greyhound, 6, Sep Palin | 1938 | 1:53 3/5 | Bret Hanover, 4, Frank Ervin | 1966 |
| 1:54 4/5 | Nevele Pride, 4, Stanley Dancer | 1969 | 1:52 | Steady Star, 4, Joe O'Brien | 1971 |
| 1:54 4/5 | Lindy's Crown, 4, Howard Beissinger | 1980 | 1:49 1/5 | Niatross, 3, Clint Galbraith | 1980 |
| 1:54 | Arndon, 3, Del Miller | 1982 | | | |

## HISTORY OF TRADITIONAL HARNESS RACING STAKES

### The Hambletonian

Three-year-old trotters. One mile. Guy McKinney won first race at Syracuse in 1926; held at Goshen, N.Y., 1930–1942, 1944–1956; at Yonkers, N.Y., 1943; at Du Quoin, Ill., 1957–1980. Since 1981, the race has been held at The Meadowland in East Rutherford, N.J.

| Year | Winner | Driver | Best time | Total purse |
|---|---|---|---|---|
| 1967 | Speedy Streak | Del Cameron | 2:00 | 122,650 |
| 1968 | Nevele Pride | Stanley Dancer | 1:59 2/5 | 116,190 |
| 1969 | Lindy's Pride | Howard Beissinger | 1:57 3/5 | 124,910 |
| 1970 | Timothy T. | John Simpson, Jr. | 1:58 2/5[1] | 143,630 |
| 1971 | Speedy Crown | Howard Beissinger | 1:57 2/5 | 129,770 |
| 1972 | Super Bowl | Stanley Dancer | 1:56 2/5 | 119,090 |
| 1973 | Flirth | Ralph Baldwin | 1:57 1/5 | 144,710 |
| 1974 | Christopher T | Billy Haughton | 1:58 3/5 | 160,150 |
| 1975 | Bonefish | Stanely Dancer | 1:59[2] | 232,192 |
| 1976 | Steve Lobell | Billy Haughton | 1:56 2/5 | 263,524 |
| 1977 | Green Speed | Billy Haughton | 1:55 3/5 | 284,131 |
| 1978 | Speedy Somolli | Howard Beissinger | 1:55[3] | 241,280 |
| 1979 | Legend Hanover | George Sholty | 1:56 1/5 | 300,000 |
| 1980 | Burgomeister | Billy Haughton | 1:56 3/5 | 293,570 |
| 1981 | Shiaway St. Pat | Ray Remmen | 2:01 1/5[4] | 838,000 |
| 1982 | Speed Bowl | Tommy Haughton | 1:56 4/5 | 875,750 |
| 1983 | Duenna | Stanley Dancer | 1:57 2/5 | 1,000,000 |
| 1984 | Historic Free | Ben Webster | 1:56 2/5 | 1,219,000 |
| 1985 | Prakas | Bill O'Donnell | 1:54 3/5 | 1,272,000 |
| 1986 | Nuclear Kosmos | Ulf Thoresen | 1:56 | 1,172,082 |

1. By Formal Notice. 2. By Yankee Bambino. 3. By Speedy Somolli and Florida Pro. 4. By Super Juan.

### Little Brown Jug

Three-year-old pacers. One Mile. Raced at Delaware County Fair Grounds, Delaware, Ohio.

| Year | Winner | Driver | Best time | Total purse |
|---|---|---|---|---|
| 1967 | Best of All | Jim Hackett | 1:59[1] | 84,778 |
| 1968 | Rum Customer | Billy Haughton | 1:59 3/5 | 104,226 |
| 1969 | Laverne Hanover | Billy Haughton | 2:00 2/5 | 109,731 |
| 1970 | Most Happy Fella | Stanley Dancer | 1:57 1/5 | 100,110 |
| 1971 | Nansemond | Herve Filion | 1:57 2/5 | 102,994 |
| 1972 | Strike Out | Keith Waples | 1:56 3/5 | 104,916 |
| 1973 | Melvin's Woe | Joe O'Brien | 1:57 3/5 | 120,000 |
| 1974 | Ambro Omaha | Billy Haughton | 1:57 | 132,630 |
| 1975 | Seatrain | Ben Webster | 1:57[2] | 147,813 |
| 1976 | Keystone Ore | Stanley Dancer | 1:56 4/5[3] | 153,799 |
| 1977 | Governor Skipper | John Chapman | 1:56 1/5 | 150,000 |
| 1978 | Happy Escort | William Popfinger | 1:55 2/5[4] | 186,760 |
| 1979 | Hot Hitter | Herve Filion | 1:55 3/5 | 226,455 |
| 1980 | Niatross | Clint Galbraith | 1:54 4/5 | 207,361 |
| 1981 | Fan Hanover | Glen Garnsey | 1:56[5] | 243,799 |
| 1982 | Merger | John Campbell | 1:56 3/5 | 328,900 |
| 1983 | Ralph Hanover | Ron Waples | 1:55 3/5 | 358,800 |
| 1984 | Colt 46 | Norman Boring | 1:53 3/5 | 366,717 |
| 1985 | Nihilator | Bill O'Donnell | 1:52 1/5 | 350,730 |
| 1986 | Barberry Spur | Bill O'Donnell | 1:52 4/5 | 407,684 |

1. By Nardin's Byrd. 2. By Armbro Ranger. 3. By Falcon Almahurst. 4. By Falcon Almahurst. 5. By Seahawk Hanover.

## HARNESS HORSE OF THE YEAR

Chosen in poll conducted by United States Trotting Association in conjunction with the U.S. Harness Writers Assn.

| | | | | | |
|---|---|---|---|---|---|
| 1959 | Bye Bye Byrd, Pacer | 1968 | Nevele Pride, Trotter | 1977 | Green Speed, Trotter |
| 1960 | Adios Butler, Pacer | 1969 | Nevele Pride, Trotter | 1978 | Abercrombie, Pacer |
| 1961 | Adios Butler, Pacer | 1970 | Fresh Yankee, Trotter | 1979 | Niatross, Pacer |
| 1962 | Su Mac Lad, Trotter | 1971 | Albatross, Pacer | 1980 | Niatross, Pacer |
| 1963 | Speedy Scot, Trotter | 1972 | Albatross, Pacer | 1981 | Fan Hanover, Pacer |
| 1964 | Bret Hanover, Pacer | 1973 | Sir Dalrae, Pacer | 1982 | Cam Fella, Pacer |
| 1965 | Bret Hanover, Pacer | 1974 | Delmonica Hanover, Trotter | 1983 | Cam Fella, Pacer |
| 1966 | Bret Hanover, Pacer | 1975 | Savoir, Trotter | 1984 | Fancy Crown, Trotter |
| 1967 | Nevele Pride, Trotter | 1976 | Keystone Ore, Pacer | 1985 | Nihilator, Trotter |

# WEIGHTLIFTING

## U.S. WEIGHTLIFTING FEDERATION
## MEN'S NATIONAL CHAMPIONSHIPS

(Jacksonville, Fla., May 3-4, 1986)

| | Snatch | C&J[1] | Total[2] |
|---|---|---|---|
| 52 kg (114 lb)—Steve Womble | 70 | 92.5 | 162.5 |
| 56 kg (123 lb)—Gene Galsdorf | 90 | 117.5 | 207.5 |
| 60 kg (132 lb)—Brian Miyamoto | 105 | 120 | 225 |
| 67.5 kg (148 lb)—Cal Schake | 120 | 142.5 | 262.5 |
| 75 kg (165 lb)—Gary Savage | 127.5 | 170 | 297.5 |
| 82.5 kg (181 lb)—Curt White | 152.5 | 185 | 337.5 |
| 90 kg (198 lb)—Mike Cohen | 147.5 | 185 | 332.5 |
| 100 kg (220 lb)—Rich Schutz | 152.5 | 180 | 332.5 |
| 110 kg (242 lb)—Mario Martinez | 167.5 | 205 | 372.5 |
| Over 110 kg—John Bergman | 165 | 207.5 | 372.5 |

1. Clean and jerk. 2. All results in kilograms.

## WOMEN'S NATIONAL CHAMPIONSHIPS

(Portland, Ore., March 1, 1986)

| | Snatch | C&J[1] | Total[2] |
|---|---|---|---|
| 44 kg (97 lb)—Carol Santandrea | 40 | 55[3] | 95[3] |
| 48 kg (105.8 lb)—No contestants totaled | | | |
| 52 kg (114.5 lb)—Danelle Markham | 50 | 60 | 110 |
| 56 kg (123 lb)—Michelle Evris | 65 | 97.5 | 162.5 |
| 60 kg (132 lb)—Colleen Colley | 67.5 | 92.5 | 160 |
| 67.5 kg (148 lb)—Arlys Kovach | 80 | 92.5 | 172.5 |
| 75 kg (165 lb)—Jody Anderson | 75 | 105 | 180 |
| 82.5 kg (181 lb)—Carol Cady | 82.5 | 105 | 187.5 |
| Over 82.5 kg—Annette Bohach | 72.5 | 97.5 | 169 |

1. Clean and jerk. 2. All results in kilograms. 3. American record.

# WRESTLING

## U.S.A. NATIONAL
## CHAMPIONSHIPS—1986

**Freestyle**

105.5 lb (48 kg)—Rich Salamone, New York Athletic Club
114.5 lb (52 kg)—Joe Gonzales, Sunkist Kids, Phoenix, Ariz.
125.5 lb (57 kg)—Kevin Darkus, Cyclone Wrestling Club, Ames, Iowa
136.5 lb (62 kg)—John Smith, Sunkist Kids
149.5 lb (68 kg)—Andre Metzger, New York Athletic Club
163.0 lb (74 kg)—Dave Schultz, Sunkist Kids
180.5 lb (82 kg)—Mark Schultz, Sunkist Kids
198.0 lb (90 kg)—Jim Scherr, Wildcat Wrestling Club, Evanston, Ill.
220.0 lb (100 kg)—Dan Severn, Sunkist Kids
Unlimited—Bruce Baumgartner, New York Athletic Club

**Greco-Roman**

105.5 lb (48 kg)—Eric Wetzel, United States Marine Corps
114.5 lb (52 kg)—Shawn Sheldon, Adirondack Wrestling Club, Albany, N.Y.
125.5 lb (57 kg)—Anthony Amado, Sunkist Kids
136.5 lb (62 kg)—Frank Famiano, Adirondack Wrestling Club
149.5 lb (68 kg)—Jim Martinez, Minnesota Wrestling Club
163.0 lb (74 kg)—David Butler, United States Navy
180.5 lb (82 kg)—Darryl Gholar, Minnesota Wrestling Club
198.0 lb (90 kg)—Derrick Waldroup, United States Army
220.0 lb (100 kg)—Dennis Koslowski, Minnesota Wrestling Club
Heavyweight—Dwayne Koslowski, Minnesota Wrestling Club

## WORLD CUP—1986

(Toledo, Ohio, April, 1986)

105.5 lb (48 kg)—Sergey Karamachakov, Soviet Union
114.5 lb (52 kg)—Vladimir Togouzov, Soviet Union
125.5 lb (57 kg)—Sergey Beloglazov, Soviet Union
136.5 lb (62 kg)—Avirmediin Enkee, Mongolia

149.5 lb (68 kg)—Arsen Fadzaev, Soviet Union
163.0 lb (74 kg)—Nate Carr, United States
180.5 lb (82 kg)—Jim Scherr, United States
198.0 lb (90 kg)—Makharbek Khadartsev, Soviet Union
220.0 lb (100 kg)—Dan Severn, United States
Heavyweight—Bruce Baumgartner, United States

## WORLD CHAMPIONSHIP—1985

(Budapest, Hungary, Oct. 10–13, 1985. Next scheduled for Budapest, Oct. 18–26, 1986, after Information Please went to press)

105.5 lb (48 kg)—Kim Chol Hwan, Republic of Korea
114.5 lb (52 kg)—Valentine Jordanov, Bulgaria
125.5 lb (57 kg)—Sergey Beloglazov, Soviet Union
136.5 lb (62 kg)—Viktor Alekseev, Soviet Union
149.5 lb (68 kg)—Arsen Fadzaev, Soviet Union
163.0 lb (74 kg)—Raul Cascaret, Cuba
180.5 lb (82 kg)—Mark Schultz, United States
198.0 lb (90 kg)—Bill Scherr, United States
220.0 lb (100 kg)—Leri Khabelov, Soviet Union
Heavyweight—David Gobedgisvila, Soviet Union

## N.C.A.A. CHAMPIONSHIPS—1986

(Iowa City, Iowa, March 13–15, 1986)

118 lb—Rick Bonomo, Bloomsburg
126 lb—Brad Penrith, Iowa
134 lb—Jim Jordan, Wisconsin
142 lb—Kevin Dresser, Iowa
150 lb—Jim Heffernan, Iowa
158 lb—Jude Skove, Ohio State
167 lb—Marty Kistler, Iowa
177 lb—Melvin Douglas, Oklahoma
190 lb—Duane Goldman, Iowa
Heavyweight—Kirk Trost, Michigan
Most Outstanding Wrestler: Marty Kistler, Iowa
Team scores: 1. Iowa 158[1] 2. Oklahoma 84.75 3. Oklahoma State 77.25

1. New NCAA record.

# GOLF

It may be that golf originated in Holland—historians believe it did—but certainly Scotland fostered the game and is famous for it. In fact, in 1457 the Scottish Parliament, disturbed because football and golf had lured young Scots from the more soldierly exercise of archery, passed an ordinance that "futeball and golf be utterly cryit doun and nocht usit." James I and Charles I of the royal line of Stuarts were golf enthusiasts, whereby the game came to be known as "the royal and ancient game of golf."

The golf balls used in the early games were leather-covered and stuffed with feathers. Clubs of all kinds were fashioned by hand to suit individual players. The great step in spreading the game came with the change from the feather ball to the guttapercha ball about 1850. In 1860, formal competition began with the establishment of an annual tournament for the British Open championship. There are records of "golf clubs" in the United

States as far back as colonial days but no proof of actual play before John Reid and some friends laid out six holes on the Reid lawn in Yonkers, N.Y., in 1888 and played there with golf balls and clubs brought over from Scotland by Robert Lockhart. This group then formed the St. Andrews Golf Club of Yonkers, and golf was established in this country.

However, it remained a rather sedate and almost aristocratic pastime until a 20-year-old ex-caddy, Francis Ouimet of Boston, defeated two great British professionals, Harry Vardon and Ted Ray, in the United States Open championship at Brookline, Mass., in 1913. This feat put the game and Francis Ouimet on the front pages of the newspapers and stirred a wave of enthusiasm for the sport. The greatest feat so far in golf history is that of Robert Tyre Jones, Jr., of Atlanta, who won the British Open, the British Amateur, the U.S. Open, and the U.S. Amateur titles in one year, 1930.

## THE MASTERS TOURNAMENT WINNERS

Augusta National Golf Club, Augusta, Ga.

| Year | Winner | Score | Year | Winner | Score | Year | Winner | Score |
|------|--------|-------|------|--------|-------|------|--------|-------|
| 1934 | Horton Smith | 284 | 1953 | Ben Hogan | 274 | 1970 | Billy Casper[1] | 279 |
| 1935 | Gene Sarazen[1] | 282 | 1954 | Sam Snead[1] | 289 | 1971 | Charles Coody | 279 |
| 1936 | Horton Smith | 285 | 1955 | Cary Middlecoff | 279 | 1972 | Jack Nicklaus | 286 |
| 1937 | Byron Nelson | 283 | 1956 | Jack Burke | 289 | 1973 | Tommy Aaron | 283 |
| 1938 | Henry Picard | 285 | 1957 | Doug Ford | 283 | 1974 | Gary Player | 278 |
| 1939 | Ralph Guldahl | 279 | 1958 | Arnold Palmer | 284 | 1975 | Jack Nicklaus | 276 |
| 1940 | Jimmy Demaret | 280 | 1959 | Art Wall, Jr. | 284 | 1976 | Ray Floyd | 271 |
| 1941 | Craig Wood | 280 | 1960 | Arnold Palmer | 282 | 1977 | Tom Watson | 276 |
| 1942 | Byron Nelson[1] | 280 | 1961 | Gary Player | 280 | 1978 | Gary Player | 277 |
| 1943–45 | No Tournaments | | 1962 | Arnold Palmer[1] | 280 | 1979 | Fuzzy Zoeller[1] | 280 |
| 1946 | Herman Keiser | 282 | 1963 | Jack Nicklaus | 286 | 1980 | Severiano Ballesteros | 275 |
| 1947 | Jimmy Demaret | 281 | 1964 | Arnold Palmer | 276 | 1981 | Tom Watson | 280 |
| 1948 | Claude Harmon | 279 | 1965 | Jack Nicklaus | 271 | 1982 | Craig Stadler[1] | 284 |
| 1949 | Sam Snead | 282 | 1966 | Jack Nicklaus[1] | 288 | 1983 | Severiano Ballesteros | 280 |
| 1950 | Jimmy Demaret | 283 | 1967 | Gay Brewer, Jr. | 280 | 1984 | Ben Crenshaw | 277 |
| 1951 | Ben Hogan | 280 | 1968 | Bob Goalby | 277 | 1985 | Bernhard Langer | 282 |
| 1952 | Sam Snead | 286 | 1969 | George Archer | 281 | 1986 | Jack Nicklaus | 279 |

1. Winner in playoff.

## U.S. OPEN CHAMPIONS

| Year | Winner | Score | Where played | Year | Winner | Score | Where played |
|------|--------|-------|--------------|------|--------|-------|--------------|
| 1895 | Horace Rawlins | 173 | Newport | 1919 | Walter Hagen[2] | 301 | Brae Burn |
| 1896 | James Foulis | 152 | Shinnecock Hills | 1920 | Edward Ray | 295 | Inverness |
| 1897 | Joe Lloyd | 162 | Chicago | 1921 | Jim Barnes | 289 | Columbia |
| 1898[3] | Fred Herd | 328 | Myopia | 1922 | Gene Sarazen | 288 | Skokie |
| 1899 | Willie Smith | 315 | Baltimore | 1923 | R. T. Jones, Jr.[1] [2] | 296 | Inwood |
| 1900 | Harry Vardon | 313 | Chicago | 1924 | Cyril Walker | 297 | Oakland Hills |
| 1901 | Willie Anderson[1] | 331 | Myopia | 1925 | Willie Macfarlane[1] | 291 | Worcester |
| 1902 | Laurie Auchterlonie | 307 | Garden City | 1926 | R. T. Jones, Jr.[2] | 293 | Scioto |
| 1903 | Willie Anderson[1] | 307 | Baltusrol | 1927 | Tommy Armour[1] | 301 | Oakmont |
| 1904 | Willie Anderson | 303 | Glen View | 1928 | Johnny Farrell[1] | 294 | Olympia Fields |
| 1905 | Willie Anderson | 314 | Myopia | 1929 | R. T. Jones, Jr.[1] [2] | 294 | Winged Foot |
| 1906 | Alex Smith | 295 | Onwentsia | 1930 | R. T. Jones, Jr.[2] | 287 | Interlachen |
| 1907 | Alex Ross | 302 | Philadelphia | 1931 | Billy Burke[1] | 292 | Inverness |
| 1908 | Fred McLeod[1] | 322 | Myopia | 1932 | Gene Sarazen | 286 | Fresh Meadow |
| 1909 | George Sargent | 290 | Englewood | 1933 | John Goodman[2] | 287 | North Shore |
| 1910 | Alex Smith[1] | 298 | Philadelphia | 1934 | Olin Dutra | 293 | Merion |
| 1911 | John McDermott[1] | 307 | Chicago | 1935 | Sam Parks, Jr. | 299 | Oakmont |
| 1912 | John McDermott | 294 | Buffalo | 1936 | Tony Manero | 282 | Baltusrol |
| 1913 | Francis Ouimet[1] [2] | 304 | Brookline | 1937 | Ralph Guldahl | 281 | Oakland Hills |
| 1914 | Walter Hagen | 290 | Midlothian | 1938 | Ralph Guldahl | 284 | Cherry Hills |
| 1915 | Jerome D. Travers[2] | 297 | Baltusrol | 1939 | Byron Nelson[1] | 284 | Philadelphia |
| 1916 | Charles Evans, Jr.[2] | 286 | Minikahda | 1940 | Lawson Little[1] | 287 | Canterbury |
| 1917–18 | No tournaments[4] | | | 1941 | Craig Wood | 284 | Colonial |

| Year | Winner | Score | Where played | Year | Winner | Score | Where played |
|---|---|---|---|---|---|---|---|
| 1942–45 | No tournaments[5] | | | 1966 | Bill Casper[1] | 278 | Olympic |
| 1946 | Lloyd Mangrum[1] | 284 | Canterbury | 1967 | Jack Nicklaus | 275 | Baltusrol |
| 1947 | Lew Worsham[1] | 282 | St. Louis | 1968 | Lee Trevino | 275 | Oak Hill |
| 1948 | Ben Hogan | 276 | Riviera | 1969 | Orville Moody | 281 | Champions G. C. |
| 1949 | Cary Middlecoff | 286 | Medinah | 1970 | Tony Jacklin | 281 | Hazeltine |
| 1950 | Ben Hogan[1] | 287 | Merion | 1971 | Lee Trevino[1] | 280 | Merion |
| 1951 | Ben Hogan | 287 | Oakland Hills | 1972 | Jack Nicklaus | 290 | Pebble Beach |
| 1952 | Julius Boros | 281 | Northwood | 1973 | Johnny Miller | 279 | Oakmont |
| 1953 | Ben Hogan | 283 | Oakmont | 1974 | Hale Irwin | 287 | Winged Foot |
| 1954 | Ed Furgol | 284 | Baltusrol | 1975 | Lou Graham[1] | 287 | Medinah |
| 1955 | Jack Fleck[1] | 287 | Olympic | 1976 | Jerry Pate | 277 | Atlanta A.C. |
| 1956 | Cary Middlecoff | 281 | Oak Hill | 1977 | Hubert Green | 278 | Southern Hills |
| 1957 | Dick Mayer[1] | 298 | Inverness | 1978 | Andy North | 285 | Cherry Hills |
| 1958 | Tommy Bolt | 283 | Southern Hills | 1979 | Hale Irwin | 284 | Inverness |
| 1959 | Bill Casper, Jr. | 282 | Winged Foot | 1980 | Jack Nicklaus | 272 | Baltusrol |
| 1960 | Arnold Palmer | 280 | Cherry Hills | 1981 | David Graham | 273 | Merion |
| 1961 | Gene Littler | 281 | Oakland Hills | 1982 | Tom Watson | 282 | Pebble Beach |
| 1962 | Jack Nicklaus[1] | 283 | Oakmont | 1983 | Larry Nelson | 280 | Oakmont |
| 1963 | Julius Boros[1] | 293 | Country Club | 1984 | Fuzzy Zoeller[1] | 276 | Winged Foot |
| 1964 | Ken Venturi | 278 | Congressional | 1985 | Andy North | 279 | Oakland Hills |
| 1965 | Gary Player[1] | 282 | Bellerive | 1986 | Ray Floyd | 279 | Shinnecock Hills |

1. Winner in playoff. 2. Amateur. 3. In 1898, competition was extended to 72 holes. 4. In 1917, Jock Hutchison, with a 292, won an Open Patriotic Tournament for the benefit of the American Red Cross at Whitemarsh Valley Country Club. 5. In 1942, Ben Hogan, with a 271 won a Hale American National Open Tournament for the benefit of the Navy Relief Society and USO at Ridgemoor Country Club.

## U.S. AMATEUR CHAMPIONS

| Year | Winner | Year | Winner | Year | Winner | Year | Winner |
|---|---|---|---|---|---|---|---|
| 1895 | Charles B. Macdonald | 1922 | Jess W. Sweetser | 1949 | Charles Coe | 1970 | Lanny Wadkins |
| 1896–97 | H. J. Whigham | 1923 | Max R. Marston | 1950 | Sam Urzetta | 1971 | Gary Cowan |
| 1898 | Findlay S. Douglas | 1924–25 | R. T. Jones, Jr. | 1951 | Billy Maxwell | 1972 | Vinny Giles 3d |
| 1899 | H. M. Harriman | 1926 | George Von Elm | 1952 | Jack Westland | 1973[3] | Craig Stadler |
| 1900–01 | Walter J. Travis | 1927–28 | R. T. Jones, Jr. | 1953 | Gene Littler | 1974 | Jerry Pate |
| 1902 | Louis N. James | 1929 | H. R. Johnston | 1954 | Arnold Palmer | 1975 | Fred Ridley |
| 1903 | Walter J. Travis | 1930 | R. T. Jones, Jr. | 1955–56 | Harvie Ward | 1976 | Bill Sander |
| 1904–05 | H. Chandler Egan | 1931 | Francis Ouimet | 1957 | Hillman Robbins | 1977 | John Fought |
| 1906 | Eben M. Byers | 1932 | Ross Somerville | 1958 | Charles Coe | 1978 | John Cook |
| 1907–08 | Jerome D. Travers | 1933 | G. T. Dunlap, Jr. | 1959 | Jack Nicklaus | 1979 | Mark O'Meara |
| 1909 | Robert A. Gardner | 1934–35 | Lawson Little | 1960 | Deane Beman | 1980 | Hal Sutton |
| 1910 | W. C. Fownes, Jr. | 1936 | John W. Fischer | 1961 | Jack Nicklaus | 1981 | Nathaniel Crosby |
| 1911 | Harold H. Hilton | 1937 | John Goodman | 1962 | Labron Harris, Jr. | 1982 | Jay Sigel |
| 1912–13 | Jerome D. Travers | 1938 | Willie Turnesa | 1963 | Deane Beman | 1983 | Jay Sigel |
| 1914 | Francis Ouimet | 1939 | Marvin H. Ward | 1964 | Bill Campbell | 1984 | Scott Verplank |
| 1915 | Robert A. Gardner | 1940 | R. D. Chapman | 1965[2] | Robert Murphy, Jr. | 1985 | Sam Randolph |
| 1916 | Charles Evans, Jr. | 1941 | Marvin H. Ward | 1966 | Gary Cowan[1] | 1986 | Buddy Alexander |
| 1919 | S. D. Herron | 1946 | Ted Bishop | 1967 | Bob Dickson | | |
| 1920 | Charles Evans, Jr. | 1947 | Robert Riegel | 1968 | Bruce Fleisher | | |
| 1921 | Jesse P. Guilford | 1948 | Willie Turnesa | 1968 | Steven Melnyk | | |

1. Winner in playoff. 2. Tourney switched to medal play through 1972. 3. Return to match play.

## U.S. P.G.A. CHAMPIONS

| Year | Winner | Year | Winner | Year | Winner | Year | Winner |
|---|---|---|---|---|---|---|---|
| 1916 | Jim Barnes | 1940 | Byron Nelson | 1957 | Lionel Hebert | 1973 | Jack Nicklaus |
| 1919 | Jim Barnes | 1941 | Victor Ghezzi | 1958[2] | Dow Finsterwald | 1974 | Lee Trevino |
| 1920 | Jock Hutchison | 1942 | Sam Snead | 1959 | Bob Rosburg | 1975 | Jack Nicklaus |
| 1921 | Walter Hagen | 1944 | Bob Hamilton | 1960 | Jay Hebert | 1976 | Dave Stockton |
| 1922–23 | Gene Sarazen | 1945 | Byron Nelson | 1961 | Jerry Barber[1] | 1977 | Lanny Wadkins[1] |
| 1924–27 | Walter Hagen | 1946 | Ben Hogan | 1962 | Gary Player | 1978 | John Mahaffey |
| 1928–29 | Leo Diegel | 1947 | Jim Ferrier | 1963 | Jack Nicklaus | 1979 | David Graham[1] |
| 1930 | Tommy Armour | 1948 | Ben Hogan | 1964 | Bobby Nichols | 1980 | Jack Nicklaus |
| 1931 | Tom Creavy | 1949 | Sam Snead | 1965 | Dave Marr | 1981 | Larry Nelson |
| 1932 | Olin Dutra | 1950 | Chandler Harper | 1966 | Al Geiberger | 1982 | Ray Floyd |
| 1933 | Gene Sarazen | 1951 | Sam Snead | 1967 | Don January[1] | 1983 | Hal Sutton |
| 1934 | Paul Runyan | 1952 | Jim Turnesa | 1968 | Julius Boros | 1984 | Lee Trevino |
| 1935 | Johnny Revolta | 1953 | Walter Burkemo | 1969 | Ray Floyd | 1985 | Hubert Green |
| 1936–37 | Denny Shute | 1954 | Chick Harbert | 1970 | Dave Stockton | 1986 | Bob Tway |
| 1938 | Paul Runyan | 1955 | Doug Ford | 1971 | Jack Nicklaus | | |
| 1939 | Henry Picard | 1956 | Jack Burke, Jr. | 1972 | Gary Player | | |

1. Winner in playoff. 2. Switched to medal play.

## U.S. WOMEN'S AMATEUR CHAMPIONS

| | | | | | | | |
|---|---|---|---|---|---|---|---|
| 1916 | Alexa Stirling | 1937 | Mrs. J. A. Page, Jr. | 1957 | JoAnne Gunderson | 1972 | Mary Ann Budke |
| 1919–20 | Alexa Stirling | 1938 | Patty Berg | 1958 | Anne Quast | 1973 | Carol Semple |
| 1921 | Marion Hollins | 1939–40 | Betty Jameson | 1959 | Barbara McIntire | 1974 | Cynthia Hill |
| 1922 | Glenna Collett | 1941 | Mrs. Frank Newell | 1960 | JoAnne Gunderson | 1975 | Beth Daniel |
| 1923 | Edith Cummings | 1946 | Mildred Zaharias | 1961 | Anne Quast Decker | 1976 | Donna Horton |
| 1924 | Dorothy Campbell | 1947 | Louise Suggs | 1962 | JoAnne Gunderson | 1977 | Beth Daniel |
| | Hurd | 1948 | Grace Lenczyk | 1963 | Anne Quast Welts | 1978 | Cathy Sherk |
| 1925 | Glenna Collett | 1949 | Mrs. D. G. Porter | 1964 | Barbara McIntire | 1979 | Carolyn Hill |
| 1926 | Helen Stetson | 1950 | Beverly Hanson | 1965 | Jean Ashley | 1980 | Juli Inkster |
| 1927 | Mrs. M. B. Horn | 1951 | Dorothy Kirby | 1966 | JoAnne Gunderson | 1981 | Juli Inkster |
| 1928–30 | Glenna Collett | 1952 | Jacqueline Pung | 1967 | Lou Dill | 1982 | Juli Inkster |
| 1931 | Helen Hicks | 1953 | Mary Lena Faulk | 1968 | JoAnne G. Carner | 1983 | Joanne Pacillo |
| 1932–34 | Virginia Van Wie | 1954 | Barbara Romack | 1969 | Catherine LaCoste | 1984 | Deb Richard |
| 1935 | Glenna Collett Vare | 1955 | Patricia Lesser | 1970 | Martha Wilkinson | 1985 | Michiko Hattori |
| 1936 | Pamela Barton | 1956 | Marlene Stewart | 1971 | Laura Baugh | 1986 | Kay Cockerill |

## U.S. WOMEN'S OPEN CHAMPIONS

| Year | Winner | Score | Year | Winner | Score | Year | Winner | Score |
|---|---|---|---|---|---|---|---|---|
| 1946 | Patty Berg (match play) | — | 1960 | Betsy Rawls | 291 | 1974 | Sandra Haynie | 295 |
| 1947 | Betty Jameson | 295 | 1961 | Mickey Wright | 293 | 1975 | Sandra Palmer | 295 |
| 1948 | Mildred D. Zaharias | 300 | 1962 | Murle Lindstrom | 301 | 1976 | JoAnne Carner | 292 |
| 1949 | Louise Suggs | 291 | 1963 | Mary Mills | 289 | 1977 | Hollis Stacy | 292 |
| 1950 | Mildred D. Zaharias | 291 | 1964 | Mickey Wright[1] | 290 | 1978 | Hollis Stacy | 289 |
| 1951 | Betsy Rawls | 293 | 1965 | Carol Mann | 290 | 1979 | Jerilyn Britz | 284 |
| 1952 | Louise Suggs | 284 | 1966 | Sandra Spuzich | 297 | 1980 | Amy Alcott | 280 |
| 1953 | Betsy Rawls[1] | 302 | 1967 | Catherine LaCoste | 294 | 1981 | Pat Bradley | 279 |
| 1954 | Mildred D. Zaharias | 291 | 1968 | Susie Berning | 289 | 1982 | Janet Alex | 283 |
| 1955 | Fay Crocker | 299 | 1969 | Donna Caponi | 294 | 1983 | Jan Stephenson | 290 |
| 1956 | Katherine Cornelius[1] | 302 | 1970 | Donna Caponi | 287 | 1984 | Hollis Stacy | 290 |
| 1957 | Betsy Rawls | 299 | 1971 | JoAnne Carner | 288 | 1985 | Kathy Baker | 280 |
| 1958 | Mickey Wright | 290 | 1972 | Susie Berning | 299 | 1986 | Jane Geddes | 287 |
| 1959 | Mickey Wright | 287 | 1973 | Susie Berning | 290 | | | |

1. Winner in playoff. 2. Amateur.

## BRITISH OPEN CHAMPIONS

(First tournament, held in 1860, was won by Willie Park, Sr.)

| Year | Winner | Score | Year | Winner | Score | Year | Winner | Score |
|---|---|---|---|---|---|---|---|---|
| 1920 | George Duncan | 303 | 1947 | Fred Daly | 294 | 1968 | Gary Player | 289 |
| 1921 | Jock Hutchison[1] | 296 | 1948 | Henry Cotton | 283 | 1969 | Tony Jacklin | 280 |
| 1922 | Walter Hagen | 300 | 1949 | Bobby Locke[1] | 283 | 1970 | Jack Nicklaus[1] | 283 |
| 1923 | A. G. Havers | 295 | 1950 | Bobby Locke | 279 | 1971 | Lee Trevino | 278 |
| 1924 | Walter Hagen | 301 | 1951 | Max Faulkner | 285 | 1972 | Lee Trevino | 278 |
| 1925 | Jim Barnes | 300 | 1952 | Bobby Locke | 287 | 1973 | Tom Weiskopf | 276 |
| 1926 | R. T. Jones, Jr. | 291 | 1953 | Ben Hogan | 282 | 1974 | Gary Player | 282 |
| 1927 | R. T. Jones, Jr. | 285 | 1954 | Peter Thomson | 283 | 1975 | Tom Watson[1] | 279 |
| 1928 | Walter Hagen | 292 | 1955 | Peter Thomson | 281 | 1976 | Johnny Miller | 279 |
| 1929 | Walter Hagen | 292 | 1956 | Peter Thomson | 286 | 1977 | Tom Watson | 268 |
| 1930 | R. T. Jones, Jr. | 291 | 1957 | Bobby Locke | 279 | 1978 | Jack Nicklaus | 281 |
| 1931 | Tommy Armour | 296 | 1958 | Peter Thomson[1] | 278 | 1979 | Severiano Ballesteros | 283 |
| 1932 | Gene Sarazen | 283 | 1959 | Gary Player | 284 | 1980 | Tom Watson | 271 |
| 1933 | Denny Shute[1] | 292 | 1960 | Kel Nagle | 278 | 1981 | Bill Rogers | 276 |
| 1934 | Henry Cotton | 283 | 1961 | Arnold Palmer | 284 | 1982 | Tom Watson | 284 |
| 1935 | A. Perry | 283 | 1962 | Arnold Palmer | 276 | 1983 | Tom Watson | 275 |
| 1936 | A. H. Padgham | 287 | 1963 | Bob Charles[1] | 277 | 1984 | Severiano Ballesteros | 276 |
| 1937 | Henry Cotton | 290 | 1964 | Tony Lema | 279 | 1985 | Sandy Lyle | 282 |
| 1938 | R. A. Whitcombe | 295 | 1965 | Peter Thomson | 285 | 1986 | Greg Norman | 280 |
| 1939 | R. Burton | 290 | 1966 | Jack Nicklaus | 282 | | | |
| 1940 | Sam Snead | 290 | 1967 | Roberto de Vicenzo | 278 | | | |

1. Winner in playoff.

## OTHER 1986 PGA TOUR WINNERS

(Through August 25, 1986)

| | |
|---|---|
| MONY Tournament of Champions—Calvin Peete (267) | $90,000 |
| Bob Hope Desert Classic—Donnie Hammond (335) | 108,000 |
| Phoenix Open—Hal Sutton (267) | 90,000 |
| AT&T Pebble Beach National Pro-Am—Fuzzy Zoeller (205) | 108,000 |
| Andy Williams Open—Bob Tway (204) | 81,000 |
| Hawaiian Open—Corey Pavin (272) | 90,000 |
| Los Angeles Open—Doug Tewell (270) | 81,000 |
| Honda Classic—Kenny Knox (270) | 90,000 |
| Doral Eastern Open—Andy Bean (276) | 90,000 |
| Bay Hill Classic—Dan Forsman (202) | 90,000 |
| USF&G Classic—Calvin Peete (269) | 90,000 |
| Tournament Players Championship—John Mahaffey (275) | 162,000 |
| Greensboro Open—Sandy Lyle (275) | 90,000 |
| Heritage Classic—Fuzzy Zoeller (276) | 81,000 |
| Houston Open—Curtis Strange (274) | 90,000 |
| Las Vegas Invitational—Greg Norman (333) | 207,000 |
| Byron Nelson Classic—Andy Bean (269) | 108,000 |
| Colonial Invitational—Dan Pohl (205) | 108,000 |
| Memorial Tournament—Hal Sutton (271) | 100,000 |
| Kemper Open—Greg Norman (277) | 90,000 |
| Westchester Classic—Bob Tway (272) | 108,000 |
| Atlantic Classic—Bob Tway (269) | 90,000 |
| Canadian Open—Bob Murphy (280) | 108,000 |
| Greater Hartford Open—Mac O'Grady (269) | 126,000 |
| Busch Classic—Fuzzy Zoeller (274) | 90,000 |
| Colorado Open—Mark Wiebe (281) | 18,000 |
| Buick Open—Ben Crenshaw (270) | 90,000 |
| Western Open—Tom Kite (286) | 90,000 |
| International—Ken Green (278) | 180,000 |

## OTHER 1986 LPGA TOUR WINNERS

(Through Aug. 25, 1986)

| | |
|---|---|
| Mazda Classic—Val Skinner (280) | $30,000 |
| Elizabeth Arden Classic—Ayako Okamoto (280) | 30,000 |
| Sarasota Classic—Patty Sheehan (279) | 30,000 |
| Turquoise Classic—M. B. Zimmerman (278) | 37,500 |
| Uniden International—M. B. Zimmerman (281) | 49,500 |
| LPGA Kemper Open—Juli Inkster (276) | 45,000 |
| Glendale Federal Classic—Chris Johnson (212) | 37,500 |
| Circle K Tucson Open—Penny Pulz (276) | 30,000 |
| Nabisco-Dinah Shore—Pat Bradley (280) | 75,000 |
| Inamori Classic—Patty Sheehan (280) | 30,000 |
| S&H Classic—Pat Bradley (272) | 30,000 |
| United Virginia Bank Classic—Muffin Spencer-Devlin (214) | 37,500 |
| Chrysler-Plymouth Classic—Becky Pearson (212) | 30,000 |
| Corning Classic—Laurie Rinker (278) | 37,500 |
| LPGA Championship—Pat Bradley (277) | 45,000 |
| McDonald's Championship—Juli Inkster (281) | 67,500 |
| Lady Keystone Open—Juli Inkster (210) | 37,500 |
| Rochester Invitational—Judy Dickinson | 38,250 |
| Mayflower Classic—Sandra Palmer | 52,500 |
| Mazda Hall of Fame—Amy Alcott (284) | 45,000 |
| Boston Five Classic—Jane Geddes (281) | 41,250 |
| Du Maurier Classic—Pat Bradley (276) | 52,500 |
| National Pro-Am—Amy Alcott (283) | 45,000 |
| Henredon Classic—Betsy King (277) | 34,500 |
| World Championship of Women's Golf—Pat Bradley (279) | 78,000 |

## JAMES E. SULLIVAN MEMORIAL AWARD WINNERS

(Amateur Athlete of Year Chosen in Amateur Athletic Union Poll)

| | | | | | |
|---|---|---|---|---|---|
| 1930 | Robert Tyre Jones, Jr. | Golf | 1958 | Glenn Davis | Track and field |
| 1931 | Bernard E. Berlinger | Track and field | 1959 | Parry O'Brien | Track and field |
| 1932 | James A. Bausch | Track and field | 1960 | Rafer Johnson | Track and field |
| 1933 | Glenn Cunningham | Track and field | 1961 | Wilma Rudolph Ward | Track and field |
| 1934 | William R. Bonthron | Track and field | 1962 | Jim Beatty | Track and field |
| 1935 | W. Lawson Little, Jr. | Golf | 1963 | John Pennel | Track and field |
| 1936 | Glenn Morris | Track and field | 1964 | Don Schollander | Swimming |
| 1937 | J. Donald Budge | Tennis | 1965 | Bill Bradley | Basketball |
| 1938 | Donald R. Lash | Track and field | 1966 | Jim Ryun | Track and field |
| 1939 | Joseph W. Burk | Rowing | 1967 | Randy Matson | Track and field |
| 1940 | J. Gregory Rice | Track and field | 1968 | Debbie Meyer | Swimming |
| 1941 | Leslie MacMitchell | Track and field | 1969 | Bill Toomey | Decathlon |
| 1942 | Cornelius Warmerdam | Track and field | 1970 | John Kinsella | Swimming |
| 1943 | Gilbert L. Dodds | Track and field | 1971 | Mark Spitz | Swimming |
| 1944 | Ann Curtis | Swimming | 1972 | Frank Shorter | Marathon |
| 1945 | Felix (Doc) Blanchard | Football | 1973 | Bill Walton | Basketball |
| 1946 | Y. Arnold Tucker | Football | 1974 | Rick Wohlhuter | Track |
| 1947 | John B. Kelly, Jr. | Rowing | 1975 | Tim Shaw | Swimming |
| 1948 | Robert B. Mathias | Track and field | 1976 | Bruce Jenner | Track and field |
| 1949 | Richard T. Button | Figure skating | 1977 | John Naber | Swimming |
| 1950 | Fred Wilt | Track and field | 1978 | Tracy Caulkins | Swimming |
| 1951 | Robert E. Richards | Track and field | 1979 | Kurt Thomas | Gymnastics |
| 1952 | Horace Ashenfelter | Track and field | 1980 | Eric Heiden | Speed skating |
| 1953 | Major Sammy Lee | Diving | 1981 | Carl Lewis | Track and field |
| 1954 | Malvin Whitfield | Track and field | 1982 | Mary Decker Tabb | Track and field |
| 1955 | Harrison Dillard | Track and field | 1983 | Edwin Moses | Track and field |
| 1956 | Patricia McCormick | Diving | 1984 | Greg Louganis | Diving |
| 1957 | Bobby Jo Morrow | Track and Field | 1985 | Joan Benoit-Samuelson | Marathon |

# SOCCER

## WORLD CUP

| | | | |
|---|---|---|---|
| 1930 Uruguay | 1946 No competition | 1962 Brazil | 1978 Argentina |
| 1934 Italy | 1950 Uruguay | 1966 England | 1982 Italy |
| 1938 Italy | 1954 West Germany | 1970 Brazil | 1986 Argentina |
| 1942 No competition | 1958 Brazil | 1974 West Germany | |

## WORLD CUP—1986

A capacity crowd of 114,500 fans filled Aztec Stadium in Mexico City on Sunday, June 29, and another 500 million were estimated to have watched on television, as Argentina defeated West Germany, 3–2, for the championship of the 13th World Cup Tournament.

Argentina's Diego Maradona was the star of the tournament. His pass to teammate Jorge Burruchaga led to the winning goal, after Argentina had squandered a 2–0 lead. He was the only unanimous selection to the post-tournament all-star team.

More than 140 world nations play soccer. The World Cup, the most popular and best attended sporting event in the world, is a quadrennial event, and will next be played in 1990. Two years of elimination precede the 52-game championship tournament.

Once again, the United States was eliminated from the 1986 tourney during preliminary play. In early action, the American team defeated the Netherlands-Antilles and Trinidad-Tobago, but on May 31, 1985, lost a 1–0 game to Costa Rica and was eliminated.

That marked the ninth consecutive World Cup tournament the United States had failed to qualify for. Not since 1950 has an American squad been part of the world's most prestigious sporting event.

The early elimination of the United States from the 1986 World Cup was a big blow to soccer in America. With the North American Soccer League out of business since the end of the 1984 season because of mounting financial losses, an American appearance in the World Cup had been counted on as a much-needed boost for the sport in this country. It was not to be.

Instead, the lone professional soccer league of significance remaining in the United States in 1986 was the Major Indoor Soccer League, a derivation of the game played indoors on hockey-sized fields. There remained, outdoors, the long-established American Soccer League, but it was a league that existed on a very low budget, low fan appeal basis.

## WORLD CUP—1986

### SEMIFINALS

1. (at Guadalajara, Mexico, June 25, 1986)

West Germany 2, France 0

2. (at Mexico City, Mexico, June 25, 1986)

Argentina 2, Belgium 0

### THIRD PLACE

(at Puebla, Mexico, June 28, 1986)

France 4, Belgium 2 (overtime)

The following are the results of matches played by the four teams which reached the semifinals:

### FINALS

(at Mexico City, Mexico, June 29, 1986)

Argentina 3, West Germany 2

| Argentina (Group A) | West Germany (Group E) | France (Group C) | Belgium (Group B) |
|---|---|---|---|
| Argentina 3, South Korea 1 | West Germany 1, Uruguay 1 | France 1, Canada 0 | Mexico 2, Belgium 1 |
| Argentina 1, Italy 1 | West Germany 2, Scotland 1 | France 1, Soviet Union 1 | Belgium 2, Iraq 1 |
| Argentina 2, Bulgaria 0 | Denmark 2, West Germany 0 | France 3, Hungary 0 | Belgium 2, Paraguay 2 |
| Argentina 1, Uruguay 0 | West Germany 1, Morocco 0 | France 2, Italy 0* | Belgium 4, Soviet Union 3 (Overtime) |
| Argentina 2, England 1 | West Germany 4, Mexico 1 | France 5, Brazil 4 | Belgium 6, Spain 5 |
| | | *Italy was defending champion. | |

## MAJOR INDOOR SOCCER LEAGUE—1986
## FINAL STANDING

### EASTERN DIVISION

| | W | L | Pct | GB |
|---|---|---|---|---|
| Cleveland Force | 27 | 21 | .563 | — |
| Minnesota Strikers | 26 | 22 | .542 | 1 |
| Dallas Sidekicks | 25 | 23 | .521 | 2 |
| Baltimore Blast | 24 | 24 | .500 | 3 |
| Chicago Sting | 23 | 25 | .479 | 4 |
| Pittsburgh Spirit | 23 | 25 | .479 | 4 |

### WESTERN DIVISION

| | W | L | Pct | GB |
|---|---|---|---|---|
| San Diego Sockers | 36 | 12 | .750 | — |
| Wichita Wings | 27 | 21 | .563 | 9 |
| Tacoma Stars | 23 | 25 | .479 | 13 |
| St. Louis Streamers | 23 | 25 | .479 | 13 |
| Kansas City Comets | 18 | 30 | .375 | 18 |
| Los Angeles Lazers | 13 | 35 | .271 | 23 |

### CHAMPIONSHIP PLAYOFFS

#### Quarterfinals

Cleveland defeated Baltimore, 3 games to 2
Minnesota defeated Dallas, 3 games to 1
San Diego defeated St. Louis, 3 games to 1
Tacoma defeated Wichita, 3 games to 1

#### Semifinals

Minnesota defeated Cleveland, 3 games to 1
San Diego defeated Tacoma, 3 games to 1

#### Final

San Diego defeated Minnesota, 4 games to 3

## MAJOR INDOOR SOCCER LEAGUE LEADING SCORERS—1986

| | G | A | Pts |
|---|---|---|---|
| Steve Zungul, Tacoma | 55 | 60 | 115 |
| Erik Rasmussen, Wichita | 67 | 41 | 108 |
| Branko Segota, San Diego | 60 | 46 | 106 |
| Craig Allen, Cleveland | 50 | 31 | 81 |
| Tatu, Dallas | 49 | 32 | 81 |
| Stan Stamenkovic, Baltimore | 37 | 44 | 81 |

## MAJOR INDOOR SOCCER LEAGUE CHAMPIONS

1979—New York Arrows
1980—New York Arrows
1981—New York Arrows
1982—New York Arrows
1983—San Diego Sockers
1984—Baltimore Blast
1985—San Diego Sockers
1986—San Diego Sockers

## NORTH AMERICAN SOCCER LEAGUE CHAMPIONS

1968—Atlanta Chiefs
1969—Kansas City Stars
1970—Rochester Lancers
1971—Dallas Tornado
1972—New York Cosmos
1973—Philadelphia Atoms
1974—Los Angeles Aztecs
1975—Tampa Bay Rowdies
1976—Toronto Metro–Croatia
1977—New York Cosmos
1978—New York Cosmos
1979—Vancouver Whitecaps
1980—New York Cosmos
1981—Chicago Sting
1982—New York Cosmos
1983—Tulsa Roughnecks
1984—Chicago Sting

# YACHTING

## AMERICA'S CUP RECORD

First race in 1851 around Isle of Wight, Cowes, England. First defense and all others through 1920 held 30 miles off New York Bay. Races since 1930 held 30 miles off Newport, R.I. Conducted as one race only in 1851 and 1870; best four-of-seven basis, 1871; best two-of-three, 1876–1887; best three-of-five, 1893–1901; best four-of-seven, since 1930. Figures in parentheses indicate number of races won.

| Year | Winner and owner | Loser and owner |
|---|---|---|
| 1851 | AMERICA (1), John C. Stevens, U.S. | AURORA, T. Le Marchant, England[1] |
| 1870 | MAGIC (1), Franklin Osgood, U.S. | CAMBRIA, James Ashbury, England[2] |
| 1871 | COLUMBIA (2), Franklin Osgood, U.S.[3] | LIVONIA (1), James Ashbury, England |
| | SAPPHO (2), William P. Douglas, U.S. | |
| 1876 | MADELEINE (2), John S. Dickerson, U.S. | COUNTESS OF DUFFERIN, Chas. Gifford, Canada |
| 1881 | MISCHIEF (2), J. R. Busk, U.S. | ATALANTA, Alexander Cuthbert, Canada |
| 1885 | PURITAN (2), J. M. Forbes-Gen. Charles Paine, U.S. | GENESTA, Sir Richard Sutton, England |
| 1886 | MAYFLOWER (2), Gen. Charles Paine, U.S. | GALATEA, Lt. William Henn, England |
| 1887 | VOLUNTEER (2), Gen. Charles Paine, U.S. | THISTLE, James Bell et al., Scotland |
| 1893 | VIGILANT (3), C. Oliver Iselin et al., U.S. | VALKYRIE II, Lord Dunraven, England |
| 1895 | DEFENDER (3), C. O. Iselin-W. K. Vanderbilt-E. D. Morgan, U.S. | VALKYRIE III, Lord Dunraven-Lord Lonsdale-Lord Wolverton, England |
| 1899 | COLUMBIA (3), J. P. Morgan-C. O. Iselin, U.S. | SHAMROCK I, Sir Thomas Lipton, Ireland |
| 1901 | COLUMBIA (3), Edwin D. Morgan, U.S. | SHAMROCK II, Sir Thomas Lipton, Ireland |
| 1903 | RELIANCE (3), Cornelius Vanderbilt et al., U.S. | SHAMROCK III, Sir Thomas Lipton, Ireland |
| 1920 | RESOLUTE (4), Henry Walters et al., U.S. | SHAMROCK IV (2), Sir Thomas Lipton, Ireland |
| 1930 | ENTERPRISE (4), Harold S. Vanderbilt et al., U.S. | SHAMROCK V, Sir Thomas Lipton, Ireland |
| 1934 | RAINBOW (4), Harold S. Vanderbilt, U.S. | ENDEAVOUR (2), T. O. M. Sopwith, England |
| 1937 | RANGER (4), Harold S. Vanderbilt, U.S. | ENDEAVOUR II, T. O. M. Sopwith, England |
| 1958 | COLUMBIA (4), Henry Sears et al., U.S. | SCEPTRE, Hugh Goodson et al., England |
| 1962 | WEATHERLY (4), Henry D. Mercer et al., U.S. | GRETEL (1), Sir Frank Packer et al., Australia |
| 1964 | CONSTELLATION (4), New York Y.C. Syndicate, U.S. | SOVEREIGN (0), J. Anthony Bowden, England |
| 1967 | INTREPID (4), New York Y.C. Syndicate, U.S. | DAME PATTIE (0), Sydney (Aust.) Syndicate |
| 1970 | INTREPID (4), New York Y.C. Syndicate, U.S. | GRETEL II (1), Sydney (Aust.) Syndicate |
| 1974 | COURAGEOUS (4), New York, N.Y. Syndicate, U.S. | SOUTHERN CROSS (0), Sydney (Aust.) Syndicate |
| 1977 | COURAGEOUS (4), New York, N.Y. Syndicate, U.S. | AUSTRALIA (0), Sun City (Aust.) Syndicate |
| 1980 | FREEDOM (4), New York, N.Y. Syndicate, U.S. | AUSTRALIA (1), Alan Bond et al, Australia |
| 1983 | AUSTRALIA II (4) Alan Bond et al., Australia, | LIBERTY (3) New York, N.Y. Syndicate, U.S. |

1. Fourteen British yachts started against America; Aurora finished second. 2. Cambria sailed against 23 U.S. yachts and finished tenth. 3. Columbia was disabled in the third race, after winning the first two; Sappho substituted and won the fourth and fifth.

## LONGEST WINNING STREAK IN SPORTS HISTORY OVER

The victory of Australia II in the 1983 America's Cup race snapped a 132-year continuous victory streak by American 12-meter yachts. The end of U.S. yachting supremacy came on September 26th in an unprecedented seventh race in the best-of-seven finals.

Australia II was the first challenger to win the 33-1/2-inch silver cup since the schooner America won the inaugural race around England's Isle of Wight in 1851. Australia is planning its first defense of the America Cup trophy, in February 1987.

# AUTO RACING

## INDIANAPOLIS 500

| Year | Winner | Car | Time | mph | Second place |
|------|--------|-----|------|-----|--------------|
| 1911 | Ray Harroun | Marmon | 6:42:08 | 74.59 | Ralph Mulford |
| 1912 | Joe Dawson | National | 6:21:06 | 78.72 | Teddy Tetzloff |
| 1913 | Jules Goux | Peugeot | 6:35:05 | 75.93 | Spencer Wishart |
| 1914 | René Thomas | Delage | 6:03:45 | 82.47 | Arthur Duray |
| 1915 | Ralph DePalma | Mercedes | 5:33:55.51 | 89.84 | Dario Resta |
| 1916[1] | Dario Resta | Peugeot | 3:34:17 | 84.00 | Wilbur D'Alene |
| 1919 | Howard Wilcox | Peugeot | 5:40:42.87 | 88.05 | Eddie Hearne |
| 1920 | Gaston Chevrolet | Monroe | 5:38:32 | 88.62 | René Thomas |
| 1921 | Tommy Milton | Frontenac | 5:34:44.65 | 89.62 | Roscoe Sarles |
| 1922 | Jimmy Murphy | Murphy Special | 5:17:30.79 | 94.48 | Harry Hartz |
| 1923 | Tommy Milton | H. C. S. Special | 5:29.50.17 | 90.95 | Harry Hartz |
| 1924 | L. L. Corum–Joe Boyer | Dusenberg Special | 5:05:23.51 | 98.23 | Earl Cooper |
| 1925 | Peter DePaolo | Dusenberg Special | 4:56:39.45 | 101.13 | Dave Lewis |
| 1926[2] | Frank Lockhart | Miller Special | 4:10:14.95 | 95.904 | Harry Hartz |
| 1927 | George Souders | Dusenberg Special | 5:07:33.08 | 97.54 | Earl DeVore |
| 1928 | Louis Meyer | Miller Special | 5:01:33.75 | 99.48 | Lou Moore |
| 1929 | Ray Keech | Simplex Special | 5:07:25.42 | 97.58 | Louis Meyer |
| 1930 | Billy Arnold | Miller–Hartz Special | 4:58:39.72 | 100.448 | Shorty Cantlon |
| 1931 | Louis Schneider | Bowes Special | 5:10:27.93 | 96.629 | Fred Frame |
| 1932 | Fred Frame | Miller–Hartz Special | 4:48:03.79 | 104.144 | Howard Wilcox |
| 1933 | Louis Meyer | Tydol Special | 4:48:00.75 | 104.162 | Wilbur Shaw |
| 1934 | Bill Cummings | Boyle Products Special | 4:46:05.20 | 104.863 | Mauri Rose |
| 1935 | Kelly Petillo | Gilmore Special | 4:42:22.71 | 106.240 | Wilbur Shaw |
| 1936 | Louis Meyer | Ring Free Special | 4:35:03.39 | 109.069 | Ted Horn |
| 1937 | Wilbur Shaw | Shaw–Gilmore Special | 4:24:07.80 | 113.580 | Ralph Hepburn |
| 1938 | Floyd Roberts | Burd Piston Ring Special | 4:15:58.40 | 117.200 | Wilbur Shaw |
| 1939 | Wilbur Shaw | Boyle Special | 4:20:47.39 | 115.035 | Jimmy Snyder |
| 1940 | Wilbur Shaw | Boyle Special | 4:22:31.17 | 114.277 | Rex Mays |
| 1941 | Floyd Davis–Mauri Rose | Noc-Out Hose Clamp Special | 4:20:36.24 | 115.117 | Rex Mays |
| 1946 | George Robson | Thorne Engineering Special | 4:21:26.71 | 114.820 | Jimmy Jackson |
| 1947 | Mauri Rose | Blue Crown Special | 4:17:52.17 | 116.338 | Bill Holland |
| 1948 | Mauri Rose | Blue Crown Special | 4:10:23.33 | 119.814 | Bill Holland |
| 1949 | Bill Holland | Blue Crown Special | 4:07:15.97 | 121.327 | Johnny Parsons |
| 1950[3] | Johnnie Parsons | Wynn's Friction Proof Special | 2:46:55.97 | 124.002 | Bill Holland |
| 1951 | Lee Wallard | Belanger Special | 3:57:38.05 | 126.244 | Mike Nazaruk |
| 1952 | Troy Ruttman | Agajanian Special | 3:52:41.88 | 128.922 | Jim Rathmann |
| 1953 | Bill Vukovich | Fuel Injection Special | 3:53:01.69 | 128.740 | Art Cross |
| 1954 | Bill Vukovich | Fuel Injection Special | 3:49:17.27 | 130.840 | Jim Bryan |
| 1955 | Bob Sweikert | John Zink Special | 3:53:59.13 | 128.209 | Tony Bettenhausen |
| 1956 | Pat Flaherty | John Zink Special | 3:53:28.84 | 128.490 | Sam Hanks |
| 1957 | Sam Hanks | Belond Exhaust Special | 3:41:14.25 | 135.601 | Jim Rathmann |
| 1958 | Jimmy Bryan | Belond A–P Special | 3:44:13.80 | 133.791 | George Amick |
| 1959 | Rodger Ward | Leader Card 500 Roadster | 3:40:49.20 | 135.857 | Jim Rathmann |
| 1960 | Jim Rathmann | Ken-Paul Special | 3:36:11.36 | 138.767 | Rodger Ward |
| 1961 | A. J. Foyt | Bowes Special | 3:35:37.49 | 139.130 | Eddie Sachs |
| 1962 | Rodger Ward | Leader Card Special | 3:33:50.33 | 140.293 | Len Sutton |
| 1963 | Parnelli Jones | Agajanian Special | 3:29:35.40 | 143.137 | Jim Clark |
| 1964 | A. J. Foyt | Offenhauser Special | 3:23:35.83 | 147.350 | Rodger Ward |
| 1965 | Jim Clark | Lotus–Ford | 3:19:05.34 | 150.686 | Parnelli Jones |
| 1966 | Graham Hill | Lola–Ford | 3:27:52.53 | 144.317 | Jim Clark |
| 1967[4] | A. J. Foyt | Coyote–Ford | 3:18:24.22 | 151.207 | Al Unser |
| 1968 | Bobby Unser | Eagle–Offenhauser | 3:16:13.76 | 152.882 | Dan Gurney |
| 1969 | Mario Andretti | STP Hawk–Ford | 3:11:14.71 | 156.867 | Dan Gurney |
| 1970 | Al Unser | P. J. Colt–Ford | 3:12:37.04 | 155.749 | Mark Donohue |
| 1971 | Al Unser | P. J. Colt–Ford | 3:10:11.56 | 157.735 | Peter Revson |
| 1972 | Mark Donohue | McLaren–Offenhauser | 3:04:05.54 | 162.962 | Al Unser |
| 1973[5] | Gordon Johncock | Eagle–Offenhauser | 2:05:26.59 | 159.036 | Bill Vukovich |
| 1974 | Johnny Rutherford | McLaren–Offenhauser | 3:09:10.06 | 158.589 | Bobby Unser |
| 1975[6] | Bobby Unser | Eagle–Offenhauser | 2:54:55.08 | 149.213 | Johnny Rutherford |
| 1976[7] | Johnny Rutherford | McLaren–Offenhauser | 1:42:52.48 | 148.725 | A. J. Foyt |
| 1977 | A. J. Foyt | Coyote–Foyt | 3:05:57.16 | 161.331 | Tom Sneva |
| 1978 | Al Unser | Lola–Cosworth | 3:05:54.99 | 161.363 | Tom Sneva |
| 1979 | Rick Mears | Penske–Cosworth | 3:08:27.97 | 158.899 | A. J. Foyt |
| 1980 | Johnny Rutherford | Chaparral–Cosworth | 3:29:59.56 | 142.862 | Tom Sneva |
| 1981[8] | Bobby Unser | Eagle–Offenhauser | 3:35:41.78 | 139.029 | Mario Andretti |

| 1982 | Gordon Johncock | Wildcat–Cosworth | 3:05:09.14 | 162.029 | Rick Mears |
| 1983 | Tom Sneva | March–Cosworth | 3:05:03.06 | 162.117 | Al Unser |
| 1984 | Rick Mears | March–Cosworth | 3:03:21.00 | 162.962 | Roberto Guerrero |
| 1985 | Danny Sullivan | March–Cosworth | 3:16:06.069 | 152.982 | Mario Andretti |
| 1986 | Bobby Rahal | March–Cosworth | 2:55:43.48 | 170.722 | Kevin Cogan |

1. 300 miles. 2. Race ended at 400 miles because of rain. 3. Race ended at 345 miles because of rain. 4. Race, postponed after 18 laps because of rain on May 30, was finished on May 31. 5. Race postponed May 28 and 29 was cut to 332.5 miles because of rain, May 30. 6. Race ended at 435 miles because of rain. 7. Race ended at 255 miles because of rain. 8. Andretti was awarded the victory the day after the race after Bobby Unser, whose car finished first, was penalized one lap and dropped from first place to second for passing other cars illegally under a yellow caution flag. Unser appealed the decision to the U.S. Auto Club and was upheld. A panel ruled the penalty was too severe and instead fined Unser $40,000, but restored the victory to him.

## U.S. AUTO CLUB
## NATIONAL CHAMPIONS

| 1910 | Ray Harroun | 1926 | Harry Hartz | 1950 | Henry Banks | 1970 | Al Unser |
| 1911 | Ralph Mulford | 1927 | Peter DePaolo | 1951 | Tony Bettenhausen | 1971–72 | Joe Leonard |
| 1912 | Ralph DePalma | 1928–29 | Louis Meyer | 1952 | Chuck Stevenson | 1973 | Roger McCluskey |
| 1913 | Earl Cooper | 1930 | Billy Arnold | 1953 | Sam Hanks | 1974 | Bobby Unser |
| 1914 | Ralph DePalma | 1931 | Louis Schneider | 1954 | Jimmy Bryan | 1975 | A. J. Foyt |
| 1915 | Earl Cooper | 1932 | Bob Carey | 1955 | Bob Sweikert | 1976 | Gordon Johncock |
| 1916 | Dario Resta | 1933 | Louis Meyer | 1956–57 | Jimmy Bryan | 1977–78 | Tom Sneva |
| 1917 | Earl Cooper | 1934 | Bill Cummings | 1958 | Tony Bettenhausen | 1979 | A. J. Foyt |
| 1918 | Ralph Mulford | 1935 | Kelly Petillo | 1959 | Rodger Ward | 1980 | Johnny Rutherford |
| 1919 | Howard Wilcox | 1936 | Mauri Rose | 1960–61 | A. J. Foyt | 1981–82 | George Snider |
| 1920 | Gaston Chevrolet | 1937 | Wilbur Shaw | 1962 | Rodger Ward | 1983 | Tom Sneva |
| 1921 | Tommy Milton | 1938 | Floyd Roberts | 1963–64 | A. J. Foyt | 1984 | Rick Mears |
| 1922 | James Murphy | 1939 | Wilbur Shaw | 1965–66 | Mario Andretti | 1985 | Danny Sullivan |
| 1923 | Eddie Hearne | 1940–41 | Rex Mays | 1967 | A. J. Foyt | | |
| 1924 | James Murphy | 1946–48 | Ted Horn | 1968 | Bobby Unser | | |
| 1925 | Peter DePaolo | 1949 | Johnnie Parsons | 1969 | Mario Andretti | | |

## NATIONAL ASSOCIATION FOR STOCK CAR AUTO RACING
## (NASCAR) GRAND NATIONAL CHAMPIONS

| 1949 | Red Byron | 1956–57 | Buck Baker | 1966 | David Pearson | 1976–78 | Cale Yarborough |
| 1950 | Bill Rexford | 1958–59 | Lee Petty | 1967 | Richard Petty | 1979 | Richard Petty |
| 1951 | Herb Thomas | 1960 | Rex White | 1968–69 | David Pearson | 1980 | Dale Earnhardt |
| 1952 | Tim Flock | 1961 | Ned Jarrett | 1970 | Bobby Isaac | 1981 | Darrell Waltrip |
| 1953 | Herb Thomas | 1962–63 | Joe Weatherly | 1971–72 | Richard Petty | 1982 | Darrell Waltrip |
| 1954 | Lee Petty | 1964 | Richard Petty | 1973 | Benny Parsons | 1983 | Bobby Allison |
| 1955 | Tim Flock | 1965 | Ned Jarrett | 1974–75 | Richard Petty | 1984 | Terry Labonte |
| | | | | | | 1985 | Darrell Waltrip |

## WORLD GRAND PRIX DRIVER CHAMPIONS

| 1950 | Giuseppe Farina, Italy, Alfa Romeo | 1968 | Graham Hill, England, Lotus-Ford |
| 1951 | Juan Fangio, Argentina, Alfa Romeo | 1969 | Jackie Stewart, Scotland, Matra-Ford |
| 1952 | Alberto Ascari, Italy, Ferrari | 1970 | Jochen Rindt, Austria, Lotus-Ford |
| 1953 | Alberto Ascari, Italy, Ferrari | 1971 | Jackie Stewart, Scotland, Tyrrell-Ford |
| 1955 | Juan Fangio, Argentina, Maserati, Mercedes-Benz | 1972 | Emerson Fittipaldi, Brazil, Lotus-Ford |
| 1955 | Juan Fangio, Argentina, Mercedes-Benz | 1973 | Jackie Stewart, Scotland, Tyrrell-Ford |
| 1956 | Juan Fangio, Argentina, Lancia-Ferrari | 1974 | Emerson Fittipaldi, Brazil, McLaren-Ford |
| 1957 | Juan Fangio, Argentina, Maserati | 1975 | Niki Lauda, Austria, Ferrari |
| 1958 | Mike Hawthorn, England, Ferrari | 1976 | James Hunt, Britain, McLaren-Ford |
| 1959 | Jack Brabham, Australia, Cooper | 1977 | Niki Lauda, Austria, Ferrari |
| 1960 | Jack Brabham, Australia, Cooper | 1978 | Mario Andretti, Nazareth, Pa., Lotus |
| 1961 | Phil Hill, United States, Ferrari | 1979 | Jody Scheckter, South Africa |
| 1962 | Graham Hill, England, BRM | 1980 | Alan Jones, Australia |
| 1963 | Jim Clark, Scotland, Lotus-Ford | 1981 | Nelson Piquet, Brazil |
| 1964 | John Surtees, England, Ferrari | 1982 | Kiki Rosberg, Finland |
| 1965 | Jim Clark, Scotland, Lotus-Ford | 1983 | Nelson Piquet, Brazil |
| 1966 | Jack Brabham, Australia, Brabham-Repco | 1984 | Nikki Lauda, Austria |
| 1967 | Denis Hulme, New Zealand, Brabham-Repco | 1985 | Alain Prost, France |

## U.S. AUTO CLUB

**1986 Major Races**

**Indianapolis 500** (Indianapolis Motor Speedway, May 31, 1986, 500 miles)—1. Bobby Rahal, Dublin, Ohio; March-Cosworth; 200 laps; time: 2:55:42.48. Average speed: 170.733 mph. First place prize: $581,062. 2. Kevin Cogan, Redondo Beach, Calif.; March-Cosworth; 200 laps; $253.352. 3. Rick Mears, Bakersfield, Calif.; March-Cosworth; 200 laps; $332,262. 4. Roberto Guerrero, Columbia; March-Cosworth; 200 laps; $139,512. 5. Al Unser Jr., Albuquerque, N.M.; Lola-Cosworth; 199 laps; $113,462.

**Pocono 500** (Long Pond, Pa., Pocono International Raceway, July 20, 1986, 500 miles)—1. Tim Richmond, Ashland, Ohio; Chevrolet; 150 laps; time: 2:41:08. Average speed: 124.218. First place prize: $46,805. 2. Ricky Rudd, Chesapeake, Va.; Ford; 150 laps; $29.500. 3. Geoff Bodine, Chemung, N.Y.; Chevrolet, 150 laps; $22,350. 4. Darrell Waltrip, Owensboro, Ky.; Chevrolet; 150 laps; $23,825. 5. Bobby Allison, Hueytown, Ala.; Buick; 150 laps; $17,525.

## FINAL 1985 NASCAR LEADING MONEY WINNERS

| | |
|---|---|
| Bill Elliott | $2,383,186 |
| Darrell Waltrip | 1,318,734 |
| Harry Gant | 804,286 |
| Terry Labonte | 694,509 |
| Geoff Bodine | 565,867 |
| Dale Earnhardt | 546,595 |
| Neil Bonnett | 530,144 |
| Ricky Rudd | 512,440 |
| Richard Petty | 306,141 |
| Lake Speed | 300,325 |

## FINAL 1985 WINSTON CUP GRAND NATIONAL POINT LEADERS

| | |
|---|---|
| Darrell Waltrip | 4292 |
| Bill Elliott | 4191 |
| Harry Gant | 4033 |
| Neil Bonnett | 3902 |
| Geoff Bodine | 3862 |
| Ricky Rudd | 3857 |
| Terry Labonte | 3683 |
| Dale Earnhardt | 3561 |
| Kyle Petty | 3528 |
| Lake Speed | 3507 |
| Tim Richmond | 3413 |
| Bobby Allison | 3312 |
| Ron Bouchard | 3267 |
| Richard Petty | 3140 |
| Bobby Hillin, Jr. | 3091 |
| Ken Schrader | 3024 |
| Buddy Baker | 2986 |
| Dave Marcis | 2871 |
| Rusty Wallace | 2867 |
| Buddy Arrington | 2780 |

# *PADDLE TENNIS*

## NATIONAL OPEN CHAMPIONS—1986

Men's singles—Mark Rifenbark, Los Angeles
Women's singles—Kathy Paben, Los Angeles
Men's doubles—Sol Hauptman, Culver City, Calif. and Marvin Silver, Los Angeles
Mixed doubles—Kathy and Don Paben, Los Angeles
Beach men's doubles—Sol Hauptman, Culver City, Calif. and Jeff Fleitman, Los Angeles

# *LACROSSE*

## NATIONAL INTERCOLLEGIATE CHAMPIONS

| | | | | | |
|---|---|---|---|---|---|
| 1946 | Navy | 1959 | Army, Johns Hopkins, Maryland | 1974 | Johns Hopkins |
| 1947–48 | Johns Hopkins | 1960 | Navy | 1975 | Maryland |
| 1949 | Johns Hopkins, Navy | 1961 | Army, Navy | 1976–77 | Cornell |
| 1950 | Johns Hopkins | 1962–66 | Navy | 1978–80 | Johns Hopkins |
| 1951 | Army, Princeton | 1967 | Johns Hopkins, Maryland, Navy | 1981 | North Carolina |
| 1952 | Virginia, R.P.I. | 1968 | Johns Hopkins | 1982 | North Carolina |
| 1953 | Princeton | 1969 | Army, Johns Hopkins | 1983 | Syracuse |
| 1954 | Navy | 1970 | Johns Hopkins, Navy, Virginia | 1984 | Johns Hopkins |
| 1955–56 | Maryland | 1971[1] | Cornell | 1985 | Johns Hopkins |
| 1957 | Johns Hopkins | 1972 | Virginia | 1986 | North Carolina |
| 1958 | Army | 1973 | Maryland | | |

1. First year of N.C.A.A. Championship Tournaments.

## N.C.A.A. CHAMPIONSHIPS—1986

**DIVISION I**
**Final**
(University of Delaware, Newark, Delaware, May 26, 1986)
North Carolina 10, Virginia 9

**DIVISION III**
(Geneva, N.Y., May 17, 1986)
Hobart 13, Washington 10

# *RODEO*

## PROFESSIONAL RODEO COWBOY ASSOCIATION, ALL AROUND COWBOY

| | | | | | |
|---|---|---|---|---|---|
| 1953 | Bill Linderman | 1963–65 | Dean Oliver | 1976–79 | Tom Ferguson |
| 1954 | Buck Rutherford | 1966–70 | Larry Mahan | 1980 | Paul Tierney |
| 1955 | Casey Tibbs | 1971–72 | Phil Lyne | 1981 | Jimmie Cooper |
| 1956–59 | Jim Shoulders | 1973 | Larry Mahan | 1982 | Chris Lybbert |
| 1960 | Harry Tompkins | 1974 | Tom Ferguson | 1983 | Roy Cooper |
| 1961 | Benny Reynolds | 1975 | Leo Camarillo and | 1984 | Dee Pickett |
| 1962 | Tom Nesmith | | Tom Ferguson | 1985 | Lewis Field |

# BASEBALL—MINOR LEAGUES—1986

## CLASS AAA

### AMERICAN ASSOCIATION
#### Eastern Division

|  | W | L | Pct | GB |
|---|---|---|---|---|
| Indianapolis (Expos) | 80 | 62 | .563 | — |
| Buffalo (Chisox) | 71 | 71 | .500 | 9 |
| Nashville (Tigers) | 68 | 74 | .479 | 12 |
| Louisville (Cards) | 64 | 78 | .451 | 16 |

#### Western Division

|  | W | L | Pct | GB |
|---|---|---|---|---|
| Denver (Reds) | 76 | 66 | .535 | — |
| Iowa (Cubs) | 74 | 68 | .521 | 2 |
| Omaha (Royals) | 72 | 70 | .507 | 4 |
| Oklahoma City (Rangers) | 63 | 79 | .444 | 13 |

#### Playoffs

League championship—Indianapolis defeated Denver, 4 games to 3

### INTERNATIONAL LEAGUE
#### Final Standings

|  | W | L | Pct | GB |
|---|---|---|---|---|
| Richmond (Braves) | 80 | 60 | .571 | — |
| Rochester (Orioles) | 75 | 63 | .543 | 4 |
| Pawtucket (Red Sox) | 74 | 65 | .532 | 5 1/2 |
| Tidewater (Mets) | 74 | 66 | .529 | 6 |
| Syracuse (Blue Jays) | 72 | 67 | .518 | 7 1/2 |
| Columbus (Yankees) | 62 | 77 | .446 | 17 1/2 |
| Toledo (Twins) | 62 | 77 | .446 | 17 1/2 |
| Maine (Indians) | 58 | 82 | .414 | 22 |

#### Playoffs

Semifinals—Richmond defeated Tidewater, 3 games to 0; Rochester defeated Pawtucket, 3 games to 1
Finals—Rochester defeated Pawtucket, 3 games to 1

### PACIFIC COAST LEAGUE
#### Final First Half
#### Northern Division

|  | W | L | Pct | GB |
|---|---|---|---|---|
| Vancouver (Brewers) | 42 | 24 | .636 | — |
| Calgary (Mariners) | 36 | 35 | .507 | 8 1/2 |
| Portland (Phillies) | 34 | 35 | .493 | 9 1/2 |
| Tacoma (A's) | 32 | 40 | .444 | 13 |
| Edmonton (Angels) | 30 | 39 | .435 | 13 1/2 |

#### Southern Division

|  | W | L | Pct | GB |
|---|---|---|---|---|
| Phoenix (Giants) | 43 | 28 | .606 | — |
| Tucson (Astros) | 38 | 33 | .535 | 5 |
| Las Vegas (Padres) | 36 | 34 | .514 | 6 1/2 |
| Hawaii (Pirates) | 32 | 40 | .444 | 11 1/2 |
| Albuquerque (Dodgers) | 28 | 43 | .394 | 15 |

#### Final Second Half
#### Northern Division

|  | W | L | Pct | GB |
|---|---|---|---|---|
| Vancouver (Brewers) | 43 | 29 | .597 | — |
| Tacoma (A's) | 40 | 32 | .556 | 3 |
| Edmonton (Angels) | 38 | 34 | .528 | 5 |
| Portland (Phillies) | 34 | 38 | .472 | 9 |
| Calgary (Mariners) | 30 | 42 | .417 | 13 |

#### Southern Division

|  | W | L | Pct | GB |
|---|---|---|---|---|
| Las Vegas (Padres) | 44 | 28 | .611 | — |
| x-Phoenix (Giants) | 38 | 33 | .535 | 5 1/2 |
| Hawaii (Pirates) | 33 | 39 | .458 | 11 |
| Tucson (Astros) | 33 | 39 | .458 | 11 |
| Albuquerque (Dodgers) | 26 | 45 | .366 | 17 1/2 |

#### Playoffs

Northern Division—Vancouver defeated Tacoma, 3 games to 0.
Southern Division—Las Vegas defeated Phoenix, 3 games to 2.
Championship playoff—Las Vegas defeated Vancouver 3 games to 2.

## CLASS AA

**Eastern League**—Regular season champion: Reading (Phillies). Playoffs: Vermont (Reds) defeated Pittsfield (Cubs), 3 games to 2; Reading (Phillies) defeated Glens Falls (Tigers), 3 games to 1. Championship—Vermont defeated Reading, 3 games to 2.
**Southern League**—Eastern Division, first half: Jacksonville (Expos); second half: Columbus (Astros); Western Division, first half: Huntsville (A's); second half: Knoxville (Blue Jays). Division championships: East—Columbus defeated Jacksonville, 3 games to 1; West—Huntsville defeated Knoxville, 3 games to 1. League championship: Columbus defeated Huntsville, 3 games to 1.
**Texas League**—Eastern Division, first half: Jackson (Mets); second half: Shreveport (Giants); Western Division, first half: El Paso (Brewers); second half: El Paso (brewers). Divisional championships: East—Jackson defeated Shreveport, 2 games to 1. West: No playoff, since same team won both halves. League championship: El Paso defeated Jackson, 4 games to 0.

## CLASS A

**California League**—Northern Division, first half: Salinas (Mariners); second half: Stockton (Brewers); Southern Division, first half: Palm Springs (Angels); second half: Visalia (Twins). Playoffs: Northern: Stockton defeated Salinas, 3 games to 0; Southern: Visalia defeated Palm Springs, 3 games to 1. League championship: Stockton defeated Visalia, 3 games to 0.
**Midwest League**—Northern Division: Madison (A's); Central Division: Waterloo (Indians); Southern Division: Springfield (Cardinals). Wild card: Peoria (Cubs). Playoffs: Semifinals—Waterloo defeated Madison, 2 games to 0; Peoria defeated Springfield, 2 games to 0. League championship: Waterloo defeatd Peoria, 3 games to 0.
**Carolina League**—Northern Division, first half: Hagerstown (Orioles); second half: Hagerstown (Orioles); Southern Division, first half: Winston-Salem (Cubs); second half: Winston-Salem (Cubs). League championship: Winston-Salem defeated Hagerstown, 3 games to 1.
**Florida State League**—Western Division, first half: St. Petersburg (Cardinals); Central Division: Winter Haven (Red Sox); Southern Division: West Palm Beach (Expos); Wild card: Tampa (Reds). Playoffs: Semifinals: St. Petersburg defeated Tampa, 2 games to 1. West Palm Beach defeated Winter Haven, 2 games to 0. League championship: St. Petersburg defeated West Palm Beach, 3 games to 1.
**South Atlantic League**—Northern Division, first half—Asheville (Astros); second half: Asheville (Astros); Southern Division, first half: Columbia (Mets); second half: Columbia (Mets); League championship: Columbia defeated Asheville, 3 games to 1.
**New York-Penn League**—Yawkey Division: Oneonta (Yankees); McNamara Division: Auburn (Astros); Wrigley Division: St. Catherines (Blue Jays). Wild card: Newark (Orioles). Playoffs: Semifinals: St. Catherines defeated Auburn, 1-0 in one game playoff; Newark defeated Oneonta, 2-1, in one-game playoff. League championship: St. Catherines defeated Newark, 2 games to 0.
**Northwest League**—Oregon Division: Eugene (Royals); Washington Division: Bellingham (Mariners). League championship: one game—Bellingham defeated Eugene, 2-1.

# SOFTBALL

*Source:* Amateur Softball Association.

## AMATEUR CHAMPIONS

| | | | | | |
|---|---|---|---|---|---|
| 1959 | Aurora (III.) Sealmasters | 1971 | Welty Way, Cedar Rapids, Iowa | 1980 | Peterbilt Western, Seattle |
| 1960 | Clearwater (Fla.) Bombers | 1972 | Raybestos Cardinals, Stratford, Conn. | 1981 | Archer Daniels Midland, Decatur, III. |
| 1961 | Aurora (III.) Sealmasters | | | | |
| 1962–63 | Clearwater (Fla.) Bombers | 1973 | Clearwater (Fla.) Bombers | 1982 | Peterbilt Western, Seattle |
| 1964 | Burch Gage & Tool, Detroit | 1974 | Santa Rosa (Calif.) | 1983 | Franklin Cardinals, West Haven, Conn. |
| 1965 | Aurora (III.) Sealmasters | 1975 | Rising Sun Hotel, Reading, Pa. | | |
| 1966 | Clearwater (Fla.) Bombers | 1976 | Raybestos Cardinals, Stratford, Conn. | 1984 | California Coors Kings, Merced, Calif. |
| 1967 | Aurora (III.) Sealmasters | | | | |
| 1968 | Clearwater (Fla.) Bombers | 1977 | Billard Barbell, Reading, Pa. | 1985 | Pay 'n Pak, Bellevue, Washington |
| 1969 | Raybestos Cardinals, Stratford, Conn. | 1978 | Reading, Pa. | 1986 | Pay 'n Pak, Bellevue, Washington |
| | | 1979 | Midland, Mich. | | |

## AMATEUR SOFTBALL ASSOCIATION CHAMPIONS—1986

Men's major fast pitch—Pay 'n Pak, Bellevue, Wash.
Women's major fast pitch—Southern California Invasion, Southern Calif.
Men's Class A fast pitch—Tubbs & Sons Electric, Manteca, Calif.
Women's Class A fast pitch—San Diego Astros, San Diego, Calif.
Men's major slow pitch—Non-Ferrous Metals, Cleveland, Ohio
Women's major slow pitch—Sur-Way Tomboys, Tifton, Ga.
Men's major industrial slow pitch—Landrum & Son, Atlanta, Ga.
Men's church slow pitch—New Covenant Christian, Oklahoma City, Okla.
Men's 16 slow pitch—The Doc's, Oaklawn, III.
Women's major industrial slow pitch—Sherriff's Stars, Pensacola, Fla.
Women's church slow pitch—Rock Creek, Graham, N.C.
Men's Class A slow pitch—Vernon's, Jacksonville, Fla.
Women's Class A slow pitch—Comfort Inn, Raleigh, N.C.
Men's Class A Industrial slow pitch—Avco Lycoming, Stratford, Conn.
Men's Class A church slow pitch—Park Avenue Covenant, Minneapolis, Minn.
Men's 16 Class A slow pitch—Edison Park Inn, Des Plaines, III.
Men's modified—Don Swann Sales, Atlanta, Ga.
Men's super slow pitch—Steele's Sports, Grafton, Ohio
Women's modified—Zerbo's Hellbenders, Staten Island, N.Y.

Men's Masters (35-and-over)—Budweiser, Warren, Mich.
Co-Ed slow pitch—Lab Petroleum, San Antonio, Texas

## YOUTH TOURNAMENTS—1986

Boys 18-and-under slow pitch—Pasadena Lake Bullfrogs, Pembroke Pines, Fla.
Boys 15-and-under slow pitch—Chemicals, Inc., Tifton, Ga.
Boys 12-and-under slow pitch—Sylvester Flames, Sylvester, Ga.
Boys 18-and-under fast pitch—The Rookies, Ruthton, New Mexico
Boys 15-and-under fast pitch—East 8th Street Merchants, Sioux Falls, S.D.
Boys 12-and-under fast pitch—Prescott Little Merchants, Prescott, Ariz.
Girls 18-and-under slow pitch—Fort Lauderdale Crush, Fort Lauderdale, Fla.
Girls 15-and-under slow pitch—Lady Zappers, Del City, Okla.
Girls 12-and-under slow pitch—Pembroke Pines Pacers, Pembroke Pines, Fla.
Girls 18-and-under fast pitch—Inland Cities Raiders, Bellflower, Calif.
Girls 15-and-under fast pitch—Gordon Panthers, Buena Vista, Calif.
Girls 12-and-under fast pitch—The Gamblers, Cypress, Calif.

## WORLD CHAMPIONS—1986

Women's fast pitch—Hi-Ho Brakettes, Stratford, Conn.
Men's fast pitch—New Zealand

# HANDBALL

## U.S.H.A. NATIONAL FOUR-WALL CHAMPIONS

### Singles

| | | | | | |
|---|---|---|---|---|---|
| 1960 | Jimmy Jacobs | 1979 | Naty Alvarado | 1969 | Lou Kramberg–Lou Russo |
| 1961 | John Sloan | 1980 | Naty Alvarado | 1970 | Karl and Ruby Obert |
| 1962–63 | Oscar Obert | 1981 | Fred Lewis | 1971 | Ray Neveau–Simie Fein |
| 1964–65 | Jimmy Jacobs | 1982 | Naty Alvarado | 1972 | Kent Fusselman–Al Drews |
| 1966–67 | Paul Haber | 1983 | Naty Alvarado | 1973–74 | Ray Neveau–Simie Fein |
| 1968 | Simon (Stuffy) Singer | 1984 | Naty Alvarado | 1975 | Marty Decatur–Steve Lott |
| 1969–71 | Paul Haber | 1985 | Naty Alvarado | 1976 | Gary Rohrer–Dan O'Connor |
| 1972 | Fred Lewis | 1986 | Naty Alvarado | 1977 | Skip McDowell–Matt Kelly |
| 1973 | Terry Muck | | | 1978 | Stuffy Singer–Marty Decatur |
| 1974 | Fred Lewis | **Doubles** | | 1979 | Stuffy Singer–Marty Decatur |
| 1975 | Jay Bilyeu | | | 1980 | Skip McDowell–Harry Robertson |
| 1976 | Vern Roberts, Jr. | 1960 | Jimmy Jacobs–Dick Weisman | 1981 | Tom Kopatich–Jack Roberts |
| 1977 | Naty Alvarado | 1961 | John Sloan–Vic Hershkowitz | 1982 | Naty Alvarado–Vern Roberts |
| 1978 | Fred Lewis | 1962–63 | Jimmy Jacobs–Marty Decatur | 1983 | Naty Alvarado–Vern Roberts |
| | | 1964 | John Sloan–Phil Elbert | 1984 | Naty Alvarado–Vern Roberts |
| | | 1965 | Jimmy Jacobs–Marty Decatur | 1985 | Naty Alvarado–Vern Roberts |
| | | 1966 | Pete Tyson–Bob Lindsay | 1986 | Jon Kembler–Pancho Monreal |
| | | 1967–68 | Jimmy Jacobs–Marty Decatur | | |

# BASEBALL

The popular tradition that baseball was invented by Abner Doubleday at Cooperstown, N.Y., in 1839 has been enshrined in the Hall of Fame and National Museum of Baseball erected in that town, but research has proved that a game called "Base Ball" was played in this country and England before 1839. The first team baseball as we know it was played at the Elysian Fields, Hoboken, N.J., on June 19, 1846, between the Knickerbockers and the New York Nine. The next fifty years saw a gradual growth of baseball and an improvement of equipment and playing skill.

Historians have it that the first pitcher to throw a curve was William A. (Candy) Cummings in 1867. The Cincinnati Red Stockings were the first all-professional team, and in 1869 they played 64 games without a loss. The standard ball of the same size and weight, still the rule, was adopted in 1872. The first catcher's mask was worn in 1875. The National League was organized in 1876. The first chest protector was worn in 1885. The three-strike rule was put on the books in 1887, and the four-ball ticket to first base was instituted in 1889. The pitch-ing distance was lengthened to 60 feet 6 inches in 1893, and the rules have been modified only slightly since that time.

The American League, under the vigorous leadership of B. B. Johnson, became a major league in 1901. Judge Kenesaw Mountain Landis, by action of the two major leagues, became Commissioner of Baseball in 1921, and upon his death (1944), Albert B. Chandler, former United States Senator from Kentucky, was elected to that office (1945). Chandler failed to obtain a new contract and was succeeded by Ford C. Frick (1951), the National League president. Frick retired after the 1965 season, and William D. Eckert, a retired Air Force lieutenant general, was named to succeed him. Eckert resigned under pressure in December, 1968. Bowie Kuhn, a New York attorney, became interim commissioner for one year in February. His appointment was made permanent with two seven-year contracts until August 1983. In August 1983, Kuhn's contract was not renewed, and a search begun for his successor. Peter Ueberroth was named new Commissioner and took office Oct. 1, 1984.

## MAJOR LEAGUE ALL-STAR GAME

| Year | Date | Winning league and manager | Runs | Losing league and manager | Runs | Winning pitcher | Losing pitcher | Site | Paid attendance |
|---|---|---|---|---|---|---|---|---|---|
| 1933 | July 6 | A.L. (Mack) | 4 | N.L. (McGraw) | 2 | Gomez | Hallahan | Chicago A.L. | 47,595 |
| 1934 | July 10 | A.L. (Cronin) | 9 | N.L. (Terry) | 7 | Harder | Mungo | New York N.L. | 48,363 |
| 1935 | July 8 | A.L. (Cochrane) | 4 | N.L. (Frisch) | 1 | Gomez | Walker | Cleveland A.L. | 69,831 |
| 1936 | July 7 | N.L. (Grimm) | 4 | A.L. (McCarthy) | 3 | J. Dean | Grove | Boston N.L. | 25,556 |
| 1937 | July 7 | A.L. (McCarthy) | 8 | N.L. (Terry) | 3 | Gomez | J. Dean | Washington A.L. | 31,391 |
| 1938 | July 6 | N.L. (Terry) | 4 | A.L. (McCarthy) | 1 | Vander Meer | Gomez | Cincinnati N.L. | 27,067 |
| 1939 | July 11 | A.L. (McCarthy) | 3 | N.L. (Hartnett) | 1 | Bridges | Lee | New York A.L. | 62,892 |
| 1940 | July 9 | N.L. (McKechnie) | 4 | A.L. (Cronin) | 0 | Derringer | Ruffing | St. Louis N.L. | 32,373 |
| 1941 | July 8 | A.L. (Baker) | 7 | N.L. (McKechnie) | 5 | E. Smith | Passeau | Detroit A.L. | 54,674 |
| 1942 | July 6 | A.L. (McCarthy) | 3 | N.L. (Durocher) | 1 | Chandler | Cooper | New York A.L. | 34,178 |
| 1943 | July 13[1] | A.L. (McCarthy) | 5 | N.L. (Southworth) | 3 | Leonard | Cooper | Philadelphia A.L. | 31,938 |
| 1944 | July 11[1] | N.L. (Southworth) | 7 | A.L. (McCarthy) | 1 | Raffensberger | Hughson | Pittsburgh N.L. | 29,589 |
| 1946 | July 9 | A.L. (O'Neill) | 12 | N.L. (Grimm) | 0 | Feller | Passeau | Boston A.L. | 34,906 |
| 1947 | July 8 | A.L. (Cronin) | 2 | N.L. (Dyer) | 1 | Shea | Sain | Chicago N.L. | 41,123 |
| 1948 | July 13 | A.L. (Harris) | 5 | N.L. (Durocher) | 2 | Raschi | Schmitz | St. Louis A.L. | 34,009 |
| 1949 | July 12 | A.L. (Boudreau) | 11 | N.L. (Southworth) | 7 | Trucks | Newcombe | Brooklyn N.L. | 32,577 |
| 1950 | July 11 | N.L. (Shotton) | 4 | A.L. (Stengel) | 3[3] | Blackwell | Gray | Chicago A.L. | 46,127 |
| 1951 | July 10 | N.L. (Sawyer) | 8 | A.L. (Stengel) | 3 | Maglie | Lopat | Detroit A.L. | 52,075 |
| 1952 | July 8 | N.L. (Durocher) | 3 | A.L. (Stengel) | 2[4] | Rush | Lemon | Philadelphia N.L. | 32,785 |
| 1953 | July 14 | N.L. (Dressen) | 5 | A.L. (Stengel) | 1 | Spahn | Reynolds | Cincinnati N.L. | 30,846 |
| 1954 | July 13 | A.L. (Stengel) | 11 | N.L. (Alston) | 9 | Stone | Conley | Cleveland A.L. | 68,751 |
| 1955 | July 12 | N.L. (Durocher) | 6 | A.L. (Lopez) | 5[3] | Conley | Sullivan | Milwaukee N.L. | 45,643 |
| 1956 | July 10 | N.L. (Alston) | 7 | A.L. (Stengel) | 3 | Friend | Pierce | Washington A.L. | 28,843 |
| 1957 | July 9 | A.L. (Stengel) | 6 | N.L. (Alston) | 5 | Bunning | Simmons | St. Louis N.L. | 30,693 |
| 1958 | July 8 | A.L. (Stengel) | 4 | N.L. (Haney) | 3 | Wynn | Friend | Baltimore A.L. | 48,829 |
| 1959[2] | July 7 | N.L. (Haney) | 5 | A.L. (Stengel) | 4 | Antonelli | Ford | Pittsburgh N.L. | 35,277 |
| | Aug. 3 | A.L. (Stengel) | 5 | N.L. (Haney) | 3 | Walker | Drysdale | Los Angeles N.L. | 55,105 |
| 1960[2] | July 11 | N.L. (Alston) | 5 | A.L. (Lopez) | 3 | Friend | Monbouquette | Kansas City A.L. | 30,619 |
| | July 13 | N.L. (Alston) | 6 | A.L. (Lopez) | 0 | Law | Ford | New York A.L. | 38,362 |
| 1961[2] | July 11 | N.L. (Murtaugh) | 5 | A.L. (Richards) | 4[6] | Miller | Wilhelm | San Francisco N.L. | 44,115 |
| | July 31 | N.L. (Murtaugh) | 1 | A.L. (Richards) | 1[7] | — | — | Boston A.L. | 31,851 |
| 1962[2] | July 10 | N.L. (Hutchinson) | 3 | A.L. (Houk) | 1 | Marichal | Pascual | Washington A.L. | 45,480 |
| | July 30 | A.L. (Houk) | 9 | N.L. (Hutchinson) | 4 | Herbert | Mahaffey | Chicago N.L. | 38,359 |
| 1963 | July 9 | N.L. (Dark) | 5 | A.L. (Houk) | 3 | Jackson | Bunning | Cleveland A.L. | 44,160 |
| 1964 | July 7 | N.L. (Alston) | 7 | A.L. (Lopez) | 4 | Marichal | Radatz | New York N.L. | 50,850 |
| 1965 | July 13 | N.L. (March) | 6 | A.L. (Lopez) | 5 | Koufax | McDowell | Minnesota A.L. | 46,706 |
| 1966 | July 12 | N.L. (Alston) | 2 | A.L. (Mele) | 1[6] | Perry | Rickert | St. Louis N.L. | 49,926 |
| 1967 | July 11 | N.L. (Alston) | 2 | A.L. (Bauer) | 1[8] | Drysdale | Hunter | Anaheim A.L. | 46,309 |
| 1968 | July 9 | N.L. (Schoendienst) | 1 | A.L. (Williams) | 0 | Drysdale | Tiant | Houston N.L. | 48,321 |
| 1969 | July 23 | N.L. (Schoendienst) | 9 | A.L. (M. Smith) | 3 | Carlton | Stottlemyre | Washington A.L. | 45,259 |
| 1970 | July 14 | N.L. (Hodges) | 5 | A.L. (Weaver) | 4 | Osteen | Wright | Cincinnati N.L. | 51,838 |
| 1971 | July 13 | A.L. (Weaver) | 6 | N.L. (Anderson) | 4 | Blue | Ellis | Detroit A.L. | 53,559 |

| | | | | | | | | | | |
|---|---|---|---|---|---|---|---|---|---|---|
| 1972 | July 25 | N.L. (Murtaugh) | 4 | A.L. (Weaver) | 3[6] | McGraw | McNally | Atlanta N.L. | 53,107 |
| 1973 | July 24[1] | N.L. (Anderson) | 7 | A.L. (Williams) | 1 | Wise | Blyleven | Kansas City A.L. | 40,849 |
| 1974 | July 23[1] | N.L. (Berra) | 7 | A.L. (Williams) | 2 | Brett | Tiant | Pittsburgh N.L. | 50,706 |
| 1975 | July 15[1] | N.L. (Alston) | 6 | A.L. (Dark) | 3 | Matlack | Hunter | Milwaukee A.L. | 51,540 |
| 1976 | July 13 | N.L. (Anderson) | 7 | A.L. (D. Johnson) | 1 | R. Jones | Fidrych | Philadelphia N.L. | 63,974 |
| 1977 | July 19[1] | N.L. (Anderson) | 7 | A.L. (Martin) | 5 | Sutton | Palmer | New York A.L. | 56,683 |
| 1978 | July 11[1] | N.L. (Lasorda) | 7 | A.L. (Martin) | 3 | Sutter | Gossage | San Diego N.L. | 51,549 |
| 1979 | July 17[1] | N.L. (Lasorda) | 7 | A.L. (Lemon) | 6 | Sutter | Kern | Seattle A.L. | 58,905 |
| 1980 | July 8[1] | N.L. (Tanner) | 4 | A.L. (Weaver) | 2 | Reuss | John | Los Angeles N.L. | 56,088 |
| 1981 | Aug. 9[1] | N.L. (Green) | 5 | A.L. (Frey) | 4 | Blue | Fingers | Cleveland* A.L. | 72,086 |
| 1982 | July 13[1] | N.L. (Lasorda) | 4 | A.L. (Martin) | 1 | Rogers | Eckersley | Montreal N.L. | 59,057 |
| 1983 | July 6[1] | A.L. (Kuenn) | 13 | N.L. (Herzog) | 3 | Steib | Soto | Chicago A.L. | 43,801 |
| 1984 | July 11[1] | N.L. (Owens) | 3 | A.L. (Altobelli) | 1 | Leg | Steib | San Francisco, N.L. | 57,756 |
| 1985 | July 16[1] | N.L. (Williams) | 6 | A.L. (Anderson) | 1 | Hoyt | Morris | Minneapolis, A.L. | 54,960 |
| 1986 | July 15[1] | A.L. (Howser) | 3 | N.L. (Herzog) | 2 | Clemens | Gooden | Houston, N.L. | 45,774 |

1. Night game. 2. Two games. 3. Fourteen innings. 4. Five innings, rain. 5. Twelve innings. 6. Ten innings. 7. Called because of rain after nine innings. 8. Fifteen innings. NOTE: No game in 1945. *Game was originally scheduled for July 14, but was put off because of players' strike.

## NATIONAL BASEBALL HALL OF FAME
Cooperstown, N.Y.

### Fielders

| Member | Active years | Member | Active years | Member | Active years |
|---|---|---|---|---|---|
| Aaron, Henry (Hank) | 1954–1976 | Eyers, John | 1902–1919 | Mathews, Edwin | 1952–1968 |
| Anson, Adrian (Cap) | 1876–1897 | Ewing, William | 1880–1897 | Mays, Willie | 1951–1973 |
| Aparicio, Luis | 1956–1973 | Flick, Elmer | 1898–1910 | McCarthy, Thomas | 1884–1896 |
| Appling, Lucius (Luke) | 1930–1950 | Foxx, James | 1925–1945 | McGraw, John J. | 1891–1906 |
| Averill, H. Earl | 1929–1941 | Frisch, Frank | 1919–1937 | McCovey, Willie | 1959–1980 |
| Baker, J. Frank | | Gehrig, H. Louis (Lou) | 1923–1939 | Medwick, Joseph | |
| (Home Run) | 1908–1922 | Gehringer, Charles | 1924–1942 | (Ducky) | 1932–1948 |
| Bancroft, David | 1915–1930 | Gibson, Josh[1] | 1929–1946 | Mize, John (The Big Cat) | 1936–1953 |
| Banks, Ernest | 1953–1971 | Goslin, Leon (Goose) | 1921–1938 | Musial, Stanley | 1941–1963 |
| Beckley, Jacob | 1888–1907 | Greenberg, Henry | | O'Rourke, James | 1876–1894 |
| Bell, James | | (Hank) | 1933–1947 | Ott, Melvin | 1926–1947 |
| (Cool Papa)[1] | 1920–1947 | Hafey, Charles (Chick) | 1924–1937 | Reese, Harold (Pee Wee) | 1940–1958 |
| Berra, Lawrence (Yogi) | 1946–1965 | Hamilton, William | 1888–1901 | Rice, Edgar (Sam) | 1915–1934 |
| Bottomley, James | 1922–1937 | Hartnett, Charles | | Robinson, Brooks | 1955–1977 |
| Boudreau, Louis | 1938–1952 | (Gabby) | 1922–1941 | Robinson, Frank | 1956–1976 |
| Bresnahan, Roger | 1897–1915 | Heilmann, Harry | 1914–1932 | Robinson, Jack | 1947–1956 |
| Brock, Lou | 1961–1980 | Herman, William | 1931–1947 | Robinson, Wilbert | 1886–1902 |
| Brouthers, Dennis | 1879–1896 | Hooper, Harry | 1909–1925 | Roush, Edd | 1913–1931 |
| Burkett, Jesse | 1890–1905 | Hornsby, Rogers | 1915–1937 | Ruth, George (Babe) | 1914–1935 |
| Campanella, Roy | 1948–1957 | Irvin, Monford (Monte)[1] | 1939–1956 | Schalk, Raymond | 1912–1929 |
| Carey, Max | 1910–1929 | Jackson, Travis | 1922–1936 | Sewell, Joseph | 1920–1933 |
| Chance, Frank | 1898–1914 | Jennings, Hugh | 1891–1918 | Simmons, Al | 1924–1944 |
| Charleston, Oscar[1] | 1915–1954 | Johnson, William (Judy)[1] | 1921–1937 | Sisler, George | 1915–1930 |
| Clarke, Fred | 1894–1915 | Kaline, Albert W. | 1953–1974 | Slaughter, Enos | 1938–1959 |
| Clemente, Roberto | 1955–1972 | Keeler, William | | Snider, Edwin D. (Duke) | 1947–1964 |
| Cobb, Tyrus | 1905–1928 | (Wee Willie) | 1892–1910 | Speaker, Tristram | 1907–1928 |
| Cochrane, Gordon | | Kell, George | 1943–1957 | Terry, William | 1923–1936 |
| (Mickey) | 1925–1937 | Kelley, Joseph | 1891–1908 | Thompson, Samuel | 1885–1906 |
| Collins, Edward | 1906–1930 | Kelly, George | 1915–1932 | Tinker, Joseph | 1902–1916 |
| Collins, James | 1895–1908 | Kelly, Michael (King) | 1878–1893 | Traynor, Harold (Pie) | 1920–1937 |
| Comiskey, Charles | 1882–1894 | Killebrew, Harmon | 1954–1975 | Vaughan, Arky | 1932–1948 |
| Combs, Earle | 1924–1935 | Kiner, Ralph | 1946–1955 | Wagner, John (Honus) | 1897–1917 |
| Connor, Roger | 1880–1897 | Klein, Charles H. (Chuck) | 1928–1944 | Wallace, Roderick | |
| Crawford, Samuel | 1899–1917 | Lajoie, Napoleon | 1896–1916 | (Bobby) | 1894–1918 |
| Cronin, Joseph | 1926–1945 | Leonard, Walter (Buck)[1] | 1933–1955 | Waner, Lloyd | 1927–1945 |
| Cuyler, Hazen (Kiki) | 1921–1938 | Lindstrom, Frederick | 1924–1936 | Waner, Paul | 1926–1945 |
| Delahanty, Edward | 1888–1903 | Lloyd, John Henry[1] | 1905–1931 | Ward, John (Monte) | 1878–1894 |
| Dickey, William | 1928–1946 | Lombardi, Ernie | 1932–1947 | Wheat, Zachariah | 1909–1927 |
| Dihigo, Martin[1] | 1923–1945 | Mantle, Mickey | 1951–1968 | Williams, Theodore | 1939–1960 |
| DiMaggio, Joseph | 1936–1951 | Manush, Henry (Heinie) | 1923–1939 | Wilson, Lewis R. (Hack) | 1923–1934 |
| Doerr, Bobby | 1937–1951 | Maranville, Walter | | Youngs, Ross (Pep) | 1917–1926 |
| Duffy, Hugh | 1888–1906 | (Rabbit) | 1912–1935 | | |

### Pitchers

| Member | Active years | Member | Active years | Member | Active years |
|---|---|---|---|---|---|
| Alexander, Grover | 1911–1930 | Brown, Mordecai | | Clarkson, John | 1882–1894 |
| Bender, Charles (Chief) | 1903–1925 | (3-Finger) | 1903–1916 | Coveleski, Stanley | 1912–1928 |
| | | Chesbro, John | 1899–1909 | Dean, Jerome (Dizzy) | 1930–1947 |

| | | | | | |
|---|---|---|---|---|---|
| Drysdale, Don | 1956–1969 | Johnson, Walter | 1907–1927 | Plank, Edward | 1901–1917 |
| Faber, Urban (Red) | 1914–1933 | Joss, Adrian | 1902–1910 | Radbourn, Charles | |
| Feller, Robert | 1936–1956 | Keefe, Timothy | 1880–1893 | (Hoss) | 1880–1891 |
| Ferrell, Rick | 1929–1947 | Koufax, Sanford | | Rixey, Eppa | 1912–1933 |
| Ford, Edward (Whitey) | 1950–1967 | (Sandy) | 1955–1966 | Roberts, Robert (Robin) | 1948–1966 |
| Foster, Andrew (Rube) | 1897–1926 | Lemon, Robert | 1946–1958 | Ruffing, Charles (Red) | 1924–1947 |
| Galvin, James (Pud) | 1876–1892 | Lyons, Theodore | 1923–1946 | Rusie, Amos | 1889–1901 |
| Gibson, Bob | 1959–1975 | Marichal, Juan | 1960–1975 | Spahn, Warren | 1942–1965 |
| Gomez, Vernon (Lefty) | 1930–1943 | Marquard, Richard | | Vance, Arthur (Dazzy) | 1915–1935 |
| Griffith, Clark | 1891–1914 | (Rube) | 1908–1924 | Waddell, George | 1897–1910 |
| Grimes, Burleigh | 1916–1934 | Mathewson, Christopher | 1900–1916 | Walsh, Edward | 1904–1917 |
| Grove, Robert (Lefty) | 1925–1941 | McGinnity, Joseph | 1899–1908 | Welch, Michael (Mickey) | 1880–1892 |
| Haines, Jesse | 1918–1937 | Nichols, Charles (Kid) | 1890–1906 | Wilhelm, Hoyt | 1952–1972 |
| Hoyt, Waite | 1918–1938 | Paige, Leroy (Satchel)[1] | 1926–1965 | Wynn, Early | 1939–1963 |
| Hubbell, Carl | 1928–1943 | Pennock, Herbert | 1912–1934 | Young, Denton (Cy) | 1890–1911 |

## Officials and Others

| | | | |
|---|---|---|---|
| Alston, Walter[2] | Evans, William G.[5][3] | Klem, William[5] | Spalding, Albert G.[5] |
| Barrow, Edward[2][3] | Frick, Ford C.[7][3] | Landis, Kenesaw M.[7] | Stengel, Charles D.[8] |
| Bulkeley, Morgan G.[3] | Giles, Warren C.[3] | Lopez, Alfonso R.[8] | Weiss, George M.[3] |
| Cartwright, Alexander[3] | Gowdy, Curt[9] | Mack, Connie[2][3] | Wright, George[6] |
| Chadwick, Henry[4] | Harridge, William[3] | MacPhail, Leland S.[3] | Wright, Harry[6][2] |
| Chandler, A.B.[7] | Harris, Stanley R.[8] | McCarthy, Joseph V.[2] | Yawkey, Thomas[3] |
| Conlan, John[3] | Hubbard, R. Calvin[5] | McKechnie, William B.[2] | |
| Connolly, Thomas[5] | Higgins, Miller J.[2] | Rickey, W. Branch[2][3] | |
| Cummings, William A.[6] | Johnson, B. Bancroft[3] | Smith, Ken[10] | |

1. Negro league player selected by special committee. 2. Manager. 3. Executive. 4. Writer-statistician. 5. Umpire. 6. Early player. 7. Commissioner. 8. Player-manager. 9. Broadcaster. 10. Sportswriter.

## OTHER LIFETIME BATTING, PITCHING, AND BASE-RUNNING RECORDS

(An asterisk indicates active player)

*Sources: Baseball Record Book,* published and copyrighted by The Sporting News, St. Louis, Mo. 63166; *The Book of Baseball Records,* published and copyrighted by Seymour Siwoff, New York, N.Y. 10036; and *The Complete Handbook of Baseball,* published and copyrighted by New American Library, New York, N.Y. 10019.

### Hits (3,000 or more)

| | |
|---|---|
| Pete Rose* | 4,256 |
| Ty Cobb | 4,191 |
| Henry Aaron | 3,771 |
| Stan Musial | 3,630 |
| Tris Speaker | 3,515 |
| Honus Wagner | 3,430 |
| Carl Yastrzemski | 3,419 |
| Eddie Collins | 3,311 |
| Willie Mays | 3,283 |
| Nap Lajoie | 3,251 |
| Paul Waner | 3,152 |
| Cap Anson | 3,081 |
| Rod Carew | 3,053 |
| Lou Brock | 3,023 |
| Al Kaline | 3,007 |
| Roberto Clemente | 3,000 |

### Earned Run Average[1]

| | |
|---|---|
| Walter Johnson | 2.37 |
| Grover Alexander | 2.56 |
| Whitey Ford | 2.74 |
| Tom Seaver* | 2.80 |
| Jim Palmer | 2.83 |
| Stanley Coveleski | 2.88 |
| Juan Marichal | 2.89 |
| Wilbur Cooper | 2.89 |
| Bob Gibson | 2.91 |
| Carl Mays | 2.92 |
| Don Drysdale | 2.95 |
| Carl Hubbell | 2.98 |
| Gaylord Perry | 2.99 |
| Bert Blyleven* | 3.00 |
| Steve Carlton* | 3.04 |

1. Through 1985 season.

### Runs Scored

| | |
|---|---|
| Ty Cobb | 2,245 |
| Henry Aaron | 2,174 |
| Babe Ruth | 2,174 |
| Pete Rose* | 2,165 |
| Willie Mays | 2,062 |
| Stan Musial | 1,949 |
| Lou Gehrig | 1,888 |
| Tris Speaker | 1,881 |
| Mel Ott | 1,859 |
| Frank Robinson | 1,829 |
| Eddie Collins | 1,816 |
| Carl Yastrzemski | 1,816 |
| Ted Williams | 1,798 |
| Charlie Gehringer | 1,774 |
| Jimmie Foxx | 1,751 |
| Honus Wagner | 1,740 |
| Willie Keeler | 1,720 |
| Cap Anson | 1,712 |
| Jesse Burkett | 1,708 |
| Billy Hamilton | 1,690 |
| Mickey Mantle | 1,677 |

| | |
|---|---|
| John McPhee | 1,674 |
| George Van Haltren | 1,650 |

*Active player through 1986

### Strikeouts, Pitching

| | |
|---|---|
| Nolan Ryan* | 4,277 |
| Steve Carlton* | 4,040 |
| Tom Seaver* | 3,640 |
| Gaylord Perry | 3,534 |
| Walter Johnson | 3,508 |
| Don Sutton* | 3,431 |
| Phil Niekro* | 3,278 |
| Ferguson Jenkins | 3,192 |
| Bob Gibson | 3,117 |
| Jim Bunning | 2,855 |
| Mickey Lolich | 2,832 |
| Cy Young | 2,819 |
| Warren Spahn | 2,583 |
| Bob Feller | 2,581 |
| Tim Keefe | 2,538 |
| Christy Mathewson | 2,505 |

### Home Runs (350 or More)

| | |
|---|---|
| Henry Aaron | 755 |
| Babe Ruth | 714 |
| Willie Mays | 660 |
| Frank Robinson | 586 |
| Harmon Killebrew | 573 |
| Reggie Jackson* | 548 |
| Mickey Mantle | 536 |
| Jimmie Foxx | 534 |
| Ted Williams | 521 |
| Willie McCovey | 521 |
| Eddie Matthews | 512 |
| Ernie Banks | 512 |
| Mel Ott | 511 |
| Mike Schmidt* | 495 |
| Lou Gehrig | 493 |
| Stan Musial | 475 |
| Willie Stargell | 475 |
| Carl Yastrzemski | 452 |
| Dave Kingman* | 442 |
| Billy Williams | 426 |
| Duke Snider | 406 |
| Al Kaline | 399 |
| Johnny Bench | 389 |
| Frank Howard | 382 |
| Orlando Cepeda | 379 |
| Norm Cash | 377 |
| Rocky Colavito | 374 |
| Tony Perez* | 371 |
| Gil Hodges | 370 |
| Ralph Kiner | 369 |
| Joe DiMaggio | 361 |

| | | | | | | | |
|---|---|---|---|---|---|---|---|
| Lee May | 360 | Ed Walsh | 58 | Lou Brock | 1,730 | Ted Williams | 2,019 |
| Johnny Mize | 359 | James Galvin | 57 | Mickey Mantle | 1,710 | Carl Yastrzemski | 1,845 |
| Yogi Berra | 358 | Don Sutton* | 57 | Harmon Killebrew | 1,699 | Joe Morgan | 1,799 |
| Dick Allen | 351 | Bob Gibson | 56 | Dick Allen | 1,556 | Mickey Mantle | 1,734 |

*Active player through 1986.

Steve Carlton* 55 — Lee May 1,552 — Mel Ott 1,708
Jim Palmer 53 — Willie McCovey 1,550 — Eddie Yost 1,614
Gaylord Perry 53 — Frank Robinson 1,532 — Stan Musial 1,599
Juan Marichal 52 — Willie Mays 1,526 — Harmon Killebrew 1,559

**Shutouts**[1]

1. Through 1984 season.

Eddie Matthews 1,487 — Lou Gehrig 1,508
Frank Howard 1,460 — Willie Mays 1,464

| | |
|---|---|
| Walter Johnson | 110 |
| Grover Alexander | 90 |
| Christy Mathewson | 83 |
| Cy Young | 77 |
| Ed Plank | 64 |
| Warren Spahn | 63 |
| Tom Seaver* | 60 |

Jim Wynn 1,427 — Jimmie Foxx 1,452
1. Through 1986 season. — Eddie Mathews 1,444

**Strikeouts, Batting**[1]

Frank Robinson 1,420
Henry Aaron 1,402

| | |
|---|---|
| Reggie Jackson* | 2,362 |
| Willie Stargell | 1,912 |
| Tony Perez* | 1,845 |
| Bobby Bonds | 1,757 |

1. Through 1984 season.

**Bases on Balls**[1]

Babe Ruth 2,056

# RECORD OF WORLD SERIES GAMES

## (Through 1985)

*Source: The Book of Baseball Records*, published by Seymour Siwoff, New York City.

Figures in parentheses for winning pitchers (WP) and losing pitchers (LP) indicate the game number in the series.

1903—Boston A.L. 5 (Jimmy Collins); Pittsburgh N.L. 3 (Fred Clarke). WP—Bos.: Dinneen (2, 6, 8), Young (5, 7); Pitts.: Phillippe (1, 3, 4). LP—Bos.: Young (1), Hughes (3), Dinneen (4); Pitts.: Leever (2, 6), Kennedy (5), Phillippe (7, 8).

1904—No series.

1905—New York N.L. 4 (John J. McGraw); Philadelphia A.L. 1 (Connie Mack). WP—N.Y.: Mathewson (1, 3, 5); McGinnity (4); Phila.: Bender (2). LP—N.Y.: McGinnity (2); Phila.: Plank (1, 4), Coakley (3), Bender (5).

1906—Chicago A.L. 4 (Fielder Jones); Chicago N.L. 2 (Frank Chance). WP—Chi.: A.L.: Altrock (1), Walsh (3, 5), White (6); Chi.: N.L.: Reulbach (2), Brown (4). LP—Chi. A.L.: White (2), Altrock. (4); Chi.: N.L.: Brown (1, 6), Pfeister (3, 5).

1907—Chicago N.L. 4 (Frank Chance); Detroit A.L. 0 (Hugh Jennings). First game tied 3–3, 12 innings. WP—Pfeister (2), Reulbach (3), Overall (4), Brown (5). LP—Mullin (2, 5), Siever (3), Donovan (4).

1908—Chicago N.L. 4 (Frank Chance); Detroit A.L. 1 (Hugh Jennings). WP—Chi.: Brown (1, 4), Overall (2, 5); Det.: Mullin (3). LP—Chi.: Pfeister (3); Det.: Summers (1, 4), Donovan (2, 5).

1909—Pittsburgh N.L. 4 (Fred Clarke); Detroit A.L. 3 (Hugh Jennings). WP—Pitts.: Adams (1, 5, 7), Maddox (3); Det.: Donovan (2), Mullin (4, 6). LP—Pitts.: Camnitz (2), Leifield (4), Willis (6); Det.: Mullin (1), Summers (3, 5), Donovan (7).

1910—Philadelphia A.L. 4 (Connie Mack); Chicago N.L. 1 (Frank Chance). WP—Phila.: Bender (1), Coombs (2, 3, 5); Chi.: Brown (4). LP—Phila.: Bender (4); Chi.: Overall (1), Brown (2, 5), McIntyre (3).

1911—Philadelphia A.L. 4 (Connie Mack); New York N.L. 2 (John J. McGraw). WP—Phila.: Plank (2), Coombs (3), Bender (4, 6); N.Y.: Mathewson (1), Crandall (5). LP—Phila.: Bender (1), Plank (5); N.Y.: Marquard (2), Mathewson (3, 4), Ames (6).

1912—Boston A.L. 4 (J. Garland Stahl); New York N.L. 3 (John J. McGraw). Second game tied, 6–6, 11 innings. WP—Bos.: Wood (1, 4, 8), Bedient (5); N.Y.: Marquard (3, 6), Tesreau (7). LP—Bos.: O'Brien (3, 6), Wood (7); N.Y.: Tesreau (1, 4), Mathewson (5, 8).

1913—Philadelphia A.L. 4 (Connie Mack); New York N.L. 1 (John J. McGraw). WP—Phila.: Bender (1, 4), Bush (3), Plank (5); N.Y.: Mathewson (2); LP—Phila.: Plank (2); N.Y.: Marquard (1), Tesreau (3), Demaree (4), Mathewson (5).

1914—Boston N.L. 4 (George Stallings); Philadelphia A.L. 0 (Connie Mack). WP—Rudolph (1, 4), James (2, 3). LP—Bender (1), Plank (2), Bush (3), Shawkey (4).

1915—Boston A.L. 4 (Bill Carrigan); Philadelphia N.L. 1 (Pat Moran). WP—Bos.: Foster (2, 5), Leonard (3), Shore (4); Phila.: Alexander (1). LP—Bos.: Shore (1); Phila.: Mayer (2), Alexander (3), Chalmers (4), Rixey (5).

1916—Boston A.L. 4 (Bill Carrigan); Brooklyn N.L. 1 (Wilbert Robinson). WP—Bos.: Shore (1, 5), Ruth (2), Leonard (4); Bklyn.: Coombs (3). LP—Bos.: Mays (3); Bklyn.: Marquard (1, 4), Smith (2), Pfeffer (5).

1917—Chicago A.L. 4 (Clarence Rowland); New York N.L. 2 (John J. McGraw). WP—Chi.: Cicotte (1), Faber (2, 5, 6); N.Y.: Benton (3), Schupp (4), LP—Chi.: Cicotte (3), Faber (4); N.Y.: Sallee (1, 5), Anderson (2), Benton (6).

1918—Boston A.L. 4 (Ed Barrow); Chicago N.L. 2 (Fred Mitchell). WP—Bos.: Ruth (1, 4), Mays (3, 6); Chi.: Tyler (2), Vaughn (5). LP—Bos.: Bush (2), Jones (5); Chi.: Vaughn (1, 3), Douglas (4), Tyler (6).

1919—Cincinnati N.L. 5 (Pat Moran); Chicago A.L. 3 (William Gleason). WP—Cin.: Ruether (1), Sallee (2), Ring (4), Eller (5, 8); Chi.: Kerr (3, 6), Cicotte (7). LP—Cin.: Fisher (3), Ring (6), Sallee (7); Chi.: Cicotte (1, 4), Williams (2, 5, 8).

1920—Cleveland A.L. 5 (Tris Speaker); Brooklyn N.L. 2 (Wilbert Robinson). WP—Cleve.: Coveleski (1, 4, 7), Bagby (5), Mails (6); Bklyn.: Grimes (2), Smith (3). LP—Cleve.: Bagby (2), Caldwell (3). Bklyn.: Marquard (1), Cadore (4), Grimes (5, 7), Smith (6).

1921—New York N.L. 5 (John J. McGraw); New York A.L. 3 (Miller Huggins). WP—N.Y. N.L.: Barnes (3, 6), Douglas (4, 7), Nehf (8); N.Y. A.L.: Mays (1), Hoyt (2, 5). LP—N.Y. N.L.: Nehf (2, 5), Douglas (1). N.Y. A.L.: Quinn (3), Mays (4, 7), Shawkey (6), Hoyt (8).

1922—New York N.L. 4 (John J. McGraw); New York A.L. 0 (Miller Huggins). Second game tied 3–3, 10 innings. WP—Ryan (1), Scott (3), McQuillan (4), Nehf (5); LP—Bush (1, 5), Hoyt (3), Mays (4).

1923—New York A.L. 4 (Miller Huggins); New York N.L. 2 (John J. McGraw). WP—N.Y. A.L.: Pennock (2, 6), Shawkey (4), Bush (5); N.Y. N.L.: Ryan (1), Nehf (3). LP—N.Y. A.L.: Bush (1), Jones (3); N.Y. N.L.: McQuillan (2), Scott (4), Bentley (5), Nehf (6).

1924—Washington A.L. 4 (Bucky Harris); New York N.L. 3 (John J. McGraw). WP—Wash.: Zachary (2, 6), Mogridge (4), Johnson (7); N.Y.: Nehf (1), McQuillan (3), Bentley (5). LP—Wash.: Johnson (1, 5), Marberry (3); N.Y.: Bentley (2, 7), Barnes (4), Nehf (6).

1925—Pittsburgh N.L. 4 (Bill McKechnie); Washington A.L. 3 (Bucky Harris). WP—Pitts.: Aldridge (2, 5), Kremer (6, 7); Wash.: Johnson (1, 4), Ferguson (3). LP—Pitts.: Meadows (1), Kremer (3), Yde (4); Wash.: Coveleski (2, 5), Ferguson (6), Johnson (7).

1926—St. Louis N.L. 4 (Rogers Hornsby); New York A.L. 3 (Miller Huggins). WP—St. L.: Alexander (2, 6), Haines (3, 7); N.Y.: Pennock (1, 5), Hoyt (4). LP—St. L.: Sherdel (1, 5), Reinhart (4); N.Y.: Shocker (2), Ruether (3), Shawkey (6), Hoyt (7).

1927—New York A.L. 4 (Miller Huggins); Pittsburgh N.L. 0 (Donie Bush). WP—Hoyt (1, 4), Pipgras (2), Pennock (3), Moore (4). LP—Kremer (1), Aldridge (2), Meadows (3), Miljus (4).

1928—New York A.L. 4 (Miller Huggins); St. Louis N.L. 0 (Bill McKechnie). WP—Hoyt (1, 4), Pipgras (2), Zachary (3). LP—Sherdel (1, 4), Alexander (2), Haines (3).

**1929**—Philadelphia A.L. 4 (Connie Mack); Chicago N.L. 1 (Joe McCarthy). WP—Phila.: Ehmke (1), Earnshaw (2), Rommel (4), Walberg (5); Chi.: Bush (3). LP—Phila.: Earnshaw (3) Chi.: Root (1), Malone (2, 5), Blake (4).

**1930**—Philadelphia A.L. 4 (Connie Mack); St. Louis N.L. 2 (Gabby Street). WP—Phila.: Grove (1, 5), Earnshaw (2, 6); St. L.: Hallahan (3), Haines (4). LP—Phila.: Walberg (3), Grove (4); St. L.: Grimes (1, 5), Rhem (2), Hallahan (6).

**1931**—St. Louis N.L. 4 (Gabby Street); Philadelphia A.L. 3 (Connie Mack). WP—St. L.: Hallahan (2, 5), Grimes (3, 7); Phila.: Grove (1, 6), Earnshaw (4). LP—St. L.: Derringer (1, 6), Johnson (4); Phila.: Earnshaw (2, 7), Grove (3), Hoyt (5).

**1932**—New York A.L. 4 (Joe McCarthy); Chicago N.L. 0 (Charles Grimm). WP—Ruffing (1), Gomez (2), Pipgras (3), Moore (4). LP—Bush (1), Warneke (2), Root (3), May (4).

**1933**—New York N.L. 4 (Bill Terry); Washington A.L. 1 (Joe Cronin.). WP—N.Y.: Hubbell (1, 4), Schumacher (2), Luque (5); Wash.: Whitehill (3). LP—N.Y.: Fitzsimmons (3); Wash.: Stewart (1), Crowder (2), Weaver (4), Russell (5).

**1934**—St. Louis N.L. 4 (Frank Frisch); Detroit A.L. 3 (Mickey Cochrane). WP—St. L.: J. Dean (1, 7), P. Dean (3, 6); Det.: Rowe (2), Auker (4), Bridges (5). LP—St. L.: W. Walker (2, 4), J. Dean (5); Det.: Crowder (1), Bridges (3), Rowe (6), Auker (7).

**1935**—Detroit A.L. 4 (Mickey Cochrane); Chicago N.L. 2 (Charles Grimm). WP—Det.: Bridges (2, 6), Rowe (3), Crowder (4); Chi.: Warneke (1, 5); LP—Det.: Rowe (1, 5), Chi.: Root (2), French (3, 6), Carleton (4).

**1936**—New York A.L. 4 (Joe McCarthy); New York N.L. 2 (Bill Terry). WP—N.Y. A.L.: Gomez (2, 6), Hadley (3), Pearson (4); N.Y. N.L.: Hubbell (1), Schumacher (5); LP—N.Y. A.L.: Ruffing (1), Malone (5); N.Y. N.L.: Schumacher (2), Fitzsimmons (3, 6), Hubbell (4).

**1937**—New York A.L. 4 (Joe McCarthy); New York N.L. 1 (Bill Terry). WP—N.Y. A.L.: Gomez (1, 5), Ruffing (2), Pearson (3); N.Y. N.L.: Hubbell (4). LP—N.Y. A.L.: Hadley (4); N.Y. N.L.: Hubbell (1), Melton (2, 5), Schumacher (3).

**1938**—New York A.L. 4 (Joe McCarthy); Chicago N.L. 0 (Gabby Hartnett). WP—Ruffing (1, 4), Gomez (2), Pearson (3) LP—Lee (1, 4), Dean (2), Bryant (3).

**1939**—New York A.L. 4 (Joe McCarthy); Cincinnati N.L. 0 (Bill McKechnie). WP—Ruffing (1), Pearson (2), Hadley (3), Murphy (4). LP—Derringer (1), Walters (2, 4), Thompson (3).

**1940**—Cincinnati N.L. 4 (Bill McKechnie); Detroit A.L. 3 (Del Baker). WP—Cin.: Walters (2, 6), Derringer (4, 7); Det.: Newsom (1, 5), Bridges (3). LP—Cin.: Derringer (1), Turner (3), Thompson (5); Det.: Rowe (2, 6), Trout (4), Newsom (7).

**1941**—New York A.L. 4 (Joe McCarthy); Brooklyn N.L. 1 (Leo Durocher). WP—N.Y.: Ruffing (1), Russo (3), Murphy (4), Bonham (5); Bklyn: Wyatt (2). LP—N.Y.: Chandler (2); Bklyn: Davis (1), Casey (3, 4), Wyatt (5).

**1942**—St. Louis N.L. 4 (Billy Southworth); New York A.L. 1 (Joe McCarthy). WP—St. L.: Beazley (2, 5), White (3), Lanier (4); N.Y.: Ruffing (1). LP—St. L.: Cooper (1); N.Y.: Bonham (2), Chandler (3), Donald (4), Ruffing (5).

**1943**—New York A.L. 4 (Joe McCarthy); St. Louis N.L. 1 (Billy Southworth). WP—N.Y.: Chandler (1, 5), Borowy (3), Russo (4); St. L.: Cooper (2). LP—N.Y.: Bonham (2); St. L.: Lanier (1), Brazle (3), Brecheen (4), Cooper (5).

**1944**—St. Louis N.L. 4 (Billy Southworth); St. Louis A.L. 2 (Luke Sewell). WP—St. L. N.L.: Donnelly (2), Brecheen (4), Cooper (5), Lanier (6); St. L. A.L.: Galehouse (1), Kramer (3). LP—St. L. N.L.: Cooper (1), Wilks (3); St. L. A.L.: Muncrief (2), Jakucki (4), Galehouse (5), Potter (6).

**1945**—Detroit A.L. 4 (Steve O'Neill); Chicago N.L. 3 (Charles Grimm). WP—Det.: Trucks (2), Trout (4), Newhouser (5, 7); Chi.: Borowy (1, 6), Passeau (3). LP—Det.: Newhouser (1), Overmire (3), Trout (6); Chi.: Wyse (2), Prim (4), Borowy (5, 7).

**1946**—St. Louis N.L. 4 (Eddie Dyer); Boston A.L. 3 (Joe Cronin). WP—St. L.: Brecheen (2, 6), Munger (4); Bos.: Johnson (1), Ferriss (3), Dobson (5). LP—St. L.: Pollet (1), Dickson (3), Brazle (5); Bos.: Harris (2, 6), Hughson (4), Klinger (7).

**1947**—New York A.L. 4 (Bucky Harris); Brooklyn N.L. 3 (Burt Shotton). WP—N.Y.: Shea (1, 5), Reynolds (2), Page (7); Bklyn.: Casey (3, 4), Branca (6). LP—N.Y.: Newsom (3), Bevens (4), Page

(6); Bklyn.: Branca (1), Lombardi (2), Barney (5), Gregg (7).

**1948**—Cleveland A.L. 4 (Lou Boudreau); Boston N.L. 2 (Billy Southworth). WP—Cleve.: Lemon (2, 6), Bearden (3), Gromek (4); Bos.: Sain (1), Spahn (5). LP—Cleve.: Feller (1, 5); Bos.: Spahn (2), Bickford (3), Sain (4), Voiselle (6).

**1949**—New York A.L. 4 (Casey Stengel); Brooklyn N.L. 1 (Burt Shotton). WP—N.Y.: Reynolds (1), Page (3), Lopat (4), Raschi (5); Bklyn.: Roe (2). LP—N.Y.: Raschi (2) Bklyn.: Newcombe (1, 4), Branca (3), Barney (5).

**1950**—New York A.L. 4 (Casey Stengel); Philadelphia N.L. 0 (Eddie Sawyer). WP—Raschi (1), Reynolds (2), Ferrick (3), Ford (4). LP—Konstanty (1), Roberts (2), Meyer (3), Miller (4).

**1951**—New York A.L. 4 (Casey Stengel); New York N.L. 2 (Leo Durocher). WP—N.Y. A.L.: Lopat (2, 5), Reynolds (4), Raschi (6); N.Y. N.L.: Koslo (1), Hearn (3). LP—N.Y. A.L.: Reynolds (1), Raschi (3); N.Y. N.L.: Jansen (2, 5), Maglie (4), Koslo (6).

**1952**—New York A.L. 4 (Casey Stengel); Brooklyn N.L. 3 (Chuck Dressen). WP—N.Y.: Raschi (2, 6), Reynolds (4, 7); Bklyn.: Black (1), Roe (3), Erskine (5). LP—N.Y.: Reynolds (1), Lopat (3), Sain (5); Bklyn.: Erskine (2), Black (4, 7), Loes (6).

**1953**—New York A.L. 4 (Casey Stengel); Brooklyn N.L. 2 (Chuck Dressen). WP—N.Y.: Sain (1), Lopat (2), McDonald (5), Reynolds (6); Bklyn.: Erskine (3), Loes (4). LP—N.Y.: Raschi (3), Ford (4); Bklyn.: Labine (1, 6), Roe (2), Podres (5).

**1954**—New York N.L. 4 (Leo Durocher); Cleveland A.L. 0 (Al Lopez). WP—Grissom (1), Antonelli (2), Gomez (3), Liddie (4). LP—Lemon (1, 4), Wynn (2), Garcia (3).

**1955**—Brooklyn N.L. 4 (Walter Alston); New York A.L. 3 (Casey Stengel). WP—Bklyn.: Podres (3, 7), Labine (4), Craig (5); N.Y.: Ford (1, 6), Byrne (2). LP—Bklyn.: Newcombe (1), Loes (2), Spooner (6); N.Y.: Turley (3), Larsen (4), Grim (5), Byrne (7).

**1956**—New York A.L. 4 (Casey Stengel); Brooklyn N.L. 3 (Walter Alston). WP—N.Y.: Ford (3), Sturdivant (4), Larsen (5), Kucks (7); Bklyn.: Maglie (1), Bessent (2), Labine (6). LP—N.Y.: Ford (1), Morgan (2), Turley (6); Bklyn.: Craig (3), Erskine (4), Maglie (5), Newcombe (7).

**1957**—Milwaukee N.L. 4 (Fred Haney); New York A.L. 3 (Casey Stengel). WP—Mil.: Burdette (2, 5, 7), Spahn (4); N.Y.: Ford (1), Larsen (3), Turley (6). LP—Mil.: Spahn (1), Buhl (3), Johnson (6); N.Y.: Shantz (2), Grim (4), Ford (5), Larsen (7).

**1958**—New York A.L. 4 (Casey Stengel); Milwaukee N.L. 3 (Fred Haney). WP—N.Y.: Larsen (3), Turley (5, 7), Duren (6); Mil.: Spahn (1, 4), Burdette (2). LP—N.Y.: Duren (1), Turley (2), Ford (4); Mil.: Rush (3), Burdette (5, 7), Spahn (6).

**1959**—Los Angeles N.L. 4 (Walter Alston); Chicago A.L. 2 (Al Lopez). WP—L.A.: Podres (2), Drysdale (3), Sherry (4, 6); Chi.: Wynn (1), Shaw (5) LP—L.A.: Craig (1), Koufax (5); Chi.: Shaw (4), Donovan (3), Staley (4), Wynn (6).

**1960**—Pittsburgh N.L. 4 (Danny Murtaugh); New York A.L. 3 (Casey Stengel). WP—Pitts.: Law (1, 4), Haddix (5, 7); N.Y.: Turley (2), Ford (3, 6). LP—Pitts.: Friend (2, 6), Mizell (3); N.Y.: Ditmar (1, 5), Terry (4, 7).

**1961**—New York A.L. 4 (Ralph Houk); Cincinnati N.L. 1 (Fred Hutchinson). WP—N.Y.: Ford (1, 4), Arroyo (3), Daley (5); Cin.: Jay (2). LP—N.Y.: Terry (2); Cin.: O'Toole (1, 4), Purkey (3), Jay (5).

**1962**—New York A.L. 4 (Ralph Houk); San Francisco N.L. 3 (Al Dark). WP—N.Y.: Ford (1), Stafford (3), Terry (5, 7); S.F. Sanford (2), Larsen (4), Pierce (6). LP—N.Y.: Terry (2), Coates (4), Ford (6); S.F.: O'Dell (1), Pierce (3), Sanford (5, 7).

**1963**—Los Angeles N.L. 4 (Walter Alston); New York A.L. 0 (Ralph Houk). WP—Koufax (1, 4), Podres (2), Drysdale (3). LP—Ford (1, 4), Downing (2), Bouton (3).

**1964**—St. Louis N.L. 4 (Johnny Keane); New York A.L. 3 (Yogi Berra). WP—St. L.: Sadecki (1), Craig (4), Gibson (5, 7); N.Y.: Stottlemyre (2), Bouton (3, 6). LP—St. L.: Gibson (2), Schultz (3), Simmons (6); N.Y.: Ford (1), Downing (4), Mikkelsen (5), Stottlemyre (7).

**1965**—Los Angeles N.L. 4 (Walter Alston); Minnesota A.L. 3 (Sam Mele). WP—L.A.: Osteen (3), Drysdale (4), Koufax (5, 7); Minn.: Grant (1, 6), Kaat (2). LP—L.A.: Drysdale (1), Koufax (2), Osteen (6); Minn.: Pascual (3), Grant (4), Kaat (5, 7).

**1966**—Baltimore A.L. 4 (Hank Bauer); Los Angeles N.L. 0 (Walter Alston). WP—Drabowsky (1), Palmer (2), Bunker (3), McNally (4). LP—Drysdale (1, 4), Koufax (2), Osteen (3).

**1967**—St. Louis N.L. 4 (Red Schoendienst); Boston A.L. 3 (Dick Williams). WP—St. L.: Gibson (1, 4, 7), Briles (3); Bos.: Lonborg (2, 5); Wyatt (6). LP—St. L.: Hughes (2), Carlton (5), Lamabe (6); Bos.: Santiago (1, 4), Bell (3), Lonborg (7).

**1968**—Detroit A.L. 4 (Mayo Smith); St. Louis N.L. 3 (Red Schoendienst). WP—Det.: Lolich (2, 5, 7), McLain (6); St. L.: Gibson (1, 4), Washburn (3), LP—Det.: McLain (1, 4), Wilson (3); St. L.: Briles (2), Hoerner (5), Washburn (6), Gibson (7).

**1969**—New York N.L. 4 (Gil Hodges); Baltimore A.L. 1 (Earl Weaver). WP—N.Y.: Koosman (2, 5), Gentry (3), Seaver (4); Balt.: Cuellar (1). LP—N.Y.: Seaver (1); Balt.: McNally (2), Palmer (3), Hall (4), Watt (5).

**1970**—Baltimore A.L. 4 (Earl Weaver); Cincinnati N.L. 1 (Sparky Anderson) 1. WP—Balt.: Palmer (1), Phoebus (2), McNally (3), Cuellar (5); Cin.: Carroll (4). LP—Cin.: Nolan (1), Wilcox (2), Cloninger (3), Merritt (5); Balt.: Watt (4).

**1971**—Pittsburgh N.L. 4 (Danny Murtaugh); Baltimore A.L. 3 (Earl Weaver). WP—Pitts.: Blass (3, 7), Kison (4), Briles (5); Balt.: McNally (1, 6), Palmer (2). LP—Pitts.: Ellis (1), R. Johnson (2), Miller (6); Balt.: Cuellar (3, 7), Watt (4) McNally (5).

**1972**—Oakland A.L. 4 (Dick Williams); Cincinnati N.L. (Sparky Anderson) 3. WP—Oakland: Holtzman (1), Hunter (2, 7), Fingers (4); Cincinnati: Billingham (3), Grimsley (5, 6). LP—Oakland: Odom (3), Fingers (5), Blue (6); Cincinnati: Nolan (1), Grimsley (2), Carroll (4), Borbon (7).

**1973**—Oakland A.L. 4 (Dick Williams): New York N.L. 3 (Yogi Berra). WP—Oakland: Holtzman (1, 7), Lindblad (3), Hunter (6). New York: McGraw (2), Matlack (4), Koosman (5). LP—Oakland: Fingers (2), Holtzman (4), Blue (5). New York: Matlack (1, 7) Parker (3), Seaver (6).

**1974**—Oakland A.L. 4 (Al Dark); Los Angeles N.L. 1 (Walter Alston). WP—Oakland: Fingers (1), Hunter (3), Holtzman (4), Odom (5). Los Angeles: Sutton (2). LP—Oakland: Blue (2), Los Angeles: Messersmith (1, 4), Downing (3), Marshall (5).

**1975**—Cincinnati N.L. 4 (Sparky Anderson); Boston A.L. 3 (Darrell Johnson). WP—Cincinnati: Eastwick (2–3), Gullett (5), Carroll (7); Boston: Tiant (1–4), Wise (6). LP—Cincinnati: Gullett (1), Norman (4), Darcy (6); Boston: Drago (2), Willoughby (3), Cleveland (5), Burton (7).

**1976**—Cincinnati N.L. 4 (Sparky Anderson); New York A.L. 0 (Billy Martin). WP—Gullett (1), Billingham (2), Zachry (3), Nolan (4). LP—Alexander (1), Hunter (2), Ellis (3), Figueroa (4).

**1977**—New York A.L. 4 (Billy Martin); Los Angeles N.L. 2 (Tom Lasorda). WP—New York: Lyle (1), Torrez (3, 6), Guidry (4); Los Angeles: Hooton (2), Sutton (5). LP—New York: Hunter (2), Gullett (5); Los Angeles: Rhoden (1), John (3), Rau (4), Hooton (6).

**1978**—New York A.L. 4 (Bob Lemon), Los Angeles N.L. 2 (Tom Lasorda); WP—New York: Guidry (3), Gossage (4); Beattie (5), Hunter (6); Los Angeles: John (1), Hooton (2). LP—New York: Figuero (1), Hunter (2); Los Angeles: Sutton (3–6), Welch (4), Hooton (5).

**1979**—Pittsburgh N.L. 4 (Chuck Tanner), Baltimore A.L. 3 (Earl Weaver); WP—Pittsburgh: D. Robinson (2), Blyleven (5), Candelaria (6), Jackson (7); Baltimore: Flanagan (1), McGregor (3), Stoddard (4). LP—Pittsburgh: Kison (1), Candelaria (3), Tekulve (4); Baltimore: Stanhouse (2), Flanagan (5), Palmer (6), McGregor (7).

**1980**—Philadelphia N.L. 4 (Dallas Green), Kansas City A.L. 2 (Jim Frey); WP—Philadelphia: Walk (1), Carlton (2), McGraw (5), Carlton (6); Kansas City: Quisenberry (3), Leonard (4). LP—Philadelphia: McGraw (3), Christenson (4); Kansas City: Leonard (1), Quisenberry (2), Quisenberry (5), Gale (6).

**1981**—Los Angeles N.L. 4 (Tom Lasorda), New York A.L. 2 (Bob Lemon); WP—Los Angeles: Valenzuela (3), Howe (4), Reuss (5), Hooton (6); New York: Guidry (1), John (2). LP—Los Angeles: Reuss (1), Hooton (2); New York: Frazier (3), Frazier (4), Guidry (5), Frazier (6).

**1982**—St. Louis N.L. 4 (Whitey Herzog), Milwaukee A.L. (Harvey Kuenn); WP—St. Louis: Sutter (2), Andujar (3), Stuper (6), Andujar (7). Milwaukee: Caldwell (1), Slaton (4), Caldwell (5). LP—St. Louis: Forsch (1), Bair (4), Forsch (5). Milwaukee: McClure (2), Vuckovich (3), Sutton (6), McClure (7).

**1983**—Baltimore A.L. 4 (Joe Altobelli), Philadelphia N.L. 1 (Paul Owens); WP—Baltimore: Boddicker (2), Palmer (3), Davis (4), McGregor (5). Philadelphia: Denny (1).

**1984**—Detroit A.L. 4 (Sparky Anderson), San Diego N.L. 1 (Dick Williams); WP—Det.: Morris (1,4), Wilcox (3), Lopez (5), San Diego: Hawkins (2). LP—Det.: Petry (2), San Diego: Thurmond (1), Lollar (3), Show (4), Hawkins (5).

**1985**—Kansas City A.L. 4 (Dick Howser), St. Louis N.L. 3 (Whitey Herzog); WP—KC: Saberhagen (3,7) Quisenberry (6), Jackson (5). St. Louis: Tudor (1,4) Dayley (2). LP—KC: Jackson (1), Leibrandt (2), Black (4); St. Louis: Andujar (3), Forsch (5), Worrell (6), Tudor (7).

## BASEBALL HALTED BY PLAYERS STRIKE FOR SECOND TIME IN FOUR YEARS

Major League baseball, after months of haggling, endured a strike by players for the second time since 1981 in August 1985. Unlike the 1981 strike, which lasted seven weeks and canceled 713 games, this one was ended quickly. The players walked on Tuesday, Aug. 6, and were back on the field three days later on Thursday, Aug. 8.

First-year baseball commissioner Peter Ueberroth's intervention in the talks was widely regarded as the turning point, although Ueberroth refused to take credit and pointed to the work of Players Association Executive Director Donald Fehr, and Lee MacPhail, president of the owners Player Relations Committee.

While in 1981 the major issue was over compensation for free agent signings to the club losing players, the 1985 strike was primarily over the pension fund, and how much of the reported $1.1 billion the owners receive through network television agreements would go into the plan.

The players were seeking an increase of $45 million over the $15 million they'd been receiving under the contract signed in 1981. The owners were adamant in refusing such a large increase.

There were other matters at question, including the issue of arbitration. Under the 1981 agreement, a player with two years of major league service who couldn't come to terms with ownership could take his case to binding arbitration. The owners were looking to increase the number of years

vested service required to three years, and pointed to substantial operating losses caused, in part, by large salaries granted by arbitrators and the increasing spiral of free agent salaries.

In the end, the players wound up with approximately $35 million for their pension fund, and the owners got their desired three years for arbitration, albeit the rule would not be scheduled to take effect until 1987.

The games canceled by the strike were rescheduled for later in the season, unlike the 1981 affair when far too many games were lost to be made up.

The 1981 strike settlement had been complicated by the decision to play a split season—awarding divisional championships to the teams in first place before the strike began, and starting a new second season to crown four additional champions. Those eight teams played off in a preliminary series. The survivors played for the league title and the right to move on to the World Series.

Former commissioner Bowie Kuhn was much criticized for this plan, as he was for not taking action to prevent or shorten the 1981 strike. That may have been Ueberroth's motivation when he decided he would step in. His initial overtures were lambasted by both sides in the conflict. But in the end, both sides agreed Ueberroth had been helpful in bringing them back to the bargaining table and pressing for a settlement.

## WORLD SERIES CLUB STANDING
### (Through 1985)

| | Series | Won | Lost | Pct. | | Series | Won | Lost | Pct. |
|---|---|---|---|---|---|---|---|---|---|
| Oakland (A) | 3 | 3 | 0 | 1.000 | Detroit (A) | 9 | 4 | 5 | .444 |
| Pittsburgh (N) | 7 | 5 | 2 | .714 | New York (N-Giants) | 14 | 5 | 9 | .357 |
| St. Louis (N) | 14 | 9 | 5 | .643 | Washington (A) | 3 | 1 | 2 | .333 |
| New York (A) | 33 | 22 | 11 | .667 | Philadelphia (N) | 4 | 1 | 3 | .250 |
| Cleveland (A) | 3 | 2 | 1 | .667 | Chicago (N) | 10 | 2 | 8 | .200 |
| Boston (A) | 8 | 5 | 3 | .625 | Brooklyn (N) | 9 | 1 | 8 | .111 |
| Philadelphia (A) | 8 | 5 | 3 | .625 | St. Louis (A) | 1 | 0 | 1 | .000 |
| Los Angeles (N) | 8 | 4 | 4 | .500 | San Francisco (N) | 1 | 0 | 1 | .000 |
| New York (N-Mets) | 2 | 1 | 1 | .500 | Minnesota (A) | 1 | 0 | 1 | .000 |
| Milwaukee (N) | 2 | 1 | 1 | .500 | Kansas City (A) | 2 | 1 | 1 | .500 |
| Boston (N) | 2 | 1 | 1 | .500 | Milwaukee (A) | 1 | 0 | 1 | .000 |
| Chicago (A) | 4 | 2 | 2 | .500 | San Diego (N) | 1 | 0 | 1 | .000 |
| Cincinnati (N) | 8 | 4 | 4 | .500 | | | | | |
| Baltimore (A) | 6 | 3 | 3 | .500 | | | | | |

**Recapitulation**

| | Won |
|---|---|
| American League | 47 |
| National League | 35 |

## SINGLE GAME AND SINGLE SERIES RECORDS
### (Through 1985)

Most hits game—5, Paul Molitor, Milwaukee A.L., first game vs. St. Louis, N.L., 1982.

Most 4-hit games, series—2, Robin Yount, Milwaukee A.L., first and fifth games vs. St. Louis N.L., 1982.

Most hits inning—2, held by many players.

Most hits series—13 (7 games) Bobby Richardson, New York A.L., 1964; Lou Brock, St. Louis N.L., 1968; 12 (6 games) Billy Martin, New York A.L., 1953; 12 (8 games) Buck Herzog, New York N.L., 1912; Joe Jackson, Chicago A.L., 1919; 10 (4 games) Babe Ruth, New York A.L., 1928; 9 (5 games) held by 8 players.

Most home runs, series—5 (6 games) Reggie Jackson, New York A.L., 1977; 4 (7 games) Babe Ruth, New York A.L., 1926; Duke Snider, Brooklyn N.L., 1952, 1955; Hank Bauer, New York A.L., 1958; Gene Tenace, Oakland A.L., 1972; 4 (4 games) Lou Gehrig, New York A.L., 1928; 3 (6 games) Babe Ruth, New York A.L., 1923; Ted Kluszewski, Chicago A.L., 1959; 3 (5 games) Donn Clendenon, New York Mets N.L., 1969.

Most home runs, game—3, Babe Ruth, New York A.L., 1926 and 1928; Reggie Jackson, New York A.L., 1977.

Most strikeouts, series—12 (6 games) Willie Wilson, Kansas City A.L., 1980; 11 (7 games) Ed Mathews, Milwaukee N.L., 1958; Wayne Garrett, New York N.L., 1973; 10 (8 games) George Kelly, New York N.L., 1921; 9 (6 games) Jim Bottomley, St. Louis N.L., 1930;

9 (5 games) Carmelo Martinez, San Diego, N.L., 1984; Duke Snider, Brooklyn N.L., 1949; 7 (4 games) Bob Muesel, New York A.L., 1927.

Most stolen bases, game—3, Honus Wagner, Pittsburgh N.L., 1909; Willie Davis, Los Angeles N.L., 1965; Lou Brock, St. Louis N.L., 1967 and 1968.

Most strikeouts by pitcher, game—17, Bob Gibson, St. Louis N.L. 1968.

Most strikeouts by pitcher in succession—6, Horace Eller, Cincinnati N.L., 1919; Moe Drabowsky, Baltimore A.L., 1966.

Most strikeouts by pitcher, series—35 (7 games) Bob Gibson, St. Louis N.L., 1968; 28 (8 games) Bill Dinneen, Boston A.L., 1903; 23 (4 games) Sandy Koufax, Los Angeles, 1963; 20 (6 games) Chief Bender, Philadelphia A.L., 1911; 18 (5 games) Christy Mathewson, New York N.L., 1905.

Most bases on balls, series—11 (7 games) Babe Ruth, New York A.L., 1926; Gene Tenace, Oakland A.L., 1973; 9 (6 games) Willie Randolph, New York A.L., 1981; 7 (5 games) James Sheckard, Chicago N.L., 1910; Mickey Cochrane, Philadelphia A.L., 1929; Joe Gordon, New York A.L., 1941; 7 (4 games) Hank Thompson, New York N.L., 1954.

Most consecutive scoreless innings one series—27, Christy Mathewson, New York N.L., 1905.

## LIFETIME WORLD SERIES RECORDS
### (Through 1985)

Most hits—71, Yogi Berra, New York A.L., 1947, 1949-53, 1955-58, 1960-63.

Most runs—42, Mickey Mantle, New York A.L., 1951-53, 1955-58, 1960-64.

Most runs batted in—40, Mickey Mantle, New York A.L., 1951-53, 1955-58, 1960-64.

Most home runs—18, Mickey Mantle, New York A.L., 1951-53, 1955-58, 1960-64.

Most bases on balls—43, Mickey Mantle, New York A.L., 1951-53, 1955-58, 1960-64.

Most strikeouts—54, Mickey Mantle, New York A.L., 1951-53, 1955-58, 1960-64.

Most stolen bases—14, Eddie Collins, Philadelphia A.L. 1910-11, 13-14; Chicago A.L., 1917, 1919. Lou Brock, St. Louis N.L., 1964, 67-68.

Most victories, pitcher—10, Whitey Ford, New York A.L., 1950, 1953, 1955-58, 1960-64.

Most times member of winning team—10, Yogi Berra, New York A.L., 1947, 1949-53, 1956, 1958, 1961-62.

Most victories, no defeats—6, Vernon Gomez, New York A.L., 1932, 1936(2), 1937(2), 1938.

Most shutouts—4, Christy Mathewson, New York N.L., 1905 (3), 1913.

Most innings pitched—146, Whitey Ford, New York A.L., 1950, 1953, 1955-58, 1960-1964.

Most consecutive scoreless innings—33 2/3, Whitey Ford, New York A.L., 1960 (18), 1961 (14), 1962 (1 2/3).

Most strikeouts by pitcher—94, Whitey Ford, New York A.L., 1950, 1953, 1955-58, 1960-64.

## AMERICAN LEAGUE HOME RUN CHAMPIONS

| Year | Player, team | No. | Year | Player, team | No. | Year | Player, team | No. |
|---|---|---|---|---|---|---|---|---|
| 1901 | Nap Lajoie, Phila. | 13 | 1932 | Jimmy Foxx, Phila. | 58 | 1964 | Harmon Killebrew, Minn. | 49 |
| 1902 | Ralph Seybold, Phila. | 16 | 1933 | Jimmy Foxx, Phila. | 48 | 1965 | Tony Conigliaro, Bost. | 32 |
| 1903 | Buck Freeman, Bost. | 13 | 1934 | Lou Gehrig, N.Y. | 49 | 1966 | Frank Robinson, Balt. | 49 |
| 1904 | Harry Davis, Phila. | 10 | 1935 | Jimmy Foxx, Phila., and | | 1967 | Carl Yastrzemski, Bost., and | |
| 1905 | Harry Davis, Phila. | 8 | | Hank Greenberg, Det. | 36 | | Harmon Killebrew, Minn. | 44 |
| 1906 | Harry Davis, Phila. | 12 | 1936 | Lou Gehrig, N.Y. | 49 | 1968 | Frank Howard, Wash. | 44 |
| 1907 | Harry Davis, Phila. | 8 | 1937 | Joe DiMaggio, N.Y. | 46 | 1969 | Harmon Killebrew, Minn. | 49 |
| 1908 | Sam Crawford, Det. | 7 | 1938 | Hank Greenberg, Det. | 58 | 1970 | Frank Howard, Wash. | 44 |
| 1909 | Ty Cobb, Det. | 9 | 1939 | Jimmy Foxx, Bost. | 35 | 1971 | Bill Melton, Chicago | 33 |
| 1910 | J. Garland Stahl, Bost. | 10 | 1940 | Hank Greenberg, Det. | 41 | 1972 | Dick Allen, Chicago | 37 |
| 1911 | Franklin Baker, Phila. | 9 | 1941 | Ted Williams, Bost. | 37 | 1973 | Reggie Jackson, Oak. | 32 |
| 1912 | Franklin Baker, Phila. | 10 | 1942 | Ted Williams, Bost. | 36 | 1974 | Dick Allen, Chicago | 32 |
| 1913 | Franklin Baker, Phila. | 12 | 1943 | Rudy York, Det. | 34 | 1975 | Reggie Jackson, Oak., and | |
| 1914 | Franklin Baker, Phila., and | | 1944 | Nick Etten, N.Y. | 22 | | George Scott, Mil. | 36 |
| | Sam Crawford, Det. | 8 | 1945 | Vern Stephens, St. L. | 24 | 1976 | Graig Nettles, N.Y. | 32 |
| 1915 | Robert Roth, Chi.-Cleve. | 7 | 1946 | Hank Greenberg, Det. | 44 | 1977 | Jim Rice, Boston | 39 |
| 1916 | Wally Pipp, N.Y. | 12 | 1947 | Ted Williams, Bost. | 32 | 1978 | Jim Rice, Boston | 46 |
| 1917 | Wally Pipp, N.Y. | 9 | 1948 | Joe DiMaggio, N.Y. | 39 | 1979 | Gorman Thomas, Milwaukee | 45 |
| 1918 | Babe Ruth, Bost., and | | 1949 | Ted Williams, Bost. | 43 | 1980 | Reggie Jackson, N.Y., and | |
| | Clarence Walker, Phila. | 11 | 1950 | Al Rosen, Cleve. | 37 | | Ben Oglivie, Mil. | 41 |
| 1919 | Babe Ruth, Bost. | 29 | 1951 | Gus Zernial, Chi.-Phila. | 33 | 1981* | Tony Armas, Oak., Dwight | |
| 1920 | Babe Ruth, N.Y. | 54 | 1952 | Larry Doby, Cleve. | 32 | | Evans, Bost., Bobby Grich, | |
| 1921 | Babe Ruth, N.Y. | 59 | 1953 | Al Rosen, Cleve. | 43 | | Calif., and Eddie Murray, | |
| 1922 | Ken Williams, St. L. | 39 | 1954 | Larry Doby, Cleve. | 32 | | Balt. (tie) | 22 |
| 1923 | Babe Ruth, N.Y. | 41 | 1955 | Mickey Mantle, N.Y. | 37 | 1982 | Gorman Thomas, Mil., and | |
| 1924 | Babe Ruth, N.Y. | 46 | 1956 | Mickey Mantle, N.Y. | 52 | | Reggie Jackson, Calif. | 39 |
| 1925 | Bob Meusel, N.Y. | 33 | 1957 | Roy Sievers, Wash. | 42 | 1983 | Jim Rice, Boston | 39 |
| 1926 | Babe Ruth, N.Y. | 47 | 1958 | Mickey Mantle, N.Y. | 42 | 1984 | Tony Armas, Boston | 43 |
| 1927 | Babe Ruth, N.Y. | 60 | 1959 | Rocky Colavito, Cleve., and | | 1985 | Darrell Evans, Detroit | 40 |
| 1928 | Babe Ruth, N.Y. | 54 | | Harmon Killebrew, Wash. | 42 | 1986 | Jesse Barfield, Toronto | 40 |
| 1929 | Babe Ruth, N.Y. | 46 | 1960 | Mickey Mantle, N.Y. | 40 | | | |
| 1930 | Babe Ruth, N.Y. | 49 | 1961 | Roger Maris, N.Y. | 61 | | | |
| 1931 | Lou Gehrig, N.Y., and | | 1962 | Harmon Killebrew, Minn. | 48 | | | |
| | Babe Ruth, N.Y. | 46 | 1963 | Harmon Killebrew, Minn. | 45 | | | |

## AMERICAN LEAGUE BATTING CHAMPIONS

| Year | Player, team | Avg | Year | Player, team | Avg | Year | Player, team | Avg. |
|---|---|---|---|---|---|---|---|---|
| 1901 | Nap Lajoie, Phila. | .422 | 1930 | Al Simmons, Phila. | .381 | 1959 | Harvey Kuenn, Det. | .353 |
| 1902 | Ed Delahanty, Wash. | .376 | 1931 | Al Simmons, Phila. | .390 | 1960 | Pete Runnels, Bost. | .320 |
| 1903 | Nap Lajoie, Cleve. | .355 | 1932 | Dale Alexander, Det.-Bost. | .367 | 1961 | Norman Cash, Det. | .361 |
| 1904 | Nap Lajoie, Cleve. | .381 | 1933 | Jimmy Foxx, Phila. | .356 | 1962 | Pete Runnels, Bost. | .326 |
| 1905 | Elmer Flick, Cleve. | .306 | 1934 | Lou Gehrig, N.Y. | .363 | 1963 | Carl Yastrzemski, Bost. | .321 |
| 1906 | George Stone, St. L. | .358 | 1935 | Buddy Myer, Wash. | .349 | 1964 | Tony Oliva, Minn. | .323 |
| 1907 | Ty Cobb, Det. | .350 | 1936 | Luke Appling, Chi. | .388 | 1965 | Tony Oliva, Minn. | .321 |
| 1908 | Ty Cobb, Det. | .324 | 1937 | Charley Gehringer, Det. | .371 | 1966 | Frank Robinson, Balt. | .316 |
| 1909 | Ty Cobb, Det. | .377 | 1938 | Jimmy Foxx, Bost. | .349 | 1967 | Carl Yastrzemski, Bost. | .326 |
| 1910 | Ty Cobb, Det. | .385 | 1939 | Joe DiMaggio, N.Y. | .381 | 1968 | Carl Yastrzemski, Bost. | .301 |
| 1911 | Ty Cobb, Det. | .420 | 1940 | Joe DiMaggio, N.Y. | .352 | 1969 | Rod Carew, Minn. | .332 |
| 1912 | Ty Cobb, Det. | .410 | 1941 | Ted Williams, Bost. | .406 | 1970 | Alex Johnson, Calif. | .329 |
| 1913 | Ty Cobb, Det. | .390 | 1942 | Ted Williams, Bost. | .356 | 1971 | Tony Oliva, Minn. | .337 |
| 1914 | Ty Cobb, Det. | .368 | 1943 | Luke Appling, Chi. | .328 | 1972 | Rod Carew, Minn. | .318 |
| 1915 | Ty Cobb, Det. | .369 | 1944 | Lou Boudreau, Cleve. | .327 | 1973 | Rod Carew, Minn. | .350 |
| 1916 | Tris Speaker, Cleve. | .386 | 1945 | George Sternweiss, N.Y. | .309 | 1974 | Rod Carew, Minn. | .364 |
| 1917 | Ty Cobb, Det. | .383 | 1946 | Mickey Vernon, Wash. | .353 | 1975 | Rod Carew, Minn. | .359 |
| 1918 | Ty Cobb, Det. | .382 | 1947 | Ted Williams, Bost. | .343 | 1976 | George Brett, Kansas City | .333 |
| 1919 | Ty Cobb, Det. | .384 | 1948 | Ted Williams, Bost. | .369 | 1977 | Rod Carew, Minn. | .388 |
| 1920 | George Sisler, St. L. | .407 | 1949 | George Kell, Det. | .343 | 1978 | Rod Carew, Minn. | .333 |
| 1921 | Harry Heilmann, Det. | .394 | 1950 | Billy Goodman, Bost. | .354 | 1979 | Fred Lynn, Boston | .333 |
| 1922 | George Sisler, St. L. | .420 | 1951 | Ferris Fain, Phila. | .344 | 1980 | George Brett, Kansas City | .390 |
| 1923 | Harry Heilmann, Det. | .403 | 1952 | Ferris Fain, Phila. | .327 | 1981* | Carney Lansford, Bost. | .336 |
| 1924 | Babe Ruth, N.Y. | .378 | 1953 | Mickey Vernon, Wash. | .337 | 1982 | Willie Wilson, Kansas City | .332 |
| 1925 | Harry Heilmann, Det. | .393 | 1954 | Bobby Avila, Cleve. | .341 | 1983 | Wade Boggs, Boston | .361 |
| 1926 | Heinie Manush, Det. | .378 | 1955 | Al Kaline, Det. | .340 | 1984 | Don Mattingly, New York | .343 |
| 1927 | Harry Heilmann, Det. | .398 | 1956 | Mickey Mantle, N.Y. | .353 | 1985 | Wade Boggs, Boston | .368 |
| 1928 | Goose Goslin, Wash. | .379 | 1957 | Ted Williams, Bost. | .388 | 1986 | Wade Boggs, Boston | .357 |
| 1929 | Lew Fonseca, Cleve. | .369 | 1958 | Ted Williams, Bost. | .328 | | | |

*Split season because of player strike.

## NATIONAL LEAGUE HOME RUN CHAMPIONS

| Year | Player, team | No. | Year | Player, team | No. | Year | Player, team | No. |
|------|-------------|-----|------|-------------|-----|------|-------------|-----|
| 1876 | George Hall, Phila. Athletics | 5 | 1913 | Cliff Cravath, Phila. | 19 | 1948 | Ralph Kiner, Pitts., and | |
| 1877 | George Shaffer, Louisville | 3 | 1914 | Cliff Cravath, Phila. | 19 | | John Mize, N.Y. | 40 |
| 1878 | Paul Hines, Providence | 4 | 1915 | Cliff Cravath, Phila. | 24 | 1949 | Ralph Kiner, Pitts. | 54 |
| 1879 | Charles Jones, Bost. | 9 | 1916 | Davis Robertson, N.Y., and | | 1950 | Ralph Kiner, Pitts. | 47 |
| 1880 | James O'Rourke, Bost., and | | | Fred Williams, Chi. | 12 | 1951 | Ralph Kiner, Pitts. | 42 |
| | Harry Stovey, Worcester | 6 | 1917 | Davis Robertson, N.Y., and | | 1952 | Ralph Kiner, Pitts., and | |
| 1881 | Dan Brouthers, Buffalo | 8 | | Cliff Cravath, Phila. | 12 | | Hank Sauer, Chi. | 37 |
| 1882 | George Wood, Det. | 7 | 1918 | Cliff Cravath, Phila. | 8 | 1953 | Ed Mathews, Mil. | 47 |
| 1883 | William Ewing, N.Y. | 10 | 1919 | Cliff Cravath, Phila. | 12 | 1954 | Ted Kluszewski, Cin. | 49 |
| 1884 | Ed Williamson, Chi. | 27 | 1920 | Cy Williams, Phila. | 15 | 1955 | Willie Mays, N.Y. | 51 |
| 1885 | Abner Dalrymple, Chi. | 11 | 1921 | George Kelly, N.Y. | 23 | 1956 | Duke Snider, Bklyn. | 43 |
| 1886 | Arthur Richardson, Det. | 11 | 1922 | Rogers Hornsby, St. L. | 42 | 1957 | Henry Aaron, Mil. | 44 |
| 1887 | Roger Conoor, N.Y., and | | 1923 | Cy Williams, Phila. | 41 | 1958 | Ernie Banks, Chi. | 47 |
| | Wm. O'Brien, Wash. | 17 | 1924 | Jacques Fournier, Bklyn. | 27 | 1959 | Ed Mathews, Mil. | 46 |
| 1888 | Roger Connor, N.Y. | 14 | 1925 | Rogers Hornsby, St. L. | 39 | 1960 | Ernie Banks, Chi. | 41 |
| 1889 | Sam Thompson, Phila. | 20 | 1926 | Hack Wilson, Chi. | 21 | 1961 | Orlando Cepeda, San Fran. | 46 |
| 1890 | Tom Burns, Bklyn, and | | 1927 | Hack Wilson, Chi., and | | 1962 | Willie Mays, San Fran. | 49 |
| | Mike Tiernan, N.Y. | 13 | | Cy Williams, Phila. | 30 | 1963 | Henry Aaron, Mil., and | |
| 1891 | Harry Stovey, Bost., and | | 1928 | Hack Wilson, Chi., and | | | Willie McCovey, San Fran. | 44 |
| | Mike Tiernan, N.Y. | 16 | | Jim Bottomley, St. L. | 31 | 1964 | Willie Mays, San Fran. | 47 |
| 1892 | Jim Holliday, Cin. | 13 | 1929 | Chuck Klein, Phila. | 43 | 1965 | Willie Mays, San Fran. | 52 |
| 1893 | Ed Delahanty, Phila. | 19 | 1930 | Hack Wilson, Chi. | 56 | 1966 | Henry Aaron, Atlanta | 44 |
| 1894 | Hugh Duffy, Bost., and | | 1931 | Chuck Klein, Phila. | 31 | 1967 | Henry Aaron, Atlanta | 39 |
| | Robert Lowe, Bost. | 18 | 1932 | Chuck Klein, Phila., and | | 1968 | Willie McCovey, San Fran. | 36 |
| 1895 | Bill Joyce, Wash. | 17 | | Mel Ott, N.Y. | 38 | 1969 | Willie McCovey, San Fran. | 45 |
| 1896 | Ed Delhanty, Phila., and | | 1933 | Chuck Klein, Phila. | 28 | 1970 | Johnny Bench, Cin. | 45 |
| | Sam Thompson, Phila. | 13 | 1934 | Mel Ott, N.Y., and | | 1971 | Willie Stargell, Pitts. | 48 |
| 1897 | Nap Lajoie, Phila. | 10 | | Rip Collins, St. L. | 35 | 1972 | Johnny Bench, Cin. | 40 |
| 1898 | James Colins, Bost. | 14 | 1935 | Wally Berger, Bost. | 34 | 1973 | Willie Stargell, Pitts. | 44 |
| 1899 | John Freeman, Wash. | 25 | 1936 | Mel Ott, N.Y. | 33 | 1974 | Mike Schmidt, Phila. | 36 |
| 1900 | Herman Long, Bost. | 12 | 1937 | Mel Ott, N.Y., and Joe | | 1975 | Mike Schmidt, Phila. | 38 |
| 1901 | Sam Crawford, Con. | 16 | | Medwick, St. L. | 31 | 1976 | Mike Schmidt, Phila. | 38 |
| 1902 | Tom Leach, Pitts. | 6 | 1938 | Mel Ott, N.Y. | 36 | 1977 | George Foster, Cin. | 52 |
| 1903 | James Sheckard, Bklyn. | 9 | 1939 | John Mize, St. L. | 28 | 1978 | George Foster, Cin. | 40 |
| 1904 | Harry Lumley, Bklyn. | 9 | 1940 | John Mize, St. L. | 43 | 1979 | Dave Kingman, Chicago | 48 |
| 1905 | Fred Odwell, Cin. | 9 | 1941 | Dolph Camilli, Bklyn. | 34 | 1980 | Mike Schmidt, Phila. | 48 |
| 1906 | Tim Jordan, Bklyn | 12 | 1942 | Mel Ott, N.Y. | 30 | 1981* | Mike Schmidt, Phila. | 31 |
| 1907 | David Brain, Bost. | 10 | 1943 | Bill Nicholson, Chi. | 29 | 1982 | Dave Kingman, N.Y. | 37 |
| 1908 | Tim Jordan, Bklyn. | 12 | 1944 | Bill Nicholson, Chi. | 33 | 1983 | Mike Schmidt, Phila. | 40 |
| 1909 | John Murray, N.Y. | 7 | 1945 | Tommy Holmes, Bost. | 28 | 1984 | Mike Schmidt, Phila. and | |
| 1910 | Fred Beck, Bost., and | | 1946 | Ralph Kiner, Pitts. | 23 | | Dale Murphy, Atlanta | 36 |
| | Frank Schulte, Chi. | 10 | 1947 | Ralph Kiner, Pitts., and | | 1985 | Dale Murphy, Atlanta | 37 |
| 1911 | Frank Schulte, Chi. | 21 | | John Mize, N.Y. | 51 | 1986 | Mike Schmidt, Phila. | 37 |
| 1912 | Henry Zimmerman, Chi. | 14 | | | | | | |

*Split season because of player strike.

## NATIONAL LEAGUE BATTING CHAMPIONS

| Year | Player, Team | Avg | Year | Player, Team | Avg | Year | Player, Team | Avg |
|------|-------------|-----|------|-------------|-----|------|-------------|-----|
| 1876 | Roscoe Barnes, Chicago | .404 | 1894 | Hugh Duffy, Boston | .438 | 1912 | Henry Zimmerman, Chicago | .372 |
| 1877 | Jim White, Boston | .385 | 1895 | Jesse Burkett, Cleveland | .423 | 1913 | Jake Daubert, Brooklyn | .350 |
| 1878 | Abner Dalrymple, Mil. | .356 | 1896 | Jesse Burkett, Cleveland | .410 | 1914 | Jake Daubert, Brooklyn | .329 |
| 1879 | Cap Anson, Chicago | .407 | 1897 | Willie Keeler, Baltimore | .432 | 1915 | Larry Doyle, New York | .320 |
| 1880 | George Gore, Chicago | .365 | 1898 | Willie Keeler, Baltimore | .379 | 1916 | Hal Chase, Cincinnati | .339 |
| 1881 | Cap Anson, Chicago | .399 | 1899 | Ed Delahanty, Phila. | .408 | 1917 | Edd Roush, Cincinnati | .341 |
| 1882 | Dan Brouthers, Buffalo | .367 | 1900 | Honus Wagner, Pittsburgh | .381 | 1918 | Jack Wheat, Brooklyn | .335 |
| 1883 | Dan Brouthers, Buffalo | .371 | 1901 | Jesse Burkett, St. Louis | .382 | 1919 | Edd Roush, Cincinnati | .321 |
| 1884 | James O'Rourke, Buffalo | .350 | 1902 | Clarence Beaumont, Pitts. | .357 | 1920 | Rogers Hornsby, St. Louis | .370 |
| 1885 | Roger Connor, N. Y. | .371 | 1903 | Honus Wagner, Pittsburgh | .355 | 1921 | Rogers Hornsby, St. Louis | .397 |
| 1886 | King Kelly, Chicago | .388 | 1904 | Honus Wagner, Pittsburgh | .349 | 1922 | Rogers Hornsby, St. Louis | .401 |
| 1887 | Cap Anson, Chicago | .421 | 1905 | Cy Seymour, Cincinnati | .377 | 1923 | Rogers Hornsby, St. Louis | .384 |
| 1888 | Cap Anson, Chicago | .343 | 1906 | Honus Wagner, Pittsburgh | .339 | 1924 | Rogers Hornsby, St. Louis | .424 |
| 1889 | Dan Brouthers, Boston | .373 | 1907 | Honus Wagner, Pittsburgh | .350 | 1925 | Rogers Hornsby, St. Louis | .403 |
| 1890 | John Glasscock, N. Y. | .336 | 1908 | Honus Wagner, Pittsburgh | .354 | 1926 | Gene Hargrave, Cincinnati | .353 |
| 1891 | William Hamilton, Phila. | .338 | 1909 | Honus Wagner, Pittsburgh | .339 | 1927 | Paul Waner; Pittsburgh | .380 |
| 1892 | Dan Brouthers, Bklyn., and | | 1910 | Sherwood Magee, | | 1928 | Rogers Hornsby, Boston | .387 |
| | Clarence Childs, Cleve. | .335 | | Philadelphia | .331 | 1929 | Lefty O'Doul, Phila. | .398 |
| 1893 | Hugh Duffy, Boston | .378 | 1911 | Honus Wagner, Pittsburgh | .334 | 1930 | Bill Terry, N.Y. | .401 |

| Year | Player, Team | Avg | Year | Player, Team | Avg | Year | Player, Team | Avg |
|---|---|---|---|---|---|---|---|---|
| 1931 | Chick Hafey, St. Louis | .349 | 1950 | Stan Musial, St. Louis | .346 | 1969 | Pete Rose, Cincinnati | .348 |
| 1932 | Lefty O'Doul, Brooklyn | .368 | 1951 | Stan Musial, St. Louis | .355 | 1970 | Rico Carty, Atlanta | .366 |
| 1933 | Chuck Klein, Phila. | .368 | 1952 | Stan Musial, St. Louis | .336 | 1971 | Joe Torre, St. Louis | .363 |
| 1934 | Paul Waner, Pittsburgh | .362 | 1953 | Carl Furillo, Brooklyn | .344 | 1972 | Billy Williams, Chicago | .333 |
| 1935 | Arky Vaughan, Pittsburgh | .385 | 1954 | Willie Mays, N. Y. | .345 | 1973 | Pete Rose, Cincinnati | .338 |
| 1936 | Paul Waner, Pittsburgh | .373 | 1955 | Richie Ashburn, Phila. | .338 | 1974 | Ralph Garr, Atlanta | .353 |
| 1937 | Joe Medwick, St. Louis | .374 | 1956 | Henry Aaron, Mil. | .328 | 1975 | Bill Madlock, Chicago | .354 |
| 1938 | Ernie Lombardi, Cin. | .342 | 1957 | Stan Musial, St. Louis | .351 | 1976 | Bill Madlock, Chicago | .339 |
| 1939 | John Mize, St. Louis | .349 | 1958 | Richie Ashburn, Phila. | .350 | 1977 | Dave Parker, Pittsburgh | .338 |
| 1940 | Debs Garms, Pittsburgh | .355 | 1959 | Henry Aaron, Mil. | .355 | 1978 | Dave Parker, Pittsburgh | .334 |
| 1941 | Pete Reiser, Brooklyn | .343 | 1960 | Dick Groat, Pittsburgh | .325 | 1979 | Keith Hernandez, St. Louis | .344 |
| 1942 | Ernie Lombardi, Boston | .330 | 1961 | Roberto Clemente, Pitts. | .351 | 1980 | Bill Buckner, Chicago | .324 |
| 1943 | Stan Musial, St. Louis | .357 | 1962 | Tommy Davis, L. A. | .346 | 1981* | Bill Madlock, Pittsburgh | .341 |
| 1944 | Dixie Walker, Brooklyn | .357 | 1963 | Tommy Davis, L. A. | .326 | 1982 | Al Oliver, Montreal | .331 |
| 1945 | Phil Cavarretta, Chicago | .355 | 1964 | Roberto Clemente, Pitts. | .339 | 1983 | Bill Madlock, Pittsburgh | .323 |
| 1946 | Stan Musial, St. Louis | .365 | 1965 | Roberto Clemente, Pitts. | .329 | 1984 | Tony Gwynn, San Diego | .351 |
| 1947 | Harry Walker, St. L.-Phila. | .363 | 1966 | Matty Alou, Pittsburgh | .342 | 1985 | Willie McGee, St. Louis | .353 |
| 1948 | Stan Musial, St. Louis | .376 | 1967 | Roberto Clemente, Pitts. | .357 | 1986 | Tim Raines, Montreal | .334 |
| 1949 | Jackie Robinson, Brooklyn | .342 | 1968 | Pete Rose, Cincinnati | .335 | | | |

## AMERICAN LEAGUE PENNANT WINNERS

| Year | Club | Manager | Won | Lost | Pct | Year | Club | Manager | Won | Lost | Pct |
|---|---|---|---|---|---|---|---|---|---|---|---|
| 1901 | Chicago | Clark C. Griffith | 83 | 53 | .610 | 1945[1] | Detroit | Steve O'Neill | 88 | 65 | .575 |
| 1902 | Philadelphia | Connie Mack | 83 | 53 | .610 | 1946 | Boston | Joseph E. Cronin | 104 | 50 | .675 |
| 1903[1] | Boston | Jimmy Collins | 91 | 47 | .659 | 1947[1] | New York | Stanley R. Harris | 97 | 57 | .630 |
| 1904[2] | Boston | Jimmy Collins | 95 | 59 | .617 | 1948[1] | Cleveland | Lou Boudreau | 97 | 58 | .626 |
| 1905 | Philadelphia | Connie Mack | 92 | 56 | .622 | 1949[1] | New York | Casey Stengel | 97 | 57 | .630 |
| 1906[1] | Chicago | Fielder A. Jones | 93 | 58 | .616 | 1950[1] | New York | Casey Stengel | 98 | 56 | .636 |
| 1907 | Detroit | Hugh A. Jennings | 92 | 58 | .613 | 1951[1] | New York | Casey Stengel | 98 | 56 | .636 |
| 1908 | Detroit | Hugh A. Jennings | 90 | 63 | .588 | 1952[1] | New York | Casey Stengel | 95 | 59 | .617 |
| 1909 | Detroit | Hugh A. Jennings | 98 | 54 | .645 | 1953[1] | New York | Casey Stengel | 99 | 52 | .656 |
| 1910[1] | Philadelphia | Connie Mack | 102 | 48 | .680 | 1954 | Cleveland | Al Lopez | 111 | 43 | .721 |
| 1911[1] | Philadelphia | Connie Mack | 101 | 50 | .669 | 1955 | New York | Casey Stengel | 96 | 58 | .623 |
| 1912[1] | Boston | J. Garland Stahl | 105 | 47 | .691 | 1956[1] | New York | Casey Stengel | 97 | 57 | .630 |
| 1913[1] | Philadelphia | Connie Mack | 96 | 57 | .627 | 1957 | New York | Casey Stengel | 98 | 56 | .636 |
| 1914 | Philadelphia | Connie Mack | 99 | 53 | .651 | 1958[1] | New York | Casey Stengel | 92 | 62 | .597 |
| 1915[1] | Boston | William F. Carrigan | 101 | 50 | .669 | 1959 | Chicago | Al Lopez | 94 | 60 | .610 |
| 1916[1] | Boston | William F. Carrigan | 91 | 63 | .591 | 1960 | New York | Casey Stengel | 97 | 57 | .630 |
| 1917[1] | Chicago | Clarence H. Rowland | 100 | 54 | .649 | 1961[1] | New York | Ralph Houk | 109 | 53 | .673 |
| 1918[1] | Boston | Ed Barrow | 75 | 51 | .595 | 1962[1] | New York | Ralph Houk | 96 | 66 | .593 |
| 1919 | Chicago | William Gleason | 88 | 52 | .629 | 1963 | New York | Ralph Houk | 104 | 57 | .646 |
| 1920[1] | Cleveland | Tris Speaker | 98 | 56 | .636 | 1964 | New York | Yogi Berra | 99 | 63 | .611 |
| 1921 | New York | Miller J. Huggins | 98 | 55 | .641 | 1965 | Minnesota | Sam Mele | 102 | 60 | .630 |
| 1922 | New York | Miller J. Huggins | 94 | 60 | .610 | 1966[1] | Baltimore | Hank Bauer | 97 | 53 | .606 |
| 1923[1] | New York | Miller J. Huggins | 98 | 54 | .645 | 1967 | Boston | Dick Williams | 92 | 70 | .568 |
| 1924[1] | Washington | Stanley R. Harris | 92 | 62 | .597 | 1968[1] | Detroit | Mayo Smith | 103 | 59 | .636 |
| 1925 | Washington | Stanley R. Harris | 96 | 55 | .636 | 1969 | Baltimore[3] | Earl Weaver | 109 | 53 | .673 |
| 1926 | New York | Miller J. Huggins | 91 | 63 | .591 | 1970[1] | Baltimore[3] | Earl Weaver | 108 | 54 | .667 |
| 1927[1] | New York | Miller J. Huggins | 110 | 44 | .714 | 1971 | Baltimore[4] | Earl Weaver | 101 | 57 | .639 |
| 1928[1] | New York | Miller J. Huggins | 101 | 53 | .656 | 1972[1] | Oakland[5] | Dick Williams | 93 | 62 | .600 |
| 1929[1] | Philadelphia | Connie Mack | 104 | 46 | .693 | 1973[1] | Oakland[6] | Dick Williams | 94 | 68 | .580 |
| 1930[1] | Philadelphia | Connie Mack | 102 | 52 | .662 | 1974[1] | Oakland[6] | Alvin Dark | 90 | 72 | .556 |
| 1931 | Philadelphia | Connie Mack | 107 | 45 | .704 | 1975 | Boston[4] | Darrell Johnson | 95 | 65 | .594 |
| 1932[1] | New York | Joseph V. McCarthy | 107 | 47 | .695 | 1976 | New York[7] | Billy Martin | 97 | 62 | .610 |
| 1933 | Washington | Joseph E. Cronin | 99 | 53 | .651 | 1977[1] | New York[7] | Billy Martin | 100 | 62 | .617 |
| 1934 | Detroit | Gordon Cochrane | 101 | 53 | .656 | 1978[1] | New York[7] | Billy Martin | | | |
| 1935[1] | Detroit | Gordon Cochrane | 93 | 58 | .616 | | | and Bob Lemon | 100 | 63 | .613 |
| 1936[1] | New York | Joseph V. McCarthy | 102 | 51 | .667 | 1979 | Baltimore[8] | Earl Weaver | 102 | 57 | .642 |
| 1937[1] | New York | Joseph V. McCarthy | 102 | 52 | .662 | 1980 | Kansas City[9] | Jim Frey | 97 | 65 | .599 |
| 1938[1] | New York | Joseph V. McCarthy | 99 | 53 | .651 | 1981 | New York[10] | Gene Michael-Bob | | | |
| 1939[1] | New York | Joseph V. McCarthy | 106 | 45 | .702 | | | Lemon | 59 | 48 | .551* |
| 1940 | Detroit | Delmar D. Baker | 90 | 64 | .584 | 1982 | Milwaukee[11] | Harvey Kuenn | 95 | 67 | .586 |
| 1941[1] | New York | Joseph V. McCarthy | 101 | 53 | .656 | 1983[1] | Baltimore[12] | Joe Altobelli | 98 | 64 | .605 |
| 1942 | New York | Joseph V. McCarthy | 103 | 51 | .669 | 1984[1] | Detroit[13] | Sparky Anderson | 104 | 58 | .642 |
| 1943[1] | New York | Joseph V. McCarthy | 98 | 56 | .636 | 1985[1] | Kansas City[14] | Dick Howser | 91 | 71 | .562 |
| 1944 | St. Louis | Luke Sewell | 89 | 65 | .578 | 1986 | Boston[11] | John McNamara | 95 | 66 | .590 |

*Split season because of player strike. 1. World Series winner. 2. No World Series. 3. Defeated Minnesota, Western Division winner, in playoff. 4. Defeated Oakland, Western Division Leader, in playoff. 5. Defeated Detroit, Eastern Division winner, in playoff. 6. Defeated Baltimore, Eastern Division winner, in playoff. 7. Defeated Kansas City, Western Division winner, in playoff. 8. Defeated California, Western Division winner, in playoff. 9. Defeated New York, Eastern Division winner, in playoff. 10. Defeated Oakland, Western Division winner, in playoff. 11. Defeated California, Western Division winner, in playoff. 12. Defeated Chicago, Western Division winner in playoff. 13. Defeated Kansas City, Western Division winner, in playoff. 14. Defeated Toronto, Eastern Division winner, in playoff.

## NATIONAL LEAGUE PENNANT WINNERS

| Year | Club | Manager | Won | Lost | Pct | Year | Club | Manager | Won | Lost | Pct |
|------|------|---------|-----|------|-----|------|------|---------|-----|------|-----|
| 1876 | Chicago | Albert G. Spalding | 52 | 14 | .788 | 1932 | Chicago | Charles J. Grimm | 90 | 64 | .584 |
| 1877 | Boston | Harry Wright | 31 | 17 | .646 | 1933 | New York[1] | William H. Terry | 91 | 61 | .599 |
| 1878 | Boston | Harry Wright | 41 | 19 | .683 | 1934 | St. Louis[1] | Frank F. Frisch | 95 | 58 | .621 |
| 1879 | Providence | George Wright | 55 | 23 | .705 | 1935 | Chicago | Charles J. Grimm | 100 | 54 | .649 |
| 1880 | Chicago | Adrian C. Anson | 67 | 17 | .798 | 1936 | New York | William H. Terry | 92 | 62 | .597 |
| 1881 | Chicago | Adrian C. Anson | 56 | 28 | .667 | 1937 | New York | William H. Terry | 95 | 57 | .625 |
| 1882 | Chicago | Adrian C. Anson | 55 | 29 | .655 | 1938 | Chicago | Gabby Hartnett | 89 | 63 | .586 |
| 1883 | Boston | John F. Morrill | 63 | 35 | .643 | 1939 | Cincinnati | William B. McKechnie | 97 | 57 | .630 |
| 1884 | Providence | Frank C. Bancroft | 84 | 28 | .750 | 1940 | Cincinnati[1] | William B. McKechnie | 100 | 53 | .654 |
| 1885 | Chicago | Adrian C. Anson | 87 | 25 | .777 | 1941 | Brooklyn | Leo E. Durocher | 100 | 54 | .649 |
| 1886 | Chicago | Adrian C. Anson | 90 | 34 | .726 | 1942 | St. Louis[1] | William H. Southworth | 106 | 48 | .688 |
| 1887 | Detroit | W. H. Watkins | 79 | 45 | .637 | 1943 | St. Louis | William H. Southworth | 105 | 49 | .682 |
| 1888 | New York | James J. Mutrie | 84 | 47 | .641 | 1944 | St. Louis[1] | William H. Southworth | 105 | 49 | .682 |
| 1889 | New York | James J. Mutrie | 83 | 43 | .659 | 1945 | Chicago | Charles J. Grimm | 98 | 56 | .636 |
| 1890 | Brooklyn | William H. McGunnigle | 86 | 43 | .667 | 1946 | St. Louis[1] | Edwin H. Dyer | 98 | 58 | .628 |
| 1891 | Boston | Frank G. Selee | 87 | 51 | .630 | 1947 | Brooklyn | Burton E. Shotton | 94 | 60 | .610 |
| 1892 | Boston | Frank G. Selee | 102 | 48 | .680 | 1948 | Boston | William H. Southworth | 91 | 62 | .595 |
| 1893 | Boston | Frank G. Selee | 86 | 44 | .662 | 1949 | Brooklyn | Burton E. Shotton | 97 | 57 | .630 |
| 1894 | Baltimore | Edward H. Hanlon | 89 | 39 | .695 | 1950 | Philadelphia | Edwin M. Sawyer | 91 | 63 | .591 |
| 1895 | Baltimore | Edward H. Hanlon | 87 | 43 | .669 | 1951 | New York | Leo E. Durocher | 98 | 59 | .624 |
| 1896 | Baltimore | Edward H. Hanlon | 90 | 39 | .698 | 1952 | Brooklyn | Charles W. Dressen | 96 | 57 | .630 |
| 1897 | Boston | Frank G. Selee | 93 | 39 | .705 | 1953 | Brooklyn | Charles W. Dressen | 105 | 49 | .682 |
| 1898 | Boston | Frank G. Selee | 102 | 47 | .685 | 1954 | New York[1] | Leo E. Durocher | 97 | 57 | .630 |
| 1899 | Brooklyn | Edward H. Hanlon | 88 | 42 | .677 | 1955 | Brooklyn[1] | Walter Alston | 98 | 55 | .641 |
| 1900 | Brooklyn | Edward H. Hanlon | 82 | 54 | .603 | 1956 | Brooklyn | Walter Alston | 93 | 61 | .604 |
| 1901 | Pittsburgh | Fred C. Clarke | 90 | 49 | .647 | 1957 | Milwaukee[1] | Fred Haney | 95 | 59 | .617 |
| 1902 | Pittsburgh | Fred C. Clarke | 103 | 36 | .741 | 1958 | Milwaukee | Fred Haney | 92 | 62 | .597 |
| 1903 | Pittsburgh | Fred C. Clarke | 91 | 49 | .650 | 1959 | Los Angeles[1] | Walter Alston | 88 | 68 | .564 |
| 1904 | New York[2] | John J. McGraw | 106 | 47 | .693 | 1960 | Pittsburgh[1] | Danny Murtaugh | 95 | 59 | .617 |
| 1905 | New York[1] | John J. McGraw | 105 | 48 | .686 | 1961 | Cincinnati | Fred Hutchinson | 93 | 61 | .604 |
| 1906 | Chicago | Frank L. Chance | 116 | 36 | .763 | 1962 | San Francisco | Alvin Dark | 103 | 62 | .624 |
| 1907 | Chicago[1] | Frank L. Chance | 107 | 45 | .704 | 1963 | Los Angeles[1] | Walter Alston | 99 | 63 | .611 |
| 1908 | Chicago[1] | Frank L. Chance | 99 | 55 | .643 | 1964 | St. Louis[1] | Johnny Keane | 93 | 69 | .574 |
| 1909 | Pittsburgh[1] | Fred C. Clarke | 110 | 42 | .724 | 1965 | Los Angeles[1] | Walter Alston | 97 | 65 | .599 |
| 1910 | Chicago | Frank L. Chance | 104 | 50 | .675 | 1966 | Los Angeles | Walter Alston | 95 | 67 | .586 |
| 1911 | New York | John J. McGraw | 99 | 54 | .647 | 1967 | St. Louis[1] | Red Schoendienst | 101 | 60 | .627 |
| 1912 | New York | John J. McGraw | 103 | 48 | .682 | 1968 | St. Louis | Red Schoendienst | 97 | 65 | .599 |
| 1913 | New York | John J. McGraw | 101 | 51 | .664 | 1969 | New York[1][3] | Gil Hodges | 100 | 62 | .617 |
| 1914 | Boston[1] | George T. Stallings | 94 | 59 | .614 | 1970 | Cincinnati[4] | Sparky Anderson | 102 | 60 | .630 |
| 1915 | Philadelphia | Patrick J. Moran | 90 | 62 | .592 | 1971 | Pittsburgh[1][5] | Danny Murtaugh | 97 | 65 | .599 |
| 1916 | Brooklyn | Wilbert Robinson | 94 | 60 | .610 | 1972 | Cincinnati[4] | Sparky Anderson | 95 | 59 | .617 |
| 1917 | New York | John J. McGraw | 98 | 56 | .636 | 1973 | New York[6] | Yogi Berra | 82 | 79 | .509 |
| 1918 | Chicago | Fred L. Mitchell | 84 | 45 | .651 | 1974 | Los Angeles[6] | Walter Alston | 102 | 60 | .630 |
| 1919 | Cincinnati[1] | Patrick J. Moran | 96 | 44 | .686 | 1975 | Cincinnati[1][4] | Sparky Anderson | 108 | 54 | .667 |
| 1920 | Brooklyn | Wilbert Robinson | 93 | 61 | .604 | 1976 | Cincinnati[7][1] | Sparky Anderson | 102 | 60 | .630 |
| 1921 | New York[1] | John J. McGraw | 94 | 59 | .614 | 1977 | Los Angeles[7] | Tom Lasorda | 98 | 64 | .605 |
| 1922 | New York[1] | John J. McGraw | 93 | 61 | .604 | 1978 | Los Angeles[7] | Tom Lasorda | 95 | 67 | .586 |
| 1923 | New York | John J. McGraw | 95 | 58 | .621 | 1979[1] | Pittsburgh[6] | Chuck Tanner | 98 | 64 | .605 |
| 1924 | New York | John J. McGraw | 93 | 60 | .608 | 1980[1] | Philadelphia[4] | Dallas Green | 91 | 71 | .562 |
| 1925 | Pittsburgh[1] | William B. McKechnie | 95 | 58 | .621 | 1981 | Los Angeles[1][9] | Tom Lasorda | 63 | 47 | .573* |
| 1926 | St. Louis[1] | Rogers Hornsby | 89 | 65 | .578 | 1982[1] | St. Louis[10] | Whitey Herzog | 92 | 70 | .568 |
| 1927 | Pittsburgh | Donie Bush | 94 | 60 | .610 | 1983 | Philadelphia[11] | Paul Owens | 90 | 72 | .556 |
| 1928 | St. Louis | William B. McKechnie | 95 | 59 | .617 | 1984 | San Diego[12] | Dick Williams | 92 | 70 | .568 |
| 1929 | Chicago | Joseph V. McCarthy | 98 | 54 | .645 | 1985 | St. Louis[11] | Whitey Herzog | 101 | 61 | .623 |
| 1930 | St. Louis | Gabby Street | 92 | 62 | .597 | 1986 | New York[8] | Dave Johnson | 108 | 54 | .667 |
| 1931 | St. Louis[1] | Gabby Street | 101 | 53 | .656 | | | | | | |

*Split season because of player strike. 1. World Series winner. 2. No World Series. 3. Defeated Atlanta, Western Division winner, in playoff. 4. Defeated Pittsburgh, Eastern Division winner, in playoff. 5. Defeated San Francisco, Western Division winner, in playoff. 6. Defeated Cincinnati, Western Division winner, in playoff. 7. Defeated Philadelphia, Eastern Division winner, in playoff. 8. Defeated Houston, Western Division winner, in playoff. 9. Defeated Montreal, Eastern Division winner, in playoff. 10. Defeated Atlanta, Western Division winner, in playoff. 11. Defeated Los Angeles, Western Division in playoff. 12. Defeated Chicago, Eastern Division champion in playoff.

# MOST VALUABLE PLAYERS
(Baseball Writers Association selections)

## American League

| | |
|---|---|
| 1931 | Lefty Grove, Philadelphia |
| 1932–33 | Jimmy Foxx, Philadelphia |
| 1934 | Mickey Cochrane, Detroit |
| 1935 | Hank Greenberg, Detroit |
| 1936 | Lou Gehrig, New York |
| 1937 | Charlie Gehringer, Detroit |
| 1938 | Jimmy Foxx, Boston |
| 1939 | Joe DiMaggio, New York |
| 1940 | Hank Greenberg, Detroit |
| 1941 | Joe DiMaggio, New York |
| 1942 | Joe Gordon, New York |
| 1943 | Spurgeon Chandler, New York |
| 1944–45 | Hal Newhouser, Detroit |
| 1946 | Ted Williams, Boston |
| 1947 | Joe DiMaggio, New York |
| 1948 | Lou Boudreau, Cleveland |
| 1949 | Ted Williams, Boston |
| 1950 | Phil Rizzuto, New York |
| 1951 | Yogi Berra, New York |
| 1952 | Bobby Shantz, Philadelphia |
| 1953 | Al Rosen, Cleveland |
| 1954–55 | Yogi Berra, New York |
| 1956–57 | Mickey Mantle, New York |
| 1958 | Jackie Jensen, Boston |
| 1959 | Nellie Fox, Chicago |
| 1960–61 | Roger Maris, New York |
| 1962 | Mickey Mantle, New York |
| 1963 | Elston Howard, New York |
| 1964 | Brooks Robinson, Baltimore |
| 1965 | Zoilo Versalles, Minnesota |
| 1966 | Frank Robinson, Baltimore |
| 1967 | Carl Yastrzemski, Boston |
| 1968 | Dennis McLain, Detroit |
| 1969 | Harmon Killebrew, Minnesota |
| 1970 | John (Boog) Powell, Baltimore |
| 1971 | Vida Blue, Oakland |
| 1972 | Dick Allen, Chicago |
| 1973 | Reggie Jackson, Oakland |
| 1974 | Jeff Burroughs, Texas |
| 1975 | Fred Lynn, Boston |
| 1976 | Thurman Munson, New York |
| 1977 | Rod Carew, Minnesota |
| 1978 | Jim Rice, Boston |
| 1979 | Don Baylor, California |
| 1980 | George Brett, Kansas City |
| 1981 | Rollie Fingers, Milwaukee |
| 1982 | Robin Yount, Milwaukee |
| 1983 | Cal RipKen, Jr., Baltimore |
| 1984 | Willie Hernandez, Detroit |
| 1985 | Don Mattingly, New York |

## National League

| | |
|---|---|
| 1931 | Frank Frisch, St. Louis |
| 1932 | Chuck Klein, Philadelphia |
| 1933 | Carl Hubbell, New York |
| 1934 | Dizzy Dean, St. Louis |
| 1935 | Gabby Hartnett, Chicago |
| 1936 | Carl Hubbell, New York |
| 1937 | Joe Medwick, St. Louis |
| 1938 | Ernie Lombardi, Cincinnati |
| 1939 | Bucky Walters, Cincinnati |
| 1940 | Frank McCormick, Cincinnati |
| 1941 | Dolph Camilli, Brooklyn |
| 1942 | Mort Cooper, St. Louis |
| 1943 | Stan Musial, St. Louis |
| 1944 | Marty Marion, St. Louis |
| 1945 | Phil Cavarretta, Chicago |
| 1946 | Stan Musial, St. Louis |
| 1947 | Bob Elliott, Boston |
| 1948 | Stan Musial, St. Louis |
| 1949 | Jackie Robinson, Brooklyn |
| 1950 | Jim Konstanty, Philadelphia |
| 1951 | Roy Campanella, Brooklyn |
| 1952 | Hank Sauer, Chicago |
| 1953 | Roy Campanella, Brooklyn |
| 1954 | Willie Mays, New York |
| 1955 | Roy Campanella, Brooklyn |
| 1956 | Don Newcombe, Brooklyn |
| 1957 | Henry Aaron, Milwaukee |
| 1958–59 | Ernie Banks, Chicago |
| 1960 | Dick Groat, Pittsburgh |
| 1961 | Frank Robinson, Cincinnati |
| 1962 | Maury Wills, Los Angeles |
| 1963 | Sandy Koufax, Los Angeles |
| 1964 | Ken Boyer, St. Louis |
| 1965 | Willie Mays, San Francisco |
| 1966 | Roberto Clemente, Pittsburgh |
| 1967 | Orlando Cepeda, St. Louis |
| 1968 | Bob Gibson, St. Louis |
| 1969 | Willie McCovey, San Francisco |
| 1970 | Johnny Bench, Cincinnati |
| 1971 | Joe Torre, St. Louis |
| 1972 | Johnny Bench, Cincinnati |
| 1973 | Pete Rose, Cincinnati |
| 1974 | Steve Garvey, Los Angeles |
| 1975–76 | Joe Morgan, Cincinnati |
| 1977 | George Foster, Cincinnati |
| 1978 | Dave Parker, Pittsburgh |
| 1979 | Willie Stargell, Pittsburgh |
| 1979 | Keith Hernandez, St. Louis |
| 1980 | Mike Schmidt, Philadelphia |
| 1981 | Mike Schmidt, Philadelphia |
| 1982 | Dale Murphy, Atlanta |
| 1983 | Dale Murphy, Atlanta |
| 1984 | Ryne Sandberg, Chicago |
| 1985 | Willie McGee, St. Louis |

# CY YOUNG AWARD

| | |
|---|---|
| 1956 | Don Newcombe, Brooklyn N.L. |
| 1957 | Warren Spahn, Milwaukee N.L. |
| 1958 | Bob Turley, New York A.L. |
| 1959 | Early Wynn, Chicago A.L. |
| 1960 | Vernon Law, Pittsburgh, N.L. |
| 1961 | Whitey Ford, New York A.L. |
| 1962 | Don Drysdale, Los Angeles N.L. |
| 1963 | Sandy Koufax, Los Angeles N.L. |
| 1964 | Dean Chance, Los Angeles A.L. |
| 1965 | Sandy Koufax, Los Angeles N.L. |
| 1966 | Sandy Koufax, Los Angeles N.L. |
| 1967 | Jim Lonborg, Boston A.L.; Mike McCormick, San Francisco N.L. |
| 1968 | Dennis, McLain, Detroit A.L.; Bob Gibson, St. Louis N.L. |
| 1969 | Mike Cuellar, Baltimore, and Dennis McLain, Detroit, tied in A.L.; Tom Seaver, N.Y. N.L. |
| 1970 | Jim Perry, Minnesota A.L.; Bob Gibson, St. Louis N.L. |
| 1971 | Vida Blue, Oakland A.L.; Ferguson Jenkins, Chicago N.L. |
| 1972 | Gaylord Perry, Cleveland A.L.; Steve Carlton, Phila. N.L. |
| 1973 | Jim Palmer, Baltimore A.L.; Tom Seaver, New York N.L. |
| 1974 | Catfish Hunter, Oakland A.L.; Mike Marshall, Los Angeles N.L. |
| 1975 | Jim Palmer, Baltimore A.L.; Tom Seaver, New York N.L. |
| 1976 | Jim Palmer, Baltimore A.L.; Randy Jones, San Diego N.L. |
| 1977 | Sparky Lyle, N.Y., A.L.; Steve Carlton, Philadelphia N.L. |
| 1978 | Ron Guidry, N.Y., A.L.; Gaylord Perry, San Diego N.L. |
| 1979 | Mike Flanagan, Baltimore, A.L.; Bruce Sutter, Chicago, N.L. |
| 1980 | Steve Stone, Baltimore, A.L.; Steve Carlton, Philadelphia, N.L. |
| 1981 | Rollie Fingers, Milwaukee, A.L.; Fernando Valenzuela, Los Angeles, N.L. |
| 1982 | Pete Vuckovich, Milwaukee, A.L.; Steve Carlton, Philadelphia, N.L. |
| 1983 | LaMarr Hoyt, Chicago, A.L.; John Denny, Philadelphia, N.L. |
| 1984 | Willie Hernandez, Detroit, A.L.; Rick Sutcliffe, Chicago, N.L. |
| 1985 | Bret Saberhagen, A.L.; Dwight Gooden, N.L. |

# ROOKIE OF THE YEAR
(Baseball Writers Association selections)

## American League

| | |
|---|---|
| 1949 | Roy Sievers, St. Louis |
| 1950 | Walt Dropo, Boston |
| 1951 | Gil McDougald, New York |
| 1952 | Harry Byrd, Philadelphia |
| 1953 | Harvey Kuenn, Detroit |
| 1954 | Bob Grim, New York |
| 1955 | Herb Score, Cleveland |
| 1956 | Luis Aparicio, Chicago |
| 1957 | Tony Kubek, New York |
| 1958 | Albie Pearson, Washington |
| 1959 | Bob Allison, Washington |
| 1960 | Ron Hansen, Baltimore |
| 1961 | Don Schwall, Boston |
| 1962 | Tom Tresh, New York |
| 1963 | Gary Peters, Chicago |
| 1964 | Tony Oliva, Minnesota |
| 1965 | Curt Blefary, Baltimore |
| 1966 | Tommy Agee, Chicago |
| 1967 | Rod Carew, Minnesota |
| 1968 | Stan Bahnsen, New York |
| 1969 | Lou Piniella, Kansas City |
| 1970 | Thurman Munson, New York |
| 1971 | Chris Chambliss, Cleveland |

| | | |
|---|---|---|
| 1972 | Carlton Fisk, Boston | |
| 1973 | Alonzo Bumbry, Baltimore | |
| 1974 | Mike Hargrove, Texas | |
| 1975 | Fred Lynn, Boston | |
| 1976 | Mark Fidrych, Detroit | |
| 1977 | Eddie Murray, Baltimore | |
| 1978 | Lou Whitaker, Detroit | |
| 1979 | Alfredo Griffin, Toronto | |
| 1979 | John Castino, Minnesota | |
| 1980 | Joe Charboneau, Cleveland | |
| 1981 | Dave Righetti, New York | |
| 1982 | Cal Ripken, Jr., Baltimore | |
| 1983 | Ron Kittle, Chicago | |
| 1984 | Alvin Davis, Seattle | |
| 1985 | Ozzie Guillen, Chicago | |

**National League**

| | |
|---|---|
| 1949 | Don Newcombe, Brooklyn |
| 1950 | Sam Jethroe, Boston |

| | |
|---|---|
| 1951 | Willie Mays, New York |
| 1952 | Joe Black, Brooklyn |
| 1953 | Jim Gilliam, Brooklyn |
| 1954 | Wally Moon, St. Louis |
| 1955 | Bill Virdon, St. Louis |
| 1956 | Frank Robinson, Cincinnati |
| 1957 | Jack Sanford, Philadelphia |
| 1958 | Orlando Cepeda, San Francisco |
| 1959 | Willie McCovey, San Francisco |
| 1960 | Frank Howard, Los Angeles |
| 1961 | Billy Williams, Chicago |
| 1962 | Ken Hubbs, Chicago |
| 1963 | Pete Rose, Cincinnati |
| 1964 | Richie Allen, Philadelphia |
| 1965 | Jim Lefebvre, Los Angeles |
| 1966 | Tommy Helms, Cincinnati |
| 1967 | Tom Seaver, New York |
| 1968 | Johnny Bench, Cincinnati |
| 1969 | Ted Sizemore, Los Angeles |

| | |
|---|---|
| 1970 | Carl Morton, Montreal |
| 1971 | Earl Williams, Atlanta |
| 1972 | Jon Matlack, New York |
| 1973 | Gary Matthews, San Francisco |
| 1974 | Bake McBride, St. Louis |
| 1975 | John Montefusco, San Francisco |
| 1976 | Pat Zachry, Cincinnati |
| 1977 | Andre Dawson, Montreal |
| 1978 | Bob Horner, Atlanta |
| 1979 | Rick Sutcliffe, Los Angeles |
| 1980 | Steve Howe, Los Angeles |
| 1981 | Fernando Valenzuela, Los Angeles |
| 1982 | Steve Sax, Los Angeles |
| 1983 | Darryl Strawberry, New York |
| 1984 | Dwight Gooden, New York |
| 1985 | Vince Coleman, St. Louis |

## BASEBALL'S PERFECTLY PITCHED GAMES[1]

(no opposing runner reached base)

| | |
|---|---|
| John Richmond—Worcester vs. Cleveland (NL) June 12, 1880 | 1-0 |
| John M. Ward—Providence vs. Buffalo (NL) June 17, 1880 | 5-0 |
| Cy Young—Boston vs. Philadelphia (AL) May 5, 1904 | 3-0 |
| Addie Joss—Cleveland vs. Chicago (AL) Oct. 2, 1908 | 1-0 |
| Ernest Shore[2]—Boston vs. Washington (AL) June 23, 1917 | 4-0 |
| Charles Robertson—Chicago vs. Detroit (AL) April 30, 1922 | 2-0 |
| Don Larsen[3]—New York (AL) vs. Brooklyn (NL) Oct. 8, 1956 | 2-0 |
| Jim Bunning—Philadelphia vs. New York (NL) June 21, 1964 | 6-0 |
| Sandy Koufax—Los Angeles vs. Chicago (NL) Sept. 9, 1965 | 1-0 |
| Jim Hunter—Oakland vs. Minnesota (AL) May 8, 1968 | 4-0 |
| Len Barker—Cleveland vs. Toronto (AL) May 15, 1981 | 3-0 |
| Mike Witt—California vs. Texas (AL) Sept. 30, 1984 | 1-0 |

1. Harvey Haddix, of Pittsburgh, pitched 12 perfect innings against Milwaukee (NL), May 26, 1959 but lost game in 13th on error and hit. 2. Shore, relief pitcher for Babe Ruth who walked first batter before being ejected by umpire, retired 26 batters who faced him and baserunner was out stealing. 3. World Series.

## MAJOR LEAGUE LIFETIME RECORDS

*Source: The Book of Baseball Records,* published and copyrighted by Seymour Siwoff, New York, N.Y. 10036.

### Leading Batters, by Average
(Over 2,000 Hits)

| | Years | At Bats | Hits | Avg |
|---|---|---|---|---|
| Ty Cobb | 24 | 11,429 | 4,191 | .367 |
| Rogers Hornsby | 23 | 8,173 | 2,930 | .358 |
| Dan Brouthers | 19 | 6,725 | 2,349 | .349 |
| Ed Delahanty | 16 | 7,493 | 2,593 | .346 |
| Tris Speaker | 22 | 10,196 | 3,515 | .345 |
| Willie Keeler | 19 | 8,564 | 2,955 | .345 |
| Ted Williams | 19 | 7,706 | 2,654 | .345 |
| Billy Hamilton | 14 | 6,262 | 2,157 | .344 |
| Harry Heilmann | 17 | 7,787 | 2,660 | .342 |
| Babe Ruth | 22 | 8,399 | 2,873 | .342 |
| Jesse Burkett | 16 | 8,389 | 2,872 | .342 |
| Bill Terry | 14 | 6,428 | 2,193 | .341 |
| Lou Gehrig | 17 | 8,001 | 2,721 | .340 |
| George Sisler | 15 | 8,267 | 2,812 | .340 |
| Nap Lajoie | 21 | 9,589 | 3,251 | .339 |
| Cap Anson | 22 | 9,084 | 3,081 | .339 |
| Sam Thompson | 15 | 6,004 | 2,016 | .336 |
| Al Simmons | 20 | 8,761 | 2,927 | .334 |
| Eddie Collins | 25 | 9,949 | 3,311 | .333 |
| Paul Waner | 20 | 9,459 | 3,152 | .333 |
| Stan Musial | 22 | 10,972 | 3,630 | .331 |
| Rod Carew | 19 | 9,214 | 3,053 | .331 |
| Heinie Manush | 17 | 7,653 | 2,524 | .330 |
| Hugh Duffy | 17 | 6,999 | 2,307 | .330 |

| | Years | At Bats | Hits | Avg |
|---|---|---|---|---|
| Honus Wagner | 21 | 10,427 | 3,430 | .329 |
| Joe DiMaggio | 13 | 6,821 | 2,214 | .325 |
| Jimmie Foxx | 20 | 8,134 | 2,646 | .325 |

### Leading Pitchers
(Over 250 Victories)

| | Years | W | L | Pct |
|---|---|---|---|---|
| Cy Young | 22 | 511 | 315 | .619 |
| Walter Johnson | 21 | 416 | 279 | .599 |
| Grover Alexander | 20 | 373 | 208 | .642 |
| Christy Mathewson | 17 | 373 | 188 | .665 |
| James Galvin | 15 | 365 | 309 | .542 |
| Warren Spahn | 21 | 363 | 245 | .597 |
| Charles Nichols | 15 | 360 | 202 | .641 |
| Tim Keefe | 14 | 346 | 225 | .606 |
| John Clarkson | 12 | 328 | 175 | .652 |
| Eddie Plank | 17 | 325 | 190 | .631 |
| Steve Carlton* | 22 | 323 | 229 | .585 |
| Mickey Welch | 13 | 316 | 214 | .596 |
| Gaylord Perry | 22 | 314 | 265 | .542 |
| Tom Seaver* | 20 | 311 | 205 | .603 |
| Phil Niekro* | 23 | 311 | 261 | .544 |

| | Years | W | L | Pct | | Years | W | L | Pct |
|---|---|---|---|---|---|---|---|---|---|
| Don Sutton* | 21 | 310 | 239 | 565 | Bob Feller | 18 | 266 | 162 | .621 |
| Hoss Radbourne | 21 | 308 | 191 | .617 | Eppa Rixey | 21 | 266 | 251 | .515 |
| Lefty Grove | 20 | 300 | 141 | .680 | Gus Weyhing | 14 | 265 | 236 | .529 |
| Early Wynn | 23 | 300 | 244 | .551 | Jim McCormick | 10 | 264 | 217 | .549 |
| Robin Roberts | 19 | 286 | 245 | .539 | Ted Lyons | 21 | 260 | 230 | .531 |
| Ferguson Jenkins | 19 | 284 | 226 | .557 | Red Faber | 20 | 254 | 212 | .545 |
| Jim Kaat | 25 | 283 | 236 | .545 | Carl Hubbell | 16 | 253 | 154 | .622 |
| Tony Mullane | 14 | 282 | 221 | .561 | Bob Gibson | 17 | 251 | 174 | .591 |
| Red Ruffing | 22 | 273 | 225 | .548 | | | | | |
| Burleigh Grimes | 19 | 270 | 212 | .560 | *Active through 1986. | | | | |
| Jim Palmer | 18 | 268 | 149 | .643 | | | | | |

## MAJOR LEAGUE ALL-TIME PITCHING RECORDS

### (Through 1985)

Most Games Won—511, Cy Young, Cleveland N.L., 1890–98, St. Louis N.L., 1899–1900, Boston A.L., 1901–08, Cleveland A.L., 1909–11, Boston N.L., 1911.

Most Games Won, Season—60, Hoss Radbourne, Providence N.L., 1884. (Since 1900—41, Jack Chesbro, New York A.L., 1904.)

Most Consecutive Games Won—24, Carl Hubbell, New York N.L., 1936 (16) and 1937 (8).

Most Consecutive Games Won, Season—19, Tim Keefe, New York N.L., 1888; Rube Marquard, New York N.L., 1912.

Most Years Won 20 or More Games—16, Cy Young, Cleveland N.L., 1891–98, St. Louis N.L., 1899–1900, Boston A.L., 1901–04, 1907–08.

Most Shutouts—113, Walter Johnson, Wash. A.L., 1907–27.

Most Shutouts, Season—16, Grover Alexander, Philadelphia N.L., 1916.

Most Consecutive Shutouts—6, Don Drysdale, Los Angeles, N.L., 1968.

Most Consecutive Scoreless Innings—58, Don Drysdale, Los Angeles, N.L., 1968.

Most Strikeouts—4,083, Nolan Ryan, New York N.L., California A.L., Houston N.L., 1968–1985 (Still active)

Most Strikeouts, Season—505, Matthew Kilroy, Baltimore A.A., 1886. (Since 1900—383, Nolan Ryan, California, A.L., 1973.)

Most Strikeouts, Game—21, Tom Cheney, Washington A.L., 1962, 16 innings. Nine innings: 20, Roger Clemens, Boston, A.L., 1986; 19, Charles McSweeney, Providence N.L., 1884; Hugh Dailey, Chicago U.A., 1884. (Since 1900—19, Steve Carlton, St. Louis N.L. vs. New York, Sept. 15, 1969; Tom Seaver, New York N.L. vs. San Diego, April 22, 1970; Nolan Ryan, California A.L. vs. Boston, Aug. 12, 1974.)

Most Consecutive Strikeouts—10, Tom Seaver, New York N.L. vs. San Diego, April 22, 1970.

Most Games, Season—106, Mike Marshall, Los Angeles, N.L., 1974.

Most Complete Games, Season—74, William White, Cincinnati N.L., 1879. (Since 1900—48, Jack Chesbro, New York A.L., 1904.)

## MAJOR LEAGUE INDIVIDUAL ALL-TIME RECORDS

### (Through 1985)

Highest Batting Average—442, James O'Neill, St. Louis, A.A., 1887; .438, Hugh Duffy, Boston, N.L., 1894 (Since 1900—.424, Rogers Hornsby, St. Louis, N.L., 1924; .422, Nap Lajoie, Phil., A.L., 1901)

Most Times at Bat—12,364, Henry Aaron, Milwaukee N.L., 1954–65; Atlanta N.L., 1966–74; Milwaukee A.L., 1975–76.

Most Years Batted .300 or Better—23, Ty Cobb, Detroit A.L., 1906–26, Philadelphia A.L., 1927–28.

Most hits—4,256, Pete Rose, Cincinnati 1963–79, Philadelphia 1980–83, Montreal 1984, Cincinnati 1984 (still active)

Most Hits, Season—257, George Sisler, St. Louis A.L., 1920.

Most Hits, Game (9 innings)—7, Wilbert Robinson, Baltimore N.L., 6 singles, 1 double, 1892. Rennie Stennett, Pittsburgh N.L., 4 singles, 2 doubles, 1 triple, 1975.

Most Hits, Game (extra innings)—9, John Burnett, Cleveland A.L., 18 innings, 7 singles, 2 doubles, 1932.

Most Hits in Succession—12, Mike Higgins, Boston A.L., in four games, 1938; Walt Dropo, Detroit A.L., in three games, 1952.

Most Consecutive Games Batted Safely—56, Joe DiMaggio, New York A.L., 1941.

Most Runs—2,244, Ty Cobb, Detroit A.L., 1905–26, Philadelphia A.L., 1927–28.

Most Runs, Season—196, William Hamilton, Philadelphia N.L., 1894. (Since 1900—177, Babe Ruth, New York A.L., 1921.)

Most Runs, Game—7, Guy Hecker, Louisville A.A., 1886. (Since 1900—6, by Mel Ott, New York N.L., 1934, 1944; Johnny Pesky, Boston A.L., 1946; Frank Torre, Milwaukee N.L., 1957.)

Most Runs Batted in—2,297, Henry Aaron, Milwaukee N.L., 1954–1965; Atlanta N.L., 1966–74; Milwaukee A.L., 1975–76.

Most Runs Batted in, Season—190, Hack Wilson, Chicago N.L., 1930.

Most Runs Batted In, Game—12, Jim Bottomley, St. Louis N.L., 1924.

Most Home Runs—755, Henry Aaron, Milwaukee N.L., 1954–1965; Atlanta N.L., 1966–74; Milwaukee A.L., 1975–76.

Most Home Runs, Season—61, Roger Maris, New York A.L., 1961 (162-game season); 60, Babe Ruth, New York A.L., 1927 (154-game season)

Most Home Runs with Bases Filled—23, Lou Gehrig, New York A.L., 1927–39.

Most 2-Base Hits—793, Tris Speaker, Boston A.L., 1907–15, Cleveland A.L., 1916–26, Washington A.L., 1927, Philadelphia A.L., 1928.

Most 2-Base Hits, Season—67, Earl Webb, Boston A.L., 1931.

Most 2-base Hits, Game—4, by many.

Most 3-Base Hits—312, Sam Crawford, Cincinnati N.L., 1899–1902, Detroit A.L., 1903–17.

Most 3-Base Hits, Season—36, Owen Wilson, Pittsburgh N.L., 1912.

Most 3-Base Hits, Game—4, George Strief, Philadelphia A.A., 1885; William Joyce, New York N.L., 1897. (Since 1900—3, by many.)

Most Games Played—3,298, Henry Aaron, Milwaukee N.L., 1954–1965; Atlanta, N.L., 1966–74; Milwaukee A.L., 1975–76.

Most Consecutive Games Played—2,130, Lou Gehrig, New York A.L., 1925–39.

Most Bases on Balls—2,056, Babe Ruth, Boston A.L., 1914–19; New York A.L., 1920–34, Boston N.L., 1935.

Most Bases on Balls, Season—170, Babe Ruth, New York A.L., 1923.

Most bases on Balls, Game—6, Jimmy Foxx, Boston A.L., 1938.

Most Strikeouts, Season—189, Bobby Bonds, San Francisco N.L., 1970.

Most Strikeouts, Game (9 innings)—5, by many.

Most Strikeouts, Game (extra innings)—6, Carl Weilman, St. Louis A.L., 15 innings, 1913; Don Hoak, Chicago N.L., 17 innings, 1956; Fred Reichardt, California A.L., 17, innings, 1966; Billy Cowan, California A.L., 20, 1971; Cecil Cooper, Boston A.L., 15, 1974.

Most pinch—hits, lifetime—150, Manny Mota, S.F., 1962; Pitt., 1963–68; Montreal, 1969; L.A., 1969–80, N.L.

Most Pinch-hits, season—25, Jose Morales, Montreal N.L., 1976.

Most consecutive pinch-hits—9, Dave Philley, Phil., N.L., 1958 (8), 1959 (1).

Most pinch-hit home runs, lifetime—18, Gerald Lynch, Pitt.-Cin. N.L., 1957–66.

Most pinch-hit home runs, season—6, Johnny Frederick, Brooklyn, N.L., 1932.

Most stolen bases, lifetime (since 1900)—938, Lou Brock, Chicago N.L. 1961–64; St. Louis, N.L. 1964–79.

Most stolen bases, season—156, Harry Stovey, Phil., A.A., 1888. Since 1900: 130, Rickey Henderson, Oak., A.L., 1982; 118, Lou Brock, St. Lou., 1974.

Most stolen bases, game—7, George Gore, Chicago N.L. 1881; William Hamilton, Philadelphia N.L. 1894. (Since 1900—6, Eddie Collins, Philadelphia A.L., 1912.)

Most time stealing home, lifetime—35, Ty Cobb, Detroit-Phil. A.L., 1905–28.

## MAJOR LEAGUE ATTENDANCE RECORDS

### (Through 1986)

Single game—78,672, San Francisco at Los Angeles (N.L.), April 18, 1958. (At Memorial Coliseum.)

Doubleheader—84,587, New York at Cleveland (A.L.), Sept. 12, 1954.

Night—78,382, Chicago at Cleveland (A.L.), Aug. 20, 1948.

Season, home—3,608,881, Los Angeles (N.L.), 1982.

Season, road—2,461,240, New York (A.L.), 1980.

Season, league—23,988,661, American League, 1983.

Season, both leagues—45,557,582, 1983.

World Series, single game—92,706, Chicago (A.L.) at Los Angeles (N.L.), Oct. 6, 1959.

World Series, all games (6)—420,784, Chicago (A.L.) and Los Angeles (N.L.), 1959.

## MOST HOME RUNS IN ONE SEASON

### (45 or More)

| HR | Player/Team | Year | HR | Player/Team | Year |
|---|---|---|---|---|---|
| 61 | Roger Maris, New York (AL) | 1961 | 48 | Jimmy Foxx, Philadelphia (AL) | 1933 |
| 60 | Babe Ruth, New York (AL) | 1927 | 48 | Harmon Killebrew, Minnesota (AL) | 1962 |
| 59 | Babe Ruth, New York (AL) | 1921 | 48 | Willie Stargell, Pittsburgh (NL) | 1971 |
| 58 | Jimmy Foxx, Philadelphia (AL) | 1932 | 48 | Dave Kingman, Chicago (NL) | 1979 |
| 58 | Hank Greenberg, Detroit (AL) | 1938 | 48 | Mike Schmidt, Philadelphia (NL) | 1980 |
| 56 | Hack Wilson, Chicago (NL) | 1930 | 47 | Babe Ruth, New York (AL) | 1926 |
| 54 | Babe Ruth, New York (AL) | 1920 | 47 | Ralph Kiner, Pittsburgh (NL) | 1950 |
| 54 | Babe Ruth, New York (AL) | 1928 | 47 | Ed Mathews, Milwaukee (NL) | 1953 |
| 54 | Ralph Kiner, Pittsburgh (NL) | 1949 | 47 | Ernie Banks, Chicago (NL) | 1958 |
| 54 | Mickey Mantle, New York (AL) | 1961 | 47 | Willie Mays, San Francisco (NL) | 1964 |
| 52 | Mickey Mantle, New York (AL) | 1956 | 47 | Henry Aaron, Atlanta (NL) | 1971 |
| 52 | Willie Mays, San Francisco (NL) | 1965 | 47 | Reggie Jackson, Oakland (AL) | 1969 |
| 52 | George Foster, Cincinnati (NL) | 1977 | 46 | Babe Ruth, New York (AL) | 1924 |
| 51 | Ralph Kiner, Pittsburgh (NL) | 1947 | 46 | Babe Ruth, New York, (AL) | 1929 |
| 51 | John Mize, New York (NL) | 1947 | 46 | Babe Ruth, New York (AL) | 1931 |
| 51 | Willie Mays, New York (NL) | 1955 | 46 | Lou Gehrig, New York (AL) | 1931 |
| 50 | Jimmy Foxx, Boston (AL) | 1938 | 46 | Joe DiMaggio, New York (AL) | 1937 |
| 49 | Babe Ruth, New York (AL) | 1930 | 46 | Ed Mathews, Milwaukee (NL) | 1959 |
| 49 | Lou Gehrig, New York (AL) | 1934 | 46 | Orlando Cepeda, San Francisco (NL) | 1961 |
| 49 | Lou Gehrig, New York (AL) | 1936 | 46 | Jim Rice, Boston (AL) | 1978 |
| 49 | Ted Kluszewski, Cincinnati (NL) | 1954 | 45 | Harmon Killebrew, Minnesota (AL) | 1963 |
| 49 | Willie Mays, San Francisco (NL) | 1962 | 45 | Willie McCovey, San Francisco (NL) | 1969 |
| 49 | Harmon Killebrew, Minnesota (AL) | 1964 | 45 | Johnny Bench, Cincinnati (NL) | 1970 |
| 49 | Frank Robinson, Baltimore (AL) | 1966 | 45 | Gorman Thomas, Milwaukee (AL) | 1979 |
| 49 | Harmon Killebrew, Minnesota (AL) | 1969 | 45 | Henry Aaron, Milwaukee (NL) | 1962 |

## MAJOR LEAGUE BASEBALL EXPANDS PLAYOFFS TO BEST 4-OF-7

After 16 years of five-game league championship playoffs, baseball expanded to a seven-game format in 1985 for the purpose of reaping a reported additional $9 million in network television revenue.

An agreement was reached between management and players to expand the series for 1985. The decision immediately increased baseball's revenue from $20 to $29 million for the playoffs.

The formula for splitting that money was part of the agreement with the players which settled the Aug. 6–8 major league players strike.

The playoffs had been a best 3-of-5 affair since 1969, when divisional play was first initiated. The World Series remained a best 4-of-7 format.

## MAJOR LEAGUE BALL PARK STATISTICS*

lf—Left-field foul line; cf—center field; rf—right-field foul line

| Club, nickname, and grounds | Distance, feet | | | Seating capacity | Record Attendance[4] | | |
|---|---|---|---|---|---|---|---|
| | lf | cf | rf | | Day game | Double-header[3] | Night game |
| **American League** | | | | | | | |
| Baltimore Orioles—Memorial Stadium | 309 | 405 | 309 | 53,208 | 51,956 | 46,796 | 51,883 |
| Boston Red Sox—Fenway Park | 315 | 390 | 302 | 33,465 | 36,388 | 41,995 | 36,228 |
| California Angels—Anaheim Stadium | 333 | 404 | 333 | 67,335 | 62,020 | 41,723 | 61,640 |
| Chicago White Sox—Comiskey Park | 341 | 401 | 341 | 43,651 | 54,215 | 55,555 | 53,940 |
| Cleveland Indians—Municipal Stadium | 320 | 400 | 320 | 74,208 | 74,420 | 84,587 | 78,382 |
| Detroit Tigers—Tiger Stadium | 340 | 440 | 325 | 52,687 | 57,888 | 58,369 | 56,586 |
| Kansas City Royals—Royals Stadium | 330 | 410 | 330 | 40,635 | 41,095 | 40,525 | 41,860 |
| Milwaukee Brewers—County Stadium | 315 | 402 | 315 | 53,192 | 55,120 | 54,630 | 55,716 |
| Minnesota Twins—Hubert H. Humphrey Metrodome | 343 | 408 | 327 | 55,122 | 46,463 | 43,419 | 52,299 |
| New York Yankees—Yankee Stadium[1] | 312 | 417 | 310 | 57,545 | 69,755 | 81,841 | 74,747 |
| Oakland A's—Oakland Coliseum | 330 | 397 | 330 | 50,219 | 48,758 | 48,562 | 49,300 |
| Seattle Mariners—Kingdome | 316 | 410 | 316 | 59,438 | 47,353 | 25,344 | 57,762 |
| Texas Rangers—Arlington Stadium | 330 | 400 | 330 | 41,284 | 40,078 | 42,163 | 41,097 |
| Toronto Blue Jays—Exhibition Stadium | 330 | 400 | 330 | 43,737 | 44,649 | 41,308 | 39,347 |
| **National League** | | | | | | | |
| Atlanta Braves—Atlanta Stadium | 330 | 402 | 330 | 52,934 | 51,275 | 46,489 | 53,775 |
| Chicago Cubs—Wrigley Field | 355 | 400 | 353 | 37,272 | 46,572 | 46,965 | No lights |
| Cincinnati Reds—Riverfront Stadium | 330 | 404 | 330 | 52,392 | 53,390 | 52,147 | 53,328 |
| Houston Astros—Astrodome | 340 | 406 | 340 | 45,000 | 49,442 | 45,115 | 50,908 |
| Los Angeles Dodgers—Dodger Stadium[2] | 330 | 400 | 330 | 56,000 | 78,672 | 53,856 | 72,140 |
| Montreal Expos—Olympic Stadium | 325 | 404 | 325 | 58,838 | 57,592 | 59,282 | 57,121 |
| New York Mets—Shea Stadium | 338 | 410 | 338 | 55,300 | 56,738 | 57,175 | 56,658 |
| Philadelphia Phillies—Veterans Stadium | 330 | 408 | 330 | 66,507 | 63,283 | 40,720 | 63,501 |
| Pittsburgh Pirates—Three Rivers Stadium | 335 | 400 | 335 | 54,598 | 51,695 | 49,341 | 48,846 |
| St. Louis Cardinals—Busch Memorial Stadium | 330 | 414 | 330 | 50,222 | 50,548 | 49,743 | 50,340 |
| San Diego Padres—Jack Murphy Stadium | 330 | 405 | 330 | 51,319 | 36,750 | 43,473 | 50,569 |
| San Francisco Giants—Candlestick Park | 335 | 400 | 335 | 58,000 | 56,197 | 50,924 | 55,920 |

*At end of 1982 season. 1. Distance and capacity after rebuilding; attendance records prior to rebuilding. 2. Played also in Los Angeles Coliseum. 3. Two day games. 4. Through 1982 season.

# PETE ROSE BREAKS TY COBB'S ALL-TIME HIT RECORD

Baseball fans in Cincinnati and all over the country waited patiently for the moment throughout the 1985 season. On Sept. 11, 1985, it finally came. Pete Rose singled to left field against San Diego Padres right-hander Eric Show at 8:01 P.M. EDT to break a record most had long thought would stand forever—Ty Cobb's career mark of 4,191 base hits.

Base hit 4,192 came before a crowd of 47,237 at Cincinnati's Riverfront Stadium in the first inning of a game the Reds would win 2–0.

Rose, 44 years old and a 23-year major league veteran, broke the record in the city and playing for the team with which he began his major league career in 1963. Rose played with the Reds through 1978, before signing with the Philadelphia Phillies in 1979 as a free agent. He stayed there until 1984, when he again signed as a free agent—this time with the Montreal Expos.

Rose's stay in Montreal was brief. In August, 1984, he was brought back to Cincinnati to serve as player-manager of a struggling, once-proud franchise. And while he pursued Cobb's record in 1985, he kept a surprising young Reds team in the chase for the National League Western Division championship most of the season.

Rose broke Cobb's record on the 57th anniversary of Cobb's last game—Sept. 11, 1928, against the Yankees at Yankee Stadium while playing for the old Philadelphia Athletics.

Ironically also, Padres first baseman Steve Garvey, second baseman Jerry Royster, and umpire Lee Weyer, who were all in Cincinnati for the historic hit, had all been in Atlanta in 1974 when Hank Aaron had broken another longtime record —Babe Ruth's mark of 714 career home runs.

Rose tied the record in Chicago on Sunday, Sept. 9, against Cubs pitcher Reggie Patterson.

His first major league base hit came on April 13, 1963. It was a triple against Pittsburgh Pirates pitcher Bob Friend. Other historic Rose hits came as follows: 1,000: June 26, 1968, against New York Mets pitcher Dick Selma; 2,000: June 19, 1973, against Ron Bryant, San Francisco Giants; 3,000: May 5, 1978, against Steve Rogers, Montreal Expos; 4,000: April 13, 1984, against Jerry Koosman, Philadelphia Phillies.

Rose also holds major league record for most games played, most at bats, most singles, most hits by a switch hitter, total bases by a switch hitter, most seasons with 200 or more hits, most consecutive seasons with 100 hits or more, most seasons 600 or more at-bats, most seasons 150 or more games played, highest fielding percentage by an outfielder, 1,000 games or more, and only player to play 500 games or more at five positions—first base, second base, third base, left field, and right field.

## MAJOR LEAGUE BASEBALL—1986

### AMERICAN LEAGUE
### (Final Standing—1986)

#### EASTERN DIVISION

| Team | W | L | Pct | GB |
|------|---|---|-----|----|
| Boston Red Sox | 95 | 66 | .590 | — |
| New York Yankees | 90 | 72 | .556 | 5 1/2 |
| Detroit Tigers | 87 | 75 | .537 | 8 1/2 |
| Toronto Blue Jays | 86 | 76 | .531 | 9 1/2 |
| Cleveland Indians | 84 | 78 | .519 | 11 1/2 |
| Milwaukee Brewers | 77 | 84 | .478 | 18 |
| Baltimore Orioles | 73 | 89 | .451 | 22 1/2 |

#### WESTERN DIVISION

| Team | W | L | Pct | GB |
|------|---|---|-----|----|
| California Angels | 92 | 70 | .568 | — |
| Texas Rangers | 87 | 75 | .537 | 5 |
| Kansas City Royals | 76 | 86 | .469 | 16 |
| Oakland Athletics | 76 | 86 | .469 | 16 |
| Chicago White Sox | 72 | 90 | .444 | 20 |
| Minnesota Twins | 71 | 91 | .438 | 21 |
| Seattle Mariners | 67 | 95 | .414 | 25 |

### NATIONAL LEAGUE
### (Final Standing—1986)

#### EASTERN DIVISION

| Team | W | L | Pct | GB |
|------|---|---|-----|----|
| New York Mets | 108 | 54 | .667 | — |
| Philadelphia Phillies | 86 | 75 | .534 | 21 1/2 |
| St. Louis Cardinals | 79 | 82 | .491 | 28 1/2 |
| Montreal Expos | 78 | 83 | .484 | 29 1/2 |
| Chicago Cubs | 70 | 90 | .438 | 37 |
| Pittsburgh Pirates | 64 | 96 | .395 | 44 |

#### WESTERN DIVISION

| Team | W | L | Pct | GB |
|------|---|---|-----|----|
| Houston Astros | 96 | 66 | .593 | — |
| Cincinnati Reds | 86 | 76 | .531 | 10 |
| San Francisco Giants | 83 | 79 | .512 | 13 |
| San Diego Padres | 74 | 88 | .457 | 22 |
| Los Angeles Dodgers | 73 | 89 | .451 | 23 |
| Atlanta Braves | 72 | 89 | .447 | 23 1/2 |

### AMERICAN LEAGUE LEADERS—1986

| | |
|---|---|
| Batting—Wade Boggs, Boston | .357 |
| Runs—Rickey Henderson, New York | 130 |
| Hits—Don Mattingly, New York | 238 |
| Runs batted in—Joe Carter, Cleveland | 121 |
| Triples—Brett Butler, Cleveland | 14 |
| Doubles—Don Mattingly, New York | 53 |
| Home runs—Jesse Barfield, Toronto | 40 |
| Stolen bases—Rickey Henderson, New York | 87 |
| Game winning RBIs—George Bell, Toronto | 15 |
| Don Mattingly, New York | 15 |
| Cal Ripkin, Baltimore | 15 |

#### Pitching

| | |
|---|---|
| Victories—Roger Clemens, Boston | 24 |
| Earned run average—Roger Clemens, Boston | 2.48 |
| Strikeouts—Mark Langston, Seattle | 245 |
| Shutouts—Jack Morris, Detroit | 6 |
| Complete games—Tom Candiotti, Cleveland | 17 |
| Saves—Dave Righetti, New York | 46[1] |

1. New major league record.

### NATIONAL LEAGUE LEADERS—1986

| | |
|---|---|
| Batting—Tim Raines, Montreal | .334 |
| Runs—Tony Gwynn, San Diego | 107 |
| Von Hayes, Philadelphia | 107 |
| Hits—Tony Gwynn, San Diego | 211 |
| Runs batted in—Mike Schmidt, Philadelphia | 119 |
| Doubles—Von Hayes, Philadelphia | 46 |
| Triples—Mitch Webster, Montreal | 13 |
| Home runs—Mike Schmidt, Philadelphia | 37 |
| Stolen bases—Vince Coleman, St. Louis | 107 |
| Game winning RBIs—Gary Carter, New York | 16 |
| Glenn Davis, Houston | 16 |

#### Pitching

| | |
|---|---|
| Victories—Fernando Valenzuela, Los Angeles | 21 |
| Earned run average—Mike Scott, Houston | 2.22 |
| Strikeouts—Mike Scott, Houston | 306 |
| Shutouts—Bob Knepper, Houston | 5 |
| Mike Scott, Houston | 5 |
| Complete games—Fernando Valenzuela, Los Angeles | 20 |
| Saves—Todd Worrell, St. Louis | 36 |

### AMERICAN LEAGUE AVERAGES—1986

#### Batting—Club

| | AB | R | H | HR | RBI | Pct |
|---|----|---|---|----|-----|-----|
| Cleveland | 5702 | 831 | 1620 | 157 | 775 | .284 |
| New York | 5569 | 797 | 1512 | 188 | 745 | .272 |
| Boston | 5498 | 794 | 1488 | 144 | 752 | .271 |
| Toronto | 5715 | 809 | 1540 | 181 | 767 | .269 |
| Texas | 5530 | 771 | 1479 | 182 | 722 | .267 |
| Detroit | 5512 | 798 | 1448 | 197 | 749 | .263 |
| Minnesota | 5531 | 741 | 1446 | 195 | 700 | .261 |
| Baltimore | 5523 | 708 | 1424 | 169 | 669 | .258 |
| California | 5434 | 786 | 1387 | 167 | 742 | .255 |
| Milwaukee | 5461 | 667 | 1393 | 127 | 625 | .255 |
| Seattle | 5498 | 718 | 1392 | 158 | 681 | .253 |
| Oakland | 5433 | 731 | 1369 | 163 | 680 | .252 |
| Kansas City | 5561 | 654 | 1403 | 137 | 618 | .252 |
| Chicago | 5406 | 644 | 1334 | 121 | 605 | .247 |

#### Batting Leaders
(350 or more at bats)

| Player/Team | AB | R | H | HR | RBI | Pct |
|-------------|----|---|---|----|-----|-----|
| Boggs, Boston | 580 | 107 | 207 | 8 | 71 | .357 |
| Mattingly, NY | 677 | 117 | 238 | 31 | 113 | .352 |
| Puckett, Minnesota | 680 | 119 | 223 | 31 | 96 | .328 |
| Tabler, Cleveland | 473 | 61 | 154 | 6 | 48 | .326 |
| Rice, Boston | 618 | 98 | 200 | 20 | 110 | .324 |
| Ward, Texas | 380 | 54 | 120 | 5 | 51 | .316 |
| Yount, Milwaukee | 522 | 82 | 163 | 9 | 46 | .312 |
| Fernndz, Toronto | 687 | 91 | 213 | 10 | 65 | .310 |
| PBradley, Seattle | 526 | 87 | 163 | 12 | 50 | .310 |
| Bell, Toronto | 641 | 101 | 198 | 31 | 108 | .309 |
| Franco, Cleveland | 599 | 80 | 183 | 10 | 74 | .306 |
| Murray, Baltimore | 495 | 61 | 151 | 17 | 84 | .305 |
| Carter, Cleveland | 663 | 108 | 200 | 29 | 121 | .302 |
| Easler, NY | 490 | 64 | 148 | 14 | 78 | .302 |
| Bernzrd, Cleveland | 562 | 88 | 169 | 17 | 73 | .301 |
| Fletcher, Texas | 530 | 82 | 159 | 3 | 50 | .300 |
| Baines, Chicago | 570 | 72 | 170 | 21 | 88 | .298 |
| MHall, Cleveland | 442 | 68 | 131 | 18 | 77 | .296 |
| Joyner, California | 592 | 82 | 172 | 22 | 100 | .291 |
| Brett, Kansas | 441 | 70 | 128 | 16 | 73 | .290 |
| OBrien, Texas | 551 | 86 | 160 | 21 | 90 | .290 |
| Barfield, Toronto | 589 | 107 | 170 | 40 | 108 | .289 |
| Jacoby, Cleveland | 583 | 83 | 168 | 17 | 81 | .288 |
| Gaetti, Minnesota | 596 | 92 | 171 | 34 | 108 | .287 |

| | | | | | | |
|---|---|---|---|---|---|---|
| LSmith, Kansas | 508 | 80 | 146 | 8 | 45 | .287 |
| Lacy, Baltimore | 491 | 77 | 141 | 11 | 47 | .287 |
| Lynn, Baltimore | 397 | 68 | 114 | 23 | 67 | .287 |

## Leading Pitchers
(10 or more decisions)

| Player/Team | IP | H | BB | SO | W | L | ERA |
|---|---|---|---|---|---|---|---|
| Eichhorn, Toronto | 157 | 104 | 45 | 166 | 14 | 6 | 1.72 |
| Clear, Milwaukee | 74 | 53 | 36 | 85 | 5 | 5 | 2.20 |
| Righetti, NY | 107 | 88 | 35 | 83 | 8 | 8 | 2.45 |
| Clemens, Boston | 254 | 179 | 67 | 238 | 24 | 4 | 2.48 |
| Candlaria, California | 92 | 68 | 26 | 80 | 10 | 2 | 2.55 |
| Quisnbry, Kansas | 82 | 92 | 24 | 36 | 3 | 7 | 2.73 |
| Higuera, Milwaukee | 248 | 225 | 74 | 207 | 20 | 11 | 2.79 |
| Harris, Texas | 111 | 103 | 42 | 94 | 10 | 8 | 2.83 |
| MWitt, California | 269 | 218 | 73 | 208 | 18 | 10 | 2.84 |
| Plesac, Milwaukee | 91 | 81 | 29 | 75 | 10 | 7 | 2.97 |
| Aase, Baltimore | 82 | 71 | 28 | 67 | 6 | 7 | 2.98 |
| Hurst, Boston | 174 | 169 | 50 | 167 | 13 | 8 | 2.99 |
| Farr, Kansas | 109 | 90 | 39 | 82 | 8 | 4 | 3.13 |
| Black, Kansas | 121 | 100 | 43 | 68 | 5 | 10 | 3.20 |
| DJackson, Kansas | 186 | 177 | 79 | 115 | 11 | 12 | 3.20 |
| Morris, Detroit | 267 | 229 | 82 | 223 | 21 | 8 | 3.27 |
| Tewksbry, NY | 130 | 144 | 31 | 49 | 9 | 5 | 3.31 |
| Henke, Toronto | 91 | 63 | 32 | 118 | 9 | 5 | 3.35 |
| McCaskill, California | 246 | 207 | 92 | 202 | 17 | 10 | 3.40 |
| CYoung, Oakland | 198 | 176 | 57 | 116 | 13 | 9 | 3.45 |
| Candiotti, Cleveland | 252 | 234 | 106 | 167 | 16 | 12 | 3.46 |
| King, Detroit | 138 | 108 | 63 | 79 | 11 | 4 | 3.51 |
| Darwin, Milwaukee | 130 | 120 | 35 | 80 | 6 | 8 | 3.52 |
| Bannister, Chicago | 165 | 162 | 48 | 91 | 10 | 14 | 3.54 |

## Pitching—Club

| | ERA | H | ER | BB | SO | ShO | SA |
|---|---|---|---|---|---|---|---|
| Kansas City | 3.83 | 1413 | 613 | 479 | 888 | 13 | 30 |
| California | 3.86 | 1356 | 624 | 478 | 954 | 12 | 40 |
| Chicago | 3.94 | 1361 | 631 | 561 | 892 | 8 | 38 |
| Boston | 3.94 | 1468 | 626 | 474 | 1029 | 6 | 41 |
| Milwaukee | 4.03 | 1477 | 641 | 494 | 946 | 12 | 32 |
| Detroit | 4.03 | 1374 | 647 | 571 | 877 | 12 | 38 |
| Toronto | 4.07 | 1467 | 667 | 488 | 1001 | 12 | 44 |
| New York | 4.10 | 1461 | 657 | 492 | 878 | 8 | 58 |
| Texas | 4.13 | 1355 | 666 | 736 | 1055 | 8 | 41 |
| Baltimore | 4.30 | 1451 | 687 | 535 | 955 | 6 | 39 |
| Oakland | 4.31 | 1333 | 687 | 667 | 931 | 8 | 37 |
| Cleveland | 4.62 | 1549 | 743 | 605 | 743 | 7 | 34 |
| Seattle | 4.66 | 1590 | 745 | 585 | 942 | 5 | 27 |
| Minnesota | 4.77 | 1579 | 759 | 503 | 931 | 6 | 24 |

# NATIONAL LEAGUE AVERAGES—1986

## Batting—Club

| | AB | R | H | HR | RBI | Pct |
|---|---|---|---|---|---|---|
| New York | 5560 | 783 | 1462 | 148 | 731 | .263 |
| San Diego | 5516 | 656 | 1440 | 136 | 629 | .261 |
| Chicago | 5468 | 677 | 1401 | 134 | 634 | .256 |
| Houston | 5424 | 650 | 1382 | 124 | 607 | .255 |
| Montreal | 5508 | 637 | 1401 | 110 | 603 | .254 |
| Cincinnati | 5537 | 732 | 1404 | 144 | 670 | .254 |
| San Francisco | 5501 | 698 | 1393 | 114 | 575 | .253 |
| Philadelphia | 5483 | 739 | 1384 | 154 | 696 | .252 |
| Los Angeles | 5471 | 638 | 1374 | 128 | 599 | .251 |
| Pittsburgh | 5441 | 661 | 1363 | 110 | 616 | .251 |
| Atlanta | 5384 | 615 | 1348 | 138 | 575 | .250 |
| St. Louis | 5377 | 601 | 1268 | 58 | 550 | .236 |

## Batting Leaders
(350 or more at bats)

| Player/Team | AB | R | H | HR | RBI | Pct |
|---|---|---|---|---|---|---|
| Raines, Montreal | 580 | 91 | 194 | 9 | 62 | .334 |
| Sax, Los Angeles | 633 | 91 | 210 | 6 | 56 | .332 |
| Gwynn, San Diego | 642 | 107 | 211 | 14 | 59 | .329 |
| Backman, NY | 387 | 67 | 124 | 1 | 27 | .320 |
| CBrown, San Francisco | 416 | 57 | 132 | 7 | 49 | .317 |
| Walling, Houston | 382 | 53 | 119 | 13 | 58 | .312 |
| Bass, Houston | 591 | 84 | 184 | 20 | 78 | .311 |
| KHerrndz, NY | 551 | 94 | 171 | 13 | 84 | .310 |
| Hayes, Philadelphia | 610 | 107 | 186 | 19 | 98 | .305 |
| Ray, Pittsburgh | 579 | 67 | 174 | 6 | 78 | .301 |
| Knight, NY | 487 | 51 | 145 | 11 | 76 | .298 |
| Dykstra, NY | 431 | 77 | 127 | 8 | 45 | .295 |
| Schmidt, Philadelphia | 552 | 97 | 160 | 37 | 119 | .290 |
| Webster, Montreal | 576 | 89 | 167 | 8 | 49 | .290 |
| MWilson, NY | 381 | 61 | 110 | 9 | 45 | .289 |
| TPena, Pittsburgh | 510 | 56 | 147 | 10 | 52 | .288 |
| McReylds, San Diego | 561 | 89 | 161 | 26 | 96 | .287 |
| WClark, San Francisco | 408 | 66 | 117 | 11 | 41 | .287 |
| Dawson, Montreal | 496 | 65 | 141 | 20 | 78 | .284 |
| Sandberg, Chicago | 627 | 68 | 178 | 14 | 76 | .284 |
| Flannery, San Diego | 368 | 47 | 103 | 3 | 28 | .280 |
| Madlock, Los Angeles | 379 | 38 | 106 | 10 | 60 | .280 |
| OSmith, St. Louis | 514 | 67 | 144 | 0 | 54 | .280 |
| Bell, Cincinnati | 568 | 89 | 158 | 20 | 75 | .278 |
| CDavis, San Francisco | 526 | 71 | 146 | 13 | 70 | .278 |
| Cruz, Houston | 479 | 48 | 133 | 10 | 72 | .278 |

## Leading Pitchers
(10 or more decisions)

| Player/Team | IP | H | BB | SO | W | L | ERA |
|---|---|---|---|---|---|---|---|
| Worrell, St. Louis | 104 | 86 | 41 | 73 | 9 | 10 | 2.08 |
| Scott, Houston | 275 | 182 | 72 | 306 | 18 | 10 | 2.22 |
| Orosco, NY | 81 | 64 | 35 | 62 | 8 | 6 | 2.33 |
| Ruffin, Philadelphia | 145 | 138 | 44 | 70 | 9 | 4 | 2.48 |
| Assnmchr, Atlanta | 68 | 60 | 26 | 56 | 7 | 3 | 2.50 |
| Ojeda, NY | 217 | 185 | 52 | 148 | 18 | 5 | 2.53 |
| Tekulve, Philadelphia | 110 | 99 | 25 | 56 | 11 | 5 | 2.54 |
| Garber, Atlanta | 78 | 76 | 20 | 56 | 5 | 5 | 2.54 |
| Kerfeld, Houston | 94 | 71 | 42 | 76 | 11 | 2 | 2.59 |
| McGffgan, Montreal | 143 | 114 | 55 | 104 | 10 | 5 | 2.65 |
| DSmith, Houston | 56 | 39 | 22 | 45 | 4 | 7 | 2.73 |
| McCllers, San Diego | 136 | 103 | 58 | 92 | 10 | 10 | 2.78 |
| Darling, NY | 237 | 203 | 81 | 184 | 15 | 6 | 2.81 |
| Rhoden, Pittsburgh | 254 | 210 | 76 | 159 | 15 | 12 | 2.84 |
| Gooden, NY | 250 | 197 | 80 | 200 | 17 | 6 | 2.84 |
| Cox, St. Louis | 220 | 189 | 60 | 108 | 12 | 13 | 2.90 |
| Tudor, St. Louis | 220 | 197 | 53 | 107 | 13 | 7 | 2.90 |
| Burke, Montreal | 101 | 103 | 46 | 82 | 9 | 7 | 2.93 |
| Franco, Cincinnati | 101 | 90 | 44 | 82 | 6 | 6 | 2.94 |
| Sebra, Montreal | 91 | 81 | 25 | 65 | 5 | 5 | 2.96 |
| Show, San Diego | 136 | 109 | 69 | 94 | 9 | 5 | 2.97 |
| Dedmon, Atlanta | 100 | 90 | 39 | 58 | 6 | 6 | 2.98 |
| MDavis, San Francisco | 84 | 63 | 34 | 90 | 5 | 7 | 2.99 |
| Lefferts, San Diego | 108 | 97 | 44 | 72 | 9 | 8 | 3.01 |
| McDwll, NY | 128 | 107 | 42 | 65 | 14 | 9 | 3.02 |

## Pitching—Club

| | ERA | H | ER | BB | SO | ShO | SA |
|---|---|---|---|---|---|---|---|
| New York | 3.11 | 1304 | 513 | 509 | 1081 | 11 | 46 |
| Houston | 3.15 | 1196 | 508 | 518 | 1155 | 19 | 51 |
| San Francisco | 3.33 | 1264 | 541 | 591 | 992 | 10 | 35 |
| St. Louis | 3.37 | 1363 | 550 | 485 | 760 | 4 | 46 |
| Los Angeles | 3.76 | 1426 | 607 | 499 | 1051 | 14 | 25 |
| Montreal | 3.77 | 1349 | 614 | 566 | 1047 | 9 | 50 |
| Philadelphia | 3.87 | 1471 | 624 | 553 | 868 | 11 | 38 |
| Pittsburgh | 3.90 | 1394 | 628 | 567 | 913 | 9 | 30 |
| Cincinnati | 3.91 | 1465 | 638 | 524 | 917 | 8 | 45 |
| Atlanta | 3.98 | 1442 | 630 | 576 | 931 | 5 | 39 |
| San Diego | 4.00 | 1404 | 641 | 607 | 929 | 7 | 33 |
| Chicago | 4.48 | 1540 | 716 | 555 | 954 | 6 | 42 |

## MAJOR LEAGUE BASEBALL—1986

### AMERICAN LEAGUE PLAYOFFS—1986

**1st game, Boston, Massachusetts, October 7**

| California | 041 | 000 | 030 | — | 8 | 11 | 0 |
|---|---|---|---|---|---|---|---|
| Boston | 000 | 001 | 000 | — | 1 | 5 | 1 |

Witt; Clemens, Sambito (8), Stanley (9).
Winner: Witt. Loser: Clemens. Attendance: 32,993

**2nd game, Boston, Massachusetts, October 8**

| California | 000 | 110 | 000 | — | 2 | 11 | 3 |
|---|---|---|---|---|---|---|---|
| Boston | 110 | 010 | 33x | — | 9 | 13 | 2 |

McCaskill, Lucas (8), Corbett (8); Hurst
Winner: Hurst. Loser: McCaskill. Home Runs: California: Joyner; Boston: Rice. Attendance: 32,786

**3rd game, Anaheim, California, October 10**

| Boston | 010 | 000 | 020 | — | 3 | 9 | 1 |
|---|---|---|---|---|---|---|---|
| California | 000 | 001 | 31x | — | 5 | 8 | 0 |

Boyd, Sambito (7), Schiraldi (8); Candelaria, Moore (8).
Winner: Candelaria. Loser: Boyd. Home Runs: California: Schofield, Pettis. Attendance: 64,206

**4th game, Anaheim, California, October 11**

| Boston | 000 | 000 | 120 | 00 | — | 3 | 6 | 1 |
|---|---|---|---|---|---|---|---|---|
| California | 000 | 000 | 003 | 01 | — | 4 | 11 | 2 |

Clemens, Schiraldi (9); Sutton, Lucas (7), Rohle (7), Finley (8), Corbett (8).
Winner: Corbett. Loser: Schiraldi. Home Runs: California: DeCinces Attendance: 64,223

**5th game, Anaheim, California, October 12**

| Boston | 020 | 000 | 004 | 01 | — | 7 | 12 | 0 |
|---|---|---|---|---|---|---|---|---|
| California | 001 | 002 | 201 | 00 | — | 6 | 13 | 0 |

Hurst, Stanley (7), Sambito (9), Crawford (9), Scharldi (11); Witt, Lucas (9), Moore (9), Finley (11)
Winner: Crawford. Loser: Moore. Home Runs: Boston: Gedman, Baylor, Henderson; California: Boone, Grich. Attendance: 64,223

**6th game, Boston, Massachusetts, October 14**

| California | 200 | 000 | 110 | — | 4 | 11 | 1 |
|---|---|---|---|---|---|---|---|
| Boston | 205 | 010 | 20x | — | 10 | 16 | 1 |

McCaskill, Lucas (3), Corbett (4), Finley (7); Boyd, Stanley (8)
Winner: Boyd. Loser: McCaskill. Home Runs: California: Downing. Attendance: 32,998

**7th game, Boston, Massachusetts, October 15**

| California | 000 | 000 | 010 | — | 1 | 6 | 2 |
|---|---|---|---|---|---|---|---|
| Boston | 030 | 400 | 10x | — | 8 | 8 | 1 |

Candelaria, Sutton (4), Moore (8); Clemens, Schiraldi (8).
Winner: Clemens. Loser: Candelaria. Home Runs: Boston: Rice (2), Evans. Attendance: 33,001

### NATIONAL LEAGUE PLAYOFFS—1986

**1st game, Houston, Texas, October 8**

| New York | 000 | 000 | 000 | — | 0 | 5 | 0 |
|---|---|---|---|---|---|---|---|
| Houston | 010 | 000 | 00x | — | 1 | 7 | 1 |

Gooden, Orosco (8); Scott
Winner: Scott. Loser: Gooden. Home Run: Houston: Davis Attendance: 44,131

**2nd game, Houston, Texas, October 9**

| New York | 000 | 230 | 000 | — | 5 | 10 | 0 |
|---|---|---|---|---|---|---|---|
| Houston | 000 | 000 | 100 | — | 1 | 10 | 2 |

Ojeda; Ryan, Andersen (6), Lopez (8), Kerfeld (9)
Winner: Ojeda. Loser: Ryan. Attendance: 44,391

**3rd game, New York, New York, October 11**

| Houston | 220 | 000 | 100 | — | 5 | 8 | 1 |
|---|---|---|---|---|---|---|---|
| New York | 000 | 004 | 002 | — | 6 | 10 | 1 |

Knepper, Kerfeld (8), Smith (9); Darling, Aguilera (6), Orosco (8)
Winner: Orosco. Loser: Smith. Home Runs: Houston: Doran; New York: Strawberry, Dykstra. Attendance: 55,052

**4th game, New York, New York, October 12**

| Houston | 020 | 010 | 000 | — | 3 | 4 | 1 |
|---|---|---|---|---|---|---|---|
| New York | 000 | 000 | 010 | — | 1 | 3 | 0 |

Scott; Fernandez, McDowell (7), Sisk (9)
Winner: Scott. Loser: Fernandez. Home Runs: Houston: Ashby, Thon. Attendance: 55,038

**5th game, New York, New York, October 14**

| Houston | 000 | 010 | 000 | 000 | — | 1 | 9 | 1 |
|---|---|---|---|---|---|---|---|---|
| New York | 000 | 010 | 000 | 001 | — | 2 | 4 | 0 |

Ryan, Kerfeld (10); Gooden, Orosco (11)
Winner: Orosco. Loser: Ryan. Home Run: New York: Strawberry (2). Attendance: 54,986

**6th game, Houston, Texas, October 15**

| New York | 000 | 000 | 003 | 000 | 010 | 3 | — | 7 | 11 | 0 |
|---|---|---|---|---|---|---|---|---|---|---|
| Houston | 300 | 000 | 000 | 000 | 010 | 2 | — | 6 | 11 | 1 |

Ojeda, Aguilera (6), McDowell (9), Orosco (14); Knepper, Smith (9), Andersen (11), Lopez (14), Calhoun (16).
Winner: Orosco. Loser: Lopez. Home Run: Houston: Hatcher. Attendance: 45,718.

## NOLAN RYAN BREAKS 4,000 STRIKEOUT MARK

The date was July 11, 1985. The opponent, his original team, the New York Mets. The batter—former teammate Danny Heap. And when Heap swung and missed at an 0-2 curve ball in the top of the sixth inning of a game between the Mets and the Houston Astros, Nolan Ryan had become the first pitcher in the history of major league baseball to strike out 4,000 batters.

At the age of 38, Ryan, who also holds the record for most strikeouts in a season at 383 and who has hurled a record five no-hitters, was pitching in his 19th major league season. His career had included stops in New York with the Mets, California with the Angels, and Houston with the Astros.

When he won his 10th and final game of the 1985 season, bringing his career win total to 241, he had recorded a total of 209 strikeouts for the season and had a career total of 4,083. It also marked the 10th time in his career that he had struck out 200 or more batters.

## HENDERSON OF A'S SETS STOLEN-BASES RECORD

Rickey Henderson of the Oakland A's broke the major league record for stolen bases in one season on Aug. 27, 1982, at Milwaukee when he stole his 119th base in the third inning. The previous record of 118 was held by Lou Brock of St. Louis and was set in 1974. Henderson had broken the American League stolen-bases mark in 1980 when he surpassed Ty Cobb's record of 96, set in 1915. Henderson finished the 1980 season with 100 stolen bases. In 1982 he completed the season with 130. The major league record for career stolen bases is held by Brock with 938.

## WORLD SERIES—1986
### New York Mets (NL) defeated Boston Red Sox (AL), 4 games to 3
### 1st Game—New York, Oct. 18

| BOSTON (A) | AB | R | H | BI | | NEW YORK (N) | AB | R | H | BI |
|---|---|---|---|---|---|---|---|---|---|---|
| Boggs, 3b | 4 | 0 | 0 | 0 | | Wilson, lf | 4 | 0 | 1 | 0 |
| Barrett, 2b | 4 | 0 | 1 | 0 | | McDowell, p | 0 | 0 | 0 | 0 |
| Buckner, 1b | 4 | 0 | 1 | 0 | | Dykstra, cf | 3 | 0 | 0 | 0 |
| Stapleton, 1b | 0 | 0 | 0 | 0 | | Hernandez, 1b | 3 | 0 | 0 | 0 |
| Rice, lf | 2 | 1 | 1 | 0 | | Carter, c | 4 | 0 | 1 | 0 |
| Evans, rf | 3 | 0 | 0 | 0 | | Strawberry, rf | 2 | 0 | 0 | 0 |
| Gedman, c | 4 | 0 | 0 | 0 | | Knight, 3b | 3 | 0 | 0 | 0 |
| Henderson, cf | 4 | 0 | 2 | 0 | | Teufel, 2b | 3 | 0 | 2 | 0 |
| Owen, ss | 2 | 0 | 0 | 0 | | Backman, 2b | 1 | 0 | 0 | 0 |
| Hurst, p | 3 | 0 | 0 | 0 | | Santana, ss | 2 | 0 | 0 | 0 |
| Greenwell, ph | 1 | 0 | 0 | 0 | | Heep, ph | 1 | 0 | 0 | 0 |
| Schiraldi, p | 0 | 0 | 0 | 0 | | Darling, p | 2 | 0 | 0 | 0 |
| | | | | | | Mitchell, lf | 1 | 0 | 0 | 0 |
| **Total** | **31** | **1** | **5** | **0** | | **Total** | **29** | **0** | **4** | **0** |

| | | | | |
|---|---|---|---|---|
| Boston | 000 000 100 | | 1 5 0 |
| New York | 000 000 000 | | 0 4 1 |

Game-winning RBI—None. E—Teufel. DP—Boston 1, New York 1. LOB—Boston 8, New York 8. SB—Wilson (1), Strawberry (1). S—Santana.

| | IP | H | R | ER | BB | SO |
|---|---|---|---|---|---|---|
| **Boston** | | | | | | |
| Hurst W, 1-0 | 8 | 4 | 0 | 0 | 4 | 8 |
| Schiraldi S, 1 | 1 | 0 | 0 | 0 | 1 | 1 |
| **New York** | | | | | | |
| Darling, L, 0-1 | 7 | 3 | 1 | 0 | 3 | 8 |
| McDowell | 2 | 2 | 0 | 0 | 2 | 0 |

WP—Darling 2. Time of game—2:59. Attendance—55,076.

### 2nd Game—New York, Oct. 19

| BOSTON (A) | AB | R | H | BI | | NEW YORK (N) | AB | R | H | BI |
|---|---|---|---|---|---|---|---|---|---|---|
| Boggs, 3b | 5 | 1 | 2 | 2 | | Dykstra, cf | 3 | 0 | 1 | 0 |
| Barrett, 2b | 5 | 0 | 2 | 1 | | Backman, 2b | 3 | 1 | 2 | 1 |
| Buckner, 1b | 5 | 0 | 2 | 1 | | Hernandez, 1b | 4 | 0 | 1 | 1 |
| Stapleton, 1b | 1 | 0 | 0 | 0 | | Carter, c | 4 | 0 | 1 | 1 |
| Rice, lf | 6 | 2 | 3 | 0 | | Strawberry, rf | 4 | 0 | 0 | 0 |
| Evans, lf | 4 | 2 | 2 | 2 | | Heep, lf | 2 | 0 | 0 | 0 |
| Gedman, c | 5 | 0 | 1 | 0 | | Aguilera, p | 0 | 0 | 0 | 0 |
| Henderson, cf | 5 | 2 | 3 | 2 | | Orosco, p | 0 | 0 | 0 | 0 |
| Owen, ss | 4 | 1 | 3 | 1 | | Mazzilli, ph | 1 | 0 | 0 | 0 |
| Romero, ss | 0 | 0 | 0 | 0 | | Fernandez, p | 0 | 0 | 0 | 0 |
| Clemens, p | 1 | 1 | 0 | 0 | | Sisk, p | 0 | 0 | 0 | 0 |
| Crawford, p | 1 | 0 | 0 | 0 | | Johnson, 3b | 4 | 0 | 0 | 0 |
| Greenwell, ph | 1 | 0 | 0 | 0 | | Santana, ss | 4 | 1 | 2 | 0 |
| Stanley, p | 1 | 0 | 0 | 0 | | Gooden, p | 2 | 1 | 1 | 0 |
| | | | | | | Wilson, lf | 2 | 0 | 0 | 0 |
| **Total** | **44** | **9** | **18** | **9** | | **Total** | **33** | **3** | **8** | **3** |

| | | | | |
|---|---|---|---|---|
| Boston | 003 120 201 | | 9 18 0 |
| New York | 002 010 000 | | 3 8 1 |

Game-winning RBI—Boggs (1). E—Hernandez. DP—New York 1. LOB—Boston 13, New York 9. 2B—Boggs 2. HR—Henderson (1), Evans (1). S—Dykstra, Clemens.

| | IP | H | R | ER | BB | SO |
|---|---|---|---|---|---|---|
| **Boston** | | | | | | |
| Clemens | 4 1/3 | 5 | 3 | 3 | 4 | 3 |
| Crawford W, 1-0 | 1 2/3 | 1 | 0 | 0 | 0 | 2 |
| Stanley S, 1 | 3 | 2 | 0 | 0 | 1 | 3 |

| **New York** | IP | H | R | ER | BB | SO |
|---|---|---|---|---|---|---|
| Gooden L, 0-1 | 5 | 8 | 6 | 5 | 2 | 6 |
| Aguilera | 1 | 5 | 2 | 2 | 1 | 1 |
| Orosco | 2 | 2 | 0 | 0 | 0 | 3 |
| Fernandez | 1/3 | 3 | 1 | 1 | 0 | 1 |
| Sisk | 2/3 | 0 | 0 | 0 | 1 | 1 |

Time of game—3:36. Attendance—55,063.

### 3rd Game—Boston, Oct. 21

| NEW YORK (N) | AB | R | H | BI | | BOSTON (A) | AB | R | H | BI |
|---|---|---|---|---|---|---|---|---|---|---|
| Dykstra, cf | 5 | 2 | 4 | 1 | | Boggs, 3b | 3 | 0 | 1 | 0 |
| Backman, 2b | 5 | 1 | 1 | 0 | | Barrett, 2b | 4 | 0 | 2 | 1 |
| Hernandez, 1b | 4 | 1 | 2 | 0 | | Buckner, 1b | 4 | 0 | 0 | 0 |
| Carter, c | 5 | 1 | 2 | 3 | | Rice, lf | 3 | 0 | 0 | 0 |
| Strawberry, rf | 4 | 1 | 1 | 0 | | Baylor, dh | 4 | 0 | 1 | 0 |
| Knight, 3b | 4 | 0 | 1 | 1 | | Evans, rf | 4 | 0 | 0 | 0 |
| Heep, dh | 3 | 0 | 1 | 2 | | Gedman, c | 4 | 0 | 1 | 0 |
| Mitchell, ph | 0 | 0 | 0 | 0 | | Henderson, cf | 2 | 1 | 1 | 0 |
| Mazzilli, ph | 1 | 0 | 0 | 0 | | Owen, ss | 3 | 0 | 0 | 0 |
| Wilson, lf | 4 | 0 | 0 | 0 | | | | | | |
| Santana, ss | 4 | 1 | 1 | 0 | | | | | | |
| **Total** | **39** | **7** | **13** | **7** | | **Total** | **31** | **1** | **5** | **1** |

| | | | | |
|---|---|---|---|---|
| New York | 400 000 210 | | 7 13 0 |
| Boston | 001 000 000 | | 1 5 0 |

Game-winning RBI—Dykstra (1). E—None. DP—New York 1, Boston 1. LOB—New York 6, Boston 6. 2B—Carter, Baylor, Knight. HR—Dykstra (1).

| | IP | H | R | ER | BB | SO |
|---|---|---|---|---|---|---|
| **New York** | | | | | | |
| Ojeda W, 1-0 | 7 | 5 | 1 | 1 | 3 | 6 |
| McDowell | 2 | 0 | 0 | 0 | 0 | 0 |
| **Boston** | | | | | | |
| Boyd L, 0-1 | 7 | 9 | 6 | 6 | 1 | 3 |
| Sambito | 0 | 2 | 1 | 1 | 0 | 0 |
| Stanley | 2 | 2 | 0 | 0 | 0 | 1 |

WP—Ojeda, Sambito. Time of game—2:58. Attendance—33,595.

### 4th Game—Boston, Oct. 22

| NEW YORK (N) | AB | R | H | BI | | BOSTON (A) | AB | R | H | BI |
|---|---|---|---|---|---|---|---|---|---|---|
| Dykstra, cf | 5 | 1 | 1 | 2 | | Boggs, 3b | 5 | 0 | 0 | 0 |
| Backman, 2b | 4 | 1 | 2 | 0 | | Barrett, 2b | 4 | 0 | 2 | 0 |
| Hernandez, 1b | 3 | 0 | 0 | 0 | | Buckner, 1b | 5 | 0 | 0 | 0 |
| Carter, c | 4 | 2 | 3 | 3 | | Rice, lf | 4 | 1 | 1 | 0 |
| Strawberry, rf | 4 | 1 | 2 | 0 | | Baylor, dh | 3 | 0 | 0 | 0 |
| Knight, 3b | 4 | 0 | 2 | 1 | | Evans, rf | 3 | 1 | 1 | 1 |
| Heep, dh | 4 | 0 | 0 | 0 | | Gedman, c | 4 | 0 | 3 | 0 |
| Wilson, lf | 4 | 1 | 2 | 0 | | Henderson, cf | 3 | 0 | 0 | 1 |
| Santana, ss | 4 | 0 | 0 | 0 | | Owen, ss | 1 | 0 | 0 | 0 |
| | | | | | | Greenwell, ph | 0 | 0 | 0 | 0 |
| | | | | | | Romero, ss | 0 | 0 | 0 | 0 |
| **Total** | **36** | **6** | **12** | **6** | | **Total** | **32** | **2** | **7** | **2** |

| | | | | |
|---|---|---|---|---|
| New York | 000 300 210 | | 6 12 0 |
| Boston | 000 000 020 | | 2 7 1 |

Game-winning RBI—Carter (1). E—Gedman. DP—Boston 2. LOB—New York 4, Boston 11. 2B—Barrett, Gedman, Strawberry, Carter, Rice. HR—Carter 2(2), Dykstra (2). SB—Backman (1), Wilson 2(3). SF—Henderson.

| New York | IP | H | R | ER | BB | SO |
|---|---|---|---|---|---|---|
| Darling W, 1-1 | 7 | 4 | 0 | 0 | 6 | 4 |
| McDowell | 2/3 | 3 | 2 | 2 | 1 | 0 |
| Orosco S, 1 | 1 1/3 | 0 | 0 | 0 | 0 | 1 |
| **Boston** | | | | | | |
| Nipper L, 0-1 | 6 | 7 | 3 | 3 | 1 | 2 |
| Crawford | 2 | 4 | 3 | 3 | 0 | 2 |
| Stanley | 1 | 1 | 0 | 0 | 0 | 0 |

Time of game—3:22. Attendance—33,920.

New York    000 020 010 3   6 8 2

Game-winning RBI—None. E—Evans, Knight, Elster Gedman, Buckner. DP—Boston 1, New York 1. LOB—Boston 14, New York 8. 2B—Evans, Boggs. HR—Henderson (2). SB—Strawberry 2 (3). S—Owen, Dykstra, Backman. SF—Carter.

| | IP | H | R | ER | BB | SO |
|---|---|---|---|---|---|---|
| **Boston** | | | | | | |
| Clemens | 7 | 4 | 2 | 1 | 2 | 8 |
| Schiraldi L, 0-1 | *2 2/3 | 4 | 4 | 3 | 2 | 1 |
| Stanley | 0 | 0 | 0 | 0 | 0 | 0 |
| **New York** | | | | | | |
| Ojeda | 6 | 8 | 2 | 2 | 2 | 3 |
| McDowell | 1 2/3 | 2 | 1 | 0 | 3 | 1 |
| Orosco | 1/3 | 0 | 0 | 0 | 0 | 0 |
| Aguilera W, 1-0 | 2 | 3 | 2 | 2 | 0 | 3 |

*Two outs when winning run scored. Stanley pitched to one batter in the 10th. HBP—Buckner by Aguilera. WP—Stanley. Time of game—4:02. Attendance—55,078.

## 5th Game—Boston, Oct. 24

| NEW YORK (N) | AB | R | H | BI |
|---|---|---|---|---|
| Dykstra, cf | 5 | 0 | 1 | 0 |
| Teufel, 2b | 4 | 1 | 2 | 1 |
| Hernandez, 1b | 4 | 0 | 1 | 0 |
| Carter, c | 4 | 0 | 0 | 0 |
| Strawberry, rf | 4 | 0 | 1 | 0 |
| Knight, 3b | 4 | 0 | 1 | 0 |
| Mitchell, dh | 4 | 0 | 1 | 0 |
| Wilson, lf | 4 | 1 | 2 | 0 |
| Santana, ss | 2 | 0 | 1 | 1 |
| **Total** | 35 | 2 | 10 | 2 |

| BOSTON (A) | AB | R | H | BI |
|---|---|---|---|---|
| Boggs, 3b | 5 | 0 | 2 | 0 |
| Barrett, 2b | 4 | 0 | 2 | 0 |
| Buckner, 1b | 5 | 1 | 1 | 0 |
| Stapleton, 1b | 0 | 0 | 0 | 0 |
| Rice, lf | 3 | 1 | 2 | 0 |
| Baylor, dh | 3 | 1 | 1 | 1 |
| Evans, rf | 4 | 0 | 2 | 1 |
| Gedman, c | 4 | 0 | 0 | 0 |
| Henderson, cf | 4 | 1 | 2 | 1 |
| Owen, ss | 3 | 0 | 0 | 1 |
| **Total** | 35 | 4 | 12 | 4 |

New York    000 000 011   2 10 1
Boston      011 020 00x   4 12 0

Game-winning RBI—Owen (1). E—Santana. DP—Boston 1. LOB—New York 8, Boston 11. 2B—Teufel, Henderson, Barrett, Wilson. 3B—Henderson. Rice. HR—Teufel (1). S—Santana. SF—Owen.

| | IP | H | R | ER | BB | SO |
|---|---|---|---|---|---|---|
| **New York** | | | | | | |
| Gooden L, 0-2 | 4 | 9 | 4 | 3 | 2 | 3 |
| Fernandez | 4 | 3 | 0 | 0 | 0 | 5 |
| **Boston** | | | | | | |
| Hurst W, 2-0 | 9 | 10 | 2 | 2 | 1 | 6 |

Gooden pitched to 3 batters in the 5th. HBP—Baylor by Gooden. Time of game—3:09. Attendance—34,010.

## 6th Game—New York, Oct. 25

| BOSTON (A) | AB | R | H | BI |
|---|---|---|---|---|
| Boggs, 3b | 5 | 2 | 3 | 0 |
| Barrett, 2b | 4 | 1 | 3 | 2 |
| Buckner, 1b | 5 | 0 | 0 | 0 |
| Rice, lf | 5 | 0 | 0 | 0 |
| Evans, rf | 4 | 0 | 1 | 2 |
| Gedman, c | 5 | 0 | 1 | 0 |
| Henderson, cf | 5 | 1 | 2 | 1 |
| Owen, ss | 4 | 1 | 3 | 0 |
| Clemens, p | 3 | 0 | 0 | 0 |
| Greenwell, ph | 1 | 0 | 0 | 0 |
| Schiraldi, p | 0 | 0 | 0 | 0 |
| Stanley, p | 0 | 0 | 0 | 0 |
| **Total** | 42 | 5 | 13 | 5 |

| NEW YORK (N) | AB | R | H | BI |
|---|---|---|---|---|
| Dykstra, cf | 4 | 0 | 0 | 0 |
| Backman, 2b | 4 | 0 | 1 | 0 |
| Hernandez, 1b | 4 | 0 | 1 | 0 |
| Carter, c | 4 | 1 | 1 | 1 |
| Strawberry, rf | 2 | 1 | 0 | 0 |
| Aguilera, p | 0 | 0 | 0 | 0 |
| Mitchell, ph | 1 | 1 | 1 | 0 |
| Knight, 3b | 4 | 2 | 2 | 2 |
| Wilson, lf | 5 | 0 | 1 | 0 |
| Santana, ss | 1 | 0 | 0 | 0 |
| Heep, ph | 1 | 0 | 0 | 0 |
| Elster, ss | 1 | 0 | 0 | 0 |
| Johnson, ss | 1 | 0 | 0 | 0 |
| Ojeda, p | 2 | 0 | 0 | 0 |
| McDowell, p | 0 | 0 | 0 | 0 |
| Orosco, p | 0 | 0 | 0 | 0 |
| Mazzilli, rf | 2 | 1 | 1 | 0 |
| **Total** | 36 | 6 | 8 | 3 |

Boston      110 000 100 2   5 13 3

## 7th Game—Boston, Oct. 27

| BOSTON (A) | AB | R | H | BI |
|---|---|---|---|---|
| Boggs, 3b | 4 | 0 | 1 | 1 |
| Barrett, 2b | 5 | 0 | 1 | 0 |
| Buckner, 1b | 4 | 1 | 2 | 0 |
| Rice, lf | 4 | 1 | 2 | 0 |
| Evans, rf | 4 | 1 | 2 | 3 |
| Gedman, c | 4 | 1 | 1 | 1 |
| Henderson, cf | 2 | 1 | 0 | 0 |
| Owen, ss | 3 | 0 | 0 | 0 |
| Baylor, ph | 1 | 0 | 0 | 0 |
| Nipper, p | 0 | 0 | 0 | 0 |
| Crawford, p | 0 | 0 | 0 | 0 |
| Hurst, p | 0 | 0 | 0 | 0 |
| Armas, ph | 1 | 0 | 0 | 0 |
| Schiraldi, p | 0 | 0 | 0 | 0 |
| Sambito, p | 0 | 0 | 0 | 0 |
| Stanley, p | 0 | 0 | 0 | 0 |
| Romero, ss | 1 | 0 | 0 | 0 |
| **Total** | 33 | 5 | 9 | 5 |

| NEW YORK (N) | AB | R | H | BI |
|---|---|---|---|---|
| Wilson, cf | 3 | 1 | 1 | 0 |
| Teufel, 2b | 2 | 0 | 0 | 0 |
| Backman, 2b | 1 | 1 | 1 | 0 |
| Hernandez, 1b | 4 | 0 | 1 | 3 |
| Carter, c | 4 | 0 | 0 | 1 |
| Strawberry, rf | 4 | 1 | 1 | 1 |
| Knight, 3b | 4 | 2 | 3 | 1 |
| Mitchell, lf | 2 | 0 | 0 | 0 |
| Dykstra, cf | 3 | 1 | 1 | 0 |
| Santana, ss | 3 | 1 | 1 | 1 |
| Darling, p | 1 | 0 | 0 | 0 |
| Fernandez, p | 0 | 0 | 0 | 0 |
| Mazzilli, ph | 1 | 1 | 1 | 0 |
| McDowell, p | 0 | 0 | 0 | 0 |
| Orosco, p | 1 | 0 | 1 | 1 |
| **Total** | 32 | 8 | 10 | 8 |

Boston      030 000 020   5 9 0
New York    000 003 32x   8 10 0

Game-winning RBI—Knight (1). LOB—Boston 6, New York 8. 2B—Evans. HR—Evans (2), Gedman (1), Knight (1), Strawberry (1). S—Hurst 2, McDowell. SF—Hernandez.

| | IP | H | R | ER | BB | SO |
|---|---|---|---|---|---|---|
| **Boston** | | | | | | |
| Hurst | 6 | 4 | 3 | 3 | 1 | 3 |
| Schiraldi L, 0-2 | 1/3 | 3 | 3 | 3 | 0 | 0 |
| Sambito | 1/3 | 0 | 0 | 0 | 2 | 0 |
| Stanley | 1/3 | 0 | 0 | 0 | 0 | 0 |
| Nipper | 1/3 | 3 | 2 | 2 | 1 | 0 |
| Crawford | 2/3 | 0 | 0 | 0 | 0 | 0 |
| **New York** | | | | | | |
| Darling | 3 2/3 | 6 | 3 | 3 | 1 | 0 |
| Fernandez | 2 1/3 | 1 | 0 | 0 | 1 | 4 |
| McDowell W, 1-0 | 1 | 3 | 2 | 2 | 0 | 1 |
| Orosco S, 2 | 2 | 0 | 0 | 0 | 0 | 2 |

McDowell pitched to 3 batters in the 8th. HBP—Henderson by Darling, Wilson by Crawford. WP—Schiraldi. Time of game—3:11. Attendance—55,032.

# CHESS

## WORLD CHAMPIONS

| | |
|---|---|
| 1894–1921 | Emanuel Lasker, Germany |
| 1921–27 | Jose R. Capablanca, Cuba |
| 1927–35 | Alexander A. Alekhine, U.S.S.R. |
| 1935–37 | Dr. Max Euwe, Netherlands |
| 1937–46 | Alexander A. Alekhine, U.S.S.R.[1] |
| 1948–57 | Mikhail Botvinnik, U.S.S.R. |
| 1957–58 | Vassily Smyslov, U.S.S.R. |
| 1958–60 | Mikhail Botvinnik, U.S.S.R. |
| 1960–61 | Mikhail Tal, U.S.S.R. |
| 1961–63 | Mikhail Botvinnik, U.S.S.R. |
| 1963–68 | Tigran Petrosian, U.S.S.R. |
| 1969–71 | Boris Spassky, U.S.S.R. |
| 1972–74 | Bobby Fischer, Los Angeles |
| 1975 | Bobby Fischer[2], Anatoly Karpov, U.S.S.R. |
| 1976–85 | Anatoly Karpov, U.S.S.R.[3] |
| 1985– | Gary Kasparov, U.S.S.R. |

1. Alekhine, a French citizen, died while champion. 2. Relinquished title. 3. In 1978, Karpov defeated Viktor Korchnoi 6 games to 5.

## UNITED STATES CHAMPIONS

| | |
|---|---|
| 1909–36 | Frank J. Marshall, New York |
| 1936–44 | Samuel Reshevsky, New York[1] |
| 1944–46 | Arnold S. Denker, New York |
| 1946 | Samuel Reshevsky, Boston |
| 1948 | Herman Steiner, Los Angeles |
| 1951–52 | Larry Evan, New York |

| | |
|---|---|
| 1954–57 | Arthur Bisguier, New York |
| 1958–61 | Bobby Fischer, Brooklyn, N.Y. |
| 1962 | Larry Evans, New York |
| 1963–67 | Bobby Fischer, New York |
| 1968 | Larry Evans, New York |
| 1969–71 | Samuel Reshevsky, Spring Valley, N.Y. |
| 1972 | Robert Byrne, Ossining, N.Y. |
| 1973 | Lubomir Kavelek, Washington; John Grefe, San Francisco |
| 1974–77 | Walter Browne, Berkeley, Calif. |
| 1978–79 | Lubomir Kavalek, New York |
| 1980 | Tie, Walter Browne, Berkeley, Calif. Larry Christiansen, Modesto, Calif. Larry Evans, Reno, Nev. |
| 1981–82[2] | Tie, Walter Browne, Berkeley, Calif. Yasser Seirawan, Seattle, Wash. |
| 1983 | Tie, Walter Browne, Berkeley, Calif. Larry Christiansen, Los Angeles, Calif., Roman Dzindzichashvili, Corona, N.Y. |
| 1984–85 | Lev Alburt, New York City[3] |

1. In 1942, Isaac I. Kashdan of New York was co-champion for a while because of a tie with Reshevsky in that year's tournament. Reshevsky won the play-off. 2. Championship not contested in 1982. 3. 1986 United States Championship tournament set for November, after *Information Please* went to press.

# GYMNASTICS

## AMERICAN CUP CHAMPIONSHIPS—1986

(Fairfax, Va., March 1-2, 1986)

### Men's Events

| | Pts |
|---|---|
| All-Around—Alexsei Tikhonkin, Soviet Union | 58.350 |
| Floor exercise—Brian Ginsberg, United States | 9.80 |
| Parallel bars—Alexsei Tikhonkin, Soviet Union | 9.90 |
| Pommel horse—Wang Chongsheng, China, and Tim Daggett, United States (tie) | 9.850 |
| Still rings—Brian Ginsberg, United States | 9.750 |
| Vault—Tikhonkin, Soviet Union, Ginsberg, United States, and Laurent Barbieri, France (tie) | 9.60 |
| Horizontal bars—Tikhonkin, Soviet Union, and Chongsheng, China (tie) | 9.90 |

### Women's events

| | Pts |
|---|---|
| All-around—Kristie Phillips, United States | 38.7750 |
| Floor exercise—Kristie Phillips, United States | 9.80 |
| Vault—Kristie Phillips, United States | 9.850 |
| Uneven bars—Irina Baraksanova, Soviet Union | 9.650 |
| Balance beam—Kristie Phillips, United States, and Borjana Stojanova, Bulgaria | 9.675 |

## WORLD CHAMPIONSHIPS—1985

(Montreal, Canada, Nov. 3-10, 1985)

### Men's Events

| | Pts |
|---|---|
| All-around—Yuri Korolev, Soviet Union | 117.850 |
| Floor exercise—Tong Fei, China | 19.750 |
| High bar—Tong Fei, China | 19.850 |

| | Pts |
|---|---|
| Still Rings—Li Ning, China, and Yuri Korolev, Soviet Union (tie) | 19.750 |
| Pommell horse—Valentin Mogilnyi, Soviet Union | 19.750 |
| Parallel bars—Sylvio Kroll, West Germany | 19.800 |
| Vault—Yuri Korolev, Soviet Union | 19.625 |
| Team—Soviet Union | |

### Women's Events

| | Pts |
|---|---|
| All-around—Elena Shoushounova, Soviet Union and Oksana Omeliantchik, Soviet Union (tie) | 78.663 |
| Floor exercise—Oksana Omeliantchik, Soviet Union | 19.900 |
| Balance beam—Daniela Silivas, Romania | 19.813 |
| Uneven bars—Gabriele Fahrnich, West Germany | 19.938 |
| Vault—Elena Shoushounova, Soviet Union | 19.826 |
| Team—Soviet Union | |

# CURLING

## UNITED STATES CHAMPIONSHIPS—1986

Men (Seattle, Wash, March 10-16, 1986)—Madison, Wisc, Steve Brown skip (defeated North Dakota, 8-5 in final)

Women (Chicago, Ill. March, 1986)—St. Paul, Minn., Gerri Tilden skip (defeated North Dakota, 9-7 in final)

## WORLD CHAMPIONSHIPS—1986

Men (Toronto, Canada, March 31-April 6) Canada, Eddie Lukowich skip (defeated Scotland, 4-3, in final)

Women (Kelowana, B.C., Canada March 24-30) Canada, Marilyn Darte skid (defeated West Germany 12-5 in final)

# CURRENT EVENTS

## What Happened in 1985-86

Highlights of the important events of the year from September 1985 to August 1986, organized month by month, in three categories for easy reference. The Countries of the World section (starting on page 144) covers specific international events, country by country.

## 1985-86

### SEPTEMBER 1985

#### International

**Pol Pot Retires From Khmer Rouge (Sept. 2):** Cambodian rebel movement says country's former ruler during reign of terror will assume military advisory role.

**Riots Strike Birmingham, England (Sept. 9):** Black youths, mostly of West Indian descent, and whites rampage through Handsworth section of northern industrial city, looting Asian-owned shops and starting fires. **(Sept. 10):** Youths hurl bottles at British Home Secretary Douglas Hurd on second straight day of violence. **(Sept. 11):** City calms down as workers clear debris. Police report 137 arrests in rioting, with more than 1,400 officers confronting youths as Asian and West Indian descent. Sporadic violence flares in other cities.

**Reagan Announces South Africa Sanctions (Sept. 9):** President adopts major reversal of position, accepting most trade and financial steps against apartheid sought by Congress, including ban on sale of computers to security forces and most loans to Pretoria.

**Eleven European Nations Order Sanctions on South Africa (Sept. 10):** Agree to trade, cultural, and military embargoes, including ban on arms and law-enforcement equipment and nuclear cooperation.

**Senate G.O.P. Blocks Tough Pretoria Curbs (Sept. 11):** Leadership turns back Democratic move for vote on Congressional version of economic sanctions.

**Three Soviet Astronauts in Orbit (Sept. 17):** Rocket to join two others who brought *Salyut 7* space station back to life. *Soyuz T-14* transport launched under command of Lieut. Col. Vladimir V. Vasyutin, 33. Also aboard are Lieut. Col. Aleksandr A. Volkov, researcher, 37, and Georgi M. Grechko, 54, veteran astronaut.

**American Hostage in Lebanon Freed (Sept. 18):** Rev. Benjamin Weir, 61, Presbyterian minister, rejoins family in U.S. after 16 months. **(Sept. 19):** Weir tells President that Shiite militants will hold remaining hostages until U.S. obtains release of 17 terrorists held prisoner by Kuwait.

**Thousands Killed in Mexican Earthquake (Sept. 19):** Shock strikes central and southwestern areas and devastates parts of Mexico City and three coastal states. Disrupts travel, commerce, and communications, with heavy toll of life and property. **(Sept. 21):** More buildings collapse in capital as second quake hits. **(Oct. 2):** Official death toll set at more than 5,500. Government faces resentment and new crises.

**Greenpeace Scandal Rocks France (Sept. 20):** Defense Minister Charles Hernu resigns and intelligence agency chief, Adm. Pierre Lacoste, is dismissed in political crisis surrounding sabotage of antinuclear protest ship in New Zealand. **(Sept. 22):** Prime Minister Laurent Fabius admits intelligence agents sank *Rainbow Warrior* but does not say who gave order.

**Russian Official Slain in Lebanon (Sept. 30):** Four Soviet diplomats abducted in West Beirut. **(Oct. 2):** Moscow identifies man found slain as one of four victims. Kremlin holds Israel indirectly responsible.

#### National

**GTE Company Accused on Pentagon Documents (Sept. 10):** Government Systems Corporation, a leading maker of electronic warfare devices, accused by U.S. of conspiring to obtain internal planning data.

**U.S. Tests First Anti-Satellite Weapon (Sept. 13):** Air Force Missile destroys orbiting derelict satellite 290 miles above Pacific. F-15 fighter launches rocket.

**U.S. Becomes a Debtor Country (Sept. 16):** Commerce Department shows nation owes foreigners more than they owe it for first time since World War I. Foreign investments rose $39.5 billion in first half of year.

**Reagan Proposes Export Subsidies (Sept. 23):** Announces plan to open foreign markets to American goods.

#### General

**Hurricane Inflicts Wide Damage on Mississippi Coast (Sept. 2):** Elena uproots trees and badly damages buildings in Biloxi and Gulfport after four days of uncertainty for millions from Sarasota, Fla., to New Orleans. Warnings prevent deaths or serious injuries when storm hits shore. Elena blamed for three deaths earlier in Florida.

**Human Heart Replaces Artificial One (Sept. 7):** Michael Drummond, 25, undergoes experimental operation at University of Arizona Medical Center after team rushes new organ to Tucson from Tyler, Tex.

**Spacecraft First to Fly Through Comet's Tail (Sept. 11):** *International Cometary Explorer* glides through magnetic turbulence and high-energy particles surrounding comet Giacobini-Zinner, relatively small object speeding from sun 44 million miles from earth, and sending back scientific data "rich in detail." **(Sept. 13):** Spacecraft detects charged water and carbon monoxide particles and sprinkling of tiny dust particles.

**Musicians Play to Aid Farmers (Sept. 22):** Top rock and country performers appear at Champaign, Ill., in 14-hour Farm Aid to raise money and stress plight.

# OCTOBER 1985

## International

**Israel Bombs P.L.O. Headquarters (Oct. 1):** Planes fly 1,500 miles for attack in Tunisia to avenge slaying of three Israelis on Cyprus. Sixty reported killed. White House calls foray "legitimate response" to terrorism. **(Oct. 2):** Backing down, U.S. calls raid "understandable" but agrees that the bombing cannot be condoned.

**Tourist Ship Hijacked; American Killed (Oct. 7):** Four armed men seize *Achille Lauro,* Italian tourist vessel, with 400 aboard, in Mediterranean. They demand release of 50 prisoners held in Israel. Threaten to kill passengers. **(Oct. 9):** Leon Klinghoffer, 69, of New York, killed and thrown overboard. Hijackers surrender in Egypt. **(Oct. 10):** U.S. Navy planes intercept Egyptian plane carrying hijackers to Tunisia and force it to land in Sicily. **(Oct. 11):** Italy charges them with murder and kidnapping. **(Oct. 12):** Mohammed Abbas, high Palestinian official suspected of involvement, leaves Italy for Yugoslavia soon after U.S. arrest warrant is issued. **(Oct. 14):** Abbas reported to have gone on to Southern Yemen.

**U.S. Limits World Court Role (Oct. 7):** Ends policy of automatic compliance with decisions of International Court of Justice. State Department charges abuse for "political ends," particularly by Nicaragua.

**U.N. Marks 40th Anniversary (Oct. 14):** Opens 10-day commemorative session designed to attract 80 heads of state and government and special envoys. Threatened with U.S. boycott, U.N. drops resolution to invite P.L.O. leader Yasir Arafat. **(Oct. 24):** On anniversary date, members fail to agree on universal declaration of purpose over Palestinian question. President Reagan, in General Assembly address, asks "fresh-start" in U.S.-Soviet relations. Links progress in East-West understanding to resolution of fighting in Afghanistan, Angola, Cambodia, Ethiopia, and Nicaragua, denouncing "Marxist-Leninism's war with the people," and calls on Soviet Union to help resolve those conflicts.

**Hijacking Topples Italian Government (Oct. 16):** Political crisis develops when small Republican Party quits five-party coalition to protest government's action in takeover by Palestinians of cruise ship *Achille Lauro* and release of Palestinian leader. **(Oct. 17):** Prime Minister Bettino Craxi resigns, bitter at U.S. over use of unauthorized plane to follow Egyptian airliner taking senior Palestinian official and associate from Sicily to Rome. **(Oct. 21):** President Francesco Cossiga asks Craxi to form new government.

**Black Activist Hanged in South Africa (Oct. 18):** Benjamin Moloise, 30, supporter of African National Congress, executed for role in 1982 murder of security policeman despite international appeals for clemency. Hundreds of blacks riot in downtown Johannesburg. Two white policemen stabbed, black man shot by security force, and whites are beaten.

**Rebels Release Duarte's Daughter (Oct. 24):** El Salvador leftists free Inés Guadalupe Duarte and companion, abducted Sept. 10, after agreement by which government of President José Napoleón Duarte releases 22 political prisoners.

**Three Russians Freed in Beirut (Oct. 30):** Moslem captors release trio from Soviet Embassy a month after abduction with fourth colleague, later slain.

## National

**Secretary Named Envoy to Ireland (Oct. 1):** President announces Mrs. Margaret M. Heckler will leave post at Health and Human Services as reward for "fine job." Denies reports of Administration dissatisfaction with her performance.

**Two Plead Guilty in Navy Spy Case (Oct. 28):** John A. Walker Jr., 48, admits charges that he spied for Soviet Union and recruited his son, Michael I. Walker, 22, a brother, and a friend into an operation called one of most damaging in U.S. history. John Walker sentenced to life in prison. Under plea agreement, federal judge in Baltimore agrees to reduced sentence of 25 years for son.

**U.S. Arrests Oregon Guru (Oct. 28):** Bhagwan Shree Rajneesh, 53, from India, held at Charlotte, N.C. He is under indictment for conspiring to violate immigration laws. Agents say he was trying to flee country.

## General

**Fourth Space Shuttle Flies Secret Mission (Oct. 3):** *Atlantis,* final craft in nation's winged spaceship fleet, takes off from Cape Canaveral, Fla., with five military officers aboard. Timing and plans for orbiting kept secret under Pentagon security rules. Commander is Air Force Col. Karol J. Bobko, flying third space shuttle mission. Air Force Lieut. Col. Ronald J. Grabe is pilot. Other crew members are: Marine Maj. David C. Hilmers; Air Force Maj. William A. Pailes, and Army Lieut. Col. Robert C. Stewart. **(Oct. 7):** *Atlantis* lands safely at Edwards Air Force Base, Calif. Primary military goal said to be launching of communications satellites for Department of Defense. Shuttle also carried civilian experiment to test effect of cosmic rays on crew and craft.

**Many Dead in Puerto Rico Landslide (Oct. 6):** One-hundred fifty estimated buried in hillside shantytown at Ponce as heavy rains pound island, starting floods. **(Oct. 9):** Gov. Rafel Hernández Colón proclaims emergency, declaring disaster "worst tragedy ever to strike island." **(Oct. 9):** Five thousand mourn dead at ceremony. Health officials seek to seal valley floor.

**U.S. Jury Upholds National Review (Oct. 25):** Mixed verdict finds that Liberty Lobby had libeled William F. Buckley, Jr.,'s publication and awards $1,000 in punitive damages and $1 in nominal damages. *National Review* had sought $16 million on four counts.

**Shuttle Flies International Mission (Oct. 30):** Largest space shuttle crew ever, five Americans, two West Germans, and a Dutchman, orbit aboard *Challenger* from Cape Canaveral, Fla. West Germany planned and directed it from control center near Munich D-1 (for Deutschland), first manned space flight managed by country other than U.S. or Soviet Union. Five Americans are: Henry W. Hartsfield, Jr., 51, commander; Lieut. Col. Steven R. Nagel, 39, of Air Force, pilot; Dr. Bonnie J. Dunbar, 36, biomedical engineer; Col. James F. Buchli, 40, of Marine Corps, and Col. Guion S. Bluford, Jr., 42, of Air Force, a doctor of aerospace engineering. Germans are: Dr. Ernst Messerschmid, 40, and Dr. Reinhard Furrer, 44, both physicists. Dr. Wubbo J. Ockels, 39, Netherlands physicist, represents 11-nation European Space Agency. **(Nov. 6):** *Challenger* lands safely at Edwards Air Force Base, Calif., after testing new nose wheel steering system. Week included complex experiments in metallurgy, crystal growth, biology, and human physiology.

# NOVEMBER 1985

## International

**South Africa Curbs Reporters (Nov. 2):** Imposes sweeping restrictions on local and foreign journalists. Government bars television crews, photographers, and radio reporters from areas of unrest covered by emergency decree and restricts press reporters. Heavy prison sentences and fines ordered.

**Roman Catholics and Jews Reach Accord (Nov. 2):** Agree in Vatican-sponsored dialogue on joint program "to overcome residues of indifference, resistance, and suspicion." Pact eases strained relations.

**Two French Agents Admit Guilt (Nov. 4):** Prosecution drops murder charges in sinking of *Greenpeace* flagship and death of crewman against Maj. Alain Mafart, 34, and Capt. Dominique Prieur, 36, after pleas on manslaughter charges.

**Defector Returning to Russia (Nov. 4):** Vitaly Yurchenko of K.G.B., described as one of most senior Soviet intelligence officers to turn to West, announces plan to go home. Tells press he was kidnapped in Rome, drugged, and held prisoner in U.S. by C.I.A.

**Dead and Missing 25,000 in Volcanic Eruption (Nov. 14):** Floods of water and mud bury thousands in Colombia as snow-capped peak, rumbling for months, explodes overnight in two blasts. Walls of mud sweep through valleys surrounding 16,200-foot Nevada de Ruiz volcano 85 miles northwest of Bogotá. Floods bury most of town of Armero and devastate Chinchiná. (**Nov. 16**): Thousands flee towns in path of cascades of mud. Dead and missing include 8,000 children. (**Nov. 17**): Search reported suspended, with many feared to be buried alive.

**Reagan and Gorbachev Meet at Summit (Nov. 19):** U.S. President and Soviet leader hold two two-hour conferences, first meeting between two nations' leaders in six years. (**Nov. 21**): Summit conference ends with leaders expressing hopes of new chapter in relations. In joint statement, they agree to step up arms negotiations and meet more regularly. Other agreements include: renewal of academic, cultural, and performing arts exchanges; new consulates in Kiev and New York; North Pacific air safety agreement. Among restatements are: prevention of nuclear spread; chemical weapons ban; mutual balances for reductions in Europe. In statement, Gorbachev admits he failed to change Reagan's commitment to space-based missile defenses. Reagan tells Congress meeting created "room for movement, action, and progress." Leaders win praise for establishing climate that could lead way to serious bargaining.

**Fifty-Nine Dead in Malta Hijacking (Nov. 23):** Three to five terrorists seize Egyptian Boeing 737 airliner after takeoff from Athens Airport for Cairo. (**Nov. 24**): Passengers killed at Valleta, Malta, as Egyptian special forces storm plane and hijackers retaliate by throwing three grenades at victims. Maltese government announces one surviving hijacker is unconscious in hospital. (**Nov. 26**): He gives his name as Omar Marzouki, 20, of Tunisia, and is identified as chief hijacker. In Cairo, Egyptian officials accuse Libya of being behind hijacking. (**Nov. 27**): Autopsies show most victims died of smoke inhalation, not bullet wounds. Official says explosions by commandos set off fire on airliner, not grenades by terrorists.

## National

**Election Breakthrough in Two States (Nov. 6):** Coalitions reformulated as moderates carry Virginia and New Jersey. Gerald L. Baliles, Governor-elect, leads Democrats to victory in Virginia. Gov. Thomas H. Kean, Republican, wins landslide in New Jersey with broad support including blacks and union members.

**Health Secretary Nominated (Nov. 7):** Reagan names Dr. Otis R. Bowen, former Governor of Indiana, to be Secretary of Health and Human Services. Dr. Bowen, a family doctor and clinical professor at Indiana University, to succeed Margaret M. Heckler.

**Royal Couple Hailed in Washington (Nov. 9):** Prince Charles and Princess Diana arrive for three-day visit to be occupied by social, commercial, and esthetic affairs. President and Mrs. Reagan greet them.

**Senate Unit Rejects Reagan Nominee (Nov. 19):** Labor and Human Resources Committee turns down Edward A. Curran for post of chairman of National Endowment for the Humanities. Questions qualifications.

**Four Charged With Espionage (Nov. 26):** Intelligence officials report damage to U.S. from series of cases. Suspects are: Larry Wu-Tai Chin, 63, accused of spying for China for more than three decades as C.I.A. analyst; Jonathan Jay Pollard, 31, Navy counter-intelligence analyst charged with spying for Israel, and his wife, Anne L. Henderson-Pollard, 25, also held on espionage charges; Ronald W. Pelton, 44, former communications specialist for National Security Agency, caught as result of information from Vitaly Yurchenko, Soviet defector who returned to Soviet Union.

## General

**Forty Dead in Middle Atlantic Floods (Nov. 6):** Record river levels cause millions in damages. Scores missing. (**Nov. 7**): Waters flood Richmond, Washington, and other major cities along half-a-dozen major rivers on Eastern seaboard.

**Mormons Choose New Leader (Nov. 11):** Ezra Taft Benson, at 86, named temporal and spiritual head of Church of Jesus Christ of Latter-Day Saints as president to succeed late Spencer W. Kimball. Benson was Secretary of Agriculture for eight years under President Dwight D. Eisenhower.

**Miami Gets First Cuban-American Mayor (Nov. 13):** Xavier Suarez, 36, Harvard law graduate, takes oath.

**Guru Pleads Guilty in U.S. Court (Nov. 14):** Bhagwan Shree Rajneesh, leader of Oregon commune, admits charges of violating immigration laws by scheme of sham marriages to let followers live in U.S.

**Shuttle Atlantis Flies Second Mission (Nov. 26):** Spaceship goes into orbit in second night launching of a space vehicle. Mission commander is Lieut. Col. Brewster H. Shaw, Jr., of Air Force, making second shuttle flight, and the pilot is Marine Lieut. Col. Bryan D. O'Connor. Others in crew are: Air Force Maj. Jerry L. Ross; Army Lieut. Col Sherwood Spring; Dr. Mary L. Cleave, biologist; Rodolfo Neri Vela, Mexican mission specialist, and Charles Walker of McDonnell Douglas Corporation. (**Dec. 3**): *Atlantis* ends successful seven-day mission with safe landing at Edwards Air Force Base, Calif. One main object was test of construction methods for building large space station. Crew also launched telecommications satellites for Mexico, Australia, and RCA.

# DECEMBER 1985

## International

**Britain Leaving UNESCO (Dec. 5):** One of key founders breaks with 160-member organization. Official charges agency is "harmfully politicized" and is inefficient and badly managed.

**Britain Signs "Star Wars" Pact (Dec. 6):** Agrees to take part in research on American missile-defense system in space, first accord with any U.S. allies.

**Plane Crash Kills 248 U.S. Soldiers (Dec. 12):** Eight crew members also perish as DC-8 operated by Arrow Airlines of Miami crashes on takeoff at international airport at Gander, Newfoundland. Soldiers are members of 101st Airborne Division returning from six-month tour of duty with international peacekeeping force in Sinai Peninsula. (**Dec. 14**): Under agreement with Canada, bodies are sent to Delaware for required autopsies.

**U.N. Condemns Hostage-Taking (Dec. 18):** Security Council unanimously votes resolution, binding on all U.N. members, calling for action to win release.

**Bomb Kills Five Whites in South Africa (Dec. 23):** Three children among victims in explosion among pre-Christmas shoppers at mall near Durban. Official blames outlawed African National Congress. (**Dec. 26**): Christmas season death toll set at 71 as six more blacks die in political violence.

**Mount Etna Erupts in Sicily (Dec. 25):** Sets off earthquakes and spews four rivers of red lava. Quakes destroy resort hotel, killing one and injuring 12.

**Airport Terrorists Kill 19 (Dec. 27):** Hurl grenades and fire submachine guns on holiday travelers at Rome and Vienna in attacks on check-in counters of El Al Israel Airlines. Five Americans among dead. Three gunmen killed; one survives. (**Dec. 28**): Survivor identifies himself as Palestinian born in Lebanon and member of renegade Palestinian group that broke with Yasir Arafat's mainstream Palestinian Liberation Army. (**Dec. 30**): As world indignation mounts, President Reagan accuses Libya of aiding the attackers and says U.S. is prepared to work with other governments to exert pressure on Libya to stop what Administration calls export of terrorism. U.S. warships alerted. (**Jan. 24**): Austrian woman dies of wounds in attack.

**Zoologist Slain in Central Africa (Dec. 28):** Dian Fossey, 53, American who studied Rwanda's rare mountain gorillas for 18 years, found dead in camp. She had been active opponent of poachers.

## National

**Ex-Navy Analyst Gets Two-Year Sentence (Dec. 4):** Samuel Loring Morison, 41, former civilian intelligence official, sentenced in Baltimore Federal Court for stealing classified documents and giving secret American satellite photographs of a Soviet aircraft carrier to British military journal.

**House Approves Tax Revision Bill (Dec. 11):** Republicans in chamber block consideration of legislation, in major rebuff to President Reagan. (**Dec. 17**): Measure passes by voice vote after President rounds up Republicans to bring it to floor. Bill sets top rate of 38 percent and limits $2,000 exemption to those not itemizing.

**Budget-Balancing Bill Enacted (Dec. 12):** President signs measure passed by Congress mandating five-year program for reducing deficit. It is designed to force a balanced budget by 1991. Measure known as Gramm-Rudman-Hollings, for sponsors.

**Congress Votes Farm Policy Change (Dec. 18):** House, 325-96, and Senate, 55-38, approve compromise measure to reduce government income and price supports for first time since 1933. Another bill voted to reorganize farm credit system. (**Dec. 23**): Reagan signs both measures, but approves costly farm bill reluctantly.

**Congress Leaves Without Deficit Vote (Dec. 20):** Ends 1985 session after failing to approve three-year $74-billion deficit-reducing package.

**White House Relaxes Polygraph Rule (Dec. 20):** Tests to be given only to officials suspected of espionage. Acts after Secretary of State George P. Shultz threatens to resign if asked to take test.

**F.B.I. Seizes New Spy Suspect (Dec. 21):** Randy Miles Jeffries, 26, employee of company that transcribes secret sessions of House of Representatives, charged with spying for Soviet Union after offering to sell undercover agent secret documents.

## General

**Cigarette Maker Wins Libel Suit (Dec. 5):** Viceroy manufacturer awarded $5.05 million by federal jury in Chicago in action against CBS Inc. and Walter Jacobson, popular commentator, for broadcast charging improper advertising methods.

**A.M.A. Urges Tobacco Advertising Ban (Dec. 10):** House of Delegates calls for federal laws making it illegal to promote or advertise tobacco products in any media. Curb on health dangers is aim.

**Twentieth Yale President Named (Dec. 10):** Benno C. Schmidt, 43, dean of Columbia University Law School, succeeds A. Bartlett Giamatti, 48.

**Nation's Largest Civil Damage Award (Dec. 10):** Texas judge accepts jury's verdict that Texaco Inc. must pay Pennzoil Company $10.53 billion for blocking Pennzoil merger with Getty Oil Company. (**Jan. 10**): Federal judge rules Texaco need not post $12-billion bond to appeal case, a major victory for Texaco in legal battle.

**G.E. Taking Over RCA Corporation (Dec. 11):** Agrees to acquire ownership of NBC television network in deal estimated at more than $6 billion.

**Shore Bird an Endangered Species (Dec. 12):** Federal ruling protects piping plover, once common on Atlantic and Gulf coasts and along Great Lakes.

**First Woman Heads an Indian Tribe (Dec. 14):** Cherokees install Wilma P. Mankiller, 40, as Principal Chief.

**First Woman with Artificial Heart (Dec. 19):** Mary Lund, 40, of Kensington, Minn., receives smaller version of Jarvik-7 pump, used previously, in operation at Abbott Northwestern Hospital, Minneapolis. (**Jan. 2, 1986**): Mrs. Lund emerges from coma. (**Jan. 31**): She is given heart of teen-age girl.

**Garden of 1680 Discovered in Virginia (Dec. 22):** Archeologists report English-style renaissance garden at Bacons Castle, earliest documented formal garden in America, with central broad walk.

**R.J. Reynolds Upheld in Smoker's Suit (Dec. 23):** California jury rejects contention that tobacco company should be liable in lung cancer death of Santa Barbara man, as argued in family's action.

**Ten Racists Convicted in Seattle (Dec. 30):** Federal jury finds members of the Order, white supremacy sect conspiring to foment white revolution, guilty of crimes under racketeering law.

**Medical Licenses "Marital Property" (Dec. 26):** New York's highest court rules their value must be divided equitably at time of a divorce.

## JANUARY 1986

### International

**Two Nations Join Common Market (Jan. 1):** European Economic Community admits Spain and Portugal as 11th and 12th members under treaty already ratified.

**U.S., Soviet Leaders Exchange Greetings (Jan. 1):** President Reagan and Mikhail S. Gorbachev extend New Year's wishes to each other's people in unusual television exchange, broadcast to both nations.

**President Freezes Libyan Assets in U.S. (Jan. 8):** Order affects bank deposits. Europeans react coolly to appeal for joint sanctions against Libya.

**South African Activist Slain (Jan. 12):** Ampie Mayisa stabbed to death hours before he was scheduled to meet with Chester A. Crocker, U.S. Assistant Secretary of State for African Affairs. Progovernment activists reportedly killed Mayisa.

**Spain Recognizes Israel (Jan. 17):** Joint statement establishes diplomatic relations 38 years after Israel's founding as a nation.

**Plans for Channel Tunnel Announced (Jan. 20):** Britain and France give go-ahead for construction of double railway running 30 miles under sea between Dover and Calais, realizing centuries-old dream.

**Blast Kills 22 in East Beirut (Jan. 21):** More than 100 wounded as car bomb explodes near headquarters of President Amin Gemayel's Christian Phalangist Party.

**Blacks Slay Two White South African Policemen (Jan. 21):** Stabbing and beating by crowd in segregated township near Johannesburg is first slaying of white policemen in more than 16 months of political violence that has claimed more than 1,050 lives, most of them blacks. **(Jan. 22):** Police kill seven blacks near Johannesburg.

**U.S. Holds Maneuvers Off Libya (Jan. 24):** Carrier jets begin Navy operations north of Gulf of Sidra, claimed by Libya as territorial waters. Libya's armed forces placed on "full alert."

### National

**F.D.A. Issues Heart Transplant Rules (Jan. 8):** Says experiments to implant artificial organs can continue but only with case-by-case U.S. approval.

**Space Shuttle Has Troubled Flight (Jan. 12):** *Columbia* soars into orbit from Cape Canaveral, Fla., after record seven postponements. Ship's mission is 24th of shuttle program. Crew members include Dr. Franklin R. Chang-Díaz, first Hispanic American to fly in space. Other members are: Navy Comdr. Robert L. Gibson, mission commander; Rep. Bill Nelson, Democrat of Florida, chairman of House subcommittee that oversees NASA budget; Marine Lieut. Col. Charles F. Bolden, Jr., pilot; Dr. Steven A. Hawley, astrophysicist; Dr. George D. Nelson, astronomer, and Robert C. Cenker, satellite engineer for RCA. Astronauts launch $50-million communications satellite for RCA Corporation. **(Jan. 18):** *Columbia* lands safely at Edwards Air Force Base, Calif., because of bad weather in Florida. Crew reports 90% success in achieving goals, which also included observing Halley's Comet, a test for President Reagan's space-based missile defense plan, and a dozen other experiments in materials science, astrophysics, and life sciences.

**Supreme Court Bars Bias in Grand Jury (Jan. 14):** Justices, 6-3, reverse 1963 murder conviction of black prisoner in California on ground members of own race were excluded from panel.

**Rev. Martin Luther King, Jr., Honored (Jan. 15):** Nation marks 57th birthday of martyred civil rights leader. President Reagan, continuing personal involvement, tells black schoolchildren Dr. King "was a great man who wrested justice from the heart of a great country."

**National Holiday for Dr. Martin Luther King, Jr. (Jan. 20):** Thousands parade in Atlanta and elsewhere across nation to mark first federal holiday honoring assassinated civil rights leader.

**Bank of America Fined $4.75 Million (Jan. 21):** Treasury imposes record civil penalty for failure to report more than 17,000 large cash deposits or transfers from 1980 to 1985.

**Shuttle Explodes, Killing Seven (Jan. 28):** *Challenger* bursts into flames minute and a quarter after launch at Cape Canaveral, Fla. Christa McAuliffe, New Hampshire teacher, chosen as first ordinary citizen in space, among victims. Others are: Francis R. (Dick) Scobee, commander; Comdr. Michael J. Smith of Navy, pilot; Dr. Judith A. Resnick; Dr. Ronald E. McNair; Lieut. Col. Ellison S. Onizuka of Air Force; Gregory B. Jarvis. Spectators horrified and nation is shocked. **(Jan. 29):** Teams of investigators organized as ships, planes, and helicopters search Atlantic Ocean for remains of *Challenger.* **(Jan. 31):** Space agency study shows right-hand solid-fuel booster suddenly experienced drop in power 10 seconds before spacecraft exploded. President Reagan mourns loss of "seven *Challenger* heroes" before audience of thousands at memorial services at Johnson Space Center, Tex. Pledges to honor them with renewed national commitment to the conquest of space.

### General

**Fatal Gas Leak at Uranium Plant (Jan. 4):** One killed and 32 injured as radioactive gas escapes when tank ruptures at Kerr-McGee Corporation subsidiary at Gore, Okla. Executive says workers were using untested process to expel gas from tank.

**Killer's Execution Stirs Protest (Jan. 10):** International objections arise against penalty for crimes committed by juvenile as South Carolina executes James Terry Roach, 25, for double murder he committed when he was only 17.

**Colonel Loses Appeal in Libel Suit (Jan. 15):** Federal Appeals Court in Manhattan rejects $44-million action by retired Army Col. Anthony Herbert against CBS charging malicious portrayal in 1973 "60 Minutes" broadcast by CBS News.

**Secrets of Uranus Discovered (Jan. 26):** *Voyager 2* spacecraft sends back detailed images revealing startling features of major moons. One, Miranda, disclosed as icy world with rugged mix of valleys, fractures, and ridges. **(Jan. 27):** Analysis of data shows rings of planet are composed primarily of blocky chunks of dark material. Among many discoveries: detection of 220-mile-an-hour winds in thick atmosphere, temperatures of 350 degrees below zero Fahrenheit, and an estimated 16 to 17 hours for planet's day. *Voyager* millions of miles beyond Uranus on way to neptune in 1989.

**Sale of Intrauterine Devices Halted (Jan. 31):** G.D. Searle & Co. takes Copper-7 and Tatum-T off market in U.S., citing unwarranted lawsuits.

# FEBRUARY 1986

## International

**Pontiff Greeted on Visit to India (Feb. 1):** John Paul II opens 10-day trip by proclaiming respect for all of country's religions. Places wreath at memorial to Mohandas K. Gandhi.

**Israelis Intercept Libyan Jet (Feb. 4):** Force civilian plane to land in Israel to capture Palestinian terrorist, but find it carried only seven Syrian politicians and two Lebanese militia officers.

**Paris Specialty Store Bombed (Feb. 5):** Nine injured, three seriously, in third incident in three days in campaign of random terrorism.

**Haiti's President Flees to France (Feb. 7):** Jean-Claude Duvalier, 34, ends 28-year grip of family after months of unrest over economic conditions. Lieut. Gen. Henri Namphy, 53, commander of armed forces, says Army will rule with six-member governing council including two civilians. Twenty killed, 75 injured in violent disorders.

**Opposition Leader Slain in Philippines (Feb. 11):** Gunmen kill Evelio Javier, 43, outspoken Marcos opponent.

**Socialist Elected Portugal President (Feb. 16):** Mário Soares, former Prime Minister, named nation's first elected civilian President in 60 years.

**Marcos Declared Philippines Victor (Feb. 17):** National Assembly proclaims President winner in Presidential election Feb. 7 over Corazon A. Aquino, widow of assassinated Benigno S. Aquino, Jr. Citizens Watch group, other observers, and supporters of Mrs. Aquino charge widespread fraud by Marcos side. **(Feb. 16):** Mrs. Aquino claims victory and announces program of strikes and boycotts in nonviolent campaign to unseat Marcos.

**King Hussein Ends Peace Campaign (Feb. 19):** Jordan monarch abandons year-long effort to achieve joint strategy for Middle East peace with Yasir Arafat, chairman of Palestine Liberation Organization.

**Soviet Launches Space Station (Feb. 20):** *Mir*, "third generation" system, is designed to be hub of permanently manned space research complex.

**Marcos Rule Ends After 20 Years (Feb. 26):** President Ferdinand E. Marcos, 68, and in ill health, flees Philippines for Guam after 20 years as President. Corazon C. Aquino, widow of assassinated Benigno S. Aquino, Jr., succeeds him. She is inaugurated to head a provisional government.

**Egypt Crushes Rebellion (Feb. 27):** Government reports suppressing uprising by paramilitary police after three days of street clashes. Thirty-six reported dead and 321 wounded.

**Prime Minister of Sweden Slain (Feb. 28):** Olof Palme 59, shot dead in street minutes after leaving movie theater with wife. Leader of country's Social Democratic Party is first European head of government in 47 years to be slain while in office. Wife, Lisbeth Palme, superficially wounded. She says she had seen assassin before. **(March 1):** Party moves to nominate acting Prime Minister Ingvar Carlsson as new leader.

## National

**Panel Named for Shuttle Inquiry (Feb. 3):** President Reagan appoints 12 to independent commission to investigate cause of *Challenger*'s explosion. Chairman is William P. Rogers, former Attorney General and Secretary of State.

**President Pledges More Decontrol (Feb. 6):** Economic Report to Congress seeks deregulation of natural gas prices and further deregulation of trucking industry. White House will seek further decontrol of banks and dismantling of farm support bureaucracy.

**Lee Iacocca Ousted From Commission (Feb. 12):** U.S. removes Chrysler chairman as head of federal advisory panel on restoring Statue of Liberty and historic buildings on Ellis Island.

**Senate Approves Ban on Genocide (Feb. 19):** Endorses United Nations convention 37 years after submission by President Truman. Convention, result of Nazi holocaust, declares genocide an international crime.

**High Court Balks Pornography Foes (Feb. 24):** Decision, without opinion, rules unconstitutional Indianapolis ordinance penalizing pornography as discrimination against women, upholding lower courts.

**Justices Approve Curb on Sex Films (Feb. 25):** Supreme Court, 7-2, rules local zoning officials have broad powers to restrict movie theaters' location.

**Nation's First Official Poet Laureate (Feb. 26):** Robert Penn Warren, 80-year-old poet, novelist and essayist appointed to recently established post.

**NASA Administrator Resigns (Feb. 26):** James M. Beggs on leave while facing fraud charges resulting from tenure as executive of General Dynamics Corporation.

**Senate to Test Television (Feb. 27):** Votes, 67-21, to televise proceedings on trial basis beginning June 1. Action follows years of heated debate.

## General

**Retired C.I.A. Analyst Guilty as Spy (Feb. 7):** Federal jury in Virginia convicts Larry Wu-Tai Chin of espionage and related charges. He had acknowledged spying for Peking over 30 years. He said he had sought friendship between U.S. and China.

**F.B.I. Presses Tylenol Death Inquiry (Feb. 14):** Gives "highest priority" to case of Diane Elsroth, 23, who died in Yonkers, N.Y., after taking Extra-Strength Tylenol laced with cyanide. Eight states ban sales of capsules. Johnson & Johnson suspends production of drug in capsule form. **(Feb. 17):** Johnson & Johnson suspends manufacture of all over-the-counter drugs in capsule form. Estimates withdrawl from capsules will cost $100 million to $150 million after taxes. **(Feb. 18):** Other drug companies decide against following Johnson's action.

**Coca-Cola Buying Dr. Pepper (Feb. 20):** Agrees to pay $470 million to acquire soft-drink company in deal representing windfall for investors in a buyout.

**Convicted Spy for China a Suicide (Feb. 21):** Larry Wu-Tai Chin, 63, retired Central Intelligence Agency analyst, suffocates himself in Virginia jail.

**Storms Ravage West Coast (Feb. 22):** About 20 dead as six-day series of storms drops record rain and snow. Floods drive thousands from homes as levees break. Damage estimated past $300 million.

**Eastern Airlines Approves Sale (Feb. 24):** Texas Air Corporation to buy nation's second-largest carrier. Texas Air bid estimated at close to $600 million.

**Naval Surgeon Convicted in Deaths (Feb. 26):** Comdr. Donal M. Billig, 55, found guilty by military court of involuntary manslaughter and negligent homicide in deaths of three heart surgery patients at Bethesda Naval Hospital, where he had been Chief of Heart Surgery.

**Seven Baseball Players Suspended Over Drugs (Feb. 28):** Commissioner Peter Ueberroth orders year's penalty for Keith Hernandez of Mets, Dale Berra of Yankees, and five others for use of cocaine.

# MARCH 1986

## International

**Full Civil Rights for Filipinos (March 2):** In first proclamation as President, Corazon Aquino restores full protection against arrest without charges.

**Gunman Kills West Bank Mayor (March 2):** Zafer el-Masri, 44, appointed by Israel as mayor of Nablus, shot dead walking from his home to City Hall. He represented alternative to radical Palestinian program.

**Kurt Waldheim Service as Nazi Revealed (March 3):** Official papers made public in Vienna say former Secretary General of United Nations was attached to German Army command in World War II that engaged in mass deportation of Greek Jews. **(March 7):** Waldheim tells World Jewish Congress that reports of links to Nazi crimes were part of "unsubstantiated and unfounded" campaign.

**South Africa Ends Emergency Rule (March 7):** Releases reported last 327 of nearly 8,000 detained since decree took effect in July 1985. Security procedure continues but with relaxed provisions.

**U.S. Orders Cut in Soviet U.N. Mission (March 7):** Administration charges espionage by Russian, Ukrainian, and Byelorussian delegations and decrees 38 percent reduction in personnel.

**Spain Votes to Stay in NATO (March 12):** In national referendum, 53 percent vote to remain in North Atlantic Treaty Organization. National ballot a victory for Prime Minister Felipe González.

**Marcos' Fortune Found Worldwide (March 13):** Philippine government identifies $800-million bank account held by former President Ferdinand E. Marcos. **(March 19):** Documents found among personal effects show Marcos and family maintained bank accounts and other holdings around the world worth hundreds of millions of dollars. **(March 25):** Swiss government freezes all bank deposits in Switzerland belonging to Marcos family.

**Moscow Extends Nuclear Test Halt (March 13):** Mikhail S. Gorbachev, Soviet leader, says moratorium will continue as long as U.S. holds off testing.

**Rightist Parties Victorious in France (March 16):** Alliance of Rally for the Republic and Union of French Democracy wins slender majority in national election to Parliament, ending Socialist rule. **(March 20):** Jacques Chirac, neo-Gallist, assumes post of Prime Minister at invitation of Socialist President François Mitterand.

**Bhopal Settlement Tentatively Reached (March 22):** Union Carbide Corporation and lawyers for victims of gas leak in India agree on tens of billions in damage claims from history's worst industrial disaster. Union Carbide to pay $350 million for deaths of more than 2,000 and injury to 200,000 from chemical leak at pesticide plant Dec. 2-3, 1984.

**U.S. Forces Clash With Libyans (March 24):** Encounter begins as U.S. Navy ships conduct maneuver in Gulf of Sidra in Mediterranean, claimed by Libya as territorial waters. Libyan ground batteries fire six missiles at American planes. U.S. Navy aircraft retaliate by attacking two Libyan vessels and a ground missile site. One patrol boat set afire, another "severely damaged." **(March 25):** U.S. forces launch additional attacks after Libyans display "hostile intentions." **(March 27):** U.S. ships and planes complete exercises south of Col. Muammar el-Qaddafi's "line of death," northern boundary of Gulf, and move north. Incidents follow allegations of Libyan link to terrorism.

**Reagan Orders Emergency Aid for Honduras (March 25):** Releases $20 million in military assistance after Western diplomats report 1,500 Nicaraguan soldiers crossed border to attack rebel camps. **(March 26):** Fourteen U.S. Army helicopters transport Honduran battalion near to area of fighting.

**Record Death Toll of 30 in South Africa (March 26):** Police fire on crowd of more than 5,000 in Bophuthatswana homeland and kill others across country in one of highest mortality totals in country in a year.

**Six Acquitted in Plot Against Pope (March 29):** Italian court frees three Bulgarians and three Turks accused of conspiring to assassinate John Paul II. Rules evidence against them is ambiguous.

**Fire Damage Hampton Court Palace (March 31):** Destroys part of Henry VIII edifice by Thames, one of Britain's most famous historical buildings. One dead, damage in millions. Queen inspects wreckage. Most of valuable paintings spared.

**Mexican Plane Crash Kills 166 (March 31):** Nine Americans among victims as Mexican Airline Boeing 727 goes down in remote central mountainous region. **(April 1):** Voice and flight data records recovered.

## National

**Reagan Accepts Peril of Acid Rain (March 19):** President endorses joint Canadian-U.S. report calling for curbs on airborne pollutants as serious environmental problem.

**Justices Affirm Curb on Yarmulke (March 23):** Supreme Court, 5-4, rules military discipline supersedes constitutional rights and holds military can bar Orthodox Jewish officer from wearing cap indoors while in uniform.

**Senate, 53-47, Votes Contras Aid (March 27):** Approves President's request for $100 million to guerrillas fighting to depose Nicaraguan government.

## General

**Philadelphia Officials Criticized (March 6):** Special inquiry reports Mayor W. Wilson Goode was negligent and irresponsible in deaths resulting from confrontation with radical group Move in May 1985. Panel calls Fire Commissioner William C. Richmond and Police Commissioner Gregore J. Sambor primarily responsible for fatalities in fire that followed dropping of aerial bomb on Move residence.

**Tornadoes Kill Two in Three States (March 10):** Storms and winds up to 87 miles an hour sweep Indiana, Kentucky, and Ohio. Twenty injured. Electricity cut off for thousands. Planes destroyed.

**Lynching Victim Pardoned Posthumously (March 11):** State of Georgia awards pardon to Leo M. Frank, Jewish businessman killed by mob in 1915 for a murder that he denied committing.

**Messenger Sentenced in Spy Case (March 13):** Randy M. Jeffries, 26, gets three to nine years in federal prison for trying to sell U.S. secrets to Soviet Union.

**Two Teams Report Finding AIDS Virus (March 26):** Competing U.S. and French scientists contend independently that each has discovered new viruses related to deadly disease.

**Volcano Erupts in Alaska (March 28):** Augustine Volcano blows ash and gas for second day in first eruption in 10 years. Health alerts sounded throughout south-central area. Debris spreads 600 miles.

# APRIL 1986

## International

**Reagan Attends Seven-Nation Economic Conference (April 26):** On Los Angeles stopover on way to Tokyo, President warns "dictators and terrorists" they face consequences of "cowardly acts." **(April 27):** In Honolulu, Reagan rejects Ferdinand E. Marcos's claim to be rightful President of Philippines. **(May 4):** Terrorists penetrate tight security and fire five rockets at Tokyo guest house during welcome for leaders of industrial nations. They overshoot mark and no one is hurt. **(May 5):** Seven-nation leaders, in joint statment, condemn terrorism and single out Libya as source of state-supported terrorism. They agree to work toward closer coordination of economic policies to assure that their currencies are fairly valued. **(May 7):** Twelth annual conference ends with leaders satisfied that they had confronted terrorism and taken important economic steps toward new trade talks and revamping of world monetary system.

**Bomb on T.W.A. Plane Kills Four (April 2):** Three Americans in group sucked from Trans World Airlines Boeing 727 carrying 121 from Rome to Athens. Nine wounded. Arab Revolutionary Cells group claims responsibility. **(April 3):** International investigation focuses on known Arab terrorist, identified as May Mansour, carrying Lebanese passport.

**Bomb Kills Two in Berlin Nightclub (April 5):** Wounds 155, including 50 to 60 Americans in discothèque popular with U.S. troops. American serviceman and Turkish woman dead. **(April 7):** German security officials, suspecting Libyan link, step up surveillance of Libyans in move to block new attacks.

**Pope Visits Rome Synagogue (April 13):** Makes first recorded papal call on central Jewish temple. Embraces world's Jews as "our elder brothers" and denounces persecution and displays of anti-Semitism.

**U.S. Planes Attack Libya (April 14):** Bombers strike five bases. Eighteen F-111 aircraft from England attack military installations, military barracks, and a training center near Tripoli. Fifteen A-6 planes from two aircraft carriers strike two targets near Benghazi. President Reagan says strikes were aimed as "terrorist" centers." Reports "irrefutable" evidence that Libya was behind terrorist bomb blast in Germany fatal to U.S. soldier and Turkish woman. **(April 15):** U.S. F-111 with two pilots only plane lost from antiaircraft fire. Libya retaliates by hurling missiles at U.S. Coast Guard station on Lampedusa island. **(April 16):** Libyans report 15 dead and 16 wounded in raids. Among dead is reported to be 15-month old adopted daughter of Libyan leader, Col. Muammar el-Qaddafi.

**Desmond Tutu Elected Archbishop (April 14):** Anglicans choose foe of apartheid, 54, Nobel peace prize winner, as first black titular head of church in South Africa.

**Three Hostages Slain in Lebanon (April 17):** Peter Kilburn, U.S. librarian, and two Britons found dead near Beirut. Note with bodies says they were killed because of U.S. bombing of Libya with British aid.

**South Africa Lifts Pass Control Laws (April 18):** President P.W. Botha says hated symbol of curbs on blacks' residence and work will no longer be enforced.

**Vladimir Horowitz Plays in Moscow (April 20):** Pianist, 81, returns to native Soviet Union for first recital since leaving 61 years previously. Audience in tears as he performs Russian music.

**British Hostage Slain in Beirut (April 23):** Pro-Libyan group reports killing of Alec Collett, 64, freelance journalist, based in New York, in retaliation for American air attack on Libya.

**South Africa Easing Travel of Blacks (April 23):** Government announces plan to abolish virtually all laws prohibiting free movement and migration into black sections of cities. "Pass laws" to end.

**Common Market Adopts Terror Pact (April 24):** Ministers of eight European Community nations agree at The Hague to step up exchange of information with U.S. and other non-member nations.

## National

**High Court Relaxes Libel Policy (April 21):** Rules, 5-4, person suing news organization must prove damaging statements are false, at least "on matters of public concern." Pennsylvania statute voided.

**Justices Uphold Blacks on Juries (April 30):** Supreme Court, 7-2, holds prosecutors may not use peremptory challenge to exclude blacks from juries from concern they may favor defendants of own race.

## General

**Union Carbide Faces $1.4-Million Fine (April 1):** Disregard for health and safety at Institute, West Va., plant charged by Occupational Safety and Health Administration. Proposed penalty largest ever sought by safety agency, Labor Department division.

**Halley's Comet on Return Visit (April 10):** Traveler from space, a sensation in 1910, disappoints viewers as it loses most of tail as it comes within 39 million miles of Earth. Astronomers succeed in learning many mysteries of comets. Developments in comet's return: **(Nov. 13, 1985):** Object displays unexpected early brightness as it emerges from space. **(March 4, 1986):** Soviet craft *Vega 1* pierces comet's atmosphere and from within 5,500 miles transmits first pictures showing icy core formed as solar system was evolving 4.6 billion years ago. **(March 9):** Soviet's *Vega 2* flies within 5,200 miles of comet's nucleus and sends data confirming that elliptical nucleus is solid. **(March 14):** European spacecraft Giotto plunges to within 335 miles of icy nucleus but dust particles interrupt transmission. Scientists report spinning Giotto revealed mysterious nucleus to be dark, rough, and irregular and bigger than had been thought.

**Sex Bias Dispute Settled (April 11):** Federal judge in Seattle approves $482-million settlement by Washington state with its employees over differences in wage differentials between men and women.

**Stalin's Daughter Back in U.S. (April 17):** Svetlana Alliluyeva, 60, lands in Chicago. Defected in 1967 and, after nearly 17 years in U.S., returned to Russia, saying she had been unhappy. A day earlier, daughter, Olga, returned to Quaker boarding school in England she had left two years earlier.

**Protein Linked to Alzheimer's Disease (April 24):** Research team finds substance that does not exist in normal brains. Discovery expected to aid diagnosis of devastating disease and discovery of cause.

**Methodists Oppose Nuclear Weapons (April 29):** United Church Council of Bishops votes unanimously to issue pastoral letter declaring "clear and unconditioned" opposition to any use of them.

## MAY 1986

### International

**Soviet Nuclear Accident Alarms World (April 28 et seq.):** Moscow announces major accident at huge Chernobyl power station at new town of Pripyat near Chernobyl and 60 miles north of Kiev. Radioactivity spreads over parts of Soviet Union, Eastern Europe, Scandinavia, and later over Western Europe. Small amounts of radioactivity sweep high over U.S. Poland announces radiation levels, bans milk from grazing cows, and issues antiradiation medicine to 11 million children. By June 5 death toll has risen to 26, including two killed in initial explosion and 24 dead of radiation. Soviet doctors also report about 18,000 suffer headaches, coughing, respiratory trouble, and some spat blood after disaster. Western nations accuse Soviet of withholding or delaying vital details.

**Twenty Killed in Sri Lanka Bomb Blast (May 3):** Tamil extremists blamed for bomb in tail section of Air Lanka craft as passengers board at Colombo.

**Spain Expels Libyan Diplomat (May 9):** Consul General Saad Ismail is fourth Libyan diplomat expelled by Spain since December. Army Col. Carlos Meer de Rivera is arrested, charged with having asked Col. Muammar el-Qaddafi for money to finance extreme right-wing activities in Spain.

**Britain Ousts Three Syrian Attachés (May 10):** Expels diplomats involved in investigation of terrorist activities, including attempt to smuggle bomb aboard Israeli jumbo jet at Heathrow Airport. Syria expels three British diplomats in retaliation.

**South Africa Attacks Three Neighbors (May 19):** Raids capitals of Botswana, Zambia, and Zimbabwe in 25-year-old war on guerrillas of African National Congress. Several dead in coordinated air attacks.

**China Returns Cargo Jet to Taiwan (May 19):** Two nations conclude first face-to-face negotiations in 37 years. (**May 23**): Under agreement, plane hijacked three weeks previously to China, and two crew members, returned to Taiwan in formal ceremony at Hong Kong. Pilot had defected to mainland.

**Former Libyan Official Slain in East Berlin (May 22):** Mohammed Ashour, 42, once member of Bonn Embassy, reported to have been informer for investigation of terrorist attacks in West Berlin.

**NATO Approves Chemical Weapons Plan (May 22):** Defense ministers back Reagan Administration project to resume production for first time since 1969 to counter Soviet Union's arsenal.

**Car Bomb Kills 11 in East Beirut (May 23):** Wounds 84 in Christian area. Bombing raises death toll to 64 and number wounded to 243 in three days of bloodshed.

**Bangladesh River Ferry With 1,000 Capsizes (May 26):** At least 80 known dead and more than 500 are missing as storm sinks ship and buffets southern coast.

**European Space Launching Crippled (May 31):** Capability threatened by destruction of *Ariane* rocket in midair. Inquiry to seek cause of fourth failure of commercial vehicle in 18 launchings.

### National

**Failures Cripple Space Missions (May 3):** *Delta* rocket with weather satellite spins out of control over Cape Canaveral, Fla., forcing destruction of $57.5-million payload. Mishap follows explosion of Air Force *Titan* rocket and loss of space shuttle *Challenger*. Incidents set back ability to lift commercial, military, and scientific satellites into space for near future.

**Death Penalty Challenge Blocked (May 5):** Supreme Court, 6-3, rules opponents may be barred from juries in capital cases, regardless of whether action increases likelihood of conviction.

**Justices Uphold Aerial Searches (May 19):** Supreme Court, 5-4, rules government investigators do not need warrants for surveillance of private areas.

**Supreme Court Rules Against Blacks (May 19):** Justices, in five separate opinions, hold unconstitutional Michigan school board's giving preference to minority teachers in layoffs. But majority finds governments may give preference to blacks in hiring to redress past discrimination.

**U.S. Abandoning Arms Limitation Pact (May 27):** President decides to dismantle two old submarines to stay within unratified 1979 treaty, but plans to deploy cruise missiles over its limits. (**May 29**): At NATO meeting in Halifax, Secretary of State Shultz makes it clear that U.S. adherence to pact will end unless Soviet policy changes drastically. Decision alarms major allies. (**June 2**): Reagan decision criticized across Western Europe as showing U.S. disdain for Allies' opinion.

### General

**Six Convicted in Smuggling of Aliens (May 1):** U.S. jury in Tucson, Ariz., finds activists guilty of plotting to bring Salvadorans and Guatemalans into United States. Five of 11 church workers cleared of that serious charge, with two found guilty on lesser charges, and three acquitted on all counts. Those convicted of conspiracy include Rev. John M. Fife, 3rd, 45, founder of church movement for church sanctuary for illegal aliens fleeing violence in Central America.

**American Indian Made a Bishop (May 6):** Rev. Donald E. Pelotte, 41, son of Algonquin laborer, ordained in Roman Catholic ceremony at Gallup. N.M.

**Oxford Dictionary Goes Modern (May 8):** Fourth and final supplement includes yuppie, self-service, Sputnik, and security blanket.

**Teamsters President Indicted (May 16):** U.S. jury in Cleveland accuses Jackie Presser, 59, head of nation's largest union, of embezzlement and racketeering in payroll-padding scheme.

**Nine Mountain Climbers Perish (May 16):** Six found dead in snow cave on Mount Hood, Ore. Two teen-agers survive three-day ordeal, probably because of being near top. Three others died earlier in climb.

**Drought Ravages Southeast (May 17):** Croplands dried up by worst dry spell in more than 100 years.

**Schooner Sinks in Atlantic; Four Lost (May 19):** Coast Guard reports two-masted *Pride of Baltimore* toppled by tornado-like winds north of Puerto Rico. She was to have joined tall ships in New York Harbor on July Fourth. Eight survivors rescued.

**Continental Human Chain Aids Homeless (May 25):** Links rich, poor, famous, and officials in 4,150-mile line organized by Hands Across America to raise 50 million to combat hunger and homelessness.

**Bus Crash Kills 18 in California (May 30):** Twenty-two injured as tour coach carrying residents of retirement home plunges from mountain road into icy river.

**Five Sikhs Linked to Plot on Airliner (May 31):** Arraigned in Montreal on charges of conspiring to blow up Air India Boeing 747 flying out of New York.

# JUNE 1986

## International

**Reagan Wins on Arms for Saudis (June 5):** Senate, by one vote, fails to override veto of resolution to block sale of advanced missiles to Saudi Arabia.

**At Least 43 Dead in Sri Lanka Bombings (June 11):** Time devices in two buses and outside a theater laid to Tamil terrorists. Seventy-three wounded.

**Bishop Tutu and President Botha Confer (June 13):** Meet for first time in six years day after South Africa imposes severest emergency decrees.

**Millions of Blacks Strike in South Africa (June 16):** In defiance of government repression of dissent, stage subdued protest marking 10th anniversary of 1976 Soweto uprising. Eight more blacks killed in segregated black townships. Government orders most sweeping press restrictions since hardline Nationalists took power in 1948. **(June 18):** Strikes and sitdowns by black supermarket workers spread across nation to protest detention of union leaders under emergency decrees.

**Lebanon Kidnappers Free Two (June 20):** Shiite Moslems release Philippe Rochot, 39, French television correspondent, and Georges Hansen, 45, his cameraman. Two others of TV crew abducted March 8 are still missing.

**Bomb Explodes at El-Al Counter in Madrid (June 26):** Suitcase blows up during security inspection after X-ray examination. Twelve persons wounded.

**Irish Voters Affirm Ban on Divorce (June 27):** Reject proposal to end it by 63% to 36%. Ballot viewed as setback for Prime Minister Garret FitzGerald.

**World Court Rules Against U.S. (June 27):** International Court of Justice at The Hague finds Reagan Administration broke international law and violated Nicaraguan sovereignty by aiding rebels.

## National

**Senate Goes on Television (June 2):** Floor debate broadcast first time in six-week trial period.

**High Court Upholds Mentally Ill (June 2):** Unanimously rejects Justice Department appeal and rules thousands of New Yorkers have right to sue government for illegally denying them disability benefits.

**Shuttle Inquiry Faults Management (June 9):** Presidential commission says failure of rocket joint was single physical cause of *Challenger* disaster, but finds fundamental responsibility lay with problems in space agency and rocket manufacturer. Final report by 13-member body cites long history of engineering and managerial mistakes. Commission lists 11 broad recommendations to improve faulty joints and management flaws.

**High Court Affirms Abortion Rights (June 11):** Justices, 5-4, uphold 1973 decision and void Pennsylvania law as unconstitutional on ground it is designed to deter some from abortions and risks health.

**U.S. Army Restricts Smoking (June 11):** Leaders issue directive designed to make "nonsmoking the norm" for military offices, barracks, vehicles, and aircraft as health measure.

**Sex Harassment at Work Outlawed (June 19):** Supreme Court rules unanimously such harassment of employee by a superior violates federal law against sex discrimination in the workplace.

**Daylight Saving Time Extended (June 24):** Bill passed by Congress would begin it first Sunday in April 1987. Time will still end last Sunday in October.

**Senate Votes Sweeping Tax Revision (June 24):** Bipartisan 97-3 vote approves lowering rates, and restricting many deductions, shelters, and other tax preferences, affecting nearly every taxpayer.

**Supreme Court Limits Libel Actions (June 25):** Rules, 6-3, federal courts must dismiss suits by public officials and figures unless evidence supports proof of libel with "convincing clarity." Ruling made in suit by Liberty Lobby Inc. and founder against Jack Anderson, the columnist, and others.

**House Votes Aid to "Contras" (June 25):** Administration wins major victory as Representatives, 221-209, approve $70 million in military assistance and $30 million in nonmilitary aid for Nicaraguan rebels. House reverses stand under intense lobbying campaign by President Reagan.

**Justices Limit Right of Privacy (June 30):** Supreme Court, 5-4, rules Constitution does not protect homosexual relations between consenting adults, even in privacy of own homes. With bitter disagreement, Court upholds Georgia law prohibiting homosexual sex. Ruling widely protested as setback for rights of homosexuals.

## General

**Ex-Navy Analyst Guilty as Spy for Israel (June 4):** In plea bargain, Jonathan Jay Pollard, 31, admits selling classified documents. Wife, Anne Henderson Pollard, pleads guilty to two lesser offenses. Justice Department names four Israelis as unindicted co-conspirators. Pollard provides information about Israeli spying in U.S.

**Ex-Official Convicted of Espionage (June 5):** Ronald W. Pelton, 44, former employee of National Security Agency, found guilty by U.S. jury of selling sensitive intelligence secrets to Soviet Union.

**Southern Baptists Name Fundamentalist (June 10):** Convention elects Rev. Adrian Rogers, Memphis preacher, as president. Fundamentalists now can control nation's largest Protestant denomination.

**Church Names Former Hostage as Head (June 11):** Rev. Benjamin Weir, 62, once missionary to Lebanon who was held captive for 16 months, elected moderator of Presbyterian Church (U.S.A.).

**Tulane Basketball Star Acquitted (June 16):** New Orleans jury clears John (Hot Rod) Williams on five counts of taking part in point-shaving scandal.

**Grand Canyon Air Crash Kills 25 (June 18):** Sight-seeing twin-engine Otter and Bell 206 turbine-powered helicopter collide and crash into mile-deep gorge, killing all aboard.

**Artificial-Heart Recipient Dies (June 19):** Murray P. Haydon, 59, wore implant 16 months and 2 days after becoming third person with artificial heart. Failure of kidneys blamed for death.

**Former F.B.I. Agent Guilty as Spy (June 19):** Richard W. Miller, 48, convicted by Federal Court in Los Angeles on six counts of espionage for Soviet Union and for bribery. Twenty-year veteran of agency charged with passing classified documents for $65,000 and sexual favors of emigrée spy.

**Cocaine Blamed in Athlete's Death (June 24):** Maryland medical examiner says Len Bias, University of Maryland basketball star, sniffed drug June 19 shortly before collapsing in dormitory room. Bias, 22, all-America forward, was second player selected in draft by Boston Celtics.

**Hurricane Hits Gulf Coast (June 26):** Bonnie kills two as 85-mile-an-hour winds and heavy rains spawn tornadoes, destroy homes, and cut off power.

**Cocaine Blamed in Player's Death (June 30):** Coroner in California announces Don Rogers, 23, Cleveland Brown defensive back, died after using drug.

# JULY 1986

## International

**Missing American Freed in Lebanon (July 2):** Steven John Donahue, 32, held 10 months by drug traffickers.

**Nicaragua Closes Newspaper (July 3):** Managua regime shuts opposition *La Prensa,* charging it favors U.S. Several hundred employees lose jobs.

**Nicaragua Expels a Bishop (July 4):** Accuses Roman Catholic prelate, Pablo Antonio Vega, of supporting anti-Sandinista rebels.

**Two Australians Hanged in Malaysia (July 7):** Kevin Barlow and Brian Chambers, both 28, executed for trafficking in heroin under stringent law.

**Paris Police Headquarters Bombed (July 9):** Kills inspector and wounds at least 22. (**July 11**): Direct Action, left-wing French terrorist group, takes responsibility for bombing.

**Terrorists Kill German Industrialist (July 9):** Remote-control bomb fatal to Karl-Heinz Beckurts, 56, director of research and technology at Siemens A.G. Red Army Faction admits guilt, calling victim a proponent of nuclear energy and "Star Wars."

**Six Killed in Clash Off Lebanon (July 10):** Two Israeli soldiers and four guerrillas, intercepted in dinghy at sea, perish in three-hour battle. Later, Israeli aircraft attack reported Palestinian bases in Lebanon, with 10 persons dead or wounded.

**Typhoon Hits South China (July 14):** At least 21 dead in China after storm rakes Philippines, killing 119. Millions of soldiers and civilians work to rescue tens of thousands stranded in Chinese province.

**Nine Killed in Madrid Blast (July 14):** Nine paramilitary Civil Guards dead and 43 others wounded. Basque separatist terrorists blamed. In Portugal five bombs explode in three cities, killing two.

**U.S. Troops Join in Bolivian Cocaine Raids (July 15):** Reagan Administration sends soldiers and aircraft to help in forays against major drug traffickers.

**Rockets Attack Madrid Defense Ministry (July 21):** Nine wounded by 12 missiles and car-bomb blast outside building. Basque separatist guerrillas blamed.

**Morocco and Israel Leaders Meet (July 23):** Prime Minister Shimon Peres ends 48-hour visit to King Hassan II. Several Arab nations condemn Hassan's meeting with Peres. (**July 24**): The two differ on success of talks, with no breakthrough in Middle East peace efforts.

**Sikhs Kill 13 Hindus in Punjab (July 25):** Extremists halt bus in rural area and shoot victims.

**American Hostage Freed in Lebanon (July 26):** Radical Shiite group, Islamic Holy War, releases Rev. Lawrence Martin Jenco, 51, Roman Catholic priest from Joliet, Ill., one of five kidnapped Americans.

**Car Bomb Kills 31 in Beirut (July 28):** Wounds 120 and devastates three-block area in Christian suburb. (**July 29**): Car bomb in Moslem area kills 25 and wounds 180. No groups take responsibility in either.

**U.S. Vetoes Anti-Contra Measure (July 31):** Eleven countries approve U.N. Security Council call for compliance with World Court ruling outlawing military and financial support for guerrillas fighting Sandinista government.

## National

**Justices Uphold Advertising Ban (July 1):** Supreme Court, 5-4, rules governments may forbid truthful advertising of products and services that are legal but are regarded as harmful.

**Supreme Court Backs Affirmative Action (July 2):** Justices, 6-3, endorse tactic to cure past discrimination against minorities when other steps do not suffice. Two rulings rebuff Administration.

**Centennial of Statue of Liberty (July 3):** Nation rededicates symbol of freedom in New York Harbor, refurbished for $66 million over four years. As fourday celebration begins, President Reagan and President Mitterand of France preside over official opening ceremonies on Governors Island in program of music, fireworks, speeches, and laser beams to relight statue. (**July 4**): Parade of oldtime tall ships joins modern warships in salute to July Fourth and statue's centennial. As 21-gun salutes echo, President Reagan reviews international armada from deck of battleship Iowa. (**July 5**): Statue open to visitors. Celebration continues with boat and air races, open houses aboard ships, and festival in lower Manhattan. (**July 6**): Liberty weekend closes with capacity crowds at statue.

**Supreme Court Voids Budget Balancing Law (July 7):** Justices, 7-2, strike down automatic mechanism for cutting spending as unconstitutional violation of separation of powers.

**Congress Votes $11.7-Billion Spending Cuts (July 17):** Ratifies reductions made under budget-balancing law's automatic spending cut mechanism voided by Supreme Court as violation of separation of powers.

**Senate Endorses Extradition Treaty (July 17):** Votes 87-10 to approve landmark pact with Britain easing extradition from U.S. of terrorism suspects.

## General

**Earthquakes Rock California Areas (July 8):** Temblor measuring 6 on Richter scale shakes Palm Springs and other communities along Mojave Desert. (**July 21**): State's fourth earthquake in two weeks rocks wide area and rattles buildings as far east as Salt Lake City, 700 miles away. No injuries reported.

**Ex-F.B.I. Agent Sentenced as Spy (July 14):** U.S. Court in Los Angeles metes two concurrent life terms to Richard W. Miller, 49, and additional 50 years to run concurrently. Espionage for Soviet Union charged.

**Litton Systems Inc. Admits Fraud Guilt (July 15):** Contracting arm of Litton Industries agrees to plead guilty to overbilling Pentagon by $6.3 million, largest case of false billing against a defense contractor. Unit, 19th largest military contractor, to pay U.S. $15 million in fines, civil penalties, interest and restitution.

**LTV Files in Bankruptcy (July 17):** In largest such action in U.S. history, corporation seeks protection from more than 20,000 creditors. Halts payments of debts of more than $4 billion. LTV is parent company of LTV Steel Company, second-largest steel manufacturer, and has energy and aerospace operations.

**Ex-Navy Radioman Convicted as Spy (July 24):** U.S. jury in San Francisco finds Jerry A. Whitworth, 46, guilty of participating in Soviet ring by stealing classified cryptographic data in exchange for $332,000.

**Drought Losses Past $2 Billion (July 25):** Heat spell destroys crops and livestock in eight Middle-Atlantic and Southern states. Farmers in North and East send hay to feed livestock.

**U.S. Football League Rebuffed (July 29):** Federal jury in New York finds National Football League violated antitrust laws, but awards only $1 in damages to U.S.F.L., which had sought $1.69 billion.

# AUGUST 1986

## International

**Senate Panel Votes South Africa Sanctions (Aug. 1):** Foreign Relations Committee, in 15-2 bipartisan action, approves economic measures, including ban on new loans or investments by U.S. business.

**South Africa Acts Against Black Nations (Aug. 5):** Plans economic countermeasures against neighbors after Commonwealth announcement of new sanctions.

**Ex-Commander of Indian Army Slain (Aug. 10):** Four gunmen kill Gen. Arun S. Vaidya, retired Chief of Staff, who had received death threats from Sikh militants.

**Sri Lankans Rescued Off Canada (Aug. 12):** Crowded into two lifeboats, 155 men, women and children are picked up by fishing boats in fog off Newfoundland. They tell authorities they had sailed from India, paying thousands for voyage.

**Pakistan Arrests Dissidents (Aug. 13):** Benazir Bhutto, 33, leader of opposition Pakistan Peoples Party, among hundreds held in widest action since martial law rule was ended in 1985.

**U.S. Agent Tortured in Mexico (Aug. 14):** Police detain overnight, interrogate, and abuse member of U.S. Drug Enforcement Administration working in Guadalajara. (Aug. 27): Mexican authorities charge 11 Jalisco state policemen in connection with detention.

**Missile Downs Sudanese Airliner; 60 Lost (Aug. 17):** Sudan rebels shoot down plane with antiaircraft weapons.

**Israel and Soviet Hold Talks (Aug. 18):** Negotiators meet in Finland in first official contact since Soviet Union broke off relations with Israel in 1967.

**Car Bomb Kills 20 in Teheran (Aug. 19):** Scores wounded in central square in second incident in four days in Iran. Car bomb in Moslem city of Qum had killed 13.

**Volcano Gas Kills 1,500 in Cameroon (Aug. 25):** Cloud from lake-bottom explosion chokes many victims to death as they sleep. Rescue workers impeded by remoteness of Lake Nios area and continuing toxic vapors. (Aug. 28): Government and U.S. officials call situation stabilized. Medical and food supplies have reached most of thousands of homeless.

**Soweto Death Toll Set at 21 (Aug. 28):** South Africa revises upward figure for political strife Aug. 26 in black township. Death toll in nation since September 1984 set at 2,200, mostly black, 270 of them since newest emergency decree was promulgated June 12.

**U.S. Correspondent Arrested in Moscow (Aug. 30):** Nicholas Daniloff, writer for U.S. News and World Report, detained after Soviet acquaintance hands him package containing two maps marked "top secret."

**Toll in Ship Collision Set at 398 (Aug. 31):** Soviet passenger vessel, Admiral Nakhimov, sinks in Black Sea 15 minutes after being hit broadside by freighter, Pyotr Vasev. Liner carried 888 passengers and 346 crew members. Rescue vessels save many.

# AUGUST 1986

## National

**Soviet Gets Subsidized Wheat (Aug. 1):** President authorizes sale, ending dispute among advisers.

**U.S. Aids Drought-Stricken Farmers (Aug. 1):** Agriculture Department announces multibillion-dollar financial relief program for tens of thousands of growers in Southern and Middle Atlantic states.

**House Votes Limit on Atomic Tests (Aug. 8):** In first move to halt nuclear weapons testing, representatives act, 234-155, to impose year's moratorium on all but smallest underground operations if Soviet Union agrees to reciprocate.

**Senate Panel Approves Rehnquist (Aug. 14):** Judiciary Committee, 13-5, votes to recommend confirmation of Reagan choice for Chief Justice of U.S., Associate Justice William H. Rehnquist. Hearings had exposed doubts about his candor and judicial ethics and disapproval of record on civil rights.

**Senate Votes South Africa Sanctions (Aug. 15):** Defies Administration and approves, 84-14, tough economic moves against racial separation. Rejects proposal similar to more stringent bill voted by House.

**House Rejects "Star Wars" Policy (Aug. 15):** By 255-152, Representatives approve 1987 military appropriations bill that defies Administration policies on arms control, new chemical weapons and space-oriented defense against missiles.

**Conferees Approve Tax Revision Bill (Aug. 16):** Congressional measure calls for most comprehensive restructuring of Federal income tax law since World War II.

**Pan Am Fined $1.95 Million (Aug. 22):** Pan American World Airways agrees to pay for violations of Federal aircraft safety regulations found in F.A.A. Audit.

**Convicted Spy Gets 365-Year Term (Aug. 28):** Jerry A. Whitworth, 47, also fined $410,000 by Federal judge in San Francisco for part in Soviet spy ring that Government termed most damaging espionage conspiracy in decades.

**Trade Deficit at $18 Billion Record (Aug. 29):** Commerce Department reports imports twice as large as exports for first time. Economists dismayed.

# AUGUST 1986

## General

**Fossils of Oldest Known Birds Found (Aug. 13):** Scientists report discovery in Texas of remains 75 million years older than any found before. Evidence supports theory of birds' evolution from dinosaurs.

**Vatican Disciplines U.S. Theologian (Aug. 18):** Rev. Charles E. Curran, major liberal theologian, stripped of authority to teach theology at Catholic University. He had opposed church's stand on sexual issues.

**Hunts Brothers Enterprise Files in Bankruptcy (Aug. 29):** Placid Oil Company, one of largest privately owned oil companies in U.S., petitions under Chapter 11 of Bankruptcy Code. Action prevents sale of oil and gas fields, land, stock and real estate. Falling oil prices blamed for crisis.

**Three Lutheran Groups Merge (Aug. 29):** Form Evangelical Lutheran Church in America, with 5.3 million members. Aim is single, more divers and effective denomination.

**Slave Descendants Hold Reunion (Aug. 30):** Hundreds who trace ancestry to 21 slave families meet at Somerset Place in Creswell, N.C., once state's second largest plantation and now a state park.

**Sixty-four on Jetliner Die in Collision (Aug. 31):** Three passengers on Piper PA-28 also perish as small plane crashes with Aeromexico DC-9 at Cerritos, Calif. Many on ground also killed, toll not set.

# Late Events

**Twenty-one Killed in Plane Hijacking (Sept. 6):** More than 100 wounded at Karachi, Pakistan, by gunmen who elude security and capture New York-bound Pan American jumbo jet Boeing 747 and begin shooting and detonating grenades in darkened cabin.

**Twenty-one Killed in Istanbul Synagogue (Sept. 6):** Jews perish as two Arab terrorists lock doors and attack Sabbath congregation. Gunmen also die.

**Miss America Crowned (Sept. 13):** Kellye Cash, a communications major at Memphis State University, becomes the 1987 title-holder. A great-niece of Johnny Cash, she is from Memphis, Tenn.

**Senate Confirms Supreme Court Justices (Sept. 17):** Justice William H. Rehnquist gains confirmation as Chief Justice by a vote of 65 to 33, receiving more negative votes than any other Justice confirmed to the Court. Antonin Scalia wins confirmation unanimously.

**Bombs Kill 10, Wound 162 in Paris (Sept. 25):** French police arrest nine after a series of explosions. Committee seeking freedom for Arab prisoners blamed. Principal explosions: inside main police headquarters (Sept. 15), one dead, 51 wounded; outside crowded department store (Sept. 17), five dead, 50 wounded.

**Senate Passes Tax Bill (Sept. 27):** By a vote of 74 to 23, the Senate approves the most sweeping changes in the Federal income tax system since World War II. The House gave its approval by a vote of 292 to 136 (Sept. 25). Reagan signs (Oct. 22).

**Daniloff Gains Freedom (Sept. 29):** The Soviet Union allows Nicholas S. Daniloff to leave the country without standing trial. (Sept. 30): Gennadi F. Zakharov pleads no contest to spying charge and leaves for Moscow. The Soviet Union also agrees to permit two dissidents, Yuri F. Orlov and his wife Irina L. Valitova, to emigrate.

**Senate Overrides President's Veto (Oct. 2):** Following the lead of the House, the Senate, in a 78 to 21 vote, rebuffs Reagan's opposition to imposing economic sanctions on South Africa.

**Soviet Sub Sinks (Oct. 6):** Following a fire and explosion (Oct. 3) in which three crewmen die, the badly damaged nuclear submarine sinks about 4 a.m. EDT. Crewmen evacuate the vessel before it sinks 600 miles off Bermuda.

**Senate Convicts Judge on Impeachment Charges (Oct. 9):** Federal District Judge Harry E. Claiborne becomes the first official to be removed from office by impeachment in 50 years.

**Strong Quakes Hit San Salvador (Oct. 10):** Two strong tremors topple buildings, sending residents into streets in San Salvador. Casualties running high. (Oct. 13): Strongest aftershock hits El Salvador.

**Iceland Summit Fails (Oct. 12):** On the brink of the most far-reaching arms agreement to date, the accord founders on "Star Wars." Gorbachev demands a 10-year ban on space testing of the Strategic Defense Initiative. Reagan refuses.

## 1986 Nobel Prize Winners

**Peace:** Elie Wiesel (American) according to the announcement, "As one of the most important spiritual leaders and guides in an age when violence, repression and racism continue to characterize the world."

**Medicine:** Dr. Rita Levi-Montalcini (dual U.S. and Italian citizenship), senior scientist at the Institute of Cell Biology in Rome, and Dr. Stanley Cohen (American), professor of biochemistry at Vanderbilt University School of Medicine in Nashville, for their major contributions to the understanding of substances that influence cell growth and the orderly development of tissues, including the nervous system.

**Physics:** Dr. Ernst Ruska (German), of the Fritz Haben Institute of the Max Planch Society in West Berlin, for his invention of the electron microscope, and Dr. Gerd Binnig (German) and Dr. Heinrich Rohrer (Swiss), both staff members of the I.B.M. Research Laboratory in Zurich, for their work on the scanning tunneling microscope.

**Chemistry:** Dudley R. Herschback (American), of Harvard University, Yuan T. Lee (American), of the University of California, and John C. Polanyi (Canadian), of the University of Toronto, for their work on "reaction dynamics."

**Economics:** James M. Buchanan (American), a professor at George Mason University in Virginia, for his pioneering development of new methods for analyzing economic and political decision-making.

**Literature:** Wole Soyinka (Nigerian), a playwright and poet. The academy citation states "in a wide cultural perspective and with poetical overtones [he] fashions the drama of existence."

## Major Emmy Awards for TV, 1986

**Drama series:** *Cagney and Lacey* (CBS)
  **Actress:** Sharon Gless, *Cagney and Lacey* (CBS)
  **Actor:** William Daniels, *St. Elsewhere* (NBC)
  **Supporting actress:** Bonnie Bartlett, *St. Elsewhere* (NBC)
  **Supporting actor:** John Karlen, *Cagney and Lacey* (CBS)

**Comedy series:** *The Golden Girls* (NBC)
  **Actress:** Betty White, *The Golden Girls* (NBC)
  **Actor:** Michael J. Fox, *Family Ties* (NBC)
  **Supporting actress:** Rhea Perlman, *Cheers* (NBC)
  **Supporting actor:** John Larroquette, *Night Court* (NBC)

**Variety, music or comedy program,** *The Kennedy Center Honors: A Celebration of the Arts* (CBS)

**Limited series or special:** *Peter the Great* (NBC)
  **Actress:** Marlo Thomas, *Nobody's Child* (CBS)
  **Actor:** Dustin Hoffman, *Death of a Salesman* (CBS)
  **Supporting actress:** Colleen Dewhurst, *Between Two Women* (ABC)
  **Supporting actor:** John Malkovich, *Death of a Salesman* (CBS)

**Drama Special:** *Love Is Never Silent* (NBC)

**Individual performance in a variety or music program:** Whitney Houston, *The 28th Annual Grammy Awards* (CBS)

**Guest performer in a dramatic series:** John Lithgow, *Amazing Stories* (NBC)

**Guest performer in a comedy series:** Roscoe Lee Browne, *The Cosby Show*, (NBC)

**Children's program:** *Wonderworks: Anne of Green Gables* (PBS)

**Governor's Award:** Red Skelton

**Network totals:** NBC 19, CBS 10, ABC 1, PBS 1

# Deaths in 1985–1986

(As of September 1, 1986)

**Addabbo, Representative Joseph P.,** 61: Queens, N.Y., Democrat, a power in shaping defense policy as chairman of a key House subcommittee. April 10, 1986.

**Aherne, Brian,** 83: British-born actor who played classic suave leading man on stage and in films. Feb. 10, 1986.

**Alda, Robert,** 72: actor who starred in Broadway musical "Guys and Dolls" and portrayed George Gershwin in film "Rhapsody in Blue." May 3, 1986.

**Arlen, Harold,** 81: composer of lasting popular tunes such as "Over the Rainbow" and "Stormy Weather." April 23, 1986.

**Armstrong, Herbert W.,** 93: broadcasting evangelist and founder and pastor of Worldwide Church of God. Jan. 16, 1986.

**Ashley, Laura,** 60: British fashion designer who founded international fabric and clothing empire. Sept. 17, 1985.

**Baxter, Anne,** 62: Academy-Award winning film and TV actress known for her roles in "All About Eve" and "The Razor's Edge." Dec. 12, 1985.

**Beauvoir, Simone de,** 78: French author of "Second Sex," seminal polemic on status of women, and figure in left-wing French intellectual circles. April 14, 1986.

**Borges, Jorge Luis,** 86: Argentine short-story writer, poet, and essayist considered one of Latin America's greatest writers. June 14, 1986.

**Bowles, Chester,** 85: adviser to four Democratic Presidents in 30-year career including service as Congressman, ambassador, and governor of Connecticut May 25, 1986.

**Brynner, Yul,** 65: Stage and film star identified with role as Siamese monarch in "The King and I" for 4,625 performances. Oct. 10, 1985.

**Cagney, James,** 86: cocky film star in gangster roles in "The Public Enemy" and in scores of other movies. Won Academy Award for portrayal of George M. Cohan in "Yankee Doodle Dandy." March 30, 1986.

**Calvino, Italo,** 61: Italy's leading contemporary novelist, master of allegorical fantasy. Sept. 19, 1985.

**Canfield, Cass,** 88: a leading book publisher, associated for more than 40 years with Harper & Row (formerly Harper & Bros.). March 27, 1986.

**Chase, Lucia,** 88: founder and for 35 years co-director of New York's American Ballet Theater. Jan. 9, 1986.

**Chase, Stuart,** 97: economist, member of Franklin D. Roosevelt's brain trust who coined phrase "New Deal." Nov. 16, 1985.

**Ciardi, John,** 69: prolific poet and professor internationally known for translation of Dante's "Inferno." March 30, 1986.

**Cohn, Roy,** 59: Chief counsel for Senator Joseph R. McCarthy's Senate investigation of Communismn in 1950s. Aug. 2, 1986.

**Collingwood, Charles,** 68: CBS News correspondent who covered World War II, the Vietnam War, and other major events over four decades. Oct. 3, 1985.

**Crawford, Broderick,** 74: film actor known as heavyweight tough guy who won Academy Award for performance in "All the King's Men." April 26, 1986.

**Crowley, Jim,** 83: one of famed Four Horsemen of Notre Dame, later coach at Fordham University. Jan. 15, 1986.

**Da Silva, Howard,** 76: actor, director, producer, and author whose show business career spanned more than 55 years. Feb. 16, 1986.

**Desmond, Johnny** (born Giovanni de Simone), 65: singer and actor famed as vocalist with Glenn Miller's swing band. Sept. 6, 1985.

**Downey, Morton,** 83: Irish tenor popular with radio and night club audiences in 1930s and 40s. Oct. 25, 1985.

**Eastland, James O.,** 81: conservative U.S. Senator from Mississippi, chairman of Judiciary Committee for 22 years. Feb. 19, 1986.

**Ellis, Perry,** 46: a top fashion designer of sportswear for men and women. May 30, 1986.

**Goodman, Benny,** 77: clarinetist and band leader known as "King of Swing," pioneer of Big Band era of 1930s. June 13, 1986.

**Gilels, Emil,** 68: one of world's greatest pianists, in 1955 first Soviet musician to perform in United States since Prokofiev in 1921. Oct. 14, 1985.

**Graves, Robert,** 90: English poet, novelist, and classical scholar known as prolific and versatile writer. Dec. 7, 1985.

**Halleck, Charles A.,** 85: Republican Representative in Congress from Indiana. The "one-hundred percent Republican" served as both majority and minority leader of House of Representatives in 34-year career. March 3, 1986.

**Harriman, W. Averell,** 94: heir to railway fortune who as businessman had major role in developing U.S.-Soviet relations. Democratic governor of New York from 1955 to 1959. Served four presidents in key diplomatic posts. July 26, 1986.

**Hayden, Sterling,** 70: screen actor who played leading-man roles in 1940s and 1950s. May 23, 1986.

**Hobson, Laura Z.,** 85: author of "Gentleman's Agreement," 1947 novel on anti-Semitism in America, and other works. Feb. 28, 1986.

**Hudson, Rock,** 59: screen actor known for handsome looks and comic talent, whose search for treatment for AIDS focussed world attention on disease. Oct. 2, 1985.

**Isherwood, Christopher,** 81: author whose stories served as basis of play and movie "I Am a Camera." Jan. 4, 1986.

**Jarvis, Gregory B.,** 41: died in shuttle explosion. Jan. 28, 1986. See page 357 for details.

**Javits, Jacob K.,** 81: U.S. Senator for 24 years and one of most respected and influential political leaders. Was minority liberal within Republican Party. March 7, 1986.

**Jessup, Philip C.,** 89: authority on international law who served in United States delegation to United Nations and as a justice on International Court of Justice. Played critical role in ending Berlin blockade. Jan. 31, 1986.

**Kekkonen, Urho K.,** 85: Finland's president for 25 years. Followed policy of neutrality and friendship with neighboring Soviet Union. Aug. 30, 1986.

**Kimball, Spencer W.,** 90: leader of Mormon church since 1973, who struck down church's 148-year policy of excluding black men from full participation. Nov. 5, 1985.

**Kraft, Joseph,** 61: syndicated Washington columnist and author of books and articles on national and foreign affairs. Jan. 10, 1986.

**Lee, Russell,** 83: key figure in American photography, known for portraits of Depression-era migrant workers, postwar coal miners, and industrial scenes. Aug. 28, 1986.

**Lerner, Alan Jay, 67:** lyricist and playwright partner of Frederick Loewe in musical theater. Works included "My Fair Lady," "Brigadoon," "Camelot." June 14, 1986.

**Lodge, John Davis, 82:** former governor of Connecticut, member of House of Representatives, and Ambassador to Spain, Argentina, and Switzerland. Oct. 29, 1985.

**Loewy, Raymond, 92:** "Father of Streamlining," who pioneered industrial development movement that changed appearance of cars and thousands of other articles. July 14, 1986.

**Lovett, Robert A., 90:** Secretary of Defense from 1951 to 1953 and former Under Secretary of State. A Republican investment banker who served under Franklin D. Roosevelt and Harry Truman.

**MacRae, Gordon, 64:** singer and actor who starred in film versions of "Oklahoma" and "Carousel." Jan. 24, 1986.

**Malamud, Bernard, 71:** novelist and short-story writer who won two National Book Awards and Pulitzer Prize. March 18, 1986.

**Maris, Roger, 51:** held baseball major league record for most home runs in a single season. Dec. 14, 1985.

**Markham, Beryl, 83:** British aviation pioneer, first person to fly solo across Atlantic from England from east to west, in 1936. Aug. 3, 1986.

**McAuliffe, Christa, 37:** died in shuttle explosion. Jan. 28, 1986. See page 357 for details.

**McNair, Ronald E., 35:** died in shuttle explosion. Jan. 28, 1986. See page 357 for details.

**Merkel, Una, 82:** veteran Hollywood actress and winner of Tony award for role in "The Ponder Heart." Jan. 2, 1986.

**Milland, Ray, 81:** film actor who won Academy Award and other honors for portrayal of alcoholic in "The Lost Weekend" in 1945. March 10, 1986.

**Miller, Merle, 67:** author of best-selling oral biographies of Presidents Harry S. Truman and Lyndon B. Johnson, June 10, 1986.

**Minnelli, Vincente, 76:** highly reputed producer of Hollywood musicals, including "Gigi," July 25, 1986.

**Moore, Henry, 88:** British sculptor and leader in twentieth century art. Represented by countless carvings, bronzes and drawings throughout the world. Aug. 31, 1986.

**Myrdal, Alva, 84:** Swedish diplomat, co-winner of Nobel Peace Prize in 1982 for her efforts to promote world disarmament. Feb. 1, 1986.

**Norkay, Tenzing, 72:** Sherpa who climbed Mount Everest with Sir Edmund Hillary in 1953. May 9, 1986.

**O'Keefe, Georgia, 98:** key figure in 20th century American painting and leader in development of American modernism. March 8, 1986.

**Onizuka, Ellison S., 39:** died in shuttle explosion. Jan. 28, 1986. See page 357 for details.

**Papanin, Ivan D., 91:** Soviet polar explorer who commanded Russians' first ice-floe station in 1937-38. Jan. 30, 1986.

**Pears, Sir Peter, 75:** British tenor known for profound musical interpretations. Personal and professional partner of composer Benjamin Britten. April 3, 1986.

**Perry, Lincoln Theodore (Stepin Fetchit), 83:** first widely known black actor in Hollywood. Nov. 19, 1985.

**Pollard, Fritz, 92:** only black head coach of a National Football League team and member of the National Football Foundation

**Hall of Fame** for college players. May 11, 1986.

**Preminger, Otto, 80:** producer and director known for such films as "Laura" and "Exodus." April 23, 1986.

**Reed, Donna, 64:** Academy-Award winning star of more than 40 movies and star of television's "Donna Reed Show" in 1950s and 1960s. Jan. 14, 1986.

**Resnick, Judith A., 36:** died in shuttle explosion. Jan. 28, 1986. See page 357 for details.

**Richter, Dr. Charles F., 85:** pioneer in seismology for whom Richter scale for measuring earthquakes is named. Sept. 30, 1985.

**Rickover, Admiral Hyman G., 86:** known as father of nuclear Navy, served 68 years, July 8, 1986.

**Romulo, Carlos P., 86:** Filipino diplomat, a leading spokesman for third world countries in early days of United Nations. Dec. 15, 1985.

**Ruffing, Charles (Red), 81:** pitcher and pinch-hitter who helped Yankees win seven pennants and six World Series championships. Feb. 17, 1986.

**Ryskind, Morrie, 89:** writer or collaborator on comedies and satires including "Of Thee I Sing" and Marx Brothers films. Aug. 24, 1985.

**Schroeder, William J., 54:** longest-surviving recipient of artifical heart after 620 days with device. Aug. 6, 1986.

**Scobee, Francis R., 46:** died in shuttle explosion. Jan. 28, 1986. See page 357 for details.

**Silvers, Phil, 73:** comedian on TV and in films, who started career as vaudeville singer. Nov. 1, 1985.

**Smith, Kate, 79:** popular singer who made "God Bless America" unofficial national anthem. June 17, 1986.

**Smith, Michael J., 40:** died in shuttle explosion. Jan. 28, 1986. See page 357 for details.

**Sobol, Louis, 90:** Broadway columnist for Hearst newspapers for four decades. Feb. 9, 1986.

**Stewart, Potter, 70:** Eisenhower Republican who served 23 years on Supreme Court and was known as conservative. Dec. 7, 1985.

**Vallee, Rudy, 84:** crooner and saxophone player, public idol of 1930s and 1940s. Famed for theme song "My Time Is Your Time." July 3, 1986.

**Van Arsdale, Harry, Jr., 80:** president of New York City Central Labor Council and one of last survivors of George Meany era. Feb. 16, 1986.

**Welles, Orson, 70:** Hollywood "boy wonder," innovator in film and theater, creator of classic "Citizen Kane." Oct. 10, 1985.

**White, E. B., 86:** essayist and stylist whose articles and poems helped set tone of *New Yorker* magazine. Author of children's classics, including "Stuart Little." Oct. 1, 1985.

**White, Theodore H., 71:** Pulitzer-prize-winning journalist, author of "Making of the President" book series. May 15, 1986.

**Williams, Cootie, 77:** trumpeter, last surviving member of Duke Ellington Orchestra of 1920s. Sept. 15, 1985.

**Williams, William B., 62:** radio personality, disk jockey in New York for 42 years, who emphasized old favorites of popular music. Aug. 3, 1986.

**Wilson, Teddy, 73:** jazz pianist known for suave and incisive touch in 50-year career. Joined Benny Goodman band in 1930s as one of first blacks to appear with white musicians. July 31, 1986.

**Windsor, Duchess of, 89:** former Wallis Warfield Simpson married King Edward VIII after his abdication in romance that threatened to shake monarchy. April 24, 1986.

1257086
ISBN 0-395-42503-4